THE 2000 ANNOTATED

TREMEEAR'S CRIMINAL CODE

And the following related statutes

Canada Evidence Act
Canadian Charter of Rights and Freedoms
Controlled Drugs and Substances Act
Food and Drugs Act
Narcotic Control Act
Young Offenders Act
Interpretation Act
Firearms Act

The Honourable Mr. Justice David Watt
of the Ontario Court (General Division)

Michelle Fuerst
of Gold & Fuerst,
Toronto, Ontario

STATUTES OF CANADA ANNOTATED

CARSWELL
Thomson Professional Publishing

Canadian Cataloguing in Publication Data

The National Library of Canada has catalogued this publication as follows:

Canada
    [Criminal Code (Tremeear)]
    The annotated . . . Tremeear's Criminal Code and the following related statutes...
Began with 1990 issue.
Annual.
"R.S.C. 1985, Chapter C-46"
Description based on: 1991.
Editors. 1990- : David Watt and Michelle K. Fuerst.
Continues: Canada. Tremeear's . . . Criminal Code and miscellaneous
statutes.
ISSN 1184-0293
ISBN 0-459-26264-5 (2000 : police)
ISBN 0-459-26262-9 (2000 : student)
ISBN 0-459-26260-2 (2000 : prof.)
1. Criminal Law — Canada. I. Tremeear, W.J., 1864-1926. II. Watt, David,
1948-. III. Fuerst, Michelle. IV. Title. V. Title: Criminal Code
(Tremeear).
KE8804.53.A18T7   345.71'002632   C91-039008-8
KF9219.C2T72

CARSWELL
Thomson Professional Publishing

One Corporate Plaza	Customer Care
2075 Kennedy Road	Toronto 1-416-609-3800
Scarborough, Ontario	Elsewhere in Canada/U.S. 1-800-387-5164
M1T 3V4	Fax 1-416-298-5094
	World Wide Web: http://www.carswell.com
	E-mail: orders@carswell.com

OTHER STATUTES OF CANADA ANNOTATED

Beach, *Canada Evidence Act and Related Statutes*
Chotalia, *Canadian Human Rights Act*
David & Pelly, *Bank Act*
Gray, *Canada Evidence Act*
Houlden & Morawetz, *Bankruptcy and Insolvency Act*
Imai & Hawley, *Indian Act*
Libman, *Contraventions Act*
MacDonald & Wilton, *Divorce Act*
Marrocco, Goslett & Désilets, *Loi sur l'immigration du Canada*
Marrocco, Goslett & Nigam, *Citizenship Act*
McFarlane, Pun & Loparco, *Unemployment Insurance Act*
Meehan, *Canadian Charter of Rights and Freedoms*
Moscowitz & Pinsonneault, *Robic-Leger Trade-marks Act*
Northey, *Canadian Environmental Assessment and EARP Guidelines Order*
Nozick, *Competition Act*
Prabhu, *Customs Act*
Sgayias, Kinnear, Rennie & Saunders, *Crown Liability and Proceedings Act*
Snyder, *Canada Labour Code*
Tamaro, *Copyright Act*
Watt, *Tremeear's Related Criminal Statutes*
Zambelli, *Refugee Convention*

TABLE OF CONTENTS

Table of Contents

PUBLISHER'S NOTE

Case Law Developments

The case law is current to May 6, 1999. This edition contains approximately 80 new annotations of the Supreme Court of Canada, Court of Appeal and provincial court decisions. These decisions include *Ewanchuk* ("no" means no; unavailability of implied consent as a defence to sexual assault; limits on the defence of honest but mistaken belief in consent (S.C.C.)); *Godoy* (police power to enter private dwelling in response to emergency 911 calls (S.C.C.)); *Rose* (scope of *Charter* right to full answer and defence; order of address prescribed by s. 651(3) of *Code* does not violate right (S.C.C.)); *M. (M.R.)* (applicability of *Charter* to school officials; modified constitutional requirements governing searches of students by school officials (S.C.C.)); *Arp* (informed consent to provision of bodily substances; absent specific agreement as to limits by police and consenting party, no limit should be imposed on subsequent use (S.C.C.)); *Thomas* (limits on powers of appellate courts to issue ancillary orders under s. 686 of the *Code* (S.C.C.)); *Warsing* (circumstances in which D may be permitted to raise NCRMD defence for first time on appeal; powers of court where defence thus raised (S.C.C.)); *Cuerrier* (non-disclosure of H.I.V.-positive status vitiates consent to sexual intercourse (S.C.C.)); and *Ruzic* (the limited defence of duress under s. 17 of the Code is unconstitutional (Ont. C.A.)).

Legislative Amendments and Developments:

With the exception of those provisions of S.C. 1999, c. 5, whose July in force date was announced by statutory instrument prior to June 1 and which appear as if in force, the legislation is current to June 1, 1999. The following significant statutory developments have been incorporated into the 2000 edition of Tremeear's:

1) *An Act to amend the Criminal Code, the Controlled Drugs and Substances Act and the Corrections and Conditional Release Act* (S.C. 1999, c. 5: see Table of Amendments for in force information): This is a wide ranging piece of legislation addressing such matters as conditional sentences and fines, proof of causation in homicide cases, execution of search warrants and removal of surveillance devices, and non-communication orders pending trial, and relating to such offences as telemarketing fraud, theft of valuable minerals, prostitution, gaming, and producing likenesses of Canadian currency.

Criminal Code amendments are detailed as follows:

- Amendments relating to conditional sentencing clarify that police officers can arrest offenders with or without warrant for alleged breach of conditional sentence, and that their arrest powers in such circumstances are equivalent to those for indictable offence. The running of a conditional sentence will now be suspended, where breach is alleged, from the time of the offender's arrest or issue of arrest warrant until the conclusion of the hearing on the breach; suspended time may later be re-credited to the offender if the court finds there was no breach, that the offender had reasonable excuse, or where there were other compelling reason.

- Amendments relating to fines allowing for the imposition of a fine in addition to, but not in lieu of, other mandatory minimum punishments, provide that the ability of an offender to pay a fine is not relevant where a mandatory minimum fine or fine in lieu of forfeiture is imposed by statute, provide, with specified exceptions, that the *Code's* fine provisions will apply to fines imposed under other federal statutes, and extend enforcement provisions to allow for the suspension of licences and permits where the offender is in default of payment.

- The s. 227 year and a day rule applicable to homicide prosecutions has been repealed.

- The electronic surveillance provisions of the *Code* have been amended to authorize surreptitious entry to premises for the purpose of removing lawfully-installed surveillance devices. Those provisions relating to search warrants, including related forms, have been amended to explicitly provide that only those with law enforcement duties can execute warrants.

- Non-communication orders may now be made upon an accused's first appearance before a justice and prior to the conclusion of a bail hearing.
- In terms of substantive offences: the proceeds of deceptive telemarketing are now subject to the *Code's* seizure and forfeiture provisions; the offence of attempting to obtain the sexual services of a person under eighteen has been replaced with the offence of communicating for that purpose and police are now authorized to use electronic surveillance to investigate several prostitution-related offences; the scope of mineral offences has been expanded by replacing references to "precious metals" with references to "valuable minerals", defined to include diamonds and other gemstones of specified value; gambling will now be allowed on bona fide international cruise ships sailing in international waters and provinces are authorized to conduct dice games; an exemption has been created to the offence of producing likenesses of Canadian currency to permit reproduction of images of bank notes by specified parties for specified purposes, and the offence has been revised to cover new methods of reproduction.

Amendments to the *Controlled Drugs and Substances Act* are detailed as follows:

- The limits on criminal liability of law enforcement officers for laundering of proceeds of certain offences in the course of the execution of their duties have been clarified;
- The court is now authorized to consider any relevant aggravating factors, including those enumerated in s. 10 (2), in sentencing an offender for a designated substance offence, and the duty of the court to give reasons where it is satisfied of the existence of specified aggravating factors, but decides not to sentence the offender to imprisonment, has been clarified.

2) *An Act to amend the Nunavut Act with Respect to the Nunavut Court of Justice and to amend other Acts in Consequence* (S.C. 1999, c. 3, in force April 1, 1999): This Act establishes a single-level trial court, at the superior court level, for the new territory of Nunavut. It amends the *Criminal Code* to delineate applicable procedures for the new Nunavut Court of Justice relating to such matters as jurisdiction of judges, summary conviction appeals, judicial interim release, elections as to mode of trial, and creates a new statutory form of review. It also amends the *Young Offenders Act* to provide appropriate procedures for a single-level trial court consistent with the new procedures in the *Code*.

3) *An Act Respecting DNA Identification and to make consequential amendments to the Criminal Code and other Acts*, S.C. 1998, c. 37, received Royal Assent on December 10, 1998. While not in force at date of publication, the consequential amendments to the *Criminal Code*, including new forms, have been incorporated as shaded text. Those amendments provide for orders authorizing the collection of bodily substances from which DNA profiles can be derived for inclusion in the DNA data bank established by the Act. The amendments further provide that such substances may be collected from offenders under sentence who meet specified criteria.

4) The greater part of the *Firearms Act*, S.C. 1995, c. 39, was brought into force on December 1, 1998: see Table of Amendments for details. As at date of publication, only the following provisions of the Act remained unproclaimed: ss. 5(3), 7(4)(e), 24(2)(c)-(d), 29(1), 32(b), part of s. 35, 36-43, and s. 97 of the *Criminal Code* as enacted by s. 139. The Act introduces a new legislative régime to govern the licensing, registration, transport, export, import, storage, display, transfer and use of firearms in Canada . It repeals and replaces the existing firearms scheme under Part III of the *Criminal Code*. A table of concordance relating to the provisions of the former Part III to the new Part III has been added to the work for ease of reference.

New Commentary

Significant new commentary has been added to the 2000 edition of *Tremeear's* in respect of Part III on "*Firearms and Other Offensive Weapons*". The provisions of the new Part III of the Code have been summarized in detail and new related provisions added. Relevant historical cases have been relocated and retained with appropriate cross-references.

Features

Please note the following when using the 2000 edition of *Tremeear's*:

Unproclaimed Legislation and Related Commentary: Legislation which has received Royal Assent but which has not yet been proclaimed in force appears as shaded text. Commentary which discusses an unproclaimed amendment to an existing section also appears as shaded text. Commentary referring to new sections or subsections which are not yet proclaimed does not appear as shaded text.

Pocket Supplement with Hardbound Edition: The first case law supplement, delivered to purchasers of the hardbound editions, contains recent case law updates to the 2000 edition which have come to the attention of the publisher and the authors subsequent to the preparation of the main work. It will cover new case law up to July 30, 1999. It is intended to serve as a convenient reference to recent developments and to provide exceptional currency for users of *Tremeear's Criminal Code*. Legislative supplements will be provided free to purchasers of the hardbound edition. Subsequent case law supplements will also be available at a nominal charge.

ACKNOWLEDGMENTS

We are delighted to introduce the eleventh edition of the *Annotated Tremeear's Criminal Code*. Over the past decade, many of our colleagues on the Bench and at the Bar have made use of the book. We are most grateful to them for their support, and for the many helpful suggestions that they have made. We have tried to incorporate these suggestions whenever it has been possible to do so. Alan Gold, our respective law school classmate and partner, has been an invaluable source of encouragement and information.

A number of individuals at Carswell have been instrumental in ensuring the manuscripts' timely completion. We particularly wish to thank Rachel Francis, Director, Major Market, and more recently, Jilean Bell, Product Development Manager. We also express our appreciation to the Production and Marketing personnel at Carswell for their tireless efforts.

Andrea Hind deserves special recognition for her tireless ongoing efforts to make the illegible, legible and the unclear, clear.

On a personal note, we are grateful to our families for their continued support. Katie and Lindsay Watt greet our frequent (and, no doubt, boring) discussions about the publication with good humour and patience. We also wish to thank Charlotte, our golden retriever, for leaving this year's manuscript relatively intact, despite her apparent fondness for paper.

David Watt
Michelle Fuerst
Toronto, June, 1999

GLOSSARY OF TERMS

To economize on space and facilitate use of the work as a quick reference tool, the annotations which follow each section of the *Criminal Code* make use of the following contractions:

D	Defendant/Accused
P	Prosecutor/Crown
V	Victim/Complainant
VFS	Victim Fine Surcharge
External circumstances	All elements in the definition of a crime except D's mental element
Mental element	D's mental element in respect of the external circumstances of a crime
NCR	not criminally responsible
S.	section(s), subsection(s), paragraph(s) or sub-paragraph(s)
CDA	Controlled Drugs and Substances Act
CEA	Canada Evidence Act
Charter	Canadian Charter of Rights and Freedoms
Code	Criminal Code
FDA	Food and Drugs Act
IA	Interpretation Act
ICA	Identification of Criminals Act
NCA	Narcotic Control Act
YOA	Young Offenders Act

TABLE OF CASES

Cases are referenced to section numbers of the *Criminal Code* unless preceded by the following: Constitution Act *CA*, Canada Evidence Act *CEA*, Firearms Act *FA*, Food and Drugs Act *FDA*, Interpretation Act *IA*, Narcotic Control Act *NCA*, Young Offenders Act *YOA*.

Table of Cases

Table of Cases

Table of Cases

Table of Cases

Table of Cases

Table of Cases

1

Table of Cases

Table of Cases

Table of Cases

Table of Cases

Table of Cases

Table of Cases

Table of Cases

Table of Cases

Table of Cases

Table of Cases

Table of Cases

TABLE OF CONCORDANCE

R.S.C. 1970, c. C-34	R.S.C. 1985, c. C-46	R.S.C. 1970, c. C-34	R.S.C. 1985, c. C-46
C-34	C-46	6(1.5)	7(3.3)
1	1	6(1.6)	7(3.4)
2	2	6(1.7)	7(3.5)
2 "court of criminal jurisdiction"	2 "court of criminal jurisdiction"	6(1.8)	7(3.6)
2 "magistrate"	2 "magistrate" [rep. R.S. 1985, c. 27 (1st. Supp.), s. 2(4)]	6(1.9)	7(3.7)
		6(1.91)	7(3.71)
		6(1.92)	7(3.72)
2 "motor vehicle"	2 "motor vehicle"	6(1.93)	7(3.73)
2 "peace officer"	2 "peace officer"	6(1.94)	7(3.74)
(d.1)	(e)	6(1.95)	7(3.75)
(e)	(f)	6(1.96)	7(3.76)
(f)	(g)	6(1.97)	7(3.77)
2 "railway equipment"	2 "railway equipment"	6(2)	7(4)
2 "superior court of criminal juridiction"	2 "superior court of criminal jurisdiction"	6(3)	7(5)
		6(3.1)	7(5.1)
(c)	(c)	6(4)	7(6)
(d)	(e)	6(5)	7(7)
(e)	(d)	6(6)	7(8)
(f)	(f)	6(7)	7(9)
(g)	(g)	6(8)	7(10)
2.1	3	6(9)	7(11)
Part I	Part I	7	8
3(1)	4	7(1)(a)	8(1)(b)
3(2)	4(1)	7(1)(b)	8(1)(a)
3(3)	4(2)	8	9
3(4)	4(3)	9	10
3(5)	4(4)	10	11
3(6)	4(5)	11	12
3(7)	4(6)	12	13
3(8)	4(7)	13	—
4	5	14	14
5	6	15	15
6	7	16	16
6(1.1)	7(2)	17	17
6(1.2)	7(3)	18	18
6(1.3)	7(3.1)	19	19
6(1.4)	7(3.2)	20	20
		21	21
		22	22

Conc.

Table of Concordance

R.S.C. 1970, c. C-34	R.S.C. 1985, c. C-46
23	23
23.1	23.1 [en. R.S. 1985, c. 24 (2nd Supp.), s. 45]
24	24
25	25
26	26
27	27
28	28
29	29
30	30
31	31
32	32
33	33
—	33.1 [en. 1995, c. 32, s. 1]
34	34
35	35
36	36
37	37
38	38
39	39
40	40
41	41
42	42
43	43
44	44
45	45
Part II	Part II
46	46
47	47
48	48
49	49
50	50
51	51
52	52
53	53
54	54
55	55
56	—
57	56
58	57
59	58
60	59
61	60
62	61
63	62

R.S.C. 1970, c. C-34	R.S.C. 1985, c. C-46
64	63
65	64
66	65
67	66
68	67
69	68
70	69
71	70
72	71
73	72
74	73
75	74
76	75
76.1	76
76.2	77
76.3	78
—	78.1 [en. 1993, c. 7, s. 4]
77	79
78	80
79	81
80	82
81	83
Part II.1	Part III

(Note: Part III, R.S.C. 1985, c. C-46 replaced by S.C. 1995, c. 39. See the end of this Table for a Table of Equivalent Sections.)

R.S.C. 1970, c. C-34	R.S.C. 1985, c. C-46
82	84
83	85
84	86
85	87
86	88
87	89
88	90
88(1)	90(1)
88(2)	90(2)
88(3)	90(3)
—	90(3.1) [en. 1991, c. 28, s. 6; rep. 1994, c. 44, s. 6]
—	90(3.2) [en. 1991, c. 40, s. 4(2)]
88(4)	90(4)
—	90.1 [en. 1991, c. 40, s. 4(3)]
89	91
—	91.1 [en. 1991, c. 40, s. 6]

Table of Concordance

R.S.C. 1970, c. C-34	R.S.C. 1985, c. C-46	R.S.C. 1970, c. C-34	R.S.C. 1985, c. C-46
90	92	106.4	112
91	93	106.5	113
92	94	106.6	114
93	95	106.7	115
—	95.1 [3n. 1991, c. 40, s. 9]	106.8	116
		106.9	117
94	96	Part III	Part IV
95	97	107	118
96	98	108	119
97	99	109	120
98	100	110	121
98(11) "appeal court"	100(11) "appeal court"	111	122
		112	123
(a)	(d)	113	124
(b)	(b.1) [rep. 1992, c. 51, s. 33(1)]	114	125
		115	126
(b.1)	(a)	116	127
(c)	(b)	117	128
(d)	(c)	118	129
(e)	—	119	130
(f)	(e)	120	131
99	101	121	132
100	102	122	133
101	103	122.1	134
102	104	123	135 [rep. R.S. 1985, c. 27 (1st. Supp.), s. 17]
103	105		
104	106		
104(1)	106(1)	124	136
104(2)	106(2)	125	137
—	106(3)	126	138
104(3)	106(4)	127	139
104(4)	106(5)	128	140
104(5)	106(6)	129	141
104(6)	106(7)	130	142
104(7)	106(8)	131	143
104(8)	106(9)	132	144
104(9)	106(10)	133	145
104(10)	106(11)	133(7)	145(7) [rep. 1985, c. 27 (1st Supp.), s. 20(2)]
104(11)	106(12)		
104(12)	106(13)		
105	107	134	146
106	108	135	147
106.1	109	136	148
—	109.1 [en. 1991, c. 40, s. 22]	137	149
		Part IV	Part V
106.2	110	138	150
106.3	111	139	150.1

R.S.C. 1970, c. C-34	R.S.C. 1985, c. C-46	R.S.C. 1970, c. C-34	R.S.C. 1985, c. C-46
140	150.1(1) [en. R.S. 1985, c. 19 (3rd Supp.), s. 1]	163	167
		164	168
—	150.1(2)	165	169
—	150.1(3)	166	170
—	150.4	167	171
—	150.5	168	172
—	151	168(1)	172(1)
—	152	168(2)	172(2) [rep. R.S. 1985, c. 19 (3rd Supp.), s. 6]
142–145	—		
—	153	168(3)	172(3)
147	154 [rep. R.S. 1985, c. 19 (3rd Supp.), s. 1]	168(4)	172(4)
		169	173
148–149	—	169(1)	173(1)
150	155	169(2)	173(2)
151–153	156–158 [rep. 1985, c. 19 (3rd Supp.), s. 2]	170	174
		171	175
154	159	172	176
155	160	173	177
156	—	174	178
157–158	161–162 [rep. 1985, c. 19 (3rd Supp.), s. 4]	175	179
—	161 [en. 1993, c. 45, s. 1]	175(1)(a)	—
		175(1)(b)	—
159	163	175(1)(c)	—
159(1)	163(1)	175(1)(d)	179(1)(a)
159(2)	163(2)	175(1)(e)	179(1)(b)
159(3)	163(3)	175(2)	179(2)
159(4)	163(4)	175(3)	—
159(5)	163(5)	176	180
159(6)	163(6) [rep. 1993, c. 46, s. 1]	177	181
		178	182
159(7)	163(7)	Part IV.1	Part VI
159(8)	163(8)	178.1	183
—	163.1 [en. 1993, c. 46, s. 2]	178.1 "offence"	183 "offence"
		—	183.1 [en. 1993, c. 40, s. 2]
160	164	178.11	184
160(8) "court"	164(8) "court"	178.11(1)	184(1)
(a)	(a)	178.11(2)	184(2)
(a.1)	(b)	178.11(3)	184(3) [rep. 1993, c. 40, s. 3(3)]
(b)	(c)		
(c)	(d)	—	184.1 [en. 1993, c. 40, s. 4]
161	165		
162	166 [rep. 1994, c. 44, s. 9]	—	184.2 [en. 1993, c. 40, s. 4]
		—	184.3 [en. 1993, c. 40, s. 4]

R.S.C. 1970, c. C-34	R.S.C. 1985, c. C-46	R.S.C. 1970, c. C-34	R.S.C. 1985, c. C-46
—	184.4 [en. 1993, c. 40, s. 4]	178.2	193
—	184.5 [en. 1993, c. 40, s. 4]	—	193.1 [en. 1993, c. 40, s. 12]
—	184.6 [en. 1993, c. 40, s. 4]	178.2(2)(e)	193(2)(e)
178.12	185	178.21	194
178.12(1)(e.1)	185(1)(f)	178.22	195
178.12(1)(f)	185(1)(g)	178.22(2)(g.1)	195(2)(h)
178.12(1)(g)	185(1)(h)	178.22(2)(h)	195(2)(i)
178.13	186	178.22(2)(i)	195(2)(j)
178.13(1.1)	186(2)	178.22(2)(j)	195(2)(k)
178.13(1.2)	186(3)	178.22(2)(k)	195(2)(l)
178.13(2)	186(4)	178.22(2)(l)	195(2)(m)
178.13(2.1)	186(5)	178.22(2)(m)	195(2)(n)
178.13(3)	186(6)	178.23	196
178.13(4)	186(7)	178.23(1)	196(1)
178.14	187	178.23(2)	—
178.15	188	178.23(3)	196(2)
178.15(1)	188(1)	178.23(4)	196(3)
178.15(2)	188(2)	178.23(5)	196(4)
178.15(3)	188(3) [rep. 1993, c. 40, s. 8]	Part V	Part VII
		179	197
178.15(4)(a)	188(4)(a)	180	198
178.15(4)(b)	188(4)(b)	181	199
178.15(4)(b.1)	188(4)(e.1)	182–183	—
178.15(4)(c)	188(4)(f.1)	184	200 [rep. R.S. 1985, c. 27 (1st Supp.), s. 30]
178.15(4)(c.1)	188(4)(d)	185	201
178.15(4)(c.2)	188(4)(c)	186	202
178.15(4)(d)	188(4)(e)	187	203
178.15(4)(e)	188(4)(f)	188	204
178.15(4)(f)	188(4)(g)	188(6.1)	204(7)
178.15(4)(g)	188(4)(h)	188(6.2)	204(8)
—	188.1 [en. 1993, c. 40, s. 9]	188(6.3)	204(8.1)
178.16	189	188(7)	204(9)
178.16(1)	189(1) [rep. 1993, c. 40, s. 10]	188(7.1)	204(9.1)
		188(8)	204(10)
178.16(2)	189(2) [rep. 1993, c. 40, s. 10]	188(9)	204(11)
178.16(3)	189(3) [rep. 1993, c. 40, s. 10]	188.1	205 [rep. 1985, c. 52 (1st Supp.), s.1]
178.16(3.1)	189(4)	189	206
178.16(4)	189(5)	190	207
178.16(5)	189(6)	191	208 [rep. R.S. 1985, c. 27 (1st Supp.), s. 32]
178.17	190		
178.18	191	192	209
178.19	192	193	210

R.S.C. 1970, c. C-34	R.S.C. 1985, c. C-46	R.S.C. 1970, c. C-34	R.S.C. 1985, c. C-46
194	211	228	244; 244.1 [en. 1995, c. 39, s. 144]
195	212		
195(2)–(4)	212	229	245
195.1	213	230	246
Part VI	Part VIII	231	247
196	214	232	248
196 "operate"	214 "operate"	233	249
197	215	233(1)(d)	249(1)(d)
198	216	234	250
199	217	235	251
200	218	235(1)(c)	251(1)(c)
201	—	235(2)(c)	251(2)(c)
202	219	235(3)	251(3)
203	220	236	252
204	221	237	253
205	222	238	254
206	223	238(2)	254(2)
207	224	238(6)	254(6)
208	225	239	255
209	226	240	256
210	227	240.1	257
211	228	241	258
212	229	241(1)(a)	258(1)(a)
213	230	242	259
214	231	242(1)	259(1)
214(1)	231(1)	242(2)	259(2)
214(2)	231(2)	242(4)	259(4)
214(3)	231(3)	242(5)(a)	259(5)(a)
214(4)	231(4)	243	260
214(5)	231(5)	243.1	261
214(6)	231(6) [rep. R.S. 1985, c. 27 (1st Supp.), s. 35]	243.2	262
		243.3	263
214(7)	231(7)	—	264 [rep. R.S. 1985, c. 27 (1st Supp.), s. 37]
215	232		
216	233		264 [en. 1993, c. 45, s. 2]
217	234		
218	235	243.4	264.1
219	236	244	265
220	237	245	266
221	238	245.1	267
222	239	245.2	268
223	240	245.3	269
224	241	245.4	269.1
225	—	246	270
226	242	246.1	271
227	243	246.1(1)	271(1)

R.S.C. 1970, c. C-34	R.S.C. 1985, c. C-46	R.S.C. 1970, c. C-34	R.S.C. 1985, c. C-46
246.1(2)	271(2) [rep. R.S. 1985, c. 19 (3rd Supp.), s. 10]	253	289 [rep. R.S. 1985, s. 27 (1st Supp.), s. 41]
246.2	272	254	290
246.3	273	255	291
—	273.1 [en. 1992, c. 38, s.1]	256	292
		257	293
—	273.2 [en. 1992, c. 38, s.1]	258	294
		259	295
—	273.3 [en. 1992, c. 38, s.1]	260	296
		261	297
246.4	274	262	298
246.5	275	263	299
246.6	276	264	300
246.6(1)	276(1)	265	301
—	276.1 [en. 1992, c. 38, s.2]	266	302
		267	303
—	276.2 [en. 1992, c. 38, s.2]	268	304
		269	305
—	276.3 [en. 1992, c. 38, s.2]	270	306
		271	307
—	276.4 [en. 1992, c. 38, s.2]	272	308
		273	309
—	276.5 [en. 1992, c. 38, s.2]	274	310
246.7	277	275	311
246.8	278	276	312
247	279	277	313
247.1	279.1 [en. R.S. 1985, c. 27 (1st Supp.), s. 40]	278	314
		279	315
248	—	280	316
		281	317
249	280	281.1	318
250	281	281.2	319
250.1	282	281.3	320
250.2	283	281.3(8) "court"	320(8) "court"
250.3	284	(a)	(a)
250.4	285	(a.1)	(b)
250.5	286	(b)	(c)
251	287	(c)	(d)
251(6) "Minister of Health"	287(6) "Minister of Health"	281.3(8) "judge"	320(8) "judge"
(a)	(a)	Part VII	Part IX
(a.1)	(d)	282	321
(b)	(c)	283	322
(c)	(b)	284	323
(d)	(e)	285	324
252	288	286	325
		287	326

Table of Concordance

R.S.C. 1970, c. C-34	R.S.C. 1985, c. C-46	R.S.C. 1970, c. C-34	R.S.C. 1985, c. C-46
287.1	327	317	359
288	328	318	360
289	329	319	361
290	330	320	362
291	331	321	363
292	332	322	364
293	333	323	365
294	334	324	366
295	335	325	367
295(1)	335(1)	325(1)	367(1)
295(2)	335(2)	325(2)	367(2) [rep. 1994, c. 44, s. 24]
296	336		
297	337	326	368
298	338	327	369
298(1.1)	338(2)	328	370
298(2)	338(3)	329	371
298(3)	338(4)	330	372
299	339	331	373 [rep. R.S. 1985, c. 27 (1st Supp.), s. 53]
300	340		
301	341	332	374
301.1	342	333	375
301.1(1)	342(1)	334	376
301.1(2)	342(2)	335	377
301.1(3)	342(3) [rep. R.S. 1985, c. 27 (1st Supp.), s. 44]	336	378
301.2	342.1 [en. R.S. 1985, c. 27 (1st Supp.), s. 45]	Part VIII	Part X
		337	379
		338	380
		339	381
302	343	340	382
303	344	341	383
304	345	342	384
305	346	343	385
305.1	347	344	386
306	348	345	387
306(3)	—	346	388
306(4)	348(3)	347	389
307	349	348	390
308	350	349	391
309	351	350	392
310	352	351	393
311	353	352	394
312	354	353	395
313	355	354	396
314	356	355	397
315	357	356	398
316	358	357	399

Table of Concordance

R.S.C. 1970, c. C-34	R.S.C. 1985, c. C-46	R.S.C. 1970, c. C-34	R.S.C. 1985, c. C-46
420.15	462.35 [en. R.S. 1985, c. 42 (4th Supp.), s.2]	423	465
		423(1)(c)	—
		423(1)(d)	465(1)(c)
420.16	462.36 [en. R.S. 1985, c. 42 (4th Supp.), s.2]	423(1)(e)	465(1)(d)
		423(2)	465(2) [rep. R.S. 1985, c. 27 (1st Supp.), s. 61(3)]
420.17	462.37 [en. R.S. 1985, c. 42 (4th Supp.), s.2]	423(3)	465(3)
420.18	462.38 [en. R.S. 1985, c. 42 (4th Supp.), s.2]	423(4)	465(4)
		423(5)	465(5)
		—	465(6)
420.19	462.39 [en. R.S. 1985, c. 42 (4th Supp.), s.2]	423(6)	465(7)
		424	466
420.2	462.4 [en. R.S. 1985, c. 42 (4th Supp.), s.2]	425	467
		Part XII	Part XIV
		426	468
420.21	462.41 [en. R.S. 1985, c. 42 (4th Supp.), s.2]	427	469
		428	470
		429	471
420.22	462.42 [en. R.S. 1985, c. 42 (4th Supp.), s.2]	429.1	472 [rep. 1985, c. 27 (1st Supp.), s. 63]
420.23	462.43 [en. R.S. 1985, c. 42 (4th Supp.), s.2]	430	473
		431	474
420.24	462.44 [en. R.S. 1985, c. 42 (4th Supp.), s.2]	431.1	475
		432	476
		433	477
420.25	462.45 [en. R.S. 1985, c. 42 (4th Supp.), s.2]	—	477.1
		—	477.2
420.26	462.46 [en. R.S. 1985, c. 42 (4th Supp.), s.2]	—	477.3
		—	477.4
		434	478
420.27	462.47 [en. R.S. 1985, c. 42 (4th Supp.), s.2]	435	479
		436	480
		437	481
420.28	462.48 [en. R.S. 1985, c. 42 (4th Supp.), s.2]	438	482
		438(1.1)	482(2)
420.29	462.49 [en. R.S. 1985, c. 42 (4th Supp.), s.2]	438(2)	482(3)
		438(3)	–
420.3	462.5 [en. R.S. 1985, c. 42 (4th Supp.), s.2]	438(4)	482(4)
		438(5)	482(5)
		Part XIII	Part XV
Part XI	Part XIII	439	483
421	463	440	484
422	464	440.1	485

Table of Concordance

R.S.C. 1970, c. C-34	R.S.C. 1985, c. C-46	R.S.C. 1970, c. C-34	R.S.C. 1985, c. C-46
455.4	508	462	529 [rep. 1994, c. 44, s. 52]
455.5	509		
455.6	510	Part XIV.1	Part XVII
456	511	462.1	530
456.1	512	462.11	530.1 [en. R.S. 1985, c. 31 (4th Supp.), s. 94]
456.2	513		
456.3	514		
457	515	462.2	531
457(2)(c.1)	515(2)(d)	462.3	532
457(2)(d)	515(2)(e)	462.4	533
457(2.1)	515(2.1)	Part XV	Part XVIII
457(3)	515(3)	463	535
457(4)	515(4)	464	536
457(5)	515(5)	465	537
457(5.1)	515(6)	465(1)(a)	—
457(5.2)	515(7)	465(1)(b)	537(1)(a)
457(5.3)	515(8)	465(1)(c)	537(1)(b)
457(6)	515(9)	465(1)(d)	537(1)(c)
457(7)	515(10)	465(1)(e)	537(1)(d)
457(8)	515(11)	465(1)(f)	537(1)(e)
457.1	516	465(1)(g)	—
457.2	517	465(1)(h)	537(1)(f)
457.3	518	465(1)(i)	537(1)(g)
457.4	519	465(1)(j)	537(1)(h)
457.5	520	465(1)(k)	537(1)(i)
457.6	521	465(2)–(4)	537(2)–(4) [rep. 1991, c. 43, s. 9, Sch. item 3(2)]
457.7	522		
457.7(2.1)	522(3)		
457.7(2.2)	522(4)	466	538
457.7(3)	522(5)	467	539
457.7(4)	522(6)	468	540
457.8	523	469	541
458	524	470	542
458(4.1)	524(5)	471	543
458(4.2)	524(6)	471.1	544
458(4.3)	524(7)	472	545
458(5)	524(8)	473	546
458(5.1)	524(9)	474	547
458(6)	524(10)	474.1	547.1 [en. R.S. 1985, c. 27 (1st Supp.), s. 100]
458(7)	524(11)		
458(8)	524(12)	475	548
458(9)	524(13)	476	549
459	525	477	550
459.1	526	478	551
460	527	479–481	—
461	528	Part XVI	Part XIX

R.S.C. 1970, c. C-34	R.S.C. 1985, c. C-46	R.S.C. 1970, c. C-34	R.S.C. 1985, c. C-46
482	552	496	566
482 "judge"	552 "judge"	497	567
(a)	(a)	498	568
(b)	(b)	499	569 [rep. R.S. 1985, c. 27 (1st Supp.), s. 111]
(c)	(c)		
(c.1)	(d)		
(d)	(g)	500	570
(e)	(e)	501	571
(f)	(h)	502	572
(g) Nfld.	(f) Nfld.	503	573 [rep. R.S. 1985, c. 27 (1st Supp.), s. 113]
(h) P.E.I.	(f) P.E.I.		
(h) Y.T., N.W.T.	(i) Y.T., N.W.T.	Part XVII	Part XX
(i) "magistrate"	(i) "magistrate" [rep. R.S. 1985, c. 27, (1st Supp.), s. 103(2)]	504	574
		505	575 [rep. R.S. 1985, c. 27 (1st Supp.), s. 113]
483	553	506	576
484	554	507	577
484(1)	554(1)	507.1	578
484(2)	554(2) [rep. R.S. 1985, c. 27 (1st Supp.), s. 105)]	508	579
		—	579.1 [en. 1994, c. 44, s. 60]
484(3)	554(3) [rep. R.S. 1985, c. 27 (1st Supp.), s. 105)]	509	580
		510	581
484(4)	554(4) [rep. R.S. 1985, c. 27 (1st Supp.), s. 105)]	511	582
		512	583
485	555	513	584
486	556	514	585
487	557	515	586
488	558	516	587
489	559	517	588
490	560	518	589
490(1)	560(1)	519	590
490(2)	560(2)	520	591
490(3)	560(3)	521	592
490(4)	560(4)	522	593
490(5)	560(5) [rep. R.S. 1985, c. 27 (1st Supp.), s. 109(2)]	523–525	594–596 [rep. R.S. 1985, c. 27 (1st Supp.), s. 120]
491	561	526	597
492	562	526.1	598
493	563	527	599
494	564 [rep. R.S. 1985, c. 27 (1st Supp.), s. 110]	527(1)	599(1)
		527(1.1)	599(2) [rep. R.S. 1985, c. 1 (4th Supp.), s. 16]
495	565	527(2)	599(3)

R.S.C. 1970, c. C-34	R.S.C. 1985, c. C-46	R.S.C. 1970, c. C-34	R.S.C. 1985, c. C-46
527(3)	599(4)	—	635 [en. 1992, c. 41, s. 2]
527(4)	599(5)		
528	600	565	636 [rep. 1992, c. 41, s. 2]
529	601		
530	602 [rep. R.S. 1985, c. 27 (1st Supp.), s. 124]	566	637 [rep. 1992, c. 41, s. 2]
		567	638
531	603	568	639
532	604	569	640
533	605	570	641
533.1	625.1 [en. R.S. 1985, c. 27 (1st Supp.), s. 127]	571	642
		572	643
		573	644
534	606	574	645
535	607	575	646
535(6)	607(6)	576	647
536	608	576.1	648
537	609	576.2	649
538	610	577	650
539	611	578	651
540	612	579	652
541	613	580	653
542–547	614–619 [rep. 1991, c. 43, s. 3]	581	654
		582	655
549	621	583	656
550	622	584	657
551	623	584.1	657.1 [en. R.S. 1985, c. 23 (4th Supp.), s. 3]
552	624		
553	625		
553.1	625.1	585	658
554	626	586	659 [rep. R.S. 1985, c. 19 (3rd Supp.), s. 15]
555	627 [rep. R.S. 1985, c. 2 (1st Supp.), ss. 1 and 3]		
		—	659 [en. 1993, c. 45, s. 9]
556	—		
557	628 [rep. R.S. 1985, c. 27 (1st Supp.), s. 129]	587	660
		588	661
		589	662
558	629	590	663
559	630	591	664
560	631	592	665
561	632	593	666
562	633	594	667
563	634	594(3.1)	667(4)
564 [rep. 1977–78, c. 36, s. 4]	635 [rep. R.S. 1985, c. 2 (1st Supp.), s. 2]	594(4)	667(5)
		595	668
		596	669

R.S.C. 1970, c. C-34	R.S.C. 1985, c. C-46	R.S.C. 1970, c. C-34	R.S.C. 1985, c. C-46
597	669.1 [en. R.S. 1985, c. 27 (1st Supp.), s. 137]	619	—
		620	692
597.1	669.2 [en. R.S. 1985, c. 27 (1st Supp.), s. 137]	620(3)(b)	692(3)(b)
		621	693
—	669.3 [en. 1994, c. 44, s. 66]	621(1)	693(1)
		622	694
598	670	622.1	694.1 [en. R.S. 1985, c. 34 (3rd Supp.), s. 13]
599	671		
600	672	622.2	694.2 [en. R.S. 1985, c. 34 (3rd Supp.), s. 13]
—	Part XX.1 [en. 1991, c. 43, s. 4]		
—	672.1–672.95 [en. 1991, c. 43, s. 4]	623	695
		624	696
Part XVIII	Part XXI	Part XIX	Part XXII
601	673	625	697
601 "sentence"	673 "sentence"	626	698
602	674	627	699
603	675	628	700
603(1.1)	675(2)	629	701
603(2)	675(3)	630	702
603(3)	675(4)	631	703
604	—	631.1	703.1 [en. R.S. 1985, c. 27 (1st Supp.), s. 149]
605	676		
606	677		
607	678	631.2	703.2 [en. R.S. 1985, c. 27 (1st Supp.), s. 149]
607.1	678.1 [en. R.S. 1985, c. 27 (1st Supp.), s. 140]		
		632	704
608	679	633	705
608.1	680	634	706
608.2	681 [rep. 1991, c. 43, s. 9, Sch., item 7]	635	707
		636	708
		637	709
609	682	638	710
610	683	639	711
610(5)	683(5)	640	712
611	684	640(1)	712(1)
612	685	640(2)	712(2)
613	686	640(3)	712(3) [rep. R.S. 1985, c. 27 (1st Supp.), s. 153]
614	687		
615	688		
616	689	641	713
616(1)	689(1)	—	713.1 [en. 1994, c. 44, s.76]
617	690		
618	691	642	714
618(1)(b)	691(1)(b)	643	715

R.S.C. 1970, c. C-34	R.S.C. 1985, c. C-46
643.1	715.1 [en. R.S. 1985, c. 19 (3rd Supp.), s. 16]
Part XX	Part XXIII
(Note: Part XXIII, R.S.C. 1985, c. 46 replaced by S.C. 1995, c. 22. See the end of this Table for a Table of Equivalent Sections.)	
644	716
645	717
646	718
646.1	718.1 [en. R.S. 1985, c. 27 (1st Supp.), s. 156]
647	719
648	720
649	721
650	722
651	723
652	724
653	725
654	726
655	727 [rep. R.S. 1985, c. 27 (1st Supp.), s. 160]
656	728
657	729
658	730
659	731
659(1)	731(1)
659(2)	731(2)
659(3)	731(3)
659(4)	731(4)
659(5)	731(5)
659(6)	731(6) [rep. 1992, c. 20, s. 200(1)]
659(6.1)	731(7) [rep. 1992, c. 20, s. 200(1)]
659(7)	731(8)
—	731.1 [en. 1992, c. 20, s. 201]
660	732
660.1	733
661	734
662	735
662(1.1)	735(1.1)
662(1.2)	735(1.2)
662(1.3)	735(1.3)
662(1.4)	735(1.4)

R.S.C. 1970, c. C-34	R.S.C. 1985, c. C-46
662(2)	735(2)
662.1	736
663	737
664	738
665	739
666	740
667	741 [rep. R.S. 1985, c. 27 (1st Supp.), s. 164]
668	741.1 [rep. R.S. 1985, c. 24 (2nd Supp.), s. 47]
—	741.2 [en. 1992, c. 20, s. 203]
669	742
—	742.1 [en. 1992, c. 11, s. 16]
670	743
—	743.1 [en. 1992, c. 11, s. 16]
671	744
—	744.1 [en. 1992, c. 11, s. 16]
672	745
672(6)(a)	745(6)
672(6)(a)(i)	745(6)(e)
672(6)(a)(ii)	745(6)(c)
672(6)(a)(iii)	745(6)(d)
672(6)(a)(iv)	—
672(6)(a)(v)	745(6)(a)
672(6)(a)(vi)	745(6)(b)
672(6)(b)	745(6)(f) part
672(6)(c)	745(6)(f) part
673	746
674	747
675–681	—
682	748
682(3.1)	748(4)
682(3.2)	748(5)
682(4)	748(6)
683	749
685	750
686	751
Part XXI	Part XXIV
687	752
688	753
689	754
690	755

R.S.C. 1970, c. C-34	R.S.C. 1985, c. C-46	R.S.C. 1970, c. C-34	R.S.C. 1985, c. C-46
691	756	725(1)	790(1)
692	757	725(2)	790(2)
693	758	725(3)	790(3) [rep. R.S. 1985, c. 27 (1st Supp.), s. 172]
694	759		
695	760		
695.1	761	725(4)	790(4) [rep. R.S. 1985, c. 27 (1st Supp.), s. 172]
Part XXII	Part XXV		
696	762	725(5)	—
697	763	726	
698	764		791 [rep. R.S. 1985, c. 27 (1st Supp.), s. 173]
699	765		
700	766	727	
701	767	728	792 [rep. 1985, c. 27 (1st Supp.), s. 174]
701.1	767.1 [en. R.S. 1985, c. 27 (1st Supp.), s. 167]	729	793 [rep. 1985, c. 27 (1st Supp.), s. 175]
702	768		
703	769		
704	770	730	794
705	771	731	795
706	772	732	796 [rep. 1985, c. 27 (1st Supp.), s. 176]
707	773		
Part XXIII	Part XXVI	732.1	797 [rep. 1985, c. 27 (1st Supp.), s. 176]
708	774		
709	775		
710	776	733	798
711	777	734	799
712	778	735	800
713	779	736	801
714	780	736(1)	801(1)
715	781	736(2)	801(2)
716	782	736(3)	801(3)
717	783	736(4)	801(4) [rep. R.S. 1985, c. 27 (1st Supp.), s. 177(2)]
718	—		
719	784	736(5)	801(5) [rep. R.S. 1985, c. 27 (1st Supp.), s. 177(2)
Part XXIV	Part XXVII		
720	785		
721	786	737	802
722	787	738	803
722(1)	787(1)	738(2)	—
722(2)	787(2)	738(3)	803(2)
722(3)–(11)	787(3)–(11) [rep. R.S. 1985, c. 27 (1st Supp.), s. 171]	738(3.1)	803(3)
723	788	738(4)	803(4)
724	789	738(5)–(8)	803(5)–(8) [rep. 1991, c. 43, s. 9, Sch., item 11]
725	790		

R.S.C. 1970, c. C-34	R.S.C. 1985, c. C-46	R.S.C. 1970, c. C-34	R.S.C. 1985, c. C-46
739	804	765	833
740	805 [rep. R.S. 1985, c. 27 (1st Supp.), s. 179]	766	834
		767	835
		768	836
741	806	769	837
742	807	770	838
743	808	771	839
744	809	772	840
745	810	Part XXV	Part XXVIII
—	810.1 [en. 1993, c. 45, s. 11]	773	841
		773(3)	841(3)
746	811	Forms 1–2	Forms 1–2
747	812	Form 3	Form 3 [rep. R.S. 1985, c. 27 (1st Supp.), s. 184(2)]
747 "appeal court"	812 "appeal court"		
747(a)	812(f)	Form 4	Form 4
747(b)	812(g)	Form 5	Form 5
747(c)	812(c)	Form 5.1	Form 5.1 [en. R.S. 1985, c. 27 (1st Supp.), s. 184(3)]
747(d)	812(b)		
747(e)	812(a)		
747(f)	812(d)	Form 5.2	Form 5.2 [en. R.S. 1985, c. 27 (1st Supp.), s. 184(3)]
747(g)	—		
747(h)	812(e) [rep. 1992, c. 51, s. 43(2)]	Form 5.3	Form 5.3 [en. R.S. 1985, c. 42 (4th Supp.), s. 6]
747(i)	812(h)		
748	813		
749	814	Form 6	Form 6
750	815	Form 7	Form 7
751	—	Form 8	Form 8
752	816	Form 8.1	Form 9
752.1	817	Form 8.2	Form 10
752.2	818	Form 8.3	Form 11
752.3	819	—	Form 11.1 [en. 1994, c. 44, s. 84]
753	820		
754	821	Form 9	Form 12
755	822	Form 9.1	Form 13
755.1	823 [rep. 1991, c. 43, s. 9, Sch., item 14]	Form 9.2	Form 14
		Form 10	Form 15
		Form 11	Form 16
756	824	Form 12	Form 17
757	825	Form 13	Form 18
758	826	Form 14	Form 19
759	827	Form 15	—
760	828	Form 16	Form 20
761	829	Form 17	—
762	830	Form 18	Form 21
763	831	Form 19	Form 22
764	832	Form 20	Form 23

Table of Concordance

R.S.C. 1970, c. C-34	R.S.C. 1985, c. C-46	R.S.C. 1970, c. C-34	R.S.C. 1985, c. C-46
Form 21	Form 24	Form 38	Form 42
Form 22	Form 25	Form 39	Form 43
Form 23	Form 26	Forms 40–41	—
Form 24	Form 27	Form 42	Form 44
Form 25	Form 28	Form 43	Form 45
Form 25.1	Form 29	Form 44	Form 46
Form 26	Form 30	Form 45	Form 47 [en. R.S. 1985, c. 42 (4th Supp.), s.8]
Form 27	Form 31		
Form 28	Form 32		
Form 29	Form 33	—	Form 48 [en. 1991, c. 43, s. 8]
Form 30	Form 34		
Form 31	Form 35	—	Form 49 [en. 1991, c. 43, s. 8]
Form 32	Form 36		
Form 33	Form 37	—	Form 50 [en. 1991, c. 43, s. 8]
Form 34	Form 38		
Form 35	Form 39	—	Form 51 [en. 1991, c. 43, s. 8]
Form 36	Form 40		
Form 37	Form 41	774	—

Part III: Firearms and Other Weapons

Table of Equivalent Sections

The *Firearms Act*, S.C. 1995, c. 39 repeals and replaces Part III of the *Criminal Code*. What follows is a table of equivalent sections and subsections which identify, insofar as possible, the substantive correspondence between sections and subsections of the new and old Part III. Note that certain of the provisions of the old Part III also correspond to the provisions of the *Firearms Act* itself.

Part III S.C. 1995, c. 39	Part III R.S.C. 1985, c. C-46 (prior to enactment of S.C. 1995, c. 39)	Part III S.C. 1995, c. 39	Part III R.S.C. 1985, c. C-46 (prior to enactment of S.C. 1995, c. 39)
84(1)	84(1)	91(5)	—
84(2)	84(1.1)	92(1)	—
84(3)	84(2)	92(2), (3)	91(1)
84(3.1)	—	92(4)	91(4)
84(4)	—	92(5), (6)	—
85	85	93	91(2)
86(1)	86(2)	94(1), (2)	90(2); 91(3)
86(2)	86(3)	94(3)	—
86(3)	86(2), (3)	94(4)	90(4); 91(5)
87	86(1)	94(5)	—
88	87	95	—
89	88	96	—
90	89	97	—
91(1)	—	98	—
91(2), (3)	90(1); 91(1)	99	93; 94; 95; 96; 97
91(4)(a)	90(3.1); 91(4)(b)	100	—
91(4)(b)	91(4)(c)		

Part III S.C. 1995, c. 39	Part III R.S.C. 1985, c. C-46 (prior to enactment of S.C. 1995, c. 39)	Part III S.C. 1995, c. 39	Part III R.S.C. 1985, c. C-46 (prior to enactment of S.C. 1995, c. 39)
101	93(1); 94; 95; 96; 97	117.011	—
		117.012	—
102	95.1	117.02	101
103	95(1)	117.03	102
104	95(1); 96(3); 97(3)	117.04	103(1), (2), (3), (3.1)
105(1)	104(1), (2); 105(2), (8)		
		117.05(1)	103(4)
105(2)	104(5); 105(8)	117.05(2)	103(4.1)
106	105(2); 105(8)	117.05(3)	103(5)
107	—	117.05(4)	103(6)
108	104(3), (3.1), (4), (5)	117.05(5)	—
		117.05(6)	—
109	100(1), (1.1), (1.3)	117.05(7)-(9)	103(8)
110	100(2), (2.1), (3)	117.06(1)	103(7)
111(1)	100(4)	117.06(2)	103(7.1)
111(2)	100(5)	117.07	92; 98(1), (3)
111(3)	100(6)	117.08	92; 98(2)
111(4)	100(9)	117.09(1), (2)	91(6); 99
111(5)	100(7)	117.09(3)	–
111(7)	—	117.09(4), (5), (6), (7)	92(2); 98(3)
111(8)-(10)	100(10)		
111(11)	100(11)	117.1	–
112	—	117.11	115(1)
113	100(1.1), (1.2)	117.12	115(2)
114	—	117.13	–
115	100(13)	117.14	91.1
116	100(7.1)	117.15	116; 84(1) "prohibited weapon"; "restrictred weapon"
117	—		
117.01	100(12); 103(10)		

Part XXIII: Sentencing

Table of Equivalent Sections

Bill C-41 (1995, c. 22) repealed and replaced the whole of Part XXIII of the *Criminal Code*, R.S.C. 1985, c. C-46. The substance of many of the sections of Part XXIII as it existed prior to the proclamation of Bill C-41 (1995, c. 22) was carried over into the new Part XXIII, but because many new sections were introduced, a complete renumbering of sections was required. What follows is a table of equivalent sections and subsections, which identifies, insofar as possible, the substantive correspondence between sections and subsections, of the "new" and "old" Part XXIII.

Part XXIII S.C. 1995, c. 22	Part XXIII R.S.C. 1985, c. C-46	Part XXIII S.C. 1995, c. 22	Part XXIII R.S.C. 1985, c. C-46
"New" section	Prior equivalent section/subsection	"New" section	Prior equivalent section/subsection
716	716	717.1	—
717	—	717.2	—

Table of Concordance

Part XXIII S.C. 1995, c. 22 "New" section	Part XXIII R.S.C. 1985, c. C-46 Prior equivalent section/subsection	Part XXIII S.C. 1995, c. 22 "New" section	Part XXIII R.S.C. 1985, c. C-46 Prior equivalent section/subsection
745.2	743	746.1(1)	747(1)
745.3	743.1	746.1(2)	747(2)
745.4	744	746.1(3)	747(2.1)
745.5	744.1	(Note: ss. 747 to 747.8 not in force at date of publication.)	
745.6	745		
745.6(2)(a)	745(2)	748	749
745.6(2)(b)	745(2)	748.1	750
745.6(2)(c)	745(2)	749	751
745.6(2)(d)	—	750	748
745.6(2)(e)	745(2)	750(1) [two years or more]	748(1) [exceeding five years]
745.6(3)	—		
745.6(4)	745(3)	750(2)	748(2)
745.6(5)	745(4)	750(3)	748(3)
745.6(6)	745(5)	750(4)	748(4)
745.6(7)	745(6)	750(5)	748(5)
745.6(8)	745(7)	750(6)	748(6)
746	746	751	728
746.1	747	751.1	729

TABLE OF AMENDMENTS

Amendments to Criminal Statutes

(Note: The references in square brackets are to the pre-revision statute numbers.)

CRIMINAL CODE, R.S., c. C-46

Amendments	*Coming Into Force*
R.S., c. 2 (1st Supp.) [1977–78, c. 36]	— in force January 1, 1990
R.S., c. 11 (1st Supp.) [1984, c. 41]	— in force January 1, 1985; *see* s. 3
R.S., c. 27 (1st Supp.) [1985, c. 19]	— ss. 1–35, 37–93, 96–126 and 128–208; ss. 249–253, 254(1) and (3)–(6) and 255(1)–(4) and 256–261, with the exception of 258(1)(c)(i) and 258(1)(g)(iii)(A) of the *Criminal Code*, as enacted by s. 36; in each of the Provinces, s. 254(2) of the *Criminal Code*, as enacted by s. 36; in the Provinces of N.B., Manitoba, P.E.I., Alberta and Saskatchewan, and in the Yukon and the N.W.T., s. 255(5) of the *Criminal Code*, as enacted by s. 36, proclaimed in force December 4, 1985; *see* SI/85-211
	— s. 94 proclaimed in force September 1, 1987 in the Provinces of N.S., P.E.I. and Saskatchewan, in respect of offences punishable on summary conviction; and in the Province of Saskatchewan, in respect of indictable offences; *see* SI/87-180
	— s. 255(5) of the *Criminal Code*, as enacted by s. 36, proclaimed in force January 1, 1988 in the Province of N.S.; *see* SI/88-24
	— s. 127, as amended by R.S., c. 1 (4th Supp.), s. 45, proclaimed in force September 1, 1988; *see* SI/88-125
R.S., c. 31 (1st Supp.) [1985, c. 26]	— s. 61 proclaimed in force October 2, 1986; *see* SI/86-192
R.S., c. 47 (1st Supp.) [1985, c. 44]	— proclaimed in force November 1, 1985; *see* SI/85-204
R.S., c. 51 (1st Supp.) [1985, c. 50]	— in force December 20, 1985
R.S., c. 52 (1st Supp.) [1985, c. 52]	— proclaimed in force December 31, 1985; *see* SI/86-5
R.S., c. 1 (2d Supp.) [1986, c. 1]	— s. 213 proclaimed in force November 10, 1986; *see* SI/86-206
R.S., c. 24 (2d Supp.) [1986, c. 32]	— ss. 45–47 proclaimed in force September 1, 1986; *see* SI/86-152
R.S., c. 27 (2d Supp.) [1986, c. 35]	— s. 10 (Schedule, items 6(2), (10) and (11) and s. 11 proclaimed in force September 2, 1986; *see* SI/86-175; s. 10 (Schedule, items 6(1), (4)–(9) and (13)–(16)) proclaimed in force October 1, 1987; *see* SI/87-221
R.S., c. 35 (2d Supp.) [1986, c. 43]	— proclaimed in force July 25, 1986; *see* SI/86-148
R.S., c. 10 (3d Supp.) [1987, c. 13]	— proclaimed in force June 1, 1987; *see* SI/87-128
R.S., c. 19 (3d Supp.) [1987, c. 24]	— proclaimed in force January 1, 1988; *see* SI/87-259
R.S., c. 30 (3d Supp.) [1987, c. 37]	— ss. 1 and 2 in force September 16, 1987
R.S., c. 34 (3d Supp.) [1987, c. 42]	— ss. 9–13 proclaimed in force April 25, 1988; see SI/88-87
R.S., c. 1 (4th Supp.) [1988, c. 2]	— in force February 4, 1988

Table of Amendments

Amendments	*Coming Into Force*
1991, c. 43	— proclaimed in force Feb. 4, 1992, except ss. 672.64, 672.65, 672.66 of the *Criminal Code* as enacted by s. 4; ss. 5, 6, and 10(8) to be proclaimed; *see* SI/92-9. Not in force as of May 1, 1997; *note* ss. 5, 6 repealed by 1995, c. 22, s. 12
1992, c. 1	— in force Feb. 28, 1992 except s. 58(1) (Schedule I, item 13) in force on day which para. 725(b) of the *Criminal Code* as enacted by s. 6 of *An act to amend the Criminal Code (victims of crime)*, R.S. 1985, c. 23 (4th Supp.) comes into force; *see* s. 58(2). *Note* ss. 58(1), (2) repealed by 1995, c. 22, ss. 14, 15
1992, c. 11	— in force May 15, 1992; *see* SI/92-82
1992, c. 20	— proclaimed in force November 1, 1992 except s. 204; *see* SI/92-197. *Note* s. 204 repealed by 1995, c. 42, s. 61
1992, c. 21	— s. 9 proclaimed in force June 30, 1992; *see* SI/92-126
1992, c. 22	— s. 12 proclaimed in force July 24, 1992; *see* SI/92-134
1992, c. 27	— s. 90 proclaimed in force November 30, 1992; see SI/92-194
1992, c. 38	— proclaimed in force August 15, 1992; *see* SI/92-136
1992, c. 41	— deemed in force July 23, 1992; *see* s. 8
1992, c. 47	— ss. 68-72 in force August 1, 1996, *see* SI/96-56. *Note*, ss. 68-72 amended by 1994, c. 44, s. 94, 1996, c. 7, ss. 38 and 42
1992, c. 51	— ss. 32 to 43 and 67 proclaimed in force January 30, 1993; see SI/93-11
1993, c. 7	— in force September 1, 1993; *see* SI/93-79
1993, c. 25	— ss. 94–96 in force June 10, 1993; s. 93 deemed in force January 1, 1993
1993, c. 28	— s. 78 in force April 1, 1999
1993, c. 34	— s. 59(1) in force December 15, 1994; *see* SI/94-137
1993, c. 37	— in force September 1, 1993; *see* SI/93-176
1993, c. 40	— in force August 1, 1993; *see* SI/93-154
1993, c. 45	— in force August 1, 1993; *see* SI/93-156
1993, c. 46	— in force August 1, 1993; *see* SI/93-155
1994, c. 12	— s. 1 in force July 1, 1994; *see* SI/94-83
1994, c. 13	— s. 7(1)(b) in force May 12, 1994
1994, c. 38	— ss. 14, 25(1)(g) in force January 12, 1995; *see* SI/95-9
1994, c. 44	— ss. 2-8(1), 9-38, 44-83, 94, 103 proclaimed in force February 15, 1995, *see* SI/95-20; ss. 8(2), 39-43 and 84 proclaimed in force April 1, 1995; *see* SI/95-20
1995, c. 5	— s. 25(1)(g) in force May 13, 1995; *see* SI/95-65
1995, c. 19	— ss. 37–41 in force December 1, 1995; *see* SI/95-116
1995, c. 22	— ss. 1-12, other than subsection 718.3(5) and ss. 747 to 747.8 of the *Criminal Code*, as enacted by s. 6 of the Act, ss. 14, 15, 18 to 24 and 26 in force September 3, 1996, *see* SI/96-79
	— subsection 718.3(5) and ss. 747 to 747.8 of the *Criminal Code*, as enacted by s. 6, not in force as of May 1, 1998
1995, c. 27	ss. 1, 3 in force July 13, 1995
1995, c. 29	ss. 39, 40 in force November 1, 1995; *see* SI/95-115
1995, c. 32	— in force September 15, 1995; *see* SI/95-101

Table of Amendments

Amendments	*Coming Into Force*
1995, c. 39	— ss. 141-150 and s. 139 as it affects s. 85 of the Code in force January 1, 1996; see SI/96-2
	— ss. 138, 139 (except to the extent that it replaces section 85 and 97 of the Code), 140, 151-157, 163, 164, 188(a), (b), 190 in force December 1, 1998; see SI/98-93 as amended by SI/98-95
1995, c. 42	— ss. 73-76, 86, 87 in force January 24, 1996; *see* SI/96-10
1996, c. 7	— ss. 38 and 42 in force July 31, 1996; *see* SI/96-57
1996, c. 8	— s. 32 in force July 12, 1996; *see* SI/96-69
1996, c. 16	— s. 60 in force July 12, 1996; *see* SI/96-67
1996, c. 19	— ss. 61, 65-76 and 93.3 in force May 14, 1997; *see* SI/97-47
1996, c. 31	— ss. 67-72 in force January 31, 1997; *see* SI/97-21
1996, c. 34	— ss. 2(2), 6-8 in force January 9, 1997; *see* SI/97-12, ss. 1, 2(1), 3-5 not in force as of May 1, 1998
1997, c. 9	— s. 124 not in force May 1, 1998
1997, c. 16	— Act in force May 26, 1997
1997, c. 17	— ss. 1-10 in force August 1, 1997; *see* SI/97-84
1997, c. 18	— ss. 107.1 and 139.1 in force May 2, 1997; *see* SI/97-60; ss. 23, 27 to 39, 99, 100, 109 and 140 in force May 14, 1997, *see* SI/97-62; ss. 2 to 22, 24 to 26, 40 to 98, 101 to 105, 108, 110 to 115 and 141 in force June 16, 1997, *see* SI/97-68, *see also* SI/97-62
	— ss. 106 and 107 not in force May 1, 1998
1997, c. 23	— Act in force May 2, 1997; *see* SI/97-61
1997, c. 30	— Act in force May 12, 1997
1997, c. 39	— ss. 1 to 3 in force December 18, 1997
1998, c. 7	— ss. 2, 3 not in force as of February 17, 1999
1998, c. 9	— ss. 2-8 in force June 30, 1998
1998, c. 15	— s. 20 in force June 11, 1998
1998, c. 30	— ss. 14, 16 not in force as of June 1, 1999
1998, c. 34	— ss. 8, 9 in force February 14, 1999; s. 11 not in force as of June 1, 1999
1998, c. 35	— ss. 119-121 not in force as of June 1, 1999
1998, c. 37	— ss. 15-24 not in force as of June 1, 1999
1999, c. 2	— s. 47 in force March 18, 1999
1999, c. 3	— ss. 25-58 in force April 1, 1999
1999, c. 5	— ss. 6, 7 in force March 15, 1999; ss. 1-5, 8, 10-24, 26-28; 43-50 in force May 1, 1999; ss. 25, 29-42 in force July 7, 1999

CANADA EVIDENCE ACT, R.S., c. C-5

Amendments	*Coming Into Force*
R.S., c. 19 (3d Supp.) [1987, c. 24]	— proclaimed in force January 1, 1988; *see* SI/87-259
1992, c. 1	— s. 142(1) (Schedule V, item 9(1)) in force Feb. 28, 1992
	— s. 142(1) (Schedule V, item 9(2)) in force on day following the day on which the *Small Loans Act*, R.S. 1970, c. S-11 is repealed. Not in force as of May 1, 1996
1992, c. 47	— s. 66 in force July 1, 1996; *see* SI/96-56
1993, c. 28	— s. 78 in force April 1, 1999
1993, c. 34	— s. 15 in force June 23, 1993

Table of Amendments

Table of Amendments

NARCOTIC CONTROL ACT, R.S., c. N-1 [Repealed 1996, c. 19, s. 94]

Amendments	Coming Into Force
R.S., c. N-1	— Part II not in force as of May 1, 1994; see s. 28
R.S., c. 27 (1st Supp.) [1985, c. 19]	— ss. 196–200 proclaimed in force December 4, 1985; see SI/85-211
R.S., c. 27 (2d Supp.) [1986, c. 35]	— s. 10 (Schedule, item 17) proclaimed in force October 1, 1987; see SI/87-221; s. 11 proclaimed in force September 2, 1986; see SI/86-175
R.S., c. 42 (4th Supp.) [1988, c. 51]	— s. 12 proclaimed in force January 1, 1989; see SI/88-230
1990, c. 16	— s. 18 proclaimed in force July 1, 1990; see SI/90-90
1990, c. 17	— s. 36 proclaimed in force September 1, 1990; see SI/90-106
1992, c. 1	— s. 98 in force Feb. 28, 1992
1992, c. 20	— ss. 215, 216 proclaimed in force November 1, 1992; see SI/92-197
1992, c. 51	— ss. 59 and 67 proclaimed in force January 30, 1993; see SI/93-11
1993, c. 28	— s. 78 in force April 1, 1999
1993, c. 37	— in force September 1, 1993; see SI/93-176
1996, c. 8	— s. 32 in force July 12, 1996; see SI/96-69
1996, c. 16	— s. 60 in force July 12, 1996; see SI/96-67
1996, c. 19	— s. 94 in force May 14, 1997; see SI/97-47

YOUNG OFFENDERS ACT, R.S., c. Y-1

Amendments	Coming Into Force
R.S., c. 27 (1st Supp.) [1985, c. 19]	— s. 187 proclaimed in force December 4, 1985; see SI/85-211
R.S., c. 24 (2d Supp.) [1986, c. 32]	— ss. 1–30, 37–51 proclaimed in force September 1, 1986 and ss. 31–36 proclaimed in force November 1, 1986; see SI/86-152
R.S., c. 1 (3d Supp.) [1987, c. 1]	— proclaimed in force June 11, 1987; see SI/87-126
R.S., c. 1 (4th) Supp.) [1988, c. 2]	— in force February 4, 1988
1991, c. 43	— ss. 31–36 proclaimed in force Feb. 4, 1992; see SI/92-9
1992, c. 1	— in force Feb. 28, 1992
1992, c. 11	— ss. 1 to 13, and 18 in force May 15, 1992; see SI/92-82
1992, c. 47	— ss. 81 to 83 not in force as of May 14, 1993
1993, c. 28	— s. 78 in force April 1, 1999
1993, c. 45	— in force August 1, 1993; see SI/93-156
1994, c. 26	— s. 76 in force June 23, 1994
1995, c. 19	— in force December 1, 1995; see SI/95-116
1995, c. 22	— ss. 16, 17, 25, 26 in force September 3, 1996; see SI/96-79
1995, c. 27	— in force July 13, 1995
1995, c. 39	— ss. 177-187 and 189 not in force as of May 1, 1997
1996, c. 19	— s. 93.1 in force May 14, 1997; see SI/97-47
1998, c. 15	— s. 41 in force April 1, 1999
1999, c. 3	— ss. 86.89 in force April 1, 1999

FIREARMS ACT, S.C. 1995, c. 39

Amendments	Coming Into Force
	— ss. 118-119 in force April 30, 1996; see P.C. 1996-644

Table of Amendments

CRIMINAL CODE
An Act respecting the criminal law

R.S.C. 1985, c. C-46, as am. R.S.C. 1985, c. 2 (1st Supp.), ss. 1–3; R.S.C. 1985, c. 11 (1st Supp.), s. 2; R.S.C. 1985, c. 27 (1st Supp.), ss. 1–187, 203; R.S.C. 1985, c. 31 (1st Supp.), s. 61; R.S.C. 1985, c. 47 (1st Supp.), s. 1; R.S.C. 1985, c. 51 (1st Supp.), s. 1; R.S.C. 1985, c. 52 (1st Supp.), ss. 1–3; R.S.C. 1985, c. 1 (2d Supp.), s. 213; R.S.C. 1985, c. 24 (2d Supp.), ss. 45–47; R.S.C. 1985, c. 27 (2d Supp.), s. 10; R.S.C. 1985, c. 35 (2d Supp.), s. 34; R.S.C. 1985, c. 10 (3d Supp.), ss. 1, 2; R.S.C. 1985, c. 19 (3d Supp.), ss. 1–16; R.S.C. 1985, c. 30 (3d Supp.), ss. 1, 2; R.S.C. 1985, c. 34 (3d Supp.), ss. 9–13; R.S.C. 1985, c. 1 (4th Supp.), ss. 13–18, 45; R.S.C. 1985, c. 23 (4th Supp.), ss. 1–5, 6 (pt.), 7, 8; R.S.C. 1985, c. 29 (4th Supp.), s. 17; R.S.C. 1985, c. 30 (4th Supp.), s. 45; R.S.C. 1985, c. 31 (4th Supp.), ss. 94–97; R.S.C. 1985, c. 32 (4th Supp.), ss. 55–62; R.S.C. 1985, c. 40 (4th Supp.), s. 2; R.S.C. 1985, c. 42 (4th Supp.), ss. 1–8; R.S.C. 1985, c. 50 (4th Supp.), s. 1; 1989, c. 2, s. 1; 1990, c. 15, s. 1; 1990, c. 16, ss. 2–7; 1990, c. 17, ss. 7–15; 1990, c. 44, s. 15; 1991, c. 1, s. 28; 1991, c. 4, ss. 1, 2; 1991, c. 28, ss. 6–12; 1991, c. 40, ss. 1–41; 1991, c. 43, ss. 1–10; 1992, c. 1, s. 58; 1992, c. 11, ss. 14–18; 1992, c. 20, ss. 199–204, 215, 216, 228, 229; 1992, c. 21, s. 9; 1992, c. 22, s. 12; 1992, c. 27, s. 90; 1992, c. 38; 1992, c. 41; 1992, c. 47, ss. 68–72; 1992, c. 51, ss. 32–43, 67; 1993, c. 7; c. 25, ss. 93–96; 1993, c. 28, s. 78; 1993, c. 34, s. 59(1); 1993, c. 37; 1993, c. 40; 1993, c. 45; 1993, c. 46; 1994, c. 12, s. 1; 1994, c. 13, s. 7; 1994, c. 38, ss. 14, 25; 1994, c. 44, ss. 1–84; 1995, c. 5, s. 25(1)(g); 1995, c. 19, ss. 37–41; 1995, c. 22, ss. 1–12, 14, 15, 19–24; 1995, c. 27, ss. 1, 3; 1995, c. 29, ss. 39, 40; 1995, c. 32, s. 33; 1995, c. 39, ss. 139, 141–150; 1995, c. 42, ss. 73–78, 86, 87; 1996, c. 8, s. 32; 1996, c. 16, s. 60; 1996, c. 19, ss. 65–76, 93.3; 1996, c. 31, ss. 68–72; 1996, c. 34, ss. 2(2), 6–8; 1997, c. 2; 1997, c. 16, ss. 1–7; 1997, c. 17, ss. 1-10; 1997, c. 18, ss. 2-115, 139.1, 140, 141; 1997, c. 17, ss. 1-10; 1997, c. 23, ss. 1–20, 26, 27; 1997, c. 30, ss. 1–3, 1997, c. 39, ss. 1–3; 1998, c. 7, ss. 2,3; 1998, c. 9, ss. 2–8; 1998, s. 15, s. 20; 1998, c. 30, ss. 14, 16; 1998, c. 34, ss. 8, 9, 11; 1998, c. 35, ss. 119–121; 1998, c. 37, ss. 15–24; 1999, c. 2, s. 47; 1999, c. 3, ss. 25–58; 1999, c. 5, ss. 1–47, 51, 52; 1999, c. 17, s. 120

See Table of Amendments for coming into force.

Short Title

1. Short title — This Act may be cited as the *Criminal Code*.

R.S., c. C-34, s. 1.

Commentary: The section provides a short title for "An Act respecting the Criminal Law", the *Criminal Code*.

Related Provisions: The *Code* consists of several Parts that define and punish criminal offences, describe the elements of criminal liability, defence, excuse and exemption, and enact procedural provisions that govern the proceedings from institution through trial to final appeal. It was first enacted as S.C. 189, c. 29 having been drafted by Burbidge J. and Sedgwick J. based on Stephen's *Digest of the Criminal Law* and the *Draft Criminal Code* of 1880, prepared by the Royal Commissioners in England but rejected there. It also consolidated several earlier Canadian statutes on criminal law and procedure.

Apart from the usual process of statutory amendment, consolidation and periodic general revision, the only substantial revision of the *Code* occurred as a result of the work of the Royal Commission appointed by Order in Council P.C. 2275 on May 10, 1951. A Draft Bill prepared by the Commission, after consideration and revision, was presented to Parliament as a Government Bill and debated in the House of Commons and Senate during the sessions of 1952–54. The Bill was passed, as amended, and received Royal Assent on June 26, 1954. It became chapter 51 of S.C. 1953–54 and came into force on April 1, 1955.

References to the *Code* in its sections describe it as "this Act".

Interpretation

2. Definitions — In this Act,

"Act" includes

    (a) an Act of Parliament,

    (b) an Act of the legislature of the former Province of Canada,

    (c) an Act of the legislature of a province, and

    (d) an Act or ordinance of the legislature of a province, territory or place in force at the time that province, territory or placebecame a province of Canada;

"Attorney General"

    (a) with respect to proceedings to which this Act applies, means the Attorney General or Solicitor General of the province in which those proceedings are taken and includes his lawful deputy, and

    (b) with respect to

        (i) the Yukon Territory, the Northwest Territories and Nunavut, or

        (ii) proceedings commenced at the instance of the Government of Canada and conducted by or on behalf of that Government in respect of a contravention of, a conspiracy or attempt to contravene or counselling the contravention of any Act of Parliament other than this Act or any regulation made under any such Act,

means the Attorney General of Canada and includes his lawful deputy;

"bank-note" includes any negotiable instrument

    (a) issued by or on behalf of a person carrying on the business of banking in or out of Canada, and

    (b) issued under the authority of Parliament or under the lawful authority of the government of a state other than Canada,

intended to be used as money or as the equivalent of money, immediately on issue or at some time subsequent thereto, and includes bank bills and bank post bills;

"bodily harm" means any hurt or injury to a person that interferes with the health or comfort of the person and that is more than merely transient or trifling in nature;

"Canadian Forces" means the armed forces of Her Majesty raised by Canada;

"cattle" means neat cattle or an animal of the bovine species by whatever technical or familiar name it is known, and includes any horse, mule, ass, pig, sheep or goat;

"clerk of the court" includes a person, by whatever name or title he may be designated, who from time to time performs the duties of a clerk of the court;

"complainant" means the victim of an alleged offence;

"counsel" means a barrister or solicitor, in respect of the matters or things that barristers and solicitors, respectively, are authorized by the law of a province to do or perform in relation to legal proceedings;

"count" means a charge in an information or indictment;

"court of appeal" means

(a) in the Province of Prince Edward Island, the Appeal Division of the Supreme Court, and

(b) in all other provinces, the Court of Appeal;

"court of criminal jurisdiction" means

(a) a court of general or quarter sessions of the peace, when presided over by a Superior Court judge,

(a.1) in the Province of Quebec, the Court of Quebec, the municipal court of Montreal and the municipal court of Quebec;

(b) a provincial court judge or judge acting under Part XIX, and

(c) in the Province of Ontario, the Ontario Court of Justice;

"criminal organization" means any group, association or other body consisting of five or more persons, whether formally or informally organized,

(a) having as one of its primary activities the commission of an indictable offence under this or any other Act of Parliament for which the maximum punishment is imprisonment for five years or more, and

(b) any or all of the members of which engage in or have, within the preceding five years, engaged in the commission of a series of such offences;

"criminal organization offence" means

(a) an offence under sectiion 467.1 or an indictable offence under this or any other Act of Parliament committed for the benefit of, at the direction of or in association with a criminal organization for which the maximum punishment is imprisonment for five years or more, or

(b) a conspiracy or an attempt to commit, being an accessory after the fact in relation to, or any counselling in relation to, an offence referred to in paragraph (a);

"day" means the period between six o'clock in the forenoon and nine o'clock in the afternoon of the same day;

"document of title to goods" includes a bought and sold note, bill of lading, warrant, certificate or order for the delivery or transfer of goods or any other valuable thing, and any other document used in the ordinary course of business as evidence of the possession or control of goods, authorizing or purporting to authorize, by endorsement or by delivery, the person in possession of the document to transfer or receive any goods thereby represented or therein mentioned or referred to;

"document of title to lands" includes any writing that is or contains evidence of the title, or any part of the title, to real property or to any interest in real property, and any notarial or registrar's copy thereof and any duplicate instrument, memorial, certificate or document authorized or required by any law in force in any part of Canada with respect to registration of titles that relates to title to real property or to any interest in real property;

"dwelling-house" means the whole or any part of a building or structure that is kept or occupied as a permanent or temporary residence, and includes

(a) a building within the curtilage of a dwelling-house that is connected to it by a doorway or by a covered and enclosed passage-way, and

(b) a unit that is designed to be mobile and to be used as a permanent or temporary residence and that is being used as such a residence;

"every one", "person", "owner", and similar expressions include Her Majesty and public bodies, bodies corporate, societies, companies and inhabitants of counties, parishes, municipalities or other districts in relation to the acts and things that they are capable of doing and owning respectively;

"explosive substance" includes

(a) anything intended to be used to make an explosive substance,

(b) anything, or any part thereof, used or intended to be used, or adapted to cause, or to aid in causing an explosion in or with an explosive substance, and

(c) an incendiary grenade, fire bomb, molotov cocktail or other similar incendiary substance or device and a delaying mechanism or other thing intended for use in connection with such a substance or device;

"firearm" means a barrelled weapon from which any shot, bullet or other projectile can be discharged and that is capable of causing serious bodily injury or death to a person, and includes any frame or receiver of such a barrelled weapon and anything that can be adapted for use as a firearm;

"Her Majesty's Forces" means the naval, army and air forces of Her Majesty wherever raised, and includes the Canadian Forces;

"highway" means a road to which the public has the right of access, and includes bridges over which or tunnels through which a road passes;

"indictment" includes

(a) information or a count therein,

(b) a plea, replication or other pleading, and

(c) any record;

"internationally protected person" means

(a) a head of state, including any member of a collegial body that performs the functions of a head of state under the constitution of the state concerned, a head of a government or a minister of foreign affairs, whenever that person is in a state other than the state in which he holds that position or office,

(b) a member of the family of a person described in paragraph (a) who accompanies that person in a state other than the state in which that person holds that position or office,

(c) a representative or an official of a state or an official or agent of an international organization of an intergovernmental character who, at the time when and at the place where an offence referred to in subsection 7(3) is committed against his person or any property referred to in section 431 that is used by him, is entitled, pursuant to international law, to special protection from any attack on his person, freedom or dignity, or

(d) a member of the family of a representative, official or agent described in paragraph (c) who forms part of his household, if the representative, official or agent, at the time when and at the place where any offence referred to in subsection 7(3) is committed against the member of his family or any property referred to in section 431 that is used by that member, is entitled, pursuant to international law, to special protection from any attack on his person, freedom or dignity;

"justice" means a justice of the peace or a provincial court judge, and includes two or more justices where two or more justices are, by law, required to act or, by law, act or have jurisdiction;

"mental disorder" means a disease of the mind;

"military" shall be construed as relating to all or any of the Canadian Forces;

"military law" includes all laws, regulations or orders relating to the Canadian Forces;

"motor vehicle" means a vehicle that is drawn, propelled or driven by any means other than muscular power, but does not include railway equipment;

"municipality" includes the corporation of a city, town, village, county, township, parish or other territorial or local division of a province, the inhabitants of which are incorporated or are entitled to hold property collectively for a public purpose;

"newly-born child" means a person under the age of one year;

"night" means the period between nine o'clock in the afternoon and six o'clock in the forenoon of the following day;

"offence-related property" means any property, within or outside Canada,

(a) by means of or in respect of which a criminal organization offence is committed,

(b) that is used any manner in connection with the commission of a criminal organization offence, or

(c) that is intended for use for the purpose of committing a criminal organization offence,

but does not include real property, other than real property built or significantly modified for the purpose of facilitating the commission of a criminal organization offence;

"offender" means a person who has been determined by a court to be guilty of an offence, whether on acceptance of a plea of guilty or on a finding of guilt;

"offensive weapon" has the same meaning as "weapon";

"peace officer" includes

(a) a mayor, warden, reeve, sheriff, deputy sheriff, sheriff's officer and justice of the peace,

(b) a member of the Correctional Service of Canada who is designated as a peace officer pursuant to Part I of the *Corrections and Conditional Release Act*, and a warden, deputy warden, instructor, keeper, jailer, guard and any other officer or permanent employee of a prison other than a penitentiary as defined in Part I of the *Corrections and Conditional Release Act*,

(c) a police officer, police constable, bailiff, constable, or other person employed for the preservation and maintenance of the public peace or for the service or execution of civil process,

(d) an officer or a person having the powers of a customs or excise officer when performing any duty in the administration of the *Customs Act* or the *Excise Act*,

(e) a person designated as a fishery guardian under the *Fisheries Act* when performing any duties or functions under that Act and a person designated as a fishery officer under the *Fisheries Act* when performing any duties or functions under that Act or the *Coastal Fisheries Protection Act,*

(f) the pilot in command of an aircraft

(i) registered in Canada under regulations made under the *Aeronautics Act,* or

(ii) leased without crew and operated by a person who is qualified under regulations made under the *Aeronautics Act* to be registered as owner of an aircraft registered in Canada under those regulations,

while the aircraft is in flight, and

(g) officers and non-commissioned members of the Canadian Forces who are

(i) appointed for the purposes of section 156 of the *National Defence Act,* or

(ii) employed on duties that the Governor in Council, in regulations made under the *National Defence Act* for the purposes of this paragraph, has prescribed to be of such a kind as to necessitate that the officers and non-commissioned members performing them have the powers of peace officers;

"prison" includes a penitentiary, common jail, public or reformatory prison, lock-up, guard-room or other place in which persons who are charged with or convicted of offences are usually kept in custody;

"property" includes

(a) real and personal property of every description and deeds and instruments relating to or evidencing the title or right to property, or giving a right to recover or receive money or goods,

(b) property originally in the possession or under the control of any person, and any property into or for which it has been converted or exchanged and anything acquired at any time by the conversion or exchange, and

(c) any postal card, postage stamp or other stamp issued or prepared for issue under the authority of Parliament or the legislature of a province for the payment to the Crown or a corporate body of any fee, rate or duty, whether or not it is in the possession of the Crown or of any person;

"prosecutor" means the Attorney General or, where the Attorney General does not intervene, means the person who institutes proceedings to which this Act applies, and includes counsel acting on behalf of either of them;

"provincial court judge" means a person appointed or authorized to act by or pursuant to an Act of the legislature of a province, by whatever title that person may be designated, who has the power and authority of two or more justices of the peace and includes his lawful deputy of that person;

"public department" means a department of the Government of Canada or a branch thereof or a board, commission, corporation or other body that is an agent of Her Majesty in right of Canada;

"public officer" includes

(a) an officer of customs or excise,

(b) an officer of the Canadian Forces,

(c) an officer of the Royal Canadian Mounted Police, and

(d) any officer while the officer is engaged in enforcing the laws of Canada relating to revenue, customs, excise, trade or navigation;

"public stores" includes any personal property that is under the care, supervision, administration or control of a public department or of any person in the service of a public department;

"railway equipment" means

(a) any machine that is constructed for movement exclusively on lines of railway, whether or not the machine is capable of independent motion, or

(b) any vehicle that is constructed for movement both on and off lines of railway while the adaptations of that vehicle for movement on lines of railway are in use;

"steal" means to commit theft;

"superior court of criminal jurisdiction"means

(a) in the Province of Ontario, the Court of Appeal or the Superior Court of Justice,

(b) in the Province of Quebec, the Superior Court,

(c) in the Province of Prince Edward Island, the Supreme Court,

(d) in the Provinces of New Brunswick, Manitoba, Saskatchewan and Alberta, the Court of Appeal or the Court of Queen's Bench,

(e) in the Provinces of Nova Scotia, British Columbia and Newfoundland, the Supreme Court or the Court of Appeal,

(f) in the Yukon Territory, the Supreme Court,

(g) in the Northwest Territories, the Supreme Court, and

(h) in Nunavut, the Nunavut Court of Justice;

"territorial division" includes any province, county, union of counties, township, city, town, parish or other judicial division or place to which the context applies;

"testamentary instrument" includes any will, codicil or other testamentary writing or appointment, during the life of the testator whose testamentary disposition it purports to be and after his death, whether it relates to real or personal property or to both;

"trustee" means a person who is declared by any Act to be a trustee or is, by the law of a province, a trustee, and, without restricting the generality of the foregoing, includes a trustee on an express trust created by deed, will or instrument in writing, or by parol;

"unfit to stand trial" means unable on account of mental disorder to conduct a defence at any stage of the proceedings before a verdict is rendered or to instruct counsel to do so, and, in particular, unable on account of mental disorder to

(a) understand the nature or object of the proceedings

(b) understand the possible consequences of the proceedings, or

(c) communicate with counsel;

"valuable mineral" means a mineral of a value of at least $100 per kilogram, and includes precious metals, diamonds and other gemstones and any rock or ore that contains those minerals;

"valuable security" includes

    (a) an order, exchequer acquittance or other security that entitles or evidences the title of any person

        (i) to a share or interest in a public stock or fund or in any fund of a body corporate, company or society, or

        (ii) to a deposit in a savings bank or other bank,

    (b) any debenture, deed, bond, bill, note, warrant, order or other security for money or for payment of money,

    (c) a document of title to lands or goods wherever situated,

    (d) a stamp or writing that secures or evidences title to or an interest in a chattel personal, or that evidences delivery of a chattel personal, and

    (e) a release, receipt, discharge or other instrument evidencing payment of money;

"weapon" means anything used, designed to be used or intended for use

    (a) in causing death or injury to any person, or

    (b) for the purpose of threatening or intimidating any person

and, without restricting the generality of the foregoing, includes a firearm;

"wreck" includes the cargo, stores and tackle of a vessel and all parts of a vessel separated from the vessel, and the property of persons who belong to, are on board or have quitted a vessel that is wrecked, stranded or in distress at any place in Canada;

"writing" includes a document of any kind and any mode in which, and any material on which, words or figures, whether at length or abridged, are written, printed or otherwise expressed, or a map or plan is inscribed.

R.S., c. C-34, s. 2; 1972, c. 13, s. 2; c. 17, s. 2; 1973–74, c. 17, s. 9; 1974–75–76, c. 19, ss. 1, 2; c. 48, s. 24; c. 93, s. 2; 1976–77, c. 35, s. 21; 1978–79, c. 11, s. 10; 1980–81–82–83, c. 125, s. 1; R.S. 1985, c. 11 (1st Supp.), s. 2; c. 27 (1st Supp.), ss. 2, 203; c. 31 (1st Supp.), s. 61; c. 1 (2d Supp.), Sched. IV; c. 27 (2d Supp.), Sched.; c. 35 (2d Supp.), s. 34; c. 28 (4th Supp.), s. 34; c. 32 (4th Supp.), s. 55; c. 40 (4th Supp.), s. 2; 1990, c. 17, s. 7; 1991, c. 1, s. 28; 1991, c. 40, s. 1; 1991, c. 43, ss. 1, 9; 1992, c. 20, s. 216(1)(a); 1992, c. 51, s. 32; 1993, c. 28, s. 78 (Sched. III, item 25) [Amended 1999, c. 3, (Sched., item 5).]; 1993, c. 34, s. 59(1); 1994, c. 44, s. 2; 1995, c. 29, ss. 39, 40; 1995, c. 39, s. 138; 1997, c. 23, s.1; 1998, c. 30, s. 14(d); 1999, c. 3, s. 25; 1999, c. 5, s. 1.

Commentary: The section defines various words and phrases which appear in the *Code*.

Definitions that use the word "means", described as *exhaustive* or *exclusive* definitions, assign to the word or phrase its exclusive or *only* meaning. Definitions that use the word "includes" are *inclusive or expansive* definitions. They *enlarge* the normal, natural everyday meaning of the term to include what would or might not otherwise be included. They are, in other words, permissive, *not* limitative, of meanings other than what is stated.

Case Law

Attorney General

R. v. Wetmore (1983), 38 C.R. (3d) 161, 7 C.C.C. (3d) 507 (S.C.C.) — Only in the case of prosecutions of the criminal law under the *Code* has authority to prosecute been assigned to the provincial Attorneys General, and then *only* by virtue of federal enactment. The Attorney General of Canada or his/her counsel consequently may prefer indictments and conduct prosecutions for *F.D.A.* violations.

Canada (A.G.) v. C.N. Transportation Ltd. (1983), 38 C.R. (3d) 97, 7 C.C.C. (3d) 449 (S.C.C.) — The vesting of prosecutorial power in the Attorney General of Canada in respect of violations of the *Combines Investigation Act* does *not* offend any constitutional principle and is within the legislative competence of Parliament.

R. v. Hauser (1979), 8 C.R. (3d) 89, 46 C.C.C. (2d) 481 (S.C.C.) — *See also*: *R. v. Sacobie* (1979), 51 C.C.C. (2d) 430 (N.B. C.A.); affirmed (1983), 1 C.C.C. (3d) 446 (S.C.C.) — The definition makes the

Attorney General of Canada the "Attorney General" in respect of all criminal proceedings instituted at the instance of the Government of Canada and conducted by or on behalf of that government in respect of an offence or conspiracy pertaining to a statute other than the *Code*. The provincial Attorney General is *excluded* from any authority in such cases. If the statute being enforced does *not* depend upon s. 91(27) criminal law powers for its constitutional validity, then it is within the competence of Parliament to exclude the provincial Attorneys General, as in the case of the *N.C.A.*

R. v. Pelletier (1974), 28 C.R.N.S. 129 (Ont. C.A.) — The Attorney General of Canada has the status and authority to prosecute a *conspiracy*, contrary to the *Code*, to violate an *indictable* offence section of the *N.C.A.* In the absence of federal action, the provincial Attorney General is also competent to prosecute.

Every one, Person, Owner

U.N.A. v. Alberta (Attorney General) (1992), 13 C.R. (4th) 1, 71 C.C.C. (3d) 225 (S.C.C.) — A union, being an unincorporated association recognized under the provincial *Labour Relations Act* as a bargaining agent and accorded powers relevant to that status, may fall within the definition of "person" in *Code* s. 2 which includes "societies".

R. v. Church of Scientology of Toronto (1997), 116 C.C.C. (3d) 1 (Ont. C.A.) — The fundamental justice guarantee of *Charter* s. 7 does *not* apply to corporations.

The identification doctrine serves as a basis upon which to impose criminal liability upon a *non-profit* corporation established for religious purposes.

R. v. Forges du Lac Inc. (1997), 117 C.C.C. (3d) 71 (Que. C.A.) — Corporate criminal liability is based on the liability of the representative who holds a position of authority in the corporate hierarchy and who, in some respects, is one of its directing minds.

Where there is an issue whether the directing mind undertook activities in *fraud* of the corporation, or for his/her own benefit, the availability of the defence depends upon the absence of a *benefit* to V. The defence avails where the company is charged with fraud, but *not* where it is charged with filing a false income tax return.

Firearm

R. v. Covin (1983), 8 C.C.C. (3d) 240 (S.C.C.); affirming (1982), 2 C.C.C. (3d) 185 (N.S. C.A.) — An inoperable air pistol used in a robbery is not a "firearm". It is not a weapon capable of causing serious bodily harm. An inoperable weapon, capable of being made readily operable, would be included in the definition.

R. v. Cairns (1963), 39 C.R. 154 (B.C. C.A.) — A weapon otherwise within the definition of "firearm" does *not* cease to be within the definition simply because it is in a state of easily curable disrepair.

R. v. Dufour (1982), 3 C.C.C. (3d) 14 (N.S. C.A.) — To be a "firearm" an object, if inoperable, must be capable of being made operable. The burden is on P to show that while the object is not in an immediate state of operation, it is capable of operation through adaptation or assembly.

R. v. Formosa (1992), 79 C.C.C. (3d) 95 (Ont. C.A.) — Any object which is a "firearm" under s. 84 is also a "weapon" under s. 2.

R. v. Belair (1981), 24 C.R. (3d) 133, 61 C.C.C. (2d) 461 (Ont. C.A.) — Although the weapon itself was inoperable at the time of the commission of the robbery, it was nevertheless a firearm within the meaning of the *Code*. The air pistol was capable of causing serious bodily harm. *Code* provisions dealing with use of firearms during the commission of an offence are aimed at the prevention not only of injury but also the causing of alarm in the commission of crimes.

R. v. Cheetham (1980), 17 C.R. (3d) 1, 53 C.C.C. (2d) 109 (Ont. C.A.) — An unloaded rifle constitutes a "firearm".

Peace Officer

R. v. Nolan (1987), 58 C.R. (3d) 335, 34 C.C.C. (3d) 289 (S.C.C.); affirming (1982), 66 C.C.C. (2d) 417 (N.S. C.A.)

A military policeman is a peace officer under s. 2(g)(ii) but *not* under s. 2(g)(i).

R. v. Whiskeyjack (1985), 17 C.C.C. (3d) 245 (Alta. C.A.) — A band constable on an Indian reserve appointed as a special constable under the provincial *Police Act* to enforce the *Indian Act* is a "peace officer".

R. v. Smith (1983), 2 C.C.C. (3d) 250 (B.C. C.A.) — Military police acting pursuant to the *Defence Establishment Trespass Regulations* are engaged in preserving and maintaining the public peace, hence are peace officers entitled to make a breathalyzer demand of a civilian on a defence establishment.

R. v. Rushton (1981), 62 C.C.C. (2d) 403 (N.B. C.A.) — A game warden appointed under the provincial *Fish and Wildlife Act* is within the definition of peace officer.

R. v. Renz (1972), 10 C.C.C. (2d) 250 (Ont. C.A.) — Conservation officers have the powers necessary to bring them within the definition of peace officer.

R. v. Rutt (1981), 59 C.C.C. (2d) 147 (Sask. C.A.) — A wildlife officer appointed under the provincial *Wildlife Act* is a "peace officer" is defined by this section.

Prosecutor [See also s. 785]

Edmunds v. R. (1981), 21 C.R. (3d) 168, 58 C.C.C. (2d) 485 (S.C.C.) — Where D, charged with a strictly indictable offence, elects trial by provincial court judge, the definition in this section is the applicable definition. A police officer who is neither the informant nor counsel cannot conduct the prosecution.

R. v. Parsons (1985), 14 C.C.C (3d) 490 (Nfld. C.A.); leave to appeal refused (November 22, 1984) (S.C.C.) — An agent of the Attorney General who communicates to the court the Attorney General's decision to proceed by way of indictment is *not* at that stage a prosecutor. A police officer may indicate the Attorney General's election.

Public Officer

Labelle v. R., [1971] Que. A.C. 641 (C.A.) — A municipal health inspector is a public officer.

Unfit to Stand Trial [See also, ss. 672.22-672.33]

R. v. Taylor (1992), 17 C.R. (4th) 371, 77 C.C.C. (3d) 551 (Ont. C.A.) — The test to be applied in determining D's ability to communicate with counsel is one of limited cognitive capacity. The inquiry is whether D can recount to counsel the necessary facts relating to the offence in such a way that counsel can properly present a defence. It is *not* necessary that D be able to act in his/her own best interests.

Valuable Security [See also s. 4]

R. v. Pennell (1965), 47 C.R. 200, [1966] 1 C.C.C. 258 (B.C. C.A.) — A *traveller's cheque* is a valuable security even though *not* yet counter-signed by its owner.

R. v. Zinck (1986), 32 C.C.C. (3d) 150 (N.B. C.A.) — A *money order* is a valuable security. Its value is the amount indicated on its face.

Weapon [See also case digests under ss. 84, 87, 90 and 91] [†Cases decided upon prior definition]

R. v. Felawka (1993), 25 C.R. (4th) 70, 85 C.C.C. (3d) 248 (S.C.C.); affirming (1991), 9 C.R. (4th) 291, 68 C.C.C. (3d) 481 (B.C.C.A.) — *See also*: *R. v. Formosa* (1992), 79 C.C.C. (3d) 95 (Ont. C.A.) — A "firearm" within s. 84(1) is always a "weapon" within s. 2, irrespective of the intention of the person who carries it.

†*R. v. Roberts* (1990), 60 C.C.C. (3d) 509 (N.S. C.A.) — *See also*: *R. v. Murray* (1991), 4 O.R. (3d) 97, 65 C.C.C. (3d) 507 (C.A.) — The definition of "weapon" in s. 2 involves a *subjective* test. D must intend to *use* the object *as a* weapon. Proof that an object was being used as a weapon will depend on all the circumstances of the case.

†*Malang v. R.* (1982), 25 C.R. (3d) 398 (Ont. C.A.) — A bomb is an offensive weapon or weapon.

Related Provisions: A word or phrase may be specifically defined in or for the purposes of the subsection, section, group of sections or Part of the *Code* where it is found, or in s. 2 for the purposes of the *Code* as a whole. It may be defined in the *Interpretation Act*, R.S.C. 1985, c. I-21 or in another federal enactment which deals with the same subject-matter. Absent statutory definition, meaning will be assigned to the word or phrase in accordance with general principles of statutory interpretation applicable to penal statutes.

3. Descriptive cross references — Where, in any provision of this Act, a reference to another provision of this Act or a provision of any other Act is followed by words in parenthesis that are or purport to be descriptive of the subject-matter of the provision referred to, the words in parenthesis form no part of the provision in which they occur but shall be deemed to have been inserted for convenience of reference only.

1976–77, c. 53, s. 2.

Commentary: The section describes the interpretative value of descriptive cross-references.

Related Provisions: Descriptive cross-references are often incomplete. For example, the reference to "section 279 (kidnapping and forcible confinement)", *fails to refer to* the unlawful imprisonment and forcible seizure offences in s. 279(2), and *misdescribes* the confinement offence as "forcible confinement", rather than "unlawful confinement".

PART I

General

4. (1) Postcard a chattel, value — For the purposes of this Act, a postal card or stamp referred to in paragraph (*c*) of the definition "property" in section 2 shall be deemed to be a chattel and to be equal in value to the amount of the postage, rate or duty expressed on its face.

(2) Value of valuable security — For the purposes of this Act, the following rules apply for the purpose of determining the value of a valuable security where value is material:

(a) where the valuable security is one mentioned in paragraph (*a*) or (*b*) of the definition "valuable security" in section 2, the value is the value of the share, interest, deposit or unpaid money, as the case may be, that is secured by the valuable security;

(b) where the valuable security is one mentioned in paragraph (*c*) or (*d*) of the definition "valuable security" in section 2, the value is the value of the lands, goods, chattel personal or interest in the chattel personal, as the case may be; and

(c) where the valuable security is one mentioned in paragraph (*e*) of the definition "valuable security" in section 2, the value is the amount of money that has been paid.

(3) Possession — For the purposes of this Act,

(a) a person has anything in "possession" when he has it in his personal possession or knowingly

(i) has it in the actual possession or custody of another person, or

(ii) has it in any place, whether or not that place belongs to or is occupied by him, for the use or benefit of himself or of another person; and

(b) where one of two or more persons, with the knowledge and consent of the rest, has anything in his custody or possession, it shall be deemed to be in the custody and possession of each and all of them.

(4) Expressions taken from other acts — Where an offence that is dealt with in this Act relates to a subject that is dealt with in another Act, the words and expressions used in this Act with respect to that offence have, subject to this Act, the meaning assigned to them in that other Act.

(5) Sexual intercourse — For the purposes of this Act, sexual intercourse is complete on penetration to even the slightest degree, notwithstanding that seed is not emitted.

(6) Proof of notifications and service of documents — For the purposes of this Act, the service of any document and the giving or sending of any notice may be proved

    (a) by oral evidence given under oath by, or by the affidavit or solemn declaration of, the person claiming to have served, given, or sent it; or

    (b) in the case of a peace office, by a statement in writing certifying that the document was served or the notice was given or sent by the peace officer, and such a statement is deemed to be a statement made under oath.

(7) Attendance for examination — Notwithstanding subsection (6), the court may require the person who appears to have signed an affidavit, solemn declaration or statement referred to in that subsection to appear before it for examination or cross-examination in respect of the issue of proof of service or the giving or sending of any notice.

R.S., c. C-34, s. 3; 1980–81–82–83, c. 125, s. 2; R.S. 1985, c. 27 (1st Supp.), s. 3; 1994, c. 44, s. 3; 1997, c. 18, s. 2.

Commentary: The several subsections bear no particular relation to one another, but are of general application in proof of material elements of certain offences and the service of documents.

Subsection (1) complements the definition of "property" in s. 2 by *deeming* a postal card or stamp to be a chattel, equal in *value* to the *amount* of the postage, rate or duty expressed on its face.

Subsection (2) describes how to value a "valuable security" as defined in s. 2, where value is material.

Subsection (3) defines *possession* for the purposes of the *Code*. In general, possession may be actual or attributed by operation of law.

Actual possession is proven where it is established that a person has the subject-matter in his/her *personal possession*.

Possession may be *attributed* to a person in three circumstances. Under s. 4(3)(a)(i), a person is in possession of a thing when s/he *knowingly* has it in the *actual* custody or possession of another. The *joint* possession of the thing is *actual* in one person and *attributed* to the other. Under s. 4(3)(a)(ii), one is in possession when s/he *knowingly* has the subject-matter in a place for the use or benefit of him/herself or another. It is of no consequence that the place neither belongs to nor is occupied by such person. Finally, possession, often described as "constructive possession", may be attributed to one, under s. 4(3)(b). Where one of two or more persons, with the knowledge and consent of the rest, has anything in his/her custody or possession, the thing is deemed to be in the custody and possession of each and all of them. The person who has custody or possession of the thing is in *actual* possession of it and P need not rely upon s. 4(3)(b) to establish such fact. Possession is attributed to the others or, to put the matter in another way, is constructed in the others upon the actual possession of one and the knowledge and consent of the rest.

Subsection (4), in defined circumstances, permits recourse to other federal enactments to assign meaning to words and expressions used in the *Code*. There must first be an offence under the *Code* that relates to a subject dealt with in another Act. The meaning of the words and expressions used in the *Code* in respect of that offence are the same as the meaning assigned to them in the other Act, subject to *Code* provisions that enact otherwise.

Subsection (5) provides that sexual intercourse is complete upon the slightest penetration. It is of no legal consequence that seed is not emitted.

Under ss. 4(6) and (7), proof of *service of any document* and the giving or sending of any notice may be made by *oral* evidence under oath, the *affidavit* or *solemn declaration* of the serving party or, in the case of a peace officer, by a statement in writing which is deemed to be made under oath. Where documentary proof of service is offered, s. 4(7) authorizes the court to require the personal attendance of the serving party for examination or cross-examination on the issue on proof of service.

Case Law

Value of Valuable Security: S. 4(2)

R. v. Pennell (1965), 47 C.R. 200, [1966] 1 C.C.C. 258 (B.C. C.A.) — The value of a traveller's cheque, even if not counter-signed, is its face value.

Possession: S. 4(3) [See also s. 354]

R. v. Lovis (1974), 17 C.C.C. (2d) 481 (S.C.C.) — Section 4(3) applies to *all* proceedings under the *Code.* It applies not only to charges of unlawful possession but also where possession is proven as an item of circumstantial evidence to establish another offence of which possession is not a material element.

Beaver v. R. (1957), 26 C.R. 193, 118 C.C.C. 129 (S.C.C.) — There is *no* possession of a thing *without knowledge* of what that thing is. *Possession* and *knowledge* must co-exist with some act of *control.*

R. v. Breau (1987), 33 C.C.C. (3d) 354 (N.B. C.A.) — Without some measure of control over an object, the presence of fingerprints do *not* lead to the sole conclusion that the handler possessed it.

R. v. Christie (1978), 41 C.C.C. (2d) 282 (N.B. C.A.) — Even though D has a right of control over an object and is aware of its presence and character, D is *not* guilty of possession without proof of an intention to exercise control over the object.

Joint Possession: S. 4(3)

R. v. Terrence (1983), 33 C.R. (3d) 193, 4 C.C.C. (3d) 193 (S.C.C.) — Control is a constituent and essential element of constructive possession.

R. v. Roan (1985), 17 C.C.C. (3d) 534 (Alta. C.A.) — *Knowledge* and *consent* are essential elements of joint possession. They do *not* exist without some measure of control.

R. v. Croft (1979), 35 N.S.R. (2d) 344 (C.A.) — The *constructive* possession deemed by *knowledge* and *consent* may be *rebutted* by credible evidence that goes either to the issue of knowledge or of consent with its attendant element of control.

Chambers v. R. (1985), 20 C.C.C. (3d) 440 (Ont. C.A.) — Where drugs were found in D's room, the fact that she was aware of their presence and could have refused to consent to the drugs being stored there by her boyfriend gave her the measure of control necessary to constitute consent.

R. v. Piaskoski (1979), 52 C.C.C. (2d) 316, 318 (Ont. C.A.) — Consent requires more than mere indifference or passive acquiescence.

Expressions Taken From Other Acts: S. 4(4)

R. v. Cumming (1962), 37 C.R. 219, 132 C.C.C. 281 (S.C.C.) — In cases of theft from the mail, definitions respecting the post office are to be sought in the *Post Office Act* [now *Canada Post Act*].

Sexual Intercourse: S. 4(5)

R. v. Johns (1956), 25 C.R. 153, 116 C.C.C. 200 (B.C. Co. Ct.) — Sexual intercourse is complete upon the penetration of the labia, no matter how little, even though there is *no* penetration of the vagina, and the hymen is *not* touched.

Related Provisions: Offences relating to counterfeit stamps are contained in s. 376(1). "Stamp" defined in s. 376(3).

Offences relating to *valuable securities* are found in ss. 340(b)(destroying, cancelling, concealing or obliterating a valuable security), 363 (obtaining execution of a valuable security by fraud) and 397 (falsification of a valuable security).

Section 358 describes when certain possession offences are complete.

In general, service or execution of process upon individuals is to be effected personally by a peace officer, subject to statutory exception. It may be made on a holiday under s. 20. Proof of service requires, *inter alia*, proof of the identity of the documents or process as well as of the person served.

---

5. Canadian Forces not affected — Nothing in this Act affects any law relating to the government of the Canadian Forces.

R.S., c. C-34, s. 4.

Commentary: The section provides that the *Code* does *not* affect any law relating to the government of the Canadian Forces. It does *not* provide that members of the Canadian Forces are, by reason of their military character, exempt from the criminal jurisdiction of the civil courts in all cases.

Case Law

Reference re Exemption of the U.S. Forces from Canadian Criminal Law (1943), 80 C.C.C. 161 (S.C.C.) — No soldiers, Canadian or foreign, are exempt from the criminal jurisdiction of the Canadian courts, absent specific legislative enactments to the contrary.

Related Provisions: "Canadian Forces", "military" and "military law" are defined in s. 2.

Sections 53, 54 and 62 prohibit certain acts in relation to members of the Canadian Forces, and ss. 419 and 420 enact similar prohibitions in relation to military uniforms, stores and certificates.

Offences under military law tried before a military tribunal are exempted from *Charter* s. 11(f) (trial by jury).

6. (1) Presumption of innocence — Where an enactment creates an offence and authorizes a punishment to be imposed in respect of that offence,

(a) a person shall be deemed not to be guilty of the offence until he is convicted or discharged under section 730 of the offence; and

(b) a person who is convicted or discharged under section 730 of the offence is not liable to any punishment in respect thereof other than the punishment prescribed by this Act or by the enactment that creates the offence.

(2) Offences outside Canada — Subject to this Act or any other Act of Parliament, no person shall be convicted or discharged under section 730 of an offence committed outside Canada.

(3) Definition of "enactment" — In this section "enactment" means

(a) an Act of Parliament, or

(b) an Act of the legislature of a province that creates an offence to which Part XXVII applies,

or any regulation made thereunder.

R.S., c. C-34, s. 5;R.S. 1985, c. 27 (1st Supp.), s. 4; 1995, c. 22, ss. 10, 18.

Commentary: Section 6(1) statutorily guarantees the presumption of innocence and, upon its displacement by a finding of guilt or conviction, punishment only in accordance with statutory enactment, as defined in s. 7(3).

Section 6(2) provides a general rule that no one shall be convicted or discharged of an offence committed outside Canada, subject to the *Code* or other federal enactment.

Case Law

Charter Considerations [See Charter s. 11(d)]

Offences Outside Canada: S. 6(2)

Libman v. R. (1985), 21 C.C.C. (3d) 206 (S.C.C.) — All that is necessary to make an offence subject to the jurisdiction of the Canadian courts is that a *significant portion* of the activities constituting the offence took place in Canada. It is sufficient if there is a *real and substantial* link between an offence and this country.

R. v. Chapman (1970), 11 C.R.N.S. 1, [1970] 5 C.C.C. 46 (Ont. C.A.) — The initiation and realization of a fraudulent scheme in Canada is an offence committed in Canada even though the inducement was extended only to persons outside Canada.

Related Provisions: The several *Code* provisions that enact presumptions respecting essential elements of an offence and/or reverse the onus of proof in relation thereto, are subject to *Charter* ss. 7 and 11(d) scrutiny.

Subsection (2) should be read together with s. 9. Sections 7, 465(1)(a) and 465(3) and (4) constitute exceptions to the general rule of s. 6(2).

7. (1) Offences committed on aircraft — Notwithstanding anything in this Act or any other Act, every one who

(a) on or in respect of an aircraft

(i) registered in Canada under regulations made under the *Aeronautics Act*, or

(ii) leased without crew and operated by a person who is qualified under regulations made under the *Aeronautics Act* to be registered as owner of an aircraft registered in Canada under those regulations,

while the aircraft is in flight, or

(b) on any aircraft, while the aircraft is in flight if the flight terminated in Canada,

commits an act or omission in or outside Canada that if committed in Canada would be an offence punishable by indictment shall be deemed to have committed that act or omission in Canada.

(2) Idem — Notwithstanding this Act or any other Act, every one who

(a) on an aircraft, while the aircraft is in flight, commits an act or omission outside Canada that if committed in Canada or on an aircraft registered in Canada under regulations made under the *Aeronautics Act* would be an offence against section 76 or paragraph 77(*a*),

(b) in relation to an aircraft in service, commits an act or omission outside Canada that if committed in Canada would be an offence against any of paragraphs 77(*b*), (*c*) or (*e*),

(c) in relation to an air navigation facility used in international air navigation, commits an act or omission outside Canada that if committed in Canada would be an offence against paragraph 77(*d*)

(d) at or in relation to an airport serving international civil aviation, commits an act or omission outside Canada that if committed in Canada would be an offence against paragraph 77(*b*) or (*f*), or

(e) commits an act or omission outside Canada that if committed in Canada would constitute a conspiracy or an attempt to commit an offence referred to in this subsection, or being an accessory after the fact or counselling in relation to such an offence,

shall be deemed to have committed that act or omission in Canada if the person is, after the commission thereof, present in Canada.

(2.1) Offences against fixed platforms or international maritime navigation — Notwithstanding anything in this Act or any other Act, every one who commits an act or omission outside Canada against or on board a fixed platform attached to the continental shelf of any state or against or on board a ship navigating or scheduled to navigate beyond the territorial sea of any state, that if committed in Canada would constitute an offence against, a conspiracy or an attempt to commit an offence against, or being an accessory after the fact or counselling in relation to an offence against, section 78.1, shall be deemed to commit that act or omission in Canada if it is committed

(a) against or on board a fixed platform attached to the continental shelf of Canada;

(b) against or on board a ship registered or licensed, or for which an identification number has been issued, pursuant to any Act of Parliament;

(c) by a Canadian citizen;

(d) by a person who is not a citizen of any state and who ordinarily resides in Canada;

(e) by a person who is, after the commission of the offence, present in Canada;

(f) in such a way as to seize, injure or kill, or threaten to injure or kill, a Canadian citizen; or

(g) in an attempt to compel the Government of Canada to do or refrain from doing any act.

(2.2) Offences against fixed platforms or navigation in the internal waters or territorial sea of another state — Notwithstanding anything in this Act or any other Act, every one who commits an act or omission outside Canada against or on board a fixed platform not attached to the continental shelf of any state or against or on board a ship not navigating or scheduled to navigate beyond the territorial sea of any state, that if committed in Canada would constitute an offence against, a conspiracy or an attempt to commit an offence against, or being an accessory after the fact or counselling in relation to an offence against, section 78.1, shall be deemed to commit that act or omission in Canada

(a) if it is committed as described in any of paragraphs (2.1)(b) to (g); and

(b) if the offender is found in the territory of a state, other than the state in which the act or omission was committed, that is

(i) a party to the Convention for the Suppression of Unlawful Acts against the Safety of Maritime Navigation, done at Rome on March 10, 1988, in respect of an offence committed against or on board a ship, or

(ii) a party to the Protocol for the Suppression of Unlawful Acts against the Safety of Fixed Platforms Located on the Continental Shelf, done at Rome on March 10, 1988, in respect of an offence committed against or on board a fixed platform.

(3) Offence against internationally protected person — Notwithstanding anything in this Act or any other Act, every one who, outside Canada, commits an act or omission against the person of an internationally protected person or against any property referred to in section 431 used by that person that if committed in Canada would be an offence against section 235, 236, 266, 267, 268, 269, 271, 272, 273, 279, 279.1, 280 to 283, 424 or 431 shall be deemed to commit that act or omission in Canada if

(a) the act or omission is committed on a ship that is registered or licensed, or for which an identification number has been issued, pursuant to any Act of Parliament;

(b) the act or omission is committed on an aircraft

(i) registered in Canada under regulations made under the *Aeronautics Act*, or

(ii) leased without crew and operated by a person who is qualified under regulations made under the *Aeronautics Act* to be registered as owner of an aircraft in Canada under those regulations;

(c) the person who commits the act or omission is a Canadian citizen or is, after the act or omission has been committed, present in Canada; or

(d) the act or omission is against

(i) a person who enjoys the status of an internationally protected person by virtue of the functions that person performs on behalf of Canada, or

(ii) a member of the family of a person described in subparagraph (i) who qualifies under paragraph (b) or (d) of the definition "internationally protected person" in section 2.

(3.1) **Offence of hostage taking** — Notwithstanding anything in this Act or any other Act, every one who, outside Canada, commits an act or omission that if committed in Canada would be an offence against section 279.1 shall be deemed to commit that act or omission in Canada if

(a) the act or omission is committed on a ship that is registered or licensed, or for which an identification number has been issued, pursuant to any Act of Parliament;

(b) the act or omission is committed on an aircraft

(i) registered in Canada under regulations made under the *Aeronautics Act*, or

(ii) leased without crew and operated by a person who is qualified under regulations made under the *Aeronautics Act* to be registered as owner of an aircraft in Canada under such regulations;

(c) the person who commits the act or omission

(i) is a Canadian citizen, or

(ii) is not a citizen of any state and ordinarily resides in Canada;

(d) the act or omission is committed with intent to induce Her Majesty in right of Canada or of a province to commit or cause to be committed any act or omission;

(e) a person taken hostage by the act or omission is a Canadian citizen; or

(f) the person who commits the act or omission is, after the commission thereof, present in Canada.

(3.2) **Offences involving nuclear material** — Notwithstanding anything in this Act or any other Act, where

(a) a person, outside Canada, receives, has in his possession, uses, transfers the possession of, sends or delivers to any person, transports, alters, disposes of, disperses or abandons nuclear material and thereby

(i) causes or is likely to cause the death of, or serious bodily harm to, any person, or

(ii) causes or is likely to cause serious damage to, or destruction of, property, and

(b) the act or omission described in paragraph (a) would, if committed in Canada, be an offence against this Act,

that person shall be deemed to commit that act or omission in Canada if paragraph (3.5)(a), (b) or (c) applies in respect of the act or omission.

(3.3) **Idem** — Notwithstanding anything in this Act or any other Act, every one who, outside Canada, commits an act or omission that if committed in Canada would constitute

   (a) a conspiracy or an attempt to commit,

   (b) being an accessory after the fact in relation to, or

   (c) counselling in relation to,

an act or omission that is an offence by virtue of subsection (3.2) shall be deemed to commit the act or omission in Canada if paragraph (3.5)(a), (b) or (c) applies in respect of the act or omission.

(3.4) **Idem** — Notwithstanding anything in this Act or any other Act, every one who, outside Canada, commits an act or omission that if committed in Canada would constitute an offence against, a conspiracy or an attempt to commit or being an accessory after the fact in relation to an offence against, or any counselling in relation to an offence against,

   (a) section 334, 341, 344 or 380 or paragraph 362(1)(a) in relation to nuclear material,

   (b) section 346 in respect of a threat to commit an offence against section 334 or 344 in relation to nuclear material,

   (c) section 423 in relation to a demand for nuclear material, or

   (d) paragraph 264.1(1)(a) or (b) in respect of a threat to use nuclear material

shall be deemed to commit that act or omission in Canada if paragraph (3.5)(a), (b) or (c) applies in respect of the act or omission.

(3.5) **Idem** — For the purposes of subsections (3.2) to (3.4), a person shall be deemed to commit an act or omission in Canada if

   (a) the act or omission is committed on a ship that is registered or licensed, or for which an identification number has been issued, pursuant to any Act of Parliament;

   (b) the act or omission is committed on an aircraft

      (i) registered in Canada under regulations made under the *Aeronautics Act*, or

      (ii) leased without crew and operated by a person who is qualified under regulations made under the *Aeronautics Act* to be registered as owner of an aircraft in Canada under such regulations; or

   (c) the person who commits the act or omission is a Canadian citizen or is, after the act or omission has been committed, present in Canada.

(3.6) **Definition of "nuclear material"** — For the purposes of this section, "nuclear material" means

   (a) plutonium, except plutonium with an isotopic concentration of plutonium-238 exceeding eighty per cent,

   (b) uranium-233,

   (c) uranium containing uranium-233 or uranium-235 or both in such an amount that the abundance ratio of the sum of those isotopes to the isotope uranium-238 is greater than 0.72 per cent,

   (d) uranium with an isotopic concentration equal to that occurring in nature, and

   (e) any substance containing anything described in paragraphs (a) to (d), but does not include uranium in the form of ore or ore-residue.

(3.7) **Jurisdiction** — Notwithstanding anything in this Act or any other Act, every one who, outside Canada, commits an act or omission that, if committed in Canada, would constitute an offence against, a conspiracy or an attempt to commit an offence against, being an accessory after the fact in relation to an offence against, or any counselling in relation to an offence against, section 269.1 shall be deemed to commit that act or omission in Canada if

(a) the act or omission is committed on a ship that is registered or licensed, or for which an identification number has been issued, pursuant to any Act of Parliament;

(b) the act or omission is committed on an aircraft

(i) registered in Canada under regulations made under the *Aeronautics Act*, or

(ii) leased without crew and operated by a person who is qualified under regulations made under the *Aeronautics Act* to be registered as owner of an aircraft in Canada under those regulations;

(c) the person who commits the act or omission is a Canadian citizen;

(d) the complainant is a Canadian citizen; or

(e) the person who commits the act or omission is, after the commission thereof, present in Canada.

(3.71) **Jurisdiction: war crimes and crimes against humanity** — Notwithstanding anything in this Act or any other Act, every person who, either before or after the coming into force of this subsection, commits an act or omission outside Canada that constitutes a war crime or a crime against humanity and that, if committed in Canada, would constitute an offence against the laws of Canada in force at the time of the act or omission shall be deemed to commit that act or omission in Canada at that time if,

(a) at the time of the act or omission,

(i) that person is a Canadian citizen or is employed by Canada in a civilian or military capacity,

(ii) that person is a citizen of, or is employed in a civilian or military capacity by, a state that is engaged in an armed conflict against Canada, or

(iii) the victim of the act or omission is a Canadian citizen or a citizen of a state that is allied with Canada in an armed conflict; or

(b) at the time of the act or omission, Canada could, in conformity with international law, exercise jurisdiction over the person with respect to the act or omission on the basis of the person's presence in Canada, and subsequent to the time of the act or omission the person is present in Canada.

(3.72) **Procedure and evidence** — Any proceedings with respect to an act or omission referred to in subsection (3.71) shall be conducted in accordance with the laws of evidence and procedure in force at the time of the proceedings.

(3.73) **Defences** — In any proceedings with respect to an act or omission referred to in subsection (3.71), notwithstanding that the act or omission is an offence under the laws of Canada in force at the time of the act or omission, the accused may, subject to subsection 607(6), rely on any justification, excuse or defence available under the laws of Canada or under international law at that time or at the time of the proceedings.

(3.74) Conflict with internal law — Notwithstanding subsection (3.73) and section 15, a person may be convicted of an offence in respect of an act or omission referred to in subsection (3.71) even if the act or omission is committed in obedience to or in conformity with the law in force at the time and in the place of its commission.

(3.75) Attorney General of Canada — Notwithstanding any other provision of this Act, no proceedings may be commenced with respect to an act or omission referred to in subsection (3.71) without the personal consent in writing of the Attorney General or Deputy Attorney General of Canada, and such proceedings may only be conducted by the Attorney General of Canada or counsel acting on behalf thereof.

(3.76) Definitions — For the purposes of this section,

"conventional international law" means

(a) any convention, treaty or other international agreement that is in force and to which Canada is a party, or

(b) any convention, treaty or other international agreement that is in force and the provisions of which Canada has agreed to accept and apply in an armed conflict in which it is involved;

"crime against humanity" means murder, extermination, enslavement, deportation, persecution or any other inhumane act or omission that is committed against any civilian population or any identifiable group of persons, whether or not it constitutes a contravention of the law in force at the time and in the place of its commission, and that, at that time and in that place, constitutes a contravention of customary international law or conventional international law or is criminal according to the general principles of law recognized by the community of nations;

"war crime" means an act or omission that is committed during an international armed conflict, whether or not it constitutes a contravention of the law in force at the time and in the place of its commission, and that, at that time and in that place, constitutes a contravention of the customary international law or conventional international law applicable in international armed conflicts.

(3.77) Meaning of "act or omission" — In the definitions "crime against humanity" and "war crime" in subsection (3.76), "act or omission" includes, for greater certainty, attempting or conspiring to commit, counselling any person to commit, aiding or abetting any person in the commission of, or being an accessory after the fact in relation to, an act or omission.

(4) Offences by public service employees — Every one who, while employed as an employee within the meaning of the *Public Service Employment Act* in a place outside Canada, commits an act or omission in that place that is an offence under the laws of that place and that, if committed in Canada, would be an offence punishable by indictment shall be deemed to have committed that act or omission in Canada.

(4.1) Offence in relation to sexual offences against children — Notwithstanding anything in this Act or any other Act, every one who, outside Canada, commits an act or omission that if committed in Canada would be an offence against section 151, 152, 153, 155 or 159, subsection 160(2) or (3), section 163.1, 170, 171 or 173 or subsection 212(4) shall be deemed to commit that act or omission in Canada if the person who commits the act or omission is a Canadian citizen or a permanent resident within the meaning of the *Immigration Act*.

(4.2) **No proceedings** — Proceedings with respect to an act or omission that if committed in Canada would be an offence against section 151, 152, 153, 155 or 159, subsection 160(2) or (3) or section 163.1, 170, 171 or 173 shall be instituted in Canada only if a request to that effect to the Minister of Justice of Canada is made by

(a) any consular officer or diplomatic agent accredited to Canada by the state where the offence has been committed; or

(b) any minister of that state communicating with the Minister through the diplomatic representative of Canada accredited to that state.

(4.3) **Consent of Attorney General** — Proceedings referred to in subsection (4.2) may only be instituted with the consent of the Attorney General.

(5) **Jurisdiction** — Where a person is alleged to have committed an act or omission that is an offence by virtue of this section, proceedings in respect of that offence may, whether or not that person is in Canada, be commenced in any territorial division in Canada and the accused may be tried and punished in respect of that offence in the same manner as if the offence had been committed in that territorial division.

(5.1) **Appearance of accused at trial** — For greater certainty, the provisions of this Act relating to

(a) requirements that an accused appear at and be present during proceedings, and

(b) the exceptions to those requirements,

apply to proceedings commenced in any territorial division pursuant to subsection (5).

(6) **Where previously tried outside Canada** — Where a person is alleged to have committed an act or omission that is an offence by virtue of this section and that person has been tried and dealt with outside Canada in respect of the offence in such a manner that, if that person had been tried and dealt with in Canada, he would be able to plead *autrefois acquit, autrefois convict* or pardon, that person shall be deemed to have been so tried and dealt with in Canada.

(7) **Consent** — No proceedings shall be instituted under this section without the consent of the Attorney General of Canada if the accused is not a Canadian citizen.

(8) **Definition of "flight" and "in flight"** — For the purposes of this section, of the definition "peace officer" in section 2 and of sections 76 and 77, "flight" means the act of flying or moving through the air and an aircraft shall be deemed to be in flight from the time when all external doors are closed following embarkation until the later of

(a) the time at which any such door is opened for the purpose of disembarkation, and

(b) where the aircraft makes a forced landing in circumstances in which the owner or operator thereof or a person acting on behalf of either of them is not in control of the aircraft, the time at which control of the aircraft is restored to the owner or operator thereof or a person acting on behalf of either of them.

(9) **Definition of "in service"** — For the purposes of this section and section 77, an aircraft shall be deemed to be in service from the time when pre-flight preparation of the aircraft by ground personnel or the crew thereof begins for a specific flight until

(a) the flight is cancelled before the aircraft is in flight,

(b) twenty-four hours after the aircraft, having commenced the flight, lands, or

(c) the aircraft, having commenced the flight, ceases to be in flight,

whichever is the latest.

(10) Certificate as evidence — If in any proceedings under this Act a question arises as to whether any person is a person who is entitled, pursuant to international law, to special protection from any attack on his person, freedom or dignity, a certificate purporting to have been issued by or under the authority of the Minister of Foreign Affairs stating any fact relevant to that question is admissible in evidence in those proceedings without proof of the signature or authority of the person appearing to have signed it and, in the absence of evidence to the contrary, is proof of the facts so stated.

(11) Idem — A certificate purporting to have been issued by or under the authority of the Minister of Foreign Affairs stating

    (a) that at a certain time any state was engaged in an armed conflict against Canada or was allied with Canada in an armed conflict,

    (b) that at a certain time any convention, treaty or other international agreement was or was not in force and that Canada was or was not a party thereto, or

    (c) that Canada agreed or did not agree to accept and apply the provisions of any convention, treaty or other international agreement in an armed conflict in which Canada was involved,

is admissible in evidence in any proceedings under this Act without proof of the signature or authority of the person appearing to have issued it, and is proof of facts so stated.

    R.S., c. C-34, s. 6; 1972, c. 13, s. 3; 1974–75–76, c. 93, s. 3; 1980–81–82–83, c. 125, s. 3; R.S. 1985, c. 27 (1st Supp.), s. 5; c. 10 (3d Supp.), s. 1; c. 30 (3d Supp.), s. 1(1), (3); 1992, c. 1, s. 58(1), Schedule I, items 1(1), (2); 1993, c. 7, s. 1; 1995, c. 5, s. 25(1)(g); 1997, c. 16, s. 1.

Commentary: This series of provisions *deems* certain acts or omissions committed *outside* Canada to have been *committed* in Canada, so as to render them justiciable by Canadian courts.

The subsections relate to offences on or in respect of an *aircraft* or in relation to an *aircraft in service* or *air navigation facility* (ss. 7(1) and (2)), against the person or certain property of an "internationally protected person" (s. 7(3)), or in respect of "nuclear material" (ss. 7(3.2)–(3.6)). Similar provision is made in respect of acts or omissions *outside* Canada that, if committed in Canada, would be the offence of hostage taking under s. 279.1 (s. 7(3.1)) or an offence or preliminary crime in relation to s. 245.4 (s. 7(3.7)). A recent enactment has added several subsections, (3.71)–(3.77), in respect of acts or omissions outside Canada that constitute a "war crime" or "crime against humanity" as defined in s. 7(3.76) and that, if committed in Canada, would constitute an offence against the laws of Canada in force at the time of the act or omission.

Sections 7(4.1)-(4.3) apply where listed sexual offences are alleged to have been committed against children outside Canada by a Canadian citizen or permanent resident. Proceedings for these offences may be instituted in Canada *only* upon *request* to the Minister of Justice of Canada under s. 7(4.2) *and*, with the *consent* of the Attorney General, under s. 7(4.3).

Under s. 7(4), "employees" within the meaning of the *Public Service Employment Act*, in a place outside Canada, who commit an act or omission there that is an offence there and would be an indictable offence, if committed in Canada, are *deemed* to have committed the act in Canada.

Subsections (5)–(7) make provision for the *trial in Canada* of offences that are *deemed* to have occurred here. Proceedings in respect of such offences may be commenced *in any territorial division in Canada*, whether or not D is present in Canada. Where D is *not* a Canadian citizen, the proceedings may *not* be instituted without the consent of the Attorney General of Canada. D may be tried and punished in respect of that offence in the same manner as if the offence had been committed in the territorial division of trial. D must appear at and be present during the proceedings, unless permitted or ordered excluded by the court. Subsection (6) applies where D has been tried and dealt with outside Canada in respect of an act or omission that is an offence by virtue of subsection (7). The foreign trial must have been held in such a manner that, if it had occurred in Canada, D could plead the special pleas of *autrefois acquit, autrefois convict* or pardon. The subsection *deems* D to have been so tried and dealt with in Canada, thereby entitling reliance upon the special plea in respect of the foreign adjudication.

Subsections (10) and (11) provide for the admission into evidence of a *certificate* issued by or under the authority of the Minister of Foreign Affairs stating certain facts described in each of the subsections. A *certificate* under s. 7(10), in *absence of evidence to the contrary*, is *proof* of the facts so stated and, under s. 7(11), is *conclusive proof* of such facts.

Case Law
War Crimes: S. 7(3.71), (3.76)

R. v. Finta (1994), 88 C.C.C. (3d) 417 (S.C.C.) — In *war crimes*, the *mental element* includes proof that D *knew* or was *aware* of, or was *wilfully blind* to the facts or circumstances which would bring the relevant actions within the definition of a "war crime". P must also prove that D *knew* that a state of war existed and that his/her actions, even in a state of war, would shock the conscience of all right-thinking people. P need *not* prove that D actually knew that the acts constituted war crimes. It suffices for P to prove that the acts, viewed objectively, constituted war crimes.

Defences: War Crimes: S. 7(3.71), (3.76)

R. v. Finta (1994), 88 C.C.C. (3d) 417 (S.C.C.) — The defence of compliance with the laws of the country where the offence is alleged to have occurred is available if the laws of that country at the relevant time are held to be valid.

Where the laws of the country where the offence is alleged to have occurred are held invalid, members of the military or police forces may nonetheless rely on the defence of superior orders or the police officer defence, provided the relevant orders were not manifestly unlawful. The police officer and superior orders defences remain available, even where the orders are manifestly unlawful, provided D had no moral choice whether to follow the order because of the air of compulsion and threat to D that D had no alternative but to obey the order.

Crimes Against Humanity: S. 7(3.71), (3.76)

R. v. Finta (1994), 88 C.C.C. (3d) 417 (S.C.C.) — In *crimes against humanity*, the *mental element* includes subjective *knowledge* by D of the factual conditions which render the relevant conduct a crime against humanity. P must prove that D was *aware* of or *wilfully blind* to the facts or circumstances which would bring the acts within the definition of a "crime against humanity". P need *not* prove that D knew the acts were inhumane, only that the actions, viewed by a *reasonable person* in the position of D, were inhumane.

P must prove more than that D's conduct would constitute a listed offence if committed in Canada. Proof of an added element of *inhumanity* is required.

Territorial Jurisdiction: S. 7(5)

R. v. Finta (1994), 88 C.C.C. (3d) 417 (S.C.C.) — Canadian courts, as a rule, do *not* try ordinary offences allegedly committed on foreign soil. It is only when the conditions of s. 7(3.71) are satisfied that Canadian courts have jurisdiction to try persons living in Canada for crimes allegedly committed on foreign soil. It is the nature of the act committed that is of critical importance in the determination of jurisdiction. The alleged crime must be a "war crime" or a "crime against humanity".

Charter Considerations

R. v. Finta (1994), 88 C.C.C. (3d) 417 (S.C.C.) — Sections 7(3.74) and (3.76) do *not* violate Charter s. 7, 11(d), 11(g) or 15.

Related Provisions: Section 6(2) enacts the general rule that, subject to the *Code* or other federal enactment, no person shall be convicted or discharged of an offence committed *outside* Canada. Section 7 constitutes a series of exceptions to this general rule. It is also a general rule of s. 478(1), subject to the *Code*, that the courts of one province do *not* try offences committed entirely in another.

Offences relating to aircraft, to which ss. 7(1) and (2) as well as the definitions in ss. 7(8) and (9) apply, are found in ss. 76–78. Under s. 424, it is an indictable offence to threaten to commit an enumerated offence against an "internationally protected person." Section 431 prohibits attacks on official premises, private accommodation or means of transport of such a person.

Special jurisdiction in relation to domestic offences is provided in ss. 476–481.

The special pleas of *autrefois acquit, autrefois convict* and pardon are governed by ss. 607–610. Section 607(6) describes the circumstances under which a plea of *autrefois convict* will *not* be available where D has been tried out of Canada in respect of a matter that is an offence in Canada under ss. 7(2)–(3.4) or s. 7(3.7) or (3.71).

8. (1) Application to territories — The provisions of this Act apply throughout Canada except

> (a) in the Yukon Territory, in so far as they are inconsistent with the *Yukon Act;*
>
> (b) in the Northwest Territories, in so far as they are inconsistent with the *Northwest Territories Act,* and
>
> (c) in Nunavut, in so far as they are inconsistent with the *Nunavut Act.*

(2) Application of criminal law of England — The criminal law of England that was in force in a province immediately before April 1, 1955 continues in force in the province except as altered, varied, modified or affected by this Act or any other Act of the Parliament of Canada.

(3) Common law principles continued — Every rule and principle of the common law that renders any circumstance a justification or excuse for an act or a defence to a charge continues in force and applies in respect of proceedings for an offence under this Act or any other Act of Parliament except in so far as they are altered by or are inconsistent with this Act or any other Act of Parliament.

R.S., c. C-34, s. 71993, c. 28, s. 78 (Sched. III, item 26).

Commentary: The section describes the application of the *Code* and the extent to which the criminal and common law of England continues to apply under the *Code.*

Under s. 8(1) the *Code* applies generally throughout Canada. For the Yukon Territory, the Northwest Territories *[and Nunavat],* the *Code* applies only to the extent that it is *not inconsistent* with the *Yukon Act, Northwest Territories Act [or the Nunavut Act], as the case may be.*

Under s. 8(2) the *criminal law of England* in force in a province immediately before April 1, 1955, the proclamation date of the 1953–54 *Code* revision, continues in force in the province, but only to the extent that it has not been *altered, varied, modified* or *affected* by the *Code* or other Federal enactment.

Under s. 8(3) every rule and principle of the *common law* that renders any circumstance a justification or excuse for an act or a *defence* to a charge continues in force to the extent that they are not *altered* by or *inconsistent* with the *Code* or other Federal enactment.

Case Law

Common Law Defences — Generally

R. v. Jobidon (1991), 7 C.R. (4th) 233, 66 C.C.C. (3d) 454 (S.C.C.) — Under s. 8(3), courts may look to pre-existing common law rules and principles to give meaning to and explain the outlines and boundaries of an existing defence or justification to indicate where they will not be held legally effective, provided there is no clear language in the *Code* to indicate its displacement of the common law.

R. v. Kirzner (1977), 1 C.R. (3d) 138, 38 C.C.C. (2d) 131 (S.C.C.) — Subsection (3) should not be construed as freezing the power of the court to recognize such new defences as they may think proper, thus enlarging upon the common law.

Abuse of Process [See also Charter ss. 7 and 11]

R. v. La (1997), 8 C.R. (5th) 156, [1997] 2 S.C.R. 680, 116 C.C.C. (3d) 97 — Whether a *stay of proceedings* is appropriate depends on the *effect* of the *conduct* which constitutes an abuse of process or other prejudice on the the *fairness* of the *trial.* It is often best assessed in the context of the trial, as it unfolds. A trial judge has a *discretion* whether to *rule* on an *application* to stay proceedings *immediately,* or after hearing some or all of the evidence. It is *preferable* for the trial judge to *reserve* on the application, unless it is clear that nothing but a stay will cure the prejudice occasioned by the underlying abuse of conduct. Where the application is dismissed at an early stage of the proceedings, it may be renewed later where there is a *material* change in circumstances.

R. v. O'Connor (1995), 44 C.R.(4th) 1, 103 C.C.C.(3d) 1 (S.C.C.) — In general, there is *no* utility in maintaining two distinct approaches to abusive conduct by P. The principles of fundamental justice both reflect and accommodate the common law doctrine of abuse of process.

R. v. Power (1994), 29 C.R. (4th) 1, 89 C.C.C. (3d) 1 (S.C.C.); reversing (1993), 81 C.C.C. (3d) 1 (Nfld. C.A.) — Courts should be cautious before attempting to second-guess the motives which underlie a decision by P. Courts should only intervene to prevent an abuse of process where there is conspicuous evidence of *improper motives* or *bad faith*, or of an act so wrong that it violates the conscience of the community such that it would be gravely unfair and indecent to proceed. Such cases will be extremely rare.

R. v. L. (W.K.) (1991), 6 C.R. (4th) 1, 64 C.C.C. (3d) 321 (S.C.C.) — *Delay* between the commission of an offence and the laying of a charge will *not per se* justify a stay of proceedings as an abuse of process or a breach of *Charter* s. 7 or 11(d). To stay proceedings based merely on the passage of time would be to impose a judicially-created limitation period for crimes. Pre-charge delay is relevant *only* insofar as it bears upon the fairness of the trial, hence a potential breach of *Charter* s. 7 and 11(d). The particular circumstances of the case must be considered and findings of fact made upon proper foundation.

R. v. Conway (1989), 70 C.R. (3d) 209, 49 C.C.C. (3d) 289 (S.C.C.) — It is only in exceptional circumstances that P's refusal to accept a plea of guilty to other than the offence charged could amount to an abuse of process.

R. v. Keyowski (1988), 40 C.C.C. (3d) 481 (S.C.C.) — *See also*: *R. v. Jans* (1990), 59 C.C.C. (3d) 398 (Alta. C.A.); *R. v. Jewitt* (1985), 47 C.R. (3d) 193, 21 C.C.C. (3d) 7 (S.C.C.); reversing (1983), 34 C.R. (3d) 193, 5 C.C.C. (3d) 234 (B.C. C.A.) — The *test* for abuse of process is whether the proceedings would violate the fundamental principles of justice which underlie the community's sense of fair play and decency, or whether the proceedings were oppressive or vexatious. The power to stay proceedings on this basis should be exercised only in the clearest of cases.

R. v. L. (P.S.) (1995), 103 C.C.C. (3d) 341 (B.C. C.A.) — Where D can establish that *missing evidence* is of such potential importance that its destruction deprived D of the ability to make full answer and defence, a judicial stay of proceedings may be warranted. The threshold is met where D shows that the missing material would have likely assisted D in meeting P's case.

R. v. Mitchelson (1992), 13 C.R. (4th) 73, 71 C.C.C. (3d) 471 (Man. C.A.) — The common law doctrine of abuse of process is available to prevent multiple proceedings, even without evidence of prosecutorial misconduct or improper motivation. The issue is *not* whether a particular accused, prominent in the community, should stand trial because of such status, but rather, whether *anyone*, in similar circumstances, ought to be subjected to that process.

R. v. Boutillier (1995), 45 C.R. (4th) 345, 104 C.C.C. (3d) 327 (N.S. C.A.) — Where P discovers a mistake in a charge after the end of the limitation period, lays a new information charging the appropriate offence and determines to proceed by indictment, notwithstanding an earlier election to proceed by summary conviction, proceedings *may* be stayed as an abuse of process.

R. v. Waugh (1985), 21 C.C.C. (3d) 80, 68 N.S.R. (2d) 247 (C.A.) — Criminal proceedings commenced *solely* to collect a civil debt are abusive of the court's process, but if there is *prima facie* evidence of a crime V can pursue concurrent criminal and civil proceedings.

R. v. Dikah (1994), 31 C.R. (4th) 105, 89 C.C.C. (3d) 321 (Ont. C.A.) — The arrangement by which payment in full to a police agent is made conditional upon the laying of charges does *not* amount to an inherent abuse of process. (per Brooke and Labrosse JJ.A.).

R. v. D. (E.) (1990), 78 C.R. (3d) 112, 57 C.C.C. (3d) 151 (Ont. C.A.) — *See also*: *R. v. Ashoona* (1988), 41 C.C.C. (3d) 255 (N.W.T. C.A.) — Where D alleges an abuse of process, the *burden* is on D to show on a *balance of probabilities* that to allow the state to proceed would violate the community's sense of fair play and decency, or that the trial would be an oppressive proceeding.

R. v. MacDonald (1990), 54 C.C.C. (3d) 97 (Ont. C.A.) — It was *not* an abuse of process for P to prosecute D for murder, where P had previously agreed D would *not* be so prosecuted if he gave a truthful statement to the police, but evidence later discovered showed that D's statement was untruthful and that he was involved in the murder.

R. v. Marostica (1988), 65 C.R. (3d) 191 (Ont. C.A.) — A stay of proceedings was *not* the appropriate remedy where a newspaper editorial urged a particular sentence during D's trial. The appearance of justice could be satisfied by a reasoned judgment supported by reference to the evidence and the law.

R. v. B. (K.R.) (1986), 53 C.R. (3d) 216, 29 C.C.C. (3d) 365 (Ont. C.A.) — Where a trial on a new charge would *not* involve the relitigation of issues decided in the first trial and would involve different facts and time periods, and where there was no improper motive in delaying the laying of a new charge, there is no abuse of process.

Automatism [See s. 16]

Drunkenness [See "Intoxication" and s. 16]

Due Diligence

R. v. Pontes (1995), 100 C.C.C. (3d) 353 (S.C.C.) — *See also*: *R. v. Chapin* (1979), 7 C.R. (3d) 225, 45 C.C.C. (2d) 333 (S.C.C.) — The essence of a *strict* liability offence is that D may avoid conviction by proving on a *balance of probabilities* either

    i. that s/he had an *honest but mistaken* belief in facts which, if true, would render the act innocent; or

    ii. that s/he exercised *all reasonable care* to avoid committing the offence.

Where neither facet of the due diligence defence is available to D, the offence is one of *absolute, not strict* liability.

R. v. City of Sault Ste. Marie (1978), 3 C.R. (3d) 30, 40 C.C.C. (2d) 353 (S.C.C.) — There are three categories of offences: (1) offences in which *mens rea* must be proved by the prosecution — offences which are *criminal* in the true sense fall in this category; (2) *offences of strict liability* in which there is no necessity for P to prove *mens rea* — the doing of the prohibited act *prima facie* imports the offence, leaving it open to D to avoid liability by proving that s/he took all reasonable care: The defence will be available if D reasonably believed in a mistaken set of facts which, if true, would render the act or omission innocent, or if D took all reasonable steps to avoid the particular event; (3) offences of *absolute liability* where it is *not* open to D to exculpate him/herself by showing that s/he is free of fault. Public welfare offences would *prima facie* fall into the second category unless words such as "wilfully", "with intent", "knowingly" or "intentionally" are used. Offences of *absolute liability* would be those in respect of which the legislature made it clear that guilt would follow proof merely of the proscribed act.

R. v. Cancoil Thermal Corp. (1986), 52 C.R. (3d) 188, 27 C.C.C. (3d) 295 (Ont. C.A.) — *Absolute liability* punishable by imprisonment violates *Charter* s. 7 even if there is statutory intention that the offence be treated as one of absolute liability. To avoid a violation of s. 7 such an offence must be treated as one of *strict liability* to which the defence of due diligence applies.

Duress

R. v. Ruzic (1998), 128 C.C.C. (3d) 97 (Ont. C.A.); additional reasons at (1998), 128 C.C.C. (3d) 481 (Ont. C.A.); leave to appeal allowed (March 25, 1999), Doc. 26930 (S.C.C.) — At common law, duress focussed on availability of a safe avenue of escape. Duress is available at common law, notwithstanding that

    i. the *threatener* is *not present* when the offence is committed;

    ii. the *threat* is of *future, not immediate* harm; and,

    iii. the *threatened harm* is directed at a *family* member, not at D.

The operative test for duress at common law is whether D had a *safe avenue* of *escape.*

Entrapment

R. v. Pearson, [1998] 3 S.C.R. 620, 21 C.R. (5th) 106, 130 C.C.C. (3d) 293 — Entrapment is concerned with police and Crown conduct. It is completely separate from guilt or innocence and is dealt with at a separate proceeding from the trial on the merits. Once D is found guilty of an offence, D alone bears the burden of establishing that the conduct of P and/or the police amounted to an abuse of process that deserves a stay of proceedings. Entrapment does *not* engage the presumption of innocence.

R. v. Barnes (1991), 63 C.C.C. (3d) 1 (S.C.C.); affirming (1990), 54 C.C.C. (3d) 368 (B.C. C.A.) — Police may *only present* the *opportunity* to commit a particular crime to one who arouses *suspicion* that s/he is already engaged in such activity. In exceptional cases, where police undertake a *bona fide* investigation directed at an *area* which is defined with sufficient precision and where it is *reasonably* suspected that criminal activity is occurring, they may present anyone associated with the area with the opportunity. Association with an area does *not* require more than being present in the area. Randomness to such an extent is permissible within the scope of a *bona fide* inquiry.

There is *random virtue-testing* only where police present a person with the opportunity to commit an offence without a reasonable suspicion, either that the person is already engaged in the particular criminal activity, or is associated with a physical location where the particular criminal activity is likely occurring.

R. v. Mack (1988), 67 C.R. (3d) 1, 44 C.C.C. (3d) 513 (S.C.C.) — *See also: R. v. Showman* (1988), 67 C.R. (3d) 61, 45 C.C.C. (3d) 289; *R. v. Meuckon* (1990), 78 C.R. (3d) 196, 57 C.C.C. (3d) 193 (B.C. C.A.); *R. v. Jewitt* (1985), 47 C.R. (3d) 193, 21 C.C.C. (3d) 7 (S.C.C.); *R. v. Ashoona* (1988), 41 C.C.C. (3d) 255 (N.W.T. C.A.) — Entrapment occurs when: (a) the authorities *provide* a person with an *opportunity* to commit an offence *without* acting on *reasonable suspicion* that this person is already engaged in criminal activity, or without making a *bona fide* inquiry; or (b) when, although having such reasonable suspicion or acting in the course of a *bona fide* inquiry, they go beyond providing an opportunity, and induce the commission of an offence. The issue of entrapment is one of law, or mixed law and fact, and should be decided by a judge, not a jury. Before making such determination, the offence for which D has been charged must have been proved beyond a reasonable doubt. The defence of entrapment is to be proved by D on the balance of probabilities, and is to be recognized in only "the clearest of cases", where the administration of justice would be brought into disrepute if the conviction were to stand. The proper remedy is a stay of proceedings.

R. v. Amato (1982), 29 C.R. (3d) 1, 69 C.C.C. (2d) 31 (S.C.C.); affirming (1979), 51 C.C.C. (2d) 401 (B.C. C.A.) — The question of entrapment arises *only* where police tactics leave no room for the formation of an independent criminal intent by D.

R. v. Kirzner (1977), 1 C.R. (3d) 138, 38 C.C.C. (2d) 131 (S.C.C.) — Before the issue of entrapment could be considered there must be evidence of police conduct which went beyond mere solicitation or decoy work and which amounted to an active scheme of entrapment for the purpose of prosecuting the person so caught.

R. v. Cahill (1992), 13 C.R. (4th) 327 (B.C. C.A.) — A *reasonable suspicion* that enables the state to provide a person with the opportunity to commit an offence means something *more* than *mere* suspicion, but *less* than *belief* based on *reasonable and probable* grounds. What will give rise to a reasonable suspicion will depend on all the circumstances. Where the reasonable suspicion is based on information provided to the authorities, the reliability of the informant is a relevant consideration, but the threshold established by such consideration is necessarily low.

R. v. Kenyon (1990), 61 C.C.C. (3d) 538 (B.C. C.A.) — When police did *not* engage in a *bona fide* investigation of a suspected offender or location, a person responding to an opportunity to commit an offence is entitled to a stay of proceedings on the basis of entrapment.

R. v. Biddulph (1987), 34 C.C.C. (3d) 544 (Man. C.A.) — P does *not* have to disprove entrapment when there is *no* evidence that D was entrapped. Mere solicitation of an offence by an undercover officer is not enough to raise the defence. There must be evidence that the accused had been pressured, threatened, or deceived, and conduct on the part of the police so shocking or outrageous as to bring the administration of justice into disrepute.

R. v. Maxwell (1990), 61 C.C.C. (3d) 289 (Ont. C.A.) — Entrapment may be raised after a plea of guilty. A plea of guilty, an admission of all the issues necessary to support a conviction, does *not* address the issue of entrapment. Where entrapment is raised, there is a *two-stage* inquiry. The court must *first* decide whether P has proven *all* of the *essential* elements of the offence beyond a reasonable doubt. The court must then determine whether proceedings should be stayed by reason of entrapment. D must prove entrapment on a balance of probabilities.

R. v. Pearson (1994), 89 C.C.C. (3d) 535 (Que. C.A.); leave to appeal refused (1994), 90 C.C.C. (3d) vi, 91 C.C.C. (3d) vi (S.C.C.) — Disclosure of material primarily or exclusively relevant to entrapment, or issues like it, which are considered after a finding of guilt, ought be made upon request.

Honest Belief (Mistake of Fact) [See also ss. 265 and 273.2]

Sansregret v. R. (1985), 45 C.R. (3d) 193, 18 C.C.C. (3d) 223 (S.C.C.); affirming (1983), 37 C.R. (3d) 45, 10 C.C.C. (3d) 164 (Man. C.A.); which reversed (1983), 34 C.R. 162 (Man. Co. Ct.) — An honest belief on the part of D, although *unreasonable*, that V was consenting to intercourse fully and *not* because of threats would entitle D to an acquittal on a charge of rape. However, if D deliberately blinds himself to the obvious, the law will presume knowledge.

Laroche (1964), 43 C.R. 228 (S.C.C.); reversing (1963), 40 C.R. 144 (Ont. C.A.) — The defence of honest belief is founded upon an honest opinion of right.

R. v. Roche (1985), 46 C.R. (3d) 160, 20 C.C.C. (3d) 524 (Ont. C.A.); affirming (1984), 40 C.R. (3d) 138 (Ont. Co. Ct.) — The common law defence of an honest belief in the existence of facts or circumstances which, if true, would make the act innocent, is preserved by this section. The defence is *not* limited to a mistake as to facts which are elements of the offence. The defence is available unless it is taken away by Parliament in language which makes that intention clear.

Intoxication [See also ss. 16 and 33.1]

R. v. Seymour (1996), 106 C.C.C. (3d) 520 (S.C.C.) — Where intoxication is raised, a trial judge should instruct the jury,

i.   that the reasonable common sense *inference* of intention of consequences of conduct may *only* be drawn after an assessment of *all* the evidence, *including* evidence of *intoxication*; and

ii.   that the inference cannot be drawn if the jury is left with a reasonable doubt of D's intention.

R. v. Robinson (1996), 105 C.C.C. (3d) 97 (S.C.C.); affirming (1984), 92 C.C.C. (3d) 193 (B.C. C.A.) — *See also*: *R. v. McMaster* (1996), 105 C.C.C. (3d) 193 (S.C.C.) — The rules of *D.P.P. v. Beard*, that,

i.   intoxication only becomes relevant for the trier of fact to consider where it removes D's *capacity* to form the requisite intent; and,

ii.   the *presumption* that a person intends the natural consequences of his/her acts cannot be rebutted by evidence falling short of incapacity

infringe *Charter* ss. 7 and 11(d) and are *not* saved by s. 1. Rule ii, *supra*, at all events, is only a common sense *inference*, not a *presumption*.

R. v. Robinson (1996), 105 C.C.C. (3d) 97 (S.C.C.); affirming (1984), 92 C.C.C. (3d) 193 (B.C. C.A.) — *See also*: *R. v. McMaster* (1996), 105 C.C.C. 193 (S.C.C.) — To be required to instruct a jury on intoxication, a trial judge must first be satisfied that the *effect* of *intoxication* was such that it *might have impaired* D's *foresight* of *consequences* sufficient to raise a reasonable doubt. Where intoxication is left to the jury, it must be made clear that the issue for the jury is whether P has satisfied them beyond a reasonable doubt that D *had* the requisite intent. A *single-step* charge on intoxication, which omits any reference to "capacity" or "capability" and focuses the jury's attention on the question of "intent in fact" is useful. In some instances, however, for example where experts testify in terms of "capacity", a two-step charge may be appropriate.

R. v. Robinson (1996), 105 C.C.C. (3d) 97 (S.C.C.); affirming (1984), 92 C.C.C. (3d) 193 (B.C. C.A.) — *See also*: *R. v. McMaster* (1996), 105 C.C.C. (3d) 193 (S.C.C.) — Where a *two-step* charge, using language of "capacity" or "capability" has been given, an appellate court must decide, in each case, whether there is a *reasonable possibility* that the jury may have been misled into believing that a determination of capacity was the only relevant inquiry. Relevant factors to be considered include, but are *not* limited to the following:

i.   the number of times that reference to capacity is used;

ii.   the number of times that reference to the real inquiry of actual intent is used;

iii. whether there is an additional "incapacity" defence;

iv.   the nature of the expert evidence;

v.   the extent of the intoxication evidence;

vi.   whether D requested that references to capacity be included; and,

vii. whether it was made clear that the primary function of the jury was to determine whether they were satisfied beyond a reasonable doubt that D possessed the requisite intent to commit the crime.

R. v. Lemky (1996), 105 C.C.C. (3d) 137 (S.C.C.) — *See also*: *R. v. Robinson* (1996), 105 C.C.C. (3d) 97 (S.C.C.) — To warrant submission of the defence of intoxication to the jury, there must be *evidence* sufficient to permit a *reasonable* inference that D did *not, in fact,* foresee the consequences of his/her act. There are cases where evidence, which falls short of establishing that D lacked the capacity to form the intent, may nonetheless leave jurors with a reasonable doubt that D did, in fact, foresee (in a case of murder) the likelihood of death when the offence was committed.

R. v. Daviault (1994), 33 C.R. (4th) 165, 93 C.C.C. (3d) 21 (S.C.C.) — D may give evidence of the amount of alcohol consumed and its effect.

R. v. MacKinlay (1986), 53 C.R. (3d) 105, 28 C.C.C. (3d) 306 (Ont. C.A.) — *See also: R. v. Dumais* (1993), 87 C.C.C. (3d) 281 (Sask. C.A.) — Intoxication causing a person to cast off restraint and act in a manner in which he would not have acted if sober affords *no* excuse for the commission of a crime while in that state if D had the intent required to constitute the offence. Where a *specific intent* is required to constitute the crime, the crime is *not* committed if D lacked the specific intent. In considering whether P has proved beyond a reasonable doubt the specific intent, the jury should take into account D's consumption of alcohol or drugs along with other facts which throw light on D's intent.

R. v. Colburne (1991), 66 C.C.C. (3d) 235 (Que. C.A.) — The offence of attempting to commit an offence is itself an offence of *specific intent* for which the defence of intoxication is available, even where the full offence attempted is itself an offence of general intent.

Necessity [See also s. 17]

R. v. Hibbert (1995), 40 C.R. (4th) 141, 99 C.C.C. (3d) 193 (S.C.C.) — The common law defences of necessity and duress apply in similar fact situations and ought to be interpreted in a similar way. *Necessity* requires that compliance with the law be demonstrably impossible. *Duress* has a similar requirement and is unavailable if a safe avenue of escape is open to D. Whether a safe avenue of escape existed must be decided on an objective basis, but taking into account D's personal circumstances.

Perka v. R. (1984), 42 C.R. (3d) 113, 14 C.C.C. (3d) 385 (S.C.C.); affirming (1982), 69 C.C.C. (2d) 405 (B.C. C.A.) — *See also: R. v. McKay* (1992), 13 C.R. (4th) 315 (B.C. C.A.) — The basic criterion of the excuse of necessity is the moral involuntariness of the penalized act. The excuse is available *only* in circumstances of imminent risk where the action was taken to avoid direct and immediate peril. The act must be inevitable, unavoidable and afford no reasonable opportunity for an alternative course of action that does not involve a breach of the law. The harm inflicted must be less than the harm sought to be avoided. Contributory fault will disentitle D to the defence only where D contemplated or ought to have contemplated that his/her actions would likely give rise to an emergency requiring the breaking of the law. However, mere negligence or the fact that D was engaged in illegal or immoral conduct when the emergency arose will not exclude the defence. Once D puts forward sufficient evidence to raise the issue of necessity, the onus is on P to meet it beyond a reasonable doubt.

MacMillan Bloedel Ltd. v. Simpson (1994), 89 C.C.C. (3d) 217 (B.C. C.A.) — The defence of necessity is available *only* in truly *emergent* circumstances when the person at risk has *no* alternative but to break the law. It cannot operate to excuse conduct which has been specifically enjoined, or to avoid a peril that is authorized by law.

R. v. Berriman (1987), 45 M.V.R. 165 (Nfld. C.A.); reversing (1984), 30 M.V.R. 1 (Nfld. Dist. Ct.) — Necessity is only available where no reasonable legal alternative to the action taken existed and the action was taken to avoid direct and immediate peril.

Res Judicata — Issue Estoppel

Grdic v. R. (1985), 46 C.R. (3d) 1, 19 C.C.C. (3d) 289 (S.C.C.) — For the purpose of applying the doctrine of *res judicata,* P is *not* necessarily estopped from relitigating all or any issues raised in the first trial, but any issue which had to be resolved in favour of D as a prerequisite to the acquittal is irrevocably deemed to have been found conclusively in D's favour.

Gushue v. R. (1980), 16 C.R. (3d) 39, 50 C.C.C. (2d) 417 (S.C.C.) — Issue estoppel could *not* be founded on false evidence where the falsity was disclosed by subsequent evidence not available at the trial from which issue estoppel was alleged to arise. Unless it could be said that a subsequent prosecution for contradictory evidence was an attempt by P to re-try D, the preferable policy was to exclude issue estoppel.

R. v. Feeley (1963), 40 C.R. 261, [1963] 3 C.C.C. 201 (S.C.C.); affirming (1962), 38 C.R. 321, [1963] 1 C.C.C. 254 (Ont. C.A.) — For the defence of *res judicata* to succeed on a second count after an acquittal on the first count, the substantial basic facts common to both counts must have been determined in favour of D in the first trial.

R. v. L. (T.W.) (1993), 87 C.C.C. (3d) 143 (Alta. C.A.) — Issue estoppel does *not* bar prosecution of D for perjury in the giving of evidence at D's previous trial which has resulted in conviction. No fundamental issue had been determined in D's favour at the first trial. No policy reason required that D be granted immunity from prosecution for unsuccessful perjury in the earlier proceeding.

Turigan v. Alberta (1988), 45 C.C.C. (3d) 136 (Alta. C.A.) — Cases cannot be reopened even where they have been decided under *Code* provisions that the Supreme Court of Canada has subsequently held to be unconstitutional. The original conviction gives rise to issue estoppel, as the validity of the offence provision was impliedly in issue.

R. v. Van Den Meerssche (1989), 74 C.R. (3d) 161, 53 C.C.C. (3d) 449 (B.C. C.A.) — Issue estoppel does *not* apply to a ruling made on a *voir dire* concerning the validity of a search warrant and the reasonableness of a search and seizure.

R. v. Wright (1965), 45 C.R. 38, [1965] 3 C.C.C. 160 (Ont. C.A.) — The defence of issue estoppel differs from the special pleas of *autrefois acquit* and *autrefois convict* in that the court may look beyond the offences charged in the counts. D may show in any admissible way and with reference to the course of previous proceedings that an element which is currently in issue was decided in D's favour in the previous proceedings.

Res Judicata — Multiple Convictions [See s. 12]

Related Provisions: This section, together with s. 9, make it plain that the primary source of the substantive and adjectival criminal law is the *Code*. It is also clear, however, that recourse may be had, to the extent described, to the criminal and common law of England.

C.E.A. s. 4(5), for example, continues the common law rule of spousal competency in addition to the specific statutory provisions to the same effect. Each is an exception to the general rule that the spouse of D is *not* a competent and compellable witness for P.

The provisions of s. 8(3) are exemplified by the continued availability of the defences of necessity and intoxication, as well as *res judicata* and issue estoppel, none of which are referred to in the *Code*.

9. Criminal offences to be under law of Canada — Notwithstanding anything in this Act or any other Act, no person shall be convicted or discharged under section 730

(a) of an offence at common law,

(b) of an offence under an Act of the Parliament of England, or of Great Britain, or of the United Kingdom of Great Britain and Ireland, or

(c) of an offence under an Act or ordinance in force in any province, territory or place before that province, territory or place became a province of Canada,

but nothing in this section affects the power, jurisdiction or authority that a court, judge, justice or provincial court judge had, immediately before April 1, 1955, to impose punishment for contempt of court.

R.S., c. C-34, s. 8;R.S. 1985, c. 27 (1st Supp.), s. 6; 1995, c. 22, ss. 10, 18.

Commentary: Notwithstanding anything in the *Code* or other federal enactment, this section prohibits conviction or finding of guilt of offences at common law or under statutes other than those of the Parliament of Canada. The single exception is that the pre-April 1, 1955, common law power of a court, judge, justice or provincial court judge to impose punishment for contempt of court is retained.

The authority to punish for contempt has been challenged under *Charter* ss. 7, 11(d) and (f).

Case Law

Contempt of Court: Essential Ingredients

U.N.A. v. Alberta (Attorney General) (1992), 13 C.R. (4th) 1, 71 C.C.C. (3d) 225 (S.C.C.) — The distinction between civil and criminal contempt lies in the concept of public defiance. Simple breach of a court order may be civil contempt. The addition of an element of *public defiance* of the court's processes in a way calculated to lessen societal respect for the courts makes a contempt criminal. It is *not* publicity *per se*, which converts civil contempt into criminal contempt. It is, rather, because it constitutes a public act of defiance of the court in circumstances where D knew, intended or was reckless as to the fact that the act would publicly bring the court into contempt.The *external circumstances* of criminal contempt require proof by P beyond reasonable doubt that D defied or disobeyed a court order in a public way. The *mental element* requires proof beyond reasonable doubt that the external circumstances were caused with *intent, knowledge* or *recklessness* as to the fact that the public disobedience will tend to depreciate the authority of the court. The mental element may be inferred from the circumstances. An open and public defiance of a court order will tend to depreciate the authority of the court. Where D must have known that his/her act of defiance will be public, it may be *inferred* that D was at least reckless as to whether the court's authority would be brought into contempt.

A union, being an unincorporated association recognized under the provincial *Labour Relations Act* as a bargaining agent and accorded powers relevant to that status, has sufficient status to be held liable for the common law criminal offence of contempt of court.

B.C.G.E.U. v. British Columbia (A.G.) (1988), 44 C.C.C. (3d) 289 (S.C.C.) — Picketing a court house constitutes criminal contempt.

R. v. Flamand (1982), 65 C.C.C. (2d) 192n (S.C.C.); reversing (1980), 57 C.C.C. (2d) 366 (Que. C.A.) — An expressed lack of confidence in a judge, if genuinely believed, even if *not* reasonable, does *not* constitute contempt.

R. v. Paul (1980), 15 C.R. (3d) 219, 52 C.C.C. (2d) 331 (S.C.C.); affirming (1978), 6 C.R. (3d) 272, 44 C.C.C. (2d) 257 (Ont. C.A.) — Allegations tending to bring the administration of justice into disrepute made in court against officers of the court may be contempt.

R. v. Doz (1985), 19 C.C.C. (3d) 434 (Alta. C.A.); reversed on other grounds (1987), 38 C.C.C. (3d) 479 (S.C.C.) — Language that was insulting and grossly offensive and that was calculated to scandalize and ridicule the judge and to bring disrespect upon him will support a conviction for contempt.

R. v. CHEK TV Ltd. (1987), 33 C.C.C. (3d) 24 (B.C. C.A.); affirming (1985), 23 C.C.C. (3d) 395 (B.C. S.C.); leave to appeal refused (1987), 33 C.C.C. (3d) 24n (S.C.C.) — A television station may be convicted of contempt for showing, during coverage of D's murder trial, a tape of a previous incident in which D had shot a prison guard.

R. v. Perkins (1980), 51 C.C.C. (2d) 369 (B.C. C.A.) — If the *effect* of the conduct was to *interfere* with the course of justice or otherwise bring the court into contempt and the conduct was intentional, then D is guilty of contempt. If conduct having the required effect was unintentional but exhibited an apparent indifference and contemptuous disregard for the consequences, then D would also be guilty of contempt. The intentional consumption of a large amount of alcohol just prior to attendance in court, can render D guilty of contempt even though D had not intended to interfere with the course of justice or otherwise act in contempt of court.

Hill v. R. (1977), 37 C.R.N.S. 380 (B.C. C.A.) — The law does *not* require proof of an intent to disrupt, hinder or delay the course of justice in order to warrant a finding of contempt, if the conduct was calculated to delay, disrupt and bring the judicial process into contempt.

R. v. Bunn, (sub nom. *R. v. Chippeway)* 94 C.C.C. (3d) 57 (Man. C.A.) — Inadvertence, without a further finding of subsequent wilful or deliberate conduct intended to frustrate, or capable of frustrating the administration of justice, does *not* constitute contempt.

Manitoba (A.G.) v. Groupe Quebecor Inc. (1987), 59 C.R. (3d) 1, 37 C.C.C. (3d) 421 (Man. C.A.) — The creation of a real risk of prejudice against persons charged with an offence before the trial constitutes contempt. It is immaterial that the trial will not take place for several months and that D may not have intended to prejudice the trial. It is only necessary that D intended to do the act, in this case publish certain information, and that the act was likely to prejudice the fair trial of the persons charged.

R. v. Pinx (1979), 50 C.C.C. (2d) 65 (Man. C.A.) — While the act of a lawyer absenting him/herself could amount to a contempt, the person so charged must be informed of the charge facing him. The fact that D, through inadvertence and negligence, did *not* appear in court was *not* sufficient to warrant a criminal conviction for contempt.

R. v. Swartz (1977), 34 C.C.C. (2d) 477 (Man. C.A.) — An attempt by counsel to withdraw from the case after being refused an adjournment, while not approved of by the court, did *not* in the circumstances constitute contempt.

R. v. Western Printing & Publishing Co. (1954), 111 C.C.C. 122 (Nfld. C.A.) — A newspaper article accusing certain judges of assuming dictatorial powers and of being parties to a campaign for suppression of a free press was a contempt of court. The owners of the paper were vicariously liable, although there was no ill intent on their part.

R. v. Anders (1982), 67 C.C.C. (2d) 138 (Ont. C.A.) — Failure of a lawyer to attend in court when required to do so constituted contempt where his actions were *not* inadvertent. His conduct was deliberate and his indifference was a direct interference with the administration of justice. His apology was relevant only to penalty.

R. v. Kopyto (1981), 21 C.R. (3d) 276, 60 C.C.C. (2d) 85 (Ont. C.A.) — D's apology is a matter to be considered along with the evidence showing that D had manifested complete indifference to, and a contemptuous disregard for, the judicial process.

R. v. Jones (1978), 42 C.C.C. (2d) 192 (Ont. C.A.) — Failure of counsel to appear due to mere inadvertence, falling short of indifference, does *not* necessarily constitute contempt, even though some degree of negligence may be attributable. Such matters as whether there have been other instances of failure to attend, and whether there has been a failure to take proper care to ensure that his/her obligations to the court and to his/her client are met will be relevant considerations.

R. v. Southam Press (Ontario) Ltd. (1976), 31 C.C.C. (2d) 205 (Ont. C.A.) — The deliberate violation of a court order prohibiting the publication of evidence on the preliminary issue of D's fitness to stand trial constituted contempt.

R. v. Carocchia (1973), 15 C.C.C. (2d) 175 (Que. C.A.) — The issuance of a press release by the accused police officer, after charges were laid against V for breach of a municipal by-law, linking the complainant to organized crime and indicating that additional charges would be brought in the near future was held to be a contempt of court. The truth of the press release was not a defence; the issue was whether the publication could prejudice V by potentially influencing the judicial proceedings, even though no jury would be involved.

Contempt — Jurisdiction

MacMillan Bloedel Ltd. v. Simpson (1995), 44 C.R. (4th) 277, 103 C.C.C. (3d) 225 (S.C.C.) — The power to punish youths for contempt of court was within the jurisdiction of superior courts at Confederation and cannot be removed without constitutional amendment. Youth courts may be given power to determine contempt of court but, *semble*, *not* exclusive jurisdiction so as to oust the authority of superior courts. It is for the superior courts to elect to hold contempt proceedings against a youth or defer to the youth court.

R. v. K. (B.) (1995), 43 C.R. (4th) 123, 102 C.C.C. (3d) 18 (S.C.C.); reversing (1994), 125 Sask. R. 183 (C.A.) — The notion of citing in contempt should *not* be used to express a finding of contempt, rather as a means to provide notice to D that s/he has been contemptuous and will be required to show cause why s/he should not be held in contempt. The *instanter* procedure is *not* justified absent circumstances which make it urgent and imperative to act immediately to convict and sentence a person in contempt.

R. v. Vermette (1987), 57 C.R. (3d) 340, 32 C.C.C. (3d) 519 (S.C.C.); affirming (1983), 6 C.C.C. (3d) 97 (Alta. C.A.) — *See also*: *R. v. Doz* (1987), 38 C.C.C. (3d) 479 (S.C.C.); reversing (1985), 19 C.C.C. (3d) 434 (Alta. C.A.) — A provincial court judge, presiding over a court of inferior jurisdiction, has *no* jurisdiction to deal with contempt *ex facie*.

C.B.C. v. Cordeau (1979), 48 C.C.C. (2d) 289 (S.C.C.) — The *superior* courts have exclusive jurisdiction at common law to punish for contempt committed *ex facie*. An *inferior* court may punish *only* for contempt committed *in* the face of the court. Inferior courts which are *not* courts of record have no power to punish for contempt unless the power is given to them by a statute. A provincial legislature does not have the constitutional jurisdiction to confer the power to punish for contempt *ex facie* on a tribunal not federally appointed.

R. v. Bubley (1976), 32 C.C.C. (2d) 79 (Alta. C.A.) — There is *no* power in a provincial judge to punish summarily for contempt a witness at a preliminary inquiry who refuses to answer relevant questions without offering reasonable excuse. His/her power is limited to the procedure set out in s. 545.

R. v. Fields (1986), 53 C.R. (3d) 260, 28 C.C.C. (3d) 353 (Ont. C.A.) — An inferior court of record has the power to punish for contempt committed *in the face* of the court. A provincial court judge sitting as a summary conviction court judge under Part XXVII is a court of record.

R. v. Dunning (1979), 50 C.C.C. (2d) 296 (Ont. C.A.) — A provincial court judge, trying indictable offences under Part XIX, has the inherent power to punish for contempt *in the face* of the court a witness who refuses to give evidence at trial when lawfully required to do so.

Contempt — Procedural Considerations

R. v. K. (B.) (1995), 43 C.R. (4th) 123, 102 C.C.C. (3d) 18 (S.C.C.); reversing (1994), 125 Sask. R. 183 (C.A.) — See digest under Contempt — Jurisdiction, *supra*.

R. v. Vermette (1987), 57 C.R. (3d) 340, 32 C.C.C. (3d) 519 (S.C.C.); affirming (1983), 6 C.C.C. (3d) 97 (Alta. C.A.) — Although fallen into disuse, procedure by indictment for the punishment of contempt *ex facie* is preserved by this section and remains available in Canada. However, this does *not* create contempt an indictable offence for the purposes of the *Code*, so as to permit D to elect trial by provincial court judge. The contempt is triable only by the superior court.

Kulyk v. Wigmore (1987), 53 Alta. L.R. (2d) 44 (C.A.) — Personal service is required on an application for citation for contempt. Furthermore, such an application cannot be based on hearsay evidence.

R. v. Froese (No. 3) (1980), 18 C.R. (3d) 75, 54 C.C.C. (2d) 315 (B.C. C.A.) — Procedure by originating notice of motion is the proper manner of proceeding in cases of contempt *ex facie curiae* where there is no urgency in the situation. The procedure can hardly be described as "summary" except to distinguish it from procedure by indictment.

R. v. Jetco Manufacturing Ltd. (1987), 31 C.C.C. (3d) 171 (Ont. C.A.) — Where there is a dispute concerning the facts relating to matters essential to a decision as to whether a party is in contempt, those facts cannot be found by an assessment of the credibility of deponents who have not been seen or heard by the trier of fact.

R. v. Carter (1975), 28 C.C.C. (2d) 219 (Ont. C.A.) — D should be given sufficient notice of the specific conduct alleged to constitute contempt and the evidence which forms the basis for the conviction should be given in D's presence and an opportunity provided for cross-examination.

Barbacki c. Lalonde (1992), (sub nom. *R. v. Barbacki*) 76 C.C.C (3d) 549 (Qué. C.A.) — In a case of contempt in the face of the court, the judge need *not* proceed immediately with the hearing where there is no urgency. Where the alleged contempt lies in remarks aimed at the judge personally, fairness and the interests of an impartial hearing require that the judge disqualify himself or herself and leave the case to be determined by another judge.

R. v. Vallieres (1973), 17 C.C.C. (2d) 375 (Que. C.A.) — D were given the opportunity to submit written arguments with respect to the issue of their bail and both wrote insulting letters to the judge. Although this constituted contempt, it was *not* contempt in the face of the court and the Crown should not have moved by summary procedure since such is available with respect to contempt *ex facie* only where there is some urgency such as where a trial in progress might be unduly delayed.

La Société de Publication Merlin Limitée v. Letourneau-Belanger (1969), 6 C.R.N.S. 308 (Que. C.A.) — Although contempt proceedings are usually taken by P or its officers, there is no rule prohibiting an ordinary citizen from launching such proceedings where they are not proceedings by way of indictment.

Contempt — Charter Considerations

U.N.A. v. Alberta (Attorney General) (1992), 13 C.R. (4th) 1, 71 C.C.C. (3d) 225 (S.C.C.) — The common law offence of criminal contempt preserved by *Code* s. 9 does *not* infringe *Charter* s. 7, 11(a) or 11(g). No principle of fundamental justice prohibits uncodified common law offences. The crime of criminal contempt is not so vague nor difficult to apply so as to violate the principle of fundamental justice that a law should be fixed, pre-determined and accessible, as well understandable by the public.

R. v. Winter (1986), 53 C.R. (3d) 372 (Alta. C.A.) — An obscene remark made in the face of the court warranted a conviction for contempt *instanter*, so as to maintain order in the courtroom. Such a conviction, rather than after a show cause hearing, is justified under *Charter* s. 1 in exceptional circumstances.

Manitoba (A.G.) v. Groupe Quebecor Inc. (1987), 59 C.R. (3d) 1, 37 C.C.C. (3d) 421 (Man. C.A.) — D charged with contempt *ex facie* is *not* charged with an "offence" within the meaning of *Charter* s. 11, so as to raise the possibility of a right to trial by jury under *Charter* s. 11(f).

R. v. Kopyto (1987), 61 C.R. (3d) 209, 39 C.C.C. (3d) 1 (Ont. C.A.) — The offence of contempt of court by scandalizing the court violates the right to freedom of speech as guaranteed by *Charter* s. 2(b) and is *not* saved by s. 1.

R. v. Martin (1985), 19 C.C.C. (3d) 248 (Ont. C.A.) — Where D's behaviour following conviction for fraud, after a trial in which the trial judge made adverse findings of credibility against D, could be characterized as contemptuous, the issue should be tried before a different judge. There would be a reasonable apprehension of bias, violating D's right under *Charter* s. 11(d).

R. v. Cohn (1984), 42 C.R. (3d) 1, 15 C.C.C. (3d) 150 (Ont. C.A.) — Contempt hearings by summary procedure do *not* violate the *Charter*. However, D is entitled to trial according to the principles of fundamental justice, including the right to be presumed innocent, to be represented by counsel, and to a fair and public hearing by an independent and impartial tribunal.

R. v. Ayres (1984), 42 C.R. (3d) 33 (Ont. C.A.) — A person who is cited for contempt for failure to testify is entitled to have the proceedings conducted in accordance with the rules of natural justice and without infringement of the rights guaranteed by the *Charter*.

Related Provisions: Although s. 9 abolishes common law *offences*, s. 8(3) preserves the rules and principles of the common law that render any circumstance a *justification* or *excuse* for an act or *defence* to a charge in respect of *Code* offences, except insofar as they are altered by or inconsistent with the *Code* or other federal enactment. Section 8(2) continues the criminal law of England that was in force in a province immediately before April 1, 1955, except as altered, varied, modified or affected by the *Code* or other federal enactment.

Section 10 authorizes appeals from conviction and sentence of contempt of court.

10. (1) Appeal — Where a court, judge, justice or provincial court judge summarily convicts a person for a contempt of court committed in the face of the court and imposes punishment in respect thereof, that person may appeal

   (a) from the conviction; or

   (b) against the punishment imposed.

(2) Idem — Where a court or judge summarily convicts a person for a contempt of court not committed in the face of the court and punishment is imposed in respect thereof, that person may appeal

   (a) from the conviction; or

   (b) against the punishment imposed.

(3) Part XXI applies — An appeal under this section lies to the court of appeal of the province in which the proceedings take place, and, for the purposes of this section, the provisions of Part XXI apply, with such modifications as the circumstances require.
                        R.S., c. C-34, s. 9; 1972, c. 13, s. 4; R.S. 1985, c. 27 (1st Supp.), s. 203.

Commentary: The section defines the *rights of appeal* from *conviction* and against *punishment* imposed for contempt of court. Subsection (1) applies to contempt *in facie curiae* and subsection (2) to contempt *ex facie curiae*. Under s. 10(3) an appeal lies to the court of appeal of the province in which the proceedings take place, in accordance with Part XXI, with such modifications as the circumstances require.

Case Law

R. v. Fields (1986), 53 C.R. (3d) 260, 28 C.C.C. (3d) 353 (Ont. C.A.) — Where a witness is convicted of contempt of court after refusing to answer a question ruled relevant by the trial judge, the witness, on appeal, may challenge the correctness of the ruling. Where the testimony sought to be introduced is *not* relevant and therefore inadmissible, refusal to answer the question does *not* constitute contempt.

Related Provisions: Appeals against conviction and sentence in proceedings by indictment are authorized by s. 675(1) and determined in accordance with ss. 686 and 687 of Part XXI.

Several *Code* provisions relate to special forms of contempt. Under s. 127 it is an offence to disobey a lawful order of the court, without lawful excuse. Under s. 545(1) a witness at a preliminary inquiry may be committed, *inter alia*, for failure or refusal to be sworn, testify, produce writings or sign his/her deposition. The general authority to punish for contempt of court any witness who fails, without lawful excuse, to attend or remain in attendance to give evidence is contained in s. 708. It is also contempt to fail to comply with the terms of an order releasing exhibits for scientific testing under s. 605(2).

11. Civil remedy not suspended — No civil remedy for an act or omission is suspended or affected by reason that the act or omission is a criminal offence.

R.S., c. C-34, s. 10.

Commentary: Under this section a civil remedy for an act or omission is neither affected nor suspended because the act or omission is a crime.

Case Law

Stay of Civil Proceedings [See also ss. 261, 683(5), (6)]

Rowe v. Brandon Packers Ltd. (1961), 35 C.R. 410 (Man. C.A.) — *See also*: *Stickney v. Trusz* (1973), 25 C.R.N.S. 257, 16 C.C.C. (2d) 25 (Ont. H.C.); affirmed (1974), 28 C.R.N.S. 125 at 126, 17 C.C.C. (2d) 478 at 480 (Ont. C.A.) — A stay of civil proceedings should be refused except under extraordinary circumstances.

Leier v. Shumiatcher (No. 2) (1962), 39 W.W.R. 446 (Sask. C.A.) — Where the continuation of the civil proceedings would prejudice the defence in the criminal prosecution, the discretion of the court should be exercised to grant a stay.

Related Provisions: The authority to stay criminal proceedings upon the ground of abuse of process is retained under s. 8(2) and given constitutional dimension under *Charter* s. 7.

12. Offence punishable under more than one Act — Where an act or omission is an offence under more than one Act of Parliament, whether punishable by indictment or on summary conviction, a person who does the act or makes the omission is, unless a contrary intention appears, subject to proceedings under any of those Acts, but is not liable to be punished more than once for the same offence.

R.S., c. C-34, s. 11.

Commentary: The section ensures that, although an act or omission may attract liability and punishment under more than one Federal enactment, unless a contrary intention appears, D may *not* be *punished* more than once for the same offence: *nemo debet bis vexari pro una et eadem causa.*

Case Law

General

R. v. Mason (1935), 63 C.C.C. 97 (S.C.C.) — Where an act may constitute an offence under each of two statutes, P may prosecute under either.

Res Judicata [See also s. 8]

R. v. Prince (1986), 54 C.R. (3d) 97, 30 C.C.C. (3d) 35 (S.C.C.) — The rule against multiple convictions is applicable only if the offence arise from the *same transaction*. The *factual nexus* requirement may be found in a single act of D but may have to be resolved by having regard to factors such as the remoteness or proximity of the events in time and place, the presence or absence of relevant intervening events, and whether D's actions were related to each other by a common objective. There must also be an adequate *relationship* between the *offences* themselves. A single act of D can involve two or more delicts against society which bear little or no connection to each other. The requirement of sufficient proximity between offences will be satisfied only if there is no additional and distinguishing element that goes to guilt contained in the offence for which a conviction is sought to be precluded. Where offence are of unequal gravity, a conviction on the lesser offence may be precluded notwithstanding that there are additional elements in the greater offence for which a conviction has been entered, provided that there are no distinct additional elements in the lesser offence. Finally, the rule against multiple convictions is subject to the manifestation of a legislative intent to increase punishment in the event that two or more offences overlap.

R. v. Terlecki (1983), 4 C.C.C. (3d) 522 (Alta. C.A.); affirmed (1985), 22 C.C.C. (3d) 224n (S.C.C.) — *See also*: *R. v. P. (D.W.)* (1989), 70 C.R. (3d) 315, 49 C.C.C. (3d) 417 (S.C.C.) — In a situation where the rule against multiple convictions precludes a conviction on both offences with which D is charged, the trial court should determine whether D is guilty of both charges and if so, enter a conviction on one charge and a conditional stay on the other. After the appeal period elapses on the first charge, the conditional stay may be lifted on the second charge and an acquittal entered. If D appeals the conviction on the first charge and it is set aside on appeal, the appellate court may, if appropriate, enter a conviction on the charge which was stayed. Wherever possible P should give notice to D that if D succeeds on appeal, P will seek to have a conviction registered on the charge which was conditionally stayed.

R. v. Loyer (1978), 3 C.R. (3d) 105, 40 C.C.C. (2d) 291 (S.C.C.) — Where D is charged with two or more offences of different degrees of gravity arising out of the same delict so as to invoke the rule against multiple convictions, the following procedure is to prevail. If D is convicted or pleads guilty to the more serious charge, then an acquittal is to be entered on the less serious charge. If D is acquitted on the more serious charge, D may be convicted on the less serious charge if that charge is proved on the merits. If D pleads guilty to the less serious charge, the guilty plea is to be held in abeyance until the outcome of the trial on the more serious charge which outcome will determine whether the plea should be accepted or whether it should be struck and an acquittal entered.

Kienapple v. R. (1974), 26 C.R.N.S. 1, 15 C.C.C. (2d) 524 (S.C.C.) — The common law doctrine of *res judicata* prevents multiple convictions for the same wrongful act even if the subject matter of that act can be the basis for two or more separate offences.

R. v. Briscoe (1992), 76 C.C.C. (3d) 563 (B.C. C.A.) — The rule against multiple convictions bars convictions for offences contrary to s. 267(1)(a) (assault with a weapon) and s. 87 (weapon dangerous) where i) the *evidence* relied upon by P to establish the assault on V and the purpose for which D possessed the weapon is the same, *viz.*, the pointing of the weapon with the threat to use it; and *ii*) substantially the same *elements* make up both offences, *viz.*, carrying the weapon as an aggravating circumstance under s. 267(1)(a) and possession of it under s. 87, and are proven by the same evidence.

R. v. Koble (1984), 29 M.V.R. 34 (B.C. C.A.) — Where the charges were alternative charges, although simultaneous convictions on both charges were precluded, a conviction on the second charge was *not* precluded simply because there had been an acquittal on the first charge.

R. v. P. (D.W.), [1987] 5 W.W.R. 374 (Man. C.A.); affirmed on other grounds (1989), 70 C.R. (3d) 315, 49 C.C.C. (3d) 417 (S.C.C.) — Where multiple charges arise out of the same delict, the trial court is to consider the question of guilt without considering the rule against multiple convictions and to enter a conviction on the most serious charge of which D is found guilty.

R. v. Hagenlocher (1982), 65 C.C.C. (2d) 101 (Man. C.A.); affirmed (1982), 70 C.C.C. (2d) 41 (S.C.C.) — There is *no* requirement that the two offences must be alternative offences before the rule against multiple convictions is applicable. Where the same elements and facts underlie both charges, a single criminal act can give rise to two offences. D can be convicted only on the charge which is more serious and carries the more severe penalty.

Res Judicata — Issue Estoppel [See also s. 8]

R. v. Van Rassel (1990), 75 C.R. (3d) 150, 53 C.C.C. (3d) 353 (S.C.C.) — The rule does *not* apply to offences involving different victims.

R. v. Andrew (1990), 78 C.R. (3d) 239, 57 C.C.C. (3d) 301 (B.C. C.A.) — To determine whether the *Kienapple* principle may be engaged, the *facts* must be examined, in the *context* of the *offences*, to determine whether only one wrongful act, in both its physical and mental elements, is involved. The *offences* must also be examined, in the *context of the facts*, to determine whether there is an additional or distinguishing element in one offence not contained in the other. Where an additional or distinguishing element exists, *Kienapple* will *not* apply unless

(a)   while there are *additional elements* in the greater offence, there are no distinct additional elements in the lesser offence;

(b)   an element of one offence is a *particularization* of essentially the same element in the other offence;

(c)   there is more than one method, embodied in more than one offence, to prove a single criminal act; or,

(d)   Parliament has *deemed* a particular element to be satisfied on proof of another element.

R. v. Furlong (1993), 22 C.R. (4th) 193, 81 C.C.C. (3d) 449 (Nfld. C.A.) — Breach of probation and breach of recognizance entail elements which are additional and distinct from one another and relate to the respective culpability of each offence. The respective breaches of the orders, even if both are grounded upon the same act, must be treated as arising from entirely different causes, matters or delicts. (Mahoney and Marshall JJ.A.)

Charter Considerations

R. v. Wigglesworth (1988), 60 C.R. (3d) 193 (S.C.C.); affirming (1984), 33 C.R. (3d) 44, 11 C.C.C. (3d) 27 (Sask. C.A.); which affirmed (1983), 35 C.R. (3d) 322, 7 C.C.C. (3d) 170 (Sask. Q.B.); which reversed (1983), 33 C.R. (3d) 44 (Sask. Prov. Ct.) — Disciplinary offences are separate and distinct from criminal offences. A finding of guilt by an R.C.M.P. service tribunal of unnecessary violence towards a prisoner did *not* preclude a prosecution for common assault under the *Code*. *Charter* s. 11(h) was *not* violated as D was not being tried and punished for the same offence.

Related Provisions: The common law doctrine or, as it is sometimes misdescribed, defence, of *res judicata*, unaffected by the section, precludes multiple *convictions* for the same delict, notwithstanding that it may form the basis of two or more separate offences. The operation of the doctrine, as well as the related concept of issue estoppel, is preserved by ss. 8(2) and (3).

Charter s. 11(h) guarantees to any one charged with an offence the right, if finally found guilty of and punished for the offence, not to be *tried* or *punished* for it again.

The special pleas of *autrefois acquit, autrefois convict* and pardon are governed by ss. 607–610.

13. Child under twelve — No person shall be convicted of an offence in respect of an act or omission on his part while that person was under the age of twelve years.

R.S., c. C-34, s. 12; 1980–81–82–83, c. 110, s. 72.

Commentary: The section, in effect, creates a *conclusive presumption*. A person under 12 years of age is *incapable*, as a matter of law, of committing a criminal offence. Under the section, sometimes described as the defence or excuse of *infancy*, no conviction may be entered in respect of any act or omission of D whilst D was under the age of 12 years.

Case Law
Child

R. v. Sawchuk (1991), 66 C.C.C. (3d) 255, [1991] 5 W.W.R. 381 (Man. C.A.) — "Child" under s. 13 refers to chronological age, *not* intellectual capacity.

Parties[See also s. 23.1]

R. v. D. (R.C.) (November 13, 1991), Doc. No. 1125/90 (Ont. C.A.) — D may be convicted of aiding or abetting the commission of a sexual offence by a child under 12, notwithstanding that the child is exempt from criminal liability.

Related Provisions: Age is determined under *I.A.* s. 30.

Under *Y.O.A.* s. 5(1), and subject to its exception, a youth court has exclusive jurisdiction in respect of any offence alleged to have been committed by a "young person", defined in s. 2 of the Act as a person who is or, in the absence of evidence to the contrary, appears to be 12 years of age or more, but under 18 years of age.

C.E.A. s. 16 provides for the manner in which a proposed witness under the age of 14 years may give evidence in criminal proceedings. For certain offences, s. 715.1 permits the introduction of a videotape, adopted by V or another witness, where either was under the age of eighteen years at the time of the offence, while testifying, as evidence in the proceedings.

14. Consent to death — No person is entitled to consent to have death inflicted on him, and such consent does not affect the criminal responsibility of any person by whom death may be inflicted on the person by whom consent is given.

R.S., c. C-34, s. 14.

Commentary: In this section two discrete, yet related, provisions describe the effect, in law, of a person consenting to have death inflicted upon him/her.

The section first provides that no one may consent to have death inflicted upon him/her. Any such consent is legally invalid. Even where consent to death has been given, it does *not* affect the criminal responsibility of any person by whom death may be inflicted upon the consenting party. In other words, V's consent to death is legally *irrelevant* to the criminal responsibility of D who causes it.

Related Provisions: Under s. 241 to counsel, aid or abet a person to commit suicide is an indictable offence.

Section 265(3) describes the circumstances which vitiate consent in *any* form of assault. Section 273.1 defines "consent" for the purposes of the sexual assault offences of ss. 271–273, and describes the circumstances in which no consent will be obtained. An honest belief in consent (*apprehended consent*) is a defence to any non-fatal offence against the person of another of which assault is an essential element, *provided* the consent which is apprehended would itself be legally effectual. Section 273.2 describes the circumstances in which apprehended consent will be vitiated in cases of sexual assault.

Under s. 150.1, the consent of V, who is under the age of 14 years, is *not* a defence to certain offences of sexual assault, interference or exploitation. It is similarly provided in s. 286 that in proceedings in respect of an offence of abduction (ss. 280–283), it is *not* a defence that a young person consented to or suggested any conduct by D.

15. Obedience to de facto law — **No person shall be convicted of an offence in respect of an act or omission in obedience to the laws for the time being made and enforced by persons in** *de facto* **possession of the sovereign power in and over the place where the act or omission occurs.**

R.S., c. C-34, s. 15.

Commentary: The section bars a conviction where D's act or omission was in obedience to the laws for the time being made and enforced by persons in *de facto* possession of the sovereign power in and over the place where the act or omission occurred. Obedience to *de facto* law, in other words, is generally a defence.

Case Law

R. v. McFall (1975), 26 C.C.C. (2d) 181 (B.C. C.A.) — The fact that the provincial censor has approved a film does *not* mean that the film is not obscene, only evidence relevant in determining whether the film is obscene.

R. v. 294555 Ontario Ltd. (1978), 39 C.C.C. (2d) 352 (Ont. C.A.) — The fact that publications had been admitted entry under the *Customs Act* affords no defence to a charge of distributing them as obscene publications. The section is irrelevant to such a charge.

R. v. Daylight Theatre Co. (1973), 24 C.R.N.S. 182, 13 C.C.C. (2d) 524 (Sask. C.A.) — Where there is no conflict between provincial and federal legislation and the citizen is properly subject to controls prescribed by both a provincial statute and the *Code*, this section has no application.

Related Provisions: Sections 7(3.7), (3.71) and (3.74) override, *inter alia*, s. 15 and permit conviction of D of torture (s. 269.1), a war crime or a crime against humanity, notwithstanding obedience to or conformity with *de facto* law.

16. (1) Defence of mental disorder — **No person is criminally responsible for an act committed or an omission made while suffering from a mental disorder that rendered the person incapable of appreciating the nature and quality of the act or omission or of knowing that it was wrong.**

(2) Presumption — **Every person is presumed not to suffer from a mental disorder so as to be exempt from criminal responsibility by virtue of subsection (1), until the contrary is proved on the balance of probabilities.**

(3) Burden of proof — The burden of proof that an accused was suffering from a mental disorder so as to be exempt from criminal responsibility is on the party that raises the issue.

R.S., c. C-34, s. 16;1991, c. 43, s. 2.

Commentary: The section describes the basis upon which D will be relieved from criminal responsibility due to *mental disorder*.

In general, everyone is *presumed not* to suffer from *mental disorder* so as to be exempt from criminal responsibility under s. 16(1). The *presumption* in s. 16(2), which carries with it responsibility for acts or omissions which constitute crimes under the *Code*, is *rebuttable*. Proof of "the contrary" on a *balance of probabilities* will rebut the presumption, and exempt D from criminal responsibility. By s. 16(3), the *burden* of establishing the exemption rests upon the party that raises the issue.

Section 16(1) describes the *extent* of mental disorder which, if established to the requisite standard of proof, will exempt D from criminal responsibility. It must first be shown that, at the *time* the *relevant act* was committed or omission made, D was suffering from a *mental disorder viz.*, a disease of the mind. The mental disorder must also be sufficiently severe to bring it within *either* branch of s. 16(1). Under the *first branch*, the mental disorder must have rendered D *incapable* of *appreciating the nature and quality of the act or omission*. Under the *second branch*, the mental disorder must have rendered D *incapable* of *knowing that the act or omission was wrong*. The first branches are alternatives. A mental disorder which meets either branch will relieve D of criminal responsibility on account of mental disorder.

Case Law

Nature of Mental Disorder [Insanity] [See now s. 16(1)]

R. v. Chaulk (1990), 2 C.R. (4th) 1 (S.C.C.) — Insanity is an exemption from criminal liability based on incapacity for criminal intent which will usually be manifested under s. 16 either as a denial of *mens rea* in the particular case, or an excuse for what otherwise would be a crime.

Mental Disorder [See also "Automatism"]

R. v. Parks (1992), 15 C.R. (4th) 289, 75 C.C.C. (3d) 287 (S.C.C.); affirming (1990), 78 C.R. (3d) 1, 56 C.C.C. (3d) 449 (Ont. C.A.) — "Disease of the mind" is a legal concept which is determined by the trial judge by adding to a *medical* component a *legal* or *policy* component. The "continuing danger" and "internal cause" theories reflect two distinct approaches to the legal or policy component. The "continuing danger" theory considers any condition likely to present a *recurring* danger to the public to be insanity (mental disorder). The "internal cause" theory regards conditions derived from the psychological or emotional make-up of D, rather than some external factor, as insanity (mental disorder). Common to both theories is a concern for recurrence. Somnambulism is a condition not well-suited to analysis under either theory.

R. v. Parks (1992), 15 C.R. (4th) 289, 75 C.C.C. (3d) 287 (S.C.C.); affirming (1990), 78 C.R. (3d) 1, 56 C.C.C. (3d) 449 (Ont. C.A.) — Somnambulism is a condition not well-suited to analysis under the "continuing danger" or "internal cause" theories. A trial judge may have to look to additional policy considerations, as for example, whether the condition is easily feigned, as well whether recognition of the condition as non-insane automatism would open the floodgates to such a defence. No compelling policy factors precluded the finding *on the evidence adduced* that the condition was non-insane automatism. Different evidence might dictate a finding that sleepwalking is a "disease of the mind".

Cooper v. R. (1979), 13 C.R. (3d) 97, 51 C.C.C. (2d) 129 (S.C.C.) — *See also*: *R. v. Rafuse* (1980), 53 C.C.C. (2d) 161 (B.C. C.A.) — "Disease of the mind" is a legal term embracing any *illness, disorder* or abnormal condition which impairs the human mind and its functioning. Excluded are self-induced states caused by alcohol or drugs or transitory mental states such as hysteria or concussion. A personality disorder may be a disease of the mind if it meets either test of s. 16(1).

R. v. Rabey (1977), 15 C.R. (3d) 225 (S.C.C.); affirming (1977), 40 C.R.N.S. 46, 37 C.C.C. (2d) 461 (Ont. C.A.) — Any malfunctioning of the mind or mental affliction that has its source primarily in some subjective weakness or condition *internal* to D may be a *disease of the mind* if it prevents D from knowing what s/he is doing. Transient disturbances of consciousness due to specific external factors are *not* within the concept of disease of the mind.

R. v. MacLeod (1980), 52 C.C.C. (2d) 193 (B.C. C.A.) — A dissociative state caused by anxiety, gives rise to insane automatism, not non-insane automatism. Anxiety, an internal factor, may constitute a disease of the mind.

R. v. Malcolm (1989), 71 C.R. (3d) 238, 50 C.C.C. (3d) 172 (Man. C.A.) — *Delirium tremens* is a disease of the mind.

R. v. Pomeroy (January 27, 1995), Doc. No. CA17668 (Ont. C.A.) — It is error to instruct the jury that "mental disorder" does *not* include impairment or incapacity brought about by the ordinary stresses or disappointments of life.

R. v. Mailloux (1985), 25 C.C.C. (3d) 171 (Ont. C.A.); affirmed (1988), 67 C.R. (3d) 75, 45 C.C.C. (3d) 193 (S.C.C.) — Toxic psychosis resulting from heavy use of cocaine is a disease of the mind.

R. v. Oakley (1986), 24 C.C.C. (3d) 351 (Ont. C.A.) — "Disease of the mind" is a legal concept which includes any medically recognized mental disorder or mental illness, prone to recur or otherwise, that could render a person incapable of appreciating the nature and quality of his act, or of knowing that the act is wrong, but does *not* include transient mental disturbances caused by external factors such as violence or drugs.

R. v. Hilton (1977), 34 C.C.C. (2d) 206 (Ont. C.A.) — Even if a disease of the mind results from self-induced intoxication, D may be found NCR if he had a disease of the mind within the meaning of s. 16(2) [now s. 2], whatever the origin or cause of such disease.

R. v. Charest (1990), 76 C.R. (3d) 63, 57 C.C.C. (3d) 312 (Que. C.A.) — An irresistible impulse may be a symptom or manifestation of a disease of the mind.

Appreciates [See also "Nature and Quality of Act"]

R. v. Kjeldsen (1981), 24 C.R. (3d) 289, 64 C.C.C. (2d) 161 (S.C.C.); affirming (1980), 53 C.C.C. (2d) 55 (Alta. C.A.) — The defence of insanity is *not* open to D merely because D had no feeling about what he was doing.

R. v. Barnier (1979), 13 C.R. (3d) 129, 51 C.C.C. (2d) 193 (S.C.C.) — "Appreciating" does *not* mean "knowing", otherwise Parliament would *not* have used the two different words. "Appreciate" embraces the act of knowing, but the converse is not necessarily true. While "know" has a positive connotation requiring a bare awareness, "appreciate" requires the analysis of knowledge or experience. To be NCR within the [now] s. 16(1) a person must be incapable of appreciating, in the analytical sense, the nature and quality of the act, or of knowing, in the positive sense, that the act was wrong.

Cooper v. R. (1979), 13 C.R. (3d) 97, 51 C.C.C. (2d) 129 (S.C.C.) — *See also: R. v. Baltzer* (1974), 27 C.C.C. (2d) 118 (N.S. C.A.) — The phrase "appreciating the nature and quality of an act or omission" is *not* synonymous with the English position of knows the nature and quality of his act. The Canadian test is: was D, by reason of disease of the mind, deprived of the mental capacity to foresee and measure the physical consequences of the act.

R. v. Simpson (1977), 35 C.C.C. (2d) 337 (Ont. C.A.) — "Appreciates" imports something more than mere knowledge of the physical quality of the act. D may be aware of the physical character of an act without necessarily having the capacity to appreciate that, in nature and quality, that act will result in the death of a human being. Where D who suffers from a personality disorder understands the nature, character and consequences of his act but merely lacks appropriate feelings of remorse or guilt for what s/he has done, the defence fails.

R. v. Lafrance (1972), 19 C.R.N.S. 80, 8 C.C.C. (2d) 22 (Ont. C.A.) — There may be cases where the meaning of appreciate, a common word of wide use, should be explained to the jury. The absence of an explanation does *not* necessarily render the instruction defective.

R. v. Charest (1990), 76 C.R. (3d) 63, 57 C.C.C. (3d) 312 (Que. C.A.) — Where D suffers from an unusual delusion of such intensity as to cause an homicidal act to assume, in D's mind, an entirely different character, D may be insane under the first branch of [now] s. 16(1).

Nature and Quality of Act [See also, "Appreciates"]

R. v. Landry (1991), 2 C.R. (4th) 268, 62 C.C.C. (3d) 117 (S.C.C.) — The first branch of [now] s. 16(1) only extends to D who, because of a disease of the mind, is incapable of appreciating the *physical consequences* of his/her act.

Knows [See also, Wrong]

R. v. Oommen (1994), 30 C.R. (4th) 195, 91 C.C.C. (3d) 8 (S.C.C.); affirming (1993), 21 C.R. (4th) 117 (Alta. C.A.) — Section 16(1) embraces not only the *intellectual ability* to know right from wrong in an abstract sense, but also the *ability to apply* that *knowledge* in a rational way to the alleged criminal act. The provision focuses upon the particular capacity of D to understand that the act was wrong at the time it was committed.

R. v. Oommen (1994), 30 C.R. (4th) 195, 91 C.C.C. (3d) 8 (S.C.C.); affirming (1993), 21 C.R. (4th) 117 (Alta. C.A.) — D is exempt from criminal responsibility where, at the time of the act, a *mental disorder* deprived D of the capacity for rational perception, hence *rational choice* about the rightness or wrongness of the act.

Wrong

R. v. Chaulk (1990), 2 C.R. (4th) 1 (S.C.C.) — *See also*: *R. v. Ratti* (1991), 62 C.C.C. (3d) 105 (S.C.C.); *R. v. Landry* (1991), 62 C.C.C. (3d) 117 (S.C.C.) — "Wrong" means "morally wrong" *not* "legally wrong". The issue is whether D, due to disease of the mind, was rendered incapable of knowing that the act committed was something that s/he ought not to have done. D may well be aware that an act is contrary to law but, by reason of a disease of the mind, at the same time, be incapable of knowing that the act is morally wrong in the circumstances, according to the moral standards of society.

R. v. W. (J.M.) (1998), 123 C.C.C. (3d) 245 (B.C. C.A.) — A person who understands society's views of what is right and wrong in particular circumstances, but either does not care, or because of a delusion chooses to act nevertheless in contravention of society's view, is *not* excused from criminal responsibility.

R. v. Worth (1995), 40 C.R. (4th) 123, 98 C.C.C. (3d) 133 (Ont. C.A.) — Mental disorder exempts D from criminal responsibility if D proves, on a balance of probabilities, s/he is suffering from a disease of the mind that renders him/her incapable of knowing that his/her act was legally or morally wrong.

Delusions as Evidence of Mental Disorder

R. v. Oommen (1994), 30 C.R. (4th) 195, 91 C.C.C. (3d) 8 (S.C.C.); affirming (1993), 21 C.R. (4th) 117 (Alta. C.A.) — D need *not* establish that the delusion permits D to raise a specific defence, as for example self-defence, to be exempt from criminal responsibility. The inability to make a rational choice may result from a variety of mental disorders, including delusions which cause D to perceive an act which is wrong as right or justifiable.

R. v. Ratti (1991), 62 C.C.C. (3d) 105 (S.C.C.) — It is not sufficient, under the second branch of [now] s. 16(1), to decide that D's act was a result of a delusion. Where D's act was motivated by a delusion, a conviction will follow where D was capable of knowing, in spite of the delusion, that the act, in the circumstances, would have been morally condemned by reasonable members of society.

R. v. Abbey (1982), 29 C.R. (3d) 193, 68 C.C.C. (2d) 394 (S.C.C.) — In order to render D incapable of appreciating the nature and quality of an act, the delusion suffered by D must be shown to have negatived an element of the crime. A delusion which renders D incapable of appreciating the nature and quality of his/her act goes to the *mens rea* of the offence, and results in a verdict of not guilty by reason of insanity. However, punishment is not an element of the offence itself, and an inability to appreciate the penal consequences of an act does not bring D within either arm of s. 16(2) [now s. 16(1)]. The inability to appreciate the nature and quality of the act refers to the physical character of the act and the second arm requires knowledge that it is wrong according to law, not appreciation of the consequences, whether physical or penal.

R. v. Budic (No. 3) (1978), 43 C.C.C. (2d) 419 (Alta. C.A.) — The fact that the specific delusions experienced by D did *not* cause him to believe in the existence of a state of things that, if it existed, would have justified the killing, did *not* preclude D suffering from a disease of the mind which rendered him incapable of knowing that the killing was wrong.

R. v. Swain (1986), 50 C.R. (3d) 97, 24 C.C.C. (3d) 385 (Ont. C.A.) — Where D did not think he was causing injury, but believed he was protecting his family from evil spirits, he was properly found not guilty by reason of insanity.

R. v. Kirkby (1985), 47 C.R. (3d) 97, 21 C.C.C. (3d) 31 (Ont. C.A.) — *See also*: *R. v. Charest* (1990), 76 C.R. (3d) 63, 57 C.C.C. (3d) 312 (Que. C.A.) — Where D appreciates the physical nature of the act and its physical consequences, that is, D knows that s/he is shooting a human being and that the shooting will cause death, D may nevertheless not appreciate the nature and quality of the act if a delusion has caused the act of killing to assume in D's mind an entirely different character.

R. v. Courville (1982), 2 C.C.C. (3d) 118 (Ont. C.A.) — Delusions resulting from self-induced intoxication by drugs which caused a loss of self-control or an irresistible impulse do not constitute a defence where the evidence indicated that D had acted voluntarily, with knowledge and appreciation of what he was doing and that it was wrong.

Presumption of No Mental Disorder: S. 16(2)

R. v. Chaulk (1990), 2 C.R. (4th) 1 (S.C.C.); — *See also: R. v. Ratti* (1991), 62 C.C.C. (3d) 105 (S.C.C.); *R. v. Romeo* (1991), 62 C.C.C. (3d) 1 (S.C.C.) — Section [now] s. 16(2), infringes but is a reasonable limitation upon the presumption of innocence guarantee in s. 11(d).

Evidentiary Considerations [See also, C.E.A. s. 7]

R. v. Jacquard (1997), [1997] 1 S.C.R. 314, 4 C.R. (5th) 280, 113 C.C.C. (3d) 1 (S.C.C.) — Evidence of concealment of flight may *not* speak, as evidence of consciousness of guilt, to a particular level of offence, but it bears upon whether D was capable of appreciating that what s/he had done was wrong.

R. v. Giesbrecht (1994), 91 C.C.C. (3d) 230, 30 C.R. (4th) 391 (S.C.C.); affirming (1993), 20 C.R. (4th) 73 (Man. C.A.) — Evidence of statements made by D to psychiatrists concerning his state of mind are hearsay on the issue of state of mind. Testimony from other witnesses that D had been observed to make statements concerning his belief that the community was out to get him, or statements to like effect, are admissible as evidence of the observed behaviour of D and may be used to decide whether D suffered from delusions.

R. v. Chaulk (1990), 2 C.R. (4th) 1 (S.C.C.) — While P must tender, as part of its case in-chief, evidence to establish the essential elements of the offence charged, evidence need *not* be adduced in-chief to challenge a defence that D might possibly raise, even if D has warned of the intent to raise the defence. To require P to adduce evidence of insanity, in its case in-chief, would defeat the purpose of s. 16(4) [now s. 16 (2)].

R. v. Abbey (1982), 29 C.R. (2d) 394, 68 C.C.C. (2d) 394 (S.C.C.) — While medical experts may, in stating their opinions, refer to what they were told by others, the party tendering the evidence is obliged to establish, through properly admissible evidence, the factual basis of their opinion. The underlying facts on which the opinion is based must be found to exist before any weight may be given to the opinion.

Bleta v. R. (1964), 44 C.R. 193 (S.C.C.) — The trial judge may, in his/her discretion, allow the evidence of a psychiatric expert to be admitted, even though the questions were not asked in hypothetical form.

R. v. Baltzer (1974), 27 C.C.C. (2d) 118 (N.S. C.A.) — *See also: R. v. Kirkby* (1985), 47 C.R. (3d) 97, 21 C.C.C. (3d) 31 (Ont. C.A.) — Evidence of conversations in which D made comments of a weird nature should *not* be rejected as hearsay. They are admissible as original evidence and are relevant to the issue of insanity.

R. v. Skrzydlewski (1995), 103 C.C.C. (3d) 467 (Ont. C.A.) — Where D denies criminal responsibility on account of mental disorder, *semble*, it is proper for the trial judge to instruct the jury

i.   that hospital records relied upon by experts do *not* suffer from the hearsay dangers associated with statements made by D to hospital personnel;

ii. that statements made by D and others to treatment personnel are *not* evidence of the truth of their contents; and,

iii. that they ought *not* consider opinions of experts who did *not* testify contained in material considered by those experts who did testify.

R. v. Worth (1995), 98 C.C.C. (3d) 133, 40 C.R. (4th) 123 (Ont. C.A.) — Where D denies criminal responsibility on account of mental disorder, and refuses to be examined by a psychiatrist retained by P, a jury may be instructed that it may infer that the defence would not withstand scrutiny. Such an instruction, coupled with a direction that D was *not* required to submit to such an examination, did *not* contravene *Charter* s. 7.

R. v. Stevenson (1990), 58 C.C.C. (3d) 464 at 496 (Ont. C.A.) — *See also: R. v. Sweeney (No.2)* (1977), 40 C.R.N.S. 37, 35 C.C.C. (2d) 245 (Ont. C.A.); *R. v. Fitzgerald* (1982), 70 C.C.C. (2d) 87 (Ont.

C.A.) — A jury should be instructed that D's refusal to discuss the circumstances of an offence with a psychiatrist retained by P was an exercise of his right to remain silent from which no inference of guilt could be drawn. It should also be made clear that, in assessing P's expert evidence in comparison to that called by D, the jury could properly consider D's refusal to discuss the offence with P's expert.

R. v. Kirkby (1985), 47 C.R. (3d) 97, 21 C.C.C. (3d) 31 (Ont. C.A.) — The jury is entitled to reject expert evidence of insanity and to conclude, from D's previous and contemporaneous conduct and utterances, that he was insane, if the facts support that conclusion.

Mental Disorder (Insanity) Raised by Prosecution

R. v. Swain (1991), 63 C.C.C. (3d) 481 (S.C.C.) — The principles of fundamental justice require that D have the right to control his/her own defence. The decision whether raise the insanity (mental disorder) defence is part and parcel of the conduct of D's overall defence. The ability of P to raise insanity (mental disorder) over and above D's wishes interferes with D's control over the conduct of his/her defence. It could interfere with other defences being advanced by D and irreversibly damage D's credibility. P may only raise the issue of insanity (mental disorder) *after* the trier of fact has concluded D was *otherwise guilty* of the offence charged. If D is then found insane (not criminally responsible) at the time of the offence, a verdict of not guilty by reason of insanity (not criminally responsible on account of mental disorder) is entered. If D is *not* found insane (not criminally responsible) a conviction is entered. The only exception to this rule is that where D's own evidence tends to put his/her mental capacity for criminal intent into question, P is entitled to put forward evidence of insanity (mental disorder) in the course of the trial and the judge is entitled to charge the jury on the insanity defence.D has the option of raising insanity (mental disorder) during the course of the trial, or of waiting until there has been a finding of guilt.

R. v. Thomson (1991), 10 C.R. (4th) 201, 69 C.C.C. (3d) 314 (Ont. C.A.) — The introduction of evidence of [now] mental disorder by P does *not, per se,* violate D's s. 7 *Charter* rights. It is only the introduction of that evidence where D does *not* wish to rely on the exemption that does so. Where the introduction of such evidence by P facilitates D's alternative defence (mental disorder) by providing an evidentiary basis therefor, *Charter* s. 7 is *not* implicated.

There is no infringement of *Charter* s. 7 where P adduces evidence of insanity (mental disorder) after D indicates that, as an alternative to another defence, insanity (mental disorder) will be advanced. An infringement of D's s. 7 rights only occurs when P attempts to adduce evidence of insanity (mental disorder) against D's wishes.

Jury Trials

Theriault v. R. (1981), 22 C.R. (3d) 138 (S.C.C.); affirming (1978), 5 C.R. (3d) 72 (Que. C.A.) — A trial judge does *not* have to translate for the jury into lay terms the terminology used by the experts when these terms have been adequately explained during the course of the testimony.

R. v. Winters (1985), 51 Nfld. & P.E.I.R. 271 (Nfld. C.A.) — The trial judge must relate the evidence bearing on the defence of insanity to the jury, explain the manner in which the evidence supports the defence in law and advise the jury how to decide what weight should be given to the evidence.

Instructions to Jury Re Nature of Verdict [Cases decided prior to enactment of Part XX.1]

R. v. Potvin (1971), 16 C.R.N.S. 233 (Que. C.A.) — The trial judge must warn the jury that, if their acquittal is based on [now] mental disorder, they must declare that reason.

Lack of Intent Due to Mental Illness or Disorder [See also s. 229]

R. v. Wright (1980), 11 C.R. (3d) 257, 48 C.C.C. (2d) 334 (Alta. C.A.); leave to appeal refused (1979), 18 A.R. 450n (S.C.C.) — In the absence of a finding of insanity, lack of intent cannot be based on a lack of mental capacity to form the requisite intent. However, evidence that is adduced on the issue of insanity may be relevant on the issue of intent, not for the purpose of showing that D did not have the capacity to form the intent, but for the limited purpose of showing D did not in fact form the requisite intent.

R. v. Baltzer (1974), 27 C.C.C. (2d) 118 (N.S. C.A.) — *See also: R. v. Hilton* (1977), 34 C.C.C. (2d) 206 (Ont. C.A.) — Although D may not have been suffering from a mental disorder of such a nature as to fall within the definition of insanity, nevertheless, where the offence charged is one requiring specific intent, the illness might have affected the ability of D to formulate the specific intent.

Amnesia

R. v. Schonberger (1960), 33 C.R. 107, 126 C.C.C. 113 (Sask. C.A.) — Amnesia itself is *not* a defence to a murder charge, but is only evidence of a state of mind that might be a defence to the charge. Emotional or hysterical amnesia would not constitute such evidence as it was effective only after the event and would be no indication of the lack of capacity to form the specific intent at the time the offence occurred. Organic amnesia, caused perhaps by injury, drugs or alcohol, would be evidence that D was deprived of the power of conscious reasoning during the commission of the offence and therefore incapable of forming the specific intent essential to constitute the offence of murder.

Automatism [See also "Mental Disorder"]

R. v. Parks (1992), 15 C.R. (4th) 289, 75 C.C.C. (3d) 287 (S.C.C.); affirming (1990), 78 C.R. (3d) 1, 56 C.C.C. (3d) 449 (Ont. C.A.) — *See also*: *R. v. Halsam* (1990), 78 C.R. (3d) 23, 56 C.C.C. (3d) 491 (B.C. C.A.) — Where D raises a defence of non-insane automatism, the trial judge must determine whether there is *some* evidence to support leaving the defence to the jury *and* whether the condition alleged is, in law, non-insane automatism.

R. v. McQuarrie (1998), 127 C.C.C. (3d) 282 (Alta. C.A.) — The mere assertion of a *lack* of *memory* of relevant events is *insufficient* to found a defence of non-insane automatism. An essential part of the foundation for the defence is the existence of some condition, or physical state, that is capable of causing involuntary, automatic behaviour. D bears an *evidential* burden of raising *some* evidence pointing to a *condition* that is, in law, non-insane automatism, before the defence may be left with the jury.

R. v. Haslam (1990), 78 C.R. (3d) 23, 56 C.C.C. (3d) 491 (B.C. C.A.) — *Semble*, it is unlikely that D's uncorroborated evidence will ever be sufficient to warrant the submission of non-insane automatism to the jury.

R. v. Rabey (1980), 15 C.R. (3d) 225 (S.C.C.); affirming (1977), 40 C.R.N.S. 46, 37 C.C.C. (2d) 461 (Ont. C.A.) — Ordinary stresses and disappointments of life cannot form the basis of a defence of non-insane automatism.

R. v. Berger (1975), 27 C.C.C. (2d) 357 (B.C. C.A.) — Automatism is unconscious, involuntary behaviour. The person, though capable of action, is *not* conscious of what he is doing. Automatism means an unconscious involuntary act where the mind does not go with what is being done.

R. v. Myers (1979), 31 N.S.R. (2d) 444 (C.A.) — There is a presumption that a person acts consciously. P, in proving beyond a reasonable doubt the commission of a conscious act, can rely upon this presumption. Automatism is a denial of this essential element. To rebut the presumption D must raise a reasonable doubt as to his/her consciousness.

R. v. King (1982), 67 C.C.C. (2d) 549 (Ont. C.A.) — Where D was fully conscious of what he was doing, the fact that his perceptions were distorted and that he felt that he was detached from his body, did *not* constitute automatism.

R. v. Hartridge (1966), 48 C.R. 389 (Sask. C.A.) — *See also*: *R. v. Szymusiak* (1972), 19 C.R.N.S. 373, 8 C.C.C. (2d) 407 (Ont. C.A.); *R. v. Revelle* (1979), 21 C.R. (3d) 161 at 162, 48 C.C.C. (2d) 267 (Ont. C.A.); affirmed (1981), 21 C.R. (3d) 161 at 167, 61 C.C.C. (2d) 575 (S.C.C.) — Where the possibility of an unconscious act depends on, and only on, *intoxication*, then, depending upon the evidence, the defence is either insanity or intoxication, but *not* automatism.

R. v. Minor (1955), 21 C.R. 377, 112 C.C.C. 29 (Sask. C.A.) — Unconsciousness from any cause which results in an inability to form any intent may constitute a defence in respect of an act performed by D while in that condition. This defence is distinct and separate from the defence of insanity.

Charter Considerations [See also, "Presumption of No Mental Disorder"]

R. v. Malcolm (1989), 71 C.R. (3d) 238, 50 C.C.C. (3d) 172 (Man. C.A.) — *See also*: *R. v. Stevenson* (1990), 58 C.C.C. (3d) 464 at 496 (Ont. C.A.) — It is *not* contrary to *Charter* s. 11(c) to direct a jury that a negative inference may be drawn from D's refusal to be examined by P's psychiatrist where D makes his sanity an issue.

Related Provisions: "Mental disorder" is defined in s. 2 as "disease of the mind".

Where the trier of fact finds that D committed the act or made the omission that formed the basis of the offence charged, but was at the time suffering a mental disorder so as to be exempt from criminal responsibility under s. 16(1), the *verdict* to be rendered under s. 672.34 is that D committed the act or made the omission but is *not criminally responsible on account of mental disorder*. The effect of the verdict is described in s. 672.35 and 672.36.

In *proceedings upon indictment*, D may *appeal* to the court of appeal from the special verdict under s. 675(3). The right of the Attorney General to appeal from such a verdict is found s. 676(1)(a). In *summary conviction proceedings*, both D and P have a right of appeal from the special verdict under s. 813(a)(iii) and (b)(iii), as does any *party to the proceedings* under s. 830 upon the grounds there stated.

Upon return of the special verdict, the *trial court* may hold a *disposition hearing* under s. 672.45. Where the court does *not* make a disposition under s. 672.45, the disposition hearing will be held before and a disposition made by the *Review Board* under s. 672.47. The procedure at the hearing is governed by s. 672.5 and the terms of the disposition by ss. 672.54–672.64. Reviews by the Board are in accordance with ss. 672.81–672.85.

Quite apart from the issue of criminal responsibility for the offence charged, a question may arise concerning D's *fitness to stand trial*. "Unfit to stand trial" is defined in s. 2. Fitness to stand trial is governed by ss. 672.22–672.33. Where D is found unfit to stand trial, the trial court may hold a disposition hearing and make a disposition under s. 672.45. Where the *court* makes no s. 672.45 disposition, the hearing will be held before and the disposition made by the *Review Board* under s. 672.47. Hearing procedure follows s. 672.5. The terms of the disposition are determined by ss. 672.44–672.64. The obligations on the Board to review dispositions appear in ss. 672.81–672.85.

In *proceedings upon indictment*, a finding of unfit to stand trial may be appealed to the court of appeal by D under s. 675(3) and by P under s. 676(3). A similar right in *summary conviction proceedings* is conferred by ss. 813(a)(iii) and (b)(iii) and s. 830.

Appeals to the court of appeal from dispositions made after a mental disorder verdict are permitted and governed by ss. 672.72–672.8.

17. Compulsion by threats — **A person who commits an offence under compulsion by threats of immediate death or bodily harm from a person who is present when the offence is committed is excused for committing the offence if the person believes that the threats will be carried out and if the person is not a party to a conspiracy or association whereby the person is subject to compulsion, but this section does not apply where the offence that is committed is high treason or treason, murder, piracy, attempted murder, sexual assault, sexual assault with a weapon, threats to a third party or causing bodily harm, aggravated sexual assault, forcible abduction, hostage taking, robbery, assault with a weapon or causing bodily harm, aggravated assault, unlawfully causing bodily harm, arson or an offence under sections 280 to 283 (abduction and detention of young persons).**

R.S., c. C-34, s. 17; 1974–75–76, c. 105, s. 29; 1980–82–83, c. 125, s. 4;R.S. 1985, c. 27 (1st Supp.), s. 40(2).

Commentary: The section defines the basis upon which *compulsion* may operate as a legal excuse when D commits an offence.

Compulsion under the section has several elements. The *threats* by which D is compelled must be of *immediate death or bodily harm*. "Bodily harm" is defined in s. 2. The threats must emanate *from* a *person* who is *present when the offence is committed*. D must *believe* the threats will be carried out. D, further must *not* be a party to a conspiracy or association, whereby s/he is subject to compulsion.

It is the effect of the section that, as a general principle, D, who has *actually* committed an offence in such circumstances, is excused from what otherwise would be criminal responsibility. Where the offence that D commits in consequence of compulsion, however, is one listed in the section, D is *not* excused in such circumstances, notwithstanding compulsion.

Case Law

General Principles

R. v. Hibbert (1995), 40 C.R. (4th) 141, 99 C.C.C. (3d) 193 (S.C.C.) — Section 17 codifies the defence of duress *only* in relation to *principals* under s. 21(1)(a). Persons who commit an offence as *parties* may invoke the *common law* defence of duress preserved by *Code* s. 8(3).

R. v. Hibbert (1995), 40 C.R. (4th) 141, 99 C.C.C. (3d) 193 (S.C.C.) — The common law defences of necessity and duress apply in similar fact situations and ought to be interpreted in a similar way. *Necessity* requires that compliance with the law be demonstrably impossible. *Duress* has a similar requirement and is unavailable if a safe avenue of escape is open to D. Whether a safe avenue of escape existed must be decided on an objective basis, but taking into account D's personal circumstances.

The fact that D committed an offence as a result of threats of death or bodily harm in certain circumstances, may be *relevant* to whether D had the *mens rea* necessary to be guilty of the offence. Where the offence is one where the presence of duress is potentially relevant to proof of *mens rea*, D is entitled to rely upon evidence of threats as a basis for a submission that P has *not* proven beyond reasonable doubt the requisite *mens rea.*

R. v. Hébert, [1989] 1 S.C.R. 233, 49 C.C.C. (3d) 59 (S.C.C.) — On charges of perjury and obstructing justice for giving false testimony on behalf of P at a preliminary inquiry, the fact that the testimony was given under a death threat did *not* support the defence of compulsion.

R. v. Keller (1998), 131 C.C.C. (3d) 59 (Alta. C.A.) — The reasonableness or safety of the legal alternative depends, to a large extent, on the quality and imminence of the threat.

R. v. Bergstrom (1980), 13 C.R. (3d) 342, 52 C.C.C. (2d) 407 (Man. C.A.); affirmed on other grounds (1981), 20 C.R. (3d) 347 (S.C.C.) — D is expected by society to resist threats or run away from them. It is only when these options were unavailable that duress affords a defence.

R. v. Hébert (1986), 3 Q.A.C. 251 (C.A.); reversed on other grounds (1989), 49 C.C.C. (3d) 59 (S.C.C.) — Compulsion is unavailable where D is able to protect him/herself against the persons threatening him/her and has the means to render the threats ineffective.

R. v. Robbins (1982), 66 C.C.C. (2d) 550 (Que. C.A.) — There must be an *immediate* threat to the person committing the offence. Fear that her child would be kidnapped was neither a threat of death nor of bodily harm to D and thus did not bring D within the section.

Parties

R. v. Hibbert (1995), 40 C.R. (4th) 141, 99 C.C.C. (3d) 193 (S.C.C.) — Duress will *not* negate the mental element required to establish accessoryship under either s. 21(1)(b) or (2). The phrase "for the purpose of" in s. 21(1)(b) means "intention". It does *not* require proof that D desired the commission of the offence. Equally, s. 21(2) does *not* require proof that D desired the commission of the unlawful purpose, only that the party and principal have in mind the same unlawful purpose.

R. v. Jasman (1985), 60 A.R. 100 (C.A.) — *See also: R. v. Misener* (1982), 51 N.S.R. (2d) 160 (C.A.) — The defence of duress is unavailable to someone who actually committed robbery. Where D is alleged to be a party, duress is a complete defence *not* only to robbery but also to any included offences.

R. v. Curran (1977), 38 C.C.C. (2d) 151 (Alta. C.A.) — *See also: R. v. Hartford* (1979), 51 C.C.C. (2d) 462 (B.C. C.A.) — The defence of duress is available to D charged as a *party* to murder as an aider or abettor.

R. v. Mena (1987), 57 C.R. (3d) 172, 34 C.C.C. (3d) 304 (Ont. C.A.) — Whether the common law defence of duress was available to D depended on whether he was a party to the offence of robbery as an aider or whether he actually committed the offence as a co-perpetrator. Co-perpetration requires acting in concert as a joint enterprise.

Charter Considerations

R. v. Ruzic (1998), 128 C.C.C. (3d) 97 (Ont. C.A.); additional reasons at (1998), 128 C.C.C. (3d) 481 (Ont. C.A.); leave to appeal allowed (March 25, 1999), Doc. 26930 (S.C.C.) — Section 17 offends *Charter* s. 7 and is *not* saved by s. 1.

R. v. Langlois (1993), 19 C.R. (4th) 87, 80 C.C.C. (3d) 28 (Que. C.A.) — The statutory defence of compulsion by threats in *Code* s. 17 is inoperative due to its infringement of *Charter* s. 7. Where D *actually* commits an offence, however, D may rely on the *common law defence* of duress. At common law, there is *no* requirement that the threats be made by a person present at the scene of D's crime. The threat, however, must be immediate or imminent and the person threatened must resort to the protection of the law if s/he can do so.

Related Provisions: The effect of the parenthetical reference "(abduction and detention of young persons)" is described in s. 3.

Section 18 abolishes the common law presumption of spousal compulsion where D commits an offence in the presence of his/her spouse. D must adduce evidence of *actual compulsion* within s. 17 in such cases.

The related excuse of necessity is preserved by s. 8(3).

18. Compulsion of spouse — **No presumption arises that a married person who commits an offence does so under compulsion by reason only that the offence is committed in the presence of the spouse of that married person.**

R.S., c. C-34, s. 18; 1980–81–82–83, c. 125, s. 4.

Commentary: The section abolishes the common law presumption of spousal compulsion where D commits an offence in the presence of his/her spouse.

Related Provisions: Evidence of *actual* compulsion within s. 17 may excuse D in the circumstances described in s. 18.

Under s. 23(2) *no* married person whose spouse has been a party to an offence is an accessory after the fact to the offence by receiving, comforting or assisting the spouse for the *purpose* of enabling the spouse to escape.

Section 278 permits one spouse to be charged with any crime of sexual assault in respect of the other committed during cohabitation. Theft between spouses is an offence in circumstances described in s. 329.

Spousal competency and compellability in criminal proceedings is governed by *C.E.A.* ss. 4(1)–(5).

19. Ignorance of the law — **Ignorance of the law by a person who commits an offence is not an excuse for committing that offence.**

R.S., c. C-34, s. 19.

Commentary: The section states the well-known principle that ignorance of the law is no excuse for the commission of crime. It follows from the principle, though it is not expressly stated, that everyone is presumed to know the law.

Case Law

R. v. Forster (1992), 70 C.C.C. (3d) 59 (S.C.C.) — An honest but mistaken belief about the legal consequences of one's own deliberate actions furnishes *no* defence to a criminal charge, even where the mistake cannot be attributed to D's negligence.

R. v. Jones (1991), 8 C.R. (4th) 137, 66 C.C.C. (3d) 512 (S.C.C.) — A mistaken belief that a law does not apply because it is inoperative on a reserve is a mistake of law, hence no defence to a charge.

R. v. MacDougall (1982), 31 C.R. (3d) 1, 1 C.C.C. (3d) 65 (S.C.C.) — Although there may be appropriate cases for a defence of *officially induced error* of law, it does *not* arise where there is no evidence that D, charged with driving while suspended under provincial law, had been misled by an error on the part of the Registrar of Motor Vehicles.

Molis v. R. (1980), 55 C.C.C. (2d) 558 (S.C.C.) — Section 11(2) of the *Statutory Instruments Act* provides that no person shall be convicted of contravening a regulation which was not published in the *Canada Gazette* unless the regulation was exempted from publication and reasonable steps had been taken to bring the regulation to the notice of those persons likely to be affected by it. Where applicable, s. 11(2) would relax the operation of s. 19. It does *not* apply, however, when the applicable regulation had been published in the *Canada Gazette*.

R. v. Cancoil Thermal Corp. (1986), 52 C.R. (3d) 188, 27 C.C.C. (3d) 295 (Ont. C.A.) — Officially induced error of law is available as a defence to an alleged violation of a regulatory statute where D has *reasonably* relied upon the erroneous legal opinion or advice of an official who is responsible for the administration or enforcement of the particular law.

R. v. MacIntyre (1983), 24 M.V.R. 67 (Ont. C.A.); reversing (1983), 24 M.V.R. 657 at 72 (Ont. Co. Ct.); which affirmed (1982), 24 M.V.R. 67 at 68 (Ont. Prov. Ct.); leave to appeal refused (1983), 2 O.A.C. 400 (S.C.C.) — The reliance by D on an erroneous judgment of an inferior court does *not* constitute a *reasonable excuse* for the failure to provide a breath sample.

Related Provisions: The section does *not* include reference to mistake of fact which remains a defence preserved by s. 8(3), subject to any statutory limitations placed upon it by the *Code* or other federal enactment.

20. Certain acts on holidays valid — **A warrant or summons that is authorized by this Act or an appearance notice, promise to appear, undertaking or recognizance issued, given or entered into in accordance with Part XVI, XXI or XXVII may be issued, executed, given or entered into, as the case may be, on a holiday.**

R.S., c. C-34, s. 20; c. 2 (2d Supp.), s. 2.

Commentary: The section authorizes the *issuance and execution* of a warrant, summons, appearance notice, promise to appear, undertaking or recognizance under Part XVI, XXI or XXVII on a holiday.

Case Law

Train v. R. (1959), 31 C.R. 139 (N.B. C.A.) — The judicial act of issuing a warrant or summons on Sunday, is validated by this section.

Related Provisions: "Holiday" is defined in *I.A.* s. 34. Provision is made for the holidays of Canada Day, Remembrance Day and Victoria Day in the *Holidays Act*, R.S.C. 1985, c. H-5.

The effect and enforcement of recognizances is governed generally by Part XXV (ss. 762–773). Part XXII (ss. 697–715.1) provides for procuring the attendance of witnesses.

Parties to Offences

21. (1) Parties to offence — **Every one is a party to an offence who**

(a) actually commits it;

(b) does or omits to do anything for the purpose of aiding any person to commit it; or

(c) abets any person in committing it.

(2) Common intention — **Where two or more persons form an intention in common to carry out an unlawful purpose and to assist each other therein and any one of them, in carrying out the common purpose, commits an offence, each of them who knew or ought to have known that the commission of the offence would be a probable consequence of carrying out the common purpose is a party to that offence.**

R.S., c. C-34, s. 21.

Commentary: The section describes the basis upon which criminal liability may be established. It eliminates common law distinctions between principals and accessories.

D may be a *party to an offence* under the section upon any or all of four discrete bases.

Where D *actually commits* the offence, viz, causes the external circumstances of the offence with the requisite mental element, D is a party to the offence under s. 21(1)(a). The *perpetrator* or *principal* may act alone or jointly with another (co-principal.

D is a *party* to an offence where s/he *does or omits* to do anything *for the purpose* of aiding another person to commit the offence. D is an *aider* under s. 21(1)(b). The person who actually commits, is the perpetrator or principal under s. 21(1)(a).

D is a party to an offence where s/he *abets* any person in committing it. Under s. 21(1)(c), D is an *abettor*. The person who actually commits it, is the *principal* or *perpetrator* under s. 21(1)(a).

Section 21(2) imposes criminal liability upon joint venturers in respect of criminal offences which each *knew or ought to have known* would be a *probable consequence* of carrying out a *common unlawful purpose*. Under the section, liability attaches equally to all for what might be described as *collateral crimes* committed by one of several joint venturers in carrying out a common unlawful purpose. To establish criminal liability upon this basis, P must first prove that two or more persons formed an *intention in common to carry out an unlawful purpose* and to assist each other therein. Further, P must establish that *one* of such persons, in carrying out the common unlawful purpose, *committed an offence*. The *unlawful purpose* and *the offence* must *not* be one and the same. The subsection imposes criminal liability for the offence of one upon *each* of the others who *knew or ought to have known* that the commission of the *offence* would be a *probable consequence* of carrying out the *common unlawful purpose*. Participation in the common unlawful purpose may attract liability for it under s. 21(1). Section 21(2) imposes criminal liability for all *collateral* crimes committed by any of several joint venturers, provided the requisite degree of foreseeability has been established.

The provisions of s. 21(2), more particularly, the imposition of liability upon the basis of objective foreseeability, in accordance with the words "ought to have known", have attracted *Charter* s. 7 scrutiny.

Case Law

General Principles of Accessoryship

R. v. Greyeyes (1997), 8 C.R. (5th) 308, 116 C.C.C. (3d) 334 (S.C.C.) — A purchaser of narcotics, by purchase alone, does *not* aid or abet the offence of trafficking. A person who incidentally assists the purchaser should be considered a purchaser, *not* a trafficker. These persons aid or abet possession, *not* trafficking. (per L'Heureux-Dubé, La Forest, Sopinka and Gonthier JJ.)

A *purchaser* of a narcotic is *not* a *trafficker*, nor *per se* an *aider* or *abettor* of a *trafficker*. (per Cory, McLachlin and Major JJ.)

R. v. Hick (1991), 7 C.R. (4th) 297 (S.C.C.) — *See also*: *Rémillard v. R.* (1921), 62 S.C.R. 21, 35 C.C.C. 227 — The acquittal of a principal, conclusive only as between P and the principal in the proceedings taken against him/her, determines nothing in respect of the liability of an aider or abettor.

R. v. Thatcher (1987), 57 C.R. (3d) 97, 32 C.C.C. (3d) 481 (S.C.C.) — There is *no* requirement of jury unanimity as to the *nature* of D's *participation* whether as principal, aider or abettor.

R. v. Isaac (1984), 9 C.C.C. (3d) 289 (S.C.C.) — Where there is evidence that more than one person participated in the commission of a crime, even though only one is charged, a direction under this section may be necessary.

R. v. Sparrow (1979), 12 C.R. (3d) 158, 51 C.C.C. (2d) 443 (Ont. C.A.) — *See also*: *R. v. Wood* (1989), 51 C.C.C. (3d) 201 (Ont. C.A.) — A trial judge should *not* charge a jury on this section where there is *no* evidence proper to be left with a jury that *more than one* person was actually involved in the commission of the offence. It is appropriate to charge the jury on this section on a joint trial where there is evidence that a crime was committed by two or more accused acting in concert, even though it was uncertain which accused was the actual perpetrator. It is also appropriate, when D is being tried alone and there is evidence that more than one person was involved, to direct the jury on this section even though the identity of the other participants is unknown, and even though the precise part played by each participant may be uncertain.

Principals: S. 21(1)(a)

R. v. Berryman (1990), 78 C.R. (3d) 376, 57 C.C.C. (3d) 375 (B.C. C.A.) — *See also*: *R. v. MacFadden* (1971), 16 C.R.N.S. 251 (N.B. C.A.) — The phrase "actually commits it" in s. 21(1)(a) includes a case where D commits an offence by causing it to be committed by an innocent agent under his/her direction. The common law doctrine of innocent agency has survived the enactment of the *Code*.

R. v. Fell (1981), 64 C.C.C. (2d) 456 (Ont. C.A.) — The fact that the acts of D corporate president were at law those of the corporation for the purpose of imposing liability on it did *not* prevent conviction of D as either a principal or as an aider or abettor as the facts might warrant.

Aids: S. 21(1)(b)

R. v. Greyeyes (1997), 8 C.R. (5th) 308, 116 C.C.C. (3d) 334 (S.C.C.) — To satisfy the *purpose* requirement of s. 21(1)(b), P need *only* prove that D *intended* the *consequences* that ensued from the aid provided. P need *not* prove that D desired or approved of the consequences. (per Cory, McLachlin and Major JJ.)

R. v. Hibbert (1995), 40 C.R. (4th) 141, 99 C.C.C. (3d) 193 (S.C.C.) — Duress will *not* negate the mental element required to establish accessoryship under s. 21(1)(b). The phrase "for the purpose of" in s. 21(1)(b) means "intention". It does *not* require proof that D desired the commission of the offence.

R. v. Morgan (1993), 80 C.C.C. (3d) 16 at 21 (Ont. C.A.) — Liability as an aider does not rest entirely on whether D's conduct has the *effect* of aiding the principal. D is only liable if s/he *intended* to assist the principal.

R. v. Barr (1975), 23 C.C.C. (2d) 116 at 124 (Ont. C.A.) — *See also*: *R. v. Madigan* (1969), 6 C.R.N.S. 180 (Ont. C.A.) — Section 21(1)(b) requires an act or omission "for the *purpose* of aiding".

R. v. F.W. Woolworth Co. (1974), 18 C.C.C. (2d) 23 (Ont. C.A.) — Even when the offence is one of strict liability, an alleged aider must know that he is aiding. It is *not* necessary that D know that the conduct aided constitutes an offence. It is necessary that D at least have known the circumstances necessary to constitute the offence. Further, s. 21 requires that an alleged party have done or omitted to do something *for the purpose* of aiding the principal to commit the offence, as opposed to incidentally and innocently assisting in the commission of the offence.

Abets: S. 21(1)(c)

R. v. Greyeyes (1997), 8 C.R. (5th) 308, 116 C.C.C. (3d) 334 (S.C.C.) — Under s. 21(1)(c), P must prove

i.   that D *encouraged* the *principal* with acts or words; and

ii.   that D *intended* to *encourage* the principal.

(per Cory, McLachlin and Major JJ.)

An *agent* for the *purchaser* who assists the purchaser in buying drugs is a *party* to the vendor's *trafficking* under s. 21(1)(b) or (c). (per Cory, McLachlin and Major JJ.)

R. v. Curran (1977), 38 C.C.C. (2d) 151 (Alta. C.A.) — D must have intended his words to be words of encouragement. P must prove that the acts or words were done *for the purpose* of abetting the principal offender.

R. v. Meston (1975), 34 C.R.N.S. 323, 28 C.C.C. (2d) 497 (Ont. C.A.) — "Abets" means to encourage and differs from aiding.

Aids or Abets: Ss. 21(1)(b), (c)

Dunlop v. R. (1979), 8 C.R. (3d) 349, 47 C.C.C. (2d) 93 (S.C.C.) — *Mere presence* at the scene of a crime is *not* sufficient to ground culpability. Something more is needed: encouragement of the principal offender; an act which facilitates the commission of the offence, such as keeping watch or enticing V away; or an act which tends to prevent or hinder interference with accomplishment of the criminal act, such as preventing the intended victim from escaping, or being ready to assist the prime culprit. A person is *not* guilty merely because s/he is present at the scene of a crime and does nothing to prevent it. If there is no evidence of encouragement by D, his/her presence at the scene will *not* suffice to render him/her liable as an aider or abettor. However, *presence* at the commission of an offence can be evidence of aiding or abetting if accompanied by other factors such as prior knowledge of the principal offender's intention to commit the offence, or attendance for the purpose of encouragement.

R. v. Roan (1985), 17 C.C.C. (3d) 534 (Alta. C.A.) — To be a party to an offence, D must have had *knowledge* that the principal was intending to commit the offence and have acted with the *intention of assisting* in the commission of the offence.

R. v. Yu (1998), 122 C.C.C. (3d) 353 (B.C. C.A.) — To establish guilt on the basis of aiding or abetting an offence, P must prove beyond a reasonable doubt that

i.   an *offence* was committed;

ii.   there was an *act* or *omission* of *assistance* concerning the offence; and,

iii. the act or omission took place for the *purpose* of *assisting* the *perpetrator* in the *commission* of the offence.

R. v. Nixon (1990), 78 C.R. (3d) 349, 57 C.C.C. (3d) 97 (B.C. C.A.) — *See also*: *R. v. Black* (1970), 10 C.R.N.S. 17, [1970] 4 C.C.C. 251 (B.C. C.A.) — Where D is present at the scene of an offence but does no act to aid or encourage its commission, s/he may nonetheless be convicted as an aider or abettor where his/her *purpose* in failing to act, in accordance with a common law or statutory duty to do so, was to aid in or encourage the commission of the offence.

R. v. Fraser (1984), 13 C.C.C. (3d) 292 (B.C. C.A.) — Intoxication may rebut the specific intent required to aid or abet, even if the offence is one of basic intent.

R. v. Black (1970), 10 C.R.N.S. 17, [1970] 4 C.C.C. 251 (B.C. C.A.) — Although mere presence at the scene of the offence is insufficient to constitute aiding or abetting, it is not "mere presence" where D's presence ensured against the escape of V.

R. v. Stevenson (1984), 11 C.C.C. (3d) 443 (N.S. C.A.) — Where D intended to assist in a fight by keeping V's friends away while V was assaulted, D was a party to the assault.

R. v. Meston (1975), 34 C.R.N.S. 323, 28 C.C.C. (2d) 497 (Ont. C.A.) — While it is common to speak of aiding *and* abetting, the two concepts are *not* the same. Either activity constitutes a sufficient basis of liability.

Aiding or Abetting in Conspiracy [See also s. 465]

R. v. McNamara (No. 1) (1981), 56 C.C.C. (2d) 193 (Ont. C.A.); affirmed on other grounds *(sub nom. R. v. Can. Dredge & Dock Co.)* 59 N.R. 241 — D can be a party to a conspiracy under the section if D became aware of the conspiracy before the attainment of its object and aided or encouraged the conspiracy to pursue its object.

R. v. Vucetic (1998), 129 C.C.C. (3d) 178 (Ont. C.A.) — To establish D's guilt of conspiracy as an *aider* or *abettor*, P must prove that D

i.   *knew* the *object* of the conspiracy;

ii. *assisted* the *conspirators*; and,

iii. *intended* to *assist* the *conspirators* in attaining their unlawful object.

Common Intention: S. 21(2)

R. v. Hibbert (1995), 40 C.R. (4th) 141, 99 C.C.C. (3d) 193 (S.C.C.) — Duress will *not* negate the mental element required under s. 21(2), which does not require proof that D desired the commission of the unlawful purpose, only that the party and principal have in mind the same unlawful purpose.

R. v. Jackson (1993), 26 C.R. (4th) 178, 86 C.C.C. (3d) 385 (S.C.C.) — The "offence" referred to in s. 21(2) is *not* confined to the offence of which the perpetrator is convicted, but extends to included offences.

R. v. Simpson (1988), 62 C.R. (3d) 137, 38 C.C.C. (3d) 481 (S.C.C.) — *See also: R. v. Light* (1993), 78 C.C.C. (3d) 221 at 253-259 (B.C. C.A.) — The "unlawful purpose" in s. 21(2) must be *different* from the offence charged. Section 21(2) makes a party to the offence someone who did not aid or abet in the commission of the offence but who knew or ought to have known that the offence was a probable consequence of carrying out the unlawful purpose in common with the actual perpetrator.

R. v. Zanini (1967), 2 C.R.N.S. 219 at 222, [1968] 2 C.C.C. 1 (S.C.C.); affirming (1965), 47 C.R. 195, [1966] 2 C.C.C. 185 (Ont. C.A.) — Section 21(2) enlarges what amounts to complicity in possession offences. P is *not* limited to reliance on the provisions of s. 4(3) with respect to the issue of possession.

R. v. Suchan (1952), 15 C.R. 310, 104 C.C.C. 193 (S.C.C.) — Common intention is rarely expressed or reduced to writing. In general, it must be found from the conduct of the parties. What takes place at the scene of the crime is material, as is the prior and subsequent conduct of the parties.

R. v. Laliberty (1997), 117 C.C.C. (3d) 97 (Ont. C.A.) — Where there is evidence of *intoxication* sufficient to be left with the jury on a charge of murder involving the application of s. 21(2) to the offence of robbery, the trial judge should relate the defence and relevant evidence to

i.   the *mental element* in *murder*

ii. the *intention* in *common* to *rob* V; and

iii. the *subjective foresight* or *knowledge* of each party that *murder* was a *probable consequence* of carrying out the robbery.

R. v. King (1974), 27 C.R.N.S. 303, 18 C.C.C. (2d) 193 (Ont. C.A.) — A mere reading of s. 21(2) to the jury without further instruction is insufficient to apprise the jury of its true meaning or of how to apply the provision to the facts of the case.

R. v. Rice (1902), 5 C.C.C. 509 (Ont. C.A.) — It is *not* necessary to determine which of two persons fired the fatal shot where each of them had a revolver and they had formed a common design to escape lawful custody and the shooting took place during their attempt to escape.

51

Abandonment of Common Intention

Miller v. R. (1976), 38 C.R.N.S. 139 (S.C.C.) — The abandonment of the common unlawful purpose requires *timely communication* of such by D to his associates amounting, where practicable and reasonable, to *unequivocal notice* prior to the commission of the crime.

Procedural Considerations

R. v. Michaud (1996), 107 C.C.C. (3d) 193 (S.C.C.) — To be confirmatory of the testimony of a tainted witness (accomplice), evidence may, but need not implicate, D.

R. v. Bevan (1993), 82 C.C.C. (3d) 310, 21 C.R. 277 (S.C.C.); reversing (1991), 63 C.C.C. (3d) 333, 4 C.R. (4th) 245 (Ont. C.A.) — *See also: R. v. Yanover* (1985), 20 C.C.C. (3d) 300 at 324 (Ont. C.A.); *R. v. Babinski* (1991), 67 C.C.C. (3d) 187 (Ont. C.A.); affirmed (1992), 76 C.C.C. (3d) 286 (S.C.C.) — A trial judge has a *discretion* to determine whether the evidence of *any* witness, not merely accomplices, is for some reason untrustworthy to such an extent that a warning to the jury is necessary. A *Vetrovec* caution is *not* required in all cases where accomplices or accessories after the fact give evidence. There are, however, some circumstances in which the caution *must* be given.

R. v. Bevan (1993), 82 C.C.C. (3d) 310, 21 C.R. (4th) 277 (S.C.C.); reversing (1991), 63 C.C.C. (3d) 333, 4 C.R. (4th) 245 (Ont. C.A.) — *See also: R. v. Yanover* (1985), 20 C.C.C. (3d) 300 at 324 (Ont. C.A.); *R. v. Babinski* (1991), 67 C.C.C. (3d) 187 (Ont. C.A.); affirmed (1992), 76 C.C.C. (3d) 286 (S.C.C.) — *Vetrovec* does *not* establish that, if a warning is given regarding a particular witness, the trial judge must always point out in detail evidence which is potentially corroborative of the witness' testimony. Such an instruction may be given in tandem with a *Vetrovec* warning, but is *not* required in all cases.It is a usual corollary of a *Vetrovec* warning that the trial judge make some reference to evidence that the jury may consider supportive of the impugned testimony. In some cases, however, some or all of the supportive evidence may be extremely prejudicial to D, to such an extent that its recitation, in tandem with the *Vetrovec* warning, may be unfair to D. In such circumstances, the trial judge has a *discretion* to decide whether the *Vetrovec* warning should be given, and if so, whether it should be accompanied by a direction concerning the supportive evidence upon which the jury may rely. The decision of the trial judge upon these issues ought not be lightly disturbed on appeal.

Vetrovec v. R. (1982), 27 C.R. (3d) 304 (S.C.C.) — There is *no* special rule of evidence for accomplices. Where, as a matter of common sense, something in the nature of confirmatory evidence should be found before the finder of fact relied upon the evidence of a key witness who was suspect as being an accomplice or complainant or of disreputable character, what was appropriate was a clear and sharp warning to attract the attention of the jury to the risks of adopting, without more, the evidence of the witness. This approach is limited to situations in which corroboration was required by common law and does not apply where corroboration is required and defined by statute. The judge may properly illustrate from the evidence what the jury may rely upon in confirmation of the testimony of the witnesses.

R. v. Koufis (1941), 76 C.C.C. 161 (S.C.C.) — Acts done or words spoken *in furtherance of* a common design are admissible against all the parties to the common design. This rule applies to all indictments for crime, not only indictments for conspiracy.

R. v. Light (1993), 78 C.C.C. (3d) 221, 255 (B.C. C.A.) — Where the existence of a particular intention in common to carry out an unlawful purpose has been established beyond a reasonable doubt, and D's probable adherence to that intention has been established by evidence of D's own acts and declarations, the acts and declarations of a co-accused in furtherance of the common intention may be admitted against D.

R. v. Glasgow (1996), 110 C.C.C. (3d) 57 (Ont. C.A.) — An appellate court ought show deference to a decision by the trial judge *not* to give a *Vetrovec* caution in relation to a certain witness. It is, a *fortiori*, wher no such direction is sought at trial. On appeal, D must demonstrate that such instruction was so essential to a fair trial that the trial judge was compelled to give such a warning.

R. v. Hoilett (1991), 4 C.R. (4th) 372 (Ont. C.A.) — The *Vetrovec* caution should only be given in relation to witnesses whose evidence assists in the demonstration of guilt. It should *not* be given in relation to the evidence of D or of defence witnesses.

R. v. Hall (1984), 12 C.C.C. (3d) 93 (Ont. C.A.) — *See also: R. v. Harder* (1956), 23 C.R. 295, 114 C.C.C. 129 (S.C.C.) — An information charging an offence *simpliciter* is capable of supporting a conviction based on the D's participation as an aider or abettor of the offence.

Principal Offender Acquitted [See also s. 23.1]

Charter Considerations

R. v. Sit (1991), 9 C.R. (4th) 126, 66 C.C.C. (3d) 449 (S.C.C.) — Since the principles of fundamental justice constitutionally require proof of subjective foresight of death to sustain a conviction of a principal of murder, the same degree of *mens rea* is required for conviction of a s. 21(2) party.

R. v. Logan (1990), 79 C.R. (3d) 169, 58 C.C.C. (3d) 391 (S.C.C.); affirming (1988), 68 C.R. (3d) 1, 46 C.C.C. (3d) 354 (Ont. C.A.) — It is *not* a principle of fundamental justice that, in all cases, the level of *mens rea* required to prove the guilt of a principal is also required in respect of a party. For certain offences, however, the *objective* ("... ought to have known ...") component of s. 21(2) will operate to restrict D's rights under *Charter* s. 7. Where the offence is one of the few for which s. 7 requires a minimum degree of *mens rea*, a party may *not* be convicted on the basis of a degree of *mens rea* below the constitutionally required minimum. In each case, it must first be determined whether fundamental justice requires a minimum degree of *mens rea* before D may be convicted as a principal in the offence. Where a minimum degree of *mens rea* is required to convict a principal, an equivalent minimum degree is required to convict a party. The words "or ought to have known" are *inoperative* when considering, under s. 21(2), whether D is a party to any offence which constitutionally *requires* that *foresight* of the *consequences* be *subjective*.

Related Provisions: D may also become a party to an offence under s. 22 by *counselling* another to be a party to an offence. D's liability is established where the person counselled becomes a party to that offence, even if the offence was committed in a way different from that counselled. Under s. 22(2), D is a party to every offence that the other commits in consequence of the counselling that D knew *or ought to have known* was likely to be committed in consequence of such counselling. Section 464 applies where the offence counselled is not committed.

Under s. 23.1 the provisions of s. 21 apply to D, notwithstanding that the person D aids or abets cannot be him/herself convicted of the offence.

In general, D's complicity in an offence may be proven on any basis described in either s. 21 or 22 supported by the evidence adduced at trial. The accessoryship provisions of ss. 21 and 22 generally apply to all offences, absent statutory provisions excluding their operation, as for example in s. 231(5), which restricts its application to the actual killer by the inclusion of the words "when the death is caused *by that person*". The participation of parties in a sexual assault aggravates the offence under s. 272(d).

22. (1) Person counselling offence — Where a person counsels another person to be a party to an offence and that other person is afterwards a party to that offence, the person who counselled is a party to that offence, notwithstanding that the offence was committed in a way different from that which was counselled.

(2) Idem — Every one who counsels another person to be a party to an offence is a party to every offence that the other commits in consequence of the counselling that the person who counselled knew or ought to have known was likely to be committed in consequence of the counselling.

(3) Definition of "counsel" — For the purposes of this Act, "counsel" includes procure, solicit or incite.

R.S., c. C-34, s. 22;R.S. 1985, c. 27 (1st Supp.), s. 7(1).

Commentary: The section describes the basis upon which criminal liability may be established for *counselling*. Under s. 22(3), "counsel" includes "procure, solicit or incite".

Section 22(1) applies where D counsels another to be a party to an offence, and the other person thereafter becomes a party to that offence. The offence counselled and that committed are one and the same, although the offence may have been committed in a way different from that which was counselled. Section 22(1) makes the counsellor a party to the offence. The basis of the criminal liability of the person counselled would depend upon the mode of his/her participation in the offence.

Under s. 22(2), the scope of the counsellor's liability is enlarged to encompass *collateral crimes* committed by the person counselled. Where D counsels another to be a party to an offence, D is a party to *every offence* that the *person counselled commits*, in consequence of the counselling, *that D knew or ought to have known* was likely to be committed in consequence of the counselling. The language, similar to s. 21(2), is subject to *Charter* scrutiny on a similar basis.

Case Law

Vallieres v. R. (1970), 9 C.R.N.S. 24 (Que. C.A.) — Where the indictment specifically charged that D unlawfully *counselled* the explosion of a bomb at certain premises, P must prove that D took part in the decision to bomb the specified premises, not merely that D advocated generally the placing of bombs in any place whatsoever.

Related Provisions: D may also become a party to an offence in any of the four ways described in s. 21.

The *external circumstances* of the offences defined in ss. 152 (sexual touching) and 241(a) expressly include counselling as an essential element.

D's complicity in an offence may be established upon any basis of s. 21 or 22 which is supported by the evidence adduced at trial, unless the operation of the section is excluded by express wording or necessary implication in the offence-creating section or otherwise. The mode of participation need not be expressly pleaded.

It is also an offence, a preliminary or inchoate crime, to counsel another to commit an offence, where the offence counselled is not in fact committed. Section 464 applies in such cases, except where it is otherwise expressly provided by law.

Under s. 23.1, the provisions of s. 22 apply to D, notwithstanding that the person whom D counselled cannot him/herself be convicted of the offence.

23. (1) Accessory after the fact — An "accessory after the fact" to an offence is one who, knowing that a person has been a party to the offence, receives, comforts or assists that person for the purpose of enabling that person to escape.

(2) Husband or wife, when not accessory — No married person whose spouse has been a party to an offence is an accessory after the fact to that offence by receiving, comforting or assisting the spouse for the purpose of enabling the spouse to escape.

R.S., c. C-34, s. 23; 1974–75–76, c. 66, s. 7.

Commentary: The section defines accessoryship after the fact and provides a spousal exemption.

Section 23(1) requires proof of three elements. D must *know* that a person has been a *party* to an offence. This element of *knowledge* extends to the *fact* of the party's *participation*, *not* the *legal character* or classification thereof. The second element is *assistance*. The alleged accessory must receive, comfort or assist the party. Third, is an element of *purpose*. The *assistance* given must be for the *purpose* of *enabling* the party to *escape*. Only this combination of external circumstances and mental element will constitute D an accessory after the fact to the party's offence.

Section 23(2) enacts a spousal exemption from the operation of s. 23(1). No married person, whose spouse is a party to an offence, is an accessory after the fact to that offence by receiving, comforting or assisting the spouse for the purpose of enabling the spouse to escape.

Case Law

Accessory

R. v. McVay (1982), 66 C.C.C. (2d) 512 (Ont. C.A.) — The acts done by the accessory must be for the *purpose* of enabling the offender to escape, *not* merely with the *effect* of assisting the offender to escape.

R. v. Dumont (1921), 37 C.C.C. 166 (Ont. C.A.) — A mere failure to disclose the fact that an offence has been committed in one's presence does *not* make one an accessory after the fact to the offence.

Young v. R. (1950), 10 C.R. 142, 98 C.C.C. 195 (Que. C.A.) — Anything done which goes beyond a mere omission to aid in the apprehension of the offender is sufficient assistance. By informing the murder suspects that the police had their names and licence number, D went beyond mere omission to aid in their apprehension and became an accessory after the fact.

Principal Offender Not Convicted [See also s. 23.1][†Cases decided prior to s. 23.1]

†R. v. Vinette (1974), 19 C.C.C. (2d) 1 (S.C.C.) — A plea of guilty by the principal offender is admissible as evidence against the accessory after the fact as proof of the principal crime.

R. v. Camponi (1993), 22 C.R. (4th) 348, 82 C.C.C. (3d) 506 (B.C. C.A.) — Whether D is an accessory after the fact to a principal's crime is determined under *Code* s. 23. In light of s. 23.1, the fact that the principal cannot be convicted does *not* bar D's conviction as an accessory after the fact.

† *R. v. McAvoy* (1981), 21 C.R. (3d) 305, 60 C.C.C. (2d) 95 (Ont. C.A.) — A person may be convicted as an accessory after the fact although the principal has neither been tried nor convicted.

R. c. Hamel (1993), 20 C.R. (4th) 68 (Que. C.A.) — Evidence of a verdict of guilt pronounced against the principal is *not* admissible on the trial of an accessory after the fact where the verdict is under appeal at the time it is sought to adduce it in evidence and the principal does *not* testify as a witness for P.

Essential Elements of Accessoryship

R. v. Duong (1998), 15 C.R. (5th) 209, 124 C.C.C. (3d) 392 (Ont. C.A.) — Section 23(1) contemplates *aid* given to the *principal* who has committed an offence by a person who *knew* that the *principal* had *committed* the offence when the assistance was provided. The charge must allege the commission of a specific offence or offences. P must prove that D, the alleged accessory, *knew* that the person assisted was a *party* to the *offence alleged,* not merely that the principal committed a criminal offence.

To prove that D *knew* that the person assisted was a party to the specific offence(s) alleged, P may prove that

i.   D had *actual* knowledge of the offence committed; or,

ii.   D actually *suspected* the offence committed and consciously decided *not* to *make inquiries* which could confirm the suspicion.

Evidentiary Issues

R. v. Duong (1998), 15 C.R. (5th) 209, 124 C.C.C. (3d) 392 (Ont. C.A.) — At the trial of an accessory after the fact, *any evidence* that would be admissible against the *principal* is admissible. Evidence of the previous *conviction* of the *principal* is admissible as *some* evidence that the principal committed the crime. Its probative value is for the trier of fact. A full exploration of the principal's guilt on the trial of an accessory is *not* foreclosed. The fact that the principal's conviction is under appeal does *not* render it inadmissible.

The prior conviction of a principal may be proven under *C.E.A.*, s. 23 by introduction of a certified copy of the indictment endorsed by the trial judge.

Related Provisions: Although evidence of the commission of an offence by the party must be adduced to establish D's accessoryship after the fact, D may nonetheless be indicted under s. 592, whether or not the principal or any other party to the offence has been indicted, convicted or is or is not amenable to justice. Section 23.1 is to a similar effect.

The general punishment provision applicable to accessories after the fact is contained in s. 463. Accessory after the fact to murder attracts a maximum punishment of imprisonment for life under s. 240.

In proving the offence of the party at D's trial as an accessory after the fact, P's proof will be in accordance with the rules of evidence applicable to the trial of the party. Proof of the party's offence is a critical element of P's case against the accessory. Section 657.2 enacts an admissibility rule permitting proof of the party's conviction or discharge.

23.1 Where one party cannot be convicted — For greater certainty, sections 21 to 23 apply in respect of an accused notwithstanding the fact that the person whom the accused aids or abets, counsels or procures or receives, comforts or assists cannot be convicted of the offence.

R.S. 1985, c. 24 (2d Supp.), s. 45.

Commentary: By this section, ss. 21–23 apply to D, even though the person who D aids, abets, counsels or procures, or receives, comforts or assists cannot be convicted of the offence. Where D's liability is determined under ss. 21–23, it matters *not* that the person in whose offence D has participated cannot be convicted. The section does *not* describe or limit the basis upon which a conviction of the principal cannot be made. The inability to locate or compel the attendance of such a person, as well as incapacity based on infancy under s. 13 are illustrative.

Case Law

R. v. S. (F.J.) (1998), 121 C.C.C. (3d) 223 (S.C.C.); affirming (1997), 115 C.C.C. (3d) 450 (N.S. C.A.) — An accessory may be convicted even where the principal is acquitted.

Sections 23.1 and 592 treat parties, including accessories after the fact, as principals. Conviction of the principal is *not* necessary in order to convict an accessory.

R. v. Camponi (1993), 22 C.R. (4th) 348, 82 C.C.C. (3d) 506 (B.C. C.A.) — The fact that the principal cannot be convicted does *not* bar D's conviction as an accessory after the fact.

Related Provisions: Under s. 592, anyone charged with being an accessory after the fact to any offence may be indicted, whether the principal or any other party has been indicted or convicted or is amenable to justice.

The substance of ss. 21–23 is described in the *Commentary* to each section.

24. (1) Attempts — **Every one who, having an intent to commit an offence, does or omits to do anything for the purpose of carrying out his intention is guilty of an attempt to commit the offence whether or not it was possible under the circumstances to commit the offence.**

(2) Question of law — **The question whether an act or omission by a person who has an intent to commit an offence is or is not mere preparation to commit the offence, and too remote to constitute an attempt to commit the offence, is a question of law.**

R.S., c. C-34, s. 24.

Commentary: The section defines the inchoate or preliminary crime of *attempt* and delineates the function of the trial judge in determining whether conduct amounts to an attempt in law.

An attempt requires proof of both *external circumstances* and a *mental element* in relation to a specific offence. There is no such thing as an attempt in the air. D must have an *intent* to commit an offence: the *mental element* of the offence attempted. With the intent to commit the offence, D must do or omit to do something. The *act or omission* constitutes the *external circumstances* of the attempt. What D does or omits to do must go *beyond mere preparation* to commit the intended offence. Where D's conduct does *not* go beyond mere preparation, the external circumstances of an attempt have *not* been established. Whether D's conduct is sufficiently proximate to constitute an attempt is, by s. 24(2), a question of law for the trial judge. D's act or omission going beyond mere preparation must be *for the purpose of carrying out the intention* to commit the substantive offence.

The *external circumstances* of an attempt, in general, consists of an *act or omission, beyond mere preparation*, to do anything. The *mental element* consists of the *intention* to commit the offence attempted, and the purposeful or intentional causing of the external circumstances to carry out that intention.

Case Law

Nature and Elements of an Attempt

United States v. Dynar (1997), [1997] 2 S.C.R. 462, 8 C.R. (5th) 79, 115 C.C.C. (3d) 481 (S.C.C.) — An attempt consists of

i.   an *intent* to commit the completed offence;

ii.   an *act, more* than merely *preparatory*, taken in furtherance of the attempt.

The distinction between factual and legal impossibility is *not* tenable under *Code* s. 24(1). The *only* relevant distinction is between attempts to commit *imaginary crimes* and attempts to do the *factually impossible*. It is *only* attempts to commit imaginary crimes which are not covered by s. 24(1).

R. v. Ward (1979), 31 N.S.R. (2d) 79 (C.A.) — There are *three* essential elements in an attempt: the *intention* to commit the offence; some *overt act or omission* toward commission of the offence; and *non-commission* of the offence. Intention, a state of mind, may be inferred from the facts proved.

R. v. Cline (1956), 24 C.R. 58, 115 C.C.C. 18 (Ont. C.A.) — There must be *actus reus* as well as *mens rea* to constitute an attempt. Although the criminality of the misconduct lies mainly in the intention of

D, criminal intention alone is insufficient to constitute an attempt. Similar act evidence which is not too remote is admissible to establish a pattern of conduct from which to infer the necessary *mens rea*. The *actus reus* must be more than mere preparation. When the preparation is complete the next step done for the purpose and with the intention of committing the crime constitutes sufficient *actus reus* for an attempt.

Intent

R. v. Colburne (1991), 66 C.C.C. (3d) 235 (Que. C.A.) — An *attempt* to commit an offence is a crime of *specific intent* for which the defence of intoxication is available, *even if* the *full offence* attempted is an offence of *general intent*.

R. v. Sorrell (1978), 41 C.C.C. (2d) 9 (Ont. C.A.) — Where D's intention has been proved by extrinsic evidence, acts which on their face are equivocal, may nonetheless, be sufficiently proximate to constitute an attempt. Where, however, D's intention is *not* otherwise proved, equivocal acts may be insufficient to show that they were done with the intent to commit the crime D is alleged to have attempted.

R. v. Gagnon (1975), 24 C.C.C. (2d) 339 (Que. C.A.) — On a charge of attempted theft P need only prove an intention to steal and acts which went beyond mere preparation. P need *not* prove what D intended to steal, nor that it would have been possible to complete the work.

Attempt or Mere Preparation

R. v. Deutsch (1986), 52 C.R. (3d) 305, 27 C.C.C. (3d) 385 (S.C.C.); affirming (1983), 5 C.C.C. (3d) 41 (Ont. C.A.) — No satisfactory general criterion has been, or can be, formulated for drawing the line between preparation and attempt. The distinction, as it applies to the facts of a particular case, must be left to common sense judgment. It is a qualitative one, involving the *relationship* between the *nature and quality* of the *act* in question and the *nature* of the completed *offence*. Consideration should be given to the *relative proximity* of the act in question to what would have been the completed offence in terms of time, location and acts under the control of D remaining to be accomplished.Relative proximity may give an act which might otherwise appear to be mere preparation, the quality of an attempt, but an act does not lose its quality as the *actus reus* of attempt simply because further acts are required to complete the offence or a significant period of time may elapse before the offence would be completed.

Detering v. R. (1982), 31 C.R. (3d) 354, 70 C.C.C. (2d) 321 (S.C.C.) — D may be convicted of an attempt where the acts went beyond mere preparation and were fully carried out in circumstances which did *not* amount to the full offence. Where D's actions went beyond mere preparation D can be convicted of attempted fraud, even though V had not been deceived.

R. v. Olhauser (1970), 11 C.R.N.S. 334 (Alta. C.A.) — The determination of intent must often be inferred from the facts in evidence. If the facts, taken by themselves, cannot support the inference that they were done with criminal intent, they are merely preparatory.

Role of Judge and Jury: S. 24(2)

R. v. Carey (1957), 25 C.R. 177, 118 C.C.C. 241 (S.C.C.) — It is for the *jury* to decide the question of intention and consider any other defence raised on behalf of D. It is for the *judge* to decide, as a question of fact and a question of law whether, on the facts found by the jury, what was done amounted to an attempt. If there is no evidence of an attempt, then the trial judge must withdraw the issue from the jury.

R. v. Dickie (No. 2) (1982), 67 C.C.C. (2d) 218 (Ont. C.A.) — The judge's function pursuant to s. 24(2) is to determine of whether an act or omission constituted attempt or mere preparation. It is for the jury to decide whether D had the necessary intention for an attempt.

Crown Election [See also s. 463(d)]

R. v. Ellerbeck (1981), 61 C.C.C. (2d) 573 (Ont. C.A.) — Where P can elect to proceed by summary conviction with respect to the completed offence, it has the same election with respect to an attempt.

Related Provisions: Section 24 articulates *no* general test to distinguish attempt from mere preparation.

Under s. 660, D may be convicted of an attempt to commit the offence charged where the evidence establishes an attempt but not the complete offence. Under s. 661(1), where D is charged with an attempt to commit an offence but the evidence establishes the commission of the complete offence, D may be convicted of the attempt or the jury discharged and D indicted for the complete offence.

Attempts are punished under s. 463, except where otherwise expressly provided by law. Under s. 239 attempted murder is punishable by imprisonment for life.

The descriptions of several offences, as for example ss. 119(1)(a)(iii), 123(2), 139(1), 71(a) and (b) and 75(c) include an attempt as part of the definition of the essential elements of the complete offence.

Protection of Persons Administering and Enforcing the Law

25. (1) Protection of persons acting under authority — Every one who is required or authorized by law to do anything in the administration or enforcement of the law

    (a) as a private person,

    (b) as a peace officer or public officer,

    (c) in aid of a peace officer or public officer, or

    (d) by virtue of his office,

is, if he acts on reasonable grounds, justified in doing what he is required or authorized to do and in using as much force as is necessary for that purpose.

(2) Idem — Where a person is required or authorized by law to execute a process or to carry out a sentence, that person or any person who assists him is, if that person acts in good faith, justified in executing the process or in carrying out the sentence notwithstanding that the process or sentence is defective or that it was issued or imposed without jurisdiction or in excess of jurisdiction.

(3) When not protected — Subject to subsections (4) and (5), a person is not justified for the purposes of subsection (1) in using force that is intended or is likely to cause death or grievous bodily harm unless the person believes on reasonable grounds that it is necessary for the self-preservation of the person or the preservation of any one under that person's protection from death or grievous bodily harm.

(4) When protected — A peace officer, and every person lawfully assisting the peace officer, is justified in using force that is intended or is likely to cause death or grievous bodily harm to a person to be arrested, if

    (a) the peace officer is proceeding lawfully to arrest, with or without warrant, the person to be arrested;

    (b) the offence for which the person is to be arrested is one for which that person may be arrested without warrant;

    (c) the person to be arrested takes flight to avoid arrest;

    (d) the peace officer or other person using the force believes on reasonable grounds that the force is necessary for the purpose of protecting the peace officer, the person lawfully assisting the peace officer or any other person from imminent or future death or grievous bodily harm; and

    (e) the flight cannot be prevented by reasonable means in a less violent manner.

(5) Power in case of escape from penitentiary — A peace officer is justified in using force that is intended or is likely to cause death or grievous bodily harm against an inmate who is escaping from a penitentiary within the meaning of subsection 2(1) of the *Corrections and Conditional Release Act*, if

    (a) the peace officer believes on reasonable grounds that any of the inmates of the penitentiary pose a threat of death or grievous bodily harm to the peace officer or any other person; and

(b) the escape cannot be prevented by reasonable means in a less violent manner.

R.S., c. C-34, s. 25;1994, c. 12, s. 1.

Commentary: The section defines the *scope of authority* which may be exercised by certain categories of persons in the *administration and enforcement of the law*, thereby the ambit of protection afforded to such persons in equivalent circumstances.

Section 25(1) applies to private persons, peace and public officers, persons acting in their aid, and anyone acting "by virtue of his office" who are *required or authorized by law* to do anything in its administration or enforcement. Each is, if acting in such capacity on *reasonable grounds*, justified, not only in *doing what s/he is required or authorized to do*, but also, *in using as much force as is necessary for that purpose*. The justification and protection of the subsection does *not* extend beyond what is required or authorized to be done, nor to the use of force beyond what is necessary for such purpose. The person claiming justification may be mistaken as to the facts which underlie the conduct sought to be justified. The justification and protection is only vitiated, however, where it is *not* based on reasonable grounds.

Section 25(2) justifies the execution of process or carrying out of a sentence, *provided* it is done *in good faith* by a person required or authorized by law to do so. The justification is extended, notwithstanding that the process or sentence is defective or that it was issued or imposed without or in excess of jurisdiction.

Sections 25(3) to (5), impose *limits* upon the justifiable use of force that is intended or likely to cause death or grievous bodily harm.

Section 25(3) applies to *every person*. The *only* justification for the use of force that is intended or likely to cause death or grievous bodily harm arises when the person who uses the force believes, on *reasonable* grounds, that its use is necessary for self-preservation or preservation of anyone under that person's protection from death or grievous bodily harm. In other words, the justification arises from a reasonably grounded belief in the necessity of self or other preservation from an equivalent fate.

Section 25(4), the "fleeing felon" rule, justifies the use of force, *intended* or *likely* to *cause death* or grievous bodily harm, by a *peace officer* and anyone who lawfully assists the peace officer in arresting another person (V). The force is justified if:

i.   the *peace officer* is proceeding *lawfully* to *arrest* V, with or without warrant;

ii.   the *offence* for which V is to be arrested is one for which V may be arrested *without* warrant;

iii.   V takes *flight* to avoid arrest;

iv.   the peace officer or assister believes, on *reasonable* grounds, that *force* is *necessary* for the preservation of self or others from imminent or future death or grievous bodily harm and,

v.   V's flight cannot be prevented by reasonable means in a less violent manner.

The requirements are cumulative.

Section 25(5) justifies the use by a peace officer of force intended or likely to cause death or grievous bodily harm against an inmate who is escaping from a penitentiary as defined in s. 2(1) *Corrections and Conditional Release Act (C.C.R.A.)*. The justification is only available where the officer has a reasonably grounded belief that any inmate poses a threat of death or grievous bodily harm to the officer or any other person, and the escape cannot be prevented by reasonable means in a less violent manner.

Case Law
Protection

R. v. Godoy (1997), 7 C.R. (5th) 216, 115 C.C.C. (3d) 272 (Ont. C.A.); affirmed (1998), 21 C.R. (5th) 205, 131 C.C.C. (3d) 129 (S.C.C.) — Police conduct which interferes with an individual's liberty or freedom is authorized by the *common law* if

i.   the police *acted in* the *course* of their *duty* when the interference was effected; and

ii.   the police *conduct* did *not* involve an *unjustifiable use of power* in the circumstances.

R. v. Cluett (1985), 21 C.C.C. (3d) 318 (S.C.C.) — Police officers are *not* justified in using force generally to carry out their duty to investigate crimes, short of arrest. However, where a police officer arrests a person who s/he had reasonable grounds for believing was assaulting another police officer, s/he is justified in using the force necessary for such purpose, as long as it is *not* excessive.

Eccles v. Bourque (1973), 22 C.R.N.S. 199 at 201, 14 C.C.C. (2d) 279 (B.C. C.A.); affirmed (1974), 27 C.R.N.S. 325 (S.C.C.) — Section 25(1) absolves of blame anyone who does something that s/he is required or authorized by law to do, and authorizes the use of as much force as is necessary to do it.

Green. v. Lawrence (1998), 127 C.C.C. (3d) 416 (Man. C.A.) — The purpose of s. 25(1) is to excuse from liability an officer who has used no more force than reasonably necessary to effect an arrest. It does *not* excuse an officer from civil negligence.

Arrests

R. v. Feeney, [1997] 2 S.C.R. 13, 115 C.C.C. (3d) 129 (S.C.C.) — The *common law* rule that a warrantless arrest after forced entry into private premises is legal if

i.   the officer has *reasonable grounds* to believe that the *person sought* is *in* the premises;

ii.   *proper announcement* is made;

iii.   the officer believes *reasonable grounds* for the arrest exist; and

iv.   there are *reasonable and probable grounds* for the arrest,

offends Charter s. 8.

In general, *warrantless arrests* in dwelling-houses are *prohibited* because the privacy interest of the occupant in the dwelling-house outweighs the interests of the police. Prior to a warrantless arrest in a dwelling-house, police must *obtain* a *warrant* to enter the dwelling-house for the purpose of arrest. The warrant may only be issued if there are reasonable grounds

i.   for arrest; and,

ii.   for the belief that the person sought will be found in the named premises.

Proper *announcement* must also be made. In cases of hot pursuit, however, police may enter a dwelling-house to make a warrantless arrest.

R. v. Dand, [1965] 4 C.C.C. 366 (B.C. C.A.) — An acquittal is *not* conclusive that the arrest was without reasonable and probable grounds.

R. v. O'Donnell (1982), 3 C.C.C. (3d) 333 (N.S. C.A.) — Police officers do *not* have the right to detain persons or to use force for that purpose short of arrest. Where they attempt to question a citizen but do not arrest him/her or give reasons why s/he is being arrested, then any detention is unlawful and the officers are *not* acting in the execution of their duties. Use of force would not be justified under s. 25.

Kennedy v. Tomlinson (1959), 126 C.C.C. 175 (Ont. C.A.) — A police officer has a duty to take preventative action and to investigate a charge of a serious nature made by a private citizen. Where, as a result, the police officer has reasonable and probable cause for believing that D is *about to commit* an indictable offence, s/he is justified in arresting D without a warrant. It is of no consequence that only a lesser charge against D is subsequently laid.

Saskatchewan (A.G.) v. Pritchard (1961), 35 C.R. 150 (Sask. C.A.) — If an arrested person is subsequently acquitted, the arresting officer is protected if s/he acted on reasonable (and probable) grounds.

Entry into Private Dwelling

R. v. Godoy (1998), 21 C.R. (5th) 205, 131 C.C.C. (3d) 129 (S.C.C.) — Whether the police have authority to enter dwelling-houses in the course of an investigation of a 911 call depends on the circumstances of each case. Where police conduct constitutes a *prima facie* interference with someone's liberty or property, courts have to consider whether the conduct

i.   falls within the general *scope* of any *statutory* or *common law* duty; and,

ii.   involves an *unjustifiable* use of *powers* associated with that duty.

Forced entry into a dwelling to ascertain the health and safety of a 911 caller is justified by the importance of the police duty to protect life. The intrusion is *limited*, however, to the *protection* of *life* and *safety*. Police may investigate the call, in particular,

i.   to *locate* the *caller*;

ii.   to determine the *reasons* for the call; and,

iii.   to provide *assistance* to the *caller*

but no more. The police do *not* have permission to search the premises or otherwise intrude on a resident's privacy or property.

A 911 call engages the common law police duty to protect life whenever it can be inferred that the caller is or may be in some distress. This includes calls that are disconnected before the operator can find out the nature of the emergency. Despite the privacy interest residents have in the sanctity of the home, *threats* to *life* and *limb* more directly engage the values of dignity, integrity and autonomy that underlie the right to privacy than does the interest in being free from the *minimal* state intrusion of police entry to investigate a potential emergency.

Searches [See also Charter s. 8]

Reynen v. Antonenko (1975), 30 C.R.N.S. 135 (Alta. T.D.); affirmed Alta. C.A. (unreported) — Police officers who caused a medical examination of the plaintiff's rectum to be carried out by a physician without unreasonable force or threat to the plaintiff's health, were protected under this section. The search had revealed two condoms containing heroin.

Scott v. R. (1975), 24 C.C.C. (2d) 261 at 265 (Fed. C.A.) — Even if a search of D for drugs was, in the circumstances, justifiable, the use of force is *only* justifiable to the extent necessary to carry out the search.

Trespass [See also Charter s. 8]

Eccles v. Bourque (1974), 27 C.R.N.S. 325 (S.C.C.) — This section does *not* authorize one to commit a trespass in the accomplishment of an authorized arrest. It merely affords justification to a person for what s/he is required or authorized by law to do in the administration or enforcement of the law, if s/he acts on reasonable (and probable) grounds, and for using necessary force for that purpose.

When Not Protected

Bottrell v. R. (1981), 22 C.R. (3d) 271, 60 C.C.C. (2d) 211 (B.C. C.A.) — A police officer is *not* in breach of s. 25(3) merely because grievous bodily harm resulted, unless he intended that result. "Grievous bodily harm" means serious hurt or pain. The circumstances that existed at the time are determinative of the issue.

Force in Preventing Escape: S. 25(4) [Cases decided under previous section]

R. v. Roberge (1983), 33 C.R. (3d) 289, 4 C.C.C. (3d) 304 (S.C.C.); reversing (1981), 22 C.R. (3d) 263, 64 C.C.C. (2d) 78 (N.B. C.A.); which reversed (1980), 31 N.B.R. (2d) 668 (Q.B.) — A peace officer who has lawful authority to arrest a person in one province and is pursuing that person retains, for the purpose of s. 25(4), his/her status of a peace officer in another province if the pursuit is still fresh. The firing of three shots at the car's tires in the middle of a municipal street was *not* disproportionate to the suspicion created by the motorist persisting in flight despite all warnings.

Priestman v. Colangelo (1959), 30 C.R. 209 (S.C.C.) — Where this subsection is raised as a defence, it must be determined whether the officers used no more force than was necessary to prevent escape and whether the escape could have been prevented by reasonable means in a less violent manner.

Related Provisions: "Peace officer" and "public officer" are defined in s. 2.

Several other provisions in this Part also protect persons who administer and enforce the law. In addition to ss. 27–31, ss. 32 and 33 permit the suppression of riots, and ss. 43–45 protect certain persons in authority. Under *I.A.* s. 31(2), where a power is given to a person or officer to do or enforce the doing of anything, all such powers as are necessary to enable the person or officer to do or enforce the doing of the thing are deemed also to have been given.

Private defence, including defence of *person* (ss. 34–37), and of *property* (ss. 38–42), affords justification to persons who are not enforcing or administering the law nor assisting those who do so.

The general authority of persons other than a peace officer to arrest without warrant is described in s. 494, whereas that of a peace officer appears in s. 495. A warrant of arrest in Form 7 is executed in accordance with ss. 28, 29, 514 and 528. Sections 529.1–529.5 govern entry of dwelling houses to effect an arrest.

Section 26 defines the circumstances under which any person, lawfully authorized to use force, is criminally responsible for any excess thereof.

26. Excessive force — **Every one who is authorized by law to use force is criminally responsible for any excess thereof according to the nature and quality of the act that constitutes the excess.**

R.S., c. C-34, s. 26.

Commentary: The section imposes *criminal responsibility* for the use of *excessive force* and defines, in general, its extent. The section holds every one who is authorized by law to use force criminally responsible for any excess thereof. There is no distinction amongst the several categories of persons, as for example in the manner described in s. 25(1), who are lawfully authorized to use force. The *nature and quality of the act* which constitutes the excess determines criminal responsibility.

Case Law [See s. 34, "Excessive Force" and s. 229, "Intention to Kill" and "Mental Element and its Proof"]

Excessive Force in Self-Defence

Reilly v. R. (1984), 42 C.R. (3d) 154, 15 C.C.C. (3d) 1 (S.C.C.) — Use of excessive force in self-defence does *not* reduce murder to manslaughter.

Brisson v. R. (1982), 29 C.R. (3d) 289, 69 C.C.C. (2d) 97 (S.C.C.) — The Australian doctrine of excessive force in self-defence does *not* apply in Canada. *Code* ss. 25–45 cover comprehensively the occasions on which the use of force is legally justified.

Related Provisions: The provision endeavours to continue the common law principle that all powers, the exercise of which may do harm to others, should be exercised in a *reasonable* way. Justification is *not* at large but rather confined within well-defined limits. Any one who exceeds the prescribed limit is liable for it, according to the nature and quality of the act that constitutes the excess.

The use of force is authorized to the extent and in the circumstances described in ss. 25–44.

Section 37(2) also emphasizes that the justification of s. 37(1) (preventing assault) does *not* permit infliction of any hurt or mischief that is excessive, having regard to the nature of the assault that the force was intended to prevent.

27. Use of force to prevent commission of offence — **Every one is justified in using as much force as is reasonably necessary**

(a) to prevent the commission of an offence

(i) for which, if it were committed, the person who committed it might be arrested without warrant, and

(ii) that would be likely to cause immediate and serious injury to the person or property of anyone, or

(b) to prevent anything being done that, on reasonable grounds, he believes would, if it were done, be an offence mentioned in paragraph (a).

R.S., c. C-34, s. 27.

Commentary: The section authorizes and defines the extent to which force may be used to *prevent* the *commission* of certain *offences* or conduct which may reasonably lead thereto.

The section is of general application. The person asserting the justification need *not* be a peace or public officer, owner or person in possession of real property or a dwelling-house or member of an otherwise restricted category or class of persons. What is justified is "as much force as is *reasonably* necessary". The inclusion of "reasonably" adds an objective element to the responsive force: it is *not* simply "as much force as is necessary". The force used must be *to prevent* the commission of an offence, as described in s. 27(a), or the doing of anything which, reasonably viewed, if done, would be such an offence. The inclusion of "on reasonable grounds" adds an objective element to s. 27(b): the subjective belief must be reasonably grounded.

Case Law [See also s. 26]

R. v. Hebert (1996), 107 C.C.C. (3d) 42 (S.C.C.) — Section 27 is of general application and *not* limited to persons who administer and enforce the law.

MacMillan Bloedel Ltd. v. Simpson (1994), 89 C.C.C. (3d) 217 (B.C. C.A.)— Section 27 does *not* justify force or other conduct which a court has already enjoined.

R. v. Scopelliti (1981), 63 C.C.C. (2d) 481 (Ont. C.A.)— The use of deadly force can *only* be justified either in self-defence or in preventing the commission of a crime *likely* to cause immediate and serious injury.

Related Provisions: The section permits the use of only "as much force as is *reasonably necessary* ..." for preventative purposes. Excessive force may attract criminal responsibility under s. 26.

Other provisions which justify the limited use of force appear in ss. 25 and 28–44.

28. (1) **Arrest of wrong person** — Where a person who is authorized to execute a warrant to arrest believes, in good faith and on reasonable grounds, that the person whom he arrests is the person named in the warrant, he is protected from criminal responsibility in respect thereof to the same extent as if that person were the person named in the warrant.

(2) **Person assisting** — Where a person is authorized to execute a warrant to arrest,

(a) every one who, being called on to assist him, believes that the person in whose arrest he is called on to assist is the person named in the warrant, and

(b) every keeper of a prison who is required to receive and detain a person who he believes has been arrested under the warrant, is protected from criminal responsibility in respect thereof to the same extent as if that person were the person named in the warrant.

R.S., c. C-34, s. 28.

Commentary: The section affords limited protection from criminal responsibility to persons who arrest, *with a warrant*, the *wrong person* or detain persons wrongly arrested in custody.

Under s. 28(1) an *arresting officer* may be protected from criminal responsibility where the wrong person has been arrested with a warrant. The person arresting must be authorized to execute the warrant of arrest and *believe*, in good faith, on *reasonable grounds*, that the person arrested is the person named in the warrant. In other words, the belief, albeit mistaken, must, nonetheless, be honestly held *and* based on reasonable grounds. The degree of protection is equivalent to that given in cases where there has been no mistake as to identity.

Section 28(2) applies to those requested to *assist* and *keepers of prisons* who are required to receive and detain persons arrested under warrant. Those who assist in the arrest are protected to the same extent as if the person were the person named in the warrant, where the persons assisting believe that the person being arrested is the person named in the warrant. There is *no* requirement that such belief be based on reasonable grounds. The prison keeper is protected to an equivalent extent, upon belief that the person has been arrested under the warrant.

Related Provisions: The duty of a person arresting under a warrant is described in s. 29. A Form 7 warrant of arrest is addressed to the peace officers in the territorial jurisdiction of its issue. It may be endorsed for execution in another jurisdiction under s. 528. A warrant is executed under ss. 514 and 528. Anyone under arrest has the rights described in *Charter* s. 10 and, when charged with an offence, s. 11.

The extent of protection afforded, *inter alia*, to the person arresting, assisting in the arrest or receiving the person arrested under a warrant, is described in s. 25. Criminal responsibility for excessive force is governed by s. 26.

Section 232(4) applies where a person being arrested illegally causes the death of another in circumstances that amount to culpable homicide under s. 222(5).

29. (1) **Duty of person arresting** — It is the duty of every one who executes a process or warrant to have it with him, where it is feasible to do so, and to produce it when requested to do so.

(2) Notice — It is the duty of every one who arrests a person, whether with or without a warrant, to give notice to that person, where it is feasible to do so, of

(a) the process or warrant under which he makes the arrest; or

(b) the reason for the arrest.

(3) Failure to comply — Failure to comply with subsection (1) or (2) does not of itself deprive a person who executes a process or warrant, or a person who makes an arrest, or those who assist them, of protection from criminal responsibility.

R.S., c. C-34, s. 29.

Commentary: The section describes the *duty* imposed upon persons who *execute process* or *arrest*, with or without a warrant.

Under s. 29(1) anyone who executes a process or warrant must have the process or warrant with him/her, *where it is feasible to do so*. Possession of the process is only required where feasible. The process or warrant must be produced upon request. The requirements, in essence, are of possession and production of the warrant.

Section 29(2) imposes a specific duty upon those who arrest another, whether with or without a warrant. Notice must be given to the person arrested, *where it is feasible to do so*, of either the process or warrant under which the arrest is made or the reason therefor.

Non-compliance with s. 29(1) or (2) does not *per se* deprive the person effecting the arrest or executing the process or those who assist them, of protection from criminal responsibility.

Case Law

Notice (Where Feasible) [See also Charter s. 10]

Gamracy v. R. (1974), 22 C.R.N.S. 224 at 226, 12 C.C.C. (2d) 209 (S.C.C.) — Section 29(2) is to be read disjunctively. Where an arrest is being made pursuant to a warrant, but without the arresting officer having possession of the warrant, the officer need *only* inform the arrested person that the reason for the arrest is the existence of an outstanding warrant.

R. v. Fielding (1967), 1 C.R.N.S. 221 at 223, [1967] 3 C.C.C. 258 (B.C. C.A.) — It is sufficient to state the substance of the offence that is the reason for the arrest without specifying the statute and section.

Related Provisions: Upon arrest, every person has, *inter alia*, the right to be informed promptly of the *reasons* therefor and, further, the right to retain and instruct counsel without delay and to be informed of that right under *Charter* ss. 10(a) and (b). Under *Charter* s. 11(a) any person charged with an offence has the right to be informed, without unreasonable delay, of the *specific* offence.

Protection from criminal responsibility is afforded to those administering and enforcing the law under *Code* ss. 25, 27, 28, 30 and 31. The use of excessive force may attract criminal responsibility in accordance with s. 26.

The general authority of persons, other than peace officers, to arrest without warrant is described in s. 494. The corresponding powers of a peace officer are described in s. 495. A warrant of arrest in Form 7 is executed in accordance with this section and ss. 514 and 528.

30. Preventing breach of peace — Every one who witnesses a breach of the peace is justified in interfering to prevent the continuance or renewal thereof and may detain any person who commits or is about to join in or to renew the breach of the peace, for the purpose of giving him into the custody of a peace officer, if he uses no more force than is reasonably necessary to prevent the continuance or renewal of the breach of the peace or than is reasonably proportioned to the danger to be apprehended from the continuance or renewal of the breach of the peace.

R.S., c. C-34, s. 30.

Commentary: The section authorizes and justifies certain conduct by persons who *witness* a breach of the peace.

Everyone who witnesses a breach of the peace is justified in *interfering* to *prevent* the *continuance* or *renewal* thereof and may *detain* anyone who *commits* or is *about to join* in or *renew* the breach of the peace, for the purpose of giving him/her into the custody of a peace officer. The interference or detention may involve the use of force, provided it is no more than is *reasonably* necessary to prevent the continuance or renewal of the breach or than is *reasonably* proportional to the danger apprehended from the continuance or renewal of the breach.

Related Provisions: "Breach of the peace" is not defined in the section, nor elsewhere in or for the purposes of the *Code*. It occurs whenever harm is actually or likely to be done to a person, or in his/her presence to his/her property, or a person is in fear of being so harmed through an assault, affray, riot, unlawful assembly or other disturbance.

The authority to arrest for breach of the peace is described in s. 31.

A breach of the peace may also engage s. 810 and require a recognizance or committal to guard against a repetition thereof.

The suppression of riots is governed by ss. 32 and 33.

31. (1) **Arrest for breach of peace** — Every peace officer who witnesses a breach of the peace and every one who lawfully assists the peace officer is justified in arresting any person whom he finds committing the breach of the peace or who, on reasonable grounds, the peace officer believes is about to join in or renew the breach of the peace.

(2) **Giving person in charge** — Every peace officer is justified in receiving into custody any person who is given into his charge as having been a party to a breach of the peace by one who has, or who on reasonable grounds the peace officer believes has, witnessed the breach of the peace.

R.S., c. C-34, s. 31.

Commentary: The section authorizes a *peace officer* to arrest and take custody of persons apparently involved in breaches of the peace.

Under s. 31(1), the authority to *arrest* is limited to a *peace officer* who *witnesses* a breach of the peace, as well as every one who is lawfully assisting the officer. The person arrested must be one whom the officer either *finds committing* the breach of the peace or who the officer *believes, on reasonable grounds*, is *about to join in or renew* the breach of the peace. The phrase "on reasonable grounds" adds an objective element to the officer's subjective belief.

Section 31(2) authorizes a peace officer to *receive into custody* anyone delivered into his/her charge as having been a party to a breach of the peace. The delivery must be made by a person who has, or, on *reasonable grounds*, the officer believes has witnessed the breach of the peace. In the latter case, it would seem incumbent upon the officer to inquire as to the basis of the delivering party's assertions.

Case Law

R. v. Biron (1975), 30 C.R.N.S. 109, 23 C.C.C. (2d) 513 (S.C.C.) — A peace officer is justified, by s. 31(2), in receiving into custody a person arrested for apparently causing a disturbance in a public place. The disturbance would constitute a breach of the peace.

Hayes v. Thompson (1985), 44 C.R. (3d) 316, 18 C.C.C. (3d) 254 (B.C.C.A.) — Under s. 31 a peace officer who has witnessed a breach of the peace is entitled to make an arrest. At common law, a peace officer may arrest for an *apprehended* breach of the peace.

R. v. Lefebvre (1982), 1 C.C.C. (3d) 241 (B.C. Co. Ct.); affirmed (1984), 15 C.C.C. (3d) 503 (B.C. C.A.) — A peace officer has a duty to *prevent* a breach of the peace, actual or anticipated. There can be no conviction for breach of the peace, but as a form of preventative justice there can be arrest for up to 24 hours or a peace bond at common law.

Brown v. Durham Regional Police Force (1998), 21 C.R. (5th) 1, 131 C.C.C. (3d) 1 (Ont. C.A.) — A breach of the peace is an act or actions that result in actual or threatened harm to someone.

To properly invoke the power to arrest or detain to prevent an apprehended breach of the peace, the apprehended breach must be imminent and the risk that the breach will occur must be substantial. The officer must have *grounds* for believing that the anticipated breach of the peace will *likely* occur if the person is *not* detained.

Related Provisions: Section 30 describes what may be done by a person who witnesses a breach of the peace and authorizes, *inter alia*, the delivery of the participants therein to the custody of a peace officer.

The general authority of persons other than peace officers to arrest without warrant is described in s. 494 and that of peace officers in s. 495.

Unlawful assemblies and riots are punishable under ss. 63–69, and various forms of disorderly conduct, under ss. 173–179. Causing a disturbance is punishable under ss. 175(1)(a) and (d).

Other related provisions are described in the corresponding note to s. 30, *supra*.

Suppression of Riots

32. (1) Use of force to suppress riot — Every peace officer is justified in using or in ordering the use of as much force as the peace officer believes, in good faith and on reasonable grounds,

    (a) is necessary to suppress a riot; and

    (b) is not excessive, having regard to the danger to be apprehended from the continuance of the riot.

(2) Person bound by military law — Every one who is bound by military law to obey the command of his superior officer is justified in obeying any command given by his superior officer for the suppression of a riot unless the order is manifestly unlawful.

(3) Obeying order of peace officer — Every one is justified in obeying an order of a peace officer to use force to suppress a riot if

    (a) he acts in good faith; and

    (b) the order is not manifestly unlawful.

(4) Apprehension of serious mischief — Every one who, in good faith and on reasonable grounds, believes that serious mischief will result from a riot before it is possible to secure the attendance of a peace officer is justified in using as much force as he believes in good faith and on reasonable grounds,

    (a) is necessary to suppress the riot; and

    (b) is not excessive, having regard to the danger to be apprehended from the continuance of the riot.

(5) Question of law — For the purposes of this section, the question whether an order is manifestly unlawful or not is a question of law.

R.S., c. C-34, s. 32.

Commentary: This section, together with s. 33, provides justification, thereby protection, for certain categories of persons in connection with the *suppression of riots*.

Section 32(1) justifies a *peace officer* using or ordering the use of *as much force* as the officer believes, *in good faith and on reasonable grounds*, is necessary to suppress a riot and is *not* excessive, having regard to the danger to be apprehended from the continuance of the riot. It may ultimately be determined, with the advantage of hindsight, that the officer was mistaken as to the nature or degree of force required. Provided the officer's belief was at once honestly held and based upon reasonable grounds the justification is established. Section 32(3) affords justification to those who obey the order of a peace officer under s. 32(1) to use force to suppress a riot.

Obedience to the order of a peace officer is justified if the person who obeys acts in good faith and the order is *not* manifestly unlawful. Similarly, every one bound by military law to obey the command of a superior officer is justified in obeying such an order for the suppression of a riot unless the order is manifestly unlawful. Whether an order is manifestly unlawful, under s. 32(5), is a question of law.

In certain circumstances, *persons other than peace officers* are justified in acting to suppress a riot before a peace officer has attended. Under s. 32(4) anyone who, *in good faith and on reasonable grounds*, believes that serious mischief will result from a riot before it is possible to secure the attendance of a peace officer is justified in using the same degree or extent of force as a peace officer may use or order others to use under s. 32(1).

Related Provisions: "Peace officer" is defined in s. 2. Under s. 64, a riot is an unlawful assembly, as defined in s. 63(1), that has begun to disturb the peace tumultuously. Taking part in a riot is an indictable offence under s. 65.

Persons administering and enforcing the law are protected under s. 25. The use of force to prevent the commission of an offence is authorized under s. 27. Criminal responsibility for the use of excessive force is determined under s. 26.

Offences relating to unlawful assemblies and riots are described in ss. 63–69. The duty of peace officers and those lawfully required to assist where rioters do not, upon the reading of the proclamation, disperse, is defined in s. 33.

33. (1) Duty of officers if rioters do not disperse — Where the proclamation referred to in section 67 has been made or an offence against paragraph 68(a) or (b) has been committed, it is the duty of a peace officer and of a person who is lawfully required by him to assist, to disperse or to arrest persons who do not comply with the proclamation.

(2) Protection of officers — No civil or criminal proceedings lie against a peace officer or a person who is lawfully required by a peace officer to assist him in respect of any death or injury that by reason of resistance is caused as a result of the performance by the peace officer or that person of a duty that is imposed by subsection (1).

(3) Section not restrictive — Nothing in this section limits or affects any powers, duties or functions that are conferred or imposed by this Act with respect to the suppression of riots.

R.S., c. C-34, s. 33.

Commentary: The section describes the *duty of peace officers* where rioters do *not* disperse upon the making of a proclamation under s. 67, or an offence under s. 68(a) or (b) has been committed. It does *not* limit or affect any powers, duties or functions conferred or imposed by the *Code* with respect to the suppression of riots.

The duties imposed on a peace officer under s. 33(1) arise when the proclamation of s. 67 has been made or an offence against s. 68(a) or (b) has been committed. The duty, also imposed upon anyone lawfully required to assist, is to disperse or arrest anyone who does not comply with the proclamation. Where any death or injury is caused by reason of resistance as a result of the performance of the duties imposed by s. 33(1), neither the peace officer, nor anyone lawfully required to assist, is civilly or criminally responsible therefor.

Related Provisions: The proclamation of s. 67 must be read by a designated official. It commands immediate dispersal and peaceable departure of rioters. The offences of ss. 68(a) and (b) relate to the reading of the proclamation and dispersal of rioters thereafter.

Under s. 69, it is an indictable offence for a peace officer who receives notice that there is a riot within his/her jurisdiction and, without reasonable excuse, to fail to take all reasonable steps to suppress it.

Section 32 also provides justification, thereby protection, for certain categories of persons in connection with the suppression of riots.

Other related provisions are described in the corresponding note to s. 32, *supra*.

Self-Induced Intoxication

33.1 (1) When defence not available — It is not a defence to an offence referred to in subsection (3) that the accused, by reason of self-induced intoxication, lacked the general intent or the voluntariness required to commit the offence, where the accused departed markedly from the standard of care as described in subsection (2).

(2) Criminal fault by reason of intoxication — For the purposes of this section, a person departs markedly from the standard of reasonable care generally recognized in Canadian society and is thereby criminally at fault where the person, while in a state of self-induced intoxication that renders the person unaware of, or incapable of consciously controlling, their behaviour, voluntarily or involuntarily interferes or threatens to interfere with the bodily integrity of another person.

(3) Application — This section applies in respect of an offence under this Act or any other Act of Parliament that includes as an element an assault or any other interference or threat of interference by a person with the bodily integrity of another person.

1995, c. 32, s. 1.

Commentary: This is the legislative response to *R. v. Daviault* (1994), 33 C.R. (4th) 165, 93 C.C.C. (3d) 21 (S.C.C.).

The provision *only* applies to offences under the *Code* or other federal enactment that include, as an element, an *assault*, or any other actual or threatened *interference* by a person with the *bodily integrity* of another. For these offences, it is *no* defence that D, by reason of self-induced intoxication, lacked the

i.   *general intent*; or,

ii.   *voluntariness*

required to commit the offence where D, in a state of self-induced intoxication that rendered D unaware or incapable of consciously controlling his/her behaviour,

iii.   voluntarily; or,

iv.   involuntarily

interfered or threatened to interfere with the bodily integrity of another.

Case Law
General Principles
R. v. C. (C.) (1999), 131 C.C.C. (3d) 552 (Ont. C.A.) — Although D may raise, on appeal, the defence of a change in the law that has occurred between the time of trial and the hearing of the appeal, s/he should *not* be permitted to raise the defence of *extreme* intoxication for the first time on appeal.
Expert Opinion Evidence
R. v. Tom (1998), 129 C.C.C. (3d) 540 (B.C. C.A.) — The *opinion* of an *expert* about the *effect* of the amount or approximate amount of alcohol consumed by a person like D, in the absence of evidence of the amount actually consumed, is speculative and of *no* value to the trier of fact.
Standard of Proof
R. v. Tom (1998), 129 C.C.C. (3d) 540 (B.C. C.A.) — The *standard* of proof required of D under s. 33.1 is proof on a *balance* of *probabilities*.

Related Provisions: Intoxication as a defence is preserved by ss. 8(2) and (3). Section 33.1 was apparently intended to apply *only* to crimes of "general intent".

Defence of Person

34. (1) Self-defence against unprovoked assault — Every one who is unlawfully assaulted without having provoked the assault is justified in repelling force by force if the force he uses is not intended to cause death or grievous bodily harm and is no more than is necessary to enable him to defend himself.

(2) Extent of justification — Every one who is unlawfully assaulted and who causes death or grievous bodily harm in repelling the assault is justified if

(a) he causes it under reasonable apprehension of death or grievous bodily harm from the violence with which the assault was originally made or with which the assailant pursues his purposes; and

(b) he believes, on reasonable grounds, that he cannot otherwise preserve himself from death or grievous bodily harm.

R.S., c. C-34, s. 34.

Commentary: The section defines the scope of lawful *self-defence* by one who has him/herself been *unlawfully assaulted*.

Subsection (1) is of general application where a person has been unlawfully assaulted, *without* having provoked the assault. Force may be repelled by force provided the responsive force is *not intended* to cause death or grievous bodily harm and is *no more* than is necessary to enable him/her to defend him/herself. No further use of force is justified.

Subsection (2), of particular application where the responsive force applied by one who has been unlawfully assaulted by another causes death or grievous bodily harm, requires that the death of or grievous bodily harm to the assailant be caused under a *reasonable* apprehension of death or grievous bodily harm from the initial assault or its pursuit. The responsive force must be inflicted in the belief, on *reasonable* grounds, that the person assaulted cannot otherwise preserve him/herself from death or grievous bodily harm. The use of "reasonable" imports an objective element.

Case Law

General Relationship of Subsections and Other Defences

R. v. Brisson (1982), 29 C.R. (3d) 289, 69 C.C.C. (2d) 97 (S.C.C.); affirming [1980] C.A. 457 (Que. C.A.) — Section 34(1) may be invoked *only* if there is no intention to cause death or grievous harm and no more force than necessary is used. Section 34(2) affords justification where there was an intention kill. D must actually and reasonably believe that s/he was going to be killed.

R. v. Westhaver (1992), 17 C.R. (4th) 401 (N.S. C.A.) — Failure to retreat does *not* necessarily preclude reliance on *Code* s. 34, D need not be reduced to a state of frenzy.

R. v. Black (1990), 55 C.C.C. (3d) 421 (N.S. C.A.) — Accident is distinct from self-defence and, in the case of an unprovoked assault, is not dependent upon *Code* s. 34.

R. v. Mulligan (1997), 115 C.C.C. (3d) 559 (Ont. C.A.) — Self-defence is available where D *honestly* and *reasonably*, albeit mistakenly, *believes* that V has assaulted him/her.

R. v. Pintar (1996), 2 C.R. (5th) 151, 110 C.C.C. (3d) 402 (Ont. C.A.) — In determining the manner in which a jury ought be instructed on self-defence, a trial judge should,

i. consider carefully the relevant evidence to determine the *essence* of the claim and the *Code provision(s) realistically available* to support the claim;

ii. *not* instruct the jury on any *provision* where one or more of its *constitutient elements lack* an air of *reality*;

iii. *encourage* P to admit the *underlying facts*, thereby avoid unnecessary legal instruction, where the evidence *clearly establishes* one or more *constitutent elements* of a particular provision; and

iv. instruct upon a provision which affords D a *wider* scope of justification than a companion and narrower provision which should only be left when supported by the evidence and unaccounted for by the wider provision.

R. v. Pintar (1996), 2 C.R. (5th) 151, 110 C.C.C. (3d) 402 (Ont. C.A.) — Sections 34(1) and (2) apply where D has been *unlawfully assaulted*. Section 34(2) applies, however, unlike s. 34(1), even if D has provoked the assault. Where death or grievous bodily harm results, unlike s. 34(1), s. 34(2) applies, notwithstanding that D intended to cause death or grievous bodily harm. Under s. 34(2), unlike s. 34(1), the issue is *not* whether the responsive force used was *no more than necessary* to enable D to self-defend, rather, whether D believed, on *reasonable* grounds, that s/he could *not* otherwise *preserve* him/herself from death or grievous bodily harm.

R. v. Baxter (1975), 33 C.R.N.S. , 27 C.C.C. (2d) 96, 111 (Ont. C.A.) — *See also*: *R. v. Bolyantu* (1975), 29 C.C.C. (2d) 174 at 175-176 (Ont. C.A.); *R. v. Nelson* (1992), 13 C.R. (4th) 359, 71 C.C.C. (3d) 449 (Ont. C.A.) — The doctrine of mistake of fact applies to ss. 34(1) and (2). D's belief that s/he was in imminent danger from an attack may be *reasonable*, *although* s/he may be *mistaken* in his/her belief. Moreover, a person defending him/herself against an attack, reasonably apprehended, cannot be expected to weigh to a nicety the exact measure of necessary defensive action.

R. v. Martin (1985), 47 C.R. (3d) 342 (Que. C.A.) — Under s. 34(1), D is *not* guilty if he was attacked by V and, in defending himself, stabbed V without intending to cause death or grievous bodily harm and used no more force than was necessary to defend himself. Under s. 34(2), D is also not guilty if he was attacked by V and, in defending himself, caused the death of V, as long as D *reasonably* feared his own death or grievous bodily harm and reasonably believed that he had no other way of avoiding his own death or grievous bodily harm. Self-defence is available even if D intended to cause death or grievous bodily harm to V.

Application of S. 34(1)

R. v. Bayard (1989), 92 N.R. 376 (S.C.C.); reversing (1988), 29 B.C.L.R. 366 (C.A.) — Section 34(1) can never provide a justification for murder under s. 229(a). It is only where the trier of fact has concluded that the intention to commit murder was *not* present that s. 34(1) becomes relevant.

R. v. Deegan (1979), 49 C.C.C. (2d) 417 (Alta. C.A.) — *See also*: *R. v. Jack* (1994), 91 C.C.C. (3d) 446 (B.C. C.A.) — The onus is on P to prove beyond a reasonable doubt that the requirements of self-defence have not been met. There is no requirement of retreat, especially when D is in his own home.

R. v. Marky, [1976] 6 W.W.R. 390 (Alta. C.A.) — The fact that the force used to protect oneself results in grievous bodily harm does not determine whether more force than necessary was used. Consideration should be given to the facts as the person using the force to protect him/herself would reasonably appreciate them.

R. v. Kandola (1993), 80 C.C.C. (3d) 481 (B.C. C.A.) — Section 34(1) justifies the use of force, *not* the consequences of it. If the force is justified under s. 34(1), *viz*, all of the conditions are met, the defence is made out, even if death or grievous bodily harm results.

R. v. Matson (1970), 1 C.C.C. (2d) 374 (B.C. C.A.) — The extent of the injuries suffered by V does *not* determine whether more force than necessary was used.

R. v. Antley (1963), 42 C.R. 384, [1964] 2 C.C.C. 142 (Ont. C.A.) — D need *not* be reduced to a state of frenzy in resisting an attack before self-defence is available. Neither must D have waited to be struck first before using any force against his attacker. D is not required to retreat where V is a trespasser. D may remove V by force, if force is necessary, provided D used no more force than was necessary for that purpose.

Application of S. 34(2)

R. v. Malott (1998), 121 C.C.C. (3d) 456 (S.C.C.) — The constituent elements under s. 34(2) where V has died are

i.   an unlawful assault;

ii.   a *reasonable apprehension* of death or grievous bodily harm; and

iii.   a *reasonable belief* that it is *not* possible to preserve oneself from harm except by killing V.

R. v. McIntosh (1995), 36 C.R.(4th) 171, 95 C.C.C. (3d) 481 (S.C.C.); affirming (1993), 84 C.C.C. (3d) 473, 24 C.R. (4th) 265, 15 O.R. (3d) 450 (C.A.) — *See also*: *R. v. Stubbs* (1988), 28 O.A.C. 14 (Ont. C.A.); *R. v. Nelson* (1992), 71 C.C.C. (3d) 449, 13 C.R. (4th) 359 (Ont. C.A.); *R. v. Cameron* (1995), 96 C.C.C. (3d) 346 (Ont. C.A.) — Section 34(2) is *available* to an *initial aggressor*. The words "without having provoked the assault", which appear in s. 34(1), are *not* to be read into s. 34(2).

R. v. Pétel (1994), 26 C.R. (4th) 145 (S.C.C.); affirming (1993), 78 C.C.C. (3d) 543 (Que. C.A.) — The constituent elements of self-defence under s. 34(2) where V has died are:

i.   an *unlawful* assault;

ii.   a *reasonable* apprehension of a risk of death or grievous bodily harm; and,

iii. a *reasonable* belief that it is not possible to preserve oneself from harm except by killing the attacker.

In each case, the trier of fact must seek to determine how D perceived the relevant facts and whether the perception was reasonable. The determination is objective.an honest but reasonable mistake as to the existence of an assault is permitted. The existence of an assault must *not* be made a kind of prerequisite for the exercise of self-defence to be assessed without regard for D's perception. D's state of mind is what is relevant and requires examination. The question to be asked is whether D *reasonably believed, in the circumstances,* that s/he was being unlawfully assaulted, *not* whether D was unlawfully assaulted.There is no formal requirement that danger to D be imminent. Imminence of danger is but a factor to be considered in determining items ii and iii, *supra*.

R. v. Lavallee (1990), 76 C.R. (3d) 329, 55 C.C.C. (3d) 97 (S.C.C.); reversing (1988), 65 C.R. (3d) 387, 44 C.C.C. (3d) 113 (Man. C.A.) — See digest under "Evidence", *infra*.

Reilly v. R. (1984), 42 C.R. (3d) 154, 15 C.C.C. (3d) 1 (S.C.C.); affirming (1982), 66 C.C.C. (2d) 146 (Ont. C.A.) — *See also: R. v. Harms* (1936), 66 C.C.C. 134 (Sask. C.A.) — Section 34(2) affords a defence to the use of force intended to cause death only if D *reasonably* apprehended death or grievous bodily harm and believed on *reasonable* grounds that he could not, otherwise than by the force used, preserve himself from death, or grievous bodily harm. Although an intoxicated person might be able to rely on s. 34(2), the *intoxication* of D is *irrelevant* to this inquiry because, while it can induce a mistake of fact, it cannot induce a mistake of something required to be based on reasonable grounds.

Northwest v. R. (1980), 22 A.R. 522 (C.A.) — A failure to retreat is *only* a factor to be considered in determining whether D believed on *reasonable* grounds that D could *not* otherwise preserve himself from death or grievous bodily harm. It does *not*, in itself, remove the availability of a defence under the subsection.

R. v. Proulx (1998), 127 C.C.C. (3d) 511 (B.C. C.A.) — The *unlawful assault* requirement of s. 34(2) is met by D's *reasonable perception* of an unlawful assault. A jury may reject D's account of an actual assault, yet find that D believed the account to be true and that there were reasonable grounds for D to have the mistaken belief.

The apprehension of harm and belief that a violent defence is the *only* available option for self-preservation are both perceptions that may be founded on *honest* mistakes by D. The inquiry is into D's state of mind, *not* what a reasonable person would have done in the circumstances.

Retreat may be an irrelevant consideration when a person is attacked at home, but it is *not* so when the attack occurs elsewhere. Although there is *no obligation* to retreat, it is a means of otherwise preserving one's self, hence should be considered under s. 34(2).

R. v. Berrigan (1998), 127 C.C.C. (3d) 120 (B.C. C.A.) — D may rely on self-defence where s/he makes a *reasonable* mistakable of fact that s/he was assaulted by V.

R. v. Kindt (1998), 15 C.R. (5th) 307, 124 C.C.C. (3d) 20 (B.C. C.A) — Section 34(2) applies even where D did *not* cause grievous bodily harm to V. (per Donald and Braidwood JJ.A.)

R. v. Siu (1992), 12 C.R. (4th) 356, 71 C.C.C. (3d) 197 (B.C. C.A.) — A trial judge should *not* instruct a jury in such a way as to invite it first to consider whether D's conduct fell within s. 34(2), then to decide whether an additional unstated prohibition against excessive force disqualified D from the benefit of the defence. If the requirements of s. 34(2) have been met, no further inquiry or consideration of the nature of the force used by D is necessary or permissible. To invite the jury to undertake such an inquiry would contravene the principle that a defender against an upraised knife cannot be expected to weigh with nicety the exact measure of responsive force.

R. v. Pintar (1996), 2 C.R. (5th) 151, 110 C.C.C. (3d) 402 (Ont. C.A.) — Section 34(2) is available to D charged with murder whether s/he intended to kill or cause grievous bodily harm or not

R. v. Jenkins (1996), 48 C.R. (4th) 213, 107 C.C.C. (3d) 440 (Ont. C.A.) — The effect of an omission to instruct a jury, in terms, that an accused who provokes an assault may rely on *Code* s. 34(2) depends upon the rest of the instructions on self-defence. Non-direction on the issue of provocation constitutes an error of law only where the instructions, taken as whole, could reasonably have misled the jury into concluding that an accused who provoked the assault could *not* rely on *Code* s. 34(2).

R. v. Nelson (1992), 13 C.R. (4th) 359, 71 C.C.C. (3d) 449 (Ont. C.A.) — *See also*: *R. v. Stubbs* (1988), 28 O.A.C. 14 (C.A.) — Provocation by D is *not* relevant to the availability of self-defence under s. 34(2).

R. v. Nelson (1992), 13 C.R. (4th) 359, 71 C.C.C. (3d) 449 (Ont. C.A.) — The *diminished intelligence* of D due to a condition of arrested intellectual or mental development, which relates to the ability to perceive and react to events, ought to be considered in the application of the standards of reasonableness required by the section.

R. v. Ward (1978), 4 C.R. (3d) 190 (Ont. C.A.) — It is *not* a requirement of self-defence that there be no other reasonable means whereby a person can retreat, nor of s. 34(2), that the force used must be proportionate to the assault against which D is defending him/herself. These factors, however, may be relevant as evidence in considering whether the actions taken by D purported to be in self-defence, were justifiable.

R. v. Mulder (1978), 40 C.C.C. (2d) 1 (Ont. C.A.) — There is *no* requirement under s. 34(2) of "proportionate force".

R. v. Bogue (1976), 30 C.C.C. (2d) 403 (Ont. C.A.) — If the jury have a reasonable doubt, that D had a *reasonable* apprehension of death or grievous bodily harm and that D had *reasonable and probable* grounds to believe that she could not otherwise preserve herself from death or grievous bodily harm, there is no further requirement that the force used by D be proportionate to the assault made upon her by V.

R. v. Setrum (1976), 32 C.C.C. (2d) 109 (Sask. C.A.) — Where there is no evidence that D was under reasonable apprehension of death or grevious bodily harm, self-defence may still be available, by virtue of s. 34(1), if D did *not* mean to cause death or grevious bodily harm and did *not* use more force than was necessary, notwithstanding that V died as a result of the injuries.

Evidence

R. v. Malott (1998), 121 C.C.C. (3d) 456 (S.C.C.) — D may be honestly but reasonably mistaken about the existence of an assault under s. 34(2). Expert evidence about the battered woman syndrome may help the jury to assess the *reasonableness* of D's perception.

Where the battered woman syndrome defence is raised, the jury should be instructed about the *use* of the *evidence* to help them understand

i.   *why* an abused woman might *remain* in an abusive relationship;

ii.   the *nature* and *effect* of the *violence* that may exist in a battering relationship;

iii.   the *ability* of D to *perceive danger* from her abuser; and,

iv.   whether D *believed*, on *reasonable grounds*, that she could not otherwise preserve herself from death or grievous bodily harm.

R. v. Pétel (1994), 26 C.R. (4th) 145 (S.C.C.); affirming (1993), 78 C.C.C. (3d) 543 (Que. C.A.) — Evidence of *prior threats* by V to D is relevant to a determination of D's state of mind at the material time, including:

i.   D's honest but reasonably mistaken *belief* as to the *existence* of an assault;

ii.   D's *apprehension* of a risk of death or grievous bodily harm; and,

iii.   D's *belief* in the need to use deadly force.

The manner in which a reasonable person would have acted cannot be assessed without taking into account prior threats.

R. v. Lavallee (1990), 76 C.R. (3d) 329, 55 C.C.C. (3d) 97 (S.C.C.); reversing (1988), 65 C.R. (3d) 387, 44 C.C.C. (3d) 113 (Man. C.A.) — Expert testimony concerning the ability of a battered wife to perceive danger from her battering partner may be relevant to whether, under s. 34(2)(a), she *reasonably apprehended death or grievous bodily harm* on a particular occasion. The testimony may also explain why D did not flee when she perceived her life to be in danger, hence assist a jury, under s. 34(2)(b), in assessing the reasonableness of D's belief that killing her batterer, V, was the only way to save her own life. The evidence is relevant, though not determinative, of the issue whether D's perceptions and actions were reasonable.

R. v. Dejong (1998), 16 C.R. (5th) 372, 125 C.C.C. (3d) 302 (B.C. C.A.) — Where evidence of V's *peaceable* character is

i.   *not* logically *probative* of any *element* of the offence charged; and,

ii.   *not* offered to *rebut evidence* of V's violent disposition adduced by D. *semble*, it is *irrelevant*.

R. v. Sims (1994), 87 C.C.C. (3d) 402 (B.C. C.A.) — Even if self-defence is *not* left to the jury, evidence of prior acts of violence by V may be admissible. Where an issue arises whether it was D or V who first produced a knife, evidence of V's violent disposition, including the propensity to resort to knives when involved in an altercation, is relevant and admissible. The evidence tends to support D's evidence that it was V who first produced the knife.

R. v. Siu (1992), 12 C.R. (4th) 356, 71 C.C.C. (3d) 197 (B.C. C.A.) — Evidence of V's violent act towards D an hour before the fatal incident is relevant to show that D had a reasonable apprehension of violence from V at the time of the fatal incident.

R. v. Trombley (1998), 126 C.C.C. (3d) 495 (Ont. C.A.); notice of appeal filed as of right (April 23, 1999), Doc. 26755 (S.C.C.) — Where expert evidence is given about the battered woman syndrome and its application to the circumstances and conduct of D, the judge should instruct the jury that the evidence

i.   could explain how D could *reasonably* be much more *apprehensive* about her safety than would otherwise be the case; and

ii.   would help the jury understand D's *reasonable* perception of *what* she had to do to *protect* herself.

R. v. Mulligan (1997), 115 C.C.C. (3d) 559 (Ont. C.A.) — Evidence of D's *disposition* for *violence* is *relevant*

i.   if *not known* to D, on the issue whether V or D was the *likely aggressor,* or

ii.   if *known* to D, on the issue of D's *state of mind.*

R. v. Scopelliti (1981), 63 C.C.C. (2d) 481 (Ont. C.A.) — Firing at a mere trespasser is *not* justified. The use of deadly force can only be justified either in self-defence or in preventing the commission of a crime likely to cause immediate and serious injury. Evidence of specific acts of violence by V, which were *not known* to D at the time of the incident, is admissible to corroborate D's evidence that he was attacked by the deceased. Evidence of specific acts *known* to D is relevant to show the reasonableness of his apprehension.

Excessive Force [See also s. 26]

R. v. Faid (1983), 33 C.R. (3d) 1, 2 C.C.C. (3d) 513 (S.C.C.) — *See also: R. v. Gee* (1982), 29 C.R. (3d) 347, 68 C.C.C. (2d) 576 (S.C.C.); *Martin v. R.* (1985), 47 C.R. (3d) 342 (Que. C.A.) — Where a killing has resulted from excessive force in self-defence, D loses the justification provided by the *Code.* There is no partial justification whereby D can be convicted only of manslaughter. A manslaughter verdict can rest only upon the fact that an unlawful killing has been committed without the intent required for murder.

R. v. Clark (1984), 5 C.C.C. (3d) 264 (Alta. C.A.) — This section is *not* available to D who used unreasonable and excessive force intended to cause bodily harm, even though D may not have known it would cause death. Lack of knowledge or foresight of death may reduce D's guilt from murder to manslaughter.

R. v. Kandola (1993), 80 C.C.C. (3d) 481 (B.C. C.A.) — Force, which is so recklessly applied in self-defence as to be excessive, will be *unnecessary* force, hence the defence will fail. What deprives D of the defence in such cases is recklessness as to the necessary measure of force, *not* recklessness as to the consequences or the risk thereof flowing from the application of that force.

R. v. Clow (1985), 44 C.R. (3d) 228 (Ont. C.A) — *See also: R. v. Desveaux* (1986), 26 C.C.C. (3d) 88 (Ont. C.A.); *R. v. Nealy* (1986), 54 C.R. (3d) 158, 30 C.C.C. (3d) 460 (Ont. C.A.) — The *cumulative effect* of consumption of alcohol or drugs, provocation and excessive force in self-defence should be related to the requisite intent required to convict for murder.

Related Provisions: Under s. 36, provocation includes provocation by blows, words or gestures. "Grievous bodily harm" is *not* defined, but may be taken to include no less than really serious bodily harm. "Bodily harm" is defined in s. 2.

An "unlawful assault" within s. 35(1) may also amount to "a wrongful act or insult" within s. 232(2) and, subject to its provisions, provocation that may reduce culpable homicide that otherwise would be murder to manslaughter under s. 232(1). Assault is defined in s. 265.

Section 37 justifies force in protection of self or another from assault. Section 35 defines the limits of self-defence where the person asserting it was initially the aggressor.

Sections 38–42 authorize prescribed force in defence of real and personal property.

Excessive force may attract criminal responsibility under s. 26.

35. Self-defence in case of aggression — Every one who has without justification assaulted another but did not commence the assault with intent to cause death or grievous bodily harm, or has without justification provoked an assault on himself by another, may justify the use of force subsequent to the assault if

(a) he uses the force

(i) under reasonable apprehension of death or grievous bodily harm from the violence of the person whom he has assaulted or provoked, and

(ii) in the belief, on reasonable grounds, that it is necessary in order to preserve himself from death or grievous bodily harm;

(b) he did not, at any time before the necessity of preserving himself from death or grievous bodily harm arose, endeavour to cause death or grievous bodily harm; and

(c) he declined further conflict and quitted or retreated from it as far as it was feasible to do so before the necessity of preserving himself from death or grievous bodily harm arose.

R.S., c. C-34, s. 35.

Commentary: The section defines the scope of lawful self-defence *by a person who* him/herself *has assaulted or provoked an assault* on him/herself *by another*. Several elements, which attempt to ensure that self-defence is founded on necessity comprise the justification.

The section applies only where the person asserting it has, *without justification*, either *assaulted* another, without commencing the assault with intent to cause death or grievous bodily harm, *or provoked* an assault upon him/herself by another in the similar absence of justification. The use of force by the aggressor in the initial assault must be under *reasonable* apprehension of death or grievous bodily harm from the violence of the person assaulted or provoked.

The force must also be used in the reasonably grounded belief that it is *necessary* to preserve the aggressor from death or grievous bodily harm. "Reasonable" imports *objective* considerations into the aggressor's apprehension and belief under s. 35(a).

The aggressor, at any time before the necessity of preserving him/herself from death or grievous bodily harm arose, must not have endeavoured to cause death or grievous bodily harm. The aggressor also must have *declined* further conflict and *quitted* or *retreated* from it, as far as it was feasible to do so, before the necessity of preserving him/herself from death or grievous bodily harm arose.

Case Law

R. v. Chamberland (1988), 65 Alta. L.R. (2d) 175 (C.A.) — "On reasonable grounds" in s. 35(a)(ii) import an objective standard. The effect of alcohol and drugs on the required belief is *not* a factor to be considered by the trier of fact.

R. v. Siu (1992), 12 C.R. (4th) 356, 71 C.C.C. (3d) 197 (B.C. C.A.) — A trial judge should *not* instruct a jury in such a way as to invite it first to consider whether D's conduct fell within s. 35, then to decide whether an additional unstated prohibition against excessive force disqualified D from the benefit of the defence. If the requirements of s. 35 have been met, no further inquiry or consideration of the nature of the force used by D is necessary or permissible.

R. v. Merson (1983), 4 C.C.C. (3d) 251 (B.C. C.A.) — Where D had *no* intent to cause death or grievous bodily harm, the use of force might be justified if the requirements of the section are satisfied.

R. v. Bolyantu (1975), 29 C.C.C. (2d) 174 (Ont. C.A.) — Where D is charged with assault, the trial judge should charge the jury with respect to the application of this section in the event that they were of the view that D had provoked an assault (either actual or believed) by V.

Related Provisions: Section 265 defines an assault and s. 36 provides that provocation includes provocation by blows, words or gestures. "Grievous bodily harm", *not* statutorily defined, means no more nor less than really serious bodily harm. "Bodily harm" is defined in s. 2.

Section 34 affords justification where the person asserting self-defence has been unlawfully assaulted. Section 34(2) is also available to an initial aggressor. Section 37 justifies force in defence of self or another from assault.

Sections 38–42 authorize prescribed force in defence of real and personal property.

Excessive force may attract criminal responsibility to the extent described in s. 26.

36. Provocation — "Provocation" includes, for the purposes of sections 34 and 35, provocation by blows, words or gestures.

R.S., c. C-34, s. 36.

Commentary: The expansive definition of provocation, applicable only to ss. 34 and 35, includes blows, words and gestures.

Case Law

R. v. Nelson (1992), 13 C.R. (4th) 359, 71 C.C.C. (3d) 449 (Ont. C.A.) — Provocation under this section is *not* confined to blows, words or gestures. It means *conduct* by D that is intended by D to provoke an assault on him/herself.

Related Provisions: Provocation, in its ordinary sense, connotes the action or an act of exciting anger, resentment or irritation. It may be given in different ways to or by different persons. Blows, words and gestures, singly or in combination, are but three modes of giving provocation.

Sections 38(2), 41(2), 42(2) and (3) make reference to assaults which are *deemed* to have been committed *without justification or provocation*, or are *deemed* to have been *provoked by* a *trespasser*, as the case may be. Since provocation is deemed either to have been given or not given, as the case may be, no definition of the term is required and the definition of s. 36 is inapplicable.

Provocation as a *defence* to murder is governed by s. 232.

37. (1) Preventing assault — Every one is justified in using force to defend himself or any one under his protection from assault, if he uses no more force than is necessary to prevent the assault or the repetition of it.

(2) Extent of justification — Nothing in this section shall be deemed to justify the wilful infliction of any hurt or mischief that is excessive, having regard to the nature of the assault that the force used was intended to prevent.

R.S., c. C-34, s. 37.

Commentary: The section defines the extent to which the use of force may be justified in defence of self or of anyone under protection from or against assault.

Under s. 37(1) the defensive force must be *no more* than is necessary to prevent the assault or its repetition. There is no express reference to an assault which is reasonably apprehended nor to any other objective element or standard. Neither is there any reference to the nature or gravity of the assault in response to which the force is administered.

Section 37(2) further defines the extent of the justification afforded by s. 37(1). The *wilful infliction* of any hurt or mischief that is *excessive*, having regard to the nature of the assault that the force used was intended to prevent is not justified under s. 37(1). The responsive force, in other words, must be proportionate to the assault which engages it.

Case Law

R. v. McIntosh (1995), 36 C.R. (4th) 171, 95 C.C.C. (3d) 481 (S.C.C.); affirming (1993), 84 C.C.C. (3d) 473, 24 C.R. (4th) 265, 15 O.R. (3d) 450 (C.A.) — At the very least, s. 37 provides a basis for self-defence where s. 34 and 35 are *not* applicable. Where the evidence does not disclose a basis for self-defence other than those in which s. 34 or 35 would apply, s. 37 need *not* be left to the jury.

R. v. Brisson (1982), 29 C.R. (3d) 289, 69 C.C.C. (2d) 97 (S.C.C.) — Section 37 need not be put to the jury in every case where self-defence is suggested. There must be some evidence, sufficient to give an air of reality to the defence, before it need be left with the jury.

R. v. Whynot (Stafford) (1983), 37 C.R. (3d) 198, 9 C.C.C. (3d) 499 (N.S. C.A.) — No person has the right, in anticipation of an assault that might or might not happen, to apply force to prevent the imaginary assault. A person seeking the justification of this section must be faced with an *actual* assault and the assault must be life-threatening before s/he could be justified in killing in defence of D's person or that of someone under D's protection.

R. v. Mulder (1978), 40 C.C.C. (2d) 1 (Ont. C.A.) — The use of force permitted by this section is "proportionate force" and must not be more than is necessary to prevent an assault.

Related Provisions: An assault, under s. 265, may be actual or constructive. In s. 37(1) it would appear limited to the definitions of ss. 265(1)(a) and (b).

Section 34 affords justification where the person asserting self-defence has been unlawfully assaulted. Section 35 is to a similar effect where the person claiming justification has assaulted or provoked assault upon him or herself by another.

Sections 38–42 authorize prescribed force in defence of real and personal property.

The use of excessive force may attract criminal responsibility under s. 26.

Defence of Property

38. (1) Defence of personal property — Every one who is in peaceable possession of personal property, and every one lawfully assisting him, is justified

    (a) in preventing a trespasser from taking it, or

    (b) in taking it from a trespasser who has taken it,

if he does not strike or cause bodily harm to the trespasser.

(2) Assault by trespasser — Where a person who is in peaceable possession of personal property lays hands on it, a trespasser who persists in attempting to keep it or take it from him or from any one lawfully assisting him shall be deemed to commit an assault without justification or provocation.

R.S., c. C-34, s. 38.

Commentary: This section justifies *defence* of *personal property*.

The justification of s. 38(1) is available, not only to the *person in peaceable possession of personal property*, but, as well, to *every one lawfully assisting* such a person. What is justified is *preventing a trespasser from taking* the personal property, as well as *retaking the property from a trespasser* who has taken it, *provided* it does *not* involve striking or causing bodily harm to the trespasser.

Subsection (2) applies where a person in peaceable possession of personal property lays hands on the property and a trespasser persists in attempting to keep or take the property from that person or any one lawfully assisting him/her. The trespasser, in such circumstances, is deemed to commit an assault without justification or provocation.

Case Law

R. v. Lei (1997), 120 C.C.C. (3d) 441 (Man. C.A.); leave to appeal refused (1998), 123 C.C.C. (3d) vi (S.C.C.) — It is only s. 38(2) that justifies the infliction of bodily harm, *provided* D is in "peaceable possession" of personal property.

R. v. Weare (1983), 4 C.C.C. (3d) 494 (N.S. C.A.) — D was justified under this section in preventing persons, who he *reasonably* believed to be trespassers, from taking his movable property by pointing a rifle and ordering them off his property, as long as he did *not* strike them or cause bodily harm to them. The test to be applied in determining whether D was justified in using force and the extent to which he used that force is not an objective test, but rather whether D used more force than D, on *reasonable* grounds, believed was necessary.

Related Provisions: "Personal property" is *not* defined. "Bodily harm" is defined in s. 2. Possession is determined under s. 4(3).

Section 39 is complementary to the present provision in respect of those in peaceable possession of personal property. Sections 40–42, in the circumstances there described, justify the use of force in defence of the dwelling or other real property.

The degree of force with which a person who has been assaulted by another without justification or provocation, here the person in peaceable possession of personal property, may respond is described in ss. 34 and 37. The extent of force justified in the case of a person who has him/herself assaulted another without justification or provocation, here the trespasser, is defined in s. 35.

Criminal responsibility for excessive force is determined under s. 26.

39. (1) Defence with claim of right — Every one who is in peaceable possession of personal property under a claim of right, and every one acting under his authority, is protected from criminal responsibility for defending that possession, even against a person entitled by law to possession of it, if he uses no more force than is necessary.

(2) Defence without claim of right — Every one who is in peaceable possession of personal property, but does not claim it as of right or does not act under the authority of a person who claims it as of right, is not justified or protected from criminal responsibility for defending his possession against a person who is entitled by law to possession of it.

R.S., c. C-34, s. 39.

Commentary: The section defines the extent of justification afforded those in *peaceable possession* of *personal property*, with and without a claim of right, who defend it against persons entitled by law to possession of the property.

Section 39(1) defines the extent to which force may be used by any one who is in peaceable possession of personal property under a claim of right, or who claims under such a person. No more force than is necessary may be used in defending possession of the property. There is *no* express reference to an objective standard, viz "no more force than is *reasonably* necessary", or "no more force than, on *reasonable* grounds, is necessary". The justifiable force may even be used against a person entitled by law to possession of the personal property.

Section 39(2) applies to those who are in peaceable possession of personal property but neither claim it nor under the authority of another who claims it as of right. The subsection denies justification and protection from criminal responsibility to such persons who defend their possession against a person who is by law entitled to possession of it.

Case Law
Claim of Right

R. v. Lei (1997), 120 C.C.C. (3d) 441 (Man. C.A.); leave to appeal refused (1998), 123 C.C.C. (3d) vi (S.C.C.) — "Claim of right" embraces an honest but mistaken belief in entitlement to the personal property, notwithstanding that the mistake is based on an error of law or fact.

Related Provisions: Neither "personal property" nor "claim of right" is defined. Possession may be established in accordance with s. 4(3).

The complementary s. 38 makes no reference to claim of right in its justification for those in peaceable possession of personal property.

Sections 40–42 justify the use of prescribed force in defence of dwelling or other real property.

Criminal responsibility for excessive force is determined under s. 26.

40. Defence of dwelling — Every one who is in peaceable possession of a dwelling-house, and every one lawfully assisting him or acting under his authority, is justified in using as much force as is necessary to prevent any person from forcibly breaking into or forcibly entering the dwelling-house without lawful authority.

R.S., c. C-34, s. 40.

Commentary: The section authorizes and limits the use of *force* to *prevent* the *forcible entry* of *a dwelling-house*.

The force may be used not only by a person in *peaceable possession* of a dwelling-house but, equally, by everyone *lawfully* assisting him/her or acting under his/her authority. The force must be used to *prevent* another from *breaking* into or *forcibly entering* the dwelling-house without lawful authority, not for some other or ulterior reason. The extent of the force justified is "as much force as is necessary" to prevent unlawful and forcible entry.

The section does *not* expressly contain an *objective* element. In effect, it justifies a householder in using *necessary force* to *prevent* anyone from forcibly breaking or entering his/her house without lawful authority.

Case Law

See cases under s. 41.

Related Provisions: This is the first of three sections which justify the use of force in respect of *real* property. Section 41 applies in respect of a dwelling-house or real property, and s. 42 has similar application.

"Dwelling-house" is defined in s. 2. Forcible entry is defined in ss. 72(1) and (1.1) and punished under s. 73. Offences relating to breaking and entering are described in ss. 348 and terms there used defined for such purposes by ss. 321 and 350.

The position of a *trespasser*, who resists attempts by a householder to prevent entry or removal or who assaults a householder in similar circumstances is described in ss. 41(2) and 42(2). In each case, the trespasser is *deemed* to commit an assault on the householder without justification or provocation. The householder's responsive force in such circumstances would be governed by ss. 34 and 37.

Criminal responsibility for excessive force is governed by s. 26.

41. (1) Defence of house or real property — Every one who is in peaceable possession of a dwelling-house or real property, and every one lawfully assisting him or acting under his authority, is justified in using force to prevent any person from trespassing on the dwelling-house or real property, or to remove a trespasser therefrom, if he uses no more force than is necessary.

(2) Assault by trespasser — A trespasser who resists an attempt by a person who is in peaceable possession of a dwelling-house or real property, or a person lawfully assisting him or acting under his authority to prevent his entry or to remove him, shall be deemed to commit an assault without justification or provocation.

R.S., c. C-34, s. 41.

Commentary: The section authorizes and limits the *use of force against trespassers*.

The justification of s. 41(1) extends to *everyone* who is in *peaceable possession* of a *dwelling-house or real property*, and everyone assisting or acting under the authority of such persons. Each is justified and protected to an equivalent degree. The force must be applied *to prevent entry* by the trespasser upon *or to effect removal* of the trespasser from the dwelling-house or real property. The force used to effect the statutorily prescribed purpose must be *no more than is necessary*. No express reference is made to objective standards or elements.

Section 41(2) defines the position of a *trespasser who resists* the attempts of a householder to prevent his/her entry or effect his/her removal. The trespasser, in such circumstances, is *deemed* to commit an assault upon the householder without justification or provocation.

Case Law
Extent of Justification

R. v. Born With a Tooth (1992), 76 C.C.C. (3d) 169 (Alta. C.A.) — The four elements of the s. 41(1) defence are:

a.   that D be in *possession* of *land*;

b.   that D's *possession* be *peaceable*;

c.   that V be a *trespasser*; and

d.   that the force used to eject V be *reasonable* in the circumstances.

Item "a" requires *control*, not necessarily exclusive control over the relevant land. Under item b, *peaceable possession* means possession not seriously challenged by others, *not* peaceful possession. Critical to it is whether the possession and challenge to it are such to be unlikely to lead to violence.Where V has a right to be on the land, even if D also has such a right, item "c" is *not* met and the defence does *not* avail D. It is unclear whether D may treat V as a trespasser where V has a right to enter the land for one purpose but enters for another unlawful purpose, before the unlawful purpose appears.Mistake is available as a defence in relation to items "a" and "b", and the factual content of item "c". D may honestly but mistakenly believe that s/he may have a measure of control over the lands, that it is unchallenged or believe in facts which, if true, would make V a trespasser.

R. v. Clark (1984), 5 C.C.C. (3d) 264 (Alta. C.A.) — The defence of property which would justify killing can only arise where the one in possession of the property is able to make out a case of self-defence within s. 34.

R. v. Dixon (1993), 26 C.R. (4th) 173 (N.B. C.A.) — The legal standard applied under s. 41(1) is that of a person of reasonable prudence in the circumstances. The *de facto* or applied standard may vary with the activity and circumstances of individual cases.

R. v. Keating (1992), 76 C.C.C. (3d) 570 (N.S. C.A.) — A person may be an invitee for one purpose but not another. The trial judge should consider whether V, an invitee for one purpose, ceases to be an invitee when he pursues another purpose and, further, whether D had reasonable grounds to believe that V was thereby a trespasser.

R. v. MacLeod (1987), 77 N.S.R. (2d) 87 (C.A.) — Defence of property is unavailable where the person assaulted had not been a trespasser at all material times.

R. v. Scopelliti (1981), 63 C.C.C. (2d) 481 (Ont. C.A.) — Section 41(1) may apply to the occupier of commercial premises, as well as a dwelling-house.

Trespasser Trying to Leave

R. v. Matson (1970), 1 C.C.C. (2d) 374 (B.C. C.A.) — Where the case involves an occupier assaulting a trespasser who is trying to leave, the issue is one under s. 34 as to whether the trespasser used more force than was necessary to defend himself. This section is inapplicable.

Refusal of Trespasser to Leave

R. v. Alkadri (1986), 29 C.C.C. (3d) 467 (Alta. C.A.); leave to appeal refused (1986), 29 C.C.C. (3d) 467n (S.C.C.) — Section 41(2) does not apply where D used unnecessary force which provoked the trespasser. The attempt to eject the trespasser must be lawful.

R. v. Tricker (1995), 21 O.R. (3d) 575 (C.A.) — The occupier of a dwelling gives implied licence to any member of the public, including a police officer on legitimate business, to come on to the property. The implied licence ends at the door of the dwelling and may be withdrawn by the property owner. Once withdrawn, the person who entered under the licence must leave the property within a reasonable time or become a trespasser.

R. v. Figueira (1981), 63 C.C.C. (2d) 409 (Ont. C.A.) — The infliction of serious injury with a knife cannot be justified merely to prevent a person from trespassing, although the circumstances may give rise to the defence of self-defence, or permit the use of force to prevent the commission of offences involving serious injury to persons or property.

R. v. Baxter (1975), 33 C.R.N.S. 22, 27 C.C.C. (2d) 96 (Ont. C.A.) — *See also*: *R. v. Scopelliti* (1981), 63 C.C.C (2d) 481 (Ont. C.A.) — The effect of s. 41(2) is *not* to convert mere passive resistance into an assault, but merely to provide that any force used by the wrongdoer in resisting an attempt to prevent his/her entry or to remove him/her is unlawful and constitutes an assault. Firing at a mere trespasser is *not* justifiable.

Assisting Homeowner

R. v. Miller (1986), 25 C.C.C. (3d) 554 (Sask. C.A.) — D will *not* be entitled to the defences provided by ss. 40 and 41 where there is *no* evidence that D was *assisting* the homeowner or acting under his authority in ejecting an individual from the homeowner's property.

Entry by Police Officer [See also Code s. 25 and Charter s. 8]

Colet v. R. (1981), 19 C.R. (3d) 84 (S.C.C.) — Police are *not* justified in making an entry unless they have first announced their presence and demonstrated their authority by stating a lawful reason for their entry. A warrant authorizing only seizure of weapons did not also authorize the police to enter and search the premises. It would be dangerous to hold that the private rights of an individual to the exclusive enjoyment of his/her own property are subject to invasion by police whenever they can be said to be acting in furtherance of the enforcement of any section of the *Code*, although they lack express authority to justify their action.

R. v. Custer (1984), 12 C.C.C. (3d) 372 (Sask. C.A.); affirming [1983] 3 W.W.R. 66 (Sask. Q.B.) — Forcible entry into private premises to prevent death or serious injury may be made by a police officer if s/he has a belief based on reasonable and probable grounds that s/he is confronted with an emergency involving the preservation of life of some person within the dwelling-house, or the prevention of serious injury to that person, and if a proper announcement is made prior to entry.

Related Provisions: Section 40 also justifies the use of necessary force by a householder to prevent forcible entry or breaking into a dwelling-house.

"Dwelling-house" is defined in s. 2. "Real property" is undefined.

The responsive force of a householder or person in peaceable possession of real property where a trespasser commits an assault without justification or provocation under s. 41(2) is described in ss. 34 and 37.

Criminal responsibility for excessive force is governed by s. 26.

42. (1) Assertion of right to house or real property — Every one is justified in peaceably entering a dwelling-house or real property by day to take possession of it if he, or a person under whose authority he acts, is lawfully entitled to possession of it.

(2) Assault in case of lawful entry — Where a person

    (a) not having peaceable possession of a dwelling-house or real property under a claim of right, or

    (b) not acting under the authority of a person who has peaceable possession of a dwelling-house or real property under a claim of right,

assaults a person who is lawfully entitled to possession of it and who is entering it peaceably by day to take possession of it, for the purpose of preventing him from entering, the assault shall be deemed to be without justification or provocation.

(3) Trespasser provoking assault — Where a person

    (a) having peaceable possession of a dwelling-house or real property under a claim of right, or

    (b) acting under the authority of a person who has peaceable possession of a dwelling-house or real property under a claim of right,

assaults any person who is lawfully entitled to possession of it and who is entering it peaceably by day to take possession of it, for the purpose of preventing him from entering, the assault shall be deemed to be provoked by the person who is entering.

R.S., c. C-34, s. 42.

Commentary: The section justifies *peaceable entry* of *real* property by those lawfully entitled to it, and defines the position in law of persons who assault those lawfully entitled to possession of such property.

Section 42(1) justifies *peaceable entry of a dwelling-house or other real property*, by day, to take possession thereof by anyone who is or acts under the authority of another who is lawfully entitled to possession of it. The entry, in other words, must be peaceable, affected by day, and lawfully authorized.

Under s. 42(2) a person, neither in peaceable possession of a dwelling-house or real property under a claim of right, nor acting under the authority of any such person, who assaults a person described in s. 42(1) to prevent such a person from peaceable entry upon the property, is *deemed* to have committed the assault *without justification or provocation*. Generally, under s. 42(3) one, either in peaceable possession of a dwelling-house or real property under a claim of right, or acting under the authority of such a person, who assaults a person lawfully entitled to possession of the property who is entering, by day, to take possession of it, to prevent such re-entry, is *deemed* to have been provoked by the party entering.

Related Provisions: Unlike this section, which does *not* authorize the use of force in connection with real property, ss. 40 and 41(1) describe the extent of force that may be justified in defence of a dwelling-house or other real property.

"Dwelling-house" is defined in s. 2. "Real property" is *not* defined.

A person who is unlawfully assaulted is justified in responding with force as described in ss. 34 and 37. Section 35 prescribes the nature of force which may be applied by one who has, without justification, assaulted another. Criminal responsibility for excessive force is determined under s. 26. The offence of forcible detainer is described in s. 72(2) and punished under s. 73.

Protection of Persons in Authority

43. Correction of child by force — **Every schoolteacher, parent or person standing in the place of a parent is justified in using force by way of correction toward a pupil or child, as the case may be, who is under his care, if the force does not exceed what is reasonable under the circumstances.**

R.S., c. C-34, s. 43.

Commentary: The section describes the extent to which the *correction* of a child or pupil *by force* may be justified.

The force may only be used by a schoolteacher, parent or person standing in the place of a parent. No other category of person is entitled to place reliance on the section. The force must be applied by way of *correction* and not for any other purpose toward a pupil or child, as the case may be, under the care of the person administering the force. The person administering the force, in other words, must stand in a defined relationship to the person who receives it. Finally, the force must *not exceed* what is *reasonable under the circumstances*.

Case Law

Person Standing in Place of Parent

R. v. Nixon (1984), 14 C.C.C. (3d) 257 (S.C.C.) — A counsellor, charged with using physical force on a mentally retarded adult, does not stand in the place of the parent or school teacher. The retarded adult was not a child or a pupil within the meaning of the section. The section provides no defence.

R. v. Ogg-Moss (1984), 41 C.R. (3d) 297, 14 C.C.C. (3d) 116 (S.C.C.); affirming (1981), 24 C.R. (3d) 264, 60 C.C.C. (2d) 127 (Ont. C.A.) — This section must be strictly construed. "Child" means a person under the age of majority and does not refer to a mentally retarded adult, however childlike. Further, a counsellor at an institution for the mentally retarded is not a person who assumes parental obligations or has parental rights delegated by a natural parent. "Pupil" is limited to a child taking instruction. "Schoolteacher" is a person who gives formal instruction in a children's school. This section authorizes the use of force only where it is for the benefit of the education of the child. The person applying the force must intend it for correction. The person being corrected must be capable of learning from the correction.

Excessive Force [See also s. 26]

R. v. Taylor (1985), 44 C.R. (3d) 263 (Alta. C.A.) — If a method used to discipline a child is "unacceptable", that method cannot be afforded the protection of this section.

R. v. Dupperon (1985), 43 C.R. (3d) 70, 16 C.C.C. (3d) 453 (Sask. C.A.) — In determining whether the force used was reasonable, the court will consider from both an objective and a subjective standpoint such matters as the nature of the offence calling for correction, the age and character of the child and the likely effect of the punishment on this particular child, the degree of gravity of the punishment, the circumstances under which it was inflicted, and the injuries, if any, suffered. Injuries endangering life, limbs, health or disfigurement would alone be sufficient to find that the punishment was unreasonable.

R. v. Haberstock (1970), 1 C.C.C. (2d) 433 (Sask. C.A.) — Force may be excused under this section if applied at the next reasonable opportunity after an actual or apprehended (on reasonable or probable grounds) breach of discipline.

Related Provisions: "Schoolteacher", "parent", "pupil" and "child" are *not* defined. Each must be accorded its normal natural everyday meaning. The definition of "child" and "parent" in *YOA* s. 2(1) is for the purposes of that *Act* and it is doubtful whether *Code* s. 4(4) would extend its application to s. 43.

The justification for the application of force which is *reasonable under the circumstances* both adds an objective element. It ensures that each case will depend upon its own circumstances. Excessive force will attract criminal responsibility under s. 26.

The receivability of evidence of persons under 14 years of age or those whose mental capacity is challenged is governed by *C.E.A.* s. 16.

44. Master of ship maintaining discipline — **The master or officer in command of a vessel on a voyage is justified in using as much force as he believes, on reasonable grounds, is necessary for the purpose of maintaining good order and discipline on the vessel.**

R.S., c. C-34, s. 44.

Commentary: The section defines the extent to which force may be used by the *master of a ship* to maintain discipline on the vessel.

The justification conferred by the section is extended to the master or officer in command of a vessel on a voyage. The degree or extent of force which is justified is "as much force as he believes, on *reasonable* grounds, is necessary for the purpose of maintaining good order and discipline on the vessel." "On *reasonable* grounds" objectifies the subjective belief of the master or commanding officer. It ensures that only reasonably necessary disciplinary force, administered for the statutory purpose, is justified.

Related Provisions: Excessive force will attract criminal responsibility under s. 26.

Jurisdiction over offences committed on vessels is governed by ss. 476(a)–(c), as well as s. 477.

45. Surgical operations — **Every one is protected from criminal responsibility for performing a surgical operation on any person for the benefit of that person if**

    (a) the operation is performed with reasonable care and skill; and

    (b) it is reasonable to perform the operation, having regard to the state of health of the person at the time the operation is performed and to all the circumstances of the case.

R.S., c. C-34, s. 45.

Commentary: The section defines the extent to which *persons performing surgical operations* for the benefit of the patient are *protected from criminal responsibility*.

There are two elements necessary to engage the protection. The *operation* must be *performed with reasonable care and skill*. It must also be *reasonable to perform the operation*, having regard to the patient's [then] state of health and all the circumstances of the case. The requirement of reasonableness, both in the necessity for and conduct of the operation, ensures that protection from criminal responsibility will only be extended to practitioners who are reasonably competent in their assessment and conduct in such matters.

Related Provisions: Under s. 216 every one who undertakes to administer surgical or medical treatment to another, except in cases of necessity, is under a legal duty to have and to use *reasonable* knowledge, skill and care in so doing. Section 217, not confined to medical matters, imposes a legal duty upon every one who undertakes to do an act, if an omission to do it is or may be dangerous to life. Criminal negligence is defined in s. 219 and punishment imposed for causing death or bodily harm thereby in ss. 220 and 221.

Section 238(2) exempts from criminal liability under s. 238(1) for causing the death of an unborn child, a person, such as a physician, who, by means that, in good faith s/he considers necessary to preserve the life of the mother of the child, causes the death of the child.

PART II — OFFENCES AGAINST PUBLIC ORDER

Treason and other Offences against the Queen's Authority and Person

46. (1) **High treason** — Every one commits high treason who, in Canada,

(a) kills or attempts to kill Her Majesty, or does her any bodily harm tending to death or destruction, maims or wounds her, or imprisons or restrains her;

(b) levies war against Canada or does any act preparatory thereto; or

(c) assists an enemy at war with Canada, or any armed forces against whom Canadian Forces are engaged in hostilities, whether or not a state of war exists between Canada and the country whose forces they are.

(2) **Treason** — Every one commits treason who, in Canada,

(a) uses force or violence for the purpose of overthrowing the government of Canada or a province;

(b) without lawful authority, communicates or makes available to an agent of a state other than Canada, military or scientific information or any sketch, plan, model, article, note or document of a military or scientific character that he knows or ought to know may be used by that state for a purpose prejudicial to the safety or defence of Canada;

(c) conspires with any person to commit high treason or to do anything mentioned in paragraph (a);

(d) forms an intention to do anything that is high treason or that is mentioned in paragraph (a) and manifests that intention by an overt act; or

(e) conspires with any person to do anything mentioned in paragraph (b) or forms an intention to do anything mentioned in paragraph (b) and manifests that intention by an overt act.

(3) **Canadian citizen** — Notwithstanding subsection (1) or (2), a Canadian citizen or a person who owes allegiance to Her Majesty in right of Canada,

(a) commits high treason if, while in or out of Canada, he does anything mentioned in subsection (1); or

(b) commits treason if, while in or out of Canada, he does anything mentioned in subsection (2).

(4) **Overt act** — Where it is treason to conspire with any person, the act of conspiring is an overt act of treason.

R.S., c. C-34, s. 46; 1974–75–76, c. 105, s. 2.

Commentary: The section defines the offences of *high treason* and *treason* and enacts ancillary evidentiary and procedural provisions.

High treason, defined in s. 46(1), may be committed in any of several ways. In essence, it involves proscribed conduct directed towards Her Majesty, levying war against Canada or doing any act preparatory thereto, or assisting an enemy or hostile forces. The *mental element* consists of the intention to cause any external circumstances of the offence. The offence is committed under s. 46(3)(a) where a Canadian citizen or person owing allegiance to Her Majesty in right of Canada does anything described in s. 46(1) either in or out of Canada.

Section 46(2) defines *treason*. Under s. 46(3)(b) the offence is committed by a Canadian citizen or person owing allegiance to Her Majesty in right of Canada who does anything described in s. 46(2) while in or out of Canada. The *external circumstances* described in ss. 46(2)(a) and (b) constitute the primary definitions of the offence. The *mental element* requires proof, not only of the *intention* to cause the external circumstances, but also the further elements of *purpose* and actual or constructive *knowledge*. The *external circumstances* of the offence described in s. 46(2)(c) require proof of a conspiracy to commit high treason or, alternatively, to do anything described in s. 46(2)(a). The *mental element* consists of the intention to cause the *external circumstances*. There is *no* requirement that P prove D manifested such intention by an overt act. Under both ss. 46(2)(d) and (e), however, the intention or conspiracy must be manifested by an overt act. Under s. 46(4), where it is treason to conspire with anyone, the act of conspiracy is itself an overt act of treason.

Related Provisions: The punishment for high treason is described in ss. 47(1), (4) and 745(a), and for treason in s. 47(2). Both offences lie within the *exclusive* trial (ss. 468 and 469(a)(i)) and judicial interim release (s. 522) jurisdiction of the *superior court* of criminal jurisdiction.

Special *evidentiary and procedural rules* apply in prosecutions for high treason and treason. Section 47(3) requires *corroboration*. Limitations are placed upon the commencement of certain proceedings for treason under s. 48. Specific pleading rules relating to the statement of overt acts in the indictment are mandatory under ss. 581(4) and 601(9). Under s. 55 no evidence is admissible of an overt act *unless* it is set out in the indictment, or where the evidence is otherwise relevant as tending to prove an overt act specified in the indictment or count. Under s. 582, no one shall be convicted of high treason unless specifically charged with it in the indictment.

Both offences are exempted from the operation of the excuse of compulsion under s. 17. Rules which confer jurisdiction on Canadian courts in respect of offences committed outside Canada appear in ss. 7(5) and 464(4) as exceptions to the general rule of s. 6(2). Related offences are described in ss. 49–54.

47. (1) Punishment for high treason — Every one who commits high treason is guilty of an indictable offence and shall be sentenced to imprisonment for life.

(2) Punishment for treason — Every one who commits treason is guilty of an indictable offence and liable

(a) to be sentenced to imprisonment for life if he is guilty of an offence under paragraph 46(2)(*a*), (*c*) or (*d*);

(b) to be sentenced to imprisonment for life if he is guilty of an offence under paragraph 46(2)(*b*) or (*e*) committed while a state of war exists between Canada and another country; or

(c) to be sentenced to imprisonment for a term not exceeding fourteen years if he is guilty of an offence under paragraph 46(2)(*b*) or (*e*) committed while no state of war exists between Canada and another country.

(3) Corroboration — No person shall be convicted of high treason or treason on the evidence of only one witness, unless the evidence of that witness is corroborated in a material particular by evidence that implicates the accused.

(4) Minimum punishment — For the purposes of Part XXIII, the sentence of imprisonment for life prescribed by subsection (1) is a minimum punishment.

R.S., c. C-34, s. 47; 1974–75–76, c. 105, s. 2.

Commentary: The section prescribes the *punishment* upon conviction of high treason and treason. It also enacts a mandatory *evidentiary rule* applicable in prosecutions for treason.

Under s. 47(3) *corroboration is mandatory*. D may *not* be convicted on the evidence of *only* one witness, *unless* the evidence is *corroborated* in a material particular by evidence that implicates D.

Related Provisions: Under s. 745(a), the *minimum punishment* upon conviction of high treason is imprisonment for life without eligibility for release on parole until after D has served 25 years of the sentence. The parole ineligibility period may be reviewed under s. 745.6 after D has served at least 15 years of the sentence. Where a sentence of life imprisonment is imposed as a maximum punishment upon conviction of treason, parole eligibility is determined in accordance with the normal rules under s. 745(d).

Other related procedural and evidentiary provisions are described in the corresponding note to s. 46, *supra*.

48. (1) Limitation — No proceedings for an offence of treason as defined by paragraph 46(2)(a) shall be commenced more than three years after the time when the offence is alleged to have been committed.

(2) Information for treasonable words — No proceedings shall be commenced under section 47 in respect of an overt act of treason expressed or declared by open and considered speech unless

(a) an information setting out the overt act and the words by which it was expressed or declared is laid under oath before a justice within six days after the time when the words are alleged to have been spoken; and

(b) a warrant for the arrest of the accused is issued within ten days after the time when the information is laid.

R.S., c. C-34, s. 48; 1974–75–76, c. 105, s. 29.

Commentary: The section imposes *limitations* upon the *commencement of proceedings* for an offence of *treason*.

Related Provisions: The section does not define *what* constitutes the *commencement* of proceedings, hence *when* they are commenced. In the usual course, criminal proceedings are commenced by and when an information has been laid under oath before a justice of the peace.

The computation of time is in accordance with *I.A.* ss. 26–30.

Other related procedural, substantive and evidentiary provisions are described in the corresponding note to s. 46, *supra*.

Prohibited Acts

49. Acts intended to alarm Her Majesty or break public peace — Every one who wilfully, in the presence of Her Majesty,

(a) does an act with intent to alarm Her Majesty or to break the public peace, or

(b) does an act that is intended or is likely to cause bodily harm to her Majesty,

is guilty of an indictable offence and liable to imprisonment for a term not exceeding fourteen years.

R.S., c. C-34, s. 49.

Commentary: The section prohibits acts in the presence of Her Majesty which are accompanied by a proscribed state of mind.

The *external circumstances* of the offence consist of *an act* by D *in the presence of Her Majesty*. The reference to "an act" is undifferentiated, qualified only by the requirement that, whatever the act, it be accompanied by the proscribed state of mind. The *mental element*, in all cases, requires proof that D's act be *wilful*. Under s. 49(a), the mental element includes the further or *ulterior* intent to alarm Her Majesty or to break the public peace. Under s. 49(b), the *mental element* requires proof that D intended the act to cause bodily harm to Her Majesty. The alternative, "is likely to cause bodily harm to Her Majesty", would appear to require at least some degree of foreseeability on the part of D, in addition to the intention to do the act which, objectively viewed, is likely to cause such harm.

Related Provisions: The offences fall within the *exclusive* trial (ss. 468 and 469(a)(ii)) and judicial interim release (s. 522) jurisdiction of the *superior court* of criminal jurisdiction.

Special procedural and evidentiary rules are applicable in prosecutions under the section. Under s. 581(4) every overt act upon which P relies must be stated in the indictment. Section 601(9) ensures that the amendment power is not used to add to the overt acts pleaded in the indictment under s. 581(4). Further, s. 55 bars the introduction of evidence of overt acts unless the overt act has been pleaded in the indictment or the evidence is otherwise relevant as tending to prove such an overt act.

50. (1) Assisting alien enemy to leave Canada, or omitting to prevent treason — Every one commits an offence who

  (a) incites or willfully assists a subject of

      (i) a state that is at war with Canada, or

      (ii) a state against whose forces Canadian Forces are engaged in hostilities, whether or not a state of war exists between Canada and the state whose forces they are,

    to leave Canada without the consent of the Crown, unless the accused establishes that assistance to the state referred to in subparagraph (i) or the forces of the state referred to in subparagraph (ii), as the case may be, was not intended thereby; or

  (b) knowing that a person is about to commit high treason or treason does not, with all reasonable dispatch, inform a justice of the peace or other peace officer thereof or make other reasonable efforts to prevent that person from committing high treason or treason.

(2) Punishment — Every one who commits an offence under subsection (1) is guilty of an indictable offence and liable to imprisonment for a term not exceeding fourteen years.

R.S., c. C-34, s. 50; 1974–75–76, c. 105, s. 29.

Commentary: These indictable offences are committed where D *incites or wilfully assists* an alien enemy to leave Canada, or *omits to prevent* the commission of treason or high treason by another person.

The *external circumstances* under of s. 50(1)(a) require proof that D, *incited or assisted* a subject of a state described in either (a)(i) or (ii) to leave Canada without the consent of the Crown. The *mental element* requires proof that D intended to cause the external circumstances of the offence. Where P alleges that D *assisted* a subject to leave Canada without the consent of the Crown, it must establish that D did so *wilfully*. It is doubtful whether *wilfully* adds anything to the *mental element* that is otherwise required. At all events, it is *not* required where it is alleged that D *incited* the subject to leave Canada. It is open to D, in defence, to assert an absence of intention to assist the state or forces described in the subparagraph. The requirement that D *establish* such defence may have ss. 7 and 11(d) *Charter* implications, especially as it would appear that an intention to assist is not an essential element of P's proof.

The *external circumstances* under s. 50(1)(b) involve *knowledge* and *omission*. D must *know* that a person is *about to commit* treason or high treason. Knowledge, extends to the facts or circumstances which underlie the intended offence, rather than its legal character of classification. *Omission* requires proof of the failure, without all reasonable dispatch, to inform a judge or other peace officer or an equivalent failure to make other reasonable efforts to prevent the person from committing treason or high treason. The *mental element* consists of the intention to cause the external circumstances of the offence and includes the requisite knowledge of the other party's intention. No further or ulterior intent is required.

Related Provisions: The *Code* does *not* define "incite", part of the expansive definition of "counsel" in s. 22(3), used in the offences of ss. 53 (incitement to mutiny) and 319 (incitement of hatred). "Assists", also *not* defined, appears in several provisions, as for example, ss. 21(2), 23 and 129(b). Each word is of common usage and bears its normal natural everyday meaning.

"Canadian Forces" is defined in s. 2. High treason and treason are described in s. 46.

Under s. 7(11) a *certificate* issued by or under the authority of the Secretary of State for External Affairs stating that, at a certain time, a state was engaged in an armed conflict with Canada is receivable in evidence in *proof* of the facts there stated.

Under s. 148 it is an indictable offence to assist a prisoner of war to escape.

The offence of this section is *not* listed in s. 469. D may elect mode of trial under s. 536(2). Judicial interim release is determined by a justice under s. 515.

The special evidentiary and procedural rules applicable to prosecutions under the section are described in the corresponding note to s. 49, *supra*.

51. Intimidating Parliament or legislature — Every one who does an act of violence in order to intimidate Parliament or the legislature of a province is guilty of an indictable offence and liable to imprisonment for a term not exceeding fourteen years.
R.S., c. C-34, s. 51.

Commentary: The gravamen of this offence rests in the purpose that underlies it.

The *external circumstances* of the offence consist of an *act of violence* by D, i.e., the exercise by D of physical force so as to inflict injury upon or damage to persons or property. The terms are unqualified by any reference to time, place, manner or other circumstance which describe or limit the act of violence. The *mental element* demands proof of an ulterior purpose "in order to intimidate Parliament or the legislature of a province".

Related Provisions: This offence comes within the *exclusive* jurisdiction of the superior court of criminal jurisdiction. It is an "offence" within s. 183 for the purposes of Part VI.

Special procedural and evidentiary rules applicable to prosecutions under this section are described in the corresponding note to s. 49, *supra*.

52. Sabotage — (1) Every one who does a prohibited act for a purpose prejudicial to

　(a) the safety, security or defence of Canada, or

　(b) the safety or security of the naval, army or air forces of any state other than Canada that are lawfully present in Canada,

is guilty of an indictable offence and liable to imprisonment for a term not exceeding ten years.

(2) **"prohibited act"** — In this section, "prohibited act" means an act or omission that

　(a) impairs the efficiency or impedes the working of any vessel, vehicle, aircraft, machinery, apparatus or other thing; or

　(b) causes property, by whomever it may be owned, to be lost, damaged or destroyed.

(3) **Saving** — No person does a prohibited act within the meaning of this section by reason only that

　(a) he stops work as a result of the failure of his employer and himself to agree on any matter relating to his employment;

(b) he stops work as a result of the failure of his employer and a bargaining agent acting on his behalf to agree on any matter relating to his employment; or

(c) he stops work as a result of his taking part in a combination of workmen or employees for their own reasonable protection as workmen or employees.

(4) **Idem** — No person does a prohibited act within the meaning of this section by reason only that he attends at or near or approaches a dwelling-house or place for the purpose only of obtaining or communicating information.

R.S., c. C-34, s. 52.

Commentary: The section defines "sabotage" by prohibition and exception.

The *external circumstances* comprise the doing of a prohibited act which is any act or omission within s. 52(2), but *not* within s. 52(3) or (4).

The *mental element* has a dual aspect. D must first *intend* to cause the external circumstances of the offence, that is to say, to do the prohibited act. P must also prove that D intentionally did the prohibited act for either *purpose* proscribed by s. 52(1).

"Sabotage" describes any malicious or wanton destruction of the property of another. In a more restrictive sense, it refers to the malicious damaging or destruction of an employer's property by workers during a strike or similar work-related activity. Sections 52(3) and (4) except or exempt certain employment-related activity, as for example lawful strikes and picketing, from the description of "prohibited act" in s. 52(2).

Related Provisions: This offence is an "offence" for the purposes of s. 183 and Part VI. Mischief in relation to property is an offence under s. 430(1). Exemptions similar to those of present ss. 52(3) and (4) appear in ss. 430(6) and (7).

Under s. 581(4) every overt act upon which P relies must be stated in the indictment. Section 55 prohibits the introduction of evidence of overt acts unless the overt act has itself has been pleaded in the indictment or the evidence is otherwise relevant as tending to prove such an overt act.

D may elect mode of trial under s. 536(2). Judicial interim release is determined under s. 515.

53. Inciting to mutiny — Every one who

(a) attempts, for a traitorous or mutinous purpose, to seduce a member of the Canadian Forces from his duty and allegiance to Her Majesty, or

(b) attempts to incite or to induce a member of the Canadian Forces to commit a traitorous or mutinous act,

is guilty of an indictable offence and liable to imprisonment for a term not exceeding fourteen years.

R.S., c. C-34, s. 53.

Commentary: The section prohibits *attempts to create disaffection* amongst members of the Canadian Forces.

The *external circumstances* of s. 53(a) are complete where D *attempts to seduce* a member of the Canadian Forces from his/her duty and allegiance to Her Majesty. The attempt need *not* succeed. In addition to proof of the intention to cause the external circumstances of the offence, P must establish that the attempted seduction was *for a traitorous or mutinous purpose*.

Under s. 53(b) P must prove an *attempt to incite or induce* a member of the Canadian Forces to commit a traitorous or mutinous act. The *mental element* does *not* extend beyond proof of the intention to cause the external circumstances of the offence, as required under s. 53(a), which include a traitorous or mutinous act.

Related Provisions: An *attempt* in law is defined in s. 24. In ordinary parlance, to "attempt" is to try to do or achieve something.

Several other sections create offences relating to the "Canadian Forces" as defined in s. 2. Section 54 prohibits the giving of assistance to a person known to be a deserter or absentee without leave from the Canadian Forces. Interferences with loyalty and discipline in the Canadian Forces are indictable under s.

62. Sections 419 and 420 create offences relating to the unlawful use of military uniforms or certificates, as well as unlawful traffic or dealing in military stores.

Special procedural and evidentiary rules applicable to prosecutions under this section are described in the corresponding note to s. 49, *supra*.

This offence falls within the *exclusive* jurisdiction of the superior court of criminal jurisdiction for trial (ss. 468 and 469(a)(iv)) and judicial interim release (s. 522) purposes.

54. Assisting deserter — **Every one who aids, assists, harbours or conceals a person who he knows is a deserter or absentee without leave from the Canadian Forces is guilty of an offence punishable on summary conviction, but no proceedings shall be instituted under this section without the consent of the Attorney General of Canada.**

R.S., c. C-34, s. 54.

Commentary: The *consent* of the Attorney General of Canada is *required* to institute proceedings in respect of this summary conviction offence, *assisting a deserter*.

The *external circumstances* require that D's conduct amount to aiding, assistance, harbouring or concealment of another, who is either a deserter or an absentee without leave from the Canadian Forces. The *mental element* requires proof that D intended to cause the external circumstances of the offence, with the *knowledge* of the status of the person aided, assisted, harboured or concealed.

Related Provisions: The definition of "Attorney General" in s. 2 includes his/her "lawful deputy". " Canadian Forces" is defined in s. 2.

Section 53 prohibits attempts to create disaffection amongst members of the Canadian Forces. Interferences with loyalty and discipline in the Canadian Forces are indictable under s. 62. Sections 419 and 420 create offences relating to the unlawful use of military uniforms or certificates as well as unlawful traffic or dealing in military stores.

Accessorial liability is determined under ss. 21–23, *supra*.

The offence is tried under Part XXVII and punished in accordance with s. 787(2).

55. Evidence of overt acts — **In proceedings for an offence against any provision in section 47 or sections 49 to 53, no evidence is admissible of an overt act unless that overt act is set out in the indictment or unless the evidence is otherwise relevant as tending to prove an overt act that is set out therein.**

R.S., c. C-34, s. 55.

Commentary: The section enacts an *evidentiary rule* which complements a specific rule of pleading applicable where D is charged with a listed offence. An *overt act* is any act manifesting the intention and tending to the accomplishment of a criminal object. It need *not* be an act which would, itself, constitute the offence.

In proceedings in respect of offences against any of s. 47 or ss. 49–53, the section admits evidence of overt acts only if the overt act is set out in the indictment (s. 581(4)), or if the evidence is otherwise relevant as tending to prove an overt act set out in the indictment.

Related Provisions: The essential elements of the listed offences are described in the *Commentary* to ss. 47 and 49–53.

Section 581(4) requires a statement in the indictment of every overt act to be relied upon by P. Section 601(9), applicable only to treason, high treason (s. 47), ss. 49–51 and 53 prohibits the use of the amendment power of s. 601 to add to the overt acts stated in the indictment.

56. Offences in relation to members of R.C.M.P — **Every one who wilfully**

(a) **persuades or counsels a member of the Royal Canadian Mounted Police to desert or absent himself without leave,**

(b) **aids, assists, harbours or conceals a member of the Royal Canadian Mounted Police who he knows is a deserter or absentee without leave, or**

(c) **aids or assists a member of the Royal Canadian Mounted Police to desert or absent himself without leave, knowing that the member is about to desert or absent himself without leave,**

is guilty of an offence punishable on summary conviction.

R.S., c. 34, s. 57;R.S. 1985, c. 27 (1st Supp.), s. 8.

Commentary: These summary conviction offences prohibit conduct which tends to produce or support desertion or absence without leave by members of the R.C.M.P.

The *external circumstances* of the offences of s. 56(a) require proof that D *persuaded or counselled* a member of the R.C.M.P. to desert or absent him/herself without leave. The persuasion or counselling may be addressed to any member, whether predisposed to desertion or absence or otherwise. It need *not* result in actual desertion or absence without leave. The *mental element* does *not* extend beyond proof of the intention to cause the external circumstances of the offence.

Under s. 56(c), the *external circumstances* involve proof that D *aided or assisted* a member to desert or absent him/herself without leave. The member must, however, be *about* to desert or absent him/herself without leave, irrespective of the aid or assistance of D. Actual desertion or absence *semble* need *not* be proven as part of the external circumstances. The *mental element* combines the intention to cause the external circumstances of the offence with *knowledge* that the member aided or assisted is about to desert or absent him/herself without leave. The offences of ss. 56(a) and (c) involve participation by D as an accessory, i.e., party, prior to or contemporaneous with the desertion or absence, should it occur.

The offence of s. 56(b) requires proof of desertion or absence without leave and makes criminal certain conduct after desertion or absence. The *external circumstances* involve aiding, assisting, harbouring or counselling of a member who has deserted or is absent without leave. The *mental element* involves proof of the intention to do so, together with *knowledge* of the status of the member.

Related Provisions: Under s. 22(3), "counsel" includes "procure, solicit or incite". "Aids, assists, harbours or conceals" also appear in s. 54.

R.C.M.P. members come within the definition of "public officer" in s. 2. Bribery of public officers is an indictable offence under s. 120 and personation a summary conviction offence under s. 130. Obstruction of a public officer and related offences are punished under s. 129.

The offence of this section is tried under Part XXVII and punished in accordance with s. 787(2).

Passports

57. (1) Forgery of or uttering forged passport — Every one who, while in or out of Canada,

(a) **forges a passport, or**

(b) **knowing that a passport is forged**

    (i) **uses, deals with or acts on it, or**

    (ii) **causes or attempts to cause any person to use, deal with, or act on it, as if the passport were genuine,**

is guilty of an indictable offence and liable to imprisonment for a term not exceeding fourteen years.

(2) False statement in relation to passport — Every one who, while in or out of Canada, for the purpose of procuring a passport for himself or any other person or for the purpose of procuring any material alteration or addition to any such passport, makes a written or an oral statement that he knows is false or misleading

(a) **is guilty of an indictable offence and liable to imprisonment for a term not exceeding two years; or**

(b) **is guilty of an offence punishable on summary conviction.**

(3) **Possession of forged, etc.**, **passport** — Every one who without lawful excuse, the proof of which lies on him, has in his possession a forged passport or a passport in respect of which an offence under subsection (2) has been committed is guilty of an indictable offence and liable to imprisonment for a term not exceeding five years.

(4) **Special provisions applicable** — For the purposes of proceedings under this section,

   (a) the place where a passport was forged is not material; and

   (b) the definition "false document" in section 321, and section 366, apply with such modifications as the circumstances require.

(5) **"passport"** — In this section, "passport" means a document issued by or under the authority of the Minister of Foreign Affairs for the purpose of identifying the holder thereof.

(6) **Jurisdiction** — Where a person is alleged to have committed, while out of Canada, an offence under this section, proceedings in respect of that offence may, whether or not that person is in Canada, be commenced in any territorial division in Canada and the accused may be tried and punished in respect of that offence in the same manner as if the offence had been committed in that territorial division.

(7) **Appearance of accused at trial** — For greater certainty, the provisions of this Act relating to

   (a) requirements that an accused appear at and be present during proceedings, and

   (b) the exceptions to those requirements,

apply to proceedings commenced in any territorial division pursuant to subsection (6).
   R.S., c. C-34, s. 58;R.S. 1985, c. 27 (1st Supp.), s. 9; 1994, c. 44, s. 4; 1995, c. 5, s. 25(1)(g).

Commentary: The section defines "passport", describes and punishes several offences relating to the making, obtaining possession and use of passports, and enacts several procedural provisions applicable to the trial of such offences.

Under s. 57(1), the *forgery* of passports, and certain dealings with passports D *knows* to be forged, are prohibited. Under s. 57(1)(a) the *external circumstances* of the offence consist of the *forgery* of the passport. The *definition* of "false document" in ss. 321 and 366 apply. Where the passport is forged is *not* material. The *mental element* is essentially a duplicate of the specific or ulterior intent of forgery in s. 366(1). The *external circumstances* in s. 57(1)(b) consist of any *dealing* with a forged passport that falls within the various modes described in the paragraph. The *mental element* requires proof of D's *knowledge* of the forged character of the passport, and the intention to deal with it in a prohibited way. "Passport" is defined in s. 57(5).

The *external circumstances* under s. 57(2) involve *making* a *false or misleading statement*, written or oral, in the context of procuring a passport or a material alteration or addition thereto. The *mental element*, a combination of intention, purpose and knowledge, requires proof that D *intended* to make the prohibited statement, with *knowledge* of its false or misleading character, for a prohibited *purpose*.

The *external circumstances* of the complementary possession offence of s. 57(3) requires proof that D was in *possession*, without lawful excuse, of a passport which is either forged or the subject of other unlawful dealings under s. 57(2). The burden of establishing a lawful excuse for the possession rests upon D, thereby invoking *Charter* s. 7 and/or s. 11(d) scrutiny. The *mental element* requires proof of the intention to cause or recklessness with respect to the external circumstances of the offence, coupled with knowledge of the spurious character of the passport.

Sections 57(6) and (7) relate to trial jurisdiction and procedure. Where the offence is alleged to have been committed *out of* Canada, s. 57(6) permits the *commencement* of proceedings in *any* territorial division in Canada, whether D is in Canada or not. In combination, ss. 57(6) and (7) permit D's trial in any territorial division in Canada and, upon conviction, punishment. *Corroboration* is mandatory under s. 367(2).

Case Law

Multiple Convictions

R. v. Berryman (1990), 78 C.R. (3d) 376, 57 C.C.C. (3d) 375 (B.C. C.A.) — A conviction under s. 57(2) of making a written statement on a passport application which D knew to be false, for the purpose of procuring a passport, does *not* bar a conviction under s. 57(1)(a) of forging a passport.

Related Provisions: Fraudulent use of a certificate of citizenship or naturalization is punishable under s. 58.

Forgery and offences resembling forgery are described and punished in ss. 366–378. Possession is defined in s. 4(3).

Authorization to intercept private communications may be given in respect of these offences under Part VI.

The requirement that D be personally present at his/her trial, together with relevant exceptions, are found in s. 650.

The indictable offences of ss. 57(1) and (3) are crimes in respect of which D may elect mode of trial under s. 536(2). Under s. 57(2), where P chooses to proceed by way of indictment, D may elect mode of trial.

58. (1) **Fraudulent use of certificate of citizenship** — **Every one who, while in or out of Canada,**

> (a) **uses a certificate of citizenship or a certificate of naturalization for a fraudulent purpose, or**

> (b) **being a person to whom a certificate of citizenship or a certificate of naturalization has been granted, knowingly parts with the possession of that certificate with intent that it should be used for a fraudulent purpose,**

is guilty of an indictable offence and liable to imprisonment for a term not exceeding two years.

(2) **"certificate of citizenship", "certificate of naturalization"** — **In this section, "certificate of citizenship" and "certificate of naturalization" respectively, mean a certificate of citizenship and a certificate of naturalization as defined by the *Citizenship Act*.**

R.S., c. C-34, s. 59; 1974–75–76, c. 108, s. 41.

Commentary: These indictable offences involve the actual or intended *fraudulent use* of *certificates of citizenship or naturalization* as defined in s. 58(2).

The offences of s. 58(1) may be committed while D is in or out of Canada. Under s. 58(1)(a), the *external circumstances* of the offence consist of the *use* of either type of certificate. The *mental element* comprises the *intention* to use the certificate and the ulterior element of *fraudulent purpose*. Under s. 58(1)(b), as principal, D must be a person to whom a certificate of citizenship or naturalization has been granted and must part with the possession of the certificate. The *mental element* requires proof that D acted *knowingly* in parting with the possession of the certificate, and, further, did so with the specific or ulterior intent that it should be used *for a fraudulent purpose*.

Related Provisions: "Certificate of citizenship" and "certificate of naturalization" are defined under s. 2(1) of the *Citizenship Act*, R.S. 1985, c. C-29.

D may elect mode of trial under s. 536(2).

Sedition

59. (1) Seditious words — Seditious words are words that express a seditious intention.

(2) Seditious libel — A seditious libel is a libel that expresses a seditious intention.

(3) Seditious conspiracy — A seditious conspiracy is an agreement between two or more persons to carry out a seditious intention.

(4) Seditious intention — Without limiting the generality of the meaning of the expression "seditious intention", every one shall be presumed to have a seditious intention who

(a) teaches or advocates, or

(b) publishes or circulates any writing that advocates,

the use, without the authority of law, of force as a means of accomplishing a governmental change within Canada.

R.S., c. C-34, s. 60.

Commentary: The section defines several constituent elements of the seditious offences described and punished in s. 61.

An essential element of seditious words, a seditious libel and a seditious conspiracy, as defined in ss. 59(1)–(3) is a "seditious intention". In terms, "seditious intention" is not defined in the section. In general, it may be said to include, *inter alia*, an intention to raise discontent or disaffection amongst the subjects of the sovereign. Under s. 59(4) a *seditious intention* will be *presumed* in everyone who teaches or advocates, or publishes or circulates any writing that advocates the use, without lawful authority, of force as a means of accomplishing a government change within Canada. The presumption of an essential element of P's case in prosecutions under s. 61, may attract *Charter* ss. 7 and 11(d) scrutiny.

Case Law

Seditious Libel: S. 59(2)

Duval v. R. (1938), 64 B.R. 270 (Que. C.A.) — Where the writings or publications complained of are of a seditious nature, the sincerity of the belief of those publishing them is irrelevant.

Seditious Intention: S. 59(4)

Boucher v. R. (1951), 11 C.R. 85, 99 C.C.C. 1 (S.C.C.) — In most cases, proof of seditious intent requires proof of an intention to incite violence, public disorder or unlawful conduct against the State.

Related Provisions: Sections 584(1) and (2) govern the manner in which counts for seditious libel may be pleaded. Section 584(3) holds sufficient, on the trial of a count of publishing a seditious libel, proof that the matter published was libellous, with or without innuendo.

The seditious offences of s. 61, under s. 469(a)(v) are within the exclusive trial and judicial interim release jurisdiction of the superior court of criminal jurisdiction.

Section 60 sets out several exceptions to the presumption of s. 59(4) concerning seditious intention.

Section 62 creates a related offence that prohibits certain conduct in relation to members of Canadian Forces or the forces of another state lawfully present in Canada.

60. Exception — Notwithstanding subsection 59(4), no person shall be deemed to have a seditious intention by reason only that he intends, in good faith,

(a) to show that Her Majesty has been misled or mistaken in her measures;

(b) to point out errors or defects in

(i) the government or constitution of Canada or a province,

(ii) Parliament or the legislature of a province, or

93

(iii) the administration of justice in Canada;

(c) to procure, by lawful means, the alteration of any matter of government in Canada; or

(d) to point out, for the purpose of removal, matters that produce or tend to produce feelings of hostility and ill-will between different classes of persons in Canada.

R.S., c. C-34, s. 61.

Commentary: The section, which operates notwithstanding the *presumption* of seditious intention in s. 59(4), excepts or exempts from liability certain conduct which otherwise may be deemed to reflect a seditious intention. Under the exemption, D is deemed *not* to have a seditious intention by reason *only* that s/he intends, in *good faith*, to show, point out or procure anything described in ss. 60(a)–(d).

Case Law

Boucher v. R. (1949), 9 C.R. 127 (S.C.C.) — D believed that hatred and ill-will towards Jehovah's Witnesses already existed in Quebec and that the plea set forth in the pamphlet would remove that hatred and ill-will. Absent evidence to contradict his good faith, D fell within the provisions of the section.

Related Provisions: See the corresponding note to s. 59, *supra*.

61. Punishment of seditious offences — Every one who

(a) speaks seditious words,

(b) publishes a seditious libel, or

(c) is a party to a seditious conspiracy,

is guilty of an indictable offence and liable to imprisonment for a term not exceeding fourteen years.

R.S., c. C-34, s. 62.

Commentary: This section, with s. 59, describes and punishes the three seditious offences under the *Code*.

Related Provisions: "Publish" is *not* expressly defined for the purposes of the section, although s. 299 provides a definition of it in respect of libel. In general, publishing involves making something publicly or generally known, accessible or available. More narrowly, it means to issue or cause to be issued for sale or other distribution to the public a book, treatise, or related publication. The *Code* also prohibits other forms of libel in ss. 296 (blasphemous libel) and 297–316 (defamatory libel).

Authorization to intercept private communications may be given in respect of these offences under Part VI.

Accessorial liability is governed by ss. 21 and 22. Special *territorial jurisdiction* provisions apply to conspiracy cases under ss. 465(3)–(7).

Other related provisions are described in the corresponding note to s. 59, *supra*.

62. (1) Offences in relation to military forces — Every one who wilfully

(a) interferes with, impairs or influences the loyalty or discipline of a member of a force,

(b) publishes, edits, issues, circulates or distributes a writing that advises, counsels or urges insubordination, disloyalty, mutiny or refusal of duty by a member of a force, or

(c) advises, counsels, urges or in any manner causes insubordination, disloyalty, mutiny or refusal of duty by a member of a force,

is guilty of an indictable offence and liable to imprisonment for a term not exceeding five years.

(2) "member of a force" — In this section, "member of a force" means a member of

(a) the Canadian Forces; or

(b) the naval, army or air forces of a state other than Canada that are lawfully present in Canada.

R.S., c. C-34, s. 63.

Commentary: The gravamen of these offences is an *interference* with the *loyalty or discipline* of members of the Canadian Forces, or the military forces of a foreign state lawfully present in Canada. A "member of a force" is defined exhaustively in s. 62(2).

The *external circumstances* of the offences are described in ss. 62(1)(a)–(c). The *mental element* requires proof that D acted "wilfully". The section requires *no* proof of any ulterior mental element.

Related Provisions: "Canadian Forces" is defined in s. 2 and "counsel" in s. 22. The meaning of "publishes", *not* expressly defined in the section or Part, is discussed in the corresponding note to s. 61, *supra*.

Other offences relating to members of the Canadian Forces include inciting to mutiny (s. 53), and assisting a deserter (s. 54). Sections 46(1)(c) and 50(1)(a) prohibit the assistance of enemies of Canada. Unlawful use of military uniforms or certificates (s. 419) and certain dealings in military stores (s. 420) are also prohibited.

D may elect mode of trial under s. 536(2).

Unlawful Assemblies and Riots

63. (1) Unlawful assembly — An unlawful assembly is an assembly of three or more persons who, with intent to carry out any common purpose, assemble in such a manner or so conduct themselves when they are assembled as to cause persons in the neighbourhood of the assembly to fear, on reasonable grounds, that they

(a) will disturb the peace tumultuously; or

(b) will by that assembly needlessly and without reasonable cause provoke other persons to disturb the peace tumultuously.

(2) Lawful assembly becoming unlawful — Persons who are lawfully assembled may become an unlawful assembly if they conduct themselves with a common purpose in a manner that would have made the assembly unlawful if they had assembled in that manner for that purpose.

(3) Exception — Persons are not unlawfully assembled by reason only that they are assembled to protect the dwelling-house of any one of them against persons who are threatening to break and enter it for the purpose of committing an indictable offence therein.

R.S., c. C-34, s. 64.

Commentary: The section defines an *unlawful assembly*.

An *unlawful assembly* under s. 63(1) requires the assembly of *three or more* persons. Further, the *manner* of assembly, or the *conduct* of its members, must be such as to cause persons in the neighbourhood of the assembly to fear, *on reasonable grounds*, that the members of the assembly will either disturb the peace tumultuously or, by that assembly, needlessly and without reasonable cause, provoke others to do so. The phrase, "on *reasonable* grounds", adds an objective element, to ensure that it is only where the neighbour's fears are *reasonably based* that liability shall follow. The *mental element* requires proof that the assembly was with *intent to carry out any common purpose*.

Under s. 63(2), a lawful assembly becomes unlawful when those assembled conduct themselves with a *common purpose* in a manner that would have made the assembly unlawful, if they had (originally) assembled in that manner for that purpose. In other words, an assembly, at first lawful, becomes unlawful when and to the extent it changes its purpose and manner to that of an unlawful assembly.

Under s. 63(3) no unlawful assembly is deemed to have occurred where the sole purpose of the assembly is the protection of the dwelling-house of any one of them against others who are threatening to break and enter for the purpose of committing an indictable offence therein.

Case Law

R. v. Berntt (1997), 11 C.R. (5th) 131, 120 C.C.C. (3d) 344 (B.C. C.A.) — A tumultuous disturbance requires an air or atmosphere of actual or constructive force or violence.

R. v. Patterson (1931), 55 C.C.C. 218 (Ont. C.A.) — This provision distinguishes between a lawful meeting and an assembly, either unlawful in its inception, or that is deemed to have become unlawful by reason of the action of those assembled, or of the improper action of others having no sympathy with the objects of the meeting.

Charter Considerations

R. v. Berntt (1997), 11 C.R. (5th) 131, 120 C.C.C. (3d) 344 (B.C. C.A.) — The section is *not* unconstitutional because of vagueness or overbreadth.

Related Provisions: Membership in an unlawful assembly is a summary conviction offence under s. 66 and, upon conviction, punishable under s. 787(1).

A *riot*, defined in s. 64, includes an unlawful assembly. Participation in a riot is an indictable offence under s. 65. Other offences relating to riots and, in particular, proclamation thereof appear in ss. 68 and 69.

Section 32 describes the degree of force which may be used to suppress a riot. Section 33 imposes certain obligations and confers equivalent protection upon peace officers where rioters do not disperse. Section 30 describes what may be done by anyone who witnesses a breach of the peace and limits the degree of force which may be used. Section 31 defines the authority of a peace officer to arrest and take custody of a person who is or has been a party to a breach of the peace.

Causing a disturbance is an offence under s. 175.

64. Riot — A riot is an unlawful assembly that has begun to disturb the peace tumultuously.

R.S., c. C-34, s. 65.

Commentary: The section describes a riot. An "unlawful assembly" is defined in s. 63.

"Tumultuously" indicates a disturbance which is disorderly and noisy, turbulent, one marked by disorderly commotion.

Case Law

Elements of Offence

R. v. Lockhart (1976), 15 N.S.R. (2d) 512 (C.A.) — A riot requires: (1) at least *three* persons; (2) *common purpose*; (3) execution or inception of the common purpose; (4) an *intent* to help one another by force if necessary, against any person who may oppose them in the execution of their common purpose; and (5) force or violence not merely used in demonstrating, but displayed in such a manner as to alarm at least one person of reasonable firmness and courage.

Tumultuously

R. v. Berntt (1997), 11 C.R. (5th) 131, 120 C.C.C. (3d) 344 (B.C. C.A.) — A tumultuous disturbance requires an air or atmosphere of actual or constructive force or violence.

R. v. Lockhart (1976), 15 N.S.R. (2d) 512 (C.A.) — "Tumultuously" means more than "disorder, confusion or uproar". There must be "some element of violence or force which may be exhibited by menaces or threats".

Charter Considerations

R. v. Berntt (1997), 11 C.R. (5th) 131, 120 C.C.C. (3d) 344 (B.C. C.A.) — The section is *not* unconstitutional because of vagueness or overbreadth.

Related Provisions: Participation in a riot is an indictable offence under s. 65.

Other related provisions are described in the corresponding note to s. 63, *supra*.

65. Punishment of rioter — **Every one who takes part in a riot is guilty of an indictable offence and liable to imprisonment for a term not exceeding two years.**

R.S., c. C-34, s. 66.

Commentary: The section makes *participation in a riot* an indictable offence. The manner of participation is neither described nor limited. The *mental element* of the offence requires proof of an intention to participate in a riot as defined in s. 64. The *external circumstances* consist of participation in a riot.

Case Law

Elements of Offence

R. v. Brien (1993), 86 C.C.C. (3d) 550 (N.W.T. S.C.) — Section 65 does *not* create a strict liability offence and does *not* infringe *Charter* s. 7 or 11(d). P must prove at least *objective foresight* of the consequences described in s. 63 in order to establish liability.

Related Provisions: Sections 21 and 22 describe the modes of participation in an offence. Nothing in s. 65, nor in the definition of riot (s. 64) or unlawful assembly (s. 63) would appear to detract from this general principle. Participation in an unlawful assembly under s. 66 would appear an included offence in this section.

D may elect mode of trial in respect of this offence under s. 536(2).

Other related provisions are described in the corresponding note to s. 63, *supra*.

66. Punishment for unlawful assembly — **Every one who is a member of an unlawful assembly is guilty of an offence punishable on summary conviction.**

R.S., c. C-34, s. 67.

Commentary: It is a summary conviction offence under this section to be a *member* of an *unlawful assembly*.

The *external circumstances* of the offence consist of the participation in an assembly of three or more persons assembled in a manner made unlawful by s. 63(1). The *mental element* requires proof of the intention to so participate, as well as the ulterior intent to carry out any common purpose.

Related Provisions: This offence is tried under Part XXVII and punished under s. 787(1).

Other related provisions are discussed in the corresponding note to ss. 63 and 65, *supra*.

67. Reading proclamation — **A person who is**

(a) **a justice, mayor or sheriff, or the lawful deputy of a mayor or sheriff,**

(b) **a warden or deputy warden of a prison, or**

(c) **the institutional head of a penitentiary, as those expressions are defined in subsection 2(1) of the *Corrections and Conditional Release Act*, or that person's deputy,**

who receives notice that, at any place within the jurisdiction of the person, twelve or more persons are unlawfully and riotously assembled together shall go to that place and, after approaching as near as is safe, if the person is satisfied that a riot is in progress, shall command silence and thereupon make or cause to be made in a loud voice a proclamation in the following words or to the like effect:

Her Majesty the Queen charges and commands all persons being assembled immediately to disperse and peaceably to depart to their habitations or to their lawful business on the pain of being guilty of an offence for which, on convic-

tion, they may be sentenced to imprisonment for life. GOD SAVE THE QUEEN.

R.S., c. C-34, s. 68;1994, c. 44, s. 5.

Commentary: The section describes the several circumstances under which the "riot act" may be read to an assembly of persons.

Notice of the prescribed activity must be received by anyone described in paragraph (a) to (c). The designated official must go to the place of the riot and approach it as near as safely s/he may do. The designated official, on location must be satisfied that a riot is in progress. The designated official may then command silence and thereupon make or cause to be made the proclamation described in the section or words to like effect.

Related Provisions: "Justice" is defined in s. 2. The persons described in paragraph (a) to (c) are included in the expansive definition of "peace officer" in s. 2. Section 68 describes and punishes a number of offences relating to the proclamation permitted under s. 67. Some overlap may exist between the offences of ss. 68(a) and 129(a).

The proclamation may only be read where an unlawful assembly within s. 63 has proceeded to a riot of the nature and extent described in s. 67.

Other related provisions are described in the corresponding notes to ss. 63 and 65, *supra*.

68. Offences related to proclamation — Every one is guilty of an indictable offence and liable to imprisonment for life who

(a) opposes, hinders or assaults, wilfully and with force, a person who begins to make or is about to begin to make or is making the proclamation referred to in section 67 so that it is not made;

(b) does not peaceably disperse and depart from a place where the proclamation referred to in section 67 is made within thirty minutes after it is made; or

(c) does not depart from a place within thirty minutes when he has reasonable grounds to believe that the proclamation referred to in section 67 would have been made in that place if some person had not opposed, hindered or assaulted, wilfully and with force, a person who would have made it.

R.S., c. C-34, s. 69.

Commentary: The section describes and punishes several offences relating to the making of a proclamation under s. 67.

The *external circumstances* of the offence of s. 68(a), *obstructing* the *making* of a proclamation under s. 67, consist of any conduct which opposes, hinders or assaults, wilfully and with force, a person beginning or making a proclamation to such an extent that the proclamation is *not* made. No ulterior *mental element* need be proven. An intention to cause the external circumstances, wilfully and with force, is sufficient.

The offences of ss. 68(b) and (c) focus upon conduct which occurs *after* the actual or attempted making of the proclamation and not in compliance therewith. The *external circumstances* of the offence under s. 68(b) consist of a *failure* peaceably to *disperse* and *depart* from the place in which the proclamation of s. 67 has been made, within 30 minutes of its making. Section 68(c) is applicable where no proclamation has been made because someone, not necessarily D, prevented it by committing an offence under s. 68(a). The *external circumstances* of the offence of s. 68(c) consist of the *failure to depart* within 30 minutes from a place where D has *reasonable* grounds to believe that the making of a proclamation would have occurred but for an offence under s. 68(a). No proof of an ulterior mental element is required. It would appear necessary, however, that P prove D's *knowledge* of the actual or abortive making of the proclamation.

Related Provisions: Section 69 imposes an obligation on peace officers who receive notice of a riot within their jurisdiction to take all reasonable steps to suppress it. Failure to do so, without reasonable excuse, is an indictable offence under s. 69.

Assault is defined in s. 265.

A person charged with an offence under this section may elect mode of trial under s. 536(2).

Other related provisions are described in the corresponding notes to ss. 63 and 65, *supra*.

69. Neglect by peace officer — **A peace officer who receives notice that there is a riot within his jurisdiction and, without reasonable excuse, fails to take all reasonable steps to suppress the riot is guilty of an indictable offence and liable to imprisonment for a term not exceeding two years.**

R.S., c. C-34, s. 70.

Commentary: The principal in this offence must be a *peace officer* who has received *notice* that there is a *riot* within his/her jurisdiction. The *external circumstances* of the offence consist of the failure of D to take all reasonable steps to suppress the riot, and the absence of reasonable excuse. No ulterior *mental element* is required, although it must be established that D had *actual* notice of the riot within his jurisdiction.

Related Provisions: "Peace officer" is defined in s. 2 and "riot" in s. 64.

D may elect mode of trial under s. 536(2).

Other related provisions are described in the corresponding notes to ss. 63 and 65, *supra*.

Unlawful Drilling

70. (1) Orders by Governor in Council — **The Governor in Council may by proclamation, make orders**

    (a) to prohibit assemblies, without lawful authority, of persons for the purpose

        (i) of training or drilling themselves,

        (ii) of being trained or drilled to the use of arms, or

        (iii) of practising military exercises; or

    (b) to prohibit persons when assembled for any purpose from training or drilling themselves or from being trained or drilled.

(2) General or special order — **An order that is made under subsection (1) may be general or may be made applicable to particular places, districts or assemblies to be specified in the order.**

(3) Punishment — **Every one who contravenes an order made under this section is guilty of an indictable offence and liable to imprisonment for a term not exceeding five years.**

R.S., c. C-34, s. 71.

Commentary: The section authorizes the proclamation of orders prohibiting certain types of assemblies and imposes criminal liability for their contravention.

Under s. 70(1), the Governor in Council is authorized, by proclamation, to make orders prohibiting assemblies of the type described in ss. 70(1)(a) and (b). Under s. 70(2), the orders may be general or specific to particular places, districts or assemblies.

It is an offence under s. 70(3) to contravene an order made under the section. The *external circumstances* of the offence consist of proof of the contravention. No ulterior *mental element* is required although it would appear necessary for P to prove D's knowledge of the order contravened.

Related Provisions: Under s. 536(2), D may *elect* mode of trial.

Duels

71. Duelling — Every one who

(a) challenges or attempts by any means to provoke another person to fight a duel,

(b) attempts to provoke a person to challenge another person to fight a duel, or

(c) accepts a challenge to fight a duel,

is guilty of an indictable offence and liable to imprisonment for a term not exceeding two years.

R.S., c. C-34, s. 72.

Commentary: The section prohibits certain conduct preliminary to a duel, although it does *not,* in terms, prevent duelling itself.

The offence of s. 71(a) is complete where D challenges or attempts by any means to provoke another to fight a duel. The challenge need not be accepted, the provocation acted upon or any duel actually take place. The *mental element* requires an intention to cause the external circumstances.

The *external circumstances* of s. 71(b) are once removed from s. 71(a) and are proven where D attempts to provoke one to challenge another to fight a duel. The *mental element* consists of the intention to cause the external circumstances.

The offence of s. 71(c) involves the acceptance of a challenge to fight a duel. The *mental element* requires proof that D intended to accept the challenge.

Case Law [See s. 234]

Related Provisions: D may elect mode of trial under s. 536(2).

Death resulting from the conduct of a duel would appear to be culpable homicide under s. 222(5)(a). Whether it is murder or manslaughter will depend on the circumstances in which death was caused and the mental element which accompanied it.

Forcible Entry and Detainer

72. (1) Forcible entry — A person commits forcible entry when that person enters real property that is in the actual and peaceable possession of another in a manner that is likely to cause a breach of the peace or reasonable apprehension of a breach of the peace.

(1.1) Matters not material — For the purposes of subsection (1), it is immaterial whether or not a person is entitled to enter the real property or whether or not that person has any intention of taking possession of the real property.

(2) Forcible detainer — A person commits forcible detainer when, being in actual possession of real property without colour of right, he detains it in a manner that is likely to cause a breach of the peace or reasonable apprehension of a breach of the peace, against a person who is entitled by law to possession of it.

(3) Questions of law — The questions whether a person is in actual and peaceable possession or is in actual possession without colour of right are questions of law.

R.S., c. C-34, s. 73;R.S. 1985, c. 27 (1st Supp.), s. 10.

Commentary: The section defines the essential elements of *forcible detainer* and *forcible entry* punished under s. 73. The essence of forcible entry is the character of the entry, whereas in forcible detainer it is the character of the detainer which may be forcible, notwithstanding that the initial entry was itself peaceable.

The *external circumstances* of *forcible entry* under s. 72(1) require entry of real property, in the actual and peaceable possession of another in a manner that is likely to cause a breach of the peace or a *reasonable* apprehension thereof. The requirement that the apprehension of a breach of the peace be reasonable adds an objective element. The real property need *not* be a dwelling-house. It is *immaterial* whether D is entitled to enter. The *mental element* consists of an intention to cause the external circumstances of the offence but does *not* require proof of intention to take possession of the property.

In *forcible detainer* under s. 72(2), D, as principal, must be a person in possession of real property, without colour of right. The *external circumstances* are complete where D detains the real property against a person entitled by law to possession thereof in a manner likely to cause a breach of the peace or a reasonable apprehension thereof. P must prove D's knowledge of the nature of his/her possession and the likelihood of a breach of the peace by the detainer, but no ulterior *mental element* need be established.

Whether a person is in actual and peaceable possession of real property (s. 72(1)) or in actual possession of real property without colour of right (s. 72(2)) are questions of law under s. 72(3).

Case Law

R. v. Czegledi (1931), 55 C.C.C. 114 at 117 (Sask. C.A.) — Forcible entry requires some violence, or threatened violence, and the presence of someone who might resist.

Related Provisions: Neither "real property" nor "breach of the peace" is defined in the *Code*. A *breach of the peace* occurs when harm is actually or likely to be done to a person, or in his/her presence to his/her property, or a person is in fear of being so harmed through an assault, affray, riot, unlawful assembly or other disturbance.

Section 30 describes the scope of authority which may be exercised to prevent the continuance or renewal of a breach of the peace. Section 31 describes the circumstances under which a peace officer may arrest persons found committing a breach of the peace or whom, on reasonable grounds, the officer believes are about to join in or renew such a breach.

Sections 348–358 prohibit breaking and entering and related preliminary crimes. Unlawful confinement and forcible seizure of other persons are punishable under s. 279(2).

73. Punishment — **Every person who commits forcible entry or forcible detainer is guilty of**

> **(a) an offence punishable on summary conviction; or**
>
> **(b) an indictable offence and liable to imprisonment for a term not exceeding two years.**
> R.S., c. C-34, s. 74;R.S. 1985, c. 27 (1st Supp.), s. 11; 1992, c. 1, s. 58(1), Schedule I, item 2.

Commentary: The section provides for the mode of procedure and punishment in cases of forcible entry and detainer.

Related Provisions: Where P elects to proceed by indictment, D may elect mode of trial under s. 536(2). Where D elects to proceed by summary conviction, the punishment upon conviction is provided by s. 787(1).

Other related provisions are described in the corresponding note to s. 72, *supra*.

Piracy

74. (1) Piracy by law of nations — **Every one commits piracy who does any act that, by the law of nations, is piracy.**

(2) Punishment — **Every one who commits piracy while in or out of Canada is guilty of an indictable offence and liable to imprisonment for life.**
R.S., c. C-34, s. 75; 1974–75–76, c. 105, s. 3.

Commentary: The section provides a general definition of *piracy* and the punishment therefor. The offence is left to be defined by international law, in essence, by reference to existing conventions to which Canada is a signatory. Piracy includes those acts of robbery and other depradation upon the high seas which, if committed on land, would have amounted to a felony at common law. A pirate is a sea-thief.

Under s. 74(2) piracy committed in or out of Canada is an indictable offence, punishable upon conviction by imprisonment for life.

Related Provisions: The excuse of compulsion under s. 17 is *not* available to D.

Section 75 describes and punishes certain piratical acts in relation to Canadian ships.

The general rule of s. 6(2) that no one shall be convicted or discharged in respect of an offence committed outside Canada is subject to exception, as for example in s. 6 itself. Section 477 enacts special territorial jurisdiction provisions concerning offences committed in the territorial sea and coastal waters of Canada.

The offence of s. 74, including the inchoate crimes of attempt and conspiracy, under s. 469(a)(vi) lies within the exclusive trial and judicial interim release jurisdiction of the superior court of criminal jurisdiction.

75. Piratical acts — Every one who, while in or out of Canada,

(a) steals a Canadian ship,

(b) steals or without lawful authority throws overboard, damages or destroys anything that is part of the cargo, supplies or fittings in a Canadian ship,

(c) does or attempts to do a mutinous act on a Canadian ship, or

(d) counsels a person to do anything mentioned in paragraph (*a*), (*b*) or (*c*),

is guilty of an indictable offence and liable to imprisonment for a term not exceeding fourteen years.

R.S., c. C-34, s. 76;R.S. 1985, c. 27 (1st Supp.) s. 7(3).

Commentary: The section describes several *piratical acts* which are indictable offences.

The offence of s. 75(a) is a form of *theft*. The subject-matter must be a Canadian ship. The ulterior or specific *mental element* of s. 322(1) must coincide with D's unlawful taking or conversion.

Under s. 75(b), the subject-matter of D's conduct may be anything that is part of cargo, supplies, or fittings in a Canadian ship. The *external circumstances* are complete where D steals or, without lawful authority, throws overboard, damages or destroys any such property. The *mental element*, save in cases of stealing the property, is complete upon proof that D intended to cause the external circumstances of the offence.

The *external circumstances* of the offence of s. 75(e) consists of the doing of or attempt at a mutinous act on a Canadian ship. The *mental element* comprises the intention to do so.

Section 75(d) would appear somewhat of a grab bag offence, perhaps unnecessary in the light of ss. 22 and 464, save in respect of penalty, where the offence counselled is *not* in fact committed. The *external circumstances* and *mental element* are those associated with counselling under s. 22 and the substantive offence of the applicable paragraph.

Related Provisions: Under s. 2 "steals" means to commit theft. Under s. 22(3), "counsel" includes procure, solicit or incite. Section 22(1) and (2) define the scope of liability where D counsels another to commit an offence. Section 464(a) is the general punishment provision where the offence counselled is not committed. Attempt is defined in s. 24.

The offences of the section including attempt and conspiracy, under s. 469(a)(vii), fall within the exclusive trial and judicial interim release jurisdiction of the superior court of criminal jurisdiction.

Other related provisions are described in the corresponding note to s. 74, *supra*.

Offences Against Air or Maritime Safety

76. Hijacking — Every one who, unlawfully, by force or threat thereof, or by any other form of intimidation, seizes or exercises control of an aircraft with intent

(a) to cause any person on board the aircraft to be confined or imprisoned against his will,

(b) to cause any person on board the aircraft to be transported against his will to any place other than the next scheduled place of landing of the aircraft,

(c) to hold any person on board the aircraft for ransom or to service against his will, or

(d) to cause the aircraft to deviate in a material respect from its flight plan,

is guilty of an indictable offence and liable to imprisonment for life.

1972, c. 13, s. 6.

Commentary: The section describes and punishes the offence of *aircraft hijacking*.

The *external circumstances* require proof that D unlawfully seized or exercised control of an aircraft, by force or threat thereof, or by any other form of intimidation. P must prove that the *external circumstances* were caused by D with the ulterior state of mind or *mental element* described in *any* of ss. 76(a)–(d).

Related Provisions: Section 77 prohibits certain conduct which *endangers* the *safety* of aircraft in flight or *renders* an aircraft *incapable* of flight. Section 78 makes it an offence to take offensive weapons or explosive substances on board a civil aircraft in certain circumstances.

Sections 7(1) and (2), as well as s. 476(d), enact special *territorial jurisdiction* provisions applicable to offences committed on or in respect of aircraft. "Flight" is defined in s. 7(8).

The offences of unlawful confinement and imprisonment are described in s. 279(2). Hostage taking is an offence under s. 279.1, and kidnapping is prohibited under s. 279(1).

D may elect mode of trial under s. 536(2). Murder committed by D while committing the offence in s. 76 is classified as first degree murder under s. 231(5)(a). It is also an offence for which authorization to intercept private communications may be given under Part VI.

77. Endangering safety of aircraft or airport — Every one who,

(a) on board an aircraft in flight, commits an act of violence against a person that is likely to endanger the safety of the aircraft,

(b) using a weapon, commits an act of violence against a person at an airport serving international civil aviation that causes or is likely to cause serious injury or death and that endangers or is likely to endanger safety at the airport,

(c) causes damage to an aircraft in service that renders the aircraft incapable of flight or that is likely to endanger the safety of the aircraft in flight,

(d) places or causes to be placed on board an aircraft in service anything that is likely to cause damage to the aircraft, that will render it incapable of flight or that is likely to endanger the safety of the aircraft in flight,

(e) causes damage to or interferes with the operation of any air navigation facility where the damage or interference is likely to endanger the safety of an aircraft in flight,

(f) using a weapon, substance or device, destroys or causes serious damage to the facilities of an airport serving international civil aviation or to any aircraft not in service located there, or causes disruption of services of the airport, that endangers or is likely to endanger safety at the airport, or

(g) endangers the safety of an aircraft in flight by communicating to any other person any information that the person knows to be false,

is guilty of an indictable offence and liable to imprisonment for life.

1972, c. 13, s. 6;1993, c. 7, s. 3.

Commentary: These offences involve interference with aircraft and airport safety.

The *external circumstances* of each offence involve an act of violence against a person, or an actual or potential interference with aircraft or airport safety. Only paragraph (g) requires that D's conduct actually endanger aircraft safety. In every other case, P need only prove D's conduct is likely to endanger the safety of the aircraft or at the airport, as the case may be.

The *mental element* involves *foresight* of the *likely* consequences of D's conduct. Under s. 77(g), P must also prove that D knows the *information* communicated is *false*.

Related Provisions: "Flight" and "in service" are defined in ss. 7(8) and (9), respectively, assault in s. 265. D may *elect* mode of trial under s. 536(2).

Authorization to intercept private communications may be given under Part VI in respect of these offences.

Other related provisions are described in the corresponding note to s. 76, *supra*.

78. (1) Offensive weapons and explosive substances — Every one, other than a peace officer engaged in the execution of his duty, who takes on board a civil aircraft an offensive weapon or any explosive substance

(a) without the consent of the owner or operator of the aircraft or of a person duly authorized by either of them to consent thereto, or

(b) with the consent referred to in paragraph (a) but without complying with all terms and conditions on which the consent was given,

is guilty of an indictable offence and liable to imprisonment for a term not exceeding fourteen years.

(2) Definition of "civil aircraft" — For the purposes of this section, "civil aircraft" means all aircraft other than aircraft operated by the Canadian Forces, a police force in Canada or persons engaged in the administration or enforcement of the *Customs Act* or the *Excise Act*.

1972, c. 13, s. 6;R.S. 1985, c. 1 (2d Supp.), Schedule III.

Commentary: The section describes the circumstances under which it is a criminal offence to take an offensive weapon or explosive substance on board a "civil aircraft" as defined in s. 78(2).

The *external circumstances* of the offence contain three elements. As principal, D must *not* be a peace officer engaged in the execution of his/her duty. D must take on board a civil aircraft an offensive weapon or explosive substance. There must further be an *absence* of any or specific *consent* to the transportation of the weapon or explosive substance. The *mental element* consists of an intention to cause the external circumstances of the offence. No ulterior *mental element* need be established, as for example, the intent to commit an indictable offence on the aircraft.

Related Provisions: "Peace officer", "offensive weapon", "weapon" and "explosive substance" are defined in s. 2.

The offence is one in respect of which authorization to intercept private communications may be given under Part VI.

Section 79 imposes a duty of care upon persons who have in their possession, care or control explosive substances. Sections 80–82.1 describe and punish certain offences involving the care, use and possession of explosive substances. Offences related to the use of firearms and other offensive weapons are described in ss. 85–92.

Under s. 536(2), D may elect mode of trial.

Other related provisions are described in the corresponding note to s. 76, *supra*.

78.1 (1) Seizing control of ship or fixed platform — Every one who seizes or exercises control over a ship or fixed platform by force or threat of force or by any other form of intimidation is guilty of an indictable offence and liable to imprisonment for life.

(2) **Endangering safety of ship or fixed platform** — Every one who

(a) commits an act of violence against a person on board a ship or fixed platform,

(b) destroys or causes damage to a ship or its cargo or to a fixed platform,

(c) destroys or causes serious damage to or interferes with the operation of any maritime navigational facility, or

(d) places or causes to be placed on board a ship or fixed platform anything that is likely to cause damage to the ship or its cargo or to the fixed platform,

where that act is likely to endanger the safe navigation of a ship or the safety of a fixed platform, is guilty of an indictable offence and liable to imprisonment for life.

(3) **False communication** — Every one who communicates information that endangers the safe navigation of a ship, knowing the information to be false, is guilty of an indictable offence and liable to imprisonment for life.

(4) **Threats causing death or injury** — Every one who threatens to commit an offence under paragraph (2)(*a*), (b) or (*c*) in order to compel a person to do or refrain from doing any act, where the threat is likely to endanger the safe navigation of a ship or the safety of a fixed platform, is guilty of an indictable offence and liable to imprisonment for life.

(5) **Definitions** — In this section,

"fixed platform" means an artificial island or a marine installation or structure that is permanently attached to the seabed for the purpose of exploration or exploitation of resources or for other economic purposes;

"ship" means every description of vessel not permanently attached to the seabed, other than a warship, a ship being used as a naval auxiliary or for customs or police purposes or a ship that has been withdrawn from navigation or is laid up.

1993, c. 7, s. 4.

Commentary: The section creates several offences which involve interference with ships and fixed platforms, as defined in s. 78.1(5), and maritime navigation facilities. Each offence is indictable and carries a maximum punishment of imprisonment for life.

The *external circumstances* of the offence of s. 78.1(1) involve the *seizure* or *exercise of control* over a ship or fixed platform. The means used include force, actual or threatened, or any other form of intimidation. The *mental element* consists of the intention to cause the external circumstances of the offence.

The *external circumstances* of the offences of s. 78.1(2) comprise prohibited conduct which, further, must be likely to endanger the safe navigation of a ship or safety of a fixed platform. The *mental element* includes the intention to cause the external circumstances, and further, foresight that the conduct is likely to cause danger of that consequence. Under s. 78.1(4), it is also an offence to threaten to commit an offence under s. 78.1(2)(a)–(c). The threat must be *likely to endanger* the safe navigation of a ship or the safety of a fixed platform. The *mental element* involves an element of purpose which underlies D's threat. P must establish that the threat was made "in order to compel a person to do or refrain from doing any act".

The offence of s. 78.1(3) involves the communication of false information that endangers the safe navigation of a ship. It is *not* sufficient that the information is only likely to endanger safe ship navigation. The *mental* element includes D's *knowledge* of the falsity of the information.

Related Provisions: Piracy, according to the law of nations, is an offence under s. 74. Section 75 prohibits certain piratical acts on or in relation to a Canadian ship.

Authorization to intercept private communications may be given in respect of these offences. Special jurisdiction provisions are included in s. 7(2.1) and (2.2) and s. 477.

D may elect mode of trial under s. 536(2).

Dangerous Substances

79. Duty of care re explosive — **Every one who has an explosive substance in his possession or under his care or control is under a legal duty to use reasonable care to prevent bodily harm or death to persons or damage to property by that explosive substance.**

R.S., c. C-34, s. 77.

Commentary: The section imposes a legal *duty of care* upon all persons who have possession, care or control of an *explosive substance*. The duty is to use *reasonable care* to prevent bodily harm or death to persons or damage to property by the explosive substance. The requirement is an objective standard in the circumstances of the possession, care or control. What a reasonable person similarly circumstanced would have done is determinative of what D should have done.

Case Law

R. v. Can. Liquid Air Ltd. (1972), 22 C.R.N.S. 208 (B.C. S.C.) — A corporation can breach the duty set out in this section.

Related Provisions: "Explosive substance" and "property" are defined in s. 2. Possession may be established under s. 4(3).

Breach of the duty of care imposed by the section may attract liability under s. 80. The use of explosives in circumstances prohibited by s. 81 is also an offence, as is unlawful possession under s. 82. Section 78 generally prohibits the taking of explosive substances on board a civil aircraft.

Section 103 authorizes the issuance of a warrant to search for and seize explosive substances in the circumstances there described. In exigent circumstances the search and seizure may be conducted by a peace officer without warrant under s. 103(2). Upon execution of a search warrant under s. 47, explosive substances may be seized and, upon conviction, forfeited in accordance with s. 492.

Section 100 authorizes a prohibition against possession, *inter alia*, of explosive substances, upon conviction of offences described in ss. 100(1) and (2).

80. Breach of duty — **Every one who, being under a legal duty within the meaning of section 79, fails without lawful excuse to perform that duty, is guilty of an indictable offence and, if as a result an explosion of an explosive substance occurs that**

(a) causes death or is likely to cause death to any person, is liable to imprisonment for life; or

(b) causes bodily harm or damage to property or is likely to cause bodily harm or damage to property, is liable to imprisonment for a term not exceeding fourteen years.

R.S., c. C-34, s. 78.

Commentary: The section imposes criminal liability where certain consequences ensue from a *failure to discharge* the legal *duty of care* imposed under s. 79.

The *external circumstances* of the offence comprise several elements. As principal, D must be under a legal *duty of care in respect of explosive substances* imposed by s. 79. D must *fail to perform* that duty. D's failure must be *without lawful excuse* and result in an explosion. The consequences of the explosion actual or probable must fall within either s. 80(a) or (b). No death, bodily harm nor damage to property need actually occur, provided it was a likely result of D's conduct. The maximum punishment upon conviction of the offence varies depending upon the consequences of the explosion.

The section does *not*, in terms, require proof of any ulterior or specific *mental element* in order to establish liability. Proof of an intention to cause the external circumstances of the offence will suffice. It is at best doubtful whether D need have knowledge of the likelihood of any specific injury or damage in consequence of the explosion caused by breach of duty.

Case Law

R. v. Yanover (No. 1) (1985), 20 C.C.C. (3d) 300 (Ont. C.A.) — If, because of a failure by D to discharge the legal duty imposed by s. 79, an explosion results, D is liable to conviction under s. 80. If the failure to use reasonable care does *not* result in an explosion, D is *not* liable under this section. A breach of s. 79 is *not* an included offence.

Related Provisions: "Explosive substance" is defined in s. 2. D may elect mode of trial under s. 536(2).

Authorization to intercept private communications in respect of this offence may be given under Part VI.

Other related provisions are described in the corresponding note to s. 79, *supra*.

81. (1) Using explosives — **Every one commits an offence who**

(a) **does anything with intent to cause an explosion of an explosive substance that is likely to cause serious bodily harm or death to persons or is likely to cause serious damage to property;**

(b) **with intent to do bodily harm to any person**

(i) **causes an explosive substance to explode,**

(ii) **sends or delivers to a person or causes a person to take or receive an explosive substance or any other dangerous substance or thing, or**

(iii) **places or throws anywhere or at or on a person a corrosive fluid, explosive substance or any other dangerous substance or thing;**

(c) **with intent to destroy or damage property without lawful excuse, places or throws an explosive substance anywhere; or**

(d) **makes or has in his possession or has under his care or control any explosive substance with intent thereby**

(i) **to endanger life or to cause serious damage to property, or**

(ii) **to enable another person to endanger life or to cause serious damage to property.**

(2) Punishment — **Every one who commits an offence under subsection (1) is guilty of an indictable offence and liable**

(a) **for an offence under paragraph (1)(a) or (b), to imprisonment for life, or**

(b) **for an offence under paragraph (1)(c) or (d), to imprisonment for a term not exceeding fourteen years.**

R.S., c. C-34, s. 79.

Commentary: The several offences of this section involve the *use or possession of explosive substances*. Each requires proof of an ulterior *mental element*.

The *external circumstances* of the offence in s. 81(1)(a) are loosely defined. They consist of the doing of anything. D's conduct must, however, be accompanied by the prohibited ulterior state of mind described in the concluding words of the paragraph including the intent to cause an explosion of an explosive substance. *Quaere* whether *knowledge* of the likelihood of bodily harm, death or damage to property is required?

Under s. 81(1)(b), the *external circumstances* of the offence must fall within *any* of ss. 81(1)(b)(i)–(iii). The *mental element* includes the specific or ulterior intent to do bodily harm to *any* person. D's state of mind need not focus upon or be exclusive to a particular individual, V.

The *external circumstances* of the offence of s. 81(1)(c) involve the *placing or throwing* of an explosive substance anywhere and the *absence of lawful excuse* therefor. The *mental element* requires proof of an ulterior or specific intent, the intent to destroy or damage property.

Under s. 81(1)(d) the *external circumstances* of the offence require proof that D made, had in his/her possession or had under his/her care or control an explosive substance. Life need not be actually endangered nor (serious) damage to property occur in consequence. The specific or ulterior *mental element* which must accompany the external circumstances is the intent to endanger life or to cause serious damage to property or the intent to enable another to do likewise.

Section 81(2) prescribes the *punishment* upon conviction of the offences of s. 81(1). Convictions under s. 81(1)(a) or (b) attract a maximum punishment of imprisonment for life. Convictions under s. 81(1)(c) or (d) carry a maximum punishment of imprisonment for a term not exceeding 14 years.

Case Law

R. v. Musitano (1985), 24 C.C.C. (3d) 65 (Ont. C.A.) — The difference between s. 81(1)(a) and s. 81(1)(d) is that (1)(a) requires the specific intention to cause an explosion whereas (1)(d) does not. Furthermore, s. 81(1)(d) does *not* deal exclusively with all instances of possession. D may be charged and convicted under s. 81(1)(a) although possession of an explosive substance is an element of the charge.

Related Provisions: "Explosive substance", "property" and "bodily harm" are defined in s. 2. Possession may be established under s. 4(3). Authorization to intercept private communications may be given in respect of these offences under Part VI.

The use of explosive or other dangerous substances in such a manner as to cause bodily harm to or endanger the life of V may also attract liability under ss. 268(1) and 269. Where death ensues from the unlawful use of explosive substances, culpable homicide has been committed under either s. 222(5)(a) or (b). It will be either murder or manslaughter, depending upon the mental element accompanying it. D's conduct may also amount to criminal negligence under s. 219(1) and, depending upon the consequences, an offence under s. 220 or 221.

Other related provisions are discussed in the corresponding note to s. 79, *supra*.

D may elect mode of trial under s. 536(2).

82. (1) Possession without lawful excuse — Every person who, without lawful excuse, the proof of which lies on the person, makes or has in the possession or under the care or control of the person any explosive substance is guilty of an indictable offence and liable to imprisonment for a term not exceeding five years.

(2) Possession in association with criminal organization — Every person who, without lawful excuse, the proof of which lies on the person, makes or has in the possession or under the care or control of the person any explosive substance for the benefit of, at the direction of or in association with a criminal organization is guilty of an indictable offence and liable to imprisonment for a term not exceeding fourteen years.

R.S., c. C-34, s. 80;R.S. 1985, c. 27 (1st Supp.), s. 12; 1997, c. 23, s. 2.

Commentary: The *external circumstances* of these offences require that D either make, have in his/her possession or under his/her care or control an explosive substance and, under s. 82(2), do so for the benefit of, at the direction of or in association with a criminal organization. D must have no lawful excuse. The shift in the onus of proving a lawful excuse to D, raises possible *Charter* ss. 7 and 11(d) implications. The *mental element* consists of the intention to cause the external circumstances of the offence.

Case Law

Lawful Excuse

Malang v. R. (1982), 25 C.R. (3d) 398 (Ont. C.A.) — Absent lawful excuse, Parliament has proscribed absolutely the possession of bombs. The fact that D had no intention of destroying any property or injuring any person, but merely wished to set a bomb off to make a loud noise, afforded no defence, in the absence of proof of "lawful excuse" for possession. "Bomb" and "grenade" are to be given their ordinary meaning.

Reverse Onus

Mongeau v. R. (1957), 25 C.R. 195 (Que. C.A.) — The reverse onus only applies after P has proven possession beyond a reasonable doubt.

Res Judicata

R. v. Clark (1951), 13 C.R. 190, 101 C.C.C. 166 (Ont. C.A.) — Possession of explosives is a separate and distinct offence from possession of housebreaking instruments. D may be convicted of both offences, if the alleged housebreaking instruments include an explosive.

Related Provisions: "Explosive substance" and "criminal organization" are defined in s. 2 and possession determined under s. 4(3). It is the unlawful having of an explosive substance that is the gravamen of these offences. Under s. 82(1), in respect of the offence of possession without lawful excuse. No breach of any duty of care need be shown, as for example under s. 80, nor any ulterior *mental element* and/or specific use, as is required under s. 81.

Authorization to intercept private communications may be given in respect of this offence under Part VI.

D may elect mode of trial under s. 536(2).

Other related provisions are described in the corresponding note to s. 79, *supra*. For an offence under s. 82(2), additional sentencing provisions are found in s. 82.1.

82.1 Sentences to be served consecutively — A sentence imposed on a person for an offence under subsection 82(2) shall be served consecutively to any other punishment imposed on the person for an offence arising out of the same event or series of events and to any other sentences to which the person is subject at the time the sentence is imposed on the person for an offence under subsection 82(2).

1997, c. 23, s. 2.

Commentary: Under this section, sentences imposed upon conviction of *possession* of *explosives* for the *benefit* of or at the *direction* of or in *association* with a *criminal organization* must be served *consecutively* to any sentence for a *related offence* and any *existing* sentence.

Related Provisions: A comparable provision appears in s. 85(4). It requires the imposition of consecutive sentences for the "use imitation firearm" offences of ss. 85(1) and (2).

The general rule with respect to cumulative punishments is stated in s. 718.3(4).

Prize Fights

83. (1) **Engaging in prize fight** — Every one who

(a) engages as a principal in a prize fight,

(b) advises, encourages or promotes a prize fight, or

(c) is present at a prize fight as an aid, second, surgeon, umpire, backer or reporter,

is guilty of an offence punishable on summary conviction.

(2) **Definition of "prize fight"** — In this section, "prize fight" means an encounter or fight with fists or hands between two persons who have met for that purpose by previous arrangement made by or for them, but a boxing contest between amateur sportsmen, where the contestants wear boxing gloves of not less than one hundred and forty grams each in mass, or any boxing contest held with the permission or under the authority of an athletic board or commission or similar body established by or under the authority of the legislature of a province for the control of sport within the province, shall be deemed not to be a prize fight.

R.S., c. C-34, s. 81;R.S. 1985, c. 27 (1st Supp.), s. 186.

Commentary: The section defines "prize fight" and prohibits certain types of participation therein. The offences of s. 83(1) are crimes which require proof of no *mental element* beyond the intention to cause the external circumstances. Under s. 83(1)(a) the *external circumstances* require proof that D engaged as a principal in a prize fight. In other words the actual participants, the fighters are criminally liable. Section 83(1)(b) attaches liability to anyone who advises, encourages or promotes a prize fight, arguably enlarging the traditional basis of accessorial liability of ss. 21 and 22. Finally, s. 83(1)(c) requires proof of actual presence at a prize fight in a designated capacity.

The definition of "prize flight" in s. 83(2) excludes bouts sanctioned by provincial athletic bodies and amateur bouts, sanctioned or otherwise, where the fighters wear boxing gloves of not less than 140 g each in mass.

Related Provisions: The offence is tried under Part XXVII and punished in accordance with s. 787(1).

PART III — FIREARMS AND OTHER WEAPONS

Interpretation

84. Definitions — (1) In this Part and subsections 491(1), 515(4.1) and (4.11) and 810(3.1) and (3.11),

"ammunition" means a cartridge containing a projectile designed to be discharged from a firearm and, without restricting the generality of the foregoing, includes a caseless cartridge and a shot shell;

"antique firearm" means

(a) any firearm manufactured before 1898 that was not designed to discharge rimfire or centre-fire ammunition and that has not been redesigned to discharge such ammunition, or

(b) any firearm that is prescribed to be an antique firearm;

"authorization" means an authorization issued under the *Firearms Act*;

"automatic firearm" means a firearm that is capable of, or assembled or designed and manufactured with the capability of, discharging projectiles in rapid succession during one pressure of the trigger;

"cartridge magazine" means a device or container from which ammunition may be fed into the firing chamber of a firearm;

"chief firearms officer" means a chief firearms officer as defined in subsection 2(1) of the *Firearms Act*;

"cross-bow" means a device with a bow and a bowstring mounted on a stock that is designed to propel an arrow, a bolt, a quarrel or any similar projectile on a trajectory guided by a barrel or groove and that is capable of causing serious bodily injury or death to a person;

"export" means export from Canada and, for greater certainty, includes the exportation of goods from Canada that are imported into Canada and shipped in transit through Canada;

"firearms officer" means a firearms officer as defined in subsection 2(1) of the *Firearms Act*;

"handgun" means a firearm that is designed, altered or intended to be aimed and fired by the action of one hand, whether or not it has been redesigned or subsequently altered to be aimed and fired by the action of both hands;

"imitation firearm" means any thing that imitates a firearm, and includes a replica firearm;

"import" means import into Canada and, for greater certainty, includes the importation of goods into Canada that are shipped in transit through Canada and exported from Canada;

"licence" means a licence issued under the *Firearms Act*,

"prescribed" means prescribed by the regulations;

"prohibited ammunition" means ammunition, or a projectile of any kind, that is prescribed to be prohibited ammunition;

"prohibited device" means

(a) any component or part of a weapon, or any accessory for use with a weapon, that is prescribed to be a prohibited device,

(b) a handgun barrel that is equal to or less than 105 mm in length, but does not include any such handgun barrel that is prescribed, where the handgun barrel is for use in international sporting competitions governed by the rules of the International Shooting Union,

(c) a device or contrivance designed or intended to muffle or stop the sound or report of a firearm,

(d) a cartridge magazine that is prescribed to be a prohibited device, or

(e) a replica firearm;

"prohibited firearm" means

(a) a handgun that

(i) has a barrel equal to or less than 105 mm in length, or

(ii) is designed or adapted to discharge a 25 or 32 calibre cartridge,

but does not include any such handgun that is prescribed, where the handgun is for use in international sporting competitions governed by the rules of the International Shooting Union,

(b) a firearm that is adapted from a rifle or shotgun, whether by sawing, cutting or any other alteration, and that, as so adapted,

(i) is less than 660 mm in length, or

(ii) is 660 mm or greater in length and has a barrel less than 457 mm in length,

(c) an automatic firearm, whether or not it has been altered to discharge only one projectile with one pressure of the trigger, or

(d) any firearm that is prescribed to be a prohibited firearm;

"prohibited weapon" means

(a) a knife that has a blade that opens automatically by gravity or centrifugal force or by hand pressure applied to a button, spring or other device in or attached to the handle of the knife, or

(b) any weapon, other than a firearm, that is prescribed to be a prohibited weapon;

"prohibition order" means an order made under this Act or any other Act of Parliament prohibiting a person from possessing any firearm, cross-bow, prohibited weapon, restricted weapon, prohibited device, ammunition, prohibited ammunition or explosive substance, or all such things;

"Registrar" means the Registrar of Firearms appointed under section 82 of the *Firearms Act*;

"registration certificate" means a registration certificate issued under the *Firearms Act*,

"replica firearm" means any device that is designed or intended to exactly resemble, or to resemble with near precision, a firearm, and that itself is not a firearm, but does not include any such device that is designed or intended to exactly resemble, or to resemble with near precision, an antique firearm;

"restricted firearm" means

(a) a handgun that is not a prohibited firearm,

(b) a firearm that

(i) is not a prohibited firearm,

(ii) has a barrel less than 470 mm in length, and

(iii) is capable of discharging centre-fire ammunition in a semi-automatic manner,

(c) a firearm that is designed or adapted to be fired when reduced to a length of less than 660 mm by folding, telescoping or otherwise, or

(d) a firearm of any other kind that is prescribed to be a restricted firearm;

"restricted weapon" means any weapon, other than a firearm, that is prescribed to be a restricted weapon;

"superior court" means

(a) in Ontario, the Superior Court of Justice, sitting in the region, district or county or group of counties where the relevant adjudication was made,

(b) in Quebec, the Superior Court,

(c) in New Brunswick, Manitoba, Saskatchewan and Alberta, the Court of Queen's Bench,

(d) in Nova Scotia, British Columbia and a territory, the Supreme Court, and

(e) in Prince Edward Island and Newfoundland, the Trial Division of the Supreme Court;

"transfer" means sell, provide, barter, give, lend, rent, send, transport, ship, distribute or deliver.

(2) **Barrel length** — For the purposes of this Part, the length of a barrel of a firearm is

(a) in the case of a revolver, the distance from the muzzle of the barrel to the breach end immediately in front of the cylinder, and

(b) in any other case, the distance from the muzzle of the barrel to and including the chamber, but does not include the length of any component, part or accessory including any component, part or accessory designed or intended to suppress the muzzle flash or reduce recoil.

(3) **Certain weapons deemed not to be firearm** — For the purposes of sections 91 to 95, 99 to 101, 103 to 107 and 117.03 of this Act and the provisions of the *Firearms Act*, the following weapons are deemed not to be firearms;

    (a) any antique firearm;

    (b) any device that is

        (i) designed exclusively for signalling, for notifying of distress, for firing blank cartridges or for firing stud cartridges, explosive-driven rivets or other industrial projectiles, and

        (ii) intended by the person in possession of it to be used exclusively for the purpose for which it is designed;

    (c) any shooting device that is

        (i) designed exclusively for the slaughtering of domestic animals, the tranquillizing of animals or the discharging of projectiles with lines attached to them, and

        (ii) intended by the person in possession of it to be used exclusively for the purpose for which it is designed; and

    (d) any other barrelled weapon, where it is proved that the weapon is not designed or adapted to discharge

        (i) a shot, bullet or other projectile at a muzzle velocity exceeding 152.4 m per second, or

        (ii) a shot, bullet or other projectile that is designed or adapted to attain a velocity exceeding 152.4 m per second.

(3.1) **Exceptions — antique firearms** — Notwithstanding subsection (3), an antique firearm is a firearm for the purposes of regulations made under paragraph 117(*h*) of the *Firearms Act* and subsection 86(2) of this Act.

(4) **Meaning of "holder"** — For the purposes of this Part, a person is the holder of

    (a) an authorization or a licence if the authorization or licence has been issued to the person and the person continues to hold it; and

    (b) a registration certificate for a firearm if

        (i) the registration certificate has been issued to the person and the person continues to hold it, or

        (ii) the person possesses the registration certificate with the permission of its lawful holder.

1995, c. 39, s. 139; 1998, c. 30, s. 16.

Commentary: This section enacts *exhaustive* definitions for terms used in Part III and certain related *Code* provisions.

Section 84(2) describes the manner in which the *barrel length* of a firearm is to be determined for the purposes of Part III.

Section 84(3) is of limited application. It *deems* certain weapons not to be *firearms* for the purpose of listed *Code* sections and the *Firearms Act (F.A.)*. The provision should be read together with s. 84(3.1), a *non obstante* provision, which makes an "antique firearm" a "firearm" for the purposes of *Code* s. 86(2) and regulations made under *F.A.* s. 117(h).

Section 84(4) defines "holder" in connection with authorizations, licences and registration certificates for the purposes of Part III.

Case Law

Prohibited Weapon

R. v. Hasselwander (1993), 20 C.R. (4th) 277, 81 C.C.C. (3d) 471 (S.C.C.); reversing (1991), 9 C.R. (4th) 281, 67 C.C.C. (3d) 426 (Ont. C.A.) — In paragraph (c) of the definition of "prohibited weapon", "capable" includes an aspect of potential capability for conversion. It should be defined as meaning capable of conversion to an automatic weapon in a relatively short period of time with relative ease. A weapon which can be quickly and readily converted to an automatic status is a "prohibited weapon".

R. v. Cook (1989), 48 C.C.C. (3d) 61 (Man. C.A.) — Although a sawed off shotgun was incapable of being fired because it lacked a firing pin and because part of the mechanism had been bent, it is a prohibited weapon if D had the capacity by himself or with the assistance of others within a reasonable time to activate the shotgun for firing.

R. v. Richard (1981), 24 C.R. (3d) 373, 63 C.C.C. (2d) 333 (N.B. C.A.) — A knife may be a prohibited weapon even though it is not designed to be used as such if in fact its blade, through wear or alteration, can be fully opened for use by applying centrifugal force or gravity to the blade. The wording of the definition should be interpreted as the application of centrifugal force to the blade, not to the handle.

R. v. Murray (1985), 24 C.C.C. (3d) 568 (Ont. C.A.) — To fall within s. 84(1)(e) of the definition of "prohibited weapon", the object must not only be subject to an Order in Council but must also fit the definition of "weapon" in *Code* s. 2. The phrase "used or intended to be used" in s. 2 refers to the user or intention of D, and imports a subjective test or element.

R. v. Archer (1983), 6 C.C.C. (3d) 129 (Ont. C.A.) — A knife which may be opened by holding the blade and applying centrifugal force to the handle is not a prohibited weapon, unless the blade might be opened by centrifugal force while holding the handle.

R. v. Vaughan (1990), 60 C.C.C. (3d) 87 (Que. C.A.) — To be a "prohibited weapon" under s. 84(1)(b) a knife blade must not only open by gravity or centrifugal force, but also automatically. Where ability and practice are required to permit automatic opening, the knife is *not* a "prohibited weapon" within the section.

Restricted Weapon

R. v. Watkins (1987), 33 C.C.C. (3d) 465 (B.C. C.A.) — Although the only way a pistol could be fired was by using two hands, it was properly regarded as a "restricted weapon" because it was "designed" to be fired by the action of one hand.

Exemptions

R. v. Tellier (1982), 67 C.C.C. (2d) 351 (Que. C.A.) — The exemptions in this section are inapplicable to a charge of using a firearm during the commission of an indictable offence.

Related Provisions: "Firearm" is defined in s. 2.

Several other provisions define terms used in particular sections. These provisions include ss. 107(3) ("report" and "statement"), 109(4) and 110(4) ("release from imprisonment"), 111(11) ("provincial court judge"), 113(5) ("competent authority") and 117.07(2) ("public officer").

Use Offences

85. (1) Using firearm in commission of offence — Every person commits an offence who uses a firearm

> **(a) while committing an indictable offence, other than an offence under section 220 (criminal negligence causing death), 236 (manslaughter), 239 (attempted murder), 244 (causing bodily harm with intent — firearm), 272 (sexual assault with a weapon), 273 (aggravated sexual assault), 279 (kidnapping), 279.1 (hostage-taking), 344 (robbery) or 346 (extortion),**
>
> **(b) while attempting to commit an indictable offence, or**

(c) during flight after committing or attempting to commit an indictable offence, whether or not the person causes or means to cause bodily harm to any person as a result of using the firearm.

(2) **Using imitation firearm in commission of offence** — Every person commits an offence who uses an imitation firearm

(a) while committing an indictable offence,

(b) while attempting to commit an indictable offence, or

(c) during flight after committing or attempting to commit an indictable offence, whether or not the person causes or means to cause bodily harm to any person as a result of using the imitation firearm.

(3) **Punishment** — Every person who commits an offence under subsection (1) or (2) is guilty of an indictable offence and liable

(a) in the case of a first offence, except as provided in paragraph (b), to imprisonment for a term not exceeding fourteen years and to a minimum punishment of imprisonment for a term of one year;

(b) in the case of a first offence committed by a person who, before January 1, 1978, was convicted of an indictable offence, or an attempt to commit an indictable offence, in the course of which or during flight after the commission or attempted commission of which the person used a firearm, to imprisonment for a term not exceeding fourteen years and to a minimum punishment of imprisonment for a term of three years; and

(c) in the case of a second or subsequent offence, to imprisonment for a term not exceeding fourteen years and to a minimum punishment of imprisonment for a term of three years.

(4) **Sentences to be served consecutively** — A sentence imposed on a person for an offence under subsection (1) or (2) shall be served consecutively to any other punishment imposed on the person for an offence arising out of the same event or series of events and to any other sentence to which the person is subject at the time the sentence is imposed on the person for an offence under subsection (1) or (2).

1995, c. 39, s. 139.

Commentary: This section prohibits *use of a firearm* during the actual or attempted commission of an *indictable* offence or *flight* therefrom, and further provides the minimum and maximum punishment therefor.

The *external circumstances* of the offence of s. 85(1) require that D commit or attempt to commit an *indictable* offence other than a listed offence. D must also *use* a firearm while committing or attempting to commit the indictable offence or during flight thereafter. Bodily harm need not ensue from such use. The *mental element* requires proof of the mental element of the indictable offence attempted or actually committed, together with the intention to contemporaneously use the firearm. P need *not* prove that D intended to cause bodily harm to any person as a result of the commission of the offence.

The *external circumstances* of the offence of s. 85(2) parallel those of s. 85(1) except that s. 85(2) involves use of an *imitation firearm* and is engaged upon the commission of *any* indictable offence.

The constitutional validity of the section has been challenged under *Charter* ss. 7 and 11(h).

Upon conviction, the minimum and maximum *punishment* provisions of ss. 85(1)(c) and (d) become engaged. Under s. 85(2), the sentence must be served consecutively to any other punishment imposed on D for an offence arising out of the same event or series of events and, further, to any other sentence to which D is then subject.

The constitutionality of the sentence provisions has been impeached under *Charter* ss. 9 and 12.

Case Law
Use of Firearm: S. 85(1)

R. v. McGuigan (1982), 26 C.R. (3d) 289 (S.C.C.); affirming (1979), 50 C.C.C. (2d) 306 (Ont. C.A.) — D may be convicted of this offence as a party under s. 21.

R. v. Cheetham (1980), 17 C.R. (3d) 1, 53 C.C.C. (2d) 109 (Ont. C.A.) — The firearm does *not* have to be pointed at the victim of a robbery to be "used" within the meaning of the section.

R. v. Langevin (No.1) (1979), 10 C.R. (3d) 193, 47 C.C.C. (2d) 138 (Ont. C.A.) — Pulling out a firearm which the offender has upon his/her person, and holding it in his/her hand to intimidate another, constitutes "use".

R. v. Fitzwilliams (1992), 79 C.C.C. (3d) 81 (Qué. C.A.) — A firearm is *not* "used" under s. 85(1) where it is found in a bag in a motor vehicle in which D is an occupant.

Commission of Indictable Offence

R. v. Pringle (1989), 70 C.R. (3d) 305, 48 C.C.C. (3d) 449 (S.C.C.) — D must be convicted of the underlying indictable offence to sustain a conviction under this section. It is not sufficient that as a matter of fact D had committed another indictable offence with which he was not charged and of which he could not be convicted.

R. v. Woods (1982), 65 C.C.C. (2d) 554 (Ont. C.A.) — A separate offence is committed by a person each time s/he uses a firearm in the commission of a separate indictable offence involving a separate transaction, notwithstanding it is the same firearm.

Second or Subsequent Offence — Increased Penalty: S. 85(1)(d)[now s.85(3)(c)]

R. v. Nicholson (1981), 24 C.R. (3d) 284 (S.C.C.); affirming (1980), 52 C.C.C. (2d) 157 (Man. C.A.) — Where D was a party to a previous offence in which a companion, not D, used a firearm in the commission of the offence, the increased penalty nevertheless applied.

R. v. Oswald (1981), 57 C.C.C. (2d) 484 (B.C. C.A.) — D is not liable to the increased penalty in a situation in which all the offences were committed prior to the first conviction. The words "second or subsequent offence" refer to an offence which is committed after a conviction for an offence of the same character.

R. v. Cheetham (1980), 17 C.R. (3d) 1, 53 C.C.C. (2d) 109 (Ont. C.A.) — To constitute a "second or subsequent offence" under this subsection, the second offence must have been committed after a previous conviction under this section for use of a firearm.

Consecutive Sentences: S. 85(2) [now s. 85(4)]

R. v. Jensen (1982), 3 C.C.C. (3d) 46 (Alta. C.A.) — The words "sentence to which he is subject" in s. 85(2) mean a sentence which is actually being served. Therefore, when an accused is being sentenced for more than one offence requiring an obligatory consecutive sentence for using a firearm, there is no requirement that the firearm sentences be consecutive to each other and the court may order that a firearm sentence together with its associated offence sentence be served concurrently with another firearm sentence and its associated offence sentence.

R. v. Cochrane (1994), 88 C.C.C. (3d) 570 (B.C. C.A.) — Section 85(2) does *not* authorize imposition of a sentence consecutive to a sentence of imprisonment for life. Where D is convicted of several s. 85 offences, the sentences for these offences ought be consecutive to each other, but concurrent to a sentence of imprisonment for life.

R. v. Goforth (1986), 24 C.C.C. (3d) 573 (B.C. C.A.) — Where D is convicted of two firearms offences arising out of the same event, the sentences for use of a firearm contrary to this section must not only be consecutive to the indictable offence to which they relate, but also consecutive to each other.

R. v. MacLean (1979), 12 C.R. (3d) 1 (N.S. C.A.); leave to appeal dismissed (1979), 35 N.S.R. (2d) 180n (S.C.C.) — Where there are multiple convictions under s. 85(1), those sentences must be consecutive to each other as well as to the indictable offence. However, s. 85(2) requires only sentences for use of a firearm to be consecutive; therefore where D is also being sentenced for multiple counts of the indictable offence, concurrent sentences may be imposed for those offences.

R. v. H. (R.) (1992), 77 C.C.C. (3d) 198 (Ont. C.A.) — A young offender convicted of an offence under *Code* s. 85 is *not* liable to the minimum punishment of imprisonment for one year prescribed by the section. The sentencing provisions of *Code* s. 85 have been superceded by *Y.O.A.* s. 20.

Multiple Convictions

Krug v. R. (1985), 48 C.R. (3d) 97, 21 C.C.C. (3d) 193 (S.C.C.) — The common law principle of *res judicata* does not apply to prevent conviction for both attempted robbery and use of a firearm. The act of using a firearm is not necessarily encompassed in the act of being armed with it. However, D cannot be convicted of use of a firearm contrary to this section and of unlawfully pointing it. It would be difficult to believe that Parliament intended to make the same objectionable behavior the subject of two separate offences.

R. v. McGuigan (1982), 26 C.R. (3d) 289 (S.C.C.); affirming (1979), 50 C.C.C. (2d) 306 (Ont. C.A.) — Parliament has shown the intention to depart from the common law principles elaborated in *Kienapple* and has intended that when, in the course of a robbery, a firearm is used, multiple convictions could follow.

R. v. Quon (1948), 6 C.R. 160, 92 C.C.C. 1 (S.C.C.) — *See also*: *R. v. Chang* (1989), 50 C.C.C. (3d) 413 (B.C. C.A.) — D could not be convicted of possession of a firearm while committing a criminal offence where an essential element of the criminal offence was the possession of a firearm.

R. v. Switzer (1987), 56 C.R. (3d) 107, 32 C.C.C. (3d) 303 (Alta. C.A.) — The rule against multiple convictions requires sufficient factual and legal *nexus* between the two offences. The charge of use of a firearm in the commission of an indictable offence has distinguishing elements from that of aggravated assault; so although there was a factual nexus between the two charges there is no legal nexus and D could be convicted of both offence.

R. v. Carlson (1984), 57 A.R. 218 (C.A.) — The offence of assault with a weapon contemplates the possibility of an assault with a weapon other than a firearm and, therefore, a conviction for that offence as well as one under this section does not breach the rule against multiple convictions.

R. v. Osbourne (1994), 94 C.C.C. (3d) 435 (Ont. C.A.) — Convictions of aggravated assault and using a firearm while committing the offence of aggravated assault do not offend the rule against multiple convictions, notwithstanding that the same delict, the discharge of a firearm, gives rise to both counts.

R. v. Poisson (1983), 8 C.C.C. (3d) 381 (Ont. C.A.) — The rule against multiple convictions precludes the invocation of this section only where the "indictable offence" makes the use, as distinct from the possession, of a firearm a constituent element of the offence. Therefore, a conviction for intent to cause bodily harm did not preclude a conviction under this section even though the bodily harm was caused by the use of a firearm.

R. v. Langevin (No.1) (1979), 10 C.R. (3d) 193, 41 C.C.C. (2d) 138 (Ont. C.A.) — Where the offender brandished the weapon to intimidate the victim, he was convicted of using a firearm while committing robbery along with robbery. "Use of a firearm" must be a constituent element of the indictable offence to preclude multiple convictions.

R. v. Pineault (1979), 12 C.R. (3d) 129 (Que. C.A.) — Parliament has intended to specifically ban the use of firearms and to punish more severely those who make use of them, and, as such, to impose a second penalty for the same set of facts. Therefore, D may be convicted of using a firearm while committing an indictable offence in addition to a conviction for discharging a firearm with intent to wound.

Charter Considerations

R. v. Brown (1994), 93 C.C.C. (3d) 97 (S.C.C); reversing (1993), 19 C.R. (4th) 140, 80 C.C.C. (3d) 275 (Man. C.A.) — Where armed robbery is the underlying offence, s. 85(2) does *not* offend *Charter* s. 12.

Krug v. R. (1985), 48 C.R. (3d) 97, 21 C.C.C. (3d) 193 (S.C.C.) — A conviction both under this section and for attempted robbery does not violate *Charter* s. 7, as Parliament created an aggravated form of robbery by punishing more severely D who uses a firearm in perpetrating that offence. Further, *Charter* s. 12 is not offended by the imposition of an additional term of imprisonment as Parliament intended to repress the use of firearms in the commission of crimes.

Related Provisions: "Firearm" is defined in s. 2 and is *not*, for the purposes of this section, restricted as in s. 84(3) and (3.1).

The offences exempted from the operation of s. 85(1) by its paragraph (a) each attract a minimum term of imprisonment of four (4) years where a firearm is used in their commission.

The language of ss. 85(1)(a) and (b) is similar to that of s. 230(d), found constitutionally deficient in other respects in *R. v. Vaillancourt*, [1987] 2 S.C.R. 636.

The general authority to impose consecutive sentences is found in s. 718.3(4).

Conviction under s. 85 attracts the mandatory prohibition of s. 109, a "sentence" for appellate purposes under s. 673.

86. (1) Careless use of firearm, etc. — Every person commits an offence who, without lawful excuse, uses, carries, handles, ships, transports or stores a firearm, a prohibited weapon, a restricted weapon, a prohibited device or any ammunition or prohibited ammunition in a careless manner or without reasonable precautions for the safety of other persons.

(2) Contravention of storage regulations, etc — Every person commits an offence who contravenes a regulation made under paragraph 117(*h*) of the *Firearms Act* respecting the storage, handling, transportation, shipping, display, advertising and mail-order sales of firearms and restricted weapons.

(3) Punishment — Every person who commits an offence under subsection (1) or (2)

  (a) is guilty of an indictable offence and liable to imprisonment

    (i) in the case of a first offence, for a term not exceeding two years, and

    (ii) in the case of a second or subsequent offence, for a term not exceeding five years; or

  (b) is guilty of an offence punishable on summary conviction.

1995, c. 39, s. 139.

Commentary: The section creates and punishes two offences that involve *handling* firearms and other regulated items in a prohibited way.

Under s. 86(1), the *external circumstances* involve a firearm or other regulated item and a prohibited form of *handling, transfer* or *storage*. The handling, transfer or storage must be *careless*, or without *reasonable precautions* for the *safety* of others. There must be *no lawful* excuse for D's conduct. The *mental element* requires that D's conduct be a *marked* departure from the standard of care of a *reasonable* person in the circumstances. No ulterior mental element is required.

The offence of s. 86(2) involves improper handling of firearms and restricted weapons. Liability is established where P proves that D's conduct *contravened* a *regulation* made under *F.A.* s. 117(h). No ulterior *mental element* has to be proven.

The offences are triable either way. There are increased penalty provisions for subsequent indictable convictions.

Case Law

Careless Use or Storage: S. 86(1)

R. v. Finlay (1993), 23 C.R. (4th) 321, 83 C.C.C. (3d) 513 (S.C.C.); reversing (1991), 6 C.R. (4th) 157, 64 C.C.C. (3d) 557 (Sask. C.A.) — *See also*: *R. v. Durham* (1992), 15 C.R. (4th) 45, 76 C.C.C. (3d) 219 (Ont. C.A.) — The objective fault requirement of s. 86(2) demands that D's conduct be a *marked departure* from the standard of care of a *reasonable person* in the circumstances. Where there is a reasonable doubt whether D's conduct constituted a marked departure from the requisite standard of care, or that reasonable precautions were taken to discharge the duty of care in the circumstances, D must be acquitted. There is *no* onus on D to establish, on a balance of probabilities, that he or she exercised due diligence in order to negate a finding of fault under s. 86(2).

R. v. Cannon (1977), 37 C.C.C. (2d) 325 (Ont. C.A.) — The safety of one person only need be endangered to fall within s. 86(2).

R. v. Smillie (1998), 20 C.R. (5th) 179, 129 C.C.C. (3d) 414 (B.C. C.A.) — The offence of s. 86(3) is a crime of *strict liability*. A reasonable doubt with respect to a *mistake* of *fact* or *due diligence* in efforts to comply with the regulation entitles D to an acquittal.

Under s. 86(3), P is required to prove that D stored firearms in a manner contrary to the requirements of the regulations. The standard by which the manner of storage is measured is objectively determined by reference to the regulations. P does *not* have to prove that D was negligent *per se*.

Included Offences

R. v. Morrison (1991), 66 C.C.C. (3d) 257 (B.C.C.A.) — Careless handling of a firearm under [now] s. 86(1) is *not* an included offence upon a charge of pointing a firearm under [now] s. 87.1.

R. v. Clements (1974), 17 C.C.C. (2d) 574 (P.E.I. C.A.) — Careless use of a firearm is an included offence in the offence of discharging a firearm with intent to endanger life.

Res Judicata

R. v. Missel (1980), 52 C.C.C. (2d) 1 (Alta. C.A.) — The offences of unlawful confinement and pointing a firearm are different delicts, and convictions can be entered for both.

Charter Considerations

R. v. Finlay (1993), 23 C.R. (4th) 321, 83 C.C.C. (3d) 513 (S.C.C.); reversing (1991), 6 C.R. (4th) 157, 64 C.C.C. (3d) 557 (Sask. C.A.) — *See also*: *R. v. Durham* (1992), 15 C.R. (4th) 45, 76 C.C.C. (3d) 219 (Ont. C.A.) — Section 86(1), as described under heading ""Careless Use or Storage, *supra*, does *not* infringe *Charter* s. 7.

Charter Considerations: S. 86(2)

R. v. Smillie (1998), 20 C.R. (5th) 179, 129 C.C.C. (3d) 414 (B.C. C.A.) — The fault element in s. 86(3) does *not* offend *Charter* s. 7.

Related Provisions: "Firearm" and "weapon" are defined in s. 2, the other regulated items in s. 84(1). An antique firearm is a "firearm" for the purposes of s. 86(2).

Conviction or discharge of an offence under s. 86 may result in a discretionary prohibition order under s. 110 or a mandatory prohibition if the conditions of s. 109(1)(d) have been met. Either order is a "sentence" for indictable appeal purposes under s. 673.

P's election to proceed by indictment allows D to elect mode of trial under s. 536(2). Punishment on summary conviction is governed by s. 787(1).

87 (1) Pointing a firearm — Every person commits an offence who, without lawful excuse, points a firearm at another person, whether the firearm is loaded or unloaded.

(2) Punishment — Every person who commits an offence under subsection (1)

   (a) is guilty of an indictable offence and liable to imprisonment for a term not exceeding five years; or

   (b) is guilty of an offence punishable on summary conviction.

1995, c. 39, s. 139.

Commentary: This is the former s. 86(1). The external circumstances require that D *point* a firearm at another person. It is of *no* legal consequence that the firearm is unloaded. D's conduct must be *without* lawful excuse. The *mental element* involves nothing more than the intention to engage in the conduct that constitutes the external circumstances of the offence. The offence is triable either way.

Related Provisions: "Firearm" is defined in s. 2.

Under s. 244, it is an indictable offence to *discharge* a *firarm* at another person with any of the states of mind described in the section. Conviction attracts a minimum punishment of imprisonment for a term of four years.

There are ten serious indictable offences that attract a minimum punishment of imprisonment for a term of four years where a firearm is used in their commission. The offences include

i.   s. 220 (criminal negligence causing death);

ii.   s. 236 (manslaughter);

iii. s. 239 (attempted murder);

iv.   s. 244 (cause bodily harm with intent);

v.   s. 272 (sexual assault with a weapon);

vi.   s. 273 (aggravated sexual assault);

vii.   s. 279 (kidnapping);

viii.   s. 279.1 (hostage-taking);

ix.   s. 343 (robbery); and,

x.   s. 346 (extortion).

Conviction or discharge may attract a discretionary prohibition order under s. 110 or, if the requisite conditions have been met, a mandatory order under s. 109(1)(d).

Where P proceeds by indictment, D may elect mode of trial under s. 536(2). Summary conviction punishment is governed by s. 787(1).

Possession Offences

88. (1) Possession of weapon for dangerous purpose — Every person commits an offence who carries or possesses a weapon, an imitation of a weapon, a prohibited device or any ammunition or prohibited ammunition for a purpose dangerous to the public peace or for the purpose of committing an offence.

(2) Punishment — Every person who commits an offence under subsection (1)

     (a) is guilty of an indictable offence and liable to imprisonment for a term not exceeding ten years; or

     (b) is guilty of an offence punishable on summary conviction.

1995, c. 39, s. 139.

Commentary: This offence was previously in s. 87 where it applied only to weapons and imitation weapons. In s. 88(1), the offence is expanded to include other regulated items. The critical element in each offence is the *purpose* for which the weapon, imitation weapon or regulated item, is carried or possessed.

The *external circumstances* of the offences are straightforward. D must carry or possess a weapon, imitation weapon or regulated item. Actual use is *not* required.

The *mental element* involves either

i.   a purpose *dangerous* to the *public peace*; or,

ii.   the purpose of *committing* an offence.

Proof of *either* ulterior state of mind, together with the basic mental element involved in possession or carriage, is sufficient.

Case Law
Weapon

R. v. Califoux (1974), 24 C.R.N.S. 314 at 316, 14 C.C.C. (2d) 526 (B.C. C.A.) — A weapon as contemplated by the section may be: (a) anything designed to be used as a weapon; (b) anything that a person uses as a weapon, whether that thing is designed as a weapon or not; or (c) anything that one intends to use as a weapon regardless of its design.

R. v. Boutilier, [1974] 4 W.W.R. 443 (B.C. C.A.) — A starting pistol is an imitation of a weapon.

R. v. Allan (1971), 4 C.C.C. (2d) 521 (N.B. C.A.) — A broken piece of glass may be a weapon.

Malang v. R. (1982), 25 C.R. (3d) 398 (Ont. C.A) — A bomb falls within the definition of offensive weapon or weapon.

Possession [See also ss. 4 and 354]

Ferland v. R., [1958] B.R. 619 (Que. C.A.) — Constructive possession is sufficient for a conviction under this section.

Purpose of Accused

R. v. Calder (1984), 11 C.C.C. (3d) 546 (Alta. C.A.) — P must prove an intention to possess for a purpose dangerous to the public peace. This intention must precede the use of the weapon for such purpose. The dangerous act must be premeditated and not a mere reaction to a situation that had developed. Where D originally possessed a knife for innocent purposes, P must prove that, at the time of the incident, D's intention had changed to one of use for a dangerous purpose.

R. v. Sulland (1982), 2 C.C.C. (3d) 68 (B.C. C.A.) — An offence under this section is not committed if a person carries a weapon for self-defence that is an appropriate instrument with which to repel, in a lawful manner, the type of attack reasonably apprehended and if the person carrying the weapon is competent to handle it and is likely to use it responsibly.

R. v. Proverbs (1983), 9 C.C.C. (3d) 249 (Ont. C.A.) — The formation of the unlawful purpose must precede its use in a manner dangerous to the public peace. Although the unlawful purpose may be inferred from the circumstances in which the weapon is used, where there is reasonable doubt that D, prior to entry of police executing a search warrant, did not have a weapon for a purpose dangerous to the public peace and only loaded the firearm in an attempt to defend himself unaware it was police seeking entry, D is entitled to an acquittal.

R. v. Chomenko (1974), 18 C.C.C. (2d) 353 (Ont. C.A.) — D must have had the intention to possess an imitation weapon for a purpose dangerous to the public peace. It is insufficient that D merely did an act which was in fact dangerous to the public peace.

R. v. Nelson (1972), 19 C.R.N.S. 88, 8 C.C.C. (2d) 29 (Ont. C.A.) — A weapon may be for defensive purposes but at the same time, in all the circumstances, for a purpose dangerous to the public peace. The subjective purpose of self-defence is only one of the factors to be considered in assessing the purpose of the possession.

Public Peace

Stavroff v. R. (1979), 48 C.C.C. (2d) 353 (S.C.C.) — Possession of a weapon in a private dwelling place does not preclude a finding of a purpose dangerous to the public peace.

Consent

R. v. Gur (1986), 27 C.C.C. (3d) 511 (N.S. C.A.) — Consent is not a defence to a charge under this section.

Multiple Convictions

R. v. Briscoe (1992), 76 C.C.C. (3d) 563 (B.C. C.A.) — The rule against multiple convictions bars convictions for offences contrary to s. 267(1)(a) (assault with a weapon) and 88 (weapon dangerous) where:

a.   the *evidence* relied upon by P to establish the assault on V and the purpose for which D possessed the weapon is the same, *viz.*, the pointing of the weapon with the threat to use it; and,

b.   substantially the same *elements* make up both offences, *viz.*, carrying the weapon as an aggravating circumstance under s. 267(l)(a) and possession of it under s. 88, and are proven by the same evidence.

Related Provisions: Except for "weapon", which is defined in s. 2, the regulated items are defined in s. 84(1).

Unless s. 109(1)(a) or (d) applies, a prohibition order is discretionary under s. 110 upon conviction or discharge for this offence, which is triable either way. D may elect mode of trial where P proceeds by indictment. The summary conviction punishment is provided in s. 787(1). Weapons used during the commission of the offence are forfeited under s. 491.

---

89. (1) Carrying weapon while attending public meeting — Every person commits an offence who, without lawful excuse, carries a weapon, a prohibited device or any ammunition or prohibited ammunition while the person is attending or is on the way to attend a public meeting.

(2) Punishment — **Every person who commits an offence under subsection (1) is guilty of an offence punishable on summary conviction.**

1995, c. 39, s. 139.

Commentary: This section is similar to former s. 88 except that the new provision extends to

i.   prohibited devices;

ii.   ammunition; and,

iii.   prohibited ammunition,

in addition to weapons.

The *external circumstances* include the *absence* of a *lawful excuse* and *carriage* of a weapon or other regulated item. The weapon need *not* be displayed or used. What is critical, however, is that D carry the weapon or regulated item

i.   while *attending*; or,

ii.   on the *way* to

a *public* meeting.

There is *no* requirement that P prove any ulterior mental element on the part of D, as for example, an intention to use the weapon in some manner at the meeting.

Case Law

Carrying

Crawford v. R. (1980), 18 C.R. (3d) 171, 54 C.C.C. (2d) 412 (Ont. C.A.) — Carrying a weapon is *not* confined to carrying on the person. It extends to a weapon concealed under the floor mat of a vehicle.

Concealment

R. v. Felawka (1993), 25 C.R. (4th) 79, 85 C.C.C. (3d) 248 (S.C.C.); affirming (1991), 9 C.R. (4th) 291, 68 C.C.C. (3d) 481 (B.C.C.A.) — To prove concealment, P must prove beyond a reasonable doubt that D took steps to hide the weapon so that it would not be observed or come to the notice of others. Carriage of a firearm in a case or tightly wrapped in canvas, as required by some provincial regualtions, does not contravene [now] s. 90. Placement of a firearm in a locked trunk, or out of sight in a locked and unattended vehicle, in compliance with federal regulations, does not breach [now] s. 90. A firearm which breaks down and is carried in a case which resembles a briefcase in not "concealed" if the carrying case is clearly marked as a firearm's case.

Mental Element

R. v. Felawka (1993), 25 C.R. (4th) 79, 85 C.C.C. (3d) 248 (S.C.C.); affirming (1991), 9 C.R. (4th) 291, 68 C.C.C. (3d) 481 (B.C. C.A.) — *See also*: *R. v. Lemire* (1980), 20 C.R. (3d) 186, 57 C.C.C. (2d) 561 (B.C. C.A.); leave to appeal refused (1980), 57 C.C.C. (2d) 561n (S.C.C.); *R. v. Formosa* (1992), 79 C.C.C. (3d) 95 (Ont. C.A.) — The *mental element* requires proof beyond a reasonable doubt that D concealed an object that D *knew* to be a weapon.

R. v. Campbell (1979), 9 C.R. (3d) 383 (B.C. C.A.) — The reason for the concealment is immaterial.

Res Judicata

R. v. Singh (1983), 8 C.C.C. (3d) 38 (Ont. C.A.) — D can be convicted of both carrying a concealed weapon and being in possession of a restricted weapon as each offence contains elements distinct from those of the other.

Charter Considerations

R. v. Conrad (1983), 8 C.C.C. (3d) 482 (N.S. C.A.) — This section does not contravene *Charter* s. 11(d).

Related Provisions: "Public meeting" is *not* defined. "Weapon" is defined in s. 2, the other regulated items in s. 84(1).

A prohibition order is discretionary upon conviction or discharge under s. 110 unless s. 109(1)(d) applies. Weapons used during the commission of offences are forfeited under *Code* s. 491.

Section 117.11 puts the onus on D to prove that s/he is the holder of any relevant authorization, licence or registration certificate.

The summary conviction provisions of Part XXVII govern this offence, including the general punishment of s. 787(1).

Carrying a concealed weapon, prohibited device, ammunition or prohibited ammunition is an offence under s. 90(1).

90. (1) Carrying concealed weapon — Every person commits an offence who carries a weapon, a prohibited device or any prohibited ammunition concealed, unless the person is authorized under the *Firearms Act* to carry it concealed.

(2) Punishment — Every person who commits an offence under subsection (1)

    (a) is guilty of an indictable offence and liable to imprisonment for a term not exceeding five years; or

    (b) is guilty of an offence punishable on summary conviction.

1995, c. 39, s. 139.

Commentary: This is the former s. 89 that has been expanded to include prohibited devices and prohibited ammunition. The offence is triable either way.

The essence of this offence is *concealment*. The *external circumstances* consist of

i. carriage;

ii. concealment

of a weapon or other regulated item; and,

iii. the absence of *F.A.* authorization to carry the weapon or other regulated item concealed.

The *mental element* requires proof that D intended to conceal what the law regards as a weapon or other regulated item.

Related Provisions: Under s. 117.11, the *onus* is on D to prove that s/he has the relevant *F.A.* authorization.

Unless s. 109(1)(d) applies, a prohibition order is discretionary under s. 110 upon conviction or discharge. Punishment in summary conviction proceedings is governed by s. 787(1).

Weapons used during the commission of offences are forfeited under s. 491.

91. (1) Unauthorized possession of firearm — Subject to subsections (4) and (5) and section 98, every person commits an offence who possesses a firearm, unless the person is the holder of

    (a) a licence under which the person may possess it; and

    (b) a registration certificate for the firearm.

(2) Unauthorized possession of prohibited weapon or restricted weapon — Subject to subsection (4) and section 98, every person commits an offence who possesses a prohibited weapon, a restricted weapon, a prohibited device, other than a replica firearm, or any prohibited ammunition, unless the person is the holder of a licence under which the person may possess it.

(3) Punishment — Every person who commits an offence under subsection (1) or (2)

    (a) is guilty of an indictable offence and liable to imprisonment for a term not exceeding five years; or

    (b) is guilty of an offence punishable on summary conviction.

(4) Exceptions — Subsections (1) and (2) do not apply to

    (a) a person who possesses a firearm, a prohibited weapon, a restricted weapon, a prohibited device or any prohibited ammunition while the person is under the direct and immediate supervision of a person who may lawfully possess it, for the purpose of using it in a manner in which the supervising person may lawfully use it; or

(b) a person who comes into possession of a firearm, a prohibited weapon, a restricted weapon, a prohibited device or any prohibited ammunition by the operation of law and who, within a reasonable period after acquiring possession of it,

(i) lawfully disposes of it, or

(ii) obtains a licence under which the person may possess it and, in the case of a firearm, a registration certificate for the firearm.

(5) **Borrowed firearm for sustenance** — Subsection (1) does not apply to a person who possesses a firearm that is neither a prohibited firearm nor a restricted firearm and who is not the holder of a registration certificate for the firearm if the person

(a) has borrowed the firearm;

(b) is the holder of a licence under which the person may possess it; and

(c) is in possession of the firearm to hunt or trap in order to sustain the person or the person's family.

1995, c. 39, s. 139.

Commentary: The offences created by this section involve unauthorized possession of firearms and other regulated items. Each offence is triable either way and subject to statutory exceptions or exemptions.

Section 91(1) relates to *firearms*. The *external circumstances* involve *possession* of a firearm and the absence of a *licence* and *registration certificate* for the weapon. The *mental element* requires proof that D knew or was reckless about the nature of the item as a firearm.

Under ss. 91(4) and 91(5), the prohibition of s. 91(1) does *not* apply to a person who

i.   has the firearm under the *supervision* of a person who may lawfully possess it and uses it in the same manner as the authorized person;

ii.   obtains the firearm by *operation* of *law* and within a reasonable time afterward lawfully disposes of it or gets the necessary documents to keep it; or,

iii. has the firearm, which is neither a prohibited nor restricted firearm, that s/he has borrowed for *sustenance* purposes and for which s/he holds a licence.

The offence of s. 91(2) relates to regulated items and is similar in structure to s. 91(1). D must *not* have a licence for the regulated items. The exceptions of items i and ii, *supra*, apply to the s. 91(2) offence, with the necessary changes.

Section 98 enacts a transitional provision for the coming into force of s. 91. Under s. 117.11, the onus is on D that s/he has the necessary licence or registration certificate.

Case Law

Weapon [See also s. 2]

R. v. K. (A.) (1991), 68 C.C.C. (3d) 135 (B.C. C.A.) — There is *no* requirement that the device come within "weapon" as defined in s. 2. D will be convicted of the offence of possession of a prohibited weapon where P proves that the Governor-In-Council has declared the device to be a prohibited weapon, and that D *knowingly* had it in his/her possession.

R. v. Ferguson (1985), 20 C.C.C. (3d) 256 (Ont. C.A.) — The nature of the offence of possession of a prohibited weapon under this section being possession, the acceptable amount of adaptation and the time span required to render an inoperable gun operable, so as to bring it within the definition of weapon for the purposes of this section, is longer than that required for a conviction for use of a firearm. In the latter case, the adaptation must be capable of being made on the scene in order to support the charge.

Restricted Weapon

R. v. Watkins (1987), 33 C.C.C. (3d) 465 (B.C. C.A.) — Although the only way a pistol could be fired was by using two hands, it was a "restricted weapon" because it was "designed" to be fired by the action of one hand.

Registration Certificate

R. v. Bibeau (1990), 1 C.R. (4th) 397, 61 C.C.C. (3d) 339 (Que. C.A.) — *See also*: *R. v. Létourneux* (1990), 62 C.C.C. (3d) 451 (Que. C.A.) — The obligation to have a registration certificate arises when D obtains possession of the weapon, not afterwards. It is no defence that D may later have intended to have the weapon registered. Section 91(4)(c) [now subsumed in s. 91(4)(b)(ii)] only applies where D, from the outset, was justified in acquiring the weapon without first having obtained a certificate.

Mental Element: S. 91(2)

R. v. Baxter (1982), 6 C.C.C. (3d) 447 (Alta. C.A.) — D's belief that the weapon was legal was a mistake of law, not fact, and afforded no defence where D was aware of the weapon's characteristics which caused it to be prohibited.

R. v. K. (A.) (1991), 68 C.C.C. (3d) 135 (B.C. C.A.) — The *mental element* involves *knowledge or recklessness* with respect to the *characteristics* of the device which make it a prohibited weapon. It is no defence that D did *not* intend to use the device for an unlawful purpose, or know that it was a prohibited weapon.

R. v. Richard (1981), 24 C.R. (3d) 373, 63 C.C.C. (2d) 333 (N.B. C.A.) — Possession of a prohibited weapon is a strict liability offence. Once P proves "possession" and that the object is a "prohibited weapon", the burden is on D to establish by a preponderance of evidence that he did not know that the knife could be opened by applying centrifugal force to the blade or that he could not have acquired such knowledge by taking reasonable care.

R. v. Archer (1983), 6 C.C.C. (3d) 129 (Ont. C.A.) — It is a defence to a charge under this section that D lacked any knowledge regarding the characteristics which rendered a knife, not designed to be such, a prohibited weapon.

R. v. Phillips (1978), 44 C.C.C. (2d) 548 (Ont. C.A.) — *Mens rea* is an essential element of the offence. Ignorance of the fact that a knife opened automatically by gravity or centrifugal force is a good defence. The necessary guilty knowledge may, however, be inferred from the possession of a knife which is, in fact, a prohibited weapon, and the burden of raising a reasonable doubt of guilty knowledge passes to D.

Res Judicata

R. v. Singh (1983), 8 C.C.C. (3d) 38 (Ont. C.A.) — A conviction of possession of a restricted weapon and of carrying a concealed weapon did not offend the rule against multiple convictions. The two offences contain elements distinct from each other. A concealed weapon need not be a restricted weapon.

Charter Considerations

R. v. Schwartz (1988), 66 C.R. (3d) 251, 45 C.C.C. (3d) 97 (S.C.C.) — A provision making it an offence to possess a weapon for which the proper registration has *not* been obtained creates a rule of evidence, and does *not* impose a reverse onus on D. D is *not* required to disprove any element of the offence or anything related to the offence. Even if such a provision infringes *Charter* s. 11(d), it is saved by s. 1.

Related Provisions: The relevant definitions, except for "firearm", are found in s. 84. Possession may be proven in accordance with s. 4(3).

Other possession offences are contained in ss. 88, 89, 90 and 92-96.

A prohibition order is discretionary under s. 110 on conviction or discharge, unless it becomes mandatory under s. 109(1)(d). Forfeiture is required under s. 491.

In summary conviction proceedings, the maximum punishment is governed by *Code* s. 787(1).

92. (1) Possession of firearm knowing its possession is unauthorized — Subject to subsections (4) and (5) and section 98, every person commits an offence who possesses a firearm knowing that the person is not the holder of

(a) a licence under which the person may possess it; and

(b) a registration certificate for the firearm.

(2) Possession of prohibited weapon, device or ammunition knowing its possession is unauthorized — Subject to subsection (4) and section 98, every person commits an offence who possesses a prohibited weapon, a restricted weapon, a prohibited device, other than a replica firearm, or any prohibited ammunition knowing that the person is not the holder of a licence under which the person may possess it.

(3) Punishment — Every person who commits an offence under subsection (1) or (2) is guilty of an indictable offence and liable

    (a) in the case of a first offence, to imprisonment for a term not exceeding ten years;

    (b) in the case of a second offence, to imprisonment for a term not exceeding ten years and to a minimum punishment of imprisonment for a term of one year; and

    (c) in the case of a third or subsequent offence, to imprisonment for a term not exceeding ten years and to a minimum punishment of imprisonment for a term of two years less a day.

(4) Exceptions — Subsections (1) and (2) do not apply to

    (a) a person who possesses a firearm, a prohibited weapon, a restricted weapon, a prohibited device or any prohibited ammunition while the person is under the direct and immediate supervision of a person who may lawfully possess it, for the purpose of using it in a manner in which the supervising person may lawfully use it; or

    (b) a person who comes into possession of a firearm, a prohibited weapon, a restricted weapon, a prohibited device or any prohibited ammunition by the operation of law and who, within a reasonable period after acquiring possession of it,

        (i) lawfully disposes of it, or

        (ii) obtains a licence under which the person may possess it and, in the case of a firearm, a registration certificate for the firearm.

(5) Borrowed firearm for sustenance — Subsection (1) does not apply to a person who possesses a firearm that is neither a prohibited firearm nor a restricted firearm and who is not the holder of a registration certificate for the firearm if the person

    (a) has borrowed the firearm;

    (b) is the holder of a licence under which the person may possess it; and

    (c) is in possession of the firearm to hunt or trap in order to sustain the person or the person's family.

(6) Evidence for previous conviction — Where a person is charged with an offence under subsection (1), evidence that the person was convicted of an offence under subsection 112(1) of the *Firearms Act* is admissible at any stage of the proceedings and may be taken into consideration for the purpose of proving that the person knew that the person was not the holder of a registration certificate for the firearm to which the offence relates.

1995, c. 39, s. 139.

Commentary: This section is remarkably similar to s. 91, both in the offences it creates and the exemptions it permits.

The inclusion of "knowing" in the liability-creating provisions of ss. 92(1) and (2) makes it plain, as s. 117.11 confirms by its omission of any reference to the section, that the *onus* of proving the *absence* of required authorization, and D's *knowledge* of it, is part of P's case. P's proof of knowledge may be helped by introduction of D's prior conviction under s. 112(1) *F.A.*

Related Provisions: The offence of s. 91 would seem to be an included offence in the crimes described in ss. 92(1) and (2), as a result of *Code* s. 662(1).

Other related provisions are described in the corresponding note to s. 91.

93. (1) Possession at unauthorized place — Subject to subsection (3) and section 98, every person commits an offence who, being the holder of an authorization or a licence under which the person may possess a firearm, a prohibited weapon, a restricted weapon, a prohibited device or prohibited ammunition, possesses the firearm, prohibited weapon, restricted weapon, prohibited device or prohibited ammunition at a place that is

(a) indicated on the authorization or licence as being a place where the person may not possess it;

(b) other than a place indicated on the authorization or licence as being a place where the person may possess it; or

(c) other than a place where it may be possessed under the *Firearms Act*.

(2) Punishment — Every person who commits an offence under subsection (1)

(a) is guilty of an indictable offence and liable to imprisonment for a term not exceeding five years; or

(b) is guilty of an offence punishable on summary conviction.

(3) Exception — Subsection (1) does not apply to a person who possesses a replica firearm.

1995, c. 39, s. 139

Commentary: This section makes it an offence, triable either way, to *possess* a firearm or regulated item at an *unauthorized place*. The provision does *not* apply to replica firearms.

The *external circumstances* consist of several elements. D must be the holder of a licence or authorization for a firearm or regulated item. D must be in *possession* of the firearm or regulated item. The *place* of possession must be some place *other* than where the authorization, licence or F.A. allows it to be.

There is *no* ulterior *mental element* required under this section.

Related Provisions: "Firearm" is defined in s. 2, the other regulated items in s. 84(1), along with "licence" and "authorization".

Under s. 117.12(2), P may file a certified copy of the licence or authorization to prove *where* D is permitted to have the firearm or item. The *onus* is on D under s. 117.11 to prove that s/he is the holder of the licence or authorization.

A prohibition is discretionary on conviction or discharge under s. 110, unless s. 109(1)(d) applies. The weapons are forfeited on conviction under s. 491.

Where P proceeds by indictment, D may elect mode of trial under s. 536(2). Summary conviction proceedings are governed by Part XXVII and punishment by s. 787(1).

94. (1) Unauthorized possession in motor vehicle — Subject to subsections (3) to (5) and section 98, every person commits an offence who is an occupant of a motor vehicle in which the person knows there is a firearm, a prohibited weapon, a restricted weapon, a prohibited device, other than a replica firearm, or any prohibited ammunition, unless

(a) in the case of a firearm,

(i) the person or any other occupant of the motor vehicle is the holder of

(A) an authorization or a licence under which the person or other occupant may possess the firearm and, in the case of a prohibited firearm or a restricted firearm, transport the prohibited firearm or restricted firearm, and

(B)   a registration certificate for the firearm,

(ii) the person had reasonable grounds to believe that any other occupant of the motor vehicle was the holder of

(A)   an authorization or a licence under which that other occupant may possess the firearm and, in the case of a prohibited firearm or a restricted firearm, transport the prohibited firearm or restricted firearm, and

(B)   a registration certificate for the firearm, or

(iii) the person had reasonable grounds to believe that any other occupant of the motor vehicle was a person who could not be convicted of an offence under this Act by reason of sections 117.07 to 117.1 or any other Act of Parliament; and

(b) in the case of a prohibited weapon, a restricted weapon, a prohibited device or any prohibited ammunition,

(i) the person or any other occupant of the motor vehicle is the holder of an authorization or a licence under which the person or other occupant may transport the prohibited weapon, restricted weapon, prohibited device or prohibited ammunition, or

(ii) the person had reasonable grounds to believe that any other occupant of the motor vehicle was

(A)   the holder of an authorization or a licence under which the other occupant may transport the prohibited weapon, restricted weapon, prohibited device or prohibited ammunition, or

(B)   a person who could not be convicted of an offence under this Act by reason of sections 117.07 to 117.1 or any other Act of Parliament.

(2) **Punishment** — Every person who commits an offence under subsection (1)

(a) is guilty of an indictable offence and liable to imprisonment for a term not exceeding ten years; or

(b) is guilty of an offence punishable on summary conviction.

(3) **Exception** — Subsection (1) does not apply to an occupant of a motor vehicle who, on becoming aware of the presence of the firearm, prohibited weapon, restricted weapon, prohibited device or prohibited ammunition in the motor vehicle, attempted to leave the motor vehicle, to the extent that it was feasible to do so, or actually left the motor vehicle.

(4) **Exception** — Subsection (1) does not apply to an occupant of a motor vehicle where the occupant or any other occupant of the motor vehicle is a person who came into possession of the firearm, prohibited weapon, restricted weapon, prohibited device or prohibited ammunition by the operation of law.

(5) **Borrowed firearm for sustenance** — Subsection (1) does not apply to an occupant of a motor vehicle where the occupant or any other occupant of the motor vehicle is a person who possesses a firearm that is neither a prohibited firearm nor a restricted firearm and who is not the holder of a registration certificate for the firearm if the person

(a) has borrowed the firearm;

(b) is the holder of a licence under which the person may possess it; and

(c) is in possession of the firearm to hunt or trap in order to sustain the person or the person's family.

1995, c. 39, s. 139.

Commentary: This section merges parts of former sections 90(2) (prohibited weapon) and 91(3) (restricted weapon) into a single crime that deals with illegal possession of firearms and other regulated items in motor vehicles. The offences are subject to the exemptions of ss. 94(3)-(5) and the transitional provisions of s. 98.

The *external circumstances* involve several elements. D must be an *occupant* of a *motor vehicle*. There must be a *firearm* or other regulated *item in* the motor vehicle. No one in the motor vehicle has the relevant authority to have the firearm or item there. The critical feature of the *mental element* is that D *knows* that a firearm or other regulated item is *in* the motor vehicle. Where the item is a restricted or prohibited weapon, D must also *know* or be *reckless* with respect to the characteristics of the item that make it a prohibited or restricted weapon.

D will *not* be found guilty of the offence under s. 94(1) if

i.   D or *any* other *occupant* of the vehicle has the requisite *authority* to have the firearm or regulated item;

ii. D *reasonably* believes that another occupant of the vehicle has the necessary authority to have the firearm or regulated item; or,

iii. D *reasonably* believes that any other occupant is a person who could *not* be convicted of a *Code* offence because of ss. 117.07 - 117.1 or another federal Act.

There are also several exceptions to the offence created by s. 94(1). Under s. 94(3), a person who leaves or tries to leave the motor vehicle, to the extent that it is feasible to do so, on learning that a firearm or regulated item is in it, is *not* liable to conviction. No liability attaches under s. 94(4) where the person comes into possession of the firearm or other regulated item by operation of law. Under s. 94(5), the prohibition does *not* apply to cases where an occupant has a firearms possession licence and borrowed the firearm for sustenance hunting purposes. The transition provisions of s. 98 also apply to this offence.

Case Law

Mental Element

R. v. Watters (1977), 18 N.B.R. (2d) 274 (C.A.) — D need not know that the weapon was restricted. It is sufficient that they were aware of its presence in the car and of the characteristics which rendered it a restricted weapon.

R. v. Green; R. v. Rawlins (1993), 5 M.V.R. (3d) 280 (Ont. C.A.) — It is an essential element of the offence under [former] s. 91(3) [now subsumed in s. 94(1)] that D is the occupant of a vehicle in which D *knows* there is a restricted weapon. D's *knowledge* may be established by direct or circumstantial evidence.

Related Provisions: "Firearm" and "motor vehicle" are defined in s. 2, the other relevant terms in s. 84(1).

Sections 117.07 - 117.1 define several categories of persons who are exempt from conviction under the *Code* and *F.A.*, notwithstanding that their conduct may constitute a *prima facie* breach.

Upon conviction or discharge of a s. 94(1) offence, D may be the subject of a prohibition order under s. 110. Where the circumstances of s. 109(1)(d) apply, a prohibition order is mandatory. Any weapons that are the subject-matter of the offence are forfeited under s. 491.

The offence of s. 94(1) is triable either way. Where P elects to proceed by indictment, D may elect mode of trial under s. 536(1). Where P proceeds by summary conviction, Part XXVII and s. 787(1) apply.

95. (1) Possession of prohibited or restricted firearm with ammunition —

Subject to subsection (3) and section 98, every person commits an offence who, in any place, possesses a loaded prohibited firearm or restricted firearm, or an unloaded pro-

129

hibited firearm or restricted firearm together with readily accessible ammunition that is capable of being discharged in the firearm, unless the person is the holder of

(a) an authorization or a licence under which the person may possess the firearm in that place; and

(b) the registration certificate for the firearm.

(2) Punishment — Every person who commits an offence under subsection (1)

(a) is guilty of an indictable offence and liable to imprisonment for a term not exceeding ten years and to a minimum punishment of imprisonment for a term of one year, or

(b) is guilty of an offence punishable on summary conviction and liable to imprisonment for a term not exceeding one year.

(3) Exception — Subsection (1) does not apply to a person who is using the firearm under the direct and immediate supervision of another person who is lawfully entitled to possess it and is using the firearm in a manner in which that other person may lawfully use it.

1995, c. 39, s. 139.

Commentary: This new offence prohibits and punishes unauthorized possession of *loaded* prohibited or restricted firearms or *unloaded* weapons of the same kind with readily *accessible ammunition* suitable for firing in them. The offence is triable either way. Conviction in indictable proceedings requires a minimum punishment of imprisonment for a term of one year.

The offence created by s. 95(1) and punished in s. 95(2) is subject to the operation of the transitional provisions in s. 98 and the supervised and authorized use exception of s. 95(3).

The *external circumstances* require proof of four elements:

i.   that D possessed a *firearm*;

ii.   that the firearm was a *prohibited* or *restricted* firearm;

iii.   that the firearm was *loaded*, or *unloaded* with *readily accessible ammunition* capable of firing in the weapon; and,

iv.   that D did *not* have an authorization, licence or registration certificate for the firearm.

The *mental element* does *not* require proof of any *ulterior* state of mind. It is necessary, however, that P prove that D *knew* or was *reckless* with respect to the characteristics of the weapon that made it a restricted or prohibited firearm.

Related Provisions: The relevant terms are defined in s. 84(1). Possession is determined in accordance with s. 4(3). A prohibition is *mandatory* upon conviction of this offence under s. 109(1)(b). The weapons are forfeited upon conviction under *Code* s. 491.

Where P proceeds by indictment, D may elect mode of trial under s. 536(2). Upon conviction, however, D is liable to a minimum punishment of imprisonment for one year. Summary conviction proceedings are governed by Part XXVII and punishment by s. 787(1).

96. (1) Possession of weapon obtained by commission of offence — Subject to subsection (3), every person commits an offence who possesses a firearm, a prohibited weapon, a restricted weapon, a prohibited device or any prohibited ammunition that the person knows was obtained by the commission in Canada of an offence or by an act or omission anywhere that, if it had occurred in Canada, would have constituted an offence.

(2) Punishment — Every person who commits an offence under subsection (1)

(a) is guilty of an indictable offence and liable to imprisonment for a term not exceeding ten years and to a minimum punishment of imprisonment for a term of one year; or

**(b) is guilty of an offence punishable on summary conviction and liable to impris-
onment for a term not exceeding one year.**

(3) Exception — Subsection (1) does not apply to a person who comes into possession of anything referred to in that subsection by the operation of law and who lawfully
disposes of it within a reasonable period after acquiring possession of it.

1995, c. 39, s. 139.

Commentary: This section creates a new offence, one whose essential elements might be characterized as a specific application of the general possession offence in s. 354. It is triable either way. On
conviction in proceedings by indictment, there is a *minimum punishment* of imprisonment for a term of
one year.

There are several constituents in the *external circumstances*. D must *possess* a firearm or other regulated
item. The item must have been *obtained* by crime. The predicate offence by which the firearm or item
was obtained may have occurred in Canada, or as a result of an act or omission some place else that
would be an offence in Canada if it had occurred here.

The critical feature of the *mental element* is *knowledge*. D must *know* or be *reckless* with respect to the
characteristics of the weapon that make it a firearm or other regulated item. D must *know* or be *reckless*
with respect to the spurious origins of the property, though *not* the legal character of the predicate offence. No ulterior mental element is required.

Section 96(3) enacts an *exception* or exemption from the offence created by s. 96(1). A person who gets
possession of a firearm or regulated item by operation of law and who doesn't have the required documentation, is exempt from liability if s/he disposes of the item within a *reasonable* time.

Related Provisions: What constitutes possession is defined in Code s. 4(3).

There are several familiar means by which P may try to prove D's *knowledge* of the spurious *origins* of
the firearm or regulated item. D may have made an *admission*. P may rely on the familiar inference a
trier of fact may draw from D's *possession* of *recently-stolen* firearms or regulated items. The provisions
of ss. 359 and 360 are *not* available to P in prosecutions under s. 96.

"Firearm" is defined in s. 2, the other relevant items in s. 84(1).

The general possession offence is contained in s. 354. In cases governed by that section, which could
include as subject-matter any of the items described in s. 96(1), the special evidentiary rules of ss. 359
and 360 apply, as does s. 358, that declares when possession is complete.

Conviction or discharge *may* attract a prohibition order under s. 110. Where the circumstances of s.
109(1)(d) apply, the order is mandatory. The *forfeiture* provisions of s. 491 apply to weapons that are the
subject-matter of the offence.

Where P proceeds by *indictment*, D may elect mode of trial. Conviction requires a *minimum* prison
sentence of one year. Summary conviction proceedings are governed by Part XXVII and punishment by
s. 787(1).

Authorization may be given in relation to this offence under Part VI.

97. (1) Delivery of firearm to person without firearms acquisition certifi-
cate — Every one who sells, barters, gives, lends, transfers or delivers any firearm to a
person who does not, at the time of the sale, barter, giving, lending, transfer or delivery
or, in the case of a mail–order sale, within a reasonable time prior thereto, produce a
firearms acquisition certificate for inspection by the person selling, bartering, giving,
lending, transferring or delivering the firearm, that that person has no reason to believe is invalid or was issued to a person other than the person so producing it,

    **(a) is guilty of an indictable offence and liable to imprisonment for a term not
exceeding two years; or**

    (b) is guilty of an offence punishable on summary conviction.

(2) **Saving provision** — Subsection (1) does not apply to a person

(a) lawfully in possession of a firearm who lends the firearm

(i) to a person for use by that person in his company and under his guidance or supervision in the same manner in which he may lawfully use it,

(ii) to a person who requires the firearm to hunt or trap in order to sustain himself or his family, or

(iii) to a person who is the holder of a permit issued under subsection 110(1), (6), or (7) permitting the lawful possession of the firearm;

(b) who returns a firearm to a person who lent it to him in circumstances described in paragraph (a);

(c) who comes into possession of a firearm in the ordinary course of a business described in paragraph 105(1)(a) and who returns the firearm to the person from whom it is received; or

(d) who is a peace officer, local registrar of firearms or firearms officer who returns a firearm to a person who had lawfully possessed the firearm and subsequently lost it or from whom it had been stolen.

(3) **Acquisistion of firearm without firearms acquisition certificate** — Every one who imports or otherwise acquires possession in any manner whatever of a firearm while he is not the holder of a firearms acquisition certificate

(a) is guilty of an indictable offence and liable to imprisonment for a term not exceeding two years; or

(b) is guilty of an offence punishable on summary conviction.

(4) **Saving provision** — Subsection (3) does not apply to a person who

(a) acquires a firearm in circumstances such that, by virtue of subsection (2), subsection (1) does not apply to the person from whom he acquires the firearm;

(b) reacquires a firearm from a person to whom he lent the firearm;

(c) imports a firearm at a time when he is not a resident of Canada;

(d) comes into possession of a firearm by operation of law and thereafter, with reasonable despatch, lawfully disposes of it or obtains a firearms acquisition certificate under which he could have lawfully acquired the firearm;

(e) comes into possession of a firearm in the ordinary course of a business described in paragraph 105(1)(a) or (b) or 105(2)(a) or (b); or

(f) has lawfully possessed a firearm and has subsequently lost it, or from whom it had been stolen, and who then reacquires it from a peace officer, local registrar of firearms or firearms officer or finds it and so reports to a peace officer, local registrar of firearms or firearms officer.

1991, c. 40, ss. 10, 38.

Proposed Amendment — 97

97. (1) **Sale of cross-bow to person without licence** — Every person commits an offence who at any time sells, barters or gives a cross-bow to another person, unless the other person produces for inspection by the person at that time a licence that the person has no reasonable grounds to believe is invalid or was issued to anyone other than the other person.

(2) Punishment — Every person who commits an offence under subsection (1)

    (a) is guilty of an indictable offence and liable to imprisonment for a term not exceeding two years; or

    (b) is guilty of an offence punishable on summary conviction.

(3) Exception — Subsection (1) does not apply to a person who lends a cross-bow to another person while that other person is under the direct and immediate supervision of a person who may lawfully possess it.

1995, c. 39, s. 139 [Not in force at date of publication.]

Commentary: This new offence governs the transfer of cross-bows. It imposes a *duty* on the transferor to make sure that the recipient has a valid licence for the cross-bow.

The offence of s. 97(1) is triable either way. The *external circumstances* involve the transfer, by sale, barter, or gift, of a cross-bow to another person. There must also be a *failure* by the recipient to *produce* a valid licence for D to inspect. Under s. 117.11, D bears the *onus* of proving that the recipient had a valid licence. D must be acquitted if s/he had *reasonable* grounds to *believe* that the *licence* was *valid*, even if it was not.

The *mental element* does *not* require proof of any ulterior state of mind.

Section 97(3) exempts from liability anyone in *lawful* possession of a cross-bow who *lends* it to another person whom s/he directly supervises.

Related Provisions: "Cross-bow" and "licence" are defined in s. 84(1).

Conviction or discharge *may* attract a prohibition order under s. 110. An order is only required where the circumstances of s. 109(1)(d) apply. Section 491 authorizes forfeiture of weapons that are the subject-matter of an offence.

Where P elects to proceed by *indictment*, D may elect mode of trial under s. 536(2). Summary conviction proceedings are governed by Part XXVII and punishment by s. 787(1).

98. (1) Transitional — licences — Every person who, immediately before the coming into force of any of subsections 91(1), 92(1), 93(1), 94(1) and 95(1), possessed a firearm without a firearm acquisition certificate because

    (a) the person possessed the firearm before January 1, 1979, or

    (b) the firearm acquisition certificate under which the person had acquired the firearm had expired,

shall be deemed for the purposes of that subsection to be, until January 1, 2001 or such other earlier date as is prescribed, the holder of a licence under which the person may possess the firearm.

(2) Transitional — licences — Every person who, immediately before the coming into force of any subsections 91(1), 92(1), 93(1), 94(1) and 95(1), possessed a firearm and was the holder of a firearm acquisition certificate shall be deemed for the purposes of that subsection to be, until January 1, 2001 or such other earlier date as is prescribed, the holder of a licence under which the person may possess the firearm.

(3) Transitional — registration certificates — Every person who, at any particular time between the coming into force of subsection 91(1), 92(1) or 94(1) and the later of January 1, 1998 and such other date as is prescribed, possesses a firearm that, as of that particular time, is not a prohibited firearm or a restricted firearm shall be deemed for the purposes of that subsection to be, until January 1, 2003 or such other earlier date as is prescribed, the holder of a registration certificate for that firearm.

1995, c. 39, s. 139.

Commentary: This section modifies certain offences to permit possession of firearms without licences and registration certificates during the transitional period.

Anyone who has a valid *F.A.C.* prior to ss. 91(1), 92(1), 93(1), 94(1) or 95(1) coming into force is *deemed* to have a *licence* until January 1, 2001, after which the person will have to get a licence to possess or acquire firearms. Anyone whose *F.A.C.* expires before the listed sections come into force, or who had the firearms before January 1, 1979, is deemed to have a licence until January 1, 2001, after which the person will have to get a licence to possess or acquire firearms.

Under s. 98(3), anyone who had a non-restricted firearm prior to ss. 91(1), 92(1), or 94(1) coming into force is *deemed* to have *registration certificates* for the firearms until January 1, 2003, after which the person will have to get a registration certificate for *each* firearm.

Related Provisions: Section 91(1) creates a new offence of unauthorized possession of a firearm. Section 92(1) makes it an offence to *knowingly* possess a firearm or other regulated item without a licence and registration certificate. The offence of s. 93(1) deals with possession of a firearm or other regulated item at an unauthorized place. Under s. 94(1), it is an offence to have unauthorized possession of a firearm or other regulated item in a motor vehicle. Section 95(1) is a new offence involving possession of loaded restricted or prohibited firearms or unloaded weapons of the same nature with readily-accessible ammunition suitable for use in them.

Sections 120-135 of the *Firearms Act* contain transitional provisions that deem certain documents issued under the previous legislation to be valid under the new regime for a specified time. In essence, people have until January 1, 2001, to get a licence to possess or acquire firearms and other regulated items. They have until January 1, 2003, to obtain a registration certificate for their firearms.

99. **(1) Weapons trafficking** — Every person commits an offence who

    (a) manufactures or transfers, whether or not for consideration, or

    (b) offers to do anything referred to in paragraph (*a*) in respect of

a firearm, a prohibited weapon, a restricted weapon, a prohibited device, any ammunition or any prohibited ammunition knowing that the person is not authorized to do so under the *Firearms Act* or any other Act of Parliament or any regulations made under any Act of Parliament.

(2) Punishment — Every person who commits an offence under subsection (1) is guilty of an indictable offence and liable to imprisonment for a term not exceeding ten years and to a minimum punishment of imprisonment for a term of one year.

1995, c. 39, s. 139.

Commentary: This section creates an offence that may generally be described as *trafficking* in firearms or other regulated items, *without* proper authorization.

The *external circumstances* involve traffic in a firearm or other regulated item. Trafficking may involve transfer, manufacture or an offer to do either. D must not be authorized to manufacture or transfer the firearm or other regulated item.

The essential feature of the *mental element* is D's *knowledge* that s/he was *not* authorized to manufacture or transfer the relevant item, or offer to do so. No ulterior state of mind is required.

Related Provisions: The relevant definitions, apart from "firearm" that is defined in s. 2, appear in s. 84(1).

The offence of s. 100 could be viewed as a preparatory or preliminary crime to the offence described in s. 99. The former could be described as *possession* for the *purpose* of *trafficking* in firearms or other regulated items.

Upon conviction, a *prohibition* order is *mandatory* under s. 109. Section 491 governs forfeiture of any weapons that are the subject-matter of the offence.

The offence is indictable only and carries a one-year minimum punishment on conviction.

100. (1) Possession for purpose of weapons trafficking — Every person commits an offence who possesses a firearm, a prohibited weapon, a restricted weapon, a prohibited device, any ammunition or any prohibited ammunition for the purpose of

(a) transferring it, whether or not for consideration, or

(b) offering to transfer it,

knowing that the person is not authorized to transfer it under the *Firearms Act* or any other Act of Parliament or any regulations made under any Act of Parliament.

(2) Punishment — Every person who commits an offence under subsection (1) is guilty of an indictable offence and liable to imprisonment for a term not exceeding ten years and to a minimum punishment of imprisonment for a term of one year.

1995, c. 39, s. 139.

Commentary: Under this section, it is an offence to possess a firearm or other regulated item for the *purpose* of transferring or offering to transfer it to another person without proper authorization.

The *external circumstances* require that D possess a firearm or other regulated item. The critical feature of the *mental element* is the *purpose* that underlies D's possession. The firearm or regulated item must be kept for the purpose of transferring or offering to transfer it. D must also *know* that the transfer or offer to transfer is unauthorized.

This offence is strictly *indictable*. Upon conviction, it attracts a *minimum* term of imprisonment of one year and a maximum of ten years.

Related Provisions: "Firearm" is defined in s. 2, the other regulated items in s. 84(1) where "transfer" is also defined.

This offence may be regarded as a preliminary or preparatory crime to the offence in s. 99. The unauthorized transfer of firearms and other weapons and regulated items is prohibited by s. 101.

A prohibition order is mandatory on conviction. Weapons that are the subject-matter of the offence are forfeited under s. 491.

101. (1) Transfer without authority — Every person commits an offence who transfers a firearm, a prohibited weapon, a restricted weapon, a prohibited device, any ammunition or any prohibited ammunition to any person otherwise than under the authority of the *Firearms Act* or any other Act of Parliament or any regulations made under an Act of Parliament.

(2) Punishment — Every person who commits an offence under subsection (1)

(a) is guilty of an indictable offence and liable to imprisonment for a term not exceeding five years; or

(b) is guilty of an offence punishable on summary conviction.

1995, c. 39, s. 139

Commentary: This section combines elements of former ss. 93, 94, 96 and 97. It prohibits unauthorized *transfer* of a firearm or other regulated item.

The *external circumstances* require proof that D *transferred* a firearm or other regulated item. It is also essential for P to prove that the *transfer* was *unauthorized*, that is to say, done in some manner *not* permitted by *F.A.* or any other federal law or regulation.

The *mental element* involves *no* ulterior state of mind.

Related Provisions: Section 84(1) defines transfer and the several regulated items described in the section. "Firearm" is defined in s. 2.

A *prohibition* order is *discretionary* upon conviction or discharge under s. 110. Where the circumstances of s. 109(1)(d) apply, the order is mandatory. The weapons are forfeited on conviction under s. 491.

Where P proceeds by *indictment*, D may elect mode of trial under s. 536(2). Summary conviction proceedings are governed by Part XXVII and punishment by s. 787(1).

Assembling Offence

102. (1) Making automatic firearm — Every person commits an offence who, without lawful excuse, alters a firearm so that it is capable of, or manufactures or assembles any firearm that is capable of, discharging projectiles in rapid succession during one pressure of the trigger.

(2) Punishment — Every person who commits an offence under subsection (1)

(a) is guilty of an indictable offence and liable to imprisonment for a term not exceeding ten years and to a minimum punishment of imprisonment for a term of one year, or

(b) is guilty of an offence punishable on summary conviction and liable to imprisonment for a term not exceeding one year.

1995, c. 39, s. 139

Commentary: This section prohibits the *making* of automatic firearms.

The *external circumstances* require proof that D *make* an automatic firearm. D's conduct may include *alteration* of an existing firearm to make it capable of rapid-fire, or *manufacture* or *assemble* the firearm with rapid-fire capacity. P must also prove that D had *no* authority to make the weapons.

The *mental element* does *not* require proof of any ulterior state of mind.

The offence of s. 102(1) is triable either way. Conviction on *indictment* carries a *minimum* punishment on imprisonment for one year.

Related Provisions: "Firearm" is defined in s. 2, as is "automatic firearm", although the term is *not* itself used in s. 102. Section 104(1)(b) prohibits import or export of components for automatic firearms without proper authority.

A prohibition order is *mandatory* upon conviction under s. 109(1)(b), likewise *forfeiture* of the weapons under s. 491.

Where P elects to proceed by indictment, D may elect mode of trial under s. 536(2). Summary conviction proceedings are governed by Part XXVII and punishment by s. 787(1).

Authorization may be given to intercept private communications in relation to this offence.

Export and Import Offences

103. (1) Importing or exporting knowing it is unauthorized — Every person commits an offence who imports or exports

(a) a firearm, a prohibited weapon, a restricted weapon, a prohibited device or any prohibited ammunition, or

(b) any component or part designed exclusively for use in the manufacture of or assembly into an automatic firearm,

knowing that the person is not authorized to do so under the *Firearms Act* or any other Act of Parliament or any regulations made under an Act of Parliament.

(2) Punishment — Every person who commits an offence under subsection (1) is guilty of an indictable offence and liable to imprisonment for a term not exceeding ten years and to a minimum punishment of imprisonment for a term of one year.

(3) Attorney General of Canada may act — Any proceedings in respect of an offence under subsection (1) may be commenced at the instance of the Government of Canada and conducted by or on behalf of that government.

1995, c. 39, s. 139

Commentary: This section makes it an indictable offence to *knowingly* import or export firearms and other regulated items *without* authorization.

The *external circumstances* require proof that D imported or exported a firearm, other regulated item or a *component* or part designed *exclusively* for use in the manufacture or assembly of a firearm into an *automatic firearm*. D must not be authorized to engage in import or export.

The essential feature of the *mental element* is D's *knowledge* that s/he was not *authorized* to import or export the relevant item.

The offence of s. 103(1) is exclusively indictable. It carries a *minimum* punishment on conviction of imprisonment for one year. Under s. 103(3), proceedings may be instituted and conducted by the Government of Canada.

Related Provisions: "Firearm" is defined in s. 2, the other relevant terms in s. 84(1).

On conviction, a *prohibition* order is mandatory under s. 109(1)(b) and a *forfeiture* order is required under s. 491. The offence is one for which authorization to intercept private communications may be given under Part VI.

Section 102(1) prohibits making an automatic firearm. The offence of s. 104(1)(b) is similar to s. 103(1)(b), except for the *mental element* that does *not* require proof of *knowledge* as in s. 103(1)(b).

D may elect mode of trial under s. 536(2).

104. (1) Unauthorized importing or exporting — **Every person commits an offence who imports or exports**

(a) a firearm, a prohibited weapon, a restricted weapon, a prohibited device or any prohibited ammunition, or

(b) any component or part designed exclusively for use in the manufacture of or assembly into an automatic firearm,

otherwise than under the authority of the *Firearms Act* or any other Act of Parliament or any regulations made under an Act of Parliament.

(2) Punishment — **Every person who commits an offence under subsection (1)**

(a) is guilty of an indictable offence and liable to imprisonment for a term not exceeding five years; or

(b) is guilty of an offence punishable on summary conviction.

(3) Attorney General of Canada may act — **Any proceedings in respect of an offence under subsection (1) may be commenced at the instance of the Government of Canada and conducted by or on behalf of that government.**

1995, c. 39, s. 139

Commentary: This offence, unauthorized importing or exporting firearms or other regulated devices, re-groups parts of former ss. 95(1), 96(3) and 97(3) and expands their subject-matter beyond prohibited weapons.

The *external circumstances* involve *import* or *export* of firearm, other regulated item or a component or part designed *exclusively* for use in the manufacture or assembly of automatic firearms. D must *not* be authorized to import or export the relevant item. Section 117.11 puts the onus of proving the relevant authority (licence, authorization and/or registration certificate) on D.

The *mental element* does *not* involve proof of any ulterior state of mind.

This offence is triable either way. It is also a crime in respect of which proceedings may be started and conducted by the Government of Canada.

Related Provisions: "Firearm" is defined in s. 2, the other relevant terms in s. 84(1).

This offence, and the crime described in s. 103, comprise the "export and import offences" in Part III. Possession offences are contained in ss. 88-101. The search and seizure provisions of the Part appear in ss. 117.02 - 117.06.

Where P proceeds by *indictment*, D may elect mode of trial. Summary conviction proceedings are governed by Part XXVII and punishment by s. 787(1).

Upon conviction, a *prohibition* order is *discretionary* under s. 110, *unless* s. 109(1)(d) applies when it becomes mandatory. Forfeiture is required under s. 491.

Offences relating to Lost, Destroyed or Defaced Weapons, etc.

105. (1) Losing or finding — Every person commits an offence who

(a) having lost a firearm, a prohibited weapon, a restricted weapon, a prohibited device, any prohibited ammunition, an authorization, a licence or a registration certificate, or having had it stolen from the person's possession, does not with reasonable despatch report the loss to a peace officer, to a firearms officer or a chief firearms officer, or

(b) on finding a firearm, a prohibited weapon, a restricted weapon, a prohibited device or any prohibited ammunition that the person has reasonable grounds to believe has been lost or abandoned, does not with reasonable despatch deliver it to a peace officer, a firearms officer or a chief firearms officer or report the finding to a peace officer, a firearms officer or a chief firearms officer.

(2) Punishment — Every person who commits an offence under subsection (1)

(a) is guilty of an indictable offence and liable to imprisonment for a term not exceeding five years; or

(b) is guilty of an offence punishable on summary conviction.

1995, c. 39, s. 139

Commentary: This is the first of several sections relating to lost, destroyed or defaced weapons or documents. The offences created are crimes of *omission*. Each imposes a *duty* upon D as the loser or finder of designated items, as the case may be.

The *external circumstances* of s. 105(1)(a) consist of the *loss* of the firearm, regulated item or authorizing document. The loss may arise because of theft or misadventure. D must *fail* to *report* the loss with *reasonable despatch* to a designated authority.

The *external circumstances* of the offence in s. 105(b) involve the *finding* of an apparently *lost* or *abandoned* firearm or regulated item. D must *fail* to report the finding or *deliver* the object found with reasonable *despatch* to a designated authority.

In each case, *no* ulterior *mental element* need be proven.

Related Provisions: Except for "firearm", which is defined in s. 2, the relevant terms are defined in s. 84(1).

Section 106(1) creates a related offence of omission. It involves the failure to report the destruction of firearms or other regulated items.

A prohibition order is *discretionary* on conviction or discharge of this offence under s. 110, *unless* s. 109(1)(d) applies to make the order mandatory.

Where P proceeds by *indictment*, D may elect mode of trial under s. 536(2). Summary conviction proceedings are governed by Part XXVII and punishment determined by s. 787(1).

106. (1) Destroying — Every person commits an offence who

(a) after destroying any firearm, prohibited weapon, restricted weapon, prohibited device or prohibited ammunition, or

(b) on becoming aware of the destruction of any firearm, prohibited weapon, restricted weapon, prohibited device or prohibited ammunition that was in the person's possession before its destruction, does not with reasonable despatch report the destruction to a peace officer, firearms officer or chief firearms officer.

(2) Punishment — Every person who commits an offence under subsection (1)

(a) is guilty of an indictable offence and liable to imprisonment for a term not exceeding five years; or

(b) is guilty of an offence punishable on summary conviction.

1995, c. 39, s. 139

Commentary: This new offence, triable either way, involves a failure to report the *destruction* of a firearm or other regulated item. The prohibitions are similar in structure to the offences of s. 105.

The *external circumstances* of each offence involve the *destruction* of a firearm or other regulated item. Under s. 106(1)(a), it is D who destroys the relevant item, whereas under s. 106(1)(b), it is D's *awareness* of the destruction that imposes the obligation to report. There must also be a failure to report with *reasonable dispatch* the destruction of the weapon to a designated authority.

A principal component in the *mental element* under s. 106(1)(b) is *knowledge* of the weapon's destruction. No ulterior mental element has to be proven under either paragraph.

Related Provisions: Section 105(1) creates a related offence of omission in connection with lost or stolen weapons or documents and found weapons.

Other related provisions are discussed in the corresponding note to s. 105, *supra*.

107. (1) False statements — Every person commits an offence who knowingly makes, before a peace officer, firearms officer or chief firearms officer, a false report or statement concerning the loss, theft or destruction of a firearm, a prohibited weapon, a restricted weapon, a prohibited device, any prohibited ammunition, an authorization, a licence or a registration certificate.

(2) Punishment — Every person who commits an offence under subsection (1)

(a) is guilty of an indictable offence and liable to imprisonment for a term not exceeding five years; or

(b) is guilty of an offence punishable on summary conviction.

(3) Definition of "report" or "statement" — In this section, "report" or "statement" means an assertion of fact, opinion, belief or knowledge, whether material or not and whether admissible or not.

1995, c. 39, s. 139

Commentary: This is a new offence that, in some respects at least, is like mischief. It involves knowingly making a false statement to a person in authority about the loss, theft or destruction of a firearm or other regulated item.

The *external circumstances* involve a *false report* or *statement* made to a peace officer, firearms officer or chief firearms officer. The falsity must relate to the *loss, theft* or *destruction* of the firearm or other regulated item. "Statement" and "report" are defined in s. 107(3).

The critical feature of the *mental element* is D's *knowledge* of the *falsity* of the statement or report: it must be *knowingly* made. No ulterior mental element has to be proven.

The offence is triable either way.

Related Provisions: Section 108 prohibits tampering with serial numbers on firearms and having a firearm with knowledge that the serial number has been altered, defaced or removed.

Public mischief under s. 140 may be committed in a variety of ways. It requires proof of an intent to mislead.

"Firearm" is defined in s. 2, the other regulated items in s. 84(1).

Where P proceeds by indictment, D may elect mode of trial. Summary conviction proceedings are governed by Part XXVII and punished under s. 787(1).

108. (1) **Tampering with serial number** — Every person commits an offence who, without lawful excuse, the proof of which lies on the person,

    (a) alters, defaces or removes a serial number on a firearm; or

    (b) possesses a firearm knowing that the serial number on it has been altered, defaced or removed.

(2) **Punishment** — Every person who commits an offence under subsection (1)

    (a) is guilty of an indictable offence and liable to imprisonment for a term not exceeding five years; or

    (b) is guilty of an offence punishable on summary conviction.

(3) **Exception** — No person is guilty of an offence under paragraph (1)(b) by reason only of possessing a firearm the serial number on which has been altered, defaced or removed, where that serial number has been replaced and a registration certificate in respect of the firearm has been issued setting out a new serial number for the firearm.

(4) **Evidence** — In proceedings for an offence under subsection (1), evidence that a person possesses a firearm the serial number on which has been wholly or partially obliterated otherwise than through normal use over time is, in the absence of evidence to the contrary, proof that the person possesses the firearm knowing that the serial number on it has been altered, defaced or removed.

1995, c. 39, s. 139

Commentary: This section creates offences relating to firearms with tampered serial numbers. Both offences are triable either way.

Section 108(1)(a) is the *tampering* offence. The *external circumstances* require proof that D altered, defaced or removed a serial number on a firearm. D must have *no* lawful excuse for doing so. The *onus* of proving a lawful excuse is on D. The *mental element* does *not* require proof of any ulterior mental state.

The offence of s. 108(1)(b) is a *possession* offence. Its *external circumstances* involve *possession* of a *firearm* with an altered, defaced or missing serial number. D must have *no* lawful excuse for having the weapon. The *onus* of proving any excuse is on D. Under s. 108(3), there is no offence committed when the altered serial number has been replaced and a registration certificate issued for the new number.

The *mental element* requires proof that D *knew* of the *altered state* of the serial number. Proof of knowledge may be helped by the *rebuttable presumption* of s. 108(4). In essence, proof of *possession* of a firearm with an *altered* serial number is *proof* of *knowledge* of the *alteration*, absent evidence to the contrary.

Related Provisions: "Firearm" is defined in s. 2.

An evidentiary provision similar to s. 108(4) appears in s. 354(2) applicable to obliterated vehicle identification numbers on motor vehicles or parts in prosecutions for possession of property obtained by crime.

In summary conviction proceedings, s. 794(2) puts the onus on D to establish a lawful excuse. The proceedings are governed by Part XXVII and punished under s. 787(1).

Whether a *prohibition* order is made on conviction is *discretionary* under s. 110, *unless* s. 109(1)(d) applies to make it mandatory. The weapons are forfeited under s. 491.

109. (1) **Mandatory prohibition order** — Where a person iis convicted, or discharged under section 730, of

        (a) an indictable offence in the commission of which violence against a person was used, threatened or attempted and for which the person may be sentenced to imprisonment for ten years or more,

(b) an offence under subsection 85(1) (using firearm in commission of offence), subsection 85(2) (using imitation firearm in commission of offence), 95(1) (possession of prohibited or restricted firearm with ammunition), 99(1) (weapons trafficking), 100(1) (possession for purpose of weapons trafficking), 102(1) (making automatic firearm), 103(1) (importing or exporting knowing it is unauthorized) or section 264 (criminal harassment),

(c) an offence relating to the contravention of subsection 6(1) or (2) or 7(1) or (2) of the *Controlled Drugs and Substances Act*, or

(d) an offence that involves, or the subject-matter of which is, a firearm, a cross-bow, a prohibited weapon, a restricted weapon, a prohibited device, any ammunition, any prohibited ammunition or an explosive substance and, at the time of the offence, the person was prohibited by any order made under this Act or any other Act of Parliament from possessing any such thing

the court that sentences the person or directs that the person be discharged, as the case may be, shall, in addition to any other punishment that may be imposed for that offence or any other condition prescribed in the order of discharge, make an order prohibiting the person from possessing any firearm, cross-bow, prohibited weapon, restricted weapon, prohibited device, ammunition, prohibited ammunition and explosive substance during the period specified in the order as determined in accordance with subsection (2) or (3), as the case may be.

(2) Duration of prohibition order — first offence — An order made under subsection (1) shall, in the case of a first conviction for or discharge from the offence to which the order relates, prohibit the person from possessing

(a) any firearm, other than a prohibited firearm or restricted firearm, and any cross-bow, restricted weapon, ammunition and explosive substance during the period that

(i) begins on the day on which the order is made, and

(ii) ends not earlier than ten years after the person's release from imprisonment after conviction for the offence or, if the person is not then imprisoned or subject to imprisonment, after the person's conviction for or discharge from the offence; and

(b) any prohibited firearm, restricted firearm, prohibited weapon, prohibited device and prohibited ammunition for life.

(3) Duration of prohibition order — subsequent offences — An order made under subsection (1) shall, in any case other than a case described in subsection (2), prohibit the person from possessing any firearm, cross-bow, restricted weapon, ammunition and explosive substance for life.

(4) Definition of "release from imprisonment" — In subparagraph (2)(a)(ii), "release from imprisonment" means release from confinement by reason of expiration of sentence, commencement of statutory release or grant of parole.

(5) Application of ss. 113 to 117 — Sections 113 to 117 apply in respect of every order made under subsection (1).

1995, c. 39, s. 190(d); 1996, c. 19, s. 65.1.

Commentary: This is the first of two sections that deals with *prohibition* orders. Under this section, the orders are *mandatory* where D is convicted or discharged of certain serious *indictable* offences, or of committing a weapons offence while bound by a prohibition order.

Section 109(1) describes the predicate offences and the scope of the prohibition order. Conviction or discharge of an offence listed or described in s. 109(1) *requires* an additional punishment that prohibits *possession* of any firearm or regulated item for periods specified and determined under ss. 109(2) and (3). "Release from imprisonment", a term of importance in s. 109(2)(a)(ii), is defined in s. 109(4). Under s. 109(5), ss. 113 - 117 apply to prohibition orders made under the section.

Case Law

Application-Jurisdiction

R. v. Myers (1984), 32 Alta. L.R. (2d) 97 (C.A.) — The court had jurisdiction to impose prohibition where D pleaded guilty to careless use of a firearm and no violence had been used or threatened. The phrase "in the commission of which violence against a person was used, threatened or attempted" refers only to offences other than offences involving the use of firearms.

R. v. Cardinal (1980), 52 C.C.C. (2d) 269, 22 A.R. 241 (C.A.) — To bring s. 100(1) into effect the offence referred to must, of itself, have an aspect of violence in its execution; whereas in s. 100(2) the offence is actually separate and independent of the violence itself, the violence being a mere incident or part of the background upon which the judge may exercise his discretion as to whether he should grant a prohibition order.

R. v. Blinch (1994), 90 C.C.C. (3d) 346 (B.C. C.A.) — A conviction of possession of a weapon for a purpose dangerous to the public peace attracts the mandatory firearms prohibition in s. 100(1), even though the weapon was a "firearm" as described in s. 100(2).

R. v. Howard (1981), 60 C.C.C. (2d) 344 (B.C. C.A.) — Section 100(1) applies even where D is not actually sentenced to a term of imprisonment or where violence is not an essential element of the offence but the violence was closely related to the commission of the offence.

R. v. Kenway (1990), 58 C.C.C. (3d) 414 (Ont. C.A.) — Section 100(1) applies where violence against a person is used, threatened or attempted in the commission of an offence. Violence need not be an ingredient of the offence of which D is convicted.

R. v. Keays (1983), 10 C.C.C. (3d) 229 (Ont. C.A.) — In determining whether for the purposes of s. 100(1) a conviction is to be considered a first conviction, convictions registered prior to the enactment of this section are to be taken into account.

R. v. Broome (1981), 24 C.R. (3d) 254, 63 C.C.C. (2d) 426 (Ont. C.A.) — *See also*: *R. v. Kenway* (1990), 58 C.C.C. (3d) 414 (Ont. C.A.) — Section 100(1) applies even where the circumstances of the indictable offence did not involve the use of firearms. The provisions of this section are mandatory and where the preconditions are met, an order of prohibition must be made.

R. v. Savard (1979), 11 C.R. (3d) 309, 55 C.C.C. (2d) 286 (Que. C.A.) — Section 100(1) applies despite the fact that the crime of violence committed did *not* involve the use of a firearm.

R. v. Bilous (1984), 34 Sask. R. 227 (C.A.) — Section 100(1) is not confined to firearm offences but extends to any indictable offence involving violence where a sentence of at least 10 years' imprisonment was possible.

Charter Considerations

R. v. Sawyer (1992), 78 C.C.C. (3d) 191 (S.C.C.) — *See also*: *R. v. Kelly* (1990), 80 C.R. (3d) 185, 59 C.C.C. (3d) 497, 4 C.R.R. (2d) 157, 41 O.A.C. 32 (C.A.); *R. v. Luke* (1994), 28 C.R. (4th) 93, 87 C.C.C. (3d) 121 (Ont. C.A.); leave to appeal refused (November 10, 1994), Doc. No. 24229 (S.C.C.) — Section 100 does *not* offend *Charter* s. 12.

Related Provisions: "Firearm", "explosive substance" and "weapon" are defined in s. 2, the other regulated items in s. 84(1).

Several other *Code* sections make provision for prohibition orders. Prohibition may be included, for example, as a condition of *judicial interim release* under s. 515(4.1) or a term of a probation order under s. 732.1. It may also be a condition of a *recognizance* under ss. 810(3.1), 810.01(5) and 810.2(5). *Preventive* prohibition orders may be made under ss. 111(5) and 117.05(4).

A *prohibition* order may be *lifted* for sustenance or employment purposes under s. 113. Section 114 requires *surrender* of items that are the subject of a prohibition order. *Forfeiture* is governed by s. 115 and *return* of otherwise forfeitable items to their lawful owner by s. 117. When a prohibition order takes effect, any lawful authority permitting possession of prohibited items is revoked or amended to the extent required by the order under s. 116.

Discretionary prohibition orders are governed by s. 110.

110. (1) Discretionary prohibition order — Where a person is convicted, or discharged under section 736, of

(a) an offence, other than an offence referred to in any of paragraphs 109(1)(a), (b) and (c), in the commission of which violence against a person was used, threatened or attempted, or

(b) an offence that involves, or the subject-matter of which is, a firearm, a cross-bow, a prohibited weapon, a restricted weapon, a prohibited device, ammunition, prohibited ammunition or an explosive substance and, at the time of the offence, the person was not prohibited by any order made under this Act or any other Act of Parliament from possessing any such thing,

the court that sentences the person or directs that the person be discharged, as the case may be, shall, in addition to any other punishment that may be imposed for that offence or any other condition prescribed in the order of discharge, consider whether it is desirable, in the interests of the safety of the person or of any other person, to make an order prohibiting the person from possessing any firearm, cross-bow, prohibited weapon, restricted weapon, prohibited device, ammunition, prohibited ammunition or explosive substance, or all such things, and where the court decides that it is so desirable, the court shall so order.

(2) Duration of prohibition order — An order made under subsection (1) against a person begins on the day on which the order is made and ends not later than ten years after the person's release from imprisonment after conviction for the offence to which the order relates or, if the person is not then imprisoned or subject to imprisonment, after the person's conviction for or discharge from the offence.

(3) Reasons — Where the court does not make an order under subsection (1), or where the court does make such an order but does not prohibit the possession of everything referred to in that subsection, the court shall include in the record a statement of the court's reasons for not doing so.

(4) Definition of "release from imprisonment" — In subsection (2), "release from imprisonment" means release from confinement by reason of expiration of sentence, commencement of statutory release or grant of parole.

(5) Application of ss. 113 to 117 — Sections 113 to 117 apply in respect of every order made under subsection (1).

1995, c. 39, s. 139, 190(e).

Commentary: This section provides for *discretionary* prohibition orders. Unlike the mandatory orders of s. 109, the discretionary prohibition in s. 110 does *not* have to be a *blanket* prohibition. Some, but *not* all of

i.   firearms;

ii.   cross-bows;

iii. prohibited weapons;

iv.   restricted weapons;

v.   prohibited devices;

vi.   ammunition; or,

vii. explosive substances

may be included.

The predicate offences on which a discretionary prohibition may be based are described in s. 110(1). They involve less serious offences than those described in s. 109(1)(a) - (c) or offences involving firearms or listed items committed when D was not bound by a prohibition. The court is required to *consider* the *desirability* of a prohibition based on *safety* concerns. The order may prohibit possession of some or all listed items. Reasons are required where no or a partial order is made.

The maximum term of a discretionary prohibition is ten (10) years from the date of conviction, discharge or "release from imprisonment", as defined in s. 110(4). Sections 113 - 117 apply to discretionary orders under s. 110(5). These provisions relate to

i.   *lifting* prohibition orders for sustenance or employment purposes (s. 113);

ii.   *surrender* of prohibited items (s. 114);

iii. *forfeiture* of prohibited items (s. 115);

iv.   *revocation* or *amendment* of documents (s. 116); and,

v.   *return* of property to lawful owner (s. 117).

Related Provisions: Related provisions are described in the corresponding note to s. 109, *supra*.

111. (1) Application for prohibition order — A peace officer, firearms officer or chief firearms officer may apply to a provincial court judge for an order prohibiting a person from possessing any firearm, cross-bow, prohibited weapon, restricted weapon, prohibited device, ammunition, prohibited ammunition or explosive substance, or all such things, where the peace officer, firearms officer or chief firearms officer believes on reasonable grounds that it is not desirable in the interests of the safety of the person against whom the order is sought or of any other person that the person against whom the order is sought should possess any such thing.

(2) Date for hearing and notice — On receipt of an application made under subsection (1), the provincial court judge shall fix a date for the hearing of the application and direct that notice of the hearing be given, in such manner as the provincial court judge may specify, to the person against whom the order is sought.

(3) Hearing of application — Subject to subsection (4), at the hearing of an application made under subsection (1), the provincial court judge shall hear all relevant evidence presented by or on behalf of the applicant and the person against whom the order is sought.

(4) Where hearing may proceed *ex parte* — A provincial court judge may proceed *ex parte* to hear and determine an application made under subsection (1) in the absence of the person against whom the order is sought in the same circumstances as those in which a summary conviction court may, under Part XXVII, proceed with a trial in the absence of the defendant.

(5) Prohibition order — Where, at the conclusion of a hearing of an application made under subsection (1), the provincial court judge is satisfied that the circumstances referred to in that subsection exist, the provincial court judge shall make an order prohibiting the person from possessing any firearm, cross-bow, prohibited weapon, restricted weapon, prohibited device, ammunition, prohibited ammunition or explosive substance, or all such things, for such period, not exceeding five years, as is specified in the order, beginning on the day on which the order is made.

(6) Reasons — Where a provincial court judge does not make an order under subsection (1), or where a provincial court judge does make such an order but does not prohibit the possession of everything referred to in that subsection, the provincial court judge shall include in the record a statement of the court's reasons.

(7) **Application of ss. 113 to 117** — Sections 113 to 117 apply in respect of every order made under subsection (5).

(8) **Appeal by person or Attorney General** — Where a provincial court judge makes an order under subsection (5), the person to whom the order relates, or the Attorney General, may appeal to the superior court against the order.

(9) **Appeal by Attorney General** — Where a provincial court judge does not make an order under subsection (5), the Attorney General, may appeal to the superior court against the decision not to make an order.

(10) **Application of Part XXVII to appeals** — The provisions of Part XXVII, except sections 785 to 812, 816 to 819 and 829 to 838, apply in respect of an appeal made under subsection (8) or (9), with such modifications as the circumstances require and as if each reference in that Part to the appeal court were a reference to the superior court.

(11) **Definition of "provincial court judge"** — In this section and sections 112, 117.011 and 117.012, "provincial court judge" means a provincial court judge having jurisdiction in the territorial division where the person against whom the application for an order was brought resides.

1995, c. 39, s. 139

Commentary: This is the first of two sections that permit a judicial officer to make *preventive prohibition* orders. The procedure involves several steps.

Section 111 becomes engaged when a *peace* officer, *firearms* officer or *chief firearms* officer applies to a *provincial court judge* in the territorial division where the respondent resides for an order of prohibition. There is no statutory form of application, but the applicant must have a *reasonably-grounded* belief that it is *not desirable* in the *interests* of the *safety* of the respondent or others that the respondent have any firearm or other regulated item listed in s. 111(1).

When the application is received, the provincial court judge must *fix* a date for hearing and *notify* the *respondent* in an appropriate manner of its time and place.

At the hearing, the provincial court judge is required to hear all *relevant* evidence that the applicant and respondent present. The hearing may be conducted in the absence of the respondent if the conditions that permit an *ex parte* summary conviction trial to be held have been met.

At the conclusion of the hearing, the judge must decide *whether* s/he is satisfied that it is *desirable* in the *interests* of the *safety* of the respondent or others that the respondent be prohibited from possessing some or all of the items listed in s. 111(1). Where the judge is so satisfied, s/he must make the prohibition order, which may incorporate ss. 113 - 117. Reasons are required under s. 111(6) where no or a partial order is made.

Appellate rights are governed by ss. 111(8) - (10). An *order* under s. 111(5) may be appealed by the Attorney General or respondent and the *failure* to make an order by the Attorney General only under ss. 111(8) and (9). The governing appellate provisions are ss. 813 - 815 and 820 - 828 of Part XXVII. The forum is the superior court of the province. Appeals are generally on the record at first instance, but s. 822(4) permits a hearing *de novo* in certain circumstances.

Case Law
Evidentiary Considerations

R. v. Zeolkowski, [1989] 4 W.W.R. 385 (S.C.C.); reversing (1987), 33 C.C.C. (3d) 231 (Man. C.A.) — Hearsay evidence is admissible at the hearing of an application under s. 100(6). It was not intended that the judge strictly apply the rules of evidence upon the hearing. The judge must simply be satisfied, on a balance of probabilities, that the peace officer had reasonable grounds for the belief. The phrase, "all relevant evidence", means all facts which are logically probative of the issue and does not exclude hearsay.

R. v. McWhirter (1982), 51 N.S.R. (2d) 181 (C.A.) — The words "all relevant evidence" in ss. 100(6) and (7) permit the admission of hearsay evidence since no accusation of a criminal offence is involved.

Exemptions: Ss. 100(1.1), (1.2)

R. v. Austin (1996), 103 C.C.C. (3d) 384 (S.C.C.); reversing (1995), 36 C.R. (4th) 241, 94 C.C.C. (3d) 252 (B.C. C.A.) — Under s. 100(1.1), a court is *not* required to make an order where D establishes that it is not in the interest of the safety of D or another that a prohibition order be made. Absent this, an order under s. 100(1) is required. Where D meets the initial requirement, the court must consider the factors in s. 100(1.2) to determine whether the order ought to be made.

Related Provisions: "Firearm", "peace officer", "superior court", "Attorney General" and "weapon" are defined in s. 2. The other regulated items are defined in s. 84(1).

Section 177.05 applies where a firearm or other regulated item has been seized for public safety reasons. At a disposition hearing, a *peace* officer may apply under s. 117.05 for an order prohibiting the respondent from possessing firearms and other regulated items. A complementary provision appears in s. 117.011.

The provisions of Part XXVII, incorporated by reference in s. 111(10), are discussed in the *Commentary* and *Related Provisions* that accompany each of the applicable sections.

Other related provisions are discussed in the corresponding note to s. 109, *supra*.

112. Revocation of prohibition order under s. 111(5) — A provincial court judge may, on application by the person against whom an order is made under subsection 111(5), revoke the order if satisfied that the circumstances for which it was made have ceased to exist.

1995, c. 39, s. 139, s. 190(e).

Commentary: This section permits a person against whom a preventive prohibition order was made under s. 111(5) to apply to a *provincial court judge* to *revoke* the order. No form of application is provided.

Where the provincial court judge is satisfied that there is *no longer* a public safety risk, the preventive prohibition order may be revoked.

Related Provisions: An application under s. 112 need *not* be made to the issuing judge, but it must be made to a judge who has jurisdiction in the territorial division where the applicant resides.

A preventive prohibition order under s. 111 is *not* a "sentence" under s. 673 or 785. Rights of appeal are governed by ss. 111(8) - (10).

113. (1) Lifting of prohibition order for sustenance or employment — Where a person who is or will be a person against whom a prohibition order is made establishes to the satisfaction of a competent authority that

    (a) the person needs a firearm or restricted weapon to hunt or trap in order to sustain the person or the person's family, or

    (b) a prohibition order against the person would constitute a virtual prohibition against employment in the only vocation open to the person,

the competent authority may, notwithstanding that the person is or will be subject to a prohibition order, make an order authorizing a chief firearms officer or the Registrar to issue, in accordance with such terms and conditions as the competent authority considers appropriate, an authorization, a licence or a registration certificate, as the case may be, to the person for sustenance or employment purposes.

(2) Factors — A competent authority may make an order under subsection (1) only after taking the following factors into account;

    (a) the criminal record, if any, of the person;

(b) the nature and circumstances of the offence, if any, in respect of which the prohibition order was or will be made; and

(c) the safety of the person and of other persons.

(3) Effect of order — Where an order is made under subsection (1),

(a) an authorization, a licence or a registration certificate may not be denied to the person in respect of whom the order was made solely on the basis of a prohibition order against the person or the commission of an offence in respect of which a prohibition order was made against the person; and

(b) an authorization and a licence may, for the duration of the order, be issued to the person in respect of whom the order was made only for sustenance or employment purposes and, where the order sets out terms and conditions, only in accordance with those terms and conditions, but, for greater certainty, the authorization or licence may also be subject to terms and conditions set by the chief firearms officer that are not inconsistent with the purpose for which it is issued and any terms and conditions set out in the order.

(4) When order can be made — For greater certainty, an order under subsection (1) may be made during proceedings for an order under subsection 109(1), 110(1), 111(5), 117.05(4) or 515(2), paragraph 732.1(3)(d) or subsection 810(3).

(5) Meaning of "competent authority" — In this section, "competent authority" means the competent authority that made or has jurisdiction to make the prohibition order.

1995, c. 39, s. 139, s. 190(e).

Commentary: This section, without equivalent in the former legislation, permits a *prohibition* order to be *lifted* in some limited circumstances.

In proceedings for a prohibition order under a provision listed in s. 113(4), that is to say,

i.   a *mandatory* prohibition (s. 109);

ii. a *discretionary* prohibition (s. 110);

iii. a *preventive* prohibition (ss. 111(5) and 117.05(4));

iv. a condition of *judicial* interim release (s. 515(2));

v.   a condition of a *probation* order (s. 732.1(3)(d)); or,

vi. a condition of a *recognizance* (s. 810(3)),

the person who is or will be the individual against whom an order is made may apply to the court for an order *lifting* the *prohibition* in certain respects.

There is *no* statutory form for the application and only two circumstances in which the application may succeed. The applicant may need a *firearm* or *restricted weapon* to hunt or trap for *sustenance* purposes. A prohibition order may constitute a virtual prohibition against employment in the *only* vocation open to the applicant.

The court is required to take into account

i.   the *applicant's* criminal record, if any;

ii. the *nature* and *circumstances* of any underlying *offence* on which the prohibition was or would be grounded; and,

iii. the *safety* of others and the applicant.

Where an order is made, it may authorize issuance of a *restricted* authority (authorization, licence or registration certificate) for sustenance or employment purposes. The authority may not be refused *only* on the basis of the prohibition order or underlying offence, although the chief firearms officer may add further terms and conditions *not* inconsistent with the judicial order.

Related Provisions: Under s. 114, a court may include a *condition* in the prohibition order requiring *surrender* of any firearm or related item prohibited by the order and any enabling authority relating to it. When a prohibition order takes effect, any enabling authority is automatically *revoked* or *amended* to the extent required under s. 116.

Sections 115 and 117 deal with forfeiture and return of forfeited items covered by prohibition orders.

Other related provisions are discussed in the corresponding note to s. 109, *supra*.

114. Requirement to surrender — **A competent authority that makes a prohibition order against a person may, in the order, require the person to surrender to a peace officer, a firearms officer or a chief firearms officer**

> **(a) any thing the possession of which is prohibited by the order that is in the possession of the person on the commencement of the order, and**

> **(b) every authorization, licence and registration certificate relating to any thing the possession of which is prohibited by the order that is held by the person on the commencement of the order.**

and where the competent authority does so, it shall specify in the order a reasonable period for surrendering such things and documents and during which section 117.01 does not apply to that person.

1995, c. 39, s. 139.

Commentary: Under this section, a court that makes a *prohibition* order may include in it a condition requiring the individual to *surrender* any firearm, regulated item and enabling authority related to the prohibited thing. Surrender may be made within a *reasonable* time specified in the order to a *peace officer, firearms officer* or chief *firearms officer*. The offence of s. 117.01(1), possession contrary to a prohibition order, does not apply during the amnesty period.

Related Provisions: Unlike s. 113(5), which defines "competent" authority for the purposes of s. 113, there is neither definition nor incorporation by reference of the term in s. 114.

When a prohibition order is made, any enabling authority relating to possession of prohibited items is revoked or amended to the extent required under s. 116.

Other related provisions are discussed in the corresponding notes to ss. 109 and 113, *supra*.

115. (1) Forfeiture — **Unless a prohibition order against a person specifies otherwise, every thing the possession of which is prohibited by the order that, on the commencement of the order, is in the possession of the person is forfeited to Her Majesty.**

(2) Disposal — **Every thing forfeited to Her Majesty under subsection (1) shall be disposed of or otherwise dealt with as the Attorney General directs.**

1995, c. 39, s. 139

Commentary: This section governs *forfeiture* of items covered by a prohibition order. The *general* rule is simple: unless otherwise specified, *everything* that the individual has that is covered by the order is *forfeited* to Her Majesty. What is forfeited is *disposed* of or otherwise dealt with as the Attorney General directs.

Related Provisions: Section 2 defines Attorney General.

Section 117 provides for the *return* of items that might otherwise be forfeited to the lawful owner.

Other related provisions are discussed in the corresponding notes to ss. 109 and 113, *supra*.

116. Authorizations revoked or amended — **Every authorization, licence and registration certificate relating to any thing the possession of which is prohibited by a prohibition order and issued to a person against whom the prohibition order is made is,**

on the commencement of the prohibition order, revoked, or amended, as the case may be, to the extent of the prohibitions in the order.

1995, c. 39, s. 139

Commentary: This section gives effect to prohibition orders by ensuring that, when the order takes effect, any enabling authority (authorization, licence or registration certificate) relating to prohibited items is *revoked* or *amended* so that it coincides with the scope of the prohibition.

Related Provisions: *Forfeiture* of items covered by a prohibition order is governed by s. 115. Forfeiture of items seized and detained as a result of being used in the commission of an offence is required by s. 491. Section 117 deals with *return* of otherwise forfeitable items to their lawful owner. Other related provisions are discussed in the corresponding notes to ss. 109 and 113, *supra*.

117. Return to owner — Where the competent authority that makes a prohibition order or that would have had jurisdiction to make the order is, on application for an order under this section, satisfied that a person, other than the person against whom a prohibition order was or will be made,

(a) is the owner of any thing that is or may be forfeited to Her Majesty under subsection 115(1) and is lawfully entitled to possess it, and

(b) in the case of a prohibition order under subsection 109(1) or 110(1), had no reasonable grounds to believe that the thing would or might be used in the commission of the offence in respect of which the prohibition order was made,

the competent authority shall order that the thing be returned to the owner or the proceeds of any sale of the thing be paid to that owner or, if the thing was destroyed, that an amount equal to the value of the thing be paid to the owner.

1995, c. 39, s. 139

Commentary: This section describes the circumstances in which otherwise forfeitable items may be *returned* to their lawful owner.

The provision is invoked by an *application* on behalf of the lawful owner or person lawfully entitled to possession of an item covered by a prohibition order. The applicant cannot be the person who is prohibited under the order. Where the prohibition order has been made under ss. 109(1) or 110(1), the applicant must also show that s/he had *no reasonable* grounds to *believe* that the item sought to be returned *would* or *might* be used in the *commission* of the predicate *offence*.

Where the requirements of the section have been met, the court is *required* to order the return of

i.   the *item*;

ii. the *proceeds* of sale, if the item has been sold; or,

iii. an amount equal to the *value* of the item, if it has been destroyed.

Related Provisions: Related provisions are discussed in the corresponding note to s. 116, *supra*.

117.01 (1) Possession contrary to order — Subject to subsection (4), every person commits an offence who possesses a firearm, a cross-bow, a prohibited weapon, a restricted weapon, a prohibited device, any ammunition, any prohibited ammunition or an explosive substance while the person is prohibited from doing so by any order made under this Act or any other Act of Parliament.

(2) Failure to surrender authorization, etc. — Every person commits an offence who wilfully fails to surrender to a peace officer, a firearms officer or a chief firearms officer any authorization, licence or registration certificate held by the person when the person is required to do so by any order made under this Act or any other Act of Parliament.

(3) **Punishment** — Every person who commits an offence under subsection (1) or (2)

    (a) is guilty of an indictable offence and liable to imprisonment for a term not exceeding ten years; or

    (b) is guilty of an offence punishable on summary conviction.

(4) **Exception** — Subsection (1) does not apply to a person who possessed a firearm in accordance with an authorization or licence issued to the person as the result of an order made under subsection 113(1).

1995, c. 39, s. 139

Commentary: This section creates and punishes two offences. The first involves *possession* of a firearm or other regulated item in *contravention* of a *prohibition* order. The second involves a *failure* to *surrender* documentation when required to do so. Each, in other words, relates to a breach of a court order.

The *external circumstances* of the *possession* offence of s. 117.01(1) require proof that D possessed a *firearm* or other regulated item. At the time, D must be *bound* by a *Code* or other federal statute *prohibition*. The *mental element* involves D's *knowledge* of or *recklessness* towards the applicable prohibition.

The *external circumstances* of the *failure* to *surrender* offence of s. 117.01(2) involve proof that D was the *holder* of an authorization, licence or registration certificate at the relevant time. There must be an order that D *surrender* the document to the relevant authority. The order must be made under the *Code* or other federal statute. D must *fail to surrender* the document as required. The *mental element* requires proof of a *wilful* failure to surrender. D must be aware of the requirement and deliberately fail to comply with it.

If D has possession under an authorization or licence issued under s. 113(1), for sustenance or employment purposes, *no* offence is committed under s. 117.01(1).

Each offence is triable either way.

Related Provisions: Section 117.12 may be invoked to prove the relevant licence, authorization or registration certificate.

The prohibition that is contravened in the offence of s. 117.01(1) may have been made on conviction or discharge of an offence (ss. 109, 110), as a preventive measure (ss. 111 and 117.05), as a term of a judicial interim release or probation order (ss. 515(4.1) and 732.1) or as a condition of a recognizance (s. 810).

On conviction or discharge under s. 117.01(1), a *prohibition* order is mandatory.

D may be required to surrender documentation under ss. 114 and 116.

Where P proceeds by indictment, D may *elect* mode of trial. Summary conviction proceedings are governed by Part XXVII and punishment by s. 787(1).

117.011 (1) Application for order — A peace officer, firearms officer or chief firearms officer may apply to a provincial court judge for an order under this section where the peace officer, firearms officer or chief firearms officer believes on reasonable grounds that

    (a) the person against whom the order is sought cohabits with, or is an associate of, another person who is prohibited by any order made under this Act or any other Act of Parliament from possessing any firearm, cross-bow, prohibited weapon, restricted weapon, prohibited device, ammunition, prohibited ammunition or explosive substance, or all such things; and

    (b) the other person would or might have access to any such thing that is in the possession of the person against whom the order is sought.

(2) **Date for hearing and notice** — On receipt of an application made under subsection (1), the provincial court judge shall fix a date for the hearing of the application

and direct that notice of the hearing be given, in such manner as the provincial court judge may specify, to the person against whom the order is sought.

(3) **Hearing of application** — Subject to subsection (4), at the hearing of an application made under subsection (1), the provincial court judge shall hear all relevant evidence presented by or on behalf of the applicant and the person against whom the order is sought.

(4) **Where hearing may proceed *ex parte*** — A provincial court judge may proceed *ex parte* to hear and determine an application made under subsection (1) in the absence of the person against whom the order is sought in the same circumstances as those in which a summary conviction court may, under Part XXVII, proceed with a trial in the absence of the defendant.

(5) **Order** — Where, at the conclusion of a hearing of an application made under subsection (1), the provincial court judge is satisfied that the circumstances referred to in that subsection exist, the provincial court judge shall make an order in respect of the person against whom the order was sought imposing such terms and conditions on the person's use and possession of anything referred to in subsection (1) as the provincial court judge considers appropriate.

(6) **Terms and conditions** — In determining terms and conditions under subsection (5), the provincial court judge shall impose terms and conditions that are the least intrusive as possible, bearing in mind the purpose of the order.

(7) **Appeal by person or Attorney General** — Where a provincial court judge makes an order under subsection (5), the person to whom the order relates, or the Attorney General, may appeal to the superior court against the order.

(8) **Appeal by Attorney General** — Where a provincial court judge does not make an order under subsection (5), the Attorney General may appeal to the superior court against the decision not to make an order.

(9) **Application of Part XXVII to appeals** — The provisions of Part XXVII, except sections 785 to 812, 816 to 819 and 829 to 838, apply in respect of an appeal made under subsection (7) or (8), with such modifications as the circumstances require and as if each reference in that Part to the appeal court were a reference to the superior court.

1995, c. 39, s. 139.

Commentary: This provision complements s. 111 and ensures that a person who is bound by a prohibition order does *not* get access to things that s/he is prohibited from possessing through cohabitation or association with others who have them.

Section 117.011 may be engaged by any *peace officer, firearms officer* or *chief firearms officer* who has a *reasonably-grounded* belief that the respondent *cohabits* or *associates* with a *person* who is *bound* by a *prohibition* order and would or might have access to any prohibited things in the respondent's possession. Application is made by the officer to a *provincial court* judge. There is *no* statutory form for the application.

When the application is received, the provincial court judge has to fix a date for hearing and *notify* the respondent, in an appropriate manner, of the time and place of hearing.

At the hearing, the provincial court judge must hear all *relevant* evidence that the applicant and respondent present. The hearing may proceed in the absence of the respondent if the conditions that permit *ex parte* summary conviction trials are met.

At the end of the hearing, the judge has to decide whether there are *reasonable* grounds to believe

i.   that the respondent *cohabits* or *associates* with someone who is bound by a prohibition order made under the *Code* or other federal statute; and,

ii.   that the prohibited person *would* or *might* have access to a prohibited item in the respondent's possession.

Where the necessary grounds are established, the provincial court judge must make an order imposing the least-intrusive terms and conditions possible on the respondent's use and possession of any item that the prohibited person must *not* possess.

Sections 117.011(7) - (9) provide appellate rights and govern the conduct and determination of appeals. The Attorney General and respondent may appeal an order made under s. 117.011(5). The Attorney General may also appeal a judge's failure to make an order under the subsection. Sections 813 - 815 and 820 - 828 of Part XXVII govern appeals to the superior court.

Related Provisions: Section 839(1)(c) authorizes appeals to the court of appeal from decisions made on appeals under s. 822. Leave to appeal is required and the appeals are limited to questions of law alone.

The definition of "provincial court judge" that applies to s. 117.011 applications is contained in s. 117(11). It requires that the application be made to a provincial court judge with jurisdiction where the respondent resides.

Section 803(2)(a) describes the circumstances in which an *ex parte* summary conviction trial may take place.

Other related provisions are discussed in the corresponding notes to ss. 109 and 111, *supra*.

117.012 Revocation of order under s. 117.011 — A provincial court judge may, on application by the person against whom an order is made under subsection 117.011(5), revoke the order if satisfied that the circumstances for which it was made have ceased to exist.

1995, c. 39, s. 139

Search and Seizure

117.02 (1) Search and seizure without warrant where offence committed — Where a peace officer believes on reasonable grounds

(a) that a weapon, an imitation firearm, a prohibited device, any ammunition, any prohibited ammunition or an explosive substance was used in the commission of an offence, or

(b) that an offence is being committed, or has been committed, under any provision of this Act that involves, or the subject-matter of which is, a firearm, an imitation firearm, a cross-bow, a prohibited weapon, a restricted weapon, a prohibited device, ammunition, prohibited ammunition or an explosive substance,

and evidence of the offence is likely to be found on a person, in a vehicle or in any place or premises other than a dwelling-house, the peace officer may, where the conditions for obtaining a warrant exist but, by reason of exigent circumstances, it would not be practicable to obtain a warrant, search, without warrant, the person, vehicle, place or premises, and seize any thing by means of or in relation to which that peace officer believes on reasonable grounds the offence is being committed or has been committed.

(2) Disposition of seized things — Any thing seized pursuant to subsection (1) shall be dealt with in accordance with sections 490 and 491.

1995, c. 39, s. 139.

Commentary: This is the first of several sections dealing with search and seizure and disposition of items seized with or without warrant.

Section 117.02 authorizes the *warrantless* search of persons and *places other* than *dwelling-houses* where the conditions for obtaining a warrant exist, but because of exigent circumstances, it would be impracticable to get one.

To engage the *warrantless* search and seizure authority of s. 117.02(1), a *peace officer* must believe on *reasonable* grounds that

i.   a weapon or other thing listed in s. 117.02(1)(a) was *used* in the commission of an *offence*; or,

ii. a *Code* offence is being or *has* been committed that *involves*, or the subject-matter of which is, a firearm or other thing described in s. 117.02(1)(b); and,

iii. *evidence* of the offence is *likely* to be *found* on a *person* or in a *place*, other than a dwelling-house.

There are two further requirements:

iv. the conditions for obtaining a *warrant* exist, that is to say, there are *reasonable* grounds to believe that it is *not desirable* in the *interests* of the *safety* of the person to be searched or anyone else that the person have a thing described in s. 117.04(1); and,

v.   it would not be *practicable* to obtain a search warrant.

Where the relevant conditions have been met, the peace officer may *search*, without warrant, the

i.   person;

ii. vehicle;

iii. place; or,

iv. premises, other than a dwelling-house

and *seize* anything by *means* of or in *relation* to which the officer believes, on *reasonable* grounds, the offence is being or has been committed.

Under s. 117.02(2), *disposition* of the seized items is governed by ss. 490 and 491.

Related Provisions: Section 117.04(2) authorizes a *warrantless* search and seizure for public safety reasons and s. 117.03 permits seizure of firearms and other regulated items from persons who fail, on demand, to produce documentation authorizing their possession. Section 117.04(1) provides for the issuance of a *warrant* to search for and seize items that s. 117.02(1) permits to be searched for and seized in exigent circumstances without a warrant. Disposition of items seized with or without warrant under ss. 117.04(1) or (2) is governed by s. 117.05. Where *no* application or finding has been made under s. 117.04, restoration or return is governed by s. 117.06.

The general search warrant provisions are found in s. 487. Other related provisions are discussed in the corresponding note to that section and ss. 488 to 490.7, *infra*.

117.03 (1) Seizure on failure to produce authorization — Notwithstanding section 117.02, a peace officer who finds

(a) a person in possession of a firearm who fails, on demand, to produce, for inspection by the peace officer, an authorization or a licence under which the person may lawfully possess the firearm and a registration certificate for the firearm, or

(b) a person in possession of a prohibited weapon, a restricted weapon, a prohibited device or any prohibited ammunition who fails, on demand, to produce, for inspection by the peace officer, an authorization or a licence under which the person may lawfully possess it,

may seize the firearm, prohibited weapon, restricted weapon, prohibited device or prohibited ammunition unless its possession by the person in the circumstances in which it is found is authorized by any provision of this Part, or the person is under the direct and immediate supervision of another person who may lawfully possess it.

(2) Return of seized thing on production of authorization — Where a person from whom any thing is seized pursuant to subsection (1) claims the thing within fourteen days after the seizure and produces for inspection by the peace officer by whom it was seized, or any other peace officer having custody of it,

(a) an authorization or a licence under which the person is lawfully entitled to possess it, and

(b) in the case of a firearm, a registration certificate for the firearm, the thing shall forthwith be returned to that person.

(3) Forfeiture of seized thing — Where any thing seized pursuant to subsection (1) is not claimed and returned as and when provided by subsection (2), a peace officer shall forthwith take the thing before a provincial court judge, who may, after affording the person from whom it was seized or its owner, if known, an opportunity to establish that the person is lawfully entitled to possess it, declare it to be forfeited to Her Majesty, to be disposed of or otherwise dealt with as the Attorney General directs.

1995, c. 39, s. 139.

Commentary: This is *not*, strictly speaking, a search provision. It does, however, authorize *seizure* of firearms and other regulated items in certain circumstances.

The authority to seize is engaged when a *peace officer finds* a person in *possession* of a firearm, prohibited weapon, device or ammunition or restricted weapon and the person *fails* to *produce* the required documentation in *answer* to the officer's *demand*. Under s. 117.03(1), the officer is entitled to *seize* the firearm, weapon or other regulated item unless its possession is otherwise permitted by Part III.

Sections 117.03(2) and (3) govern *return* and *forfeiture* of things seized under s. 117.03(1). In essence, if the person from whom the thing was seized produces the necessary documentation within *fourteen* days after seizure, the item is returned. Where *no* claim is made, a peace officer has to take the thing before a provincial court judge. The person from whom the thing has been taken or its owner is given an opportunity to establish lawful entitlement to it. Where *entitlement* is not shown, the item is *forfeited* and *disposed* of according to the direction of the Attorney General.

Related Provisions: Section 117.04(1) authorizes issuance of a *warrant* to search for and seize weapons and related items on public safety grounds. Warrantless searches for similar items are permitted by s. 117.04(2).

Section 117.02 authorizes the *warrantless* search of persons and places other than dwelling-houses, if the conditions for getting a warrant exist, but exigent circumstances make it impractical to get one.

Section 117.03 operates *notwithstanding* the warrantless search authority of s. 117.02.

"Peace officer", "firearm" and "person" are defined in s. 2, the other relevant terms of s. 84(1).

Other related provisions are discussed in the corresponding note to s. 117.02, *supra*.

117.04 (1) Application for warrant to search and seize — Where, pursuant to an application made by a peace officer with respect to any person, a justice is satisfied that there are reasonable grounds to believe that it is not desirable in the interests of the safety of the person, or of any other person, for the person to possess any weapon, prohibited device, ammunition, prohibited ammunition or explosive substance, the justice may issue a warrant authorizing a peace officer to search for and seize any such thing, and any authorization, licence or registration certificate relating to any such thing, that is held by or in the possession of the person.

(2) Search and seizure without warrant — Where, with respect to any person, a peace officer is satisfied that there are reasonable grounds to believe that it is not desirable, in the interests of the safety of the person or any other person, for the person to possess any weapon, prohibited device, ammunition, prohibited ammunition or explosive substance, the peace officer may, where the grounds for obtaining a warrant under subsection (1) exist but, by reason of a possible danger to the safety of that person or any other person, it would not be practicable to obtain a warrant, search for and seize any such thing, and any authorization, licence or registration certificate relating to any such thing, that is held by or in the possession of the person.

(3) Return to justice — A peace officer who executes a warrant referred to in subsection (1) or who conducts a search without a warrant under subsection (2) shall forthwith make a return to the justice who issued the warrant or, if no warrant was issued, to a justice who might otherwise have issued a warrant, showing

(a) in the case of an execution of a warrant, the things or documents, if any, seized and the date of execution of the warrant; and

(b) in the case of a search conducted without a warrant, the grounds on which it was concluded that the peace officer was entitled to conduct the search, and the things or documents, if any, seized.

(4) **Authorizations etc., revoked** — Where a peace officer who seizes any thing under subsection (1) or (2) is unable at the time of the seizure to seize an authorization or a licence under which the person from whom the thing was seized may possess the thing and, in the case of a seized firearm, a registration certificate for the firearm, every authorization, licence and registration certificate held by the person is, as at the time of the seizure, revoked.

1995, c. 39, s. 139.

Commentary: This section is rooted in public safety concerns. It permits warranted and warrantless searches for listed items on the basis that public safety may be at risk if the items remain in the possession of unsuitable persons.

Section 117.04(1) provides for *warranted* searches. The procedure begins with an application by a *peace officer* to a *justice* for a *warrant* to search for and seize a weapon, prohibited device, ammunition, prohibited ammunition or explosive substance in the possession of a person. The form of application is *not* described, nor does the section insist that the material be presented on oath or its equivalent.

The *justice* must be satisfied that there are *reasonable* grounds to believe that it is *not desirable* in the *interests* of the *safety* of the person or of anyone else that the person possess a listed item. The warrant authorizes a peace officer to *search* for and *seize*, not only any weapon or other regulated item, but also any enabling authority (authorization, licence or registration certificate) relating to the weapon or item.

Section 117.04(2) governs *warrantless* searches and seizures of weapons, ammunition, explosive substances and prohibited devices and ammunition. The authority may be exercised where the *peace officer* has *reasonable* grounds to *believe* that the *grounds* required to obtain a *warrant* exist, but it would be *impractical* to get a warrant because of a *possible* danger to the safety of any person. The scope of the search and seizure authority is the equivalent of what is given by warrant under s. 117.04(1).

Section 117.04(3) requires the peace officer who has seized any item under or without a warrant to make a *return* to the issuing or another justice. The report must show what things or documents were seized and, in the case of a warrantless search, the grounds on which the search and seizure were based.

Section 117.04(4) governs documents that permit possession of seized items, but that cannot be seized contemporaneously with the items. The documents are revoked as of the time the other things are seized.

Related Provisions: Disposition of things and documents seized under s. 117.04(1) and (2) is governed by ss. 117.05 and 117.06.

Other search and seizure authority is conferred by ss. 117.02 and 117.03. What is permitted in each case is discussed in the *Commentary* that accompanies each section.

Other related provisions are discussed in the corresponding note to ss. 117.02 and 117.03, *supra*.

117.05 (1) Application for disposition — Where any thing or document has been seized under subsection 117.04(1) or (2), the justice who issued the warrant authorizing the seizure or, if no warrant was issued, a justice who might otherwise have issued a warrant, shall, on application for an order for the disposition of the thing or document so seized made by a peace officer within thirty days after the date of execution of the warrant or of the seizure without a warrant, as the case may be, fix a date for the hearing of the application and direct that notice of the hearing be given to such persons or in such manner as the justice may specify.

(2) Ex parte hearing — A justice may proceed *Ex parte* to hear and determine an application made under subsection (1) in the absence of the person from whom the thing or document was seized in the same circumstances as those in which a summary conviction court may, under Part XXVII, proceed with a trial in the absence of the defendant.

(3) Hearing of application — At the hearing of an application made under subsection (1), the justice shall hear all relevant evidence, including evidence respecting the value of the thing in respect of which the application was made.

(4) Forfeiture and prohibition order on finding — Where, following the hearing of an application made under subsection (1), the justice finds that it is not desirable in the interests of the safety of the person from whom the thing was seized or of any other person that the person should possess any weapon, prohibited device, ammunition, prohibited ammunition and explosive substance, or any such thing, the justice shall

(a) order that any thing seized by forfeited to Her Majesty or be otherwise disposed of; and

(b) where the justice is satisfied that the circumstances warrant such an action, order that the possession by that person of any weapon, prohibited device, ammunition, prohibited ammunition and explosive substance, or of any such thing, be prohibited during any period, not exceeding five years, that is specified in the order, beginning on the making of the order.

(5) Reasons — Where a justice does not make an order under subsection (4), or where a justice does make such an order but does not prohibit the possession of all of the things referred to in that subsection, the justice shall include in the record a statement of the justice's reasons.

(6) Application of ss. 113 to 117 — Sections 113 to 117 apply in respect of every order made under subsection (4).

(7) Appeal by person — Where a justice makes an order under subsection (4) in respect of a person, or in respect of any thing that was seized from a person, the person may appeal to the superior court against the order.

(8) Appeal by Attorney General — Where a justice does not make a finding as described in subsection (4) following the hearing of an application under subsection (1), or makes the finding but does not make an order to the effect described in paragraph (4)(b), the Attorney General may appeal to the superior court against the failure to make the finding or to make an order to the effect so described.

(9) Application of Part XXVII to appeals — The provisions of Part XXVII, except sections 785 to 812, 816 to 819 and 829 to 838, apply in respect of an appeal made under subsection (7) or (8) with such modifications as the circumstances require and as if each reference in that Part to the appeal court were a reference to the superior court.
1995, c. 39, s. 139.

Commentary: This section and s. 117.06 provide for *disposition* of things and documents seized with or without a warrant on public safety grounds under ss. 117.04(1) and (2). The structure of the section parallels ss. 111 and 117.011.

Disposition proceedings are started by an application to the authorizing or another justice within thirty days after the warrant has been executed or seizure made. The applicant must be a *peace officer*. When the application is received, the justice must fix a date for hearing and direct that notice of it be given to appropriate parties in an appropriate way.

At the hearing, the justice is required to receive and consider all *relevant* evidence, *including* evidence about the value of the things that are the subject-matter of the application. If the respondent fails to appear, the justice may proceed *ex parte*.

The issue on the hearing is framed by s. 117.05(4). The justice must decide whether it is *not* desirable, in the *interests* of anyone's *safety*, that the respondent *possess* any or all of the things seized. An affirmative finding requires the justice to order that anything seized be forfeited and, where warranted, that the respondent be subject to a prohibition order for *not* more than five years. Under s. 117.05(5), the justice must give reasons for *not* making an order of forfeiture or making an order in connection with some but not all of the items seized. Sections 113 - 117 apply to these orders.

Appellate rights are governed by ss. 117.05(7) - (9). The respondent may appeal a s. 117.05(4) order to the superior court. The Attorney General may appeal the failure to make the threshold finding required by s. 117.05(4) or a prohibition order under s. 117.05(4)(b). The summary conviction appeal provisions incorporated by exclusion in s. 117.05(9) apply.

Related Provisions: Things seized under s. 117.02(1) are *disposed* of in accordance with ss. 490 and 491. Section 117.03 permits *seizure* on failure to produce authorization, but neither contains nor incorporates by reference any provisions for disposition of the seized items.

Section 117.06(1) applies where there is *no* application for disposition under s. 117.05(1) within the prescribed time period, or no finding has been made under s. 117.05(4). The things or documents seized must be *returned* to the person from whom they have been seized. Any authorizations revoked under s. 117.04(4) may be restored under s. 117.06(2).

Other related provisions are discussed in the corresponding notes to ss. 117.02 and 117.03, *supra*.

117.06 (1) Where no finding or application — Any thing or document seized pursuant to subsection 117.04(1) or (2) shall be returned to the person from whom it was seized if

(a) no application is made under subsection 117.05(1) within thirty days after the date of execution of the warrant or of the seizure without a warrant, as the case may be; or

(b) an application is made under subsection 117.05(1) within the period referred to in paragraph (a), and the justice does not make a finding as described in subsection 117.05(4).

(2) Restoration of authorizations — Where, pursuant to subsection (1), any thing is returned to the person from whom it was seized and an authorization, a licence or a registration certificate, as the case may be, is revoked pursuant to subsection 117.04(4), the justice referred to in paragraph (1)(b) may order that the revocation be reversed and that the authorization, licence or registration certificate be restored.

1995, c. 39, s. 139

Commentary: This section governs what happens when a peace officer has *failed* to apply to a justice for disposition of seized items within thirty days of their seizure under or without warrant under ss. 117.04(1) or (2), where the application has been unsuccessful. The result is that the items are returned to the person from whom they were seized and any authorization revoked under s. 117.04(4) may be restored under s. 117.06(2).

Related Provisions: Section 117.04(1) governs *warranted* seizures of weapons and other regulated items and s. 117.04(2) applies to *warrantless* seizures. Disposition proceedings are governed by s. 117.05.

Other related provisions are discussed in the corresponding note to ss. 117.02 - 117.05, *supra*.

Exempted Persons

117.07 (1) Public officers — Notwithstanding any other provision of this Act, but subject to section 117.1, no public officer is guilty of an offence under this Act or the *Firearms Act* by reason only that the public officer

(a) possesses a firearm, a prohibited weapon, a restricted weapon, a prohibited device, any prohibited ammunition or an explosive substance in the course of or for the purpose of the public officer's duties or employment;

(b) manufactures or transfers, or offers to manufacture or transfer, a firearm, a prohibited weapon, a restricted weapon, a prohibited device, any ammunition or any prohibited ammunition in the course of the public officer's duties or employment;

(c) exports or imports a firearm, a prohibited weapon, a restricted weapon, a prohibited device or any prohibited ammunition in the course of the public officer's duties or employment;

(d) exports or imports a component or part designed exclusively for use in the manufacture of or assembly into an automatic firearm in the course of the public officer's duties or employment;

(e) in the course of the public officer's duties or employment, alters a firearm so that it is capable of, or manufactures or assembles any firearm with intent to produce a firearm that is capable of, discharging projectiles in rapid succession during one pressure of the trigger;

(f) fails to report the loss, theft or finding of any firearm, prohibited weapon, restricted weapon, prohibited device, ammunition, prohibited ammunition or explosive substance that occurs in the course of the public officer's duties or employment or the destruction of any such thing in the course of the public officer's duties or employment; or

(g) alters a serial number on a firearm in the course of the public officer's duties or employment.

(2) Definition of "public officer" — In this section, "public officer" means

(a) a peace officer;

(b) a member of the Canadian Forces or of the armed forces of a state other than Canada who is attached or seconded to any of the Canadian Forces;

(c) an operator of a museum established by the Chief of the Defence Staff or a person employed in any such museum;

(d) a member of a cadet organization under the control and supervision of the Canadian Forces;

(e) a person training to become a police officer or a peace officer under the control and supervision of

(i) a police force, or

(ii) a police academy or similar institution designated by the Attorney General of Canada or the lieutenant governor in council of a province;

(f) a member of a visiting force, within the meaning of section 2 of the *Visiting Forces Act*, who is authorized under paragraph 14(a) of that Act to possess and carry explosives, ammunition and firearms;

(g) a person, or member of a class of persons, employed in the public service of Canada or by the government of a province or municipality who is prescribed to be a public officer; or

(h) a chief firearms officer and any firearms officer.

1995, c. 39, s. 139

Commentary: This is the first of four sections that define the categories of persons who are *exempt* from conviction for conduct that would otherwise offend liability-creating provisions of the *Criminal Code* or *Firearms Act*.

The *exemption* in s. 117.07(1) applies to *public officers* as defined in s. 117.07(2). The exemption is confined to possession in the *course* of the officer's *duties* or *employment* and the circumstances described in the applicable paragraph. There is *no* exemption if the officer is subject to a *prohibition* order and acts contrary to it or to an authorization or licence issued by an order made under s. 113(1).

Related Provisions: Section 117.08 exempts persons who engage in certain conduct on behalf of and under the authority of a police force, the Canadian Forces, a visiting force or a department of the federal or a provincial government. Employees of businesses with licences, of carriers and of museums are exempted in circumstances described in s. 117.09.

Several other provisions also furnish specific or more general exceptions. They include the transitional provisions of s. 98, supervised possession, for example, under s. 95(3), and sustenance hunting, for example, under s. 91(4).

"Public officer" is generally defined in s. 2, as is "Canadian Forces".

117.08 Individuals acting for police force, Canadian Forces and visiting forces — Notwithstanding any other provision of this Act, but subject to section 117.1, no individual is guilty of an offence under this Act or the *Firearms Act* by reason only that the individual

(a) possesses a firearm, a prohibited weapon, a restricted weapon, a prohibited device, any prohibited ammunition or an explosive substance,

(b) manufactures or transfers, or offers to manufacture or transfer, a firearm, a prohibited weapon, a restricted weapon, a prohibited device, any ammunition or any prohibited ammunition,

(c) exports or imports a firearm, a prohibited weapon, a restricted weapon, a prohibited device or any prohibited ammunition,

(d) exports or imports a component or part designed exclusively for use in the manufacture of or assembly into an automatic firearm,

(e) alters a firearm so that it is capable of, or manufactures or assembles any firearm with intent to produce a firearm that is capable of, discharging projectiles in rapid succession during one pressure of the trigger,

(f) fails to report the loss, theft or finding of any firearm, prohibited weapon, restricted weapon, prohibited device, ammunition, prohibited ammunition or explosive substance or the destruction of any such thing, or

(g) alters a serial number on a firearm,

if the individual does so on behalf of, and under the authority of, a police force, the Canadian Forces, a visiting force, within the meaning of section 2 of the *Visiting Forces Act*, or a department of the Government of Canada or of a province.

1995, c. 39, s. 139

Commentary: Exemption under this section relates to individuals who engage in conduct on *behalf* and under the *authority* of

i.   a police force;

ii.   the Canadian Forces;

159

iii.   a visiting force; or,

iv.   a department of the federal or a provincial government.

The exemption of the section extends to Code and *F.A.* offences, but does *not* apply if the individual is subject to and contravenes a prohibition order or acts contrary to an authorization or licence issued in accordance with s. 113(1).

Related Provisions: The related provisions are discussed in the corresponding note to s. 117.07, *supra.*

117.09 (1) Employees of business with licence — Notwithstanding any other provision of this Act, but subject to section 117.1, no individual who is the holder of a licence to possess and acquire restricted firearms and who is employed by a business as defined in subsection 2(1) of the *Firearms Act* that itself is the holder of a licence that authorizes the business to carry out specified activities in relation to prohibited firearms, prohibited weapons, prohibited devices or prohibited ammunition is guilty of an offence under this Act or the *Firearms Act* by reason only that the individual, in the course of the individual's duties or employment in relation to those specified activities,

    (a) possesses a prohibited firearm, a prohibited weapon, a prohibited device or any prohibited ammunition;

    (b) manufactures or transfers, or offers to manufacture or transfer, a prohibited weapon, a prohibited device or any prohibited ammunition;

    (c) alters a firearm so that it is capable of, or manufactures or assembles any firearm with intent to produce a firearm that is capable of, discharging projectiles in rapid succession during one pressure of the trigger, or

    (d) alters a serial number on a firearm.

(2) Employees of business with licence — Notwithstanding any other provision of this Act, but subject to section 117.1, no individual who is employed by a business as defined in subsection 2(1) of the *Firearms Act* that itself is the holder of a licence is guilty of an offence under this Act or the *Firearms Act* by reason only that the individual, in the course of the individual's duties or employment, possesses, manufactures or transfers, or offers to manufacture or transfer, a partially manufactured barrelled weapon that, in its unfinished state, is not a barrelled weapon from which any shot, bullet or other projectile can be discharged and that is capable of causing serious bodily injury or death to a person.

(3) Employees of carriers — Notwithstanding any other provision of this Act, but subject to section 117.1, no individual who is employed by a carrier, as defined in subsection 2(1) of the *Firearms Act*, is guilty of an offence under this Act or that Act by reason only that the individual, in the course of the individual's duties or employment, possesses any firearm, cross-bow, prohibited weapon, restricted weapon, prohibited device, ammunition or prohibited ammunition or transfers, or offers to transfer any such thing.

(4) Employees of museums handling functioning imitation antique firearm — Notwithstanding any other provision of this Act, but subject to section 117.1, no individual who is employed by a museum as defined in subsection 2(1) of the *Firearms Act* that itself is the holder of a licence is guilty of an offence under this Act or the *Firearms Act* by reason only that the individual, in the course of the individual's duties or employment, possesses or transfers a firearm that is designed or intended to exactly resemble, or to resemble with near precision, an antique firearm if the individual has been trained to handle and use such a firearm.

(5) **Employees of museums handling firearms generally** — Notwithstanding any other provision of this Act, but subject to section 117.1, no individual who is employed by a museum as defined in subsection 2(1) of the *Firearms Act* that itself is the holder of a licence is guilty of an offence under this Act or the *Firearms Act* by reason only that the individual possesses or transfers a firearm in the course of the individual's duties or employment if the individual is designated, by name, by a provincial minister within the meaning of subsection 2(1) of the *Firearms Act*.

(6) **Public safety** — A provincial minister shall not designate an individual for the purpose of subsection (4) where it is not desirable, in the interests of the safety of any person, to designate the individual.

(7) **Conditions** — A provincial minister may attach to a designation referred to in subsection (4) any reasonable condition that the provincial minister considers desirable in the particular circumstances and in the interests of the safety of any person.

1995, c. 39, s. 139.

Commentary: The exemptions of s. 117.09 apply to three separate groups or categories of persons:

i. employees of *weapons-related businesses*;

ii. employees of *carriers*; and,

iii. employees of *museums*.

The exemptions or exceptions do not apply if the person is subject to and contravenes a *prohibition* order or breaches the condition of a s. 113 authorization, licence or registration certificate issued on the partial lifting of a prohibition order for employment or sustenance purposes.

The exemptions of ss. 117.09(1) and (2) apply to employees of licenced weapons- related businesses. Licenced employees are governed by s. 117.09(1) and those who are unlicenced by s. 117.09(2). In each case, the employee must be acting in the *course* of his/her *duties* or *employment*.

Under s. 117.09(3), unlicenced employees of *carriers* can have or transfer weapons or other regulated items if they are acting in the course of their *duties* or *employment*.

Sections 117.09(4) - (7) create exemptions for *museum* employees. They may have and transfer firearms that resemble antiques in the *course* of their *duties*, provided they have the necessary training, are *not* subject to a prohibition and work for a licenced museum. Any museum employee designated by the relevant provincial Minister may have and transfer firearms in the course of his/her duties or employment.

Related Provisions: "Business", "carrier" and "museum" are defined in s. 2(1) *F.A.*

Other related provisions are discussed in the corresponding notes to ss. 117.02 - 117.05 and 117.08, *supra*.

117.1 Restriction — Sections 117.07 to 117.09 do not apply if the public officer or the individual is subject to a prohibition order and acts contrary to that order or to an authorization or a licence issued under the authority of an order made under subsection 113(1).

1995, c. 39, s. 139

Commentary: This section *limits* the exemptions from liability under the *Code* and *F.A.* that ss. 117.07 - 117.09 create. The exemptions do *not* operate where the public officer or employee is subject to and contravenes a *prohibition* order or acts *contrary* to an authorization or licence issued on the partial *lifting* of a prohibition order for employment or sustenance purposes.

Related Provisions: The exemptions of ss. 117.07 - 117.09 are discussed in the *Commentary* that accompanies each section.

Section 113 permits a court to *lift* a prohibition order if the individual bound by it can establish that the order would constitute a virtual bar against employment in the *only* vocation open to the person, or that s/he needs a firearm or restricted weapon for sustenance hunting.

Other related provisions are discussed in the corresponding notes to ss. 117.02 - 117.05 and 117.08, *supra*.

General

117.11 Onus on the accused — **Where, in any proceedings for an offence under any of sections 89, 90, 91, 93, 97, 101, 104 and 105, any question arises as to whether a person is the holder of an authorization, a licence or a registration certificate, the onus is on the accused to prove that the person is the holder of the authorization, licence or registration certificate.**

1995, c. 39, s. 139.

Commentary: This section shifts the onus of proving certain *lawful* authority to D, the person who claims to have it, in proceedings for listed offences. It is likely to attract *Charter* scrutiny.

Section 117.11 applies to several possession, assembling, export and import offences, as well as an offence relating to lost, destroyed or defaced weapons. Where any issue arises about whether D was the *holder* of an authorization, licence or registration certificate at the relevant time, the *onus* of proving the essential authority is on D.

Case Law
Charter Considerations

R. v. Schwartz (1988), 66 C.R. (3d) 251, 45 C.C.C. (3d) 97 (S.C.C.) — Section 115(1) is valid because it is a rule of evidence, and does not impose a reverse onus on D on a charge of possession of an unregistered weapon. D is not required to prove or disprove any element of the offence or anything related to the offence. Even if s. 115(1) infringes *Charter* s. 11(d), it is saved by s. 1.

Related Provisions: "Authorization", "licence" and "registration certificate" are defined in s. 84(1), "holder" in s. 84(4).

The essential elements of each listed offence are discussed in the *Commentary* that accompanies the section.

The evidentiary effect of documents that claim to be an authorization, licence or registration certificate is described in s. 117.12.

117.12 (1) Authorizations, etc. as evidence — **In any proceedings under this Act or any other Act of Parliament, a document purporting to be an authorization, a licence or a registration certificate is evidence of the statements contained therein.**

(2) Certified copies — **In any proceedings under this Act or any other Act of Parliament, a copy of any authorization, licence or registration certificate is, if certified as a true copy by the Registrar or a chief firearms officer, admissible in evidence and, in the absence of evidence to the contrary, has the same probative force as the authorization, licence or registration certificate would have had if it had been proved in the ordinary way.**

1995, c. 39, s. 139.

Commentary: This section states the *evidentiary effect* of documents that purport to be an authorization, licence or registration certificate.

Under s. 117.12(1), any document that claims to be an authorization, licence or registration certificate is *evidence* of the *statements* contained in it. Any copy *certified* by the Registrar or chief firearms officer as a *true* copy is admissible in evidence in any proceeding under a federal statute. In the *absence* of *evidence* to the *contrary*, the copy has the same probative force as the original.

Related Provisions: Section 117.11 puts the onus on D to prove lawful authority in prosecutions under listed sections.

Section 117.13 permits reception of a *certificate* of an analyst in prosecutions under the *Code* and another listed statute. Leave is required to permit the analyst to be called for cross-examination.

Section 117.12 contains *no* notice provisions. Relevant terms, such as "authorization", "licence", "Registrar", "registration certificate" and "chief firearms officer" are defined in s. 84(1).

117.13 (1) Certificate of analyst — A certificate purporting to be signed by an analyst stating that the analyst has analyzed any weapon, prohibited device, ammunition, prohibited ammunition or explosive substance, or any part or component of such a thing, and stating the results of the analysis is evidence in any proceedings in relation to any of those things under this Act or under section 19 of the *Export and Import Permits Act* in relation to subsection 15(2) of that Act without proof of the signature or official character of the person appearing to have signed the certificate.

(2) Attendance of analyst — The party against whom a certificate of an analyst is produced may, with leave of the court, require the attendance of the analyst for the purposes of cross-examination.

(3) Notice of intention to produce certificate — No certificate of an analyst may be admitted in evidence unless the party intending to produce it has, before the trial, given to the party against whom it is intended to be produced reasonable notice of that intention together with a copy of the certificate.

(4) Proof of service — For the purposes of this Act, service of a certificate of an analyst may be proved by oral evidence given under oath by, or by the affidavit or solemn declaration of, the person claiming to have served it.

(5) Attendance for examination — Notwithstanding subsection (4), the court may require the person who appears to have signed an affidavit or solemn declaration referred to in that subsection to appear before it for examination or cross-examination in respect of the issue of proof of service.

1995, c. 39, s. 139

Commentary: This section enacts an *admissibility* rule that permits the *results* of *analysis* to be established in *Code* and other proceedings by introduction of a *certificate*.

Section 117.13(1) creates the basic rule. To prove the *results* of *analysis* of any

i.   weapon;
ii. prohibited device;
iii. ammunition or prohibited ammunition; or,
iv. explosive substance

a *certificate* of an analyst stating the *results* is evidence of them without any need to prove the signature or official character of the analyst. The certificate may *not* be admitted unless reasonable notice of the *intention* to adduce it, together with a *copy* of the *certificate*, has been provided to the party against whom it is tendered. The notice required by s. 117.13(3) appears to apply to both P and D. Service of the certificate may be proved by oral evidence, or *affidavit* or *solemn declaration* of the serving party under s. 117.13(4).

The party against whom the certificate is tendered may obtain *leave* to *cross-examine* the *analyst* under s. 117.13(2). The court may also require the *party* who *served* the *certificate* to attend for examination or cross-examination on the issue of *proof* of *service*.

Related Provisions: Proof by certificate with leave to cross-examine is a common method of proof under the *Code*.

"Analyst" is *not* defined in Part III, nor in s. 2(1) *F.A.* It is a term defined for difference purposes in s. 254(1) of the *Criminal Code* and s. 2(1) C.D.S.A. In common language, it is a person who analyzes a particular thing or subject-matter.

117.14 (1) Amnesty period — The Governor in Council may, by order, declare for any purpose referred to in subsection (2) any period as an amnesty period with respect to any weapon, prohibited device, prohibited ammunition, explosive substance or component or part designed exclusively for use in the manufacture of or assembly into an automatic firearm.

(2) Purposes of amnesty period — An order made under subsection (1) may declare an amnesty period for the purpose of

(a) permitting any person in possession of any thing to which the order relates to do anything provided in the order, including, without restricting the generality of the foregoing, delivering the thing to a peace officer, a firearms officer or a chief firearms officer, registering it, destroying it or otherwise disposing of it; or

(b) permitting alterations to be made to any prohibited firearm, prohibited weapon, prohibited device or prohibited ammunition to which the order relates so that it no longer qualifies as a prohibited firearm, a prohibited weapon, a prohibited device or prohibited ammunition, as the case may be.

(3) Reliance on amnesty period — No person who, during an amnesty period declared by an order made under subsection (1) and for a purpose described in the order, does anything provided for in the order, is, by reason only of the fact that the person did that thing, guilty of an offence under this Part.

(4) Proceedings are a nullity — Any proceedings taken under this Part against any person for anything done by the person in reliance of this section are a nullity.

1995, c. 39, s. 139.

Commentary: This section authorizes the proclamation of an amnesty period with respect to certain items for a statutorily-prescribed purpose.

Under s. 117.14(1), the Governor-in-Council may declare an amnesty period for any listed item. The purpose of the period must be to permit

* anyone in possession of the relevant item to do anything provided in the order; or,
* anyone to *alter* any prohibited firearm, weapon, device or ammunition so that it no longer qualifies as such.

Sections 117.14(3) and (4) state the *effect* of an amnesty period. No one who does anything during the amnesty period for the specified purpose commits an offence simply by compliance. Under s. 117.14(4), any proceedings taken against someone for conduct in compliance with the amnesty period are a nullity.

Related Provisions: Section 98 enacts transitional provisions that have an effect similar to that of an amnesty period.

117.15 (1) Regulations — Subject to subsection (2), the Governor in Council may make regulations prescribing anything that by this Part is to be or may be prescribed.

(2) Restriction — In making regulations, the Governor in Council may not prescribe any thing to be a prohibited firearm, a restricted firearm, a prohibited weapon, a restricted weapon, a prohibited device or prohibited ammunition if, in the opinion of the Governor in Council, the thing to be prescribed is reasonable for use in Canada for hunting or sporting purposes.

1995, c. 39, s. 139

Commentary: The section authorizes the Governor-in-Council to make regulations prescribing anything that must or may be prescribed. The scope of authority provided by s. 117.15(1) is cut down by s. 117.15(2): *nothing* may be prescribed as

i.   a *prohibited* firearm, weapon, device or ammunition; or,

ii. a *restricted* firearm or weapon

that it is *reasonable* to use in Canada for *hunting* or *sporting* purposes.

Related Provisions: Sections 117 - 119 *F.A.* permit regulations to be made under that *Act* for defined purposes and in relation to specified subject-matter.

PART IV — OFFENCES AGAINST THE ADMINISTRATION OF LAW AND JUSTICE

Interpretation

118. Definitions — In this Part

"evidence" or "statement" means an assertion of fact, opinion, belief or knowledge whether material or not and whether admissible or not;

"government" means

(a) the Government of Canada,

(b) the government of a province, or

(c) Her Majesty in right of Canada or a province;

"judicial proceeding" means a proceeding

(a) in or under the authority of a court of justice

(b) before the Senate or House of Commons or a committee of the Senate or House of Commons, or before a legislative council, legislative assembly or house of assembly or a committee thereof that is authorized by law to administer an oath,

(c) before a court, judge, justice, provincial court judge or coroner,

(d) before an arbitrator or umpire, or a person or body of persons authorized by law to make an inquiry and take evidence therein under oath, or

(e) before a tribunal by which a legal right or legal liability may be established, whether or not the proceeding is invalid for want of jurisdiction or for any other reason;

"office" includes

(a) an office or appointment under the government,

(b) a civil or military commission, and

(c) a position or an employment in a public department;

"official" means a person who

(a) holds an office, or

(b) is appointed to discharge a public duty;

"witness" means a person who gives evidence orally under oath or by affidavit in a judicial proceeding, whether or not he is competent to be a witness, and includes a child of tender years who gives evidence but does not give it under oath, because, in the opinion of the person presiding, the child does not understand the nature of an oath.

R.S., c. C-34, s. 107; R.S. 1985, c. 27 (1st Supp.), ss. 15, 203.

Commentary: The section defines several terms used in the offences of this *Part*.

Case Law

Judicial Proceeding

R. v. Wijesinha (1995), 42 C.R. (4th) 1, 100 C.C.C. (3d) 410 (S.C.C.) — Law Society disciplinary proceedings are included in "judicial proceeding" in s. 118(d) and (e).

Re Shumiatcher (1961), 36 C.R. 171, 131 C.C.C. 259 (S.C.C.) — An examination under oath before the registrar of the provincial Securities Commission is a "judicial proceeding".

R. v. Hewson (1976), 35 C.C.C. (2d) 407 (Ont. C.A.); affirming (1976), 30 C.C.C. (2d) 126 (Ont. Co. Ct.) — A bail review hearing is a "judicial proceeding".

Foster v. R. (1982), 69 C.C.C. (2d) 484 (Sask. C.A.) — An examination for discovery is a "judicial proceeding".

Official

R. v. Sheets (1971), 15 C.R.N.S. 232, 1 C.C.C. (2d) 508 (S.C.C.) — An elected municipal "official" is an "official".

R. v. Martineau (1965), 48 C.R. 209, [1966] 4 C.C.C. 327 (S.C.C.) — A member of the Legislative Council of the Province of Quebec is an "official".

Sommers v. R. (1959), 31 C.R. 36, 124 C.C.C. 241 (S.C.C.) — "Official" includes a Minister of the Crown.

Witness

R. v. Hewson (1976), 35 C.C.C. (2d) 407 (Ont. C.A.); affirming (1976), 30 C.C.C. (2d) 126 (Ont. Co. Ct.) — A person who gives evidence on a bail review hearing is a "witness".

Related Provisions: Section 123(3) defines "municipal official" for the purposes of that section, and s. 136(2) restricts the definition of "evidence" in s. 118 to evidence that is material in prosecutions under s. 136. Section 149(3) contains an exhaustive definition of "escape" for the purposes of s. 149(1).

The definition of "witness" in s. 118 "includes a *child of tender years* who gives evidence but does *not* give it under oath, because, in the opinion of the person presiding the child does not understand the nature of an oath". *C.E.A.* s. 16 does *not* use the phrase "child of tender years", and imposes a slightly different test than did its predecessor in determining whether a proposed witness "under 14 years of age or a person whose mental capacity is challenged" may testify on promising to tell the truth.

Other sources of interpretative assistance are described in the corresponding note to s. 2, *supra*.

Corruption and Disobedience

119. (1) Bribery of judicial officers, etc. — Every one who

(a) being the holder of a judicial office, or being a member of Parliament or of the legislature of a province, corruptly

(i) accepts or obtains,

(ii) agrees to accept, or

(iii) attempts to obtain,

any money, valuable consideration, office, place or employment for himself or another person in respect of anything done or omitted or to be done or omitted by him in his official capacity, or

(b) gives or offers, corruptly, to a person mentioned in paragraph (a) any money, valuable consideration, office, place or employment in respect of anything done or omitted or to be done or omitted by him in his official capacity for himself or another person,

is guilty of an indictable offence and liable to imprisonment for a term not exceeding fourteen years.

(2) Consent of Attorney General — No proceedings against a person who holds a judicial office shall be instituted under this section without the consent in writing of the Attorney General of Canada.

R.S., c. C-34, s. 108.

Commentary: The corruption or bribery offence described and punished in this section is a bilateral offence. It requires and punishes both a *donor* and *recipient*. The conduct of of each must be *corrupt*. The *external circumstances* of the *recipient* offence in s. 119(1)(a) require that D be the holder of a judicial office, a member of Parliament or of a provincial legislature. D must *corruptly* accept, agree to accept, obtain or attempt to obtain money, valuable consideration, office, place or employment for him/herself or another person. What is obtained or accepted by D must be *in respect of anything* done or omitted or to be done or omitted by D in his/her official capacity. The *mental element* includes the intent to cause the external circumstances of the offence. Under s. 119(2), the Attorney General of Canada must consent *in writing* to the institution of proceedings under this section against the holder of a judicial office.

The *external circumstances* of the *donor* offence in s.119(1)(b) require that D give or offer, *corruptly*, to the holder of the judicial office, member of Parliament or of a provincial legislature any money, valuable consideration, office, place or employment. What is given or offered must be *in respect of anything* done or omitted or to be done or omitted by the recipient in his/her official capacity, for the donor or another person. The *mental element* consists of the intention to cause the external circumstances of the offence.

Case Law
Official Capacity
Arseneau v. R. (1979), 45 C.C.C. (2d) 321 (S.C.C.) — A cabinet minister, in the absence of evidence to the contrary, is to be taken as acting in his/her official capacity as a member of the Legislature when taking ministerial actions connected with the administration of the department.

R. v. Bruneau (1963), 42 C.R. 93, [1964] 1 C.C.C. 97 (Ont. C.A.) — An M.P. who agrees to accept money for the use of his influence to bring about the purchase by the Government of certain lands is acting in his official capacity.

R. v. Yanakis (1981), 64 C.C.C. (2d) 374 (Que. C.A.) — It is *no* defence to a charge that D, an M.P., used money received for "non-reimbursable expenses" he or she incurred as an M.P. The use made of the payments is immaterial. P must prove, however, that D did or omitted to do something in his/her official capacity in return for the money. Mere provision of documents that the donor could have obtained from the relevant government department is *not* something done by D in his or her official capacity.

Related Provisions: "Office" is defined in s. 118.

Other bribery and corruption offences are found in ss. 120–125, 139(3) and 426.

This offence is an "enterprise crime offence" under s. 462.3 and Part XII.2, and an "offence" under s. 183 for the purposes of Part VI.

Where D is the holder of a judicial office, this offence, listed in s. 469(c), falls within the exclusive trial and judicial interim release jurisdiction of the superior court of criminal jurisdiction.

The preliminary crimes of attempt and conspiracy to commit the offence in relation to the holder of a judicial office, do *not* fall within s. 469. In all other respects, D may elect mode of trial under s. 536(2).

The disabilities of ss. 750(1) and (2) will ensue where D is the holder of an office under the Crown or other public employment and, upon conviction, is sentenced to imprisonment for a term exceeding five years.

120. Bribery of officers — Every one who
(a) being a justice, police commissioner, peace officer, public officer or officer of a juvenile court, or being employed in the administration of criminal law, corruptly
(i) accepts or obtains,
(ii) agrees to accept, or

   (iii) attempts to obtain,
**for himself or any other person any money, valuable consideration, office, place or
employment with intent**
   (iv) to interfere with the administration of justice,
   (v) to procure or facilitate the commission of an offence, or
   **(vi) to protect from detection or punishment a person who has committed or
   who intends to commit an offence, or**
**(b) gives or offers, corruptly, to a person mentioned in paragraph (a) any money,
valuable consideration, office, place or employment with intent that the person
should do anything mentioned in subparagraph (a)(iv), (v) or (vi),**
**is guilty of an indictable offence and liable to imprisonment for a term not exceeding
fourteen years.**
                                                                R.S., c. C-34, s. 109.

Commentary: This corruption or bribery offence, a bilateral crime, requires and punishes both a
donor and *recipient*. In each case, D's conduct must be *corrupt* and accompanied by an ulterior mental
element.

The *external circumstances* of the *recipient* offence of s. 120(a) require that D be a justice, police commissioner, peace or public officer, officer of a juvenile court or a person employed in the administration
of the criminal law. D must, in other words, be a member of the designated group of persons or act in a
particular capacity. D must *corruptly*, accept or agree to accept, obtain or attempt to obtain, for
him/herself or any other person, any money, valuable consideration, office, place or employment. There
is *no* requirement that what is obtained or accepted be in respect of anything done or omitted to be done
or omitted by D in his/her official capacity as under s. 119(1). P must, however, prove that one of the
ulterior *mental elements* listed in ss. 120(a)(iv)–(vi) accompanied the external circumstances.

The *external circumstances* of the *donor* offence in s. 120(b) consist of the giving or offering by D to a
person described in s. 120(a) of any money, valuable consideration, office, place or employment. The
offer or gift must be made *corruptly*. The *mental element* comprises not only the intention to cause the
external circumstances of the offence but, further, the *intent* that the recipient should *do anything* described in ss. 120(a)(iv)–(vi).

Case Law
Officer
R. v. Smith (1921), 38 C.C.C. 21 (Ont. C.A.) — There can be *no* corruption unless the person bribed is
an officer and the person bribing knows or believes them to be so.

Offence
R. v. Sommervill (1963), 40 C.R. 384, [1963] 3 C.C.C. 240 (Sask. C.A.) — "Offence" includes breach
of a valid provincial statute.

Mental Element
R. v. Dees (1978), 40 C.C.C. (2d) 58 (Ont. C.A.) — Character evidence is to be considered in assessing
whether D was of such good character that D was *unlikely* to have committed the offence unless intoxicated to an incapacitating extent.

Administration of Justice
R. v. Kalick (1920), 36 C.C.C. 159 (S.C.C.) — An attempt to induce a police officer to refrain from
prosecuting an offence is an attempt to interfere with the due administration of justice.

Related Provisions: "Justice", "peace officer", and "public officer" are defined in s. 2, "office" in
s. 118. The reference to "juvenile court" is anachronistic.

Section 128 prohibits misconduct by peace officers in the execution of a process. Section 129 describes
and punishes several offences involving misconduct towards a peace or public officer, and s. 130 prohibits impersonation of a peace officer. Under s. 140(1) public mischief is committed where D, with
intent to mislead, causes a peace officer to enter upon or continue on an investigation by doing or reporting certain things or events.

This offence is an "enterprise crime offence" under Part XII.2, and an "offence" for the purposes of Part VI.

Under s. 536(2), D may elect mode of trial.

Other related provisions appear in the corresponding note to s. 119, *supra*.

121. (1) Frauds on the government — Every one commits an offence who

(a) directly or indirectly

(i) gives, offers, or agrees to give or offer to an official or to any member of his family, or to any one for the benefit of an official, or

(ii) being an official, demands, accepts or offers or agrees to accept from any person for himself or another person,

a loan, reward, advantage or benefit of any kind as consideration for cooperation, assistance, exercise of influence or an act or omission in connection with

(iii) the transaction of business with or any matter of business relating to the government, or

(iv) a claim against Her Majesty or any benefit that Her Majesty is authorized or is entitled to bestow,

whether or not, in fact, the official is able to cooperate, render assistance, exercise influence or do or omit to do what is proposed, as the case may be;

(b) having dealings of any kind with the government, pays a commission or reward to or confers an advantage or benefit of any kind on an employee or official of the government with which he deals, or to any member of his family, or to any one for the benefit of the employee or official, with respect to those dealings, unless he has the consent in writing of the head of the branch of government with which he deals, the proof of which lies on him;

(c) being an official or employee of the government, demands, accepts or offers or agrees to accept from a person who has dealings with the government a commission, reward, advantage or benefit of any kind directly or indirectly, by himself or through a member of his family or through any one for his benefit, unless he has the consent in writing of the head of the branch of government that employs him or of which he is an official, the proof of which lies on him;

(d) having or pretending to have influence with the government or with a minister of the government or an official, demands, accepts or offers or agrees to accept for himself or another person a reward, advantage or benefit of any kind as consideration for cooperation, assistance, exercise of influence or an act or omission in connection with

(i) anything mentioned in subparagraph (*a*)(iii) or (iv), or

(ii) the appointment of any person, including himself, to an office;

(e) gives, offers, or agrees to give or offer to a minister of the government or an official a reward, advantage or benefit of any kind as consideration for cooperation, assistance, exercise of influence or an act or omission in connection with

(i) anything mentioned in subparagraph (*a*)(iii) or (iv), or

(ii) the appointment of any person, including himself, to an office; or

(f) having made a tender to obtain a contract with the government

(i) gives, offers or agrees to give or offer to another person who has made a tender or to a member of his family, or to another person for the benefit of that person, a reward, advantage or benefit of any kind as consideration for the withdrawal of the tender of that person, or

(ii) demands, accepts or offers or agrees to accept from another person who has made a tender a reward, advantage or benefit of any kind as consideration for the withdrawal of his tender.

(2) Contractor subscribing to election fund — Every one commits an offence who, in order to obtain or retain a contract with the government, or as a term of any such contract, whether express or implied, directly or indirectly subscribes or gives, or agrees to subscribe or give, to any person any valuable consideration

(a) for the purpose of promoting the election of a candidate or a class or party of candidates to Parliament or the legislature of a province; or

(b) with intent to influence or affect in any way the result of an election conducted for the purpose of electing persons to serve in Parliament or the legislature of a province.

(3) Punishment — Every one who commits an offence under this section is guilty of an indictable offence and liable to imprisonment for a term not exceeding five years.

R.S., c. C-34, s. 110.

Commentary: The section creates a number of offences, generally described as "frauds upon the government". Each involves a donor and recipient.

The offence of s. 121(1)(a) is *influence peddling*. The *external circumstances* of the *donor* offence require that D, directly or indirectly, give, offer or agree to give or offer to an official, a member of his/her family or anyone for the benefit of the official, a loan, reward, advantage or benefit of any kind. What is given must be as *consideration* for co-operation, assistance, exercise of influence or an act or omission *in connection with* a business or claim as described in s. 121(1)(a)(iii) or (iv). It is of no legal moment whether the official is, in fact, able to fulfill the expectations of the donor. The *mental element* consists of the intention to cause the external circumstances of the offence. The provision does *not* explicitly require proof of any ulterior mental element. The *external circumstances* and *mental element* of the *recipient* offence mirror that of the donor, save that D must demand, accept or offer or agree to accept from another, for him/herself or another person, the prohibited subject-matter for the self-same consideration in connection with the same type of business or claim. Likewise, it is of no legal consequence whether D, is in fact, able to fulfil the expectations of the donor. The *mental element* requires proof that D intended to cause the external circumstances of the offence.

The offences of ss. 121(1)(b) and (c), in essence, prohibit unauthorized payments to or for the benefit of government officials by or on behalf of those who have dealings with the government.

The *external circumstances* of the *donor* offence of s. 121(1)(b) require that D have dealings of any kind with the government. D must, further, pay a commission or reward to or confer an advantage or benefit of any kind on an employee or official of the government with which D deals, to any member of D's family or to anyone for the benefit of the employee or official. What is paid or conferred must be *with respect to the dealings* D has with the government. Finally, the payment or conferment must be *without* the *consent* in *writing* of the head of the branch of the government with which D is dealing. The *mental element* consists of the intention to cause the external circumstances of the offence.

The *external circumstances* of the *recipient* offence of s. 121(1)(c) require that D is an official or employee of the government. D must demand, accept or offer or agree to accept from a person who has dealings with the government a commission, reward, advantage or benefit of any kind. D's demand or acceptance may be directly or indirectly by D or through a family member or a third party for D's benefit. Finally, what D demands or accepts must be *without* the *consent* in *writing* of the head of the branch of the government which employs D or of which s/he is an official. The *mental element* consists of the intention to cause the external circumstances of the offence.

The offences of ss. 121(1)(d) and (e) contain common elements.

The *external circumstances* of the *recipient* offence of s. 121(1)(d) require proof that D have or pretend to have influence with the government, a minister or official thereof. D must demand, accept or offer or

agree to accept for him/herself or another person, a reward, advantage or benefit of any kind. The reward, advantage or benefit which D demands or accepts (as earlier described) must be *as consideration
for* co-operation, assistance, exercise of influence or an act or omission in connection with any of the
matters described in s. 121(1)(d)(i) or (ii). The *mental element* consists of the intention to cause the
external circumstances of the offence.

The *external circumstances* of the *donor* offence, of s. 121(1)(e), require that D must give, offer or agree
to give or offer to a minister or official of the government a reward, advantage or benefit of any kind.
What is given, offered or agreed upon must be as consideration for co-operation, assistance, the exercise
of influence or an act or omission in connection with anything described in s. 121(1)(e)(i) or (ii). The
mental element, consists of the intention to cause the external circumstances of the offence.

The bilateral offence of s. 121(1)(f) involves the making of tenders to obtain government contracts. In
both the donor and recipient offence, D, as principal, must have made a tender to obtain a government
contract.

The *external circumstances* of the *donor* offence of s. 121(1)(f)(i) require that D, having made a tender
to obtain a contract with the government, give, offer or agree to give or offer to another who has made a
tender, a member of his/her family or a third party for the benefit of the rival tender, a *reward, advantage or benefit of any kind*. The reward advantage or benefit must be as consideration for withdrawal of
the tender of the competitor or *recipient*. The *external circumstances* of the recipient offence in s.
121(1)(f)(ii) require proof that D, having made a tender to obtain a government contract, demand, accept, or offer or agree to accept from another who has made a tender a reward, advantage or benefit of
any kind. The demand, acceptance or offer must be as consideration for the recipient's withdrawal of
tender. The *mental element* of each offence requires proof of the intention to cause the external
circumstances.

The offence of subsection (2) prohibits certain conduct by government contractors in which there is a
nexus between the contract and the election of political candidates. The *external circumstances* are complete where D, directly or indirectly, subscribes or gives or agrees to subscribe or give, to any person
any valuable consideration. There is no requirement *per se*, that D be a contractor with the government
at the time valuable consideration is given, though the initial purpose element in the section, *viz*, "in
order to obtain or retain a contract with the government, or as a term of any such contract" would seem
to suggest that more likely than not D will be an actual or putative contractor with the government. The
excerpted portion would seem more aptly characterized as a part of the *mental element* which must also
include proof of either the specific purpose of s. 121(2)(a) or intent of s. 121(2)(b) to establish liability.

Under s. 121(3) all offences under the section are indictable and, upon conviction, punishable by imprisonment for a term not exceeding five years.

Case Law
Nature and Elements of Offence

R. v. Cogger (1997), 116 C.C.C. (3d) 322 (S.C.C.) — An *intention* to commit a *prohibited act*, together
with *knowledge* of the *relevant* circumstances, is an acceptable basis of criminal liability. It is *not* strict
liability.

Section 121(1)(a) does *not* require the *recipient* to accept the benefit *qua* government employee, and *not*
in some other capacity. Section 121(1)(a)(ii) is designed to prevent government officials from undertaking, for consideration, to act on another's behalf in conducting business with the government. P is *not*
required to prove

i.   that the *benefit* was conferred *because* of D's position; or

ii.   that the *recipient knew* of the purpose of item i.

The *object* of s. 121(1)(a) is to prevent government *officials* from taking *benefits* from a third party in
exchange for conducting some form of business on the donor's behalf with the government. D must
agree to deal with the government on another's behalf for consideration. It is not necessary that the
official believe that his/her integrity has been compromised. It is the official's position in dealing with
the government, while a member of government, that makes it criminal. "Corruption" is *not* an essential
element, nor does it matter that the official purports to act in another capacity.

R. v. Hinchey (1996), 111 C.C.C. (3d) 353 (S.C.C.) — The purpose of s. 121(1)(c) in *not* merely to
preserve the integrity of government, but also to preserve the *appearance* of integrity. It is *not* necessary

for there to be a *corrupt* practice in order for the appearance of integrity to be harmed. What is made criminal is the conduct of a government official or employee under certain circumstances accepting a benefit from a person who has dealings with the government.

The *actus reus* of the s. 121(1)(c) offence comprises,

     i. the *giving* of a commission, reward, advantage or benefit of any kind *by* a person who has *dealings* with the *government*;

     ii. the *receipt* of item i by a *government employee*; and

     iii. the *absence* of *consent* of the employee's *superior* to the receipt.

What is given and received need *not* be something of value which constituted a *profit* to the employee derived, at least in part, from the employee's relation to or position with the government. "A person who has dealings with the government" contemplates a donor who is *in the process* of having *commercial dealings* with the government at the material time. "Commission, reward, advantage or benefit of any kind" includes diverse forms of benefits that amount to a material or substantial gain.

The *mental element* in s. 121(1)(c) requires proof that D *knew* of the relevant *conduct* and of the *circumstances* in which it occurred. P is required to prove,

     i. that D consciously decided to *accept* what, in all of the circumstances, is found to be "a commission, reward, advantage or benefit of any kind";

     ii. that D *knew* or was *wilfully blind* that, at the time of the receipt, the donor had *dealings* with the government; and

     iii. that D *knew* or was *wilfully blind* that, at the time of the receipt, his/her *superior* had *not* consented to the receipt.

P need *not* prove that D knew the benefit was received because of D's position in government.

R. v. Giguere (1983), 37 C.R. (3d) 1, 8 C.C.C. (3d) 1 (S.C.C.) — Proof of an agreement that D co-operate, assist or exercise influence is an essential element of the offence.

Martineau v. R. (1965), 48 C.R. 209, [1966], 4 C.C.C. 327 (S.C.C.) — A member of the Quebec Legislative Council is an "official", being "appointed to discharge a public duty", and, as such, may be properly convicted of influence peddling. Under s. 121(1)(a), it need *not* be shown that D was acting in his/her official capacity when contravening the section.

R. v. Greenwood (1991), 8 C.R. (4th) 235, 67 C.C.C. (3d) 435 (Ont. C.A.) — "Commission" and "reward" connote compensation for services rendered. "Advantage" and "benefit" have a wider meaning, which includes gifts which do not relate to any service provided by the recipient. A government employee receives an "advantage" or "benefit" when the employee receives something of value which, in all the circumstances, the trier of fact concludes constitutes a profit to the employee (or a family member), derived at least in part because the employee is a government employee, or because of the nature of the work done by the employee for the government.

Mental Element

R. v. Cogger (1997), 116 C.C.C. (3d) 322 (S.C.C.) — The essence of the s. 121(1)(a) offence is that D *intentionally* committed the prohibited act with the *knowledge* of the *circumstances* which are *necessary* elements of the offence.

P must prove that D

i.   *knew* that s/he was an *official*;

ii.   *intentionally* demanded or accepted a loan, reward, advantage or benefit for D or another; and

iii.   *knew* that the *reward* was in *consideration* for co-operation, assistance or exercise of influence *in connection with* the transaction of business with or relating to the government.

R. v. Cooper (1977), 37 C.R.N.S. 1, 34 C.C.C. (2d) 18 (S.C.C.) — An "intention" to confer a benefit "with respect to" dealings with the government is a necessary element of a charge under s. 121(1)(b). The offence is *not* one of strict liability.

R. v. Fisher (1994), 28 C.R. (4th) 63, 88 C.C.C. (3d) 103 (Ont. C.A.); leave to appeal refused (1995), 35 C.R. (4th) 401 (note), 94 C.C.C. (3d) vii (note) (S.C.C.) — P is required to prove *knowledge* or *wilful blindness* of the existence of the relevant circumstances constituting a blameworthy state of mind which makes D's voluntary conduct criminal, even if there is *no* requirement of an ulterior or corrupt *motive* in receiving the benefit.

Dealings

R. v. Achtem (1978), 13 C.R. (3d) 199 (Alta. C.A.) — Dealings with an official of the Alberta Housing Corporation, an arm or agency of the government, constitute dealings with the government.

R. v. Greenwood (1991), 8 C.R. (4th) 235, 67 C.C.C. (3d) 435 (Ont. C.A.) — The *mental element* of the offences created by s. 121(2) and the provisions of s. 121 other than s. 121(1)(c), requires that the doing of the prohibited act be accompanied by a purpose or intent. The *mental element* of s. 121(1)(c) is the employee's conscious decision to accept the thing offered, made with knowledge or wilful blindness that the giver was having dealings with the government and that the employee's superior had *not* consented to the employee's receipt of the thing.

Person

R. v. Barrow (1984), 14 C.C.C. (3d) 470 (N.S. C.A.) — A unincorporated political association constitutes a "person" within s. 121(1)(d).

Cooperation, Assistance, Exercise of Influence

R. v. Giguere (1983), 37 C.R. (3d) 1, 8 C.C.C. (3d) 1 (S.C.C.) — "Influence" requires the actual affecting of a decision, such as the awarding of a contract. " Cooperation" and "assistance" are *not* so limited. The opening of doors or arranging of meetings does *not* constitute exercise of influence. It does constitute assistance or co-operation.

Charter Considerations

R. v. Fisher (1994), 28 C.R. (4th) 63, 88 C.C.C. (3d) 103 (Ont. C.A.); leave to appeal refused (1995), 35 C.R. (4th) 401n, 94 C.C.C. (3d) viin (S.C.C.) — The shift to D of the *onus* of proving the existence of the relevant written consent offends *Charter* s. 11(d) and is *not* saved by s. 1. The section ought be read as if the phrase "the proof of which lies on him" were deleted.

R. v. Fisher (1994), 28 C.R. (4th) 63, 88 C.C.C. (3d) 103 (Ont. C.A.); leave to appeal refused (1995), 35 C.R. (4th) 401n, 94 C.C.C. (3d) viin (S.C.C.) — The failure of s. 121(1)(c) to define the mental element required to be proven, as well the substantial breadth of the provision, does *not* offend *Charter* s. 7.

Related Provisions: "Government", "office" and "official" are defined in s. 118.

Section 122 punishes fraud or breach of trust committed by any official, in connection with the duties of their office. Municipal corruption is prohibited under s. 123. Section 124 makes it an indictable offence to sell or purchase offices and s. 125 bars influencing or negotiating appointments, as well as dealing in offices.

Upon conviction of a s. 121 offence, D, under s. 750(3), lacks capacity to contract or receive any benefit under a contract with or to hold office under Her Majesty. Section 750(4) permits application for restoration of any one or more of the capacities lost upon conviction.

This offence is an "enterprise crime offence" under s. 462.3 and an "offence" under s. 183 for the purposes of Parts XII.2 and VI, respectively.

D may *elect* mode of trial under s. 536(2).

---

122. Breach of trust by public officer — Every official who, in connection with the duties of his office, commits fraud or a breach of trust is guilty of an indictable offence and liable to imprisonment for a term not exceeding five years, whether or not the fraud or breach of trust would be an offence if it were committed in relation to a private person.

R.S., c. C-34, s. 111.

Commentary: The section describes and punishes *fraud* and *breach of trust* by persons who hold an *office*, or are appointed to discharge *public duty*. The *external circumstances* and *mental element* of the offence are the external circumstances and mental elements of the offence of fraud or breach of trust, as the case may be. Liability under the section would seem to be somewhat more expansive, in that it may nonetheless be established even where a case of fraud or breach of trust cannot be made out in relation to a private person.

Case Law

Nature and Elements of Offence

R. v. Leblanc (1982), 44 N.R. 150 (S.C.C.) — The actions of a municipal treasurer, who accepted money in exchange for greater cooperation with a town planner, constitute misconduct in the execution of his functions at common law and a breach of trust under the *Code*.

R. v. Sheets (1971), 15 C.R.N.S. 232, 1 C.C.C. (2d) 508 (S.C.C.) — An elected municipal official may be convicted under this section.

R. v. Campbell (1967), 50 C.R. 270, [1967] 3 C.C.C. 250 (Ont. C.A.), affirmed, *(*sub nom. *Campbell v. R)* 2 C.R.N.S. 403 — This section applies to a breach of trust by an official in connection with the duties of his office, *not* a breach of trust in respect of trust property.

R. v. Lippi (1996), 2 C.R. (5th) 32, 111 C.C.C. (3d) 187 (Que. C.A.) — The essential elements of the offence are,

    i. the *status* of a *public official*;

    ii. an *act* committed in the context of the *carrying out* of the duties; and

    iii. an *act* constituting *fraud* or *breach of trust*.

R. v. Perreault (1992), 75 C.C.C. (3d) 425 (Que. C.A.); leave to appeal refused (1993), 77 C.C.C. (3d) vi (note), 149 N.R. 239 (note) (S.C.C.) — The offence requires proof:

    i. that D is an "official" within s. 118;

    ii. that the acts alleged were committed in the general *context* of the execution of D's duties; and

    iii. that the acts constituted a *fraud* or *breach of trust*.

Where it is alleged that the acts constituted a breach of trust, it is *not* necessary to prove *corruption*. It must be shown in such cases, however, that D did or failed to do an act *contrary* to the *duty* imposed upon him/her by statute, regulation, employment contract or official directive and that the act gave D some personal benefit, directly or indirectly. The *benefit* could be payment of money, hope of promotion, or a mere desire to please a superior. The criminal law prohibits acts done in furtherance of personal ends, the use of D's office in a public service for the promotion of private ends or to obtain, directly or indirectly, some benefit. It is *not* used to punish technical breaches, nor acts of administrative indiscipline or fault.

R. v. Hébert, [1986] R.J.Q. 236 (C.A.) — This section does *not* require dishonesty or corruption, nor concealment of the illegal act. Absence of monetary prejudice to the government is no defence.

Quebec (P.G.) v. Cyr, [1984] C.A. 254 (Que. C.A.) — Corporations are capable of breach of trust.

Parties [See also s. 21]

R. v. Robillard (1985), 18 C.C.C. (3d) 266 (Que. C.A.) — Assistance to a public officer in a breach of trust may make D a party to the offence.

R. v. Lippi (1996), 2 C.R. (5th) 32, 111 C.C.C. (3d) 187 (Que. C.A.) — The section does *not* offend *Charter* s. 7.

Related Provisions: "Official" and "office" are defined in s. 118. The general offence of fraud is described in s. 380(1) and criminal breach of trust in s. 336. "Trustee" is defined in s. 2.

This offence is an "enterprise crime offence" under s. 462.3 and an "offence" under s. 183 for the purposes of Parts XII.2 and VI, respectively.

Under s. 536(2), D may elect mode of trial.

123. (1) Municipal corruption — Every one who

    (a) gives, offers or agrees to give or offer to a municipal official, or

    (b) being a municipal official, demands, accepts or offers or agrees to accept from any person, a loan, reward, advantage or benefit of any kind as consideration for the official

(c) **to abstain from voting at a meeting of the municipal council or a committee thereof,**

(d) **to vote in favour of or against a measure, motion or resolution,**

(e) **to aid in procuring or preventing the adoption of a measure, motion or resolution, or**

(f) **to perform or fail to perform an official act,**

is guilty of an indictable offence and liable to imprisonment for a term not exceeding five years.

(2) **Influencing municipal official** — Every one who

(a) **by suppression of the truth, in the case of a person who is under a duty to disclose the truth,**

(b) **by threats or deceit, or**

(c) **by any unlawful means, influences or attempts to influence a municipal official to do anything mentioned in paragraphs (1)(c) to (f)**

is guilty of an indictable offence and liable to imprisonment for a term not exceeding five years.

(3) **"municipal official"** — In this section "municipal official" means a member of a municipal council or a person who holds an office under a municipal government.

R.S., c. C-34, s. 112; R.S. 1985, c. 27 (1st Supp.), s. 16.

Commentary: The section describes and punishes the bilateral offence of *municipal corruption*. It creates a further offence which prohibits the actual or attempted improper influence of municipal officials. In each case, the actual or intended recipient of the consideration or object of influence, as the case may be, is a "municipal official" as defined in s. 123(3).

The *external circumstances* of the *donor* offence of *municipal corruption* requires proof that D gave, offered or agreed to give or offer to a municipal official a loan, reward, advantage or benefit of any kind. What is given, offered or agreed upon must be *as consideration for* the official doing or failing to do anything described in ss. 123(1)(c)–(f). The *external circumstances* of the *recipient* offence require proof that D, a municipal official under s. 123(3), demand, accept or offer or agree to accept from another a loan, reward, advantage or benefit of any kind. What is demanded, accepted or agreed upon must be *as consideration for* D, the official, doing or failing to do anything described in ss. 123(1)(c)–(f). In each case the *mental element* requires proof of the intention to cause the external circumstances of the offence.

The *influence* offence of s. 123(2) is directed solely at the conduct of the person who seeks to exert influence on a "municipal official". The *external circumstances* of the offence consist of the influence, actual or attempted, of a municipal official, as defined in s. 123(3), to do anything described in ss. 123(1)(c)–(f) by any means prohibited in ss. 123(2)(a)–(c). The *mental element* does *not* require proof of any intention beyond the intention to cause the external circumstances of the offence.

Case Law

Essential Elements

R. v. Leblanc (1982), 44 N.R. 150 (S.C.C.) — The simple fact that the actions of a municipal treasurer, in accepting money in exchange for greater cooperation with a town planner, were preferential treatment was sufficient for them to constitute an offence.

R. v. Sheets (1971), 15 C.R.N.S. 232, 1 C.C.C. (2d) 508 (S.C.C.) — The offences of this section, dealing with municipal corruption and the influencing of municipal officials, require the involvement of at least two persons. An offence under s. 122 may be committed by the act or omission of a single person.

Municipal Official

Belzberg v. R. (1961), 36 C.R. 368, 131 C.C.C. 281 (S.C.C.) — The position of Chief Building Inspector is an "office" under s. 123(3).

R. v. St. Pierre, [1971] Que. C.A. 758 (C.A.) — A police officer, within the *Code's* definition of peace officer, is also through his/her employment by the city, a municipal official.

Related Provisions: Related corruption or bribery offences are described in ss. 119 and 120. Frauds upon the government are punished under s. 121 and breach of trust or fraud by "officials", as described in s. 118, by s. 122. Certain conduct involving the sale, purchase or other dealings in offices is prohibited under ss. 124 and 125. Section 128 prohibits misconduct by peace officers or coroners in the execution of a process.

The offence is an "offence" under s. 183 for the purposes of Part VI.

Under s. 536(2), D may *elect* mode of trial.

124. Selling or purchasing office — Every one who

(a) purports to sell or agrees to sell an appointment to or resignation from an office, or a consent to any such appointment or resignation, or receives or agrees to receive a reward or profit from the purported sale thereof, or

(b) purports to purchase or gives a reward or profit for the purported purchase of any such appointment, resignation or consent, or agrees or promises to do so,

is guilty of an indictable offence and liable to imprisonment for a term not exceeding five years.

R.S., c. C-34, s. 113.

Commentary: This section prohibits certain transactions involving the *purchase and sale of offices*, as defined in s. 118. Both the vendor and purchaser are subject to criminal liability.

The *external circumstances* of the *vendor* offence in s. 124(a) are complete when D purports or agrees to sell an appointment to or resignation from an office or a consent thereto. They are also established where D receives or agrees to receive a reward or profit from the purported sale of such appointment, resignation or consent. No actual sale need take place. Neither is it necessary to show that D had the actual authority to complete such a transaction. The *mental element* requires proof only of the intent to cause the external circumstances of the offence.

In the *purchaser* offence in s. 124(b), the *external circumstances* are proven where D purports to purchase or gives a reward or profit for the purported purchase of any appointment to or resignation from an office, or consent thereto. They are equally proven where D agrees or promises to do so. No actual purchase need take place. The *mental element* consists of the intent to cause the external circumstances of the offence.

Related Provisions: "Office" is defined in s. 118.

Section 125 prohibits the influence or negotiation of appointments, as well as certain dealings in offices. The offences of ss. 121(1)(d) and (e) also prohibit the sale and purchase of influence, *inter alia*, in connection with appointments to an "office" as defined in s. 118.

Under s. 536(2), D may *elect* mode of trial.

Sections 750(3) and (4) apply upon conviction.

125. Influencing or negotiating appointments or dealing in offices — Every one who

(a) receives, agrees to receive, gives or procures to be given, directly or indirectly, a reward, advantage or benefit of any kind as consideration for cooperation, assistance or exercise of influence to secure the appointment of any person to an office,

(b) solicits, recommends or negotiates in any manner with respect to an appointment to or resignation from an office, in expectation of a direct or indirect reward, advantage or benefit, or

(c) keeps without lawful authority, the proof of which lies on him, a place for transacting or negotiating any business relating to

(i) the filling of vacancies in offices,

(ii) the sale or purchase of offices, or

(iii) appointments to or resignations from offices,

is guilty of an indictable offence and liable to imprisonment for a term not exceeding five years.

R.S., c. C-34, s. 114.

Commentary: The section prohibits certain transactions involving influence or dealing in, as well as negotiation of, appointment to or resignation from offices.

The bilateral *influence* offence of s. 125(a) involves a *recipient* and donor, a *transaction*, actual or intended, prohibited *subject-matter* and an element of *consideration* or purpose. The *mental element* consists of the intention to cause the external circumstances.

The *external circumstances* of the *negotiation* offence of s. 125(b), involve, *inter alia, conduct* "in expectation of a direct or indirect reward, advantage or benefit" for D as a result of solicitation, recommendation or negotiation. The *mental element* requires proof of *no* ulterior state of mind.

The offence of s. 125(c), *dealing in offices*, requires proof that D keeps, without lawful authority, a place for transacting or negotiating any business relating to any subject-matter described in ss. 125(c)(i)–(iii). The shift of the onus of proving lawful authority to D, may invoke scrutiny under *Charter* ss. 7 and 11(d). No ulterior *mental element* need be proven.

Related Provisions: "Office" is defined in s. 118.

Under s. 536(2), D may elect mode of trial.

Other related provisions are described in the corresponding note to s. 124, *supra*.

126. (1) Disobeying a statute — Every one who, without lawful excuse, contravenes an Act of Parliament by wilfully doing anything that it forbids or by wilfully omitting to do anything that it requires to be done is, unless a punishment is expressly provided by law, guilty of an indictable offence and liable to imprisonment for a term not exceeding two years.

(2) Attorney General of Canada may act — Any proceedings in respect of a contravention of or conspiracy to contravene an Act mentioned in subsection (1), other than this Act, may be instituted at the instance of the Government of Canada and conducted by or on behalf of that Government.

R.S., c. C-34, s. 115; 1974–75–76, c. 93, s. 4.

Commentary: The section punishes contraventions of Acts of Parliament *in the absence of other provisions* and provides for the institution of proceedings in such cases by the Attorney General of Canada.

For liability under s. 126(1), D must contravene an Act of Parliament, either by wilfully *doing anything* the Act forbids, or by wilfully *omitting to do anything* the Act requires. There must be *no* lawful excuse for D's conduct and *no* punishment expressly provided by law for such contravention. The precise elements that together constitute the *external circumstances* and *mental element* of D's offence will vary with the requirements of the Act contravened.

Section 126(2) is procedural. It authorizes the institution and conduct of proceedings in respect of a contravention or conspiracy to contravene an Act described in s. 126(1) other than the *Code*, by the Government of Canada, but is *not* limitative of the prosecutorial authority which may conduct such proceedings.

Case Law
Act of Parliament

R. v. Singer (1940), 75 C.C.C. 1 (S.C.C.) — A violation of an Order-in-Council is *not* a violation of an Act of Parliament.

Without Lawful Excuse

R. v. Parrot (1979), 51 C.C.C. (2d) 539 (Ont. C.A.); leave to appeal refused (1980), 51 C.C.C. (2d) 539n (S.C.C.) — A mistaken belief as to a legal obligation affords no basis for a defence of lawful excuse.

Application of Section

Vapor Can. Ltd. v. MacDonald, [1977] 2 S.C.R. 134 — This section is a default provision, engaged only when no penalty or punishment is expressly provided. It cannot provide a basis on which to support the validity, under the criminal law power, of a completely independent civil remedy, which lies only at the behest of private parties claiming some private injury.

Related Provisions: The language, "an Act of Parliament", limits the expansive definition of "Act" in s. 2 for the purposes of this section.

Section 126(2) parallels, to some extent, part of the definition of "Attorney General" in s. 2 and the general scope of federal prosecutorial authority and responsibility.

Semble, D may *elect* a mode of trial.

127. (1) Disobeying order of court — **Every one who, without lawful excuse, disobeys a lawful order made by a court of justice or by a person or body of persons authorized by any Act to make or give the order, other than an order for the payment of money, is, unless a punishment or other mode of proceeding is expressly provided by law, guilty of an indictable offence and liable to imprisonment for a term not exceeding two years.**

(2) Attorney General of Canada may act — **Where the order referred to in subsection (1) was made in proceedings instituted at the instance of the Government of Canada and conducted by or on behalf of that Government, any proceedings in respect of a contravention of or conspiracy to contravene that order may be instituted and conducted in like manner.**

R.S., c. C-34, s. 116; 1974–75–76, c. 93, s. 5.

Commentary: The section authorizes proceedings for *disobedience of a lawful order* of a court or other duly authorized tribunal *where no other mode of proceeding or punishment is provided* and, further, describes the circumstances under which such proceedings may be instituted and conducted on behalf of the Government of Canada.

Section 127(1) only applies where a punishment or other mode of proceeding is *not* expressly provided by law. In general, the *external circumstances* of the offence consist of the disobedience by D of a lawful order made by a court of justice or by a person or body of persons authorized by any Act to make or give the order. The order disobeyed must *not* be an order for the payment of money. D must disobey the order *without a lawful excuse*. P must prove the lawfulness of the underlying order and the authority of the court or other tribunal to make it. The *mental element* of the offence consists of the intention to cause its external circumstances.

Under s. 127(2) the Government of Canada has the authority to institute and conduct proceedings under s. 127(1) where the underlying order was made in the circumstances described.

Case Law
Lawful Order

R. v. Clement (1981), 23 C.R. (3d) 193, 61 C.C.C. (2d) 449 (S.C.C.) — The words "a lawful order made by a court of justice" refer to an order of the court, either criminal or civil in nature. The power of a court to control its own process through the mechanism of contempt, while recognized at common law as an inherent right of a court, is *not* another mode of proceeding expressly provided by law, so as to bar a conviction under s. 127(1).

Re Gerson (1946), 87 C.C.C. 143 (S.C.C.) — The section does *not* supersede the inherent power of a court of justice to punish summarily for contempt committed in the face of the court.

R. v. Gaudreault (1992), 76 C.C.C. (3d) 188 (Que. C.A.) — Civil contempt may constitute "a punishment or other mode of proceeding" within s. 127(1).

Punishment or Other Mode of Proceeding

R. v. Gaudreault (1995), 105 C.C.C. (3d) 270 (Que. C.A.) — Where D's conduct could have been the object of proceedings under the *Code of Civil Procedure*, there is no breach of *Code*, s. 127.

Related Provisions: "Act" is expansively defined in s. 2 to include Federal and Provincial enactments both prior and subsequent to Confederation.

The section does not purport to supersede or otherwise limit the inherent power or authority of a court of record to punish summarily for contempt *in facie curiae*, a power, jurisdiction and authority expressly preserved by *Code* s. 9.

Under s. 536(2), D may *elect* mode of trial.

128. Misconduct of officers executing process — Every peace officer or coroner who, being entrusted with the execution of a process, wilfully

(a) misconducts himself in the execution of the process, or

(b) makes a false return to the process,

is guilty of an indictable offence and liable to imprisonment for a term not exceeding two years.

R.S., c. C-34, s. 117.

Commentary: The section prohibits misconduct by those who execute a process.

The *external circumstances* require that D, as principal, be a peace officer or coroner who is entrusted with the execution of a process. Further, D must either misconduct him/herself in the execution of the process, or make a false return thereto. The *mental element* consists of the intention to cause the external circumstances of the offence. No ulterior *mental element*, as for example, an intent to mislead or obstruct the course of justice, need be proven.

Related Provisions: "Peace officer" is expansively defined in s. 2. "Coroner" is not defined. Provision is made in s. 529 for the issuance of a coroner's warrant and recognizance.

Other corruption and disobedience offences in relation to peace officers are found in s. 120. Sections 146 and 147 prohibit conduct by peace officers which permits or assists the escape of persons in lawful custody.

Sections 25–31 provide protection, equally authority, for persons administering and enforcing the law.

Under s. 536(2), D may *elect* mode of trial.

129. Offences relating to public or peace officer — Every one who

(a) resists or wilfully obstructs a public officer or peace officer in the execution of his duty or any person lawfully acting in aid of such an officer,

(b) omits, without reasonable excuse, to assist a public officer or peace officer in the execution of his duty in arresting a person or in preserving the peace, after having reasonable notice that he is required to do so, or

(c) resists or wilfully obstructs any person in the lawful execution of a process against lands or goods or in making a lawful distress or seizure,

is guilty of

(d) an indictable offence and liable to imprisonment for a term not exceeding two years, or

(e) an offence punishable on summary conviction.

R.S., c. C-34, s. 118; 1972, c. 13, s. 7.

Commentary: The gravamen of these offences is the unlawful interference with peace or public officers in the execution of their duties. The *external circumstances* of the offences of ss. 129(a) and (c) involve *resistance* or *obstruction*. Under s. 129(a), the person resisted or obstructed must be a peace or a public officer *in the execution* of his/her duty or anyone *lawfully* acting in aid of the officer. Under s. 129(c), V may be *any* person in the lawful execution of a process against lands or goods or in making a lawful distress or seizure. In each case the *mental element* requires that D intend to cause the external circumstances of the offence. The *obstruction* mode requires proof that D's conduct be *wilful*.

The offence of s. 129(b) is one of *omission*. The *external circumstances* require proof that D omitted to assist a public or peace officer in the execution of his/her duty in arresting someone or preserving the peace, after D had reasonable notice that such assistance was required. P must also prove that there was *no* reasonable excuse for such omission to assist.

The *mental element* requires proof that D's act or omission was intentional.

Case Law

Wilfully

R. v. Goodman (1951), 12 C.R. 65, 99 C.C.C. 366 (B.C. C.A.) — "Wilfully" implies that D, being a free agent, knew what s/he was doing and intended to do what s/he did.

Obstruction: S. 129(a); (c)

R. v. Moore (1979), 5 C.R. (3d) 289, 43 C.C.C. (2d) 833 (S.C.C.) — D's refusal to identify himself to a police officer, who observed him going through a red light on a bicycle, was an obstruction of the officer in the performance of his duties, namely, the duty of enforcing the law.

R. v. Kephart (1988), 44 C.C.C. (3d) 97 (Alta. C.A.) — As an officer has no statutory or common law right to enter a dwelling house without a warrant, a refusal to permit him entry does not constitute an obstruction.

R. v. Guthrie (1982), 28 C.R. (3d) 395, 69 C.C.C. (2d) 216 (Alta. C.A.) — Where there is no evidence of the commission of any offence, in the absence of statutory compulsion, there is no legal obligation to respond to police questions. The refusal to identify oneself does *not* amount to obstruction.

R. v. Soltys (1980), 56 C.C.C. (2d) 43 (B.C. C.A.) — D's attempt to drink a glass of whiskey immediately after a demand was made by a police officer for a breathalyzer constituted an attempt to obstruct the officer in the performance of his duty.

R. v. Watkins (1972), 7 C.C.C. (2d) 513 (Ont. H.C.); appeal dismissed without reasons (1972), 7 C.C.C. (2d) 513n (Ont. C.A.) — The continued presence of D, in defiance of a proper order by the police to disperse, is an obstruction of the police in the execution of their duty.

R. v. Lavin (1992), 16 C.R. (4th) 112, 76 C.C.C. (3d) 279 (Que. C.A.) — D may *not* be convicted of obstructing a peace officer merely by doing nothing, absent a common law or statutory duty to do so. Wilful obstruction requires some positive act, such as concealment of evidence, or an omission to do something which D is legally obliged to do. (per Vallerand and Tyndale JJ.A.)

In the Execution of His Duty: S. 129(a); (b)

R. v. Biron (1975), 30 C.R.N.S. 109, 23 C.C.C. (2d) 513 (S.C.C.) — Even where D is subsequently found *not* guilty of the offence for which he was arrested, D may be convicted of resisting an officer in the execution of his duty where D resisted the officer into whose custody he was delivered. The *lawfulness* of the arrest is to be determined in relation to the *circumstances* which were *apparent* to the peace officer at the *time* of arrest. The peace officer was entitled to arrest an accused whom he found "apparently" committing a criminal offence. In any event, the second officer who received D into custody was in the execution of his duty as he reasonably believed that the first officer had witnessed a breach of the peace.

Knowlton v. R. (1973), 21 C.R.N.S. 344, 10 C.C.C. (2d) 377 (S.C.C.) — Police officers refusing admittance to a cordoned-off area of a public street were acting in the execution of their duty. D's conduct in pushing his way past, despite warnings, amounted to obstruction.

R. v. Houle (1986), 48 C.R. (3d) 284, 24 C.C.C. (3d) 57 (Alta. C.A.) — A peace officer is *not* acting in the lawful execution of his duty when seeking to enforce a non-existent law, even if he honestly and reasonably believes it to exist.

R. v. Noel (1995), 101 C.C.C. (3d) 183 (B.C. C.A.) — To be "in the execution of his duty", a peace officer does *not* have to be involved in the investigation of a specific crime with an identifiable subject. If, whilst on duty, a peace officer's activities fall within the duties or responsibilities of a police officer under statute or common law, the peace officer will be engaged "in the execution of his duty". More than simply being "on duty" or "at work" is required.

R. v. Thomas (1991), 67 C.C.C. (3d) 81 (Nfld. C.A.); affirmed (1993), 78 C.C.C. (3d) 575 (S.C.C.) — A police officer *unlawfully* on the premises is *not* acting in the *execution* of duty, at least in relation to persons lawfully in possession of the premises. Resistance offered in response to an officer's conduct in such circumstances is *not* obstruction. Entry upon the property of another may *not* be made by anyone, including police officers, unless authorized by statute, the common law or on behalf of the owner.

R. v. Tortolano (1975), 28 C.C.C. (2d) 562 (Ont. C.A.) — The obstruction must relate to the execution of the officer's duty and not merely take place while the officer is on duty. D need not completely frustrate, but only affect the officer in the execution of his/her duty.

R. v. Quist (1981), 61 C.C.C. (2d) 207 (Sask. C.A.) — D is *not* entitled to leave before an officer has an opportunity to exercise his/her duty, such as where after failing to produce a driver's licence and to respond to questions as to alcohol consumption, D fled before the officer had the opportunity to make a breathalyzer demand. In that instance, D has obstructed a peace officer in the execution of his/her duty.

The Mental Element

R. v. Noel (1995), 101 C.C.C. (3d) 183 (B.C. C.A.) — Section 129(a) proscribes conduct undertaken with the *intention* that it obstruct an individual in the execution of his/her duty. The *circumstances* of the offence include that the individual obstructed is

i.   a peace officer; and,

ii.   engaged in the execution of his/her duty.

Items i and ii are *circumstances* of the offence. *Knowledge* of items i and ii is an essential element of *mens rea*. Intention to obstruct need *not* be tied to a specifically defined duty. D need only know or be aware, at the time of the obstructive conduct, that the peace officer was engaged in the execution of a duty not the specifics it.

Res Judicata [See also s. 8]

R. v. Georgieff (1955), 20 C.R. 142, 111 C.C.C. 3 (Ont. C.A.) — D should *not* be convicted both of obstructing and of assaulting police officers if the charges arise out of the same series of events and the evidence shows that the obstruction constitutes the assault.

Related Provisions: "Peace officer" and "public officer" are defined in s. 2. The *Code* does not contain an exhaustive statement of the duties and authority of a peace or public officer, although several provisions implicitly or explicitly define or limit certain aspects of their authority and/or duty. Sections 25–31 define the limits of protection, hence authority, of persons administering and enforcing the law, and ss. 32 and 33 relate to the suppression of riots. Specific authority to arrest without a warrant is given by s. 495. Section 494(3) allows reception of a person arrested by another without warrant.

Section 120 prohibits, *inter alia*, the bribery of peace or public officers, and s. 270 prohibits assaults upon such persons. Impersonation of a peace or public officer is an offence under s. 130.

Sections 146 and 147 prohibit conduct by peace officers which permits or assists the escape of persons in lawful custody. Section 128 renders criminal certain misconduct by peace officers in the execution or return of process.

These offences are triable either way. Where P proceeds by indictment, D may *elect* mode of trial under s. 536(2).

130. Personating peace officer — Every one who

(a) falsely represents himself to be a peace officer or a public officer, or

(b) not being a peace officer or public officer, uses a badge or article of uniform or equipment in a manner that is likely to cause persons to believe that he is a peace officer or a public officer, as the case may be,

is guilty of an offence punishable on summary conviction.
R.S., c. C-34, s. 119.

Commentary: The essence of each offence is a *representation* by D of a *specific* false character, namely, that s/he is a peace or public officer.

The *external circumstances* of the offence of s. 130(a) are proven where D falsely represents him/herself to be a peace or public officer. There is *no* restriction on the means of the false representation. D must intentionally make such representation in the *knowledge* of its falsity. No ulterior *mental element*, as for example, "with intent to gain advantage for himself or another person", is required.

The *external circumstances* of s. 130(b) require that, as principal, D *not* be a peace or public officer. The *means* of misrepresentation must be a badge or article of uniform or equipment. The *manner* of misrepresentation must be likely to cause persons to believe that D is a peace or public officer, i.e., produce a likelihood of mischief. The *mental element* comprises the intention to cause the external circumstances of the offence including, *semble*, knowledge of the likelihood that such mischief will ensue from use of the prohibited means.

Related Provisions: "Peace officer" and "public officer" are defined in s. 2.

Several impersonation offences are described and punished in ss. 403–405 of Part X.

Other offences relating to peace and public officers are described in the corresponding note to s. 129, *supra*.

The offence is tried under Part XXVII and punished in accordance with s. 787(1).

Misleading Justice

131. (1) Perjury — Subject to subsection (3), every one commits perjury who, with intent to mislead, makes before a person who is authorized by law to permit it to be made before him, a false statement under oath or solemn affirmation, by affidavit, solemn declaration or deposition or orally, knowing that the statement is false.

(2) Idem — Subsection (1) applies whether or not a statement referred to in that subsection is made in a judicial proceeding.

(3) Application — Subsection (1) does not apply to a statement referred to in that subsection that is made by a person who is not specially permitted, authorized or required by law to make that statement.
R.S., c. C-34, s. 120; R.S. 1985, c. 27 (1st Supp.), s. 17.

Commentary: This section defines perjury.

The *external circumstances* of perjury comprise several elements. D must make a *false statement*. The false statement must be made *before* a *person* who is *authorized* by law to permit it to be made before him. It is *not* essential under s. 131(2) that the false statement be made in a judicial proceeding, but it must be made under oath or *solemn affirmation*, by *affidavit, solemn declaration* or deposition or orally. The section does *not* apply to statements made by a person who is *not* specially permitted, authorized or required by law to make such a statement. In other words, D must be a person who is so permitted, authorized or required by law.

The *mental element* in perjury requires proof that D intended to do the acts which constitute the external circumstances of the offence, further that D made such statement in the express *knowledge of its falsity, with intent to mislead.*

The constitutional integrity of the section has been challenged under *Charter* s. 11(h).

Case Law
Nature and Elements of Offence

Wolf v. R. (1974), 27 C.R.N.S. 150, 17 C.C.C. (2d) 425 (S.C.C.) — Where a witness falsely testifies that he does *not* remember, such that the failure of recollection is dishonest and deliberately asserted to prevent the court from arriving at a decision upon credible evidence, the witness commits perjury. An intent to mislead must be proved.

Calder v. R. (1960), 129 C.C.C. 202 (S.C.C.) — P must prove that the evidence given by D was *false*, that D *knew* it to be false, and that D gave the evidence with *intent to mislead* the court.

Farris v. R., [1965] 3 C.C.C. 245 (Ont. C.A.) — Even though an answer may be literally true if the question is understood in a certain sense, if D knew that *another sense* was intended by the question and that the answer in that context was false, then the result is perjury.

R. v. Regnier (1955), 21 C.R. 374, 112 C.C.C. 79 (Ont. C.A.) — To constitute perjury, it is *not* necessary that the false statement actually mislead the court, but only that D intended it to mislead the court.

Abuse of Process [See also s. 8]

Grdic v. R. (1985), 46 C.R. (3d) 1, 19 C.C.C. (3d) 289 (S.C.C.); reversing (1982), 29 C.R. (3d) 395, 3 C.C.C. (3d) 379 (B.C. C.A.) — *See also: R. v. Tracey* (1984), 9 C.C.C. (3d) 352 (Ont. C.A.) — On a charge of perjury arising from testimony by D at his trial, P is estopped from relitigating issues decided in favour of D unless P tenders, in addition to or in lieu of the evidence previously adduced, evidence that was not at the time of the first trial available by the exercise of reasonable diligence.

R. v. Skanes (1988), 44 C.C.C. (3d) 273 (Nfld. C.A.); reversing (1987), 62 Nfld. & P.E.I.R. 340 (Nfld. T.D.) — Although P became aware during an adjournment of the trial that D had committed perjury, P did *not* present evidence to challenge the false evidence. D was convicted on the original charge and subsequently charged with perjury. A stay of proceedings was *not* warranted as the perjury charge did not amount to a retrial or relitigation of an issue which has been resolved.

Res Judicata [See s. 8]

Related Provisions: "Statement" and "judicial proceeding" are defined in s. 118. Oaths and solemn affirmations are provided for under *C.E.A.* ss. 13–16.

Under s. 133, corroboration is *mandatory* in perjury cases. The evidence of a single witness is insufficient for conviction: it must be corroborated in a material particular by evidence that implicates D. Upon conviction, punishment is imposed in accordance with s. 132. D may elect mode of trial under s. 536(2).

A complementary summary conviction offence, applicable where D is *not* specially permitted, authorized or required by law to make a statement under oath or a solemn affirmation, appears in s. 134. The giving of contradictory evidence is an offence under s. 136. Fabricating evidence and certain offences relating to affidavits are prohibited under ss. 137 and 138. Obstructing justice is an offence under s. 139.

Section 585 contains special provisions respecting the sufficiency of counts charging, *inter alia*, perjury. Section 587(1)(a) permits the ordering of particulars of what is relied upon in support of a charge of perjury.

Neither the objection to answer incriminating questions under *C.E.A.* s. 5(2), the corresponding obligation to answer, nor *Charter* s. 13 render inadmissible the responses given in subsequent prosecutions for perjury.

132. Punishment — Every one who commits perjury is guilty of an indictable offence and liable to imprisonment for a term not exceeding fourteen years, but if a person commits perjury to procure the conviction of another person for an offence punishable by death, the person who commits perjury is liable to a maximum term of imprisonment for life.

Proposed Amendment — 132.

132. Punishment — Every one who commits perjury is guilty of an indictable offence and liable to imprisonment for a term not exceeding fourteen years.

> 1998, c. 35, s. 119 [Not in force at date of publication.],
> R.S., c. C-34, s. 121; R.S. 1985, c. 27 (1st Supp.), s. 17.

Commentary: The section makes perjury an indictable offence and provides the penalty upon conviction.

Related Provisions: Perjury, defined in s. 131, is an offence in respect of which D may *elect* mode of trial under s. 536(2), and an "offence" under s. 183 for the purposes of Part VI.

Other Related Provisions are discussed in the corresponding note to s. 131, *supra*.

133. Corroboration — No person shall be convicted of an offence under section 132 on the evidence of only one witness unless the evidence of that witness is corroborated in a material particular by evidence that implicates the accused.

> R.S., c. C-34, s. 122; R.S. 1985, c. 27 (1st Supp.), s. 17.

Commentary: *Corroboration* is *mandatory* in cases of perjury. The rule constitutes an exception to the general principle of evidentiary law that the testimony of a single witness, if believed with the requisite degree of certainty, is capable of proving P's case beyond a reasonable doubt. The section prohibits conviction of perjury upon the evidence of a single witness, unless that evidence is corroborated *in a material particular by evidence that implicates D.*

Case Law

R. v. Kyling (1970), 14 C.R.N.S. 257, 2 C.C.C. (2d) 79 (S.C.C.) — Corroboration is *not* required for the offence of inciting a person to commit perjury.

R. v. Van Straten (1994), 89 C.C.C. (3d) 470 (Alta. C.A.) — *See also*: *R. v. Doz* (1984), 12 C.C.C. (3d) 200 (Alta. C.A.) — Corroboration need only be of "a *material* particular", *not* of a contested issue.

R. v. Brewer (1921), 34 C.C.C. 341 (Alta. C.A.) — *See also*: *R. v. Nash* (1914), 23 C.C.C. 38 (Alta. C.A.); affirmed 8 W.W.R. 632n (S.C.C.) — When the falsity of the statement is proved by D's own sworn statement, made on another occasion, this section does *not* apply. It *only* applies where *one* witness is produced at trial to contradict D's sworn statement.

R. v. Thind (1991), 64 C.C.C. (3d) 301 (B.C. C.A.) — The section requires more than one witness to the falsehood of D's statement which is alleged to be incorrect. The evidence of the second witness need *not* confirm the evidence of the first witness. It must, however, contradict some part, not necessarily all of what D has sworn falsely.

R. v. Moore (1980), 52 C.C.C. (2d) 202 (B.C. C.A.) — Although there is a common element of giving false evidence, knowing that it is false, in both perjury and wilfully attempting to obstruct justice, there is an additional element required in a perjury charge. Corroboration is *not* required for an obstruction charge.

R. v. Evans (1995), 101 C.C.C. (3d) 369 (Man. C.A.) — To satisfy s. 133, the evidence of the other witnesses must, at least in total, deal with the *falsity* of the statement alleged to be false, not merely constitute "corroboration" as defined in cases relating to unsavory witnesses.

Bouchard v. R. (1982), 26 C.R. (3d) 178, 66 C.C.C. (2d) 338 (Man. C.A.); reversing (1981), 61 C.C.C. (2d) 242 (Man. Co. Ct.) — There is some doubt whether an admission of perjury, not made on oath and made out of court, must be corroborated.

Related Provisions: Other *Code* provisions which require corroboration before a finding of guilt may be made include s. 292(2) (procuring a feigned marriage) and s. 47(3) (treason and high treason).

Section 658(2) mentions corroboration of evidence concerning the age of a child or young person but does *not* appear to require it. Corroboration is *not* required under *C.E.A.* s. 16 (*unsworn* evidence), or *Code* s. 274 (listed offences of sexual assault, interference or exploitation).

134. (1) **Idem** — Subject to subsection (2), every one who, not being specially permitted, authorized or required by law to make a statement under oath or solemn affirmation, makes such a statement, by affidavit, solemn declaration or deposition or orally before a person who is authorized by law to permit it to be made before him, knowing that the statement is false, is guilty of an offence punishable on summary conviction.

(2) **Application** — Subsection (1) does not apply to a statement referred to in that subsection that is made in the course of a criminal investigation.

1974–75–76, c. 93, s. 6; R.S. 1985, c. 27 (1st Supp.), s. 17.

Commentary: This summary conviction offence is complementary to the crime of perjury in s. 131.

The *external circumstances* require that D be a person who is *not* specially permitted, authorized or required by law to make a statement under oath or solemn affirmation. D must make the statement by affidavit, solemn declaration or deposition or orally, before a person *authorized by law* to permit it to be made before him/her. Under s. 135(2), the statement must *not* be made in the course of a criminal investigation. It must also be false. The *mental element* comprises the intention to do the acts which constitute the external circumstances of the offence, as well as proof of *knowledge by D that the statement is false*.

Related Provisions: "Statement" is defined in s. 118.

Conduct which falls within the exception of s. 134(2) may also attract liability under s. 140(1) as public mischief. Perjury is defined in s. 131 and punished under s. 132.

Other related offences are described in the corresponding note to s. 131, *supra*.

The offence is tried under Part XXVII and punished under s. 787(1).

135. [Repealed R.S. 1985, c. 27 (1st Supp.), s. 17.]

136. (1) **Witness giving contradictory evidence** — Every one who, being a witness in a judicial proceeding, gives evidence with respect to any matter of fact or knowledge and who subsequently, in a judicial proceeding, gives evidence that is contrary to his previous evidence is guilty of an indictable offence and liable to imprisonment for a term not exceeding fourteen years, whether or not the prior or later evidence or either is true, but no person shall be convicted under this section unless the court, judge or provincial court judge, as the case may be, is satisfied beyond a reasonable doubt that the accused, in giving evidence in either of the judicial proceedings, intended to mislead.

(2) **"Evidence"** — Notwithstanding the definition "evidence" in section 118, "evidence", for the purposes of this section, does not include evidence that is not material.

(2.1) **Proof of former trial** — Where a person is charged with an offence under this section, a certificate specifying with reasonable particularity the proceeding in which that person is alleged to have given the evidence in respect of which the offence is charged, is evidence that it was given in a judicial proceeding, without proof of the signature or official character of the person by whom the certificate purports to be signed if it purports to be signed by the clerk of the court or other official having the custody of the record of that proceeding or by his lawful deputy.

(3) **Consent required** — No proceedings shall be instituted under this section without the consent of the Attorney General.

R.S., c. C-34, s. 124; R.S. 1985, c. 27 (1st Supp.), ss. 18, 203.

Commentary: The section describes and punishes the giving of *contradictory evidence*, provides for *proof* of certain of its essential elements *by certificate*, and imposes limitations upon the institution of proceedings.

The essential elements of the offence of s. 136(1) are restricted by the definition of "evidence" contained in s. 136(2). The *external circumstances* require that D must first have been a witness in a judicial proceeding where s/he gave evidence with respect to a matter of fact or knowledge. D must thereafter give evidence in a subsequent judicial proceeding. The latter evidence must be *contrary* to the evidence earlier given. In each case, s. 136(2) requires that the evidence given must be *material* in the proceedings. It matters not whether any of the evidence is true. In essence, the external circumstances consist of the giving of contradictory evidence of knowledge or fact in respect of material matters in separate judicial proceedings. In addition to the intention to cause the external circumstances of the offence, the *mental element* requires proof that, in either proceeding, D intended to mislead. Under s. 136(3), proceedings in respect of this offence may only be instituted with the consent of the Attorney General.

Section 136(2.1) permits the introduction of a *certificate* in *proof* of the fact that the contradictory evidence was given in judicial proceedings. The *certificate* must specify, with reasonable particularity, the proceeding in which D is alleged to have given the evidence in respect of which the offence is charged. The certificate should be signed by the clerk of the court, other custodian of the records of the court or the lawful deputy of either. The certificate is *evidence* that the evidence was given in a judicial proceeding, without proof of the signature or official character of the person who has signed it. The subsection contains *no* notice provision.

Case Law
Consent of Attorney General: S. 136(3)

R. v. Falkenberg (1974), 25 C.R.N.S. 374, 16 C.C.C. (2d) 525 (Ont. C.A.) — The consent of the Attorney General is *not* a mere formality. No amendment is permissible which alleges an offence other than the offence with respect to which the Attorney General consented.

Res Judicata

R. v. Gushue (1976), 35 C.R.N.S. 304, 32 C.C.C. (2d) 189 (Ont. C.A.); affirmed (1979), 50 C.C.C. (2d) 417 (S.C.C.) — A conviction for perjury cannot stand along with a conviction for giving contradictory evidence arising out of the same false testimony.

Related Provisions: "Judicial proceeding" and "witness" are defined in s. 118 but the definition of "evidence" there given is restricted by s. 136(2) to exclude evidence that is *not* material, thereby making materiality of the evidence an essential element of P's proof. "Attorney General" is defined in s. 2.

The special provision relating to the sufficiency of counts charging perjury and related offences is *not* expressly made applicable to a prosecution under this section, nor is s. 587(1)(a), authorizing the supply of particulars of what is relied upon in support of such a charge.

C.E.A. s. 5(2) involving incriminating questions does *not* include giving contradictory evidence as an exception to the general rule against subsequent evidentiary use of responses given after objection. The offence is included with perjury in the exception contained in *Charter* s. 13.

Under s. 536(2), D may *elect* mode of trial. Other related provisions are described in the corresponding note to s. 131.

137. Fabricating evidence — **Every one who, with intent to mislead, fabricates anything with intent that it shall be used as evidence in a judicial proceeding, existing or proposed, by any means other than perjury or incitement to perjury is guilty of an indictable offence and liable to imprisonment for a term not exceeding fourteen years.**
R.S., c. C-34, s. 125.

Commentary: This offence, directed at *real* rather than testimonial evidence, further complements the offence of perjury and related crimes which impose criminal liability upon those who give false evidence in judicial proceedings to induce the tribunal to reach an erroneous determination.

The *external circumstances* require proof that D "fabricates anything". To "fabricate", in context, involves making up, framing or inventing. The essence of the offence rests in its *mental element*, which combines two ulterior mental states beyond the intention to cause the external circumstances of the offence. D must *intend* to *mislead*. The fabrication must be with *intent* that what is fabricated shall be *used* as *evidence* in a judicial proceeding, existing or proposed, by some means other than perjury or incitement to perjury.

Case Law

R. v. Sevick (1930), 54 C.C.C. 92 (N.S. S.C.) — It is *not* necessary that the proceedings should have begun or be pending when the evidence is fabricated.

R. v. Boyko (1945), 83 C.C.C. 295 (Sask. C.A.) — An intent to mislead is essential. There can be *no* conviction based upon the writing of notes which could *not* be admitted in evidence.

Related Provisions: "Evidence" and "judicial proceeding" are defined in s. 118, the essential elements of perjury described in s. 131.

In some cases there may be an overlap between this offence and the general offence of obstructing justice under s. 139(2), as well as of public mischief under s. 140(1)(b). Section 138 creates several offences relating to affidavits.

The special provisions of s. 585(c) respecting the sufficiency of the description contained in an indictment or count and the authority to order particulars under s. 587(1)(a) apply.

Under s. 536(2), D may *elect* mode of trial.

138. Offences relating to affidavits — Every one who

(a) signs a writing that purports to be an affidavit or statutory declaration and to have been sworn or declared before him when the writing was not so sworn or declared or when he knows that he has no authority to administer the oath or declaration,

(b) uses or offers for use any writing purporting to be an affidavit or statutory declaration that he knows was not sworn or declared, as the case may be, by the affiant or declarant or before a person authorized in that behalf, or

(c) signs as affiant or declarant a writing that purports to be an affidavit or statutory declaration and to have been sworn or declared by him, as the case may be, when the writing was not so sworn or declared,

is guilty of an indictable offence and liable to imprisonment for a term not exceeding two years.

R.S., c. C-34, s. 126.

Commentary: The essence of each offence is the creation of a spurious or pretended affidavit or statutory declaration. In each case, D must either *sign* the writing in a particular *capacity* (ss. 138(a) and (c)) or *use* or *offer* it for *use* in a particular *manner* (s. 138(b)). In no case is proof required of an ulterior or specific *mental element,* as for example, the intent to mislead.

Under s. 138(a), the *external circumstances* require that D sign a writing which purports to be an affidavit or statutory declaration sworn or declared before D. The writing must either *not* have been so sworn or declared, that is to say, before D, or D must have *no* authority to administer the oath or declaration. The *mental element* requires proof of an intention to cause the external circumstances of the offence including, where applicable, specific knowledge of the lack of authority to administer the oath or declaration.

The *external circumstances* of the offence of s. 138(b) involve the *use or offer for use* of a writing which purports to be an affidavit or statutory declaration. The writing must either *not* be sworn or declared by the affiant or declarant, or *not* before an authorized person. The *mental element* is the intention to cause the external circumstances of the offence and includes *knowledge* of the spurious character of the affidavit or statutory declaration.

The offence of s. 138(c) is similar to s. 138(a). Its *external circumstances* require that D sign as affiant or declarant a writing which purports to be an affidavit or statutory declaration. The writing must also purport to have been sworn or declared by D when it was in fact not so.

Case Law

Falsely Swearing Affidavit

R. v. Chow (1978), 41 C.C.C. (2d) 143 (Sask. C.A.) — Falsely swearing an affidavit is *not* an offence of strict liability. P must establish *mens rea* to found a conviction. An honest, but mistaken, belief that sufficient formalities to constitute swearing of an affidavit have been met to justify the completion of the jurat is a defence to a charge under s. 138(a).

Use of False Affidavit

Stevenson v. R. (1980), 19 C.R. (3d) 74 (Ont. C.A.) — Use of a sham affidavit by police officers in order to obtain an incriminating statement from a suspect fell within the scope of s. 138(b). Section 138 is *not* restricted to affidavits which are to be relied upon in judicial, administrative or business proceedings. The gravamen of the offences is the creation of a sham affidavit, *not* its use or intended use in judicial proceedings. The word "uses" in s. 138(b) should be given its ordinary dictionary meaning of "employs for a purpose". It clearly extends to a use intended to bring about a result which would adversely affect another's legal position, irrespective of the user's motives. The use of a photocopy of the affidavit was sufficient to bring the user within the prohibition.

Related Provisions: Under *C.E.A.* s. 41 anyone authorized to take affidavits to be used in either provincial or federal courts may receive statutory declarations in the form described in the section. The *Code* itself permits the use of affidavits in proof of various matters, as for example, the ownership and value of property under s. 657.1(2) or the service of any documents under ss. 4(6) and (7), but this section is not restricted to such cases.

Other Related Provisions are described in the corresponding note to s. 131, *supra.*

Under s. 536(2), D may *elect* mode of trial.

139. (1) Obstructing justice — Every one who wilfully attempts in any manner to obstruct, pervert or defeat the course of justice in a judicial proceeding,

    (a) by indemnifying or agreeing to indemnify a surety, in any way and either in whole or in part, or

    (b) where he is a surety, by accepting or agreeing to accept a fee or any form of indemnity whether in whole or in part from or in respect of a person who is released or is to be released from custody,

is guilty of

    (c) an indictable offence and is liable to imprisonment for a term not exceeding two years, or

    (d) an offence punishable on summary conviction.

(2) Idem — Every one who wilfully attempts in any manner other than a manner described in subsection (1) to obstruct, pervert or defeat the course of justice is guilty of an indictable offence and liable to imprisonment for a term not exceeding ten years.

(3) Idem — Without restricting the generality of subsection (2), every one shall be deemed wilfully to attempt to obstruct, pervert or defeat the course of justice who in a judicial proceeding, existing or proposed,

    (a) dissuades or attempts to dissuade a person by threats, bribes or other corrupt means from giving evidence;

    (b) influences or attempts to influence by threats, bribes or other corrupt means a person in his conduct as a juror; or

    (c) accepts or obtains, agrees to accept or attempts to obtain a bribe or other corrupt consideration to abstain from giving evidence, or to do or to refrain from doing anything as a juror.

R.S., c. C-34, s. 127; c. 2 (2nd Supp.), s. 3; 1972, c. 13, s. 8.

Commentary: The section describes and punishes the offence of *obstructing justice*, a crime complete upon proof of an attempt without the necessity of success or actual completion. The offence may be committed in a number of ways.

The offence of s. 139(1) involves conduct of or in relation to a *surety*. The *external circumstances* require that D attempt *in any manner* to obstruct, pervert or defeat the course of justice in a judicial proceeding. As a *donor* or offeror, D must indemnify or agree to indemnify a surety in any way and, in whole or in part. As a *recipient* surety, D must accept or agree to accept a fee or any form of whole or partial indemnity from or in respect of a person who is released or to be released from custody. The *mental element* requires proof of an intention to cause the external circumstances of the offence, including the specific *purpose* of obstructing justice, by such conduct.

The more expansive s. 139(2) proscribes any and all attempts to obstruct, pervert or defeat the course of justice in a manner *not* described in s. 139(1). The gist of the *external circumstances* is the doing of any act, other than as described in s. 139(1), which has a tendency to obstruct, defeat or pervert the course of justice. The *mental element* requires that the external circumstances be intentionally caused for such purpose.

Section 139(3) should be read with s. 139(2) whose generality it does *not* restrict. Conduct within s. 139(3) is *deemed* to be obstructing justice. The *mental element* is the intention to cause the external circumstances.

Case Law

Nature and Elements of Offence

R. v. Wijesinha (1995), 42 C.R. (4th) 1, 100 C.C.C. (3d) 410 (S.C.C.) — It is *not* an essential element of an offence under s. 139(2) that declarations be, in fact, statutory declarations. The essence of the offence is that D *knowingly* tendered false documents which purported to have been duly executed.

R. v. Vermette (1987), 57 C.R. (3d) 340 (S.C.C.); affirming (1983), 6 C.C.C. (3d) 97 (Alta. C.A.) — The common law offence of contempt is preserved. A court is *not* precluded from relying on its power to punish for contempt merely because P may also have proceeded under this section.

R. v. Vermette (1983), 6 C.C.C. (3d) 97 (Alta. C.A.); affirmed on other grounds (1987), 57 C.R. (3d) 340 (S.C.C.) — Section 139(2) is sufficiently broad in its scope to include all acts of contempt at common law not specifically covered in other *Code* offences.

R. v. Kotch (1990), 61 C.C.C. (3d) 132 (Alta. C.A.) — The gravamen of the s. 139(2) offence is the corrupt attempt itself. Any attempt to pay any form of compensation to a witness that has, as its purpose, a direct tendency to influence the witness not to give evidence in a judicial proceeding is a corrupt attempt to obstruct justice. Equally, any attempt to pay compensation to V or the perceived cause of V, in order to influence the proceeding, is also a corrupt attempt to obstruct justice. Negotiations for the withholding, withdrawal or reduction of a charge, conducted with a Crown law officer, is *not* an offence, nor is honestly approaching a witness who has made a false or mistaken statement and, by reasoned arguments, trying to persuade him/her from giving perjured or erroneous testimony.

R. v. Hearn (1989), 48 C.C.C. (3d) 376 (Nfld. C.A.); affirmed (1989), 53 C.C.C. (3d) 352 (S.C.C.) — It is *irrelevant* that the wilful *attempt* to obstruct justice is *unsuccessful*, or that the intention could not be satisfied by the act undertaken by D.

R. v. Poulin (1998), 127 C.C.C. (3d) 115 (Que. C.A.) — Refusal to testify at a preliminary inquiry may constitute the basis of a charge under s. 139(2) where a provincial court judge has *not* exercised jurisdiction under s. 545.

R. v. Charbonneau (1992), 13 C.R. (4th) 191, 74 C.C.C. (3d) 49, 60–63 (Que. C.A.); leave to appeal refused (1992), 75 C.C.C. (3d) vi (note), 145 N.R. 90 (note) (S.C.C.) — The *mental element* of the s. 139(2) offence is the specific intent to obstruct justice. Where the external circumstances involve the submission of an affidavit which is alleged to be false, D may *not* be convicted if there is a reasonable doubt whether D *honestly believed* the affidavit to be true, even if it is, in fact, false.

Obstruction

R. v. Rousseau (1988), 65 C.R. (3d) 275, 43 C.C.C. (3d) 347 (S.C.C.) — To be found guilty, D must perform an act amounting to an attempt to obtain the desired results.

R. v. Graham (1985), 20 C.C.C. (3d) 210 (Ont. C.A.); affirmed (1988), 38 C.C.C. (3d) 574 (S.C.C.) — The gist of the offence is the doing of an act which has a *tendency* to obstruct the course of justice and which is done for that purpose. The writing of a letter by D, while awaiting trial in jail, requesting assistance in intimidating V to refrain from testifying, although confiscated and never posted, was sufficient basis for a conviction.

R. v. Mercer (1988), 65 C.R. (3d) 275, 43 C.C.C. (3d) 347 (Alta. C.A.) — Where a recalcitrant witness at a preliminary inquiry is jailed for refusing to be sworn and testify, the witness cannot subsequently be charged under this section with obstructing justice.

R. v. Doz (1984), 12 C.C.C. (3d) 200 (Alta. C.A.) — D solicitor's conduct of knowingly misleading the court by presenting a client's friend as the person charged with the offence, where the client had given the friend's name to police when arrested, constituted an obstruction of justice.

R. v. Savinkoff (1962), 39 C.R. 306, [1963] 1 C.C.C. 163 (B.C. C.A.) — If the charge is that D attempted to induce another "to give false evidence", P must prove that D *knew* that the evidence he was requesting would be *false*. *Mens rea* is a necessary element, requiring proof of knowledge of the falsity of the statement.

R. v. Hoggarth (1956), 25 C.R. 174 (B.C. C.A.) — An essential element of the offence, when based on a statement to police, is that the *purpose* of giving the statement was to *obstruct* anything which, in the circumstances of the case, could be said to be "the course of justice".

R. v. Hanneson (1989), 71 C.R. (3d) 249, 49 C.C.C. (3d) 467 (Ont. C.A.) — A breach of *Charter* s. 10(b) does *not* insulate the person detained from subsequent criminal responsibility by rendering inadmissible statements which are the *actus reus* of the offence.

R. v. Zeck (1980), 53 C.C.C. (2d) 551 (Ont. C.A.) — D's actions in removing and destroying parking tags from cars previously tagged by the police were held to constitute obstruction of the normal enforcement by police of by-law contraventions, which came within the term "the course of justice".

R. v. Simon (1979), 45 C.C.C. (2d) 510 (Ont. C.A.) — P is entitled to proceed under this section on a charge of attempt to obstruct justice rather than on a charge of perjury, which would require corroboration, where the intent of D was to procure a mistrial by a concocted story and the perjury was only incidental to the purpose of D.

R. v. Spezzano (1977), 34 C.C.C. (2d) 87 (Ont. C.A.) — The right to remain silent does *not* also confer a right to mislead a police officer investigating a crime by false information, simply because the false statements are made by a person to shield himself from prosecution.

The Course of Justice

R. v. Wijesinha (1995), 42 C.R. (4th) 1, 100 C.C.C. (3d) 410 (S.C.C.) — "The course of justice" in s. 139(2) *includes* the *investigatory* stage. The investigation is an essential first step in any judicial or quasi-judicial proceeding which may result in a prosecution. To knowingly mislead during the first step of the investigation perverts the course of justice as much as would bribing a witness to change testimony at trial.

R. v. Wijesinha (1995), 42 C.R. (4th) 1, 100 C.C.C. (3d) 410 (S.C.C.) — "The course of justice" applies to disciplinary proceedings of the Law Society and is *not* limited to the judicial proceedings described in s. 139(1) and (3). It includes all judicial proceedings defined in *Code* s. 118.

"The course of justice" includes any decision-making body which

i.   judges;

ii.   derives its authority to judge from a statute; and

iii. is required, by statute, to act in a judicial manner.

R. v. Spezzano (1977), 34 C.C.C. (2d) 87 (Ont. C.A.) — The expression "the course of justice" includes judicial proceedings existing or proposed but is *not* limited to such proceedings. The offence also includes attempts by a person to obstruct, pervert or defeat a prosecution which he contemplates may take place, even if no decision to prosecute has been made.

Judicial Proceeding

R. v. Wijesinha (1995), 42 C.R. (4th) 1, 100 C.C.C. (3d) 410 (S.C.C.) — Law Society disciplinary proceedings are included in paragraphs (d) and (e) of the definition "judicial proceeding" in *Code* s. 118.

R. v. Heater (1996), 111 C.C.C. (3d) 445 (Ont. C.A.) — Proceedings to determine whether parole should be revoked constitute a "judicial proceeding".

Conspiracy

R. v. May (1984), 13 C.C.C. (3d) 257 (Ont. C.A.); leave to appeal refused (1984), 56 N.R. 239n (S.C.C.) — Although the section is framed in the language of an attempt, it in fact creates a substantive offence. D may be convicted of conspiring to commit the substantive offence of attempting to obstruct the course of justice.

Related Provisions: "Judicial proceeding" is defined in s. 118. Section 24 defines what, in law, constitutes an attempt.

Several *Code* provisions create offences where D's conduct amounts to actual obstruction, as for example in ss. 129 (obstructing a peace or public officer in the execution of his duty), 423(1)(g) (obstructing a highway), and 438(1) and (2) (interfering with the saving of a wrecked vessel or wreck). Section 127 makes it an offence to disobey the lawful order of a court.

The offences of ss. 140 (public mischief), 141 (compounding an indictable offence) and, to a lesser extent, perhaps, 142 (corruptly taking a reward for recovery of goods) and 143 (advertising reward and immunity) are cognate offences. Accessoryship after the fact, as described in s. 23, may also have a similar effect.

This offence is an "offence" for the purposes of Part VI.

Under s. 139(1), where P proceeds by indictment and, under s. 139(2), in all cases, D may *elect* mode of trial under s. 536(2).

140. (1) Public mischief — **Every one commits public mischief who, with intent to mislead, causes a peace officer to enter on or continue an investigation by**

(a) making a false statement that accuses some other person of having committed an offence;

(b) doing anything that is intended to cause some other person to be suspected of having committed an offence that the other person has not committed, or to divert suspicion from himself;

(c) reporting that an offence has been committed when it has not been committed; or

(d) reporting or in any other way making it known or causing it to be made known that he or some other person has died when he or that other person has not died.

(2) Punishment — **Every one who commits public mischief**

(a) is guilty of an indictable offence and liable to imprisonment for a term not exceeding five years; or

(b) is guilty of an offence punishable on summary conviction.
> R.S., c. C-34, s. 128; 1972, c. 13, s. 8; R.S. 1985, c. 27 (1st Supp.), s. 19.

Commentary: The section imposes criminal liability for causing a peace officer to enter on or continue an investigation by conveying certain false information with an intent to mislead the officer.

The *external circumstances* require the conveyance of false information, by words or conduct, in *any* manner described in ss. 140(1)(a)–(d). It would *not* appear that the information need be directly communicated to the peace officer, although such frequently occurs. D must, by the conveyance of such false information, cause a peace officer to enter upon or continue an investigation. There must be a causal *nexus* between the police investigation and the false information. The *mental element* requires proof of the intention to cause the external circumstances of the offence, together with the further or ulterior intent to mislead.

Case Law
Causes . . . An Investigation
Stapleton v. R. (1982), 26 C.R. (3d) 361, 66 C.C.C. (2d) 231 (Ont. C.A.) — *See also: R. v. J.(J.)* (1988), 65 C.R. (3d) 371, 43 C.C.C. (3d) 257 (Ont. C.A.) — Section 140(1)(c) requires that D "cause" an investigation to be conducted. Although a complaint by D's mother of mistreatment of her son by police caused the police to enter upon an investigation, D was convicted because his false detailed statements

to the police substantially caused the ultimate investigation. The statements were properly admitted in evidence without the necessity of a *voir dire*, since they constituted the *actus reus* of the offence.

"Offence"

R. v. Howard (1972), 18 C.R.N.S. 395, 7 C.C.C. (2d) 211 (Ont. C.A.) — "Offence" as used in this section, is equivalent to a "breach of law involving penal sanction", whether federal law, provincial law or otherwise. It is *not* limited to offences under the *Code*.

Related Provisions: "Peace officer" is defined in s. 2. "Offence" is not defined.

Other forms of *mischief* prohibited in the *Code* include the offences of ss. 430 and 431. Spreading false news under s. 181 also contains an element of mischief. Related offences are found in ss. 141 (compounding an indictable offence), 142 (corruptly taking reward for recovery of goods) and 143 (advertising reward and immunity).

The offence of the section is triable either way under s. 140(2). Where P proceeds by indictment, D may *elect* mode of trial under s. 536(2).

141. (1) Compounding indictable offence — Every one who asks for or obtains or agrees to receive or obtain any valuable consideration for himself or any other person by agreeing to compound or conceal an indictable offence is guilty of an indictable offence and liable to imprisonment for a term not exceeding two years.

(2) Exception for diversion agreements — No offence is committed under subsection (1) where valuable consideration is received or obtained or is to be received or obtained under an agreement for compensation or restitution or personal services that is

(a) entered into with the consent of the Attorney General; or

(b) made as part of a program, approved by the Attorney General, to divert persons charged with indictable offences from criminal proceedings.

R.S., c. C-34, s. 129; R.S. 1985, c. 27 (1st Supp.), s. 19.

Commentary: The section describes and punishes the offence of *compounding* an indictable offence. It, in essence, involves an exchange of concealment of criminal activity in return for valuable consideration.

The *external circumstances* of the offence of s. 141(1) comprise essentially two elements. D must agree to compound or conceal an indictable offence. To *compound* means simply to settle or discharge a debt or other form of liability by an agreement for the payment of a sum of money or similar consideration. D must ask for, or obtain or agree to receive or obtain *valuable consideration* for him/herself or any other person by making such agreement. Valuable consideration need *not* actually pass. A request for or agreement to receive or obtain it is sufficient. The *mental element* consists of the intention to cause the external circumstances of the offence. It includes *knowledge* of the facts which constitute the underlying offence, though not its legal character.

Section 141(2) *excepts* from what would otherwise be criminal liability under s. 141(1), receiving or obtaining valuable consideration under an agreement for compensation, restitution or personal services, provided the agreement is entered into with the consent of the Attorney General or is part of an approved diversion programme.

Related Provisions: "Attorney General" is defined in s. 2. Restitution orders are governed by ss. 738–741.2. Section 736 provides for the establishment of fine option programmes whereby, in certain circumstances, a fine may be discharged, in whole or in part, by earning credits for work performed over a specified period in accordance with an approved plan.

Under *I.A.* s. 34(1)(a), an offence is deemed to be an indictable offence, if the enactment provides that an offender may be prosecuted therefor by indictment.

Related offences are described in ss. 142 (corruptly taking reward for recovery of goods) and 143 (advertising reward and immunity). The elements of accessoryship after the fact are described in s. 23.

Under s. 536(2), D may elect mode of trial.

142. Corruptly taking reward for recovery of goods — Every one who corruptly accepts any valuable consideration, directly or indirectly, under pretence or on account of helping any person to recover anything obtained by the commission of an indictable offence is guilty of an indictable offence and liable to imprisonment for a term not exceeding five years.

R.S., c. C-34, s. 130.

Commentary: The *external circumstances* of this offence consist of two elements. D must accept *valuable consideration*, directly or indirectly. The *acceptance* must be under pretence or on account of helping any person to recover anything obtained by the commission of an indictable offence. There must, then, be a *nexus* between the pretence or representation of assistance and the actual receipt of valuable consideration. The *mental element* consists of the intention to cause what amounts to the external circumstances of the offence, as well as the further requirement expressed in the compendious term "corruptly". "Corruptly" connotes not only *knowledge* by D that what is being done is *wrong*, but, further, that it is done with an evil *object*.

Related Provisions: The related offence of advertising reward and immunity appears in s. 143. Compounding an indictable offence is punishable under s. 141, and the elements of accessoryship after the fact described in s. 23.

Under *I.A.* s. 34(1)(a), an offence is *deemed* to be an indictable offence if the enactment provides that an offender may be prosecuted therefor by indictment.

Under s. 536(2), D may elect mode of trial.

143. Advertising reward and immunity — Every one who

(a) publicly advertises a reward for the return of anything that has been stolen or lost, and in the advertisement uses words to indicate that no questions will be asked if it is returned,

(b) uses words in a public advertisement to indicate that a reward will be given or paid for anything that has been stolen or lost, without interference with or inquiry about the person who produces it,

(c) promises or offers in a public advertisement to return to a person who has advanced money by way of loan on, or has bought, anything that has been stolen or lost, the money so advanced or paid, or any other sum of money for the return of that thing, or

(d) prints or publishes any advertisement referred to in paragraph (*a*), (*b*) or (*c*),

is guilty of an offence punishable on summary conviction.

R.S., c. C-34, s. 131.

Commentary: This summary conviction offence prohibits *advertisement of reward and immunity* for return of stolen or lost property.

The *external circumstances* are described in ss. 143(a)–(d). Sections 143(a) and (b) impose liability upon advertisers of reward and immunity, whereas s. 143(c) attaches liability to the person who promises or offers in any public advertisement to return the property. Paragraph (d) relates to the printer or publisher of any such advertisement. The *mental element* consists of the intention to cause what amounts to the external circumstances of the offence.

Related Provisions: "Reward" is *not* defined. It encompasses a return or recompense made to another for some service or merit.

Related offences appear in ss. 141 (compounding an indictable offence) and 142 (corruptly taking a reward for recovery of goods). Section 23 defines the elements in accessoryship after the fact.

The offence of this section is tried in accordance with Part XXVII, and punished under s. 787(1).

Escapes and Rescues

144. Prison breach — Every one who

(a) **by force or violence breaks a prison with intent to set at liberty himself or any other person confined therein, or**

(b) **with intent to escape forcibly breaks out of, or makes any breach in, a cell or other place within a prison in which he is confined,**

is guilty of an indictable offence and liable to imprisonment for a term not exceeding ten years.

R.S., c. C-34, s. 132; 1976–77, c. 53, s. 5.

Commentary: The section describes the indictable offence of *prison breach* and provides the punishment upon conviction. The offence may be committed in either of two ways. Each involves a specific or ulterior mental element.

Under s. 144(a), the *external circumstances* are complete where D, by force or violence, breaks a *prison*. P must prove, as the essential *mental element*, that D intended to cause the external circumstances of the offence, with the further or ulterior *intent to set at liberty* him/herself or another person there confined.

The *external circumstances* of the offence of s. 144(b) are complete where D forcibly breaks out of a cell or other place within a prison in which s/he is confined, or where D makes any breach in a cell or other place within a prison in which he is confined. In addition to the intention to cause the external circumstances of the offence, P must further prove that D did so with *intent to escape*.

Related Provisions: "Prison" is expansively defined in s. 2. "Break" is *not* defined. Its definition in s. 321 is for the purposes of Part IX "Offences Against Rights of Property" only.

Section 145(1) describes and punishes the related offences of escaping from lawful custody and being unlawfully at large. Service of a term of imprisonment for the offence of escaping lawful custody is governed by s. 149. Sections 146 and 147 prohibit permitting or assisting escape and rescue from lawful custody.

This offence is an "offence" for the purposes of Part VI.

Under s. 536(2), D may *elect* mode of trial.

145. (1) Escape and being at large without excuse — Every one who

(a) **escapes from lawful custody, or**

(b) **is, before the expiration of a term of imprisonment to which he was sentenced, at large in or out of Canada without lawful excuse, the proof of which lies on him,**

is guilty of an indictable offence and liable to imprisonment for a term not exceeding two years or is guilty of an offence punishable on summary conviction.

(2) Failure to attend court — Every one who,

(a) **being at large on his undertaking or recognizance given to or entered into before a justice or judge, fails, without lawful excuse, the proof of which lies on him, to attend court in accordance with the undertaking or recognizance, or**

(b) **having appeared before a court, justice or judge, fails, without lawful excuse, the proof of which lies on him, to attend court as thereafter required by the court, justice or judge,**

or to surrender himself in accordance with an order of the court, justice or judge, as the case may be, is guilty of an indictable offence and liable to imprisonment for a term not exceeding two years or is guilty of an offence punishable on summary conviction.

(3) Failure to comply with condition of undertaking or recognizance — Every person who is at large on an undertaking or recognizance given to or entered into before a justice or judge and is bound to comply with a condition of that undertaking or recognizance directed by a justice or judge, and every person who is bound to comply with a direction ordered under subsection 515(12) or 522(2.1), and who fails, without lawful excuse, the proof of which lies on that person, to comply with that condition or direction, is guilty of

    (a) an indictable offence and is liable to imprisonment for a term not exceeding two years; or

    (b) an offence punishable on summary conviction.

(4) **Failure to appear or to comply with summons** — Every one who is served with a summons and who fails, without lawful excuse, the proof of which lies on him, to appear at a time and place stated therein, if any, for the purposes of the *Identification of Criminals Act* or to attend court in accordance therewith, is guilty of

    (a) an indictable offence and is liable to imprisonment for a term not exceeding two years; or

    (b) an offence punishable on summary conviction.

(5) **Failure to comply with appearance notice or promise to appear** — Every person who is named in an appearance notice or promise to appear, or in a recognizance entered into before an officer in charge or another peace officer, that has been confirmed by a justice under section 508 and who fails, without lawful excuse, the proof of which lies on the person, to appear at the time and place stated therein, if any, for the purposes of the *Identification of Criminals Act*, or to attend court in accordance therewith, is guilty of

    (a) an indictable offence and is liable to imprisonment for a term not exceeding two years; or

    (b) an offence punishable on summary conviction.

(5.1) **Failure to comply with conditions of undertaking** — Every person who, without lawful excuse, the proof of which lies on the person, fails to comply with any condition of an undertaking entered into pursuant to subsection 499(2) or 503(2.1)

    (a) is guilty of an indictable offence and is liable to imprisonment for a term not exceeding two years; or

    (b) is guilty of an offence punishable on summary conviction.

(6) **Idem** — For the purposes of subsection (5), it is not a lawful excuse that an appearance notice, promise to appear or recognizance states defectively the substance of the alleged offence.

(7) [Repealed R.S. 1985, c. 27 (1st Supp.), s. 20(2).]

(8) For the purposes of subsections (3) to (5), it is a lawful excuse to fail to comply with a condition of an undertaking or recognizance or to fail to appear at a time and place stated in a summons, an appearance notice, a promise to appear or a recognizance for the purposes of the *Identification of Criminals Act* if before the failure the Attorney General, within the meaning of the *Contraventions Act*, makes an election under section 50 of that Act.

(9) **Proof of certain facts by certificate** — In any proceedings under subsection (2), (4) or (5), a certificate of the clerk of the court or a judge of the court before which the accused is alleged to have failed to attend or of the person in charge of the place at

which it is alleged the accused failed to attend for the purposes of the *Identification of Criminals Act* stating that,

    (a) in the case of proceedings under subsection (2), the accused gave or entered into an undertaking or recognizance before a justice or judge and failed to attend court in accordance therewith or, having attended court, failed to attend court thereafter as required by the court, justice or judge or to surrender in accordance with an order of the court, justice or judge, as the case may be,

    (b) in the case of proceedings under subsection (4), a summons was issued to and served on the accused and the accused failed to attend court in accordance therewith or failed to appear at the time and place stated therein for the purposes of the *Identification of Criminals Act*, as the case may be, and

    (c) in the case of proceedings under subsection (5), the accused was named in an appearance notice, a promise to appear or a recognizance entered into before an officer in charge or another peace officer, that was confirmed by a justice under section 508, and the accused failed to appear at the time and place stated therein for the purposes of the *Identification of Criminals Act*, failed to attend court in accordance therewith or, having attended court, failed to attend court thereafter as required by the court, justice or judge, as the case may be,

is evidence of the statements contained in the certificate without proof of the signature or the official character of the person appearing to have signed the certificate.

(10) Attendance and right to cross-examination — An accused against whom a certificate described in subsection (9) is produced may, with leave of the court, require the attendance of the person making the certificate for the purposes of cross-examination.

(11) Notice of intention to produce — No certificate shall be received in evidence pursuant to subsection (9) unless the party intending to produce it has, before the trial, given to the accused reasonable notice of his intention together with a copy of the certificate.

R.S., c. C-34, s. 133; c. 2 (2nd Supp.), s. 4; 1974–75–76, c. 93, s. 7;R.S. 1985, c. 27 (1st Supp.), s. 20; 1992, c. 47, s. 68; 1994, c. 44, s. 8; 1996, c. 7, s. 38; 1997, c. 18, s. 3.

Commentary: The section describes the offences of *escaping* and being *unlawfully at large* from lawful custody, as well as *failure to comply* with the terms of a release form. It further makes provision for proof by certificate of certain essential elements of the failure to comply offences.

The offences of *escaping* from lawful custody and being *unlawfully at large* are described and punished in s. 145(1). Under s. 145(1)(a), the *external circumstances* are complete where D escapes from lawful custody. The *mental element* requires proof that D intended to do so. Under s. 145(1)(b), D must be under a term of imprisonment which has *not* expired. Further, D must be, prior to the expiration of such term, at large in or out of Canada. Finally, D's absence must be *without lawful excuse*. The shift of the *onus* of proof of lawful excuse to D, engages *Charter* ss. 7 and 11(d) scrutiny. The *mental element* consists of the intention to cause the external circumstances.

The offences of ss. 145(2) and (3) may conveniently be considered together. The *external circumstances* of the offences of ss. 145(2)(a) and (3) require that D be at large upon an undertaking or recognizance given to or entered into before a judge or justice. Under s. 145(2)(a), D must *fail to attend* court in accordance with the release form. Under s. 145(3), D must *fail to comply* with a condition of the release form or a direction. In each case, there must be no lawful excuse for the failure to attend or comply, as the case may be. The *onus* of establishing a lawful excuse rests upon D, thereby attracting *Charter* ss. 7 and 11(d) scrutiny. The *mental element* consists of an intention to cause the external circumstances of the offence.

Section 145(2)(b) is enacted in more general terms without reference to a particular form of judicial interim release. The offence might be compendiously described as "failure to remain". The *external circumstances* of the offence require that D has appeared before a court, justice or judge (in accordance with some form of release). D must then fail to attend court as thereafter required, or fail to surrender in accordance with the terms of the order. There must further be the absence of lawful excuse. The *onus* of proving lawful excuse rests upon D, thereby attracting *Charter* ss. 7 and 11(d) scrutiny.

The offences of ss. 145(4), (5) and (5.1) are in parallel terms, the difference being in the form of release or process upon which D is at liberty. The *external circumstances* require proof of the underlying summons or confirmed appearance notice, promise to appear or recognizance entered into before the officer in charge. There must, further, be proof that D failed to attend court for the purposes of the *I.C.A.*, or to comply with a specified condition, as the case may be. At all events, such failure of attendance must be *without lawful excuse*. The *onus* of proof of lawful excuse is shifted to D, thereby engaging *Charter* ss. 7 and 11(d) scrutiny. It is not a lawful excuse under s. 145(5) or (5.1) that the release form states defectively the substance of the alleged offence.

Sections 145(9)–(11) permit *proof* of non-attendance in court or for the purpose of the *I.C.A.* by *certificate*, upon reasonable notice of the intention to adduce such evidence, together with a copy of the certificate. The certificates, completed in accordance with s. 145(9), essentially record the form of release or process issued, together with the relevant failure of appearance. The certificate is evidence of the statements there contained without proof of the signature or official character of the person who has signed it. Section 145(10) permits leave to be given to cross-examine the maker of the certificate.

Case Law

Lawful Custody

R. v. Whitfield (1969), 9 C.R.N.S. 59, [1970] 1 C.C.C. 129 (S.C.C.) — An arrest is effected by actual seizure or touching of a person's body, with a view to his detention; or, by words of arrest, if the person arrested submits to the process and goes with the arresting officer.

R. v. Huff (1979), 50 C.C.C. (2d) 324 (Alta. C.A.) — The lawfulness of the custody depends on the validity of the initial arrest. Where the peace officer did *not* have the authority to arrest D for the offence stated at the time of the arrest, it is *immaterial* that the officer might have lawfully arrested D for a different offence.

R. v. Zajner (1977), 36 C.C.C. (2d) 417 (Ont. C.A.) — D was present in court to hear his sentence pronounced and was in lawful custody from the moment he submitted to arrest by following the officer towards the prisoner's bench and submitting to the officer's authority.

R. v. C.A. (1986), 25 C.C.C. (3d) 133 (Sask. C.A.) — There is *no* distinction between custody occurring after arrest and before sentence and a custodial term. Both present situations of custody allowing for the possibility of escape.

Escape

R. v. M. (1985), 21 C.C.C. (3d) 191 (Man. C.A.) — "Escape" cannot be interpreted as "at large". Section 145(1)(a) deals with escapes from custody, s. 145(1)(b) with being unlawfully at large. Failure to return from a day pass is a breach of s. 145(1)(b).

R. v. Folchito (1986), 26 C.C.C. (3d) 253 (Que. C.A.) — There is no escape from lawful custody while D is benefitting from legally granted release from prison. D should be charged with being unlawfully at large contrary to s. 145(1)(b).

Unlawfully at Large

R. v. McKay (1985), 21 C.C.C. (3d) 191 (Man. C.A.) — Secure and open custody under *Y.O.A.* is tantamount to a form of imprisonment, hence can found a conviction for being unlawfully at large.

R. v. B.D. (1986), 49 C.R. (3d) 283, 24 C.C.C. (3d) 187 (Ont. C.A.) — A young offender, found guilty of an offence and sentenced to *open custody* for a specified period has been "sentenced to a term of imprisonment" and may be convicted under s. 145(1)(b).

R. v. Seymour (1980), 52 C.C.C. (2d) 305 (Ont. C.A.) — There must be a wilful breach of a condition of temporary absence which shows an intention to withdraw from the control of the correctional authorities to be rendered "at large". Where D's intoxication was *not* a wilful breach of a condition of his temporary absence pass, D must be acquitted of a charge under s. 145(1)(b).

R. v. C.A. (1986), 25 C.C.C. (3d) 133 (Sask. C.A.) — When dealing with a young offender, s. 145(1)(b) should be modified to read "before the expiration of a period of custodial committal which he is serving under the Young Offenders Act". Although *Y.O.A.* provides a procedure for dealing with young persons who escape custody, P, nevertheless, has the option to proceed under this section and the person is liable to be dealt with as provided by *Y.O.A.* s. 51.

Failure to Comply

R. v. Legere (1995), 95 C.C.C. (3d) 555 (Ont. C.A.) — In a prosecution for breach of a recognizance term that required D to abstain from communication with any person under the age of 16 years except in the company of an adult, an attempt to initiate communication by an act or gesture is not sufficient to establish liability. Communication, as in the definition of "private communication" in s. 183, involves the imparting of information, by act, gesture or words, from one to another.

R. v. Simanek (1993), 82 C.C.C. (3d) 576 (Ont. C.A.) — Section 145(3) does *not* apply to a charge which alleges a breach of a recognizance entered into under s. 810 (see now s. 811).

R. v. Smith (1975), 27 C.C.C. (2d) 257 (Ont. C.A.) — D must attend court in answer to a summons. No method is provided for avoiding that obligation except for procedures under provincial legislation whereby D may plead guilty, pay a fine and avoid a court appearance.

R. v. Gaudreault (1995), 105 C.C.C. (3d) 270 (Que. C.A.) — A subsequent judgment which sets aside a conviction which gave rise to an undertaking does *not* justify a violation of the undertaking which occurred prior to the conviction being set aside.

Failure to Appear

R. v. Okanee (1981), 59 C.C.C. (2d) 149 (Sask. C.A.) — A defendant who appears by counsel in a summary conviction court has complied with his undertaking to appear and may *not* be charged with failing to attend court.

Failure to Appear for Fingerprints

R. v. Gauthier (1983), 35 C.R. (3d) 159 (Que. C.A.) — Where on the date set for the appearance of D for *I.C.A.* purposes, the appearance notice had *not* yet been confirmed, D must be acquitted of failure to appear.

Multiple Convictions

R. v. Furlong (1993), 22 C.R. (4th) 193, 81 C.C.C. (3d) 449 (Nfld. C.A.) — Breach of probation and breach of recognizance entail elements which are additional and distinct from one another and relate to the respective culpability of each offence. The respective breaches of the orders, even if both are grounded upon the same act, must be treated as arising from entirely different causes, matters or delicts. (Mahoney and Marshall JJ.A.)

Related Provisions: "Justice" is defined in s. 2. The various forms of release and process, define in s. 493, but only for the purpose of Part XVI, appear in Part XXVIII.

The offences of s. 145(1) are crimes in respect of which authorization to intercept private communications may be given under Part VI.

The offences of the section are triable either way. Where P proceeds by indictment, D may *elect* mode of trial under s. 536(2). Sections 475 and 544 describe the remedies available where D absconds *during the course of the trial* (s. 475) or *preliminary inquiry* (s. 544). A summary conviction trial may proceed *ex parte* under s. 803(2) where D fails to appear or to remain in attendance.

146. Permitting or assisting escape — Every one who

    (a) permits a person whom he has in lawful custody to escape, by failing to perform a legal duty,

    (b) conveys or causes to be conveyed into a prison anything, with intent to facilitate the escape of a person imprisoned therein, or

    (c) directs or procures, under colour of pretended authority, the discharge of a prisoner who is not entitled to be discharged,

is guilty of an indictable offence and liable to imprisonment for a term not exceeding two years.

R.S., c. C-34, s. 134.

Commentary: Permitting or assisting prisoners to escape is prohibited under the section.

The *permitting* offence, one of omission, is described in s. 146(a). As principal, D must have a person in his/her lawful custody. D must permit the prisoner to escape and, further, do so by failing to perform a legal duty. D's conduct must be intentional.

The *assisting* offence of s. 146(b) requires proof that D conveyed or caused to be conveyed into a prison *anything* with the ulterior *mental element* or intent to facilitate the escape of a prisoner. "Anything" is a phrase of comprehensive import, would include the components of explosive substances or other devices designed to effect a prison or cell breach.

The offence of s. 146(c) involves the discharge of a prisoner under false pretence of authority. The *external circumstances* require that D direct or procure the discharge of a prisoner, under colour of pretended authority. The prisoner must *not* be entitled to be discharged. The *mental element* requires proof that D intentionally cause the external circumstances of the offence. It would include *knowledge* of the spurious character of the authority and, further, that the prisoner was *not* entitled to be discharged.

Related Provisions: "Prison" is defined in s. 2. "Procures" is included in the definition of "counsel" in s. 22(3).

There would appear to be some overlap between this offence and the crimes of prison breach (s. 144) and rescue or permitting escape under s. 147, particularly in combination with ss. 21(1)(b) and 22.

Under s. 536(2), D may *elect* mode of trial.

147. Rescue or permitting escape — Every one who

(a) **rescues any person from lawful custody or assists any person in escaping or attempting to escape from lawful custody,**

(b) **being a peace officer, wilfully permits a person in his lawful custody to escape, or**

(c) **being an officer of or an employee in a prison, wilfully permits a person to escape from lawful custody therein,**

is guilty of an indictable offence and liable to imprisonment for a term not exceeding five years.

R.S., c. C-34, s. 135.

Commentary: The section creates offences involving the rescue of persons from lawful custody, as well as peace or prison officers or employees permitting their escape.

The *rescue* offence of s. 147(a) requires that D rescue another from lawful custody. "Rescue" connotes the recovery or saving of someone from some evil or harm, or the delivery of one out of the hands of assailants or enemies. The *external circumstances* are also established where D assists any person in escaping or attempting to escape. The *mental element* consists of the intention to cause the external circumstances.

The offences of ss. 147(b) and (c) both fall within the description of "permitting escape". Each requires that, as principal, D hold a particular position. Under s. 147(b), D must be a *peace officer*, having a prisoner in his/her lawful custody. Under s. 147(c), D must be an *officer or employee in a prison*, where another person is lawfully confined. In each case, D must permit the prisoner to escape from lawful custody. The *mental element* in each offence is encompassed by the compendious term "wilfully". No ulterior state of mind need be proved to establish liability.

Case Law

R. v. Harrer (1998), 124 C.C.C. (3d) 368 (B.C. C.A.) — Section 147(a) does *not* require that D's *assistance* be a *necessary* factor in a completed escape. If D's act joins in the enterprise of escape, assistance is proven, even if the act does *not* materially contribute to the escape.

R. v. Stutt (1979), 52 C.C.C. (2d) 53 (B.C. C.A.) — An escape is *not* necessarily complete when a prisoner first gains his/her freedom. When, on the day following an escape from custody, D1 transported the prisoner to the home of D2, both have assisted in the prisoner's escape.

Related Provisions: "Peace officer" is defined in s. 2.

There would appear to be some overlap between these offences and the crimes of prison breach (s. 144), escaping lawful custody (s. 145(1)(a)) and permitting or assisting escape (s. 146), particularly when ss. 21(1)(b) and 22 are considered.

Under s. 536(2), D may elect mode of trial.

148. Assisting prisoner of war to escape — Every one who knowingly and wilfully

    (a) assists a prisoner of war in Canada to escape from a place where he is detained, or

    (b) assists a prisoner of war, who is permitted to be at large on parole in Canada, to escape from the place where he is at large on parole,

is guilty of an indictable offence and liable to imprisonment for a term not exceeding five years.

R.S., c. C-34, s. 136.

Commentary: The section creates the offence of assisting a prisoner of war to escape. The *external circumstances* of the offence are described in ss. 148(a) and (b). The *mental element* is expressed in the compendious phrase "knowingly and wilfully". D must have *knowledge* of the prisoner's status and intentionally assist the escape.

Related Provisions: It is high treason under s. 46(1)(c), *inter alia*, to assist an enemy at war with Canada or any armed forces against whom Canadian Forces are engaged in hostilities. Section 50(1)(a) prohibits incitement or wilful assistance of an alien enemy to leave Canada without the consent of P in the circumstances there described.

Under s. 536(2),D may elect mode of trial.

149. (1) Service of term for escape — Notwithstanding section 743.1, a court that convicts a person for an escape committed while undergoing imprisonment may order that the term of imprisonment be served in a penitentiary, even if the time to be served is less than two years.

(2) Definition of "escape" — In this section, "escape" means breaking prison, escaping from lawful custody or, without lawful excuse, being at large before the expiration of a term of imprisonment to which a person has been sentenced.

R.S., c. C-34, s. 137; 1972, c. 13, s. 9; 1976–77, c. 53, s. 6;R.S. 1985, c. 27 (1st Supp.), s. 203; 1992, c. 20, s. 199; 1995, c. 22, s. 1.

Commentary: The section authorizes an order requiring that a sentence of less than two (2) years for an "escape" as defined in s. 149(2) be served in a penitentiary.

Related Provisions: The general authority to impose consecutive or cumulative punishment is found in s. 718.3(4). Section 85(4) requires that any sentence imposed for conviction of using a firearm during the commission of an offence be served consecutively to any other punishment imposed on D for an offence arising out of the same event or series of events and to any other sentence to which s/he is subject at the time the sentence is imposed on him/her for the s. 85(1) offence.

The place and manner of service of a sentence of imprisonment are determined in accordance with ss. 743.1-743.5.

PART V — SEXUAL OFFENCES, PUBLIC MORALS AND DISORDERLY CONDUCT

Interpretation

150. Definitions — In this Part,

"guardian" includes any person who has in law or in fact the custody or control of another person;

"public place" includes any place to which the public have access as of right or by invitation, express or implied;

"theatre" includes any place that is open to the public where entertainments are given, whether or not any charge is made for admission.

R.S., c. C-34, s. 138.

Commentary: This section expansively defines "guardian", "public place" and "theatre", for use in this Part.

Case Law
Public Place

R. v. Lavoie, [1968] 1 C.C.C. 265 (N.B. C.A.) — The definition of "public place" is *not* exhaustive. A private road adjacent to but *not* visible from a public highway that was used by the public without objection is a "public place".

Related Provisions: Section 153(2) exhaustively defines "young person", and s. 155(4) expansively defines "brother" and "sister", as used in their respective sections. Section 163(7) defines "crime comic" as used in the section, and s. 163(8) deems certain publications to be obscene under the *Code*. Section 164(8) defines "court", "crime comic" and "judge" for the purposes of the section.

Other sources of assistance in determining the meaning of words and phrases used in the *Code* are described in the *Related Provisions* note to s. 2, *supra*.

Sexual Offences

150.1 (1) Consent no defence — Where an accused is charged with an offence under section 151 or 152 or subsection 153(1), 160(3) or 173(2) or is charged with an offence under section 271, 272 or 273 in respect of a complainant under the age of fourteen years, it is not a defence that the complainant consented to the activity that forms the subject-matter of the charge.

(2) Exception — Notwithstanding subsection (1), where an accused is charged with an offence under section 151 or 152, subsection 173(2) or section 271 in respect of a complainant who is twelve years of age or more but under the age of fourteen years, it is not a defence that the complainant consented to the activity that forms the subject-matter of the charge unless the accused

(a) is twelve years of age or more but under the age of sixteen years;

(b) is less than two years older than the complainant; and

(c) is neither in a position of trust or authority towards the complainant nor is a person with whom the complainant is in a relationship of dependency.

(3) Exemption for accused aged twelve or thirteen — No person aged twelve or thirteen years shall be tried for an offence under section 151 or 152 or subsection

173(2) unless the person is in a position of trust or authority towards the complainant or is a person with whom the complainant is in a relationship of dependency.

(4) Mistake of age — It is not a defence to a charge under section 151 or 152, subsection 160(3) or 173(2), or section 271, 272 or 273 that the accused believed that the complainant was fourteen years of age or more at the time the offence is alleged to have been committed unless the accused took all reasonable steps to ascertain the age of the complainant.

(5) Idem — It is not a defence to a charge under section 153, 159, 170, 171 or 172 or subsection 212(2) or (4) that the accused believed that the complainant was eighteen years of age or more at the time the offence is alleged to have been committed unless the accused took all reasonable steps to ascertain the age of the complainant.

R.S. 1985, c. 19 (3d Supp.), s. 1.

Commentary: The section describes the circumstances that determine whether *consent* or *mistaken belief* as to V's *age* will constitute a defence to a listed offence of sexual assault, interference or exploitation.

Sections 150.1(1) and (2) concern the defence of *consent*. Section 150.1(1) enacts the general rule that, where D is *charged* with a *listed offence* of sexual interference, invitation to sexual touching, sexual exploitation, bestiality, exposure, or sexual assault in respect of V under the age of 14 years, V's consent to the activity said to constitute the offence is *not* a defence to the charge. The vitiating element is V's age and concurrent mental immaturity. Section 150.1(2) enacts a limited *exception* to the general rule. It applies where D is charged with an offence listed in s. 150.1(2). V must be 12 years of age or more, but under the age of 14 years. D must be 12 years of age or more but under the age of 16 years, less than two years older than V and *not* in a position of trust or authority towards V, nor a person with whom V is in a relationship of dependency. Section 150.1(2) does *not* shift the onus of proof to D on the consent issue, nor expressly impose any burden of proof upon D. The subsection reinforces the general rule that consent of V under 14 years of age is *no* defence, subject to the limited exception there created.

Section 150.1(3) *prohibits* the trial of D, aged 12 or 13 years, for a listed offence, *unless* D is in a position of trust or authority towards V, or a person with whom V is in a relationship of dependency.

Sections 150.1(4) and (5), enacted in parallel terms, describe the circumstances under which a *mistaken belief* as to V's *age* may constitute a defence to a charge of a listed offence. The *general rule* of each subsection is that mistaken belief as to age is *no* defence where D is charged with a listed offence. The relevant age for s. 150.1(4) is 14 years of age or more and, under s. 150.1(5), 18 years of age or more. D falls within the exception, whereby mistaken belief as to age will constitute a defence, where D has taken *all reasonable steps* to ascertain V's age. There is no express statutory shift in the onus of proof in respect of these exceptions.

The subsections may attract scrutiny under *Charter* ss. 7 and 15 due to their general abrogation of the defence of consent and mistaken belief as to age for the listed offences.

Case Law

Exception for Age [See also ss. 13 and 23.1]

Cardinal v. R. (1984), 18 C.C.C. (3d) 96 (S.C.C.); affirming (1983), 3 C.C.C. (3d) 376 (Alta. C.A.) — D, a party to an act of rape committed by a 13-year-old, can be convicted of rape even though the 13-year-old is immune from prosecution.

R. v. Thompson (1992), 16 C.R. (4th) 168, 76 C.C.C. (3d) 142 (Alta. C.A.) — Notwithstanding the absence of a provision like s. 749(2), the *onus* of establishing age proximity, hence the consent exception of s. 749(2), rests upon D.

Proof of D's age is *not* an essential element of the offence.

R. v. P. (L.T.) (1997), 113 C.C.C. (3d) 42 (B.C. C.A.) — Where a defence of honest but mistaken belief in V's age arises in circumstances where s. 150.1(4) applies, P must prove beyond a reasonable doubt

i.   that D did *not* take *all reasonable* steps to ascertain V's age; or

ii.   that D did *not* have an *honest* belief that V's age was more than 14 years.

For the defence to succeed, there must be evidence which raises a *reasonable doubt*

i.   that D *held* the requisite *belief*; and,

ii.   that D took *all reasonable steps* to *ascertain* V's age.

To determine whether P has proven beyond a reasonable doubt that D did *not* take *all* reasonable steps to ascertain V's age, a trial judge must consider what *steps* it would have been *reasonable* for D to have taken in the circumstances. A *visual observation* may be sufficient in some cases. Whether *further* steps would be reasonable depends upon the apparent *indicia* of V's age and D's knowledge of it, including

i.   V's *physical appearance*;

ii.   V's *behaviour*;

iii. the *ages* and *appearance* of those in whose company V was found;

iv.   the relevant *activities*; and

v.   the times, places and other circumstances in which D observed V and V's conduct.

The trial judge should ask whether, considering the *indicia*, a *reasonable* person would *believe* that V was 14 years of age or more without further inquiry. If a reasonable person would *not* believe that V was 14 years or more without further inquiry, the trial judge should ask what further steps a reasonable person would take in the circumstances to ascertain V's age. Evidence of D's *actual* state of mind is relevant, but *not* dispositive.

R. v. K. (R.A.) (1996), 106 C.C.C. (3d) 93 (N.B. C.A.) — What constitutes "reasonable steps" depends upon the circumstances of each case, but may include,

i.   the association of D and V with older persons;

ii.   the relative age differential between D and V;

iii. the demeanour of V;

iv.   the appearance of V; and

v.   V's lack of curfew.

R. v. Osborne (1992), 17 C.R. (4th) 350 (Nfld. C.A.) — Section 150.1(4) limits the application of the defence of honest but mistaken belief to cases where D has taken *all reasonable steps to ascertain V's age*. The section places *no* persuasive burden on D. It requires only that there be evidence which, if true, would entitle D to an acquittal. The evidence need only raise a reasonable doubt.The evidence D relies upon to establish a reasonable doubt must be directed to "all" [reasonable steps], as much as any other part of the subsection. It is expected that those who engage in sexual activity with the young will make reasonable efforts to ascertain the age of prospective partners. The requirement is more than causal. There must be an earnest inquiry or some other compelling factor that negates the need for inquiry.

Charter Considerations

R. v. Brooks (1989), 47 C.C.C. (3d) 276 (Alta. C.A.) — Former s. 146(1), which made it an offence for a male to have sexual intercourse with a female under the age of 14 years "whether or not he believes that she is 14 years of age or more", is inconsistent with *Charter* s. 7 and of no force or effect, in that it fails to provide for the defence of honest mistake about V's age.

R. v. Hann (1992), 15 C.R. (4th) 355, 75 C.C.C. (3d) 355 (Nfld. C.A.) — Section 150.(1) does *not* contravene *Charter* s. 7 or 15(1) in the case of a teacher charged with an offence under s. 153(1)(a) in relation to V, a student aged 15 years.

R. v. McLeod (1989), 51 C.C.C. (3d) 257 (Ont. C.A.) — Rather than declaring former s. 146(1) unconstitutional in its entirety, the appropriate remedy is to *delete* the words "whether or not he believes she is 14 years of age or more".

R. v. M. (R.S.) (1991), 69 C.C.C. (3d) 223 (P.E.I. C.A.) — Section 150.1(1) is not contrary to s. 7 of the *Charter*. The section does *not* create an offence of absolute liability, as s. 150.1(4) provides a defence of due diligence.

Related Provisions: "Complainant" is defined in s. 2. Age is determined in accordance with *I.A.* s. 30. The *Code* does not define "position of trust or authority" nor "relationship of dependency".

"Consent" for the purposes of the sexual assault offences in ss. 271–273 is defined in s. 273.1(1) Sections 273.1(2) and (3) describe the circumstances in which *no* consent is obtained in cases of sexual assault. Section 273.2 describes the circumstances in which *apprehended* consent affords no defence to a charge of sexual assault.

In general, where P must establish the absence of consent, or that V was a member of an age-limited class of persons, D may assert that V consented, was not a member of the age-limited class or, at all events, D had a mistaken belief of either. The reasonableness or otherwise of D's belief is but an item of evidence of the honesty or lack thereof with which it was held. Where assault is an element of the offence, apprehended consent is governed by s. 265(4). Consent may be vitiated in such cases by any matter enumerated in s. 265(3).

C.E.A. s. 4(2) provides for spousal competence and compellability for P where D is charged with certain offences listed in s. 150.1, as well as attempts to commit such offences. Other special evidentiary rules are made applicable to certain of the offences under ss. 274–277 and 715.1.

Other related provisions are discussed in the corresponding notes to each of the listed sections.

151. Sexual interference — **Every person who, for a sexual purpose, touches, directly or indirectly, with a part of the body or with an object, any part of the body of a person under the age of fourteen years is guilty of an indictable offence and is liable to imprisonment for a term not exceeding ten years or is guilty of an offence punishable on summary conviction.**

R.S. 1985, c. 19 (3d Supp.), s. 1.

Commentary: The section creates and punishes the offence of *sexual interference* and provides the punishment upon finding of guilt.

The *external circumstances* of the offences are complete where D *touches* any part of the body of V, who is under the age of 14 years. D's touching may be *direct or indirect*. It may be with a part of the body or with an object. The touching must be *for a sexual purpose*. The offence requires proof of an intention to cause the external circumstances of the offence, including proof of sexual purpose.

Case Law
Elements of Offence

R. v. Bone (1993), 21 C.R. (4th) 218, 81 C.C.C. (3d) 389 (Man. C.A.) — The offence involves an act committed for "a sexual purpose". It is a crime of *specific* intent. Intoxication is a defence.

R. v. Sears (1990), 58 C.C.C. (3d) 62 (Man. C.A.) — D "touches" V where s/he intends sexual interaction of any kind with V and, with such intent, makes contact with V's body, notwithstanding that V offered sexual favours in return for money.

Proof of Age [See also, Code s. 658]

R. v. Johnson (1993), 80 C.C.C. (3d) 199 (N.S. C.A.) — In a prosecution under s. 151, V may testify as to her age. The evidence, strictly speaking, is hearsay, but may be admitted if it is reliable and necessary in the circumstances of the case.

Related Provisions: The offence is also an *element* in the *sexual exploitation* offence of s. 153(1)(a).

The defence of *consent*, equally *mistaken belief* that V was more than 14 years of age, has limited or no application to this offence as a result of s. 150.1. The evidentiary rules of ss. 274–277 and 715.1, as well as the spousal competence and compellability rules of *C.E.A.* s. 4(2), apply to proceedings under this section. V's age is determined under *I.A.* s. 30.

The offence of the section is triable either way. Where P proceeds by indictment, D may *elect* mode of trial under s. 536(2).

152. Invitation to sexual touching — **Every person who, for a sexual purpose, invites, counsels or incites a person under the age of fourteen years to touch, directly or indirectly, with a part of the body or with an object, the body of any person, including the body of the person who so invites, counsels or incites and the body of the person under the age of fourteen years, is guilty of an indictable offence and is liable to impris-**

onment for a term not exceeding ten years or is guilty of an offence punishable on summary conviction.

R.S. 1985, c. 19 (3d Supp.), s. 1.

Commentary: Under this section, invitation to sexual touching is an offence triable either way.

The *external circumstances* consist of several elements. D must *incite, counsel* or *invite* V, a person under the age of 14 years, to touch the *body* of any person. The proposed touching may be *direct* or *indirect*, with a *part* of the *body* or with an *object*. The body which it is proposed that V touch may be of *any* person, including D and V. D's conduct must be *for a sexual purpose*. The offence requires proof of the intention to do what constitutes the external circumstances of the offence, including the critical element of a sexual purpose.

Case Law

R. v. Fong (1994), 92 C.C.C. (3d) 171 (Alta. C.A.) — The section should be construed purposively, in a manner consistent with the philosophy and rationale underlying Parliament's objectives. It includes both actual and indirect touching. The offence is made out where D invites a young child to act as a sexual repository by holding in his hand a tissue onto which D ejaculated.

Related Provisions: This offence is also an essential element of sexual exploitation in s. 153(1)(b). Under s. 22(3), "counsel" includes, *inter alia*, "incite". V's age is determined under *I.A.* s. 30.

The defence of *consent*, as well as the *mistaken belief* that V was more than 14 years of age, has limited or no application to this offence as a result of the provisions of s. 150.1. The evidentiary rules of ss. 274–277 and 715.1, as well as the spousal competence and compellability rule of *C.E.A.* s. 4(2), apply to proceedings under this section.

Where P proceeds by indictment, D may *elect* mode of trial under s. 536(2). Summary conviction proceedings are governed by Part XXVII.

153. (1) Sexual exploitation — Every person who is in a position of trust or authority towards a young person or is a person with whom the young person is in a relationship of dependency and who

(a) for a sexual purpose, touches, directly or indirectly, with a part of the body or with an object, any part of the body of the young person, or

(b) for a sexual purpose, invites, counsels or incites a young person to touch, directly or indirectly, with a part of the body or with an object, the body of any person, including the body of the person who so invites, counsels or incites and the body of the young person,

is guilty of an indictable offence and liable to imprisonment for a term not exceeding five years or is guilty of an offence punishable on summary conviction.

(2) Definition of "young person" — In this section, "young person" means a person fourteen years of age or more but under the age of eighteen years.

R.S. 1985, c. 19 (3d Supp.), s. 1.

Commentary: This section combines elements of sexual interference and invitation to sexual touching with other circumstances to constitute the crime of *sexual exploitation*.

The *external circumstances* require that D, as principal, stand in a *particular relationship* to V, namely, in a position of *trust or authority* towards V, or be a person with whom V is in a *relationship of dependency*. V must be a young person, as defined in s. 153(2). D must commit the offence of sexual interference or invitation to sexual touching with or upon V. The *mental element*, in each case, is that of the offence of sexual interference or invitation to sexual touching, as the case may be. It is an offence of specific intent.

Case Law
Elements of Offences

R. v. Audet (1996), 106 C.C.C. (3d) 481 (S.C.C.) — The essential elements of the offence are,

i.   that V is a "young person" within s. 153(2);

ii.   that D engaged in the conduct prohibited in s. 153(1);

iii. that D was in a position of trust/authority towards V, or V in a relationship of dependency with D; and,

iv.   that D had the *mens rea* required for each element of the offence.

P is *not* required to prove that D *exploited* his/her privileged position with respect to V. The offence of s. 153(1) is a specific intent offence.

"Authority" and "trust" should to be given their ordinary meaning. "Position of authority" is *not* restricted to cases where the relationship of authority derives from D;s *role*, rather, extends to any relationship where D actually exercises such a power. The analysis is directed to the nature of the relationship between V and D, *not* their status in relation to each other.

To determine whether D is in a position of trust/authority in relation to V, or V in a relationship of dependency with D, requires a consideration of all the factual circumstances relevant to the characterization of the relationship. Relevant factors include, but are *not* restricted to,

i.   the *age difference* between D and V;

ii.   the *evolution* of the *relationship* between D and V; and

iii. the *status* of D in relation to V.

Teachers are *not* in a *de jure* position of trust/authority towards their students. They are, however, in such a position, in fact, in most cases. Absent evidence which raises a reasonable doubt in the mind of the trier of fact of the evidence of a relationship of trust/authority, a teacher is in such a relationship.

R. v. Bone (1993), 21 C.R. (4th) 218, 81 C.C.C. (3d) 389 (Man. C.A.) — The offence involves an act committed for "a sexual purpose", hence it is a crime of *specific* intent. A person too drunk to form such intent cannot be convicted of the offence.

R. v. Hann (1992), 15 C.R. (4th) 355, 75 C.C.C. (3d) 355 (Nfld. C.A.) — It is a defence to a charge under s. 153(1)(a) if D had a *reasonable* belief that V was *over* eighteen, if D took all reasonable steps to ascertain V's age. It is also a defence where it appears that D:

i.   did *not* know s/he was in a position of trust;

ii.   did *not* mean to touch V; or,

iii. did *not* intend the touching for sexual purposes.

R. v. Galbraith (1994), 30 C.R. (4th) 230, 90 C.C.C. (3d) 76 (Ont. C.A.) — A "relationship of dependency" is a relationship in which there is a *de facto* reliance by a young person on a figure who has assumed a position of power, such as trust or authority, over the young person along non-traditional lines. The category is *ejusdem generis* to the other categories of the section, positions of trust or authority. Whether such a relationship exists in any case is a question of fact decided after consideration of all of the circumstances.

R. v. G. (T.F.) (1992), 11 C.R. (4th) 221 (Ont. C.A.); leave to appeal refused (1992), 145 N.R. 391, 62 O.A.C. 160 (S.C.C.) — The purpose of s. 153 is to make it clear that a person in a position of authority or trust towards a young person is *not* to engage in sexual activity with the young person, even where there is apparent consent. P need establish no *nexus* between D's position of authority and the young person's consent to the sexual activity.

Included Offences

R. v. Nelson (1989), 51 C.C.C. (3d) 150 (Ont. H.C.) — Sexual exploitation is *not* an included offence of sexual assault.

Relationship of Dependency

R. v. Galbraith (1994), 30 C.R. (4th) 230, 90 C.C.C. (3d) 76 (Ont. C.A.) — See digest under *Elements of Offence supra.*

Position of Trust

R. v. L. (D.B.) (1995), 43 C.R. (4th) 252, 101 C.C.C. (3d) 406 (Ont. C.A.) — The *test* for whether D is in a *position of trust* in relation to V must be, in general, the same regardless of their respective ages. Where V is under 14 and D is over 12 but less than two years older than V, however, the meaning of "position of trust", of necessity, must accommodate the ages and age differential of D and V. A large age differential may support a conclusion that D was in a position of trust or authority towards V, or V in a position of dependency upon D. An age differential of less than two years between D and V may support the opposite conclusion.

R. v. L. (D.B.) (1995), 43 C.R. (4th) 252, 101 C.C.C. (3d) 406 (Ont. C.A.) — A person in a position of trust will be in a particular position in relation to the other person which imposes on him/her a duty of care in relation to that person. The relationship is often, but need not be accompanied by an authority by the dominant person over the other. The existence of a trust relationship between D and V will frequently result in a relationship of dependency between V and D. The closer the ages of D and V, the more ambiguous may be their relationship. It is only infrequently that a young person close in age to V will be entrusted with sufficient resposibility to create a position of trust towards V.

Related Provisions: Age is determined under *I.A.* s. 30. The essential elements of sexual interference and invitation to sexual touching are described in the *Commentary* to ss. 151 and 152, respectively.

For other related provisions, see the corresponding note to s. 151, *supra*.

153.1 (1) Sexual exploitation of person with disability — Every person who is in a position of trust or authority towards a person with a mental or physical disability or who is a person with whom a person with a mental or physical disability is in a relationship of dependency and who, for a sexual purpose, counsels or incites that person to touch, without that person's consent, his or her own body, the body of the person who so counsels or incites, or the body of any other person, directly or indirectly, with a part of the body or with an object, the body of any person, including the body of the person who so invites, counsels or incites and the body of the person with the disability is guilty of

(a) an indictable offence and liable to imprisonment for a term not exceeding five years; or

(b) an offence punishable on summary conviction and liable to imprisonment for a term not exceeding eighteen months.

(2) Definition of "consent" — Subject to subsection (3), "consent" means, for the purposes of this section, the voluntary agreement of the complainant to engage in the sexual activity in question.

(3) When no consent obtained — No consent is obtained, for the purposes of this section, if

(a) the agreement is expressed by the words or conduct of a person other than the complainant;

(b) the complainant is incapable of consenting to the activity;

(c) the accused counsels or incites the complainant to engage in the activity by abusing a position of trust, power or authority;

(d) the complainant expresses, by words or conduct, a lack of agreement to engage in the activity; or

(e) the complainant, having consented to engage in sexual activity, expresses, by words or conduct, a lack of agreement to continue to engage in the activity.

(4) Subsection (3) not limiting — Nothing in subsection (3) shall be construed as limiting the circumstances in which no consent is obtained.

(5) **When belief in consent not a defence** — It is not a defence to a charge under this section that the accused believed that the complainant consented to the activity that forms the subject-matter of the charge if

    (a) the accused's belief arose from the accused's

        (i) self-induced intoxication, or

        (ii) recklessness or wilful blindness; or

    (b) the accused did not take reasonable steps, in the circumstances known to the accused at the time, to ascertain that the complainant was consenting.

(6) **Accused's belief as to consent** — If an accused alleges that he or she believed that the complainant consented to the conduct that is the subject-matter of the charge, a judge, if satisfied that there is sufficient evidence and that, if believed by the jury, the evidence would constitute a defence, shall instruct the jury, when reviewing all the evidence relating to the determination of the honesty of the accused's belief, to consider the presence or absence of reasonable grounds for that belief.

1998, c. 9, s. 2.

154. [Repealed R.S. 1985, c. 19 (3d Supp.), s. 1.]

155. (1) Incest — Every one commits "incest" who, knowing that another person is by blood relationship his or her parent, child, brother, sister, grandparent or grandchild, as the case may be, has sexual intercourse with that person.

(2) **Punishment** — Every one who commits incest is guilty of an indictable offence and liable to imprisonment for a term not exceeding fourteen years.

(3) **Defence** — No accused shall be determined by a court to be guilty of an offence under this section if the accused was under restraint, duress or fear of the person with whom the accused had the sexual intercourse at the time the sexual intercourse occurred.

(4) **"brother", "sister"** — In this section,"brother" and "sister", respectively, include half-brother and half-sister.

R.S., c. C-34, s. 150; 1972, c. 13, s. 10; R.S. 1985, c. 27 (1st Supp.), s. 21.

Commentary: This section describes and punishes the offence of *incest*.

In essence, incest consists of *sexual intercourse* between persons within a *defined blood relationship* to each other. The *external circumstances* are complete upon proof of sexual intercourse between D and a listed relation. Under s. 155(4) "brother" and "sister" include half-brother and half-sister. The *mental element* requires proof that D intentionally had sexual intercourse with a person within the defined relationship, with the *knowledge* thereof.

Section 155(3) provides a *defence* to or *exemption* from liability. D must *not* be convicted where s/he was under restraint, duress or fear of the person with whom D had sexual intercourse, at the time sexual intercourse occurred.

Case Law

Charter **Considerations**

R. v. S. (M.) (1996), 111 C.C.C. (3d) 467 (B.C. C.A.) — The section does *not* contravene *Charter* ss. 2(a), 2(d), 7 or 15.

Related Provisions: Whether an act of sexual intercourse has occurred is determined by s. 4(5). The *Code* does *not* define nor otherwise limit the phrase "restraint, duress or fear", leaving its meaning to be determined in accordance with the everyday usage of the terms.

The special evidentiary rules of ss. 274–277 and 715.1, as well as the rule of spousal competence and compellability under *C.E.A.* s. 4(2), apply.

Under s. 536(2), D may elect mode of trial.

156. [Repealed R.S. 1985, c. 19 (3d Supp.), s. 2.]

157. [Repealed R.S. 1985, c. 19 (3d Supp.), s. 2.]

158. [Repealed R.S. 1985, c. 19 (3d Supp.), s. 2.]

159. (1) Anal intercourse — Every person who engages in an act of anal intercourse is guilty of an indictable offence and liable to imprisonment for a term not exceeding ten years or is guilty of an offence punishable on summary conviction.

(2) Exception — Subsection (1) does not apply to any act engaged in, in private, between

(a) husband and wife, or

(b) any two persons, each of whom is eighteen years of age or more, both of whom consent to the act.

(3) Idem — For the purposes of subsection (2),

(a) an act shall be deemed not to have been engaged in in private if it is engaged in in a public place or if more than two persons take part or are present; and

(b) a person shall be deemed not to consent to an act

(i) if the consent is extorted by force, threats or fear of bodily harm or is obtained by false and fraudulent misrepresentations respecting the nature and quality of the act, or

(ii) if the court is satisfied beyond a reasonable doubt that the person could not have consented to the act by reason of mental disability.

R.S. 1985, c. 19 (3d Supp.), s. 3.

Commentary: This section, by prohibition and exception, creates an offence of *anal intercourse*.

The *external circumstances* consist of an act of anal intercourse. The *mental element* requires proof of the intention to engage in such conduct. No ulterior mental element need be established.

Section 159(2) exempts specified acts of anal intercourse from liability. In each case, the act must occur *in private*. Under s. 159(3)(a) acts are deemed *not* to have occurred in private, either if they occurred in a public place, as defined in s. 150, or if more than two persons took part or were present. Private acts of anal intercourse between husband and wife are exempt from liability under s. 159(2)(a). Private acts of anal intercourse between any two persons, each of whom is 18 years of age or more and *both* of whom consent to the act are exempt under s. 159(2)(b). There is no consent where the circumstances in s. 159(3)(b) obtain.

Case Law

Exception [These cases were decided under the precedessor section]

R. v. Volk (1973), 24 C.R.N.S. 166, 12 C.C.C. (2d) 395 (Alta. C.A.) — *See also: Duchesne v. R.* (1976), 36 C.R.N.S. 365 (Que. C.A.) — The burden of proof that the exception operates in favour of D is on D and must be established on a balance of probabilities.

Public Place [See also s. 173]

R. v. Goguen (1977), 36 C.C.C. (2d) 570 (B.C. C.A.) — The definition of "public place" is *not* exhaustive. An alcove, open and accessible to the public and located near a beach used by the public both day and night, is a public place.

R. v. Hogg (1970), 15 C.R.N.S. 106 (Ont. C.A.) — A locked cubicle in a public washroom is a public place.

Charter **Considerations**

R. v. M. (C.) (1995), 41 C.R. (4th) 134, 98 C.C.C. (3d) 481 (Ont. C.A.) — Section 159 infringes *Charter* s. 15 on the basis of *age* (per Goodman, Catzman and Abella JJ.A.) and sexual *orientation* (per Abella J.A.) and is *not* saved by *Charter* s. 1.

R. v. Roy (1998), 125 C.C.C. (3d) 442 (Que. C.A.) — Section 159 offends *Charter* s. 15 and is *not* saved by s. 1.

Related Provisions: Consent under s. 159(3)(b) may be actual or apprehended. The nature of consent ineffectual to vitiate a charge of assault is found in s. 265(3).

The special evidentiary rules of ss. 274–277 and 715.1, as well as the rule of spousal competence and compellability in *C.E.A.* s. 4(2), apply.

Under s. 536(2), D may elect mode of trial.

160. (1) Bestiality — Every person who commits bestiality is guilty of an indictable offence and is liable to imprisonment for a term not exceeding ten years or is guilty of an offence punishable on summary conviction.

(2) Compelling the commission of bestiality — Every person who compels another to commit bestiality is guilty of an indictable offence and is liable to imprisonment for a term not exceeding ten years or is guilty of an offence punishable on summary conviction.

(3) Bestiality in presence of or by child — Notwithstanding subsection (1), every person who commits bestiality in the presence of a person who is under the age of fourteen years or who incites a person under the age of fourteen years to commit bestiality is guilty of an indictable offence and is liable to imprisonment for a term not exceeding ten years or is guilty of an offence punishable on summary conviction.

R.S. 1985, c. 19 (3d Supp.), s. 3.

Commentary: This section describes and punishes various *bestiality* offences. Bestiality is *not* itself defined.

In general, bestiality is committed where D, a *human* being, carries out *intercourse*, in any way, with a *beast* or *bird*. This form of unnatural sexual indulgence, as well as sodomy, is comprised under the general description "buggery".

The offence of s. 160(2) also requires proof of bestiality as an essential element. Its *external circumstances* consist of D's compulsion of another to commit bestiality. The means of compulsion are *not* specified nor statutorily limited. The *mental element* requires proof that D intentionally caused the external circumstances of the offence.

Under s. 160(3), the *external circumstances* consist of D committing bestiality in the *presence* of a person *under 14* years of age. The *external circumstances* are also established where D *incites* a person under the age of 14 years to commit bestiality. The *mental element* consists of the intention to cause the external circumstances of the offence.

Related Provisions: Age is determined under *I.A.* s. 30. Under s. 22(3), "counsel" includes "incite". The accessoryship provisions of s. 22 provide some overlap between ss. 160(1) and (3) where V is under the age of 14 years. There is *no* difference in penalty.

Offences relating to sexual activity involving persons under the age of 18 years are described in ss. 170–172.

Under s. 150.1(4), it is *no* defence to a charge under s. 160 that D believed V was 14 years of age or more at the time of the offence, *unless* D took *all* reasonable steps to ascertain V's age. The special evidentiary rules of ss. 274–277 are applicable in prosecutions under ss. 160(2) and (3) as are the spousal competence and compellability rules of *C.E.A.* s. 4(2) and *Code* s. 715.1 (video-taped evidence).

Each offence is triable either way. Where P proceeds by indictment, D may *elect* mode of trial under s. 536(2).

161. **(1) Order of prohibition** — Where an offender is convicted, or is discharged on the conditions prescribed in a probation order under section 730, of an offence under section 151, 152, 155 or 159, subsection 160(2) or (3) or section 170, 171, 271, 272, 273 or 281, in respect of a person who is under the age of fourteen years, the court that sentences the offender or directs that the accused be discharged, as the case may be, in addition to any other punishment that may be imposed for that offence or any other condition prescribed in the order of discharge, shall consider making and may make, subject to the conditions or exemptions that the court directs, an order prohibiting the offender from

(a) attending a public park or public swimming area where persons under the age of fourteen years are present or can reasonably be expected to be present, or a daycare centre, schoolground, playground or community centre; or

(b) seeking, obtaining or continuing any employment, whether or not the employment is remunerated, or becoming or being a volunteer in a capacity, that involves being in a position of trust or authority towards persons under the age of fourteen years.

(2) Duration of prohibition — The prohibition may be for life or for any shorter duration that the court considers desirable and, in the case of a prohibition that is not for life, the prohibition begins on the later of

(a) the date on which the order is made; and

(b) where the offender is sentenced to a term of imprisonment, the date on which the offender is released from imprisonment for the offence, including release on parole, mandatory supervision or statutory release.

(3) Court may vary order — A court that makes an order of prohibition or, where the court is for any reason unable to act, another court of equivalent jurisdiction in the same province, may, on application of the offender or the prosecutor, require the offender to appear before it at any time and, after hearing the parties, that court may vary the conditions prescribed in the order if, in the opinion of the court, the variation is desirable because of changed circumstances after the conditions were prescribed.

(4) Offence — Every person who is bound by an order of prohibition and who does not comply with the order is guilty of

(a) an indictable offence and is liable to imprisonment for a term not exceeding two years; or

(b) an offence punishable on summary conviction.

1993, c. 45, s. 1; 1995, c. 22, s. 18 (Sch. IV); 1997, c. 18, s. 4.

Commentary: This section *requires* a sentencing court to *consider*, and *permits* it to *impose*, an order of *prohibition* upon conviction or conditional discharge of a listed offence in respect of a person under the age of 14 years. It also provides for *variation* of the conditions of the order and creates an *offence* for failure to comply with its terms.

Subsections (1) and (2) should be considered together. The obligation to consider and discretion to impose an order of prohibition in the terms described in s. 161(1)(a) and (b) is engaged where a sentencing court has *convicted* or *conditionally discharged* an offender of a *listed* offence in respect of a person under 14 years of age. The order of prohibition is *in addition to* any other punishment that may be imposed. It may be subject to such *conditions* or exemptions as the sentencing judge directs. The order would appear designed to eliminate, at all events limit, the opportunities for contact between the offender and persons under the age of 14 years in recreational, educational and custodial premises or locations, as well employment and voluntary associations. Under s. 161(2), the prohibition may be for life or specified time and commences on the date made or on the offender's release from imprisonment, including conditional release, whichever is later.

Under s. 161(3), the *conditions* of an order of prohibition may be *varied* by the sentencing court or another court of equivalent jurisdiction in the same province (where the sentencing court is unable to act). Either D or P may apply for the variation and are entitled to be heard on the application. Variation may be made if, in the opinion of the court, a *change* in *circumstances* since the original order make it desirable.

Under s. 161(4), *failure to comply* with the terms of an order of prohibition is an *offence* triable either way.

Related Provisions: An order made under this section is a "sentence" under s. 673. It appears somewhat incongruous that the offence of s. 163.1 (child pornography) is *not* listed as a predicate crime.

The scope of prohibition contemplated by the section, in particular its duration and prospective bar of both voluntary and remunerated employment, may render it overinclusive, hence subject to *Charter* review, especially where the predicate crime is a summary conviction offence.

Sections 161(3) and (4) are analogous to ss. 732.2(3) and 733.1(1) which apply to conventional probation orders the length of which must not exceed three years.

Sections 179(1)(b) and (2) punish loitering in or near a school ground, playground, public park or bathing area by a person convicted of a listed crime.

162. [Repealed R.S. 1985, c. 19 (3d Supp.), s. 4.]

Offences Tending to Corrupt Morals

163. (1) **Corrupting morals** — Every one commits an offence who

(a) makes, prints, publishes, distributes, circulates, or has in his possession for the purpose of publication, distribution or circulation any obscene written matter, picture, model, phonograph record or other thing whatever; or

(b) makes, prints, publishes, distributes, sells or has in his possession for the purpose of publication, distribution or circulation a crime comic.

(2) **Idem** — Every one commits an offence who knowingly, without lawful justification or excuse,

(a) sells, exposes to public view or has in his possession for such a purpose any obscene written matter, picture, model, phonograph record or other thing whatever;

(b) publicly exhibits a disgusting object or an indecent show;

(c) offers to sell, advertises or publishes an advertisement of, or has for sale or disposal any means, instructions, medicine, drug or article intended or represented as a method of causing abortion or miscarriage; or

(d) advertises or publishes an advertisement of any means, instructions, medicine, drug or article intended or represented as a method for restoring sexual virility or curing venereal diseases or diseases of the generative organs.

(3) **Defence of public good** — No person shall be convicted of an offence under this section if the public good was served by the acts that are alleged to constitute the offence and if the acts alleged did not extend beyond what served the public good.

(4) **Question of law and question of fact** — For the purposes of this section, it is a question of law whether an act served the public good and whether there is evidence

that the act alleged went beyond what served the public good, but it is a question of fact whether the acts did or did not extend beyond what served the public good.

(5) Motives irrelevant — For the purposes of this section, the motives of an accused are irrelevant.

(6) [Repealed 1993, c. 46, s. 1.]

(7) "crime comic" — In this section, "crime comic" means a magazine, periodical or book that exclusively or substantially comprises matter depicting pictorially

(a) the commission of crimes, real or fictitious; or

(b) events connected with the commission of crimes, real or fictitious, whether occurring before or after the commission of the crime.

(8) Obscene publication — For the purposes of this Act, any publication a dominant characteristic of which is the undue exploitation of sex, or of sex and any one or more of the following subjects, namely, crime, horror, cruelty and violence, shall be deemed to be obscene.

R.S., c. C-34, s. 159; 1993, c. 46, s. 1.

Commentary: The offences of this section relate to the actual or intended *distribution* of obscene material, crime comics and related goods and services. It further provides whether certain matters of excuse shall constitute a defence to the charge and includes definitions of "obscenity" and "crime comic." The prohibitions have attracted *Charter* s. 2(b) scrutiny.

In general, the offences of s. 163(1) prohibit the *production and distribution*, actual or intended, of obscene material and crime comics. The *external circumstances* require proof of prohibited subject-matter. Whether the subject-matter is obscene is determined under s. 163(8). "Crime comic" is defined in s. 163(7). The *external circumstances* also require proof of a prohibited method of production or distribution. The *mental element* requires proof that D intentionally caused the external circumstances of the offence.

The offences of s. 163(2) require proof of a proscribed method of exhibition, prohibited subject-matter and the *absence* of *lawful excuse*. The *mental element* expressed in the compendious term "knowingly" requires *no* proof of any ulterior state of mind, but *semble* includes knowledge of the presence and character of the material. To constitute a defence, D's acts must serve and *not* extend beyond what served the public good.

Sections 163(3) and (4) provide for a *defence of public good*. Under s. 163(4) it is a question of law whether an act served the public good and whether there is evidence that the act alleged went beyond what served the public good. The question whether the acts did or did not extend beyond what served the public good is a question of fact. D's motives are irrelevant to the issue of liability under s. 163(5).

Case Law

Nature and Elements of Offence

R. v. Jorgensen (1995), 43 C.R. (4th) 137, 102 C.C.C. (3d) 97 (S.C.C.) — In general, "knowingly" applies to *all* elements of the *actus reus*. Nothing in s. 163(2) or its legislative history supports a restricted meaning for "knowingly" in the section. It sets an onerous standard of proof in relation to sellers/retailers. To prove *mens rea*, P must establish that the seller/retailer

i. was aware that the *subject-matter* of the material had, as its dominant characteristic, the exploitation of sex; and

ii. knew of the *specific acts* which make the material obscene in law.

Material which involves explicit sex

i. with violence; or

ii. which is degrading or dehumanizing

is generally obscene. Where a film is alleged to be obscene, "overall", rather than in any particular scene, P must prove that the seller/retailer was aware of the "overall" obscene nature of the film.

A retailer is *not* immunized from conviction merely because s/he does *not* know how the law defines obscenity.

Proof of a retailer's "knowledge" of the sale of obscene material does *not* necessarily require P to prove the retailer actually viewed the obscene material. P may rely on wilful blindness to prove knowledge. A deliberate choice *not* to know something when there are reasons to believe further inquiry is necessary may establish the requisite mental element. Approval of a film by a provincial Censor Board may be relevant to the issue of wilful blindness.

Reliance on provincial Censor Board approval of a film does *not* negate *mens rea*. Provincial Censor Board approval may be relevant to a determination of community standards of tolerance, but is *not* relevant to D's knowledge of the nature of the film. P need *not* prove that D knew that a film exceeded community standards.

Approval of a film by a provincial Censor Board does *not* constitute a lawful justification or excuse.

Hawkshaw v. R. (1986), 51 C.R. (3d) 289, 26 C.C.C. (3d) 129 (S.C.C.) — Publication is *not* a necessary element of every offence created by s. 163(1)(a). A separate offence of making an obscene picture exists. Where, as here, the indictment alleged an element of publication, evidence of publication, or an intent to publish, was required.

R. v. Metro News Ltd. (1986), 53 C.R. (3d) 289, 29 C.C.C. (3d) 35 (Ont. C.A.), leave to appeal refused, *ibid* (S.C.C.) — *Charter* s. 2(b) protects freedom of expression in all forms, whether they be oral, written, pictorial, sculpture, music, dance or film.

"Publishes"

Germain v. R. (1985), 21 C.C.C. (3d) 289 (S.C.C.) — Signs at a sex boutique gave the articles sold within a public character so that they came within the meaning of "publication" without the need for any accompanying written description.

R. v. Small (1973), 26 C.R.N.S. 77, 12 C.C.C. (2d) 145 (B.C. C.A.) — "Publication" refers to a tangible thing, such as a book, not a threatical performance.

"Distributes"

R. v. Fraser, [1967] 2 C.C.C. 43 (S.C.C.); affirming [1966] 1 C.C.C. 110 (B.C. C.A.) — "Distribution" is a wider term than "sale" and includes sale.

R. v. Harris (1987), 57 C.R. (3d) 356, 35 C.C.C. (3d) 1 (Ont. C.A.) — The activities of duplicating video cassettes and retaining copies for rental constitute distribution.

R. v. Sudbury News Services Ltd. (1978), 39 C.C.C. (2d) 1 (Ont. C.A.) — The act of distribution is complete upon the allocation and delivery of magazines to confectionery stores.

R. v. Dorosz (1971), 14 C.R.N.S. 357, 4 C.C.C. (2d) 203 (Ont. C.A.) — A retail sales clerk who sells or exposes for view obscene matter, or has in his/her possession these things for such purposes, is *not* a distributor.

"Circulates": S. 163(1)

R. v. Rioux (1969), 8 C.R.N.S. 21, [1970] 3 C.C.C. 149 (S.C.C.) — "Circulate" means to pass around from hand to hand. A private showing of obscene films does *not* constitute circulation.

Possession for Distribution: S. 163(1)

R. v. Fraser (1967), [1967] 2 C.C.C. 43 (S.C.C.); affirming [1966] 1 C.C.C. 110 (B.C. C.A.) — Where D was in possession of the material for sale, D may be charged with either possession for the purpose of distribution under s. 163(1)(a), or possession for the purpose of sale under s. 163(2)(a).

R. v. Householders T.V. & Appliances (1985), 10 C.C.C. (3d) 571 (Ont. C.A.) — Possession for the purpose of distribution requires *more* than the mere rental of copies of movie video cassettes to individual memebers of the public.

Public Good: S. 163(3)[Cases decided under previous subsection.]

R. v. American News Co. (1957), 25 C.R. 374, 118 C.C.C. 152 (Ont. C.A.) — Public good is that which is "necessary or advantageous to religion, or morality, to the administration of justice, the pursuit of science, literature or art, or other objects of general interest".

R. v. National News Co. (1953), 16 C.R. 369, 106 C.C.C. 26 (Ont. C.A.) — Section 163(3) does *not* alter the test of obscenity. It merely provides that D, who would otherwise be guilty, shall *not* be convicted if

D *proves* that the *public good* was served by what was done which did not exceed what the public good required.

Delorme v. R. (1973), 21 C.R.N.S. 305 (Que. C.A.) — Section 163(3) provides a defence if the acts alleged to constitute the offence serve the public good and do not extend beyond what serves the public good. In this case, although the book was beneficial to sexology students, it was available in a public bookstore, and therefore, it could not be said that the public good was being served.

Obscenity: S. 163(8)

R. v. Butler (1992), 11 C.R. (4th) 137 (S.C.C.) — The portrayal of sex coupled with violence will almost always constitute the undue exploitation of sex. Explicit sex which is degrading or dehumanizing may be undue if the risk of harm is substantial. Explicit sex that is not violent, nor degrading or dehumanizing, will not constitute the undue exploitation of sex unless it employs children in its production. Material which is not obscene under this framework does not become so by reason of the person to whom it is shown, or the place of manner in which it is shown.

R. v. Video World Ltd. (1986), 22 C.C.C. (3d) 331 (Man. C.A.); affirmed (1987), 35 C.C.C. (3d) 191 (S.C.C.) — The fact that films are to be viewed at home does *not* change the legal definition of obscenity. The films in question were held to be obscene as they were wholly destitute of plot and, although free of violence, portrayed degrading and dehumanizing sexual acts.

Hawkshaw v. R. (1986), 51 C.R. (3d) 289, 26 C.C.C. (3d) 129 (S.C.C.) — The *test* of obscenity in s. 163(8) applies to the issue of obscenity in all *Code* charges, whether based on publication or not.

Germain v. R. (1985), 21 C.R. (3d) 289 (S.C.C.) — In determining whether an article is obscene, the audience or market to which it is restricted is irrelevant.

Towne Cinema Theatres Ltd. v. R. (1985), 45 C.R. (3d) 1, 18 C.C.C. (3d) 193 (S.C.C.) — The proper test of undueness is not what Canadians think is right for themselves but whether they would object to others seeing the film because to allow them to see it would be beyond the contemporary Canadian standard of tolerance.

Brodie v. R. (1962), 37 C.R. 120, 132 C.C.C. 161 (S.C.C.) — The definition of obscene is exhaustive. A publication is *not* obscene unless it falls within the definition of "obscene" in s. 163(8) and it cannot be confiscated unless it is found to be obscene. There is *no* undue exploitation of sex in a novel if there is no more emphasis on the theme than is required in its serious treatment.

R. v. Wagner (1985), 43 C.R. (3d) 318 (Alta. Q.B.); affirmed on other grounds (1986), 50 C.R. (3d) 175, 26 C.C.C. (3d) 242 (Alta. C.A.); leave to appeal refused (1986), 50 C.R. (3d) 175n (S.C.C.) — "Undue" is that which exceeds the contemporary Canadian standard of tolerance. The nature of the material does not change according to the age of the possessor or the location where it is shown. Intolerable is pornography which is sexually explicit with violence, or sexually explicit without violence but dehumanizing or degrading. Sexually explicit erotica which portrays positive and affectionate human sexual interaction between consenting individuals participating on a basis of equality is tolerable no matter how explicit.

R. v. Penthouse Int. Ltd. (1979), 46 C.C.C. (2d) 111 (Ont. C.A.); leave to appeal refused (1979), 46 C.C.C. (2d) 111n (S.C.C.) — A magazine is to be judged in a somewhat different way than a novel. In novels, passages which deal in explicit terms with sex must be judged against the entire work, and in the context of its theme. A magazine, however, has no theme. Each page must be looked at more or less in isolation from the others. Offensive passages or pictorial presentations in a magazine cannot be saved merely be surrounding them with profound articles on foreign policy.

R. v. Kiverago (1973), 11 C.C.C. (2d) 463 (Ont. C.A.) — It is the *standard* of the *contemporary* Canadian community that should be applied in deciding the question of obscenity, *not* that of a small segment such as *one community.*

Evidence of Community Standards

Towne Cinema Theatres Ltd. v. R. (1985), 45 C.R. (3d) 1, 18 C.C.C. (3d) 193 (S.C.C.) — Censor board approval can be considered as evidence of the community standard of tolerance. P need *not* adduce expert evidence as to community standards.

R. v. Prov. News Co. (1974), 20 C.C.C. (2d) 129 (Alta. C.A.) — The onus is *not* on P to lead evidence of community standards, P can rely on the production or the publication itself to support the allegation of obscenity.

R. v. McFall (1975), 26 C.C.C. (2d) 181 (B.C. C.A.) — The criteria employed by the film classification director in determining whether to approve, prohibit or regulate the showing of a particular film is admissible as evidence relevant to show what is the standard of the community with respect to teh acceptance of the film in question for display to the public.

R. v. Great West News (1970), 10 C.R.N.S. 42, [1970] 4 C.C.C. 307 (Man. C.A.) — Expert evidence is admissible to describe the community standards of tolerance, but not necessarily essential.

Charter Considerations [See also Charter s. 2(b)]

R. v. Butler (1992), 11 C.R. (4th) 137, 18 C.C.C. (3d) 1 (B.C. C.A.); affirming (1984), 38 C.R. (3d) 275, 11 C.C.C. (3d) 389 (B.C. Co. Ct.) — *See also:R. v. Wagner* (1985), 43 C.R. (3d) 318 (Alta. Q.B.); affirmed on other grounds (1986), 50 C.R. (3d) 175, 26 C.C.C. (3d) 242 (Alta. C.A.); leave to appeal refused (1986), 50 C.R. (3d) 175n (S.C.C.) — The use of the community standard test in its interpretation is *not* so vague and overly broad as to violate *Charter* s. 7. The limitation on the right to freedom of expresssion is reasonable and demonstrably justified in a free and democratic society.

R. v. Video World (1986), 22 C.C.C. (3d) 331 (Man. C.A.) — *See also:Ontario Film & Video Appreciation Society v. Ontario Board of Censors* (1984), 38 C.R. (3d) 271 (Ont. C.A.) — *Charter* s. 2(b) protects freedom of expression in all forms, whether they be oral, written, pictoral, sculpture, music, dance or film.

Related Provisions: "Possession" is determined by s. 4(3).

Related offences appear in ss. 165 (tied sale), 167 (immoral theatrical performance) and 168 (mailing obscene matter). Section 166(1) prohibits the publication of certain matters disclosed in judicial proceedings and s. 163.1 possession of child pornography.

Section 164 provides for the issuance of a warrant to seize copies of publications said to be obscene or crime comics. *In rem* proceedings may thereafter be taken under the section.

In addition to the general provisions of s. 583, holding certain omissions in an indictment or count do *not* vitiate a pleading, s. 584(1) provides that no count for selling or exhibiting an obscene book, pamphlet, newspaper or other written matter is insufficient by reason only that it does not set out the writing that is alleged to be obscene. Particulars of such passages may, however, be ordered under s. 587(1)(d).

Section 169 provides that the offences described in s. 163 are triable either way. Where P proceeds by indictment, D may elect mode of trial under s. 536(2). The offences of this section are an "enterprise crime offence" for the purpose of Part XII.2 and the offence of s. 163(1)(a) is an "offence" for the purposes of Part VI (Invasion of Privacy).

163.1 (1) Definition of "child pornography" — In this section, "child pornography" means

    (a) a photographic, film, video or other visual representation, whether or not it was made by electronic or mechanical means,

        (i) that shows a person who is or is depicted as being under the age of eighteen years and is engaged in or is depicted as engaged in explicit sexual activity, or

        (ii) the dominant characteristic of which is the depiction, for a sexual purpose, of a sexual organ or the anal region of a person under the age of eighteen years; or

    (b) any written material or visual representation that advocates or counsels sexual activity with a person under the age of eighteen years that would be an offence under this Act.

(2) Making child pornography — Every person who makes, prints, publishes or possesses for the purpose of publication any child pornography is guilty of

    (a) an indictable offence and liable to imprisonment for a term not exceeding ten years; or

    (b) an offence punishable on summary conviction.

(3) Distribution or sale of child pornography — Every person who imports, distributes, sells or possesses for the purpose of distribution or sale any child pornography is guilty of

(a) an indictable offence and liable to imprisonment for a term not exceeding ten years; or

(b) an offence punishable on summary conviction.

(4) Possession of child pornography — Every person who possesses any child pornography is guilty of

(a) an indictable offence and liable to imprisonment for a term not exceeding five years; or

(b) an offence punishable on summary conviction.

(5) Defences — It is not a defence to a charge under subsection (2) in respect of a visual representation that the accused believed that a person shown in the representation that is alleged to constitute child pornography was or was depicted as being eighteen years of age or more unless the accused took all reasonable steps to ascertain the age of that person and took all reasonable steps to ensure that, where the person was eighteen years of age or more, the representation did not depict that person as being under the age of eighteen years.

(6) Defences — Where the accused is charged with an offence under subsection (2), (3) or (4), the court shall find the accused not guilty if the representation or written material that is alleged to constitute child pornography has artistic merit or an educational, scientific or medical purpose.

(7) Other provisions to apply — Subsections 163(3) to (5) apply, with such modifications as the circumstances require, with respect to an offence under subsection (2), (3) or (4).

1993, c. 46, s. 1.

Commentary: This section exhaustively defines "child pornography", creates several offences relating to it and provides for general and specific defences.

The *definition* in s. 163.1(1)(a) applies to photographic, film, video or other visual representations. Section 163.1(1)(b) defines "child pornography" in the form of written material or visual representation.

The *offence* of s. 163.1(2), triable either way, is concerned with *publication* of child pornography. Its *external circumstances* include making, printing, publishing or possessing for the purpose of publication any child pornography. The *mental element* includes an intention to cause the relevant external circumstances and knowledge of the character of the subject-matter. The defences of public good in s. 163(3) and (4), incorporated by s. 163.1(7), and artistic merit/legitimate purpose under s. 163.1(6) are available to D. Under s. 163(5), also incorporated by s. 163.1(7), D's motives are irrelevant. D's assertion of a belief that a person depicted in a visual representation alleged to be child pornography was, or was depicted to be, 18 years of age or more is circumscribed as a defence by s. 163.1(5).

The *external circumstances* of the offence of s. 163.1(3) include importing, distribution, sale or possession for the purpose of distribution or sale. The *mental element* includes not only an *intention* to cause the external circumstances of the offence and *knowledge* of the character of the subject-matter, but also, where charged, proof of the *purpose* of D's possession. The offence is triable either way. D may rely on the defence described in s. 163.1(6) (artistic merit/legitimate purpose), as well as s. 163(3) and (4) (public good), but D's motives are irrelevant under s. 163(5).

The *offence* of s. 163.1(4) involves *possession* of child pornography. The *external circumstances* consist of possession of the prohibited subject-matter. The *mental element* includes *knowledge* of the character of the subject-matter. The defences of artistic merit/legitimate purpose [s. 163.1(6)] and public good [s. 163(3), (4)] are available, but D's motives are irrelevant under s. 163(5).

Related Provisions: Section 164 authorizes issuance of a special search and seizure *warrant* for "child pornography". The offences of this section are ones in respect of which *authorization* to intercept private communications may be given. Summary conviction proceedings are governed by Part XXVII. Possession is determined under s. 4(3). Other related provisions are described in the corresponding note to s. 163.

164. (1) **Warrant of seizure** — A judge who is satisfied by information on oath that there are reasonable grounds for believing that

(a) any publication, copies of which are kept for sale or distribution in premises within the jurisdiction of the court, is obscene or a crime comic, within the meaning of section 163, or

(b) any representation or written material, copies of which are kept in premises within the jurisdiction of the court, is child pornography within the meaning of section 163.1

may issue a warrant authorizing seizure of the copies.

(2) **Summons to occupier** — Within seven days of the issue of a warrant under subsection (1), the judge shall issue a summons to the occupier of the premises requiring him to appear before the court and show cause why the matter seized should not be forfeited to Her Majesty.

(3) **Owner and maker may appear** — The owner and the maker of the matter seized under subsection (1), and alleged to be obscene, a crime comic or child pornography, may appear and be represented in the proceedings in order to oppose the making of an order for the forfeiture of the matter.

(4) **Order of forfeiture** — If the court is satisfied that the publication, representation or written material referred to in subsection (1) is obscene, a crime comic or child pornography, it shall make an order declaring the matter forfeited to Her Majesty in right of the province in which the proceedings take place, for disposal as the Attorney General may direct.

(5) **Disposal of matter** — If the court is not satisfied that the publication, representation or written material referred to in subsection (1) is obscene, a crime comic or child pornography, it shall order that the matter be restored to the person from whom it was seized forthwith after the time for final appeal was expired.

(6) **Appeal** — An appeal lies from an order made under subsection (4) or (5) by any person who appeared in the proceedings

(a) on any ground of appeal that involves a question of law alone,

(b) on any ground of appeal that involves a question of fact alone, or

(c) on any ground of appeal that involves a question of mixed law and fact,

as if it were an appeal against conviction or against a judgment or verdict of acquittal, as the case may be, on a question of law alone under Part XXI and sections 673 to 696 apply with such modifications as the circumstances require.

(7) **Consent** — Where an order has been made under this section by a judge in a province with respect to one or more copies of a publication, representation or written material, no proceedings shall be instituted or continued in that province under section 163 or 163.1 with respect to those or other copies of the same publication, representation or written material without the consent of the Attorney General.

(8) **Definitions** — In this section

"court" means

> **(a) in the Province of Quebec, the Court of Quebec, the municipal court of Montreal and the municipal court of Quebec;**
>
> **(a.1) in the Province of Ontario, the Superior Court of Justice,**
>
> **(b) in the Provinces of New Brunswick, Manitoba, Saskatchewan and Alberta, the Court of Queen's Bench;**
>
> **(c) in the Provinces of Prince Edward Island and Newfoundland, the Trial Division of the Supreme Court;**
>
> **(d) in the Provinces of Nova Scotia and British Columbia, the Yukon Territory and the Northwest Territories, the Supreme Court; and**
>
> **(e) in Nunavut, the Nunavut Court of Justice;**

"crime comic" has the same meaning as in section 163;

"judge" means a judge of a court.

R.S., c. C-34, s. 160; 1974–75–76, c. 48, s. 25; 1978–79, c. 11, s. 10;R.S. 1985, c. 27 (2d Supp.), Sched.; c. 40 (4th Supp.), s. 2; 1990, c. 16, s. 3; 1990, c. 17, s. 9; 1992, c. 1, s. 58(1), Sched. 1, item 3; 1992, c. 51, s. 34; 1993, c. 28, s. 78 (Sched. III, item 28) [Repealed 1999, c. 3, (Sched., item 6).]; 1993, c. 46, s. 3; 1997, c. 18, s. 5; 1998, c. 30, s. 14(d); 1999, c. 3, s. 27.

Commentary: The section authorizes the issuance of a *warrant to seize* obscene publications, child pornography and crime comics and, thereafter, the taking of *in rem* proceedings in respect of the publications to determine whether what has been seized ought to be ordered forfeited.

Section 164(1) authorizes the issuance of a *warrant of seizure* by a "judge" as defined in s. 164(8). An information on oath laid before the judge must disclose that there are *reasonable grounds* for believing that *any publication*, copies of which are kept for sale or distribution in premises within the jurisdiction of the court as defined in s. 164(8), *is obscene, a crime comic, or child pornography*. A judge who is satisfied that there *are* such reasonable grounds, may issue a warrant authorizing *seizure* of the copies. No statutory forms are prescribed.

The *procedure* to be followed in determining whether the objects of seizure shall be ordered forfeited, and the effect of any order made in that respect, are described in s. 164(2)–(7). Under s. 164(2), within seven days of the issue of the warrant, the authorizing judge must issue a summons to the occupier of the premises from which the objects were seized requiring his/her appearance before the court to *show cause* why the objects of seizure ought not to be forfeited to Her Majesty. Under s. 164(3) the owner and maker of the seized matter have status to appear and make representations in opposition to an order of forfeiture. Upon the show-cause hearing, the court may declare the object of seizure forfeited (if satisfied the matter is obscene, a crime comic, or child pornography) or restored to the person from whom it has been seized after the expiration of the appeal period described in s. 164(6) (if not so satisfied). Once an order has been made under this section by a judge in a province with respect to one or more copies of a publication, proceedings under s. 163 or s. 163.1 may only be instituted or continued in that province with respect to those or other copies of the same publication with the consent of the Attorney General.

An order of forfeiture under s. 164(4) and restoration under s. 164(5) may be appealed under s. 164(6), subject to the limitations there imposed.

Case Law

Jurisdiction

R. v. Penthouse Int. Ltd. (1979), 46 C.C.C. (2d) 111 (Ont. C.A.); leave to appeal refused (1979), 46 C.C.C. (2d) 111n (S.C.C.) — It must be shown that copies of the publication are kept for sale or distribution. Mere possession of an obscene publication is not a basis for proceeding under this section.

Show Cause

R. v. Marshall (1982), 69 C.C.C. (2d) 197 (N.S. C.A.) — *See also:Benjamin News (Montreal) Reg'd v. R.* (1978), 6 C.R. (3d) 281 (Que. C.A.) — On an application for forfeiture under this section the onus is on P to offer evidence in support of the application and to satisfy the court that the publication is obscene, despite the fact that the owner is required to "show cause" why the matter seized should not be forfeited.

Right of Appeal

Prov. News v. R. (1974), 20 C.C.C. (2d) 385 (S.C.C.) — Subsection (6) only provides for an appeal to a court of appeal. It authorizes a further appeal to the Supreme Court of Canada only on a question of law.

Related Provisions: "Attorney General" is defined in s. 2. Offences relating to the publication and distribution of obscene matter are found in ss. 163 and 168 in s. 169.

The general *Code* provisions relating to the issuance and execution of search warrants are found in ss. 487–492. Other specialized warrants authorizing search for and/or seizure of certain materials are exemplified by ss. 320(8) (hate propaganda), 395 (minerals and precious metals) and 101–103 (weapons and ammunition).

Other related offences are described in the corresponding note to s. 163, *supra*.

165. Tied sale — Every one commits an offence who refuses to sell or supply to any other person copies of any publication for the reason only that the other person refuses to purchase or acquire from him copies of any other publication that the other person is apprehensive may be obscene or a crime comic.

R.S., c. C-34, s. 161.

Commentary: The *external circumstances* of this offence are complete where D refuses to sell or supply to another, copies of a publication. The sole reason for the refusal must be that the prospective purchaser *refuses to purchase or acquire* from D copies of any other publication which the prospective purchaser is apprehensive may be obscene or a crime comic. In other words, the refusal to sell or supply publication X is exclusively *tied* to or connected with the failure to purchase or acquire publication Y on defined grounds. The *mental element* involves proof of the intention to cause what amounts to the external circumstances of the offence.

Related Provisions: Obscenity is defined in s. 163(8) and "crime comic" in s. 163(7).

Under s. 169 the offence of this section is triable either way. The punishment is there prescribed. Where P proceeds by indictment, D may elect mode of trial.

The publication and distribution of obscene matter and crime comics is prohibited under s. 163. Section 168 prohibits the use of the mails to transmit or deliver anything that is obscene, indecent, immoral or scurrilous.

166. [Repealed 1994, c. 44, s. 9.]

167. (1) Immoral theatrical performance — Every one commits an offence who, being the lessee, manager, agent or person in charge of a theatre, presents or gives or allows to be presented or given therein an immoral, indecent or obscene performance, entertainment or representation.

(2) Person taking part — Every one commits an offence who takes part or appears as an actor, a performer or an assistant in any capacity, in an immoral, indecent or obscene performance, entertainment or representation in a theatre.

R.S., c. C-34, s. 163.

Commentary: The section prohibits certain participation in an immoral, indecent or obscene performance, entertainment or representation. The *external circumstances* of the offence consist of an immoral, indecent or obscene performance, entertainment or representation, together with a proscribed mode of participation. Under s. 167(1), D must be a lessee, manager, agent or person in charge of the theatre who has presented, given or allowed to be presented or given the proscribed entertainment. Under s. 167(2) the mode of participation is established where D takes part or appears as an actor, performer, or assistant in any capacity, in such an entertainment. The *mental element*, in each case, requires proof that D intentionally participated in the proscribed performance.

Case Law
Immoral

Johnson v. R. (1975), 23 C.R.N.S. 273, 13 C.C.C. (2d) 402 (S.C.C.) — A dance before a public audience, which would have been unexceptional if performed when fully or partly clad, does *not* become "immoral" on the sole ground that it is performed in the nude. Although Parliament has made nudity an offence, it does *not* necessarily follow that it is "immoral".

R. v. Maclean (No. 2) (1982), 1 C.C.C. (3d) 412 (Ont. C.A.) — The *community standard of tolerance* determines whether a performance is immoral. In determining this standard, evidence as to D's purpose in giving the performance should be considered. The locale of the performance, the forewarning of the public of the performance's nature, the conditions of admission, the audience's size and nature as well as the "extent" of the audience's reception of the particular performance and of similar performances are other factors to be considered. If the performance is found to exceed the community standard of tolerance, then the performance was immoral regardless of D's purpose.

Indecent

R. v. Mara (1997), 115 C.C.C. (3d) 539 (S.C.C.) — The *tolerance* basis of the *community standards* test is the *same* in *indecency* and *obscenity* cases. Indecency, unlike obscenity, entails an assessment of the surrounding circumstances in applying the community standards test. A performance is indecent if the social harm engendered by the performance, having regard to the circumstances in which it took place, is such that the community would not tolerate its occurrence.

Obscene

Nova Scotia Board of Censors v. McNeil (1978), 44 C.C.C. (2d) 316 (S.C.C.) — There is no constitutional reason why a prosecution could not be brought under this section even though a provincial Board of Censors has approved the film.

R. v. Graham (1977), 45 C.C.C. (2d) 245 (Alta. C.A.) — Although the question of obscenity is one of fact, P need *not* lead evidence of community standards. A judge is competent to declare community standards without the necessity of evidence to support P's case.

R. v. Small (1973), 26 C.R.N.S. 77, 12 C.C.C. (2d) 145 (B.C. C.A.) — The definition of obscene in s. 163(8) does *not* apply to a theatrical performance. It is applicable only to "publications".

Mental Element

R. v. Mara (1997), 115 C.C.C. (3d) 539 (S.C.C.) — Section 167 requires that D "allow" the indecent performance. There must be at least

i.   concerted acquiescence; or

ii.   wilful blindness

on the part of D. "Allow" is the equivalent of "knowingly". It is a *full mens rea* offence.

Related Provisions: "Theatre" is defined in s. 150 and obscenity determined, in some instances at least, under s. 163(8).

Related offences appear in ss. 173 (indecent acts), 174 (public nudity), and 175(1)(b) (indecent exhibition).

Section 169 permits this offence to be tried either way and prescribes the punishment which may be imposed. Where P proceeds by indictment, D may elect mode of trial under s. 536(2).

168. Mailing obscene matter — (1) Every one commits an offence who makes use of the mails for the purpose of transmitting or delivering anything that is obscene, indecent, immoral or scurrilous.

(2) **Exception** — Subsection (1) does not apply to a person who

(a) prints or publishes any matter for use in connection with any judicial proceedings or communicates it to persons who are concerned in the proceedings;

(b) prints or publishes a notice or report under the direction of a court; or

(c) prints or publishes any matter

(i) **in a volume or part of a genuine series of law reports that does not form part of any other publication and consists solely of reports of proceedings in courts of law, or**

(ii) **in a publication of a technical character that is intended, in good faith, for circulation among members of the legal or medical profession.**

R.S., c. C-34, s. 164; 1999, c. 5, s. 2.

Commentary: The section prohibits the use of the mails for the purpose of transmitting or delivering anything that is obscene, indecent, immoral or scurrilous. The *external circumstances* of the offence, involve any prohibited use of the mails. The *mental element* requires proof that such use was intentional, for a proscribed purpose. The section does *not* apply to use of the mails for transmitting or delivering anything described in s. 166(4).

Case Law

Popert v. R. (1981), 19 C.R. (3d) 393 (Ont. C.A.) — This section applies to the distribution by mail of magazines or journals to subscribers and to everyone who makes use of the mails in a prohibited manner. It is *not* limited to individuals who, rather than indulging in obscene telephone calls, indulge in obscene mailings.

R. v. Pink Triangle Press (1980), 51 C.C.C. (2d) 485 (Ont. Co. Ct.), affirmed, (sub nom. *Popert v. R)* 19 C.R. (3d) 393, 58 C.C.C. (2d) 505 — Although a magazine must be considered as a whole, it is *not* necessary that an entire issue be indecent, immoral, or scurrilous. A single passage or article may be properly found offensive and such a passage cannot be saved by surrounding it with more edifying ones.

Related Provisions: The determination of whether a publication is obscene is made under s. 163(8).

Jurisdiction over offences committed in respect of the mail in the course of its door-to-door delivery, is governed by s. 476(e). Section 381 prohibits the use of the mails to defraud the public or to obtain money under false pretences. It is also an offence under s. 372(1) to convey a false message by letter.

Under s. 169 this offence is triable either way and punished according to the section. Where P proceeds by indictment, D may elect mode of trial under s. 536(2).

169. Punishment — **Every one who commits an offence under section 163, 165, 167 or 168 is guilty of**

(a) **an indictable offence and is liable to imprisonment for a term not exceeding two years; or**

(b) **an offence punishable on summary conviction.**

R.S., c. C-34, s. 165; 1999, c. 5, s. 3.

Commentary: The section prescribes the *punishment* upon conviction of any listed offence. The offences are triable either way.

Related Provisions: Where P proceeds by summary conviction, the offences are tried in accordance with Part XXVII and punished under s. 787(1).

Where P proceeds by indictment, D may *elect* mode of trial under s. 536(2).

170. Parent or guardian procuring sexual activity — **Every parent or guardian of a person under the age of eighteen years who procures that person for the purpose of engaging in any sexual activity prohibited by this Act with a person other than the parent or guardian is guilty of an indictable offence and liable to imprisonment for a term not exceeding five years, if the person procured for that purpose is under the age of fourteen years or to imprisonment for a term not exceeding two years if the person so procured is fourteen years of age or more but under the age of eighteen years.**

R.S., c. C-34, s. 166; R.S. 1985, c. 19 (3d Supp.), s. 5.

Commentary: The section imposes criminal liability upon a parent or guardian who *procures* certain *sexual activity* by a person under the age of 18 years and provides the punishment.

The *external circumstances* require proof that D, as principal, be a parent or guardian of a person under the age of 18 years. D must procure the young person for the purpose of engaging in any sexual activity prohibited by the *Code* with someone other than D. The *mental element* requires proof that D intentionally procured the young person for the proscribed purpose.

Related Provisions: "Guardian" is defined in s. 150 and age determined under *I.A.* s. 30. Under s. 22(3), "counsel" includes "procure".

Sexual offences are described in ss. 150.1–160, and sexual assaults in ss. 272–274. Procuring is an offence under s. 212. Offences in relation to prostitution are described in s. 213. Related offences appear in ss. 171 (householder permitting sexual activity) and 172 (corrupting children).

The special evidentiary rules of ss. 274–277 and 715.1 apply. D's spouse is a competent and compellable witness for P under *C.E.A.* s. 4(2).

The *punishment* upon conviction is dependent upon the age of the young person procured for sexual activity at the time of the procuring. D may elect mode of trial under s. 536(2).

171. Householder permitting sexual activity — Every owner, occupier or manager of premises or other person who has control of premises or assists in the management or control of premises who knowingly permits a person under the age of eighteen years to resort to or to be in or on the premises for the purpose of engaging in any sexual activity prohibited by this Act is guilty of an indictable offence and is liable to imprisonment for a term not exceeding five years if the person in question is under the age of fourteen years or to imprisonment for a term not exceeding two years if the person in question is fourteen years of age or more but under the age of eighteen years.

R.S., c. C-34, s. 167; R.S. 1985, c. 19 (3d Supp.), s. 5.

Commentary: The section describes the basis upon which criminal liability may be established in respect of a person who, in control of premises, *permits* certain sexual activity to take place thereon.

The *external circumstances* require that, as principal, D be an owner, occupier, or manager of premises or other person who has control or assists in the management or control of premises. D must *permit* a person under the age of 18 years to resort to or be in or on the premises for the purpose of engaging in any sexual activity prohibited by the *Code*. The *mental element* requires proof that such permission was "knowingly" given by D.

Related Provisions: "Owner" is defined in s. 2.

Other related provisions are described in the corresponding note for s. 170.

172. (1) Corrupting children — Every one who, in the home of a child, participates in adultery or sexual immorality or indulges in habitual drunkenness or any other form of vice, and thereby endangers the morals of the child or renders the home an unfit place for the child to be in, is guilty of an indictable offence and liable to imprisonment for a term not exceeding two years.

(2) [Repealed R.S. 1985, c. 19 (3d Supp.), s. 6]

(3) Definition of "child" — For the purposes of this section, "child" means a person who is or appears to be under the age of eighteen years.

(4) Who may institute prosecutions — No proceedings shall be commenced under subsection (1) without the consent of the Attorney General, unless they are instituted by or at the instance of a recognized society for the protection of children or by an officer of a juvenile court.

R.S., c. C-34, s. 168; R.S. 1985, c. 19 (3d Supp.), s. 6.

Commentary: The section prohibits certain conduct tending to *corrupt* children and imposes limitations upon the institution of proceedings.

The *external circumstances* of the offence of s. 172(1) require that the prohibited conduct occur in the home of a child, as defined in s. 172(3). D must participate in adultery or sexual immorality or indulge in drunkenness or any other form of vice. D's conduct must *endanger* the morals of the child, or render the home an unfit place for the child. The *mental element* consists of the intention to participate or indulge in the designated conduct which has the deleterious effect.

Section 172(4) in effect, prohibits private prosecutions by requiring that proceedings *only* be commenced with the *consent* of the Attorney General, unless instituted by or at the instance of a designated agency or officer.

Related Provisions: "Attorney General" is defined in s. 2 and the age of the child determined under *I.A.* s. 30. Proof of age may be made under s. 658.

Section 215, *inter alia*, imposes a duty to provide necessaries of life for a child under the age of 16 years and criminal liability upon proof of failure to do so. Section 218 creates the offence of abandoning a child.

The special evidentiary rules of ss. 274–277, and s. 715.1 apply. D's spouse is a competent and compellable witness for P under *C.E.A.* s. 4(2).

Under s. 536(2), D may *elect* mode of trial.

Disorderly Conduct

173. (1) Indecent acts — **Every one who wilfully does an indecent act**

(a) in a public place in the presence of one or more persons, or

(b) in any place, with intent thereby to insult or offend any person, is guilty of an offence punishable on summary conviction.

(2) Exposure — **Every person who, in any place, for a sexual purpose, exposes his or her genital organs to a person who is under the age of fourteen years is guilty of an offence punishable on summary conviction.**

R.S., c. C-34, s. 169; R.S. 1985, c. 19 (3d Supp.), s. 7.

Commentary: The section creates two offences, compendiously described as *indecent acts* and *sexual exposure*.

An *indecent act*, may be a crime in either of two ways. Under s. 173(1)(a), the *external circumstances* require proof that D did an indecent act in a public place in the presence of one or more persons. The *mental element* is expressed in the term "wilfully". No ulterior mental element need be proven. Under s. 172(1)(b), the *external circumstances* comprise the doing of an indecent act in any place. The *mental element*, however, requires not only that the indecent act be wilfully done but, further, that it be done with the further or ulterior intent to insult or offend any person.

The recently-enacted *sexual exposure* offence of s. 173(2) combines elements of purpose, exposure and place or audience. The *external circumstances* require, initially, that D, in any place, expose genital organs. The *display* must be to a *person* under the age of 14 years and *for a sexual purpose*. The *mental element* consists of the intention to cause the external circumstances, including the critical element of *purpose*.

Case Law

Essential Elements of Offence

R. v. Mailhot (1996), 108 C.C.C. (3d) 376 (Que. C.A.) — Under s. 173(1)(a), P must prove D,

i.   *wilfully* committed an indecent act; and,

ii. *wilfully* committed the act in a public place in the presence of one or more persons, excluding the participants.

R. v. Jacob (1996), 112 C.C.C. (3d) 1 (Ont. C.A.) — The language of s. 173(1)(a) does *not* require that an indecent act have a sexual context. Indecency concerns, but is *not* restricted to, sexual behaviour. The *community* standard of *tolerance* test is relevant to acts alleged to be criminally indecent. In the application of the test, a court must consider what harm will accrue from exposure to the allegedly obscene act or material. Tolerance *cannot* be assessed independently of harm. The corollation is inverse: the greater the potential harm, the less tolerant of its exposure will be the community. The surrounding circumstances in any resultant harm ought be considered solely within the community standard of tolerance analysis. (per Osborne and Austin JJ.A.)

Public Place [See also s. 159]

Hutt v. R. (1978), 1 C.R. (3d) 164 (S.C.C.) — A police officer's car is *not* a public place, rather a private place over which he had the sole control. To interpret the words "by invitation, express or implied" otherwise would mean that if someone were to invite a person to enter their home then that home would be a public place.

R. v. Buhay (1986), 30 C.C.C. (3d) 30 (Man. C.A.) — A public place is *not* restricted to a place to which the public has access by right. It includes a place in which the public could witness indecent acts.

Related Provisions: "Public place" is expansively defined in s. 150. Age is determined under *I.A.* s. 30 and may be proven, *inter alia*, under s. 658.

The related offences of public nudity and indecent exhibition appear in ss. 174 and 175(1)(b). Immoral theatrical performances are punishable under s. 167. Public exhibition of an indecent show is prohibited by s. 163(2)(b).

The special evidentiary rules of ss. 274–277 and 715.1 apply to prosecutions under the section and D's spouse is a competent and compellable witness for P under *C.E.A.* s. 4(2).

The offences are tried in accordance with Part XXVII and punished under s. 787(1).

174. (1) Nudity — Every one who, without lawful excuse,

(a) is nude in a public place, or

(b) is nude and exposed to public view while on private property, whether or not the property is his own,

is guilty of an offence punishable on summary conviction.

(2) Nude — For the purposes of this section, a person is nude who is so clad as to offend against public decency or order.

(3) Consent of Attorney General — No proceedings shall be commenced under this section without the consent of the Attorney General.

R.S., c. C-34, s. 170.

Commentary: The section describes the offence of *public nudity* and imposes certain limitations upon commencement of its prosecution.

The *external circumstances* of the offence require proof either that D is nude in a public place or that D is nude and exposed to public view whilst on private property. It matters *not* that the property belongs to D. There must also be an *absence of lawful excuse* for D's conduct. Under s. 174(2) nude is *not* synonymous with naked. D may be nude whilst clad, provided s/he is so clad as to offend against public decency or order. The *mental element* of which proof is required is simply the intention to cause the external circumstances of the offence.

Under s. 174(3), the commencement of proceedings requires the consent of the Attorney General.

Case Law

Nature and Elements of Offence

R. v. Verrette (1978), 3 C.R. (3d) 132, 40 C.C.C. (2d) 273 (S.C.C.) — Where there is complete nudity without lawful excuse in a public place, the offence is committed whether or not the nudity offends against public decency or order. Proof that the nudity offended against public decency or order is *not* required from P.

Nude

R. v. Verrette (1978), 3 C.R. (3d) 132, 40 C.C.C. (2d) 273 (S.C.C.) — Section 174(2) does not apply to a situation of complete nudity. "Nude" in s. 174(1) retains its normal dictionary meaning of total bareness. The definition is notionally extended by s. 174(2) to certain ways of being clothed. "Nude" in s. 174(1), however, simply means "completely bare", without reference to public decency or order.

R. v. Giambalvo (1982), 70 C.C.C. (2d) 324 (Ont. C.A.) — The performance of a dance in a public place by a performer who is not completely unclothed contravenes this section only if the dancer is so clad as to offend against public decency or order. The proper *test* to be applied is the standard of community tolerance in the circumstances in which the dance was performed.

R. v. Sidey (1980), 52 C.C.C. (2d) 257 (Ont. C.A.) — Where the case falls within the ambit of s. 174(2), it is not necessary that P lead evidence that the conduct offended against public decency or order. The trial judge may make such a finding without such evidence.

R. v. McCutcheon (1977), 1 C.R. (3d) 39, 40 C.C.C. (2d) 555 (Que. C.A.) — Notwithstanding that D could have been charged with an immoral theatrical performance, since a theatre is a public place, a person giving a performance in a theatre may be charged with nudity in a public place. Where D at all times wore a transparent veil fastened at her throat while performing D was *not* "so clad as to offend against public decency or order" under s. 174(2).

Related Provisions: See the corresponding note to s. 173, *supra*.

175. (1) Causing disturbance, indecent exhibition, loitering, etc. — Every one who

    (a) not being in a dwelling-house, causes a disturbance in or near a public place,

        (i) by fighting, screaming, shouting, swearing, singing or using insulting or obscene language,

        (ii) by being drunk, or

        (iii) by impeding or molesting other persons,

    (b) openly exposes or exhibits an indecent exhibition in a public place,

    (c) loiters in a public place and in any way obstructs persons who are in that place, or

    (d) disturbs the peace and quiet of the occupants of a dwelling-house by discharging firearms or by other disorderly conduct in a public place or who, not being an occupant of a dwelling-house comprised in a particular building or structure, disturbs the peace and quiet of the occupants of a dwelling-house comprised in the building or structure by discharging firearms or by other disorderly conduct in any part of a building or structure to which, at the time of such conduct, the occupants of two or more dwelling-houses comprised in the building or structure have access as of right or by invitation, express or implied,

is guilty of an offence punishable on summary conviction.

(2) Evidence of peace officer — In the absence of other evidence, or by way of corroboration of other evidence, a summary conviction court may infer from the evidence of a peace officer relating to the conduct of a person or persons, whether ascertained or not, that a disturbance described in paragraph (1)(a) or (d) or an obstruction described in paragraphs (1)(c) was caused or occurred.

R.S., c. C-34, s. 171; 1972, c. 13, s. 11; 1974–75–76, c. 93, s. 9.1997, c. 18, s. 6.

Commentary: This section describes several summary conviction offences, generally described as disorderly conduct.

The offences of ss. 175(1)(a) and (d) involve *causing a disturbance*. Under s. 175(1)(a) the *external circumstances* demand that D *not* be in a dwelling-house. D must *cause a disturbance* in or near a public place. The disturbance must be caused by a means described in ss. 175(1)(a)(i)–(iii). Under s. 175(1)(d) the essence of the offence is the disturbance of the peace of the occupants of a dwelling-house. The *means* of disturbance must involve the discharge of firearms or other disorderly conduct in a public place or part of a building or structure to which the public have access. The *mental element*, in each case, does not extend beyond proof of the intention to cause external circumstances of the offence.

Section 175(2) assists P in proof of the requirement of ss. 175(1)(a), (c) and (d) that a disturbance or obstruction was caused or occurred. The summary conviction court, *in the absence of other evidence or as corroboration* thereof, may infer the requisite disturbance or obstruction from the evidence of a peace officer relating to the conduct of others, whether ascertained or not.

The *external circumstances* of the offence in s. 175(1)(b) require proof of the open exposure or exhibition of an indecent exhibition in a public place. Under s. 175(1)(c), the *external circumstances* require that D *loiter* in a public place and there *obstruct* in some way, persons who are in that public place. No ulterior *mental element* need be proven in either case.

Case Law
A Disturbance: S. 175(1)(a)

R. v. Lohnes (1992), 10 C.R. (4th) 125, 69 C.C.C. (3d) 289 (S.C.C.) — *See also*: *R. v. Reed* (1992), 76 C.C.C. (3d) 204 (B.C. C.A.) — The offence of s. 175(1)(a)(i) requires proof of an externally-manifested disturbance of the public peace, in the sense of an interference with the ordinary or customary use of the premises by the public. There may be direct evidence of the effect or interference, or it may be inferred from the evidence of a police officer under s. 175(2). The disturbance may consist of the impugned act itself, or it may flow as a consequence thereof. It must be one which may *reasonably* have been foreseen in the particular circumstances of time and place. An interference with the ordinary and customary conduct in or near the public place may consist of something as minor as being distracted from one's work, but the interference must be at once present and externally-manifested.

R. v. C.D. (1973), 22 C.R.N.S. 326, 13 C.C.C. (2d) 206 (N.B. C.A.) — Annoyance or emotional upset is insufficient to constitute a disturbance in the absence of tumult, uproar or disorder.

Swinamer v. R. (1978), 3 C.R. (3d) 165 (N.S. C.A.) — The offence is complete if the doing of *any* of the specified acts causes, or might reasonably cause, someone to be disturbed. It does not matter if the person disturbed is in a public or non-public place.

Shouting: s. 175(1)(a)(i)

R. v. Reed (1992), 76 C.C.C. (3d) 204 (B.C. C.A.) — "Shouting" does *not* include the amplification by a sound device of the normal speaking voice. (per Hutcheon J.A.)Speaking into an electronic megaphone in a normal tone of voice can constitute "shouting". (per Southin J.A.)

Swearing: S. 175(1)(a)(i)

R. v. Clothier (1975), 13 N.S.R. (2d) 141 (C.A.) — Swear means to use bad, profane or obscene language and is not limited to profane language.

Loiters: S. 175(1)(c)

R. v. Gauvin (1984), 11 C.C.C. (3d) 229 (Ont. C.A.) — Loitering requires an element of idly standing around. Purposeful activity is the antithesis of idleness.

R. v. Munroe (Mota) (1983), 34 C.R. (3d) 268, 5 C.C.C. (3d) 217 (Ont. C.A.); affirming (1982), 30 C.R. (3d) 263, 1 C.C.C. (3d) 305 (Ont. Co. Ct.) — Purposeful soliciting by a prostitute does *not* constitute loitering or obstruction. The use of this section as a blanket weapon against prostitutes constitutes abuse of process.

Evidentiary Considerations: S. 175(2)

Peters v. R. (1982), 27 C.R. (3d) 246, 65 C.C.C. (2d) 83 (B.C. C.A.) — Section 175(2) is evidentiary in nature and does *not* alter the elements of proof that must be found before a conviction can be entered for a breach of s. 175(1). P must still prove that a disturbance was caused. There is no need to call as witnesses individual members of the public to establish that they were in fact disturbed. A disturbance may be inferred from the evidence of a peace officer of D's conduct.

Attempt

R. v. Kennedy (1973), 21 C.R.N.S. 251, 11 C.C.C. (2d) 263 (Ont. C.A.) — D may be convicted of an attempt to cause a disturbance.

Related Provisions: "Dwelling-house" is defined in s. 2, "public place" in s. 150. The definition of "firearm" in s. 84(1), as well as the exclusions of s. 84(2), are, in terms, limited to the offences of Part III and, accordingly, are not applicable to the present section.

Section 173 prohibits the doing of indecent acts in the circumstances there defined and s. 174 public nudity. Trespassing by night is an offence under s. 177. An assault is committed under s. 265(1)(c) when D, while openly wearing or carrying a real or imitation weapon, accosts or impedes another person or begs.

Sections 30 and 31 afford protection to peace officers and other persons who intercede to prevent a breach of the peace or arrest those who participate therein.

The offences are tried under Part XXVII and punished under s. 787(1).

176. (1) Obstructing or violence to or arrest of officiating clergyman —
Every one who

    (a) by threats or force, unlawfully obstructs or prevents or endeavours to obstruct or prevent a clergyman or minister from celebrating divine service or performing any other function in connection with his calling, or

    (b) knowing that a clergyman or minister is about to perform, is on his way to perform or is returning from the performance of any of the duties or functions mentioned in paragraph (a)

        (i) assaults or offers any violence to him, or

        (ii) arrests him on a civil process, or under the pretence of executing a civil process,

is guilty of an indictable offence and liable to imprisonment for a term not exceeding two years.

(2) Disturbing religious worship or certain meetings — Every one who wilfully disturbs or interrupts an assemblage of persons met for religious worship or for a moral, social or benevolent purpose is guilty of an offence punishable on summary conviction.

(3) Idem — Every one who, at or near a meeting referred to in subsection (2), wilfully does anything that disturbs the order or solemnity of the meeting is guilty of an offence punishable on summary conviction.

                                        R.S., c. C-34, s. 172.

Commentary: The section creates a number of offences involving *interference with religious ceremonies.*

The *external circumstances* of the offence of s. 176(1)(a) require proof that D unlawfully obstructed or prevented, or endeavoured to obstruct or prevent a member of the clergy or a minister from celebrating divine service or performing any other function in connection with his/her calling. D must do so with threats or force. The *mental element* requires proof that D intended to cause the external circumstances of the offence.

The *external circumstances* of the offence of s. 176(1)(b) are described in its subparagraphs. Either will suffice. The *mental element* comprises the intention to cause the external circumstances, together with the *knowledge* described in the introductory words of the paragraph.

The summary conviction offences of ss. 176(2) and (3) may conveniently be considered together. Under s. 176(2), the *external circumstances* require that there be an assemblage of persons met for religious worship or a moral, social or benevolent purpose. D must disturb or interrupt such an assemblage. The *mental element* is expressed in the compendious term "wilfully". The companion offence of s. 176(3) imposes liability for conduct at or near the meeting that disturbs its order or solemnity. The *external circumstances* consist of a meeting of the type described in s. 176(2). D must be at or near the meeting. Further, D must do anything, at or near the meeting, that disturbs its order or solemnity. The *mental element* involves proof that D's act is "wilful".

The section has been impeached under *Charter* ss. 2(a) and (b).

Case Law

Elements of Offence: S.176(3)

R. v. Reed (1994), 91 C.C.C. (3d) 481 (B.C. C.A.) — Under s. 176(3),

i.   two people are "an assemblage of persons";

ii.   a "meeting" occurs when people meet for religious worship; and

iii.   the period prior to the formal ceremony is included in the "order or solemnity of the meeting". (per McEachern C.J.B.C., Proudfoot J.A.)

R. v. Reed (1994), 91 C.C.C. (3d) 481 (B.C. C.A.) — Where D's conduct is more than a brief temporary annoyance and constitutes a deliberate continuing annoyance which also obstructs or partially obstructs, or causes parishioners to refrain from using the principal regular entrance to their place of worship, the offence is proven. (per McEachern C.J.B.C., Proudfoot J.A.)

Charter Considerations

R. v. Reed (1985), 19 C.C.C. (3d) 180 (B.C. C.A.) — The *motive* for the disruption is *irrelevant*. The section does *not* interfere with a person's freedom of expression and other rights guaranteed by the *Charter*. Without the protection afforded by this section, such things as freedom of assembly and association could be meaningless.

Related Provisions: Assault is defined in s. 265(1).

D may elect mode of trial under s. 536(2) in respect of the offences of s. 176(1). The summary conviction offences of ss. 176(2) and (3) are tried under Part XXVII and punished under s. 787(1).

177. Trespassing at night — Every one who, without lawful excuse, the proof of which lies on him, loiters or prowls at night on the property of another person near a dwelling-house situated on that property is guilty of an offence punishable on summary conviction.

R.S., c. C-34, s. 173.

Commentary: The *external circumstances* of these summary conviction offences striking at the "peeping tom" consist of three elements. D must *loiter or prowl* on property of another near a dwelling-house situated on the property. D's conduct must occur *at night* and *without lawful excuse*. The onus of proving a lawful excuse rests upon D. The *mental element* requires that D intend to cause the external circumstances of the offence.

The statutory shift to D of the onus of proof of lawful excuse may attract *Charter* ss. 7 and 11(d) scrutiny.

Case Law [See also, s. 179]

R. v. Cloutier (1991), 66 C.C.C. (3d) 149 (Que. C.A.) — The section creates two separate offences: loitering and prowling. The essence of *loitering* is D's conduct in wandering about, apparently without precise destination. It is conduct which essentially has nothing reprehensible about it, provided it does *not* take place on private property where, in principle, D has no business. *Prowling* involves some notion of evil. The actions of a prowler are purposeful and would lead someone to believe that D was going to do some specific act.

Related Provisions: "Dwelling-house", "night" and "property" are defined in s. 2.

Sections 348–351 create several offences of break and entry and related crimes, including being unlawfully in a dwelling-house (s. 349) and possession of break-in instruments (s. 351). Forcible entry is an offence under ss. 72(1) and 73.

The authority of the owner or person in lawful possession of property or anyone authorized on their behalf to arrest without a warrant a person whom they find committing a criminal offence on or in relation to the property is described in s. 494(2). Sections 40–42 define the scope of protection afforded to persons in peaceable possession of a dwelling-house or other real property who prevent unlawful entry and remove trespassers therefrom.

This summary conviction offence is tried under Part XXVII and punished under s. 787(1).

178. Offensive volatile substance — Every one other than a peace officer engaged in the discharge of his duty who has in his possession in a public place or who deposits, throws or injects or causes to be deposited, thrown or injected in, into or near any place,

(a) an offensive volatile substance that is likely to alarm, inconvenience, discommode or cause discomfort to any person or to cause damage to property, or

(b) a stink or stench bomb or device from which any substance mentioned in paragraph (*a*) is or is capable of being liberated,

is guilty of an offence punishable on summary conviction.

R.S., c. C-34, s. 174.

Commentary: The section prohibits certain conduct in relation to an *offensive volatile substance* or related device.

To establish the *external circumstances* of the offence, P must prove that D, as principal, is *not* a peace officer engaged in the discharge of his/her duty. D must have in his/her *possession*, in a public place, an offensive volatile substance or other device of a nature described in s. 178(a) or (b). Liability will also be established where D deposited, threw, or injected or caused to be deposited, thrown or injected in, into or near any place, a similar substance or device. No ulterior *mental element* need be established.

Related Provisions: "Peace officer" is defined in s. 2, "public place" in s. 150. Possession is determined under s. 4(3).

This offence is, in essence, a form of mischief or nuisance and could have been included within the general prohibitions of s. 180(1) and/or s. 430(1).

The offence is prosecuted under Part XXVII and punished under s. 787(1).

179. (1) Vagrancy — Every one commits vagrancy who

(a) supports himself in whole or in part by gaming or crime and has no lawful profession or calling by which to maintain himself; or

(b) having at any time been convicted of an offence under section 151, 152 or 153, subsection 160(3) or 173(2) or section 271, 272 or 273, or of an offence under a provision referred to in paragraph (*b*) of the definition "serious personal injury offence" in section 687 of the *Criminal Code*, chapter C-34 of the Revised Statutes of Canada, 1970, as it read before January 4, 1983, is found loitering in or near a school ground, playground, public park or bathing area.

(2) Punishment — Every one who commits vagrancy is guilty of an offence punishable on summary conviction.

R.S., c. C-34, s. 175; 1972, c. 13, s. 12; 1984, c. 40, s. 20; R.S. 1985, c. 27 (1st Supp.), s. 22; c. 19 (3d Supp.), s. 8.

Commentary: The section defines and punishes vagrancy.

Under s. 179(1)(a) the *external circumstances* require that D support him/herself, in whole or in part, by gaming or crime. No proof of prior convictions is required. Further, it must be established that D has *no* lawful profession or calling by which to maintain him/herself. In essence, the offence is a condition or state that derives from specified acts or omissions by D. Put otherwise, the offence consists *not in doing* but rather in *being*.

Under s. 179(1)(b), the *external circumstances* require that D has previously been convicted of a listed offence and must be loitering in or near a school ground, playground, public park or bathing area. Nothing more than loitering in or near a specified area need be proven.

The offence requires no proof of any ulterior or specific *mental element*. In most instances proof of the causing of the external circumstances of the offence will supply proof of the necessary mental element.

Case Law
Essential Elements

R. v. Heywood (1994), 34 C.R. (4th) 133, 94 C.C.C. (3d) 481, 24 C.R.R. (2d) 189 (S.C.C.); affirming (1992), 18 C.R. (4th) 63, 77 C.C.C. (3d) 502 (B.C. C.A.) — "Loitering" means to stand idly around, hang around, linger, tarry, saunter, delay or dawdle. It does *not* require proof of any malevolent intent.

Charter Considerations

R. v. Heywood (1994), 94 C.C.C. (3d) 481, 34 C.R. (4th) 133 (S.C.C.); affirming (1992), 18 C.R. (4th) 63, 77 C.C.C. (3d) 502 (B.C. C.A.) — Section 179(1)(b) violates *Charter* s. 7 and is *not* saved by s. 1.

Related Provisions: Offences relating to gaming and betting are described in ss. 201–209 of Part VII.

Section 161 authorizes the making of an order, *inter alia*, prohibiting persons convicted or conditionally discharged of certain listed offences from attending certain premises or locations, including public parks, swimming areas, schoolgrounds and playgrounds. Failure to comply with an order made under the section is an offence under s. 161(4).

Prior to January 4, 1983, para. (b) of the definition "serious personal injury offence" in s. 687 read as follows:

> "an offence mentioned in section 144 (rape) or 145 (attempted rape) or an offence or attempt to commit an offence mentioned in section 146 (sexual intercourse with a female under fourteen or between fourteen and sixteen), 149 (indecent assault on the female), 156 (indecent assault on the male) or 157 (gross indecency)."

The wife or husband of D is a competent and compellable witness for P without D's consent under *C.E.A.* s. 4(2).

Proceedings are governed by Part XXVII and punishment by s. 787(1).

Nuisances

180. (1) Common nuisance — Every one who commits a common nuisance and thereby

    (a) endangers the lives, safety or health of the public, or

    (b) causes physical injury to any person,

is guilty of an indictable offence and liable to imprisonment for a term not exceeding two years.

(2) Definition — For the purposes of this section, every one commits a common nuisance who does an unlawful act or fails to discharge a legal duty and thereby

    (a) endangers the lives, safety, health, property or comfort of the public; or

    (b) obstructs the public in the exercise or enjoyment of any right that is common to all the subjects of Her Majesty in Canada.

R.S., c. C-34, s. 176.

Commentary: The section defines and punishes the offence of *common nuisance*. In general, a common or public nuisance is one which materially affects the public by substantially annoying fellow citizens.

The *external circumstances* of a common nuisance, as described in s. 180(2), consist of an act or omission and certain defined consequences. D's act must be unlawful, the omission, a failure to discharge a legal duty. The consequences of such act or omission must be *either* those described in s. 180(2)(a) or (b). The *mental element* requires proof of the intention to cause the act or omission which underlies the offence.

To constitute the indictable offence of s. 180(1), P must further establish that, by commission of a common nuisance, D endangered the lives, safety or health of the public or caused physical injury to any person. These additional consequences would *not* seem to require any further *mental element*.

Case Law
External Circumstances

R. v. Schula (1956), 23 C.R. 403, 115 C.C.C. 382 (Alta. C.A.) — The acts which endanger health must be directed at the public. Anonymous, obscene telephone calls directed at three individuals were *not* sufficient to sustain a conviction.

Legal Duty

R. v. Thornton (1991), 3 C.R. (4th) 381 (C.A.); affirmed (1993), 21 C.R. (4th) 215, 82 C.C.C. (3d) 350 (S.C.C.) — The "legal duty" of s. 180(2) may be one imposed by *statute or* one which arises at *common law*. The common law recognized a fundamental duty to refrain from conduct which could cause injury to another. It is a duty which requires, at a minimum, that everyone refrain from conduct which, it is reasonably foreseeable, *could* cause serious harm to others. Donating blood which D knows to be HIV-contaminated, to an organization whose purpose is to make blood available for transfusion to others, constitutes a breach of this common law duty, hence a failure to discharge "a legal duty" under s. 180(2). When the gravity of potential harm from D's conduct is great, the public is *endangered* under s. 180(2)(a), even where the risk of harm actually occurring is slight, or minimal, due to screening techniques used by the recipient agency.

Related Provisions: Sections 181 (spreading false news) and 182 (unlawful conduct in relation to a dead body) are specific nuisance offences.

Mischief is described in s. 430(1) and punished in ss. 430(2), (4) and (5.1).

Sections 215–218, describe and punish a number of offences involving the failure to perform various duties which tend to the preservation of life. Sections 219–221, define criminal negligence and create the offences of causing death or bodily harm by criminal negligence.

Section 78 imposes a legal duty upon those having possession, care or control of an explosive substance and s. 80 imposes criminal liability for breach of such duty.

Under s. 536(2), D may elect mode of trial.

181. Spreading false news — **Every one who wilfully publishes a statement, tale or news that he knows is false and that causes or is likely to cause injury or mischief to a public interest is guilty of an indictable offence and liable to imprisonment for a term not exceeding two years.**

R.S., c. C-34, s. 177.

Commentary: This offence involves the *spreading* of *false news* likely to cause mischief or injury to a public interest.

The *external circumstances* require that D publish a statement, tale or news. What is published must be *false*. The false statement, tale or news published must cause or be likely to cause injury or mischief to a public interest. The *mental element* consists of the intention to cause the external circumstances of the offence, including *wilfulness* in relation to the publication and knowledge of the falsity of the statement, tale or news when published.

The section has been held constitutionally invalid under *Charter* s. 2(b).

Case Law
Charter Considerations

R. v. Zundel (1992), 16 C.R. (4th) 1, 75 C.C.C. (3d) 449 (S.C.C.); reversing on constitutional grounds (sub nom. *R. v. Zundel (No. 2))* 53 C.C.C. (3d) 161 — Section 181 infringes the fundamental freedoms of thought, belief, opinion and expression guaranteed by *Charter* s. 2(b) and cannot be saved by s. 1.

Related Provisions: The general common nuisance offence is described in s. 180. The cognate offence of public mischief appears in s. 140.

Several other *Code* provisions prohibit the publication of certain matter, as for example, ss. 296 (blasphemous libel), 298–301 (defamatory libel), 163 (obscene matter and crime comics) and 59 (seditious libel). On occasion, this offence may overlap with the hate propaganda provisions of ss. 318 and 319.

Under s. 536(2), D may elect mode of trial.

182. Dead body — Every one who

(a) neglects, without lawful excuse, to perform any duty that is imposed on him by law or that he undertakes with reference to the burial of a dead human body or human remains, or

(b) improperly or indecently interferes with or offers any indignity to a dead human body or human remains, whether buried or not,

is guilty of an indictable offence and liable to imprisonment for a term not exceeding five years.

R.S., c. C-34, s. 178.

Commentary: The gravamen of this offence rests in certain acts or omissions in relation to a *dead* human *body* or human remains.

The offence of s. 182(a) is one of *omission*. Its *external consequences* consist of a neglect by D to perform any legal or voluntarily assumed *duty* with reference to the *burial* of a dead human body or human remains. P must also establish the absence of lawful excuse.

Under s. 182(b), the offence is one of *commission*. P must establish that D *interfered* with a dead human body or human remains. The interference must be improper or indecent in all of the circumstances. The *external circumstances* are equally established where D offers an indignity to a dead human body or human remains. In neither case is it of any legal consequence whether the body or remains are buried.

The *mental element* in each case requires proof of the intent to cause what amounts to the external circumstances of the offence. It is, however, essential that D know, at the material time, that the body is dead.

Case Law

R. v. Moyer (1994), 92 C.C.C. (3d) 1 (S.C.C.); reversing (1993), 25 C.R. (4th) 115, 83 C.C.C. (3d) 280 (Ont. C.A.) — Under s. 182(b), proof of *physical interference* with a dead body or human remains is *not* required.

R. v. Moyer (1994), 92 C.C.C. (3d) 1 (S.C.C.); reversing (1993), 25 C.R. (4th) 115, 83 C.C.C. (3d) 280 (Ont. C.A.) — While s. 182(b) does *not* apply to offering indignities to monuments *per se*, it does apply to offering indignities to monuments that mark human remains.

R. v. Mills (1993), 25 C.R. (4th) 69, 84 C.C.C. (3d) 352 (S.C.C.); reversing (1992), 16 C.R. (4th) 390, 77 C.C.C. (3d) 318 (Man. C.A.) — The purposeful destruction of coffins by a grave-digger using a backhoe to refill a grave, which resulted in the disruption of the peaceful laying to rest of human remains, constitutes an offence under s. 182. D's conduct was disrespectful, dishonourable and callous.

R. v. Ladue (1965), 45 C.R. 287, [1965] 4 C.C.C. 264 (Y.T. C.A.) — Only if D's actions would have been innocent and lawful had the body been alive would lack of knowledge that the body was dead be a defence to a charge under this section.

Related Provisions: The general offence of common nuisance is found in s. 180.

Section 243 prohibits concealment of the dead body of a child as defined in s. 214.

Under s. 536(2), D may elect mode of trial.

PART VI — INVASION OF PRIVACY

Definitions

183. Definitions — In this Part,

"authorization" means an authorization to intercept a private communication given under section 186 or subsection 184.2(3), 184.3(6) or 188(2);

"electro-magnetic, acoustic, mechanical or other device" means any device or apparatus that is used or is capable of being used to intercept a private communication, but

does not include a hearing aid used to correct subnormal hearing of the user to not better than normal hearing;

"intercept" includes listen to, record or acquire a communication or acquire the substance, meaning or purport thereof;

"offence" means an offence contrary to, any conspiracy or attempt to commit or being an accessory after the fact in relation to an offence contrary to, or any counselling in relation to an offence contrary to section 47 (high treason), 51 (intimidating Parliament or a legislature), 52 (sabotage), 57 (forgery, etc.), 61 (sedition), 76 (hijacking), 77 (endangering safety of aircraft or airport), 78 (offensive weapons, etc., on aircraft), 78.1 (offences against maritime navigation or fixed platforms), 80 (breach of duty), 81 (using explosives), 82 (possessing explosive), 96 (possession of weapon obtained by commission of offence), 99 (weapons trafficking), 100 (possession for purpose of weapons trafficking), 102 (making automatic firearm), 103 (importing or exporting knowing it is unauthorized), 104 (unauthorized importing or exporting), 119 (bribery, etc.), 120 (bribery, etc.), 121 (fraud on government), 122 (breach of trust), 123 (municipal corruption), 132 (perjury), 139 (obstructing justice), 144 (prison breach), 163.1 (child pornography), 184 (unlawful interception), 191 (possession of intercepting device), 235 (murder), 264.1 (uttering threats), 267 (assault with a weapon or causing bodily harm), 268 (aggravated assault), 269 (unlawfully causing bodily harm), 271 (sexual assault), 272 (sexual assault with a weapon, threats to a third party or causing bodily harm), 273 (aggravated sexual assault), 279 (kidnapping), 279.1 (hostage taking), 280 (abduction of person under sixteen), 281 (abduction of person under fourteen), 282 (abduction in contravention of custody order), 283 (abduction), 318 (advocating genocide), 327 (possession of device to obtain telecommunication facility or service), 334 (theft), 342 (theft, forgery, etc., or credit card), 342.1 (unauthorized use of computer), 342.2 (possession of device to obtain computer service), 344 (robbery), 346 (extortion), 347 (criminal interest rate), 348 (breaking and entering), 354 (possession of property obtained by crime), 356 (theft from mail), 367 (forgery), 368 (uttering forged document), 372 (false messages), 380 (fraud), 381 (using mail to defraud), 382 (fraudulent manipulation of stock exchange transactions), 424 (threat to commit offences against internationally protected person), 426 (secret commissions), 430 (mischief), 431 (attack on premises, residence or transport of internationally protected person), 433 (arson), 434 (arson), 434.1 (arson), 435 (arson for fraudulent purposes), 449 (making counterfeit money), 450 (possession, etc., of counterfeit money), 452 (uttering, etc., counterfeit money), 462.31 (laundering proceeds of crime), 467.1 (participation in criminal organization), subsection 145(1) (escape, etc.), 201(1) (keeping gaming or betting house), 210(1) (keeping common bawdy house), 212(1) (procuring), 212(2) (procuring), 212(2.1) (aggravated offence in relation to living on the avails of prostitution of a person under the age of eighteen years), 212(4) (offence — prostitution of person under eighteen) or 462.33(11) (acting in contravention of restraint order) or paragraph 163(1)(a) (obscene materials), or 202(1)(e) (pool-selling, etc.) of this Act, section 45 (conspiracy) of the *Competition Act* in relation to any of the matters referred to in paragraphs 45(4)(a) to (d) of that Act, section 47 (bid-rigging) or subsection 52.1 (3) (deceptive telemarketing) of that Act, or section 5 (trafficking), 6 (importing and exporting), 7 (production), 8 (possession of property obtained by designated substance offences) or 9 (laundering proceeds of designated substance offences of the *Controlled Drugs and Substances Act*, section 153 (false statements), 159 (smuggling), 163.1 (possession of property obtained by smuggling, etc.) or 163.2 (laundering proceeds of smuggling, etc.) of the *Customs Act*, sections 94.1 and 94.2 (organizing entry into Canada), 94.4 (disembarking persons at sea) and 94.5 (counselling false statements) of the *Immigration Act*, section 126.1 (possession of property obtained by excise offences), 126.2 (laundering proceeds of excise offences), 158 (unlawful distillation of spirits) or 163 (unlawful selling of spirits) or subsection 233(1) (unlawful packaging or stamping) or 240(1) (unlawful possession or sale of manufactured tobacco or cigars) of the *Excise Act*, section 198 (fraudulent bankruptcy) of the *Bankruptcy and Insolvency Act*, section 3 (bribing a foreign public official), section 4 (possession of property) or section 5 (laundering proceeds of the offence) of the *Corruption of Foreign Public Officials Act*, section 3 (spying) of the *Official Secrets Act*, section 13 (export or attempt to export), 14 (import or attempt to import), 15 (diversion, etc.), 16 (no transfer or permits), 17 (false information) or 18 (aiding or abetting) of the *Export and Import Permits Act* or any other offence created by this Act for which an offender may be sentenced to imprisonment for five years or more that there are reasonable grounds to believe is part of a pattern of criminal activity planned and organized by a number of persons acting in concert, or any other offence created by this or any other Act of Parliament for which an offender may be sentenced to imprisonment for five years or more that there are reasonable grounds to believe is committed for the benefit of, at the direction of or in association with a criminal organization;

"private communication" means any oral communication, or any telecommunication, that is made by an originator who is in Canada or is intended by the originator to be received by a person in Canada and that is made under circumstances in which it is reasonable for the originator to expect that it will not be intercepted by any person other than the person intended by the originator to receive it, and includes any radio-based telephone communication that is treated electronically or otherwise for the purpose of preventing intelligible reception by any person other than the person intended by the originator to receive it;

"public switched telephone network" means a telecommunication facility the primary purpose of which is to provide a land line-based telephone service to the public for compensation;

"radio-based telephone communication" means any radiocommunication within the meaning of the *Radiocommunication Act* that is made over apparatus that is used primarily for connection to a public switched telephone network;

"sell" includes offer for sale, expose for sale, have in possession for sale or distribute or advertise for sale;

"solicitor" means, in the Province of Quebec, an advocate or a notary and, in any other province, a barrister or solicitor.

1973–74, c. 50, s. 2; 1976–77, c. 53, s. 7; 1980–81–82–83, c. 125, s. 10; 1984, c. 21, s. 76; R.S. 1985, c. 27 (1st Supp.), ss. 7(2), 23; c. 1 (2d Supp.), s. 213(1), Schedule I, item 2; c. 1 (4th Supp.), s. 20; c. 29 (4th Supp.), s. 17; c. 42 (4th Supp.), s. 1; 1991, c. 28, s. 12; 1992, c. 27, s. 90(1); 1993, c. 7, s. 5; c. 25, s. 94; c. 40, s. 1; c. 46, s. 4; 1995, c. 39, s. 140; 1997, c. 18, s. 7; c. 23, s. 3; 1998, c. 34, s. 8; 1999, c. 2, s. 47; 1999, c. 5, s. 4.

Commentary: The section defines various words and phrases used in the Part.

Case Law [See also, ss. 487.01 and 492.2]

Intercept

R. v. McQueen (1975), 25 C.C.C. (2d) 262 (Alta. C.A.) — "Intercept" suggests an *interference* by a third party *between* the place of *origination* and the place of *destination* of the communication.

R. v. Singh (1998), 127 C.C.C. (3d) 429 (B.C. C.A.) — There is *no* breach of Part VI when a police officer, executing a search warrant at the residence of a suspected drug user, answers the telephone and persuades D, a drug trafficker, to meet her to complete a drug transaction.

Private Communication   [All cases decided under prior definition]

R. v. Monachan (1985), 16 C.C.C. (3d) 576 (S.C.C.); affirming (1981), 22 C.R. (3d) 1, 60 C.C.C. (2d) 286 (Ont. C.A.) — A message to a police station to convey a threat to a police officer cannot reasonably be considered a "private communication", as it would be unreasonable to expect that it would not be listened to or recorded by anyone other than the switchboard operator.

Goldman v. R. (1979), 13 C.R. (3d) 228 (S.C.C.) — There is a distinction between "private communication" and "private conversation". A "communication" involves the passing of thoughts, ideas, words or information from one person to another, whereas "conversation" is a broader term and would include an interchange of a series of separate communications. The "originator" of the private communication is the person who makes the remark or series of remarks which P seeks to adduce in evidence.

R. v. Lubovac (1989), 52 C.C.C. (3d) 551 (Alta. C.A.) — Pager messages are *not* private communications. The originator has no control over who may hear the messages and can not reasonably expect the communications to remain private.

R. v. Davie (1980), 17 C.R. (3d) 72, 54 C.C.C. (2d) 216 (B.C. C.A.) — A prayer to God is *not* a private communication between two persons. "Person" refers to a human being having legal rights and duties and does not include God.

R. v. Fegan (1993), 21 C.R. (4th) 65, 80 C.C.C. (3d) 356 (Ont. C.A.) — A digital number recorder (DNR) installed by Bell Canada, an investor-owned utility, which records electronic impulses emitted from a monitored telephone on a computer printout tape which discloses the number dialled in an outgoing call, but does *not* indicate whether the call is answered or the fact or substance of the communication, does *not* intercept a "private communication" within Part VI. A "communication" contemplates the exchange of information between persons. The initiation of a communication process by dialling a number does *not* constitute a "communiction", at least until the originator is in a position to deliver the message. The DNR only records the fact that a means of communication has been engaged, *not* the communication itself. A "communication" in s. 183 does *not* embrace the action of an originator lifting a telephone receiver and dialling a number [now see s. 492.2].

Related Provisions: "Agent of the state" is defined in s. 184.1(4) for the purposes of the section. Section 188(4) defines "chief justice" for similar purposes. "Tracking device" and "number recorder" are defined in s. 492.2(4) and 492.2(4) for the purposes of their respective sections.

Other Related Provisions are discussed in the corresponding note to s. 2, *supra*.

183.1 Consent to interception — **Where a private communication is originated by more than one person or is intended by the originator thereof to be received by more than one person, a consent to the interception thereof by any one of those persons is sufficient consent for the purposes of any provision of this Part.**

1993, c. 40, s. 2.

Commentary: This section describes and delimits who may *consent* to the *interception* of private communications for Part VI purposes. Where there are *several* originators or intended recipients of a private communication, the consent to its interception by *any* originator or intended recipient is sufficient for the purposes of any provision of Part VI.

Related Provisions: What constitutes a valid consent is *not* defined in Part VI.

Consent interceptions are saved from criminal liability under s.184(2)(a). The consent given to the interception may be express or implied.

Under s. 184.1, an agent of the state may intercept a private communication without judicial authorization in order to prevent bodily harm provided, *inter alia*, either the originator or intended recipient of the private communication has consented to the interception. Authorized consent interceptions may be made after successful application under s. 184.2 or 184.3. Consent to interception and disclosure is relevant to the use and disclosure offences of s. 193 and 193.1.

Interception of Communications

184. (1) **Interception** — Every one who, by means of any electro-magnetic, acoustic, mechanical or other device, wilfully intercepts a private communication is guilty of an indictable offence and liable to imprisonment for a term not exceeding five years.

(2) **Saving provision** — Subsection (1) does not apply to

(a) a person who has the consent to intercept, express or implied, of the originator of the private communication or of the person intended by the originator thereof to receive it;

(b) a person who intercepts a private communication in accordance with an authorization or pursuant to section 184.4 or any person who in good faith aids in any way another person who the aiding person believes on reasonable grounds is acting with an authorization or pursuant to section 184.4;

(c) a person engaged in providing a telephone, telegraph or other communication service to the public who intercepts a private communication,

(i) if the interception is necessary for the purpose of providing the service,

(ii) in the course of service observing or random monitoring necessary for the purpose of mechanical or service quality control checks, or

(iii) if the interception is necessary to protect the person's rights or property directly related to providing the service; or

(d) an officer or servant of Her Majesty in right of Canada who engages in radio frequency spectrum management, in respect of a private communication intercepted by that officer or servant for the purpose of identifying, isolating or preventing an unauthorized or interfering use of a frequency or of a transmission.

(3) [Repealed 1993, c. 40, s. 3(3).]

1973–74, c. 50, s. 20; 1993, c. 40, s. 3.

Commentary: The section defines and punishes the *interception* offence, and delineates its statutory exceptions.

The *external circumstances* of the offence of s. 184(1) are an amalgam of an interception, a private communication and a prohibited device. D's conduct must amount to an *interception*. What is intercepted must be a *private communication*. The interception must be effected *by means of an electro-magnetic, acoustic, mechanical or other device*. The italicized terms are all defined in s. 183. The *mental element* is expressed in the compendious term "wilfully". No ulterior mental element need be established.

Section 184(2) *exempts* from criminal liability conduct which would, *prima facie*, contravene s. 184(1). The subsection, in effect, renders lawful any interceptional activity falling within it.

Consent interceptions are saved by s. 184(2)(a). An interceptor must have the *express or implied* consent of an originator or intended recipient *to the interception* of the private communication. Where there are multiple originators or intended recipients, the consent of *any* originator or intended recipient to the interception is sufficient under s. 183.1.

Authorized interceptions are saved from liability under s. 184(2)(b), provided they are made by a person who intercepts a private communication *in accordance with an authorization* or by any person who *in good faith* aids, in any way, a person who s/he believes, on reasonable grounds, is acting with an authorization. The saving provision only avails to the extent of compliance with the court-ordered interceptional authority. It extends, however, not only to those who intercept but, equally, to those who assist, provided that the assistance is given *bona fide* to one reasonably believed to be acting under judicial authority. Interceptions made without authorization in the exceptional circumstances described in s. 184.4 are also saved from liability under s. 184(2)(b).

Service interceptions do *not* attract liability under s. 184(1), provided they are made by a person and in circumstances described in s. 184(2)(c) or (d).

Case Law

Consent Interceptions: S. 184(2)(a)

Goldman v. R. (1979), 13 C.R. (3d) 228 (S.C.C.) — The consent referred to in s. 184(2)(a) is a consent to the interception. The consent must be *voluntary*, in the sense that it is free from coercion. It must be made *knowingly*, in that the consenter must be *aware* of what he is doing and aware of the significance of his act and the use which the police may be able to make of the consent. Although the consent must *not* be procured by intimidating conduct or by force or threats of force by the police, coercion, in the sense in which the word applies here, does not arise merely because the consent is given because of promised or expected leniency or immunity from prosecution.

R. v. Fegan (1993), 80 C.C.C. (3d) 356 (Ont. C.A.) — Even if a DNR installed by an investor-owned utility, which records electronic impulses emitted from a monitored telephone on a computer printout tape which discloses the number dialled in an outgoing call, but does *not* indicate whether the call is answered or the fact or substance of the communication constitutes the interception of a private communication, the interception is lawful under s. 184(2)(a) and (c).

Charter Considerations

R. v. Thompson (1990), 80 C.R. (3d) 129, 59 C.C.C. (3d) 225 (S.C.C.); reversing (1986), 53 C.R. (3d) 56, 29 C.C.C. (3d) 516 (B.C. C.A.) — *See also*: *R. v. Duarte*, supra; *R. v. Garofoli* (1990), 80 C.R. (3d) 317, 60 C.C.C. (3d) 161 (S.C.C.) — Electronic surveillance constitutes a "search and seizure" within *Charter* s. 8.

R. v. Duarte (1990), 74 C.R. (3d) 281, 53 C.C.C. (3d) 1 (S.C.C.) — *See also*: *R. v. Wiggins* (1990), 74 C.R. (3d) 281, 53 C.C.C. (3d) 476 (S.C.C.) — The interception of private communications by an instrumentality of the state *with* the *consent* of one of the participants, but *without* prior judicial *authorization*, violates *Charter* s. 8.

Related Provisions: "Electro-magnetic, acoustic, mechanical or other device", "intercept" and "private communication" are defined in s. 183, but "originator" is neither there nor elsewhere defined. Section 184.5 creates a similar offence relating to the interception of radio-based telephone communications.

This offence is an "offence" under s. 183 for the purposes of this Part.

Judicial *authorization* to intercept private communications may be given under s. 184.2 and 184.3 (authorized consent), 185 and 186 (conventional authorizations and renewals) and 188 (emergency authorizations). "Authorization" is defined in s. 183. Confidentiality and disclosure of documents relating to applications under Part VI are governed by s. 187.

The interception of private communications is a search or seizure which is subject to the requirement of reasonableness inherent in *Charter* s. 8. The *admissibility* of evidence obtained by a s. 8 *Charter* infringement is governed by *Charter* s. 24(2). Notice of P's intention to adduce intercepted private communications as evidence, together with disclosure in the appropriate form, is required by s. 189(5).

Possession of interception devices is an offence under s. 191 and disclosure of private communications intercepted without the consent of a party thereto is prohibited in the circumstances described in s. 193. Disclosure of information received from interception of radio-based telephone communications is prohibited in the circumstances described in s. 193.1. It is also an offence to intercept, by means of an electro-magnetic, accoustic, mechanical or other device, any function of a computer system under s. 342.1(1)(b).

Under s. 536(2), D may *elect* mode of trial. Upon conviction, the device by means of which the offence was committed may be ordered forfeited unde s. 192 and a punitive damage award made against D under s. 194.

184.1 (1) Interception to prevent bodily harm — An agent of the state may intercept, by means of any electro-magnetic, acoustic, mechanical or other device, a private communication if

    (a) either the originator of the private communication or the person intended by the originator to receive it has consented to the interception;

    (b) the agent of the state believes on reasonable grounds that there is a risk of bodily harm to the person who consented to the interception; and

    (c) the purpose of the interception is to prevent the bodily harm.

(2) **Admissibility of intercepted communicaiton** — The contents of a private communication that is obtained from an interception pursuant to subsection (1) are inadmissible as evidence except for the purposes of proceedings in which actual, attempted or threatened bodily harm is alleged, including proceedings in respect of an application for an authorization under this Part or in respect of a search warrant or a warrant for the arrest of any person.

(3) **Destruction of recording and transcripts** — The agent of the state who intercepts a private communication pursuant to subsection (1) shall, as soon as is practicable in the circumstances, destroy any recording of the private communication that is obtained from an interception pursuant to subsection (1), any full or partial transcript of the recording and any notes made by that agent of the private communication if nothing in the private communication suggests that bodily harm, attempted bodily harm or threatened bodily harm has occurred or is likely to occur.

(4) **Definition of "agent of the state"** — For the purposes of this section, "agent of the state" means

    (a) a peace officer; and

    (b) a person acting under the authority of, or in cooperation with, a peace officer.

1993, c. 40, s. 4.

Commentary: The section provides exceptional authority for an *agent of the state*, as defined in s. 184.1(4), to intercept private communications *without* judicial authorization. It enacts unique provisions for the admissibility in evidence and the preservation of records of the interceptions made.

An *agent of the state* is a peace officer or anyone acting under the authority of, or in cooperation with, a peace officer. Under s. 184.1(1), an agent of the state may intercept a private communication by means of an electro-magnetic, acoustic, mechanical or other device if

i.   an *originator* or *intended recipient* of the private communication has consented to the interception;

ii.   the agent of the state has a *reasonably grounded* belief that there is a risk of bodily harm to the consenting party; and,

iii.   the *purpose* of the interception is to *prevent* the *bodily harm*.

The requirements are cumulative. No judicial authorization is required. Interceptional authority is founded upon participant consent, the agent's reasonably grounded belief and the preventative purpose of the interception.

Section 184.1(2) enacts a rule of *admissibility* for *primary evidence* obtained by interception under s. 184.1(1). The rule appears founded upon the nature of the allegation made in the proceedings in which the primary evidence is sought to be used. The rule excludes primary evidence obtained under s. 184.1(1) except for proceedings in which actual, attempted or threatened bodily harm is alleged. "Proceedings" include applications for authorization under Part VI and, further, for search or arrest warrants.

Section 184.1(3) governs maintenance and destruction of records made of private communications intercepted under s. 184.1(1). Where nothing in the intercepted private communication suggests that actual, attempted or threatened bodily harm has occurred or is likely to occur, the intercepting agent is required, as soon as is practicable in the circumstances, to destroy any recordings, transcripts and notes made of the intercepted private communication. It would seem logically to follow that where such suggestion does appear in the intercepted private communications, the records are to be maintained by the agent of the state. (S. 184.1)

Related Provisions: "Authorization", "intercept", "private communication" and "electro-magnetic, acoustic, mechanical or other device" are defined in s. 183. "Bodily harm" is defined in s. 2.

Authorization to intercept private communications may be given under s. 184.2 and 184.3 (consent authorization), 186 (conventional authorizations) and 188 (emergency authorizations). Authorizations may also permit the interception of radio-based telephone communications, as well as private communications, under s. 184.5(2) and 184.6.

Section 184.4 also permits interception of private communications to be made without judicial authorization. A peace officer who makes unauthorized interceptions under s. 184.4 is saved from criminal liability by s. 184(2)(b). The applicable saving provision for s. 184.1 unauthorized interceptions is s. 184.(2)(a) and is based upon participant consent.

The direction of s. 184.1(3) that records of the intercepted private communications be destroyed, absent defined circumstances, is problematic. It appears designed to ensure that no investigative use is made of primary evidence gathered for a purpose which does not materialize. *Quaere* whether a rule of admissibility, as in s. 184.1(2), or the conjoint effect of *Charter* s. 8 and 24(2), would not suffice? The requirement of destruction may also conflict with provincial regulations concerning the maintenance of police notes.

184.2 (1) Interception with consent — A person may intercept, by means of any electro-magnetic, acoustic, mechanical or other device, a private communication where either the originator of the private communication or the person intended by the originator to receive it has consented to the interception and an authorization has been obtained pursuant to subsection (3).

(2) Application for authorization — An application for an authorization under this section shall be made by a peace officer, or a public officer who has been appointed or designated to administer or enforce any federal or provincial law and whose duties include the enforcement of this or any other Act of Parliament, ex parte and in writing to a provincial court judge, a judge of a superior court of criminal jurisdiction or a judge as defined in section 552, and shall be accompanied by an affidavit, which may be sworn on the information and belief of that peace officer or public officer or of any other peace officer or public officer, deposing to the following matters:

    (a) that there are reasonable grounds to believe that an offence against this or any other Act of Parliament has been or will be committed;

    (b) the particulars of the offence;

    (c) the name of the person who has consented to the interception;

    (d) the period for which the authorization is requested; and

    (e) in the case of an application for an authorization where an authorization has previously been granted under this section or section 186, the particulars of the authorization.

(3) Judge to be satisfied — An authorization may be given under this section if the judge to whom the application is made is satisfied that

    (a) there are reasonable grounds to believe that an offence against this or any other Act of Parliament has been or will be committed;

    (b) either the originator of the private communication or the person intended by the originator to receive it has consented to the interception; and

(c) there are reasonable grounds to believe that information concerning the offence referred to in paragraph (a) will be obtained through the interception sought.

(4) Content and limitation of authorization — An authorization given under this section shall

(a) state the offence in respect of which private communications may be intercepted;

(b) state the type of private communication that may be intercepted;

(c) state the identity of the persons, if known, whose private communications are to be intercepted, generally describe the place at which private communications may be intercepted, if a general description of that place can be given, and generally describe the manner of interception that may be used;

(d) contain the terms and conditions that the judge considers advisable in the public interest; and

(e) be valid for the period, not exceeding sixty days, set out therein.

1993, c. 40, s. 4.

Commentary: This section, and s. 184.3, provide for judicially *authorized consent* interception of private communications. The provisions represent the parliamentary response to *R. v. Duarte* (1990), 53 C.C.C. (3d) 1 (S.C.C.). What is permitted is interception of private communications with the consent of a participant and under judicial authorization.

Section 184.2(2) governs the application for authorization and supportive affidavit. The applicant must be a peace officer, or a public officer whose duties include, *inter alia*, the enforcement of the *Criminal Code* or other federal statute. No further or special designation is required. The application made *ex parte* and in writing to a *provincial court* judge, a judge of the *superior court* of criminal jurisdiction or a judge as defined in *Code* s. 552. It must be accompanied by an *affidavit*, which may be sworn on the *information and belief* of the applicant or any other peace or public officer, which is compliant with s. 184.2(2). A simple recital of the fact of probable cause, hence literal compliance with s. 184.2(2)(a), would seem constitutionally inadvisable. The affiant should display the facts which underlie the belief asserted, as in s. 184(1)(c), thereby permitting the authorizing judge independently to decide whether probable cause has been made out. The offence, particulars of which must be included under s. 184.2(2)(b), may be an offence against the *Code* or other federal statute which has been or will be committed. The affiant must also disclose the *name* of the *consenting* originator or intended recipient. Where available, it is suggested that a signed and witnessed consent be exhibited to the affidavit. Authorization history need *only* be disclosed under s. 184.2(2)(e) where authorization has earlier been given under the section or s. 186.

The *affidavit content* requirements of s. 184.2(2) do *not* coincide with the *findings* required to be made under s. 184.2(3)(c) before authorization may be given, or the terms of the order under s. 184.2(4)(b) and (c). The authorizing judge may only make the necessary findings on the basis of evidence, likewise the inclusion of terms. The affidavit constitutes the evidentiary basis for the authorization, hence ought include a statement of facts which will permit the finding of s. 184.2(3)(c) and the inclusion of the mandatory terms of s. 184.2(4)(b) and (c).

Section 184.2(3) articulates the *conditions precedent* to be satisfied, or findings to be made, before judicial authorization may be given. What must be established is a *reasonably* grounded belief that an offence against the *Code* or other federal statute *has been* or *will be* committed and, further, that *information* concerning the offence *will* be obtained through the interception sought. Information is a word of comprehensive import. It includes, but is *not* restricted to, evidence which may be admissible in subsequent proceedings. The authorizing judge must also be satisfied that a *party* to the private communication to be intercepted has *consented* to the interception.

The terms of an authorization given under s. 184.2 are described in s. 184.2(4). They duplicate what is required in the case of conventional authorizations by s. 186(4).

Related Provisions: Consent is *not* defined in or for the purposes of this section or Part. Under s. 183.1, *any* originator or intended recipient of a private communication may consent to its interception. "Peace officer" and "public officer" are defined in s. 2, as is "provincial court judge" and "superior court of criminal jurisdiction".

Application for authorization may also be made by telephone or other means of telecommunication in the circumstances described and subject to the requirements of s. 184.3. Under s. 184.5(2) and 184.6, authorizations under s. 184.2 and 184.3 may permit interception of *radio-based telephone communications*, as well as private communications. One authorization will suffice. The authorizations may be executed anywhere in Canada under s. 188.1(1), although "backing" in another jurisdiction may be required in the circumstances described in s. 188.1(2). An assistance order may be made under s. 487.02.

The disclosure scheme of s. 187 applies to applications for consent authorization under s. 184.2.

Conventional authorizations are obtained and may be renewed under s. 185 and 186. Section 188 governs emergency authorizations. The *Commentary* which accompanies each section describes the procedure to be followed, the basis upon which authorization may be given and the terms and conditions to be included in the order.

184.3 (1) Application by means of telecommunication — Notwithstanding section 184.2, an application for an authorization under subsection 184.2(2) may be made ex parte to a provincial court judge, a judge of a superior court of criminal jurisdiction or a judge as defined in section 552, by telephone or other means of telecommunication, if it would be impracticable in the circumstances for the applicant to appear personally before a judge.

(2) Application — An application for an authorization made under this section shall be on oath and shall be accompanied by a statement that includes the matters referred to in paragraphs 184.2(2)(a) to (e) and that states the circumstances that make it impracticable for the applicant to appear personally before a judge.

(3) Recording — The judge shall record, in writing or otherwise, the application for an authorization made under this section and, on determination of the application, shall cause the writing or recording to be placed in the packet referred to in subsection 187(1) and sealed in that packet, and a recording sealed in a packet shall be treated as if it were a document for the purposes of section 187.

(4) Oath — For the purposes of subsection (2), an oath may be administered by telephone or other means of telecommunication.

(5) Alternative to oath — An applicant who uses a means of telecommunication that produces a writing may, instead of swearing an oath for the purposes of subsection (2), make a statement in writing stating that all matters contained in the application are true to the knowledge or belief of the applicant and such a statement shall be deemed to be a statement made under oath.

(6) Authorization — Where the judge to whom an application is made under this section is satisfied that the circumstances referred to in paragraphs 184.2(3)(a) to (c) exist and that the circumstances referred to in subsection (2) make it impracticable for the applicant to appear personally before a judge, the judge may, on such terms and conditions, if any, as are considered advisable, give an authorization by telephone or other means of telecommunication for a period of up to thirty-six hours.

(7) Giving authorization — Where a judge gives an authorization by telephone or other means of telecommunication, other than a means of telecommunication that produces a writing,

(a) the judge shall complete and sign the authorization in writing, noting on its face the time, date and place at which it is given;

(b) the applicant shall, on the direction of the judge, complete a facsimile of the authorization in writing, noting on its face the name of the judge who gave it and the time, date and place at which it was given; and

(c) the judge shall, as soon as is practicable after the authorization has been given, cause the authorization to be placed in the packet referred to in subsection 187(1) and sealed in that packet.

(8) Giving authorization where telecommunication produces writing — Where a judge gives an authorization by a means of telecommunication that produces a writing, the judge shall

(a) complete and sign the authorization in writing, noting on its face the time, date and place at which it is given;

(b) transmit the authorization by the means of telecommunication to the applicant, and the copy received by the applicant shall be deemed to be a facsimile referred to in paragraph (7)(b); and

(c) as soon as is practicable after the authorization has been given, cause the authorization to be placed in the packet referred to in subsection 187(1) and sealed in that packet.

1993, c. 40, s. 4.

Commentary: This section provides a further basis upon which *judicially-authorized consent* interceptions of private communications may be made.

The authority provided by the section differs from that in s. 184.2 in several respects. Under s. 184.3(1), the *application* for authorization is made *by telephone or other means of telecommunication*, rather than in writing, as under s. 184.2(1). The application may only be made under s. 184.3(1) if it would be impracticable for the applicant to appear personally before the authorizing judge. In both cases, the applicant must be a peace officer, or a public officer whose duties include federal law enforcement. The authorizing judge, as under s. 184.2(2), is a provincial court judge, a judge of the superior court of criminal jurisdiction, or a judge as defined in *Code* s. 552.

Under s. 184.3(2), the *application* must be *on oath* and accompanied by a *statement* that complies with s. 184.2(2) and further describes the circumstances that make it *impracticable* for the applicant to *appear personally* before the authorizing judge. Under s. 184.3(4), the oath may be administered by telephone or other means of telecommunication. Section 184.3(5) permits the applicant, instead of swearing an oath, to make a *statement in writing* stating that all matters contained in the application are true to the best of the applicant's knowledge or belief, and *deems* the statement to be under *oath*.

The *findings* required before an authorization may issue under s. 184.3(6) are those required by s. 184.2(3) and, further, that it is *impracticable* for the applicant to attend personally before the authorizing judge. The authorization may *not* exceed a period of 36 hours. Completion of the authorization and custody of it are governed by s. 184.3(7) and (8).

Related Provisions: An information to obtain a search warrant may also be submitted by telephone or by other means of telecommunication under s. 487.1.

Other *Related Provisions* are described in the corresponding note to s. 184.2, *supra*.

184.4 Interception in exceptional circumstances — A peace officer may intercept, by means of any electro-magnetic, acoustic, mechanical or other device, a private communication where

    (a) the peace officer believes on reasonable grounds that the urgency of the situation is such that an authorization could not, with reasonable diligence, be obtained under any other provision of this Part;

    (b) the peace officer believes on reasonable grounds that such an interception is immediately necessary to prevent an unlawful act that would cause serious harm to any person or to property; and

    (c) either the originator of the private communication or the person intended by the orginator to receive it is the person who would perform the act that is likely to cause the harm or is the victim, or intended victim, of the harm.

1993, c. 40, s. 4.

Commentary: This exceptional provision permits unauthorized interception of private communications by a peace officer. It is bound to attract *Charter* scrutiny.

Under this section, a peace officer may intercept a private communication by means of an electro-magnetic, acoustic, mechanical or other device, provided:

i.   the peace officer has a *reasonably grounded belief* that the *urgency* of the situation is such that *no authorization* could be obtained, with *reasonable diligence*, under any provision of Part VI;

ii.   the peace officer has a *reasonably grounded belief* that the interception is *immediately necessary* to *prevent* an unlawful act that would seriously harm a person or property; and,

iii.   either the *originator* or the *intended recipient* of the private communication is the *person* who would *do* the act likely to cause harm or is the actual or intended *victim* of it.

The section imposes *no* time limit on the interception. They would appear permitted only so long as the required states of mind continue.

Related Provisions: "Peace officer" is defined in s. 2, "intercept", "electro-magnetic, acoustic, mechanical or other device" and "private communication" by s. 183. Interceptions may also be made of *radio-based telephone communications* under s. 184.5(2) and 184.6.

The absence of formal application, judicial determination and written authorization render several provisions of Part VI inapplicable to interceptions made under s. 184.4. The *confidentiality* rule of s. 187 does *not* apply, nor is there any requirement of *notification* of the objects of interception under s. 196. The provisions of s. 188.1 which permit Canada-wide execution of authorizations and of s. 487.02, which permit inclusion of assistance orders in authorizations are *inapplicable* since no authorization is given under s. 184.4.

Section 184.1 permits consent interception by agents of the state to prevent bodily harm or the risk of it to the consenting party.

A person who intercepts a private communication, pursuant to s. 184.4, or any person who aids in good faith another whom the aider reasonably believes is acting under s. 184.4, is saved from liability for interception by s. 184(2)(b) and, more generally, under s. 188.2.

184.5 (1) Interception of radio-based telephone communications — Every person who intercepts, by means of any electro-magnetic, acoustic, mechanical or other device, maliciously or for gain, a radio-based telephone communication, if the originator of the communication or the person intended by the originator of the communication to receive it is in Canada, is guilty of an indictable offence and liable to imprisonment for a term not exceeding five years.

(2) Other provisions to apply — Section 183.1, subsection 184(2) and sections 184.1 to 190 and 194 to 196 apply, with such modifications as the circumstances require, to interceptions of radio-based telephone communications referred to in subsection (1).

1993, c. 40, s. 4.

Commentary: The section creates an interception offence in relation to radio-based telephone communications and makes other provisions of the Part applicable to these interceptions.

The *external circumstances* of the offence of s. 184.5(1) comprise an interception, by means of a prohibited device of a radio-based telephone communication whose originator or intended recipient is in Canada. The *mental element* requires that D intentionally cause the external circumstances "maliciously or for gain". The offence is indictable and punishable by imprisonment for a term *not* exceeding five years.

Section 184.5(2) incorporates by reference several provisions of Part VI the effect of which is to ensure similar treatment of "private communications" and "radio-based telephone communications" under the Part. In particular, radio-based telephone communications may be intercepted in accordance with authorized consents (s. 184.2 and 184.3), conventional authorizations and renewals (s. 186) and emergency authorizations (s. 188). They may also be intercepted without authorization under s. 184.1 (agent of the state) and 184.4 (peace officer).

Related Provisions: "Intercept", "electro-magnetic, acoustic, mechanical or other device" and "radio-based telephone communication" are defined in s. 183.

Section 184(1) prohibits wilful interception of private communications by means of an electro-magnetic, acoustic, mechanical or other device, but does *not* require that it be "maliciously or for gain" as under s. 184.5(1). Related use and disclosure offences are contained in s. 193 (private communications) and 193.1 (radio-based telephone communications). Punitive damage awards may be made upon conviction of the interception (s. 184 and 184.5) and use and disclosure offences (s. 193 and 193.1).

Under s. 184.6, any authorization granted under Part VI may permit interception of both private communications and radio-based telephone communications.

Other related provisions are described in the corresponding note to s. 184.2, *supra*.

184.6 One application for authorization sufficient — For greater certainty, an application for an authorization under this Part may be made with respect to both private communications and radio-based telephone communications at the same time.

1993, c. 40, s. 4.

Commentary: This section permits *any* application for authorization under Part VI to include both *private* communications and *radio-based* telephone communications.

Related Provisions: "Authorization", "private communication" and "radio-based telephone communication" are defined in s. 183.

Conventional (60-day) authorizations may be given and renewed under s. 186. Emergency authorizations are governed by s. 188. Authorized consent interceptions may be made under s. 184.2 and 184.3. Execution of authorizations may be carried out anywhere in Canada in accordance with s. 188.1 and assistance orders made under s. 487.02.

Indictable offences relating to the interception of radio-based telephone communications and their use and disclosure are enacted by s. 184.5 and 193.1. A punitive damage award may be made upon conviction of either offence under s. 194(1).

185. (1) Application for authorization — An application for an authorization to be given under section 186 shall be made ex parte and in writing to a judge of a superior court of criminal jurisdiction or a judge as defined in section 552 and shall be signed by the Attorney General of the province in which the application is made or the Solicitor General of Canada or an agent specially designated in writing for the purposes of this section by

    (a) the Solicitor General of Canada personally or the Deputy Solicitor General of Canada personally, if the offence under investigation is one in respect of which

245

proceedings, if any, may be instituted at the instance of the Government of Canada and conducted by or on behalf of the Attorney General of Canada, or

(b) the Attorney General of a province personally or the Deputy Attorney General of a province personally, in any other case,

and shall be accompanied by an affidavit, which may be sworn on the information and belief of a peace officer or public officer deposing to the following matters:

(c) the facts relied on to justify the belief that the authorization should be given together with particulars of the offence,

(d) the type of private communication proposed to be intercepted,

(e) the names, addresses and occupations, if known, of all persons, the interception of whose private communications there are reasonable grounds to believe may assist the investigation of the offence, a general description of the nature and location of the place, if known, at which private communications are proposed to be intercepted and a general description of the manner of interception proposed to be used,

(f) the number of instances, if any, on which an application has been made under this section in relation to the offence and a person named in the affidavit pursuant to paragraph (e) and on which the application was withdrawn or no authorization was given, the date on which each application was made and the name of the judge to whom each application was made,

(g) the period for which the authorization is requested, and

(h) whether other investigative procedures have been tried and have failed or why it appears they are unlikely to succeed or that the urgency of the matter is such that it would be impractical to carry out the investigation of the offence using only other investigative procedures.

(1.1) Exception for criminal organizations — Notwithstanding paragraph (1)(h), that paragraph does not apply where the application for an authorization is in relation to

(a) an offence under section 467.1; or

(b) an offence committed for the benefit of, at the direction of or in association with a criminal organization.

(2) Extension of period for notification — An application for an authorization may be accompanied by an application, personally signed by the Attorney General of the province in which the application for the authorization is made or the Solicitor General of Canada if the application for the authorization is made by him or on his behalf, to substitute for the period mentioned in subsection 196(1) such longer period not exceeding three years as is set out in the application.

(3) Where extension to be granted — Where an application for an authorization is accompanied by an application referred to in subsection (2), the judge to whom the applications are made shall first consider the application referred to in subsection (2) and where, on the basis of the affidavit in support of the application for the authorization and any other affidavit evidence submitted in support of the application referred to in subsection (2), the judge is of the opinion that the interests of justice warrant the granting of the application, he shall fix a period, not exceeding three years, in substitution for the period mentioned in subsection 196(1).

(4) Where extension not granted — Where the judge to whom an application for an authorization and an application referred to in subsection (2) are made refuses to fix a period in substitution for the period mentioned in subsection 196(1) or where the judge fixes a period in substitution therefor that is less than the period set out in the application referred to in subsection (2), the person appearing before the judge on the application for the authorization may withdraw the application for the authorization and thereupon the judge shall not proceed to consider the application for the authorization or to give the authorization and shall return to the person appearing before him on the application for the authorization both applications and all other material pertaining thereto.

1973–74, c. 50, s. 2; 1976–77, c. 53, s. 8; 1993, c. 40, s. 5; 1997, c. 18, s. 8; c. 23, s. 4.

Commentary: The section defines the *basis* upon which *application* may be made for conventional (60 day) judicial *authorization* to intercept private communications and for *extension* of the period within which *notice* of interception must be given to the object thereof under s. 196(1).

Section 185(1) defines *who* may bring an application for authorization, the *court* before which it may be brought and *what* must be filed in support.

The initiating document, an *application in writing*, must be signed personally by the Attorney General of the province in which the application is made, or the Solicitor General of Canada, or an agent of either specially designated in writing for such purpose under s. 185(1)(a) or (b), as the case may be.

The application must be accompanied by an *affidavit* compliant with ss. 185(1)(c)–(h). The section permits *no* other material to be filed in support of the application. The supportive affidavit of the peace or public officer may be sworn upon information and belief, but must depose to the matters enumerated in ss. 185(1)(c)–(h).

Section 185(1)(c) requires delineation of *the facts* upon which, and *particulars of the offence* in respect of which authorization is sought. The offence must be an "offence" in s. 183.

Under s. 185(1)(d), the *type of private communication* proposed to be intercepted must be identified. *What* it is proposed to intercept must be a "private communication" in s. 183.

Section 185(1)(e) contains three requirements relating to the *who* (objects), *where* (location) and *how* (manner) of interception. An *object of interception* is any person interception of whose private communications there are reasonable grounds to believe *may* assist the investigation of a specified offence. The *identification* requirement demands inclusion of names, addresses and occupations, *if known*, in the affidavit. The *location of interception* requirement necessitates a general description of the nature and location of the place, *if known*, at which it is proposed to make interceptions. The object and location of interception requirements are closely related to the provisions of ss. 186(2) and (3). The *manner of interception* requirement is unconditional: the affidavit must contain a general description of the manner of interception proposed to be used.

Section 185(1)(f) requires *disclosure* in detail of any *previous applications* for authorization in relation to the offence and the person named in the affidavit which have been either withdrawn or unsuccessful.

Section 185(1)(g) requires a designation of the *period* for which the authorization is requested. The period must not exceed 60 days.

Section 185(1)(h) requires an assertion of *investigative necessity*. The affidavit must depose to the inadequacy, impracticality or unavailability of investigative procedures other than judicially authorized electronic surveillance unless s. 185(1.1) applies. Subsection 185(1.1) waives the requirement for an assertion of investigative necessity in s. 185(1)(h) where the application for authorization is in relation to a criminal organization.

Sections 185(2)–(4), permit an application for authorization to be accompanied by an application to substitute for the statutory *notification* period of s. 196(1) a longer period, not exceeding three years. The application must be personally signed by the Attorney General or Solicitor General of Canada, as the case may be, and, under s. 185(2), must be considered first, prior to any determination of the application for authorization. The judge to whom the applications are made is to consider the affidavit filed in support of the application for authorization and any other affidavits submitted in support of the application for deferral of notification. The criterion to be applied is whether the *interests of justice* warrant the granting of the application. Where the application for deferral of notice is refused, or a period fixed less than that requested in the application, the applicant, under s. 185(4), may withdraw the application for authorization and the judge shall *not* determine it. Both applications must then be returned to the applicant. Where an application for deferral of notification is successful, a period, not exceeding three years, is fixed in the order in substitution for the statutory period of s. 196(1).

Case Law

Jurisdiction

R. v. Cordes (1979), 10 C.R. (3d) 186 (S.C.C.); affirming (1978), 40 C.C.C. (2d) 442 (Alta. C.A.) — The jurisdiction accorded to a judge is to be exercised *qua* judge, not as a *persona designata*. Authorization to intercept private communications with respect to an *N.C.A.* offence is obtainable on the application of an agent of the Solicitor General of Canada.

R. v. Hancock (1976), 36 C.R.N.S. 102 (B.C. C.A.) — The offences mentioned in s. 185(1)(a) which might be instituted at the instance of the Government of Canada and conducted by or on behalf of the Attorney General of Canada refer to federal statute offences designated in s. 183, and not to *Code* offences. Only the provincial Attorney General may commence proceedings under the *Code* and, consequently, only the provincial Attorney General may designate an agent for applications with respect to *Code* offences enumerated in s. 183.

R. v. Barbeau (1996), 50 C.R. (4th) 357, 110 C.C.C. (3d) 69 (Que. C.A.) — An applicant's *self-description* as a duly authorized agent of the relevant authority is *sufficient* to establish the condition precedent. There is *no* requirement that a written authorization be included in the packet.

R. c. Bujold (1987), 4 Q.A.C. 148 (C.A.) — Designated representatives of the provincial Attorneys General have the power to seek wiretap authorizations in narcotics investigations. They are not restricted by the concurrent authority of the federal Solicitor General.

Affidavits: S. 185(1) [See also Charter, s. 8]

R. v. Garofoli (1990), 80 C.R. (3d) 317, 60 C.C.C. (3d) 161 (S.C.C.); reversing (1988), 41 C.C.C. (3d) 97, 64 C.R. (3d) 193 (Ont. C.A.) — Hearsay statements of an informant *can* provide *reasonable and probable grounds* to justify a search, but evidence of an informant's tip, by itself, is insufficient to establish reasonable and probable grounds. The reliability of a tip is to be assessed by having regard to the totality of the circumstances, including the degree of detail, source of knowledge and *indicia* of reliability or confirmation. The results of a search cannot, *ex post facto*, provide evidence of the reliability of the information.

R. v. Cheung (1997), 119 C.C.C. (3d) 507 (B.C. C.A.); leave to appeal refused (1998), 122 C.C.C. (3d) vi (S.C.C.) — There is *no* requirement that the affiant have a *subjective* belief of the *reasonableness* of the grounds relied upon in support of the application. The authorizing judge may reach such a conclusion based on the facts set out in the affidavit.

R. v. Moore, R. v. Bogdanich (1993), 21 C.R. (4th) 387, 81 C.C.C. (3d) 161 (B.C. C.A.) — Section 186(6), applicable to renewals, does *not* apply to applications for fresh authorization. The requirements of an application for authorization are found in s. 185. The supportive affidavit must disclose the facts relied on to justify the belief that an authorization should be given. Each and every investigative step taken by the police up to the time of the application need *not* be disclosed. There must be, however, full, fair and frank disclosure of the investigative steps taken by the police, including disclosure of relevant intercepted private communications up to the time of the application.

Once a premises has been identified as a place to which named targets resorted during the first authorization, it should be disclosed to the authorizing judge on an application for a second authorization under *Code* s. 185(1)(e). The "resort to" clause of the first authorization cannot be relied upon to continue interceptions at the identified premises under the second authorization.

R. v. Gill (1980), 18 C.R. (3d) 390, 56 C.C.C. (2d) 169 (B.C. C.A.) — The supporting affidavit must comply with the provisions of the *Code* frankly, fully and fairly. The applicant should *not* try to conceal his true intentions. It is *not* the formality of compliance that is required but real compliance with the true intent of the *Code*.

R. v. Smyk (1993), 86 C.C.C. (3d) 63 (Man. C.A.) — The authorizing judge, at a minimum, should be told of the nature, progress and difficulties in an investigation to ensure that interception of private communications is more than just a useful tool. (per Scott C.J.M., Philp J.A.)

R. v. Shayesteh (1996), 111 C.C.C. (3d) 225 (Ont. C.A.) — An affiant is *not* required to ignore evidence probative of the commission of the authorized offence simply because there may exist some alternative explanation. It is the judicial officer who must be satisfied of the grounds, *not* the affiant.

Known Persons: S. 185(1)(a)

R. v. Chesson (1988), 65 C.R. (3d) 193, 43 C.C.C. (3d) 353 (S.C.C.) — A *known* person is someone whose *existence* is known to the police and whose *private communications* there are *reasonable grounds* to believe *may assist* the investigation of the offence. If a person meets the criteria of a "known person" at the time of the authorization, then s/he must be named as a target. His/her communications cannot be intercepted under a "basket clause", even where the communications are made with a named "known person".

Places of Interception: S. 185(1)(c)

R. v. Moore, R. v. Bogdanich (1993), 21 C.R. (4th) 387, 81 C.C.C. (3d) 161 (B.C. C.A.) — See digests under "Affidavits: s. 185(1)", *supra*.

Other Investigative Procedures: S. 185(1)(h)

R. v. Grant (1998), 130 C.C.C. (3d) 53 (Man. C.A.) — To satisfy s. 185(1)(h), an affiant should assert

i.   the specific reasons for surveillance;

ii. why surveillances failed; and,

iii. what evidence the interceptions are expected to produce.

Related Provisions: "Superior court of criminal jurisdiction", "Attorney General", "peace officer" and "public officer" are defined in s. 2.

Sections 186(1)–(4), describe the *basis* upon which an *authorization* may be given, as well as the terms which must be included in it. Renewals are governed by ss. 186(6) and (7). Section 186.1 governs time-limits in respect of authorizations for s. 467.1 offences and for criminal organization offences. Section 187 describes the manner in which the documents relating to an application for authorization under s. 185 or renewal under s. 186(6) are to be kept confidential and the circumstances under which they may be opened, copied and disclosed. Emergency authorizations, a form of s. 186 authorization, are governed by s. 188.

Consent authorizations may be sought and obtained in accordance with ss. 184.2 and 184.3. Under s. 184.6, any application for authorization under Part VI may include both private communications and radio-based telephone communications. The authorization issued may do likewise.

Authorizations to intercept private communications may be executed anywhere in Canada under s. 188.1 and may include assistance orders under s. 487.02.

The *general* rule respecting *notification* of the objects of interception is contained in s. 196(1). The period is subject to extension under ss. 196(2)–(5).

The persons who intercept private communications in accordance with authorizations, as well as those who, *bona fide*, aid in any way a person believed, on reasonable grounds, to be acting with an authorization are saved from criminal liability for interception under s. 184(2)(b) and for possession of interception devices under s. 191(2)(b).

186. (1) Judge to be satisfied — An authorization under this section may be given if the judge to whom the application is made is satisfied

(a) that it would be in the best interests of the administration of justice to do so; and

(b) that other investigative procedures have been tried and have failed, other investigative procedures are unlikely to succeed or the urgency of the matter is such that it would be impractical to carry out the investigation of the offence using only other investigative procedures.

(1.1) Exception for criminal organizations — Notwithstanding paragraph (1)(*b*), that paragraph does not apply where the judge is satisfied that the application for an authorization is in relation to

(a) an offence under section 467.1; or

(b) an offence committed for the benefit of, at the direction of or in association with a criminal organization.

(2) Where authorization not to be given — No authorization may be given to intercept a private communication at the office or residence of a solicitor, or at any other place ordinarily used by a solicitor and by other solicitors for the purpose of consultation with clients, unless the judge to whom the application is made is satisfied that there are reasonable grounds to believe that the solicitor, any other solicitor practising with him, any person employed by him or any other such solicitor or a member of the solicitor's household has been or is about to become a party to an offence.

(3) Terms and conditions — Where an authorization is given in relation to the interception of private communications at a place described in subsection (2), the judge by whom the authorization is given shall include therein such terms and conditions as he considers advisable to protect privileged communications between solicitors and clients.

(4) Content and limitation of authorization — An authorization shall

(a) state the offence in respect of which private communications may be intercepted;

(b) state the type of private communication so that may be intercepted;

(c) state the identity of the persons, if known, whose private communications are to be intercepted, generally describe the place at which private communications may be intercepted, if a general description of that place can be given, and generally describe the manner of interception that may be used;

(d) contain such terms and conditions as the judge considers advisable in the public interest; and

(e) be valid for the period, not exceeding sixty days, set out therein.

(5) Persons designated — The Solicitor General of Canada or the Attorney General, as the case may be, may designate a person or persons who may intercept private communications under authorizations.

(5.1) Installation and removal of device — For greater certainty, an authorization that permits interception by means of an electro-magnetic, acoustic, mechanical or other device includes the authority to install, maintain or remove the device covertly.

(5.2) Removal after expiry of authorization — On an *ex parte* application, in writing, supported by affidavit, the judge who gave an authorization referred to in subsection (5.1) or any other judge having jurisdiction to give such an authorization may give a further authorization for the covert removal of the electro-magnetic, acoustic, mechanical or other device after the expiry of the original authorization

(a) under any terms or conditions that the judge considers advisable in the public interest; and

(b) during any specified period of not more than sixty days.

(6) Renewal of authorization — Renewals of an authorization may be given by a judge of a superior court of criminal jurisdiction or a judge as defined in section 552 on receipt by him of an *ex parte* application in writing signed by the Attorney General of the province in which the application is made or the Solicitor General of Canada or an agent specially designated in writing for the purposes of section 185 by the Solicitor

General of Canada or the Attorney General, as the case may be, accompanied by an affidavit of a peace officer or public officer deposing to the following matters:

(a) the reason and period for which the renewal is required,

(b) full particulars, together with times and dates, when interceptions, if any, were made or attempted under the authorization, and any information that has been obtained by any interception, and

(c) the number of instances, if any, on which, to the knowledge and belief of the deponent, an application has been made under this subsection in relation to the same authorization and on which the application was withdrawn or no renewal was given, the date on which each application was made and the name of the judge to whom each application was made,

and supported by such other information as the judge may require.

(7) Renewal — A renewal of an authorization may be given if the judge to whom the application is made is satisfied that any of the circumstances described in subsection (1) still obtain, but no renewal shall be for a period exceeding sixty days.

1973–74, c. 50, s. 2; 1976–77, c. 53, s. 9; 1993, c. 40, s. 6; 1997, c. 23, s. 5; 1999, c. 5, s. 5.

Commentary: The section describes the *basis* upon which and *form* in which *conventional authorizations* and *renewals* thereof may be granted by competent judicial authority.

The *conditions precedent* are described in s. 186. The authorizing judge must be satisfied that it would be in the *best interests of the administration of justice* to authorize such interceptions. This finding has *no* analogue in the affidavit requirements of ss. 185(1)(c)–(h). It is a determination to be made upon the whole of the affidavit material. The authorizing judge must also be satisfied that *one* of the conditions of *investigative necessity*, as described in s. 186(1)(b), has been met unless s. 186(1.1) applies. Subsection 186(1.1) waives the requirement that one of the conditions of investigative necessity in s. 186(1)(b) be met where the judge is satisfied that the application for authorization is in relation to a *criminal organization*. This finding is based on the affidavit material included by s. 185(1)(h).

Authorization *content* is governed by s. 186(4), a provision which, in large measure, tracks the affidavit requirements of ss. 185(1)(c)–(h).

The *offence* to be stated under s. 186(4)(a) must be an "offence" within s. 183. The *type of communication* to be intercepted must come within "private communication" as defined in the same section.

The requirements of s. 186(4)(c) are threefold. The *identity* of the objects of interception must be stated, *if known*. The provisions of s. 185(1)(e) may assist in this respect but are *not* mandatory. The *place of interception* must be generally described, if a general description may be given. The *manner of interception* must, in all cases, be generally described.

Under s. 186(4)(e) the authorization must state its *duration*, a period not exceeding 60 days. The authorizing judge may under s. 186(4)(d) impose such *terms and conditions* as s/he considers advisable in the public interest.

Section 186(2) generally prohibits authorization to intercept private communications at the office or residence of a *solicitor*, or at any other place generally used by solicitors for consultation with their clients. Exceptionally, however an authorization may be given to intercept such private communications where there are reasonable grounds of probable complicity of the nature described. In such circumstances s. 186(3) requires the inclusion of any conditions considered advisable to protect privileged communications between solicitors and clients.

Sections 186(6) and (7) describe the basis upon which *renewals* of authorizations to intercept private communications may, from time to time, be given. Under s. 186(6) application is made in writing to and by a competent authority, accompanied by an affidavit of a peace or public officer deposing to the matters described in ss. 186(6)(a)–(c). Further information may be required by the judge to whom the application is made. There is no express requirement concerning the form or substance of this information. Under s. 186(7), a renewal may be given where the judge is satisfied that *any* of the circumstances required to justify the granting of the original authorization continue to obtain.

The constitutional integrity of the section under *Charter* s. 8 has been sustained.

Case Law

Conditions Precedent: S. 186(1) [See also s. 185, "Affidavits", supra.]

R. v. Garofoli (1990), 80 C.R. (3d) 317, 60 C.C.C. (3d) 161 (S.C.C.); reversing (1988), 64 C.R. (3d) 193, 41 C.C.C. (3d) 97 (Ont. C.A.) — The statutory requirements of s. 186(1)(a) are identical to the constitutional requirements of *Charter* s. 8 which are applicable to the interception of private communications. The issuing judge must be satisfied that there are *reasonable and probable grounds*, established under oath, to *believe* that an *offence is being or has been committed* and that the interceptions proposed *will afford evidence* thereof. An applicant must also satisfy the investigative necessity requirement of s. 186(1)(b).

R. v. Rosebush (1992), 77 C.C.C. (3d) 241 (Alta. C.A.) — The fact that other investigative means were proceeding successfully in that a police informer was continually co-operative and promised to testify at any forthcoming trial did *not* mean that the investigative necessity requirement could not be met. Investigative necessity may anticipate the vicissitudes of proof at any forthcoming trial. The testimony of a police informer would predictably be attacked and contradicted by such evidentiary means as were available. The witness may not appear for trial and it is not inevitable that the evidence given at the preliminary inquiry could be read in under *Code* s. 715.P may resort to authorized interceptions to gather independent confirmatory, even corroborative evidence, where such evidence will be required by the realities of a forthcoming trial. Investigative necessity may include the gathering of independent and confirming evidence not reasonably available otherwise than by interception of private communications.

R. v. Araujo (1998), 127 C.C.C. (3d) 315 (B.C. C.A.); leave to appeal allowed (April 22, 1999), Doc. 26898, 26899, 26904, 26943, 26968 (S.C.C.) — The credibility of the police officer affiant does *not* impact on the objectively identifiable reasonable and probable grounds, or on the sufficiency of the evidence on the record as amplified on the review.

R. v. Cheung (1997), 119 C.C.C. (3d) 507 (B.C. C.A.); application for leave to appeal filed (November 19, 1997), Doc. No. 26327 (S.C.C.) — There is *no* requirement that the affiant have a *subjective* belief of the *reasonableness* of the grounds relied upon in support of the application. The authorizing judge may reach such a conclusion based on the facts set out in the affidavit.

R. v. Paulson (1995), 97 C.C.C. (3d) 344 (B.C. C.A.) — Investigative necessity under s. 186(1)(b) must be approached on a practical basis. That investigators have enough information to justify a charge does not *bar* continuation of the investigation upon showing proper grounds. An authorization is *not* barred because support for or corroboration of existing evidence might be obtained by future interceptions of private communications, provided there are reasonable, practical grounds to permit continuation of the investigation by interception of private communications. It is *a fortiori* where there is a reasonable expectation that evidence of a further offence may be obtained.

R. v. Smyk (1993), 86 C.C.C. (3d) 63 (Man. C.A.) — The authorizing judge, at a minimum, should be told of the nature, progress and difficulties in an investigation to ensure that interception of private communications is more than just a useful tool. (per Scott C.J.M., Philp J.A.)

R. v. Grant (1998), 130 C.C.C. (3d) 53 (Man. C.A.) — The issuing judge must be satisfied that there are reasonable and probable grounds to believe that a specific crime or conspiracy has been or is being committed prior to issuing an authorization. The judge must also be satisfied, on reasonable and probable grounds, that the authorization [*sic*] will provide evidence of that offence.

R. v. Tahirkheli (1998), 130 C.C.C. (3d) 19 (Ont. C.A.) — The authorizing judge need *only* be satisfied that investigative necessity has been shown with respect to the investigation as a whole, *not* with respect to each named object of interception.

Anticipated Offences: S. 186(1)

R. v. Grant (1998), 130 C.C.C. (3d) 53 (Man. C.A.) — An authorization may *not* be granted to *prevent* future criminal activity or uncover evidence of unknown crimes.

Solicitor-Client Conditions: Ss. 186(2), (3)

R. v. Taylor (1997), 121 C.C.C. (3d) 353 (B.C. C.A.); affirmed [1998] 1 S.C.R. 26, 121 C.C.C. (3d) 353 — Interception, at a cellular telephone distribution centre, of a call between a third party on a cellular telephone and D, a lawyer, does *not* violate s. 186(2).

R. v. Chambers (1983), 37 C.R. (3d) 128, 9 C.C.C. (3d) 132 (B.C. C.A.); affirmed on other grounds (1986), 52 C.R. (3d) 394, 26 C.C.C. (3d) 353 (S.C.C.) — A judge is *not required* but may impose terms protecting privileged solicitor-client communications.

R. v. Lyons (1979), 52 C.C.C. (2d) 113 (B.C. Co. Ct.); affirmed on other grounds (1982), 69 C.C.C. (2d) 318 (B.C. C.A.); which was affirmed (1985), 43 C.R. (3d) 97, 15 C.C.C. (3d) 318 (S.C.C.) — The onus is on D to lead evidence of a breach of the prohibition relating to solicitors. There is no onus on P to prove there has been no breach when primary evidence is tendered.

R. v. Paterson (1985), 44 C.R. (3d) 150, 18 C.C.C. (3d) 137 (Ont. C.A.) — Where an authorization permits the interception of private communications at the offices of a solicitor, the judge is *not* obliged to impose terms and conditions to protect privileged communications.

Authorization Content: S. 186(4) [See also ss. 188.1, 487.02]

R. v. Thompson (1990), 80 C.R. (3d) 129, 59 C.C.C. (3d) 225 (S.C.C.); reversing (1986), 53 C.R. (3d) 56, 29 C.C.C. (3d) 516 (B.C. C.A.) — Where the police are aware, prior to seeking an authorization, that the targets make extensive use of pay telephones, the authorizations, to comply with *Charter* s. 8 must, at a minimum, provide that conversations at *pay telephones* should *not* be intercepted *unless* there are *reasonable and probable grounds* to believe that a *target* is *using* the telephone at the time that the listening device is activated.

R. v. Thompson (1990), 80 C.R. (3d) 129, 59 C.C.C. (3d) 225 (S.C.C.); reversing (1986), 53 C.R. (3d) 56, 29 C.C.C. (3d) 516 (B.C. C.A.) — An authorizing judge's determination whether there are reasonable and probable grounds to believe the interception of an individual's private communication will assist the investigation can be made with respect to certain *classes of places* under s. 186.

R. v. Papalia (1988), 65 C.R. (3d) 226, 43 C.C.C. (3d) 129 (S.C.C.) — Although an *automobile* is a *place* within the meaning of s. 186(2)(c), an authorization that provided for the installation of devices at "locations both stationary or mobile for which there are reasonable and probable grounds to believe such locations may be used by any person or persons" was sufficient to cover the interception of communications in D's automobile.

R. v. Chesson (1988), 65 C.R. (3d) 193, 43 C.C.C. (3d) 353 (S.C.C.) — All "*known* persons" must be named as targets in the authorization or their private communications cannot be intercepted; the police cannot rely on the "basket clause" for interceptions of "known persons".

R. v. Paterson (1985), 44 C.R. (3d) 150 (Ont. C.A.); affirmed (1987), 60 C.R. (3d) 107 (S.C.C.) — A "basket clause" giving the police the discretion to intercept the private communications of any or all persons if reasonable grounds exist for a belief that an interception would assist the investigation of any offence specified in the authorization is invalid as constituting a delegation of the judge's function to the police. The clause, however, was severable and did not affect the validity of the balance of the authorization.

R. v. Grabowski (1985), 22 C.C.C. (3d) 449 (S.C.C.) — *See also*: *R. v. Lachance* (1990), 80 C.R. (3d) 374 (S.C.C.); reversing (1988), 27 O.A.C. 45 (C.A.) — An authorization employing the phrase "any other place or locality" effectively contains no limitation as to *persons* or *place* and is, therefore, invalid. However, where there is a clear dividing line between the good and the bad parts of an authorization, and the bad part is not so interwoven with the good part that it cannot be separated, the court may sever the authorization and preserve the valid portion.

Reference re an Application for an Authorization (1985), 15 C.C.C. (3d) 466 (S.C.C.) — A judge in issuing an authorization has jurisdiction, expressly to authorize any person acting under the authorization to enter any place at which private communications are proposed to be intercepted for the purpose of implementing the particular authorization.

Lyons v. R. (1985), 43 C.R. (3d) 97, 15 C.C.C. (3d) 318 (S.C.C.) — Although a court, in issuing an authorization, should, in the exercise of its supervisory function, designate the type of device or devices which may be employed and the procedures and conditions which, in the circumstances revealed in the application, are necessary or advisable in the public interest, the absence of such detail does not go to the validity of the order because in many circumstances only the general clauses of the subsections themselves will be appropriate.

R. v. Willock (1998), 127 C.C.C. (3d) 346 (Alta. C.A.) — An authorization may permit the interception of private communications of unknown persons who communicate over telephone lines at a place described in the authorization, even if the person was *not* present at the location, rather, only communicated from elsewhere.

R. v. Braithwaite (1986), 30 C.C.C. (3d) 348 (Alta. C.A.) — Authorizations providing for the interception of communications of *any* person at any place to which the person *may* resort are invalid as containing insufficient description. Such an authorization is *not* severable where, in addition to severance, an amendment would also be required, as the good and bad parts are so interwoven that they cannot be separated.

R. v. Newall (No. 1), [1984] 2 W.W.R. 131 (B.C. C.A.) — Authorizations that permit the interception of private communications of named persons at places they have "resorted to" are sufficient provided that evidence is led that the person in fact "resorted to" that place.

R. v. Murphy (1982), 69 C.C.C. (2d) 152 (B.C. C.A.); leave to appeal refused (1982), 43 N.R. 450n (S.C.C.) — There is *no* requirement that the authorization set forth a specific number of identifiable days to constitute a period of validity. An authorization stating that it was valid for a period not exceeding 30 days commencing on a specific date is valid.

Diamond v. R. (1982), 70 C.C.C. (2d) 148 (Man. C.A.); affirming *(*sub nom. *Glesby v. R.)* 66 C.C.C. (2d) 332 — An authorization which provides for the interception of "private communications as hereunder specified and for such purposes to take all steps as are reasonably necessary to install, make use of, monitor and remove any electro-magnetic, acoustic, mechanical and other device as may be required to implement this authorization" complies with s. 186(4)(c) in that it substantially and generally describes the *manner of interception* that was to be used, namely, a telephone or telecommunication interception.

R. v. Musitano (1985), 24 C.C.C. (3d) 65 (Ont. C.A.); leave to appeal refused (1987), 79 N.R. 79n (S.C.C.) — An authorization containing a *basket* clause which included other *persons* who *might act* in concert with any of those persons specifically named in the authorization in the commission of specified offences was held to be valid with respect to the interception of communications between D and his former girlfriend. The girlfriend had *not* been specifically named in the authorization because the police were under the impression that D had separated from her. There was *no* improper delegation to the police of the power to select whose communications should be intercepted or where the interception should be made.

R. v. Samson (1983), 36 C.R. (3d) 126 (Ont. C.A.) — A judge may grant an authorization which includes the interception of unnamed and unknown persons.

R. v. Mathurin (1978), 41 C.C.C. (2d) 263 (Que. C.A.) — The "offence" may be described in generic terms.

Place of Interception: S. 186(4)(c) [Now see s. 188.1]

R. v. Thompson (1990), 80 C.R. (3d) 129, 59 C.C.C. (3d) 225 (S.C.C.); reversing (1986), 53 C.R. (3d) 56, 29 C.C.C. (3d) 516 (B.C. C.A.) — *See also: R. v. Niles* (1978), 40 C.C.C. 512 (Ont. C.A.) — An intercepted private communication cannot itself provide evidence that a person "resorted to" a place of interception, thereby justify its own admission. Other evidence must be adduced, including prior lawfully intercepted private communications, to indicate that the location was a place resorted to or used by the target.

R. v. Moore, R. v. Bogdanich (1993), 21 C.R. (4th) 387, 81 C.C.C. (3d) 161 (B.C. C.A.) — Once a premises has been identified as a place to which named targets resorted to during the first authorization, it should be disclosed to the authorizing judge on an application for a second authorization under *Code* s. 185(1)(e). The "resort to" clause of the first authorization cannot be relied upon to continue interceptions at the identified premises under the second authorization.

Designation of Interceptors: S. 186(5)

R. v. Shaw (1983), 4 C.C.C. (3d) 348 (N.B. C.A.) — An "interceptor" need *not* be designated in an authorization. Persons who participate in the interceptions must be acting under the authority of the designated "interceptor". It is *not* necessary for a person to be present at all times to monitor the equipment. Interceptions automatically made by the equipment are admissible.

R. v. Vrany (1979), 46 C.C.C. (2d) 14 (Ont. C.A.) — The designation of the Commanding Officer of "O" Division of the R.C.M.P. or any person acting under his/her authority does not require that the person so acting under his/her authority be specifically and personally authorized by the Commanding

Officer. Such a designation is broad enough to include a person acting within the scope or ambit of the general authority conferred on him/her by the Commanding Officer.

Renewal of Authorization: Ss. 186(6), (7)

R. v. Thompson (1990), 80 C.R. (3d) 129, 59 C.C.C. (3d) 225 (S.C.C.); reversing (1986), 53 C.R. (3d) 56, 29 C.C.C. (3d) 516 (B.C. C.A.) — *Renewal* of an existing authorization is appropriate where it is sought to extend its term but leave its provisions otherwise unchanged. *Fresh authorization* should be obtained where an authorization has expired or it is sought to extend the scope of the surveillance.

R. v. Moore, R. v. Bogdanich (1993), 21 C.R. (4th) 387, 81 C.C.C. (3d) 161 (B.C. C.A.) — Section 186(6), applicable to renewals, does *not* apply to applications for *fresh* authorization. The requirements of an application for authorization are found in s. 185. The supportive affidavit must disclose the facts relied on to justify the belief that an authorization should be given. Each and every investigative step taken by the police up to the time of the application need *not* be disclosed. There must be, however, full, fair and frank disclosure of the investigative steps taken by the police, including disclosure of relevant intercepted private communications up to the time of the application.

R. v. Turangan (1976), 32 C.C.C. (2d) 249 (B.C. S.C.), appeal dismissed on jurisdictional grounds 32 C.C.C. (2d) 254n (B.C. C.A.) — The provincial Attorney General cannot apply to renew an authorization given to the federal authorities, nor can the federal representatives apply to renew an authorization given to the province.

R. v. Dass (1979), 8 C.R. (3d) 29, 47 C.C.C. (2d) 194 (Man. C.A.); leave to appeal refused (1979), 30 N.R. 609n (S.C.C.) — It is proper to *renew* the original authorization in respect of one named individual but not renew concerning others named in the original order. Similarly, with respect to locations, the renewal may be made for some of the locations but not for all. However, the renewal may not add a new location by changing one of the addresses.

R. v. Dubois (1986), 27 C.C.C. (3d) 325 (Ont. C.A.) — A renewal cannot add terms to the authorization sought to be renewed; it can only extend the period of time within which it is effective. Where it is necessary to broaden the terms of an authorization, a new authorization may be obtained which covers not only the original offences but adds new ones.

R. v. Pleich (1980), 16 C.R. (3d) 194, 55 C.C.C. (2d) 13 (Ont. C.A.) — A renewal can be made only during the period of the authorization, otherwise a new authorization is required. In the application for a new authorization reference must be made to the previous authorization and the interceptions made thereunder.

R. v. Nicolucci (1990), 53 C.C.C. (3d) 546 (Que. C.A.) — It is not unlawful to seek a new authorization, as opposed to a renewal, when new locations are sought to be added to the original authorization.

Review of Authorization [See s. 189]

Charter Considerations

R. v. Garofoli (1990), 80 C.R. (3d) 317, 60 C.C.C. (3d) 161 (S.C.C.); reversing (1988), 64 C.R. (3d) 193, 41 C.C.C. (3d) 97 (Ont. C.A.) — *See also*: *R. v. Thompson* (1990), 80 C.R. (3d) 129, 59 C.C.C. (3d) 225 (S.C.C.); reversing (1986), 53 C.R. (3d) 56, 29 C.C.C. (3d) 516 (B.C. C.A.) — The interception of private communications constitutes a search or seizure under *Charter* s. 8. The statutory requirements of s. 186(1)(a) are, however, identical to those demanded by s. 8 in that there must be *reasonable and probable grounds*, established under oath, to believe that an *offence is being or has been committed* and that the *interceptions* proposed *will afford evidence* thereof.

Related Provisions: "Intercept", "offence", "private communication" and "solicitor" are defined in s. 183, "Attorney General" in s. 2.

Section 188 describes the circumstances under which emergency (36-hour) authorization may be given. Section 187 provides the manner in which documents relating to an application under s. 185 are to be kept, opened, copied, and distributed.

Consent authorizations may be sought and obtained in accordance with s. 184.2 and 184.3. Under s. 184.6, any application for authorization under Part VI may include both private communications and radio-based telephone communications. The authorization issued may do likewise.

Authorizations to intercept private communications may be executed anywhere in Canada under s. 188.1 and may include assistance orders under s. 487.02.

The interception of private communications in accordance with an authorization relieves the interceptor, as well as any person who in good faith aids in any way a person who s/he believes, on reasonable grounds, is acting with an authorization, of criminal liability for the interception under s. 184(2)(b). Under s. 191(2)(b), possession of an electro-magnetic, acoustic, mechanical or other device, for the purpose of using it to make authorized interceptions, is not an offence. Disclosure of authorized interceptions may, however, attract liability under s. 193.

The *interception* of private communications is a *search or seizure*, hence is subject to *Charter* s. 8. Admissibility is governed by *Charter* s. 24(2). Section 189(5) enacts a *notice* requirement when primary evidence is tendered for admission. Section 189(6) preserves any existing *privilege* that would otherwise have been destroyed upon interception.

Other *Related Provisions* are described in the corresponding note to s. 185, *supra*.

186.1 Time limitation in relation to criminal organizations — Notwithstanding paragraph 184.2(4)(*e*) and 186(4)(*e*) and subsection 186(7), an authorization or any renewal of an authorization may be valid for one or more periods specified in the authorization exceeding sixty days, each not exceeding one year, where the authorization is in relation to

(a) an offence under section 467.1; or

(b) an offence committed for the benefit of, at the direction of or in association with criminal organization.

1997, c. 23, s. 6.

Commentary: This section overrides the general rules that prescribe the periods for which consent and conventional authorizations and renewals may be in force.

When the authorizations or renewals relate to a *criminal organization offence* (s. 467.1), or an offence committed for the *benefit* or at the *direction* of or in *association* with a criminal organization, the relevant interception period is one year, not sixty days.

Related Provisions: The offences described in ss. 186.1(a) and (b) are contained in the definition of "offence" in s. 183.

Sections 185(1.1) and 186(1.1) remove any requirement that the supportive *affidavit* contain reference to or the authorizing judge make a discrete *finding* of investigate necessity as a condition precedent to granting a conventional authorization in relation to criminal organization offences.

The provision seems ripe for s. 8 *Charter* challenge.

187. (1) Manner in which application to be kept secret — All documents relating to an application made pursuant to any provision of this Part are confidential and, subject to subsection (1.1), shall be placed in a packet and sealed by the judge to whom the application is made immediately on determination of the application, and that packet shall be kept in the custody of the court in a place to which the public has no access or in such other place as the judge may authorize and shall not be dealt with except in accordance with subsections (1.2) to (1.5).

(1.1) **Exception** — An authorization given under this Part need not be placed in the packet except where, pursuant to subsection 184.3(7) or (8), the original authorization is in the hands of the judge, in which case that judge must place it in the packet and the facsimile remains with the applicant.

(1.2) **Opening for further applications** — The sealed packet may be opened and its contents removed for the purpose of dealing with an application for a further authorization or with an application for renewal of an authorization.

(1.3) **Opening on order of judge** — A provincial court judge, a judge of a superior court of criminal jurisdiction or a judge as defined in section 552 may order that the sealed packet be opened and its contents removed for the purpose of copying and examining the documents contained in the packet.

(1.4) Opening on order of trial judge — A judge or provincial court judge before whom a trial is to be held and who has jurisdiction in the province in which an authorization was given may order that the sealed packet be opened and its contents removed for the purpose of copying and examining the documents contained in the packet if

(a) any matter relevant to the authorization or any evidence obtained pursuant to the authorization is in issue in the trial; and

(b) the accused applies for such an order for the purpose of consulting the documents to prepare for trial.

(1.5) Order for destruction of documents — Where a sealed packet is opened, its contents shall not be destroyed except pursuant to an order of a judge of the same court as the judge who gave the authorization.

(2) Order of judge — An order under subsection (1.2), (1.3), (1.4) or (1.5) made with respect to documents relating to an application made pursuant to section 185 or subsection 186(6) or 196(2) may only be made after the Attorney General or the Solicitor General by whom or on whose authority the application for the authorization to which the order relates was made has been given an opportunity to be heard.

(3) Idem — An order under subsection (1.2), (1.3), (1.4) or (1.5) made with respect to documents relating to an application made pursuant to subsection 184.2(2) or section 184.3 may only be made after the Attorney General has been given an opportunity to be heard.

(4) Editing of copies — Where a prosecution has been commenced and an accused applies for an order for the copying and examination of documents pursuant to subsection (1.3) or (1.4), the judge shall not, notwithstanding those subsections, provide any copy of any document to the accused until the prosecutor has deleted any part of the copy of the document that the prosecutor believes would be prejudicial to the public interest, including any part that the prosecutor believes could

(a) compromise the identity of any confidential informant;

(b) compromise the nature and extent of ongoing investigations;

(c) endanger persons engaged in particular intelligence-gathering techniques and thereby prejudice future investigations in which similar techniques would be used; or

(d) prejudice the interests of innocent persons.

(5) Accused to be provided of documents — After the prosecutor has deleted the parts of the copy of the document to be given to the accused under subsection (4), the accused shall be provided with an edited copy of the document.

(6) Original documents to be returned — After the accused has received an edited copy of a document, the prosecutor shall keep a copy of the original document, and an edited copy of the document and the original document shall be returned to the packet and the packet resealed.

(7) Deleted parts — An accused to whom an edited copy of a document has been provided pursuant to subsection (5) may request that the judge before whom the trial is to be held order that any part of the document deleted by the prosecutor be made available to the accused, and the judge shall order that a copy of any part that, in the

opinion of the judge, is required in order for the accused to make full answer and defence and for which the provision of a judicial summary would not be sufficient, be made available to the accused.

1973–74, c. 50, s. 2; R.S. 1985, c. 27 (1st Supp.), s. 24; 1993, c. 40, s. 7.

Commentary: This section enacts a comprehensive scheme of disclosure of the contents of documents relating to applications under Part VI. In many respects, it gives statutory effect to the decisions in *R. v. Garofoli* (1990), 80 C.R. (3d) 317, 60 C.C.C. (3d) 161 (S.C.C.) and *Dersch v. Canada (Attorney General)* (1990), 80 C.R. (3d) 299, 60 C.C.C. (3d) 132 (S.C.C.).

Under s. 187(1), all documents relating to any application under Part VI are *confidential*. Upon determination of the application, the documents are to be placed in a packet and sealed by the judge to whom the application was made. Under s. 187(1.1), an *authorization* need *not* be placed in the packet unless granted under s. 184.3(7) or (8), in which case the original authorization is placed in the packet and the facsimile given to the applicant. The packets are kept in the custody of the court in a place to which the public has no access or as otherwise directed by the authorizing judge.

The procedure for opening the packet, removing, copying, examining and disclosing its contents involves several steps.

Under s. 187(1.2), the *sealed* packet may be *opened* and its *contents removed* to deal with applications for *further authorization or renewal* of an authorization. Section 187(1.5) prohibits destruction of the contents without an order of a judge of the authorizing court. Where the application is made with respect to documents relating to a conventional authorization or renewal, or deferral of notification of the objects of interception, an opportunity must be given to the Attorney General or Solicitor General under whose authority the original application for authorization was made to be heard. Where the order sought under s. 187(1.2) relates to documents relating to an application for consent authorization under ss. 184.2 or 184.3, the Attorney General must be given an opportunity to be heard under s. 187(3).

Under s. 187(1.3), *a provincial court* judge, judge of the *superior court* of criminal jurisdiction or a judge as defined in *Code* s. 552 may order the *opening* of a sealed packet and the *removal* of its contents for the *purpose* of *copying and examining* them. The subsection is silent concerning the basis upon which the order may be sought and/or made. The provisions of s. 187(2) and (3) ensure that the Attorney General or Solicitor General has the opportunity to be heard before an order is made under s. 187(1.3).

Section 187(1.4) also authorizes application for an order opening a sealed packet and removing its contents for *copying and examining*. Application must be made to a *provincial court* judge or *judge* before whom a *trial* is to be held and who has jurisdiction in the province where the authorization was given. The order may be made if the judge is satisfied that the requirements of s. 187(1.4)(a) and (b) have been met. In essence, the discretion is engaged where D is the applicant and seeks the order to consult the documents to prepare for trial where any matters relevant to the authorization or evidence obtained under it are at issue. The purpose of the order would appear to be to ensure that D is able to challenge the admissibility of primary, perhaps derivative evidence at trial. The Attorney General or Solicitor General must be given the opportunity to be heard under s. 187(2) or (3), as the case may be.

In most cases, an order will be sought under either s. 187(1.3) or (1.4) after a prosecution has commenced against the applicant, D. Under s. 187(4), D will *not* be provided a copy of any document until P has deleted from it any part which P believes would be prejudicial to the public interest. What may be deleted may include, but is not limited to, any part that P believes could

i.   compromise the *identity* of any *confidential informant*;

ii.   compromise the *nature and extent* of ongoing *investigations*;

iii.   endanger persons engaged in particular *intelligence-gathering techniques* and thereby prejudice future investigations in which similar techniques would be used; or,

iv.   prejudice the interests of *innocent* persons.

The subsection, while elucidating the *factors* which P may consider in editing, provides *no* guidance concerning the *procedure* to be followed. When P's editing has been completed, D will receive an edited copy of the affidavit under s. 187(5). P is to retain a copy of the original document. An edited copy of the document and the original are returned to the packet and the packet resealed under s. 187(6).

Under s. 187(7), having received an edited copy of the documents relating to the Part VI application, D may request of the trial judge further disclosure of the edited material. The trial judge must decide whether what is sought is required for D to make full answer and defence and, further, whether a judicial summary of the edited material would be sufficient. D will receive the edited material if it is required to make full answer and defence and a judicial summary would be inadequate. *Semble*, if the material is required and a judicial summary would be adequate for such purpose, D will be provided with the judicial summary.

Case Law

Opening of Sealed Packet: General Principles [*Decided under former law]

*Michaud v. Quebec (Attorney General) (1996), 109 C.C.C. (3d) 289 (S.C.C.) — The pre-*Charter* interpretation of [former] s. 187(1)(a)(ii) prevails in relation to former surveillance targets who are *not* accused. The predominant consideration in such cases is packet confidentiality. To obtain access, an interested non-accused party must *demonstrate more than* a mere *suspicion* of police wrongdoing. The applicant, as a rule, must produce some evidence which suggests that the authorization was procured through *fraud* or *wilful* non-disclosure by police. The imposition of such a standard in relation to non-accused targets does *not* contravene *Charter* s. 8. (per Lamer C.J., L'Heureux-Dubé, Gonthier, McLachlin, Iacobucci JJ.)

A judge may examine the contents of the packets in private in order to determine an application under [former] s. 187(1)(a)(ii). The confidentiality interests which underlie the provision are *not* implicated when a competent judicial authority examines the packet contents *in camera*. (per Lamer C.J., L'Heureux-Dubé, Gonthier, McLachlin and Iacobucci JJ.)

Under [former] s. 187, Parliametn conferred an unlimited *discretion* on courts to determine the circumstances in which access to the sealed packet is justified and the extent to which it should be authorized. Access is *not* limited to accused targets. *Charter* s. 8 affords an equivalent right of access to sealed packets to all targets, accused and non-accused, subject to the authority to edit on grounds of public policy. (per La Forest, Sopinka, Cory and Major JJ.)

The right of *any* target to access to the sealed packet is not absolute. It may be limited when it is in the *public's interest* to do so. Documents in the sealed packet may be edited in accordance with the *Garofoli* criteria and procedure. (per La Forest, Sopinka, Cory and Major JJ.)

The non-accused former surveillance target has *no Code* procedure to obtain disclosure of recording materials. Disclosure of packet contents under [former] s. 187(1)(a)(ii) does *not* include recording materials. A non-accused target who obtains access to the packet under [former] s. 187(1)(a)(ii) may seek access to the recording materials upon a new motion in a subsequent proceeding. (per Lamer C.J., L'Heureux-Dubé, Gonthier, McLachlin and Iacobucci JJ.)

Access to the sealed packet does *not* entail access to the recordings. Where an authorization has been declared invalid, however, wiretaps carried out pursuant to it are unlawful and in breach of *Charter* s. 8. Once an applicant has demonstrated that a wiretap was unauthorized, s/he is entitled to access to any communications to which the target was a party unlawfully intercepted by the state through,

i.   the recordings;

ii.   a transcript of the recordings; or

iii.   any other equivalent source.

All traces of such unlawful interceptions are to be destroyed by the state.

Where a court finds that,

i.   the authorization complies with the *Code* requirements; and,

ii.   the non-accused targets' arguments based on the contents of the sealed packet do *not* disclose any other cause of unlawfulness,

Charter s. 8 requires further examination whether the wiretaps complied with the authorization. The rights of *Charter* s. 8 are adequately protected by granting the non-accused target indirect access to the recordings. Access to the recordings is rarely given. The challenge to the validity of the wiretap must be made through the affidavits, relevant documents and by cross-examination of the affiants. Where the wiretap is found to be unlawful for failure to comply with the authorization, the target may obtain access to the recordings to which s/he is a party.

Section 187 does *not* limit access to the sealed packets to accused targets. The legislative framework imposed on the exercise of discretion applies *only* with respect to applications for access by accused targets, *not* to applications by other persons. (per La Forest, Sopinka, Cory and Major JJ.)

*R. v. Garofoli (1988), 64 C.R. (3d) 193, 41 C.C.C. (3d) 97 (Ont. C.A.); reversed on other grounds (1990), 80 C.R. (3d) 317, 60 C.C.C. (3d) 161 (S.C.C.) — Under s. 683(1)(a) the court of appeal has jurisdiction to open the sealed packet on an appeal from conviction.

Editing Procedure

R. v. Laws (1998), 18 C.R. (5th) 257, 128 C.C.C. (3d) 516 (Ont. C.A.) — Submissions to the trial judge about *editing* wiretap affidavits are to be made in *open court*, unless D consents under *Code* s. 650(2)(b). Where D is wrongly excluded, s. 650(1) is breached. Section 686(1)(b)(iv) does *not* apply, at all events, because of the perceived unfairness of the procedure.

Related Provisions: Under Part VI, application may be made for authorization to intercept private communications or radio-based telephone communications under ss. 184.2 and 184.3 (consent authorizations), 186 (conventional authorizations and renewals) and 188 (emergency authorizations). Application may also be made under s. 196(2) and (5) to defer notification of the objects of interception made under conventional authorization.

The phrase "a judge ... before whom a trial is to be held ..." in s. 187(1.4) appears sufficiently expansive to permit early designation of a trial judge to hear and determine the s. 187 application, as for example, under s. 645(5), thereby reducing trial discontinuity. Where D seeks disclosure *prior to preliminary* inquiry in order to develop an evidentiary basis for exclusion of primary evidence at trial, application should be made to a provincial court judge under s. 187(1.3) who will apply s. 187(4)–(6), but *not* s. 187(7) which gives jurisdiction to the trial judge only. D will *not* be entitled to *Charter* relief at the inquiry, however, under *R. v. Mills* (1986), 52 C.R. (3d) 1, 26 C.C.C. (3d) 481 (S.C.C.).

Consent authorizations given under ss. 184.2 and 184.3 are *not* commenced by an application of an agent of the Attorney General of the province or Solicitor General of Canada. The Attorney General must, nonetheless, be afforded an opportunity to be heard under s. 187(3).

The evidentiary rules applicable to evidence obtained by authorization are described in *Commentary* to s. 189, *infra*.

188. (1) Authorizations in emergency — Notwithstanding section 185, an application made under that section for an authorization may be made *ex parte* to a judge of a superior court of criminal jurisdiction, or a judge as defined in section 552, designated from time to time by the Chief Justice, by a peace officer specially designated in writing, by name or otherwise, for the purposes of this section by

(a) the Solicitor General of Canada, if the offence is one in respect of which proceedings, if any, may be instituted by the Government of Canada and conducted by or on behalf of the Attorney General of Canada, or

(b) the Attorney General of a province, in respect of any other offence in the province,

if the urgency of the situation requires interception of private communications to commence before an authorization could, with reasonable diligence, be obtained under section 186.

(2) Certain interceptions deemed not lawful — Where the judge to whom an application is made pursuant to subsection (1) is satisfied that the urgency of the situation requires that interception of private communications commence before an authorization could, with reasonable diligence, be obtained under section 186, he may, on such terms and conditions, if any, as he considers advisable, give an authorization in writing for a period of up to thirty-six hours.

(3) [Repealed 1993, c 40, s. 8.]

(4) Definition of "chief justice" — In this section, "Chief Justice" means

(a) in the Province of Ontario, the Chief Justice of the Ontario Court;

(b) in the Province of Quebec, the Chief Justice of the Superior Court;

(c) in the Provinces of Nova Scotia and British Columbia, the Chief Justice of the Supreme Court;

(d) in the Provinces of New Brunswick, Manitoba, Saskatchewan and Alberta, the Chief Justice of the Court of Queen's Bench;

(e) in the Provinces of Prince Edward Island and Newfoundland, the Chief Justice of the Supreme Court, Trial Division; and;

(f) in the Yukon Territory, the Northwest Territories and Nunavut, the senior judge within the meaning of subsection 22(3) of the *Judges Act.*

(5) Inadmissibility of evidence — The trial judge may deem inadmissible the evidence obtained by means of an interception of a private communication pursuant to a subsequent authorization given under this section, where he finds that the application for the subsequent authorization was based on the same facts, and involved the interception of the private communications of the same person or persons, or related to the same offence, on which the application for the original authorization was based.

1973–74, c. 50, s. 2; 1974–75–76, c. 19, s. 1; 1978–79, c. 11, s. 10;R.S. 1985, c. 27 (1st Supp.), s. 25; c. 27 (2d Supp.), Sched., item 6; 1990, c. 17, s. 10; 1992, c. 1, s. 58(1), Sched. I, item 4; 1992, c. 51, s. 35; 1993, c. 28, s. 78 (Sched. III, item 29) [Repealed 1999, c. 3, (Sched., item 6).]; 1993, c. 40, s. 8; 1999, c. 3, s. 28.

Commentary: The section describes the basis upon which application may be made and order given authorizing the interception of private communications in circumstances of *emergency*.

Subsection (1) furnishes the authority to apply for an *emergency authorization*. The procedure is initiated by an *ex parte* application to a judge of the superior court of criminal jurisdiction or as defined in s. 552 designated from time to time by the Chief Justice, as defined in s. 188(4). The applicant must be a peace or public officer, specially designated in writing for the purposes of the section by the Solicitor General of Canada or Attorney General of a province, in accordance with ss. 188(1)(a) and (b). The application may be made *if* the urgency of the situation requires interception of private communications to commence before a conventional authorization could, with reasonable diligence, be obtained.

Section 188(2) describes the basis upon which an emergency authorization may be given and, to a lesser extent, its terms. The authorizing judge must be satisfied that the *urgency* of the situation *requires* that *interception commence before a conventional (60-day) authorization could, with reasonable diligence, be obtained.* An emergency authorization must be *in writing*, may be for a period of *up to 36 hours*, and may include such terms and conditions, if any, as the authorizing judge considers advisable.

Section 188(5) enacts an *evidentiary rule* which relates to *primary* evidence obtained under a subsequent *emergency* authorization. The rule permits exclusion of the primary evidence where the trial judge finds that the application for the subsequent emergency authorization under which the evidence was obtained was based on the same facts, and involved the same object(s) of interception, or related to the same offence, as the original authorization.

Case Law [Cases decided prior to amendment]

R. v. Galbraith (1989), 70 C.R. (3d) 392, 49 C.C.C. (3d) 178 (Alta. C.A.) — *See also: R. v. Laudicina* (1990), 53 C.C.C. (3d) 281 (Ont. H.C.) — Although the section does *not* require that the *information* provided to the issuing judge be *on oath*, an authorization obtained *without* oral testimony on oath or confirmation of the written information under oath is *invalid* under *Charter* s. 8.

Section 188 must be strictly construed. The applicant officer, rather than the position he occupies, must be designated by the Solicitor General.

Related Provisions: "Superior court criminal jurisdiction" and "peace officer" are defined in s. 2, "authorization", "intercept", "offence" and "private communication" in s. 183.

The reference in s. 188(1) to s. 185 and "an application made under *that* section" would appear intended to make an emergency authorization a form of conventional authorization which is given in circumstances of urgency for a limited time. It would seem to follow that an affidavit compliant with s. 185(1)(c)–(h), ought to be submitted in support of the application for emergency authorization. The supportive affidavit should also disclose the circumstances of urgency which will support the finding necessary under s. 188(2). The mandatory terms of a conventional authorization are described in s. 186(4) and should appear in a s. 188 order. An emergency authorization may also permit interception of radio-based telephone communications under ss. 184.5(2) and 184.6. The order may be executed anywhere in Canada under s. 188.1 and include an assistance order under s. 487.02.

The provisions of s. 188(3) deeming certain interceptions *not* to have been *lawfully* made is for section 189 evidentiary purposes only. Section 184(2)(b) excepts such interceptional activity from liability under s. 184(1). A similar result is achieved by s. 191(2)(b) in relation to the possession offence under s. 191(1). Liability for unlawful disclosure may nonetheless be established under s. 193(1).

The evidentiary rules which apply in cases of primary evidence are described in the *Commentary* to s. 189, *infra*.

188.1 (1) Execution of authorizations — Subject to subsection (2), the interception of a private communication authorized pursuant to section 184.2, 184.3, 186 or 188 may be carried out anywhere in Canada.

(2) Execution in another province — Where an authorization is given under section 184.2, 184.3, 186 or 188 in one province but it may reasonably be expected that it is to be executed in another province and the execution of the authorization would require entry into or upon the property of any person in the other province or would require that an order under section 487.02 be made with respect to any person in that other province, a judge in the other province may, on application, confirm the authorization and when the authorization is so confirmed, it shall have full force and effect in that other province as though it had originally been given in that other province.

1993, c. 40, s. 9.

Commentary: This section permits *execution* of any authorization given under Part VI *anywhere* in Canada.

The general rule is stated in s. 188.1(1). Authorized interception of private communications may be carried out anywhere in Canada. In terms, s. 188.1(1) is subservient to s. 188.1(2) which requires that an authorization given in one province be "backed" to permit execution in another province in defined circumstances. "Backing" is required where an authorization given in one province may reasonably be expected to be executed in another province and the execution in the other province

i.   would require entry into or upon the property of any person in the other province; or,

ii.   would require a s. 487.02 assistance order with respect to any person in the other province.

"Backing" consists of confirmation of the authorization given by a judge in the other province in which it is to be executed. Its effect is to give the authorization elsewhere issued the same force and effect as though it had originally been given in the province of execution. Absent the circumstances described in items i and ii, *supra*, extra-provincial execution is permitted under s. 188.1(1) without "backing".

Case Law

General Principles

R. v. Pham (1997), 122 C.C.C. (3d) 90 (B.C. C.A.); leave to appeal refused (1998), 128 C.C.C. (3d) vi (S.C.C.) — To implement in British Columbia an Ontario authorization which permits interception in British Columbia, a *confirmation* order under s. 188.1 is *only* required where execution of the authorization would require

i.   *entry* into or upon the property of someone in British Columbia; or

ii.   an *assistance* order under s. 487.2.

No confirmation order is required where telephone company personnel are prepared to help without an assistance order.

Related Provisions: The procedure described in s. 188.1(2) is analogous to that of s. 487(2) in relation to search warrants and s. 487.03 in relation to general investigative (s. 487.01), tracking (s. 492.1) and number recorder (s. 492.2) warrants. The endorsement for extra-provincial execution should appear on the relevant warrant or authorization.

No statutory provision expressly permits the inclusion of an entry clause in an authorization. Neither does the Part describe the materials to be filed in support of an application for an order for extra-provincial execution under s. 188.1(2). An assistance order may be made under s. 487.02.

The general rule of s. 188.1(1) and the specific provisions of s. 188.1(2) apply to all authorizations issued under Part VI.

188.2 No civil or criminal liability — No person who acts in accordance with an authorization or under section 184.1 or 184.4 or who aids, in good faith, a person who he or she believes on reasonable grounds is acting in accordance with an authorization or under one of those sections incurs any criminal or civil liability for anything reasonably done further to the authorization or to that section.

1993, c. 40, s. 9.

Commentary: This provision saves from civil and criminal liability anyone who acts in accordance with any authorization given under Part VI, and further anyone who aids, in good faith, a person the aider believes, on reasonable grounds, is acting in accordance with an authorization, to the extent of anything reasonably done further to the authorization. Equivalent protection is offered to those who intercept without authorization under ss. 184.1 and 184.4, as well those who aid them on the basis just discussed.

Related Provisions: Authorization to intercept private communications may be granted under ss. 184.2 and 184.3 (consent authorizations), 186 (conventional authorizations and renewals) and 188 (emergency authorizations). A single authorization may permit interception of both private communications and radio-based telephone communications under ss. 184.5(2) and 184.6. Authorizations may be executed anywhere in Canada in accordance with s. 188.1 and include assistance orders under s. 487.02.

Interceptions made in accordance with judicial authorization, or under s. 184.4 are exempt from criminal liability under s. 184(2)(b). Those made with the consent of a party to the communication, as for example under s. 184.1, are exempt under s. 184(2)(a).

Use or disclosure of intercepted private communications may attract liability under s. 193(1). The comparable offence in respect of radio-based telephone communications is s. 193.1(1).

189. (1)–(4) [Repealed 1993, c. 40, s. 10.]

(5) Notice of intention to produce evidence — The contents of a private communication that is obtained from an interception of the private communication pursuant to any provision of, or pursuant to an authorization given under, this Part shall not be received in evidence unless the party intending to adduce it has given to the accused reasonable notice of the intention together with

(a) a transcript of the private communication, where it will be adduced in the form of a recording, or a statement setting out full particulars of the private communication, where evidence of the private communication will be given *viva voce*; and

(b) a statement respecting the time, place and date of the private communication and the parties thereto, if known.

(6) Privileged evidence — Any information obtained by an interception that, but for the interception, would have been privileged remains privileged and inadmissible as evidence without the consent of the person enjoying the privilege.

1973–74, c. 50, s. 2; 1976–77, c. 53, s. 10; R.S. 1985, c. 27 (1st Supp.), s. 203; 1993, c. 40, s. 10.

Commentary: The *notice* provisions of s. 189(5) apply whenever *primary* evidence is tendered for admission. They are *not* limited, as had earlier been the case, to private communications that were lawfully intercepted. The rule is generally exclusionary. It bars reception of the contents of *any* private communication that has been obtained by interception pursuant to any authorization or other provision of Part VI *unless* the party intending to adduce the evidence has given *reasonable notice* to D of the *intention* to do so, together with the form of *disclosure* required by s. 189(5)(a) or (b), whichever is applicable.

Section 189(6) preserves the privileged character of any primary evidence to which a recognized privilege attaches. The subsection does *not* itself create privilege where none exists, rather preserves what otherwise would be lost through the process of interception.

The *interception* of private communications is a *search* or *seizure*, hence is subject to the requirement of reasonableness inherent in *Charter* s. 8. Where D asserts that primary evidence should be excluded for *Charter* infringement, D is required to establish, on a balance of probabilities,

i.   that the *interceptions* made were in *breach* of *Charter* s. 8;

ii.   that the *primary* evidence was *obtained* in a *manner* that infringed s. 8 *Charter* rights; and,

iii.   that the *admission* of the evidence *could* bring the administration of justice into disrepute.

Case Law [All cases decided under former section (except *)]

General Principles of Review and Editing

R. v. Durette (1994), 28 C.R. (4th) 1, 88 C.C.C. (3d) 1 (S.C.C.) — When determining whether the contents of the supportive affidavit should be disclosed to D, full disclosure should be the rule, subject only to certain exceptions based on overriding public interests that may justify non-disclosure. Editing should only be to the extent necessary to protect the overriding public interest.

R. v. Durette (1994), 28 C.R. (4th) 1, 88 C.C.C. (3d) 1 (S.C.C.) — Where *over-editing* of the supportive affidavit is demonstrated, D have established, *prima facie*, that their ability to make full answer and defence has been prejudiced. Denial of the opportunity to test fully the validity of the authorization prejudices D's right to make full answer and defence. D is *not* required to demonstrate the specific use to be made of the undisclosed information which D has not seen.

R. v. Garofoli (1990), 80 C.R. (3d) 317, 60 C.C.C. (3d) 161 (S.C.C.); reversing (1987), 64 C.R. (3d) 193, 41 C.C.C. (3d) 97 (Ont. C.A.) — It is the *trial judge* who must determine whether a search or seizure is reasonable and evidence thereof admissible. To determine whether a search was reasonable under *Charter* s. 8, the *trial judge* must decide whether the *Code* requirements, identical to those of s. 8, have been met. The trial judge does *not*, however, substitute his/her view for that of the authorizing judge. If, based on the record before the authorizing judge as *amplified on the review*, the trial judge concludes that the authorization *could* have been granted, s/he should *not* interfere. Upon review, the existence of fraud, non-disclosure, misleading disclosure and new evidence are all relevant to a determination whether there remains a basis for the decision of the authorizing judge, but are *not* prerequisites to review. The order should *not* be set aside unless the reviewing judge is satisfied, on the whole of the material, that there was *no basis* for the authorization.

R. v. Garofoli (1990), 80 C.R. (3d) 317, 60 C.C.C. (3d) 161 (S.C.C.); reversing (1987), 64 C.R. (3d) 193, 41 C.C.C. (3d) 97 (Ont. C.A.) — Where editing renders an authorization unsupportable, P may apply to the *trial judge* to consider so much of the excised material as is required to support the authorization. The trial judge should only accede to such a request if satisfied that D is sufficiently aware of the nature of the excised material, from a judicial summary thereof prepared by the trial judge, to challenge it by evidence or argument.

R. v. Araujo (1998), 127 C.C.C. (3d) 315 (B.C. C.A.); leave to appeal allowed (April 22, 1999), Doc. 26898, 26899, 26904, 26943, 26968 (S.C.C.) — Evidence tendered on a *voir dire* to determine the admissibility of primary evidence obtained under an authorization is also evidence that the reviewing court may properly consider to *amplify* material that was originally presented in the application for authorization.

R. v. Morrison (1989), 72 C.R. (3d) 332, 50 C.C.C. (3d) 353 (Ont. C.A.) — The court of appeal has jurisdiction to consider whether the authorization was invalid because of non-disclosure or misleading disclosure, to satisfy itself that there has been no miscarriage of justice because of the admission of the intercepted communications. Where there has been non-disclosure or misleading disclosure, the court can examine the parts of the affidavit which have not been impugned to determine whether or not the authorization would still have been granted. A doubtful or marginal case should be resolved in favour of the person attacking the authorization.

R. v. Bisson (1994), 87 C.C.C. (3d) 440 (Que. C.A.); affirmed (1994), 94 C.C.C. (3d) 94, 173 N.R. 237 (S.C.C.) — An authorization is *not* automatically set aside upon proof of fraud, non-disclosure or misleading disclosure. The reviewing judge ought to consider whether, taking into account the non-disclosure, the authorizing judge *could have* granted the authorization. The misleading element may affect *some* of the facts set out in the affidavit, but what remains may suffice to support the conclusion that the authorizing judge *could have* granted the authorization.

R. v. Hiscock (1991), 68 C.C.C. (3d) 182 (Que. C.A.) — Where a court of appeal determines that an affiant should be cross-examined, it should direct that the cross-examination take place before a person designated by the Chief Justice. The transcript of the cross-examination may be filed with the trial record and the appeal further considered on its merits.

Opening of Packet [See s. 187]

Right of Cross-Examination

R. v. Garofoli (1990), 80 C.R. (3d) 317, 60 C.C.C. (3d) 161 (S.C.C.); reversing (1987), 64 C.R. (3d) 193, 41 C.C.C. (3d) 97 (Ont. C.A.) — D has *no absolute right* to cross-examine an affiant on an application to the trial judge to find interceptions unreasonable, hence unlawful, and to exclude them as evidence under *Code* s. 189. A trial judge, however, should grant *leave* to cross-examine the affiant when satisfied that cross-examination is *necessary* to enable D to make *full answer* and *defence*. D must show a basis for the view that the cross-examination will elicit testimony tending to *discredit* the existence of one of the *pre-conditions* to the authorization, for example, the existence of reasonable and probable grounds. The cross-examination should nonetheless be limited to questions directed to establish that there was *no* basis upon which authorization could have been granted.

R. v. Garofoli (1990), 80 C.R. (3d) 317, 60 C.C.C. (3d) 161 (S.C.C.); reversing (1987), 64 C.R. (3d) 193, 41 C.C.C. (3d) 97 (Ont. C.A.) — There is no right to cross-examine an informant who is neither a witness nor a person who can be identified unless D establishes the case is within the "innocence at stake" exception.

R. v. Lachance (1990), 80 C.R. (3d) 374 (S.C.C.); reversing (1987), 27 O.A.C. 45 (C.A.) — Where an affidavit describes an informant and a named person as different people, when they are, in fact, one and the same person, it is misleading on a matter which bears directly on the requirement of s. 186(1)(b) that the only practical investigative technique is the interception of private communications. In such circumstances, cross-examination of the affiant should be permitted.

R. v. Starr (1998), 123 C.C.C. (3d) 145 (Man. C.A.); notice of appeal as of right filed , Doc. 26514 (S.C.C.) — D is *not* permitted to cross-examine the affiant unless s/he establishes an evidentiary basis that cross-examination would elicit testimony tending to discredit the affiant on the existence of a condition precedent.

R. v. Hiscock (1991), 68 C.C.C. (3d) 182 (Que. C.A.) — Where the affidavit only generally describes the nature of the police investigation, mentions nothing about the sources of the affiant's information, fails to disclose the nature of the information provided and supplies but limited detail, the affiant may be cross-examined.

Voir Dire : [Former S. 189(1)]

R. v. Parsons (1977), 40 C.R.N.S. 202, 37 C.C.C. (2d) 497 (Ont. C.A.), affirmed, (sub nom. *Charette v. R.*) 14 C.R. (3d) 191, 51 C.C.C. (2d) 350 — The *voir dire* is for determining the *admissibility* of the intercepted communications. Where an *authorization* is relied upon for admissibility, the determination of whether the *statutory conditions* precedent have been fulfilled is properly dealt with in a *voir dire*. This would include such matters as the validity of the authorization, compliance with the authorization, and compliance with the statutory notice requirements. Matters such as the *integrity* of the tape, its *continuity, voice identification,* and lack of tampering go to the weight of the evidence and are matters dealt with before the jury, *not* on a *voir dire.*

R. v. Barbeau (1996), 110 C.C.C. (3d) 69 (Que. C.A.) — An applicant's self-description as a duly authorized agent of the relevant authority is sufficient to establish the condition precedent. There is *no* requirement that a written authorization be included in the packet.

Lawfully Made : [Former S. 189(1)(a)]

R. v. Thompson (1990), 80 C.R. (3d) 129, 59 C.C.C. (3d) 225 (S.C.C.); reversing (1986), 53 C.R. (3d) 97, 29 C.C.C. (3d) 516 (B.C. C.A.) — Interceptions obtained by means of surreptitious entry into residential premises that were *not* specifically mentioned on the face of the authorization violate *Charter* s. 8.

R. v. Chesson (1988), 65 C.R. (3d) 193, 43 C.C.C. (3d) 353 (S.C.C.) — Even though an entry might otherwise amount to unlawful conduct, the interception is lawfully made since this Part contemplates by necessary implication a covert or surreptitious entry into private property for the purpose of installing an authorized listening device, including devices which depend for their operation on an external power source such as an electrical socket or a car battery.

R. v. Chesson (1988), 65 C.R. (3d) 193, 43 C.C.C. (3d) 353 (S.C.C.) — Intercepted telephone communications were inadmissible against a person who, while known, was *not* named in the authorization. The interceptions in such case cannot be made under an unknown person's clause.

R. v. Paterson (1985), 44 C.R. (3d) 150, 18 C.C.C. (3d) 137 (Ont. C.A.); affirmed (1987), 60 C.R. (3d) 107 (S.C.C.) — A basket clause giving the police the discretion to intercept the private communications of any or all persons if reasonable grounds exist for a belief that an interception would assist the investigation of any offence specified in the authorization is invalid as constituting a delegation of the judge's function to the police. The "basket clause", however, is severable and did *not* affect the validity of the balance of the authorization.

R. v. Grabowski (1985), 22 C.C.C. (3d) 449 (S.C.C.) — *See also*: *R. v. Lachance* (1990), 80 C.R. (3d) 374, 60 C.C.C. (3d) 449 (S.C.C.) — Where an offending "basket clause" is severable, a court can divide the authorization and preserve the valid portion such that interceptions made under the valid authorization are admissible.

Lyons v. R. (1985), 43 C.R. (3d) 97, 15 C.C.C. (3d) 417 (S.C.C.); affirming (1982), 69 C.C.C. (2d) 318 (B.C. C.A.) — Nowhere in the *Code* is a distinction made between "interception" of a private communication and entry for the purpose of effecting the interception. Although there is *no* express authority for the entry of premises under surveillance, Parliament should *not* be taken to have authorized the use of the procedures and equipment without having also permitted the appropriate means to carry them out. The necessary result of the legislation is the express and implied recognition of the invasion of citizens' rights and the authorized conduct would not in law amount to trespass. Primary evidence is not, thereby, rendered inadmissible.

R. v. Ritch (1982), 69 C.C.C. (2d) 289 (Alta. C.A.); affirmed (1984), 16 C.C.C. (3d) 191 (S.C.C.) — A wiretap authorization which fails to state the identity of the person whose private communications are to be intercepted, but only provides for an interception of communications in respect of a particular telephone number at a particular residence, is unlawful.

R. v. Jean (1979), 7 C.R. (3d) 338, 46 C.C.C. (2d) 176 (Alta. C.A.); affirmed (1979), 16 C.R. (3d) 193 (S.C.C.) — Where neither of the parties to a conversation were the named objects of interception, and there was no basket clause in respect of telecommunications, the conversation was not admissible.

R. v. Munroe (1985), 19 C.C.C. (3d) 486 (Alta. C.A.) — Invalid portions of an authorization do not render the entire order invalid. P is required to show that what remains after the excision is valid and authorized the interception in question.

R. v. LeClerc (1985), 20 C.C.C. (3d) 173 (B.C. C.A.) — Where the authorization permitting the interception referred to any place "resorted to" and the police had seen D use a public pay phone on previous occasions, conversations intercepted by a device subsequently installed at that phone were lawfully intercepted.

R. v. Lloyd (1980), 16 C.R. (3d) 221, 53 C.C.C. (2d) 121 (B.C. C.A.); reversed on other grounds (1981), 31 C.R. (3d) 157 (S.C.C.) — An authorization did not become inoperative during the period for which it was granted just because the identity of a person whose identity was not known when the authorization was granted became known during that period. The authorization had contained a basket clause which ended with the words: "The private communications of such persons as described whose identities are unknown at that date hereof may be intercepted during the period for which this authorization is valid notwithstanding that during such period their identities may become known."

R. v. Shayesteh (1996), 111 C.C.C. (3d) 225 (Ont. C.A.) — Where D's communications have been intercepted because of his participation in calls with a third party, the interceptions are lawful, *provided* they were lawful in relation to the third party.

R. v. Shayesteh (1996), 111 C.C.C. (3d) 225 (Ont. C.A.) — Where an authorization is *overbroad* with respect to others, but sufficient with respect to D, the breach of the third party's rights does *not* render unlawful the interceptions concerning D.

R. v. Fegan (1993), 80 C.C.C. (3d) 356 (Ont. C.A.) — Where Bell Canada, an investor-owned utility, installs a DNR, *otherwise* than at the request or direction of the police to facilitate a criminal investigation, *Charter* s. 8 is *not* implicated since the utility is *not* an instrument of the State.

R. v. Musitano (1985), 24 C.C.C. (3d) 65 (Ont. C.A.); leave to appeal refused (1987), 79 N.R. 79n (S.C.C.) — An authorization containing a *basket clause* which included other persons who might act in concert with any of those persons specifically named in the authorization in the commission of specified offences was held to be valid with respect to the interception of communications between D and his former girlfriend. The girlfriend had not been specifically named in the authorization because the police were under the impression that the accused had separated from her. Furthermore, there was no improper delegation to the police of the power to select whose communications should be intercepted or where the interception should be made.

R. v. McCafferty (1984), 16 C.C.C. (3d) 224 (Ont. C.A.) — An interception was *not* lawfully made where the transmitting device was installed during the execution of a search warrant prior to the obtaining of an authorization, notwithstanding that no communications were recorded until after the authorization was obtained.

R. v. Crease (No. 2) (1980), 53 C.C.C. (2d) 378 (Ont. C.A.) — At the time of the application for the original authorization "S" was known to be a person whose private communications might assist in the investigation and at the time of the first renewal the appellants' identities were similarly known. They were not named in the original authorization or any of the renewals nor were fresh authorizations obtained applying to them. The interceptions of their communications were *not* lawful.

R. v. Niles (1978), 40 C.C.C. (2d) 512 (Ont. C.A.) — Where an authorization permitted interceptions only at places or premises "resorted to or used by" D, P must prove that the interception was made at such a place before the evidence of the conversation is admissible. P cannot use the communication itself as proof that the place was one resorted to or used by D.

R. v. Welsh (No. 6) (1977), 32 C.C.C. (2d) 363 (Ont. C.A.) — If an authorization does *not* include either as a named or unnamed person any of the parties to a communication, the interception cannot be characterized as lawful.

Different Offence [Former S. 189(4)]

R. v. Commisso (1983), 36 C.R. (3d) 105, 7 C.C.C. (3d) 1 (S.C.C.) — Once the court has authorized the interception of a conversation, evidence in support of any criminal offence incidentally disclosed is admissible, even though the authorization did not specifically authorize an interception for that offence and, assuming no material non-disclosure, whether or not the offence was anticipated or unanticipated.

Application of New Rules of Evidence

R. v. Gallego (1993), 85 C.C.C. (3d) 178 (Ont. Gen. Div.) — The amendments to s. 189 are *retrospective* in their operation.

Admissibility Under *Charter* S. 24(2)

R. v. Pope (1998), 20 C.R. (5th) 173, 129 C.C.C. (3d) 59 (Alta. C.A.) — Intercepted private communications are *non-conscriptive* evidence. D is *not* compelled to participate in the creation or discovery of the evidence. Compulsion requires more than passive observation or eavesdropping by the state.

Surreptitious monitoring and recording has nothing to do with their utterance by D who speaks without any form of state coercion or inducement. The evidence exists in a usable form independently of any

Charter violation. It consists of oral statements that could be introduced through the other party or by compliance with Part VI of the *Code*.

Notice of Intention to Introduce Primary Evidence: S. 189(5) [Cases decided under former section]

R. v. Dunn (1977), 38 C.R.N.S. 383, 36 C.C.C. (2d) 495 (Sask. C.A.), affirmed (1979), 52 C.C.C. (2d) 127 (S.C.C.) — The transcript need *not* be "an official writing or an official copy" of the proceedings. Nor is it required to be certified by a court stenographer. It need only be a "transcript of the private communication".

R. v. Montoute (1991), 62 C.C.C. (3d) 481 (Alta. C.A.) — *See also*: *R. v. McDonald* (1981), 22 C.R. (3d) 15, 60 C.C.C. (2d) 336 (Alta. C.A.); *R. v. Banas* (1982), 65 C.C.C. (2d) 224 (Ont. C.A.) — Where interceptions have been made of a co-conspirator's private communications with an undercover police officer, with the consent of the officer, the interceptions, while lawfully made under Part VI, violate *Charter* s. 8. In such a case, D has status to seek exclusion of the evidence under *Charter* s. 24(2). The evidence should be excluded to prevent the administration of justice being brought into further disrepute by admission of evidence obtained by constitutional infringement. (per Harradence and Belzil JJ.A.).

R. v. Chevarie (1985), 3 W.W.R. 394 (Alta. C.A.) — The object of the subsection is to give D sufficient notice so that he can inquire into the veracity and admissibility of evidence proposed to be introduced. The subsection does *not* apply where no question of admissibility arises under s. 189(1), such as where the accused was neither the originator nor the intended recipient of the communication.

R. v. Cordes (1978), 40 C.C.C. (2d) 442 (Alta. C.A.); affirmed on other grounds (1979), 10 C.R. (3d) 186, 47 C.C.C. (2d) 46 (S.C.C.) — The tendering of the authorization at the preliminary was, of itself, notice that the prosecution intended to rely on and to produce the authorization at trial.

R. v. Filby (1983), 1 C.C.C. (3d) 159 (Ont. C.A.) — Reasonable notice means sufficient time to prepare a case for trial. The notice and the transcripts need *not* be served simultaneously. "Together with" should be read as meaning "and" a transcript.

R. v. Douglas (1977), 1 C.R. (3d) 238, 33 C.C.C. (2d) 395 (Ont. C.A.) — The purpose of this subsection is to give D adequate notice of the details of the evidence intended to be used against him. This section is mandatory in its terms but is procedural only and can be waived by D or counsel.

R. v. Viscount (1977), 37 C.C.C. (2d) 533 (Ont. G.S.P.) — P must give *reasonable notice* of its intention to adduce into evidence a lawfully intercepted private communication to *all* D at a joint trial and not merely to those who were a party to the communication.

Privileged Communications: S. 189(6)

Lloyd v. R. (1981), 31 C.R. (3d) 157 (S.C.C.) — A communication between spouses is privileged within the meaning of s. 189(6).

R. v. Jean (1979), 7 C.R. (3d) 338, 46 C.C.C. (2d) 176 (Alta. C.A.); affirmed (1979), 16 C.R. (3d) 193 (S.C.C.) — A conversation between spouses which was overheard on a lawful interception was properly excluded as evidence where the recipient spouse was not a competent and compellable witness for P. The privilege is not destroyed upon interception.

Tapes and Transcripts as Exhibits

R. v. Shayesteh (1996), 111 C.C.C. (3d) 225 (Ont. C.A.) — Where intercepted private communications have been audiotaped, the tapes should be produced and filed if otherwise admissible. It is of *no* momoent whether the communciations are in an official language. It is matter for the *discretion* of the trial judge,

i.   whether *foreign language* tapes will be *played* for the jury; and,

ii.   whether foreign language tapes should be left with the jury during their deliberations.

Where *foreign language interceptions* have been made, *secondary evidence* which is relevant may be admitted to assist the trier of fact in understanding the primary evidence and its full impact. Translations will be essential. The secondary opinion evidence of translators may be adduced *viva voce* or by admission. Where translations are in transcript form, they should be filed as exhibits. Reading them or leaving them with the jury is a matter of judicial discretion.

R. v. Rowbotham (1988), 63 C.R. (3d) 113, 41 C.C.C. (3d) 1 (Ont. C.A.); affirming on this issue (1984), 42 C.R. (3d) 179 (Ont. H.C.) — The trial judge has a discretion whether a transcript of intercepted communications should be left with the jury during their deliberations. If there are only one or two brief communications, the transcript should, in all probability, *not* be left with the jury. If the communications are lengthy or numerous, or in need of translation, a transcript should be left with the jury.

R. v. Pleich (1980), 16 C.R. (3d) 194, 55 C.C.C. (2d) 13 (Ont. C.A.) — The *authorizations* themselves should *not* be admitted into evidence as exhibits and, in particular, should *not* be left with the jury for use in their deliberations. There is no error, however, in allowing tapes of intercepted private communications to go to the jury room. If the trial judge believes that allowing the jury to play the tapes during their deliberations might result in their being given undue emphasis, s/he may withhold them from the jury.

Related Provisions: Sections 184.1(2) and 188(5) enact special evidentiary rules. Under s. 190, a judge of the trial court may order that *further particulars* be given of the private communication that is intended to be adduced as evidence and of which notice has been given under s. 189(5).

Section 187 enacts a comprehensive scheme of disclosure of documents relating to applications under any provision of Part VI in order that D may challenge the admissibility of primary evidence.

Section 184(1) prohibits wilful interception of private communications by means of an electro-magnetic, acoustic, mechanical or other device. Section 184(2) exempts certain conduct from liability, including interceptions made in accordance with an authorization or pursuant to s. 184.4. Authorizations may be obtained under ss. 184.2 and 184.3 (consent authorizations), 186 (conventional authorizations and renewals) and 188 (emergency authorizations). Section 184.4 permits unauthorized interception by a peace officer in defined circumstances. Section 188.2 also exempts interceptions made by an agent of the state under s. 184.1, *inter alia*, from criminal liability.

190. Further particulars — **Where an accused has been given notice pursuant to subsection 189(5), any judge of the court in which the trial of the accused is being or is to be held may at any time order that further particulars be given of the private communication that is intended to be adduced in evidence.**

1973–74, c. 50, s. 2.

Commentary: The section authorizes the supply of *further particulars* to D of the private communication which it is intended to adduce as primary evidence. The order may be made by any judge of the court in which D's trial is to be or is being held, at any time after D has been given notice under s. 189(5) of P's intention to adduce primary evidence.

Related Provisions: The *notice* provisions of s. 189(5) enact a twofold requirement. There must be *reasonable notice* of P's *intention* to adduce primary evidence. There must also be either a *transcript* or fully *particularized statement* of the intercepted private communication proposed to be adduced as primary evidence and a statement of time, date and place of the private communication and the parties thereto, if known. It is the second requirement of s. 189(5) that s. 190 is designed to further particularize or amplify.

There is *no* corresponding provision respecting the notice of interception given under s. 196(1) or (2).

This provision should not be confused with the authority to order particulars under section 587 in respect of a count contained in an information or indictment.

191. (1) Possession, etc. — **Every one who possesses, sells or purchases any electro-magnetic, acoustic, mechanical or other device or any component thereof knowing that the design thereof renders it primarily useful for surreptitious interception of private communications is guilty of an indictable offence and liable to imprisonment for a term not exceeding two years.**

(2) Exemptions — Subsection (1) does not apply to

(a) a police officer or police constable in possession of a device or component described in subsection (1) in the course of his employment;

(b) a person in possession of such a device or component for the purpose of using it in an interception made or to be made in accordance with an authorization;

(b.1) a person in possession of such a device or component under the direction of a police officer or police constable in order to assist that officer or constable in the course of his duties as a police officer or police constable;

(c) an officer or a servant of Her Majesty in right of Canada or a member of the Canadian Forces in possession of such a device or component in the course of his duties as such an officer, servant or member, as the case may be; and

(d) any other person in possession of such a device or component under the authority of a licence issued by the Solicitor General of Canada.

(3) Terms and conditions of licence — **A licence issued for the purpose of paragraph (2)(*d*) may contain such terms and conditions relating to the possession, sale or purchase of a device or component described in subsection (1) as the Solicitor General of Canada may prescribe.**

1973–74, c. 50, s. 2; R.S. 1985, c. 27 (1st Supp.), s. 26.

Commentary: The section defines the *possession* offence, provides the general punishment upon finding of guilt and lists the circumstances under which liability will not be attracted.

The *external circumstances* of the offence of s. 191(1) require proof of D's possession, sale or purchase of a prohibited device. The device must be an electro-magnetic, acoustic, mechanical or other device or component thereof the design of which renders it primarily useful for the surreptitious interception of private communications. The *mental element* consists of the intention to engage in conduct which amounts to the external circumstances of the offence and requires P to establish D's *knowledge* of the character or capability of the device.

Section 191(2) lists the *exemptions from liability* under s. 191(1). Sections 191(2)(a)–(b.1) involve *investigative possession*. Under s. 191(2)(a) there need be no actual investigation ongoing in which the device is or is to be used, provided the person in possession is a police officer or constable in the course of his/her employment. Section 191(2)(b) exempts *anyone* whose possession is for the purpose of use in *authorized interceptions*. Section 191(2)(b.1) exempts any person whose possession is under the direction of a police officer or constable and in order to assist the officer or constable in the performance of his/her duties.

The exemption of s. 191(2)(c) applies *only* to an officer or servant of Her Majesty in right of Canada, or a member of the Canadian Forces who is in possession in the course of his/her duties.

Licenced possession is exempt under s. 191(2)(d), provided it falls within the authority given by a general or specific licence under s. 191(3).

Related Provisions: "Authorization", "electro-magnetic, acoustic, mechanical or other device", "interception", "private communication", and "sell" are defined in s. 183, "Canadian Forces" in section 2. Possession is determined under s. 4(3). Neither "police officer" nor "police constable" is defined, though each is part of the expansive definition of "peace officer" in s. 2. The offence is an "offence" under s. 183 for the purposes of Part VI.

The interception offence is defined in s. 184(1) and its exemptions in s. 184(2). The exemptions of ss. 191(2)(b) and (c) track the interception exemptions in ss. 184(2)(b) and (d), respectively. The exemption of s. 191(2)(b.1) has been used most frequently in consensual interceptions exempted under s. 184(2)(a) to avoid the need to obtain a licence for the wired civilian informant, a constitutionally endangered species.

In addition to the punishment provided upon conviction under s. 191(1), forfeiture may be ordered under s. 192.

D may *elect* mode of trial under s. 536(2).

192. (1) Forfeiture — **Where a person is convicted of an offence under section 184 or 191, any electro-magnetic, acoustic, mechanical or other device by means of which the offence was committed or the possession of which constituted the offence, on the conviction, in addition to any punishment that is imposed, may be ordered forfeited to Her Majesty whereupon it may be disposed of as the Attorney General directs.**

(2) Limitation — No order for forfeiture shall be made under subsection (1) in respect of telephone, telegraph or other communication facilities or equipment owned by a person engaged in providing telephone, telegraph or other communication service to the public or forming part of the telephone, telegraph or other communication service or system of that person by means of which an offence under section 184 has been committed if that person was not a party to the offence.

1973–74, c. 50, s. 2.

Commentary: The section authorizes *forfeiture* of any electro-magnetic, acoustic, mechanical or other device by means of which an offence under s. 184 (unlawful interception) was committed or the possession of which constituted the offence under s. 191 (unlawful possession).

Under s. 192(1) forfeiture may be ordered upon conviction under s. 184 or 191, in addition to any punishment which might otherwise might be imposed. The device is forfeited to Her Majesty to be disposed of as the Attorney General directs. The order of forfeiture may not extend to the facilities or equipment described in s. 192(2), unless the owner thereof was a party to the interception offence of s. 184.

Related Provisions: "Electro-magnetic, acoustic, mechanical or other device" is defined in s. 183, "Attorney General" in s. 2.

A person engaged in providing a telephone, telegraph or other communication service to the public is exempt from liability in respect of interceptional activity which falls within s. 184(2)(c).

The *Code* contains several other forfeiture provisions which may become engaged upon conviction of specified offences. Sections 327(2) and (3) (possession of device to obtain telecommunication facility or service) and ss. 199(3) and (6) (lottery and gaming material) are most similar to the present section.

A further penalty that may be attracted upon conviction under s. 184 (unlawful interception) or 193 (unlawful disclosure) is an award of punitive damages under s. 194.

193. (1) Disclosure of information — Where a private communication has been intercepted by means of an electro-magnetic, acoustic, mechanical or other device without the consent, express or implied, of the originator thereof or of the person intended by the originator thereof to receive it, every one who, without the express consent of the originator thereof or of the person intended by the originator thereof to receive it, wilfully

   (a) uses or discloses the private communication or any part thereof or the substance, meaning or purport thereof or of any part thereof, or

   (b) discloses the existence thereof,

is guilty of an indictable offence and liable to imprisonment for a term not exceeding two years.

(2) Exemptions — Subsection (1) does not apply to a person who discloses a private communication or any part thereof or the substance, meaning or purport thereof or of any part thereof or who discloses the existence of a private communication

   (a) in the course of or for the purpose of giving evidence in any civil or criminal proceedings or in any other proceedings in which the person may be required to give evidence on oath;

   (b) in the course of or for the purpose of any criminal investigation if the private communication was lawfully intercepted;

   (c) in giving notice under section 189 or furnishing further particulars pursuant to an order under section 190;

   (d) in the course of the operation of

      (i) a telephone, telegraph or other communication service to the public, or

(ii) a department or an agency of the Government of Canada,

if the disclosure is necessarily incidental to an interception described in paragraph 184(2)(c) or (d); or

(e) where disclosure is made to a peace officer or prosecutor in Canada or to a person or authority with responsibility in a foreign state for the investigation or prosecution of offences and is intended to be in the interests of the administration of justice in Canada or elsewhere; or

(f) where the disclosure is made to the Director of the Canadian Security Intelligence Service or to an employee of the Service for the purpose of enabling the Service to perform its duties and functions under section 12 of the *Canadian Security Intelligence Service Act.*

(3) Publishing of prior lawful disclosure — Subsection (1) does not apply to a person who discloses a private communication or any part thereof or the substance, meaning or purport thereof or of any part thereof or who discloses the existence of a private communication where that which is disclosed by him was, prior to the disclosure, lawfully disclosed in the course of or for the purpose of giving evidence in proceedings referred to in paragraph (2)(a).

1973–74, c. 50, s. 2; 1976–77, c. 53, s. 11; 1984, c. 21, s. 77; R.S. 1985, c. 30 (4th Supp.), s. 45; 1993, c. 40, s. 11.

Commentary: The section defines the *elements* of the "disclosure" offence, lists the *exemptions* and provides the general *punishment* upon conviction.

In general, an offence is committed where there is *disclosure or use* without the consent of a participant in a private communication which has been intercepted without consent. The *external circumstances* of the offence consist of three elements. There must be an *interception* of a private communication by means of an electro-magnetic, acoustic, mechanical or other device, *without* the *consent* of an or the originator or intended recipient thereof. D need not be proven to have made the interception. The interception need not be unlawful, only non-consensual. There must be *use or disclosure* of the private communication, any part thereof, or its substance, meaning purport or existence thereof. The disclosure or use must be *without the express consent of a party* to the intercepted communication. The *mental element* is expressed in the compendious term "wilfully". It would also seem incumbent upon P, in accordance with general principle, to establish D's *knowledge* of the absence of consent to intercept and to use or disclosure.

Sections 193(2) and (3) contain a lengthy list of *exemptions* from the liability-creating provisions of s. 193(1), which may be sub-divided into three groups.

Sections 193(2)(a) and (c) and (3) exempt *evidentiary use or disclosure*. Under s. 193(2)(a) disclosure in the course or for the purpose of giving evidence in any proceedings in which D may be required to give evidence under oath is exempt. Section 193(3) protects from liability subsequent disclosure of what has earlier been disclosed under s. 193(2)(a). Under s. 193(2)(c) *disclosure* made in giving *notice* of intention to introduce primary evidence under s. 189(5) or in furnishing *particulars* under s. 190 is *exempt* from criminal liability.

Sections 193(2)(b), (e) and (f) exempt *law enforcement use or disclosure*. Under s. 193(2)(b), use may be made or disclosure given without liability in the course or for the purpose of any criminal investigation, provided the interception was lawful. Any disclosure made to a peace officer or prosecutor, domestic or foreign, and intended to be in the interests of the administration of justice is exempt under s. 193(2)(e). Disclosure to CSIS personnel to enable them to carry out their functions and perform their duties under s. 12 of the *Canadian Security Intelligence Service Act* is *not* culpable under s. 193(2)(f).

The remaining *service exemption*, s. 193(2)(d), is incidental to the interception exemptions of ss. 184(2)(c) and (d).

Case Law

R. v. Nygaard (1987), 59 C.R. (3d) 37, 36 C.C.C. (3d) 199 (Alta. C.A.); reversed on other grounds (1989), 72 C.R. (3d) 257, 51 C.C.C. (3d) 417 (S.C.C.) — D may disclose for the purpose of cross-examination prior inconsistent statements made by the witness and obtained through an interception of a private communication.

Related Provisions: "Private communication", "intercept" and "electro-magnetic, acoustic, mechanical or other device" are defined in s. 183. "Peace officer" is defined in s. 2, but "criminal investigation" is neither defined nor, perhaps, capable of precise definition. Under s. 184(2)(a), the interception of a private communication with the consent, express or implied, of an originator or intended recipient is not unlawful.

The interception offence is described in s. 184, the crime of possession of interception devices in s. 191.

A conviction under s. 193(1) carries a maximum punishment of imprisonment for a term not exceeding two years. In addition, D may be ordered to pay to a person aggrieved an amount not exceeding $5,000 as punitive damages under s. 194. Under s. 536(2), D may *elect* mode of trial.

193.1 (1) Disclosure of information received from interception of radio-based telephone communications — Every person who wilfully uses or discloses a radio-based telephone communication or who wilfully discloses the existence of such a communication is guilty of an indictable offence and liable to imprisonment for a term not exceeding two years, if

(a) the originator of the communication or the person intended by the originator of the communication to receive it was in Canada when the communication was made;

(b) the communication was intercepted by means of an electromagnetic, acoustic, mechanical or other device without the consent, express or implied, of the originator of the communication or of the person intended by the originator to receive the communication; and

(c) the person does not have the express or implied consent of the originator of the communication or of the person intended by the originator to receive the communication.

(2) Other provisions to apply — Subsections 193(2) and (3) apply, with such modifications as the circumstances require, to disclosures of radio-based telephone communications.

1993, c. 40, s. 12.

Commentary: The section creates an *indictable* offence which prohibits the *use* or *disclosure* of an intercepted radio-based telephone communication. The crime is similar to that described in s. 193 in relation to private communications.

The *external circumstances* of the offence include several elements. A radio-based telephone communication, originated or intended to be received by a person in Canada, must have been intercepted by means of an electro-magnetic, acoustic, mechanical or other device without the express or implied consent of any party to it. D must use or disclose the intercepted radio-based telephone communication, or its existence, without the express or implied consent of any party to it. The *mental element* requires that D act *wilfully* in making use or disclosure and have knowledge of the absence of consent.

Under s. 193.1(2), the saving provisions of s. 193(2) and (3) apply to disclosure of radio-based telephone communications.

Related Provisions: "Intercept", "electro-magnetic, acoustic, mechanical or other device" and "radio-based telephone communication" are defined in s. 183. Section 183.1 describes *who* may consent to an interception, but does not define what constitutes a valid consent.

Section 184.5(1) describes the circumstances in which the interception of radio-based telephone communications is an offence. The conjoint effect of ss. 184.5(2) and 184.6 is to permit any authorization granted under Part VI to permit the interception of both private communications and radio-based telephone communications. Unauthorized interception of radio-based telephone communications may also be made under ss. 184.1 and 184.4.

Upon conviction of an offence under s. 184.5 or 193.1, D may be required to pay punitive damages to a person aggrieved under s. 194(1).

194. (1) Damages — Subject to subsection (2), a court that convicts an accused of an offence under section 184, 184.5, 193 or 193.1 may, on the application of a person aggrieved, at the time sentence is imposed, order the accused to pay to that person an amount not exceeding five thousand dollars as punitive damages.

(2) No damages where civil proceedings commenced — No amount shall be ordered to be paid under subsection (1) to a person who has commenced an action under Part II of the *Crown Liability Act.*

(3) Judgment may be registered — Where an amount that is ordered to be paid under subsection (1) is not paid forthwith, the applicant may, by filing the order, enter as a judgment, in the superior court of the province in which the trial was held, the amount ordered to be paid, and that judgment is enforceable against the accused in the same manner as if it were a judgment rendered against the accused in that court in civil proceedings.

(4) Moneys in possession of accused may be taken — All or any part of an amount that is ordered to be paid under subsection (1) may be taken out of moneys found in the possession of the accused at the time of his arrest, except where there is a dispute respecting ownership of or right of possession to those moneys by claimants other than the accused.

1973–74, c. 50, s. 2; 1993, c. 40, s. 13.

Commentary: The section authorizes and prescribes the conditions under which an award of *punitive damages* may be made upon conviction of a designated offence under this Part.

The general authority to award *punitive damages*, described in ss. 194(1) and (2), permits such an award only upon the application of a person aggrieved, where D has been convicted of an interception (ss. 184, 184.5) or disclosure (ss. 193, 193.1) offence. The *convicting court* is authorized, upon application therefor, to make an award in an amount *not exceeding $5,000.* The award must be made *at the time sentence is imposed.* To prevent double recovery, no amount may be awarded as punitive damages to a person who has commenced an action under Part II of the *Crown Liability Act.*

Sections 194(3) and (4) make provision for payment of an award of punitive damages under s. 194(1). Under s. 194(3), the failure to pay forthwith an amount ordered to be so paid entitles the applicant, by filing the order, to enter as a judgment in the superior court of the province in which the trial was held, the amount ordered to be paid as punitive damages. Thereafter, the judgment is enforceable against D in the same manner as if it were a judgment against him/her in that court in civil proceedings. Section 194(4) permits moneys found in D's possession at the time of his/her arrest to be applied in payment of an award of punitive damages, except where there is a dispute concerning ownership of or right of possession to the moneys by claimants other than D.

Related Provisions: "Person aggrieved" is not defined in the section, Part, nor elsewhere in the *Code.*

The enforcement mechanism described in s. 194(3) is also available to recover fines levied against, but not paid by, corporations (s. 735) and, subject to certain limitations, fines, pecuniary penalties, or forfeitures imposed by law, where no other mode of recovery is provided therefor (s.734.6).

The additional penalty of forfeiture of any electro-magnetic, acoustic, mechanical or other device by means of which an interception offence (s. 184) was committed or the possession of which constituted an offence (s. 191) is provided for in s. 192.

An award of punitive damages under s. 194(1) is a "sentence" for appellate purposes under s. 673 and Part XXI.

195. (1) **Annual report** — The Solicitor General of Canada shall, as soon as possible after the end of each year, prepare a report relating to

(a) authorizations for which he and agents to be named in the report who were specially designated in writing by him for the purposes of section 185 made application, and

(b) authorizations given under section 188 for which peace officers to be named in the report who were specially designated by him for the purposes of that section made application,

and interceptions made thereunder in the immediately preceding year.

(2) **Information respecting authorizations** — The report referred to in subsection (1) shall, in relation to authorizations and interceptions made thereunder, set out

(a) the number of applications made for authorizations;

(b) the number of applications made for renewal of authorizations;

(c) the number of applications referred to in paragraphs (a) and (b) that were granted, the number of those applications that were refused and the number of applications referred to in paragraph (a) that were granted subject to terms and conditions;

(d) the number of persons identified in an authorization against whom proceedings were commenced at the instance of the Attorney General of Canada in respect of

(i) an offence specified in the authorization,

(ii) an offence other than an offence specified in the authorization but in respect of which an authorization may be given, and

(iii) an offence in respect of which an authorization may not be given;

(e) the number of persons not identified in an authorization against whom proceedings were commenced at the instance of the Attorney General of Canada in respect of

(i) an offence specified in such an authorization,

(ii) an offence other than an offence specified in such an authorization but in respect of which an authorization may be given, and

(iii) an offence other than an offence specified in such an authorization and for which no such authorization may be given,

and whose commission or alleged commission of the offence became known to a peace officer as a result of an interception of a private communication under an authorization;

(f) the average period for which authorizations were given and for which renewals thereof were granted;

(g) the number of authorizations that, by virtue of one or more renewals thereof, were valid for more than sixty days, for more than one hundred and twenty days, for more than one hundred and eighty days and for more than two hundred and forty days;

(h) the number of notifications given pursuant to section 196;

(i) the offences in respect of which authorizations were given, specifying the number of authorizations given in respect of each of those offences;

(j) a description of all classes of places specified in authorizations and the number of authorizations in which each of those classes of places was specified;

(k) a general description of the methods of interception involved in each interception under an authorization;

(l) the number of persons arrested whose identity became known to a peace officer as a result of an interception under an authorization;

(m) the number of criminal proceedings commenced at the instance of the Attorney General of Canada in which private communications obtained by interception under an authorization were adduced in evidence and the number of those proceedings that resulted in a conviction; and

(n) the number of criminal investigations in which information obtained as a result of the interception of a private communication under an authorization was used although the private communication was not adduced in evidence in criminal proceedings commenced at the instance of the Attorney General of Canada as a result of the investigations.

(3) Other information — The report referred to in subsection (1) shall, in addition to the information referred to in subsection (2), set out

(a) the number of prosecutions commenced against officers or servants of Her Majesty in right of Canada or members of the Canadian Forces for offences under section 184 or 193; and

(b) a general assessment of the importance of interception of private communications for the investigation, detection, prevention and prosecution of offences in Canada.

(4) Report to be laid before Parliament — The Solicitor General of Canada shall cause a copy of each report prepared by him under subsection (1) to be laid before Parliament forthwith on completion thereof, or if Parliament is not then sitting, on any of the first fifteen days next thereafter that Parliament is sitting.

(5) Report by Attorneys General — The Attorney General of each province shall, as soon as possible after the end of each year, prepare and publish or otherwise make available to the public a report relating to

(a) authorizations for which he and agents specially designated in writing by him for the purposes of section 185 made application, and

(b) authorizations given under section 188 for which peace officers specially designated by him for the purposes of that section made application,

and interceptions made thereunder in the immediately preceding year setting out, with such modifications as the circumstances require, the information described in subsections (2) and (3).

1973–74, c. 50, s. 2; 1976–77, c. 53, s. 11.1; R.S. 1985, c. 27 (1st Supp.), s. 27.

Commentary: The section describes the yearly reporting requirements imposed upon the Solicitor General of Canada (s. 195(1)–(4)) and the Attorney General of the province (s. 195(5)) in respect of conventional and emergency authorizations obtained upon the application of agents or peace officers designated by the respective authorities. The details of the report are described in ss. 195(2) and (3).

Related Provisions: "Authorization" is defined in s. 183 and "Attorney General" in s. 2. Authorizations to intercept private communications are granted in accordance with the provisions of ss. 185, 186 and 186.1 (conventional authorizations and renewals) and 188 (emergency authorizations).

196. (1) **Written notification to be given** — The Attorney General of the province in which an application under subsection 185(1) was made or the Solicitor General of Canada if the application was made by or on behalf of the Solicitor General of Canada shall, within ninety days after the period for which the authorization was given or renewed or within such other period as is fixed pursuant to subsection 185(3) or subsection (3) of this section, notify in writing the person who was the object of the interception pursuant to the authorization and shall, in a manner prescribed by regulations made by the Governor in Council, certify to the court that gave the authorization that the person has been so notified.

(2) **Extension of period for notification** — The running of the ninety days referred to in subsection (1), or of any other period fixed pursuant to subsection 185(3) or subsection (3) of this section, is suspended until any application made by the Attorney General or the Solicitor General to a judge of a superior court of criminal jurisdiction or a judge as defined in section 552 for an extension or a subsequent extension of the period for which the authorization was given or renewed has been heard and disposed of.

(3) **Where extension to be granted** — Where the judge to whom an application referred to in subsection (2) is made, on the basis of an affidavit submitted in support of the application, is satisfied that

(a) the investigation of the offence to which the authorization relates, or

(b) a subsequent investigation of an offence listed in section 183 commenced as a result of information obtained from the investigation referred to in paragraph (a),

is continuing and is of the opinion that the interests of justice warrant the granting of the application, the judge shall grant an extension, or a subsequent extension, of the period, each extension not to exceed three years.

(4) **Application to be accompanied by affidavit** — An application pursuant to subsection (2) shall be accompanied by an affidavit deposing to

(a) the facts known or believed by the deponent and relied on to justify the belief that an extension should be granted; and

(b) the number of instances, if any, on which an application has, to the knowledge or belief of the deponent, been made under that subsection in relation to the particular authorization and on which the application was withdrawn or the application was not granted, the date on which each application was made and the judge to whom each application was made.

(5) **Exception for criminal organization** — Notwithstanding subsection (3) and 185(3), where the judge to whom an application referred to in subsection (2) or 185(2) is made, on the basis of an affidavit submitted in support of the application, is satisfied that the investigation is in relation to

(a) an offence under section 467.1, or

(b) an offence committed for the benefit of, at the direction of or in association with a criminal organization,

and is of the opinion that the interests of justice warrant the granting of the application, the judge shall grant an extension, or a subsequent extension, of the period, but no extension may exceed three years.

1973–74, c. 50, s. 2; 1976–77, c. 53, s. 12; R.S. 1985, c. 27 (1st Supp.), s. 28; 1993, c. 40, s. 14; 1997, c. 23, s. 7.

Commentary: The section requires that *written notification* be given to persons who have been the *objects of authorized interception* and, thereafter, that *certification* of such notification be given to the authorizing court.

Section 196(1) imposes the obligation of *notification* upon the Solicitor General of Canada or the Attorney General of the province, as the case may be, upon whose behalf authorization was sought and given. The notification must be given *in writing* to the person who was *object of the interception pursuant to the authorization*, within 90 days after the period for which the authorization was given or renewed, or such other period as is fixed in substitution therefor under s. 185(3) or 196(3). In all cases, the Solicitor General of Canada or Attorney General of the province, as the case may be, must certify to the authorizing court, in a manner prescribed by regulations made by the Governor in Council, that the object of interception has been so notified.

Sections 196(2)–(5) permit a court of competent jurisdiction to *substitute* a longer period within which the notification of s. 196(1) is given. The application under subsection (2) must be made by the Attorney General of the province or Solicitor General of Canada, as the case may be, on whose behalf the authorization was granted to a judge of the superior court of criminal jurisdiction or as defined in s. 552. Under s. 196(2) the running of the 90 day or extended period is suspended until any initial or subsequent extension application is heard and determined. The application may seek the substitution of a specified (further) period, not exceeding three years, in substitution for the statutory or earlier substituted period. Under s. 196(4) the application must be accompanied by an affidavit deposing to the matters described in ss. 196(4)(a) and (b). The affidavit may depose to the facts known or believed by one deponent. Section 196(3) describes the findings which must be made in order to engage the authority to fix the substitute notification period. A judge must be satisfied that the *investigation* of an authorized offence *or* the subsequent investigation of an offence listed in s. 183 commenced as a result of information obtained from the investigation of an authorized offence is *continuing and*, further, that the *interests of justice* warrant the granting of the application unless s. 196(5) applies. Subsection 196(5) waives the requirement in s. 195(3) that a judge must be satisfied that the *investigation* is *continuing* where the judge is satisfied that the application is in relation to a criminal organization. Where such findings have been made, the judge must fix a period, not exceeding three years, in substitution for the statutory period or the period earlier fixed under s. 185(3).

Case Law

Zaduk v. R. (1979), 46 C.C.C. (2d) 327 (Ont. C.A.) — This section requires only that the person who was the object of an interception be notified; it does not require that the person be provided with the contents or details of the authorization.

R. v. Welsh (No. 6) (1977), 32 C.C.C. (2d) 363 (Ont. C.A.) — A failure to comply with this section does *not* retrospectively characterize an otherwise lawful interception as unlawful.

Related Provisions: An application for a conventional authorization may also be accompanied, under s. 185(2) by an application to substitute for the statutory period of s. 196(1) a longer period not exceeding three years, set out in the application. The procedure to be followed and findings made to engage this jurisdiction are set out in ss. 185(3) and (4). There is no corresponding provision for emergency authorizations under s. 186. The substituted periods under ss. 185(3) and 196(3) and 196(5) would appear cumulative.

The documents relating to an application under s. 196(2) come within the confidentiality rule of s. 187, as well as the exceptions thereto.

The *Protection of Privacy Regulations* that describe the certificate required under s. 196(1) are as follows:

2. For the purposes of subsection 196(1) of the *Criminal Code*, the Attorney General of a province who gave a notice required to be given by that subsection, or the Solicitor General of Canada where the notice was given by him, shall certify to the court that issued the authorization that such notice was given by filing with a judge of the court a certificate signed by the person who gave the notice specifying

(a) the name and address of the person who was the object of the interception;

(b) the date on which the authorization and any renewal thereof expired;

(c) if any delay for the giving of notice was granted under section 196 or subsection 185(3) of the *Criminal Code*, the period of such delay; and

(d) the date, place and method of the giving of the notice.

3. [Revoked. SOR/81-859.]

4. A certificate filed pursuant to section 2 shall be treated as a confidential document, shall be placed in a packet, sealed by the judge with whom it is filed and kept with the packet sealed pursuant to section 187 of the *Criminal Code* that relates to the authorization to which the certificate relates. C.R.C. 1978, c. 440; SOR/81-859, Can. Gaz. Pt. II, 26/10/81, p. 3153.

PART VII — DISORDERLY HOUSES, GAMING AND BETTING

Interpretation

197. (1) Definitions — In this Part

"bet" means a bet that is placed on any contingency or event that is to take place in or out of Canada, and without restricting the generality of the foregoing, includes a bet that is placed on any contingency relating to a horse-race, fight, match or sporting event that is to take place in or out of Canada;

"common bawdy-house" means a place that is

(a) kept or occupied, or

(b) resorted to by one or more persons

for the purpose of prostitution or the practice of acts of indecency;

"common betting house" means a place that is opened, kept or used for the purpose of

(a) enabling, encouraging or assisting persons who resort thereto to bet between themselves or with the keeper, or

(b) enabling any person to receive, record, register, transmit or pay bets or to announce the results of betting;

"common gaming house" means a place that is

(a) kept for gain to which persons resort for the purpose of playing games, or

(b) kept or used for the purpose of playing games

(i) in which a bank is kept by one or more but not all of the players,

(ii) in which all or any portion of the bets on or proceeds from a game is paid, directly or indirectly, to the keeper of the place,

(iii) in which, directly or indirectly, a fee is charged to or paid by the players for the privilege of playing or participating in a game or using gaming equipment, or

(iv) in which the chances of winning are not equally favourable to all persons who play the game, including the person, if any, who conducts the game;

"disorderly house" means a common bawdy-house, a common betting house or a common gaming house;

"game" means a game of chance or mixed chance and skill;

"gaming equipment" means anything that is or may be used for the purpose of playing games or for betting;

"keeper" includes a person who

(a) is an owner or occupier of a place,

(b) assists or acts on behalf of an owner or occupier of a place,

(c) appears to be, or to assist or act on behalf of an owner or occupier of a place,

(d) has the care or management of a place, or

(e) uses a place permanently or temporarily, with or without the consent of the owner or occupier;

"place" includes any place, whether or not

(a) it is covered or enclosed,

(b) it is used permanently or temporarily, or

(c) any person has an exclusive right of user with respect to it;

"prostitute" means a person of either sex who engages in prostitution;

"public place" includes any place to which the public have access as of right or by invitation, express or implied.

(2) **Exception** — A place is not a common gaming house within the meaning of paragraph (*a*) or subparagraph (*b*)(ii) or (iii) of the definition "common gaming house" in subsection (1) while it is occupied and used by an incorporated genuine social club or branch thereof, if

(a) the whole or any portion of the bets on or proceeds from games played therein is not directly or indirectly paid to the keeper thereof; and

(b) no fee is charged to persons for the right or privilege of participating in the games played therein other than under the authority of and in accordance with the terms of a licence issued by the Attorney General of the province in which the place is situated or by such other person or authority in the province as may be specified by the Attorney General thereof.

(3) **Onus** — The onus of proving that, by virtue of subsection (2), a place is not a common gaming house is on the accused.

(4) **Effect when game partly played on premises** — A place may be a common gaming house notwithstanding that

(a) it is used for the purpose of playing part of a game and another part of the game is played elsewhere;

(b) the stake that is played for is in some other place, or

(c) it is used on only one occasion in the manner described in paragraph (*b*) of the definition "common gaming house" in subsection (1), if the keeper or any person acting on behalf of or in concert with the keeper has used another place on another occasion in the manner described in that paragraph.

R.S., c. C-34, s. 179; 1972, c. 13, s. 13; 1980–81–82–83, c. 125, s. 11;R.S. 1985, c. 27 (1st Supp.), s. 29.

Commentary: The section defines several words and phrases used in this Part.

The *exhaustive* definition "common gaming house" in s. 197(1) should be read together with the exemption of s. 197(2) relating to incorporated genuine social clubs or branches thereof and s. 197(4). Section

197(3) shifts the *onus* of establishing the exemption of s. 197(2) to D, thereby attracting *Charter* ss. 7 and 11(d) scrutiny.

Case Law

Bet: S. 197(1)

R. v. Benwell (1972), 9 C.C.C. (2d) 158 (Ont. C.A.); affirmed (1973), 10 C.C.C. (2d) 503n (S.C.C.) — "Bet", used in the *Code*, does *not* have the same connotation as in the civil law of contract.

Common Bawdy-House: S. 197(1) [See also s. 210]

Patterson v. R. (1967), 3 C.R.N.S. 23, [1968] 2 C.C.C. 247 (S.C.C.) — *See also: R. v. Ikeda* (1978), 3 C.R. (3d) 382, 42 C.C.C. (2d) 195 (Ont. C.A.); *R. v. Lahaie* (1990), 55 C.C.C. (3d) 572 (Que. C.A.) — P must prove frequent or habitual use of a place for the purposes of prostitution in order to justify a conviction.

R. v. McLellan (1980), 55 C.C.C. (2d) 543 (B.C. C.A.) — Not every room must be used for the purposes of prostitution to make a hotel a common bawdy-house, nor does a particular room have to be used exclusively for prostitution in order to qualify.

R. v. Sorko, [1969] 4 C.C.C. 241 (B.C. C.A.) — It is *not* essential to prove that actual acts of prostitution or intercourse took place, provided an inference can be drawn from the circumstances that the premises were continually kept and occupied for that purpose.

R. v. Turkiewich (1962), 38 C.R. 220, 133 C.C.C. 301 (Man. C.A.) — To constitute prostitution for the purpose of the definition of common bawdy-house there need *not* be an element of monetary payment or gain. Illicit or promiscuous sexual intercourse is sufficient.

R. v. Pierce (1982), 66 C.C.C. (2d) 388 (Ont. C.A.) — A *parking lot* can qualify as a common bawdy-house. Any defined space is capable of being a common bawdy-house if there was localization of a number of acts of prostitution within specified boundaries.

R. v. Worthington (1972), 22 C.R.N.S. 34, 10 C.C.C. (2d) 311 (Ont. C.A.) — A prostitute can be convicted of keeping a common bawdy-house provided her premises were resorted to or occupied for the purpose of prostitution.

R. v. Laliberté (1973), 12 C.C.C. (2d) 109 (Que. C.A.) — An *indecent* act is an act which offends the general standards that decency permits. A physical act performed for gain on complete strangers for their sexual satisfaction constitutes an indecent act.

Common Betting House: S. 197(1)

R. v. Silvestro (1964), 45 C.R. 76, [1965] 2 C.C.C. 253 (S.C.C.) — The recording of bets is *not* an essential element of keeping a common betting house.

R. v. Ruskoff (1979), 45 C.C.C. (2d) 504 (Ont. C.A.) — Evidence that a place was equipped with "gaming equipment" but which was not, or may not, "be used for betting" was *not* proof that the place was a common betting house.

R. v. Grainger (1978), 42 C.C.C. (2d) 119 (Ont. C.A.) — The nature of the activity encompassed by the word "opened" must be taken to be the same as that included by the words "kept or used" which requires proof that the activity was frequent or habitual in nature. Use of a hotel room on only one occasion does *not* come within the subsection.

Common Gaming House: S. 197(1)

R. v. DiPietro (1986), 50 C.R. (3d) 266, 25 C.C.C. (3d) 100 (S.C.C.); reversing (1982), 1 C.C.C. (3d) 458 (Ont. C.A.) — The necessary element of gaming is that the participants stand to win or lose money or money's worth. The custom of losers buying drinks for the winners did *not* meet that requirement, where no money changed hands among the players. They were *not* putting up stakes on the outcome of the game.

Rockert v. R. (1978), 2 C.R. (3d) 97, 38 C.C.C. (2d) 438 (S.C.C.) — A single or isolated use of premises for the prohibited purpose is insufficient to constitute the premises a common gaming house.

R. v. Monroe (1970), 1 C.C.C. (2d) 68 (B.C. C.A.) — To be a "bank" as contemplated by the section, some advantage over the other players must accrue to the banker because of his position.

R. v. Irwin (1982), 1 C.C.C. (3d) 212 (Ont. C.A.) — On a charge of *keeping* a common gaming house, P has to prove that the game's *participants* and *operators* have a *chance* of both winning or losing money, or money's worth, by participating in a game of chance or mixed chance and skill.

R. v. Karavasilis (1980), 54 C.C.C. (2d) 530 (Ont. C.A.) — Premises leased by D for the purpose of operating a club to which members resorted nightly to play rummy was capable of constituting a common gaming house even though the membership fees were donated to a *bona fide* soccer club and D received no money from the games.

R. v. LeFrancois (1981), 63 C.C.C. (2d) 380 (Que. C.A.) — It is enough that a room was kept for the purpose of gain for it to be found to be a common gaming house, and it is *not* necessary that in the end there was a gain. The deficit incurred by a gaming house does not absolve the owner of the offence committed.

Game: S. 197(1)

Ross v. R. (1968), 4 C.R.N.S. 233, [1969] 1 C.C.C. 1 (S.C.C.) — The words used to define "game" are *not* ambiguous and apply to any game of chance only or of mixed chance and skill regardless of the respective proportions of the two elements. Bridge falls within the subsection.

R. v. Cosmopolitan Club (1948), 5 C.R. 100 (Alta. T.D.) — Bingo is a game of chance but not a lottery.

R. v. LeFrancois (1981), 63 C.C.C. (2d) 380 (Que. C.A.) — Neutral objects which are *not* generally considered as gaming equipment if actually used for gaming and betting, are gaming equipment.

Keeper: S. 197(1) [See also ss. 201 and 210]

R. v. Corbeil (1991), 5 C.R. (4th) 62, 64 C.C.C. (3d) 272 (S.C.C.); affirming (1990), 57 C.C.C. (3d) 554 (Que. C.A.) — A "keeper" under s. 197(1) does *not* necessarily "keep" a common bawdy-house for the purposes of s. 210(1). To be guilty of *keeping* a common bawdy-house, D must

i. have *some* degree of *control* over the *care and management* of the premises; and

ii. *participate*, to some extent, in the "illicit" activities of the common bawdy-house.

D need *not* personally participate in the sexual acts which occur in the house, provided he or she participates in the use of the house as a common bawdy-house.

Rockert v. R. (1978), 2 C.R. (3d) 97, 38 C.C.C. (2d) 438 (S.C.C.) — "Keeps" connotes frequent or habitual behaviour. A place used once for gaming is not a common gaming house.

R. v. McLellan (1980), 55 C.C.C. (2d) 543 (B.C. C.A.) — Where there was no evidence that D, a prostitute, provided the accommodation at a hotel which she used on four occasions, or that she rented the room from the hotel, she was acquitted of keeping a common bawdy-house.

R. v. Monroe (1970), 1 C.C.C. (2d) 68 (B.C. C.A.) — Mere possession of the fund which constitutes the bank does *not* make the possessor the keeper of a common gaming house.

R. v. Howden Social Club, [1968] 1 C.C.C. 41 (B.C. C.A.) — The manager of a social club who actively arranged for persons to act as "trustees" of prize moneys from bingo games held on the premises, is a "keeper".

R. v. Lamolinara (1989), 53 C.C.C. (3d) 250 (Que. C.A.) — While a place must be used frequently or habitually for gaming to be a common gaming house, it is *not* essential on a charge of keeping to prove that D also was repeatedly present there.

R. v. Poo How Do, [1965] 2 C.C.C. 51 (Que. C.A.) — A person who acted as dealer and stakeholder and kept a portion of the bets was considered a "keeper". In addition, the possession of a key to the premises was sufficient to make one a "keeper".

Place: S. 197(1)

R. v. Rubenstein (1960), 32 C.R. 20, 126 C.C.C. 312 (Ont. C.A.) — A public park at which a game is operated on a picnic table is a "place".

Vincent v. R. (1962), 38 C.R. 259 (Que. C.A.) — Part of a building, or even a room, may be a common gaming house although the building or room as a whole could *not* be so considered. It is also important whether D has exclusive use of the entire building or room.

Public Place: S. 197(1)

Hutt v. R. (1978), 1 C.R. (3d) 164, 38 C.C.C. (2d) 418 (S.C.C.) — A plainclothes police officer's car is *not* a public place.

Exception for Genuine Social Club: S. 197(2)

R. v. MacDonald (1965), 47 C.R. 37, [1966] 2 C.C.C. 307 (S.C.C.) — A "social club", open to the public on payment of an admission fee, where persons could participate in bingo games, the whole or a portion of the proceeds which were directly or indirectly paid to the keeper, is *not* a *bona fide* social club.

Related Provisions: Other sources of assistance in determining the meaning of words and phrases used in the *Code* are described in the *Related Provisions* note to s. 2, *supra*.

Presumptions

198. (1) Presumptions — In proceedings under this Part,

(a) evidence that a peace officer who was authorized to enter a place was wilfully prevented from entering or was wilfully obstructed or delayed in entering is, in the absence of any evidence to the contrary, proof that the place is a disorderly house;

(b) evidence that a place was found to be equipped with gaming equipment or any device for concealing, removing or destroying gaming equipment is, in the absence of any evidence to the contrary, proof that the place is a common gaming house or a common betting house, as the case may be;

(c) evidence that gaming equipment was found in a place entered under a warrant issued pursuant to this Part, or on or about the person of anyone found therein, is, in the absence of any evidence to the contrary, proof that the place is a common gaming house and that the persons found therein were playing games, whether or not any person acting under the warrant observed any persons playing games therein; and

(d) evidence that a person was convicted of keeping a disorderly house is, for the purpose of proceedings against any one who is alleged to have been an inmate or to have been found in that house at the time the person committed the offence of which he was convicted, in the absence of any evidence to the contrary, proof that the house was, at that time, a disorderly house.

(2) Conclusive presumption from slot machine — For the purpose of proceedings under this Part, a place that is found to be equipped with a slot machine shall be conclusively presumed to be a common gaming house.

(3) "slot machine" defined — In subsection (2), "slot machine" means any automatic machine or slot machine

(a) that is used or intended to be used for any purpose other than vending merchandise or services, or

(b) that is used or intended to be used for the purpose of vending merchandise or services if

(i) the result of one of any number of operations of the machine is a matter of chance or uncertainty to the operator,

(ii) as a result of a given number of successive operations by the operator the machine produces different results, or

(iii) on any operation of the machine it discharges or emits a slug or token

but does not include an automatic machine or slot machine that dispenses as prizes only one or more free games on that machine.

R.S., c. C-34, s. 180; 1974–75–76, c. 93, s. 10.

Commentary: The section creates several *presumptions* applicable in proceedings under Part VII and enacts an exhaustive definition of "slot machine", for the purposes of the presumption of s. 198(2).

The presumptions of s. 198(1) require evidence of (a> basic fact(s) of the nature described. The *presumed* fact (*"proof* that ...") follows from the *evidentiary* or proven fact (*"evidence* that ...") unless rebutted by evidence to the contrary.

The *rebuttable* presumptions of subsection (1) may be contrasted with the *irrebuttable* presumption of s. 198(2), which *conclusively* presumes a place to be a common gaming house, upon proof that it is equipped with a slot machine as defined in s. 198(3).

Sections 198(1) and (2) have attracted *Charter* ss. 7 and 11(d) scrutiny.

Case Law

Application

R. v. Wong (1950), 9 C.R. 46 (Ont. C.A.) — The presumptions do *not* apply to premises of an incorporated *bona fide* social club.

R. v. DiSerio (1974), 28 C.R.N.S. 256 (Que. C.A.) — Once a place is found to be equipped with gaming equipment, there is *no* need for P to lead any further evidence establishing the premises as a common gaming house. D must rebut the presumption by leading evidence to the contrary.

Presumptions and Evidence to the Contrary

Theirlynck v. R. (1931), 56 C.C.C. 156 (S.C.C.) — Delay in opening the premises to police officers on demand was *prima facie* evidence of guilt.

R. v. Zippilli (1980), 54 C.C.C. (2d) 481 (Ont. C.A.) — A pinball machine in which the only prizes for high scores were free games is *not* a slot machine.

R. v. LeFrancois (1981), 63 C.C.C. (2d) 380 (Que. C.A.) — Twenty-five cent pieces used to play "heads or tails" constituted "gaming equipment" since the evidence established that the pieces were actually being used for gaming and betting. The presumption in s. 198(1)(b) applied.

R. v. Ball (1957), 26 C.R. 142 (Que. C.A.) — Being found playing cards does not constitute *prima facie* evidence that the place is a common betting house.

Lewis v. R. (1949), 9 C.R. 36, 97 C.C.C. 268 (Que. C.A.) — Where the presumption contained in s. 198(1)(b) is relied upon, P must show that the equipment was used for betting.

Charter Considerations

R. v. Shisler (1990), 53 C.C.C. (3d) 531 (Ont. C.A.) — The conclusive presumption in s. 198(2) violates *Charter* s. 11(d) and is *not* saved by s. 1.

R. v. Janoff (1991), 8 C.R. (4th) 265, 68 C.C.C. (3d) 454 (Que. C.A.) — Section 198(1)(d) is of *no* force and effect on account of its impermissible infringement of *Charter* s. 7 and 11(d).

Related Provisions: "Common betting house", "common gaming house" and "disorderly house" are defined in s. 197(1).

Sections 201–203, create several gaming, betting and cognate offences, s. 204 certain exemptions therefrom. Section 199 confirms special powers of entry, search, seizure, apprehension and forfeiture in relation to designated offences contained in this Part.

Search

199. (1) Warrant to search — A justice who is satisfied by information on oath that there are reasonable grounds to believe that an offence under section 201, 202, 203, 206, 207 or 210 is being committed at any place within the jurisdiction of the justice may issue a warrant authorizing a peace officer to enter and search the place by day or night and seize anything found therein that may be evidence that an offence under section 201, 202, 203, 206, 207 or 210, as the case may be, is being committed at that

place, and to take into custody all persons who are found in or at that place and requiring those persons and things to be brought before that justice or before another justice having jurisdiction, to be dealt with according to law.

(2) **Search without warrant, seizure and arrest** — A peace officer may, whether or not he is acting under a warrant issued pursuant to this section, take into custody any person whom he finds keeping a common gaming house and any person whom he finds therein, and may seize anything that may be evidence that such an offence is being committed and shall bring those persons and things before a justice having jurisdiction, to be dealt with according to law.

(3) **Disposal of property seized** — Except where otherwise expressly provided by law, a court, judge, justice or provincial court judge before whom anything that is seized under this section is brought may declare that the thing is forfeited, in which case it shall be disposed of or dealt with as the Attorney General may direct if no person shows sufficient cause why it should not be forfeited.

(4) **When declaration or direction may be made** — No declaration or direction shall be made pursuant to subsection (3) in respect of anything seized under this section until

(a) it is no longer required as evidence in any proceedings that are instituted pursuant to the seizure; or

(b) the expiration of thirty days from the time of seizure where it is not required as evidence in any proceedings.

(5) **Conversion into money** — The Attorney General may, for the purpose of converting anything forfeited under this section into money, deal with it in all respects as if he were the owner thereof.

(6) **Telephones exempt from seizure** — Nothing in this section or in section 489 authorizes the seizure, forfeiture or destruction of telephone, telegraph or other communication facilities or equipment that may be evidence of or that may have been used in the commission of an offence under section 201, 202, 203, 206, 207 or 210 and that is owned by a person engaged in providing telephone, telegraph or other communication service to the public or forming part of the telephone, telegraph or other communication service or system of that person.

(7) **Exception** — Subsection (6) does not apply to prohibit the seizure, for use as evidence, of any facility or equipment described in that subsection that is designed or adapted to record a communication.

R.S., c. C-34, s. 181; R.S. 1985, c. 27 (1st Supp.), s. 203; 1994, c. 44, s. 10.

Commentary: The section permits the issuance of a *warrant* authorizing the *entry* and *search* of premises, the *seizure* there of anything that *may afford evidence* of the commission of a designated offence and its subsequent *forfeiture* and *disposal*. Persons found in or keeping such places may also be taken into custody under the section.

The authority to issue a *disorderly house warrant* under s. 199(1) requires the submission by a peace officer to a justice of an *information on oath*. The information must disclose that the *officer believes, on reasonable grounds*, that a *designated offence* contrary to ss. 201–203, s. 206, 207 or 209 *is being committed* at any place within the territorial jurisdiction of the justice. Satisfaction of these conditions precedent engages the discretion to issue a warrant authorizing a peace officer to *enter* and *search* the place, by day or night, and there *seize* anything that may be evidence that an offence under a designated section is being committed at that place. Sections 199(6) and (7) prohibit or limit the facilities or equipment which may be seized under such a warrant. The warrant further authorizes the peace officer to *take into custody all persons found in or at the searched premises*. Under the warrant, both the persons taken into custody and the things taken as evidence must be brought before the issuing justice or another justice of concurrent jurisdiction to be dealt with according to law.

Section 199(2) confers upon a peace officer the authority to *take into custody* any person whom s/he *finds keeping* or *in a common betting house* and the ancillary authority to *seize anything* that may be evidence that such an offence is being committed. The officer is obliged to bring the things and persons before a justice to be dealt with according to law. The authority of s. 199(2) may be exercised by a peace officer, whether or not s/he is acting under a warrant issued pursuant to s. 199(1). The provisions of ss. 199(6) and (7) prohibit or limit the facilities or equipment which may be seized under this subsection.

Sections 199(3)–(5) provide for the *forfeiture* and subsequent *disposal* of anything seized under s. 199(1) or (2). Under s. 199(3), applicable except where otherwise expressly provided by law, a court, justice or provincial court judge before whom anything seized under the section has been brought may declare it forfeited. An order of forfeiture may be made only where no one shows sufficient cause why the property should not be forfeited. Once ordered forfeited, the thing may be disposed of or dealt with as the Attorney General may direct. Under s. 199(5), the Attorney General may, for the purpose of converting forfeited property into money, deal with it in all respects as if s/he were the owner thereof. Under s. 199(4), no declaration of forfeiture may be made nor an order for disposal given until *either* of the conditions of s. 199(4)(a) or (b) have been met.

Case Law

Declaration of Forfeiture

R. v. Harb (1994), 88 C.C.C. (3d) 204 (N.S. C.A.) — Gambling devices seized under a s. 487 search warrant may be ordered forfeited under s. 199(3).

R. v. Owens (1972), 5 C.C.C. (2d) 125 (Ont. C.A.) — Where *no* evidence is offered to suggest that the money was *not* associated with the illegal operation, the order of forfeiture was proper, P need *not* prove the identity of the monies with a particular offence of which D is guilty to justify an order of forfeiture.

R. v. Duval (1962), 37 C.R. 305 (Que. C.A.) — Once the court deems that the seized object may be evidence of the commission of the offence, the onus is upon D to show sufficient cause why it should *not* be forfeited.

R. v. Anderson (1983), 10 C.C.C. (3d) 183 (Y.T. C.A.) — A declaration of forfeiture must await the outcome of any trial proceedings instituted pursuant to the seizure, but not appellate proceedings.

Appeal From Forfeiture [See also s. 673.]

R. v. Carmichael (1983), 6 C.C.C. (3d) 572 (Que. C.A.) — An appeal of a forfeiture order lies to the court of appeal notwithstanding that D was only found guilty of being "found in" a common gaming house.

Charter Considerations

R. v. Harb (1994), 88 C.C.C. (3d) 204 (N.S. C.A.) — A forfeiture order under s. 199(3) is *not* a seizure under *Charter* s. 8.

Related Provisions: "Justice", "peace officer", "day", "night" and "Attorney General" are defined in s. 2.

A declaration under s. 199(3) is a "sentence" within s. 673 and s. 785(1) for appellate purposes under Parts XXI and XXVII, respectively.

The general *Code* provisions relating to the issuance and execution of *search warrants* are found in ss. 487–492. Other *specialized warrants* which authorize search for and/or seizure of certain materials include ss. 320 (hate propaganda), 395 (minerals and precious metals) and 101–103 (firearms and ammunition).

The general authority to *arrest without warrant* is described in ss. 494 (anyone and owners or others in lawful possession of property) and 495 (peace officers).

Sections 25–31 define the limits of protection from criminal responsibility afforded those who administer or enforce the law. Under s. 26, criminal responsibility follows according to the nature and quality of the act which constitutes the excessive force.

200. [Repealed R.S. 1985, c. 27 (1st Supp.), s. 30.]

Gaming and Betting

201. (1) **Keeping gaming or betting house** — Every one who keeps a common gaming house or common betting house is guilty of an indictable offence and liable to imprisonment for a term not exceeding two years.

(2) **Person found in or owner permitting use** — Every one who

    (a) is found, without lawful excuse, in a common gaming house or common betting house, or

    (b) as owner, landlord, lessor, tenant, occupier or agent, knowingly permits a place to be let or used for the purposes of a common gaming house or common betting house,

is guilty of an offence punishable on summary conviction.

R.S., c. C-34, s. 185.

Commentary: The offences of this section relate to the *operation* of *common gaming* and *betting* houses and are distinguished by the nature or mode of D's participation therein.

The "keeper" or "keeping" offence of s. 201(1) requires proof that D *kept* a common gaming or betting house, as the case may be. In essence, what is required is some act of participation by D in the unlawful use of the premises as a specified type of disorderly house. P need prove no ulterior *mental element* to establish D's liability.

The *external circumstances* of the "found in" offence of s. 201(2)(a) combines elements of presence, prohibited character of the premises and the absence of lawful excuse. The premises must be a *common gaming* or *common betting house*, as the case may be. D must be *found in* the premises and be there *without lawful excuse*.

The offence of s. 201(2)(b) is generally described as "permitting". The *external circumstances* require proof that D is the owner, landlord, lessor, tenant, occupier or agent of a place. Further, D must permit the place to be let or used for a prohibited purpose. The *mental element* requires that P establish that D intentionally caused the external circumstances of the offence and, in particular, that s/he *knowingly* permitted the place to be let or used for a proscribed purpose.

Case Law

Keeper [See also ss. 197 and 202]

Silvestro v. R. (1964), 45 C.R. 76, [1965] 2 C.C.C. 253 (S.C.C.) — The recording of bets is *not* an essential element of *keeping* a common betting house. D does *not* actually have to receive a bet, but only keep the premises *for the purpose of* enabling persons to receive or record bets.

R. v. Kerim (1963), 39 C.R. 390, [1963] 1 C.C.C. 233 (S.C.C.) — The offence of *keeping* a common gaming house, requires something more than the keeping of a place whose use, by someone other than D, makes it a common gaming house.

Keeper

R. v. Bragdon (1996), 112 C.C.C. (3d) 91 (N.B. C.A.) — Participation in illegal gaming activities on a premises does *not* make D a *keeper* of the presmises.

R. v. Volante (1993), 83 C.C.C. (3d) 558 (Ont. C.A.) — *See also*: *R. v. Karavasilis* (1980), 54 C.C.C. (2d) 530 (Ont. C.A.) — To prove a charge of keeping a common gaming house, P must establish some degree of *control* by D over the *care* and *management* of the premises, as well participation, to some extent, in the illicit activities carried out there.

Related Provisions: "Common betting house" is exhaustively defined in s. 197(1). The exhaustive definition of "common gaming house" in s. 197(1) must be read together with the exception of s. 201(2), onus of s. 201(3) and the "notwithstanding" provisions of s. 201(4). "Keeper" and "place" are expansively defined in s. 197(1). Section 198 enacts a series of presumptions that aid P in its proof of the character of the premises. Sections 204(1)–(3) provide exemptions from what otherwise would be criminal liability under the section.

Under ss. 199(1) and (2) special entry, search, seizure, apprehension and forfeiture provisions apply in respect of the offences of s. 201. What is seized may be ordered forfeited and disposed of at the direction of the Attorney General under ss. 199(3)–(7).

The offence of s. 201(1) is an "enterprise crime offence" in s. 462.3 and an "offence" under s. 183 for the purposes of Part VI. Related offences are described in ss. 202–203, 206 and 209.

The *indictable* offence of subsection (1), *keeping* a common gaming or betting house, falls within the *absolute* trial jurisdiction of a provincial court judge under s. 553(c)(i). The offences of s. 201(2) are tried in accordance with Part XXVII and punished under s. 787(1).

202. (1) Betting, pool-selling, book-making, etc. — Every one commits an offence who

    (a) uses or knowingly allows a place under his control to be used for the purposes of recording or registering bets or selling a pool;

    (b) imports, makes, buys, sells, rents, leases, hires or keeps, exhibits, employs or knowingly allows to be kept, exhibited or employed in any place under his control any device or apparatus for the purpose of recording or registering bets or selling a pool, or any machine or device for gambling or betting;

    (c) has under his control any money or other property relating to a transaction that is an offence under this section;

    (d) records or registers bets or sells a pool;

    (e) engages in book-making or pool-selling, or in the business or occupation of betting, or makes any agreement for the purchase or sale of betting or gaming privileges, or for the purchase or sale of information that is intended to assist in book-making, pool-selling or betting;

    (f) prints, provides or offers to print or provide information intended for use in connection with book-making, pool-selling or betting on any horse-race, fight, game or sport, whether or not it takes place in or outside Canada or has or has not taken place;

    (g) imports or brings into Canada any information or writing that is intended or is likely to promote or be of use in gambling, book-making, pool-selling or betting on a horse-race, fight, game or sport, and where this paragraph applies it is immaterial

        (i) whether the information is published before, during or after the race, fight, game or sport, or

        (ii) whether the race, fight, game or sport takes place in Canada or elsewhere,

but this paragraph does not apply to a newspaper, magazine or other periodical published in good faith primarily for a purpose other than the publication of such information;

    (h) advertises, prints, publishes, exhibits, posts up, or otherwise gives notice of any offer, invitation or inducement to bet on, to guess or to foretell the results of a contest, or a result of or contingency relating to any contest;

    (i) wilfully and knowingly sends, transmits, delivers or receives any message by radio, telegraph, telephone, mail or express that conveys any information relating to book-making, pool-selling, betting or wagering, or that is intended to assist in book-making, pool-selling, betting or wagering; or

    (j) aids or assists in any manner in anything that is an offence under this section.

(2) Punishment — Every one who commits an offence under this section is guilty of an indictable offence and liable

(a) for a first offence, to imprisonment for not more than two years;

(b) for a second offence, to imprisonment for not more than two years and not less than fourteen days; and

(c) for each subsequent offence, to imprisonment for not more than two years and not less than three months.

R.S., c. C-34, s. 186; 1974–75–76, c. 93, s. 11.

Commentary: The section describes and punishes several offences relating to *betting, pool-selling, book-making* and *wagering*. It should be read in conjunction with the exemptions of ss. 204(1)–(3).

The offences are of two types. As exemplified by ss. 202(1)(a), (b) and (d)–(i), there are several discrete and specific offences the essential elements of which are set out in the applicable paragraph. For example, under s. 202(1)(d) liability is established where it is proven that D *recorded* or *registered* bets or *sold* a *pool*. The *mental element* generally demands proof only of the intention to cause the external circumstances of the offence but, in some instances, for example, under s. 202(1)(a), the inclusion of "*knowingly*" requires proof of specific knowledge. As ss. 202(1)(c) and (j) illustrate, there are *general* offences which proscribe certain forms of accessoryship in relation to the specific crimes of other paragraphs. The offence of s. 202(1)(c), for example, requires proof that D has under his/her control any *money or other property* relating to a transaction that is an offence under the section. The provision, for example, would prohibit D from becoming a custodian or depository of a proscribed wager. The offence of s. 202(1)(j), a form of accessoryship, requires proof that D, in any manner, aided or assisted in *anything* that is *an offence under the section*. No ulterior mental element need be established in either case, but it is necessary that P prove *knowing* participation in the underlying offence.

Section 202(2) prescribes the *punishment* for the indictable offences described in s. 202(1). Second and subsequent offences attract a minimum punishment, as well as being subject to the statutory maximum applicable in all cases.

Case Law
Keeping: S. 202(1)(b)
R. v. Kent (1994), 92 C.C.C. (3d) 344 (S.C.C.); reversing (1993), 122 N.S.R. (2d) 348 (N.S. C.A.) — The essential elements of the "keeping" offence of s. 202(1)(b) are:

i. that D *kept devices* in a place under D's control;

ii. that the devices were *gambling devices*; and,

iii. that D *knew* the devices were gambling devices and *knowingly* kept them.

P is *not* required to prove that the machines were *actually* used for the purpose of gambling. The prohibition of s. 202(1)(b) is against the *keeping* of gambling machines, regardless of how they are used.

Gambling Machines or Devices: S. 202(1)(b)
R. v. Kent (1994), 92 C.C.C. (3d) 344 (S.C.C.); reversing (1993), 122 N.S.R. (2d) 348 (N.S. C.A.) — *See digest above.*

R. v. Mozel, [1973] 5 W.W.R. 333 (B.C. C.A.) — In order to establish that D is keeping a common betting house, it must be shown that D was the *owner* or *occupier* of the place or was *involved* in the *care* or *management* of the premises, or assisted the owner or occupier in that way. This does not have to be proved to establish a charge of engaging in bookmaking. That offence can be committed on the streets of a city and without D being the keeper of a common betting house.

Keeping vs. Engage in the Business: Ss. 201(1) and 202(1)(e)
R. v. Fialkow (1963), 40 C.R. 151, [1963] 2 C.C.C. 42 (Ont. C.A.) — There is a clear *distinction* between *keeping* a common betting house and being *engaged* in the *business* of betting. On the former charge it must be shown, (1) that the bets are recorded at the place, (2) that the place is kept for that purpose, and (3) that D was involved in the care, management or control of that place. In the latter charge the only question is proof that D was engaged in the business of betting.

Providing Bookmaking Information: S. 202(1)(f); (g)

R. v. Ede (1993), 84 C.C.C. (3d) 447 (Ont. C.A.) — Sections 202(1)(f) and (g) do *not* require that the gambling activities to which the information relates be criminal, *per se*, in the foreign jurisdiction.

Lotteries [See also s. 206]

Canada (A.G.) v. Loto-Que (1983), 9 C.C.C. (3d) 508 (Que. C.A.) — A permitted lottery is lawful regardless of whether it constitutes betting, bookmaking or pool-selling.

Aids or Assists: S. 202(1)(j)

R. v. Michael (1974), 18 C.C.C. (2d) 282 (Alta. C.A.) — "Aids or Assists" means "aids or assists in selling a pool" and not merely making it possible for the offence to be committed by the seller by buying a ticket. Similarly, to aid or assist in recording a bet does not mean to make it possible for a bet to be recorded by writing down one's own bet and handing it to a bookmaker. Parliament has not made it a crime to buy a pool ticket or place a bet with a bookmaker.

Related Provisions: "Bet" and "place" are defined in s. 197(1). "Property" is defined in s. 2. There would appear to be some overlap between the offence of s. 202(1)(j) and the accessoryship provisions of ss. 21(1)(b) and (c).

The *exemptions* of ss. 204(1)–(3) apply to the offences under s. 201(1) and have the effect of excusing from criminal liability conduct which would, *prima facie*, attract it.

The special entry, search, seizure, and apprehension provisions of ss. 199(1) and (2) apply to the offences of this section. The objects of seizure may be ordered forfeited and disposed of upon the direction of the Attorney General under ss. 199(3)–(7).

Related offences are described in ss. 201, 203, 206 and 209. The offence of this section is an "enterprise crime offence" in s. 462.3 and that of s. 202(1)(e) an "offence" under s. 183 for the purposes of Part VI.

The *indictable* offences of the section fall within the *absolute* trial jurisdiction of a provincial court judge under s. 553(c)(ii). The minimum punishment provisions of ss. 202(2)(b) and (c) become engaged upon proof of a prior offence under *any* paragraph of subsection (1). Sections 727 and 667 provide a method to prove previous convictions.

203. Placing bets on behalf of others — Every one who

(a) places or offers or agrees to place a bet on behalf of another person for a consideration paid or to be paid by or on behalf of that other person,

(b) engages in the business or practice of placing or agreeing to place bets on behalf of other persons, whether for a consideration or otherwise, or

(c) holds himself out or allows himself to be held out as engaging in the business or practice of placing or agreeing to place bets on behalf of other persons, whether for a consideration or otherwise,

is guilty of an indictable offence and liable

(d) for a first offence, to imprisonment for not more than two years,

(e) for a second offence, to imprisonment for not more than two years and not less than fourteen days, and

(f) for each subsequent offence, to imprisonment for not more than two years and not less than three months.

R.S., c. C-34, s. 187; 1974–75–76, c. 93, s. 11.

Commentary: The section imposes liability for certain off-track betting schemes.

The *external circumstances* of the offence of s. 203(a) combine two elements: D must *place or offer or agree to place* a bet on behalf of another. In all cases, in other words, a bet need *not* be placed. What is done, whether actually, offered or agreed upon, must be *for a consideration* paid or to be paid by or on behalf of the person for whom the bet is or is to be placed.

The *external circumstances* of the offence of s. 203(b) are complete where D *engages in the business or practice* of *placing* or *agreeing* to place bets on behalf of others. It is immaterial whether consideration is actually paid or agreed upon.

The offence of s. 203(c) is an extension of s. 203(b). Liability is attracted where D *holds him/herself out or allows him/herself to be held out* as engaging in the practice of placing or agreeing to place bets on behalf of others.

Proof of an ulterior mental element is *not* required under any of the paragraphs.

Sections 203(d)–(f) are *punishment* provisions. Second and subsequent offences attract a minimum punishment, as well as being subject to the same statutory maximum.

Related Provisions: "Bet" is defined in s. 197(1) and "person" in s. 2.

Special entry, search, seizure and apprehension provisions in ss. 199(1) and (2) are applicable to the offences of this section. The objects of seizure may be ordered forfeited and disposed of upon the direction of the Attorney General under ss. 199(3)–(7).

The offences of the section fall within the definition of "enterprise crime offence" in s. 462.3.

The *indictable* offences of the section fall within the *absolute* trial jurisdiction of a *provincial court judge* under s. 553(c)(iii).

The minimum punishment provisions of ss. 203(e) and (f) become engaged upon proof of a prior offence under *any* of ss. 203(a)–(c). D's previous conviction may be proven under ss. 727 and 667.

204. (1) Exemption — Sections 201 and 202 do not apply to

(a) any person or association by reason of his or their becoming the custodian or depository of any money, property or valuable thing staked, to be paid to

(i) the winner of a lawful race, sport, game or exercise,

(ii) the owner of a horse engaged in a lawful race, or

(iii) the winner of any bets between not more than ten individuals;

(b) a private bet between individuals not engaged in any way in the business of betting;

(c) bets made or records of bets made through the agency of a pari-mutuel system on running, trotting or pacing horse-races if

(i) the bets or records of bets are made on the race-course of an association in respect of races conducted at that race-course or another race-course in or out of Canada, and, in the case of a race conducted on a race-course situated outside Canada, the governing body that regulates the race has been certified as acceptable by the Minister of Agriculture and Agri-Food or a person designated by that Minister pursuant to subsection (8.1) and that Minister or person has permitted pari-mutuel betting in Canada on the race pursuant to that subsection, and

(ii) the provisions of this section and the regulations are complied with.

(1.1) Exception — For greater certainty, a person may, in accordance with the regulations, do anything described in section 201 or 202, if the person does it for the purposes of legal pari-mutuel betting.

(2) Presumption — For the purposes of paragraph (1)(c), bets made, in accordance with the regulations, in a betting theatre referred to in paragraph 8(e), or by telephone calls to the race-course of an association or to such a betting theatre, are deemed to be made on the race-course of the association.

(3) Operation of pari-mutuel system — No person or association shall use a pari-mutuel system of betting in respect of a horse-race unless the system has been approved by and its operation is carried on under the supervision of an officer appointed by the Minister of Agriculture and Agri-Food.

(4) **Supervision of pari-mutuel system** — Every person or association operating a pari-mutuel system of betting in accordance with this section in respect of a horse-race, whether or not the person or association is conducting the race-meeting at which the race is run, shall pay to the Receiver General in respect of each individual pool of the race and each individual feature pool one-half of one per cent, or such greater fraction not exceeding one per cent as may be fixed by the Governor in Council, of the total amount of money that is bet through the agency of the pari-mutuel system of betting.

(5) **Percentage that may be deducted and retained** — Where any person or association becomes a custodian or depository of any money, bet or stakes under a pari-mutuel system in respect of a horse-race, that person or association shall not deduct or retain any amount from the total amount of money, bets or stakes unless it does so pursuant to subsection (6).

(6) **Idem** — An association operating a pari-mutuel system of betting in accordance with this section in respect of a horse-race, or any other association or person acting on its behalf, may deduct and retain from the total amount of money that is bet through the agency of the pari-mutuel system, in respect of each individual pool of each race or each individual feature pool, a percentage not exceeding the percentage prescribed by the regulations plus any odd cents over any multiple of five cents in the amount calculated in accordance with the regulations to be payable in respect of each dollar bet.

(7) **Stopping of betting** — Where an officer appointed by the Minister of Agriculture and Agri-Food is not satisfied that the provisions of this section and the regulations are being carried out in good faith by any person or association in relation to a race meeting, he may, at any time, order any betting in relation to the race meeting to be stopped for any period that he considers proper.

(8) **Regulations** — The Minister of Agriculture and Agri-Food may make regulations

(a) prescribing the maximum number of races for each race-course on which a race meeting is conducted, in respect of which a pari-mutuel system of betting may be used for the race meeting or on any one calendar day during the race meeting, and the circumstances in which the Minister of Agriculture and Agri-Food or a person designated by him for that purpose may approve of the use of that system in respect of additional races on any race-course for a particular race meeting or on a particular day during the race meeting;

(b) prohibiting any person or association from using a pari-mutuel system of betting for any race-course on which a race meeting is conducted in respect of more than the maximum number of races prescribed pursuant to paragraph (a) and the additional races, if any, in respect of which the use of a pari-mutuel system of betting has been approved pursuant to that paragraph;

(c) prescribing the maximum percentage that may be deducted and retained pursuant to subsection (6) by or on behalf of a person or association operating a pari-mutuel system of betting in respect of a horse-race in accordance with this section and providing for the determination of the percentage that each such person or association may deduct and retain;

(d) respecting pari-mutuel betting in Canada on horse-races conducted on a race-course situated outside Canada; and

(e) authorizing pari-mutuel betting and governing the conditions for pari-mutuel betting, including the granting of licences therefor, that is conducted by an association in a betting theatre owned or leased by the association in a province in which the Lieutenant Governor in Council, or such other person or authority in the province as may be specified by the Lieutenant Governor in Council thereof, has issued a licence to that association for the betting theatre.

(8.1) **Approvals** — The Minister of Agriculture and Agri-Food or a person designated by that Minister may, with respect to a horse-race conducted on a race-course situated outside Canada,

(a) certify as acceptable, for the purposes of this section, the governing body that regulates the race; and

(b) permit pari-mutuel betting in Canada on the race.

(9) **Regulations** — The Minister of Agriculture and Agri-Food may make regulations respecting

(a) the supervision and operation of pari-mutuel systems related to race meetings, and the fixing of the dates on which and the places at which an association may conduct such meetings;

(b) the method of calculating the amount payable in respect of each dollar bet;

(c) the conduct of race-meetings in relation to the supervision and operation of pari-mutuel systems, including photo-finishes, video patrol and the testing of bodily substances taken from horses entered in a race at such meetings, including, in the case of a horse that dies while engaged in racing or immediately before or after the race, the testing of any tissue taken from its body;

(d) the prohibition, restriction or regulation of

(i) the possession of drugs or medicaments or of equipment used in the administering of drugs or medicaments at or near race-courses, or

(ii) the administering of drugs or medicaments to horses participating in races run at a race meeting during which a pari-mutuel system of betting is used; and

(e) the provision, equipment and maintenance of accommodation, services or other facilities for the proper supervision and operation of pari-mutuel systems related to race meetings, by associations conducting those meetings or by other associations.

(9.1) **900 metre zone** — For the purposes of this section, the Minister of Agriculture and Agri-Food may designate, with respect to any race-course, a zone that shall be deemed to be part of the race-course, if

(a) the zone is immediately adjacent to the race-course;

(b) the farthest point of that zone is no more than 900 metres from the nearest point on the race track of the race-course; and

(c) all real property situated in that zone is owned or leased by the person or association that owns or leases the race-course.

(10) **Contravention** — Every person who contravenes or fails to comply with any of the provisions of this section or of any regulations made under this section is guilty of

(a) an indictable offence and is liable to imprisonment for a term not exceeding two years, or

(b) an offence punishable on summary conviction.

(11) Definition of "association" — For the purposes of this section "association" means an association incorporated by or pursuant to an Act of the Parliament or of the legislature of a province that owns or leases a race-course and conducts horse-races in the ordinary course of its business and, to the extent that the applicable legislation requires that the purposes of the association be expressly stated in its constating instrument, having as one of its purposes the conduct of horse-races.

R.S., c. C-34, s. 188; 1980–81–82–83, c. 99, s. 1; R.S. 1985, c. 47 (1st Supp.), s. 1; 1989, c. 2, s. 1; 1994, c. 38, s. 25(1)(g).

Commentary: The section provides *exemption* from the liability-creating provisions of ss. 201 and 202 and, further, provides for the operation and supervision of a system of pari-mutuel betting.

The *exemptions* of s. 204(1) are threefold. Under s. 204(1)(a), any person or association which becomes the custodian or depository of any money, property or valuable thing staked, to be paid to any person described in ss. 204(1)(i)–(iii), does *not* contravene either s. 201 or 202. "Association" is defined in s. 204(11). Section 204(1)(b) exempts a private bet between individuals, not engaged in any way in the business of betting. Under s. 204(1)(c), bets made or records of bets made through the agency of a *pari-mutuel system* on running, trotting or pacing horse-races do not attract liability, provided compliance is made with ss. 204(1)(i) and (ii). Section 204(2) deems bets made by telephone calls to the race-course of an association, in accordance with the applicable regulations, to be made on the race-course of the association.

Section 204(1.1) creates a further exemption which permits anything described in s. 201 or 202 to be done without criminal liability, provided it is done in accordance with the regulations and for the purpose of legal pari-mutuel betting.

Sections 204(3)-(9.1) provide for the organization and operation of *pari-mutuel systems* of betting in respect of horse-races under the approval and supervision of the Minister of Agriculture and his/her designates. Regulations may be passed for such purpose. Under s. 204(3), no such system of betting may be used by any person or association as defined in s. 204(11), unless it has been approved by, and its operation carried on under, the supervision of an officer appointed by the Minister.

Under s. 204(10), it is an offence, triable either way, to contravene or fail to comply with any of the provisions of the section or regulations made thereunder.

Case Law

R. v. Gula (1971), 17 C.R.N.S. 129 (Ont. Prov. Ct.); affirmed (1971), 17 C.R.N.S. 129, 136 (Ont C.A.) — It is for D to satisfy the court, or at least raise a reasonable doubt, that an exemption applies

Related Provisions: "Person" and "property" are defined in s. 2.

Section 201 describes and punishes offences relating to the operation of common gaming or betting houses. The prohibition of s. 202 is directed against betting, pool-selling, book-making and other unlawful forms of wagering. The special entry, search, seizure and apprehension provisions of ss. 199(1) and (2) are *not* applicable to offences under s. 204(10).

P's election to proceed by way of indictment under s. 204(10)(a) would appear to confer upon D a right to elect mode of trial under s. 536(2). The offence is *not* listed in s. 553. Summary conviction proceedings under s. 204(10)(b) are tried under Part XXVII and punished under s. 787(1).

205. [Repealed R.S. 1985, c. 52 (1st Supp.), s. 1.]

206. (1) Offence in relation to lotteries and games of chance — Every one is guilty of an indictable offence and liable to imprisonment for a term not exceeding two years who

(a) makes, prints, advertises or publishes, or causes or procures to be made, printed, advertised or published, any proposal, scheme or plan for advancing, lending, giving, selling or in any way disposing of any property by lots, cards, tickets or any mode of chance whatever;

(b) sells, barters, exchanges or otherwise disposes of, or causes or procures, or aids or assists in, the sale, barter, exchange or other disposal of, or offers for sale, barter or exchange, any lot, card, ticket or other means or device for advancing, lending, giving, selling or otherwise disposing of any property by lots, tickets or any mode of chance whatever;

(c) knowingly sends, transmits, mails, ships, delivers or allows to be sent, transmitted, mailed, shipped or delivered, or knowingly accepts for carriage or transport or conveys any article that is used or intended for use in carrying out any device, proposal, scheme or plan for advancing, lending, giving, selling or otherwise disposing of any property by any mode of chance whatever;

(d) conducts or manages any scheme, contrivance or operation of any kind for the purpose of determining who, or the holders of what lots, tickets, numbers or chances, are the winners of any property so proposed to be advanced, lent, given, sold or disposed of;

(e) conducts, manages or is a party to any scheme, contrivance or operation of any kind by which any person, on payment of any sum of money, or the giving of any valuable security, or by obligating himself to pay any sum of money or give any valuable security, shall become entitled under the scheme, contrivance or operation to receive from the person conducting or managing the scheme, contrivance or operation, or any other person, a larger sum of money or amount of valuable security than the sum or amount paid or given, or to be paid or given, by reason of the fact that other persons have paid or given, or obligated themselves to pay or give any sum of money or valuable security under the scheme, contrivance or operation;

(f) disposes of any goods, wares or merchandise by any game of chance or any game of mixed chance and skill in which the contestant or competitor pays money or other valuable consideration;

(g) induces any person to stake or hazard any money or other valuable property or thing on the result of any dice game, three-card monte, punch board, coin table or on the operation of a wheel of fortune;

(h) for valuable consideration carries on or plays or offers to carry on or to play, or employs any person to carry on or play in a public place or a place to which the public have access, the game of three-card monte;

(i) receives bets of any kind on the outcome of a game of three-card monte; or

(j) being the owner of a place, permits any person to play the game of three-card monte therein.

(2) **"three-card monte"** — In this section "three-card monte" means the game commonly known as three-card monte and includes any other game that is similar to it, whether or not the game is played with cards and notwithstanding the number of cards or other things that are used for the purpose of playing.

(3) **Exemption for fairs** — Paragraphs (1)(f) and (g), in so far as they do not relate to a dice game, three-card monte, punch board or coin table, do not apply to the board of an annual fair or exhibition, or to any operator of a concession leased by that board within its own grounds and operated during the fair or exhibition on those grounds.

(3.1) **Definition of "fair or exhibition"** — For the purposes of this section, "fair or exhibition" means an event where agricultural or fishing products are presented or where activities relating to agriculture or fishing take place.

(4) Offence — Every one who buys, takes or receives a lot, ticket or other device mentioned in subsection (1) is guilty of an offence punishable on summary conviction.

(5) Lottery sale void — Every sale, loan, gift, barter or exchange of any property, by any lottery, ticket, card or other mode of chance depending on or to be determined by chance or lot, is void, and all property sold, lent, given, bartered or exchanged is forfeited to Her Majesty.

(6) Bona fide exception — Subsection (5) does not affect any right or title to property acquired by any *bona fide* purchaser for valuable consideration without notice.

(7) Foreign lottery included — This section applies to the printing or publishing, or causing to be printed or published, of any advertisement, scheme, proposal or plan of any foreign lottery, and the sale or offer for sale of any ticket, chance or share, in any such lottery, or the advertisement for sale of such ticket, chance or share, and the conducting or managing of any such scheme, contrivance or operation for determining the winners in any such lottery.

(8) Saving — This section does not apply to

(a) the division by lot or chance of any property by joint tenants or tenants in common, or persons having joint interests in any such property;

(b) the distribution by lot of premiums given as rewards to promote thrift by punctuality in making periodical deposits of weekly savings in any chartered savings bank; or

(c) bonds, debentures, debenture stock or other securities recallable by drawing of lots and redeemable with interest and providing for payment of premiums on redemption or otherwise.

R.S., c. C-34, s. 189; R.S. 1985, c. 52 (1st Supp.), s. 2.

Commentary: The section creates a number of offences relating to *lotteries* and specified *games of chance*. It should be read together with the exemption of s. 207.

Section 206(1) creates several indictable offences which proscribe certain conduct in relation to lotteries and specified games of chance. The *external circumstances* of each may be established in a variety of ways. None requires proof of any ulterior *mental element*. Section 206(2) provides a definition of "three-card monte", an expression used in ss. 206(1)(g)–(j).

Sections 206(3) and (8) provide *exceptions* to the liability created by s. 206(1). The exception of s. 206(8) is of general application, whereas that of s. 206(3) applies only to ss. 206(1)(f) and (g), insofar as they do not relate to a dice game, three-card monte, punch board or coin table and only excepts certain operations at an annual fair or exhibition as described in s. 206(3.1). Section 206(7), on the other hand, describes the application of the provisions of the section to a foreign lottery.

Under s. 206(5), transactions in property, by any lottery, ticket, card or other mode of chance depending on or to be determined by chance or lot are void. The property that is the subject of the transactions is forfeited to Her Majesty. Subsection (6) exempts rights or title to property acquired by any *bona fide* purchaser for valuable consideration without notice from the operation of s. 206(5).

Case Law

Lottery or Mode of Chance: Ss. 206(1)(a)-(c)

Roe v. R. (1949), 8 C.R. 135, 94 C.C.C. 273 (S.C.C.) — The scheme must be one of pure chance. A scheme of skill or mixed skill and chance does *not* contravene the section.

R. v. Wallace (1954), 20 C.R. 39 (Alta. C.A.) — Although some participants in the scheme may be contestants in a contest of skill, where the outstanding and controlling factor is that thousands of ticket holders will be eliminated through some type of draw or other pure mode of chance with no opportunity to enter the purported contest of skill, the scheme must be characterized as the disposition of property by mode of chance.

R. v. Young (1957), 27 C.R. 226, 119 C.C.C. 389 (B.C. C.A.) — The selection of contestants by chance who were required to answer a question to test their skill and knowledge in order to win a prize circumvents of the section.

R. v. Robert Simpson (Regina) Ltd. (1958), 121 C.C.C. 39 (Sask. C.A.) — Where the skill-testing question is only a device to circumvent the section, a conviction is apt.

Sells

R. v. Groulx (1982), 67 C.C.C. (2d) 382 (Que. C.A.) — Neither the statute nor the regulations expressly or implicitly prohibit persons from buying tickets from a retailer for resale at a higher price.

Pyramid Schemes: S. 206(1)(e)

Dream Home Contests (Edmonton) Ltd. v. R. (1960), 33 C.R. 47, 126 C.C.C. 241 (S.C.C.) — It is irrelevant to a charge under s. 206(1)(e) that the scheme involves skill only rather than chance.

R. v. Golden Can. Products (1973), 26 C.R.N.S. 199, 15 C.C.C. (2d) 1 (Alta. C.A.) — The larger sum of money than that paid in that the participant is entitled to receive need not be in existence at the time the participant pays into the scheme. Nor does the imposition upon the participants of qualifications over and beyond a willingness to pay a sum of money take the scheme outside the section, where the qualifications do not really affect the essence of the scheme but rather involve subordinate and collateral matters.

R. v. Fehr (1983), 4 C.C.C. (3d) 382 (B.C. C.A.) — Subparagraph (e) embraces a scheme where D was entitled to receive money from other participants as well as from the person conducting or managing the scheme.

R. v. MacKenzie (1982), 66 C.C.C. (2d) 528 (Ont. C.A.) — On a charge of conducting a pyramid scheme the essential element is the scheme itself. The scheme must contemplate that a participant would receive a *larger* sum than he paid in as a result of the *participation* of others.

R. v. Canus of North Amer. Ltd. (1964), 43 C.R. 321, [1965] 1 C.C.C. 91 (Sask. C.A.) — Chance and skill are not necessary to constitute an offence under subpara. (e). The issue is whether or not, under the scheme, the participant stands to receive a larger amount paid back than he paid in because other persons have contributed.

Exceptions

R. v. Jones (1991), 8 C.R. (4th) 137, 66 C.C.C. (3d) 512 (S.C.C.) — Colour of right affords no defence to a charge under s. 206(1)(d). A mistaken belief that the section has no application because it is inoperative on a reserve is a mistake of law which affords no defence to the charge.

R. v. Cross (1978), 40 C.C.C. (2d) 505 (Alta. C.A.) — On a charge of keeping a common gaming house in relation to slot machines, D may *not* on the exemptions of s. 206.

R. v. Andrews (1976), 32 C.R.N.S. 358, 28 C.C.C. (2d) 450 (Sask. C.A.) — *See also: R. v. Grayland* (1960), 34 C.R. 211, 128 C.C.C. 428 (B.C. C.A.) — If a charge may have been laid under a different section on the same facts, D is entitled to the protection of any exemption set out in that section. D, charged under s. 201(1) with keeping a common gaming house, is entitled to the benefit of the exemption afforded by this section if he was able to bring himself within its terms.

***Charter* Considerations**

R. v. Stromberg (1999), 131 C.C.C. (3d) 546 (B.C. C.A.) — Section 206(7) is *not* unconstitutionally vague.

Related Provisions: "Property" and "valuable security" are defined in s. 2, "bet" in s. 197(1).

The special entry, search, seizure, apprehension and forfeiture provisions of s. 199 are applicable to the offences of this section.

Section 207 permits the conduct of specified lotteries, thereby exempting their operation from the liability-creating provisions of this section. Section 201 describes and punishes offences relating to the operation of common gaming or common betting houses. Section 202 proscribes certain conduct relating to betting, pool-selling, book-making and other unlawful forms of wagering. Section 203 imposes criminal liability for placing bets on behalf of others.

The offences lie within the *absolute* trial jurisdiction of a provincial court judge under s. 553(c)(iv).

207. **(1) Permitted lotteries** — Notwithstanding any of the provisions of this Part relating to gaming and betting, it is lawful

(a) for the government of a province, either alone or in conjunction with the government of another province, to conduct and manage a lottery scheme in that province, or in that and the other province, in accordance with any law enacted by the legislature of that province;

(b) for a charitable or religious organization, pursuant to a licence issued by the Lieutenant Governor in Council of a province or by such other person or authority in the province as may be specified by the Lieutenant Governor in Council thereof, to conduct and manage a lottery scheme in that province if the proceeds from the lottery scheme are used for a charitable or religious object or purpose;

(c) for the board of a fair or of an exhibition or an operator of a concession leased by that board, to conduct and manage a lottery scheme in a province where the Lieutenant Governor in Council of the province or such other person or authority in the province as may be specified by the Lieutenant Governor in Council thereof has

(i) designated that fair or exhibition as a fair or exhibition where a lottery scheme may be conducted and managed, and

(ii) issued a licence for the conduct and management of a lottery scheme to that board or operator;

(d) for any person, pursuant to a licence issued by the Lieutenant Governor in Council of a province or by such other person or authority in the province as may be specified by the Lieutenant Governor in Council thereof, to conduct and manage a lottery scheme at a public place of amusement in that province if

(i) the amount or value of each prize awarded does not exceed five hundred dollars, and

(ii) the money or other valuable consideration paid to secure a chance to win a prize does not exceed two dollars;

(e) for the government of a province to agree with the government of another province that lots, cards or tickets in relation to a lottery scheme that is by any of paragraphs (*a*) to (*d*) authorized to be conducted and managed in that other province may be sold in the province;

(f) for any person, pursuant to a licence issued by the Lieutenant Governor in Council of a province or such other person or authority in the province as may be designated by the Lieutenant Governor in Council thereof, to conduct and manage in the province a lottery scheme that is authorized to be conducted and managed in one or more other provinces where the authority by which the lottery scheme was first authorized to be conducted and managed consents thereto;

(g) for any person, for the purpose of a lottery scheme that is lawful in a province under any of paragraphs (*a*) to (*f*), to do anything in the province, in accordance with the applicable law or licence, that is required for the conduct, management or operation of the lottery scheme or for the person to participate in the scheme; and

(h) for any person to make or print anywhere in Canada or to cause to be made or printed anywhere in Canada anything relating to gaming and betting that is to be used in a place where it is or would, if certain conditions provided by law are met, be lawful to use such a thing, or to send, transmit, mail, ship, deliver or allow to be sent, transmitted, mailed, shipped or delivered or to accept for carriage or transport or convey any such thing where the destination thereof is such a place.

(2) **Terms and conditions of licence** — Subject to this Act, a licence issued by or under the authority of the Lieutenant Governor in Council of a province as described in paragraph (1)(*b*), (*c*), (*d*), or (*f*) may contain such terms and conditions relating to the conduct, management and operation of or participation in the lottery scheme to which the licence relates as the Lieutenant Governor in Council of that province, the person or authority in the province designated by the Lieutenant Governor in Council thereof or any law enacted by the legislature of that province may prescribe.

(3) **Offence** — Every one who, for the purposes of a lottery scheme, does anything that is not authorized by or pursuant to a provision of this section

(a) in the case of the conduct, management or operation of that lottery scheme

(i) is guilty of an indictable offence and liable to imprisonment for a term not exceeding two years, or

(ii) is guilty of an offence punishable on summary conviction; or

(b) in the case of participating in that lottery scheme, is guilty of an offence punishable on summary conviction.

(4) **Definition of "lottery scheme"** — In this section, "lottery scheme" means a game or any proposal, scheme, plan, means, device, contrivance or operation described in any of paragraphs 206(1)(*a*) to (*g*), whether or not it involves betting, pool selling or a pool system of betting other than

(a) three-card monte, punch board or coin table;

(b) bookmaking, pool selling or the making or recording of bets, including bets made through the agency of a pool or pari-mutuel system, on any race or fight, or on a single sport event or athletic contest; or

(c) for the purposes of paragraphs (1)(b) to (f), a game or proposal, scheme, plan, means, device, contrivance or operation described in any of paragraphs 206(1)(a) to (g) that is operated on or through a computer, video device or slot machine, within the meaning of subsection 198(3), or a dice game.

(5) **Exception re: pari-mutuel betting** — For greater certainty, nothing in this section shall be construed as authorizing the making or recording of bets on horse-races through the agency of a pari-mutuel system other than in accordance with section 204.

R.S., c. C-34, s. 190; 1974–75–76, c. 93, s. 12; R.S. 1985, c. 27 (1st Supp.), s. 31; c. 52 (1st Supp.), s. 3; 1999, c. 5, s. 6.

Commentary: The section operates notwithstanding the provisions of the Part relating to gaming and betting and, by describing what is permitted in relation to the conduct and management of a lottery scheme, defines the limits of *permissible lottery schemes*. "Lottery scheme" is defined in s. 207(4).

Under s. 207(1), *lawful lottery schemes* may be conducted by the *government* of a *province*, a *charitable* or *religious organization*, a board of a fair or exhibition, or operator of a concession leased by the board or by anyone in accordance with the terms of a licence. Section 207(2) authorizes the issuance of a *licence* by the Lieutenant Governor in Council, subject to the terms of the *Code*. The licence may contain such *terms and conditions* relating to the conduct, management and operation of or participation in the lottery scheme as the licensing authority may prescribe. The *government* of a *province* does *not* require a *licence* to manage a lottery scheme. Section 207(5) makes it clear that nothing in the section authorizes the making or recording of bets on horse races through a pari-mutuel system, otherwise than in accordance with s. 204.

Section 207(3) creates *offences* which prohibit unlawful conduct, management or operation of or participation in a lottery scheme. The *external circumstances* consist of doing anything not authorized by or pursuant to a provision of the section for the purposes of a lottery scheme. The *mental element* consists of the intention to cause the external circumstances of the offence. The mode of D's participation in the unauthorized activity determines the potential penalty. Under s. 207(3)(a), where the unauthorized activity relates to the conduct, management or operation of the lottery scheme, the offence is triable either way. Unauthorized participation in the scheme is a summary conviction offence under s. 207(1)(b).

Case Law
Constitutional Validity

R. v. Furtney (1991), 8 C.R. (4th) 121, 66 C.C.C. (3d) 498 (S.C.C.) — Sections 207(1)(b) and (2) are *not* constitutionally invalid as an impermissible delegation to the province of the authority to make criminal law, nor offend *Charter* s. 11(g).

Related Provisions: "Lieutenant Governor in Council" and "province" are defined in *I.A.* s. 35(1), "person" and "bet" in *Code* ss. 2 and 97(1).

The special entry, search, seizure, apprehension and forfeiture provisions of s. 199 apply to the offences of this section.

Section 206 creates several offences relating to lotteries and specified games of chance.

The offence of s. 207(3)(a) is triable *either* way. Where P elects to proceed by indictment, D may *elect* mode of trial under s. 536(2). The offence of s. 207(3)(b) is tried under Part XVII and punished under s. 787(1).

Other related provisions are discussed in the corresponding note to s. 206, *supra*.

207.1 (1) Exemption — lottery scheme on an international cruise ship —
Despite any of the provisions of this Part relating to gaming and betting, it is lawful for the owner or operator of an international cruise ship, or their agent, to conduct, manage or operate and for any person to participate in a lottery scheme during a voyage on an international cruise ship when all of the following conditions are satisfied:

    (a) all the people participating in the lottery scheme are located on the ship;

    (b) the lottery scheme is not linked, by any means of communication, with any lottery scheme, betting, pool selling or pool system of betting located off the ship;

    (c) the lottery scheme is not operated within five nautical miles of a Canadian port at which the ship calls or is scheduled to call; and

    (d) the ship is registered

        (i) in Canada and its entire voyage is scheduled to be outside Canada, or

        (ii) anywhere, including Canada, and its voyage includes some scheduled voyaging within Canda and the voyage

            (A) is of at least forty-eight hours duration and includes some voyaging in international waters and at least one non-Canadian port of call including the port at which the voyage begins or ends, and

            (B) is not scheduled to disembark any passengers at a Canadian port who have embarked at another Canadian port, without calling on at least one non-Canadian port between the two Canadian ports.

(2) Paragraph 207(1)(h) and subsection 207(5) apply — For greater certainty, paragraph 207(1)(h) and subsection 207(5) apply for the purposes of this section.

(3) Offence — Every one who, for the purpose of a lottery scheme, does anything that is not authorized by this section

(a) in the case of the conduct, management or operation of the lottery scheme,

(i) is guilty of an indictable offence and liable to imprisonment for a term of not more than two years, or

(ii) is guilty of an offence punishable on summary conviction; and

(b) in the case of participating in the lottery scheme, is guilty of an offence punishable on summary conviction.

(4) Definitions — The definitions in this subsection apply in this section

"international cruise ship means a passenger ship that is suitable for continuous ocean voyages of at least forty-eight hours duration, but does not include such a ship that is used or fitted for the primary purpose of transporting cargo or vehicles.

"lottery scheme" means a game or any proposal, scheme, plan, means, device, contrivance or operation described in any of paragraphs 206(1)(a) to (g), whether or not it involves betting, pool selling or a pool system of betting. It does not include

(a) three-card monte, punch board or coin table; or

(b) bookmaking, pool selling or the making or recording of bets, including bets made through the agency of a pool or pari-mutuel system, on any race or fight, or on a single sporting event or athletic contest.

1999, c. 5, s. 7.

208. [Repealed R.S. 1985, c. 27 (1st Supp.), s. 32.]

209. Cheating at play — Every one who, with intent to defraud any person, cheats while playing a game or in holding the stakes for a game or in betting is guilty of an indictable offence and liable to imprisonment for a term not exceeding two years.

R.S., c. C-34, s. 192.

Commentary: The *external circumstances* of this offence involve two elements. D must *cheat*. D's cheating must take place whilst s/he is *playing a game in holding the stakes for a game or in betting*. The *external circumstances* must be accompanied by a concurrent ulterior *mental element*, the *intent to defraud any person*, to establish liability. The person whom it is intended to defraud need not be ascertained.

Case Law

McGarey v. R. (1974), 19 C.R.N.S. 82, 6 C.C.C. (2d) 525 (S.C.C.) — In holding that the operator of a milk bottle toss game was an active participant, and *not* a mere passive bystander, the court noted that D solicited players, collected money, placed the bottles in the proper position and would have had to part with a prize should the player have won. If the bottle toss had been what it appeared to be, it would have been a game of pure skill. By the device of differing weights the game had been turned into one of mixed chance and skill. If the varying weight of the bottles were indicated such would merely have been a raising of the degree of skill necessary. The false visual impression was the perpetrating of a fraud which constituted cheating.

R. v. Reilly (1979), 48 C.C.C. (2d) 286 (Ont. C.A.) — Inflating a basketball to higher than ordinary pressures for use in a game at a carnival is simply a measure taken to increase the degree of skill required. It did not change the character of the game from one of skill to one of mixed skill and chance.

Related Provisions: "Bet" and "game" are defined in s. 197(1), "person" in s. 2. The general offence of *fraud* is described in s. 380(1). What constitutes a false pretence is defined in s. 361. Section 362(1) creates several offences involving the use of false pretences.

S. 209 Criminal Code

The special entry, search, seizure, forfeiture and apprehension provisions of s. 199 are *not* applicable to the offences of this section.

The offence, listed in s. 553(c)(v), falls within the *absolute* trial jurisdiction of a provincial court judge.

Other related provisions are described in the corresponding note to s. 206, *supra*.

Bawdy-houses

210. (1) **Keeping common bawdy-house** — Every one who keeps a common **bawdy-house is guilty of an indictable offence and liable to imprisonment for a term not exceeding two years.**

(2) **Landlord, inmate, etc.** — Every one who

   (a) **is an inmate of a common bawdy-house,**

   (b) **is found, without lawful excuse, in a common bawdy-house, or**

   (c) **as owner, landlord, lessor, tenant, occupier, agent or otherwise having charge or control of any place, knowingly permits the place or any part thereof to be let or used for the purposes of a common bawdy-house,**

is guilty of an offence punishable on summary conviction.

(3) **Notice of conviction to be served on owner** — Where a person is convicted of an offence under subsection (1), the court shall cause a notice of the conviction to be served on the owner, landlord or lessor of the place in respect of which the person is convicted or his agent, and the notice shall contain a statement to the effect that it is being served pursuant to this section.

(4) **Duty of landlord on notice** — Where a person on whom a notice is served under subsection (3) fails forthwith to exercise any right he may have to determine the tenancy or right of occupation of the person so convicted, and thereafter any person is convicted of an offence under subsection (1) in respect of the same premises, the person on whom the notice was served shall be deemed to have committed an offence under subsection (1) unless he proves that he has taken all reasonable steps to prevent the recurrence of the offence.

R.S.,c. C-34, s. 193.

Commentary: The offences of this section prohibit certain conduct relating to the operation of common bawdy-houses and are distinguished by the manner of D's participation therein. Sections 210(3) and (4) entitle P to make consequential use of convictions recorded under s. 210(1).

The "keeper" or "keeping" offence of s. 210(1) requires proof that D *kept* a common bawdy-house, as defined in s. 197(1). There should be established some *act* of *participation* by D in the unlawful use of the premises as the specified type of disorderly house. No ulterior *mental element* need be established.

The "inmate" offence of s. 210(2)(a) requires proof that D, at the material time, was an *inmate* of a common bawdy-house. "Inmate" is *not* defined but, in general, refers to an occupant, perhaps along with others, of a premises, or one who dwells therein.

The "found-in" offence of s. 210(2)(b) involves three elements. D must be found in a premises. There must be no lawful excuse for D's presence. The premises must be a common bawdy-house. Neither paragraph requires proof of any ulterior *mental element*.

The "permitting" offence of s. 210(2)(c) requires proof that D is an owner, landlord, lessor, tenant, occupier or otherwise has the charge or control of any place. The place or a part thereof must be let or used for the purposes of a common bawdy-house. D must permit the letting or use of such premises. The *mental element* is expressed in the compendious term"knowingly" which requires proof of knowledge of the character of the premises or the applicable part thereof.

302

Sections 210(3) and (4) should be considered together. Upon conviction under s. 210(1), the court must cause a notice of conviction to be served upon the owner, landlord, or lessor of the premises, or his/her agent, stating that it is being served under the subsection. Service of the notice of conviction under s. 210(3) imposes a duty upon the owner, landlord, lessor or agent, as the case may be, to forthwith exercise any right s/he may have to determine the tenancy. A subsequent conviction of anyone under s. 210(1) in respect of the same premises, under s. 210(4), deems the person served to have committed an offence under s. 210(1). The person served may only be excused from liability where s/he proves that s/he took all reasonable steps to prevent the recurrence of the offence.

The reversal of onus of proof in respect of this defence of due diligence may engage *Charter* ss. 7 and 11(d) scrutiny.

Case Law
Keeps: s. 210(1) [See also s. 197]

R. v. Corbeil (1991), 5 C.R. (4th) 62, 64 C.C.C. (3d) 272 (S.C.C.); affirming (1990), 57 C.C.C. (3d) 554 (Que. C.A.) — A "keeper" under s. 197(1) does *not* necessarily "keep" a common bawdy-house for the purposes of s. 210(1). To be guilty of *keeping* a common bawdy-house, D must

a.   have *some* degree of *control* over the care and management of the premises; and,

b.   *participate*, to some extent, in the "illicit" activities of the common bawdy-house.

D need *not* personally participate in the sexual acts which occur in the house, provided D participates in the use of the house as a common bawdy-house.

R. v. McLellan (1980), 55 C.C.C. (2d) 543 (B.C. C.A.) — The provision of accommodation is the essence of keeping.

R. v. Woszczyna (1983), 6 C.C.C. (3d) 221 (Ont. C.A.) — There is *no* requirement that P prove participation in the day-to-day running of the premises. D was the owner and directing mind of a steambath and knew of the activities on the premises. He participated in the management, received the proceeds from the business, hired staff and paid the operating expenses.

R. v. Catalano (1977), 37 C.C.C. (2d) 255 (Ont. C.A.) — There is a distinction between one who "keeps a common bawdy-house" and a "keeper of a common bawdy-house". The latter is *not* an offence known to law, since not every "keeper" as defined in s. 197 is one who "keeps a common bawdy-house".

Common Bawdy-House [See also s. 197]

R. v. Tremblay (1993), 23 C.R. (4th) 98, 84 C.C.C. (3d) 97 (S.C.C.) — On a charge of keeping a common bawdy-house for the purpose of the practice of acts of indecency, a test of *community standard of tolerance*, similar to that used in obscenity cases, should be applied.

Theirlynck v. R. (1931), 56 C.C.C. 156 (S.C.C.) — Evidence of the general reputation of a house is admissible to show that it is a bawdy-house.

R. v. Pierce (1982), 66 C.C.C. (2d) 388 (Ont. C.A.) — A parking lot or any defined space can qualify as a common bawdy-house, if there is localization of a number of acts of prostitution within specified boundaries. The mere presence of D in the parking lot on a number of occasions is not sufficient to establish them as "keepers" absent some measure of control over the lot or a particular space.

R. v. Worthington (1972), 22 C.R.N.S. 34, 10 C.C.C. (2d) 311 (Ont. C.A.) — An accused who used her residence alone for the purpose of prostitution kept a common bawdy-house.

Labelle v. R., [1957] B.R. 81 (Que. C.A.) — The offence of being "found in" a common bawdy-house is *not* an included offence within the offence of keeping a common bawdy-house.

Found In: s. 210(2)(b)

R. v. Lemieux (1991), 11 C.R. (4th) 224, 70 C.C.C. (3d) 434 (Que. C.A.) — Section 210(2)(b) requires that D be *found in*, *not* merely present at, a common bawdy-house. Proof of mere presence on the premises at an earlier time is *not* sufficient to establish liability. D must have been perceived there or seen by someone.

Permits: S. 210(2)(c)

R. v. Wong (1977), 33 C.C.C. (2d) 6 (Alta. C.A.) — This section is directed at landlords who have actual charge or control and *not* those who have merely the right to acquire or control through termination of the lease.

Charter Considerations

Reference re ss. 193 & 195.1(1)(c) of the Criminal Code (1990), 77 C.R. (3d) 1, 56 C.C.C. (3d) 65 (S.C.C.) — The "keeping" offence of s. 193(1) [now 210(1)] does *not* infringe *Charter* s. 2(b) or 7, either alone or in combination with s. 195.1(1)(c) [now 213(1)(c)].

Related Provisions: "Common bawdy-house", "prostitute", "place" and "keeper" are defined in s. 197(1), "owner" and "person" in s. 2. Related offences are described in ss. 211 (transporting person to a common bawdy-house), 212 (procuring) and 213 (offence in relation to prostitution).

The special entry, search, seizure, forfeiture and apprehension provisions of s. 199 apply in respect of offences under this section. The offence of s. 210(1), "keeping", is listed in s. 553(c)(vi) as being within the *absolute* trial jurisdiction of a provincial court judge. The offences of subsection (2) are tried under Part XXVII and punished under s. 787(1).

The definition of "enterprise crime offence" in s. 462.3 includes an offence against s. 210.

211. Transporting person to bawdy-house — Every one who knowingly takes, transports, directs, or offers to take, transport, or direct any other person to a common bawdy-house is guilty of an offence punishable on summary conviction.

R.S., c. C-34, s. 194.

Commentary: The *external circumstances* of this summary conviction offence may be established in a number of ways. They are equally complete upon D taking, transporting or directing another person to a common bawdy-house or upon D's mere offer to do so. "Knowingly" requires proof of D's knowledge of the character of the premises as an essential component of the *mental element* of the offence.

Related Provisions: "Common bawdy-house" is defined in s. 197(1).

Related offences are described in ss. 210 (keeping common bawdy-house), 212 (procuring) and 213 (offence in relation to prostitution).

The special entry, search, seizure, forfeiture and apprehension provisions of s. 199 do *not* apply to this offence.

The offence is tried under Part XXVII and punished under s. 787(1).

Procuring

212. (1) Procuring — Every one who

(a) procures, attempts to procure or solicits a person to have illicit sexual intercourse with another person, whether in or out of Canada,

(b) inveigles or entices a person who is not a prostitute to a common bawdy-house for the purpose of illicit sexual intercourse or prostitution,

(c) knowingly conceals a person in a common bawdy-house,

(d) procures or attempts to procure a person to become, whether in or out of Canada, a prostitute,

(e) procures or attempts to procure a person to leave the usual place of abode of that person in Canada, if that place is not a common bawdy-house, with intent that the person may become an inmate or frequenter of a common bawdy-house, whether in or out of Canada,

(f) on the arrival of a person in Canada, directs or causes that person to be directed or takes or causes that person to be taken, to a common bawdy-house,

(g) procures a person to enter or leave Canada, for the purpose of prostitution,

(h) for the purposes of gain, exercises control, direction or influence over the movements of a person in such manner as to show that he is aiding, abetting or compelling that person to engage in or carry on prostitution with any person or generally,

(i) applies or administers to a person or causes that person to take any drug, intoxicating liquor, matter or thing with intent to stupefy or overpower that person in order thereby to enable any person to have illicit sexual intercourse with that person, or

(j) lives wholly or in part on the avails of prostitution of another person,

is guilty of an indictable offence and liable to imprisonment for a term not exceeding ten years.

(2) **Idem** — Notwithstanding paragraph (1)(j), every person who lives wholly or in part on the avails of prostitution of another person who is under the age of eighteen years is guilty of an indictable offence and liable to imprisonment for a term not exceeding fourteen years.

(2.1) **Aggravated offence in relation to living on the avails of prostitution of a person under the age of eighteen years** — Notwithstanding paragraph (1)(j) and subsection (2), every person who lives wholly or in part on the avails of prostitution of another person under the age of eighteen years, and who

(a) for the purposes of profit, aids, abets, counsels or compels the person under that age to engage in or carry on prostitution with any person or generally, and

(b) uses, threatens to use or attempts to use violence, intimidation or coercion in relation to the person under that age,

is guilty of an indictable offence and liable to imprisonment for a term not exceeding fourteen years but not less than five years.

(3) **Presumption** — Evidence that a person lives with or is habitually in the company of a prostitute or lives in a common bawdy-house is, in the absence of evidence to the contrary, proof that the person lives on the avails of prostitution, for the purposes of paragraph (1)(j) and subsections (2) and (2.1).

(4) **Offence — prostitution of person under eighteen** — Every person who, in any place, obtains for consideration, or communicates with anyone for the purpose of obtaining for consideration, the sexual services of a person who is under the age of eighteen years is guilty of an indictable offence and liable to imprisonment for a term not exceeding five years.

(5) [Repealed 1999, c. 5, s. 8.]

R.S., c. C-34, s. 195; 1972, c. 13, s. 14; 1980–81–82–83, c. 125, s. 13;R.S. 1985, c. 19 (3d Supp.), s. 9; 1997, c. 16, s. 2; 1999, c. 5, s. 8.

Commentary: The section creates a number of discrete offences conveniently grouped as "procuring" and enacts an evidentiary presumption, engaged upon evidence of a preliminary fact, applicable to the offences of s. 212(1)(j), (2) and (2.1). In most, though not all instances, D's conduct must be accompanied by an element of purpose or ulterior intent.

The offence of s. 212(1)(a) requires that D procure, attempt to procure or solicit a person to have illicit sexual intercourse with another person. It matters not whether the illicit sexual intercourse is to take place in or out of Canada. "Illicit" means not sanctioned by law, rule or custom. The *mental element* engages proof of the intention to cause the external circumstances of the offence.

Under s. 212(1)(b), a form of corruption is proscribed. The *external circumstances* are established where D inveigles or entices a person, who is *not* a prostitute to a common bawdy-house. The inveiglement or enticement must be for the *purpose* of illicit sexual intercourse or prostitution. The *mental element* comprises the intent to cause the external circumstances of the offence, including their unlawful purpose.

The offence of s. 212(1)(c) consists of the *concealment* of a person in a common bawdy-house. The *mental element*, expressed in the compendious term "knowingly", involves proof of knowledge by D of the character of the concealment.

Under s. 212(1)(d), the *external circumstances* require proof of *actual* or *attempted* procurement of another to become, in or out of Canada, a prostitute. Actual procurement need *not* occur. The *mental element* is established upon proof of the intention to cause the external circumstances of the offence.

The offence of s. 212(1)(e) is complementary to that of s. 212(1)(d). The *actual* or *attempted* procurement must be of a person to leave their usual Canadian abode which must not be a common bawdy-house. Proof of an ulterior *mental element*, the intent that the person procured may become an inmate or frequenter of a common bawdy-house in Canada or elsewhere, is also required.

Under s. 212(1)(f), the offence must occur upon the arrival of a person in Canada. It is complete where D directs or causes a person, upon his/her arrival in Canada, to be directed, or takes or causes the person to be taken, to a common bawdy-house. No ulterior *mental element* need be established, though it would seem to accord with general principle to require proof of D's knowledge of the character of the place to which V is to be taken.

The complementary offence of s. 212(1)(g) proscribes procurement of a person to enter or leave Canada for the purposes of prostitution. Under s. 212(1)(h), the *external circumstances* consist of the exercise of control, direction or influence by D over the movements of a person in a manner demonstrative of aiding, abetting or compelling such person to engage in or carry on prostitution with any person or generally. D's conduct must be accompanied by a proscribed purpose, namely, "gain".

The offence of s. 212(1)(i) requires that D apply or administer to a person or cause such a person to take any drug, intoxicating liquor, matter or thing. D's conduct must be accompanied by the ulterior *mental element* described in the remainder of the paragraph.

Under s. 212(1)(j), D's offence is complete where D lives, wholly or in part, on the avails of the prostitution of another. The *mental element* consists of the intention to do so. Section 212(2) creates a distinct offence and punishment where the person on the avails of whose prostitution D lives, in whole or in part, is under the age of 18 years. Section 212(2.1) creates an *aggravated* version of s. 212(2). If D lives, in whole or in part, on the avails of prostitution of a person under eighteen *and if* D, for the purpose of profit, aids, abets, counsels or compels that person to engage in or carry on prostitution *and* uses, threatens to use or attempts to use violence, intimidation or coercion against that person, the *external circumstances* of the offence are proven. The *mental element* is the intent to cause the external circumstances. P's proof of any of these offences is assisted by s. 212(3). It converts *evidence* that D lives with or is habitually in the company of a prostitute or lives in a common bawdy-house into *proof* that D is living on the avails of prostitution, *in the absence of evidence to the contrary*. It is also aided by the presumption in s. 212(5) [Editor's Note: Subsection 212(5) repealed 1999, c. 5, s. 8]. Where there is evidence that the person from whom sexual services were obtained was represented to D as being under eighteen. This is *proof* in absence of evidence to the contrary, there is proof that D believed that person to be under eighteen.

Case Law

Procure [See also s. 22]

R. v. Babcock (1974), 18 C.C.C. (2d) 175 (B.C. C.A.) — Solicitation of two men for illicit sexual intercourse with another person is procuring.

R. v. Gruba, [1969] 2 C.C.C. 365 (B.C. C.A.) — It is a necessary ingredient of the offence of procuring illicit sexual intercourse that the intercourse take place.

Attempts to Procure [See also s. 24]

R. v. Deutsch (1983), 5 C.C.C. (3d) 41 (Ont. C.A.); affirmed (1986), 52 C.R. (3d) 305, 27 C.C.C. (3d) 385 (S.C.C.) — D contemplated that sexual intercourse with business clients would be required and a normal incident of employment. By holding out the lure of a financial reward, D intended to induce women to accept such employment and this would have been sufficient to constitute an attempt to procure. A conviction for attempting to procure the commission of a proscribed act was not precluded because the invitation was to commit the proscribed act with a person, not yet ascertained, falling within a specified class.

R. v. Cline (1982), 65 C.C.C. (2d) 214 (Alta. C.A.) — Belief that the woman is a prostitute negates the *mens rea* for attempting to procure. "Procure" points to active persuasion by D. It does *not* apply where the woman becomes a prostitute of her own free will.

Control, Direct or Influence Movements: S. 212(1)(h)

R. v. Perreault (1996), 113 C.C.C. (3d) 573 (Que. C.A.) — In order to establish liability under s. 212(1)(h), P must prove beyond a reasonable doubt

i. that D exercised *control, direction* or *influence* over the movements of a person;

ii. that D *aided, abetted* or *compelled* the person *to engage in or carry on* prostitution with another person, or generally; and

iii. that D's conduct was for the *purpose* of *gain.*

Illicit Sexual Intercourse

R. v. Deutsch (1986), 52 C.R. (3d) 305, 27 C.C.C. (3d) 385 (S.C.C.) — The word "illicit" is to be given the meaning that has been assigned by the weight of judicial opinion to the word "unlawful" in comparable legislative texts *viz.*, sexual intercourse not authorized or sanctioned by lawful marriage.

Lives on the Avails of Prostitution: S. 212(1)(j)

R. v. Murphy (1981), 21 C.R. (3d) 39, 60 C.C.C. (2d) 1 (Alta. C.A.) — The offence of living on the avails of prostitution contemplates two separate persons: the offender and the prostitute. The subsection cannot be construed as including the prostitute herself as an offender, nor can the prostitute be guilty of the principal offence as a party. However, the fact that one of the parties to the agreement is immune from liability for the substantive offence and, thus, immune from liability for conspiring to commit the substantive offence does not affect the liability of the co-conspirator. Consequently, the immunity of a prostitute is irrelevant to the pimp's liability for conspiring with the prostitute to live on the avails of her prostitution.

R. v. Celebrity Enterprises Ltd. (1978), 41 C.C.C. (2d) 540 (B.C. C.A.) — To live on the avails of prostitution D must receive either in kind all or part of the proceeds from the prostitution or have the proceeds applied in some way to support his living. Indirect benefits, such as admission fees or tips paid to a nightclub, are *not* the avails of prostitution.

R. v. Grilo (1991), 5 C.R. (4th) 113, 64 C.C.C. (3d) 53 (Ont. C.A.) — *See also*: *R. v. Bramwell* (1993), 86 C.C.C. (3d) 418 (B.C. C.A.) — The element of exploitation inherent in the parasitic aspect of the relationship is essential to the concept of living on the avails of prostitution. The issue is whether D and the prostitute had entered into a normal and legitimate living arrangement, which included sharing expenses for their mutual benefit, or whether D was living parasitically on the prostitute's earnings for his/her own benefit.

Presumption: S. 212(3)

R. v. Downey (1992), 13 C.R. (4th) 129, 72 C.C.C. (3d) 1 (S.C.C.) — Section 212(3) enacts a mandatory presumption which requires the trier of fact to conclude from proof of the *basic fact* (that D lives with or is habitually in the company of prostitutes), the *presumed fact* (that D lives on the avails of prostitution). This mandatory conclusion results in an evidential burden which requires D to call evidence, unless there is already evidence to the contrary in P's case.

Limitation Period [Formerly s. 195(3)]

R. v. Ford (1993), 84 C.C.C. (3d) 544 (Ont. C.A.) — D, who could *not* be prosecuted for an offence because a statutory limitation period had run, may *not* be prosecuted for it if the limitation period is subsequently repealed.

Charter Considerations

R. v. Boston (June 15, 1988), Vancouver Doc. No. CA006712 (B.C. C.A.) — Section 212(1)(j) does *not* violate *Charter* s. 2(d).

R. v. Downey (1992), 13 C.R. (4th) 129, 72 C.C.C. (3d) 1 (S.C.C.) — The mandatory presumption of s. 212(3) infringes *Charter* s. 11(d), but is saved by s. 1.

Related Provisions: "Common bawdy-house", "place" and "prostitute" are defined in s. 197(1). Under s. 22(3), "procure" is included in "counsel". Although an act of sexual intercourse need *not* take place to establish liability in most, if not all, of the offences of the section, whether such an act is complete is determined in accordance with s. 4(5). Age is determined under *I.A.* s. 30 and may be proven, *inter alia*, under *Code* s. 658.

Section 150.1(5) limits the availability of a defence of mistaken belief as to V's age under s. 150.1(2) and (4): it will only avail where D took all reasonable steps to ascertain the age of V.

Under *C.E.A.* s. 4(2), D's spouse is a competent and compellable witness for P without the consent of D. Corroboration is *not* required under s. 274.

Related offences are described in ss. 170 (parent or guardian procuring sexual activity), 171 (householder permitting sexual activity) and 172 (corrupting children). The offence of this section is an "enterprise crime offence" in s. 462.3 and s. 212(1) is an "offence" in s. 183 in respect of which authorization to intercept private communications may be given.

Under s. 536(2), D may *elect* mode of trial.

Offence in Relation to Prostitution

213. (1) Offence in relation to prostitution — Every person who in a public place or in any place open to public view

(a) stops or attempts to stop any motor vehicle,

(b) impedes the free flow of pedestrian or vehicular traffic or ingress to or egress from premises adjacent to that place, or

(c) stops or attempts to stop any person or in any manner communicates or attempts to communicate with any person

for the purpose of engaging in prostitution or of obtaining the sexual services of a prostitute is guilty of an offence punishable on summary conviction.

(2) Definition of "public place" — In this section, "public place" includes any place to which the public have access as of right or by invitation, express or implied, and any motor vehicle located in a public place or in any place open to public view.

1972, c. 13, s. 15;R.S. 1985, c. 51 (1st Supp.), s. 1.

Commentary: The section defines the circumstances under which certain aspects of the public practice of prostitution is a summary conviction offence.

In each case, D's conduct must either be *in a public place*, as defined in s. 213(2), or in *any place open to public view*. Equally, in every case, D's conduct must be for either *purpose* prohibited by s. 213(1), namely, for the purpose of *engaging in prostitution* or of *obtaining the sexual services of a prostitute*. This element of purpose makes it clear that the prohibitions are directed equally at both vendors and purchasers of the services of a prostitute. An actual act of prostitution need not take place to establish liability.

Under s. 213(1)(a), in addition to the elements common to all offences, D must *stop or attempt* to *stop* a motor vehicle. The offence of s. 213(1)(b), is only established where, in addition, D *impedes* the free flow of pedestrian or vehicular traffic, or ingress to or egress from premises adjacent to a public place or place open to public view. The offence of s. 213(1)(c) is committed where D stops or attempts to stop another, in a proscribed place, for a prohibited purpose. It is equally established where D, in any manner, communicates or attempts to communicate with another in the circumstances and for the purpose common to each offence. Actual stopping and/or communication is not required to establish liability: an attempt at either will suffice.

The constitutional validity of s. 213(1)(c) has been challenged under *Charter* ss. 2(b) and (d), 7 and 15(1).

Case Law

Elements of Offence

R. v. Pake (1995), 45 C.R. (4th) 117, 103 C.C.C. (3d) 524 (Alta. C.A.) — Section 213(1)(c) requires proof of an *intention* to *engage* the sexual services of a prostitute.

R. v. Smith (1989), 49 C.C.C. (3d) 127 (B.C. C.A.) — "Public place": includes a motor vehicle whether stationary or mobile.

R. v. Head (1987), 59 C.R. (3d) 80, 36 C.C.C. (3d) 562 (B.C. C.A.) — It is an offence under s. 213(1)(c) to stop or attempt to stop any person "or" in any manner to communicate or attempt to communicate with any person for the purpose of engaging in prostitution or of obtaining the sexual services of a prostitute. There is *no* requirement that D both stop "and" communicate.

R. v. Ruest (1991), 7 C.R. (4th) 48, 67 C.C.C. (3d) 476 (Que. C.A.) — The section is intended to prohibit street solicitation of sex for money from a person who the offender believes to be a prostitute. It does not require that the recipient of the communication be a prostitute.

Charter Considerations

Reference re ss. 193 & 195.1(1)(c) of the Criminal Code (1990), 77 C.R. (3d) 1, 56 C.C.C. (3d) 65 (S.C.C.) — *See also*: *R. v. Skinner* (1990), 77 C.R. (3d) 84, 56 C.C.C. (3d) 1 (S.C.C.) — Freedom of expression extends to the activity of communication for the purpose of engaging in prostitution, hence s. 213(1)(c) constitutes a *prima facie* infringement of *Charter* s. 2(b). The infringement, however, is justified as a reasonable limit under s. 1. "Prostitution", "communicate" and "attempts to communicate" are terms that, given the benefit of judicial interpretation, are *not* so vague in their meaning to offend principles of fundamental justice.

R. v. Stagnitta (1990), 56 C.C.C. (3d) 17 (S.C.C.) — Communicating in a public place for the purpose of engaging in prostitution is the nature of the activity to which s. 213(1)(c) is directed. Its target is expressive conduct, not conduct of an associational nature. The mere fact that it limits the possibility of commercial activities or agreements is not sufficient to show a *prima facie* interference with *Charter* s. 2(d). The subsection does, however, infringe the freedom of expression guarantee in s. 2(b), but is justifiable under s. 1.

Related Provisions: "Place" and "prostitute" are defined in s. 197(1). The definition of "public place" in s. 213(2) is expansive and would appear to supplement the definition of the same term in s. 197(1). To attempt is simply to try or to make an effort or endeavour to do or accomplish some action. In a legal sense, an attempt is defined in s. 24(1).

Related offences appear in several paragraphs of s. 212(1), as well as in its ss. and (4). Sections 170 (parent or guardian procuring sexual activity), 171 (householder permitting sexual activity) and 172 (corrupting children) describe kindred offences.

Under s. 2 of R.S.C. 1985, c. 51 (1st. Supp.), three years after the coming into force of this section (December 20, 1985), a comprehensive review was to have been undertaken of its provisions by a committee designated or established by the House of Commons for that purpose. Within one year of that review, the committee was to have submitted a report to the House, including a statement of any changes the committee recommends to the legislation.

The offence is tried under Part XXVII and punished under s. 787(1).

PART VIII — OFFENCES AGAINST THE PERSON AND REPUTATION

Interpretation

214. Definitions — In this Part,

"abandon" or "expose" includes

(a) a wilful omission to take charge of a child by a person who is under a legal duty to do so, and

(b) dealing with a child in a manner that is likely to leave that child exposed to risk without protection;

"aircraft" does not include a machine designed to derive support in the atmosphere primarily from reactions against the earth's surface of air expelled from the machine;

"child" includes an adopted child and an illegitimate child;

"form of marriage" includes a ceremony of marriage that is recognized as valid

(a) by the law of the place where it was celebrated, or

(b) by the law of the place where an accused is tried, notwithstanding that it is not recognized as valid by the law of the place where it was celebrated;

"guardian" includes a person who has in law or in fact the custody or control of a child.

"operate"

(a) means, in respect of a motor vehicle, to drive the vehicle,

(b) means, in respect of railway equipment, to participate in the direct control of its motion, whether

(i) as a member of the crew of the equipment,

(ii) as a person who, by remote control, acts in lieu of such crew, or

(iii) as other than a member or person described in subparagraphs (i) and (ii), and

(c) includes, in respect of a vessel or an aircraft, to navigate the vessel or aircraft;

"vessel" includes a machine designed to derive support in the atmosphere primarily from reactions against the earth's surface of air expelled from the machine.

R.S., c. C-34, s. 196; R.S. 1985, c. 27 (1st Supp.), s. 33; c. 32 (4th Supp.), s. 56.

Commentary: The section defines several terms used in various provisions of the Part.

Related Provisions: Several other provisions of the Part enact definitions that apply to a particular section or group of sections. See, for example ss. 219(2), 254(1), 260(7), 269.1, 276(6), 280(2), 287(6) and 297.

Other sources of assistance in determining the meaning of words and phrases used in the *Code* are described in the *Related Provisions* note to s. 2, *supra*.

Duties Tending to Preservation of Life

215. (1) Duty of persons to provide necessaries — Every one is under a legal duty

(a) as a parent, foster parent, guardian or head of a family, to provide necessaries of life for a child under the age of sixteen years;

(b) as a married person, to provide necessaries of life to his spouse; and

(c) to provide necessaries of life to a person under his charge if that person

(i) is unable, by reason of detention, age, illness, mental disorder or other cause, to withdraw himself from that charge, and

(ii) is unable to provide himself with necessaries of life.

(2) Offence — Every one commits an offence who, being under a legal duty within the meaning of subsection (1), fails without lawful excuse, the proof of which lies on him, to perform that duty, if

(a) with respect to a duty imposed by paragraph (l)(*a*) or (*b*),

(i) the person to whom the duty is owed is in destitute or necessitous circumstances, or

(ii) the failure to perform the duty endangers the life of the person to whom the duty is owed, or causes or is likely to cause the health of that person to be endangered permanently; or

(b) with respect to a duty imposed by paragraph (1)(*c*), the failure to perform the duty endangers the life of the person to whom the duty is owed or causes or is likely to cause the health of that person to be injured permanently.

(3) Punishment — Every one who commits an offence under subsection (2) is guilty of

(a) an indictable offence and is liable to imprisonment for a term not exceeding two years; or

(b) an offence punishable on summary conviction.

(4) Presumptions — For the purpose of proceedings under this section,

(a) evidence that a person has cohabited with a person of the opposite sex or has in any way recognized that person as being his spouse is, in the absence of any evidence to the contrary, proof that they are lawfully married;

(b) evidence that a person has in any way recognized a child as being his child is, in the absence of any evidence to the contrary, proof that the child is his child;

(c) evidence that a person has left his spouse and has failed, for a period of any one month subsequent to the time of his so leaving, to make provision for the maintenance of his spouse or for the maintenance of any child of his under the age of sixteen years is, in the absence of any evidence to the contrary, proof that he has failed without lawful excuse to provide necessaries of life for them; and

(d) the fact that a spouse or child is receiving or has received necessaries of life from another person who is not under a legal duty to provide them is not a defence.

R.S., c. C-34, s. 197; 1974-75-76, c. 66, s. 8; 1991, c. 43, s. 9, Schedule, item 2.

Commentary: The section defines the circumstances under which a *legal duty to provide necessaries of life* will arise, and creates offences for *failure or neglect* to perform the duty. Subsection (4) creates several *rebuttable presumptions* that may assist P in proof of some essential elements of the offence.

Section 215(1) imposes a *legal duty* to provide necessaries of life in the circumstances of a described relationship. Under s. 215(1)(a), the duty is imposed upon a parent, foster parent, guardian or head of a family. These persons must provide the necessaries of life for a child, including an adopted and illegitimate child, under 16 years of age. Section 215(1)(b) imposes a similar duty upon a married person in respect of a spouse. The legal duty of s. 215(1)(c) is imposed where one person has another under his/her charge, who is unable, by reason of detention, age, illness, mental disorder or other cause to withdraw him/herself from that charge and, further, is unable to provide him/herself with such necessaries.

Section 215(2) creates *offences* triable either way. The elements vary somewhat but otherwise have common features. In each case, D must be under a *legal duty* imposed by s. 215(1). D must *fail* to perform that duty. D's failure must be *without lawful excuse*. The proof of lawful excuse is statutorily shifted to D, thereby attracting *Charter* ss. 7 and 11(d) scrutiny.

Where the duty is that of a parent, foster parent, guardian, head of a family or married person imposed by ss. 215(1)(a) and (b), P must also establish that the beneficiary of the duty is in *destitute* or *necessitous* circumstances. The *external circumstances* of the offence will also be complete where D's omission endangered the beneficiary's life or caused or was likely to cause his/her health to be permanently endangered. For the duty imposed by s. 215(1)(c), P must further establish that D's omission *endangered* the beneficiary's life or caused or was likely to cause his/her health to be permanently injured.

Sections 215(4)(a)–(c) convert *evidence* of the matters described in the opening words of each paragraph to *proof* of the conclusions later stated, *in the absence of any evidence to the contrary.*

Under s. 215(4)(d) the supply of necessaries by another person does *not* relieve D of liability for failure to perform a legal duty imposed upon him/her in the same respect.

Case Law

General

R. v. Wilson (1933), 60 C.C.C. 309 (Alta. C.A.) — A person receiving charity or relief from a public authority is *not* necessarily in "necessitous circumstances".

R. v. Brooks (1902), 5 C.C.C. 372 (B.C. C.A.) — "Necessaries of life" mean such necessaries as tend to preserve life, and *not* necessaries in their ordinary legal sense.

R. v. Yuman (1910), 17 C.C.C. 474 (Ont. C.A.) — Financial inability to provide necessaries may be a lawful excuse.

Mental Element

R. v. Naglik (1993), 23 C.R. (4th) 335, 83 C.C.C. (3d) 526 (S.C.C.) — Section 215(2) imposes liability on an *objective* basis. In considering what D ought to have known, the trier of fact must determine the conduct or a reasonable person when engaging in the particular activity in the specific circumstances of the case. The circumstances do *not* include the personal characteristics of D, short of those which deprive D of the capacity to appreciate the risk.

Charter Considerations

R. v. Naglik (1993), 23 C.R. (4th) 335, 83 C.C.C. (3d) 526 (S.C.C.) — Section 215(2) imposes liability on an objective basis, but does not contravene *Charter* s. 7.

R. v. Curtis (1998), 123 C.C.C. (3d) 178 (Ont. C.A.) — The clause ". . . the proof of which lies upon him . . ." in s. 215(2) is a reverse onus provision that contravenes *Charter* s. 11(d) and is *not* saved by. s. 1.

R. v. Tutton (1985), 44 C.R. (3d) 193, 18 C.C.C. (3d) 328 (Ont. C.A.); affirmed on other grounds (1989), 69 C.R. (3d) 289, 48 C.C.C. (3d) 129 (S.C.C.) — The statutory duty to provide the necessaries of life applies to all parents. The fact that it is *not* a lawful excuse for a parent, who knowing that a child is in need of medical assistance, refuses to obtain such assistance because to do so would be contrary to a tenet of his/her own particular faith does *not* offend the guarantee of freedom of conscience and religion under *Charter* s. 2(a).

Related Provisions: "Necessaries of life" is *not* defined. It is determined in the circumstances of each case.

Breach of a duty imposed under s. 215(1), which shows wanton or reckless disregard for the lives or safety of others, may amount to criminal negligence under s. 219(1). Culpable homicide is defined in s. 222(5) and characterized as murder, manslaughter or infanticide by s. 222(4). Murder is defined in s. 229 and classified for sentencing purposes by s. 231.

Sections 216 and 217 also impose legal duties upon persons in various circumstances. Abandoning a child is an offence under s. 218.

Under *C.E.A.* s. 4(2), D's spouse is a competent and compellable witness for P without D's consent on a charge under s. 215(3).

Where P elects to proceed by indictment under s. 215(3)(a), D may elect mode of trial under s. 536(2). The offence of s. 215(3)(b) is tried under Part XXVII, and punished under s. 787(1).

216. Duty of persons undertaking acts dangerous to life — Every one who undertakes to administer surgical or medical treatment to another person or to do any other lawful act that may endanger the life of another person is, except in cases of necessity, under a legal duty to have and to use reasonable knowledge, skill and care in so doing.

R.S., c. C-34, s. 198.

Commentary: The section imposes a *legal duty* upon those who undertake specified conduct. The substance or standard of the legal duty imposed, except in cases of necessity, is to have and to use *reasonable knowledge, skill* and *care* in so doing.

Case Law

R. v. Rogers (1968), 4 C.R.N.S. 303, [1968] 4 C.C.C. 278 (B.C. C.A.) — *See also*: *R. v. Watson* (1936), 66 C.C.C. 233 (B.C. C.A.) — The *standard* under this section is *not* subjective, but *objective*. It is based on the *reasonable* knowledge and skill possessed by members of the medical profession generally.

Related Provisions: The section does *not* itself create an offence for breach of duty. Section 45 describes the scope of protection from criminal responsibility afforded in the performance of surgical operations.

Section 215(1) imposes a duty upon certain persons to provide necessaries of life to others within a defined relationship. Sections 215(2) and (3) describe the circumstances under which a failure to perform such duties may attract criminal liability. Section 217 also imposes a legal duty upon persons who undertake to do acts in the described circumstances.

Other related provisions are described in the corresponding note to s. 216, *supra*.

217. Duty of persons undertaking acts — Every one who undertakes to do an act is under a legal duty to do it if an omission to do the act is or may be dangerous to life.

R.S., c. C-34, s. 199.

Commentary: The section imposes a *legal* duty. The *undertaking* of an act, imposes a legal duty, where the omission to do the act is or may be dangerous to life, but not otherwise.

Case Law

R. v. Browne (1997), 116 C.C.C. (3d) 183 (Ont. C.A.) — The legal duty of s. 217 does not flow from the relationship between the parties, but from D's undertaking, something in the nature of a commitment, upon which reliance may be reasonably placed. The mere expression of words indicative of a willingness to act does not suggest a legal duty.

Related Provisions: The section does *not* itself create an offence for breach of duty.

Other related provisions are described in the corresponding note to s. 216, *supra*.

218. Abandoning child — Every one who unlawfully abandons or exposes a child who is under the age of ten years, so that its life is or is likely to be endangered or its health is or is likely to be permanently injured, is guilty of an indictable offence and liable to imprisonment for a term not exceeding two years.

R.S., c. C-34, s. 200.

Commentary: The section describes and provides the punishment for the indictable offence of abandoning a child.

The *external circumstances* require that D unlawfully abandon or expose a child, who must be under the age of 10 years. The abandoning or exposure must be such that the life of the child is, or is *likely* to be, endangered or its health is, or is likely to be, *permanently* injured. The *mental element* consists of the intention to abandon or expose the child in the circumstances.

Related Provisions: "Child" is defined in s. 214. Age, determined under *I.A.* s. 30, may also be established, *inter alia*, in accordance with *Code* s. 658.

Killing an unborn child in the act of birth is an offence under s. 238. Neglect to obtain assistance in childbirth is punishable under s. 242, and concealing the body of a child under s. 243.

Other related provisions are described in the corresponding notes to ss. 215–217, *supra*.

Under *C.E.A.* s. 4(2), D's spouse is a competent and compellable witness for P without D's consent.

D may *elect* mode of trial under s. 536(2)

Criminal Negligence

219. (1) Criminal negligence — Every one is criminally negligent who

(a) in doing anything, or

(b) in omitting to do anything that it is his duty to do,

shows wanton or reckless disregard for the lives or safety of other persons.

(2) "duty" — For the purposes of this section, "duty" means a duty imposed by law.

R.S., c. C-34, s. 202.

Commentary: The section defines *criminal negligence*.

Criminal negligence is established where D, in *doing* anything or *in omitting to do anything* that it is his/her duty imposed by law to do, shows wanton or reckless disregard for the lives or safety of other persons. *The mental element* is the same in cases of act and omission.

Case Law

Duty Imposed By Law: S. 219(1)(b); (2)

Leblanc v. R. (1975), 29 C.C.C. (2d) 97 (S.C.C.) — *See also*: *R. v. Titchner* (1961), 35 C.R. 111 (Ont. C.A.) — Mere proof of breach of a duty imposed by law is insufficient to support a conviction for criminal negligence, unless accompanied by wanton or reckless disregard for the lives or safety of others.

R. v. Coyne (1958), 31 C.R. 335, 124 C.C.C. 176 (N.B. C.A.) — The "law" in "duty imposed by law" may be a duty at common law or by statute.

R. v. Popen (1981), 60 C.C.C. (2d) 232 (Ont. C.A.) — The *common law* imposes a legal duty upon a *parent* to take reasonable steps to protect his child from illegal violence used by the other parent or a third person towards the child which the parent foresees or ought to foresee. That parent is criminally liable under the *Code* for failing to discharge that duty in circumstances which show a wanton or reckless disregard for the child's safety where the failure to discharge the legal duty has contributed to the death or caused bodily harm to the child.

Wanton or Reckless Disregard: S. 219(1)

R. v. Tutton (1985), 44 C.R. (3d) 193, 18 C.C.C (3d) 328 (Ont. C.A.); affirmed (1989), 69 C.R. (3d) 289, 48 C.C.C. (3d) 129 (S.C C.) — A loving and caring parent who omits to seek medical assistance because of the honest but mistaken belief that the child is *not* in need of assistance should not be found to have shown a wanton or reckless disregard for the child's safety *merely* because it can be said that reasonable parents would have responded differently.

R. v. Lebedynski (1984), 28 M.V.R. 20 (B.C. C.A.) — *See also*: *R. v. Walker* (1974), 26 C.R.N.S. 268, 18 C.C.C. (2d) 179 (N.S. C.A.); leave to appeal refused (1974), 18 C.C.C. (2d) 179n (S.C.C.) — To constitute "criminal negligence", D's conduct need be reckless or wanton, but *not* necessarily both.

R. v. Barron (1985), 48 C.R. (3d) 334, 23 C.C.C. (3d) 544 (Ont. C.A.); reversing (1984), 39 C.R. 379 (Ont. H.C.) — The test for criminal negligence is whether there has been a *marked* departure from the standard of the reasonable person.

Mental Element: S. 219(1)

R. v. Anderson (1990), 75 C.R. (3d) 50, 53 C.C.C. (3d) 481 (S.C.C.) — Whether an objective or subjective test is applied, a finding that the impugned conduct is a marked departure from the norm is central. In some cases the actions of D and the consequences of them are so interwoven that the consequences are relevant in characterizing the conduct of D.

R. v. Tutton (1989), 69 C.R. (3d) 289 (S.C.C.) — [Per Dickson CJ., Wilson and LaForest JJ.] — "Wanton or reckless disregard for the lives or safety of other persons" signifies more than gross negligence in the objective sense. P must establish some degree of awareness or advertence by D to the threat to the lives or safety of others, or alternatively a wilful blindness to the threat which is culpable in light of the gravity of the risk assumed. Malice or intent, in the sense of a mind directed to a purpose, are *not* elements of the offence.[Per McIntyre and L'Heureux-Dubé JJ.] — The objective test must be applied in determining criminal negligence since it is D's conduct which must be examined. There is no distinction in principle between acts of commission and omission. The test is reasonableness, and the surrounding circumstances and D's perception of them must be considered to determine whether D's conduct was reasonable. The honestly-held belief in circumstances which would support a defence must, to be effective, be reasonably held.[Per Lamer J.] — In applying the objective test, generous allowance should be made for factors particular to D such as youth, mental development and education.

R. v. Waite (1989), 69 C.R. (3d) 323, 48 C.C.C. (3d) 1 (S.C.C.) — [Per Dickson C.J., Wilson and La Forest JJ.] — Criminal negligence requires both the *conduct* addressed by the objective test and a subjective *mental element* which is the minimal intent of awareness of the prohibited risk or wilful blindness to the risk.[Per McIntyre and L'Heureux-Dubé JJ.] — Criminal negligence is shown where P proves conduct on D's part which shows a marked and substantial departure from the standard of behaviour expected of a reasonably prudent person in the circumstances. The objective test is to be applied whether the acts are ones of commission or omission. The offence does *not* involve a subjective element. (See also Lamer J.'s decision here and in *Tutton, supra*.)

R. v. Ubhi (1994), 27 C.R. (4th) 332 (B.C. C.A.) — Objective *mens rea* suffices for criminal negligence, unqualified by reference to D's personal characteristics. Evidence of D's mental retardation, however, is relevant to D's *capacity* to understand or appreciate the risk.

R. v. Gingrich (1991), 6 C.R. (4th) 197, 65 C.C.C. (3d) 188 (Ont. C.A.) — The *mens rea* for criminal negligence in the operation of a motor vehicle involves an objective assessment of D's conduct. The crime of criminal negligence is negligence, the tort of civil negligence. It is elevated to a crime by the magnitude of the omissions or commissions of D which show a wanton or reckless disregard for the lives and safety of others.

R. v. Nelson (1990), 75 C.R. (3d) 70, 54 C.C.C. (3d) 285 (Ont. C.A.) — *See also: R. v. Cabral* (1990), 54 C.C.C. (3d) 317 (Ont. C.A.) — Absent further clarification by the Supreme Court of Canada, the mental element required to establish criminal negligence involves an objective standard. In practical terms, in most cases which involve the operation of a motor vehicle, little difference exists between the objective and subjective standard.

R. v. Sharp (1984), 39 C.R. 367, 12 C.C.C. (3d) 428 (Ont. C.A.) — To prove criminal negligence, P is *not* required to prove intention or deliberation. Indifference, in the sense of a negative state of mind, will suffice. Where driving is involved, it must be a marked and substantial departure from the standard of a reasonable driver. The driver must have either run an obvious and serious risk to the lives and safety of others, or have given no thought to that risk.

Charter Considerations

R. v. Gingrich (1991), 6 C.R. (4th) 197, 65 C.C.C. (3d) 188 (Ont. C.A.) — *Charter* s. 7 does *not* require that a subjective intent be proven to establish guilt.

R. v. Nelson (1990), 75 C.R. (3d) 70, 54 C.C.C. (3d) 285 (Ont. C.A.) — *See also: R. v. Cabral* (1990), 54 C.C.C. (3d) 317 (Ont. C.A.) — *Charter* s. 7 does *not* require that P prove subjective foresight of the consequences of conduct to found a conviction of criminal negligence causing death or bodily harm.

Related Provisions: Sections 79 (explosive substance), 215(1) (provide necessaries), 216 (undertaking acts dangerous to life) and 217 (duty of persons undertaking acts) impose legal duties. Section 45 defines the extent to which those who perform beneficial surgical operations are protected from criminal responsibility. Section 26 describes the extent of criminal responsibility for the use of excessive force.

Sections 220 and 221 create offences where death or bodily harm (s. 221) is caused by criminal negligence. The punishment varies with the consequence.

Under s. 222(5)(b), culpable homicide is committed where D causes the death of a human being by criminal negligence. It is characterized as murder, manslaughter or infanticide by s. 221(4). Murder is defined in s. 229 and classified for sentencing purposes, in s. 231.

220. Causing death by criminal negligence — Every person who by criminal negligence causes death to another person is guilty of an indictable offence and liable

(a) where a firearm is used in the commission of the offence, to imprisonment for life and to a minimum punishment of imprisonment for a term of four years; and

(b) in any other case, to imprisonment for life.

R.S., c. C-34, s. 203; 1995, c. 39, s. 141.

Commentary: The section creates the indictable offence of *causing death by criminal negligence*. P must prove D's criminal negligence and a *nexus* or causal connection between the criminal negligence and V's death.

Case Law

Another Person

R. v. Sullivan (1991), 63 C.C.C. (3d) 97 (S.C.C.) — A fetus is *not* a "person" within this section.

Criminal Negligence [See also s. 219]

R. v. Lockhart (1993), 19 C.R. (4th) 263 (B.C. C.A.) — Notwithstanding an acquittal of an impaired driving offence arising from the same events, the trier of fact may still consider D's evidence of drinking as part of the conduct which establishes criminal negligence.

R. v. Thomas (1990), 75 C.R. (3d) 64, 53 C.C.C. (3d) 245 (B.C. C.A.) — Driving a defective car which cannot be controlled properly can constitute criminal negligence.

Causation

R. v. Rotundo (1993), 47 M.V.R. (2d) 90 (Ont. C.A.) — There is no requirement that there be physical contact between D's car and that of V in order that D may be convicted of criminal negligence causing death. Liability may be established where it is proven that V was killed in a collision with a car driven by another person with whom D was engaged in a joint venture (racing) which amounted to criminal negligence.

Multiple Convictions

R. v. Plante (1997), 120 C.C.C. (3d) 323 (Que. C.A.) — The rule against multiple convictions does *not* bar convictions for

i.   criminal negligence causing death; and,

ii.   impaired driving causing death

because the element of intoxication is *not* necessary to establish criminal negligence in the operation of a motor vehicle, at all events where there is evidence of excessive speed and place of impact.

Charter Considerations [See also s. 219]

R. v. Morrisey (1998), 14 C.R. (5th) 365, 124 C.C.C. (3d) 38 (N.S. C.A.); motion for leave to appeal filed (1998), 232 N.R. 195 (note) (S.C.C.) — Section 220(a) does *not* contravene *Charter* s. 12.

Related Provisions: Criminal negligence is defined in s. 219 and may be established upon proof of an act or omission of the nature required. Causing bodily harm by criminal negligence is an offence under s. 221.

Section 223 defines when a child becomes a human being. Issues of causation are described in ss. 224–227. In particular, no offence is committed under this section unless V's death occurs within one year and a day from the occurrences described in s. 227.

Under s. 662(5), a count charging an offence under this section arising out of the operation of a motor vehicle or the navigation of a vessel or aircraft *includes* an offence under s. 249. The general provisions of s. 662(1) would include the offence of s. 221 in a count charging a breach of this section.

Under *C.E.A.* s. 4(4), D's spouse is a competent and compellable witness for P without D's consent where V is under the age of 14. Age is determined in accordance with *I.A.* s. 30 and may be established, *inter alia*, under *Code* s. 658.

Under s. 536(2) D may *elect* mode of trial. Where D is convicted or discharged of an offence under this section committed by means of a motor vehicle, vessel or aircraft, the sentencing court may, in addition to any other punishment that may be imposed for the offence, make an order prohibiting D from operating a motor vehicle on a street, road, highway or any other public place, or a vessel or an aircraft, as the case may be, during the period described in s. 259(2). The order may be stayed pending appeal under s. 261.

Other related provisions are described in the corresponding note to s. 219, *supra*.

221. Causing bodily harm by criminal negligence — Every one who by criminal negligence causes bodily harm to another person is guilty of an indictable offence and liable to imprisonment for a term not exceeding ten years.

R.S., c. C-34, s. 204.

Commentary: The section creates the indictable offence of causing bodily harm by criminal negligence. P must prove D's criminal negligence and a *nexus* or causal connection between that negligence and V's bodily harm.

Case Law

Another Person [See s. 220]

Mental Element [See s. 219]

Causation [See s. 220]

Charter Considerations [See. s. 219]

Related Provisions: "Bodily harm" is defined in s. 2.

Under s. 662(5), a count charging an offence under this section arising out of the operation of a motor vehicle or the navigation of a vessel or aircraft includes an offence under s. 249.

Other related provisions are described in the corresponding note to s. 220, *supra*.

Homicide

222. (1) Homicide — A person commits homicide when, directly or indirectly, by any means, he causes the death of a human being.

(2) Kinds of homicide — Homicide is culpable or not culpable.

(3) Non culpable homicide — Homicide that is not culpable is not an offence.

(4) Culpable homicide — Culpable homicide is murder or manslaughter or infanticide.

(5) Idem — A person commits culpable homicide when he causes the death of a human being,

    (a) by means of an unlawful act,

    (b) by criminal negligence,

    (c) by causing that human being, by threats or fear of violence or by deception, to do anything that causes his death, or

    (d) by wilfully frightening that human being, in the case of a child or sick person.

(6) Exception — Notwithstanding anything in this section, a person does not commit homicide within the meaning of this Act by reason only that he causes the death of a human being by procuring, by false evidence, the conviction and death of that human being by sentence of the law.

R.S., c. C-34. s. 205.

Commentary: Section 222 defines homicide and divides it into two kinds or types. Homicide which is *not* culpable is *not* an offence. *Culpable homicide*, defined in s. 222(5) will be murder, manslaughter or infanticide, depending upon the *external circumstances* of the killing and the *mental element* which accompanies it.

Case Law
Causation: S. 222(1) [See also s. 219]

Smithers v. R. (1977), 40 C.R.N.S. 79, 34 C.C.C. (2d) 427 (S.C.C.) — The fact that death would not ordinarily result from the unlawful act is no defence to a manslaughter charge. One who assaults another must take the victim as he finds him. Causation is a question of fact for the jury, not experts, to determine on all the evidence before them, both lay and expert. In order to establish causation, P need only establish that the cause was at least a contributing cause of death, outside the *de minimis* range.

R. v. Klassen (1997), 113 C.C.C. (3d) 97 (B.C. C.A.) — For an "opportunity" to constitute an "intervening act", there must be evidence of an act separate from the act of D by a person other than D. The "intervening act" must be of a nature which results in D being no longer substantially connected to the death. (per Macfarlane and Gibbs JJ.A.)

R. v. Cribbin (1994), 28 C.R. (4th) 137, 89 C.C.C (3d) 67 (Ont. C.A.) — The common law test for causation, *viz.*, an unlawful act that is at least a contributing cause of death outside the *de minimis* range, does *not* offend *Charter* s. 7.

A Human Being: S. 222(1)

R. v. Sullivan (1991), 63 C.C.C. (3d) 97 (S.C.C.) — A fetus is *not* a "human being" within *Code* s. 222(1).

Culpable Homicide by an Unlawful Act: S. 222(5)(a) [See also s. 234]

R. v. Creighton (1993), 23 C.R. (4th) 189, 83 C.C.C. (3d) 346 (S.C.C.) — See digest under s. 234.

R. v. Gosset (1993), 23 C.R. (4th) 280, 83 C.C.C (3d) 494 (S.C.C.) — See digest under s. 234.

R. v. Jobidon (1991), 7 C.R. (4th) 233, 66 C.C.C. (3d) 454 (S.C.C.) — For policy reasons, the common law limited the legal effectiveness of consent to a fist fight. The limit persists in s. 265, vitiating consent between adults intentionally to apply force causing serious hurt or non-trivial bodily harm to each other in the course of a fist fight or brawl. The common law rule will *not* vitiate freely-given consent to participate in rough sporting activities, providing the intentional application of force to which consent is given, is within the customary norms and rules of the game. Neither will the limitations vitiate consent to medical treatment, appropriate survical intervention or the activities of stuntmen whose advance agreement to perform risky activities creates a socially valuable cultural product.

R. v. Adkins (1987), 39 C.C.C (3d) 346 (B.C. C.A.) — An "unlawful act" must be likely to cause harm in the eyes of the reasonable person. Where there is no dispute about this additional test, it is not necessary to instruct the jury about it.

R. v. Fraser (1984), 16 C.C.C (3d) 250 (N.S. C.A.) — Culpable homicide can be based on the unlawful acts of assault or pointing a firearm without the necessity of a finding that the acts were dangerous. However, the pointing of a firearm is not unlawful if done accidentally or in self-defence.

R. v. Carpenter (1993), 83 C.C.C. (3d) 193 (Ont. C.A.) — It is preferable to instruct the jury that, if they are satisfied or have a reasonable doubt whether D acted in self-defence in causing the death of V, there is no unlawful act committed by D.

R. v. Cole (1981), 64 C.C.C (2d) 119 (Ont. C.A.) — Where the unlawful act is *not* criminal, the act must be an *intentional* one which, viewed objectively, was *dangerous* and *likely* to subject another person to harm or injury.

R. v. Vaillancourt (1995), 105 C.C.C. (3d) 552 (Que. C.A.) — The phrase "by means of" in s. 222(5)(a) requires a *causal connection* between V's death and D's unlawful act. The deliberate pointing of a firearm which D believed to be unloaded did *not* amount to causing death by means of any unlawful act.

Culpable Homicide by Threats or Fear of Violence: S. 222(5)(c)

Graves v. R. (1913), 21 C.C.C. 44 (S.C.C.) — If V himself did the act which resulted in *his* death being induced thereto by a fear of violence inspired by D, the homicide is one for which D is responsible.

Related Provisions: "Person" is defined in s. 2 and "criminal negligence" in s. 219. Section 223 determines when a child becomes a human being, *inter alia*, for the purposes of this section.

Sections 223(2) and 224–226 describe specific instances in which D's conduct will be held to have caused V's death for the purposes of the law of homicide. Under s. 227, *inter alia*, culpable homicide is *not* committed unless V's death occurs within one year and a day from the time of the occurrence of the last event by means of which D caused or contributed to the cause of death. Section 228 describes the circumstances under which causing death solely by influence on the mind or by any disorder resulting from influence on the mind may constitute culpable homicide.

Murder is defined in ss. 229. It is classified for sentencing purposes as first degree murder and second degree murder by s. 231. Infanticide is defined in s. 233 and manslaughter in s. 234.

Causing death by criminal negligence is an offence under s. 220.

223. (1) **When child becomes human being** — A child becomes a human being within the meaning of this Act when it has completely proceeded, in a living state, from the body of its mother whether or not

    (a) it has breathed,

    (b) it has an independent circulation, or

    (c) the navel string is severed.

(2) Killing child — A person commits homicide when he causes injury to a child before or during its birth as a result of which the child dies after becoming a human being.

R.S., c. C-34, s. 206.

Commentary: In general, homicide occurs *only* when the deceased is a human being. Section 223(1) defines when a child becomes a human being for such purposes, thereby defining one of the outer limits of the law of homicide. The express enactment in s. 223(2) that it is nonetheless homicide where the injuries caused to a *child* prior to or during birth caused death after the child has become a *human being* duplicates the requirement of s. 222(1) that the victim of a homicide be a human being.

Case Law
Human Being

R. v. Sullivan (1988), 65 C.R. (3d) 256, 43 C.C.C. (3d) 65 (B.C. CA.) — "Person" within the meaning of s. 219 does *not* include a child that has not been born alive. A child still in the birth canal remains part of the mother. Midwives engaged to deliver a baby, which was born dead having been asphyxiated before birth, may be convicted of criminal negligence causing bodily harm to the mother, but not criminal negligence causing the death of the infant.

R. v. Prince (1988), 44 C.C.C. (3d) 510 (Man. C.A.) — A person who attacks an obviously pregnant woman with intent to harm her is guilty of at least manslaughter if the fetus, subsequently born alive, dies from injuries or disease resulting from the attack.

Related Provisions: Under s. 222(1), homicide occurs when a person, directly or indirectly, by any means, causes the death of a *human being*. Killing an unborn child in the act of birth is an offence under s. 238. Offences relating to neglect in childbirth and concealing the dead body of a child are described in ss. 242 and 243.

The expansive definition of "child" in s. 214 has greater relevance for the offences of ss. 215(1) and (2) (failure to provide necessaries) and 218 (abandoning child) than for the offences of ss. 238 (killing unborn child in act of birth), 242 (neglect to obtain assistance in child-birth) and 243 (concealing dead body of child).

224. Death which might have been prevented — Where a person, by an act or omission, does any thing that results in the death of a human being, he causes the death of that human being notwithstanding that death from that cause might have been prevented by resorting to proper means.

R.S., c. C-34, s. 207.

Commentary: This section, one of several *Code* provisions relating to *causation* in cases of homicide, requires that P establish an adequate causal *nexus* between D's acts or omissions and V's death. Under s. 222(1), homicide is committed only when D, by any means, directly or indirectly, causes V's death. Section 224 maintains the required causal *nexus* where D has, by act or omission, done any thing that results in V's death, notwithstanding that the death might have been prevented by resort to proper means.

Related Provisions: Section 223(1) describes when a child becomes a human being for the purposes of the law of homicide. Section 223(2) also makes it homicide to cause injury to a child before or during birth which results in death after the child becomes a human being.

Under s. 222(1) homicide is committed where D, directly or indirectly, causes the death of a human being. All homicide is culpable or not culpable. Section 222(5) defines culpable homicide. All culpable homicide is either murder, manslaughter or infanticide under s. 222(4). Murder is defined in s. 229 and the constitutionally deficient s. 230 and classified for sentencing purposes in s. 231. Infanticide is defined in s. 233. Under s. 234, all culpable homicide that is neither murder nor infanticide is manslaughter.

Other causation provisions appear in ss. 225 (death from treatment of injury), 226 (acceleration of death), 227 (death within a year and a day) and 228 (killing by influence on the mind).

225. Death from treatment of injury — Where a person causes to a human being a bodily injury that is of itself of a dangerous nature and from which death results, he causes the death of that human being notwithstanding that the immediate cause of death is proper or improper treatment that is applied in good faith.

R.S., c. C-34, s. 208.

Commentary: Section 225 preserves the causal *nexus* requisite in homicide cases between D's conduct and V's death in cases of an intervening and immediate cause of death. The section becomes engaged upon proof that D caused V an inherently dangerous bodily injury from which V's death resulted. It is of no legal consequence to D's potential criminal liability that the immediate cause of D's death was the *bona fide* application of proper or improper treatment.

Case Law

R. v. Kitching (1976), 32 C.C.C. (2d) 159 (Man. C.A.) — *See also*: *R. v. Malcherek* (1981), 73 Cr. App. R. 173 (C.A.) — There may be two or more independent operative causes of death. The conduct of the doctors in shutting off the life support systems and removing the kidneys of V was irrelevant as it did *not* exonerate D unless there was a reasonable doubt that the actions of D constituted an operative cause of death.

R. v. Torbiak (1978), 40 C.C.C. (2d) 193 (Ont. C.A.) — The fact that doctors followed a conservative course of non-interventional treatment and V died three weeks later on the operating table after his condition deteriorated, did *not* prevent the gunshot wound from being the operative cause of death.

Related Provisions: "Bodily injury" is not defined in the *Code*. "Bodily harm" is defined, however, in s. 2.

Other causation provisions are found in ss. 224 (death that might have been prevented), 226 (acceleration of death), 227 (death within a year and a day) and 228 (killing by influence on the mind).

Other related provisions are discussed in the corresponding note to s. 224, *supra*.

226. Acceleration of death — Where a person causes to a human being a bodily injury that results in death, he causes the death of that human being notwithstanding that the effect of the bodily injury is only to accelerate his death from a disease or disorder arising from some other cause.

R.S., c. C-34, s. 209.

Commentary: Under this section, D causes V's death if D caused V bodily injury from which death resulted, even though the only effect of such bodily injury was to accelerate V's inevitable death from another cause.

Related Provisions: The section should be read in conjunction with s. 223(1), which defines when a child becomes a human being. Section 223(2) declares it to be homicide where D causes injury to a child before or during birth as a result of which the child dies after becoming a human being. Under s.

227, culpable homicide is committed only where V's death occurs within a year and a day from the time of the occurrence of the last event by means of which D caused or contributed to the cause of death.

Other causation provisions appear in ss. 224 (death that might have been prevented), 225 (death from treatment of injury) and 228 (killing by influence on the mind).

Other related provisions are discussed in the corresponding note to s. 224, *supra*.

227. Death within year and a day — No person commits culpable homicide or the offence of causing the death of a person by criminal negligence or by means of the commission of an offence under subsection 249(4) or 255(3) unless the death occurs within one year and one day from the time of the occurrence of the last event by means of which the person caused or contributed to the cause of death.

R.S., c. C-34, s. 210; R.S. 1985, c. 27 (1st Supp.), s. 34; 1997, c. 18, s. 9.

Commentary: The section codifies the arbitrary common law rule which arose from the difficulty of tracing the causative link when a substantial period intervened between the infliction of the injury and V's death. It would now seem justified solely upon the footing that one who has injured another ought not to remain indefinitely at risk of prosecution for culpable homicide or an enumerated statutory offence.

Related Provisions: The offence of s. 249(4) is causing death by dangerous operation of a motor vehicle, vessel or aircraft. Section 255(3) prohibits impaired operation of a motor vehicle, vessel or aircraft causing death.

Other related provisions are discussed in the corresponding notes to ss. 224 and 226, *supra*.

228. Killing by influence on the mind — No person commits culpable homicide where he causes the death of a human being

(a) by any influence on the mind alone, or

(b) by any disorder or disease resulting from influence on the mind alone,

but this section does not apply where a person causes the death of a child or sick person by wilfully frightening him.

R.S. c. C-34, s. 211.

Commentary: The section excepts from what otherwise would be culpable homicide acts or omissions of D that caused V's death solely by influence on the mind or by any disorder or disease resulting therefrom. The exception is not itself unqualified. It remains culpable homicide to cause the death of a child or sick person by wilfully frightening him/her.

Case Law

R. v. Powder (1981), 29 C.R. (3d) 183 (Alta. C.A.) — V, who had a pre-existing heart disease, died from a heart attack apparently brought on by the stress and fright of a break-in by D and another. There had been a scuffle, but no evidence of physical injury. D's conviction for manslaughter was quashed on the basis that the evidence established that stress and fright, *not* the assault, caused the death, and that the assault was only a contributing factor to the stress and fright.

Related Provisions: Under s. 222(5)(d), D commits culpable homicide where D causes the death of a human being by wilfully frightening V who is a child or sick person. "Child" under s. 214 includes an adopted and illegitimate child but is not otherwise defined.

Other related provisions are described in the corresponding *note* to ss. 224 and 226, *supra*.

Murder, Manslaughter and Infanticide

229. Murder — Culpable homicide is murder

(a) where the person who causes the death of a human being

(i) means to cause his death, or

(ii) means to cause him bodily harm that he knows is likely to cause his death, and is reckless whether death ensues or not;

(b) where a person, meaning to cause death to a human being or meaning to cause him bodily harm that he knows is likely to cause his death, and being reckless whether death ensues or not, by accident or mistake causes death to another human being, notwithstanding that he does not mean to cause death or bodily harm to that human being; or

(c) where a person, for an unlawful object, does anything that he knows or ought to know is likely to cause death, and thereby causes death to a human being, notwithstanding that he desires to effect his object without causing death or bodily harm to any human being.

R.S., c. C-34, s. 212.

Commentary: The section provides three *definitions* of *murder*.

Section 229(a) provides the *primary* definition of murder. It requires proof of an ulterior intention to kill or closely related state of mind which combines elements of *intention* (to cause bodily harm), *foresight or knowledge* (that the bodily harm is *likely* to cause death) and *recklessness* (whether death ensues or not).

Section 229(b), a further definition of *murder*, requires proof of the same *mental element* described in s. 229(a), *supra*. Under s. 229(b), however, liability for murder is established where P proves that, at the time of the acts that unlawfully caused the death of AV (the actual victim) D had the requisite state of mind in relation to IV (the intended victim). P must prove such a coincidence or concurrence of the *external circumstances* and *mental element* to establish D's liability.

Section 229(c) enacts a definition of *constructive murder*. It constructs the crime of murder out of a death that occurs in D's prosecution of a (further) unlawful object beyond the (immediate) unlawful act(s) which causes V's death. There is substituted for the specific *mental element* required in cases of actual murder an amalgam of *purpose* ("... for an unlawful object, does anything") and *objective foresight* of the *likelihood of death*. Murder is nonetheless proven where D does not desire to cause death or bodily harm to anyone. The paragraph is, in part ("... ought to have known"), constitutionally deficient under *Charter* s. 7.

Case Law

Mental Element and its Proof [See also s. 8: Intoxication]

R. v. Seymour (1996), 106 C.C.C. (3d) 520 (S.C.C.) — Where *intoxication* is raised, a trial judge should instruct the jury

i.   that the reasonable common sense *inference* of intention of consequences of conduct may *only* be drawn after an assessment of *all* the evidence, including evidence of *intoxication*; and

ii.   that the inference cannot be drawn if the jury is left with a reasonable doubt of D's intention.

R. v. Robinson (1996), 105 C.C.C. (3d) 97 (S.C.C.); affirming (1984), 92 C.C.C. (3d) 193 (B.C. C.A.) — *See also*: *R. v. McMaster* (1996), 105 C.C.C. (3d) 193 (S.C.C.) — To be required to instruct a jury on *intoxication*, a trial judge must first be satisfied that the *effect* of intoxication was such that it *might have impaired* D's *foresight* of *consequences* sufficient to raise a reasonable doubt. Where intoxication is left to the jury, it must be made clear that the issue for the jury is whether P has satisfied them beyond a reasonable doubt that D had the requisite intent.A single-step charge on intoxication, which omits any reference to "capacity" or "capability" and focuses the jury's attention on the question of "intent in fact" is useful. In some instances, however, for example where experts testify in terms of "capacity", a two-step charge may be appropriate.

R. v. Lemky (1996), 105 C.C.C. (3d) 137 (S.C.C.) — *See also*: *R. v. Robinson* (1996), 105 C.C.C. (3d) 97 (S.C.C.) — To warrant submission of the defence of intoxication to the jury, there must be evidence sufficient to permit a reasonable inference that D did *not, in fact* foresee the consequences of his/her act. There are cases where evidence, which falls short of establishing that D lacked the capacity to form the intent, may nonetheless leave jurors with a reasonable doubt that D did, in fact, foresee (in a case of murder) the likelihood of death when the offence was committed.

R. v. Cooper (1993), 78 C.C.C. (3d) 289 (S.C.C.) — There is only a slight relaxation in the *mental element* required to prove murder under s. 229(a)(ii) compared to 229(a)(i).The *mental element* in s. 229(a)(ii) has two aspects:

i.   *subjective intent* to cause bodily harm; and

ii. *subjective knowledge* that the bodily harm is of such a nature that it is *likely* to *result* in *death*.

The *mental element* must not only be present, but must also be at some point *concurrent* with the impugned act. An act which may be innocent, or no more than careless at the outset may become criminal later when D acquires *knowledge* of its nature, yet refuses to change his/her course of action. Whether the mental element coincides with the wrongful act will depend to a large extent upon the nature of the act.It is *not* necessary that the requisite mental element *continue throughout* the entire time required to cause V's death. If V's death results from a series of wrongful acts that are part of a single transaction, P must establish that the requisite mental element coincided at some point with the wrongful acts.

R. v. Stewart (1995), 41 C.R. (4th) 102 (B.C. C.A.) — *Semble*, it is *not* error to fail to instruct the jury on the cumulative effects of drugs, provocation and instinctive reaction absent evidence of intoxication and of D's psychological make-up.

R. v. Naldzil (1991), 9 C.R. (4th) 112, 68 C.C.C. (3d) 350 (B.C.C.A.) — The *mental element* of s. 229(a)(ii), which requires proof of subjective foresight of death, does *not* infringe *Charter* s. 7.

R. v. Rathwell (1998), 130 C.C.C. (3d) 302 (Ont. C.A.); application for leave to appeal filed , Doc. 27039 (S.C.C.) — A trial judge who makes reference to the sane and sober person should tell the jury that the *inference* that a person intends the natural and probable consequences of his/her acts applies *only* when the person being considered is

i.   *sane* and *sober*; and,

ii. in *possession* of otherwise *intact* mental faculties.

The judge should tell the jury that *all* of the evidence bearing on the issue of intent should be considered while dealing with the intent required for murder.

It is preferable that trial judges avoid language that isolates intoxication as a "defence". The issue is not so much whether D was intoxicated, but rather, whether D's *consumption* of alcohol, when taken with *other factors* relevant to the issue of intent, raises a *reasonable doubt* of the issue of intent for murder.

R. v. Nealy (1986), 54 C.R. (3d) 158, 30 C.C.C. (3d) 460 (Ont. C.A.) — *See also*: *R. v. Desveaux* (1986), 51 C.R. (3d) 173, 26 C.C.C. (3d) 88 (Ont. C.A.); *R. v. Clow* (1985), 44 C.R. (3d) 228 (Ont. C.A.); *R. v. Bob* (1990), 78 C.R. (3d) 102 (Ont. C.A.); *R. v. Settee* (1990), 55 C.C.C. (3d) 431 (Sask. C.A.) — All of the circumstances surrounding the act of killing must be taken into account in determining whether D had the requisite intent for murder, including consumption of alcohol and provocation.

R. v. Hilton (1977), 34 C.C.C. (2d) 206 (Ont. C.A.) — *See also*: *R. v. Browning* (1976), 34 C.C.C. (2d) 200 (Ont. C.A.); *R. v. Leblanc* (1991), 4 C.R. (4th) 98 (Que. C.A.); leave to appeal refused (July 4, 1991), Doc. No. 22426 (S.C.C.); *Lechasseur v. R.* (1977), 1 C.R. (3d) 190, 38 C.C.C. (2d) 319 (Que. C.A.); *R. v. Meloche* (1975), 34 C.C.C. (2d) 184 (Que. C.A.); *R. v. Stevenson* (1990), 58 C.C.C. (3d) 464, 488, (Ont. C.A.); *R. v. Baltzer* (1974), 27 C.C.C. (2d) 118 (N.S. C.A.) — Evidence of mental disorder or illness falling short of insanity should be considered along with all other evidence in determining whether D had the requisite intent for murder. If there is a reasonable doubt on the issue of intent, the verdict should be manslaughter.

Molleur v. R. (1948), 6 C.R. 375, 93 C.C.C. 36 (Que. C.A.) — "The use of the word 'likely' connotes a substantial degree of probability, and to make the section applicable it must be established that the illegal act was such that D knew, or should have known, that its commission would probably result in death".

Intoxication as a Defence [See s. 8]

Intention to Kill: S. 229(a)(i) [See also Mental Element and its Proof, supra]

Young v. R. (1981), 20 C.R. (3d) 325, 25 C.R. (3d) 193, 59 C.C.C. (2d) 305 (S.C.C.) — Where the defence raised only one issue at trial, namely, whether D was too intoxicated to form the requisite intent for murder, it was not necessary to leave before the jury the defence of whether or not D, apart from drunkenness, did not know that the bodily harm inflicted was likely to cause death. The trial judge made it clear to the jury that a manslaughter verdict was available if they had a doubt D had formed the requisite intent.

R. v. Ferber (1987), 36 C.C.C. (3d) 157 (Alta. C.A.) — There is *no* requirement that the trial judge direct the jury that the evidence of provocation and self defence should be considered cumulatively to determine whether or not D had formed the specific intent as long as the judge has directed the jury on the necessity to prove intent.

Intention to Cause Bodily Harm: S. 229(a)(ii) [See also Mental Element and its Proof, supra]

R. v. Murray (1994), 93 C.C.C. (3d) 70, 20 O.R. (3d) 156, 73 O.A.C. 321 (Ont. C.A.) — Where there is an issue whether D knew that the bodily harm inflicted on V was likely to cause death, an illustration based on the common sense inference that a sane and sober person intends the natural consequences of an act such as pointing a loaded firearm at the head of a person has the effect of blending the mental element in s. 229(a)(i) with that of s. 229(a)(ii), thereby confusing the real issue and deflecting the jury's attention from it.

Manslaughter as Possible Verdict

R. v. Wade (1994), 29 C.R. (4th) 327, 89 C.C.C. (3d) 39 (Ont. C.A.); reversed (1995), 98 C.C.C. (3d) 97 (S.C.C.) — Manslaughter need only be left as a possible verdict at trial upon a charge of second degree murder where there is an air of reality to the verdict. In determining whether there is an *air of reality*, the trial judge must consider the entirety of the evidence in the context of the conduct of the case to decide whether manslaughter is a realistic option open to the jury performing their task in accordance with their oath.

Transferred Intent: S. 229(b)

Brown v. R. (1983), 4 C.C.C. (3d) 571 (Ont. H.C.) — This section applies where D kills someone else while attempting to kill himself.

R. v. Droste (1979), 18 C.R. (3d) 64, 49 C.C.C. (2d) 52 (Ont. C.A.) — P must establish, notwithstanding this paragraph, that the *external circumstances* and the *mental element* are *concurrent*.

"Unlawful Object" Murder: S. 229(c)

R. v. Martineau (1990), 79 C.R. (3d) 129, 58 C.C.C. (3d) 353 (S.C.C.); affirming (1988), 43 C.C.C. (3d) 417 (Alta. C.A.) — *See also*: *R. v. Rodney* (1990), 79 C.R. (3d) 187, 58 C.C.C. (3d) 408 (S.C.C.), additional reasons to 1988), 46 C.C C. (3d) 323 (B.C. C.A.); *R. v. J. (J.T.)* (1990), 79 C.R. (3d) 219, 59 C.C.C. (3d) 1 (S.C.C.); reversing in part (1988), 40 C.C.C. (3d) 97 (Man. C.A.); *R. v. Luxton* (1990), 79 C.R. (3d) 193, 58 C.C.C. (3d) 449 (S.C.C.); *R. v. Arkell* (1990), 79 C.R. (3d) 207, 59 C.C.C. (3d) 65 (S.C.C.); affirming (1988), 64 C.R. (3d) 340, 43 C.C.C. (3d) 402 (B.C. C.A.) — Since subjective fore-sight of death must be proven beyond a reasonable doubt to sustain a conviction for murder, the phrase "ought to know is likely to cause death" in s. 229(c) *probably* infringes *Charter* ss. 7 and 11(d) and would *not* likely be saved under s. 1.

R. v. Vasil (1981), 20 C.R. (3d) 193, 58 C.C.C. (2d) 97 (S.C.C.); affirming (1977), 37 C.C.C. (2d) 199 (Ont. C.A.) — The "anything" under s. 229(c) is a dangerous act which may or may not be in itself unlawful. If the dangerous act is itself unlawful then there must be a further unlawful object clearly distinct from the immediate object of the dangerous (unlawful) act to fall within the ambit of subsection (c). The unlawful object must be that which, if prosecuted fully, would amount to an indictable offence requiring *mens rea*.

R. v. Tousignant (1986), 51 C.R. (3d) 84 (Ont. C.A.) — *See also*: *R. v. De Wolfe* (1976), 31 C.C.C. (2d) 23 (Ont. C.A.) — *Contra*: *R. v. Blackmore* (1967), 1 C.R.N.S. 286 (N.S. C.A.) — An *unlawful object* must be something *other than* the *unlawful act*. There must be a further unlawful object the pursuit of which led to V's death.

R. v. O'Connor (1989), 49 C.C.C (3d) 371 (Sask. C.A.) — Section 229(c) was intended to protect inno-cent victims of the further unlawful object and does *not* apply where one of the participants is killed.

Self-Defence [See ss. 27, 34, 35]

Accessoryship to Murder [See also s. 21]

R. v. Kirkness (1990), 60 C.C.C. (3d) 97 (S.C.C.) — *See also*: *R. v. Jackson* (1993), 26 C.R. (4th) 178, 86 C.C.C. (3d) 385 (S.C.C.) — To be guilty of murder as an aider or abettor, D must have the same mental element as is required of the principal. D must either intend that V's death ensue or intend that he or the principal cause bodily harm of a kind likely to result in death and be reckless whether death ensues or not.

R. v. Yu (1998), 122 C.C.C. (3d) 353 (B.C. C.A.) — To be found guilty of *murder* as an aider or abettor requires proof that

i.   D's acts, omissions or words *assisted* or *encouraged* the principal; and

ii.   D, as well as the principal, *knew* and *intended* that V would die.

D may be convicted of *manslaughter* as an aider or abettor if P proves beyond a reasonable doubt that the principal intend to kill V, but fails to prove beyond a reasonable doubt that D intended to do so.

R. v. Kent (1986), 27 C.C.C. (3d) 405 (Man. C.A.) — *See also*: *R. v. Trudeau* (1985), 49 C.R. (3d) 234, 23 C.C.C. (3d) 445 (Ont. C.A.) — Participation in the common plan is *not* sufficient to prove murder. If D lacked the intent to cause bodily harm of a kind likely to cause death, only a conviction for manslaughter is possible.

R. v. Laliberty (1997), 117 C.C.C. (3d) 97 (Ont. C.A.) — Where liability for murder depends upon the application of s. 21(2) to the underlying offence of robbery involving possession of knives, P must prove that D had *actual* foresight or knowledge that another accused would stab V with the *intent* to kill.

Where there is evidence of *intoxication* sufficient to be left with the jury on a charge of murder involving the application of s. 21(2) to the offence of robbery, the trial judge should relate the defence and relevant evidence to

i.   the *mental element* in *murder*,

ii.   the intention in *common* to rob V; and

iii. the *subjective foresight* or *knowledge* of each party that *murder* was a *probable consequence* of carrying out the robbery.

R. v. Cribbin (1994), 89 C.C.C. (3d) 67 (Ont. C.A.) — D may only be found guilty of murder as an aider or abettor if D *knew* of the principal's intention to kill V or to cause V bodily harm that the principal knew was likely to cause V's death and if D intended to aid or abet the principal.

R. v. Jackson (1991), 9 C.R. (4th) 57, 68 C.C.C. (3d) 385 (Ont. C.A.); affirmed (1993), 26 C.R. (4th) 178, 86 C.C.C. (3d) 385 (S.C.C.) — D may be found guilty of second degree murder as a s. 21(2) *party* arising out of a *robbery* where P proves beyond a reasonable doubt that:

i.   D and the co-accused (or principal) formed an *intention in common to rob* V and to *assist each other* in such purpose;

ii.   the co-accused (or principal) in carrying out that common intention *committed murder* under s. 229(a) on V; and,

iii. D *knew* that it was a *probable consequence* of carrying out the common intention to rob that the co-accused (or principal) would commit *murder* as defined in s. 229(a) on V.

Related Provisions: Homicide is defined in s. 222(1) and the means whereby culpable homicide may be committed in s. 222(5). The other forms of culpable homicide are infanticide, defined in s. 233, and manslaughter in s. 234. Section 223(1) describes when a child becomes a human being for the purposes of the law of homicide and s. 223(2) makes it homicide to cause injury to a child before or during birth that results in death after the child becomes a human being. Sections 224–228 contain a number of causation provisions.

Murder is classified for sentencing purposes by s. 231 and is punished under ss. 235 and 745–745.5. It is an offence expressly exempted from the definition of "serious personal injury offence" in s. 752 for the purposes of Part XXIV but is included in the definition of "enterprise crime offence" in s. 462.3 for the purposes of Part XII.2 and of "offence" in s. 183 for the purposes of obtaining authorization to intercept private communications under Part VI. Under *C.E.A.* s. 4(4), the spouse of D charged with murder is a competent and compellable witness for P, without D's consent, where V is under the age of 14 years.

The offence of murder, in either degree, falls within the exclusive trial and judicial interim release jurisdiction of the superior court of criminal jurisdiction under ss. 469(a)(viii) and 522.

Section 589 discusses the circumstances in which a count charging an offence other than murder may be joined in an indictment to a count charging murder.

Murder by one who has actually committed the offence under s. 21(1)(a) is exempted from the operation of the excuse of compulsion in s. 17.

The effect of a conviction or acquittal of murder on a subsequent prosecution of the same homicide as manslaughter or infanticide is described in ss. 610(2) and (3).

A conviction of murder will attract prohibition against possession of firearms, ammunition and explosive substances of s. 100(1).

There are special provisions enacted in ss. 662(2)–(4), which define the included offences of which D may be convicted upon an indictment for first degree murder (s. 229(2)), murder (s. 229(3)) and the murder of a child or infanticide (s. 224(4)).

230. Murder in commission of offences — Culpable homicide is murder where a person causes the death of a human being while committing or attempting to commit high treason or treason or an offence mentioned in section 52 (sabotage), 75 (piratical acts), 76 (hijacking an aircraft), 144 or subsection 145(1) or sections 146 to 148 (escape or rescue from prison or lawful custody), section 270 (assaulting a peace officer), section 271 (sexual assault), 272 (sexual assault with a weapon, threats to a third party or causing bodily harm), 273 (aggravated sexual assault), 279 (kidnapping and forcible confinement), 279.1 (hostage taking), 343 (robbery), 348 (breaking and entering) or 433 or 434 (arson), whether or not the person means to cause death to any human being and whether or not he knows that death is likely to be caused to any human being, if

(a) he means to cause bodily harm for the purpose of

(i) facilitating the commission of the offence, or

(ii) facilitating his flight after committing or attempting to commit the offence,

and the death ensues from the bodily harm;

(b) he administers a stupefying or overpowering thing for a purpose mentioned in paragraph (*a*), and the death ensues therefrom; or

(c) he wilfully stops, by any means, the breath of a human being for a purpose mentioned in paragraph (*a*), and the death ensues therefrom,

and the death ensues as a consequence.

R.S., c. C-34, s. 213; 1974–75–76, c. 93, s. 13; c. 105, s. 29; 1980–81–82–83, c. 125, s. 15; R.S. 1985, c. 27 (1st Supp.), s. 40(2); 1991, c. 4, s. 1.

Commentary: The section *defines* murder on a *constructive* basis. Culpable homicide is murder where V's death is caused in defined circumstances arising out of the commission of a listed primary crime or predicate offence, and notwithstanding the absence of an intention to cause death, as well as objective foresight of its likelihood.

Sections 230(a) and (c) have been declared constitutionally invalid by the Supreme Court of Canada. There is substantial reason to doubt the validity of s. 230(b).

Case Law

Charter Considerations

R. v. Sit (1991), 9 C.R. (4th) 126, 66 C.C.C. (3d) 449 (S.C.C.) — Sections 230(a) and (c) infringe *Charter* s. 7 and are not saved by *Charter* s. 1.

R. v. Martineau (1990), 79 C.R. (3d) 129, 58 C.C.C. (3d) 353 (S.C.C.); affirming (1988), 43 C.C.C. (3d) 417 (Alta. C.A.) — *See also*: *R. v. Rodney* (1990), 79 C.R. (3d) 187, 58 C.C.C. (3d) 408 (S.C.C.), additional reasons to (1988), 46 C.C.C. (3d) 323 (B.C. C.A.); *R. v. J. (J.T.)* (1990), 79 C.R. (3d) 219, 59 C.C.C. (3d) 1 (S.C.C.); reversing in part (1988), 40 C.C.C. (3d) 97 (Man. C.A.); *R. v. Luxton* (1990), 79 C.R. (3d) 193, 58 C.C.C. (3d) 449 (S.C.C.); *R. v. Arkell* (1990), 79 C.R. (3d) 207, 59 C.C.C. (3d) 65 (S.C.C.); affirming (1988), 64 C.R. (3d) 340, 43 C.C.C. (3d) 402 (B.C. C.A.) — [Per Dickson C.J., Lamer C.J., Wilson Gonthier and Cory JJ.] — It is a principle of fundamental justice that a conviction for murder cannot rest on anything less than proof beyond a reasonable doubt of *subjective foresight of death.* The express elimination by s. 230 of the requirement of proof of subjective foresight of death renders the section, in particular s. 230(a), an infringement of *Charter* ss. 7 and 11(d) which is not justified by s. 1.

R. v. Favel (1988), 43 C.C.C. (3d) 481 (Alta. C.A.); leave to appeal refused (1989), 97 A.R. 80n, 101 N.R. 234n (S.C.C.) — *See also: R. v. Johnston* (1988), 44 C.C.C. (3d) 15 (Man. C.A.) — The constitutional argument does not apply to homicides which took place before the proclamation of the *Charter.*

Related Provisions: Murder is also defined in s. 229, where the basis of liability is actual rather than constructive, except under s. 229(c). It is classified for sentencing purposes under s. 231, *infra.*

Other related substantive, procedural and evidentiary provisions are described in the corresponding note to s. 229, *supra.*

231. (1) Classification of murder — Murder is first degree murder or second degree murder.

(2) Planned and deliberate murder — Murder is first degree murder when it is planned and deliberate.

(3) Contracted murder — Without limiting the generality of subsection (2), murder is planned and deliberate when it is committed pursuant to an arrangement under which money or anything of value passes or is intended to pass from one person to another, or is promised by one person to another, as consideration for that other's causing or assisting in causing the death of anyone or counselling another person to do any act causing or assisting in causing that death.

(4) Murder of peace officer, etc. — Irrespective of whether a murder is planned and deliberate on the part of any person, murder is first degree murder when the victim is

(a) a police officer, police constable, constable, sheriff, deputy sheriff, sheriff's officer or other person employed for the preservation and maintenance of the public peace, acting in the course of his duties;

(b) a warden, deputy warden, instructor, keeper, jailer, guard or other officer or a permanent employee of a prison, acting in the course of his duties; or

(c) a person working in a prison with the permission of the prison authorities and acting in the course of his work therein.

(5) Hijacking, sexual assault or kidnapping — Irrespective of whether a murder is planned and deliberate on the part of any person, murder is first degree murder in respect of a person when the death is caused by that person while committing or attempting to commit an offence under one of the following sections:

(a) section 76 (hijacking an aircraft);

(b) section 271 (sexual assault);

(c) section 272 (sexual assault with a weapon, threats to a third party or causing bodily harm);

(d) section 273 (aggravated sexual assault);

(e) section 279 (kidnapping and forcible confinement); or

(f) section 279.1 (hostage taking).

(6) Criminal harassment — Irrespective of whether a murder is planned and deliberate on the part of any person, murder is first degree murder when the death is caused by that person while committing or attempting to commit an offence under section 264 and the person committing that offence intended to cause the person murdered to fear for the safety of the person murdered or the safety of anyone known to the person murdered.

(6.1) Using explosives in association with criminal organization — Irrespective of whether a murder is planned and deliberate on the part of a person, murder is first degree murder when the death is caused while committing or attempting to commit an offence under section 81 for the benefit of, at the direction of or association with a criminal organization.

(7) Second degree murder — All murder that is not first degree murder is second degree murder.

R.S., c. C-34, s. 214; c. C-35, s. 4; 1973–74, c. 38, s. 2; 1974–75–76, c. 105, s. 4; 1980–81–82–83, c. 125, s. 16; R.S. 1985, c. 27 (1st Supp.), ss. 7(2), 35, 40(2); 1997, c. 16, s. 3; c. 23, s. 8.

Transitional Provision (S.C. 1992, c. 11, s. 18):

18. Where a young person is alleged to have committed first degree murder or second degree murder within the meaning of section 231 of the *Criminal Code* before the coming into force of this Act and

(a) an application was made in respect of the young person under subsection 16(1) of the Young Offenders Act, as that subsection read immediately before the coming into force of this Act, but no decision made under that subsection had been issued before teh coming into force of this Act, or

(b) an application is made in respect of the young person under subsection 16(1) of the Young Offenders Act after the coming into force of this Act, the provisions of the Young Offenders Act enacted by this Act shall apply to the young person as if the offence had occurred after the coming into force of this Act.

Commentary: The section classifies, for sentencing purposes, murder, as defined in s. 229, as either first degree murder or second degree murder. Sections 231(2)–(6.1) describe the only circumstances under which murder shall be classified as first degree murder.

In its primary sense, first degree murder is *planned and deliberate* murder under s. 231(2). Section 231(3) imputes planning and deliberation to contracted murder. Subsections (4), (5) and (6.1) *deem* certain murders to be first degree murder, notwithstanding the absence of actual or imputed planning and deliberation. Under s. 231(4) it is the status of the deceased which makes murder first degree murder. Section 231 (5) *classifies* murder as first degree murder when the person causing death as a sole or co-principal does so while committing or attempting to commit an enumerated primary crime. Section 231(6) *deems* murder to be first degree when the death is caused by that person while committing or attempting to commit an offence under s. 264, *criminal harassment*, and intending to cause the murder victim to fear for their own safety or the safety of a person known to the victim. Section 231(6.1) stipulates that murder is first degree murder when the death is caused by that person while committing or attempting to commit an offence under s. 81 for the *benefit* of, at the *direction* of or in *association* with a *criminal organization*. In each and every case there must first be established murder before it can be classified as first degree murder. All murder that is not first degree murder is, by s. 231(7), second degree murder.

Case Law

Classification of Murder: Ss. 231(1), (7)

Droste v. R. (1984), 39 C.R. (3d) 26, 10 C.C.C. (3d) 404 (S.C.C.) — This section does *not* create a separate substantive offence of first degree murder. It classifies for sentencing purposes the substantive offence of murder as defined in ss. 229 and 230. Murder committed in any one of the relevant ways defined by the *Code* is first degree murder if it is planned and deliberate.

R. v. Farrant (1983), 32 C.R. (3d) 289, 4 C.C.C. (3d) 354 (S.C.C.); reversing (1981), 9 Sask. R. 7 (C.A.) — If so charged, D may be convicted of second degree murder, notwithstanding the evidence may prove first degree murder. This section merely serves to classify the sentence for the offence of murder.

R. v. Quesnel (1991), 4 C.R. (4th) 118 (Man. C.A.) — Where first degree murder is charged, a trial judge should ordinarily instruct the jury to decide first whether murder was committed and, then, if it decides that murder was committed, to classify it as murder in the first or second degree.

Planned and Deliberate Murder: S. 231(2)

R. v. Jacquard, [1997] 1 S.C.R. 314, 4 C.R. (5th) 280, 113 C.C.C. (3d) 1 (S.C.C.) — A trial judge need *not* instruct the jury on the finer distinctions of the manner in which D's *mental incapacity* can undermine his/her capacity to intend, as opposed to the capacity to plan and deliberate. It is sufficient if the instructions, read as a whole,

i.   apprise the jury that the evidence of D's *mental disorder* should be considered on each issue; and

ii.   *not* mislead the jury to conclude that a finding of planning and deliberation necessarily follows from a finding of intention.

R. v. Aalders (1993), 82 C.C.C. (3d) 215 (S.C.C.); affirming (1991), 69 C.C.C. (3d) 154 (Que. C.A.) — Planning and deliberation are separate concepts. Both must be established in respect of a murder before it may be classified as first degree murder under *Code* s. 231(2).

R. v. Wallen (1990), 75 C.R. (3d) 328, 54 C.C.C. (3d) 383 (S.C.C.); reversing (1988), 84 A.R. 12 (C.A.) — [Per La Forest, L'Heureux-Dube, and McLachlin JJ, *contra* Lamer C.J. and Cory J.] — A jury should be instructed to consider the effect of intoxication upon the requirement that a murder be planned and deliberate to be first degree murder under s. 231(2). This instruction should be in addition to and separate from an instruction which relates evidence of intoxication to the mental element of murder in s. 229(a). *Semble*, it is *not* an absolute rule that the jury be *expressly* instructed that a lesser degree of intoxication will suffice to negate planning and deliberation than is required to negate the mental element of s 229(a).

R. v. Nygaard (1989), 72 C.R. (3d) 257, 51 C.C.C. (3d) 417 (S.C.C.) — The essence of s. 229(a)(ii) is an intention to cause bodily harm of such a serious nature D knew it was likely to result in death and yet persisted in the assault. There is nothing incompatible in that mental state and the planning and deliberation required for first degree murder. D may be convicted of first degree murder where the killing constitutes murder under s. 229(a)(ii).

R. v. Droste (1984), 39 C.R. (3d) 26, 10 C.C.C. (3d) 404 (S.C.C.); affirming (sub nom. *R. v. Droste (No. 2)*) 63 C.C.C. (2d) 418 — Planning and deliberation with respect to the killing of a specific person makes the offence first degree murder even if, in the course of carrying out the plan, D in fact kills someone else.

R. v. Mitchell (1965), 43 C.R. 391 (S.C.C.) — The questions of provocation and drunkenness must be considered separately both as a defence to murder and in deciding whether the murder was planned and deliberate. Planning and deliberation involves the exercise of mental processes and in almost every case the determination must be made on the basis of circumstantial evidence. The rule in *Hodge's Case* does not apply to this determination. The circumstances include not only evidence of D's actions, but also of D's condition, state of mind as affected by real or imaginary insults and provoking actions of the victim and by D's consumption of alcohol.

More v. R. (1963), 41 C.R. 98, [1963] 3 C.C.C. 289 (S.C.C.) — Psychiatric evidence that D was suffering from a depressive psychosis at the time of pulling the trigger is admissible and relevant to the issue of whether the murder was planned and deliberate, since the court must determine whether D's acts were considered rather than impulsive.

R. v. Strong (1990), 60 C.C.C. (3d) 516 (Alta C.A.) — Where V's death is caused while D is committing a planned robbery, P must further show that causing bodily harm of the nature described in s. 229(a)(ii) was a necessary part of D's scheme, as distinct from an intention to carry out a robbery with a maximum degree of intimidation, in order to prove D guilty of planned and deliberate first degree murder.

R. v. Knuff (1980), 52 C.C.C. (2d) 523 (Alta. C.A.) — *See also*: *R. v. Kematch* (1979), 9 C.R. (3d) 331, 48 C.C.C. (2d) 179 (Sask. C.A.); *R. v. Howard* (1986), 29 C.C.C. (3d) 544 (Ont. C.A.) — Where there is evidence of drinking, the jury should be instructed that evidence falling short of negativing intent for murder may nevertheless negative planning and deliberation.

R. v. Brown (1995), 102 C.C.C. (3d) 422 (N.S. C.A.) — .There is no requirement that D participate in the formulation of the relevant plan, provided D *knew about, adopted and executed the plan*

R. v. Smith (1986), 71 N.S.R. (2d) 229 (C.A.) — *See also: R. v. Ruptash* (1982), 68 C.C.C. (2d) 182 (Alta. C.A.); *R. v. Smith* (1979), 51 C.C.C. (2d) 381 (Sask. C.A.); *R. v. Reynolds* (1978), 44 C.C.C. (2d) 129 (Ont. C.A.) — The planning and deliberation must precede the commencement of the homicide. "Planned" means a calculated scheme or design which has been carefully thought out and the nature and consequences of which have been considered and weighed. The plan may be very simple. "Deliberate" means more than intentional since it is only if D's acts are intentional that he can be found guilty of murder. "Deliberate" means carefully thought out, not hasty or rash. The doer has taken the time to weigh the pros and cons of his intended action.

R. v. Palmer (1986), 24 C.C.C. (3d) 557 (Ont. C.A.) — Although a robbery had been planned and the killing intentional, it does *not* inevitably follow that the killing was planned, hence first degree murder under s. 231(2).

R. v. Kirkby (1985), 47 C.R. (3d) 97, 21 C.C.C. (3d) 31 (Ont. C.A.) — *See also: R. v. Charest* (1990), 76 C.R. (3d) 63, 57 C.C.C. (3d) 312 (Que. C.A.) — D, notwithstanding the existence of a mental disorder, may have had the capacity to plan and deliberate. However, the jury is entitled to consider subjective factors personal to D, namely mental disorder and possible intoxication at the time of the offence, in deciding whether the murder was, in fact, planned and deliberate.

R. v. Chabot (1985), 44 C.R. (3d) 70, 16 C.C.C. (3d) 483 (Ont. C.A.) — *See also: R. v. Brigham* (1988), 44 C.C.C. (3d) 379 (Que. C.A.) — Murder is *not* first degree murder solely because the unlawful object under s. 229(c) was planned and deliberate. Just as it is impossible to conclude that a person may intend to commit an unintentional killing as described in s. 229(c), it is *not* possible to conclude that a person planned and deliberated such a killing.

R. v. Reynolds (1978), 44 C.C.C. (2d) 129 (Ont. C.A.) — *Intoxication* is relevant to the issue of planning and deliberation in two respects. D, due to intoxication may be unable to plan and deliberate or D may have acted *impulsively* due to intoxication even though he still had the ability to plan and deliberate.

R. v. Allard (1990), 57 C.C.C. (3d) 397 (Que. C.A.) — The jury should be instructed to consider all the evidence, including evidence of D's mental condition not sufficient to establish mental disorder under s. 16(2), in relation to the mental element in murder and the requirement that murder be planned and deliberate to be first degree murder under s. 231(2).

R. v. Smith (1979), 51 C.C.C. (2d) 381 (Sask. C.A.) — *See also: R. v. Belowitz* (1990), 56 C.C.C. (3d) 402 at 407 (Ont. C.A.) — For a murder to be "planned" there must be some evidence that the killing was the result of a scheme or design previously formulated or designed by D and that the killing was its implementation. A murder committed on a sudden impulse and without prior consideration will not constitute a planned murder, even though the intent to kill is clearly proved.

Murder of Law Enforcement Personnel: S. 231(4)

R. v. Collins (1989), 69 C.R. (3d) 235, 48 C.C.C. (3d) 343 (Ont. C.A.) — *See also: R. v. Shand* (1971), 3 C.C.C. (2d) 8 (Man. C.A); affirmed (1971), 4 C.C.C. (2d) 173n (S.C.C.); *R. v. Lefebvre* (1992), 72 C.C.C. (3d) 162 (Que. C.A.); leave to appeal refused (1992), 72 C.C.C. (3d) vi (note) (S.C.C.) — Under s. 231(4)(a), there is an onus on P to establish beyond a reasonable doubt that V was a person designated therein acting in the course of his duties to the *knowledge* of D or with *recklessness* on the part of D as to whether V was such a person so acting. So interpreted, the section does *not* offend *Charter* s. 7.

R. v. Prevost (1988), 64 C.R. (3d) 188, 42 C.C.C. (3d) 314 (Ont. C.A.) — "Acting in the course of his duties" is a wider term than "engaged in the execution of his duty". It includes any activity which is related to the performance of a duty or the ability of the officer to perform his duty.

R. v. Fitzgerald (1982), 70 C.C.C. (2d) 87 (Ont. C.A.) — It is *not* necessary for P to lead evidence of a police officer's exact activities at the time of his death in establishing whether he was acting in the course of his duties. It is sufficient to prove that he was in uniform, assigned to a police cruiser, part of a detachment and performing his duties before death.

Constructive First Degree Murder: S. 231(5)

R. v. Harbottle (1993), 24 C.C.C. (4th) 137, 84 C.C.C. (3d) 1 (S.C.C.); affirming (1992), 14 C.R. (4th) 363, 72 C.C.C. (3d) 257 (Ont. C.A.) — *See also: R. v. McGill* (1986), 15 O.A.C. 266 (C.A.) — The phrase "... when the death is caused by that person" includes both perpetrators and those who assist in the murder in that they are a *substantial cause* of V's death. Liability is *not* limited to a person who diagnostically occasions V's death. The test for causation, however, is a strict one and more limited than the *de minimis* test which suffices for liability for manslaughter.In a case under s. 231(5), P must prove beyond a reasonable doubt

i.   that D committed or attempted to commit the *underlying crime* of domination;

ii.   that D committed *murder* on V;

iii.   that D *participated in the murder* in such a manner that s/he was a *substantial cause* of V's *death*;

iv.   that there was *no intervening act* of another which resulted in D no longer being substantially connected to V's death; and,

v.   that the crimes of domination and murder were part of the *same transaction, i.e.,* the death was caused while committing the offence of domination as part of the same series of events.

R. v. Pare (1987), 60 C.R. (3d) 346, 38 C.C.C. (3d) 97 (S.C.C.) — *See also*: *R. v. Gunton* (1992), 77 C.C.C. (3d) 259 (Sask. C.A.) — The phrase "while committing" does *not* require that the underlying offence and the murder occur simultaneously. It is sufficient if the murder and the underlying offence are connected and form part of the same transaction.

R. v. Strong (1990), 60 C.C.C. (3d) 516 (Alta. C.A.) — Violence, actual or threatened, is an essential element of robbery, hence every robbery involves some measure of restraint upon V, however transitory. Parliament, however, omitted robbery from the list of predicate offences in s. 231(5)(e) and, accordingly, could *not* have intended that the transitory restraint inherent in the actual or threatened violence of every robbery would engage the section, on the basis of unlawful confinement, and make the killing first degree murder.

R. v. Green (1987), 36 C.C.C. (3d) 137 (Alta. C.A.) — There is *no* requirement that V also be the victim of the confinement.

R. v. Beaulac (1997), 120 C.C.C. (3d) 12 (B.C. C.A.) — Placing V, unconscious, into the trunk of a car for transport to a place where V was killed constitutes unlawful confinement for the purposes of s. 231(5).

R. v. Peer (1995), 100 C.C.C. (3d) 251 (B.C. C.A.) — Where the victims of a robbery are held facedown on the floor so that they are not merely prevented from interfering with the theft of property, but also forced to assume a defenceless position so that they might be dealt with whenever and however their captors please, a murder committed in such circumstances is first degree murder under s. 231(5)(c).

R. v. Stevens (1984), 11 C.C.C. (3d) 518 (Ont. C.A.) — *See also*: *R. v. Sargent* (1983), 5 C.C.C. (3d) 429 (Sask. C.A.) — Where death is caused *after* the underlying offence is *complete* and the act causing death is committed for the purpose of facilitating the flight of D the murder is not first degree murder. However, where the act causing death and the acts constituting the underlying offence are all part of one *continuous sequence* of events forming a single transaction, the death may well have been caused during the commission of the offence even though the underlying offence could, in a sense, be said to be complete.

R. v. Dollan (1982), 25 C.R. (3d) 308, 65 C.C.C. (2d) 240 (Ont. C.A.); leave to appeal refused (1982), 42 N.R. 351 (S.C.C) — *See also*: *R. v. Gourgon* (1979), 19 C.R. (3d) 272 (B.C. C.A.) — For the purposes of determining whether the offence is first degree murder, it is of no consequence that an unlawful confinement may have been *incidental* to the commission of some other crime as long as there was an unlawful confinement contrary to the *Code.*

R. v. Kingsley (1995), 45 C.R. (4th) 381, 105 C.C.C. (3d) 85 (Que. C.A.) — Under s. 231(5)(e), in addition to evidence of murder, there must also be specific evidence of unlawful domination by forcible [*sic*] confinement which goes beyond the violence inherent in robbery.

Accessoryship: Ss. 231(2) and 21(1)(b), (c)

R. v. Wong (1992), 71 C.C.C. (3d) 490 (B.C. C.A.); leave to appeal refused (1992), 74 C.C.C. (3d) vi (note) (S.C.C.) — D may be convicted of planned and deliberate first degree murder as an aider under s. 21(1)(b) if it is proven beyond reasonable doubt that D *participated* in the planning and deliberation (of the murder) or, aided the killing, *knowing* that it was one that had been planned and deliberated upon by the person who actually killed V.

R. v. Storry (1992), 71 C.C.C. (3d) 501 (B.C. C.A.) — A trial judge should make it clear in a case in which D is said to be an aider or abettor of a planned and deliberate first degree murder, that it is the planned and deliberate *murder* which D must aid or abet, *not* some preliminary or underlying crime.

R. v. Gray (1992), 66 C.C.C. (3d) 6, 4 O.R. (3d) 33 (C.A.); leave to appeal refused (1992), 69 C.C.C. (3d) vi (note), 6 O.R. (3d) xiii (note) (S.C.C.) — D cannot be convicted of planned and deliberate first degree murder as an aider or abettor unless D *knew* that the principal had planned to kill V.

R. v. Peters (1985), 23 C.C.C. (3d) 171 (B.C. C.A.) — To be convicted of first degree murder as an aider and abettor it is not enough that the actions of the principal were planned and deliberate. There must be evidence of planning and deliberation by D.

Charter Considerations: S. 231(4) and (5)

R. v. Arkell (1990), 79 C.R. (3d) 207, 59 C.C.C. (3d) 65 (S.C.C.); affirming (1988), 64 C.R. (3d) 340, 43 C.C.C. (3d) 402 (B.C. C.A.) — *See also*: *R. v. Luxton* (1990), 79 C.R. (3d) 193, 58 C.C.C. (3d) 449 (S.C.C.) — The classification of murder as first degree murder in s. 231(5) is neither arbitrary nor irrational, hence does *not* infringe *Charter* s. 7 or 11(d). No principle of fundamental justice prevents classification of murder done while committing certain underlying offences as more serious, thereby attracting more substantial penalty.

R. v. Luxton (1990), 79 C.R. (3d) 193, 58 C.C.C. (3d) 449 (S.C.C.) — The combined effect of ss. 231(5)(e) and 742(a) accords with the principles of fundamental justice, does *not* demonstrate arbitrariness in violation of s. 9 and does *not* constitute cruel and unusual punishment under *Charter* s. 12.

R. v. Bowen (1990), 59 C.C.C. (3d) 515 (Alta. C.A.) — *See also*: *R. v. Lefebvre* (1992), 72 C.C.C. (3d) 162 (Que. C.A.); leave to appeal refused (1992), 72 C.C.C. (3d) vi (note) (S.C.C.) — The sentence for murder of law enforcement personnel classified as first degree murder by s. 231(4) does *not* offend *Charter* s . 7, 9, 12 or 15.

Related Provisions: Liability for murder may be *actual* under ss. 229(a) and (b), or *constructive* under ss. 229(c) and 230. The constructive basis of liability under ss. 230(a) and (c) has been held constitutionally impermissible and s. 229(c) is, at best, of doubtful validity.

Other related substantive, evidentiary and procedural provisions are described in the corresponding note to s. 229, *supra*.

232. (1) Murder reduced to manslaughter — Culpable homicide that otherwise would be murder may be reduced to manslaughter if the person who committed it did so in the heat of passion caused by sudden provocation.

(2) What is provocation — A wrongful act or insult that is of such a nature as to be sufficient to deprive an ordinary person of the power of self-control is provocation for the purposes of this section if the accused acted on it on the sudden and before there was time for his passion to cool.

(3) Questions of fact — For the purposes of this section, the questions

    (a) whether a particular wrongful act or insult amounted to provocation, and

    (b) whether the accused was deprived of the power of self-control by the provocation that he alleges he received,

are questions of fact, but no one shall be deemed to have given provocation to another by doing anything that he had a legal right to do, or by doing anything that the accused incited him to do in order to provide the accused with an excuse for causing death or bodily harm to any human being.

(4) Death during illegal arrest — Culpable homicide that otherwise would be murder is not necessarily manslaughter by reason only that it was committed by a person who was being arrested illegally, but the fact that the illegality of the arrest was known to the accused may be evidence of provocation for the purpose of this section.

R.S., c. C-34, s. 215.

Commentary: This section expressly defines the circumstances under which what otherwise would be murder shall be reduced to manslaughter. This type of manslaughter is generally designated "voluntary manslaughter". The presence of a statutorily-defined mitigating circumstance, sudden provocation, reduces the proven and more serious form of culpable homicide, murder, to a less serious form, manslaughter. The permissive "may" is read as "shall".

Provocation under s. 232 has two aspects. The first, the *objective test test*, considers the effect of the alleged provocation, the wrongful act(s) and/or insult(s) upon an *ordinary person*. The second, only to be considered where there exists an evidentiary basis in support of the objective test, is *subjective* and determines whether the *accused* actually acted upon the provocation, on the sudden, and before there was time for his/her passion to cool. Suddenness must characterize not only the alleged provocation but, equally, D's response thereto.

The ultimate determination of whether there was provocation and D acted upon it in the statutorily prescribed manner is, by s. 232(3), reserved to the trier of fact. There is, however, a preliminary question for the trial judge, *viz.*, whether there is *any evidence* upon the basis of which a reasonable jury, properly instructed, could find provocation within the section.

Under s. 232(3), no provocation is given where what was done was something the party provoking had a legal right to do or was incited to do by D. Section 232(4) describes under what circumstances an illegal arrest may amount to provocation.

Case Law
General Principles

R. v. Gilling (1997), 117 C.C.C. (3d) 444 (Ont. C.A.) — The jury should be instructed that they need only consider provocation if otherwise satisfied beyond a reasonable doubt that D has committed murder. It is error to instruct the jury that provocation is only applicable if D did not have the intent necessary for murder.

Burden of Proof

Latour v. R. (1951), 11 C.R. 1, 98 C.C.C. 258 (S.C.C.) — *See also*: *Linney v. R.* (1977), 32 C.C.C. (2d) 294 (S.C.C.) — It is unnecessary for D to "establish" provocation. If the jury find affirmatively or are left in doubt, they must reduce murder to manslaughter. The trial judge must, expressly or by necessary implication, relate the principle of reasonable doubt to the "defence" of provocation.

R. v. LeBlanc (1985), 22 C.C.C. (3d) 126 (Ont. C.A.) — "May" in s. 232(1) means "shall".

Nature and Source of Provocation: Ss. 232(2)–(4)

R. v. Louison (1975), 26 C.C.C. (2d) 266 (Sask. C.A); affirmed [1979] 1 S.C.R. 100 — Provocation cannot consist of the predictable response of V to D's own unlawful conduct.

Parnerkar v. R. (1973), 21 C.R.N.S. 129 (S.C.C.) — Provocation is, (1) a wrongful act or insult, (2) which must satisfy (a) the *objective* test of being sufficient to deprive an ordinary person, confronted with all the same circumstances as D of the power of self-control, and (b) the *subjective* test of having caused D himself to actually act upon it, (3) on the sudden and before there was time for his passion to cool.

Wright v. R., [1969] 3 C.C.C. 258 (S.C.C.) — *See also*: *Taylor v. R.* (1947), 3 C.R. 475, 89 C.C.C. 209 (S.C.C.) — Provocation involves two inquiries. The first, the strictly *objective* standard of the average or normal man, whether the provocation was such to deprive that ordinary person of the power of self control. The character, background, temperament, idiosyncrasies, or drunkenness of D are *not* relevant to this inquiry. However, these factors may be considered on the second inquiry which involves the *subjective* test of whether D was, in fact, provoked and acted upon it on the sudden and before there was time for his passion to cool.

R. v. Tripodi (1955), 21 C.R 192, 112 C.C.C. 66 (S.C.C) — The expression "sudden provocation" means that "the wrongful act or insult must strike upon a mind unprepared for it, that it must make an unexpected impact that takes the understanding by surprise and sets the passions aflame".

R. v. Manchuk (1938), 69 C.C.C 172 (S.C.C) — *See also*: *R. v. Davies* (1975), 60 Cr. App. R. 253 (C.A.) — Provocation received from one person which becomes the occasion of an act of homicide against another who, as D knows and fully realizes, was *not* in any way concerned in the provocation is *not* contemplated by this section. However, acts of provocation committed by a third person, which might be sufficient to reduce the offence to manslaughter V *had* participated in them, may have the same effect where the offence against V is committed by D under the belief that V was a party to those acts. Provocation by V in any degree does *not* justify his death, but if there was provocation, whether coming from V or from another, then, to some extent, the offence is mitigated.

R. v. Hansford (1987), 55 C.R. (3d) 347, 33 C.C.C. (3d) 74 (Alta. C.A.); leave to appeal refused (1987), 79 A.R. 239n (S.C.C.) — Mistake of fact can be relevant to the *objective* branch of provocation. It is open to D to say that an ordinary person would have misinterpreted the facts which confronted D.

R. v. Ly (1987), 33 C.C.C (3d) 31 (B.C. C.A.) — In the absence of racial slurs, evidence of D's own cultural background is not to be considered in determining whether a reasonable man would have been provoked. It is relevant, however, to the second stage of provocation, the subjective test, where D's mental condition, background and temper, character and idiosyncrasies may be considered.

R. v. Bakun (1966), 50 C.R. 178, [1967] 2 C.C.C. 214 (B.C. C.A.) — *See also*: *R. v. Oickle* (1984), 11 C.C.C. (3d) 180 (N.S. C.A.) — It is the provocation itself, *not* the absence of intent, which reduces the crime from murder to manslaughter.

R. v. Young (1993), 78 C.C.C. (3d) 538 (N.S. C.A.) — *Semble*, a termination of a relationship is *not* a wrongful act or insult capable of constituting provocation.

R. v. Droste (No. 2), (sub nom. *R. v. Droste)* 63 C.C.C. (2d) 418 (Ont. C.A.); affirmed on other grounds (1984), 39 C.R. (3d) 26, 10 C.C.C. (3d) 404 (S.C.C.)) — D, acting under such provocation as would reduce murder to manslaughter, shoots at one person with the intention of killing him, but accidentally kills another, intention extenuated by provocation is transferred from the intended victim to the actual victim. In those circumstances, D is guilty of manslaughter only.

R. v. Haight (1976), 30 C.C.C. (2d) 168 (Ont. C.A.) — *See also*: *R. v. Galgay* (1972), 6 C.C.C. (2d) 539 (Ont. C.A.) — The term "legal right" in this section means a right which is sanctioned by law, for example the right to use lawful force in self-defence, not merely something that a person may do without incurring legal liability. The law does not approve of everything which it does not forbid.

Objective Standard: S. 232(2)

R. v. Thibert (1996), 104 C.C.C. (3d) 1 (S.C.C.) — In the *objective* element or test of provocation, the "ordinary person" must be of the same age and sex and share with D those other factors which would give the act or insult a special significance and have experienced that same series of acts or insults as D. The past history and relationship between V and D is also relevant.

R. v. Hill (1986), 51 C.R. (3d) 97, 25 C.C.C. (3d) 322 (S.C.C.) — The ordinary person has a normal temperament and level of self control and is not exceptionally excitable or pugnacious or in a state of drunkenness. Particular features such as sex, age or race which do not detract from a person's characterization as ordinary and are not peculiar or idiosyncratic can be ascribed to an ordinary person without subverting the logic of the objective test. The "collective good sense" of the jury will lead it to ascribe to the ordinary person any general characteristics relevant to the provocation in question.

R. v. Newman, (April 16, 1993), Doc. No. CA C7071 (Ont. C.A.) — *See also*: *R. v. Carpenter* (1993), 83 C.C.C. (3d) 193 (Ont. C.A.) — A jury ought *not* be instructed that the question to be decided on the objective test of provocation is whether "an ordinary person would lose his control and do what the accused did ...". The alleged provocation need only be sufficient to deprive the ordinary person of the power of self-control. It is not necessary that the ordinary person would have lost self-control and have done what D did.

R. v. Cameron (1992), 12 C.R (4th) 396, 71 C.C.C. (3d) 272 (Ont. C.A.); leave to appeal refused (1992), 75 C.C.C (3d) vi (note) (S.C.C.) — *See also*: *R. v. Conway* (1985), 17 C.C.C. (3d) 481 (Ont. C.A.); *R. v. Carpenter* (1993), 83 C.C.C. (3d) 193 (Ont. C.A.) — Earlier conduct involving D and V may be relevant to the jury's assessment whether an *ordinary person* would have lost self-control as a result of V's conduct immediately before the infliction of the fatal injury.

Subjective Standard: S. 232(2)

R. v. Thibert (1996), 104 C.C.C. (3d) 1 (S.C.C.) — The *subjective* element or test of provocation requires that D act upon the insult on the sudden and before there was time for D's passion to cool. Sudden provocation requires that the wrongful act or insult strike upon a mind unprepared for it, make an unexpected impact that takes the understanding by surprise and sets the passions aflame. The past history and relationship between V and D is also relevant.

Olbey v. R. (1979), 14 C.R (3d) 44, 50 C.C.C. (2d) 257 (S.C.C.) — *See also*: *Taylor v. R.* (1947), 3 C.R. 475, 89 C.C.C. 209 (S.C.C.) — The jury is entitled to consider the effect of D's intoxication in determining the subjective issue.

Functions of Judge and Jury: S. 232(3)

R. v. Thibert (1996), 104 C.C.C. (3d) 1 (S.C.C.) — While the objective and subjective elements of provocation are questions of fact for the jury, the trial judge must decide whether there is *any* evidence upon which a reasonable jury properly instructed and acting judicially could find provocation. The standard is met where there is *some* evidence that both elements may be satisfied. The trial judge should consider the *nature* of the wrongful act or insult and how it should be viewed in the context of the case, but must *not* weigh the sufficiency of the evidence.

R. v. Squire (1976), 29 C.C.C. (2d) 497 (S.C.C.) — *See also*: *R. v. Kuzmack* (1954), 20 C.R. 365, 110 C.C.C. 338 (Alta. C.A.); affirmed (1955), 20 C.R. 377, 111 C.C.C. 1 (S.C.C.) — Where there is no evidence on which a reasonable jury could find provocation and where the defence was not advanced by D, the trial judge is under no duty to leave the defence of provocation with the jury.

Parnerkar v. R. (1973), 21 C.R.N.S. 129, 10 C.C.C. (2d) 253 (S.C.C.) — As a matter of law it is within the trial judge's exclusive area to decide if there is no evidence potentially enabling a reasonable jury acting judicially to find a wrongful act or insult under subsection (3). Where the judge so decides it is his/her duty not to put provocation to the jury. The issue of sufficiency of evidence of provocation is a question of fact for the jury to decide.

Charter Considerations

R. v. Cameron (1992), 12 C.R. (4th) 396, 71 C.C.C. (3d) 272 (Ont. C.A.); leave to appeal refused (1992), 75 C.C.C. (3d) vi (note) (S.C.C.) — The imposition of an *objective* standard as a threshold test for provocation does *not* offend *Charter* s. 7.

Related Provisions: Under *C.E.A.* s. 4(4), the wife or husband of D is a competent and compellable witness for P without D's consent, where V is under the age of 14 years. Manslaughter may also be a "serious personal injury offence" under para. (a) of the definition in s. 752 for the purposes of Part XXIV. Manslaughter, however, is *not* an "offence" within s. 183 for which judicial authorization to intercept private communications may be given, nor is it excepted from the excuse of compulsion described in s 17. It is not an "enterprise crime offence" as defined in s. 462.3 for the purposes of Part XII.2.

A previous conviction or acquittal on an indictment for manslaughter bars a subsequent indictment for the same homicide charging it as infanticide under s. 610(4).

Manslaughter is an offence in respect of which D may elect mode of trial under s. 536(2). A conviction may attract prohibition against possession of firearms, ammunition or explosive substances under s. 100(1), and where the offence is committed by means of a motor vehicle, vessel or aircraft, may further attract a discretionary prohibition under s. 259(2) which may be stayed pending appeal under s. 261. The punishment for manslaughter is set out in s. 236.

The special pleading rules of ss. 582 and 589, as well as the included offence provisions of ss. 662(2)–(4) are inapplicable where the principal offence is manslaughter. Section 662(5), however, permits conviction of an offence under s. 249 (dangerous operation of a motor vehicle, vessel or aircraft) where the principal charge is manslaughter arising out of the operation of a motor vehicle or the navigation or operation of a vessel or aircraft.

It is also manslaughter under s. 263(3)(a) where death results from the failure to guard an opening in ice or an excavation on land.

Other related provisions are described in the corresponding note to s. 229, *supra*.

233. Infanticide — A female person commits infanticide when by a wilful act or omission she causes the death of her newly-born child, if at the time of the act or omission she is not fully recovered from the effects of giving birth to the child and by reason thereof or of the effect of lactation consequent on the birth of the child her mind is then disturbed.

R.S., c. C-34, s. 216.

Commentary: The section defines *infanticide*, a form of culpable homicide.

Infanticide is committed when a female principal, D, by a wilful act or omission, causes the death of her newly-born child, a person under the age of one year, when D is not fully recovered from the effects of giving birth. It is necessary, further, to prove that the mind of D was disturbed, either because of the effects of giving birth or of lactation consequent upon such birth. It is the only form of culpable homicide that does not attract a minimum or maximum punishment of imprisonment for life.

Case Law

Nature and Elements of Offence

R. v. Marchello (1951), 12 C.R. 7, 100 C.C.C. 137 (Ont. H.C.) — "The elements of the offence of infanticide would appear to be: (a) D must be a woman; (b) she must have caused the death of a child; (c) the child must have been newly born; (d) the child must have been a child of D; (e) the death must have been caused by a wilful act or omission of D; (f) at the time of the wilful act or omission D must not have fully recovered from the effect of giving birth to the child; and (g) by reason of giving birth to the child the balance of her mind must have been then disturbed"

Related Provisions: "Newly-born child" is defined in s. 2. Section 223 determines, for the purposes of the law of homicide, when a child becomes a human being.

Under s. 222(4), infanticide is a form of culpable homicide. Section 222(1) defines homicide and s. 222(5) culpable homicide. The other forms of culpable homicide are murder, as defined in s. 229 and the constitutionally deficient s. 230, and classified for sentencing purposes in s. 231, and manslaughter, as described in s. 234.

Sections 224–228 contain several provisions relating to causation in homicide cases.

Killing an unborn child in the act of birth is an offence under s. 238. Sections 242 and 243 create offences relating to neglect in childbirth and concealing the dead body of a child. Sections 215 and 218 create offences for failure to provide necessaries of life and abandoning a child.

The husband or wife of D is a competent and compellable witness for P under *C.E.A.* s. 4(4) without D's consent. The special included offence provisions of ss. 662(3) and (4) are applicable where D is charged with murder and the evidence proves infanticide, or with the murder of a child or infanticide and the evidence proves an offence under s. 243. Further, ss. 610(2) and (4) describe the circumstances under which a conviction or acquittal of murder, manslaughter or infanticide will bar subsequent indictment for another form of culpable homicide.

Section 663, which permits conviction upon proof of certain matters, unless the evidence establishes that the act or omission was *not* wilful, applies to cases of infanticide. The punishment for infanticide is described in s. 236. A finding of guilt may attract the discretionary prohibition or s. 100(2).

Under s. 536(2), D may elect mode of trial.

234. Manslaughter — Culpable homicide that is not murder or infanticide is manslaughter.

R.S., c. C-34, s. 217.

Commentary: Manslaughter, unlike the other forms of culpable homicide, murder and infanticide, is not expressly defined. It is a residual category of culpable homicide, namely, that which is neither murder nor infanticide.

Manslaughter is either "voluntary" or "involuntary" manslaughter. In *voluntary* manslaughter, the mental element of murder is proven, but the presence of a reasonable doubt of some defined mitigating circumstance, as for example provocation under s. 232, reduces what otherwise would be murder to manslaughter. *Involuntary* manslaughter includes any culpable homicide that lacks the *mental element* of murder. It may be committed, in any way described in s. 222(5).

Case Law

Burden of Proof

R. v. Kuzmack (1955), 20 C.R. 377, 111 C.C.C. 1 (S.C.C.) — *See also*: *R. v. Otis* (1978), 39 C.C.C. (2d) 304 (Ont C.A.) — If the jury concludes upon the evidence that the homicide was culpable, it is then necessary to decide, as a fact, with what intent D inflicted the wound. If there is a reasonable doubt that

D possessed the requisite intent for murder, D must be given the benefit of the doubt and convicted only of manslaughter.

Mental Element [See also s. 229 Mental Element and its ProofS

R. v. Creighton (1993), 23 C.R. (4th) 189, 83 C.C.C. (3d) 346 (S.C.C.) — *See also: R. v. Reyat* (1993), 20 C.R. (4th) 149, 80 C.C.C. (3d) 210 (B.C. C.A.); leave to appeal refused (1993), 25 C.R. (4th) 125 (S.C.C.) — In *unlawful act manslaughter* under s. 222(5)(a), the *mens rea* comprises

i.   the *mens rea* of the underlying offence: and

ii. objective foreseeability of the risk of bodily harm which is neither trivial nor transitory, in the context of the dangerous act.

Foreseeability of death is *not* required. (per McLachlin, La Forest, L'Heureux-Dubé, Gonthier and Cory JJ.A.)

R. v. Gosset (1993), 23 C.R. (4th) 280, 83 C.C.C. (3d) 494 (S.C.C.) — A conviction of unlawful act manslaughter may be based on careless use of a firearm under *Code* s. 86(2). Where D's conduct constitutes a *marked departure* from the standard of care of a reasonably prudent person in the circumstances, a jury may find that the necessary external circumstances and mental element have been proven, absent evidence of incapacity to appreciate the risk involved in the conduct.

Smithers v. R. (1977), 40 C.R.N.S. 79, 34 C.C.C. (2d) 427 (S.C.C.) — There is *no* requirement that P prove an intention to cause death or injury. It is *not* a defence to manslaughter that the fatality was not anticipated or that death would not ordinarily result from the unlawful act.

Intoxication [See also ss. 8 and 229]

R. v. Mack (1975), 29 C.R.N.S. 270, 22 C.C.C. (2d) 257 (Alta. C.A.) — Murder requires a specific intent; manslaughter does not. Intent, however, is an essential element of manslaughter. When the only defence offered is voluntary intoxication, falling short of insanity, the mental element is established by proof that D did the prohibited act.

Party to Manslaughter

R. v. Jackson (1993), 26 C.R. (4th) 178, 86 C.C.C. (3d) 385 (S.C.C.) — D may be convicted of unlawful act manslaughter through ss. 21(1)(b) or (c) without proof of a subjective appreciation of the consequences of the relevant act. The test is objective. The risk of death need not be foreseeable. Provided the unlawful act is inherently dangerous and harm to another which is neither trivial nor transitory is its foreseeable consequence, the resultant death amounts to manslaughter.Where D aids or abets another in the offence of murder, D may be convicted of manslaughter if a reasonable person, in all of the circumstances, would have appreciated that bodily harm was a foreseeable consequence of the dangerous act which was being undertaken.

Where a *common unlawful purpose* has been proven and a party to it has committed murder, another party to the purpose may be convicted of murder or manslaughter under s. 21(2). The "offence" referred to in s. 21(2) is not confined to the offence of which the perpetrator is convicted, but extends to included offences.The appropriate *mens rea* for manslaughter under s. 21(2) is objective awareness of the risk of harm. Proof of foreseeability of death is *not* required, only foreseeability of harm, which, in fact, results in death. A party to a common intention to carry out an unlawful purpose within s. 21(2) may be guilty of manslaughter, notwithstanding the principal is guilty of murder, where the party did not foresee the probability of murder, but where a reasonable person, in all of the circumstances, would have foreseen at least the risk of harm to another as a result of carrying out the common intention.

R. v. Kirkness (1990), 60 C.C.C. (3d) 97 (S.C.C.) — Where the intent of D is insufficient to establish liability for murder, D may be convicted of manslaughter, as an aider or abettor, if the unlawful act causing death which was aided or abetted by D is one which D knew was likely to cause some harm to V short of death.

Cluett v. R. (1985), 21 C.C.C. (3d) 318 (S.C.C.) — On a charge of aiding and abetting manslaughter, P is not required to prove the intention to kill, or to cause bodily harm of the type described in s. 229(a)(ii).

R. v. Barbeau (1998), 127 C.C.C. (3d) 104 (Que. C.A.) — Where D *arranges* to have a third party *present* at a meeting with V, whom D *knew* to be *aggressive* and likely to fight, D may be convicted of manslaughter if s/he *foresaw*, as a *reasonable* person would appreciate, an unlawful and inherently dangerous physical confrontation that risked bodily harm to V.

Accident

R. v. Tennant (1975), 31 C.R.N.S. 1, 23 C.C.C. (2d) 80 (Ont. C.A.) — *See also*: *R. v. Lelievre* (1962), 37 C.R. 83, 132 C.C.C. 288 (Ont. C.A.) — Where death is caused by the accidental discharge of a firearm in the commission of an unlawful act and the act is such that any reasonable person would inevitably realize that it would subject another to the risk of at least some harm, albeit not serious harm, the death would amount to manslaughter. Where D is engaged in a lawful purpose and death is caused by the accidental discharge of a pistol, then, in the absence of criminal negligence, accident is a complete defence.

Charter Considerations

R. v. Creighton (1993), 23 C.R. (4th) 189, 83 C.C.C. (3d) 346 (S.C.C.) — *See also*: *R. v. Reyat* (1993), 20 C.R. (4th) 149, 80 C.C C. (3d) 210 (B.C. C.A.); leave to appeal refused (September 16, 1993), Doc. No. 23606 (S.C.C.) — Unlawful act manslaughter does *not* contravene *Charter* s. 7.

Related Provisions: See the corresponding note to s. 232, *supra*.

235. (1) Punishment for murder — Every one who commits first degree murder or second degree murder is guilty of an indictable offence and shall be sentenced to imprisonment for life.

(2) Minimum punishment — For the purposes of Part XXIII, the sentence of imprisonment for life prescribed by this section is a minimum punishment.

R.S., c. C-34, s. 218; 1973–74, c. 38; s. 3; 1974–75–76, c. 105, s. 5.

Commentary: The section prescribes the punishment upon conviction of murder. The minimum punishment of imprisonment for life includes a parole ineligibility period.

Case Law

Charter Considerations [See also s. 231]

R. v. Bowen (1990), 59 C.C.C. (3d) 515 (Alta. C.A.) — The sentence for first degree murder of law enforcement personnel under s. 231(4) does *not* offend *Charter* s. 7, 9, 12 or 15.

R. v. Mitchell (1987), 39 C.C.C. (3d) 141 (N.S. C.A.) — The mandatory minimum sentence for second degree murder does *not* violate *Charter* s. 7, 9 or 12.

Related Provisions: See the corresponding notes to ss. 229–231, *supra*.

236. Manslaughter — Every person who commits manslaughter is guilty of an indictable offence and liable

(a) where a firearm is used in the commission of the offence, to imprisonment for life and to a minimum punishment of imprisonment for a term of four years; and

(b) in any other case, to imprisonment for life.

R.S., c. C-34, s. 219; 1995, c. 39, s. 142.

Commentary: The section does not distinguish voluntary from involuntary manslaughter. The punishment for manslaughter is not a minimum punishment except in cases where a firearm is used. A period of parole ineligibility may be fixed under s. 741.2.

Case Law

Basis for Sentencing

R. v. Braun (1995), 95 C.C.C. (3d) 443 (Man. C.A.) — Where D is convicted of manslaughter by a jury, a trial judge ought *not* impose sentence on the basis of facts contained in D's inculpatory statement which were inconsistent with the manslaughter verdict.

R. v. Cooney (1995), 98 C.C.C. (3d) 196 (Ont. C.A.) — Where manslaughter has been left to the jury on the basis of both ss. 21(1) and 21(2), the sentencing judge will be required to reach his/her own conclusions as to D's participation in light of the jury's verdict. Where facts are disputed on the issue of sentence, the burden of establishing aggravating facts rests upon P.

Related Provisions: See the corresponding note to s. 232, *supra*.

237. Punishment for infanticide — Every female person who commits infanticide is guilty of an indictable offence and liable to imprisonment for a term not exceeding five years.

R.S., c. C-34, s. 220.

Commentary: The section provides the punishment upon finding of guilt of infanticide, the only form of culpable homicide which does *not* carry a minimum or maximum punishment of imprisonment for life.

Related Provisions: See the corresponding note to s. 233, *supra*.

238. (1) Killing unborn child in act of birth — Every one who causes the death, in the act of birth, of any child that has not become a human being, in such a manner that, if the child were a human being, he would be guilty of murder, is guilty of an indictable offence and liable to imprisonment for life.

(2) Saving — This section does not apply to a person who, by means that, in good faith, he considers necessary to preserve the life of the mother of a child, causes the death of that child.

R.S., c. C-34, s. 221.

Commentary: This offence requires proof of *murder* during the act of birth of a child who has *not* become a human being under s. 223. Although proof of *murder* of V is necessary to establish D's liability, V's status as a *child* removes the offence from the category of homicide, hence culpable homicide, which requires, under s. 222(1), that V be a human being. Notwithstanding proof that D has committed murder upon V, a child, the exception of s. 238(2) applies where D has done so, by means that, in good faith, D considers necessary to preserve the life of V's mother.

Related Provisions: Section 223(1) defines when a child becomes a human being for the purposes of the law of homicide. Section 223(2) provides that it is homicide where D causes injury to a child before or during its birth as a result of which the child dies after becoming a human being. Murder is defined in s. 229. It is classified for sentencing purposes by s. 231.

Infanticide is defined in s. 233. Offences relating to neglect in childbirth and concealing the dead body of a child are described in ss. 242 and 243.

Under s. 536(2), D may elect mode of trial. *Quaere* whether, upon conviction, the order of s. 100(1) may be made since V, under the section, is not a "human being" hence, presumably, *not* a "person"?

239. Attempt to commit murder — Every person who attempts by any means to commit murder is guilty of an indictable offence and liable

  (a) where a firearm is used in the commission of the offence, to imprisonment for life and to a minimum punishment of imprisonment for a term of four years; and

  (b) in any other case, to imprisonment for life.

R.S., c. C-34, s. 222;1995, c. 39, s. 143.

Commentary: This section does *not* specify nor otherwise describe the means by which the offence may be committed, hence its external circumstances. The *mental element* requires proof of the intent to kill.

Case Law
Mental Element

R. v. Logan (1990), 79 C.R. (3d) 169, 58 C.C.C. (3d) 391 (S.C.C.); affirming (1988), 68 C.R. (3d) 1, 46 C.C.C. (3d) 354 (Ont. C.A.) — The *mental element* in attempted murder cannot, without infringing

Charter s. 7, require less than the *subjective foresight* demanded in cases of murder under s. 229(a)(i). The subjective foresight necessary to convict a principal of attempted murder is also constitutionally required to convict a party under s. 21(2). The words "or ought to have known" are inoperative when considering the liability of the party.

R. v. Ancio (1984), 39 C.R. (3d) 1, 10 C.C.C. (3d) 385 (S.C.C.) — The *mental element* in attempted murder is specific intent to kill.

R. v. Marshall (1986), 25 C.C.C. (3d) 151 (N.S. C.A.) — The *mental element* required for attempted murder is the specific intent to kill someone. The *actus reus* is anything done for the purpose of carrying out that murder. It is not necessary for P to prove that the specific intent related to the named victims where D shoots randomly at a number persons crowded into an area, even though those persons were not the original targets of D's intent to murder.

R. v. Adams (1989), 49 C.C.C. (3d) 100 (Ont. C.A.) — On a charge of attempted murder where D is alleged to be an aider or abettor under s. 21(1), it must be shown that D knew of the principal's intention to kill. Knowledge that the principal only intended to commit an act of violence is *not* sufficient.

R. v. Campbell (1977), 1 C.R. (3d) 309, 38 C.C.C. (2d) 6 (Ont. C.A.) — Provocation and excessive force in self-defence will *not* reduce a charge of attempted murder to attempted manslaughter. The evidence may be considered on the issue of whether D had the requisite intent for attempted murder. Provocation may produce in D a state of excitement, anger or disturbance, as a result of which D might not contemplate the consequences of his/her acts hence, might not intend their consequences.

Included Offences [See also s. 662]

R. v. Wigman (1987), 56 C.R. (3d) 289, 33 C.C.C. (3d) 97 (S.C.C.) — The offence of causing bodily harm with intent to endanger life may be an included offence in attempted murder.

R. v. Simpson (No. 2) (1981), 20 C.R. (3d) 36, 58 C.C.C. (2d) 122 (Ont. C.A.) — The description of the offence of attempted murder in this section does *not* include the offences of causing bodily harm with intent to wound, assault causing bodily harm, and unlawfully causing bodily harm. They are not, therefore, included offences unless described as such in the specific indictment. An indictment that states that D attempted to cause the death of V, without specifying the means, is *not* such a description, although it may include an attempt to unlawfully cause bodily harm.

R. v. Colburne (1991), 66 C.C.C. (3d) 235 (Que. C.A.) — Attempted murder, as described in the section, includes attempting unlawfully to cause bodily harm.

Charter Considerations

R. v. Logan (1990), 79 C.R. (3d) 169, 58 C.C.C. (3d) 391 (S.C.C.); affirming (1988), 68 C.R. (3d) 1, 46 C.C.C. (3d) 354 (Ont. C.A.) — See digest under "Mental Element", *supra*

Related Provisions: An attempt is defined in s. 24. Murder is defined in s. 229 and classified for sentencing purposes in s. 231.

Attempted murder is an "offence" within s. 183 for the purposes of Part VI. It is also an "enterprise crime offence" for the purposes of Part XII.2 and may also fall within para. (a) of the definition "serious personal injury offence" in s. 752 for the purposes of Part XXIV. The wife or husband of D charged with attempted murder in respect of a complainant under the age of 14 years is a competent and compellable witness for P without D's consent. The excuse of compulsion is *not* available to D in the circumstances described in s. 17.

Related non-fatal offences against the person appear in ss. 244–248, 264.1, 267(1)(b), 268 and 269.

Section 662(2) expressly permits conviction of attempted (second degree) murder on an indictment for first degree murder. Section 661 provides for the comparatively rare instance where an attempt is charged but the evidence proves the complete offence.

Attempted murder is an offence in respect of which D may *elect* mode of trial under s. 536(2). It is *not* an offence described in s. 469(d) which falls within the exclusive trial or judicial interim release jurisdiction of the superior court of criminal jurisdiction. A conviction may attract the prohibition of s. 109.

240. Accessory after fact to murder — Every one who is an accessory after the fact to murder is guilty of an indictable offence and liable to imprisonment for life.

R.S., c. C-34, s. 223.

Commentary: This section, an exception to the general provisions of s. 463(a), expressly provides for the punishment which may be imposed, upon conviction as an accessory after the fact to murder.

The essential elements of accessoryship after the fact, defined in s. 23(1), include both *external circumstances* and elements of knowledge and purpose. Accessoryship after the fact to murder requires proof:

i.   that A (accessory) *received, comforted* or *assisted* P (principal);

ii.   that A did so with the *knowledge* that P was a party to murder, and

iii.   that A did so for the *purpose* of *enabling* P to *escape* liability therefor.

Case Law [See ss. 23, 23.1, 592]

R. v. Camponi (1993), 22 C.R. (4th) 348, 82 C.C.C. (3d) 506 (B.C. C.A.) — D may be convicted of being an accessory after the fact to murder, notwithstanding that proceedings against the principal have been stayed.

Related Provisions: Murder is defined in s. 229 and classified for sentencing purposes in section 231.

Accessory after the fact to murder is an "offence" for the purposes of Part VI and an "enterprise crime offence" under s. 462.3 for the purposes of Part XII.2. It is unlikely that the offence would come within para. (a) of the definition of "serious personal injury offence" in s. 752 for the purposes of Part XXIV. The wife or husband of D charged with being an accessory after the fact to murder in respect of V under the age of 14 years is a competent and compellable witness for P without D's consent under *C.E.A.* s. 4(4).

Under s. 23.1, D may be convicted of being an accessory after the fact to murder (or any other offence) upon proper proof, notwithstanding that the principal or other party cannot be convicted. Section 592 permits the indictment of an accessory whether or not the principal or any other party has been indicted, convicted, or is or is not amenable to justice.

Accessory after the fact to murder falls within the *exclusive* trial and judicial interim release jurisdiction of the superior court of criminal jurisdiction. *Quaere* whether, upon conviction, the provisions of s. 109(1) would be applicable?

Suicide

241. Counselling or aiding suicide — Every one who

(a) counsels a person to commit suicide, or

(b) aids or abets a person to commit suicide,

whether suicide ensues or not, is guilty of an indictable offence and liable to imprisonment for a term not exceeding fourteen years.

R.S., c. C-34, s. 224; R.S. 1985, c. 27 (1st Supp.), s. 7(3).

Commentary: The offence is somewhat unusual. Suicide is *not* itself a crime, nor is its attempt. Under s. 225 of the 1970 Statutory Revision and s. 213 of the 1953–54 *Code*, attempted suicide was a summary conviction offence. It was repealed by S.C. 1972, c. 13, s. 16.

Case Law

R. v. Gagnon (1993), 24 C.R (4th) 369, 84 C.C.C. (3d) 143 (Que. C.A.) — When the parties to a suicide pact are in such a mental state that they have formed a common and irrevocable intent to commit suicide together, simultaneously, by the same act, and where the risk of death is identical and equal for both, the surviving party has a defence to murder, but may be guilty of counselling or aiding suicide under s. 241.

Related Provisions: Under s. 22(3), "counsel" includes procure, solicit or incite. Participation in an offence by aiding or abetting is governed by ss. 21(1)(b) and (c).

Liability by counselling, is described in ss. 22(1) and (2). Under s. 23.1, D, the counsellor, may be convicted, notwithstanding that the principal cannot him/herself be convicted of the offence. The general rules respecting the liability and punishment of persons who counsel another to commit an offence that is *not* in fact committed are found in s. 464.

S. 241 Criminal Code

Under s. 536(2), D may *elect* mode of trial.

Neglect in Child-birth and Concealing Dead Body

242. Neglect to obtain assistance in child-birth — A female person who, being pregnant and about to be delivered, with intent that the child shall not live or with intent to conceal the birth of the child, fails to make provision for reasonable assistance in respect of her delivery is, if the child is permanently injured as a result thereof or dies immediately before, during or in a short time after birth, as a result thereof, guilty of an indictable offence and is liable to imprisonment for a term not exceeding five years.

R.S., c. C-34, s. 226.

Commentary: As principal, D must be a female person, pregnant and about to be delivered of her child. The offence can only be committed at or immediately before the birth of a child and, as a principal, only by the child's mother. The *external circumstances* of the crime combine an *omission* by D ("fails to make provision for reasonable assistance in her delivery") and certain *consequences* ("the child is permanently injured as a result thereof or dies immediately before, during or in a short time after birth, as a result thereof"). The *mental element* of the offence requires proof of either *an intent that the child shall not live* or an intent to conceal the birth of the child.

Case Law

R. v. Bryan (1959), 123 C.C.C. 160 (Ont. C.A.) — This section does *not* apply to a death which resulted from acts subsequent to the delivery and which did *not* result from a failure to obtain reasonable assistance in respect to the delivery itself. Death or injury must be a direct result of a deliberate failure to obtain reasonable assistance at birth.

Related Provisions: Section 223(1) defines when a "child" becomes a human being for the purposes of the law of homicide. Section 223(2) declares a person to have committed homicide where s/he causes injury to a child before or during its birth as a result of which the child dies after becoming a human being. Section 222(5) defines what constitutes culpable homicide. Under s. 222(4), culpable homicide is murder, manslaughter or infanticide. Murder is defined, *inter alia*, in s. 229 and is classified for sentencing purposes in s. 231. Infanticide is defined in s. 233 and is punished under s. 237.

Killing an unborn child in the act of birth is an offence under s. 238. Concealing the dead body of a child is an offence under s. 243, and administering a noxious thing to another is a crime under s. 245. D may *elect* mode of trial under s. 536(2).

243. Concealing body of child — Every one who in any manner disposes of the dead body of a child, with intent to conceal the fact that its mother has been delivered of it, whether the child died before, during or after birth, is guilty of an indictable offence and liable to imprisonment for a term not exceeding two years.

R.S., c. C-34, s. 227.

Commentary: As principal, D may be anyone. The *external circumstances* require proof of the disposal of the *dead body* of a child. It matters not whether the child has died before, during or after birth. It is, however, essential that the disposal of the dead body of the child be with intent to conceal the fact that its mother has been delivered of it. Mere concealment of the body, in other words, will not suffice to establish liability.

Related Provisions: Section 223(1) determines when a "child" becomes a human being for the purposes of the law of homicide.

Neglect to obtain assistance in childbirth is an offence under s. 242, and killing an unborn child in the act of birth a crime under s. 238. Improper interference with a dead body or its burial is prohibited under s. 182.

Infanticide is a form of culpable homicide defined in s. 233, and punished under s. 237. The substantive, evidentiary and procedural provisions applicable in such cases are discussed in the corresponding note to

s. 233, *supra.* Upon an indictment for infanticide or murder of a child, s. 662(4) permits conviction of an offence under s. 243 upon evidence adequate to sustain proof thereof but insufficient to establish the offence charged.

Under s. 536(2), D may *elect* mode of trial.

Bodily Harm and Acts and Omissions Causing Danger to the Person

244. Causing bodily harm with intent — firearm — Every person who, with intent

(a) to wound, maim or disfigure any person,

(b) to endanger the life of any person, or

(c) to prevent the arrest or detention of any person,

discharges a firearm at any person, whether or not that person is the person mentioned in paragraph (*a*), (*b*) or (*c*), is guilty of an indictable offence and liable to imprisonment for a term not exceeding fourteen years and to a minimum punishment of imprisonment for a term of four years.

R.S., c. C-34, s. 228; 1980–81–82–83, c. 125, s. 17;1995, c. 39, s. 144

Commentary: The *external circumstances* of this offence require proof of the *discharge* of a *firearm* at another person. The gravamen of the offence, however, rests in the *mental element. One* of the ulterior *mental elements* specified in ss. 244(a)–(c) must accompany the discharge of the weapon.

Case Law

Intent

R. v. Angevine (1984), 61 N.S.R. (2d) 263 (C.A.) — The intent to wound, maim or disfigure is *not* the same and is a separate offence from the intent to endanger the life of any person.

Wound

R. v. Littletent (1985), 17 C.C.C. (3d) 520 (Alta. C.A.) — A breaking of the skin is necessary to constitute wounding.

Maim

R. v. Schultz (1962), 38 C.R. 76, 133 C.C.C. 174 (Alta. C.A.); leave to appeal refused [1962] S.C.R. x (S.C.C.) — *See also*: *R. v. Innes* (1972), 7 C.C.C. (2d) 544 (B.C. C.A.) — A person is maimed when he is injured to the extent that he is less able to fight. To break V's leg is sufficiently serious to amount to maiming.

Disfigure

R. v. Innes (1972), 7 C.C.C. (2d) 544 (B.C. C.A.) — Disfigure denotes "more than a temporary marring of the figure or appearance of a person".

Firearm

R. v. Roberts (1998), 125 C.C.C. (3d) 471 (N.B. C.A.) — The definition of "firearm" in s. 84(1) does *not* apply to an offence under this section. (see now *Code* s. 2.)

Included Offences

R. v. Colburne (1991), 66 C.C.C. (3d) 235 (Que. C.A.) — Assault is an included offence in a count which charges unlawfully discharging a firearm in the direction of another person, even if the shot misses the intended target who is unaware of it. Included in a count which charges discharging a firearm with intent to wound are the offences of pointing a firearm without lawful excuse (s. 86(1)(a)) and attempting to cause bodily harm (s. 269).

Charter Considerations

R. v. Roberts (1998), 125 C.C.C. (3d) 471 (N.B. C.A.) — The minimum punishment provided for by this section does *not* offend *Charter* s. 12.

R. v. Benoit (1985), 56 Nfld. & P.E.I.R. 55 (Nfld. C.A.) — A conviction for *discharging* a firearm with intent to endanger life and for *using* a firearm while committing an indictable offence would punish D twice for the same offence and offend *Charter* s. 11(h).

Related Provisions: "Firearm" is defined in s. 2.

"Wounds", "maims", "disfigures" or "endangers the life" also appear in the related offence of aggravated assault (s. 268). Assault with a 'weapon', as defined in s. 2, is an offence under s. 267(1)(a). Assault causing bodily harm and unlawfully causing bodily harm are offences under ss. 267(1)(b) and 269, respectively. "Bodily harm" is defined in s. 2.

This section is analogous to s. 229(b) in that, in each case, D's intent may relate to V_1, and the external circumstances of the offence to V_2, although s. 244 does *not* require the discharge to strike anyone as a condition precedent to liability.

This offence would appear to fall within para. (a) of the definition of "serious personal injury offence" in s. 752, for the purposes of Part XXIV.

D may *elect* mode of trial under s. 536(2). A conviction under the section may attract the prohibitions of s. 109.

244.1 Causing bodily harm with intent — air gun or pistol — Every person who, with intent

(a) to wound, maim or disfigure any person,

(b) to endanger the life of any person, or

(c) to prevent the arrest or detention of any person,

discharges an air or compressed gas gun or pistol at any person, whether or not that person is the person mentioned in paragraph (*a*), (*b*) or (*c*), is guilty of an indictable offence and liable to imprisonment for a term not exceeding fourteen years.

1995, c. 39, s. 144.

Commentary: The *external circumstances* of this offence involve the *discharge* of an air or compressed gas gun or pistol *at another* person. The *mental element* requires proof of an ulterior mental state, any of ss. 244.1(a)-(c).

Related Provisions: The *Code* does not define the weapons described in the section. Except for the nature of the weapon used, the section is a duplicate of s. 244.

Other related provisions are discussed in the corresponding notes to s. 244.

245. Administering noxious thing — Every one who administers or causes to be administered to any person or causes any person to take poison or any other destructive or noxious thing is guilty of an indictable offence and liable

(a) to imprisonment for a term not exceeding fourteen years, if he intends thereby to endanger the life of or to cause bodily harm to that person; or

(b) to imprisonment for a term not exceeding two years, if he intends thereby to aggrieve or annoy that person.

R.S., c. C-34, s. 229.

Commentary: The *external circumstances* require proof that D administered, caused to be administered or caused anyone to take poison, or any other destructive or noxious thing. It would seem necessary that the drug be noxious in the quantity administered.

The description of the offence itself makes no reference to any specific or ulterior *mental element*. Under paras. (a) and (b), however, the nature of the specific or ulterior mental element proven determines the maximum punishment for the offence.

Case Law

R. v. Burkholder (1977), 34 C.C.C. (2d) 214 (Alta. C.A.) — P must prove that the substance administered by D was a noxious thing, as administered, and that D *intended* to cause bodily harm thereby. P need *not* prove that D knew the substance was noxious.

Related Provisions: "Poison", "destructive thing" and "noxious thing" are *not* defined in nor for the purposes of the section. "Bodily harm" is defined in s. 2.

Section 246 creates the offence of overcoming resistance to the commission of an indictable offence. Unlawfully causing bodily harm is an offence under s. 269. Assault causing bodily harm is an offence under s. 267(1)(b), and aggravated assault is defined in s. 268(1). Discharging a firearm, air gun or air pistol is a crime in circumstances described in s. 244 and s. 244.1. The supply of noxious things with knowledge of their intended use or employment to procure a miscarriage is prohibited by s. 288. Other related offences are found in ss. 212(1)(i) (procuring) and 287(1) (procuring miscarriage).

Where death ensues from the administration of poison or any other destructive or noxious thing, D may have committed culpable homicide under s. 222(5)(a) or (b). Culpable homicide is either murder, manslaughter or infanticide

The offences of the section permit D to *elect* mode of trial under s. 536(2).

246. Overcoming resistance to commission of offence — Every one who, with intent to enable or assist himself or another person to commit an indictable offence,

    (a) attempts, by any means, to choke, suffocate or strangle another person, or by any means calculated to choke, suffocate or strangle, attempts to render another person insensible, unconscious or incapable of resistance, or

    (b) administers, or causes to be administered to any person, or attempts to administer to any person, or causes or attempts to cause any person to take a stupefying or overpowering drug, matter or thing,

is guilty of an indictable offence and liable to imprisonment for life.

R.S., c. C-34, s. 230; 1972, c. 13, s. 70.

Commentary: D's liability under this section is established by proof of the *external circumstances* of either para. (a) or (b), together with the specific or ulterior *mental element* described in the section.

Related Provisions: Under *I.A.* s. 34(1)(a), an *indictable* offence is any offence that *may* be prosecuted by indictment. An attempt is defined in s. 24.

Where death ensues from the external circumstances of these offences, D may have committed culpable homicide under s. 222(5)(a) and/or (b). Culpable homicide is either murder, manslaughter or, infanticide.

Related non-fatal offences against the person may include attempted murder (s. 239), administering a noxious thing (s. 245), assault (s. 266), assault causing bodily harm (s. 267(1)(b)), aggravated assault (s. 268) and unlawfully causing bodily harm (s. 269).

D may *elect* mode of trial under s. 536(2). A conviction may engage a prohibition under s. 100(1). The offence would also seem to fall within para. (a) of the definition of "serious personal injury offence" in s. 752, for the purposes of Part XXIV.

247. (1) Traps likely to cause bodily harm — Every one who, with intent to cause death or bodily harm to persons, whether ascertained or not, sets or places or causes to be set or placed a trap, device or other thing whatever that is likely to cause death or bodily harm to persons is guilty of an indictable offence and liable to imprisonment for a term not exceeding five years.

(2) Permitting traps on premises — A person who, being in occupation or possession of a place where anything mentioned in subsection (1) has been set or placed,

S. 247(2)   Criminal Code

knowingly and wilfully permits it to remain at that place, shall be deemed, for the purposes of that subsection, to have set or placed it with the intent mentioned therein.

R.S., c. C-34, s. 231.

Commentary: The *external circumstances* of the offence of s. 247(1) must be accompanied by proof of an ulterior or specific *mental element*, that is to say the "intent to cause death or bodily harm to persons, whether ascertained or not ..." in order to establish liability.

Section 247(2) creates a statutory *presumption* whereby the *mental element* of the offence of s. 247(1) is deemed established upon proof that D, in occupation or possession of a place where anything mentioned in s. 247(1) has been set or placed, knowingly and wilfully permits it to remain. *Semble*, at least indirectly, the subsection shifts the onus of disproof in respect of the *mental element* to D, thereby potentially raising a *Charter* s. 11(d) issue.

Related Provisions: "Bodily harm" is defined in s. 2. "Place" is *not* defined for the purposes of the section.

Where death ensues from the external circumstances of the offences described in the section D may have committed culpable homicide under s. 222(5)(a) and/or (b) which may be murder, manslaughter or, rarely, infanticide.

Related non-fatal offences against the person include attempted murder (s. 239) and unlawfully causing bodily harm (s. 269), if not the various levels of assault on account of the definition in s. 265(1)(a).

D may elect mode of trial under s. 536(2). A conviction may engage the prohibition of s. 100(2), provided the setting or placing of traps, in the circumstances, could be said to be an offence "in the commission of which *violence* against a person is *used, threatened or attempted* ...".

248. Interfering with transportation facilities — Every one who, with intent to endanger the safety of any persons, places anything on or does anything to any property that is used for or in connection with the transportation of persons or goods by land, water or air that is likely to cause death or bodily harm to persons is guilty of an indictable offence and liable to imprisonment for life.

R.S., c. C-34, s. 232.

Commentary: The *external circumstances* of the offence, namely, "places anything on or does anything to any property that is used for or in connection with the transportation of persons or goods by land, water or air that is likely to cause death or bodily harm to persons" must be accompanied by the specific *intent* to endanger the safety of *any person* to establish D's liability.

Related Provisions: "Property" and "bodily harm" are defined in s. 2.

Where death occurs in consequence of conduct prohibited by this section, D may have committed culpable homicide under s. 222(5)(a) or (b) or criminal negligence, as defined in s. 219(1)(a). To cause bodily harm in the circumstances may amount to an offence under s. 269.

Section 430 defines and punishes several offences of mischief which consist of various wilful and forbidden acts in respect of certain property. Mischief that causes actual danger to life is punishable under s. 430(2).

D may elect mode of trial under s. 536(2).

Motor Vehicles, Vessels and Aircraft

249. (1) Dangerous operation of motor vehicles, vessels and aircraft — Every one commits an offence who operates

(a) a motor vehicle in a manner that is dangerous to the public, having regard to all the circumstances, including the nature, condition and use of the place at which the motor vehicle is being operated and the amount of traffic that at the time is or might reasonably be expected to be at that place;

346

Part VIII — Offence Against Person

(b) a vessel or any water skis, surf-board, water sled or other towed object on or over any of the internal waters of Canada or the territorial sea of Canada, in a manner that is dangerous to the public, having regard to all the circumstances, including the nature and condition of those waters or sea and the use that at the time is or might reasonably be expected to be made of those waters or sea;

(c) an aircraft in a manner that is dangerous to the public, having regard to all the circumstances, including the nature and condition of that aircraft or the place or air space in or through which the aircraft is operated; or

(d) railway equipment in a manner that is dangerous to the public, having regard to all the circumstances, including the nature and condition of the equipment or the place in or through which the equipment is operated.

(2) Punishment — Every one who commits an offence under subsection (1)

(a) is guilty of an indictable offence and liable to imprisonment for a term not exceeding five years; or

(b) is guilty of an offence punishable on summary conviction.

(3) Dangerous operation causing bodily harm — Every one who commits an offence under subsection (1) and thereby causes bodily harm to any other person is guilty of an indictable offence and liable to imprisonment for a term not exceeding ten years.

(4) Dangerous operation causing death — Every one who commits an offence under subsection (1) and thereby causes the death of any other person is guilty of an indictable offence and liable to imprisonment for a term not exceeding fourteen years.
R.S., c. C-34, s. 233; R.S. 1985, c. 27 (1st Supp.), s. 36; c. 32 (4th Supp.), s. 57; 1994, c. 44, s. 11.

Commentary: The section defines the essential elements of the offence of *dangerous operation* of motor vehicles, vessels and related towed objects, aircraft, and railway equipment and provides the punishment in respect of the offence in its simple and aggravated forms.

The *external circumstances* of the *motor vehicle* offence in s. 249(1)(a) require that D *operate* a motor vehicle. The *manner* in which D operates the motor vehicle must be *dangerous to the public* having regard to all the circumstances, including, but not limited to those listed in the paragraph.

The *vessel* or related towed object offence of s. 249(1)(b) requires that D *operate* a vessel, water skis, surf-board, water sled or other towed object. The operation must be over or on any of the internal waters or territorial sea of Canada. The operation, further, must be in any manner that is dangerous to the public, having regard to all the circumstances, including, but not limited to those enumerated in the paragraph.

The *aircraft* and *railway equipment* offences are contained in ss. 249(1)(c) and (d). The *external circumstances* are established where D *operates* an aircraft or railway equipment in a manner dangerous to the public, having regard to all of the circumstances, including, but not limited to those listed in the paragraph.

There has always been some dispute as to the nature of the *mental element* involved in the dangerous operation offence, more specifically its characterization in terms of advertent or inadvertent negligence. It would seem clear, at all events, that no ulterior *mental element* need be established.

The general offence is triable either way under s. 249(2).

Sections 249(3) and (4) provide punishment for dangerous operation where bodily harm or death has been caused thereby. There must be a causal *nexus* or link between the manner of D's operation and bodily harm (s. 249(3)) or death (s. 249(4)) to attract liability for the aggravated offence. The *mental element* remains the same.

Case Law
Nature and Elements of Offence

R. v. MacGillivray, 37 C.R. (4th) 221, 97 C.C.C. (3d) 13, [1995] 1 S.C.R. 890 (S.C.C.); affirming (1993), 126 N.S.R. (2d) 275, 352 A.P.R. 275 (N.S. C.A.) — The *actus reus* of dangerous operation of a vessel is conduct which, viewed objectively, constitutes a *significant departure* from the standard of a reasonably prudent person. There is no real difference between "significant departure" and "marked departure".

R. v. Hundal (1993), 19 C.R. (4th) 169, 79 C.C.C. (3d) 97 (S.C.C.) — The *mental element* in dangerous driving is to be assessed objectively, but *in the context of all the events* surrounding the incident. The objective test meets the requirements of *Charter* s. 7.Section 249 requires an *objective* standard. D, whose conduct was objectively dangerous, should *not* be acquitted because s/he was *not* thinking of his/her manner of driving at the time of an accident. The question to be asked, given that liability under s. 249 is based on negligence, is whether, viewed objectively, D exercised the appropriate standard of care, *not* whether D subjectively intended the consequences of his/her action. D may still raise a reasonable doubt that a reasonable person would have been aware of the risks of the conduct. The test is to be applied flexibly in the context of the events surrounding the incident.The trier of fact must be satisfied that the conduct amounted to a *marked departure* from the standard of care that a reasonable person would observe in D's situation. If D offers an explanation, such as a sudden and unexpected onset of illness, the trier of fact, in order to convict, must be satisfied that a *reasonable* person in *similar circumstances ought to have been aware* of the *risk* and of the *danger* involved in the conduct manifested by D. A jury charge in such terms is adequate.

Peda v. R. (1969), 7 C.R.N.S. 243, [1969] 4 C.C.C. 245 (S.C.C.) — The essence of the offence is the manner or character of D's driving. The trier of fact must determine the actual behaviour of the driver in light of the section, but it is not necessary to determine that a given state of mind of D exists in order to convict. A jury need not be instructed as to the difference between "advertent" and "inadvertent" negligence.

Binus v. R. (1967), 2 C.R.N.S. 118, [1968] 1 C.C.C. 227 (S.C.C.) — Instructions to the effect that the alleged offence constituted a form of criminal conduct, that it meant something more than mere civil negligence, and that the jury might disregard the matter of intent if, on the facts, they found D's manner of driving to have been dangerous were adequate.

R. v. Hnatiuk (1983), 22 M.V.R. 53 (Alta. C.A.) — *Mens rea* is required for both criminal negligence and dangerous driving, but there is a greater moral fault for criminal negligence, often exemplified by some gross feature in the manner of driving such as greatly excessive speed or impairment by alcohol or drugs.

R. v. Quesnel (1996), 20 M.V.R. (3d) 46 (B.C. C.A.) — Evidence of speed alone will *not* necessarily found a conviction of dangerous driving. Where speed, however, together with other circumstances, elevates D's driving to the culpable level required of dangerous driving, a conviction may follow.

R. v. Piluke (1993), 86 C.C.C. (3d) 1 (B.C. C.A.) — *See also*: *R. v. Rai* (1993), 86 C.C.C. (3d) 122 (B.C. C.A.); *R. v. Blenner-Hassett* (1993), 50 M.V.R. (2d) 241, 86 C.C.C. (3d) 199 (B.C. C.A.); *R. v. Topping* (1993), 50 M.V.R. (2d) 274, 26 C.R. (4th) 396 (B.C. C.A.) — P must prove that D's driving amounted to a *marked departure* from the standard of care which a reasonable person would observe in D's situation. Driving which falls below that standard is, absent an explanation which raises a reasonable doubt for its occurrence, an offence. The trier of fact must consider not only D's conduct with the vehicle, but also other factors or circumstances affecting D's situation. P need not prove that D knew of the danger the driving created or that D was reckless or deliberate in the conduct. The only guilty intention that need be proven is that which may reasonably be inferred from D's conduct. (per Finch and Proudfoot JJ.A.)

R. v. Fortin (1971), 4 C.C.C. (2d) 535 (B.C. C.A.) — In determining whether the driving was dangerous to the public, all the circumstances must be considered including: (a) the nature, condition and use of the place; (b) the amount of traffic in the place at the time; and (c) the amount of traffic which at the time might reasonably be expected to be in the place.

R. v. Bartlett (1998), 15 C.R. (5th) 35, 124 C.C.C. (3d) 417 (Ont. C.A.) — It is error to equate dangerous driving to the failure to exercise the standard of care of a prudent driver.

R. v. Rajic (1993), 80 C.C.C. (3d) 533 (Ont. C.A.) — The degree of negligence required for dangerous driving is a *marked departure* from prudent conduct.

R. v. Beaudoin (1973), 12 C.C.C. (2d) 81 (Ont. C.A.) — In order to support a charge of dangerous driving P must prove that: (1) the lives or safety of others were endangered by D's driving; and (2) such jeopardizing resulted from the driver's departing from the standard of care that a prudent driver would have exercised, having regard to what actually was or might reasonably have been expected to be the condition, nature or use of the place where he was driving, including the amount of traffic there.

R. v. Arsenault (1992), 16 C.R. (4th) 301 (P.E.I. C.A.) — Evidence of D's actual mental state is *not* always a prerequisite to a conviction of dangerous driving. The trier of fact *may*, but is not required to, infer the necessary mental element from D's conduct which is found to depart from the standard of care that a prudent drier would have exercised in all of the circumstances. P must prove beyond a reasonable doubt that D did *not* drive with the care that a prudent person would exercise in the circumstances having regard to the factors of s. 249(4).The proper test on causation is whether D's conduct was a contributing cause beyond the *de minimis* range. P need *not* prove that D's driving was a *substantial* rather than minimal or insignificant cause.

Manner Dangerous

R. v. Fotti (1979), 45 C.C.C. (2d) 353 (Man. C.A.); affirmed (1980), 50 C.C.C. (2d) 479 (S.C.C.) — Speeding through a red light and striking a motorcycle carrying two passengers at an intersection, thereby causing a fatal accident, constituted dangerous driving.

Belanger v. R. (1970), 10 C.R.N.S. 373, [1970] 2 C.C.C. 206 (S.C.C.) — A person who seizes the wheel of a motor vehicle, which is being driven carefully and lawfully by another, causing the vehicle to be driven in a manner dangerous to the public, is within the ambit of the section.

R. v. F. (D.) (1989), 73 C.R. (3d) 391, 52 C.C.C. (3d) 357 (Alta. C.A.) — The proper approach is to consider the sum of the driving pattern, rather than to analyze each blameworthy facet of the driving pattern. The test is would an ordinary, prudent bystander have perceived an obvious risk that lives or safety would be endangered by the driving or impaired condition.

R. v. Mounsey (1991), 28 M.V.R. (2d) 191 (B.C. C.A.) — Failure to anticipate the adverse reaction of another driver to common driving conduct does *not* constitute operating a motor vehicle in a manner dangerous to the public.

Prima Facie Dangerous

R. v. Mason (1990), 60 C.C.C. (3d) 338 (B.C. C.A.); leave to appeal refused (1990), 60 C.C.C. (3d) 338n (S.C.C.) — Evidence of D's actual mental state is not always a prerequisite to conviction. In an appropriate case, evidence of a marked departure from the norm will be sufficient to establish liability. Driving on a busy highway at night, in an exhausted state with a blood alcohol content of 50 mg, is evidence of such a departure which, when coupled with evidence that D fell asleep and veered over to the wrong side of the road, will support a conviction under s. 249(3).

R. v. Lamont (1982), 14 M.V.R. 266 (Ont. C.A.) — Retrograde amnesia could not stand in place of the requisite explanation where the only inference available from the fact that D struck a pedestrian on or near the shoulder of the road was that D had been driving in a dangerous manner.

R. v. Lowe (1974), 21 C.C.C. (2d) 193 (Ont. C.A.) — Fault is an essential element of dangerous driving. The presence of the requisite degree of fault may be inferred from the factual situation, if, when viewed objectively, the driving is such as to endanger the lives of others. An evidential burden passes to D to rebut the inference which flows from the factual situation by raising a reasonable doubt on the issue of fault. This can be done by explanation or arise on the whole of the evidence. Appropriate consideration must be given to the fact that D through no fault of his own, has no memory of events immediately prior to the accident and was thereby precluded from giving an explanation with respect to them.

Ryan v. R., [1968] 1 C.C.C. 78 (Que. C.A.) — Evidence of a fatality is not, in itself, proof of dangerous driving.

Intoxication

R. v. Peda (1969), 4 C.R.N.S. 161 (Ont. C.A.); affirmed (1969), 7 C.R.N.S. 243, [1969] 4 C.C.C. 245 (S.C.C.) — Evidence of alcohol consumption by the driver "is always admissible on a charge of dangerous driving. It is relevant to show the cause of the dangerous driving and to negate any defence that the driving was the result of something beyond the control of the accused".

R. v. Nash (1986), 40 M.V.R. 173 (B.C. C.A.) — Breathalyzer results are admissible on a charge of dangerous driving if they are introduced by a qualified expert.

R. v. McDowell (1980), 52 C.C.C. (2d) 298 (Ont. C.A.) — If D has consumed alcohol when he knew or ought to have known his ability to operate a motor vehicle would be impaired, then the fault required to constitute the offence is present. Recklessness is not necessary to provide the requisite element of fault.

Public Place

R. v. Hartman (1992), 35 M.V.R. (2d) 143 (Ont. C.A.) — A driveway to which members of the public have free access is a "public place" and the purpose of the complainant in attending there is irrelevant.

R. v. Gaudreault (1978), 44 C.C.C. (2d) 235 (Ont. C.A.) — The object of the section is to protect members of the public from dangerous driving in places to which the public has ready access. Therefore, the front of a school to which the public, including the students and teachers, had access and in which motor vehicles could be driven was a "public place".

R. v. Widder (1971), 2 C.C.C. (2d) 224 (Ont. C.A.) — Most school grounds are "public places" but the fact has to be proved in each case.

R. v. English, [1970] 1 C.C.C 358 (Ont. C.A.) — A privately owned driveway and parking area, designed for customer accommodation and, accessible to the public, comes within "or other public place".

R. v. Mailloux (1969), 8 C.R.N.S. 1, [1970] 1 C.C.C. 338 (Que. C.A.) — "Public place" includes the parking lot of a shopping centre, to which the public has access.

Dangerous to the Public

R. v. Edlund (1990), 23 M.V.R. (2d) 21 (Alta. C.A.) — *See also: R. v. MacPhee* (1977), 38 C.C.C. (2d) 49 (N.S. C.A.) — The "public" contemplated in s. 249(1)(a) includes D's passenger and the police officer giving chase.

R. v. Mueller (1975), 32 C.R.N.S. 188, 29 C.C.C. (2d) 243 (Ont. C.A.) — *See also: R. v. Beaudoin* (1973), 12 C.C.C. (2d) 81 (Ont. C.A.) — Dangerous driving is proved by driving which is dangerous to the public, that is either the public actually present at the scene of the offence, or the public which might reasonably have been expected to be in the particular vicinity at the time the driving took place.

Causation

R. v. F. (D.) (1989), 73 C.R. (3d) 391, 52 C.C.C. (3d) 357 (Alta. C.A.) — *See also: R. v. Ewart* (1990), 53 C.C.C. (3d) 153 (Alta. C.A.); *R. v. Colby* (1989), 52 C.C.C. (3d) 321 (Alta. C.A.) — There must at least be proof that the unlawful operation of the vehicle was a real and truly contributing cause of, or a real factor in bringing about, any ensuing injury or death.

R. v. Arsenault (1992), 16 C.R. (4th) 301 (P.E.I. C.A.) — The proper test on causation is whether D's conduct was a contributing cause beyond the *de minimis* range. P need *not* prove that D's driving was a *substantial* rather than minimal or insignificant cause.

Included Offences

R. v. Rodgers (1952), 15 C.R. 55, 103 C.C.C. 97 (B.C. C.A.) — Impaired driving is *not* an included offence in dangerous driving.

Res Judicata

R. v. Colby (1989), 52 C.C.C. (3d) 321 (Alta. C.A.) — Where the act which amounted to dangerous driving was operating a motor vehicle while the ability to do so was impaired by alcohol, conviction for both dangerous driving causing death and impaired driving causing death is precluded and the offences being of equal gravity, the conviction should be entered on the impaired driving charge because it more accurately describes the delict.

R. v. Andrew (1990), 78 C.R. (3d) 239, 57 C.C.C. (3d) 301 (B.C. C.A.) — Where the charge of impaired driving is based upon the impairment of capacity followed by driving and does *not* encompass the manner of driving which forms part of the sequence of acts constituting criminal negligence, the accused can be convicted of both impaired driving causing bodily harm and criminal negligence causing bodily harm.

R. v. Haubrich (1978), 5 C.R. (3d) 221, 43 C.C.C. (2d) 190 (Sask. C.A.) — D can be convicted of both impaired driving and dangerous driving arising out of the same incident.

Sentencing Principles

R. v. Brown (1991), 6 C.R. (4th) 353, 66 C.C.C. (3d) 1 (S.C.C.) — The sentencing judge is bound by the express and implied factual implications of a jury verdict. Where, on counts of dangerous driving causing death and bodily harm, a jury finds guilt of dangerous driving *simpliciter*, they have negated the causal *nexus* required in the more serious charges. Since Parliament chose to make dangerous driving a consequence related crime, the consequence of death or bodily harm must be taken to be excluded under a finding of guilt of dangerous driving *simpliciter*.

Charter Considerations

R. v. Hundal (1993), 19 C.R. (4th) 169, 79 C.C.C. (3d) 97 (S.C.C.) — The *mental element* in dangerous driving, one which is objective, satisfies *Charter* s. 7.

R. v. Demeyer (1986), 27 C.C.C. (3d) 575 (Alta. C.A.); leave to appeal refused (1986), 74 A.R. 400n (S.C.C.) — This section does not offend *Charter* s. 7.

Related Provisions: "Motor vehicle", "railway equipment" and "bodily harm" are defined in s. 2, "vessel", "operate" and "aircraft" in s. 214. Special territorial jurisdiction provisions relating to aircraft, vehicles and vessels are found in ss. 476(a), (c) and (d). Section 477 makes provision for jurisdiction over offences on the territorial sea or on internal waters between the territorial sea and coast of Canada.

Under s. 662(5), the offence of this section is an included offence in a count charging a breach of ss. 220 (criminal negligence causing bodily harm), 221 (criminal negligence causing death) and 236 (manslaughter), arising out of the operation of a motor vehicle or navigation or operation of a vessel or aircraft. It would also seem to accord with general principle as expressed in s. 662(1), that the offences of s. 249(4) would include the offences of ss. 249(1) and (3) and that of s. 249(3), the offence of s. 249(1).

Under s. 227, no offence is committed under subsection (4) unless V's death occurred within a year and a day of one of the occurrences there described.

The basic offence of s. 249(1) is, under s. 249(2), triable either way. Where P elects to proceed by indictment, D may elect mode of trial under s. 536(2). Where P elects to proceed by summary conviction, the offence is tried under Part XXVII and punished under s. 787(1). In addition to any other punishment that may be imposed the sentencing court may make an order prohibiting operation of a conveyance under s. 259(2). The order may be stayed pending appeal under s. 261. D may elect mode of trial for the offences of ss. 249(3) and (4).

250. (1) Failure to keep watch on person towed — Every one who operates a vessel while towing a person on any water skis, surf-board, water sled or other object, when there is not on board such vessel another responsible person keeping watch on the person being towed, is guilty of an offence punishable on summary conviction.

(2) Towing of person after dark — Every one who operates a vessel while towing a person on any water skis, surf-board, water sled or other object during the period from one hour after sunset to sunrise is guilty of an offence punishable on summary conviction.

R.S., c. 34, s. 234; 1974–75–76, c. 93, ss. 14, 102;R.S. 1985, c. 27 (1st Supp.), s. 36.

Commentary: The section creates two summary conviction offences which relate to the towing of persons on listed objects behind a vessel.

The *external circumstances* of the offence of s. 250(1) require that D, as principal, operate a vessel while towing another person on water skis, surf-board, water sled or other object. There must *not* be on board the vessel another responsible person keeping watch on the person being towed.

The offence of s. 250(2) duplicates the first element of the *external circumstances* of the offence of s. 250(1) and further requires that the towing occur during the period from one hour after sunset to sunrise.

No ulterior *mental element* need be proven to establish liability under either subsection.

Related Provisions: "Vessel" is defined in s. 214. Special territorial jurisdiction provisions relating to vessels are found in ss. 476(a) and (c), as well as in s. 477.

Dangerous operation of a vessel is an offence under s. 249. Failure to stop at the scene of an accident is punishable under s. 252. Operation or having the care or control of a vessel while impaired or with more than 80 mg of alcohol in 100 ml of blood is an offence under s. 253.

The offences of this section are tried under Part XXVII, and punished under s. 787(1). Under s. 259(2), the sentencing court may prohibit D from operating a vessel in accordance with the terms of the section. The operation of the order may be stayed pending appeal under s. 261.

251. (1) Unseaworthy vessel and unsafe aircraft — Every one who knowingly

(a) sends or being the master takes a vessel that is registered or licensed, or for which an identification number has been issued, pursuant to any Act of Parliament and that is unseaworthy

(i) on a voyage from a place in Canada to any other place in or out of Canada, or

(ii) on a voyage from a place on the inland waters of the United States to a place in Canada,

(b) sends an aircraft on a flight or operates an aircraft that is not fit and safe for flight, or

(c) sends for operation or operates railway equipment that is not fit and safe for operation

and thereby endangers the life of any person, is guilty of an indictable offence and liable to imprisonment for a term not exceeding five years.

(2) Defences — An accused shall not be convicted of an offence under this section where the accused establishes that,

(a) in the case of an offence under paragraph (1)(*a*),

(i) the accused used all reasonable means to ensure that the vessel was seaworthy, or

(ii) to send or take the vessel while it was unseaworthy was, under the circumstances, reasonable and justifiable;

(b) in the case of an offence under paragraph (1)(*b*),

(i) the accused used all reasonable means to ensure that the aircraft was fit and safe for flight, or

(ii) to send or operate the aircraft while it was not fit and safe for flight was, under the circumstances, reasonable and justifiable; and

(c) in the case of an offence under paragraph (1)(c),

(i) the accused used all reasonable means to ensure that the railway equipment was fit and safe for operation, or

(ii) to send the railway equipment for operation or to operate it while it was not fit and safe for operation was, under the circumstances, reasonable and justifiable.

(3) Consent of Attorney General — No proceedings shall be instituted under this section in respect of a vessel or aircraft, or in respect of railway equipment sent for operation or operated on a line of railway that is within the legislative authority of Parliament, without the consent in writing of the Attorney General of Canada.

1974–75–76, c. 93, ss. 15, 102; R.S. 1985, c. 27 (1st Supp.), s. 36; c. 32 (4th Supp.), s. 58.

Commentary: This section defines the extent of criminal liability for sending or taking unseaworthy vessels on a voyage, unsafe aircraft on a flight, or unsafe railway equipment for an operation. Limitations are imposed upon the institution of proceedings.

The *unseaworthy vessel* offence is described in s. 251(1)(a). The *external circumstances* require proof that D sent or, if the master, took a vessel of Canadian registry or licence on a voyage described in s. 251(i) or (ii). The vessel must be unseaworthy at the time. D's conduct must *endanger the life* of any person.

The *unsafe aircraft* offence of s. 251(1)(b) requires proof that D sent an aircraft on a flight or operated an aircraft. The aircraft must *not* be fit and safe for the flight. Further, D's conduct must *endanger the life* of any person. The *unsafe railway equipment* offence of s. 251(1)(c) embodies similar requirements.

No ulterior *mental element* need be proven to establish liability. "Knowingly" requires that P establish, however, that D knew of the unseaworthy or unfit and unsafe character of the vessel or aircraft, as the case may be.

Section 251(2) provides to D two statutory defences to a charge under s. 251(1), but obliges D to *establish* each defence. This shift in onus of proof may attract scrutiny under *Charter* ss. 7 and 11(d). D must prove that s/he took *all reasonable steps* to ensure that the vessel was seaworthy or the aircraft fit and safe for flight, as the case may be. D will also *not* be held liable where D establishes that to send or take the vessel or aircraft in its then unsuitable condition was *reasonable and justifiable*.

Under s. 251(3), proceedings may be instituted only with the consent in writing of the Attorney General of Canada.

Related Provisions: "Aircraft" and "vessel" are defined in s. 214. The definition of "flight" in s. 7(8) is of assistance for jurisdictional purposes as are the special territorial jurisdiction provisions of ss. 476(a), (c) and (d) and s. 477.

Under s. 536(2), D may elect mode of trial. Under s. 259(2), the sentencing court may prohibit D from operating an aircraft, vessel or railway equipment in accordance with the terms of the subsection. The operation of the order may be stayed pending appeal under s. 261.

Other related provisions are described in the corresponding notes to ss. 249 and 250, *supra*.

252. (1) **Failure to stop at scene of accident** — Every person who has the care, charge or control of a vehicle, vessel or aircraft that is involved in an accident with

(a) another person,

(b) a vehicle, vessel or aircraft, or

(c) in the case of a vehicle, cattle in the charge of another person,

and with intent to escape civil or criminal liability fails to stop the vehicle, vessel or, where possible, the aircraft, give his or her name and address and, where any person has been injured or appears to require assistance, offer assistance, is guilty of an indictable offence and liable to imprisonment for a term not exceeding five years or is guilty of an offence punishable on summary conviction.

(2) **Evidence** — In proceedings under subsection (1), evidence that an accused failed to stop his vehicle, vessel or, where possible, his aircraft, as the case may be, offer assistance where any person has been injured or appears to require assistance and give his name and address is, in the absence of evidence to the contrary, proof of an intent to escape civil or criminal liability.

R.S., c. C-34, s. 235; 1974–75–76, c. 93, s. 16; R.S. 1985, c. 27 (1st Supp.), s. 36; 1994, c. 44, s. 12.

Commentary: The section creates the dual procedure offence of *failure to stop* at the scene of an accident and enacts a rebuttable presumption of fact that assists P in proof of its ulterior mental element.

The *external circumstances* of the offences of s. 252(1) consist of a combination of act and omission. D must have the *care, charge* or *control* of a vehicle, vessel or aircraft, which must be involved in an accident with an object or person described in any of ss. 252(1)(a)–(c). D must *fail to stop* the vehicle, vessel or, where possible, aircraft. Further, D must *fail to give* his/her *name* and *address*. Finally, where any person has been injured or appears to require assistance, D must also *fail to offer assistance*. The *mental element* requires proof of the intentional causing of the *external circumstances* of the offence, including the requirement that D have contemporaneous knowledge of involvement in an accident. The section also requires proof of the ulterior intent to escape civil or criminal liability.

Under s. 252(2), *evidence* that D caused the external circumstances of the offence is, in the absence of evidence to the contrary, *proof* of the required ulterior *mental element* that s. 252(1) requires. The subsection has been challenged under *Charter* ss. 7 and 11(d).

Case Law

Care, Charge or Control

R. v. Shea (1982), 17 M.V.R. 40 (Nfld. C.A.) — An owner of a motor vehicle who does not have care or control at the time of an accident may nevertheless be guilty under this section if he causes the vehicle to be driven off in contravention of the section. Where, however, it was the original driver who drove the vehicle from the accident scene, albeit only a short distance, the owner may be properly acquitted.

R. v. Slessor (1969), 7 C.R.N.S. 379, [1970] 2 C.C.C. 247 (Ont. C.A.) — The owner of the car, sitting asleep beside the driver at the time of impact, did not have "care, charge or control". *Quaere* whether a passenger-owner may be liable under this section.

Accident

R. v. Mihalick (1991), 28 M.V.R. (2d) 114 (B.C. C.A.); leave to appeal refused (1991), 30 M.V.R. (2d) 41 (note) (S.C.C.) — "Accident" is not restricted to circumstances where there is an impact between the vehicle and a specified person. It includes any sort of incident causing injury or death.

R. v. Hansen (1988), 46 C.C.C. (3d) 504 (B.C. C.A.) — Accident means any incident in which a person operates a vehicle so as to cause injury to another person or vehicle, whether the striking is intentional or unintentional.

Intent to Escape Liability

Fournier v. R. (1978), 8 C.R. (3d) 248, 43 C.C.C. (2d) 468 (Que. C.A.) — The civil or criminal liability a person must intend to escape from in failing to remain at the scene must be a liability in connection with the accident, not any liability such person may have incurred prior to the accident such as being arrested for robbery.

R. v. Hofer (1982), 2 C.C.C. (3d) 236 (Sask. C.A.); reversing (1982), 67 C.C.C. (2d) 134 (Sask. Q.B.) — The intent must be to escape criminal or civil liability for the accident. The intent to escape outstanding warrants for failure to pay fines did not constitute the necessary intent. D was, nevertheless, required to negate the presumption arising with respect to the accident from the failure to stop.

Presumption of Intent

R. v. Roche (1983), 34 C.R. (3d) 14, 3 C.C.C. (3d) 193 (S.C.C.) — The presumption of section 252(2) should be read disjunctively. It applies on proof of breach of any one of the three duties.

R. v. Proudlock (1978), 5 C.R. (3d) 21, 43 C.C.C. (2d) 321 (S.C.C.) — A presumption of intent merely establishes a *prima facie* case. The burden of proof does not shift. D does not have to "establish" a defence or an excuse, only raise a reasonable doubt. Evidence disbelieved by the trier of fact is not "evidence to the contrary".

R. v. Guay (1978), 44 C.C.C. (2d) 116 (Que. C.A.) — Where D rebuts the *prima facie* evidence by offering a plausible explanation to the effect that he had no criminal intent, P must then prove criminal intent beyond a reasonable doubt.

Evidence to the Contrary

R. v. Smaggus (1973), 5 N.S.R. (2d) 409 (C.A.) — Evidence that D had stopped and examined the vehicle he had struck, that there was no one in the vicinity and that he drove on with the intention of reporting the accident in the morning and did later report it, was held to indicate lack of intent to escape liability.

R. v. Nolet (Charette) (1980), 4 M.V.R. 265 (Ont. C.A.) — *See also*: *R. v. Gosselin* (1988), 67 C.R. (3d) 349, 45 C.C.C. (3d) 568 (Ont. C.A.); *R. v. Colby* (1989), 52 C.C.C. (3d) 321 (Alta. C.A.) — Evidence to the contrary is evidence which is *not* rejected by the trier of fact and which tends to show D may not have had the requisite intent. Evidence of drunkenness can constitute "evidence to the contrary". Where there is such evidence the onus shifts to P to prove the guilty intent beyond a reasonable doubt.

R. v. Adler (1981), 59 C.C.C. (2d) 517 (Sask. C.A.) — The presumption of intent was raised where D failed to provide his name and address. Evidence that D was impaired by alcohol and had wandered to a nearby residence constituted "evidence to the contrary".

Statements

R. v. Smith (1973), 25 C.R.N.S. 246, 15 C.C.C. (2d) 113 (Alta. C.A.) — A statement provided by the driver of a motor vehicle involved in an accident as required by provincial legislation, is admissible without the necessity of a *voir dire* to determine voluntariness.

R. v. Fex (1973), 23 C.R.N.S. 368, 14 C.C.C. (2d) 188 (Ont. C.A.); leave to appeal refused (1973), 14 C.C.C. (2d) 188n (S.C.C.) — The existence of the statutory duty under this section does not dispense with the onus upon P to establish that a statement made pursuant to that duty was not otherwise involuntary.

Charter Considerations

R. v. T. (S.D.) (1985), 43 C.R. (3d) 307, 18 C.C.C. (3d) 125 (N.S. C.A.) — *See also*: *R. v. Gosselin* (1988), 67 C.R. (3d) 349, 45 C.C.C. (3d) 568 (Ont. C.A.) — The presumption created by s. 252(2) violates *Charter* s. 11(d), but is saved by s. 1.

Related Provisions: "Vessel" and "aircraft" are defined in s. 214, "motor vehicle" in s. 2, but no definition of "vehicle", applicable to Part VIII, is there or elsewhere given.

Dangerous operation of motor vehicles, vessels and aircraft is prohibited and punished under s. 249. Their operation or care or control thereof whilst impaired, or with more than 80 mg of alcohol in 100 ml of blood is proscribed under s. 253. Criminal negligence is defined in s. 219(1), and is punished, according to its consequences, under ss. 220 and 221. Manslaughter is described in s. 234 and punished under s. 236. There is no discrete offence of criminal negligence or manslaughter in the operation of a motor vehicle, vessel or aircraft.

The offence of s. 252(1) is triable either way. By indictment, D may elect mode of trial under s. 536(2). Upon summary conviction, the offence is tried under Part XXVII and punished under s. 787(1). A conviction or discharge in respect of this offence may attract an order of prohibition under s. 259(2), which may be stayed pending appeal under s. 261.

253. Operation while impaired — Every one commits an offence who operates a motor vehicle or vessel or operates or assists in the operation of an aircraft or of railway equipment or has the care or control of a motor vehicle, vessel, aircraft or railway equipment, whether it is in motion or not,

(a) while the person's ability to operate the vehicle, vessel, aircraft or railway equipment is impaired by alcohol or a drug; or

(b) having consumed alcohol in such a quantity that the concentration in the person's blood exceeds eighty milligrams of alcohol in one hundred millilitres of blood.

R.S., c. C-34, s. 236; 1974–75–76, c. 93, ss. 17, 102; R.S. 1985, c. 27 (1st Supp.), s. 36; c. 32 (4th Supp.), s. 59.

Commentary: The section creates the companion offences of operation, or having the care or control of a motor vehicle, vessel, aircraft or railway equipment whilst impaired or with more than 80 mg of alcohol in 100 ml of blood.

The *external circumstances* of the *operation* offences combine elements of operation with *impairment of ability by alcohol or drug* or with a *prohibited blood-alcohol concentration*. In each case D must operate a motor vehicle or vessel or operate or assist in the operation of an aircraft or railway equipment. Further, D's ability to operate the conveyance must be impaired by alcohol or a drug, or the concentration of alcohol in D's blood must exceed the concentration described in s. 253(b), as the case may be. The *mental element* in respect of the *operation* offences is the intent to operate the conveyance after voluntary consumption of alcohol or a drug, as the case may be.

The *external circumstances* of the *care or control* offence combine elements of care or control with *impairment of ability*, by alcohol or a drug, or with a *prohibited blood-alcohol concentration*. In each case, D must have the care or control of a motor vehicle, vessel, aircraft or railway equipment. It matters not whether the conveyance is in motion. Further, D's ability to operate the conveyance must be impaired by alcohol or a drug, or the concentration of alcohol in D's blood must exceed the concentration described in s. 253(b), as the case may be. The *mental element* consists of the intention to assume care or control after the voluntary consumption of alcohol or a drug, as the case may be.

Case Law

Nature and Elements of Offence

R. v. Stellato (1994), 31 C.R. (4th) 60, 90 C.C.C. (3d) 160 (S.C.C.); affirming (1993), 18 C.R. (4th) 127, 78 C.C.C. (3d) 380 (Ont. C.A.) — *See also*: *R. v. Aube* (1993), 2 M.V.R. (3d) 127 (Que. C.A.); *R. v. Campbell* (1991), 26 M.V.R. (2d) 319 (P.E.I. C.A.); *R. v. Smith* (1994), 4 M.V.R. (3d) 130 (B.C. C.A.) — The offences of impaired operation or impaired care or control are established by proof of any degree of impairment ranging from slight to great. P need *not* establish a marked departure from normal behaviour. Impairment is an issue of fact for the trial judge.

R. v. Polturak (1988), 9 M.V.R. (2d) 89 (Alta. C.A.) — Proof of bad driving is not a necessary element under this section. The charge is directed at D's ability to drive, not to the nature of the operation of the vehicle.

R. v. Jones (1961), 35 C.R. 306, 130 C.C.C. 190 (Alta. C.A.) — The application of this section is not limited to highways and public places.

Beals v. R. (1956), 25 C.R. 85, 117 C.C.C. 22 (N.S. C.A.) — There need not be factual evidence of physical impairment while driving in order to justify a conviction. The fact that there appeared to be nothing wrong with D's driving while it was under observation is not conclusive.

R. v. Grosse (1996), 107 C.C.C. (3d) 97 (Ont. C.A.) — Where the opinion of a toxicologist called by P is based on an *assumption* that D did *not* drink large quantities of alcohol immediately before being stopped, P is required to adduce evidence to support the assumption. In the absence of such evidence, whether direct or circumstantial, including D's failure to testify to an unusual drinking pattern in the face of contradictory circumstantial evidence, the opinion ought to be disregarded.

R. v. MacCannell (1980), 54 C.C.C. (2d) 188 (Ont. C.A.); reversing (1979), 3 M.V.R. 264 (Ont. Co. Ct.) — The *actus reus* of the offence consists of: (1) the consumption of alcohol, followed by, (2) the act of driving or being in care or control of a motor vehicle, and (3) the performance of the act at a time when the proportion of alcohol in the driver's blood exceeded 80 mg of alcohol in 100 ml of blood.

Impaired by Alcohol or Drug

Graat v. R. (1982), 31 C.R. (3d) 289 (S.C.C.); affirming (1980), 17 C.R. (3d) 55, 55 C.C.C. (2d) 429 (Ont. C.A.) — Non-expert opinion evidence is admissible to determine the degree of D's impairment. Intoxication and impairment are questions of fact and conditions which do not require medical expertise to identify. Most people should be able to express an opinion on impairment from their own experience and their evidence would be admissible. Opinion evidence given by police officers would not necessarily be given more weight than that given by a lay witness.

R. v. Polturak (1988), 9 M.V.R. (2d) 89 (Alta. C.A.) — The admissibility of the opinion of a police officer or other nonexpert witness who observed D should not be limited to cases where impairment is by alcohol only. The rationale that impairment by alcohol is a matter about which most people would be able to express an opinion from their ordinary daily life experience is equally applicable to impairment by drugs.

R. v. Rogers (1976), 55 C.C.C. (2d) 181 (B.C. C.A.) — Evidence of D's blood-alcohol reading may be used to corroborate evidence of impairment.

R. v. McBurney (1975), 21 C.C.C. (2d) 207 (Man. C.A.) — *See also*: *R. v. Stevenson* (1972), 14 C.C.C. (2d) 412 (B.C. C.A.) — The trial judge cannot take judicial notice of the progressive absorption of alcohol into the blood for the purpose of proving "over 80" without either the statutory presumption or expert evidence relating the reading back to the time of driving.

R. v. MacAulay (1975), 25 C.C.C. (2d) 1 (N.B. C.A.) — It is unnecessary for P to prove whether alcohol or a drug was primarily responsible for the impairment.

R. v. Laprise (1996), 113 C.C.C. (3d) 87 (Que. C.A.) — Impairment of the ability to operate a motor vehicle may be proven, *inter alia*, by

i. the evidence of a police officer or another person of the characteristics of D's driving;

ii.   inference from physical signs, including odour of alcohol, unsteady gait or glassy eyes; and

iii.   evidence of the results of *analysis* of bodily fluids.

The results of scientific analysis of bodily fluids may corroborate other evidence of impairment of ability to drive, but do *not* permit an inference as to the

i.   *amount* of alcohol consumed; or

ii.   *effect* of alcohol consumed

without expert evidence of a correlation between results of analysis and possible impairment of faculties. A court will *not* take judicial notice of these facts.

R. v. Marionchuk (1978), 4 C.R. (3d) 178, 42 C.C.C. (2d) 573 (Sask. C.A.) — The gravamen of the offence of impaired driving is impairment, not the consumption of alcohol or drugs. Therefore "drug" is to be given a broad and reasonable meaning and thus includes any substance or chemical agent, the consumption of which will bring about impairment.

Motor Vehicle

Saunders v. R. (1967), 1 C.R.N.S. 249 (S.C.C.) — The definition of motor vehicle in s. 2 applies to this section and refers only to the type, not the actual operability or effective functioning of the vehicle and makes irrelevant any consideration of internal or external conditions which might affect its operability or functioning.

Operates

R. v. Ernst (1979), 50 C.C.C. (2d) 320 (N.S. C.A.) — A vessel is being operated for the purposes of this section even if the engine is turned off and the boat is simply drifting.

Care or Control

Ford v. R. (1982), 65 C.C.C. (2d) 392 (S.C.C.); affirming (1979), 4 M.V.R. 231 (P.E.I. C.A.) — Care or control may be exercised without an intent to set the car in motion such as where D performs some act or series of acts involving the use of the car, its fittings or equipment, whereby the vehicle may unintentionally be set in motion.

Saunders v. R. (1967), 1 C.R.N.S. 249, [1967] 3 C.C.C. 278 (S.C.C.) — There is no requirement that the impairment cause actual or potential danger.

Archer v. R. (1955), 20 C.R. 181, 110 C.C.C. 321 (S.C.C.) — One may have the care or control of a motor vehicle whether it is in motion or not without being the driver. Similarly, one may be the driver of a motor vehicle under the direct supervision and instruction of another without having the care or control of it.

R. v. Donald (1971), 14 C.R.N.S. 17, 3 C.C.C. (2d) 146 (B.C. C.A.) — P can establish "care or control" either by showing *actual* care or control or by relying on the *presumption* created by the *Code* once it was shown that D was in the seat ordinarily occupied by the driver.

R. v. Blair (1987), 5 M.V.R. (2d) 291 (N.S. C.A.) — Care or control could be established by showing that D was in the immediate vicinity of the car while possessing the means of setting it in motion or controlling it.

R. v. Pilon (1998), 131 C.C.C. (3d) 236 (Ont. C.A.) — A course of conduct associated with a vehicle that would involve a *risk* of putting the vehicle in motion so that it could become dangerous may constitute care or control.

Mental Element — Care or Control

R. v. Penno (1990), 80 C.R. (3d) 97, 59 C.C.C. (3d) 344 (S.C.C.); affirming (1986), 30 C.C.C. (3d) 533 (Ont. C.A.) — Intoxication is *not* a defence to a charge of having care or control of a motor vehicle while impaired.

R. v. Toews (1985), 47 C.R. (3d) 213, 21 C.C.C. (3d) 24 (S.C.C.) — The *mens rea* for the offence of having care or control of a motor vehicle while impaired is the intent to assume care or control after the voluntary consumption of alcohol or a drug. There is no requirement of intent to drive. The *actus reus* is the assumption of care or control of a motor vehicle when the voluntary consumption of alcohol or a drug has impaired the ability to drive. In the absence of the presumption of care or control, P must establish some act which involves the use of the car or its fittings and equipment, or some course of conduct which would involve the risk of putting the vehicle in motion so that it could become dangerous.

Ford v. R. (1982), 65 C.C.C. (2d) 392 (S.C.C.); affirming (1979), 4 M.V.R. 231 (P.E.I. C.A.) — P need only establish an intention to assume some measure of active control over, or with respect to, the vehicle, notwithstanding the absence of any intention to drive. "Care or control" is established where D had the immediate capacity and means of driving the vehicle, regardless of his intention not to do so upon entering it or otherwise assuming its physical management.

R. v. McNeil (1991), 25 M.V.R. (2d) 165 (N.S. C.A.) — The *mens rea* for "over 80" is the general intent of assuming control over the vehicle. It is not a defence that D honestly believed the vehicle was under police control at the time of its operations.

R. v. Rousseau (1997), 121 C.C.C. (3d) 571 (Que. C.A.) — Where D occupies the driver's seat of a motor vehicle, which he has parked but left the motor running, in order to sleep off the effects of excess consumption of alcohol, D has care or control of the motor vehicle.

Mental Element — Impairment

R. v. Stellato (1994), 31 C.R. (4th) 60, 90 C.C.C. (3d) 160 (S.C.C.); affirming (1993), 18 C.R. (4th) 127, 78 C.C.C. (3d) 380 (Ont. C.A.) — *See also: R. v. Aube* (1993), 2 M.V.R. (3d) 127, (Que. C.A.); *R. v. Campbell* (1991), 26 M.V.R. (3d) 319 (P.E.I. C.A.) — The offences of impaired operation or impaired care or control are established by proof of any degree of impairment ranging from slight to great. P need *not* establish a marked departure from normal behaviour. Impairment is an issue of fact for the trial judge.

R. v. King (1962), 38 C.R. 52, 133 C.C.C. 1 (S.C.C.) — Although when it has been proven that D was driving a motor vehicle while his ability to do so was impaired by alcohol or drug a rebuttable presumption arises that his condition was voluntary, nevertheless, the necessary *mens rea* would not be established if there is a reasonable doubt that D voluntarily consumed a drug which he knew or ought to have known would likely impair his ability to drive.

R. v. Andrews (1996), 46 C.R. (4th) 74, 104 C.C.C. (3d) 392 (Alta. C.A.) — There is a distinction between "slight impairment" generally and "slight impairment of one's ability to operate a motor vehicle". The issue is whether D's *ability* to *drive* is impaired to any degree, *not* whether D's functional ability is impaired to any degree.

Pitre v. R. (1971), 16 C.R.N.S. 226, 3 C.C.C. (2d) 380 (B.C. C.A.) — Where a person is found to be impaired by alcohol, a presumption arises that his condition results from his own voluntary act, and the presumption can only be rebutted by evidence which raises a reasonable doubt whether his condition was brought about through no fault of his own.

Penner v. R. (1974), 16 C.C.C. (2d) 334 (Man. C.A.) — A rebuttable presumption of *mens rea* arises once it is established that D drove with an excessive amount of alcohol in his system. D's mistaken belief that the amount of alcohol consumed would not put him "over 80" is no defence.

R. v. Mavin (1997), 119 C.C.C. (3d) 38 (Nfld. C.A.) — D has the *mens rea* to support a conviction of impaired driving where his/her impairment results from self-induced voluntary intoxication from *voluntary* ingestion of alcohol or a drug

i.   *intentionally*, for the purpose of becoming intoxicated; or,

ii.   *recklessly*, aware that impairment could result, but persisting despite the risk.

R. v. Lynch (1982), 69 C.C.C. (2d) 88 (Nfld. C.A.) — The fact that D was unaware that an earlier operation would have the effect of producing a high blood-alcohol level after the consumption of a relatively small amount of alcohol was not a defence.

R. v. Patterson (1982), 69 C.C.C. (2d) 274 (N.S. C.A.) — *See also: R. v. MacCannell* (1980), 54 C.C.C. (2d) 188 (Ont. C.A.); *R. v. Daynard* (1991), 28 M.V.R. (2d) 42 (Ont. C.A.) — *Mens rea* is supplied by the voluntary consumption of alcohol. It is not necessary to prove that when D drove the vehicle he either knew that his blood-alcohol level exceeded the permissible amount or that he was reckless with respect to his blood-alcohol level being in excess of that permitted.

R. v. Murray (1985), 22 C.C.C. (3d) 502 (Ont. C.A.) — The voluntary ingesting of a sedative drug that D knew might impair his ability to drive was sufficient *mens rea*. The over-estimation by D of the time it would take for the drug to take effect did not negate the *mens rea*.

Necessity

R. v. Roberts (1987), 65 Nfld. & P.E.I.R. 343 (P.E.I. C.A.) — The defence of necessity failed where D drove his mother, who had developed a pain below her heart, to hospital while intoxicated. Reasonable legal alternatives were open to D to get his mother to the hospital.

Included Offences — Driving and Care or Control

R. v. Mullins (1977), 35 C.C.C. (2d) 295 (N.B. C.A.) — *See also*: *R. v. Mitchelmore* (1984), 27 M.V.R. 68 (Nfld. C.A.); *R. v. Pitcher* (1988), 6 M.V.R. (2d) 51 (Nlfd. C.A.) — This section creates two separate offences of care or control with blood-alcohol level over .08 and of driving with blood-alcohol level over .08. The offence of care or control is not included in the offence of driving with excessive alcohol.

R. v. Plank (1986), 28 C.C.C. (3d) 386 (Ont. C.A.) — *See also*: *R. v. Morton* (1975), 37 C.R.N.S. 42, 29 C.C.C. (2d) 518 (N.S C.A.); *R. v. Handy* (1971), 15 C.R.N.S. 239, 3 C.C.C. (2d) 298 (Alta. C.A.) — The *Code* creates two separate offences of driving and of having care or control while "over 80". However, the offence of care or control is an included offence to the offence of driving while "over 80".

R. v. Miller, [1953] O.W.N. 334 (C.A.) — *See also*: *R. v. Coultis* (1982), 29 C.R. (3d) 189 (Ont. C.A.); *R. v. Stevenot* (1992), 33 M.V.R. (2d) 297 (B.C. C.A.) — A person having care or control of a motor vehicle includes the driver.

R. v. MacInnis (1982), 16 M.V.R. 70 (P.E.I. C.A.) — *See also*: *R. v. Young* (1979), 4 M.V.R. 38 (P.E.I. C.A.); *R. v. Drolet* (1990), 26 M.V.R. (2d) 169 (S.C.C.); affirming (1988), 14 M.V.R. (2d) 50 (Que. C.A.) — Everyone who drives must be in care or control. Therefore, the offence of care or control is included in the offence of driving.

R. v. Faer (1975), 26 C.C.C. (2d) 327 (Sask. C.A.) — *See also*: *R. v. Fischer*, [1968] 2 C.C.C. 86 (Ont. C.A.) — *Contra*: *R. v. Plank, supra*

This section creates two distinct and separate offences of driving and of having care or control neither of which is included in the other.

Included Offences — Criminal Negligence and Impaired Driving

R. v. Lapierre (1974), 29 C.R.N.S. 353 (Ont. C.A.) — *See also*: *R. v. Rabouin* (1976), 35 C.R.N.S. 173 (Que. C.A.) — Impaired driving is not an included offence in a charge of criminal negligence.

Res Judicata

R. v. Casson (1976), 30 C.C.C. (2d) 506 (Alta. C.A.) — *See also*: *R. v. Koble* (1984), 29 M.V.R. 34 (B.C. C.A) — D may be acquitted of impaired driving but convicted of driving while the percentage of alcohol in the blood exceeded .08.

R. v. Houchen (1976), 31 C.C.C. (2d) 274 (B.C. C.A.) — D cannot be convicted of both impaired driving and driving while "over 80" when the counts arise out of the same cause or matter.

R. v. Pendleton (1982), 1 C.C.C. (3d) 228 (Ont. C.A.) — Where P attempts to prove "care or control" on evidence of finding D in the driver's seat, it is not possible for the court to convict on the basis of an admission by D that at some time prior to that he had driven the vehicle. P is bound by the particulars of the charge it presents.

R. v. Boivin (1976), 34 C.R.N.S. 227, 34 C.C.C. (2d) 203 (Que. C.A.) — Convictions for both impaired driving and driving "over 80" alleged to have been committed at the same time and place and under the same circumstances, will not be sustained.

R. v. Haubrich (1978), 5 C.R. (3d) 221, 43 C.C.C. (2d) 190 (Sask. C.A.); reversing (1977), 38 C.R.N.S. 257 (Sask. Dist. Ct.) — An accused may be convicted of both impaired driving and dangerous driving.

Double Punishment

R. v. Art (1987), 61 C.R. (3d) 204, 39 C.C.C. (3d) 563 (B.C. C.A.); affirming (1987), 48 M.V.R. 99 (B.C. S.C.) — A 24-hour licence suspension under provincial legislation is not a criminal punishment and, therefore, when coupled with a sentence for impaired driving, does not constitute double punishment.

R. v. Huber (1985), 36 M.V.R. 10 (Ont. C.A.); leave to appeal refused (1985), 36 M.V.R. xxxviii (S.C.C.) — A 12-hour driving suspension under a provincial *Highway Traffic Act* does not constitute a conviction or charging of an offence so as to support a plea of *autrefois convict*.

Duplicity

R. v. Meisner (1980), 9 M.V.R. 134 (N.S. C.A.) — "Care or control" describes one offence which may be composed of one or both of the acts. Therefore a charge of "care and control" is not duplicitous.

R. v. Hawryluk (1967), 1 C.R.N.S. 143, [1967] 3 C.C.C. 356 (Sask. C.A.) — A conviction on the basis of an information using the wording of the *Code* "that he while his ability to drive a motor vehicle was impaired by alcohol or drug did unlawfully drive a motor vehicle" was valid in that it charged only one offence which might be committed in two different ways. It was not duplicitous.

Charter Considerations [See also s. 254]

R. v. Penno (1990), 80 C.R. (3d) 97, 59 C.C.C. (3d) 344 (S.C.C.); affirming (1986), 30 C.C.C. (3d) 553 (Ont. C.A.) — The exclusion of intoxication as a defence to a charge of having care or control of a motor vehicle while impaired does *not* infringe *Charter* s. 7 or 11(d) (per Wilson, La Forest, L'Heureux-Dube, Sopinka, Gonthier and McLachlin JJ.).

R. v. Gillis (1994), 91 C.C.C. (3d) 575 (Alta. C.A.) — A person required to comply with the breathalyzer demand does *not* have the right to view the readings as the breathalyzer is taken. D's right to make full answer and defence under *Charter* s. 7 does *not* include the right to observe or participate in the collection of evidence during an investigation to determine whether a crime has been committed.

R. v. McLennan (1988), 41 C.C.C. (3d) 379 (B.C. C.A.) — D must be informed of his right to counsel prior to being required to perform roadside physical tests.

R. v. Selig (1991), 4 C.R. (4th) 20, 27 M.V.R. (2d) 166 (N.S. C.A.) — Refusal to permit D to observe the breathalyzer gauge during the tests infringes *Charter* ss. 7 and 11(d), and requires exclusion of the readings.

Related Provisions: "Motor vehicle" is defined in s. 2, "vessel" and "aircraft" in s. 214.

To assist P in its proof of the essential elements of the offences, ss. 254(2)–(4) authorize the making of demands by police officers, thereafter, the taking of samples of breath or blood for the purposes of alcohol content analysis. Section 256 describes the circumstances under which a warrant may issue to take samples of blood for alcohol content analysis. Section 258 enacts a series of presumptions which become engaged upon the introduction of evidence or proof of certain preliminary facts and assist P in its proof of the essential elements of the offences of s. 253.

The general punishment provisions of ss. 255(1) and (5) apply. Whether D's offence is a second or subsequent offence for such purposes is determined under s. 255(4). Sections 255(2) and (3) punish aggravated forms of the offences of s. 253 where bodily harm or death has been caused thereby. Section 259(1) requires the making of a prohibition order upon conviction or discharge of an offence under the section and prescribes the terms thereof. Sections 260(1)–(3) describe the manner in which the order is made and executed. An operating prohibition under s. 259(1) is a "sentence" for the purposes of ss. 673 and 785(1) and may be stayed pending appeal under s. 261.

The offences of the section are triable either way. Upon indictment, D may elect mode of trial under s. 536(2). By summary conviction, the offence is tried under Part XXVII and punished under s. 787(1). Each of the aggravated forms of the offence, punishable under ss. 255(2) and (3), is exclusively indictable and affords D an election as to mode of trial.

254. (1) Definitions — In this section and sections 255 to 258,

"analyst" means a person designated by the Attorney General as an analyst for the purposes of section 258;

"approved container" means

   (a) in respect of breath samples, a container of a kind that is designed to receive a sample of the breath of a person for analysis and is approved as suitable for the purposes of section 258 by order of the Attorney General of Canada, and

   (b) in respect of blood samples, a container of a kind that is designed to receive a sample of the blood of a person for analysis and is approved as suitable for the purposes of section 258 by order of the Attorney General of Canada;

"approved instrument" means an instrument of a kind that is designed to receive and make an analysis of a sample of the breath of a person in order to measure the concentration of alcohol in the blood of that person and is approved as suitable for the purposes of section 258 by order of the Attorney General of Canada;

"approved screening device" means a device of a kind that is designed to ascertain the presence of alcohol in the blood of a person and that is approved for the purposes of this section by order of the Attorney General of Canada;

"qualified medical practitioner" means a person duly qualified by provincial law to practise medicine.

"qualified technician" means,

(a) in respect of breath samples, a person designated by the Attorney General as being qualified to operate an approved instrument, and

(b) in respect of blood samples, any person or person of a class of persons designated by the Attorney General as being qualified to take samples of blood for the purposes of this section and sections 256 and 258.

(2) **Testing for presence of alcohol in the blood** — Where a peace officer reasonably suspects that a person who is operating a motor vehicle or vessel or operating or assisting in the operation of an aircraft or of railway equipment or who has the care or control of a motor vehicle, vessel, aircraft or railway equipment, whether it is in motion or not, has alcohol in the person's body, the peace officer may, by demand made to that person, require the person to provide forthwith such a sample of breath as in the opinion of the peace officer is necessary to enable a proper analysis of the breath to be made by means of an approved screening device and, where necessary, to accompany the peace officer for the purpose of enabling such a sample of breath to be taken.

(3) **Samples of breath or blood where reasonable belief of commission of offence** — Where a peace officer believes on reasonable and probable grounds that a person is committing, or at any time within the preceding two hours has committed, as a result of the consumption of alcohol, an offence under section 253, the peace officer may, by demand made to that person forthwith or as soon as practicable, require that person to provide then or as soon thereafter as is practicable

(a) such samples of the person's breath as in the opinion of a qualified technician, or

(b) where the peace officer has reasonable and probable grounds to believe that, by reason of any physical condition of the person,

(i) the person may be incapable of providing a sample of his breath; or

(ii) it would be impracticable to obtain a sample of his breath,

such samples of the person's blood, under the conditions referred to in subsection(4), as in the opinion of the qualified medical practitioner or qualified technician taking the samples

are necessary to enable proper analysis to be made in order to determine the concentration, if any, of alcohol in the person's blood, and to accompany the peace officer for the purpose of enabling such samples to be taken.

(4) **Exception** — Samples of blood may only be taken from a person pursuant to a demand made by a peace officer under subsection (3) if the samples are taken by or under the direction of a qualified medical practitioner and the qualified medical practi-

tioner is satisfied that the taking of those samples would not endanger the life or health of the person.

(5) Failure or refusal to provide sample — Every one commits an offence who, without reasonable excuse, fails or refuses to comply with a demand made to him by a peace officer under this section.

(6) Only one determination of guilt for failure to comply with demand — A person who is convicted of an offence committed under subsection (5) for a failure or refusal to comply with a demand made under subsection (2) or paragraph (3)(a) or (b) in respect of any transaction may not be convicted of another offence committed under subsection (5) in respect of the same transaction.

1974–75–76, c. 93, s. 17; R.S. 1985, c. 27 (1st Supp.), s. 36; c. 1 (4th Supp.), s. 14; c. 32 (4th Supp.), s. 60.

Regulations: The following regulations apply undersection 254:

Approved Blood Sample Container Order

2. Approved Container — The container, Vacutainer ™ XF947, being a container of a kind that is designed to receive a sample of the blood of a person for analysis, is hereby approved as suitable, in respect of blood samples, for the purposes of section 241 of the *Criminal Code*.

SI/85-199

Approved Breath Analysis Instruments Order

2. Approved Instruments — The following instruments, each being an instrument of a kind that is designed to receive and make an analysis of a sample of the breath of a person in order to measure the concentration of alcohol in the blood of that person, are hereby approved as suitable for the purposes of section 258 of the *Criminal Code*:

(a) Breathalyzer ™, Model 800;

(b) Breathalyzer ™, Model 900;

(c) Breathalyzer ™, Model 900A;

(d) Intoximeter Mark IV;

(e) Alcolmeter AE-D1;

(f) Intoxilyzer 4011AS;

(g) Alcotest ™ 7110;

(h) Intoxilyzer ™ 5000 C;

(i) Breathalyzer ™, Model 900B;

(j) Intoxilyzer 1400;

(k) BAC Datamaster C; and

(l) Alco-Sensor IV-RBT IV.

SI/85-201; SI/92-105; SI/92-167; SI/93-61; SI/93-175; SOR/94-422; SOR/94-572; SOR/95-312.

Approved Screening Devices Order

2. Approved Screening Devices — The following devices, each being a device of a kind that is designed to ascertain the presence of alcohol in the blood of a person, are hereby approved for the purposes of section 254 of the *Criminal Code*:

(a) Alcolmeter S-L2;

(b) Alco-Sûr;

(c) Alcotest ™ 7410 PA3;

(d) Alcotest ™ 7410 GLC;

(e) Alco-Sensor IV DWF;

(f) Alco-Sensor IV PWF; and

(g) Intoxilyzer 400D.

SI/85-200; SI/88-136; SOR/93-263; SOR/94-193; SOR/94-423; SOR/96-81; SOR/97-116.

Commentary: The effect of this section is threefold.

Section 254(1) exhaustively defines terms used in this section and in ss. 255–258.

Sections 254(2) and (3) should be considered together and in conjunction with s. 254(4). The former sections delineate the circumstances under which a peace officer may demand a sample of breath or blood from another person. The latter circumscribes the manner in which blood samples shall be taken.

A demand under s. 254(2) may be made upon the *reasonable suspicion* of a peace officer that a person who is operating a motor vehicle or vessel or operating or assisting in the operation of an aircraft or railway equipment, or who *has the care or control* of any such conveyance has alcohol in his/her body. The demand *will require* the person to provide forthwith such a sample of breath as in the opinion of the officer is necessary to enable a proper analysis to be made by an approved screening device. The demand *may also require* that, where necessary, the person accompany the officer to enable the sample to be taken.

The authority to make the demands of s. 254(3) varies with the nature of the sample requested. In every case, a peace officer must believe, on reasonable and probable grounds, that a person is committing or at any time within the preceding two hours has committed, as a result of alcohol consumption, an offence under s. 253. Upon a basis of such belief the officer may, by demand made to the person forthwith or as soon as practicable, require the person *to provide* then, or as soon thereafter as is practicable, such *samples of breath* as in the opinion of a qualified technician are necessary to enable a proper blood-alcohol analysis to be performed and *to accompany* the officer for such purpose. Upon the basis of such belief *and* the belief described in s. 254(3)(b)(i) or (ii), the officer may, by demand, require the taking of a *blood sample* in accordance with s. 254(4). Blood samples may only be taken under s. 254(4) pursuant to a peace officer's demand if the samples are taken by or under the direction of a qualified medical practitioner and the qualified medical practitioner is satisfied that the taking of those samples would not endanger the life or health of the person.

Section 254(5) creates an offence of non-compliance with the demand of a peace officer to provide a breath or blood sample, as the case may be. The *external circumstances* consist of a demand by a peace officer authorized under the section, and a failure or refusal of compliance by D in the absence of reasonable excuse. The *mental element* consists of intentional non-compliance.

Section 254(6), ancillary to the offence-creating provisions of s. 254(5), proscribes multiple convictions under s. 254(5) for repeated failures or refusals of compliance in respect of the same transaction.

Case Law

Approved Instrument: S. 254(1)

R. v. Janes (1987), 40 C.C.C. (3d) 209 (N.S. C.A.) — Where the technician testified that he used a "Breathalyzer, Model 900A" in administering the test, the technician's later reference to the instrument as a Borkenstein did not invalidate the evidence that the instrument was approved.

R. v. Bebbington (1988), 43 C.C.C. (3d) 456 (Ont. C.A.) — The words "is approved as suitable" refer to the "kind" of instrument used. Where the breathalyzers used were of the kind Model 900A, the fact that they had been, or might have been, modified by capacitors to prevent radio frequency interference did not affect their designation as an "approved instrument" since the modification in issue did not change the kind or nature of the breathalyzer itself.

R. v. Alatyppo (1983), 4 C.C.C. (3d) 514 (Ont. C.A.) — The words "breathalyzer instrument" are insufficient to rely on the presumption created by the certificate.

R. v. Kelly (1987), 7 M.V.R. (2d) 121 (P.E.I. C.A.) — A certificate using the term "Borkenstein Breathalyzer, model 900A" is admissible in evidence, where it also contained the critical *Code* wording, "an approved instrument".

Qualified Technician: S. 254(1)

R. v. De Young (1987), 4 M.V.R. (2d) 131 (B.C. C.A.) — The testimony of the breathalyzer technician that "someone in the Attorney General's department" had designated him was sufficient evidence to establish the fact of designation.

Reference re ss. 222, 224 and 224A of the Criminal Code (1971), 3 C.C.C. (2d) 243 (N.B. C.A.) — A qualified technician designated by the Attorney General is an expert witness competent to give opinion evidence in relation to matters pertaining to the analysis of the breath, the approved instrument, and the substances and procedures used in the making of a test and of the conclusion to be drawn from such a test, including the weight per milligrams of alcohol present in 100 ml of the blood of the accused at the time the breath sample test was taken.

R. v. Marcoux (1990), 26 M.V.R. (2d) 262 (Ont. C.A.) — A police officer's evidence that he was designated as a breathalyzer operator was sufficient basis for the trial judge to find he was a qualified technician.

R. v. Novis (1987), 36 C.C.C. (3d) 275 (Ont. C.A.) — *See also*: *R. v. Bouchard*, (November 30, 1987), Doc. No. CA640/87 (Ont. C.A.) — Publication of the designation of a technician in a provincial Gazette is not a prerequisite for legal effect. Furthermore, P may prove an offence by calling a qualified technician or by way of certificate. If the latter route is taken it is unnecessary to introduce independent proof of the designation of the technician.

Peace Officer

R. v. Nolan (1987), 58 C.R. (3d) 335, 34 C.C.C. (3d) 289 (S.C.C.) — *See also*: *R. v. Courchene* (1989), 52 C.C.C. (3d) 375 (Ont. C.A.); *R. v. Haynes* (1994), 4 M.V.R. (3d) 317 (N.S. C.A.) — A military policeman is *not* a peace officer for all the purposes of the *Code*. Where the arresting military policeman was a peace officer, he had authority to demand a breath sample of a civilian after following the civilian off a military base to a public highway.

R. v. Telford (1979), 50 C.C.C. (2d) 322 (Alta. C.A.) — There is nothing to restrict the term "peace officer" so as to mean that only the first officer on the scene can make the demand or administer the test.

R. v. Harvey (1979), 5 M.V.R. 41 (Alta. C.A.); leave to appeal refused (1979), 20 A.R. 266 (S.C.C.) — A military policeman with the rank of private was not empowered to stop a private citizen on a highway not within a military base and demand a breath sample. However, once the sample was voluntarily given this amounted to a waiver of the shortcoming of the demand and the certificate was admissible.

R. v. Arsenault (1980), 55 C.C.C. (2d) 38 (N.B. C.A.) — *See also*: *R. v. Soucy* (1975), 36 C.R.N.S. 129, 23 C.C.C. (2d) 561 (N.B. C.A.) — A demand made by a constable outside his territorial jurisdiction is of no effect. The officer is *not* a peace officer for *Code* purposes when acting outside of his own jurisdiction.

R. v. Cogswell (1979), 2 M.V.R. 34 (N.B. C.A.) — A demand made by a military policeman on a Canadian Forces Base was a proper one.

Reasonably Suspects

R. v. Gilroy (1987), 3 M.V.R. (2d) 123 (Alta. C.A.) — The test is one of consumption alone, not of amount of consumption or the behavioural consequences of consumption. It is no defence that D's thought, coordination or awareness did not seem to be impaired.

Reasonable and Probable Grounds

R. v. Knox, 1 C.R. (5th) 254, 109 C.C.C. (3d) 481, [1996] 3 S.C.R. 199 (S.C.C.) — P need *not* prove D's consent to the giving of a blood sample under *Code* s. 254(3). The provision is mandatory, *not* consensual, P need only establish

i.   that there were *reasonable* and *probable* grounds to believe that D committed an offence of impaired driving;

ii.   that it was *impractical* to obtain a *breathalyzer* sample; and

iii. that a *demand* was made to obtain a *blood* sample.

There is a distinction between consent and compliance. *Consent* involves agreement and co-operation. It connotes a decision to allow the police to do something which they could not otherwise do. *Compliance* signals only a failure to object. It may be vitiated by trickery. No one can be forced to provide a blood sample.

R. v. Oduneye (1995), 15 M.V.R. (3d) 161 (Alta. C.A.); leave to appeal refused (February 8, 1996), Doc. No. 25000 (S.C.C.) — Evidence of close observation of D's physical behaviour and condition may constitute reasonable and probable grounds for a breathalyzer demand, even if the officer decides it is unnecessary to administer an R.S.D. demand.

R. v. Chisholm (1995), 14 M.V.R. (3d) 190 (N.S. C.A.) — In the absence of evidence that the police officer had knowledge that the A.L.E.R.T. 3JA had been modified and might no longer be an approved screening device, or that its results might not be reliable, he was entitled to consider those results in arriving at reasonable and probable grounds for a breathalyzer demand.

R. v. Bernshaw (1994), 35 C.R. (4th) 201, 95 C.C.C. (3d) 193, [1995] 3 W.W.R. 457, 176 N.R. 81 (S.C.C.); reversing (1993), 85 C.C.C. (3d) 404, 48 M.V.R. (2d) 246 (B.C. C.A.) — The requirement of s. 254(3) that reasonable and probable grounds exist is both a statutory and constitutional requirement under *Charter* s. 8.

R. v. Bernshaw (1994), 35 C.R. (4th) 201, 95 C.C.C. (3d) 193, [1995] 3 W.W.R. 457, 176 N.R. 81 (S.C.C.); reversing (1993), 85 C.C.C. (3d) 404, 48 M.V.R. (2d) 246 (B.C. C.A.) — Where there is evidence that a peace officer knew that a suspect had recently consumed alcohol and expert evidence shows that the subsequent screening test would be unreliable due to the presence of alcohol in the mouth, it cannot be said, as a matter of law, that both the subjective and objective tests of s. 254(3) have been satisfied.

R. v. Bernshaw (1994), 35 C.R. (4th) 201, 95 C.C.C. (3d) 193, [1995] 3 W.W.R. 457, 176 N.R. 81 (S.C.C.); reversing (1993), 85 C.C.C. (3d) 404, 48 M.V.R. (2d) 246 (B.C. C.A.) — Under s. 254(3), a peace officer must subjectively have an honest belief that the suspect has committed the offence and objectively there must be reasonable grounds for the belief. A "fail" result on a screening may be considered, together with any other *indicia* of impairment, to provide the peace officer with the necessary reasonable and probable grounds to demand a breathalyzer test. A "fail" result *per se*, however, may not provide such grounds.

R. v. McClelland (1995), 98 C.C.C. (3d) 509 (Alta. C.A.) — The question whether a peace officer had reasonable and probable grounds must be based upon facts known by or available to the officer at the time s/he formed the requisite belief, *not* on information acquired thereafter. The officer's understanding of the facts must be a reasonable one. (per McClung and McFadyen JJ.A.).

R. v. Huddle (1990), 21 M.V.R. (2d) 150 (Alta. C.A.) — It is an error in law to test individual pieces of evidence which are offered to establish the existence of reasonable and probable grounds. The question is whether, on an objective standard, the totality of the evidence provided reasonable and probable grounds.

R. v. Yurechuk, [1983] 1 W.W.R. 460 (Alta. C.A.) — *See also: R. v. Meade* (1990), 23 M.V.R. (2d) 12 (Alta. C.A.) — Where D fails an A.L.E.R.T. test, proof that the A.L.E.R.T. device is approved is not required to find that the police officer had reasonable and probable grounds for requesting a breath sample.

R. v. Johnson (1987), 46 M.V.R. 226 (Man. C.A.) — *See also: R. v. Phillips* (1992), 35 M.V.R. (2d) 167 (Alta. C.A.) — The words "is driving" have a past as well as a present significance. The suspicion to ground a demand for a breath sample does not have to exist almost contemporaneously with D's actual cessation of driving.

Babineau v. R. (1981), 11 M.V.R. 204 (N.B. C.A.); affirming (1981), 36 N.B.R. (2d) 72 (Q.B.) — Objective evidence of impairment or consumption of alcohol such as red eyes, unsteadiness or admission of alcohol consumption is sufficient evidence upon which an officer may acquire reasonable and probable grounds.

R. v. Warford (1981), 61 C.C.C. (2d) 489 (Nfld. C.A.) — There is no requirement that the reasonable and probable grounds exist before the vehicle is stopped. The only requirement is that the proper grounds exist before the breath test is demanded.

R. v. Hurley (1980), 9 M.V.R. 46 (Nfld. C.A.) — *See also: R. v. Denney* (1985), 34 M.V.R. 111 (N.S. C.A.); *R. v. Arthurs* (1981), 25 C.R. (3d) 83 (Sask. C.A.); *R. v. Beech* (1993), 144 M.V.R. (2d) 273 (Ont. C.A.) — Failure of a roadside screening test amounts to reasonable grounds for demanding a breath sample. P need not establish proper functioning of the screening device.

R. v. Trask (1987), 3 M.V.R. (2d) 6 (N.S. C.A.) — The test is not whether the belief was correct, but rather whether it was reasonable.

R. v. Feener (1986), 74 N.S.R. (2d) 164 (C.A.) — To justify giving a breathalyzer demand a police officer does not have to establish that D was driving or had control of a motor vehicle. He must have had reasonable and probable grounds to believe that D was or had been within the preceding two hours in violation of the *Code* section. Reasonable and probable grounds is a question of fact or mixed law and fact.

R. v. Pavel (1989), 74 C.R. (3d) 195, 53 C.C.C. (3d) 296 (Ont. C.A.) — The demand for the breath or blood sample must be made by the same officer who formed the belief on reasonable and probable grounds that the subject committed the offence within the two hours preceding the formation of the belief.

R. v. Gavin (1993), 50 M.V.R. (2d) 302 (P.E.I. C.A.) — The data the officer relies on at the time s/he makes the demand must, when taken as a whole, have sufficient objective persuasiveness as would lead a reasonable person similarly situated to conclude that more likely than not D had committed an offence under s. 253 within the preceding two hours. Indicia of impairment discovered *ex post facto* cannot rehabilitate an invalid or premature demand.

R. v. Farrar (1993), 80 C.C.C. (3d) 381 (P.E.I. C.A.) — A s. 254(3) demand is *not* valid if its only supportive grounds are those which have been acquired by a s. 8 *Charter* breach by investigating officers.

R. v. Strongquill (1978), 4 C.R. (3d) 182 (Sask. C.A.) — *See also*: *R. v. Chetwynd* (1977), 25 N.S.R. (2d) 492 (C.A.); *R. v. Sesula* (1991), 31 M.V.R. (2d) 15 (Sask. C.A.) — A police officer testifying as to the grounds for making a breathalyzer demand may testify as to information received from another person used as a basis for the demand, even though it is hearsay. It is not admissible for proof of the facts stated, however.

Demand for Breath or Blood Sample

R. v. Knox, 1 C.R. (5th) 254, 109 C.C.C. (3d) 481, [1996] 3 S.C.R. 199 (S.C.C.) — A *demand* is deficient if it fails to provide the s. 254(4) assurances that the samples would only be taken by a qualified medical practitioner who was satisfied that taking them would neither harm D's health, nor endanger D's life. A sample taken absent such assurances contravenes *Charter* ss. 7 and 8. A constitutionally-flawed demand means that D cannot be convicted under s. 254(5) for failure to comply.

R. v. Knox, 1 C.R. (5th) 254, 109 C.C.C. (3d) 481, [1996] 3 S.C.R. 199 (S.C.C.) — Section 254(5) is concerned with the adequacy of the demand, *not* with whether D actually complied with the request.

R. v. Bernshaw (1994), 35 C.R. (4th) 201, 95 C.C.C. (3d) 193, [1995] 3 W.W.R. 457, 176 N.R. 81 (S.C.C.) — While a screening test should be administered as soon as possible, the statutory provisions allow the time required to take a proper test. Under s. 254(2), a peace officer is specifically entitled to demand a breath sample which enables a proper analysis of the breath. Waiting fifteen minutes is permitted under s. 254(2) when it accords with the exigencies of the use of the equipment.

R. v. Deruelle (1992), 15 C.R. (4th) 215, 75 C.C.C. (3d) 118 (S.C.C.) — Section 254(3) requires only that a peace officer form a belief that an impaired driving offence has been committed by the suspect within the past two hours. A demand made pursuant to such belief must follow forthwith or as soon as practicable, but may fall *outside* the two-hour limit. There is no need for the formulation of the belief and the resultant demand to be concurrent.

R. v. Green (1992), 70 C.C.C. (3d) 285 (S.C.C.) — A demand for blood samples pursuant to s. 254(3) of the *Code* must incorporate the assurances of s. 254(4), that the samples of blood will only be taken by or under the direction of a qualified medical practitioner, and that the taking of those samples will not endanger the life or health of the patient. Where the demand made to D was not validly made under s. 254(3), D could not be convicted under s. 254(5) for the offence of failing to comply with a demand under s. 254.

R. v. Grant (1991), 7 C.R. (4th) 388, 67 C.C.C. (3d) 268 (S.C.C.) — A demand to provide a sample of breath when the screening device arrives, rather than forthwith, is not a demand within s. 254(2). D is under no obligation to comply with such a demand, and does not commit an offence in refusing to do so.

R. v. Forsyth (1974), 15 C.C.C. (2d) 23 (Man. C.A.) — A demand, once lawfully made, is to be considered as a continuing demand and it covers not only the first sample furnished but also any subsequent samples.

R. v. Mathews (1974), 14 C.C.C. (2d) 1 (Man. C.A.) — *See also: R. v. Kitchemonia* (1973), 12 C.C.C. (2d) 225 (Sask. C.A.) — The fact that at the time and place the demand is made proper equipment is not immediately available to receive and analyze the sample is irrelevant. If the demand is there and then refused, the offence created is complete.

R. v. Langdon (1993), 74 C.C.C. (3d) 570, 40 M.V.R. (2d) 1 (Nfld. C.A.) — *See also: R. v. Johns* (1994), 7 M.V.R. (3d) 67 (Alta. C.A.) — The failure of a police officer to include the s. 254(4) assurances in a demand for blood samples is relevant in the case of a refusal to comply with the demand, but not where there is consent to the demand.

R. v. Latour (1997), 116 C.C.C. (3d) 279 (Ont. C.A.) — In s. 254(2), "forthwith" means in circumstances such that there is no reasonable opportunity to contact counsel. A valid demand does *not* require a peace officer *reasonably* believe that a sample can be provided before D has a realistic opportunity to consult counsel. Where a peace officer in all of the circumstances, including the time elapsed between the demand and sample, is in a position to require D to provide a sample before D has a realistic opportunity to consult counsel, the statutory requirements are met.

R. v. Nagy (1997), 115 C.C.C. (3d) 473 (Ont. C.A.) — Where D is detained for the purpose of complying with a lawful demand for a blood sample, D need not be apprised of the specific charge under investigation. The nature of the charge is irrelevant to the validity of the demand.

R. v. Cote (1992), 11 C.R. (4th) 214, 70 C.C. (3d) 280 (Ont. C.A.) — *See also: R. v. Misasi* (1993), 79 C.C.C. (3d) 339 (Ont. C.A.); *R. v. Higgins* (1994), 88 C.C.C. (3d) 232 (Man. C.A.); *R. v. Payne* (1994), 5 M.V.R. (3d) 189 (Nfld. C.A.) — The requirement in s. 254(2) that the breath sample be provided "forthwith" means immediately or very shortly after D has been requested to accompany the officer for the purpose of providing the sample, usually at roadside or in the immediate vicinity. If the officer is not in a position to require that a breath sample be provided before any realistic opportunity to consult counsel, then the demand is not a demand made under s. 254(2), and D is entitled to refuse to comply with the demand.

R. v. Lemieux (1990), 24 M.V.R. (2d) 157 (Ont. C.A.) — On a charge of refusal under s. 254(5), P need not establish that the device to be used was an approved screening device.

R. v. Campbell (1988), 66 C.R. (3d) 150, 44 C.C.C. (3d) 502 (Ont. C.A.) — *See also: R. v. Courchene* (1989), 52 C.C.C. (3d) 375 (Ont C.A.) — A demand for a roadside breath sample which is not made as soon as is reasonably possible in the circumstances, such that D's care or control of the vehicle has ended by the time the demand is made, is invalid.

R. v. Angelantoni (1975), 31 C.R.N.S. 342 (Ont. C.A.) — A demand by a peace officer to give a sample of breath, and the agreement or acceptance by D to give the sample, does not create an obligation to administer the test, so that a failure to do so would not vitiate a trial based on other evidence.

R. v. Farrar (1993), 80 C.C.C. (3d) 381 (P.E.I. C.A.) — A s. 254(3) demand is *not* valid if its only supportive grounds are those which have been acquired by a s. 8 *Charter* breach by investigating officers.

R. v. Knox (1995), 39 C.R. (4th) 362 (C.A. Que.) — When the law prescribes that a sample of blood should be provided after a valid demand under s. 254(3), P need *not* establish that the person complying with the order has consented to it.

R. v. Flegel (1972), 7 C.C.C. (2d) 55 (Sask. C.A.) — No particular words are necessary in making a demand as long as the words and surrounding circumstances convey to the person that the demand is being made pursuant to the section.

Forthwith

R. v. Deruelle (1992), 15 C.R. (4th) 215, 75 C.C.C. (3d) 118 (S.C.C.) — Section 254(3) requires only that a peace officer form a belief that an impaired driving offence has been committed by the suspect within the past two hours. A demand made pursuant to such belief must follow forthwith or as soon as practicable, but may fall *outside* the two-hour limit. There is no need for the formulation of the belief and the resultant demand to be concurrent.

Brownridge v. R. (1972), 18 C.R.N.S. 308, 7 C.C.C. (2d) 417 (S.C.C.); reversing (1972), 15 C.R.N.S. 387, 4 C.C.C. (2d) 463 (Ont. C.A.) — For all practical purposes, "without delay" and "forthwith" are interchangeable. Whatever leeway of time each allows is particular to its own setting.

R. v. MacKinnon (1989), 48 C.C.C. (3d) 442 (N.S. C.A.) — Where an approved screening device demand is made, there is no requirement that the test be administered at roadside and the motorist may be required to go to a police station for the test, as long as it is administered as soon as possible under the circumstances.

R. v. MacGillivray (1971), 4 C.C.C. (2d) 244 (Ont. C.A.) — The use of the phrase "forthwith or as soon as practicable" does not cut down or restrict the meaning of the word "forthwith" had that word alone appeared in the statute. "Forthwith" means within a reasonable time.

As Soon as Practicable [See s. 258]

Samples Necessary to Enable Proper Analysis

R. v. Schimpf (1980), 7 M.V.R. 161 (Alta. C.A.) — Once D supplies breath, the opinion of the qualified technician, or perhaps an expert, is required to determine whether the sample is adequate for a proper analysis to be made.

R. v. Ralloff, [1977] 1 W.W.R. 391 (B.C. C.A.) — The technician is not required to stipulate in the certificate that the breath samples taken were sufficient for him to form the opinion as to the number of samples necessary to enable a proper analysis to be made.

R. v. Pierman (1994), 19 O.R. (3d) 704, 92 C.C.C. (3d) 160 (Ont. C.A.) — "Proper analysis" incorporates an element of accuracy. Where there are facts which cause the officer to conclude that a short delay is required to obtain an accurate result, the officer acts within s. 254(2) in delaying the taking of the sample.

Failure or Refusal to Comply With Demand

R. v. Knox, 1 C.R. (5th) 254, 109 C.C.C. (3d) 481, [1996] 3 S.C.R. 199 — *See also:R. v. Green* (1992), 70 C.C.C. (3d) 285 (S.C.C.) — A *demand* is deficient if it fails to provide the s. 254(4) assurances that the samples would only be taken by a qualified medical practitioner who was satisfied that taking them would neither harm D's health, nor endanger D's life. A sample taken absent such assurances contravenes *Charter* ss. 7 and 8. A constitutionally-flawed demand means that D cannot be convicted under s. 254(5) for failure to comply.

R. v. Grant (1991), 7 C.R. (4th) 388, 67 C.C.C. (3d) 268 (S.C.C.) — A demand to provide a sample of breath when the screening device arrives, rather than forthwith, is not a demand within s. 254(2). D is under no obligation to comply with such a demand, and does not commit an offence in refusing to do so.

R. v. Jumaga (1976), 34 C.R.N.S. 172, 29 C.C.C. (2d) 269 (S.C.C.) — Where on the facts the first refusal was in effect a request for counsel, such that the police allowed D access to counsel, no offence is made out.

R. v. Brunet (1968), 4 C.R.N.S. 202, [1969] 1 C.C.C. 297 (S.C.C.) — *See also: R. v. MacLennan* (1973), 13 C.C.C. (2d) 217 (N.S. C.A.); *R. v. Kitchemonia* (1973), 12 C.C.C. (2d) 225 (Sask. C.A.) — Non-compliance with a breathalyzer demand constitutes one offence. It is immaterial whether the non-compliance arises from a failure or a refusal without reasonable excuse to supply a sample of breath.

R. v. Sullivan (1992), 65 C.C.C. (3d) 541, 32 M.V.R. (2d) 92 (B.C. C.A.) — Once a proper demand is made, it continues in full force and need not be repeated. Where D, to whom a demand has been made, indicates that he will not provide a breath sample until he has spoken to his lawyer, but gives no indication after consulting counsel that he is willing to provide a sample, his conditional refusal becomes a refusal by his silence.

R. v. Quiring (1979), 7 C.R. (3d) 180, 46 C.C.C. (2d) 51 (B.C. C.A.) — *See also: R. v. Hatt* (1978), 41 C.C.C. (2d) 442 (N.B. C.A.); *R. v. Hazzard* (1978), 51 C.C.C. (2d) 344 (N.W.T. C.A.) — It is not sufficient for D to give a single sample to constitute compliance with this section. This is true even if the technician testifies that he can make an analysis with one sample only.

R. v. McGauley (1974), 16 C.C.C (2d) 419 (B.C. C.A.) — An offence under this section is complete upon the refusal being made. It is no defence that, after consulting with his lawyer, D changed his mind and was prepared to take the test.

R. v. Rowe (1973), 12 C.C.C. (2d) 24 (B.C. C.A.) — The offence is complete once D refuses to provide a sample. D is not entitled to further time in which to change his mind.

R. v. Gesner (1979), 46 C.C.C. (2d) 252 (N.B. C.A.) — The word "refuses" used in subsection (5) is fully comprised within the word "fails" such that a verbal refusal of a demand for a sample does not preclude conviction on a charge of "failing" to comply with a lawful demand without reasonable excuse.

R. v. Hurley (1980), 9 M.V.R. 46 (Nfld. C.A.) — *See also: R. v. Dunn* (1978), 43 C.C.C. (2d) 519 (P.E.I. C.A.) — The statement "my lawyer advises me not to take the test" was held to be a refusal to take the test.

R. v. Bowman (1978), 40 C.C.C. (2d) 525 (N.S. C.A.) — *See also: R. v. Butt* (1983), 23 M.V.R. 273 (Nfld. C.A.) — A person is entitled to a reasonable time in which to decide whether or not he is going to comply with a demand but, once a person decides he is not going to comply and makes that decision known to the officer, the offence is made out regardless of a subsequent change of mind.

R. v. MacNeil (1978), 41 C.C.C. (2d) 46 (Ont. C.A.) — The section creates one offence of failing or refusing to comply with a demand. The offence can be committed by refusing to provide a sample or by refusing to accompany the officer. Where the information sets forth both manners and one is proved, the additional averment is not essential and is mere surplusage.

R. v. Brotton (1983), 24 M.V.R. 76 (Sask. C.A.) — The section did not require the accused to comply forthwith with the demand and the word comply must be interpreted to mean within a reasonable time having regard to all the circumstances, including D's opportunity to speak with counsel.

Reasonable Excuse

Taraschuk v. R. (1977), 30 C.R.N.S. 321, 25 C.C.C. (2d) 108 (S.C.C.) — The fact that a court subsequently concludes that D was not, in fact, impaired or did not, while impaired, have care or control of a motor vehicle, does not provide a reasonable excuse for failure to provide a sample of breath.

Rilling v. R. (1975), 31 C.R.N.S. 142, 24 C.C.C. (2d) 81 (S.C.C.) — While the absence of reasonable and probable grounds for belief of impairment may afford a defence to a charge of refusal to submit to a breathalyzer test, it does not render the certificate inadmissible once the demand has been acceded to.

Brownridge v. R. (1972), 18 C.R.N.S. 308, 7 C.C.C. (2d) 417 (S.C.C.) — Failure to give D access to counsel may constitute a "reasonable excuse".

R. v. Pittendreigh (1994), 9 M.V.R. (3d) 236 (Alta. C.A.) — Concern about sanitation of an unwrapped mouthpiece is a reasonable excuse.

R. v. Campbell (1978), 40 C.C.C. (2d) 570 (Alta. C.A.) — A correct belief on the part of D that blood in his mouth would be a contaminant and therefore affect the result of a breath test is not a reasonable excuse. It would be open to D to lead the contamination evidence as "evidence to the contrary" under s. 258.

R. v. Crossman (1991), 28 M.V.R. (2d) 221 (B.C. C.A.); leave to appeal refused (1991), 31 M.V.R. (2d) 221 (note) (S.C.C.) — Failure of the police to inform D that a non-lawyer was en route to assist her is not a reasonable excuse for failure to provide a breath sample.

R. v. Dunn (1980), 8 M.V.R. 198 (B.C. C.A.) — A fear on the part of a person to whom a demand is made that the breathalyzer readings may be inaccurate is not a reasonable excuse for refusing the demand.

R. v. Chomokowski (1973), 11 C.C.C. (2d) 562 (Man. C.A.) — Religious belief, genuinely held, cannot form the basis of immunity from the requirement of providing a sample of breath.

R. v. MacDougall (1975), 15 N.B.R. (2d) 279 (C.A.) — The burden of proof of a reasonable excuse is on D on a preponderance of probabilities.

R. v. Nadeau (1974), 19 C.C.C. (2d) 199 (N.B. C.A.) — Reasonable excuse as envisaged by the section must be some circumstance which renders compliance with the demand either extremely difficult or likely to involve substantial risk to the health of the person on whom the demand is made. The fact that D did not drive or have the care or control of a motor vehicle within the two hours of the demand is no excuse.

R. v. Warford (1981), 61 C.C.C. (2d) 489 (Nfld. C.A.) — The fact that a peace officer had no grounds for a random stopping of D is not a reasonable excuse for refusal to provide a sample. In this case, after stopping D the officer did have grounds for a demand.

R. v. Rector (1987), 81 N.S.R (2d) 55 (C.A.) — D is entitled to acquittal on a charge of refusing to provide a breath sample where there is no evidence to indicate that D was driving or had the care or control of a motor vehicle within the 2-hour period preceding the breathalyzer demand.

R. v. Bauditz (1981), 12 M.V.R. 200 (N.S. C.A.); leave to appeal refused (1981), 41 N.R. 264n (S.C.C.) — *See also*: *R. v. Warnica* (1980), 56 C.C.C. (2d) 100 (N.S. C.A.) — Voluntary intoxication rendering D incapable of comprehending a demand for a sample does not amount to a defence.

R. v. Phinney (1979), 49 C.C.C (2d) 81 (N.S. C.A.) — There is no all-inclusive definition of reasonable excuse. The proper test lies somewhere between the narrow view which justifies refusal on physical grounds and the broad view which would allow the judge to decide whether the excuse was reasonable in all the circumstances. In this case, D's honest belief that the machine was not functioning properly afforded a reasonable excuse because it was based on objective evidence that there may have been a problem with the machine in question.

R. v. Swietorzecki (1995), 97 C.C.C. (3d) 285 (Ont. C.A.) — It is a defence to a charge of refusing to provide a roadside sample that the police had only reasonable suspicion and did not have reasonable and probable grounds to believe that the accused was driving or had care or control of the vehicle.

R. v. Moser (1992), 13 C.R. (4th) 96, 71 C.C.C. (3d) 165 (Ont. C.A.) — "Reasonable excuse" is *not* confined to matters in the mind of D. It includes situations where there is reason at the time not to make the demand or require compliance under threat of prosecution, but that reason is not fully known, either to the investigating officer or to the suspect.

R. v. MacIntyre (1983), 24 M.V.R. 67 (Ont. C.A.); reversing (1983), 24 M.V.R. 67 at 72 (Ont. Co. Ct.) — Mistake of law is *not* a reasonable excuse for refusing to provide a breath sample.

R. v. Giroux (1981), 24 C.R. (3d) 101, 63 C.C.C. (2d) 555 (Que. C.A.) — D, on the advice of his lawyer refused to provide a second sample. The lawyer insisted on being present for the test, and also on checking the machine after the first test. Both requests were denied. It was held that the failure to take the second test on the advice of counsel was not a lawful excuse.

R. v. Wall (1974), 19 C.C.C. (2d) 146 (Sask. C.A.) — *See also*: *R. v. Richardson* (1993), 80 C.C.C. (3d) 287 (Ont. C.A.); *R. v. Taylor* (1993), 43 M.V.R. (2d) 240 (B.C. C.A.); *R. v. Weir* (1993), 79 C.C.C. (3d) 538 (N.S. C.A.) — It is not a reasonable excuse for failing to provide a breath sample that D instead offered to provide a sample of his breath.

Procedural Considerations

R. v. Schilbe (1976), 30 C.C.C. (2d) 113 (Ont. C.A.) — The offences of impaired driving and refusal to comply with a demand are separate and distinct acts or delicts. D may be convicted of both offences even though they arise out of the same incident.

Charter Considerations — Arbitrary Detention [See also, Charter s. 9]

Dedman v. R. (1985), 46 C.R. (3d) 193, 20 C.C.C. (3d) 97 (S.C.C.) — A well-publicized police programme of random spot checks is in furtherance of the general police duties to prevent crime and to preserve life and property. The random stopping is reasonable and a necessary exercise of police powers.

Charter Considerations — Right to Counsel — Roadside Screening

R. v. Grant (1991), 7 C.R. (4th) 388, 67 C.C.C. (3d) 268 (S.C.C.) — Where D is suspected of operating a motor vehicle with alcohol in his/her system and is required to await the arrival of an A.L.E.R.T. machine, s/he is detained and must be given the s. 10(b) warning.

R. v. Thomsen (1988), 63 C.R. (3d) 1, 40 C.C.C. (3d) 411 (S.C.C.) — The limitation on the right to retain and instruct counsel at the roadside testing stage is a reasonable one, demonstrably justified in a free and democratic society, having regard to the fact that the right to counsel is available at the more serious breathalyzer stage.

R. v. Yuskow (1989), 73 C.R. (3d) 159, 52 C.C.C. (3d) 382 (Alta. C.A.) — The change in wording from "road-side" to "approved screening device" and the elimination of the requirement that both samples be taken within two hours does not impose a right to counsel.

R. v. Haché (1993), 1 M.V.R. (3d) 172 (N.B. C.A.) — The *Charter* does not require that D be informed that s/he has a right to be advised of the right to counsel and the breathalyzer demand, in his/her choice of official language.

R. v. Sadlon (1992), 36 M.V.R. (2d) 127, 9 C.R.R. (2d) 191 (Ont. C.A.); leave to appeal refused (1992), 11 C.R.R. (2d) 384 (note) (S.C.C.) — *See also*: *R. v. Mitchell* (1994), 35 C.R. (4th) 282 (Alta. C.A.) — Where a valid demand is made for an immediate breath sample by means of an approved screening device, there is no right to counsel imposed by the fact that D has a cellular telephone in his vehicle.

R. v. Farrell (1992), 76 C.C.C. (3d) 201 (P.E.I. C.A.) — There is no obligation on the police officer who makes a roadside screening demand to tell D that s/he has the right to remain silent under s. 7 of the *Charter*, in addition to informing him/her of the right to counsel.

R. v. Bacon (1990), 60 C.C.C (3d) 446, 26 M.V.R. (2d) 165 (Sask. C.A.) — The present section is to be construed as its predecessor was, and there is no right to counsel when a demand for a roadside sample is made.

Charter Considerations — Right to Counsel — Breathalyzer Test

R. v. Mohl (1989), 69 C.R. (3d) 399, 47 C.C.C. (3d) 575 (S.C.C.) — Assuming it was a violation of D's right to counsel for the police to advise him of his rights at a time when he was so drunk that he did not understand, the admission of the breathalyzer results would not bring the administration of justice into disrepute.

R. v. Baig (1987), 61 C.R. (3d) 97, 37 C.C.C. (3d) 181 (S.C.C.) — Following the advisement of D's right to counsel, there are no correlative duties triggered and cast upon the police until D indicates a desire to exercise such right. In the absence of proof of circumstances indicating that D did not understand his right to retain counsel upon being informed of it, the onus is on D to prove that he asked for the right but was denied, or that he was denied any opportunity to even ask for it.

R. v. Trask (1985), 45 C.R. (3d) 137, 18 C.C.C. (3d) 514 (S.C.C.) — Where D has been denied the right to retain and instruct counsel without delay, evidence of the breathalyzer test should be excluded because its admission would, in all the circumstances, bring the administration of justice into disrepute.

R. v. Rahn (1985), 45 C.R. (3d) 134, 18 C.C.C. (3d) 516 (S.C.C.) — When a breathalyzer demand was made, D was detained within the meaning of the *Charter*. D had been denied the right to retain and instruct counsel without delay. Evidence of the breathalyzer test should be excluded because its admission would in all the circumstances bring the administration of justice into disrepute.

R. v. Therens (1985), 45 C.R. (3d) 97, 18 C.C.C. (3d) 481 (S.C.C.) — When a police officer gives a breathalyzer demand, D is "detained" within the meaning of *Charter* s. l0 and therefore entitled to retain and instruct counsel without delay and to be advised of that right prior to complying with the demand.

R. v. Gyori (1993), 50 M.V.R. (2d) 82 (Alta. C.A.) — The opportunity to consult counsel must be provided at the police facility to which D is taken for the *bona fide* purpose of continuing the investigation. The police are not obliged to take D to the nearest police facility for the purpose of contacting counsel where there is no other reason to go to that location.

R. v. Therrien (1993), 49 M.V.R. (2d) 81 (Alta. C.A.) — Where D, arrested for an impaired driving offence, is advised of the right to retain and instruct counsel without delay, but is *not* advised of the right to free and immediate legal advice from duty counsel, there is a breach of s. 10(b) of the *Charter*. It is *not* necessary for D to call evidence to show that s/he is indigent, or that s/he would have called duty counsel if properly advised.

R. v. Top (1989), 48 C.C.C. (3d) 493 (Alta. C.A.) — *See also*: *R. v. Nelson* (1991), 28 M.V.R. (2d) 4 (B.C. C.A.) — After initial attempts to reach D's counsel of choice have failed, the police need not delay further in requiring compliance with the breathalyzer demand if the delay is unlikely to assist D.

R. v. Elefante (1986), 47 Alta. L.R. (2d) 139 (C.A.) — D tried to contact a lawyer from a list of lawyers for 20 minutes without success. The police then demanded that D provide a breath sample which he refused to do. The police had stopped the process of D contacting a lawyer and had thereby breached D's rights under the *Charter* and thus D was acquitted.

R. v. Stebbings (1993), 49 M.V.R. (2d) 90 (B.C. C.A.) — *See also*: *R. v. Bailey* (1993), 50 M.V.R. (2d) 134 (Y. C.A.) — The police were under no further obligation where D, after placing four telephone calls in an attempt to reach his lawyer, then complied with the breathalyzer demand without indicating whether or not he had been able to obtain advice.

R. v. Ferron (1989), 49 C.C.C. (3d) 432 (B.C. C.A.) — Where D fails to tell the police he has been unable to reach counsel and is requesting further time to do so, he has no reasonable excuse for refusing to comply with the breathalyzer demand.

R. v. Dunnett (1990), 62 C.C.C. (3d) 14 (N.B. C.A.) — Where D was diligent in attempting to contact a lawyer and there was no urgency, he did not waive his right to counsel when he asked to be taken to hospital to obtain insulin.

R. v. Stark (1984), 27 M.V.R. 161 (N.S. C.A.) — D was afforded reasonable opportunity to contact counsel. His inability to do so was not attributable to the police. D was not entitled to the presence of a lawyer either for the purposes of consultation or to observe any breathalyzer test that might be performed and he did not have two hours in which to decide whether to comply with the breathalyzer demand.

R. v. Wills (1992), 12 C.R. (4th) 58, 70 C.C.C. (3d) 529 (Ont. C.A.) — The taking of a breath sample can, in some circumstances, constitute a seizure, such as where there was no consent, or no valid consent, given by D. The taking of a breath sample constituted a seizure where D, because of the misinformation and non-disclosure of information, failed to realize both his potential jeopardy and the potential criminal consequences of taking the breathalyzer test.

R. v. Pavel (1989), 74 C.R. (3d) 195, 53 C.C.C. (3d) 296 (Ont. C.A.) — It is an infringement of *Charter* s. 10(b) to tell D he could make only one telephone call.

R. v. Vanstaceghem (1987), 58 C.R. (3d) 121, 36 C.C.C. (3d) 142 (Ont. C.A.) — The right to be informed of one's right to counsel has a logical corollary, the right to be informed in a language which one comprehends.

R. v. Marshall (1987), 50 M.V.R. 278 (Ont. C.A.) — It was a violation of D's right to counsel for the police officer to imply that D had a right to counsel only if he wished to have counsel present when the breath samples were taken.

Charter Considerations — Right to Counsel — Refusal to Comply

R. v. Peck (1994), 1 M.V.R. (3d) 197 (N.S. C.A.) — The expression "without reasonable cause" creates a reverse onus which is contrary to s. 11(d) of the *Charter*, but it is saved under s. 1.

R. v. Williams (1992), 17 C.R. (4th) 277, 78 C.C.C. (3d) 72, 11 O.R. (3d) 300 (C.A.) — Denial of the right to counsel is *not a reasonable excuse* for refusal to comply with a breathalyzer demand under *Code* s. 254(5). Where a s. 10(b) *Charter* breach is demonstrated by D, the remedies available are those of *Charter* s. 24, in particular s. 24(2).

R. v. MacKinnon (1985), 47 C.R. (3d) 1 (P.E.I. C.A.) — A failure to advise D of his right to counsel is a reasonable excuse for failing to comply with a breathalyzer demand.

Charter Considerations — Right to Counsel — Privacy [See also, Charter s. 10]

R. v. Jumaga (1976), 34 C.R.N.S 172, 29 C.C.C. (2d) 269 (S.C.C.) — Where D accepted the telephone facilities as provided and did not object to speaking with his lawyer by telephone within hearing distance of police officers, he could not complain later at trial of the inadequacy of the facilities in order to justify his refusal to provide a sample.

R. v. Penner (1973), 22 C.R.N.S. 35, 12 C.C.C. (2d) 468 (Man. C.A.) — Privacy is an essential element of the right to retain and instruct counsel. Not allowing one who has been detained to confer with his lawyer in private when at the police station is a reasonable excuse for refusing to provide a sample on demand.

R. v. Makismchuk (1974), 15 C.C.C. (2d) 208 (Man. C.A.) — The presence of the police while D was telephoning his lawyer afforded a reasonable excuse for failure to comply.

R. v. Young (1987), 6 M.V.R. (2d) 295 (N.B. C.A.) — Where a police officer overheard "bits and pieces" of D's telephone conversation with his lawyers, after being requested to give the accused privacy, D's right to counsel was violated. However, s. 24(2) did not operate to exclude evidence of D's refusal to provide a sample in such circumstances.

R. v. Miller (1991), 25 M.V.R. (2d) 171 (Nfld. C.A.) — D has sufficient privacy when he speaks to counsel from an enclosed glass booth that is in sight of the police officer.

R. v. Dempsey (1987), 46 M.V.R. 179 (N.S. C.A.) — The right to consult a lawyer in private does not include complete seclusion from police surveillance. It was sufficient that if D had called his lawyer, a radio would have been turned on to cover the conversation.

R. v. Jackson (1993), 48 M.V.R. (2d) 277, 25 C.R. (4th) 265, 86 C.C.C. (3d) 233 (Ont. C.A.) — Although there is no obligation on the police to advise D that the right to retain and instruct counsel is a right to do so in privacy, if D indicates that s/he does not understand that there is such a right, or is concerned about whether privacy will be given, then there is an obligation on the police to advise D of the right to privacy.

R. v. Olak (1990), 56 C.C.C. (3d) 257 (Ont. C.A.) — Where, despite the presence of a police officer during his telephone conversation with counsel, D is able to consult with counsel, obtain the necessary advice and act on it, the admission of the breathalyzer test results will not bring the administration of justice into disrepute.

R. v. McKane (1987), 58 C.R. (3d) 130, 35 C.C.C. (3d) 481 (Ont. C.A.) — *See also: R. v. Ginther* (1986), 54 Sask. R. 303 (C.A.) — A police officer was present while D was speaking to his lawyer on the telephone and refused to leave despite D's request for greater privacy. This was a violation of D's *Charter* rights as the right to retain and instruct counsel necessarily includes the right to do so in private.

R. v. Panchyshyn (1985), 38 Sask. R. 239 (C.A.) — D who was informed of his right to counsel both after a roadside breath test and before a station breathalyzer test had been adequately allowed his *Charter* right despite the continued presence of a police officer during a telephone conversation with his father.

Charter Considerations — Right to Counsel — Waiver

R. v. Rackow (1986), 54 C.R. (3d) 185, 30 C.C.C. (3d) 250 (Alta. C.A.) — D's position is not prejudiced, where after being informed of his right to counsel, he shows no interest in exercising it.

R. v. Dunnett (1990), 62 C.C.C. (3d) 14, 26 M.V.R. (2d) 194 (N.B. C.A.) — Where D was diligent in attempting to contact a lawyer and there was no urgency, he did not waive his right to counsel when he asked to be taken to hospital to obtain insulin.

R. v. Nugent (1988), 63 C.R. (3d) 351, 42 C.C.C. (3d) 431 (N.S. C.A.); reversing (1987), 80 N.S.R. (2d) 281 (T.D.) — To constitute a valid waiver, D must have a true *appreciation* of the *consequences* of not exercising the right to counsel.

LePage v. R. (1986), 54 C.R. (3d) 371, 32 C.C.C. (3d) 171 (N.S. C.A.) — Where an officer allows D to telephone a lawyer from D's house then advises D that the officer would have to keep him under observation at all times, D's right to privacy in consulting with counsel is violated. D could not be said to have waived his rights, given the officer's unilateral imposition of conditions on the exercise of such rights.

R. v. Pearson (1987), 55 Sask. R. 122 (C.A.) — The duty of a police officer to inform D of his right to counsel does not include a duty to discover whether or not D is waiving that right.

Charter Considerations — Roadside Screening

R. v. Warren (1994), 2 M.V.R. (3d) 113 (N.S. Prov. Ct.) — *See also: R. v. Speller* (1993), 47 M.V.R. (2d) 129 (Ont. Prov. Ct.); *R. v. Gole* (1994), 1 M.V.R. (3d) 257 (Ont. Gen. Div.); *R. v. Gatley* (1993), 50 M.V.R. (2d) 153 (Ont. Gen. Div.) — A breathalyzer demand based solely on an unapproved ALERT result amounts to a demand made merely on suspicion and violates s. 8 of the *Charter.*

R. v. Tanner (1986), 41 M.V.R. 92 (N.S. C.A.) — D is not entitled to observe the operation of the ALERT test.

R. v. O'Halloran (1993), 47 M.V.R. (2d) 88 (P.E.I. C.A.) — Section 254(2) does not violate s. 7 or 8 of the *Charter.* Even if it did so, it would be saved under s. 1.

Charter Considerations — Breathalyzer Test

R. v. Gillis (1994), 91 C.C.C. (3d) 575 (Alta. C.A.) — Failure to permit D to view the readings as a breathalyzer is taken does *not* infringe *Charter* s. 7.

R. v. Altseimer (1982), 29 C.R. (3d) 276, 1 C.C.C. (3d) 7 (Ont. C.A.) — The *Charter* does not confer a broad privilege against self-incrimination, but confers specific protection solely against testimonial compulsion, which has no relevance to compulsory breath tests. Detention for failure to pass a roadside breath test is in no way arbitrary.

Drobot v. R. (1985), 35 M.V.R. 233 (Sask. C.A.) — The fact that the officer who had arrested D also administered the breathalyzer test did not violate D's rights under *Charter* s. 7.

R. v. Gaff (1984), 36 Sask. R. 1 (Sask. C.A.); leave to appeal refused (1984), 15 C.C.C. (3d) 126n (S.C.C.) — Compulsory breath tests pursuant to the *Code* do not violate *Charter* s. 7 which guar the right to life, liberty and security of the person.

Charter Considerations — Blood Samples [See s. 256]

R. v. Knox, 1 C.R. (5th) 254, 109 C.C.C. (3d) 481, [1996] 3 S.C.R. 199 (S.C.C.) — There is a significant distinction between compliance and refusal for *Charter* s. 24(2) purposes. Where D actually complies with a demand, constitutionally flawed for failure to include the s. 254(4) assurances, adducing evidence of the blood sample is unlikely to bring the administration of justice in disrepute. It is *a fortiori* when the conditions stipulated by the provision have been met.

R. v. Knox, 1 C.R. (5th) 254, 109 C.C.C. (3d) 481, [1996] 3 S.C.R. 199 (S.C.C.) — There is *no* requirement in *Charter* s. 8 that P prove D's *consent* to give a blood sample to make the sample admissible at D's trial on driving charges. P need only establish

i.   that there *reasonable and probable grounds* to believe that D had committed the *offence* of impaired driving;

ii.   that it was *impracticable* to obtain a *breathalyzer* sample; and

iii.   that a *demand* to obtain the *blood* sample was *made*.

R. v. Lunn (1990), 61 C.C.C. (3d) 193, 26 M.V.R. (2d) 209 (B.C. C.A.) — A failure to make the demand for a blood sample under s. 254(3) does not render a sample taken by medical personnel inadmissible, where the police have obtained it by executing a search warrant at the hospital, nor is there a breach of the *Charter* where medical personnel confirm to the police the existence of such a sample so that a warrant can be executed.

R. v. Harder (1989), 49 C.C.C. (3d) 565 (B.C. C.A.) — Where the demand for blood samples was made at the hospital, D was detained and entitled to be given his right to counsel under *Charter* s. 10(b).

R. v. Fowler (1990), 3 C.R. (4th) 225, 61 C.C.C. 505 (Man. C.A.) — A consent to obtain a blood sample following the reading of the demand is not a true consent, but is a consent in response to a demand backed by the authority of the law. Where the officer who made the demand had no reasonable or probable grounds for believing D to be impaired, the obtaining of the blood sample in response to the demand was an unreasonable search or seizure.

R. v. Greene (1991), 62 C.C.C. (3d) 344, 27 M.V.R. (2d) 212 (Nfld. C.A.) — In addition to advising D of his right to counsel where a demand for blood samples has been made, the police must provide him/her with the opportunity to contact counsel.

R. v. Brown (1991), 69 C.C.C. (3d) 139 (N.S. C.A.) — Even though a blood sample is self-incriminating evidence emanating from D, the results of its analysis may be admissible under *Charter* s. 24(2) where the evidence would have been obtained in any event, the *Charter* breach was technical, and the police did not act in bad faith.

Charter Considerations — Physical Tests

R. v. Bonogofski (1987), 39 C.C.C. (3d) 457 (B.C. C.A.) — *See also*: *R. v. Gallant* (1989), 70 C.R. (3d) 139, 48 C.C.C. (3d) 329 (Alta. C.A.); leave to appeal refused (1990), 73 C.R. (3d) xxviin (S.C.C.); *R. v. Baroni* (1989), 49 C.C.C. (3d) 553 (N.S. C.A.) — D is "detained" upon being asked to perform roadside physical sobriety tests, because the officer's purpose was to investigate a suspected offence. Therefore D must be informed of his right to counsel before performing the tests.

R. v. Boucher (1990), 26 M.V.R. (2d) 48 (N.B. Q.B.) — The failure to advise D of his right to counsel prior to having him perform sobriety tests violates s. 10(b) of the *Charter*, but where the request is authorized at common law, the violation is justified under s. 1.

R. v. Saunders (1988), 63 C.R. (3d) 37, 41 C.C.C. (3d) 532 (Ont. C.A.) — A driver who acquiesces to a demand by a police officer to pull over and perform co-ordination tests is "detained" and entitled to counsel under *Charter* s. 10(b). However, provincial highway legislation authorizing officers to demand such tests without informing the driver of his right to counsel constitutes a reasonable limit on the driver's constitutional rights under *Charter* s. 1.

Related Provisions: "Peace officer", "motor vehicle" and "railway equipment" are defined in s. 2, "vessel" and "aircraft" in s. 214. Section 253 prohibits the operation or having the care or control of a motor vehicle, vessel or aircraft while impaired or with more than 80 mg of alcohol in 100 ml of blood.

Section 256 describes the procedure to be followed to obtain a warrant in accordance with which blood samples may be taken from a person believed to have recently committed an offence under s. 253 in an accident resulting in the death of or bodily harm to another person.

The provisions of this section should be read together with ss. 258(1)(d)–(i), which describe the evidentiary effect of analysis performed upon samples of breath or blood taken in accordance with this section. The failure or refusal of D, without reasonable excuse, to comply with a demand made under this section is admissible in evidence under s. 258(3), and the court may draw an inference therefrom adverse to D. The offence of s. 254(5) is triable either way. By indictment, D may elect mode of trial under s. 536(2). Upon summary conviction, the offence is tried in accordance with Part XXVII and punished under s. 787(1). The offence is also a "previous offence" for the purposes of s. 255(4) in prosecutions under not only s. 254(5) but also ss. 253(a) and (b). A conviction or discharge under this section attracts the mandatory prohibition order of s. 259(1). Its operation may be stayed pending appeal under s. 261.

255. (1) Punishment — Every one who commits an offence under section 253 or 254 is guilty of an indictable offence or an offence punishable on summary conviction and is liable,

     (a) whether the offence is prosecuted by indictment or punishable on summary conviction, to the following minimum punishment, namely,

         (i) for a first offence, to a fine of not less than three hundred dollars,

         (ii) for a second offence, to imprisonment for not less than fourteen days, and

         (iii) for each subsequent offence, to imprisonment for not less than ninety days;

     (b) where the offence is prosecuted by indictment, to imprisonment for a term not exceeding five years; and

     (c) where the offence is punishable on summary conviction, to imprisonment for a term not exceeding six months.

(2) Impaired driving causing bodily harm — Every one who commits an offence under paragraph 253(a) and thereby causes bodily harm to any other person is guilty of an indictable offence and liable to imprisonment for a term not exceeding ten years.

(3) Impaired driving causing death — Every one who commits an offence under paragraph 253(a) and thereby causes the death of any other person is guilty of an indictable offence and liable to imprisonment for a term not exceeding fourteen years.

(4) Previous convictions — Where a person is convicted of an offence committed under paragraph 253(a) or (b) or subsection 254(5), that person shall, for the purposes of this Act, be deemed to be convicted for a second or subsequent offence, as the case may be, if the person has previously been convicted of

     (a) an offence committed under any of those provisions;

     (b) an offence under subsection (2) or (3); or

     (c) an offence under section 250, 251, 252, 253, 259 or 260 or subsection 258(4) of this Act as this Act read immediately before the coming into force of this subsection.

(5) Conditional discharge — Notwithstanding subsection 736(1), a court may, instead of convicting a person of an offence committed under section 253, after hearing medical or other evidence, if it considers that the person is in need of curative treatment in relation to his consumption of alcohol or drugs and that it would not be contrary to the public interest, by order direct that the person be discharged under section 730 on the conditions prescribed in a probation order, including a condition respecting the person's attendance for curative treatment in relation to his consumption of alcohol or drugs.

R.S., c. C-34, s. 237; 1974–75–76, c. 93, ss. 18, 102; R.S. 1985, c. 27 (1st Supp.), s. 36; 1995, c. 22, s. 18, Sch. IV, item 26.

S. 255(5) has been proclaimed in force in the provinces of Alberta, Manitoba, New Brunswick, Nova Scotia, Prince Edward Island, Saskatchewan and in Yukon Territory and Northwest Territories.

Commentary: The section determines the punishment which may be imposed upon conviction of offences under ss. 253 and 254.

Section 255(1) prescribes both the minimum and maximum punishment for the *general* offences of s. 253 and the offence of s. 254 and permits the offences to be tried either way. The minimum punishment prescribed by s. 255(1)(a) is the same, irrespective of the mode of procedure and is determined by whether it is D's first, second or a subsequent offence. Subsection (4) determines what constitutes an "offence" for the purposes of the enhanced punishment provisions of s. 255(1)(a). Sections 255(1)(b) and (c) provide the maximum punishment for the general offences of s. 253 and the offence of s. 254. The mandatory term of incarceration has attracted *Charter* s. 7 scrutiny. The maximum punishment is determined by the mode of procedure.

Sections 255(2) and (3) describe *aggravated* forms of impaired operation or care or control (the offence of s. 253(a)), declare each offence to be exclusively indictable and provide the maximum punishment therefor. Under s. 255(2), impaired operation *causing bodily harm* to a person other than D is punishable by imprisonment for a term not exceeding 10 years. P must demonstrate a causal *nexus* between the impaired operation and the bodily harm to V. Under s. 255(3), the causal *nexus* which must be demonstrated is as between the impaired operation or care or control and the death of V. The offence, exclusively indictable, carries a maximum imprisonment for a term not exceeding 14 years.

Section 255(5) operates notwithstanding the general provisions applicable to discharges, s. 730(1), and permits conditional discharges for curative treatment in the circumstances there described. The selective proclamation of the subsection has attracted *Charter* s. 15(1) scrutiny.

Case Law

Causation

R. v. Ewart (1989), 53 C.C.C. (3d) 153 (Alta. C.A.) — The underlying impaired driving must be a *real factor* in bringing about any bodily harm or death.

R. v. Andrew (1994), 91 C.C.C. (3d) 97 (B.C. C.A.) — D may be convicted of impaired operation causing death where the impaired driving ability as evidenced by driving conduct, or failure to react or to make a certain judgment constitutes a *contributing cause* of V's death beyond the *de minimis* range. (per Cumming and Goldie JJ.A.) Impairment is *not* a contributing causative factor in death unless it first leads to faulty driving which, in turn, causes death. The driving must be such that, by omission or commission, there was fault on D's part. The faulty conduct must *not* be conduct that would have been engaged in by a reasonable person in all the circumstances. It must also be a contributing cause, beyond *de minimis*, of V's death. The departure from the standard of a reasonable driver need *not* be marked, as in the case of dangerous driving. (per Lambert J.A., dissenting in part)

R. v. Fisher (1992), 13 C.R. (4th) 222, 36 M.V.R. (2d) 6 (B.C. C.A.) — The fact that a collision may be combined with breathalyzer readings in excess of the legal limit, without evidence of anything unusual in the operation of D's vehicle prior to the collision, is not sufficient to establish that D's impairment was at least a contributing cause outside the *de minimis* range.

R. v. Laprise (1996), 113 C.C.C. (3d) 87 (Que. C.A.) — On a charge of impaired driving causing death, P need only prove that D's condition *contributed* to the smallest degree to V's death. It is *not* necessary for P to prove that the decrease in D's ability to drive was the *only* cause of V's death. Proof of impairment, *per se* does not usually suffice to establish causation, but

i.   evidence of unusual conduct by D;

ii.   expert evidence that D's intoxication could have contributed in more than a minor way to V's death; and

iii.   the absence of an explanation by D

may support the requisite finding.

Where D is charged with impaired operation causing death, the trial judge ought first determine whether P has proven beyond a reasonable doubt that D operated a motor vehicle whilst his/her ability to do so was impaired. It is only where P has impaired ability that the issue of causation need be considered. *R. v. Powell* (1989), 52 C.C.C. (3d) 403 (Sask. C.A.) — *See also*: *R. v. Stephens* (1991), 27 M.V.R. (2d) 24 (Ont. C.A.); *R. v. White* (1994), 3 M.V.R. (3d) 283 (N.S. C.A.); *R. v. Deprez* (1994), 94 C.C.C. (3d) 29 (Man. C.A.) — The test of causation under this section is whether D's impaired condition was at least a contributing cause outside the *de minimis* range, ·

Subsequent Offences

R. v. Skolnick (1982), 29 C.R. (3d) 143, 68 C.C.C. (2d) 385 (S.C.C.) — Convictions for impaired driving and refusing to provide a breathalyzer sample, where both charges arise out of the same incident, are only to be treated as a single conviction for purposes of sentencing on subsequent convictions.

R. v. Morris (1978), 6 C.R. (3d) 36 (S.C.C.) — D's juvenile record could be considered a prior record for purposes of sentencing him as a third-time offender under the drinking and driving penalties.

R. v. Robertson (1998), 124 C.C.C. (3d) 558 (Nfld. C.A.); application for leave to appeal refused (January 7, 1999), Doc. 26614 (S.C.C.) — Two prior convictions entered at the same time, but arising out of separate incidents, are properly considered as a single prior conviction for sentencing purposes under s. 255.

R. v. Negridge (1980), 17 C.R. (3d) 14, 54 C.C.C. (2d) 304 (Ont. C.A.) — A conviction registered prior to the enactment of s. 234.1 [later s. 239(4), now s. 255(4)] is properly taken into account as a "first" offence. Second or subsequent offences must occur after conviction for an earlier offence for the minimum penalty to be invoked.

Res Judicata

R. v. Andrew (1990), 78 C.R. (3d) 239, 57 C.C.C. (3d) 301 (B.C. C.A.) — Where the charge of impaired driving is based upon the impairment of capacity followed by driving and does not encompass the manner of driving which forms part of the sequence of acts constituting criminal negligence, the accused can be convicted of both impaired driving causing bodily harm and criminal negligence causing bodily harm.

Multiple Convictions

R. v. Plante (1997), 120 C.C.C. (3d) 323 (Que. C.A.) — The rule against multiple convictions does *not* bar convictions for

i.   criminal negligence causing death; and

ii. impaired driving causing death

because the element of intoxicaiton is *not* necessary to establish criminal negligence in the operation of a motor vehicle, at all events where there is evidence of excessive speed and place of impact.

Curative Treatment [See also "Charter Considerations — Non-Proclamation"]

R. v. Storr (1995), 14 M.V.R. (3d) 34 (Alta. C.A.) — In assessing whether a curative discharge would be contrary to the public interest, the court should consider the circumstances of the offence and whether the accused was involved in an accident which caused death, bodily harm or significant property damage; the *bona fides* of the offender; the criminal record of the accused as it relates to alcohol-driving offenses; whether the accused was subject to a driving prohibition at the time of the offence; and whether the accused has received the benefit of a prior curative discharge.

R. v. Morrell-Russell (1991), 28 M.V.R. (2d) 209 (N.B. Q.B.) — The non-availability of the discharge provision for persons convicted of failing to provide breath samples does not violate *Charter* s. 15.

R. v. Ashberry (1989), 68 C.R. (3d) 341, 47 C.C.C. (3d) 138 (Ont. C.A.) — A prior drinking and driving record alone should not preclude the granting of a discharge pursuant to subsection (5), particularly where the evidence establishes genuine motivation and the likelihood of rehabilitation.

Sentence

R. v. Stubel (1991), 25 M.V.R. (2d) 118 (Alta. C.A.) — A fine alone may not be imposed in respect of a conviction for impaired driving causing bodily harm but may only be imposed in addition to any other authorized punishment.

Charter Considerations — Minimum Penalty

R. v. Kumar (1993), 85 C.C.C. (3d) 417 (B.C. C.A.) — In general, the minimum punishment provisions of s. 255(1)(a)(ii) applicable to second offenders do not infringe *Charter* s. 12. In the rare case where imposition of the minimum punishment would be grossly disproportionate to the gravity of D's offence, a court may grant D a constitutional exemption. Although the provisions contravene *Charter* s. 7, they are saved by *Charter* s. 1. (per Taylor and Carrothers JJ.A.)

R. v. Aucoin (1987), 48 M.V.R. 154 (N.S. C.A.) — *See also*: *R. v. Stewart* (1991), 27 M.V.R. (2d) 187 (B.C. S.C.) — The mandatory minimum penalty of imprisonment for those found guilty of a second or subsequent drinking and driving offence does not violate *Charter* s. 15.

R. v. Chabot (1992), 77 C.C.C. (3d) 371 (Que. C.A.) — In the absence of a challenge to the constitutional validity of the minimum punishment provisions of s. 255(1), the sentencing judge had no authority to impose a sentence less than the statutory minimum. *Charter* s. 24(1) does *not* provide a basis to order P to pay damages to D in criminal proceedings.

R. v. Tardif (1983), 37 C.R. (3d) 95, 9 C.C.C. (3d) 223 (Sask. C.A.) — The mandatory jail sentence for a second offence of failing to provide a sample does not contravene *Charter* s. 7. Such an offender is not morally innocent, and the provision is not unreasonable considering the element of the protection of the public.

Charter Considerations — Non-Proclamation

R. v. Van Vliet (1988), 45 C.C.C. (3d) 481 (B.C. C.A.) — D's equality rights under the *Charter* are not violated by the failure to proclaim subsection (5) into force in British Columbia. The *Charter* may be used to enact legislation.

R. v. Jackson (1993), 80 C.C.C. (3d) 22 (Nfld. C.A.) — The failure to proclaim in force in all provinces *Code* s. 255(5) does *not* violate the equality rights of D in Newfoundland where the provision has not been proclaimed.

R. v. Alton (1989), 74 C.R. (3d) 124, 53 C.C.C. (3d) 252 (Ont. C.A.) — Lack of universal proclamation of s. 255 does not offend *Charter* s. 15. The section *not* having been proclaimed in Ontario, curative treatment is not available in Ontario.

R. v. Ellsworth (1988), 46 C.C.C. (3d) 442 (Que. C.A.) — Unequal application of s. 255(5) resulting from the failure to proclaim it in all provinces, including Quebec, does not constitute discrimination.

R. v. Schneider (1986), 43 M.V.R. 223 (Sask. C.A.) — The failure to proclaim the section in all provinces does not infringe the *Charter*.

Related Provisions: By s. 227, no offence is committed under subsection (3) unless V's death occurs within one year and a day of the occurrence of the events described in the section.

Under s. 255(1), where P proceeds by indictment, D may elect mode of trial under s. 536(2). Where P proceeds by summary conviction, the offence is tried under Part XXVII, but is subject to the punishment provided in s. 255(1)(a) or (c), as the case may be, not the general punishment of s. 787(1). D may elect mode of trial under s. 536(2) in respect of the offences of ss. 255(2) and (3).

Several provisions in this group of sections assist P in its proof of the essential elements of the offences described in the section. Sections 254(2)–(4) authorize the making of demands by peace officers, thereafter, the taking of samples of breath or blood for the purposes of alcohol content analysis. Section 256 describes the circumstances under which a warrant may issue to take samples of blood for alcohol content analysis. Section 258 enacts a series of presumptions which become engaged upon the introduction of evidence or proof of certain preliminary facts and assist P in its proof of the essential elements of the offences of s. 253, hence ss. 255(2) and (3) of this section. Previous convictions may be proven in accordance with ss. 727 and 667.

Convictions, as well as discharges, under ss. 253 and 254 attract the mandatory operating prohibition order of s. 259(1). Similar dispositions under ss. 255(2) and (3) engage the discretionary authority of s. 259(2). Either order may be stayed pending appeal under s. 261.

256. (1) Warrants to obtain blood samples — Subject to subsection (2), where a justice is satisfied, on an information on oath in Form 1 or on an information on oath submitted to the justice pursuant to section 487.1 by telephone or other means of tele-communication, that there are reasonable grounds to believe that

(a) a person has, within the preceding four hours, committed, as a result of the consumption of alcohol, an offence under, section 253 and the person was involved in an accident resulting in the death of another person or in bodily harm to himself or herself or to any other person, and

(b) a qualified medical practitioner is of the opinion that

(i) by reason of any physical or mental condition of the person that resulted from the consumption of alcohol, the accident or any other occurrence related to or resulting from the accident, the person is unable to consent to the taking of samples of his blood, and

(ii) the taking of samples of blood from the person would not endanger the life or health of the person,

the justice may issue a warrant authorizing a peace officer to require a qualified medical practitioner to take, or to cause to be taken by a qualified technician under the direction of the qualified medical practitioner, such samples of the blood of the person as in the opinion of the person taking the samples are necessary to enable a proper analysis to be made in order to determine the concentration, if any, of alcohol in his blood.

(2) **Form** — A warrant issued pursuant to subsection (1) may be in Form 5 or 5.1 varied to suit the case.

(3) **Information on oath** — Notwithstanding paragraphs 487.1(4)(*b*) and (*c*), an information on oath submitted by telephone or other means of telecommunication for the purposes of this section shall include, instead of the statements referred to in those paragraphs, a statement setting out the offence alleged to have been committed and identifying the person from whom blood samples are to be taken.

(4) **Duration of warrant** — Samples of blood may be taken from a person pursuant to a warrant issued pursuant to subsection (1) only during such time as a qualified medical practitioner is satisfied that the conditions referred to in subparagraphs (1)(*b*)(i) and (ii) continue to exist in respect of that person.

(5) **Facsimile to person** — Where a warrant issued pursuant to subsection (1) is executed, the peace officer shall, as soon as practicable thereafter, give a copy or, in the case of a warrant issued by telephone or other means of telecommunication, a facsimile of the warrant to the person from whom the blood samples were taken.

R.S., c. C-34, s. 238; 1972, c. 13, s. 18; 1974–75–76, c. 93, s. 19;R.S. 1985, c. 27 (1st Supp.), s. 36; 1992, c. 1, s. 58(1); 1994, c. 4, s. 13.

Commentary: The section authorizes the issuance and execution of a warrant to take blood samples. Under s. 256(1), information on oath in Form 1 or by telephone or other means of telecommunication pursuant to s. 487.1, must be submitted to a justice. Under s. 256(3) the information must include a statement setting out the alleged offence and identifying the person whose blood samples it is proposed to take. The justice must be satisfied upon the basis of the information that there are reasonable grounds to believe that the conditions of ss. 256(1)(a) and (b) have been met. The requirements of the paragraphs are cumulative and involve both *probable participation* in an alcohol related offence under s. 253 that involves an accident resulting in death or bodily harm to another person (s. 256(a)) and *medical necessity*. The warrant issued may be in Form 5 or 5.1, varied to suit the case. It authorizes a peace officer to require a qualified medical practitioner to take, or to cause to be taken by a qualified technician under the direction of a qualified medical practitioner such samples of the blood of the person as in the opinion of the person taking the samples are necessary to enable a proper alcohol content analysis to be made.

The warrant is executed under ss. 256(4) and (5). Under s. 256(4), the samples may be taken only during such time as a qualified medical practitioner remains satisfied that the conditions of s. 256(1)(b) continue to exist in respect of the subject. As soon as practicable after the execution of the warrant, a peace officer is required by s. 256(5) to provide to the person whose blood samples have been taken an actual or facsimile copy of the warrant.

The subsection is subject to *Charter* s. 8 scrutiny.

Case Law

Charter Considerations [See also case digests under "Charter Considerations — Blood Samples", s. 255]

R. v. Colarusso (1994), 26 C.R. (4th) 289 (S.C.C.); affirming (1991), 28 M.V.R. (2d) 7 (Ont. C.A.) — The use by the police of blood samples, taken for medical purposes and seized by the coroner without warrant pursuant to his statutory authority, which the police had been given by the coroner for transport to a lab only, is a seizure which violates *Charter* s. 8. However, the admission of the results of the blood alcohol analysis would not bring the administration of justice into disrepute.

R. v. Dersch (1993), 25 C.R. (4th) 88, 85 C.C.C. (3d) 1 (S.C.C.); reversing (1992), 65 C.C.C. (3d) 252 (B.C. C.A.) — Although the taking of a blood sample by a physician solely for medical purposes is not subject to *Charter* scrutiny, the taking of the sample over D's objection was improper. Further, the provision to the police of the results of a blood alcohol test performed on the sample, without D's consent to disclose, violated the doctor's common law duty of confidentiality to D. The obtaining of that information by the police without a search warrant violated *Charter* s. 8 and it should be excluded under s. 24(2).

R. v. Erickson (1993), 81 C.C.C. (3d) 447 (S.C.C.); affirming (1992), 72 C.C.C. (3d) 75 (Alta. C.A.) — The seizure of blood samples and hospital records pursuant to search warrants obtained after a doctor showed the police officer the alcohol screen results, violated s. 8 of the *Charter*, but as the evidence was real evidence it should not be excluded under s. 24(2).

R. v. Dyment (1988), 66 C.R. (3d) 348, 45 C.C.C. (3d) 244 (S.C.C.) — A warrantless seizure by the police of a blood sample taken at hospital by a physician for medical purposes was unreasonable and a contravention of *Charter* s. 8.

R. v. Pohoretsky (1987), 58 C.R. (3d) 113, 33 C.C.C. (3d) 398 (S.C.C.) — The taking of a blood sample, without a warrant or statutory authority, while D was unconscious after a motor vehicle accident constituted an unreasonable seizure contrary to *Charter* s. 8, and the admission of the blood sample as evidence was likely to bring the administration of justice into disrepute.

R. v. Lunn (1990), 61 C.C.C. (3d) 193, 26 M.V.R. (2d) 209 (B.C. C.A.) — A failure to make the demand for a blood sample under s. 254(3) does not render a sample taken by medical personnel inadmissible, where the police have obtained it by executing a search warrant at the hospital, nor is there a breach of the *Charter* where medical personnel confirm to the police the existence of such a sample so that a warrant can be executed.

R. v. McGrath (1994), 30 C.R. (4th) 132, 3 M.V.R. (3d) 192 (Nfld. C.A.) — Where the police obtained a warrant authorizing the taking of blood rather than the seizure of results of blood tests performed for medical reasons, *Charter* s. 8 was violated but the test results were admissible.

R. v. Katsigiorgis (1987), 4 M.V.R. (2d) 102, 39 C.C.C. (3d) 256 (Ont. C.A.) — A police officer who asked a doctor if he could put a seal for continuity purposes on one of the vials of blood that had been taken under routine hospital procedure was held to have had reasonable and probable grounds to protect the blood samples in the course of his investigation of a fatal accident where alcohol was suspected to have been involved, in order to effectively execute the search warrant that was subsequently issued.

Related Provisions: "Peace officer" and "justice" are defined in s. 2, "qualified medical practitioner" and "qualified technician" in s. 254(1).

The general provisions relating to conventional search warrants and telewarrants are found in ss. 487 and 487.1.

In proceedings under s. 255(1) in respect of an offence under s. 253, as well as in proceedings under ss. 255(2) and (3), the provisions of ss. 258(1)(d), (h) and (i) may become engaged to assist P in the proof of the concentration of alcohol in D's blood at the material time. Upon summary application under s. 258(4), D may obtain one of the blood samples for examination or analysis, subject to appropriate terms to ensure its safeguarding and preservation for subsequent use. Samples taken under s. 256 may also be tested for the presence of drugs under s. 258(5).

The notice requirements of s. 258(7) and the extent to which cross examination may be permitted under s. 258(6) apply in respect of the certificates of ss. 258(1)(h) and (i) only.

Section 257(1) exempts qualified medical practitioners from criminal liability in respect of any refusal to take or cause to be taken blood samples under this section. Section 257(2) exempts qualified medical practitioners and qualified technicians from criminal and civil liability for anything necessarily done with reasonable care and skill in the taking of a blood sample under the section.

257. (1) No offence committed — No qualified medical practitioner or qualified technician is guilty of an offence only by reason of his refusal to take a sample of blood from a person for the purposes of section 254 or 256 and no qualified medical practitioner is guilty of an offence only by reason of his refusal to cause to be taken by a qualified technician under his direction a sample of blood from a person for such purposes.

(2) No criminal or civil liability — No qualified medical practitioner by whom or under whose direction a sample of blood is taken from a person pursuant to a demand made under subsection 254(3) or a warrant issued under section 256 and no qualified technician acting under the direction of a qualified medical practitioner incurs any criminal or civil liability for anything necessarily done with reasonable care and skill in the taking of such a sample of blood.

R.S., c. C-34, s. 239; R.S. 1985, c. 27 (1st Supp.), s. 36.

Commentary: The section describes the circumstances under which criminal and civil liability will not be incurred by a qualified medical practitioner or qualified technician, as the case may be, involved in the taking of blood samples.

Section 257(1) applies where the qualified medical practitioner or qualified technician refuses to take a blood sample from a person for the purposes of s. 254 or 256. In neither case is an offence committed only by reason of such refusal.

Section 257(2) applies where a qualified medical practitioner or qualified technician, under the direction of a qualified medical practitioner, has taken a sample of blood pursuant to a demand made under s. 254(3) or a warrant under s. 256. Neither the qualified technician acting under the direction of the qualified medical practitioner nor the qualified medical practitioner himself incurs any criminal or civil liability for anything necessarily done with reasonable care and skill in the taking of the blood sample.

Related Provisions: "Qualified medical practitioner" and "qualified technician" are defined in s. 254(1).

Section 25 affords general protection to persons administering and enforcing the law and defines the limits within which such persons may use force. Excessive force attracts criminal responsibility under s. 26, according to the nature and quality of the act that constitutes the excess.

258. (1) Proceedings under section 255 — In any proceedings under subsection 255(1) in respect of an offence committed under section 253 or in any proceedings under subsection 255(2) or (3),

(a) where it is proved that the accused occupied the seat or position ordinarily occupied by a person who operates a motor vehicle, vessel, aircraft or railway equipment or who assists in the operation of an aircraft or of railway equipment, the accused shall be deemed to have had the care or control of the vehicle, vessel, aircraft or railway equipment, as the case may be, unless the accused establishes that the accused did not occupy that seat or position for the purpose of setting the vehicle, vessel, aircraft or railway equipment in motion or assisting in the operation of the aircraft or railway equipment, as the case may be;

(b) the result of an analysis of a sample of the breath or blood of the accused (other than a sample taken pursuant to a demand made under subsection 254(3)) or of the urine or other bodily substance of the accused may be admitted in evidence notwithstanding that, before the accused gave the sample, he was not warned that he need not give the sample or that the result of the analysis of the sample might be used in evidence;

(c) where samples of the breath of the accused have been taken pursuant to a demand made under subsection 254(3), if

Proposed Addition — 258(1)(c)

(i) at the time each sample was taken, the person taking the sample offered to provide to the accused a specimen of the breath of the accused in an approved container for his own use, and, at the request of the accused made at thet time, such a specimen was thereupon provided to the accused,

R.S. 1985, c. 27 (1st Supp.), s. 36. [Not in force at date of publication.]

(ii) each sample was taken as soon as practicable after the time when the offence was alleged to have been committed and, in the case of the first sample, not later than two hours after that time, with an interval of at least fifteen minutes between the times when the samples were taken,

(iii) each sample was received from the accused directly into an approved container or into an approved instrument operated by a qualified technician, and

(iv) an analysis of each sample was made by means of an approved instrument operated by a qualified technician,

evidence of the results of the analyses so made is, in the absence of evidence to the contrary, proof that the concentration of alcohol in the blood of the accused at the time when the offence was alleged to have been committed was, where the results of the analyses are the same, the concentration determined by the analyses and, where the results of the analyses are different, the lowest of the concentrations determined by the analyses;

(d) where a sample of the blood of the accused has been taken pursuant to a demand made under subsection 254(3) or otherwise with the consent of the accused or pursuant to a warrant issued under section 256, if

(i) at the time the sample was taken, the person taking the sample took an additional sample of the blood of the accused and one of the samples was retained, to permit an analysis thereof to be made by or on behalf of the accused and, in the case where the accused makes a request within six months from the taking of the samples, one of the samples was ordered to be released pursuant to subsection (4),

(ii) both samples referred to in subparagraph (i) were taken as soon as practicable after the time when the offence was alleged to have been committed and in any event not later than two hours after that time,

(iii) both samples referred to in subparagraph (i) were taken by a qualified medical practitioner or a qualified technician under the direction of a qualified medical practitioner,

(iv) both samples referred to in subparagraph (i) were received from the accused directly into, or placed directly into, approved containers that were subsequently sealed, and

(v) an analysis was made by an analyst of at least one of the samples that was contained in a sealed approved container,

evidence of the result of the analysis is, in the absence of evidence to the contrary, proof that the concentration of alcohol in the blood of the accused at the time when the offence was alleged to have been committed was the concentration determined by the analysis or, where more than one sample was analyzed and results of the analyses are the same, the concentration determined by the analyses and, where the results of the analyses are different, the lowest of the concentrations determined by the analyses;

(d.1) where samples of the breath of the accused or a sample of the blood of the accused have been taken as described in paragraph (c) or (d) under the conditions described therein and the results of the analyses show a concentration of alcohol in blood exceeding eighty milligrams of alcohol in one hundred millilitres of blood, evidence of the result of the analyses is, in the absence of evidence tending to show that the concentration of alcohol in the blood of the accused at the time when the offence was alleged to have been committed did not exceed eighty milligrams of alcohol in one hundred millilitres of blood, proof that the concentration of alcohol in the blood of the accused at the time when the offence was alleged to have been committed exceeded eighty milligrams of alcohol in one hundred millilitres of blood;

(e) a certificate of an analyst stating that the analyst has made an analysis of a sample of the blood, urine, breath or other bodily substance of the accused and stating the result of that analysis is evidence of the facts alleged in the certificate without proof of the signature or the official character of the person appearing to have signed the certificate;

(f) a certificate of an analyst stating that the analyst has made an analysis of a sample of an alcohol standard that is identified in the certificate and intended for use with an approved instrument and that the sample of the standard analyzed by the analyst was found to be suitable for use with an approved instrument, is evidence that the alcohol standard so identified is suitable for use with an approved instrument without proof of the signature or the official character of the person appearing to have signed the certificate;

(g) where samples of the breath of the accused have been taken pursuant to a demand made under subsection 254(3), a certificate of a qualified technician stating

(i) that the analysis of each of the samples has been made by means of an approved instrument operated by the technician and ascertained by the technician to be in proper working order by means of an alcohol standard, identified in the certificate, that is suitable for use with an approved instrument,

(ii) the results of the analyses so made, and

(iii) if the samples were taken by the technician,

Proposed Addition — 258(1)(g)(iii)

(A) that at the time each sample was taken the technician offered to provide the accused with a specimen of the breath of the accused in an approved container for his own use and, at the request of the accused made at that time, the accused was thereupon provided with such a specimen,

R.S. 1985, c. 27 (1st Supp.), s. 36. [Not in force at date of publication.]

(B) the time when and place where each sample and any specimen described in clause (A) was taken, and

(C) that each sample was received from the accused directly into an approved container or into an approved instrument operated by the technician,

is evidence of the facts alleged in the certificate without proof of the signature or the official character of the person appearing to have signed the certificate;

(h) where a sample of the blood of the accused has been taken pursuant to a demand made under subsection 254(3) or otherwise with the consent of the accused or pursuant to a warrant issued under section 256,

(i) a certificate of a qualified medical practitioner stating that

(A) the medical practitioner took the sample and that before the sample was taken he was of the opinion that the taking of blood samples from the accused would not endanger the life or health of the accused and, in the case of a demand made pursuant to a warrant issued pursuant to section 256, that by reason of any physical or mental condition of the accused that resulted from the consumption of alcohol, the accident or any other occurrence related to or resulting from the accident, the accused was unable to consent to the taking of his blood,

(B) at the time the sample was taken, an additional sample of the blood of the accused was taken to permit analysis of one of the samples to be made by or on behalf of the accused,

(C) the time when and place where both samples referred to in clause (B) were taken, and

(D) both samples referred to in clause (B) were received from the accused directly into, or placed directly into, approved containers that were subsequently sealed and that are identified in the certificate,

(ii) a certificate of a qualified medical practitioner stating that the medical practitioner caused the sample to be taken by a qualified technician under his direction and that before the sample was taken the qualified medical practitioner was of the opinion referred to in clause (i)(A), or

(iii) a certificate of a qualified technician stating that the technician took the sample and the facts referred to in clauses (i)(B) to (D)

is evidence of the facts alleged in the certificate without proof of the signature or official character of the person appearing to have signed the certificate; and

(i) a certificate of an analyst stating that the analyst has made an analysis of a sample of the blood of the accused that was contained in a sealed approved container identified in the certificate, the date on which and place where the sample was analyzed and the result of that analysis is evidence of the facts alleged in the certificate without proof of the signature or official character of the person appearing to have signed it.

(2) **No obligation to give sample except as required under s. 254** — No person is required to give a sample of urine or other bodily substance for analysis for the purposes of this section except breath or blood as required under section 254, and evidence that a person failed or refused to give such a sample or that such a sample was not taken is not admissible nor shall such a failure or refusal or the fact that a sample was not taken be the subject of comment by any person in the proceedings.

(3) Evidence of failure to comply with demand — In any proceedings under subsection 255(1) in respect of an offence committed under paragraph 253(*a*) or in any proceedings under subsection 255(2) or (3), evidence that the accused, without reasonable excuse, failed or refused to comply with a demand made to him by a peace officer under section 254 is admissible and the court may draw an inference therefrom adverse to the accused.

(4) Release of specimen for testing — A judge of a superior court of criminal jurisdiction or a court of criminal jurisdiction shall, on the summary application of the accused made within six months from the day on which samples of the blood of the accused were taken, order the release of one of the samples for the purpose of an examination or analysis thereof, subject to such terms as appear to be necessary or desirable to ensure the safeguarding of the sample and its preservation for use in any proceedings in respect of which it was retained.

(5) Testing blood for presence of drugs — Where a sample of blood of an accused has been taken pursuant to a demand made under subsection 254(3) or otherwise with the consent of the accused or pursuant to a warrant issued under section 256, the sample may be tested for the presence of drugs in the blood of the accused.

(6) Attendance and right to cross-examine — A party against whom a certificate described in paragraph (1)(*e*), (*f*), (*g*), (*h*) or (*i*) is produced may, with leave of the court, require the attendance of the qualified medical practitioner, analyst or qualified technician, as the case may be, for the purposes of cross-examination.

(7) Notice of intention to produce certificate — No certificate shall be received in evidence pursuant to paragraph (1)(*e*), (*f*), (*g*), (*h*) or (*i*) unless the party intending to produce it has, before the trial, given to the other party reasonable notice of his intention and a copy of the certificate.

R.S., c. C-34, s. 240; 1972, c. 13, s. 19; R.S. 1985, c. 27 (1st Supp.), s. 36; c. 32 (4th Supp.), s. 61; 1994, c. 44, s. 14; 1997, c. 18, s. 10.

Paragraphs 258(1)(f) and (g) [incorrectly noted in R.S. 1985, c. 27 (1st Supp.), s. 204 as paragraphs 255(1)(f) and (g)] of the Code, as they read immediately before the coming into force of the amendments to those paragraphs, as enacted by s. 36 of the Criminal Law Amendment Act, 1985, R.S. 1985, c. 27 (1st Supp.), continue to apply to any proceedings in respect of which a certificate referred to in those paragraphs was issued prior to the coming into force of the amendments to those paragraphs.

Commentary: The section enacts a number of evidentiary and procedural provisions applicable to the trial of offences created by this group of sections. The evidentiary rules assist P in its proof of the essential elements of the offences.

Section 258(1) applies only in prosecutions for listed offences. Sections 258(1)(e)–(i) permit proof by certificate of matters there asserted and certified by an analyst, qualified medical practitioner or qualified technician, as the case may be. Proof of the signature or official character of the person appearing to have signed the certificate is not required. Section 258(6) permits D, with leave of the court, to require the attendance of the qualified medical practitioner, analyst or qualified technician, as the case may be, for the purposes of cross-examination. Section 258(7) imposes a two-part notice requirement as a condition precedent to the reception of the certificate into evidence. D must be given *reasonable notice* of P's *intention* to adduce the certificate as evidence and *a copy of the certificate*.

Sections 258(1)(c) and (d) permit the reception of evidence of the results of analysis made of breath or blood samples taken in accordance with the requirements of the applicable paragraphs. Compliance with such requirements compels proof of the matters stated in the applicable paragraphs, in the absence of evidence to the contrary.

Section 258(1)(d.1) compels proof, in the absence of evidence tending to show a reading under the prohibited concentration, that the accused had a blood alcohol concentration of eighty milligrams of alcohol in one hundred milliliters of blood at the time when the offence was alleged to have been committed, where samples have been taken in accordance with s. 258(1)(c) and (d) and the results of the analyses show such a concentration.

P's proof of the essential element of care or control of a conveyance in prosecutions under ss. 253 and 255(2) and (3) is assisted by the provisions of s. 258(1)(a). Upon *proof* that D occupied the seat or position ordinarily occupied by the operator of a motor vehicle, vessel or aircraft or one who assists in the operation of an aircraft or railway equipment, D is presumed to have had the care or control of the conveyance, unless D establishes that s/he did not occupy that seat or position for the purpose of setting the vehicle, vessel, aircraft or railway equipment in motion or assisting in the operation of the aircraft or railway equipment, as the case may be.

Section 258(1)(b) permits the reception of evidence of the results of an analysis of a breath or blood sample, other than a sample taken pursuant to a s. 254(3) demand, as well as a sample of urine or other bodily substance, upon the trial of a listed offence, notwithstanding that D was *not* warned that s/he need not give the sample or that the result might be given in evidence. Section 258(2) makes it clear that there is no general obligation to give a sample of urine or other bodily substance for analysis, apart from breath or blood under s. 254. The section further provides that D's refusal or failure to provide such a sample of urine or other bodily substance is not admissible in evidence. Neither may the failure or refusal or the fact that no such sample was taken be the subject of *any* comment in the proceedings. Under s. 258(3), however, in proceedings under s. 255(1) in respect of an offence under s. 253(a), as well as in proceedings under ss. 255(2) and (3), evidence that D, without reasonable excuse, failed or refused to comply with a s. 254 demand is admissible and may be used to found an inference adverse to D. Section 258(5) permits a blood sample taken pursuant to a s. 254(3) demand, on consent or by warrant under s. 256 to be tested for drugs as well.

Section 258(4) permits D, upon summary application to a judge of a superior court of criminal jurisdiction within six months of the date of the taking of the samples, to obtain one of the *blood* samples for examination or analysis, subject to appropriate terms regarding preservation.

The sections which create presumptions have been challenged under *Charter* ss. 7 and 11(d).

Case Law
Presumption of Care or Control

Ford v. R. (1982), 65 C.C.C. (2d) 392 (S.C.C.) — Subsection (1)(a) does *not* create a defence to the charge, as its effect is only evidentiary. Where D establishes that he did not mount the vehicle for the purpose of setting it in motion, the burden of proof shifts back to P without the aid of the statutory presumption. However, it is not an essential element of the offence that D had the purpose or intention of setting the vehicle in motion, as care or control may be exercised where D performs some act or series of acts involving the use of the car, its fittings or equipment whereby the vehicle may unintentionally be set in motion.

R. v. Bennett (1970), 11 C.R.N.S. 180, [1970] 5 C.C.C. 4 (N.S. C.A.) — P does *not* need to rely on the presumption, and, if it can prove care or control without the presumption, the fact that the evidence does not fall within the ambit of the presumption is of no consequence.

Rebutting the Presumption of Care or Control

R. v. Appleby (1971), 16 C.R.N.S. 35, 3 C.C.C. (2d) 354 (S.C.C.) — The standard of proof required to rebut the presumption of care or control is by a preponderance of evidence or by a balance of probabilities, and in the absence of such proof the presumption will prevail.

R. v. George (1994), 90 C.C.C. (3d) 502, 5 M.V.R. (3d) 1 (Nfld. C.A.) — Proof of indecision on the part of D as to whether or not to set the vehicle in motion does not rebut the presumption.

R. v. Hatfield (1997), 115 C.C.C. (3d) 47 (Ont. C.A.) — The fact that the driver's seat was fully reclined does *not* rebut the statutory presumption where there is evidence that D drove to the place where the seat position was altered.

R. v. McGuigan (1974), 7 Nfld. & P.E.I.R. 190 (P.E.I. C.A.) — The presumption can be rebutted by evidence establishing that D did not enter the vehicle for the purpose of setting it in motion. If, however, in giving that evidence, D "establishes" also that he had care or control, he will rebut the presumption but may well provide sufficient evidence to warrant a conviction.

R. v. Johnson (1986), 29 C.C.C. (3d) 395 (Sask. C.A.); reversing (1985), 37 M.V.R. 122 (Sask. Q.B.) — The presumption is not applicable if it is proved that D did not enter the vehicle for the purpose of setting it in motion.

Presumption of Care or Control — Charter Considerations

R. v. Whyte (1988), 64 C.R. (3d) 123, 42 C.C.C. (3d) 97 (S.C.C.) — This section requires the trier of fact to accept as proven that D had care or control of a vehicle, an essential element of the offence, by virtue of his occupancy of the driver's seat in spite of a reasonable doubt about the existence of that element. This violates the presumption of innocence guaranteed by *Charter* s. 11(d). However, the provision is saved by *Charter* s. 1 since the objective of protecting the public against drunk drivers is sufficiently important to override a constitutionally protected right and the means used is proportional to the objective.

Presumption of Alcohol Concentration

R. v. St. Pierre, 36 C.R. (4th) 273, 96 C.C.C. (3d) 385, [1995] 1 S.C.R. 791 (S.C.C.); reversing (1992), 76 C.C.C. (3d) 249, 16 C.R. (4th) 220 (Ont. C.A.) — The presumption of identity in s. 258(1)(c) assists P over the hurdle of having to prove in every case that D's blood alcohol level at the time of driving was the same as at the time of testing.

R. v. Deruelle (1992), 15 C.R. (4th) 215, 75 C.C.C. (3d) 118 (S.C.C.) — The two-hour limit of s. 254(3) contributes to the objective of the broader breathalyzer scheme in the *Code* by forcing prompt police investigation, and further by requiring the police to take the sample as soon as practicable. This purpose goes to the *admissibility* of the sample as evidence, and is distinguishable from the purpose of the time limit in the presumption of s. 258(1)(c), which provides a procedural shortcut for the police, but only where the sample has been obtained within two hours of the alleged offence.

Lightfoot v. R. (1981), 24 C.R. (3d) 323 (S.C.C.) — The statutory presumption is available to P upon proof, by certificate or by oral evidence, of the three requirements specified in the section. P is not required to prove the suitability of the substance or solution used in the breathalyzer.

R. v. Noble (1978), 40 C.R.N.S. 19 (S.C.C.); affirming (1976), 32 C.C.C. (2d) 68 (N.B. C.A.) — A certificate is inadmissible and the presumption is unavailable if only one sample is mentioned in it. However, P may prove its case by calling expert evidence to compliment the *viva voce* evidence of the technician.

R. v. Aujla (1989), 47 C.C.C. (3d) 481 (B.C. C.A.) — Where D does not see the certificate of analysis for almost four months after the giving of blood samples, the three-month period within which D could apply under subsection (4) for release of one of the samples having expired, P fails to meet the conditions precedent in subsection (1)(d)(i) for admission of the certificate.

R. v. Ross (1996), 108 C.C.C. (3d) 168 — Failure to give notice of the existence of a second blood sample only disentitles P's reliance on the *presumption* of blood alcohol concentration. P is entitled to adduce *viva voce* evidence of a doctor and analyst to prove the blood alcohol level.

R. v. Grosse (1996), 107 C.C.C. (3d) 97 (Ont. C.A.) — Where P *cannot* rely on s. 258(1)(c) *Code* presumption, the case against D must be proven in the ordinary way.

Presumption of Alcohol Concentration — Charter Considerations

R. v. Duke (1972), 18 C.R.N.S. 302, 7 C.C.C. (2d) 474 (S.C.C.) — The refusal or omission by P to give D a specimen of his breath for analysis did not deprive D of a fair hearing.

R. v. Lefebvre (1988), 9 M.V.R. (2d) 304 (Alta. Q.B.) — P is not required to provide the defence with a random sampling of ampoules used in the breathalyzer tests. The technician will be available for cross-examination at trial, and D's rights under *Charter* s. 7 are not infringed.

R. v. Alexander (1988), 93 N.B.R. (2d) 77 (C.A.) — Putting D in a cell immediately after obtaining a breath sample instead of releasing him in accordance with ss. 497 and 498, without providing a justification for such detention and knowing that the continued detention would have effectively prevented D from his announced intention of obtaining independent blood samples, violated D's rights under *Charter* ss. 7, 9 and 11(d).

R. v. Langille (1992), 42 M.V.R (2d) 116 (N.S. C.A.) — The non-proclamation of the "container clauses" in ss. 258(1)(c)(i) and 258(1)(g)(iii)(A) does not offend s. 7 of the *Charter.*

R. v. Eagles (1989), 68 C.R. (3d) 271, 47 C.C.C. (3d) 129 (N.S. C.A.) — *See also: R. v. Hodgson* (1991), 24 M.V.R. (2d) 42 (B.C. C.A.); *R. v. Dunn* (1990), 26 M.V.R. (2d) 34 (Ont. Gen. Div.) — D's right under *Charter* s. 7 to make full answer and defence was not infringed by the nonproduction of a representative ampoule, where it was not shown that its production and examination would have any meaningful capacity to advance the defence.

R. v. Phillips (1988), 64 C.R. (3d) 154, 42 C.C.C. (3d) 150 (Ont. C.A.) — Although this provision infringes *Charter* s. 11(d), *Charter* s. 1 operates to save it. The three components of the Supreme Court's proportionality test are satisfied in that the provision is carefully designed to achieve the objective of controlling drunk driving, it impairs the *Charter* right as little as possible, and its effects are proportional to its objectives.

R. v. Potma (1983), 31 C.R. (3d) 231, 2 C.C.C. (3d) 383 (Ont. C.A.); leave to appeal refused (1983), 33 C.R. (3d) xxv (S.C.C.) — The failure of the police to turn over the test and reference ampoules used in D's breathalyzer tests to her lawyer for independent testing did not violate D's rights to fundamental justice and a fair trial.

R. v. Bourget (1987), 56 C.R. (3d) 97, 35 C.C.C. (3d) 371 (Sask. C.A.) — P is required to provide sample ampoules upon request by D. Failure to provide such samples constitutes a violation of D's rights under *Charter* s. 7 as well as the opportunity to make full answer and defence.

R. v. Kalafut (1988), 8 M.V.R (2d) 185 (Sask Q.B.) — A *bona fide* request by defence counsel for a sample ampoule of the standard alcohol solution used in the breathalyzer five months after the alleged offence took place is not untimely. Where the request cannot be granted as the solution lot was completely used up in other tests, a stay of proceedings is appropriate to protect D's *Charter* right to make full answer and defence.

Presumption of Alcohol Concentration — As Soon As Practicable

R. v. Hafermehl (1993), 50 M.V.R. (2d) 78 (Alta. C.A) — The test is whether the breath tests were administered "within a reasonably prompt time under the circumstances". Where a police officer *reasonably* believes a vehicle poses a danger to the travelling public or that there is a risk to the security of the vehicle or its contents, a reasonable delay is justified.

R. v. Rasmussen (1981), 64 C.C.C. (2d) 304 (B.C. C.A.); leave to appeal refused (1982), 42 N.R. 122 (S.C.C.) — *See also: R. v. Carter* (1980), 55 C.C.C. (2d) 405 (B.C. C.A.) — The trial judge must consider what was reasonably possible in light of all the circumstances. P is not required to account for every minute of the time that elapses.

R. v. Myrick (1995), 13 M.V.R. (3d) 1 (Nfld. C.A.) — Whether a breathalyzer test has been administered as soon as practicable is a question of law.

R. v. Altseimer (1982), 29 C.R. (3d) 276, 1 C.C.C. (3d) 7 (Ont. C.A.) — *See also: R. v. Payne* (1990), 56 C.C.C. (3d) 548 (Ont. C.A.); *R. v. Clarke* (1991), 27 M.V.R. (2d) 1 (Ont. C.A.) — "As soon as practicable" does not mean as soon as possible.

R. v. Carter (1981), 59 C.C.C. (2d) 450 (Sask. C.A.) — The requirement that the sample be taken as soon as practicable must be applied with reason. Only where a delay is not satisfactorily explained, or where such delay prejudices D should the certificate be inadmissible.

Presumption of Alcohol Concentration — Fifteen Minutes Apart

R. v. Perry (1978), 41 C.C.C. (2d) 182 (B.C. C.A.); affirmed (1980), 51 C.C.C. (2d) 576n (S.C.C.) — At least 15 minutes means 15 minutes or more. Breath samples taken at 3:00 a.m. and 3:15 a.m. complied with the requirement of a 15-minute interval.

R. v. Kornak (1984), 12 C.C.C. (3d) 182 (Alta. C.A.) — It is the taking of the samples, not their reading or analysis, that must be separated by at least 15 minutes.

R. v. Moore (1984), 13 C.C.C. (3d) 281 (B.C. C.A.) — *See also: R. v. DeCoste* (1984), 15 C.C.C. (3d) 289 (N.S. C.A.) — The *Code* does not require that the certificate state the time at which the taking of the first sample was completed and the time the taking of the second sample was commenced. A statement in the certificate that one sample was taken at a certain time and a second sample was taken 15 minutes later is conclusive and final.

R. v. Andrushko (1977), 40 C.R.N.S. 216, 37 C.C.C. (2d) 273 (Man. C.A.) — Non-compliance with the 15-minute requirement does not render a certificate inadmissible, but merely precludes P from relying on the presumption.

R. v. Atkinson (1986), 42 M.V.R. 78 (N.S. C.A.) — It is not necessary to state on a certificate the time when any of the breath tests were concluded. The test is taken when D blows into the machine and this takes no more than a moment.

R. v. Hayes (1985), 19 C.C.C. (3d) 569 (Ont. C.A.) — *See also: R. v. Daly* (1985), 32 M.V.R. 213 (Ont. C.A.); *R. v. Hogg* (1990), 25 M.V.R. (2d) 1 (Ont. C.A.) — The taking of a breath sample is completed when D's breath sample is inside the breathalyzer machine and that is the point in time from which to calculate the 15-minute interval. The period of time required to complete the analysis and obtain the result is not included in the measurement of the interval.

R. v. Perrier (1984), 15 C.C.C. (3d) 506 (Ont. C.A.) — The words "each sample" do not include any sample of which a proper analysis cannot be made; proper samples must satisfy the time constraints.

MacKay v. R. (1985), 32 M.V.R. 115 (P.E.I. C.A.) — *See also: R. v. Taylor* (1983), 7 C.C.C. (3d) 293 (Ont. C.A.) — The 15-minute interval is to be measured from the completion of the taking of the first sample to the beginning of the taking of the second. If the certificate states the time from the beginning of the taking of the first sample, evidence concerning the time involved in the taking of the sample must also be introduced.

Dawson v. R. (1984), 12 C.C.C. (3d) 152 (P.E.I. C.A.) — Each sample takes a different length of time to complete and without evidence as to the length of time it took for the breath samples to be taken it cannot be concluded beyond a reasonable doubt that an exact 15-minute interval occurred when the time was measured from completion of each sample.

Presedo v. R. (1984), 37 M.V.R. 134 (Que. C.A.) — When a certificate indicates a 20-minute interval between the taking of breath samples it is not necessary to specify the precise times when the first sample was completed and the second sample commenced because the taking of a single sample does not require more than 2 1/2 minutes.

Presumption of Alcohol Concentration — No Later Than Two Hours

R. v. Deruelle (1992), 15 C.R. (4th) 215, 75 C.C.C. (3d) 118 (S.C.C.) — Where a sample is taken more than two hours after the commission of the alleged offence, P loses the benefit of the presumption in s. 258(1)(c), but nothing more. The evidence obtained is nonetheless admissible *provided* the demanding officer formed a belief that, within the preceding two hours, D had committed an alcohol-driving offence.

R. v. Crawford (1979), 4 M.V.R. 1 (B.C. C.A.) — Where there was insufficient evidence that D had been driving within two hours of the time the tests were administered, evidence of the rate of removal of alcohol from the system of D was acceptable given by a police corporal whose training and experience as a technician rendered him qualified to give such an opinion.

R. v. Gale (1992), 65 C.C.C. (3d) 373, 32 M.V.R. (2d) 107 (Nfld. C.A.) — Where a blood sample is taken more than two hours after the alleged time of the offence, the presumption of alcohol concentration in s. 258(1)(d) does not apply. P can adduce evidence of the result of the analysis, but must adduce additional evidence to relate that result to the alleged time of the offence.

R. v. Montgomery (1992), 11 C.R. (4th) 313, 70 C.C.C. (3d) 229 (Ont. C.A.) — If P intends to rely on the presumption of alcohol concentration in s. 258, it must comply with all the conditions imposed by the section. Where D is not made aware of the charges against him/her, and the certificate evidence upon which P relies within three months of the taking of the samples, D is denied the opportunity of obtaining the statutorily mandated production of a sample for independent examination. A condition of s. 258 has not been complied with, and P cannot rely on the presumption.

Presumption of Alcohol Concentration — Lowest Reading

R. v. Adams (1982), 15 M.V.R. 152 (N.S. C.A.) — In the absence of evidence to the contrary, the lowest reading must be accepted as the proportion of alcohol in D's blood at the time of the alleged offence.

Evidence to the Contrary

R. v. St. Pierre, 36 C.R. (4th) 273, 96 C.C.C. (3d) 385, [1995] 1 S.C.R. 791 (S.C.C.); reversing (1992), 76 C.C.C. (3d) 249, 16 C.R. (4th) 220 (Ont. C.A.) — "Evidence to the contrary" in s. 258(1)(c) means evidence that shows that D's blood alcohol level at the time of driving was different from the level at the time of testing. It need not show that the level at the time of driving was below .08.

R. v. St. Pierre, 36 C.R. (4th) 273, 96 C.C.C. (3d) 385, [1995] 1 S.C.R. 791 (S.C.C.); reversing (1992), 76 C.C.C. (3d) 249, 16 C.R. (4th) 220 (Ont. C.A.) — The presumption of identity is a shortcut for P, a temporal presumption designed to simplify the evidentiary necessity of bridging the time gap between the breathalyzer test and the offence. If D is able to show that the shortcut ought not apply, and that his/her blood alcohol level was different at the time of driving than at the time of testing, the presumption of identity would be rebutted.

R. v. St. Pierre, 36 C.R. (4th) 273, 96 C.C.C. (3d) 385, [1995] 1 S.C.R. 791 (S.C.C.); reversing (1992), 76 C.C.C. (3d) 249, 16 C.R. (4th) 220 (Ont. C.A.) — The effect of normal biological processes of absorption and elimination of alcohol cannot by and of itself constitute "evidence to the contrary".

R. v. Crosthwait (1980), 52 C.C.C. (2d) 129 (S.C.C.) — In challenging the proper functioning of the breathalyzer machine, a mere possibility of some inaccuracy is not sufficient. Evidence tending to show an actual inaccuracy in the breathalyzer or in the manner of its operation is necessary.

R. v. Moreau (1979), 42 C.C.C. (2d) 525 (S.C.C.) — Evidence to the contrary has to be evidence which tends to establish that the proportion of alcohol in the blood of D at the time when the offence was alleged to have been committed was not the same as that indicated by the result of the chemical analysis. Evidence as to the inherent infallibility of the breathalyzer instrument or the possible uncertainty of elements of the legislative scheme is not evidence to the contrary.

R. v. Proudlock (1978), 5 C.R. (3d) 21, 43 C.C.C. (2d) 321 (S.C.C.) — To overcome the statutory presumption of fact all that is necessary is evidence raising a reasonable doubt. D may do this by giving evidence which, if believed, provides an explanation that may reasonably be true.

R. v. Hay (1991), 25 M.V.R. (2d) 121 (B.C. C.A.) — Evidence to the contrary is to be considered with all the other evidence for and against P's case and the ultimate question is whether it and everything else favourable to D raises a reasonable doubt on the whole of the case against D.

R. v. Mitchell (1987), 1 M.V.R. (2d) 220 (Nfld. C.A.) — The "evidence to the contrary" must be weighed by the court to determine if it is sufficient to support an inference of a reasonable doubt concerning the guilt of D.

R. v. Marcelli (1990), 54 C.C.C. (3d) 313 (N.S. C.A.) — Evidence to the contrary is not restricted to expert evidence.

R. v. Latour (1997), 116 C.C.C. (3d) 279 (Ont. C.A.) — Where there is *no* evidence of D's tolerance to alcohol, opinion evidence that normal, average persons with the same breathalyzer readings should exhibit stronger *indicia* of impairment than D is *not* capable of being "evidence to the contrary".

R. v. Auld (1987), 38 C.C.C (3d) 43 (Ont. Dist. Ct.); affirmed (1989), 49 C.C.C. (3d) 128n (Ont. C.A.) — Evidence which is rejected by the trier of fact does not constitute evidence to the contrary.

R. v. Kaminski (1992), 36 M.V.R. (2d) 169 (Sask. C.A.) — Once the trial judge finds "evidence to the contrary", s/he should find that the statutory presumption does not apply, and then weigh the whole of the evidence with a view to determining whether there is a reasonable doubt about D's blood alcohol concentration being in excess of the legal limit at the relevant time.

Actual Alcohol Consumption

R. v. Weir (1983), 56 A.R. 144 (C.A.) — Evidence from an expert witness that, considering the size of D the amount of alcohol D drank would produce a level below 80 mg of alcohol per 100 ml of blood was merely hypothetical and as such insufficient to rebut the presumption of his blood-alcohol level. It is necessary to present evidence of D's actual blood-alcohol level.

R. v. Hughes (1982), 30 C.R. (3d) 2, 70 C.C.C. (2d) 42 (Alta. C.A.) — *See also*: *R. v. St. Pierre* (1982), 70 C.C.C. (2d) 453 (Alta C.A.) — Simulation evidence based on D's own statements as to the quantity and rate of consumption of alcohol is admissible as evidence to the contrary. If the evidence is believed and not rejected and raises a reasonable doubt in the mind of the trier of fact as to whether D's blood-alcohol content was over .08, D should be acquitted.

R. v. Beauchesne (1987), 48 M.V.R. 52 (B.C. C.A.) — Expert evidence as to the effect of alcohol on D which was based solely on D's evidence as to how much he had to drink, which latter evidence the trial judge did not accept, did not constitute evidence to the contrary.

R. v. MacDonald (1988), 5 M.V.R. (2d) 187 (N.S. C.A.) — It is improper for a trial judge to conduct his own experiments as to the amount of alcohol consumed.

R. v. Andrews (1987), 3 M.V.R. (2d) 203 (N.S. C.A.); reversing (1987), 79 N.S.R. (2d) 267 (Co. Ct.) — Although the trial judge may take judicial notice of the fact that consumption of alcohol increases rather than decreases the blood alcohol level of an individual, he cannot take judicial notice of the extent to which consumption of a given amount of alcohol would have raised or lowered a subsequent reading.

R. v. Star (1983), 10 C.C.C. (3d) 363 (N.S. C.A) — Expert evidence showing that D's blood-breath alcohol partition ratio was substantially lower than the average measurement adopted for breathalyzer analysis had no probative value when unaccompanied by evidence and test results relating to what D actually ate and drank on the night in question.

Carter v. R. (1985), 19 C.C.C. (3d) 174 (Ont. C.A.) — Where the blood sample reading does not reflect the alcohol consumption testified to by D and D's testimony is believed, he has raised a doubt as to the accuracy of the reading, and he is not obliged to speculate where the error may have occurred.

Presumption of Alcohol Concentration — Post-Driving Alcohol Consumption

R. v. St. Pierre, 36 C.R. (4th) 273, 96 C.C.C. (3d) 385, [1995] 1 S.C.R. 791 (S.C.C.); reversing (1992), 76 C.C.C. (3d) 249, 16 C.R. (4th) 220 (Ont. C.A.) — The effect of normal biological processes of absorption and elimination of alcohol cannot by and of itself constitute "evidence to the contrary".

R. v. Kizan (1981), 58 C.C.C. (2d) 444 (B.C. C.A.) — Evidence of consumption of alcohol after the offence and before giving a breath sample is evidence to the contrary tending to show that the certificate reading does not reflect the condition of D at the time of the offence.

Gallagher v. R. (1981), 64 C.C.C. (2d) 533 (N.B. C.A.) — *See also*: *R. v. Creed* (1987), 7 M.V.R. (2d) 184 (P.E.I. C.A.) — Evidence of consumption of a quantity of liquor immediately prior to a breathalyzer demand, standing alone, did not constitute "evidence to the contrary". Some evidence of the effect of the alcohol on the result of the breathalyzer test was needed.

R. v. White (1986), 41 M.V.R. 82 (Nfld. C.A.) — "Evidence to the contrary" means evidence that the blood-alcohol level of D who claims he started consuming alcohol after his driving ceased, was increased to the extent that doubt remained as to whether D's blood-alcohol level was over the allowable limit at the time of the offence.

R. v. Batley (1985), 19 C.C.C. (3d) 382 (Sask. C.A.) — Evidence of alcohol consumption subsequent to the commission of the alleged offence is capable of constituting, but is not, in itself, evidence to the contrary.

Presumption of Alcohol Concentration — Inaccurate Breath Analysis

R. v. McMullen (1985), 19 C.C.C. (3d) 495 (B.C. C.A.) — Evidence of the technician concerning the possible effects of radio frequencies on the accuracy of the breathalyzer machine was nothing more than a basis for conjecture and speculation and was not capable of raising a reasonable doubt. Therefore, it was not evidence to the contrary.

R. v. Stewart (1984), 8 C.C.C. (3d) 368 (B.C. C.A.) — Evidence of the susceptibility of a breathalyzer machine to error caused by radio frequency interference is evidence capable of raising a reasonable doubt where it is shown that there was a possibility of such interference on the occasion that the readings were taken. In such a case the evidence is more than mere conjecture.

R. v. Underwood (1982), 3 C.C.C (3d) 94 (B.C. C.A.) — *See also*: *R. v. Westman* (1973), 11 C.C.C. (2d) 355 (Sask. C.A.) — Differences in the two breathalyzer readings does not constitute evidence to the contrary.

R. v. Raymond (1987), 77 N.S.R. (2d) 334 (C.A.) — The question as to whether burping constituted "evidence to the contrary" was one of fact to be decided by the trial judge. In this case the trial judge had rejected D's argument that a burp had resulted in a falsely high breathalyzer test.

R. v. Hatfield (1986), 75 N.S.R. (2d) 101 (C.A.) — Mere speculation as to the cause of a variation in breathalyzer readings does not constitute evidence to the contrary.

R. v. Fraser (1983), 6 C.C.C. (3d) 273 (N.S. C.A.) — The passing results of an A.L.E.R.T. test did not constitute "evidence to the contrary". The breathalyzer had been tested for accuracy, but there was no evidence that the A.L.E.R.T. device had been calibrated properly.

R. v. Kozun (1981), 64 C.C.C. (2d) 62 (Sask. C.A.) — The fact that three tests were taken but only two results recorded on the certificate did not by itself constitute "evidence to the contrary", causing the certificate to lose its probative value.

Inaccurate Blood Sample Analysis

R. v. Egger (1993), 82 C.C.C. (3d) 193 (S.C.C.); reversing (1991), 69 C.C.C. (3d) 97 (Alta. C.A.) — For the s. 258(1)(d) presumption to arise, D must have notice within the 3-month period that she/he is charged with an impaired driving offence, that P has had a sample of D's blood analyzed, and that a second sample was taken and is available for analysis by D. The most appropriate way to notify D is by service of the CQT (or CQMP). If notice is given by other means, it must be proven beyond a reasonable doubt. If not served when the samples are taken, the CQT or other notice should be given when the summons is served. The availability of the presumption is not dependent upon a court ordering the release of the second sample at D's request, but rather is available even if D takes no steps to obtain the second sample.

R. v. Smeltzer (1986), 40 M.V.R. 216 (N.S. C.A.); leave to appeal refused (1986), 74 N.S.R. (2d) 360 (S.C.C.) — *See also: R. v. Beers* (1985), 21 C.C.C. (3d) 417 (P.E.I. C.A.) — Where D was unable to adduce evidence concerning the properties of white powder which was observed at the bottom of vials in which samples of D's blood was placed and its possible effects on the accuracy of blood analysis, the existence of the white powder did not constitute evidence to the contrary.

R. v. Swinimer (1983), 25 M.V.R. 222 (N.S. C.A.) — To rebut the presumption in this section, the accused's evidence must tend to show that the sample was contaminated. There is no requirement that P prove that the sample of D's blood was not contaminated

Presumption of Alcohol Concentration — Certificate of Analysis as Proof

R. v. St. Pierre, 36 C.R. (4th) 273, 96 C.C.C. (3d) 385, [1995] 1 S.C.R. 791 (S.C.C.); reversing (1992), 76 C.C.C. (3d) 249, 16 C.R. (4th) 220 (Ont. C.A.) — The presumption of accuracy in s. 258(1)(g), together with s. 25 of the *Interpretation Act*, establishes a presumption that the reading received on the breathalyzer provides an accurate determination of D's blood alcohol level at the time of the testing.

R. v. Johnson (1985), 37 M.V.R. 306 (Alta. C.A.) — The identification of the solution by lot number in the certificate of analysis constitutes sufficient compliance with the *Code*.

R. v. Taylor (1985), 38 M.V.R. 263 (B.C. C.A.) — The description of the solution is required to include a reference to a lot number. Where a certificate of analysis does not adequately identify the solution, P is not entitled to supplement the omissions in the certificate with oral evidence.

R. v. Pearce (1984), 27 M.V.R. 128 (B.C. C.A.) — It was implicit in the certificate of analysis that the test was satisfactory, and, therefore, the presumption of alcoholic content was applicable.

Hache v. R. (1985), 36 M.V.R. 119 (N.B. C.A.) — A certificate stated that at (1) 5:50 p.m. and (2) 6:10 p.m. "... I did take breath samples from the accused". Use of the active rather than the passive voice contained in the *Code* section was held not to be ambiguous and the use of numerical figures to record the time when the samples were taken is a matter of form and not substance.

R. v. Ziemer (1994), 5 M.V.R. (3d) 34 (N.S. C.A.) — Where the lot number of the solution used in the breathalyzer test is incorrectly stated on the certificate of analysis, it can be corrected by *viva voce* evidence.

R. v. Forbes (1986), 40 M.V.R. 224 (N.S. C.A.) — The certificate of analysis is required to identify the solution in a manner sufficient to be capable of later identification and recognition by D for the purpose of further investigation. As such the identification of the solution is required to include a reference to the lot number.

R. v. McEwen (1988), 39 C.C.C. (3d) 572 (Ont. C.A.) — The *Code* does not require that the solution be described, but only that it be identified. Manufacturer, type and lot number is sufficient.

R. v. Walsh (1980), 53 C.C.C. (2d) 568 (Ont. C.A.) — It is a permissible inference to be drawn that a qualified technician's certificate will not be forthcoming for use as evidence unless the technician is satisfied that it is based on a suitable sample.

R. v. Kroeger (1992), 36 M.V.R. (2d) 55 (Sask. C.A.) — *See also: R. v. Squires* (1994), 87 C.C.C. (3d) 430 (Nfld. C.A.); *R. v. Harding* (1994), 88 C.C.C. (3d) 97 (Ont. C.A.) — Section 258(1)(f) is not a prerequisite to the introduction into evidence of the technician's certificate under s. 258(1)(g). It is sufficient that the technician states s/he has ascertained the breathalyzer to be in proper working order by means of an alcohol standard.

R. v. Janzen (1986), 41 M.V.R. 1 (Sask. C.A.) — A solution is adequately identified if the description enables D to pursue an independent investigation as to the suitability of the solution.

R. v. Dookhun (1985), 24 C.C.C. (3d) 16 (Sask. C.A.); leave to appeal refused (1986), 38 M.V.R. xxxviin (S.C.C.) — A solution or substance is adequately described for the purpose of the section by the use of the generic name alone.

R. v. Workman (1974), 2 Y.R. 1 (C.A.); affirming (1974), 2 Y.R. 8 (S.C.) — It is only necessary that the solution be identified in the certificate of analysis. It is not necessary to identify the elements going to make up the solution or to give a quantitative analysis of the solution.

Presumption of Alcohol Concentration — Admissibility of Certificate

R. v. St. Pierre, 36 C.R. (4th) 273, 96 C.C.C. (3d) 385, [1995] 1 S.C.R. 791 (S.C.C.); reversing (1992), 76 C.C.C. (3d) 249, 16 C.R. (4th) 220 (Ont. C.A.) — The mere fact that the presumption of identity is rebutted does not render the certificate of analysis inadmissible. It, together with expert evidence on alcohol absorption rates and other relevant evidence, may sustain a conviction of impaired driving if not of "over 80".

R. v. Noble (1977), 40 C.R.N.S. 19, 37 C.C.C. (2d) 193 (S.C.C.) — A certificate is not admissible as proof of D's blood-alcohol level when only one sample was taken. The provisions in this section, designed to assist P in proving its case and restricting D's normal rights, are to be strictly construed and, where ambiguous, interpreted in favour of D.

R. v. Ryden (1994), 86 C.C.C. (3d) 57 (Alta. C.A.) — *See also*: *R. v. Bykowski* (1980), 54 C.C.C. (2d) 398 (Alta. C.A.); *R. v. Baptiste* (1980), 9 M.V.R. 216 (Alta. C.A.) — A typographical error on the certificate of analysis which is corrected by *viva voce* evidence will not render the certificate inadmissible, where the error was not of such a nature as to have misled D or interfered with his/her right to make full answer and defence.

R. v. Cosgrove (1993), 46 M.V.R. (2d) 99 (Alta. C.A.) — All carbon copies of a certificate of analysis on which the word "original" is stamped are themselves originals for the purposes of s. 258(1)(c).

R. v. Pilarski (1993), 46 M.V.R. (2d) 142 (Alta. C.A.) — The absence of reasonable and probable grounds to make a breathalyzer demand does not affect the admissibility of the certificate of analysis.

R. v. Morgan (1995), 104 C.C.C. (3d) 342 (Nfld. C.A.) — Absent evidence to the contrary, service of a copy of a pre-printed form with legible insertions made by carbon is *prima facie* evidence of service of a copy. There is *no* requirement that there be comparison of the pre-printed portions of the form.

R. v. Cyr (1983), 25 M.V.R. 62 (N.S. C.A.) — A certificate of analysis that is admissible in connection with the offence specified in the indictment is also admissible for any other offence properly included therein.

R. v. Saulnier (1979), 50 C.C.C. (2d) 350 (N.S. C.A.) — A certificate is not inadmissible because it is not provided in both English and French.

Presumption of Alcohol Concentration — Notice of Intention to Produce Certificate

R. v. Hamm (1976), 33 C.R.N.S. 339, 28 C.C.C. (2d) 257 (S.C.C.) — The court did not find it necessary for the purposes of the appeal to make any finding as to the propriety of effecting service on someone in an advanced stage of intoxication. In this particular case, the alcohol level recorded in the technician's certificate did not automatically rebut the presumption that D understood what was going on when he was served at the time of the taking of the breathalyzer readings with the notice of intention under this section.

R. v. Spreen (1987), 40 C.C.C. (3d) 190 (Alta. C.A.) — P is permitted to establish service of the notice of intention and a copy of the certificate by an affidavit of service.

R. v. Nickerson (1984), 27 M.V.R. 124 (N.S. C.A.) — Notice of intention served prior to D's first trial was effective notice for the purposes of a subsequent trial.

R. v. McCullagh (1990), 53 C.C.C. (3d) 130 (Ont. C.A.) — Superfluous reference to another charge does not invalidate a notice of intention which does refer to the charge on which D is tried.

R. v. Brebner (1989), 49 C.C.C. (3d) 97 (Ont. C.A.) — A notice is not invalid by reason of it specifying an offence different than that with which D is charged.

R. v. Winter (1986), 38 M.V.R. 311 (Ont. C.A.) — The notice of intention need *not* be served "together" or simultaneously with a copy of the certificate served.

R. v. Koback (1986), 43 M.V.R. 272 (Sask. C.A.); affirming (1986), 43 M.V.R. 264 (Sask. Q.B.) — Where an accused alleges non-compliance with this subsection the sole issue is whether D had reasonable notice of P's intention to rely on the certificate.

Providing Alcohol Concentration — Blood Samples

R. v. Gale (1992), 65 C.C.C. (3d) 373, 32 M.V.R. (2d) 107 (Nfld. C.A.) — The result of an analysis of a blood sample obtained pursuant to a demand which was out of time may be admissible under s. 258(1)(b).

R. v. Redmond (1990), 54 C.C.C. (3d) 273 (Ont. C.A.) — Evidence of hospital technologists as to the results of analysis of the alcohol concentration in D's blood was admissible where they could testify the machine was capable of making the required measurements, in good working order and was properly used.

Charter Considerations — Adverse Inference from Evidence of Refusal

R. v. Van Den Elzer (1983), 10 C.C.C. (3d) 352 (B.C. C.A.) — The adverse inference authorized by this section does not infringe D's guarantee to the presumption of innocence as set out in *Charter* s. 11(d).

Related Provisions: "Superior court of criminal jurisdiction" and "court of criminal jurisdiction" are defined in s. 2; "qualified medical practitioner", "analyst", "qualified technician", "approved container", "approved instrument" in s. 254(1).

The essential elements of the offences of ss. 253 and 255 are described in the *Commentary* accompanying each section.

Sections 254(2)–(4) describe the circumstances under which a peace officer may demand a breath or blood sample from a person suspected of committing or having committed a listed offence. Section 256 prescribes the basis upon which a warrant may be issued to obtain blood samples and provides for the manner in which it is to be executed. Section 257 affords protection to qualified medical practitioners and qualified technicians for their conduct in taking or failing to take blood samples under ss. 254 and 256.

259. (1) Mandatory order of prohibition — Where an offender is convicted of an offence committed under section 253 or 254 or discharged under section 730 of an offence committed under section 253 and, at the time the offence was committed or, in the case of an offence committed under section 254, within the two hours preceding that time, was operating or had the care or control of a motor vehicle, vessel, aircraft or railway equipment or was assisting in the operation of an aircraft or of railway equipment, the court that sentences the offender shall, in addition to any other punishment that may be imposed for that offence, make an order prohibiting the offender from operating a motor vehicle on any street, road, highway or other public place, or from operating a vessel, aircraft or railway equipment, as the case may be,

(a) for a first offence, during a period of not more than three years plus any period to which the offender is sentenced to imprisonment, and not less than three months;

(b) for a second offence, during a period of not more than three years plus any period to which the offender is sentenced to imprisonment, and not less than six months; and

(c) for each subsequent offence, during a period of not more than three years plus any period to which the offender is sentenced to imprisonment, and not less than one year.

(2) Discretionary order of prohibition — Where an offender is convicted or discharged under section 730 of an offence under section 220, 221, 236, 249, 250, 251 or 252, subsection 255(2) or (3) or this section committed by means of a motor vehicle, vessel, aircraft or railway equipment, the court that sentences the offender may, in addition to any other punishment that may be imposed for that offence, make an order prohibiting the offender from operating a motor vehicle on any street, road, highway or other public place, or from operating a vessel, aircraft or railway equipment, as the case may be,

> (a) during any period that the court considers proper, if the offender is liable to imprisonment for life in respect of that offence;

> (b) during any period not exceeding ten years plus any period to which the offender is sentenced to imprisonment, if the offender is liable to imprisonment for more than five years but less than life in respect of that offence; and

> (c) during any period not exceeding three years plus any period to which the offender is sentenced to imprisonment, in any other case.

(3) Saving — No order made under subsection (1) or (2) shall operate to prevent any person from acting as master, mate or engineer of a vessel that is required to carry officers holding certificates as master, mate or engineer.

(4) Operation while disqualified — Every one who operates a motor vehicle, vessel, aircraft or railway equipment in Canada while disqualified from doing so

> (a) is guilty of an indictable offence and liable to imprisonment for a term not exceeding two years; or

> (b) is guilty of an offence punishable on summary conviction.

(5) Definition of "disqualification" — For the purposes of this section, "disqualification" means

> (a) a prohibition from operating a motor vehicle, vessel, aircraft or railway equipment ordered pursuant to subsection (1) or (2); or

> (b) a disqualification or any other form of legal restriction of the right or privilege to operate a motor vehicle, vessel or aircraft imposed

>> (i) in the case of a motor vehicle, under the law of a province, or

>> (ii) in the case of a vessel or an aircraft, under an Act of Parliament,

in respect of a conviction or discharge under section 730 of any offence referred to in subsection (1) or (2).

1972, c. 13, s. 20; 1974–75–76, c. 93, s. 20; R.S. 1985, c. 27 (1st Supp.), s. 36; c. 32 (4th Supp.), s. 62; 1995, c. 22, ss. 10, 18; 1997, c. 18, s. 11.

Commentary: The section authorizes, or requires, the making of an order prohibiting D from operating a motor vehicle, vessel, aircraft or railway equipment upon conviction or discharge of an enumerated offence. It further creates the offence of operating a motor vehicle, vessel, aircraft or railway equipment in Canada whilst disqualified from so doing and provides the punishment therefor.

Sections 259(1)–(3) govern orders of prohibition. Under s. 259(1), an order is *mandatory* where D has been convicted or discharged of an offence under s. 253 (operation or care or control whilst impaired or with more than 80 mg of alcohol in 100 ml of blood) or 254 (failure or refusal to comply with demand for breath or blood sample), and, either at the time the offence was committed, or in the case of the s. 254 offence, within the two hours preceding, was operating or had the care or control of a motor vehicle, vessel, aircraft or railway equipment or assisted in the operation of an aircraft or railway equipment. The term of the prohibition will vary under ss. 259(1)(a)–(c), depending upon whether the conviction or discharge is for a first, second or subsequent offence. There is, in each case, a minimum and maximum term of prohibition.

The *discretionary* prohibition of s. 259(2) also requires that D be convicted or discharged of a listed offence. The offence must have been committed by means of a motor vehicle, vessel, aircraft or railway equipment. The term or period of the prohibition is governed by ss. 259(2)(a)–(c), and is dependent upon the maximum provided for the underlying offence.

The prohibitions of ss. 259(1) and (2) prevent D from operating a motor vehicle, vessel, aircraft or railway equipment for the term thereof. Under s. 259(3), the order does not operate to prevent D from acting as a master, mate or engineer of a vessel of the nature there described.

The *external circumstances* of the offence of s. 259(4) require that D operate a motor vehicle, vessel, aircraft or railway equipment in Canada. At the time of operation, D must be disqualified from so doing. Disqualification is defined in s. 259(5). The *mental element* requires proof of D's knowledge of the fact of disqualification at the relevant time. It is generally established by inference from proof of the *external circumstances* of the offence.

Case Law

Driving While Disqualified — Nature and Elements of Offence

R. v. Mansour (1979), 47 C.C.C. (2d) 129 (S.C.C.) — D whose licence is suspended by virtue of provincial legislation should only be convicted of driving while disqualified if he is driving in a place where a licence is required by provincial legislation.

Driving While Disqualified — Mental Element

R. v. Prue (1979), 8 C.R. (3d) 68, 46 C.C.C. (2d) 257 (S.C.C.) — The offence requires proof of *mens rea*. The existence of a suspension from driving is a question of fact and ignorance of that fact is a valid defence.

R. v. Lock (1974), 18 C.C.C. (2d) 477 (Ont. C.A.) — Once P has proved that D drove while disqualified, it has made out a *prima facie* case although it has not shown that D knew of the disqualification. The onus then shifts to D to produce evidence of lack of knowledge.

R. v. Larsen (1992), 71 C.C.C. (3d) 335 (Sask. C.A.) — Where provincial legislation and the *Code* require that, upon conviction of an offence, D be informed by the court that s/he is disqualified from driving, and, under provincial legislation, a resident D is to surrender the licence to the convicting judge and will not be entitled to re-instatement so long as the disqualification remains, the presumption of regularity applies to *presume* D was notified of the disqualification. The conjoint effect of the registrar's certificate and the presumption of regularity constitutes *prima facie* proof of the mental element, i.e., that D *knew* s/he was disqualified from driving. Absent evidence of lack of knowledge, D runs the risk of conviction.

Prohibition Order

R. v. Girard (1993), 79 C.C.C. (3d) 174 (N.B. C.A.) — A judge may not impose an exception to a prohibition order.

R. v. Laycock (1989), 51 C.C.C. (3d) 65 (Ont. C.A.) — The period of driving prohibition commences on the day the order is made and the sentencing judge has no authority to order that it commence at some later date.

Charter Considerations

R. v. Buchanan (1989), 46 C.C.C. (3d) 468 (N.S. C.A.) — Subsections (4) and (5)(b)(i) are constitutionally valid as they were enacted for the attainment of a valid federal objective. Any inequality which exists from province to province is reasonably justified in a federal state.

R. v. Lepage (1993), 46 M.V.R. (2d) 167 (Que. C.A.) — The application of the mandatory driving prohibition in s. 259(1) to persons convicted of refusing to provide a breath sample does not offend s. 7, 11(d) or 12.

Related Provisions: "Motor vehicle", "highway" and railway equipment are defined in s. 2, "operate", "aircraft" and "vessel" in s. 214(1). Previous convictions may be established in accordance with ss. 727 and 667. The procedure to be followed upon the making of an order of prohibition is described in ss. 260(1) and (2). D's failure to endorse receipt and acknowledge explanation of the order does *not* affect the validity of the order. A prohibition order under either s. 259(1) or (2) is a "sentence" for the purposes of ss. 673 and 785. A judge of the court to which an appeal is taken may, under s. 261, direct that a prohibition order be stayed pending the final disposition of the appeal or until otherwise ordered by the court.

Sections 260(4)–(7), assist P in proof of the essential elements of the offence of s. 259(4).

The offence of s. 259(4) is triable either way. Where P proceeds by indictment under s. 259(4)(a), it is unclear whether the offence lies within the absolute jurisdiction of a provincial court judge under s. 553(c)(vii) as did its unconstitutional predecessor. The lack of clarity is perhaps best resolved by affording D an election as to his mode of trial under s. 536(2). Where P proceeds by summary conviction, the offence is tried under Part XXVII and punished under s. 787(1). It is an "offence" for the purpose of the second and subsequent offence provisions of s. 255(4).

260. **(1) Proceedings on making of prohibition order** — Where a court makes a prohibition order under subsection 259(1) or (2) in relation to an offender, it shall cause

(a) the order to be read by or to the offender;

(b) a copy of the order to be given to the offender; and

(c) the offender to be informed of subsection 259(4).

(2) Endorsement by offender — After subsection (1) has been complied with in relation to an offender who is bound by an order referred to in that subsection, the offender shall endorse the order, acknowledging receipt of a copy thereof and that the order has been explained to him.

(3) Validity of order not affected — The failure of an offender to endorse an order pursuant to subsection (2) does not affect the validity of the order.

(4) Onus — In the absence of evidence to the contrary, where it is proved that a disqualification referred to in paragraph 259(5)(*b*) has been imposed on a person and that notice of the disqualification has been mailed by registered or certified mail to that person, that person shall, after five days following the mailing of the notice, be deemed to have received the notice and to have knowledge of the disqualification, of the date of its commencement and of its duration.

(5) Certificate admissible in evidence — In proceedings under section 259, a certificate setting out with reasonable particularity that a person is disqualified from

(a) driving a motor vehicle in a province, purporting to be signed by the registrar of motor vehicles for that province, or

(b) operating a vessel or aircraft, purporting to be signed by the Minister of Transport or any person authorized by the Minister of Transport for that purpose

is evidence of the facts alleged therein without proof of the signature or official character of the person by whom it purports to be signed.

(6) Notice to accused — Subsection (5) does not apply in any proceedings unless at least seven days notice in writing is given to the accused that it is intended to tender the certificate in evidence.

(7) Definition of "registrar of motor vehicles" — In subsection (5), "registrar of motor vehicles " includes the deputy of that registrar and any other person or body, by whatever name or title designated, that from time to time performs the duties of superintending the registration of motor vehicles in the province.

1972, c. 13, s. 20;R.S. 1985, c. 27 (1st Supp.), s. 36.

Commentary: The section describes the procedure to be followed upon the making of a prohibition order under s. 259 and enacts evidentiary rules to help P prove the s. 259(4) offence.

Sections 260(1)–(3) describe the procedure to be followed upon the making of a prohibition order under s. 259(1) or (2). The sentencing court must cause the order to be read by or to D and D to be informed of the provisions of s. 259(4) (operation whilst disqualified). D must also be given a copy of the order.

Section 260(3) requires D to acknowledge receipt of a copy of the order and explanation thereof but, by s. 260(3), the failure of D to so endorse the order does *not* affect its validity.

Sections 260(4)–(7) facilitate P's proof of a s. 259(4) offence. Under s. 260(4), upon proof of imposition of a disqualification under s. 259(5)(b) and notice sent by registered or certified mail to D, after five days following the mailing of notice, D is deemed to have received the notice and to have had knowledge of the fact and particulars of the disqualification, in the absence of evidence to the contrary. The subsection, in other words, assists proof of D's knowledge of disqualification. Under ss. 260(5)–(7) proof of D's disqualification at the material time may be made by certificate as described in s. 260(5). Notice is required under s. 260(6) to make the certificate of the registrar of motor vehicles receivable as evidence of the facts alleged therein.

Case Law

R. v. Tatomir (1989), 51 C.C.C. (3d) 321 (Alta. C.A.); leave to appeal refused (1990), 70 Alta. L.R. (2d) liiin (S.C.C.) — Even though P has not complied with ss. 260(5) and (6), it is entitled at common law to tender without notice the official order of driving prohibition against D as an exemplification under the seal of the court.

R. v. Vollman (1989), 52 C.C.C. (3d) 379 (Sask. C.A.) — A letter to D's lawyer constitutes notice to D.

R. v. Materi (1987), 35 C.C.C. (3d) 273 (Sask. C.A.); reversing (1986), 56 Sask. R. 5 (Q.B.) — The functions set out in this section cannot be delegated by the trial judge to an agent of D. The delegation must be to a court official. The purpose of the section is to ensure that D understands the nature of the prohibition order and the consequences of its breach.

Related Provisions: "Motor vehicle" is defined in s. 2, "operate", "vessel" and "aircaft" in s. 214(1). The calculation of the notice period provided in s. 260(6) is made under *I.A.* ss. 26 and 27.

Section 261 authorizes the stay of a prohibition order pending the final disposition of an appeal relating to the conviction or discharge of a listed offence.

261. (1) Stay of order pending appeal — Where an appeal is taken against a conviction or discharge under section 730 for an offence committed under any of sections 220, 221, 236, 249 to 255 and 259, a judge of the court being appealed to may direct that any order under subsection 259(1) or (2) arising out of the conviction or discharge shall, on such conditions as the judge or court may impose, be stayed pending the final disposition of the appeal or until otherwise ordered by that court.

(2) Effect of conditions — Where conditions are imposed pursuant to a direction made under subsection (1) that a prohibition order under subsection 259(1) or (2) be stayed, the direction shall not operate to decrease the period of prohibition provided in the order made under subsection 259(1) or (2).

1972, c. 13, s. 20;R.S. 1985, c. 27 (1st Supp.), s. 36; 1994, c. 44, s. 15; 1994, c. 44. s. 103; 1997, c. 18, ss. 12, 141(a).

Commentary: The section authorizes the stay of a prohibition order pending appeal in certain circumstances. There must be an appeal taken against a conviction or discharge for a listed offence. The stay may only be directed by a judge of "the court being appealed to", may be of any order under s. 259(1) or (2) arising out of the conviction or discharge and may be made pending the final disposition of the appeal or until otherwise ordered by the court to which the appeal has been taken. Any conditions imposed on the stay of a prohibition order, by s. 261(2) do *not decrease* the *period* of the prohibition.

Case Law [Cases decided under earlier provision]

R. v. Smith (1993), 50 M.V.R. (2d) 307 (B.C. C.A.) — There is power in an appellate court to stay a driving prohibition order in part, for example to permit D to drive only for the purpose of going to and from work.

R. v. Jay (1987), 50 M.V.R. 137 (P.E.I. S.C.) — Discretionary relief under the section may be invoked where D shows that the appeal is not frivolous, that there is at least some arguable point to be made, that the prohibition is *not* necessary in the public interest and that a stay would not detrimentally affect the confidence of the public in the enforcement and administration of criminal law.

Related Provisions: A prohibition order under s. 259(1) or (2) is a "sentence" under ss. 673 and 785 which may be appealed in accordance with the applicable provisions of Part XXI or Part XXVII. Section 261 would seem, however, to permit the entry of a stay where the underlying conviction or discharge is being appealed under either Part XXI or XXVII. The general stay authority of the court of appeal in indictable matters under s. 683(5) would not appear to include a prohibition under s. 259(1) or (2). The provisions of s. 683(5) are not incorporated into appeals under s. 813 on account of s. 822(1).

262. Impeding attempt to save life — Every one who

(a) **prevents or impedes or attempts to prevent or impede any person who is attempting to save his own life, or**

(b) **without reasonable cause prevents or impedes or attempts to prevent or impede any person who is attempting to save the life of another person,**

is guilty of an indictable offence and liable to imprisonment for a term not exceeding ten years.

R.S., c. C-34, s. 241.

Commentary: The section defines the extent to which criminal liability will be imposed for impeding attempts to save the life of another person.

Section 262(a) applies where V is attempting to save his/her *own life*. D must actually or attempt to prevent or impede V in his/her own life saving attempt.

Section 262(b) applies where D's interference is directed at one who is trying to save the *life of another* person (V). Further, D must actually or attempt to prevent or impede the rescue efforts and do so without reasonable cause.

Neither s. 262(a) nor (b) requires proof of any ulterior *mental element*.

Related Provisions: The nature of D's intervention may also attract liability for assault under s. 266. Where the person whose rescue is impeded by D dies, D's conduct may amount to culpable homicide under s. 222(5)(a) or (b). Whether such culpable homicide will amount to murder, manslaughter or infanticide will depend upon the external circumstances and accompanying mental element.

Under s. 536(2), D may *elect* mode of trial.

263. (1) Duty to safeguard opening in ice — Every one who makes or causes to be made an opening in ice that is open to or frequented by the public is under a legal duty to guard it in a manner that is adequate to prevent persons from falling in by accident and is adequate to warn them that the opening exists.

(2) Excavation on land — Every one who leaves an excavation on land that he owns or of which he has charge or supervision is under a legal duty to guard it in a manner that is adequate to prevent persons from falling in by accident and is adequate to warn them that the excavation exists.

(3) Offences — Every one who fails to perform a duty imposed by subsection (1) or (2) is guilty of

(a) **manslaughter, if the death of any person results therefrom;**

(b) **an offence under section 269, if bodily harm to any person results therefrom; or**

(c) **an offence punishable on summary conviction.**

R.S., c. C-34, s. 242; 1980–81–82–83, c. 125, s. 18.

Commentary: The section imposes *legal duties* in connection with *openings in ice* and *excavations on land* and describes the circumstances under which criminal liability may be attracted for failure to perform either duty.

The legal duty of s. 263(1), imposed upon everyone who makes or causes to be made an *opening in ice* that is open to or frequented by the public, is twofold. The opening must be guarded in a manner that is adequate to *prevent* persons from falling in accidentally. The guarding must be adequate to *warn* persons that the opening exists.

The legal duty of s. 263(2), imposed upon everyone who leaves an *excavation on land* which s/he owns, has charge or supervises, is the equivalent of the duty imposed under subsection (1).

The *mental element* requires proof of nothing more than the intention to cause the external circumstances of the offence. Knowledge of the excavation or opening would seem, however, an essential element of P's proof.

Section 263(3) defines the nature and extent to which criminal liability will be imposed for failure to perform the duty of either s. 263(1) or (2). Under s. 263(3)(a), the failure to perform the duty is *manslaughter* if the death of any person results therefrom. Under s. 263(3)(b), the failure to perform the duty is a breach of s. 269 (unlawfully causing bodily harm) if bodily harm to any person results therefrom. Under s. 263(3)(c), where neither death nor bodily harm results from such failure, D's offence is punishable on summary conviction.

Case Law

R. v. Aldergrove Competition Motorcycle Assn. (1983), 5 C.C.C. (3d) 114 (B.C. C.A.) — This section creates a legal duty to guard an excavation not just in a manner which is *adequate* to *warn* but also in a manner which is *adequate* to *prevent* persons falling in by accident. D who breaches that duty will be guilty of manslaughter if death results from the breach. P need *not* prove criminal negligence as defined in s. 219.

Related Provisions: Manslaughter is culpable homicide that is neither murder nor infanticide. Culpable homicide is defined in s. 222(5). The offence of s. 269 generally occurs as a result of an act by D. The offences of s. 263(3) are statutory forms of manslaughter and unlawfully causing bodily harm which occur by omission.

The offences of ss. 263(3)(a) and (b) are exclusively indictable. D may elect mode of trial. The offence of s. 263(3)(c) is tried under Part XXVII and punished under s. 787(1).

264. (1) Criminal harassment — No person shall, without lawful authority and knowing that another person is harassed or recklessly as to whether the other person is harassed, engage in conduct referred to in subsection (2) that causes that other person reasonably, in all the circumstances, to fear for their safety or the safety of anyone known to them.

(2) Prohibited conduct — The conduct mentioned in subsection (1) consists of

(a) repeatedly following from place to place the other person or anyone known to them;

(b) repeatedly communicating with, either directly or indirectly, the other person or anyone known to them;

(c) besetting or watching the dwelling-house, or place where the other person, or anyone known to them, resides, works, carries on business or happens to be; or

(d) engaging in threatening conduct directed at the other person or any member of their family.

(3) Punishment — Every person who contravenes this section is guilty of

(a) an indictable offence and is liable to imprisonment for a term not exceeding five years; or

(b) an offence punishable on summary conviction.

(4) **Factors to be considered** — Where a person is convicted of an offence under this section, the court imposing the sentence on the person shall consider as an aggravating factor that, at the time the offence was committed, the person contravened

(a) the terms or conditions of an order made pursuant to section 161 or a recognizance entered into pursuant to section 810, 810.1 or 810.2; or

(b) the terms or conditions of any other order or recognizance made or entered into under the common law or a provision of this or any other Act of Parliament or of a province that is similar in effect to an order or recognizance referred to in paragraph (*a*)

(5) **Reasons** — Where the court is satisfied of the existence of an aggravating factor referred to in subsection (4), but decides not to give effect to it for sentencing purposes, the court shall give reasons for its decision.

R.S. 1985, c. 27 (1st Supp.), s. 37; 1993, c. 45, s. 2; 1997, c. 16, s. 4; c. 17, s. 9(3).

Commentary: The section creates a new offence, "criminal harassment", often described as "stalking" which may be prosecuted by indictment or upon summary conviction.

The *external circumstances* of the offence involve conduct by D that comes within any paragraph of s. 264(2). The conduct must be without lawful authority and cause V, reasonably in all the circumstances, to fear for his/her own safety or the safety of anyone known to V. The *mental element* comprises the intention to cause the external circumstances of the offence, as well *knowledge* that or *recklessness* whether V is harassed by the conduct.

Sections 264(4) and (5) apply to the sentencing of persons convicted of offences under s. 264. Under s. 264(4), a sentencing court is *required* to consider the fact that D *contravened* the terms or conditions of a listed or otherwise described order or recognizance when committing a s. 264 offence as an aggravating factor on sentence. Where the sentencing court decides not to give effect to the aggravating factor of s. 264(4) in imposing sentence, reasons must be given under s. 264(5).

Case Law

Essential Elements

R. v. Sillipp (1997), 120 C.C.C. (3d) 384 (Alta. C.A.); leave to appeal refused (1998), 228 N.R. 195 (note) (S.C.C.) — The *external circumstances* of criminal harassment are set out in s. 264(2):

i.   repeated following from place to place;

ii.   repeated communication with V; or

iii. besetting or watching the dwelling-house or place of business of V.

The *mental element* includes knowledge that, or recklessness or wilfull blindness whether, V was harassed.

A jury should be instructed that to find D guilty of criminal harassment, they must be satisfied beyond a reasonable doubt that

i.   D engaged in any of the conduct described in s. 264(2)(a)-(d);

ii.   V was harassed;

iii. D knew or was reckless or wilfully blind whether V was harassed;

iv.   the conduct caused V to fear his/her safety, or the safety of anyone known to V; and

v.   V's fear, in all of the circumstances, was reasonable.

R. v. Ryback (1996), 105 C.C.C. (3d) 24 (B.C. C.A); leave to appeal refused (1996), 107 C.C.C. (3d) vi (note) (S.C.C.) — "Repeatedly" means repeated on more than one occasion.

R. v. Lamontagne (1998), 129 C.C.C. (3d) 181 (Que. C.A.) — Section 264(1) articulates the *constituent elements* of the offence of criminal harassment. Section 264(2) describes the four types of prohibited conduct to which s. 264(1) refers.

Harassment is not limited to the classic and restricted definition of "to subject without respite to repeated little attacks, to incessant rapid assaults". It may include "bothering someone with requests, solicitations, incitements". D's conduct must have the *effect* of bothering someone because of its continuity or repetition in the sense of "vex, trouble, annoy continually or chronically".

Under s. 264(2)(d), P must prove

i.   that D *engaged* in *threatening conduct directed* at V;

ii. that the threatening conduct caused V to *reasonably* fear for his/her *safety*;

iii. that V was *harassed*; and

iv. that D *knew* or was *reckless* whether V was *harassed*.

Evidence

R. v. Ryback (1996), 105 C.C.C. (3d) 24 (B.C. C.A.); leave to appeal refused (1996), 107 C.C.C. (3d) vi (note) (S.C.C.) — Evidence of D's conduct which occurred prior to the enactment of the section is relevant to a determination whether V had *reasonable* fear for safety and D's *knowledge* of or *recklessness* as to whether the conduct harassed V. To admit the evidence does *not* offend *Charter* s. 11(g).

Charter Considerations

R. v. Sillipp (1997), 120 C.C.C. (3d) 384 (Alta. C.A.); leave to appeal refused (1998), 228 N.R. 195 (note) (S.C.C.) — The offence of criminal harassment does *not* offend Charter s. 7.

Related Provisions: Intimidation is a summary conviction offence under s. 423(1). Uttering threats an offence triable either way under s. 264.1. Upon conviction or conditional discharge of certain listed offences, a sentencing judge under s. 161 may prohibit D from attending certain premises or areas where persons under 14 years of age are or can reasonably be expected to be present. Failure to comply with an order of prohibition is an offence under s. 161(4). A related crime is described in s. 179(1)(b).

Where P proceeds by indictment, D may *elect* mode of trial under s. 536(2). Summary conviction proceedings are governed by Part XXVII and punishment by s. 787(1).

A prohibition is *mandatory* under s. 109(1)(b).

Assaults

264.1 (1) Uttering threats — **Every one commits an offence who, in any manner, knowingly utters, conveys or causes any person to receive a threat**

   (a) to cause death or bodily harm to any person;

   (b) to burn, destroy or damage real or personal property; or

   (c) to kill, poison or injure an animal or bird that is the property of any person.

(2) Punishment — **Every one who commits an offence under paragraph (1)(a) is guilty of**

   (a) an indictable offence and liable to imprisonment for a term not exceeding five years; or

   (b) an offence punishable on summary conviction and liable to imprisonment for a term not exceeding eighteen months.

(3) Idem — **Every one who commits an offence under paragraph (1)(b) or (c)**

   (a) is guilty of an indictable offence and liable to imprisonment for a term not exceeding two years; or

   (b) is guilty of an offence punishable on summary conviction.

R.S. 1985, c. 27 (1st Supp.), s. 38; 1994, c. 44, s. 16.

Commentary: The section describes the circumstances under which uttering threats may attract criminal liability and relates the maximum punishment to the nature of the threat.

Section 264.1(1) defines the elements of the offence. The *external circumstances* are complete where D utters, conveys or causes a person to receive a threat of any nature described in ss. 264.1(a)–(c). The *mental element* consists of the intent to utter the prohibited threat.

Sections 264.1(2) and (3) desribe the punishment which may be imposed upon conviction and characterize the nature of the offence.

Case Law

Knowingly

R. v. LeBlanc (1989), 70 C.R. (3d) 94, 50 C.C.C. (3d) 192 (S.C.C.); reversing (1988), 66 C.R. (3d) 134, 44 C.C.C. (3d) 18 (N.B. C.A.) — A threat is a menace or denunciation that will befall the recipient. Although a threat innocently made is not a threat, it is not material whether D intended to carry out the threat.

R. v. Bone (1993), 21 C.R. (4th) 218, 81 C.C.C. (3d) 389 (Man. C.A.) — In deciding whether to infer the specific intent to instil fear in someone, the trier of fact must consider evidence of D's intoxication, together with all the other circumstances in which the threat is uttered.

Elements of Offence

R. v. Clemente (1994), 31 C.R. (4th) 28, 91 C.C.C. (3d) 1 (S.C.C.); affirming (1993), 27 C.R. (4th) 281, 86 C.C.C. (3d) 398 (Man. C.A.) — The *external circumstances* of the offence of s. 264.1(1)(a) comprise the uttering of threats of death or serious bodily harm. The *mental element* is that the words be spoken or written as a threat to cause serious bodily harm, i.e., that they were meant to intimdiate or to be taken seriously.

R. v. Kafé (1996), 45 C.R. (4th) 389, 106 C.C.C. (3d) 569 (Que. C.A.) — In a jury trial, it is for the trial judge to decide

i.   whether, as a matter of law, the threat alleged in the indictment *can* constitute a threat under the section; and,

ii. whether there is *any* evidence that it was D who made or caused to the threat to be received.

It is for the jury to determine whether the essential elements of the offence have been proven beyond a reasonable doubt, in particular whether, as a matter of fact, the words uttered amount to a threat.

Threat

R. v. Clemente (1994), 31 C.R. (4th) 28, 91 C.C.C. (3d) 1 (S.C.C.); affirming (1993), 27 C.R. (4th) 281, 86 C.C.C. (3d) 398 (Man. C.A.) — *See also*: *R. v. Carons* (1978), 42 C.C.C. (2d) 19 (Alta. C.A.) — It is *not* essential that P prove that the intended victim was aware of the threat.

It is a crime under s. 264.1(1)(a) to issue threats without any further action being taken beyond the threat itself. It is the meaning conveyed by the words that is important. Words spoken in jest are beyond the scope of the section.

Under s. 264.1(1)(a), P must prove that D intended to intimidate and instill fear in V. The threats need *not* cause actual fear in V.

R. v. McCraw (1991), 7 C.R. (4th) 314, 66 C.C.C. (3d) 517 (S.C.C.) — Whether particular words constitute a threat to cause serious bodily harm is an issue of law. In each case, the issue is whether, viewed objectively in the context of all the words written or spoken, and having regard to the person to whom they were addressed, the questioned words would convey a threat of serious bodily harm to a *reasonable person*. A threat to commit rape, depending on the context and circumstances, may contravene the section.

R. v. Tibando (1994), 88 C.C.C. (3d) 229 (Ont. C.A.) — P need *not* prove that D intended that the threat be conveyed to V nor that V was threatened or put in fear. Liability is established where the evidence proves that, in the context in which they were uttered and having regard to the person to whom they were directed, the words would have conveyed to a *reasonable* person a threat of serious bodily harm and that D intended the threat to be taken seriously.

R. v. Ross (1986), 50 C.R. (3d) 391, 26 C.C.C. (3d) 413 (Ont. C.A.) — A threat includes a threat conditional upon some course of conduct.

Henry v. R. (1981), 24 C.R. (3d) 261 (Ont. C.A.) — This section does *not* apply where there is no evidence that D intended that the person(s) hearing the threat should act as messengers or intermediaries to convey the threat to the intended victim.

R. v. Thompson (1981), 22 C.R. (3d) 389, 59 C.C.C. (2d) 514 (Ont. C.A.) — The intended victim need not be the direct recipient of the threat.

R. v. Rémy (1993), 82 C.C.C. (3d) 176 (Que. C.A.) — The fact that V was unknown when a threat was made does *not* bar conviction. A threat to cause death to a member of an ascertained group of persons contravenes s. 264.1. The offence is complete upon the threat being uttered. P need *not* prove any element of fear in any person created by the threat.

R. v. Payne-Binder (1991), 7 C.R. (4th) 308 (Y.T. C.A.) — To determine whether words uttered constitute a threat, various factors must be considered objectively, including the context of all the written or spoken words in which they occurred and the situation of the recipient of the alleged threat.

Serious Bodily Harm

R. v. McCraw (1991), 7 C.R. (4th) 314, 66 C.C.C. (3d) 517 (S.C.C.) — "Serious bodily harm" means any hurt or injury, whether physical or psychological, that interferes in a substantial way with the physical or psychological integrity, health or well-being of V.

Form of Indictment

R. v. Rémy-Mercier (1993), 82 C.C.C. (3d) 176 (Que. C.A.) — An indictment charging the offence is *not* insufficient because it fails to specify the means by which the threat was conveyed. Since the offence is proven when the threats are conveyed "in any manner", specification of the means is *not* an essential element of the offence.

Mental Element

R. v. Clemente (1994), 31 C.R. (4th) 28, 91 C.C.C. (3d) 1 (S.C.C.); affirming (1993), 27 C.R. (4th) 281, 86 C.C.C. (3d) 398 (Man. C.A.) — In the absence of any explanation by D, a determination whether either mental element has been proven involves consideration of

i.   the words used;

ii.   the context in which the words were used or spoken; and,

iii.   the person to whom the words were directed.

R. v. Neve (1993), 87 C.C.C. (3d) 190 (Alta C.A.); leave to appeal refused (1994), 87 C.C.C. (3d) vi (note) (S.C.C) — *See also*: *R. v. Shaw* (1992), 135 A.R. 161 (C.A.) — The mental element requires proof that D intended that the uttered threat be taken seriously.

Charter Considerations

R. v. Clemente (1993), 27 C.R. (4th) 281, 86 C.C.C. (3d) 398 (Man. C.A.); affirmed (1994), 31 C.R. (4th) 281, 91 C.C.C. (3d) 1 (S.C.C.) — Section 264.1(1) infringes *Charter* s. 2(b), but is saved by s. 1.

Related Provisions: "Person", "property" and "bodily harm" are defined in s. 2.

Extortion is an offence under s. 346 and extortion by libel under s. 302. Indecent and harassing telephone calls are punishable under ss. 372(2) and (3). Threats to commit an offence against an internationally protected person is an offence under s. 424. Arson and other fires are governed by ss. 433–436. Injury to or endangering cattle or other animals are offences under ss. 444 and 445.

The offences of s. 264.1(1)(a) and 264.1(1)(b), (c) allow D to elect mode of trial. Where P proceeds by summary conviction under s. 264.1(3)(b), Part XXVII governs, except as to penalty.

This offence is an "offence" in s. 183 for the purposes of Part VI.

265. (1) Assault — A person commits an "assault" when

(a) without the consent of another person, he applies force intentionally to that other person, directly or indirectly;

(b) he attempts or threatens, by an act or a gesture, to apply force to another person, if he has, or causes that other person to believe on reasonable grounds that he has, present ability to effect his purpose; or

(c) while openly wearing or carrying a weapon or an imitation thereof, he accosts or impedes another person or begs.

(2) **Application** — This section applies to all forms of assault, including sexual assault, sexual assault with a weapon, threats to a third party or causing bodily harm and aggravated sexual assault.

(3) **Consent** — For the purposes of this section, no consent is obtained where the complainant submits or does not resist by reason of

(a) the application of force to the complainant or to a person other than the complainant;

(b) threats or fear of the application of force to the complainant or to a person other than the complainant;

(c) fraud; or

(d) the exercise of authority.

(4) **Accused's belief as to consent** — Where an accused alleges that he believed that the complainant consented to the conduct that is the subject-matter of the charge, a judge, if satisfied that there is sufficient evidence and that, if believed by the jury, the evidence would constitute a defence, shall instruct the jury, when reviewing all the evidence relating to the determination of the honesty of the accused's belief, to consider the presence or absence of reasonable grounds for that belief.

R.S., c. C-34, s. 244; 1974-75-76, c. 93, s. 21; 1980-81-82-83, c. 125, s. 19.

Commentary: An assault may be actual or constructive. In its primary sense, an assault under s. 265(1)(a) is the intentional application of force, directly or indirectly, to the person of V, without consent. Consent may be real or apprehended. Whether V consented is in each case a question of fact. Evidence of submission or lack of resistance by V may found a defence of consent, provided it is *not* vitiated under s. 265(3). D may also assert an honest belief that V consented to what is said to constitute the external circumstances of the offence. D must adduce some evidence to raise the issue of apprehended consent, thereafter P must prove beyond a reasonable doubt that D had no such honest belief. Under s. 265(4) the trier of fact may consider the presence or absence of reasonable grounds for D's belief as an item of evidence in determining the honesty with which the asserted belief was held. Constructive assaults are described in ss. 265(1)(b), (c).

Under s. 265(2) the definition of assault applies to all forms of assault, including the several levels of sexual assault.

Case Law

Nature and Elements of Offence: S. 265(1)

R. v. Burden (1981), 25 C.R. (3d) 283 (B.C. C.A.) — A touching of V may constitute an intentional application of force. The strength of the force is immaterial.

R. v. Byrne (1968), 3 C.R.N.S. 190 (B.C. C.A.) — *See also*: *R. v. Judge* (1957), 118 C.C.C. 410 (Ont. C.A.) — Although physical violence is *not* necessary, there must be a threatening act or gesture. Mere words can not amount to an assault.

R. v. Horncastle (1972), 19 C.R.N.S. 362, 8 C.C.C. (2d) 253 (N.B. C.A.) — *See also*: *R. v. Cadden* (1989), 70 C.R. (3d) 340, 48 C.C.C. (3d) 122 (B.C. C.A.) — Assault is committed when a threat is intentionally made to apply force to the person of another and there is the present ability to carry out that threat. Neither the degree of alarm felt by the person threatened, nor the intent of D to carry out the threat are involved in the determination.

Mental Element

R. v. Deakin (1974), 26 C.R.N.S. 236, 16 C.C.C. (2d) 1 (Man. C.A.) — Where D in attempting to strike P, struck and broke a glass ornament which injured the eye of P's wife, the general intent to apply force was transferred to P's wife. Lack of specific intent or hostility is irrelevant.

R. v. Wolfe (1974), 20 C.C.C. (2d) 382 (Ont. C.A.) — A reflex action lacks the necessary intent to constitute an assault.

R. v. Starratt (1971), 5 C.C.C. (2d) 32 (Ont. C.A.) — An application of force by a police officer in the course of duty through carelessness lacks the requisite intention for assault

Accessoryship

R. v. Nurse (1993), 83 C.C.C. (3d) 546 (Ont. C.A.) — Where D intends to aid and [*sic*] abet conduct that amounts to an assault, D is guilty of assault.

Consent: Ss. 265(1), (3) [See also s. 273.1]

R. v. Ewanchuk (1999), 22 C.R. (5th) 1, 131 C.C.C. (3d) 481 (S.C.C.) — The *absence* of *consent* is subjective. It is determined by reference to V's internal state of mind towards the touching *when* the touching takes place. V's statement of non-consent is a matter of credibility for the trier of fact. It is to be considered in light of *all* of the evidence *including* any ambiguous conduct by V. If the trier of fact accepts V's assertion of absence of consent, no matter how strongly V's conduct may contradict the assertion, absence of consent is established. Implied consent is *not* a defence to sexual assault.

There is no consent where V agrees to sexual activity *only* because s/he believes that s/he will otherwise suffer physical violence. The approach is *subjective*. The *plausibility* of the alleged fear and any *overt expressions* of it are relevant to assessing V's *credibility*. A trial judge need only consult *Code* s. 265(3) where V

i.   has chosen to participate in sexual activity; or,

ii.   by ambiguous conduct or submission, has raised a doubt about the absence of consent.

R. v. M. (M.L.) (1994), 30 C.R. (4th) 153, 89 C.C.C. (3d) 96 (S.C.C.); reversing (1992), 18 C.R. (4th) 186, 78 C.C.C. (3d) 318 (N.S. S.C.) — There is no requirement that V must offer some minimal word or gesture of objection in order to demonstrate non-consent. Lack of resistance is *not* equivalent to consent.

R. v. Jobidon (1991), 7 C.R. (4th) 233, 66 C.C.C. (3d) 454 (S.C.C.) — For policy reasons, the common law limited the legal effectiveness of consent to a fist fight. The limit persists in s. 265, vitiating consent between adults intentionally to apply force causing serious hurt, or non-trivial bodily harm to each other in the course of a fist fight or brawl. The common law rule will *not* vitiate freely-given consent to participate in rough sporting activities, providing the intentional application of force to which consent is given is within the customary norms and rules of the game. The limitations will also not vitiate consent to medical treatment, appropriate surgical intervention or the activities of stuntmen whose advance agreement to perform risky activities creates a socially valuable cultural product.

R. v. Caskenette (1993), 80 C.C.C. (3d) 439 (B.C. C.A.) — *Contra: R. v. Guerrero* (1988), 64 C.R. (3d) 65 (Ont. C.A.) — Section 265(3) is *not* exhaustive of the circumstances in which consent may be vitiated.

R. v. Stanley (1977), 36 C.C.C. (2d) 216 (B.C. C.A.) — *See also: R. v. Maher* (1987), 63 Nfld. & P.E.I.R. 30 (Nfld. C.A.) — Genuine consent to an assault must be freely given with an appreciation of the risks. It cannot be extracted by threats or violence nor forced as a submission to or acceptance of an inevitable confrontation.

R. v. W. (G.) (1994), 30 C.R. (4th) 393, 90 C.C.C. (3d) 139 (Ont. C.A.) — Where D, a young offender, intends to cause serious harm to V, a young person, and does so, D's youth affords no basis upon which to found a "defence" of consent to a charge of assault causing bodily harm.

R. v. Leclerc (1991), 7 C.R. (4th) 282, 67 C.C.C. (3d) 563 (Ont. C.A.) — Hockey players impliedly consent to some bodily contact necessarily incidental to the game, but not to overtly violent attacks. Conduct which, according to objective criteria, evinces a deliberate purpose to inflict injury is generally outside the scope of immunity provided by the doctrine of implied consent. While a "no contact" rule is relevant in ascertaining the scope of implied consent, it is *not* dispositive of the issue.

R. v. McIlwaine (1996), 111 C.C.C. (3d) 426 (Que. C.A.) — That bodily harm *resulted* from the application of force does *not* vitiate V's consent. To vitiate consent, the bodily harm must be *intended*.

R. v. Saint-Laurent (1994), 90 C.C.C. (3d) 291 (Que. C.A.), leave to appeal refused (May 5, 1994), Doc. No. 23982 (S.C.C.) — Consent in the context of sexual relationships implies a reasonably informed choice, freely exercised. There is no such choice where V, because of her mental state, is incapable of understanding the sexual nature of the act or of realizing that she may choose to decline participation. A significant power imbalance between V and D may have an effect on apparent consent. (per Fish J.A.)

Consent — Fraud: S. 265(3)(c)

R. v. Cuerrier (1998), 127 C.C.C. (3d) 1 (S.C.C.) — The failure of D to disclose that he is HIV-positive is a type of fraud which may vitiate consent to sexual intercourse under s. 265(3)(c).

The dishonest action or behaviour that vitiates consent must *relate* to obtaining *consent* to *engage* in unprotected sexual intercourse. D's actions must be assessed objectively to determine whether a *reasonable* person would find them to be *dishonest*. The dishonest act is either

i.   deliberate *deceit* respecting HIV status; or,

ii.   *non-disclosure* of HIV status.

There is *no* consent without disclosure of HIV status since the consent must be to have intercourse with a partner who is HIV-positive.

The extent of the duty to disclose HIV status increases with the risks attendant on the act of intercourse. There is, however, a *positive* duty to disclose. The nature and extent of the duty must be considered in the context of the facts of the case. (per Cory, Major, Bastarache and Binnie JJ.)

Fraud that will vitiate consent under s. 265(3)(c) involves not only *dishonesty*, but also *deprivation*.

Deprivation may consist of *actual harm or the risk* of *harm*. P must prove that the *dishonest* act had the *effect* of exposing the consenting party to a *significant risk* of *bodily harm*. The risk of contracting Aids from unprotected intercourse meets this test.

P must also prove beyond a reasonable doubt that V *would* have refused to have unprotected sexual intercourse with D *if* V had been told that D was HIV-positive. V's consent may be vitiated by fraud under s. 265(3)(c) if D's failure to disclose his HIV-positive status

i.   is *dishonest*; and,

ii.   *result* in *deprivation* by putting V at a *significant risk* of *suffering serious* bodily harm. (per Cory, Major, Bastarache and Binnie JJ.)

R. v. Cuerrier (1996), 111 C.C.C. (3d) 261 (B.C. C.A.) — The *only* fraud that will vitiate consent under s. 265(3)(c) is fraud concerning

i.   the nature and quality of the act; or

ii.   the identity of D.

R. v. Petrozzi (1987), 58 C.R. (3d) 320, 35 C.C.C. (3d) 528 (B.C. C.A.) — D's failure to pay a prostitute for sexual services did not vitiate her consent. Fraud, in this context is restricted to fraud as to the nature and quality of the act or the identity of the offender. It does not cover fraud which has a causal connection with the giving of consent.

Consent — Exercise of Authority: S. 265(3)(d)

R. v. J. (R.H.) (1993), 27 C.R. (4th) 40, 86 C.C.C. (3d) 354 (B.C. C.A.) — The fact of the relationship between a common law step-father and 17-year-old V does *not* establish a conclusive presumption of lack of consent. Section 265(3)(d) ought *not* be expanded on the basis of public policy

R. v. Saint-Laurent (1994), 90 C.C.C. (3d) 291 (Que. C.A.); leave to appeal refused (May 5, 1994), Doc. No. 23982 (S.C.C.) — A significant power imbalance between V and D, as for example, where D is a psychiatrist and V a patient undergoing psychotherapy, may vitiate consent under s. 265(3)(d). (per Tourigny and Fish JJ.A.)

R. v. Saint-Laurent (1994), 90 C.C.C. (3d) 291 (Que. C.A.); leave to appeal refused (May 5, 1994), Doc. No. 23982 (S.C.C.) — Under s. 265(3)(d), "authority" is *not* limited to relationships where there is a right to issue orders and to enforce obedience. (per Fish J.A.)

Consent — Honest Belief S. 265(4) ["Apprehended Consent"][See also s. 273.2]

R. v. Ewanchuk (1999), 22 C.R. (5th) 1, 131 C.C.C. (3d) 481 (S.C.C.) — There is *no* burden on D in connection with the defence of mistake. Support for it may arise from *any* of the evidence, including P's case in-chief and V's testimony.

To raise the defence of honest but mistaken belief, D must show that s/he *believed* that V *affirmatively communicated,* by words or action, *consent* to engage in the relevant *sexual activity.*

A belief that

i.   silence;

ii.   passivity; or,

iii.   ambiguous conduct

constitutes consent is *not* a defence.

D may *not* rely upon his/her purported belief that V's express lack of agreement to sexual touching actually constituted an invitation to more persistent and aggressive contact. Once V has expressed his/her unwillingness to engage in sexual contact, D should make certain that V has truly changed his/her mind before proceeding with further intimacies. D may *not* rely on a mere lapse of time or V's silence or equivocal conduct to indicate that V has had a change of heart, hence consents. D is also *not* able to engage in further sexual touching to "test the waters".

R. v. Esau (1997), 7 C.R. (5th) 357, 116 C.C.C. (3d) 289 (S.C.C.) — To permit consideration of apprehended consent by the trier of fact, there must be some plausible evidence adduced in support so as to give it an air of reality. The evidence may consist of a combination of

i.   V's evidence;

ii.   D's evidence; and

iii. evidence of the circumstances surrounding the commission of the offence.

R. v. Park (1995), 39 C.R. (4th) 287, 99 C.C.C. (3d) 1 (S.C.C.) — Before any defence can be left with a jury, it must have an "air of reality". The test is a legal, not a factual, threshold. The trial judge must decide if the evidence put forward is such that, if believed, a reasonable jury properly charged could acquit. The trial judge is not concerned with the weight of the evidence or assessments of credibility.

R. v. Park (1995), 39 C.R. (4th) 287, 99 C.C.C. (3d) 1 (S.C.C.) — There is no air of reality to a particular defence, hence no need to put it to the jury, where the totality of evidence for D is

i.   incapable of amounting to the defence asserted; or,

ii.   clearly, logically inconsistent with the totality of evidence which is not materially in dispute.

The standards ought to be viewed realistically, not evaluated to purely speculative or hypothetical extremes. What is of importance is that the evidence which is said to provide a basis for the defence must actually relate to, and support, the defence.

R. v. Osolin (1993), 26 C.R. (4th) 1, 86 C.C.C (3d) 481 (S.C.C.); reversing (1991), 10 C.R. (4th) 159 (B.C. C.A.) — Section 265(4), applicable to all assaults, codifies the common law defence of mistake of fact. As in the case of all defences, apprehended consent must be put to the jury if a reasonable jury, properly instructed, could acquit D on the evidence adduced in support of the defence. The *trial judge* must canvass the evidence and decide whether it is sufficient to warrant submission of the defence to the jury. Where the evidence meets this threshold, the defence must be put. It is for the *jury* then to decide whether the evidence raises a reasonable doubt as to D's guilt.

R. v. Osolin (1993), 26 C.R. (4th) 1, 86 C.C.C. (3d) 481 (S.C.C.); reversing (1991), 10 C.R. (4th) 159 (B.C. C.A) — *See also*: *R. v. Reddick* (1991), 5 C.R. (4th) 389, 64 C.C.C. (3d) 257 (S.C.C.) — Under s. 265(4), there must be evidence that gives an air of reality to D's assertion of a belief that V consented before apprehended consent need be put to the jury. There must be evidence beyond the mere assertion of the belief, but it need *not* be evidence independent of D.

R. v. Bulmer (1987), 58 C.R. (3d) 48, (sub nom. *Laybourn v. R.)* 33 C.C.C. (3d) 385 — *See also*: *R. v. Pappajohn* (1980), 14 C.R. (3d) 243 (S.C.C.); *R. v. White* (1986), 24 C.C.C. (3d) 1 (B.C. C.A.); leave to appeal refused 69 N.R. 80n (S.C.C.) — While the presence or absence of reasonable grounds for a belief in consent may assist a jury in determining whether it was honestly held, a mistaken belief in consent, if honestly held, need not be based on reasonable grounds.

R. v. Robertson (1987), 58 C.R. (3d) 28 (S.C.C.) — *See also*: *R. v. Guthrie* (1985), 20 C.C.C. (3d) 73 (Ont. C.A.) — There must be evidence that gives an air of reality to D's submission that he believed that V was consenting before the issue goes to the jury. In cases where there is nothing in P's case to indicate that D honestly believed in V's consent, D bears an evidentiary burden to introduce sufficient evidence if he wishes the issue to reach the jury. Where there is sufficient evidence to put the issue before the jury, P bears the burden of persuading the jury beyond a reasonable doubt that D knew V was not consenting or was reckless as to whether she was consenting or not.

Sansregret v. R. (1985), 45 C.R. (3d) 193, 18 C.C.C. (3d) 223 (S.C.C.) — An honest belief by D, even though unreasonably held, that V freely consented to intercourse would entitle D to an acquittal. However, where D deliberately blinded himself to reality, he is deemed to have had knowledge of the forced nature of the consent. The defence of honest though unreasonable mistake of fact is not available in circumstances of wilful blindness.

R. v. S. (A.W.) (1998), 122 C.C.C. (3d) 442 (Man. C.A.) — The "air of reality" test is a legal *not* a factual threshold. Although an ongoing sexual relationship may be evidence that provides an "air of reality" to a defence of apprehended consent, the trial judge must determine, in the particular circumstances, whether the "air of reality" does exist, as a matter of law.

R. v. M. (S) (1995), 39 C.R. (4th) 60, 97 C.C.C. (3d) 281 (Ont. C.A.) — Where V's consent could afford a defence to a charge of assault causing bodily harm, D's honest belief in the existence of that consent is likewise a defence.

Intoxication [See also ss. 8, 33.1 and 273.2]

R. v. Moreau (1986), 51 C.R. (3d) 209, 26 C.C.C. (3d) 359 (Ont. C.A.) — *See also: R. v. M. (R.D.)* (1986), 31 C.C.C. (3d) 323 (N.S. C.A.) — Where a mistaken belief in consent exists because of the voluntary intoxication of D, such a mistake does not exempt D from liability for sexual assault. Sexual assault is a crime of general intent Where D relies on mistaken belief and there is also evidence of his intoxication, the issue is whether D would have made the same mistake if sober.

Charter Considerations

R. v. Osolin (1993), 26 C.R. (4th) 1, 86 C.C.C. (3d) 481 (S.C.C.); reversing (1991), 10 C.R. (4th) 159 (B.C. C.A.) — Section 265(4) violates neither *Charter* s. 11(d) nor 11(f).

Related Provisions: "Weapon", "complainant" and "bodily harm" are defined in s. 2.

Assault, punishable under s. 266, is an essential ingredient of the offences of ss. 267 (assault with a weapon or causing bodily harm), 268 (aggravated assault), 270 (assaulting a peace officer), 271 (sexual assault), 272 (sexual assault with a weapon, threats to third party or causing bodily harm), 273 (aggravated sexual assault) and 343(a)–(c) (robbery). It is an included offence in all such crimes. Other related non-fatal offences against the person include ss. 269 (unlawfully causing bodily harm), 244 (causing bodily harm with intent) and 239 (attempted murder).

The intentional application of force to the person of another may be justified in the administration and enforcement of the law (ss. 25–31), the suppression of riots (ss. 32–33), private defence of person or property (ss. 34–42) and, in some instances, by designated persons in authority (ss. 43–45).

Where death ensues as a consequence *of an assault*, D may have committed culpable homicide under s. 222(5)(a). The offence committed, may be murder, manslaughter or infanticide.

Under s. 266, simple assault is an offence triable either way. Where P proceeds by indictment, D may *elect* mode of trial. Where P proceeds by summary conviction, the offence is tried under Part XXVII and punished under s. 787(1).

266. Assault — **Every one who commits an assault is guilty of**

   (a) an indictable offence and is liable to imprisonment for a term not exceeding five years; or

   (b) an offence punishable on summary conviction.
R.S., c. C-34, s. 245; 1972, c. 13, s. 21; 1974–75–76, c. 93, s. 22; 1980–81–82–83, c. 125, s. 19.

Commentary: Assault is an offence triable either way at P's election.

Related Provisions: An assault is defined in s. 265(1). Related offences in which assault is an essential element and justification of the intentional application of force are described in the corresponding note to s. 265.

Where P proceeds by indictment under s. 266(a), D may elect mode of trial. Where P proceeds by summary conviction, the offence is tried under Part XXVII and punished under s. 787(1).

Under *C.E.A.* s. 4(4), the wife or husband of D is a competent and compellable witness for P without D's consent, where V is under the age of 14 years.

S. 267 Criminal Code

267. Assault with a weapon or causing bodily harm — Every one who, in committing an assault,

(a) carries, uses or threatens to use a weapon or an imitation thereof, or

(b) causes bodily harm to the complainant,

is guilty of an indictable offence and liable to imprisonment for a term not exceeding ten years or an offence punishable on summary conviction and liable to imprisonment for a term not exceeding eighteen months.

1980–81–82–83, c. 125, s. 19; 1994, c. 44 s. 17.

Commentary: This section describes assault offences which differ from simple assault in their external circumstances and mental element. The offences are triable either way.

The *external circumstances* under s. 267(1)(a) involve the carriage or use, actual or threatened, of a real or imitation weapon, in addition to those of an assault. The *mental element* includes the mental element of simple assault and the intention to do that which constitutes the particular carriage or use described in the information or indictment.

Under s. 267(1)(b), the *external circumstances* comprise those of a simple assault and a resultant "bodily harm". The *mental element* is that required for simple assault and *objective foresight* that the assault would subject V to the risk of bodily harm.

Case Law
Uses Weapon: S. 267(1)(a)
Rowe v. R (1951), 12 C.R. 148, 100 C.C.C. 97 (S.C.C.) — "Using" a firearm includes pulling out a firearm which D has upon his person and holding it in his hand to intimidate another.

R. v. Richard (1992), 72 C.C.C. (3d) 349 (N.S. C.A.) — A beer bottle may be a "weapon" if D intended to use it to cause injury to V. P need *not* prove that the weapon actually caused injuries to V.

R. v. McLeod (1993), 84 C.C.C. (3d) 336 (Y.T. C.A.) — "Weapon" is *not* confined to inanimate objects, but may include the use of a dog to attack V.

Causing Bodily Harm: S. 267(1)(b)
R. v. Brooks (1988), 64 C.R. (3d) 322, 41 C.C.C. (3d) 157 (B.C. C.A.) — Where D pulled V from a vehicle into the path of an oncoming car, there is sufficient proximate cause to constitute assault causing bodily harm.

R. v. Nurse (1993), 83 C.C.C. (3d) 546 (Ont. C.A.) — Under s. 267(1)(b), *semble*, the *external circumstances* consist of:

i. the external circumstances of an assault under s. 265(1)(a) or (b); and,

ii. the resultant "bodily harm" within s. 267(2).

The *mental element, semble*, requires proof of:

i. the mental element required for the offence of assault; and,

ii. objective foreseeability that the assault would subject V to the risk of bodily harm.

R. v. Swenson (1994), 91 C.C.C. (3d) 541 (Sask. C.A.) — *See also: R. v. Brooks* (1988), 64 C.R. (3d) 322, 41 C.C.C. (3d) 157 (B.C. C.A.) — The essential elements of assault causing bodily harm are:

i. the *mental element* of assault, *viz.*, the intention to apply force to the person of V; and,

ii. *bodily harm* resulting from the force applied.

R. v. Dupperon (1984), 43 C.R. (3d) 70 (Sask. C.A.) — Where it was *not* proved that the bruises inflicted were more than merely transient or trifling in nature, a conviction for assault was substituted.

Consent [See s. 265]
Mental Element [See also Causing Bodily Harm: s. 267(1)(b), supra]
R. v. Janvier (1979), 11 C.R. (3d) 399 (Alta. C.A.) — *See also: R. v. Lee* (1988), 29 O.A.C. 379 (C.A.) — Assault causing bodily harm is a crime of general, *not* specific, intent. The words "commits an assault that causes bodily harm to any person" merely deal with the consequences of the assault.

R. v. Vandergraaf (1994), 34 C.R. (4th) 266, 93 C.C.C. (3d) 286, 95 Man. R. (2d) 315 (C.A.) — Assault with a weapon requires proof that D intended to apply force, directly or indirectly, to another person. Where D throws an object, intending it to strike the ice surface of an arena, but the object accidentally strikes and injures a fellow spectator, the offence is not made out.

Multiple Convictions

R. v. Briscoe (1992), 76 C.C.C. (3d) 563 (B.C. C.A.) — The rule against multiple convictions bars convictions for offences contrary to s. 267(1)(a) (assault with a weapon) and 87 (weapon dangerous) where:

i.   the *evidence* relied upon by P to establish the assault on V and the purpose for which D possessed the weapon is the same, *viz.*, the pointing of the weapon with the threat to use it; and,

ii. substantially the same *elements* make up both offences, *viz.*, carrying the weapon as an aggravating circumstance under s. 267(1)(a) and possession of it under s. 87, and are proven by the same evidence.

Related Provisions: "Weapon", "complainant" and "bodily harm" are defined in s. 2 and assault in s. 265.

Simple assault is an offence under s. 266 and aggravated assault likewise under section 268. Attempted murder is punishable under s. 239. The related offences of unlawfully causing bodily harm (s. 269), discharging a firearm with intent (s. 244) and uttering threats (s. 264.1) do *not* necessarily include commission of the present offence. The sexual assault offence of s. 272 includes the offence of this section. Use of a firearm while committing an indictable offence is also an offence under s. 85(1).

This offence is an "offence" for the purpose of Part VI, and would also appear to fall within para. (a) of the definition of "serious personal injury offence" in s. 752 for the purposes of Part XXIV. In any prosecution under the section, D's wife or husband is a competent and compellable witness for P without D's consent where V is under 14 years of age. The offence is excepted from the operation of the excuse of duress in s. 17.

Under s. 536(2), D may *elect* mode of trial. Conviction may engage the prohibition of s. 109 or 110.

268. (1) Aggravated assault — Every one commits an "aggravated assault" who wounds, maims, disfigures or endangers the life of the complainant.

(2) Punishment — Every one who commits an aggravated assault is guilty of an indictable offence and liable to imprisonment for a term not exceeding fourteen years.

(3) Excision — For greater certainty, in this section, "wounds" or "maims" includes to excise, infibulate or mutilate, in whole or in part, the labia majora, labia minora or clitoris of a person, except where

(a) a surgical procedure is performed, by a person duly qualified by provincial law to practise medicine, for the benefit of the physical health of the person or for the purpose of that person having normal reproductive functions or normal sexual appearance or function; or

(b) the person is at least eighteen years of age and there is no resulting bodily harm.

(4) Consent — For the purposes of this section and section 265, no consent to the excision, infibulation or mutilation, in whole or in part, of the labia majora, labia minora or clitoris of a person is valid, except in the cases described in paragraphs (3)(a) and (b)

1980–81–82–83, c. 125, s. 19; 1997, c. 16, s. 5.

Commentary: Aggravated assault differs from simple assault in its external circumstances and mental element.

The *external circumstances* consist of an assault and resultant harm to V that comes within the phrase "wounds, maims, disfigures or endangers the life".

Section 268(3) elaborates on the definitions of "wounds" and "maims" to include what is commonly referred to as "female genital mutilation". Excision, infibulation, or mutilation of female genitalia, except where it is done by a duly qualified medical practitioner in the circumstances of s. 268(3)(a), or where the person is eighteen or older and there is no bodily harm, constitutes an offence under s. 268. Consent is no defence for the purposes of this section or s. 265, except in the aforementioned circumstances.

The *mental element* comprises the mental element of an assault and *objective foresight* of the risk of a consequence described in the section.

Case Law

Nature and Elements of Offence

R. v. Cuerrier (1998), 127 C.C.C. (3d) 1 (S.C.C.) — The essential elements of aggravated assault are that

i.   D's act *endangered* the *life* of V; and,

ii. D *intentionally* applied force to V *without* V's *consent*.

Element is established by the *significant* risk to the *lives* of victims caused by an act of unprotected intercourse. P does *not* have to prove that the victims were infected with the HIV virus to satisfy this element.

In connection with element ii, it is *not* necessary when considering whether consent is vitiated under s. 265(3)(c), to consider whether the fraud relates to "the nature and quality of the act". (per Cory, Major, Bastarache and Binnie JJ.)

R. v. Cuadra (1998), 125 C.C.C. (3d) 289 (B.C. C.A.) — The *mental element* required to establish liability for aggravated assault as an *aider* is *objective foresight* of *bodily harm*. P is *not* required to prove

i.   *objective* foresight of the *specific* wounds inflicted; or,

ii. *subjective* awareness of the principal's possession of a weapon or its intended use.

R. v. Godin (1994), 31 C.R. (4th) 33, 89 C.C.C. (3d) 574 (S.C.C.); reversing (1993), 22 C.R. (4th) 265, 82 C.C.C. (3d) 44 (N.B. C.A.) — *See also*: *R. v. Leclerc* (1991), 7 C.R. (4th) 282, 67 C.C.C. (3d) 563 (Ont. C.A.) — The *mental element* is objective foresight of bodily harm, *not* an intent to wound, maim or disfigure.

R. v. Carriere (1987), 56 C.R. (3d) 257, 35 C.C.C. (3d) 276 (Alta. C.A.) — P must prove an assault as defined by the *Code*. Consent is *not* a defence to aggravated assault where the injuries were caused by stabbing with a knife.

R. v. Scharf (1988), 42 C.C.C. (3d) 378 (Man. C.A.) — *Contra*: *R. v. Parish* (1990), 60 C.C.C. (3d) 350 (N.B. C.A.) — This section does *not* require a specific intent above the general intent required for simple assault. An intent to endanger life is *not* an essential element of the offence. D who commits an assault which endangers the life of V is guilty of aggravated assault whether or not the nature and extent of V's injuries were reasonably foreseeable.

R. v. Nurse (1993), 83 C.C.C. (3d) 546 (Ont. C.A.) — The *external circumstances* of aggravated assault include an assault as defined in s. 265(1)(a) or (b) and, *inter alia*, a resultant wounding which is objectively foreseeable.

R. v. L. (S.R.) (1992), 16 C.R. (4th) 311, 76 C.C.C. (3d) 502 (Ont. C.A.) — This offence is a crime of general intent, not of absolute liability. It requires proof of the external circumstances and mental element of an assault, as well as a causal connection between the assault and the resultant harm or danger to V. P must also establish some further *nexus* which warrants the imposition of criminal liability based on the occurrence of that harm or danger. P must prove *objective foresight* of the risk of wounding, maiming, disfiguring or endangering the life of V. The trier of fact must decide whether a reasonable person would inevitably have realized that the assault would subject another to the risk of one of the specified results. P need *not* prove, however, some subjectively determined culpable mental state with respect to the consequences of the assault.

Wound, Maim, Disfigure [See s. 244]

Included Offences

R. v. St. Clair (1994), 88 C.C.C. (3d) 402 (Ont. C.A.) — An indictment which charges *aggravated assault* without particularization of the means by which the assault is alleged to have been committed does *not* contain assault with a weapon as an included offence.

R. v. Lucas (1987), 34 C.C.C. (3d) 28 (Que. C.A.) — The offence of assault causing bodily harm is included in the offence of aggravated assault.

Multiple Convictions

R. v. Osbourne (1994), 94 C.C.C. (3d) 435, 21 O.R. (3d) 97, 75 O.A.C. 315 (C.A.) — Convictions of aggravated assault and using a firearm while committing the offence of aggravated assault do not offend the rule against multiple convictions, notwithstanding that the same delict, the discharge of a firearm, gives rise to both counts.

Related Provisions: "Complainant" is defined in s. 2 and assault in s. 265. "Wounds", "maims", "disfigures" and "endangers ... life", are not defined in or for the purposes of the section.

Simple assault (s. 266), assault causing bodily harm (s. 267(1)(b)) and/or unlawfully causing bodily harm (s. 269) appear included in this offence, which is itself included in aggravated sexual assault described in s. 273. It may also be included in attempted murder under s. 239. The related offence of discharging a firearm, with intent is found in s. 244.

Where death ensues as a consequence of an assault *under this* section D may have committed culpable homicide under s. 222(5)(a). The offence committed, may be murder, manslaughter or infanticide.

This offence is an "offence" in s. 183 for the purposes of Part VI and would appear to fall within para. (a) of the definition of "serious personal injury offence" in s. 752 for the purposes of Part XXIV. The wife or husband of D is a competent and compellable witness for P, without the consent of D, under *C.E.A.* s. 4(4), where V is under 14 years of age. The offence is excepted from the excuse of duress in s. 17. D may *elect* mode of trial under s. 536(2). Conviction under the section engages the prohibition of s. 109.

269. Unlawfully causing bodily harm — Every one who unlawfully causes bodily harm to any person is guilty of

    (a) an indictable offence and liable to imprisonment for a term not exceeding ten years; or

    (b) an offence punishable on summary conviction and liable to imprisonment for a term not exceeding eighteen months.

1980–81–82–83, c. 125, s. 19; 1994, c. 44, s. 18.

Commentary: The *external circumstances* of this offence require proof of an act that is unlawful as a federal or provincial offence other than one of absolute liability. The act must also be *likely* to subject another to danger of bodily harm that is more than merely trivial or transitory in nature.

The *mental element* comprises the mental element required of the underlying unlawful act and objective foresight of bodily harm.

Case Law

Essential Elements

R. v. DeSousa (1992), 15 C.R. (4th) 66, 76 C.C.C. (3d) 124 (S.C.C.) — "Unlawfully" in s. 269 requires proof of an act that is unlawful as a federal or provincial offence. This underlying offence must *not* be an offence of absolute liability. Its mental element must itself be constitutionally sufficient.*Objective foresight* of *bodily harm* is also required for all underlying offences. D's act. unlawful in the sense earlier described, must also be one likely to subject another person to danger of bodily harm that is more than merely trivial or transitory in nature. In most cases, this will involve an act of violence done deliberately to another.

Relationship With Assault Bodily Harm: Ss. 267(1)(b) and 269

R. v. Glowacki (1984), 16 C.C.C. (3d) 574 (B.C. C.A.) — The fact that the findings on a charge under this section would also support a conviction for assault causing bodily harm is irrelevant.

Charter Considerations

R. v. DeSousa (1992), 15 C.R. (4th) 66, 76 C.C.C. (3d) 124 (S.C.C.) — Section 269, as interpreted *supra*, does *not* infringe *Charter* s. 7. It is *not* an offence which, due to its stigma and penalty, requires proof of fault based on a subjective standard.

Related Provisions: "Bodily harm" is defined in s. 2. There is no precise equivalent to this offence in the sexual assault trilogy of ss. 271–273, as each requires a sexual assault, *a fortiori*, an assault as an essential element.

An attempt to commit this offence is probably included in a count of attempted murder *simpliciter*. The offence may also be included in any assault or sexual assault offence involving proof of at least bodily harm to V where P's proof of an assault, sexual assault or the circumstances of aggravation described in ss. 268(1) and 273(1) is found deficient.

Related offences which include causing bodily harm as an essential element are criminal negligence causing bodily harm (s. 221), dangerous operation of a motor vehicle, vessel or aircraft causing bodily harm (ss. 249(1) and (3)), impaired operation of a motor vehicle, vessel or aircraft causing bodily harm (ss. 253(a), 255(2)) and breach of duty concerning explosive substances causing bodily harm (s. 80(b)). Failure to guard an opening in the ice or an excavation on land which causes bodily harm under s. 263(3)(b) is an offence under this section. Administering a noxious thing under s. 245(a) includes the intent to cause bodily harm as part of the mental element. The offences of ss. 247(1), 248 and 422 include, *inter alia*, foresight of bodily harm as an essential aspect of the mental element.

This offence is an "offence" under s.183 for the purposes of Part VI. Further, the offence would, in many instances at least, fall within para. (a) of definition of "serious personal injury offence" in s. 752 for the purposes of Part XXIV.

D may elect mode of trial under s. 536(2) where P proceeds by indictment. Where V is a person under 14 years of age, the wife or husband of D is a competent and compellable witness for P without D's consent. The offence is excepted from the excuse of duress in s. 17. Upon conviction, the mandatory provisions of s. 109(1) may become engaged, provided the bodily harm caused amounts to "violence" within the subsection.

269.1 (1) Torture — Every official, or every person acting at the instigation of or with the consent or acquiescence of an official, who inflicts torture on any other person is guilty of an indictable offence and is liable to imprisonment for a term not exceeding fourteen years.

(2) Definitions — For the purposes of this section,

"official" means

    (a) a peace officer,

    (b) a public officer,

    (c) a member of the Canadian Forces, or

    (d) any person who may exercise powers, pursuant to a law in force in a foreign state, that would, in Canada be exercised by a person referred to in paragraph (*a*), (*b*), or (*c*),

whether the person exercises powers in Canada or outside Canada;

"torture" means any act or omission by which severe pain or suffering, whether physical or mental, is intentionally inflicted on a person

    (a) for a purpose including

        (i) obtaining from the person or from a third person information or a statement,

(ii) **punishing the person for an act that the person or a third person has committed or is suspected of having committed, and**

(iii) **intimidating or coercing the person or a third person, or**

(b) **for any reason based on discrimination of any kind,**

but does not include any act or omission arising only from, inherent in or incidental to lawful sanctions.

(3) **No defence** — It is no defence to a charge under this section that the accused was ordered by a superior or a public authority to perform the act or omission that forms the subject-matter of the charge or that the act or omission is alleged to have been justified by exceptional circumstances, including a state of war, a threat of war, internal political instability or any other public emergency.

(4) **Evidence** — In any proceedings over which Parliament has jurisdiction, any statement obtained as a result of the commission of an offence under this section is inadmissible in evidence except as evidence that the statement was so obtained.

R.S. 1985, c. 10 (3d Supp.), s. 2.

Commentary: This section, creates the offence of torture, eliminates the defence of superior orders and enacts an ancillary evidentiary provision which excludes evidence of statements obtained in breach of the section, save for limited purposes.

Sections 269.1(1) and (2) should be read together. Section 269.1(1) requires that, as principal, D be a member of a defined class of persons, namely, an official or person acting at the instigation of or with the consent or acquiescence of an official. "Official" is exhaustively defined in s. 269.1(2). It is of no consequence to liability that the exercise of the official's powers took place in or outside Canada. The *external circumstances* also involve proof that D inflicted torture, as defined by s. 269.1(2), upon another person. The description of the offence in s. 269.1(1) would not itself require proof by P of an ulterior *mental element* but the definition of "torture" in s. 269.1(2) requires that the intentional infliction of severe physical or mental pain or suffering be for a proscribed purpose, thereby demanding proof of such ulterior purpose as an essential part of P's case.

Section 269.1(3) removes *superior orders* as a *defence*. It is further no defence for D to assert that what would otherwise amount to an offence is justified by exceptional circumstances, as for example, a state or threat of war, internal political instability or any other public emergency.

Section 269.1(4), an evidentiary rule applicable to all proceedings over which Parliament has legislative competence, generally bars the introduction of any statement obtained as a result of the commission of an offence under the section. Its sole exception permits reception of the statement as evidence that it was obtained in breach of the section.

Related Provisions: "Peace officer", "public officer" and "Canadian Forces" are defined in s. 2.

The section is subject to special territorial jurisdiction provisions in s. 6(1.9) and would appear to fall within para. (a) of the definition of "serious personal injury offence" in s. 752 for the purposes of Part XXIV.

It is doubtful whether it would be a a defence, in any event, for D to assert that his/her acts were done in obedience to the orders of a superior, whether civil or military, at least in times of peace.

D may elect mode of trial under s. 536(2). Conviction engages the prohibition of s. 109(1).

270. (1) Assaulting a peace officer — Every one commits an offence who

(a) **assaults a public officer or peace officer engaged in the execution of his duty or a person acting in aid of such an officer;**

(b) **assaults a person with intent to resist or prevent the lawful arrest or detention of himself or another person; or**

(c) assaults a person

> **(i) who is engaged in the lawful execution of a process against lands or goods or in making a lawful distress or seizure, or**
>
> **(ii) with intent to rescue anything taken under lawful process, distress or seizure.**

(2) Punishment — Every one who commits an offence under subsection (1) is guilty of

> **(a) an indictable offence and is liable to imprisonment for a term not exceeding five years; or**
>
> **(b) an offence punishable on summary conviction.**
>
> R.S., c. C-34, s. 246; 1972, c. 13, s. 22; 1980–81–82–83, c. 125, s. 19.

Commentary: Each offence requires proof of an assault. In some cases, V must also be one of a defined group of persons [ss. 270(1)(a) and (c)(i)]. In others [ss. 270(1)(b) and (c)(ii)], there is no such requirement. The *mental element* is in some cases [ss. 270(1)(b) and (c)(ii)], ulterior to the external circumstances of the crime. Under ss. 270(1)(a) and (c)(i), no such specific *mental element* is required. *Quaere* whether P must prove D's knowledge of V's status in such cases?

Case Law

In the Execution of His Duty [See s. 129]

R. v. Stenning (1970), 11 C.R.N.S. 68, [1970] 3 C.C.C. 145 (S.C.C.) — A peace officer investigating a possible unlawful entry was engaged in the lawful execution of his duty whether or not he was technically a trespasser on private property.

R. v. Berriault (1985), 43 Alta. L.R. (2d) 163 (C.A.) — A sheriff's officer effecting a seizure under a landlord's warrant of distress was exercising his authority by virtue of his public office and accordingly, was a peace officer acting in the execution of his duty.

R. v. Plamondon (1997), 12 C.R. (5th) 385, 121 C.C.C. (3d) 314 (B.C. C.A.) — If the actions of a peace officer exceed his/her powers, the external circumstances of the offence under s. 270 are *not* proven.

R. v. Cottam (1969), 7 C.R.N.S. 179, [1970] 1 C.C.C. 117 (B.C. C.A.) — To determine whether arresting officers were engaged in the execution of their duty the jury required instruction (1) as to the circumstances in which the arrest would be lawful, and (2) if the arrests were not lawful, whether the officers had so far exceeded their duty and authority as to be no longer engaged in the execution of their duty.

R. v. Corrier (1972), 7 C.C.C. (2d) 461 (N.B. C.A.) — In the course of investigating a theft, while attempting to seize D's car against his objections and without arresting him, a police officer exceeded his powers and therefore was not acting in the execution of his duty. D's use of excessive force, however, led to his conviction on the included offence of common assault.

Arrest

Gamracy v. R. (1974), 22 C.R.N.S. 224, 12 C.C.C. (2d) 209 (S.C.C.) — An arrest was lawful where the assaulted officer acted pursuant to an outstanding warrant not in his possession. His duty was fully discharged, without showing the warrant or ascertaining its contents, by telling D that the outstanding warrant was the reason for the arrest.

Mental Element [See also case digests for s. 231(4)]

R. v. Tom (1992), 18 C.R. (4th) 203, 79 C.C.C. (3d) 84 (B.C. C.A.) — Assault with intent to resist arrest is a specific intent offence which requires proof, *inter alia*, that D was *aware* that s/he was, or about to be placed, under arrest.

R. v. McLeod (1954), 20 C.R. 281, 111 C.C.C. 106 (B.C. C.A.) — *See also*: *R. v. Vlcko* (1972), 10 C.C.C. (2d) 139 (Ont. C.A.) — *Knowledge* that the person assaulted is, in fact, a police officer is an essential element of the offence.

Related Provisions: "Peace officer" and "public officer" are defined in s. 2, assault in s. 265.

The *Code* does not exhaustively define the powers or authority of a peace or public officer. Sections 25–31 protect persons administering and enforcing the law. Sections 32 and 33 justify the use of force in the suppression of riots and the dispersal of rioters. The scope of protection afforded, to some extent at least, defines the ambit of authority given. Other provisions, as for example s. 495 (arrest without warrant by a peace officer), furnish specific authority to be exercised by a peace officer, in given circumstances.

Other offences relating to peace or public officers include ss. 120 (bribery), 129 (obstruction, failure to assist), 140 (inducing investigation by false statement) and 130 (impersonation). The present offence is a primary crime in the constitutionally deficient definition of murder found in s. 230. Murder of a police officer or police constable is first degree murder under s. 231(4)(a). Other assault offences, liability for which is not dependent upon V being a peace or public officer, are described in ss. 265–268. Simple assault under s. 266 would appear an included offence.

The offence is triable either way. Where P proceeds by indictment, D may elect mode of trial under s. 536(2). Where P proceeds by summary conviction, the offence is tried under Part XXVII and punished under s, 787(1). A finding of guilt may attract the discretionary prohibition of s. 110.

271. (1) Sexual assault — **Every one who commits a sexual assault is guilty of**

(a) an indictable offence and is liable to imprisonment for a term not exceeding ten years; or

(b) an offence punishable on summary conviction and liable to imprisonment for a term not exceeding eighteen months.

(2) [Repealed R.S. 1985, c. 19 (3d Supp.), s. 10.]
   1980–81–82–83, c. 125, s. 19; R.S. 1985, c. 19 (3d Supp.), s. 10; 1994, c. 44, s. 19.

Commentary: Sexual assault is not defined, although an essential element, assault, is elsewhere defined for such purposes. In general, it is an assault under s. 265(1) committed in circumstances of a sexual nature such as to violate the sexual integrity of V. The *mental element* requires proof of a general intent only. Sexual assault, like assault, is both itself a crime and an essential element of the external circumstances of its more aggravated forms, ss. 272 and 273.

Case Law
Elements of Offence

R. v. Ewanchuk (1999), 22 C.R. (5th) 1, 131 C.C.C. (3d) 481 (S.C.C.) — The *external circumstances* of sexual assault include

i.   *touching*;
ii. *sexual* nature; and,
iii. *absence* of *consent*.

The *mental element* in sexual assault has two components:

i.   the *intention* to *touch*; and,
ii. *knowledge* or *recklessness* of or *wilful blindness* towards lack of consent.

R. v. Daigle, [1998] 1 S.C.R. 1220, 127 C.C.C. (3d) 129 (S.C.C.); affirming (1997), 127 C.C.C. (3d) 130 (Que. C.A.) — An assault that is sexual in nature does *not* always appear hostile in the same way as an ordinary assault. Hostility may arise from lack of consent.

R. v. Litchfield (1993), 25 C.R. (4th) 137, 86 C.C.C. (3d) 97 (S.C.C.) — Sexual assault is a crime of general intent. P need not prove a specific intent with respect to the sexual nature of the assault since it forms part of the *actus reus*. The test is objective. All the circumstances surrounding the relevant conduct are relevant to the issue whether the conduct was of a sexual nature and violated V's sexual integrity. Unnecessary barriers to a consideration of all of the circumstances surrounding conduct alleged to constitute a sexual assault ought not be created, especially where V has consented to some touching not of a sexual nature.

R. v. V. (K.B.) (1993), 82 C.C.C. (3d) 382 (S.C.C.); affirming (1992), 13 C.R. (4th) 87, 71 C.C.C. (3d) 65 (Ont. C.A.) — To determine whether sexual assault has been committed, a court should consider a number of factors, including the body part touched, the nature of the contact, any words or gestures including threats accompanying the conduct, and D's intent or purpose, including the presence or absence of sexual gratification. Sexual assault does *not*, however, require sexuality or sexual gratification. A misguided and primitive disciplinary exercise which is an aggressive act of domination which violates the sexual integrity of V and constitutes an assault may be a sexual assault. (per Robins and Osborne JJ.A.)

R. v. S. (P.L.) (1991), 5 C.R. (4th) 351, 64 C.C.C. (3d) 193 (S.C.C.) — Sexual assault is a crime of basic or general intent. The intent of D is but one factor to consider in deciding whether the overall conduct had a sexual context.

R. v. Chase (1987), 59 C.R. (3d) 193, 37 C.C.C. (3d) 97 (S.C.C.) — *See also*: *R. v. Moreau* (1986), 51 C.R. (3d) 209, 26 C.C.C. (3d) 359 (Ont. C.A.) — Sexual assault is an assault committed in circumstances of a sexual nature, such that the sexual integrity of V is violated. The test to be applied in determining whether the impugned conduct has the requisite sexual nature is objective. The intent or purpose of the assault, as well as a motive if such motive of sexual gratification, may also be factors in considering whether the conduct is sexual.

R. v. Taylor (1985), 44 C.R. (3d) 263 (Alta. C.A.) — The term "sexual assault" includes an act which is intended to degrade or demean another person for sexual gratification. The carnal or sexual aspect that is required is *not* restricted to acts of force involving the sexual organs.

R. v. Ricketts (1985), 61 A.R. 175 (C.A.) — A lascivious suggestion accompanied by an expression of force sufficient to amount to an assault, constitutes, without more, a sexual assault.

R. v. Cook (1985), 46 C.R. (3d) 129, 20 C.C.C. (3d) 18 (B.C. C.A.) — The elements that turn a simple assault into a sexual assault are not solely a matter of anatomy. An affront to sexual integrity and sexual dignity may be sufficient.

R. v. Alderton (1985), 44 C.R. (3d) 254, 17 C.C.C. (3d) 204 (Ont. C.A.) — Intentional and forced contact with the genital organs of another person is *not* required for a conviction for sexual assault. "Sexual assault" includes an assault with the intention of having sexual intercourse with V without her consent, or an assault made upon a victim for the purpose of sexual gratification.

R. v. Bernier, [1998] 1 S.C.R. 975, 124 C.C.C. (3d) 383 (S.C.C.); affirming (1997), 119 C.C.C. (3d) 467 (Que. C.A.) — A sexual assault is committed where there is voluntary touching by D of V's breasts and testicles without V's consent. No hostility is required.

Actual and Apprehended Consent [See s. 265, 273.1 and 273.2]

Expert Evidence [See also CEA s. 7]

R. v. Kliman (1996), 47 C.R. (4th) 137, 107 C.C.C. (3d) 549 (S.C.C.) — Expert evidence that V suffers from fleeting delusions and borderline personality disorder, disabilities that affect V's ability to testify reliably, is admissible. The evidence is not limited to the opinion, rather, extends to the facts and circumstances on which the diagnosis is based and the extent to which V's credibility is affected.

R. v. Burns (1992), 74 C.C.C. (3d) 124 (B.C. C.A.); reversed on other grounds (1994), 29 C.R. (4th) 113, 89 C.C.C. (3d) 193 (S.C.C.) — Expert evidence of a psychologist may be admitted notwithstanding that it tends to show that V was assaulted by another person in addition to D. P is entitled to lead from the psychologist the history of abuse as given by V, because the history is often the basis for the expert's opinion. P may also ask the expert whether, at any time, so far as the expert was aware, V had told him/her something that was untrue. The expert is entitled to support the credibility of his/her opinion to such an extent. To do so is *not* to give evidence in support of the credibility of V.

R. v. Jmieff (1994), 94 C.C.C. (3d) 157 (B.C. C.A.) — Experts such as a psychologist are competent to give evidence about human conduct, such as delayed complaints or recantations in sexual matters, in order to explain V's conduct, notwithstanding that the evidence may indirectly support V's credibility. Experts cannot give evidence, however, which purports directly to confirm the credibility of a witness. Evidence tendered for the specific purpose of bolstering the credibility of a witness is inadmissible.

R. v. C. (R.A.) (1990), 78 C.R. (3d) 390, 57 C.C.C. (3d) 522 (B.C. C.A.) — *See also*: *R. v. P. (C.)* (1992), 74 C.C.C. (3d) 481, 484–5 (B.C. C.A.) — In cases of alleged sexual abuse of children, where credibility is in issue, the evidence of a duly qualified expert, such as a sexual abuse therapist, may be received since, in its absence, a jury might well draw an inference adverse to V due to failure of or delay in complaint.

R. v. R. (R.) (1994), 30 C.R. (4th) 293, 91 C.C.C. (3d) 193 (Ont. C.A.) — An expert qualified to give opinion evidence with respect to the behavioural patterns of sexually-abused children is *not* entitled to testify that it is *highly likely* that the assault occurred as alleged by V.

R. v. R. (S.) (1992), 15 C.R. (4th) 102, 73 C.C.C. (3d) 225 (Ont. C.A.) — In a case of alleged sexual abuse of children, evidence that the expert *believed* the story told to him/her by V is not admissible, as it offends the rule against oath-helping. An expert may not express the opinion that V had been subjected to sexual abuse.

R. v. Garfinkle (1992), 15 C.R. (4th) 254 (Que. C.A.) — Psychiatric evidence with respect to personality traits of D is admissible provided that it is:

i.   relevant;

ii.   not excluded by policy; and,

iii. properly within the sphere of expert evidence.

Since pedophilia is an abnormal disposition, expert psychiatric evidence is admissible to show that D does *not* have such disposition. Policy rules prevent P from adducing psychiatric evidence to establish that D had such a propensity.

R. v. Silva (1994), 31 C.R. (4th) 361 (Sask. C.A.); leave to appeal refused (September 15, 1994), Doc. No. 24203 (S.C.C.) — A general medical practitioner with a residency in obstetrics and gynaecology may testify that V's vaginal injuries are consistent with forced sexual intercourse.

Hearsay Evidence of Children's Statements [See also C.E.A. s. 16]

R. v. Rockey (1996), 111 C.C.C. (3d) 481 (S.C.C.) — Where hearsay evidence is tendered for admission, the trial judge ought formally rule on

i.   necessity; and

ii.   reliability.

There is no presumption of necessity. Where the hearsay declarant is a child. P must decide whether to tender the child as a witness. Where the child is not tendered as a witness, the trial judge ought decide whether the child could not have testified, hence the necessity of calling a hearsay recipient as a substitute witness.

Necessity may be established in relation to a child hearsay declarant where

i.   the child is *incompetent* to testify;

ii.   the child is *unable* to testify;

iii. the child is *unavailable* to testify;

iv.   the trial judge is satisfied, based on psychological assessments, that testimony in court might be traumatic or cause harm to the child; or,

v.   if the child testifies, the trial judge is satisfied that the admission of the hearsay statements is reasonably necessary to put a full and frank account of the child's version of relevant events before the trier of fact.

Disclosure of Medical Records [See now ss. 278.1-278.91]

R. v. O'Connor (1995), 44 C.R. (4th) 1, 103 C.C.C. (3d) 1 (S.C.C.) — The intensely private nature of therapeutic records does *not* affect P's obligation to disclose to D those records already in P's possession. Privacy and privilege concerns disappear where the documents have come into P's possession. There is no privacy interest to be balanced against D's right to make full answer and defence. P's disclosure obligations are *not* affected by the confidential nature of therapeutic records in P's possession.

R. v. O'Connor (1995), 44 C.R. (4th) 1, 103 C.C.C. (3d) 1 (S.C.C.) — Where D seeks production and disclosure of records in the possession of a third party, a two-stage procedure is to be followed. The procedure is commenced by a formal written application supported by an affidavit describing the specific grounds for production. Notice should be given to third party custodians of the documents and the persons who have a privacy interest in the records. The custodian and records should be subpoenaed to ensure their attendance or presence. The initial application ought to be made to the judge seized of the trial but may be brought, with other pre-trial motions, before the jury is empanelled. At the *first* stage in the production procedure, D has the *onus* of satisfying the judge that the information sought is *likely* to be *relevant.* Every case does *not* require evidence and a *voir dire.* There is an initial threshold to provide a basis for production. It may be met by oral submissions of counsel. If the matter cannot be resolved on the basis of oral submissions, evidence and a *voir dire* may be required.The test of *likely relevance* requires that the judge be satisfied that there is a *reasonable possibility* that the information sought is *logically probative* on an *issue* at trial *or* the *competence* of a witness to testify. The *issues at trial* include:

i.   the *matters in issue* in the case;

ii.   the *credibility* of witnesses; and,

iii. the *reliability* of *other evidence* in the case.

The burden on D should *not* be considered onerous, nor should it be assumed that private, therapeutic or counselling records are irrelevant to full answer and defence. The records may be *relevant*, in cases of sexual assault, because they:

i.   contain information concerning the *unfolding of events* underlying the complaint;

ii.   reveal the use of a *therapy* which *influenced* V's *memory* of the alleged offence; or,

iii. contain information relevant to V's *credibility*, including testimonial factors like the quality of V's perception of the events at the time of offence and V's memory thereafter.

At the *second* stage, the judge ought examine the records produced to determine whether, and to what extent, they ought be produced to D. The judge must weigh and examine the salutary and deleterious effects of a production order, as well decide whether a non-production order would constitute a reasonable limit on D's right to make full answer and defence. The judge may be able to provide a judicial summary of the records for counsel to assist in the determination.In balancing the competing rights, the judge ought consider:

i.   the extent to which the record is *necessary* for D to make full answer and defence;

ii.   the *probative value* of the record;

iii. the nature and extent of the *reasonable expectation of privacy* vested in the record;

iv.   whether production would be premised on any discriminatory belief or bias; and,

v.   the potential *prejudice* of V's dignity, privacy or personal security occasioned by production.

R. v. Beharriell (1995), 44 C.R. (4th) 91, 103 C.C.C. (3d) 92 (S.C.C.) — Third parties, for example V and providers of sexual abuse counselling services to V, may challenge interlocutory court orders.An order made by a *provincial court judge* should be challenged by an enlarged remedy of *certiorari* with its applicable rights of appeal. An order of a *judge of the superior court of criminal jurisdiction* may be challenged by third parties by seeking leave to appeal directly to the Supreme Court of Canada under s. 40(1) of the *Supreme Court Act.* Both P and V have standing in third party appeals brought by counselling organizations.

R. v. Kliman (1996), 47 C.R. (4th) 137, 107 C.C.C. (3d) 549 (B.C. C.A.) — It is error for the trial judge to require D to lead expert evidence in support of an application for production of records relevant to the possible impact of a therapeutic process on memory recovery by V.

R. v. L. (P.S.) (1995), 103 C.C.C. (3d) 341 (B.C. C.A.) — If D can establish that missing evidence was of such importance that it deprived D of the ability to make full answer and defence, a stay of proceedings may be warranted. The threshold will be met where D shows that the missing material *would likely have assisted* D in meeting P's case.

Blood Samples [See also s. 487.05]

R. v. Borden (1994), 33 C.R. (4th) 147, 92 C.C.C. (3d) 404 (S.C.C.); affirming (1993), 24 C.R. (4th) 184, 84 C.C.C. (3d) 380 (N.S. C.A.) — There is no statutory authorization for the seizure of a blood sample in relation to the offence of sexual assault.

Charter Considerations

R. v. Piercey (1986), 60 Nfld. & P.E.I.R. 76 (Nfld. C.A.) — The term "sexual" in sexual assaultis not so vague as to offend *Charter* ss. 7 or 9.

Historic Offences: Rape

R. v. O'Connor (1998), 123 C.C.C. (3d) 487 (B.C. C.A.) — On a charge of rape, s. 135(b) of the *Criminal Code*, S.C. 1953-54, c. 51 defines the circumstances in which *consent*, if obtained, may be considered impaired or vitiated:

i.   by threats of bodily harm;

ii. by personation of V's husband; or,

iii. by fraud as to the nature of the act.

The exercise of authority does *not* vitiate consent, although it is a circumstance which may be considered in deciding whether V consented, and if V did not consent, to explain the lack of resistance.

A subjective absence of consent is sufficient to establish the "without consent" element in rape. Evidence of failure of V to resist is a circumstance for the trier of fact to consider in deciding whether to believe V's assertion of non-consent and, if the evidence were accepted, whether D was honestly mistaken about V's consent due to her passivity.

Prior to 1983, "consent" means the same thing for both rape and indecent assault.

Related Provisions: Assault, defined in s. 265(1), is an included offence.

Consent, actual and apprehended, is generally a defence to this crime. "Consent" is defined in s. 273.1(1) for the purposes of the sexual assault offences. It may be vitiated by any of the matters or factors in ss. 273.1(2) or (3) or 265(3). Equally, under s. 150.1(1), it is not a defence that V, under the age of 14 years, consented, save in the limited circumstances of s. 150.1(2), nor that D believed that V was 14 years of age or more unless, in the latter case, under s. 150.1(4), D took all reasonable steps to ascertain V's age. An honest belief in consent, "apprehended consent", is also a defence. Under s. 265(4), D's belief in V's consent need not be both honest and *reasonable*, but the presence or absence of reasonable grounds for the belief are factors for the trier of fact to consider in assessing the honesty of the belief. The belief must not be one which discloses a state of affairs, which, if true, would be an invalid consent, as for example under s. 265(3). Apprehended consent is not a defence where s. 273.2 applies.

This offence is an essential element of, hence is included in the offences of ss. 272 (sexual assault with a weapon, threats to a third party, causing bodily harm or involving parties) and 273 (aggravated sexual assault). Other sexual offences appear in ss. 150.1–153, 155, 159, 160 and 170–172. Under s. 231(5)(b), murder is first degree murder where D causes V's death while committing or attempting to commit an offence under s. 271. The offence also falls within para. (b) of the definition of "serious personal injury offence" in s. 752 for the purposes of Part XXIV and is an "offence" in s. 183, for the purposes of Part VI.

The special evidentiary rules of ss. 274 (corroboration), 275 (recent complaint), 276 (other sexual activity), 277 (sexual reputation) and 715.1 (videotaped evidence of V or other witness) are applicable to proceedings under the section. S. 4(2) *C.E.A.* makes D's wife or husband a competent and compellable witness for P without D's consent. Under s. 278, D may be charged with the offence even where V is her husband or his wife, as the case may be. D may not rely on the excuse of compulsion under s. 17. Production of third party records is governed by ss. 278.1-278.91.

The offence is triable either way upon P's election. In proceedings upon indictment, D may elect mode of trial under s. 536(2). Proceedings upon summary conviction are governed by Part XXVII. The circumstances of the offence and mode of procedure, upon finding of guilt or conviction, may engage either s. 109 or 110.

---

272. (1) Sexual assault with a weapon, threats to a third party or causing bodily harm — Every person commits an offence who, in committing a sexual assault,

(a) carries, uses or threatens to use a weapon or an imitation of a weapon;

(b) threatens to cause bodily harm to a person other than the complainant;

(c) causes bodily harm to the complainant; or

(d) is a party to the offence with any other person.

(2) Punishment — Every person who commits an offence under subsection (1) is guilty of an indictable offence and liable

   (a) where a firearm is used in the commission of the offence, to imprisonment for a term not exceeding fourteen years and to a minimum punishment of imprisonment for a term of four years; and

   (b) in any other case, to imprisonment for a term not exceeding fourteen years.
                                                   1980–81–82–83, c. 125, s. 19;1995, c. 39, s. 145.

Commentary: This sexual assault offence, one of an intermediate level of gravity, is punishable only upon indictment. When a firearm is used, it carries a minimum term of imprisonment.

The *external circumstances* consist of a sexual assault coupled with *any* of the aggravating features of weapons, bodily harm or parties as described in ss. 272(a)-(d). The *mental element* remains one of general intent, subject to the specific accessoryship requirement of s 272(d).

Case Law
Essential Elements [See also ss. 33.1 and 267]

R. v. Daviault (1994), 33 C.R. (4th) 165, 93 C.C.C. (3d) 21 (S.C.C.) — D may give evidence of the amount of alcohol consumed and its effect.

R. v. Bernard (1988), 67 C.R. (3d) 113, 45 C.C.C. (3d) 1 (S.C.C.) — The offence of sexual assault causing bodily harm is one of general intent. In establishing the mental element, P must only prove the intention of D to apply force.

R. v. Welch (1995), 43 C.R. (4th) 225, 101 C.C.C. (3d) 216 (Ont. C.A.) — P must prove conduct which, viewed objectively, is such that it would be likely to cause bodily harm to V.

Consent as Defence

R. v. Welch (1995), 43 C.R. (4th) 225, 101 C.C.C. (3d) 216 (Ont. C.A.) — Consent is *not* a defence to a charge of sexual assault causing bodily harm.

Related Provisions: "Weapon", "complainant" and "bodily harm" are defined in s. 2, assault in s. 265. The general accessoryship provisions are found in ss. 21 and 22.

Assault (s. 266) and sexual assault (s. 271) are included offences. The offences of ss. 267(1)(a) and (b) are included in the offences of ss. 272(a) and (c), respectively.

The other related provisions discussed in the corresponding note to s. 271, *supra*, also apply to this offence, subject to four exceptions. The age differential defence of s. 150.1(2) does *not* apply to a charge under this section. This offence is exclusively indictable. D may elect mode of trial under s. 536(2). The applicable reference in the classification of murder as first degree murder is s 231(5)(c). A conviction under ss. 272(a), (b) and (c) would probably engage the provisions of s. 109, s. 272(d) less obviously so.

273. (1) Aggravated sexual assault — Every one commits an aggravated sexual assault who, in committing a sexual assault, wounds, maims, disfigures or endangers the life of the complainant.

(2) Aggravated sexual assault — Every person who commits an aggravated sexual assault is guilty of an indictable offence and liable

   (a) where a firearm is used in the commission of the offence, to imprisonment for life and to a minimum punishment of imprisonment for a term of four years; and

   (b) in any other case, to imprisonment for life.
                                                   1980–81–82–83, c. 125, s. 19; 1995, c. 39, s. 146.

Commentary: This offence aggravated sexual assault adds to the *external circumstances* of sexual assault "wounds, maims, disfigures or endangers the life of the complainant". None of these elements is statutorily defined.

Semble the *mental element* of aggravated sexual assault does *not* extend beyond what is required in cases of sexual assault *simpliciter*. The distinguishing features of aggravated sexual assault lie in its external circumstances, in particular the consequences.

Related Provisions: "Complainant" is defined in s. 2, assault in s. 265.

Assault (s. 266) and sexual assault (s. 271) are included offences. Assault causing bodily harm under s. 267(1)(b) and sexual assault causing bodily harm under s. 272(c) are likely included, since it is difficult to envisage assaultive behaviour that amounts to "wounds, maims, disfigures or endangers the life of the complainant" which does not also cause V "bodily harm", as defined in s. 267(2).

The other related provisions discussed in the corresponding note to s. 271, *supra*, have equal application to the present offence with four exceptions. The age differential defence of s. 150.1(2) does not avail D charged under this section. The applicable reference in the classification of murder as first degree murder is s. 231(5)(d). This offence is exclusively indictable. D may elect mode of trial under s. 536(2). Conviction under this section engages the prohibition of s. 109.

273.1 (1) Meaning of "consent" — Subject to subsection (2) and subsection 265(3), "consent" means, for the purposes of sections 271, 272 and 273, the voluntary agreement of the complainant to engage in the sexual activity in question.

(2) Where no consent obtained — No consent is obtained, for the purposes of sections 271, 272 and 273, where

   (a) the agreement is expressed by the words or conduct of a person other than the complainant;

   (b) the complainant is incapable of consenting to the activity;

   (c) the accused induces the complainant to engage in the activity by abusing a position of trust, power or authority;

   (d) the complainant expresses, by words or conduct, a lack of agreement to engage in the activity; or

   (e) the complainant, having consented to engage in sexual activity, expresses, by words or conduct, a lack of agreement to continue to engage in the activity.

(3) Subsection (2) not limiting — Nothing in subsection (2) shall he construed as limiting the circumstances in which no consent is obtained.

1992, c. 38, s. 1.

Commentary: This section defines "consent" for the purposes of the sexual assault offences in ss. 271–273.

"Consent" in s. 273.1(1) is defined exhaustively and specifically related to the external circumstances of the sexual assault offences. For the purposes of ss. 271–273, "consent" means the *voluntary agreement* of V to engage in the *sexual activity in question*. V's agreement, in other words, must not only be *voluntary*, but also activity specific. The definition is subject to s. 273.1(2) and 265(3).

Sections 273.1(2) and (3) should be read and considered together. Each describes circumstances in which no consent is obtained for the purposes of ss. 271–273. No consent is obtained in *any* of the circumstances enumerated ss. 273.1(2).

Section 273.1(3) enacts that s. 273.1(2) is *not* limitative of the circumstances in which no consent is obtained.

Case Law[See also, s. 265]

R. v. Ewanchuk (1999), 22 C.R. (5th) 1, 131 C.C.C. (3d) 481 (S.C.C.) — There is no consent where V agrees to sexual activity *only* because s/he believes that s/he will otherwise suffer physical violence. The approach is *subjective*. The *plausibility* of the alleged fear and any *overt expressions* of it are *relevant* to assessing V's *credibility*. A trial judge need only consult *Code* s. 265(3) where V

i.   has chosen to participate in sexual activity; or,

ii.   by ambiguous conduct or submission, has raised a doubt about the absence of consent.

The *absence* of *consent* is *subjective*. It is determined by reference to V's internal state of mind towards the touching *when* the touching takes place. V's statement of non-consent is a matter of credibility for the trier of fact. It is to be considered in light of *all* of the evidence *including* any ambiguous conduct by V. If the trier of fact accepts V's assertion of absence of consent, no matter how strongly V's conduct may contradict the assertion, absence of consent is established. Implied consent is *not* a defence to sexual assault.

R. v. Jensen (1996), 47 C.R. (4th) 363, 106 C.C.C. (3d) 430 (Ont. C.A.) — V's actual state of mind is determinative of the issue of consent. The approach is *subjective*. (per Brooke and Rosenberg JJ.A.)

R. v. Welch (1995), 43 C.R. (4th) 225, 101 C.C.C. (3d) 216 (Ont. C.A.) — The definition of consent in s. 273.1 is *not* exhaustive. For public policy reasons, V cannot consent to the infliction of bodily harm upon her/himself, except where D acts in the course of a generally-approved social purpose when inflicting the harm. Notwithstanding legal recognition of individual freedom and autonomy, when an activity involves pursuit of sexual gratification by deliberate infliction of pain upon another that gives rise to bodily harm, the personal interests of the individuals involved must yield to the more compelling societal interests challenged by such behaviour.

Charter Considerations

R. v. Darrach (1998), 13 C.R. (5th) 283, 122 C.C.C. (3d) 225 (Ont. C.A.); application for leave to appeal allowed (1998), 124 C.C.C. (3d) vi (S.C.C.) — Section 273.1(2)(d) is *not* void for vagueness.

Related Provisions: "Consent" is *not* elsewhere defined, as for example, in or for the purposes of the definition of assault in s. 265(1). No consent is obtained where V submits or does not resist by reason of any circumstance described in s. 265(3), which is applicable to sexual assaults under S. 265(2), as well as s. 273.1(1). Sections 150.1(1) and (2) and 286 also remove consent as a defence to certain listed crimes. Under s. 14, no person is entitled to consent to have death inflicted on him/her.

Apprehended consent is a defence, *inter alia*, to the crimes of sexual assault. It is governed, in part, by s. 265(4) and restricted in its application by s. 273.2.

The *Code* provides no definition of "... a position of trust, power or authority ..." as used in s. 273.1(2)(c). The phrase "a position of trust or authority" also appears in *Code* s. 153(1), but is neither there nor elsewhere defined.

273.2 Where belief in consent not a defence — **It is not a defence to a charge under section 271, 272 or 273 that the accused believed that the complainant consented to the activity that forms the subject-matter of the charge, where**

   (a) the accused's belief arose from the accused's

      (i) self-induced intoxication, or

      (ii) recklessness or wilful blindness; or

   (b) the accused did not take reasonable steps, in the circumstances known to the accused at the time, to ascertain that the complainant was consenting.

1992, c. 38, s. 1.

Commentary: The section restricts the availability of *apprehended consent* as a defence to charges of sexual assault under ss. 271–273.

In general, it is open to D on a charge of sexual assault to assert an *honest* belief that V consented to the sexual activity said to constitute the crime charged. Section 273.2(a), however, removes apprehended consent as a defence where D's belief arises from D's:

i.   self-induced *intoxication*;

ii.   *recklessness*; or,

iii. *wilful blindness*.

Further, under s. 273.2(b), apprehended consent is no defence where D did *not* take *reasonable* steps in the circumstances known to D at the time, to ascertain that V was consenting.

Apprehended consent induced by any prohibited source or the *failure* to take *reasonable steps* will disentitle D to the benefit of the defence. Both are *not* required. The disentitling factors are alternative not cumulative.

Case Law

R. v. Ewanchuk (1999), 22 C.R. (5th) 1, 131 C.C.C. (3d) 481 (S.C.C.) — There is *no* burden on D in connection with the defence of *mistake*. Support for it may arise from *any* of the evidence, including P's case in-chief and V's testimony.

To raise the defence of honest but mistaken belief, D must show that s/he *believed* that V *affirmatively communicated*, by words or action, *consent* to engage in the relevant *sexual activity*. A belief that

i.   silence;

ii.   passivity; or,

iii.   ambiguous conduct

constitutes consent is *not* a defence.

D may *not* rely upon his/her purported belief that V's express lack of agreement to sexual touching actually constituted an invitation to more persistent and aggressive contact. Once V has expressed his/her unwillingness to engage in sexual contact, D should make certain that V has truly changed his/her mind before proceeding with further intimacies. D may *not* rely on a mere lapse of time or V's silence or equivocal conduct to indicate that V has had a change of heart, hence consents. D is also *not* able to engage in further sexual touching to "test the waters".

R. v. Daigle, [1998] 1 S.C.R. 1220, 127 C.C.C. (3d) 129; affirming (1997), 127 C.C.C. (3d) 130 (Que. C.A.) — A defence of *apprehended* consent is *not* available where D does *not* take *reasonable* steps to ascertain whether V is consenting.

R. v. G. (R.) (1994), 38 C.R. (4th) 123 (B.C. C.A.) — Section 273.2(b) does *not* restrict apprehended consent to those accused who first "determined unequivocally" that V was consenting. It requires that D meet the evidentiary burden of establishing that s/he took reasonable steps in the circumstances which he knew to determine whether V was consenting. There is a proportionate relationship between what will be required as reasonable steps and the circumstances known to D. (per Macfarlane and Wood JJ. A.)

Charter Considerations

R. v. Darrach (1998), 13 C.R. (5th) 283, 122 C.C.C. (3d) 225 (Ont. C.A.); application for leave to appeal allowed (1998), 124 C.C.C. (3d) vi (S.C.C.) — Notwithstanding s. 273.2(b), sexual assault is an offence based substantially on a constitutionally sufficient level of subjective fault. There is *no* breach of *Charter* s. 11(c).

Related Provisions: "Consent" is defined in s. 273.1(1) and may be vitiated by any of the matters described in ss. 273.1(2) or (3) or in s. 265(3). Sections 150.1(1) and (2) also remove consent as a defence to certain listed crimes including sexual assaults.

Section 265(4) describes the obligation of a trial judge when *apprehended consent* is raised as a defence before a jury.

273.3 (1) Removal of child from Canada — No person shall do anything for the purpose of removing from Canada a person who is ordinarily resident in Canada and who is

(a) under the age of fourteen years, with the intention that an act be committed outside Canada that if it were committed in Canada would be an offence against section 151 or 152 or subsection 160(3) or 173(2) in respect of that person;

(b) fourteen years of age or more but under the age of eighteen years, with intention that an act be committed outside Canada that if it were committed in Canada would be an offence against section 153 in respect of that person; or

(c) under the age of eighteen years, with the intention that an act be committed outside Canada that if it were committed in Canada would be an offence against section 155 or 159, subsection 160(2) or section 170, I71, 267, 268, 269, 271, 272 or 273 in respect of that person.

(2) **Punishment** — **Every person who contravenes this section is guilty of**

  (a) an indictable offence and is liable to imprisonment for a term not exceeding five years; or

  (b) an offence punishable on summary conviction.

1993, c. 45, s. 3; 1997, c. 18, s. 13.

Commentary: The section creates three offences which relate to the purposeful removal from Canada of a young person who is ordinarily resident here.

The *external circumstances* of each offence comprise conduct by D ("... *do* anything ...") in relation to V who is a member of the group of persons described in the applicable paragraph and is ordinarily resident in Canada. There need be no actual removal of V from Canada. D's conduct is rather preliminary to, albeit for the purpose of, actual removal.

The *mental element* of each offence includes the intention to cause the external circumstances for the purpose of removing V, ordinarily a Canadian resident and a member of the protected group of young persons, from Canada. It is necessary that P establish further that the purposeful removal was with the intention that an act be committed outside Canada that if it were committed in Canada would be a listed offence in respect of the young person. Under s. 273.3(2), the offences of s. 273.3(1) are triable either way at the option of P.

Related Provisions: The essential elements of the listed offences are described in the *Commentary* which accompanies each section.

Where P proceeds by indictment, D may elect mode of trial under s. 536(2). Summary conviction proceedings are governed by Part XXVII.

274. Corroboration not required — **Where an accused is charged with an offence under section 151, 152, 153, 155, 159, 160, 170, 171, 172, 173, 212, 271, 272 or 273, no corroboration is required for a conviction and the judge shall not instruct the jury that it is unsafe to find the accused guilty in the absence of corroboration.**

1980–81–82–83, c. 125, s. 19; R.S. 1985, c. 19 (3d Supp.), s. 11.

Commentary: The section provides *a rule of evidence*. No corroboration is *required* for a conviction in respect of a listed offence. It is not a prerequisite to conviction in such cases. A trial judge is also expressly prohibited from instructing the jury that it is *unsafe* to find D guilty in the absence of corroboration.

Case Law

Requirement of Caution

R. v. K. (V.) (1991), 4 C.R. (4th) 338, 68 C.C.C. (3d) 18 (B.C. C.A.) — There is no statutory requirement nor rule of practice that a judge caution him/herself against the risks associated with relying solely upon the unsupported evidence of a *child* witness. Further, there is no rule of practice which requires such caution in the case of *sexual offences*, due to the nature of the offence alleged. Cautions, matters within the discretion of the trial judge, are dependent upon the circumstances of individual cases.

Corroboration

R. v. R. (B.W.) (1987), 82 A.R. 319 (C.A.) — A direction that it was unsafe to convict in the absence of supporting evidence amounted to a direction requiring corroboration and constitued a misdirection.

R. v. Saulnier (1989), 48 C.C.C. (3d) 301 (N.S. C.A.) — In a case of a sexual offence involving a child V, it is open to the trial judge to direct the jury that they would ordinarily look for confirmative evidence which would support the evidence of V, even though the legal requirement for corroboration has been removed.

R. v. D. (D.) (1991), 65 C.C.C. (3d) 511 (Ont. C.A.) — Where a trial judge chooses to refer to corroborative evidence, (s)he should indicate to the jury that there is evidence *capable of* corroborating or confirming V's testimony, but that it is for them to decide whether it, in fact, does so. It is preferable to identify the evidence which bears corroborative potential. V cannot provide corroboration through an earlier statement *not* admissible in proof of its contents.

Charter Considerations

R. v. Johnstone (1986), 26 C.C.C. (3d) 401 (N.S. C.A.) — The provisions of the *Code* concerning sexual assault do not require corroboration of the complainant's evidence while the *Y.O.A.* requires corroboration where a young person is charged with the same offence. The different procedural rules for young persons were created for their protection, hence inequality is not necessarily discriminatory. Even assuming the scheme was discriminatory, it was justified under *Charter* s. 1. P was still required to establish proof beyond a reasonable doubt for both age groups.

Related Provisions: Corroboration is required in respect of the offences of perjury (s. 133), treason and high treason and procuring a feigned marriage. It is mentioned but *not* required in respect of the age of a child in s. 658(2).

The section does not appear to limit the well-established right of a trial judge to comment upon the evidence, and to assist the jury in determining what weight, if any, to attribute to it. Neither does it exempt the trial judge from the duty, in appropriate cases, while commenting upon the weight to be assigned to V's evidence, to caution the jury in simple terms of the risks of relying exclusively upon the evidence of a single witness, and to explain the reasons for such caution.

The related evidentiary rules of ss. 274 (recent complaint), 275 (sexual activity), 276 (sexual reputation) and 715.1(1) (videotaped evidence of V or other witness), as well as *C.E.A.* s. 4(2) (spousal competence and compellability) have application to some, though not all, of the offences listed in the section. Under ss. 486(2.1)–(5), special provision is made for the manner in which the evidence of a youthful complainant may be received in prosecutions under listed sections. *C.E.A.* s. 16 governs *inter alia*, the manner in which the evidence of a witness under 14 years of age or of defective mental capacity may be received. No corroboration is required in respect of such testimony, even where the witness is permitted to give evidence on promising to tell the truth.

275. Rules respecting recent complaint abrogated — **The rules relating to evidence of recent complaint are hereby abrogated with respect to offences under sections 151, 152, 153, 155 and 159, subsections 160(2) and (3), and sections 170, 171, 172, 173, 271, 272 and 273.**

1980–81–82–83, c. 125, s. 19; R.S. 1985, c. 19 (3d Supp.), s. 11.

Commentary: As a general rule, evidence of a statement made by a witness on an earlier occasion and consistent with his/her evidence at trial is *not* admissible in criminal proceedings. The principal basis for such a rule, variously known as the rule against self-serving statements, self-confirmation or narrative, is that evidence of a prior consistent statement is superfluous in a system emphasizing *viva voce* testimony as the principal means of proof. The recent complaint doctrine, an exception to this rule, in the case of certain sexual offences, permitted, in defined circumstances, evidence of both the fact and details of a recent complaint by V to be received in support of V's credibility *qua* witness in the proceedings.

This section *abrogates* the doctrine of *recent complaint*, thereby excluding its reception as evidence. It does not, *semble*, affect the operation of other principles of evidentiary law, as for example *res gestae* and recent fabrication, which may permit the reception of evidence of contemporaneous outcry or previous consistent statement.

Case Law

R. v. M. (T.E.) (1996), 110 C.C.C. (3d) 179 (Alta. C.A.) — A jury should be instructed that there is *no* inviolable rule how persons who are the victims of trauma, like sexual assault, will behave. Reactions vary. In deciding whether V acted after the incident in a manner consistent with his/her story, the jury ought consider *inter alia*,

i.   V's *state of mind* at the time;

ii.   V's *age* and level of *maturity*;

iii. V's sense of *confidence* and composure; and

iv.   the *relationship* between V and the abuser.

The jury should be warned, in cases where there is little or no evidence of prompt complaint that, as a matter of law, it cannot be said that a complainant who is wronged will always complain at the first opportunity.

R. v. Ay (1994), 93 C.C.C. (3d) 456 (B.C. C.A.) — To achieve the full purpose of the abrogation of the recent complaint doctrine by s. 275, P may lead evidence of

    i. *when* a complaint was first made;

    ii. *why* a complaint was not made at the first reasonable opportunity; and,

    iii. what precipitated the making of the complaint.

This evidence is receivable as part of the narrative to ensure the jury has all the evidence of V's conduct necessary to help them draw the right inference with respect to V's credibility.The prior complaint, admissible under the narrative exception to the rule against prior consistent statements, is *not* admissible to gauge the consistency, hence credibility of V's evidence at trial. Absent a need to provide the context for some other circumstances relevant to the jury's consideration, the actual content of the complaint is irrelevant, hence inadmissible. P may elicit evidence which describes the complaint in general terms and relates the fact of the complaint to the allegations made, without details of what was said.

R. v. George (1985), 23 C.C.C. (3d) 42 (B.C. C.A.) — The fact of the complaint may be admissible, where it is a necessary part of the background of the case for example, in order to explain D's admissions.

R. v. Henrich (1996), 108 C.C.C. (3d) 97 (Ont. C.A.) — Evidence of a delayed complaint is different from evidence of prior sexual activity since it relates to the "timing" of disclosure of the very allegations that are being tried. Explanation of the timeliness of complaint is *not* unduly intrusive and may have probative value. A *voir dire* is *not* unduly intrusive and may have probative value. A *voir dire* is not always required before D may raise the issue of the timeliness of V's complaint.

R. v. Henrich (1996), 108 C.C.C. (3d) 97 (Ont. C.A.) — The timeliness of V's complaint is an issue which both D and P may explore, thereby leaving the trier of fact to determine what to make of the explanation. P should be permitted to adduce evidence of prior complaint that falls within the narrative exception, and D allowed to explore the issue of timing.

R. v. F. (J.E.) (1993), 26 C.R. (4th) 220, 85 C.C.C. (3d) 457 (Ont. C.A.) — Section 275 prohibits P from adducing evidence of recent complaint during its case in-chief, but does not bar cross-examination by D on the issue of lack of recent complaint. Prior consistent statements may be admissible as part of P's case in-chief if they fall within an existing exception to the rule which generally bars their introduction, as for example, to rebut an allegation of recent fabrication, as part of the *res gestae* or as part of the narrative.

R. v. M. (P.S.) (1992), 77 C.C.C. (3d) 402, 408–9 (Ont. C.A.) — *See also*: *R. v. W. (R.)* (1992), 13 C.R. (4th) 257, 74 C.C.C. (3d) 134, 145 (S.C.C.) — The significance of V's failure to make timely complaint must *not* be the subject of any presumptive adverse inference based on now-rejected stereotypical assumptions of how persons (particularly children) react to acts of sexual abuse. The importance to V's credibility of the failure to make timely complaint will vary from case to case and be dependent upon the trier of fact's assessment of the evidence relevant to such failure.

R. v. Owens (1986), 55 C.R. (3d) 386, 33 C.C.C. (3d) 275 (Ont. C.A.) — This section does *not* render inadmissible in all cases evidence of recent complaint. Previous consistent statements are admissible, not to prove the truth of the statements, but to rebut an allegation of recent fabrication.

Related Provisions: The section should be read together with s. 715.1, which in the circumstances there described, permits reception of videotaped evidence by V or the other witness, under 18 years of age when the offence was committed, the contents of which V or the other witness has adopted while testifying.

Other related evidentiary and procedural provisions are described in the corresponding note to s. 274, *supra*. The substantive offences to which the section applies are described in the Commentary which accompanies each.

276. (1) **Evidence of complainant's sexual activity** — In proceedings in respect of an offence under section 151, 152, 153, 155 or 159, subsections 160(2) or (3), or

section 170, 171, 172, 173, 271, 272 or 273, evidence that the complainant has engaged in sexual activity, whether with the accused or with any other person, is not admissible to support an inference that, by reason of the sexual nature of that activity, the complainant

(a) is more likely to have consented to the sexual activity that forms the subject-matter of the charge; or;

(b) is less worthy of belief.

(2) **Idem** — In proceedings in respect of an offence referred to in subsection (1), no evidence shall be adduced by or on behalf of the accused that the complainant has engage in sexual activity other than the sexual activity that forms the subject-matter of the charge, whether with the accused or with any other person, unless the judge, provincial court judge or justice determines, in accordance with the procedures set out in sections 276.1 and 276.2, that the evidence

(a) is of specific instances of sexual activity;

(b) is relevant to an issue at trial; and

(c) has significant probative value that is not substantially outweighed by the danger of prejudice to the proper administration of justice.

(3) **Factors that judge must consider** — In determining whether evidence is admissible under subsection (2), the judge, provincial court judge or justice shall take into account

(a) the interests of justice, including the right of the accused to make a full answer and defence;

(b) society's interest in encouraging the reporting of sexual assault offences;

(c) whether there is a reasonable prospect that the evidence will assist in arriving at a just determination in the case;

(d) the need to remove from the fact-finding process any discriminatory belief or bias;

(e) the risk that the evidence may unduly arouse sentiments of prejudice, sympathy or hostility in the jury;

(f) the potential prejudice to the complainant's personal dignity and right of privacy;

(g) the right of the complainant and of every individual to personal security and to the full protection and benefit of the law; and

(h) any other factor that the judge, provincial court judge or justice considers relevant.

1980–81–82–83, c. 125, s. 19; R.S. 1985, c. 19 (3d Supp.), s. 12; 1992, c. 38, s. 2.

Commentary: The section enacts a rule of *admissibilty* which generally *excludes sexual activity evidence* tendered for a specified purpose in proceedings in respect of listed offences. The general prohibition of s. 276(1) is subject to the *exception* of s. 276(2) application which is determined by a consideration of the factors listed in s. 276(3).

The general exclusionary rule of s. 276(1) is *not*, in terms, limited to the *trial* of listed offences. It has application "in *proceedings* in respect of an offence" listed in the subsection. It excludes "evidence that the complainant has engaged in sexual activity, whether *with the accused* or with any other person". The italicized words represent an expansion of the exclusionary rule from what had been barred by its unconstitutional predecessor. The rule of s. 276(1), however, does *not* bar *all* evidence that V has engaged in sexual activity with D or another. To attract the exclusionary rule, the evidence must be tendered to support an *inference* that, by reason of *the sexual nature of the activity*, V:

i.   is *more likely to have consented* to the sexual activity that forms the subject-matter of the charge; or,

ii.   is *less worthy of belief.*

What is required to engage the rule of inadmissibility enacted by s. 276(1), in other words, is the proffer of a particular *kind of evidence* (that V has engaged in sexual activity with D or another) for a *specified purpose* (to support an inference that by reason of the sexual nature of the activity, V is more likely to have consented to the sexual activity that forms the subject-matter of the charge or is less worthy of belief) in proceedings in respect of a *listed offence.*

Sections 276(2) and (3), read together, enact an *exception* to the general exclusionary rule of s. 276(1), articulate the *basis* upon which sexual activity evidence may be *admitted* and list the *factors* to be considered in determining whether the evidence ought to be received. It is s. 276(2) which defines the basis upon which sexual activity evidence may be admitted as an exception to s. 276(1). The re-statement of the exclusionary rule in s. 276(2), however, is in different terms than those of s. 276(1), in that it is limited to sexual activity evidence "adduced by or on behalf of the accused", excepts out "other than the sexual activity that forms the subject-matter of the charge", and makes no reference to the purpose for which the evidence is tendered. The evidence, otherwise barred, may be received where the presiding judicial officer, after conducting a hearing in accordance with s. 276.1 and 276.2, determines that the evidence:

i.   is of *specific instances* of sexual activity;

ii.   is *relevant* to an issue at trial; and,

iii.   has *significant probative value* that is *not substantially outweighed* by the *danger of prejudice* to the proper administration of justice.

In deciding whether the proposed evidence may be admitted under s. 276(2), the presiding judicial officer is required to consider the factors listed in s. 276(3).

The offences to which s. 276 applies are as follows:

     s.151 (sexual interference);

     s. 152 (invitation to sexual touching);

     s. 153 (sexual exploitation);

     s. 155 (incest);

     s. 159 (anal intercourse);

     s. 160(2) (compelling bestiality);

     s. 160(3) (bestiality in presence of or by child);

     s. 170 (parent or guardian procuring sexual activity);

     s. 171 (householder permitting sexual activity);

     s. 172 (corrupting children);

     s. 173 (indecent acts);

     s. 271 (sexual assault);

     s. 272 (sexual assault with a weapon, threats to third party or causing bodily harm); and,

     s. 273 (aggravated sexual assault)

Case Law

Principles Governing Admissibility [Cases decided under former s. 276]

R. v. Crosby (1995), 39 C.R. (4th) 315, 98 C.C.C. (3d) 225 (S.C.C.); reversing (1994), 88 C.C.C. (3d) 353 (N.S. C.A.) — Section 276 cannot be interpreted to deprive D of a fair defence. It does not mean, however, that D is entitled to the most beneficial procedures possible. Under s. 276, the judge must undertake a balancing excercise which is sensitive to many differing and potentially conflicting interests.

R. v. Nicholson (1998), 129 C.C.C. (3d) 198 (Alta. C.A.) — Where D does *not* assert apprehended consent based on prior sexual activity with V some years earlier, evidence of the prior sexual conduct is *irrelevant* on the issue of *consent.* D is also *not* entitled to cross-examine V on prior sexual history to obtain denials, which D would seek to disprove.

Where a trial judge decides that evidence of prior sexual activity is *irrelevant* and its *probative value* is *outweighed* by its *prejudicial effect,* there is *no* requirement of a step-by-step consideration of the balancing factors articulated in *Code* s. 276(3).

R. v. Brothers (1995), 40 C.R. (4th) 250, 99 C.C.C. (3d) 64 (Alta. C.A.) — Section 276 does *not* exclude evidence that V was a virgin. It only refers to V who has engaged in sexual activity and specific instances of sexual activity.

R. v. Morden (1991), 9 C.R. (4th) 315, 69 C.C.C. (3d) 123 (B.C. C.A.) — Where P adduced from V that she had terminated her previous relationship with D because she preferred women, P created the inference that V was the sort of person who would *not* have consented to sexual relations with D. The defence was entitled to rebut that inference by adducing evidence of V's sexual activity with a man days prior to the alleged assault by D.

R. v. B. (O.) (1995), 45 C.R. (4th) 68, 103 C.C.C. (3d) 531 (N.S. C.A.) — The rules of ss. 276, 276.1 and 277 do not apply to determine the admissibility of evidence concerning other alleged sexual assaults upon V. The admissibility of such evidence is to be decided by the application of the common law rules.

R. v. Bell (1998), 126 C.C.C. (3d) 94 (N.W.T. C.A.) — There is a heavy burden on counsel to be forthright and candid concerning the nature and purpose of evidence tendered for admission under s. 276.

R. v. Darrach (1998), 13 C.R. (5th) 283, 122 C.C.C. (3d) 225 (Ont. C.A.); application for leave to appeal allowed (1998), 124 C.C.C. (3d) vi (S.C.C.) — Neither the common law nor the *Charter* require that any specific procedure be followed to determine the admissibility of evidence.

In s. 276(1), ". . . by reason of the sexual nature of that activity" should be read as meaning ". . . solely to support the inference that the complainant is by reason of such conduct. . .".

R. v. Harris (1997), 10 C.R. (5th) 287, 118 C.C.C. (3d) 498 (Ont. C.A.) — There is no general rule that a single prior incident of consensual sexual activities between the parties is not probative of the issue of apprehended consent. Each case must be decided on its own facts including, but not only,

i.   the viability of the defence;

ii.   the nature and extent of the prior activity compared to the activity that forms the subject-matter of the charge;

iii. the time period between the incidents; and,

iv.   the nature of the relationship between the parties.

Reasonable Notice

Forsythe v. R. (1980), 15 C.R. (3d) 280, 53 C.C.C. (2d) 225 (S.C.C.) — What is reasonable notice is a question of fact in each case.

R. v. B. (G.S.), (November 4, 1987), Doc. No. CA005051 (B.C. C.A.) — Where no notice of intention to cross-examine V on her prior sexual conduct had been given, it was improper to ask V if she had ever made other complaints of sexual assault.

R. v. Blondheim (1980), 54 C.C.C. (2d) 36 (Ont. C.A.) — *See also*: *R. v. Lawson* (1978), 39 C.C.C. (2d) 85 (B.C. C.A.) — Where the notice suggested "a fishing expedition" and was totally deficient in the particulars necessary to enable P to prepare, a hearing *in camera* was unnecessary.

Procedure to Determine Admissibility

R. v. Ecker (1995), 37 C.R. (4th) 51, 96 C.C.C. (3d) 161 (Sask. C.A.) — When application is made to adduce evidence of other sexual activity, the judge must first determine, in accordance with s. 276.1 and on the face of the matter, whether the proposed evidence is capable of admissibility under s. 276(2). If the proposed evidence is capable of admissibility, the judge must next decide, in a hearing conducted under s. 276.2, whether and to what extent the evidence itself is admissible. (per Cameron, Vancise and Lane JJ.A.)

Evidence of Sexual Activity

R. v. Drakes (1998), 122 C.C.C. (3d) 498 (B.C. C.A.) — *Semble,* a prior conviction of communicating for the purposes of prostitution is evidence of "sexual activity" under s. 276.

R. v. Gauthier (1995), 100 C.C.C. (3d) 563 (B.C. C.A.) — Sections 276-276.2 have no application to evidence which tends to show that V fabricated stories of sexual activity in which V admittedly never engaged.

R. v. C. (R.C.) (1996), 107 C.C.C. (3d) 362 (N.S. C.A.) — Section 276 limits the use D may make of evidence of V's prior sexual activity, but does not apply to non-consensual sexual activity.

R. v. Bell (1998), 126 C.C.C. (3d) 94 (N.W.T. C.A.) — In some cases, evidence of V's sexual activity with a third party may be so intertwined with V's evidence of how she came to recollect the alleged assault by D, that it is admissible.

Charter Considerations

R. v. Darrach (1998), 13 C.R. (5th) 283, 122 C.C.C. (3d) 225 (Ont. C.A.); application for leave to appeal allowed (1998), 124 C.C.C. (3d) vi (S.C.C.) — Section 276(2)(a) and (c) do *not* contravene *Charter* ss. 7, 11(c) or 11(d).

Related Provisions: "Complainant", "provincial court judge" and "justice" are defined in s. 2, and "newspaper" in s. 297. "Consent" is defined in s. 273.1(1) for the purposes of the sexual assault offences of ss. 271–273. It may be vitiated by any of the matters or factors described in ss. 273.1(2) or (3) or in s. 265(3). Sections 150.1(1) and (2) also remove consent as a defence in respect of certain of the offences listed in s. 276(1).

The hearing to determine admissibility under s. 276(2) proceeds in two stages or steps. Under s. 276.1, a *preliminary hearing* is held to determine under s. 276.1(4) whether the application is in proper form under s. 276.1(2), if adequate notice has been given to P and the clerk of the court and whether the proposed evidence is *capable* of being admissible under s. 276(2). An applicant who succeeds on the preliminary hearing under s. 276.1 is entitled to an *evidentiary hearing* under s. 276.2. An applicant who is unsuccessful on the preliminary hearing is *not* entitled to an evidentiary hearing under s. 276.2.

A determination made on an evidentiary hearing under s. 276.2 is *deemed* a question of law by s. 276.5 for the purposes of s. 675 and 676. Where evidence is admitted under s. 276.2, the judge is required by s. 276.4 to instruct the jury as to the uses the jury may and may not make of the evidence.

Section 276.3 imposes restrictions on publication of certain matters disclosed in the preliminary and evidentiary hearings of s. 276.1 and 276.2.

276.1 (1) Application for hearing — Application may be made to the judge, provincial court judge or justice by or on behalf of the accused for a hearing under section 276.2 to determine whether evidence is admissible under subsection 276(2).

(2) Form and content of application — An application referred to in subsection (1) must be made in writing and set out

    (a) detailed particulars of the evidence that the accused seeks to adduce, and

    (b) the relevance of that evidence to an issue at trial,

and a copy of the application must be given to the prosecutor and to the clerk of the court.

(3) Jury and public excluded — The judge, provincial court judge or justice shall consider the application with the jury and the public excluded.

(4) Judge may decide to hold hearing — Where the judge, provincial court judge or justice is satisfied

    (a) that the application was made in accordance with subsection (2),

    (b) that a copy of the application was given to the prosecutor and to the clerk of the court at least seven days previously, or such shorter interval as the judge, provincial court judge or justice may allow where the interests of justice so require, and

(c) that the evidence sought to be adduced is capable of being admissible under subsection 276(2),

the judge, provincial court judge or justice shall grant the application and hold a hearing under section 276.2 to determine whether the evidence is admissible under subsection 276(2).

1992, c. 38, s. 2.

Commentary: The section authorizes *application* for a *hearing* to *determine admissibility* of sexual activity evidence under the exception of s. 276(2) and describes the *procedure* to be followed to determine whether an evidentiary hearing will be held under s. 276.2. The hearing authorized by this section may be conveniently designated the *preliminary hearing*.

Under s. 276.1(1), an application by D to have sexual activity evidence admitted under s. 276(2) is to be made to "the judge, provincial court judge or justice". By s. 276.1(2), the application is to be *in writing* and set out:

i.   *detailed particulars* of the proposed evidence; and

ii.   the *relevance* of the proposed evidence to an issue at trial.

A *copy* of the application is to be provided to P and the clerk of the court. As a result of s. 276.1(4)(b), it would seem advisable to provide the clerk of the court with a copy of the application at least seven days prior to its return.

The preliminary hearing of the application is held under s. 276.1(3) with the jury and public excluded. The issues to be decided on the hearing, as framed by s. 276.1(4), are whether:

i.   the *application* complies with s. 276.1(2);

ii.   *adequate notice* of the application has been given to P and the clerk of the court; and

iii. the proposed *evidence* is *capable* of *admission* under s. 276(2).

The notice described in item ii, *supra*, is generally required to be "at least seven days", but s. 276.1(4)(b) permits the presiding judicial officer to allow a shorter interval "where the interests of justice so require". Satisfaction of items i–iii, *supra, requires* that an *evidentiary hearing* be held under s. 276.2. Failure to satisfy any of items i–iii, *supra*, denies D an evidentiary hearing.

Case Law

Procedure

R. v. Ecker (1995), 37 C.R. (4th) 51, 96 C.C.C. (3d) 161 (Sask. C.A.) — Section 276.1 entails only a *facial consideration* of the matter and a *tentative decision* concerning the *capability* of the evidence being *admissible*. Courts should be cautious in limiting D's rights to cross-examine and adduce evidence. Unless the evidence clearly appears to be incapable of admissibility, having regard to the criteria of s. 276(2) and the indicia of s. 276(3), the judge should proceed to an evidentiary hearing under s. 276.2. Any doubts under s. 276.1 are better left for decision on the evidentiary hearing under s. 276.2. (per Cameron, Vancise and Lane JJ.A.)

Related Provisions: "Provincial court judge", "justice", "prosecutor" and "clerk of the court" are defined in s. 2.

Section 276.2 governs the conduct of an evidentiary hearing required after a favourable determination has been made at the preliminary hearing under s. 276.1(4). The evidentiary rules which apply when sexual activity evidence is proposed for admission are set out in s. 276.

Section 276.5 does *not* deem a determination made under s. 276.1 a question of law for the purposes of *Code* s. 675 and 676.

Section 276.1 contains no reference, as in s. 276.2(2), to the non-compellability of V at the preliminary hearing. At all events, in view of the issues framed for determination by s. 216.1(4), it would seem unlikely that V would have any material evidence to give on the preliminary hearing.

Other related provisions are described in the corresponding note to s. 276.

276.2 (1) Jury and public excluded — At a hearing to determine whether evidence is admissible under subsection 276(2), the jury and the public shall be excluded.

(2) Complainant not compellable — The complainant is not a compellable witness at the hearing.

(3) Judge's determination and reasons — At the conclusion of the hearing, the judge, provincial court judge or justice shall determine whether the evidence, or any part thereof, is admissible under subsection 276(2) and shall provide reasons for that determination, and

(a) where not all of the evidence is to be admitted, the reasons must state the part of the evidence that is to be admitted;

(b) the reasons must state the factors referred to in subsection 276(3) that affected the determination; and

(c) where all or any part of the evidence is to be admitted, the reasons must state the manner in which that evidence is expected to be relevant to an issue at trial.

(4) Record of reasons — The reasons provided under subsection (3) shall be entered in the record of the proceedings or, where the proceedings are not recorded, shall be provided in writing.

1992, c. 38, s. 2.

Commentary: The section authorizes an *evidentiary hearing* to determine the admissibility of sexual activity evidence under s. 276(2) and describes the procedure to be followed on the hearing.

Under s. 276.2(1), the evidentiary hearing is to be held with the jury and public excluded. Upon the hearing, V is *not* a compellable witness. The mandatory exclusion of the public under s. 276.2(1) may attract *Charter* scrutiny under ss. 2(b), 7 and 11(d).

Sections 276.2(3) and (4) require the presiding judicial officer to give *reasons* for any determination made concerning the admissibility of sexual activity evidence under s. 276(2) and, to some extent, describe the matters to which reference must be made in the reasons where at least some sexual activity evidence is to be admitted. Under s. 276.2(4), the reasons provided under s. 276.2(3) are to be entered in the record of the proceedings, or absent their recording, provided in writing.

Case Law

R. v. Potvin (1998), 124 C.C.C. (3d) 568 (Que. C.A.) — Evidence of possible consensual intercourse *after* the date of the alleged offence may become relevant to V's credibility.

Related Provisions: "Complainant", "provincial court judge" and "justice" are defined in s. 2. Section 540 provides for the taking of evidence at preliminary inquiry. It applies to the trial of indictable offences by ss. 557, 572 and 646 and to summary conviction proceediongs by s. 801(3).

The admissibility rules that govern the reception of sexual activity evidence are found in s. 276. Section 276.1 requires that a preliminary hearing be conducted at which it will be determined whether an evidentiary hearing under s. 276.2 is required.

Other related provisions are described in the corresponding note to s. 276.

276.3 (1) Publication prohibited — No person shall publish in a newspaper, as defined in section 297, or in a broadcast, any of the following:

(a) the contents of an application made under section 276.1;

(b) any evidence taken, the information given and the representations made at an application under section 276.1 or at a hearing under section 276.2;

(c) the decision of a judge, provincial court judge or justice under subsection 276.1(4), unless the judge, provincial court judge or justice, after taking into account the complainant's right of privacy and the interests of justice, orders that the decision may be published; and

(d) the determination made and the reasons provided under section 276.2, unless

(i) that determination is that evidence is admissible, or

(ii) the judge, provincial court judge or justice, after taking into account the complainant's right of privacy and the interests of justice, orders that the determination and reasons may be published.

(2) Offence — Every person who contravenes subsection (1) is guilty of an offence punishable on summary conviction.

1992, c.38, s. 2.

Commentary: The section restricts *newspaper publication* and *broadcast* of certain matters relating to applications to have sexual activity evidence admitted in criminal proceedings. Contravention of a prohibition on publication is made a summary conviction offence under s. 276.3(2).

Under ss. 276.3(1)(a) and (b), the prohibition on publication and broadcast is absolute. Publication or broadcast of the *contents* of an *application* under s. 276.1 (preliminary hearing) and any *evidence* taken, *information* given and *representations* made upon the preliminary hearing or at an evidentiary hearing under s. 276.2 is absolutely barred.

The prohibitions of ss. 276.3(1)(c) and (d) are *not* absolute. In general, publication and broadcast of the *decision* at preliminary hearing under s. 276.1(4) and the *determination* made and *reasons* provided on the evidentiary hearing of s. 276.2 is prohibited. An order permitting publication may be made, however, after consideration of:

i.   V's *right of privacy*; and,

ii.   the *interests of justice*

or, on an evidentiary hearing under s. 276.2, where the evidence is ruled admissible.

Related Provisions: The section may attract scrutiny under *Charter* s. 2(b).

Restrictions on newspaper publication and broadcast of evidence taken in criminal proceedings may also be imposed under ss. 486(3) and (4) (testimony of youthful complainants of sexual offences), s. 539 (preliminary inquiries), s. 175 (judicial interim release hearings), and s. 648 (proceedings in absence of jury). "Newspaper" is defined in s. 297.

The summary conviction offence of s. 276.3(2) is punished under s. 787(1).

Other related provisions are described in the corresponding notes to ss. 276 and 276.1.

276.4 Judge to instruct jury re use of evidence — Where evidence is admitted at trial pursuant to a determination made unde section 276.2, the judge shall instruct the jury as to the uses that the jury may and may not make of that evidence.

1992, c. 38, s. 2.

Commentary: The section *requires* a trial judge to instruct the jury as to the *permitted* and *prohibited* uses of sexual activity evidence admitted under s. 276.2. It does *not*, however, describe the instructions to be given.

Related Provisions: The admissibility rules which govern the reception of sexual activity evidence appear in s. 276. The evidence may only be admitted under s. 276(2), after consideration of the factors listed in s. 276(3) and in accordance with the procedural requirements of ss. 276.1 and 276.2. Section 276(1) enacts the general rule of admissibility.

Section 276.4 replicates existing common law when evidence received at trial may be used by the trier of fact for one purpose but not another. It is a salutary practice for a trial judge to instruct the jury as to the permitted and prohibited use of the evidence, not only in the summing-up or charge at the end of the case but, equally, if not more importantly, at the time the evidence is received.

Other related provisions are described in the corresponding notes to s. 276 and 276.1.

276.5 Appeal — For the purposes of sections 675 and 676, a determination made under section 276.2 shall be deemed to be a question of law.

1992, c. 38, s. 2.

Commentary: This section *deems* a *determination* made under s. 276.2 regarding the *admissibility of sexual activity evidence* to be a *question of law* for the purposes of ss. 675 and 676, hence appeals taken in proceedings in respect of indictable offences.

Related Provisions: Under s. 675(1)(a)(i), D may appeal to the provincial court of appeal against conviction on any ground of appeal that involves a question of law alone. The Attorney General or counsel instructed by him/her for the purpose may also appeal to the provincial court of appeal against a judgment or verdict of acquittal or not criminally responsible by account of mental disorder on any ground of appeal that involves a question of law alone under s. 676(1)(a). Leave to appeal is *not* required in either case. A dissent on a question of law alone may found an appeal to the Supreme Court of Canada as of right under ss. 691(1)(a), 692(3)(a) and 693(1)(a). Appeals to the Supreme Court of Canada may also be taken on any question of law upon which the court grants leave to appeal under ss. 691(1)(b), 692(3)(b) and 693(1)(b).

Under s. 601(6), the question whether to amend an indictment or count thereof is also a question of law.

277. Reputation evidence — In proceedings in respect of an offence under section 151, 152, 153, 155 or 159, subsection 160(2) or (3), or section 170, 171, 172, 173, 271, 272 or 273, evidence of sexual reputation, whether general or specific, is not admissible for the purpose of challenging or supporting the credibility of the complainant.

1980–81–82–83, c. 125, s. 19; R.S. 1985, c. 19 (3d Supp.), s. 13.

Commentary: This section first appeared as s. 246.7 under S.C. 1980–81–82–83, c. 125, s. 19, and was later enlarged to cover additional offences.

The *exclusionary* rule is only engaged where evidence of general or specific sexual reputation is tendered to challenge or support V's credibility. There are no statutory exceptions. Evidence of sexual reputation tendered for other than a proscribed purpose is *not* excluded under the section, although it may engage the exclusionary rule of s. 276.

Case Law

Application of section

R. v. Brothers (1995), 40 C.R. (4th) 250, 99 C.C.C. (3d) 64 (Alta. C.A.) — Section 277 does *not* exclude evidence that V was a virgin since it is evidence of a physical fact, not of reputation.

Charter Considerations

R. v. Seaboyer, (sub nom. *R. v. Gayme)* 7 C.R. (4th) 117, 66 C.C.C. (3d) 321 — The section does not exclude relevant evidence. There is neither a logical nor practical link between V's sexual reputation and V's truthfulness as a witness. There is no breach of *Charter* s. 7.

Related Provisions: "Complainant" is defined in s. 2.

This section should be read together with s. 276, which generally excludes evidence of V's sexual activity with any person other than D, but is subject to inclusionary exception.

Other related evidentiary and procedural provisions are described in the corresponding note to s. 274, *supra*. Substantive offences to which the section applies are described in the *Commentary* which accompanies s. 276.

Where D has adduced evidence of good character at trial, s. 666 permits P to adduce evidence of D's previous convictions in answer thereto. Section 667 may be used to prove previous convictions.

278. Spouse may be charged — A husband or wife may be charged with an offence under section 271, 272 or 273 in respect of his or her spouse, whether or not the spouses were living together at the time the activity that forms the subject-matter of the charge occurred.

1980–81–82–83, c. 125, s. 19.

Commentary: Under this section, spouses, whether living together or separate and apart, may be charged with any sexual assault offence in respect of the complainant spouse.

Related Provisions: The complainant spouse may also provide evidence against D. Under *C.E.A.* s. 4(2), D's spouse is a competent and compellable witness for P without D's consent. See also *C.E.A.* s. 4(5).

Theft between spouses is governed by ss. 329(1) and (2). Offences relating to the failure to provide necessaries, *inter alia*, to a spouse, and evidentiary provisions applicable at the trial of such offences, appear in s. 215.

Under s. 18, there is *no* presumption that a married person commits an offence under compulsion by reason only that the offence is committed in the presence of D's spouse. Under s. 23(2), no married person whose spouse has been a party to an offence is an accessory after the fact by receiving, comforting or assisting the spouse for the purpose of enabling the spouse to escape.

The evidentiary and procedural provisions which govern the trial of the sexual assault offences of ss. 271–273 as well as their elements are described in the *Commentary* which accompanies each.

278.1 Definition of "record" — **For the purposes of sections 278.2 to 278.9, "record" means any form of record that contains personal information for which there is a reasonable expectation of privacy and includes, without limiting the generality of the foregoing, medical, psychiatric, therapeutic, counselling, education, employment, child welfare, adoption and social services records, personal journals and diaries, and records containing personal information the production or disclosure of which is protected by any other Act of Parliament or a provincial legislature, but does not include records made by persons responsible for the investigation or prosecution of the offence.**

1997, c. 30, s. 1.

Commentary: The section exhaustively defines "record" for applications under ss. 278.2-278.9. It does so by general description, express inclusion and specific exclusion.

In general, any form of record that contains *personal information* for which there is a *reasonable expectation* of privacy is a record under s. 278.1. Several types of records are included by express enumeration or general description. Records made by investigators or prosecutors of the offence are excluded.

Related Provisions: Section 278.2 enacts a general rule which bars disclosure of any "record" relating to V, or a witness in proceedings in respect of a listed offence. Sections 278.3-278.9 govern applications for production of the records.

278.2 Production of record to accused — **(1) No record relating to a complainant or a witness shall be produced to an accused in any proceedings in respect of**

(a) an offence under section 151, 152, 153, 153.1, 155, 159, 160, 170, 171, 172, 173, 210, 211, 212, 213, 271, 272 or 273,

(b) an offence under section 144, 145, 149, 156, 245 or 246 of the *Criminal Code*, chapter C-34 of the Revised Statutes of Canada, 1970, as it read immediately before January 4, 1983, or

(c) an offence under section 146, 151, 153, 155, 157, 166 or 167 of the *Criminal Code*, chapter C-34 of the Revised Statutes of Canada, 1970, as it read immediately before January 1, 1988,

or in any proceedings in respect of two or more offences that include an offence referred to in any of paragraphs (a) to (c), except in accordance with sections 278.3 to 278.91.

(2) Application of provisions — **Section 278.1, this section and sections 278.3 to 278.91 apply where a record is in the possession or control of any person, including the prosecutor in the proceedings, unless, in the case of a record in the possession or con-**

trol of the prosecutor, the complainant or witness to whom the record relates has expressly waived the application of those sections.

(3) Duty of prosecutor to give notice — In the case of a record in respect of which this section applies that is in the possession or control of the prosecutor, the prosecutor shall notify the accused that the record is in the prosecutor's possession but, in doing so, the prosecutor shall not disclose the record's contents.

1997, c. 30, s. 1, 1998, c. 9, s. 3.

Commentary: The section enacts a general rule which prohibits production of records of any V, or witness in proceedings for a listed offence, whether charged alone or with an unlisted offence. Where production is ordered under ss. 278.3-278.9, the general rule does not apply.

The rule against record production applies to records in the possession or control of any person. Where the record is in the possession or control of P, s. 278.2(3) requires P to notify D of P's custody without disclosing the contents of the record.

Section 278.2(2) permits V, or the witness to expressly waive the requirements of ss. 278.3-278.91, hence consent to production and disclosure, but only in relation to records of which P is the custodian.

Related Provisions: Under ss. 278.2-278.9, there is a two-step procedure to obtain production and disclosure of s. 278.1 records. Step one involves production to the trial judge for review. Step two involves disclosure to D.

Sections 278.3-278.5 govern the first step. Under s. 278.3, the application must be in writing and set out certain requirements. It must be served in a particular manner. The application may only be made to the trial judge, actual or designated. Sections 278.4 and 278.5 govern the procedure of the production hearing and articulate the basis upon which production to the trial judge may be ordered.

Sections 278.6-278.9 apply to the second step, disclosure. Section 278.6 imposes a requirement of judicial review of the records ordered produced and provides for the manner of hearing. Section 278.7 describes the basis upon which disclosure may be ordered.

Under s. 278.8, the judge is required to give reasons on applications for production and disclosure. By s. 278.91, the decisions made are questions of law for appellate purposes.

Section 278.9 bans publication of listed matters. Contravention of the prohibition is a summary conviction offence.

278.3 (1) Application for production — An accused who seeks production of a record referred to in subsection 278.2(1) must make an application to the judge before whom the accused is to be, or is being, tried.

(2) No application in other proceedings — For greater certainty, an application under subsection (1) may not be made to a judge or justice presiding at any other proceedings, including a preliminary inquiry.

(3) Form and content of application — An application must be made in writing and set out

    (a) particulars identifying the record that the accused seeks to have produced and the name of the person who has possession or control of the record; and

    (b) the grounds on which the accused relies to establish that the record is likely relevant to an issue at trial or to the competence of a witness to testify.

(4) Insufficient grounds — Any one or more of the following assertions by the accused are not sufficient on their own to establish that the record is likely relevant to an issue at trial or to the competence of a witness to testify:

    (a) that the record exists;

    (b) that the record relates to medical or psychiatric treatment, therapy or counselling that the complainant or witness has received or is receiving;

(c) that that record relates to the incident that is the subject-matter of the proceedings;

(d) that the record may disclose a prior inconsistent statement of the complainant or witness;

(e) that the record may relate to the credibility of the complainant or witness;

(f) that the record may relate to the reliability of the testimony of the complainant or witness merely because the complainant or witness has received or is receiving psychiatric treatment, therapy or counselling;

(g) that the record may reveal allegations of sexual abuse of the complainant by a person other than the accused;

(h) that the record relates to the sexual activity of the complainant with any person, including the accused;

(i) that the record relates to the presence or absence of a recent complaint;

(j) that the record relates to the complainant's sexual reputation; or

(k) that the record was made close in time to a complaint or to the activity that forms the subject-matter of the charge against the accused.

(5) Service of application and subpoena — The accused shall serve the application on the prosecutor, on the person who has possession or control of the record, on the complainant or witness, as the case may be, and on any other person to who, to the knowledge of the accused, the record relates, at least seven days before the hearing referred to in subsection 278.4(1) or any shorter interval that the judge may allow in the interests of justice. The accused shall also serve a subpoena issued under Part XXII in Form 16.1 on the person who has possession or control of the record at the same time as the application is served.

(6) Service on other persons — The judge may at any time order that the application be served on any person to whom the judge considers the record may relate.

1997, c. 30, s. 1.

Commentary: This section governs application for production of s. 278.1 records for judicial review. The application is a necessary first step for D to obtain disclosure of the records in order to make full answer and defence.

Sections 278.3(1) and (2) determine to whom the application may be brought. It must be made to the trial judge, not merely a judge of the trial court. Section 278.3(2) emphasizes the rule of s. 278.3(1) and forecloses applications at preliminary inquiry.

Sections 278.3(3), (5) and (6) govern the form and content of applications and service of the relevant documents.

Under s. 278.3(3), applications must be in writing and set out particulars of the record and its custodian, and the grounds upon which D relies to establish the likely relevance of the record to an issue at trial, or the testimonial competence of a witness. Section 278.3(4) itemizes several grounds that individually and in combination are not sufficient to establish likely relevance.

Sections 278.3(5) and (6) articulate the requirements of service. D must serve the application on the prosecutor, custodian of the record, V, or the witness and any other person to whom, to D's knowledge, the record relates. Service must be made at least seven (7) days before the hearing of the application for production, unless ordered otherwise by the trial judge. The custodian of the record must be served at the same time with a subpoena in Form 16.1. The judge may order service on other persons under s. 278.3(6).

Related Provisions: The conduct of the "production" hearing is governed by s. 278.4 and the criteria to be applied to decide it are contained in s. 278.5. Judicial review of the records ordered produced is controlled by s. 278.6. Section 278.7 describes the basis upon which disclosure may be ordered.

Other related provisions are discussed in the corresponding note to s. 278.2.

278.4 (1) Hearing *in camera* — The judge shall hold a hearing *in camera* to determine whether to order the person who has possession or control of the record to produce it to the court for review by the judge.

(2) Persons who may appear at hearing — The person who has possession or control of the record, the complainant or witness, as the case may be, and any other person to whom the record relates may appear and make submissions at the hearing, but they are not compellable as witnesses at the hearing.

(3) Costs — No order for costs may be made against a person referred to in subsection (2) in respect of their participation in the hearing.

1997, c. 30, s. 1.

Commentary: Section 278.4 outlines the nature of the hearing to determine whether the record will be produced for judicial review.

The production hearing is an *in camera* proceeding. Its purpose is to determine whether the custodian should produce the record for judicial review. The custodian, V, or witness, and anyone else to whom the record relates, may appear and make submissions. None are compellable witnesses. No costs may be awarded against any hearing participant.

Related Provisions: To order production for review, the trial judge must be satisfied of the matters contained in s. 278.5(1), after consideration of the factors listed in s. 278.5(2).

Other related provisions are discussed in the corresponding note to s. 278.2.

278.5 (1) Judge may order production of record for review — The judge may order the person who has possession or control of the record to produce the record or part of the record to the court for review by the judge if, after the hearing referred to in subsection 278.4(1), the judge is satisfied that

(a) the application was made in accordance with subsections 278.3(2) to (6);

(b) the accused has established that the record is likely relevant to an issue at trial or to the competence of a witness to testify; and

(c) the production of the record is necessary in the interests of justice.

(2) Factors to be considered — In determining whether to order the production of the record or part of the record for review pursuant to subsection (1), the judge shall consider the salutary and deleterious effects of the determination on the accused's right to make a full answer and defence and on the right to privacy and equality of the complainant or witness, as the case may be, and any other person to whom the record relates. In particular, the judge shall take the following factors into account:

(a) the extent to which the record is necessary for the accused to make a full answer and defence;

(b) the probative value of the record;

(c) the nature and extent of the reasonable expectation of privacy with respect to the record;

(d) whether production of the record is based on a discriminatory belief or bias;

(e) the potential prejudice to the personal dignity and right to privacy of any person to whom the record relates;

(f) society's interest in encouraging the reporting of sexual offences;

(g) society's interest in encouraging the obtaining of treatment by complainants of sexual offences; and

(h) the effect of the determination on the integrity of the trial process.

1997, c. 30, s. 1.

Commentary: The section describes the standard which the trial judge is to apply to decide whether to order production of a s. 278.1 record for judicial review.

Under s. 278.5(1), the trial judge may order production of a record, or part of it, if satisfied that

i.   the application conforms with the requirements of ss. 278.3(2)-(6);

ii.   the record is likely relevant to an issue at trial, or testimonial competence of a witness; and,

iii. the production of the record is necessary in the interests of justice.

To decide the applicaiton, the trial judge must consider the salutary and deleterious effects of the determination on

i.   D's right to make full answer and defence; and,

ii.   the right of V, the witness, or any other person to whom the record relates to privacy and equality.

In making the decision, the trial judge must consider the factors listed in ss. 278.5(2)(a)-(h).

Related Provisions: Section 278.8 requires the trial judge to give reasons for deciding the application for production.

Where D is successful under s. 278.5, the trial judge will review the record to determine whether to order disclosure to D. This review is governed by s. 278.6. Whether disclosure will be ordered is determined by s. 278.7. The factors of s. 278.5(2) are replicated in s. 278.7(2).

278.6 (1) Review of record by judge — Where the judge has ordered the production of the record or part of the record for review, the judge shall review it in the absence of the parties in order to determine whether the record or part of the record should be produced to the accused.

(2) Hearing *in camera* — The judge may hold a hearing *in camera* if the judge considers that it will assist in making the determination.

(3) Provisions re hearing — Subsections 278.4(2) and (3) apply in the case of a hearing under subsection (2).

1997, c. 30, s. 1.

Commentary: Where production of a s. 278.1 record for judicial review has been ordered, s. 278.6 applies.

As a general rule, judicial review to determine whether the record or part of it should be disclosed to D occurs in the absence of the parties. Under s. 278.6(2), however, the trial judge may conduct an *in camera* hearing if s/he considers it will assist in making the determination. Standing at the hearing and the absence of authority to award costs follow ss. 278.4(2) and (3), the procedure on the preliminary or production application.

Related Provisions: The test to be applied in deciding whether disclosure will be ordered is contained in s. 278.7, as are the factors to be considered and the conditions which may be imposed.

Other related provisions are discussed in the corresponding note to s. 278.2.

278.7 (1) Judge may order production of record to accused — Where the judge is satisfied that the record or part of the record is likely relevant to an issue at trial or to the competence of a witness to testify and its production is necessary in the interests of justice, the judge may order that the record or part of the record that is likely relevant be produced to the accused, subject to any conditions that may be imposed pursuant to subsection (3).

(2) Factors to be considered — In determining whether to order the production of the record or part of the record to the accused, the judge shall consider the salutary and deleterious effects of the determination on the accused's right to make a full an-

441

swer and the defence and on the right to privacy and equality of the complainant or witness, as the case may be, and any other person to whom the record relates and, in particular, shall take the factors specified in paragraphs 278.5(2)(a) to (h) into account.

(3) **Conditions on production** — Where the judge orders the production of the record or part of the record to the accused, the judge may impose conditions on the production to protect the interest of justice and, to the greatest extent possible, the privacy and equality interests of the complainant or witness, as the case may be, and any other person to whom the record relates, including, for example, the following conditions:

(a) that the record be edited as directed by the judge;

(b) that a copy of the record, rather than the original, be produced;

(c) that the accused and counsel for the accused not disclose the contents of the record to any other person, except with the approval of the court;

(d) that the record be viewed only at the offices of the court;

(e) that no copies of the record be made or that restrictions be imposed on the number of copies of the record that may be made; and

(f) that information regarding any person named in the record, such as their address, telephone number and place of employment, be severed from the record.

(4) **Copy to prosecutor** — Where the judge orders the production of the record or part of the record to the accused, the judge shall direct that a copy of the record or part of the record be provided to the prosecutor, unless the judge determines that it is not in the interests of justice to do so.

(5) **Record not to be used in other proceedings** — The record or part of the record that is produced to the accused pursuant to an order under subsection (1) shall not be used in any other proceedings.

(6) **Retention of record by court** — Where the judge refuses to order the production of the record or part of the record to the accused, the record or part of the record shall, unless a court orders otherwise, be kept in a sealed package by the court until the later of the expiration of the time for any appeal and the completion of any appeal in the proceedings against the accused, whereupon the record or part of the record shall be returned to the person lawfully entitled to possession or control of it.

1997, c. 30, s. 1.

Commentary: The section defines the standard which the trial judge must apply to decide whether to order disclosure to D of a s. 278.1 record.

Sections 278.7(1) and (2), in combination, set the standard and list the factors to be considered in deciding whether disclosure should be ordered. The trial judge must be satisfied that the record, or part of it

i.   is likely relevant to an issue at trial, or the testimonial competence of a witness; and,

ii.   is necessary to be produced in the interests of justice.

To make the decision s. 278.7(2) requires the trial judge to consider the salutary and deleterious effects of the determination on the competing interests

i.   of D, to make full answer and defence; and

ii.   of V, the witness, or other person to whom the record relates, to privacy and equality,

as well as the factors listed in s. 278.5(2)(a)-(h).

Where disclosure is ordered, conditions may be imposed under s. 278.7(3). The guiding principles are protection of the interests of justice and, to the greatest extent possible, the privacy and equality interests of V, the witness, or others to whom the record relates. Under s. 278.7(4), a copy of what is disclosed to

D must also be disclosed to P. Section 278.7(5) forbids use of the disclosed record in any other proceedings.

Where disclosure is not ordered, s. 278.7(6) requires that the record be sealed and preserved until after relevant appeal periods have expired when it is to be returned to its custodian.

Related Provisions: Section 278.8 requires that reasons be given for any determination made under s. 278.7(1). Publication is prohibited under s. 278.9.

Other related provions are discussed in the corresponding note to s. 278.2.

278.8 (1) Reasons for decision — **The judge shall provide reasons for ordering or refusing to order the production of the record or part of the record pursuant to subsection 278.5(1) or 278.7(1).**

(2) Record of reasons — **The reasons referred to in subsection (1) shall be entered in the record of the proceedings or, where the proceedings are not recorded, shall be provided in writing.**

1997, c. 30, s. 1.

Commentary: The section requires that reasons be given for decisions made on production and disclosure hearings and describes the manner in which they are to be recorded.

Related Provisions: Section 278.9 governs publication of the reasons given as required by this section.

Other related provisions are discussed in the corresponding note to s. 278.2.

278.9 (1) Publication prohibited — **No person shall publish in a newspaper, as defined in section 297, or in a broadcast, any of the following:**

(a) the contents of an application made under section 278.3;

(b) any evidence taken, information given or submissions made at a hearing under subsection 278.4(1) or 278.6(2); or

(c) the determination of the judge pursuant to subsection 278.5(1) or 278.7(1) and the reasons provided pursuant to section 278.8, unless the judge, after taking into account the interests of justice and the right to privacy of the person to whom the record relates, orders that the determination may be published.

(2) Offence — **Every person who contravenes subsection (1) is guilty of an offence punishable on summary conviction.**

1997, c. 30, s. 1.

Commentary: The section prohibits publication of the items listed subject to one exception. The determination of the judge on the production application, or on disclosure after the judicial review may be published, if the judge decides it should be after considering the interests of justice and the right to privacy of the person to whom the application relates.

Under s. 278.9(2), contravention of the publication ban is a summary conviction offence.

Related Provisions: Similar non-publication provisions are found in ss. 286(3)(identity of complainant or witness) and 487.2(1)(warranted searches).

Other related provisions are discussed in the corresponding note to s. 278.2.

278.91 Appeal — **For the purposes of sections 675 and 676, a determination to make or refuse to make an order pursuant to subsection 278.5(1) or 278.7(1) is deemed to be a question of law.**

1997, c. 30, s. 1.

Commentary: This section is concerned with appellate review of decisions made under ss. 278.5(1) (production) and 278.7(1) (disclosure). For appellate purposes, the decisions are deemed to be questions of law.

Related Provisions: The effect of this provision is to enable appellate review, not only by the provincial court of appeal, but also, under ss. 691-693, by the Supreme Court of Canada.

Kidnapping, Hostage Taking and Abduction

279. (1) Kidnapping — Every person commits an offence who kidnaps a person with intent

    (a) to cause the person to be confined or imprisoned against the person's will;

    (b) to cause the person to be unlawfully sent or transported out of Canada against the person's will; or

    (c) to hold the person for ransom or to service against the person's will.

(1.1) Punishment — Every person who commits an offence under subsection (1) is guilty of an indictable offence and liable

    (a) where a firearm is used in the commission of the offence, to imprisonment for life and to a minimum punishment of imprisonment for a term of four years; and

    (b) in any other case, to imprisonment for life.

(2) Forcible confinement — Every one who, without lawful authority, confines, imprisons or forcibly seizes another person is guilty of

    (a) an indictable offence and liable to imprisonment for a term not exceeding ten years; or

    (b) an offence punishable on summary conviction and liable to imprisonment for a term not exceeding eighteen months.

(3) Non-resistance — In proceedings under this section, the fact that the person in relation to whom the offence is alleged to have been committed did not resist is not a defence unless the accused proves that the failure to resist was not caused by threats, duress, force or exhibition or force.

R.S., c. C-34, s. 247; R.S. 1985, c. 27 (1st Supp.), s. 39; 1995, c. 39. s. 147; 1997, c. 18, s. 14.

Commentary: Section 279(1) does *not* describe the *external circumstances* of kidnapping. "Kidnap", in common usage, connotes a taking, stealing or carrying off by force or fraud of one by another. This element, the asportation of a human being, has become substantially attenuated in recent times. The *mental element* which must accompany the external circumstances requires proof of *any* of the ulterior states of mind of ss. 279(1)(a)–(c).

Section 279(2) creates the discrete offences of unlawful confinement, imprisonment and forcible seizure. The absence of lawful authority is a critical element in the *external circumstances* of each offence. Lawful authority may derive from either civil or criminal law and may be actual or apprehended. No ulterior state of mind need be proven.

Section 279(3) defines the circumstances under which a lack of resistance by V may afford a defence under either s. 279 (1) or (2): It is only a defence where D proves, on a balance of probabilities, that the failure to resist was not caused by threats, duress, force or exhibition of force. This statutory reversal of the onus of proof is constitutionally vulnerable under *Charter* s. 11(d).

Case Law

Kidnaps

R. v. Oakley (1977), 39 C.R.N.S. 105 (Alta. C.A.) — *Contra: R. v. Welland*, [1978] 1 W.L.R. 921 (C.A.) — In order to make out an offence of kidnapping rather than one of imprisonment, a taking of the person from one place to another is required.

R. v. Kear (1989), 51 C.C.C. (3d) 574 (Ont. C.A.) — Foreign contracts or common law rights recognized in a foreign country which authorize a surety to seize an absconding accused and deliver him to court in the foreign jurisdiction are of *no* effect in Canada.

Against His Will

R. v. Metcalfe (1983), 10 C.C.C. (3d) 114 (B.C. C.A.); leave to appeal refused (1984), 54 N.R. 320n (S.C.C.) — *See also*: *R. v. Brown* (1972), 8 C.C.C. (2d) 13 (Ont. C.A.); *R. v. Johnson* (1984), 65 N.S.R. (2d) 54 (C.A.); leave to appeal refused (1985), 67 N.S.R. (2d) 180 (S.C.C.) — It is *not* necessary that V be *forcibly* conveyed to the place of confinement. It is sufficient if V is induced by fraud to accompany D.

Ransom

R. v. Robertson (1982), 39 A.R. 273 (Alta. C.A.) — The absence of a demand for ransom or any other demand is irrelevant.

Unlawful Confinement

R. v. Gratton (1985), 18 C.C.C. (3d) 462 (Ont. C.A.); leave to appeal refused (1985), 18 C.C.C. (3d) 462n (S.C.C.) — Confinement does *not* require proof of total physical restraint of V. Further, it is not necessary for V to have been confined for the entire time that V was together with D. If V was restrained against her wishes for any significant period of time, then a confinement had taken place.

R. v. Lemaigre (1987), 56 Sask. R. 300 (C.A.) — Confinement consists of restricting V's liberty, but *not* V's ability to escape. V need *not* be restricted to a particular place.

Relationship Between Sections 279(1) and (2)

R. v. Tremblay (1997), 117 C.C.C. (3d) 86 (Que. C.A.) — A kidnapping necessarily entails an unlawful confinement, but the converse is not always so. Unlawful confinement deprives V of the liberty to move from point to point. Kidnapping consists of taking control of V and carrying V away from one point to another.

Charter Considerations

R. v. Pete (1998), 131 C.C.C. (3d) 233 (B.C. C.A.) — Section 279(3) is unconstitutional.

R. v. Gough (1985), 43 C.R. (3d) 297, 18 C.C.C. (3d) 453 (Ont. C.A.) — Section 279(3) contravenes *Charter* s. 11(d) and is *not* saved by *Charter*, s. 1.

Related Provisions: "Forcible abduction" is an offence to which the excuse of compulsion in s. 17 is *not* applicable. *Semble*, the offences of ss. 279(1) and (2), at least in part, would fall within this description.

Under s. 536(2), D may *elect* mode of trial. The expanded territorial jurisdiction provisions of s. 7(3) are applicable where V is an "internationally protected person" as defined in s. 2.

The offences of ss. 279(1) and (2) are primary crimes within the classification of murder as first degree murder under s. 231(5)(e). Each is an "offence" in s. 183 for the purposes of Part VI.

279.1 (1) Hostage taking — Every one takes a person hostage who

(a) confines, imprisons, forcibly seizes or detains that person, and

(b) in any manner utters, conveys or causes any person to receive a threat that the death of, or bodily harm to, the hostage will be caused or that the confinement, imprisonment or detention of the hostage will be continued with intent to induce any person, other than the hostage, or any group of persons or any state or international or intergovernmental organization to commit or cause to be committed any act or omission as a condition, whether express or implied, of the release of the hostage.

(2) Hostage–taking — Every person who takes a person hostage is guilty of an indictable offence and liable

(a) where a firearm is used in the commission of the offence, to imprisonment for life and to a minimum punishment of imprisonment for a term of four years; and

(b) in any other case, to imprisonment for life.

(3) Non—resistance — Subsection 279(3) applies to proceedings under this section as if the offence under this section were an offence under section 279.

R.S. 1985, c. 27 (1st Supp.), s. 40(1); 1995, c. 39, s. 148.

Commentary: The section first appeared as s. 247.1 upon enactment by S.C. 1985, c. 19, s. 41(1).

The *external circumstances* combine an *unlawful confinement*, as described in s. 279.1(a), with a *threat* of the nature described in s. 279.1(1)(b). The *mental element*, ulterior to the external circumstances, requires proof of an intent to *induce a third party* to take a course of action, by act, omission or direction, as a condition, express or implied, of the release of the hostage. The third party whom D seeks to induce to act by taking V hostage may be a person, group of persons, state, international or inter-governmental organization, but must *not* be V.

Section 279.1(3) incorporates s. 279(3), which defines the circumstances under which lack of resistance by V may amount to a defence. It is only a defence where D proves, on a balance of probabilities, that the failure to resist was not caused by threats, duress, force or exhibition of force. This statutory reversal of the onus of proof is constitutionally vulnerable under *Charter* s. 11(d).

Related Provisions: The excuse of compulsion is *not* available to D in the circumstances described in s. 17.

D may elect mode of trial under s. 536(2). The expanded territorial jurisdiction provisions of ss. 7(3) and (4) are applicable where V is an "internationally protected person" as defined in s. 2.

Hostage taking is a primary crime for the classification of murder as first degree murder under s. 231(5)(f). It is also an "offence" under s. 183 for the purposes of Part VI.

280. (1) Abduction of person under sixteen — Every one who, without lawful authority, takes or causes to be taken an unmarried person under the age of sixteen years out of the possession of and against the will of the parent or guardian of that person or of any other person who has the lawful care or charge of that person is guilty of an indictable offence and liable to imprisonment for a term not exceeding five years.

(2) Definition of "guardian" — In this section and sections 281 to 283, "guardian" includes any person who has in law or in fact the custody or control of another person.

R.S., c. C-34, s. 249; 1980–81–82–83, c. 125, s. 20.

Commentary: Unlike several abduction offences, s. 280 does *not* require that, as principal D be a member of a defined class or stand in a particular relationship to V. The *external circumstances* of this offence occur when D, without lawful authority, takes or causes to be taken V, an unmarried person under 16 years of age, out of the possession of and against the will of V's parents, guardian or other custodian. The gravamen of the offence consists in the *taking* of the young person out of the possession and *against the will* of the parents, guardian or other custodian. The description of the offence, also the provisions of s. 286, render V's consent to the taking immaterial, although the consent of V's parent, guardian or custodian from whom V was taken will negate an essential element of P's proof. Further, if the court is *satisfied* that the taking was necessary to protect V from danger of imminent harm, or if D was escaping from a similar danger, s. 285 provides a defence. The *mental element* requires proof of an intent to cause the external circumstances of the offence.

Section 280(2) furnishes an expansive definition of "guardian" for this and other abduction offences.

Case Law

R. v. Cox (1969), 5 C.R.N.S. 395, [1969] 4 C.C.C. 321 (Ont. C.A.) — Consent obtained by fraud or trick is *not* a valid consent.

R. v. Langevin (1962), 38 C.R. 421 (Ont. C.A.) — Persuasion by D is *not* an essential ingredient of this offence.

Related Provisions: D may elect mode of trial under s. 536(2), but may be tried under the expanded territorial jurisdiction provisions of s. 7(3) where V is an "internationally protected person" as defined in s. 2.

D's spouse is a competent and compellable witness for P under *C.E.A.* s. 4(2) without D's consent. The offence is exempted from the excuse of duress under s. 17.

281. Abduction of person under fourteen — Every one who, not being the parent, guardian or person having the lawful care or charge of a person under the age of fourteen years, unlawfully takes, entices away, conceals, detains, receives or harbours that person with intent to deprive a parent or guardian, or any other person who has the lawful care or charge of that person, of the possession of that person is guilty of an indictable offence and liable to imprisonment for a term not exceeding ten years.

R.S., c. C-34, s. 250; 1980-81-82-83, c. 125, s. 20.

Commentary: The *external circumstances* of this offence require that, as principal, D be someone other than V's parent, guardian or custodian. V must be under 14 years of age. The means of abduction must be one of the statutory alternatives, *viz.* "unlawfully takes, entices away, conceals, detains, receives or harbours". Each term is accorded its normal natural everyday meaning.

The ulterior *mental element* requires proof of an intent to *deprive* the parent, guardian, or custodian of *possession* of V.

It is *not* a defence that V consented to or suggested the conduct said to constitute the offence (s. 286). It is a defence where D *establishes* parental, guardian or custodian consent on a balance of probabilities (s. 284), or where the court is *satisfied* that the abduction was necessary to protect V from danger of imminent harm or if D was escaping from a similar danger (s. 285). The reversal of the onus of proof by ss. 284 and 285 may require reassessment under *Charter* s. 11(d).

Case Law
Elements of Offence

R. v. Chartrand (1994), 31 C.R. (4th) 1, 91 C.C.C. (3d) 396 (S.C.C.) — There is *no* requirement that P prove an additional *unlawful* element or some element of unlawfulness beyond the taking of a child by a person who did not have lawful authority over that child. "Unlawfully", absent from the French text, is surplusage and merely indicates the existence of general defences, justifications and excuses under the *Code*.

R. v. Chartrand (1994), 31 C.R. (4th) 1, 91 C.C.C. (3d) 396 (S.C.C.) — Proof of the *mental element* may be made by proof of an intentional and purposeful deprivation of the parents' control over the child. It may also be established by the mere fact of the deprivation of the possession of the child through a taking, provided the trier of fact infers that the consequences of the taking are foreseen by D as a certain or substantially certain result of the taking.

R. v. Adams (1993), 19 C.R. (4th) 277, 79 C.C.C. (3d) 193 (Ont. C.A.) — The trial judge should define "guardian" for the jury.

Bigelow v. R. (1982), 69 C.C.C. (2d) 204 (Ont. C.A.); leave to appeal refused (1982), 69 C.C.C. (2d) 204n (S.C.C.) — "Detains" should be given its dictionary meaning of withhold. The intentional withholding of a child from its mother, with the effect of depriving her of her custodial rights, constitutes detention. An Ontario court had jurisdiction to try the offence where D's act deprived the mother in Ontario of custody.

Related Provisions: See the *Related Provisions* note to s. 280, *supra*.

282. (1) Abduction in contravention of custody order — Every one who, being the parent, guardian or person having the lawful care or charge of a person under the age of fourteen years, takes, entices away, conceals, detains, receives or harbours that person, in contravention of the custody provisions of a custody order in relation to that person made by a court anywhere in Canada, with intent to deprive a parent or guardian or any other person who has the lawful care or charge of that person, of the possession of that person is guilty of

(a) an indictable offence and is liable to imprisonment for a term not exceeding ten years; or

(b) an offence punishable on summary conviction.

(2) Where no belief in validity of custody order — Where a count charges an offence under subsection (1) and the offence is not proven only because the accused did not believe that there was a valid custody order but the evidence does prove an offence under section 283, the accused may be convicted of an offence under section 283.

1980–81–82–83, c. 125, s. 20; 1993, c. 45, s. 4.

Commentary: The *external circumstances* of this abduction offence require that, as principal, D be the parent, guardian or custodian of V, who must be under the age of 14 years. The means of abduction must be one of the statutory alternatives of "... unlawfully takes, entices away, conceals, detains, receives or harbours" as such terms are used in normal natural everyday language. The abduction must be in contravention of the custody provisions of a Canadian custody order respecting V.

The *mental element* is the intent to deprive a parent, guardian or custodian of possession of V and, *semble, inter alia, knowledge* of the custody order.

Section 282(2) permits conviction of D of an offence under s. 283 in a prosecution under s. 282(1). Where D is charged with a s. 282(1) offence and is found not guilty only because D did not believe that there was a valid custody order in relation to V, D may be convicted of an offence under s. 283 provided its essential elements have been proven. In other words, on a trial under s. 282(1), where the trier of fact has a reasonable doubt whether D had knowledge of a valid custody order in relation to V, D may be found not guilty of the offence charged, but guilty of an offence under s. 283 where the existence of a custody order is irrelevant to liability.

Case Law
General

R. v. Van Herk (1984), 40 C.R. (3d) 264, 12 C.C.C. (3d) 359 (Alta. C.A.) — P must prove that D was the *parent* of the child *under 14*, that D took the child with *intent* to deprive the *other parent* of the child, that the other parent was the person who by the custody order had *lawful care or charge* of the child, and that the taking was in *breach of the custody order*.

R. v. Petropoulos (1990), 59 C.C.C. (3d) 393 (B.C. C.A.) — A clause in a custody order prohibiting either parent from removing any of the children without consent of the other parent or a court order, is a custody provision of a custody order. Its effect is to restrict the custody rights of the custodial parent by limiting the geographic area within which the parent is free to move the child. An *access* provision may also involve transfer of the lawful care or charge of the child to a parent for the duration of the access. Where the parent entitled to access has been prevented from the exercise of the right to lawful care or charge of the child during such access periods, s/he has been denied possession of the child for that period.

Mental Element

R. v. Hammerbeck (1991), 68 C.C.C. (3d) 161 (B.C. C.A.) — Per Southin and Gibbs JJ.A.: *Semble*, a *mistake* by D that a custody order which police would not enforce was invalid, should be treated as a mistake of fact which may afford a defence to a charge under this section. Per Locke, Southin and Gibbs JJ.A.: To constitute a defence under the section, D's mistaken belief must be honestly held. It need *not* be honest *and* reasonable. The reasonableness or otherwise of D's belief may be considered by the trier of fact in determining whether the belief was honestly held.

R. v. McDougall (1990), 1 O.R. (3d) 247 (Ont. C.A.) — The *mental element* must coincide with common notions of abduction and be sufficiently culpable to warrant criminal sanction. The deprivation intended must be something more than the detention or withholding of the child. D must intend to put the child beyond the reach of the physical control or custody of the other parent. The mental element is not established upon proof of an intention by D not to assist or co-operate in the return of the child to the other parent.

R. v. Ilczyszyn (1988), 45 C.C.C. (3d) 91 (Ont. C.A.); leave to appeal granted (1989), 36 O.A.C. 215n (S.C.C.) — The *mental element* of the offence is an intent to deprive the person with lawful care of possession of the child and an intent to do so in contravention of a valid and subsisting custody order. It is a defence to the charge that D mistakenly believes on reasonable grounds that the order was no longer in existence.

External Circumstances

R. v. McDougall (1990), 1 O.R. (3d) 247 (C.A.) — "Detains" means witholds. Merely keeping a child beyond a prescribed access period does not *per se* constitute a withholding, hence detention of the child. There must be some actual or constructive refusal by D to turn over a child before the child has been "withheld", hence detained.

Related Provisions: This offence is triable either way but, if prosecuted by indictment, D may elect mode of trial under s. 536(2). Unlike s. 283, it does not require consent of the Attorney General or counsel instructed by him/her for the purpose in order to commence proceedings. The extended territorial jurisdiction provisions of s. 7(3) apply where V is an "internationally protected person" as defined in s. 2.

It is not a defence to the charge that V consented or suggested the conduct said to constitute the offence (s. 286), but is a defence where D *establishes* parental, guardian or custodian consent on a balance of probabilities (s. 284). It is equally a defence where the court is *satisfied* that the abduction was necessary to protect V from danger of imminent harm or D was escaping from a similar danger (s. 285). A reversal of the onus of proof by ss. 284 and 285 may require reassessment in light of *Charter* s. 11(d).

D's spouse is a competent and compellable witness for P without D's consent under *C.E.A.* s. 4(2).

This offence is also exempted from the excuse of duress in s. 17.

Section 662 enacts general and specific rules concerning included offences. Section 660 permits conviction of attempts when a completed offence is charged but not proven.

283. (1) Abduction — Every one who, being the parent, guardian or person having the lawful care or charge of a person under the age of fourteen years, takes, entices away, conceals, detains, receives or harbours that person, whether or not there is a custody order in relation to that person made by a court anywhere in Canada, with intent to deprive a parent or guardian, or any other person who has the lawful care or charge of that person, of the possession of that person, is guilty of

(a) an indictable offence and is liable to imprisonment for a term not exceeding ten years; or

(b) an offence punishable on summary conviction.

(2) Consent required — No proceedings may be commenced under subsection (1) without the consent of the Attorney General or counsel instructed by him for that purpose.

1980-81-82-83, c. 125, s. 20; 1993, c. 45, s. 5.

Commentary: The *external circumstances* require that D, as principal, be V's parent, guardian or custodian. V must be under the age of 14 years. The manner of abduction must amount to "... unlawfully takes, entices away, conceals, detains, receives or harbours" as such terms are understood in normal natural everyday usage. It is immaterial whether a Canadian custody order is in force in relation to V.

The *mental element* of the offence requires proof of the ulterior *intent to deprive* a parent, guardian or custodian of the *possession* of V.

Under s. 283(2) *no* proceedings may be commenced in respect of this offence without the *consent* of the provincial Attorney General or counsel instructed by him for such purpose.

Case Law

R. v. Dawson, [1996] 3 S.C.R. 783, 111 C.C.C. (3d) 1, 2 C.R. (5th) 121 — The essence of the s. 283 offence is an *intentional interference* with a parent's ability to exercise control over his/her child.A "taking" occurs where D causes the child to come or go with him/her, thereby excluding the authority of another with the lawful care/charge of the child. It need *not* be proven that the custodial parent had *actual* possession of the child at the *moment* of the *taking*. To "deprive" means, *inter alia*, to keep a person from that which s/he would otherwise have. "Possession" extends to the ability to exercise control over the child, *not* merely actual, physical possession.The *mental element*, the intent to deprive of possession, is proven where D *knows* or *foresees* that his/her actions would be certain or substantially certain to result in the custodial parent being deprived of the ability to exercise control over V. D will *not* be convicted without proof that D intended to deprive the person entitled to possession of the child of that possession.

Related Provisions: The consent of the provincial Attorney General, or counsel instructed by him/her for such purposes to the commencement of proceedings is required irrespective of the mode of procedure followed. If prosecuted by indictment, D will elect mode of trial under s. 536(2). The extended territorial jurisdiction provisions of s. 7(3) apply where V is an "internationally protected person" as defined in s. 2.

It is *not* a defence to the charge that V consented to or suggested the conduct said to constitute the offence (s. 286). It is a defence where D *establishes* parental, guardian or custodian consent on a balance of probabilities (s. 284) or where the court is *satisfied* that the abduction was necessary to protect V from danger of imminent harm or D is escaping from a similar danger (s. 285). The reversal of the onus of proof by ss. 284 and 285 may require reassessment in light of *Charter* s. 11(d).

D's spouse is a competent and compellable witness for P under *C.E.A.* s. 4(2) without D's consent.

This offence is also exempted from the excuse of duress in s. 17.

284. Defence — No one shall be found guilty of an offence under sections 281 to 283 if he establishes that the taking, enticing away, concealing, detaining, receiving or harbouring of any young person was done with the consent of the parent, guardian or other person having the lawful possession, care or charge of that young person.

1980–81–82–83, c. 125, s. 20.

Commentary: This section, applicable to the abduction offences of ss. 281–283, provides a *defence of consent* in certain circumstances. The consent must be given by V's parent, guardian or custodian. The consent of V is ineffectual under s. 286, *infra*. It would further appear that the consent must be to what would otherwise constitute the external circumstances of the offence and, *semble*, not otherwise be vitiated, as for example by threats.

No express mention is made of apprehended consent as a defence. On general principle, however, it would appear available, provided that what was apprehended would, in law, amount to an effectual consent.

The onus of proof is statutorily shifted to D to be established, *semble*, on a balance of probabilities. This aspect of the provision may engage the operation of *Charter* ss. 7 and 11(d).

Case Law

R. v. Dawson, [1996] 3 S.C.R. 783, 111 C.C.C. (3d) 1, 2 C.R. (5th) 121 — The consent must emanate from the person whom D intended to deprive of possession of the child.

Related Provisions: See the corresponding notes to ss. 280–283, *supra*.

285. Defence — No one shall be found guilty of an offence under sections 280 to 283 if the court is satisfied that the taking, enticing away, concealing, detaining, receiving or harbouring of any young person was necessary to protect the young person from danger of imminent harm or if the person charged with the offence was escaping from danger of imminent harm.

1980–81–82–83, c. 125, s. 20; 1993, c. 45, s. 6.

Commentary: This section, applicable to the abduction offences of ss. 280–283, provides a limited *defence of necessity*. No offence is committed if V's abduction is necessary to protect V from danger of imminent harm or D is escaping from similar harm. No lesser necessity will suffice, nor is any greater necessity required. Although the language of the section is not so clear as appears in s. 284 it would also appear to shift the onus of proof in respect of the defence to D on a balance of probabilities, thereby engaging *Charter* ss. 7 and 11(d) scrutiny.

Quaere whether apprehended necessity would also constitute a defence without any shift in the onus of proof?

Case Law

R. v. Mendez (1997), 113 C.C.C. (3d) 304 (Ont. C.A.) — The second branch of *Code* s. 285 is only engaged where the non-custodial parent is escaping from the danger of imminent harm. There must be a nexus between taking of the child and the non-custodial parent's escape from the danger of imminent harm.

R. v. Adams (1993), 19 C.R. (4th) 277, 79 C.C.C (3d) 193 (Ont. C.A.) — Section 285 introduces a statutory scheme which provides a defence to what otherwise would be a crime on the grounds of *qualified necessity*. The qualification is that the "taking" of V must be in response to the perceived danger of imminent harm.The section provides its own elements of proportionality and avoids wholesale access to self-help in response to an honest belief or perception (even if mistaken) that V is in danger of imminent harm. To be *necessary* within s. 285, a "taking" in response to the belief must be a proportional response, viewed objectively, but in light of the circumstances honestly (even if mistakenly) believed by D.

R. v. Adams (1993), 19 C.R. (4th) 277, 79 C.C.C. (3d) 193 (Ont. C.A.) — The doctrine of *mistake of fact* is applicable to the defence provided by s. 285. An honest (but mistaken) belief that V was in danger of imminent harm may be raised under the section. The belief need *not* be both honest and reasonable. The trier of fact ought to be instructed, however, that the reasonableness of any mistaken belief as to the danger of imminent harm ought to be considered in deciding whether the belief was honestly held.D's honest belief in the danger of imminent harm to V does not, *per se*, afford a defence under s. 285. The taking of V must also be *necessary* in an *objective* sense based on the circumstances as D honestly believed them to be. The trier of fact ought be instructed to consider on this issue other remedial steps which might have been taken.

Related Provisions: See the corresponding notes to ss. 280–283, *supra*.

286. No defence — In proceedings in respect of an offence under sections 280 to 283, it is not a defence to any charge that a young person consented to or suggested any conduct of the accused.

1980–81–82–83, c. 125, s. 20.

Commentary: It is *not* a defence to an abduction charge under any of ss. 280–283, that V consented to or suggested any of D's conduct. *Semble*, apprehension of such consent would also *not* amount to a defence.

The words, actions, conduct and demeanour of V which do not afford a defence of consent, actual or apprehended, may disclose to D the basis for the qualified necessity defence described in s. 285, *supra*.

Related Provisions: See the corresponding notes to ss. 280–283, *supra*.

Abortion

287. (1) Procuring miscarriage — Every one who, with intent to procure the miscarriage of a female person, whether or not she is pregnant, uses any means for the purpose of carrying out his intention is guilty of an indictable offence and liable to imprisonment for life.

(2) Woman procuring her own miscarriage — Every female person who, being pregnant, with intent to procure her own miscarriage, uses any means or permits any

means to be used for the purpose of carrying out her intention is guilty of an indictable offence and liable to imprisonment for a term not exceeding two years.

(3) **"means"** — In this section, "means" includes

(a) the administration of a drug or other noxious thing;

(b) the use of an instrument; and

(c) manipulation of any kind.

(4) **Exceptions** — Subsections (1) and (2) do not apply to

(a) a qualified medical practitioner, other than a member of a therapeutic abortion committee for any hospital, who in good faith uses in an accredited or approved hospital any means for the purpose of carrying out his intention to procure the miscarriage of a female person, or

(b) a female person who, being pregnant, permits a qualified medical practitioner to use in an accredited or approved hospital any means for the purpose of carrying out her intention to procure her own miscarriage,

if, before the use of those means, the therapeutic abortion committee for that accredited or approved hospital, by a majority of the members of the committee and at a meeting of the committee at which the case of the female person has been reviewed,

(c) has by certificate in writing stated that in its opinion the continuation of the pregnancy of the female person would or would be likely to endanger her life or health, and

(d) has caused a copy of that certificate to be given to the qualified medical practitioner.

(5) **Information requirement** — The Minister of Health of a province may by order

(a) require a therapeutic abortion committee for any hospital in that province, or any member thereof, to furnish him with a copy of any certificate described in paragraph (4)(c) issued by that committee, together with such other information relating to the circumstances surrounding the issue of that certificate as he may require, or

(b) require a medical practitioner who, in that province, has procured the miscarriage of any female person named in a certificate described in paragraph (4)(c), to furnish him with a copy of that certificate, together with such other information relating to the procuring of the miscarriage as he may require.

(6) **Definitions** — For the purposes of subsections (4) and (5) and this subsection

"accredited hospital" means a hospital accredited by the Canadian Council on Hospital Accreditation in which diagnostic services and medical, surgical and obstetrical treatment are provided;

"approved hospital" means a hospital in a province approved for the purposes of this section by the Minister of Health of that province;

"board" means the board of governors, management or directors, or the trustees, commission or other person or group of persons having the control and management of an accredited or approved hospital;

"Minister of Health" means

    (a) in the Provinces of Ontario, Quebec, New Brunswick, Prince Edward Island, Manitoba, and Newfoundland, the Minister of Health,

    (b) in the Provinces of Nova Scotia and Saskatchewan, the Minister of Public Health, and

    (c) in the Province of British Columbia, the Minister of Health Services and Hospital Insurance,

    (d) in the Province of Alberta, the Minister of Hospitals and Medical Care,

    (e) in the Yukon Territory, the Northwest Territories and Nunavut, the Minister of National Health and Welfare;

"qualified medical practitioner" means a person entitled to engage in the practice of medicine under the laws of the province in which the hospital referred to in subsection (4) is situated;

"therapeutic abortion committee" for any hospital means a committee, comprised of not less than three members each of whom is a qualified medical practitioner, appointed by the board of that hospital for the purpose of considering and determining questions relating to terminations of pregnancy within that hospital.

(7) Requirement of consent not affected — Nothing in subsection (4) shall be construed as making unnecessary the obtaining of any authorization or consent that is or may be required, otherwise than under this Act, before any means are used for the purpose of carrying out an intention to procure the miscarriage of a female person.

R.S., c. C-34, s. 251; 1974–75–76, c. 93, s. 22.11993, c. 28, s. 78 (Sched. III, item 30); 1996, c. 8, s. 32(1)(d).

Commentary: The section has been declared unconstitutional in *Morgentaler v. R.* (1988), 62 C.R. (3d) 1, 37 C.C.C. (3d) 449 (S.C.C.).

Related Provisions: Several *Code* sections describe and punish offences relating to childbirth and the death of children. Infanticide and the related offence of killing an unborn child in the act of birth are described in ss. 233, 237 and 238. Neglect in childbirth and concealment of the dead body of a child are described and punished in ss. 242 and 243.

288. Supplying noxious things — Every one who unlawfully supplies or procures a drug or other noxious thing or an instrument or thing, knowing that it is intended to be used or employed to procure the miscarriage of a female person, whether or not she is pregnant, is guilty of an indictable offence and liable to imprisonment for a term not exceeding two years.

R.S., c. C-34, s. 252.

Commentary: This section imposes criminal liability for supply of an abortifacient to a female, in the *knowledge* that it is to be used or employed to procure her miscarriage. The *external circumstances* of the offence consist in the unlawful supply or procurement of the abortifacient. It would seem unnecessary that the means actually be given or sold to the female, at all events where the allegation is one of procurement. The female need *not* be pregnant. The critical *mental element* under the section is proof of D's *knowledge* of the intended use or employment of that which is supplied to procure the miscarriage of the female.

Case Law
Mental Element

R. v. Irwin (1968), 3 C.R.N.S. 377 (S.C.C.); affirming [1968] 2 C.C.C. 50 (Alta. C.A.) — If the person who supplied the drug believes that the person to whom he is supplying it intends to use it to procure a miscarriage, that is sufficient for a conviction under the section. It does not matter that the person to whom the drug was supplied did not in fact intend to use it, as where it is supplied to an undercover policewoman.

Related Provisions: The indictable offence created by s. 288 permits D to elect mode of trial under s. 536(2).

Other related provisions are described in the corresponding note to s. 287, *supra*.

289. [Repealed R.S. 1985, c. 27 (1st Supp.), s. 41.]

Offences Against Conjugal Rights

290. (1) **Bigamy** — Every one commits "bigamy" who

(a) in Canada,

(i) being married, goes through a form of marriage with another person,

(ii) knowing that another person is married, goes through a form of marriage with that person, or

(iii) on the same day or simultaneously, goes through a form of marriage with more than one person; or

(b) being a Canadian citizen resident in Canada leaves Canada with intent to do anything mentioned in subparagraphs (a)(i) to (iii) and, pursuant thereto, does outside Canada anything mentioned in those subparagraphs in circumstances mentioned therein.

(2) **Matters of defence** — No person commits bigamy by going through a form of marriage if

(a) that person in good faith and on reasonable grounds believes that his spouse is dead,

(b) the spouse of that person has been continuously absent from him for seven years immediately preceding the time when he goes through the form of marriage, unless he knew that his spouse was alive at any time during those seven years,

(c) that person has been divorced from the bond of the first marriage, or

(d) the former marriage has been declared void by a court of competent jurisdiction.

(3) **Incompetency no defence** — Where a person is alleged to have committed bigamy, it is not a defence that the parties would, if unmarried, have been incompetent to contract marriage under the law of the place where the offence is alleged to have been committed.

(4) **Validity presumed** — Every marriage or form of marriage shall, for the purpose of this section, be deemed to be valid unless the accused establishes that it was invalid.

(5) **Act or omission by accused** — No act or omission on the part of an accused who is charged with bigamy invalidates a marriage or form of marriage that is otherwise valid.

R.S., c. C-34, s. 254.

Commentary: Bigamy renders criminal multiple marriages. In general, it occurs when a spouse marries again during the life of an earlier or current spouse. This simultaneous plurality of spouses is more accurately designated polygamy. The *external circumstances* are defined in ss. 290(1)(a) and (b).

The *mental element* of the offence described in s. 290(1)(a) requires no proof of an ulterior state of mind though specific knowledge of the partner's marital status is critical under s. 290(a)(ii). An ulterior state of mind, namely, the intent to do anything described in s. 290(1)(a), is essential in prosecutions under (1)(b).

Section 290(2) provides several *defences* to a charge of bigamy, including an honest and reasonably grounded belief in the death of the duplicate spouse, the continuous absence of the duplicate spouse for seven years, without knowledge that such person was alive, divorce and annulment of the former marriage. Under s. 290(3) it is no defence that the parties would, if unmarried, have been incompetent to marry under domestic or foreign law, as the case may be, nor can D rely upon his/her own act or omission, for example, non-consummation, to invalidate an otherwise valid marriage or form of marriage.

Section 290(4) *presumes* all marriages to be valid unless D *establishes* that it was invalid. The degree of proof required, if constitutionally sustainable, is upon a balance of probabilities.

Case Law
Nature and Elements of Offence
Queneau v. R. (1949), 8 C.R. 235, 95 C.C.C. 187 (Que. C.A.) — To obtain a conviction for bigamy P must establish three *essential elements*: (1) that D was previously married; (2) that the first wife was still living when the second form of marriage was entered into; and (3) the fact of the second form of marriage.

Form of Marriage
R. v. Grant (1924), 42 C.C.C. 344 (N.S. C.A.) — "Form of marriage" is synonymous with "ceremony of marriage".

Mental Element
R. v. Brinkley (1907), 12 C.C.C. 454 (Ont. C.A.) — It is not a defence to a charge of bigamy that D believed in good faith that a valid decree of divorce had been granted and that he was legally free to marry again. Ignorance of the law is no excuse. The section requires that a valid divorce be proved.

R. v. Haugen, [1923] 2 W.W.R. 709 (Sask. C.A.) — If D believed in good faith and on reasonable grounds that at the time he "married" his first wife she then had a husband living such that the "marriage" was a nullity, this would be a valid defence to a charge of bigamy based on a "second" marriage.

Related Provisions: Proof of the marriage or form of marriage may be made by a certificate of marriage under s. 291(2) *semble*, coupled with proof of identity. The marriage so proven is presumed valid under s. 290(4). D's spouse is a competent and compellable witness for P without D's consent under *C.E.A.* s. 4(2).

D may elect mode of trial under s. 536(2).

291. (1) Punishment — Every one who commits bigamy is guilty of an indictable offence and liable to imprisonment for a term not exceeding five years.

(2) Certificate of marriage — For the purposes of this section, a certificate of marriage issued under the authority of law is evidence of the marriage or form of marriage to which it relates without proof of the signature or official character of the person by whom it purports to be signed.

R.S., c. C-34, s. 255.

Commentary: Under s. 291(1), bigamy is an indictable offence punishable by imprisonment for a term not exceeding five years.

Section 291(2) facilitates proof of bigamy by permitting the reception of a *certificate of marriage* as evidence of the marriage or form of marriage to which it relates. There is no express notice requirement. Under s. 290(4), the marriage or form of marriage so certified is presumed valid. Absent an admission, evidence would be required to establish the identity of the parties to the marriage described in the certificate.

Related Provisions: See the corresponding note to s. 290, *supra*.

292. (1) **Procuring feigned marriage** — Every person who procures or knowingly aids in procuring a feigned marriage between himself and another person is guilty of an indictable offence and liable to imprisonment for a term not exceeding five years.

(2) **Corroboration** — No person shall be convicted of an offence under this section on the evidence of only one witness unless the evidence of that witness is corroborated in a material particular by evidence that implicates the accused.

R.S., c. C-34, s. 256; 1980–81–82–83, c. 125, s. 21.

Commentary: As principal, D may be either male or female. The *external circumstances* include not only procuring a feigned marriage between D and another, but also knowingly aiding in such procuring. In each case the subject-matter procured is a feigned marriage between D and another. The *mental element* does *not* extend beyond the intent to cause the external circumstances of the offence and does *not* require, for example, proof of an intent to defraud others in consequence of the feigned marriage.

Section 292(2) requires *corroboration* as a condition precedent to conviction. The corroboration must be evidence which, in a material particular, implicates D in the offence charged.

Related Provisions: D may elect mode of trial under s. 536(2).

Under *C.E.A.* s. 4(2), D's spouse is a competent and compellable witness for P without D's consent.

293. (1) **Polygamy** — Every one who

     (a) practises or enters into or in any manner agrees or consents to practise or enter into

         (i) any form of polygamy, or

         (ii) any kind of conjugal union with more than one person at the same time, whether or not it is by law recognized as a binding form of marriage; or

     (b) celebrates, assists or is a party to a rite, ceremony, contract or consent that purports to sanction a relationship mentioned in subparagraph (a)(i) or (ii),

is guilty of an indictable offence and liable to imprisonment for a term not exceeding five years.

(2) **Evidence in case of polygamy** — Where an accused is charged with an offence under this section, no averment or proof of the method by which the alleged relationship was entered into, agreed to or consented to is necessary in the indictment or on the trial of the accused, nor is it necessary on the trial to prove that the persons who are alleged to have entered into the relationship had or intended to have sexual intercourse.

R.S., c. C-34, s. 257.

Commentary: *Polygamy*, under s. 293(1), does *not* require proof that D actually practised or entered into a polygamous conjugal union. The *external circumstances* are equally established where D, in any manner, agrees or consents to practice or enter into such form of union. There must, however, be agreement, consent or practice of some form of union in the guise of marriage. Adultery *per se*, even where both parties are married to other spouses at the time, is not polygamy. Under s. 293(1)(b) any who are knowingly parties to a ceremony sanctioning a polygamous relationship are parties to the offence. The *mental element* of the offence does not extend beyond the intention to bring about its external circumstances with the requisite degree of knowledge.

Section 293(2) is an amalgam of procedural, evidentiary and substantive rules applicable in polygamy prosecutions. P need *not* plead in the indictment, nor prove at trial, the method by which the alleged polygamous relationship was entered into, agreed or consented to by the parties. Further, P need not prove the parties had or intended to have sexual intercourse. The offence is complete upon proof of the agreement, consent or practice of multiple conjugal unions.

Related Provisions: D may elect mode of trial under s. 536(2).

Under *C.E.A.* s. 4(2), D's spouse is a competent and compellable witness for P without D's consent.

The pleading provision in s. 293(2) is consistent with the general principles of s. 583(f).

Unlawful Solemnization of Marriage

294. Pretending to solemnize marriage — Every one who

(a) solemnizes or pretends to solemnize a marriage without lawful authority, the proof of which lies upon him, or

(b) procures a person to solemnize a marriage knowing that he is not lawfully authorized to solemnize the marriage,

is guilty of an indictable offence and liable to imprisonment for a term not exceeding two years.

R.S., c. C-34, s. 258.

Commentary: The *external circumstances* of this offence vary. Under s. 294(a), there must be actual or feigned solemnization of marriage by D who lacks the authority to do so. It is not incumbent upon P to establish want of lawful authority but rather upon D to establish, on a balance of probabilities, actual lawful authority. Under s. 294(b), P must establish that D has procured someone to solemnize a marriage who, to the knowledge of D, is not lawfully authorized to do so. Proof of actual or pretended solemnization of the marriage is not an essential element of the *external circumstances* of the offence of s. 294(b). The offence rests in the procurement of one for such purpose with knowledge of his/her lack of lawful authority.

The *mental element* to be established in either case does not extend beyond the intention to cause the external circumstances of the offence.

Quaere whether the reverse onus clause of s. 294(a) infringes *Charter* ss. 7 and 11(d)?

Related Provisions: D has an election as to mode of trial under s. 536(2).

Under *C.E.A.* s. 4(2), D's spouse is a competent and compellable witness for P without D's consent.

The section naturally complements s. 295, which enjoins the unlawful solemnization of marriage by one who is lawfully authorized to perform marriage ceremonies.

295. Marriage contrary to law — Every one who, being lawfully authorized to solemnize marriage, knowingly and wilfully solemnizes a marriage in contravention of the laws of the province in which the marriage is solemnized is guilty of an indictable offence and liable to imprisonment for a term not exceeding two years.

R.S., c. C-34, s. 259.

Commentary: This prohibition enjoins the unlawful solemnization of marriage by one who is lawfully authorized to perform marriage ceremonies. The *external circumstances* require proof that D is lawfully authorized to solemnize marriage under the laws of the province in which the ceremony occurred. P must also prove that D solemnized a marriage and, further, that the solemnization of the marriage by D was knowingly and wilfully in contravention of the laws of the province in which it occurred.

The *mental element* consists of proof that D intended to cause the external circumstances of the offence.

Related Provisions: The section naturally complements s. 294, which prohibits the actual or intended solemnization of marriage by unauthorized persons or procuring such a person to do so.

D may elect mode of trial under s. 536(2).

Unlike s. 294, this offence is not one to which the exception of *C.E.A.* s. 4(2) applies.

Blasphemous Libel

296. (1) **Offence** — Every one who publishes a blasphemous libel is guilty of an indictable offence and liable to imprisonment for a term not exceeding two years.

(2) **Question of fact** — It is a question of fact whether or not any matter that is published is a blasphemous libel.

(3) **Saving** — No person shall be convicted of an offence under this section for expressing in good faith and in decent language, or attempting to establish by argument used in good faith and conveyed in decent language, an opinion on a religious subject.

R.S., c. C-34, s. 260.

Commentary: Subsection (1) punishes *publication* of a *blasphemous libel*.

The *external circumstances* of the offence consist of two elements: publishing and subject-matter. "Publishing" is not expressly defined for the purposes of this section but would seem to entail making publicly or generally known, by exhibition, display or delivery, in written or spoken words, matter that amounts to a blasphemous libel. Under s. 296(2), whether what is published constitutes a blasphemous libel is a question of fact, but it would seem to require something beyond what is excepted by s. 296(3) in order to establish the offence. The *mental element* consists of D's intention to publish the words said to be libellous.

The offence would seem rarely prosecuted and likely to attract a challenge under *Charter* ss. 2(a) and (b).

Related Provisions: The *Code* also punishes *seditious* libel under ss. 59–61 and *defamatory* libel under ss. 298–302. Provision is *not* made for justification or privilege, as it is for defamatory libel under ss. 303(3)–316. The special provisions of s. 584 relating to the sufficiency of counts charging libel are, however, applicable to prosecutions under this section.

D may elect mode of trial under s. 536(2).

Defamatory Libel

297. **"Newspaper"** — In sections 303, 304 and 308, "newspaper" means any paper, magazine or periodical containing public news, intelligence or reports of events, or any remarks or observations thereon, printed for sale and published periodically or in parts or numbers, at intervals not exceeding thirty-one days between the publication of any two such papers, parts or numbers, and any paper, magazine or periodical printed in order to be dispersed and made public, weekly or more often, or at intervals not exceeding thirty-one days, that contains advertisements, exclusively or principally.

R.S., c. C-34, s. 261.

Commentary: "Newspaper" is exhaustively defined for the purposes of ss. 303 (vicarious liability of proprietor), 304 (exemption for seller or servant) and 308 (exemption for fair report of public meeting). To qualify, the publication must be a paper, magazine or periodical of specified content printed for sale and published periodically within the terms of the section.

Related Provisions: See the corresponding note to s. 298, *infra*.

298. (1) **Definition** — A "defamatory libel" is matter published, without lawful justification or excuse, that is likely to injure the reputation of any person by exposing him to hatred, contempt or ridicule, or that is designed to insult the person of or concerning whom it is published.

(2) **Mode of expression** — A defamatory libel may be expressed directly or by insinuation or irony

(a) in words legibly marked upon any substance, or

(b) by any object signifying a defamatory libel otherwise than by words.

R.S., c. C-34, s. 262.

Commentary: The *external circumstances* of *defamatory libel* include several elements. There must be a *matter* which is *published*, as defined in s. 299. It may be expressed either directly or by innuendo, as described in s. 298(2). The publishing must be *without lawful justification or excuse*. It is only defamatory libel that provides for a defence of truth or justification. A series of excuses, provided in s. 303(3) and 304–315 will avail D and require negation by P, upon P's introduction of evidence in support. P must also prove that the published matter was either *likely to injure the reputation* of someone in a manner proscribed in s. 298(1), or, *designed to insult* the person of or concerning whom it was published. The *mental element* consists of D's intention to publish the allegedly libellous matter.

The offence may attract a *Charter* s. 2(b) challenge.

Case Law

Charter Considerations

R. v. Lucas (1998), 14 C.R. (5th) 237, 123 C.C.C. (3d) 97 (S.C.C.) — The provisions are *not* so vague that they offend *Charter* s. 7. Although they infringe *Charter* s. 2(b), they are saved by s. 1.

The section is *not* so vague that it infringes *Charter* s. 7. It does, however, offend *Charter* s. 2(b) but, except for the phrase, ". . . by the person whom it defames or . . .", in s. 299(c), is saved by s. 1. Section 299(c) should be read:

> A person publishes a libel when he . . . shows or delivers it, or causes it to be shown or delivered, with an intent that it should be read or seen by any other person.

Related Provisions: The offence attracts a maximum punishment of two years' imprisonment. Where it is also proven that D *knew* the defamatory libel to be *false*, the maximum is five years. The related crime of extortion by libel is described in s. 302. Section 303, in part, and subject to exception, imposes vicarious liability upon the proprietor of a newspaper which contains defamatory matter. Sections 303(3) and 304(1) excuse sellers of newspapers and other publications, absent knowledge of defamatory contents. Sections 305–315 provide a series of excuses for publication of material that would otherwise attract the prohibition.

Special *pleading* provisions apply to trials of cases of defamatory libel. Section 584 makes special provision for the sufficiency of counts alleging defamatory libel, as well as the manner in which such counts may be pleaded and proven. Sections 611 and 612 expressly permit D to plead justification. A private prosecutor, under s. 637, has no authority to stand prospective jurors by. Costs are recoverable by the party in whose favour judgment is given under ss. 728 and 729.

Under s. 478(2), D's trial for a defamatory libel published in a newspaper may be held either where D resides or the newspaper is printed. D will elect mode of trial under s. 536(2). Under s. 317, the jury may return a general verdict of not guilty upon the whole matter, and shall not be directed to find D guilty merely on proof of publication by him/her, and of the writing bearing the meaning ascribed to it in the indictment. The judge is entitled to state his/her opinion to the jury, as in other cases, and the jury may, if it desires, return a special verdict.

299. Publishing — A person publishes a libel when he

    (a) exhibits it in public,

    (b) causes it to be read or seen, or

    (c) shows or delivers it, or causes it to be shown or delivered, with intent that it should be read or seen by the person whom it defames or by any other person.

R.S., c. C-34, s. 263.

Commentary: The section embodies the common law definition of "publishing" and includes publication to the person defamed. It would seem implicit in the section that either wide-spread or restricted display, reading or viewing will amount to "publishing". Under s. 299(c) the display or delivery, actual or caused, must be accompanied by the ulterior intention that the defamatory material be read or seen by the person it defames or any other person. No such ulterior mental element is required under either s. 299(a) or (b).

Related Provisions: See the corresponding note to s. 298, *supra*.

300. Punishment of libel known to be false — Every one who publishes a defamatory libel that he knows is false is guilty of an indictable offence and liable to imprisonment for a term not exceeding five years.

R.S., c. C-34, s. 264.

Commentary: The *external circumstances* consist of publishing a defamatory libel. A defamatory libel is defined in s. 298 and publishing in s. 299. The element added by the punishment provisions of this section requires P to prove that D knew the defamatory libel to be false. The *mental element* consists of the intention to publish the matter with knowledge of its falsity.

It is D's *knowledge* of the *falsity* of the defamatory libel that distinguishes this offence from that punished under s. 301 by a maximum term of imprisonment not exceeding two years.

Case Law

Essential Elements

R. v. Lucas (1998), 14 C.R. (5th) 237, 123 C.C.C. (3d) 97 (S.C.C.) — The mental element in s. 300 includes both an *intention* to *defame* V and *knowledge* of the *falsity* of the statement.

Charter Considerations

R. v. Lucas (1998), 14 C.R. (5th) 237, 123 C.C.C. (3d) 97 (S.C.C.) — The provisions are *not* so vague that they offend *Charter* s. 7. Although they infringe *Charter* s. 2(b), they are saved by s. 1.

Related Provisions: See the corresponding note to s. 298, *supra*.

301. Punishment for defamatory libel — Every one who publishes a defamatory libel is guilty of an indictable offence and liable to imprisonment for a term not exceeding two years.

R.S., c. C-34, s. 265.

Commentary: The *external circumstances* require proof that D published a defamatory libel under the definitions enacted by ss. 298 and 299. The *mental element* requires proof of the intention to publish the material alleged to be defamatory. This offence appears included in the crime punished under s. 300.

Related Provisions: See the corresponding note to s. 298, *supra*.

302. (1) Extortion by libel — Every one commits an offence who, with intent

    (a) to extort money from any person, or

    (b) to induce a person to confer on or procure for another person an appointment or office of profit or trust,

publishes or threatens to publish or offers to abstain from publishing or to prevent the publication of a defamatory libel.

(2) Idem — Every one commits an offence who, as the result of the refusal of any person to permit money to be extorted or to confer or procure an appointment or office of profit or trust, publishes or threatens to publish a defamatory libel.

(3) Punishment — Every one who commits an offence under this section is guilty of an indictable offence and liable to imprisonment for a term not exceeding five years.

R.S., c. C-34, s. 266.

Commentary: *Extortion by libel*, a specific form of blackmail or extortion, may be committed in several ways.

Under s. 302(1), the *external circumstances* are proven where D publishes or threatens to publish, offers to abstain from publishing or to prevent the publication of defamatory libel. No publishing of a defamatory libel need actually occur. Defamatory libel is defined in s. 298 and publishing in s. 299. The *mental element* consists of *either* of the ulterior states of mind described in ss. 302(1)(a) and (b).

The *external circumstances* of the offence of s. 302(2), a natural complement to s. 302(1), require that D publish or threaten to publish a defamatory libel as a result of the refusal of another person to permit money to be extorted, or to confer or procure an appointment or office of profit or trust. In other words, there must be a failure to extort the money or office sought and, in consequence, an actual or threatened publication of the original defamatory libel. The *mental element* is the intention to cause the external circumstances of the offence.

Section 302(3) punishes the offence.

Related Provisions: Extortion, defined in more general terms in s. 346(1), is punishable by imprisonment for life. Other provisions, for example ss. 264.1(1), 423(1)(b) and 424, make it an offence to utter threats, to intimidate by threats and to threaten to commit specified offences against an "internationally protected person" as defined in s. 2.

For related procedural and evidentiary provisions see the corresponding note to s. 298, *supra*.

303. (1) Proprietor of newspaper presumed responsible — The proprietor of a newspaper shall be deemed to publish defamatory matter that is inserted and published therein, unless he proves that the defamatory matter was inserted in the newspaper without his knowledge and without negligence on his part.

(2) General authority to manager when negligence — Where the proprietor of a newspaper gives to a person general authority to manage or conduct the newspaper as editor or otherwise, the insertion by that person of defamatory matter in the newspaper shall, for the purposes of subsection (1), be deemed not to be negligence on the part of the proprietor unless it is proved that

(a) he intended the general authority to include authority to insert defamatory matter in the newspaper; or

(b) he continued to confer general authority after he knew that it had been exercised by the insertion of defamatory matter in the newspaper.

(3) Selling newspapers — No person shall be deemed to publish a defamatory libel by reason only that he sells a number or part of a newspaper that contains a defamatory libel, unless he knows that the number or part contains defamatory matter or that defamatory matter is habitually contained in the newspaper.

R.S., c. C-34, s. 267.

Commentary: The section only applies to newspapers as defined in s. 297. In general, s. 303(1) holds the *proprietor* of a newspaper criminally liable for any and all defamatory matter that is published in it. Liability may be escaped if D proves, *semble*, on a balance of probabilities, that the defamatory matter was inserted without his *knowledge* and *negligence*. Whether D has discharged the onus is a question of fact.

A proprietor may well assert that the management and conduct of the newspaper has been left to an editor whose responsibility it is to oversee content. Under s. 303(2), it is *presumed* that D was *not* acting negligently in so doing, unless P proves that such general authority included authority to insert defamatory matter or was continued after D knew it had been exercised to insert defamatory matter in the paper. *Semble*, the onus cast upon P could only be discharged by proof beyond a reasonable doubt.

The criminal liability of *sellers of newspapers* which contain defamatory matter is governed by s. 303(3). In essence, no seller is liable, absent proof of *actual knowledge* of the defamatory matter or knowledge that such matter is habitually contained in the newspaper.

Related Provisions: Sections 21 and 22 establish the basis of criminal liability. Limitations or expansions upon the basis of liability may appear, however, in respect of specified offences or groups of offences.

The reverse onus provisions of subsection (1) may require re-examination under *Charter* s. 11(d).

For other related procedural and evidentiary provisions, see the corresponding note to s. 298, *supra*.

304. (1) **Selling book containing defamatory libel** — No person shall be deemed to publish a defamatory libel by reason only that he sells a book, magazine, pamphlet or other thing, other than a newspaper that contains defamatory matter if, at the time of the sale, he does not know that it contains the defamatory matter.

(2) **Sale by servant** — Where a servant, in the course of his employment, sells a book, magazine, pamphlet or other thing, other than a newspaper, the employer shall be deemed not to publish any defamatory matter contained therein unless it is proved that the employer authorized the sale knowing that

(a) defamatory matter was contained therein; or

(b) defamatory matter was habitually contained therein, in the case of a periodical.

R.S., c. C-34, s. 268.

Commentary: This section applies only to sellers of materials other than a newspaper, in which defamatory matter is contained, as well, their employers. There is no reversal of the onus of proof. In general, liability could be established under s. 299(a) or (b).

Section 304(1), by exempting from liability all sellers of defamatory material, other than newspapers, who do not know of such contents, in effect, requires P to prove, in the case of *sellers*, actual *knowledge* that what is sold, other than newspapers, contains defamatory material. This would seem to accord with general principle.

Section 304(2) applies to employers of servants who sell materials, other than newspapers, containing defamatory matter. The employer will only be held liable in respect of such sales where P proves that D authorized the sale with knowledge of the actual defamatory contents or that such material was habitually contained in the periodical.

Related Provisions: See the corresponding note to s. 298, *supra*.

305. Publishing proceedings of courts of justice — No person shall be deemed to publish a defamatory libel by reason only that he publishes defamatory matter

(a) in a proceeding held before or under the authority of a court exercising judicial authority; or

(b) in an inquiry made under the authority of an Act or by order of Her Majesty, or under the authority of a public department or a department of the government of a province.

R.S., c. C-34, s. 269.

Commentary: The section *excuses* in cases where D's liability for publishing a defamatory libel would otherwise be established. D does not publish a defamatory libel *only* by publishing defamatory matter disclosed in judicial proceedings, as described in s. 305(a), or in federally or provincially sanctioned inquiries, as described in s. 305(b).

Related Provisions: In some instances, the publication of proceedings of courts of justice may attract prosecution for contempt or constitute one of the statutory offences in s. 276(5), 486(4), 517(2), 539(3) or 648(2).

See also the corresponding note to s. 298, *supra*.

306. Parliamentary papers — No person shall be deemed to publish a defamatory libel by reason only that he

(a) publishes to the Senate or House of Commons or to a legislature of a province defamatory matter contained in a petition to the Senate or House of Commons or to the legislature of a province, as the case may be;

(b) publishes by order or under the authority of the Senate or House of Commons or of the legislature of a province a paper containing defamatory matter; or

(c) publishes, in good faith and without ill-will to the person defamed, an extract from or abstract of a petition or paper mentioned in paragraph (a) or (b).

R.S., c. C-34, s. 270.

Commentary: This section *excuses* those who publish defamatory matter contained in parliamentary or legislative papers either to or under the authority of the parliamentary or legislative body. The excuse extends to the publication of an extract from or abstract of a parliamentary or legislative petition or paper, provided it is done in good faith and without ill-will to the person defamed. There is no shift in the onus of proof. It would, however, seem incumbent on D to adduce evidence of good faith and lack of ill-will, thereafter, the burden of P to negate it beyond a reasonable doubt.

Related Provisions: Section 307, in part, allows for the fair reporting of parliamentary or legislative proceedings and is a natural complement of the present section. Section 316(1) affords a means of proof.

See also the corresponding note to s. 298, *supra*.

307. (1) Fair reports of Parliamentary or judicial proceedings — No person shall be deemed to publish a defamatory libel by reason only that he publishes in good faith, for the information of the public, a fair report of the proceedings of the Senate or House of Commons or the legislature of a province, or a committee thereof, or of the public proceedings before a court exercising judicial authority, or publishes, in good faith, any fair comment on any such proceedings.

(2) Divorce proceedings an exception — This section does not apply to a person who publishes a report of evidence taken or offered in any proceeding before the Senate or House of Commons or any committee thereof, on a petition or bill relating to any matter of marriage or divorce, if the report is published without authority from or leave of the House in which the proceeding is held or is contrary to any rule, order or practice of that House.

R.S., c. C-34, s. 271.

Commentary: Section 307(1) extends the *excuse* for the publication of defamatory material originating in parliamentary, legislative or judicial proceedings to *fair reports of* and *fair comments upon* such proceedings. It is not limited by manner of reporting. The excuses have several aspects. A *fair report* of parliamentary, legislative or public judicial proceedings must be published in good faith for the information of the public. A *fair comment* on any such proceedings must simply be published in good faith.

The excuse of s. 307(1) is *not*, however, unqualified. Under s. 307(2), it does not extend to reports of evidence taken or offered in petitions or bills relating to matters of marriage or divorce before either House of Parliament or a committee thereof, if the report is unauthorized or contrary to any rule, order or practice of the House. Authorized reporting would seem to be excused.

Where D seeks to rely on the excuse of s. 307(1) it would be necessary to introduce evidence to raise such an issue, thereafter leaving P to disprove it beyond reasonable doubt.

Related Provisions: The publication of defamatory matter originating in judicial proceedings and authorized inquiries is excused under s. 305. Section 306 excuses publication of defamatory matter prepared for, originating in or derived from parliamentary or legislative proceedings. Fair reporting of public meetings and fair comment on a public person or work of art are excused under ss. 308 and 310.

For other related provisions, see the corresponding note to s. 298, *supra*.

308. Fair report of public meeting — No person shall be deemed to publish a defamatory libel by reason only that he publishes in good faith, in a newspaper, a fair report of the proceedings of any public meeting if

    (a) the meeting is lawfully convened for a lawful purpose and is open to the public;

    (b) the report is fair and accurate;

    (c) the publication of the matter complained of is for the public benefit; and

    (d) he does not refuse to publish in a conspicuous place in the newspaper a reasonable explanation or contradiction by the person defamed in respect of the defamatory matter.

R.S., c. C-34, s. 272.

Commentary: *Fair newspaper reporting* of public meetings may be excused from liability in respect of defamatory matters contained therein, provided certain criteria are met. The public meeting reported must be lawfully convened for a lawful purpose and open to the public. The report itself must be fair and accurate. The publication in the newspaper must be in good faith and for the public benefit. There must be no refusal of publication in a conspicuous place in the newspaper of a reasonable explanation or contradiction by the person defamed in respect of the defamatory matter.

Where D seeks to rely on this excuse, applicable only to reporting in *newspapers* as defined in s. 297, it is necessary that some evidence be adduced of the requisite elements of the excuse before it will become necessary for P to prove beyond a reasonable doubt that it is unavailing.

Related Provisions: See the corresponding note to s. 298, *supra*.

309. Public benefit — No person shall be deemed to publish a defamatory libel by reason only that he publishes defamatory matter that, on reasonable grounds, he believes is true, and that is relevant to any subject of public interest, the public discussion of which is for the public benefit.

R.S., c. C-34, s. 273.

Commentary: The section, unrestricted in the type of publication to which it may apply, affords an *excuse of public benefit*. It will only avail, however, where D believes, on reasonable grounds, that the defamatory matter is true. The defamatory matter need not, in fact, be true, provided D has a reasonably grounded belief that it is so. It is further necessary that the defamatory matter be relevant to a subject of public interest, the public discussion of which is for the public benefit. It is unclear whether this requirement is to be tested objectively or based upon D's belief. It would seem, at all events, that an honest belief by D in such public benefit may nonetheless afford a defence. There is no express or implied shift in the onus of proof in respect of this excuse. P would only be required to negate the excuse in the event of evidentiary support therefor.

Related Provisions: The circumstances under which truth will be a defence upon a charge of publishing a defamatory libel are described in s. 311.

For other related provisions, see the corresponding note to s. 298, *supra*.

310. Fair comment on public person or work of art — No person shall be deemed to publish a defamatory libel by reason only that he publishes fair comments

    (a) upon the public conduct of a person who takes part in public affairs; or

    (b) upon a published book or other literary production, or on any composition or work of art or performance publicly exhibited, or on any other communication made to the public on any subject, if the comments are confined to criticism thereof.

R.S., c. C-34, s. 274.

Commentary: The *excuse of fair comment*, unrestricted by the medium in which it may appear, is nonetheless of narrow application. In essence, it is limited to fair and critical comment upon persons, art, literature and communications in the public domain. It applies in two discrete situations. Fair and critical comment on the public conduct of a person who takes part in public affairs is excused under s. 310(a). It would seem logically to follow that equally fair comment on the *private conduct* of such a person would not be excused. Under s. 310(b), a fair comment upon books, other literature, works of art or public performances are excused, as are fair and critical comments on public communications on any subject. Whether what is said to be fair comment falls within the statutory excuse is a question of fact.

Related Provisions: Fair reporting of defamatory matter in certain circumstances is excused under ss. 307(1) and 308.

For further related provisions see the corresponding note to s. 298, *supra*.

311. When truth a defence — No person shall be deemed to publish a defamatory libel where he proves that the publication of the defamatory matter in the manner in which it was published was for the public benefit at the time when it was published and that the matter itself was true.

R.S., c. C-34, s. 275.

Commentary: This justification must be specially pleaded so that the truth of the matter said to be defamatory may be inquired into, other than where D is charged under s. 300. The justification has two elements: public benefit and truth. The publication, in manner and time, must be for the *public benefit*. The defamatory matter must itself be *true*. A reasonably grounded belief in truth is inadequate to found this justification.

The section expressly shifts the onus of proof. D must prove the justification on a balance of probabilities. This statutory reversal of onus may require re-examination under *Charter* s. 11(d).

Related Provisions: Section 309 also provides for an excuse which combines elements of public benefit and truth but in which a reasonably grounded belief in the truth of the allegedly defamatory matter will suffice.

The special plea of justification is provided for in ss. 611–612.

For further related provisions see the corresponding note to s. 298, *supra*.

312. Publication invited or necessary — No person shall be deemed to publish a defamatory libel by reason only that he publishes defamatory matter

(a) on the invitation or challenge of the person in respect of whom it is published, or

(b) that it is necessary to publish in order to refute defamatory matter published in respect of him by another person,

if he believes that the defamatory matter is true and it is relevant to the invitation, challenge or necessary refutation, as the case may be, and does not in any respect exceed what is reasonably sufficient in the circumstances.

R.S., c. C-34, s. 276.

Commentary: Subject to the limitations of the section, D will not be criminally liable only for publishing defamatory matter at the invitation or upon the challenge of another or in refutation of matter defamatory of D earlier published.

The limitations are threefold. D must believe that the matter is true. Such belief need not be founded upon reasonable, or reasonable and probable grounds, though their existence may afford cogent evidence of the honesty of D's belief. The matter need not actually be true. Further, the matter must be relevant to that to which it responds. It must not, in any respect, exceed what is reasonably sufficient in the circumstances. It is unclear whether the requirements of relevance and reasonable sufficiency are discrete, objective requirements or must equally be part of D's belief. At all events, the apprehension by D would seem to excuse on general principle.

There is no express or implied shift in the onus of proof in respect of this excuse. P is required to negate it only where there is evidence to raise the issue.

Related Provisions: Related excuses and justifications are described in ss. 313–315, *infra*. See also the corresponding note to s. 298, *supra*.

313. Answer to inquiries — No person shall be deemed to publish a defamatory libel by reason only that he publishes, in answer to inquiries made to him, defamatory matter relating to a subject-matter in respect of which the person by whom or on whose behalf the inquiries are made has an interest in knowing the truth or who, on reasonable grounds, the person who publishes the defamatory matter believes has such an interest, if

(a) the matter is published, in good faith, for the purpose of giving information in answer to the inquiries;

(b) the person who publishes the defamatory matter believes that it is true;

(c) the defamatory matter is relevant to the inquiries; and

(d) the defamatory matter does not in any respect exceed what is reasonably sufficient in the circumstances.

R.S., c. C-34, s. 277.

Commentary: In certain circumstances, D will be excused from criminal liability for publishing a defamatory libel in answer to inquiries made of him.

The defamatory matter must be published in good faith in answer to inquiries of D. It must be relevant to the inquiries and not, in any respect, exceed what is reasonably sufficient in the circumstances. The matter must also relate to a subject-matter in respect of which the person by whom or on whose behalf the inquiries are made has an interest in knowing the truth or whom D believes, on reasonable grounds, has such an interest. D must also believe, though not on reasonable, nor on reasonable and probable grounds, that the defamatory answers are true.

There is neither an express nor implied shift in the onus of proof in respect of this excuse. It requires negation by P only where there is evidence to warrant leaving the issue to the trier of fact.

Related Provisions: Related excuses are described in ss. 312, 314 and 315. See also the corresponding note to s. 298, *supra*.

314. Giving information to person interested — No person shall be deemed to publish a defamatory libel by reason only that he publishes to another person defamatory matter for the purpose of giving information to that person with respect to a subject-matter in which the person to whom the information is given has, or is believed on reasonable grounds by the person who gives it to have, an interest in knowing the truth with respect to that subject-matter if

(a) the conduct of the person who gives the information is reasonable in the circumstances;

(b) the defamatory matter is relevant to the subject-matter; and

(c) the defamatory matter is true, or if it is not true, is made without ill-will toward the person who is defamed and is made in the belief, on reasonable grounds, that it is true.

R.S., c. C-34. s. 278.

Commentary: This section provides a limited excuse where defamatory matter is published by giving it, as information, to a person interested.

The *recipient* of the defamatory matter must be one who has, or, on reasonable grounds D believes to have, an interest in knowing the truth about the subject-matter. The defamatory matter must be *relevant* to such subject-matter and published to give information to the recipient about it. The defamatory matter must be true or, if not, made without ill-will and in the reasonably-grounded belief that it is true. D's conduct in providing such information must be reasonable in the circumstances. There need be no request for or necessity of disclosure of such information.

The section does *not* alter the onus of proof upon this issue. The excuse will only require negation by P where there is evidence to warrant its consideration by the trier of fact.

Related Provisions: Related excuses and justifications are described in ss. 312, 313 and 315. See also the corresponding note to s. 298, *supra*.

315. Publication in good faith for redress of wrong — No person shall be deemed to publish a defamatory libel by reason only that he publishes defamatory matter in good faith for the purpose of seeking remedy or redress for a private or public wrong or grievance from a person who has, or who on reasonable grounds he believes has, the right or is under an obligation to remedy or redress the wrong or grievance, if

(a) he believes that the defamatory matter is true;

(b) the defamatory matter is relevant to the remedy or redress that is sought; and

(c) the defamatory matter does not in any respect exceed what is reasonably sufficient in the circumstances.

R.S., c. C-34, s. 279.

Commentary: The section defines the circumstances in which publication of defamatory matter in good faith to remedy or redress a wrong may be excused. In defined circumstances the publication of defamatory matter by D to obtain a remedy from another is permitted.

The defamatory matter must be published *in good faith* for the defined purpose of seeking remedy or redress for a private or public wrong or grievance from one who has, or is reasonably believed to have, the right or obligation to remedy or redress it. The defamatory matter must be *relevant* to the remedy sought and must not, in any respect, exceed what is reasonably sufficient in the circumstances. D must also believe that the defamatory matter is true, though such belief need not rest on reasonable or reasonable and probable grounds. The matter itself need not actually be true.

There is *no* shift in the onus of proof or in P's burden where there is evidence to warrant consideration of the excuse by the trier of fact.

Related Provisions: Related excuses and justifications appear in ss. 312–314. Other provisions are described in the corresponding note to s. 298, *supra*.

316. (1) Proving publication by order of legislature — An accused who is alleged to have published a defamatory libel may, at any stage of the proceedings, adduce evidence to prove that the matter that is alleged to be defamatory was contained in a paper published by order or under the authority of the Senate or House of Commons or the legislature of a province.

(2) Directing verdict — Where at any stage in proceedings referred to in subsection (1) the court, judge, justice or provincial court judge is satisfied that the matter alleged to be defamatory was contained in a paper published by order or under the authority of the Senate or House of Commons or the legislature of a province, he shall direct a verdict of not guilty to be entered and shall discharge the accused.

(3) Certificate of order — For the purposes of this section, a certificate under the hand of the Speaker or clerk of the Senate or House of Commons or the legislature of a province to the effect that the matter that is alleged to be defamatory was contained in a paper published by order or under the authority of the Senate, House of Commons or the legislature of a province, as the case may be, is conclusive evidence thereof.

R.S., c. C-34, s. 280; R.S. 1985, c. 27 (1st Supp.), s. 203.

Commentary: This section relates primarily to the excuse of s. 306(b).

Section 316(1) gives D a positive right, at any stage of the proceedings, to adduce evidence of publication of the defamatory matter in a paper published by order or under the authority of the Senate, House of Commons or provincial legislature. Proof made by certificate under s. 316(3) is *conclusive* of the issue. It would appear that the matter could be dealt with upon preliminary application at the outset of the proceedings and, in most instances, it would seem prudent to do so. No notice is required.

The effect of proof of authorized publication is described in s. 316(2). *Satisfactory* proof of authorized publication requires the direction of a verdict of not guilty and the discharge of D. The use of "satisfied", in s. 316(2), may connote some obligation on D to do more than raise a reasonable doubt upon the issue of authorized publication. In the usual case of a directed verdict, it is the absence of evidence in P's case that dictates such result, rather than the introduction of *any evidence*, let alone proof, by D. The apparent effect of including "satisfied" with its consequent shift in onus of proof is largely eliminated by the conclusive nature of the documentary evidence permitted under s. 316(3).

Related Provisions: The section is a natural complement of s. 306, which, *inter alia*, excuses defamatory matter published under parliamentary or legislative authority or order.

See the corresponding note to s. 298, *supra*.

Verdicts

317. Verdicts in cases of defamatory libel — Where, on the trial of an indictment for publishing a defamatory libel, a plea of not guilty is pleaded, the jury that is sworn to try the issue may give a general verdict of guilty or not guilty on the whole matter put in issue on the indictment, and shall not be required or directed by the judge to find the defendant guilty merely on proof of publication by the defendant of the alleged defamatory libel, and of the sense ascribed thereto in the indictment, but the judge may, in his discretion, give a direction or opinion to the jury on the matter in issue as in other criminal proceedings, and the jury may, on the issue, find a special verdict.

R.S., c. C-34, s. 281.

Commentary: The section authorizes both *general and special verdicts* in cases of defamatory libel where the plea has been not guilty, *semble*, not justification.

On a plea of not guilty, the jury may return a *general verdict* of not guilty upon the whole matter, and may not be directed to find D guilty merely on proof of publication by him/her, and of the writing bearing the meaning ascribed to it in the indictment. The judge is entitled to state his/her opinion to the jury, as in other cases, and the jury may, if it desires, return a special verdict.

The section was derived from the controversy in England, finally settled by the Imperial Statute of 1792, c. 60, as to the respective provinces of judge and jury in libel actions. This section, which is taken from that Act, eliminates the possibility of a renewal of the old contention that it is for the judge, and not for the jury, to determine whether or not the document published is libellous, after the jury has found that it was published, and that it bears the meaning alleged by P.

Related Provisions: Provision is made in s. 672.34 for the special verdict of not criminally responsible on account of mental disorder and in s. 672.31 of unfit to stand trial.

See the corresponding note to s. 298, *supra*.

Hate Propaganda

318. (1) Advocating genocide — Every one who advocates or promotes genocide is guilty of an indictable offence and liable to imprisonment for a term not exceeding five years.

(2) Definition of "genocide" — In this section "genocide" means any of the following acts committed with intent to destroy in whole or in part any identifiable group, namely,

    (a) killing members of the group; or

(b) deliberately inflicting on the group conditions of life calculated to bring about its physical destruction.

(3) Consent — No proceeding for an offence under this section shall be instituted without the consent of the Attorney General.

(4) Definition of "identifiable group" — In this section "identifiable group" means any section of the public distinguished by colour, race, religion or ethnic origin.

R.S., c. 11 (1st Supp.), s. 1.

Commentary: The *external circumstances* of the offence of s. 318(1) require proof that D's conduct amounted to advocating or promoting genocide. To "advocate" means to argue in favour of or to recommend publicly a particular course of action or conduct. To "promote" is to further, advance, encourage or actively support a course of action or conduct. That which must be advocated or promoted as an object is genocide, exhaustively defined in s. 318(2). Genocide itself involves *acts* and an ulterior state of mind. The *acts* may be killing the members of an identifiable group or deliberately inflicting upon them conditions of life calculated to bring about its physical destruction. The *mental element* is the intention to destroy, in whole or in part, the identifiable group. It is this intentional extinction of the whole or part of a group in a specified manner that constitutes the gravamen of genocide, the object whose promotion or advocation is punishable under s. 318(1). "Identifiable group" is defined in s. 318(4). The *mental element* consists of the intention to cause the external circumstances of the offence.

The conjoint effect of s. 318(3) and the definition of "Attorney General" in s. 2 requires *the* consent of the Attorney General of the province to the institution of proceedings.

The section may attract *Charter* s. 2(b) scrutiny.

Related Provisions: Section 320 makes special provision for the issuance of a warrant to seize, *inter alia*, any writing, sign or visible representation that advocates or promotes genocide. The material may be ordered forfeited after a post-seizure hearing, subject to review on appeal, or upon conviction of D under s. 319(4). This offence is an "offence" under s. 183 for the purposes of Part VI.

319. (1) Public incitement of hatred — Every one who, by communicating statements in any public place, incites hatred against any identifiable group where such incitement is likely to lead to a breach of the peace is guilty of

(a) an indictable offence and is liable to imprisonment for a term not exceeding two years; or

(b) an offence punishable on summary conviction.

(2) Wilful promotion of hatred — Every one who, by communicating statements, other than in private conversation, wilfully promotes hatred against any identifiable group is guilty of

(a) an indictable offence and is liable to imprisonment for a term not exceeding two years; or

(b) an offence punishable on summary conviction.

(3) Defences — No person shall be convicted of an offence under subsection (2)

(a) if he establishes that the statements communicated were true;

(b) if, in good faith, he expressed or attempted to establish by argument an opinion upon a religious subject;

(c) if the statements were relevant to any subject of public interest, the discussion of which was for the public benefit, and if on reasonable grounds he believed them to be true; or

(d) if, in good faith, he intended to point out, for the purpose of removal, matters producing or tending to produce feelings of hatred towards an identifiable group in Canada.

(4) Forfeiture — Where a person is convicted of an offence under section 318 or subsection (1) or (2) of this section, anything by means of or in relation to which the offence was committed, on such conviction, may, in addition to any other punishment imposed, be ordered by the presiding provincial court judge or judge to be forfeited to Her Majesty in right of the province in which that person is convicted, for disposal as the Attorney General may direct.

(5) Exemption from seizure of communication facilities — Subsections 199(6) and (7) apply with such modifications as the circumstances require to section 318 or subsection (1) or (2) of this section.

(6) Consent — No proceeding for an offence under subsection (2) shall be instituted without the consent of the Attorney General.

(7) Definitions — In this section,

"communicating" includes communicating by telephone, broadcasting or other audible or visible means;

"identifiable group" has the same meaning as in section 318;

"public place" includes any place to which the public have access as of right or by invitation, express or implied;

"statements" includes words spoken or written or recorded electronically or electromagnetically or otherwise, and gestures, signs or other visible representations.

R.S., c. 11 (1st Supp.), s. 1.

Commentary: The section creates two separate offences, each triable either way. The offence of s. 319(2) requires the consent of the Attorney General of the province to institute proceedings. Anything except communication facilities by means of or in relation to which the offence was committed may be ordered forfeited. The definitions of s. 319(7) are common to each offence.

The *external circumstances* of the offence of s. 319(1), *public incitement of hatred*, involve a number of factors. There must be a *communication of statements* in a *public place*, as the terms are defined in s. 319(7). By communicating such statements in a public place, D must *incite* hatred against an *identifiable group* as defined in ss. 319(7) and 318(4). The incitement must be likely to lead to a breach of the peace. The *mental element* consists of the intention to cause the external circumstances of the offence.

Some of the *external circumstances* of the wilful promotion of hatred under s. 319(2) duplicate those of the offence in s. 319(1). The offence equally requires the communication of statements as the means whereby hatred is promoted. The statements must, however, be communicated, *other than in private conversation*. A public place is not required, as under s. 319(1). The promotion of hatred must be against *any identifiable group*. The *mental element* consists of the intention to promote hatred.

Section 319(3) describes a series of defences to a charge of wilfully promoting hatred under s. 319(2). The defences, in terms, do not apply to the offence of s. 319(1).

The section has attracted *Charter* s. 2(b) scrutiny.

Case Law

Charter Considerations

R. v. Keegstra (1990), 1 C.R. (4th) 129, 61 C.C.C. (3d) 1 (S.C.C.) — *See also*: *R. v. Andrews* (1990), 1 C.R. (4th) 266, 61 C.C.C. (3d) 490 (S.C.C.) — Although s. 319(2) offends the freedom of expression guarantee in *Charter* s. 2(b), it constitutes a reasonable limit on the freedom within *Charter* s. 1.

General

R. v. Buzzanga (1979), 49 C.C.C. (2d) 369 (Ont. C.A.) — D "wilfully" promoted hatred only if (a) their conscious *purpose* in distributing the document was to promote hatred, or (b) they *foresaw* that the promotion of hatred was certain or almost certain to result, but distributed the document as a means of achieving their purpose of obtaining a school.

Related Provisions: Section 320 makes special provision for the issuance of a warrant to seize, *inter alia*, any writing, sign or visible representation whose communication by any person would constitute an offence under s. 319. The material may be ordered forfeited after a post-seizure hearing, subject to review on appeal, or upon conviction of D under s. 319(4).

320. (1) **Warrant of seizure** — A judge who is satisfied by information on oath that there are reasonable grounds for believing that any publication, copies of which are kept for sale or distribution in premises within the jurisdiction of the court, is hate propaganda shall issue a warrant under his hand authorizing seizure of the copies.

(2) **Summons to occupier** — Within seven days of the issue of a warrant under subsection (1), the judge shall issue a summons to the occupier of the premises requiring him to appear before the court and show cause why the matter seized should not be forfeited to Her Majesty.

(3) **Owner and author may appear** — The owner and the author of the matter seized under subsection (1) and alleged to be hate propaganda may appear and be represented in the proceedings in order to oppose the making of an order for the forfeiture of the matter.

(4) **Order of forfeiture** — If the court is satisfied that the publication referred to in subsection (1) is hate propaganda, it shall make an order declaring the matter forfeited to Her Majesty in right of the province in which the proceedings take place, for disposal as the Attorney General may direct.

(5) **Disposal of matter** — If the court is not satisfied that the publication referred to in subsection (1) is hate propaganda, it shall order that the matter be restored to the person from whom it was seized forthwith after the time for final appeal has expired.

(6) **Appeal** — An appeal lies from an order made under subsection (4) or (5) by any person who appeared in the proceedings

    (a) on any ground of appeal that involves a question of law alone,

    (b) on any ground of appeal that involves a question of fact alone, or

    (c) on any ground of appeal that involves a question of mixed law and fact,

as if it were an appeal against conviction or against a judgment or verdict of acquittal, as the case may be, on a question of law alone under Part XXI, and sections 673 to 696 apply with such modifications as the circumstances require.

(7) **Consent** — No proceeding under this section shall be instituted without the consent of the Attorney General.

(8) **Definitions** — In this section

"court" means

    (a) in the Province of Quebec, the Court of Quebec;

    (a.1) in the Province of Ontario, the Superior Court of Justice;

    (b) in the Provinces of New Brunswick, Manitoba, Saskatchewan and Alberta, the Court of Queen's Bench;

    (c) in the Provinces of Prince Edward Island and Newfoundland, the Supreme Court, Trial Division;

    (d) in the Provinces of Nova Scotia and British Columbia, the Yukon Territory and Northwest Territories, the Supreme Court; and

(e) in Nunavut, the Nunavut court of Justice;

"genocide" has the same meaning as it has in section 318;

"hate propaganda" means any writing, sign or visible representation that advocates or promotes genocide or the communication of which by any person would constitute an offence under section 319;

"judge" means a judge of a court.
> R.S., c. 11 (1st Supp.), s. 1; 1974–75–76, c. 48, s. 25; 1978–79, c. 11, s. 10; R.S. 1985, c. 27 (2d Supp.), Schedule, item 6; c. 40 (4th Supp.), s. 2; 1990, c. 16, s. 4; c. 17, s. 11; 1992, c. 1, s. 58(1), (Sched. 1, item 6); 1993, c. 28, s. 78 (Sched. III, item 30) [Repealed 1999, c. 3, (Sched., item 7).]; 1998, c. 30, s. 14(d); 1999, c. 3, s. 29.

Commentary: The section permits the *seizure of hate propaganda* under the prior authorization of judicial warrant. No formal prosecution need ever be brought. Section 320(1) requires a judge, as defined in s. 320(8), who is satisfied, by information on oath, that there are reasonable grounds for believing that hate propaganda is kept for sale or distribution in premises within the jurisdiction of the court, to issue a warrant authorizing its seizure.

Sections 320(2)–(5) enact a procedure to determine what shall be done with the matter seized. Within seven days after the issue of the warrant, the judge will issue a show cause summons to the occupier of the premises where the seizure was made. The owner and author of the material may appear to oppose a forfeiture order. Whether forfeiture is ordered is wholly dependent upon whether the judge determines the seized material to be hate propaganda. If the material is determined to be hate propaganda, as defined in s. 320(8), it is ordered forfeited to Her Majesty in right of the province for disposal as the Attorney General may direct. If not, it is restored to the person from whom it was seized. Appellate rights are provided under s. 320(6).

Section 320(7) requires the consent of the Attorney General to the institution of proceedings under this section. The only "proceedings", in the usual sense of the term, are those held to determine whether the seized matter shall be forfeited.

Related Provisions: The general provisions relating to search warrants are found in s. 487. Detention of objects of seizure is dealt with under s. 490.

PART IX — OFFENCES AGAINST RIGHTS OF PROPERTY

Interpretation

321. Definitions — In this Part,

"break" means

> (a) to break any part, internal or external, or

> (b) to open any thing that is used or intended to be used to close or to cover an internal or external opening;

"credit card" means any card, plate, coupon book or other device issued or otherwise distributed for the purpose of being used

> (a) on presentation to obtain, on credit, money, goods, services or any other thing of value, or

> (b) in an automated teller machine, a remote service unit or a similar automated banking device to obtain any of the services offered through the machine, unit or device;

"document" means any paper, parchment or other material on which is recorded or marked anything that is capable of being read or understood by a person, computer system or other device, and includes a credit card, but does not include trade marks on articles of commerce or inscriptions on stone or metal or other like material;

"exchequer bill" means a bank note, bond, note, debenture or security that is issued or guaranteed by Her Majesty under the authority of Parliament or the legislature of a province;

"exchequer bill paper" means paper that is used to manufacture exchequer bills;

"false document" means a document

(a) the whole or a material part of which purports to be made by or on behalf of a person

(i) who did not make it or authorize it to be made, or

(ii) who did not in fact exist,

(b) that is made by or on behalf of the person who purports to make it but is false in some material particular,

(c) that is made in the name of an existing person, by him or under his authority, with a fraudulent intention that it should pass as being made by a person, real or fictitious, other than the person who makes it or under whose authority it is made;

"revenue paper" means paper that is used to make stamps, licences or permits or for any purpose connected with the public revenue.

R.S., c. C-34, s. 282; R.S. 1985, c. 27 (1st Supp.), s. 42.

Commentary: The section exhaustively *defines* critical elements in the *external circumstances* of several offences created in this Part, solely for the purpose of this Part.

Case Law

"False Document" [See also s. 366]

R. v. Foley (1994), 30 C.R. (4th) 238, 90 C.C.C. (3d) 390 (Nfld. C.A.) — *Authorized signings*, including those which do *not* indicate on their face that the signatory is acting as the proxy of another, are excluded from the offence of forgery. Such documents may be misleading, but they lack the falsity which is inherent in a forgery.

R. v. Ogilvie (1993), 81 C.C.C. (3d) 125 (Que. C.A.) — *See also*: *R. v. Nuosci* (1991), 10 C.R. (4th) 332, 69 C.C.C. (3d) 64 (Ont. C.A.); leave to appeal refused (1992), 71 C.C.C. (3d) vii (S.C.C.) — A document which merely contains a lie is *not* always a "false document", hence a forgery under ss. 366 and 368. A document which is false in reference to the very purpose for which it was created is one that is false in a material particular within s. 321, hence may be a forgery. (per Fish and Baudouin JJ.A.)

Related Provisions: Other related provisions are described in the corresponding note to s. 2, *supra.*

Theft

322. (1) Theft — Every one commits theft who fraudulently and without colour of right takes, or fraudulently and without colour of right converts to his use or to the use of another person, anything, whether animate or inanimate, with intent,

(a) to deprive, temporarily or absolutely, the owner of it, or a person who has a special property or interest in it, of the thing or of his property or interest in it;

(b) to pledge it or deposit it as security;

(c) to part with it under a condition with respect to its return that the person who parts with it may be unable to perform; or

(d) to deal with it in such a manner that it cannot be restored in the condition in which it was at the time it was taken or converted.

(2) Time when theft completed — A person commits theft when, with intent to steal anything, he moves it or causes it to move or to be moved, or begins to cause it to become movable.

(3) Secrecy — A taking or conversion of anything may be fraudulent notwithstanding that it is effected without secrecy or attempt at concealment.

(4) Purpose of taking — For the purposes of this Act, the question whether anything that is converted is taken for the purpose of conversion, or whether it is, at the time it is converted, in the lawful possession of the person who converts it is not material.

(5) Wild living creature — For the purposes of this section, a person who has a wild living creature in captivity shall be deemed to have a special property or interest in it while it is in captivity and after it has escaped from captivity.

R.S., c. C-34, s. 283.

Commentary: The *external circumstances* of theft, defined in s. 322(1), permit the *subject-matter* to be *anything*, which is *not* defined in the section but is informed by the expansive definition of "property" in s. 2. The *manner* of the theft may be by *taking* or *conversion* by D, to D's or another's use, and must be *fraudulent* and *without colour of right*. Under s. 322(3) the taking or conversion may be nonetheless fraudulent, though effected without secrecy or attempt at concealment. Under s. 322(4) it is *not* material whether the subject-matter was taken for the purpose of conversion or was in the lawful possession of D when converted. The offence is complete under s. 322(2) when, with intent to steal, D moves the thing, causes it to move or be moved or begins to cause it to become movable.

The *mental element* in theft does not consist merely in the intention to cause the *external circumstances*. It requires proof of *one* of the ulterior mental states of ss. 322(1)(a)–(d).

Section 322(5) provides for the rare case of a wild living creature, kept in captivity, being stolen. For the purposes of the law of theft, its captor is deemed to have a special property or interest in it, both before and after its theft.

Case Law
Takes or Converts

R. v. Milne (1992), 12 C.R. (4th) 175, 70 C.C.C. (3d) 481 (S.C.C.); reversing (1990), 59 C.C.C. (3d) 372 (Alta. C.A.) — Where a transferor mistakenly transfers property to a recipient, who knows of the mistake, property does *not* pass for the purpose of the criminal law if the law of property creates a right of recovery, no matter whether the original transfer is said to be void or voidable. If the recipient then *converts* the property to his/her own use, fraudulently and without colour of right, and with *intent* to deprive the transferor of the property, the recipient is guilty of theft.

R. v. Lafrance (1973), 23 C.R.N.S. 100 (S.C.C.) — Where the evidence reveals an *intentional* taking, with *no* mistake, of the vehicle of another, the taking is fraudulent and theft is made out. An intention to return the vehicle is irrelevant.

R. v. Bates (1989), 94 A.R. 238 (C.A.) — The repainting of a mortgaged helicopter and the exchange of its registration and serial plates with those of a dismantled helicopter to conceal its identity from the bank, and subsequent use of the disguised helicopter constituted theft by conversion.

R. v. Johnson (1978), 42 C.C.C. (2d) 249 (Man. C.A.) — Where D *knew* that money had been erroneously placed in D's bank account, D's conduct in converting it to D's own use without colour of right constituted theft. The issue of whether the conversion by D fell within the definition of "theft" was a question of law and not of fact.

R. v. Nelson (1997), 120 C.C.C. (3d) 1 (Ont. C.A.) — The *actus reus* of theft by conversion is D's conversion of the property of another.

R. v. Smith (1992), 77 C.C.C. (3d) 182 (Ont. C.A.) — If V has the right to recover civilly the goods which V has transferred to D, then D may be convicted of theft by conversion. The *mental element* in theft by conversion is proven where D *knows* that V mistakenly transferred the property yet D retains it.

Questions of civil law relating to the various modes of transfer of title in property have no application to a charge of theft under the *Code* (per Finlayson and Abella JJ.A.).

Anything, Whether Animate or Inanimate

R. v. Stewart (1988), 63 C.R. (3d) 305, 41 C.C.C. (3d) 481 (S.C.C.); reversing (1983), 35 C.R. (3d) 105, 5 C.C.C. (3d) 481 (Ont. C.A.), which reversed (1982), 68 C.C.C. (2d) 305 (Ont. H.C.) — The word "anything" in this section includes intangible objects which are capable of being converted in a way that deprives the owner, in some way, of the owner's proprietary interest. Intangible confidential information should *not* be considered property for the purposes of theft since it is incapable of being taken and cannot be converted, except in a few exceptional circumstances, in a way that would deprive the owner of it.

Fraudulent Intent

R. v. Laroche (1964), 43 C.R. 228 (S.C.C.) — The defence of lack of fraudulent intent, based on D's claim that D had taken money from the municipal offices, of which D was treasurer, on the orders of the mayor, would have succeeded if D honestly believed that D was justified in obeying the mayor's orders, even though D did *not* have to do so, and even though the belief was without foundation.

R. v. Pace, [1965] 3 C.C.C. 55 (N.S. C.A.) — A belief by the taker that the object taken will be of *no* use or value to the owner is nonetheless a depriving of the owner.

R. v. Nelson (1997), 120 C.C.C. (3d) 1 (Ont. C.A.) — Where failure to observe accepted commercial practice is relied upon to prove fraudulent intent or dishonesty, P bears the onus of leading evidence of the practice, at all events where it is not clear that what D did was not in conformity with general industy practices.

R. v. DeMarco (1973), 22 C.R.N.S. 258 (Ont. C.A.) — *See also*: *R. v. Dalzell* (1983), 6 C.C.C. (3d) 112 (N.S. C.A.) — Conduct is *not* "fraudulent" unless it is morally wrong. Where D, lessee of a motor vehicle, honestly believed that the lessor would allow D to keep the car for a period beyond the rental term and pay the rent owing when D returned it, which D honestly intended to do, the element of "fraudulently and without colour of right" was *not* established.

Colour of Right

R. v. Lilly (1983), 34 C.R. (3d) 297, 5 C.C.C. (3d) 1 (S.C.C.) — The defence of "colour of right" is dependent on whether D, at the time of the transfer of money, had an honest belief that D had the right to the money. It is *not* dependent on what the jury thinks D's actual rights were.

R. v. Shymkowich (1954), 19 C.R. 401 (S.C.C.) — *See also*: *R. v. Howson* (1966), 47 C.R. 322, [1966] 3 C.C.C. 348 (Ont. C.A.) — The claim of right must be an honest one, though it may be unfounded in law or in fact.

R. v. Hardiman (1979), 31 N.S.R. (3d) 232 (C.A.) — *See also*: *R. v. Hemmerly* (1976), 30 C.C.C. (2d) 141 (Ont. C.A.) — A *belief* in a *moral* right to take something is *not* a defence to theft. A genuine *belief* in a *legal* right to take things *may* be a defence.

Special Property or Interest [See also s. 328]

R. v. Kane (1982), 68 C.C.C. (2d) 1 (B.C. C.A.) — The NRC has "special property or interest" in a grant to a professor which included conditions on how the money was to be utilized.

R. v. Smith (1962), 38 C.R. 378, [1963] 1 C.C.C. 68 (Ont. C.A.) — The words "special property or interest" are broad enough to *include* an equitable interest of a *cestui que trust* in shares of a company.

Res Judicata [See also ss. 8 and 12]

R. v. Rosen (1985), 44 C.R. (3d) 232, 16 C.C.C. (3d) 481 (S.C.C.), — There was *no* conflict between a conviction for fraud and one for theft where the fraud had been committed prior to the commencement of the theft.

R. v. Hammerling (1982), 31 C.R. (3d) 204, 1 C.C.C. (3d) 353 (S.C.C.); affirming (1981), 9 E.T.R. 84 (Man. C.A.) — D, a lawyer, *not* could be convicted of both theft and breach of trust where D had improperly used D's client's trust fund for D's own personal benefit.

Doctrine of Recent Possession [See also s. 354]

R. v. Kowlyk (1988), 65 C.R. (3d) 97, 43 C.C.C. (3d) 1 (S.C.C.); affirming (1986), 51 C.R. (3d) 65, 27 C.C.C. (3d) 61 (Man C.A.) — The unexplained possession of recently stolen property is sufficient to allow an *inference* of guilt of both theft and offences incidental thereto, even in the absence of other evidence of guilt. The inference is permissive, *not* mandatory. P must, of course, establish that the goods were stolen and, where relevant, that a break-in occurred. If the question arises as to whether D actually stole the goods or was merely a possessor, then it is up to the trier of fact to decide which, if either, inference is to be drawn.

R. v. Newton (1976), 34 C.R.N.S. 161, 28 C.C.C. (2d) 286 (S.C.C.) — Where P has proven possession of recently stolen goods, the jury *may*, but *not* must, in the absence of any reasonable explanation, find D guilty. If the jury thinks that the explanation may *reasonably* be true, though they are *not* convinced that it is true, D is entitled to an acquittal. Where *no* explanation whatever has been advanced, the jury should be instructed that the evidence of such possession, standing alone, raises a *prima facie* case upon which they are entitled to bring in a guilty verdict. This instruction to the jury does *not* amount to a comment on the failure of the accused to testify.

Charter Considerations

Russell v. R. (1983), 32 C.R. (3d) 307, 4 C.C.C. (3d) 460 (N.S. C.A.) — The doctrine of recent possession does *not* offend *Charter* s. 11(d).

Related Provisions: The punishment for theft under s. 334, varies according to the nature or value of the property stolen and, in some cases, the manner in which P chooses to proceed.

Sections 323–328 and 330–333 describe several specific forms of theft defined by reference to subject-matter or the relationship between D and V. Section 329 delineates the circumstances in which one spouse may be criminally liable for thefts from the other. Sections 335–342 create a series of offences resembling theft.

Section 588 assists in the pleading and proof of ownership, *inter alia*, for the purposes of the law of theft. The real and personal property of which a person has lawful management, control or custody is *deemed* to be the property of that person.

The forum of trial depends upon the value or nature of the property stolen. Where the property stolen is a *testamentary instrument* or of a value *exceeding $5,000*, D may choose the mode of trial under s. 536(2). Where the property is neither a testamentary instrument nor of a value exceeding $5,000, P may elect mode of procedure but, in every case, subject to the exceptions of ss. 555(1) and (2), D shall be tried before a provincial court judge under s. 553.

The value of postal cards, stamps and valuable securities is ascertained under ss. 4(1) and (2).

Upon conviction, D may be required to pay compensation under ss. 738 and 739.

323. Oysters — **(1) Where oysters and oyster brood are in oyster beds, layings or fisheries that are the property of any person and are sufficiently marked out or known as the property of that person, that person shall be deemed to have a special property or interest in them.**

(2) Oyster bed — **An indictment is sufficient if it describes an oyster bed, laying or fishery by name or in any other way, without stating that it is situated in a particular territorial division.**

R.S., c. C-34, s. 284.

Commentary: The section contains two discrete but related provisions.

Section 323(1) creates a *special property or interest* in oysters and oyster brood in oyster beds, layings or fisheries that are V's property and are either sufficiently marked out or known as such. In a charge of theft of oysters, for example, the indictment would allege the property to be in V.

Section 323(2) is a rule of criminal pleading concerning the *description* of an oyster bed, laying or fishery. Description by name, or in any other way, is sufficient. There is no requirement that the location be described as situate in a particular territorial division.

Related Provisions: Section 588 enacts a general rule concerning pleading and proof of ownership of property.

The general provisions concerning criminal pleading, in particular the sufficiency of counts, are contained in ss. 581–583.

324. Theft by bailee of things under seizure — Every one who is a bailee of anything that is under lawful seizure by a peace officer or public officer in the execution of the duties of his office, and who is obliged by law or agreement to produce and deliver it to that officer or to another person entitled thereto at a certain time and place, or on demand, steals it if he does not produce and deliver it in accordance with his obligation, but he does not steal it if his failure to produce and deliver it is not the result of a wilful act or omission by him.

R.S., c. C-34, s. 285.

Commentary: The section defines when it is theft for a *bailee* to fail to produce and deliver that which s/he holds under an obligation.

The *external circumstances* require that D be a bailee of something lawfully seized by a peace or public officer. There must be an *obligation*, by law or agreement, *to produce and deliver* that which is held, on prescribed terms of time and place, or on demand. D must *wilfully* fail to produce and deliver the subject-matter in accordance with his/her obligation. The *mental element* consists of the intention to cause the external circumstances of the offence.

The reference to "steals", defined in s. 2 as "commits theft", makes this offence a species of theft.

Case Law

Nature and Elements of Offence

R. v. Brown (1984), 53 A.R. 147 (C.A.) — An essential element of the offence is the lawfulness of the seizure by the public officer.

R. v. Vroom (1975), 23 C.C.C. (2d) 345 (Alta. C.A.) — P must establish beyond a reasonable doubt that the goods in question, which it alleges were the subject of a lawful seizure, were on the premises when the purported seizure was made.

Related Provisions: The general punishment provisions of s. 334 apply to this species of theft.

For other related provisions see the corresponding note to s. 322, *supra*.

325. Agent pledging goods, when not theft — A factor or an agent does not commit theft by pledging or giving a lien on goods or documents of title to goods that are entrusted to him for the purpose of sale or for any other purpose, if the pledge or lien is for an amount that does not exceed the sum of

(a) the amount due to him from his principal at the time the goods or documents are pledged or the lien is given; and

(b) the amount of any bill of exchange that he has accepted for or on account of his principal.

R.S., c. C-34, s. 286.

Commentary: Under this section, an *agent or factor* will *not* be guilty of theft by pledging or giving a lien on goods or documents of title to goods entrusted to him/her for sale. The section does *not*, in terms, describe a species of theft committed by a factor or agent in pledging goods in contravention of the justification there given. It would seem logically to follow, however, that theft may be committed where the agent's or factor's conduct falls outside what statutorily does not amount to theft. In essence, D is permitted to pledge or give a lien on the goods for an amount that does *not* exceed the sum of the amounts described in ss. 325(a) and (b).

Related Provisions: This species of theft, if such be the result of a pledge or lien in an amount beyond what is statutorily permitted, would seem punishable under s. 334.

For other related provisions, see the corresponding note to s. 322, *supra*.

326. (1) Theft of telecommunication service — Every one commits theft who fraudulently, maliciously, or without colour of right,

> (a) abstracts, consumes or uses electricity or gas or causes it to be wasted or diverted; or
>
> (b) uses any telecommunication facility or obtains any telecommunication service.

(2) Definition of "telecommunication" — In this section and section 327, "telecommunication" means any transmission, emission or reception of signs, signals, writing, images or sounds or intelligence of any nature by wire, radio, visual, or other electro-magnetic system.

R.S., c. C-34, s. 287; 1974–75–76, c. 93, s. 23.

Commentary: This section prohibits theft of public utilities services. The *external circumstances* consist of the elements described in s. 326(1)(a) or (b). Telecommunication, an integral part of "telecommunication facility" in s. 326(1)(b), is exhaustively defined in s. 326(2). The *mental element* does *not* require proof of any ulterior state of mind. D must, however, be acting fraudulently, maliciously, or without colour of right in causing the external circumstances of the offence. These states of mind are stated in the alternative. To demonstrate liability P need *not* prove that the taking or conversion was both fraudulent and without colour of right as required under the general definition of theft in s. 322(1).

Case Law
Fraudulently [See also s. 322]

R. v. Miller (1984), 12 C.C.C. (3d) 466 (Alta. C.A.) — D designed and attached a "tunable stub" to their television to correct the reception of their cable service. It also perfected pay T.V. reception to which they did not subscribe. Absent fraud, *no* offence is committed.

R. v. Renz (1974), 18 C.C.C. (2d) 492 (B.C. C.A.) — *See also*: *R. v. Brais* (1972), 20 C.R.N.S. 190, 7 C.C.C. (2d) 301 (B.C. C.A.) — "Fraudulently" requires that D act intentionally and deliberately with knowledge that he was *not* permitted to obtain the service in the way that it was obtained.

Telecommunication Facility [See also s. 327]

R. v. McLaughlin (1980), 18 C.R. (3d) 339 (S.C.C.) — A *computer terminal* is *not* a telecommunication facility. Telecommunication connotes some type of external transmission or reception and the existence of a sender and a receiver.

Related Provisions: Section 327(1) defines and punishes the related preparatory offence of unlawful possession of devices to obtain telecommunication facilities or services.

Since s. 326(1) describes a particular species of theft without reference to penalty, s. 344 applies. Under s. 327(2), subject to the exception of s. 322(3), any instrument or device in relation to which the offence was committed may be ordered forfeited.

Further related provisions are discussed in the corresponding note to s. 322, *supra*.

327. (1) Possession of device to obtain telecommunication facility or service — Every one who, without lawful excuse, the proof of which lies on him, manufactures, possesses, sells or offers for sale or distributes any instrument or device or any component thereof, the design of which renders it primarily useful for obtaining the use of any telecommunication facility or service, under circumstances that give rise to a reasonable inference that the device has been used or is or was intended to be used to obtain the use of any telecommunication facility or service without payment of a lawful charge therefor, is guilty of an indictable offence and liable to imprisonment for a term not exceeding two years.

(2) Forfeiture — Where a person is convicted of an offence under subsection (1) or paragraph 326(1)(*b*), any instrument or device in relation to which the offence was committed or the possession of which constituted the offence, upon such conviction, in addition to any punishment that is imposed, may be ordered forfeited to Her Majesty, whereupon it may be disposed of as the Attorney General directs.

(3) Limitation — No order for forfeiture shall be made under subsection (2) in respect of telephone, telegraph or other communication facilities or equipment owned by a person engaged in providing telephone, telegraph or other communication service to the public or forming part of the telephone, telegraph or other communication service or system of such a person by means of which an offence under subsection (1) has been committed if such person was not a party to the offence.

1974–75–76, c. 93, s. 24.

Commentary: This offence parallels the interception device prohibition of s. 191(1).

The *external circumstances* require an instrument, device or a component thereof, the design of which renders it *primarily* useful for *obtaining* the use of any telecommunication facility or service. D must manufacture, possess, sell, offer for sale or distribute this device, instrument or component. The circumstances of the possession or other dealing must be such as to give rise to a *reasonable inference* of past or intended unlawful use of the device. D must have no lawful excuse for such possession or other dealing. D must establish a lawful excuse, a reversal of onus which may attract *Charter* s. 11(d) scrutiny.

The *mental element* consists of the intention to have possession etc. of a proscribed device, *semble*, with *knowledge* of its character. To require proof of knowledge of the nature and character of the device accords with general principle. Inclusion of words, as in s. 191(1), *viz.* "... *knowing that the design thereof* ... " would leave no doubt of the requirement.

Section 327(2) provides for forfeiture of the instrument or device upon conviction under s. 327(1), subject to the limitation of s. 327(3) in respect of property of telecommunication common carriers who are not parties to the offence.

Case Law

R. v. Ross (1988), 32 O.A.C. 47 (C.A.) — The fact that the devices *could* be modified to achieve some other purpose did *not* answer a charge under s. 327(1), without adequate proof that such modification had been made, where the devices had in fact been modified in a manner which achieved the unlawful purpose. P was *not* required to prove that the devices were intended to be used by the accused personally for the unlawful purpose.

R. v. Fulop (1988), 46 C.C.C. (3d) 427 (Ont. C.A.) — Subsection (1) applies where D possesses the devices for storage purposes under circumstances giving rise to a reasonable inference that he *knows* the *intended* use of the devices by other persons is to unlawfully obtain television signals. The intended use need *not* be by D.

Related Provisions: This offence is a natural complement to the theft of telecommunications under s. 326(1), being frequently preliminary to it. "Possession" is defined in s. 4(3) and "telecommunication" in s. 326(2).

D may elect *mode* of trial in respect of this offence under s. 536(2).

328. Theft by or from person having special property or interest — A person may be convicted of theft notwithstanding that anything that is alleged to have been stolen was stolen

(a) by the owner of it from a person who has a special property or interest in it;

(b) by a person who has a special property or interest in it from the owner of it;

(c) by a lessee of it from his reversioner;

(d) by one of several joint owners, tenants in common or partners of or in it from the other persons who have an interest in it; or

(e) by the directors, officers or members of a company, body corporate, unincorporated body or of a society associated together for a lawful purpose from the company, body corporate, unincorporated body or society, as the case may be.

R.S., c. C-34, s. 288.

Commentary: This section permits conviction of theft, notwithstanding that the subject-matter thereof, the "anything" of s. 322(1), was stolen by D, who, alone or with another or others, stands in a defined relation to V, whereby each, D and V, whether alone or with others, has an interest in the property. In other words, D may be convicted of theft even where D and V stand in a defined relationship to one another in respect of the property that is stolen.

Case Law

R. v. Chinook (1986), 43 Alta L.R. (2d) 241 (C.A.) — Sale of a bale wagon knowing of a bank's chattel mortgage and special interest in it is theft.

Related Provisions: Section 322(1) defines theft. It is punished under s. 344.

Theft by spouses is governed by s. 329.

For other related provisions see the corresponding note to s. 322, *supra*.

329. (1) Husband or wife — Subject to subsection (2), no husband or wife, during cohabitation, commits theft of anything that is by law the property of the other.

(2) Theft by spouse while living apart — A husband or wife commits theft who, intending to desert or on deserting the other or while living apart from the other, fraudulently takes or converts anything that is by law the property of the other in a manner that, if it were done by another person, would be theft.

(3) Assisting or receiving — Every one commits theft who, during cohabitation of a husband and wife, knowingly

(a) assists either of them in dealing with anything that is by law the property of the other in a manner that would be theft if they were not married, or;

(b) receives from either of them anything that is by law the property of the other and has been obtained from the other by dealing with it in a manner that would be theft if they were not married.

R.S., c. C-34, s. 289.

Commentary: Sections 329(1) and (2) describe the circumstances under which one *spouse* may commit *theft* in relation to the property of the other. In general, as s. 329(1) enacts, what would otherwise be theft is *not* so where the property of one spouse is stolen by the other *during cohabitation*. Section 329(2), however, describes the circumstances under which theft may be committed by one spouse in respect of the property of the other, cohabitation notwithstanding. It is theft where D spouse, intending to desert, on deserting, or living apart from V spouse, commits what otherwise would be theft of V's property. The liability of third parties, strangers to the marriage, would be determined under ss. 21(1)(b), (c), (2) and s. 22.

A third party may also be convicted of theft, where D spouse could *not* be found guilty as a principal. Under s. 329(3), D will commit theft by *assisting* one spouse, during cohabitation, to commit what otherwise would be theft in relation to the property of the other. It is equally theft where D *receives* from a spouse property of the other spouse obtained by what otherwise would be theft in the absence of marriage.

The inclusion of "knowingly" in s. 329(3) requires proof by P of *knowledge* of the *external circumstances* of either s. 329(3)(a) or (b). The assistance or receipt, as the case may be, must be intentional under general accessoryship principles.

Quaere whether the spouse assisted or from whom the property of the other is received may be liable, under general accessoryship principles, for the offence of another under s. 329(3), notwithstanding the spouse could not be convicted as a principal under s. 329(1)?

Related Provisions: Absent reference to punishment, s. 334 applies.

Under *C.E.A.* s. 4(2), D's spouse is a competent and compellable witness for P without D's consent. This provision would seem applicable chiefly to a charge of theft founded upon s. 329(2) and would only be applicable under s. 329(3) if D's spouse can be and is a co-accused of a third party assister or receiver.

330. (1) Theft by person required to account — Every one commits theft who, having received anything from any person on terms that require him to account for or pay it or the proceeds of it or a part of the proceeds to that person or another person, fraudulently fails to account for or pay it or the proceeds of it or the part of the proceeds of it accordingly.

(2) Effect of entry in account — Where subsection (1) otherwise applies, but one of the terms is that the thing received or the proceeds or part of the proceeds of it shall be an item in a debtor and creditor account between the person who receives the thing and the person to whom he is to account for or to pay it, and that the latter shall rely only on the liability of the other as his debtor in respect thereof, a proper entry in that account of the thing received or the proceeds or part of the proceeds of it, as the case may be, is a sufficient accounting therefor, and no fraudulent conversion of the thing or the proceeds or part of the proceeds of it thereby accounted for shall be deemed to have taken place.

R.S., c. C-34, s. 290.

Commentary: This species of theft requires a defined relationship between D and V. The *external circumstances* involve the receipt by D of anything from V, *on terms* requiring an accounting or repayment, as described in s. 330(1), and the fraudulent failure of D to do so. The *mental element* consists of the intention to cause the external circumstances of the offence.

Section 330(2) enacts a special provision applicable to cases of debtor and creditor accounts. Proper accounting entries of the thing, proceeds or part thereof being received is a sufficient accounting and, to such extent, no fraudulent conversion is deemed to have taken place.

Case Law
Nature and Elements of Offence

R. v. McKenzie (1972), 16 C.R.N.S. 374, 4 C.C.C. (2d) 296 (S.C.C.) — P must prove upon what terms D was to account for or pay the sum of money in question. Absent such proof, P has *not* proved that D failed to comply with the terms.

Related Provisions: Absent specific reference to penalty, s. 334 applies.

For further related provisions see the corresponding note to s. 332, *supra*.

331. Theft by person holding power of attorney — Every one commits theft who, being entrusted, whether solely or jointly with another person, with a power of attorney for the sale, mortgage, pledge or other disposition of real or personal property, fraudulently sells, mortgages, pledges or otherwise disposes of the property or any part of it, or fraudulently converts the proceeds of a sale, mortgage, pledge or other disposition of the property, or any part of the proceeds, to a purpose other than that for which he was entrusted by the power of attorney.

R.S., c. C-34, s. 291.

Commentary: This section involves the *breach* of a *trust* relationship of a more specific nature than described in s. 330 or 332.

The *external circumstances* require that D be entrusted solely, or jointly, with a *power of attorney*. The power of attorney must be for a *specified purpose*, namely the sale, mortgage, pledge or other disposition of real or personal property. The essence of the offence lies in the *fraudulent* sale, mortgage, pledge or other disposition of the property, in whole or in part, or the *fraudulent* conversion of the proceeds or any part thereof, to a *purpose other* than that for which D was *entrusted* under the power of attorney. The *mental element* consists of the intention to cause the external circumstances of the offence.

Related Provisions: Related theft offences appear in ss. 330 and 332. Section 336 creates an offence of criminal breach of trust.

The general penalty provisions of s. 334 apply.

For other related provisions see the corresponding note to s. 322, *supra*.

332. (1) Misappropriation of money held under direction — Every one commits theft who, having received, either solely or jointly with another person, money or valuable security or a power of attorney for the sale of real or personal property, with a direction that the money or a part of it, or the proceeds or a part of the proceeds of the security or the property shall be applied to a purpose or paid to a person specified in the direction, fraudulently and contrary to the direction applies to any other purpose or pays to any other person the money or proceeds or any part of it.

(2) Effect of entry in account — This section does not apply where a person who receives anything mentioned in subsection (1) and the person from whom he receives it deal with each other on such terms that all money paid to the former would, in the absence of any such direction, be properly treated as an item in a debtor and creditor account between them, unless the direction is in writing.

R.S., c. C-34, s. 292.

Commentary: Section 332(1) creates a discrete species of theft, in some respects similar to the offences of ss. 330 and 331. P must establish, initially, that D, solely or jointly, *received* money, valuable security or a power of attorney for the sale of real or personal property. The receipt must be accompanied by a *direction* that the money or proceeds, in whole or in part, be applied to a defined purpose or paid to a specified person. It must finally be established that, *fraudulently and contrary to the direction*, D applied to another purpose or paid to another person the money, proceeds or part thereof. The gist of the offence lies in the misappropriation of the money or proceeds in a manner inconsistent with D's direction. The *mental element* consists of the intention to cause the external circumstances of the offence, *fraudulently and contrary to the direction*.

Section 332(2) holds the provisions of s. 332(1) inapplicable to ongoing debtor-creditor relationships, unless the direction is in writing.

Case Law

Nature and Elements of Offence

R. v. Skalbania (1997), 120 C.C.C. (3d) 217 (S.C.C.) — An intentional misappropriation, without mistake, establishes the mental element required by s. 332(1).

R. v. Lowden (1981), 59 C.C.C. (2d) 1 (Alta. C.A.); affirmed (1982), 68 C.C.C. (2d) 531 (S.C.C.) — The gist of the offence is the receipt of money with a direction for application and the fraudulent application contrary to that direction. The direction is an essential averment in the charge and its proof is necessary to constitute the offence.

Related Provisions: "Valuable security" is defined in s. 2 and its value determined under s. 4(2). For further related provisions, see the corresponding notes to ss. 322, 330 and 331, *supra*.

333. Taking ore for scientific purpose — No person commits theft by reason only that he takes, for the purpose of exploration or scientific investigation, a specimen of ore or mineral from land that is not enclosed and is not occupied or worked as a mine, quarry or digging.

R.S., c. C-34, s. 293.

Commentary: *Prima facie*, the taking of a specimen of ore or mineral from land, neither enclosed, occupied nor worked as a mine, quarry or digging, for exploration or scientific investigation, would be theft. This section enacts that it shall *not* be theft, provided the taking is for *scientific or exploratory* purposes and the land from which it was taken is as described. Taking for another purpose, *semble*, would attract liability for theft.

Related Provisions: Section 394 creates the offence of fraud in relation to minerals and s. 396 creates a similar offence in relation to mines and samples taken therefrom. Section 395 provides for a special warrant to search for precious metals.

For further related theft provisions see the corresponding note to s. 322, *supra*.

334. Punishment for theft — Except where otherwise provided by law, every one who commits theft

(a) is guilty of an indictable offence and liable to imprisonment for a term not exceeding ten years, where the property stolen is a testamentary instrument or the value of what is stolen exceeds five thousand dollars; or

(b) is guilty

(i) of an indictable offence and is liable to imprisonment for a term not exceeding two years, or

(ii) of an offence punishable on summary conviction,

where the value of what is stolen does not exceed five thousand dollars.

R.S., c. C-34, s. 294; 1972, c. 13, s. 23; 1974–75–76, c. 93, s. 25;R.S. 1985, c. 27 (1st Supp.), s. 43; 1994, c. 44, s. 20.

Commentary: This section *classifies* the offence of theft for *sentencing* purposes and provides the punishment therefor.

The offence of s. 334(a) is exclusively *indictable*. It applies to thefts (under the general or any specific definition of the offence) where the property stolen is a testamentary instrument or of a value exceeding $5,000. Both "testamentary instrument" and "property" are expansively defined in s. 2.

The classification of s. 334(b), applies to thefts that are *not* included in s. 334(a). The offence is triable either way.

Related Provisions: Theft is an "enterprise crime offence" under s. 462.3 for the purposes of Part XII.2, but only an "offence" under s. 183 for Part VI where it falls within s. 334(a).

The value of a "valuable security" is determined under s. 4(2).

D may *elect* mode of trial under s. 536(2) for the offence of s. 334(a). Where P elects to proceed by indictment under s. 334(b)(i), D will be tried by a provincial court judge under s. 553(a)(i). Summary conviction proceedings under s. 334(b)(ii) are governed by Part XXVII and punished under s. 787(1).

For further related provisions, see the corresponding note to s. 322, *supra*.

Offences Resembling Theft

335. (1) Taking motor vehicle or vessel or found therein without consent — Subject to subsection (1.1), every one who, without the consent of the owner, takes a motor vehicle or vessel with intent to drive, use, navigate or operate it or cause it to be driven, used, navigated or operated, or is an occupant of a motor vehicle or vessel knowing that it was taken without the consent of the owner, is guilty of an offence punishable on summary conviction.

(1.1) Exception — Subsection (1) does not apply to an occupant of a motor vehicle or vessel who, on becoming aware that it was taken without the consent of the owner, attempted to leave the motor vehicle or vessel, to the extent that it was feasible to do so, or actually left the motor vehicle or vessel.

(2) Definition of "vessel" — **For the purposes of subsection (1), "vessel" has the meaning assigned by section 214.**

R.S., c. C-34, s. 295; 1972, c. 13, s. 23; R.S. 1985, c. 1 (4th Supp.), s. 22; 1997, c. 18, s. 15.

Commentary: This summary conviction offence has recently been expanded to include vessels as well as motor vehicles, and occupants as well as principals.

The *external circumstances* of the "taking" offence involve the taking of a motor vehicle or vessel and the absence of consent from the owner. The taking must be intentional. The *mental element* also requires proof of any ulterior intent specified in s. 335(1).

The external circumstances of the "occupant" offence require that D be an *occupant* in a motor vehicle or vessel which has been *taken without* the owner's consent. The crux of the *mental element* is D's *knowledge* that the *conveyance* was *taken without* the owner's *consent*. An occupant who attempts to leave or actually leaves the conveyance, to the extent it is feasible to do so, on becoming aware that it was taken without consent, is *not* liable because of the exception in s. 335(1.1).

An honest belief that the owner consented to the taking would afford a defence for both the "taker" and "occupant".

The "occupant" offence is likely to attract *Charter* challenge.

Case Law

Included Offences

R. v. Lafrance (1973), 23 C.R.N.S. 100 (S.C.C.) — The offence of taking a motor vehicle without consent is *not* included in the offence of theft.

Related Provisions: "Motor vehicle" is exhaustively defined in s. 2 which also includes an expansive definition of "owner". Section 588 also provides for ownership of property.

The general summary conviction punishment provisions of s. 787(1) apply.

336. Criminal breach of trust — **Every one who, being a trustee of anything for the use or benefit, whether in whole or in part, of another person, or for a public or charitable purpose, converts, with intent to defraud and in contravention of his trust, that thing or any part of it to a use that is not authorized by the trust is guilty of an indictable offence and liable to imprisonment for a term not exceeding fourteen years.**

R.S., c. C-34, s. 296.

Commentary: The essence of this offence lies in the contravention by a trustee of an *express* trust of a defined type by conversion with intent to defraud.

The *external circumstances* require that D be a *trustee*, as exhaustively defined in s. 2, of anything for the use or benefit, in whole or in part, of another, or for a public or charitable purpose. D must *convert* the trust property, in whole or in part, to an unauthorized use. The conversion must be *in* contravention of the trust. The specific *mental element* that must accompany D's intentional act of conversion is the *intent* to *defraud*.

Case Law

R. v. Rosen (1985), 44 C.R. (3d) 232, 16 C.C.C. (3d) 481 (S.C.C.); reversing in part (1980), 55 C.C.C. (2d) 342n (Ont. C.A.) — Failure to prove the averment that D was a trustee, is fatal to a conviction for breach of trust. It was insufficient to prove that D, alleged to be the principal, was a party to the offence committed by the actual trustee, a corporate entity.

R. v. Hammerling (1982), 31 C.R. (3d) 204, 1 C.C.C. (3d) 353 (S.C.C.); affirming (1981), 9 E.T.R. 84 (Man. C.A.) — The element of *deprivation* is satisfied on proof of *detriment*, *prejudice* or *risk* of *prejudice* to the economic interests of V. There need *not* be actual economic loss.

Related Provisions: Breach of trust by an "official", as defined in s. 118, is an offence under s. 122. The *express* trust required under s. 336 is absent from the related specific theft offences of ss. 330–332, *supra*.

D may *elect* mode of trial under s. 536(2).

337. Public servant refusing to deliver property — Every one who, being or having been employed in the service of Her Majesty in right of Canada or in right of a province, or in the service of a municipality, and entrusted by virtue of that employment with the receipt, custody, management or control of anything, refuses or fails to deliver it to a person who is authorized to demand it and does demand it is guilty of an indictable offence and liable to imprisonment for a term not exceeding fourteen years.

R.S., c. C-34, s. 297.

Commentary: The *external circumstances* of this seldom-prosecuted offence comprise four elements. D must be or have been a *federal, provincial or municipal employee*. By virtue of that employment, D must be or have been *entrusted* with receipt, custody, management or control of "anything". D must *refuse or fail to deliver* the "anything", that is, the subject-matter with which D was entrusted in an official capacity. The refusal or failure of delivery must be to someone who is not only authorized to demand it but has in fact done so. The *mental element* consists of the intention to cause the external circumstances of the offence.

Related Provisions: Breach of trust by an "official", as defined in s. 118, is an offence under s. 122 punishable by five years' imprisonment. Section 336 applies only in respect of an express trust and, further, requires proof of conversion with intent to defraud, neither of which is an essential element under s. 337.

D may elect mode of trial under s. 536(2).

338. (1) Fraudulently taking cattle or defacing brand — Every one who, without the consent of the owner,

(a) fraudulently takes, holds, keeps in his possession, conceals, receives, appropriates, purchases or sells cattle that are found astray, or

(b) fraudulently, in whole or in part,

(i) obliterates, alters or defaces a brand or mark on cattle, or

(ii) makes a false or counterfeit brand or mark on cattle,

is guilty of an indictable offence and liable to imprisonment for a term not exceeding five years.

(2) Punishment for theft of cattle — Every one who commits theft of cattle is guilty of an indictable offence and liable to imprisonment for a term not exceeding ten years.

(3) Evidence of property in cattle — In any proceedings under this Act, evidence that cattle are marked with a brand or mark that is recorded or registered in accordance with any Act is, in the absence of any evidence to the contrary, proof that the cattle are owned by the registered owner of that brand or mark.

(4) Presumption from possession — Where an accused is charged with an offence under subsection (1) or (2), the burden of proving that the cattle came lawfully into the possession of the accused or his employee or into the possession of another person on behalf of the accused is on the accused, if the accused is not the registered owner of the brand or mark with which the cattle are marked, unless it appears that possession of the cattle by an employee of the accused or by another person on behalf of the accused was without the knowledge and authority, sanction or approval of the accused.

R.S., c. C-34, s. 298; 1974–75–76, c. 93, s. 26.

Commentary: The section combines substantive, evidentiary and procedural provisions.

Section 338(1) creates two offences, each requiring proof of *fraudulent* conduct by D. The offence of s. 338(1)(a), fraudulent dealing in stray cattle, is committed only where D's conduct falls within "takes, holds, keeps in his possession, conceals, receives, appropriates, purchases or sells". The subject-matter must be "cattle that are found astray". D's dealings must be *fraudulent* and intentionally so. The offence of s. 338(1)(b) also requires fraudulent conduct by D. The *external circumstances* involve either the entire or partial obliteration, alteration, or defacing of a brand or mark on cattle, or alternatively, the making of a false or counterfeit mark thereon. The *mental element* requires proof that D did so *fraudulently*.

Section 338(3) creates a *rebuttable presumption of ownership* upon proof of the preliminary fact that cattle have been marked with a brand or mark recorded or registered under any Act. Upon such preliminary proof, ownership is presumed to be in the owner of the brand or mark. The presumption may be rebutted by *evidence* to the contrary and is applicable in any *Code* proceedings in which such evidence is relevant. The provision may attract *Charter* s. 11(d) scrutiny.

The effect of s. 338(4), particularly when considered conjointly with s. 338(3), would appear to be to create, somewhat indirectly, a further *rebuttable presumption* applicable only in prosecutions under ss. 338(1) and (2). It must first be shown that D, either personally or through an employee or agent, is in possession of cattle. The cattle must be *marked* with a brand or mark of which D is *not* the registered owner. D must then prove D's *actual or imputed possession* is lawful. In other words, upon proof of the preliminary fact of possession of cattle so marked, it is presumed *unlawful*. D's rebuttal may include a demonstration of unknown or unauthorized possession by D's agents or employees as provided in s. 338(4). This exception accords with general principle, although it may be vulnerable to attack under *Charter* s. 11(d) due to the reversal of the onus of proof.

Section 338(2) makes theft of cattle punishable by imprisonment for a term not exceeding 10 years. The value of the cattle is immaterial.

Related Provisions: "Cattle" is exhaustively defined in s. 2. Section 4(3) describes the circumstances under which D may be found in *possession* of anything.

339. (1) Taking possession, etc., of drift timber — Every one is guilty of an indictable offence and liable to imprisonment for a term not exceeding five years who, without the consent of the owner,

    (a) fraudulently takes, holds, keeps in his possession, conceals, receives, appropriates, purchases or sells,

    (b) removes, alters, obliterates or defaces a mark or number on, or

    (c) refuses to deliver up to the owner or to the person in charge thereof on behalf of the owner or to a person authorized by the owner to receive it,

any lumber or lumbering equipment that is found adrift, cast ashore or lying on or embedded in the bed or bottom, or on the bank or beach, of a river, stream or lake in Canada, or in the harbours or any of the coastal waters of Canada.

(2) Dealer in second-hand goods — Every one who, being a dealer in second-hand goods of any kind, trades or traffics in or has in his possession for sale or traffic any lumbering equipment that is marked with the mark, brand, registered timber mark, name or initials of a person, without the written consent of that person, is guilty of an offence punishable on summary conviction.

(3) Search for timber unlawfully detained — A peace officer who suspects, on reasonable grounds, that any lumber owned by any person and bearing the registered timber mark of that person is kept or detained in or on any place without the knowledge or consent of that person, may enter into or on that place to ascertain whether or not it is detained there without the knowledge or consent of that person.

(4) Evidence of property in timber — Where any lumber or lumbering equipment is marked with a timber mark or a boom chain brand registered under any Act, the mark or brand is, in proceedings under subsection (1), and, in the absence of any evidence to the contrary, proof that it is the property of the registered owner of the mark or brand.

(5) **Presumption from possession** — Where an accused or his servants or agents are in possession of lumber or lumbering equipment marked with the mark, brand, registered timber mark, name or initials of another person, the burden of proving that it came lawfully into his possession or into possession of his servants or agents is, in proceedings under subsection (1), on the accused.

(6) **Definitions** — In this section

"coastal waters of Canada" includes all of Queen Charlotte Sound, all the Strait of Georgia and the Canadian waters of the Strait of Juan de Fuca;

"lumber" means timber, mast, spar, shingle bolt, sawlog or lumber of any description;

"lumbering equipment" includes a boom chain, chain, line and shackle.

R.S., c. C-34, s. 299.

Commentary: This section provides substantive, evidentiary and procedural provisions in respect of certain lumber and lumbering equipment. Several definitions appear in s. 339(6).

Section 339(1) creates three discrete offences. In each case, P must establish the *absence* of the *consent* of the *owner* to D's conduct. The subject-matter of D's conduct must be lumber or lumbering equipment of the kind or nature described in the concluding words of the subsection.

The offence of s. 339(1)(a) may generally be described as *unlawful dealing* in lumber or lumbering equipment of the specified type in any manner proscribed. The dealing must be *fraudulent* on D's part. Neither s. 339(1)(b) nor (c) requires proof of fraudulent conduct. Though such an inference could arise upon proof of the *external circumstances*. The gravamen of the offence under s. 339(1)(b) consists of the *concealment* of proper numbers or marks on lumber or lumbering equipment. The concealment may be effected in any way described in the paragraph. Under s. 339(1)(c), the gist of the offence is the *refusal* to deliver up the subject matter to the owner or other authorized person.

Sections 339(4) and (5) assist P in its *proof* of *ownership* and the *nature* of D's *possession*. Under s. 339(4), lumber or lumbering equipment marked with a registered timber-mark or boom-chain brand is *proof* that it is the property of the registered owner of the mark or brand, absent evidence to the contrary. Under s. 339(5), *evidence* that D, D's servants or agents came into possession of lumber or lumbering equipment with the mark, brand, registered timber-mark, name or initials of another engages a *reverse onus* provision putting the onus on D to prove the lawful character of such possession. The conjoint effect of the subsections is, upon *evidence* of D's *possession* of lumber or lumbering equipment with designated markings, to deem or *presume* that D is in *unlawful possession* of the property of the registered owner. The *onus* of proving the lawful character of such possession falls upon D. These provisions only apply to prosecutions under s. 339(1).

The summary conviction offence of s. 339(2) requires *no* proof of fraudulent intent. The *external circumstances* require that D be a dealer in second-hand goods of any kind, who trades or traffics in or has possession for sale or traffic lumbering equipment marked in a manner described in the subsection without the *written* consent of the person whose mark appears on the equipment. The *mental element* consists of the intention to cause the external circumstances, with knowledge of the absence of specified consent. Apprehended consent would constitute a valid defence.

Section 339(3) *permits* a *non-warranted* search and entry for marked lumber by a peace officer on reasonably grounded suspicion as described. There is no express power of seizure given. This provision may attract s. 8 *Charter* scrutiny.

Case Law

Mental Element

R. v. Shymkowich (1954), 19 C.R. 401 (S.C.C.) — A *mistaken belief* by D that D is *entitled to take* sawlogs belonging to another person is *no* defence when D is fully aware to whom the logs belong and the circumstances under which the other person has possession of them.

Watts v. R. (1953), 16 C.R. 290, 105 C.C.C. 193 (S.C.C.) — *Mens rea* is an essential element of the offence of refusing to deliver up drift timber. Where D acts with an honest and reasonable belief that what is done is right and involves no breach of the law, D commits no offence.

Related Provisions: D may *elect* mode of trial for the offence of s. 339(1). The offence of s. 339(2) is tried under Part XXVII and punished under s. 787(1).

340. Destroying documents of title — Every one who, for a fraudulent purpose, destroys, cancels, conceals or obliterates

   (a) a document of title to goods or lands,

   (b) a valuable security or testamentary instrument, or

   (c) a judicial or official document,

is guilty of an indictable offence and liable to imprisonment for a term not exceeding ten years.

R.S., c. C-34, s. 300.

Commentary: This section prohibits improper dealings in relation to a defined class of instruments and documents for prohibited purpose.

The *external circumstances* of this offence require that D's conduct relate to a document or instrument within any of ss. 340(a)–(c). D must destroy, conceal, cancel or obliterate a document or instrument. The *mental element* requires proof of a *fraudulent* purpose.

Related Provisions: Section 2 defines "document of title to goods", "document of title to lands", "valuable security" and "testamentary instrument". There is *no* general definition of "document", nor specific definition of the type of documents described in s. 340(c).

Section 341, a more general provision, prohibits, *inter alia*, the concealment of *anything* for a fraudulent purpose. Section 385 creates the specific offence of fraudulent concealment of title documents.

D may elect mode of trial under s. 536(2).

341. Fraudulent concealment — Every one who, for a fraudulent purpose, takes, obtains, removes or conceals anything is guilty of an indictable offence and liable to imprisonment for a term not exceeding two years.**

R.S., c. C-34, s. 301.

Commentary: The scope of this offence is substantial. Its *external circumstances* involve any conduct of D that amounts to "takes, obtains, removes or conceals". The subject-matter may be "anything", *semble*, irrespective of whether it is capable of being stolen, as had been previously required. The *mental element* requires proof of an ulterior *fraudulent purpose*, as for example, a bankrupt's concealment of assets to defraud creditors.

Related Provisions: The offence of s. 340 is of more restricted application, as is s. 385 (fraudulent concealment of title documents). "Anything" which is not defined, is generally regarded as a word of wide and unrestricted use.

D may *elect* mode of trial under s. 536(2).

342. (1) Theft, forgery, etc., of credit card — Every person who

   (a) steals a credit card,

   (b) forges or falsifies a credit card,

   (c) possesses, uses or traffics in a credit card or a forged or falsified credit card, knowing that it was obtained, made or altered

      (i) by the commission in Canada of an offence, or

      (ii) by an act or omission anywhere that, if it had occurred in Canada, would have constituted an offence, or

(d) uses a credit card knowing that it has been revoked or cancelled,

is guilty of

(e) an indictable offence and is liable to imprisonment for a term not exceeding ten years, or

(f) an offence punishable on summary conviction.

(2) Jurisdiction — **An accused who is charged with an offence under subsection (1) may be tried and punished by any court having jurisdiction to try that offence in the place where the offence is alleged to have been committed or in the place where the accused is found, is arrested or is in custody, but where the place where the accused is found, is arrested or is in custody is outside the province in which the offence is alleged to have been committed, no proceedings in respect of that offence shall be commenced in that place without the consent of the Attorney General of that province.**

(3) Unauthorized use of credit card data — Every person who, fraudulently and without colour of right, possesses, uses, traffics in or permits another person to use credit card data, whether or not authentic, that would enable a person to use a credit card or to obtain the services that are provided by the issuer of a credit card to credit card holders is guilty of

(a) an indictable offence and is liable to imprisonment for a term not exceeding ten years; or

(b) an offence punishable on summary conviction.

(4) Definition of"traffic" — In this section, "traffic" means, in relation to a credit card or credit card data, to sell, export from or import into Canada, distribute or deal with in any other way.

(3) [Repealed R.S. 1985, c. 27 (1st Supp.), s. 44.]

1974–75–76, c. 93, s. 27; R.S. 1985, c. 27 (1st Supp.), s. 44; 1997, c. 18, s. 16.

Commentary: This section prohibits unlawful dealing in *credit cards* and *credit card data*. It also provides for where trials may be held, and defines "traffic".

Each paragraph of s. 342(1) creates a discrete offence. Under s. 342(1)(a), *theft* of a credit card, the *external circumstances* and *mental element* are those of s. 322(1), *supra*. The credit card, as defined in s. 321, is the "anything" of s. 322(1). Proof of *actual* use is *not* an essential ingredient of P's case. The *external circumstances* of the offence in s. 342(1)(b) are the *forgery* or *falsification* of a credit card. "Forgery", defined in s. 366, requires proof of an ulterior mental element. It is *not* clear whether such proof is required here where the offence would seem complete by the creation of a false credit card, at least where "falsifies" is alleged.

The offences of ss. 342(1)(c) and (d) require proof of *knowledge* by D of the character of the credit card or forged or falsified credit card used, possessed or trafficked in. Under s. 342(1)(c), P must prove that D *knew* the credit card or forged or falsified credit card was obtained, made or altered in the manner specified in either s. 342(1)(c)(i) or (ii). The *external circumstances* consist of possession, use or trafficking in the card. Under s. 342(1)(d), actual use must be proven. The *mental element* includes *knowledge* that the card has been revoked or cancelled at the time of such use.

Under s. 342(3), an offence is created with respect to the *unauthorized use of credit card data*. The *external circumstances* of the offence consist of possessing, using, trafficking in or permitting another person to use credit card data, whether or no authentic, that would enable a person to use a credit card or to obtain the services that are provided by the issuer of a credit card to credit card holders. The *mental element* requires D's actions to be *fraudulent* and *without colour of right*.

The offences are triable either way. Upon indictment, the maximum penalty is imprisonment for a term not exceeding 10 years, irrespective of whether any goods, money, services or other things of value were actually obtained. Under s. 342(2), the offence may be tried by a court of competent jurisdiction where the offence occurred or where D is found. Section 342(4) defines "traffic" for the purposes of s. 342.

Case Law
Nature and Elements of Offence

R. v. Costello (1982), 1 C.C.C. (3d) 403 (B.C. C.A.) — *See also*: *R. v. Elias* (1986), 33 C.C.C. (3d) 476 (Que. C.A.) — D *obtains* a credit card by the commission of an offence when, after innocently obtaining it by finding it, D forms the intent to *convert* it to his/her own use, thereby committing theft.

Res Judicata

R. v. Colman, [1981] 3 W.W.R. 572 (Alta. Q.B.) — *Contra*: *R. v. McKay* (1978), 3 C.R. (3d) 1 (Y.T. C.A.) — The English version of s. 342(1)(c) creates three offences. The French version creates only one. The court must adopt the version most favourable to D. D, acquitted of unlawfully using or dealing with a credit card, cannot be convicted of unlawfully possessing a credit card.

Related Provisions: "Steal" is exhaustively defined in s. 2 as "commit theft". The general possession offence is found in s. 354(1) and possession defined in s. 4(3). Possession is complete under s. 358 when D has, alone or jointly with another, possession of or control over a credit card or when D aids in concealing or disposing of it, as the case may be. Section 359 may permit P to show D was in possession of other recently stolen property. The evidence is receivable on the issue of D's knowledge that the subject-matter of the s. 342 proceedings was stolen.

Section 315 prohibits bringing into Canada anything obtained by an act that, if committed in Canada, would have been an offence, *inter alia*, under s. 342.

The general summary conviction punishment provisions of s. 787(1) apply where P proceeds by summary conviction.

342.01 (1) Making having or dealing in instruments for forging or falsifying credit cards — Every person who, without lawful justification or excuse,

    (a) makes or repairs,

    (b) buys or sells,

    (c) exports from or imports into Canada, or

    (d) possesses

any instrument, device, apparatus, material or thing that the person knows has been used or knows is adapted or intended for use in forging or falsifying credit cards is guilty of an indictable offence and liable to imprisonment for a term not exceeding ten years, or is guilty of an offence punishable on summary conviction.

(2) Forfeiture — Where a person is convicted of an offence under subsection (1), any instrument, device, apparatus, material or thing in relation to which the offence was committed or the possession of which constituted the offence may, in addition to any other punishment that may be imposed, be ordered forfeited to Her Majesty, whereupon it may be disposed of as the Attorney General directs.

(3) Limitation — No order of forfeiture may be made under subsection (2) in respect of any thing that is the property of a person who was not a party to the offence under subsection (1).

1997, c. 18, s. 17.

Commentary: The *preliminary* offence of s. 342.01 prohibits certain conduct in relation to instruments for forging or falsifying credit cards. Provision is also made for *forfeiture* of the instruments or property used to commit the offence.

It is s. 342.01(1) which creates the offence. The *external circumstances* involve the absence of lawful justificaton or excuse, conduct which falls within any of ss. (1)(a)-(d) and an instrument, device, apparatus, material or thing of the nature described. Actual use is *not* required, provided the instrument is adapted or intended for use in forging or falsifying credit cards.

The most critical feature of the *mental element* is D's *knowledge* of the *character* of the device.

Sections 342.01(2) and (3) describe the circumstances in which a person convicted of an offence under the section may be ordered to forfeit the instrument in relation to which the offence was committed, or possession of which constituted the offence. Anything that is the property of a person who was not a party to the offence may not be ordered forfeited.

Related Provisions: Sections 342(1) and (3) create several offences relating to credit cards, a term defined in s. 321. Trial jurisdiction is governed by s. 342(2). Sections 657.1(1) and (2)(c.1) permit introduction of evidence by affidavit or solemn declaration to prove various requirements under s. 342.

Forgery and offences resembling forgery are contained in s. 366-378. "Document" and "false document" are defined in s. 321, making a false document in s. 366(2).

Forfeiture may only be ordered where D is convicted, not where D is found guilty of the offence and given an absolute or conditional discharge under Code s. 730.

342.1 (1) Unauthorized use of computer — Every one who, fraudulently and without color of right,

(a) obtains, directly or indirectly, any computer service,

(b) by means of an electro-magnetic, acoustic, mechanical or other device, intercepts or causes to be intercepted, directly or indirectly, any function of a computer system,

(c) uses or causes to be used, directly or indirectly, a computer system with intent to commit an offence under paragraph (a) or (b) or an offence under section 430 in relation to data or a computer system, or

(d) uses, possesses, traffics in or permits another person to have access to a computer password that would enable a person to commit an offence under paragraph (a), (b) or (c)

is guilty of an indictable offence and liable to imprisonment for a term not exceeding ten years, or is guilty of an offence punishable on summary conviction.

(2) Definitions — In this section,

"computer password" means any data by which a computer service or computer system is capable of being obtained or used;

"computer program" means data representing instructions or statements that, when executed in a computer system, causes the computer system to perform a function;

"computer service" includes data processing and the storage or retrieval of data;

"computer system" means a device that, or a group of interconnected or related devices one or more of which,

(a) contains computer programs or other data, and

(b) pursuant to computer programs,

(i) performs logic and control, and

(ii) may perform any other function;

"data" means representations of information or of concepts that are being prepared or have been prepared in a form suitable for use in a computer system;

"electro-magnetic, acoustic, mechanical or other device" means any device or apparatus that is used or is capable of being used to intercept any function of a computer system, but does not include a hearing aid used to correct subnormal hearing of the user to not better than normal hearing;

"function" includes logic, control, arithmetic, deletion, storage and retrieval and communication or telecommunication to, from or within a computer system;

"intercept" includes listen to or record a function of a computer system, or acquire the substance, meaning or purport thereof.

"traffic" means, in respect of a computer password, to sell, export from or import into Canada, distribute or deal with in any other way.

R.S. 1985, c. 27 (1st Supp.), s. 45; 1997, c. 18, s. 18.

Commentary: The section creates four separate offences relating to the unauthorized use of a computer service or system.

The *external circumstances* of the *obtaining* offence of s. 342.1(1)(a) comprise the direct or indirect obtaining of any "computer service", as defined in s. 342.1(2).

The *external circumstances* of the *interception* offence of s. 342.1(1)(b) require that D *intercept* or cause to be *intercepted any* function of a computer system. The interception must be made by means of an *electro-magnetic, acoustic, mechanical or other device*. The italicized elements are either exhaustively or expansively defined in s. 342.1(2).

The *enabling* offence of s. 342.1(1)(d) requires that P prove that D used, possessed, trafficked in or permitted another person to have access to a *computer password* that would *enable* a person to commit an offence under the three previous paragraphs. In each case the *mental element* includes proof caused the external circumstances that D did fraudently and without colour of right.

The *user* offence of s. 342.1(1)(c) requires proof that D use or cause to be used, directly or indirectly, a "computer system". The *mental element* requires that D's conduct be *fraudulent* and *without colour* of *right*, further the intent to commit a listed offence.

The offences are triable either way.

Related Provisions: Section 430(1.1) describes the offence of mischief in relation to data.

Where P elects to proceed by indictment, D may *elect* mode of trial under s. 536(2). The general punishment provisions of s. 787(1) apply where P proceeds by summary conviction.

342.2 (1) Possession of device to obtain computer service — Every person who, without lawful justification or excuse, makes, possesses, sells, offers for sale or distributes any instrument or device or any component thereof, the design of which renders it primarily useful for committing an offence under section 342.1, under circumstances that give rise to a reasonable inference that the instrument, device or component has been used or is or was intended to be used to commit an offence contrary to that section,

> (a) is guilty of an indictable offence and liable to imprisonment for a term not exceeding two years; or
>
> (b) is guilty of an offence punishable on summary conviction.

(2) Forfeiture — Where a person is convicted of an offence under subsection (1), any instrument or device, in relation to which the offence was committed or the possession of which constituted the offence, may, in addition to any other punishment that may be imposed, be ordered forfeited to Her Majesty, whereupon it may be disposed of as the Attorney General directs.

(3) Limitation — No order of forfeiture may be made under subsection (2) in respect of any thing that is the property of a person who was not a party to the offence under subsection (1).

1997, c. 18, s. 19.

Commentary: This section prohibits *possession* of devices to obtain a computer service and provides for *forfeiture* of the devices upon conviction.

The *external circumstances* consist of several elements. They include

i. absence of lawful justification or excuse;

ii. conduct

iii. subject-matter; and,

iv. circumstances.

The conduct requirement includes *any* of ". . .makes, possesses, sells, offers for sale or distributes. . .". The subject-matter must be an ". . .instrument, device or a component . . ." of a prohibited design. The conduct must take place in *circumstances* which give rise to a *reasonable inference* of the nature described in the section.

The critical feature of the *mental element* involves *knowledge* of the *character* of the subject-matter.

Sections 342.2(2) and (3) permit a court to make an order of *forfeiture* of the instrument or device involved in the offence of which D is convicted, provided it is *not* the property of a person who was *not* a party to the offence.

Related Provisions: Unauthorized use of a computer service is an offence under s. 342.1(1). Several relevant terms are defined in s. 342.1(2). Mischief in relation to data is an offence under s. 430(1.1), punishable under s. 430(5).

Search of a computer system may be authorized under warrant issued under s. 487(2.1). The duties of persons in possession or control of premises where searches of computer systems are conducted are described in s. 487(2.2).

The phrase "primarily useful. . ." also appears in s. 191(1) in relation to interception devices.

343. Robbery — Every one commits "robbery" who

(a) steals, and for the purpose of extorting whatever is stolen or to prevent or overcome resistance to the stealing, uses violence or threats of violence to a person or property;

(b) steals from any person and, at the time he steals or immediately before or immediately thereafter, wounds, beats, strikes or uses any personal violence to that person;

(c) assaults any person with intent to steal from him; or

(d) steals from any person while armed with an offensive weapon or imitation thereof.

R.S., c. C-34, s. 302.

Commentary: Robbery may be committed by any means described in s. 343.

Theft is an essential ingredient of the *external circumstances* of robbery ss. 343(a), (b) and (d). The additional elements vary. Under s. 343(a), P must prove the *use or threat of violence* by D to a person or property *for a specified purpose*. Section 343(b) demands proof of the *infliction* of *personal violence* upon V, within the time specified. Under s. 343(d), P must establish that D stole while *armed* with an offensive weapon or imitation thereof.

The *mental element* that P must establish under ss. 343(a), (b) and (d) consists of the intention to cause the external circumstances described in each of the paragraphs. "Steal", defined in s. 2 to mean "commit theft", requires proof of the ulterior *mental element* described in s. 322(1) in cases of robbery falling within those paragraphs. Under s. 343(a), P must also prove the use or threat of violence was for the defined purpose.

The *external circumstances* of s. 343(c) are complete upon proof of an assault upon V. No theft is required. P must, however, prove that an ulterior *mental element* accompanied the assault, namely, the intent to steal from V.

493

Case Law

Nature and Elements of Offence

R. v. Trudel (1984), 12 C.C.C. (3d) 342 (Que. C.A.) — Section 343(a) requires violence or the threat of violence for the *purpose* extorting the thing stolen or to prevent or overcome resistance. The force used need not be strong or be an assault causing bodily harm. Section 343(b) specifies certain acts of violence. It is *not* necessary that the violence be used with the intention of facilitating the offence. The violence requires more than the mere assault referred to in s. 343(c).

Uses Violence or Threats of Violence: S. 343(a)

R. v. George (1960), 34 C.R. 1 (S.C.C.) — D intoxicated so as to have been incapable of forming the intent to commit theft, may be convicted of common assault if he knew he was applying force to the person of another.

R. v. Sayers (1983), 8 C.C.C. (3d) 572 (Ont. C.A.) — While violence or a reasonable apprehension of violence is required to constitute robbery, the *totality* of D's conduct has to be considered in determining whether a reasonable apprehension of violence was present.

Personal Violence: S. 343(b)

R. v. Doliente (1997), [1997] 2 S.C.R. 11, 115 C.C.C. (3d) 352 (S.C.C.); reversing (1996), 108 C.C.C. (3d) 137 (Alta. C.A.) — Where D stabs V in the course of a robbery, the multiple convictions rule bars conviction of both aggravated assault and robbery under s. 343(b).

R. v. Oakley (1986), 24 C.C.C. (3d) 351 (Ont. C.A.) — *See also*: *R. v. Lew* (1978), 40 C.C.C. (2d) 140 (Ont. C.A.) — A mere technical assault by D does *not* constitute the personal violence required by para. (b). Merely nudging V to steal a purse is *not* sufficient. Fraudulent intent, an element in theft, must also be proven because of the definition of "steal" in s. 2.

R. v. Downer (1978), 40 C.C.C. (2d) 532 (Ont. C.A.) — *See also*: *R. v. Lieberman*, [1970] 5 C.C.C. 300 (Ont. C.A.) — Robbery, as defined in para. (b) contemplates personal violence to V which accompanies the act of stealing or immediately precedes or follows the theft. The *purpose* for which the violence is inflicted is immaterial provided it accompanies, *immediately precedes*, or follows the act of stealing.

Armed With An Offensive Weapon: S. 343(d)

R. v. Sloan (1974), 19 C.C.C. (2d) 190 (B.C. C.A.) — One who *pretends* to have a gun, but is really unarmed, cannot be convicted under para. (d). "Armed" means equipped with or possessed of an instrument.

Tremblay v. Quebec (A.G.) (1984), 43 C.R. (3d) 92 (Que. C.A.); reversed on other grounds (1988), 67 C.R. (3d) 207 (S.C.C.) — There is *no* requirement that V be in any way frightened or intimidated by the sight of the offensive weapon, or that D intended to use it.

Included Offences [See also s. 662]

R. v. Luckett (1981), 20 C.R. (3d) 393, 50 C.C.C. (2d) 489 (S.C.C.); affirming (1978), 3 C.R. (3d) 315, 42 C.C.C. (2d) 390 (B.C. C.A.) — Assault is an included offence on a charge of robbery. The fact that robbery as defined may be committed without involving an assault does *not* alter the fact that robbery, as described in the enactment creating the offence, does include the offence of assault.

R. v. Horsefall (1990), 61 C.C.C. (3d) 245 (B.C. C.A.) — Where an indictment alleges "... did commit robbery", D may be convicted of the included offence of assault causing bodily harm. Under s. 662, an offence may be included in another if it is included in the enactment creating it. The inclusion of "wounds" and the description of robbery in s. 343(b) makes assault causing bodily harm an included offence in a charge of robbery.

R. v. McPhee (1978), 45 C.C.C. (2d) 89 (N.S. C.A.) — Where the words used in the indictment for robbery sufficiently described the offence of assault causing bodily harm, it is an included offence.

R. v. Boisvert (1991), 68 C.C.C. (3d) 478 (Que. C.A.) — On an indictment for robbery, particularized as an assault with intent to steal under s. 343(c), D may be convicted of attempted theft through s. 662(1)(b), where the evidence fails to prove an assault, but does prove attempted theft (and theft).

Duress [See also s. 17]

R. v. Jasman (1985), 60 A.R. 100 (C.A.) — *See also*: *R. v. Misener* (1982), 51 N.S.R. (2d) 160 (C.A.) — If a robbery was committed, the defense of duress is *not* available. If D committed theft, *not* robbery, then duress is a complete defence. If the involvement of D is as a party, duress is a complete defence not only to the robbery but to any included offences.

R. v. Mena (1987), 57 C.R. (3d) 172, 34 C.C.C. (3d) 304 (Ont. C.A.) — Whether the *common law* defence of duress is available to D depends on whether D is a party to the offence of robbery as an aider or whether D actually committed the offence as a co-perpetrator. Co-perpetration requires acting in concert as a joint enterprise. The defence was open to D who testified that he aided in the robbery only under threats from the armed perpetrator.

Related Provisions: Section 2 defines "steal", "offensive weapon", "weapon" and "property". Section 265(1) defines "assault". "Theft" is described in s. 322(1).

Assault with a weapon and assault causing bodily harm under s. 267(1), as well as unlawfully causing bodily harm under s. 269, are related offences.

Section 588 assists in the pleading and proof of ownership, *inter alia*, for the purposes of the offence of robbery. The real and personal property of which a person has lawful management, control or custody is *deemed* to be the property of such person.

In some of its definitions, robbery qualifies as a "serious personal injury offence" in s. 752, for the purpose of dangerous offender proceedings. A s. 100(1) order may be imposed upon conviction. Robbery is an "offence" under s. 183 for the purposes of Part VI, and an "enterprise crime offence" under s. 462.3 for the purpose of Part XII.2.

The offence is exempted from the excuse of compulsion or duress in s. 17.

Under s. 536(2), D may elect mode of trial.

344. Robbery — **Every person who commits robbery is guilty of an indictable offence and liable**

    (a) where a firearm is used in the commission of the offence, to imprisonment for life and to a minimum punishment of imprisonment for a term of four years; and

    (b) in any other case, to imprisonment for life.

R.S., c. C-34, s. 303; 1972, c. 13, s. 70; 1995, c. 39, s. 149.

Commentary: The section provides the punishment for robbery. The maximum punishment remains the same irrespective of the value or nature of the property, if any, stolen. Where a *firearm* is used in the commission of robbery, the *minimim* punishment is imprisonment for a term of four (4) years.

Case Law

Minimum Punishment

R. v. Alain (1997), 119 C.C.C. (3d) 177 (Que. C.A.) — A trial judge may *not* take pre-trial custody into account to reduce a sentence below the statutory minimum.

R. v. Wust (1998), 17 C.R. (5th) 45, 125 C.C.C. (3d) 43 (B.C. C.A.) — There is no conflict between s. 344(a) and ss. 719(1) and (3). In sentencing for robbery where a firearm has been used, a judge must impose a minimum sentence of four years. Time served must *not* be taken into account if it results in a sentence less than the statutory minimum.

R. v. McDonald (1998), 17 C.R. (5th) 1, 127 C.C.C. (3d) 57 (Ont. C.A.) — The language of s. 344(a), in particular the distinction between "punishment" and "sentence", permits a court to consider *pre-sentence custody* as directed by s. 719(3). It is the total *punishment* that must add up to at least four years imprisonment.

In calculating the total *punishment* and taking into account the *pre-sentence custody* as permitted by s. 719(3), a trial judge *may deduct* from the four years any periods of the *pre-sentence custody* that s/he considers appropriate. The final number is the sentence that commences when imposed.

Charter Considerations

R. v. Lapierre (1998), 123 C.C.C. (3d) 332 (Que. C.A) — Section 344(a) does *not* violate the guarantee of *Charter* s. 12 against grossly disproportionate sentences. *Semble*, any s. 12 violation arising from the combined effect of pre-trial custody, *Code* ss. 719(1) and (3), and the mandatory minimum sentence of s. 344(a) may be remedied by constitutional exemption.

Related Provisions: See the corresponding note to s. 343, *supra*.

345. Stopping mail with intent — Every one who stops a mail conveyance with intent to rob or search it is guilty of an indictable offence and liable to imprisonment for life.

R.S., c. C-34, s. 304.

Commentary: This offence is infrequently prosecuted.

The *external circumstances* involve stopping a mail conveyance. P need *not* prove that either a robbery or search of the conveyance actually took place, after it had been stopped. The *mental element* includes the intention to stop the conveyance, and the ulterior intent to rob or search it.

Related Provisions: "Mail conveyance" is *not* defined in the section nor elsewhere in the *Code*. In ordinary parlance, it would include any means whereby mail is transported from the point of mailing until final delivery.

Robbery of the conveyance is punishable as robbery, *simpliciter*, under s. 343. Theft from the mail is punished under s. 356(1). The use of the mails for certain prohibited purposes is contrary to ss. 168 and 381.

D may elect mode of trial under ss. 536(2).

346. (1) Extortion — Every one commits "extortion" who, without reasonable justification or excuse and with intent to obtain anything, by threats, accusations, menaces or violence induces or attempts to induce any person, whether or not he is the person threatened, accused or menaced or to whom violence is shown, to do anything or cause anything to be done.

(1.1) Extortion — Every person who commits extortion is guilty of an indictable offence and liable

(a) where a firearm is used in the commission of the offence, to imprisonment for life and to a minimum punishment of imprisonment for a term of four years; and

(b) in any other case, to imprisonment for life.

(2) Saving — A threat to institute civil proceedings is not a threat for the purposes of this section.

R.S., c. C-34, s. 305; R.S. 1985, c. 27 (1st Supp.), s. 46; 1995, c. 39, s. 150.

Commentary: The *external circumstances* of this offence require that D induce or attempt to induce *any* person to do anything or cause anything to be done. No words suggest omission, as for example, "or to abstain from doing anything". "Anything" and "any person", words of wide and unrestricted use are neither qualified nor defined in the section. The *means* must be "threats, accusations, menaces or violence". The only qualification upon these words appears in s. 346(2), where a threat to institute civil proceedings is *not* a "threat" for the purposes of the subsection. There must finally be the *absence of reasonable justification or excuse*. There is no shift in the burden of proof of this element.

The *mental element* extends beyond proof of the intention to cause the *external circumstances* of the offence. P must prove that D did so "with intent to extort or gain anything".

Case Law

Reasonable Justification or Excuse

R. v. Nattarelli (1967), 1 C.R.N.S. 302, [1968] 1 C.C.C. 154 (S.C.C.) — A right or honest belief of a right to the thing demanded does *not*, by itself, constitute a defence. There must be *reasonable* justification or excuse not only for the demand, but also for the making of threats or menaces to compel compliance with the demand. Once it is proved that threats were made for which there could be *no* justification or excuse, and that they were made with *intent to gain* something or to *induce* the person threatened to do something, the offence is established.

Anything

R. v. Bird (1969), 9 C.R.N.S. 1, [1970] 3 C.C.C. 340 (B.C. C.A.) — The word "anything" is *not* restricted to some tangible material thing. It may include the extortion from a woman of the use of her body for sexual intercourse.

Threats

R. v. Rousseau (1985), 21 C.C.C. (3d) 1 (S.C.C.) — A demand by a lawyer, representing security firm employees who were suspected of theft and receiving the stolen goods of a customer, for money from the firm to avoid publicity relating to the offence and for arranging for charges to be dropped did *not* constitute extortion.

R. v. Swartz (1977), 37 C.C.C. (2d) 409 (Ont. C.A.); affirmed on other grounds (1979), 7 C.R. (3d) 185, 45 C.C.C. (2d) 1 (S.C.C.) — It is *not* necessary that D threaten to injure V personally. A false representation by D of a threat by a third party is sufficient to constitute the offence.

Related Provisions: The offences described in ss. 279(1) and 302(1) include reference to extortion or similar conduct. The use of threats is an element of several offences, including ss. 264.1, 423(1)(a), (b) and 424, as well as the definition of assault in s. 265(1)(b). Threats will also vitiate consent where it is a material element in an offence.

A conviction may attract a s. 100(1) order, provided the means used in the extortion, *viz.*, "... threats, accusations, menaces or violence" fall within the phrase "... violence against a person is used, threatened or attempted ..." in s. 100(1). Extortion is both an "offence" under s. 183 for the purposes of Part VI and an "enterprise crime offence" under s. 462.3 for the purposes of Part XII.2.

D may *elect* mode of trial under s. 536(2).

Criminal Interest Rate

347. (1) Criminal interest rate — **Notwithstanding any Act of Parliament, every one who**

(a) enters into an agreement or arrangement to receive interest at a criminal rate, or

(b) receives a payment or partial payment of interest at a criminal rate,

is guilty of

(c) an indictable offence and is liable to imprisonment for a term not exceeding five years, or

(d) an offence punishable on summary conviction and is liable to a fine not exceeding twenty-five thousand dollars or to imprisonment for a term not exceeding six months or to both.

(2) Definitions — **In this section,**

"credit advanced" means the aggregate of the money and the monetary value of any goods, services or benefits actually advanced or to be advanced under an agreement or arrangement minus the aggregate of any required deposit balance and any fee, fine, penalty, commission and other similar charge or expense directly or indirectly incurred under the original or any collateral agreement or arrangement;

"criminal rate" means an effective annual rate of interest calculated in accordance with generally accepted actuarial practices and principles that exceeds sixty per cent on the credit advanced under an agreement or arrangement;

"insurance charge" means the cost of insuring the risk assumed by the person who advances or is to advance credit under an agreement or arrangement, where the face amount of the insurance does not exceed the credit advanced;

"interest" means the aggregate of all charges and expenses, whether in the form of a fee, fine, penalty, commission or other similar charge or expense or in any other form, paid or payable for the advancing of credit under an agreement or arrangement, by or on behalf of the person to whom the credit is or is to be advanced, irrespective of the person to whom any such charges and expenses are or are to be paid or payable, but does not include any repayment of credit advanced or any insurance charge, official fee, overdraft charge, required deposit balance or, in the case of a mortgage transaction, any amount required to be paid on account of property taxes;

"official fee" means a fee required by law to be paid to any governmental authority in connection with perfecting any security under an agreement or arrangement for the advancing of credit;

"overdraft charge" means a charge not exceeding five dollars for the creation of or increase in an overdraft, imposed by a credit union or caisse populaire the membership of which is wholly or substantially comprised of natural persons or a deposit taking institution the deposits in which are insured, in whole or in part, by the Canada Deposit Insurance Corporation or guaranteed, in whole or in part, by the Quebec Deposit Insurance Board;

"required deposit balance" means a fixed or an ascertainable amount of the money actually advanced or to be advanced under an agreement or arrangement that is required, as a condition of the agreement or arrangement, to be deposited or invested by or on behalf of the person to whom the advance is or is to be made and that may be available, in the event of his defaulting in any payment, to or for the benefit of the person who advances or is to advance the money.

(3) **Presumption** — Where a person receives a payment or partial payment of interest at a criminal rate, he shall, in the absence of evidence to the contrary, be deemed to have knowledge of the nature of the payment and that it was received at a criminal rate.

(4) **Proof of effective annual rate** — In any proceedings under this section, a certificate of a Fellow of the Canadian Institute of Actuaries stating that he has calculated the effective annual rate of interest on any credit advanced under an agreement or arrangement and setting out the calculations and the information on which they are based is, in the absence of evidence to the contrary, proof of the effective annual rate without proof of the signature or official character of the person appearing to have signed the certificate.

(5) **Notice** — A certificate referred to in subsection (4) shall not be received in evidence unless the party intending to produce it has given to the accused or defendant reasonable notice of that intention together with a copy of the certificate.

(6) **Cross examination with leave** — An accused or a defendant against whom a certificate referred to in subsection (4) is produced may, with leave of the court, require the attendance of the actuary for the purposes of cross-examination.

(7) **Consent required for proceedings** — No proceedings shall be commenced under this section without the consent of the Attorney General.

(8) **Application** — This section does not apply to any transaction to which the *Tax Rebate Discounting Act* applies.

1980–81–82–83, c. 43, s. 9.

Commentary: The section creates two offences triable either way. Exhaustive definitions of relevant terms appear in s. 347(2). The section operates notwithstanding any Act of Parliament, but does *not* apply to any transaction to which the *Tax Rebate Discounting Act* applies.

Under s. 347(1)(a), P must prove D entered into an agreement or arrangement to receive interest *at a criminal rate* as defined in s. 347(2). The essence of the offence lies in the making of the prohibited agreement or arrangement. D need *not* actually receive any payment or partial payment of interest to establish liability, though evidence of it may assist in P's proof. The *mental element* consists of the intention to enter into the agreement or arrangement to receive interest at the proscribed rate.

Under s. 347(1)(b), the *external circumstances* involve the actual *receipt* of a payment or partial payment of interest at a criminal rate. *Semble*, D, the recipient, need *not* be a party to the original agreement or arrangement under s. 347(1)(a), as for example where D is simply a collector of accounts. The *mental element* requires proof of D's *knowledge* of the nature of the payment. P's proof is aided by the *presumption* of s. 347(3) engaged where D receives a payment or part payment of interest at a criminal rate. In the *absence of evidence to the contrary*, such receipt imputes to D *knowledge* of the nature of the payment and that it was received at a criminal rate.

Sections 347(4)–(6) permit *proof* of effective annual rate of interest on credit advanced under an agreement or arrangement by introduction of a *certificate* of a Fellow of the Canadian Institute of Actuaries setting out the calculations and the information on which they are based. Under s. 347(5) *reasonable notice* of the intention to produce the certificate must be given to D, together with a *copy* of the certificate. Under s. 347(6), the actuary may be cross-examined only with leave of the court. The certificate is, in the *absence of evidence to the contrary, proof* of the effective annual rate of interest.

Proceedings may be instituted under this section only with the *consent* of the Attorney General of the province in which they originate.

Case Law

Nature and Elements of the Offence

Degelder Construction v. Dancorp Developments Ltd., [1998] 3 S.C.R. 90, 20 C.R. (5th) 77, 129 C.C.C. (3d) 129 — *See also*: *Garland v. Consumers Gas Co.*, [1998] 3 S.C.R. 112, 20 C.R. (5th) 44, 129 C.C.C. (3d) 97 — Section 347 defines two offences. Under s. 347(1)(a), it is illegal to enter into an *agreement or arrangement* to *receive* interest at a criminal rate. Under s. 347(1)(b), it is unlawful to *receive* a *payment* or *partial payment* of interest at a criminal rate.

Section 347(1)(a) should be *narrowly* construed. The offence is complete where there is an *agreement* or *arrangement* for credit, and provable by its terms. The section is violated if a credit agreement *expressly* imposes an annual rate of interest above sixty percent, or if the agreement requires payment of interest charges over a period that necessarily gives rise to an annual rate that exceeds the legal limit.

Whether an agreement or arrangement violates s. 347(1)(a) is decided as of the *time* the *transaction* is entered into. If the agreement or arrangement permits but does *not* require payment at a criminal rate, there is *no* violation of s. 347(1)(b), although s. 347(1)(a) may apply.

Section 347(1)(b) should be *broadly* construed. A payment of interest may be illegal under s. 347(1)(b), even if the loan agreement did *not* violate s. 347(1)(a) when it was reached. The relevant time period for calculation of the interest rate is the period over which credit is actually re-paid. In some instances, a wait-and-see approach is required. Lenders who agree to receive interest under ambiguous terms, however, run the risk that the agreement, in its operation, may contravene s. 347.

R. v. McRobb (1986), 32 C.C.C. (3d) 479n (Ont. C.A.); varying (1984), 20 C.C.C. (3d) 493 (Ont. Co. Ct.) — The *mental element* required with respect to the offence of entering into an agreement to receive a criminal rate of interest is the *intentional* entering into an agreement which provides for the receiving of a criminal interest rate with full *knowledge* of the terms of the agreement. There is *no* requirement that P prove that D knew that the rate charged in the agreement was unlawful, nor that D acted dishonestly or preyed on others by usury or was engaged in swindling or other trickery.

Proof of Offence

R. v. Duzan (1993), 79 C.C.C. (3d) 552 (Sask. C.A.) — Where P proceeds summarily, evidence of payments made prior to the six-month limitation period and actuarial certificates based upon such payments are admissible. P is nonetheless required to prove that the offence was committed within the limitation period.

Charter Considerations

R. v. McRobb (1986), 32 C.C.C. (3d) 479n (Ont. C.A.); varying (1984), 20 C.C.C. (3d) 493 (Ont. Co. Ct.) — This section does *not* infringe *Charter* s. 7.

Related Provisions: The offence is often associated with extortion under s. 346(1). The maximum punishment on summary conviction is, *inter alia*, a fine of not more than $25,000. It is also an "offence" under s. 183 for the purposes of Part VI.

Breaking and Entering

348. (1) **Breaking and entering with intent, committing offence or breaking out** — Every one who

(a) breaks and enters a place with intent to commit an indictable offence therein,

(b) breaks and enters a place and commits an indictable offence therein, or

(c) breaks out of a place after

(i) committing an indictable offence therein, or

(ii) entering the place with intent to commit an indictable offence therein,

is guilty

(d) if the offence is committed in relation to a dwelling-house, of an indictable offence and liable to imprisonment for life, and

(e) if the offence is committed in relation to a place other than a dwelling-house, of an indictable offence and liable to imprisonment for a term not exceeding ten years or of an offence punishable on summary conviction.

(2) **Presumptions** — For the purposes of proceedings under this section, evidence that an accused

(a) broke and entered a place or attempted to break and enter a place is, in the absence of any evidence to the contrary, proof that he broke and entered the place or attempted to do so, as the case may be, with intent to commit an indictable offence therein; or

(b) broke out of a place is, in the absence of any evidence to the contrary, proof that he broke out after

(i) committing an indictable offence therein, or

(ii) entering with intent to commit an indictable offence therein.

(3) **Definition of "place"** — For the purposes of this section, and section 351, "place" means

(a) a dwelling-house;

(b) a building or structure or any part thereof, other than a dwelling-house;

(c) a railway vehicle, a vessel, an aircraft or a trailer; or

(d) a pen or an enclosure in which fur-bearing animals are kept in captivity for breeding or commercial purposes.

R.S., c. C-34, s. 306; 1972, c. 13, s. 24; R.S. 1985, c. 27 (1st Supp.), s. 47; 1997, c. 18, s. 20.

Commentary: The section creates indictable offences if the offences are committed in relation to a dwelling-house and dual procedure offences if the offences are committed in relation to a place other than a dwelling-house. It also provides for the application of certain presumptions in their prosecution, and defines "place", an essential element of each offence.

Under s. 348(1)(a) the *external circumstances* consist of the *break and entry of a place*. "Break" is defined in s. 321 and "entry", which may be actual or constructive, in s. 350. "Place" is defined in s.

348(3). The offence requires proof of an ulterior *mental element*, namely, the *intent to commit an indictable offence in the place* which has been broken and entered. No offence need actually be committed in the premises to establish liability. P's proof of the requisite *mental element* is assisted by the *presumption* of s. 348(2)(a) which, upon *evidence that D broke and entered* a place, and the *absence of evidence to the contrary*, is *proof* that D broke and entered with the *state of mind* requisite to conviction under s. 348(1)(a).

Under s. 348(1)(b), the *external circumstances* include the break and entry of a place and *the commission of an indictable offence therein*. The last italicized words, critical to P's case, distinguish the external circumstances of this offence from those of s. 348(1)(a). The *mental element* requires *no* proof of an ulterior intent unless the indictable offence committed is itself a crime which requires such proof.

The offence of s. 348(1)(c), shortly described as *breaking out*, requires proof that D broke out of a place after *either committing an indictable offence therein or entering with intention* to do so. The *mental element* is ulterior to an intention to commit the *external circumstances*, except where the indictable offence committed therein requires no such proof. P's proof of this issue is assisted by s. 348(2)(b), which, upon *evidence that D broke out* of a place, in the *absence of evidence* to the *contrary*, is *proof* that D broke out *after committing or entering with the intent* to commit an indictable offence therein.

The provisions of s. 348(2) may attract *Charter* s. 11(d) scrutiny.

Case Law
Mental Element: Ss. 348(1)(a); (b)

R. v. Quin (1988), 67 C.R. (3d) 162, 44 C.C.C. (3d) 570 (S.C.C.); affirming (1983), 36 C.R. (3d) 394, 9 C.C.C. (3d) 94 (Ont. C.A.) — Intoxication is *not* a defence to a charge under s. 348(1)(b), an offence of general intent, but is a defence under s. 348(1)(a).

Breaks: S. 321

R. v. Farbridge (1984), 42 C.R. (3d) 385, 15 C.C.C. (3d) 521 (Alta. C.A.) — The entering of a large retail store by D through the public entrance during business hours did *not* constitute "breaking", even though D's sole purpose for entering was to hide until after the store closed and then steal a large quantity of clothing.

R. v. Jewell (1974), 28 C.R.N.S. 331 (Ont. C.A.); leave to appeal refused (1974), 22 C.C.C. (2d) 252n (S.C.C.) — Entry through a door open sufficiently wide to permit D to enter the building, without further displacement of the door, does *not* constitute "breaking".

Place: S. 348(3)

R. v. Fajtl (1986), 53 C.R. (3d) 396 (B.C. C.A.); leave to appeal refused (1987), 55 C.R. (3d) xxxiin (S.C.C.) — *See also: R. v. Thibault* (1982), 66 C.C.C. (2d) 422 (N.S. C.A.) — An area enclosed by a permanent fence and building is a "structure", hence a "place".

R. v. Howe (No. 2) (1983), 57 N.S.R. (2d) 325 (C.A.) — A tent is a "place". Used as a temporary residence by persons to sleep, it is a "dwelling house".

Presumptions and Evidence to the Contrary: S. 348(2)

R. v. Proudlock (1978), 5 C.R. (3d) 21 at 24 (B.C. C.A.) — The presumption in subsection (2) merely establishes a *prima facie* case. The burden of proof does *not* shift. D does *not* have to "establish" a defence or an excuse, but only raise a reasonable doubt. Evidence disbelieved by the trier of fact is *not* "evidence to the contrary", and the *prima facie* case remains.

R. v. Campbell (1974), 17 C.C.C. (2d) 320 (Ont. C.A.) — *See also: R. v. Swan*, (May 9, 1991), Doc. No. V01045 (B.C. C.A.) — Evidence of D's *consumption* of *alcohol* and *drugs* and D's *irrational behaviour* was "evidence to the contrary" as it was evidence which tended to negative the existence of the requisite intent. The onus was then on P to prove the existence of the necessary intent beyond a reasonable doubt and without the assistance of the presumption.

Recent Possession [See also s. 322]

R. v. Kowlyk (1988), 65 C.R. (3d) 97, 43 C.C.C. (3d) 1 (S.C.C.) — *See also: R. v. Newton* (1976), 34 C.R.N.S. 161 (S.C.C.); *Riendeau v. R.* (1947), 2 C.R. 493 (S.C.C.) — The unexplained possession of recently stolen property is sufficient to allow an inference of guilt of both theft and offences incidental thereto, even in the absence of other evidence of guilt. The inference is permissive, not mandatory. P must, of course, establish that the goods were stolen and, where relevant, that a break-in occurred. If the question arises as to whether D actually stole the goods or was merely a possessor, then it is up to the trier of fact to decide which, if either, inference is to be drawn.

Included Offences [See also s. 662(6)]

R. v. Miller (1948), 5 C.R. 415, 91 C.C.C. 270 (Alta. C.A.) — A charge of breaking and entering *with intent* to commit an indictable offence includes a charge of being *unlawfully* in a dwelling-house.

R. v. Rivet (1975), 29 C.R.N.S. 301 (Ont. C.A.) — *Contra*: *R. v. L'Hirondelle* (1992), 72 C.C.C. (3d) 254 (Alta. C.A.) — A charge of breaking and entering and theft does *not* include the offence of possession of property obtained by crime.

Charter Considerations

R. v. Slavens (1991), 5 C.R. (4th) 204, 64 C.C.C. (3d) 29 (B.C. C.A.) — Section 348(2)(b) contravenes s. 11(d) of the *Charter*, but is saved by s. 1.

Related Provisions: "Dwelling-house", a "place" under s. 348(3)(a), is defined in s. 2. The nature of the premises entered determines the maximum punishment. "Break" is defined in s. 321, and whether entry has occurred is determined under s. 350.

Under *I.A.* s. 34(1)(a), "indictable offences" includes not only those offences which *must* be prosecuted by indictment, but also those which *may* be so.

Related offences appear in ss. 177 (trespassing at night) and 349(1) (being unlawfully in a dwelling-house). The preparatory or preliminary crime of possession of break-in instruments is defined in s. 351(1).

The offences of s. 348(1) are an "offence" within s. 183 for the purposes of Part VI.

Under s. 662(6), inadequate proof of an offence under s. 348(1)(b) may result in conviction under s. 348(1)(a).

D may *elect* mode of trial under s. 536(2).

349. (1) Being unlawfully in dwelling-house — Every person who, without lawful excuse, the proof of which lies on that person, enters or is in a dwelling-house with intent to commit an indictable offence in it is guilty of an indictable offence and liable to imprisonment for a term not exceeding ten years or of an offence punishable on summary conviction.

(2) Presumption — For the purposes of proceedings under this section, evidence that an accused, without lawful excuse, entered or was in a dwelling-house is, in the absence of any evidence to the contrary, proof that he entered or was in the dwelling-house with intent to commit an indictable offence therein.

R.S., c. C-34, s. 307; 1997, c. 18, s. 21.

Commentary: The *external circumstances* of this offence require proof that D entered or was in a dwelling-house *without lawful excuse*. D must prove on a balance of probabilities, that D's presence or entry was lawful. The *mental element* consists of the intention to cause the *external circumstances*, together with the ulterior intent to commit an indictable offence *in the premises*. Section 349(2) assists P in proof of the mental element. *Evidence* that D, without lawful excuse, entered or was in a dwelling-house, *absent any evidence to the contrary*, is *proof* of the requisite mental element. The reverse onus clause of s. 349(1) and rebuttable presumption of s. 349(2) may attract *Charter* s. 11(d) scrutiny.

Case Law

Presumption: S. 349(2)

Austin v. R. (1968), 4 C.R.N.S. 338, [1969] 1 C.C.C. 97 (S.C.C.) — Even where P relies on the presumption, there is *no* onus on D to explain D's presence on the premises. The totality of the evidence may raise a doubt as to D's intention which is an essential ingredient for P to establish.

R. v. Proudlock (1978), 43 C.C.C. (2d) 321 (S.C.C.); reversing 5 C.R. (3d) 21 at 24 (B.C. C.A.) — A change in the wording of the section was merely a substitution of an equivalent expression in the English and French languages for the Latin words "*prima facie*". Where a presumption merely establishes a *prima facie* case, the burden of proof does *not* shift. D need only raise a reasonable doubt by giving evidence of an explanation that may reasonably be true. However, an explanation which is *not* believed is *not* "any evidence to the contrary".

R. v. Bernard (1989), 90 N.S.R. (2d) 10 (C.A.) — D may rebut the presumption by raising a reasonable doubt. It is *not* necessary to establish D's lack of intent. Where evidence tending to negate the existence of the necessary intent is adduced, the onus is on P to prove intent beyond a reasonable doubt.

Included Offences

R. v. E. (S.) (1993), 80 C.C.C. (3d) 502 (N.W.T. C.A.) — On a charge of entering a dwelling-house without lawful excuse with intent to commit an indictable offence therein, mischief, under s. 430(1)(d) of the *Code*, is an included offence.

Charter Considerations

R. v. Nagy (1988), 67 C.R. (3d) 329, 45 C.C.C. (3d) 350 (Ont. C.A.) — Before the presumption of intent is allowed to become effective, entry or presence without lawful excuse must be established. The presumption is mandatory, and requires conviction in the absence of any evidence which if believed raises a reasonable doubt as to the existence of intent. Although subsection (2) violates *Charter* s. 11(d), it is saved by s. 1.

Related Provisions: "Dwelling house" is defined in s. 2. Section 350(a) describes when "entry" *actually* occurs.

There are several distinctions between this offence and that of s. 348(1)(a). No breaking is involved under s. 349(1). It is an essential element of the *external circumstances* in s. 348(1)(a). Under s. 349(1), the entry need *not* have been made with intent to commit an indictable offence therein, provided such intent is formulated while D is *in* the dwelling. Similar rebuttable presumptions of intent arise, however, upon proof of unlawful entry [s. 349(2)] or break and entry [s. 348(2)(a)]. Under s. 348(1), what is broken and entered must be a "place". Section 349(1) applies only to a "dwelling-house", a subdivision of "place".

Related offences are described in ss. 177 (trespassing at night) and 348(1) (breaking and entering with intent, committing offence or breaking out). The preparatory crime of possession of break-in instruments described in s. 351(1) is more related to the offences of s. 348(1).

350. Entrance — For the purposes of sections 348 and 349,

    (a) a person "enters" as soon as any part of his body or any part of an instrument that he uses is within any thing that is being entered; and

    (b) a person shall be deemed to have broken and entered if

        (i) he obtained entrance by a threat or artifice or by collusion with a person within, or

        (ii) he entered without lawful justification or excuse, the proof of which lies on him, by a permanent or temporary opening.

R.S., c. C-34, s. 308.

Commentary: For the purposes of ss. 348 and 349 *only*, this section describes when actual entry occurs and defines constructive break and entry.

Under s. 350(a), *actual entry* is *not* limited to the earliest moment at which D's body enters the dwelling house or other place. Actual entry also occurs when *any part* of an *instrument* used by D is within anything being entered. What constitutes an actual "break and entry" is *not* defined, but the descriptions of "entry", *supra*, and "break" as defined in s. 321, have a similar effect.

Under s. 350(b), D is *deemed* to have *broken and entered* in either of the circumstances there described. Section 350(b)(i) applies in respect of *consensual entries* (artifice or collusion), as well as to those where entrance is gained by a "threat". "Threat" is *not* qualified, as for example, by words such as "of bodily harm or damage to property". Under s. 350(b)(ii), entry, without lawful justification or excuse, *by a temporary or permanent opening*, is *deemed* a break and entry, absent proof of D's justification or excuse.

The presumption of s. 350(b)(ii) may attract *Charter* s. 11(d) scrutiny.

Case Law
Deemed to Have Broken and Entered: S. 350(b)

R. v. Farbridge (1984), 42 C.R. (3d) 385, 15 C.C.C. (3d) 521 (Alta. C.A.) — The *Code deems* a person to have broken and entered if that person entered without "lawful justification or excuse". The time of entry is relevant when considering whether such justification exists since the object of the legislation is to strike at intruding strangers. There is *no* "breaking" where D entered a large retail store by the public entrance during business hours, even though the sole purpose for doing so was to hide until after the store closed and then steal clothing.

By Artifice: S. 350(b)(i)

R. v. Leger (1976), 31 C.C.C. (2d) 413 (Ont. C.A.) — Where D waited outside of an underground parking garage of an apartment building and, without the knowledge of the driver, followed a car in after the driver opened the door with his key, D obtained entrance into the building by "artifice".

Permanent or Temporary Opening: S. 350(b)(ii)

Johnson v. R. (1977), 37 C.R.N.S. 370, 34 C.C.C. (2d) 12 (S.C.C.) — An *open* doorway, for which the *door* has *not* yet been *installed*, leading to a dwelling-house under construction is "a permanent or temporary opening".

Related Provisions: See the corresponding notes to ss. 348 and 349, *supra*.

351. (1) Possession of break-in instrument — Every one who, without lawful excuse, the proof of which lies on him, has in his possession any instrument suitable for the purpose of breaking into any place, motor vehicle, vault or safe under circumstances that give rise to a reasonable inference that the instrument has been used or is or was intended to be used for any such purpose, is guilty of an indictable offence and liable to imprisonment for a term not exceeding ten years.

(2) Disguise with intent — Every one who, with intent to commit an indictable offence, has his face masked or coloured or is otherwise disguised is guilty of an indictable offence and liable to imprisonment for a term not exceeding ten years.

R.S., c. C-34, s. 309; 1972, c. 13, s. 25; R.S. 1985, c. 27 (1st Supp.), s. 48.

Commentary: The two indictable offences of the section frequently are preliminary to the commission of other substantive offences against rights of property or the person of another.

The gravamen of the offence of s. 351(1) consists of the *unlawful possession* of proscribed instruments in designated circumstances. The *external circumstances* comprise several elements. D must be *in possession of an instrument*; a term which is *not* defined, and is of wide significance. D's possession must be *without a lawful excuse*. The *burden* of proving such excuse rests upon D. The instrument must be *suitable for the purpose of breaking into any place, motor vehicle, vault or safe*. Further, D's possession must be *under circumstances that give rise to a reasonable inference that the instrument has been used or is or was intended to be used for any such purpose*. A reasonable doubt upon any element of the *external circumstances*, namely, possession of the instruments, their suitability and circumstances supporting a reasonable inference of actual or intended unlawful use, will result in an acquittal. The *mental element* requires proof of an intention to have possession of such instruments. Section 351(1) has been challenged under *Charter* s. 11(d).

The offence of s. 351(2), often preliminary to other substantive crimes, differs substantially from that in s. 351(1). Its *external circumstances* require proof that D's face was, at the material time, masked, coloured, or otherwise disguised. No definitions are provided, but each is a word of common every day usage. P must prove an ulterior *mental element*: D's intent to commit a specified indictable offence to establish liability.

Case Law
Elements of Offence

R. v. Holmes (1988), 64 C.R. (3d) 97, 41 C.C.C. (3d) 497 (S.C.C.) — The *elements* to be proven by P beyond a reasonable doubt are *possession* by D of specified instruments, the *suitability* of the instruments for the prohibited purpose, and an *intention* to *use* the instruments for a prohibited purpose.

R. v. K. (S.) (1995), 103 C.C.C. (3d) 572 (B.C. C.A.) — P need *not* establish a *nexus* between D's possession of instruments and a target motor vehicle. The absence of a *nexus* in time and place is a factor to consider in deciding whether the circumstances, taken as a whole, support a reasonable inference that the instruments had been or were intended to be used for a prohibited purpose.

Instrument

R. v. Benischek (1963), 39 C.R. 285, [1963] 3 C.C.C. 286 (Ont. C.A.) — "Instrument" refers essentially to any substantial thing which possesses the physical characteristics which would enable it to be used or handled by a person to facilitate a breaking or opening. The ingredients for nitro-glycerine are instruments.

Evidence of Explanation

R. v. Crossley (1997), 117 C.C.C. (3d) 533 (B.C. C.A.) — Where D is charged under *Code* s. 351(1), it may be reasonable to allow D to adduce evidence of the excuse s/he gave upon apprehension without examining whether there was an opportunity for concoction. (per Esson and Prowse JJ.A.)

Where D, charged with a possession offence, seeks to introduce an exculpatory statement made *contemporaneously* with discovery or arrest, factors other than reliability are relevant. The emphasis is on contemporaneity. (per Rowles J.A.)

Charter Considerations

R. v. Holmes (1988), 64 C.R. (3d) 97, 41 C.C.C. (3d) 497 (S.C.C.) — The provisions of s. 351(1) do *not* violate the presumption of innocence guarantee of *Charter* s. 11(d).

Related Provisions: "Motor vehicle" is defined in s. 2. The definition of "place" in s. 348(3) does *not* apply to the offence of s. 351(1). Possession is defined in s. 4(3).

Breaking into a motor vehicle, vault or safe is not *per se* an offence. Break and entry of the place wherein each is stored or located may attract liability under s. 348(1).

Related offences include ss. 82 (possession of explosives) and 352 (instruments for coin-operated or currency exchange devices). Others are described in the corresponding notes to ss. 348 and 349, *supra*.

The "indictable offence" described in s. 351(2) is, under *I.A.* s. 34(1)(a), any offence that *may* be prosecuted by indictment.

D may *elect* mode of trial under s. 536(2).

352. Possession of instruments for breaking into coin-operated or currency exchange devices — Every one who, without lawful excuse, the proof of which lies on him, has in his possession any instrument suitable for breaking into a coin-operated device or a currency exchange device, under circumstances that give rise to a reasonable inference that the instrument has been used or is or was intended to be used for breaking into a coin-operated device or a currency exchange device, is guilty of an indictable offence and liable to imprisonment for a term not exceeding two years.

R.S., c. C-34, s. 310; 1972, c. 13, s. 26; 1974-75-76, c. 93, s. 28.

Commentary: This offence duplicates the structure of s. 351(1), but in respect of instruments which are *suitable for breaking into a coin-operated device or currency exchange device*. Neither type of device is defined.

The *external circumstances* require that D be *in possession of an instrument*, a term which is *not* defined and is of wide significance. D's possession must be *without lawful excuse*. The instrument must be *suitable for the purpose of breaking into a coin-operated device or a currency exchange device*. Further, D's possession must be *under circumstances that give rise to a reasonable inference that the instrument has been used or is or was intended to be used for breaking into a coin-operated device or currency exchange device*. A reasonable doubt upon any essential element will result in an acquittal. The *mental element* requires proof of an intention to have possession of such instruments.

The provision, which requires D to prove lawful excuse, may attract *Charter* s. 11(d) scrutiny.

Case Law

R. v. Stanziale (1979), 9 C.R. (3d) 281, 47 C.C.C. (2d) 348 (Ont. C.A.) — D, with a key that s/he used to break into a parking meter, could be convicted of theft or of the offence of s. 352, but *not* both, unless it could be shown that D had used, or intended to use, the key to break into another parking meter.

Related Provisions: Breaking into a coin-operated or currency exchange device, *per se*, is *not* an offence. Possession is defined under s. 4(3).

D may elect mode of trial under s. 536(2).

353. (1) Selling, etc., automobile master key — Every one who

(a) sells, offers for sale or advertises in a province an automobile master key otherwise than under the authority of a licence issued by the Attorney General of that province, or

(b) purchases or has in his possession in a province an automobile master key otherwise than under the authority of a licence issued by the Attorney General of that province, is guilty of an indictable offence and liable to imprisonment for a term not exceeding two years.

(1.1) Exception — A police officer specially authorized by the chief of the police force to possess an automobile master key is not guilty of an offence under subsection (1) by reason only that the police officer possesses an automobile master key for the purposes of the execution of the police officer's duties.

(2) Terms and conditions of licence — A licence issued by the Attorney General of a province as described in paragraph (1)(*a*) or (*b*) may contain such terms and conditions relating to the sale, offering for sale, advertising, purchasing, having in possession or use of an automobile master key as the Attorney General of that province may prescribe.

(2.1) Fees — The Attorney General of a province may prescribe fees for the issue or renewal of licences as described in paragraph (1)(*a*) or (*b*).

(3) Record to be kept — Every one who sells an automobile master key

(a) shall keep a record of the transaction showing the name and address of the purchaser and particulars of the licence issued to the purchaser as described in paragraph (1)(*b*); and

(b) shall produce the record for inspection at the request of a peace officer.

(4) Failure to comply with subsection (3) — Every one who fails to comply with subsection (3) is guilty of an offence punishable on summary conviction.

(5) Definitions — The definitions in this subsection apply in this section.

"automobile master key" includes a key, pick, rocker key or other instrument designed or adapted to operate the ignition or other switches or locks of a series of motor vehicles.

"licence" includes any authorization,

R.S., c. C-34, s. 311; 1997, c. 18, s. 22.

Commentary: This section prohibits certain dealings with or in what s. 353(5) defines as an "automobile master key". Two separate offences are created.

The *external circumstances* of the s. 353(1) offence require that D's conduct amounts to "sells, offers for sale, advertises ... purchases or has in his possession ..." an automobile master key. The seller, putative seller, advertiser and purchaser, or anyone *in possession* of an automobile master key may be liable. D's conduct must *not* be *authorized* by a *licence* issued by the Attorney General of the province in which it occurs. The *mental element* does *not* extend beyond the intention to cause the external circumstances of the offence, *semble*, including *knowledge* of the *nature* of the article and *absence* of *authority* therefor. The onus of proving *absence* of licensed authority would appear to fall on P.

Section 353(1.1) creates an *exception* to the offences of s. 353(1) for police officers authorized by the chief of police who have the key to carry out thier duties.

A *licence* may be issued by the Attorney General of a province under s. 353(2) and fees for issue or renewal of such a licence may be prescribed by the Attorney General under s. 353(2.1). It may contain such terms and conditions relating to transactions in dealings with or use of an automobile master key as the Attorney General of the province may prescribe. Under s. 353(3), specified *records* must be maintained and produced for inspection at the request of a peace officer. Failure to maintain or produce the prescribed records is a summary conviction offence under s. 353(4). In addition to "automobile master key", s. 353(5) also defines "licence" for the purposes of this section.

Case Law
Automobile Master Key: S. 353(5)

R. v. Young (1983), 3 C.C.C. (3d) 395 (Ont. C.A.) — A coat hanger, even if adapted for use to enter a vehicle, is *not* an "automobile master key". The definition contemplates manufactured devices that could be the subject of advertising and commerce.

Related Provisions: Section 4(3) may be invoked to establish possession.

D may *elect* mode of trial in respect of the indictable offence of s. 353(1). The summary conviction offence of s. 353(4) is tried under Part XXVII, and punished under s. 787(1).

Having in Possession

354. (1) Possession of property obtained by crime — Every one commits an offence who has in his possession any property or thing or any proceeds of any property or thing knowing that all or part of the property or thing or of the proceeds was obtained by or derived directly or indirectly from

(a) the commission in Canada of an offence punishable by indictment; or

(b) an act or omission anywhere that, if it had occurred in Canada, would have constituted an offence punishable by indictment.

(2) Obliterated vehicle identification number — In proceedings in respect of an offence under subsection (1), evidence that a person has in his possession a motor vehicle the vehicle identification number of which has been wholly or partially removed or obliterated or a part of a motor vehicle being a part bearing a vehicle identification number that has been wholly or partially removed or obliterated is, in the absence of any evidence to the contrary, proof that the motor vehicle or part, as the case may be, was obtained, and that such person had the motor vehicle or part, as the case may be, in his possession knowing that it was obtained,

(a) by the commission in Canada of an offence punishable by indictment; or

(b) by an act or omission anywhere that, if it had occurred in Canada, would have constituted an offence punishable by indictment.

(3) "vehicle identification number" defined — For the purposes of subsection (2), "vehicle identification number "means any number or other mark placed on a motor vehicle for the purpose of distinguishing the motor vehicle from other similar motor vehicles.

(4) Exception — A peace officer or a person acting under the direction of a peace officer is not guilty of an offence under this section by reason only that the peace officer

**or person possesses property or a thing or the proceeds of property or a thing men-
tioned in subsection (1) for the purposes of an investigation or otherwise in the execution of the peace officer's duties.**

R.S., c. C-34, s. 312; 1972, c. 13, s. 27; 1974–75–76, c. 93, s. 29; 1997, c. 18, s. 23.

Commentary: The section describes and punishes the offence of *possession* of *property* or *proceeds* of criminal origin and enacts an evidentiary provision to assist P in its proof.

The *external circumstances* of the offence under s. 354(1) require that D have in his/her *possession* any *property, thing or proceeds* thereof. The subject-matter in whole or in part, must have been *obtained by or derived directly or indirectly from a source* described in s. 354(1)(a) or (b). The *mental element* comprises the intention to possess the subject-matter, as well as specific *knowledge* of its spurious *character*.

Section 354(2) creates two *rebuttable presumptions of fact* which assist P in its proof. The presumptions arise upon *evidence* that D has *possession* of a motor vehicle or part thereof, the vehicle identification number of which has been wholly or partially removed or obliterated. "Vehicle identification number" is defined in s. 354(3). Such evidence, in the *absence of evidence* to the *contrary*, constitutes *proof* of the spurious *character* of the motor vehicle or part, as well as D's *knowledge* thereof. Put shortly, *evidence* of possession of the specified subject-matter constitutes *proof* of its spurious *character* and D's *knowledge* thereof, absent evidence to the contrary.

Section 354(4) creates an *exception* to an offence under this section for a peace officer or person acting under his/her direction who possesses property or a thing derived from a source described in s. 354(1) or the proceeds of such property or thing, for investigatory purposes or otherwise in the *execution* of the officer's *duty*.

Case Law
Obtained by Crime

R. v. Geauvreau (1979), 51 C.C.C. (2d) 75 (Ont. C.A.); affirmed (1982), 28 C.R. (3d) 1, 66 C.C.C. (3d) 375 (S.C.C.) — Subsection (1) creates a single offence based on the possession of property. P must allege as a necessary element of the offence the unlawful source of the goods. Where P has alleged in the indictment that the goods were "obtained" by D through unlawful means, it could *not* amend the indictment on appeal to allege that the goods had been "derived directly or indirectly" by crime.

R. v. Hayes (1985), 46 C.R. (3d) 393, 20 C.C.C. (3d) 385 (Ont. C.A.) — A person who comes into the possession of property lawfully, but subsequently steals it by converting it to his/her own use and continues in possession of it is guilty of having property in his/her possession knowing it was obtained by the commission of an indictable offence.

R. v. Epp (1988), 42 C.C.C. (3d) 572 (Sask. C.A.) — The purchase of property from the owner whom D knew, had made a false insurance claim for loss of the property as stolen, does *not* constitute an offence under this section. The property was not obtained by or derived directly or indirectly from the commission of an indictable offence.

Mental Element

R. v. L'Heureux (1985), 47 C.R. (3d) 221, 21 C.C.C. (3d) 574 (S.C.C.) — The trial judge must be convinced beyond a reasonable doubt that D *knew* the property was *stolen* and must acquit if the explanation offered for possession *could* be true, even if not convinced that it is true.

R. v. Hewitt (1984), 27 Man. R. (2d) 11 (Co. Ct.); affirmed (1986), 55 C.R. (3d) 41, 32 C.C.C. (3d) 54 (Man. C.A.) — Under suspicious circumstances, failure to inquire as to proof of ownership is wilful blindness.

R. v. Blentzas (1984), 62 N.S.R. (2d) 336 (C.A.) — D, has an onus as a pawnshop owner, to ensure that he was making legitimate purchases. The purchase of valuable items from a teenager may exemplify wilful blindness.

Possession [See also s. 4(3)]

R. v. Terrence (1983), 33 C.R. (3d) 193, 4 C.C.C. (3d) 193 (S.C.C.); affirming (1980), 17 C.R. (3d) 390, 55 C.C.C. (2d) 183 (Ont. C.A.) — A constituent and essential element of "possession" of a stolen car is *control* of the vehicle by D.

Recent Possession [See also s. 322]

R. v. Kowlyk (1988), 65 C.R. (3d) 97, 43 C.C.C. (3d) 1 (S.C.C.); affirming (1986), 51 C.R. (3d) 65, 27 C.C.C. (3d) 61 (Man. C.A.) — See digest under s. 322.

R. v. Graham (1972), 19 C.R.N.S. 117, 7 C.C.C. (2d) 93 (S.C.C.) — P need *not* prove that no explanation was given before trial, or that any explanation given could *not* reasonably be true, if it wishes to rely on the presumption flowing from possession of recently stolen goods. Explanatory statements made by D upon first being found "in possession" constitute part of the *res gestae* and are admissible in any description of the circumstances under which the crime was committed. They may be adduced in cross-examination. Self-serving statements made by D several hours after the discovery *cannot* be adduced by the defence during cross-examination.

Tremblay v. R., [1970] 4 C.C.C. 120 (S.C.C.) — A trial judge, in summing up, must avoid leaving the impression that the onus of proof passes to D once P establishes recent possession on D's part. The jury must be told that they must acquit D if D's explanation *could* be true, even if they are *not* convinced that it is, and that, when relying on the doctrine of recent possession, they have the right, but not the obligation, to convict D if they do not believe D's explanation or find it unreasonable to believe.

Obliterate

R. v. Hodgkins (1985), 19 C.C.C. (3d) 109 (Ont. C.A.) — "Obliterate" includes destroying the integrity of the original identification number to produce a spurious number.

Origin

R. v. Leslie (1975), 23 C.C.C. (2d) 343 (Ont. C.A.) — Where the indictment alleges that the goods were obtained through the commission of a particular offence, P must prove that offence was committed, without benefit of the statutory presumption on the issue.

Charter Considerations: S. 354(2)

Russell v. R. (1983), 32 C.R. (3d) 307, 4 C.C.C. (3d) 460 (N.S. C.A.) — The doctrine of recent possession does *not* offend *Charter* s. 11(d).

Boyle v. R. (1983), 35 C.R. (3d) 34, 5 C.C.C. (3d) 193 (Ont. C.A.) — The first presumption in subsection (2) (*spurious character*) is reasonable, hence, constitutionally valid. The second presumption (guilty *knowledge*) is unreasonable as it infringes *Charter* s. 11(d) and is *not* justifiable under s. 1.

Related Provisions: The requisite elements of possession are described in s. 4(3). Section 358 declares when possession is complete.

What constitutes "proceeds" is *not* disclosed in the section or elsewhere. The term itself and the nature of the causal link described suggest considerable latitude in the tracing of origins. "Obtained" is equally a term of comprehensive import.

The offence is an "offence" in s. 183 and "enterprise crime offence" in s. 462.3 for the purposes of Parts VI and XII.2, respectively.

The phrase "punishable by indictment", interpreted in the light of *I.A.* s. 34(1)(a), includes offences triable either way.

Sections 359 and 360 permit the reception of evidence of D's possession of other unlawfully obtained property, as well as previous convictions of offences involving theft or possession (s. 354) upon a charge under s. 354(1). The evidence is receivable upon the issue of D's *knowledge* of the spurious character of the property which is the subject of the s. 354(1) charge, an essential element of P's proof. Section 657.2(1) permits admission of evidence of conviction or discharge of another of *theft* of the property as evidence against D charged with possession. Absent evidence to the contrary, it is *proof* the *property* was *stolen*.

Section 356(1)(b) creates a specific offence of possession of property stolen from or relating to the *mail* and s. 357 makes it an offence to bring into Canada anything obtained outside Canada by an act that, committed in Canada, would have been theft or an offence under s. 354. Several offences make possession of defined subject-matter a crime.

Special rules of criminal pleading and joinder including ss. 583(b) (naming the owner or holder of a special property or interest in the count) and 593 (joint trials of several accused who have possession of subject-matter at different times or places) apply to prosecutions for possession.

355. Punishment — Every one who commits an offence under section 354

(a) is guilty of an indictable offence and liable to imprisonment for a term not exceeding ten years, where the subject-matter of the offence is a testamentary instrument or the value of the subject-matter of the offence exceeds five thousand dollars; or

(b) is guilty

(i) of an indictable offence and is liable to imprisonment for a term not exceeding two years, or

(ii) of an offence punishable on summary conviction,

where the value of the subject-matter of the offence does not exceed five thousand dollars.

R.S., c. C-34, s. 313; 1972, c. 13, s. 28; 1974–75–76, s. 30;1985, c. 27 (1st Supp.), s. 49; 1994, c. 44, s. 21.

Commentary: Possession of property or its proceeds obtained by crime is *classified* for *sentencing* purposes by this section.

The classification of s. 355(a) is exclusively indictable. It applies to possession offences where the property obtained is a testamentary instrument or in excess of the described value. Both "testamentary instrument" and "property" are expansively defined in s. 2.

The classification of s. 355(b), applies to possession offences where the value of the property obtained does *not* exceed the designated value. The offence is triable either way.

Case Law

Nature and Elements of Offence

R. v. Gillis (1977), 35 C.C.C. (2d) 418 (N.S. C.A.) — *See also*: *R. v. Norcross* (1957), 27 C.R. 220, 120 C.C.C. 108, 110 (B.C. C.A.) — The value of the stolen article is *not* an essential ingredient of the offence. If the evidence does *not* establish that the value of the goods exceeds the value in s. 355, then the court may sentence D under s. 355.

Value [See also s. 4(2)]

R. v. Belanger (1972), 6 C.C.C. (2d) 210 (B.C. C.A.) — An article's retail value is, *prima facie*, its intrinsic value.

Related Provisions: Similar classification provisions exist for theft, false pretences , and fraud.

The forum of trial depends upon the value or nature of the property obtained. On a charge under s. 355(a), D may elect mode of trial under s. 536(2). On a charge under s. 355(b), P may elect mode of procedure. Where P proceeds by indictment, subject to the exceptions of s. 555(2), D is tried before a provincial court judge under s. 553(a)(iii). Summary conviction proceedings take place under Part XXVII, and are punished under s. 787(1).

The value of a "valuable security" is determined by s. 4(2).

For further related provisions see the corresponding note to s. 354, *supra*.

356. (1) Theft from mail — Every one who

(a) steals

(i) any thing sent by post, after it is deposited at a post office and before it is delivered,

(ii) a bag, sack or other container or covering in which mail is conveyed, whether or not it contains mail, or

(iii) a key suited to a lock adopted for use in the Canada Post Corporation, or

(b) has in his possession anything in respect of which he knows that an offence has been committed under paragraph (*a*),

is guilty of an indictable offence and liable to imprisonment for a term not exceeding ten years.

(2) Allegation of value not necessary — In proceedings for an offence under this section it is not necessary to allege in the indictment or to prove on the trial that anything in respect of which the offence was committed had any value.

R.S., c. C-34, s. 314; 1980–81–82–83, c. 54, s. 56.

Commentary: The section describes and punishes two separate offences and provides, in s. 356(2), that neither an allegation nor proof of value is essential under the section.

Section 356(1)(a) is a particular species of *theft*. The "anything" of s. 322(1) is the property described in any of ss. 356(1)(a)(i)–(iii). The *external cicumstances* and *mental element* of the offence duplicate those of the general definition of theft and only differ in their requirement of proof of specific subject-matter.

The offence of s. 356(1)(b) is a specific application of the general *possession* offence of s. 354(1). The subject-matter of the possession, the spurious character of which D must know so as to establish liability, is *anything* in respect of which an offence has been committed under s. 356(1)(a).

Case Law

R. v. Weaver (1980), 55 C.C.C. (2d) 564 (Ont. C.A.) — On a charge under s. 356(1)(a)(i) an article deposited in a letter box is in the course of post until it is forwarded to a place where the addressee of the article has access, and is *not* "delivered" until then.

R. v. Wendland (1970), 1 C.C.C. (2d) 382 (Sask. C.A.) — Mailable matter which has been deposited at a post office is *deemed* to be the property of the Postmaster General.

Related Provisions: Other offences relating to the mail include stopping a mail conveyance with intent to rob or search it (s. 345), mailing obscene matter (s. 168), and using the mails to defraud the public (s. 381). Provision is made in s. 476(e) for expanded trial jurisdiction where offences are committed in respect of mail in the course of door-to-door delivery.

Possession may be established under s. 4(3) and is complete in accordance with s. 358. The special evidentiary rules of ss. 359 and 360 apply to prosecutions under s. 356(1)(b).

Judicial authorization to intercept private communications in respect of this "offence" may be given under s. 183 of Part VI.

D may *elect* mode of trial under s. 536(2).

357. Bringing into Canada property obtained by crime — Every one who brings into or has in Canada anything that he has obtained outside Canada by an act that, if it had been committed in Canada, would have been the offence of theft or an offence under section 342 or 354, is guilty of an indictable offence and liable to a term of imprisonment not exceeding ten years.

R.S., c. C-34, s. 315; R.S. 1985, c. 27 (1st Supp.), s. 50.

Commentary: In general, this section prevents importation into Canada as well as domestic possession of certain foreign contraband. It appears rarely invoked.

The *external circumstances* of the *importation* offence require that D bring "anything" *into Canada* that has been *obtained outside Canada*. "Anything", a word of wide and unrestricted use is nowhere defined, but, *semble*, would include at least "property" as defined in s. 2. The "anything" obtained outside Canada must have been obtained by an act that, if it had been committed in Canada, would have amounted to theft or an offence under s. 342 (theft, forgery of credit card) or 354 (possession). The *mental element*, while requiring the intention to commit the external circumstances, hence knowledge of the spurious character of the property, requires proof of no further ulterior intention.

The *external circumstances* are also proven where D "has in Canada" the "anything" just described. Liability is *not* restricted to the actual importer. The remaining elements of the *external circumstances*, as well as the *mental element*, are identical with that earlier mentioned.

Quaere whether "has" limits the external circumstances to *actual* possession by D?

Related Provisions: The essential elements of the offences of theft and possession are described in the commentary to ss. 322 and 354.

D may elect mode of trial under s. 536(2).

358. Having in possession when complete — For the purposes of sections 342 and 354 and paragraph 356(1)(*b*), the offence of having in possession is complete when a person has, alone or jointly with another person, possession of or control over anything mentioned in those sections or when he aids in concealing or disposing of it, as the case may be.

R.S., c. C-34, s. 316; R.S. 1985, c. 27 (1st Supp.), s. 50.

Commentary: The section declares when *possession* is *complete* in respect of the general possession offences of ss. 354, 356(1)(b) and 342.

Possession is complete when D, alone or jointly with another, has possession of or control over the relevant subject-matter. Possession, equally, is complete when D aids in concealing or disposing of the property, for example where D assists another in selling the property to another party. General principle would require proof of D's *knowledge* of the spurious character of the property, together with the intention to possess, or aid in concealment or disposal, as the case may be.

Case Law [See also s. 4(3) and s. 335]

Terrence v. R. (1980), 17 C.R. (3d) 390, 55 C.C.C. (2d) 183 (Ont. C.A.); affirmed (1983), 33 C.R. (3d) 193, 4 C.C.C. (3d) 193 (S.C.C.) — The mere act of getting into a vehicle knowing it to be stolen, is *not* sufficient to establish the measure of control necessary for a conviction of having possession of property obtained by crime.

Related Provisions: For related provisions, see the corresponding notes to ss. 342, 354 and 356, *supra*.

359. (1) Evidence — Where an accused is charged with an offence under section 342 or 354 or paragraph 356(1)(*b*), evidence is admissible at any stage of the proceedings to show that property other than the property that is the subject-matter of the proceedings

    (a) was found in the possession of the accused, and

    (b) was stolen within twelve months before the proceedings were commenced,

and that evidence may be considered for the purpose of proving that the accused knew that the property that forms the subject-matter of the proceedings was stolen property.

(2) Notice to accused — Subsection (1) does not apply unless

    (a) at least three days notice in writing is given to the accused that in the proceedings it is intended to prove that property other than the property that is the subject-matter of the proceedings was found in his possession; and

    (b) the notice sets out the nature or description of the property and describes the person from whom it is alleged to have been stolen.

R.S., c. C-34, s. 317; R.S. 1985, c. 27 (1st Supp.), s. 51.

Commentary: This section allows P to prove an essential element of any listed offence in part by the introduction of *evidence of other similar misconduct*. D must first be *charged* with an offence under s. 342, 354 or 356(1)(b). Evidence is then admissible, at *any stage of the proceedings*, to show that property, *other* than the subject-matter of the charge, was found in D's possession, having been stolen within 12 months before the proceedings in which it is tendered as evidence were commenced. D need *not* have put his/her character in issue or denied knowledge of the spurious origins of the subject-matter of the charge to permit the reception of this evidence. Proceedings need *not* have been instituted nor, *a fortiori* convictions registered in respect of the collateral misconduct. The evidence would *not* seem to be required to meet the rigours of the similar act rule. The other misconduct need *not* relate to property *similar* to that alleged in the indictment. The property, which is the subject of the collateral misconduct, may have been stolen and found in D's possession *after* the subject-matter of the indictment, provided it qualifies under the time limit imposed by s. 359(1)(b). The evidence of collateral misconduct is admissible to prove D's *knowledge* of the spurious *character of the property* described in the indictment.

The evidence of collateral misconduct is receivable upon compliance with the *written notice and disclosure* requirements of s. 359(2). The conditions precedent do *not* include a requirement that D first be shown to be in possession of the subject-matter alleged in the indictment on which D is being tried.

This provision has been impeached under *Charter* s. 7.

Case Law

Charter Considerations

R. v. Hewitt (1986), 55 C.R. (3d) 41, 33 C.C.C. (3d) 54 (Man. C.A.); affirming (1984), 27 Man. R. (2d) 11 (Co. Ct.) — *See also*: *R. v. Guyett* (1989), 72 C.R. (3d) 383, 51 C.C.C. (3d) 368 (Ont. C.A.) — The admission of irrelevant and prejudicial evidence contravenes *Charter* s. 7. This section must be read down in order to coexist with the *Charter*. The evidence must be *relevant* for a reason *other* than to merely show that D is a person of *bad character*.

Related Provisions: Proceedings are generally commenced by the laying of an information.

For related provisions, see the corresponding notes to ss. 342, 354 and 356, *supra*.

360. (1) Evidence of previous conviction — **Where an accused is charged with an offence under section 354 or paragraph 356(1)(b) and evidence is adduced that the subject-matter of the proceedings was found in his possession, evidence that the accused was, within five years before the proceedings were commenced, convicted of an offence involving theft or an offence under section 354 is admissible at any stage of the proceedings and may be taken into consideration for the purpose of proving that the accused knew that the property that forms the subject-matter of the proceedings was unlawfully obtained.**

(2) Notice to accused — **Subsection (1) does not apply unless at least three days notice in writing is given to the accused that in the proceedings it is intended to prove the previous conviction.**

R.S., c. C-34, s. 318.

Commentary: This section permits the reception of evidence of D's *previous convictions* of certain offences in *proof* of *knowledge* of the spurious *character of the property* in the offence charged.

Section 360(1) only applies where D is charged under s. 354 or 356(1)(b). Evidence must first be adduced of D's *possession* of the subject-matter alleged in the indictment. Thereafter, evidence may be adduced, *at any stage of the proceedings*, that D, within a period of five years before the subject proceedings were commenced, had been convicted under s. 354 or of a theft offence. The subject-matter of the previous conviction need *not* be similar to that alleged in the indictment, nor is there any requirement that D first put his/her character in issue or deny knowledge of the spurious character of the property which is the subject of the charge. Once the evidence is received, it assists in P's proof of D's knowledge of the unlawful character of the property described in the indictment, an essential element of P's proof.

Section 360(2) requires P to give D at least three days notice in writing of the intention to adduce such evidence. No further disclosure is required by the subsection.

This section has also attracted *Charter* s. 7 challenge.

Case Law

Hewson v. R. (1978), 5 C.R. (3d) 155 (S.C.C.) — A previous conviction is *not* rendered inadmissible under this section solely on the basis that it is under appeal.

Related Provisions: Previous convictions may be proven, *inter alia*, under s. 667.

For other related provisions, see the corresponding notes to ss. 354, 356 and 359, *supra*.

False Pretences

361. (1) False pretence — A "false pretence" is a representation of a matter of fact either present or past, made by words or otherwise, that is known by the person who makes it to be false and that is made with a fraudulent intent to induce the person to whom it is made to act on it.

(2) Exaggeration — Exaggerated commendation or depreciation of the quality of anything is not a false pretence unless it is carried to such an extent that it amounts to a fraudulent misrepresentation of fact.

(3) Question of fact — For the purposes of subsection (2), it is a question of fact whether commendation or depreciation amounts to a fraudulent misrepresentation of fact.

R.S., c. C-34, s. 319.

Commentary: A false pretence requires a *representation* of a *matter of fact*. The expression of an opinion is *not* sufficient. The representation must be of a matter of fact, *present or past*. Representations as to the *future*, as for example by promise or statement of intention, do *not* come within the definition. The representation may be made by *words or otherwise*, as for example, wholly or partly by conduct. The *maker* of the representation, D, must *know it to be false*. The representation must also be made with a *fraudulent intent to induce the person to whom it is made to act on it*.

Sections 361(2) and (3) further assist in defining "false pretence". As a general rule, exaggerated commendation or depreciation of the quality of anything is *not* a false pretence. Under s. 361(2), such commendation or depreciation is a false pretence only when it amounts to a fraudulent misrepresentation of fact. Whether it is carried to such an extent is, under s. 361(3), a question of fact.

Case Law

R. v. Reid (1940), 74 C.C.C. 156 (B.C. C.A.) — *See also*: *R. v. Godfrey* (1972), 9 C.C.C. (2d) 386 (Ont. C.A.) — A mere promise to pay for goods in the future which does *not* involve the necessary and irresistible representation of a present fact is *not* a false pretence within the section.

Related Provisions: A false pretence is an essential element of the offences of ss. 362 and 363. Related offences involving fraudulent representations are found in ss. 364 and 365. Fraudulent transactions relating to contracts and trade are found in Part X, ss. 379–427, *infra*.

362. (1) False pretence or false statement — Every one commits an offence who

(a) by a false pretence, whether directly or through the medium of a contract obtained by a false pretence, obtains anything in respect of which the offence of theft may be committed or causes it to be delivered to another person;

(b) obtains credit by a false pretence or by fraud;

(c) knowingly makes or causes to be made, directly or indirectly, a false statement in writing with intent that it should be relied on, with respect to the financial condition or means or ability to pay of himself or any person, firm or corporation that he is interested in or that he acts for, for the purpose of procuring, in any form whatever, whether for his benefit or the benefit of that person, firm or corporation,

  (i) the delivery of personal property,

  (ii) the payment of money,

  (iii) the making of a loan,

  (iv) the grant or extension of credit,

  (v) the discount of an account receivable, or

(vi) the making, accepting, discounting or endorsing of a bill of exchange, cheque, draft or promissory note; or

(d) knowing that a false statement in writing has been made with respect to the financial condition or means or ability to pay of himself or another person, firm or corporation that he is interested in or that he acts for, procures on the faith of that statement, whether for his benefit or for the benefit of that person, firm or corporation, anything mentioned in subparagraphs (c)(i) to (vi).

(2) **Punishment** — Every one who commits an offence under paragraph (1)(a)

(a) is guilty of an indictable offence and liable to a term of imprisonment not exceeding ten years, where the property obtained is a testamentary instrument or the value of what is obtained exceeds five thousand dollars; or

(b) is guilty

(i) of an indictable offence and is liable to imprisonment for a term not exceeding two years, or

(ii) of an offence punishable on summary conviction,

where the value of what is obtained does not exceed five thousand dollars.

(3) **Idem** — Every one who commits an offence under paragraph (1)(b), (c) or (d) is guilty of an indictable offence and liable to imprisonment for a term not exceeding ten years.

(4) **Presumption from cheque issued without funds** — Where, in proceedings under paragraph (1)(a), it is shown that anything was obtained by the accused by means of a cheque that, when presented for payment within a reasonable time, was dishonoured on the ground that no funds or insufficient funds were on deposit to the credit of the accused in the bank or other institution on which the cheque was drawn, it shall be presumed to have been obtained by a false pretence, unless the court is satisfied by evidence that when the accused issued the cheque he believed on reasonable grounds that it would be honoured if presented for payment within a reasonable time after it was issued.

(5) **Definition of "cheque"** — In this section, "cheque" includes, in addition to its ordinary meaning, a bill of exchange drawn on any institution that makes it a business practice to honour bills of exchange or any particular kind thereof drawn on it by depositors.

R.S., c. C-34, s. 320; 1972, c. 13, s. 29; 1974–75–76, c. 93, s. 31;R.S. 1985, c. 27 (1st Supp.), s. 52; 1994, c. 44, s. 22.

Commentary: This section combines substantive and evidentiary provisions relating to the crime of *obtaining by false pretences*. Common to each mode of commission is the *means* of obtaining: a false pretence, statement or fraud.

The *general* obtaining offence of s. 362(1)(a) requires that D obtain or cause to be delivered to another, *by a false pretence*, anything capable of being stolen. The false pretence may be the direct or indirect means by which the "anything" is obtained. P's proof is assisted in NSF cheque cases by the *rebuttable presumption* of s. 362(4). Upon proof of obtaining by a cheque that was dishonoured upon presentation in the usual course on the ground that *no*, or *insufficient*, funds were on deposit to the credit of D in the institution upon which it was drawn, a rebuttable presumption of false pretence arises. The *presumption* may be *rebutted* where the court is *satisfied* that D had a reasonably grounded belief of payment upon presentation in the usual course. The subsection may attract *Charter* s. 11(d) scrutiny. "Cheque" is expansively defined in s. 362(5).

Sections 362(1)(b)-(d), represent *specific* forms of obtaining, distinguished by the nature of the representations made or the property obtained. Under s. 362(1)(b) the means of obtaining credit may be either a "false pretence" or "fraud". "Fraud" is *not* restricted in its meaning to what is a "false pretence" in s. 361(1), and, *semble*, includes representations as to the future. The complementary offences of ss. 362(1)(c) and (d) require proof of a "false statement in writing" in relation to a particular subject-matter which is sought or procured. Although such statements are, not infrequently, a "false pretence" within s. 361(1), it would seem that it is not necessary that they be so.

Sections 362(2) and (3) are *punishment* provisions. The maximum penalty for the general obtaining offence of s. 362(1)(a) varies, depending upon the nature and value of the property obtained and, in some cases, upon the mode of procedure followed. The specific obtaining offences of ss. 362(1)(b)-(d) are punishable under s. 362(3).

Case Law
Nature and Elements of Offence

R. v. Scheer (1923), 39 C.C.C. 82 (Man C.A.) — The essential distinction between theft by a trick and obtaining by false pretences is that in theft the owner, if he voluntarily parts with the possession of the goods, does *not* intend to part with the ownership. In obtaining by false pretences the owner's intention must be to actually part with the ownership.

R. v. Cohen (1984), 15 C.C.C. (3d) 231 (Que. C.A.) — Knowledge of the falsity of the information on the part of the recipient does *not* constitute a defence for D. Evidence of loss or detriment to the recipient is *not* a necessary element of the offence.

Obtains [See also s. 354]

R. v. Hemingway (1955), 22 C.R. 275, 112 C.C.C. 321 (S.C.C.) — *See also*: *R. v. Vallilee* (1974), 24 C.R.N.S. 319, 15 C.C.C. (2d) 409 (Ont. C.A.) — One who obtains delivery of goods under a conditional sales agreement may be properly convicted of obtaining the goods by false pretences notwithstanding that the agreement expressly provides that ownership of the goods is to remain in the seller until payment in full of the purchase price.

Obtains Credit: S. 362(1)(b); (c)

R. v. Hall (1957), 27 C.R. 92 (N.S. S.C.) — *See also*: *R. v. Dvornek* (1962), 37 C.R. 344, 132 C.C.C. 231 (B.C. C.A.) — "Obtaining credit" means obtaining something on a promise to do something in the future. Obtaining an article from a merchant *on approval*, by giving a false name, is obtaining credit by a false pretence. The credit need *not* be that of D.

Extension of Credit: S. 362(1)(c)

R. v. Cohen (1984), 15 C.C.C. (3d) 231 (Que. C.A.) — The phrase "extension of credit" in s. 362(1)(c)(iv) must be read in the same sense as the French "ouverture d'un credit": granting or according credit. False statements which merely serve to keep open an existing line of credit do *not* fall within the subsection.

Abuse of Process [See also s. 8]

R. v. Waugh (1985), 21 C.C.C. (3d) 80, 68 N.S.R. (2d) 247 (N.S. C.A.) — Criminal proceedings commenced solely to collect a civil debt are an abuse of process. If there is *prima facie* evidence of a crime however, V may pursue concurrent criminal and civil proceedings.

Charter Considerations

R. v. Driscoll (1987), 60 C.R. (3d) 88, 38 C.C.C. (3d) 28 (Alta. C.A.) — *See also*: *R. v. Ferguson* (1992), 12 C.R. (4th) 198, 70 C.C.C. (3d) 330 (P.E.I. T.D.) — *Contra*: *R. v. Bunka* (1984), 12 C.C.C. (3d) 437 (Sask. Q.B.) — Subsection (4) breaches the presumption of innocence in *Charter* s. 11(d).

Related Provisions: For related offences see the corresponding note to s. 361, *supra*.

Where the property obtained is a testamentary instrument or of a value exceeding the specified amount, D will *elect* mode of trial under s. 536(2). Where the value of what is obtained does not exceed the specified amount, P will *elect* mode of procedure but, irrespective of the election, D will be tried by a provincial court judge, under s. 553(a)(ii), subject to an order being made under s. 555(1) or (2), if P proceeds by indictment, and under Part XXVII, where P proceeds by summary conviction.

Section 583 makes certain omissions of detail *not* grounds for objection, provided the count otherwise complies with the requirements of s. 581. Under s. 586, no false pretences count is insufficient by reason only that it does not set out in detail the nature of the false pretence. Section 587(1)(b) permits the ordering of particulars of any false pretence that is alleged.

Upon conviction, D may be ordered to pay compensation to V (s. 738) or to a *bona fide* purchaser of property that D has obtained by false pretences (s. 739).

363. Obtaining execution of valuable security by fraud — Every one who, with intent to defraud or injure another person, by a false pretence causes or induces any person

  (a) to execute, make, accept, endorse or destroy the whole or any part of a valuable security, or

  (b) to write, impress or affix a name or seal on any paper or parchment in order that it may afterwards be made or converted into or used or dealt with as a valuable security,

is guilty of an indictable offence and liable to imprisonment for a term not exceeding five years.

R.S., c. C-34, s. 321.

Commentary: This *specific* form of *obtaining by false pretences* carries a maximum punishment of imprisonment for a term not exceeding five years.

The *external circumstances* consist of D causing or inducing V to do what is described in either s. 363(a) or (b). The acts caused or induced in s. 363(a) relate to an existing valuable security. Under s. 363(b), the acts induced or caused relate to paper or parchment so that it may later become, be used or be dealt with as valuable security. In every case, the means used to induce the conduct must be a *false pretence*.

In addition to the intention to cause the external circumstances of the offence, P must prove that D did so *with intent to defraud or injure another person*. Such person need not be the person induced or caused by the false pretences to engage in the conduct described in ss. 363(a) and (b). "Injure" is a word of comprehensive import.

Related Provisions: A "false pretence" is defined in s. 361(1). "Valuable security" is defined in s. 2 and its value determined under s. 4(2). Related offences are described in the corresponding note to s. 361, *supra*. In particular, such offences appear in ss. 340 and 397. Other related provisions are described in the corresponding note to s. 362.

364. (1) Fraudulently obtaining food, beverage or accommodation — Every one who fraudulently obtains food, a beverage or accommodation at any place that is in the business of providing those things is guilty of an offence punishable on summary conviction.

(2) Presumption — In proceedings under this section, evidence that the accused obtained food, a beverage or accommodation at a place that is in the business of providing those things and did not pay for it and

  (a) made a false or fictitious show or pretence of having baggage,

  (b) had any false or pretended baggage,

  (c) surreptitiously removed or attempted to remove his baggage or any material part of it,

  (d) absconded or surreptitiously left the premises,

  (e) knowingly made a false statement to obtain credit or time for payment, or

  (f) offered a worthless cheque, draft or security in payment for the food, beverage or accommodation,

is, in the absence of any evidence to the contrary, proof of fraud.

517

(3) Definition of "cheque" — In this section "cheque" includes, in addition to its ordinary meaning, a bill of exchange drawn on any institution that makes it a business practice to honour bills of exchange or any particular kind thereof drawn on it by depositors.

R.S., c. C-34, s. 322; 1994, c. 44, s. 23.

Commentary: The summary conviction offence of s. 364(1) contains no express reference to a "false pretence", though it would appear most likely the means whereby the specified subject-matter is obtained.

The *external circumstances* consist of the obtaining of food, beverage or accommodation at any place that is in the business of providing those things. Proof of the concurrent *mental element*, described in the compendious term "fraudulently", is aided by the *presumption* of s. 364(2), which becomes engaged when any of the circumstances of ss. 364(2)(a)-(f), accompany *evidence* that D obtained the specified services at a designated location without payment therefor. Absent evidence to the contrary, *evidence* of the matters described in s. 364(2) is *proof* of *fraud*. The subsection may be open to scrutiny under *Charter* s. 11(d).

Under s. 364(3), "cheque", used in s. 364(2)(f), is expansively defined as in s. 362(5).

Case Law

Food

R. v. Tremblay (1987), 57 C.C.C. (3d) 427 (Que. C.A.); affirming (1986), 57 C.C.C. (3d) 427 (Que. S.C.) — "Food", and its French equivalent, "aliments", includes not only solid food but also alcoholic beverages sold in a hotel bar.

Related Provisions: Punishment is governed by s. 787(1).

Other related provisions are described in the corresponding notes to ss. 361 and 362, *supra*.

365. Pretending to practise witchcraft, etc. — Every one who fraudulently

    (a) pretends to exercise or to use any kind of witchcraft, sorcery, enchantment or conjuration,

    (b) undertakes, for a consideration, to tell fortunes, or

    (c) pretends from his skill in or knowledge of an occult or crafty science to discover where or in what manner anything that is supposed to have been stolen or lost may be found,

is guilty of an offence punishable on summary conviction.

R.S., c. C-34, s. 323.

Commentary: This summary conviction offence also makes no express reference to a "false pretence" as the means whereby the offence is committed.

The *external circumstances* are those of any of ss. 365(a)-(c). A specified pretence is necessary under ss. 365(a) and (c). The paid undertaking to tell fortunes will satisfy s. 365(b).

The *mental element* in all cases requires proof that D acted "fraudulently", that is to say, with an intention to deceive V.

Case Law

R. v. Labrosse (1984), 17 C.C.C. (3d) 283 (Que. C.A.); affirmed (1987), 33 C.C.C. (3d) 220 (S.C.C.) — Although D did *not* expressly claim the power to predict the future, the essential element, "fraudulently", may arise from the gestures, actions and words of D to make V believe in D's power to predict the future. It was *not* necessary to prove that the predictions were, in fact, false.

Related Provisions: The offence is punishable under s. 787(1).

Forgery and Offences Resembling Forgery

366. (1) Forgery — Every one commits forgery who makes a false document, knowing it to be false, with intent

(a) that it should in any way be used or acted on as genuine, to the prejudice of any one whether within Canada or not, or

(b) that a person should be induced, by the belief that it is genuine, to do or to refrain from doing anything, whether within Canada or not.

(2) Making false document — Making a false document includes

(a) altering a genuine document in any material part;

(b) making a material addition to a genuine document or adding to it a false date, attestation, seal or other thing that is material; or

(c) making a material alteration in a genuine document by erasure, obliteration, removal or in any other way.

(3) When forgery complete — Forgery is complete as soon as a document is made with the knowledge and intent referred to in subsection (1), notwithstanding that the person who makes it does not intend that any particular person should use or act on it as genuine or be induced, by the belief that it is genuine, to do or refrain from doing anything.

(4) Forgery complete though document incomplete — Forgery is complete notwithstanding that the false document is incomplete or does not purport to be a document that is binding in law, if it is such as to indicate that it was intended to be acted on as genuine.

R.S., c. C-34, s. 324.

Commentary: The section describes the offence of *forgery* and when it is complete.

Under s. 366(1), the *external circumstances* of forgery consist of the *making of a false document*, expansively defined in s. 366(2) to refer *only* to alterations of and additions to a genuine document. A "false document" is exhaustively defined for the purposes of Part IX, including s. 366(1), in s. 321.

Under s. 366(3), forgery is *complete* as soon as the document is made with the proscribed purpose and intent, notwithstanding that D, its maker, does *not* intend a particular victim to act upon it. The offence is also complete under s. 366(4), notwithstanding incompleteness or absence of represented legal effect of the document, *provided* it appears to indicate it was intended to be acted upon as genuine.

The *mental element* of forgery requires proof of the *intention* to make a false document, *knowledge* of its *falsity* and the specific intention of either s. 366(1)(a)or (b).

Case Law

"False Document" [See also ss. 321 and 368]

Gaysek v. R. (1971), 15 C.R.N.S. 345, 2 C.C.C. (2d) 545 (S.C.C.) — D makes a "false document" where D prepares a document which is false in some material particular, including the very purpose for which it was created.

R. v. Foley (1994), 30 C.R. (4th) 238, 90 C.C.C. (3d) 390 (Nfld. C.A.) — Authorized signings, including those which do *not* indicate on their face that the signatory is acting as the proxy of another, are excluded from the offence of forgery. Such documents may be misleading, but they lack the falsity which is inherent in a forgery.

R. v. Ogilvie (1993), 81 C.C.C. (3d) 125 (Que. C.A.) — *See also: R. v. Nuosci* (1991), 10 C.R. (4th) 332, 69 C.C.C. (3d) 64 (Ont. C.A.); leave to appeal refused (1992), 71 C.C.C. (3d) vii (note) (S.C.C.) — A document which merely contains a lie is *not* always a "false document", hence a forgery under ss. 366

and 368. A document which is false in reference to the very purpose for which it was created is one that is false in a *material particular* within s. 321, and hence may afford a basis for conviction of forgery. (per Fish and Baudouin JJ.A.)

Mental Element

R. v. Cowan (1961), 36 C.R. 313 (Ont. C.A.); affirmed (1962), 37 C.R. 151 (S.C.C.) — It is sufficient that D made the false document with the *intent* that it should be acted upon to the prejudice of anyone. It is unnecessary for P to prove that it was in fact acted upon to the prejudice of anyone.

R. v. Couture (1991), 64 C.C.C. (3d) 227 (Que. C.A.) — The intent to cause prejudice required by s. 366(1)(a) requires an element of moral blameworthiness going beyond mere negligence or incompetence.

Material Addition: S. 366(2)(b)

R. v. Paquette (1979), 45 C.C.C. (2d) 575 (S.C.C.); reversing (1977), 42 C.C.C. (2d) 59 (Que. C.A.) — A notary makes a false document under s. 366(2)(b) by attesting in an affidavit to the signature of a witness on a power of attorney without ever having met the purported witness. P is not required to prove the notary was aware that the entire document was a forgery.

Related Provisions: Under s. 367, forgery is an indictable offence punishable by a term of imprisonment not exceeding 10 years or an offence punishable on summary conviction.

Uttering a forged document is an offence under s. 368(1). Sections 369–371 and 374–378 describe and punish the creation or use of specific forms or types of false documents. Offences relating to the forgery of trademarks and trade descriptions appear in ss. 406–414, and those relating to spurious currency in ss. 448–460.

D may elect mode of trial under s. 536(2).

367. Punishment for forgery — Every one who commits forgery

(a) **is guilty of an indictable offence and liable to imprisonment for a term not exceeding ten years; or**

(b) **is guilty of an offence punishable on summary conviction.**

1994, c. 44, s. 24; 1997, c. 18, s. 24.

Commentary: Section 367 punishes forgery, an offence triable either way.

Related Provisions: Forgery is an "offence" for the purposes of s. 183 and Part VI and an "enterprise crime offence" under s. 462.3 and Part XII.2.

368. (1) Uttering forged document — Every one who, knowing that a document is forged,

(a) **uses, deals with or acts upon it, or**

(b) **causes or attempts to cause any person to use, deal with or act upon it,**

as if the document were genuine,

(c) **is guilty of an indictable offence and liable to imprisonment for a term not exceeding ten years; or**

(d) **is guilty of an offence punishable on summary conviction.**

(2) **Wherever forged** — For the purposes of proceedings under this section, the place where a document was forged is not material.

R.S., c. C-34, s. 326; 1994, c. 44, s. 24; 1997, c. 18, s. 25.

Commentary: The section describes the dual procedure offence of *uttering*. Liability is attracted not only in cases where D *actually* uses, deals with or acts upon a forged document, but equally where D *causes* or *attempts* to cause another person to do so.

The *external circumstances* of s. 368(1)(a) require proof that D used, dealt with or acted upon a *forged* document, *as if it were genuine*. Under s. 368(1)(b), P need not prove any actual use of or dealing with the document by D. The *external circumstances* of s. 368(1)(b) are complete where D causes or attempts to cause another to use, deal with or act upon a forged document, as if it were genuine. An *attempt* to cause another to act in a proscribed manner is as much unlawful as it is to actually cause such action to be undertaken. In each case, P must prove that D knew the document to be forged.

Under s. 368(2), it is immaterial where the document was forged.

Case Law

Forged Document [See also s. 366]

R. v. Valois (1983), 35 C.R. (3d) 166 (Que. C.A.); affirmed (1986), 51 C.R. (3d) 243, 25 C.C.C. (3d) 97 (S.C.C.) — The document must be "forged", *not* merely false. Documents, although false, are *not* "forged" within the meaning of s. 366, absent evidence of prejudice or of intent to cause prejudice.

R. v. Jones (1970), 11 C.R.N.S. 219 (Ont. C.A.) — *See also*: *R. v. Elkin* (1978), 42 C.C.C. (2d) 185 (B.C. C.A.); *R. v. Keshane* (1974), 20 C.C.C. (2d) 542 (Sask. C.A.) — A valid cheque becomes a forged document when an unauthorized endorsement is placed upon it.

Uttering

R. v. Valois (1986), 51 C.R. (3d) 243, 25 C.C.C. (3d) 97 (S.C.C.); affirming (1983), 35 C.R. (3d) 166 (Que. C.A.) — D must have done something beyond preparing or conspiring to utter the forged documents. To be guilty, D must have begun uttering the documents or dealt with or acted upon them as genuine documents in relation to someone else.

R. v. Paquette (1979), 45 C.C.C. (2d) 575 (S.C.C.) — A notary's actions in annexing a false attestation to a deed of loan, *knowing* it to be forged, constituted *uttering* a forged document.

Mental Element

R. v. Sebo (1988), 64 C.R. (3d) 388, 42 C.C.C. (3d) 536 (Alta. C.A.) — This offence requires only an *intent to deceive*, *not* an intent to cause prejudice or to defraud.

Related Provisions: Forgery is described in s. 366. "Document" and "false document" are defined in s. 321.

Sections 369–371 and 374–378 describe and punish the creation or use of specific forms or types of false documents. Further offences relating to forgery of trade marks and descriptions appear in ss. 406–414. Several offences relating to spurious currency are found in ss. 448–460.

Authorization to intercept private communications in respect of this "offence" may be given under Part VI. It is also an "enterprise crime offence" under Part XII.2.

D may *elect* mode of trial under s. 536(2), where P proceeds by indictment.

---

369. Exchequer bill paper, public seals, etc. — Every one who, without lawful authority or excuse, the proof of which lies on him,

(a) makes, uses or knowingly has in his possession

(i) any exchequer bill paper, revenue paper or paper that is used to make bank notes, or

(ii) any paper that is intended to resemble paper mentioned in subparagraph (i),

(b) makes, offers or disposes of or knowingly has in his possession any plate, die, machinery, instrument or other writing or material that is adapted and intended to be used to commit forgery, or

(c) makes, reproduces or uses a public seal of Canada or of a province, or the seal of a public body or authority in Canada, or of a court of law,

is guilty of an indictable offence and liable to imprisonment for a term not exceeding fourteen years.

R.S., c. C-34, s. 327.

Commentary: This section generally prohibits the unlawful use, making, possession or disposal of certain materials.

The *external circumstances* of the offences consist of the *absence of lawful authority or excuse*, together with the conduct specified in s. 369(a), (b) or (c), as the case may be. In each case, there are alternative modes in which D may participate in the *external circumstances*. Under s. 369(a), D must make, use or *knowingly* have in D's possession a prohibited paper or any paper intended to resemble it. Under s. 369(b), D must make, offer, dispose of or knowingly have in D's possession prohibited materials *adapted and intended to be used to commit forgery*. Both adaptation for and intended use are required. The *external circumstances* in s. 369(c) must amount to "makes, reproduces or uses" a public or court seal. In each case, there is a prohibited manner of dealing and a prohibited subject-matter.

The *mental element* consists of the intentional conduct of D which constitutes the external circumstances of the offence. The requirement that P prove D "knowingly" has in his/her possession defined subject-matter probably adds little to the general requirement of *knowledge* of the character of subject-matter required in possession cases.

It is necessary that D establish lawful authority or excuse for D's conduct. This reversal of onus in respect of an essential element of P's proof may attract *Charter* s. 11(d) scrutiny.

Related Provisions: The offences of ss. 369(a)–(c) do *not* require, in all cases, actual use of the prohibited subject-matter to the detriment of V.

The manner in which D may be in possession of anything is described in s. 4(3). "Bank note" and "writing" are defined in s. 2, "exchequer bill paper" and "revenue paper" in s. 321.

Other related offences are described in the corresponding note to s. 366, *supra*.

D may *elect* mode of trial under s. 536(2).

370. Counterfeit proclamation, etc. — Every one who knowingly

(a) prints a proclamation, order, regulation or appointment, or notice thereof, and causes it falsely to purport to have been printed by the Queen's Printer for Canada, or the Queen's Printer for a province, or

(b) tenders in evidence a copy of a proclamation, order, regulation or appointment that falsely purports to have been printed by the Queen's Printer for Canada or the Queen's Printer for a province,

is guilty of an indictable offence and liable to imprisonment for a term not exceeding five years.

R.S., c. C-34, s. 328.

Commentary: The section creates two offences relating to counterfeit proclamations or other defined official documents.

The *external circumstances* under s. 370(a) combine elements of printing and false representation. D must print a proclamation, order, regulation, appointment or notice thereof. D must further cause the subject-matter falsely to purport to have been officially printed. The spurious is printed and represented as genuine.

The *external circumstances* under s. 370(b) relate to a specified use of a copy of what has been described in s. 370(a). It is the tendering of such a spurious and unauthorized document in *evidence* that constitutes the *external circumstances* of the offence.

In each case, P must prove that D's conduct was *knowingly* done. An honest belief in the genuine character of the document would be a defence to the charge. P need *not* prove an intent to defraud or other ulterior mental element to establish liability.

Related Provisions: Fabricating evidence is an offence under s. 137. Forgery is defined in s. 366 and punished in s. 367. Uttering a forged document is an offence under s. 368.

Section 781(2) requires that *judicial notice* be taken of certain proclamations, orders, rules, regulations and by-laws. Provision is also made in ss. 19–22 *C.E.A.* for proof of proclamations, orders, regulations and appointments.

D may *elect* mode of trial under s. 536(2).

371. Telegram, etc., **in false name** — Every one who, with intent to defraud, causes or procures a telegram, cablegram or radio message to be sent or delivered as being sent by the authority of another person, knowing that it is not sent by his authority and with intent that the message should be acted on as being sent by his authority, is guilty of an indictable offence and liable to imprisonment for a term not exceeding five years.

R.S., c. C-34, s. 329.

Commentary: The *external circumstances* are proven where it is shown that D caused or procured a telegram, cablegram or radio message to be sent or delivered, apparently under the authority of another. The *mental element* requires proof that D *intended* to cause the external circumstances of the offence, intended that the message be *acted upon* as *genuine*, knew it was not sent with the authority as described, and intended thereby to defraud.

Related Provisions: The offence of forgery is defined in s. 366 and punished in s. 367. Uttering a forged document is an offence under s. 368.

D may *elect* mode of trial under s. 536(2).

372. (1) False messages — Every one who, with intent to injure or alarm any person, conveys or causes or procures to be conveyed by letter, telegram, telephone, cable, radio or otherwise information that he knows is false is guilty of an indictable offence and liable to imprisonment for a term not exceeding two years.

(2) Indecent telephone calls — Every one who, with intent to alarm or annoy any person, makes any indecent telephone call to that person is guilty of an offence punishable on summary conviction.

(3) Harassing telephone calls — Every one who, without lawful excuse and with intent to harass any person, makes or causes to be made repeated telephone calls to that person is guilty of an offence punishable on summary conviction.

R.S., c. C-34, s. 330.

Commentary: The offences of the section relate to certain types of communications and require proof of a specific or ulterior mental element.

Under s. 372(1), P must prove D conveyed or caused or procured to be conveyed *information*. To "convey" is simply to transmit, communicate, impart or express, in words, information. The *means* of conveyance must be letter, telegram, cable, telephone, radio or "otherwise". The *mental element* requires proof that D *knew* that the information conveyed was *false* and, further, that it was conveyed with *intent to injure or alarm any person*. The "any person" whom D intends to injure or alarm need *not* be the recipient of the false information.

The *external circumstances* of s. 372(2) are that D make an *indecent telephone call* to V. The *mental element* requires proof that such indecent telephone call was made *with intent to alarm or annoy*. An indecent telephone call made to A, intended *only to annoy* B, would escape the prohibition.

Under s. 372(3), the *external circumstances* consist of *repeated telephone calls* which D either makes or causes to be made to V. The calls must be made without lawful excuse. The *mental element* requires proof of the specific *intent to harass* V.

Case Law

R. v. Manicke (1992), 79 C.C.C. (3d) 191 (Sask. Q.B.); affirmed (1993), 81 C.C.C. (3d) 255 (Sask. C.A.) — The offence of s. 372(2) does *not* require that the words spoken be heard contemporaneously with their speech by D. The offence is also made out where D makes the call to V with the *knowledge* that it is being recorded and would later be heard by V.

Related Provisions: D may *elect* mode of trial under s. 536(2) in respect of the offence of s. 372(1). The offences of ss. 372(2) and (3) are tried under Part XXVII and punished under s. 787(1).

Uttering threats is punishable under s. 264.1.

"Radio" is defined in *I.A.* s. 35(1).

373. [Repealed R.S. 1985, c. 27 (1st Supp.), s. 53.]

374. Drawing document without authority, etc. — Every one who

    (a) with intent to defraud and without lawful authority makes, executes, draws, signs, accepts or endorses a document in the name or on the account of another person by procuration or otherwise, or

    (b) makes use of or utters a document knowing that it has been made, executed, signed, accepted or endorsed with intent to defraud and without lawful authority, in the name or on the account of another person, by procuration or otherwise,

is guilty of an indictable offence and liable to imprisonment for a term not exceeding fourteen years.

R.S., c. C-34, s. 332.

Commentary: These offences involve both the creation of a spurious document and its subsequent use.

The *external circumstances* of s. 374(a) are proven where D, *without lawful authority*, makes, executes, draws, signs, accepts or endorses a document in the name or on the account of another whether by procuration, *viz.*, by delegated authority or otherwise. The *mental element* requires proof of an *intent to defraud*.

Section 374(b) is applicable where D, with *knowledge* of the unlawful origins of the document described in s. 374(a), as well as its intended fraudulent use, makes use of or utters the document.

Related Provisions: "Document" is exhaustively defined in s. 321 for the purposes of this Part.

D may *elect* mode of trial under s. 536(2).

For further related provisions, see the corresponding notes to ss. 366–368, *supra*.

375. Obtaining, etc., by instrument based on forged document — Every one who demands, receives or obtains anything, or causes or procures anything to be delivered or paid to any person under, on or by virtue of any instrument issued under the authority of law, knowing that it is based on a forged document, is guilty of an indictable offence and liable to imprisonment for a term not exceeding fourteen years.

R.S., c. C-34, s. 333.

Commentary: This "obtaining" offence is rarely prosecuted.

P must prove that D demanded, received or obtained *anything*, or caused or procured anything to be delivered or paid to any person upon the *basis* of any instrument issued under the authority of law. "Anything" is a word of wide and comprehensive import. Nothing need change hands provided it be demanded by D. If *anything* is delivered or paid, D need *not* be the recipient. The *mental element* requires proof that D *knew* that the legal instrument under which he was acting had itself been based upon a forged document.

Related Provisions: This offence may be compared with the general uttering offence of s. 368(1). Under this provision a forged document has been first used to obtain a legal instrument. The legal instrument, thereby obtained, is itself used to demand or obtain something further.

"Instrument" is not defined for the purposes of this Part or otherwise. "Documents" and "false document" are defined in s. 321, and the latter is further described in s. 366.

D may elect mode of trial under s. 536(2).

376. (1) Counterfeiting stamp, etc. — Every one who

    (a) fraudulently uses, mutilates, affixes, removes or counterfeits a stamp or part thereof,

(b) knowingly and without lawful excuse, the proof of which lies on him, has in his possession

    (i) a counterfeit stamp or a stamp that has been fraudulently mutilated, or

    (ii) anything bearing a stamp of which a part has been fraudulently erased, removed or concealed, or

(c) without lawful excuse, the proof of which lies on him, makes or knowingly has in his possession a die or instrument that is capable of making the impression of a stamp or part thereof,

is guilty of an indictable offence and liable to imprisonment for a term not exceeding fourteen years.

(2) **Counterfeiting mark** — Every one who, without lawful authority,

(a) makes a mark,

(b) sells, or exposes for sale, or has in his possession a counterfeit mark,

(c) affixes a mark to anything that is required by law to be marked, branded, sealed or wrapped other than the thing to which the mark was originally affixed or was intended to be affixed, or

(d) affixes a counterfeit mark to anything that is required by law to be marked, branded, sealed or wrapped,

is guilty of an indictable offence and liable to imprisonment for a term not exceeding fourteen years.

(3) **Definitions** — In this section

"mark" means a mark, brand, seal, wrapper or design used by or on behalf of

(a) the Government of Canada or a province,

(b) the government of a state other than Canada, or

(c) any department, board, commission or agent established by a government mentioned in paragraph (*a*) or (*b*) in connection with the service or business of that government;

"stamp" means an impressed or adhesive stamp used for the purpose of revenue by the Government of Canada or of a province or by the government of a state other than Canada.

R.S., c. C-34, s. 334.

Commentary: The offences of this section relate to the improper use or counterfeiting of *stamps* and *marks*. The critical terms are exhaustively defined in s. 376(3).

The *stamp* offences are described and punished in s. 376(1). The offences of ss. 376(1)(a) and (b) relate specifically to "stamps", as defined in s. 376(3) or counterfeits thereof. The offence of s. 376(1)(c) is more preparatory: it involves the unauthorized use or possession of stamp-making dies or instruments. Any mode of commission of the offence which involves possession as an essential element requires proof by P of D's *knowledge* of the unlawful character of the stamps and shifts the onus of proof of lawful excuse to D, thereby attracting potential *Charter* s, 11(d) scrutiny. The *mental element* which must accompany the *external circumstances* of s. 376(1)(a) requires proof D acted "fraudulently".

The *external circumstances* of the offence relating to *marks* are set out in ss. 376(2)(a)–(c). Proof of *any* of the matters there described will establish the *external circumstances* of the offence. P must also prove in each case that D acted without lawful authority. There is no reversal of the usual onus of proof in respect of this *mental element* under s. 376(2).

Related Provisions: Possession is defined in s. 4(3). Several offences prohibit conduct in relation to public seals and marks, for example, ss. 369(c) and 417(1). Currency offences are described and punished in ss. 448–462.

D may *elect* mode of trial under s. 536(2).

377. (1) Damaging documents — Every one who unlawfully

(a) destroys, defaces or injures a register, or any part of a register of births, baptisms, marriages, deaths or burials that is required or authorized by law to be kept in Canada, or a copy or any part of a copy of such a register that is required by law to be transmitted to a registrar or other officer,

(b) inserts or causes to be inserted in a register or copy referred to in paragraph (*a*) an entry, that he knows is false, of any matter relating to a birth, baptism, marriage, death or burial, or erases any material part from that register or copy,

(c) destroys, damages or obliterates an election document or causes an election document to be destroyed, damaged or obliterated, or

(d) makes or causes to be made an erasure, alteration or interlineation in or on an election document,

is guilty of an indictable offence and liable to imprisonment for a term not exceeding five years.

(2) Definition of "election document" — In this section, "election document" means any document or writing issued under the authority of an Act of Parliament or the legislature of a province with respect to an election held pursuant to the authority of that Act.

R.S., c. C-34, s. 335.

Commentary: The section creates offences relating to official registers and "election documents".

Sections 377(1)(a) and (b) relate to the destruction, defacing or falsification of defined registers, kept to record certain data under legal authority. The *external circumstances* of the offences are described in ss. 377(1)(a) and (b). In general, the *mental element* requires proof of only the intent to cause the *external circumstances*. Under s. 377(1)(b), however, D must *know* that the entry inserted is *false*. An honest belief in its truth would exculpate D.

The offences of ss. 377(1)(c) and (d) relate to "election documents" as defined in s. 377(2). The *external circumstances* are described in the paragraphs. The *mental element* requires proof that D intended to cause them. No ulterior *mental element* need be established.

Related Provisions: Section 378 also prohibits certain conduct in relation to registers.

D may *elect* mode of trial under s. 536(2).

378. Offences in relation to registers — Every one who

(a) being authorized or required by law to make or issue a certified copy of, extract from or certificate in respect of a register, record or document, knowingly makes or issues a false certified copy, extract or certificate,

(b) not being authorized or required by law to make or issue a certified copy of, extract from or certificate in respect of a register, record or document, fraudulently makes or issues a copy, extract or certificate that purports to be certified as authorized or required by law, or

(c) being authorized or required by law to make a certificate or declaration concerning any particular required for the purpose of making entries in a register, record or document, knowingly and falsely makes the certificate or declaration,

is guilty of an indictable offence and liable to imprisonment for a term not exceeding five years.

R.S., c. C-34, s. 336.

Commentary: The section creates and punishes three offences in relation to *registers*. Considerations of accessoryship aside, D must, in each case. fall within a defined class of principal.

Under ss. 378(a) and (c), D must be *authorized* or required by law to make or issue certain documents. P must prove that D has done so *falsely* and *knowingly*, that is to say, in full *knowledge* of the falsity of the copy, extract, certificate or declaration given.

Under s. 378(b), D must *not* be *authorized* or required by law to make or issue a document described in s. 378(a), but nonetheless, make or issue a copy or extract or certificate that purports to be certified as authorized or required by law. The *mental element* is expressed in the term "fraudulently", an element lacking in the offences of ss. 378(a) and (c), but often motivating D's conduct.

The section would appear aimed at preserving the integrity of public registers. Such preservation is to be achieved by making criminal the release of false information as to their contents.

Related Provisions: "Document" is defined in s. 321. "Register" is *not* statutorily defined. In everyday language, it is an official or authoritative record, or books of records, kept by an official appointed for such purpose. In a traditional sense, matters such as births, deaths, and burials are commonly recorded. The term, as used in this section, is left unqualified, *a fortiori*, in light of the specific provisions of s. 377(1)(a) and (b).

D may *elect* mode of trial under s. 536(2).

PART X — FRAUDULENT TRANSACTIONS RELATING TO CONTRACTS AND TRADE

Interpretation

379. Definitions — In this Part,

"goods"means anything that is the subject of trade or commerce;

"trading stamps"includes any form of cash receipt, receipt, coupon, premium ticket or other device, designed or intended to be given to the purchaser of goods by the vendor thereof or on his behalf, and to represent a discount on the price of the goods or a premium to the purchaser thereof

> **(a) that my be redeemed**
>
>> **(i) by any person other than the vendor, the person from whom the vendor purchased the goods or the manufacturer of the goods,**
>>
>> **(ii) by the vendor, the person from whom the vendor purchased the goods or the manufacturer of the goods in cash or in goods that are not his property in whole or in part, or**
>>
>> **(iii) by the vendor elsewhere than in the premises where the goods are purchased, or**
>
> **(b) that does not show on its face the place where it is delivered and the merchantable value thereof, or**
>
> **(c) that may not be redeemed on demand at any time,**

but an offer, endorsed by the manufacturer on a wrapper or container in which goods are sold, of a premium or reward for the return of that wrapper or container to the manufacturer is not a trading stamp.

R.S., c. C-34, s. 337.

Commentary: The section defines "goods" and "trading stamps" for Part X purposes.

Related Provisions: Section 389 prohibits the fraudulent disposal of *goods* upon which money has been advanced. Unlawful dealings in trading stamps are an offence under s. 427.

Fraud

380. (1) Fraud — Every one who, by deceit, falsehood or other fraudulent means, whether or not it is a false pretence within the meaning of this Act, defrauds the public or any person, whether ascertained or not, of any property, money or valuable security or any service.

(a) is guilty of an indictable offence and liable to a term of imprisonment not exceeding ten years, where the subject-matter of the offence is a testamentary instrument or the value of the subject-matter of the offence exceeds five thousand dollars; or

(b) is guilty

(i) of an indictable offence and is liable to imprisonment for a term not exceeding two years, or

(ii) of an offence punishable on summary conviction,

where the value of the subject-matter of the offence does not exceed five thousand dollars.

(2) Affecting public market — Every one who, by deceit, falsehood or other fraudulent means, whether or not it is a false pretence within the meaning of this Act, with intent to defraud, affects the public market price of stocks, shares, merchandise or anything that is offered for sale to the public, is guilty of an indictable offence and liable to imprisonment for a term not exceeding ten years.

R.S., c. C-34, s. 338; 1974–75–76, c. 93, s. 32; R.S. 1985, c. 27 (1st Supp.), s. 54; 1994, c. 44, s. 25; 1997, c. 18, s. 26.

Commentary: The section describes the general offence of *fraud* and creates the specific offence of fraudulently affecting the public market price of stocks, shares, merchandise or anything offered for sale to the public. The essence of fraud is *dishonest deprivation*.

The *external circumstances* of the offence of s. 380(1) consist of several elements. D must *defraud the public or any person, ascertained or not*. V must be defrauded of *property, money, valuable security or any service*. Actual economic loss is *not* an essential element of the offence, though P must prove an actual risk of prejudice to V's economic interest. The fraud must be committed by *deceit, falsehood or other fraudulent means* which need *not be* a "false pretence" within s. 361. The *mental element* requires proof of subjective *knowledge* of the prohibited act and that its performance could have, as a consequence, the deprivation (including the putting at risk of V's pecuniary interests) of another.

The *external circumstances* of the offence of s. 380(2) require proof by P that D, *by deceit falsehood or other fraudulent means*, which need *not* be a "false pretence" under s. 361, *affected the public market price of stocks, shares, merchandise or anything offered for sale to the public*. The *mental element*, in addition to the intent to cause the external circumstances of the offence, involves proof of an *intent to defraud*. The section, designed to protect the investing public against fraudulent stock exchange transactions, is cast in much wider language and is plainly not so limited in its reach.

Case Law
Deceit

R. v. Sebe (1987), 57 C.R. (3d) 348, 35 C.C.C. (3d) 97 (Sask. C.A.) — The words "deceit, falsehood or other fraudulent means" connote an element of subjective or deliberate dishonesty.

Other Fraudulent Means

R. v. Zlatic (1993), 19 C.R. (4th) 230, 79 C.C.C. (3d) 466 (S.C.C.) — Fraud by "other fraudulent means" encompasses *all* other *means* which can properly be stigmatized as *dishonest*. Dishonesty is determined objectively by reference to what a reasonable person would consider to be a dishonest act. The essence of dishonesty is the wrongful use of something in which another has an interest in such a manner that the other's interest is extinguished or put at risk.

R. v. Théroux (1993), 19 C.R. (4th) 194, 79 C.C.C. (3d) 449 (S.C.C.) — As is the case with "deceit" and "falsehood", the external circumstances of fraud by "other fraudulent means" is determined objectively, by reference to what a reasonable person would consider to be a dishonest act.

R. v. Olan (1978), 5 C.R. (3d) 1, 41 C.C.C. (2d) 145 (S.C.C.) — *See also*: *R. v. Cox* (1963), 40 C.R. 52, 2 C.C.C. 148 (S.C.C.); *R. v. Renard* (1974), 17 C.C.C. (2d) 355 (Ont. C.A.) — Proof of deceit is *not* an essential element to support a conviction under subsection (1). The words "other fraudulent means" include means which are *not* in the nature of a falsehood or a deceit: they encompass all other means which can properly be stigmatized as dishonest.

R. v. Gatley (1992), 74 C.C.C. (3d) 468 (B.C. C.A.) — Where P relies on "other fraudulent means", it is *not* sufficient that the jury be instructed that "other fraudulent means" is dishonest conduct and that the jury decide whether what D did was dishonest. The jury should be instructed that they should determine honesty or dishonesty, *not* necessarily in accordance with their own personal views but, rather, in the way they believe the *community* would consider that question.

R. v. Wendel (1992), 78 C.C.C. (3d) 279, [1993] 2 W.W.R. 481 (Man. C.A.) — P is *not* required to establish deceit or misrepresentation to prove fraud under s. 380. Fraud may also be committed by "other fraudulent means" *viz.*, means that are considered dishonest by ordinary people. P must also prove that D was *subjectively aware* of his/her dishonest act.

R. v. Émond (1997), 117 C.C.C. (3d) 276 (Que. C.A.) — "Other fraudulent means" refers to *any* means that can be stigmatized as *dishonest*. The falsehood may consist of a *positive act*, or an *omission*, as for example, through silence about a fundamental and essential matter. The omission must be of such a nature, however, that it would mislead a reasonable person.

R. v. Sebe (1987), 57 C.R. (3d) 348, 35 C.C.C. (3d) 97 (Sask. C.A.) — To constitute "other fraudulent means", the means must have an objective aspect or intrinsic quality of dishonesty. D must also *know* that the acts were dishonest.

Defrauds

R. v. Gaetz (1993), 84 C.C.C. (3d) 351 (S.C.C.); affirming (1992), 77 C.C.C. (3d) 445 (N.S. C.A.) — It is sufficient that V be deprived of that to which it would or might, but for the fraud, be entitled. Fraudulent withholding or diversion of that which is due to V will satisfy the test for fraud.

R. v. Théroux (1993), 19 C.R. (4th) 194, 79 C.C.C. (3d) 449 (S.C.C.) — The *external circumstances* of fraud are established by proof of:

i. a prohibited *act* of deceit, falsehood or other fraudulent means; and,

ii. *deprivation* caused by the prohibited act.

Item ii, *supra*, may consist of *actual* loss or the placing of V's pecuniary interests at *risk*. As is the case with "deceit" and "falsehood", the external circumstances of fraud by "other fraudulent means" is determined objectively, by reference to what a *reasonable* person would consider to be a *dishonest* act.

R. v. Campbell (1986), 29 C.C.C. (3d) 97 (S.C.C.) — *See also*: *R. v. Knelson* (1962), 38 C.R. 181, 133 C.C.C. 210 (B.C. C.A.) — An essential element of fraud is actual *risk* of *prejudice* to the *economic interests* of V. There need *not* be *actual* economic *loss*.

R. v. Olan (1978), 5 C.R. (3d) 1, 41 C.C.C. (2d) 145 (S.C.C.) — There is no exhaustive definition of "defraud". Two elements "dishonesty" and "deprivation" are essential.

Scott v. Commissioner of Police for the Metropolis, [1974] 3 All E.R. 1032 (H.L.) — To defraud is to deprive, by dishonest means, a person of something which is his/hers or to which, but for the fraud, they would be entitled.

London v. Globe Finance Corp., [1900–03] All E.R. 891 (Ch. D.) — *See also*: *R. v. Littler* (1972), 13 C.C.C. (2d) 530 (Que. S.P.); affirmed (1974), 27 C.C.C. (2d) 216 (Que. C.A.) — To *deceive* is to induce a person to believe that a thing is true which is false, and which the person practicing the deceit knows or believes to be false. To *defraud* is to deprive by deceit, or by deceit to induce a person to act to his/her injury. To *deceive* is by falsehood to induce a state of mind, and to defraud is by deceit to induce a course of action.

United States of America v. Schrang (1997), 114 C.C.C. (3d) 553 (B.C. C.A.); application for leave to appeal filed (1997), Doc. No. 25880 (S.C.C.) — Risk of economic loss only occurs when a prospective victim actually transfers assets.

R. v. Long (1990), 61 C.C.C. (3d) 156 (B.C. C.A.) — The *external circumstances* of s. 380(1) consist of dishonest conduct which causes deprivation. Dishonesty is conduct which ordinary, decent people would feel was discreditable, as being clearly at variance with straightforward or honourable dealings. The conduct need *not* also amount to a deceit or falsehood.

R. v. Ruhland (1998), 123 C.C.C. (3d) 262 (Ont. C.A.) — Accounts receivable are debt obligations owed to a person or entity, hence assets of that person or entity. To transfer these receivables from one corporation to another, as security for a loan obtained for D's benefit, constitutes dishonest deprivation.

R. v. Moffat (1988), 30 O.A.C. 4 (C.A.) — *Charter* s. 7 does *not* limit the language of subsection (1) to require proof of a specific and purely subjective intent to defraud.

R. v. Doren (1982), 66 C.C.C. (2d) 448 (Ont. C.A.) — *See also*: *R. v. Thornson* (1977), 39 C.R.N.S. 7, 36 C.C.C. (2d) 171 (Man. C.A.) — Conduct falling short of being the highest standard of straightforward or honourable business dealings will *not* always amount to "dishonesty" for the purposes of the law of fraud.

R. v. Wagman (1981), 60 C.C.C. (2d) 23 (Ont. C.A.) — *See also*: *R. v. Knowles* (1979), 51 C.C.C. (2d) 237 (Ont. C.A.) — A conviction for fraud requires proof of *dishonest deprivation*. Potential *risk of* prejudice is sufficient deprivation. It is *not* essential that there be actual economic loss. Deprivation is made out by proof of detriment, prejudice or risk of prejudice to V's economic interests.

R. v. Lacombe (1990), 60 C.C.C. (3d) 489 (Que. C.A.) — The *external circumstances* of fraud under s. 380(1) require, *inter alia*, that V's deprivation be caused by D's conduct which, by the ordinary standards of reasonable and honest people, would be regarded as dishonest. D must act knowingly and intentionally in the sense of being aware that his conduct would be considered dishonest and result in deprivation. Honesty is a function of community standards, not personal morality.

The Public Or Any Person

R. v. Campbell (1986), 29 C.C.C. (3d) 97 (S.C.C.) — A sole proprietorship is *not*, in and of itself, a person capable of being defrauded.

Vezina v. R. (1986), 49 C.R. (3d) 351, (sub nom. *R. v. Côté*) 23 C.C.C. (3d) 481 — It is *not* necessary to particularize V in a charge of fraud. V may be unascertained.

R. v. Fitzpatrick (1984), 11 C.C.C. (3d) 46 (B.C. C.A.) — *See also*: *R. v. Kirkwood* (1983), 35 C.R. (3d) 97, 5 C.C.C. (3d) 393 (Ont. C.A.) — The offence of fraud by counterfeiting videotapes does *not* require proof of a relationship between D and the owner of a copyright. D must be aware that his dishonest conduct could subject the owner of the copyright to the risk of economic loss.

R. v. Chris (1984), 3 O.A.C. 142 (C.A.) — *See also*: *R. v. Kribbs*, [1968] 1 C.C.C. 345 (Ont. C.A.) — A causal connection between the deception and the loss sustained by V, in this case OHIP, was established where D feigned ailments in order to obtain prescriptions to support his drug addiction. Athough the deceit had been practiced upon the physicians, it had been the operative cause of the loss suffered by OHIP.

Mental Element

R. v. Théroux (1993), 19 C.R. (4th) 194, 79 C.C.C. (3d) 449 (S.C.C.) — The *mental element* of fraud is established by proof of subjective *knowledge*:

i.   of the prohibited act; and,

ii.   that performance of the prohibited act could have as a consequence the deprivation, including the putting at risk of the pecuniary interests, of another.

In some cases, item ii, *supra*, may be inferred from the prohibited act itself, absent some explanation which casts doubt upon the inference.Where the external circumstances and mental element are established, D's guilt is made out, whether D actually intended the deprivation or was reckless as to its occurrence. D's belief that the conduct is not wrong or that no one will be hurt in the end affords *no* defence.

R. v. Zlatic (1993), 19 C.R. (4th) 230, 79 C.C.C. (3d) 466 (S.C.C.) — The *mental element* in fraud by "other fraudulent means" does *not* require that D subjectively appreciated the dishonesty of the relevant acts. D must *knowingly, viz.*, subjectively:

i.   undertake the conduct which constitutes the dishonest act; and,

ii. appreciate that the consequences of such conduct could be deprivation, *viz.*, causing another to lose his/her interest in the property or placing the interest at risk.

R. v. Gatley (1992), 74 C.C.C. (3d) 468 (B.C. C.A.) — D's honest belief that s/he was doing no wrong or lacked fraudulent intent is no defence. Where D is aware of all relevant circumstances and the only issue is whether D's conduct is dishonest, mistake of fact need *not* be left to the jury. The *mental element* of fraud is awareness of the relevant circumstances, but it is for the jury, not D, to characterize D's conduct as dishonest.

R. v. Long (1990), 61 C.C.C. (3d) 156 (B.C. C.A.) — The *mental element* of s. 380(1) is a general intent which is proven when the trier of fact is satisfied that D's conduct was deliberate, in that it was the product of an operating mind with *knowledge* of the relevant facts. An assessment of the mental element is *not* based on what D thought about the honesty or otherwise of his/her conduct, but rather, on what D knew were the facts of the transaction, the circumstances in which it was undertaken and what the consequences might be if carried out. The trier of fact may infer D intended the natural and probable consequences of his/her acts.

R. v. Monk, (February 3, 1988), Doc. Nos. CA 1029/84, CA 102/85 (Ont. C.A.) — A mistake of civil law is a defence to an offence requiring fraudulent intent.

R. v. Lacombe (1990), 60 C.C.C. (3d) 489 (Que. C.A.) — The *mental element* embraces a subjective component similar to that required for theft, i.e., proof that D acted *fraudulently* and *without colour of right*.

Related Provisions: "Deceit", "falsehood" or "other fraudulent means", are *not* statutorily defined. "Property", "testamentary instrument" and "valuable security" are defined in s. 2, and the latter is valued in accordance with s. 4(2). "False pretence" is defined in s. 361. Related offences of which fraud is an essential element are found in ss. 363–365, 381–394 and 396.

Fraud is an "offence" for the purposes of Part VI and an "enterprise crime offence" under Part XII.2.

Special pleading provisions are applicable in fraud cases. Section 583 makes certain omissions of detail not grounds for objection, *provided* the count otherwise complies with the requirements of s. 581. Under s. 586, no fraud count is insufficient by reason only that it does *not* set out in detail the nature of the fraud. Sections 587(1)(b) and (c) permit the ordering of particulars of any alleged fraud, attempt, or conspiracy by fraudulent means. Section 588 assists in allegations and proof of ownership.

Where the property obtained is a testamentary instrument or of a value exceeding $5,000, D will elect mode of trial under s. 536(2). Where the value of what is obtained does *not* exceed $5,000, P will elect mode of procedure. Where P proceeds by indictment, D will be tried by a provincial court judge under s. 553(a)(iv), subject to an order under s. 555(1) or (2). Where P proceeds by summary conviction, D will be tried under Part XXVII, and punished under s. 787(1).

Upon conviction, D may be ordered to pay restitution to V (s. 738) or to a *bona fide* purchaser of property which D has obtained by fraud (s. 739).

381. Using mails to defraud — **Every one who makes use of the mails for the purpose of transmitting or delivering letters or circulars concerning schemes devised or intended to deceive or defraud the public, or for the purpose of obtaining money under false pretences, is guilty of an indictable offence and liable to imprisonment for a term not exceeding two years.**

R.S., c. C-34, s. 339.

Commentary: The section is designed to prohibit the use of a public communications facility, the mail, for *fraudulent* purposes.

The offence requires both *use of the mails* and an ulterior purpose therefor. Use of the mail for the purpose of transmitting or delivering letters or circulars concerning schemes devised or intended to deceive or defraud the public is prohibited. The scheme need *not* be successful, provided the mails have been engaged to publicize the scheme, itself designed or intended to deceive or defraud the public. Equally, the section enjoins use of the mail for the purpose of obtaining money under false pretences, notwithstanding that no money may in fact be obtained thereby.

Related Provisions: Authorization to intercept private communications may be given in respect of this "offence" under Part VI.

Mailing obscene, indecent, immoral or scurrilous matter is an offence under s. 168. Theft from the mail is prohibited by s. 356.

D may *elect* mode of trial under s. 536(2).

For other related substantive, procedural and evidentiary provisions, see the corresponding note to s. 380, *supra*.

382. Fraudulent manipulation of stock exchange transactions — Every one who, through the facility of a stock exchange, curb market or other market, with intent to create a false or misleading appearance of active public trading in a security or with intent to create a false or misleading appearance with respect to the market price of a security,

(a) effects a transaction in the security that involves no change in the beneficial ownership thereof,

(b) enters an order for the purchase of the security, knowing that an order of substantially the same size at substantially the same time and at substantially the same price for the sale of the security has been or will be entered by or for the same or different persons, or

(c) enters an order for the sale of the security, knowing that an order of substantially the same size at substantially the same time and at substantially the same price for the purchase of the security has been or will be entered by or for the same or different persons,

is guilty of an indictable offence and liable to imprisonment for a term not exceeding five years.

R.S., c. C-34, s. 340.

Commentary: The section prohibits what is commonly called "wash trading" or "wash sales".

The *external circumstances* consist of certain transactions through the facility of a stock exchange, curb or other market. The precise transactions which constitute the essence of the external circumstances are described in ss. 382(a)–(c). Section 382(a) encompasses transactions in securities *without changes in their beneficial ownership*. Sections 382(b) and (c) involve the *matching of purchase and sale orders* of substantially the same size, at substantially the same time and price. The entering of purchase and sale orders with substantial correspondence in time, place and quantity is not *per se* a crime.

The *mental element* comprises not only the intention to engage in the transactions which constitute the external circumstances of the offence, but further, the ulterior intent to *create a false or misleading appearance* of either *active public trading in a security or with respect to the market price of the security*. In cases falling within s. 382(b) or (c), D must also *know* of the matching order of the type there described.

Proof of economic loss is *not* an essential element of P's case. The gravamen of the offence consists of the use of prohibited means with the intention to create a false and misleading impression or appearance of actual public interest or with respect to the market price of the security.

Case Law
Mental Element

R. v. MacMillan, [1969] 2 C.C.C. 289 (Ont. C.A.) — Effecting the kind of transactions described in paras. (a)–(c), with either special intent is a fraudulent misrepresentation made to members of the public trading on the Exchange. The transaction need *not* contain any element or be the result of a fraudulent conspiracy to be criminal.

R. v. Jay, [1966] 1 C.C.C. 70 (Ont. C.A.) — The entering of a purchase order and also a sale order corresponding substantially as to time, quantity and price is not *per se* a crime. It must be shown that the orders were made with the *intent* to create a false or misleading appearance of active public trading. The selling of shares for the purpose of stabilizing the market price to one's own advantage is legitimate.

Other Market

Bluestein v. R. (1982), 36 C.R. (3d) 46, 70 C.C.C. (2d) 336 (Que. C.A.) — The over-the-counter market is an "other market" within the meaning of the section. The sale of unlisted securities taking place in a broker's office falls within the section.

Related Provisions: Authorization to intercept private communications may be given in respect of this "offence" under Part VI. It is also an "enterprise crime offence" under Part XII.2.

D may *elect* mode of trial under s. 536(2).

For other related provisions, see the corresponding note to s. 380, *supra*.

---

383. (1) **Gaming in stocks or merchandise** — Every one is guilty of an indictable offence and liable to imprisonment for a term not exceeding five years who, with intent to make gain or profit by the rise or fall in price of the stock of an incorporated or unincorporated company or undertaking, whether in or outside Canada, or of any goods, wares or merchandise,

(a) makes or signs, or authorizes to be made or signed, any contract or agreement, oral or written, purporting to be for the purchase or sale of shares of stock or goods, wares or merchandise, without the *bona fide* intention of acquiring the shares, goods, wares or merchandise or of selling them, as the case may be, or

(b) makes or signs, or authorizes to be made or signed, any contract or agreement, oral or written, purporting to be for the sale or purchase of shares of stock or goods, wares or merchandise in respect of which no delivery of the thing sold or purchased is made or received, and without the *bona fide* intention of making or receiving delivery thereof, as the case may be,

but this section does not apply where a broker, on behalf of a purchaser, receives delivery, notwithstanding that the broker retains or pledges what is delivered as security for the advance of the purchase money or any part thereof.

(2) **Onus** — Where, in proceedings under this section, it is established that the accused made or signed a contract or an agreement for the sale or purchase of shares of stock or goods, wares or merchandise, or acted, aided or abetted in the making or signing thereof, the burden of proof of a *bona fide* intention to acquire or to sell the shares, goods, wares or merchandise or to deliver or to receive delivery thereof, as the case may be, lies on the accused.

R.S., c. C-34, s. 341.

Commentary: The section was enacted to suppress the operation of "bucket shops", establishments conducted nominally for the transaction of a stock exchange or similar business, but in reality, for the registration of bets or wagers for small amounts on the rise or fall of the prices of stock or other commodities. There is neither transfer nor delivery of the stock or commodity in which the nominal dealings were conducted.

In general, the *external circumstances* consist of the making or authorizing of any contract or agreement, purporting to be for the sale or purchase of shares of stock or goods, wares or merchandise, *without* the acquisition or disposal of such items. The *mental element* comprises not only the intent to enter into such an agreement without the *bona fide* intention of acquisition or disposal, but further, the specific or ulterior intent to make gain or profit by the rise or fall in price of the stock, goods, wares, or merchandise.

P's proof of the absence of *bona fide* intention to acquire, sell or deliver the shares, goods, wares or merchandise, is assisted by s. 383(2), which, upon *proof* that D made or signed or acted, aided or abetted in the making or signing of a contract or agreement, shifts the onus of proving *bona fides* to D. Put shortly, proof of a prohibited agreement or participation therein raises a *rebuttable presumption* of unlawful *intention*, an essential element of P's proof. This provision may attract *Charter* s. 11(d) scrutiny.

The section is inapplicable where a *broker* receives delivery on behalf of a purchaser, even though a broker may retain or pledge what it delivered as security for the advance of the purchase money.

Related Provisions: "Goods" are defined in s. 379. "Broker" is *not* defined. Ordinarily, it refers to one employed as a middleman to transact business, in particular, one who, for compensation, acts as an agent of a buyer or seller to buy or sell stock, bonds, commodities or services, usually on a commission basis. Provincial securities legislation generally requires that brokers be licensed.

D may *elect* mode of trial under s. 536(2).

For related evidentiary, procedural and substantive provisions, see the corresponding note to s. 380, *supra*.

384. Broker reducing stock by selling for his own account — Every one is guilty of an indictable offence and liable to imprisonment for a term not exceeding five years who, being an individual, or a member or an employee of a partnership, or a director, an officer or an employee of a corporation, where he or the partnership or corporation is employed as a broker by any customer to buy and carry on margin any shares of an incorporated or unincorporated company or undertaking, whether in or out of Canada, thereafter sells or causes to be sold shares of the company or undertaking for any account in which

(a) he or his firm or a partner thereof, or

(b) the corporation or a director thereof,

has a direct or indirect interest, if the effect of the sale is, otherwise than unintentionally, to reduce the amount of those shares in the hands of the broker or under his control in the ordinary course of business below the amount of those shares that the broker should be carrying for all customers.

R.S., c. C-34, s. 342.

Commentary: This particular species of fraud was enacted to protect the purchasers of shares or stocks on margin.

The *external circumstances* consist of several elements. As principal, D must be employed as a *broker* by any customer to buy and carry on margin shares of a company or undertaking. The company may be incorporated or unincorporated, and it or its undertaking in or out of Canada. D may act as a broker in an individual capacity, or as a member or an employee of a partnership, or a director, officer or employee of a corporation. D must thereafter sell or cause to be sold the shares bought and carried on margin for any account in which D, D's firm, partner, corporation or a director thereof has a direct or indirect interest. The *effect* of the sale must be the reduction of the amount of those shares in the hands of the broker or under the broker's control in the ordinary course of business below the amount of those shares that the broker should be carrying for all customers.

The *mental element* requires proof that D intentionally reduced the amount of shares below the necessary minimum.

Related Provisions: D may elect mode of trial under s. 536(2).

Other related provisions are discussed in the corresponding note to s. 380, *supra*.

385. (1) Fraudulent concealment of title documents — Every one who, being a vendor or mortgagor of property or of a chose in action or being a solicitor for or agent of a vendor or mortgagor of property or a chose in action, is served with a written demand for an abstract of title by or on behalf of the purchaser or mortgagee before the completion of the purchase or mortgage, and who

(a) with intent to defraud and for the purpose of inducing the purchaser or mortgagee to accept the title offered or produced to him, conceals from him any settlement, deed, will or other instrument material to the title, or any encumbrance on the title, or

(b) falsifies any pedigree on which the title depends,

is guilty of an indictable offence and liable to imprisonment for a term not exceeding two years.

(2) Consent required — No proceedings shall be instituted under this section without the consent of the Attorney General.

R.S., c. C-34, s. 343.

Commentary: This section prohibits fraudulent transactions or conduct in respect of real property or documents of title thereto. The *consent* of the *Attorney General* of the *province* in which the proceedings arise is required under s. 385(2) to prevent frivolous prosecutions.

The *external circumstances* of the offence of s. 385(1) require that, as principal, D be a vendor or mortgagor of property or a chose in action or act as a solicitor or agent for such a person. D must be served with a written demand for an abstract of title to the property by or on behalf of the purchaser or mortgagee before the completion of the purchase or mortgage. D must either conceal from the purchaser or mortgagee any instruments material to or encumbrances on the title, or falsify any pedigree on which title depends.

Under s. 385(1)(a), the *mental element*, in addition to proof of the intention to cause the external circumstances of the offence, requires proof of *both* an *intent to defraud* and *a prohibited purpose*, namely, to induce the purchaser or mortgagee to accept the tide offered or produced. There is no such requirement under s. 385(1)(b) where the *mental element* is *not* ulterior to the external circumstances of the offence.

Related Provisions: Falsification of pedigree may or may not require that false entries be made in an account or register of a line of ancestors. Offences relating to registers are described in ss. 377–378, *supra*.

D may *elect* mode of trial under s. 536(2).

For related provisions, see the corresponding note to s. 380, *supra*.

386. Fraudulent registration of title — Every one who, as principal or agent, in a proceeding to register title to real property, or in a transaction relating to real property that is or is proposed to be registered, knowingly and with intent to deceive,

(a) makes a material false statement or representation,

(b) suppresses or conceals from a judge or registrar, or any person employed by or assisting the registrar, any material document, fact, matter or information, or

(c) is privy to anything mentioned in paragraph (*a*) or (*b*),

is guilty of an indictable offence and liable to imprisonment for a term not exceeding five years.

R.S., c. C-34, s. 344.

Commentary: The essence of this offence lies in the *fraudulent registration of title* to real property, *not* in the nature of the underlying transaction which is registered.

The *external circumstances* require proof that D was acting, as a principal or agent, in a proceeding to register title to real property, or in a transaction relating to real property that is or is proposed to be registered. The remaining elements of the external circumstances are described in ss. 386(a) and (b). Both need not be proven. Either will suffice. D may also be liable if privy to anything described in either s. 386(a) or (b).

In addition to the intention to cause the external circumstances of the offences, whether as principal or privy, D must be shown to have done so *knowingly and with intent to deceive*.

Case Law

External Circumstances

R. v. Sonntag, (October 10, 1991), Doc. No. 1168/88 (Ont. C.A.) — A false representation of the amount of consideration specified in the affidavits required by the *Land Transfer Tax Act* falls within the scope of "in a transaction relating to real property that is or is proposed to be registered". Under s. 386(a), P is *not* required to prove that there has been, in fact, a dishonest deprivation.

Related Provisions: Sections 385 and 387 also describe offences relating to the sale or mortgage of real property.

The phrase "is privy to", in s. 386(c), is *not* defined in the section nor elsewhere in the *Code*. In general, one is "privy to" the actions or conduct of another if one partakes or has any part or interest in such action, conduct matter or thing. The term would seem to comprehend, at least, the traditional notions of accessoryship found in ss. 21 and 22.

D may elect mode of trial under s. 536(2).

Related provisions are discussed in the corresponding note to s. 380, *supra*.

387. Fraudulent sale of real property — Every one who, knowing of an unregistered prior sale or of an existing unregistered grant, mortgage, hypothec, privilege or encumbrance of or on real property, fraudulently sells the property or any part thereof is guilty of an indictable offence and liable to imprisonment for a term not exceeding two years.

R.S., c. C-34, s. 345.

Commentary: This section prohibits the *fraudulent sale of real property*.

The *external circumstances* consist of the sale of real property or any part thereof. The *mental element* requires proof of a specific *knowledge* on the part of D, namely, of an unregistered prior sale or of an existing unregistered grant, mortgage, hypothec, privilege or encumbrance of or on the subject real property.

Case Law
Sale

Lawrence v. R. (1949), 9 C.R. 5 (Que. C.A.) — A sale includes a contract for the transfer of property from one person to another for valuable consideration.

Related Provisions: Sections 385 and 386 also describe offences relating to the sale or mortgage of real property. D may *elect* mode of trial under s. 536(2).

The corresponding note to s. 380, *supra*, describes related provisions.

388. Misleading receipt — Every one who wilfully

    (a) with intent to mislead, injure or defraud any person, whether or not that person is known to him, gives to a person anything in writing that purports to be a receipt for or an acknowledgment of property that has been delivered to or received by him, before the property referred to in the purported receipt or acknowledgment has been delivered to or received by him, or

    (b) accepts, transmits or uses a purported receipt or acknowledgment to which paragraph (*a*) applies,

is guilty of an indictable offence and liable to imprisonment for a term not exceeding two years.

R.S., c. C-34, s. 346.

Commentary: The *external circumstances* of this offence occur when D gives to another anything *in writing* that purports to be a receipt for or acknowledgement of property that has been delivered to or received by D. The writing need *not* be in any particular commercial form. Its purport must be as described in s. 388(a). The property described as delivered to or received by D must *not* have been so at the time of the giving of the writing to V. Under s. 388(a), as principal, D must be the person who gives the purported receipt of acknowledgment. Under s. 388(b), as principal D must accept, transmit or use a receipt or acknowledgment described in s. 388(a). In other words, s. 388(a) relates to the donor, s. 388(b) to the recipient of the fraudulent receipt or acknowledgment.

The *mental element* involves the intention to cause the external circumstances of the offence *wilfully*. Under s. 388(b), this would include *knowledge* of the character of the purported receipt or acknowledgement. Section 388(a) also requires proof of an ulterior mental element, namely, the intent to mislead, injure or defraud any person. The object of this intention need *not* be the person to whom the spurious document has been given. This ulterior mental element is neither expressly nor impliedly carried into the offence described in s. 388(b).

Related Provisions: Closely related provisions appear in s. 390.

Under s. 391, special provision is made where an offence under this section has been committed by D acting in the name of a corporation, firm or partnership. It is only the *person who actually does the act* and anyone who is *secretly privy to the doing of such act* who are liable. The phrase "secretly privy" is *not* defined, but connotes participation in the act in a clandestine or concealed way. "Secretly", at all events, adds a notion of secrecy to the accessoryship.

D may *elect* mode of trial under s. 536(2).

Other related provisions are discussed in the corresponding note to s. 380, *supra*.

389. (1) Fraudulent disposal of goods on which money advanced — Every one who

(a) having shipped or delivered to the keeper of a warehouse or to a factor, an agent or a carrier anything on which the consignee thereof has advanced money or has given valuable security, thereafter, with intent to deceive, defraud or injure the consignee, disposes of it in a manner that is different from and inconsistent with any agreement that has been made in that behalf between him and the consignee, or

(b) knowingly and wilfully aids or assists any person to make a disposition of anything to which paragraph (*a*) applies for the purpose of deceiving, defrauding or injuring the consignee,

is guilty of an indictable offence and liable to imprisonment for a term not exceeding two years.

(2) Saving — No person is guilty of an offence under this section where, before disposing of anything in a manner that is different from and inconsistent with any agreement that has been made in that behalf between him and the consignee, he pays or tenders to the consignee the full amount of money or valuable security that the consignee has advanced.

R.S., c. C-34, s. 347.

Commentary: This specific fraud offence contains its own accessoryship provisions.

The *exteral circumstances* of s. 389(1)(a) require that D ship or deliver to a warehouse keeper, factor, agent or carrier, anything on which the consignee has advanced money or given security. After shipping or delivery, D must then dispose of the subject-matter in a manner that is different from *and* inconsistent with the agreement with the consignee. The disposal need *not* be in any particular manner, for example by sale or delivery to another party, but must be otherwise than and inconsistent with the agreement between D and the consignee. This intentional conduct by D in disposing of the property must be with the further intent to deceive, defraud or injure the consignee. "Injure", in this sense, connotes the doing of harm or damage to V.

Under s. 389(1)(b), specific provision is made for *accessorial liability*. The *external circumstances* are complete where D aids or assists another to make a disposition of anything to which s. 389(a) applies. The *mental element* has two components. D must *knowingly and wilfully* render the aid or assistance which constitutes the external circumstances of the offence. In addition, D must do so for the ulterior purpose of deceiving, defrauding or injuring the consignee.

Related Provisions: "Valuable security" is defined in s. 2.

General accessoryship provisions are found in ss. 21 and 22. Under s. 391, it is necessary in cases were D is acting in the name of a corporation, firm or partnership to establish that D actually did the act by means of which the offence was committed, namely, disposed of the property in a prohibited manner, or was secretly privy to it.

Related offences are described in ss. 388 and 390. Other related substantive, procedural and evidentiary provisions are described in the corresponding note to s. 380, *supra*. D may elect mode of trial under s. 536(2).

390. Fraudulent receipts under Bank Act — **Every one is guilty of an indictable offence and liable to imprisonment for a term not exceeding two years who**

    (a) wilfully makes a false statement in any receipt, certificate or acknowledgment for anything that may be used for a purpose mentioned in the *Bank Act*; or

    (b) wilfully,

        (i) after giving to another person,

        (ii) after a person employed by him has, to his knowledge, given to another person, or

        (iii) after obtaining and endorsing or assigning to another person,

any receipt, certificate or acknowledgment for anything that may be used for a purpose mentioned in the *Bank Act*, without the consent in writing of the holder or endorsee or the production and delivery of the receipt, certificate or acknowledgment, alienates or parts with, or does not deliver to the holder or owner the property mentioned in the receipt, certificate or acknowledgment.

R.S., c. C-34, s. 348.

Commentary: The section deals specifically with receipts and similar documents which may be used for a purpose mentioned in the *Bank Act*, as for example, the advancement of monies upon the security of warehouse receipts, bills of lading and other valuable securities.

The *external circumstances* in s. 390(a), in essence, consist of the making of a false statement in the receipt or similar document, whereas under s. 390(b), it is the disposal or non-delivery of the property described therein. The *mental element* in each case consists of the *wilful* causing of the external circumstances of the offence.

Case Law

R. v. Dubois (1979), 45 C.C.C. (2d) 531 (Ont. C.A.) — The expression "receipt, certificate or acknowledgment for anything that may be used for a purpose mentioned in the *Bank Act*" refers to documents acquired as collateral security that are evidence of title to property and that may be transferred by endorsement or delivery. This section does *not* make it an offence to make a false statement in any document that may be used in relation to the business of the bank.

Related Provisions: "Receipt", "certificate" and "acknowledgment" are not defined in the *Code*, but are words of common usage. "Property" is expansively defined in s. 2.

Under s. 391, it is necessary in cases where D is acting in the name of a corporation, firm or partnership to establish that D actually did the act by means of which the offence was committed, that is to say, made the false statement or disposed of or failed to deliver the property, or was secretly privy to it.

Related offences are described in ss. 388 and 389 and related substantive, evidentiary and procedural provisions in the corresponding note to s. 380.

D may *elect* mode of trial under s. 536(2).

391. Saving — **Where an offence is committed under section 388, 389 or 390 by a person who acts in the name of a corporation, firm or partnership, no person other**

than the person who does the act by means of which the offence is committed or who is secretly privy to the doing of that act is guilty of the offence.

R.S., c. C-34, s. 349.

Commentary: This accessoryship provision applies *only* to the special forms of agency in ss. 388–390.

Where D's conduct is *not* in his/her personal capacity, but rather as an agent, liability shall only be established where P proves that D did the act by means of which the offence charged was committed or was secretly privy thereto. Although "secretly", forms *no* part of the general accessoryship provisions of ss. 21 and 22, it would appear somewhat more limitative than is the general rule in accessoryship cases.

Related Provisions: The *Commentary* to ss. 388–390, describes the essential elements of each offence to which this section applies.

392. Disposal of property to defraud creditors — Every one who,

(a) **with intent to defraud his creditors,**

    (i) **makes or causes to be made any gift, conveyance, assignment, sale, transfer or delivery of his property, or**

    (ii) **removes, conceals or disposes of any of his property, or**

(b) **with intent that any one should defraud his creditors, receives any property by means of or in relation to which an offence has been committed under paragraph (*a*),**

is guilty of an indictable offence and liable to imprisonment for a term not exceeding two years.

R.S., c. C-34, s. 350.

Commentary: These offences prohibit the *disposal of property to defraud creditors*, not only by the debtor, but also by those who, in the circumstances described, receive property from the debtor.

The *external circumstances* of the debtor's offence in s. 392(a) consist of the *disposal* by the debtor of any or all of its property in a manner described. The *mental element* consists of the intention to so dispose of the property, with the further or ulterior intent to *defraud* his/her creditors. The reference to *creditors* does not include "or any of them".

The *receiver's* offence in s. 392(b), demands proof that D *received* any property by means of or in relation to which an offence has been committed by the debtor under s. 392(a). The *mental element* requires that D intended to receive the property and, in accord with general principle, that D knew of or was reckless as to the unlawful origins of the property. Finally, D must further intend that anyone, as for example the debtor, should defraud his/her creditors.

Case Law
Assignment

R. v. Ehresman (1979), 31 C.B.R. (N.S.) 209 (B.C. Co. Ct.); affirmed (1980), 58 C.C.C. (2d) 574 (B.C. C.A.) — The granting of a third mortgage to a friend for *no* consideration was an "assignment" with intent to defraud creditors.

"Conceals"

R. v. Goulis (1981), 20 C.R. (3d) 360 (Ont. C.A.) — "Conceals" requires a positive act done for the purpose of secreting the debtor's property, *not* mere non-disclosure of assets.

Related Provisions: This section originally preceded the enactment of any Federal bankruptcy legislation and read "defraud his creditors *or any of them*". In general, the *Bankruptcy Act*, R.S.C. 1985, c. B-2, only becomes engaged where there is a bankruptcy, whether by receiving order, petition or authorized assignment. Certain conduct by a *bankrupt* may attract liability and be prosecuted under both the *Act* and the *Code*. Where the conduct is not that of a bankrupt, s. 392 may apply.

"Property" is defined in s. 2 and given no more specific or restricted meaning in this Part. "Receives", in its normal everyday usage, means to get or come into possession of a particular subject-matter.

Fraudulent concealment is an offence under s. 341. The offence of s. 397(2) makes special reference to the intent to defraud creditors.

Other related provisions are described in the corresponding note to s. 380, *supra*.

D may *elect* mode of trial under s. 536(2).

393. (1) Fraud in relation to fares, etc. — Every one whose duty it is to collect a fare, toll, ticket or admission who wilfully

    (a) fails to collect it,

    (b) collects less than the proper amount payable in respect thereof, or

    (c) accepts any valuable consideration for failing to collect it or for collecting less than the proper amount payable in respect thereof,

is guilty of an indictable offence and liable to imprisonment for a term not exceeding two years.

(2) Idem — Every one who gives or offers to a person whose duty it is to collect a fare, toll, ticket or admission fee, any valuable consideration

    (a) for failing to collect it, or

    (b) for collecting an amount less than the amount payable in respect thereof,

is guilty of an indictable offence and liable to imprisonment for a term not exceeding two years.

(3) Fraudulently obtaining transportation — Every one who, by any false pretence or fraud, unlawfully obtains transportation by land, water or air is guilty of an offence punishable on summary conviction.

R.S., c. C-34, s. 351.

Commentary: This section describes and punishes three separate, albeit related, species of fraud.

Under s. 393(1), as principal, D must be under a *duty to collect* a fare, toll, ticket or admission. The *external circumstances* consist of D's failure to collect, collection of less or acceptance of valuable consideration for failing to collect or collecting less than the amount payable. D's conduct, a breach of duty, must be "wilful".

Under s. 393(2), as principal, D must be a *patron or customer*. The *external circumstances* consist of the giving or offering of valuable consideration by D to a fare, toll, ticket or admission collector for a purpose described in s. 393(2)(a) or (b). The *mental element* consists of the intention to cause the external circumstances.

The offence of s. 393(3) requires that D *obtain transportation* by land, water or air. The means whereby such transportation was obtained must be fraud or a false pretence. No ulterior *mental element* is specifically required by the section, although one would seem inherent in the use of fraud or a false pretence.

Related Provisions: Sections 393(1) and (2) deal with the offences of employees who fail in a specified duty, as well as those who are parties to such failure. Each would appear to be a party to the other's offence, at all events, upon general principles of accessorial liability under s. 21 or 22. The failure of the collector to turn over to his/her employer the money collected is not an offence under this section, but would be under s. 330(1). The giving or receipt of valuable consideration may also amount to an offence under ss. 426(1)(a) and (2).

The offences of ss. 393(1) and (2) fall within the *absolute* trial jurisdiction of a provincial court judge under s. 553(c)(viii), irrespective of the amount involved, subject to an order under s. 555(1).

The offence of s. 393(3) is tried in accordance with Part XXVII.

394. (1) **Fraud in relation to valuable minerals** — No person who is the holder of a lease or licence issued under an Act relating to the mining of valuable minerals, or by the owner of land that is supposed to contain valuable minerals, shall

   (a) by a fraudulent device or contrivance, defraud or attempt to defraud any person of

      (i) any valuable minerals obtained under or reserved by the lease or licence, or

      (ii) any money or valuable interest or thing payable in respect of valuable minerals obtained or rights reserved by the lease or licence; or

   (b) fraudulently conceal or make a false statement with respect to the amount of valuable minerals obtained under the lease or licence.

(2) **Sale of valuable minerals** — No person, other than the owner or the owner's agent or someone otherwise acting under lawful authority, shall sell any valuable mineral that is unrefined, partly refined, uncut or otherwise unprocessed.

(3) **Purchase of valuable minerals** — No person shall buy any valuable mineral that is unrefined, partly refined, uncut or otherwise unprocessed from anyone who the person has reason to believe is not the owner or the owner's agent or someone otherwise acting under lawful authority.

(4) **Presumption** — In any proceeding in relation to subsection (2) or (3), in the absence of evidence raising a reasonable doubt to the contrary, it is presumed that

   (a) in the case of a sale, the seller is not the owner of the valuable mineral or the owner's agent or someone otherwise acting under lawful authority; and

   (b) in the case of a purchase, the purchaser, when buying the valuable mineral, had reason to believe that the seller was not the owner of the mineral or the owner's agent or someone otherwise acting under lawful authority.

(5) **Offence** — A person who contravenes subsection (1), (2) or (3) is guilty of an indictable offence and liable to imprisonment for a term of not more than five years.

(6) **Forfeiture** — If a person is convicted of an offence under this section, the court may order anything by means of or in relation to which the offence was committed, on such conviction, to be forfeited to Her Majesty.

(7) **Exception** — Subsection (6) does not apply to real property other than real property built or significantly modified for the purpose of facilitating the commission of an offence under this section.

R.S., c. C-34, s. 352; R.S. 1985, c. 27 (1st Supp.), s. 186; 1999, c. 5, s. 10.

Commentary: Sections 394–396 enact substantive, evidentiary and procedural provisions respecting *fraud in relation to mines and minerals.*

Under s. 394(1)(a), as principal, D must be a lease or licence holder, as described, whose conduct amounts to the several elements of the *external circumstances.* D must defraud or attempt to defraud V of any precious metal or money payable or reserved by the lease or licence. The fraud or attempt must be by a fraudulent device or contrivance. Alternatively, P may prove that D fraudulently concealed or made a false statement with respect to the amount of precious metals D procured. The *mental element* is the intention to cause the external circumstances.

The offence of s. 394(1)(b) proscribes the sale or purchase of a rock, mineral or other substance that contains precious metals in the described state. The *mental element* consists of the intention to purchase or sell the proscribed subject-matter. The requirement that D establish lawful authority for the purchase or sale has failed *Charter* s. 11(d) scrutiny.

541

Under s. 394(1)(c), the gravamen of the offence consists of *possession* of defined subject-matter. The *external circumstances* require proof that D had in his/her possession, or on his/her premises, any of the items described in ss. 394(1)(c)(i)–(iii). There must be *reasonable grounds to believe* that the subject-matter has been *stolen* or otherwise dealt with contrary to the section. The *mental element* involves D's intention to possess, or knowledge that the subject-matter is on D's premises, together with his/her *knowledge* of its unlawful nature.

The statutory shift in the onus of proof of lawful authority, with its necessary implication of absence of such authority upon proof of possession, sale or purchase, as the case may be, may attract *Charter* s. 11(d) scrutiny.

Under s. 394(2), there is a discretionary authority, upon conviction, to order forfeiture of anything by means of or in relation to which the offence was committed.

Case Law

R. v. Laba (1994), 94 C.C.C. (3d) 385, 34 C.R. (4th) 360, 25 C.R.R. (2d) 92, 120 D.L.R. (4th) 175, 174 N.R. 34, 76 O.A.C. 241 (S.C.C.); reversing in part (1992), 12 O.R. (3d) 239 (Ont. C.A.) — The reverse onus clause in s. 394(1)(b) violates *Charter* s. 11(d) and cannot be saved by s. 1.The appropriate remedy is to strike down the *persuasive* burden and read in words to *substitute* an *evidentiary* burden. The clause "unless he establishes that..." should be struck down and "in the absence of evidence which *raises a reasonable doubt*" read in.

Related Provisions: Possession is determined under s. 4(3). Neither "precious metal" nor "mineral" is defined in the *Code*. Section 4(4) allows the meaning assigned to such terms in another Act to be used in determining their meaning under the *Code*.

Section 396 creates a further offence relating to mines, and s. 341, a general offence of fraudulent concealment. Section 395 provides a procedure whereby a warrant may be issued to search places or persons and seize precious metals.

Other related provisions are described in the corresponding note to s. 380, *supra*.

D may *elect* mode of trial under s. 536(2).

394.1 (1) Possession of stolen or fraudulently obtained valuable minerals — No person shall possess any valuable mineral that is unrefined, partly refined, uncut or otherwise unprocessed that has been stolen or dealt with contrary to section 394.

(2) Evidence — Reasonable grounds to believe that the valuable mineral has been stolen or dealt with contrary to section 394 are, in the absence of evidence raising a reasonable doubt to the contrary, proof that the valuable mineral has been stolen or dealt with contrary to section 394.

(3) Offence — A person who contravenes subsection (1) is guilty of an indictable offence and liable to imprisonment for a term of not more than five years.

(4) Forfeiture — If a person is convicted of an offence under this section, the court may, on that conviction, order that anything by means of or in relation to which the offence was committed be forfeited to Her Majesty.

(5) Exception — Subsection (4) does not apply to real property, other than real property built or significantly modified for the purpose of facilitating the commission of an offence under subsection (3).

1999, c. 5, s. 10.

395. (1) Search for valuable minerals — If an information in writing is laid under oath before a justice by a peace officer or by a public officer who has been appointed or designated to administer or enforce a federal or provincial law and whose duties include the enforcement of this Act or any other Act of Parliament and the jus-

tice is satisfied that there are reasonable grounds to believe that, contrary to this Act or any other Act of Parliament, any valuable mineral is deposited in a place or held by a person, the justice may issue a warrant authorizing a peace officer or a public officer, if the public officer is named in it, to search any of the places or persons mentioned in the information.

(2) **Power to seize** — Where, on search, anything mentioned in subsection (1) is found, it shall be seized and carried before the justice who shall order

    (a) that it be detained for the purposes of an inquiry or a trial; or

    (b) if it is not detained for the purposes of an inquiry or a trial,

        (i) that it be restored to the owner, or

        (ii) that it be forfeited to Her Majesty in right of the province in which the proceedings take place if the owner cannot be ascertained.

(3) **Appeal** — An appeal lies from an order made under paragraph (2)(*b*) in the manner in which an appeal lies in summary conviction proceedings under Part XXVII and the provisions of that Part relating to appeals apply to appeals under this subsection.

R.S., c. C-34, s. 353; 1999, c. 5, s. 11.

Commentary: The section authorizes the issuance of a *warrant to search for and seize precious metals*, in a natural or refined state.

Under s. 395(1), an *information in writing and under oath* must be presented to a justice. The informant must be a person who has an interest in a mining claim and must swear that a precious metal, rock, mineral or other substance containing precious metals is unlawfully deposited in any place or held by any person contrary to law. No statutory form of information is prescribed. The subsection does *not* require that the informant's belief be reasonably grounded, nor that such grounds as may exist for the asserted belief be displayed in the information to obtain the warrant. The justice is given a *discretion* to issue a warrant to search any of the places or persons mentioned in the information. No form is prescribed for the warrant.

Section 395(2) provides for the *seizure* of precious metals, rock, mineral or other substance containing precious metals upon search, their *return* before the issuing justice, and the orders that may be made upon such return. Where forfeiture or restoration to the owner is ordered under s. 395(2)(b), an appeal lies under s. 395(3), in accordance with Part XXVII.

Related Provisions: The general provisions relating to search warrants are found in s. 487. The information to obtain such a warrant is in Form 1, the warrant itself may be in Form 5.

Two separate rights of appeal exist under Part XXVII. Further appeals may be taken to the court of appeal under s. 839(1), with leave, on a question of law alone.

The provisions apply to the offence of s. 394 and, *semble*, would assist in the gathering of evidence for a prosecution under s. 396, *infra*.

396. (1) Offences in relation to mines — Every one who

    (a) adds anything to or removes anything from any existing or prospective mine, mining claim or oil well with a fraudulent intent to affect the result of an assay, a test or a valuation that has been made or is to be made with respect to the mine, mining claim or oil well, or

    (b) adds anything to, removes anything from or tampers with a sample or material that has been taken or is being or is about to be taken from any existing or prospective mine, mining claim or oil well for the purpose of being assayed, tested or otherwise valued, with a fraudulent intent to affect the result of the assay, test or valuation,

is guilty of an indictable offence and liable to imprisonment for a term not exceeding ten years.

(2) Presumption — For the purposes of proceedings under subsection (1), evidence that

    (a) something has been added to or removed from anything to which subsection (1) applies, or

    (b) anything to which subsection (1) applies has been tampered with,

is, in the absence of any evidence to the contrary, proof of a fraudulent intent to affect the result of an assay, test or a valuation.

R.S., c. C-34, s. 354.

Commentary: The section deals with the practices of "highgrading" and "salting".

The *external circumstances* under s. 396(1)(a) are complete where D *adds or removes* anything from an existing or prospective mine, mining claim or oil well. The *mental element* requires that D cause the external circumstances with the fraudulent intent to affect the result of an assay, test or valuation that had been made or is to be made with the respect to the mine, mining claim or oil well.

Under s. 396(1)(b), the *external circumstances* consist of the addition to, removal from or tampering with a sample or material which has been, is being or is about to be taken from any existing or prospective mine, mining claim or oil well to be assayed, tested or otherwise valued. The *mental element*, ulterior to the intention to cause the external circumstances, requires proof of a fraudulent intent to affect the result of the assay, test or valuation.

Section 396(2) enacts a *rebuttable presumption* of fact to assist P in proof of the requisite *mental element*. The introduction of *evidence* of adulteration of the sample, by addition, removal or tampering, *proves* the requisite fraudulent *intent, absent evidence to the contrary*. The provision may attract *Charter* s. 11(d) review.

Related Provisions: Section 394 creates a related offence of fraud in relation to minerals, and s. 341, the general offence of fraudulent concealment. The general fraud offence is described in s. 380(1). The corresponding note to s. 380 discusses substantive, evidentiary and procedural provisions applicable in fraud prosecutions.

Specific authority to search persons and places for precious metals is conferred by s. 395.

D may *elect* mode of trial under s. 536(2).

Falsification of Books and Documents

397. (1) Books and documents — Every one who, with intent to defraud,

    (a) destroys, mutilates, alters, falsifies, or makes a false entry in, or

    (b) omits a material particular from, or alters a material particular in, a book, paper, writing, valuable security or document is guilty of an indictable offence and liable to imprisonment for a term not exceeding five years.

(2) Privy — Every one who, with intent to defraud his creditors, is privy to the commission of an offence under subsection (1) is guilty of an indictable offence and liable to imprisonment for a term not exceeding five years.

R.S., c. C-34, s. 355.

Commentary: The section generally prohibits the destruction, alteration or falsification of certain documents or records with *intent to defraud* and provides for accessorial liability in specific terms.

The offence of s. 397(1) requires proof that D did anything described in s. 397(1)(a) or (b) in relation to a book, paper, writing, valuable security or document. The ulterior *mental element*, "with intent to defraud", is unrestricted as to V. It would seem, in most instances, that V would be a person who has placed reliance on a falsified or altered documents.

Section 397(2) affixes liability upon D as a principal, where s/he is privy to an offence under s. 397(1) with the specific intent to defraud his/her creditors. "Creditors" formerly included "or any of them".

Related Provisions: "Writing" and "valuable security" are defined in s. 2. The general accessory-ship provisions of ss. 21 and 22 would seem included in "privy" in s. 397(2).

The making of a false document is forgery within s. 366 and its use, "uttering", under s. 368. There is some further overlap between this offence and false pretences (s. 362), fraud (s. 380) and the more specific offences of ss. 363, 392 and 401. See the corresponding notes to those sections.

D may *elect* mode of trial under s. 536(2).

398. Falsifying employment record — Every one who, with intent to deceive, falsifies an employment record by any means, including the punching of a time clock, is guilty of an offence punishable on summary conviction.

R.S., c. C-34, s. 356.

Commentary: The falsification of an employment record, *simpliciter*, is *not* a crime under this section. It must be done *with intent to deceive*.

The *external circumstances* consist of the *falsification* of an *employment record*. The falsification may be *by any means*, including, but *not* limited to, punching a time clock. D need *not* be the person whose employment record is falsified. The specific *mental element* is expressed by the phrase "with intent to deceive". V is *not* specified and, *semble*, need *not* be the employer. To intend to deceive is frequently, though not always, to intend to defraud.

Related Provisions: In some circumstances, as for example, where D falsifies an employment record to show presence at a place of employment rather than elsewhere in order to provide an alibi for crime, the offence may be a breach of s. 139(2).

Related evidentiary, substantive and procedural provisions are described in the corresponding note to s. 397, *supra*. The records which constitute an essential element of P's proof may be received under *C.E.A.* s. 30.

The offence is tried and punished under Part XXVII and s. 787(1).

399. False return by public officer — Every one who, being entrusted with the receipt, custody or management of any part of the public revenues, knowingly furnishes a false statement or return of

(a) any sum of money collected by him or entrusted to his care, or

(b) any balance of money in his hands or under his control,

is guilty of an indictable offence and liable to imprisonment for a term not exceeding five years.

R.S., c. C-34, s. 357.

Commentary: This offence is a specific form of breach of trust by a public official.

The *external circumstances* require proof that D, as principal, was entrusted with the receipt custody or management of any part of the public revenues. It also must be established that D furnished a false statement or return of the nature described in s. 399(a) or (b). The *mental element* requires proof that the false statement or return was furnished *knowingly*, thereby affording D a defence of honest belief. There is no requirement that P prove an intent to defraud.

Related Provisions: Criminal breach of trust, an offence under s. 336, is not restricted to public servants. The offence of s. 337 is applicable where a public servant refuses or fails to deliver up property entrusted to him/her by virtue of employment. Section 122 describes the offence of breach of trust by an "official" who holds "office" within s. 118.

D may *elect* mode of trial under s. 536(2).

400. (1) False prospectus, etc. — **Every one who makes, circulates or publishes a prospectus, statement or an account, whether written or oral, that he knows is false in a material particular, with intent**

(a) **to induce persons, whether ascertained or not, to become shareholders or partners in a company,**

(b) **to deceive or defraud the members, shareholders or creditors, whether ascertained or not, of a company, or**

(c) **to induce any person to**

(i) **entrust or advance anything to a company, or**

(ii) **enter into any security for the benefit of a company,**

is guilty of an indictable offence and liable to imprisonment for a term not exceeding ten years.

(2) **Definition of "company"** — **In this section, "company" means a syndicate, body corporate or company, whether existing or proposed to be created.**

R.S., c. C-34, s. 358; 1994, c. 44, s. 26.

Commentary: The section creates a single offence whose essence is an attempt to induce persons to advance monies to a company on the basis of a *false prospectus*. The offence, both in its external circumstances and mental element, may be committed in a number of ways.

The *external circumstances* of the offence consist of making, circulating or publishing a prospectus, statement or account. D need not occupy any particular position, but is usually a promoter, director, officer or agent of a company acting in such capacity. The prospectus, statement or account may be oral or written. It must be *false in a material particular*. The manner in which the falsity may arise, as for example by positive statement or omission, is neither specified nor restricted.

In addition to proving that D intentionally caused the external circumstances of the offence, P must also prove that D *knew* the statement, prospectus or account to be false in a material particular and, further, that one of the ulterior mental elements of ss. 400(1)(a)–(c) accompanied the external circumstances. Proof of an intent to defraud or deceive is but one of the several mental elements. It is *not*, in every case, required. An *honest belief* in the *truth* of the allegedly false material particular is a *defence*. The reasonableness or otherwise of the belief is an item of evidence in deciding whether the belief was honestly held.

"Company" is exhaustively defined in s. 400(2).

Case Law [See also s. 380]

Cox v. R. (1963), 40 C.R. 52, [1963] 2 C.C.C. 148 (S.C.C.) — The section creates only one offence, the essence of which is an attempt to induce persons to advance monies to a company by means of a false prospectus. Making, circulating and publishing are not separate offences but modes in which one offence may be committed. The test is *not* whether the statement amounted, strictly speaking, to a false pretence, but rather whether the conduct of D in making it was fraudulent.

R. v. Scallen (1974), 15 C.C.C. (2d) 441 (B.C. C.A.) — An intent to defraud is *not* an essential element under s. 400(1)(a). P need only prove a false material particular, *knowledge* of the falsity and the intent to induce persons to become shareholders.

R. v. Davidson (1971), 3 C.C.C. (2d) 509 (B.C. C.A.) — Where D claims that he honestly believed the false statement, the trial judge must leave the issue whether D's belief was honest, hence negatived guilty knowledge. Whether reasonable grounds existed for the belief is merely relevant evidence to be weighed by the jury.

R. v. Colucci (1965), 46 C.R. 256, [1965] 4 C.C.C. 56 (Ont. C.A.) — Deceit includes an omission of a material particular.

Related Provisions: "Person" is expansively defined in s. 2.

Related offences are found in ss. 380 (fraud) and 381 (using mails to defraud), where other evidentiary, procedural and substantive provisions are discussed. False statements of the type described in s. 400(1) may also amount to a false pretence as defined in s. 361(1).

D may elect mode of trial under s. 536(2).

401. (1) Obtaining carriage by false billing — Every one who, by means of a false or misleading representation, knowingly obtains or attempts to obtain the carriage of anything by any person into a country, province, district or other place, whether or not within Canada, where the importation or transportation of it is, in the circumstances of the case, unlawful is guilty of an offence punishable on summary conviction.

(2) Forfeiture — Where a person is convicted of an offence under subsection (1), anything by means of or in relation to which the offence was committed, on such conviction, in addition to any punishment that is imposed, is forfeited to Her Majesty and shall be disposed of as the court may direct.

R.S., c. C-34, s. 359.

Commentary: The essence of this offence consists of the use of *deceit* to obtain or attempt to obtain the *unlawful carriage* of anything.

The *external circumstances* require D to obtain or attempt to obtain another to carry anything to a destination. The transportation or importation of the subject-matter to its destination must, in the circumstances, be unlawful. D must obtain or attempt to obtain such carriage by a false or misleading representation. The nature of the false or misleading representation is neither described nor limited. The *mental element* involves proof that D intentionally caused the external circumstances of the offence with *knowledge* of the falsity or misleading character of the representations and, *semble*, the unlawful character of the transport.

Under s. 401(2), upon conviction, anything by means of or in relation to which the offence was committed is forfeited.

Related Provisions: This offence is tried and punished under Part XXVII.

402. (1) Trader failing to keep accounts — Every one who, being a trader or in business,

(a) is indebted in an amount exceeding one thousand dollars,

(b) is unable to pay his creditors in full, and

(c) has not kept books of account that, in the ordinary course of the trade or business in which he is engaged, are necessary to exhibit or explain his transactions,

is guilty of an indictable offence and liable to imprisonment for a term not exceeding two years.

(2) Saving — No person shall be convicted of an offence under this section

(a) where, to the satisfaction of the court or judge, he

(i) accounts for his losses, and

(ii) shows that his failure to keep books was not intended to defraud his creditors; or

(b) where his failure to keep books occurred at a time more than five years prior to the day on which he was unable to pay his creditors in full.

R.S., c. C-34, s. 360.

Commentary: This offence has been largely supplanted by the introduction of federal bankruptcy legislation.

Its *external circumstances* require that, as principal, D be a trader or in business, indebted in an amount exceeding $1,000, and unable to pay his/her creditors. D must also fail to maintain the books of account described in s. 402(1)(c). No ulterior *mental element*, as for example, an intent to defraud creditors generally, or a specific creditor, need be proven.

Section 402(2) is a saving provision that, in s. 402(2)(a) only, imposes a burden of proof on D. Under s. 402(2)(a)(ii) D must negate an intent to defraud creditors which is not an element of P's proof. No onus of proof associated with s. 402(2)(b).

Related Provisions: Neither "trader" nor "business" is defined in the section, nor elsewhere in the *Code*. In many instances, the failure to keep books of account may afford cogent evidence of an offence under ss. 341 and 392. See the corresponding note accompanying each of those sections.

D may elect mode of trial under s. 536(2).

Personation

403. Personation with intent — Every one who fraudulently personates any person, living or dead,

    (a) with intent to gain advantage for himself or another person,

    (b) with intent to obtain any property or an interest in any property, or

    (c) with intent to cause disadvantage to the person whom he personates or another person,

is guilty of an indictable offence and liable to imprisonment for a term not exceeding ten years or an offence punishable on summary conviction.

R.S., C-34, s. 361;1994, c. 44, s. 27.

Commentary: The *external circumstances* of this dual procedure offence consist of *personation* by D of any living or deceased person. The *mental element* requires proof that D acted fraudulently, as well as with one of the ulterior mental elements described in ss. 403(a)–(c).

Neither "advantage" nor "disadvantage" is defined for the purposes of the section or generally. Each bears its ordinary meaning without restriction to an economic or proprietary advantage or disadvantage. Although "person" is defined in s. 2 to include natural as well as artificial persons, the context of this section is limited to natural persons.

Case Law

R. v. Northrup (1982), 1 C.C.C. (3d) 210 (N.B. C.A.) — Personation involves the assumption for fraudulent purposes of the identity of another person either in existence or who has existed. The use of a fictitious name does *not* meet this requirement.

R. v. Hetsberger (1980), 51 C.C.C. (2d) 257 (Ont. C.A.) — *See also*: *Rozon v. R.* (1974), 28 C.R.N.S. 232 (Que. C.A.) — "Advantage" is *not* confined to monetary advantage. It extends to any better position or favourable circumstance.

Related Provisions: Personation of a peace officer is a summary conviction offence under s. 130. Sections 404 and 405 prohibit certain forms of personation relating to examinations and the acknowledgment of instruments in a false name. In many instances, personation may be a component of fraud (s. 380) or obtaining by false pretences (s. 362).

D may elect mode of trial under s. 536(2).

404. Personation at examination — Every one who falsely, with intent to gain advantage for himself or some other person, personates a candidate at a competitive or qualifying examination held under the authority of law or in connection with a university, college or school or who knowingly avails himself of the results of such personation is guilty of an offence punishable on summary conviction.

R.S., c. C-34, s. 362.

Commentary: This summary conviction offence includes not only personation at defined examinations, but, further, advantaging oneself of the results thereof.

In the *personation* offence D must *personate* a candidate at a competitive or qualifying examination. The examination must be held under the authority of law, or in connection with a university, college or school. The *mental element* requires proof that the personation be done falsely, not fraudulently as under s. 403, and with the specific intent to gain advantage for D or another.

An offence is also committed where D avails him/herself of the result of the personation offence of another. The *mental element* requires proof that D "knowingly" availed him/herself of such personation. In many instances, the person advantaged by the personation offence would be a party to its commission under s. 21 and/or 22.

Related Provisions: This offence is tried and punished under Part XXVII.

Related provisions are discussed in the corresponding note to s. 403, *supra*.

405. Acknowledging instrument in false name — Every one who, without lawful authority or excuse, the proof of which lies on him, acknowledges, in the name of another person before a court or a judge or other person authorized to receive the acknowledgment, a recognizance of bail, a confession of judgment, a consent to judgment or a judgment, deed or other instrument is guilty of an indictable offence and liable to imprisonment for a term not exceeding five years.

R.S., c. C-34, s. 363.

Commentary: The gravamen of this offence rests in the *acknowledgment*, in the *name of another*, of certain court documents or other instruments.

The *external circumstances* require that D *acknowledge*, in the *name of another* person, a specified instrument. There is no express requirement that the person in whose name the acknowledgment is given be living. The acknowledgment must be before a court, judge or other person authorized to receive it and made *without* lawful authority or excuse. The onus of proof of lawful authority or excuse rests upon D.

Unlike most other personation offences, this offence requires proof of *no* ulterior *mental element* beyond the intent to cause the external circumstances.

Case Law

R. v. Gendron (1985), 22 C.C.C. (3d) 312 (Ont. C.A.) — On a charge of acknowledging in the name of another person a recognizance of bail, P must prove not only that D *acknowledged* the recognizance in a *name other* than his own but, where the recognizance purports to be issued by an officer in charge, that it was in fact acknowledged before a peace officer who had been duly designated as the officer in charge of the lock-up or place when D was taken there to be detained in custody.

Related Provisions: The listed documents are *not* statutorily defined, but little practical difficulty should be encountered in determining the application of the section.

Other related provisions are discussed in the corresponding note to s. 403, *supra*.

D may *elect* mode of trial under s. 536(2).

Forgery of Trade-marks and Trade Descriptions

406. Forging trade-mark — For the purposes of this Part, every one forges a trade-mark who

(a) without the consent of the proprietor of the trade-mark, makes or reproduces in any manner that trade-mark or a mark so nearly resembling it as to be calculated to deceive; or

(b) falsifies, in any manner, a genuine trade-mark.

R.S., c. C-34, s. 364.

Commentary: This section describes what constitutes *forgery of a trade-mark.*

Under s. 406(a), D must make or reproduce in any manner, a trade-mark, or a mark so nearly resembling a trade-mark as to be *calculated to deceive.* D's conduct must be without the consent of the proprietor of the trade-mark. The *mental element* consists of an intention to make or reproduce the trade-mark or near resemblance, which must be calculated to deceive. An intent to defraud is not essential.The similarity must be sufficient to be likely to create confusion and calculated to deceive.

Under s. 406(b), P must prove that D falsified, in any manner, a genuine trade-mark.

Related Provisions: "Trade-mark" is not defined in the *Code* but, under s. 4(4), has the meaning assigned to it in the *Trade Marks Act*, R.S.C. 1985, c. T-13, s. 2.

Forgery is defined in s. 366 and punished in s. 367(1). Fraud is described and punished in s. 380(1).

Related trade-mark offences appear in ss. 407 and 409–411. In addition to the punishment provided for those offences, anything by means of or in relation to which D commits an offence under, *inter alia*, ss. 407 and 409–411 is forfeited upon conviction.

407. Offence — **Every one commits an offence who, with intent to deceive or defraud the public or any person, whether ascertained or not, forges a trade-mark.**
                    R.S., c. C-34, s. 365.

Commentary: This section describes the circumstances in which forgery of a trade-mark will constitute an offence.

The *external circumstances* consist of the forgery of a trade-mark, as described in s. 406. The *mental element* is ulterior to that required in forgery, *simpliciter.* The forgery must be with intent to deceive or defraud the public or any person. The person need not be ascertained, actually deceived or defrauded.

Related Provisions: Forgery of a trade-mark is defined in s. 406. The offence of this section is punished under s. 412(1). Forfeiture of the means of or in relation to which the offence is committed is generally ordered under s. 412(2).

Under s. 412(1), P may *elect* mode of procedure. Where P proceeds by indictment, D may *elect* mode of trial under s. 536(2). Summary conviction proceedings are governed by Part XXVII.

Other related provisions are described in the corresponding note in s. 406, *supra.*

408. Passing off — **Every one commits an offence who, with intent to deceive or defraud the public or any person, whether ascertained or not,**

    (a) passes off other wares or services as and for those ordered or required; or

    (b) makes use, in association with wares or services, of any description that is false in a material respect regarding

        (i) the kind, quality, quantity or composition,

        (ii) the geographical origin, or

        (iii) the mode of the manufacture, production or performance

    of those wares or services.
                  R.S., c. C-34, s. 366.

Commentary: The *external circumstances* of this offence, "passing off", are proven where P establishes what is described in either s. 408(a) or (b). Under s. 408(a), D must *pass off* other wares or services as and for those ordered or required. The essence of passing-off is the supply of something represented to be what was ordered or required, which is not in fact so. Under s. 408(b), the *external circumstances* are complete where D made use of a description in association with wares or services that was *false, in a material respect* regarding any matter described in any of ss. 408(b)(i)–(iii).

The *mental element* is the same ulterior mental element found in s. 407 described, *supra.*

Case Law
Included Offences

R. v. Ferjo (1994), 58 C.P.R. (3d) 223 (Ont. C.A.) — The offence of s. 408(b) is *not* an included offence in s. 408(a).

Related Provisions: To "pass off" is to cause something to be accepted in a false character, to give something out as that which it is not, or to pretend to be.

Related substantive, evidentiary and procedural provisions are described in the corresponding notes to ss. 406 and 407, *supra*.

409. (1) Instruments for forging trade-mark — Every one commits an offence who makes, has in his possession or disposes of a die, block, machine or other instrument designed or intended to be used in forging a trade-mark.

(2) Saving — No person shall be convicted of an offence under this section where he proves that he acted in good faith in the ordinary course of his business or employment.

R.S., c. C-34, s. 367.

Commentary: This offence, often preliminary to the offence of s. 407, prohibits dealings in instruments by which trade-marks may be forged.

The *external circumstances* under s. 409(1) may be proven in several ways. D must make, have in his/her possession or dispose of one of a defined class of item (a die, block, machine or other instrument designed or intended to be used in forging a trade-mark). It need *not* be proven that the instrument is both designed and intended to be used in forging a trade-mark. Either will suffice. The *mental element* consists of the intention to cause the external circumstances of the offence, as well, D's *knowledge* of the character of the instruments and further, where applicable, of possession of them.

In general, s. 409(2) preserves a defence of *good faith*. The subsection, however, requires that D act in good faith in the ordinary course of his/her business or employment and, further, that D prove s/he so acted. The shift in onus of proof may attract *Charter* s. 11(d) review. The phrase "in the ordinary course of his business or employment" would appear to impose a limitation upon what would otherwise he a general defence of good faith.

Case Law

R. v. Strong Cobb Arner of Canada Ltd. (1973), 16 C.C.C. (2d) 150 (Ont. C.A.) — "Trade-mark" in this section means a trade-mark as defined in the *Trade Marks Act*. Although registration of a trade-mark results in a presumption of validity, where D establishes the invalidity of the trade-mark D has a valid defence to a charge under s. 409(1).

Related Provisions: Possession may be established under s. 4(3).

Neither "die" nor "block" is defined in the *Code*. A "die" might be described as an engraved stamp for impressing a design or figure on some other, often softer material. A "block", on the other hand, is generally a piece of wood or other material on which lines, figures or letters are engraved, in order to be printed from it or to be stamped on another material through the application of pressure.

Similar preparatory or preliminary crimes are found, for example, in ss. 351(1), 352 and 458.

Related provisions are described in the corresponding notes to ss. 406 and 407, *supra*.

410. Other offences in relation to trade-marks — Every one commits an offence who, with intent to deceive or defraud,

(a) defaces, conceals or removes a trade-mark or the name of another person from anything without the consent of that other person; or

(b) being a manufacturer, dealer, trader or bottler, fills any bottle or siphon that bears the trade-mark or name of another person, without the consent of that other

person, with a beverage, milk, by-product of milk or other liquid commodity for the purpose of sale or traffic.

R.S., c. C-34, s. 368.

Commentary: The section, as its heading implies, describes other offences relating to trademarks. In each case, P must prove the ulterior or specific intent to deceive or defraud. Actual deception or fraud need *not* be established, provided the *external circumstances* described in s. 410(a) or (b) are accompanied by the proscribed specific *mental element*. Both ss. 410(a) and (b) require proof that the holder of the trade-mark or other person whose name appears on the article did *not* consent to D's conduct.

Related Provisions: Related provisions are discussed in the corresponding notes to ss. 406 and 407, *supra*.

411. Used goods sold without disclosure — Every one commits an offence who sells, exposes or has in his possession for sale, or advertises for sale, goods that have been used, reconditioned or remade and that bear the trade-mark or the trade-name of another person, without making full disclosure that the goods have been reconditioned, rebuilt or remade for sale and that they are not then in the condition in which they were originally made or produced.

R.S., c. C-34, s. 369.

Commentary: The section, in essence a form of passing off, prohibits certain dealings in *used goods* without full disclosure of their history. It may be committed in a variety of ways.

The *external circumstances* require that D sell, expose or have in possession or advertise for sale, goods which are used, reconditioned or remade and, further, bear the trade-mark or trade-name of another. D must fail to make full disclosure that the goods have been reconditioned, rebuilt or remade for sale and, further, that the goods are not then in the condition in which they were originally made or produced. The *mental element* requires proof of the intention to cause the external circumstances and, in particular, includes *knowledge* of the nature of the goods, as well as the intention not to make full disclosure of their history. It is not necessary to prove that D intended to deceive or defraud anyone, though such an inference might easily arise upon proof of the elements of the offence.

Related Provisions: "Goods" is exhaustively defined in s. 379 to mean anything that is the subject of trade or commerce. The corresponding notes to ss. 406–408 describe related provisions.

412. (1) Punishment — Every one who commits an offence under section 407, 408, 409, 410 or 411 is guilty of

    (a) an indictable offence and is liable to imprisonment for a term not exceeding two years; or

    (b) an offence punishable on summary conviction.

(2) Forfeiture — Anything by means of or in relation to which a person commits an offence under section 407, 408, 409, 410 or 411 is, unless the court otherwise orders, forfeited on the conviction of that person for that offence.

R.S., c. C-34, s. 370.

Commentary: Section 412(1) provides the punishment for the offences of ss. 407-411, and allows P to elect mode of procedure. Where P proceeds by indictment, D may elect mode of trial. Summary conviction proceedings are governed by Part XXVII.

Section 412(2) enacts a general rule that anything by means of or in relation to which D commits an offence under ss. 407–411 is forfeited upon conviction, absent contrary order by the trial court.

Related Provisions: The corresponding notes to ss. 406-411 describe related provisions.

413. Falsely claiming royal warrant — Every one who falsely represents that goods are made by a person holding a royal warrant, or for the service of Her Majesty, member of the Royal Family or public department is guilty of an offence punishable on summary conviction.

R.S., c. C-34, s. 371.

Commentary: The *external circumstances* of this rarely-prosecuted summary conviction offence consist of a *representation* that goods are made by a person holding a royal warrant or for the service of Her Majesty, a member of the Royal Family or a public department. The representation must be *false*. The *mental element* requires proof of the intention to so represent the goods, including *knowledge* of the *falsity* of such representations.

Related Provisions: "Public department" is defined in s. 2, and "goods" in s. 379.

Certain transactions relating to public stores are prohibited in ss. 417–418. The corresponding notes to ss. 406-411 describe other related provisions.

The offence is tried under Part XXVII.

414. Presumption from port of shipment — Where, in proceedings under this Part, the alleged offence relates to imported goods, evidence that the goods were shipped to Canada from a place outside Canada is, in the absence of any evidence to the contrary, proof that the goods were made or produced in the country from which they were shipped.

R.S., c. C-34, s. 372.

Commentary: The section creates a *rebuttable presumption of fact* applicable in prosecutions under Part X. It would appear to facilitate proof that otherwise might be difficult due to the absence of essential witnesses.

The presumption becomes engaged when an offence under Part X relates to imported goods. *Evidence* that the goods were shipped to Canada from a place outside the country constitutes *proof*, in the absence of any evidence to the contrary, that the goods were made or produced in the country from which they were shipped.

Related Provisions: "Goods" are defined in s. 379 as anything that is the subject of trade or commerce.

Offences in which importing is an essential element include ss. 357 and 401. The presumption applies where "the alleged offence relates to imported goods", not only where importing goods is an essential element of the external circumstances of the offence.

Wreck

415. Offences in relation to wreck — Every one who

(a) secretes wreck, defaces or obliterates the marks on wreck, or uses any means to disguise or conceal the fact that anything is wreck, or in any manner conceals the character of wreck, from a person who is entitled to inquire into the wreck,

(b) receives wreck, knowing that it is wreck, from a person other than the owner thereof or a receiver of wreck, and does not within forty-eight hours thereafter inform the receiver of wreck thereof,

(c) offers wreck for sale or otherwise deals with it, knowing that it is wreck, and not having a lawful authority to sell or deal with it,

(d) keeps wreck in his possession knowing that it is wreck, without lawful authority to keep it, for any time longer than the time reasonably necessary to deliver it to the receiver of wreck, or

(e) boards, against the will of the master, a vessel that is wrecked, stranded or in distress unless he is a receiver of wreck or a person acting under orders of a receiver of wreck,

553

is guilty of

(f) an indictable offence and is liable to imprisonment for a term not exceeding two years, or

(g) an offence punishable on summary conviction.

R.S., c. C-34, s. 373.

Commentary: The section creates a number of offences in relation to "wreck", as defined in s. 2. The *external circumstances* of each offence appear in ss. 415(a)-(e). The *mental element*, in each case, consists of an *intention* to cause the external circumstances, as well, *knowledge* of the nature described in the applicable paragraph.

Related Provisions: Possession is determined under s. 4(3).

Section 4(4) permits the meaning assigned to words and expressions in other Acts, for example, "receiver of wreck" as used in the *Canada Shipping Act*, R.S.C. 1985, c. S-9, to be used under the *Code*.

These offences are triable either way. In prosecutions by indictment, D may *elect* mode of trial under s. 536(2). Summary conviction prosecutions are governed by Part XXVII.

Public Stores

416. Distinguishing mark on public stores — The Governor in Council may, by notice to be published in the *Canada Gazette*, prescribe distinguishing marks that are appropriate for use on public stores to denote the property of Her Majesty therein, whether the stores belong to Her Majesty in right of Canada or to Her Majesty in any other right.

R.S., c. C-34, s. 374.

Commentary: The section authorizes the Governor in Council to prescribe distinguishing marks that are appropriate for use on public stores. Notice thereof must be published in the *Canada Gazette*. The marks denote the property of Her Majesty, whether in right of Canada or otherwise.

Related Provisions: "Public stores" is defined in s. 2. Definitions of "Governor in Council" and "Her Majesty" appear in *I.A.* s. 35(1).

Section 417(1) creates offences relating to the unlawful application or removal of marks appropriated for use in public stores.

417. (1) Applying or removing marks without authority — Every one who,

(a) without lawful authority, the proof of which lies on him, applies a distinguishing mark to anything, or

(b) with intent to conceal the property of Her Majesty in public stores, removes, destroys or obliterates, in whole or in part, a distinguishing mark,

is guilty of an indictable offence and liable to imprisonment for a term not exceeding two years.

(2) Unlawful transactions in public stores — Every one who, without lawful authority, the proof of which lies on him, receives, possesses, keeps, sells or delivers public stores that he knows bear a distinguishing mark is guilty of

(a) an indictable offence and is liable to imprisonment for a term not exceeding two years; or

(b) an offence punishable on summary conviction.

554

(3) Definition of "distinguishing mark" — For the purposes of this section, "distinguishing mark" means a distinguishing mark that is appropriated for use on public stores pursuant to section 416.

R.S., c. C-34, s. 375.

Commentary: The section prohibits certain conduct in relation to *public stores*.

Section 417(1) creates two separate offences. Under s. 417(1)(a), the *external circumstances* consist of the unauthorized application of a distinguishing mark, as defined in s. 417(3), to anything. The *mental element* requires proof of the intention to do so. Proof of lawful authority rests with D. Under s. 417(1)(b), the *external circumstances* consist of the removal, destruction or obliteration, in whole or in part, of a distinguishing mark on public stores. The *mental element* includes proof of an ulterior intent, namely, the intent to conceal the property of Her Majesty in public stores.

The offence of s. 417(2) requires proof that D received, possessed, kept, sold or delivered public stores which bear a distinguishing mark as described in s. 417(3). The transactions must he *without lawful authority*. Proof of lawful authority rests upon D. The *mental element* requires no proof of any ulterior intent, as under s. 417(1), but P must prove D's knowledge that the public stores bear a distinguishing mark.

The shift of the onus of proof to D may attract *Charter* s. 11(d) scrutiny.

Related Provisions: Section 416 authorizes the Governor in Council to prescribe distinguishing marks for "public stores", as defined in s. 2. Possession may be established under s. 4(3).

Section 421(2), applicable only in prosecutions under s. 417(2), creates a presumption of knowledge in D that the public stores bore a distinguishing mark at the material time, where D was in the service or employment of Her Majesty or was a dealer in marine stores or old metals.

Under s. 417(1), D may *elect* mode of trial. The offence of s. 417(2) is triable either way. Where P proceeds by indictment, D may *elect* mode of trial under s. 536(2). Summary conviction proceedings are governed by Part XXVII.

418. (1) Selling defective stores to Her Majesty — Every one who knowingly sells or delivers defective stores to Her Majesty or commits fraud in connection with the sale, lease or delivery of stores to Her Majesty or the manufacture of stores for Her Majesty is guilty of an indictable offence and liable to imprisonment for a term not exceeding fourteen years.

(2) Offences by officers and employees of corporations — Every one who, being a director, an officer, an agent or an employee of a corporation that commits, by fraud, an offence under subsection (1),

(a) knowingly takes part in the fraud, or

(b) knows or has reason to suspect that the fraud is being committed or has been or is about to be committed and does not inform the responsible government, or a department thereof, of Her Majesty,

is guilty of an indictable offence and liable to imprisonment for a term not exceeding fourteen years.

R.S., c. C-34, s. 376.

Commentary: The section creates two offences relating to the *delivery of stores* to Her Majesty.

The first offence deals with the sale or delivery of *defective military stores*. The sale or delivery of defective military stores to Her Majesty constitutes the *external circumstances*. The *mental element* requires proof that D *knowingly* made such a sale or delivery.

The second offence of s. 418(1) is concerned with acts of dishonesty, fraud or deception in connection with transactions in public stores. The *external circumstances* consist of the sale, lease or delivery of stores to or the manufacture of stores for Her Majesty, D must commit fraud in relation to such transactions. The *mental element, semble,* includes the specific intent to commit fraud in relation to the transaction.

Neither general principle nor the terms of s. 418(1) would appear to limit liability to persons who *actually* commit the offence. General accessoryship principles (ss. 21 and 22) would apply. Section 418(2), however, contains its own accessoryship provisions which apply only where D is a director, officer, agent or employee of a corporation that commits by fraud, an offence under s. 418(1). D, in such circumstances, will be liable, *semble*, as an accessory, if his/her conduct falls within either s. 418(2)(a) or (b).

Related Provisions: The general offence of fraud is described in s. 380(1).

D may *elect* mode of trial under s. 536(2).

419. Unlawful use of military uniforms or certificates — Every one who without lawful authority, the proof of which lies on him,

(a) wears a uniform of the Canadian Forces or any other naval, army or air force or a uniform that is so similar to the uniform of any of those forces that it is likely to be mistaken therefor,

(b) wears a distinctive mark relating to wounds received or service performed in war, or a military medal, ribbon, badge, chevron or any decoration or order that is awarded for war services, or any imitation thereof, or any mark or device or thing that is likely to be mistaken for any such mark, medal, ribbon, badge, chevron, decoration or order,

(c) has in his possession a certificate of discharge, certificate of release, statement of service or identity card from the Canadian Forces or any other naval, army or air force that has not been issued to and does not belong to him, or

(d) has in his possession a commission or warrant or a certificate of discharge, certificate of release, statement of service or identity card issued to an officer or a person in or who has been in the Canadian Forces or any other naval, army or air force, that contains any alteration that is not verified by the initials of the officer who issued it, or by the initials of an officer thereto lawfully authorized,

is guilty of an offence punishable on summary conviction.

R.S., c. C-34, s. 377.

Commentary: The section creates four separate summary conviction offences. Their essence is the *unlawful use* of military *uniforms, decorations* and *certificates*.

The *external circumstances* of the offences are described in ss. 419(a)–(d). Sections 419(a) and (b) prohibit the *wearing* of certain *uniforms* and military *decorations*, whereas ss. 419(c) and (d) forbid *possession* of *certificates* of the types there described. The offences are only committed where D lacks lawful authority to wear or possess the items described. The *onus* of proving lawful authority is, however, statutorily shifted to D.

The section does not require proof of any ulterior *mental element*.

Related Provisions: Under s. 421(1), *evidence* that a person was, at any time, performing duties in the Canadian Forces is, in the *absence of evidence to the contrary, proof* that his/her prior enrolment in the Canadian Forces was regular. Section 420(1) creates offences relating to military stores.

In some instances, conduct falling within s. 419, accompanied by the requisite mental element and representations, may amount to fraud, obtaining by false pretences or personation.

The offences are tried and punished under Part XXVII.

420. (1) Military stores — (1) Every one who buys, receives or detains from a member of the Canadian Forces or a deserter or an absentee without leave therefrom any

military stores that are owned by Her Majesty or for which the member, deserter or absentee without leave is accountable to Her Majesty is guilty of

> (a) an indictable offence and is liable to imprisonment for a term not exceeding five years; or
>
> (b) an offence punishable on summary conviction.

(2) Exception — No person shall be convicted of an offence under this section where he establishes that he did not know and had no reason to suspect that the military stores in respect of which the offence was committed were owned by Her Majesty or were military stores for which the member, deserter or absentee without leave was accountable to Her Majesty.

R.S., c. C-34, s. 378.

Commentary: The section prohibits certain *dealings in military stores*.

Under s. 420(1), D must buy, receive or detain from a member of or deserter or absentee without leave from the Canadian Forces, military stores. The stores must either be owned by Her Majesty or be ones for which the member, deserter or absentee is accountable to Her Majesty. The *mental element* requires proof of knowledge of the character of the property.

Section 420(2) provides an *exception* to the offence of s. 420(1) which may generally be described as a good faith defence. It requires not only absence of knowledge of the unlawful character of the stores, but, equally, absence of reason to suspect that the stores were owned by or returnable to Her Majesty. The onus of proof in respect of such exception is statutorily placed upon D, thereby raising *Charter* s. 11(d) implications.

Related Provisions: Section 419 creates summary conviction offences involving the unlawful use of military uniforms. The enlistment presumption of s. 421(1) is applicable to prosecutions under this section.

The offence of s. 420(1) is triable either way. Proceedings by indictment allow D to elect mode of trial. Summary conviction proceedings are governed by Part XXVII.

"Canadian Forces" is defined in s. 2.

421. (1) Evidence of enlistment — In proceedings under sections 417 to 420, evidence that a person was at any time performing duties in the Canadian Forces is, in the absence of any evidence to the contrary, proof that his enrolment in the Canadian Forces prior to that time was regular.

(2) Presumption when accused a dealer in stores — An accused who is charged with an offence under subsection 417(2) shall be presumed to have known that the stores in respect of which the offence is alleged to have been committed bore a distinguishing mark within the meaning of that subsection at the time the offence is alleged to have been committed if he was, at that time, in the service or employment of Her Majesty or was a dealer in marine stores or in old metals.

R.S., c. C-34, s. 379.

Commentary: The section enacts two *rebuttable presumptions of fact* applicable in prosecutions for designated offences.

Section 421(1) is applicable in proceedings under ss. 417–420. *Evidence of performance* of duties in the Canadian Forces is, in the absence of evidence to the contrary, *proof* of prior *regular enrolment*.

Section 421(2), applicable only in prosecutions under s. 417(2), creates a *presumption* of *knowledge* in D that the public stores bore a distinguishing mark at the material time where D was in the service or employment of Her Majesty, or was a dealer in marine stores or old metals. The subsection makes no reference to the "evidence to the contrary", thereby apparently providing an irrebuttable presumption of knowledge.

557

Related Provisions: Related provisions are discussed in the corresponding notes to ss. 416–420, *supra*.

Breach of Contract, Intimidation and Discrimination Against Trade Unionists

422. (1) **Criminal breach of contract** — Every one who wilfully breaks a contract, knowing or having reasonable cause to believe that the probable consequences of doing so, whether alone or in combination with others, will be

(a) to endanger human life,

(b) to cause serious bodily injury,

(c) to expose valuable property, real or personal, to destruction or serious injury,

(d) to deprive the inhabitants of a city or place, or part thereof, wholly or to a great extent, of their supply of light, power, gas or water, or

(e) to delay or prevent the running of any locomotive engine, tender, freight or passenger train or car, on a railway that is a common carrier,

is guilty of

(f) an indictable offence and is liable to imprisonment for a term not exceeding five years, or

(g) an offence punishable on summary conviction.

(2) **Saving** — No person wilfully breaks a contract within the meaning of subsection (1) by reason only that

(a) being the employee of an employer, he stops work as a result of the failure of his employer and himself to agree on any matter relating to his employment, or,

(b) being a member of an organization of employees formed for the purpose of regulating relations between employers and employees, he stops work as a result of the failure of the employer and a bargaining agent acting on behalf of the organization to agree on any matter relating to the employment of members of the organization,

if, before the stoppage of work occurs, all steps provided by law with respect to the settlement of industrial disputes are taken and any provision for the final settlement of differences, without stoppage of work, contained in or by law deemed to be contained in a collective agreement is complied with and effect given thereto.

(3) **Consent required** — No proceedings shall be instituted under this section without the consent of the Attorney General.

R.S., c. C-34, s. 380.

Commentary: The section describes the circumstances under which breach of contract may amount to a crime and, further, requires the Attorney General's *consent* to the institution of proceedings.

The *external circumstances* of the offence of s. 422(1) consist of a breach of contract. The *mental element* requires proof of a combination of *intention, knowledge* and *foresight*. The breach of contract must be wilful. Further, D must know or have *reasonable* cause to believe that the probable consequence of the contractual breach will be any result in ss. 422(1)(a)–(e). No such consequence need ever ensue, provided the requisite knowledge or reasonably grounded belief is established.

The effect of s. 422(2) is to *excuse* from liability employees who, as individuals or members of a union, stop work as a result of contractual disputes, provided the requisite dispute mechanisms have first been engaged and exhausted.

Section 422(3) requires the *consent* of the Attorney General of the province to the institution of proceedings under the section, apparently to prevent the criminal process being used to settle industrial disputes.

Related Provisions: "Attorney General", defined in s. 2, here means the Attorney General of the province in which the proceedings are taken. "Property" is also defined in S. 2.

The offence of sabotage, defined in ss. 52(1) and (2), has an exemption similar to present s. 422(2) in its s. 52(3). Conspiracy in restraint of trade is an offence under s. 466(l),with exemptions provided in ss. 466(2) and 467. Intimidation is an offence under s. 423(1), with an exception made for obtaining or communicating information under s. 423(2). Section 425 creates an offence in relation to employers.

The offence of s. 422(1) is triable either way. In proceedings by indictment, D may *elect* mode of trial. Summary conviction proceedings are tried under Part XXVII.

423. (1) Intimidation — **Every one who, wrongfully and without lawful authority, for the purpose of compelling another person to abstain from doing anything that he has a lawful right to do, or to do anything that he has a lawful right to abstain from doing,**

    (a) uses violence or threats of violence to that person or his spouse or children, or injures his property,

    (b) intimidates or attempts to intimidate that person or a relative of that person by threats that, in Canada or elsewhere, violence or other injury will be done to or punishment inflicted on him or a relative of his, or that the property of any of them will be damaged,

    (c) persistently follows that person about from place to place,

    (d) hides any tools, clothes or other property owned or used by that person, or deprives him of them or hinders him in the use of them,

    (e) with one or more other persons, follows that person, in a disorderly manner, on a highway,

    (f) besets or watches the dwelling-house or place where that person resides, works, carries on business or happens to be, or

    (g) blocks or obstructs a highway,

is guilty of an offence punishable on summary conviction.

(2) Exception — **A person who attends at or near or approaches a dwelling-house or place, for the purpose only of obtaining or communicating information, does not watch or beset within the meaning of this section.**

R.S., c. C-34, s. 381; 1980–81–82–83, c. 125,.s. 22.

Commentary: This summary conviction offence, compendiously designated "intimidation," was intended to apply to industrial disputes. Its language, however, is capable of and has been accorded wider meaning.

Under s. 423(1), the *external circumstances* consist of the *absence of lawful authority*, together with words or conduct that fall within any of ss. 423(1)(a)–(g). It is doubtful whether "wrongfully" adds substantially to "without lawful authority". The *mental element* requires proof that D intended to cause the external circumstances for a prohibited purpose, that is to say, to compel another to abstain from doing anything s/he has a lawful right to do or to do anything that s/he has a lawful right to abstain from doing.

The exception of s. 423(2) relates specifically to the external circumstances described in s. 423(1)(f). D does not watch or beset where s/he attends at or near or approaches a dwelling-house solely to obtain or communicate information. The exception does *not* extend to other conduct which may constitute the external circumstances described in another paragraph of s. 423(1).

Case Law

R. v. Basaraba (1976), 24 C.C.C. (2d) 296 (Man. C.A.) — The section is *not* limited in application to intimidation in the context of industrial disputes.

559

R. v. Branscombe (1956), 25 C.R. 88 (Ont. C.A.) — The *purpose* in watching or besetting a place is an essential ingredient of the offence.

R. v. Lenton (1947), 3 C.R. 41, 88 C.C.C. 1 (Ont. C.A.) — "Violence", as used in this section, is *not* to be limited in its application to instances of actual physical contact with the person. It includes occurrences which may be described as "forcibly interfering with personal freedom", "undue restraint applied to some natural process, habit, etc. so as to prevent its free development or exercise", "force or strength of physical action".

Related Provisions: "Property", "highway" and "dwelling-house" are defined in s. 2.

In some circumstances, conduct which amounts to a breach of s. 423(1) may also contravene the provisions relating to unlawful assemblies and riots (ss. 63–68), causing a disturbance (s. 175(1)), trespassing by night (s. 177) or various forms of assault (ss. 265–269).

The offence is governed by Part XXVII. Under s. 810, D may be required by a justice of the peace to enter into a recognizance to keep the peace for a specified period not to exceed, 12 months.

424. Threat to commit offence against internationally protected person — Every one who threatens to commit an offence under section 235, 266, 279 or 279.1 against an internationally protected person or who threatens to commit an offence under section 431 is guilty of an indictable offence and liable to imprisonment for a term not exceeding five years.

1974-75-76, c. 93, s. 33; R.S. 1985, c. 27 (1st Supp.), s. 55.

Commentary: The section punishes *threats* to commit listed offences against an *internationally protected person*, as well as threats to attack the *official premises*, private accommodation or means of transport of such a person.

The *external circumstances* of the offence consist of a threat. The threat must be to murder (s. 235), assault (s. 266), kidnap (s. 279) or take hostage (s. 279.1) an internationally protected person, or to attack his/her official premises, private accommodation or means of transport. The *mental element* consists of the intention to convey such a threat.

Related Provisions: "Internationally protected person" is defined in s. 2. A related offence-appears in s. 431.

Uttering threats of certain consequences is an offence under s. 264.1. Extortion is a crime under s. 346. Authorization to intercept private communications may be given under Part VI in respect of this offence.

The excuse of compulsion by threats (duress) is described in s. 17.

D may *elect* mode of trial under s. 536(2).

425. Offences by employers — Every one who, being an employer or the agent of an employer, wrongfully and without lawful authority

(a) refuses to employ or dismisses from his employment any person for the reason only that the person is a member of a lawful trade union or of a lawful association or combination of workmen or employees formed for the purpose of advancing, in a lawful manner, their interests and organized for their protection in the regulation of wages and conditions of work,

(b) seeks by intimidation, threat of loss of position or employment, or by causing actual loss of position or employment, or by threatening or imposing any pecuniary penalty, to compel workmen or employees to abstain from belonging to a trade union, association or combination to which they have a lawful right to belong, or

(c) conspires, combines, agrees or arranges with any other employer or his agent to do anything mentioned in paragraph (*a*) or (*b*),

is guilty of an offence punishable on summary conviction.

R.S., c. C-34, s. 382.

Commentary: This section applies principally to industrial disputes.

As principal, D must be an employer or the agent of an employer who acts wrongfully and without lawful authority. Under s. 425(a), D must refuse to employ or dismiss from employment any person, by reason only of what may shortly be described as union membership. Under s. 425(b), D must intimidate, threaten or cause defined consequences. The proscribed conduct must be for an ulterior purpose, namely, to compel workers or employees to abstain from lawful union membership. Under s. 425(c), the *external circumstances* consist of a conspiracy, combination, agreement or arrangement between D and another employer or agent. The agreement must be for a purpose proscribed in s. 425(a) or (b).

Each offence requires proof of a *mental element* which includes an intention to do the prohibited acts for the proscribed reason or purpose.

Case Law

Canadair Ltd. v. R. (1947), 5 C.R. 67 (Que. C.A.) — P must prove that the sole reason for the dismissal was membership in a lawful trade union. "Sole reason" means the principal or real reason or determining cause.

Related Provisions: Conspiracy in restraint of trade is an offence under s. 466(1). A saving provision appears in s. 467.

The offence is tried under Part XXVII.

Secret Commissions

426. (1) **Secret commissions** — Every one commits an offence who

(a) corruptly

(i) gives, offers or agrees to give or offer to an agent, or

(ii) being an agent, demands, accepts or offers or agrees to accept from any person,

any reward, advantage or benefit of any kind as consideration for doing or forbearing to do, or for having done or forborne to do, any act relating to the affairs or business of his principal or for showing or forbearing to show favour or disfavour to any person with relation to the affairs or business of his principal; or

(b) with intent to deceive a principal, gives to an agent of that principal, or, being an agent, uses with intent to deceive his principal, a receipt, account or other writing

(i) in which the principal has an interest,

(ii) that contains any statement that is false or erroneous or defective in any material particular, and

(iii) that is intented to mislead the principal.

(2) **Privity to offence** — Every one commits an offence who is knowingly privy to the commission of an offence under subsection (1).

(3) **Punishment** — A person who commits an offence under this section is guilty of an indictable offence and liable to imprisonment for a term not exceeding five years.

(4) **Definitions of "agent" and "principal"** — In this section "agent" includes an employee, and "principal" includes an employer.

R.S., c. C-34, s. 383; R.S. 1985, c. 27 (1st Supp.), s. 56.

Commentary: This section, concerned with *secret transactions* with an agent relating to the affairs of his/her principal, imposes liability not only upon the agent, but equally upon the third party with whom s/he has dealings. "Agent" is expansively defined in s. 426(4).

Under s. 426(1)(a)(i), D must give, offer, or agree to give or offer to an agent, a *reward, advantage* or *benefit* of any kind. Under s. 426(1)(a)(ii), D, the *agent*, must demand, accept or offer or agree to accept from a third party, a reward, advantage or benefit of any kind. The *mental element* requires proof of D's intention to do the prohibited acts, *corruptly*, and as consideration of the type described. Proof of this ulterior mental element is necessary, irrespective of whether D is an agent or the third party.

The offences of s. 426(1)(b) may also be committed by an agent or a third party. The *external circumstances* of the *third party's offence* consist of giving to an agent a receipt, account or other writing in which the principal has an interest which contains any false, erroneous or materially defective statement intended to mislead the principal. The *external circumstances* of the *agent's offence* consist of the use of a receipt, account or other writing of the nature described. In each case, in addition to proof of an intent to cause the external circumstances of the offence, P must prove that D, whether agent or third party, *intended to deceive the principal.*

On general principle, the general accessoryship provisions of ss. 21–22 should apply to D's offence. Section 426(2), however, extends liability to anyone "who is knowingly privy to" D's offence, thereby enacting its own accessoryship rule. Critical to P's case of accessoryship under s. 426(2) is proof of knowledge and privity by D. On general accessoryship principles, it would seem that the agent and third party are parties to each other's offence.

Case Law

R. v. Kelly (1992), 14 C.R. (4th) 181, 73 C.C.C. (3d) 385 (S.C.C.) — *See also*: *R. v. Arnold* (1992), 73 C.C.C. (3d) 31 (S.C.C.) — The *external circumstances* of the *recipient* offence in s. 426(1)(a)(ii), as they apply to an accused agent/recipient with regard to the acceptance of a commission, are:

i.   the existence of an *agency relationship*;

ii.   *acceptance* by the agent of a *benefit* as *consideration* for doing or forebearing to do any act *in relation to* the *affairs* of the agent's *principal*; and,

iii.   failure by the agent to make adequate and timely disclosure of the source, amount and nature of the benefit.

"Corruptly" means *secretly* or *without* the requisite *disclosure*. P is *not* required to prove the existence of a corrupt bargain between donor and recipient. The recipient may be convicted, notwithstanding the innocence of the donor.The *mental element* of the recipient offence in s. 426(1)(a)(ii) must be established for each element of the external circumstances. The agent/recipient must:

i.   be *aware* of the agency *relationship*;

ii.   *knowingly* accept the benefit as *consideration* for an act to he undertaken in relation to the affairs of the principal; and,

iii.   be *aware* of the exent of the disclosure to the principal or lack thereof.

Where D is aware *some* disclosure has been made, the court must decide whether, in all the circumstances, the disclosure was adequate and timely.

R. v. Wile (1990), 58 C.C.C. (3d) 85, 79 C.R. (3d) 32 (Ont. C.A.) — The gravamen of the donor offence of s. 426(1)(a)(i) is the offer to the agent and the corrupt intention which accompanies it. P must prove that the recipient of the offer was, in fact, an agent but need *not* further prove either that the agent had a specific principal at the relevant time, or that the agent intended to carry out the purpose of the offer.

R. v. Atkinson (1980), 30 N.B.R. (2d) 649 (Q.B.); varied (1981), 57 C.C.C. (2d) 489 (N.B. C.A.); leave to appeal refused (1981), 36 N.B.R. (2d) 358 (S.C.C.) — *See also*: *R. v. Reid*, [1969] 2 C.C.C. 31 (Ont. C.A.) — Corrupt intention may be inferred from proven facts. The fact that practices may have been common is no defence.

R. v. Brown (1956), 24 C.R. 404, 116 C.C.C. 287 (Ont. C.A.) — Everyone is prohibited from entering into secret transactions under which he offers consideration to an agent for services with relation to the affairs of his principal. The act of doing the very thing which the statute prohibits is a "corrupt" act. Furthermore, it is *not* an answer for a person to say that he believed he had a right to have a certain thing done by the agent or that he believed that the agent ought to have done the act in question with relation to the affairs or business of his principal.

Related Provisions: "Corruptly" in common usage connotes a giving or receipt which is *mala fide* and designed, in whole or in part, to bring about a prohibited effect.

"Reward", "advantage" and "benefit" are given no specific meaning in the section. Each is a word of wide and comprehensive import.

This offence is sometimes associated with other fraudulent transactions relating to contracts and trade (ss. 380–396) or offences against rights of property under Part IX. The offence is essentially a form of breach of trust by an agent and may, in some circumstances, amount to an offence under s. 336. Corruption and disobedience offences are described in ss. 119–129.

Authorization to intercept private communications may be given in respect of this "offence" which is also an "enterprise crime offence" under Part XII.2.

D may *elect* mode of trial under s. 536(2).

Trading Stamps

427. (1) Issuing trading stamps — Every one who, by himself or his employee or agent, directly or indirectly issues, gives, sells or otherwise disposes of, or offers to issue, give, sell or otherwise dispose of trading stamps to a merchant or dealer in goods for use in his business is guilty of an offence punishable on summary conviction.

(2) Giving to purchaser of goods — Every one who, being a merchant or dealer in goods, by himself or his employee or agent, directly or indirectly gives or in any way disposes of, or offers to give or in any way dispose of, trading stamps to a person who purchases goods from him is guilty of an offence punishable on summary conviction.

R.S., c. C-34, s. 384.

Commentary: The section prohibits certain transactions in "trading stamps" as defined in s. 379.

Section 427(1), in general, prohibits the actual or proposed *supply* of trading stamps *to* a merchant or dealer in goods for use in his/her business. The *mental element* is the intention to cause the external circumstances of the offence.

Section 427(2), in general, forbids the actual or proposed *supply* of trading stamps *by* a merchant or dealer in goods to a purchaser of goods. The *mental element* consists of the intention to do so.

Related Provisions: "Goods" is also defined in s. 379.

The offence is tried and punished under Part XXVII.

PART XI — WILFUL AND FORBIDDEN ACTS IN RESPECT OF CERTAIN PROPERTY

Interpretation

428. "Property" — In this Part, "property" means real or personal corporeal property.

R.S., c. C-34, s. 385.

Commentary: The section exhaustively defines "property" for Part XI purposes.

Related Provisions: The definition, more restrictive than in s. 2 which is applicable generally under the *Code*, is necessary due to the nature of the acts forbidden under Part XI.

429. (1) Wilfully causing event to occur — Every one who causes the occurrence of an event by doing an act or by omitting to do an act that it is his duty to do, knowing that the act or omission will probably cause the occurrence of the event and being reckless whether the event occurs or not, shall be deemed, for the purposes of this Part, "wilfully" to have caused the occurrence of the event.

(2) Colour of right — No person shall be convicted of an offence under sections 430 to 446 where he proves that he acted with legal justification or excuse and with colour of right.

(3) Interest — Where it is an offence to destroy or to damage anything,

(a) the fact that a person has a partial interest in what is destroyed or damaged does not prevent him from being guilty of the offence if he caused the destruction or damage; and

(b) the fact that a person has a total interest in what is destroyed or damaged does not prevent him from being guilty of the offence if he caused the destruction or damage with intent to defraud.

R.S., c. C-34, s. 386.

Commentary: The section assists in proof of several Part XI offences.

"Wilfully", an essential ingredient of many offences in Part XI, is defined in s. 429(1) by *deeming* D *wilfully* to have caused the occurrence of an event in certain circumstances. D must cause the occurrence of an event by *doing* an act *or omitting* to do an act that it is his/her duty to do. Further, D must *know* that the act or omission will *probably cause* the occurrence of the event. Finally, D must be *reckless* as to the occurrence of the event. The definition, in other words, combines elements of *conduct* (act or omission), *knowledge* (of probable consequences) and *recklessness*.

Under s. 429(2), D is excused from liability under ss. 430–446, where D *proves* s/he acted *with lawful justification or excuse and with colour of right*. This onus shift may attract *Charter* s. 11(d) scrutiny.

Section 429(3) applies where it is an offence to destroy or damage anything and D has an interest in what is destroyed or damaged. A *partial* interest in what is damaged or destroyed will not in any case bar D's conviction. A *total* interest in what is destroyed or damaged will not bar D's conviction, if D caused the damage or destruction *with intent to defraud*.

Case Law

Wilfully: S. 429(1)

R. v. Muma (1989), 51 C.C.C. (3d) 85 (Ont. C.A.) — "Wilfully" in s. 429(1) has an extended meaning. It includes recklessness.

Colour of Right: S. 429(2) [See also s. 322]

R. v. Shymkowich (1954), 19 C.R. 401, 110 C.C.C. 97 (S.C.C.) — The claim of right must be an honest one, though it may be unfounded in law or in fact.

R. v. Creaghan (1982), 31 C.R. (3d) 277, 1 C.C.C. (3d) 449 (Ont. C.A.) — Section 429(2) does *not* require the establishment of *both* colour of right and legal justification. The word "and" preceding the words "with colour of right" is to be read disjunctively, as "or", instead of conjunctively. "Colour of right" in this context means an honest belief in a state of facts which, if it existed, would be a legal justification or excuse.

Partial or Total Interest: S. 429(3)

R. v. Rothe, [1966] 4 C.C.C. 400 (B.C. C.A.) — It is *not* an offence for the *sole* owner to destroy or damage his own property unless the act was done with intent to defraud.

R. v. Surette (1993), 82 C.C.C. (3d) 36 (N.S. C.A.) — An *honest* belief by D, based on *reasonable* grounds, that s/he had a total interest in the damaged property, is a defence to a charge under s. 430(4)(b). A person is legally justified in damaging their own property, provided there is *no* intent to defraud.

R. v. Bernardi (1974), 20 C.C.C. (2d) 523 (Ont. C.A.); leave to appeal refused (1974), 20 C.C.C. (2d) 523n (S.C.C.) — An interest in a building, subject to a mortgage, is a "partial" *not* a "total" interest. The owner of a "partial" interest is liable if he caused the destruction or damage, whether or not there was an "intent to defraud".

Charter Considerations

R. v. Gamey (1993), 80 C.C.C. (3d) 117 (Man. C.A.) — *Semble*, s. 429(2) violates the presumption of innocence guarantee of *Charter* s. 11(d) and is *not* saved by s. 1. The section need *not* be declared inoperative, however, as there was *no* evidence upon which a colour of right defence could be founded. (Huband, J.A., Kroft, J.A. concurring)

Related Provisions: In general, "wilfully" means not merely to commit an act voluntarily, but to commit it purposely, with an evil intention. In other words, something is done deliberately, intentionally, corruptly and without any justifiable excuse. The definition of s. 429(2), *semble*, is an extension of the usual meaning of the term.

Mischief

430. (1) **Mischief** — Every one commits "mischief" who wilfully

(a) destroys or damages property;

(b) renders property dangerous, useless, inoperative or ineffective;

(c) obstructs, interrupts or interferes with the lawful use, enjoyment or operation of property; or

(d) obstructs, interrupts or interferes with any person in the lawful use, enjoyment or operation of property.

(1.1) **Mischief in relation to data** — Every one commits "mischief" who wilfully

(a) destroys or alters data;

(b) renders data meaningless, useless or ineffective;

(c) obstructs, interrupts or interferes with the lawful use of data; or

(d) obstructs, interrupts or interferes with any person in the lawful use of data or denies access to data to any person who is entitled to access thereto.

(2) **Punishment** — Every one who commits mischief that causes actual danger to life is guilty of an indictable offence and liable to imprisonment for life.

(3) **Idem** — Every one who commits mischief in relation to property that is a testamentary instrument or the value of which exceeds five thousand dollars

(a) is guilty of an indictable offence and liable to imprisonment for a term not exceeding ten years; or

(b) is guilty of an offence punishable on summary conviction.

(4) **Idem** — Every one who commits mischief in relation to property, other than property described in subsection (3),

(a) is guilty of an indictable offence and liable to imprisonment for a term not exceeding two years; or

(b) is guilty of an offence punishable on summary conviction.

(5) **Idem** — Everyone who commits mischief in relation to data

(a) is guilty of an indictable offence and liable to imprisonment for a term not exceeding ten years; or

(b) is guilty of an offence punishable on summary conviction.

(5.1) Offence — Every one who wilfully does an act or wilfully omits to do an act that it is his duty to do, if that act or omission is likely to constitute mischief causing actual danger to life, or to constitute mischief in relation to property or data,

> (a) is guilty of an indictable offence and liable to imprisonment for a term not exceeding five years; or
>
> (b) is guilty of an offence punishable on summary conviction.

(6) Saving — No person commits mischief within the meaning of this section by reason only that

> (a) he stops work as a result of the failure of his employer and himself to agree on any matter relating to his employment;
>
> (b) he stops work as a result of the failure of his employer and a bargaining agent acting on his behalf to agree on any matter relating to his employment; or
>
> (c) he stops work as a result of his taking part in a combination of workmen or employees for their own reasonable protection as workmen or employees.

(7) Idem — No person commits mischief within the meaning of this section by reason only that he attends at or near or approaches a dwelling-house or place for the purpose only of obtaining or communicating information.

(8) Definition of "data" — In this section, "data" has the same meaning as in section 342.1.

R.S., c. C-34, s. 387; 1972, c. 13, s. 30; R.S. 1985, c. 27 (1st Supp.), s. 57; 1994, c. 44, s. 28.

Commentary: *Mischief* may be committed in a number of ways. Its *punishment* varies with the *consequences* which ensue from the mischief or the value or nature of the property in relation to which it is committed.

The *external circumstances* of the mischief offence of s. 430(1), mischief in relation to *property*, are described in ss. 430(1)(a)-(d). The *mental element* requires proof that D acted "wilfully", but no ulterior intent need be proven.

The offence of s. 430(1.1), mischief in relation to *data*, as defined in ss. 430(8) and 342.1 has *external circumstances* described in ss. 430(1.1)(a)-(d). The *mental element* requires proof that D acted "wilfully" but not with any ulterior intent.

The offence of s. 430(5.1) is preliminary to the actual commission of mischief in relation to property or data. The *external circumstances* consist of the doing of an act, or the omission to do an act that it is D's duty to do. The act or omission must *likely* to constitute mischief causing actual danger to life, or mischief in relation to property or data. The act or omission must he wilful, but it would appear that no ulterior *mental element* need be proven.

The *saving* provisions of ss. 430(6) and (7) apply chiefly to labour disputes, though s. 430(7) is capable of wider application.

Case Law

Mischief: S. 430(1)

United States of America v. Schrang (1997), 114 C.C.C. (3d) 553 (B.C. C.A.); application for leave to appeal filed (1997), Doc. No. 25880 (S.C.C.) — An offence under s. 430(1)(b) may be made out where barrels containing hazardous waste are left in premises and leak their contents including flammable substances.

While destruction or damage to property is an essential element of mischief under s. 430(1)(a), it is *not* required under s. 430(1)(b) where the offence is complete upon proof of wilfully rendering property dangerous.

R. v. Maddeaux (1997), 6 C.R. (5th) 176, 115 C.C.C. (3d) 122 (Ont. C.A.) — "Enjoyment of property" is *not* limited to mere *possession*, but includes activities such as presence for the purpose of

i.   cooking;

ii.   eating;

iii.   cleaning;

iv.   resting;

v.   sleeping;

vi.   listening to the radio; or

vii.   watching television.

R. v. Drapeau (1995), 37 C.R. (4th) 180, 96 C.C.C. (3d) 554 (Que. C.A.) — The terms "use", "enjoyment" and "operation" in s. 430(1)(d) merely describe the different ways in which a person can physically profit from property that the person legally possesses. (per Beauregard J.A.)The term "enjoyment" is restricted to the entitlement or excercise of a right, *not* the purely subjective state such as the nature or intensity of the pleasure derived from a property by its owner. (per Fish J.A.)The term "enjoyment" is *not* restricted in its meaning to refer only to interference in relation to the fact or right of possessing property. The term includes the action of obtaining from property, which a person lawfully holds, the satisfaction that the property can provide to this person. (per Chamberland J.A., dissenting)

R. v. Quickfall (1993), 78 C.C.C. (3d) 563 (Que. C.A.) — The offence of s. 430(1)(a) requires proof that property was rendered *less suitable* for its intended purpose or that, at least temporarily, the *usefulness* or value of the property was *impaired*. Putting a poster on a piece of public property neither impairs the use or value of the property nor renders it less suited for its intended purpose. (per Proulx J.A., Le Bel J.A. concurring).There is *no* minimum amount of damage which must be proved to establish the offence of s. 430(1)(a). Even if only the appearance of property is affected, the offence is nonetheless established. (per McCarthy J.A. dissenting)

R. v. Lebrun (1988), 65 C.R. (3d) 280 (Que. C.A.) — There is now only one offence of mischief, which is defined by subsection (1). After the offence has been proved, it is then classified for sentencing purposes by application of subsection (2), (3) or (4).

Any Person [See also s. 2]

R. v. Biggin (1980), 55 C.C.C. (2d) 408 (Ont. C.A.) — "Any person" is *not* limited to an owner or leaseholder. Employees or invitees of an owner or leaseholder would ordinarily fall within the description of "any person in the lawful use, enjoyment or operation of property".

Obstructs [See also s. 139]

R. v. Mammolita (1983), 9 C.C.C. (3d) 85 (Ont. C.A.) — D may be guilty as a principal of committing mischief under subsection (1)(c) if he forms part of a group which constitutes a human barricade or other obstruction, even if he only stands shoulder to shoulder with the other persons and neither says nor does anything further.

Danger to Life: S. 430(2)

R. v. Humphrey (1986), 21 O.A.C. 36 (C.A.) — *See also*: *R. v. Nairn* (1955), 112 C.C.C. 272 (Nfld. C.A.) — The "actual danger to life" can be caused by the act which caused the damage as well as he caused by the damage. However, the danger must be the direct result of a deliberate act of mischief and not just merely incidental thereto.

Mischief: Defences

R. v. Surette (1993), 82 C.C.C. (3d) 36 (N.S. C.A.) — An *honest* belief by D, based on *reasonable* grounds, that s/he had a total interest in the property damaged, affords a defence to a charge under s. 430(4)(b). A person is legally justified in damaging their own property, provided there is no intent to defraud.

Intoxication [See also ss. 8 and 16]

R. v. Schmidtke (1985), 44 C.R. (3d) 392, 19 C.C.C. (3d) 390 (Ont. C.A.) — *See also*: *R. v. St. Pierre* (1987), 61 Sask. R. 80 (C.A.) — Self-induced intoxication is *not* a defence to a charge under s. 430(1)(a) since the offence is a crime of general intent. The requisite mental element is an intentional or reckless causing of the external circumstances.

Related Provisions: "Property" is defined in s. 428.

Mischief in relation to property is classified for sentencing purposes in accordance with the consequences thereof or the nature or value of the property in relation to which it has been committed.

Mischief in relation to property that causes *actual danger to life* attracts a maximum punishment of imprisonment for life under s. 430(2). Mischief in relation to property that is a testamentary instrument or of a value exceeding $5,000 is punishable under s. 430(3) on indictment or upon summary conviction. P may elect mode of procedure and D, mode of trial, where P elects to proceed by indictment. Mischief in relation to property that is neither a testamentary instrument nor of a value exceeding $5,000 is, under s. 430(4), triable either way. Where P proceeds by indictment, the trial will be before a provincial court judge under s. 553(a)(v), subject to an order under s. 555(1) or (2). Summary conviction proceedings are governed by Part XXVII.

Mischief in relation to *data* and the preliminary offence of s. 430(5.1) are also triable either way. In proceedings by indictment, D may *elect* mode of trial under s. 536(2).

Sabotage under s. 52, in some respects, an aggravated form of mischief.

Public mischief is also an offence under s. 140.

431. Attack on premises, residence or transport of internationally protected person — Every one who commits an attack on the official premises, private accommodation or means of transport of an internationally protected person that is likely to endanger the life or liberty of such person is guilty of an indictable offence and liable to imprisonment for a term not exceeding fourteen years.

1974-75-76, c. 93, s. 34; R.S. 1985, c. 27 (1st Supp.), s. 58.

Commentary: The *external circumstances* of this offence require proof that D attacked the official premises, private accommodation or means of transport of an "internationally protected person" in such a manner as was *likely* to endanger the life or liberty of V. The *mental element* requires proof of an intent to commit such an attack.

Related Provisions: "Intenationally protected person" is defined in s. 2. Special jurisdiction provisions apply in the trial of such cases under s. 7(3). Other offences in relation to internationally protected persons appear in s. 424.

432. [Repealed R.S. 1985, c. 27 (1st Supp.), s. 58.]

Arson and Other Fires

433. Arson — disregard for human life — Every person who intentionally or recklessly causes damage by fire or explosion to property, whether or not that person owns the property, is guilty of an indictable offence and liable to imprisonment for life where

(a) the person knows that or is reckless with respect to whether the property is inhabited or occupied; or

(b) the fire or explosion causes bodily harm to another person.

R.S., c. C-34, s. 389; 1990, c. 15, s. 1.

Commentary: This indictable offence is the most serious of the several arson offences.

The *external circumstances* require proof that, as principal, D caused damage to property by fire or explosion. Under s. 433(b) P must further show that the fire or explosion caused *bodily harm* to a person other than D. It is legally irrelevant whether D owned the damaged property.

The *mental element* in each case requires proof that D intentionally or recklessly caused the external circumstances of the offence. Under s. 433(b) no further mental element need be proven, but s. 433(a) demands proof that D *knew* or was *reckless* whether the damaged property was inhabited or occupied.

Case Law
Included Offences
R. v. Pascal (1994), 90 C.C.C. (3d) 575 (Man. C.A.) — On its face, s. 433(a) does *not* include an offence under s. 434. D may be convicted, however, of an included offence under s. 430.

Related Provisions: "Property" is defined in s. 428. "Bodily harm", not defined in or for the purposes of the section, includes any hurt or injury that interferes with the health or comfort of V and that is more than merely transient or trifling in nature.

This offence is an offence for which authorization to intercept private communications may be given under Part VI, an "enterprise crime offence" under Part XII.2 and, in some cases, a "serious personal injury offence" under Part XXIV.

Sections 433–436 describe other arson offences and s. 436.1, a related preparatory crime. Offences relating to an "explosive substance," as defined in s. 2, are described in ss. 79–82.1.

D may *elect* mode of trial under s. 536(2).

434. Arson — damage to property — **Every person who intentionally or recklessly causes damage by fire or explosion to property that is not wholly owned by that person is guilty of an indictable offence and liable to imprisonment for a term not exceeding fourteen years.**

R.S., c. C-34, s. 390; 1990, c. 15, s. 1.

Commentary: The *external circumstances* of this indictable offence require proof that D, as principal, caused damage, by fire or explosion, to property which D does *not* wholly own. Nothing further is required.

The basic *mental element* consists of either intention or recklessness by D to cause the external circumstances. No further or ulterior state of mind need be established.

Case Law

Damage

R. v. V. (M.) (1998), 123 C.C.C. (3d) 138 (Ont. C.A.); notice of application for leave to appeal filed , Doc. 36527 (S.C.C.) — "Damage" means "causing harm". It may be proven by evidence of *reduction* in *value* or of real *physical harm*.

Related Provisions: Some elements of this offence are constituent elements of the crimes in ss. 433, 434.1 and 435(1). The additional external circumstances or mental element of each offence, as well as the related preparatory crime of s. 436.1, are described in the *Commentary* which accompanies each.

Where D is a *part* owner of the damaged property, liability under the present section is established without proof that the fire or explosion seriously threatened the health, safety or property of another person as is required under s. 434.1.

This offence is an "offence" for the purposes of s. 183 and Part VI, but not an "enterprise crime offence" within Part XII.2. It is *not, per se*, a "serious personal injury offence" under Part XXIV.

"Property" is defined in s. 428 and "explosive substance" in s. 2.

D may elect mode of trial under s. 536(2).

434.1 Arson — own property — **Every person who intentionally or recklessly causes damage by fire or explosion to property that is owned, in whole or in part, by that person is guilty of an indictable offence and liable to imprisonment for a term not exceeding fourteen years, where the fire or explosion seriously threatens the health, safety or property of another person.**

1990, c. 15, s. 1.

Commentary: The *external circumstances* of this indictable offence comprise three elements. D, as principal, must cause damage by fire or explosion to property. The property must be owned, *in whole or in part*, by D. The fire or explosion must *seriously threaten* the health, safety or property of someone other than D.

The *mental element* is established where D intentionally or recklessly caused damage by fire or explosion to property. The section does *not*, in terms, require proof of intention, recklessness or foresight of the consequences of the fire or explosion.

Related Provisions: Where D partly owns the damaged property, this offence is distinguished from s. 434 only by its requirement that the fire or explosion seriously threaten the health, safety or property of another person. The constitutent elements of the related offences of ss. 433, 434, 435 and 436 and the preparatory crime of s. 436.1 are described in their accompanying *Commentary*.

The offence may be the subject of judicial *authorization* under Part VI.

Other related provisions are described in the corresponding note to s. 434, *supra*.

435. (1) Arson for fraudulent purpose — Every person who, with intent to defraud any other person, causes damage by fire or explosion to property, whether or not that person owns, in whole or in part, the property, is guilty of an indictable offence and liable to imprisonment for a term not exceeding ten years.

(2) Holder or beneficiary of fire insurance policy — Where a person is charged with an offence under subsection (1), the fact that the person was the holder of or was named as a beneficiary under a policy of fire insurance relating to the property in respect of which the offence is alleged to have been committed is a fact from which intent to defraud may be inferred by the court.

R.S., c. C-34, s. 391; 1990, c. 15, s. 1.

Commentary: The section creates an indictable *offence* and a statutory *inference* which assists in its proof.

The *external circumstances* under s. 435(1) are complete where D causes damage to property, by fire or explosion. It is irrelevant to liability that D is the sole or a part owner of the property.

The *mental element* consists not only of the basic intent or recklessness as to the external circumstances but, further, the ulterior "intent to defraud any other person".

Proof of an "intent to defraud any other person" may be assisted by the permissive *inference* of s. 435(2), by which the *fact* that D was the holder or a named beneficiary under a policy of fire insurance relating to the damaged property *may* support an *inference* of *intent to defraud*.

Case Law
Elements of Offence
R. v. D. (R.N.) (1994), 89 C.C.C. (3d) 449 (B.C. C.A.) — A fraudulent purpose under s. 435(2) imports dishonesty in accord with community standards.

Related Provisions: As a matter of general principle, the omission of the alternatives "intentionally or recklessly" from s. 435(1) would appear of no legal or practical significance.

Other arson offences, and the related preparatory crime of possession of incendiary material, are described in the *Commentary* to ss. 433–434.1, 436 and 436.1 respectively.

Other related provisions are described in the corresponding note to s. 434, *supra*.

436. (1) Arson by negligence — Every person who owns, in whole or in part, or controls property is guilty of an indictable offence and liable to imprisonment for a term not exceeding five years where, as a result of a marked departure from the standard of care that a reasonably prudent person would use to prevent or control the spread of fires or to prevent explosions, that person is a cause of a fire or explosion in that property that causes bodily harm to another person or damage to property.

(2) Non-compliance with prevention laws — Where a person is charged with an offence under subsection (1), the fact that the person has failed to comply with any law respecting the prevention or control of fires or explosions in the property is a fact from which a marked departure from the standard of care referred to in that subsection may be inferred by the court.

R.S., c. C-34, s. 392; 1990, c. 15, s. 1.

Commentary: The section creates an indictable offence, shortly described as *arson by negligence*, and a statutory *inference* which assists in its *proof*.

The *external circumstances* comprise several elements. As principal, D must own, *in whole or in part*, or control property in which there is a fire or explosion. D must be *a cause* of the fire or explosion as a result of a marked departure from the standard of care which a reasonably prudent person would use to prevent or control the spread of fires or prevent explosions. The fire or explosion must cause *bodily harm* to another person or *damage* to the *property*.

The *mental element* consists of an intention to act or a failure to act in a manner which, viewed objectively, constitutes the necessary departure from the standard of care of a reasonably prudent person in the circumstances. This aspect may attract a *Charter* s. 7 challenge.

Under s. 436(2) *proof* that D's *act* or omission constituted the *marked departure* required by s. 436(1) *may* be *inferred* from the *fact* of *failure* of *compliance* with any law respecting the prevention or control of fires or explosions in the property.

Case Law

Essential Elements

R v. Harricharan (1995), 98 C.C.C. (3d) 145, 23 O.R. (3d) 233 (C.A.) — Under s. 436(1), P must prove a causal connection between

i.   D's *breach of duty* under s. 436(1);

ii.   the resulting *spread* of the fire; and

iii. the *causing* of either *property damage* or *bodily harm* by its spread.

R v. Harricharan (1995), 98 C.C.C. (3d) 145, 23 O.R. (3d) 233 (C.A.) — Section 436(1) does *not* require proof that D's actions were a cause of the fire. It imposes a duty on a person to control the spread of a fire that, in turn, causes bodily harm or property damage. (per Morden A.C.J.O., Catzman J.A.).

Related Provisions: Other arson offences and the preparatory crime of possession of incendiary material are described in the *Commentary* which accompanies ss. 433–435 and 436.1 respectively. Other related provisions are described in the corresponding note to s. 434, *supra*.

Authorization to intercept private communications may be given in respect of this offence.

436.1 Possession of incendiary material — Every person who possesses any incendiary material, incendiary device or explosive substance for the purpose of committing an offence under any of sections 433 to 436 is guilty of an indictable offence and liable to imprisonment for a term not exceeding five years.

1990, c. 15, s. 1.

Commentary: This offence is often *preliminary* to the arson crimes of ss. 433–435.

The *external circumstances* consist of the possession of any incendiary material or device or explosive substance. The *mental element* comprises the intention to have such possession for the proscribed *purpose* of committing a listed arson offence.

Related Provisions: "Incendiary device" and "incendiary material" are not defined in or for the purposes of the section. "Explosive substance" is defined in s. 2 and possession established under s. 4(3).

It is difficult to envisage circumstances in which D could be said to have possession of incendiary material, an incendiary device, or an explosive substance for the purpose of committing an offence under s. 436(1), a crime of negligence.

The arson offences of ss. 433–436 are described in their *Commentary*. Other related provisions are described in the corresponding note to s. 434, *supra*.

D may *elect* mode of trial under s. 536(2).

Other Interference with Property

437. False alarm of fire — Every one who wilfully, without reasonable cause, by outcry, ringing bells, using a fire alarm, telephone or telegraph, or in any other manner, makes or circulates or causes to be made or circulated an alarm of fire is guilty of

    (a) an indictable offence and is liable to imprisonment for a term not exceeding two years; or

    (b) an offence punishable on summary conviction.

R.S., c. C-34, s. 393; 1972, c. 13, s. 31.

Commentary: The gravamen of this offence is the raising of a *false alarm of fire*.

The *external circumstances* in each case involve the making or circulation or causing to be made or circulated an alarm of fire. The *means* by which such alarm may be raised may be "by outcry, ringing bells, using a fire alarm, telephone or telegraph or in any other manner". The alarm must be raised *without reasonable cause*.

The *mental element* requires proof that D acted *wilfully*. No ulterior mental element need be proven.

Related Provisions: The absence of reasonable cause for raising an alarm of fire is an essential element of P's proof. A reasonable doubt upon the issue will entitle D to an acquittal without the necessity of making compliance with the more onerous requirements of s. 429(2). The *mental element, wilfully*, may be established under s. 429(1).

The raising of a false alarm of fire may sometimes constitute mischief, as for example under s. 430(1)(c) or (d), and be punishable under s. 430(2) or (5.1).

The offence is triable either way. In proceedings by indictment, D may *elect* mode of trial. Summary conviction proceedings are governed by Part XXVII.

438. (1) Interfering with saving of wrecked vessel — Every one who wilfully prevents or impedes, or who wilfully endeavours to prevent or impede,

    (a) the saving of a vessel that is wrecked, stranded, abandoned or in distress, or

    (b) a person who attempts to save a vessel that is wrecked, stranded, abandoned or in distress,

is guilty of an indictable offence and liable to imprisonment for a term not exceeding five years.

(2) Interfering with saving of wreck — Every one who wilfully prevents or impedes or wilfully endeavours to prevent or impede the saving of wreck is guilty of an offence punishable on summary conviction.

R.S., c. C-34, s. 394.

Commentary: These offences involve *interferences* with wrecked vessels, persons attempting to save them and "wreck".

Under s. 438(1), D must prevent or impede or endeavour to prevent or impede the saving of a vessel or a person who attempts to save a vessel that is wrecked, stranded or in distress. The *mental element* requires proof that D acted *wilfully* but not expressly with any ulterior state of mind.

The *external circumstances* of the offence of s. 438(2) consist of D preventing or impeding, or endeavouring to prevent or impede the saving of wreck. D must have acted *wilfully*, but there is *no* express requirement of proof of an ulterior state of mind.

Related Provisions: "Wreck" is defined in s. 2. The definition of "vessel" in s. 214 applies only to Part VIII. "Wilfully" may be established under s. 429(1).

The defence of legal justification or excuse and colour of right under s. 429(2) is available to D under this section.

In some circumstances there may be an overlap between the offence of s. 438(1) and that of impeding an attempt to save life under s. 262.

The offence of s. 438(1) is triable either way. Where P proceeds by indictment, D may *elect* mode of trial. Summary conviction proceedings are governed by Part XXVII.

439. (1) Interfering with marine signal, etc. — **Every one who makes fast a vessel or boat to a signal, buoy or other sea-mark that is used for purposes of navigation is guilty of an offence punishable on summary conviction.**

(2) Idem — **Every one who wilfully alters, removes or conceals a signal, buoy or other sea-mark that is used for purposes of navigation is guilty of an indictable offence and liable to imprisonment for a term not exceeding ten years.**

R.S., c. C-34, s. 395.

Commentary: The two offences of this section prohibit *interference* with marine signals or marks. Under s. 439(1), the *external circumstances* consist of making fast a vessel or boat to a buoy, signal or other sea-mark used for navigation purposes. The *mental element* consists of the intention to cause the external circumstances. Neither "wilfully" nor any ulterior state of mind is an essential element of the offence.

Under s. 439(2), the *external circumstances* comprise the alteration, removal, or concealment of a signal, buoy or other sea-mark used for the purposes of navigation. P must also prove D acted *wilfully*.

Related Provisions: The absence of legal justification or excuse and colour of right is *not* expressly made an essential element of P's proof under either subsection although s. 429(2) is applicable.

"Wilfully" may be proven under s. 429(1). Under s. 4(4), the meanings assigned to words and expressions used in other Acts may be assigned to the same words under the *Code*.

Part XXVII applies to the summary conviction offence of subsection (1). D may *elect* mode of trial for the offence of subsection (2).

440. Removing natural bar without permission — **Every one who wilfully and without the written permission of the Minister of Transport, the burden of proof of which lies on the accused, removes any stone, wood, earth or other material that forms a natural bar necessary to the existence of a public harbour, or that forms a natural protection to such a bar, is guilty of an indictable offence and liable to imprisonment for a term not exceeding two years.**

R.S., c. C-34, s. 396.

Commentary: The *external circumstances* require proof that D removed stone, wood, earth or other material that formed a natural bar necessary to the existence of a public harbour or that forms a natural protection to such a bar. The removal must be without the written permission of the Minister of Transport. D has the *onus* of proving that the requisite *written* permission has been obtained. The *mental element* requires proof that D acted *wilfully*.

Related Provisions: "Wilfully" may be established under s. 429(1). Under s. 4(4), the meanings assigned to words and expressions in other Acts may be assigned to the same words under the *Code*.

The section does *not*, in terms, require that P prove D to have acted *without legal justification or excuse and without colour of right*. Although s. 429(2) applies to this offence, it is difficult to envisage what is added thereby in light of D's obligation to prove the conduct was with the written permission of the Minister of Transport.

D may *elect* mode of trial under s. 536(2).

441. Occupant injuring building — **Every one who, wilfully and to the prejudice of a mortgagee or an owner, pulls down, demolishes or removes, all or any part of a dwelling-house or other building of which he is in possession or occupation, or severs**

from the freehold any fixture fixed therein or thereto is guilty of an indictable offence and liable to imprisonment for a term not exceeding five years.

R.S., c. C-34, s. 397.

Commentary: The section prohibits an occupant from causing certain harm to a building.

The *external circumstances* require that D be in possession or occupation of a dwelling-house or other building. D must pull down, demolish or remove all or any part of the premises or sever from the freehold any fixture fixed therein or thereto. The harm also must be to the prejudice of a mortgagee or owner of the property. The *mental element* requires proof that D acted wilfully and with knowledge of prejudice to V.

Case Law
Nature and Elements of Offence

R. v. Lundgard (1991), 63 C.C.C. (3d) 368, [1991] 4 W.W.R. 259 (Alta. C.A.); leave to appeal refused 66 C.C.C. (3d) vi, [1991] 6 W.W.R. lxvii (S.C.C.) — The section creates a discrete offence, separate from those of mischief and theft, intended to protect the mortgagee. P must prove D's acts reduced the property value. The offence is established where any specified act, done with the requisite intent, negatively affected the mortgagee's security interest.

Related Provisions: "Dwelling-house" is defined in s. 2. "Wilfully" may be established under s. 429(1). The provisions of ss. 429(2) and (3) are also applicable.

Theft of a fixture or other property left with the building would be punishable as theft under ss. 322 and 334.

D may *elect* mode of trial under s. 536(2).

---

442. Interfering with boundary lines — Every one who wilfully pulls down, defaces, alters or removes anything planted or set up as the boundary line or part of the boundary line of land is guilty of an offence punishable on summary conviction.

R.S., c. C-34, s. 398.

Commentary: The section prohibits *interference* with *boundary lines*.

The *external circumstances* require proof that D pulled down, defaced, altered or removed anything planted or set up as the boundary line of land or part thereof. The interference, in other words, must be of one of the types described. The *mental element* requires proof that D acted *wilfully*. No ulterior mental element is expressly required by the section.

Related Provisions: A related offence, interference with boundary marks, is described in s. 443(1). "Wilfully" may be established under s. 429(1).

The application of s. 429(2) to this offence permits a defence of legal justification or excuse and colour of right. The onus of proof in respect of such defence is statutorily shifted to D. Its application, however, may have the added effect of including lack of justification or excuse and colour of right in the essential elements of the offence. Section 429(3) also applies.

In certain circumstances, the offence may also amount to mischief under s. 430(1).

The offence is tried and punished under Part XXVII.

---

443. (1) Interfering with international boundary marks, etc. — Every one who wilfully pulls down, defaces, alters or removes

    (a) a boundary mark lawfully placed to mark an international, provincial, county or municipal boundary, or

    (b) a boundary mark lawfully placed by a land surveyor to mark any limit, boundary or angle of a concession, range, lot or parcel of land,

is guilty of an indictable offence and liable to imprisonment for a term not exceeding five years.

(2) Saving provision — A land surveyor does not commit an offence under subsection (1) where, in his operations as a land surveyor,

    (a) he takes up, when necessary, a boundary mark mentioned in paragraph (1)(*b*) and carefully replaces it as it was before he took it up, or

    (b) he takes up a boundary mark mentioned in paragraph (1)(*b*) in the course of surveying for a highway or other work that, when completed, will make it impossible or impracticable for that boundary mark to occupy its original position, and he establishes a permanent record of the original position sufficient to permit that position to be ascertained.

R.S., c. C-34, s. 399.

Commentary: The section prohibits *interference* with official *boundary marks*.

Under s. 443(1), the *external circumstances* consist of the pulling down, defacing, altering or removing of a boundary mark of the nature described in either s. 443(1)(a) or (b). The *mental element* requires proof that D acted *wilfully*. No ulterior mental element need be proven according to the definition of the offence.

Section 443(2) is a *saving* provision applicable to certain conduct by *land surveyors*. The conduct, which is not criminal under ss. 443(2)(a) and (b), must take place in D's operations as a land surveyor.

Related Provisions: The *mental element* in the statutory definition of the offence, *wilfully*, may be established under s. 429(1). No proof of an ulterior *mental element* is expressly required. Under s. 429(2) D may assert a defence of legal justification or excuse and colour of right. It is D's onus to establish the defence but, where raised, it would seem to add an element to P's proof, or disproof.

In some circumstances, the offence may also amount to mischief under ss. 430(1)(c) and (d).

D may *elect* mode of trial under s. 536(2).

Cattle and Other Animals

444. Injuring or endangering cattle — Every one who wilfully

    (a) kills, maims, wounds, poisons or injures cattle, or

    (b) places poison in such a position that it may easily be consumed by cattle,

is guilty of an indictable offence and liable to imprisonment for a term not exceeding five years.

R.S., c. C-34, s. 400.

Commentary: These offences prohibit *injuring* or *endangering cattle*.

Under s. 444(a), the *external circumstances* occur when D kills, wounds, maims, poisons or injures cattle. Under s. 444(b), no injury nor, *a fortiori*, death, wounding or maiming need occur, provided D places poison in such a position that it may easily be consumed by cattle. The *mental element*, in each case, requires proof that D acted *wilfully*.

Case Law

R. v. Brown (1984), 11 C.C.C. (3d) 191 (B.C. C.A.) — This section applies to all cattle, whether or not ownership is proved.

Related Provisions: "Cattle" is defined in s. 2, and "wilfully" may be established under s. 429(1).

The terms "wounds" and "maims" also appear in relation to a human victim in ss. 268(1) and 273(1). "Wounds", in general, involves an intentional injury which cuts or tears the flesh or skin. "Maims" means to deprive of the use of some member, to mutilate or cripple and involves a more permanent or lasting type of injury.

Semble, an interest in the cattle affords D *no* defence under this section because of s. 429(3).

The offence of s. 445 is a natural complement to the present section. Its application is confined to dogs, birds or animals that are not cattle and are kept for a lawful purpose.

D may elect mode of trial under s. 536(2).

445. Injuring or endangering other animals — Every one who wilfully and without lawful excuse

    (a) **kills, maims, wounds, poisons or injures dogs, birds or animals that are not cattle and are kept for a lawful purpose, or**

    (b) **places poison in such a position that it may easily be consumed by dogs, birds or animals that are not cattle and are kept for a lawful purpose,**

is guilty of an offence punishable on summary conviction.

R.S., c. C-34, s. 401.

Commentary: The section is similar to s. 444.

Under s. 445(a), the *external circumstances* occur when D kills, wounds, maims, poisons or injures dogs, birds or animals that are *not* cattle and *are kept for lawful purpose*. Under s. 445(b), D's conduct need not result in injury, *a fortiori* death, but must constitute the placing of poison in such a position that it may easily be consumed by a member of the statutorily delimited class. In each case, D must have *no lawful excuse* for the conduct.

The *mental element* in each case is comprised in the term "wilfully". No ulterior mental element need be proven.

Related Provisions: The *mental element*, described as "wilfully", may be proven under s. 429(1). The meaning of "wounds" and "maims" is discussed in the corresponding note to s. 444, *supra*.

An interest in the birds or animals will *not* bar D's conviction due to s. 429(3).

Under s. 429(2), the onus of proving a legal justification or excuse and colour of right rests upon D, though proof of absence of lawful excuse is an essential element of P's proof. The subsection may, accordingly, attract *Charter* s. 11(d) scrutiny.

The offence of s. 444, in similar terms, applies to cattle.

This offence is tried under Part XXVII.

Cruelty to Animals

446. (1) Causing unnecessary suffering — Every one commits an offence who

    (a) **wilfully causes or, being the owner, wilfully permits to be caused unnecessary pain, suffering or injury to an animal or bird;**

    (b) **by wilful neglect causes damage or injury to animals or birds while they are being driven or conveyed;**

    (c) **being the owner or the person having the custody or control of a domestic animal or a bird or an animal or a bird wild by nature that is in captivity, abandons it in distress or wilfully neglects or fails to provide suitable and adequate food, water, shelter and care for it;**

    (d) **in any manner encourages, aids or assists at the fighting or baiting of animals or birds;**

    (e) **wilfully, without reasonable excuse, administers a poisonous or an injurious drug or substance to a domestic animal or bird or an animal or a bird wild by nature that is kept in captivity or, being the owner of such an animal or a bird, wilfully permits a poisonous or an injurious drug or substance to be administered to it;**

    (f) **promotes, arranges, conducts, assists in, receives money for or takes part in any meeting, competition, exhibition, pastime, practice, display, or event at or in** the course of which captive birds are liberated by hand, trap, contrivance or any other means for the purpose of being shot when they are liberated; or

(g) being the owner, occupier, or person in charge of any premises, permits the premises or any part thereof to be used for a purpose mentioned in paragraph (f).

(2) **Punishment** — Every one who commits an offence under subsection (1) is guilty of an offence punishable on summary conviction.

(3) **Failure to exercise reasonable care as evidence** — For the purposes of proceedings under paragraph (1)(a) or (b), evidence that a person failed to exercise reasonable care or supervision of an animal or a bird thereby causing it pain, suffering, damage or injury is, in the absence of any evidence to the contrary, proof that the pain, suffering, damage or injury was caused or was permitted to be caused wilfully or was caused by wilful neglect, as the case may be.

(4) **Presence at baiting as evidence** — For the purpose of proceedings under paragraph (1)(d), evidence that an accused was present at the fighting or baiting of animals or birds is, in the absence of any evidence to the contrary, proof that he encouraged, aided or assisted at the fighting or baiting.

(5) **Order of prohibition** — Where an accused is convicted of an offence under subsection (1), the court may, in addition to any other sentence that may be imposed for the offence, make an order prohibiting the accused from owning or having the custody or control of an animal or bird during any period not exceeding two years.

(6) **Breach of order** — Every one who owns or has the custody or control of an animal or a bird while he is prohibited from doing so by reason of an order made under subsection (5) is guilty of an offence punishable on summary conviction.

R.S., c. C-34, s. 402; 1974–75–76, c. 93, s. 35.

Commentary: This summary conviction offence prohibits causing *unnecessary suffering* to birds or animals, enacts evidentiary provisions applicable in certain prosecutions, and permits prohibition orders to be made upon conviction.

The summary conviction offence of s. 446(1), causing *unnecessary suffering* to birds or animals, may be committed in any way described in the subsection. Proof of an ulterior *mental element* is not required. Wilful conduct need be established under many, though not all, descriptions of the offence.

The *presumption* of s. 446(3), applicable only in cases under ss. 446(1)(a) and (b), is engaged by the introduction of *evidence* that D *failed to exercise reasonable care or supervision* of an animal or bird, thereby causing it pain, suffering, damage or injury. The introduction of such evidence, *absent any evidence to the contrary*, is *proof* that the pain, suffering, damage or injury was caused or was permitted to be caused *wilfully* or was caused by wilful neglect, as the case may be. Section 446(4) only applies in cases under s. 446(1)(d). *Evidence* that D was *present* at the fighting or baiting of animals or birds is, in the *absence of any evidence to the contrary, proof* that D *encouraged, aided* or *assisted* at the fighting or baiting.

Under s. 446(5) a court may prohibit D from owning or having the custody or control of an animal or bird for a period not exceeding two years upon conviction under s. 446(1). A breach by D of the prohibition is itself a summary conviction offence under s. 446(6).

Case Law

R. v. McHugh (1965), 50 C.R. 263, [1966] 1 C.C.C. 170 (N.S. C.A.) — "Wilfully" includes reckless acts, as well as acts done with a bad motive or evil intent, or acts done by anyone as a free agent who knows what he is doing and intends to do it.

R. v. Menard (1978), 4 C.R. (3d) 333, 43 C.C.C. (2d) 458 (Que. C.A.) — The amount of the pain inflicted is *not* the issue if it is inflicted unnecessarily. The magnitude of the pain will be relevant when

577

determining the necessity for its infliction. It is unnecessary if another less painful means of obtaining the end result exists known to D and not of prohibitive cost.

Related Provisions: Proof of "wilfully" may be made under s. 429(1).

D may assert the defence of legal justification or excuse and colour of right under s. 429(2).

In general, mere presence by D at the scene of an offence, at all events without evidence of prior agreement or encouragement, would not render D liable as an aider or abettor under s. 21(1)(b) or (c). Subsection (4) would seem to reverse this general proposition.

Related offences appear in ss. 444, 445 and 447.

This offence is tried under Part XXVII.

447. (1) Keeping cockpit — Every one who builds, makes, maintains or keeps a cockpit on premises that he owns or occupies, or allows a cockpit to be built, made, maintained or kept on such premises is guilty of an offence punishable on summary conviction.

(2) Confiscation — A peace officer who finds cocks in a cockpit or on premises where a cockpit is located shall seize them and take them before a justice who shall order them to be destroyed.

R.S., c. C-34, s. 403.

Commentary: The *external circumstances* of the offence of s. 447(1) may be established by proof of acts or omissions by D. They are proven where D builds, makes, maintains or keeps a cockpit on premises he owns or occupies, as well where D allows a cockpit to be built, made, maintained or kept on the premises. No ulterior *mental element* need be proven. The intention to cause or allow the external circumstances to be committed will suffice. Knowledge is a critical element.

Section 447(2) obliges a *peace officer* who finds cocks in a cockpit, or on premises where a cockpit is located, to seize them and take them before a justice. The justice must order the birds destroyed.

Related Provisions: A related offence appears in s. 446(1)(d).

This offence is tried under Part XXVII.

PART XII — OFFENCES RELATING TO CURRENCY

Interpretation

448. Definitions — In this Part,

"counterfeit money" includes

    (a) false coin or false paper money that resembles or is apparently intended to resemble or pass for a current coin or current paper money,

    (b) a forged bank note or forged blank bank note, whether complete or incomplete,

    (c) a genuine coin or genuine paper money that is prepared or altered to resemble or pass for a current coin or current paper money of a higher denomination,

    (d) a current coin from which the milling is removed by filing or cutting the edges and on which new milling is made to restore its appearance,

    (e) a coin cased with gold, silver or nickel, as the case may be, that is intended to resemble or pass for a current gold, silver or nickel coin, and

    (f) a coin or a piece of metal or mixed metals washed or coloured by any means with a wash or material capable of producing the appearance of gold, silver or nickel and that is intended to resemble or pass for a current gold, silver or nickel coin;

"**counterfeit token of value**" means a counterfeit excise stamp, postage stamp or other evidence of value, by whatever technical, trivial or deceptive designation it may be described, and includes genuine coin or paper money that has no value as money;

"**current**" means lawfully current in Canada or elsewhere by virtue of a law, proclamation or regulation in force in Canada or elsewhere as the case may be;

"**utter**" includes sell, pay, tender and put off.

R.S., c. C-34, s. 406.

Commentary: The section defines terms used in this Part.

Related Provisions: "Bank-note" is defined in s. 2, and forgery in s. 366.

A related offence in respect of exchequer bill paper, as defined in s. 321, appears in s. 369.

Making

449. Making — Every one who makes or begins to make counterfeit money is guilty of an indictable offence and liable to imprisonment for a term not exceeding fourteen years.

R.S., c. C-34, s. 407.

Commentary: The *external circumstances* are established where D makes or begins to make counterfeit money. No counterfeit money need actually be made, provided the process of making it has commenced. *Quaere* whether to begin to make counterfeit D need go beyond what would otherwise be mere preparation? The *mental element* consists of the intention to make counterfeit money.

Related Provisions: There is *no* express definition of "makes" or "begins to make", although s. 461(1) provides when offences relating to counterfeit money are deemed complete. "Counterfeit money" is defined in s. 448. Its character may be proven, *inter alia*, by the certificate of an examiner of counterfeit under s. 461(2). The offence is one in respect of which authorization to intercept private communications may be given under Part VI and also an "enterprise crime offence" under Part XII.2.

Section 458 creates the preliminary or preparatory offence of making, having or dealing in instruments for counterfeiting.

D may *elect* mode of trial under s. 536(2).

Possession

450. Possession, etc., of counterfeit money — Every one who, without lawful justification or excuse, the proof of which lies on him,

    (a) buys, receives or offers to buy or receive,

    (b) has in his custody or possession, or

    (c) introduces into Canada,

counterfeit money is guilty of an indictable offence and liable to imprisonment for a term not exceeding fourteen years.

R.S., c. C-34, s. 408.

Commentary: This section prohibits certain *transactions* in *counterfeit money.*

Under s. 450(a), the *external circumstances* are complete when D buys, receives, or offers to buy or receive counterfeit money. No actual receipt or purchase need be established: the offer to do either is sufficient.

The offence of s. 450(b) is committed when D has in his/her *custody or possession* counterfeit money.

Under s. 450(c) the *external circumstances* require that D *introduce into Canada* counterfeit money.

The *external circumstances* also require proof that D's transactions are *without lawful justification or excuse*, a matter which D must prove on the balance of probabilities. The *onus* shift may attract *Charter* s. 11(d) scrutiny.

The *mental element* comprises the intention to cause the external circumstances of the offence, together with *knowledge* of the counterfeit nature of the money.

Case Law

Nature and Elements of Offence

R. v. Freng (1993), 86 C.C.C. (3d) 91 (B.C. C.A.) — *See also: R. v. Sagliocco* (1978), 39 C.C.C. (2d) 514 (B.C. C.A.) — On a charge of *possession* of counterfeit money, P must prove beyond a reasonable doubt that D *knew* of the *counterfeit character* of the money. Lack of knowledge is *not* "a legal justification or excuse", the burden of proof of which is on D under s. 450.

R. v. Santeramo (1976), 36 C.R.N.S. 1, 32 C.C.C. (2d) 35 (Ont. C.A.) — *Contra: R. v. Caccamo* (1973), 21 C.R.N.S. 83, 11 C.C.C. (2d) 249 (Ont. C.A.); affirmed on other grounds (1975), 29 C.R.N.S. 78 (S.C.C.) — *Knowledge* that the bill or coin was counterfeit at the time of possession is an essential element of the offence to be proved by P.

Lawful Justification or Excuse

R. v. Duane (1984), 12 C.C.C. (3d) 368 (Alta. C.A.); affirmed (1985), 22 C.C.C. (3d) 448 (S.C.C.) — An intention to spend the money is neither an essential element of nor a lawful excuse for the possession of counterfeit money.

Robinson v. R. (1974), 10 C.C.C. (2d) 505 (S.C.C.) — Where the coins resemble current coin, the fact that D does not intend to use the coins as currency, but rather to sell them as numismatic curiosities does *not* make their possession otherwise than that of counterfeit money.

Charter Considerations

R. v. Burge (1987), 55 C.R. (3d) 131 (B.C. C.A.) — This section is *not* inconsistent with *Charter* s. 11(d). Lack of knowledge of the counterfeit nature of the money is a complete defence. To place the onus of proof on D does *not* violate s. 11(d).

Related Provisions: "Counterfeit money" is defined in s. 448, and s. 461(1) provides when offences relating to counterfeit money are complete. The counterfeit character of the money may be established by the certificate of an examiner of counterfeit under s. 461(2).

Possession, an essential element of the offence described in s. 450(b), may be proven under s. 4(3).

Section 449 prohibits making counterfeit money, and s. 458 describes the preparatory or preliminary offence of making, having or dealing in instruments for counterfeiting.

Authorization to intercept private communications may be given in respect of this "offence" under s. 183 and Part VI. It is also an "enterprise crime offence" under s. 462.3 and Part XII.2.

D may *elect* mode of trial under s. 536(2).

451. Having clippings, etc. — Every one who, without lawful justification or excuse, the proof of which lies on him, has in his custody or possession

(a) gold or silver filings or clippings,

(b) gold or silver bullion, or

(c) gold or silver in dust, solution or otherwise,

produced or obtained by impairing, diminishing or lightening a current gold or silver coin, knowing that it has been so produced or obtained, is guilty of an indictable offence and liable to imprisonment for a term not exceeding five years.

R.S., c. C-34, s. 409.

Commentary: This section prohibits *possession* of gold or silver of a specified origin.

The *external circumstances* require that D have in his/her *custody or possession* gold or silver, in any state or form described in ss. 451(a)–(c). The gold or silver must be *produced or obtained* by *impairing*, *diminishing* or *lightening* a current gold or silver coin. D's custody or possession must be *without lawful justification or excuse*. The shift to D of the onus of proving a lawful justification or excuse, on a balance of probabilities, may be vulnerable under *Charter* s. 11(d).

No ulterior *mental element*, as for example an intent to defraud, need be proven. P must prove however, that D intended to cause the external circumstances of the offence and, in particular, had *knowledge* of the nature of the subject-matter and its origins.

Related Provisions: The circumstances under which D may be found in possession are described in s. 4(3). "Current" is defined in s. 448.

Related offences appear in ss. 455 and 456.

D may *elect* mode of trial under s. 536(2).

Uttering

452. Uttering, etc., counterfeit money — Every one who, without lawful justification or excuse, the proof of which lies on him,

    (a) utters or offers to utter counterfeit money or uses counterfeit money as if it were genuine, or

    (b) exports, sends or takes counterfeit money out of Canada,

is guilty of an indictable offence and liable to imprisonment for a term not exceeding fourteen years.

R.S., c. C-34, s. 410.

Commentary: The section prohibits certain transactions in counterfeit money.

Under s. 452(a), the *external circumstances* require that D *utter* or *offer to utter* counterfeit money, or *use* counterfeit money as if it were genuine. An actual uttering need *not* be established. Under s. 452(b), the *external circumstances* relate to exportation or transfer of counterfeit money: D must export, send or take counterfeit money out of Canada. D's conduct must be without lawful justification or excuse. The onus of proving lawful justification or excuse is on D.

The *mental element* requires proof that D intended to cause the external circumstances of the offence. P must also establish D's *knowledge* of the counterfeit character of the money. No ulterior mental element, as for example intent to defraud, need be established.

Case Law
Nature and Elements of Offence
R. v. Freng (1993), 86 C.C.C. (3d) 91 (B.C. C.A.) — P must prove that D *knew* of the *counterfeit character* of the money. Lack of knowledge is *not* "a legal justification or excuse", the burden of proof of which is on D under s. 452.

R. v. Kelly (1979), 48 C.C.C. (2d) 560 (Ont. C.A.) — The sale of counterfeit money as counterfeit, to be put in circulation as currency, falls within the concept of "uttering," notwithstanding that the immediate purchaser is not deceived.

Charter Considerations — Reverse Onus
R. v. Burge (1987), 55 C.R. (3d) 131 (B.C. C.A.) — This section does not offend *Charter* s. 11(d).

Related Provisions: Section 448 expansively defines "counterfeit money" and "utter". "Utter" includes sell, pay, tender and put off. "Utter" ordinarily means to pass or circulate as legal tender or to put forth upon the market.

Other uttering offences in relation to currency appear in ss. 452–456. Uttering a forged document is punishable under s. 368.

The counterfeit character of the money may be proven by the certificate of a designated examiner of counterfeit under s. 461(2). Section 461(1) describes when the offence is complete. The money itself is forfeited to Her Majesty under s. 462(1), and may be seized and detained by a peace officer pending such forfeiture under s. 462(2).

Authorization to intercept private communications may be given in respect of this "offence" under Part VI. It is also an "enterprise crime offence" under Part XII.2.

D may elect mode of trial under s. 536(2).

453. Uttering coin — Every one who, with intent to defraud, knowingly utters

(a) a coin that is not current, or

(b) a piece of metal or mixed metals that resembles in size, figure or colour a current coin for which it is uttered,

is guilty of an indictable offence and liable to imprisonment for a term not exceeding two years.

R.S., c. C-34, s. 411.

Commentary: This *uttering* offence relates to *coins* and *metallic resemblances.*

The *external circumstances* consist of uttering a coin that is *not* current, or a metallic piece that resembles in size, figure or colour a current coin for which it is uttered. The section meets cases where noncurrent domestic or foreign coin or metals similar in size, colour or figure to a current coin are passed off as current coin. Nothing is said of the absence of lawful justification or excuse.

The *mental element* has several components. D must intend to cause the external circumstances of the offence. The uttering must be done "knowingly": P must establish D's *knowledge* of the spurious *character* of the coin or metal. P must also prove an ulterior *mental element*, the *intent* to *defraud.*

Related Provisions: "Current" and "utter" are defined in s. 448. "Utter" ordinarily means to pass or circulate as legal tender, or to put forth upon the market.

Other uttering offences appear in ss. 452–456. Uttering a forged document is punishable under s. 368.

Unlike the offence of s. 452(a), where the external circumstances are complete upon proof of an offer to utter, the offence of this section requires an actual uttering to establish liability. The coin of s. 453(a) need *not* be counterfeit, provided it is not current.

D may *elect* mode of trial under s. 536(2).

454. Slugs and tokens — Every one who without lawful excuse, the proof of which lies on him,

(a) manufactures, produces or sells, or

(b) has in his possession

anything that is intended to be fraudulently used in substitution for a coin or token of value that any coin or token-operated device is designed to receive is guilty of an offence punishable on summary conviction.

R.S., c. C-34, s. 412; 1972, c. 13, s. 32.

Commentary: The section prohibits certain transactions in items used in substitution for coins or tokens of value in certain devices.

The *external circumstances* are established when D manufactures, produces, sells, or has in his/her possession certain items. The items may be anything, but must be intended for fraudulent use in substitution for a coin or token of value that any coin or token-operated device is designed to receive. There must be no lawful excuse for D's conduct. The *onus* of proving lawful excuse is shifted to D, thereby engaging s. 11(d) *Charter* concerns.

The *mental element* consists of the intention to cause the external circumstances of the offence. P must prove D's *knowledge* of the character of the items and, further, that they are *intended for fraudulent use* in substitution for genuine coins or tokens of value in coin or token operated device.

The section, for example, would apply in cases where metal slugs are inserted in coin-operated telephones, or in machines which sell or receive tokens for public transportation.

Related Provisions: Possession may be established under s. 4(3). Neither "token of value", "coin-operated device" nor "token-operated device" is defined, although "counterfeit token of value" is exhaustively defined in s. 448.

This offence may overlap with the offences of theft of a telecommunications service (s. 326), and transportation fraud (s. 393(3)). It is also an offence to possess instruments for breaking into coin-operated or currency exchange devices under s. 352.

This offence is tried under Part XXVII.

Defacing or Impairing

455. Clipping and uttering clipped coin — Every one who

(a) impairs, diminishes or lightens a current gold or silver coin with intent that it should pass for a current gold or silver coin, or

(b) utters a coin, knowing that it has been impaired, diminished or lightened contrary to paragraph (a),

is guilty of an indictable offence and liable to imprisonment for a term not exceeding fourteen years.

R.S., c. C-34, s. 413.

Commentary: These offences involve the *impairment* and *uttering* of impaired coin.

The *external circumstances* of the *impairment* offence of s. 455(a) are complete when D impairs, diminishes or lightens a current gold or silver coin. The *mental element* consists of the intention to cause the external circumstances with the further or ulterior intent that the impaired coin should pass for current gold or silver coin. The *external circumstances* of the *uttering* offence of s. 455(b) require proof that D uttered a coin impaired in a manner described in s. 455(a). The *mental element* consists of an intention to utter a coin in the *knowledge* of its spurious character or origins. No further mental element need be established.

Related Provisions: "Current" and "utter" are defined in s. 448. "Utter" ordinarily means pass or circulate as legal tender or put forth something on the market. Other uttering offences in relation to currency appear in ss. 452, 453 and 456 and in relation to forged documents generally, in s. 368. The offence of s. 456 prohibits the defacing and uttering of defaced coins.

D may *elect* mode of trial.

456. Defacing current coins — Every one who

(a) defaces a current coin, or

(b) utters a current coin that has been defaced,

is guilty of an offence punishable on summary conviction.

R.S., c. C-34, s. 414.

Commentary: This section is similar to s. 455.

The *external circumstances* under s. 456(a) consist of *defacing* a current coin and, under s. 456(b), of *uttering* a current coin that has been defaced. The *mental element* consists of the intention to cause the external circumstances and, *semble*, under s. 456(b), includes D's *knowledge* of the character of the coin uttered.

Related Provisions: The offences of s. 455 are closely related to the present offence. Other crimes of uttering in respect of currency appear in ss. 452, 453 and 455. Uttering forged documents is punishable under s. 368.

This offence is tried under Part XXVII.

457. (1) Likeness of bank-notes — No person shall make, publish, print, execute, issue, distribute or circulate, including by electronic or computer-assisted means, anything in the likeness of

(a) a current bank-note; or

(b) an obligation or a security of a government or bank.

(2) Exception — Subsection (1) does not apply to

(a) the Bank of Canada or its employees when they are carrying out their duties;

(b) the Royal Canadian Mounted Police or its members or employees when they are carrying out their duties; or

(c) any person acting under a contract or licence from the Bank of Canada or Royal Canadian Mounted Police.

(3) Offence — A person who contravenes subsection (1) is guilty of an offence punishable on summary conviction.

(4) Defence — No person shall be convicted of an offence under subsection (3) in relation to the printed likeness of a Canadian bank-note if it is established that the length or width of the likeness is less than three-fourths or greater than one-and-one-half times the length or width, as the case may be, of the bank-note and

(a) the likeness is in black-and-white only; or

(b) the likeness of the bank-note appears on only one side of the likeness.

R.S., c. C-34, s. 415; 1999, c. 5, s. 12.

Commentary: The section was enacted to stifle the increasing tendency towards photographic and other reproductions of Bank of Canada notes, either for commercial advertising or other purposes, or simply as a matter of interest or curiosity. There is generally no intention of passing them off as currency or of making any wrongful use of the negatives or plates used in their production.

The *external circumstances* of each offence are described in ss. 457(1) and (2) respectively. The *mental element* is an intention to cause the external circumstances of the offence. No ulterior mental element need be proven.

Under s. 457(3), D will *not* be convicted where it is *established* that in publishing anything to which s. 457(2) applies, *all* of the elements of ss. 457(3)(a)–(e) are applicable. It would appear likely that the onus of proving compliance with s. 457(3) rests with D, thereby engaging s. 11(d) *Charter* review.

Related Provisions: Unlike the particular material on which the likeness or appearance must be printed under s. 457(1), the subject-matter of s. 457(2) may be "anything", a word of wide and comprehensive import.

"Current" is defined in s. 448 and "bank-note" in s. 2.

The offences are tried under Part XXVII.

Instruments or Materials

458. Making, having or dealing in instruments for counterfeiting — Every one who, without lawful justification or excuse, the proof of which lies on him,

(a) makes or repairs,

(b) begins or proceeds to make or repair,

(c) buys or sells, or

(d) has in his custody or possession,

any machine, engine, tool, instrument, material or thing that he knows has been used or that he knows is adapted and intended for use in making counterfeit money or counterfeit tokens of value is guilty of an indictable offence and liable to imprisonment for a term not exceeding fourteen years.

R.S., c. C-34, s. 416.

Commentary: The section makes it an offence to make, repair, have or deal in counterfeiting instruments. The offence is often preliminary to other crimes under this Part. No counterfeit money or tokens of value need ever be produced to attract liability.

The *external circumstances* require that D's conduct fall within any of ss. 458(a)–(d) and be in respect of a machine, engine, tool, instrument, material or thing. The subject-matter further must have been used or be *adapted* and *intended* for use in making counterfeit money or tokens of value. D's conduct must be without lawful justification or excuse. The *onus* of proving a lawful justification or excuse is shifted to D, thereby relieving P of the initial burden in respect of the issue and attracting *Charter* s. 11(d) challenge.

The section does *not* demand proof of any ulterior *mental element*, only the intention to cause the external circumstances and, in particular, knowledge of the previous, adapted or intended use of the subject-matter.

Related Provisions: "Counterfeit money" and "counterfeit token of value" are defined in s. 448 and "bank-note" in s. 2. Possession may be established under s. 4(3). Offences relating to counterfeit money appear in ss. 449, 450, 452 and 460.

Section 369(a) creates a similar offence in relation to exchequer bill and revenue paper as defined in s. 321.

D may *elect* mode of trial under s. 536(2).

459. Conveying instruments for coining out of mint — Every one who, without lawful justification or excuse, the proof of which lies on him, knowingly conveys out of any of Her Majesty's mints in Canada,

(a) any machine, engine, tool, instrument, material or thing used or employed in connection with the manufacture of coins,

(b) a useful part of anything mentioned in paragraph (a), or

(c) coin, bullion, metal or a mixture of metals,

is guilty of an indictable offence and liable to imprisonment for a term not exceeding fourteen years.

R.S., c. C-34, s. 417.

Commentary: The section seeks to prevent coinage out of mint by prohibiting the conveying of instruments for coining. The offence, quite often, is preliminary to other offences relating to coins. No coining out of mint need ever occur to establish liability.

The *external circumstances* require that D *convey out* of any of Her Majesty's mints in Canada anything described in ss. 459(a)–(c), *without lawful justification or excuse*. As is common in this Part, the onus of proof of lawful justification or excuse is shifted to D, a matter which may attract *Charter* s. 11(d) scrutiny.

The *mental element* requires that P prove that D intended to cause the external circumstances of the offence and, in particular, that the conveyance was done *knowingly* by D.

Related Provisions: Other offences relating to coins appear in ss. 451, 453, 455 and 456.

D may *elect* mode of trial under s. 536(2).

Advertising and Trafficking in Counterfeit Money or Counterfeit Tokens of Value

460. (1) Advertising and dealing in counterfeit money, etc. — Every one who

(a) by an advertisement or any other writing, often to sell, procure or dispose of counterfeit money or counterfeit tokens of value or to give information with respect to the manner in which or the means by which counterfeit money or counterfeit tokens of value may be sold, procured or disposed of, or

(b) purchases, obtains, negotiates or otherwise deals with counterfeit tokens of value, or offers to negotiate with a view to purchasing or obtaining them,

is guilty of an indictable offence and liable to imprisonment for a term not exceeding five years.

(2) Fraudulent use of money genuine but valueless — No person shall be convicted of an offence under subsection (1) in respect of genuine coin or genuine paper money that has no value as money unless, at the time when the offence is alleged to have been committed, he knew that the coin or paper money had no value as money and he had a fraudulent intent in his dealings with or with respect to the coin or paper money.

R.S., c. C-34, s. 418.

Commentary: Section 460(1) prohibits advertising and other transactions in counterfeit money and tokens of value.

The *external circumstances* are described in ss. 460(1)(a) and (b). The gravamen of the offence of s. 460(1)(a) rests in the *advertising* of means for disposal of counterfeit money or tokens of value. Under s. 460(1)(b), a *dealing in* counterfeit money or tokens of value must be shown.

The *mental element* of each offence consists of the intention to cause its external circumstances.

Section 460(2) enacts a *saving* provision, applicable in prosecutions under s. 460(1), where the subject-matter is genuine, but valueless, coin or paper money. D may only be convicted of an offence where P proves that, at the time of the offence, D *knew* that the coin or paper money was valueless. P must also prove that at such time, D had a fraudulent intent in such dealings.

It would seem difficult to envisage how conduct described in s. 460(2) could amount to an offence under s. 460(1), at all events because genuine, but valueless, coin or paper money would *not* seem to fall within the definition of "counterfeit money" in s. 448. Conduct described in s. 460(2) would only amount to an offence under s. 460(1), if s. 460(2) is both a liability-creating and a saving provision.

Related Provisions: "Counterfeit money" and "counterfeit token of value" are defined in s. 448, and "writing" in s. 2.

Section 461(1) describes when offences relating to counterfeit money or tokens of value are deemed complete.

D may *elect* mode of trial under s. 536(2).

Special Provisions as to Proof

461. (1) When counterfeit complete — Every offence relating to counterfeit money or counterfeit tokens of value shall be deemed to be complete notwithstanding that the money or tokens of value in respect of which the proceedings are taken are not finished or perfected or do not copy exactly the money or tokens of value that they are apparently intended to resemble or for which they are apparently intended to pass.

(2) Certificate of examiner of counterfeit — In any proceedings under this Part, a certificate signed by a person designated as an examiner of counterfeit by the Solicitor General of Canada, stating that any coin, paper money or bank note described therein is counterfeit money or that any coin, paper money or bank note described therein is genuine and is or is not, as the case may be, current in Canada or elsewhere, is evidence of the statements contained in the certificate without proof of the signature or official character of the person appearing to have signed the certificate.

(3) Cross-examination and notice — Subsections 258(6) and (7) apply, with such modification as the circumstances require, in respect of a certificate described in subsection (2).

R.S., c. C-34, s. 419; 1992, c. 1, s. 58(1), Schedule I, item 7.

Commentary: The section describes *when* offences relating to counterfeit money or tokens of value are *complete*, and authorizes *proof* of the *counterfeit* nature of designated subject-matter by *certificate* of an *examiner* of counterfeit.

Under s. 461(1), *offences* relating to counterfeit money or tokens of value are *complete* notwithstanding that the money or tokens are *not* finished or perfected, or do *not* copy exactly the genuine money or tokens they are apparently intended to resemble or for which they are apparently intended to pass.

Section 461(2) enables *proof by certificate* of the counterfeit character of any coin, paper money or bank-note in prosecutions under Part XII. The certificate must be signed by an *examiner of counterfeit* designated by the Solicitor General of Canada, must describe the coin, paper money or bank-note in respect of which the opinion is given, and further disclose whether it is counterfeit, genuine and current or not in Canada or elsewhere. The certificate is *evidence* of the statements contained therein without proof of the signature or official character of the designated examiner of counterfeit.

The reference to ss. 258(6) and (7) permits *cross-examination* of the examiner and require P to give D *reasonable notice* of the intention to adduce the certificate, as well as a *copy* of the certificate, in order that the certificate may be receivable in evidence. Attendance and cross-examination of the examiner is only permitted with leave of the court.

Case Law

R. v. Serratore (1980), 53 C.C.C. (2d) 106 (Ont. C.A.) — An R.C.M.P. officer, designated as an examiner of counterfeit money under s. 461(2), was qualified, by training and experience, to give evidence, *viva voce* or by certificate, as to whether forged bills were current legal tender in the United States.

R. v. MacIntosh (1972), 16 C.R.N.S. 119, 5 C.C.C. (2d) 239 (Ont. C.A.) — Testimony by a police examiner of counterfeit that certain counterfeit bills are imitations of current paper money is *prima facie* evidence of what is lawfully current in Canada. P need *not* produce a certificate under this section.

Related Provisions: "Counterfeit money" and "counterfeit token of value" are defined in s. 448, as is "current". "Bank-note" is defined in s. 2.

Forfeiture

462. (1) Ownership — Counterfeit money, counterfeit tokens of value and anything that is used or is intended to be used to make counterfeit money or counterfeit tokens of value belong to Her Majesty.

(2) Seizure — A peace officer may seize and detain

    (a) counterfeit money,

    (b) counterfeit tokens of value, and

    (c) machines, engines, tools, instruments, materials or things that have been used or that have been adapted and are intended for use in making counterfeit money or counterfeit tokens of value, and anything seized shall be sent to the Minister of Finance to be disposed of or dealt with as he may direct, but anything that is required as evidence in any proceedings shall not be sent to the Minister until it is no longer required in those proceedings.

R.S., c. C-34, s. 420.

Commentary: Section 462(1) makes all counterfeit money, counterfeit tokens of value and anything used or intended to be used to make either the property of Her Majesty.

Under s. 462(2), a peace officer may seize *without* warrant and detain counterfeit money, counterfeit tokens of value and anything used or adapted and intended for use in making either. This aspect of the subsection may attract s. 8 *Charter* scrutiny. Anything seized and not or no longer required as evidence in any proceedings must be sent to the Minister of Finance for disposal.

Related Provisions: "Counterfeit money" and "counterfeit token of value" are defined in s. 448. The general search warrant provisions are found in s. 487.

PART XII.1 — INSTRUMENTS AND LITERATURE FOR ILLICIT DRUG USE

Interpretation

462.1 "Consume" — In this Part,

"consume", "consumption" includes smoking, inhaling, masticating and injecting into the human body;

"illicit drug" means a controlled substance or precursor the import, export, production, sale or possession of which is prohibited or restricted pursuant to the *Controlled Drugs and Substances Act*;

"illicit drug use" means the importation, exportation, production, sale or possession of a controlled substance or precursor contrary to the *Controlled Drugs and Substances Act* or a regulation made under that Act;

"instrument for illicit drug use" means anything designed primarily or intended under the circumstances for consuming or to facilitate the consumption of an illicit drug, but does not include a "device" as that term is defined in section 2 of the *Food and Drugs Act*;

"literature for illicit drug use" means any printed matter or video describing or depicting, and designed primarily or intended under the circumtances to promote, encourage or advocate the production, preparation or consumption of illicit drugs;

"sell" includes offer for sale, expose for sale, have in possession for sale and distribute, whether or not the distribution is made for consideration.

R.S. 1985, c. 50 (4th Supp.), s. 1; 1996, c. 19, s. 67.

Commentary: The section defines terms which are essential elements of the offence of s. 462.2.

Related Provisions: Other related provisions are described in the corresponding note to s. 2, *supra*.

Offence

462.2 Offence — **Every one who knowingly imports into Canada, exports from Canada, manufactures, promotes or sells instruments or literature for illicit drug use is guilty of an offence and is liable on summary conviction**

(a) **for a first offence, to a fine not exceeding one hundred thousand dollars or to imprisonment for a term not exceeding six months or to both; or**

(b) **for a second or subsequent offence, to a fine not exceeding three hundred thousand dollars or to imprisonment for a term not exceeding one year or to both.**

R.S. 1985, c. 50 (4th Supp.), s. 1.

Commentary: The section prohibits certain transactions in instruments or literature for illicit drug use.

The *external circumstances* include any of several transactions involving instruments or literature for *illicit drug use*. The unlawful transactions include *importation* into Canada, *exportation* from Canada, *manufacture, promotion* or *sale* of instruments or literature for illicit drug use.

The *mental element*, expressed as "knowingly", requires no proof of any ulterior or specific mental element.

Related Provisions: "Instrument for illicit drug use", "literature for illicit drug use", "illicit drug" and "sell" are defined in s. 462.1.

The summary conviction offence created by this section is tried under Part XXVII. Sections 462.2(a) and (b) apply to penalty, however, not the general punishment provisions of s. 787(1).

PART XII.2 — PROCEEDS OF CRIME

Interpretation

462.3 Definitions — **In this Part,**

[Repealed 1996, c. 19, s. 68(1).]

"designated substance offence" means

(a) **an offence under Part I of the** *Controlled Drugs and Substances Act*, **except subsection 4(1) of that Act, or**

(b) **a conspiracy or an attempt to commit, being an accessory after the fact in relation to, or any counselling in relation to, an offence referred to in paragraph (a);**

"enterprise crime offence" means

(a) **an offence against any of the following provisions, namely,**

(i) **subsection 99(1) (weapons trafficking),**

(i.1) **subsection 100(1) (possession for purpose of weapons trafficking),**

(i.2) **subsection 102(1) (making automatic firearm),**

(i.3) **subsection 103(1) (importing or exporting knowing it is unauthorized),**

(i.4) **subsection 104(1) (unauthorized importing or exporting),**

(i.5) **section 119 (bribery of judicial officers, etc.),**

(ii) section 120 (bribery of officers),

(iii) section 121 (frauds on the government),

(iv) section 122 (breach of trust by public officer),

(iv.1) section 123 (municipal corruption),

(iv.2) section 124 (selling or purchasing office),

(iv.3) section 125 (influencing or negotiating appointments or dealing in offices),

(v) section 163 (corrupting morals),

(v.1) section 163.1 (child pornography),

(vi) subsection 201(1) (keeping gaming or betting house),

(vii) section 202 (betting, pool-selling, book-making, etc.),

(vii.1) paragraph 206(1)(e) (money increment schemes, etc.),

(viii) section 210 (keeping common bawdy-house),

(ix) section 212 (procuring),

(x) section 235 (punishment for murder),

(xi) section 334 (punishment for theft),

(xii) section 344 (punishment for robbery),

(xiii) section 346 (extortion),

(xiii.1) section 347 (criminal interest rate),

(xiv) section 367 (punishment for forgery),

(xv) section 368 (uttering forged document),

(xvi) section 380 (fraud),

(xvii) section 382 (fraudulent manipulation of stock exchange transactions),

(xvii.1) section 394 (fraud in relation to valuable minerals),

(xvii.2) section 394.1 (possession of stolen or fraudulently obtained valuable minerals),

(xviii) section 426 (secret commissions),

(xix) section 433 (arson),

(xx) section 449 (making counterfeit money),

(xxi) section 450 (possession, etc., of counterfeit money),

(xxii) section 452 (uttering, etc., counterfeit money),

(xxiii) section 462.31 (laundering proceeds of crime), or

(xxiv) section 467.1 (participation in criminal organization),

(a.1) any indictable offence under this or any other Act of Parliament committed for the benefit of, at the direction of or in association with a criminal organization for which the maximum punishment is imprisonment for five years or more,

(b) an offence against subsection 96(1) (possession of weapon obtained by commission of offence) or section 354 (possession of property obtained by crime), committed in relation to any property, thing or proceeds obtained or derived directly or indirectly as a result of

(i) the commission in Canada of an offence referred to in paragraph (a) or (a.1) or a designated substance offence, or

(ii) an act or omission anywhere that, if it has occurred in Canada, would have constituted an offence referred to in paragraph (*a*) or (*a.*1) or a designated substance offence,

(**b.**1) an offence against section 126.1 or 126.2 or subsection 233(1) or 240(1) of the *Excise Act*, section 153, 159, 163.1 or 163.2 of the *Customs Act* or subsection 52.1(9) of the *Competition Act*, or

Conditional Amendment — 462.3(b.1)

If Bill C-20, entitled *An Act to amend the Competition Act and to make consequential and related amendments to other Acts* [Assented to March 11, 1999.], and Bill C-51, entitled *An Act to amend the Criminal Code, the Controlled Drugs and Substances Act and the Corrections and Conditional Release Act* [Assented to March 11, 1999.], introduced during the first session of the thirty-sixth Parliament, are assented to, then, on the latest of the coming into force of

(a) subsection 9(2) of this Act,

(b) section 13 of Bill C-20, and

(c) section 53 of Bill C-51,

paragraph (b.1) of the definition 'enterprise crime offence' in section 462.3 of the *Criminal Code* is replaced by the following:

(**b.**1) an offence against section 126.1 or 126.2 or subsection 233(1) or 240(1) of the *Excise Act*, section 153, 159, 163.1 or 163.2 of the *Customs Act*, subsection 52.1(9) of the *Competition Act* or section 3, 4 or 5 of the *Corruption of Foreign Public Officials Act*, or

1998, c. 34, s. 11 [Not in force at date of publication.]

(c) a conspiracy or an attempt to commit, being an accessory after the fact in relation to, or any counselling in relation to, an offence referred to in paragraph (*a*), (*a.*1), (*b*) or (*b.1*);

"judge" means a judge as defined in section 552 or a judge of a superior court of criminal jurisdiction;

"proceeds of crime" means any property, benefit or advantage, within or outside Canada, obtained or derived directly or indirectly as a result of

(a) the commission in Canada of an enterprise crime offence or a designated substance offence,

(b) an act or omission anywhere that, if it had occurred in Canada, would have constituted an enterprise crime offence or a designated substance offence.

R.S. 1985, c. 42 (4th Supp.), s. 2; 1993, c. 25, s. 95; 1993, c. 37, s. 32; 1993, c. 46, s. 5; 1994, c. 44, s. 29; 1995, c. 39, s. 151; 1996, c. 19, ss. 68, 70(a), (b); 1997, c. 18, s. 27; c. 23, s. 9; 1998, c. 34, s. 9; 1999, c. 5, ss. 13, 52.

Commentary: The section defines several terms for the purposes of this Part.

The definitions of "designated substance offence" and "enterprise crime offence" include not only listed *substantive* offences, but also the *preliminary* crimes of conspiracy, attempt and counselling as well as accessoryship after the fact in relation to their commission.

Related Provisions: "Superior court of criminal jurisdiction" and "property" are defined in s. 2, "counsel" in s. 22(3). Liability for counselling is determined under ss. 22(1) and (2). Accessoryship after the fact is provided for in s. 23. An accused to whom ss. 21–23 apply may be convicted, notwithstanding that the person whom D has aided or abetted, counselled, or procured, or received, comforted or assisted cannot be convicted of the offence. Whether conduct amounts in law to an attempt is determined in accordance with s. 24.

The effect of the descriptive parenthetical cross-references is described in s. 3.

Other related provisions are described in the corresponding note to s. 2, *supra*.

Offence

462.31 (1) Laundering proceeds of crime — Every one commits an offence who uses, transfers the possession of, sends or delivers to any person or place, transports, transmits, alters, disposes of or otherwise deals with, in any manner and by an means, any property or any proceeds of any property with intent to conceal or convert that property or those proceeds, knowing or believing that all or a part of that property or of those proceeds was obtained or derived directly or indirectly as a result of

(a) the commission in Canada of an enterprise crime offence or a designated substance offence; or

(b) an act or omission anywhere that, if it had occurred in Canada, would have constituted an enterprise crime offence or a designated substance offence.

(2) Punishment — Every one who commits an offence under subsection (1)

(a) is guilty of an indictable offence and liable to imprisonment for a term not exceeding ten years; or

(b) is guilty of an offence punishable on summary conviction.

(3) Exception — A peace officer or a person acting under the direction of a peace officer is not guilty of an offence under subsection (1) if the peace officer or person does any of the things mentioned in that subsection for the purposes of an investigation or otherwise in the execution of the peace officer's duties.

R.S. 1985, c. 42 (4th Supp.), s. 2; 1996, c. 19, s. 70(c); 1997, c. 18, s. 28.

Commentary: The section defines an offence generally described as *laundering proceeds of crime* and provides for its punishment.

The *external circumstances* comprise a prohibited *transaction* and *subject-matter*. The *subject-matter* is any property or any proceeds of any property, all or part of which was obtained or derived directly or indirectly as a result of the commission in Canada of an enterprise crime or designated substance offence, or as a result of an act or omission anywhere that, had it occurred in Canada, would have constituted either offence. The prohibited *transaction* by D must amount to "... uses, transfers ... by any means ...". The *mental element* includes the basic requirement that D intentionally engage in the conduct which constitutes the external circumstances of the offence. D must have *knowledge or belief* of the spurious or derivative *character* of the property or proceeds. P must prove that D had the further or ulterior *intent to conceal or convert* the property or proceeds.

Section 462.31(2) provides that the offence of s. 462.31(1) is triable either way.

Section 462.31(3) creates an *exception* to an offence under s. 462.31(1) for a peace officer or a person acting under his/her direction. To come within the exception the acts mentioned in subsection (1) must be done for investigatory purposes or must be otherwise pursuant to the execution of the peace officer's duties.

Case Law
Nature and Elements of Offence

United States v. Dynar, [1997] 2 S.C.R. 462, 8 C.R. (5th) 79, 115 C.C.C. (3d) 481 (S.C.C.) — Knowledge is *not* the *mens rea* of the money-laundering offences. There are *two* constituents of knowledge

i.   *truth*; and

ii.   *belief*.

It is only *belief* that is mental or subjective and is the *mens rea* of the money-laundering offences. The truth of the belief is one of the attendant circumstances of the *actus reus*.

Related Provisions: "Enterprise crime offence" and "designated substance offence" are defined in s. 462.3, "person" and "property" in s. 2. The phrase "proceeds of crime" is *not* used, as such, in s. 462.31(1) but the introductory words of the definition *viz.* "*any property, benefit or advantage ...*" may assist in attributing meaning to "proceeds" as there used. Possession is determined under s. 4(3).

This offence, itself an "enterprise crime offence" within s. 462.3, may be the subject of a special search warrant under section 462.32, restraint order under s. 462.33 or, upon conviction or discharge, order of forfeiture under s. 462.37. An order of forfeiture under s. 462.37 is a "sentence" for the purposes of s. 673 and appeals under Part XXI. It is also an "offence" for which authorization to intercept private communications may be given under Part VI.

Where P proceeds by indictment under s. 462.31(2)(a), D may *elect* mode of trial under s. 536(2). Where P proceeds by summary conviction under s. 462.31(2)(b), D is tried and punished under Part XXVII.

Search, Seizure and Detention of Proceeds of Crime

462.32 (1) Special search warrant — Subject to subsection (3), where a judge, on application of the Attorney General, is satisfied by information on oath in Form 1 that there are reasonable grounds to believe that there is in any building, receptacle or place, within the province in which the judge has jurisdiction or any other province, any property in respect of which an order of forfeiture may be made under subsection 462.37(1) or 462.38(2), in respect of an enterprise crime offence alleged to have been committed within the province in which the judge has jurisdiction, the judge may issue a warrant authorizing a person named therein or a peace officer to search the building, receptacle or place for that property and to seize that property and any other property in respect of which that person or peace officer believes, on reasonable grounds, that an order of forfeiture may be made under that subsection.

(2) Procedure — An application for a warrant under subsection (1) may be made *ex parte*, shall be made in writing and shall include a statement as to whether any previous applications have been made under subsection (1) with respect to the property that is the subject of the application.

(2.1) Execution of warrant — Subject to subsection (2.2), a warrant issued pursuant to subsection (1) may be executed anywhere in Canada.

(2.2) Execution in another province — Where a warrant is issued under subsection (1) in one province but it may be reasonably expected that it is to be executed in another province and the execution of the warrant would require entry into or on the property of any person in the other province, a judge in the other province may, on *ex parte* application, confirm the warrant, and when the warrant is so confirmed it shall have full force and effect in that other province as though it had originally been issued in that province.

(3) Execution of warrant in other territorial jurisdictions — Subsections 487(2) to (4) and section 488 apply, with such modifications as the circumstances require, to a warrant issued under this section.

(4) Detention and record of property seized — Every person who executes a warrant issued by a judge under this section shall

(a) detain or cause to be detained the property seized, taking reasonable care to ensure that the property is preserved so that it may be dealt with in accordance with the law;

(b) as soon as practicable after the execution of the warrant but within a period not exceeding seven days thereafter, prepare a report in Form 5.3, identifying the property seized and the location where the property is being detained, and cause the report to be filed with the clerk of the court; and

(c) cause a copy of the report to be provided, on request, to the person from whom the property was seized and to any other person who, in the opinion of the judge, appears to have a valid interest in the property.

(5) Notice — Before issuing a warrant under this section in relation to any property, a judge, may require notice to be given to and may hear any person who, in the opinion of the judge, appears to have a valid interest in the property unless the judge is of the opinion that giving such notice before the issuance of the warrant would result in the disappearance, dissipation or reduction in value of the property or otherwise affect the property so that all or a part thereof could not be seized pursuant to the warrant.

(6) Undertakings by Attorney General — Before issuing a warrant under this section, a judge shall require the Attorney General to give such undertakings as the judge considers appropriate with respect to the payment of damages or costs, or both, in relation to the issuance and execution of the warrant.

R.S. 1985, c. 42 (4th Supp.), s. 2; 1997, c. 18, s. 29.

Commentary: Under this section, a special *search warrant* may be issued authorizing the *search* for and *seizure* of any property in respect of which an order of forfeiture may be made under s. 462.37(1) or 462.38(2) in respect of an enterprise crime offence alleged to have been committed within the province in which the judge in receipt of the application for authorization has jurisdiction.

The procedure to obtain the warrant is commenced by an *application in writing* by the Attorney General, made to a judge as defined in s. 462.3. Under s. 462.32(2), the application may be made *ex parte*, but it must be accompanied by an *information on oath* in Form 1, which must satisfy the judge that there *is* in a building, receptacle or place in the province in which the judge has jurisdiction or any other province, any *property* in respect of which an *order of forfeiture* may be made under s. 462.37(1) or 462.38(2) in respect of an enterprise crime offence alleged to have been committed within the province in which the judge has jurisdiction before a warrant may issue. Before issuing a warrant the judge, under s. 462.32(6), *must* require the Attorney General to give such *undertakings* as the judge considers appropriate with respect to the payment of damages and/or costs in relation to the issuance and execution of the warrant and, under s. 462.32(5), *may* require *notice* to be given to and hear any person who appears to have a valid interest in the property, *unless* of the opinion that pre-warrant notice would result in the disappearance, dissipation or reduction in the value of the property or otherwise affect the property so that all or a part thereof could not be seized pursuant to the warrant.

The warrant may be in Form 5, varied to suit the case, and may be *endorsed* for *execution* in another territorial division, under ss. 487(2) and (4). Under s. 462.32(1), the warrant will authorize a *named* person or a peace officer to *search* the building, receptacle or place for the property and, further, to *seize* the property and any *other* property in respect of which the named person or peace officer believes, *on reasonable grounds*, that an order of forfeiture may be made under s. 462.37(1) or 462.38(2). The warrant must be executed by day unless the issuing judge has *expressly* authorized its execution by night.

Execution of the warrant engages the tripartite requirements of s. 462.32(4): *detention, report* and *notice*. Under s. 462.32(4)(a), the property seized must be *detained* with *reasonable care* to *ensure* its *preservation* for subsequent proceedings. The obligation of s. 462.32(4)(b) requires the preparation of a Form 5.3 report as soon as practicable after the execution of the warrant, but within a period *not* exceeding seven days thereafter. The report identifying the property seized and the location of its detention, must be filed with the clerk of the court. Under s. 462.32(4)(c), upon request, a copy of the report must be provided to the person from whom the property has been seized. A judge may make a similar order in respect of *any other person* whom the judge determines *appears* to have a *valid interest* in the property.

The section is subject to the constitutional requirement of reasonableness in *Charter* s. 8.

Related Provisions: "Judge" is defined in s. 462.3, "Attorney General", "day", "peace officer" and "property" in s. 2.

Under s. 462.37(1), an *order of forfeiture* may be made in respect of any property, upon conviction or discharge of D of an "enterprise crime offence", as defined in s. 462.3, where the court is satisfied, on a balance of probabilities, that the property is "proceeds of crime" as defined in s. 462.3 and that the enterprise crime offence was committed in relation to that property. Section 462.38(2) provides for an *in rem* forfeiture hearing and forfeiture of property which is proceeds of crime where proceedings in respect of an enterprise crime offence committed in relation to the property have been commenced and D has either died or absconded. *Relief from forfeiture* may be extended under s. 462.42. It is these provisions which define the scope of *property* which may be subject to seizure under special warrant under this section.

The general *Code* provisions relating to search warrants are found in ss. 487, 488 and 489. Telewarrants are governed by s. 487.1. Other specialized warrants which authorize search for and/or seizure of certain materials or property are exemplified by ss. 199 (disorderly house), 320 (hate propaganda), 395 (minerals and precious metals) and 101–103 (firearms and ammunition).

Sections 25–31 define the limits of protection from criminal responsibility afforded those who administer or enforce the law. Under s. 26, criminal responsibility follows according to the nature and quality of any act which constitutes excessive force.

Section 462.34 authorizes *review* of, *inter alia*, warrants issued under s. 462.32 and describes what orders may be made upon such applications. Section 462.35 provides for the automatic expiry of warrants six months after the time of seizure, subject to the exceptions of the section.

462.33 (1) Application for restraint order — The Attorney General may make an application in accordance with subsection (2) for a restraint order under subsection (3) in respect of any property.

(2) Procedure — An application made under subsection (1) for a restraint order under subsection (3) in respect of any property may be made *ex parte* and shall be made in writing to a judge and be accompanied by an affidavit sworn on the information and belief of the Attorney General or any other person deposing to the following matters, namely,

(a) the offence or matter under investigation;

(b) the person who is believed to be in possession of the property;

(c) the grounds for the belief that an order of forfeiture may be made under subsection 462.37(1) or 462.38(2) in respect of the property;

(d) a description of the property; and

(e) whether any previous applications have been made under this section with respect to the property.

(3) Restraint order — Where an application for a restraint order is made to a judge under subsection (1), the judge may, if satisfied that there are reasonable grounds to believe that there exists within the province in which the judge has jurisdiction or any other province, any property in respect of which an order of forfeiture may be made under subsection 462.37(1) or 462.38(2), in respect of an enterprise crime offence alleged to have been committed within the province in which the judge has jurisdiction, make an order

(a) prohibiting any person from disposing of, or otherwise dealing with any interest in, the property specified in the order otherwise than in such manner as may be specified in the order; and

(b) at the request of the Attorney General, where the judge is of the opinion that the circumstances so require,

(i) appointing a person to take control of and to manage or otherwise deal with all or part of that property in accordance with the directions of the judge, which power to manage or otherwise deal with all or part of that property includes, in the case of perishable or rapidly depreciating property, the power to make an interlocutory sale of that property, and

(ii) requiring any person having possession of that property to give possession of the property to the person appointed under subparagraph (i).

(3.01) Execution in another province — Subsections 462.32(2.1) and (2.2) apply, with such modifications as the circumstances require, in respect of a restraint order.

(3.1) Appointment of minister of public works and government services — Where the Attorney General of Canada so requests, a judge appointing a person under subparagraph 462.33(3)(*b*)(*i*) shall appoint the Minister of Public Works and Government Services.

(4) Idem — An order made by a judge under subsection (3) may be subject to such reasonable conditions as the judge thinks fit.

(5) Notice — Before making an order under subsection (3) in relation to any property, a judge may require notice to be given to and may hear any person who, in the opinion of the judge, appears to have a valid interest in the property unless the judge is of the opinion that giving such notice before making the order would result in the disappearance, dissipation or reduction in value of the property or otherwise affect the property so that all or a part thereof could not be subject to an order of forfeiture under subsection 462.37(1) or 462.38(2).

(6) Order in writing — An order made under subsection (3) shall be made in writing.

(7) Undertakings by Attorney General — Before making an order under subsection (3), a judge shall require the Attorney General to give such undertakings as the judge considers appropriate with respect to the payment of damages or costs, or both, in relation to the making and execution of the order.

(8) Service of order — A copy of an order made by a judge under subsection (3) shall be served on the person to whom the order is addressed in such manner as the judge directs or as may be prescribed by rules of court.

(9) Registration of order — A copy of an order made under subsection (3), shall be registered against any property in accordance with the laws of the province in which the property is situated.

(10) Continues in force — An order made under subsection (3) remains in effect until

(a) it is revoked or varied under subsection 462.34(4) or revoked under paragraph 462.43(*a*);

(b) it ceases to be in force under section 462.35; or

(c) an order of forfeiture or restoration of the property is made under subsection 462.37(1), 462.38(2) or 462.41(3) or any other provision of this or any other Act of Parliament.

(11) Offence — Any person on whom an order made under subsection (3) is served in accordance with this section and who, while the order is in force, acts in contravention of or fails to comply with the order is guilty of an indictable offence or an offence punishable on summary conviction.

R.S. 1985, c. 42 (4th Supp.), s. 2; 1996, c. 16, s. 60(1)(d); 1997, c. 18, s. 30.

Commentary: The section authorizes the making of a *restraint order* proscribing certain dealings in property which is subject thereto, defines the basis upon which such orders may be made, and describes the manner in which they shall be executed and enforced.

Sections 462.33(1) and (2) authorize the making of an *application* for a restraint order and describe the materials which must be filed in support thereof. The application must be made *in writing* by the Attorney General *to a judge* as defined in s. 462.3, and may be made *ex parte*. It must be made in respect of any property liable to forfeiture under s. 462.37(1) or 462.38(2). The application must be accompanied by an *affidavit*, sworn on the information and belief of the Attorney General or any other person, deposing to the five matters described in ss. 462.33(2)(a)–(e).

Under s. 462.33(3), the *affidavit* material must satisfy the judge that there are *reasonable grounds* to believe that there *exists* within the province in which the judge has jurisdiction or any other province, any property in respect of which an order of forfeiture may be made under s. 462.37(1) or 462.38(2), in respect of an enterprise crime offence alleged to have been committed within the province in which the judge has jurisdiction. Such a finding permits an order to be made in accordance with s. 462.33(3)(a) and, upon further showing, ss. 462.33(3)(b) and (3.1). Section 462.33(3.01) stipulates that the same provisions with respect to executing a special search warrant in another province apply to executing a restraint order in another province. Prior to making a restraint order, the judge, under s 462.33(7), *must* require the Attorney General to give such *undertakings* as the judge considers appropriate with respect to the payment of damages or costs, or both, in relation to the making and execution of the order, and, under s. 462.33(5), *may* require *notice* to be given to and hear any person who appears to have a valid interest in the property, *unless* of the opinion that pre-order notice would result in the disappearance, dissipation or reduction in value of the property or otherwise affect the property so that all or a part thereof could not be subject to an order of forfeiture under s. 462.37(1) or 462.38(2).

A restraint order under s. 462.33(6) must be in *writing* and may be subject to such reasonable *terms* as the issuing judge thinks fit under s. 462.33(4).

The *execution and enforcement* of a restraint order is governed by ss. 462.33(8)–(11). A copy of the order must be *served* on the person to whom it is addressed as directed by the issuing judge or prescribed by rules of court. Under s. 462.33(9) a copy of the order must be *registered* against the subject property in accordance with provincial law. Under s. 462.33(10), the order will remain in effect until it is revoked or varied under s. 462.34(4), reversed under s. 462.43(a), ceases to be in force under s. 462.35, or an order of forfeiture or restoration of the property is made under s. 462.37(1), 462.38(2) or 462.31(3) or under any other Federal enactment.

Under s. 462.33(11), it is an offence, triable either way, for anyone upon whom a restraint order has been served to act in contravention of or fail to comply with the order.

Case Law

Serrano v. Canada (1992), 73 C.C.C. (3d) 437 (Ont. Gen. Div.) — A *restraint* order may *only* be issued upon the basis of an *affidavit* setting out, *inter alia*, the grounds for belief that a s. 462.37 order of forfeiture may be made. No restraint order may be made merely on the basis of a "reasonable possibility".

A s. 462.33 restraint order against property that may be forfeited as proceeds of crime under s. 462.37 does *not* authorize a seizure within *Charter* s. 8.

Related Provisions: Possession is determined in accordance with *Code* s. 4(3).

Property which may be the subject of a restraint order under this section may also be the subject of a special warrant authorizing seizure under s. 462.32.

Section 462.34 authorizes review of, *inter alia*, restraint orders issued under s. 462.33 and describes what orders may be made upon such applications. Section 462.35 provides for the automatic expiry of warrants six months after the time of seizure, subject to the exceptions of the section.

Under s. 462.4(b), where a restraint order has been served under s. 462.33(8), a court may set aside any conveyance or transfer of the property occurring *after* service of the order, unless the conveyance or transfer was for valuable consideration for a person acting in good faith and with notice.

Where a restraint order has been made in relation to property and D is ordered to stand trial in respect of an enterprise crime offence, a copy of the restraint order is filed with the clerk of the trial court under s. 462.36.

Any *person* with an *interest* in the restrained property may *apply* to a judge as defined in s. 462.3 to *examine* it under ss. 462.34(1)(b) and (3) or for its *release* from the order under ss. 462.34(1) and (4)–(6). Section 462.43 furnishes a residual power to remove property from a restraint order upon application of the Attorney General, any person having an interest in the property, or upon the judge's own motion. The requisite notice must be given and the judge satisfied that the property will no longer be required for any forfeiture proceedings or investigative or evidentiary purpose, and that its possession is lawful in the person to whom it is returned. Where a recognizance has been substituted for the property under s. 462.34(4)(a), or the property placed under the control of a receiver under ss. 462.33(3)(b)(i) and (3.1), the recognizance may be cancelled and the property returned upon a similar basis. Any person who considers him/herself aggrieved by an order under s. 462.43 may appeal in accordance with the provisions of s. 462.44, which incorporates the indictable appeal provisions of Part XXI. The operation of an order of forfeiture or restoration under s. 462.43 is suspended under s. 462.45 pending an appeal under s. 462.44 and any other proceeding in which the right of seizure of the property is questioned.

The offence of s. 462.33(11) is one in respect of which *authorization* to intercept private communications may be given under Part VI.

Other related provisions are discussed in the corresponding note to s. 462.32, *supra*.

462.34 (1) Application for review of special warrants and restraint orders — Any person who has an interest in property that was seized under a warrant issued pursuant to section 462.32 or in respect of which a restraint order was made under subsection 462.33(3) may, at any time, apply to a judge

    (a) for an order under subsection (4); or

    (b) for permission to examine the property.

(2) Notice to Attorney General — Where an application is made under paragraph (1)(*a*),

    (a) the application shall not, without the consent of the Attorney General, be heard by a judge unless the applicant has given to the Attorney General at least two clear days notice in writing of the application; and

    (b) the judge may require notice of the application to be given to and may hear any person who, in the opinion of the judge, appears to have a valid interest in the property.

(3) Terms of examination order — A judge may, on an application made to the judge under paragraph (1)(*b*), order that the applicant be permitted to examine property subject to such terms as appear to the judge to be necessary or desirable to ensure that the property is safeguarded and for any purpose for which it may subsequently be required.

(4) Order of restoration of property or revocation or variation of order — On an application made to a judge under paragraph (1)(*a*) in respect of any property and after hearing the applicant and the Attorney General and any other person to whom notice was given pursuant to paragraph (2)(*b*), the judge may order that the property or a part thereof be returned to the applicant or, in the case of a restraint order made under subsection 462.33(3), revoke the order, vary the order to exclude the property or any interest in the property or part thereof from the application of the order or make the order subject to such reasonable conditions as the judge thinks fit,

    (a) if the applicant enters into a recognizance before the judge, with or without sureties, in such amount and with such conditions, if any, as the judge directs and, where the judge considers it appropriate, deposits with the judge such sum of money or other valuable security as the judge directs;

    (b) if the conditions referred to in subsection (6) are satisfied; or

(c) for the purpose of

(i) meeting the reasonable living expenses of the person who was in possession of the property at the time the warrant was executed or the order was made or any person who, in the opinion of the judge, has a valid interest in the property and of the dependants of that person.

(ii) meeting the reasonable business and legal expenses of a person referred to in subparagraph (i), or

(iii) permitting the use of the property in order to enter into a recognizance under Part XVI,

if the judge is satisfied that the applicant has no other assets or means available for the purposes set out in this paragraph and that no other person appears to be the lawful owner of or lawfully entitled to possession of the property.

(5) **Hearing** — For the purpose of determining the reasonableness of legal expenses referred to in subparagraph (4)(c)(ii), a judge shall hold an *in camera* hearing, without the presence of the Attorney General, and shall take into account the legal aid tariff of the province.

(5.1) **Expenses** — For the purpose of determining the reasonableness of expenses referred to in paragraph (4)(c), the Attorney General may

(a) at the hearing of the application, make representations as to what would constitute the reasonableness of the expenses, other than legal expenses; and

(b) before or after the hearing of the application held *in camera* pursuant to subsection (5), make representations as to what would constitute reasonable legal expenses referred to in subparagraph (4)(c)(ii).

(5.2) **Taxing legal fees** — The judge who made an order under paragraph (4)(c) may, and on the application of the Attorney General shall, tax the legal fees forming part of the legal expenses referred to in subparagraph (4)(c)(ii) and, in so doing, shall take into account

(a) the value of property in respect of which an order of forfeiture may be made;

(b) the complexity of the proceedings giving rise to those legal expenses;

(c) the importance of the issues involved in those proceedings;

(d) the duration of any hearings held in respect of those proceedings;

(e) whether any stage of those proceedings was improper or vexatious;

(f) any representations made by the Attorney General; and

(g) any other relevant matter.

(6) **Conditions to be satisfied** — An order under paragraph (4)(b) in respect of property may be made by a judge if the judge is satisfied

(a) where the application is made by

(i) a person charged with an enterprise crime offence or a designated substance offence, or

(ii) any person who acquired title to or a right of possession of that property from a person referred to in subparagraph (i) under circumstances that give rise to a reasonable inference that the title or right was transferred from that person for the purpose of avoiding the forfeiture of the property, that a warrant should not have been issued pursuant to section 462.32 or a restraint order under subsection 462.33(3) should not have been made in respect of that property, or

(b) in any other case, that the applicant is the lawful owner of or lawfully entitled to possession of the property and appears innocent of any complicity in an enterprise crime offence or designated substance offence or of any collusion in relation to such an offence, and that no other person appears to be the lawful owner of or lawfully entitled to possession of the property,

and that the property will no longer be required for the purpose of any investigation or as evidence in any proceeding.

(7) Saving provision — Section 354 of this Act and subsection 8(1) of the *Controlled Drugs and Substances Act* do not apply to a person who comes into possession of any property or thing that, pursuant to an order made under paragraph 4(c), was returned to any person after having been seized or was excluded from the application of a restraint order made under subsection 462.33(3).

(8) Form of recognizance — A recognizance entered into pursuant to paragraph (4)(*a*) may be in Form 32.

R.S. 1985, c. 42 (4th Supp.), s. 2; 1996, c. 19, ss. 69, 70(d), (e); 1997, c. 18, s. 31.

Commentary: The section describes the circumstances under which application may be made to a court of competent jurisdiction for an *order to examine or have returned* some or all of the property seized under a s. 462.32 warrant or made the subject of a s. 462.33(3) restraint order.

Under s. 462.34(1) the review mechanism may be invoked by *any person who has an interest in property* that was *seized* under a s. 462.32 *warrant* or the subject of a s. 462.33(3) *restraint order*. The application may be made *at any time* to *a judge as defined in s. 462.3*, either for permission to *examine* the property under ss. 462.34(1)(b) and (3), or for a *return* of all or part of the property under ss. 462.34(1)(a) and (4)–(6).

On applications to *examine* property under s. 462.34(3), the judge may *permit examination*, subject to such *terms* as may be necessary or desirable to ensure the safeguarding and preservation of the property, for any purpose for which it may subsequently be required.

Applications for *return* of the property under s. 462.34(1)(a) must be on *notice* under s. 462.34(2). In general, the Attorney General must be given at least two clear days' notice in writing of the application. Under s. 462.34(2)(b), the hearing judge *may* require notice of the application to be given to, and may hear on the application, any person who, in the opinion of the judge, has a valid interest in the property.

On s. 462.34(1)(a) applications, the judge, under s. 462.34(4), may order the *return* of all or part of the property to the applicant, or *revoke* the restraint order, *vary* it, so as to exclude the property or any interest in it, or part thereof, from the application of the order, or make the order subject to such reasonable *conditions* as the judge thinks fit.

The *return* of the property, in whole or in part, to the applicant may be made in four instances. The applicant, under ss. 462.34(4)(a) and (8), may be required to enter into a *recognizance* in Form 28 which may include sureties, conditions and deposit of a sum of money or valuable security, as the judge directs, in effect in substitution for the actual property. Under ss. 462.34(4)(b) and (6)(a) the property may be returned, in whole or in part, to a person charged with a designated drug or enterprise crime offence, or to a person who acquired the property under circumstances giving rise to a reasonable inference of collusion to avoid forfeiture of the property, where the hearing judge, is of the view that the *warrant* should *not* have *issued* or *restraint order* should *not* have been *made*, as the case may be, and the *property* is *no longer required* for investigative or evidentiary purposes. Under ss. 462.34(4)(b) and (6)(b), full or partial return of the property may be ordered in any other case where the judge is satisfied that the *applicant* is the *lawful owner or possessor* of the property, appears *innocent of complicity or collusion* in an enterprise crime or designated substance offence, the *property is no longer required* for investigative or evidentiary purposes and *no other person appears to be the lawful owner or lafully entitled to possession of the property*. Under s. 462.34(4)(c), provided the judge is satisfied that the applicant has no other assets or means available for the enumerated purposes and that no other person appears to lawfully own or be lawfully entitled to possession of the property, full or partial return of the property may be ordered to meet the *reasonable living or business and legal expenses* of the person in possession of the property at the time the warrant was issued or restraint order made, any person who has a valid interest in the property and his/her dependants or to permit the use of the property in a recognizance under Part XVI. Under s. 462.34(5), the reasonableness of legal expenses are determined in an *in camera* hearing, in the absence of the Attorney General. Section 462.34(5.1) permits the Attorney General, within the guidelines set out therein, to make representations regarding the reasonableness of the expenses referred to in s. 462.34(4)(c). Section 462.34(5.2) allows a judge who made an order under s. 462.34(4)(c) to tax the legal fees forming part of the legal expenses in s. 462.34(4)(c)(ii), and in doing so, take into account the listed criteria. On an application of the Attorney General, the judge *must* tax these legal fees.

The possession of proceeds of crime offences in *Code* s. 354 and *C.D.A.* s. 8 do *not* apply to those whose possession originates in the return of property under s. 462.34(4)(c).

Case Law

Giles v. Canada (Department of Justice) (1991), 63 C.C.C. (3d) 184 (B.C. S.C.) — *See also*: *R. v. Wilson* (1994), 25 C.R. (4th) 239, 86 C.C.C. (3d) 464 (Ont. C.A.); affirming (1991), 68 C.C.C. (3d) 569 (Ont. Gen. Div.) — Unless property is seized under Part XII.2, its remedial measures cannot be invoked to seek its return or partial release to meet "reasonable legal expenses" under s. 462.34(4)(c)(ii).

Morra v. R. (1992), 77 C.C.C. (3d) 380 (Ont. Gen. Div.) — An application to vary a restraint order to pay reasonable legal expenses out of property said to be proceeds of crime must be supported by evidence of personal knowledge. D may file an affidavit particularizing assets and debts to demonstrate absence of sufficient funds to pay reasonable legal expenses. P is entitled to cross-examine D on the affidavit, but *not* to determine the *source* of the funds which is immaterial on the application, nor to obtain information which may assist P to prosecute D on further criminal charges in other proceedings.

R. v. Gaudreau (1994), 90 C.C.C. (3d) 436 (Sask. C.A.) — This provision does *not* apply where the money has been seized under a s. 487 search warrant and *not* under the special warrant of s. 462.32.

Related Provisions: "Person", "property" and "Attorney General" are defined in s. 2, "judge", "enterprise crime offence" and "designated substance offence" in s. 462.3.

The *basis* upon which a *warrant* may be *issued* under s. 462.32 or a *restraint order* made under s. 462.33(3) are described in the commentary which accompanies each section. The expiry of such orders is governed by s. 462.35.

Section 462.43 provides a residual authority to *return* property seized under a s. 462.32 warrant, the subject of a s. 462.33 restraint order, or a recognizance under s. 462.34(4)(a). An order may be made, under the terms of the section, by a judge as defined in s. 462.3, upon the application of the Attorney General, of any person having an interest in the property, or upon the judge's own motion. An order is only permissible where the judge is satisfied that the property will no longer be required for forfeiture proceedings, or investigative or evidentiary use and, further, that possession of the property in the person to whom it is returned is lawful.

The *forfeiture* of proceeds of crime is governed by the provisions of ss. 462.37, 462.371 and 462.38. Interested parties may claim relief from forfeiture under s. 462.42 and appeal orders made under ss. 462.38(2), 462.41(3) and 462.43 under s. 462.44. The operation of an order of forfeiture or restoration is suspended pending appeal or other application in accordance with s. 462.45.

462.341 Application of property restitution provisions — Subsection 462.34(2), paragraph 462.34(4)(*c*) and subsections 462.34(5), (5.1) and (5.2) apply, with any modifications that the circumstances require, to a person who has an interest in money or bank-notes that are seized under this Act or the *Controlled Drugs and Substances Act* and in respect of which proceedings may be taken under subsection 462.37(1) or 462.38(2).

1997, c. 18, ss. 32, 140(a); 1999, c. 5, s. 14.

Commentary: This section extends certain aspects of s. 462.34 to cases where the seized or restrained property in which an interest is asserted is money or bank notes seized under the *Code* or *CDSA*.

The incorporated provisions ensure that the Attorney General receives notice of applications to restore seized property or to revoke or vary a restraint order made in relation to money or bank notes. They also ensure that the hearing and adjudication is conducted in the same way as under ss. 462.34(4)(c), (5), (5.1) and (5.2).

Related Provisions: "Bank-note" is defined in s. 2 but "money" is *not* defined there nor elsewhere. The relevant provisions in ss. 462.34, 462.37 and 462.38 are discussed in the *Commentary* that accompanies each section.

462.35 (1) Expiration of special warrants and restraint orders — Subject to this section, where property has been seized under a warrant issued pursuant to section 462.32 or a restraint order has been made under section 462.33 in relation to property, the property may be detained or the order may continue in force, as the case may be, for a period not exceeding six months from the seizure or the making of the order, as the case may be.

(2) Where proceedings instituted — The property may continue to be detained, or the order may continue in force, for a period that exceeds six months if proceedings are instituted in respect of which the thing detained may be forfeited.

(3) Where application made — The property may continue to be detained or the order may continue in force for a period or periods that exceed six months if the continuation is, on application made by the Attorney General, ordered by a judge, where the judge is satisfied that the property is required, after the expiration of the period or periods, for the purpose of section 462.37 or 462.38 or any other provision of this or any other Act of Parliament respecting forfeiture or for the purpose of any investigation or as evidence in any proceeding.

R.S. 1985, c. 42 (4th Supp.), s. 2; 1997, c. 18, s. 33.

Commentary: The section imposes *time limits*, subject to certain exceptions, upon the *detention of property* seized under a s. 462.32 warrant or ordered restrained under s. 462.33.

As a general rule, the property may *not* be detained, or transactions therein restrained, for a period of *more than six months* after its seizure or the making of the restraint order, as the case may be. Detention or restraint of the property for a longer period is permissible where proceedings are instituted in respect of which the thing detained may be forfeited or where the Attorney General, upon application to a judge as defined in s. 462.3 prior to the expiration of the period, establishes that the property may be required after the expiration of the six-month period for forfeiture proceedings or investigative or evidentiary use.

Related Provisions: Under s. 462.33(10), a restraint order remains in *effect* until it is revoked or varied under s. 462.34(4) or revoked under s. 462.43(a), ceases to be enforced under s. 462.35, or an order of forfeiture or restoration of the property has been made under s. 462.37(1), 462.38(2) or 462.41(3) or any other similar provision. Property seized under warrant may be returned under ss. 462.34(4)–(6), or the residual power of s. 462.43(c). Any person who considers him/herself aggrieved by an order under s. 462.43 may appeal from the order under s. 462.44.

Forfeiture proceedings in respect of proceeds of crime may be undertaken after conviction or discharge of an enterprise crime offence in accordance with s. 462.37. *In rem* proceedings are permitted under s. 462.38. Each is subject to the *notice* requirements of s. 462.41. The operation of an order of forfeiture may be suspended under s. 462.45 and relief from forfeiture claimed under s. 462.42.

Section 462.46 permits *copying* and provides for the *admissibility* of such copies in evidence upon return or forfeiture ordered under various provisions of this Part.

The Part confers *no* right of appeal from an order made under this section.

462.36 Forwarding to clerk where accused to stand trial — Where a judge issues a warrant under section 462.32 or makes a restraint order under section 462.33 in respect of any property, the clerk of the court shall, when an accused is ordered to

stand trial for an enterprise crime offence, cause to be forwarded to the clerk of the court to which the accused has been ordered to stand trial a copy of the report filed pursuant to paragraph 462.32(4)(*b*) or of the restraint order in respect of the property.

R.S. 1985, c. 42 (4th Supp.), s. 2.

Commentary: Under this section, the clerk of the court in which a preliminary inquiry has been held must forward to the clerk of the court in which D has been ordered to stand trial for an enterprise crime offence a copy of the Form 5.3 report filed under s. 462.32(4)(b), where property has been seized under a s. 462.32 warrant, or a copy of the restraint order under s. 462.33, in relation to the property, where such an order is the basis of its retention.

Related Provisions: "Judge" and "enterprise crime offence" are defined in s. 462.3, "property" and "clerk of the court" in s. 2.

Under s. 551 the record, including the information, evidence, exhibits, D's statement, if any, under s. 541, any release form given or entered into under Part XVI, or any evidence taken before a coroner that is in the possession of the justice must be forwarded by the justice to the proper officer of the trial court.

Section 462.32 warrants and s. 462.33 restraint orders may be reviewed under s. 462.34. Their expiry is governed by s. 462.35. The forfeiture of proceeds of crime is governed by ss. 462.37–462.46.

Forfeiture of Proceeds of Crime

462.37 (1) Order of forfeiture of property on conviction — Subject to this section and sections 462.39 to 462.41, where an offender is convicted or discharged under section 730 of an enterprise crime offence and the court imposing sentence on the offender, on application of the Attorney General, is satisfied, on a balance of probabilities, that any property is proceeds of crime and that the enterprise crime offence was committed in relation to that property, the court shall order that the property be forfeited to Her Majesty to be disposed of as the Attorney General directs or otherwise dealt with in accordance with the law.

(2) Proceeds of crime derived from other offences — Where the evidence does not establish to the satisfaction of the court that the enterprise crime offence of which the offender is convicted, or discharged under section 730, was committed in relation to property in respect of which an order of forfeiture would otherwise be made under subsection (1) but the court is satisfied, beyond a reasonable doubt, that that property is proceeds of crime, the court may make an order of forfeiture under subsection (1) in relation to that property.

(3) Fine instead of forfeiture — Where a court is satisfied that an order of forfeiture under subsection (1) should be made in respect of any property of an offender, but that that property or any part thereof or interest therein cannot be made subject to such an order and, in particular,

(a) cannot, on the exercise of due diligence, be located,

(b) has been transferred to a third party,

(c) is located outside Canada,

(d) has been substantially diminished in value or rendered worthless, or

(e) has been commingled with other property that cannot be divided without difficulty,

the court may, instead of ordering that property or part thereof or interest therein to be forfeited pursuant to subsection (1), order the offender to pay a fine in an amount equal to the value of that property, part or interest.

(4) Imprisonment in default of payment of fine — Where a court orders an offender to pay a fine pursuant to subsection (3), the court shall

    (a) impose, in default of payment of that fine, a term of imprisonment

        (i) not exceeding six months, where the amount of the fine does not exceed ten thousand dollars,

        (ii) of not less than six months and not exceeding twelve months, where the amount of the fine exceeds ten thousand dollars but does not exceed twenty thousand dollars,

        (iii) of not less than twelve months and not exceeding eighteen months, where the amount of the fine exceeds twenty thousand dollars but does not exceed fifty thousand dollars,

        (iv) of not less than eighteen months and not exceeding two years, where the amount of the fine exceeds fifty thousand dollars but does not exceed one hundred thousand dollars,

        (v) of not less than two years and not exceeding three years, where the amount of the fine exceeds one hundred thousand dollars but does not exceed two hundred and fifty thousand dollars,

        (vi) of not less than three years and not exceeding five years, where the amount of the fine exceeds two hundred and fifty thousand dollars but does not exceed one million dollars, or

        (vii) of not less than five years and not exceeding ten years, where the amount of the fine exceeds one million dollars; and

    (b) direct that the term of imprisonment imposed pursuant to paragraph (a) be served consecutively to any other term of imprisonment imposed on the offender or that the offender is then serving.

(5) Fine option not available to offender — Section 736 does not apply to an offender against whom a fine is imposed pursuant to subsection (3).

R.S. 1985, c. 42 (4th Supp.), s. 2; 1995, c. 22, s. 18.

Commentary: The section authorizes the *forfeiture of proceeds of crime*, where D has been convicted or found guilty of an enterprise crime offence, and defines the basis upon which a fine may be imposed in lieu of forfeiture.

The *mandatory* forfeiture order of s. 462.37(1) requires that D first be *convicted or discharged* of an *enterprise crime offence*, as defined in s. 462.3. Application for an order of forfeiture must be made by the Attorney General, to the sentencing court. *Notice* must be given under s. 462.41. The sentencing judge must be satisfied, on a balance of probabilities, that property is "proceeds of crime". In deciding the matter, the court is entitled to rely, *inter alia*, upon the *inference* from net worth contained in s. 462.39. The court must equally be satisfied that the enterprise crime offence was committed in *relation to the property*. Satisfaction of these conditions precedent *requires* an order that the property be forfeited to Her Majesty, to be disposed of as the Attorney General directs, or otherwise dealt with in accordance with the law. Prior to a forfeiture order, the court may, under s. 462.4, *set aside* any conveyance or transfer of the property that occurred after its seizure, or the service of the order under s. 462.33, unless the conveyance or transfer was for valuable consideration to a person acting in good faith and without notice. Section 462.41(3) *permits* a *restoration order* to be made in respect of the lawful owner or possessor of property who is neither a person charged with an enterprise crime or designated substance offence nor a person who acquired title to or possession of property from such a person in circumstances giving rise to a reasonable inference of collusion. The property or part thereof that would otherwise be forfeited under s. 462.37(1) may be restored to the innocent party.

In the circumstances described in s. 462.37(3), a *fine* may be imposed where the forfeited or forfeitable property is inaccessible to a forfeiture order. The court must first be satisfied that an order of forfeiture, under s. 462.37(1), should be made in respect of property. Further, the court must be satisfied that property, or any part thereof or interest therein, cannot be made subject to such an order and, in particular, that *any* of the conditions of ss. 462.37(3)(a)–(e) obtain. The court *may* then order the payment of a fine, in an amount equal to the value of the property, part or interest, instead of making a forfeiture order under s. 462.37(1). Under s. 462.37(5), the fine option program of s. 736 does not apply to a fine imposed under s. 462.37(3). Section 462.37(4) requires the imposition of a term of imprisonment in default of payment of a s. 462.37(3) fine, and provides a schedule of default terms.

Under s. 462.37(2), a forfeiture order *may* be made in respect of property, notwithstanding that the conditions of s. 462.37(1) have *not* been met. A discretionary order may be made where the sentencing court is *not* satisfied that the enterprise crime offence of which D was convicted or discharged was committed in relation to property, which would otherwise be the subject of a s. 462.37(1) forfeiture order, but is satisfied, *beyond a reasonable doubt*, that the property is proceeds of crime as defined in s. 462.3. In other words, the absence of a *nexus* between the property and enterprise crime offence of which D has been convicted or discharged is not dispositive against a forfeiture order. An order *may* nonetheless be made where the evidence establishes *beyond a reasonable doubt* that the property *is* proceeds of crime.

Case Law

R. v. Rosenblum (1998), 130 C.C.C. (3d) 481 (B.C. C.A.) — "Property" under s. 2 permits a court to determine whether property has been converted into personalty or realty and to follow it as the evidence permits.

It is *only* where an order of forfeiture cannot be made in respect of the property required to be forfeited under s. 462.37(1) that a trial judge may impose a fine.

Where the necessary election has been made and plea taken, a provincial court judge may make an order of forfeiture under s. 462.37(1), or impose a fine in lieu of forfeiture under s. 462.37(3).

R. v. Garoufalis (1998), 131 C.C.C. (3d) 242 (Man. C.A.) — The ability of D to pay is irrelevant to the question whether a fine should be imposed in lieu of forfeiture under *Code* s. 462.37.

R. v. Wilson (1994), 25 C.R. (4th) 239, 86 C.C.C. (3d) 464 (Ont. C.A.); affirming (1991), 68 C.C.C. (3d) 569 (Ont. Gen. Div.) — Forfeiture of property under s. 462.37 is part of the sentencing process. It is mandatory where D has been found guilty of an enterprise crime, and P has established on a balance of probabilities that the property in question is the proceeds of crime, and that the enterprise crime of which D was found guilty was committed in relation to that property.

Related Provisions: The definition of "sentence" in s. 673 includes a forfeiture order under s. 462.37.

Section 462.42 permits application by persons with a defined interest in forfeited property for *relief from forfeiture* and describes the nature of declaratory order that may be made upon such application. Appellate rights are also given.

Section 462.38 describes the circumstances under which the Attorney General may apply for an *in rem* forfeiture hearing where an order may be made forfeiting property to Her Majesty to be disposed of as the Attorney General directs or otherwise dealt with in accordance with the law. An appeal may be taken under s. 462.44 and the suspension provisions of s. 462.45 apply with respect thereto.

Where property has been seized under a s. 462.32 warrant, made subject to a s. 462.33 restraint order or a s. 462.34(4)(a) recognizance substituted therefor, a judge, as defined in s. 462.3, has residual authority to dispose of it under s. 462.43, upon application by the Attorney General, anyone having an interest in the property or upon the judge's own motion. An appeal may be taken from such an order under s. 462.44 and the suspension provisions of s. 462.45 apply in such cases.

Under s. 462.46, documents forfeited, returned or otherwise dealt with under the section may be copied by the Attorney General. A certified true copy of the document is receivable in evidence and, in the absence of evidence to the contrary, has the same probative value as the original proven in the ordinary course. The section may well attract *Charter* ss. 7 and 8 scrutiny.

The post-disposition forfeiture provisions of the section are incorporated by *C.D.A.* s. 23 and the repealed *F.D.A.* ss. 44.4 (controlled drugs) and 51 (restricted drugs) and *N.C.A.* s. 19.3.

462.371 (1) Definition of "order" — In this section, "order" means an order made under section 462.36 or 462.38.

(2) Execution — An order may be executed anywhere in Canada.

(3) Filing of order from another province — Where the Attorney General of a province in which property that is the subject of an order made in another province is situated receives a certified copy of the order and files it with the superior court of criminal jurisdiction of the province in which the property is situated, the order shall be entered as a judgment of that court.

(4) Attorney General of Canada — Where the Attorney General of Canada receives a certified copy of an order made in a province in respect of property situated in another province and files the order with the superior court of criminal jurisdiction of the province in which the property is situated, the order shall be entered as a judgment of the court.

(5) Effect of registered order — An order has, from the date it is filed in a court of a province under subsection (3) or (4), the same effect as if it had been an order originally made by that court.

(6) Notice — Where an order has been filed in a court under subsection (3) or (4), it shall not be executed before notice in accordance with subsection 462.41(2) is given to every person who, in the opinion of the court, appears to have a valid interest in the property.

(7) Application of section 462.42 — Section 462.42 applies, with such modifications as the circumstances require, in respect of a person who claims an interest in property that is the subject of an order filed under subsection (3) or (4).

(8) Application under section 462.42 to be made in one province — No person may make an application under section 462.42 in relation to property that is the subject of an order filed under subsection (3) or (4) if that person has previously made an application in respect of the same property in another province.

(9) Finding in one court binding — The finding by a court of a province in relation to property that is the subject of an order filed under subsection (3) or (4) as to whether or not an applicant referred to in subsection 462.42(4) is affected by the forfeiture referred to in that subsection or declaring the nature and extent of the interest of the applicant under that subsection is binding on the superior court of criminal jurisdiction of the province where the order is entered as a judgment.

1997, c. 18, s. 34.

Commentary: This section provides for the enforcement or execution of orders of forfeiture made upon conviction or during *in rem* proceedings.

Section 462.371(2) states the general rule. Forfeiture orders may be executed anywhere in Canada. Where the relevant property is located in a province other than the one in which the forfeiture order with the superior court of criminal jurisdiction in the province where the property is located. Under s. 462.371(5), filing the order gives it the same effect as it would have if it had originally been made by that court.

No forfeiture order may be executed on property in another province unless a s. 462.41(2) notice is given to *every* person who, in the opinion of the court, *appears* to have a *valid interest* in the property. An interested party who wants relief from forfeiture may apply under s. 462.42, but only once. Under s. 462.371(9), the finding made on the application for relief from forfeiture binds the superior court of any other province where the order is filed.

Related Provisions: "Superior court of criminal jurisdiction" is defined in s. 2. The order to which s. 462.36 refers is a restraint order under s. 462.33. Section 462.38 governs order of forfeiture made in *in rem* proceedings.

Section 462.42 permits a person who claims an interest in forfeited property to apply for a declaration that his/her interest is *not* subject to forfeiture. Section 462.44 provides a right of appeal for any person who considers her/himself aggrieved by forfeiture order.

462.38 (1) Application for forfeiture — Where an information has been laid in respect of an enterprise crime offence, the Attorney General may make an application to a judge for an order of forfeiture under subsection (2) in respect of any property.

(2) Order of forfeiture of property — Subject to sections 462.39 to 462.41, where an application is made to a judge under subsection (1), the judge shall, if the judge is satisfied that

(a) any property is, beyond a reasonable doubt, proceeds of crime,

(b) proceedings in respect of an enterprise crime offence committed in relation to that property were commenced, and

(c) the accused charged with the offence referred to in paragraph (*b*) has died or absconded,

order that the property be forfeited to Her Majesty to be disposed of as the Attorney General directs or otherwise dealt with in accordance with the law.

(3) Person deemed absconded — For the purposes of this section, a person shall be deemed to have absconded in connection with an enterprise crime offence if

(a) an information has been laid alleging the commission of the offence by the person,

(b) a warrant for the arrest of the person or a summons in respect of a corporation has been issued in relation to that information,

(c) reasonable attempts to arrest the person pursuant to the warrant or to serve the summons have been unsuccessful during the period of six months commencing on the day the warrant or summons was issued, or, in the case of a person who is not or never was in Canada, the person cannot be brought within that period to the jurisdiction in which the warrant or summons was issued,

and the person shall be deemed to have so absconded on the last day of that period of six months.

R.S. 1985, c. 42 (4th Supp.), s. 2; 1997, c. 18, s. 35(2).

Commentary: The section permits the Attorney General to take *in rem* forfeiture proceedings in respect of property that is proceeds of crime, but belongs to D who has died or absconded after being charged with an enterprise crime offence in relation to the property.

Sections 462.38(1) and (2) describe the circumstances in which a *forfeiture order* may be made in proceedings under the section. The incorporation, by s. 462.38(2), of s. 462.41 requires that the *notice* of s. 462.41(1), be given to *any* person who appears to have an interest in the property, preliminary to any order of forfeiture being made under s. 462.38(2). Further, the incorporation of s. 462.4 permits the court to *set aside* any conveyance or transfer of property which occurred after seizure or service of a restraint order unless made for valuable consideration to a person acting in good faith and without notice.

There are three discrete *findings* under s. 462.38(2) before forfeiture may be ordered. The *property* must be "proceeds of crime", as defined in s. 462.3. The inference from net worth provisions of s. 462.39 may be relied upon in its proof. *Proceedings* in respect of an enterprise crime offence committed in relation to that property must have been *commenced*. D, charged with the enterprise crime offence in relation to the property, must have either *died or absconded*. Proof that D has absconded is assisted by the *presumption* of s. 462.38(3). D is *deemed* to have absconded in connection with an enterprise crime offence, if an information has been laid alleging the commission of the offence, a warrant issued for D's arrest or a summons issued in respect of a corporation and reasonable efforts to arrest D under the warrant or to serve the summons have been unsuccessful during the six months immediately following the issuance of the warrant or summons or, if D is not or never was in Canada, where D cannot be brought within that period to the jurisdiction in which the warrant or summons was issued. D is deemed to have absconded on the last day of the six-month period.

Proof of these matters will result in forfeiture of the property to Her Majesty, to be dealt with as the Attorney General directs, or otherwise in accordance with the law. The incorporation by s. 462.38(2) of, *inter alia*, s. 462.41(3) permits the return of property that would otherwise be forfeited to persons lawfully entitled thereto not complicit in D's offence.

Related Provisions: Any *person* who considers him/herself *aggrieved* by forfeiture order under s. 462.38(2) may *appeal* from the order under and in accordance with s. 462.44. Under s. 462.45, the operation of the *order* of forfeiture under s. 462.38(2) or restoration under s. 462.41(3), as incorporated by s. 462.38(2), is *suspended* pending appellate proceedings. Documents ordered returned, forfeited or otherwise dealt with under s. 462.38(2) or 462.41(3) may he copied by the Attorney General and received in evidence as an original, where certified by the Attorney General under s. 462.46. Relief from forfeiture may be sought under s. 462.42.

The section is incorporated by *C.D.A.* s. 23.

Property seized under a s. 462.32 warrant or the subject of a s. 462.33 restraint order may also he disposed of under s. 462.43. Appeals from these dispositions are authorized by s. 462.44. Sections 462.45 (suspension of forfeiture pending appeal) and 462.46 (admissibility of copy documents) also apply.

462.39 Inference — **For the purpose of subsection 462.37(1) or 462.38(2), the court may infer that property was obtained or derived as a result of the commission of an enterprise crime offence where evidence establishes that the value, after the commission of that offence, of all the property of the person alleged to have committed the offence exceeds the value of all the property of that person before the commission of that offence and the court is satisfied that the income of that person from sources unrelated to enterprise crime offences or designated substance offences committed by that person cannot reasonably account for such an increase in value.**

R.S. 1985, c. 42 (4th Supp.), s. 2; 1996, c. 19, s. 70(f).

Commentary: The section facilitates *proof* on forfeiture applications that *property* has been *obtained* or *derived* as a result of the commission of an *enterprise crime* offence, by enacting a statutory *inference from net worth*.

Proof of certain preliminary facts is required before the inference of unlawful origin may be drawn in relation to property in forfeiture proceedings under s. 462.37(1) or 462.38(2). Evidence must establish that the *value, after* the commission of the enterprise crime *offence*, of all the property of the person alleged to have committed the offence *exceeds* the *value* of all the property of that person *before* the commission of the *offence*. The court must be *satisfied* that the *income* of that person from sources *unrelated* to the enterprise crime offence or designated substance offence committed by that person *cannot reasonably account* for such an increase in value. *Proof* of these two preliminary facts engages the permissive *inference* of the section in forfeiture proceedings under ss. 462.37(1) (post-disposition forfeiture) and 462.38(2) (*in rem* forfeiture). In essence, what the inference establishes, if drawn, is that the property is "proceeds of crime", as defined in s. 462.3.

Related Provisions: The section is incorporated by *C.D.A.* s. 23.

462.4 Voidable transfers — **A court may,**

    (a) prior to ordering property to be forfeited under subsection 462.37(1) or 462.38(2), and

(b) in the case of property in respect of which a restraint order was made under section 462.33, where the order was served in accordance with subsection 462.33(8),

set aside any conveyance or transfer of the property that occurred after the seizure of the property or the service of the order under section 462.33, unless the conveyance or transfer was for valuable consideration to a person acting in good faith.

R.S. 1985, c. 42 (4th Supp.), s. 2; 1997, c. 18, s. 36.

Commentary: The section authorizes a court, in certain circumstances, to *set aside conveyances or transfers of property*, preliminary to a forfeiture order being made, as well after a restraint order has been served. Any conveyance or transfer of property that occurred *after* the property had been seized or after a restraint order in respect of the property had been served under s. 462.33(8), may be set aside by a court, *unless* the conveyance or transfer was for *valuable consideration*, to a person acting in *good faith*. The order voiding the transfer or conveyance may be made prior to ordering forfeiture of the property under s. 462.37(1) or 462.38(2) and also after a restraint order in respect of the property has been served under s. 462.33(8).

Related Provisions: "Property" is defined in s. 2 and may be seized by special warrant issued under s. 462.32 or made the subject of a restraint order under s. 462.33 in the circumstances there defined.

Forfeiture of property which is proceeds of crime may be ordered upon disposition of an enterprise crime offence under s. 462.37(1) or in an *in rem* forfeiture hearing under s. 462.38(2). Notice is required under s. 462.41. Relief from forfeiture may be sought under s. 462.42. Section 462.43 confers a residual authority to dispose of property seized under special warrant or the subject of a restraint order.

The section is also incorporated by *C.D.A.* s. 23.

462.41 (1) Notice — Before making an order under subsection 462.37(1) or 462.38(2) in relation to any property, a court shall require notice in accordance with subsection (2) to be given to and may hear any person who, in the opinion of the court, appears to have a valid interest in the property.

(2) Manner of giving notice — A notice given under subsection (1) shall

(a) be given or served in such manner as the court directs or as may be prescribed by the rules of the court;

(b) be of such duration as the court considers reasonable or as may be prescribed by the rules of the court; and

(c) set out the enterprise crime offence charged and a description of the property.

(3) Order of restoration of property — Where a court is satisfied that any person, other than

(a) a person who is charged with, or was convicted of, an enterprise crime offence or a designated substance offence, or

(b) a person who acquired title to or a right of possession of that property from a person referred to in paragraph (*a*) under circumstances that give rise to a reasonable inference that the title or right was transferred for the purpose of avoiding the forfeiture of the property,

is the lawful owner or is lawfully entitled to possession of any property or any part thereof that would otherwise be forfeited pursuant to subsection 462.37(1) or 462.38(2) and that the person appears innocent of any complicity in an offence referred to in paragraph (*a*) or of any collusion in relation to such an offence, the court may order that the property or part thereof be returned to that person.

R.S. 1985, c. 42 (4th Supp.), s. 2; 1996, c. 19, s. 70(g); 1997, c. 18, ss. 37, 140(d)(ii).

Commentary: The section enacts *notice* provisions applicable to *forfeiture* hearings under ss. 462.37(1) and 462.38(2) and also permits *restoration* of property, otherwise forfeitable, to "innocent parties" in accordance with the terms of s. 462.41(3).

The *notice* requirement of ss. 462.41(1) and (2) is *mandatory* before any order under s. 462.37(1) (post-disposition forfeiture) or 462.38(2) (*in rem* forfeiture) may be made. Subsection (1) also *permits* the court to hear any person on the return of the forfeiture application, who appears to have a valid interest in the property. The *form of notice*, governed by s. 462.41(2), must be given or served in such manner as the court directs, or the rules of court, if any, prescribe. The notice must be of such duration as the court considers *reasonable*, or the rules of court, if any, prescribe, and must set out the enterprise crime offence charged and describe the property that is the subject of the forfeiture application.

Section 462.41(3) permits *relief from forfeiture* for a specified class of persons who are *not* charged with, convicted of or otherwise complicit in the predicate offence, or have colluded in taking the property to avoid its forfeiture. To obtain *restoration* of the property or part thereof, an applicant must *not* be charged with, convicted of or otherwise complicit or collusive in an enterprise crime or designated substance offence. Section 462.41 (3)(a) does *not* restrict such complicity or collusion to an enterprise crime or designated substance offence committed in relation to the forfeitable property. An applicant must *not* be a person acquiring title to or possession of the property from a person charged with an enterprise crime or designated substance offence, under circumstances from which it may reasonably be inferred that such transfer was to avoid forfeiture of the property. The applicant must be the lawful owner or, at least, lawfully entitled to possession of the property or part thereof restoration of which is sought. The property or part itself must otherwise be forfeitable under s. 462.37(1) or 462.38(2).

Case Law

R. v. Wilson (1994), 25 C.R. (4th) 239, 86 C.C.C. (3d) 464 (Ont. C.A.); affirming (1991), 68 C.C.C. (3d) 569 (Ont. Gen. Div.) — An innocent third party may seek the return of property under s. 462.41 *before* the property is ordered forfeited, as part of the forfeiture application. A lawyer who holds a contingent interest in seized funds should assert his/her claim under s. 462.41, before an order of forfeiture is made.

Related Provisions: Forfeiture of proceeds of crime may be ordered under s. 462.37(1) (post disposition forfeiture) or 462.38(2) (*in rem* forfeiture).

Relief from forfeiture by a person claiming an interest in forfeited property may also be sought and granted under s. 462.42. A general residual remedy is available under and in accordance with s. 462.43.

Rules of court may be made under, and subject to, the limitations of s. 482.

The order does not fall within the definition of "sentence" in s. 673 or 785(1). An order of restoration under s. 462.41(3) may be appealed under s. 462.44 and is suspended under s. 462.45, pending further proceedings. Any documents restored under s. 462.41(3) may be copied by the Attorney General, prior to restoration, and, properly certified, are receivable in evidence as if the original under s. 462.46.

The section is also incorporated by *C.D.A.* s. 23.

462.42 (1) Application by person claiming interest for relief from forfeiture — Where any property is forfeited to Her Majesty under subsection 462.37(1) or 462.38(2), any person who claims an interest in the property, other than

(a) a person who is charged with, or was convicted of, an enterprise crime offence or a designated substance offence that was committed in relation to the property forfeited, or

(b) a person who acquired title to or a right of possession of that property from a person referred to in paragraph (a) under circumstances that give rise to a reasonable inference that the title or right was transferred from that person for the purpose of avoiding the forfeiture of the property,

may, within thirty days after that forfeiture, apply by notice in writing to a judge for an order under subsection (4).

(2) **Fixing day for hearing** — The judge to whom an application is made under subsection (1) shall fix a day not less than thirty days after the date of filing of the application for the hearing thereof.

(3) **Notice** — An applicant shall serve a notice of the application made under subsection (1) and of the hearing thereof on the Attorney General at least fifteen days before the day fixed for the hearing.

(4) **Order declaring interest not subject to forfeiture** — Where, on the hearing of an application made under subsection (1), the judge is satisfied that the applicant is not a person referred to in paragraph (1)(*a*) or (*b*) and appears innocent of any complicity in any enterprise crime offence or designated substance offence that resulted in the forfeiture or of any collusion in relation to any such offence, the judge may make an order declaring that the interest of the applicant is not affected by the forfeiture and declaring the nature and extent of the interest.

(5) **Appeal from order under subsection (4)** — An applicant or the Attorney General may appeal to the court of appeal from an order under subsection (4) and the provisions of Part XXI with respect to procedure on appeals apply, with such modifications as the circumstances require, to appeals under this subsection.

(6) **Return of property** — The Attorney General shall, on application made to the Attorney General by any person who has obtained an order under subsection (4) and where the periods with respect to the taking of appeals from that order have expired and any appeal from that order taken under subsection (5) has been determined,

(a) direct that the property or the part thereof to which the interest of the applicant relates be returned to the applicant; or

(b) direct that an amount equal to the value of the interest of the applicant, as declared in the order, be paid to the applicant.

R.S. 1985, c. 42 (4th Supp.), s. 2; 1996, c. 19, s. 70(h), (i); 1997, c. 18, s. 38(1), 140(d)(iii).

Commentary: The section authorizes *relief from forfeiture* of property ordered under s. 462.37(1) or 462.38(2).

Under s. 462.42(1) an *applicant* may be any person who claims an interest in the property, other than a person charged with an enterprise crime or designated substance offence committed in relation to the property, or a person whose title or possession of the property was acquired from such a person in circumstances giving rise to a reasonable inference that such transfer was for the purpose of avoiding forfeiture of the property. The application must be commenced by *notice* thereof, in writing, to a "judge" as defined in s. 462.3, within 30 days after the forfeiture.

After notice has been given under s. 462.42(1), the judge to whom the application is made, under s. 462.42(2) must fix a *date for hearing*, not less than 30 days after the filing of the application. Section 462.42(3) requires the applicant to serve notice of the application and hearing on the Attorney General, at least 15 days before the date fixed for hearing.

Section 462.42(4) defines the *authority* of the judge *upon the hearing* of the application. Where the judge is satisfied that the applicant is *not* disentitled to relief under s. 462.42(1), and further appears innocent of any complicity or collusion in the underlying enterprise crime or designated substance offence, the judge *may* make an order *declaring* the nature and extent of the applicant's interest, and that it is *not* affected by the forfeiture. Section 462.42(5) permits the applicant or the Attorney General to appeal an order under subsection (4), in accordance with the procedural provisions of Part XXI, *mutatis mutandis*.

Where a declaratory order has been made under s. 462.42(4), the applicant will apply to the Attorney General for the return of the property or interest. Upon such application, where the appeal periods have expired and any appeal taken has been determined, s. 462.42(6) requires the Attorney General to direct that the property or part to which the applicant's interest relates be returned to the applicant or its value repaid as the case may be. The subsection contains no provision to inform the discretion of the Attorney

General or mechanism whereby the value of an applicant's interest in property may finally be determined.

Case Law

R. v. Pawlyk (1991), 4 C.R. (4th) 388, 65 C.C.C. (3d) 63 (Man. C.A.) — A person claiming interest in property may only make a claim under s. 462.42 to a judge as defined in s. 552, or of the superior court of criminal jurisdiction *after* the property has been ordered forfeited under s. 462.37(1).

R. v. Wilson (1994), 25 C.R. (4th) 239, 86 C.C.C. (3d) 464 (Ont. C.A.); affirming (1991), 68 C.C.C. (3d) 569 (Ont. Gen. Div.) — An application under s. 462.42 is made *after* the property has been ordered forfeited. A judge may decline to make an order in favour of an innocent third party, even if the preconditions of s. 462.42 are met. A forfeiture order made under s. 462.37 extinguishes any contingent interest in seized funds which D's lawyers may have had as a result of a prior assignment given to them by D. The lawyers should have asserted their claim under s. 462.41, *before* the order of forfeiture was made.

Lumen Inc. v. Canada (Attorney General) (1997), 119 C.C.C. (3d) 91 (Que. C.A.) — Ordinary creditors, who do *not* have enforceable interest in any particular asset of the debtor, have *no* valid interest in proceeds of any enterprise crime offence committed by the debtor, hence *no* entitlement under s. 462.42(4).

Related Provisions: Complicity in an offence may be established under ss. 21–23.

Any person who considers him/herself aggrieved by an order of forfeiture under s. 462.38(2) may appeal, in accordance with s. 462.44. The operation of the order will be stayed pending appeal under s. 462.45.

Property seized under a s. 462.32 warrant, made the subject of a s. 462.33 restraint order, or for which a recognizance has been substituted under s. 462.34(4)(a), may also be disposed of by a judge under s. 462.43. The provisions of ss. 462.44 (appeals), 462.45 (stay pending appeal) and 462.46 (admissibility of copies) apply to such dispositions.

The section is incorporated by *C.D.A.* s. 23 and the repealed *F.D.A.* ss. 44.4 (controlled drugs) and 51 (restricted drugs) and *N.C.A.* s. 19.3.

462.43 Residual disposal of property seized or dealt with pursuant to special warrants or restraint orders — Where property has been seized under a warrant issued pursuant to section 462.32, a restraint order has been made under section 462.33 in relation to any property or a recognizance has been entered into pursuant to paragraph 462.34(4)(a) in relation to any property and a judge, on application made to the judge by the Attorney General or any person having an interest in the property or on the judge's own motion, after notice given to the Attorney General and any other person having an interest in the property, is satisfied that the property will no longer be required for the purpose of section 462.37, 462.38 or any other provision of this or any other Act of Parliament respecting forfeiture or for the purpose of any investigation or as evidence in any proceeding, the judge

(a) in the case of a restraint order, shall revoke the order;

(b) in the case of a recognizance, shall cancel the recognizance; and

(c) in the case of property seized under a warrant issued pursuant to section 462.32 or property under the control of a person appointed pursuant to subparagraph 462.33(3)(b)(i),

(i) if possession of it by the person from whom it was taken is lawful, shall order that it be returned to that person,

(ii) if possession of it by the person from whom it was taken is unlawful and the lawful owner or person who is lawfully entitled to its possession is known, shall order that it be returned to the lawful owner or the person who is lawfully entitled to its possession, or

(iii) if possession of it by the person from whom it was taken is unlawful and the lawful owner or person who is lawfully entitled to its possession is not known, may order that it be forfeited to Her Majesty, to be disposed of as the Attorney General directs, or otherwise dealt with in accordance with the law.

R.S. 1985, c. 42 (4th Supp.), s. 2.

Commentary: The section confers a general *residual power* upon a judge as defined in s. 462.3, to *dispose of property seized* under a s. 462.32 warrant, the subject of a s. 462.33 restraint order, or for which a recognizance has been substituted under s. 462.34(4)(a).

An *application* may be initiated by the Attorney General, any person having an interest in the property, or upon the judge's own motion. The property in respect of which the application is brought must have been seized under a s. 426.32 warrant, the subject of a s. 462.33 restraint order, or for which a recognizance has been substituted under s. 462.34(4)(a). The residual authority of the section only becomes engaged where the judge is satisfied that the property will no longer be required for *forfeiture* purposes under the *Code* or other federal enactment, or for *investigative* or *evidentiary* purposes in any proceeding.

The *disposition* of the application depends upon the nature of the authority which is impeached. Where the underlying authority is a *restraint order*, it is *revoked* under s. 462.43(a). A *recognizance* must be *cancelled* under s. 462.43(b). Where the property was seized under a s. 462.32 warrant, or placed under the control of a person appointed under s. 462.33(3)(b)(i), the disposal is governed by para. (c). Where possession of it by the person from whom it was taken is *unlawful*, and the lawful owner or person who is lawfully entitled to its possession is known, the judge must order that it be *returned* to the lawful owner or person lawfully entitled to its possession. If possession of it by the person by whom it was taken is *unlawful*, and the lawful owner or person lawfully entitled to its possession is not known, the judge may order that it be *forfeited* to Her Majesty, to be disposed of as the Attorney General directs, or otherwise dealt with in accordance with the law under s. 462.43.

Related Provisions: Any person who considers him/herself aggrieved by an order made under the section may appeal under and in accordance with s. 462.44. Under s. 462.45, the application of the order is stayed pending appeal. Documents returned or ordered returned, forfeited or otherwise dealt with under s. 462.43 may first be copied by the Attorney General and, upon proper certification and proof, are receivable in evidence and, absent evidence to the contrary, have the same probative force as the original under s. 462.46.

The provisions are incorporated by *C.D.A.* s. 23.

The *general* authority to order *forfeiture* of property that is proceeds of crime under s. 462.43 is found in ss. 462.37 and 462.38, *supra*.

462.44 Appeals from certain orders — Any person who considers that they are aggrieved by an order made under subsection 462.38(2) or 462.41(3) or section 462.43 may appeal from the order as if the order were an appeal against conviction or against a judgment or verdict of acquittal, as the case may be, under Part XXI, and that Part applies, with such modifications as the circumstances require, to such an appeal.

R.S. 1985, c. 42 (4th Supp.), s. 2; 1997, c. 18, s. 39.

Commentary: Under this section any *person* who considers him/herself *aggrieved* by an order made on an *in rem* forfeiture hearing under s. 462.38(2) or under s. 462.43 or by an order of restoration under s. 462.41(3), may *appeal*, as if the order were a conviction or a judgment or verdict of acquittal, as the case may be, under Part XXI. Appellate procedure and disposition is governed by Part XXI, *mutatis mutandis*.

Related Provisions: "Person", is defined in s. 2. It includes both real and artificial persons and Her Majesty.

Rights of *appeal* against *conviction* are found in s. 675(1)(a) and (1.1) and against a judgment or verdict of *acquittal* or not criminally responsible on account of mental disorder in s. 676(1)(a) and (1.1). The dispositive *powers* of the court of appeal are described in s. 686 and *ancillary* powers exercised on the hearing of the appeal in s. 683. The operation of orders that are subject to appeal under s. 462.45 is suspended pending appeal under s. 462.46.

An order made in a post-disposition forfeiture hearing under s. 462.37 is a "sentence" for the purposes of s. 683 (indictable appeals) and s. 785(1) (summary conviction appeals). The operation of an order of forfeiture under s. 462.37(1) is suspended pending appeal under s. 689(1).

Relief from forfeiture may also be sought under s. 462.42. The section contains its own appeal provisions which make the procedural provisions of Part XXI applicable.

462.45 Suspension of forfeiture pending appeal — Notwithstanding anything in this Part, the operation of an order of forfeiture or restoration of property under subsection 462.34(4), 462.37(1), 462.38(2) or 462.41(3) or section 462.43 is suspended pending

(a) any application made in respect of the property under any of those provisions or any other provision of this or any other Act of Parliament that provides for the restoration or forfeiture of such property,

(b) any appeal taken from an order of forfeiture or restoration in respect of the property, or

(c) any other proceeding in which the right of seizure of the property is questioned, and property shall not be disposed of within thirty days after an order of forfeiture is made under any of those provisions.

R.S. 1985, c. 42 (4th Supp.), s. 2.

Commentary: The section, which operates notwithstanding anything in Part XII.2, mandates *suspension* of the operation of certain orders *pending further or other proceedings* contesting their validity.

The orders of forfeiture or restoration of property whose operation is suspended under the section are those of ss. 462.34(4), 462.37(1), 462.38(2) and 462.41(3), as well as s. 462.43. Their operation is suspended, pending any application made in respect of the property under the listed provisions or other Federal enactment relating to forfeiture or restoration, any appeal taken from an order of forfeiture or restoration, or any other proceeding in which the right of seizure of the property is questioned. The section also prohibits disposal of the property within 30 days after an order of forfeiture is made under any enumerated section.

Related Provisions: Under s. 689(1), the operation of an order of forfeiture under s. 462.37(1) is suspended until the expiration of the relevant appeal period and, where an appeal has been taken, pending the determination of the appeal.

The stay authority of s. 462.45 is incorporated by *C.D.A.* s. 23.

The remedies available in respect of each of the listed forfeiture and restoration provisions are described in the corresponding note to each of the sections.

462.46 (1) Copies of documents returned or forfeited — Where any document is returned or ordered to be returned, forfeited or otherwise dealt with under subsection 462.34(3) or (4), 462.37(1), 462.38(2) or 462.41(3) or section 462.43, the Attorney General may, before returning the document or complying with the order, cause a copy of the document to be made and retained.

(2) **Probative force** — Every copy made under subsection (1) shall, if certified as a true copy by the Attorney General, be admissible in evidence and, in the absence of evidence to the contrary, shall have the same probative force as the original document would have had if it had been proved in the ordinary way.

R.S. 1985, c. 42 (4th Supp.), s. 2.

Commentary: The section authorizes *copying* of returned or forfeited documents and provides for their *admissibility* in certain circumstances, as if they were originals. Under subsection (1), the Attorney General, before returning any document or complying with an order that it be returned, forfeited or otherwise dealt with under s. 462.34(3) or (4), 462.37(1), 462.38(2), 462.41(3) or 462.3, may cause the document to be copied and retained.

Section 462.47(2) authorizes the reception in evidence of a *certified true copy* of any document described in s. 462.47(1). The certification is to be completed by the Attorney General. The probative force of the document is the *same as the original* would have had, if proven in the ordinary way, *absent evidence to the contrary*.

The section appears, in some measure, to permit the reception of documentary evidence, irrespective of the manner is which it has been obtained. To such extent it fails to take cognizance of *Charter* s. 8 and s. 24(2).

Related Provisions: "Attorney General" is defined in s. 2.

Section 491.2 authorizes reception of a certified photograph of property in proceedings in respect of listed property offences, in lieu of the property itself.

The provisions of s. 462.46 are incorporated by *C.D.A.* s. 23.

Disclosure Provisions

462.47 No civil or criminal liability incurred by informants — For greater certainty but subject to section 241 of the *Income Tax Act*, a person is justified in disclosing to a peace officer or the Attorney General any facts on the basis of which that person reasonably suspects that any property is proceeds of crime or that any person has committed or is about to commit an enterprise crime offence or a designated substance offence.

R.S. 1985, c. 42 (4th Supp.), s. 2; 1996, c. 19, s. 70(j).

Commentary: The section provides protection, by way of statutory justification, for informants who furnish information concerning proceeds of crime or the prior or anticipated commission of an enterprise crime or designated substance offence.

The justification of the section applies where any person discloses to a peace officer or the Attorney General any facts upon the basis of which the informant *reasonably suspects* that any property is proceeds of crime, or that any person has committed or is about to commit an enterprise crime or designated substance offence. The section, in terms, is subject to s. 241 of the *Income Tax Act*, which is itself amended to permit disclosure under s. 462.48.

Related Provisions: "Peace officer" and "Attorney General" are defined in s. 2.

Disclosure of income tax information must be made in accordance with s. 462.48, *not* under this provision of general application.

462.48 (1) Disclosure of income tax information — The Attorney General may, for the purposes of an investigation in relation to

(a) a designated substance offence,

(b) an offence against section 354 or 462.31 where the offence is alleged to have been committed in relation to any property, thing or proceeds obtained or derived directly or indirectly as a result of

(i) the commission in Canada of a designated substance offence, or

(ii) an act or omission anywhere that, if it had occurred in Canada, would have constituted a designated substance offence, or

(c) an offence against section 467.1 or a conspiracy or an attempt to commit, being an accessory after the fact in relation to, or any counselling in relation to, such an offence,

make an application in accordance with subsection (2) for an order for disclosure of information under subsection (3).

(2) Application — An application under subsection (1) shall be made *ex parte* in writing to a judge and be accompanied by an affidavit sworn on the information and belief of the Attorney General or a person specially designated by the Attorney General for that purpose deposing to the following matters, namely,

(a) the offence or matter under investigation;

(b) the person in relation to whom the information or documents referred to in paragraph (c) are required;

(c) the type of information or book, record, writing, return or other document obtained by or on behalf of the Minister of National Revenue for the purposes of the *Income Tax Act* to which access is sought or that is proposed to be examined or communicated; and

(d) the facts relied on to justify the belief, on reasonable grounds, that the person referred to in paragraph (b) has committed or benefited from the commission of an offence referred to in paragraph (1)(a), (b) or (c) and that the information or documents referred to in paragraph (c) are likely to be of substantial value, whether alone or together with other material, to the investigation for the purposes of which the application is made.

(3) Order for disclosure of information — Where the judge to whom an application under subsection (1) is made is satisfied

(a) of the matters referred to in paragraph (2)(d), and

(b) that there are reasonable grounds for believing that it is in the public interest to allow access to the information or documents to which the application relates, having regard to the benefit likely to accrue to the investigation if the access is obtained,

the judge may, subject to such conditions as the judge considers advisable in the public interest, order the Deputy Minister of National Revenue or any person specially designated in writing by that Deputy Minister for the purposes of this section

> **Proposed Amendment — 462.48(3)(b)**
>
> (b) that there are reasonable grounds for believing that it is in the public interest to allow access to the information or documents to which the application relates, having regard to the benefit likely to accrue to the investigation if the access is obtained,
>
> the judge may, subject to any conditions that the judge considers advisable in the public interest, order the Commissioner of Customs and Revenue or any person specially designated in writing by the Commissioner for the purposes of this section
>
> 1999, c. 17, s. 120(1) [Not in force at date of publication.]

(c) to allow a police officer named in the order access to all such information and documents and to examine them, or

(d) where the judge considers it necessary in the circumstances, to produce all such information and documents to the police officer and allow the police officer to remove the information and documents,

within such period as the judge may specify after the expiration of seven clear days following the service of the order pursuant to subsection (4).

(4) Service of order — A copy of an order made by a judge under subsection (3) shall be served on the person to whom the order is addressed in such manner as the judge directs or as may be prescribed by rules of court.

(5) Extension of period for compliance with order — A judge who makes an order under subsection (3) may, on application of the Minister of National Revenue, extend the period within which the order is to be complied with.

(6) Objection to disclosure of information — The Minister of National Revenue or any person specially designated in writing by that Minister for the purposes of this section may object to the disclosure of any information or document in respect of which an order under subsection (3) has been made by certifying orally or in writing that the information or document should not be disclosed on the ground that

(a) the Minister of National Revenue is prohibited from disclosing the information or document by any bilateral or international treaty, convention or other agreement respecting taxation to which the Government of Canada is signatory;

(b) a privilege is attached by law to the information or document;

(c) the information or document has been placed in a sealed package pursuant to law or an order of a court of competent jurisdiction; or

(d) disclosure of the information or document would not, for any other reason, be in the public interest.

(7) Determination of objection — Where an objection to the disclosure of information or a document is made under subsection (6), the objection may be determined, on application, in accordance with subsection (8), by the Chief Justice of the Federal Court, or by such other judge of that court as the Chief Justice may designate to hear such applications.

(8) Judge may examine information — A judge who is to determine an objection pursuant to subsection (7) may, if the judge considers it necessary to determine the objection, examine the information or document in relation to which the objection is made and shall grant the objection and order that disclosure of the information or document be refused where the judge is satisfied of any of the grounds mentioned in subsection (6).

(9) Limitation period — An application under subsection (7) shall be made within ten days after the objection is made or within such greater or lesser period as the Chief Justice of the Federal Court, or such other judge of that court as the Chief Justice may designate to hear such applications, considers appropriate.

(10) Appeal to federal court of appeal — An appeal lies from a determination under subsection (7) to the Federal Court of Appeal.

(11) Limitation period for appeal — An appeal under subsection (10) shall be brought within ten days from the date of the determination appealed from or within such further time as the Federal Court of Appeal considers appropriate in the circumstances.

(12) Special rules for hearing — An application under subsection (7) or an appeal brought in respect of that application shall

(a) be heard in *camera*; and

(b) on the request of the person objecting to the disclosure of information, be heard and determined in the National Capital Region described in the schedule to the *National Capital Act*.

(13) Ex parte representations — During the hearing of an application under subsection (7) or an appeal brought in respect of that application, the person who made the

S. 462.48(13)

Criminal Code

objection in respect of which the application was made or the appeal was brought shall, on the request of that person, be given the opportunity to make representations *ex parte*.

(14) Copies — Where any information or document is examined or provided under subsection (3), the person by whom it is examined or to whom it is provided or any officer of the Department of National Revenue may make, or cause to be made, one or more copies thereof and any copy purporting to be certified by the Minister of National Revenue or an authorized person to be a copy made pursuant to this subsection is evidence of the nature and content of the original information or document and has the same probative force as the original information or document would have had if it had been proved in the ordinary way.

Proposed Amendment — 462.48(14)

(14) Copies — When any information or document is examined or provided under subsection (3), the person by whom it is examined or to whom it is provided or any officer of the Canada Customs and Revenue Agency may make, or cause to be made, one or more copies of it, and any copy purporting to be certified by the Minister of National Revenue or an authorized person to be a copy made under this subsection is evidence of the nature and content of the original information or document and has the same probative force as the original information or document would have had if it had been proved in the ordinary way.

1999, c. 17, s. 120(2) [Not in force at date of publication.]

(15) Further disclosure — No person to whom information or documents have been disclosed or provided pursuant to this subsection or pursuant to an order made under subsection (3) shall further disclose the information or documents except for the purposes of the investigation in relation to which the order was made.

(16) Form — An order made under subsection (3) may be in Form 47.

(17) Definition of "police officer" — In this section, "police officer" means any officer, constable or other person employed for the preservation and maintenance of the public peace.

R.S. 1985, c. 42 (4th Supp.), s. 2; 1994, c.13, s. 7(1)(b); 1996, c. 19, s. 70(k); 1997, c. 23, s. 10(2).

Commentary: The section authorizes *disclosure of income tax information* for the purposes of certain investigations and defines the basis upon which such disclosure may be ordered.

Sections 462.48(1) and (2) authorize *application for disclosure* and describe the material to be filed in support thereof. Application for disclosure of income tax information may be made by the Attorney General, for the purposes of an investigation in relation to a designated substance offence or a proceeds of crime offence described in s. 354 (possession of property obtained by crime) or 462.31 (laundering proceeds of crime) or derived from a designated substance offence or an offence in the context of a criminal organization under s. 467.1. Under s. 462.48(2), the application must be made *ex parte*, in writing, to a judge as defined in s. 462.3 and accompanied by an affidavit sworn by the Attorney General, or a person specially designated by the Attorney General for such a purpose. The affiant must depose to the matters described in ss. 462.48(2)(a)–(d). A critical component of the affidavit is a statement of the facts relied upon by the affiant to justify the reasonably grounded belief that the person in relation to whom the information or documents are required, has committed or benefitted from the commission of an offence described in s. 462.48(1)(a), (b) or (c), and that the information or documents described in s. 462.48(2)(c) are likely to be of substantial value, alone or together with other material, to the investigation for the purposes of which the application is made.

The *basis* on which an order may be granted and, to some extent, its terms, are described in s. 462.48(3). The judge must first be satisfied of the matters described in s. 462.48(2)(d), a combination of *probable complicity* and *substantial investigative value*. The judge must further be satisfied that there are *reasona-*

618

ble grounds to believe that it is in the *public interest* to allow the requested access, having regard to the benefit likely to accrue to the investigation if access is obtained. Where such findings have been made, the judge *may*, subject to such conditions as the judge considers advisable in the public interest, make the order requested. The order, which may be in Form 45, is directed to the Deputy Minister of National Revenue, or any person specially designated in writing by the Deputy Minister. The order may allow a named police officer, as defined in s. 462.48(17), *access* to all such information and documents, as well as *examination* of them. Alternatively, where the judge considers it necessary in the circumstances, the Deputy Minister or his/her designate may be ordered to produce the information and documents to the police officer for *removal* by the officer. In either case, the order may specify a period for access, examination or removal, as the case may be, commencing after the expiration of seven clear days following service of the order, in such manner as the judge directs or rules of courts prescribe, as the case may be, under s. 462.48(4). The period of compliance specified in the order may be extended under s. 462.48(5) on application of the Minister of National Revenue. Under s. 462.48(15), further disclosure of information or documents is limited to the purposes of the investigation in relation to which the order was made.

Sections 462.48(6)–(9) authorize revenue officials to *object to disclosure* on certain grounds and provide the *procedure* to *determine* the *validity* of their objection. The objection must be taken, under s. 462.48(6) by the Minister of National Revenue, or anyone specially designated in writing for such a purpose by the Minister, by oral or written certification refusing disclosure upon any ground described in ss. 462.48(6)(a)–(d). Under s. 462.48(7) the validity of the objection to disclosure may be determined, on application to the Chief Justice of the Federal Court or other designated judge of that court. The application, under s. 462.48(12), must be heard *in camera* and, at the request of the party taking objection, shall be heard and determined in the National Capital Region, as described in the schedule to the *National Capital Act*. The party objecting to disclosure, under s. 462.48(13), may request and shall be given the opportunity to make representations *ex parte*. Under s. 462.48(9), the application for determination must be made within 10 days of the objection or within such greater or lesser period as the Chief Justice of the Federal Court or his/her designate considers appropriate.

Upon the *hearing* of the application to determine the objection, the judge may examine the information or document if s/he considers it necessary to determine the matter. Section 462.48(8) requires the judge to grant the objection and refuse disclosure where satisfied of *any* of the grounds upon which disclosure may be refused under s. 462.48(6).

An *appeal* lies to the Federal Court of Appeal, under s. 462.48(10), from a determination made under s. 462.48(7). It must be brought, under s. 462.48(11), within 10 days of the determination or such further time as the Federal Court of Appeal considers appropriate under the circumstances. The secrecy provisions of ss. 462.48(12) and (13) apply to appeals.

Section 462.48(14) authorizes *copying* of documents or information examined or provided under s. 462.48(3) by the person examining, to whom it is provided or an officer of the Department of National Revenue. Any copy certified as true by the Minister of National Revenue or his/her designate is *receivable* as evidence of its nature and content as if the original were proven and received in the ordinary way.

Related Provisions: Section 241(4)(i) of the *Income Tax Act* permits an official or authorized persons under the Act to communicate or allow to be communicated information obtained under the Act pursuant to an order under *Code* s. 462.48(3).

The provisions of the section are incorporated by *C.D.A.* s. 23 and the repealed *F.D.A.* ss. 44.4 (controlled drugs) and 51 (restricted drugs), but are extended by ss. 43.1 (controlled drugs) and 50.1 (restricted drugs) so that the underlying or predicate offence includes the inchoate and accessorial-related offences. Similar extended incorporation is made by the repealed *N.C.A.* ss. 19.2 and 19.3.

Specific Rules of Forfeiture

462.49 (1) Specific forfeiture provisions unaffected by this part — This Part does not affect the operation of any other provision of this or any other Act of Parliament respecting the forfeiture of property.

(2) Priority for restitution to victims of crime — The property of an offender may be used to satisfy the operation of a provision of this or any other Act of Parliament respecting the forfeiture of property only to the extent that it is not required to satisfy the operation of any other provision of this or any other Act of Parliament respecting the restitution or compensation of persons affected by the commission of offences.

R.S. 1985, c. 42 (4th Supp.), s. 2.

Commentary: The purpose of this section is twofold. Section 462.49(1) makes it plain that Part XII.2 is *not* exhaustive of the forfeiture of property, and does *not* affect the operation of any other provision of the *Code* or other federal enactment respecting forfeiture. Section 462.49(2) assigns priority in the distribution of an offender's property to satisfaction of claims of restitution or compensation of persons affected by the commission of offences. Thereafter, the property may be applied to satisfy the operation of forfeiture provisions.

Related Provisions: "Property" is defined in s. 2.

Restitution orders may be made under ss. 491.1 and 738–741.2.

The provisions of this section are incorporated by *C.D.A.* s. 23 and the repealed *F.D.A.* ss. 44.4 (controlled drugs) and 51 (restricted drugs), but are extended by ss. 43.1 (controlled drugs) and 50.1 (restricted drugs), so that the underlying or predicate offence includes the inchoate and accessorial-related offences. Similar extended incorporation is made by the repealed *N.C.A.* ss. 19.2 and 19.3.

Regulations

462.5 Regulations — The Attorney General may make regulations governing the manner of disposing of or otherwise dealing with, in accordance with the law, property, forfeited under this Part.

R.S. 1985, c. 42 (4th Supp.), s. 2.

Commentary: The section authorizes the Attorney General to make regulations in accordance with which property forfeited under Part XII.2 may be disposed of or otherwise dealt with in accordance with the law.

Related Provisions: The section is incorporated by *C.D.A.* s. 23 and the repealed *F.D.A.* ss. 44.4(2) (controlled drugs) and 51 (restricted drugs) and by the repealed *N.C.A.* s. 19.3(2). In each case, the incorporation is, with such modifications as the circumstances require, and substitutes "Minister of Justice" for Attorney General as appears in s. 462.5.

PART XIII — ATTEMPTS — CONSPIRACIES — ACCESSORIES

463. Attempts, accessories — Except where otherwise expressly provided by law, the following provisions apply in respect of persons who attempt to commit or are accessories after the fact to the commission of offences:

(a) every one who attempts to commit or is an accessory after the fact to the commission of an indictable offence for which, on conviction, an accused is liable to be sentenced to death or to imprisonment for life is guilty of an indictable offence and liable to imprisonment for a term not exceeding fourteen years;

Proposed Amendment — 463(a)

(a) every one who attempts to commit or is an accessory after the fact to the commission of an indictable offence for which, on conviction, an accused is liable to be sentenced to imprisonment for life is guilty of an indictable offence and liable to imprisonment for a term not exceeding fourteen years;

1998, c. 35, s. 120 [Not in force at date of publication.]

(b) every one who attempts to commit or is an accessory after the fact to the commission of an indictable offence for which, on conviction, an accused is liable to imprisonment for fourteen years or less is guilty of an indictable offence and liable to imprisonment for a term that is one-half of the longest term to which a person who is guilty of that offence is liable;

(c) every one who attempts to commit or is an accessory after the fact to the commission of an offence punishable on summary conviction is guilty of an offence punishable on summary conviction; and

(d) every one who attempts to commit or is an accessory after the fact to the commission of an offence for which the offender may be prosecuted by indictment or for which he is punishable on summary conviction

    (i) is guilty of an indictable offence and liable to imprisonment for a term not exceeding a term that is one-half of the longest term to which a person who is guilty of that offence is liable, or

    (ii) is guilty of an offence punishable on summary conviction.

R.S., c. C-34, s. 421; R.S. 1985, c. 27 (1st Supp.), s. 59.

Commentary: This section provides a general *punishment* structure upon conviction of *attempt* and *accessory after the fact* to certain offences which applies *except where otherwise expressly provided by law*. The punishments, which are identical, are determined by reference to that imposed upon conviction of the substantive offence.

Under s. 463(a), where the *substantive* offence attracts a penalty of imprisonment for *life*, an attempt or accessoryship after the fact is an indictable offence punishable by imprisonment for a term not exceeding 14 years.

Under s. 463(b), where the maximum punishment upon conviction of a *substantive* indictable offence is 14 years or less, an attempt or accessoryship after the fact is an indictable offence a maximum term of imprisonment of *one-half* of the maximum for the substantive offence.

Under s. 463(c), an attempt or accessoryship after the fact to a *summary conviction* offence is itself summary conviction offence punishable under the general provisions of Part XXVII.

Section 463(d) applies to *attempts* and *accessoryship after the fact* to offences triable either way. Where P proceeds by *indictment*, the punishment is one-half of the maximum for the substantive offence. Where P proceeds by *summary conviction*, the punishment is in accordance with the provisions of Part XXVII.

Case Law [See ss. 23 and 24]

Related Provisions: An attempt is defined in s. 24 and accessoryship after the fact in s. 23. Under s. 23.1, an accessory may be convicted even where the principal cannot be, for example on account of infancy, death or absence from the jurisdiction.

General punishment provisions for counselling an offence which is *not* committed and conspiracy appear in ss. 464 and 465(1).

Both attempted murder (s. 239) and accessory after the fact to murder (s. 240) carry a maximum punishment of imprisonment for life.

Trial jurisdiction, hence rights of election, follow those applicable to the substantive offence. Accessoryship after the fact to high treason, treason or murder and attempts to commit any offence listed in s. 469, except murder and bribery by the holder of a judicial office, must be tried in the *superior court* of criminal jurisdiction. Attempts and accessoryship after the fact in relation to s. 553 offences are within the *absolute* jurisdiction of a provincial court judge.

464. Counselling offence that is not committed — Except where otherwise expressly provided by law, the following provisions apply in respect of persons who counsel other persons to commit offences, namely,

(a) every one who counsels another person to commit an indictable offence is, if the offence is not committed, guilty of an indictable offence and liable to the same punishment to which a person who attempts to commit that offence is liable; and

(b) every one who counsels another person to commit an offence punishable on summary conviction is, if the offence is not committed, guilty of an offence punishable on summary conviction.

R.S., c. C-34, s. 422; R.S. 1985, c. 27 (1st Supp.), s. 60.

Commentary: The section enacts a general *punishment* provision applicable upon conviction for *counselling* others to commit offences which are *not* in fact committed, *except where otherwise expressly provided by law*.

Case Law

Nature and Elements of Offence [See also s. 22]

R. v. Glubisz (No. 2) (1979), 9 C.R. (3d) 300, 47 C.C.C. (2d) 232 (B.C. C.A.) — The fact that the person procured at no time had the intention to commit the offence is *not* a defence to the charge, nor does it reduce the charge to an attempt to procure the commission of an offence.

R. v. Walia (No. 1) (1975), 9 C.R. (3d) 293 (B.C. C.A.) — The offence charged under this section is complete the moment D persuades another to commit an indictable offence. It does *not* matter that the person procured agrees to commit the offence and later changes his mind; nor does it matter if the person procured says that he agrees to commit the offence but really has no intention to do so.

R. v. Gonzague (1983), 34 C.R. (3d) 169, 4 C.C.C. (3d) 505 (Ont. C.A.) — The offence of procuring is complete the moment the solicitation or incitement occurs, even though it is immediately rejected by the person solicited, or the person solicited pretends to assent to the commission of the offence but really has no intention of committing it. A subsequent renunciation of the criminal purpose by the procurer does *not* constitute a defence to the charge, although it may be relevant evidence on the issue whether D because of intoxication, had the necessary intent.

Related Provisions: Counselling is defined in s. 22(3). A person who counsels an offence which is committed is a party to the offence counselled under s. 22(1). Under s. 22(2), the counsellor may also be liable to conviction of certain collateral crimes committed by the person counselled.

The section contains *no* provision similar to s. 463(d) where the offence counselled but not committed is triable either way. It would appear that under *I.A.* s. 34(1)(a) such counselling would be an indictable offence.

Counselling an offence listed in s. 553 is within the *absolute* jurisdiction of a provincial court judge under the section. Counselling a s. 469 offence which is not in fact committed, as well as other indictable offences not listed in s. 553, permits D to *elect* mode of trial under s. 536(2).

465. (1) Conspiracy — Except where otherwise expressly provided by law, the following provisions apply in respect of conspiracy:

(a) every one who conspires with any one to commit murder or to cause another person to be murdered, whether in Canada or not, is guilty of an indictable offence and liable to a maximum term of imprisonment for life;

(b) every one who conspires with any one to prosecute a person for an alleged offence, knowing that he did not commit that offence, is guilty of an indictable offence and liable

(i) to imprisonment for a term not exceeding ten years, if the alleged offence is one for which, on conviction, the person would be liable to be sentenced to death or to imprisonment for life or for a term not exceeding fourteen years, or

Proposed Amendment — 465(1)(b)(i)

(i) to imprisonment for a term not exceeding ten years, if the alleged offence is one for which, on conviction, that person would be liable to be sentenced to imprisonment for life or for a term not exceeding fourteen years, or

1998, c. 35, s. 121 [Not in force at date of publication.]

(ii) to imprisonment for a term not exceeding five years, if the alleged offence is one for which, on conviction, that person would be liable to imprisonment for less than fourteen years; and

(c) every one who conspires with any one to commit an indictable offence not provided for in paragraph (*a*) or (*b*) is guilty of an indictable offence and liable to the same punishment as that to which an accused who is guilty of that offence would, on conviction, be liable; and

(d) every one who conspires with any one to commit an offence punishable on summary conviction is guilty of an offence punishable on summary conviction.

(2) [Repealed R.S. 1985, c. 27 (1st Supp.), s. 61(3).]

(3) **Conspiracy to commit offences** — Every one who, while in Canada, conspires with any one to do anything referred to in subsection (1) in a place outside Canada that is an offence under the laws of that place shall be deemed to have conspired to do that thing in Canada.

(4) **Idem** — Every one who, while in a place outside Canada, conspires with any one to do anything referred to in subsection (1) in Canada shall be deemed to have conspired in Canada to do that thing.

(5) **Jurisdiction** — Where a person is alleged to have conspired to do anything that is an offence by virtue of subsection (3) or (4), proceedings in respect of that offence may, whether or not that person is in Canada, be commenced in any territorial division in Canada, and the accused may be tried and punished in respect of that offence in the same manner as if the offence had been committed in that territorial division.

(6) **Appearance of accused at trial** — For greater certainty, the provisions of this Act relating to

(a) requirements that an accused appear at and be present during proceedings, and

(b) the exceptions to those requirements,

apply to proceedings commenced in any territorial division pursuant to subsection (5).

(7) **Where previously tried outside Canada** — Where a person is alleged to have conspired to do anything that is an offence by virtue of subsection (3) or (4) and that person has been tried and dealt with outside Canada in respect of the offence in such a manner that, if the person had been tried and dealt with in Canada, he would be able to plead *autrefois acquit, autrefois convict* or pardon, the person shall be deemed to have been so tried and dealt with in Canada.

R.S., c. C-34, s. 423; 1974–75–76, c. 93, s. 36; 1980–81–82–83, c. 125, s. 23; R.S. 1985, c. 27 (1st Supp.), s. 61.

Commentary: The provisions of this section describe and punish various *conspiracy* offences and determine trial jurisdiction.

Section 465(1) contains general *punishment* provisions applicable to specified conspiracy offences, *except where otherwise expressly provided by law*. Although s. 465(1)(a) makes express reference to conspiracy to commit murder, the remaining paragraphs describe the offence object of the conspiracy by reference to the mode of procedure and/or the maximum penalty provided for the substantive offence. In large measure, the maximum punishment for conspiracy does *not* materially differ from that imposed upon conviction of the substantive offence.

Sections 465(3) and (4) enact *special jurisdiction provisions* applicable where the unlawful agreement or its objects take or are to take place outside Canada. Under s. 465(3), a conspiracy in Canada to do anything described in s. 465(1) outside Canada that is an offence in such place is *deemed* to be a conspiracy to do that thing in Canada. Under s. 465(4), where the conspiratorial agreement occurs outside Canada to do anything described in s. 465(1) inside Canada, D is *deemed* to have conspired in Canada. In other words, the provisions combine domestic and foreign elements of agreement and object to make the conspiracy cognizable by Canadian courts.

Sections 465(5) and (6) define *trial jurisdiction* and, to some extent, venue in respect of ss. 465(3) and (4) conspiracies. Proceedings in respect of such conspiracies may be commenced in any territorial division in Canada, whether D is or is not present in this country. D may be tried and punished in respect of the offence, as if the offence had been committed in the territorial division of trial. Section 465(6) makes it clear that the general requirement of D's presence at trial (s. 650) applies under s. 465(5), subject to the usual exceptions.

Section 465(7) also applies to ss. 465(3) and (4) conspiracies. It *deems* D, tried in a foreign jurisdiction in respect of the offence in a manner that would, if tried in Canada give rise to a special plea, to have been tried in Canada. The provision in this respect mirrors *Charter* s. 11(h).

Case Law

Nature and Elements of Offence

United States v. Dynar (1997), [1997] 2 S.C.R. 462, 8 C.R. (5th) 79, 115 C.C.C. (3d) 481 (S.C.C.) — The essential elements of a *conspiracy* are

i.   the *intention* to agree;

ii.   *completion* of the *agreement*; and

iii.   a *common design* to do something unlawful.

The offence is *complete* before any acts which go beyond mere preparation are taken to put the design into effect. Conspiracy is a more "preliminary" crime than is attempt.

Impossibility affords *no* defence to conspiracy. The distinction between factual and legal possibility is as unsound in relation to conspiracy as it is in connection with attempts. Conspiracy is a crime of intention which requires only an intention to commit the substantive offence, not the actual commission of it.

R. v. Douglas (1991), 63 C.C.C. (3d) 29 (S.C.C.) — The *essence* of conspiracy is the *agreement* to perform an *illegal act*. The overt acts taken to carry out the agreement are merely elements going to prove the agreement.

Belyea v. R. (1932), 57 C.C.C. 318 (S.C.C.) — It is *not* essential that D participate in the overt acts if he has been involved in the formation of the conspiracy.

R. v. Lindquist (1985), 40 Alta. L.R. (2d) 392 (C.A.) — P need only prove participation of D with at least one other participant named in the indictment.

R. v. Carvery (1991), 10 C.R. (4th) 228 (N.S. C.A.) — The sale of a narcotic does *not* necessarily involve a conspiracy between the vendor and purchaser. Conspiracy requires proof of an *agreement* and a *common object* to act upon the agreement. The involvement of an intermediary between the vendor and purchaser may take the transaction beyond a simple purchase and sale, as for example, where the intermediary purports to have a degree of control over the actions of the purchaser and undertakes to exercise that control in favour of expediting the transaction. The vendor and intermediary in such a case have conspired together towards the criminal object of a sale of narcotic from the vendor to the purchaser.

R. v. Gassyt (1998), 127 C.C.C. (3d) 546 (Ont. C.A.) — A conspiracy may be proven by evidence of overt acts and statements of the conspirators from which the prior agreement may be logically inferred.

R. v. Dungey (1979), 51 C.C.C. (2d) 86 (Ont. C.A.) — There is no such offence as an attempt to conspire to commit fraud which would punish guilty intention alone. It was unnecessary to decide whether one could attempt to commit the substantive offence of conspiracy.

R. v. Trudel (1984), 12 C.C.C. (3d) 342 (Que. C.A.) — It is *not* necessary for the crime contemplated to be committed. A conspiracy exists without perpetration of the contemplated offence.

R. v. Kotyszyn (1949), 8 C.R. 246, 95 C.C.C. 261 (Que. C.A.) — A criminal conspiracy requires two or more persons; agreement between the parties on a common intent; and, an unlawful purpose. A design which rests in intention only is *not* indictable.

Mental Element

R. v. Genser (1986), 27 C.C.C. (3d) 264 (Man. C.A.); affirmed (1987), 39 C.C.C. (3d) 576 (S.C.C.) — *See also*: *R. v. Roebuck* (1985), 36 Man. R. (2d) 270 (C.A.) — The gist of a conspiracy is the unlawful agreement. It is *not* necessary for all the conspirators to intend to commit the offence upon which the agreement is reached. Where it was shown that one party agreed to supply cocaine to another, knowing that party would use the cocaine for resale, an agreement to traffic in cocaine could be inferred.

R. v. O'Brien (1954), 19 C.R. 371, 110 C.C.C. 1 (S.C.C.) — There must be a genuine common design to do something unlawful to constitute a criminal conspiracy, and an intention by both or all parties to put the common design into effect. If *one* of two parties to the alleged agreement merely *pretends* to agree, without any intention of carrying the agreement into effect, there *cannot* be a conviction for conspiracy.

R. v. Randall (1983), 7 C.C.C. (3d) 363 (N.S. C.A.) — A drug trafficker who buys from an importer does *not* become an importer or a member of a conspiracy to import. Mere knowledge or discussion of, or passive acquiescence in a plan of criminal conduct is *not* sufficient to prove membership in a conspiracy.

R. v. Lessard (1982), l0 C.C.C. (3d) 61 (Que. C.A.) — Where a variety of activities were discussed at the time the agreement was reached, P must prove more than recklessness as to the object of the conspiracy. Intention to enter into an agreement to commit a particular offence is required. Recklessness is sufficient only regarding the method of executing the agreement.

Agreement

R. v. Vucetic (1998), 129 C.C.C. (3d) 178 (Ont. C.A.) — To establish D's guilt of conspiracy as an aider or abettor, P must prove that D

i. knew the object of the conspiracy;

ii. assisted the conspirators; and,

iii. intended to assist the conspirators in attaining their unlawful object.

R. v. McNamara (No. 1) (1981), 56 C.C.C. (2d) 193 (Ont. C.A.); affirmed on other grounds (1985), 45 C.R. (3d) 289, (sub nom. *Cdn. Dredge & Dock Co. v. R.)* 19 C.C.C. (3d) 1 — For a conspiracy to exist, it is *not* sufficient for two or more persons to agree. They must agree to do something. Mere knowledge or discussion of, or a passive acquiescence in a plan of criminal conduct is not sufficient. The *Code* provisions concerning aiding and abetting apply only if the accused abetted or encouraged any conspirators to pursue its object.

Co-Conspirators

Guimond v. R. (1979), 8 C.R. (3d) 185, 44 C.C.C. (2d) 481 (S.C.C.) — Where two alleged co-conspirators are tried separately the acquittal of one does not necessarily invalidate the conviction of the other. It is safer to have separate trials where the evidence against one co-accused is substantially stronger than against the other, particularly when P is tendering in evidence a damaging statement made by one under circumstances which made it inadmissible against the other.

R. v. B. (T.L.) (1989), 52 C.C.C. (3d) 72 (N.S. C.A.) — Failure to name the person(s) with whom D allegedly conspired does *not* invalidate the indictment.

Spouses

Kowbel v. R. (1954), 18 C.R. 380 (S.C.C.) — Spouses cannot be found guilty of conspiring together. Judicially speaking, they form but one person, and have but one will.

Companies

R. v. Fane Robinson Ltd. (1941), 76 C.C.C. 196 (Alta. C.A.) — Conspiracy is one of the crimes that a company can commit. The necessary *mens rea* may be found in an officer, servant or agent authorized by the company to act for it.

R. v. Ash-Temple Co. (1949), 8 C.R. 66, 93 C.C.C. 267 (Ont. C.A.) — Where a company is charged with conspiracy, if the act relied on is that of an officer, servant or agent of the company, there must be evidence that he had authority from the company to perform the act.

Outside Canada [See also s. 6]

R. v. Rowbotham (1992), 76 C.C.C. (3d) 542 (Ont. C.A.); affirmed (1993), 85 C.C.C. (3d) 575 (S.C.C.) — *See also*: *Libman v. R.* (1985), 21 C.C.C. (3d) 206 (S.C.C.) — Where an indictment alleges conspiracy to traffic in a narcotic in Toronto, Ontario and Austin, Texas, P need *not* rely on s. 465(3) nor adduce evidence of Texas law where there is evidence from which a jury could find that the conspiracy took place in Canada. The evidence disclosed

i.   that all the *planning* and *preparatory* acts regarding the sale took place in *Canada*;

ii.   that one of the *accused* was to receive his *share* of the proceeds in *Canada*; and,

iii.   that both accused anticipated that the police agent would *take* the *narcotics* from *Texas* back *to Canada*.

There was, accordingly, a *real and substantial link* with Canada and no requirement of international comity that Canada refrain from exercising jurisdiction.

Bolduc v. Quebec (P.G.) (1982), 28 C.R (3d) 193, 68 C.C.C. (2d) 413 (S.C.C.); affirming (1980), 20 C.R. (3d) 372, (sub nom. *R. v. Bolduc)* 60 C.C.C. (2d) 357 — In order for s. 465(3) to apply, the *object* of the conspiracy must he an offence both in Canada and in the country where it is to be carried out. The essential averments of the two *offences* must be identical, so that the act, if committed in Canada, would be an offence in Canada.

R. v. Gunn (1982), 27 C.R. (3d) 120, 66 C.C.C. (2d) 294 (S.C.C.); reversing (sub nom. *R. v. Apaya and Gunn)* 54 C.C.C. (2d) 163 — The statutory fiction of conspiracy in Canada in violation of foreign law can only become operative if a particular breach of foreign law is charged.

R. v. Baldini (1984), 39 C.R. (3d) 43 (Alta. C.A.) — Subsections (3) and (4) require the place of the conspiracy to be in a different country than the place of the intended offence.

R. v. Douglas (1989), 72 C.R. (3d) 309, 51 C.C.C. (3d) 129 (Ont. C.A.); affirmed on other grounds (1991), 63 C.C.C. (3d) 29 (S.C.C.) — As long as there is a *substantial link* between the offence alleged and this country, the charge is properly triable in Canada. Where D agree in Canada to supply narcotics to the United States, they are properly tried in Canada pursuant to s. 465(1) for conspiracy to traffic.

Evidentiary Considerations: The Co-conspirators' Rule

R. v. Carter (1982), 31 C.R. (3d) 97, 67 C.C.C. (2d) 568 (S.C.C.) — *See also*: *R. v. Duff* (1994), 32 C.R. (4th) 153, 90 C.C.C. (3d) 460 (Man. C.A.) — On a charge of conspiracy, the trial judge must instruct the jury to consider whether on *all* the evidence they are satisfied *beyond a reasonable doubt* that the *conspiracy* charged *existed*. If they are *not* so satisfied, there must be an *acquittal*. If they are so satisfied, they must decide whether, on evidence *directly* admissible against the *accused*, a *probability* is raised that he was a *member* of the conspiracy. Only if they conclude that there is such evidence can they apply the *hearsay exception* in determining whether guilt has been shown beyond a reasonable doubt. In the course of the trial it is not necessary to adduce the evidence in this sequence.

R. v. Desgroseilliers (1986), 13 O.A.C. 225 (C.A.); leave to appeal refused (1985), 21 O.A.C. 236n (S.C.C.) — In a conspiracy trial, where one of the conspirators pleads guilty to the charge, the trial judge should instruct the jury that the guilty plea is *not* evidence against the other accused.

R. v. Filiault (1981), 63 C.C.C. (2d) 321 (Ont. C.A.); affirmed (1984), 15 C.C.C. (3d) 352n (S.C.C.) — There must be *some* evidence properly admissible against D of some conduct or utterance by which permits the inference that D was a participant in the conspiracy. This inference may be drawn from viewing the acts of D against the picture provided of the acts of the co-conspirators, but there must be some evidence of the D's own acts and declarations which make D a participant in the conspiracy.

R. v. Viandante (1995), 40 C.R. (4th) 353 (Man. C.A.) — When a jury finds that a *two-person* conspiracy exists beyond a reasonable doubt, then at least one of the co-conspirators must be found to be a member of the conspiracy beyond a reasonable doubt. In determining the *existence* of the conspiracy, the jury is entitled to consider *direct* evidence of the *conspiracy*, but *not* hearsay. If the alleged conspirator makes a *declaration* that s/he is involved in the alleged conspiracy with others, the declaration is

i.   *direct* evidence of the existence of the conspiracy; and

ii. *hearsay* evidence of the participation of the others.

R. v. Gassyt (1998), 127 C.C.C. (3d) 546 (Ont. C.A.) — Acts and declarations by one co-conspirator *in furtherance* of the common design are admissible against another co-conspirator, *even if* the actor or declarant is *unindicted.*

R. v. Falahatchian (1995), 99 C.C.C. (3d) 420 (Ont. C.A.) — The co-conspirator's exception to the hearsay rule is also applicable to *substantive* charges where there is evidence of common design and intention.

R. v. Baron (1976), 31 C.C.C. (2d) 525 (Ont. C.A.) — The trial judge in a conspiracy trial should proceed as follows:

i.   At the end of the whole case the judge must decide as a matter of law, whether there is *any admissible* evidence against an *accused* from his *own acts and declarations*, that he is a *participant* in the conspiracy charged;

ii. If there is *no* evidence directly admissible against an accused connecting him with the conspiracy the judge must direct the jury to *acquit* that accused;

iii. If the judge concludes that there is *some* evidence admissible directly against an accused that s/he was a party to the conspiracy, s/he will instruct the jury that they must first find from evidence admissible *directly* against an accused (that is by evidence other than the acts and declarations of alleged co-conspirators) that he was a party to the conspiracy charged. The judge will then instruct the jury that if they find from such evidence that the accused was a party to the conspiracy the acts and declarations of alleged co-conspirators in *furtherance* of the conspiracy may be used against him;

iv. As a general rule, the judge should then *refer* the jury to the *principal* evidence admissible *directly* against each accused from which they may find that such accused was a party to the conspiracy but the jury should be instructed that it is for them to say if the evidence has this effect;

v.   Finally, the judge must instruct the jury that on the whole of the evidence they must be satisfied beyond a reasonable doubt that the accused was a member of the conspiracy.

Duplicity and Multiple Conspiracies

R. v. Douglas (1991), 63 C.C.C. (3d) 29 (S.C.C.) — The issue in conspiracy cases is whether P has proven the conspiracy alleged. Proof of more than one conspiracy is *not* necessarily fatal, provided what is alleged has been proven. Where the conspiracy proven includes fewer members than the number of accused, or extends over any part of the period alleged, the conspiracy proven may nonetheless be that alleged. A specific conspiracy lies within the scope of the indictment where the evidence adduced establishes that the conspiracy proven included some of the accused, occurred at some time within the time frame alleged in the indictment and had, as its object, the type of crime alleged.

R. v. Paterson (1985), 44 C.R. (3d) 150, 18 C.C.C. (3d) 137 (Ont. C.A.); affirmed (1987), 60 C.R. (3d) 107 (S.C.C.) — *See also*: *R. v. Patten* (1990), 61 C.C.C. (3d) 332 (B.C. C.A.) — A single conspiracy may have more than one illegal object and it is proper to allege in one count a conspiracy to commit several crimes. If P proves a conspiracy to do any one of the prohibited acts alleged in the indictment, that is sufficient for a conviction. Where there is only one agreement, not separate agreements as to the different unlawful objects, there can be only one conviction. P must prove the conspiracy alleged. Where the count alleges that D conspired together for a common purpose but P proves only that some of D had conspired with one of their number for their own purposes, no common purpose as alleged has been proved. Where the evidence establishes the conspiracy alleged against two or more accused, it is immaterial that the evidence also discloses another and wider conspiracy to which D belonged.

R. v. Cotroni (1979), 7 C.R. (3d) 185, 45 C.C.C. (2d) 1 (S.C.C.) — There is a distinction between a conspiracy count which charges two or more conspiracies and one which charges one conspiracy only, but is supported by proof of more than one conspiracy. The former gives rise to questions of duplicity. The latter raises the question whether P has proven the conspiracy charged against two or more of D notwithstanding evidence of a second conspiracy. In interpreting the charge, it must be assumed that the indictment was intended to relate to a crime over which the court had jurisdiction, rather than a crime over which it had no jurisdiction.

R. v. Addison, [1970] 1 C.C.C. 127 (Ont. C.A.) — An indictment charging a single conspiracy to commit numerous offences is *not* duplicitous. A conspiracy may have as its *object* the commission of *more* than *one* offence. The charge relates to the conspiracy itself, *not* the substantive offences which are the object of the conspiracy.

Res Judicata [See also ss. 8, 12]

Sheppe v. R. (1980), 15 C.R. (3d) 381, 51 C.C.C. (2d) 481 (S.C.C.) — D was properly convicted of trafficking and of conspiracy to traffic where the substantive offence occurred during the conspiracy period and the conspiracy had a wider object than the substantive offence. The conspiracy charge depended on proof of a prior illegal agreement and transcended any dependence on the trafficking transactions and therefore it was not a case of two convictions for the same cause or matter or involving the same or substantially the same elements to establish criminality.

Koury v. R. (1964), 42 C.R. 210, [1964] 2 C.C.C. 97 (S.C.C.) — There is no general rule that an acquittal on a count of conspiracy to commit certain offences and a conviction on other counts in the same indictment charging those specific offences, are necessarily inconsistent verdicts.

R. v. Kravenia (1955), 21 C.R. 232, 112 C.C.C. 81 (S.C.C.) — Conspiracy is separate and distinct from the offence that is the object of the conspiracy. Once the agreement is made, conspiracy is committed. It does not matter whether the agreement is carried out.

Related Provisions: "Territorial division" is defined in s. 2.

Specific provision is made for conspiracy in restraint of trade in ss. 466 and 467. Extended jurisdiction is given under ss. 7(3.2)–(3.5) in respect of conspiracy in relation to nuclear material as defined in s. 7(3.6).

The *Code* contains *no* express definition of conspiracy. At common law, it consisted not merely in the intention of two or more persons, but rather in their *agreement* to do an unlawful act or a lawful act by unlawful means. The *unlawful act, semble*, must now be an indictable or summary conviction offence. The repeal of the "common law conspiracy" provisions of former subsection (2) would not seem to leave open a prosecution for conspiracy to do a lawful act by unlawful means. The *external circumstances* of conspiracy consist of the unlawful agreement and the *mental element* of the intention to enter into such an agreement.

Conspiracy to commit an offence listed in s. 469(a) falls within the exclusive trial jurisdiction of the superior court of criminal jurisdiction. Conspiracy to commit any other indictable offence permits D to elect mode of trial under s. 536(2). Conspiracy to commit a summary conviction offence is tried and punished under Part XXVII.

There is *no* special statutory rule of pleading applicable to conspiracy counts nor their joinder with substantive counts.

466. (1) Conspiracy in restraint of trade — A conspiracy in restraint of trade is an agreement between two or more persons to do or to procure to be done any unlawful act in restraint of trade.

(2) Trade union, exception — The purposes of a trade union are not, by reason only that they are in restraint of trade, unlawful within the meaning of subsection (1).

R.S., c. C-34, s. 424.

Commentary: The section defines *conspiracy in restraint of trade* and enacts a trade union exception.

Under s. 466(1), the *external circumstances* of a conspiracy in restraint of trade consist of an agreement between two or more people to do or procure to be done any unlawful act in restraint of trade. The unlawful act need not be done, *a fortiori*, actually restrain trade. The *mental element* requires proof that D intended to enter into the proscribed agreement.

The *exception* of s. 466(2) holds the purposes of a trade union *not* to be unlawful, only because they are in restraint of trade. A trade union is *not, per se*, a conspiracy in restraint of trade. In other words, if nothing more than restraint of trade as is described in s. 466(2) is shown as the purpose of a trade union, the members are *not*, by reason *only* of their membership, guilty of conspiracy in restraint of trade.

Related Provisions: Section 466(1) does *not* actually create an offence. The only conspiracy offences are those specifically mentioned in s. 465(1). Section 466(2) seems to have been inserted *ex abundante cautela*. Another saving provision is contained in s. 467.

467. **(1) Saving** — **No person shall be convicted of the offence of conspiracy by reason only that he**

    (a) refuses to work with a workman or for an employer; or

    (b) does any act or causes any act to be done for the purpose of a trade combination, unless such act is an offence expressly punishable by law.

(2) "trade combination" — **In this section, "trade combination" means any combination between masters or workmen or other persons for the purpose of regulating or altering the relations between masters or workmen, or the conduct of a master or workman in or in respect of his business, employment or contract of employment or service.**

R.S., c. C-34, s. 425.

Commentary: The section enacts a further saving provision applicable in conspiracy cases and provides an exhaustive definition of "trade combination".

Under s. 467(1), proof by P that D did the acts described in either paragraph is *not* sufficient to establish D's liability for conspiracy.

Related Provisions: Conspiracy, not defined in the *Code*, is punished under s. 465 (1). Another saving provision in respect of trade combinations is contained in s. 466(2).

467.1 (1) Participation in criminal organization — Every one who

    (a) participates in or substantially contributes to the activities of a criminal organization knowing that any or all of the members of the organization engage in or have, within the preceding five years, engaged in the commission of a series of indictable offence under this or any other Act of Parliament for each of which the maximum punishment is imprisonment for five years or more, and

    (b) is a party to the commission of an indictable offence for the benefit of, at the direction of or in association with the criminal organization for which the maximum punishment is imprisonment for five years or more

is guilty of an indictable offence and liable to imprisonment for a term not exceeding fourteen years.

(2) Sentences to be served consecutively — **A sentence imposed on a person for an offence under subsection (1) shall be served consecutively to any other punishment imposed on the person for an offence arising out of the same event or series of events and to any other sentence to which is subject at the time the sentence is imposed on the person for an offence under subsection (1).**

1997, c. 23, s. 11.

Commentary: This section prohibits participation in the *activities* and *offences* of a *criminal organization*. It also requires that any sentence imposed upon conviction be served consecutively to any other punishment imposed for a related offence, and to any existing sentence.

The *external circumstances* of the offence include two components. The first involves *participation* in the *activities* of a *criminal organization*. D must participate in or *substantially* contribute to the activities of the organization. The second relates to participation in a *specific indictable* offence in defined circumstances. D must be a *party* to an indictable offence, punishable by imprisonment for five years or more. The offence must be committed

i.   for the *benefit* of;

ii.   the *direction* of; or,

iii.   in *association* with
the criminal organization.

The *mental element* extends beyond the intention to engage in the relevant conduct and participate in the commission of the particular indictable offence. P must also prove knowledge, or recklessness with respect to the activities of members of the organization as described in s. 467.1(a) and a similar state of mind with respect to the purpose or source of the conduct described in s. 467.1(b).

Section 467.1(2) is *mandatory*. Where D is punished for an offence which arises from the same event or series of events that forms the basis of the charge under s. 467.1(1), or is serving a sentence for another crime, the s. 467.1(1) sentence must be served consecutively to the other sentence(s).

Related Provisions: "Criminal organization" and "criminal organization offence" are defined in s.2. Prosecutorial responsibility is governed by s. 467.2 and the definition of "Attorney General" in s. 2.

Anyone who has a reasonably grounded fear that someone will commit a criminal organization offence may lay an information before a provincial court judge under s. 810.01. The consent of the Attorney General is required.

Sections 490.1-490.9 govern forfeiture, transfer and, in some cases, return or restoration of "offence related property", as defined in s. 2. Restraint orders may be made under s. 490.8.

The offence of s. 467.1 is an "offence" for the purposes of s. 183 and Part VI. There are several exceptions in Part VI relating to the activities of criminal organizations and the offences of s. 467.1. Section 185(1.1) removes the investigative necessity requirement of s. 185(1)(h) for affidavits relating to s. 467.1 offences and offences committed for the benefit or at the direction of, or in association with a criminal organization. Section 186(1.1) does likewise for the findings required before an authorization may be given. Section 186.1 permits conventional authorizations and renewals to be for one (1) year, not the usual sixty (60) days. Section 196(5) eliminates the usual requirements to secure an extension of the post-interception notification period under ss. 196(3) and 185(3).

467.2 (1) Powers of the Attorney General of Canada — Notwithstanding the definition of "Attorney General" in section 2, the Attorney General of Canada may conduct proceedings in respect of a criminal organization offence where the alleged offence arises out of conduct that in whole or in part is in relation to an alleged contravention of an Act of Parliament or a regulation made under such an Act, other than this Act or a regulation made under this Act, and, for that purpose, the Attorney General of Canada may exercise all the powers and perform all the duties and functions assigned to the Attorney General by or under this Act.

(2) Powers of Attorney General of a province — Subsection (1) does not affect the authority of the Attorney General of a province to conduct proceedings in respect of an offence referred to in subsection 467.1(1) or to exercise any of the powers or perform any of the duties and functions assigned to the Attorney General by or under this Act.

1997, c. 23, s. 11.

Commentary: This section governs prosecutorial responsibility for criminal organization offences.

Section 467.2(1) overrides the definition of "Attorney General" in s. 2. It *permits* the Attorney General of Canada to conduct proceedings for criminal organization offences arising from conduct which is alleged to be in violation of a federal statute or regulation other than the *Criminal Code* or a regulation made under it. The authority of the Attorney General of the province to conduct the same proceedings is maintained by s. 467.2(2).

Related Provisions: See the corresponding note to s. 467.1, *supra*.

PART XIV — JURISDICTION

General

468. Superior court of criminal jurisdiction — Every superior court of criminal jurisdiction has jurisdiction to try any indictable offence.

R.S., c. C-34, s. 426.

Commentary: This section gives the *superior* court of criminal jurisdiction — jurisdiction to try *any* indictable offence, an authority which is neither diminished nor qualified elsewhere.

Case Law

R. v. Holliday (1973), 26 C.R.N.S. 279, 12 C.C.C. (2d) 56 (Alta. C.A.) — The "absolute jurisdiction" of a provincial court judge is *not* "exclusive jurisdiction". A superior court of criminal jurisdiction may try *any* indictable offence, even those within the absolute jurisdiction of a provincial court judge.

Related Provisions: "Superior court of criminal jurisdiction" is defined in s. 2. In addition to offences which are exclusively indictable, as described in the provisions creating or punishing the offence, *I.A.* s. 34(1)(a) deems indictable those offences triable either way, unless and until P elects to proceed by summary conviction.

The *indictable offence trial jurisdiction* of the superior court of criminal jurisdiction is *exclusive* in respect of the offences listed in s. 469. No other court can try such offences. Jurisdiction is *not* dependent on D's election. An *election* by D for trial, other than before a provincial court judge, may also lead to a trial before the superior court of criminal jurisdiction.

The *jurisdiction over the person* exercised by the superior court of criminal jurisdiction is described in s. 470. The form of trial is regulated by ss. 471 and 473, and in some cases, by the election of D.

469. Court of criminal jurisdiction — Every court of criminal jurisdiction has jurisdiction to try an indictable offence other than

(a) an offence under any of the following sections:

(i) section 47 (treason),

(ii) section 49 (alarming Her Majesty),

(iii) section 51 (intimidating Parliament or a legislature),

(iv) section 53 (inciting to mutiny),

(v) section 61 (seditious offences),

(vi) section 74 (piracy),

(vii) section 75 (piratical acts), or

(viii) section 235 (murder),

(b) **Accessories** — the offence of being an accessory after the fact to high treason or treason or murder,

(c) **Corrupting justice** — an offence under section 119 (bribery) by the holder of a judicial office,

(d) **Attempts** — the offence of attempting to commit any offence mentioned in subparagraphs (a)(i) to (vii), or

(e) **Conspiracy** — the offence of conspiring to commit any offence mentioned in paragraph (a).

R.S., c. C-34, s. 427; 1972, c. 13, s. 33; 1974–75–76, c. 93, s. 37; c. 105, s. 29; R.S. 1985, c. 27 (1st Supp.), s. 62.

Commentary: This section defines the *indictable* offence *trial* jurisdiction of a *court of criminal jurisdiction* and, by necessary implication, defines the exclusive indictable offence trial jurisdiction of the superior court of criminal jurisdiction.

A court of criminal jurisdiction has jurisdiction to try *any* indictable offence, *except* those listed in ss. 469(a)–(e), which must be tried in the superior court of criminal jurisdiction.

Under s. 469(b), it is *only* the trial of accessories after the fact to high treason, treason or murder that must be held in the superior court of criminal jurisdiction. In all other prosecutions of accessoryship after the fact in respect of an indictable offence, D may *elect* mode of trial. The bribery offence of s. 119 is *only* exclusive to the superior court of criminal jurisdiction when D is the holder of a judicial office.

Under s. 469(d), attempted murder is *not* included in the *exclusive* jurisdiction of the superior court of criminal jurisdiction, hence D may *elect* mode of trial.

Case Law

R. v. Coupland (1978), 45 C.C.C. (2d) 437 (Alta. C.A.) — Absolute jurisdiction does *not* mean exclusive jurisdiction. Every court of criminal jurisdiction can try indictable offences, except those listed in this section, including those within the absolute jurisdiction of a provincial court judge.

Related Provisions: "Court of criminal jurisdiction" is defined in s. 2. "Indictable offence" refers to offences which are exclusively indictable or triable either way, unless and until P elects to proceed by summary conviction.

The *superior court of criminal jurisdiction* has *exclusive* jurisdiction in respect of the indictable offences listed in s. 469 and, under s. 468, jurisdiction to try *any* indictable offence. A *provincial court judge*, as defined in s. 2, has *absolute* jurisdiction in respect of indictable offences listed in s. 553. The jurisdiction is *not* exclusive, since either the superior court of criminal jurisdiction or a court of criminal jurisdiction, other than a provincial court judge, has jurisdiction to try such offences. A *court of criminal jurisdiction* has neither absolute nor exclusive jurisdiction in respect of any indictable offences, although it may try *any* indictable offence *not* listed in s. 469.

The jurisdiction of the superior court of criminal jurisdiction and a court of criminal jurisdiction over the person of an accused is described in s. 470.

Under s. 471, trial by *jury* is compulsory in respect of indictable offences, except where otherwise expressly provided by law, and, at all events, is constitutionally guaranteed under *Charter* s. 11(f), where the maximum punishment is imprisonment for five years or a more severe punishment.

Judicial interim release jurisdiction in respect of s. 469 offences is also exclusive to the superior court of criminal jurisdiction under s. 522.

Under s. 3 the parenthetical references are deemed to have been inserted for convenience of reference only.

470. Jurisdiction over person — Subject to this Act, every superior court of criminal jurisdiction and every court of criminal jurisdiction that has power to try an indictable offence is competent to try an accused for that offence

    (a) if the accused is found, is arrested or is in custody within the territorial jurisdiction of the court; or

    (b) if the accused has been ordered to be tried by

        (i) that court, or

        (ii) any other court, the jurisdiction of which has by lawful authority been transferred to that court.

                 R.S., c. C-34, s. 428; R.S. 1985, c. 27 (1st Supp.), s. 101(3).

Commentary: The section describes the jurisdiction of a court of criminal jurisdiction and the superior court of criminal jurisdiction over the *person* of one charged with an indictable offence.

To acquire jurisdiction over the person of D requires that D be *charged* with an indictable offence within the offence jurisdiction of the court and be *found, arrested* or in *custody* within the territorial jurisdiction of the court. Alternatively, D must be *ordered* to be tried by the court in which s/he appears or any other court whose jurisdiction has been lawfully transferred to it.

Case Law

Re Falkner (1977), 40 C.C.C. (2d) 117 (B.C. C.A.) — Where D is found, arrested, or in custody in the Province of British Columbia, a provincial court judge has jurisdiction to conduct a preliminary hearing, notwithstanding the fact that the alleged offence was committed in a county other than the one in which the preliminary hearing is being held.

R. v. Rice, [1968] 3 C.C.C. 85 (Man. C.A.); leave to appeal refused [1968] 3 C.C.C. 90n (S.C.C.) — Where an offence was committed beyond the territorial jurisdiction of the [now] provincial court judge, but within the province for which the judge held his appointment, the judge had jurisdiction under s. 470(a) to try the case by virtue of D's conduct in appearing and entering a plea. Furthermore, if an objection to the court's jurisdiction is overruled, then the court has jurisdiction, since by virtue of s. 470(b) the court has ordered D to be tried by that court.

R. v. Hardimon (1979), 31 N.S.R. (2d) 232 (C.A.) — Where, on the day of trial, D is present before the magistrate [provincial court judge], the court is entitled to exercise jurisdiction over the person of D.

R. v. Abbott (1944), 81 C.C.C. 174 (Ont. C.A.); leave to appeal refused (1944), 82 C.C.C. 14 (S.C.C.) — *See also: Gordon v. R.* (1980), 55 C.C.C. (2d) 197 (B.C. C.A.) — Although the offence may have been committed outside the territorial limits of the jurisdiction of the court in which the trial is held, the fact that D is in custody within these limits gives the court jurisdiction to try the charge.

Related Provisions: "Superior court of criminal jurisdiction" and "court of criminal jurisdiction" are defined in s. 2. An indictable offence is an offence which must or may be prosecuted by indictment (where P has not elected to proceed by summary conviction).

Sections 468 and 469 define the *indictable* offence *trial* jurisdiction of both the superior court of criminal jurisdiction and a court of criminal jurisdiction. The *territorial* jurisdiction of the court is a function of provincial enabling legislation and the scope of the incumbent's appointment. The territorial jurisdiction of the superior court of criminal jurisdiction is province-wide. Courts of limited jurisdiction may have authority only in respect of certain territorial divisions.

There are several special provisions relating to both offence and territorial jurisdiction, as for example, ss. 7, 465(4)–(7) and 476–481.

This provision deals with territorial jurisdiction not venue. The venue of trial is, *prima facie*, the territorial division in which the offence occurred, subject to an order under s. 599(1) changing the venue of trial.

471. Trial by jury compulsory — **Except where otherwise expressly provided by law, every accused who is charged with an indictable offence shall be tried by a court composed of a judge and jury.**

R.S., c. C-34, s. 429.

Commentary: The section enacts a general rule that *except* where otherwise expressly provided by law, indictable offences are tried by a court composed of a judge and jury.

Related Provisions: The right to a jury trial in respect of offences that attract a maximum punishment of five years imprisonment or a more severe punishment is constitutionally guaranteed by *Charter* s. 11(f).

The *Code* contains several provisions that permit or require non-jury trials of indictable offences. Under s. 473(1), D and the Attorney General may consent to a non-jury trial in respect of offences listed in s. 469. Section 553 lists several offences that are within the *absolute* jurisdiction of a provincial court judge, and s. 554(1) allows D to *elect* trial by provincial court judge in respect of any offence not listed in ss. 469 and 553. Rights of election are given under s. 536(2) and re-election under ss. 561 and 562. Part XIX (ss. 552–573) governs trials without jury.

The Attorney General, in some instances, may require a jury trial under s. 568.

472. [Repealed R.S. 1985, c. 27 (1st Supp.), s. 63.]

473. (1) Trial without jury — Notwithstanding anything in this Act, an accused charged with an offence listed in section 469 may, with the consent of the accused and the Attorney General, be tried without a jury by a judge of a superior court of criminal jurisdiction.

(1.1) Joinder of other offences — Where the consent of the accused and the Attorney General is given in accordance with subsection (1), the judge of the superior court of criminal jurisdiction may order that any offence be tried by that judge in conjunction with the offence listed in section 469.

(2) Withdrawal of consent — Notwithstanding anything in this Act, where the consent of an accused and the Attorney General is given in accordance with subsection (1), such consent shall not be withdrawn unless both the accused and the Attorney General agree to the withdrawal.

R.S., c. C-34, s. 430; R.S. 1985, c. 27 (1st Supp.), s. 63; 1994, c. 44, s. 30.

Commentary: The section permits trial of any s. 469 offence (*exclusive* jurisdiction of a superior court of criminal jurisdiction) without a jury hence is an exception to the general rule of compulsory jury trial of indictable offences. Section 473(1) operates notwithstanding any other *Code* provision, for example, s. 471. It applies in every province. Trial of s. 469 offences without a jury may only occur where *both* D and the Attorney General *consent*.

Section 473(1.1) permits the superior court judge to order that any other offence be tried with the s. 469 offence which is the subject of trial by consent under s. 473.

Section 473(2) ensures that, once given, consent to a non-jury trial of s. 469 offences is *not* easily withdrawn. The withdrawal of consent is only effectual where both D and the Attorney General agree to the withdrawal. Neither party can give or withdraw consent unilaterally. Where D and the Attorney General agree to withdraw consent to a non-jury trial, D will be tried by a judge of the superior court of criminal jurisdiction sitting with a jury.

Case Law

R. v. Turpin (1989), 69 C.R. (3d) 97, 48 C.C.C. (3d) 8 (S.C.C.) — The section does *not* violate *Charter* s. 11(f) or 15(1).

R. v. Davis (No. 2) (1977), 35 C.C.C. (2d) 464 (Alta C.A.); leave to appeal refused [1977] 1 S.C.R. vii (S.C.C.) — There is *no* obligation on a judge to inquire into D's understanding of the consent to be tried by judge alone where D is represented by counsel.

Related Provisions: "Attorney General" is exhaustively defined in s. 2 and includes "his lawful deputy". Nothing expressly or implicitly requires the personal consent of the Attorney General under s. 473. "Superior court of criminal jurisdiction" is exhaustively defined in s. 2.

There is some tension between the new s. 473(1.1) and s. 589 which imposes limitations upon the joinder of counts other than murder in an indictment which charges murder. *Quaere* the effect of s. 591 concerning joinder of counts? "Any offence" would seem to include a summary conviction offence. The problem may be circumvented by D's consent under s. 589(b).

The general *re-election* provisions of s. 561 are inapplicable, since D neither had, made, nor was deemed to have elected trial by jury in respect of the s. 469 offence.

474. (1) Adjournment when no jury summoned — Where the competent authority has determined that a panel of jurors is not to be summoned for a term or sittings of the court for the trial of criminal cases in any territorial division, the clerk of the court may, on the day of the opening of the term or sittings, if a judge is not present to preside over the court, adjourn the court and the business of the court to a subsequent day.

(2) Adjournment on instructions of judge — A clerk of the court for the trial of criminal cases in any territorial division may, at any time, on the instructions of the

presiding judge or another judge of the court, adjourn the court and the business of the court to a subsequent day.

R.S., c. C-34, s. 431; 1994, c. 44, s. 31.

Commentary: Section 474(1) permits an adjournment of criminal jury sittings in any territorial division where no panel of jurors has been summoned therefor. In the absence of a judge, the clerk of the court, on the opening day of the term or sittings, may adjourn the court and its business to a subsequent day.

Under s. 474(2), a clerk of the court for the trial of criminal cases may adjourn the court and its business to another day, provided the adjournment is upon the instructions of the presiding or another judge of the court. The provision seems designed to overcome arguments about loss of jurisdiction when a judicial officer does not attend.

Related Provisions: Section 474(1) should be read together with s. 599(1)(b) which permits a change of venue to be ordered where no jury is to be summoned in the territorial division where the trial would otherwise be held.

D's recognizance remains binding under s. 763, where the sittings of the court or proceedings are adjourned or the venue of trial changed.

"Territorial division" and "clerk of the court" are both defined in s. 2.

475. (1) Accused absconding during trial — Notwithstanding any other provision of this Act, where an accused, whether or not he is charged jointly with another, absconds during the course of his trial,

(a) he shall be deemed to have waived his right to be present at his trial, and

(b) the court may

(i) continue the trial and proceed to a judgment or verdict and, if it finds the accused guilty, impose a sentence on him in his absence, or

(ii) if a warrant in Form 7 is issued for the arrest of the accused, adjourn the trial to await his appearance,

but where the trial is adjourned pursuant to subparagraph (b)(ii), the court may, at any time, continue the trial if it is satisfied that it is no longer in the interests of justice to await the appearance of the accused.

(2) Adverse inference — Where a court continues a trial pursuant to subsection (1), it may draw an inference adverse to the accused from the fact that he has absconded.

(3) Accused not entitled to re-opening — Where an accused reappears at his trial that is continuing pursuant to subsection (1), he is not entitled to have any part of the proceedings that was conducted in his absence re-opened unless the court is satisfied that because of exceptional circumstances it is in the interests of justice to re-open the proceedings.

(4) Counsel for accused may continue to act — Where an accused has absconded during the course of his trial and the court continues the trial, counsel for the accused is not thereby deprived of any authority he may have to continue to act for the accused in the proceedings.

1974–75–76, c. 93, s. 39.

Commentary: The section defines the powers of the trial judge where D *absconds during the course of the trial*. It has *no* application where D fails to appear for trial. It applies notwithstanding any other provision of the *Code*, and whether D is charged alone or jointly with another.

Under s. 475(1)(a), an absconding accused is *deemed* to have *waived* his/her right to be present at trial. Under s. 475(1)(b), the trial court may *continue* the trial in D's absence, proceed to judgment or verdict and, where a finding of guilt has been made, pass *sentence* in D's absence. The court may also issue a *warrant* for D's arrest, and *adjourn* the trial to await D's reappearance. Where an *adjournment* has been given to await D's reappearance, the court may, *at any time, continue* the trial, if satisfied that it is *no* longer in the interests of justice to await D's reappearance.

In any case where the trial has been continued, whether *ab initio* or notwithstanding an initial adjournment, the court may, under s. 475(2), draw an *inference* adverse to D from the fact s/he has absconded. Under s. 475(4), the mere fact that D has absconded during the course of the trial does *not* deprive D's counsel of any authority he may have to continue to act for D where the proceedings continue.

Where D has absconded, but later reappears to attend the continuation of the trial, s/he is not entitled to have any part of the proceedings conducted in his/her absence reopened, absent a finding under s. 475(4) that, because of exceptional circumstances, it is in the interests of justice to do so.

Case Law

"Absconds"

R. v. Garofoli (1988), 64 C.R. (3d) 193, 41 C.C.C. (3d) 97 (Ont. C.A.); reversed on other grounds (1990), 80 C.R. (3d) 317, 60 C.C.C. (3d) 161 (S.C.C.) — The word "absconds" imports that D has *voluntarily* absented himself for the purpose of impeding or frustrating the trial, or with the intention of avoiding its consequences.

Inference Adverse to the Accused: S. 475(2)

R. v. Garofoli (1988), 64 C.R. (3d) 193, 41 C.C.C. (3d) 97 (Ont. C.A.); reversed on other grounds (1990), 80 C.R. (3d) 317, 60 C.C.C (3d) 161 (S.C.C.) — *See also*: *R. v. Tzimopoulos* (1986), 54 C.R. (3d) 1, 29 C.C.C. (3d) 304 (Ont. C.A.); leave to appeal refused (1987), 54 C.R. (3d) xxviin (S.C.C.) — The question whether D has absconded is for the trial judge to decide. There is *no* requirement that the jury be satisfied that D has absconded before an adverse inference can be drawn.

Counsel for Accused Continuing to Act: S. 475(4)

R. v. Garofoli (1988), 64 C.R. (3d) 193, 41 C.C.C. (3d) 97 (Ont. C.A.); reversed on other grounds (1990), 80 C.R. (3d) 317, 60 C.C.C. (3d) 161 (S.C.C.) — Although s. 475(4) makes it clear that the continuation of the trial in D's absence does *not* terminate any authority counsel may have to continue to act for the absconding accused, nonetheless, counsel may properly cease to act in accordance with professional standards and the provincial authorities may withdraw Legal Aid.

Charter Considerations

R. v. Tzimopoulos (1986), 54 C.R. (3d) 1, 29 C.C.C. (3d) 304 (Ont. C.A.); leave to appeal refused (1987), 54 C.R. (3d) xxviin (S.C.C) — *See also*: *R. v. Czuczman* (1986), 49 C.R. (3d) 385, 26 C.C.C. (3d) 43 (Ont. C.A.) — This section violates neither *Charter* s. 7 nor s. 11(d).

Related Provisions: Section 650(1) requires that D, other than a corporation, *shall* be present in court during the whole of the trial. No distinction is drawn between those who are charged alone or jointly. By absconding during the course of a trial, D is *deemed* to have waived the statutory right of presence under s. 650(1), now given constitutional dimension under *Charter* s. 7. No issue of exception under s. 650(2) arises because of the over-riding effect of the waiver under s. 475(1)(a).

The *inference* to which s. 475(2) makes reference, though not expressly stated, would seem to be one of *consciousness of guilt* based upon flight. In general, it is always subject to explanation. Its weight is an issue for the jury.

Special Jurisdiction

476. Special jurisdictions — For the purposes of this Act,

    (a) where an offence is committed in or on any water or on a bridge between two or more territorial divisions, the offence shall be deemed to have been committed in any of the territorial divisions;

    (b) where an offence is committed on the boundary of two or more territorial divisions or within five hundred metres of any such boundary, or the offence was

commenced within one territorial division and completed within another, the offence shall be deemed to have been committed in any of the territorial divisions;

(c) where an offence is committed in or on a vehicle employed in a journey, or on board a vessel employed on a navigable river, canal or inland water, the offence shall be deemed to have been committed in any territorial division through which the vehicle or vessel passed in the course of the journey or voyage on which the offence was committed, and where the center or other part of the road, or navigable river, canal or inland water on which the vehicle or vessel passed in the course of the journey or voyage is the boundary of two of more territorial divisions, the offence shall be deemed to have been committed in any of the territorial divisions;

(d) where an offence is committed in an aircraft in the course of a flight of that aircraft, it shall be deemed to have been committed

(i) in the territorial division in which the flight commenced,

(ii) in any territorial division over which the aircraft passed in the course of the flight, or

(iii) in the territorial division in which the flight ended; and

(e) where an offence is committed in respect of a mail in the course of its door-to-door delivery, the offence shall be deemed to have been committed in any territorial division through which the mail was carried on that delivery.

R.S., c. C-34, s. 432; R.S. 1985, c. 27 (lst Supp.), s. 186; 1992, c. 1, s. 58(1), Schedule I, item 8.

Commentary: This section provides for *exceptional* cases where issues of *territorial* jurisdiction, absent special provisions, might occasion difficulty. In general, the *Code deems* the offence to have been committed in several territorial divisions, thereby conferring *concurrent* territorial jurisdiction on the courts of each division with competent offence authority.

Special territorial jurisdiction is established for offences committed in or on any *water*, or on a *bridge* between two or more territorial divisions [s. 432(a)], on or within 500 m of the *boundary* of two or more territorial divisions [s. 432(b)], in or on a *vehicle or vessel* employed in a journey or on a navigable river, canal or inland water [s. 432(c)], in an *aircraft* in the course of flight [s. 432(d)] and in respect of the *mail* in the course of its door-to-door delivery [s. 432(e)].

Case Law

R. v. L. (D.A.) (1996), 107 C.C.C. (3d) 178 (B.C. C.A.) — Where an offence is alleged to have occurred in a number of provinces or territories, it is a convenient practice for the trial judge to ask the jury to specify the location of any offence of which D is found guilty.

R. v. Moore (1970), 1 C.C.C. (2d) 521 (B.C. C.A.) — "Deemed" means deemed conclusively, *not* "until the contrary is proved". The purpose of the section is to prevent a charge failing because of some uncertainty of the location. The purpose would be defeated if a charge were to fail merely because of defence evidence that the occurrence took place in an adjoining jurisdiction.

R. v. O'Blenis, [1965] 2 C.C.C. 165 (N.B. C.A.) — There is no presumption of jurisdiction in an inferior court. The onus is on P to prove jurisdiction over D.

R. v. B. (O.) (1997), 116 C.C.C. (3d) 189 (Ont. C.A.) — Section 476(c) does *not* expand the jurisdiction of a Canadian court where none of the constituent elements occurred in Canada.

Re Bigelow (1982), 69 C.C.C. (2d) 204 (Ont. C.A.); leave to appeal refused (1982), 69 C.C.C. (2d) 204n (S.C.C.) — This section establishes jurisdiction on a broad basis over interprovincial offences. If any element or part of it may have been committed in a province, the province has jurisdiction over the offence.

Related Provisions: "Territorial division" is defined in s. 2.

Other special territorial jurisdiction provisions appear in ss. 477–481 *infra*. Section 7 contains similar provisions in respect of offences committed on or in relation to an *aircraft*, as well as in respect of an *internationally protected person* and *nuclear material*. Special provision is also made in respect of *crimes against humanity* and *war crimes*. Subject to certain limitations, the offences are *deemed* to have been committed in Canada. Sections 465(3)–(5) enact similar provisions in relation to conspiracy offences.

477. (1) Definition of "ship" — In sections 477.1 to 477.4, "ship" includes any description of vessel, boat or craft designed, used or capable of being used solely or partly for marine navigation, without regard to method or lack of propulsion.

(2) Saving — Nothing in sections 477.1 to 477.4 limits the operation of any other Act of Parliament or the jurisdiction that a court may exercise apart from those sections.

R.S., c. C-34, s. 433; 1990, c. 44, s. 15; 1996, c. 31, s. 67.

Commentary: Section 477(1) defines terms used in ss. 477–477.4 by incorporating definitions in other federal enactments.

Section 477(2) makes it clear that ss. 477.1–477.4 do *not* limit the operation of any other federal act, nor the jurisdiction that a court may otherwise exercise. It there by ensures the operation, as well the paramountcy, of other relevant federal legislation.

Related Provisions: The note to s. 2 describes other sources of definitions.

The effect of ss. 477.1–477.4 is described in the *Commentary* which accompanies each.

The reference to "Attorney General of Canada" would appear to include his/her lawful deputy, under s. 2.

Section 583(g) (imprecise description of place) may have especial relevance to an information alleging an offence committed on the territorial sea. Similar provision appears in s. 323(2) respecting oyster beds, laying or fishery.

477.1 (1) Offences outside of Canada — Every person who commits an act or omission that, if it occurred in Canada, would be an offence under a federal law, within the meaning of section 2 of the *Oceans Act*, is deemed to have committed that act or omission in Canada if it is an act or omission

   (a) in the exclusive economic zone of Canada that

      (i) is committed by a person who is in the exclusive economic zone of Canada in connection with exploring or exploiting, conserving or managing the natural resources, whether living or non-living, of the exclusive economic zone of Canada, and

      (ii) is committed by or in relation to a person who is a Canadian citizen or a permanent resident within the meaning of the *Immigration Act*,

   (b) that is committed in a place in or above the continental shelf of Canada and that is an offence in that place by virtue of section 20 of the *Oceans Act*,

   (c) that is committed outside Canada on board or by means of a ship registered or licensed, or for which an identification number has been issued, pursuant to any Act of Parliament;

   (d) that is committed outside Canada in the course of hot pursuit; or

   (e) that is committed outside the territory of any state by a Canadian citizen.

1990, c. 44, s. 15; 1996, c. 31, s. 68.

Commentary: Under this section, acts or omissions that would be federal offences, if committed in Canada, are *deemed* to have been committed in Canada in certain circumstances.

The circumstances which engage the deeming provision of s. 477.1(1) are twofold. The act or omission must be one which would be an *offence under federal law*, if committed in Canada. The act or omission must also have occurred in circumstances or places described in *any* of ss. 477.1(1)(a)–(e). The circumstances of s. 477.1(1)(b) are limited by s. 477.1(2).

Related Provisions: Section 477 defines terms used in the section. Other related provisions are described in the corresponding note to s. 477.

477.2 (1) Consent of Attorney General of Canada — No proceedings in respect of an offence committed in or on the territorial sea of Canada shall be continued unless the consent of the Attorney General of Canada is obtained not later than eight days after the proceedings are commenced, if the accused is not a Canadian citizen and the offence is alleged to have been committed on board any ship registered outside Canada.

(1.1) Exception — Subsection (1) does not apply to proceedings by way of summary conviction.

(2) Consent of Attorney General of Canada — No proceedings in respect of which courts have jurisdiction by virtue only of paragraph 477.1(*a*) or (*b*) shall be continued unless the consent of the Attorney General of Canada is obtained not later than eight days after the proceedings are commenced, if the accused is not a Canadian citizen and the offence is alleged to have been committed on board any ship registered outside Canada.

(3) Consent of Attorney General of Canada — No proceedings in respect of which courts have jurisdiction by virtue only of paragraph 477.1(*d*) or (*e*) shall be continued unless the consent of the Attorney General of Canada is obtained not later than eight days after the proceedings are commenced.

(4) Consent to be filed — The consent of the Attorney General required by subsection (1), (2) or (3) must be filed with the clerk of the court in which the proceedings have been instituted.

1990, c. 44, s. 15; 1994, c. 44, s. 32; 1996, c. 31, s. 69.

Commentary: The section regulates the continuation of certain proceedings including those in respect of offences committed by a person in or on the territorial sea and those in respect of which Canadian courts acquire jurisdiction under s. 477.1(1)(a), (b), (d) and (e).

Under s. 477.2(1), except in the case of summary conviction proceedings, the consent of the Attorney General of Canada must be obtained no later than eight days after proceedings have been instituted. The section applies to proceedings in respect of an offence committed in or on the territorial sea by a person who is *not* a Canadian citizen on board any ship registered outside of Canada.

Similar consents must be obtained within the same time period in cases in respect of which Canadian courts have jurisdiction under s. 477.1(a), (b), (d) and (e). In cases governed by s. 477.1(a) and (b), s. 477.2(2) only requires consent where D is not a Canadian citizen and the offence is alleged to have been committed on board a ship registered outside Canada.

Section 477.2(4) does not provide a form for the consent of the Attorney General. It requires, however, that the consent be filed with the clerk of the court in which the proceedings have been instituted.

Case Law

Consent Requirement [Cases decided under previous section]

R. v. Ford (1956), 115 C.C.C. 113 (B.C. C.A.) — The prohibition of the prosecution of an offence committed in territorial waters where D is *not* a Canadian citizen, unless the Attorney General has consented, is unrestricted. It applies to any tribunal, including assize courts and magistrates.

Status to Consent

R. v. Sunila (1987), 35 C.C.C. (3d) 289 (N.S. C.A.) — The Attorney General cannot delegate to another official the decision whether to give consent under this section. A consent form signed by the Deputy Attorney General may suffice where the court is satisfied that the Attorney General in fact consented to the prosecution.

Related Provisions: Proceedings are instituted by the laying of an information.

The consent of the Attorney General should be endorsed on the information which institutes proceedings, or a copy of the consent attached to a certified copy of the information.

The authority of the Attorney General of Canada to stay proceedings is found in newly enacted s. 579.1. Other related provisions appear in the corresponding note to s. 477.

477.3 (1) Exercising powers of arrest, entry, etc. — Every power of arrest, entry, search or seizure or other power that could be exercised in Canada in respect of an act or omission referred to in section 477.1 may be exercised, in the circumstances referred to in that section,

    (a) at the place or on board the ship or marine installation or structure, within the meaning of section 2 of the *Oceans Act*, where the act or omission occurred; or

    (b) where hot pursuit has been commenced, at any place on the seas, other than a place that is part of the territorial sea of any other state.

(2) Arrest, search, seizure, etc. — A justice or judge in any territorial division in Canada has jurisdiction to authorize an arrest, entry, search or seizure or an investigation or other ancillary matter related to an offence

    (a) committed in or on the territorial sea of Canada or any area of the sea that forms part of the internal waters of Canada, or

    (b) referred to in section 477.1

in the same manner as if the offence had been committed in that territorial division.

(3) Limitation — Where an act or omission that is an offence by virtue only of section 477.1 is alleged to have been committed on board any ship registered outside Canada, the powers referred to in subsection (1) shall not be exercised outside Canada with respect to that act or omission without the consent of the Attorney General of Canada.

1990, c. 44, s. 15; 1996, c. 34, s. 70.

Commentary: The section extends powers of *arrest, entry, search* or *seizure* and related powers to offences cognizable by Canadian courts under s. 477.1 and imposes *limitations* upon their use.

Under s. 477.3(1), domestic powers of arrest, entry, search or seizure or other powers are extended to acts or omissions cognizable by Canadian courts under s. 477.1. They may be exercised at the *locus* of the offence or, in cases of hot pursuit, anywhere on the seas, other than a place that is part of the territorial sea of another state. Subsection (3) requires the consent of the Attorney General of Canada to the exercise of such powers outside Canada where the act or omission cognizable under s. 477.1(1) is alleged to have been committed on board a ship of foreign registry.

The *effect* of s. 477.3(2) is to permit a justice or judge in any territorial division in Canada to authorize an arrest, entry, search or seizure, investigation or other ancillary matter in respect of an offence described in s. 477.1(1) committed in or on the territorial sea, or any part of the sea that is part of Canada's internal waters. In other words, defined domestic authority is extended to s. 477.1(1) offences, as well as to those which occur in the territorial sea or part of the sea included in Canada's internal waters.

Related Provisions: "Justice" and "territorial division" are defined in s. 2.

Related provisions are described in the corresponding note to s. 477.

477.4 (1) [Repealed, 1996, c. 31, s. 71(1)]

(2) [Repealed, 1996, c. 31, s. 71(1)]

(3) Evidence — In proceedings in respect of an offence,

    (a) a certificate referred to in subsection 23(1) of the *Oceans Act*, or

(b) a certificate issued by or under the authority of the Minister of Foreign Affairs containing a statement that any geographical location specified in the certificate was, at any time material to the proceedings, in an area of a fishing zone of Canada that is not within the internal waters of Canada or the territorial sea of Canada or outside the territory of any state.

is conclusive proof of the truth of the statement without proof of the signature or official character of the person appearing to have issued the certificate.

(4) Certificate cannot be compelled — A certificate referred to in subsection (3) is admissible in evidence in proceedings referred to in that subsection but its production cannot be compelled.

1990, c. 44, s. 15; 1995, c. 5, s. 25(1)(g); 1996, c. 31, s. 71.

Commentary: The section enacts *evidentiary provisions* applicable to certain certificates issued under defined statutory or ministerial authority.

Section 474.4(3) permits proof of certain matters by *certificate*. Although a certificate authorized by subsection (3) is admissible under subsection (4), its production cannot be compelled. When received as evidence, it is *conclusive proof* of the truth of the statements in it, without proof of the signature or authority of its maker.

Related Provisions: Related provisions are described in the corresponding note to s. 477.

478. (1) Offence committed entirely in one province — Subject to this Act, a court in a province shall not try an offence committed entirely in another province.

(2) Exception — Every proprietor, publisher, editor or other person charged with the publication of a defamatory libel in a newspaper or with conspiracy to publish a defamatory libel in a newspaper shall be dealt with, indicted, tried and punished in the province where he resides or in which the newspaper is printed.

(3) Idem — An accused who is charged with an offence that is alleged to have been committed in Canada outside the province in which the accused is may, if the offence is not an offence mentioned in section 469 and

(a) in the case of proceedings instituted at the instance of the Government of Canada and conducted by or on behalf of that Government, if the Attorney General of Canada consents, or

(b) in any other case, if the Attorney General of the province where the offence is alleged to have been committed consents,

appear before a court or judge that would have had jurisdiction to try that offence if it had been committed in the province where the accused is, and where the accused consents to plead guilty and pleads guilty to that offence, the court or judge shall determine the accused to be guilty of the offence and impose the punishment warranted by law, but where the accused does not consent to plead guilty and does not plead guilty, the accused shall, if the accused was in custody prior to appearance, be returned to custody and shall be dealt with according to law.

(4) Where accused committed to stand trial — Notwithstanding that an accused described in subsection (3) has been ordered to stand trial or that an indictment has been preferred against the accused in respect of the offence to which he desires to plead guilty, the accused shall be deemed simply to stand charged of that offence without a preliminary inquiry having been conducted or an indictment having been preferred with respect thereto.

(5) "newspaper" — In this section "newspaper" has the same meaning that it has in section 297.

R.S., c. C-34, s. 434; 1974–75–76, c. 93, s. 40; R.S. 1985, c. 27 (1st Supp.), ss. 64, 101(3); 1994, c. 44, s. 33.

Commentary: Subsection (1) enacts a *general rule* that offences committed *entirely in one province* shall *not* be *tried* by the courts of *another* province. The rule is "subject to this Act" including the other subsections of this section. The jurisdiction may be engaged before any court of competent offence jurisdiction.

Under s. 478(2) anyone charged with publishing or conspiracy to publish a *defamatory libel* in a newspaper as defined in ss. 478(5) and 297, may be tried in the province in which s/he resides or the newspaper is published. Section 478(3) equally constitutes a qualified exception to the general rule of s. 478(1) in that, while it permits the courts of a province other than that in which an offence has been wholly committed to make a disposition in respect of the offence, it only authorizes the acceptance of the *plea of guilty, not* the conduct of trial proceedings in respect of such an offence. To invoke s. 478(3), D must be charged with an offence, *not* listed in s. 469 alleged to be committed in Canada, *outside* the province in which D is, by virtue of residence or otherwise. D must, further, appear before a court of competent offence jurisdiction in his/her province of residence and there indicate his/her consent to plead guilty and plead guilty to the offence. The Attorney General under whose authority the proceedings were instituted in the province of offence must consent to the transfer of jurisdiction to the province of residence.

Under s. 478(4), even where D has been ordered to stand trial or an indictment has been preferred against him/her in the province of offence, D is *deemed* simply to *stand charged* with the offence without a preliminary inquiry having been held or indictment preferred. This provision enables the majority of such offences to be dealt with by a provincial court judge.

Sections 478(3) and (4) afford D the opportunity to enter *pleas of guilty* in the province of residence or incarceration to offences outstanding in other provinces, thereby to receive a single sentence in respect of all outstanding matters and, upon release from prison, *not* to be required to face further outstanding offences alleged to have been committed at some previous time. From the point of view of P, the necessity of re-arrest and transportation out of province is also avoided.

Case Law

R. v. L. (D.A.) (1996), 107 C.C.C. (3d) 178 (B.C. C.A.) — Where an offence is alleged to have occurred in a number of provinces or territories, it is a convenient practice for the trial judge to ask the jury to specify the location of any offence of which D is found guilty.

R. v. Parisien (1971), 3 C.C.C. (2d) 433 (B.C. C.A.) — *See also*: *R. v. Burke*, [1968] 2 C.C.C. (2d) 124 (Ont. C.A.) — To take advantage of s. 478(3), D must know what warrants have been issued against him. To withhold the information is unfair.

R. v. Horbas (1968), 5 C.R.N.S. 342, (sub nom. *R. v. Trudel)* [1969] 3 C.C.C. 95 — The principles applicable to the formation of a civil contract are *not* determinative of an inquiry about where a criminal act took place. Some criminal acts are of a continuing character and might be deemed to occur in more than one jurisdiction.

Related Provisions: Defamatory libel is described in s. 298 and punished in ss. 300 and 301.

Under the definition of "Attorney General" in s. 2, the consent required by subsection (3) may be given by his/her lawful deputy. The Attorney General of the province in which D resides or is in custody is *not* required to consent to the transfer of outstanding charges.

The entry of extra-provincial guilty pleas are exceptions to the general rule that courts in one province cannot take cognizance of nor assert jurisdiction over offences committed entirely in another province. There are *not*, and s. 478 does not authorize, extra-provincial trials on the basis of *forum conveniens*. There are no extra-provincial changes of venue. Neither can D enter a plea of guilty to "any other offence arising out of the same transaction" as the offence charged pursuant to s. 606(4). The plea must be to the offence charged, unless a fresh information is laid in respect of the other offence, and the necessary consent given.

Probation orders may also be transferred to other provinces under s. 379.

479. Offence outstanding in same province — Where an accused is charged with an offence that is alleged to have been committed in the province in which he is, he may, if the offence is not an offence mentioned in section 469, and

(a) in the case of proceedings instituted at the instance of the Government of Canada and conducted by or on behalf of that Government, the Attorney General of Canada consents, or

(b) in any other case, the Attorney General of the province where the offence is alleged to have been committed consents,

appear before a court or judge that would have had jurisdiction to try that offence if it had been committed in the place where the accused is, and where the accused consents to plead guilty and pleads guilty to that offence, the court or judge shall determine the accused to be guilty of the offence and impose the punishment warranted by law, but where the accused does not consent to plead guilty and does not plead guilty, the accused shall, if the accused was in custody prior to appearance, be returned to custody and shall be dealt with according to law.

R.S., c. C-34, s. 435; 1974–75–76, c. 93, s. 41; R.S. 1985, c. 27 (1st Supp.), s. 65; 1994, c. 44, s. 34.

Commentary: This section authorizes the entry of *pleas of guilty* in territorial divisions of the *same province, other* than the *territorial division* in which the *offence* is alleged to have been *committed.*

D must be charged with a non-s. 469 offence, alleged to have been committed in the province but in a different territorial division than where D is. D must *appear* before a court of competent offence jurisdiction in the territorial division where D is, there signify his/her *consent to plead* guilty and, in fact, *plead* guilty to the offence charged. The Attorney General under whose authority the prosecution is being conducted must *consent* to the transfer of jurisdiction. The court in the territorial division where D is may then find D guilty of the offence and impose a fit sentence. Without a plea of guilty the procedure cannot be invoked.

Related Provisions: "Attorney General" is defined in s. 2 as including "the lawful deputy". No form of consent is provided, though it should clearly appear on the record. The consent of P conducting the proceedings should be sufficient.

It would appear that D may *not* enter a plea of guilty to "any other offence arising out of the same transaction" as the offence charged under s. 606(4). The plea must be to the offence charged, unless a fresh information is laid which charges the other offence and the required consent given.

Upon application by P, under s. 733, probation orders may also be transferred to other territorial divisions within the same province. No further consent is required.

480. (1) Offence in unorganized territory — Where an offence is committed in an unorganized tract of country in any province or on a lake, river or other water therein, not included in a territorial division or in a provisional judicial district, proceedings in respect thereof may be commenced and an accused may be charged, tried and punished in respect thereof within any territorial division or provisional judicial district of the province in the same manner as if the offence had been committed within that territorial division or provisional judicial district.

(2) New territorial division — Where a provisional judicial district or a new territorial division is constituted in an unorganized tract referred to in subsection (1), the jurisdiction conferred by that subsection continues until appropriate provision is made by law for the administration of criminal justice within the provisional judicial district or new territorial division.

R.S., c. C-34, s. 436.

Commentary: This section determines *territorial jurisdiction* where an offence is committed in an *unorganized* tract of country in any province or on a lake, river or other water therein which is *not* included in a territorial division or provisional judicial district. Section 480(1) provides concurrent territorial jurisdiction in respect of these offences in courts of competent offence jurisdiction in any territorial division or provisional judicial district in the province where the offence is alleged to have been committed.

Section 480(2) is a *transitional* provision which continues the territorial jurisdiction of s. 480(1) where a provisional judicial district or new territorial division is constituted in an unorganised tract of country until provision is made for the administration of justice within the provisional judicial district or new territorial division.

Related Provisions: "Territorial division" is defined in s. 2. "Province", under *I.A.* s. 35(1), includes the Yukon Territory, Northwest Territories and Nunavut. Provisional judicial districts and new territorial divisions are created by provincial legislation. A related provision in respect of offences committed in a part of Canada, not in a province, appears in s. 481, *infra*.

481. Offence not in a province — Where an offence is committed in a part of Canada not in a province, proceedings in respect thereof may be commenced and the accused may be charged, tried and punished within any territorial division in any province in the same manner as if that offence had been committed in that territorial division.

R.S., c. C-34, s. 437.

Commentary: This section determines territorial jurisdiction in respect of offences committed in a part of Canada which is *not* in a province. Concurrent territorial jurisdiction exists in every court of competent offence jurisdiction and any territorial division in *any* province.

Related Provisions: See the corresponding note to s. 480, *supra*.

The practical course for the trial which this provision facilitates but does not compel, would be to try D in the territorial division of that province of Canada as is most convenient to the place of offence.

481.1 Offence in Canadian waters — Where an offence is committed in or on the territorial sea of Canada or any area of the sea that forms part of the internal waters of Canada, proceedings in respect thereof may, whether or not the accused is in Canada, be commenced and an accused may be charged, tried and punished within any territorial division in Canada in the same manner as if the offence had been committed in that territorial division.

1996, c. 31, s. 72.

Commentary: This section permits proceedings for offences committed in or on

i.   the *territorial sea* of Canada; or

ii. any area of the *sea* that forms part of the *internal waters* of Canada

to be commenced and conducted anywhere in Canada.

Related Provisions: The *Code* does *not* define "territorial sea" or "internal waters", but s. 2 defines "territorial division".

There are special jurisdiction provisions in ss. 476-481.3 and in s. 7 of the *Code*. As a general rule, D may *not* be found guilty of any offence committed outside Canada. This rule, stated in *Code* s. 6(2), is subject to exception, for example, in the circumstances described in s. 481.2.

481.2 Offence outside Canada — Subject to this or any other Act of Parliament, where an act or omission is committed outside Canada and the act or omission, when committed in those circumstances, is an offence under this or any other Act of Parliament, proceedings in respect thereof may, whether or not the accused is in Canada, be commenced, and an accused may be charged, tried and punished within any territorial division in Canada in the same manner as if the offence had been committed in that territorial division.

1996, c. 31, s. 72.

Commentary: The section permits proceedings to be commenced and conducted in Canada for conduct, acts or omissions, which took place outside Canada but which, in the circumstances, would contravene a federal statute. The jurisdiction may be exercised whether D is in Canada or not, anywhere in Canada. Charge, trial and punishment are all permitted.

Related Provisions: The rules concerning D's attendance at trial, for example, *Code* s. 650, are preserved by s. 481.3. Offences committed in Canadian waters are governed by s. 481.1.

Other related provisions are discussed in the corresponding note to s. 481.1, *supra*.

481.3 Appearance of accused at trial — For greater certainty, the provisions of this Act relating to

(a) the requirement of the appearance of an accused at proceedings, and

(b) the exceptions to that requirement

apply to proceedings commenced in any territorial division pursuant to section 481, 481.1 or 481.2

1996, c. 31, s. 72.

Commentary: The section makes the *Code* provisions which govern D's attendance in domestic proceedings applicable to proceedings commenced under any listed section.

Related Provisions: Several *Code* sections govern the presence of D at various proceedings. In indictable proceedings, the general requirement that D be present throughout his/her trial is contained in s. 650(1). An appearance by video links is permitted by ss. 650(1.1) and (1.2) and D's exclusion governed by s. 650(2). The requirements for the presence of a corporate accused are found in ss. 556, 620 and 623.

Sections 800(2)-(3) state the general rule and exceptions in summary conviction proceedings for both individual and corporate accused.

Where D *absconds* during the preliminary inquiry or trial, ss. 544 and 475 permit proceedings to continue and provide, *inter alia*, for the drawing of inferences adverse to D in the result.

Rules of Court

482. (1) Power to make rules — Every superior court of criminal jurisdiction and every court of appeal may make rules of court not inconsistent with this or any other Act of Parliament, and any rules so made apply to any prosecution, proceeding, action or appeal, as the case may be, within the jurisdiction of that court, instituted in relation to any matter of a criminal nature or arising from or incidental to any such prosecution, proceeding, action or appeal.

(2) Idem — Every court of criminal jurisdiction for a province and every appeal court within the meaning of section 812 that is not a court referred to in subsection (1) may, subject to the approval of the lieutenant governor in council of the province, make rules of court not inconsistent with this Act or any other Act of Parliament, and any rules so made apply to any prosecution, proceeding, action or appeal, as the case may be, within the jurisdiction of that court, instituted in relation to any matter of a criminal nature or arising from or incidental to any such prosecution, proceeding, action or appeal.

(3) Purpose of rules — Rules under subsection (1) or (2) may be made

(a) generally to regulate the duties of the officers of the court and any other matter considered expedient to attain the ends of justice and carry into effect the provisions of the law;

(b) to regulate the sittings of the court or any division thereof, or of any judge of the court sitting in chambers, except in so far as they are regulated by law;

(c) to regulate in criminal matters the pleading, practice and procedure in the court including pre-hearing conferences held pursuant to section 625.1 and proceedings with respect to judicial interim release and, in the case of rules under subsection (1), proceedings with respect to *mandamus, certiorari, habeas corpus,* prohibition and *procedendo* and proceedings on an appeal under section 830; and

(d) to carry out the provisions of this Act relating to appeals from conviction, acquittal or sentence and, without restricting the generality of this paragraph,

(i) for furnishing necessary forms and instructions in relation to notices of appeal or applications for leave to appeal to officials or other persons requiring or demanding them,

(ii) for ensuring the accuracy of notes taken at a trial and the verification of any copy or transcript,

(iii) for keeping writings, exhibits or other things connected with the proceedings on the trial,

(iv) for securing the safe custody of property during the period in which the operation of an order with respect to that property is suspended under subsection 689(1), and

(v) for providing that the Attorney General and counsel who acted for the Attorney General at the trial be supplied with certified copies of writings, exhibits and things connected with the proceedings that are required for the purposes of their duties.

(4) Publication — Rules of court that are made under the authority of this section shall be published in the *Canada Gazette.*

(5) Regulations to secure uniformity — Notwithstanding anything in this section, the Governor in Council may make such provision as he considers proper to secure uniformity in the rules of court in criminal matters, and all uniform rules made under the authority of this subsection prevail and have effect as if enacted by this Act.

R.S., c. C-34, s. 438; 1974–75–76, c. 93, s. 42; R.S. 1985, c. 27 (1st Supp.), s. 66; 1994, c. 44, s. 35.

Commentary: This section authorizes designated courts to pass *rules* of court relating to criminal proceedings before them.

Under s. 482(1) *superior courts of criminal jurisdiction and courts of appeal* may make rules of court, *not* inconsistent with the *Code* or other federal enactment. The rules will apply to any *prosecution, proceeding, action* or *appeal* within the jurisdiction of the court, instituted in relation to any matter of a criminal nature or arising from or incidental to any such prosecution, proceeding, action or appeal. Under s. 482(4), the rules must be published in the *Canada Gazette* and are subject to over-riding uniform rules made by the Governor in Council under s. 482(5).

Under s. 482(2), a *court of criminal jurisdiction and every appeal court* as defined in s. 812, that is *not* a superior court of criminal jurisdiction or court of appeal, may also make rules applicable as under s. 482(1). The rules must, however, be approved by the Lieutenant Governor in Council of the province, and published in the *Canada Gazette* under s. 482(4). The rules are subject to the enactment of overriding uniform rules made by the Governor in Council under s. 482(5).

The subject-matter of the rules is described in s. 482(3).

Case Law

Jurisdiction

R. v. Johnson (1994), 31 C.R. (4th) 262, 91 C.C.C. (3d) 21 (Y.T. C.A.) — Rules may be made and published under s. 482(2) to provide for sentencing circles to assist trial judges in imposing sentence in certain kinds of cases. The rules will inform those involved of the kinds of cases to which sentencing circles apply and what the parties may expect in such cases.

Stays Pending Appeal [See ss. 261, 675, 683 and 732.2]

Habeas Corpus

Quebec (A.G.) v. Cronier (1981), 23 C.R. (3d) 97, 63 C.C.C. (2d) 437 (Que. C.A.) — In the absence of a legislative provision allowing the imposition of costs in *habeas corpus* proceedings with *certiorari* in aid in criminal matters, and in view of the fact that there are no costs in criminal matters, s. 482(3)(c) and the rules of practice adopted pursuant to that section cannot create such a right. The superior court does have inherent supervisory powers to award costs to uphold its authority and control its process. Those powers should *not* be used arbitrarily and without limits, rather only with the greatest reluctance and anxiety.

Related Provisions: "Superior court of criminal jurisdiction", "court of appeal" and "court of criminal jurisdiction" are defined in s. 2, "appeal court" in s. 812. "Governor in Council" and "Lieutenant Governor in Council" are defined in *I.A.* s. 35(1).

The rule-making powers for which provision is made in this section do *not* permit the enactment of substantive law, nor in any way derogate from the distribution of legislative powers set out in head 27 of s. 91 and head 14 of s. 92 of the *Constitution Act, 1867*.

PART XV — SPECIAL PROCEDURE AND POWERS

General Powers of Certain Officials

483. Officials with powers of two justices — Every judge or provincial court judge authorized by the law of the province in which he is appointed to do anything that is required to be done by two or more justices may do alone anything that this Act or any other Act of the Parliament authorizes two or more justices to do.

R.S., c. C-34, s. 439;R.S. 1985, c. 27 (1st Supp.), s.203

Commentary: The section empowers a judge or provincial court judge, who is authorized by provincial legislation to do anything that is required to be done by two or more justices, to do *alone* anything which the *Code* or other federal enactment authorizes two or more justices to do.

Related Provisions: "Provincial court judge" and "justice" are defined in s. 2. "Judge" is *not* defined for the purposes of Part XV, nor generally in s. 2.

484. Preserving order in court — Every judge or provincial court judge has the same power and authority to preserve order in a court over which he presides as may be exercised by the superior court of criminal jurisdiction of the province during the sittings thereof.

R.S., c. C-34, s. 440;R.S. 1985, c. 27 (1st Supp.), s.203

Commentary: The section confers upon judges and provincial court judges the same power and authority to preserve order in their respective courts as that which may be exercised by a judge of the superior court of criminal jurisdiction during the sittings of that court.

Case Law [See ss. 9, 10]

Related Provisions: "Provincial court judge" and "superior court of criminal jurisdiction" are defined in s. 2.

It is indispensable to the due administration of justice that the presiding judicial officer have control of the proceedings. The section endeavours to ensure the same degree of control in each level of court and is most frequently engaged to found the authority to commit for *contempt* in the *face* of the court. It does *not* purport to incorporate the wider authority of the superior court of criminal jurisdiction to punish for contempt committed out of the face of the court.

Jurisdiction to impose punishment for contempt of court is expressly preserved under s. 9. Appellate rights from conviction and punishment for contempt in the face of the court are given by s. 10(1).

485. (1) Procedural irregularities — Jurisdiction over an offence is not lost by reason of the failure of any court, judge, provincial court judge or justice to act in the exercise of that jurisdiction at any particular time, or by reason of a failure to comply with any of the provisions of this Act respecting adjournments or remands.

(1.1) Where accused not present — Jurisdiction over an accused is not lost by reason of the failure of the accused to appear personally, so long as paragraph 537(1)(j) or subsection 650(1.1) applies and the accused is to appear by counsel.

(2) Summons or warrant — Where jurisdiction over an accused or a defendant is lost and has not been regained, a court, judge, provincial court judge or justice may, within three months after the loss of jurisdiction, issue a summons, or if it or he considers it necessary in the public interest, a warrant for the arrest of the accused or defendant.

(3) Dismissal for want of prosecution — Where no summons or warrant is issued under subsection (2) within the period provided therein, the proceedings shall be deemed to be dismissed for want of prosecution and shall not be recommenced except in accordance with section 485.1.

(4) Adjournment and order — Where, in the opinion of the court, judge, provincial court judge or justice, an accused or a defendant who appears at a proceeding has been misled or prejudiced by reason of any matter referred to in subsection (1), the court, judge, provincial court judge or justice may adjourn the proceeding and may make such order as it or he considers appropriate.

(5) Part XVI to apply — The provisions of Part XVI apply with such modifications as the circumstances require where a summons or warrant is issued under subsection (2).

1974–75–76, c. 93, s. 43;R.S. 1985, c. 27 (1st Supp.), ss. 67, 203; 1997, c. 18, s. 40.

Commentary: The section deals with the effect on *jurisdiction over* an *offence* and the *person* of D in cases of certain procedural irregularities or where D is not present.

Under s. 485(1), there is *no loss of jurisdiction* over an *offence* for failure of the court to exercise jurisdiction at a particular time, or to comply with any *Code* requirements concerning adjournments or remands. Neither *failure to act, nor failure to comply* with the adjournment and remand requirements of the *Code* deprive the court of *offence jurisdiction*. Where D has been prejudiced or misled by any such failure, the court *may* adjourn the proceedings under s. 485(4) and make such order as is considered appropriate.

Under s. 485(1.1), jurisdiction over an *offence* is lost if D does not appear personally *unless* the "video links" provisions of s. 537(1)(j) or s. 650(1.1) apply and D is to appear by counsel.

Section 485(2) deals with cases in which *jurisdiction over* the *person* of D has been *lost* and *not* regained. The court may, *within three months after the loss of jurisdiction*, issue a summons or, if it is considered necessary in the public interest, a warrant, for D's arrest. Under s. 485(4), the issuance of a summons or warrant to compel D's appearance invokes Part XVI. Failure to issue a summons or warrant within the three-month period described in s. 485(2) has the effect, under s. 485(3), of deeming the proceedings to have been dismissed for want of prosecution. Recommencement may be only in accordance with s. 485.1.

Case Law

Jurisdiction not Lost: S. 485(1)

R. v. Petersen (1982), 30 C.R. (3d) 165, 69 C.C.C. (2d) 385 (S.C.C.) — The curative provisions of this section prevent loss of the summary conviction court's jurisdiction where proceedings are adjourned for more than eight days without D's consent. The court remained a court of competent jurisdiction, even though the judge decided, in error, that he had no jurisdiction.

R. v. Chisan (1988), 62 Alta. L.R. (2d) 359 (C.A.) — The provincial court does *not* lose jurisdiction by failing to call D's case on the return date. Subsection (1) applies to all actions in all cases by judges and justices, including matters under provincial summary convictions legislation.

C.N. Transportation Ltd. v. Canada (A.G.) (1985), 60 A.R. 380 (C.A.); affirmed [1986] 2 S.C.R. 711 (S.C.C.) — This section was used to cure an irregularity resulting when, on the date for fixing a date for a preliminary hearing, the information was *not* at hand as it had been forwarded for a prohibition application and the proceedings were adjourned to an undefined future date to await the outcome of the prohibition application.

Lévesque v. R. (1983), 36 C.R. (3d) 149 (Que. C.A.) — The adjournment of the trial to a Sunday was a minor error which caused no prejudice to anyone, hence did *not* result in a loss of jurisdiction over the offence.

Jurisdiction Lost

R. v. Krannenburg (1980), 17 C.R. (3d) 357, 51 C.C.C. (2d) 205 (S.C.C.) — A predecessor did *not* save jurisdiction over an *offence* when the court failed to proceed or attend on the date to which the case was adjourned. Loss of jurisdiction over the *person* differs from loss of jurisdiction over an offence. Failure to comply with *Code* provisions respecting adjournments or remands results in a loss of jurisdiction over the *person*. Failure to proceed or attend results in a loss of jurisdiction over the *offence*. Under the 1985 amendment, jurisdiction over an offence is *not* lost due to the failure to act in the exercise of that jurisdiction at any particular time.

R. v. Thompson (1980), 51 C.C.C. (2d) 212 (S.C.C.) — This section can *not* cure the loss of jurisdiction when the informations were lost but subsequently found.

R. v. Belton (1981), 61 C.C.C. (2d) 499 (Man. C.A.) — Jurisdiction over the offences was lost when, without consent or notice to D, informations that were expected to be dealt with in pre-trial "C" court were placed on "A" court's docket for hearing.

Jurisdiction Regained

R. v. Pearson (1982), 66 C.C.C. (2d) 485 (Que. C.A.); leave to appeal refused (1982), 44 N.R. 628 (S.C.C.) — *See also*: *R. v. Fogarty* (1988), 46 C.C.C. (3d) 289 (N.S. C.A.) — Loss of jurisdiction over the person may be regained by the subsequent voluntary appearance of D.

Charter Considerations

R. v. Jarvis (1986), 76 N.S.R. (2d) 268 (C.A.); leave to appeal refused (1987), 78 N.S.R. (2d) 360n (S.C.C.) — The section does *not* violate *Charter*, s. 7.

Related Provisions: Several *Code* provisions relate to *adjournments*. The general authority of a *justice* to adjourn a *preliminary inquiry* is found in s. 537(1)(a). Special provision is made in s. 547 to adjourn the inquiry where D has been deceived, misled or prejudiced by certain irregularities or variances in the process compelling appearance or information in which D is charged and the evidence adduced at the inquiry.

In *trials by jury*, the general authority to adjourn proceedings is found in ss. 645(1)–(3) and the specific authority to do so where the indictment is amended, under s. 601(5). Where *no* jury panel has been summoned the sittings may be adjourned under s. 474.

In *trials without a jury* under Part XIX, s. 571 empowers a judge or a provincial court judge to adjourn trial proceedings, from time to time, until the trial is finally terminated. Section 572 makes the provisions of Part XX, "Procedure in Jury Trials and General Provisions", applicable, with such modifications as the circumstances require, to non-jury trials.

The recommencement of proceedings deemed dismissed for want of prosecution under s. 485(3) is governed by s. 485.1.

An appellate court may dismiss an appeal under s. 686(1)(b)(iv), notwithstanding *any* procedural irregularity at trial, where the trial court had jurisdiction over the class of offence of which the appellant was convicted and the court is of the opinion that the appellant suffered no prejudice thereby.

485.1 Recommencement where dismissal for want of prosecution —

Where an indictment in respect of a transaction is dismissed or deemed by any provision of this Act to be dismissed for want of prosecution, a new information shall not be laid and a new indictment shall not be preferred before any court in respect of the same transaction without

> **(a) the personal consent in writing of the Attorney General or Deputy Attorney General, in any prosecution conducted by the Attorney General or in which the Attorney General intervenes; or**

> **(b) the written order of a judge of that court, in any prosecution conducted by a prosecutor other than the Attorney General and in which the Attorney General does not intervene.**

R.S. 1985, c. 27 (1st Supp.), s. 67.

Commentary: The section describes the circumstances under which proceedings may be recommenced where an indictment in respect of a transaction has been or is deemed to have been dismissed for want of prosecution. The recommencement may be by a new information or upon a fresh indictment.

In prosecutions conducted by the Attorney General, or in which the Attorney General intervenes, *no* new information may be laid, nor new indictment preferred, before any court in respect of the same transaction for which an indictment has been or is deemed to have been dismissed for want of prosecution, without the *personal written consent of the Attorney General or Deputy Attorney General*. In prosecutions neither conducted by the Attorney General, nor in which the Attorney General intervenes, there must be *the written order of a judge of the court* in which the new information is laid or new indictment preferred before proceedings may recommence in similar circumstances.

Case Law

R. v. Richardson (1987), 39 C.C.C. (3d) 262 (N.S. C.A.) — This section only applies where the original indictmentwas quashed for want of prosecution, not for non-compliance with s. 581.

Procter & Gamble Inc. v. Alberta (A.G.) (1993), (sub nom. *R. v. Procter & Gamble Inc.)* 82 C.C.C. (3d) 477 (Alta. C.A.); leave to appeal refused (1993), 11 Alta. L.R. (3d) li (note), 11 C.E.L.R. (N.S.) 23 1n (S.C.C.) — Where charges initiated by a private complaint have been dismissed for want of prosecution, a new information laid by an agent of the Crown may be laid with the consent of the Attorney General or Deputy Attorney General. The written order of a judge under s. 485. 1(b) is *not* required.

Related Provisions: "Indictment" is defined in s. 2 to include "information". Generally, the definition of "Attorney General" in s. 2 includes any lawful deputy but this provision, like s. 577(c), is limitative of it. Agents of the Attorney General are *not* authorized by this section to give such consent. Section 485.1(a) expressly requires that the consent be personal, in writing, and by the Attorney General or Deputy Attorney General.

An information may be laid under ss. 504 and 505 following the procedure set out in ss. 507, 508 and 508.1. An indictment may be preferred under ss. 566 (non-jury) and 574–577 (jury).

The *Code* contains no express provision authorizing the dismissal of an indictment for want of prosecution.

486. (1) Exclusion of public in certain cases — Any proceedings against an accused shall be held in open court, but where the presiding judge, provincial court judge or justice, as the case maybe, is of the opinion that it is in the interest of public morals, the maintenance of order or the proper administration of justice to exclude all or any members of the public from the court room for all or part of the proceedings, he may so order.

(1.1) Protection of child witnesses — For the purposes of subsections (1) and (2.3) and for greater certainty, the "proper administration of justice" includes ensuring that the interests of witnesses under the age of fourteen years are safeguarded in proceedings in which the accused is charged with a sexual offence, an offence against any of sections 271, 272 and 273 or an offence in which violence against the person is alleged to have been used, threatened or attempted.

(1.2) Support person — In proceedings referred to in subsection (1.1), the presiding judge, provincial court judge or justice may, on application of the prosecutor or a witness who, at the time of the trial or preliminary hearing, is under the age of fourteen years, order that a support person of the witness' choice be permitted to be present and to be close to the witness while testifying.

(1.3) Witness not to be a support person — The presiding judge, provincial court judge or justice shall not permit a witness in the proceedings referred to in subsection (1.1) to be a support person unless the presiding judge, provincial court judge or justice is of the opinion that the proper administration of justice so requires.

(1.4) No communication while testifying — The presiding judge, provincial court judge or justice may order that the support person and the witness not communicate with each other during the testimony of the witness.

(2) Reasons to be stated — Where an accused is charged with an offence mentioned in section 274 and the prosecutor or the accused makes an application for an order under subsection (1), the presiding judge, provincial court judge or justice, as the case may be, shall, if no such order is made, state, by reference to the circumstances of the case, the reason for not making an order.

(2.1) Testimony outside court room — Notwithstanding section 650, where an accused is charged with an offence under section 151, 152, 153, 155 or 159, subsection 160(2) or (3), or section 163.1, 170, 171, 172, 173, 210, 211, 212, 213, 266, 267, 268, 271, 272 or 273 and the complainant or any witness, at the time of the trial or preliminary inquiry, is under the age of eighteen years or is able to communicate evidence but may have difficulty doing so by reason of a mental or physical disability, the presiding judge or justice, as the case may be, may order that the complainant or witness testify outside the court room or behind a screen or other device that would allow the complainant or witness not to see the accused, if the judge or justice is of the opinion that the exclusion is necessary to obtain a full and candid account of the acts complained of from the complainant or witness.

(2.11) Same procedure for opinion — Where the judge or justice is of the opinion that it is necessary for the complainant or witness to testify in order to determine whether an order under subsection (2.1) should be made in respect of that complainant or witness, the judge or justice shall order that the complainant or witness testify pursuant to that subsection.

(2.2) Condition of exclusion — A complainant or witness shall not testify outside the court room pursuant to subsection (2.1) or (2.11) unless arrangements are made for the accused, the judge or justice and the jury to watch the testimony of the complainant or other witness by means of closed-circuit television or otherwise and the accused is permitted to communicate with counsel while watching the testimony.

(2.3) Accused not to cross-examine child witness — In proceedings referred to in subsection (1.1), the accused shall not personally cross-examine a witness who at the time of the proceedings is under the age of fourteen years, unless the presiding judge, provincial court judge or justice is of the opinion that the proper administration of justice requires the accused to personally conduct the cross-examination and, where the accused is not personally conducting the cross-examination, the presiding judge, provincial court judge or justice shall appoint counsel for the purpose of conducting the cross-examination.

(3) **Order restricting publication** — Subject to subsection (4), where an accused is charged with

(a) an offence under section 151, 152, 153, 155, 159, 160, 170, 171, 172, 173, 210, 211, 212, 213, 271, 272, 273, 346 or 347,

(b) an offence under section 144, 145, 149, 156, 245 or 246 of the *Criminal Code*, chapter C-34 of the Revised Statutes of Canada, 1970, as it read immediately before January 4, 1983, or

(c) an offence under section 146, 151, 153, 155, 157, 166 or 167 of the *Criminal Code*, chapter C-34 of the Revised Statutes of Canada, 1970, as it read immediately before January 1, 1988,

the presiding judge or justice may make an order directing that the identity of the complainant or of a witness and any information that could disclose the identity of the complainant or witness shall not be published in any document or broadcast in any way.

(3.1) **Limitation** — An order made under subsection (3) does not apply in respect of the disclosure of information in the course of the administration of justice where it is not the purpose of the disclosure to make the information known in the community.

(4) **Mandatory order on application** — The presiding judge or justice shall

(a) at the first reasonable opportunity, inform any witness under the age of eighteen years and the complainant to proceedings in respect of an offence mentioned in subsection (3) of the right to make an application for an order under subsection (3); and

(b) on application made by the complainant, the prosecutor or any such witness, make an order under that subsection.

(5) **Failure to comply with order** — Every one who fails to comply with an order made pursuant to subsection (3) is guilty of an offence punishable on summary conviction.

(6) [Repealed R.S. 1985, c. 19 (3d Supp.), s. 14(2).]

R.S., c. C-34, s. 442; 1974–75–76, c. 93, s. 44;1980–81–82–83, c. 110, s. 74; c. 125, s. 25;R.S. 1985, c.27 (1st Supp.), s. 203; c. 19 (3d Supp.), s. 14; c. 23 (4th Supp.), s. 1; 1992, c. 21, s. 9; 1993, c. 45, s. 7; 1997, c. 16, s. 6.

Commentary: The section describes the circumstances under which a judge may *exclude* any or all *members of the public* from the courtroom during all or any part of criminal proceedings. It further makes provision for *obstructed view and videotape testimony* in respect of certain offences of sexual assault, interference and exploitation and limits what may be reported of such and other testimony.

Section 486(1) states the *general rule* that any proceedings against D are to be held in *open court* and describes the exceptions thereto. *Any or all members of the public* may be excluded from the courtroom, for *all or any part of the proceedings*, only where the presiding judge is of the opinion that it is in *the interests of public morals, maintenance of order or the proper administration of justice* to do so. The presiding judge, in other words, has a statutorily defined discretion to limit or eliminate public accessibility to criminal proceedings. No special rule is enacted in respect of the offences of sexual assault, interference or exploitation described in s. 274 but, in the event of application by P or D for an order under s. 486(1), s. 486(2) obliges the presiding judge to give reasons for refusing such an order.

Sections 486(1.1)–(1.4) and (2.3) enact protection for child witnesses while they testify in certain proceedings.

Section 486(1.1) provides assistance in interpreting the phrase "proper administration of justice" which is critical to a decision under s. 486(1). In proceedings in which D is charged with "a sexual offence", any crime of sexual assault or an offence in which violence against the person is alleged to have been used, threatened or attempted, the "proper administration of justice" under s. 486(1) includes ensuring that the interests of witnesses under 14 years of age are safeguarded in the proceedings. There would appear no requirement that the witness whose interests are to be safeguarded be the complainant in the offence charged. The effect of the section is to require consideration of the interests of youthful witnesses in determining whether the proper administration of justice warrants an order under s. 486(1) where D is charged with a designated offence.

Sections 486(1.2)–(1.4) provide for the presence of a *support person* for youthful witnesses in cases where D is charged with an offence described in s. 486(1.1). Under s. 486(1.2), P or any witness under 14 years of age may apply at trial or preliminary hearing for an order that a support person of the witness' choice be permitted to be present and close to the witness while testifying. Unless the proper administration of justice requires it, s. 486(1.3) bars another witness in a proceeding serving as the support person for the youthful witness. The presiding judge or justice may also order, under s. 486(1.4), that the support person and youthful witness not communicate with each other during the witness' testimony.

Section 486(2.3) governs *cross-examination* by D of youthful witnesses and proceedings in respect of offences described in s. 486(1.1). It appears applicable *only* in cases where D is *not* represented by counsel, although the subsection contains no express statement to this effect. In general, s. 486(2.3) prohibits D from personally cross-examining a youthful witness in designated proceedings. There is no prohibition against examination-in-chief, hence summoning witnesses. Where D is not personally conducting the cross-examination, the presiding judge must appoint counsel to do so. D may personally conduct the cross-examination only where the proper administration of justice requires that D do so. The denial to an unrepresented accused of the right personally to cross-examine a youthful witness, absent exceptional circumstances, and the appointment of counsel for such purpose, may be constitutionally suspect.

Sections 486(2.1)–(4) are a series of provisions applicable *inter alia* in proceedings in respect of listed offences. Under s. 486(2.1), the presiding judge or justice may order that V, under 18 years of age at the time of the proceedings, or with difficulty communicating evidence due to mental or physical disability, testify outside the courtroom or behind a screen or other device that would allow V *not* to see D. The presiding judge or justice must first be satisfied that the *exclusion is necessary to obtain a full and candid account of the acts complained of from* V. Where the presiding judge or justice is of the opinion that s/he must first hear V testify in order to determine whether an order under s. 486(2.1) should issue, then the judge or justice must order that V testify pursuant to s. 486(2.1). Under s. 486(2.2), V may *only* testify outside the court room where arrangements can be made for D, the presiding judge or justice and the jury to watch the testimony of V, by means of closed-circuit television or otherwise, and where D is permitted to communicate with counsel while watching the testimony.

Sections 486(3), (3.1) and (4) deal with *publication bans* in respect of the testimony of V or a witness who gives evidence in proceedings in respect of listed offences. The ban is *mandatory* upon application by V, P or a witness and *discretionary* upon the motion of the presiding judge or justice. The ban prohibits publication or broadcast of the *identity* of V or the witness, as well as any *information* that would *disclose* that *identity*, subject to the disclosure exception in s. 486(3.1). Failure to comply with a non-publication order is a summary conviction offence under s. 486(5). Under s. 486(4) it is the duty of the presiding judge or justice, at the first reasonable opportunity, to inform V or a witness under 18 years of age of the right to make an application for an order under s. 486(3). The listed offences also include extortion (s. 346) and criminal interest rate (s. 347).

The absolute nature of the publication ban under s. 486(3) upon application by P, V or the witness has attracted *Charter* s. 2(b) scrutiny. The provisions of ss. 486(2.1) and (2.2) are likely to attract *Charter* ss. 7 and 11(d) scrutiny.

Case Law

Inherent Jurisdiction

R. v. Létourneau (1994), 87 C.C.C. (3d) 481, 517–21 (B.C. C.A.) — A *superior* court of criminal jurisdiction has *inherent* jurisdiction to permit an adult witness to testify from behind a sequestration *screen* where legitimate concerns arise about the witness' security. The jury should be instructed that the erection of the screen is in *no* way evidence against D.

The General Rule: S. 486(1)

C.B.C. v. New Brunswick (Attorney General) (1996), 110 C.C.C. (3d) 193 (S.C.C.) — The *discretion* of s. 486(1) must be exercised in conformity with the *Charter*. The presiding judge should

i.   consider *available options*, including other reasonable and effective alternatives;

ii.   consider whether the *order* is as *limited* in scope as possible; and

iii.   weigh the *importance* of the *objectives* and *probable effects* of the order *against* the *importance* of *openness* and the *expression* that will be limited.

C.B.C. v. New Brunswick (Attorney General) (1996), 110 C.C.C. (3d) 193 (S.C.C.) — Under s. 486(1), the party who seeks an order displacing the general rule of openness bears the *burden* of proving that

i.   the particular order is *necessary* to the proper administration of justice;

ii.   the order is as *limited* as possible; and

iii.   the *salutary* effects are *proportionate* to the *deleterious* effects of the order.

The application should be grounded on an adequate evidentiary basis to found the exercise of judical discretion.

Vickery v. Prothonotary of the Supreme Court of Nova Scotia at Halifax (1991), 64 C.C.C. (3d) 65 (S.C.C.) — The court, as custodian of exhibits produced at trial, is entitled to regulate their use and may deny public access to them once the trial has been completed, where there is a need to protect the innocent.

F.P. Publications (Western) Ltd. v. R. (1980), 51 C.C.C. (2d) 110 (Man. C.A.) — Publicity is the hallmark of justice. Trial in open court is the instrument through which publicity is effectively obtained. The section should *not* be used to prohibit conduct which was not wrongful and was an expression of freedom of the press, on the basis of the proper administration of justice. Reporters could not be barred from the courtroom in order to prevent newspapers from publishing the names of witnesses who were patrons of a massage parlour respecting a charge of keeping a common bawdy-house.

R. v. Laws (1998), 18 C.R. (5th) 257, 128 C.C.C. (3d) 516 (Ont. C.A.) — The discretion to exclude members of the public when circumstances warrant should *not* be exercised arbitrarily or in the absence of an evidentiary foundation. It must be exercised in accordance with the *Charter*.

R. v. Vandevelde (1994), 89 C.C.C. (3d) 161 (Sask. C.A.) — While a discretion exists to exclude some or all members of the public under s. 486(1), the overriding principle is that trials are to be held in open court. There must be a sufficient evidentiary foundation upon which to order exclusion. The applicant bears the burden of proof.

Procedure on Hearing

R. v. Vandevelde (1994), 89 C.C.C. (3d) 161 (Sask. C.A.) — Where there is *no dispute* on the facts or information presented to the trial judge, the matter may be determined on the basis of this information which could include:

i.   the age of the witness;

ii.   what took place at preliminary inquiry;

iii.   the nature of the evidence; and,

iv.   the effect of the presence of the general public on the ability of the witness to testify.

Where there is *a dispute* concerning the essential facts, however, the party seeking the exclusion order must place sufficient evidence before the trial judge to warrant the order sought. The evidence may be adduced on a *voir dire* which may be held *in camera*.

In Camera Hearings: S. 486(1)

Canadian Broadcasting Corp. v. New Brunswick (Attorney General) (1996), 2 C.R. (5th) 1, 110 C.C.C. (3d) 193 (S.C.C.) — In exercising the discretion of s. 486(1), a judge should conclude,

i. that there are *no reasonable* and *effective* alternatives;

ii. that the order is as *limited* as possible; and,

iii. that the *salutary* effects are *proportionate* to its *deleterious* effects.

There is *no per se* rule that an order should be made in cases of sexual assault on young females. Undue hardship to persons involved may be sufficient to warrant an order excluding the public, but apart from exceptional cases, *not* an accused who has pleaded guilty.

R. v. Brint (1979), 6 C.R. (3d) 377, 45 C.C.C. (2d) 560 (Alta. C.A.) — The fact that under 486(2) the judge is required to give reasons for *not* closing the courtroom does *not* enlarge the grounds under 486(1) for closing a courtroom. When an application is made under 486(2), the judge should close the court only if there be real and weighty reasons for exercising his power to exclude the public from all or part of the proceedings.

R. v. Warawuk (1978), 42 C.C.C. (2d) 121 (Alta. C.A.) — A trial may be held in *camera* either to protect public morals, *i.e.* when the making public of details of a trial might havean adverse or corrupting effect on public morals, or in the pursuance of the proper administration of justice, as when giving evidence in public may put an intolerable strain on a witness. The discretion given must be exercised with caution and only as the exigencies demand.

R. v. Musitano (1985), 24 C.C.C. (3d) 65 (Ont. C.A.) — It was a proper exercise of discretion to exclude the public in the interest of the proper administration of justice for a trial judge to hold an *in camera* inquiry, in the presence of D and their counsel, to determine the impartiality of three members of the jury.

R. v. Quesnel (1979), 51 C.C.C. (2d) 270 (Ont. C.A.) — It is an insufficient basis upon which to grant an *in camera* hearing that a witness who has to testify as to sexual behavior may be embarrassed. There must be some further reason such that the truth is more difficult or unlikely or that the witness will be too frightened to testify so as to justify an order on the basis of the proper administration of justice.

R. v. Douglas (1977), 1 C.R. (3d) 238, 33 C.C.C. (2d) 395 (Ont. C.A.) — D has no right to make full answer and defence in private. Trials conducted wholly or in part *in camera* are to be avoided except in the circumstances set out in this section. The fact that D's testimony would reveal that she had been a police informer in the past and that she intended to do it again would not add in any substantial way to whatever danger was alleged to attend her testifying in open court. However, it may be preferable in certain cases that the trial judge listen *in camera* to counsel's reasons for wishing exclusion.

R. v. Lefebvre (1984), 17 C.C.C. (3d) 277 (Que. C.A.) — An order may be made excluding the public where V is unable to testify because of the stress caused by the presence of too many persons in the courtroom.

R. v. Vandevelde (1994), 89 C.C.C. (3d) 161 (Sask. C.A.) — If the capacity of a witness to testify in the presence of the general public is rendered impossible or so difficult that the witness is unwilling or unable to testify, or that the witness' evidence would be rendered practically useless, thereby threatening or endangering the proper administration of justice, the right to a public trial must yield to the interests of justice.

Testimony Outside Courtroom: Ss. 486(2.1), (2.2)

R. v. H. (B.C.) (1990), 58 C.C.C. (3d) 16 (Man. C.A.) — A trial judge may hold a *voir dire* to determine whether a witness may testify out of the courtroom under s. 486(2.1), but may *not* receive opinion evidence from non-experts upon the issue.

R. v. R. (M.E.) (1989), 71 C.R. (3d) 113, 49 C.C.C. (3d) 475 (N.S. C.A.) — The right of D to be present at his trial is *not* absolute. A trial judge has a discretion to permit the child complainant in a sexual assault case to testify from outside the courtroom on video camera.

Obstructed View Testimony: S. 486(2.1)

R. v. M. (P.) (1990), 1 O.R. (3d) 341 (C.A.) — *See also: R. v. Levogiannis* (1990), 2 C.R. (4th) 355, 62 C.C.C. (3d) 59 (C.A.); affirmed (1993), 25 C.R. (4th) 325, 85 C.C.C. (3d) 327 (S.C.C.) — An order for obstructed view testimony under s. 486(2.1) should only be made upon the basis of evidence capable of supporting the preliminary findings required by the section. Evidence that V did *not* want to see D, because she disliked him, will *not* suffice. The jury should *not* be instructed that the use of a screen tells against V's credibility.

Non-Publication Orders: S. 486(3)

Dagenais v. Canadian Broadcasting Corp. (1994), 34 C.R. (4th) 269, 94 C.C.C. (3d) 289, [1994] 3 S.C.R. 835 — An applicant who seeks a publication ban in the context of criminal proceedings under a judge's common law or legislated discretionary authority must apply to the trial judge, if one has been appointed, or to a judge of the court at the level the case will be heard if it may be determined by reference to the applicable statutory provisions. If the level of court has not been established and cannot be determined by reference to statutory provisions, the appliation ought to be made to a judge of the superior court of criminal jurisdiction, the highest court that could hear the case.

Dagenais v. Canadian Broadcasting Corp. (1994), 34 C.R. (4th) 269, 94 C.C.C. (3d) 289, [1994] 3 S.C.R. 835 — To seek or challenge a publication ban on appeal, D and P must follow regular *Code* appeal provision. Some flexibility in the rule against collateral attacks must be made to permit these appeals.

Dagenais v. Canadian Broadcasting Corp. (1994), 34 C.R. (4th) 269, 94 C.C.C. (3d) 289, [1994] 3 S.C.R. 835 — Applications for a publication ban under a judge's common law or legislated discretionary authority should be heard in the absence of the jury. The presiding judge has the discretion to direct that third parties, such as the media, be given notice under the applicable rules of criminal procedure, granted standing and to determine what rights the third parties should have on the hearing of the application.

Dagenais v. Canadian Broadcasting Corp. (1994), 34 C.R. (4th) 269, 94 C.C.C. (3d) 289, [1994] 3 S.C.R. 835 — The common law rule authorizing publication bans must be modified to give effect to the equal status of the freedom of expression under *Charter* s. 2(b) and the right to a fair trial under s. 11(d). A publication ban should only be ordered when

i.   it is necessary to prevent a real and substantial risk to the fairness of the trial, because reasonably available alternatives will not prevent the risk; and,

ii.   the salutary effects of the ban outweigh the deleterious.

The *Charter* does *not* require that all conceivable steps be taken to remove even the most speculative risks to a fair trial.

R. v. Paterson (1998), 122 C.C.C. (3d) 254 (B.C. C.A.) — Whether an order should be made banning publication of witnesses' names should be decided on the basis of the statements of counsel, *not* on *vivo voce* testimony from the witnesses and experts on a *voir dire*.

R. v. K. (V.) (1991), 4 C.R. (4th) 338, 68 C.C.C. (3d) 18 (B.C. C.A.) — Once made, an order of non-publication of the identity of V continues in effect until varied by a court having jurisdiction to do so.

Southam Inc. v. R. (1989), 47 C.C.C. (3d) 21 (Ont. C.A.) — Although no evidentiary support was required on an application for an order prohibiting the disclosure of the name of V in sexual assault proceedings, the court is without jurisdiction to prohibit the naming of D or other persons or places on the ground that such information would disclose the identity of V without evidence to that effect.

R. v. Unnamed Person (1985), 22 C.C.C. (3d) 284 (Ont. C.A.) — A superior court has the jurisidiction to make an order prohibiting the publication of the identity of D where such an order is necessary to protect a trial which is being conducted before it. It also has the jurisdiction to render assistance to an inferior court to enable it to administer justice effectively and fully. It is not within a superior court's inherent jurisdiction, however, to make an order prohibiting the publication of the name of D, on trial before an inferior court, solely for the purpose of protecting the privacy of D and D's family.

R. v. Calabrese (No. 3) (1981), 64 C.C.C. (2d) 71 (Que. S.C.) — An application for an order directing that the identity of V and her evidence not be published or broadcast must be made no later than the time V begins her testimony.

Reviewability

R. v. Adams (1995), 44 C.R. (4th) 195, 103 C.C.C. (3d) 262 (S.C.C.) — There is nothing in s. 486(4) which authorizes revocation of an order where the circumstances which make an order mandatory continue in force. Where both V and P consent to revocation of the ban, the circumstances which make the order mandatory are no longer present and, subject to D's rights under s. 486(3), the order may be revoked.

Dagenais v. Canadian Broadcasting Corp. (1994), 34 C.R. (4th) 269, 94 C.C.C. (3d) 289, [1994] 3 S.C.R. 835 — Third parties affected by publication bans, as for example the media, may also apply to review the order made.Where a publication ban has been made by a *provincial court judge*, the third party may apply by *certiorari* to the superior court, thereafter follow *Code* appellate routes. The remedial powers available on *certiorari* include the remedies available under *Charter* s. 24(1). A publication ban unauthorized by the common law is an error of law on the face of the record which is remediable on *certiorari*Where the order has been made by a *judge of the superior court of criminal jurisdiction*, the third party may apply for leave to appeal to the Supreme Court of Canada under s. 40 of the *Supreme Court Act*.

Jury Instructions

R. v. Levogiannis (1990), 2 C.R. (4th) 355, 62 C.C.C. (3d) 59 (Ont. C.A.); affirmed on other grounds (1993), 25 C.R. (4th) 325, 85 C.C.C. (3d) 327 (S.C.C.) — As a general rule, a jury should be instructed that the use of a sequestration screen (obstructed view testimony) is a procedure permitted, due to the age of the witness, and further, that, since it has nothing to do with D's guilt or innocence, *no* adverse inference should be drawn from its use.

R. v. Tierney (1982), 31 C.R. (3d) 66, 70 C.C.C. (2d) 481 (Ont. C.A.) — Where the existence of an order prohibiting publication of V's identity or evidence is disclosed to the jury, an explanation that the order should have no adverse effect on the complainant's credibility is desirable.

Breach of Orders: S. 486(5)

R. v. Publications Photo-Police Inc. (1988), 42 C.C.C. (3d) 220 (Que. C.A.) — By limiting the court's powers in subsection (5) to punish those who breach an order made under subsection (3), Parliament has ousted theinherent jurisdiction of the superior court to cite for contempt for breaching the order.

Charter Considerations

C.B.C. v. New Brunswick (Attorney General) (1996), 2 C.R. (5th) 1, 110 C.C.C. (3d) 193 (S.C.C.) — By its facial purpose, *Code* s. 486(1) restricts expressive activity: *viz*, the free flow of ideas and information, hence violates *Charter* s. 2(b). It is nonetheless saved by *Charter* s. 1.

R. v. Levogiannis (1993), 25 C.R. (4th) 325, 85 C.C.C. (3d) 327 (S.C.C.); affirming (1990), 2 C.R. (4th) 355, 62 C.C.C. (3d) 59 (Ont. C.A.) — *See also: R. v. M. (P.)* (1990), 1 O.R. (3d) 341 (C.A.) — The provision for obstructed view testimony in s. 486(2.1) contravenes neither *Charter* s. 7 nor s. 11(d).

R. v. Cdn. Newspapers Co. (1988), 65 C.R. (3d) 50, (sub nom. *Cdn. Newspapers Co. v. Canada (A.G.)*) 43 C.C.C. (3d) 24 — Although s. 486(3) infringes the freedom of the press as guaranteed by *Charter* s. 2(b) to the extent it makes the order mandatory on the application of P or a complainant, it is a justifiable limit under s.1 where the application has been made on behalf of the complainant and the order is discretionary. Furthermore, the subsection does *not* infringe D's right to a public hearing under *Charter* s. 11(d) since the mandatory ban on publication does *not* prevent the public or the press from attending the trial proceedings, but only restricts publication of facts disclosing the complainant's identity.

Related Provisions: "Provincial court judge" and "prosecutor" are defined in s. 2. Age is determined under *I.A.* s. 30.

Most of the offences listed in ss. 486(2.1) and (3) are the subject of special evidentiary rules under ss. 274–277. The competence of witnesses under the age of 14 years is determined under *C.E.A.* s. 16."Sexual offences" are described in ss. 150.1–161.

Counsel may be appointed for an accused who is a party to an appeal to the court of appeal (s. 684) or Supreme Court of Canada (s. 694.1) in indictable proceedings. Section 684 is incorporated by s. 839(2) in appeals to the court of appeal in summary conviction matters. Under s. 672.24, counsel may also be appointed for an unrepresented accused where the court has reasonable grounds to believe that the accused is unfit to stand trial.

The offences listed in s. 274, as well as ss. 486(2.1) and (3) of the present section, are described in the corresponding note which accompanies each section.

487. (1) Information for search warrant — A justice who is satisfied by information on oath in Form 1 that there are reasonable grounds to believe that there is in a building, receptacle or place

(a) anything on or in respect of which any offence against this Act or any other Act of Parliament has been or is suspected to have been committed,

(b) anything that there are reasonable grounds to believe will afford evidence with respect to the commission of an offence, or will reveal the whereabouts of a person who is believed to have committed an offence, against this Act or any other Act of Parliament,

(c) anything that there are reasonable grounds to believe is intended to be used for the purpose of committing any offence against the person for which a person may be arrested without warrant,

(c.1) any offence-related property, or

may at any time issue a warrant authorizing a peace officer or a public officer who has been appointed or designated to administer or enforce a federal or provincial law and whose duties include the enforcement fo this Act or any other Act of Parliament and who is named in the warrant

(d) to search the building, receptacle or place for any such thing and to seize it, and

(e) subject to any other Act of Parliament, to, as soon as practicable, bring the thing seized before, or make a report in respect thereof to, the justice or some other justice for the same territorial division in accordance with section 489.1.

(2) Endorsement of search warrant — Where the building, receptacle, or place in which anything mentioned in subsection (1) is believed to be is in any other territorial division, the justice may issue his warrant in like form modified according to the circumstances, and the warrant may be executed in the other territorial division after it has been endorsed, in Form 28, by a justice having jurisdiction in that territorial division.

(2.1) Operation of computer system and copying equipment — A person authorized under this section to search a computer system in a building or place for data may

(a) use or cause to be used any computer system at the building or place to search any data contained in or available to the computer system;

(b) reproduce or cause to be reproduced any data in the form of a print-out or other intelligible output;

(c) seize the print-out or other output for examination or copying; and

(d) use or cause to be used any copying equipment at the place to make copies of the data.

(2.2) Duty of person in possession or control — Every person who is in possession or control of any building or place in respect of which a search is carried out under this section shall, on presentation of the warrant, permit the person carrying out the search

(a) to use or cause to be used any computer system at the building or place in order to search any data contained in or available to the computer system for data that the person is authorized by this section to search for;

(b) to obtain a hard copy of the data and to seize it; and

(c) to use or cause to be used any copying equipment at the place to make copies of the data.

(3) **Form** — A search warrant issued under this section may be in the form set out as Form 5 in Part XXVIII, varied to suit the case.

(4) **Effect of endorsement** — An endorsement that is made on a warrant as provided for in subsection (2) is sufficient authority to the peace officers or public officers to whom it was originally directed, and to all peace officers within the jurisdiction of the justice by whom it is endorsed, to execute the warrant and to deal with the things seized in accordance with section 489.1 or as otherwise provided by law.

R.S., c. C-34, s. 443;R.S. 1985, c. 27 (1st Supp.), s. 68; 1994, c. 44, s. 36; 1997, c. 18, s. 41; 1997, c. 23, s. 12; 1999, c. 5, s. 16.

Commentary: The section authorizes the issuance of *search warrants* and prescribes the conditions precedent. The right to search and seize thereby given is in derogation of the common law rights of a person in possession of real property.

Under s. 487(1), an *information on oath*, in Form 1, must be presented to a "justice" who must be satisfied that there are *reasonable grounds to believe* that there is in a *building, receptacle* or *place anything* described in s. 487(1)(a), (b) or (c) or any offence-related property under s. 487(1)(c.1). Upon being so satisfied, the justice *may* issue a warrant which, under s. 487(3) may be in Form 5. The warrant signed by the justice will *authorize* a person named therein, or a peace officer, to *search* the building, receptacle or place for the things described in the warrant, and to *seize* them. The warrant will also require that the objects of seizure be returned before, or made the subject of a report to, the issuing justice or another justice for the same territorial division. The provisions of s. 489.1 govern the report and return procedure.

Sections 487(2) and (4) permit the issuance of a warrant to search a building, receptacle or place in a territorial division beyond the jurisdiction of the issuing justice. The same procedure is followed and standard applied to determine whether the warrant should issue. The form of the warrant is modified to describe the location of the building receptacle or place to be searched and may be executed in the other territorial division when endorsed or "backed" in Form 28 by a justice having jurisdiction in the territorial division where it is to be executed. Section 487(4) describes who is authorized to execute a warrant endorsed in Form 28.

Section 487(2.1) outlines the actions that a person who has been authorized under s. 487 to search a computer system in a building or place for data may take in that respect. Section 487(2.2) directs that a person who is in possession or control of any building or place in respect of which a search is carried out under s. 487 *must*, on presentation of the warrant, allow a person authorized to search for and seize computer data to do so within the strictures of the subsection.

Those who may lawfully execute the warrant and deal with the things seized, in accordance with s. 489.1 or as otherwise provided by law, include the peace officers or persons to whom the warrant was originally directed and all peace officers in the jurisdiction of the endorsing justice.

Case Law

Application of Section: S. 487(1)

R. v. Grant (1993), 24 C.R. (4th) 1, 84 C.C.C. (3d) 173 (S.C.C.); reversing (1992), 14 C.R. (4th) 260, 73 C.C.C. (3d) 315 (B.C. C.A.) — A s. 487 warrant may be used to search for narcotics, even in a dwelling-house. The warrant need only comply with s. 487, *not* the special requirements of an *NCA* warrant. It does *not*, however, give the executing officer the special search powers provided by the *NCA*.

Multiform Manufacturing Co. v. R. (1990), 79 C.R. (3d) 390, (sub nom. *R. v. Multiform Manufacturing Co.*) 58 C.C.C. (3d) 257 (S.C.C.); affirming (1988), 42 C.C.C. (3d) 174 (Que. C.A.); affirming (1987), 33 C.C.C.(3d) 521 (Que. S.C.) — The section applies to proceedings under *any* federal statute, irrespective of whether the statute itself contains search and seizure provisions.

Canadian Oxy Chemicals Ltd. v. Canada (A.G.) (1997), 114 C.C.C. (3d) 537 (B.C. C.A.) — "Things" in s. 487 are only those relating to the commission of an offence. There is no authorization of a search for and seizure of evidence of a defence, as for example, due diligence in a regulatory offence.

Duty of Justice: S. 487(1)

Canadian Broadcasting Corp. v. New Brunswick (Attorney General) (1991), 9 C.R. (4th) 192, 67 C.C.C. (3d) 554 (S.C.C.) — *See also*: *Canadian Brunswick Corp. v. Lessard* (1991), 9 C.R. (4th) 133, 67 C.C.C. (3d) 517 (S.C.C.) — Even where all the statutory prerequisites to the issuance of a search warrant have been met, the justice has a *discretion* as to whether a warrant should issue in all of the circumstances. The justice should strike a balance between the interest of the state in investigating and prosecuting crime, and the right of the media to privacy in gathering and disseminating news. The information in support of the application should ordinarily disclose whether there are *alternative sources* of the information and whether they have been exhausted. If the information sought already has been disseminated by the media, this will weigh in favour of issuing the warrant. Consideration should be given to attaching conditions to the warrant so that the media are not unduly impeded.

R. v. Johnson & Franklin Wholesale Distributors Ltd. (1971), 16 C.R.N.S. 107, 3 C.C.C. (2d) 484 (B.C. C.A.) — The commission of the offence alleged does *not* have to be proved before or at the time of the issuing of the warrant. It is *not* the duty of the justice who is asked to grant the warrant to adjudicate upon that question.

R. v. Gray (1993), 22 C.R. (4th) 114, 81 C.C.C. (3d) 174 (Man. C.A.) — The practice of the issuing justice assisting police with the preparation of an information to obtain a search warrant violates *Charter* s. 8. It is *not* proper for police to present a judicial officer with an unsigned or incomplete information to obtain a search warrant and, having received inappropriate direction with respect to both its technical language and content, to swear it in its altered form before the justice.

Purdy v. R. (1972), 8 C.C.C. (2d) 52 (N.B. C.A.) — An honest belief on the part of the informant is insufficient grounds for the issuance of a search warrant. The justice, *not* the informant, must be satisfied that there are reasonable grounds for the issuance of the warrant.

CHUM Ltd. v. Newfoundland (1989), 74 Nfld. & P.E.I.R. 26 (Nfld. C.A.) — In an application for a search warrant, the taking of additional evidence by the justice only for the purposes of clarification did not have the effect of destroying a valid information, even if the justice had no jurisdiction to take such additional evidence.

Times Square Book Store v. R. (1985), 48 C.R. (3d) 132, (sub nom. *Marquis Video Corp. v. R.)* 21 C.C.C. (3d) 503 — Before issuing a search warrant for the seizure of obscene magazines, the justice must be satisfied, on reasonable and probable grounds, that the magazines to be seized are obscene and can be found at the specified premises. Neither the information nor the warrant need specify the title of each magazine or book it is proposed to seize.

Re Worrall (1964), 44 C.R. 151, [1965] 2 C.C.C. 1 (Ont. C.A.); leave to appeal refused [1965] S.C.R. ix (S.C.C.) — The justice must consider whether the production of the articles will afford evidence which would be relevant to the issue; the articles need *not* afford evidence sufficient to result in a conviction.

Reasonable Grounds to Believe: S. 487(1)

R. v. Carroll (1989), 88 N.S.R. (2d) 165 (C.A.) — The fact that a person was in the company of D several hours after the commission of a murder for which D is charged does *not* justify the issuance of a search warrant for the person's premises.

R. v. Moran (1987), 36 C.C.C. (3d) 225 (Ont. C.A.) — Where the justice of the peace did *not* make a judicial determination that there were reasonable grounds to believe that evidence of an offence would be found at the premises to be searched, the warrant was invalid.

R. v. Debot (1986), 54 C.R. (3d) 120, 30 C.C.C. (3d) 207 (Ont. C.A.); affirmed (1989), 73 C.R. (3d) 129, 52 C.C.C. (3d) 193 (S.C.C.) — *See also*: *Joly c. Bourdeau* (1989), 51 C.C.C. (3d) 394 (Que. S.C.) — Information supplied by a reliable informer, though hearsay, may in some circumstances provide the necessary "reasonable grounds to believe" to justify the granting of a search warrant. On an application for a search warrant, the informant must set out the grounds for his belief in order to satisfy the justice that there are reasonable grounds for believing what is alleged. A mere conclusory statement made by a police informer is insufficient.

Jurisdiction to Issue Warrant: S. 487(1)

R. v. Waterford Hospital (1983), 35 C.R. (3d) 348, 6 C.C.C. (3d) 481 (Nfld. C.A.); reversing (1981), 23 C.R. (3d) 48, 61 C.C.C. (2d) 337 (Nfld. T.D.) — A justice has *no* jurisdiction to issue a search warrant for medical files generated by a court-ordered remand for psychiatric assessment. It is fundamental to the remand procedure that the assessment be conducted in a confidential atmosphere and without the fear that factual admissions could become matters of evidence at trial. To permit the search warrant to stand would be to destroy the efficacy of the remand procedure.

I.M.P. Group Ltd. v. R. (1981), (sub nom. *I.M.P. Group Ltd. v. Webb)* 58 C.C.C. (2d) 510 (N.S. C.A.); reversing (1980), 55 C.C.C. (2d) 301 (N.S. T.D.) — The search and seizure provisions of the *Export and Import Permits Act* and the *Customs Act* do *not* exclude the use of the *Code* provisions with respect to a search for documents.

R. v. Tomaso (1989), 70 C.R. (3d) 152 (Ont. C.A.) — The section does *not* empower the issue of a warrant to obtain a blood sample from D.

R. v. Benz (1986), 51 C.R. (3d) 363, (sub nom. *R. v. Haley)* 27 C.C.C. (3d) 454 (Ont. C.A.) — *Contra*: *Ciment Indépendant v. LaFrenière* (1985), 47 C.R. (3d) 83, 21 C.C.C. (3d) 429 (Que. C.A.) — The requirement under s. 487(2) that a search warrant be *backed* where it is to be executed in another territorial division does *not* require the backing of the warrant where the issuing justice has province-wide jurisdiction.

Royal Bank v. Bourque (1985), 44 C.R. (3d) 387, (sub nom. *Quebec (A.G.) v. Royal Bank)* 18 C.C.C. (3d) 98 (Que. C.A.); leave to appeal refused (1985), 18 C.C.C. (3d) 98n (S.C.C.) — This section does *not* permit the seizure of monies deposited in a bank account.

Privilege [See also s. 488.1]

Descôteaux v. Mierzwinski (1982), 28 C.R. (3d) 289, 70 C.C.C. (2d) 385 (S.C.C.) — See digest under s. 488.1, *infra*.

Canadian Broadcasting Corp. v. New Brunswick (Attorney General) (1991), 9 C.R. (4th) 192, 67 C.C.C. (3d) 554 (S.C.C.) — *See also: Canadian Broadcasting Corp. v. Lessardo* (1991), 9 C.R. (4th) 133, 67 C.C.C. (3d) 517 (S.C.C.); *R. v. Pacific Press Ltd.* (1977), 38 C.R.N.S. 295, 37 C.C.C. (2d) 487 (B.C. S.C.) — See digest under Duty of Justice: s. 487(1), *supra*.

Warrant: S. 487(3)

Alder v. R. (1977), 37 C.C.C. (2d) 234 (Alta. T.D.) — In describing an offence a search warrant need *not* refer to the *Code* section number. It must, however, make clear the nature of the offence. A warrant which merely sets out a conspiracy to defraud without disclosing how the fraud took place or precisely what parties were defrauded is deficient in the particularization of the offence.

Goguen v. Shannon (1989), 50 C.C.C. (3d) 45 (N.B. C.A.) — A warrant which does *not* provide for a return to a justice of the peace is defective.

R. v. B. (J.E.) (1989), 52 C.C.C. (3d) 224 (N.S. C.A.) — A police officer executing a search warrant may be assisted by a person who is not a peace officer provided the officer is in control of the search.

R. v. Jamieson (1989), 48 C.C.C. (3d) 287 (N.S. C.A) — A search warrant on which the date has expired cannot be revived by the policer officer requesting and the justice granting a change of date on the warrant. The officer's only recourse is to apply by way of information for a new warrant.

R. v. Church of Scientology (1987), (sub nom. *R. v. Zaharia)* 31 C.C.C. (3d) 449 (Ont. C.A.); leave to appeal refused (1987), 23 O.A.C. 320n (S.C.C.) — Since it is very difficult to describe business and financial documents with a great deal of particularity, the warrant is to be viewed as a whole and should not fail as a result of relatively minor defects.

R. v. Benz (1986), 51 C.R. (3d) 363, (sub nom. *R. v. Haley)* 27 C.C.C. (3d) 454 (Ont. C.A.) — There is *no* requirement that a warrant be directed to any specifically named peace officer.

R. v. Fekete (1985), 44 C.R. (3d) 92, 17 C.C.C. (3d) 188 (Ont. C.A.) — A search warrant is *not* invalidated where only one of several persons actually engaging in a search and seizure is named in the warrant. The named officer may not delegate his power to invade private property, but he may execute it assisted by others.

Disclosure [See also s. 487.3]

MacIntyre v. Nova Scotia (A.G.) (1982), 26 C.R. (2d) 193, 65 C.C.C. (2d) 129 (S.C.C.) — There is no right to access by the public to proceedings leading to the issuance of a warrant nor to executed warrants where a search was made and nothing found to seize. However, where objects have been seized as a result of the search a member of the public in general is entitled to inspect the warrant and the information upon which it has been issued, unless the ends of justice would be subverted by disclosure or the judicial documents might be used for an improper purpose.

R. v. Hunter (1987), 57 C.R. (3d) 1, 34 C.C.C. (3d) 14 (Ont. C.A.) — The common law principle that information that might tend to identify informers is privileged and ought not to be disclosed is subject to one exception: where disclosure could help to show that D is innocent of the offence. There should be *reasonable* disclosure of the information used to obtain a search warrant, if needed and requested even though the informant's identity may be disclosed. The trial judge should first review the information with the object of deleting any references to the identity of the informer. D should have enough information to enable the court to determine whether reasonable and probable grounds for the issuance of the warrant have been demonstrated. If the editing does not protect the identity of the informer, P may preserve the privilege by not proceeding or by proceeding on the basis of a warrantless search. In such circumstances, the trial judge has the discretion to exclude the evidence under *Charter* s. 24(2).

Review of Warrant [See also Charter, s. 8]

R. v. Grant (1993), 24 C.R. (4th) 1, 84 C.C.C. (3d) 173 (S.C.C.); reversing (1992), 14 C.R. (4th) 260, 73 C.C.C. (3d) 315 (B.C. C.A.) — See digest under *Charter*, s. 8

R. v. Wiley (1993), 24 C.R. (4th) 34, 84 C.C.C. (3d) 161 (S.C.C.) — See digest under *Charter*, s. 8

Kourtessis v. M.N.R., [1993] 4 W.W.R. 225 (S.C.C.) — The *Criminal Code* provides no right of appeal from an order issuing a search warrant.

R. v. Tanner (1989), 46 C.C.C. (3d) 513 (Alta. C.A.) — *See also: R. v. Williams* (1987), 38 C.C.C. (3d) 319 (Y.T. C.A.); *R. v. Jamieson* (1989), 48 C.C.C. (3d) 287 (N.S. C.A.) — The *trial* is the appropriate forum in which to *attack* a *search warrant* where the ultimate *goal* is *exclusion* of *evidence* under *Charter* s. 24(2).

R. v. Sismey (1990), 55 C.C.C. (3d) 281 (B.C. C.A.) — A paragraph in an information to obtain a search warrant, though *not* intentionally misleading, may nonetheless be misleading through incompleteness and, if of sufficient significance to the information as a whole, may vitiate the warrant.

R. v. Jackson (1983), 9 C.C.C. (3d) 125 (B.C. C.A.) — Where evidence existed from which a justice acting judicially could conclude that there were reasonable grounds for issuing a warrant, a reviewing court is *not* entitled to substitute its view for that of the justice.

R. v. Komadowski (1986), 27 C.C.C. (3d) 319 (Man. C.A.); leave to appeal refused (1986), 27 C.C.C. (3d) 319n (S.C.C.) — A search warrant which is valid on its face is *not* subject to collateral attack. It should only be attacked in proceedings which have as their object the reversal, variation or nullification of the order.

R. v. Breton (1994), 93 C.C.C. (3d) 171, 74 O.A.C. 99 (Ont. C.A.) — Mere absence from the supportive information of complete details concerning surveillance activities is not a sufficient basis to set aside a search warrant.

R. v. Collins (1989), 69 C.R. (3d) 235, 48 C.C.C. (3d) 343 (Ont. C.A.) — A motion may be made by way of *certiorari* to quash a search warrant, but if it is desired to adduce evidence from the informant or other witnesses in support of such an application, there must be established a *prima facie* case of deliberate falsehood or omission, or reckless disregard for the truth on the part of the affiant to the information with respect to the material used to obtain the issuance of the warrant.

R. v. Zevallos (1987), 59 C.R. (3d) 153, 37 C.C.C. (3d) 79 (Ont. C.A.) — The pre-trial quashing of a search warrant because of non-compliance with *Charter* s. 8 is in a sense, an idle exercise. Even if the warrant is invalid in substance, evidence obtained thereby is still presumptively admissible unless D satisfies the requirements of *Charter* s. 24(2). Because the decision on the pre-trial application is appealable, possibly to the Supreme Court of Canada, the administration of justice is better served by having the trial judge decide all aspects of the issue of admissibility of the seizure.

R. v. Church of Scientology (1987), (sub nom. *R. v. Zaharia*) 31 C.C.C. (3d) 449 (Ont. C.A.); leave to appeal refused (1987), 23 O.A.C. 320n (S.C.C.) — The scope of review on an application to quash a search warrant is limited to *jurisdictional* error, and this has *not* been altered by the enactment of the *Charter*. The proper test is whether evidence existed upon which the justice could determine that a warrant should be issued. After disregarding false allegations, omissions and personal opinions, could the remaining evidence satisfy the justice that a warrant should issue. As well, the justice may have been without jurisdiction if the jurisdiction of the court was invoked by fraudulent means.

Times Square Book Store v. R. (1985), 48 C.R. (3d) 132, (sub nom. *Marquis Video Corp. v. R.)* 21 C.C.C. (3d) 503 (Ont. C.A.) — *See also: Quebec (A.G.) v. Mathieu* (1986), 50 C.R. (3d) 156 (Que. C.A.) — A judge on an application to quash a search warrant may *not* substitute his/her opinion as to the sufficiency of the evidence for that of the justice. The review is restricted to whether there was evidence upon which a justice, acting judicially, could determine that a search warrant should be issued and whether the warrant contains sufficient particulars of the items to be seized.

Model Power v. R. (1981), 21 C.R. (3d) 195 (Ont. C.A.); affirming (1979), 21 C.R. (3d) 195 (Ont. H.C.) — The applicant had no *locus standi* to challenge the validity of the search warrants at the third-party premises because he had demonstrated *no* possessory or proprietary interest in the premises or the documents seized there. Prejudice, or the possibility of prejudice, to the applicant in the event that criminal proceedings were initiated involving evidence seized from the third-party premises was not a sufficient basis of standing for *certiorari*.

R. v. Couture (1998), 129 C.C.C. (3d) 302 (Que. C.A.) — A false statement in an information to obtain a search warrant does *not per se* vitiate the warrant. It does so, however, where it affects the *whole* of the information.

Liberal Party of Quebec v. Mierzwinski (1978), 46 C.C.C. (2d) 118 (Que. S.C.) — The court is *not* entitled to look at the results of the search when considering the validity of a search warrant or the information sworn in support of the warrant.

R. v. Turcotte (1987), 39 C.C.C. (3d) 193 (Sask. C.A.) — On an application to review the issuance of a search warrant the court must determine whether there was evidence before the justice of the peace upon which he *could* have determined that a warrant should be issued. Although the justice has a discretion, he must act judicially. He only has jurisdiction to issue the warrant if, from the information provided by the informant, he is satisfied on reasonable and probable grounds that an offence has been or is suspected of being committed, the location of the search is a building, receptacle or place, the item sought will provide evidence of the commission of an offence, the grounds are current so as to lend credence to the reasonable and probable grounds, and there is a nexus between the various considerations set out.

Severance of Parts of a Warrant

Dobney Holdings v. R. (1985), 18 C.C.C. (3d) 238 (B.C. C.A.) — A judge has *no* power to *amend* a search warrant on a *certiorari* application.

R. v. Johnson & Franklin Wholesale Distributors Ltd. (1971), 16 C.R.N.S. 107, 3 C.C.C. (2d) 484 (B.C. C.A.) — The good part of a warrant may be severable from the bad part.

Return of Documents Seized Under Invalid Warrant

Bergeron v. Deschamps (1977), 33 C.C.C. (2d) 461 (S.C.C.) — When an illegal warrant is quashed on *certiorari* for vagueness, all documents seized and all extracts and copies must be returned to their owners. It is improper, in such a case, for P to be permitted to specify certain documents as required for use as evidence.

Dobney Foundry Ltd. v. Canada (A.G.) (No. 3) (1987), 29 C.C.C. (3d) 285 (B.C. C.A.); leave to appeal refused (1986), 29 C.C.C. (3d) 285n (S.C.C.) — Where search warrants were quashed by the court of appeal, it was appropriate to allow P 10 days to obtain a new search warrant before the documents were returned to their owners, as the owners had no need of the documents and P would have to obtain the documents from a number of locations if they were released and a new search warrant obtained.

Dobney Foundry Ltd. (No. 2) v. R. (1985), (sub nom. *Dobney Foundry Ltd. v. Canada A.G.))* 19 C.C.C. (3d) 465 (B.C. C.A.) — A reviewing court, on quashing a search warrant, has power to order *return* of any goods seized under the warrant. If P shows that the items seized are required to be retained for the purposes of a prosecution, either under a charge already laid or one intended to be laid in respect of a specified chargeable offence, the court may refuse to order the return.

Chapman v. R. (1984), 12 C.C.C. (3d) 1 (Ont. C.A.) — The court has a *discretion* after considering the circumstances surrounding the execution of an invalid warrant to order the *return* of items seized even if a charge has been laid and the item is required as evidence This authority existed prior to the *Charter* but is also available as a remedy under *Charter* s. 24(1).

Charter Considerations [See also Charter s. 8]

R. v. Wiley (1993), 24 C.R. (4th) 34, 84 C.C.C. (3d) 161 (S.C.C.) — See digest under *Charter*, s. 8, *infra*

R. v. Grant (1993), 24 C.R. (4th) 1, 84 C.C.C. (3d) 173 (S.C.C.); reversing (1992), 14 C.R. (4th) 260, 73 C.C.C. (3d) 315 (B.C. C.A.) — See digest under *Charter*, s. 8, *infra*

R. v. Debot (1986), 54 C.R. (3d) 120, 30 C.C.C. (3d) 207 (Ont. C.A.); affirmed (1989), 73 C.R. (3d) 129, 52 C.C.C. (3d) 193 (S.C.C.) — Although a mere conclusory statement made by an informer to a police officer would *not* constitute reasonable grounds, information supplied by a reliable informer, even though hearsay, may in some circumstances, provide the necessary "reasonable ground to believe" to justify a warrantless search where a warrantless search is authorized by law.

Hunter v. Southam Inc., (sub nom. Dir. of Investigation & Research, Combines Investigation Branch v. Southam Inc.) 41 C.R. (3d) 97, 14 C.C.C. (3d) 97 — A warrantless search is *prima facie* an unreasonable search under *Charter* s. 8. The party seeking to justify this warrantless search must rebut this presumption of unreasonableness. The prior authorization procedures mandated for searches under the *Combines Investigation Act* did not meet the minimum standards under the *Charter* for reasonableness and consequently a search under its authority was invalid under the *Charter*.

R. v. Gray (1993), 22 C.R. (4th) 114, 81 C.C.C. (3d) 174 (Man. C.A.) — See digest under "Duty of Justice: s. 487(1)", *supra*.

R. v. Tomaso (1989), 70 C.R. (3d) 152 (Ont. C.A.) — The collecting of a blood sample by a police officer by holding a collection chamber to D's ear while D was unconscious in hospital contravened s. 8. The sample results were excluded.

R. v. Zevallos (1987), 59 C.R. (3d) 153, 37 C.C.C. (3d) 79 (Ont. C.A.) — The issue of the sufficiency of the information to obtain a search warrant should be raised at trial as part of a general application to have the search found to be unreasonable contrary to *Charter* s. 8 and for the evidence to be excluded under *Charter* s. 24(2). A pre-trial quashing of the warrant may be appropriate if brought to prevent a search and seizure or to obtain the return of property seized.

R. v. Morrison (1987), 58 C.R. (3d) 63, 35 C.C.C. (3d) 437 (Ont. C.A.); reversing (1985), 45 C.R. (3d) 284, 20 C.C.C. (3d) 180 (Ont. H.C.) — *See also*: *R. v. Dombrowski* (1985), 44 C.R. (3d) 1, 18 C.C.C. (3d) 164 (Sask. C.A.) — A search is reasonable under *Charter* s. 8 if authorized by law, the law itself is reasonable and the manner of search was reasonable. As part of a lawful arrest, a peace officer has the right to search the arrested person and take any property which he reasonably believes is connected to the offence charged or may be used as evidence against the arrested person, or any instrument or weapon found upon the arrested person. The peace officer does not need to have reasonable grounds to believe that such weapons or evidence will be found.

R. v. Harris (1987), 57 C.R. (3d) 356, 35 C.C.C. (3d) 1 (Ont. C.A.); leave to appeal refused (1987), 61 C.R. (3d) xxixn, 38 C.C.C. (3d) vin (S.C.C.) — A search conducted under warrant issued upon information that did not set out facts upon which a justice acting judicially could be satisfied there were grounds for issuing the warrant or wholly failing to meet the minimum requirements of particularity respecting the things to be searched for and seized is also unreasonable under *Charter* s. 8. However, where the police acted in good faith believing that they were following proper procedures, and did not knowingly infringe D's constitutional rights, the administration of justice would not be brought into disrepute by admitting evidence seized under the invalid warrant.

R. v. Church of Scientology (1987), *(sub nom. R. v. Zaharia)* 31 C.C.C. (3d) 449 (Ont. C.A.); leave to appeal refused (1987), 23 O.A.C. 320n (S.C.C.) — The *Charter* does not specifically require particularity of description of the place to be searched and the persons or things to be seized. In this case there was no basis for requiring a rule of scrupulous exactitude simply because the search might involve intrusion into the protected area of freedom of religion.

Times Square Book Store v. R. (1985), 48 C.R. (3d) 132, *(sub nom. Marquis Video Corp. v. R.)* 21 C.C.C. (3d) 503 (Ont. C.A.) — This section complies with *Charter* s. 8 since a justice, an independent judicial officer, must be satisfied, on a balance of probabilities, that there is to be found, on specified premises, *evidence* that a criminal offence has been committed.

Kami-Mark (Marketing) Inc. v. Quebec (Procureur General) (1997), 118 C.C.C. (3d) 80 (Que. C.A.) — The absence of other sources of information is only one of many factors to consider in determining whether a search is unreasonable. It is not a condition imposed by *Charter* s. 8 for the issuance of a search warrant.

Related Provisions: "Justice" is defined in s. 2, but neither "building", "receptacle" or "place" is defined generally or for the purposes of Part XV.

Several sections authorize the issuance of specialized warrants, as for example, in respect of child pornography and obscene matter (s. 164), hate propaganda (s. 320), minerals and precious metals (s. 395) and weapons and ammunition (ss. 101–103). Provision is made for telewarrants in s. 487.1. Tracking warrants may be issued under s. 492.1 and number recorder warrants under s. 492.2. General investigative warrants, including video surveillance, may be obtained under s. 487.01.

The sections immediately following, ss. 488–492, deal with the execution of search warrants and disposal or detention of the things seized.

All searches and seizures must be reasonable to comply with *Charter* s. 8.

Articles seized, whether under warrant or otherwise, and retained as exhibits may be inspected by D without charge, after an order to stand trial has been made under s. 603. Scientific testing is permissible under s. 605.

487.01 (1) Information for general warrant — A provincial court judge, a judge of a superior court of criminal jurisdiction or a judge as defined in section 552 may issue a warrant in writing authorizing a peace officer to, subject to this section, use any device or investigative technique or procedure or do any thing described in the warrant that would, if not authorized, constitute an unreasonable search or seizure in respect of a person or a person's property if

(a) the judge is satisfied by information on oath in writing that there are reasonable grounds to believe that an offence against this or any other Act of Parliament has been or will be committed and that information concerning the offence will be obtained through the use of the technique, procedure or device or the doing of the thing;

(b) the judge is satisfied that it is in the best interests of the administration of justice to issue the warrant; and

(c) there is no other provision in this or any other Act of Parliament that would provide for a warrant, authorization or order permitting the technique, procedure or device to be used or the thing to be done.

(2) Limitation — Nothing in subsection (1) shall be construed as to permit interference with the bodily integrity of any person.

(3) Search or seizure to be reasonable — A warrant issued under subsection (1) shall contain such terms and conditions as the judge considers advisable to ensure that any search or seizure authorized by the warrant is reasonable in the circumstances.

(4) Video surveillance — A warrant issued under subsection (1) that authorizes a peace officer to observe, by means of a television camera or other similar electronic device, any person who is engaged in activity in circumstances in which the person has a reasonable expectation of privacy shall contain such terms and conditions as the judge considers advisable to ensure that the privacy of the person or of any other person is respected as much as possible.

(5) Other provisions to apply — The definition "offence" in section 183 and sections 183.1, 184.2, 184.3 and 185 to 188.2, subsection 189(5), and sections 190, 193 and 194 to 196 apply, with such modifications as the circumstances require, to a warrant referred to in subsection (4) as though references in those provisions to interceptions of private communications were read as references to observations by peace officers by means of television cameras or similar electronic devices of activities in circumstances in which persons had reasonable expectations of privacy.

(5.1) Notice after covert entry — A warrant issued under subsection (1) that authorizes a peace officer to enter and search a place covertly shall require, as part of the terms and conditions referred to in subsection (3), that notice of the entry and search be given within any time after the execution of the warrant that the judge considers reasonable in the circumstances.

(5.2) Extension of period for giving notice — Where the judge who issues a warrant under subsection (1) or any other judge having jurisdiction to issue such a warrant is, on the basis of an affidavit submitted in support of an application to vary the period within which the notice referred to in subsection (5.1) is to be given, is satisfied that the interests of justice warrant the granting of the application, the judge may grant an extension, or a subsequent extension, of the period, but no extension may exceed three years.

(6) Provisions to apply — Subsections 487(2) and (4) apply, with such modifications as the circumstances require, to a warrant issued under subsection (1).

(7) Telewarrant provisions to apply — Where a peace officer believes that it would be impracticable to appear personally before a judge to make an application for a warrant under this section, a warrant may be issued under this section on an information submitted by telephone or other means of telecommunication and, for that purpose, section 487.1 applies, with such modifications as the circumstances require, to the warrant.

1997, c. 18, s. 42; c. 23, s. 13.

Commentary: The section authorizes the issuance of a warrant which permits a peace officer to use any *device, investigative technique* or *procedure*, including video surveillance, which otherwise would constitute an unreasonable search or seizure. The descriptive "general warrant" conjures up visions of *carte blanche* authority, but an examination of the provision discloses nothing of the sort.

The procedure to obtain a s. 487.01 warrant is commenced by an *information on oath in writing* being laid before a *judge* of the *provincial* or *superior* court of criminal jurisdiction, or as defined in *Code* s. 552. There is *no* requirement that the informant be a peace or public officer, nor have any special designation to seek a warrant under this section. There is *no* prescribed form for the information, nor does the section expressly articulate what it shall contain.

Under s. 487.01(1), the judge to whom application is made must be satisfied by the *information on oath in writing* submitted that

i.   there are *reasonable grounds to believe* that an *offence* against the *Code* or other federal Act has been or will be committed;

ii.   there are *reasonable grounds to believe* that *information* concerning the offence will be obtained through the use of the technique, procedure or device, or the doing of the thing sought;

iii. it is in the *best interests of the administration of justice* to issue a warrant; and,

iv.   *no other* federal statutory *provision* authorizes what is sought.

The findings required should form the contents of the information on oath in writing since it constitutes the evidentiary predicate for the issuance of the warrant.

An investigative warrant issued under s. 487.01(1) must be in *writing* and directed to a peace officer. It authorizes the use of any device, investigative technique or procedure or the doing of any thing specified in the warrant which would constitute an unreasonable search or seizure in respect of a person or person's property if not authorized under the section. Under s. 487.01(2), it must *not* permit interference with the *bodily integrity* of any person. Section 487.01(3) permits inclusion of terms and conditions considered advisable to ensure the reasonableness of any search or seizure conducted.

In every covert entry warrant issued under s. 487.01(1), s. 487.01(5) requires that *notice* of the entry and search be given within whatever time *after* execution of the warrant that the authorizing judge considers *reasonable* in the circumstances. The period of notice may be varied by the authorizing or another judge on application under s. 487.01(5.2). The judge must be satisfied by an affidavit filed in support that the *interests of justice* warrant granting the application. No extension of further extension may exceed three years.

Specific provision is made in s. 487.01(4) and (5) for *video surveillance* warrants. The warrant is a species of s. 487.01(1) warrant. It authorizes a peace officer to observe, by means of a *television camera* or *other similar electronic device*, any person engaged in an activity in circumstances in which the person has a reasonable expectation of privacy. Section 487.01(5) incorporates by reference substantial portions of Part VI to video surveillance warrants as though references to interception of private communications were read as references to video surveillance observations. The purpose of the referential incorporation would appear to be to ensure parallel schemes for audio and video surveillance.

Section 487.01(7) permits recourse to informations submitted by telephone or other means of telecommunication where it is impracticable for the peace officer to appear personally before the authorizing judge. The telewarrant provisions of s. 487.1 apply.

Case Law

R. v. Noseworthy (1997), 116 C.C.C. (3d) 376 (Ont. C.A.) — A warrant under s. 487.01 may authorize re-seizure of items previously seized, but returned under another s. 487 warrant.

Related Provisions: In the absence of prescribed forms for informations and warrants under the section, Forms 1 and 5 may be adapted. The warrant may also include an *assistance order* under s. 487.02. Execution beyond the province of issue is governed by s. 487.03. The additional seizure and restitution provisions of ss. 489 and 489.1 apply to warrants issued under s. 487.01.

The provisions of Part VI incorporated by s. 487.01(5) in cases of video surveillance warrants include the specific definition of "offence" in s. 183, the effect of which is to limit such warrants to an "offence" as there described, rather than as in s. 487.01(1)(a). The other incorporated provisions of Part VI are, as follows:

i.   s. 183.1 *consent to interception*;

ii.   s. 184.2 *authorized consent* to interception;

iii.   s. 184.3 *tele-authorized consent* to interception;

iv.   s. 185 *application* and *affidavit* requirements for conventional authorization;

v.   s. 186 conventional authorization and renewals;

vi.   s. 187 *confidentiality* and disclosure of affidavit material;

vii.   s. 188 *emergency* authorization;

viii.   s. 188.1 *execution* of authorization;

ix.   s. 188.2 *protection* against civil or criminal liability;

ix.1   s. 189(5) *notice* of intention to produce evidence;

x.   s. 190 further *particulars* of evidence to be adduced;

xi.   s. 193 *disclosure* offence;

xii.   s. 194 punitive *damages*;

xiii.   s. 195 annual *report* of interception activity; and,

xiv.   s. 196 *notification* to objects of interception.

487.02 Assistance order — Where an authorization is given under section 184.2, 184.3, 186 or 188, a warrant is issued under this Act or an order is made under subsection 492.2(2), the judge or justice who gives the authorization, issues the warrant or makes the order may order any person to provide assistance, where the person's assis-

tance may reasonably be considered to be required to give effect to the authorization, warrant or order.

1993, c. 40, s. 15; 1997, c. 18, s. 43.

Commentary: The section permits designated authorizations, warrants and orders to include a term which orders any person to *provide assistance* where the person's assistance may *reasonably* be considered to be *required* to *give effect* to the authorization, warrant or order.

An assistance order is made by the judge who issues the authorization, warrant or order and should be based on facts disclosed in the supportive affidavit or information on oath.

Related Provisions: An assistance order under s. 487.02 may be included in any authorization issued under Part VI (s. 184.2, 184.3, 186 and 188), investigative, impression video surveillance, tracking and number recorder warrants under s. 487.01, 487.091, 492.1 and 492.2(1) or any other warrant under any other section of the *Code* and an order for production of telephone records under s. 492.2(2). Execution of assistance orders in provinces other than where the authorization or warrant was originally issued is governed by s. 188.1(2) and 487.03.

"Person" is defined in *Code* s. 2.

487.03 Execution in another province — Where

(a) a warrant is issued under section 487.01, 487.05 or 492.1 or subsection 492.2(1) in one province,

(b) it may reasonably be expected that the warrant is to be executed in another province, and

(c) the execution of the warrant would require entry into or on the property of any person in the other province or would require that an order be made under section 487.02 with respect to any person in that other province,

a judge or justice, as the case may be, in the other province may, on application, endorse the warrant and the warrant, after being so endorsed, has the same force in that other province as though it had originally been issued in that other province.

1993, c. 40, s. 15; 1995, c. 27, s. 1

Commentary: This provision governs *execution* of general investigative (including video surveillance), DNA and tracking warrants and orders for production of telephone records in provinces other than where issued, where entry or assistance orders are required.

The procedure involves "backing" the warrant or order in the province where it is to be executed. The provision applies to general investigative (including video surveillance), DNA and tracking warrants issued under s. 487.01, 487.05 and 492.1, as well as orders for delivery of telephone records under s. 492.2(2). "Backing" is required where it is *reasonable* to *expect* that the warrant issued in one province may be *executed* in *another*, where execution would require either entry into or upon the property of another person or a s. 487.02 assistance order in respect of any person.

"Backing" consists of *confirmation* of the warrant or order on application to a judge or justice in the province of execution. When "backed", the warrant or order has the same (full) force and effect in the province of execution as if issued there.

Related Provisions: The procedure is analogous to that of s. 487(2), in its effect similar to that provided in s. 487(4) in relation to conventional search warrants. A corresponding provision appears in s. 188.1(2) in relation to authorizations granted under Part VI, although s. 188.1(1) enacts a general rule that authorizations may be executed anywhere in Canada.

The *Code* provides no express authority to enter property or premises under s. 487.01, 492.1 or to make authorized interceptions under Part VI.

Forensic DNA Analysis

487.04 Definitions — In this section and sections 487.05 to 487.09, "adult" has the meaning assigned by subsection 2(1) of the *Young Offenders Act*;

"designated offence" means

(a) an offence under any of the following provisions of this Act, namely,

(i) section 75 (piratical acts),

(ii) section 76 (hijacking),

(iii) section 77 (endangering safety of aircraft or airport),

(iv) section 78.1 (seizing control of ship or fixed platform),

(v) paragraph 81(2)(a) (using explosives),

(vi) section 151 (sexual interference),

(vii) section 152 (invitation to sexual touching),

(viii) section 153 (sexual exploitation),

(ix) section 155 (incest),

(x) subsection 212(4) (offence in relation to juvenile prostitution),

(xi) section 220 (causing death by criminal negligence),

(xii) section 221 (causing bodily harm by criminal negligence),

(xiii) section 231 (murder),

(xiv) section 236 (manslaughter),

(xv) section 244 (causing bodily harm with intent),

(xvi) section 252 (failure to stop at scene of accident),

(xvii) section 266 (assault),

(xviii) section 267 (assault with a weapon or causing bodily harm),

(xix) section 268 (aggravated assault),

(xx) section 269 (unlawfully causing bodily harm),

(xxi) section 269.1 (torture),

(xxii) paragraph 270(1)(a) (assaulting a peace officer),

(xxiii) section 271 (sexual assault),

(xxiv) section 272 (sexual assault with a weapon, threats to a third party or causing bodily harm),

(xxv) section 273 (aggravated sexual assault),

(xxvi) section 279 (kidnapping),

(xxvii) section 279.1 (hostage taking),

(xxviii) section 344 (robbery),

(xxix) subsection 348(1) (breaking and entering with intent, committing offence or breaking out),

(xxx) subsection 430(2) (mischief that causes actual danger to life),

(xxxi) section 433 (arson — disregard for human life), and

(xxxii) section 434.1 (arson — own property),

(b) an offence under any of the following provisions of the *Criminal Code*, as they read from time to time before July 1, 1990, namely,

(i) section 433 (arson), and

(ii) section 434 (setting fire to other substance),

(c) an offence under the following provision of the *Criminal Code*, chapter C-34 of the Revised Statutes of Canada, 1970, as it read from time to time before January 1, 1988, namely, paragraph 153(1)(a) (sexual intercourse with stepdaughter, etc.),

(d) an offence under any of the following provisions of the *Criminal Code*, chapter C-34 of the Revised Statutes of Canada, 1970, as they read from time to time before January 4, 1983, namely,

   (i) section 144 (rape),

   (ii) section 146 (sexual intercourse with female under fourteen and between fourteen and sixteen), and

   (iii) section 148 (sexual intercourse with feeble-minded, etc.), and

(e) an attempt to commit an offence referred to in any of paragraphs (a) to (d);

Proposed Amendment — 487.04 "designated offence"

"designated offence" means a primary designated offence or a secondary designated offence;

1998, c. 37, s. 15 [Not in force at date of publication.]

"DNA" means deoxyribonucleic acid;

"forensic DNA analysis", in relation to a bodily substance that is obtained in execution of a warrant, means forensic DNA analysis of the bodily substance and the comparison of the results of that analysis with the results of the analysis of the DNA in the bodily substance referred to in paragraph 487.05(1)(b) and includes any incidental tests associated with that analysis;

Proposed Amendment — 487.04 "forensic DNA analysis"

"forensic DNA analysis"

   (a) in relation to a bodily substance that is taken from a person in execution of a warrant under section 487.05, means forensic DNA analysis of the bodily substance and the comparison of the results of that analysis with the results of the analysis of the DNA in the bodily substance referred to in paragraph 487.05(1)(b), and includes any incidental tests associated with that analysis, and

   (b) in relation to a bodily substance that is provided voluntarily in the course of an investigation of a designated offence or taken from a person in execution of an order under section 487.051 or 487.052 or under an authorization under section 487.055 or 487.091, or a bodily substance referred to in paragraph 487.05(1)(b), means forensic DNA analysis of the bodily substance;

1998, c. 38, s. 15 [Not in force at date of publication.]

Proposed definition — 487.04 "primary designated offence"

"primary designated offence" means

   (a) an offence under any of the following provisions, namely,

      (i) section 151 (sexual interference),

      (ii) section 152 (invitation to sexual touching),

      (iii) section 153 (sexual exploitation),

      (iv) section 155 (incest),

      (v) subsection 212(4) (offence in relation to juvenile prostitution),

      (vi) section 233 (infanticide),

(vii) section 235 (murder),

(viii) section 236 (manslaughter),

(ix) section 244 (causing bodily harm with intent),

(x) section 267 (assault with a weapon or causing bodily harm),

(xi) section 268 (aggravated assault),

(xii) section 269 (unlawfully causing bodily harm),

(xiii) section 271 (sexual assault),

(xiv) section 272 (sexual assault with a weapon, threats to a third party or causing bodily harm),

(xv) section 273 (aggravated sexual assault), and

(xvi) section 279 (kidnapping),

(b) an offence under any of the following provisions of the Criminal Code, chapter C-34 of the Revised Statutes of Canada, 1970, as they read from time to time before January 4, 1983, namely,

(i) section 144 (rape),

(ii) section 146 (sexual intercourse with female under fourteen and between fourteen and sixteen), and

(iii) section 148 (sexual intercourse with feeble-minded, etc.),

(c) an offence under paragraph 153(1)(a) (sexual intercourse with step-daughter, etc.) of the Criminal Code, chapter C-34 of the Revised Statutes of Canada, 1970, as it read from time to time before January 1, 1988, and

(d) an attempt to commit or, other than for the purposes of subsection 487.05(1), a conspiracy to commit an offence referred to in any of paragraphs (a) to (c);

1998, c. 38, s. 15 [Not in force at date of publication.]

"provincial court judge", in relation to a young person, includes a youth court judge within the meaning of subsection 2(1) of the *Young Offenders Act*.

Proposed definition — 487.04 "secondary designated offence"

"secondary designated offence" means

(a) an offence under any of the following provisions, namely,

(i) section 75 (piratical acts),

(ii) section 76 (hijacking),

(iii) section 77 (endangering safety of aircraft or airport),

(iv) section 78.1 (seizing control of ship or fixed platform),

(v) paragraph 81(1)(a) or (b) (using explosives),

(vi) subsection 160(3) (bestiality in the presence of or by child),

(vii) section 163.1 (child pornography),

(viii) section 170 (parent or guardian procuring sexual activity),

(ix) section 173 (indecent acts),

(x) section 220 (causing death by criminal negligence),

(xi) section 221 (causing bodily harm by criminal negligence),

(xii) subsection 249(3) (dangerous operation causing bodily harm),

(xiii) subsection 249(4) (danagerous operation causing death),

(xiv) section 252 (failure to stop at scene of accident),

(xv) subsection 255(2) (impaired driving causing bodily harm),

(xvi) subsection 255(3) (impaired driving causing death),

(xvii) section 266 (assault)

(xviii) section 269.1 (torture),

(xix) paragraph 270(1)(a) (assaulting a peace officer),

(xx) section 279.1 (hostage taking),

(xxi) section 344 (robbery),

(xxii) subsection 348(1) (breaking and entering with intent, committing offence or breaking out),

(xxiii) subsection 430(1) (mischief that causes actual danger to life),

(xxiv) section 433 (arson — disregard for human life), and

(xxv) section 434.1 (arson — own property),

(b) an offence under any of the following provisions of the *Criminal Code*, as they read from time to time before July 2, 1990, namely,

(i) section 433 (arson), and

(ii) section 434 (setting fire to other substance), and

(c) an attempt to commit or, other than for the purposes of subsection 487.05(1), a conspiracy to commit an offence referred to in paragraph (a) or (b);

1998, c. 37, s. 15 [Not in force at date of publication.]

"young person" has the meaning assigned by subsection 2(1) of the *Young Offenders Act.*

1995, c. 27, s. 1.

Commentary: This section defines terms used in sections 487.05–487.09

Related Provisions: Related provisions are described in the corresponding note to s. 487.05, *infra*.

487.05 (1) Information for warrant to obtain bodily substances for forensic DNA analysis — A provincial court judge who on *ex parte* application is satisfied by information on oath that there are reasonable grounds to believe

(a) that a designated offence has been committed,

(b) that a bodily substance has been found

(i) at the place where the offence was committed,

(ii) on or within the body of the victim of the offence,

(iii) on anything worn or carried by the victim at the time when the offence was committed, or

(iv) on or within the body of any person or thing or at any place associated with the commission of the offence,

(c) that a person was a party to the offence, and

(d) that forensic DNA analysis of a bodily substance from the person will provide evidence about whether the bodily substance referred to in paragraph (b) was from that person and who is satisfied that it is in the best interests of the administration of justice to do so may issue a warrant in writing authorizing a peace officer to obtain, or cause to be obtained under the direction of the peace officer, a bodily substance from that person, by means of an investigative procedure described in subsection 487.06(1), for the purpose of forensic DNA analysis.

Proposed Amendment — 487.05(1)

487.05 (1) Information for warrant to take bodily substances for forensic DNA analysis — A provincial court judge who on *ex parte* application made in Form 5.01 is satisfied by information on oath that there are reasonable grounds to believe

(a) that a designated offence has been committed,

(b) that a bodily substance has been found or obtained

(i) at the place where the offence was committed,

(ii) on or within the body of the victim of the offence,

(iii) on anything worn or carried by the victim at the time when the offence was committed, or

(iv) on or within the body of any person or thing or at any place associated with the commission of the offence,

(c) that a person was a party to the offence, and

(d) that forensic DNA analysis of bodily substance from the person will provide evidence about whether the bodily substance referred to in paragraph (b) was from that person

and who is satisfied that it is in the best interest of the administration of justice to do so may issue a warrant in Form 5.02 authorizing the taking, from that person, for the purpose of forensic DNA analysis, of any number of samples of one or more bodily substances that is reasonably required for that purpose, by means of the investigative procedures described in subsection 487.06(1).

1998, c. 37, s. 16(1) [Not in force at date of publication.]

(2) Criteria — In considering whether to issue the warrant, the provincial court judge shall have regard to all relevant matters, including

(a) the nature of the designated offence and the circumstances of its commission; and

(b) whether there is

(i) a peace officer who is able, by virtue of training or experience, to obtain a bodily substance from the person, by means of an investigative procedure described in subsection 487.06(1), or

(ii) another person who is able, by virtue of training or experience, to obtain under the direction of a peace officer a bodily substance from the person, by means of such an investigative procedure.

Proposed Amendment — 487.05(2)(i), (ii)

(i) a peace office who is able, by virtue of training or experience, to take samples of bodily substances from the person, by means of the investigative procedures described in subsection 487.06(1), or

> **(ii) another person who is able, by virtue of training or experience, to take, under the direction of a peace officer, samples of bodily substances from the person, by means of those investigative procedures.**
>
> 1998, c. 37, s. 16(2) [Not in force at date of publication.]

(3) Telewarrant — Where a peace officer believes that it would be impracticable to appear personally before a judge to make an application for a warrant under this section, a warrant may be issued under this section on an information submitted by telephone or other means of telecommunication and, for that purpose, section 487.1 applies, with such modifications as the circumstances require, to the warrant.

1995, c. 27, s. 1; 1997, c. 18, s. 44.

Commentary: This section describes the basis upon which a *warrant* may be issued to obtain a *bodily substance* from a person by means of an *investigative procedure* for the purpose of forensic DNA analysis.

Under s. 487.05(1), application for a DNA warrant is made *ex parte* to a *provincial court judge*, as defined in s. 487.04. The evidentiary basis of the application is an *information on oath*. Its contents must be sufficient to permit the provincial court judge to have a *reasonably grounded belief* of the matters described in paragraphs (1)(a)–(d), and that it would be in the *best interests* of the *administration* of *justice* to issue the warrant. In determining whether to issue the warrant, the provincial court judge is required to consider *all relevant* matters including, but *not* limited to those described in s. 487.05(2).

A warrant issued under s. 487.05(1) must be *in writing* and authorize a peace officer to obtain or cause to be obtained a *bodily substance* by a defined investigative procedure for the purpose of forensic DNA analysis.

Section 487.05(3) permits a warrant to be issued on an information submitted by telephone or other means of telecommunication. The provisions governing "telewarrants" in s. 487.1 apply for this purpose.

Related Provisions: "Designated offence", "DNA", "forensic DNA analysis" and "provincial court judge" are defined in s. 487.04.

Section 487.06 describes the investigative procedures which may be authorized under warrant. Execution of the warrant is governed by s. 487.07 and s. 487.03 which permits execution in another province in accordance with the "backing" procedure provided in the section. Section 487.08 imposes limitations upon the use of bodily substances and the results of forensic DNA analysis of substances obtained in execution of a DNA warrant. Destruction of the bodily substances and results of forensic DNA analysis is governed by s. 487.09.

Proposed Addition — 487.051- 487.058

487.051 Order — (1) Subject to section 487.053, if a person is convicted, discharged under section 730 or, in the case of a young person, found guilty under the *Young Offenders Act*, of a designated offence, the court

> **(a) shall, subject to subsection (2), in the case of a primary designated offence, make an order in Form 5.03 authorizing the taking, from that person, for the purpose of forensic DNA analysis, of any number of samples of one or more bodily substances that is reasonably required for that purpose, by means of the investigative procedures described in subsection 487.06(1); or**
>
> **(b) may, in the case of a secondary designated offence, make an order in Form 5.04 authorizing the taking of such samples if the court is satisfied that it is in the best interests of the administration of justice to do so.**

(2) Exception — The court is not required to make an order under paragraph (1)(a) if it is satisfied that the person or young person has established that, were the order made, the impact on the person's or young person's privacy and security of the person would be grossly disproportionate to the public interest in the protection of society and the proper administration of justice, to be achieved through the early detection, arrest and conviction of offenders.

(3) Criteria — In deciding whether to make an order under paragraph (1)(b), the court shall consider the criminal record of the person or young person, the nature of the offence and the circumstances surrounding its commission and the impact such an order would have on the person's or young person's privacy and security of the person and shall give reasons for its decision.

1998, c. 37, s. 17 [Not in force at date of publication.]

487.052 (1) Offences committed before DNA Identification Act in force — Subject to section 487.053, if a person is convicted, discharged under section 730 or, in the case of a young person, found guilty under the *Young Offenders Act*, of a designated offence committed before the coming into force of subsection 5(1) of the *DNA Identification Act* the court may, on application by the prosecutor, make an order in Form 5.04 authorizing the taking, from that person or young person, for the purpose of forensic DNA analysis, of any number of samples of one or more bodily substances that is reasonably required for that purpose, by means of the investigative procedures described in subsection 487.06(1), if the court is satisifed that it is in the best interests of the administration of justice to do so.

(2) Criteria — In deciding whether to make the order, the court shall consider the criminal record of the person or young person, the nature of the offence and the circumstances surrounding its commission and the impact such an order would have on the person's or young person's privacy and security of the person and shall give reasons for its decision.

1998, c. 37, s. 17 [Not in force at date of publication.]

487.053 No order — No court may make an order under section 487.051 or 487.052 in respect of a person or young person if the crout has been advised

(a) by the prosecutor, that a DNA profile, within the meaning of the *DNA Identification Act*, is not required for the purposes of that Act; or

(b) by the person or young person, that they consent to the entry, in the convicted offenders index of the national DNA data bank established under that Act, of the results of DNA analysis of bodily substances that were provided voluntarily in the course of the investigation of, or taken from them in execuction of a warrant that was issued under section 487.05 in respect of, the designated offence of which the person has been convicted, discharged under section 730 or, in the case of a young person, found guilty under the *Young Offenders Act*, or another designated offence in respect of the same transaction.

1998, c. 37, s. 17 [Not in force at date of publication.]

487.054 Appeal — The offender or the prosecutor may appeal from a decision of the court made under subsection 487.051(1) or 487.052(1).

1998, c. 37, s. 17 [Not in force at date of publication.]

487.055 (1) Offenders serving sentences — A provincial court judge may, on *ex parte* application made in Form 5.05, authorize, in Form 5.06, the taking, from a person who

(a) before the coming into force of this subsection, had been declared a dangerous offender under Part XXIV,

(b) before the coming into force of this subsection, had been convicted of more than one murder committed at different times, or

(c) before the coming into force of this subsection, had been convicted of more than one sexual offence within the meaning of subsection (3) and, on the date of the application, is serving a sentence of imprisonment of at least two years for one or more of those offences,

for the purpose of forensic DNA analysis, of any number of samples of one or more bodily substances that is reasonably required for that purpose, by means of the investigative procedures described in subsection 487.06(1).

(2) **Certificate** — The application shall be accompanied by a certificate referred to in paragraph 667(1)(a) establishing that the person is a person referred to in paragraph (1)(a) or (b), as the case may be,

(3) **Definition of "sexual offence"** — For the purposes of subsection (1), "sexual offence" means

(a) an offence under any of the following provisions, namely,

(i) section 151 (sexual interference),

(ii) section 152 (invitation to sexual touching),

(iii) section 153 (sexual exploitation),

(iv) section 155 (incest),

(v) subsection 212(4) (offence in relation to juvenile prostitution),

(vi) section 271 (sexual assault),

(vii) section 272 (sexual assault with a weapon, threats to a third party or causing bodily harm), and

(viii) section 273 (aggravated sexual assault);

(b) an offence under any of the following provisions of the *Criminal Code*, chapter C-34 of the Revised Statutes of Canada, 1970, as they read from time to time before January 4, 1983, namely,

(i) section 144 (rape),

(ii) section 146 (sexual intercourse with female under fourteen or between fourteen and sixteen), or

(iii) section 148 (sexual intercourse with feeble-minded, etc.);

(c) an offence under paragraph 153(1)(a) (sexual intercourse with step-daughter, etc.) of the *Criminal Code*, chapter C-34 of the Revised Statutes of Canada, 1970, as it read from time to time before January 1, 1988; and

(d) an attempt to commit an offence referred to in any of paragraphs (a) to (c).

(3.1) **Criteria** — In deciding whether to grant an authorization under subsection (1), the court shall consider the criminal record of the person, the nature of the offence and the circumstances surrounding its commission and the impact such an order would have on the person's privacy and security of the person and shall give reasons for its decision.

(4) **Summons** — A summons shall be directed to a person referred to in subsection (1), who is on conditional release requiring the person to report at the place, day and time set out in the summons in order to submit to the taking from the person of samples of bodily substances under an authorization granted under that subsection and setting out the matters referred to in paragraphs 487.07(1)(b) to (e).

(5) Service on individual — The summons shall be accompanied by a copy of the authorization referred to in subsection (1) and be served by a peace officer who shall either deliver it personally to the person to whom it is directed or, if that person cannot conveniently be found, leave it for the person at their latest or usual place of residence with any person found there who appears to be at least sixteen years of age.

(6) Proof of service — Service of a summons may be proved by the oral evidence, given under oath, of the peace officer who served it or by the peace officer's affidavit made before a justice of the peace or other person authorized to administer oaths or to take affidavits.

(7) Content of summons — The text of subsection (8) shall be set out in the summons.

(8) Failure to appear — If the person to whom a summons is directed does not report at the place, day and time set out in the summons, a justice of the peace may issue a warrant for the arrest of the person in order to allow the taking of samples of bodily substances from the person under the authorization.

(9) Contents of warrant to arrest — The warrant shall name or describe the person and order that the person be arrested without delay for the purpose of allowing the taking from them of samples of bodily substances under the authorization.

(10) No return day — A warrant issued under subsection (8) remains in force until it is executed and need not be made returnable at any particular time.

1998, c. 37, s. 17 [Not in force at date of publication.]

487.056 (1) When collection to take place — Samples of bodily substances referred to in sections 487.051 and 487.052 shall be taken at the time the person is convicted, discharged under section 730 or, in the case of a young person, found guilty under the *Young Offenders Act,* or as soon as is feasible afterwards, even though an appeal may have been taken.

(2) Collection under authorization — Samples of bodily substances referred to in section 487.055 shall be taken as soon as is feasible after the authorization referred to in that section is granted.

(3) Who collects — Samples of bodily substances referred to in sections 487.051, 487.052 and 487.055 shall be taken by a peace officer, or another person, who is able, by virtue of training or experience, to take them by means of the investigative procedures described in subsection 487.06(1).

1998, c. 37, s. 17 [Not in force at date of publication.]

487.057 (1) Report of peace officer — A peace officer who is authorized to take, or cause to be taken under the direction of the peace officer, samples of bodily substances from a person in execution of a warrant under section 487.05 or an order under section 487.051 or 487.052 or under an authorization under section 487.055 shall, as soon as is feasible after the samples have been so taken, make a written report in Form 5.07 and cause the report to be filed with

(a) the provincial court judge who issued the warrant or granted the authorization, or another judge of that provincial court; or

(b) the court that made the order.

(2) Contents of report — The report shall include

(a) a statement of the time and date the samples were taken; and

(b) a description of the bodily substances that were taken.

1998, c. 37, s. 17 [Not in force at date of publication.]

487.058 No criminal or civil liability — No peace officer or person acting under the direction of a peace officer incurs any criminal or civil liability for anything necessarily done with reasonable care and skill in the taking of samples of bodily substances from a person in execution of a warrant under section 487.05 or an order under section 487.051 or 487.052 or under an authorization under section 487.055.

1998, c. 37, s. 17 [Not in force at date of publication.]

487.06 (1) Investigative procedures — The warrant authorizes a peace officer or another person under the direction of a peace officer to obtain and seize a bodily substance from the person by means of

(a) the plucking of individual hairs from the person, including the root sheath;

(b) the taking of buccal swabs by swabbing the lips, tongue and inside cheeks of the mouth to collect epithelial cells; or

(c) the taking of blood by pricking the skin surface with a sterile lancet.

Proposed Amendment — 487.06(1)

487.06 (1) Investigative procedures — A peace officer or another person under the direction of a peace officer is authorized to take samples of bodily substances from a person by a warrant under section 487.05 or an order under section 487.051 or 487.052 or an authorization under section 487.055, by any of the following means:

1998, c. 37, s. 18 [Not in force at date of publication.]

(2) Terms and conditions — The warrant shall include any terms and conditions that the provincial court judge considers advisable to ensure that the seizure of a bodily substance authorized by the warrant is reasonable in the circumstances.

Proposed Amendment — 487.06(2)

(2) Terms and conditions — The warrant, order or authorization shall include any terms and conditions that the provincial court judge or court, as the case may be considers advisable to ensure that the taking of the samples authorized by the warrant, order or authorization is reasonable in the circumstances.

1998, c. 37, s. 18(3) [Not in force at date of publication.]

1995, c. 27, s. 1.

Commentary: This section describes what investigative procedures may be authorized under a s. 487.05 DNA warrant.

Under s. 487.06(1), a DNA warrant may authorize a peace officer or another person under his/her direction to obtain and seize a *bodily* substance from a person. The only investigative procedures which may be used are

i.   the *plucking* of individual *hairs*;

ii.   the *taking* of *buccal swabs*; or

iii. the *taking* of *blood*

in the manner described. The provincial court judge is required by s. 487.06(2) to include in the warrant any *terms* and *conditions* considered advisable to ensure that the seizure authorized is *reasonable* in the circumstances.

Related Provisions: The provisions eschew the approach of s. 186(4) which lists the contents of a conventional authorization to intercept private communications, and of s. 487(3) which permit the use of Form 5, varied to suit the case, for a conventional search warrant. It would seem desirable that a DNA warrant contain similar provisions which reflect, *inter alia*, the findings made, investigative procedures permitted and advice required by s. 487.07.

Other related provisions are discussed in the corresponding note to s. 487.05, *supra*.

487.07 (1) Execution of warrant — Before executing a warrant, a peace officer shall inform the person against whom it is to be executed of

(a) the contents of the warrant;

(b) the nature of the investigative procedure by means of which a bodily substance is to be obtained from that person;

(c) the purpose of obtaining a bodily substance from that person;

(d) the possibility that the results of forensic DNA analysis may be used in evidence;

(e) the authority of the peace officer and any other person under the direction of the peace officer to use as much force as is necessary for the purpose of executing the warrant; and

(f) in the case of a young person, the rights of the young person under subsection (4).

Proposed Amendment — 487.07(1)

(1) Duty to inform — Before taking samples of bodily substances from a person, or causing samples of bodily substances to be taken from a person under the direction of the peace officer, in execution of a warrant under section 487.05 or an order under section 487.051 or 487.052 or under an authorization under section 487.055, a peace officer shall inform the person from whom the samples are to be taken of

(a) the contents of the warrant, order or authorization;

(b) the nature of the investigative procedures by means of which the samples are to be taken;

(c) the purpose of taking the samples;

(d) the authority of the peace officer and any other person under the direction of the peace officer to use as much force as is necessary for the purpose of taking the samples;

(d.1) the possibility for the person to state their preference as to the bodily substance to be taken from the person; and

(e) in the case of samples of bodily substances taken in execution of a warrant,

(i) the possibility that the results of forensic DNA analysis may be used in evidence, and

(ii) if the sample is taken from a young person, the rights of the young person under subsection (4).

1998, c. 37, s. 19 [Not in force at date of publication.]

(2) Detention of person under warrant — A person against whom a warrant is executed

    (a) may be detained for the purpose of executing the warrant for a period that is reasonable in the circumstances for the purpose of obtaining a bodily substance from the person; and

    (b) may be required by the peace officer who executes the warrant to accompany the peace officer.

Proposed Amendment — 487.07(2)

(2) Detention of person — A person from whom samples of bodily substances are to be taken may

    (a) be detained for that purpose for a period that is reasonable in the circumstances; and

    (b) be required to accompany a peace officer for that purpose.

1998, c. 37, s. 19 [Not in force at date of publication.]

(3) Respect of privacy — A peace officer who executes a warrant against a person or a person who obtains a bodily substance from the person under the direction of the peace officer shall ensure that the privacy of that person is respected in a manner that is reasonable in the circumstances.

Proposed Amendment — 487.07(3)

(3) Respect of privacy — A peace officer who takes samples of bodily substances from a person, or a person who takes such samples from the person under the direction of a peace officer

    (a) shall ensure that the person's privacy is respected in a manner that is reasonable in the circumstances; and

    (b) shall take the person's preference into account as to the bodily substance to be taken before taking a bodily substance from the person.

1998, c. 37, s. 19 [Not in force at date of publication.]

(4) Execution of warrant against young person — A young person against whom a warrant is executed has, in addition to any other rights arising from his or her detention under the warrant,

    (a) the right to a reasonable opportunity to consult with, and

    (b) the right to have the warrant executed in the presence of

counsel and a parent or, in the absence of a parent, an adult relative or, in the absence of a parent and an adult relative, any other appropriate adult chosen by the young person.

(5) Waiver of rights of young person — A young person may waive his or her rights under subsection (4) but any such waiver

    (a) must be recorded on audio tape or video tape or otherwise; or

    (b) must be made in writing and contain a statement signed by the young person that he or she has been informed of the right being waived.

1995, c. 27, s. 1, 3.

Commentary: This section governs the execution of a warrant issued under s. 487.05.

Section 487.07(1) imposes upon the peace officer who executes a DNA warrant the *obligation to inform* the person against whom the warrant is executed of the matters described in the subsection. In the case of a *young person*, the informational obligations of the executing officer extend to the advice required by s. 487.07(1)(f) and (4).

Under s. 487.07(2), a peace officer may require the person who is the subject of the warrant to *accompany* the officer for the purpose of its execution. The officer may also *detain* the person for a period that is *reasonable in the circumstances* to obtain the relevant bodily substance. The executing officer, or his/her designate, is obliged by s. 487.07(3) to ensure that the subject's privacy is respected in a manner that is *reasonable* in the circumstances.

Related Provisions: The procedure to obtain a DNA warrant and the basis upon which it may be issued are described in s. 487.05.

Other related provisions are described in the corresponding note to s. 487.05, *supra*.

Proposed Addition — 487.01

487.071 (1) Transmission of results ot Commissioner — There shall be transmitted to the Commissioner of the Royal Canadian Mounted Police for entry in the convicted offenders index of the national DNA data bank established under the *DNA Identification Act* results of forensic DNA analysis of bodily substances that are

(a) Provided voluntarily in the course of an investigation of a designated offence by any person who is later convicted, discharged under section 730 or, in the case of a young person, found guilty under the *Young Offenders Act* of the designated offence or another designated offence in respect of the same transaction and who, having been so convicted, discharged or found guilty, consents to having the results entered in the convicted offenders index;

(b) taken in exeution of a warrant under section 487.05 from a person who is later convicted, discharged under section 730 or, in the case of young person, found guilty under the *Young Offenders Act* of the designated offence in respect of which the warrant was issued or another designated offence in respect of the same transaction and who, having been so convicted, discharged or found guilty, consents to having the results entered in the convicted offenders index;

(c) taken from a person in execution of an order under section 487.051 or 487.052; or

(d) taken from a person under an authorization under section 487.055 or 487.091.

(2) Transmission of bodily substances — Any portions of samples of bodily substances referred to in subsection (1) that are not used in forensic DNA analysis shall be transmitted to the Commission of the Royal Canadian Mounted Police for the purposes of the *DNA Identification Act*.

1998, c. 37, s. 20 [Not in force at date of publication.]

487.08 (1) Limitations on use of bodily substances — No person shall use a bodily substance that is obtained in execution of a warrant except in the course of an investigation of the designated offence for the purpose of forensic DNA analysis.

Proposed Amendment — 487.08(1), (1.1)

(1) Use of bodily substances — warrant — No person shall use bodily substances that are taken from a person in execution of a warrant under section 487.05 except

(a) to use them for the purpose of forensic DNA analysis in the course of an investigation of the designated offence; or

(b) to transmit any portions of samples of those bodily substances that are not used in forensic DNA analysis to the Commissioner of the Royal Canadian Mounted Police under subsection 487.071(2).

(1.1) Use of bodily substances — order, etc. — No person shall use bodily substances that are taken from a person in execution of an order under section 487.051 or 487.052 or under an authorization under section 487.055 except

(a) to use them for the purpose of forensic DNA analysis; or

(b) to transmit any portions of samples of those bodily substances that are not used in forensic DNA analysis to the Commissioner of the Royal Canadian Mounted Police under subsection 487.071(2).

1998, c. 37, s. 2(1) [Not in force at date of publication.]

(2) Limitations on use of results of forensic DNA analysis — No person shall use the results of forensic DNA analysis of a bodily substance that is obtained in execution of a warrant except in the course of an investigation of the designated offence or any other designated offence in respect of which a warrant was issued or a bodily substance found in the circumstances described in paragraph 487.05(1)(b) or in any proceeding for such an offence.

Proposed Amendment — 487.08(2), (2.1)

(2) Use of results — warrant — No person shall use the results of forensic DNA analysis of bodily substances that are taken from a person in execution of a warrant under section 487.05 except

(a) to use them

(i) in the course of an investigation of the designated offfence or any other designated offence in respect of which a warrant was issued or a bodily substance found in the circumstances described in paragraph 487.05(1)(b), or

(ii) in any proceeding for such an offence;

or

(b) to transmit them to the Commissioner of the Royal Canadian Mounted Police under subsection 487.071(1).

(2.1) Use of results — order, etc. — No person shall use the results of forensic DNA analysis of bodily substances that are taken from a person in execution of an order under section 487.051 or 487.052 or under an authorization under section 487.055 except to transmit them to the Commissioner of the Royal Canadian Mounted Police under subsection 487.071(1).

1998, c. 37, s. 2(1) [Not in force at date of publication.]

(3) Offence — Every person who contravenes subsection (1) or (2) is guilty of an offence punishable on summary conviction.

Proposed Addition — 487.08(4)

(4) Offence — Every person who contravenes subsection (1.1) or (2.1)

(a) is guilty of an indicatable offence and liable to imprisonment for a term not exceeding two years; or

(b) is guilty of an offence punishable on summary conviction and liable to a fine not exceeding $2,000 or to imprisonment for a term not exceeding six months, or to both.

1998, c. 37, s. 2(2) [Not in force at date of publication.]

1995, c. 27, s. 1.

Commentary: The section *restricts* investigative *use* of substances obtained under DNA warrant, as well the results of forensic DNA analysis. Contravention of the provisions, enacted to curtail DNA banking, is a summary conviction offence.

Section 487.08(1) prohibits use of *bodily substances* obtained in the execution of a DNA warrant. The use permitted by exception is offence and purpose specific. The bodily substance may be used in the course of an *investigation* of the *designated offence* for the *purpose* of forensic DNA analysis.

The prohibition of s. 487.08(2) is directed at the use of the *results of forensic DNA analysis*. The use permitted by exception is offence and a purpose specific, yet more expansive than that allowed for bodily substances. In addition to use in the course of an investigation of the designated offence, the *results* of forensic DNA analysis may be used in the course of

i.   an *investigation* of *any other designated offence* in respect of which a warrant was issued or a bodily substance found in a place, location or circumstances described in s. 487.05(1)(b); or

ii.   any *proceeding* for such an offence.

Related Provisions: "Designated offence" and "forensic DNA analysis"are defined in s. 487.04. Neither "investigation" nor "proceeding" is defined.

Destruction of bodily substances obtained under warrant and the results of forensic DNA analysis is governed by s. 487.09.

Other related provisions are described in the corresponding note to s. 487.05.

487.09 (1) **Destruction of bodily substances, etc.** — A bodily substance that is obtained from a person in execution of a warrant and the results of forensic DNA analysis shall be destroyed forthwith after

Proposed Amendment — 487.09(1)

487.09 (1) Destruction of bodily substances, etc. — warrant — Subject to subsection (2), bodily substances that are taken from a person in execution of a warrant under section 487.05 and the results of forensic DNA analysis shall be destroyed or, in the case of results in electronic form, access to those results shall be permanently removed, without delay after

1998, c. 37, s. 22 [Not in force at date of publication.]

(a) the results of that analysis establish that the bodily substance referred to in paragraph 487.05(1)(b) was not from that person;

(b) the person is finally acquitted of the designated offence and any other offence in respect of the same transaction otherwise than by reason of a verdict of not criminally responsible on account of mental disorder; or

Proposed Amendment — 487.09(1)(b)

(b) the person is finally acquitted of the designated offence and any other offence in respect of the same transaction; or

1998, c. 37, s. 22 [Not in force at date of publication.]

(c) the expiration of one year after

(i) the person is discharged after a preliminary inquiry into the designated offence or any other offence in respect of the same transaction,

(ii) the dismissal, for any reason other than acquittal, or the withdrawal of any information charging the person with the designated offence or any other offence in respect of the same transaction, or

(iii) any proceeding against the person for the offence or any other offence in respect of the same transaction is stayed under section 579 or under that section as applied by section 572 or 795,

unless during that year a new information is laid or an indictment is preferred charging the person with the designated offence or any other offence in respect of the same transaction or the proceeding is recommenced.

(2) **Exception** — Notwithstanding subsection (1), a provincial court judge may order that a bodily substance that is obtained from a person and the results of forensic DNA analysis not be destroyed during any period that the provincial court judge considers appropriate if the provincial court judge is satisfied that the bodily substance or results might reasonably be required in an investigation or prosecution of the person for another designated offence or of another person for the designated offence or any other offence in respect of the same transaction.

Proposed Amendment — 487.09(2), (3)

(2) **Exception** — A provincial court judge may order that the bodily substances that are taken from a person and the results of forensic DNA analysis not be destroyed during any period that the provincial court judge considers appropriate if the provincial court judge is satisfied that the bodily substances or results might reasonably be required in an investigation or prosecution of the person for another designated offence or of another person for the designated offence or any other offence in respect of the same transaction.

(3) **Destruction of bodily substances, etc. voluntarily given** — Bodily substances that are provided voluntarily by a person and the results of forensic DNA analysis shall be destroyed or, in the case of results in electronic form, access to those results shall be permanently removed, without delay after the results of that analysis establish that the bodily substance referred to in paragraph 487.05(1)(b) was not from that person.

1998, c. 37, s. 22(3) [Not in force at date of publication.]

1995, c. 27, s. 1.

Commentary: The section governs the *destruction* of bodily substances obtained under DNA warrant and the results of subsequent forensic DNA analysis.

Section 487.09(1) enacts the general rule. It requires *destruction* of the *bodily substance* and the *results of forensic DNA analysis* forthwith after *any* of the circumstances described in the section have occurred. No destruction is to occur, however, at the conclusion of the time period described in s. 487.09(1)(c), if a *new information* is laid or *indictment preferred* or *proceedings recommenced* charging the person whose bodily substance was seized with the designated offence, or any other offence in respect of the same transaction.

Section 487.09(2) permits a *provincial court judge* to make an order prohibiting destruction of

i. the *bodily substance*; and,

ii. the results of *forensic DNA analysis*

during a period considered appropriate, if the judge is satisfied that the bodily substance or results might *reasonably* be required in an *investigation* or a *prosecution* of the person for *another designated offence* or of *another person* for the designated offence or any other offence in respect of the same transaction.

Related Provisions: Section 487.08 imposes limitations on use of bodily substances obtained under DNA warrant and the results of forensic DNA analysis. Contravention of the limitations is a summary conviction offence under s. 487.08(3).

The phrase " ...any other offence in respect of the same transaction... " is similar to the language used in ss. 535 and 548(1), in relation to the inquiry and committal powers of a justice at preliminary inquiry, and s. 606(4) which authorizes pleas of guilty to offences other than those charged in a count.

Other related provision are described in the corresponding note to s. 487.05, *supra*.

487.091 (1) Information for impression warrant — A justice may issue a warrant in writing authorizing a peace officer to do any thing, or cause any thing to be done under the direction of the peace officer, described in the warrant in order to obtain any handprint, fingerprint, footprint, foot impression, teeth impression or other print or impression of the body or any part of the body in respect of a person if the justice is satisfied

(a) by information on oath in writing that there are reasonable grounds to believe that an offence against this or any other Act of Parliament has been committed and that information concerning the offence will be obtained by the print or impression; and

(b) that it is in the best interests of the administration of justice to issue the warrant.

(2) Search or seizure to be reasonable — A warrant issued under subsection (1) shall contain such terms and conditions as the justice considers advisable to ensure that any search or seizure authorized by the warrant is reasonable in the circumstances.

(3) Provisions to apply — Subsections 487(2) and (4) apply, with such modifications as the circumstances require, to a warrant issued under subsection (1).

(4) Telewarrant — Where a peace officer believes that it would be impracticable to appear personally before a justice to make an application for a warrant under this section, a warrant may be issued under this section on an information submitted by telephone or other means of telecommunication and, for that purpose, section 487.1 applies, with such modifications as the circumstances require, to the warrant.

1997, c. 18, s. 45.

Proposed Amendment — 487.091

Section 487.091 as enacted by 1997, c. 18, s. 45 is renumbered as section 487.092.

1998, c. 37, s. 23 [Not in force at date of publication.]

Commentary: The section authorizes a justice to issue a *print* or *impression* warrant.

Application for the warrant is based upon an *information on oath* in *writing* or, where personal *attendance* of the informant is *impracticable*, an information submitted by *telephone* or other means of telecommunication. The information of the peace officer must satisfy the justice that

i.   there are *reasonable grounds* to believe that an *offence* against the *Code* or other federal statute has been committed;

ii.   there are *reasonable grounds* to believe that *information* concerning the offence *will* be obtained by the print or impression sought; and,

iii. it is in the *best interests* of the administration of justice to issue the warrant.

The warrant may be in Form 5, varied to suit the case. It may authorize a peace officer, or someone under the direction of a peace officer, to do or cause anything to be done in order to obtain any listed or other print or impression of the body or part of the body of a person. Section 487.091(2) requires the warrant to contain such *terms* and *conditions* as the justice considers advisable to ensure the reasonableness of the search or seizure.

Section 487.091(3) and 487(2) permit a print or impression warrant to be issued for a person who is believed to be in a territorial division other than where the warrant is issued. The warrant may be executed in the other jurisdiction when endorsed by a justice there in Form 28.

Related Provisions: Issuance of a conventional search warrant is governed by s. 487 and a telewarrant by s. 487.1.

"Information concerning the offence. . .", as used in s. 487.091(1)(a), is a broader term than "evidence", a *fortiori* "admissible evidence".

Other specialized warrants are discussed in the corresponding note to s. 487, *supra*.

Proposed Addition — 487.091

Note section 487.091 as enacted by 1997, c. 18, s. 45 is renumbered as section 487.092 by 1998, c. 37, s. 23 and a new section 487.091 enacted.

487.091 (1) Collection of additional bodily substances — If a DNA profile could not be derived from the bodily substances that were taken from a person in execution of an order under section 487.051 or 487.052 or under an authorization under section 487.055, a provincial court judge may, on *ex parte* application made in Form 5.08 within a reasonable time after it is determined that the DNA profile could not be derived, grant an authorization in Form 5.09 authorizing the taking, from that person, for the purpose of forensic DNA analysis, of any number of additional samples of bodily substances that is required for that purpose, by means of the investigative procedures described in subsection 487.06(1).

(2) Reasons — The application shall state the reasons why a DNA profile could not be derived from the bodily substances that were taken from the person under the initial order or authorization.

(3) Application of certain provisions — The following provisions apply, with any modifications that the circumstances require, in respect of an authorization under this section:

(a) subsections 487.055(4) to (10);

(b) subsections 487.056(2) and (3);

(c) sections 487.057, 487.058 and 487.06;

(d) subsections 487.07(1) to (3);

(e) section 487.071; and

(f) subsections 487.08(1.1) and (2.1) and (4).

1998, c. 37, s. 23 [Not in force at date of publication.]

487.1 (1) Telewarrants — Where a peace officer believes that an indictable offence has been committed and that it would be impracticable to appear personally before a justice to make application for a warrant in accordance with section 256 or 487, the peace officer may submit an information on oath by telephone or other means of telecommunication to a justice designated for the purpose by the chief judge of the provincial court having jurisdiction in the matter.

(2) Information on oath and record — An information submitted by telephone or other means of telecommunication, other than a means of telecommunication that produces a writing, shall be on oath and shall be recorded verbatim by the justice, who shall, as soon as practicable, cause to be filed, with the clerk of the court for the territorial division in which the warrant is intended for execution, the record or a transcription of it, certified by the justice as to time, date and contents.

(2.1) Information submitted by other means of telecommunication — The justice who receives an information submitted by a means of telecommunication that produces a writing shall, as soon as practicable, cause to be filed, with the clerk of the court for the territorial division in which the warrant is intended for execution, the information certified by the justice as to time and date of receipt.

(3) Administration of oath — For the purposes of subsection (2), an oath may be administered by telephone or other means of telecommunication.

(3.1) Alternative to oath — A peace officer who uses a means of telecommunication referred to in subsection (2.1) may, instead of swearing an oath, make a statement in writing stating that all matters contained in the information are true to his or her knowledge and belief and such a statement is deemed to be a statement made under oath.

(4) Contents of information — An information submitted by telephone or other means of telecommunication shall include

(a) a statement of the circumstances that make it impracticable for the peace officer to appear personally before a justice;

(b) a statement of the indictable offence alleged, the place or premises to be searched and the items alleged to be liable to seizure;

(c) a statement of the peace officer's grounds for believing that items liable to seizure in respect of the offence alleged will be found in the place or premises to be searched; and

(d) a statement as to any prior application for a warrant under this section or any other search warrant, in respect of the same matter, of which the peace officer has knowledge.

(5) Issuing warrant — A justice referred to in subsection (1) who is satisfied that an information submitted by telephone or other means of telecommunication

(a) is in respect of an indictable offence and conforms to the requirements of subsection (4),

(b) discloses reasonable grounds for dispensing with an information presented personally and in writing, and

(c) discloses reasonable grounds, in accordance with subsection 256(1) or paragraph 487(1)(a), (b) or (c), as the case may be, for the issuance of a warrant in respect of an indictable offence,

may issue a warrant to a peace officer conferring the same authority respecting search and seizure as may be conferred by a warrant issued by a justice before whom the peace officer appears personally pursuant to subsection 256(1) or 487(1), as the case may be, and may require that the warrant be executed within such period as the justice may order.

(6) Formalities respecting warrant and facsimiles — Where a justice issues a warrant by telephone or other means of telecommunication, other than a means of telecommunication that produces a writing,

(a) the justice shall complete and sign the warrant in Form 5.1, noting on its face the time, date and place of issuance;

(b) the peace officer, on the direction of the justice, shall complete, in duplicate, a facsimile of the warrant in Form 5.1, noting on its face the name of the issuing justice and the time, date and place of issuance; and

(c) the justice shall, as soon as practicable after the warrant has been issued, cause the warrant to be filed with the clerk of the court for the territorial division in which the warrant is intended for execution.

(6.1) **Issuance of warrant where telecommunication produces writing** — Where a justice issues a warrant by a means of telecommunication that produces a writing,

(a) the justice shall complete and sign the warrant in Form 5.1, noting on its face the time, date and place of issuance;

(b) the justice shall transmit the warrant by the means of telecommunication to the peace officer who submitted the information and the copy of the warrant received by the peace officer is deemed to be a facsimile within the meaning of paragraph (6)(*b*);

(c) the peace officer shall procure another facsimile of the warrant; and

(d) the justice shall, as soon as practicable after the warrant has been issued, cause the warrant to be filed with the clerk of the court for the territorial division in which the warrant is intended for execution.

(7) **Providing facsimile** — A peace officer who executes a warrant issued by telephone or other means of telecommunication, other than a warrant issued pursuant to subsection 256(1), shall, before entering the place or premises to be searched or as soon as practicable thereafter, give a facsimile of the warrant to any person present and ostensibly in control of the place or premises.

(8) **Affixing facsimile** — A peace officer who, in any unoccupied place or premises, executes a warrant issued by telephone or other means of telecommunication, other than a warrant issued pursuant to subsection 256(1), shall, on entering the place or premises or as soon as practicable thereafter, cause a facsimile of the warrant to be suitably affixed in a prominent place within the place or premises.

(9) **Report of peace officer** — A peace officer to whom a warrant is issued by telephone or other means of telecommunication shall file a written report with the clerk of the court for the territorial division in which the warrant was intended for execution as soon as practicable but within a period not exceeding seven days after the warrant has been executed, which report shall include

(a) a statement of the time and date the warrant was executed or, if the warrant was not executed, a statement of the reasons why it was not executed;

(b) a statement of the things, if any, that were seized pursuant to the warrant and the location where they are being held; and

(c) a statement of the things, if any, that were seized in addition to the things mentioned in the warrant and the location where they are being held, together with a statement of the peace officer's grounds for believing that those additional things had been obtained by, or used in, the commission of an offence.

(10) **Bringing before justice** — The clerk of the court shall, as soon as practicable, cause the report, together with the information and the warrant to which it pertains, to be brought before a justice to be dealt with, in respect of the things seized referred to in the report, in the same manner as if the things were seized pursuant to a warrant is-

sued, on an information presented personally by a peace officer, by that justice or another justice for the same territorial division.

(11) Proof of authorization — In any proceeding in which it is material for a court to be satisfied that a search or seizure was authorized by a warrant issued by telephone or other means of telecommunication, the absence of the information or warrant, signed by the justice and carrying on its face a notation of the time, date and place of issuance, is, in the absence of evidence to the contrary, proof that the search or seizure was not authorized by a warrant issued by telephone or other means of telecommunication.

(12) Duplicates and facsimiles acceptable — A duplicate or a facsimile of an information or a warrant has the same probative force as the original for the purposes of subsection (11).

R.S. 1985, c. 27 (1st Supp.), s. 69; 1992, c. 1, s. 58(1), Schedule I, items 9, 18; 1994 c. 44 s. 37.

Commentary: The section provides a self-contained code authorizing the *issuance* and *execution* of *telewarrants*.

The *issuance of a telewarrant* is founded upon an *information on oath*, submitted by telephone or other means of telecommunication under s. 487.1(1), containing the matters described in s. 487.1(4). The *oath* may be administered, under s. 487.1(3), by telephone or other means of telecommunication. The warrant must relate to an indictable *offence* the officer believes *has* been committed. The information must be submitted to and recorded verbatim by the justice who has been designated for the purpose by the chief judge of the provincial court having jurisdiction under ss. 487.1(1) and (2). The application is made in accordance with the provisions of s. 256 or 487. Under s. 487.1(2) the justice must, as soon as practicable, cause to be filed with the clerk of the court for the territorial division where the warrant is intended for execution, the record or transcription of the information on oath, including a certification by the justice of time, date and contents.

Where the means of telecommunications used produces a writing, s. 487.1(3.1) permits a statement in writing to substitute for an oath. Where the statement indicates that all matters contained in the information are true to the officer's knowledge and belief, the statement is deemed to be a statement made under oath. Section 487.1(2.1) requires the justice to file the information in writing certified by the justice as to time and date of receipt.

The *findings* requisite to permit the issuance of a telewarrant are described in s. 487.1(5). The telewarrant confers the same search and seizure authority as is given under ss. 256 and 487(1).

The determination to issue a telewarrant requires the completion of the warrant, a facsimile thereof and the expeditious filing of the original warrant in Form 5.1 with the clerk of the court in the territorial division in which it was issued under s. 487.1(6).

Where the warrant has been issued by means of a telecommunication that produces a writing, the justice and peace officer must comply with the requirements of s. 487.1(6.1).

Sections 487.1(7) and (8) describe the *manner* in which the telewarrant is to be *executed* in occupied (s. 487.1(7)) and unoccupied (s. 487.1(8)) premises. A report must then be made under s. 487.1(9) and, together with the information on oath and warrant, be brought by the clerk of the court before a justice under s. 487.1(10).

Section 487.1(11) enacts an *evidentiary presumption* applicable in proceedings where it is material for a court to be satisfied that a search or seizure was authorized by telewarrant. The *absence* of the information on oath, transcribed and certified by the justice under s. 487.1(2), or of the original warrant, signed and completed under s. 487.1(6), is, in the *absence of evidence* to the *contrary, proof* that the search or seizure was *not authorized* by telewarrant.

Section 487.1(12) equates the *probative force* of duplicate or facsimile informations and warrants with that of the original.

Related Provisions: "Peace officer", "justice" and "clerk of the court" are defined in s. 2. "Telecommunication" is defined in *I.A.* s. 35(1).

An "indictable offence" for the purposes of ss. 487.1(1), (4) and (5) includes offences triable either way under s. *I.A.* s. 35(1)(a).

All searches must be *reasonable* to comply with *Charter* s. 8.

487.11 Where warrant not necessary — A peace officer, or a public officer who has been appointed or designated to administer or enforce any federal or provincial law and whose duties include the enforcement of this or any other Act of Parliament, may, in the course of his or her duties, exercise any of the powers described in subsection 487(1) or 492.1(1) without a warrant if the conditions for obtaining a warrant exist but by reason of exigent circumstances it would be impracticable to obtain a warrant.
1997, c. 18, s. 46.

Commentary: The section enacts an exigent circumstances exception to the warrant requirements of s. 487 (conventional search warrant) and s. 492.1 (tracking warrant).

Provided the conditions for obtaining the relevant warrant exist, but it is impracticable to do so because of exigent circumstances, a peace or public officer whose duties include federal statute enforcement may exercise any of the powers usually given under the warrant.

Related Provisions: The scope of authority furnished by ss. 487 and 492.1 warrants is discussed in the *Commentary* to each section.

Similar "exigent circumstances" provisions appear in s. 529.3 which permits a non-warranted entry into a dwelling-house to arrest or apprehend a person without warrant. The definition of "exigent circumstances" contained in s. 529.3(2) is limited in its application to the section.

487.2 (1) Restriction on publicity — Where a search warrant is issued under section 487 or 487.1 or a search is made under such a warrant, every one who publishes in any newspaper or broadcasts any information with respect to

   (a) the location of the place searched or to be searched, or

   (b) the identity of any person who is or appears to occupy or be in possession or control of that place or who is suspected of being involved in any offence in relation to which the warrant was issued,

without the consent of every person referred to in paragraph (*b*) is, unless a charge has been laid in respect of any offence in relation to which the warrant was issued, guilty of an offence punishable on summary conviction.

(2) Definition of "newspaper" — In this section, "newspaper" has the same meaning as in section 297.
R.S. 1985, c. 27 (1st Supp.), s. 69.

Commentary: The section prohibits publication or broadcast of certain information relating to warranted searches.

The *prohibition* of s. 487.2(1) applies with equivalent force where a conventional search warrant or telewarrant has been issued, or a search actually made under such a warrant. There must be *no* newspaper publication or broadcast of *any* information with respect to the matters described in s. 487.2(a) or (b), without the consent of everyone described in s. 487.2(b). In general, the information suppressed relates to the *location* of the place of search and the *identity* of anyone in occupation, possession or control thereof or suspected of involvement in an offence described in the warrant. The prohibition does *not* apply, however, where a charge has been laid in respect of *any offence in relation to which the warrant was issued.*

Section 487.2(2) defines "newspaper" in the same terms as it is described in s. 297 (defamatory libel). The section has attracted *Charter* s. 2(b) scrutiny.

Case Law

Cdn. Newpapers Co. v. Canada (A.G.) (1986), 53 C.R. (3d) 203, 29 C.C.C. (3d) 109 (Ont. H.C.) — *See also*: *Cdn. Newpapers Co. v. Canada (A.G.)* (1986), 28 C.C.C. (3d) 379 (Man. Q.B.) — Subsection (1) violates the freedom of expression guarantee of *Charter* s. 2(b) and is *not* justified under *Charter* s. 1.

Related Provisions: This section *only* applies to search warrants issued under ss. 487 and 487.1. It does *not* apply to any other form of warrant, for example the special warrants of ss. 199(1), 320(1) and 395(1).

487.3 (1) Order denying access to information used to obtain any warrant — A judge or justice may, on application made at the time of issuing a warrant under this or any other Act of Parliament or of granting an authorization to enter a dwelling-house under section 529 or an authorization under section 529.4 or at any time thereafter, make an order prohibiting access to and the disclosure of any information relating to the warrant or authorization on the ground that

(a) the ends of justice would be subverted by the disclosure for one of the reasons referred to in subsection (2) or the information might be used for an improper purpose; and

(b) the ground referred to in paragraph (*a*) outweighs in importance the access to the information.

(2) Reasons — For the purposes of paragraph (1)(*a*), an order may be made under subsection (1) on the ground that the ends of justice would be subverted by the disclosure

(a) if disclosure of the information would

(i) compromise the identity of a confidential informant,

(ii) compromise the nature and extent of an ongoing investigation,

(iii) endanger a person engaged in particular intelligence-gathering techniques and thereby prejudice future investigations in which similar techniques would be used, or

(iv) prejudice the interests of an innocent person; and

(b) for any other sufficient reason.

(3) Procedure — Where an order is made under subsection (1), all documents relating to the application shall, subject to any terms and conditions that the justice or judge considers desirable in the circumstances, including, without limiting the generality of the foregoing, any term or condition concerning the duration of the prohibition, partial disclosure of a document, deletion of any information or the occurrence of a condition, be placed in a packet and sealed by the justice or judge immediately on determination of the application, and that packet shall be kept in the custody of the court in a place to which the public has no access or in any other place that the justice or judge may authorize and shall not be dealt with except in accordance with the terms and conditions specified in the order or as varied under subsection (4).

(4) Application for variance of order — an application to terminate the order or vary any of its terms and conditions may be made to the justice or judge who made the order or a judge of the court before which any proceedings arising out of the investigation in relation to which the warrant was obtained maybe held.

1997, c. 23, s. 14; c. 39, s. 1.

Commentary: The section permits sealing orders in relation to warrants issued under the *Code* and other federal statutes and authorizations to enter dwelling-houses under ss. 529 and 529.4.

A *sealing* order prohibits access to and disclosure of any information relating to a warrant. All documents relating to the application are to be placed in a packet and sealed by the judge or justice immediately on deciding the application. The packet is then kept in the custody of the court in a place which is not publicly accessible, or as otherwise ordered. Section 487.3(3) permits the imposition of terms or conditions in the sealing order.

The order may be granted by a judge or justice at the *time* the warrant is *issued*, or *at any time thereafter*, and varied or terminated by the issuing or other authority under s. 487.3(4).

The *grounds* upon which a sealing order may be made are described in ss. 487.3(1) and (5). They involve, first, a determination that the *ends of justice* would be subverted by disclosure for any reason described in s. 487.3(2), or that the information might be used for an *improper purpose*. The judge or justice must then balance the interest just described against (public) interest in access to the information, and conclude that the interest in non-disclosure prevails.

Case Law

General Principles

R. v. Flahiff (1998), 123 C.C.C. (3d) 79 (Que. C.A.); application for leave to appeal , Doc. 26502 (S.C.C.) — A judge's discretion under s. 487.3 must be judicially exercised in accordance with the section's requirements and with due regard for

i.   D's right to a fair trial; and

ii.   freedom of the pres..

Any Other Sufficient Reason

R. v. Flahiff (1998), 123 C.C.C. (3d) 79 (Que. C.A.); application for leave to appeal , Doc. 26502 (S.C.C.) — A serious threat to the fairness of a trial constitutes a "sufficient reason" for a publication ban.

Related Provisions: The section applies to warrants issued under any federal statute, as well as s. 529 authorizations. Authorizations to intercept private communications are governed by the secrecy provisions of s. 187.

Cases which consider disclosure of material filed in support of a search warrant are digested under s. 487 "Disclosure", *supra*.

488. Execution of search warrant — **A warrant issued under section 487 or 487.1 shall be executed by day, unless**

    (a) the justice is satisfied that there are reasonable grounds for it to be executed by night;

    (b) the reasonable grounds are included in the information; and

    (c) the warrant authorizes that it be executed by night.

R.S., c. C-34, s. 44;R.S. 1985, c. 27 (1st Supp.), s.70; 1997, c. 18, s. 47.

Commentary: A conventional search warrant or telewarrant must generally be executed by day. Execution by night, however, is permissible, where the issuing justice is satisfied that there are reasonable grounds, that these grounds are in the information and that the issuing justice has expressly so authorized.

Case Law

Extended Period

R. v. Coull (1986), 33 C.C.C. (3d) 186 (B.C. C.A.) — A search warrant may be issued for an extended period of time where it authorizes only one search. The effect of the extended warrant is to give the police greater latitude as to when to execute the warrant, as for example at a time when the suspect was present.

Expiry of Warrant

R. v. Moran (1987), 36 C.C.C. (3d) 225 (Ont. C.A.) — When the warrant expires or the search is completed, the right of the police to be on the D's premises terminates. They become, thereafter, trespassers at common law.

Related Provisions: "Day" and "night" are defined in s. 2.

This section, like s. 487.2, only applies in respect of the general search warrants or telewarrants given under ss. 487 and 487.1. It has no application to specialized warrants.

488.1 (1) Definitions — In this section,

"custodian" means a person in whose custody a package is placed pursuant to subsection (2);

"document" for the purposes of this section, has the same meaning as in section 321;

"judge" means a judge of a superior court of criminal jurisdiction of the province where the seizure was made;

"lawyer" means, in the Province of Quebec, an advocate, lawyer or notary and, in any other province, a barrister or solicitor;

"officer" means a peace officer or public officer.

(2) Examination or seizure of certain documents where privilege claimed — Where an officer acting under the authority of this or any other Act of Parliament is about to examine, copy or seize a document in the possession of a lawyer who claims that a named client of his has a solicitor-client privilege in respect of that document, the officer shall, without examining or making copies of the document,

(a) seize the document and place it in a package and suitably seal and identify the package; and

(b) place the package in the custody of the sheriff of the district or county in which the seizure was made or, if there is agreement in writing that a specified person act as custodian, in the custody of that person.

(3) Application to judge — Where a document has been seized and placed in custody under subsection (2), the Attorney General or the client or the lawyer on behalf of the client, may

(a) within fourteen days from the day the document was so placed in custody apply, on two days notice of motion to all other persons entitled to make application to a judge for an order

(i) appointing a place and a day, not later than twenty-one days after the date of the order, for the determination of the question whether the document should be disclosed, and

(ii) requiring the custodian to produce the document to the judge at that time and place;

(b) serve a copy of the order on all other persons entitled to make application and on the custodian within six days of the date on which it was made; and

(c) if he has proceeded as authorized by paragraph (b), apply, at the appointed time and place, for an order determining the question.

(4) Disposition of application — On an application under paragraph (3)(c), the judge

(a) may, if the judge considers it necessary to determine the question whether the document should be disclosed, inspect the document;

(b) where the judge is of the opinion that it would materially assist him in deciding whether or not the document is privileged, may allow the Attorney General to inspect the document;

(c) shall allow the Attorney General and the person who objects to the disclosure of the document to make representations; and

(d) shall determine the question summarily and,

(i) if he is of the opinion that the document should not be disclosed, ensure that it is repackaged and resealed and order the custodian to deliver the document to the lawyer who claimed the solicitor-client privilege or to his client, or

(ii) if he is of the opinion that the document should be disclosed, order the custodian to deliver the document to the officer who seized the document or some other person designated by the Attorney General, subject to such restrictions or conditions as the judge deems appropriate,

and shall, at the same time, deliver concise reasons for the determination in which the nature of the document is described without divulging the details thereof.

(5) Privilege continues — Where the judge determines pursuant to paragraph (4)(*d*) that a solicitor-client privilege exists in respect of a document, whether or not he has, pursuant to paragraph (4)(*b*), allowed the Attorney General to inspect the document, the document remain privileged and inadmissible as evidence unless the client consents to its admission in evidence or the privilege is otherwise lost.

(6) Order to custodian to deliver — Where a document has been seized and placed in custody under subsection (2) and a judge, on the application of the Attorney General, is satisfied that no application has been made under paragraph (3)(*a*) or that following such an application no further application has been made under paragraph (3)(*c*), the judge shall order the custodian to deliver the document to the officer who seized the document or to some other person designated by the Attorney General.

(7) Application to another judge — Where the judge to whom an application has been made under paragraph (3)(*c*) cannot act or continue to act under this section for any reason, subsequent applications under that paragraph may be made to another judge.

(8) Prohibition — No officer shall examine, make copies of or seize any document without affording a reasonable opportunity for a claim of solicitor-client privilege to be made under subsection (2).

(9) Authority to make copies — At any time while a document is in the custody of a custodian under this section, a judge may, on an *ex parte* application of a person claiming a solicitor-client privilege under this section, authorize that person to examine the document or make a copy of it in the presence of the custodian or the judge, but any such authorization shall contain provisions to ensure that the document is repackaged and that the package is resealed without alteration or damage.

(10) Hearing in private — An application under paragraph (3)(*c*) shall be heard in private.

(11) Exception — This section does not apply in circumstances where a claim of solicitor-client privilege may be made under the *Income Tax Act*.

R.S. 1985, c. 27 (1st Supp.), s. 71.

Commentary: The section enacts a *procedure* to determine *claims of solicitor-client privilege* in relation to documents seized by a peace or public officer under authority of any federal statute, except the *Income Tax Act* which contains its own provisions.

Under s. 488.1(2), an officer acting under federal authority who is *about to* examine, copy or seize a document *in the possession of a lawyer* who asserts, on behalf of a *named client*, solicitor-client privilege in respect of such document, is obliged, *without examining or copying* the document, to *seize* the document, place it in a suitably *sealed and identified* package and turn it over to the *custody* of the *sheriff* of the county or district of seizure, or to a *custodian* designated in writing by *agreement* of the parties. Under s. 488.1(8), the officer must first afford a *reasonable opportunity* to *assert a claim* of solicitor-client privilege before examining, making copies or seizing any document in the possession of a lawyer.

The *procedure* to be followed to determine a claim of solicitor-client privilege involves a series of steps under ss. 488.1(3)–(6) *after seizure* of the document *and* its *delivery* to the custodian. Initially, the Attorney General, client or lawyer on behalf of the client, may bring an *application* to a judge of the superior court of criminal jurisdiction in the province of seizure, for an *order* appointing a *place and date* for *determination* of the issue, and *requiring* the *custodian* to *produce* the document to the judge. Service of the order fixing a place and date for determination must be made on all others entitled to apply under s. 488.1(3)(b). Upon the application to determine the issue of solicitor-client privilege the judge may *inspect* the document, as well as allow the Attorney General to do so, if it would materially assist the determination of the issue. Representations are required of the Attorney General and the person objecting to disclosure. Summary determination is made, with *concise reasons* describing the nature of the document but not the details thereof. Under s. 488.1(10) the application is heard *in private*.

A determination that a document is *privileged* requires that it be repackaged, resealed and delivered by the custodian to the lawyer or client who has asserted privilege. Under subsection (5), earlier disclosure to the Attorney General does *not* alter the privileged character of the document. It remains privileged and inadmissible as evidence unless the client consents to its admission in evidence or the privilege is otherwise lost.

A determination that a document is *not privileged* requires the custodian to deliver it to the seizing officer or other designate of the Attorney General, subject to such restrictions or conditions as the judge deems appropriate.

Where, after seizure and delivery to the custodian, there has been either *no* application to fix a date for determination of the solicitor-client issue, or further application to make such determination, the Attorney General, under s. 488.1(6), may apply for and the judge will order a return of the documents to the seizing officers or other designate of the Attorney General.

Under s. 488.1(9), the claimant of privilege may apply *ex parte* to a judge to examine or copy the document in the possession of the custodian. Authorization may be given, subject to terms.

Case Law

General

Descôteaux v. Mierzwinski (1982), 28 C.R. (3d) 289, 70 C.C.C. (2d) 385 (S.C.C.) *[Note this case was decided prior to the enactment of this section]* — The search and seizure provisions of the *Code*, which have the potential to breach confidentiality, must be exercised restrictively, and only to the extent necessary to fulfill the purpose of the enabling provision. The right to confidentiality does *not* prevent someone other than the lawyer, his agent or the client's agent from introducing into evidence confidential communications between a lawyer and his client. However, such evidence can be admitted only if, and to the extent that, the trial judge is persuaded that the fact sought to be proven is essential and that there is no other reasonable way of proving it.

Bloski v. R. (1987), 39 C.C.C. (3d) 248 (Sask. Q.B.) — *See also: Joly v. Bourdeau* (1989), 51 C.C.C. (3d) 394 (Que. S.C.) — This section codifies the law respecting the procedures to be followed for the issuance of a search warrant against a lawyer's office. The concerns of solicitor-client privilege in relation to searches of law offices are sufficiently dealt with under this section. There is *no* legal requirement that the justice he satisfied that alternative methods of obtaining the information have been canvassed and attempted before the issuance of the search warrant.

Procedure on Applications

R. v. Morra (1991), 68 C.C.C. (3d) 273 (Ont. Gen. Div.) — The mere assertion of a privilege claim under the section will *not* suffice. An applicant should adduce reasonable evidence, either *viva voce* or affidavit, to support an inference of solicitor/client relationship and privilege.

Rights of Appeal

R. v. Wilder (1996), 110 C.C.C. (3d) 186 (B.C. C.A.) — There is *no* right of appeal from a decision made under s. 488.1 upon an application to determine whether certain seized items are protected by solicitor-client privilege.

King v. Prince Edward Island (Sheriff of Queens County) (1992), 74 C.C.C. (3d) 191 (P.E.I. C.A.) — There is *no* right of appeal from a determination made on an application under s. 488.1(3)(c).

Related Provisions: Subsection (1) defines "custodian", "document" (with s. 321), "judge" (with s. 2), "lawyer" and "officer" (with s. 2). "Attorney General" is defined in s. 2 and includes his/her lawful deputy.

489. (1) Seizure of things not specified — Every person who executes a warrant may seize, in addition to the things mentioned in the warrant, any thing that the person believes on reasonable grounds

    (a) has been obtained by the commission of an offence against this or any other Act of Parliament;

    (b) has been used in the commission of an offence against this or any other Act of Parliament; or

    (c) will afford evidence in respect of an offence against this or any other Act of Parliament.

(2) Seizure without warrant — Every peace officer, and every public officer who has been appointed or designated to administer or enforce any federal or provincial law and whose duties include the enforcement of this or any other Act of Parliament, who is lawfully present in a place pursuant to a warrant or otherwise in the execution of duties may, without a warrant, seize any thing that the officer believes on reasonable grounds

    (a) has been obtained by the commission of an offence against this or any Act of Parliament;

    (b) has been used in the commission of an offence against this or any other Act of Parliament; or

    (c) will afford evidence in respect of an offence against this or any other Act of Parliament.

R.S., c. C-34, s. 445;R.S. 1985, c. 27 (1st Supp.), s. 72; c. 42(4th Supp.), s. 3; 1993, c. 40, s. 16; 1997, c. 18, s. 48.

Commentary: Section 489(1) describes the circumstances under which a person executing a warrant may seize things *in addition to* what is mentioned in the warrant. The person executing the warrant may seize *anything* that, on *reasonable grounds*, s/he believes has been *obtained by* or *used in* the commission of an *offence* or *will afford evidence in respect of* an *offence*. The offence may be against any federal Act.

Section 489(2) describes the circumstances under which a peace officer or other public officer who has been appointed or designated to enforce the law may seize things *without a warrant*. The officer must be *lawfully present* in a place *pursuant to a warrant* or *otherwise in the execution of duties*. If so, the officer may, without a warrant, seize *anything* that on *reasonable* grounds, s/he believes has been *obtained* or *used* in the commission of an offence or will afford *evidence* in respect of the offence. The offence may be against any federal Act.

Related Provisions: Section 492 expressly authorizes the seizure of explosives upon the execution of a conventional search warrant or telewarrant.

Post-seizure procedure is governed by ss. 489.1 to 490.9.

The words, "an offence" include any indictable, summary conviction or dual procedure offence.

489.1 (1) Restitution of property or report by peace officer — Subject to this or any other Act of Parliament, where a peace officer has seized anything under a warrant issued under this Act or under section 487.11 or 489 or otherwise in the execution of duties under this or any other Act of Parliament, the peace officer shall, as soon as is practicable,

(a) where the peace officer is satisfied,

(i) that there is no dispute as to who is lawfully entitled to possession of the thing seized, and

(ii) that the continued detention of the thing seized is not required for the purposes of any investigation or a preliminary inquiry, trial or other proceeding,

return the thing seized, on being issued a receipt therefor, to the person lawfully entitled to its possession and report to the justice who issued the warrant or some other justice for the same territorial division or, if no warrant was issued, a justice having jurisdiction in respect of the matter, that he has done so; or

(b) where the peace officer is not satisfied as described in subparagraphs (a)(i) and (ii),

(i) bring the thing seized before the justice referred to in paragraph (a), or

(ii) report to the justice that he has seized the thing and is detaining it or causing it to be detained

to be dealt with by the justice in accordance with subsection 490(1).

(2) Idem — Subject to this or any other Act of Parliament, where a person, other than a peace officer, has seized anything under a warrant issued under this Act or under section 487.11 or 489 or otherwise in the execution of duties under this or any other Act of Parliament, that person shall, as soon as is practicable,

(a) bring the thing seized before the justice who issued the warrant, or some other justice for the same territorial division or, if no warrant was issued, before a justice having jurisdiction in respect of the matter, or

(b) report to the justice referred to in paragraph (a) that he has seized the thing and is detaining it or causing it to be detained,

to be dealt with by the justice in accordance with subsection 490(1).

(3) Form — A report to a justice under this section shall be in the form set out as Form 5.2 in Part XXVIII, varied to suit the case and shall include, in the case of a report in respect of a warrant issued by telephone or other means of telecommunication, the statements referred to in subsection 487.1(9).

R.S. 1985, c. 27 (1st Supp.), s. 72; 1993, c. 40, s. 17; 1997, c. 18, s. 49.

Commentary: The section provides for the *restitution* of seized property *and reports* by peace officers and others concerning the execution of warranted searches.

Section 489.1(1) describes the duties of a *peace officer* who has seized anything under a *Code* warrant, ss. 487.11, 489 or otherwise. The officer must first determine whether s/he is satisfied:

(a) that there is a *dispute* as to whom is *lawfully entitled* to the thing seized; and,

(b) that the thing seized is required for the purpose of any *investigation or legal proceeding*.

Section 489.1(2) imposes similar obligations upon persons other than peace officers who have seized anything in similar circumstances, except that, in *all* cases, there must be a *return* or *report* to a justice so that the matter may be dealt with under s. 490(1).

An officer who is *not* satisfied of items (a) and (b), *supra*, must *return* the thing seized, on being issued a receipt therefor, to the person lawfully entitled to possession *and* report having done so, in Form 5.2, to the issuing or another justice in the same territorial division. An officer who is satisfied as described in items (a) and (b), *supra*, must, as soon as practicable, *bring* the things seized before or *report* in Form 5.2 to the justice. The justice will deal with the matter under s. 490(1).

Related Provisions: The report in Form 5.2 is addressed to the issuing justice or another justice in the same territorial division. It specifies the authority under which the seizure was made and identifies the premises searched, describes each thing which has been seized and the disposition thereof. It is signed by the peace officer or other person.

Section 490 authorizes the detention of seized items, as well as their return in certain circumstances.

490. (1) Detention of things seized — Subject to this or any other Act of Parliament, where, pursuant to paragraph 489.1(1)(*b*) or subsection 489.1(2), anything that has been seized is brought before a justice or a report in respect of anything seized is made to a justice, he shall,

(a) where the lawful owner or person who is lawfully entitled to possession of the thing seized is known, order it to be returned to that owner or person, unless the prosecutor, or the peace officer or other person having custody of the thing seized, satisfies the justice that the detention of the thing seized is required for the purposes of any investigation or a preliminary inquiry, trial or other proceeding; or

(b) where the prosecutor, or the peace officer or other person having custody of the thing seized, satisfies the justice that the thing seized should be detained for a reason set out in paragraph (*a*), detain the thing seized or order that it be detained, taking reasonable care to ensure that it is preserved until the conclusion of any investigation or until it is required to be produced for the purposes of a preliminary inquiry, trial or other proceeding.

(2) Further detention — Nothing shall be detained under the authority of paragraph (1)(*b*) for a period of more than three months after the day of the seizure, or any longer period that ends when an application made under paragraph (*a*) is decided, unless

(a) a justice, on the making of a summary application to him after three clear days notice thereof to the person from whom the thing detained was seized, is satisfied that, having regard to the nature of the investigation, its further detention for a specified period is warranted and he so orders; or

(b) proceedings are instituted in which the thing detained may be required.

(3) Idem — More than one order for further detention may be made under paragraph (2)(*a*) but the cumulative period of detention shall not exceed one year from the day of the seizure, or any longer period that ends when an application made under paragraph (*a*) is decided, unless

(a) a judge of a superior court of criminal jurisdiction or a judge as defined in section 552, on the making of a summary application to him after three clear days notice thereof to the person from whom the thing detained was seized, is satisfied, having regard to the complex nature of the investigation, that the further detention of the thing seized is warranted for a specified period and subject to such other conditions as the judge considers just, and he so orders; or

(b) proceedings are instituted in which the thing detained may be required.

(3.1) Detention without application where consent — A thing may be detained under paragraph (1)(*b*) for any period, whether or not an application for an order under subsection (2) or (3) is made, if the lawful owner or person who is lawfully entitled to possession of the thing seized consents in writing to its detention for that period.

(4) When accused ordered to stand trial — When an accused has been ordered to stand trial, the justice shall forward anything detained pursuant to subsections (1) to (3) to the clerk of the court to which the accused has been ordered to stand trial to be detained by the clerk and disposed of as the court directs.

(5) Where continued detention no longer required — Where at any time before the expiration of the periods of detention provided for or ordered under subsections (1) to (3) in respect of anything seized, the prosecutor, or the peace officer or other person having custody of the thing seized, determines that the continued detention of the thing seized is no longer required for any purpose mentioned in subsection (1) or (4), the prosecutor, peace officer or other person shall apply to

    (a) a judge of a superior court of criminal jurisdiction or a judge as defined in section 552, where a judge ordered its detention under subsection (3), or

    (b) a justice, in any other case,

who shall, after affording the person from whom the thing was seized or the person who claims to be the lawful owner thereof or person entitled to its possession, if known, an opportunity to establish that he is lawfully entitled to the possession thereof, make an order in respect of the property under subsection (9).

(6) Idem — Where the periods of detention provided for or ordered under subsections (1) to (3) in respect of anything seized have expired and proceedings have not been instituted in which the thing detained may be required, the prosecutor, peace officer or other person shall apply to a judge or justice referred to in paragraph (5)(*a*) or (*b*) in the circumstances set out in that paragraph, for an order in respect of the property under subsection (9) or (9.1).

(7) Application for order of return — A person from whom anything has been seized may, after the expiration of the periods of detention provided for or ordered under subsections (1) to (3) and on three clear days notice to the Attorney General, apply summarily to

    (a) a judge of a superior court of criminal jurisdiction or a judge as defined in section 552, where a judge ordered the detention of the thing seized under subsection (3), or

    (b) a justice, in any other case,

for an order under paragraph (9)(*c*) that the thing seized be returned to the applicant.

(8) Exception — A judge of a superior court of criminal jurisdiction or a judge as defined in section 552, where a judge ordered the detention of the thing seized under subsection (3), or a justice, in any other case, may allow an application to be made under subsection (7) prior to the expiration of the periods referred to therein where he is satisfied that hardship will result unless such application is so allowed.

(9) Disposal of things seized — Subject to this or any other Act of Parliament, if

    (a) a judge referred to in subsection (7), where a judge ordered the detention of anything seized under subsection (3), or

    (b) a justice, in any other case,

is satisfied that the periods of detention provided for or ordered under subsections (1) to (3) in respect of anything seized have expired and proceedings have not been instituted in which the thing detained may be required or, where such periods have not expired, that the continued detention of the thing seized will not be required for any purpose mentioned in subsection (1) or (4), he shall

> (c) if possession of it by the person from whom it was seized is lawful, order it to be returned to that person; or

> (d) if possession of it by the person from whom it was seized is unlawful and the lawful owner or person who is lawfully entitled to its possession is known, order it to be returned to the lawful owner or to the person who is lawfully entitled to its possession,

any may, if possession of it by the person from whom it was seized is unlawful, or if it was seized when it was not in the possession of any person, and the lawful owner or person who is lawfully entitled to its possession is not known, order it to be forfeited to Her Majesty, to be disposed of as the Attorney General directs, or otherwise dealt with in accordance with the law.

(9.1) Exception — Notwithstanding subsection (9), a judge or justice referred to in paragraph (9)(*a*) or (*b*) may, if the periods of detention provided for or ordered under subsections (1) to (3) in respect of a thing seized have expired but proceedings have not been instituted in which the thing may be required, order that the thing continue to be detained for such period as the judge or justice considers necessary if the judge or justice is satisfied

> (a) that the continued detention of the thing might reasonably be required for a purpose mentioned in subsection (1) or (4); and

> (b) that it is in the interests of justice to do so.

(10) Application by lawful order — Subject to this or any other Act of Parliament, a person, other than a person who may make an application under subsection (7), who claims to be the lawful owner or person lawfully entitled to possession of anything seized and brought before or reported to a justice under section 489.1 may, at any time, on three clear days notice to the Attorney General and the person from whom the thing was seized, apply summarily to

> (a) a judge referred to in subsection (7), where a judge ordered the detention of the thing seized under subsection (3), or

> (b) a justice, in any other case,

for an order that the thing detained be returned to the applicant.

(11) Order — Subject to this or any other Act of Parliament, on an application under subsection (10), where a judge or justice is satisfied that

> (a) the applicant is the lawful owner or lawfully entitled to possession of the thing seized, and

> (b) the periods of detention provided for or ordered under subsections (1) to (3) in respect of the thing seized have expired and proceedings have not been instituted in which the thing detained may be required or, where such periods have not expired, that the continued detention of the thing seized will not be required for any purpose mentioned in subsection (1) or (4),

the judge shall order that

> (c) the thing seized be returned to the applicant; or

(d) except as otherwise provided by law, where, pursuant to subsection (9), the thing seized was forfeited, sold or otherwise dealt within such a manner that it cannot be returned to the applicant, the applicant be paid the proceeds of sale or the value of the thing seized.

(12) Detention pending appeal, etc. — Notwithstanding anything in this section, nothing shall be returned, forfeited or disposed of under this section pending any application made, or appeal taken, thereunder in respect of the thing or proceeding in which the right of seizure thereof is questioned or within thirty days after an order in respect of the thing is made under this section.

(13) Copies of documents returned — The Attorney General, the prosecutor or the peace officer or other person having custody of a document seized may, before bringing it before a justice or complying with an order that the document be returned, forfeited or otherwise dealt with under subsection (1), (9) or (11), make or cause to be made, and may retain, a copy of the document.

(14) Probative force — Every copy made under subsection (13) that is certified as a true copy by the Attorney General, the person who made the copy or the person in whose presence the copy was made is admissible in evidence and, in the absence of evidence to the contrary, has the same probative force as the original document would have if it had been proved in the ordinary way.

(15) Access to anything seized — Where anything is detained pursuant to subsections (1) to (3.1), a judge of a superior court of criminal jurisdiction, a judge as defined in section 552 or a provincial court judge may, on summary application on behalf of a person who has an interest in what is detained, after three clear days notice to the Attorney General, order that the person by or on whose behalf the application is made be permitted to examine anything so detained.

(16) Conditions — An order that is made under subsection (15) shall be made on such terms as appear to the judge to be necessary or desirable to ensure that anything in respect of which the order is made is safeguarded and preserved for any purpose for which it may subsequently be required.

(17) Appeal — A person who feels aggrieved by an order made under subsection (8),(9), (9.1) or (11) may appeal from the order to the appeal court, as defined in section 812, and for the purposes of the appeal the provisions of sections 814 to 828 apply with such modifications as the circumstances require.

(18) Waiver of notice — Any person to whom three days notice must be given under paragraph (2)(a) or (3)(a) or subsection (7), (10) or (15) may agree that the application for which the notice is given be made before the expiration of the three days.

R.S., c. C-34, s. 446;R.S. 1985, c. 27 (1st Supp.), s. 73; 1994, c. 44, s. 38; 1997, c. 18, s. 50.

Commentary: The section describes the *procedure* to be followed *after an initial return or report* has been made under s. 489.1.

Under s. 490(1), anything seized and brought before or reported to a justice under s. 489.1(1)(b) or (2) is to be returned to its lawful owner, or the person lawfully entitled to possession thereof, *unless* P, a peace officer or other custodian of the thing *establishes* that its *detention* is *required* for the purposes of any *investigation* or *judicial proceeding*. Upon such proof, the justice must order detention, taking reasonable care to ensure preservation of the things seized until the conclusion of the investigation or proceedings.

The initial order of detention must *not* exceed three months from the date of seizure. Section 490(2), however, permits an *extension* of the initial period in cases where application is made therefor to the justice under s. 490(2)(a), or where proceedings have been instituted in which the thing seized may be required. The cumulative period of detention under s. 490(2) must not, however, exceed one year from the date of seizure or any longer period that ends when an application under s. 490(2)(a) is decided, unless proceedings are instituted in which the thing may be required, or an order has been obtained under s. 490(3)(a) authorizing further detention, or s. 490(3.1) applies to permit detention for a specific period with written consent of the owner or person in lawful possession.

Sections 490(5)–(12) provide for the *return* of things seized both during and after the expiration of periods of initial or extended detention. Section 490(5) imposes a duty upon P, the peace officer or custodian to apply, in accordance with its terms, for an order under s. 490(9) where P is satisfied the continued detention of the thing seized is no longer required. A similar obligation is imposed by s. 490(6) in cases where initial or extended periods of detention have expired, without the institution of the proceedings. A person from whom anything has been seized may apply under s. 490(7), after the expiration of the detention period and, in exceptional circumstances, under s. 490(8) before such period, for a return of the things seized. The authority to order return or forfeiture upon applications under ss. 490(5)–(8), is contained in s. 490(9).

Section 490(9.1), an overriding provision, permits a judge or justice to order *continued detention* of things seized, *notwithstanding* the *expiration* of periods of detention provided for or ordered under s. 490(1) – (3), and the *failure* to *institute proceedings* in which the thing seized may be required. The period of continued detention may be as long as the judge or justice considers necessary. No order may be made unless the judge or justice is satisfied

i.   that continued detention might *reasonably* be required for a purpose described in s. 490(1) – (4); and,

ii.   that it is in the *interests of justice* to do so.

Sections 490(10) and (11) authorize *applications, at any time*, by persons *other* than those from whom anything has been seized, as for example the lawful owner or person lawfully entitled to possession thereof, *for* the *return* of the thing seized, its value or proceeds of its sale, if forfeited or otherwise dealt with so as to render it incapable of return.

Section 490(12) is an overriding provision which prohibits return, forfeiture or disposal of seized property pending applications made or appeals taken under the section or other proceedings where the right of seizure is questioned, or within 30 days after disposition thereof. Section 490(17) gives any *person aggrieved* by an order under ss. 490(8), (9) and (11) a*right of appeal* to the (summary conviction) appeal court as defined in s. 812, in accordance with ss. 814–828.

Sections 490(13) and (14) must be read together. Section 490(13) authorizes the Attorney General, the prosecutors, the peace officer or other custodian to make and retain a *copy* of any document before returning it or otherwise complying with an order under s. 490(1), (9) or (11). Under s. 490(14), a copy of the document, *certified* as true by the Attorney General or the person who made or was present at the making of a copy, is *admissible* in evidence and, *absent evidence to the contrary*, has the same probative force as the original proven in the ordinary way.

Sections 490(15) and (16) permit *interested parties* to *apply to examine* any things detained under ss. 490(1)–(3.1), subject to terms necessary to safeguard and preserve the items for any purpose for which they may subsequently be required.

Under s. 490(17), a person who feels aggrieved by an order made under a listed subsection may appeal from the order to the "appeal court" as defined in s. 812. The appellate procedure of s. 814–828 applies.

Under s. 490(18), the *notice* requirements under s. 490(2)(a), (3)(a), (7), (10) or (15) may be waived.

Case Law

Parties

Filion v. Savard (1988), 42 C.C.C. (3d) 182 (Que. C.A.) — A police officer is entitled to apply personally for an extension of a detention order where the investigation is *not* yet complete, and the Attorney General is yet a party to the proceedings.

Jurisdiction

Canada (Attorney General) v. Mandate Erectors and Welding Ltd. (1995), 99 C.C.C. (3d) 187 (N.B. C.A.) — Section 490(12) does *not* have the effect of suspending the time limits in s. 490(2)(a) pending the hearing of an application for further detention.

Filion v. Savard (1988), 42 C.C.C. (3d) 182 (Que. C.A.) — A justice has *no* authority to hear an application for a further extension, hence may not order detained documents to be photocopied and copies given to their owner. By s. 490(15), only superior court or sessions of the peace judge may make such an order.

Return of Articles Seized: Ss. 490(7), (9)

R. v. Mac (1995), 97 C.C.C. (3d) 115 (Ont. C.A.) — To establish entitlement to return of monies seized after search under s. 490, D need only establish possession at the time of seizure. The onus rests upon P to establish that the monies were tainted by criminality.

"May Be Required": S. 490(9)

R. v. Church of Scientology of Toronto (1991), 63 C.C.C. (3d) 328 (Ont. C.A.); leave to appeal refused (1991), 67 C.C.C. (3d) vi (note) (S.C.C.) — Documents "may be required" in a pending trial, notwithstanding that they may not be required as proof of the commission of the offence alleged.

An Interest in What is Detained: S. 490(15)

Canequip Exports Ltd. v. Smith (1972), 8 C.C.C. (2d) 360 (Man. Q.B.) — An interest in what is detained is *not* limited to a proprietary interest in the documents or a connection with contemplated litigation, but includes a legal concern in the matters referred to in the documents being detained.

Examine Anything so Detained: S. 490(15)

Sutherland v. R. (1977), 38 C.C.C. (2d) 252 (Ont. Co. Ct.) — "Examine" includes making copies. It is *not* restricted to a visual examination.

Right of Appeal: S. 490(17)

R. v. Ferroclad Fishery Ltd., (April 28, 1992), Doc. No. CA C8102 (Ont. C.A.) — There is *no* appeal under s. 490(17) or otherwise from an order detaining seized articles under *Code* s. 490(2).

R. v. Church of Scientology of Toronto (1991), 63 C.C.C. (3d) 328 (Ont. C.A.); leave to appeal refused (1991), 67 C.C.C. (3d) vi (note) (S.C.C.) — The decision of a judge of the appeal court under s. 490(17) is "a decision of a court in respect of an appeal under section 822" for the purpose of s. 839(1)(a) which permits appeals to the court of appeal with leave of the court or a judge thereof.

R. v. Stewart (1970), 71 W.W.R. 768 (Sask. C.A.) — This section gives no right of appeal from an order made under s. 490(15).

Charter Considerations

R. v. Church of Scientology (1987), (sub nom. *R. v. Zaharia*) 31 C.C.C. (3d) 449 (Ont. C.A.); leave to appeal refused (1987), 23 O.A.C. 320n (S.C.C.) — This section does *not* violate *Charter* ss. 7 and 8 by reason that it provides for the *ex parte* detention if items seized under a search warrant. The *Charter* sections do *not* apply to detention orders because the *Charter* does not protect property rights, and especially not rights respecting the retention or use of property. A detention order should *not* be treated as an extension of the initial judicial process authorizing the search warrant. Retention of the things seized does *not* constitute a mere extension of the seizure.

Related Provisions: "Prosecutor", "Attorney General", "justice" and "superior court of criminal jurisdiction" are defined in s. 2. The s. 321 definition of "document" is not applicable to Part XV, except s. 488(1).

Section 603 entitles D to inspect and receive copies of certain documents or evidence after an order to stand trial has been made. Under s. 605, D may apply to obtain any exhibit for scientific or other test or examination.

Section 491.1 provides for restitution or forfeiture of property obtained by crime and overrides the provisions of s. 490 at trial.

490.01 Perishable things — Where any thing seized pursuant to this Act is perishable or likely to depreciate rapidly, the person who seized the thing or any other person having custody of the thing

    (a) may return it to its lawful owner or the person who is lawfully entitled to possession of it; or

(b) where, on *ex parte* application to a justice, the justice so authorizes, may

    (i) dispose of it and give the proceeds of disposition to the lawful owner of the thing seized, if the lawful owner was not a party to an offence in relation to the thing or, if the identity of that lawful owner cannot be reasonably ascertained, the proceeds of disposition are forfeited to Her Majesty, or

    (ii) destroy it.

1997, c. 18, s. 51; 1999, c. 5, s. 17.

Commentary: Under this section, a person who has seized or has custody of any perishable or quickly-depreciable things seized under the *Code* may dispose of them in certain circumstances. Judicial approval is usually required.

Without the approval of a justice, the seized thing may be returned to its lawful owner or the person lawfully entitled to possess it.

With the authorization of a justice, obtained on *ex parte* application, the thing may be disposed of and its proceeds distributed under s. 490.1(b)(i), or it may be destroyed.

Related Provisions: The section applies to anything of the nature described seized under the *Code*. No distinction is drawn between seizures under and those without warrant or other authorization.

Sections 488-492 govern execution of a conventional search warrant, as well as the restitution, detention and disposal of things seized.

Sections 490.1-490.9, *infra*, deal with forfeiture of offence-related property upon charge or conviction of a criminal organization offence. Provision is also made for relief from forfeiture and making restraint orders in relation to the property.

490.1 (1) Order of forfeiture of property on conviction — Subject to section 490.3 and 490.4, where a person is convicted of a criminal organization offence and, on application of the Attorney General, the court is satisfied, on a balance of probabilities, that any property is offence-related property and that the offence was committed in relation to that property, the court shall

    (a) where the prosecution of the offence was commenced at the instance of the government of a province and conducted by or on behalf of that government, order that the property be forfeited to Her Majesty in right of that province and disposed of by the Attorney General or Solicitor General of that province in accordance with the law; and

    (b) in any other case, order that the property be forfeited to Her Majesty in right of Canada and disposed of by the member of the Queen's Privy Council for Canada that may be designated for the purpose of this paragraph in accordance with the law.

(2) Property related to other offence — Where the evidence does not establish to the satisfaction of the court that the criminal organization offence of which a person has been convicted was committed in relation to property in respect of which an order of forfeiture would otherwise be made under subsection (1) but the court is satisfied, beyond a reasonable doubt, that the property is offence-related property, the court may make an order of forfeiture under subsection (1) in relation to that property.

(3) Appeal — A person who has been convicted of a criminal organization offence or the Attorney General may appeal to the court of appeal from an order or a failure to make an order under subsection (1) as if the appeal were an appeal against the sentence imposed on the person in respect of the offence.

1997, c. 23, s. 15.

Commentary: This section governs *forfeiture* of *offence-related property* where D is convicted of a *criminal organization offence*. It is subjected to the provisions of ss. 490.3 (voidable transfers) and 490.4 (notice).

Where D has been *convicted* of a criminal organization offence, the Attorney General may *apply* to the court for an *order* that *offence-related property* be *forfeited* to Her Majesty in accordance with s. 490.1(1). Anyone who appears to have valid interest in the property must be notified under s. 490.4. To succeed on the application, P must establish on a balance of probabilities that

i. the property is *offence-related property*; and,

ii. the *criminal organization offence* was committed *in relation* to the property.

Where P fails to satisfy item ii, but proves item i beyond a reasonable doubt, the court may make forfeiture order in relation to the property. Proof of items i and ii on a balance of probabilities requires an order of forfeiture. Proof of item i only, beyond a reasonable doubt, permits it.

Section 490.1(3) permits appeals by D and P from a forfeiture order or failure to make the order as if the disposition were a sentence imposed on conviction for the criminal organization offence.

Related Provisions: "Criminal organization offence", "offence-related property" and "property" are defined in s. 2. Prosecutorial responsibility in connection with criminal organization offences is determined under s. 467.2. The rights of appeal against sentence are contained in ss. 675(1)(b) and 676(1)(d) and the dispositive authority of the court of appeal on sentence appeals in s. 687.

Before ordering forfeiture, a court may *set aside* transfers or conveyances of offence-related property under s. 490.3. Restraint orders may also be made under s. 490.8.

Prior to conviction, the Attorney General may apply to a judge as defined in s. 490.2(5) for an order of *in rem* forfeiture of offence-related property under ss. 490.2(1) and (2). Notice under s. 490.4 is required. Sections 489.1 and 490 apply to offence-related property that is subject to a restraint order.

The circumstances in which the operation of a forfeiture order may be suspended are described in s. 490.7.

490.2 (1) Application for *in rem* forfeiture — Where an information has been laid in respect of a criminal organization offence, the Attorney General may make an application to a judge for an order of forfeiture under subsection (2).

(2) Order of forfeiture of property — Subject to sections 490.3 and 490.4, where an application is made to a judge under subsection (1) and the judge is satisfied

(a) beyond a reasonable doubt that any property is offence-related property,

(b) that proceedings in respect of a criminal organization offence in relation to the property referred to in paragraph (*a*) were commenced, and

(c) that the accused charged with the criminal organization offence has died or absconded,

the judge shall order that the property be forfeited and disposed of in accordance with subsection (4).

(3) Accused deemed absconded — For the purpose of subsection (2), an accused is deemed to have absconded in connection with a criminal organization offence if

(a) an information has been laid alleging the commission of the offence by the accused,

(b) a warrant for the arrest of the accused has been issued in relation to that information, and

(c) a reasonable attempts to arrest the accused under the warrant have been unsuccessful during a period of six months beginning on the day on which the warrant was issued, and the accused is deemed to have so absconded on the last day of that six month period.

(4) Who may dispose of forfeited property — For the purpose of subsection (2), the judge shall

(a) where the prosecution of the offence was commenced at the instance of the government of a province and conducted by or on behalf of that government, order that the property be forfeited to Her Majesty in right of that province and disposed of by the Attorney General or Solicitor General of that province in accordance with the law; and

(b) in any other case, order that the property be forfeited to Her Majesty in right of Canada and disposed of by the member of the Queen's Privy Council for Canada that may be designated for the purpose of this paragraph in accordance with the law.

(5) Definition of "judge" — In this section and sections 490.5 and 490.8, "judge" means a judge as defined in section 552 or a judge of a superior court of criminal jurisdiction.

1997, c. 23, s. 15.

Commentary: Under this section, the Attorney General may apply to a judge for an order of forfeiture of offence-related property.

At any time after an information has been laid charging a criminal organization offence, the Attorney General may apply to a judge as defined in s. 490.2(5), on *notice* to interested parties in accordance with s. 490.4. There is no prescribed form of application, nor listing or other description of supporting materials.

Before granting the order, the judge must be satisfied beyond a reasonable doubt that the property is offence-related property. The judge must also be satisfied, though *not* beyond a reasonble doubt, that proceedings for a criminal organization offence have been commenced in relation to the property and that D, charged with the offence, has died or absconded. D is deemed to have absconded where the conditions of s. 490.2(3) have been met.

Where forfeiture is ordered, s. 490.2(4) governs disposition of the property.

Related Provisions: Related provisions are discussed in the corresponding note to 490.1 (as enacted by 1997, c. 23, s. 15), *supra*.

490.3 Voidable transfers — A court may, before ordering that offence-related property be forfeited under subsection 490.1(1) or 490.2(2), set aside any conveyance or transfer of the property that occurred after the seizure of the property, or the making of a restraint order in respect of the property, unless the conveyance or transfer was for valuable consideration to a person acting in good faith.

1997, c. 23, s. 15.

Commentary: Under this section, a court may *set aside* a *transfer* or *conveyance* of offence-related property that occurred after seizure, or the making of a restraint order in relation to the property, *unless* the transaction was for *valuable consideration* to a person acting in *good faith*. The order may be made prior to forfeiture under either ss. 490.1(1) or 490.2(2).

The provision protects legitimate and thwarts illegitimate transfer of offence-related property which has been seized or made the subject of a restraint order. It authorizes the fraudulent to be set aside so that forfeiture orders cannot be frustrated by illegitimate transfer.

Related Provisions: Forfeiture may be ordered upon conviction of a criminal organization offence, but not on discharge, under s. 490.1(1), or in *in rem* proceedings under s. 490.2(2).

Other related provisions are discussed in the corresponding note to s. 490.1 (as enacted by 1997, c. 23, s. 15).

490.4 (1) Notice — Before making an order under subsection **490.1(1)** or **490.2(2)** in relation to any property, a court shall require notice in accordance with subsection (2) to be given to, and may hear, any person who, in the opinion of the court, appears to have a valid interest in the property.

(2) Manner of giving notice — A notice given under subsection (1) shall

(a) be given or served in the manner that the court directs or that may be specified in the rules of the court;

(b) be of any duration that the court considers reasonable or that may be specified in the rules of the court; and

(c) set out the criminal organization offence charged and a description of the property.

(3) Order of restoration of property — Where a court is satisfied that a person, other than

(a) a person who was charged with a criminal organization offence, or

(b) a person who acquired title to or a right of possession of the property from a person referred to in paragraph (*a*) under circumstances that give rise to a reasonable inference that the title or right was transferred for the purpose of avoiding the forfeiture of the property,

is the lawful owner or is lawfully entitled to possession of any property or a part of any property that would otherwise be forfeited pursuant to an order made under subsection 490.1(1) or 490.2(2) and that the person appears innocent of any complicity in an offence referred to in paragraph (*a*) or of any collusion in relation to such an offence, the court may order that the property or part be returned to the person.

1997, c. 23, s. 15.

Commentary: Under this provision, persons with a *valid* interest in offence-related property are entitled to *notice* of and the right to be *heard* in applications for forfeiture of the property.

Section 490.4(2) governs the manner of giving notice. It must be given or served as directed by the court or prescribed by the court's rules. It must also be reasonable. Notice must set out the criminal organization offence charged and describe the property that is the subject of the application.

Section 490.4(3) describes the circumstances in which otherwise forfeitable property may be returned, in whole or in part, to its lawful owner or custodian. The court must be satisfied that the applicant is not charged with or complicit in a criminal organization offence and has not acquired title to or possession of the property as part of a forfeiture avoidance scheme.

Related Provisions: Section 482 empowers courts to make rules concerning proceedings within their jurisdiction.

Other related provisions are described in the corresponding note to s. 490.1 (as enacted by 1997, c. 23, s. 15).

490.5 (1) Application — Where any offence-related property is forfeited to Her Majesty pursuant to an order made under subsection 490.1(1) or 490.2(2), any person who claims an interest in the property, other than

(a) in the case of property forfeited pursuant to an order made under subsection 490.1(1), a person who was convicted of the criminal organization offence in relation to which the property was forfeited,

(b) in the case of property forfeited pursuant to an order made subsection 490.2(2), a person who was charged with the criminal organization offence in relation to which the property was forfeited, or

(c) a person who acquired title to or a right of possession of the property from a person referred to in paragraph (*a*) or (*b*) under circumstances that give rise to a reasonable inference that the title or right was transferred from that person for the purpose of avoiding the forfeiture of the property,

may, within thirty days after the forfeiture, apply by notice in writing to a judge for an order under subsection (4).

(2) **Fixing day for hearing** — The judge to whom an application is made under subsection (1) shall fix a day not less than thirty days after the date of the filing of the application for the hearing of the application.

(3) **Notice** — An applicant shall serve a notice of the application made under subsection (1) and of the hearing of it on the Attorney General at least fifteen days before the day fixed for the hearing.

(4) **Order declaring interest not affected by forfeiture** — Where, on the hearing of an application made under subsection (1), the judge is satisfied that the applicant

(a) is not a person referred to in paragraph (1)(*a*), (*b*) or(*c*) and appears innocent of any complicity in any criminal organization offence that resulted in the forfeiture of the property or of any collusion in relation to such an offence, and

(b) exercised all reasonable care to be satisfied that the property was not likely to have been used in connection with the commission of an unlawful act by the person who was permitted by the applicant to obtain possession of the property or from whom the applicant obtained possession or, where the applicant is a mortgagee or lienholder, by the mortgagor or lien-giver,

the judge may make an order declaring that the interest of the applicant is not affected by the forfeiture and declaring the nature and the extent or value of the interest.

(5) **Appeal from order made under subsection (4)** — An applicant or the Attorney General may appeal to the court of appeal from an order made under subsection (4), and the provisions of Part XXI with respect to procedure on appeals apply, with any modifications that the circumstances require, in respect of appeals under this subsection.

(6) **Return of property** — The Attorney General shall, on application made to the Attorney General by any person in respect of whom a judge has made an order under subsection (4), and where the periods with respect to the taking of appeals from that order under subsection (4), and where the periods with respect to the taking of appeals from that order have expired and any appeal from that order taken under subsection (5) has been determined, direct that

(a) the property, or the part of it to which the interest of the applicant relates, be returned to the applicant; or

(b) an amount equal to the value of the interest of the applicant, as declared in the order, be paid to the applicant.

1997, c. 23, s. 15.

Commentary: Under this section, an innocent third party may apply for a declaration that his/her interest in property is not affected by an order of forfeiture made upon conviction of a criminal organization offence or in *in rem* proceedings.

An applicant must apply *in writing* to a judge within thirty days of the forfeiture order from whose application s/he seeks to be relieved. Notice must be given to the Attorney General under s. 490.5(3). The applicant must not be a person charged with or convicted of the underlying criminal organization offence in relation to which the property was ordered forfeited, or a person who has acquired title to or possession of the property as part of a forfeiture avoidance scheme. The judge to whom the application is made is required to fix a date for hearing under s. 490.5(2) with notice to the Attorney General under s. 490.5(3).

The section makes no reference to the materials which must or may be filed on the application. What is filed should demonstrate, however, the applicant's status to bring the application, in other words show what is required by s. 490.5(1). The materials should also satisfy the judge that the applicant

i.   is innocent of any complicity or collusion in the underlying criminal organization offence; and

ii. exercised the degree of care required by s. 490.5(4)(b).

Where satisfied of the requirements of s. 490.5(4), the judge may give a declaration that the interest of the applicant in the property, to the extent specified in the order, is not affected by the forfeiture. Return of the property is governed by s. 490.5(6).

The applicant and Attorney General may appeal from any order made under s. 490.5(4) in accordance with the indictable appeal procedure in Part XXI.

Related Provisions: The language of s. 490.5(4) is somewhat unsatisfactory. It fails to specify whether the applicable appeal procedure is "as if" the order were a "sentence", "conviction", or "judgment or verdict of acquittal". Compare s. 490.6.

The opeartion of an order made under s. 490.5(4) is suspended under s. 490.7 in accordance with its terms.

Other related provisions are discussed in the corresponding note to s. 490.1 (as enacted by 1997, c. 23, s. 15).

490.6 Appeals from orders under subsection 490.2(2) — Any person who, in their opinion, is aggrieved by an order made under subsection 490.2(2) may appeal from the order as if the order were an appeal against conviction or against a judgment or verdict of acquittal, as the case may be, under Part XXI, and that Part applies, with any modifications that the circumstances require, in respect of such an appeal.

1997, c. 23, s. 15.

Commentary: This section creates a *right* of *appeal* from *orders* made during *in rem* forfeiture proceedings under s. 490.2(2). Anyone who feels *aggrieved* by the order may appeal, as if the order were a conviction or judgment or verdict of acquittal in proceedings by indictment. Part XXI applies.

Related Provisions: Suspension of the operation of an order made in *in rem* forfeiture proceedings is governed by s. 490.7.

490.7 Suspension of order pending appeal — Notwithstanding anything in this Act, the operation of an order made in respect of property under subsection 490.1(1), 490.2(2) or 490.5(4) is suspended pending

(a) any application made in respect of the property under of those provisions or any other provision of this or any other Act of Parliament that provides for restoration or forfeiture of the property, or

(b) any appeal taken from an order of forfeiture or restoration in respect of the property,

and the property shall not be disposed of or otherwise dealt with until thirty days have expired after an order is made under any of those provisions.

1997, c. 23, s. 15.

Commentary: This section provides for and governs *suspension* of orders made in forfeiture and related proceedings concerning interest in offence-related property.

The *suspension* of the orders described is *automatic*. It requires *no* discrete application, nor judicial *fiat*. Operation of the order is suspended *pending applications* for *forfeiture* or *restoration* and *appeals* taken from any order. The property may *not* be disposed of or otherwise dealt with until thirty days after the relevant order.

Related Provisions: Section 490.7 operates notwithstanding any other *Code* provision, as for example, ss. 683(5) and (6).

Other provisions which stay the operation of various orders, or revoke stays which have been granted are found in ss. 261 (driving prohibitions), 683(5) (fines, victim fine surcharges, restitution and probation orders, forfeiture or disposition of forfeited property), and 686(6) (revocation of s. 686(5) stays).

Other related provisions are discussed in the corresponding note to s. 490.1 (as enacted by 1997, c. 23, s. 15).

490.8 (1) Application for restraint order — The Attorney General may make an application in accordance with this section for a restraint order under this section in respect of any offence-related property.

(2) Procedure — An application made under subsection (1) for a restraint order in respect of any offence-related property may be made *ex parte* and shall be made in writing to a judge and be accompanied by an affidavit sworn on the information and belief of the Attorney General or any other person deposing to the following matters:

(a) the criminal organization offence to which the offence-related property relates;

(b) the person who is believed to be in possession of the offence-related property; and

(c) a description of the offence-related property.

(3) Restraint order — Where an application for a restraint order is made to a judge under subsection (1), the judge may, if satisfied that there are reasonable grounds to believe that the property is offence-related property, make a restraint order

(a) prohibiting any person from disposing of, or otherwise dealing with any interest in, the offence-related property specified in the order otherwise than in the manner that may be specified in the order; and

(b) at the request of the Attorney General, where the judge is of the opinion that the circumstances so require,

(i) appointing a person to take control of and to manage or otherwise deal with all or part of the property in accordance with the directions of the judge, and

(ii) requiring any person having possession of the property to give possession of it to the person appointed under subparagraph (i).

(4) Conditions — A restraint order made by a judge under this section may be subject to any reasonable conditions that the judge thinks fit.

(5) Order in writing — A restraint order made under this section shall be made in writing.

(6) Service of order — A copy of a restraint order made under this section shall be served on the person to whom the order is addressed in any manner that the judge making the order directs or in accordance with the rules of the court.

(7) Registration of order — A copy of a restraint order made under this section shall be registered against any property in accordance with the laws of the province in which the property is situated.

(8) Order continues in force — A restraint order made under this section remains in effect until

(a) an order is made under subsection 490(9) or (11) in relations to the property; or

(b) an order of forfeiture of the property is made under section 490 or subsection 490.1(1) or 490.2(2).

(9) Offence — Any person on whom a restraint order made under this section is served in accordance with this section and who, while the order is in force, acts in contravention of or fails to comply with the order is guilty of an indictable offence or offence punishable on summary conviction.

1997, c. 23, s. 15.

Commentary: This section permits the Attorney General to apply for a *restraint order* for offence-related property, describes the *procedure* to be followed on applications and defines the *scope* of the order.

An *application* under s. 490.8(2) is *ex parte*, in writing and made to a *judge*. An *affidavit*, sworn on the information and belief of the Attorney General, or anyone else, must

i.   state the criminal organization *offence* to which the offence-related property relates;

ii.   identify the *person* in possession of the property; and,

iii.   describe the *property*.

Where the judge is satisfied that there are *reasonable* grounds to believe that the property is offence-related property, s/he may make a restraint order in writing in the terms described in s. 490.8(3), including any reasonable conditions that the judge thinks fit.

Service, registration and effect of the order are governed by ss. 490.8(6)-(8). Anyone served with the order who contravenes or fails to comply with it commits an offence under s. 490.8(9).

Related Provisions: A restraint order may also be made in connection with property obtained by an enterprise crime offence under s. 462.33.

Other related provisions are discussed in the corresponding note to s. 490.1 (as enacted by 1997, c. 23, s. 15).

490.9 (1) Sections 489.1 and 490 applicable — Subject to sections 490.1 to 490.7 sections 489.1 and 490 apply, with any modifications that the circumstances require, to any offence-related property that is the subject of a restraint order made under section 490.8.

(2) Recognizance — Where, pursuant to subsection (1), an order is made under paragraph 490(9)(c) for the return of any offence-related property that is the subject of a restraint order under section 490.8, the judge or justice making the order may require the applicant for the order to enter into a recognizance before the judge or justice, with or without sureties, in any amount and with any conditions that the judge or justice directs and, where the judge or justice considers it appropriate, require that applicant to deposit with the judge or justice any sum of money or other valuable security that the judge or justice directs.

1997, c. 23, s. 15.

Commentary: As a result of this section, the provisions of ss. 489.1 and 490 apply to offence-related property that is under a s. 490.8 restraint order.

Section 489.1 provides for the return of seized (restrained) property, or a report to a justice concerning its detention. Section 490 governs detention of things seized (ordered restrained). Where offence-related property is returned under s. 490(9)(c), an applicant may be required to enter into a recognizance under s. 490.9(2).

Related Provisions: The requirements of ss. 489.1 and 490 are described in the *Commentary* which accompanies each section.

Other related provisions are discussed in the corresponding note to s. 490.1 (as enacted by 1997, c. 23, s. 15).

491. (1) Forfeiture of weapons and ammunition — Subject to subsection (2) where it is determined by a court that

(a) a weapon, an imitation firearm, a prohibited device, any ammunition, any prohibited ammunition or an explosive substance was used in the commission of an offence and that thing has been seized and detained, or

(b) that a person has committed an offence that involves, or the subject-matter of which is, a firearm, a cross-bow, a prohibited weapon, a restricted weapon, a prohibited device, ammunition, prohibited ammunition or an explosive substance and any such thing has been seized and detained,

the thing so seized and detained is forfeited to Her Majesty and shall be disposed of as the Attorney General directs.

(2) Return to lawful owner — If the court by which a determination referred to in subsection (1) is made is satisfied that the lawful owner of any thing that is or may be forfeited to Her Majesty under subsection (1) was not a party to the offence and had no reasonable grounds to believe that the thing would or might be used in the commission of an offence, the court shall order that the thing be returned to that lawful owner, that the proceeds of any sale of the thing be paid to that lawful owner or, if the thing was destroyed, that an amount equal to the value of the thing be paid to the owner.

(3) Application of proceeds — Where any thing in respect of which this section applies is sold, the proceeds of the sale shall be paid to the Attorney General or, where an order is made under subsection (2), to the person who was, immediately prior to the sale, the lawful owner of the thing.

1991, c. 40, s. 30; 1995, c. 39, s. 152.

Commentary: The section authorizes *forfeiture of any listed weapon* used in the commission of an offence.

In general, where a court determines that a listed item, which has been seized and detained, was used in the commission of an offence or that a person has committed an offence that involves a listed item, the item is forfeited and dealt with as the Attorney General directs, subject to an order to return being made under s. 491(2). An item used in the commission of an offence, proceeds of its sale, or its value if destroyed, will only be returned to its lawful owner under s. 491(2) where the court is satisfied that the lawful owner was *not* a party to the offence in which the item was used, and had *no* reason to believe that the item would or might be used in the commission of *an offence*.

Proceeds from the sale of weapons forfeited under s. 491(1) are paid to the Attorney General, absent an order under s. 491(2) that they be paid to the lawful owner.

Case Law

R. v. Parsons (1996), 113 C.C.C. (3d) 216 (B.C. C.A.) — Carrying a firearm in a careless manner under s. 86(2) does *not* involve the use of a weapon in the commission of an offence, hence cannot found an order of forfeiture and destruction under s. 491.

Related Provisions: The relevant items, except "firearm" and "explosive substance" are defined in s. 84. The latter and "Attorney General" are defined in s. 2. Accessoryship is governed by ss. 21 and 22.

"Offence" includes indictable, summary conviction and dual procedure conviction offences. The use of a weapon in the commission of an offence may also attract an order of prohibition under ss. 109 or 110.

491.1 (1) Order for restitution or forfeiture of property obtained by crime — Where an accused or defendant is tried for an offence and the court determines that an offence has been committed, whether or not the accused has been convicted or discharged under section 730 of the offence, and at the time of the trial any property obtained by the commission of the offence

(a) is before the court or has been detained so that it can be immediately dealt with, and

(b) will not be required as evidence in any other proceedings,

section 490 does not apply in respect of the property and the court shall make an order under subsection (2) in respect of the property.

(2) Idem — In the circumstances referred to in subsection (1), the court shall order, in respect of any property,

(a) if the lawful owner or person lawfully entitled to possession of the property is known, that it be returned to that person; and

(b) if the lawful owner or person lawfully entitled to possession of the property is not known, that it be forfeited to Her Majesty, to be disposed of as the Attorney General directs or otherwise dealt with in accordance with the law.

(3) When certain orders not to be made — An order shall not be made under subsection (2)

(a) in the case of proceedings against a trustee, banker, merchant, attorney, factor, broker or other agent entrusted with the possession of goods or documents of title to goods, for an offence under section 330, 331, 332 or 336; or

(b) in respect of

(i) property to which a person acting in good faith and without notice has acquired lawful title for valuable consideration,

(ii) a valuable security that has been paid or discharged in good faith by a person who was liable to pay or discharge it,

(iii) a negotiable instrument that has, in good faith, been taken or received by transfer or delivery for valuable consideration by a person who had no notice and no reasonable cause to suspect that an offence had been committed, or

(iv) property in respect of which there is a dispute as to ownership or right of possession by claimants other than the accused or defendant.

(4) By whom order executed — An order made under this section shall, on the direction of the court, be executed by the peace officers by whom the process of the court is ordinarily executed.

R.S.C. 1985, c. 27 (1st Supp.), s. 74; 1995, c. 22, (Sched. IV, item 26)

Commentary: The section authorizes trial courts to order the *restitution or forfeiture* of property obtained by crime.

The authority of the section is engaged where a trial court determines that an offence has been committed and that, at the time of trial, any property obtained by the commission of the offence is either before the court, or has been elsewhere detained for immediate disposal and is *not* required as *evidence* in any other proceedings. In such circumstances, s. 491.1(1) *suspends* the operation of s. 490 in relation to the property and *requires* an order of *restitution* or *forfeiture* in accordance with s. 491.1(2), provided the property is *not* exempted under s. 491.1(3).

Section 491.1(4) provides for the execution of the order by peace officers who ordinarily execute the process of the court.

Related Provisions: "Attorney General", "property", "valuable security" and "peace officer" are defined in s. 2. An order under this section is a "sentence" under s. 673.

"Court" is *not* defined either generally or for the purposes of Part XV. *Quaere* who determines whether "an offence has been committed" in the case of a jury verdict of not guilty?

Sections 738 and 739 authorize *restitution* to be made for loss of property or to innocent purchasers thereof.

491.2 (1) Photographic evidence — Before any property that would otherwise be required to be produced for the purposes of a preliminary inquiry, trial or other proceeding in respect of an offence under section 334, 344, 348, 354, 362 or 380 is returned or ordered to be returned, forfeited or otherwise dealt with under section 489.1 or 490 or is otherwise returned, a peace officer or any person under the direction of a peace officer may take and retain a photograph of the property.

(2) Certified photograph admissible in evidence — Every photograph of property taken under subsection (1), accompanied by a certificate of a person containing the statements referred to in subsection (3), shall be admissible in evidence and, in the absence of evidence to the contrary, shall have the same probative force as the property would have had if it had been proved in the ordinary way.

(3) Statements made in certificate — For the purposes of subsection (2), a certificate of a person stating that

(a) the person took the photograph under the authority of subsection (1),

(b) the person is a peace officer or took the photograph under the direction of a peace officer, and

(c) the photograph is a true photograph

shall be admissible in evidence and, in the absence of evidence to the contrary, is evidence of the statements contained in the certificate without proof of the signature of the person appearing to have signed the certificate.

(4) Secondary evidence of peace officer — An affidavit or solemn declaration of a peace officer or other person stating that the person has seized property and detained it or caused it to be detained from the time that person took possession of the property until a photograph of the property was taken under subsection (1) and that property was not altered in any manner before the photograph was taken shall be admissible in evidence and, in the absence of evidence to the contrary, is evidence of the statements contained in the affidavit or solemn declaration without proof of the signature or official character of the person appearing to have signed the affidavit or solemn declaration.

(5) Notice of intention to produce certified photograph — Unless the court orders otherwise, no photograph, certificate affidavit or solemn declaration shall be received in evidence at a trial or other proceeding pursuant to subsection (2), (3) or (4) unless the prosecutor has, before the trial or other proceeding, given to the accused a copy thereof and reasonable notice of intention to produce it in evidence.

(6) Attendance for examination — Notwithstanding subsection (3) or (4), the court may require the person who appears to have signed a certificate, an affidavit or a solemn declaration referred to in that subsection to appear before it for examination or cross-examination in respect of the issue of proof of any of the facts contained in the certificate, affidavit or solemn declaration.

(7) Production of property in court — A court may order any property seized and returned pursuant to section 489.1 or 490 to be produced in court or made available for examination by all parties to a proceeding at a reasonable time and place, notwithstanding that a photograph of the property has been received in evidence pursuant to subsection (2), where the court is satisfied that the interests of justice so require and that it is possible and practicable to do so in the circumstances.

(8) Definition of "photograph" — In this section, "photograph" includes a still photograph, a photographic film or plate, a microphotographic film, a photostatic negative, an X-ray film, a motion picture and a videotape.

R.S. 1985, c. 23 (4th Supp.), s. 2; 1992, c. 1, s. 58(1), Schedule 1, item 10.

Commentary: The section provides the basis upon which a property *authenticated photograph* and *supporting documents* may be received as *evidence* in proceedings in respect of listed offences and have the *same probative value* as the *property*, which otherwise would have been produced. The secondary evidence receivable includes a *photograph, authenticating certificate,* and an *affidavit* or solemn declaration attesting to the unaltered condition of the property.

Section 491.2(1) authorizes a peace officer, or any person under the direction of a peace officer, (as for example, the property owner or a civilian photographer) to take and retain a *photograph* of any property that would otherwise be required to be produced for the purposes of trial, preliminary inquiry or other proceedings in respect of a listed offence. "Photograph" is defined in s. 491.2(8). The photograph, taken at any time before the property has been returned, forfeited or otherwise dealt with under either s. 489.1 or 490, is authenticated by a certificate under s. 491.2(3) which confirms that the photograph was taken in accordance with s. 491.2(1) and is a true depiction of the property.

Provision is made in ss. 491.2(2) and (3) for the admissibility of the s. 491.2(1) *photograph* and s. 491.2(3) *certificate*. By s. 491.2(2), the photograph, accompanied by a s. 491.2(3) certificate, is *admissible* in evidence and, in the *absence of evidence to the contrary*, has the same probative force as would the property, if proven in the ordinary way. Under s. 491.2(3) the *certificate* is *admissible* in evidence and, in the *absence of evidence to the contrary*, is *evidence of* the *statements* contained therein without proof of the signature of its author.

Section 491.2(4) authorizes the preparation of an *affidavit or solemn declaration* verifying the *bodily integrity* of the photographed property from the time of its original seizure. The affidavit is *admissible* in evidence, and, in the *absence of evidence to the contrary, evidence* of the *statements* contained therein, without proof of the signature or official character of the affiant or deponent. In common parlance, "continuity" is established.

The photograph, certificate, affidavit or solemn declaration rendered admissible in evidence in proceedings in respect of a listed offence by ss. 491.2(2)–(4), may only be received upon compliance with the dual *notice and disclosure* requirements of s. 491.2(5). P must give to D, before the trial or other proceeding, *reasonable notice of intention to produce* the photograph, certificate, affidavit or solemn declaration and, further, a *copy* of the material tendered for reception.

The reception of secondary evidence under the section does *not* mean that in every case the author of a certificate, affiant or declarant, as the case may be, may *not* be required to appear for examination or cross-examination in respect of the issue of proof of any of the contents thereof. Section 491.2(6) authorizes the court in which proceedings are taken to require attendance of the author for examination or cross-examination about relevant matters. Further, where property has been seized and returned under s. 489.1 or 490, the court *may* order its production in court or for examination by all parties at a reasonable time and place, where the court is satisfied that the interests of justice require production which is possible and practicable in the circumstances. The order for production may be made notwithstanding that a photograph of the property has been received in evidence.

Related Provisions: The listed offences include ss. 334 (theft), 344 (robbery), 348 (breaking and entering), 354 (possession of property obtained by crime), 362 (false pretences) and 380 (fraud).

Section 489.1 provides for the *restitution* of property seized by a peace officer under specified types of warrants or otherwise in his/her duties under federal enactment and reports by the officers and others concerning the execution of warranted searches. Section 490 describes the *procedure* to be followed after the initial return or a report has been made under s. 489.1.

Several other *Code* provisions permit proof by certificate of matters essential to P's case, as for example, in ss. 145(9) (failure to attend court or for *I.C.A.* purposes), 258(1)(e)–(i) (analysis of concentration of alcohol in blood and related manners), 461(2) (counterfeit nature of coin, paper money or bank note) and 667(1)(c) (identity of fingerprint).

In addition to *Code* provisions which permit the reception of documentary evidence as a means of proof in certain proceedings, *C.E.A.* ss. 19–36 enact provisions of more general application, as for example, s. 30, which permits the reception of *business records* where oral evidence in respect of a matter would be admissible, and s. 24, which authorizes the reception of certified copies of certain documents where the original record could be admitted in evidence.

492. (1) Seizure of explosives — **Every person who executes a warrant issued under section 487 may seize any explosive substance that he suspects is intended to be used for an unlawful purpose, and shall, as soon as possible, remove to a place of safety anything that he seizes by virtue of this section and detain it until he is ordered by a judge of a superior court to deliver it to some other person or an order is made pursuant to subsection (2).**

(2) Forfeiture — **Where an accused is convicted of an offence in respect of anything seized by virtue of subsection (1), it is forfeited and shall be dealt with as the court that makes the conviction may direct.**

(3) Application of proceeds — **Where anything to which this section applies is sold, the proceeds of the sale shall be paid to the Attorney General.**
R.S., c. C-34, s. 447;R.S. 1985, c. 27 (1st Supp.), s.70.

Commentary: The section authorizes the *seizure, removal* to a place of safety and, upon conviction, *forfeiture* of explosive substances.

Under s. 492(1), where a conventional search warrant or telewarrant is being executed, any explosive substance observed, that the executing officer *suspects* is intended for an unlawful purpose may be seized and must be removed to a place of safety, until further order by a judge of a superior court or under s. 492(2).

Upon *conviction*, any explosive substance seized under s. 492(1) is, by s. 492(2), forfeited and dealt with as the convicting court directs. Any proceeds of the sale, under s. 492(3) are payable to the Attorney General.

Related Provisions: "Explosive substance" and "Attorney General" are defined in s. 2. Neither "conviction" nor "superior court" are defined, though some assistance may be derived from decisions interpreting "conviction" under *C.E.A.* s. 12 and the definition of "superior court of criminal jurisdiction" under *Code* s. 2.

Offences relating to explosives are found in ss. 78–82.1. Prohibition orders under s. 100(1) or (2) apply to explosive substances.

492.1 (1) Information for tracking warrant — **A justice who is satisfied by information on oath in writing that there are reasonable grounds to suspect that an offence under this or any other Act of Parliament has been or will be committed and that information that is relevant to the commission of the offence, including the whereabouts of any person, can be obtained through the use of a tracking device, may at any time issue a warrant authorizing a peace officer or public officer who has been appointed or designated to administer or enforce a federal or provincial law and whose duties include the enforcement of this Act or any other Act of Parliament and who is named in the warrant**

(a) to install, maintain and remove a tracking device in or on any thing, including a thing carried, used or worn by any person; and

(b) to monitor, or to have monitored, a tracking device installed in or on any thing.

(2) **Time limit for warrant** — A warrant issued under subsection (1) is valid for the period, not exceeding sixty days, mentioned in it.

(3) **Further warrants** — A justice may issue further warrants under this section.

(4) **Definition of "tracking device"** — For the purposes of this section, "tracking device" means any device that, when installed in or on any thing, may be used to help ascertain, by electronic or other means, the location of any thing or person.

(5) **Removal after expiry of warrant** — On *ex parte* application in writing supported by affidavit, the justice who issued a warrant under subsection (1) or a further warrant under subsection (3) or any other justice having jurisdiction to issue such warrants may authorize that the tracking device be covertly removed after the expiry of the warrant

   (a) under any terms or conditions that the justice considers advisable in the public interest; and

   (b) during any specified period of not more than sixty days.

1993, c. 40, s. 18; 1999, c. 5, s. 18.

Commentary: The section, responding to the legislative *lacunae* identified in *R. v. Wise* (1992), 70 C.C.C. (3d) 193 (S.C.C.), permits warranted use of a "tracking device", as defined in s. 492.1(4), to obtain *information relevant* to the *commission* of an offence, including the *whereabouts* of any person.

The procedure to obtain a tracking device warrant is commenced by laying an *information* on *oath in writing* before a *justice*. The applicant need *not* be a peace or public officer, nor have any special designation to bring the application, or, for that matter, to swear the information. No statutory form is prescribed for the information.

Under s. 492.1(1), a tracking device warrant may be issued provided the justice is satisfied by the *information on oath in writing* that

i. there are *reasonable grounds to suspect* that an *offence* under the *Code* or other federal Act has been or will be committed; and,

ii. there are *reasonable grounds to suspect* that *information* that is relevant to the commission of the offence, including the whereabouts of any person, *can be obtained* through the use of the device.

Information is *not* the equivalent of evidence, or admissible evidence but includes both.

Under s. 492.1(1), the warrant may be issued to a *peace officer* or *person named* therein and permit installation, maintenance, monitoring and removal of a tracking device. A warrant may be valid for a specified period not exceeding 60 days under s. 492.1(2). Further warrants may be issued under s. 492.1(3), but there is no provision for renewals.

Related Provisions: An assistance order may be made under s. 487.02. Extra-provincial execution of a tracking device warrant is governed by s. 487.03. There is no general rule which permits extra-provincial execution as in s. 188.1(1).

The scheme of s. 492.1 is similar to that of s. 492.2 in relation to number recorder warrants.

Forms 1 and 5 may be adapted for use under this section.

492.2 (1) Information re number recorder — A justice who is satidfied by information on oath in writing that there are reasonable grounds to suspect that an offence under this or any other Act of Parliament has been or will be committed and that information that would assist in the investigation of the offence could be obtained through the use of a number recorder, may at any time issue a warrant authorizing a peace officer or a public officer who has been appointed or designated to administer or enforce a federal or provincial law and whose duties include the enforcement of this Act or any other Act of Parliament and who is named in the warrant

> (a) to install, maintain and remove a number recorder in relation to any telephone or telephone line; and

> (b) to monitor, or to have monitored, the number recorder.

(2) **Order re telephone records** — When the circumstances referred to in subsection (1) exist, a justice may order that any person or body that lawfully possesses records of telephone calls originated from, or received or intended to be received at, any telephone give the records, or a copy of the records, to a person named in the order.

(3) **Other provisions to apply** — Subsections 492.1(2) and (3) apply to warrants and orders issued under this section, with such modifications as the circumstances require.

(4) **Definition of "number recorder"** — For the purposes of this section, "number recorder" means any device that can be used to record or identify the telephone number or location of the telephone from which a telephone call originates, or at which it is received or is intended to be received.

1993, c. 40, s. 18; 1999, c. 5, s. 19.

Commentary: This section provides for issuance of a number recorder warrant, which authorizes installation, maintenance, monitoring and removal of a "number recorder", as defined in s. 492.2(4), in relation to any telephone or telephone line.

Under s. 492.2(1), *application* for a number recorder warrant is commenced by laying an *information on oath in writing* before a *justice*. No special designation or status is required of the applicant/informant. No statutory form of information is prescribed.

Under s. 492.2(1), a number recorder warrant may be issued where the justice has been satisfied by the *information on oath in writing* that

i.   there are *reasonable grounds to suspect* that a *Code* or other federal *offence* has been or will be committed; and,

ii.   there are *reasonable grounds to suspect* that *information* that would assist in the investigation of the offence *could be obtained* through the use of a number recorder.

Information includes, but is *not* limited to, evidence or admissible evidence. The findings required under s. 492.2(1) should inform the contents of the information, which should be sufficient to permit a detached neutral arbiter to make the required findings.

The referential incorporation by s. 492.2(3) of s. 492.1(2) and (3) has the effect of *limiting* the *period* for which a number recorder warrant may be valid to 60 days, *but permitting further* warrants to be issued.

Section 492.2(2) also permits a justice to order that any person or body in lawful possession of records of telephone calls to give the records or copies to any person named in the order.

Related Provisions: An *assistance* order may be made under s. 487.02. Extra-provincial execution of a number recorder warrant is governed by s. 487.03. There is, however, *no* general rule that permits extra-provincial execution as in s. 188.1(1).

The scheme of s. 492.2 is similar to that in s. 492.1 for tracking device warrants.

Forms 1 and 5 may be adapted for use under this section.

PART XVI — COMPELLING APPEARANCE OF AN ACCUSED BEFORE A JUSTICE AND INTERIM RELEASE

Interpretation

493. Definitions — In this Part

"accused" includes

(a) a person to whom a peace officer has issued an appearance notice under section 496, and

(b) a person arrested for a criminal offence;

"appearance notice" means a notice in Form 9 issued by a peace officer;

"judge" means

(a) in the Province of Ontario, a judge of the superior court of criminal jurisdiction of the Province,

(b) in the Province of Quebec, a judge of the superior court of criminal jurisdiction of the province or three judges of the Court of Quebec,

(c) [Repealed 1992, c. 51, s. 37.],

(d) in the Provinces of Nova Scotia, New Brunswick, Manitoba, British Columbia, Prince Edward Island, Saskatchewan, Alberta and Newfoundland, a judge of the superior court of criminal jurisdiction of the Province,

(e) in the Yukon Territory and the Northwest Territories, a judge of the Supreme Court of the territory, and

(f) in Nunavut, a judge of the Nunavut Court of Justice;

"officer in charge" means the officer for the time being in command of the police force responsible for the lock-up or other place to which an accused is taken after arrest or a peace officer designated by him for the purposes of this Part who is in charge of that place at the time an accused is taken to that place to be detained in custody;

"promise to appear" means a promise in Form 10

"recognizance", when used in relation to a recognizance entered into before an officer in charge, or other peace officer, means a recognizance in Form 11, and when used in relation to a recognizance entered into before a justice or judge, means a recognizance in Form 32;

"summons" means a summons in Form 6 issued by a justice or a judge;

"undertaking" means an undertaking in Form 11.1 or 12;

"warrant", when used in relation to a warrant for the arrest of a person, means a warrant in Form 7 and, when used in relation to a warrant for the committal of a person, means a warrant in Form 8.

R.S., c. C-34, s. 448; c. 2 (2d Supp.), s. 5; 1972, c. 17, s. 3; 1974–75–76, c. 48, s. 25(1); 1978–79, c. 11, s. 10;R.S. 1985, c. 11 (1st Supp.), Sched.; c. 27 (2d Supp.), Sched., item 6; c. 40 (4th Supp.), Sched.; 1990, c. 16, s. 5; c. 17, s. 12; 1992, c. 51, s. 37; 1993, c. 28, s. 78 (Sched. III, item 32) [Repealed 1999, c. 3, (Sched., item 7).]; 1994, c. 44, s. 39; 1999, c. 3, s. 30.

Commentary: The section defines several terms that appear in this Part.

Case Law

Officer in Charge

R. v. Gendron (1985), 22 C.C.C. (3d) 312 (Ont. C.A.) — "Officer in charge" requires an appropriate delegation of authority to the officer in charge of the police division to which D is taken to be detained in custody by the officer then in charge of the police force.

Related Provisions: Part XVI deals with the process and means to compel D's appearance before a court of competent jurisdiction.

"Peace officer", "justice" and "superior court of criminal jurisdiction" are defined in s. 2, as is "property". The various forms of release and process to compel attendance appear in Part XXVIII immediately following s. 841. Under *I.A.* s. 34(1)(a), an indictable offence is any offence that either must, or may, be prosecuted by indictment, unless and until P elects to proceed by summary conviction.

Section 145 describes and punishes several offences relating to failures to appear or comply under the terms of the various forms of release for which provision is made in this Part.

Arrest without Warrant and Release from Custody

494. (1) Arrest without warrant by any person — Any one may arrest without warrant

    (a) a person whom he finds committing an indictable offence; or

    (b) a person who, on reasonable grounds, he believes

        (i) has committed a criminal offence, and

        (ii) is escaping from and freshly pursued by persons who have lawful authority to arrest that person.

(2) Arrest by owner, etc., of property — Any one who is

    (a) the owner or a person in lawful possession of property, or

    (b) a person authorized by the owner or by a person in lawful possession of property may arrest without warrant a person whom he finds committing a criminal offence on or in relation to that property.

(3) Delivery to peace officer — Any one other than a peace officer who arrests a person without warrant shall forthwith deliver the person to a peace officer.

R.S., c. C-34, s. 449; c. 2 (2d Supp.), s. 5.

Commentary: This section defines the authority of *persons other than peace officers* to *arrest without warrant*.

The authority of s. 494(1) may be exercised by "any one". It is restricted to the circumstances described in either s. 494(1)(a) or (b). The authority of s. 494(2) may *only* be exercised by a *person who falls within either* s. 494(2)(a) or (b). It is further limited by the requirement that the person arrested be *found committing* a criminal offence *on or in relation to* that property.

Under s. 494(3), there is an obligation upon anyone, other than a peace officer, who arrests another without warrant, forthwith to deliver the arrested person to a peace officer.

Case Law

Indictable Offence [See also Interpretation Act, s. 34(1)(a)]

R. v. Huff (1979), 50 C.C.C. (2d) 324 (Alta. C.A.) — Hybrid offences, *deemed* to be indictable until P elects otherwise, are indictable for the purposes of s. 494(1)(a).

Charter Considerations

R. v. Lerke (1986), 49 C.R. (3d) 324, 24 C.C.C. (3d) 129 (Alta. C.A.) — When one citizen arrests another, the arrest is the exercise of a governmental function to which the *Charter* applies. The right to search on arrest is *not* automatic. The search must be reasonable. In the case of a private citizen, a search for evidence would usually be unreasonable.

Related Provisions: An *indictable* offence under *I.A.* s. 34(1)(a) is any offence that must or may be prosecuted by indictment. A *criminal* offence includes both summary conviction and indictable offences created under the federal criminal law power. "Peace officer" is defined in s. 2.

495. (1) Arrest without warrant by peace officer — A peace officer may arrest without warrant

(a) a person who has committed an indictable offence or who, on reasonable grounds, he believes has committed or is about to commit an indictable offence,

(b) a person whom he finds committing a criminal offence, or

(c) a person in respect of whom he has reasonable grounds to believe that a warrant of arrest or committal, in any form set out in Part XXVIII in relation thereto, is in force within the territorial jurisdiction in which the person is found.

(2) Limitation — A peace officer shall not arrest a person without warrant for

(a) an indictable offence mentioned in section 553,

(b) an offence for which the person may be prosecuted by indictment or for which he is punishable on summary conviction, or

(c) an offence punishable on summary conviction,

in any case where

(d) he believes on reasonable grounds that the public interest, having regard to all the circumstances including the need to

(i) establish the identity of the person,

(ii) secure or preserve evidence of or relating to the offence, or

(iii) prevent the continuation or repetition of the offence or the commission of another offence,

may be satisfied without so arresting the person, and

(e) he has no reasonable grounds to believe that, if he does not so arrest the person, the person will fail to attend court in order to be dealt with according to law.

(3) Consequences of arrest without warrant — Notwithstanding subsection (2), a peace officer acting under subsection (1) is deemed to be acting lawfully and in the execution of his duty for the purposes of

(a) any proceedings under this or any other Act of Parliament; and

(b) any other proceedings, unless in any such proceedings it is alleged and established by the person making the allegation that the peace officer did not comply with the requirements of subsection (2).

R.S., c. C-34, s. 450; c. 2 (2d Supp.), s. 5;R.S. 1985, c. 27 (1st Supp.), s. 75.

Commentary: The section describes the authority of a *peace officer to arrest without warrant.*

The *general* authority of a peace officer under s. (1) extends beyond the authority given to *anyone* under s. 494(1), and to persons in possession of property, or those authorized by them under s. 494(2). Under s. 495(1)(a) an officer may arrest, *inter alia*, anyone in respect of whom the officer believes, on *reasonable* grounds, is *about to commit* an indictable offence. Under s. 495(1)(c), a peace officer may arrest *without* warrant anyone in respect of whom s/he has *reasonable* grounds to believe that an *arrest* or *committal* warrant is *in force* in the territorial jurisdiction in which the person is found.

Section 495(1) is circumscribed by s. 495(2). An officer is obliged *not* to arrest without a warrant in respect of certain categories of offences, where s/he believes, on *reasonable* grounds, that the *public interest* may be satisfied **without** such an arrest, and s/he has *no* reasonable grounds to believe that, absent arrest, D will fail to **attend court.**

Section 495(3) *deems* an officer acting under s. 495(1) to be acting *lawfully and in the execution of his/her duty* for the purposes of ss. 495(3), notwithstanding noncompliance with s. 495(2).

Case Law

Reasonable Grounds [formerly "Reasonable and Probable Grounds"]

R. v. Storrey (1990), 75 C.R. **(3d)** 1, 53 C.C.C. (3d) 316 (S.C.C.) — An officer arresting without warrant must *subjectively* have **reasonable (and probable)** grounds for the arrest. The grounds must also be *objectively* justifiable.

Chartier v. Quebec (A.G.) **(1979), 9 C.R.** (3d) 97 (S.C.C.) — In order to arrest without warrant, a peace officer must have **reasonable and probable** grounds for believing in the person's guilt and that belief must take into account **all the information** available to him. The officer is entitled to disregard only that information which he has **good reason** to believe is not reliable.

Eccles v. Bourque (1974), 27 **C.R.N.S.** 325, 19 C.C.C. (2d) 129 (S.C.C.) — An entry does *not* become unlawful merely because the fugitive is not found on the premises. The question of reasonable (and probable) grounds depends upon a *bona fide* reasonable belief in a state of facts that if true, would justify the course pursued. **That the supposed fact** does *not* exist does *not* render the belief unreasonable.

R. v. Golub (1997), 117 **C.C.C. (3d)** 193 (Ont. C.A.) — In deciding whether reasonable grounds exist, a police officer must conduct **the inquiry** which the circumstances reasonably permit. It is *not* necessary to get confirmation of information **provided** by a witness outside the police force whom the officer does not know. The officer **must take into** account all available information, and may only disregard what s/he has good **reason to believe** is unreliable.

R. v. Bennett (1996), 49 **C.R. (4th)** 206, 108 C.C.C. (3d) 175 (Que. C.A.) — An anonymous tip is *not* sufficient to constitute reasonable grounds for an arrest without warrant. The arresting officer must also be satisfied of the *reliability* **of the** information assessed in light of *all* the circumstances, in particular as it relates to a suspect's *participation* in the offence. (per Proulx and Rothman JJ.A.)

R. v. Proulx (1993), 81 **C.C.C. (3d)** 48 (Que. C.A.) — Information sufficient to constitute reasonable **(and probable) grounds for an arrest** need *not* constitute *prima facie* evidence of D's guilt, *a fortiori*, need *not* be sufficient for **conviction.**

Has Committed: S. 495(1)(a)

R. v. Klimchuk (1991), 8 **C.R. (4th)** 327, 67 C.C.C. (3d) 385 (B.C. C.A.) — Under s. 495(1)(a), the authority to arrest without warrant "a person who *has committed* an indictable offence" requires the arresting officer to have *witnessed* the indictable offence occurring. The authority to arrest without warrant a person who, on **reasonable grounds** a police officer believes has committed or is about to commit an indictable offence, **requires that the** officer's *subjective* belief be based on grounds which, *objectively* viewed, are reasonable **(per Wood** and Taylor JJ.A.).

Finds Committing: S. 495(1)(b)

R. v. Biron (1975), 30 C.R.N.S. 109, 23 C.C.C. (2d) 513 (S.C.C.) — *See also*: *R. v. Miller* (1986), 25 C.C.C. (3d) 554 (Sask. **C.A.); affirmed** (1988), 39 C.C.C. (3d) 288; and, *R. v. Vance* (1979), 10 C.R. (3d) 1 (Y.T. C.A.) — The **power to arrest** without warrant is given when the peace officer finds the accused "apparently" committing a criminal offence. Therefore, an arrest may be found lawful even though the person arrested is **acquitted** of the offence for which the arrest was made. It is the *circumstances* apparent to the officer at the *time* of the *arrest* that determine the validity of the arrest.

A Criminal Offence: S. 495(1)(b) [See also s. 31]

R. v. Kephart (1988), 44 C.C.C. (3d) 97 (Alta. C.A.) — Paragraphs (1)(a) and (b) do *not* authorize police officers forcibly to enter a **private dwelling** to apprehend juvenile runaway wards of a province. There is, *no* common law authority **to do so.**

Warrant of Arrest in Force: S. 495(1)(c)

Gamracy v. R. (1974), 22 **C.R.N.S.** 224, 12 C.C.C. (2d) 209 (S.C.C.) — A police officer is under no duty to obtain the warrant **or to ascertain** its contents. He need only inform the person arrested that an outstanding warrant is the **reason for the** arrest.

Hot Pursuit

R. v. Macooh (1993), 22 C.R. (4th) 70, 82 C.C.C. (3d) 481 (S.C.C.) — "Hot pursuit" is a *continuous* pursuit conducted with *reasonable diligence* so that pursuit and capture, along with the commission of the offence, comprise part of a single transaction. The offence for which pursuit is made need not have been committed in the officer's presence.

Entry on Private Property to Arrest [Formerly "Reasonable and Probable Grounds"] [See also s. 25]

R. v. Feeney (1997), [1997] 2 S.C.R. 13, 115 C.C.C. (3d) 129 (S.C.C.) — The *common law* rule that a warrantless arrest after forced entry into private premises is legal if

i.   the officer has reasonable grounds to believe that the person sought is in the premises;

ii.   proper announcement is made;

iii.   the officer believes reasonable grounds for the arrest exist; and,

iv.   there are reasonable and probable grounds for the arrest

offends *Charter* s. 8

In general, *warrantless* arrests in dwelling-houses are *prohibited* because the privacy interest of the occupant in the dwelling-house outweighs the interests of the police. Prior to the warrantless arrest in a dwelling-house, police must obtain a *warrant* to *enter* the dwelling-house for the *purpose* of *arrest*. The warrant may only be issued if there are reasonable grounds

i.   for the arrest; and

ii.   for the belief that the person sought *will* be found in the named premises.

Proper announcement must also be made. In cases of hot pursuit, however, police may enter a dwelling-house to make a warrantless arrest.

Except for exigent circumstances, the police should give notice

i.   of *presence*, by knocking or ringing the doorbell;

ii.   of *authority*, by self-identification as law enforcement police officers; and,

iii.   of *purpose*, by stating a lawful reason for *entry*.

An arrest may *not* be made for the *sole* purpose of investigation. If grounds for arrest exist, on both a subjective and objective basis, the fact that the police intend to continue investigation does *not* vitiate the arrest.

Warrantless searches for persons are *not* permissible, nor is an arrest warrant alone a sufficient protection of a suspect's privacy rights in occupation of his/her dwelling. In general, police must obtain *prior judicial authorization* for *entry* into a dwelling-house in order to *arrest* a person there. In the absence of express *Code* authority to issue a warrant to enter a dwelling in order to arrest, such a provision should be read into the existing statutory scheme.

R. v. Macooh (1993), 22 C.R. (4th) 70, 82 C.C.C. (3d) 481 (S.C.C.) — The broad basic principle of sanctity of the home is subject to the exception that, upon proper demand, a police officer may break down doors to arrest. Entry may be made against the will of the householder if there are *reasonable* grounds for the belief that the person sought is within the premises and *proper announcement* has been made prior to entry. The power of entry exists when officers are seeking to apprehend someone pursuant to an outstanding warrant, as well as when an attempt is made to arrest without warrant for an indictable offence.

R. v. Landry (1986), 50 C.R. (3d) 55, 25 C.C.C. (3d) 1 (S.C.C.) — A peace officer is entitled to enter private premises without consent to arrest a person without a warrant, and is acting in the execution of his duty, if the offence in question is indictable, if the person committed the offence, or the officer believes on reasonable and probable grounds that the person has committed or is about to commit the offence, if the peace officer believed on reasonable and probable grounds that the person sought was within the premises, and if proper announcement was made before entry.

Eccles v. Bourque (1974), 27 C.R.N.S. 325, 19 C.C.C. (2d) 129 (S.C.C.) — Police officers generally must make an announcement prior to entry, including at a minimum a request for and denial of admission. However, in exigent circumstances, for example saving someone within the premises from death or injury or to prevent destruction of evidence or if in hot pursuit, notice may not be required.

R. v. Delong (1989), 47 C.C.C. (3d) 402 (Ont. C.A.) — The four requirements of *Landry, supra*, apply not only to forcible entry by the police, but where the police enter through an open door. An arrest is *not* lawful if the police were trespassing at the time they arrested or initiated the arrest of the accused.

R. v. Wong (1987), 56 C.R. (3d) 352, 34 C.C.C. (3d) 51 (Ont. C.A.) — The police have the power to arrest in private premises without a warrant if the offence was indictable, they had reasonable (and probable) grounds for believing that the persons sought had been committing the offence and were on the premises, and a proper announcement was made before entry. Where evidence could be destroyed or removed, an announcement is not required.

Shall Not Arrest: S. 495(2)

Moore v. R. (1978), 5 C.R. (3d) 289, 43 C.C.C. (2d) 83 (S.C.C.) — A police officer has the power, under s. 495(2), to arrest an accused whom he *finds* committing a *summary* conviction offence *only* if the arrest is necessary, *inter alia*, to establish the accused's identity. An officer is carrying out his duty when he requests such person to identify himself. An accused who refuses to accede to the request for identification is guilty of obstructing a police officer in the performance of his duties.

Resisting Arrest [See also s. 129]

R. v. Stevens (1976), 33 C.C.C. (2d) 429 (N.S. C.A.) — Where *no* grounds exist for a lawful arrest, the arrest is unlawful. D who resists such an arrest is *not* guilty of resisting a police officer in the execution of his duty.

Koechlin v. Waugh (1956), 118 C.C.C. 24 (Ont. C.A.) — D is entitled in law to resist the efforts of police officers to arrest him where the police officers exceed their powers and infringe the rights of D without justification.

Deemed to be Acting Lawfully: S. 495(3)

R. v. Delong (1989), 47 C.C.C. (3d) 402 (Ont. C.A.) — Section 495(3) relates only to the consequences of the failure to comply with s. 495(2). It has no relevance to other situations.

R. v. Adams (1973), 21 C.R.N.S. 257 (Sask. C.A.) — *See also*: *R. v. McKibbon* (1973), 12 C.C.C. (2d) 66 (B.C. C.A.) — Section 495(3) must be construed as denying the right to use a defence, based on non-compliance with s. 495(2), in any proceedings under the *Code* or under any other Act of Parliament. Therefore, one who resists arrest for an offence referred to in s. 495(2), is guilty of obstructing a police officer in the execution of his duty where the officer was acting pursuant to his powers of arrest under s. 495(1) even though the officer did not satisfy the requirements of s. 495(2).

Notice of Reason for Arrest [See also s. 29 and Charter s. 10(a)]

R. v. Storrey (1990), 75 C.R. (3d) 1, 53 C.C.C. (3d) 316 (S.C.C.) — An arrest which is lawfully made does *not* become unlawful or contravene *Charter* s. 9 simply because the officer intends to continue the investigation after the arrest.

Campbell v. Hudyma (1985), 42 Alta. L.R. (2d) 59 (C.A.) — The plaintiff's action for false imprisonment, wrongful arrest, and assault succeeded where the officer's failure to inform the plaintiff of the reason for the arrest invalidated what was initially a supportable arrest.

Koechlin v. Waugh (1956), 118 C.C.C. 24 (Ont. C.A.) — *See also*: *R. v. Beaudette* (1957), 118 C.C.C. 295 (Ont. C.A.) — A police officer after making an arrest should always *inform* the person detained of the *reason* why he is detained. It is not, however, necessary to state any reason for an arrest where it is obvious that the person under arrest is well aware of the reasons for arrest.

Charter Considerations — Arbitrary Detention [See also Charter s. 9]

R. v. Duguay (1989), 67 C.R. (3d) 252, 46 C.C.C. (3d) 1 (S.C.C.) — The issue of whether D is arbitrarily detained will depend on the extent of the departure from the standard of reasonable (and probable) grounds for the arrest, the honesty of the belief in the existence of reasonable (and probable) grounds and the basis for such belief. An honest but mistaken belief in the existence of reasonable (and probable) grounds and a basis therefor will *not* make an arrest arbitrary, even if unlawful.

R. v. Cayer (1988), 66 C.R. (3d) 30 — *See also*: *R. v. Sieben* (1989), 73 C.R. (3d) 33, 51 C.C.C. (3d) 343 (Alta. C.A.); *R. v. Scott* (1990), 24 M.V.R. (2d) 204 (B.C. C.A.) — An *arbitrary detention* is a detention which is capricious, despotic or unjustifiable. The arrest of an impaired driver in the act or virtually in the act of driving, pursuant to a police policy or a policy adopted by the individual officer, does *not* make the arrest or detention arbitrary where, in the circumstances of the particular case, the arrest is reasonable in the public interest to prevent the continuation or repetition of the offence.

Right to Counsel [See also s. 254 and Charter s. 10]

Clarkson v. R. (1986), 50 C.R. (3d) 289, 25 C.C.C. (3d) 207 (S.C.C.) — See digest under *Charter*, s. 10, *infra*.

R. v. Gilbert (1981), 61 C.R. (3d) 149, 40 C.C.C. (3d) 423 (Ont. C.A.) — *See also*: *R. v. Playford* (1987), 61 C.R. (3d) 101, 40 C.C.C. (3d) 142 (Ont. C.A.) — The right to counsel carries with it the right to consult with counsel *in private*, even if privacy is *not* requested by D. As well, although D may be questioned by police before consulting counsel, this is the case only in urgent situations.

R. v. Dombrowski (1985), 44 C.R. (3d) 1, 18 C.C.C. (3d) 164 (Sask. C.A.) — Where a telephone was readily available, nothing justifies limiting or delaying until arrival at police headquarters the opportunity of consulting counsel which D wished to exercise.

Search or Seizure Incident to Arrest [See also Charter s. 8]

Eccles v. Bourque (1973), 22 C.R.N.S. 199 (B.C. C.A.); affirmed (1974), 27 C.R.N.S. 325, 19 C.C.C. (2d) 129 (S.C.C.) — Where a police officer has the right to enter a house to make an arrest, if the person to be arrested is *not* immediately there to be seen, he has the right to go through the house to find the person. The making of the search is incidental, and may be essential, to the effecting of the arrest.

R. v. Morrison (1987), 58 C.R. (3d) 63, 35 C.C.C. (3d) 437 (Ont C.A.) — *See also*: *R. v. Miller* (1987), 38 C.C.C. (3d) 252 (Ont. C.A.) — As part of a lawful arrest, a peace officer has the right to search D and take any property which he reasonably believes is connected to the offence charged or may be used as evidence against D, or any instrument or weapon found upon the arrested person. The peace officer need *not* have reasonable grounds to believe that such weapons or evidence *will* be found.

R. v. Alderton (1985), 44 C.R. (3d) 254, 17 C.C.C. (3d) 204 (Ont. C.A.) — *See also*: *R. v. Wong* (1987), 56 C.R. (3d) 352, 34 C.C.C. (3d) 51 (Ont. C.A.); *R. v. Plourde* (1985), 23 C.C.C. (3d) 463 (Que. C.A.) — Following a valid arrest, police may search D and seize, *inter alia*, whatever reasonably afforded evidence related to the commission of an offence without breach of *Charter* s. 8. The search includes D's *immediate* surroundings.

Related Provisions: "Peace officer" is defined in s. 2. What constitutes an "indictable offence" and a "criminal offence" are discussed in the corresponding note to s. 494.

Territorial jurisdiction is *not* defined in this Part, nor elsewhere in the *Code*, though a definition of "territorial division" is found in s. 2.

Sections 25–31 afford protection to persons administering and enforcing the law.

Charter s. 10 rights arise, *inter alia*, upon *arrest*, and the right of s. 11 where D is *charged* with an offence.

The provisions of s. 496 apply where a peace officer, under s. 495(2), has not arrested a subject. After an appearance notice has been issued, ss. 505, 506 and 508 apply. Where an arrest has been made without warrant, release may be made, prior to a judicial interim release hearing, under s. 497 or 498.

496. Issue of appearance notice by peace officer — Where, by virtue of subsection 495(2), a peace officer does not arrest a person, he may issue an appearance notice to the person if the offence is

(a) an indictable offence mentioned in section 553,

(b) an offence for which the person may be prosecuted by indictment or for which he is punishable on summary conviction, or

(c) an offence punishable on summary conviction.

R.S., c. C-34, s. 451; c. 2 (2d Supp.), s. 5.

Commentary: The section applies where a peace officer does not arrest a person, without warrant, by virtue of s. 495(2). Where the offence is a s. 553 indictable, an offence triable either way or a summary conviction offence, the officer may issue an *appearance notice*, as a means whereby to ensure D's attendance at trial.

Related Provisions: "Peace officer" is defined in s. 2 and "appearance notice" (Form 9) in s. 493. Confirmation of an appearance notice issued by a peace officer is necessary to compel D's attendance in court. The procedure is governed by ss. 505 and 508. Failure to appear in court or, to comply with its terms, is an offence under s. 145(5).

497. (1) Release from custody by peace officer — Where a peace officer arrests a person without warrant for

    (a) an indictable offence mentioned in section 553,

    (b) an offence for which the person may be prosecuted by indictment or for which he is punishable on summary conviction, or

    (c) an offence punishable on summary conviction,

he shall, as soon as practicable,

    (d) release the person from custody with the intention of compelling his appearance by way of summons, or

    (e) issue an appearance notice to the person and thereupon release him,

unless

    (f) he believes on reasonable grounds that it is necessary in the public interest, having regard to all the circumstances including the need to

        (i) establish the identity of the person,

        (ii) secure or preserve evidence of or relating to the offence, or

        (iii) prevent the continuation or repetition of the offence or the commission of another offence,

    that the person be detained in custody or that the matter of his release from custody be dealt with under another provision of this Part, or

    (g) he believes on reasonable grounds that, if the person is released by him from custody, the person will fail to attend court in order to be dealt with according to law.

(2) Where subsection (1) does not apply — Subsection (1) does not apply in respect of a person who has been arrested without warrant by a peace officer for an offence described in subsection 503(3).

(3) Consequences of non-release — A peace officer who has arrested a person without warrant for an offence described in subsection (1) and who does not release the person from custody as soon as practicable in the manner described in paragraph (d) or (e) of that subsection shall be deemed to be acting lawfully and in the execution of his duty for the purposes of

    (a) any proceedings under this or any other Act of Parliament; and

    (b) any other proceedings, unless in any such proceedings it is alleged and established by the person making the allegation that the peace officer did not comply with the requirements of subsection (1).

R.S., c. C-34, s. 452; c. 2 (2d Supp.), s. 5.

Commentary: The section defines the *obligation* of a *peace officer* to *release* a *person arrested without a warrant* for a s. 553 indictable, offence triable either way or summary conviction offence.

Under s. 497(1), a *duty* is imposed upon the *peace officer* who makes a non-warranted arrest in respect of a designated offence, as soon as practicable, either to *release* D, with the intention of compelling D's appearance by *summons*, or to issue an *appearance notice*, unless the requirements of either s. 497(1)(f) or (g) are met. Section 497(1)(f) engages *public interest* considerations which require either that D be detained in custody or that release be dealt with under another provision of Part XVI, whereas s. 497(1)(g) involves custody to ensure attendance. The officer's belief must be based "on reasonable grounds".

Under s. 497(2), s. 497(1) does *not* apply to non-warranted arrest for extra-provincial offences which are dealt with by a justice under s. 503(3).

Section 497(3) *deems* an officer who has failed to comply with the release provisions of ss. 497(1)(d) and (e) to be nonetheless acting lawfully and in the execution of his/her duties, for the purposes specified.

Case Law

Charter Considerations — Arbitrary Detention [See also Charter s. 9]

R. v. Cutforth (1987), 61 C.R. (3d) 187, 40 C.C.C. (3d) 253 (Alta. C.A.) — Where P does *not* seek to introduce any evidence obtained through an alleged arbitrary detention, the detention is collateral to the issue of guilt or innocence. It is *not* a defence to the charge, nor does it provide, alter or destroy evidence relating to the sole issue at trial. The trial court is *not* a court of competent jurisdiction where the *Charter* infringement is foreign to the issue raised by the indictment and does *not* engage the exclusionary authority of s. 24(2).

R. v. McIntosh (1984), 29 M.V.R. 50 (B.C. C.A.) — *See also*: *R. v. Pashovitz* (1987), 59 C.R. (3d) 396 (Sask. C.A.) — Where there are reasonable and probable grounds for detaining D to prevent further driving while intoxicated, D's detention is *not* arbitrary.

Related Provisions: Sections 25–31 afford protection to persons administering and enforcing the law.

Section 498 describes the wider authority of the *officer in charge*, as defined in s. 493, or another peace officer to release a person who has been arrested without a warrant by or delivered to a peace officer. Section 499 confers similar authority where the arrest has been made with a warrant.

Sections 503(3) and (3.1) describe the procedure to be followed when the arrest without warrant is in respect of an indictable offence alleged to have been committed in Canada outside the province where D is in custody.

The *confirmation* procedure to be followed where D is released under s. 497(1)(e) upon the issuance of an appearance notice is set out in ss. 505 and 508. Failure to appear, as required for *I.C.A.* purposes, may result in the issuance of an arrest warrant under s. 502. Such a failure to attend or to attend court may also result in the prosecution under s. 145(5).

498. (1) Release from custody by officer in charge — Where a person who has been arrested without warrant by a peace officer is taken into custody, or where a person who has been arrested without warrant and delivered to a peace officer under subsection 494(3) is detained in custody under subsection 503(1) for

Proposed Amendment — 498(1)

498. (1) Release from custody by officer in charge — Where a person who has been arrested without warrant by a peace officer is taken into custody, or where a person who has been arrested without warrant and delivered to a peace officer under subsection 494(3) or placed in the custody of a peace officer under subsection 163.5(3) of the *Customs Act* is detained in custody under subsection 503(1) for

1998, c. 7, s. 2. Not in force at date of publication.

(a) an indictable offence mentioned in section 553,

(b) an offence for which the person may be prosecuted by indictment or for which he is punishable on summary conviction,

(c) an offence punishable on summary conviction, or

(d) any other offence that is punishable by imprisonment for five years or less, and has not been taken before a justice or released from custody under any other provision of this Part, the officer in charge or another peace officer shall, as soon as practicable,

> (e) release the person with the intention of compelling his appearance by way of summons,

> (f) release the person on his giving his promise to appear,

> (g) release the person on the person's entering into a recognizance before the officer in charge or another peace officer without sureties in such amount not exceeding five hundred dollars as the officer directs, but without deposit of money or other valuable security, or

> (h) if the person is not ordinarily resident in the province in which the person is in custody or does not ordinarily reside within two hundred kilometres of the place in which the person is in custody, release the person on the person's entering into a recognizance before the officer in charge or another peace officer without sureties in such amount not exceeding five hundred dollars as the officer directs and, if the officer so directs, on depositing with the officer such sum of money or other valuable security not exceeding in amount or value five hundred dollars, as the officer directs,

unless

> (i) he believes on reasonable grounds that it is necessary in the public interest, having regard to all the circumstances including the need to

>> (i) establish the identity of the person,

>> (ii) secure or preserve evidence of or relating to the offence, or

>> (iii) prevent the continuation or repetition of the offence or the commission of another offence,

> that the person be detained in custody or that the matter of his release from custody be dealt with under another provision of this Part, or

> (j) he believes on reasonable grounds that, if the person is released by him from custody, the person will fail to attend court in order to be dealt with according to law.

(2) Where subsection (1) does not apply — Subsection (1) does not apply in respect of a person who has been arrested without warrant by a peace officer for an offence described in subsection 503(3).

(3) Consequences of non-release — An officer in charge or another peace officer who has the custody of a person taken into or detained in custody for an offence described in subsection (1) and who does not release the person from custody as soon as practicable in the manner described in paragraph (1)(e), (f), (g) or (h) shall be deemed to be acting lawfully and in the execution of the officer's duty for the purpose of

> (a) any proceedings under this or any other Act of Parliament; or

> (b) any other proceedings, unless in any such proceedings it is alleged and established by the person making the allegation that the officer in charge or other peace officer did not comply with the requirements of subsection (1).

R.S., c. C-34, s. 453; c. 2 (2d Supp.), s. 5;R.S. 1985, c. 27 (1st Supp.), s. 186; 1997, c. 18, s. 52.

Commentary: The section describes the authority of an *officer in charge or another peace officer* to *release* a person who has been *arrested without a warrant* by or delivered to a peace officer under s. 494(3), but who has neither been taken before a justice, nor released from custody otherwise under Part XVI.

In general, s. 498(1) requires the officer to release D upon a form of release described in ss. 498(1)(e)–(h). The officer may only detain D where s/he has a reasonably grounded belief in the necessity therefor, upon either public interest grounds or in order to ensure D's attendance at trial.

Under s. 498(2), s. 498(1) does *not* apply where D has been arrested without warrant for an extraprovincial offence which will be dealt with by a justice under s. 503(3).

Section 498(3) *deems* an officer who has failed to comply with the release provisions of ss. 498(1)(e)–(h) to be, nonetheless, acting lawfully and in the execution of his/her duties for the specified purposes.

Related Provisions: "Peace officer" and "justice" are defined in s. 2 and "officer in charge", "summons", "promise to appear", "recognizance" and "warrant" in s. 493. Sections 25–31 afford general protection to persons administering and enforcing the law.

Section 497 describes the more restrictive authority of a "peace officer" to release a person arrested without warrant by or delivered to such an officer. Section 499 describes the release authority of the officer in charge where D has been arrested with a warrant.

The procedure followed where the arrest without warrant is in respect of an indictable offence alleged to have been committed in Canada outside the province where D is in custody is described in ss. 503(3) and (3.1).

Sections 505 and 508 set out the *confirmation* procedure where D has been released under this section. Failure to appear for *I.C.A.* purposes may result in the issuance of an arrest warrant under s. 502. Such a failure to attend, or attend court, may also result in a prosecution under s. 145(5).

499. (1) Release from custody by officer in charge where arrest made with warrant — Where a person who has been arrested with a warrant by a peace officer is taken into custody for an offence other than one mentioned in section 522, the officer in charge may, if the warrant has been endorsed by a justice under subsection 507(6),

(a) release the person on the person's giving a promise to appear;

(b) release the person on the person's entering into a recognizance before the officer in charge without sureties in the amount not exceeding five hundred dollars that the officer in charge directs, but without deposit of money or other valuable security; or

(c) if the person is not ordinarily resident in the province in which the person is in custody or does not ordinarily reside within two hundred kilometres of the place in which the person is in custody, release the person on the person's entering into a recognizance before the officer in charge without sureties in the amount not exceeding five hundred dollars that the officer in charge directs and, if the officer in charge so directs, on depositing with the officer in charge such sum of money or other valuable security not exceeding in amount or value five hundred dollars, as the officer in charge directs.

(2) Additional conditions — In addition to the conditions for release set out in paragraphs (1)(*a*), (*b*) and (*c*), the officer in charge may also require the person to enter into an undertaking in Form 11.1 in which the person, in order to be released, undertakes to do one or more of the following things:

(a) to remain within a territorial jurisdiction specified in the undertaking;

(b) to notify a peace officer or another person mentioned in the undertaking of any change in his or her address, employment or occupation;

(c) to abstain from communicating with any witness or other person mentioned in the undertaking, or from going to a place mentioned in the undertaking, except in accordance with the conditions specified in the undertaking;

(d) to deposit the person's passport with the peace officer or other person mentioned in the undertaking.

(e) to abstain from possessing a firearm and to surrender any firearm in the possession of the person and any authorization, licence or registration certificate or other document enabling that person to acquire or possess a firearm;

(f) to report at the times specified in the undertaking to a peace officer or other person designated in the undertaking; and

(g) to abstain from

   (i) the consumption of alcohol or other intoxicating substances, or

   (ii) the consumption of drugs except in accordance with a medical prescription.

(3) Application to justice — A person who has entered into an undertaking under subsection (2) may, at any time before or at his or her appearance pursuant to a promise to appear or recognizance, apply to a justice for an order under subsection 515(1) to replace his or her undertaking, and section 515 applies, with such modifications as the circumstances require, to such a person.

(4) Application by prosecutor — Where a person has entered into an undertaking under subsection (2), the prosecutor may

   (a) at any time before the appearance of the person pursuant to a promise to appear or recognizance, after three days notice has been given to that person, or

   (b) at the appearance.

apply to a justice for an order under subsection 515(2) to replace the undertaking, and section 515 applies, with such modifications as the circumstances require, to such a person.

R.S., c. 2 (2d Supp.), s. 5;R.S. 1985, c. 27 (1st Supp.), s. 186; 1994, c. 44, s. 40; 1997, c. 18, s. 53.

Commentary: The *officer in charge* may release *any* person arrested with a warrant by a peace officer and taken into custody *except* a person arrested for a s. 522 offence, provided the justice who issued the arrest warrant has endorsed it in Form 29. The authority to release is *discretionary*.

Where the *officer in charge* decides to release D, the release form may be a promise to appear or recognizance entered into before the officer in charge in accordance with ss. 499(1), (a) – (c). Section 499(2) authorizes the officer in charge to require D to enter into an undertaking in Form 11.1 in order to be released. The *terms* that may be required are listed in ss. 499(2), (a) – (g).

Under s. 499(3), *before* or *at* D's appearance, pursuant to the original form of release, D may apply to a justice under s. 515(1) to replace the undertaking. Section 515 governs the application. P may also do likewise under ss. 499(4) and 515(2).

Related Provisions: "Peace officer" and "justice" are defined in s. 2 and "warrant", "officer in charge", "promise to appear" and "recognizance" in s. 493.

The release authority of the officer in charge or another officer in respect of persons arrested without warrant by or delivered to a peace officer is described in s. 498. A peace officer has a more restricted release authority under s. 497. In each case the confirmation procedure of ss. 505 and 508 must be followed to validate the process.

The contents of an arrest warrant are described in ss. 511 and 513. Its execution is governed by s. 514. Sections 25–31 protect persons administering and enforcing the law.

Judicial interim release for offences listed in s. 522 may only be ordered by a judge of the superior court of criminal jurisdiction. Section 515 describes the basis upon which a justice may order D's release pending trial. Failure to comply with an undertaking under s. 499(2) will attract liability under s. 145(5.1). The undertaking may be varied under s. 515.1.

500. Money or other valuable security to be deposited with justice — If a person has, under paragraph 498(1)(h) or 499(1)(c), deposited a sum of money or other valuable security with the officer in charge, the officer in charge shall, without delay after the deposit, cause the money or valuable security to be delivered to a justice for deposit with the justice.

R.S., c. 2 (2d Supp.), s. 5; 1999, c. 5, s. 20.

Commentary: The section imposes a *duty* upon an *officer in charge* with whom D has deposited any sum of money or other valuable security, upon entering into a recognizance under s. 498(1)(h) or 499(g), forthwith after deposit, to cause the money or valuable security to be *delivered* to a *justice* for deposit with the justice.

Related Provisions: "Justice" and "valuable security" are defined in s. 2, "officer in charge" in s. 493. The procedure followed to confirm D's release by the officer in charge on a recognizance under s. 498(1)(h) is set out in ss. 505 and 508. Under s. 499(g), release on a recognizance after an arrest with warrant may occur only where the warrant has been first endorsed by a justice under s. 507(6).

501. (1) Contents of appearance notice, promise to appear and recognizance — An appearance notice issued by a peace officer or a promise to appear given to, or a recognizance entered into before, an officer in charge or another peace officer shall

(a) set out the name of the accused;

(b) set out the substance of the offence that the accused is alleged to have committed; and

(c) require the accused to attend court at a time and place to be stated therein and to attend thereafter as required by the court in order to be dealt with according to law.

(2) Idem — An appearance notice issued by a peace officer or a promise to appear given to, or a recognizance entered into before, an officer in charge or another peace officer shall set out the text of subsections 145(5) and (6) and section 502.

(3) An appearance notice issued by a peace officer or a promise to appear given to, or a recognizance entered into before, an officer in charge or another peace officer may require the accused to appear at a time and place stated in it for the purposes of the *Identification of Criminals Act*, where the accused is alleged to have committed an indictable offence and, in the case of an offence designated as a contravention under the *Contraventions Act*, the Attorney General, within the meaning of that Act has not made an election under section 50 of that Act.

(4) Signature of accused — An accused shall be requested to sign in duplicate his appearance notice, promise to appear or recognizance and, whether or not he complies with that request, one of the duplicates shall be given to the accused, but if the accused fails or refuses to sign, the lack of his signature does not invalidate the appearance notice, promise to appear or recognizance, as the case may be.

(5) Proof of issue of appearance notice — The issue of an appearance notice by any peace officer may be proved by the oral evidence, given under oath, of the officer who issued it or by the officer's affidavit made before a justice or other person authorized to administer oaths or to take affidavits.

R.S., c. 2 (2d Supp.), s. 5; R.S. 1985, c. 27 (1st Supp.), s. 76; 1992, c. 47, s. 69; 1994, c. 44, s. 41; 1996, c. 7, s. 38.

Commentary: The section describes the *contents* of the various *release forms* issued by a peace officer and either given to or entered into before an officer in charge; or another peace officer

Under ss. 501(1) and (2), each *appearance notice, promise to appear*, and *recognizance* entered into before an officer in charge, or another peace officer, must set out D's name, the substance of the alleged offence, the text of ss. 145(5) and (6) and s. 502, and require D to attend court at a specified time and place, and thereafter as required by the court. Where the offence alleged is *indictable*, the release document, under s. 501(3), may also require D's attendance at a specified time and place for *I.C.A.* purposes. D is then *deemed* to be in *lawful custody* charged with an indictable offence.

Under s. 501(4), D must be requested to sign the release form in duplicate. D will receive a duplicate, signed or otherwise. The absence of D's signature does *not* invalidate the release form.

Section 501(5) describes the manner in which *proof* may be made of the issuance of an appearance notice. Proof by affidavit or by oral evidence is permissible.

Case Law

Contents of Release Form

Powers v. R. (1973), 21 C.R.N.S. 116, 10 C.C.C. (2d) 395 (N.B. S.C.) — An appearance notice that mentions a section number but fails to specify the statute or the substance of the alleged offence is defective.

R. v. Gougeon (1980), 55 C.C.C. (2d) 218 (Ont. C.A.); leave to appeal refused (1980), 35 N.R. 83n (S.C.C.) — The omission in a promise to appear of the full text of s. 145(5) is *not* a jurisdictional defect. Where D appears, "under protest" or not, the court has jurisdiction to proceed.

Attend Court

Anderson v. R. (1983), 37 C.R. (3d) 67, 9 C.C.C. (3d) 539 (Alta. C.A.) — Attendance in court means more than being physically present. Attendance in court necessarily involves making one's presence known to the presiding justice.

R. v. Simons (1976), 34 C.R.N.S. 273, 30 C.C.C. (2d) 162 (Ont. C.A.) — There is *no* authority for an officer in charge to direct in a promise to appear that the person in custody attend before a provincial judge presiding in another territorial jurisdiction. When D is arrested and *not* released by the officer in charge, D must be brought before a justice within the territorial jurisdiction of arrest. The summons must require appearance within the territorial jurisdiction of the arrest.

Charter Considerations

R. v. Beare (1988), 66 C.R. (3d) 97, 45 C.C.C. (3d) 57 (S.C.C.) — To the extent that s. 501(3) and *I.C.A.* authorize the fingerprinting of a person who has been arrested but *not* convicted of an indictable offence, they do *not* contravene *Charter* s. 7.

Related Provisions: "Appearance notice", "promise to appear", "recognizance" and "officer in charge" are defined in s. 493, "peace officer" and "justice" in s. 2.

The *release authority* of a *peace officer* is defined in ss. 497 and 498 and of an officer in charge in ss. 498 and 499. The procedure to be followed in the confirmation of the forms of release described in this section is set out in ss. 505 and 508.

Under s. 502, *failure to appear* at a specified time and place for *I.C.A.* purposes may result in the issuance of a warrant for D's arrest, where the release process has been confirmed. Such failure, as well as a failure to attend court, may attract liability under s. 145(5).

Under *I.A.* s. 34(1)(a), an "indictable offence" includes an offence triable either way, at least prior to an election by P to proceed by summary conviction.

502. Failure to appear — **Where an accused who is required by an appearance notice or promise to appear or by a recognizance entered into before an officer in charge or another peace officer to appear at a time and place stated therein for the purposes of the *Identification of Criminals Act* does not appear at that time and place, a justice may, where the appearance notice, promise to appear or recognizance has been confirmed by a justice under section 508, issue a warrant for the arrest of the accused for the offence with which the accused is charged.**

R.S., c. 2 (2d Supp.), s. 5; 1992, c. 44, s. 70; 1994, c. 44; 1997, c. 18, s. 54.

Commentary: The section authorizes the issuance of a warrant of arrest for the offence charged where D has failed to appear at a specified time and place for *I.C.A.* purposes, in accordance with a specified form of release.

Case Law

R. v. Gauthier (1983), 35 C.R. (3d) 159 (Que. C.A.) — Where, on the date set for the appearance of D for *I.C.A.* purposes, the appearance notice had *not* yet been confirmed, D could not be guilty of failure to appear without lawful excuse, for the purposes of identification.

Related Provisions: The release form is confirmed under ss. 505 and 508.

The warrant issued under s. 502, on account of a defined failure to appear, is in respect of the offence described in the original form of release subsequently confirmed by a justice. The failure to appear may also attract *liability* under s. 145(5).

Appearance of Accused before Justice

503. (1) Taking before justice — A peace officer who arrests a person with or without warrant or to whom a person is delivered under subsection 494(3) shall cause the person to be detained in custody and, in accordance with the following provisions, to be taken before a justice to be dealt with according to law, namely:

Proposed Amendment — 503(1)

503. (1) Taking before justice — A peace officer who arrests a person with or without warrant or to whom a person is delivered under subsection 494(3) or into whose custody a person is placed under subsection 163.5(3) of the *Customs Act* shall cause the person to be detained in custody and, in accordance with the following provisions, to be taken before a justice to be dealt with according to law:

1998, c. 7, s. 3. Not in force at date of publication.

(a) where a justice is available within a period of twenty-four hours after the person has been arrested by or delivered to the peace officer, the person shall be taken before a justice without unreasonable delay and in any event within that period, and

(b) where a justice is not available within a period of twenty-four hours after the person has been arrested by or delivered to the peace officer, the person shall be taken before a justice as soon as possible,

unless, at any time before the expiration of the time prescribed in paragraph (*a*) or (*b*) for taking the person before a justice,

(c) the peace officer or officer in charge releases the person under any other provision of this Part, or

(d) the peace officer or officer in charge is satisfied that the person should be released from custody, whether unconditionally under subsection (4) or otherwise conditionally or unconditionally, and so releases him.

(2) Conditional release — Where a peace officer or an officer in charge is satisfied that a person described in subsection (1) should be released from custody conditionally, the officer may, unless the person is detained in custody for an offence mentioned in section 522, release that person on the person's giving a promise to appear or entering into a recognizance in accordance with paragraphs 498(1)(*f*) to (*h*) and subsection (2.1).

(2.1) Undertaking — In addition to the conditions referred to in subsection (2), the peace officer or officer in charge may, in order to release the person, require the person to enter into an undertaking in Form 11.1 in which the person undertakes to do one or more of the following things:

(a) to remain within a territorial jurisdiction specified in the undertaking;

(b) to notify the peace officer or another person mentioned in the undertaking of any change in his or her address, employment or occupation;

(c) to abstain from communicating with any witness or other person mentioned in the undertaking, or from going to a place mentioned in the undertaking, except in accordance with the conditions specified in the undertaking;

(d) to deposit the person's passport with the peace officer or other person mentioned in the undertaking;

(e) to abstain possessing a firearm and to surrender any firearm in the possession of the person and any authorization, licence or registration certificate or other document enabling that person to acquire or possess a firearm;

(f) to report at the times specified in the undertaking to a peace officer or other person designated in the undertaking; or

(g) to abstain from

(i) the consumption of alcohol or other intoxicating substances, or

(ii) the consumption of drugs except in accordance with a medical prescription.

(2.2) Application to justice — A person who has entered into an undertaking under subsection (2.1) may, at any time before or at his or her appearance pursuant to a promise to appear or recognizance, apply to a justice for an order under subsection 515(1) to replace his or her undertaking, and section 515 applies, with such modifications as the circumstances require, to such a person.

(2.3) Application by prosecutor — Where a person has entered into an undertaking under subsection (2.1), the prosecutor may

(a) at any time before the appearance of the person pursuant to a promise to appear or recognizance, after three days notice has been given to that person, or

(b) at the appearance,

apply to justice for an order under subsection 515(2) to replace the undertaking, and section 515 applies, with such modifications as the circumstances require, to such a person.

(3) Remand in custody for return to jurisdiction where offence alleged to have been committed — Where a person has been arrested without warrant for an indictable offence alleged to have been committed in Canada outside the territorial division where the arrest took place, the person shall, within the time prescribed in paragraph (1)(a) or (b), be taken before a justice within whose jurisdiction the person was arrested unless, where the offence was alleged to have been committed within the province in which the person was arrested, the person was taken before a justice within whose jurisdiction the offence was alleged to have been committed, and the justice within whose jurisdiction the person was arrested

(a) if the justice is not satisfied that there are reasonable grounds to believe that the person arrested is the person alleged to have committed the offence, shall release that person; or

(b) if the justice is satisfied that there are reasonable grounds to believe that the person arrested is the person alleged to have committed the offence, may

(i) remand the person to the custody of a peace officer to await execution of a warrant for his or her arrest in accordance with section 528, but if no warrant is so executed within a period of six days after the time he or she is remanded to such custody, the person in whose custody he or she then is shall release him or her, or

(ii) where the offence was alleged to have been committed within the province in which the person was arrested, order the person to be taken before a justice having jurisdiction with respect to the offence.

(3.1) **Interim release** — Notwithstanding paragraph (3)(*b*), a justice may, with the consent of the prosecutor, order that the person referred to in subsection (3), pending the execution of a warrant for arrest of that person, be released

(a) unconditionally, or

(b) on any of the following terms to which the prosecutor consents, namely,

(i) giving an undertaking, including an undertaking to appear at a specified time before the court that has jurisdiction with respect to the indictable offence that the person is alleged to have committed, or

(ii) entering into a recognizance described in any of paragraphs 515(2)(*a*) to (*e*)

with such conditions described in subsection 515(4) as the justice considers desirable and to which the prosecutor consents.

(4) **Release of person about to commit indictable offence** — A peace officer or officer in charge having the custody of a person who has been arrested without warrant as a person about to commit an indictable offence shall release that person unconditionally as soon as practicable after he is satisfied that the continued detention of that person in custody is no longer necessary in order to prevent the commission by him of an indictable offence.

(5) **Consequences of non-release** — Notwithstanding subsection (4), a peace officer or officer in charge having the custody of a person referred to in that subsection who does not release the person before the expiration of the time prescribed in paragraph (1)(*a*) or (*b*) for taking the person before the justice shall be deemed to be acting lawfully and in the execution of his duty for the purposes of

(a) any proceedings under this or any other Act of Parliament; or

(b) any other proceedings, unless in such proceedings it is alleged and established by the person making the allegation that the peace officer or officer in charge did not comply with the requirements of subsection (4).

R.S., c. C-34, s. 454; c. 2 (2d Supp.), s. 5;1974–75–76, c. 93, s. 46;R.S. 1985, c. 27 (1st Supp.), s. 77; 1994, c. 44 s. 42; 1997, c. 18, s. 55.

Commentary: The section describes the circumstances under which D, arrested with or *without* warrant, must be taken before a justice to be dealt with according to law. Special provision is made for cases where D has been arrested *without* warrant for an offence alleged to have been committed in *another province*.

Section 503(1) requires a *peace officer* who has arrested D with or without warrant, or to whom D has been delivered under s. 494(3), to take D before a justice, in accordance with s. 503(1)(a) or (b). *Where a justice is available within 24 hours* of arrest or delivery, D must be taken before the justice without unreasonable delay and, in any event, within the 24-hour period. *Where a justice is not available* in such period, D must be taken before a justice as soon as possible. The obligation of a peace officer to take D before a justice under s. 503(1)(a) or (b) does *not* arise where D is released prior to the expiration of the relevant time period, by either the peace officer or officer in charge, under any other provision of Part XVI. The officer in charge may *not* release D charged with an offence listed in s. 522.

Where the officer in charge or peace officer decides that D should be released conditionally, s. 503(2) provides for the form of release. D may be released on a promise to appear or a recognizance in accordance with s. 498(1)(f) – (h). The officer may also require D to enter into a Form 11.1 undertaking which includes one or more of the requirements of s. 503(2.1). This provision is *not* available in respect of s. 522 offences. Under s. 503(2.2.), where D has been required to enter into an undertaking under s. 503(2.1), D may apply to a justice under s. 515 to replace the undertaking. The application may be made at any time before or after D's appearance, purusant to the original form of release. Section 515 applies to the application. Under s. 503(2.3), before D's appearance, subject to three days notice, or at D's appearance, P may apply to a justice under s. 515(2) to replace the undertaking. Section 515 governs the application.

Under s. 503(4), a peace officer or officer in charge having the custody of one arrested without warrant as a person *about to commit* an indictable offence, is obliged to release the person unconditionally, as soon as practicable, when satisfied continued detention is no longer necessary to prevent the apprehended offence.

Sections 503(3) and (3.1) describe the *duties of the justice* in respect of an accused arrested without warrant for an *out-of-territorial division* offence. The justice must first determine whether s/he is satisfied that there are reasonable grounds to believe D is the person alleged to have committed the offence. Upon being satisfied of D's *identity*, the justice may remand D into custody under s. 503(3)(b)(i) or, where the offence was alleged to have been committed in the jurisdiction in which D was arrested, order the person taken before a justice having jurisdiction with respect to the offence or, with the consent of P under s. 503(3.1), order D released pending execution of the warrant. Failure to *execute* the warrant within *six* days of remand requires that D be released. If the justice is *not* satisfied that there are *reasonable grounds* to believe D is the person alleged to have committed the offence, D must be released.

Section 503(5) *deems* a peace officer or officer in charge to be acting lawfully and in the execution of his/her duties for the purposes described, notwithstanding non-compliance with s. 503(1)(a) or (b).

Case Law

Appearance Before Justice

R. v. Ings (1985), 56 Nfld & P.E.I.R. 53 (Nfld. C.A.) — *See also*: *Ex parte Venlerberghe* (1973), 24 C.R.N.S. 113, 13 C.C.C. (2d) 84 (B.C. S.C.) — The proper remedy, if any, for a denial of the right to be brought before a justice within the required time is to be determined by the trial court.

R. v. Koszulap (1974), 27 C.R.N.S. 226 (Ont. C.A.) — The obligation of the arresting officer is to bring D before a justice "without unreasonable delay". Twenty four hours is the outer limit of what is a reasonable period where a justice is available. The officer does not have an unqualified right to keep D in custody for the purposes of investigation for a 24-hour period before taking him before a justice.

Charter Considerations See also, Charter, s. 9

R. v. Charles (1987), 59 C.R. (3d) 94, 36 C.C.C. (3d) 286 (Sask. C.A.) — Failure to bring D before a justice within 24 hours of arrest, constitutes an arbitrary detention.

Related Provisions: "Justice", "peace officer" and "prosecutor" are defined in s. 2, "officer in charge" and "warrant" in s. 493.

The release authority of the *peace officer* is described in ss. 497 and 498, that of the *officer in charge* in ss. 498 and 499. A person charged with an offence listed in s. 522 may only be released by a judge of the superior court of criminal jurisdiction.

Section 528 to which reference is made in s. 503(3)(b) permits endorsement of a warrant for execution out of the jurisdiction of its issuance. Failure to comply with an undertaking under s. 503(2.1) will attract liability under s. 145(5.1). The undertaking may be varied under s. 515.1.

Information, Summons and Warrant

504. In what cases justice may receive information — Any one who, on reasonable grounds, believes that a person has committed an indictable offence may lay an information in writing and under oath before a justice, and the justice shall receive the information, where it is alleged

(a) that the person has committed, anywhere, an indictable offence that may be tried in the province in which the justice resides, and that the person

(i) is or is believed to be, or

(ii) resides or is believed to reside,

within the territorial jurisdiction of the justice;

(b) that the person, wherever he may be, has committed an indictable offence within the territorial jurisdiction of the justice;

(c) that the person has, anywhere, unlawfully received property that was unlawfully obtained within the territorial jurisdiction of the justice; or

(d) that the person has in his possession stolen property within the territorial jurisdiction of the justice.

R.S., c. C-34, s. 455; c. 2 (2d Supp.), s. 5.

Commentary: The section describes the circumstances under which anyone may lay and a justice must receive an information alleging the commission of an *indictable offence.*

The informant may be *anyone* who, on *reasonable* grounds, believes that another has committed an *indictable offence.* The information must be *in writing* and *under oath,* taken *before* the *justice.* The justice is obliged to receive the information, provided it is in proper form and alleges an offence within ss. 504(a)–(d).

Case Law

Quebec (A.G.) v. Lechasseur (1981), 63 C.C.C. (2d) 301 (S.C.C.) — This section permits *any* person, who has *reasonable* grounds, to lay an information charging an indictable offence. The provision is *intra vires* Parliament.

R. v. Southwick (1967), 2 C.R.N.S. 46 (Ont. C.A.) — Criminal proceedings commence upon the swearing of an information before a justice. The inquiry can be held and summons issued by a different justice after the expiry of the six-month limitation period for summary conviction offences as long as the information was "laid", i.e., the written complaint was sworn before a justice, within the limitation period.

Related Provisions: "Justice" is defined in s. 2. The territorial jurisdiction of a justice is determined by the terms of his/her appointment. An indictable offence under *I.A.* s. 34(1)(a) is any offence which may be prosecuted by indictment and includes offences triable either way, unless and until P elects to proceed by summary conviction.

An information laid under this section may be in Form 2, and upon receipt, the justice will follow s. 507 to determine whether or what process shall issue to compel D's attendance in court. Sections 509–514 describe the forms of process, summons and warrant, as well as the manner in which each may be served or executed.

Proceedings in respect of indictable offences may also be initiated through the confirmation procedure of ss. 505 and 507 in or, in rare cases, by direct indictment under ss. 577(a) and (c) without first laying an information.

Form 2 is also used under s. 788(1) to commence proceedings for summary conviction offences under Part XXVIII. It may include reference D's date of birth.

505. Time within which information to be laid in certain cases — Where

(a) an appearance notice has been issued to an accused under section 496, or

(b) an accused has been released from custody under section 497 or 498,

an information relating to the offence alleged to have been committed by the accused or relating to an included or other offence alleged to have been committed by him shall be laid before a justice as soon as practicable thereafter and in any event before the time stated in the appearance notice, promise to appear or recognizance issued to or given or entered into by the accused for his attendance in court.

R.S., c. 2 (2d Supp.), s. 5.

Commentary: The section describes the procedure to *confirm* the *process* by which D has been released by a peace officer or officer in charge under ss. 496–498.

An *information* relating to the offence alleged in the release form to have been committed by D, or an included or other offence, must be laid before a justice *as soon as practicable* after the form of release has been issued to, given or entered into by D. The information must *not* be laid *after* the time D's *appearance* is required in the release form.

Case Law
As Soon As Practicable

R. v. Brown (1982), 44 Nfld. & P.E.I.R. 38 (Nfld. C.A.) — Where D was released on December 11, 1981 on an appearance notice which required a court attendance on January 25, 1982, laying the information on January 4, 1982 is not "as soon as practicable".

Time Stated in Appearance Notice

R. v. Naylor (1978), 42 C.C.C. (2d) 12 (Ont. C.A.) — *See also*: *R. v. Hrankowski* (1980), 54 C.C.C. (2d) 174 (Alta. C.A.); leave to appeal refused (1980), 54 C.C.C. (2d) 174n (S.C.C.) — "Time" means "time of day" stated in the appearance notice. An information laid on the day marked for the promise to appear but before the "hour" of the court appearance is valid. The section also requires however, that the information be laid *as soon as practicable*. Where either of these time limits are *not* met, D cannot be charged with failure to appear nor can the court issue a warrant of arrest under s. 512(2). The information remains valid, however, and the court does *not* lose jurisdiction over the offence. If D appears, the court has jurisdiction over the person.

Mandatory Time Requirements

R. v. Tremblay (1982), 28 C.R. (3d) 262, 68 C.C.C. (2d) 273 (B.C. C.A.) — Once the return date on the appearance notice passes, without the information having been laid, the appearance notice is of no further force or effect. When an information is subsequently sworn, it is the only proceeding facing D. A justice then has the power to issue a summons or warrant for the arrest of D based on that information.

Harnish v. R. (1979), 49 C.C.C. (2d) 190 (N.S. C.A.) — The criminal law does not recognize "conditional appearances". An appearance by counsel on the date specified in the appearance notice, even if only to object to jurisdiction, waives any defect which may have resulted from the information not being laid as soon as practicable.

Riley v. R. (1981), 60 C.C.C. (2d) 193 (Ont. C.A.) — *See also*: *R. v. Gagné* (1989), 53 C.C.C. (3d) 89 (Que. C.A.) — Non-compliance with the requirement that the information be laid as soon as practicable after the issuance of the appearance notice renders the process which precedes the laying of the information ineffective to obligate attendance by D in court. The laying of a second information and the consequent issuance of a summons or warrant is not barred, unless the subsequent proceedings constitute an abuse of process.

R. v. Gougeon (1980), 55 C.C.C. (2d) 218 (Ont. C.A.); leave to appeal refused (1980), 35 N.R. 83n (S.C.C.) — A defect in the process by which D is brought to court, unless of a jurisdictional nature, does not affect the court's jurisdiction even if D appears under protest. Failure to meet the mandatory requirement that the information be laid as soon as practicable is not of a jurisdictional nature, hence does not affect the validity of the information.

Defective Appearance Notice

R. v. Thomson (1984), 11 C.C.C. (3d) 435 (Alta. C.A.) — An information laid after the issuance of an unsigned, hence defective appearance notice, was *not* invalidated. The defect was merely procedural. P had the option of issuing a summons on the basis of the information or laying a new information.

R. v. MacAskill (1981), 58 C.C.C. (2d) 361 (N.S. C.A.) — *See also: Kennedy v. British Columbia (A.G.)* (1983), 8 C.C.C. (3d) 322 (B.C. C.A.); leave to appeal refused (1983), 8 C.C.C. (3d) 322n (S.C.C.) — Jurisdiction cannot be lost over an information until the court has become seized of jurisdiction. Where an appearance notice was, by error, made returnable on Thanksgiving Day, jurisdiction was *not* lost, even though D attended at the court-house but no court was sitting. It is only when D has presented himself before a judge capable of taking his election and plea that the court assumes jurisdiction. Until then any error in the method of bringing D before the court, or any change in the time or place of his first appearance can be made by the issuance of a new summons or warrant.

Related Provisions: The reference to "an included or other offence", is less restrictive than "any other *indictable offence in respect of the same transaction*" as used in s. 548(1)(a), or "any charge founded on the facts disclosed by the evidence taken ..." in s. 574(1)(b).

Under s. 506, the information may be in Form 2. The justice will follow the procedure of s. 508 to determine whether to confirm or cancel the original release form or issue other process to compel D's attendance.

Proceedings in respect of indictable offences where D has *not* been released by a peace officer or officer in charge are traditionally initiated by the laying of an information under s. 504 and the issuance of process under s. 507. Exceptionally, however, an indictment may be preferred directly under ss. 577(a) or (c) without an information being first laid.

506. Form — An information laid under section 504 or 505 may be in Form 2.

R.S., c. 2 (2d Supp.), s. 5.

Commentary: The section prescribes the *form of information* that is permissible under ss. 504 and 505.

Case Law [See also s. 841]

R. v. Eddy (1982), 69 C.C.C. (2d) 568 (B.C. S.C.) — An information that lacks the name and occupation of the informant is valid. The omissions did not affect the substance of the charge. This section is permissive or directory, *not* mandatory.

Mandelbaum v. Denstedt (1968), 5 C.R.N.S. 307, [1969] 3 C.C.C. 119 (Man. C.A.) — It is necessary to distinguish a prosecution from an information. A prosecution must be taken on behalf of Her Majesty. An information may be laid in the name of the complainant alone.

Related Provisions: Form 2 is required in respect of summary conviction proceedings under s. 788(1).

The form includes reference to the territorial division in which it is laid and requires the name and occupation of the informant, as well as disclosure whether the informant has personal knowledge of the offence or believes, on reasonable grounds, that the specified offence has been committed. The information, signed by the informant, is sworn before the justice. D's date of birth may be mentioned on the information.

507. (1) Justice to hear informant and witnesses — Subject to subsection 523(1.1), a justice who receives an information, other than an information laid before the justice under section 505, shall, except where an accused has already been arrested with or without a warrant,

    (a) hear and consider, *ex parte*,

        (i) the allegations of the informant, and

        (ii) the evidence of witnesses, where he considers it desirable or necessary to do so; and

    (b) where he considers that a case for so doing is made out, issue, in accordance with this section, either a summons or a warrant for the arrest of the accused to compel the accused to attend before him or some other justice for the same territorial division to answer to a charge of an offence.

(2) Process compulsory — No justice shall refuse to issue a summons or warrant by reason only that the alleged offence is one for which a person may be arrested without warrant.

(3) Procedure when witnesses attend — A justice who hears the evidence of a witness pursuant to subsection (1) shall

    (a) take the evidence on oath; and

    (b) cause the evidence to be taken in accordance with section 540 in so far as that section is capable of being applied.

(4) Summons to be issued except in certain cases — Where the justice considers that a case is made out for compelling an accused to attend before him to answer to a charge of an offence, he shall issue a summons to the accused unless the allegations of the informant or the evidence of any witness or witnesses taken in accordance with subsection (3) disclose reasonable grounds to believe that it is necessary in the public interest to issue a warrant for the arrest of the accused.

(5) No process in blank — A justice shall not sign a summons or warrant in blank.

(6) Endorsement of warrant by justice — A justice who issues a warrant under this section or section 508 or 512 may, unless the offence is one mentioned in section 522, authorize the release of the accused pursuant to section 499 by making an endorsement on the warrant in Form 29.

(7) Promise to appear or recognizance deemed to have been confirmed — Where, pursuant to subsection (6), a justice authorizes the release of an accused pursuant to section 499, a promise to appear given by the accused or a recognizance entered into by the accused pursuant to that section shall be deemed, for the purposes of subsection 145(5), to have been confirmed by a justice under section 508.

(8) Issue of summons or warrant — Where, on an appeal from or review of any decision or matter of jurisdiction, a new trial or hearing or a continuance or renewal of a trial or hearing is ordered, a justice may issue either a summons or a warrant for the arrest of the accused in order to compel the accused to attend at the new or continued or renewed trial or hearing.

R.S., c. 2 (2d Supp.), s. 5; 1972, c. 13, s. 35;R.S. 1985, c. 27 (1st Supp.), s. 78; 1994, c. 44, s. 43.

Commentary: The section enacts the procedure followed where a justice receives an information, *other than* one which is laid to confirm a release form previously issued by a peace officer or an officer in charge, in cases where D has *not* already been arrested with or without a warrant.

Under s. 507(1), the justice must hear and consider, *ex parte*, the allegations of the informant and, if it is desirable or necessary to do so, the evidence of witnesses, thereby to determine whether or what process should issue to compel D's appearance. Any evidence must be taken under oath and recorded in the manner described in ss. 507(3) and 540.

Under s. 507(4) a justice, who has determined that process shall issue, must issue a *summons* to compel D's attendance, *unless* the allegations of the informant or evidence of witnesses discloses *reasonable grounds* to believe that it is in the public interest to issue a *warrant*. Under s. 507(6), in respect of all but s. 522 offences, the justice may authorize D's release under s. 499 by endorsing the warrant in Form 29. Any subsequent release forms, by s. 507(7), are *deemed* to have been confirmed by a justice under s. 508.

Under s. 507(8), upon a new trial, hearing or continuance or renewal of a trial, a justice may issue a summons or warrant for D's arrest to compel attendance. Where a fresh information is laid charging the same or an included offence, s. 523(1.1) applies and any previous order for release or detention continues to govern without recourse to s. 507.

Under s. 507(2), it is *not* a ground to refuse to issue a summons or warrant that the alleged offence is one for which D may be arrested without warrant. Section 507(5) prohibits the signing of summonses or warrants in blank.

Case Law

R. v. Pottle (1978), 49 C.C.C. (2d) 113 (Nfld. C.A.) — *See also*: *R. v. Bachman*, [1979] 6 W.W.R. 468 (B.C. C.A.) — A justice's failure to hold a hearing under s. 507(1)(a) does *not* affect *jurisdiction* over the *offence* when D is subsequently brought before him.

Southam Inc. v. Ontario (1990), 60 C.C.C. (3d) 267 (Ont. C.A.) — The inquiry conducted by a justice under s. 507(1) must be held *in camera*.

R. v. Whitmore (1987), 41 C.C.C. (3d) 555 (Ont. H.C.); affirmed (1989), 51 C.C.C. (3d) 294 (Ont. C.A.) — Section 507(1)(b) permits the pre-inquiry justice to consider both the allegations of the informant and the evidence of other witnesses, and to apply the *prima facie* standard in deciding whether to issue process against D. The justice does *not* review the informant's grounds for belief.

Buchbinder v. Venner (1985), 47 C.R. (3d) 135, 20 C.C.C. (3d) 481 (Ont. C.A.) — An adequate description in the information of D or the class of which he is a member is a minimum requirement. A justice has no jurisdiction to upgrade the quality of the information after hearing evidence. An information that is a nullity cannot be converted into an effective instrument for commencing legal proceedings.

R. v. Allen (1974), 20 C.C.C. (2d) 447 (Ont. C.A.) — If a justice refuses to issue a summons based on the evidence presented, the information remains. The complainant is entitled to attend before the same or another justice later with additional evidence, and to request the issue of a summons on the basis of the further evidence.

R. v. Southwick (1967), 2 C.R.N.S. 46 (Ont. C.A.) — An information may be laid before and a summons issued by different justices of the peace.

R. v. Mercure (1992), 78 C.C.C. (3d) 476 (C.A. Qué.) — Where a judge of the appeal court does *not* order a new trial, s. 507(8) affords *no* authority for the issuance of a summons.

R. v. Manseau (1992), 73 C.C.C. (3d) 476 (Que. C.A.) — Section 507(1)(b) does *not* require that the justice who has received an information, as well filled out and dated a summons, also sign the summons.

Quebec (A.G.) v. Cohen (1976), 34 C.R.N.S. 362, (sub nom. *Cohen v. R.)* 32 C.C.C. (2d) 446 (Que. C.A.); reversed on other grounds (1979), 13 C.R. (3d) 36, 46 C.C.C. (2d) 473 (S.C.C.) — Although the "pre-inquiry" must be held *ex parte* and *in camera*, there is *no* reason why the transcript of these proceedings should *not* be given to D once he has appeared before a justice to answer to the charge. The justice at a preliminary inquiry cannot, however, order production of the transcript. If the defence already has the transcripts of the depositions at the "pre-inquiry", the transcripts may be used for the purposes of cross-examination.

Re Bahinipaty (1983), 5 C.C.C. (3d) 439 (Sask. C.A.) — The failure of an information to comply with the requirements of the *Code* respecting sufficiency of detail does *not* render the information void *ab initio*, hence to deprive a justice of jurisdiction under this section to issue a summons.

Charter Considerations

Southam Inc. v. Ontario (1990), 60 C.C.C. (3d) 267 (Ont. C.A.) — The restrictions inherent in s. 507(1) on the freedoms of expression and of the press under *Charter* s. 2(b) are justifiable under s. 1.

R. v. Whitmore (1987), 41 C.C.C. (3d) 555 (Ont. H.C.); affirmed (1989), 51 C.C.C. (3d) 294 (Ont. C.A.) — The provision for an *ex parte* hearing does *not* offend *Charter* s. 7.

Related Provisions: "Justice" is defined in s. 2, the various forms of release and process in s. 493. Sections 509–514 describe the contents of summonses and warrants including the manner in which they may be served or executed.

The procedure followed where a confirmatory information is laid under s. 505 is described in s. 508.

Failure to appear under a summons for *I.C.A.* purposes may result in the issuance of a warrant for D's arrest on the original charge under s. 510, and/or prosecution for failure to appear under s. 145(4).

508. (1) Justice to hear informant and witnesses — A justice who receives an information laid before him under section 505 shall

(a) hear and consider, *ex parte*,

(i) the allegations of the informant, and

(ii) the evidence of witnesses, where he considers it desirable or necessary to do so;

(b) where he considers that a case for so doing is made out, whether the information relates to the offence alleged in the appearance notice, promise to appear or recognizance or to an included or other offence,

(i) confirm the appearance notice, promise to appear or recognizance, as the case may be, and endorse the information accordingly, or

(ii) cancel the appearance notice, promise to appear or recognizance, as the case may be, and issue, in accordance with section 507, either a summons or a warrant for the arrest of the accused to compel the accused to attend before him or some other justice for the same territorial division to answer to a charge of an offence and endorse on the summons or warrant that the appearance notice, promise to appear or recognizance, as the case may be, has been cancelled; and

(c) where he considers that a case is not made out for the purposes of paragraph (*b*), cancel the appearance notice, promise to appear or recognizance, as the case may be, and cause the accused to be notified forthwith of such cancellation.

(2) Procedure when witnesses attend — A justice who hears the evidence of a witness pursuant to subsection (1) shall

(a) take the evidence upon oath; and

(b) cause the evidence to be taken in accordance with section 540 in so far as that section is capable of being applied.

R.S., c. 2 (2d Supp.), s. 5;R.S. 1985, c. 27 (1st Supp.), s. 79.

Commentary: The section describes the procedure followed upon receipt of an information under s. 505 to *confirm* D's *release* by a peace officer or officer in charge.

Under s. 508(1)(a), the justice who receives an information under s. 505 must hear and consider, *ex parte*, the allegations of the informant and the evidence of such witnesses, if any, where s/he considers it desirable or necessary to do so, taken in accordance with s. 508(2). The justice must then consider *whether* a case for *confirmation* has been made out, either in respect of the offence alleged in the release form, or an included or other offence. If a case has been made out, the justice must *confirm* the original *release* form and *endorse* the *information* accordingly or, *cancel* the original *release* form, issue a summons or warrant, and endorse thereon that the earlier form of release has been cancelled. Where the justice considers that *no* case for confirmation has been made out, the original release form must be *cancelled* and D advised accordingly, forthwith.

Case Law

R. v. McGinnis (1979), 51 C.C.C. (2d) 301 (Alta. C.A.) — *See also*: *Kennedy v. British Columbia (A.G.)* (1983), 8 C.C.C. (3d) 322 (B.C. C.A.); leave to appeal refused (1983), 8 C.C.C. (3d) 322n (S.C.C.); *R. v. Maximick* (1979), 10 C.R. (3d) 97, 48 C.C.C. (2d) 417 (B.C. C.A); *R. v. Wetmore* (1976), 32 C.C.C. (2d) 347 (N.S. C.A.) — The reason for the requirement that the appearance notice be confirmed is to make it an offence for the person *not* to attend court. If D attends and there is a properly sworn information, the court has jurisdiction to proceed, notwithstanding the failure to confirm the appearance notice.

R. v. Tremblay (1982), 28 C.R. (3d) 262, 68 C.C.C. (2d) 273 (B.C. C.A.) — Once the time for attendance in court specified in the appearance notice has passed without an information being laid, a justice has no jurisdiction under the section to cancel the notice. The appearance notice is of no further force and effect. An information may be subsequently sworn and valid process issued.

Related Provisions: "Justice" is defined in s. 2, the various forms of release in s. 493.

The procedure followed where an information is laid and an initiating process sought under s. 504 is described in s. 507.

Failure to appear under a confirmed appearance notice, promise to appear or recognizance entered into before an officer in charge for *I.C.A.* purposes may result in the issuance of a warrant for D's arrest on the original charge under s. 502 and/or prosecution under s. 145(5).

508.1 (1) Information laid otherwise than in person — For the purposes of sections 504 to 508, a peace officer may lay an information by any means of telecommunication that produces a writing.

(2) Alternative to oath — A peace officer who uses a means of telecommunication referred to in subsection (1) shall, instead of swearing an oath, make a statement in writing stating that all matters contained in the information are true to the officer's knowledge and belief, and such a statement is deemed to be a statement made under oath.

1997, c. 18, s. 56.

Commentary: This section permits use of a means of telecommunication that produces a writing to lay an information to initiate criminal proceedings or confirm the issuance of process. A statement by a peace officer that the matters alleged are true is *deemed* to be a statement under oath.

Related Provisions: Sections 504 and 507 govern the institution of proceedings by the laying of an information and the issuance of process to compel D's attendance. Sections 505 and 508 apply where D has already been released from custody by a peace officer, the officer in charge, or on an appearance notice under s. 496. An information is laid to institute proceedings and confirm the issuance of prior process to compel D's attendance.

Other provisions permit the use of telecommunications where personal attendance is impracticable, as for example, in ss. 184.3 (consent authorizations), 487.1 (search warrants under ss. 256 and 487), 487.05 (DNA warrants), and 487.091 (print and impression warrants). Under s. 708.1, electronically-transmitted copies have the same force as originals for *Code* purposes.

509. (1) Summons — A summons issued under this Part shall

    (a) be directed to the accused;

    (b) set out briefly the offence in respect of which the accused is charged; and

    (c) require the accused to attend court at a time and place to be stated therein and to attend thereafter as required by the court in order to be dealt with according to law.

(2) Service on individual — A summons shall be served by a peace officer who shall deliver it personally to the person to whom it is directed or, if that person cannot conveniently be found, shall leave it for him at his latest or usual place of abode with an inmate thereof who appears to be at least sixteen years of age.

(3) Proof of service — Service of a summons may be proved by the oral evidence, given under oath, of the peace officer who served it or by his affidavit made before a justice or other person authorized to administer oaths or to take affidavits.

(4) Content of summons — There shall be set out in every summons the text of subsection 145(4) and section 510.

(5) Attendance for purposes of Identification of Criminals Act — A summons may require the accused to appear at a time and place stated in it for the purposes of the *Identification of Criminals Act*, where the accused is alleged to have committed an indictable offence and, in the case of an offence designated as a contravention

under the *Contraventions Act*, the Attorney General, within the meaning of that Act, has not made an election under section 50 of that Act.

R.S., c. 2 (2d Supp.), s. 5;R.S. 1985, c. 27 (1st Supp.), s.80; 1992, c. 47, s. 71; 1996, c. 7, s. 38.

Commentary: The section prescribes the contents of a *summons*, the *manner* in which it is to be *served* and its *service proven*.

In combination, ss. 509(1) and (4) require that a summons be directed to D, set out *briefly* the offence charged and *require* D to *attend* court at a specified time and place, thereafter as required by the court, to be dealt with according to law. The summons must also set out the *text* of ss. 145(4) and 510, which advise D of the *consequences* of non-appearance. Where D is alleged to have committed an *indictable* offence, the summons *may* require attendance for *I.C.A.* purposes. When D appears for such purposes, s/he is *deemed* to be in lawful custody charged with an indictable offence for the purposes of that Act. Under s. 509(2), the *general* rule is that a peace officer serve D *personally* with the summons. If D cannot conveniently be found, the officer must leave the summons at D's last or usual place of abode with an inmate, apparently *at least* 16 years old. Section 509(3) permits proof of service by oral evidence or the affidavit of the serving officer.

Case Law

R. v. Beare (1988), 66 C.R. (3d) 97, 45 C.C.C. (3d) 57 (S.C.C.) — To the extent that s. 509(5) authorizes the fingerprinting of a person who has been arrested but *not* convicted of an indictable offence, it does *not* contravene *Charter* s. 7.

Shulman v. R. (1975), 23 C.C.C. (2d) 242 (B.C. C.A.) — In penal proceedings a summons cannot properly be served on a person outside Canada without statutory authority. No *Code* provision expressly or implicitly authorizes the service of a summons *ex juris*.

Related Provisions: "Peace officer" is defined in s. 2, "summons" and "accused" in s. 493.

Section 20 permits issuance and service of a summons on a holiday. Sections 4(6) and (7) permit examination or cross-examination of an affiant in respect of the issue of proof of service or sending of any notice.

Section 546 is a remedial provision which does *not* hold invalid, any proceeding at or subsequent to a preliminary inquiry, on account of any irregularity or defect in the summons or variance between the charge set out there and that in the information or evidence adduced at the preliminary inquiry.

Failure to appear for *I.C.A.* purposes may result in the issuance of a warrant of arrest on the original charge under s. 510 and/or prosecution under s. 145(4).

510. Failure to appear — Where an accused who is required by a summons to appear at a time and place stated in it for the purposes of the *Identification of Criminals Act* does not appear at that time and place and, in the case of an offence designated as a contravention under the *Contraventions Act*, the Attorney General, within the meaning of that Act, has not made an election under section 50 of that Act, a justice may issue a warrant for the arrest of the accused for the offence with which the accused is charged.

R.S., c. 2 (2d Supp.), s. 5; 1992, c. 47, s. 72; 1996, c. 7, s. 38.

Commentary: The section authorizes the issuance of a warrant of arrest for D who, required by a summons to appear at a specified time and place for *I.C.A.* purposes, fails so to do. The warrant is issued in respect of the offence upon which D has been summonsed.

Related Provisions: The warrant may be in Form 7.

Failure, without lawful excuse, to appear at a time and place stated in a summons for *I.C.A.* purposes, is an offence triable either way under s. 145(4).

Other related provisions are described in the corresponding note to s. 511, *infra*.

511. (1) Contents of warrant to arrest — A warrant issued under this Part shall

   (a) name or describe the accused;

   (b) set out briefly the offence in respect of which the accused is charged; and

(c) order that the accused be forthwith arrested and brought before the judge or justice who issued the warrant or before some other judge or justice having jurisdiction in the same territorial division, to be dealt with according to law.

(2) **No return day** — A warrant issued under this Part remains in force until it is executed, and need not be made returnable at any particular time.

(3) **Discretion to postpone execution** — Notwithstanding paragraph (1)(c), a judge or justice who issues a warrant may specify in the warrant the period before which the warrant shall not be executed, to allow the accused to appear voluntarily before a judge or justice having jurisdiction in the territorial division in which the warrant was issued.

(4) **Deemed execution of warrant** — Where the accused appears voluntarily for the offence in respect of which the accused is charged, the warrant is deemed to be executed.

R.S., c. C-34, s. 456; c. 2 (2d Supp.), s. 5;R.S. 1985, c. 27 (1st Supp.), s. 81; 1997, c. 18, s. 57.

Commentary: The section describes the *contents* of an *arrest warrant*.

An arrest warrant must name or otherwise describe D to whom it relates, and briefly set out the offence charged. It need *not* contain a return date and will remain in force until executed. The warrant directs those executing it to arrest D forthwith, thereafter returning D before the issuing judge or justice, or another of equivalent jurisdiction in the territorial division of its issuance, unless the judge or justice issuing the warrant exercises his/her discretion in specifying in the warrant the period of time before which the warrant must not be executed so that D may be allowed to appear voluntarily. If D appears voluntarily, the warrant is deemed executed.

Related Provisions: "Justice" is defined in s. 2, "warrant" and "accused" in s. 493.

A warrant of arrest in Form 7 is *directed* to the peace officers in the territorial jurisdiction of the justice under s. 513 and orders them to *arrest* the accused described therein in respect of the designated offence and to *convey* D before a specified court, judge or justice to be dealt with according to law. The basis upon which the warrant has been issued is included by way of recital.

A warrant of arrest may be issued and executed under s. 20 on a holiday. Section 514 describes the circumstances under which it may be executed. Sections 25–29 protect persons administering and enforcing the law. In particular, s. 29 describes the duties of a person executing a warrant.

Sections 704–708 authorize the issuance of warrants for witnesses who abscond or otherwise fail to attend court as required. Provision is also made for detention or release of such witnesses, upon execution of the warrant and attendance in court. Section 527 describes the procedure to be followed to procure the attendance of a prisoner for purposes specified in the section.

512. (1) Certain actions not to preclude issue of warrant — A justice may, where the justice has reasonable grounds to believe that it is necessary in the public interest to issue a summons or a warrant for the arrest of the accused, issue a summons or a warrant notwithstanding that

(a) an appearance notice or a promise to appear or a recognizance entered into before an officer in charge or another peace officer has been confirmed or cancelled under subsection 508(1);

(b) a summons has previously been issued under subsection 507(4);or

(c) the accused has been released unconditionally or with the intention of compelling his appearance by way of summons.

(2) **Warrant in default of appearance** — Where

(a) service of a summons is proved and the accused fails to attend court in accordance with the summons,

(b) an appearance notice or a promise to appear or a recognizance entered into before an officer in charge or another peace officer has been confirmed under subsection 508(1) and the accused fails to attend court in accordance therewith in order to be dealt with according to law, or

(c) it appears that a summons cannot be served because the accused is evading service,

a justice may issue a warrant for the arrest of the accused.

R.S., c. 2 (2d Supp.), s. 5;R.S. 1985, c. 27 (1st Supp.), s.82; 1997, c. 18, s. 58.

Commentary: The section preserves the authority to issue an *arrest warrant*, notwithstanding the issuance of, default upon or evasion of other process to compel D's attendance.

Under s. 512(1), a *summons or warrant* may be issued, where the justice has *reasonable* grounds to believe that it is *necessary* to do so to compel D's attendance. It is of no consequence that the issuance of a previous form of release has been confirmed under s. 508(1), a summons previously issued under s. 507(4) or D has been released unconditionally or with intention of compelling appearance under summons. Under s. 512(2), a *warrant* may issue on non-attendance under a summons, or other confirmed form of release or upon proof that D is evading service of a summons.

Case Law

R. v. Anderson (1983), 37 C.R. (3d) 67, 9 C.C.C. (3d) 539 (Alta. C.A.) — On the date specified in the promise to appear D went to court and made his presence known to court officials. D's case was neither called nor adjourned. Jurisdiction over the information was *not* lost since D's promise to "attend" necessarily required that he make his presence known to the presiding justice which he did not. The subsequent issuance of a summons and the appearance by D on the date specified in the summons remedied any loss of jurisdiction over D.

Ex parte Chung (1976), 26 C.C.C. (2d) 497 (B.C. C.A.) — A justice has jurisdiction under this section to issue a warrant for arrest whenever it is in the *public interest* to do so. The section applies at any stage of proceedings, *not* only upon initial receipt of the information, including after D's release on a 90-day review under s. 525.

R. v. DeMelo (1994), 92 C.C.C. (3d) 52 (Ont. C.A.) — Grounds upon which a summons may be issued under s. 512(1), rather than a warrant, include information concerning the whereabouts or medical condition of D, or the nature of the offence charged.

R. v. DeMelo (1994), 92 C.C.C. (3d) 52 (Ont. C.A.) — Where a case comes within s. 512(2)(b), the justice may only issue a warrant for D's arrest.

R. v. DeMelo (1994), 92 C.C.C. (3d) 52 (Ont. C.A.) — Service of the appearance notice must be verified at the time of its confirmation, *not* later.

R. v. Gougeon (1980), 55 C.C.C. (2d) 218 (Ont. C.A.); leave to appeal refused (1980), 35 N.R. 83n (S.C.C.) — *See also*: *Siller v. R.* (1980), 59 C.C.C. (2d) 169 (B.C. C.A.) — This section gives a justice the residual power to issue a warrant where D fails to appear after an initial appearance under a defective process. Once D is subject to the jurisdiction of the court, it is in the public interest that s/he be compelled to honour the terms of a lawful adjournment.

Inverarity v. R. (1984), 18 C.C.C. (3d) 74 (Sask. Q.B.) — *Contra*: *Hartmann v. R.* (1986), 30 C.C.C. (3d) 286 (Ont. H.C.) — The issuance of a bench warrant against D already in custody, whom the authorities failed to bring to provincial court on a day specified for an appearance, was clearly an attempt to preserve the jurisdiction of the court, and as such was unjustifiable.

Related Provisions: The *contents* of an arrest warrant are described in ss. 511 and 513. The warrant in Form 7, may be executed in accordance with ss. 29 and 514 and, under s. 703(2), executed anywhere in the province in which it has been issued. Execution may be postponed under s. 597(4). Sections 25–29 protect persons administering and enforcing the law.

513. Formalities of warrant — A warrant in accordance with this Part shall be directed to the peace officers within the territorial jurisdiction of the justice, judge or court by whom or by which it is issued.

R.S., c. 2 (2d Supp.), s. 5.

Commentary: The section requires an arrest warrant to be directed to the peace officers within the territorial jurisdiction of the issuing justice, judge or court.

Related Provisions: The other *contents* of an arrest warrant are described in s. 511 and appear on the face of the warrant in Form 7.

Execution of the warrant is governed by ss. 29, 514 and 703. Sections 25–29 protect persons administering and enforcing the law.

514. (1) Execution of warrant — A warrant in accordance with this Part may be executed by arresting the accused

(a) wherever he is found within the territorial jurisdiction of the justice, judge or court by whom or by which the warrant was issued; or

(b) wherever he is found in Canada, in the case of fresh pursuit.

(2) By whom warrant may be executed — A warrant in accordance with this Part may be executed by a person who is one of the peace officers to whom it is directed, whether or not the place in which the warrant is to be executed is within the territory for which the person is a peace officer.

R.S., c. 2 (2d Supp.), s. 5.

Commentary: The section declares *where* an arrest warrant may be *executed*.

Under s. 514(1), an arrest warrant may be executed *wherever* D is found within the territorial jurisdiction of the issuing justice, judge or court, or anywhere in Canada, if D is *freshly pursued*. Section 514(2) permits execution of the warrant anywhere by any peace officer to whom it is directed, even though the place of execution may be beyond the territorial jurisdiction of the executing officer.

Related Provisions: "Fresh pursuit" is *not* defined in the *Code*.

This provision should be read together with ss. 29 and 703 which govern the manner and place in which arrest warrants may be executed. Section 20 permits execution of warrants on a holiday and ss. 25–29 protect those enforcing or administering the law.

Judicial Interim Release

515. (1) Order of release — Subject to this section, where an accused who is charged with an offence other than an offence listed in section 469 is taken before a justice the justice shall, unless a plea of guilty by the accused is accepted, order, in respect of that offence, that the accused be released on his giving an undertaking without conditions, unless the prosecutor, having been given a reasonable opportunity to do so, shows cause, in respect of that offence, why the detention of the accused in custody is justified or why an order under any other provision of this section should be made and where the justice makes an order under any other provision of this section, the order shall refer only to the particular offence for which the accused was taken before the justice.

(2) Release on undertaking with conditions, etc. — Where the justice does not make an order under subsection (1), he shall, unless the prosecutor shows cause why the detention of the accused is justified, order that the accused be released

(a) on his giving an undertaking with such conditions as the justice directs;

(b) on his entering into a recognizance before the justice, without sureties, in such amount and with such conditions, if any, as the justice directs but without deposit of money or other valuable security;

(c) on his entering into a recognizance before the justice with sureties in such amount and with such conditions, if any, as the justice directs but without deposit of money or other valuable security;

(d) with the consent of the prosecutor, on his entering into a recognizance before the justice, without sureties, in such amount and with such conditions, if any, as the justice directs and on his depositing with the justice such sum of money or other valuable security as the justice directs, or

(e) if the accused is not ordinarily resident in the province in which the accused is in custody or does not ordinarily reside within two hundred kilometres of the place in which he is in custody, on his entering into a recognizance before the justice with or without sureties in such amount and with such conditions, if any, as the justice directs, and on his depositing with the justice such sum of money or other valuable security as the justice directs.

(2.1) Power of justice to name sureties in order — Where, pursuant to subsection (2) or any other provision of this Act, a justice, judge or court orders that an accused be released on his entering into a recognizance with sureties, the justice, judge or court may, in the order, name particular persons as sureties.

(2.2) Alternative to physical presence — Where, by this Act, the appearance of an accused is required for the purposes of judicial interim release, the appearance shall be by actual physical attendance of the accused but the justice may, subject to subsection (2.3), allow the accused to appear by means of any suitable telecommunication device, including telephone, that is satisfactory to the justice.

(2.3) Where consent required — The consent of the prosecutor and the accused is required for the purposes of an appearance if the evidence of a witness is to be taken at the appearance and the accused cannot appear by closed-circuit television or any other means that allow the court and the accused to engage in simultaneous visual and oral communication.

(3) Release on undertaking with conditions etc. — The justice shall not make an order under any of paragraphs (2)(*b*) to (*e*) unless the prosecution shows cause why an order under the immediately preceding paragraph should not be made.

(4) Conditions authorized — The justice may direct as conditions under subsection (2) that the accused shall do any one or more of the following things as specified in the order:

(a) report at times to be stated in the order to a peace officer or other person designated in the order;

(b) remain within a territorial jurisdiction specified in the order;

(c) notify the peace officer or other person designated under paragraph (*a*) of any change in his address or his employment or occupation;

(d) abstain from communicating with any witness or other person expressly named in the order, or refrain from going to any place expressly named in the order, except in accordance with the conditions specified in the order that the justice considers necessary;

(e) where the accused is the holder of a passport, deposit his passport as specified in the order; and

(f) comply with such other reasonable conditions specified in the order as the justice considers desirable.

(4.1) Condition prohibiting possession of firearms, etc. — When making an order under subsection (2), in the case of an accused who is charged with

(a) an offence in the commission of which violence against a person was used, threatened or attempted,

(b) an offence under section 264 (criminal harassment),

(c) an offence relating to the contravention of subsection 5(3) or (4) or 6(3) or 7(2) of the *Controlled Drugs and Substances Act*, or

(d) an offence that involves, or the subject-matter of which is, a firearm, a cross-bow, a prohibited weapon, a restricted weapon, a prohibited device, ammunition, prohibited ammunition or an explosive substance,

the justice shall add to the order a condition prohibiting the accused from possessing any firearm, cross-bow, prohibited weapon, restricted weapon, prohibited device, ammunition, prohibited ammunition or explosive substance, or all such things, until the accused is dealt with according to law unless the justice considers that such a condition is not required in the interests of the safety of the accused or of any other person.

(4.11) Surrender, etc. — Where the justice adds a condition described in subsection (4.1) to an order made under subsection (2), the justice shall specify in the order the manner and method by which

(a) the things referred to in subsection (4.1) that are in the possession of the accused shall be surrendered, disposed of, detained, stored or dealt with; and

(b) the authorizations, licences and registration certificates held by the person shall be surrendered.

(4.12) Reasons — Where the justice does not add a condition described in subsection (4.1) to an order made under subsection (2), the justice shall include in the record a statement of the reasons for not adding the condition.

(4.2) Idem — Before making an order under subsection (2), in the case of an accused who is charged with an offence described in section 264, or an offence in the commission of which violence against a person was used, threatened or attempted, the justice shall consider whether it is desirable, in the interests of the safety of any person, to include as a condition of the order that the accused abstain from communicating with any witness or other person expressly named in the order, or be prohibited from going to any place expressly named in the order.

(5) Detention in custody — Where the prosecutor shows cause why the detention of the accused in custody is justified, the justice shall order that the accused be detained in custody until he is dealt with according to law and shall include in the record a statement of his reasons for making the order.

(6) Order of detention — Notwithstanding any provision of this section, where an accused is charged

    (a) with an indictable offence, other than an offence listed in section 469,

        (i) that is alleged to have been committed while at large after being released in respect of another indictable offence pursuant to the provisions of this Part or section 679 or 680, or

        (ii) that is an offence under section 467.1 or an offence under this or any other Act of Parliament alleged to have been committed for the benefit of, at the direction of or in association with a criminal organization for which the maximum punishment is imprisonment for five years or more,

    (b) with an indictable offence, other than an offence listed in section 469 and is not ordinarily resident in Canada,

    (c) with an offence under any of subsections 145(2) to (5) that is alleged to have been committed while he was at large after being released in respect of another offence pursuant to the provisions of this Part or section 679, 680 or 816, or

    (d) with having committed an offence punishable by imprisonment for life under subsection 5(3), 6(3) or 7(2) of the *Controlled Drugs and Substances Act* or the offence of conspiring to commit such an offence,

the justice shall order that the accused be detained in custody until he is dealt with according to law, unless the accused, having been given a reasonable opportunity to do so, shows cause why his detention in custody is not justified, but where the justice orders that the accused be released, he shall include in the record a statement of his reasons for making the order.

(7) Order of release — Where an accused to whom paragraph 6(*a*), (*c*) or(*d*) applies shows cause why the accused's detention in custody is not justified, the justice shall order that the accused be released on giving an undertaking or entering into a recognizance described in any of paragraphs (2)(*a*) to (*e*) with the conditions described in subsections (4) to (4.2) or, where the accused was at large on an undertaking or recognizance with conditions, the additional conditions described in subsections (4) to (4.2), that the justice considers desirable, unless the accused, having been given a reasonable opportunity to do so, shows cause why the conditions or additional conditions should not be imposed.

(8) Idem — Where an accused to whom paragraph (6)(*b*) applies shows cause why the accused's detention in custody is not justified, the justice shall order that the accused be released on giving an undertaking or entering into a recognizance described in any of paragraphs (2)(*a*) to (*e*) with the conditions, described in subsections (4) to (4.2), that the justice considers desirable.

(9) Sufficiency of record — For the purposes of subsections (5) and (6), it is sufficient if a record is made of the reasons in accordance with the provisions of Part XVIII relating to the taking of evidence at preliminary inquiries.

(10) Justification for detention in custody — For the purposes of this section, the detention of an accused in custody is justified only on one or more of the following grounds:

    (a) where the detention is necessary to ensure his or her attendance in court in order to be dealt with according to law;

    (b) where the detention is necessary for the protection or safety of the public, having regard to all the circumstances including any substantial likelihood that the accused will, if released from custody, commit a criminal offence or interfere with the administration of justice; and

(c) on any other just cause being shown and without limiting the generality of the foregoing, where the detention is necessary in order to maintain confidence in the administration of justice, having regard to all the circumstances, including the apparent strength of the prosecution's case, the gravity of the nature of the offence, the circumstances surrounding its commission and the potential for a lengthy term of imprisonment.

(11) Detention in custody for offence mentioned in s. 469 — Where an accused who is charged with an offence mentioned in section 469 is taken before a justice, the justice shall order that the accused be detained in custody until he is dealt with according to law and shall issue a warrant in Form 8 for the committal of the accused.

(12) Order re no communication — A justice who orders that an accused be detained in custody under this section may include in the order a direction that the accused abstain from communicating with any witness or other person named in the order, except in accordance with such conditions specified in the order as the justice deems necessary.

R.S., c. C-34, s. 457; c. 2 (2nd Supp.), s. 5;1974–75–76, c. 93, s. 47;R.S. 1985, c. 27 (1st Supp.), ss. 83,186; 1991, c. 40, s. 31; 1993, c. 45, s. 8; 1994, c. 44, s. 44; 1995, c. 39, ss. 153, 188(b); 1996, c. 19, ss. 71, 93.3; 1997, c. 18, s. 59; c. 23, s. 16; 1999, c. 5, s. 21.

Commentary: The section describes the basis upon which D, charged with an offence *not* listed in s. 469 and who does *not* plead guilty, may be released from custody pending trial. In the usual course, D's appearance for judicial interim release purposes is by actual physical attendance. The justice, under s. 515(2.2), may allow D to appear by means of any suitable telecommunication device, including telephone, that is satisfactory to the justice. Where the evidence of a witness is to be taken, the consent of P and D is required for the absence of D unless D can appear by closed-circuit television or any other means that allow the court and D to communicate simultaneously, both visually and orally.

Section 515(1) requires a justice to *release* D in respect of the offence charged upon an undertaking without conditions *unless* P, afforded a *reasonable opportunity* to do so, shows cause why D should be detained or another form of release ought to be ordered. Under s. 515(3), P must show cause why a particular form of order should be made. Where the release order is a recognizance with sureties, s. 515(2.1) permits the justice to name the sureties. The conditions that may be attached are described in s. 515(4) and, in specified cases, ss. 515(4.1), (4.11), (4.12) and (4.2).

In general, D's detention in custody pending trial will only be justified where P shows cause under one or more of the grounds of s. 515(10), which include ensuring attendance in court, the safety of the public or any other just cause. Where detention is ordered, the justice must record reasons therefor under ss. 515(5) and (9). A non-communication term may be included where D is detained under s. 515(12).

Sections 515(6)–(8) define when D will be required to show cause why s/he should be *released* from custody pending trial upon a charge not listed in s. 469, nor one to which a plea of guilty is being entered. Section 515(6) describes four cases in which the onus of proof is shifted to D. D will be detained unless D shows cause why detention is *not justified*. Constitutional challenges to ss. 515(6)(a) and (d) under *Charter* ss. 7, 9, 11(d) and (e) have failed. Where D shows cause, the form of release is governed by ss. 515(7) and (8).

Under s. 515(11), a justice must order D, charged with an offence listed in s. 469, to be detained in custody, until s/he is dealt with according to law by a judge of the superior court of criminal jurisdiction.

Case Law

Application for Release

R. v. Quinn (1977), 34 C.C.C. (2d) 473 (N.S. Co. Ct.) — *See also*: *Re Batson* (1977), 21 N.B.R. (2d) 275 (C.A.) — Prior to conviction, persons are detained *only* if it is necessary to ensure their attendance in court or if they constitute a danger to the public or the public interest so requires. There is *no* residual discretion in a justice to refuse bail and, even where the onus is on D to show cause why detention is not justified, the justice must consider *only* those grounds in determining whether the onus has been met.

Jurisdiction

R. v. Garoufalis (1996), 107 C.C.C. (3d) 173 (Man. C.A.) — A prior recognizance does *not* continue in force after D has been *indicted directly* by the Attorney General. A fresh application for judicial interim release under Code s. 515(1) is required. Any determination made under s. 515 is reviewable under ss. 520 or 521.

R. v. Jones (1997), 5 C.R. (5th) 364, 113 C.C.C. (3d) 225 (Ont. C.A.) — Proceedings upon a *direct* indictment are new proceedings, hence invoke the judicial interim release provisions of the *Code*. D may be brought before the *trial* court to have a judicial interim release hearing in at least three ways

i.   where D is in custody, by a *judge's order* under *Code* s. 527;

ii.   by a *summons* or *warrant* issued by a judge of the *trial* court under *Code* s. 578; or

iii.   by being *arrested* by a peace officer and taken before a *justice* under *Code* s. 503.

The hearing should be conducted by a judge of the *trial* court.

The mere *signing* of a direct indictment does *not* invalidate or nullify an earlier detention or release order made in relation to the *same* charges which remain in effect until the charges are disposed of according to law.

R. v. Wakelin (1991), 71 C.C.C. (3d) 115 (Sask. C.A.) — *See also*: *R. v. Allen* (1985), 18 C.C.C. (3d) 155 (Ont. C.A.) — *Contra*: *Mac Ausland v. Pyke* (1995), 37 C.R. (4th) 321, 96 C.C.C. (3d) 373 (N.S. S.C.) — A person against whom an information has been laid under s. 810 may be subject to the judicial interim release provisions of s. 515, pending the determination of the s. 810 proceedings.

R. v. Yarema (1991), 5 C.R. (4th) 125, 64 C.C.C. (3d) 260 (Ont. C.A.); affirming (1989), 52 C.C.C. (3d) 242 (Ont. H.C.) — A justice of the peace may conduct a show cause hearing where D is charged with failure to comply with a recognizance entered under s. 522(1).

Keenan v. R. (1979), 57 C.C.C. (2d) 267 (Que. C.A.) — A condition that D see a doctor and "undergo any appropriate medical treatment which the said doctor might suggest", exceeded the justice's powers.

Reverse Onus: S. 515(6)

R. v. Morales (1992), 17 C.R. (4th) 74, 77 C.C.C. (3d) 91 (S.C.C.) — Section 515(6)(a) is valid as constituting "just cause" to deny bail under *Charter* s. 11(e). The section does *not* offend *Charter* s. 9.

R. v. Pearson (1992), 17 C.R. (4th) 1, 77 C.C.C. (3d) 124 (S.C.C.) — Section 515(6)(d) is a constitutionally valid exception to *Charter* s. 11(e). The section does *not* violate *Charter* s. 9.

Public Interest: S. 515(10)(b)

R. v. Morales (1992), 17 C.R. (4th) 74, 77 C.C.C. (3d) 91 (S.C.C.) — The "public interest" criterion of s. 515(10)(b) authorizes detention in terms that are vague and imprecise, hence in violation of *Charter* s. 11(e). They cannot be upheld as a reasonable limit within *Charter* s. 1. The "public safety" component of the subsection is, however, constitutionally valid since it is sufficiently narrow to satisfy the requirements of *Charter* s. 11(e).

Extradition

Re Smith (1984), 38 C.R. (3d) 209, (sub nom. *Global Communications v. Canada (A.G.)*) 10 C.C.C. (3d) 97 — A judge presiding over the issue of bail in an extradition proceeding should apply the *Code* bail provisions "in the same manner, as nearly as may be" as would a justice acting under the *Code*.

Habeas Corpus

R. v. Pearson (1992), 17 C.R. (4th) 1, 77 C.C.C. (3d) 124 (S.C.C.) — *Habeas corpus* is available as a remedy against denial of judicial interim release where D claims that the reverse onus provisions of s. 515(6)(d) are unconstitutional and seeks a new hearing in accordance with constitutionally valid criteria. In most instances, however, *habeas corpus* is *not* a remedy against refusal to grant judicial interim release.

Charter Considerations

R. v. Morales (1992), 17 C.R. (4th) 74, 77 C.C.C. (3d) 91 (S.C.C.) — See digests under *Reverse Onus: S. 515(6)* and *Public Interest: S. 515(10)(b),supra.*

R. v. Pearson (1992), 17 C.R. (4th) 1, 77 C.C.C. (3d) 124 (S.C.C.) — See digests under *Reverse Onus: S. 515(6), supra.*

R. v. Dewsbury (1989), 50 C.C.C. (3d) 163 (Ont. H.C.) — The procedure adopted in Ontario whereby P approves sureties offends *Charter* s. 7.

R. v. Lamothe (1990), 58 C.C.C. (3d) 530 (Que. C.A.) — The discretion of s. 515(10) must be exercised judicially, in conformity with the general rules and principles of the criminal law, including guarantees of *Charter* ss. 11(d) and (e).

Related Provisions: Section 516 provides for *adjournment* of judicial interim release hearings and s. 517 permits orders to be made directing that, in certain circumstances, there be no *publication* or *broadcast* for specified periods of the evidence taken, representations made and information and reasons given. Section 518 regulates the hearing by its specification of the nature of the inquiries which may be made and description of the evidence which may be received. The formal release of D is regulated by s. 519 and the duration of the release orders or forms by s. 523.

An order made by a justice under s. 515 may be *reviewed*, at any time prior to trial, by a "judge", as defined in s. 493, upon application by D (s. 520) or P (s. 521) or under ss. 523(2) and (3). Where D's trial is delayed beyond specified periods of time, there is an automatic review of detention under s. 525. Directions may be given at any time under s. 526 to expedite any proceedings in respect of D.

Section 524 describes the circumstances under which D may be arrested for actual or anticipated misconduct or breaches while at liberty on judicial interim release.

Where D is charged with a s. 469 offence, release may *only* be ordered by a judge of the *superior court* of criminal jurisdiction under s. 522. Review of such orders is only in accordance with s. 680.

A recognizance is in Form 32, an undertaking in Form 12 and a warrant in Form 8 or 19. An undertaking or recognizance entered into under s. 515 may be varied under s. 515.1.

515.1 Variation of undertaking or recognizance — An undertaking or recognizance pursuant to which the accused was released that has been entered into under section 499, 503 or 515 may, with the written consent of the prosecutor, be varied, and where so varied, is deemed to have been entered into pursuant to section 515.

1997, c. 18, s. 60.

Commentary: This section is of practical significance. It permits an *undertaking* or *recognizance* entered into before an *officer in charge* or *justice* to be varied with the written consent of the prosecutor. When varied, the undertaking or recognizance is deemed to have been entered into under s. 515.

Related Provisions: "Prosecutor" is defined in s. 2. There is no form of consent provided.

In the usual course, variations of the terms of release imposed by a justice under s. 515 are made by a judge on application under s. 510 or 521, as the case may be. Variation is also permitted under s. 523(2).

This provision does not apply to s. 469 offences. Release in those cases is governed by s. 522, review by s. 680.

516. (1) Remand in custody — A justice may, before or at any time during the course of any proceedings under section 515, on application by the prosecutor or the accused, adjourn the proceedings and remand the accused to custody in prison by warrant in Form 19, but no adjournment shall be for more than three clear days except with the consent of the accused.

(2) Detention pending bail hearing — A justice who remands an accused to custody under subsection (1) or subsection 515(11) may order that the accused abstain from communicating with any witness or other person named in the order, except in accordance with any conditions specified in the order that the justice deems necessary.

R.S., c. 2 (2d Supp.), s. 5; 1999, c. 5, s. 22.

Commentary: The section authorizes *adjournment* of judicial interim release (show cause) hearings under s. 515, both *prior* to their commencement and *during* their course, on application by P or D, but *limits* the adjournments to *not* more than *three clear days, except* with D's consent. Where an adjournment is granted, D is remanded in custody by warrant in Form 19 to re-appear on the return date.

Case Law

R. v. Precourt (1976), 36 C.R.N.S. 150, 39 C.C.C. (2d) 311 (Ont. C.A.); leave to appeal refused (1977), 39 C.C.C. (2d) 311n (S.C.C.) — When remanded in custody, D is to be held in a custodial facility separate from mere holding cells connected with the police function, where such a prison is available. Where there were no circumstances which justified the delay in conveying D to a provincial jail, detention at police headquarters was *not* in compliance with the warrant remanding D into custody.

Related Provisions: The section is *not* made expressly applicable to proceedings under ss. 520–522, s. 524 or 525. Sections 520(4) and 521(4), however, are enacted in similar terms.

---

517. (1) Order directing matters not to be published for specified period — Where the prosecutor or the accused intends to show cause under section 515, he shall so state to the justice and the justice may, and shall on application by the accused, before or at any time during the course of the proceedings under that section, make an order directing that the evidence taken, the information given or the representations made and the reasons, if any, given or to be given by the justice shall not be published in any newspaper or broadcast before such time as

(a) if a preliminary inquiry is held, the accused in respect of whom the proceedings are held is discharged; or

(b) if the accused in respect of whom the proceedings are held is tried or committed for trial, the trial is ended.

(2) Failure to comply — Every one who fails without lawful excuse, the proof of which lies on him, to comply with an order made under subsection (1) is guilty of an offence punishable on summary conviction.

(3) "newspaper" — In this section, "newspaper" has the same meaning as in section 297.

R.S., c. 2 (2d Supp.), s. 5; 1974–75–76, c. 93, s. 48;R.S. 1985, c. 27 (1st Supp.), s. 101(2).

Commentary: This section restricts *publication* in newspapers and *broadcast* of certain matters disclosed in judicial interim release hearings under s. 515, where either P or D, as the case may be, intends to show cause why detention or release is justified.

Under s. 517(1), jurisdiction to *restrict* publication or broadcast requires that P or D declare that cause will be shown. An order may be made, either before or at any time during the course of the proceedings, that is *mandatory* upon application by D. The order prohibits publication in any newspaper, as defined in s. 517(3), or broadcast of the *evidence* taken, *representations* made and *information* and *reasons* given, until the expiry of the time periods described in s. 517(1)(a) or (b), as the case may be. The prohibition, which does *not* extend to publication or broadcast of either the fact or result of the application, has been impeached under *Charter* s. 2(b).

Under s. 517(2), it is a summary conviction offence to *fail, without lawful excuse*, to *comply* with an order made under s. 517(1). Proof of lawful excuse rests upon D, thereby attracting *Charter* s. 11(d) scrutiny.

Case Law

Jurisdiction

R. v. Forget (1982), 65 C.C.C. (2d) 373 (Ont. C.A.) — While this section gives a justice the power to prohibit the publication of the reasons for the granting or refusal of a bail application, it does not confer the power to prohibit the publication of the decision itself.

Charter Considerations

Re Smith (1984), 38 C.R. (3d) 209, *(*sub nom. *Global Communications v. Canada (A.G.))* 10 C.C.C. (3d) 97 — While the section conflicts with the enjoyment of freedom of the press, it represents a reasonable limit within the meaning of *Charter* s. 1.

Related Provisions: "Newspaper" is defined in s. 297.

The provision also applies to review proceedings under ss. 520, 521, 523(2) and 525, as well as misconduct hearings under s. 524. Under s. 522(5), the section applies to judicial interim release hearings in respect of s. 469 offences, but is not incorporated in the review provisions of s. 680.

518. (1) **Inquiries to be made by justice and evidence** — In any proceedings under section 515,

(a) the justice may, subject to paragraph (*b*), make such inquiries, on oath or otherwise, of and concerning the accused as he considers desirable;

(b) the accused shall not be examined by the justice or any other person except counsel for the accused respecting the offence with which the accused is charged, and no inquiry shall be made of the accused respecting that offence by way of cross-examination unless the accused has testified respecting the offence;

(c) the prosecutor may, in addition to any other relevant evidence, lead evidence

(i) to prove that the accused has previously been convicted of a criminal offence,

(ii) to prove that the accused has been charged with and is awaiting trial for another criminal offence,

(iii) to prove that the accused has previously committed an offence under section 145, or

(iv) to show the circumstances of the alleged offence, particularly as they relate to the probability of conviction of the accused;

(d) the justice may take into consideration any relevant matters agreed on by the prosecutor and the accused or his counsel;

(d.1) the justice may receive evidence obtained as a result of an interception of a private communication under and within the meaning of Part VI, in writing, orally or in the form of a recording and, for the purposes of this section, subsection 189(5) does not apply to such evidence; and

(e) the justice may receive and base his decision on evidence considered credible or trustworthy by him in the circumstances of each case.

(2) **Release pending sentence** — Where, before or at any time during the course of any proceedings under section 515, the accused pleads guilty and that plea is accepted, the justice may make any order provided for in this Part for the release of the accused until the accused is sentenced.

R.S., c. 2 (2d Supp.), s. 5; 1974–75–76, c. 93, s. 49;R.S. 1985, c. 27 (1st Supp.), s. 84; 1994, c. 44 s. 45.

Commentary: The section describes the nature of the *inquiries* which may be made and *evidence* which may be received in judicial interim release hearings under s. 515.

In general, a justice is authorized to make such inquiries, on oath or otherwise, of and concerning D, as s/he considers desirable. The *issues* upon the hearing are defined by s. 515(10), which describes the sole basis upon which detention may be justified. Under s. 518(1)(b), only counsel for D may examine D respecting the offence charged. Where D does testify respecting the offence, however, cross-examination is permitted.

Sections 518(1)(c)–(e) describe the nature of the evidence which may be received upon the hearing. All evidence relevant to the issue of detention or release in light of the criteria of s. 515(10), is *prima facie* receivable, as is any evidence considered by the justice to be credible or trustworthy in the circumstances. Relevant matters may be agreed upon by counsel under s. 518(1)(d), and intercepted private communications may be received without the usual notice being given under s. 518(1)(d.1). Section 518(1)(c) confirms the admissibility of relevant evidence and enlarges the scope of what may be received, by permitting evidence of the matters there described to be adduced, although a strict application of the rules of evidence would seem to render it inadmissible.

Section 518(2) authorizes D's release pending sentence where a plea of guilty is entered during the course of proceedings under s. 515.

Case Law

Evidence as to Offence: S. 518(1)(b)[†Decided under previous provision]

† *R. v. Paonessa* (1983), 34 C.R. (3d) 96, 3 C.C.C. (3d) 384n (S.C.C.) — *See also*: †*Deom v. R.* (1981), 64 C.C.C. (2d) 222 (B.C. S.C.) — Section 518(1)(b) prohibits the subsequent admissibility of any evidence given *contrary* to the provision.

Evidence Considered Credible or Trustworthy: S. 518(1)(e)

R. v. Hajdu (1984), 14 C.C.C. (3d) 563 (Ont. H.C.) — *See also*: *Powers v. R.* (1972), 20 C.R.N.S. 23, 9 C.C.C. (2d) 533 (Ont. H.C.); *R. v. Woo* (1994), 90 C.C.C. (3d) 404 (B.C. S.C.), varied on reconsideration (1994), 90 C.C.C. (3d) 404 at 415 (B.C. S.C.) — Section 518(1)(e) permits a justice to act upon direct evidence found to be credible, or hearsay which is considered to be trustworthy. A statement read by P does *not* constitute evidence.

Related Provisions: "Prosecutor" is defined in s. 2.

These provisions also apply to *review* hearings under ss. 520, 521, 523(2) and 525, including *misconduct* hearings under s. 524 and, under s. 522(5), judicial interim release hearings for s. 469 offences, but not to review hearings under s. 680.

519. (1) Release of accused — **Where a justice makes an order under subsection 515(1), (2), (7) or (8),**

    (a) if the accused thereupon complies with the order, the justice shall direct that the accused be released

        (i) forthwith, if the accused is not required to be detained in custody in respect of any other matter, or

        (ii) as soon thereafter as the accused is no longer required to be detained in custody in respect of any other matter; and

    (b) if the accused does not thereupon comply with the order, the justice who made the order or another justice having jurisdiction shall issue a warrant for the committal of the accused and may endorse thereon an authorization to the person having the custody of the accused to release the accused when the accused complies with the order

        (i) forthwith after the compliance, if the accused is not required to be detained in custody in respect of any other matter, or

        (ii) as soon thereafter as the accused is no longer required to be detained in custody in respect of any other matter

    and if the justice so endorses the warrant, he shall attach to it a copy of the order.

(2) Discharge from custody — **Where the accused complies with an order referred to in paragraph (1)(*b*), and is not required to be detained in custody in respect of any other matter, the justice who made the order or another justice having jurisdiction shall, unless the accused has been or will be released pursuant to an authorization referred to in that paragraph, issue an order for discharge in Form 39.**

(3) Warrant for committal — Where the justice makes an order under subsection 515(5) or (6) for the detention of the accused, he shall issue a warrant for the committal of the accused.

R.S., c. 2 (2d Supp.), s. 5; 1974–75–76, c. 93, s. 50;R.S. 1985, c. 27 (1st Supp.), s. 85.

Commentary: The section enacts the formal *procedure* for D's *release from custody* upon compliance with the release order under s. 515(1), (2), (7) or (8).

Under s. 519(1)(a), where D *immediately complies* with a release order, the justice will order D's *release forthwith, unless* D is required to be detained in custody in respect of another matter, in which event D will be released when such other detention is no longer required.

Under s. 519(1)(d), where D *does not immediately comply* with the release order, the justice will issue a *warrant of committal* which may be endorsed with an authorization to release D upon compliance or when detention in respect of other matters is no longer required, as the case may be. If no release authorization is endorsed on the warrant, under s. 519(2) a justice will issue an order for D's discharge in Form 39.

Where *detention* is ordered under s. 515(5) or (6) a warrant of committal is issued under s. 519(3).

Related Provisions: A warrant of committal is in Form 8.

The period for which release orders continue in force is described in s. 523(1). An undertaking is in Form 12 and a recognizance in Form 32.

520. (1) Review of order — If a justice, or a judge of the Nunavut Court of Justice, makes an order under subsection 515(2), (5), (6), (7), (8) or (12) or makes or vacates any order under paragraph 523(2)(*b*), the accused may, at any time before the trial of the charge, apply to a judge for a review of the order.

(2) Notice to prosecutor — An application under this section shall not, unless the prosecutor otherwise consents, be heard by a judge unless the accused has given to the prosecutor at least two clear days notice in writing of the application.

(3) Accused to be present — If the judge so orders or the prosecutor or the accused or his counsel so requests, the accused shall be present at the hearing of an application under this section and, where the accused is in custody, the judge may order, in writing, the person having the custody of the accused to bring him before the court.

(4) Adjournment of proceedings — A judge may, before or at any time during the hearing of an application under this section, on application by the prosecutor or the accused, adjourn the proceedings, but if the accused is in custody no adjournment shall be for more than three clear days except with the consent of the accused.

(5) Failure of accused to attend — Where an accused, other than an accused who is in custody, has been ordered by a judge to be present at the hearing of an application under this section and does not attend the hearing, the judge may issue a warrant for the arrest of the accused.

(6) Execution — A warrant issued under subsection (5) may be executed anywhere in Canada.

(7) Evidence and powers of judge on review — On the hearing of an application under this section, the judge may consider

(a) the transcript, if any, of the proceedings heard by the justice and by any judge who previously reviewed the order made by the justice,

(b) the exhibits, if any, filed in the proceedings before the justice, and

(c) such additional evidence or exhibits as may be tendered by the accused or the prosecutor, and shall either

   (d) dismiss the application, or

   (e) if the accused shows cause, allow the application, vacate the order previously made by the justice and make any other order provided for in section 515 that he considers is warranted.

(8) **Limitation of further applications** — Where an application under this section or section 521 has been heard, a further or other application under this section or section 521 shall not be made with respect to that same accused, except with leave of a judge, prior to the expiration of thirty days from the date of the decision of the judge who heard the previous application.

(9) **Application of ss. 517, 518 and 519** — The provisions of sections 517, 518 and 519 apply with such modifications as the circumstances require in respect of an application under this section.
R.S., c. 2 (2d Supp.), s. 5; 1974–75–76, c. 93, s. 51;R.S. 1985, c. 27 (1st Supp.), s. 86; 1994, c. 44, s. 46; 1999, c. 3, s. 31.

Commentary: The section permits D to apply to *review* the order of a justice relating to pre-trial release or detention.

Under s. 520(1) D may bring a review application to a "judge", as defined in s. 493, at *any time prior to trial*, where an order has been made by a justice under s. 515(2), (5)–(8), (12), or s. 523(2)(b). P is entitled, under s. 520(2), to at least *two clear days* notice in writing of the application, although consent may be given to shorter notice. D's attendance is *not* mandatory, but s. 520(3) requires his/her presence, where the judge so orders, or D or P so requests. Under s. 515(2.2), *semble*, D's attendance could be by telecommunication device. If D is out of custody and fails to attend as ordered, a warrant may be issued for D's arrest under s. 520(5) and executed anywhere in Canada under s. 520(6). Before or at any time during the review, the presiding judge may *adjourn* proceedings under s. 520(4). Where D is in custody, the adjournment may *not* be for more than *three* clear days without D's consent.

Section 520(7) describes the *material* which may be considered on the review application and, further, defines the available *dispositions*. Upon the hearing, consideration may be given to the *transcript* of the judicial interim release and any earlier review proceedings, any *exhibits* filed at the initial hearing and, further, any *additional evidence or exhibits* tendered by either party on the review hearing. The *onus* is placed upon the applicant, D, to show cause why the order below should be vacated. Where cause is shown, the reviewing judge will vacate the order made at first instance, and make *any other order in s. 515 that s/he considers warranted*. Where cause is *not* shown, the application must be dismissed.

Section 520(1) places *no* limit upon the number of applications which D may make to review a decision of a justice under a listed provision. Section 520(8) confirms that more than one application may be brought to review an order made at a judicial interim release hearing. Leave of the reviewing judge is required if an application is brought within 30 days of an earlier decision upon a review under s. 520 or 521.

Under s. 520(9), ss. 517 (restriction on publication and broadcast), 518 (scope of inquiry and evidence) and 519 (release of accused) apply to review hearings.

Case Law

Jurisdiction

R. v. Mallett (1992), 75 C.C.C. (3d) 251 (Man. C.A.) — *See also*: *R. v. Semenick*, [1985] 2 W.W.R. 132 (Man. C.A.) — Although a provincial court of appeal may be included in the definition of "superior court of criminal jurisdiction" in s. 2 of the *Code*, an application to a single justice of appeal made within thirty days of an order of a superior court judge requires special circumstances and leave. In the usual course, the remedy should be pursued before a judge of the Court of Queen's Bench.

Review

R. v. Carrier (1979), 51 C.C.C. (2d) 307 (Man. C.A.) — A review under this section should *not* be categorized as an ordinary appeal, nor is it similar to an appeal by way of trial *de novo*. Parliament intended the review to be conducted with due consideration for the initial order but, depending on the circumstances, with an independent discretion to be exercised by the review court. While it is necessary for the review court to establish rules of practice, an inflexible rule requiring transcripts in all cases might defeat the intent of the legislation to encourage expeditious disposition. Where no evidence was called at the original hearing and the judge's reasons were not extensive, and where a transcript cannot be obtained in a reasonable time, neither the transcript nor an agreed statement of facts is necessary for a review hearing.

Related Provisions: Section 521 authorizes a similar application by P where D has been released from custody under s. 515(1), (2), (7) or (8) or 523(2)(b). "Judge" is defined in s. 593.

On a *review* hearing, the presiding judge, under s. 526, may give directions for expediting any proceedings in respect of D.

The *forms* of order which are permissible where cause is shown under s. 520(7)(e) are described in ss. 515(2), (2.1) and (4). The basis upon which cause may be shown is described in s. 515(10).

521. (1) Review of order — If a justice, or a judge of the Nunavut Court of Justice, makes an order under subsection 515(1), (2), (7), (8) or (12) or makes or vacates any order under paragraph 523(2)(*b*), the prosecutor may, at any time before the trial of the charge, apply to a judge for a review of the order.

(2) Notice to accused — An application under this section shall not be heard by a judge unless the prosecutor has given to the accused at least two clear days notice in writing of the application.

(3) Accused to be present — If the judge so orders or the prosecutor or the accused or his counsel so requests, the accused shall be present at the hearing of an application under this section and, where the accused is in custody, the judge may order, in writing, the person having the custody of the accused to bring him before the court.

(4) Adjournment of proceedings — A judge may, before or at any time during the hearing of an application under this section, on application of the prosecutor or the accused, adjourn the proceedings, but if the accused is in custody no such adjournment shall be for more than three clear days except with the consent of the accused.

(5) Failure of accused to attend — Where an accused, other than an accused who is in custody, has been ordered by a judge to be present at the hearing of an application under this section and does not attend the hearing, the judge may issue a warrant for the arrest of the accused.

(6) Warrant for detention — Where, pursuant to paragraph (8)(*e*), the judge makes an order that the accused be detained in custody until he is dealt with according to law, he shall, if the accused is not in custody, issue a warrant for the committal of the accused.

(7) Execution — A warrant issued under subsection (5) or (6) may be executed anywhere in Canada.

(8) Evidence and powers of judge on review — On the hearing of an application under this section, the judge may consider

(a) the transcript, if any, of the proceedings heard by the justice and by any judge who previously reviewed the order made by the justice,

(b) the exhibits, if any, filed in the proceedings before the justice, and

(c) such additional evidence or exhibits as may be tendered by the prosecutor or the accused,

and shall either

    (d) dismiss the application, or

    (e) if the prosecutor shows cause, allow the application, vacate the order previously made by the justice and make any other order provided for in section 515 that he considers to be warranted.

(9) Limitation of further applications — Where an application under this section or section 520 has been heard, a further or other application under this section or section 520 shall not be made with respect to the same accused, except with leave of a judge, prior to the expiration of thirty days from the date of the decision of the judge who heard the previous application.

(10) Application of ss. 517, 518 and 519 — The provisions of sections 517, 518 and 519 apply with such modifications as the circumstances require in respect of an application under this section.

R.S., c. 2 (2d Supp.), s. 5; 1974–75–76, c. 93, s. 52;R.S. 1985, c. 27 (1st Supp.), s. 87; 1994, c. 44, s. 47; 1999, c. 3, s. 32.

Commentary: This section mirrors s. 520. It authorizes P to apply to *review* the order of a justice releasing D pending trial.

Under s. 521(1) P may bring a *review* application to a "judge", as defined in s. 493, at any time prior to trial, where an order has been made relating to D's release under s. 515(1), (2), (7) or (8) or under s. 523(2)(b) by a justice. The provision also applies to the new s. 515(12), a non-communication term which may only be ordered where D is detained in custody. *Semble*, it would be the failure to make such an order that P would seek to review. D is entitled, under s. 521(2), to at least two clear days *notice* in writing of the application. There is *no* provision for consent to be given to shorter notice. D's attendance is *not* mandatory, but s. 521(3) requires D's presence where the judge so orders or P or D so requests. *Semble*, s. 515(2.2) would permit D to appear by telecommunication device. If D is out of custody and *fails to attend* as required, a warrant may be issued for D's arrest under s. 521(5), and may be executed anywhere in Canada under s. 521(7). Before, or at any time during the review hearing, the presiding judge may adjourn proceedings under s. 521(4), but where D is in custody, the adjournment may not be for more than three clear days without D's consent.

Section 521(8) describes the *material* which may be considered on the *review* application and, further, defines the available dispositions. Upon the hearing, consideration may be given to the *transcript* of the judicial interim release and any earlier review proceedings, any *exhibits* filed at the initial hearing, and, further, any *additional evidence or exhibits* tendered by either party on the review. The *onus* rests upon the applicant, P, to show cause why the order below should be vacated. Where *cause* is *shown*, the reviewing judge will vacate the order made at first instance, and make *any other order* in s. 515 that s/he considers to be warranted. Where D, previously on judicial interim release, is ordered detained in custody on the review hearing, s. 521(6) requires the reviewing judge to issue a warrant for D's committal. Where *cause* is not *shown*, the application will be dismissed.

The enabling authority of s. 521(1) does *not* limit the number of applications that P may make to review a decision of a justice under a listed provision. Section 521(9) confirms that more than one application may be brought, but requires leave of the review judge, if brought within 30 days of an earlier decision upon a review under this section or s. 520.

Section 521(10) makes ss. 517 (restriction on publication and broadcast), 518 (scope of inquiry and evidence) and 519 (release of accused) applicable to review hearings.

Case Law

Jurisdiction

R. v. Sanita (1981), 60 C.C.C. (2d) 184 (B.C. C.A.) — *Contra: R. v. Cook* (1986), 26 C.C.C. (3d) 188 (Ont. C.A.) — A single judge of the court of appeal can review an order of a judge of the superior court allowing D's release pending trial.

R. v. Saracino (1989), 47 C.C.C. (3d) 185 (Ont. H.C.) — Where D is detained at his show cause hearing but ordered released on a review, P may apply to have the release order reviewed on the grounds of changed circumstances or error in principle.

R. v. Mallett (1992), 75 C.C.C. (3d) 251 (Man. C.A.) — *See also: R. v. Semenick*, [1985] 2 W.W.R. 132 (Man. C.A.) — See digest under s. 520, *supra*.

Related Provisions: Section 520 authorizes a similar application by D from an order of release or detention made by a justice under s. 515(2) or (5)–(8), (12), or under s. 523(2)(b).

On a review hearing, the presiding judge, under s. 526, may give directions for expediting any proceedings in respect of D.

The basis upon which P will endeavour to show cause are described in s. 515(10). If P fails to show cause for a detention order, the review judge may order release on more stringent terms under ss. 515(2), (2.1) and (4).

522. (1) Interim release by judge only — Where an accused is charged with an offence listed in section 469, no court, judge or justice, other than a judge of or a judge presiding in a superior court of criminal jurisdiction for the province in which the accused is so charged, may release the accused before or after the accused has been ordered to stand trial.

(2) Idem — Where an accused is charged with an offence listed in section 469, a judge of or a judge presiding in a superior court of criminal jurisdiction for the province in which the accused is charged shall order that the accused be detained in custody unless the accused, having been given a reasonable opportunity to do so, shows cause why his detention in custody is not justified within the meaning of subsection 515(10).

(2.1) Order re no communication — A judge referred to in subsection (2) who orders that an accused be detained in custody under this section may include in the order a direction that the accused abstain from communicating with any witness or other person named in the order except in accordance with such conditions specified in the order as the judge deems necessary.

(3) Release of accused — Where the judge does not order that the accused be detained in custody pursuant to subsection (2), the judge may order that the accused be released on giving an undertaking or entering into a recognizance described in any of paragraphs 515(2)(a) to (e) with such conditions described in subsections 515(4) and (4.1) as the judge considers desirable.

(4) Order not reviewable except under s. 680 — An order made under this section is not subject to review, except as provided in section 680.

(5) Application of ss. 517, 518 and 519 — The provisions of sections 517, 518 except subsection (2) thereof, and 519 apply with such modifications as the circumstances require in respect of an application for an order under subsection (2).

(6) Other offences — Where an accused is charged with an offence mentioned in section 469 and with any other offence, a judge acting under this section may apply the provisions of this Part respecting judicial interim release to that other offence.

R.S., c. 2 (2d Supp.), s. 5; 1972, c. 13, s. 36; 1974–75–76, c. 93, s. 53; R.S. 1985, c. 27 (1st Supp.), s. 88; 88; 1991, 1991, c. 40, s. 32; 1994, c. 44, s. 48.

Commentary: The section provides for judicial interim release hearings where D is charged with a s. 469 offence.

It is *only* a judge of or presiding in a *superior court of criminal jurisdiction* in the province where D is charged who may conduct a judicial interim release hearing and release D, charged with a s. 469 offence. The order may be made under s. 522(1) before or after D has been ordered to stand trial. Under s.

522(6), where D is at the same time charged with another offence, *not* listed in s. 469, the judge of the superior court of criminal jurisdiction conducting the s. 522(1) judicial interim release hearing may also deal with the non-s. 469 offence.

Section 522(2) places the *onus* upon D, charged with a s. 469 offence, to *show cause* why detention in custody is *not* justified under s. 515(10). In other words, the *general* rule of s. 515(1) that P must justify pre-trial detention is *reversed* for those charged with s. 469 offences so that D will be detained in custody, unless D shows cause why release should be ordered. Under s. 522(2.1), a detention order may include a non-communication term. This reverse onus provision has been challenged under *Charter* s. 7, 11(d) and 11(e).

The provisions of ss. 517 (restriction on publication and broadcast), 518 (scope of inquiry and evidence) except subsection (2), and 519 (release of accused) apply to hearings under this section. Subsection (3) describes the form of release order that may be made.

Under s. 522(4), orders made under the section are *only* reviewable under s. 680.

Case Law

Archer v. R. (1981), 21 C.R. (3d) 352, 59 C.C.C. (2d) 384 (Ont. C.A.) — Where D charged with first degree murder, is committed for trial on a charge of second degree murder only, a detention order made in respect of D pursuant to this section does *not* lapse and can be reviewed only by the court of appeal.

R. v. Rondeau (1996), 108 C.C.C. (3d) 474 (Que. C.A.) — Release is *not* to be refused to a person who may pose a risk or re-offending or interferring with the administration of justice whilst at liberty, but *only* where a person poses a *substantial likelihood* of doing so and the substantial likelihood endangers the protection or safety of the public. Relevant factors include:

i.   the *nature* of the *offence*;

ii.   the *circumstances* of the *offence*, including prior and subsequent events;

iii.   the *likelihood* of *conviction*;

iv.   the *degree* of *participation* by D;

v.   the *relationship* between D and V;

vi.   the *profile* of D, including occupation, lifestyle, criminal record, family situation and mental state;

vii.   D's conduct prior to the alleged offence; and

viii.   the *danger* which D's release represents for the community specifically affected by the matter.

R. v. Thatcher (No. 1) (1984), 37 Sask. R. 114 (C.A.) — The Court of Queen's Bench has jurisdiction to hear a second application for judicial interim release notwithstanding the absence of specific *Code* provision.

Charter Considerations [See also s. 515 "Reverse Onus"]

Pugsley v. R. (1982), 31 C.R. (3d) 217, 2 C.C.C. (3d) 266 (N.S. C.A.) — *Contra*: *Bray v. R.* (1983), 32 C.R. (3d) 316, 2 C.C.C. (3d) 325 (Ont. C.A.) — The reverse onus provisions contravene *Charter* s. 11(e). The burden is on P to show cause why D should be detained.

R. v. Lamothe (1990), 58 C.C.C. (3d) 530 (Que. C.A.) — The reversal of the onus of proof to establish cause for release does *not* reverse nor vary the meaning of the presumption of innocence which exists at all stages of the criminal process.

Related Provisions: The same court which has exclusive jurisdiction to try offences listed in s. 469, the superior court of criminal jurisdiction, as defined in s. 2, has authority to release D from custody prior to the trial of such charges.

The adjournment provisions of s. 516 are not expressly made applicable to s. 522 hearings.

Any release order made under s. 522(3) remains in force until D's trial is completed. The trial delay review provisions of s. 525 do not apply to s. 469 offences. *Misconduct* hearings are governed by ss. 524(4)–(7). A limited review is also available under ss. 523(2)(a) and 523(2)(c)(ii) and (iii).

523. (1) Period for which appearance notice, etc., continues in force — Where an accused, in respect of an offence with which he is charged, has not been taken into custody or has been released from custody under or by virtue of any provi-

sion of this Part, the appearance notice, promise to appear, summons, undertaking or recognizance issued to, given or entered into by the accused continues in force, subject to its terms, and applies in respect of any new information charging the same offence or an included offence that was received after the appearance notice, promise to appear, summons, undertaking or recognizance was issued, given or entered into,

(a) where the accused was released from custody pursuant to an order of a judge made under subsection 522(3), until his trial is completed; or

(b) in any other case,

(i) until his trial is completed, and

(ii) where the accused is, at his trial, determined to be guilty of the offence, until a sentence within the meaning of section 673 is imposed on the accused unless, at the time the accused is determined to be guilty, the court, judge or justice orders that the accused be taken into custody pending such sentence.

(1.1) **Where new information charging same offence** — Where an accused, in respect of an offence with which he is charged, has not been taken into custody or is being detained or has been released from custody under or by virtue of any provision of this Part and after the order for interim release or detention has been made, or the appearance notice, promise to appear, summons, undertaking or recognizance has been issued, given or entered into, a new information charging the same offence or an included offence, is received, section 507 or 508, as the case may be, does not apply in respect of the new information and the order for interim release or detention of the accused and the appearance notice, promise to appear, summons, undertaking or recognizance, if any, applies in respect of the new information.

(2) **Order vacating previous order for release or detention** — Notwithstanding subsections (1) and (1.1),

(a) the court, judge or justice before whom an accused is being tried, at any time,

(b) the justice, on completion of the preliminary inquiry in relation to an offence for which an accused is ordered to stand trial, other than an offence listed in section 469, or

(c) with the consent of the prosecutor and the accused or, where the accused or the prosecutor applies to vacate an order that would otherwise apply pursuant to subsection (1.1), without such consent, at any time

(i) where the accused is charged with an offence other than an offence listed in section 469, the justice by whom an order was made under this Part or any other justice,

(ii) where the accused is charged with an offence listed in section 469, a judge of or a judge presiding in a superior court of criminal jurisdiction for the province, or

(iii) the court, judge or justice before which or whom an accused is to be tried,

may, on cause being shown, vacate any order previously made under this Part for the interim release or detention of the accused and make any other order provided for in this Part for the detention or release of the accused until his trial is completed that the court, judge or justice considers to be warranted.

(3) **Provisions applicable to proceedings under subsection (2)** — The provisions of sections 517, 518 and 519 apply, with such modifications as the circumstances require, in respect of any proceedings under subsection (2), except that subsec-

tion 518(2) does not apply in respect of an accused who is charged with an offence listed in section 469.

R.S., c. 2 (2d Supp.), s. 5; 1974–75–76, c. 93, s. 54;R.S. 1985, c. 27 (1st Supp.), s. 89.

Commentary: The section prescribes the *period* for which the various forms of *release* are in effect and authorizes *variations* to be made at various times including trial.

Under s. 523(1), a *release* order made in respect of a *s. 469 offence* remains in force until D's trial is completed. Any *other release order* remains in force until D's trial is completed and sentence is imposed, *unless* the trial judge orders that D be detained pending sentence. Under s. 523(1.1), where a *new information* charging the same or an included offence is laid, the original release form continues to apply, without the need to confirm previous or issue fresh process.

Section 523(2) operates notwithstanding ss. 523(1) and (1.1) and, under the circumstances there described and upon cause being shown, permits any order of release or detention to be vacated, and any other order authorized under Part XVI that the court, judge or justice considers warranted, to be substituted therefor, until the trial is completed.

Under s. 523(3), the procedural provisions of ss. 517–519 apply to hearings under s. 523(2), except that s. 518(2) relating to acceptance of a plea of guilty does *not* apply where D is charged with a s. 469 offence.

Case Law

Application of Section

R. v. Jones (1997), 5 C.R. (5th) 364, 113 C.C.C. (3d) 225 (Ont. C.A.) — Sections 523(1) and (1.1) apply only to informations, *not* to indictments.

Review

R. v. Bukmeier (1996), 107 C.C.C. (3d) 272 (B.C. C.A.) — An order detaining D made by the *trial* judge under s. 532(2)(a) is *not* reviewable by a provincial appellate court, rather, only by the Supreme Court of Canada with leave under s. 40 of the *Supreme Court Act*.

Remand for Sentencing

R. v. Lenart (1998), 123 C.C.C. (3d) 353 (Ont. C.A.) — A trial judge may remand an accused in custody pending sentence under *Code* s. 523(1)(b)(ii) and may also order a pre-sentence report. Under provincial mental health legislation, a psychiatric facility is required to receive an accused, and report on his or her condition. The report may be considered in imposing sentence.

The Same Offence: S. 523(1)

R. v. Royer (1991), 50 O.A.C. 359 (C.A.) — A new information which charges first degree murder charges "the same offence" as the original information, which had alleged second degree murder. The original recognizance continues in force in respect of the new charge of first degree murder.

Vacate Order Previously Made: S. 523(2)

R. v. Patterson (1985), 36 Alta. L.R. (2d) 332 (C.A.) — When an order for release is granted or denied under s. 522 and new circumstances subsequently arise, the court may rehear the application for release pursuant to this section. It is *not* necessary to appeal the original order.

R. v. Braithwaite (1980), 57 C.C.C. (2d) 351 (N.S. C.A.) — To *vacate* an order for release, the judge must be satisfied that *cause* has been shown. Where the only new circumstance is D's committal for trial, cause has *not* been shown.

Related Provisions: Orders made under s. 523(2)(b) are reviewable by D under s. 520(1) and by P under s. 521(1).

The court, judge or justice acting under s. 523(2) may make an order expediting any proceedings in respect of D under s. 526.

The various forms of release are defined in s. 493.

Arrest of Accused on Interim Release

524. (1) **Issue of warrant for arrest of accused** — Where a justice is satisfied that there are reasonable grounds to believe that an accused

(a) has contravened or is about to contravene any summons, appearance notice, promise to appear, undertaking or recognizance that was issued or given to him or entered into by him, or

(b) has committed an indictable offence after any summons, appearance notice, promise to appear, undertaking or recognizance was issued or given to him or entered into by him,

he may issue a warrant for the arrest of the accused.

(2) **Arrest of accused without warrant** — Notwithstanding anything in this Act, a peace officer who believes on reasonable grounds that an accused

(a) has contravened or is about to contravene any summons, appearance notice, promise to appear, undertaking or recognizance that was issued or given to him or entered into by him, or

(b) has committed an indictable offence after any summons, appearance notice, promise to appear, undertaking or recognizance was issued or given to him or entered into by him,

may arrest the accused without warrant.

(3) **Hearing** — Where an accused who has been arrested with a warrant issued under subsection (1), or who has been arrested under subsection (2), is taken before a justice, the justice shall

(a) where the accused was released from custody pursuant to an order made under subsection 522(3) by a judge of the superior court of criminal jurisdiction of any province, order that the accused be taken before a judge of that court; or

(b) in any other case, hear the prosecutor and his witnesses, if any, and the accused and his witnesses, if any.

(4) **Detention of accused** — Where an accused described in paragraph (3)(*a*) is taken before a judge and the judge finds

(a) that the accused has contravened or had been about to contravene his summons, appearance notice, promise to appear, undertaking or recognizance, or

(b) that there are reasonable grounds to believe that the accused has committed an indictable offence after any summons, appearance notice, promise to appear, undertaking or recognizance was issued or given to him or entered into by him,

he shall cancel the summons, appearance notice, promise to appear, undertaking or recognizance and order that the accused be detained in custody unless the accused, having been given a reasonable opportunity to do so, shows cause why his detention in custody is not justified within the meaning of subsection 515(10).

(5) **Release of accused** — Where the judge does not order that the accused be detained in custody pursuant to subsection (4), he may order that the accused be released upon his giving an undertaking or entering into a recognizance described in any of paragraphs 515(2)(*a*) to (*e*) with such conditions described in subsection 515(4) or, where the accused was at large on an undertaking or a recognizance with conditions, such additional conditions, described in subsection 515(4), as the judge considers desirable.

(6) Order not reviewable — Any order made under subsection (4) or (5) is not subject to review, except as provided in section 680.

(7) Release of accused — Where the judge does not make a finding under paragraph (4)(*a*) or (*b*), he shall order that the accused be released from custody.

(8) Powers of justice after hearing — Where an accused described in subsection (3), other than an accused to whom paragraph (*a*) of that subsection applies, is taken before the justice and the justice finds

   (a) that the accused has contravened or had been about to contravene his summons, appearance notice, promise to appear, undertaking or recognizance, or

   (b) that there are reasonable grounds to believe that the accused has committed an indictable offence after any summons, appearance notice, promise to appear, undertaking or recognizance was issued or given to him or entered into by him,

he shall cancel the summons, appearance notice, promise to appear, undertaking or recognizance and order that the accused be detained in custody unless the accused, having been given a reasonable opportunity to do so, shows cause why his detention in custody is not justified within the meaning of subsection 515(10).

(9) Release of accused — Where the accused shows cause why his detention in custody is not justified within the meaning of subsection 515(10), the justice shall order that the accused be released on his giving an undertaking or entering into a recognizance described in any of paragraphs 515(2)(a) to (e) with such conditions, described in subsection 515(4), as the justice considers desirable.

(10) Reasons — Where the justice makes an order under subsection (9), he shall include in the record a statement of his reasons for making the order, and subsection 515(9) is applicable with such modification as the circumstances require in respect thereof.

(11) Where justice to order that accused be released — Where the justice does not make a finding under paragraph (8)(*a*) or (*b*), he shall order that the accused be released from custody.

(12) Provisions applicable to proceedings under this section — The provisions of sections 517, 518 and 519 apply with such modifications as the circumstances require in respect of any proceedings under this section, except that subsection 518(2) does not apply in respect of an accused who is charged with an offence mentioned in section 522.

(13) Certain provisions applicable to order under this section — Section 520 applies in respect of any order made under subsection (8) or (9) as though the order were an order made by a justice or a judge of the Nunavut Court of Justice under subsection 515(2) or (5), and section 521 applies in respect of any order made under subsection (9) as though the order were an order made by a justice or a judge of the Nunavut Court of Justice under subsection 515(2).

R.S., c. C-34, s. 458; c. 2 (2d Supp.), s. 5;1974–75–76, c. 93, s. 55; 1999, c. 3, s. 33.

Commentary: The section describes the circumstances under which D may be *arrested* for alleged *misconduct* on judicial interim release and provides the procedural mechanism to determine whether or on what terms release should continue.

In *general*, D may be arrested *with or without* a *warrant* and returned before a justice, to be dealt with according to law. Under s. 524(1), a *warrant* may be issued for D's arrest where a justice is satisfied there are *reasonable* grounds to believe that, since release, D has either contravened or been about to contravene his/her release form or has committed an indictable offence. Under s. 524(2), D may be arrested *without warrant* by any peace officer who has the same belief *on reasonable grounds*. The operation of s. 524 is unaffected by the fact that D is not or cannot be formally charged with a further offence as a result of the conduct that caused the arrest.

Upon arrest, D must be taken before a *justice* under s. 524(3). Where D's release was *not* under s. 522(3), the justice must conduct a hearing under s. 524(3)(b). Where the justice *finds* on the hearing that D has *contravened*, or had been *about to contravene* his/her release form, or that there are *reasonable* grounds to believe that D has *committed* an *indictable* offence since release, under s. 524(8), the original release form must be cancelled and D detained unless, given a *reasonable* opportunity to do so, D shows cause why a detention is *not* justified under s. 515(10). Where D shows cause and release is ordered, the form of release is governed by s. 524(9). *Reasons* are required under s. 524(10). Where the justice does *not* find on the hearing that D has contravened or had been about to contravene the release form or that there are reasonable grounds to believe D committed an indictable offence since release, s. 524(11) requires that D be released. Detention and release orders made under ss. 524(8) and (9) are reviewable by D under s. 520 and by P under s. 521.

Sections 524(4), (5) and (7) establish a similar procedure where the original release order was in respect of a s. 469 offence. Subsection (5), however, authorizes the imposition of additional conditions where D had been at large on an undertaking or recognizance with conditions. Orders made under subsections (4) and (5) are reviewable only under s. 680.

Sections 517 (restrictions on publication and broadcast), 518 (procedure and evidence on hearing) and 519 (formal release of accused) apply to all hearings under this section.

Case Law
Jurisdiction
R. v. Kinger (1982), 28 C.R. (3d) 282, 65 C.C.C. (2d) 483 (Alta. C.A.) — A provincial court judge has jurisdiction under s. 524(3) to determine whether a violation of a recognizance issued under s. 520 has occurred, notwithstanding that D was ordered released by a judge of the Court of Queen's Bench.

R. v. Yarema (1991), 5 C.R. (4th) 125, 64 C.C.C. (3d) 260 (Ont. C.A.); affirming (1989), 52 C.C.C. (3d) 242 (Ont. H.C.) — Conduct of a show cause hearing by a justice of the peace with respect to a discrete charge against D who has been ordered released by a judge of the superior court of criminal jurisdiction, does *not* thereafter preclude resort to a s. 524 review of the earlier release order by a judge of the superior court of criminal jurisdiction.

Related Provisions: No further charges need actually be laid in respect of the alleged misconduct in order to engage the section. Where further charges are laid, however, as for example under ss. 145(2)–(5.1) or otherwise, the onus will shift to D to show cause why detention is not justified.

The duration of the release form is governed by s. 523.

The contents of a warrant of arrest are described in ss. 511 and 513, its execution in s. 514. Sections 25–29 afford general protection to persons administering and enforcing the law.

Under s. 526, *directions* may be given to *expedite* any proceedings in respect of D on a hearing under s. 524.

Review of Detention where Trial Delayed

525. (1) Time for application to judge — Where an accused who has been charged with an offence other than an offence listed in section 469 and who is not required to be detained in custody in respect of any other matter is being detained in custody pending his trial for that offence and the trial has not commenced

(a) in the case of an indictable offence, within ninety days from

(i) the day on which the accused was taken before a justice under section 503, or

(ii) where an order that the accused be detained in custody has been made under section 521 or 524, or a decision has been made with respect to a review under section 520, the later of the day on which the accused was taken into custody under that order and the day of the decision, or

(b) in the case of an offence for which the accused is being prosecuted in proceedings by way of summary conviction, within thirty days from

(i) the day on which the accused was taken before a justice under subsection 503(1), or

(ii) where an order that the accused be detained in custody has been made under section 521 or 524, or a decision has been made with respect to a review under section 520, the later of the day on which the accused was taken into custody under that order and the day of the decision,

the person having the custody of the accused shall, forthwith on the expiration of those ninety or thirty days, as the case may be, apply to a judge having jurisdiction in the place in which the accused is in custody to fix a date for a hearing to determine whether or not the accused should be released from custody.

(2) **Notice of hearing** — On receiving an application under subsection (1), the judge shall

(a) fix a date for the hearing described in subsection (1) to be held in the jurisdiction

(i) where the accused is in custody, or

(ii) where the trial is to take place; and

(b) direct that notice of the hearing be given to such persons, including the prosecutor and the accused, and in such manner, as the judge may specify.

(3) **Matters to be considered on hearing** — On the hearing described in subsection (1), the judge may, in deciding whether or not the accused should be released from custody, take into consideration whether the prosecutor or the accused has been responsible for any unreasonable delay in the trial of the charge.

(4) **Order** — If, following the hearing described in subsection (1), the judge is not satisfied that the continued detention of the accused in custody is justified within the meaning of subsection 515(10), the judge shall order that the accused be released from custody pending the trial of the charge on his giving an undertaking or entering into a recognizance described in any of paragraphs 515(2)(a) to (e) with such conditions described in subsection 515(4) as the judge considers desirable.

(5) **Warrant of judge for arrest** — Where a judge having jurisdiction in the province where an order under subsection (4) for the release of an accused has been made is satisfied that there are reasonable grounds to believe that the accused

(a) has violated or is about to violate the undertaking or recognizance on which he has been released, or

(b) has, after his release from custody on his undertaking or recognizance, committed an indictable offence,

he may issue a warrant for the arrest of the accused.

(6) **Arrest without warrant by peace officer** — Notwithstanding anything in this Act, a peace officer who believes on reasonable grounds that an accused who has been released from custody under subsection (4)

(a) has contravened or is about to contravene the undertaking or recognizance on which he has been released, or

(b) has, after his release from custody on his undertaking or recognizance, committed an indictable offence,

may arrest the accused without warrant and take him or cause him to be taken before a judge having jurisdiction in the province where the order for his release was made.

(7) **Hearing and order** — A judge before whom an accused is taken pursuant to a warrant issued under subsection (5) or pursuant to subsection (6) may, where the accused shows cause why his detention in custody is not justified within the meaning of subsection 515(10), order that the accused be released on his giving an undertaking or entering into a recognizance described in any of paragraphs 515(2)(a) to (e) with such conditions, described in subsection 515(4), as the judge considers desirable.

(8) **Provisions applicable to proceedings** — The provisions of sections 517, 518 and 519 apply with such modifications as the circumstances require in respect of any proceedings under this section.

(9) **Directions for expediting trial** — Where an accused is before a judge under any of the provisions of this section, the judge may give directions for expediting the trial of the accused.

R.S., c. C-34, s. 459; c. 2 (2d Supp.), s. 5; 1974–75–76, c. 93, s. 56;R.S. 1985, c. 27 (1st Supp.), s. 90; 1994, c. 44, s. 49; 1997, c. 18, s. 61.

Commentary: The section provides an automatic *review of detention* where D's *trial*, in respect of an offence *not listed in s. 469*, has been *delayed* for more than a specified number of days after first appearance or a detention order made under s. 521 or 524, or a review decision under s. 520.

Under s. 525(1), the *person* having the *custody* of D must, forthwith after expiration of the fixed time periods, *apply* to a judge having jurisdiction in the territorial division of custody, to fix a date for a hearing to determine whether D should be released. The time periods are 90 days for indictable offences and 30 days for summary conviction offences, after first appearance before a justice, or detention order under s. 521 or 524, or review decision under s. 520. Upon receipt of the application, the judge must *fix* a *date* for hearing at a place described in s. 525(2)(a) and give the *notice* required under s. 525(2)(b) to interested parties.

The *issue* on the hearing is *whether* the *continued detention* of D in custody is *justified* under s. 515(10). In determining this issue, the judge, under s. 525(3), may consider who is responsible for any unreasonable delay in the trial of the charge. If the judge is *not* satisfied that the continued detention of D is justified under s. 515(10), D must be released in accordance with s. 525(4).

Sections 525(5) and (6) authorize the *arrest* of D, with or without warrant, where there are *reasonable* grounds to believe that, since release under s. 525(4), D either has or is about to contravene the form of release, or has committed an indictable offence. Upon arrest, D must be taken before a judge who will conduct a hearing under s. 525(7). The *onus* is on D to show cause why his/her detention in custody is not justified under s. 515(10). If release is ordered, it will be in accordance with ss. 515(2)(a)–(e) and 515(4).

In all proceedings under the section, the provisions of ss. 517 (restriction on publication and broadcast), 518 (procedure and evidence on hearing) and 519 (formal release of D) apply. Section 525(9) authorizes the presiding judge to give directions for expediting D's trial.

Case Law

Review of Detention

R. v. Neill (1990), 60 C.C.C. (3d) 26 (Alta. C.A.) — Section 525 applies notwithstanding that D's detention has already been reviewed by a superior court judge. The section requires that the court interest itself in a prompt trial, as well as needless detention.

Vukelich v. Vancouver Pre-Trial Centre (1993), 27 C.R. (4th) 15, 87 C.C.C. (3d) 32 (B.C. C.A.) — "Forthwith" in s. 525(1) means "as soon as practicable". D's detention does *not* become unlawful merely upon the expiration of 90 days. D's custodian is statutorily obliged to seek a hearing as soon as practicable after the expiration of the 90-day period. What is an acceptable lapse of time after the expiration of this period is determined objectively.

R. v. Burton (1993), 25 C.R. (4th) 167, 84 C.C.C. (3d) 311 (B.C. C.A.) — D is entitled to a s. 525 review, notwithstanding an earlier review under *Code* s. 520.

R. v. Burton (1993), 25 C.R. (4th) 167, 84 C.C.C. (3d) 311 (B.C. C.A.) — A s. 525 review is required to ensure that D is *not* unnecessarily detained and that directions are given to expedite the trial. Failure to conduct a s. 525 review renders continued detention beyond the 90-day period unlawful.

Gagliardi v. R. (1981), 60 C.C.C. (2d) 267 (B.C. C.A.); leave to appeal refused (1981), 60 C.C.C. (2d) 267n (S.C.C.) — A failure to proceed due to an administrative error on the date set for a hearing under this section, does *not* result in a loss of jurisdiction as a review under this section is a collateral matter.

Ferreira v. R. (1981), 58 C.C.C. (2d) 147 (B.C. C.A.) — An accused in custody pursuant to both a detention order and a warrant for breach of recognizance is entitled to have his detention reviewed upon the expiration of the later of the two 90-day periods.

R. v. Srebot (1975), 33 C.R.N.S. 73, 28 C.C.C. (2d) 160 (B.C. C.A.) — The section applies only where D has been denied interim release or whose order for release has been cancelled, not where D has been ordered released but has been unable to meet the order made.

R. v. Dass (1978), 39 C.C.C. (2d) 365 (Man. C.A.) — This section does *not* apply where there has already been a review of a bail application. Where D has had an unsuccessful bail review, the remedy is by further application after 30 days have elapsed and if circumstances have changed.

Prerogative Remedies

*Ex parte Cordes, (*sub nom. *R. v. Cordes)* 31 C.C.C. (2d) 279 — Where D, lawfully in custody, considers there has been a failure on the part of the custodian to make the required application, s/he may apply for *mandamus* to require the custodian to make the application or *habeas corpus*.

Vukelich v. Vancouver Pre-Trial Centre (1993), 27 C.R. (4th) 15, 87 C.C.C. (3d) 32 (B.C. C.A.) — Where D's custodian has applied for a s. 525 hearing, a claim for release on *habeas corpus* should be referred to the judge who conducts the s. 525 hearing. Where the custodian has made *no* application under s. 525, D may seek *habeas corpus* to determine whether the lapse of time has tainted the legality of D's detention, or *mandamus* to compel the custodian to comply with s. 525.

Ex parte Mitchell (1975), 23 C.C.C. (2d) 473 (B.C. C.A.) — D may apply for *habeas corpus* to secure his release where there has been a failure to review his detention within 90 days. The unlawful detention cannot be made lawful by a subsequent attempt by P to hold a review hearing.

R. v. Dass (1978), 39 C.C.C. (2d) 365 (Man. C.A.) — The duty of the jailer to apply for a bail hearing may be enforced by *mandamus*. The availability of the remedy of *mandamus* does not necessarily oust the remedy of *habeas corpus*.

Charter Considerations

R. v. Pomfret (1990), 53 C.C.C. (3d) (Man. C.A.) — *But see: R. v. Reimer* (1987), 47 Man. R. (2d) 156 (C.A.) — D's detention did not become arbitrary and contrary to *Charter* s. 9 where more than 90 days elapsed without the jailer applying for a review.

Related Provisions: D's right to be tried within a reasonable time is guaranteed by *Charter* s. 11(b). Section 525 endeavours to ensure, without constitutional guarantee, that D will not be unjustifiably detained for an extended period prior to trial.

Pre-trial detention may also be reviewed on application by D under s. 520. Section 523(2) provides rights of review up to and including the time of trial.

The arrest authority of ss. 525(5) and (6) is, in large measure, identical to the general authority under ss. 524(1) and (2). The hearing under s. 525(7), however, is quite dissimilar to what is required under ss. 524(4) and (8), in that it neither requires a preliminary finding of contravention, reasonably grounded belief in the commission of an indictable offence, nor expressly authorizes cancellation of the form of release.

Section 525(9) *permits* directions to expedite D's trial in the event of delay. Section 526 *permits* directions to expedit *any proceedings* in respect of D.

"Judge" is defined in s. 493.

526. Directions for expediting proceedings — Subject to subsection 525(9), a court, judge or justice before which or whom an accused appears pursuant to this Part may give directions for expediting any proceedings in respect of the accused.

R.S., c. 2 (2d Supp.), s. 5;R.S. 1985, c. 27 (1st Supp.), s. 91.

Commentary: Under this section any judge, court or justice before whom D appears under Part XVI may give *directions expediting* any proceedings in respect of D.

Related Provisions: Where D's trial has *not* commenced within a specified time, a judge *must* give directions expediting the trial under s. 525(9).

Procedure to Procure Attendance of a Prisoner

527. (1) Procuring attendance — A judge of a superior court of criminal jurisdiction may order in writing that a person who is confined in a prison be brought before the court, judge, justice or provincial court judge before whom the prisoner is required to attend, from day to day as may be necessary, if

(a) the applicant for the order sets out the facts of the case in an affidavit and produces the warrant, if any; and

(b) the judge is satisfied that the ends of justice require that an order be made.

(2) Provincial court judge's order — A provincial court judge has the same powers for the purposes of subsection (1) or (7) as a judge has under that subsection where the person whose attendance is required is within the province in which the provincial court judge has jurisdiction.

(3) Conveyance of prisoner — An order that is made under subsection (1) or (2) shall be addressed to the person who has custody of the prisoner, and on receipt thereof that person shall

(a) deliver the prisoner to any person who is named in the order to receive him; or

(b) bring the prisoner before the court, judge, justice or provincial court judge, as the case may be, upon payment of his reasonable charges in respect thereof.

(4) Detention of prisoner required as witness — Where the prisoner is required as a witness, the judge or provincial court judge shall direct, in the order, the manner in which the prisoner shall be kept in custody and returned to the prison from which he is brought.

(5) Detention in other cases — Where the appearance of the prisoner is required for the purposes of paragraph (1)(a) or (b), the judge or provincial court judge shall give appropriate directions in the order with respect to the manner in which the prisoner is

(a) to be kept in custody, if he is committed for trial; or

(b) to be returned, if he is discharged upon a preliminary inquiry or if he is acquitted of the charge against him.

(6) Application of sections respecting sentence — Sections 718.3 and 743.1 apply where a prisoner to whom this section applies is convicted and sentenced to imprisonment by the court, judge, justice or provincial court judge.

(7) Transfer of prisoner — On application by the prosecutor, a judge of a superior court of criminal jurisdiction may, if a prisoner or a person in the custody of a peace officer consents in writing, order the transfer of the prisoner or other person to the custody of a peace officer named in the order for a period specified in the order, where the judge is satisfied that the transfer is required for the purpose of assisting a peace officer acting in the execution of his or her duties.

(8) Conveyance of prisoner — An order under subsection (7) shall be addressed to the person who has custody of the prisoner and on receipt thereof that person shall deliver the prisoner to the peace officer who is named in the order to receive him.

(9) Return — When the purposes of any order made under this section have been carried out, the prisoner shall be returned to the place where he was confined at the time the order was made.

R.S., c. C-34, s. 460;R.S. 1985, c. 27 (1st Supp.), ss. 92, 101(2), 203; 1994, c. 44, s. 50; 1995, c. 22, s. 18; 1997, c. 18, s. 62.

Commentary: This section defines the procedure to procure the attendance of a prisoner in court or elsewhere for certain purposes.

Under s. 527(1), application may be made to a judge of the *superior court of criminal jurisdiction* for an order that a prisoner *appear* before a court, judge, provincial court judge or justice from day to day as may be necessary. The applicant must set out in an *affidavit* the facts upon which the application is based and produce the warrant, if any, under which the prisoner is detained. Where the judge is satisfied that the *ends of justice* require it, the order may be made. Under s. 527(2), a *provincial court judge* has the same authority to compel attendance of a prisoner under s. 527(1), where the prisoner or person in custody is within the same province.

The *order* and the *manner* in which it is to be *executed* are described in ss. 527(3)–(6). After the purposes of the order have been carried out, s. 527(9) requires that the prisoner be returned to his/her place of confinement.

Under s. 527(7), P may apply to a judge of the *superior court of criminal jurisdiction*, subject to s. 527(2), for an order, sometimes described as an *"Olson* order", transferring a prisoner or person in the custody of a peace officer to the *custody of a designated peace officer*, for a specified period, to assist the officer acting in the execution of his/her duties. The order may be made by a provincial court judge where the prisoner or person in custody is in the same province. The application may *only* be granted where the prisoner consents *in writing* and the judge is satisfied that the transfer is *required* to *assist* the officer acting in the *execution* of his/her *duties*. Upon receipt of the order, the custodian will deliver up custody of the prisoner to the designated officer. The prisoner or person in custody will be returned to his/her place of confinement or previous custody when the purposes of the order have been carried out.

Case Law

R. v. Ayres (1984), 42 C.R. (3d) 33 (Ont. C.A.) — This section authorizes an order that a prisoner be brought before the court. The presiding judge has the inherent power to require him, once in court, to testify. No *subpoena* need be served on the prisoner.

Related Provisions: Part XXII, ss. 696–707, applies where a person is required to attend to give evidence in any proceeding to which the *Code* applies.

The procedure of ss. 527(1)–(6) is available both to P and D and may relate to prisoners confined outside the province in which attendance is sought. Sections 527(7) and (8) are available only upon application by P.

Endorsement of Warrant

528. (1) Endorsing warrant — Where a warrant for the arrest or committal of an accused, in any form set out in Part XXVIII in relation thereto, cannot be executed in accordance with section 514 or 703, a justice within whose jurisdiction the accused is or is believed to be shall, on application and proof on oath or by affidavit of the signature of the justice who issued the warrant, authorize the arrest of the accused within his jurisdiction by making an endorsement, which may be in Form 28, on the warrant.

(1.1) Copy of affidavit or warrant — A copy of an affidavit or warrant submitted by a means of telecommunication that produces a writing has the same probative force as the original for the purposes of subsection (1).

(2) Effect of endorsement — An endorsement that is made upon a warrant pursuant to subsection (1) is sufficient authority to the peace officers to whom it was originally directed, and to all peace officers within the territorial jurisdiction of the justice by whom it is endorsed, to execute the warrant and to take the accused before the justice who issued the warrant or before any other justice for the same territorial division.

R.S., c. C-34, s. 461; 1974–75–76, c. 93, s. 57;R.S.1985, c. 27 (1st Supp.), s. 93; 1994, c. 44, s. 51.

Commentary: The section authorizes *endorsement* of an arrest or committal *warrant* to permit execution in a territorial division beyond the jurisdiction of the issuing justice.

Under s. 528(1), where an arrest or committal warrant cannot be executed under s. 514 or 703, application may be made to a justice within whose jurisdiction D is, or is believed to be, for an order, in Form 28, authorizing the arrest of D within his/her jurisdiction. The application must be accompanied by an affidavit or proof on oath of the signature of the issuing justice. Where the application and requisite proof are made, authorization must be given by endorsement of the warrant. The procedure is commonly described as "backing the warrant".

Under s. 528(1.1), a copy of an affidavit or warrant submitted by means of a telecommunication that produces a writing has the same probative force as the original for these purposes.

Under s. 528(2), the endorsement authorizes execution of the warrant by peace officers in the jurisdiction of its issuance and endorsement and the return of D to the jurisdiction of issuance.

Related Provisions: " Justice" and "peace officer" are defined in s. 2, "warrant" in s. 493.

Section 20 authorizes the execution of a warrant on a holiday and ss. 25–29 protect those administering or enforcing the law. Under s. 546, an irregularity or variance between the warrant, information and evidence adduced at the preliminary inquiry does not invalidate any proceeding at or subsequent to a preliminary inquiry. The manner in which warrants for committal are executed is described in s. 744. A similar "backing" procedure exists under ss. 487(2) for search warrants and 487.03 for general investigative, tracking, DNA and number recorder warrants.

529. (1) Including authorization to enter in warrant of arrest — A warrant to arrest or apprehend a person issued by a judge or justice under this or any other Act of Parliament may authorize a peace officer, subject to subsection (2), to enter a dwelling-house described in the warrant for the purpose of arresting or apprehending the person if the judge or justice is satisfied by information on oath in writing that there are reasonable grounds to believe that the person is or will be present in the dwelling house.

(2) Execution — An authorization to enter a dwelling-house granted under subsection (1) is subject to the condition that the peace officer may not enter the dwelling-house unless the peace officer has, immediately before entering the dwelling-house, reasonable grounds to believe that the person to be arrested or apprehended is present in the dwelling-house.

1997, c. 39, s. 2.

Commentary: This section permits a *warrant* of *arrest* or *apprehension* issued under the *Code* or other federal Act to include *authorization* to *enter* a *dwelling-house* to arrest or apprehend the subject and describe the circumstances in which it may be done.

To obtain entry authorization, application must be made to a judge or justice by *information on oath in writing*. The judge or justice must be satisfied that there are *reasonable* grounds to believe that the *person* to be arrested or apprehended *is* or *will be present* in the dwelling-house. Where authorization is given, s. 529(2) makes it subject to the condition that the executing officer, immediately before entering, have reasonable grounds to believe that the subject of the warrant is then present in the dwelling-house.

Related Provisions: The authorization of s. 529 is *not* free-standing. It is, rather, an "add-on" to an existing warrant of arrest or apprehension. It may also be subject to such reasonable terms and conditions as the judge or justice considers advisable to ensure reasonable entry under s. 529.2.

A free-standing warrant to enter a dwelling-house to arrest or apprehend may be issued under s. 529.1. It is in Form 7.1 and may also be subject to the terms and conditions of s. 529.2.

Entry may be made for similar purposes without warrant in exigent circumstances as described in s. 529.3

As a general rule, prior announcement must precede entry. Sections 529.4(1) and (2) describe the circumstances in which no announcement entry may be authorized and made.

Section 529.5 permits application to be made by telephone or other means of telecommunication to obtain s. 529 or s. 529.4 authorization, or a s. 529.1 warrant.

529.1 Warrant to enter dwelling-house — **A judge or justice may issue a warrant in Form 7.1 authorizing a peace officer to enter a dwelling-house described in the warrant for the purpose of arresting or apprehending a person identified or identifiable by the warrant if the judge or justice is satisfied by information on oath that there are reasonable grounds to believe that the person is or will be present in the dwelling-house and that**

> **(a) a warrant referred to in this or any other Act of Parliament to arrest or apprehend the person is in force anywhere in Canada;**
>
> **(b) grounds exist to arrest the person without warrant under paragraph 495(1)(a) or (b); or**
>
> **(c) grounds exist to arrest or apprehend without warrant the person under an Act of Parliament, other than this Act.**

1997, c. 39, s. 2.

Commentary: The section provides for a free-standing entry warrant which authorizes entry into a dwelling-house to arrest or apprehend a subject identified or identifiable by the warrant.

A s. 529.1 warrant may be issued by a judge or justice. The material submitted, an information on *oath*, must satisfy the issuing authority that there are *reasonable* grounds to believe that the *person is* or *will be present* in the dwelling-house and that *any* of the circumstances described in s. 529.1(a)-(c) are met. The warrant is in Form 7.1.

Related Provisions: Unlike the "add-on" authorization of s. 529, there is *no* requirement in s. 529.1 that the information on oath be *in writing*. No form is provided for either information.

Section 529.2 requires inclusion of terms and conditions in the warrant to ensure the entry under it is reasonable in the circumstances. Where the conditions of s. 529.4 have been met, no announcement entry may be authorized and made.

An application for a s. 529.1 entry warrant may be made under s. 529.5 by telephone or other means of telecommunication.

Other related provisions are discussed in the corresponding note to s. 529.

529.2 Reasonable terms and conditions — **Subject to section 529.4, the judge or justice shall include in a warrant referred to in section 529 or 529.1 any terms and conditions that the judge or justice considers advisable to ensure that the entry into the dwelling-house is reasonable in the circumstances.**

1997, c. 39, s. 2.

Commentary: Under this section, a judge or justice who gives an *entry authorization* under s. 529, or issues an *entry warrant* under s. 529.1, may include in it any *terms* and *conditions* which s/he conditions advisable to *ensure* that the authorized *entry* is *reasonable* in the circumstances.

The provision is subject to s. 529.4 which permits no announcement entry in certain circumstances when authorized by a judge or justice and supported by current grounds.

Related Provisions: Related provisions are discussed in the corresponding note to s. 529.

529.3 (1) Authority to enter dwelling without warrant — Without limiting or restricting any power a peace officer may have to enter a dwelling-house under this or any other Act or law, the peace officer may enter the dwelling-house for the purpose of arresting or apprehending a person, without a warrant referred to in section 529 or 529.1 authorizing the entry, if the peace officer has reasonable grounds to believe that the person is present in the dwelling-house, and the conditions for obtaining a warrant under section 529.1 exist but by reason of exigent circumstances it would be impracticable to obtain a warrant.

(2) Exigent circumstances — For the purposes of subsection (1), exigent circumstances include circumstances in which the peace officer

> **(a) has reasonable grounds to suspect that entry into the dwelling-house is necessary to prevent imminent bodily harm or death to any person; or**

> **(b) has reasonable grounds to believe that evidence relating to the commission of an indictable offence is present in the dwelling-house and that entry into the dwelling-house is necessary to prevent the imminent loss or imminent destruction of evidence.**

1997, c. 39, s. 2.

Commentary: This section permits a peace officer to enter a dwelling-house to arrest or apprehend a person *without* warrant and defines the circumstances in which s/he may do so. It imposes no restriction on any existing statutory or common law entry power.

Under s. 529.3(1), a peace officer may enter a dwelling-house to arrest or apprehend a person *without* a s. 529 authorization or a s. 529.1 warrant. To permit the entry, the officer must have *reasonable* grounds to believe the *person is* present and that the *conditions* for obtaining a s. 529.1 entry *warrant* exist. It must also be *impracticable* to obtain a warrant because of "exigent circumstances" as defined in s. 529.3(2).

The definition of "exigent circumstnaces" in s. 529.3(2) is expansive, *not* exhaustive. It includes two types of necessity, based on reasonably grounded suspicion or belief, as the case may be. Exigent circumstances *include* a reasonably grounded suspicion that *entry* is *necessary* to *prevent imminent* bodily harm or death to any person. They also exist where the officer has a reasonably grounded belief that *evidence* relating to the commission of an indictable offence is in a dwelling-house and that *entry* is *necessary* to *prevent* its *imminent* loss or destruction.

Case Law

R. v. Godoy (1998), 21 C.R. (5th) 205, 131 C.C.C. (3d) 129 (S.C.C.) — A 911 call engages the common law police duty to protect life whenever it can be inferred that the caller is or may be in some distress. This includes calls that are disconnected before the operator can find out the nature of the emergency. Despite the privacy interest residents have in the sanctity of the home, *threats* to *life* and *limb* more directly engage the values of dignity, integrity and autonomy that underlie the right to privacy than does the interest in being free from the *minimal* state intrusion of police entry to investigate a potential emergency.

Whether the police have authority to enter dwelling-houses in the course of an investigation of a 911 call depends on the circumstances of each case. Where police conduct constitutes a prima facie interference with someone's liberty or property, courts have to consider whether the conduct

i.   falls within the general scope of any *statutory* or *common* law duty; and,

ii.   involves an *unjustifiable* use of *powers* associated with that duty.

Forced entry into a dwelling to ascertain the health and safety of a 911 caller is justified by the importance of the police duty to protect life. The intrusion is *limited*, however, to the *protection* of *life* and *safety*. Police may investigate the call, in particular,

i.   to *locate* the *caller*;

ii.   to determine the *reasons* for the call; and,

iii.   to provide *assistance* to the caller

but no more. The police do *not* have permission to search the premises or otherwise intrude on a resident's privacy or property.

Related Provisions: The "exigent circumstances" exception to the authorization/warrant requirement is likely to attract *Charter* challenge, especially s. 529.3(2)(b).

In determining whether "exigent circumstances" make it impracticable to obtain an entry warrant, it may be of importance that authorization/warrant may be obtained by telephone or other means of telecommunication under s. 529.5.

The requirement of announcement prior to entry also applies to s. 529.3 entries without authorization or warrant. It is, however, subject to exception under s. 529.4(3).

Other related provisions are discussed in the corresponding note to s. 529.

529.4 (1) Omitting announcement before entry — A judge or justice who authorizes a peace officer to enter a dwelling-house under section 529 or 529.1, or any judge or justice, may authorize the peace officer to enter the dwelling-house without prior announcement if the judge or justice is satisfied by information on oath that there are reasonable grounds to believe that prior announcement of the entry would

    (a) expose the peace officer or any other person to imminent bodily harm or death; or

    (b) result in the imminent loss or imminent destruction of evidence relating to the commission of an indictable offence.

(2) Execution of authorization — An authorization under this section is subject to the condition that the peace officer may not enter the dwelling-house without prior announcement despite being authorized to do so unless the peace officer has, immediately before entering the dwelling-house,

    (a) reasonable grounds to suspect that prior announcement of the entry would expose the peace officer or any other person to imminent bodily harm or death; or

    (b) reasonable grounds to believe that prior announcement of the entry would result in the imminent loss or imminent destruction of evidence relating to the commission of an indictable offence.

(3) Exception — A peace officer who enters a dwelling-house without a warrant under section 529.3 may not enter the dwelling-house without prior announcement unless the peace officer has, immediately before entering the dwelling-house,

    (a) reasonable grounds to suspect that prior announcement of the entry would expose the peace officer or any other person to imminent bodily harm or death; or

    (b) reasonable grounds to believe that prior announcement of the entry would result in the imminent loss or imminent destruction of evidence relating to the commission of an indictable offence.

1997, c. 39, s. 2.

Commentary: This section describes the circumstances in which *no announcement entry* may be made into dwelling-houses to *arrest or apprehend* an occupant. It is implicit in the section that, except as otherwise permitted, prior announcement is required.

Sections 529.4(1) and (2) govern entries under s. 529 authorizations and s. 529.1 warrants. There are two requirements: *prior authorization* and *contemporaneous necessity*.

Under s. 529.4(1), the judge or justice who gave the authorization or issued the warrant to enter, or any other judge or justice, may authorize no announcement entry. To do so, the judicial officer must be satisfied by *information on oath* that there are *reasonable* grounds to believe that *prior announcement* of the entry would

i. *expose* the *officer* or *anyone* else to *imminent bodily harm or death; or*

ii. result in the imminent loss or destruction of evidence relating to the commission of an indictable offence.

The second requirement seeks to ensure that, at the time of execution, the *necessity* for no announcement entry *continues*. Despite authorization, the officer may *not* enter without announcement *unless*, immediately prior to entry, s/he has a reasonably grounded *suspicion* or *belief* that the consequences of prior announcement described in s. 529.4(2) still prevail.

In cases of entry without warrant/authorization under the exigent circumstances provision of s. 529.3, there must be prior announcement unless the officer, immediately before entry, has the reasonably grounded suspicion and belief described in s. 529.3(3). The requirement is a duplicate of s. 529.3(2).

Related Provisions: An entry warrant under s. 529.1 is in Form 7.1.

Other related provisions are discussed in the corresponding note to s. 529.

529.5 Telewarrant — **If a peace officer believes that it would be impracticable in the circumstances to appear personally before a judge or justice to make an application for a warrant under section 529.1 or an authorization under section 529 or 529.4, the warrant or authorization may be issued on an information submitted by telephone or other means of telecommunication and, for that purpose, section 487.1 applies, with any modifications that the circumstances require, to the warrant or authorization.**

1997, c. 39, s. 2.

Commentary: This section permits the use of a telephone or other means of telecommunication to obtain a s. 529.1 entry *warrant* or *authorization* to enter (s. 529) or to enter *without* prior *announcement* (s. 529.4). *Code* s. 487.1 applies with the necessary modifications. This alternative to *personal attendance* before the authorizing judge would be *impracticable* in the circumstances.

Related Provisions: Similar provisions appear in ss. 184.3 (consent authorizations), 487.091(4) (DNA warrants) and 487.1 (search warrants). Section 508.1 permits similar applications to lay an information, but does *not* require that personal attendance of the informant be impracticable before doing so.

Other related provisions are discussed in the corresponding note to s. 529.

PART XVII — LANGUAGE OF ACCUSED

530. (1) Language of accused — **On application by an accused whose language is one of the official languages of Canada, made not later than**

(a) **the time of the appearance of the accused at which his trial date is set, if**

(i) **he is accused of an offence mentioned in section 553 or punishable on summary conviction, or**

(ii) **the accused is to be tried on an indictment preferred under section 557,**

(b) **the time of the accused's election, if the accused elects under section 536 to be tried by a provincial court judge or under section 536.1 to be tried by a judge without a jury and without having a preliminary inquiry, or**

(c) **the time when the accused is ordered to stand trial, if the accused**

(i) **is charged with an offence listed in section 469,**

     (ii) has elected to be tried by a court composed of a judge or a judge and jury, or

     (iii) is deemed to have elected to be tried by a court composed of a judge and jury,

a justice of the peace, provincial court judge or judge of the Nunavut Court of Justice shall grant an order directing that the accused be tried before a justice of the peace, provincial court judge, judge or judge and jury, as the case may be, who speak the official languange of Canada that is the language of the accused or, if the circumstances warrant, who speak both official languages of Canada.

(2) **Idem** — On application by an accused whose language is not one of the official languages of Canada, made not later than whichever of the times referred to in paragraphs (1)(*a*) to (*c*) is applicable, a justice of the peace or provincial court judge may grant an order directing that the accused be tried before a justice of the peace, provincial court judge, judge or judge and jury, as the case may be, who speak the official language of Canada in which the accused, in the opinion of the justice or provincial court judge, can best give testimony or, if the circumstances warrant, who speak both official languages of Canada.

(3) **Accused to be advised of right** — The justice of the peace or provincial court judge before whom an accused first appears shall, if the accused is not represented by counsel, advise the accused of his right to apply for an order under subsection (1) or (2) and of the time before which such an application must be made.

(4) **Remand** — Where an accused fails to apply for an order under subsection (1) or (2) and the justice of the peace, provincial court judge or judge before whom the accused is to be tried, in this Part referred to as "the court", is satisfied that it is in the best interests of justice that the accused be tried before a justice of the peace, provincial court judge, judge or judge and jury who speak the official language of Canada that is the language of the accused or, if the language of the accused is not one of the official languages of Canada, the official language of Canada in which the accused, in the opinion of the court, can best give testimony, the court may, if it does not speak that language, by order remand the accused to be tried by a justice of the peace, provincial court judge, judge or judge and jury, as the case may be, who speak that language or, if the circumstances warrant, who speak both official languages of Canada.

(5) **Variation of order** — An order under this section that an accused be tried before a justice of the peace, provincial court judge, judge or judge and jury who speak the official language of Canada that is the language of the accused or the official language of Canada in which the accused can best give testimony may, if the circumstances warrant, be varied by the court to require that the accused be tried before a justice of the peace, provincial court judge, judge or judge and jury who speak both official languages of Canada.

          1977–78, c. 36, s. 1; R.S. 1985, c. 27 (1st Supp.), ss. 94, 203; 1999, c. 3, s. 34.

Commentary: The section authorizes application to be made to determine the official language of Canada in which trial proceedings should be conducted.

Where D's language is *one of the official languages* of Canada, D may apply under s. 530(1), within the times prescribed, to a justice of the peace or provincial court judge for an order that the trial be held before a court that speaks the same official language as D or, if the circumstances warrant, that speaks both official languages. The order is *mandatory*.

Where D's language is *not one of the official languages* of Canada, a similar application may be made for an order under s. 530(2) to have the trial conducted by a court that speaks the official language of Canada in which D, in the opinion of the justice of the peace or provincial court judge, can best give testimony or, if the circumstances warrant, in both official languages. An order under this section is *discretionary.*

Section 530(3) requires the justice of the peace or provincial court judge before whom D, unrepresented by counsel, first appears, to advise D of his/her right to make application under s. 530(1) or (2).

Under s. 530(4), authority is given to the court before whom D is to be tried to make an order in the same terms as authorized by ss. 530(1) and (2), where D has failed to comply with s. 530(1) or (2). Any order of a unilingual trial may be varied to a bilingual trial under s. 530(5).

Case Law

General Principles

R. v. Beaulac (1997), 120 C.C.C. (3d) 16 (B.C. C.A.) — The "best interests of justice" include consideration of

i.   D's right to be *present* at trial;

ii.   D's right to make *full answer and defence*; and,

iii. the requirement that jurors *understand* the *evidence.*

Any doubt should be resolved in favour of granting an application under s. 530(4).

R. v. Cross (1998), 128 C.C.C. (3d) 161 (Que. C.A.); leave to appeal allowed (March 25, 1999), Doc. 26944 (S.C.C.) — When an order is made under s. 530, D is entitled to a judge and prosecutor who speak the *same* official language as D, *except* where there is a *private* prosecutor. Once a trial has begun, however, the trial judge cannot prohibit the prosecutor who wishes to do so, from speaking French, even if D had earlier obtained an order that s/he be tried by a judge and jury who speak the official language of D, English.

Charter Considerations

Ringuette v. R. (1987), 33 C.C.C. (3d) 509 (Nfld. C.A.); leave to appeal refused (1987), 65 Nfld. & P.E.I.R. 270n (S.C.C.) — *See also: Paquette v. Canada (No. 2)* (1988), 38 C.C.C. (3d) 353 (Alta. C.A.) — Failure to proclaim this section in Newfoundland is *not* arbitrary, capricious or irrational, but due to the inability to set up the mechanism for hearing trials in French and to hire the appropriate personnel. The failure to provide a trial in French does *not* infringe *Charter* s. 15(1).

Failure to Proclaim [See also Charter s. 15]

Reference re French in Criminal Proceedings (1987), 36 C.C.C. (3d) 353 (Sask. C.A.) — The continued failure to proclaim the language provisions of this Part in force in Saskatchewan violates the equality rights provisions of *Charter* s. 15.

Related Provisions: Section 530(1) came into force in New Brunswick, Manitoba, Ontario, the Yukon Territory and the Northwest Territories on June 20, 1985. It was proclaimed in force with respect to summary conviction matters in Nova Scotia, Prince Edward Island and Saskatchewan on September 1, 1987 and in respect of indictable offences in Saskatchewan on September 1, 1987.

The remainder of the section was proclaimed in force in New Brunswick, the Yukon Territory and the Northwest Territories on May 1, 1979. In Ontario, it was proclaimed on December 31, 1979, and in Manitoba on July 1, 1982.

Related provisions appear in ss. 531–533.

530.1 Where order granted under section 530 — Where an order is granted under section 530 directing that an accused be tried before a justice of the peace, provincial court judge, judge or judge and jury who speak the official language that is the language of the accused or in which the accused can best give testimony,

   (a) the accused and his counsel have the right to use either official language for all purposes during the preliminary inquiry and trial of the accused;

   (b) the accused and his counsel may use either official language in written pleadings or other documents used in any proceedings relating to the preliminary inquiry or trial of the accused;

(c) any witness may give evidence in either official language during the preliminary inquiry or trial;

(d) the accused has a right to have a justice presiding over the preliminary inquiry who speaks the official language that is the language of the accused;

(e) except where the prosecutor is a private prosecutor, the accused has a right to have a prosecutor who speaks the official language that is the language of the accused;

(f) the court shall make interpreters available to assist the accused, his counsel or any witness during the preliminary inquiry or trial;

(g) the record of proceedings during the preliminary inquiry or trial shall include

(i) a transcript of everything that was said during those proceedings in the official language in which it was said,

(ii) a transcript of any interpretation into the other language of what was said, and

(iii) any documentary evidence that was tendered during those proceedings in the official language in which it was tendered; and

(h) any trial judgment, including any reasons given therefor, issued in writing in either official language, shall be made available by the court in the official language that is the language of the accused.

R.S. 1985, c. 31 (4th Supp.), s. 94.

Commentary: The section describes the effect of an order granted under s. 530 directing that D be tried by a court which speaks the official language that is that of D, or in which D can best give testimony.

Case Law

R. v. Cross (1998), 128 C.C.C. (3d) 161 (Que. C.A.); leave to appeal allowed (March 25, 1999), Doc. 26944 (S.C.C.) — Where a s. 530 order has been granted, s. 530.1 requires the Attorney General of Quebec to choose a prosecutor who is capable and agrees to conduct the trial in D's official language. If, during the course of the trial, the prosecutor feels unable to do justice to his/her mandate in a language other than his/her own, and wishes to speak French or English, as is permitted by s. 133 of the *Constitution Act, 1867*, the trial judge should

i.   *adjourn* the trial and *permit* the Attorney General to find a *replacement* to conduct the case in D's language; or,

ii.   if *not* possible in a reasonable time, to *declare* a *mis-trial*.

Section 530.1 is valid and applicable in Quebec.

Related Provisions: Section 530 authorizes an application to be made to determine the official language of Canada in which D's trial proceedings shall be conducted.

Other related provisions appear in ss. 531–533 and are described in the *commentary* which accompanies each.

531. Change of venue — Notwithstanding any other provision of this Act but subject to any regulations made pursuant to section 533, the court shall order that the trial of an accused be held in a territorial division in the same province other than that in which the offence would otherwise be tried if an order has been made that the accused be tried before a justice of the peace, provincial court judge, judge or judge and jury who speak the official language of Canada that is the language of the accused or the official language of Canada in which the accused can best give testimony or both official languages of Canada and such order cannot be conveniently complied with in the territorial division in which the offence would otherwise be tried.

1977–78, c. 36, s. 1; R.S. 1985, c. 27 (1st Supp.), s. 203.

Commentary: Subject to any regulations made under s. 533, a *change of venue* must be ordered where an order for a unilingual or bilingual trial has been made under s. 530, and the order cannot be conveniently met in the territorial division where the offence would otherwise be tried.

Related Provisions: The section which operates "notwithstanding any other provision of this Act ...", overrides the general authority to order a change of venue under s. 599. It was proclaimed in force in New Brunswick, the Yukon Territory and Northwest Territories on May 1, 1979, in Ontario on December 31, 1979, and in Manitoba on July 1, 1982.

532. Saving — **Nothing in this Part or the *Official Languages Act* derogates from or otherwise adversely affects any right afforded by a law of a province in force on the coming into force of this Part in that province or thereafter coming into force relating to the language of proceedings or testimony in criminal matters that is not inconsistent with this Part or that Act.**

1977–78, c. 36, s. 1.

Commentary: This section ensures that no *Official Languages Act* or Part XVII provision derogates from or otherwise adversely affects any rights concerning the language of proceedings or testimony in criminal matters afforded by any existing or future provincial law that is not inconsistent with either federal enactment.

Related Provisions: This section was proclaimed in force in New Brunswick, the Yukon Territory and the Northwest Territories on May 1, 1979, in Ontario on December 31, 1979, and in Manitoba on July 1, 1982. Under s. 534(3), now repealed, the section came into force in all provinces on January 1, 1990.

533. Regulations — **The Lieutenant Governor in Council of a province may make regulations generally for carrying into effect the purposes and provisions of this Part in the province and the Commissioner of the Yukon Territory, the Commissioner of the Northwest Territories and the Commissioner of Nunavut may make regulations generally for carrying into effect the purposes and provisions of this Part in the Yukon Territory, the Northwest Territories and Nunavut, respectively.**

1977–78, c. 36, s. 11993, c. 28, s. 78 (Sched. III, item 33)

Commentary: The section authorizes the Lieutenant Governor in Council of a province and the Commissioner of each of the territories to make regulations generally for carrying into effect the purposes and provisions of Part XVII.

Related Provisions: This section was proclaimed in force in New Brunswick, the Yukon Territory and the Northwest Territories on May 1, 1979, in Ontario on December 31, 1979, and in Manitoba on July 1, 1982. Under s. 534(3), now repealed, the section came into force in all provinces on January 1, 1990.

534. [Repealed 1997, c. 18, s. 63.]

PART XVIII — PROCEDURE ON PRELIMINARY INQUIRY

Jurisdiction

535. Inquiry by justice — **Where an accused who is charged with an indictable offence is before a justice, the justice shall, in accordance with this Part, inquire into that charge and any other indictable offence, in respect of the same transaction, founded on the facts that are disclosed by the evidence taken in accordance with this Part.**

R.S.,c. C-34, s. 463;R.S. 1985, c. 27 (1st Supp.), s. 96.

Commentary: The section imposes a *duty* on the *justice* at the preliminary inquiry to inquire into the *offence charged*, and into *any other indictable offence, in respect of the same transaction, founded on the facts disclosed by the evidence* taken upon the inquiry.

Case Law

Jurisdiction [See also s. 601]

Danchella v. R. (1985), 19 C.C.C. (3d) 490 (B.C. C.A.) — A justice does *not* become seized of the matter by taking D's election.

R. v. R (L.) (1995), 39 C.R. (4th) 390, 100 C.C.C. (3d) 329 (Ont. C.A.) — A judge presiding at preliminary inquiry has authority to make all necessary evidentiary rulings, including claims of privildge. The judge may compel witnesses to testify and to bring relevant documents.

R. v. R (L.) (1995), 39 C.R. (4th) 390, 100 C.C.C. (3d) 329 (Ont. C.A.) — The determination of what is relevant evidence at preliminary inquiry is *not* exclusive of all matters of credibility. Relevance is *not* governed solely by the narrow test for committal, rather is a broader concept because of the discovery function of the inquiry.

R. v. R (L.) (1995), 39 C.R. (4th) 390, 100 C.C.C. (3d) 329 (Ont. C.A.) — A provincial statute cannot override the *Code* and render inadmissible evidence which is relevant to the defence of a criminal charge. Where provincial legislation provides a procedure for disclosure of mental health records, the procedure should be followed in a *Code* prosecution. Such a procedure ensures adequate protection of the privacy interests of V, as does the law of privilege which may apply in the absence of provincial legislation.

R. v. Hislop (1983), 36 C.R. (3d) 29, 7 C.C.C. (3d) 240 (Ont. C.A.); reversing (1983), 34 C.R. (3d) 256 (Ont. H.C.); leave to appeal refused (1983), 52 N.R. 238 (S.C.C.) — The justice at a preliminary inquiry does *not* have the jurisdiction to inquire into the validity of the allegation based on reasonable and probable grounds contained in the information, only the power to consider whether the evidence adduced is sufficient to warrant committal for trial. The information can be quashed *only* where it discloses no offence.

Bolduc v. Quebec (A.G.) (1980), 20 C.R. (3d) 372, 60 C.C.C. (2d) 357 (Que. C.A.); affirmed (1982), 28 C.R. (3d) 193, 68 C.C.C. (2d) 413 (S.C.C.) — It is only where D is charged with an indictable offence that the justice is obliged to enquire into the charge. A justice may discharge D before taking evidence, if the information is an absolute nullity as it does *not* reveal an indictable offence known to law.

Presence of Accused [See also ss. 475, 537 and 544]

McLachlan v. R. (1986), 24 C.C.C. (3d) 255 (Ont. C.A.); affirming (1984), 18 C.C.C. (3d) 478 (Ont. H.C.); leave to appeal refused (1986), 18 O.A.C. 159n (S.C.C.) — The right of D to be present at the preliminary hearing is not only for the benefit of D but of P as well. Consequently, D does *not* have the power to absent himself from a preliminary inquiry, nor does the judge have the power to authorize his absence.

Charter Remedies at Preliminary Inquiry [See also Charter s. 24]

R. v. Seaboyer; R. v. Gayme (1991), 7 C.R. (4th) 117, 66 C.C.C. (3d) 321 — *See also: R. v. Moore* (1989), 73 C.R. (3d) 120, 51 C.C.C. (3d) 566 (P.E.I. S.C.) — The *Code* provides *no* authority for a justice presiding at a preliminary inquiry to hear and determine the constitutionality of an evidentiary provision of the *Code*.

R. v. Mills (1986), 52 C.R. (3d) 1, 26 C.C.C. (3d) 481 (S.C.C.) — A justice at a preliminary inquiry is *not* "a court of competent jurisdiction" under *Charter* s. 24, hence lacks jurisdiction to determine questions whether *Charter* rights have been infringed and evidence should be excluded under *Charter*, s. 24(2).

R. v. Morrison (1984), 44 C.R. (3d) 85, 14 C.C.C. (3d) 320 (Ont. C.A.); leave to appeal refused (1985), 58 N.R. 338n (S.C.C.) — *See also: R. v. Seaboyer* (1987), (sub nom. *R. v. Gayme*) 58 C.R. (3d) 289, 37 C.C.C. (3d) 53 (Ont. C.A.); affirmed (1991), 7 C.R. (4th) 117, 66 C.C.C. (3d) 321 (S.C.C.) — A provincial court judge conducting a preliminary inquiry is *not* a court of competent jurisdiction under *Charter* s. 24(1), hence cannot invoke abuse of process, at least as part of a complaint of *Charter* infringement, to stay proceedings.

Related Provisions: "Indictable offence", under *I.A.* s. 34(1)(a), includes an offence triable either way.

Other provisions in this Part describe the powers of the justice on the inquiry (ss. 537–538), the manner in which evidence may be taken (ss. 539–542) and the procedure to be followed where D absconds (s. 544) or a witness refuses to testify (s. 545).

Section 548 defines the *adjudicative authority* of a justice at the preliminary inquiry. The justice must consider whether D should stand trial *for the offence charged or any other indictable offence in respect of the same transaction* disclosed by the evidence taken on the preliminary inquiry. The authority of P to prefer indictments where there has been an order to stand trial is described in s. 574.

536. (1) Remand by justice to provincial court judge in certain cases —
Where an accused is before a justice other than a provincial court judge charged with an offence over which a provincial court judge has absolute jurisdiction under section 553, the justice shall remand the accused to appear before a provincial court judge having jurisdiction in the territorial division in which the offence is alleged to have been committed.

(2) Election before justice in certain cases — Where an accused is before a justice charged with an offence, other than an offence listed in section 469, and the offence is not one over which a provincial court judge has absolute jurisdiction under section 553, the justice shall, after the information has been read to the accused, put the accused to his election in the following words:

> You have the option to elect to be tried by a provincial court judge without a jury and without having had a preliminary inquiry; or you may elect to have a preliminary inquiry and to be tried by a judge without a jury; or you may elect to have a preliminary inquiry and to be tried by a court composed of a judge and jury. If you do not elect now, you shall be deemed to have elected to have a preliminary inquiry and to be tried by a court composed of a judge and jury. How do you elect to be tried?

(3) Procedure where accused elects trial by provincial court judge —
Where an accused elects to be tried by a provincial court judge, the justice shall endorse on the information a record of the election and shall

(a) where the justice is not a provincial court judge, remand the accused to appear and plead to the charge before a provincial court judge having jurisdiction in the territorial division in which the offence is alleged to have been committed; or

(b) where the justice is a provincial court judge, call on the accused to plead to the charge and if the accused does not plead guilty, proceed with the trial or fix a time for the trial.

(4) Procedure where accused elects trial by judge alone or by judge and jury or deemed election — Where an accused elects to have a preliminary inquiry and to be tried by a judge without a jury or by a court composed of a judge and jury or does not elect when put to his election, the justice shall hold a preliminary inquiry into the charge and if the accused is ordered to stand trial, the justice shall endorse on the information and, where the accused is in custody, on the warrant of committal, a statement showing the nature of the election of the accused or that the accused did not elect, as the case may be.

(5) Jurisdiction — Where a justice before whom a preliminary inquiry is being or is to be held has not commenced to take evidence, any justice having jurisdiction in the

province where the offence with which the accused is charged is alleged to have been committed has jurisdiction for the purposes of subsection (4).
R.S., c. C-34, s. 464; R.S. 1985, c. 27 (1st Supp.), ss. 96, 203.

Commentary: The section describes the procedure followed where D appears before a justice charged with an indictable offence.

Under s. 536(1), a justice before whom D appears, who is *not* also a provincial court judge, must remand D to appear before a provincial court judge where the offence charged is listed in s. 553 and within the *absolute* jurisdiction of a provincial court judge under Part XIX.

Where the offence charged is *not* listed in s. 553 or 469, the justice must require D to elect mode of trial under s. 536(2). Where D elects to be tried by a provincial court judge, the election is recorded and the matter proceeds under s. 536(3). Where D elects to have a preliminary inquiry or fails to elect, the election is recorded and the procedure of s. 536(4) is followed.

Section 536(5) authorizes *any* justice with jurisdiction in the province where the offence is alleged to have occurred to conduct a preliminary inquiry under s. 536(4), provided *no* evidence has been taken. The same justice who records the election need *not*, in other words, conduct the preliminary inquiry.

Case Law
Election: S. 536(2) [For re-election see. s. 561]

Doyle v. R. (1976), 35 C.R.N.S. 1, 29 C.C.C. (2d) 177 (S.C.C.) — Where D must be given an election under this section, nothing authorizes a justice to adjourn the case for more than eight days prior to election without the consent of D.

Caccamo v. R. (1975), 29 C.R.N.S. 78 (S.C.C.) — The right to the proper forum is a major one belonging to D. The choice is *not* vitiated if made before D learns the substance of all the evidence to be adduced against him. When D chooses to be tried by a judge or judge and jury, the law does *not* expect D to make that decision in light of the evidence but rather in the light of the charge.

R. v. Drysdale (1986), 26 C.C.C. (3d) 286 (Alta. C.A.); leave to appeal refused (1986), 69 N.R. 320n (S.C.C.) — A provincial court judge does *not* have jurisdiction to quash an information before hearing D's election where the offence is one over which he does *not* have absolute jurisdiction.

R. v. Leske (1967), 2 C.R.N.S. 95, [1968] 1 C.C.C. 347 (Alta. C.A.) — The election must be put to D in the words prescribed by this section or substantially so in order to confer jurisdiction on the justice to conduct a preliminary inquiry.

R. v. Bobyk (1962), 39 C.R. 27, [1963] 2 C.C.C. 91 (Alta. C.A.) — The consent by which D foregoes the right of trial by jury must be given in a manner which makes it clear beyond doubt that D has so consented. The consent must be expressly given in open court and cannot be inferred.

R. v. Garcia (1990), 75 C.R. (3d) 250 (B.C. C.A.) — Upon an information containing several counts, D is *not* entitled to elect different modes of trial on each count. The election is also made on the basis that, after the preliminary inquiry, P may add or substitute counts under s. 574(1)(b).

Geszthelyi v. R. (1977), 38 C.R.N.S. 15 at 19, 33 C.C.C. (2d) 543 (B.C. C.A.) — *See also: Chaisson v. R.* (1984), 15 C.C.C. (3d) 50 (Ont. H.C.); *Aeillo v. R.* (1977), 33 C.C.C. (2d) 280 (Ont. H.C.) — A provincial judge does *not* lose jurisdiction by failing to put D to his election on the first appearance in court.

R. v. Mitchell (1997), 121 C.C.C. (3d) 139 (Ont. C.A.) — The failure to arraign D is a procedural error which may be cured by s. 686(1)(b)(iv).

Without waiver of the procedural requirement of s. 536(2), the failure to put D to an election, in terms which substantially comply with the section, is a procedural error which results in a *loss* of *jurisdiction* to conduct the preliminary inquiry or trial and is *not* curable under s. 686(1)(b)(iv).

Endorsement of Election: S. 536(3)

R. v. Sagutch (1991), 63 C.C.C. (3d) 569 (B.C. C.A.) — The failure of the presiding justice to record D's election under s. 536(4) is a jurisdictional error.

R. v. Squires (1977), 35 C.C.C. (2d) 325 (Nfld. C.A.) — There is sufficient compliance with this section if a memorandum as to how D elected is endorsed on the information. There is *no* need to set out the entire election and, in the absence of evidence to the contrary, this endorsement is sufficient proof that the election was properly given, even though the election does not appear in the transcript.

Related Provisions: For s. 469 offences, a preliminary inquiry is automatically held (absent waiver), since the offences must be tried in the superior court of criminal jurisdiction without right of election. Elections may arise in connection with offences listed in s. 553 in the circumstances described in s. 555(2).

536.1 (1) Remand by justice — Nunavut — If an accused is before a justice of the peace charged with an indictable offence mentioned in section 553, the justice of the peace shall remand the accused to appear before a judge.

(2) Election before justice in certain cases — Nunavut — If an accused is before a justice of the peace or a judge charged with an indictable offence, other than an offence mentioned in section 469 or 553, the justice of the peace or judge shall after the information has been read to the accused, put the accused to an election in the following words:

> You have the option to elect to be tried by a judge without a jury and without having had a preliminary inquiry; or you may elect to have a preliminary inquiry and to be tried by a judge without a jury; or you may elect to have a preliminary inquiry and to be tried by a court composed of a judge and jury. If you do not elect now, you shall be deemed to have elected to have a preliminary inquiry and to be tried by a court composed of a judge and jury. How do you elect to be tried?

(3) Procedure if accused elects trial by judge — Nunavut — If an accused elects to be tried by a judge without a jury and without having had a preliminary inquiry, the justice of the peace or judge shall endorse on the information a record of the election and,

> (a) if the accused is before a justice of the peace, the justice of the peace shall remand the accused to appear and plead to the charge before a judge; or

> (b) if the accused is before a judge, the judge shall call on the accused to plead to the charge and if the accused does not plead guilty, proceed with the trial or fix a time for the trial.

(4) Procedure if accused elects trial by judge alone or by judge and jury or deemed election — Nunavut — If an accused elects to have a preliminary inquiry and to be tried by a judge without a jury or by a court composed of a judge and jury or does not elect when put to an election, the justice of the peace or judge shall hold a preliminary inquiry into the charge and if the accused is ordered to stand trial, the justice of the peace or judge shall endorse on the information and, if the accused is in custody, on the warrant of committal, a statement showing the nature of the election of the accused or that the accused did not elect, as the case may be.

(5) Jurisdiction — Nunavut — If a justice of the peace before whom a preliminary inquiry is being or is to be held has not commenced to take evidence, any justice of the peace having jurisdiction in Nunavut has jurisdiction for the purposes of subsection (4).

(6) Application to Nunavut — This section, and not section 536, applies in repect of criminal proceedings in Nunavut.

1999, c. 3, s. 35.

Powers of Justice

537. (1) Powers of justice — A justice acting under this Part may

(a) adjourn an inquiry from time to time and change the place of hearing, where it appears to be desirable to do so by reason of the absence of a witness, the inability of a witness who is ill to attend at the place where the justice usually sits or for any other sufficient reason;

(b) remand the accused to custody for the purposes of the *Identification of Criminals Act*;

(b) [Repealed 1991, c. 43, s. 9, Schedule, item 3(1).]

(c) except where the accused is authorized pursuant to Part XVI to be at large, remand the accused to custody in a prison by warrant in Form 19;

(d) resume an inquiry before the expiration of a period for which it has been adjourned with the consent of the prosecutor and the accused or his counsel;

(e) order in writing, in Form 30, that the accused be brought before him, or any other justice for the same territorial division, at any time before the expiration of the time for which the accused has been remanded;

(f) grant or refuse permission to the prosecutor or his counsel to address him in support of the charge, by way of opening or summing up or by way of reply on any evidence that is given on behalf of the accused;

(g) receive evidence on the part of the prosecutor or the accused, as the case may be, after hearing any evidence that has been given on behalf of either of them;

(h) order that no person other than the prosecutor, the accused and their counsel shall have access to or remain in the room in which the inquiry is held, where it appears to him that the ends of justice will be best served by so doing;

(i) regulate the course of the inquiry in any way that appears to him to be desirable and that is not inconsistent with this Act;

(j) where the prosecutor and the accused so agree, permit the accused to appear by counsel or by closed-circuit television or any other means that allow the court and the accused to engage in simultaneous visual and oral communication, for any part of the inquiry other than a part in which the evidence of a witness is taken; and

(k) for any part of the inquiry other than a part in which the evidence of a witness is taken require an accused who is confined in prison to appear by closed-circuit television or any other means that allow the court and the accused to engage in simultaneous visual and oral communication, if the accused is given the opportunity to communicate privately with counsel, in a case in which the accused is represented by counsel.

(2) Change of venue — Where a justice changes the place of hearing under paragraph (1)(a) to a place in the same province, other than a place in territorial division in which the justice has jurisdiction, any justice who has jurisdiction in the place to which the hearing is changed may continue the hearing.

(2)–(4) [Repealed 1991, c. C-43, s. 9 (Sched., item 3(2)).]

R.S., c. C-34, s. 465; c. 2 (2d Supp.), s. 6; 1972, c. 13, s. 38; 1974–75–76, c. 93, s. 58; 1991, c. 43, s. 9, Schedule, item 3; 1994, c. 44, s. 53; 1997, c. 18, s. 64.

Commentary: The section defines the *non-adjudicative powers* of a justice conducting a preliminary inquiry.

Under ss. 537(1)(a), (h), (j) and (k), *specific* authority permits certain orders to be made during the course of the inquiry. Section 537(1)(i), on the other hand, confers a more *general* authority to regulate the course of the inquiry, in any way that appears to the justice to be desirable and not inconsistent with the *Code*.

Sections 537(1)(a)–(e) authorize a justice to *adjourn* a preliminary inquiry from time to time and *remand* D in custody during such adjournments, including for *ICA* purposes, unless D has been ordered released under Part XVI. The inquiry may be resumed, on consent, prior to the expiration of the period of adjournment and D returned from custody for such purposes. Where P and D agree, under s. 537(1)(j), the justice may permit D to appear by counsel, closed-circuit television or any other means that allow simultaneous oral and visual communication between D and the court. Where D is confined in prison, s. 537(1)(k) permits the justice to require that D appear by closed-circuit television or similar means allowing other simultaneous oral and visual communication, where no evidence of a witness is to be taken during such appearance and provided D is represented by counsel and is afforded opportunity to communicate privately with counsel.

Under s. 537(1)(f), the presiding justice may allow P to open, sum up or reply to any defence evidence. Section 537(1)(g) permits either P or D to adduce further evidence after evidence has been given on behalf of either.

Under s. 537(1)(h) the courtroom may be closed to persons other than D, D's counsel and P, where the ends of justice will be best served by so doing. The section may attract *Charter* ss. 11(d) and 2(b) scrutiny.

Under s. 537(2), where a justice changes the place of hearing under s. 537(1)(a), to another place in the same province, any justice who has jurisdiction may continue the hearing.

Case Law

General Authority

Doyle v. R. (1976), 35 C.R.N.S. 1, 29 C.C.C. (2d) 177 (S.C.C.) — Whatever inherent powers may be possessed by a superior court judge in controlling the process of the court, the powers and functions of a justice are entirely statutory and must be found to have been conferred by the *Code* either expressly or by necessary implication. The careful and detailed procedural directions contained in the *Code* are exhaustive.

Absence of Accused [See ss. 475, 535 and 544]

Adjournments: S. 537(1)(a)

R. v. Solloway (1930), 53 C.C.C. 180 (Alta. C.A.) — The grant or refusal of an adjournment at preliminary hearing is a matter of discretion. The superior court will *not* interfere unless the refusal amounts to a violation of D's rights.

R. v. Gougeon (1980), 55 C.C.C. (2d) 218 (Ont. C.A.); leave to appeal refused (1980), 35 N.R. 83n (S.C.C.) — A *hybrid* offence is to be treated as *indictable until* P otherwise elects. P is *not* obliged to so elect on the first appearance of D, hence a provincial court judge has jurisdiction to adjourn the proceedings under para. (1)(a).

Permission to Make Submissions: S. 537(1)(f)

R. v. Taillefer (1978), 3 C.R. (3d) 357 (Ont. C.A.) — It is a denial of natural justice *not* to give counsel for D the opportunity to submit argument before committal for trial.

Receiving Evidence: S. 537(1)(g)

R. v. Skogman (1984), 41 C.R. (3d) 1 (S.C.C.) — The *purpose* of a preliminary hearing is to protect D from an unnecessary trial where P lacks evidence to warrant the continuation of the process. In addition, the preliminary hearing has become a forum where D is afforded an opportunity to discover and to appreciate the case to be presented at trial.

Caccamo v. R. (1975), 29 C.R.N.S. 78 (S.C.C.) — The *sole purpose* of the preliminary inquiry is to satisfy the justice that there is sufficient evidence to put D on trial. P, therefore, has the discretion to present only that evidence which makes out a *prima facie* case. If the introduction of new evidence at the trial takes D by surprise, an adjournment may be given.

R. v. Richards (1997), 115 C.C.C. (3d) 377 (Ont. C.A.) — Where a public interest immunity claim at preliminary inquiry is based upon a substantiated assertion of police informer privilege, effect ought be given to the claim. The innocence at stake exception

i.   does not operate at preliminary inquiry; or

ii. the public interest in non-disclosure exceeds D's interest in disclosure in preliminary inquiry in most cases.

Exclusion of Public: S. 537(1)(h)

Morgentaler v. Fauteux (1970), 13 C.R.N.S. 50, 3 C.C.C. (2d) 187 (Que. Q.B.); affirmed [1972] C.A. 219 (Que. C.A.) — *See also*: *Armstrong v. State of Wisconsin* (1972), 7 C.C.C. (2d) 331 (Ont. H.C.) — The court has discretion to order an *in camera* proceeding where witnesses might be hindered or prevented from testifying by the public presence.

Regulate the Course of the Inquiry: S. 537(1)(i)

R. v. McNeill (1996), 49 C.R. (4th) 131, 108 C.C.C. (3d) 364 (Ont. C.A.) — A preliminary inquiry judge has jurisdiction to determine whether D ought to remain handcuffed during the inquiry.

R. v. Robillard (1986), 28 C.C.C. (3d) 22 (Ont. C.A.) — A justice acting under his power to regulate the course of the inquiry may disqualify counsel from acting on the basis of conflict of interest.

Particulars [For amendment powers, see s. 601(11)]

R. v. Chew, [1968] 2 C.C.C. 127 (Ont. C.A.) — There is *no* power to order P to furnish particulars at a preliminary inquiry.

Related Provisions: A preliminary inquiry may be continued under s. 544 where D has absconded during the course of the proceedings.

The adjudicative authority of the justice conducting the preliminary inquiry is described in ss. 548 and 549. The manner in which evidence may be received is set out in ss. 539–542.

A justice at preliminary inquiry may exercise the amendment powers of s. 601 under s. 601(11).

538. Corporation — Where an accused is a corporation, subsections 556(1) and (2) apply, with such modifications as the circumstances require.

R.S., c. C-34, s. 466.

Commentary: The section incorporates ss. 556(1) and (2) relating to the appearance and non-appearance of corporations with such modifications as the circumstances require.

At the preliminary inquiry D corporation must appear *by counsel or agent*. Where corporate D does *not* appear, though duly served with a summons, the presiding justice may proceed with a preliminary inquiry in the absence of corporate D.

Related Provisions: Under s. 2, "everyone", "person", "owner" and similar expressions include bodies corporate and companies, in relation to the acts and things that they are capable of doing and owning, respectively.

Service of process on a corporation is governed by s. 703.2.

The appearance of corporations in proceedings on indictment is described in ss. 620–623, and in summary conviction matters in s. 800(3). The punishment of convicted corporations is provided for in s. 735, its execution in s. 735(2).

Taking Evidence of Witnesses

539. (1) Order restricting publication of evidence taken at preliminary inquiry — Prior to the commencement of the taking of evidence at a preliminary inquiry, the justice holding the inquiry

(a) may, if application therefor is made by the prosecutor, and

(b) shall, if application therefor is made by any of the accused, make an order directing that the evidence taken at the inquiry shall not be published in any newspaper or broadcast before such time as, in respect of each of the accused,

    (c) he is discharged; or

    (d) if he is ordered to stand trial, the trial is ended.

(2) Accused to be informed of right to apply for order — Where an accused is not represented by counsel at a preliminary inquiry, the justice holding the inquiry shall, prior to the commencement of the taking of evidence at the inquiry, inform the accused of his right to make application under subsection (1).

(3) Failure to comply with order — Every one who fails to comply with an order made pursuant to subsection (1) is guilty of an offence punishable on summary conviction.

(4) "Newspaper" — In this section, "newspaper" has the same meaning as in section 297.

R.S., c. C-34, s. 467; R.S. 1985, c. 27 (1st Supp.), s. 97.

Commentary: The section authorizes orders *restricting* newspaper *publication* and *broadcast* of the *evidence taken* at a preliminary inquiry for specified time periods. Failure to comply with the order is a summary conviction offence under s. 539(3).

Under s. 539(1), the justice conducting the preliminary inquiry, *prior* to the commencement of the *taking* of evidence, *may*, on P's application, and *shall* on D's application, make an order directing that the evidence taken *not* be *published* in any newspaper or broadcast in respect of each accused until discharge or the conclusion of trial. Where D is *unrepresented* by counsel, the presiding justice, under s. 539(2), must *inform* D, prior to the commencement of the taking of evidence, of the *right* to make such an application. The manifest purpose of the legislation is to prevent the reporting of evidence prior to trial in the community from which jurors may be selected, thereby endeavouring to ensure a fair trial. The subsection has attracted *Charter* s. 2(b) scrutiny.

Section 539(4) defines "newspaper" as having the same meaning as it does in s. 297.

Case Law [See ss. 276.3, 486, 517, 648 and Charter s. 2(b)]

Related Provisions: The restriction on publication in s. 539(1) would appear narrower in scope than in s. 517(1). Other restrictions on publication appear in s. 276.3 (sexual offences) as well as in ss. 486(3) and (4) (identity of complainants and witnesses in sexual assault, interference, exploitation and other listed offences). Section 648 restricts newspaper publication and broadcast of matters heard in the absence of the jury until after the retirement of the jury to consider its verdict. Section 542(2) prohibits newspaper publication or broadcast of any admission, confession or statement by D, tendered in evidence at the preliminary inquiry irrespective of an order under this section.

540. (1) Taking evidence — Where an accused is before a justice holding a preliminary inquiry, the justice shall

    (a) take the evidence under oath, in the presence of the accused, of the witnesses called on the part of the prosecution and allow the accused or his counsel to cross-examine them; and

    (b) cause a record of the evidence of each witness to be taken

        (i) in legible writing in the form of a deposition, in Form 31, or by a stenographer appointed by him or pursuant to law, or

        (ii) in a province where a sound recording apparatus is authorized by or under provincial legislation for use in civil cases, by the type of apparatus so authorized and in accordance with the requirements of the provincial legislation.

(2) Reading and signing depositions — Where a deposition is taken down in writing, the justice shall, in the presence of the accused, before asking the accused if he wishes to call witnesses,

(a) cause the deposition to be read to the witness;

(b) cause the deposition to be signed by the witness; and

(c) sign the deposition himself.

(3) Authentication by justice — Where depositions are taken down in writing, the justice may sign

(a) at the end of each deposition; or

(b) at the end of several or of all the depositions in a manner that will indicate that his signature is intended to authenticate each deposition.

(4) Stenographer to be sworn — Where the stenographer appointed to take down the evidence is not a duly sworn court stenographer, he shall make oath that he will truly and faithfully report the evidence.

(5) Authentication of transcript — Where the evidence is taken down by a stenographer appointed by the justice or pursuant to law, it need not be read to or signed by the witnesses, but, on request of the justice or of one of the parties, shall be transcribed, in whole or in part, by the stenographer and the transcript shall be accompanied by

(a) an affidavit of the stenographer that it is a true report of the evidence; or

(b) a certificate that it is a true report of the evidence if the stenographer is a duly sworn court stenographer.

(6) Transcription of record taken by sound recording apparatus — Where, in accordance with this Act, a record is taken in any proceedings under this Act by a sound recording apparatus, the record so taken shall, on request of the justice or of one of the parties, be dealt with and transcribed, in whole or in part, and the transcription certified and used in accordance with the provincial legislation, with such modifications as the circumstances require mentioned in subsection (1).

R.S., c. C-34, s. 468; R.S. 1985, c. 27 (1st Supp.), s. 98; 1997, c. 18, s. 65.

Commentary: The section authorizes three methods of *recording the evidence* given at a *preliminary inquiry*.

Under s. 540(1), the justice presiding at the preliminary inquiry must take the evidence of P's witnesses under oath and in the presence of D, thereafter allowing D or him/her counsel to cross-examine the witnesses. The justice must cause *a record* of the evidence of each witness to be taken, either by way of *deposition* in Form 31, by a *stenographer* appointed by him/her or according to law, or by means of a *sound recording apparatus* in accordance with provincial legislation.

Sections 540(2) and (3) set out the procedure to be followed in taking and authenticating evidence in the form of a deposition. Sections 540(4) and (5) apply where the evidence is taken by a stenographer, and s. 540(6) governs where the evidence is taken by a sound recording apparatus.

Case Law
Recording the Evidence

R. v. Czyszczon (1963), 41 C.R. 17, [1963] 3 C.C.C. 106 (Alta. C.A.) — Where there is no sound recording apparatus or stenographer present, the justice should record the evidence of the witnesses in the form of depositions, in Form 31.

R. v. Lacasse (1972), 8 C.C.C. (2d) 270 (B.C. C.A.) — The requirements of s. 540(1) are mandatory.

R. v. MacLeod (1994), 93 C.C.C. (3d) 339, 34 C.R. (4th) 69 (N.B. C.A.) — There is *no* statutory authority for a court reporter to destroy or erase a recording of evidence taken at preliminary inquiry within 90 days' of D's discharge. The *Code* requires a permanent record of the proceedings and its indiscriminate destruction is *not* permitted. The consequence of the unavailability of a transcript of a preliminary inquiry on D's right to make full answer and defence is assessed on a case-by-case basis.

R. v. Goupil (1985), 65 N.B.R. (2d) 162 (N.B. C.A.) — The absence of a transcript of the preliminary injury is irrelevant when the committal for trial was based on D's consent, *not* on the evidence.

Rupert v. R. (1978), 3 C.R. (3d) 351, 43 C.C.C. (2d) 34 (Ont. H.C.); affirmed without written reasons January 23, 1979 (Ont. C.A.) — *Contra*: *R. v. Boylan* (1979), 8 C.R. (3d) 36 (Sask. C.A.)*R. v. Trotchie* (1982), 66 C.C.C. (2d) 396 (Sask. C.A.) — The provisions of s. 540(1) requiring a record of the evidence at a preliminary inquiry are directory only. The court refused to quash a committal for trial on the basis that the recordings of the preliminary inquiry were lost and a transcript, therefore, unavailable.

Evidence [See also s. 537, Receiving Evidence and s. 548, Review of Committal or Discharge]

Re Ponak (1969), 7 C.R.N.S. 82 (B.C. C.A.) — A justice in a proper case, may allow a witness to be recalled to correct any wrong evidence he had given. The justice, in conducting the hearing, is governed by the ordinary rules of evidence.

R. v. R. (L.) (1995), 39 C.R. (4th) 390, 100 C.C.C. (3d) 329 (Ont. C.A.) — In a criminal prosecution, the admissibility of mental health records must be determined by the *Criminal Code*. At a perliminary inquiry, a provincial court judge is competent to make all evidentiary rulings, including those which relate to privilege claims. Admissibility is decided on the basis of *relevance* which is *not* soley governed by the narrow test for committal for trial. The preliminary inquiry also serves a discovery function. It includes the right to explore at an early stage the credibility of P's witnesses and the availability of potential defences

R. v. R. (L.) (1995), 39 C.R. (4th) 390, 100 C.C.C. (3d) 329 (Ont. C.A.) — It may be necessary to follow procedural steps in provincial mental health legisaltion, as for example, s. 35 of the *Mental Health Act*, R.S.O. 1990, c. M.7, before mental health records may be disclosed. A provincial court judge at preliminary inquiry is a court of competent jurisdiction within s. 35 of the *Act*.

R. v. Greenwood (1992), 70 C.C.C. (3d) 260 (Ont. C.A.) — *See also*: *R. v. Gray* (1991), 68 C.C.C. (3d) 193 (Ont. Gen. Div.) — Section 540(1)(a) does *not* deprive a justice of the authority to receive and order D to stand trial upon the basis of the unsworn evidence of a child under fourteen years of age. Subsection 16(3) *C.E.A.* creates an exception to the general rule of s. 540(1)(a) and permits the reception of unsworn evidence at preliminary.

Cross-Examination: S. 540(1)(a)

R. v. Forsythe (1979), 43 C.C.C. (2d) 545n (Ont. C.A.); affirmed (1980), 15 C.R. (3d) 280 (S.C.C.) — The judge at the preliminary inquiry was within his jurisdiction to refuse to let defence counsel cross-examine a police officer on the contents of his note book. As a ruling on the admissibility of evidence, the decision, even if wrong, did not support an order of *certiorari* because it did not amount to a denial of natural justice.

R. v. Roussel (1979), 10 C.R. (3d) 184 (Alta. C.A.) — *See also*: *Depagie v. R.* (1976), 32 C.C.C. (2d) 89 (Alta. C.A.) — A possible error in the exercise of jurisdiction, such as restricting the right of D to cross-examine witnesses at a preliminary inquiry, does *not* cause a loss of jurisdiction in the presiding justice.

R. v. Dawson (1998), 123 C.C.C. (3d) 385 (Ont. C.A.) — *Semble*, a justice at preliminary inquiry has jurisdiction to grant leave to cross-examine the deponent of an affidavit filed in support of an application for an authorization to intercept private communications. The entitlement of D to disclosure does *not* diminish the discovery aspect of the preliminary inquiry.

R. v. George (1991), 69 C.C.C. (3d) 148 (Ont. C.A.) — *See also*: *Zappa v. Zappa* (1981), 34 N.B.R. (2d) 358 (C.A.) — While D may *not* be substantially deprived of the right to cross-examine on a preliminary hearing, there is *no* jurisdictional error if the opportunity for full discovery is incidentally curtailed by the mere disallowance of a question or questions.

Zaor v. R. (1984), 12 C.C.C. (3d) 265 (Que. C.A.) — *See also*: *Durette v. R.* (1979), 47 C.C.C. (2d) 170 (Ont. H.C.) — Where the justice presiding at the preliminary inquiry refused D's request to cross-examine the remaining witnesses himself, jurisdiction was lost. The choice as to whether witnesses are to be cross-examined by D or by counsel belongs solely to D.

Production of Documents [See also C.E.A. s. 10]

Patterson v. R. (1970), 10 C.R.N.S. 55 (S.C.C.) — The power given to a judge by the *C.E.A.*, s. 10, to compel production of a written statement extends only to the trial. A justice conducting a preliminary hearing is not empowered to make such an order. A preliminary hearing is not a trial and should not be allowed to become one.

R. v. Goupil (1985), 65 N.B.R. (2d) 162 (N.B. C.A.) — The absence of a transcript of the preliminary inquiry is irrelevant when the committal for trial is based on D's consent, *not* on the evidence.

Re Martin (1977), 41 C.C.C. (2d) 308 (Ont. C.A.) — *See also*: *R. v. Hislop* (1983), 36 C.R. (3d) 29, 7 C.C.C. (3d) 240 (Ont. C.A.); leave to appeal refused (1983), 52 N.R. 238 (S.C.C.) — The refusal of a justice at a preliminary inquiry to order production of a police witness' notebook to defence counsel is not reviewable on *certiorari*. The refusal does not amount to a denial of natural justice or of the right to cross-examine.

Charter Remedies at Preliminary [See s. 535 and Charter s. 24]

Related Provisions: Similar provisions are made for *taking evidence at* the *trial* of indictable offences before a provincial court judge (s. 557), a jury (s. 646), and judge alone trials under Part XIX (s. 572). In summary conviction matters, s. 801(3) applies.

Section 715 describes the basis upon which evidence given at the preliminary inquiry may be admitted as evidence at D's trial upon the charge.

Section 541 requires that D be addressed after P's evidence has been taken down. Section 542(1) authorizes reception of an admission, statement or confession by D at the preliminary inquiry in accordance with the law of evidence.

541. (1) Hearing of witnesses — **When the evidence of the witnesses called on the part of the prosecution has been taken down and, where required by this Part, has been read, the justice shall, subject to this section, hear the witnesses called by the accused.**

(2) Contents of address to accused — **Before hearing any witness called by an accused who is not represented by counsel, the justice shall address the accused as follows or to the like effect:**

"Do you wish to say anything in answer to these charges or to any other charges which might have arisen from the evidence led by the prosecution? You are not obliged to say anything. but whatever you do say may be given in evidence against you at your trial. You should not make any confession or admission of guilt because of any promise or threat made to you but if you do make any statement it may be given in evidence against you at your trial in spite of the promise or threat."

(3) Statement of accused — **Where the accused who is not represented by counsel says anything in answer to the address made by the justice pursuant to subsection (2), the answer shall be taken down in writing and shall be signed by the justice and kept with the evidence of the witnesses and dealt with in accordance with this Part.**

(4) Witnesses for accused — **Where an accused is not represented by counsel, the justice shall ask the accused if he or she wishes to call any witnesses after subsections (2) and (3) have been complied with.**

(5) Depositions of such witnesses — **The justice shall hear each witness called by the accused who testifies to any matter relevant to the inquiry, and for the purposes of this subsection, section 540 applies with such modifications as the circumstances require.**

R.S., c. C-34, s. 469; R.S. 1985, c. 27 (1st Supp.) s. 99; 1994, c. 44, s. 54.

Commentary: The section enacts the *procedure* to be followed after the evidence of P's witnesses has been taken down under s. 540.

After the evidence of P's witnesses has been taken down, and where required read, the justice must hear the witnesses called by D who testify concerning any matter relevant to the inquiry. The evidence is taken down in accordance with s. 540.

Where D is *not* represented by counsel, the presiding justice is required to address D in the words of s. 541(2), or to like effect, before hearing any witnesses that D may call. Under s. 541(3), D;s answer to the justice's address must be taken down in writing, signed by the justice and kept with the evidence of other witnesses. After the address and D's answer, if any, the justice must ask D whether s/he wishes to call any witnesses. Where witnesses are called, s. 541(5) applies to the taking of their evidence.

Semble, the address of s. 541(2) is *not* required where D is represented by counsel.

Prior to its recent amendment, s. 541 required that D be addressed in terms similar to present s. 541(2) in all cases.

Case Law

Repetition of Address: S. 541(1)

Bayne v. R. (1970), 14 C.R.N.S. 130 (Alta. C.A.) — Where D on a preliminary hearing consents to have evidence in respect of one information applied in respect of additional informations, the justice must repeat the form of address and the question whether D wishes to call any witnesses. Failure to do so is jurisdictional error.

Eusler v. R. (1978), 43 C.C.C. (2d) 501 (N.B. C.A.) — The justice is required to address D *only* on the information as a whole, *not* on each separate count, provided that P has presented its case on all counts.

Opportunity to Call Witnesses: Ss. 541(3), (4)

R. v. Ward (1976), 35 C.R.N.S. 117, 31 C.C.C. (2d) 466 (Ont. H.C.); affirmed (1977), 31 C.C.C. (2d) 466n (Ont. C.A.) — *See also*: *Zastawny v. R.* (1970), 10 C.R.N.S. 155 (Sask. Q.B.) — The justice may *not* commit for trial once a *prima facie* case has been established by P without first giving D an opportunity to call witnesses and hearing those witnesses which D indicates he wishes to call. Sections 541(3) and (4) are mandatory in their effect. Noncompliance will result in a quashing of the order to stand for trial.

Related Provisions: Section 657 authorizes the use of D's s. 541(2) statement at trial, subject to the application of *Charter* s. 13.

Section 715 describes the basis upon which evidence given upon the preliminary inquiry may be received at trial on a charge.

542. (1) Confession or admission of accused — Nothing in this Act prevents a prosecutor giving in evidence at a preliminary inquiry any admission, confession or statement made at any time by the accused that by law is admissible against him.

(2) Restriction of publication of reports of preliminary inquiry — Every one who publishes in any newspaper, or broadcasts, a report that any admission or confession was tendered in evidence at a preliminary inquiry or a report of the nature of such admission or confession so tendered in evidence unless

(a) the accused has been discharged, or

(b) if the accused has been committed for trial, the trial has ended, is guilty of an offence punishable on summary conviction.

(3) "Newspaper" — In this section "newspaper" has the same meaning as in section 297.

R.S., c. C-34, s. 470; R.S. 1985, c. 27 (1st Supp.), s. 101(2).

Commentary: Section 542(1) authorizes the reception in evidence at the preliminary inquiry of any admission, confession or statement of D, which is, by law, admissible against D. Any conditions precedent to admissibility must be established in the same manner and to the same extent as required at trial.

Section 542(2) prohibits newspaper *publication or broadcast* of any report of the fact that or the nature of a confession or admission which was received at a preliminary inquiry, until discharge or the conclusion of trial. "Newspaper" is defined in s. 297.

Case Law
Voluntariness of Statement and its Determination

Park v. R. (1981), 21 C.R. (3d) 182, 59 C.C.C. (2d) 385 (S.C.C.) — Voluntariness may be determined without the necessity of a *voir dire*, if the *voir dire* is expressly waived by D or D's counsel. Silence or mere lack of objection will *not* constitute a valid waiver.

R. v. Pickett (1975), 31 C.R.N.S. 239, 28 C.C.C. (2d) 297 (Ont. C.A.) — *See also*: *R. v. Norgren* (1973), 25 C.R.N.S. 358, 15 C.C.C. (2d) 30 (B.C. C.A.); reversed on other grounds (1975), 31 C.R.N.S. 247, 27 C.C.C. (2d) 488 (B.C. C.A.); *R. v. Pearson* (1957), 117 C.C.C. 249 (Alta. C.A.); *R. v. Leboeuf* (1979), 57 C.C.C. (2d) 257 (Que. C.A.) — The burden of proving a statement voluntary is the same at a preliminary inquiry as at trial. The *standard* is proof beyond a reasonable doubt. In the absence of waiver, a *voir dire* must be held at a preliminary inquiry, as at a trial, to prove voluntariness.

Related Provisions: There is no corresponding provision applicable at trial.

The phrase "that by law is admissible against him" would also seem to require consideration of constitutional infringement, as for example under *Charter* s. 7, 10(a) or (b). The availability of *Charter* exclusionary remedy at a preliminary inquiry is problematic under *R. v. Mills*, noted under s. 535, *supra*.

Remand Where Offence Committed in Another Jurisdiction

543. (1) Order that accused appear or be taken before justice where offence committed — Where an accused is charged with an offence alleged to have been committed out of the limits of the jurisdiction in which he has been charged, the justice before whom he appears or is brought may, at any stage of the inquiry after hearing both parties,

    (a) order the accused to appear, or

    (b) if the accused is in custody, issue a warrant in Form 15 to convey the accused

before a justice having jurisdiction in the place where the offence is alleged to have been committed, who shall continue and complete the inquiry.

(2) Transmission of transcript and documents and effect of order or warrant — Where a justice makes an order or issues a warrant pursuant to subsection (1), he shall cause the transcript of any evidence given before him in the inquiry and all documents that were then before him and that are relevant to the inquiry to be transmitted to a justice having jurisdiction in the place where the offence is alleged to have been committed and

    (a) any evidence the transcript of which is so transmitted shall be deemed to have been taken by the justice to whom it is transmitted; and

    (b) any appearance notice, promise to appear, undertaking or recognizance issued to or given or entered into by the accused under Part XVI shall be deemed to have been issued, given or entered into in the jurisdiction where the offence is alleged to have been committed and to require the accused to appear before the justice to whom the transcript and documents are transmitted at the time provided in the order made in respect of the accused under paragraph (1)(*a*).

R.S., c. C-34, s. 471; c. 2 (2d Supp.), s. 7.

Commentary: The section applies where D appears for a preliminary inquiry in respect of an offence alleged to have been committed out of the limits of the jurisdiction in which D is charged. The provision is now anachronistic because most provincial court judges, who act as justices under this Part, have province-wide jurisdiction.

Under s. 543(1), the justice *may*, at any time after having heard the parties, order D to appear or be conveyed before a justice having jurisdiction in the place where the offence is alleged to have been committed. Under s. 543(2), the transcript of any evidence given before the original justice, as well as any documents before him/her that are relevant to the inquiry, are transferred to the jurisdiction of the offence where they are *deemed* to be taken by the justice to whom transferred. Release forms are *deemed* to require attendance in the jurisdiction to which the matter is transferred.

Case Law

Territorial Jurisdiction of Appearance

R. v. Simons (1976), 34 C.R.N.S. 273, 30 C.C.C. (2d) 162 (Ont. C.A.) — This section only applies where D is before a provincial judge according to law. There is *no* authority for an officer in charge to direct in a promise to appear that D attend before a provincial judge presiding in another territorial jurisdiction. When D is arrested and *not* released by the officer in charge, D must be brought before a justice within the territorial jurisdiction. Where the officer in charge summons D to appear, D must be summonsed to appear within the territorial jurisdiction of the arrest.

Related Provisions: Special provisions relating to territorial jurisdiction are contained in ss. 476–481, as well as in s. 7. An offence is generally tried by a court of competent jurisdiction in the territorial jurisdiction in which it occurs.

Under s. 537(1)(a), a justice under Part XVIII may change the place of an inquiry, where it appears desirable to do so for specified reasons relating to the attendance of witnesses.

Absconding Accused

544. (1) Accused absconding during inquiry — Notwithstanding any other provision of this Act, where an accused, whether or not he is charged jointly with another, absconds during the course of a preliminary inquiry into an offence with which he is charged,

  (a) he shall be deemed to have waived his right to be present at the inquiry; and

  (b) the justice

   (i) may continue the inquiry and, when all the evidence has been taken, shall dispose of the inquiry in accordance with section 548, or

   (ii) if a warrant is issued for the arrest of the accused, may adjourn the inquiry to await his appearance,

  but where the inquiry is adjourned pursuant to subparagraph (b)(ii), the justice may continue it at any time pursuant to subparagraph(b)(i) if he is satisfied that it would no longer be in the interests of justice to await the appearance of the accused.

(2) Adverse inference — Where the justice continues a preliminary inquiry pursuant to subsection (1), he may draw an inference adverse to the accused from the fact that he has absconded.

(3) Accused not entitled to re-opening — Where an accused reappears at a preliminary inquiry that is continuing pursuant to subsection (1), he is not entitled to have any part of the proceedings that was conducted in his absence re-opened unless the justice is satisfied that because of exceptional circumstances it is in the interests of justice to re-open the inquiry.

(4) Counsel for accused may continue to act — Where the accused has absconded during the course of a preliminary inquiry and the justice continues the inquiry, counsel for the accused is not thereby deprived of any authority he may have to continue to act for the accused in the proceedings.

(5) Accused calling witnesses — Where, at the conclusion of the evidence on the part of the prosecution at a preliminary inquiry that has been continued pursuant to

subsection (1), the accused is absent but counsel for the accused is present, he or she
shall be given an opportunity to call witnesses on behalf of the accused and subsection
541(5) applies with such modifications as the circumstances require.

1974–75–76, c. 93, s. 59; 1994, c. 44, s. 55.

Commentary: The section enacts the procedure to be followed where D *absconds* during the *course*
of the *preliminary inquiry*.

Under s. 544(1), which operates notwithstanding any other *Code* provision, where D absconds during
the course of the preliminary inquiry, D is *deemed* to have *waived* the *right* to be *present* at the inquiry.
The justice may simply *continue* with the *inquiry*, in the absence of D, and determine whether to make
an order to stand trial under s. 548. The justice may also issue a *warrant* for D's arrest and *adjourn* the
inquiry, thereafter resuming it in D's absence at any time, if satisfied it would no longer be in the
interests of justice to await D's appearance.

Where the inquiry is *continued* in D's *absence*, the justice, under s. 544(2), may draw an *inference*
adverse to D from the fact that s/he has absconded. The mere fact that D absconded does *not* deprive
his/her counsel of the authority to act at the continued proceedings. Under s. 544(3), it is only exceptionally that any part of the proceedings in D's absence will be re-opened upon his/her return. The principles
of ss. 544(2)–(4), would appear equally to apply whether the inquiry is continued under s. 544(1)(b)(i)
or resumed under s. 544(1)(b)(ii).

Where D is absent at the conclusion of P's case at the preliminary inquiry, s. 544(5) permits defending
counsel to call witnesses whose evidence will be recorded under s. 541(4).

The section may be subject to challenge under *Charter* ss. 7 and 11(d).

Case Law [See also s. 475]

Plummer v. R. (1983), 5 C.C.C. (3d) 17 (B.C. C.A.); reversing (1982), 1 C.C.C. (3d) 174 (B.C. S.C.) —
Where D elected trial by jury, the holding of a preliminary inquiry was an inevitable consequence. Acts
done following the election were "in the course of a preliminary inquiry" and, when D failed to appear
at the date set for the preliminary inquiry, the judge had jurisdiction to make a finding under this section
that D had absconded.

Related Provisions: A similar authority to proceed in D's absence at trial appears in s. 475 a
provision that operates notwithstanding the general right to be present under s. 650, which is itself subject to certain exceptions.

Section 544(2) does *not* describe the nature of the "inference adverse to the accused from the fact that he
has absconded" but, *semble*, it is an inference of consciousness of guilt, based upon flight. Such conduct
is always open to explanation on behalf of D.

Procedure where Witness Refuses to Testify

545. (1) Witness refusing to be examined — Where a person, being present at a
preliminary inquiry and being required by the justice to give evidence,

(a) refuses to be sworn,

(b) having been sworn, refuses to answer the questions that are put to him,

(c) fails to produce any writings that he is required to produce, or

(d) refuses to sign his deposition,

without offering a reasonable excuse for his failure or refusal, the justice may adjourn
the inquiry and may, by warrant in Form 20, commit the person to prison for a period
not exceeding eight clear days or for the period during which the inquiry is adjourned,
whichever is the lesser period.

(2) Further commitment — Where a person to whom subsection (1) applies is
brought before the justice on the resumption of the adjourned inquiry and again refuses to do what is required of him, the justice may again adjourn the inquiry for a

period not exceeding eight clear days and commit him to prison for the period of adjournment or any part thereof, and may adjourn the inquiry and commit the person to prison from time to time until the person consents to do what is required of him.

(3) **Saving** — Nothing in this section shall be deemed to prevent the justice from sending the case for trial on any other sufficient evidence taken by him.

R.S., c. C-34, s. 472.

Commentary: The section describes the procedure to be followed by the justice where a *witness*, present at a preliminary inquiry and required to give evidence, *fails or refuses* to do so in a manner described in s. 545(1).

Where the witness refuses to be sworn, to answer questions, to sign his/her deposition, or fails to produce any required writings, *without reasonable excuse*, the justice may commit the witness to prison for successive periods, not exceeding eight clear days, and adjourn the inquiry from time to time until the recalcitrant witness consents to do what is required. Under s. 545(3), the justice may order D to stand trial on the basis of any other sufficient evidence which satisfies the test of s. 548(1)(a).

Case Law [See also s. 9]

Lacroix v. R. (1987), 59 C.R. (3d) 92, 34 C.C.C. (3d) 94 (S.C.C.) — Where the justice does *not* exercise the powers of this section to imprison a witness for refusing to testify, an obstruction of justice charge may be laid.

R. v. McKenzie (1978), 41 C.C.C. (2d) 394 (Alta. C.A.) — The procedure of this section, *not* the general power to proceed by indictment for contempt of court, should be used where a witness refuses to testify at a preliminary inquiry.

R. v. Bubley (1976), 32 C.C.C. (2d) 79 (Alta. C.A.); leave to appeal refused (1976), 32 C.C.C. (2d) 79n (S.C.C.) — A justice may *not* resort to contempt of court proceedings against a person who refuses to testify at a preliminary inquiry.

R. v. Poulin (1998), 127 C.C.C. (3d) 115 (Que. C.A.) — Refusal to testify at a preliminary inquiry may constitute the basis of a charge under s. 139(2) where a provincial court judge has *not* exercised jurisdiction under s. 545.

Related Provisions: Under s. 550 the justice who orders D to stand trial may require any witness whose evidence is material to enter into a recognizance to give evidence at trial. Failure to comply with a recognizance may result in committal until the witness does what is required or the trial is concluded.

Part XXII "Procuring Attendance" deals with the means whereby the attendance of witnesses may be compelled.

Conduct described in s. 545(1) at trial may attract the power of the trial court to punish for contempt in the face of the court.

Remedial Provisions

546. Irregularity or variance not to affect validity — The validity of any proceeding at or subsequent to a preliminary inquiry is not affected by

(a) any irregularity or defect in the substance or form of the summons or warrant,

(b) any variance between the charge set out in the summons or warrant and the charge set out in the information, or

(c) any variance between the charge set out in the summons, warrant or information and the evidence adduced by the prosecution at the inquiry.

R.S., c. C-34, s. 473.

Commentary: The section ensures that some *variances, irregularities* and *defects do not affect* the *validity* of any proceeding at or after a preliminary inquiry. To be remediable, the irregularity, defect or variance must be in the *process* compelling *attendance*, as between the process and the information, or as between the process or information and the evidence adduced at the preliminary inquiry.

Related Provisions: Where D has been misled or deceived by any irregularity, defect or variance in s. 546, an adjournment of the inquiry may be ordered under s. 547.

Wide powers of amendment are given in both indictable (s. 601) and summary conviction (s. 795) trial proceedings. Section 601(11) permits amendment at preliminary inquiry.

547. Adjournment if accused misled — Where it appears to the justice that the accused has been deceived or misled by any irregularity, defect or variance mentioned in section 546, he may adjourn the inquiry and may remand the accused or grant him interim release in accordance with Part XVI.

R.S., c. C-34, s. 474; 1974–75–76, c. 93, s. 59.1.

Commentary: Under this section a justice may *adjourn* the preliminary inquiry where it appears that D has been misled or deceived by any irregularity, defect or variance described in s. 546. Upon adjournment, D may be remanded in custody or granted interim release under Part XVI.

Related Provisions: The general authority to adjourn proceedings at a preliminary inquiry is found in s. 537(1)(a).

See also the corresponding note to s. 546, *supra*.

547.1 Inability of justice to continue — Where a justice acting under this Part has commenced to take evidence and dies or is unable to continue for any reason, another justice may

(a) continue taking the evidence at the point at which the interruption in the taking of the evidence occurred, where the evidence was recorded pursuant to section 540 and is available; or

(b) commence taking the evidence as if no evidence had been taken, where no evidence was recorded pursuant to section 540 or where the evidence is not available.

R.S. 1985, c. 27 (1st Supp.), s. 100.

Commentary: The section provides a remedy where a justice dies or is unable, for any other reason, to continue after commencing to take evidence upon a preliminary inquiry.

Where the evidence already given has been recorded under s. 540 and is available, another justice may continue taking the evidence at the point of interruption. Where the evidence already taken is either not recorded under s. 540 or is not available, another justice may commence taking the evidence *ab initio*.

Related Provisions: Sections 547.1(a) and (b) would *not* appear mutually exclusive. Under s. 547.1(a), another justice may determine to hear *all* the evidence previously given, notwithstanding compliance with s. 540 and availability of transcript.

Section 669.2 provides authority to continue trial proceedings where the presiding judge dies or is, for any other reason, unable to continue.

Adjudication and Recognizances

548. (1) Order to stand trial or discharge — When all the evidence has been taken by the justice, he shall,

(a) if in his opinion there is sufficient evidence to put the accused on trial for the offence charged or any other indictable offence in respect of the same transaction, order the accused to stand trial; or

(b) discharge the accused, if in his opinion on the whole of the evidence no sufficient case is made out to put the accused on trial for the offence charged or any other indictable offence in respect of the same transaction.

(2) Endorsing charge — Where the justice orders the accused to stand trial for an indictable offence, other than or in addition to the one with which the accused was charged, the justice shall endorse on the information the charges on which he orders the accused to stand trial.

(2.1) Where accused ordered to stand trial — A justice who orders that an accused is to stand trial has the power to fix the date for the trial or the date on which the accused must appear in the trial court to have that date fixed.

(3) Defect not to affect validity — The validity of an order to stand trial is not affected by any defect apparent on the face of the information in respect of which the preliminary inquiry is held or in respect of any charge on which the accused is ordered to stand trial unless, in the opinion of the court before which an objection to the information or charge is taken, the accused has been misled or prejudiced in his defence by reason of that defect.

R.S., c. C-34, s. 475. c. 2 (2d Supp.), s. 8; R.S. 1985, c. 27 (1st Supp.), s. 101(1); 1994, c. 44, s. 56.

Commentary: The section sets the *standard* by which the justice at a preliminary inquiry must *determine* whether D ought to be *ordered to stand trial* in respect of the offence charged or any other indictable offence in respect of the same transaction.

Under s. 548(1)(a), D will be ordered to stand trial only where the justice is of the opinion that there is *sufficient evidence to put D on trial* in respect of the offence charged or any other indictable offence in respect of the same transaction. Where D is ordered to stand trial in respect of any other indictable offence in respect of the same transaction, s. 548(2) requires the justice to *endorse* on the information the charges in respect of which such order is made, irrespective of whether D is ordered to stand trial in relation to the offence alleged. Section 548(2.1) permits the justice to fix the trial date or a date to set the trial date. Under s. 548(3), *defects* apparent on the *face* of the information, in respect of the offence alleged, or any charge on which D is ordered to stand trial, do *not* affect the validity of the order to stand trial, unless the trial court decides that D has been misled or prejudiced by the defect.

Under s. 548(1)(b), D must be discharged where there is *not* sufficient evidence to put D on trial for the offence charged or any other indictable offence in respect of the same transaction.

Case Law
Burden of Proof

U.S.A. v. Sheppard (1976), 34 C.R.N.S. 207, 30 C.C.C. (2d) 424 (S.C.C.) — The duty imposed upon a justice under this section is the same that governs a trial judge sitting with a jury in deciding whether the evidence is "sufficient" to justify him withdrawing the case from the jury. Thus, D should be committed for trial where there is admissible evidence which could, if it were believed, result in a conviction.

Re Rosenberg (1918), 29 C.C.C. 309 (Man. C.A.) — In preliminary hearings, the usual rule of the criminal law is reversed. Any doubt as to the sufficiency of the evidence should be resolved in favour of committal rather than of discharge.

R. v. Herman (1984), 38 C.R. (3d) 284, 11 C.C.C. (3d) 102 (Sask. C.A.) — *See also: Garton v. Whelan* (1984), 14 C.C.C. (3d) 449 (Ont. H.C.) — A committing judge should *not* test the evidence to see whether it could satisfy the rule in *Hodge's Case* nor weigh the evidence and determine what inference he himself would draw if sitting as a trial judge. He should commit if he concludes that a reasonable jury properly instructed could infer guilt from the evidence.

"The Same Transaction": S. 548(1)

R. v. Panzevecchia (1997), 7 C.R. (5th) 94, 115 C.C.C. (3d) 476 (Ont. C.A.) — A threat to kill a third party who witnessed the final part of a protracted assault by D on V is an ". . . other indictable offence in respect of the same transaction . . ." as the offence charged under s. 548(1)(a).

R. v. Stewart (1988), 44 C.C.C. (3d) 109 (Ont. C.A.) — The fact that evidence given in a preliminary inquiry discloses the commission of a second offence closely interwoven with or related to the offence charged in the information is not a sufficient condition for ordering D to stand trial on both offences. The issue is whether the second offence is a component part of the transaction relating to the original offence charged.

R. v. Goldstein (1988), 64 C.R. (3d) 360, 42 C.C.C. (3d) 548 (Ont. C.A.) — The words "the same transaction" mean the series of connected acts extending over a period of time which P alleges prove the commission of the offence charged in the information.

Gratton v. Québec (Juge de la cour du Québec) (1994), 35 C.R. (4th) 393 (Que. C.A.) — An act/transaction, though separate and distinct from other acts/transactions of violence, may form part of a pattern of violent acts without forming part of the transaction compromising the other acts. There is a difference between

i.   a pattern of independent and unconnected violent acts/transactions; and

ii. a series of connected and interwoven violent acts which form part of the same event/transaction.

Special Pleas

Schmidt v. R. (1984), 10 C.C.C. (3d) 564 (Ont. C.A.); affirmed on other grounds (1987), 58 C.R. (3d) 1, 33 C.C.C. (3d) 193 (S.C.C.) — The plea of *autrefois acquit* and the defence of *res judicata* cannot be considered at a preliminary inquiry.

Review of Committal or Discharge [See also s. 774]

R. v. Dubois (1986), 51 C.R. (3d) 193, 25 C.C.C. (3d) 221 (S.C.C.) — *See also*: *R. v. Idlout*, [1988] N.W.T.R. 5 (C.A.); leave to appeal refused [1988] N.W.T.R. 5n (S.C.C.) — *Certiorari* is available to P to quash a discharge at preliminary inquiry on the ground of jurisdictional error. The mere application of the wrong test for sufficiency of evidence, is not a jurisdictional error. Where the judge assumes the function of the ultimate trier of fact by applying the reasonable doubt test and dismissing the charge, there is jurisdictional error.

Skogman v. R. (1984), 41 C.R. (3d) 1, 13 C.C.C. (3d) 161 (S.C.C.) — *See also*: *Quebec (P.G.) v. Hamel* (1987), 60 C.R. (3d) 174 (Que. C.A.) — The committal of D at a preliminary inquiry in the absence of evidence on an essential element of the offence is a reviewable jurisdictional error.

Forsythe v. R. (1980), 15 C.R. (3d) 280 (S.C.C.); affirming (1978), 43 C.C.C. (2d) 545n (Ont. C.A.) — *Certiorari* may be invoked to quash a committal for trial. Committals for trial are not appealable and can be challenged only by *certiorari* or motion to quash. The only basis upon which to invoke *certiorari* is lack of jurisdiction, which includes not only initial jurisdiction but loss of jurisdiction. Jurisdiction will be lost if the justice fails to observe the mandatory provisions of the *Code*. A denial of natural justice also goes to jurisdiction. In the case of a preliminary hearing, however, this arises only by a complete denial of D's right to cross-examine or to call witnesses. The refusal of the justice to allow cross-examination on a police officer's notes, even if wrong, does not result in a loss of jurisdiction.

Quebec (A.G.) v. Cohen (1979), 13 C.R. (3d) 36 (S.C.C.) — *See also*: *R. v. Seguin* (1982), 31 C.R. (3d) 271 (Ont. C.A.) — *Certiorari* is only available for lack of jurisdiction. Decisions concerning the admissiblity of evidence, even if erroneous, do *not* affect jurisdiction.

Re Martin (1978), 41 C.C.C. (2d) 342 (S.C.C.) — The scope of an application for *habeas corpus* with *certiorari* in aid to review an order for committal is the same as an application by way of *certiorari* alone. The pre-Confederation *Habeas Corpus Act* could not enlarge the authority to review the determination of the committing justice. A review as to the sufficiency of evidence must be a review as to whether the committal was made arbitrarily, or, at the most, whether there was some evidence upon which an opinion could be formed that D should stand trial.

Patterson v. R. (1970), 10 C.R.N.S. 55 (S.C.C.) — Lack of jurisdiction is the only ground upon which a committal for trial may be attacked. The refusal of a justice conducting a preliminary inquiry to order production of a statement made by a Crown witness does *not* go to jurisdiction.

R. v. Pike (1992), 77 C.C.C. (3d) 155 (Nfld. C.A.) — An order that D stand trial under *Code* s. 548(1), once signed and lodged with the trial court without facial defect and in good faith, raises a presumption of regularity that constitutes a valid order until set aside or quashed. The presumption remains notwithstanding subsequent discovery of a malfunction of the sound recording apparatus, hence a breach of *Code* s. 540(1).

Martin v. R. (1977), 41 C.C.C. (2d) 308 (Ont. C.A.); affirmed on other grounds (1978), 41 C.C.C. (2d) 342 (S.C.C.) — *See also*: *R. v. Kendall* (1984), 3 O.A.C. 294 (C.A.) — *Certiorari* is available to quash a committal only where there was an excess or want of jurisdiction in the inferior court. A justice acts within his jurisdiction unless he commits D without *any* evidence at all, in the sense of an entire absence of proper material as a basis for the formation of a judicial opinion that the evidence was sufficient to put D on trial.

Charter Considerations

R. v. Cancor Software Corp. (1990), 79 C.R. (3d) 22, 58 C.C.C. (3d) 53 (Ont. C.A.) — The authority of s. 548(1)(a) to order D to stand trial for any other indictable offence, in respect of the same transaction as the offence charged does *not* offend *Charter* s. 11(a).

R. v. Till (1984), 30 Sask. R. 261 (C.A.) — *Charter* s. 11(d) is *not* applicable to a preliminary hearing. Since the committing justice was not determining the guilt or innocence of D, the presumption of innocence was not affected by a committal for trial.

Related Provisions: Section 549 permits an order to stand trial to be made at any stage of the preliminary inquiry, with the *consent* of P and D. The section is not explicit but may permit a consent order to be made in respect of both the offence charged and "any other indictable offence in respect of the same transaction", as permitted in s. 548(1)(a).

The authority of P to prefer an indictment based upon an order to stand trial is described in s. 574. Section 577 authorizes direct indictments, where D has been discharged at the preliminary inquiry or no preliminary inquiry has been held.

The amendment authority of s. 601 is available at the preliminary inquiry under s. 601(11).

549. (1) **Order to stand trial at any stage of inquiry with consent** — Notwithstanding any other provision of this Act, the justice may, at any stage of the preliminary inquiry, with the consent of the accused and the prosecutor, order the accused to stand trial in the court having criminal jurisdiction, without taking or recording any evidence or further evidence.

(2) **Procedure** — Where an accused is ordered to stand trial under subsection (1), the justice shall endorse on the information a statement of the consent of the accused and the prosecutor, and the accused shall thereafter be dealt with in all respects as if ordered to stand trial under section 548.

R.S., c. C-34, s. 476; R.S. 1985, c. 27 (1st Supp.), s. 101(3).

Commentary: Under this section an order to stand trial may be made at any stage of the preliminary inquiry, with the *consent* of P and D, without taking or recording any or further evidence. Section 549(2) requires the justice to *endorse* on the information a statement that D was ordered to stand trial with the consent of P and D. D is dealt with thereafter, as if ordered to stand trial under s. 548.

Related Provisions: The general authority to order D to stand trial is found in s. 548.

The section, though not explicit, may permit a consent order to be made in respect of the offence charged, or "any other indictable offence in respect of the same transaction". There would seem no reason in principle why s. 549(1) could *not* be invoked in both cases. As a practical matter, a fresh information may be laid charging the other offence and a consent order made as "the offence charged".

550. (1) **Recognizance of witness** — Where an accused is ordered to stand trial, the justice who held the preliminary inquiry may require any witness whose evidence is, in his opinion, material to enter into a recognizance to give evidence at the trial of the accused and to comply with such reasonable conditions prescribed in the recognizance as the justice considers desirable for securing the attendance of the witness to give evidence at the trial of the accused.

(2) **Form** — The recognizance entered into pursuant to this section may be in Form 32, and may be set out at the end of a deposition or be separate therefrom.

(3) Sureties or deposit for appearance of witness — A justice may, for any reason satisfactory to him, require any witness entering into a recognizance pursuant to this section.

(a) to produce one or more sureties in such amount as he may direct; or

(b) to deposit with him a sum of money sufficient in his opinion to ensure that the witness will appear and give evidence.

(4) Witness refusing to be bound — Where a witness does not comply with subsection (1) or (3) when required to do so by a justice, he may be committed by the justice, by warrant in Form 24, to a prison in the territorial division where the trial is to be held, there to be kept until he does what is required of him or until the trial is concluded.

(5) Discharge — Where a witness has been committed to prison pursuant to subsection (4), the court before which the witness appears or a justice having jurisdiction in the territorial division where the prison is situated may, by order in Form 39, discharge the witness from custody when the trial is concluded.

R.S., c. C-34, s. 477; 1974-75-76, c. 39, s. 60; R.S. 1985, c. 27 (1st Supp.), s. 101(3).

Commentary: Under this section a justice presiding at a preliminary inquiry may require a material witness to enter into a recognizance to give evidence at trial. The process is described as "binding over a material witness".

Under s. 550(1), where D has been ordered to stand trial, the presiding justice *may* require any *witness* whose *evidence* is, in the opinion of the justice, *material*, to enter into a *recognizance* to give evidence at trial. The recognizance, in Form 32, may also contain any other reasonable condition which the justice considers desirable to secure the witness' attendance to give evidence at trial. More specifically, under s. 550(3), sureties and a deposit may be ordered. Where the witness *fails to comply* with the terms of the recognizance, to produce the necessary sureties or make the required deposit, s. 550(4) authorizes the justice to commit the witness to prison by warrant in Form 24 until the witness either does what is required or the trial is concluded. The trial court, or a justice having jurisdiction where the prison is located, may discharge the witness by order in Form 39 when the trial is concluded.

Related Provisions: The general authority to compel the attendance of witnesses appears in Part XXII, ss. 696-707. Part XXV, ss. 762-773, describes the procedure to enforce recognizances.

Transmission of Record

551. Transmitting record — Where a justice orders an accused to stand trial, the justice shall forthwith send to the clerk or other proper officer of the court by which the accused is to be tried, the information, the evidence, the exhibits, the statement if any of the accused taken down in writing under section 541, any promise to appear, undertaking or recognizance given or entered into in accordance with Part XVI, or any evidence taken before a coroner, that is in the possession of the justice.

R.S. 1985, c. 27 (1st Supp.), s. 102.

Commentary: The section defines the *record* to be *transmitted* by the justice to the clerk or other proper officer of the *trial court* where D has been ordered to stand trial. It includes the information, evidence, including any statement made by D under s. 541, exhibits, form of release and any evidence taken before a coroner that is in the possession of the justice.

Related Provisions: "Clerk of the court" is defined in s. 2. The reference to "any evidence taken before a coroner that is in the possession of the justice" refers to the evidence transmitted by a coroner under s. 529(2), where the coroner has directed a warrant be issued or recognizance be entered into to compel a person, alleged by the verdict of a coroner's inquisition to have committed murder or manslaughter but who is not charged with the offence, to be conveyed or appear before a justice.

PART XIX — INDICTABLE OFFENCES — TRIAL WITHOUT A JURY

Interpretation

552. Definitions — In this Part

"judge" means,

(a) in the Province of Ontario, a judge of the superior court of criminal jurisdiction of the Province,

(b) in the Province of Quebec, a judge of the Court of Quebec,

(c) in the Province of Nova Scotia, a judge of the superior court of criminal jurisdiction of the Province,

(d) in the Province of New Brunswick, a judge of the Court of Queen's Bench,

(e) in the Province of British Columbia, the Chief Justice or a puisne judge of the Supreme Court,

(f) in the Provinces of Prince Edward Island and Newfoundland, a judge of the Supreme Court,

(g) in the Province of Manitoba, the Chief Justice, or a puisne judge of the Court of Queen's Bench,

(h) in the Provinces of Saskatchewan and Alberta, a judge of the superior court of criminal jurisdiction of the province,

(i) in the Yukon Territory and the Northwest Territories, a judge of the Supreme Court of the territory, and

(j) in Nunavut, a judge of the Nunavut Court of Justice;

R.S., c. C-34, s. 482; 1972, c. 13, s. 39; c. 17, s. 2; 1974–75–76, c. 48, s. 25; c. 93, s. 61; 1978–79, c. 11, s. 10; R.S. 1985, c. 11 (1st Supp.), s. 2; c. 27 (1st Supp.), s. 103(1); c. 27 (2d Supp.), Schedule, item 6; c. 40 (4th Supp.), s. 2; 1990, c. 16, s. 6; 1990, c. 17, s. 13; 1992, c. 51, s. 38; 1993, c. 28, s. 78 (Sched. III, item 33) [Repealed 1999, c. 3, (Sched., item 8).]; 1999, c. 3, s. 36.

Commentary: The section defines "judge" for purposes of Part XIX.

Related Provisions: Subsection 536(2) requires that D, charged with an offence *not* listed in s. 469 nor in 553, be put to an election as to *mode of trial* in the terms of the subsection. A "judge", as defined in s. 552, has neither absolute nor exclusive jurisdiction over any indictable offence. *Offence jurisdiction* is acquired by D's election as to mode of trial and the preferment of the indictment by P. Election and re-election provisions are found in ss. 560–565.

The *absolute jurisdiction* of a "provincial court judge", as defined in s. 2 is found in s. 553, subject to the provisions of s. 555. The consent offence jurisdiction of a provincial court judge is described in s. 554(1).

Jurisdiction of Provincial Court Judges

Absolute Jurisdiction

553. Absolute jurisdiction — The jurisdiction of a provincial court judge, or in Nunavut, of a judge of the Nunavut Court of Justice, to try an accused is absolute and

does not depend on the consent of the accused where the accused is charged in an information

  (a) with

    (i) theft, other than theft of cattle,

    (ii) obtaining money or property by false pretences,

    (iii) unlawfully having in his possession any property or thing or any proceeds of any property or thing knowing that all or a part of the property or thing or of the proceeds was obtained by or derived directly or indirectly from the commission in Canada of an offence punishable by indictment or an act or omission anywhere that, if it had occurred in Canada, would have constituted an offence punishable by indictment,

    (iv) having, by deceit, falsehood or other fraudulent means, defrauded the public or any person, whether ascertained or not, of any property, money or valuable security, or

    (v) mischief under subsection 430(4),

  where the subject-matter of the offence is not a testamentary instrument and the alleged value of the subject-matter of the offence does not exceed five thousand dollars;

  (b) with counselling or with a conspiracy or attempt to commit or with being an accessory after the fact to the commission of

    (i) any offence referred to in paragraph (a) in respect of the subject-matter and value thereof referred to in that paragraph, or

    (ii) any offence referred to in paragraph (c); or

  (c) with an offence under

    (i) section 201 (keeping gaming or betting house),

    (ii) section 202 (betting, pool-selling, book-making, etc.),

    (iii) section 203 (placing bets),

    (iv) section 206 (lotteries and games of chance),

    (v) section 209 (cheating at play),

    (vi) section 210 (keeping common bawdy-house),

    (vii) subsection 259(4) (driving while disqualified),

    (viii) section 393 (fraud in relation to fares),

    (viii.1) section 811 (breach of recognizance).

    (ix) subsection 733.1(1) (failure to comply with probation order),

    (x) paragraph 4(4)(a) of the *Controlled Drugs and Substances Act*, or

    (xi) subsection 5(4) of the *Controlled Drugs and Substances Act*.

R.S., c. C-34, s. 483; 1972, c. 13, s. 40; 1974–75–76, c. 93, s. 62;R.S. 1985, c. 27 (1st Supp.), s. 104; 1992, c. 1, s. 58(1), Schedule I, item 11; 1994, c. 44, s. 57; 1995, c. 22, s. 2; 1996, c. 19, s. 72; 1997, c. 18, s. 66; 1999, c. 3, s. 37.

Commentary: The section defines the *absolute offence jurisdiction* of a *provincial court judge*.

Where D is charged with an offence listed in s. 553(a), (b) or (c), the jurisdiction of a provincial court judge to try D upon the charge is absolute and does *not* depend upon D's consent.

The jurisdiction includes, not only the substantive offence, but also counselling, attempting or being an accessory after the fact to its commission. *Conspiracy* to commit a listed offence is *not* within the absolute jurisdiction of a provincial of court judge under this section.

Case Law

Jurisdiction Not Exclusive

R. v. Coupland (1978), 45 C.C.C. (2d) 437 (Alta. C.A.) — *See also*: *R. v. Scherbank* (1966), 50 C.R. 170, [1967] 2 C.C.C. 279 (Ont. C.A.) — Absolute jurisdiction does *not* mean exclusive jurisdiction. Every court of criminal jurisdiction can try indictable offences, *except* those listed in s. 469, including indictable offences falling under this section.

R. v. Holliday (1973), 26 C.R.N.S. 279, 12 C.C.C. (2d) 56 (Alta. C.A.) — The fact that a provincial judge has "absolute jurisdiction" means only that D has *no* right of election as to manner of trial and that the provincial judge can proceed with the trial without giving D any option to elect to be tried elsewhere. It does *not* mean that he has exclusive jurisdiction to deal with the offence. This section does *not* operate to oust the jurisdiction of the superior court of criminal jurisdiction.

Alleged Value Does Not Exceed Prescribed Amount

R. v. Miller (1973), 24 C.R.N.S. 109, 14 C.C.C. (2d) 370 (Ont. C.A.) — For a provincial judge to have absolute jurisdiction on a charge of possession of stolen property, the information must allege that the property stolen had a value *under* that of the amount prescribed.

Related Provisions: The jurisdiction of a provincial court judge under s. 553 is absolute *not* exclusive. The superior court of criminal jurisdiction and a court of criminal jurisdiction may also try any listed offence. Under s. 555(1), a provincial court judge may determine that "the charge should be prosecuted by indictment" and continue proceedings as a preliminary inquiry. Section 555(2) affords D a right of election where, on a trial for an offence listed in s. 553(a), the evidence establishes value in excess of $5,000.

The reference to "counselling" in s. 553(b) appears to apply to an offence *not* committed under s. 464. Where the offence is committed, D is a party under s. 22 and liable to conviction under s. 23.1, even where the principal cannot be so.

Provincial Court Judge's Jurisdiction with Consent

554. (1) Trial by provincial court judge with consent — Subject to subsection (2), if an accused is charged in an information with an indictable offence other than an offence that is mentioned in section 469, and the offence is not one over which a provincial court judge has absolute jurisdiction under section 553, a provincial court judge may try the accused if the accused elects to be tried by a provincial court judge.

(2) Nunavut — With respect to criminal proceedings in Nunavut, if an accused is charged in an information with an indictable offence other than an offence that is mentioned in section 469, and the offence is not one over which a judge of the Nunavut Court of Justice has absolute jurisdiction under section 553, a judge of the Nunavut Court of Justice may try the accused if the accused elects to be tried by a judge without a jury and without having a preliminary inquiry.

(3) [Repealed R.S. 1985, c. 27 (1st Supp.), s. 105.]

(4) [Repealed R.S. 1985, c. 27 (1st Supp.), s. 105.]

R.S., c. C-34, s. 484; R.S. 1985, c. 27 (1st Supp.), ss. 105, 203; 1999, c. 3, s. 38.

Commentary: The section defines the scope of the *consent offence jurisdiction* of a provincial court judge.

Case Law

Election to be Tried by Provincial Judge [For re-elections see ss. 561–563]

Edmunds v. R. (1981), 21 C.R. (3d) 168, 58 C.C.C. (2d) 485 (S.C.C.) — Although D elects trial before a provincial court judge, the offence remains an indictable offence. Part XXVII does not apply.

R. v. Hawryluk (1975), 29 C.C.C. (2d) 41 (N.B. C.A.) — *See also*: *R. v. Robert* (1973), 13 C.C.C. (2d) 43 (Ont. C.A.) — Where the offence charged is a hybrid offence, P fails to elect mode of procedure and the provincial court judge, a summary conviction court, tries D without election under this section, the offence is *deemed* to have been tried as a summary conviction offence.

R. v. Gougeon (1980), 55 C.C.C. (2d) 218 (Ont. C.A.) — P is *not* obliged to elect its manner of proceeding at D's first appearance before the court, so as to allow the court to determine whether an election is available to D.

R. v. Wardley (1978), 11 C.R. (3d) 282, 43 C.C.C. (2d) 345 (Ont. C.A.) — If D, charged with the indictable offence of trafficking, elects trial by provincial court judge and pleads not guilty to the offence as charged but guilty to possession, a hybrid offence, D is *deemed* to plead guilty to the indictable offence of possession. There is *no* provision for P to elect to proceed by summary conviction after plea. D cannot be sentenced as if P had proceeded summarily.

R. v. Wiseberg (1973), 15 C.C.C. (2d) 26 (Ont. C.A.) — If the election is put to D in substantially the language of the *Code*, this is sufficient compliance. The provincial judge who takes D's election to be tried before a judge of the provincial court and also takes D's plea of not guilty, does *not* become seized with the matter.

Trial of Separate Informations Together [See case digests under s. 591 "General Principles of Joinder"]

Related Provisions: D elects in accordance with s. 536(2) and may also elect under s. 555(2). Sections 560–565 describe the rights and procedure of election and re-election. D's election as to mode of trial may be over-ridden by the judicial officer recording the election (s. 567) or, in some instances, by the Attorney General (s. 568).

Under s. 572, Part XX, "Procedure in Jury Trials and General Provisions", applies to trials before a provincial court judge under Part XIX, with such modification as the circumstances require.

In respect of *offences triable either way*, P will first elect mode of procedure and, thereafter, if proceedings are taken by indictment, D will elect mode of trial under s. 536(2).

555. (1) Provincial court judge may decide to hold preliminary inquiry — Where in any proceedings under this Part an accused is before a provincial court judge and it appears to the provincial court judge that for any reason the charge should be prosecuted by indictment, he may, at any time before the accused has entered upon his defence, decide not to adjudicate and shall thereupon inform the accused of his decision and continue the proceedings as a preliminary inquiry.

(2) Where subject-matter is a testamentary instrument or exceeds $5,000 in value — Where an accused is before a provincial court judge charged with an offence mentioned in paragraph 553(*a*) or subparagraph 553(*b*)(i), and, at any time before the provincial court judge makes an adjudication, the evidence establishes that the subject-matter of the offence is a testamentary instrument or that its value exceeds five thousand dollars, the provincial court judge shall put the accused to his or her election in accordance with subsection 536(2).

(3) Continuing proceedings — Where an accused is put to his election pursuant to subsection (2), the following provisions apply, namely,

    (a) if the accused elects to be tried by a judge without a jury or a court composed of a judge and jury or does not elect when put to his election, the provincial court judge shall continue the proceedings as a preliminary inquiry under Part XVIII and, if he orders the accused to stand trial, the provincial court judge shall comply with subsection 536(4); and

    (b) if the accused elects to be tried by a provincial court judge, the provincial court judge shall endorse on the information a record of the election and continue with the trial.

R.S., c. C-34, s. 485; 1972, c. 13, s. 41; R.S. 1985, c. 27 (1st Supp.), ss. 106, 203; 1994, c. 44, s. 58

Commentary: Under s. 555(1), a provincial court judge, in any proceedings under Part XIX, at any time before D has entered upon his/her defence, may decide *not* to adjudicate, thereupon *inform* D of the decision and *continue* the proceedings as a preliminary inquiry, where it appears to the judge that *for any reason* the charge should be *prosecuted by indictment*.

Section 555(2) governs where D is charged with an offence listed in s. 553(a) or (b) and the evidence, prior to adjudication, establishes that the subject-matter of the offence is either a testamentary instrument or of a value exceeding $5,000. The provincial court judge must then require D to elect under s. 536(2). Under s. 555(3), the proceedings will continue as a preliminary inquiry or trial, in accordance with D's election.

Case Law
Judicial Discretion: S. 555(1)

R. v. Turton (1988), 44 C.C.C. (3d) 49 (Alta. C.A.) — The power granted by s. 555(1) applies only to trials of *indictable* offences under [now] Part XIX of the *Code*. Where P is proceeding summarily, the provincial court judge does *not* have jurisdiction to exercise such power.

R. v. Babcock (1989), 68 C.R. (3d) 285 (Ont. C.A.) — The conversion of a trial into a preliminary inquiry by a provincial court judge *suo motu* solely to clear the docket was improper. Such a purpose was *not* a valid consideration.

Entered Upon His Defence: S. 555(1)

R. v. Nadeau (1971), 3 C.C.C. (2d) 276 (N.B.C.A.); leave to appeal refused [1971] S.C.R. x (S.C.C.) — D has not "entered upon his defence" until he/she calls a witness or makes known to the court after P has closed its case an intention not to do so.

Evidence Establishes: S. 555(2)

R. v. Anderson (1972), 5 N.B.R. (2d) 851 (C.A.) — The subsection does *not* require an election to be given immediately on evidence being led of a value in excess of the statutory amount, but only after evidence "establishes" that the value of what was stolen or had been in possession exceeds the statutory amount.

Related Provisions: Section 567 permits a justice, provincial court judge or judge recording the elections of several accused charged with the same offence in the circumstances there described to decline to record certain elections, re-elections or deemed elections and hold a preliminary inquiry. Under s. 568, the Attorney General may *require* a jury trial in respect of indictable offences punishable by imprisonment for more than five years.

555.1 (1) Decision to hold preliminary inquiry — Nunavut — If in any criminal proceedings under this Part an accused is before a judge of the Nunavut Court of Justice and it appears to the judge that for any reason the charge should be prosecuted by indictment, the judge may, at any time before the accused has entered a defence, decide not to adjudicate and shall then inform the accused of the decision and continue the proceedings as a preliminary inquiry.

(2) If subject-matter is a testamentary instrument or exceeds $5,000 in value — Nunavut — If an accused is before a judge of the Nunavut Court of Justice charged with an indictable offence mentioned in paragraph 553(a) or subparagraph 553(b)(i), and, at any time before the judge makes an adjudication, the evidence establishes that the subject-matter of the offence is a testamentary instrument or that its value exceeds five thousand dollars, the judge shall put the accused to an election in accordance with subsection 536.1(2).

(3) Continuation as preliminary inquiry — Nunavut — If an accused is put to an election under subsection (2) and the accused elects to have a preliminary inquiry and to be tried by a judge without a jury or a court composed of a judge and jury or does not elect when put to the election, the judge shall continue the proceedings as a preliminary inquiry under Part XVIII and, if the judge orders the accused to stand trial, the judge shall endorse on the information and, if the accused is in custody, on the warrant of committal, a statement showing the nature of the election of the acccused or that the accused did not elect, as the case may be.

(4) Continuing proceedings — Nunavut — If an accused is put to an election under subsection (2), and the accused elects to be tried by a judge without a jury and without having a preliminary inquiry, the judge shall endorse on the information a record of the election and continue with the trial.

(5) Application to Nunavut — This section and not section 555, applies in respect of criminal proceedings in Nunavut.

1999, c. 3, s. 39.

556. (1) Corporation — An accused corporation shall appear by counsel or agent.

(2) Non-appearance — Where an accused corporation does not appear pursuant to a summons and service of the summons on the corporation is proved, the provincial court judge, or in Nunavut, the judge of the Nunavut Court of Justice

(a) may, if the charge is one over which he has absolute jurisdiction, proceed with the trial of the charge in the absence of the accused corporation; and

(b) shall, if the charge is not one over which he has absolute jurisdiction, hold a preliminary inquiry in accordance with Part XVIII in the absence of the accused corporation.

(3) Corporation not electing — Where an accused corporation appears but does not elect when put to an election under subsection 536(2) or 536.1(2), the provincial court judge or judge of the Nunavut Court of Justice shall hold a preliminary inquiry in accordance with Part XVIII.

R.S., c. C-34, s. 486; R.S. 1985, c. 27 (1st Supp.), s. 107; 1999, c. 3, s. 40.

Commentary: The section governs elections and appearances by *corporate accused*. Under s. 556(1), a corporate accused must appear by *counsel or agent*. Where a corporate accused fails to elect under s. 536(2), the provincial court judge must hold a preliminary inquiry under Part XVIII. Where a corporate accused, proven to have been duly summoned, fails to appear by counsel or agent for trial, a provincial court judge *may* proceed with a trial in D's absence, where the offence is listed in s. 553, but *shall* hold a preliminary inquiry in D's absence otherwise.

Case Law

R. v. Black & Decker (1974), 15 C.C.C. (2d) 193 (S.C.C.) — An amalgamated corporation is liable for an offence committed by the amalgamating companies prior to the amalgamation.

Related Provisions: Process is served on a corporation under s. 703.2. Sections 620–623, applicable to Part XIX under s. 572, described the trial procedure in relation to corporate accused. The applicable punishment provisions appear in s. 735.

The provisions of the section are applicable to preliminary inquiries under s. 538, with such modification as the circumstances require.

557. Taking evidence — If an accused is tried by a provincial court judge or a judge of the Nunavut Court of Justice in accordance with this Part, the evidence of witnesses for the prosecutor and the accused shall be taken in accordance with the provisions of Part XVIII relating to preliminary inquiries.

R.S., c. C-34, s. 487; R.S. 1985, c. 27 (1st Supp.), s. 203; 1999, c. 3, s. 41.

Commentary: The section requires that evidence given in trials before a provincial court judge under Part XIX be taken in accordance with Part XVIII relating to preliminary inquiries.

Related Provisions: Section 540 provides for the manner in which evidence shall be taken when given upon a preliminary inquiry. It also applies to jury trials under Part XX by s. 646.

Jurisdiction of Judges

Judge's Jurisdiction with Consent

558. Trial by judge without a jury — If an accused who is charged with an indictable offence, other than an offence mentioned in section 469, elects under section 536 or 536.1 or re-elects under section 561 or 561.1 to be tried by a judge without a jury, the accused shall, subject to this Part, be tried by a judge without a jury.

R.S., c. C-34, s. 488; R.S. 1985, c. 27 (1st Supp.), s. 108; 1999, c. 3, s. 41.

Commentary: Under this section, D, charged with an indictable offence *not* listed in s. 469, who elects under s. 536 or re-elects under s. 561 to be tried by a *judge without a jury*, will be tried according to Part XIX.

Related Provisions: The general rule that mode of trial follows D's election or re-election in relation to non-s. 469 indictable offences may be defeated under s. 567 (differing elections by several jointly charged accused), and under s. 568 (Attorney General requires jury trial).

Charter s. 11(f) guarantees the right to a jury trial, where the maximum punishment for the offence is imprisonment for five years or a more severe punishment. D's election of trial by provincial court judge or judge alone in respect of such offences presumably constitutes a waiver of such right. Where s. 567 is applicable, D is *deemed* to have elected trial by judge and jury.

Under s. 566, D will be tried on an indictment in Form 4, including counts authorized by ss. 574 and 576(1). D may not be indicted directly under s. 577.

"Judge" is defined in s. 552.

559. (1) Court of record — A judge who holds a trial under this Part shall, for all purposes thereof and proceedings connected therewith or relating thereto, be a court of record.

(2) Custody of records — The record of a trial that a judge holds under this Part shall be kept in the court over which the judge presides.

R.S., c. C-34, s. 489.

Commentary: The section makes a judge conducting a trial under Part XIX a *court of record* for all purposes. Under s. 559(2), the records are kept in the court where the judge presides.

Case Law

Vickery v. Nova Scotia (Prothonotary of the Supreme Court) (1991), 64 C.C.C. (3d) 65 (S.C.C.) — The court, as custodian of exhibits produced at trial, is entitled to regulate their use. It may deny public access after once the trial has been completed, where there is a need to protect the innocent.

Related Provisions: "Court of record" is *not* defined under this Part nor generally for the purposes of the *Code*. "Judge" is defined in s. 552. Although a "provincial court judge" is authorized to conduct trials under Part XIX (ss. 553–554), there is no mention of "provincial court judge" in s. 559, unless "judge" is accorded a generic rather than its defined meaning.

Election

560. (1) Duty of judge — If an accused elects, under section 536 or 536.1 to have a preliminary inquiry and to be tried by a judge without a jury, a judge having jurisdiction shall,

    (a) on receiving a written notice from the sheriff or other person having custody of the accused stating that the accused is in custody and setting out the nature of the charge against him, or

    (b) on being notified by the clerk of the court that the accused is not in custody and of the nature of the charge against him,

fix a time and place for the trial of the accused.

(2) Notice by sheriff, when given — The sheriff or other person having custody of the accused shall give the notice mentioned in paragraph (1)(*a*) within twenty-four hours after the accused is ordered to stand trial, if he is in custody pursuant to that order or if, at the time of the order, he is in custody for any other reason.

(3) Duty of sheriff when date set for trial — Where, pursuant to subsection (1), a time and place is fixed for the trial of an accused who is in custody, the accused

    (a) shall be notified forthwith by the sheriff or other person having custody of the accused of the time and place so fixed; and

    (b) shall be produced at the time and place so fixed.

(4) Duty of accused when not in custody — Where an accused is not in custody, the duty of ascertaining from the clerk of the court the time and place fixed for the trial, pursuant to subsection (1), is on the accused, and he shall attend for his trial at the time and place so fixed.

(5) [Repealed R.S. 1985, c. 27 (1st Supp.), s. 109(2).]

        R.S., c. C-34, s. 490; R.S. 1985, c. 27 (1st Supp.), ss. 101(3), 109; 1999, c. 3, s. 42.

Commentary: The section describes the procedure to fix a *time* and *place* for a trial by judge *alone*, after election under s. 536(2).

Where D is *in custody*, for any reason, a sheriff or jailer must, within 24 hours of the order to stand trial, advise a judge having trial jurisdiction of the fact of custody and the nature of the offence charged. Where D is *not in custody*, the clerk of the court is obliged to so notify a judge and further disclose the nature of the charge against D. Receipt of notification obliges the judge, under s. 560(1), to fix a time and place for D's trial.

Under s. 560(3), where D is *in custody*, the time and place fixed for trial under s. 560(1) is to be conveyed to D forthwith by the sheriff or gaoler. D must be produced at the time and place so fixed. Where D is *not in custody*, s. 560(4) requires D to ascertain and attend at the time and place fixed for trial.

Related Provisions: *Re-election* rights are given under s. 561 and the procedure to be followed thereafter under ss. 562–563. The offences which may be included in the indictment are described in ss. 574 and 576(1), applicable to Part XIX by ss. 566(3) and 572.

561. (1) Right to re-elect — An accused who elects or is deemed to have elected a mode of trial other than trial by a provincial court judge may re-elect,

    (a) at any time before or after the completion of the preliminary inquiry, with the written consent of the prosecutor, to be tried by a provincial court judge;

    (b) at any time before the completion of the preliminary inquiry or before the fifteenth day following the completion of the preliminary inquiry, as of right, another mode of trial other than trial by a provincial court judge; and

(c) on or after the fifteenth day following the completion of the preliminary inquiry, any mode of trial with the written consent of the prosecutor.

(2) **Idem** — An accused who elects to be tried by a provincial court judge may, not later than fourteen days before the day first appointed for the trial, re-elect as of right another mode of trial, and may do so thereafter with the written consent of the prosecutor.

(3) **Notice** — Where an accused wishes to re-elect under subsection (1) before the completion of the preliminary inquiry, the accused shall give notice in writing that he wishes to re-elect, together with the written consent of the prosecutor, where that consent is required, to the justice presiding at the preliminary inquiry who shall on receipt of the notice,

(a) in the case of a re-election under paragraph (1)(b), put the accused to his re-election in the manner set out in subsection (7); or

(b) where the accused wishes to re-elect under paragraph (1)(a) and the justice is not a provincial court judge, notify a provincial court judge or clerk of the court of the accused's intention to re-elect and send to the provincial court judge or clerk the information and any promise to appear, undertaking or recognizance given or entered into in accordance with Part XVI, or any evidence taken before a coroner, that is in the possession of the justice.

(4) **Idem** — Where an accused wishes to re-elect under section (2), the accused shall give notice in writing that he wishes to re-elect together with the written consent of the prosecutor, where that consent is required, to the provincial court judge before whom the accused appeared and pleaded or to a clerk of the court.

(5) **Notice and transmitting record** — Where an accused wishes to re-elect under subsection (1) after the completion of the preliminary inquiry, the accused shall give notice in writing that he wishes to re-elect, together with the written consent of the prosecutor, where such consent is required, to a judge or clerk of the court of his original election who shall, on receipt of the notice, notify the judge or provincial court judge or clerk of the court by which the accused wishes to be tried of the accused's intention to re-elect and send to that judge or provincial court judge or clerk the information, the evidence, the exhibits and the statement, if any, of the accused taken down in writing under section 541 and any promise to appear, undertaking or recognizance given or entered into in accordance with Part XVI, or any evidence taken before a coroner, that is in the possession of the first-mentioned judge or clerk.

(6) **Time and place for re-election** — Where a provincial court judge or judge or clerk of the court is notified under paragraph (3)(b) or subsection (4) or (5) that the accused wishes to re-elect, the provincial court judge or judge shall forthwith appoint a time and place for the accused to re-elect and shall cause notice thereof to be given to the accused and the prosecutor.

(7) **Proceedings on re-election** — The accused shall attend or, if he is in custody, shall be produced at the time and place appointed under subsection (6) and shall, after

(a) the charge on which he has been ordered to stand trial or the indictment, where an indictment has been preferred pursuant to section 566, 574 or 577 or is filed with the court before which the indictment is to be preferred pursuant to section 577, or

(b) in the case of a re-election under subsection (1) before the completion of the preliminary inquiry or under subsection (2), the information has been read to the accused, be put to his re-election in the following words or in words to the like effect: You have given notice of your wish to re-elect the mode of your trial. You now have the option to do so. How do you wish to re-elect?

R.S., c. C-34, s. 491; R.S. 1985, c. 27 (1st Supp.), s. 110.

Commentary: The section defines the *rights and procedure of re-election.*

Sections 561(1), (3) and (5) describe the rights and procedure of re-election where the actual or deemed *election* by D is a mode of trial *other than trial by a provincial court judge.* Under s. 561(1), and subject to its terms, D may *re-elect* to be tried by a *provincial court judge or another mode* of trial. Where D wishes to re-elect under s. 561(1) to be tried by a provincial court judge or a mode of trial other than the original election, compliance must be made with s. 561(3). Where D wishes to re-elect any mode of trial after the completion of the preliminary inquiry, D must comply with s. 561(5).

Sections 561(2) and (4) designate the rights and procedure of *re-election* where D's *original* election was trial by a *provincial court judge.*

The formal re-election process of ss. 561(6) and (7) requires that the relevant charge be read from the indictment or information, as the case may be, and D asked about his re-election in the words of s. 561(7), or words to like effect.

Case Law
Consent of Prosecutor

R. v. Newsom, (February 22, 1988), Doc. No. CA006911 (B.C. C.A.) — P's decision *not* to consent to re-election is *not* reviewable where the refusal reflects a concern that re-election might necessitate an adjournment of the trial.

R. v. E. (L.) (1994), 94 C.C.C. (3d) 228 (Ont. C.A.) — There is *no* common law or *Code* authoritiy for a trial judge to disregard the requirements of s. 561 concerning re-election.

P's discretion to withhold consent to re-election under s. 561(1)(c) is *not* an unfettered right. It cannot be reviewed unless there has been an abuse of process through oppressive proceedings by P. D must show that the exercise of discretion is arbitrary, capricious or based upon some improper motive to invite consideration whether there has been an abuse of process, hence infringement of *Charter* s. 7.

Procedural Considerations

Korponey v. Canada (A.G.) (1982), 26 C.R. (3d) 343, 65 C.C.C. (2d) 65 (S.C.C.) — D may waive the procedural steps enacted for his benefit if the *waiver* is *clear* and *unequivocal* that D is doing so with full *knowledge* of the rights the procedure was enacted to protect and of the effect the waiver would have on those rights in the process.

R. v. Garcia (1990), 75 C.R. (3d) 250 (B.C. C.A.) — A re-election, like the original election, is made in recognition of P's right, under s. 574(1)(b), to add or substitute counts based upon evidence given at the preliminary inquiry. A re-election on the original charge is deemed to be a re-election in respect of any other charge included under s. 574(1)(b).

Charter Considerations

R. v. Forbes (1987), 89 A.R. 76 (Q.B.) — The refusal to permit a re-election by D to judge alone on the date of the trial by judge and jury does *not* violate D's rights under *Charter* s. 11.

Koleff v. R. (1987), 33 C.C.C. (3d) 460 (Man. Q.B.) — The requirement that consent to re-election during the preliminary inquiry violates neither *Charter* s. 7 nor s. 15.

Related Provisions: Section 565 describes the circumstances in which D is deemed to have elected trial by judge and jury. Sections 561(2) and (3), afford rights of re-election.

Sections 562 and 563 describe the procedure to be followed after re-election.

561.1 (1) Right to re-elect — Nunavut — An accused who has elected or is deemed to have elected a mode of trial may re-elect any other mode of trial at any time with the written consent of the prosecutor, except that an accused who has had a preliminary inquiry may not elect to be tried by a judge without a jury and without having had a preliminary inquiry.

(2) **Right to re-elect — Nunavut** — An accused who has elected to be tried by a judge without a jury and without a preliminary inquiry may, as of right, re-elect to be tried by any other mode of trial at any time up to 14 days before the day first appointed for the trial.

(3) **Right to re-elect — Nunavut** — An accused who has elected to be tried by a judge and jury or to have a preliminary inquiry and to be tried by a judge without jury may, as of right, re-elect to be tried by the other mode of trial at any time before the completion of the preliminary inquiry or before the fifteenth day following its completion.

(4) **Notice of re-election under subsection (1) or (3) — Nunavut** — If an accused wishes to re-elect under subsection (1) or (3), before the completion of the preliminary inquiry, the accused shall give notice in writing of the wish to re-elect, together with the written consent of the prosecutor, if that consent is required, to the justice of the peace or judge presiding at the preliminary inquiry who shall on receipt of the notice put the accused to a re-election in the manner set out in subsection (9).

(5) **Notice of re-election under subsection (1) — Nunavut** — If an accused wishes to re-elect under subsection (1) to be tried by a judge without a jury and without having had a preliminary inquiry and a justice of the peace is presiding at the preliminary inquiry, the justice of the peace shall notify a judge or a clerk or the Nunavut Court of Justice of the accused's intention to re-elect and send to the judge or clerk the information and any promise to appear, undertaking or recognizance given or entered into in accordance with Part XVI, or any evidence taken before a coroner, that is in the possession of the justice of the peace.

(6) **Notice of re-election under subsection (1) or (3) — Nunavut** — If an accused wishes to re-elect under subsection (1) or (3) after the completion of a preliminary inquiry or after having elected a trial by judge without a jury and without having had a preliminary inquiry, the accused shall give notice in writing of the wish to re-elect together with the written consent of the prosecutor, if that consent is required, to the judge before whom the accused appeared and pleaded or to a clerk of the Nunavut Court of Justice.

(7) **Notice of re-election under subsection (2) — Nunavut** — If an accused wishes to re-elect under subsection (2), the accused shall give notice in writing of the wish to re-elect to the judge before whom the accused appeared and pleaded or to a clerk of the Nunavut Court of Justice.

(8) **Time and place for re-election — Nunavut** — On receipt of a notice given under any of subsections (4) to (7) that the accused wishes to re-elect, a judge shall immediately appoint a time and place for the accused to re-elect and shall cause notice of the time and place to be given to the accused and the prosecutor.

(9) **Proceedings on re-election — Nunavut** — The accused shall attend or, if in custody, shall be produced at the time and place appointed under subsection (8) and shall, after

(a) the charge on which the accused has been ordered to stand trial or the indictment, if an indictment has been preferred pursuant to section 566, 574 or 577 or is filed with the court before which the indictment is to be preferred pursuant to section 577, or

(b) in the case of a re-election under subsection (1) or (3), before the completion of the preliminary inquiry or under subsection (2), the information

has been read to the accused, be put to a re-election in the following words or in words
to the like effect:

> You have given notice of your wish to re-elect the mode of your trial. You now
> have the option to do so. How do you wish to re-elect?

(10) **Application to Nunavut** — This section, and not section 561, applies in respect
of criminal proceedings in Nunavut.

1999, c. 3, s. 43.

562. (1) **Proceedings following re-election** — Where the accused re-elects under
paragraph 561(1)(*a*) before the completion of the preliminary inquiry or under subsection 561(1) after the completion of the preliminary inquiry, the provincial court judge
or judge, as the case may be, shall proceed with the trial or appoint a time and place for
the trial.

(2) **Idem** — Where the accused re-elects under paragraph 561(1)(*b*) before the completion of the preliminary inquiry or under subsection 561(2), the justice shall proceed
with the preliminary inquiry.

R.S., c. C-34, s. 492; R.S. 1985, c. 27 (1st Supp.), s. 110.

Commentary: Under s. 562(1), where D *re-elects* to be tried by a *provincial court judge* under s.
561(1)(a) *before* the *completion* of the preliminary inquiry, or under s. 561(1) *after* the *completion* of the
preliminary inquiry, the provincial court judge or judge must either proceed with the *trial* or fix a date
for trial.

Under s. 562(2), where the re-election is for a mode of trial other than a trial by a provincial court judge,
the justice must proceed to hold a *preliminary inquiry*.

Related Provisions: Section 563 enacts the procedure to be followed on re-election for trial by a
provincial court judge.

Trial procedure under Part XIX is, in practical terms, the trial procedure of Part XX, incorporated by s.
572.

562.1 (1) Proceedings following re-election — Nunavut — If the accused re-elects under subsection 561.1(1) to be tried by a judge without a jury and without a
preliminary inquiry, the judge shall proceed with the trial or appoint a time and place
for the trial.

(2) **Proceedings following re-election — Nunavut** — If the accused re-elects
under section 561.1 before the completion of the preliminary inquiry to be tried by
judge and jury or to have a preliminary inquiry and to be tried by a judge without a
jury, the justice of the peace or judge shall proceed with the preliminary inquiry.

(3) **Application to Nunavut** — This section, and not section 562, applies in respect
of criminal proceedings in Nunavut.

1999, c. 3, s. 44.

**563. Proceedings on re-election to be tried by provincial court judge
without jury** — Where an accused re-elects under section 561 to be tried by a
provincial court judge,

> (a) the accused shall be tried on the information that was before the justice at the
> preliminary inquiry, subject to any amendments thereto that may be allowed by
> the provincial court judge by whom the accused is tried; and

814

(b) the provincial court judge before whom the re-election is made shall endorse on the information a record of the re-election.

R.S., c. C-34, s. 493; R.S. 1985, c. 27 (1st Supp.), s. 110.

Commentary: Where D *re-elects* under s. 561 to be tried by *a provincial court judge*, the trial is held on the original information, subject to any amendments made at trial by the presiding judge. The provincial court judge before whom D re-elects must record the re-election on the information.

Case Law

Matheson v. R. (1981), 22 C.R. (3d) 289, 59 C.C.C. (2d) 289 (S.C.C.) — D may be convicted *only* on evidence legally adduced before the trier of fact in the course of the trial. Evidence *not* actually adduced before the trial judge cannot form part of the trial. Where D re-elects trial by provincial court judge during the preliminary inquiry and after the taking of evidence, the evidence adduced prior to the re-election cannot be considered at the trial without the *consent* of D and P. The evidence must be entered into the record of the trial by filing the transcripts or by making some reference to them in the trial proceedings.

Related Provisions: The authority to *amend* an information at trial is found in s. 601, applicable to Part XIX trials under s. 572.

Re-election for trial before a provincial court judge may be made under ss. 561(1)(a) and (c). The procedure is described in ss. 561(3) and (5)–(7).

563.1 (1) Proceedings on re-election to be tried by judge without jury — Nunavut — If an accused re-elects under section 561.1 to be tried by a judge without a jury and without having a preliminary inquiry,

(a) the accused shall be tried on the information that was before the justice of the peace or judge at the preliminary inquiry, subject to any amendments that may be allowed by the judge by whom the accused is tried; and

(b) the judge before whom the re-election is made shall endorse on the information a record of the re-election.

(2) Application to Nunavut — This section, and not section 563 applies in respect of criminal proceedings in Nunavut.

1999, c. 3, s. 45.

564. [Repealed R.S. 1985, c. 27 (1st Supp.), s. 110.]

565. (1) Election deemed to have been made — Subject to subsection (1.1), if an accused is ordered to stand trial for an offence that, under this Part, may be tried by a judge without a jury, the accused shall, for the purposes of the provisions of this Part relating to election and re-election, be deemed to have elected to be tried by a court composed of a judge and jury if

(a) he was ordered to stand trial by a provincial court judge who, pursuant to subsection 555(1), continued the proceedings before him as a preliminary inquiry;

(b) the justice, provincial court judge or judge, as the case may be, declined pursuant to section 567 to record the election or re-election of the accused; or

(c) the accused does not elect when put to an election under section 536.

(1.1) Nunavut — With respect to criminal proceedings in Nunavut, if an accused is ordered to stand trial for an offence that, under this Part, may be tried by a judge without a jury, the accused shall, for the purposes of the provisions of this Part relating to election and re-election, be deemed to have elected to be tried by a court composed of a judge and jury if

    (a) the accused was ordered to stand trial by a judge who, under subsection 555.1(1), continued to the proceedings as a preliminary inquiry;

    (b) the justice of the peace or judge, as the case may be, declined pursuant to subseciton 567.1(1) to record the election or re-election of the accused; or

    (c) the accused did not elect when put to an election under section 536.1.

(2) Where direct indictment preferred — Where an accused is to be tried after an indictment has been preferred against him pursuant to a consent or order given under section 577, the accused shall, for the purposes of the provisions of this Part relating to election and re-election, be deemed to have elected to be tried by a court composed of a judge and jury and may, with the written consent of the prosecutor, re-elect to be tried by a judge without a jury.

(3) Notice of re-election — Where an accused wishes to re-elect under subsection (2), he shall give notice in writing that he wishes to re-elect, together with the written consent of the prosecutor, to a judge or clerk of the court where the indictment has been filed or preferred who shall, on receipt of the notice, notify a judge having jurisdiction or clerk of the court by which the accused wishes to be tried of the accused's intention to re-elect and send to that judge or clerk the indictment and any promise to appear, undertaking or recognizance given or entered into in accordance with Part XVI, any summons or warrant issued under section 578, or any evidence taken before a coroner, that is in the possession of the first-mentioned judge or clerk.

(4) Application — Subsections 561(6) and (7), or subsections 561.1(8) and (9), as the case may be, apply to a re-election made under subsection (3).

           R.S., c. C-34, s. 495; R.S. 1985, c. 27 (1st Supp.), s. 111; 1999, c. 3, s. 46.

Commentary: The section describes the circumstances under which D shall be *deemed* to have *elected* trial by *judge and jury*, for the purposes of the election and re-election provisions of Part XIX, and makes further provision for re-election.

Under ss. 565(1) and (2), D is *deemed* to have elected trial by *judge and jury* where

(a)   D was *ordered to stand trial* by a provincial court judge in *proceedings continued as* a *preliminary inquiry* under s. 555(1);

(b)   D's *election* was *not recorded* under s. 567;

(c)   D *failed to elect* under s. 536; or,

(d)   a *direct indictment* was preferred against D, by consent or order under s. 577.

Under s. 565(2), where D has been *indicted directly* under s. 577, *re-election* may be made for trial by a judge without a jury, with the *written consent* of P. The procedural steps necessary to give effect to this right of re-election are described in ss. 565(3) and (4) and ss. 561(6) and (7).

Related Provisions: An indictment is *filed* when lodged with the clerk of the trial court but is *preferred* only when it is lodged with the trial court at the opening of D's trial with a court ready to proceed with the trial.

Trial

566. (1) Indictment — The trial of an accused for an indictable offence, other than a trial before a provincial court judge, shall be on an indictment in writing setting forth the offence with which he is charged.

(2) Preferring indictment — Where an accused elects under section 536 or re-elects under section 561 to be tried by a judge without a jury, an indictment in Form 4 may be preferred.

(3) What counts may be included and who may prefer indictment — Section 574 and subsection 576(1) apply, with such modifications as the circumstances require, to the preferring of an indictment pursuant to subsection (2).

R.S., c. C-34, s. 496; R.S. 1985, c. 27 (1st Supp.), s. 111; 1997, c. 18, s. 67.

Commentary: The section describes the charging document on which D will be tried where the trial is *not* before a provincial court judge.

Where D is tried under Part XIX, upon election or re-election for trial before a judge alone, the trial will take place on an *indictment*, in writing, in Form 4, setting forth the offence charged. The charges which may be included in the indictment are determined by s. 574, made applicable to Part XIX trials by s. 566(3). No direct indictment may be preferred under s. 577.

Case Law

Preferment Authority: S. 566(3)

R. v. Tapaquon (1993), 26 C.R. (4th) 193, 87 C.C.C. (3d) 1 (S.C.C.); reversing (1992), 71 C.C.C. (3d) 50 (Sask. C.A.) — In *non-jury* trials, P may *prefer* an *indictment* on *any* charge on which D has been ordered to stand trial, as well as on any charge founded on the facts disclosed by the evidence given at the preliminary inquiry, provided it is *not* an offence charged in the information on which D was *not* ordered to stand trial.

Where D has elected trial by judge alone, s. 566 prevents P from preferring an indictment under s. 577 in respect of any offence upon which D has been discharged. Where P wishes to have D stand trial on a charge upon which D has been discharged after preliminary inquiry, P may invoke s. 568 which requires a jury trial and renders s. 577 applicable. In other instances, a new information may be laid, subject to the application of the doctrine of abuse of process.

Related Provisions: The applicable rules of pleading are found in ss. 581–593 and 601.

Trials before a provincial court judge are held on an information, in accordance with s. 563.

566.1 (1) Indictment — Nunavut — The trial of an accused for an indictable offence, other than an indictable offence mentioned in section 553 or an offence in respect of which the accused has elected or re-elected to be tried by a judge without a jury without having had a preliminary inquiry, shall be on an indictment in writing setting forth the offence with which the accused is charged.

(2) Preferring indictment — Nunavut — If an accused elects under section 536.1 or re-elects under section 561.1 to have a preliminary inquiry and to be tried by a judge without a jury, an indictment in Form 4 may be preferred.

(3) What counts may be included and who may prefer indictment — Nunavut — Section 574 and subsection 576(1) apply, with any modifications that the circumstances require, to the preferring of an indictment under subsection (2).

(4) Application to Nunavut — This section, and not section 566, applies in respect of criminal proceedings in Nunavut.

1999, c. 3, s. 47.

General

567. Mode of trial where two or more accused — Notwithstanding any other provision of this Part, where two or more persons are charged with the same offence, unless all of them elect or re-elect or are deemed to have elected, as the case may be, the same mode of trial, the justice, provincial court judge or judge

    (a) may decline to record any election, re-election or deemed election for trial by a provincial court judge or a judge without a jury; and

    (b) if he declines to do so, shall hold a preliminary inquiry unless a preliminary inquiry has been held prior to the election, re-election or deemed election.

R.S., c. C-34, s. 497; R.S. 1985, c. 27 (1st Supp.), s. 111.

Commentary: The section operates notwithstanding any other provision in Part XIX and applies to cases where two or more persons are charged with the same offence. Unless all accused elect, re-elect or are deemed to have elected the same mode of trial, the justice, provincial court judge or judge, as the case may be, *may* decline to record any election, re-election or deemed election for trial by provincial court judge or judge alone and, having declined to do so, must hold a preliminary inquiry, unless one has already been held.

The section guards against the unnecessary duplication of proceedings in respect of accused jointly charged with the same offence, absent traditional grounds for separate trials. The language of the section, however, would *not* appear limited to charges contained in a single information.

Case Law

British Columbia (A.G.) v. Niedzwieki (1981), 57 C.C.C. (2d) 184 (B.C. S.C.) — The preliminary hearing of one accused may not be combined with the trial of another accused jointly charged, even without objection by D.

Related Provisions: The exercise of the authority of this section deems D to have elected trial by judge and jury under s. 565(1)(b). D's right of re-election, in the usual case of deemed elections set out in s. 561(1), may not be operative, depending upon the effect to be given to the introductory words "notwithstanding any other provisions of this Part ..." in s. 567.

567.1 (1) Mode of trial if two or more accused — Nunavut — Despite any other provision of this Part, if two or more persons are charged with the same indictable offence, unless all of them elect or re-elect or are deemed to have elected, as the case may be, the same mode of trial, the justice of the peace or judge

    (a) may decline to record any election, re-election or deemed election

        (i) for trial by a judge without a jury and without having a preliminary inquiry, or

        (ii) to have a preliminary inquiry and to be tried by a judge without a jury; and

    (b) if the justice of the peace or judge declines to do so, shall hold a preliminary inquiry unless a preliminary inquiry has been held prior to the election, re-election or deemed election.

(2) Application to Nunavut — This section, and not section 567, applies in respect of criminal proceedings in Nunavut.

1999, c. 3, s. 48.

568. Attorney General may require trial by jury — The Attorney General may, notwithstanding that an accused elects under section 536 or re-elects under section 561 to be tried by a judge or provincial court judge, as the case may be, require the accused to be tried by a court composed of a judge and jury, unless the alleged offence is one that is punishable with imprisonment for five years or less, and where the Attorney General so requires, a judge or provincial court judge has no jurisdiction to try the accused under this Part and a preliminary inquiry shall be held before a justice unless a preliminary inquiry has been held prior to the requirement by the Attorney General that the accused be tried by a court composed of a judge and jury.

R.S., c. C-34, s. 498; R.S. 1985, c. 27 (1st Supp.), s. 111.

Commentary: Under this section the *Attorney General* may *require* a *jury trial* notwithstanding D's election (s. 536) or re-election (s. 561) to be tried by a court composed of a judge sitting without a jury, or a provincial court judge.

The authority of the Attorney General may only be exercised where D has first elected or re-elected another mode of trial. It cannot, for example, be invoked where the offence is listed in s. 553. Further, the offence must *not* be one *punishable* with *imprisonment* of five years or less. The requirement of the Attorney General ousts the jurisdiction of a judge or provincial court judge to try D, in accordance with his/her election or re-election, and requires the holding of a preliminary inquiry into the charge, unless one has already been held. Unless D is discharged at the conclusion of the preliminary inquiry, the trial will be held before a court composed of a judge and jury.

The section may be vulnerable to *Charter* ss. 7 and 15 challenge.

Case Law

R. v. Tapaquon (1993), 26 C.R. (4th) 193, 87 C.C.C. (3d) 1 (S.C.C.); reversing (1992), 71 C.C.C. (3d) 50 (Sask. C.A.) — See digest under s. 566, *supra*.

Related Provisions: D has *no* right of re-election where the Attorney General has acted under this section. "Attorney General" is defined in s. 2.

Trial procedure is governed by Part XX, incorporated by s. 572.

569. (1) Attorney General may require trial by jury — Nunavut — The Attorney General may, despite that an accused elects under section 536.1 or re-elects under section 561.1 to be tried by a judge without a jury and without having had a preliminary inquiry or to have a preliminary inquiry and to be tried by a judge without a jury, require the accused to be tried by a court composed of a judge and jury, unless the alleged offence is one that is punishable with imprisonment for five years or less, and if the Attorney General so requires, a judge has no jurisdiction to try the accused under this Part and a preliminary inquiry shall be held before a justice of the peace or a judge unless a preliminary inquiry has been held prior to the requirement by the Attorney General that the accused be tried by a court composed of a judge and jury.

(2) Application to Nunavut — This section, and not section 568, applies in respect of criminal proceedings in Nunavut.

1999, c. 3, s. 49

570. (1) Record of conviction or order — Where an accused who is tried under this Part is determined by a judge or provincial court judge to be guilty of an offence on acceptance of a plea of guilty or on a finding of guilt, the judge or provincial court judge, as the case may be, shall endorse the information accordingly and shall sentence the accused or otherwise deal with the accused in the manner authorized by law and, on request by the accused, the prosecutor, a peace officer, or any other person, shall cause a conviction in Form 35 and a certified copy of it, or an order in Form 36 and a certified copy of it, to be drawn up and shall deliver the certified copy to the person making the request.

(2) Acquittal and record of acquittal — Where an accused who is tried under this Part is found not guilty of an offence with which the accused is charged, the judge or provincial court judge, as the case may be, shall immediately acquit the accused in respect of that offence and shall cause an order in Form 37 to be drawn up, and on request shall make out and deliver to the accused a certified copy of the order.

(3) **Transmission of record** — Where an accused elects to be tried by a provincial court judge under this Part, the provincial court judge shall transmit the written charge, the memorandum of adjudication and the conviction, if any, into such custody as the Attorney General may direct.

(4) **Proof of conviction order or acquittal** — A copy of a conviction in Form 35 or of an order in Form 36 or 37, certified by the judge or by the clerk or other proper officer of the court, or by the provincial court judge, as the case may be, or proved to be a true copy, is, on proof of the identity of the person to whom the conviction or order relates, sufficient evidence in any legal proceedings to prove the conviction of that person or the making of the order against that person or his acquittal, as the case may be, for the offence mentioned in the copy of the conviction or order.

(5) **Warrant of committal** — Where an accused other than a corporation is convicted, the judge or provincial court judge, as the case may be, shall issue or cause to be issued a warrant of committal in Form 21, and section 528 applies in respect of a warrant of committal issued under this subsection.

(6) **Admissibility of certified copy** — Where a warrant of committal is issued by a clerk of a court, a copy of the warrant of committal, certified by the clerk, is admissible in evidence in any proceeding.

R.S., c. C-34, s. 500; R.S. 1985, c. 27 (1st Supp.), ss. 112, 203; 1994, c. 44, s. 59.

Commentary: The section describes the *record* made upon adjudication in trials under Part XIX.

Under s. 570(1), where D is *convicted*, the presiding judge or provincial court judge must endorse the information accordingly and sentence or otherwise deal with D according to law. Upon request by D, P, peace officer or any other person, a conviction in Form 35 or order in Form 36, as well as a certified copy, will be drawn up and delivered to the requesting party.

In provincial court trials, s. 570(3) requires delivery of the charge, memo of adjudication and any conviction to such custody as the Attorney General of the province directs. Upon conviction of an individual accused, a *warrant of committal* may be prepared under s. 570(5).

Section 570(4) authorizes the use of a conviction in Form 35 or order in Form 36 in proof of the facts there contained. The conviction or order must be certified by the judge, provincial court judge, clerk or other proper officer of the court, or otherwise be established to be a true copy of the original. Upon proof of D's identity, the *certified copy* is sufficient evidence in any legal proceedings to prove D's conviction or the making of such an order in relation to D for the offence described. By s. 570(6) a copy of the warrant of committal issued and certified by a clerk of a court is admissible in any proceeding.

Under s. 570(2), where D is found *not guilty*, the presiding judge or provincial court judge must immediately, cause an order in Form 37 to be drawn up and, on request, make out and deliver to D a certified copy of it.

Case Law
Shall Sentence The Accused

R. v. Nunner (1976), 30 C.C.C. (2d) 199 (Ont. C.A.) — There is a discretion to postpone sentencing if the postponement is for a legal purpose, as for example to ascertain the progress of an accused at school.

Warrant of Committal

R. v. Fuller (1968), 5 C.R.N.S. 148, [1969] 3 C.C.C. 348 (Man. C.A.) — The judicial function ends when the provincial court judge causes the conviction to be drawn up and sentences D. Issuance of the warrant of committal is a "mere ministerial act".

Ex parte Le Clerc (1973), 21 C.C.C. (2d) 16 (Que C.A.) — A warrant of committal which is in the form of a minute of conviction rather than the conventional for is valid if it contains all the essential elements of a warrant.

Related Provisions: Similar provisions in respect of summary conviction proceedings appear in ss. 804–808.

Records of conviction or acquittal may be relevant in subsequent proceedings for a variety of reasons, including the special pleas described in ss. 607–610. Proof of previous convictions may be adduced under s. 666 where D leads evidence of good character. Proof may be made under ss. 667 and 727, as well as under *C.E.A.* s. 12(2).

571. Adjournment — **A judge or provincial court judge acting under this Part may from time to time adjourn a trial until it is finally terminated.**

R.S., c. C-34, s. 501R.S. 1985, c. 27 (1st Supp.), s. 203.

Commentary: The section authorizes a judge or provincial court judge conducting a trial under Part XIX, to *adjourn* the trial from time to time until it is finally terminated.

Case Law [See also s. 650]

R. v. Heminger, [1969] 3 C.C.C. 201 (Man. C.A.) — A summary trial of an indictable offence may be adjourned for more than eight days without D's consent .

Related Provisions: The authority is not so restricted as that of a justice on a preliminary inquiry under s. 537(1)(a). In jury proceedings the authority to adjourn is found in ss. 645(2) and (3), with specific authority in cases of amendment in s. 601(5).

The general curative provisions of s. 485(1) hold jurisdiction over an offence *not* to be lost, *inter alia*, by failure to comply with the *Code* adjournment provisions.

The provision in s. 669.2 for the continuation of trial proceedings where the presiding judge or provincial court judge dies, or is, for any reason, unable to continue applies to Part XIX under s. 572.

572. Application of Parts XVI, XVIII, XX and XXIII — **The provisions of Part XVI, the provisions of Part XVIII relating to transmission of the record by a provincial court judge where he holds a preliminary inquiry, and the provisions of Parts XX and XXIII, in so far as they are not inconsistent with this Part, apply, with such modifications as the circumstances require to proceedings under this Part.**

R.S., c. C-34, s. 502; c. 2 (2d Supp.), s. 10; R.S. 1985, c. 27 (1st Supp.), s. 203.

Commentary: This section makes several other parts of the *Code* applicable to proceedings under Part XIX. Part XVI "Compelling Appearance of an Accused before a Justice and Interim Release", Part XVIII relating to the transmission of the record after preliminary inquiry (s. 551), Part XX, "Procedure in Jury Trials and General Provisions", and Part XXIII "Punishments, Fines, Forfeitures, Costs and Restitution of Property", to the extent they are not inconsistent with Part XIX, apply, with such modification as the circumstances require, to trials without jury.

Case Law

R. v. Prentice (1965), 47 C.R. 231, [1965] 4 C.C.C. 118 (B.C. C.A.) — By this section, a provincial court judge has the authority to hold a view under s. 652.

Related Provisions: The incorporated provisions apply to trials before a *provincial court judge* as defined in s. 2 and a "judge" as defined in s. 552. The procedure to be followed in non-jury trials, essentially duplicates the procedure in jury trials under Part XX, modified accordingly, and absent inconsistency with Part XIX.

PART XIX.1 — NUNAVUT COURT OF JUSTICE

573. (1) Nunavut Court of Justice — **The powers to be exercised and the duties and functions to be performed under this Act by a court of criminal jurisdiction, a summary conviction court, a judge, a provincial court judge, a justice or a justice of the peace may be exercised or performed by a judge of the Nunavut Court of Justice.**

(2) Status when exercising power — A power exercised or a duty or function performed by a judge of the Nunavut Court of Justice under subsection (1) is exercised or performed by that judge as a judge of a superior court.

(3) Interpretation — Subsection (2) does not authorize a judge of the Nunavut Court of Justice who is presiding at a preliminary inquiry to grant a remedy under section 24 of the *Canadian Charter of Rights and Freedoms*.

1999, c. 3, s. 50.

573.1 (1) Application for review — Nunavut — An application for review may be made by the Attorney General or the accused, or by any person directly affected by the decision or order, to a judge of the Court of Appeal of Nunavut in respect of a decision or order of a judge of the Nunavut Court of Justice

    (a) relating to a warrant or summons;

    (b) relating to the conduct of a preliminary inquiry, including an order under subsection 548(1);

    (c) relating to a subpoena;

    (d) relating to the publication or broadcasting of information or access to the court room for all or part of the proceedings;

    (e) to refuse to quash an information or indictment; or

    (f) relating to the detention, disposal or forfeiture of any thing seized under a warrant or order.

(2) Limitation — A decision or order may not be reviewed under this section if

    (a) the decision or order is of a kind that could only be made in a province or a territory other than Nunavut by a superior court of criminal jurisdiction or a judge as defined in section 552; or

    (b) another statutory right of review is available.

(3) Grounds of review — The judge of the Court of Appeal of Nunavut may grant relief under subsection (4) only if the judge is satisfied that

    (a) in the case of any decision or order mentioned in subsection (1),

        (i) the judge of the Nunavut Court of Justice failed to observe a principle of natural justice or failed or refused to exercise the judge's jurisdiction, or

        (ii) the decision or order was made as a result of an irrelevant consideration or for an improper purpose;

    (b) in the case of a decision or order mentioned in paragraph (1)(a), that

        (i) the judge failed to comply with a statutory requirement for the making of the deciaion or order,

        (ii) the decision or order was made in the absence of any evidence that a statutory requirement for the making of the decision or order was met,

        (iii) the decision or order was made as a result of reckless disregard for the truth, fraud, intentional misrepresentation of material facts or intentional omission to state material facts,

        (iv) the warrant is so vague or lacking in particularity that it authorizes an unreasonable search, or

        (v) the warrant lacks a material term or condition that is required by law;

(c) in the case of a decision or order mentioned in paragraph (1)(b), that the judge of the Nunavut Court of Justice

(i) failed to follow a mandatory provision of this Act relating to the conduct of a preliminary inquiry,

(ii) ordered the accused to stand trial when there was no evidence adduced on which a properly instructed jury acting reasonably could convict, or

(iii) discharged the accused when there was some evidence adduced on which a properly instructed jury acting reasonably could convict;

(d) in the case of a decision or order mentioned in paragraph (1)(c) or (d), that the judge of the Nunavut Court of Justice erred in law;

(e) in the case of a decision or order mentioned in paragraph (1)(e), that

(i) the information or indictment failed to give the accused notice of the charge,

(ii) the judge of the Nunavut Court of Justice did not have jurisdiction to try the offence, or

(iii) the provision creating the offence alleged to have been committed by the accused is unconstitutional; or

(f) in the case of a decision or order mentioned in paragraph (1)(f), that

(i) the judge failed to comply with a statutory requirement for the making of the decision or order,

(ii) the decision or order was made in the absence of any evidence that a statutory requirement for the making of the decision or order was met, or

(iii) the decision or order was made as a result of reckless disregard for the truth, fraud, intentional misrepresentation of material facts or intentional omission to state material facts.

(4) **Powers of judge** — On the hearing of the application for review, the judge of the Court of Appeal of Nunavut may do one or more of the following:

(a) order a judge of the Nunavut Court of Justice to do any act or thing that the judge or any other judge of that court failed or refused to do or has delayed in doing;

(b) prohibit or restrain a decision, order or proceeding of a judge of the Nunavut Court of Justice;

(c) declare invalid or unlawful, quash or set aside, in whole or in part, a decision, order or proceeding of a judge of the Nunavut Court of Justice;

(d) refer back for determination in accordance with any directions that the judge considers to be appropriate, a decision, order or proceeding of a judge of the Nunavut Court of Justice;

(e) grant any remedy under subsection 24(1) of the *Canadian Charter of Rights and Freedoms*;

(f) refuse to grant any relief if the judge is of the opinion that no substantial wrong or miscarriage of justice has occurred or that the subject-matter of the application should be determined at trial or on appeal; and

(g) dismiss the application.

(5) Interim orders — If an application for review is made, a judge of the Court of Appeal of Nunavut may make any interim order that the judge considers appropriate pending the final disposition of the application for review.

(6) Rules — A person who proposes to make an application for review shall do so in the manner and within the period that may be directed by rules of court, except that a judge of the Court of Appeal of Nunavut may at any time extend any period specified in the rules.

(7) Appeal — An appeal lies to the Court of Appeal of Nunavut against a decision or order made under subsection (4). The provisions of Part XXI apply, with any modifications that the circumstances require, to the appeal.

1999, c. 3, s. 50.

573.2 (1) Habeas corpus — *Habeas corpus* proceedings may be brought before a judge of the Court of Appeal of Nunavut in respect of an order made or warrant issued by a judge of the Nunavut Court of Justice, except where

(a) the order or warrant is of a kind that could only be made or issued in a province or a territory other than Nunavut by a superior court of criminal jurisdiciton or a judge as defined in section 552; or

(b) another statutory right of review or appeal is available.

(2) Exception — Despite subsection (1), *habeas corpus* proceedings may be brought before a judge of the Court of Appeal of Nunavut with respect to an order or warrant of a judge of the Nunavut Court of Justice if the proceedings are brought to challenge the constitutionality of a person's detention or confinement.

(3) Provisions apply — Subsections 784(2) to (6) apply in respect of any proceedings brought under subsection (1) or (2).

1999, c. 3, s. 50

PART XX — PROCEDURE IN JURY TRIALS AND GENERAL PROVISIONS

Preferring Indictment

574. (1) Prosecutor may prefer indictment — Subject to subsection (3) and section 577, the prosecutor may prefer an indictment against any person who has been ordered to stand trial in respect of

(a) any charge on which that person was ordered to stand trial, or

(b) any charge founded on the facts disclosed by the evidence taken on the preliminary inquiry, in addition to or in substitution for any charge on which that person was ordered to stand trial,

whether or not the charges were included in one information.

(2) Consent to inclusion of other charges — An indictment preferred under subsection (1) may, if the accused consents, include any charge that is not referred to in paragraph (1)(*a*) or (*b*), and the offence charged may be dealt with, tried and determined and punished in all respects as if it were an offence in respect of which the accused had been ordered to stand trial, but if the offence was committed wholly in a

province other than that in which the accused is before the court, subsection 478(3) applies.

(3) **Private prosecutor requires consent** — In any prosecution conducted by a prosecutor other than the Attorney General and in which the Attorney General does not intervene, an indictment shall not be preferred under subsection (1) before any court without the written order of a judge of that court.

R.S., c. C-34, s. 504; R.S. 1985, c. 27 (1st Supp.), s. 113.

Commentary: The section, applicable where there has been a *preliminary inquiry* at which D has been ordered to stand trial, describes *who* may prefer an indictment and *what* charges may be included therein.

The *general rule* of s. 574(1) is that P may prefer an indictment against D, who has been ordered to stand trial, upon *any charge* on which D has been *ordered to stand trial* or, in *addition* thereto *or* in *substitution* therefor, *any charge founded upon the facts disclosed by the evidence taken upon the preliminary inquiry*. This preferment authority requires *no* consent. The section expressly authorizes the joinder in a single indictment of charges contained in separate informations, thereby obviating a multiplicity of proceedings. The general rule of the subsection is, however, expressly made subject to the provisions of s. 574(3), in cases of private prosecutions, and s. 577 in relation to direct indictments.

In any indictment preferred under s. 574(1), s. 574(2) authorizes the inclusion of *any other charge* to which D *consents*, except that, where the other offence was committed in another province, s. 478(3) applies to permit proceedings in respect thereof only where the offence is *not* listed in s. 469 and D pleads guilty thereto. An offence added under s. 574(2) is dealt with, tried, determined and, where applicable, punished, as if it were an offence in respect of which D had been ordered to stand trial.

Section 574(3) applies to *private prosecutions*, i.e., where an agent of the Attorney General neither prosecutes nor intervenes in the proceedings. An indictment may be preferred under s. 574(1) by a private prosecutor upon the *written* order of a judge of the trial court.

Case Law

Preferment Authority: S. 574(1)(b)

R. v. Tapaquon (1993), 26 C.R. (4th) 193, 87 C.C.C. (3d) 1 (S.C.C.); reversing (1992), 71 C.C.C. (3d) 50 (Sask. C.A.) — The refusal of a justice to order D to stand trial after preliminary inquiry in respect of an offence charged in an information amounts to a judicial determination that the charge is *not* founded on the facts disclosed by the evidence for the purpose of *Code* s. 574. The requirement that a justice specify the charges in respect of which D is ordered to stand trial means that, with respect to other charges contained in the information, D is *discharged*.

R. v. Tapaquon (1993), 26 C.R. (4th) 193, 87 C.C.C. (3d) 1 (S.C.C.); reversing (1992), 71 C.C.C. (3d) 50 (Sask. C.A.) — Under s. 574(1)(b), P may prefer an indictment upon a charge in respect of which a provincial court judge ordered D to stand trial. Provided the charge is *founded on the facts* disclosed by the evidence taken on preliminary inquiry, P may prefer an indictment in respect of a charge, as long as it is *not* an offence originally charged in respect of which D was discharged.

R. v. Litchfield (1993), 25 C.R. (4th) 137, 86 C.C.C. (3d) 97 (S.C.C.) — An indictment is preferred *only* when it is lodged with the trial judge. It may be preferred, however, once the trial judge has been assigned. D may apply to the assigned trial judge to divide or sever the counts *after* the indictment has been preferred, but *before* the court has been constituted to begin hearing evidence. It is the trial judge who should hear such applications.

R. v. Barbeau (1992), 15 C.R. (4th) 169, 75 C.C.C. (3d) 129 (S.C.C.) — Under s. 574(1)(b), P may prefer an indictment on any charge disclosed by the evidence taken at preliminary inquiry. The consent of the Attorney General under s. 577(c) is *not* required in such cases.

R. v. Chabot (1980), 18 C.R. (3d) 258, 55 C.C.C. (2d) 385 (S.C.C.) — D may apply by way of *habeas corpus* with *certiorari* in aid to quash the committal for trial until such time as the indictment is preferred. An indictment based upon a committal for trial is *not* preferred until it is lodged with the trial court at the opening of D's trial, with a court ready to proceed with the trial. The placing of an indictment before a judge in Assignment Court does *not* constitute preferment.

R. v. Garcia (1990), 75 C.R. (3d) 250 (B.C. C.A.) — P may exercise the authority of para. (1)(b) at any time after committal and prior to plea.

R. v. Hampton (1990), 60 C.C.C. (3d) 308 (Man. C.A.) — The only limitation upon P's power of preferment under s. 574(1)(b) is the requirement of s. 577(b) applicable where D is discharged at the preliminary inquiry. D is "discharged" only where there is no evidence of the offence charged or of any other indictable offence in respect of the same transaction.

R. v. D. (A.) (1990), 60 C.C.C. (3d) 407 (Ont. C.A.) — The quashing of an indictment preferred under s. 574(1)(a) on the basis of an order to stand trial under s. 548(1)(a) does *not* engage s. 577(b) to require the consent of the Attorney General to preferment of a subsequent indictment.

R. v. Guyett (1989), 72 C.R. (3d) 383, 51 C.C.C. (3d) 368 (Ont. C.A.) — A judge presiding at a trial cannot purport to conduct a preliminary inquiry on an additional charge and then, on consent, commit D to stand trial before him. The proper procedure is to add the offence to the indictment on consent of D, pursuant to s. 574(2).

R. v. Scherbank (1966), 50 C.R. 170, [1966] 4 C.C.C. 338 (Ont. C.A.) — An indictable offence within the absolute jurisdiction of a provincial court judge may be added to an indictment for an offence for which D has been committed to trial under s. 574(1)(b).

Added Counts: S. 574(2)

Canada (Procureur général) c. Bélair (1991), 10 C.R. (4th) 209 (C.A. Qué.); leave to appeal refused (1992), 144 N.R. 242 (note) (S.C.C.) — Section 574(2) authorizes the addition of new counts in an indictment in cases to be tried by a jury, if D consents.

Related Provisions: "Prosecutor", "indictment" and "Attorney General" are defined in s. 2. The section also applies to non-jury trials under ss. 566(3) and 572.

The section represents what is often described as the *ordinary mode* of procedure. It involves the *laying* of an *information*, the issuance of process to compel D's attendance, the election or requirement of trial other than before a provincial court judge, an order to stand trial, the filing and preferment of an indictment based upon the order to stand trial and trial under Part XX or XIX. Section 577 authorizes an extraordinary mode of procedure, namely, the filing and preferment of an indictment, notwithstanding the absence of preliminary inquiry and/or order to stand trial. There is no difference in trial procedure.

Proceedings on an indictment may be stayed, thereafter recommenced under s. 579. The Attorney General may intervene in what is initiated as a private prosecution after process has issued or been confirmed to compel D's appearance in answer to a charge.

The general rules respecting the jurisdiction of the courts in one province of to try offences committed entirely in another are found in s. 478.

575. [Repealed R.S. 1985, c. 27 (1st Supp.), s. 113.]

576. (1) Indictment — **Except as provided in this Act, no indictment shall be preferred.**

(2) Criminal information and bill of indictment — **No criminal information shall be laid or granted and no bill of indictment shall be preferred before a grand jury.**

(3) Coroner's inquisition — **No person shall be tried on a coroner's inquisition.**

R.S., c. C-34, s. 506; R.S. 1985, c. 27 (1st Supp.), s. 114.

Commentary: An indictment may *only* be preferred under the *Code*. Proceedings before a grand jury are no longer permissible. No one may be tried upon a coroner's inquisition.

Related Provisions: An "indictment" is defined in s.2 and preferred when it is lodged with the trial court at the opening of D's trial with a court ready to proceed with the trial.

Although s. 576(3) prohibits a trial upon a coroner's inquisition, s. 529 authorizes a coroner, in certain circumstances, to direct a person's appearance before a justice where the verdict of the coroner's inquisition finds such person to have committed murder or manslaughter.

An indictment may be preferred under either s. 574 or 577. Only s. 574 applies to trials without a jury under Part XIX.

577. Direct indictments — In any prosecution,

(a) where a preliminary inquiry has not been held, an indictment shall not be preferred, or

(b) where a preliminary inquiry has been held and the accused has been discharged, an indictment shall not be preferred or a new information shall not be laid

before any court without,

(c) where the prosecution is conducted by the Attorney General or the Attorney General intervenes in the prosecution, the personal consent in writing of the Attorney General or Deputy Attorney General, or

(d) where the prosecution is conducted by a prosecutor other than the Attorney General and the Attorney General does not intervene in the prosecution, the written order of a judge of that court.

R.S., c. C-34, s. 507; 1974–75–76, c. 93, s. 63; 1984, c. 40, s. 20(2);R.S. 1985, c. 27 (1st Supp.) s. 115.

Commentary: The section authorizes the preferment of an indictment, notwithstanding the absence of or discharge at a preliminary inquiry, and describes the procedure to be followed in both public and private prosecutions.

In a *public prosecution*, one in which the prosecution is either conducted by the Attorney General or in which the Attorney General intervenes, where *no preliminary* inquiry has been held, an indictment shall *not* be preferred, except with the *personal written consent* of the Attorney General or Deputy Attorney General. A similar consent is required where a preliminary inquiry has been held and D discharged, whether proceedings are continued by preferment of an indictment or the laying of a new information. The section has attracted *Charter* s. 7 scrutiny, especially where it is alleged that preferment in public prosecutions is coupled with no or inadequate disclosure.

In *private* prosecutions similar circumstances require the written order of a judge of the court in which the continuation is sought, whether by preferment of an indictment or the laying of a fresh information.

Case Law

Application to Judge Alone Trials

R. v. Tapaquon (1993), 26 C.R. (4th) 193, 87 C.C.C. (3d) 1 (S.C.C.); reversing (1992), 71 C.C.C. (3d) 50 (Sask. C.A.) — Where D has elected trial by judge alone, s. 566 prevents P from preferring an indictment under s. 577 in respect of any offence upon which D has been discharged. Where P wishes to have D stand trial on a charge upon which D has been discharged after preliminary inquiry, P may invoke s. 568 which requires a jury trial and renders s. 577 applicable. In other instances, a new information may be laid, subject to the application of the doctrine of abuse of process.

Preliminary Inquiry Not Held: S. 577(a)

R. v. Charlie (1998), 126 C.C.C. (3d) 513 (B.C. C.A.) — A direct indictment may be preferred after a committal for trial has been quashed. The phrase "not been held" in s. 577(a) means "not been legally concluded".

Stewart v. R. (No.2) (1977), 35 C.C.C. (2d) 281 (Ont. C.A.) — A preliminary inquiry which has begun but *not* been completed cannot be said to have been held.

Accused Discharged: S. 577(b)

Canada (Procureur général) c. Bélair (1991), 10 C.R. (4th) 209 (C.A. Qué.); leave to appeal refused (1992), 144 N.R. 242 (note) (S.C.C.) — "Discharged" is to be interpreted liberally. It includes a discharge pronounced by a judge of the superior court of criminal jurisdiction on *certiorari*.

R. v. Hampton (1990), 60 C.C.C. (3d) 308 (Man. C.A.) — D is only "discharged" at a preliminary inquiry within s. 577(b) where there is *no* evidence of the offence charged or of any other indictable offence in respect of the same transaction.

R. v. Myers (1991), 65 C.C.C. (3d) 135 (Nfld. C.A.) — "Discharged" means *not* ordered to stand trial on the charge laid and upon which the preliminary inquiry has been conducted.

R. v. D. (A.) (1990), 60 C.C.C. (3d) 407 (Ont. C.A.) — The quashing of an indictment preferred under s. 574(1)(a) on the basis of an order to stand trial under s. 548(1)(a) does *not* constitute a *discharge* under s. 574(1)(b) to require the consent of the Attorney General to preferment of a subsequent indictment.

Discretion of Attorney General

R. v. Chabot (1985), 44 C.R. (3d) 70, 16 C.C.C. (3d) 483 (Ont. C.A.) — Where the information had merely charged "murder" without specifying "first degree murder", the Supreme Court of Canada had ordered the committal for trial to be on a charge of second degree murder. The Attorney General, shortly thereafter, preferred an indictment on a charge of first degree murder. It was held that the Attorney General was entitled to exercise his discretion to do so and this did *not* amount to an abuse of process.

Consent of Attorney General: S. 577(c)

R. v. Barbeau (1992), 15 C.R. (4th) 169, 75 C.C.C. (3d) 129 (S.C.C.) — Under s. 574(1)(b), P may prefer an indictment on any charge disclosed by the evidence taken at preliminary inquiry. The consent of the Attorney General under s. 577(c) is *not* required.

R. v. Philbin (1978), 37 C.C.C. (2d) 528 (Alta. C.A.) — Where an indictment is preferred without a preliminary inquiry having been held, the Attorney General need *not* appear in court personally to prefer the indictment.

R. v. Rooke (1988), 40 C.C.C. (3d) 484 (B.C. C.A.) — The consent of the Attorney General was valid, by virtue of the *Interpretation Act*, notwithstanding the fact that the person who was Attorney General at the time the indictment was signed was no longer Attorney General when the indictment was preferred at the beginning of the trial.

R. v. Myers (1991), 65 C.C.C. (3d) 135 (Nfld. C.A.) — Section 577(c) permits the Deputy Attorney General to prefer an indictment for sexual assault where D has been discharged of the offence at a preliminary inquiry, but ordered to stand trial on a lesser charge of simple assault.

R. v. Dwyer (1978), 42 C.C.C. (2d) 83 (Ont. C.A.); reversed on other grounds (1980), 10 C.R. (3d) 20, 14 C.R. (3d) 136, 47 C.C.C. (2d) 1 (S.C.C.) — In order to properly prefer an indictment under subsection (c), as a safeguard against vexatious prosecution, the Attorney General, if he does not personally sign the indictment, must at least in a written direction personally signed by him and preferably endorsed on the indictment, clearly, direct that the indictment be preferred or state that he prefers the indictment. The Attorney General cannot delegate this responsibility by consent or otherwise to any other person.

Judicial Review of Preferment

Patrick v. Canada (A.G.) (1986), 28 C.C.C. (3d) 417 (B.C. S.C.), appeal dismissed (1987), 56 C.R. (3d) 378 (B.C. C.A.); leave to appeal refused (1987), 80 N.R. 160 (S.C.C.) — The decision of the Attorney General to prefer an indictment where D has been discharged after a preliminary inquiry is reviewable to determine whether it infringes upon a constitutionally protected right, although the decision-making process itself is not reviewable.

R. v. Moore (1986), 50 C.R. (3d) 243, 26 C.C.C. (3d) 474 (Man. C.A.); leave to appeal refused (1986), 50 C.R. (3d) 243n (S.C.C.) — Preferment of a direct indictment by the Attorney General where no preliminary inquiry has been held is *not* subject to court review.

Balderstone v. R. (1983), 8 C.C.C. (3d) 532 (Man. C.A.); affirming (1982), 2 C.C.C. (3d) 37 (Man. Q.B.); leave to appeal refused (1983), 8 C.C.C. (3d) 532n (S.C.C.) — A decision of the Attorney General to prefer a direct indictment is not subject to court review despite D's discharge at a preliminary inquiry.

R. v. Ertel (1987), 58 C.R. (3d) 252, 35 C.C.C. (3d) 398 (Ont. C.A.); leave to appeal refused (1987), 61 C.R. (3d) xxixn (S.C.C.) — The discretionary powers of the Attorney General may be reviewed by a court of competent jurisdiction if it results in a denial or infringement of a constitutionally protected right in a particular case.

Charter Considerations

R. v. Moore (1986), 50 C.R. (3d) 243, 26 C.C.C. (3d) 474 (Man. C.A.); leave to appeal refused 50 C.R. (3d) 243n (S.C.C.) — The Attorney General's decision to prefer an indictment can become reviewable only if D's rights under *Charter* s. 7 have been violated.

Stolar v. R. (1983), 32 C.R. (3d) 342, 4 C.C.C. (3d) 333 (Man. C.A.) — The preferring of a direct indictment against D, where no preliminary inquiry had been held and another person who had previously been charged and committed for trial following a preliminary inquiry, does not violate *Charter* s. 7.

R. v. Ertel (1987), 58 C.R. (3d) 252, 35 C.C.C. (3d) 398 (Ont. C.A.); leave to appeal refused (1987), 61 C.R. (3d) xxixn (S.C.C.) — *See also*: *R. v. Sterling* (1993), 84 C.C.C. (3d) 65 (Sask. C.A.); *R. v. Daniels* (1991), 65 C.C.C. (3d) 366, 6 C.R. (4th) 375 (Sask. C.A.); leave to appeal refused (1992), 69 C.C.C. (3d) vi (S.C.C.) — The direct preferment of an indictment by the Attorney General does *not* violate *Charter* s. 9 since it does *not* give rise to "detention" within the meaning of that section. Where D receives full disclosure of P's case, the direct preferment of an indictment does not violate *Charter* s. 7. Where D has had the benefit of a preliminary hearing, the direct preferment does *not* violate *Charter* s. 15. However, the direct preferment is subject to the requirement of fairness. It may also be challenged as an abuse of process, and, in individual cases as a breach of s. 7, if it results in a denial or infringement of a constitutionally protected right.

R. v. Arviv (1985), 45 C.R. (3d) 354, 19 C.C.C. (3d) 395 (Ont. C.A.); leave to appeal refused (1985), 19 C.C.C. (3d) 395n (S.C.C.) — The preferring of a direct indictment without a preliminary hearing, thereby denying D the opportunity to cross-examine a key witness prior to the witness giving evidence at trial does *not*, *per se*, violate *Charter* s. 7, where full disclosure of P's case and the witness' evidence have been made.

Related Provisions: "Indictment" and "Attorney General" are defined in s. 2.

In *public prosecutions* it is the *Attorney General or Deputy Attorney General* who must personally *consent in writing* to the preferment of the indictment or the laying of a new information, as the case may be. The consent of an agent or counsel instructed for the purpose of the section is not sufficient to regularize continuation of the proceedings. The actual prosecution may be conducted by such an agent. The plain wording of s. 577(c) is more restrictive than the general definition of "Attorney General" in s. 2 or the language of s. 579(1).

Under s. 577(d), applicable in *private prosecutions*, the authorizing mechanism is the written order, not consent, of a judge of the court in which the continuation is proposed or sought.

Stay and recommencement of proceedings is authorized under s. 579.

578. (1) Summons or warrant — Where notice of the recommencement of proceedings has been given pursuant to subsection 579(2) or an indictment has been filed with the court before which the proceedings are to commence or recommence, the court, if it considers it necessary, may issue

    (a) a summons addressed to, or

    (b) a warrant for the arrest of,

the accused or defendant, as the case may be, to compel him to attend before the court to answer the charge described in the indictment.

(2) Part XVI to apply — The provisions of Part XVI apply with such modifications as the circumstances require where a summons or warrant is issued under subsection (1).

1974–75–76, c. 93, s. 64; R.S. 1985, c. 27 (1st Supp.), s. 116.

Commentary: Under s. 578(1) a summons or warrant may be issued to compel D's appearance in answer to a charge described in a notice of recommencement under s. 579(2) or contained in an indictment filed with the court before which proceedings are to commence or recommence. The judicial interim release provisions of Part XVI, modified accordingly, apply to D.

Case Law
Compelling Attendance
Stolar v. R. (1983), 32 C.R. (3d) 342, 4 C.C.C. (3d) 333 (Man. C.A.); leave to appeal refused (1983), 4 C.R.R. 252n (S.C.C.) — A summons is an acceptable method of alerting D to the fact of trial by direct indictment. It will *not* be quashed merely because the application for it has been made *ex parte*.

Related Provisions: Execution of the warrant and service of the summons may be in accordance with ss. 703 and 703.1.

579. (1) Attorney General may direct stay — The Attorney General or counsel instructed by him for that purpose may, at any time after any proceedings in relation to an accused or a defendant are commenced and before judgment, direct the clerk or other proper officer of the court to make an entry on the record that the proceedings are stayed by his direction, and such entry shall be made forthwith thereafter, whereupon the proceedings shall be stayed accordingly and any recognizance relating to the proceedings is vacated.

(2) Recommencement of proceedings — Proceedings stayed in accordance with subsection (1) may be recommenced, without laying a new information or preferring a new indictment, as the case may be, by the Attorney General or counsel instructed by him for that purpose giving notice of the recommencement to the clerk of the court in which the stay of the proceedings was entered, but where no such notice is given within one year after the entry of the stay of proceedings, or before the expiration of the time within which the proceedings could have been commenced, whichever is the earlier, the proceedings shall be deemed never to have been commenced.

R.S., c. C-34, s. 508; 1972, c. 13, s. 43; R.S. 1985, c. 27 (1st Supp.), s. 117.

Commentary: The section authorizes the *stay and recommencement* of proceedings.

Under s. 579(1), a *stay* may be directed by the *Attorney General* or *counsel instructed* by him/her *for such purpose*. The procedure may be invoked at *any time* after proceedings have been commenced and before judgment. A *stay* is effected by a direction from the Attorney General, or counsel instructed by him/her for the purpose, to the clerk or other proper officer of the court, to make an entry on the record that the proceedings are stayed by his/her direction. The entry on the record must be made forthwith after the direction has been given. The entry stays proceedings and vacates any existing recognizances.

Under s. 579(2), proceedings stayed under s. 579(1) may be *recommenced within one year* from the entry of the stay by the Attorney General or counsel instructed by him/her for the purpose giving notice of the recommencement to the clerk of the court in which the stay was entered. No new information need be laid nor new indictment preferred. The failure to give notice of recommencement within the year, or before the expiration of the time within which the proceedings could have been commenced, whichever is earlier, *deems* the proceedings *never* to have been *commenced*.

Case Law
General Principles
R. v. Scott (1990), 2 C.R. (4th) 153, 61 C.C.C. (3d) 300 (S.C.C.) — P may direct the entry of a stay of proceedings to avoid improper disclosure of the identity of an informant. The timely *re-institution* of the proceedings does *not* constitute an *abuse* of process.

Dowson v. R. (1983), 35 C.R. (3d) 289, 7 C.C.C. (3d) 527 (S.C.C.) — Proceedings may be stayed as *soon* as an information has been laid.

R. v. Smith (1992), 79 C.C.C. (3d) 70 (B.C. C.A.) — Once P has exercised its right under s. 579 to direct a stay of proceedings, the judge hearing the prosecution is *functus* and without jurisdiction to proceed further. The s. 579 direction to the clerk of the court to enter a stay is a statutory administrative discretion given by the Attorney General and is beyond the direction or control of the trial judge.

R. v. Catagas (1977), 2 C.R. (3d) 328, 38 C.C.C. (2d) 296 (Man. C.A.) — The discretionary power to stay proceedings under this section is to be used in individual cases. P has *no* right to generally dispense with the application of a statute in favour of a particular group or race.

R. v. Jones (1997), 5 C.R. (5th) 364, 113 C.C.C. (3d) 225 (Ont. C.A.) — A stay of proceedings under *Code* s. 579 *terminates* any detention or release order made in relation to the stayed charges.

R. v. Carr (1984), 58 N.B.R. (2d) 99 (C.A.); affirming (1984), 54 N.B.R. (2d) 138 (Q.B.) — P has a right of withdrawal separate and distinct from the right of the Attorney General to order a stay of proceedings. P may withdraw an information after a plea of not guilty.

R. v. Pardo (1990), 62 C.C.C. (3d) 371 (Que. C.A.) — A stay of proceedings may be directed *after* an information has been laid but *prior* to the issuance of process.

Benloulou c. Le Greffier de la Couronne de Montréal (1976), 38 C.R.N.S. 359 (Que. C.A.) — The Attorney General may stay a non-jury trial. [See s. 572]

R. v. McKay (1979), 9 C.R. (3d) 378 (Sask. C.A.) — An agent of the Attorney General is vested by virtue of his general authority with sufficient authority to direct a stay of proceedings without specific instructions from the Attorney General.

Review of Discretion of Attorney General

Campbell v. Ontario (A.G.) (1987), 35 C.C.C. (3d) 480 (Ont. C.A.); leave to appeal refused (1987), 35 C.C.C. (3d) 480n (S.C.C.) — The exercise by the Attorney General of his prosecutorial discretion to stay proceedings is *not* subject to review by a court, *except* possibly where there is a flagrant impropriety on the part of the Attorney General.

Abuse of Process by Recommencement of Proceedings [See case digest under Code s. 8]

Charter Considerations

Chartrand v. Quebec (Min. of Justice) (1987), 59 C.R. (3d) 388, 40 C.C.C. (3d) 270 (Que. C.A.) — The Attorney General is justified in staying a prosecution where related proceedings are pending before the Supreme Court of Canada. Nevertheless, the discretion of the Attorney General to enter a stay is subject to judicial review under the *Charter*. However absolute that discretion might have been in the past, it cannot be used to override the rights guaranteed by the *Charter*. In this instance, the Attorney General did not violate *Charter* s. 15 in treating private prosecutors seeking to lay abortion charges differently from private prosecutors seeking enforcement of other *Code* provisions.

Related Provisions: "Clerk of the court" and "Attorney General" are defined in s. 2.

Proceedings are generally commenced by and upon the laying of an information under oath before a justice. It is, however, the issuance of process or its confirmation that compels D's attendance before a court of competent jurisdiction and it is only thereafter that P may stay proceedings.

The section would appear to have *no* impact on the authority of P to withdraw charges prior to arraignment and plea, nor the authority of a court to stay proceedings, as for example, on account of an abuse of process or *Charter* infringement. The *Code* makes no provision for either withdrawal of an information by P, or the entry of a judicial stay of proceedings, the latter at least contemplated in *Code* ss. 676(1)(d) and (c).

579.1 (1) Intervention by Attorney General of Canada — The Attorney General of Canada or counsel instructed by him or her for that purpose may intervene in proceedings in the following circumstances:

(a) the proceedings are in respect of a contravention of, a conspiracy or attempt to contravene or counselling the contravention of an Act of Parliament or a regulation made under that Act, other than this Act or a regulation made under this Act;

(b) the proceedings have not been instituted by an Attorney General;

(c) judgment has not been rendered; and

(d) the Attorney General of the province in which the proceedings are taken has not intervened.

(2) Section 579 to apply — **Section 579 applies, with such modifications as the circumstances require, to proceedings in which the Attorney General of Canada intervenes pursuant to this section.**

1994, c. 44, s. 60.

Commentary: Section 579.1(1) describes the circumstances in which the Attorney General of Canada, or counsel instructed by him/her for the purpose, may intervene in proceedings. The intervention must take place *before judgment* is rendered in proceedings that have *not* been instituted by an Attorney General and in which the Attorney General of the province has *not intervened*. The proceedings must also be in respect of

i.   a *contravention*;

ii.   a *conspiracy* or *attempt* to contravene; or

iii.   *counselling* the *contravention* of

an Act of Parliament or a regulation made under an Act of Parliament, *other than* the *Code* or regulation made under the *Code*.

The referential incorporation of s. 579 by s. 579.1(2) ensures that the authority of the Attorney General of Canada or counsel instructed by him/her for the purpose to stay proceedings is the same in cases where there is a s. 579.1 intervention as is the situation otherwise.

Related Provisions: The definition of "Attorney General" in s. 2 has the effect of including the Attorney General of Canada in the general authority to stay proceedings enacted by s. 579.

It is generally accepted that proceedings are instituted when an information is laid under oath before a justice. In the usual course, it seems unlikely that proceedings may be said to have been instituted by an Attorney General.

580. Form of indictment — **An indictment is sufficient if it is on paper and is in Form 4.**

R.S., c. C-34, s. 509; R.S. 1985, c. 27 (1st Supp.), s. 117.

Commentary: The section prescribes a statutory form of indictment.

Related Provisions: An indictment in Form 4 may include reference to D's date of birth.

The formal requirements of criminal pleading are found in the general and specific rules respecting counts in ss. 581–593 and 601, *infra.*

Sections 574, 576 and 577 describe the circumstances in which an indictment may be preferred, s. 579, when and how it may be stayed.

General Provisions respecting Counts

581. (1) Substance of offence — **Each count in an indictment shall in general apply to a single transaction and shall contain in substance a statement that the accused or defendant committed an indictable offence therein specified.**

(2) Form of statement — **The statement referred to in subsection (1) may be**

(a) in popular language without technical averments or allegations of matters that are not essential to be proved;

(b) in the words of the enactment that describes the offence or declares the matters charged to be an indictable offence; or

(c) in words that are sufficient to give to the accused notice of the offence with which he is charged.

(3) Details of circumstances — **A count shall contain sufficient detail of the circumstances of the alleged offence to give to the accused reasonable information with respect to the act or omission to be proved against him and to identify the transaction**

referred to, but otherwise the absence or insufficiency of details does not vitiate the count.

(4) Indictment for treason — Where an accused is charged with an offence under section 47 or sections 49 to 53, every overt act that is to be relied on shall be stated in the indictment.

(5) Reference to section — A count may refer to any section, subsection, paragraph or subparagraph of the enactment that creates the offence charged, and for the purpose of determining whether a count is sufficient, consideration shall be given to any such reference.

(6) General provisions not restricted — Nothing in this Part relating to matters that do not render a count insufficient shall be deemed to restrict or limit the application of this section.

R.S., c. C-34, s. 510; R.S. 1985, c. 27 (1st Supp.), s. 118.

Commentary: Each count in an indictment must meet the requirements of this section to be legally sufficient. The primacy of the section in matters of criminal pleading is ensured by s. 581(6).

Section 581(1) contains two requirements. Each count must, *in general*, apply to a *single transaction*. The rule is of general, though *not* universal application. Each count must contain in *substance* a *statement* that D committed a *specified offence*. The statement or specification of the offence may be in any manner authorized by s. 581(2) and under s. 581(5), may refer to any section, subsection, paragraph or subparagraph of the enactment.

The dual requirements of s. 581(3) define the amount or *degree* of circumstantial *detail* required to render a count legally sufficient. There must first be *sufficient detail* of the *circumstances* of the alleged offence to give D *reasonable information* with respect to the *act or omission to be proven against him/her*. The detail must also be sufficient to *identify the transaction* to which reference will be made. Provided the detail contained in the count is sufficient to satisfy both aspects of the requirement, the absence or insufficiency of detail otherwise will *not* vitiate the count.

Section 581(4) enacts a special rule relating to treason, high treason and certain other prohibited acts (ss. 47, 49–53) requiring the statement in the indictment of every *overt act* upon which P relies.

Case Law

Single Transaction: S. 581(1)

R. v. Cotroni (1979), 7 C.R. (3d) 185, 45 C.C.C. (2d) 1 (S.C.C.) — A distinction must be drawn between a conspiracy count which charges two or more conspiracies, and a count which charges one conspiracy only but is supported by proof of more than one conspiracy. The former gives rise to questions of duplicity; the latter raises the question of whether P has proven the conspiracy charged against two or more of the accused, notwithstanding evidence of a second conspiracy.

R. v. Cook (1985), 46 C.R. (3d) 129, 20 C.C.C. (3d) 18 (B.C. C.A.) — Where incidents are sufficiently connected by time, place and circumstances, each is not a "separate transaction".

R. v. Goler (1985), 67 N.S.R. (2d) 200 (C.A.) — The word "transaction" is *not* synonymous with "offence". The purpose of the single transaction rule is to prevent charging the offence in the disjunctive so that D knows with precision with what he is charged.

Barnes v. R. (1975), 2 C.R. (3d) 310, 26 C.C.C. (2d) 112 (N.S. C.A.) — A count may *not* charge more than one offence but a number of occurrences or acts taking place over a period of time may properly be charged in one count as one continuing offence or transaction. So long as the evidence is directed to the continuing offence contained in the charge, the validity of that charge is not affected by the fact that *not* all of the acts or occurrences alleged are proved.

R. v. Selles (1997), 116 C.C.C. (3d) 435 (Ont. C.A.) — A "single transaction" is *not* synonymous with a single incident, occurrence or offence. Separate acts which are successive and cumulative and which comprise a continuous series of acts may be considered a "single transaction".

R. v. Deutsch (1983), 5 C.C.C. (3d) 41 (Ont. C.A.); affirmed on other grounds (1986), 52 C.R. (3d) 305, 27 C.C.C. (3d) 385 (S.C.C.) — Counts which encompass *more* than one transaction contravene this section.

R. v. Burke (1988), 71 Nfld. & P.E.I.R 217 (P.E.I. C.A.) — The word "transaction" in the section refers to a pattern of conduct, as opposed to the individual incidents or occurrences, which make up that transaction or pattern.

R. v. Fischer (1987), 31 C.C.C. (3d) 303 (Sask. C.A.) — A single count indictment which refers to a continuing course of conduct is not factually duplicitous and does *not* offend the "single transaction" rule.

Statement of an Offence: Ss. 581(1), (2), (5)

R. v. Saunders (1990), 77 C.R. (3d) 397 (S.C.C.), 56 C.C.C. (3d) 220; affirming (1987), 58 C.R. (3d) 83, 35 C.C.C. (3d) 385 (B.C. C.A.) — Although the gravamen of the offence is conspiracy to import a narcotic, P may particularize the narcotic as a means of identifying the transaction which is the basis of the alleged conspiracy. Where, however, P particularizes the offence, as for example, a conspiracy to import heroin, it must prove the offence as particularized.

R. v. Cote (1977), 33 C.C.C. (2d) 353 (S.C.C.) — *See also: R. v. Lessard* (1972), 6 C.C.C. (2d) 239n (Ont. C.A.) — — A reference to the section of the *Code* creating the offence charged is sufficient to cure the omission from the charge of an element of the offence, such as "without reasonable excuse".

R. v. McKenzie (1972), 16 C.R.N.S. 374, 4 C.C.C. (2d) 296 (S.C.C.) — Theft which may be committed in several different ways, may properly be charged in the words of the general theft section.

R. v. Kostiuk (1984), 35 Sask. R. 90 (C.A.) — Incorrect statement of the section number will *not* invalidate a cound if it otherwise met the requirements of the section.

Detail of the Circumstances: Ss. 581(3), (6)

R. v. Douglas (1991), 63 C.C.C. (3d) 29 (S.C.C.) — Whether an indictment is sufficient will depend on the offence charged and the facts of the case. Time need *not* be stated with precision, unless it is an essential part of the offence charged, and D is *not* misled or prejudiced by any variation in time that arises. In general, a charge is proven if the evidence discloses the commission of the offence within the time period specified in the indictment.

R. v. B. (G.) (1990), 77 C.R. (3d) 347, 56 C.C.C. (3d) 200 (S.C.C.); affirming (1988), 65 Sask. R. 134 (Sask. C.A.) — What constitutes reasonable or adequate information with respect to the act or omission to be proven against D will vary as the factual matters which underlie some offences permit greater descriptive precision than do others. A significant factor in assessing the reasonableness of the information provided is the nature and legal character of the offence charged.In general, an information will *not* be quashed for failure to specify the exact time of the commission of an offence. A difference between the date alleged in the information and the evidence given is only of consequence where the time of the offence is critical and D may be misled by such variance, thereby suffering prejudice in his/her defence.

R. v. Saunders (1990), 77 C.R. (3d) 397, 56 C.C.C. (3d) 220 (S.C.C.); affirming (1987), 58 C.R. (3d) 83, 35 C.C.C. (3d) 385 (B.C. C.A.) — See digest under *Statement of an Offence*: ss. 581(1), (2), (5), *supra*.

R. v. WIS Developments Corp. (1984), 40 C.R. (3d) 97 (S.C.C.) — A charge is no less vitiated by insufficiencies under subsection (3) than under subsection (1).

Bolduc v. Quebec (P.G.) (1982), 28 C.R. (3d) 193 (S.C.C.) — An information which indicated the *place* and *date* of the conspiracy, the *names* of the conspirators, the object of the conspiracy and the reference to the *section* which created the offence is valid.

Brodie v. R. (1936), 65 C.C.C. 289 (S.C.C.) — The imperative requirement is that a count "shall contain" a statement that D has committed an indictable offence and that such offence must be "specified". Although a count is sufficient if it contains such statement "in substance", this does *not* mean merely classifying or characterizing the offence; it calls for specifying time, place and matter, and for stating the facts alleged to constitute the offence.

R. v. Goldstein (1986), 70 A.R. 324 (C.A.) — The original count in the information does *not* need to contain all the material required to reasonably inform D. Rather, a preliminary inquiry and the *Code* provisions regarding particulars are available to D.

R. v. Fox (1986), 50 C.R. (3d) 370, 24 C.C.C. (3d) 366 (B.C. C.A.); leave to appeal refused (1986), 50 C.R. (3d) xxvn (S.C.C.) — The count must provide *sufficient* information to allow D to make full answer and defence and to ensure a fair trial.

R. v. Babineau (1985), 66 N.B.R. (2d) 158 (C.A.) — An information will *not* be quashed when it complies with this section. Absence of details can be remedied by an order for further particulars.

R. v. Milberg (1987), 35 C.C.C. (3d) 45 (Ont. C.A.); leave to appeal refused (1987), 35 C.C.C. (3d) 45n (S.C.C.) — *See also*: *R. v. Billion-Rey* (1990), 57 C.C.C. (3d) 223 (Que. C.A.) — While the offence of keeping a bawdy-house could be perpetrated in different ways, such ways were *not* diverse or unrelated. The charge was only required to be specific enough so that D would know of the charge against him.

R. v. R.I.C. (1986), 32 C.C.C. (3d) 399 (Ont. C.A.) — The *sufficiency* of the details contained in the charge *depends* upon the facts of the case and the nature of the charge. A relevant fact is that D has been given information other than through the language of the count, such as access to P's brief or particulars.

R. v. Ryan (1985), 23 C.C.C. (3d) 1 (Ont. C.A.); leave to appeal refused (1986), 65 N.R. 244n (S.C.C.) — While it is necessary to specify time, place and matter in an information, there is *no* rigid formula as to the kind of detail that is required before that specification is met. The test is whether the information contains *sufficient* detail to give D reasonable information as to the act to be proved and to identify the transactions referred to.

R. v. Ryan (1985), 19 C.C.C. (3d) 231 (Ont. H.C.); affirmed on other grounds (1985), 23 C.C.C. (3d) 1 (Ont. C.A.); leave to appeal refused (1986), 65 N.R. 244n (S.C.C.) — *See also*: *R. v. Pawliw* (1973), 13 C.C.C. (2d) 356 (Sask. C.A.) — The fact that D might be entitled to further particulars does not void the original information if it otherwise complies in with this section. The fact that a date is described as "on or about" a particular day does not necessarily introduce a fatal ambiguity. While the date of an offence should always be alleged, an error in it is *not* material unless it is actually an essential part of the offence.

Hoffmann-La Roche Ltd. v. R. (1981), 24 C.R. (3d) 193, 62 C.C.C. (2d) 118 (Ont. C.A.) — Where P alleged a combined offence of six years' duration, it was sufficient for it to prove that the offence had been committed at some point within the time period alleged.

Review of Validity: Authority and Extraordinary Remedies [See also s. 774]

Canada (A.G.) v. ITT Industries of Can. Ltd. (1987), 39 C.C.C. (3d) 268 (B.C. C.A.) — A provincial judge has jurisdiction on arraignment and prior to election to entertain an application to *quash* the information for failure to comply with this section.

R. v. Volpi (1987), 34 C.C.C. (3d) 1 (Ont. C.A.); leave to appeal refused (1987), 23 O.A.C. 397n (S.C.C.) — A provincial court judge has jurisdiction when dealing with an indictable offence to hear a motion to quash the indictment, prior to the election by D as to the mode of trial.

R. v. Jarman (1972), 10 C.C.C. (2d) 426 (Ont. C.A.) — Where the offence charged is one within the jurisdiction of the trial judge, he has exclusive jurisdiction to determine the validity of the information. An error with respect to that determination does *not* deprive him of jurisdiction. The decision may only be challenged on an appeal against his final disposition of the charge.

Re Pouliot (1978), 41 C.C.C. (2d) 93 (Que. C.A.) — *Certiorari* does *not* lie against an interlocutory judgment dismissing a motion to quash an information. The trial judge has jurisdiction to decide the preliminary motion to quash. There is *no* right of immediate appeal.

Related Provisions: "Count" and "indictment" are defined in s. 2. The principles governing joinder or severance of counts are contained in ss. 589–591. Counts are distinguished in the manner shown in Form 4.

The general purpose of this section and others related to criminal pleading, as for example, ss. 582–593 and 601, is to ensure that D is apprised of the offence charged and to secure to D, in advance of and in preparation for trial, such reasonable and precise information respecting the charge as to ensure D's ability to make full answer and defence thereto. The sections also nullify the extreme technicality of the old forms of criminal pleading, and thereby facilitate the administration of criminal justice by ensuring trial upon the merits of a properly framed and sufficiently identified allegation of crime.

The primacy of s. 581, more particularly of s. 581(3), is reinforced by the provision of s. 583 holding certain omissions *not* to be grounds for objection, *where the count otherwise fulfils the requirements of s. 581.* Special provisions respecting counts are found in ss. 584–586. Particulars may be ordered under s. 587 and amendments made in accordance with s. 601.

The section applies to summary conviction proceedings under s. 795.

582. High treason and first degree murder — No person shall be convicted for the offence of high treason or first degree murder unless in the indictment charging the offence he is specifically charged with that offence.

R.S., c. C-34, s. 511; 1973–74, c. 38, s. 4; 1974–75–76, c. 105, s. 6.

Commentary: The section, in effect, a rule of criminal pleading, bars conviction for high treason or first degree murder, except in cases where the indictment charges D with having committed either specific offence.

Related Provisions: High treason is defined in s. 46(1) and is punished in ss. 47(1) and 47(2)(a).

Murder is *defined* in ss. 229 and *classified* for sentencing purposes as first degree murder and second degree murder in s. 231. Murder is first degree murder where it comes within ss. 231(2)–(5). All other murder is, by s. 231(7), second degree murder. First degree murder is punished under ss. 235(1), 745(a) and 745.1.

High treason and first degree murder, similarly treason and second degree murder, are within the *exclusive* trial and judicial interim release jurisdiction of the superior court of criminal jurisdiction under ss. 469(a) and 522(1).

583. Certain omissions not grounds for objection — No count in an indictment is insufficient by reason of the absence of details where, in the opinion of the court, the count otherwise fulfils the requirements of section 581 and, without restricting the generality of the foregoing, no count in an indictment is insufficient by reason only that

(a) it does not name the person injured or intended or attempted to be injured,

(b) it does not name the person who owns or has a special property or interest in property mentioned in the count;

(c) it charges an intent to defraud without naming or describing the person whom it was intended to defraud;

(d) it does not set out any writing that is the subject of the charge;

(e) it does not set out the words used where words that are alleged to have been used are the subject of the charge;

(f) it does not specify the means by which the alleged offence was committed;

(g) it does not name or describe with precision any person, place or thing; or

(h) it does not, where the consent of a person, official or authority is required before proceedings may be instituted for an offence, state that the consent has been obtained.

R.S., c. C-34, s. 512.

Commentary: The section enacts a *general rule* concerning the effect of the absence of or inadequacy in *detail* in a count in an indictment.

The saving provisions of the section only become engaged where the count otherwise satisfies the requirements of s. 581, in particular the sufficiency of details standard set by s. 581(3). In general, absence of detail does *not* vitiate a count that is valid under s. 581. In particular, the absence of details of the nature described in ss. 583(a)–(h), will *not* vitiate a count held sufficient under s. 581.

Case Law
Intent to Defraud: S. 583(c)

Vézina v. R. (1986), 49 C.R. (3d) 351, 23 C.C.C. (3d) 481 (S.C.C.) — A charge of fraud need *not* set out the intended victim. The identification of the victim is surplusage. However, although particulars which are surplusage need not be proved, this does not apply where D is prejudiced in his defence.

Description of Person, Place or Thing: S. 583(g)

Little v. R. (1975), 30 C.R.N.S. 90, 19 C.C.C. (2d) 385 (S.C.C.) — If ownership of the stolen object as alleged in the indictment is *not* proved and there are no circumstances to indicate to D the true nature of the charge, D is entitled to an acquittal. However, if there is *no* possibility for D to fail to identify the transaction about which he is charged, D is *not* entitled to an acquittal solely on the basis that the owner mentioned in the indictment has *not* been mentioned in the evidence.

Budovitch v. R. (1969), 8 C.R.N.S. 280, [1970] 4 C.C.C. 156 (N.S. C.A.) — The *place* of an offence is an essential averment which must be proved

Related Provisions: In addition to the *general* rule of s. 583 relating to the legal effect of absence of detail, the *special* provisions of ss. 584–586 may sustain the validity of a count, notwithstanding the absence of designated details in counts charging specific offences or groups of offences.

Section 587 permits *particulars* to be ordered where a court is satisfied that it is necessary to do so for a fair trial. In many instances the substance of the particular is an enumerated deficiency in detail in s. 583 or ss. 584–586.

Similar provisions apply in summary conviction proceedings under s. 795.

Special Provisions Respecting Counts

584. (1) Sufficiency of count charging libel — No count for publishing a blasphemous, seditious or defamatory libel, or for selling or exhibiting an obscene book, pamphlet, newspaper or other written matter, is insufficient by reason only that it does not set out the words that are alleged to be libellous or the writing that is alleged to be obscene.

(2) Specifying sense — A count for publishing a libel may charge that the published matter was written in a sense that by innuendo made the publication thereof criminal, and may specify that sense without any introductory assertion to show how the matter was written in that sense.

(3) Proof — It is sufficient, on the trial of a count for publishing a libel, to prove that the matter published was libellous, with or without innuendo.

R.S., c. C-34, s. 513.

Commentary: The section applies to counts charging the *publishing of a libel* and, in part only, to counts charging the sale or exhibition of *obscene written matter*.

Section 584(1), applicable to both libel and obscenity counts, does *not* require the count to set out the allegedly libellous words or obscene writing to be legally valid.

Under s. 584(2), where the basis of an alleged libel is innuendo, the count *may* specify the sense that, by innuendo, made the publication criminal, without any introductory assertion to show how the matter was written in that sense.

Section 584(3) is *not* a provision relating to criminal pleading. It describes what is sufficient to prove an allegation of publishing a libel, namely that the matter published was libellous, with or without innuendo.

Related Provisions: Particulars of passages said to be obscene and further describing any writing or words that are the subject of a charge may be ordered under ss. 587(1)(d) and (e).

The several offences of *criminal libel*, include blasphemous libel (s. 296), defamatory libel (ss. 297–316) and seditious libel (ss. 59–61). There are special provisions for evidence in cases of defamatory libel (s. 317) and for the plea of justification (ss. 611–612).

585. Sufficiency of count charging perjury, etc. — No count that charges

(a) perjury,

(b) the making of a false oath or a false statement,

(c) fabricating evidence, or

(d) procuring the commission of an offence mentioned in paragraph (*a*), (*b*) or (*c*)

is insufficient by reason only that it does not state the nature of the authority of the tribunal before which the oath or statement was taken or made, or the subject of the inquiry, or the words used or the evidence fabricated, or that it does not expressly negative the truth of the words used.

R.S., c. C-34, s. 514.

Commentary: The section makes *special provisions* for counts charging any listed offence. It is *not* a condition precedent to sufficiency that the count state the nature of the authority of the tribunal before which the oath was taken or made, or the subject of the inquiry. Further, it is *not* necessary to allege in the count either the words used or evidence fabricated. The pleading need *not* expressly negative the truth of the words used.

Related Provisions: Particulars of what is relied upon in support of the charge of perjury (s. 131), the making of a false oath or a false statement (s. 134), fabricating evidence (s. 137) or counselling their commission, and further describing any words that are a subject of a charge may be ordered under ss. 587(1)(a) and (e).

A person who procures another to commit an offence which is, in fact, committed is a party to that offence under s. 22. Under s. 23.1, the procurer (counsellor) may be convicted, notwithstanding that the person procured cannot be convicted of the offence. Where the offence procured is *not* committed, s. 464 applies.

586. Sufficiency of count relating to fraud — No count that alleges false pretences, fraud or any attempt or conspiracy by fraudulent means is insufficient by reason only that it does not set out in detail the nature of the false pretence, fraud or fraudulent means.

R.S., c. C-34, s. 515.

Commentary: This *special provision* applies *only* to counts alleging false pretences, fraud or an attempt or conspiracy by fraudulent means. The failure to set out *in detail* the nature of the false pretence, fraud or fraudulent means does *not* vitiate the count, provided it otherwise satisfies s. 581(1) and (3).

Case Law

Shumiatcher v. Saskatchewan (A.G.) (1962), 38 C.R. 411, 133 C.C.C. 69 (Sask. C.A.) — This section does *not* detract from or override the obligation to include in the charge sufficient details of the circumstances of the alleged offence to identify the transaction referred to.

Related Provisions: *General provisions* as to counts are found in ss. 581–583. Section 581 is the principal provision on account of s. 581(6). Further special provisions respecting counts charging particular offences are included in ss. 584 and 585.

Under ss. 587(1)(c) and (d), *particulars* may be ordered of any false pretence, fraud, attempt or conspiracy by fraudulent means alleged in the count.

A false pretence is defined in s. 361. Offences involving their use are described in s. 362. Fraud is described and punished in s. 380.

Particulars

587. (1) What may be ordered — A court may, where it is satisfied that it is necessary for a fair trial, order the prosecutor to furnish particulars and, without restricting the generality of the foregoing, may order the prosecutor to furnish particulars

(a) of what is relied on in support of a charge of perjury, the making of a false oath or of a false statement, fabricating evidence or counselling the commission of any of those offences;

(b) of any false pretence or fraud that is alleged;

(c) of any alleged attempt or conspiracy by fraudulent means;

(d) setting out the passages in a book, pamphlet, newspaper or other printing or writing that are relied on in support of a charge of selling or exhibiting an obscene book, pamphlet, newspaper, printing or writing;

(e) further describing any writing or words that are the subject of a charge;

(f) further describing the means by which an offence is alleged to have been committed; or

(g) further describing a person, place or thing referred to in an indictment.

(2) Regard to evidence — For the purpose of determining whether or not a particular is required, the court may give consideration to any evidence that has been taken.

(3) Particular — Where a particular is delivered pursuant to this section,

(a) a copy shall be given without charge to the accused or his counsel,

(b) the particular shall be entered in the record, and

(c) the trial shall proceed in all respects as if the indictment had been amended to conform with the particular.

R.S., c. C-34, s. 516; R.S. 1985, c. 27 (1st Supp.), s. 7(2).

Commentary: Under this section, a court *may* order P to furnish *particulars* relating to a count or counts contained in an indictment, where the court considers it necessary for a fair trial. In determining whether a particular is required, the court, under s. 587(2), may consider any evidence that has been taken, *semble* not only the evidence at trial. The matters described in ss. 587(1)(a)–(g) may be the subject of an order of particulars but are not exhaustive of what might be ordered.

Where particulars are ordered and delivered under the section, a copy *must* be given without charge to D or D's counsel. Particulars are entered in the record. The trial proceeds, thereafter, as if the indictment had been amended to conform with the particular.

Case Law

Purpose of Particulars

R. v. Colgan (1987), 61 C.R. (3d) 290, 38 C.C.C. (3d) 576 (S.C.C.) — Where no essential element of the charge is missing, greater detail is a matter for an application for particulars.

R. v. Buck (1932), 57 C.C.C. 290 (Ont. C.A.) — The true function of particulars is to give further information to D of that which it is intended to prove against him, so that he may have a fair trial. It is *not* the function of particulars to bolster up or complete an invalid count, by supplying what should have appeared in the indictment itself.

Right to Particulars at Preliminary Inquiry

R. v. Chew, [1968] 2 C.C.C. 127 (Ont. C.A.) — There is no jurisdiction to order P to furnish particulars at the time of the preliminary inquiry prior to a committal for trial.

Nature and Effect of Particulars

R. v. McCune (1998), 131 C.C.C. (3d) 152, 21 C.R. (5th) 247 (B.C. C.A.) — P's theory of a case is *not* the same as the particularized indictment. It is only the indictment that defines the factual transaction that P must prove to obtain a conviction.

R. v. H. (J.A.) (1998), 124 C.C.C. (3d) 221 (B.C. C.A.) — Particularization of a count in an indictment does *not* always require the filing of a new indictment.

R. v. Bengert (1980), 15 C.R. (3d) 114 (B.C. C.A.); leave to appeal refused , (sub nom. *R. v. Robertson)* 34 N.R. 350n — *See also*: *R. v. Govedarov* (1974), 25 C.R.N.S. 1, 16 C.C.C. (2d) 238 (Ont. C.A.) — P's opening address does *not* constitute particulars.

R. v. Groot (1998), 129 C.C.C. (3d) 293 (Ont. C.A.); leave to appeal refused (March 4, 1999), Doc. 26929 (S.C.C.) — There is a difference between particulars furnished under s. 587 and particulars of P's theory. P is bound to prove *formal* particulars, subject to the surplusage rule, but not particulars of the theory advanced to establish liability.

R. v. May (1984), 13 C.C.C. (3d) 257 (Ont. C.A.) — The furnishing of particulars by P did *not* have the effect of amending the indictment, where the particulars were merely information as to incidents in which P alleged D was personally involved, and which constituted major overt acts of D to support allegations of his participation in a conspiracy.

Appeal From Refusal to Order

R. v. Hunter (1985), 23 C.C.C. (3d) 331 (Alta. C.A.); leave to appeal refused (1986), 66 N.R. 319n (S.C.C.) — An appellate court will *not* interfere with the judicial exercise of discretion dismissing an application for particulars.

Related Provisions: Particulars give further information to D of what P intends to prove against D, so that D may have a fair trial. It is *not* their function to convert an indictment or count which is legally insufficient, for want of compliance with s. 581, into one which meets such requirements: particulars supplement a count which, technically sufficient, is *not* too informative.

Section 601(2) authorizes the amendment of particulars furnished under s. 587 to make the particular conform to the evidence, where there is a variance between the evidence and count, as it would have been if amended in conformity with the particular furnished under s. 587.

The section, unlike s. 601(11) governing amendments, does *not* apply to preliminary inquiries.

Ownership of Property

588. Ownership — **The real and personal property of which a person has, by law, the management, control or custody shall, for the purposes of an indictment or proceeding against any other person for an offence committed on or in respect of the property, be deemed to be the property of the person who has the management, control or custody of it.**

R.S., c. C-34, s. 517.

Commentary: The section is *not* wholly a matter of criminal pleading.

In general, the real and personal property of which a person has, by law, the *management custody* or *control* is, by this section, *deemed* to be the *property* of such a person. In other words, upon *proof* that V, by law, has management, custody or control of certain property, V is *deemed*, in popular language, to be the "owner thereof". The *presumption* applies "for the purposes of an indictment or proceedings against any other person for an offence committed on or in respect of the property". In practical terms, the section enables P to allege in the indictment that the real or personal property is "the property of V" and to prove that allegation by evidence that V, at the material time, had, by law, the custody, management or control of the property.

Case Law

R. v. Scott (1968), 6 C.R.N.S. 17 (Alta, C.A.) — *See also: R. v. Wright* (1990), 60 C.C.C. (3d) 321 (Alta. C.A.) — The phrase "by law" in this section applies *only* where, by reason of statute or common law, a person was invested or charged with the management, control or custody of another's property and contemplates persons occupying such capacities as administrator, liquidator or trustee in bankruptcy.

Related Provisions: "Property" and "person" are defined in s. 2.

Section 583(b) does *not* require a count, which otherwise fulfils the requirements of s. 581, to name the person who owns or has a special property or interest in property described in the count.

Theft and offences resembling theft are described in ss. 322–342.1

Joinder or Severance of Counts

589. Count for murder — No count that charges an indictable offence other than murder shall be joined in an indictment to a count that charges murder unless

    (a) the count that charges the offence other than murder arises out of the same transaction as a count that charges murder; or

    (b) the accused signifies consent to the joinder of the counts.

R.S., c. C-34, s. 518; 1991, c. 4, s. 2.

Commentary: The section describes the circumstances in which a count charging an offence *other than murder* may be joined in an indictment to a count charging *murder*.

The joinder permitted is exceptional. The basic rule is, that *no* count charging an indictable offence *other than murder* shall be *joined* in an indictment to a count that charges *murder*. Joinder is *only* authorized where the non-murder count is an *indictable offence* which *arises out of the same transaction* as the count that charges murder, or where D signifies *consent* to the joinder. Where consent is the basis of the joinder, it should be endorsed on the indictment.

The section does *not* bar the joinder of multiple counts of murder in the same indictment.

Related Provisions: Murder is defined in ss. 229 and classified, for sentencing purposes, in s. 231. The classification of murder charged should be specifically pleaded in the count, as for example, "... and did thereby commit second degree murder ...". Section 582 bars conviction for first degree murder, unless the offence is specifically alleged in the count.

The *general rule* respecting the joinder of counts is s. 591. It permits, subject to an order of severance under s. 591(3), the joinder of any number of counts for any number of offences in the same indictment, provided that they are properly distinguished as in Form 4. In certain circumstances, separate indictments may be tried together.

Section 574 describes the counts which may be contained in an indictment preferred under the section. Section 577, which permits direct preferment, contains no similar provision.

The phrase "*in respect of* the same transaction" appears in ss. 535, 541 and 548(1) applicable to the preliminary inquiry. In s. 589, the italicized words are replaced by "arises out of ...".

590. (1) Offences may be charged in the alternative — A count is not objectionable by reason only that

    (a) it charges in the alternative several different matters, acts or omissions that are stated in the alternative in an enactment that describes as an indictable offence the matters, acts or omissions charged in the count; or

    (b) it is double or multifarious.

(2) Application to amend or divide counts — An accused may at any stage of his trial apply to the court to amend or to divide a count that

(a) charges in the alternative different matters, acts or omissions that are stated in the alternative in the enactment that describes the offence or declares that the matters, acts or omissions charged are an indictable offence, or

(b) is double or multifarious,

on the ground that, as framed, it embarrasses him in his defence.

(3) Order — The court may, where it is satisfied that the ends of justice require it, order that a count be amended or divided into two or more counts, and thereupon a formal commencement may be inserted before each of the counts into which it is divided.

R.S., c. C-34, s. 519.

Commentary: Under s. 590(1), no count is objectionable *only* because it charges, in the alternative, several different matters, acts or omissions, or is double or multifarious. The remedy under s. 590(2), is for D to apply, at *any stage of the trial*, for an order *amending or dividing* the count, on the ground that it embarrasses him/her in his/her defence. An order may be made under s. 590(3), where the *ends of justice* require it, dividing or amending the count, and inserting a formal commencement before each of the counts into which it is subdivided. Each is then treated as a separate count.

Case Law
General Principles

R. v. Litchfield (1993), 25 C.R. (4th) 137, 86 C.C.C. (3d) 97 (S.C.C.) — Division or severance of counts requires the exercise of substantial discretion by the *trial* judge who must be satisfied that the ends of justice require the order.

Division of Counts: S. 590(2)

R. v. Litchfield (1993), 25 C.R. (4th) 137, 86 C.C.C. (3d) 97 (S.C.C.) — D may apply to the assigned trial judge to divide or sever the counts *after* the indictment has been preferred, but *before* the court has been constituted to begin hearing evidence. It is the *trial judge* who should hear the applications.

Lilly v. R. (1983), 34 C.R. (3d) 297, 5 C.C.C. (3d) 1 (S.C.C.) — Where P charged theft involving several transactions in a single count and it became apparent from the evidence that D had different defences for certain transactions, it would have been preferable, at that stage, to divide the count.

R. v. Hulan (1969), 6 C.R.N.S. 296, [1970] 1 C.C.C. 36 (Ont. C.A.) — The power of the court to order that a single count be divided into two or more counts contemplates that a number of acts, each in itself capable of constituting an offence, might be before the court in one count. The trial on that count might properly proceed, unless the court is satisfied that the ends of justice require a division of the count.

Related Provisions: The general rules respecting counts are contained in ss. 581–583. Special provisions as to counts charging certain offences appear in ss. 584–586.

Once a count is amended or divided, D may apply under s. 591 for an order for a separate trial on one or more of the counts.

591. (1) Joinder of counts — Subject to section 589, any number of counts for any number of offences may be joined in the same indictment, but the counts shall be distinguished in the manner shown in Form 4.

(2) Each count separate — Where there is more than one count in an indictment, each count may be treated as a separate indictment.

(3) Severance of accused and counts — The court may, where it is satisfied that the interests of justice so require, order

(a) that the accused or defendant be tried separately on one or more of the counts; and

(b) where there is more than one accused or defendant, that one or more of them be tried separately on one or more of the counts.

(4) Order for severance — An order under subsection (3) may be made before or during the trial but, if the order is made during the trial, the jury shall be discharged from giving a verdict on the counts

(a) on which the trial does not proceed; or

(b) in respect of the accused or defendant who has been granted a separate trial.

(5) Subsequent procedure — The counts in respect of which a jury is discharged pursuant to paragraph (4)(*a*) may subsequently be proceeded on in all respects as if they were contained in a separate indictment.

(6) Idem — Where an order is made in respect of an accused or defendant under paragraph (3)(*b*), the accused or defendant may be tried separately on the counts in relation to which the order was made as if they were contained in a separate indictment.

R.S., c. C-34, s. 520; R.S. 1985, c. 27 (1st Supp.), s. 119.

Commentary: The section enacts the general rule of *joinder of counts* in an indictment and the basis upon which severance may be ordered.

Under s. 591(1), any number of *counts* for any number of offences may be joined in the same indictment, but must be distinguished as in Form 4. This general rule is subject to exception as, for example, in s. 589 relating to charges of murder. Each count may be treated as a separate indictment under s. 591(2).

The *standard* to be applied in applications for severance of counts, as well as the procedure to be followed thereafter, is described in ss. 591(3)–(6). D, whether charged alone or jointly with others, may apply to the court, *before or during trial*, for an order that D be tried separately on one or more of the *counts*. An order of severance may be made where the court is satisfied that the *interests of justice* so require.

Where an order for a separate trial is made during trial, s. 591(4) requires that the jury be discharged from giving a verdict on the counts or in relation to the accused in respect of which or whom a separate trial has been ordered. The severed counts and/or accused may later be separately tried, as if those matters or persons were dealt with or contained in a separate indictment.

Case Law

General Principles of Joinder

R. v. Litchfield (1993), 25 C.R. (4th) 137, 86 C.C.C. (3d) 97 (S.C.C.) — See digest under s. 590 *General Principles, supra.*

R. v. Clunas (1992), 70 C.C.C. (3d) 115 (S.C.C.) — The court may order two or more indictments or informations to be tried together, where it is in the interests of justice and D, or where the offences could have been jointly charged. The court should seek the consent of both D and P, and where consent is withheld, explore the reasons. A court may order joinder whether or not D consents, providing the foregoing criteria for joinder are met. Summary conviction offences should be joined with indictable offences *only* where the trial on the indictable offence is to take place in provincial court. In the event of any conflict as to the applicable procedure, indictable procedures should apply.

R. v. Cassidy (1963), 40 C.R. 171 (Alta. C.A.) — The application for severance should be made at the *outset* of the trial, although there are circumstances where the refusal to grant a severance after the commencement of the trial might result in a miscarriage of justice.

R. v. Cuthbert (1996), 106 C.C.C. (3d) 28 (B.C. C.A.) — Where application to sever counts is made later in a trial on the ground of prejudice, it should be based on some prejudice which has arisen in the trial but which was *not* apparent at the outset. (Per Lambert and Goldie JJ.A.)

R. v. Massick (1985), 47 C.R. (3d) 148, 21 C.C.C. (3d) 128 (B.C. C.A.) — An information may charge a summary conviction offence under the *Code* and a summary conviction offence under a provincial statute, if the practice is *not* prohibited by provincial legislation.

R. v. Grant (1992), 52 O.A.C. 244 (C.A.) — The joint trial of indictable and summary conviction offence is *not* authorized by law. It is a procedural irregularity that may be subject to the application of either s. 686(1)(b)(iii) or s. 686(1)(b)(iv), where D has suffered *no* prejudice.

R. v. McNamara (No. 1) (1981), 56 C.C.C. (2d) 193 (Ont. C.A.); affirmed (1985), 45 C.R. (3d) 289, 19 C.C.C. (3d) 1 (S.C.C.) — The policy of the *Code* is to avoid multiplicity of proceedings.

R. v. Mazur (1986), 27 C.C.C. (3d) 359 (Y.T. C.A.); leave to appeal refused (1986), 27 C.C.C. (3d) 359n (S.C.C.) — A provincial court judge has no jurisdiction to amend an information to join the accused and a co-accused in one information. Crown counsel has untrammelled discretion, absent abuse of process, to decide when to proceed jointly or separately against accused persons.

Joinder and Severance of Accused: S. 591(3)

R. v. Crawford (1995), 37 C.R. (4th) 197, 96 C.C.C. (3d) 481 (S.C.C.); reversing (sub nom. *R. v. Creighton*) 80 C.C.C. (3d) 421, 20 C.R. (4th) 331 — Co-accused have the right to cross-examine each other in making full answer and defence. Restrictions that apply to P may *not* apply to restrict this right of a co-accused.The right to make full answer and defence is *not* absolute. Assertion of the right in a joint trial requires regard for the effect of the public interest in joint trials with respect to charges arising out of a common enterprise. The discretion to order separate trials must be exercised on the basis of legal principle, including the principle that severance ought not be ordered unless it is established that a joint trial will work an injustice to the accused. Their mere assertion of a "cut-throat" defence is *not* sufficient to warrant separate trials.

Guimond v. R. (1979), 8 C.R. (3d) 185, 44 C.C.C. (2d) 481 (S.C.C.) — Whenever it is apparent that the evidence at the joint trial of two alleged co-conspirators is *substantially* stronger against one than the other, the safer course is to direct the separate trial of each, and this is particularly the case when the prosecution is tendering in evidence a damaging statement made by one under circumstances which made it inadmissible against the other.

R. v. Nielsen (1984), 16 C.C.C. (3d) 39 (Man. C.A.); reversed on other grounds (1988), 62 C.R. (3d) 313, 40 C.C.C. (3d) 1 (S.C.C.) — An indictment may join two accused even though one was ordered to stand trial and the other was named by way of direct indictment.

R. v. Giesecke (1993), 82 C.C.C. (3d) 331 (Ont. C.A.); leave to appeal refused (1994), 86 C.C.C. (3d) viin (S.C.C.) — *See also*: *R. v. Unger* (1993), 83 C.C.C. (3d) 228 (Man. C.A.) — Severance may be required where D, in a joint trial, suffers cumulative prejudice due to the admission of evidence otherwise inadmissible against her but for the fact of a joint trial, from increasingly antagonistic defences and, in particular, from the closing address of counsel for a co-accused.

R. v. McLeod (1983), 6 C.C.C. (3d) 29 (Ont. C.A.); affirmed (1986), 27 C.C.C. (3d) 383 (S.C.C.) — The *general* rule with respect to joinder or severance of trial favours joint indictment and trial. The law presumes the jury's ability to disregard the statements of the co-accused. The general rule will be reinforced where the trial judge considers all the statements, gives the jury proper instruction and properly exercises his discretion with respect to ruling against separate trials.

R. v. Torbiak (1978), 40 C.C.C. (2d) 193 (Ont. C.A.) — Where a joint trial would deprive D1 of the benefit of the evidence of D2, which evidence might reasonably affect the verdict by creating a reasonable doubt as to the guilt of D1, separate trials may be required, notwithstanding that the evidence of D2 would be merely corroborative of the evidence of D1.

R. v. Agawa (1975), 31 C.R.N.S. 293, 28 C.C.C. (2d) 379 (Ont. C.A.) — Although *prima facie*, accused who are jointly indicted should be jointly tried where it is alleged that they acted in concert, the fact that one co-accused can give evidence on behalf of another co-accused and would be a compellable witness on a separate trial constitutes a proper foundation, in appropriate circumstances, for the exercise of the trial judge's discretion to order a separate trial.

R. v. Quiring (1974), 27 C.R.N.S. 367 (Sask. C.A.) — Where the essence of the case is that D were engaged in a common enterprise, as a general rule it is right and proper that they be jointly indicted and jointly tried, unless it can be shown that by so doing one of the accused would be prejudiced in his defence or denied the opportunity of a fair trial. It is *not* mandatory that separate trials be granted merely on the allegation that one accused may give evidence in defence of the other, but is a matter of discretion for the trial judge to determine.

Joinder and Severance of Counts: S. 591(3)

R. v. Rarru (1996), 107 C.C.C. (3d) 53 (S.C.C.); reversing (1996), 107 C.C.C. (3d) 53 at 54 (B.C. C.A.) — To be charged in the same indictment, offences need *not* meet the standard required to justify the reception of evidence of similar acts. Joinder of counts does *not* make the evidence on one count admissible on the trial of others.

Where counts are tried together and evidence on one count is *not* admissible as evidence of similar acts in relation to other counts, a trial judge ought to warn the jury

i.   that the evidence on one count ought *not* be considered in relation to other counts; and

ii. of the dangers of the potential influence of other alleged criminal acts which are *not* the subject of a particular count.

R. v. B. (M.O.) (1998), 123 C.C.C. (3d) 270 (B.C. C.A.) — In determining whether to sever *counts*, a trial judge should consider

i.   the factual and legal nexus between the counts;

ii. general prejudice to D;

iii. D's wish to testify on some, but not other counts;

iv. the possibility of inconsistent verdicts; and

v.   the desirability of avoiding several trials.

R. v. Kelly (1916), 27 C.C.C. 140 (Man. C.A.); affirmed (1916), 27 C.C.C. 282 (S.C.C.) — The mere fact that some of the evidence to be adduced is admissible only on one count is not necessarily a ground for ordering separate trials. The jury must be warned that they are to apply to each count only the evidence properly referable to, and admissible under, it.

R. v. Simpson (1977), 35 C.C.C. (2d) 337 (Ont. C.A.) — Where the evidence on one count is admissible on the other count, it is proper to try the counts together.

R. v. Cross (1996), 112 C.C.C. (3d) 410 (Que. C.A.) — The "interests of justice" refers to notions of fairness and justice and requires the judge to weigh the interest of D and of society. D has the constitutional right to make full answer and defence and the right to a fair trial. The proper administration of justice requires, in general, that a multiplicity of proceedings be avoided and costs limited.

To obtain a separate trial, D must demonstrate on a *balance of probabilities* that the interests of justice require separate trials.

Forum for Application: S. 591(4)

R. v. Litchfield (1993), 25 C.R. (4th) 37, 86 C.C.C. (3d) 97 (S.C.C.) — An indictment is preferred only when it is lodged with the trial judge. It may be preferred, however, once the trial judge has been assigned. D may apply to the assigned trial judge to divide or sever the counts after the indictment has been preferred, but before the court has been constituted to begin hearing evidence. It is the *trial* judge who should hear such applications.

Appellate Review

R. v. Litchfield (1993), 25 C.R. (4th) 37, 86 C.C.C. (3d) 97 (S.C.C.) — An appellate court should *not* interfere with the exercise of this discretion unless it is shown that the judge acted injudiciously or the order made resulted in an injustice.

Related Provisions: The charges which may be included as counts in an indictment after D has been ordered to stand trial are described in s. 574. It matters not whether the charges were contained in one information. Section 577 authorizes the preferment of a direct indictment, but does not specify what charges may be included as counts therein.

The authority of P to prefer joint indictments alleging joint liability of several accused is unquestioned, even in cases where the several accused were initially charged individually, in separate informations. Under *Clunas, supra*, it may be permissible to conduct a joint trial upon separate informations or indictments. The right of P to prefer joint indictments is, of course, subject to the authority of this section which authorizes a court to order separate trials.

Sections 592 and 593 permit the joinder of accused, in certain cases, although s. 592 and its companion provision, s. 23.1, are not, strictly speaking, rules of criminal pleading.

The provision also applies in summary conviction proceedings under s. 795.

Joinder of Accused in Certain Cases

592. Accessories after the fact — Any one who is charged with being an accessory after the fact to any offence may be indicted, whether or not the principal or any other party to the offence has been indicted or convicted or is or is not amenable to justice.

R.S., c. C-34, s. 521.

Commentary: The section *permits* the *indictment* of an *accessory after the fact*, irrespective of whether the principal or another, accused of the offence, has been indicted, convicted or is amenable to justice. At common law, an accessory could *not* be convicted, unless the principal had been first convicted, so that where the principal could not be found, the accessory would not be triable at all.

Case Law [See also case digests under s. 23]

R. v. Vinette (1974), 19 C.C.C. (2d) 1 (S.C.C.) — Evidence admissible against the principal is equally admissible against an accessory after the fact. Since a plea of guilty is admissible against the person who made it, a plea of guilty by the principal offender is admissible as evidence against the accessory after the fact as proof of the principal crime. (See now s. 657.2)

R. v. S. (F.J.) (1998), 121 C.C.C. (3d) 223 (S.C.C.); affirming (1997), 115 C.C.C. (3d) 450 (N.S. C.A.) — Sections 23.1 and 592 treat parties, including accessories after the fact, as principals. Conviction of the principal is *not* necessary in order to convict an accessory.

An accessory may be convicted even where the prinipal is acquitted.

Related Provisions: Accessoryship may be proven under ss. 21 and 22. What must be proven to make D an accessory after the fact to an offence is described in s. 23. Under s. 23.1, the principles of ss. 21–23, apply, *inter alia*, even though the principal/another party cannot him/herself be convicted of the offence. The conjoint effect of ss. 591 and 23.1 is that an accessory after the fact may be indicted, tried and convicted, notwithstanding that the principal or another party neither has been nor could be.

Section 657.2(2) permits P to prove the principal's conviction or discharge on the trial of the accessory. The evidence proves the commission of the principal offence.

The offences of being an accessory after the fact to high treason, treason or murder must be tried by the superior court of criminal jurisdiction under s. 469(b). The trial of accessories after the fact to offences listed in s. 553(a) is within the absolute jurisdiction of a provincial court judge under Part XIX. The general punishment provisions are found in s. 463.

593. (1) Trial of persons jointly for having in possession — Any number of persons may be charged in the same indictment with an offence under section 354 or paragraph 356(1)(*b*), notwithstanding that

  (a) the property was had in possession at different times; or

  (b) the person by whom the property was obtained

   (i) is not indicted with them, or

   (ii) is not in custody or is not amenable to justice.

(2) Conviction of one or more — Where, pursuant to subsection (1), two or more persons are charged in the same indictment with an offence referred to in that subsection, any one or more of those persons who separately committed the offence in respect of the property or any part of it may be convicted.

R.S., c. C-34, s. 522.

Commentary: The section applies only in prosecutions under ss. 354 and 356(1)(b) and describes who may be indicted and upon what basis convictions may be registered.

Under s. 593(1) *any number of persons* may be charged in the same indictment with an offence under s. 354 or 356(1)(b), notwithstanding the circumstances described in s. 593(1).

Under s. 593(2), *convictions* may be registered in cases under s. 593(1) of any one or more accused who are proven to have *separately* committed the offence in relation to the property or any part of it.

The section avoids the necessity of multiple indictments and trials. It emphasizes the general principle that the liability of any accused, jointly indicted, may be severally proven.

Related Provisions: The mere fact that the section permits joinder, and articulates the basis upon which any accused may be convicted, does *not* necessarily require a joint trial. D may apply for severance, for example, under s. 591(3)(b).

Possession may be established under s. 4(3). "Property" is defined in s. 2.

594. [Repealed R.S. 1985, c. 27 (1st Supp.), s. 120.]

595. [Repealed R.S. 1985, c. 27 (1st Supp.), s. 120.]

596. [Repealed R.S. 1985, c. 27 (1st Supp.), s. 120.]

Proceedings when Person Indicted is at Large

597. (1) Bench warrant — Where an indictment has been preferred against a person who is at large, and that person does not appear or remain in attendance for his trial, the court before which the accused should have appeared or remained in attendance may issue a warrant in Form 7 for his arrest.

(2) Execution — A warrant issued under subsection (1) may be executed anywhere in Canada.

(3) Interim release — Where an accused is arrested under a warrant issued under subsection (1), a judge of the court that issued the warrant may order that the accused be released on his giving an undertaking that he will do any one or more of the following things as specified in the order, namely,

(a) report at times to be stated in the order to a peace officer or other person designated in the order;

(b) remain within a territorial jurisdiction specified in the order;

(c) notify the peace officer or other person designated under paragraph (*a*) of any change in his address or his employment or occupation;

(d) abstain from communicating with any witness or other person expressly named in the order except in accordance with such conditions specified in the order as the judge deems necessary;

(e) where the accused is the holder of a passport, deposit his passport as specified in the order; and

(f) comply with such other reasonable conditions specified in the order as the judge considers desirable.

(4) Discretion to postpone execution — A judge who issues a warrant may specify in the warrant the period before which the warrant shall not be executed, to allow the accused to appear voluntarily before a judge having jurisdiction in the territorial division in which the warrant was issued.

(5) Deemed execution of warrant — Where the accused appears voluntarily for the offence in respect of which the accused is charged, the warrant is deemed to be executed.

R.S., c. C-34, s. 526; c. 2 (2d Supp.), s. 11; 1974–75–76, c. 93, s. 64.1; R.S. 1985, c. 27 (1st Supp), s. 121; 1997, c. 18, s. 68.

Commentary: Where D, at large pending trial, *fails to appear or remain in attendance* at trial, the trial court may issue an arrest warrant in Form 7, which may be executed anywhere in Canada.

A judge of a court that issued the warrant for D's arrest *may* order that D be released, after execution of the warrant, upon an undertaking containing any or all of the conditions described in ss. 597(3)(a)–(f).

Under s. 597(4) a judge issuing a warrant may postpone its execution to allow D to appear voluntarily, thereby deeming the warrant executed.

Case Law
Right of Review

R. v. Rodriques (1998), 123 C.C.C. (3d) 93 (Man. C.A. Chambers) — The decision of a superior court judge refusing release under s. 597(3) may be reviewed by another judge of the same court.

Related Provisions: Failure to appear or remain in attendance may affect the *mode* of D's trial under s. 598. Section 475 authorizes, *inter alia*, the continuance of the trial in D's absence, where D has absconded during the course of the trial. The section does *not* permit trial in *absentia* where D fails to appear at the outset of trial proceedings.

Failure to appear or remain in attendance, as required by a release order, may attract liability under ss. 145(2) and (5).

598. (1) Election deemed to be waived — Notwithstanding anything in this Act, where a person to whom subsection 597(1) applies has elected or is deemed to have elected to be tried by a court composed of a judge and jury and, at the time he failed to appear or to remain in attendance for his trial, he had not re-elected to be tried by a court composed of a judge without a jury or a provincial court judge without a jury, he shall not be tried by a court composed of a judge and jury unless

    (a) he establishes to the satisfaction of a judge of the court in which he is indicted that there was a legitimate excuse for his failure to appear or remain in attendance for his trial; or

    (b) the Attorney General requires pursuant to section 568 or 569 that the accused be tried by a court composed of a judge and jury.

(2) Election deemed to be waived — An accused who, pursuant to subsection (1), may not be tried by a court composed of a judge and jury is deemed to have elected under section 536 or 536.1 to be tried by a judge without a jury and section 561 or 561.1, as the case may be, does not apply in respect of the accused.

1974–75–76, c. 93, s. 65; R.S. 1985, c. 27 (1st Supp.), ss. 122, 203; 1999, c. 3, s. 51.

Commentary: The section describes the procedural consequences of D's failure to appear or remain in attendance on the mode of trial. Where the failure to appear or remain in attendance occurs in respect of a jury trial, prior to any re-election by D of another mode of trial, D loses his/her right to a jury trial except in two instances. Where D establishes, to the satisfaction of a judge of the trial court, a legitimate excuse for the failure to appear or remain in attendance, the proceedings will continue as a jury trial, as they will where the Attorney General so requires under, s. 568. In all other cases s. 598(2) deems D to have elected trial by judge alone in the court in which D is indicted, without right of re-election under s. 561.

The section has attracted *Charter* s. 11(f) scrutiny.

Case Law

Legitimate Excuse: S. 598(1)(a)

R. v. Papalia (1983), 48 B.C.L.R. 187 (C.A.) — The right to trial by judge and jury cannot be taken away *except* in strict accordance with the provisions of the *Code*. As the right to proffer a legitimate excuse does not expire with the passage of time, where D had not had an opportunity to provide a legitimate reason for his failure to appear at trial, D was entitled to renew his application for trial by judge and jury.

R. v. Harris (1991), 66 C.C.C. (3d) 536 (Ont. C.A.) — *See also*: *R. v. McNabb* (1987), 55 C.R. (3d) 369, 33 C.C.C. (3d) 266 (B.C. C.A.) — An honest mistake as to the date of trial is a legitimate excuse under s. 598, perhaps even if D did *not* exercise due diligence. Nothing less than an *intentional avoidance* of appearance at trial for the *purpose* of impeding or frustrating the trial or avoiding its consequences, or failure to appear due to a mistake based upon wilful blindness will deprive D of his/her *Charter* s. 11(f) rights.

Charter Considerations

R. v. Lee (1989), 73 C.R. (3d) 257, 52 C.C.C. (3d) 289 (S.C.C.) — *See also*: *R. v. Crate* (1983), 7 C.C.C. (3d) 127 (Alta. C.A.); *R. v. McNabb* (1987), 55 C.R. (3d) 369, 33 C.C.C. (3d) 266 (B.C. C.A.) — Although s. 598 restricts the right to trial by jury and is contrary to *Charter* s. 11(f), it constitutes a reasonable limit within s. 1.

Related Provisions: Under s. 597, the failure to appear or remain in attendance may result in the issuance of a warrant in Form 7 for D's arrest. Upon execution of the warrant and return of D, release may be ordered under s. 597(3).

Section 475 authorizes, *inter alia*, the continuation of the trial in D's absence where D has absconded *during the course of the trial*, but does *not* permit trial *in absentia*, where D has failed to appear at the outset of trial proceedings.

Failure to appear or remain in attendance as required may also attract liability under ss. 145(2) and (5).

Change of Venue

599. (1) Reasons for change of venue — A court before which an accused is or may be indicted, at any term or sittings thereof, or a judge who may hold or sit in that court, may at any time before or after an indictment is found, on the application of the prosecutor or the accused, order the trial to be held in a territorial division in the same province other than that in which the offence would otherwise be tried if

(a) it appears expedient to the ends of justice; or

(b) a competent authority has directed that a jury is not to be summoned at the time appointed in a territorial division where the trial would otherwise by law be held.

(2) [Repealed 1988, c. 2, s. 23.]

(3) Conditions as to expense — The court or judge may, in an order made on an application by the prosecutor under subsection (1), prescribe conditions that he thinks proper with respect to the payment of additional expenses caused to the accused as a result of the change of venue

(4) Transmission of record — Where an order is made under subsection (1), the officer who has custody of the indictment, if any, and the writings and exhibits relating to the prosecution, shall transmit them forthwith to the clerk of the court before which the trial is ordered to be held, and all proceedings in the case shall be held or, if previously commenced, shall be continued in that court.

(5) Idem — **Where the writings and exhibits referred to in subsection (4) have not been returned to the court in which the trial was to be held at the time an order is made to change the place of trial, the person who obtains the order shall serve a true copy thereof on the person in whose custody they are and that person shall thereupon transmit them to the clerk of the court before which the trial is to be held.**

R.S., c. C-34, s. 527; 1974–75–76, c. 93, s. 66; R.S. 1985, c. 1 (4th Supp.), s. 23.

Commentary: The section describes the basis upon which a *change of venue* may be ordered.

The authority of s. 599(1) to order a change of venue, may be invoked by D or P, at *any time before or after an indictment is found*. The authority may be exercised by a court before which D is or may be indicted, or any judge who may sit in that court, at any term or sittings of the court. The *basis* upon which an order may be granted are that it *appears expedient to the ends of justice* to do so, or that a competent authority has directed that no jurors will be summoned at the time and place appointed for D's trial. The italicized words constitute the principal basis upon which applications are made.

Under s. 599(3), a judge who orders a change of venue upon application by P, may prescribe conditions considered proper respecting the payment of additional expenses caused D by such an order. It is not uncommon for P to so undertake in its application for a change of venue.

The provisions of ss. 599(4) and (5) ensure the transmission of the indictment, writings and exhibits to the new place of trial for use in the trial proceedings.

Case Law
Grounds: S. 599(1)

R. v. Alward (1976), 39 C.R.N.S. 281, 32 C.C.C. (2d) 416 (N.B. C.A.) — A change of venue is justified only where there is strong evidence of a general prejudicial attitude in the community as a whole.

Successive Applications

R. v. Hutchinson (1975), 26 C.C.C. (2d) 423 (N.B. C.A.); affirmed (sub nom. *Ambrose v. R.)* 30 C.C.C. (2d) 97 — There is no right to bring successive applications for a change of venue before different judges, except where new grounds have arisen since the previous applications.

R. v. Noël (1996), 110 C.C.C. (3d) 168 (Que. C.A.) — There is *no* right of appeal from an order changing the venue of a trial and ordering P to pay an additional amount of money to counsel for D over and above the Legal Aid tariff. (per Chouinard and Nuss JJ.A.)

Related Provisions: "Territorial division" is defined in s. 2. Special territorial jurisdiction provisions appear in ss. 7 and 476–481.

In the usual course, the venue in criminal matters is laid in the county, district or region in which the offence is alleged to have been committed. An order for a change of venue directs that the trial *not* be there held, but rather take place in another territorial division in the same province. The trial procedure in all other respects remains the same. A change of venue may also be ordered where it is necessary for the purpose of the language of trial under s. 531.

The subsection affords no authority to change the venue of trial to another province and, in terms, provides expressly to the contrary. The general rule is expressed in s. 478(1).

600. Order is authority to remove prisoner — **An order that is made under section 599 is sufficient warrant, justification and authority to all sheriffs, keepers of prisons and peace officers for the removal, disposal and reception of an accused in accordance with the terms of the order, and the sheriff may appoint and authorize any peace officer to convey the accused to a prison in the territorial division in which the trial is ordered to be held.**

R.S., c. C-34, s. 528.

Commentary: Under this section, an order for a change of venue under s. 599 authorizes designated officials to remove D from a prison in the territorial division where the case would otherwise be tried, to a prison in the territorial division to which the venue of the trial has been changed, and there to confine him/her, in accordance with the terms of the order.

Related Provisions: A change of venue may be ordered under s. 599(1). The transmission of the records (indictment, writings and exhibits) to the clerk of the court before which the trial is ordered to be held is made under ss. 599(4) and (5).

Amendment

601. (1) Amending defective indictment or count — An objection to an indictment or to a count in an indictment for a defect apparent on the face thereof shall be taken by motion to quash the indictment or count before the accused has pleaded, and thereafter only by leave of the court before which the proceedings take place, and the court before which an objection is taken under this section may, if it considers it necessary, order the indictment or count to be amended to cure the defect.

(2) Amendment where variance — Subject to this section, a court may, on the trial of an indictment, amend the indictment or a count therein or a particular that is furnished under section 587, to make the indictment, count or particular conform to the evidence, where there is a variance between the evidence and

(a) a count in the indictment as preferred; or

(b) a count in the indictment

(i) as amended, or

(ii) as it would have been if it had been amended in conformity with any particular that has been furnished pursuant to section 587.

(3) Amending indictment — Subject to this section, a court shall, at any stage of the proceedings, amend the indictment or a count therein as may be necessary where it appears

(a) that the indictment has been preferred under a particular Act of Parliament instead of another Act of Parliament;

(b) that the indictment or a count thereof

(i) fails to state or states defectively anything that is requisite to constitute the offence,

(ii) does not negative an exception that should be negatived,

(iii) is in any way defective in substance,

and the matters to be alleged in the proposed amendment are disclosed by the evidence taken on the preliminary inquiry or on the trial; or

(c) that the indictment or a count thereof is in any way defective in form.

(4) Matters to be considered by the court — The court shall, in considering whether or not an amendment should be made to the indictment or a count in it, consider

(a) the matters disclosed by the evidence taken on the preliminary inquiry;

(b) the evidence taken on the trial, if any;

(c) the circumstances of the case;

(d) whether the accused has been misled or prejudiced in his defence by any variance, error or omission mentioned in subsection (2) or (3); and

(e) whether, having regard to the merits of the case, the proposed amendment can be made without injustice being done.

(4.1) Variance not material — A variance between the indictment or a count therein and the evidence taken is not material with respect to

(a) the time when the offence is alleged to have been committed, if it is proved that the indictment was preferred within the prescribed period of limitation, if any; or

(b) the place where the subject-matter of the proceedings is alleged to have arisen, if it is proved that it arose within the territorial jurisdiction of the court.

(5) Adjournment if accused prejudiced — Where, in the opinion of the court, the accused has been misled or prejudiced in his defence by a variance, error or omission in an indictment or a count therein, the court may, if it is of the opinion that the misleading or prejudice may be removed by an adjournment, adjourn the proceedings to a specified day or sittings of the court and may make such an order with respect to the payment of costs resulting from the necessity for amendment as it considers desirable.

(6) Question of law — The question whether an order to amend an indictment or a count thereof should be granted or refused is a question of law.

(7) Endorsing indictment — An order to amend an indictment or a count therein shall be endorsed on the indictment as part of the record and the proceedings shall continue as if the indictment or count had been originally preferred as amended.

(8) Mistakes not material — A mistake in the heading of an indictment shall be corrected as soon as it is discovered but, whether corrected or not, is not material.

(9) Limitation — The authority of a court to amend indictments does not authorize the court to add to the overt acts stated in an indictment for high treason or treason or for an offence against any provision in sections 49, 50, 51 and 53.

(10) Definition of "court" — In this section, "court" means a court, judge, justice or provincial court judge acting in summary conviction proceedings or in proceedings on indictment.

(11) Application — This section applies to all proceedings, including preliminary inquiries, with such modifications as the circumstances require.

R.S., c. C-34, s. 529; 1974–75–76, c. 105, s. 29; R.S. 1985, c. 27 (1st Supp.), s. 123; 1999, c. 5, s. 23.

Commentary: The section defines when *objection* may be taken to a count or indictment on the basis of facial deficiency and describes the *circumstances* under which the count or indictment may or shall be amended.

Under s. 601(1) any *objection* to an indictment or count, for a *defect apparent on the face*, must be taken on a *motion to quash*, prior to plea, thereafter, only with leave of the court. The indictment or count may be *amended* under ss. 601(2) and (3) to cure the defect. "Court" is defined in s. 601(10). Section 601(11) makes the section applicable to all proceedings, including preliminary inquiries.

The *amending* authority of s. 601(2) is *discretionary*. *On the trial* of an indictment, it authorizes amendment of the indictment, count or particular furnished under s. 587 to *conform to the evidence* adduced. Section 601(4.1) describes those variances concerning *time* and *place* which are *not* material.

The *amending* authority of s. 601(3) is *mandatory* and available *at any stage of the proceedings*. It requires amendment of defects of *form*, misdescription of statutory preferment authority, omissions or defective statements of the essential elements of the offence and defects in *substance*. Under s. 601(8), a mistake in the heading of the indictment is *not* material but must be corrected as soon as it is discovered. Subsection (4) describes what must be considered in determining whether an amendment will be made. The authority to amend an indictment does *not* authorize adding to the overt acts stated in an indictment for treason, high treason or an offence under ss. 49–51, or s. 53.

Under s. 601(7), all orders amending an indictment or count must be *endorsed* on the indictment. The proceedings thereafter continue, subject to the authority of s. 601(5) to *adjourn* where D has been prejudiced or misled by the variance, error or omission that was amended, as if the count or indictment had been originally preferred as amended.

Under s. 601(6), questions concerning the amendment of an indictment or count are questions of law.

Case Law

Timing of Motion: Ss. 601(1), (10), (11)

R. v. W. (A.G.) (1993), 17 C.R. (4th) 393, 78 C.C.C. (3d) 302 (S.C.C.) — *See also*: *R. v. Moore* (1988), 65 C.R. (3d) 1, 41 C.C.C. (3d) 289 (S.C.C.) — A provincial court judge conducting a preliminary inquiry has jurisdiction under *Code* s. 601 to determine the validity of an information.

R. v. Volpi (1987), 34 C.C.C. (3d) 1 (Ont. C.A.); leave to appeal refused (1987), 23 O.A.C. 397n (S.C.C.) — Since a properly worded information is necessary to enable D to exercise freely the right of election, an application to quash an indictment may be made *prior* to being required to elect.

R. v. Dallas (1986), 25 C.C.C. (3d) 287 (Ont. C.A.) — D is entitled to move to quash the information at the preliminary inquiry on the ground that it does *not* contain sufficient information to identify the subject of the charge.

R. v. Leclair (1956), 23 C.R. 216, 115 C.C.C. 297 (Ont. C.A.) — An objection based on the omission from the indictment of an *essential averment* should be taken by motion to quash *before* D pleads or during the course of the trial. It cannot be taken in the court of appeal unless that court is of the opinion that D has in some way been misled or prejudiced by the omission.

Authority to Amend: Ss. 601(2), (3), (4.1), (8), (9)

R. v. Tremblay (1993), 23 C.R. (4th) 98, 84 C.C.C. (3d) 97 (S.C.C.) — Section 601 does *not* permit amendments which would cause D irreparable prejudice, nor where the evidence does *not* support the proposed amendment.

R. v. B. (G.) (1990), 77 C.R. (3d) 347, 56 C.C.C. (3d) 200 (S.C.C.); affirming (1988), 58 C.R. (3d) 83, 35 C.C.C. (3d) 385 (B.C. C.A.) — What constitutes reasonable or adequate information with respect to the act or omission to be proven against D will vary as the factual matters which underlie some offences permit greater descriptive precision than do others. A significant factor in assessing the reasonableness of the information provided is the nature and legal character of the offence charged. In general, an information will *not* be quashed for failure to specify the exact *time* of the commission of an offence. A difference between the date alleged in the information and the evidence given is *only* of consequence where the time of the offence is critical and D may be misled by such variance, thereby suffering prejudice in his or her defence.

R. v. Côté (1986), 49 C.R. (3d) 351, 23 C.C.C. (3d) 481 (S.C.C.); affirming (1982), 32 C.R. (3d) 47, 3 C.C.C. (3d) 557 (Que. C.A.) — On a charge of conspiracy to defraud the Bank of Montreal where the evidence indicated an attempt to defraud the Bank of Canada, an amendment should have been permitted.

R. v. Rinnie (1970), 9 C.R.N.S. 81, [1970] 3 C.C.C. 218 (Alta. C.A.) — This section does *not* allow an amendment in order to broaden a charge to include an offence *not* originally included.

R. v. Stewart (1979), 7 C.R. (3d) 165 (B.C. C.A.) — A charge which lacks an essential averment may be amended. Where the objection is taken *after* plea, the focus is on prejudice, injustice or substantial wrong, *not* upon technicalities.

R. v. Powell, [1965] 4 C.C.C. 349 (B.C. C.A.) — Amendment of a charge to conform to the evidence, before D gave evidence but after he had made a motion for dismissal, is proper.

R. v. Greene (1976), 33 C.C.C. (2d) 251 (Nfld. C.A.) — The trial judge has *no* duty to amend the date specified in the information *suo motu*.

R. v. Wright (1987), 79 N.S.R. (2d) 52 (C.A.) — Where the information set out the incorrect name of D and D raised no objection prior to the commencement of the trial, the trial judge should have permitted P the opportunity to present its case and apply for an amendment.

R. v. Casey (1985), 71 N.S.R. (2d) 271 (C.A.) — Where a reference to an incorrect section of the *Code* was a typographical error that did *not* mislead D, an amendment was entirely proper.

R. v. Melo (1986), 29 C.C.C. (3d) 173 (Ont. C.A.) — Where D disputes the identity of V, he will *not* be misled or prejudiced in his defence by an amendment to an information that substitutes "male person" for a named victim.

R. v. R.I.C. (1986), 32 C.C.C. (3d) 399 (Ont. C.A.) — It is error for a provincial court judge to quash an information *suo motu* after D has pleaded. The absence of a motion to quash by D indicated that the information provided him with sufficient information to identify the transaction.

R. v. Wiley (1982), 65 C.C.C. (2d) 190 (Ont. C.A.) — Where D elected to call no evidence, but the trial judge amended the information to conform to P's evidence, a new trial was ordered as D may have been prejudiced in his defence.

R. v. Sault Ste. Marie (City) (1976), 30 C.C.C. (2d) 257 (Ont. C.A.); affirmed on other grounds (1978), 40 C.C.C. (2d) 353 (S.C.C.) — An information which is duplicitous or multifarious contains a defect on its face which may be amended.

Yanovitch v. R. (1958), 28 C.R. 220 (Que. C.A.) — An indictment may be amended so as to supply an essential ingredient.

Dupont v. R. (1958), 28 C.R. 146 (Que. C.A.) — An indictment may *not* be amended so as to substitute a different offence.

Considerations: S. 601(4)

R. v. Geary (1960), 33 C.R. 103, 126 C.C.C. 325 (Alta. C.A.) — In considering whether to amend the indictment, it is mandatory to consider the evidence at the preliminary inquiry.

R. v. P. (M.B.) (1992), 13 C.R. (4th) 302, 72 C.C.C. (3d) 121 (Ont. C.A.); affirmed (1994), 89 C.C.C. (3d) 289 (S.C.C.) — Under s. 601(4), the court must consider whether D will be prejudiced in his/her defence by the proposed amendment. The availability of an alibi is a significant factor to consider in assessing prejudice to D when an amendment is sought to the date of an offence of sexual assault against young children. An amendment ought *not* be made where its effect would be to deny D a significant procedural safeguard, as is the case where it would deprive D of the ability to put forward an independent assertion of innocence to the charge as laid.

R. v. Smith (1961), 35 C.R. 323 (Ont. C.A.); reversed on other grounds (1961), 36 C.R. 384 (S.C.C.) — The power of amendment may be exercised by the *trial* judge where D has been indicted without a preliminary inquiry.

Remedies: Ss. 601(5), (6)

R. v. W. (A.G.) (1993), 17 C.R. (4th) 393, 78 C.C.C. (3d) 302 (S.C.C.) — *See also*: *R. v. Moore* (1988), 65 C.R. (3d) 1, 41 C.C.C. (3d) 289 (S.C.C.) — A provincial court judge conducting a preliminary inquiry has jurisdiction under *Code* s. 601 to determine the validity of an information. The correctness of the ruling cannot generally be challenged by *certiorari*.

Vézina v. R. (1986), 49 C.R. (3d) 351, 25 C.C.C. (3d) 481 (S.C.C.) — Under s. 601(6), the decision to refuse an amendment to the information is a question of law, hence, reviewable by the court of appeal on a Crown appeal. When the decision is based upon a finding of irreparable prejudice, however, it should *not* be interfered with lightly keeping in mind the trial judge's privileged position as regards the effect on the fairness of a trial of events taking place in the courtroom.

R. v. Moore (1988), 65 C.R. (3d) 1, 41 C.C.C. (3d) 289 (S.C.C.); affirming (1984), 9 C.C.C. (3d) 1 (B.C. C.A.) — After entry of a plea of not guilty, but prior to the calling of evidence, an information was quashed as not disclosing an offence in law. It was held that D had been placed in jeopardy. Notwithstanding that the judge erred in quashing the information rather than amending it, the dismissal of the charge entitled D to a plea of *autrefois acquit* on a subsequent charge. P should have appealed the quashing of the information rather than laying a new information.

R. v. Haynen (1985), 33 Man. R. (2d) 222 (C.A.) — Where the information was quashed on the basis of uncertainty, P was *not* precluded from laying a proper information as the judge's decision had not been a final determination on the merits of the case.

R. v. Cousineau (1982), 1 C.C.C. (3d) 293 (Ont. C.A.) — Where the error is purely technical, an amendment is appropriate. Any prejudice to D is curable by an adjournment.

R. v. Jarman (1972), 10 C.C.C. (2d) 426 (Ont. C.A.) — Where the offence charged is one within the jurisdiction of the trial judge, he/she has exclusive jurisdiction to determine the validity of the information. An error with respect to that determination does *not* deprive the judge of jurisdiction. The decision may *only* be challenged on an *appeal* against the *final* disposition of the charge.

Shumiatcher v. Elliott (1961), 36 C.R. 322, 131 C.C.C. 112 (Sask. C.A.) — If D's motion to quash is denied by the trial judge in a superior court of criminal jurisdiction, *certiorari* is *not* available to quash the indictment.

Related Provisions: The sufficiency of a count or indictment is determined under s. 581. Sections 582 and 583 also contain general provisions as to counts, while special provisions respecting counts charging certain offences are found in ss. 584–586.

The authority of a *court of appeal* to amend an indictment or count derives from s. 686(4) and (8). *Quaere* whether s. 686(1)(b)(iv) adds anything to this authority?

602. [Repealed R.S. 1985, c. 27 (1st Supp.), s. 124.]

Inspection and Copies of Documents

603. Right of accused — An accused is entitled, after he has been ordered to stand trial or at his trial,

(a) to inspect without charge the indictment, his own statement, the evidence and the exhibits, if any; and

(b) to receive, on payment of a reasonable fee determined in accordance with a tariff of fees fixed or approved by the Attorney General of the province, a copy

(i) of the evidence,

(ii) of his own statement, if any, and

(iii) of the indictment;

but the trial shall not be postponed to enable the accused to secure copies unless the court is satisfied that the failure of the accused to secure them before the trial is not attributable to lack of diligence on the part of the accused.

R.S., c. C-34, s. 531; 1974–75–76, c. 93, s. 67; R.S. 1985, c. 27 (1st Supp.), s. 101(2).

Commentary: The section entitles D, after an order to stand trial or at trial, to *inspect*, without charge, and to *receive*, upon payment of a reasonable fee as fixed by the provincial tariff, a copy of the *evidence*, his/her own *statement* and the *indictment*. A trial generally will not be postponed to enable D to secure the relevant copies but it may be so, provided the court is satisfied such failure is *not* attributable to lack of D's diligence.

Case Law [See also s. 651, Remedies for Disclosure]
Disclosure

R. v. Dixon, [1998] 1 S.C.R. 244, 13 C.R. (5th) 217, 122 C.C.C. (3d) 1 — The right to full disclosure is only one component of the right to make full answer and defence. The *Charter* right to make full answer and defence is *not* necessarily impaired solely because the right to disclosure was violated.

To determine whether the right to make full answer and defence was impaired by P's failure to disclose, there are two steps to be followed. The *reliability* of the *result* must be assessed first. The undisclosed information should be examined to determine its impact on the decision to convict. If an appellate court is satisfied that there is a *reasonable possibility* that, on its face, the undisclosed information affects the reliability of the conviction, a new trial should be ordered.

The effect of non-disclosure on the *overall fairness* of the *trial process* should be considered, even if the undisclosed information does *not* affect the reliability of the trial result. What is assessed, on the basis of *reasonable possibility*, are the lines of inquiry with witnesses and the opportunities to garner additional evidence that could have been available to D if the relevant information had been disclosed. The diligence of defence counsel in pursuing disclosure from P is a factor to be considered.

Where D demonstrates a *reasonable possibility* that *undisclosed information* could have been used

i.   in *meeting* P's case;

ii.   *advancing* a defence; or,

iii.   *making* a *decision* which could have affected the *conduct* of the *defence*,

D has established that his/her *Charter* right to disclosure has been impaired.

In cases of incomplete disclosure by P, D is required to demonstrate on appeal from conviction

i.   that it is *reasonably possible* that the non-disclosed material *affected* the *reliability* of D's *conviction*; or

ii.   that it is *reasonably possible* that the non-disclosed material affected the overall fairness of the trial

in order to obtain a new trial.

R. v. La (1997), 8 C.R. (5th) 155, [1997] 2 S.C.R. 680, 116 C.C.C. (3d) 97 — The *duty* of P and the police to *preserve* the fruits of an investigation imposes an *obligation* on P to explain the loss of evidence. Where the explanation offered satisfies the trial judge that the evidence has not been destroyed or lost due to unacceptable negligence, there is no breach of the duty to disclose. Where the explanation offered fails to satisfy the judge, however, P has failed to meet its disclosure obligations and *Charter* s. 7 has been breached.

Whether a *stay of proceedings* is appropriate depends on the effect of the conduct which constitutes an abuse of process or other prejudice on the fairness of the trial. It is often best assessed in the context of the trial, as it unfolds. A trial judge has a discretion whether to rule on an application to stay proceedings immediately or after hearing some or all of the evidence. It is preferable for the trial judge to reserve on the application, unless it is clear that nothing but a stay will cure the prejudice occasioned by the underlying abuse of conduct. Where the application is dismissed at an early stage of the proceedings, it may be renewed later where there is a material change in circumstances.

The disclosure obligations of P give rise to an obligation to *preserve* relevant evidence.

Where P has *lost* evidence that should have been disclosed, P owes the duty to explain the loss or destruction. If the explanation satisfies the trial judge that the evidence has *not* been lost or destroyed due to *unacceptable negligence,* there is no breach of the duty to disclose. If P's explanation fails to satisfy the trial judge, however, there is a breach of D's disclosure obligations, perhaps an abuse of process.

To determine whether P's *explanation* for lost or destroyed evidence is satisfactory, the trial judge should consider *all* the circumstances, including

i.   whether the police took *reasonable steps* to preserve the evidence for disclosure; and

ii.   the apparent relevance of the evidence at the time of loss or destruction.

Item i is the principal considercation.

The loss of relevant evidence will *not* constitute a breach of P's disclosure obligation, provided the conduct of the police is reasonable.

R. v. Carosella (1997), 112 C.C.C. (3d) 289 (S.C.C.) — The foundation for P's obligation to produce material which may affect the conduct of the defence is that failure to do so would breach D's constitutional right to make full answer and defence. The right to disclosure of material which meets the *Stinchcombe* standard is a component of the right to make full answer and defence, hence a principle of fundamental justice under *Charter,* s. 7. Breach of the obligation is a breach of *Charter,* s. 7 without the requirement of an additional demonstration of prejudice. Where destroyed material meets the threshold test for disclosure/production, D's Charter right has been infringed. No additional prejudice has been shown.

Where D alleges a breach of the right to make full answer and defence due to

i.   non-disclosure; or

ii.   non-production,

it is *not* necessary to show *actual prejudice* to the conduct of the defence. The degree of prejudice suffered is *not* a *relevant* consideration in determining *whether* a substantive *Charter* right has been *breached,* although it is relevant in deciding what *remedy* is appropriate.

A *stay* of *proceedings* may be granted where the destruction of evidence has resulted in a breach of D's constitutional right to make full answer and defence where

i.   *no alternative remedy* would *cure* the *prejudice* to D's ability to make full answer and defence; or

ii. *irreparable prejudice* would be caused to the *integrity* of the *judicial system* if the prosecution were to continue.

R. v. O'Connor (1995), 44 C.R. (4th) 1, 103 C.C.C. (3d) 1 (S.C.C.) — Where D seeks production and disclosure of *records* in the possession of a *third party*, a two-stage procedure is to be followed.The procedure is commenced by a formal written application supported by an affidavit describing the specific grounds for production. Notice should be given to third party custodians of the documents and the persons who have a privacy interest in the records. The custodian and records should be subpoenaed to ensure their attendance or presence. The initial application ought be made to the judge seized of the trial but may be brought, with other pre-trial motions, before the jury is empanelled.At the first stage in the production procedure, D has the onus of satisfying the judge that the information sought is *likely* to be *relevant*. Every case does *not* require evidence and a *voir dire*. There is an initial threshold to provide a basis for production. It may be met by oral submissions of counsel. If the matter cannot be resolved on the basis of oral submissions, evidence and a *voir dire* may be required.The test of *likely relevance* requires that the judge be satisfied that there is a *reasonable possibility* that the information sought is *logically probative* on an *issue* at trial *or* the *competence* of a witness to testify. The *issues at trial* include,

i.   the *matters in issue* in the case;

ii. the *credibility* of witnesses; and,

iii. the *reliability* of *other evidence* in the case.

The burden on D should *not* be considered onerous, nor should it be assumed that private, therapeutic or counselling records are irrelevant to full answer and defence. The records may be *relevant*, in cases of sexual assault, because they

i.   contain information concerning the *unfolding of events* underlying the complaint;

ii. reveal the use of a *therapy* which *influenced* V's *memory* of the alleged offence; or,

iii. contain information relevant to V's *credibility*, including testimonial factors like the quality of V's perception of the events at the time of offence and V's memory thereafter.

At the second stage, the judge ought examine the records produced to determine whether, and to what extent, they ought be produced to D. The judge must weigh and examine the salutary and deleterious effects of a production order, as well decide whether a non-production order would constitute a reasonable limit on D's right to make full answer and defence. The judge may be able to provide a judicial summary of the records for counsel to assist in the determination.In balancing the competing rights, the judge ought consider,

i.   the extent to which the record is *necessary* for D to make full answer and defence;

ii. the *probative value* of the record;

iii. the nature and extent of the *reasonable expectation of privacy* vested in the record;

iv. whether production would be premised on any discriminatory belief or bias; and,

v.   the potential *prejudice* of V's dignity, privacy or personal security occasioned by production.

R. v. Khela (1995), 43 C.R. (4th) 368, 102 C.C.C. (3d) 1 (S.C.C.) — Failure by P to comply with a disclosure obligation may impair D's right to make full answer and defence, thereby infringing *Charter* s. 7.

P's disclosure obligation does *not* extend to production of P's witnesses for oral discovery. P's witnesses, even informants, are *not* P's property whom P can control and produce for examination by the defence.

Where new evidence which may warrant a change in the terms of P's obligation to disclose comes into P's possession, the appropriate procedure is an application to the trial judge, at the earliest opportunity, to vary the terms of the disclosure. The trial judge, has a discretion to vary an order for disclosure on the basis of evidence which shows that the factual foundation of the order is changed. Difficulties in compliance with disclosure orders should be resolved by application to vary *not* by non-compliance and attempted *ex post facto* justification on the basis of change to circumstances.

R. v. Chaplin (1995), 36 C.R. (4th) 201, 96 C.C.C. (3d) 225 (S.C.C.); affirming (1993), 145 A.R. 153, 20 C.R.R. (2d) 152 (Alta. C.A.) — P's disclosure obligation is shaped by the principles of fundamental justice, in particular the right to make full answer and defence, included in *Charter* s. 7.

In general, P must disclose *all* information, inculpatory or exculpatory, *except* evidence that is

i.   beyond P's control;

ii.   clearly irrelevant; or

iii.   privileged.

P must exercise the utmost good faith in determining which information must be disclosed and in providing ongoing disclosure. Failure to comply with the initial and ongoing obligation to disclose relevant and non-privileged evidence may result in a stay of proceedings or other redress against P. Further, it may constitute a serious breach of ethical standards.

P's obligation to disclose is *not* absolute. P must err on the side of inclusion, but need *not* produce the clearly irrelevant. Relevance is determined in relation to is use by the defence. It means a reasonable possibility of being useful to D in making full answer and defence.

Where D contends that P ought to have disclosed identified and existing material, P must justify non-disclosure by demonstrating that the information sought is

i.   beyond P's control;

ii.   clearly irrelevant; or,

iii.   privileged.

Justification of non-disclosure on the basis of public interest immunity or other privilege may involve special procedures to protect the confidentiality of the information.

Where P disputes the existence of material which D alleges to be relevant, P cannot be required to justify the non-disclosure of material the existence of which P is unaware or denies. D must establish a basis which could enable the presiding judge to conclude that there is in existence further material which is potentially relevant. The existence of the disputed material must be sufficiently identified, not only to reveal its nature, but also to permit the presiding judge to conclude that it may meet the test required for prosecutorial disclosure. Oral submissions may suffice. *Viva voce* evidence and a *voir dire* may be required where the presiding judge cannot determine the matter based on the submissions of counsel.Where D establishes a basis for the conclusion that the evidence may exist, P must justify the continuing refusal to disclose by demonstrating that the evidence is

i.   beyond P's control

ii.   clearly irrelevant; or

iii.   privileged.

Confidential information may require an in camera hearing, private inspection by the judge or procedures such as s. 37(2) *C.E.A.* or a *Garofoli* hearing.

R. v. Stinchcombe (1995), 38 C.R. (4th) 42, 96 C.C.C. (3d) 318 (S.C.C.) — P can only produce what is in its possession/control. D has *no* absolute right to have original material produced. If P has the originals of documents which should be produced, P should either produce the originals or allow their inspection. If the originals which had been in P's possession are not available, P should explain their absence. Where satisfactory explanation is given, P has discharged its obligations unless the conduct which resulted in absence/loss of the original is itself unconstitutional conduct.

R. v. Stinchcombe (1991), 8 C.R. (4th) 277, 68 C.C.C. (3d) 1 (S.C.C.) — D's right to make full answer and defence, which is one of the principles of fundamental justice, imposes on P a duty in the context of indictable offences, to disclose all relevant material to the imposes on P a duty in the context of indictable offences, to disclose *all* relevant material to the defence whether the material is inculpatory or exculpatory and whether or not P intends to introduce it at trial. The obligation is triggered by a request by D. Initial disclosure should occur before D is called upon to elect or plead, but there is a continuing obligation to disclose when additional material is received. P has a discretion to withhold or delay disclosure in some circumstances, for example to protect the identity of informers, but that discretion is reviewable by the trial judge.

R. v. C. (M.H.) (1991), 4 C.R. (4th) 1, 63 C.C.C. (3d) 385 (S.C.C.) — Where P's failure to disclose relevant material to defence counsel results in an unfair trial, a conviction may be set aside on appeal, as for example, where that which was not disclosed may have a material bearing on the credibility of P's principal witness, V.

Lemay v. R. (1951), 14 C.R. 89, 102 C.C.C. 1 (S.C.C.) — Although P must not hold back evidence because it would assist D, P is, nevertheless, free to exercise his discretion to determine who are material witnesses. A material witness is *not* identical with a witness who is essential to the unfolding of the narrative.

R. v. Gillis (1994), 91 C.C.C. (3d) 575 (Alta. C.A.) — The right to full disclosure does *not* arise until a charge has been laid. It does *not* entail D observing the collection of evidence by the police.

R. v. Siemens (1998), 122 C.C.C. (3d) 552 (Alta. C.A.) — Although P bears the ultimate responsibility for decisions regarding relevance and disclosure of evidence, P is *not* required to personally examine and catalogue every item of evidence. P may rely on information provided by investigators and other staff concerning document contents, especially material considered to have no relevance.

R. v. Baxter (1997), 115 C.C.C. (3d) 64 (B.C. C.A.) — Statutory declarations obtained by P from former co-accused who pleaded guilty during trial which P undertook *not* to disclose to anyone unless the declarant testified for D are relevant and disclosable to D.

R. v. Mitchell (1998), 123 C.C.C. (3d) 521 (B.C. C.A.); additional reasons at (1998), 123 C.C.C. (3d) 540 (B.C. C.A.) — The fact that a sample taken by hospital staff for medical purposes might also have been tested for a forensic purpose does *not* create a duty on P to ensure that it be kept.

R. v. W. (D.D.) (1997), 114 C.C.C. (3d) 506 (B.C. C.A.) — Crown agencies or departments involved in the investigation of a criminal case with respect to D ought disclose documents relating to the investigation to P who should take steps to obtain all such documentation of which s/he is aware.

Where a provincial ministry is not involved in the investigation of a case, rather, is only in possession of records which D seeks to further the defence, P has no greater access to the records than D. It is a *fortiori* where the records are subject to statutory obligation of non-disclosure.

R. v. Fisk (1996), 108 C.C.C. (3d) 63 (B.C. C.A.) — Where investigators are apprised of information in the possession of a third party concerning the commission of the offence charged, but decline to investigate it, P is obliged to disclose to D before trial that a third party might have important evidence relevant to the defence.

R. v. Wicksted (1996), 106 C.C.C. (3d) 385 (Ont. C.A.), notice of appeal filed (June 4, 1996), Doc. No. 25350 (S.C.C.) — A stay of proceedings is a remedy of last resort for late or failure of disclosure.

R. v. Bramwell (1996), 106 C.C.C. (3d) 365 (B.C. C.A.) — The failure of D's counsel to pursue disclosure in a timely way is a factor to consider in determining whether a stay of proceedings is an appropriate remedy.

R. v. Anutooshkin (1994), 92 C.C.C. (3d) 59 (B.C. C.A.) — D is *not* entitled to disclosure merely upon demand. The right to disclosure is dependent upon the *relevance* of the material sought. The test is whether there is a *reasonable possibility* that the requested material *could assist* the defence.

In determining whether to exclude evidence due to non-disclosure, a trial judge should consider whether counsel for D sought to obtain the evidence by all reasonable means, including a timely request for direction by the trial judge.

R. v. Lawson (1978), 39 C.C.C. (2d) 85 (B.C. C.A.) — P was under no obligation to disclose to defence counsel misconduct by the complainants during the course of the trial. In any event, D had not been prevented from making full answer and defence since the character of the complainants had been adequately placed before the jury by the evidence, the address of defence counsel, and the remarks of the judge.

R. v. Arsenault (1994), 93 C.C.C. (3d) 111 (N.B. C.A.) — When a prosecutor takes charge of a case, he/she assumes responsibility for the file and its contents extant and those which will become part of the file. In general, material in the file will have been generated or compiled through police investigation. When disclosure is sought, P also has a duty to make reasonable inquiries of other Crown agencies or departments that could reasonably be considered to be in possession of evidence. Failure to make reasonable inquiries cannot be excused where P or the police know another Crown agency has been involved in the investigation. Where P has denied access to the file of the other Crown agency, P ought notify defence counsel who may pursue such course as advised.

R. v. Petten (1993), 21 C.R. (4th) 81, 81 C.C.C. (3d) 347 (Nfld. C.A.) — P's legal duty to disclose all relevant information to the defence does *not* necessarily mean all information in the hands of P. P has a discretion to withhold information which may be sensitive, as well as to determine relevance and the manner of its release. Where certain information is not to be made available to the defence, P must make the defence aware of its existence. The defence may then apply to a judge for release of the information. The judge, guided by the general principle that information ought to be made available if there is a reasonable possibility its non-disclosure would impair D's ability to make full answer and defence, will decide the manner of disclosure and to whom it might be made.

R. v. Miaponoose (1996), 110 C.C.C. (3d) 445 (Ont. C.A.) — In an eyewitness identification case, it is essential that P ensure that *all relevant* circumstances surrounding pre-trial eyewitness identification procedures are fully disclosed to D.

R. v. Wilson (1994), 87 C.C.C. (3d) 115 (Ont. C.A.) — P is *not* required to disclose in advance of trial information whose relevance first becomes apparent during trial.

R. v. Hutter (1993), 86 C.C.C. (3d) 81 (Ont. C.A.) — P is required to disclose information in its possession concerning D's bad character.

R. v. T. (L.A.) (1993), 84 C.C.C. (3d) 90 (Ont. C.A.) — There is a duty on P to make full disclosure which includes a duty to obtain from the police, and a corresponding duty on the police to provide to P, all relevant information and material concerning the case. What must be disclosed includes information that cannot be adduced as evidence by P, but that may be used by D in cross-examination or otherwise.

R. v. Lore (1997), 7 C.R. (5th) 190, 116 C.C.C. (3d) 255 (Que. C.A.) — P is *not* required to disclose what it neither has nor controls, as for example, material which is under foreign control in a foreign jurisdiction.

R. v. Pearson (1994), 89 C.C.C. (3d) 535 (Que. C.A.); leave to appeal refused (1994), 90 C.C.C (3d) C.C.C. (3d) vi (note) (S.C.C.) — Disclosure of material primarily or exclusively relevant to entrapment, or issues like it, which are considered after a finding of guilt, should be made upon request.

Defence Disclosure

R. v. Cleghorn (1995), 41 C.R. (4th) 282, 100 C.C.C. (3d) 393 (S.C.C) — There are two components to proper disclosure of an *alibi, viz.,*

i.   adequacy; and

ii.   timeliness.

Failure of proper disclosure of an alibi *permits* the trier of fact to draw an adverse inference when weighing the alibi evidence at trial. Alibi evidence may be weakened but *not* excluded by improper disclosure. The rule is intended to guard against alibis fabricated during testimony at trial. Disclosure is proper when it allows P and the police to investigate the alibi evidence prior to trial. Disclosure at the earliest possible moment is *not* required. Disclosure by D is *not* required. Third party disclosure will suffice.

Related Provisions: "Statement" is not defined in the section nor elsewhere in the *Code*.

The section does not afford any general right to disclosure of P's case beyond what is expressly described.

Section 605 authorizes the release of exhibits for scientific or other testing or examination.

604. [Repealed 1997, c. 18, s. 69.]

605. (1) Release of exhibits for testing — A judge of a superior court of criminal jurisdiction or a court of criminal jurisdiction may, on summary application on behalf of the accused or the prosecutor, after three days notice to the accused or prosecutor, as the case may be, order the release of any exhibit for the purpose of a scientific or other test or examination, subject to such terms as appear to be necessary or desirable to ensure the safeguarding of the exhibit and its preservation for use at the trial.

(2) Disobeying orders — Every one who fails to comply with the terms of an order made under subsection (1) is guilty of contempt of court and may be dealt with summarily by the judge or provincial court judge who made the order or before whom the trial of the accused takes place.

R.S., c. C-34, s. 533; R.S. 1985, c. 27 (1st Supp.), s. 203.

Commentary: Section 605(1) authorizes the *release of exhibits* for the purpose of *scientific or other testing or examination*. An order may be made by a judge of a superior court of criminal jurisdiction or a court of criminal jurisdiction, upon *summary application* by either D or P, upon three days' notice. The subsection also authorizes the imposition of such *terms* as appears *necessary* or desirable to *ensure the safeguarding* of the exhibit *and* its *preservation* for use at trial.

Failure to comply with the terms of an order under s. 605(1) is, under subsection (2), *contempt* and may be dealt with summarily by the authorizing or trial judge.

Case Law

R. v. O'Quinn (1976), 36 C.C.C. (2d) 364 (B.C. C.A.) — This section applies *only* to objects in existence. The fact that the drug sample had been destroyed by the analyst in the course of conducting his testing did *not* deprive D of the right to make full answer and defence where the analyst had been under *no* duty to preserve the sample.

Savion v. R. (1980), 13 C.R. (3d) 259, 52 C.C.C. (2d) 276 (Ont. C.A.) — This section would permit release for testing of a tape-recording ordered produced at trial but *not* entered as an exhibit.

Related Provisions: "Exhibit", as used in the section, is *not* defined but, presumably, means real evidence that has been filed and designated as an exhibit in preliminary inquiry or earlier trial proceedings.

The section does *not* enact a rule of evidence. It makes no reference to the admissibility of the results of the scientific or other testing or examination. Admissibility is determined at trial, in accordance with the general principles of the applicable evidentiary law.

Pleas

606. (1) Pleas permitted — An accused who is called on to plead may plead guilty or not guilty, or the special pleas authorized by this Part and no others.

(2) Refusal to plead — Where an accused refuses to plead or does not answer directly, the court shall order the clerk of the court to enter a plea of not guilty.

(3) Allowing time — An accused is not entitled as of right to have his trial postponed but the court may, if it considers that the accused should be allowed further time to plead, move to quash, or prepare for his defence or for any other reason, adjourn the trial to a later time in the session or sittings of the court, or to the next of any subsequent session or sittings of the court, on such terms as the court considers proper.

(4) Included or other offence — Notwithstanding any other provision of this Act, where an accused or defendant pleads not guilty of the offence charged but guilty of any other offence arising out of the same transaction, whether or not it is an included offence, the court may, with the consent of the prosecutor, accept that plea of guilty and, if the plea is accepted, the court shall find the accused or defendant not guilty of the offence charged and find him guilty of the offence in respect of which the plea of guilty was accepted and enter those findings in the record of the court.

R.S., c. C-34, s. 534; 1974–75–76, c. 105, s. 7; R.S. 1985, c. 27 (1st Supp.), s. 125.

Commentary: This section describes the *pleas* available to D in criminal proceedings.

The general rule, of s. 606(1) is that the pleas available to D are the *general* pleas of guilty and not guilty, the *special* pleas (*autrefois acquit, autrefois convict* and pardon) and no others. Where D refuses to plead or does not answer directly, a plea of not guilty is entered under s. 606(2).

Section 606(4) is an overriding provision. It permits entry of a plea of *not guilty* of the offence charged but *guilty* of "any other offence arising out of the same transaction, whether or not it is an included offence". This plea is only effectual where P consents and it is accepted by the court. Where the plea is effectual, D is found *not* guilty of the offence charged, but guilty of the offence in respect of which the plea of guilty was accepted. Where P does *not* consent to the plea or the court does not accept it, the only plea made and recorded is a plea of not guilty to the offence charged.

Section 606(3) authorizes the presiding judge to *adjourn* D's trial to a later time in the session or sittings, or thereafter to provide D with further time to plead, move to quash, prepare D's defence or for any other reason. The adjournment may be on such terms as the court considers proper, but it is not as of right.

Case Law

Plea of Guilty — General Principles

Adgey v. R. (1973), 23 C.R.N.S. 298, 13 C.C.C. (2d) 177 (S.C.C.) — When a plea of guilty is entered by D or his/her counsel, the trial judge may or may not accept the plea. S/he is not bound as a matter of law in all cases to conduct an inquiry after a plea of guilty has been entered. If the judge chooses to hear evidence to be satisfied that the charges are well founded, or in order to have a factual background prior to imposing sentence, the evidence may indicate that D never intended to admit to a fact which is an essential element of the offence charged, or that s/he may have misapprehended the effect of the guilty plea or never intended to plead guilty at all. In any such event, the judge may, in his/her discretion, direct that a plea of not guilty be entered or permit D to withdraw his/her original plea and enter a new one. The discretion of the trial judge is one which, if exercised judicially, will not be lightly interfered with.

R. v. Corkum (1984), 64 A.R. 354 (C.A.) — When a guilty plea is offered, P should be asked to outline the facts. The facts are P's allegations. As a bare minimum, the facts must justify the plea which has been entered. D should be asked if the facts are admitted. If the facts as set out, or enough of them to sustain the plea, are admitted, the plea may then be accepted. If the essential facts are not clearly admitted, the plea of guilty should not be accepted.

R. v. Newman (1993), 79 C.C.C. (3d) 394 (Ont. C.A.) — A trial judge should *not* accept a plea of guilty if *not* satisfied that D is fully aware of the facts upon which P relies in support of the conviction.

Withdrawal of Guilty Plea [See also ss. 675 and 686]

R. v. Atlay (1992), 70 C.C.C. (3d) 553 (B.C. C.A.) — *See also*: *Thibodeau v. R.*, [1955] S.C.R. 646, 21 C.R. 265 — A trial judge has the discretion to permit a guilty plea to be withdrawn at any time before sentence is completed.

R. v. Santos (1985), 34 Man. R. (2d) 9 (C.A.) — The court's right to permit a withdrawal of a guilty plea is *not* limited to situations of error or inducement. Where D never intended to admit to an essential element of the offence, the denial of the application to withdraw was unreasonable.

R. v. Paiero (1986), 71 N.S.R. (2d) 268 (C.A.) — Where D is represented by counsel at the time a guilty plea is entered, D will be *presumed* to have been fully familiar with the circumstances surrounding the offence and to have been aware of the consequences of entering a guilty plea.

R. v. Newman (1993), 79 C.C.C. (3d) 394 (Ont. C.A.) — A court of appeal may permit D to withdraw a plea of guilty, set aside the conviction and order a new trial where the court is satisfied that D was deprived of his/her right to effective counsel and that the plea of guilty embraced a factual foundation that D was not prepared to accept for the purposes of sentencing, so that D was deprived of a fair trial.

R. v. Rubenstein (1987), 41 C.C.C. (3d) 91 (Ont. C.A.) — A trial judge has the discretion to allow the withdrawal of a plea of guilty to charges under the *Code*. It was *not* an error for a judge to refuse to allow the withdrawal by D of a plea of guilty on the basis of the judge's refusal to go along with a joint submission on sentencing.

Effect of Guilty Plea

R. v. Lucas (1983), 9 C.C.C. (3d) 71 (Ont. C.A.); leave to appeal refused (1984), 9 C.C.C. (3d) 71n (S.C.C.) — A plea of guilty is an admission by D of all the legal ingredients necessary to constitute the crime charged and dispenses with proof of the ingredients. A conditional plea of guilty is *not* open to D.

Guilty Plea to Other Offence: S. 606(4)

R. v. Rowbotham (1994), 30 C.R. (4th) 141, 90 C.C.C. (3d) 449 (S.C.C.) — Where D wishes to plead guilty with prosecutorial consent under s. 606(4), after having been given in charge of the jury, the trial judge should consider the appropriateness of the plea and decide on its acceptability in the absence of the jury. Where the plea is acceptable, the jury may be discharged and the court "now consisting of the judge alone" may record the verdict of not guilty of the offence charged and guilty of the lesser offence admitted.

Bennett v. R. (1982), 70 C.C.C. (2d) 575 (S.C.C.) — There is *no* error in law in deciding that a person can plead guilty to, and be convicted of, the lesser and included offence of second degree murder on an indictment of first degree murder, without the intervention of a jury.

R. v. Naraindeen (1990), 80 C.R. (3d) 66, 75 O.R. (2d) 120 (C.A.) — Section 606(4) moves to the commencement of trial a decision which, in the absence of the section, in a jury trial, would require a jury verdict based on the evidence adduced. While P's primary responsibility for the enforcement of the criminal law includes the power to decide whether and what charges shall be laid, as well the authority to withdraw charges prior to commencement of trial, once a matter is before a court, D has pleaded and what is sought involves something more than merely not proceeding with a charge, namely, D's acquittal of the offence alleged, the court has a legitimate role to play in the decision to be made. While a trial judge may strike a s. 606(4) plea of guilty where the facts read would support the full offence charged, great weight should be assigned to P's decision to accept a plea of guilty to an included or other offence.

R. v. Pentiluk (1974), 28 C.R.N.S. 324, 21 C.C.C. (2d) 87 (Ont. C.A.) — Where P did *not* consent to D's plea to a lesser included offence, the plea should not have been recorded. The only plea was not guilty to the offence charged.

R. v. St. Jean (1970), 15 C.R.N.S. 194 (Que. C.A.) — Where D pleads guilty to a lesser charge, the trial judge is *not* bound to accept the plea and acquit on the other charge, but may proceed with a trial on the more serious offence.

Change of Plea

R. v. Rowbotham (1994), 30 C.R. (4th) 141, 90 C.C.C. (3d) 449 (S.C.C.) — See digest under *Guilty Plea to Other Offence*: s. 606(4) *supra*.

Related Provisions: The special pleas of *autrefois acquit, autrefois convict*, pardon and, in cases of libel, justification, are determined under ss. 607–612. The applicability of a special plea is determined first, prior to D entering a general plea.

The language of s. 606(4), namely, "any other offence arising out of the same transaction, whether or not it is an included offence" is somewhat wider than the adjudicative authority of a justice at a preliminary inquiry under s. 548(1)(a) ("any other *indictable* offence in respect of the same transaction"). Under s. 574(1)(b) P may prefer an indictment on ("any charge founded on the facts disclosed by the evidence taken on the preliminary inquiry ...").

607. (1) Special pleas — An accused may plead the special pleas of

    (a) *autrefois acquit*;

    (b) *autrefois convict*; and

    (c) pardon.

(2) In case of libel — An accused who is charged with defamatory libel may plead in accordance with sections 611 and 612.

(3) Disposal — The pleas of *autrefois acquit, autrefois convict* and pardon shall be disposed of by the judge without a jury before the accused is called on to plead further.

(4) Pleading over — When the pleas referred to in subsection (3) are disposed of against the accused, he may plead guilty or not guilty.

(5) Statement sufficient — Where an accused pleads *autrefois acquit* or *autrefois convict*, it is sufficient if he

(a) states that he has been lawfully acquitted, convicted or discharged under subsection 730(1), as the case may be, of the offence charged in the count to which the plea relates; and

(b) indicates the time and place of the acquittal, conviction or discharge under subsection 730(1).

(6) Exceptions: foreign trials in absentia — A person who is alleged to have committed an act or omission outside Canada that is an offence in Canada by virtue of any of subsections 7(2) to (3.4) or subsection 7(3.7) or (3.71), and in respect of which that person has been tried and convicted outside Canada, may not plead *autrefois convict* with respect to a count that charges that offence if

(a) at the trial outside Canada the person was not present and was not represented by counsel acting under the person's instructions, and

(b) the person was not punished in accordance with the sentence imposed on conviction in respect of the act or omission,

notwithstanding that the person is deemed by virtue of subsection 7(6) to have been tried and convicted in Canada in respect of the act or omission.

R.S., c. C-34, s. 535; 1974–75–76, c. 105, s. 8; R.S. 1985, c. 27 (1st Supp.), s. 126; c. 30 (3d Supp.), s. 2; 1995, c. 22, s. 10.

Commentary: The section describes the *special pleas* available to D and the manner of their determination.

Sections 607(1) and (2) authorize the special pleas of *autrefois acquit, autrefois convict* or pardon or, in cases of defamatory libel, justification. A special plea of *autrefois acquit, autrefois convict* or pardon under s. 607(3) is disposed of by the judge *without* a jury, and if unsuccessful, requires D to be called upon under s. 607(4) to enter a general plea of guilty or not guilty.

Section 607(5) describes the requisites of a plea of *autrefois acquit* or *autrefois convict*. D must state that he/she has been lawfully acquitted, convicted or discharged under s. 736(1), as the case may be, of the offence charged to which the plea relates and indicate the time and place of such earlier disposition. Section 607(6) constitutes an exception in respect of a special plea of *autrefois convict* where the conviction relied upon was a foreign conviction registered *in absentia* without counsel acting on D's instructions and D was further not punished in accordance with the sentence imposed upon conviction. The special plea is unavailable, notwithstanding that the offence is deemed to have been committed in Canada under the special jurisdiction provisions of ss. 7(1)–(3.4), s. 7(3.7) or (3.71).

Case Law

Res Judicata [See ss. 8 and 12]

Autrefois Acquit: S. 607(1)(a)

R. v. Van Rassel (1990), 75 C.R. (3d) 150, 53 C.C.C. (3d) 353 (S.C.C.) — Although the charges need *not* be identical, the plea of *autrefois acquit* is not appropriate if the charges are different in nature. The principle may apply where the acquittal took place in a foreign jurisdiction.

R. v. Moore (1988), 65 C.R. (3d) 1, 41 C.C.C. (3d) 289 (S.C.C.) — If a charge is a nullity, *no* cure is available since the matter goes to the very jurisdiction of the judge. In such a case, the doctrine of *autrefois acquit* is never a bar to the relaying of the charge, because D was never in jeopardy. If the charge is only voidable, the judge has the jurisdiction to amend. Even a failure to state something that is an essential element of the offence is not fatal, and the judge should amend. However, if the judge has determined as a matter of law that an amendment cannot be made without causing irreparable prejudice, the quashing of the charge at trial is tantamount to an acquittal, and a plea of *autrefois acquit* is appropriate. If a charge is voidable and the judge errs in refusing an amendment, then the proper procedure is an appeal by P, *not* the laying of a new charge.

Petersen v. R. (1982), 30 C.R. (3d) 165, 69 C.C.C. (2d) 385 (S.C.C.) — When a court dismisses charges in the erroneous belief that it lacks jurisdiction, its determination of the issue will bar further proceedings on the same charge, whether further proceedings are taken summarily or by indictment. P's remedy is to appeal or to apply for a prerogative writ.

R. v. Riddle (1980), 48 C.C.C. (2d) 365 (S.C.C.) — The plea of *autrefois acquit* is available in a summary conviction proceeding. It is also available where the same charge was dismissed after D entered a plea of not guilty and P called no evidence.

R. v. Feeley (1962), 38 C.R. 321 (Ont. C.A.); affirmed (1963), 40 C.R. 261 (S.C.C.) — The plea of *autrefois acquit* is to be distinguished from the defence of *res judicata*. In determining the validity of a plea of *autrefois acquit*, the test is the "substantial identity" of the *offence* of which D was acquitted with that with which D is now charged. The defence of *res judicata* relies on a determination, favourable to D, in earlier proceedings of a question of fact vital to new charge.

R. v. Tateham (1982), 70 C.C.C. (2d) 565 (B.C. C.A.) — A stay of proceedings is *not* a final determination of the matter leading to a plea of *autrefois acquit*.

R. v. Maramba (1995), 42 C.R. (4th) 177, 104 C.C.C. (3d) 85 (Ont. C.A.) — *See also*: *R. v. Karpinski* (1957), 25 C.R. 365, 117 C.C.C. 241 (S.C.C.); *R. v. Selhi* (1990), 53 C.C.C. (3d) 576 (S.C.C.) — Withdrawal by P of an information upon which P had elected to proceed by summary conviction because it was statute-barred, does *not* constitute an acquittal, hence cannot support a plea of *autrefois acquit*. P may,

i.   lay a new information; or

ii.   have D re-arraigned and elect mode of trial on the new information.

R. v. Belair (1988), 64 C.R. (3d) 179, 41 C.C.C. (3d) 329 (Ont. C.A.) — In the case of a *hybrid* offence, the quashing of an information before plea, following P's election to proceed by way of summary conviction, on the ground that summary conviction proceedings are barred, does not give rise to the plea of *autrefois acquit*.

R. v. Côté (1986), 1 Q.A.C. 47 (C.A.) — Where the trial judge refused to grant P's request for an adjournment and dismissed the charges against D, P was *not* entitled to simply ignore a just dismissal of the prior charges and begin new proceedings. D was entitled to plead *autrefois acquit*.

R. v. Gould, [1985] 5 W.W.R. 430 (Sask. C.A.); affirmed [1987] 1 S.C.R. 499 (S.C.C.) — *See also*: *R. v. Pretty* (1989), 47 C.C.C. (3d) 70 (B.C. C.A.) — For a plea of *autrefois acquit* to succeed, D had to show that he was placed in jeopardy on the same matter on an earlier occasion and that there was an acquittal or a dismissal of the charge by a court of competent jurisdiction. Although an order, made before plea, quashing a committal for trial and setting aside an indictment was an acquittal for purposes of P's right to appeal, it was not an acquittal which would support the plea of *autrefois acquit*.

Bonli v. Gosselin (1981), 25 C.R. (3d) 303 (Sask. C.A.) — Withdrawal of an information prior to trial does not give rise to a plea of *autrefois acquit*.

Autrefois Convict: S. 607(1)(b)

R. v. Ko (1977), 38 C.R.N.S. 243, 36 C.C.C. (2d) 32 (B.C. C.A.) — The plea of *autrefois convict* was available where D might have been convicted on the first trial of all the offences for which they might be convicted on the second trial. Although the facts could have resulted in two separate indictments and convictions, it would have necessitated an amendment to the indictment separating the acts alleged to constitute each offence.

Related Provisions: *Charter* s. 11(h), adds a constitutional dimension to the special pleas of *autrefois acquit* and *autrefois convict*.

The manner in which the special pleas of *autrefois acquit* and *autrefois convict* are determined appears in ss. 608–610.

608. Evidence of identity of charges — Where an issue on a plea of *autrefois acquit* or *autrefois convict* is tried, the evidence and adjudication and the notes of the judge and official stenographer on the former trial and the record transmitted to the

court pursuant to section 551 on the charge that is pending before that court are admissible in evidence to prove or to disprove the identity of the charges.

R.S., c. C-34, s. 536.

Commentary: The section describes what is admissible to prove or disprove the *identity* of the past and present *charges* where an issue of *autrefois acquit* or *autrefois convict* is tried. The evidence, adjudication, notes of the trial judge and official stenographer, as well as the record transmitted to the court under s. 551 at the conclusion of the preliminary inquiry, are receivable as evidence on the issue of identity.

Case Law

R. v. Gee (1973), 14 C.C.C. (2d) 538 (Ont. C.A.) — It is an error to hold that a previous conviction is a bar without receiving evidence that the present charge and the one on which D was previously convicted, were founded on the same transaction.

Related Provisions: Identity is generally determined under s. 609, but, in some cases, the special rules of s. 610 apply to bar subsequent indictments in light of a previous conviction or acquittal.

Evidence taken in earlier proceedings is recorded under s. 540.

609. (1) What determines identity — Where an issue on a plea of *autrefois acquit* or *autrefois convict* to a count is tried and it appears

(a) that the matter on which the accused was given in charge on the former trial is the same in whole or in part as that on which it is proposed to give him in charge, and

(b) that on the former trial, if all proper amendments had been made that might then have been made, he might have been convicted of all the offences of which he may be convicted on the count to which the plea of *autrefois acquit* or *autrefois convict* is pleaded,

the judge shall give judgment discharging the accused in respect of that count.

(2) Allowance of special plea in part — The following provisions apply where an issue on a plea of *autrefois acquit* or *autrefois convict* is tried:

(a) where it appears that the accused might on the former trial have been convicted of an offence of which he may be convicted on the count in issue, the judge shall direct that the accused shall not be found guilty of any offence of which he might have been convicted on the former trial; and

(b) where it appears that the accused may be convicted on the count in issue of an offence of which he could not have been convicted on the former trial, the accused shall plead guilty or not guilty with respect to that offence.

R.S., c. C-34, s. 537.

Commentary: The section enacts general rules for the determination of the *issue of identity* for the special pleas of *autrefois acquit* and *autrefois convict*.

Under s. 609(1), D will be discharged on a plea of *autrefois acquit* or *autrefois convict* where the matter on which D had been given in charge in the earlier trial was the same, in whole or in part, as that on which D is to be again given in charge. It must appear that, on the former trial, if all proper amendments had been made that might have been made, D might have been convicted of *all* of the offences of which he may be convicted on the count to which the special plea relates.

Under s. 609(2), the trial judge in subsequent proceedings must direct that D *not* be found guilty of any offence of which D might have been convicted on the former trial. In respect of any offence of which D could not have been convicted on the former trial, D must enter a general plea of guilty or not guilty.

Case Law [See also s. 607]

R. v. Rinnie (1970), 9 C.R.N.S. 81, [1970] 3 C.C.C. 218 (Alta. C.A.) — Where a lesser offence is included in a principal offence as a matter of law, an acquittal on the principal offence gives rise to a plea of *autrefois acquit* as an answer to a new indictment on the included offence. Where the original indictment as worded included a lesser offence, an acquittal on the principal offence gives rise to a plea of *autrefois acquit* on the lesser charge. Where a proper amendment to the original indictment might have resulted in a conviction on the charge with which D is now faced, the plea of *autrefois acquit* is available. After D has pleaded and the trial commenced, there is no proper amendment which would permit the broadening of the charge for the sole purpose of embracing included offences.

R. v. Pederson (1935), 63 C.C.C. 262 (Alta. C.A.) — It is *not* the similarity in language of the charges but the identity of the offences in respect of which P has proceeded and proposes to proceed that is of importance in deciding whether a special plea will succeed.

R. v. Plank (1986), 28 C.C.C. (3d) 386 (Ont. C.A.) — The plea of *autrefois acquit* is available to D charged with an offence which was an included offence in a charge of which he has been previously acquitted. The plea is available to D notwithstanding an erroneous acquittal on the principal charge without a determination respecting the included offence.

Related Provisions: Section 610 describes the circumstances under which a previous disposition will bar a subsequent indictment for substantially the same offence, as well as in respect of specific forms of culpable homicide.

Section 12 bars punishment, though *not* proceedings, under different statutes, where an act or omission is an offence under more than one Act of Parliament.

Sections 660–662 provide for the verdicts which may be rendered where something other than the full offence charged has been proven at trial.

The provisions of this section appear somewhat wider than the guarantee of *Charter* s. 11(h), which simply refers to "the offence".

610. (1) Circumstances of aggravation — Where an indictment changes substantially the same offence as that charged in an indictment on which an accused was previously convicted or acquitted, but adds a statement of intention or circumstances of aggravation tending, if proved, to increase the punishment, the previous conviction or acquittal bars the subsequent indictment.

(2) Effect of previous charge of murder or manslaughter — A conviction or an acquittal on an indictment for murder bars a subsequent indictment for the same homicide charging it as manslaughter or infanticide, and a conviction or acquittal on an indictment for manslaughter or infanticide bars a subsequent indictment for the same homicide charging it as murder.

(3) Previous charges of first degree murder — A conviction or an acquittal on an indictment for first degree murder bars a subsequent indictment for the same homicide charging it as second degree murder, and a conviction or acquittal on an indictment for second degree murder bars a subsequent indictment for the same homicide charging it as first degree murder.

(4) Effect of previous charge of infanticide or manslaughter — A conviction or an acquittal on an indictment for infanticide bars a subsequent indictment for the same homicide charging it as manslaughter, and a conviction or acquittal on an indictment for manslaughter bars a subsequent indictment for the same homicide charging it as infanticide.

R.S., c. C-34, s. 538; 1973–74, c. 38, s. 5; 1974–75–76, c. 105, s. 9.

Commentary: The section describes the circumstances under which a previous disposition will bar a subsequent indictment for a more aggravated form of the same offence and in certain cases of culpable homicide.

The bar created by s. 610(1) prevents a subsequent indictment charging *substantially the same offence* as that of which D has earlier been acquitted or convicted but adding a statement of intention or circumstances of aggravation tending, if proved, to increase punishment.

Sections 610(2)–(4) enact special provisions applicable to the various forms of culpable homicide. In general, a conviction or acquittal of one form of culpable homicide, murder, manslaughter or infanticide, bars a subsequent indictment for any another form of culpable homicide in respect of the same killing.

Related Provisions: Section 609 enacts the general rule by which the issue of identity is determined for the special pleas of *autrefois acquit* and *autrefois convict*.

Sections 660–662 describe the verdicts which may be rendered where something other than the full offence charged has been proven at trial.

Murder is defined in s. 229 and classified for sentencing purposes in s. 231. Infanticide is defined in s. 233. Manslaughter is *not* expressly defined but, under s. 234, is any culpable homicide which is neither murder nor infanticide.

611. (1) Libel, plea of justification — An accused who is charged with publishing a defamatory libel may plead that the defamatory matter published by him was true, and that it was for the public benefit that the matter should have been published in the manner in which and at the time when it was published.

(2) Where more than one sense alleged — A plea that is made under subsection (1) may justify the defamatory matter in any sense in which it is specified in the count, or in the sense that the defamatory matter bears without being specified, or separate pleas justifying the defamatory matter in each sense may be pleaded separately to each count as if two libels had been charged in separate counts.

(3) Plea in writing — A plea that is made under subsection (1) shall be in writing and shall set out the particular facts by reason of which it is alleged to have been for the public good that the matter should have been published.

(4) Reply — The prosecutor may in his reply deny generally the truth of a plea that is made under this section.

R.S., c. C-34, s. 539.

Commentary: The section authorizes and provides the procedure for a *plea of justification* in cases of *defamatory libel*.

Under s. 611(1), a *plea of justification* involves an assertion that the defamatory matter was *true* and, further, that it was for the *public benefit* that the matter be published as and when it was. The plea must be *in writing* and, under s. 611(3), set out the *facts which underlie* the assertion of public good. P, by *reply*, may deny generally the truth of D's plea.

Under s. 611(2), the plea may justify the defamatory matter in any sense in which it is specified in the count, or in the sense that the defamatory matter bears without being specified. Separate pleas of separate justification may be made in relation to each count in an indictment.

Related Provisions: Defamatory libel is governed by ss. 297–317. Under s. 317, the jury may find a special or general verdict.

A plea of justification is generally required before there may be an inquiry into the truth of the matters charged in an alleged libel, unless D is charged with publishing a libel knowing it to be false.

Sections 728 and 729 make provision for the award and recovery of costs to and by the successful party in cases of defamatory libel.

612. (1) Plea of justification necessary — The truth of the matters charged in an alleged libel shall not be inquired into in the absence of a plea of justification under section 611 unless the accused is charged with publishing the libel knowing it to be false, in which case evidence of the truth may be given to negative the allegation that the accused knew that the libel was false.

(2) **Not guilty, in addition** — The accused may, in addition to a plea that is made under section 611, plead not guilty and the pleas shall be inquired into together.

(3) **Effect of plea on punishment** — Where a plea of justification is pleaded and the accused is convicted, the court may, in pronouncing sentence, consider whether the guilt of the accused is aggravated or mitigated by the plea.

R.S., c. C-34, s. 540.

Commentary: The section describes the matters which may be raised under a plea of justification in cases of defamatory libel, as well as the other pleas available in such cases.

In cases of *defamatory libel*, there is no inquiry into the truth of the matters charged in the alleged libel unless a plea of justification is made under s. 611, or D is charged with publishing the libel knowing it to be false. D may enter a plea of not guilty, in addition to a plea of justification. Both pleas are inquired into together.

Where D is convicted after justification has been pleaded, the sentencing judge may consider whether guilt is aggravated or mitigated by the plea.

Related Provisions: A plea of justification in cases of defamatory libel is authorized by s. 611. Defamatory libel is governed by ss. 297–317, and may be the subject of a special verdict.

Sections 751 and 751.1 provide for the award and recovery of costs to and by the successful party in cases of defamatory libel.

613. Plea of not guilty — Any ground of defence for which a special plea is not provided by this Act may be relied on under the plea of not guilty.

R.S., c. C-34, s. 541.

Commentary: The section authorizes a *general plea* of *not guilty* and expressly provides that any ground of defence for which a special plea is not provided may be raised under such a plea.

Case Law

Res Judicata [See also ss. 8 and 12]

Rourke v. R. (1977), 38 C.R.N.S. 268, 35 C.C.C. (2d) 129 (S.C.C.) — *Res judicata* is a defence on the merits, *not* a preliminary plea.

Related Provisions: In combination, this section and s. 8(3) permit any *justification, excuse* or *defence* at common law or by statute to be raised under a general plea of not guilty. The only *special pleas* for which provision is made are *autrefois acquit, autrefois convict*, pardon and, in cases of defamatory libel, *justification*. Neither mental disorder nor *res judicata*, for example, are special pleas but like all defences of exemptions are raised under a general mental disorder plea of not guilty.

Under s. 606(4), D may plead not guilty to the offence charged but guilty to any other offence arising out of the same transaction, whether or not it is an included offence.

Sections 660–662 provide for the verdicts which may be rendered where P's proof does not establish the offence charged beyond a reasonable doubt.

614. [Repealed 1991, c. 43, s. 3.]

615. [Repealed 1991, c. 43, s. 3.]

616. [Repealed 1991, c. 43, s. 3.]

617. [Repealed 1991, c. 43, s. 3.]

618. [Repealed 1991, c. 43, s. 3.]

619. [Repealed 1991, c. 43, s. 3.]

Transitional Provisions (S.C. 1991, c. 43, s. 10(1)): Section 10 of 1991, c. 43 reads:

10. (1) **Lieutenant Governor warrants or orders remain in force** — Any order for the detention of an accused or accused person made under section 614, 615 or 617 of the *Criminal Code* or section 200 or 201 of the *National Defence Act*, as those sections read immediately before the coming into force of section 3 or 18 of this Act, shall continue in force until the coming into force of section 672.64 of the *Criminal Code*, subject to any order made by a court or Review Board under section 672.54 of the *Criminal Code*.

Sections 614, 615 and 617 appear as follows immediately before they were repealed by S.C. 1991, c. 43, s. 3:

Defence of Insanity

614. (1) **Insanity of accused when offence committed** — Where, on the trial of an accused who is charged with an indictable offence, evidence is given that the accused was insane at the time the offence was committed and the accused is acquitted,

(a) the jury, or

(b) the judge or provincial court judge, where there is no jury,

shall find whether the accused was insane at the time the offence was committed and shall declare whether he is acquitted on account of insanity.

(2) **Custody after finding** — Where the accused is found to have been insane at the time the offence was committed, the court, judge or provincial court judge before whom the trial is held shall order that he be kept in strict custody in the place and in the manner that the court, judge or provincial court judge directs, until the decision of the lieutenant governor of the province is known.

R.S., c. C-34, s. 542; R.S. 1985, s. 27 (1st. Supp.), s. 203.

Case Law [See case digests under Code s. 16]

615. (1) **Insanity at time of trial** — A court, judge or provincial court judge may, at any time before verdict, where it appears that there is sufficient reason to doubt that the accused is, on account of insanity, capable of conducting his defence, direct that an issue be tried where the accused is then, on account of insanity, unfit to stand his trial.

(2) **Direction or remand for observation** — A court, judge or provincial court judge may, at any time before verdict or sentence, when of the opinion, supported by the evidence or, where the prosecutor and the accused consent, by the report in writing, of at least one duly qualified medical practitioner, that there is reason to believe that

(a) an accused is mentally ill, or

(b) the balance of the mind of an accused is disturbed, where the accused is a female person charged with an offence arising out of the death of her newly-born child,

by order in writing

(c) direct the accused to attend, at a place or before a person specified in the order and within a time specified therein, for observation, or

(d) remand the accused to such custody as the court, judge or provincial court judge directs for observation for a period not exceeding thirty days.

(3) **Idem** — Notwithstanding subsection (2), a court, judge or provincial court judge may remand an accused in accordance with that subsection

(a) for a period not exceeding thirty days without having heard the evidence or considered the report of a duly qualified medical practitioner where compelling circumstances exist for so doing and where a medical practitioner is not readily available to examine the accused and give evidence or submit a report; and

(b) for a period of more than thirty days but not exceeding sixty days where he is satisfied that observation for such a period is required in all the circumstances of the case and his opinion is supported by the evidence or, where the prosecutor and the accused consent, by the report in writing, of at least one duly qualified medical practitioner.

(4) **Court shall assign counsel** — Where it appears that there is sufficient reason to doubt that the accused is, on account of insanity, capable of conducting his defence, the court, judge or provincial court judge shall, if the accused is not represented by counsel, assign counsel to act on behalf of the accused.

(5) **Trial of issue** — For the purposes of subsection (1), the following provisions apply:

(a) where the issue arises before the close of the case of the prosecution, the court, judge or privincial court judge may postpone directing the trial of the issue until any time up to the opening of the case for the defence;

(b) where the trial is held or is to be held before a court composed of a judge and jury,

(i) if the judge directs the issue to be tried before the accused is given in charge to a jury for trial on the indictment, it shall be tried by twelve jurors, or in the Yukon Territory and the Northwest Territories, by six jurors, and

(ii) if the judge directs the issue to be tried after the accused has been given in charge to a jury for trial on the indictment, the jury shall be sworn to try that issue in addition to the issue on which they are already sworn; and

(c) where the trial is held before a judge or provincial court judge, he shall try the issue and render a verdict.

(6) **If sane, trial proceeds** — Where the verdict is that the accused is not unfit on account of insanity to stand his trial, the arraignment or the trial shall proceed as if no such issue had been directed.

(7) **If sane, order for custody** — Where the verdict is that the accused is unfit on account of insanity to stand his trial, the court, judge or provincial court judge shall order that the accused be kept in custody until the pleasure of the lieutenant governor of the province is known, and any plea that has been pleaded shall be set aside and the jury shall be discharged.

(8) **Where accused acquitted** — Where the court, judge or provincial court judge has postponed directing the trial of the issue pursuant to paragraph (5)(a) and the accused is acquitted at the close of the case for the prosecution, the issue shall not be tried.

(9) **Subsequent trial** — No proceeding pursuant to this section shall prevent the accused from being tried subsequently on the indictment unless the trial of the issue was postponed pursuant to paragraph (5)(a) and the accused was acquitted at the close of the case for the prosecution.

R.S., c. C-34, s. 543; 1972, c. 13, s. 44; 1974-75-76, c. 93, s. 68; R.S. 1985, c. 27 (1st Supp.), s. 203.

Case Law [See new Ss. 672.22-672.33]

617. (1) **Supervision of insane persons** — Where an accused is, pursuant to this Part, found to be insane, the lieutenant governor of the province in which he is detained may make an order

(a) for the safe custody of the accused in a place and manner directed by him; or

(b) if in his opinion it would be in the best interest of the accused and not contrary to the interest of the public, for the discharge of the accused either absolutely or subject to such conditions as he prescribes.

(2) **Warrant for transfer** — An accused to whom paragraph (1)(a) applies may, by warrant signed by an officer authorized for that purpose by the lieutenant governor of the province in which he is detained, be transferred for the purposes of his rehabilitation to any other place in Canada specified in the warrant with the consent of the person in charge of that other place.

(3) **Transfer of accused** — A warrant mentioned in subsection (2) is sufficient authority for any person who has custody of the accused to deliver the accused to the person in charge of the place specified in the warrant and for the last mentioned person to detain the accused in the manner specified in the order mentioned in subsection (1).

(4) **Arrest of accused** — A peace officer who believes on reasonable grounds that an accused to whom paragraph (1)(b) applies has contravened any condition prescribed in the order for his discharge may arrest the accused without warrant.

(5) **Taking before a justice** — Where an accused has been arrested pursuant to subsection (4), he shall be dealt with in accordance with the following provisions:

(a) where a justice having jurisdiction in the territorial division in which the accused has been arrested is available within a period of twenty-four hours after the arrest of the accused by a peace officer, the accused shall be taken before a justice without unreasonable delay and in any event within that period; and

(b) where a justice having jurisdiction in the territorial division in which the accused has been arrested is not available within a period of twenty-four hours after the arrest of the accused by a peace officer, the accused shall be taken before a justice as soon as possible.

(6) **Order of justice** — A justice before whom an accused is taken pursuant to subsection (5) may make any order that to him seems desirable in the circumstances respecting the detention of the accused pending a decision of the lieutenant governor of the province referred to in subsection (1) and shall cause notice of the order to be given to that lieutenant governor.

R.S., c. C-34, s. 545; 1972, c. 13, s. 45; 1974-75-76, c. 93, s. 69.

S.C. 1991, c. 43, s. 10(2)-(7) provides as follows:

10. (2) **Review of inmates held in custody on lieutenant governor warrants or orders** — The Review Board of a province shall, within twelve months after coming into force of this section, review the case of every person detained in custody in the province by virtue of an order of detention referred to in subsection (1).

(3) **Application of sections 672.5 to 672.85 to reviews under subsection (2)** — Sections 672.5 to 672.85 of the Criminal Code apply, with such modifications as the circumstances require, to a review under subsection (2) as if

(a) the review were a review of a disposition conducted pursuant to section 672.81 of that Act;

(b) the warrant issued by the lieutenant governor pursuant to which the person is being detained in custody were a disposition made under section 672.54 of that Act;

(c) there were included in the definition designated offence in subsection 672.64(1) of that Act a reference to any offence under and Act of Parliament, as that Act read at the time of the commission of the alleged offence for which ther person is in custody, involving violence or a threat of violence to a person or danger to the safety or security of the public, including, without limiting the generality of the foregoing, a reference to the following sections of the Criminal Code, as those section read immediately before January 4, 1983, namely,

(i) section 144 (rape),

(ii) section 145 (attempt to commit rape),

(iii) section 149 (indecent assault on female),

(iv) section 156 (indecent assault on male),

(v) section 245 (common assault)

(vi) section 246 (assault with intent);

(d) there were included in the offences mentioned in paragraph 672.64(3)(a) a reference to any of the following offences under any Act of Parliament, as that Act read at the time of the commission of the alleged offence for which the person is in custody, namely,

(i) murder punishable by death or punishable by imprisonment for life, capital murder, non-capital murder and any offence of murder, however it had been described or classified by the provisions of the Criminal Code that were in force at that time, and

(ii) any other offence under any Act of Parliament for which a minimum punishment of imprisonment for life had been prescribed by law.

(4) **Commissioner to review whether any inmate is a dangerous mentally disordered accused** — The Attorney General of Canada shall appoint a Commissioner from among the judges of superior courts of criminal jurisdiction to review and determine, before the coming into force of section 672.64 of the Criminal Code, whether any person detained in custody by virtue of an order of detnetion described in subsection (1) would have been a dangerous mentally disordered accused under section 672.65 of the Criminal Code, if that section were in force at the time the order of detention was made.

(5) **Review of application of provincial Attorney General** — Where an order of detention referred to in subsection (1) was issued against a person found not fuilty by reason of insanity of an offence that is a designated offence as defined in subsection 672.64(1) of the Criminal Code or that is included as a designated offence under paragraph (3)(c), the Attorney General of the province where the order was made, or of the province where the person is detained in custody, may apply to the Commissioner for review and determination of whether the person would be a dangerous mentally disordered accused.

(6) **Criminal Code provisions apply to hearing of application** — Section 672.65 and 672.66 of the Criminal Code apply to an application made under subsection (5) with such modifications as the circumstances require, and

(a) in addition to the evidence described in paragraph 672.65(3)(a), the Commissioner shall consider any relevant evidence subsequent to the detention of the person in respect of whom the application is made; and

(b) where the Commissioner determines that the person would be a dangerous mentally disordered accused, the Commissioner may make an order that the person be detained in custody for a maximum of life.

(7) **Effect of commissioner's orders** — An order made by the Commissioner in respect of an application under this section shall have effect on the coming into foce of section 672.64 of the Criminal Code and be subject to the rights of appeal described in sections 672.79 and 672.8 as if the order were an order of a court under section 672.65 of that Act.

Corporations

620. Appearance by attorney — Every corporation against which an indictment is filed shall appear and plead by counsel or agent.

R.S., c. C-34, s. 548; 1997, c. 18, s. 70.

Commentary: The section requires a corporation to appear and plead by counsel or agent.

Related Provisions: "Counsel" is defined in s. 2.

Similar provision is made for the *appearance* of a corporate accused at preliminary inquiry (s. 538), at trial before a provincial court judge (s. 556) and in summary conviction proceedings (s. 800(3)). Service of process on a corporation is effected under s. 703.2.

The *punishment* of a convicted corporation by fine, and its enforcement, is set out in s. 735.

Notice to a corporate accused of the finding of an indictment is given under s. 621. Trial procedure is governed by ss. 622 and 623.

621. (1) Notice to corporation — The clerk of the court or the prosecutor may, where an indictment is filed against a corporation, cause a notice of the indictment to be served on the corporation.

(2) Contents of notice — A notice of an indictment referred to in subsection (1) shall set out the nature and purport of the indictment and advise that, unless the corporation appears on the date set out in the notice or the date fixed pursuant to subsection 548(2.1), and enters a plea, a plea of not guilty will be entered for the accused by the court, and that the trial of the indictment will be proceeded with as though the corporation had appeared and pleaded.

R.S., c. C-34, s. 549; 1997, c. 18, s. 71.

Commentary: The section describes the procedure followed where an indictment is found against a corporate accused. A *notice of indictment*, describing the nature and purport of the indictment, may be served on D. The notice must advise D that, unless it appears and pleads on the date set out on the notice or date fixed pursuant to s. 548(2.1), a plea of not guilty will be entered and the trial will proceed, as if it had appeared and pleaded.

Related Provisions: Section 622 describes the procedure followed where there is no appearance and plea under the section. Section 623 provides for the trial of the corporate accused on appearance and plea, or on account of s. 622.

See the corresponding note to s. 620, *supra*.

622. Procedure on default of appearance — Where a corporation does not appear in accordance with the notice referred to in section 621, the presiding judge may, on proof of service of the notice, order the clerk of the court to enter a plea of not guilty on behalf of the corporation, and the plea has the same force and effect as if the corporation had appeared by its counsel oar agent and pleaded that plea.

R.S., c. C-34, s. 550; 1997, c. 18, s. 72.

Commentary: The section authorizes the entry of the *plea of not guilty* on behalf of a corporate accused who, duly served with the notice of indictment, *fails to appear* by counsel or agent to enter a plea in accordance with the notice. A plea of not guilty, entered at the direction of the presiding judge, has the same effect as if D had appeared and pleaded by counsel or agent.

Related Provisions: See the corresponding notes to ss. 620 and 621, *supra*.

623. Trial of corporation — Where a corporation appears and pleads to the indictment or a plea of not guilty is entered by order of the court pursuant to section 622, the court shall proceed with the trial of the indictment and, where the corporation is convicted, section 735 applies.

R.S., c. C-34, s. 551; 1995, c. 22, s. 10.

Commentary: The section authorizes the trial of a corporate accused which has appeared and pleaded, or where a plea of not guilty has been entered under s. 622. Where a corporate accused is convicted, s. 719 is the applicable punishment provision.

Related Provisions: Section 727(4) authorizes the imposition of greater punishment upon a corporate accused by reason of previous convictions, notwithstanding lack of notice of the intention of P to do so, where the trial has proceeded under s. 623 without appearance or plea by D.

See the corresponding notes to ss. 620 and 621, *supra*.

Record of Proceedings

624. (1) **How recorded** — It is sufficient, in making up the record of a conviction or acquittal on an indictment, to copy the indictment and the plea that was pleaded, without a formal caption or heading.

(2) **Record of proceedings** — The court shall keep a record of every arraignment and of proceedings subsequent to arraignment.

R.S., c. C-34, s. 552.

Commentary: Under s. 624(2), records must be kept of every arraignment and proceedings subsequent thereto. A record of conviction or acquittal is sufficient if the indictment and plea is copied without formal caption or heading.

Related Provisions: The record is transmitted to the trial court under s. 551. Under s. 559 of Part XIX, a record of the trial proceedings must be kept. A record of conviction, finding of guilt or acquittal in such cases is made in accordance with s. 570 and may be in Forms 35–37.

Section 625 applies where an indictment has been amended under s. 601.

The method by which *previous convictions* may be established, the basis upon which they may be received in evidence and the use which may be made of them are described in ss. 664–667, and *C.E.A.* s. 12.

625. Form of record in case of amendment — Where it is necessary to draw up a formal record in proceedings in which the indictment has been amended, the record shall be drawn up in the form in which the indictment remained after the amendment, without reference to the fact that the indictment was amended.

R.S., c. C-34, s. 553.

Commentary: Where a formal record is required in cases where the indictment has been amended, the record is simply drawn up in the form of the indictment, as amended, without reference to the fact of amendment.

Related Provisions: The authority to amend an indictment or count is found in s. 601. Section 601(7) requires that the amendment be endorsed on the indictment as part of the record.

Pre-hearing Conference

625.1 (1) Pre-hearing conference — Subject to subsection (2), on application by the prosecutor or the accused or on its own motion, the court, or a judge of the court, before which, or the judge, provincial court judge or justice before whom, any proceedings are to be held may order that a conference between the prosecutor and the accused or counsel for the accused, to be presided over by the court, judge, provincial court judge or justice, be held prior to the proceedings to consider the matters that, to promote a fair and expeditious hearing, would be better decided before the start of the proceedings, and other similar matters, and to make arrangements for decisions on those matters.

(2) **Mandatory pre-trial hearing for jury trials** — In any case to be tried with a jury, a judge of the court before which the accused is to be tried shall, prior to the trial, order that a conference between the prosecutor and the accused or counsel for the ac-

cused, to be presided over by a judge of that court, be held in accordance with the rules of court made under section 482 to consider such matters as will promote a fair and expeditious trial.

R.S. 1985, c. 27 (1st Supp.), s. 127; 1997, c. 18, s. 73.

Commentary: The section provides for holding *pre-hearing conferences* in respect of matters to be tried in every level of trial court.

In cases to be tried with a *jury*, s. 625.1(2) *requires* that a pre-hearing conference be held prior to trial. The conference, between P and D or counsel for D, is presided over by a judge of the trial court and held, in accordance with the applicable rules of court under s. 482, to consider such matters as will *promote* a *fair and expeditious trial*.

In *all cases except jury trials*, a pre-hearing conference is *not* mandatory. On application by P, D, or on its own motion, the court before which, or the judge, provincial court judge or justice before whom, *any proceedings* are be held, *may* order that a pre-hearing conference be held. The conference, between P and D or counsel for D, presided over by the relevant judicial officer, prior to the proceedings, will consider such matters as will *promote* a *fair and expeditious hearing*. Terms such as "any proceedings" and "fair and expeditious hearing" would seem to permit the holding of *such* conferences prior to preliminary inquiry.

Related Provisions: Section 482(3)(c) specifically authorizes the making of rules of court regulating pre-hearing conferences under s. 625.1.

Section 625.1 does *not* itself furnish authority to order pre-trial disclosure of P's case nor, for example, to deal with matters that could be considered under s. 645(5).

Juries

626. (1) Qualification of jurors — A person who is qualified as a juror according to, and summoned as a juror in accordance with, the laws of a province is qualified to serve as a juror in criminal proceedings in that province.

(2) No disqualification based on sex — Notwithstanding any law of a province referred to in subsection (1), no person may be disqualified, exempted or excused from serving as a juror in criminal proceedings on the grounds of his or her sex.

R.S., c. C-34, s. 554; 1972, c. 13, s. 46; R.S. 1985, c.27 (1st Supp.), s. 128.

Commentary: The section describes the *qualifications of jurors* to try criminal cases.

The general rule of s. 626(1) is that persons qualified as jurors according to, and summoned as jurors in accordance with, *provincial law* may serve as jurors in criminal cases. The qualifications and summoning of jurors for criminal cases, in other words, is left generally to provincial legislation.

Section 626(2), an over-riding provision, ensures, whatever may be the provincial law respecting qualifications of jurors, that no one may be disqualified, exempted or excused from serving as a juror in a criminal case on the grounds of sex.

Case Law [See s. 629]

Related Provisions: In some cases under ss. 530–533, a further language qualification may be necessary for jurors empanelled for D's trial.

The jury selection process is described in ss. 629–644.

627. Support for juror with physical disability — The judge may permit a juror with a physical disability who is otherwise qualified to serve as a juror to have technical, personal, interpretative or other support services.

1998, c. 9, s. 4.

Commentary: This section permits a *physically disabled*, but *otherwise qualified* juror, to have

i.   technical;

ii.   personal;

iii. interpretative; or,

iv.   other

support services.

Related Provisions: Under s. 631(4), the support person must be sworn (or affirmed) with the members of the jury. The support person is also subject to the rule of *Code* s. 649 that prohibits disclosure of certain jury proceedings.

In cases to which s. 627 applies, the trial judge should clearly define the scope of the support person's role. S/he is to provide a defined service for the physically disabled juror, *not* decide the case for him, her or other jurors. The support person is *not* a decision-maker.

Section 486(1.2) permits a judge to order that a support person be present and close to a witness under fourteen years of age while the witness is testifying. Section 627 contains no provision similar to s. 486(1.3) that bars a witness in the proceedings from being a support person. Section 627 also contains no provision relating to the placement of the support person.

628. [Repealed R.S. 1985, c. 27 (1st Supp.), s. 129.]

629. (1) Challenging the jury panel — The accused or the prosecutor may challenge the jury panel only on the ground of partiality, fraud or wilful misconduct on the part of the sheriff or other officer by whom the panel was returned.

(2) In writing — A challenge under subsection (1) shall be in writing and shall state that the person who returned the panel was partial or fraudulent or that he wilfully misconducted himself, as the case may be.

(3) Form — A challenge under this section may be in Form 40.

R.S., c. C-34, s. 558; R.S. 1985, c. 27 (1st Supp.), s. 130.

Commentary: The section authorizes a *challenge to the jury panel* and specifies the grounds upon which the challenge may be made.

Under s. 629(1), either P or D may challenge the jury panel upon the *ground* of *partiality, fraud*, or *wilful misconduct* on the part of the sheriff or other officer by whom the panel was returned. No other ground of challenge to the jury panel is permissible.

The challenge, which must be *in writing*, may be in Form 40. It must specify that the person who returned the panel was partial, fraudulent or wilfully misconducted him/herself, as the case may be.

Case Law
Partiality

R. v. Butler (1984), 3 C.R. (4th) 174, 63 C.C.C. (3d) 243 (B.C. C.A.) — A policy which excludes even the possibility of native Indians being selected by the sheriff from the voters' lists breaches the principle that all persons, not exempted or disqualified under provincial law, have the right to serve as jurors. Such a deliberate exclusion amounts to partiality on the part of the sheriff, hence can be the basis of a challenge to the array under s. 629.

Charter and Bill of Rights Considerations

R. v. Kent (1986), 27 C.C.C. (3d) 405 (Man. C.A.) — D is *not* entitled under *Charter* ss. 15, 25 or 27 to insist upon a jury composed entirely or proportionately of persons belonging to the same race as himself, or even that the jury include a member of his race. Absence of members of a particular race from a jury does *not* constitute proof of discrimination, particularly where there has been no deliberate exclusion of persons of a particular race and origin throughout the jury selection process.

R. v. Laws (1998), 128 C.C.C. (3d) 516 (Ont. C.A.) — The citizenship requirement in the *Justice Act of Ontario* does not contravene *Charter* s. 15.

Related Provisions: The challenge of s. 629 is to the array of jurors from which the trial jury shall be selected. Exception is taken to the entire jury panel upon a basis articulated in the section and specified in the formal written challenge in Form 40.

Exception may also be taken to individual jurors, as they are called to the book to be sworn. This form of challenge, generally described as a challenge to the polls, may be either peremptory or for cause specifically alleged and statutorily permitted. Empanelling the jury is described in ss. 631–643.

In Form 40, P or D must identify the person whose alleged misconduct has vitiated the jury panel and, further, set out the statutory basis of the challenge. There is no requirement that the factual underpinnings of the allegation be specified in the Form.

A challenge under s. 629 is tried by the judge under s. 630.

630. Trying ground of challenge — **Where a challenge is made under section 629, the judge shall determine whether the alleged ground of challenge is true or not, and where he is satisfied that the alleged ground of challenge is true, he shall direct a new panel to be returned.**

R.S., c. C-34, s. 559.

Commentary: A challenge to the jury panel, or challenge to the array as it is usually termed, is determined by the *trial judge*, who must decide whether the alleged ground of challenge is true. Where the alleged ground of challenge is found to be true, the judge will direct that a new panel be returned.

Related Provisions: Section 629 furnishes the authority for and describes the basis upon which P or D may challenge the jury panel. No other grounds are permissible.

Sections 670–672 describe the impact of formal defects in the jury process upon the trial disposition.

Empanelling Jury

631. (1) Names of jurors on cards — **The name of each juror on a panel of jurors that has been returned, his number on the panel and his address shall be written on a separate card, and all the cards shall, as far as possible, be of equal size.**

(2) To be placed in box — **The sheriff or other officer who returns the panel shall deliver the cards referred to in subsection (1) to the clerk of the court who shall cause them to be placed together in a box to be provided for the purpose and to be thoroughly shaken together.**

(3) To be drawn by clerk of court — **Where**

    (a) the array of jurors is not challenged, or

    (b) the array of jurors is challenged but the judge does not direct a new panel to be returned,

the clerk of the court shall, in open court, draw out the cards referred to in subsection (1), one after another, and shall call out the name and number on each card as it is drawn, until the number of persons who have answered to their names is, in the opinion of the judge, sufficient to provide a full jury after allowing for orders to excuse, challenges and directions to stand by.

(4) Juror and other persons to be sworn — **The clerk of the court shall swear each member of the jury in the order in which the names of the jurors were drawn and shall swear any other person providing technical, personal, interpretative or other support services to a juror with a physical disability.**

(5) Drawing additional names if necessary — **Where the number of persons who answer to their names under subsection (3) is not sufficient to provide a full jury,**

the clerk of the court shall proceed in accordance with subsections (3) and (4) until twelve jurors are sworn.

R.S., c. C-34, s. 560; R.S. 1985, c. 27 (1st Supp.), s. 131, 1992, c. 41, s. 1; 1998, c. 9, s. 5.

Commentary: The section prescribes the manner in which the names of jury panel members are chosen for jury selection at trial.

Where a jury panel has been returned, the name, number and address of each juror must be written on a separate card of similar size.

The sheriff, or other officer returning the panel, must deliver the cards of the jurors to the clerk of the court who must place them in a box provided for such purpose. The box and its contents are thoroughly shaken.

Where there has been no or an unsuccessful challenge to the array, the clerk must draw out the jurors' cards, in open court one after another. The name and number of each juror whose card has been drawn is called out as directed by the trial judge. The procedure is repeated as often as required until 12 jurors, and any support persons, have been sworn/affirmed by the clerk.

Case Law

R. v. Alward (1976), 39 C.R.N.S. 281, 32 C.C.C. (2d) 416 (N.B.C.A.); affirmed (1978), 39 C.R.N.S. 281, 35 C.C.C. (2d) 392 (S.C.C.) — It is improper for the judge to direct the clerk to draw only four names of jurors at a time. The procedure in the *Code* must be followed and a sufficient number of names to provide a full jury after allowing for challenges and stand asides must be called.

Related Provisions: Under s. 626 jurors are qualified and summoned under provincial law. The procedure to challenge the array is described in ss. 629–630.

The basis upon which and procedure in accordance with which individual jurors may be excused, directed to stand by or challenged is described in ss. 632–635, and ss. 638–643.

Under s. 643(3), *failure to comply* with the directions of ss. 631, 635, 641 or 643 does *not* affect the validity of the proceeding.

632. Excusing jurors — The judge may, at any time before the commencement of a trial, order that any juror be excused from jury service, whether or not the juror has been called pursuant to subsection 631(3) or any challenge has been made in relation to the juror, for reasons of

(a) personal interest in the matter to be tried;

(b) relationship with the judge, prosecutor, accused, counsel for the accused or a prospective witness; or

(c) personal hardship or any other reasonable cause that, in the opinion of the judge, warrants that the juror be excused.

R.S., c. C-34, s. 561; 1992, c. 41, s. 2.

Commentary: The section expressly authorizes and specifies the grounds for *judicial excusal of prospective jurors.*

A prospective juror may be *excused* from jury service *at any time before the commencement of a trial*. It matters *not* whether the prospective juror's card has been drawn from the box and name called, or whether any challenge has been made in relation to the juror. The *grounds* upon which a prospective juror may be excused by the presiding judge are:

i.   *personal interest* in the case to be tried;

ii. *relationship* with the trial judge, prosecutor, accused, defence counsel or a prospective witness; or,

iii. *personal hardship* or *any other reasonable cause* that, in the opinion of the presiding judge, *warrants excusal.*

The section contains no reference to the nature of the material upon which the presiding judge may act, or the procedure to be followed in ascertaining whether any ground(s) of excusal have been established.

Case Law

R. v. Mid Valley Tractor Sales Ltd. (1995), 101 C.C.C. (3d) 253 (N.B. C.A.) — A judge may *not* delegate the power to excuse jurors nor exercise it in private.

R. v. Betker (1997), 7 C.R. (5th) 238, 115 C.C.C. (3d) 421 (Ont. C.A.) — A trial judge may alert the jury panel to the nature of the charges and invite those prospective jurors who, because of their own victimization or close association with other victims, would find it too difficult to sit as a juror to identify themselves. The prospective juror may then be excused under *Code* s. 632(c).

Related Provisions: The phrase "before the commencement of a trial" would appear sufficiently expansive to permit some pruning of the jury list in advance of the return date on the jurors' summons.

The reference to s. 631(3) is to the procedure followed by the clerk of the court in withdrawing one after another of the juror's cards and reading out their name and juror number preliminary to beginning the challenge process.

Challenges to the *array* are governed by ss. 629 and 630. The right of *peremptory* challenge is given by s. 634 and the order of such challenges by s. 635. Challenges for *cause* are permitted and regulated by ss. 638–640.

The phrase "other reasonable cause" also appears in s. 644, which authorizes the discharge of jurors and, together with "personal hardship", in s. 633, which permits the presiding judge to direct prospective jurors to stand by on equivalent grounds.

633. Stand by — **The judge may direct a juror whose name has been called pursuant to subsection 631(3) to stand by for reasons of personal hardship or any other reasonable cause.**

R.S., c. C-34, s. 562; 1974–75–76, c. 105, s. 10, 1992, c. 41, s. 2.

Commentary: The section authorizes a *judge* to *direct* that a prospective juror, whose name has been drawn and called out by the clerk under s. 631(3), *stand by* for reasons of *personal hardship* or *any other reasonable cause.*

Related Provisions: The *Code* provides *no* other authority to direct that a prospective juror stand by. The basis upon which the direction may be made replicates s. 632(c) which permits a judge to *excuse* a prospective juror from jury service.

Section 641(1) permits the re-call of jurors directed to stand by where a full jury has *not* been sworn and no names remain in the box to be called. Section 641(2) governs where other jurors become available before a juror is sworn under s. 641(1).

634. (1) Peremptory challenges — A juror may be challenged peremptorily whether or not the juror has been challenged for cause pursuant to section 638.

(2) Maximum number — Subject to subsections (3) and (4), the prosecutor and the accused are each entitled to

(a) **twenty peremptory challenges, where the accused is charged with high treason or first degree murder;**

(b) **twelve peremptory challenges, where the accused is charged with an offence, other than an offence mentioned in paragraph (*a*), for which the accused may be sentenced to imprisonment for a term exceeding five years; or**

(c) **four peremptory challenges, where the accused is charged with an offence that is not referred to in paragraph (*a*) or (*b*).**

(3) Where there are multiple counts — Where two or more counts in an indictment are to be tried together, the prosecutor and the accused are each entitled only to the number of peremptory challenges provided in respect of the count for which the greatest number of peremptory challenges is available.

(4) Where there are joint trials — Where two or more accused are to be tried together,

(a) each accused is entitled to the number of peremptory challenges to which the accused would be entitled if tried alone; and

(b) the prosecutor is entitled to the total number of peremptory challenges available to all the accused.

R.S., c. C-34, s. 563, 1992, c. 41, s. 2.

Commentary: This section authorizes *peremptory challenges* of prospective jurors, fixes their number and ensures their availability irrespective of a challenge for cause under s. 638.

There are two kinds of challenge: challenges for cause and peremptory challenges. They are neither mutually exclusive nor mutually dependent.

Sections 634(2)–(4) should be read together. The *general rule* of s. 634(2) is that both P and D have the *number* of peremptory challenges specified in the applicable paragraph according to the specific crime or category of offence with which D is charged. Section 634(3) governs the trial of *multiple counts* and limits both P and D to the *greatest number* of peremptory challenges available in respect of a *single count*. In other words, peremptory challenges are *not* cumulative where D is charged with several counts with differing numbers of peremptory challenges. The lesser merges in the greater. Where, for example, D is charged with one count of first degree murder and two counts of attempted murder, both P and D would be entitled to challenge twenty jurors peremptorily, not forty-four as would be the case if the rights of peremptory challenge were cumulative.

Section 634(4) applies to the trial of *multiple accused*. The effect of s. 634(4)(a) is that each accused jointly tried is treated as if he/she were being tried alone, hence is entitled to the number of peremptory challenges to which he/she would be entitled if tried alone. Subsection 634(3) would govern the number of peremptory challenges available in the case of multiple counts. Under s. 634(4)(b), P is entitled to the total number of peremptory challenges available to *all* accused. Where D-1 and D-2 are jointly charged and to be jointly tried upon an indictment containing one count of first degree murder and two counts of attempted murder, the conjoint effect of ss. 634(3) and (4)(a) is to entitle *each* of D-1 and D-2 to twenty peremptory challenges, the greatest number available in respect of a single count. The combination of ss. 634(3) and (4)(b) would entitle P to forty peremptory challenges, the total number of peremptory challenges available to D-1 *and* D-2.

Related Provisions: Prospective jurors may be challenged *for cause* under s. 638 in accordance with the procedure enacted by ss. 639 and 640. The presiding judge may *excuse* prospective jurors from service under s. 632, or direct that they *stand by* until the selection process is otherwise completed under s. 633. A challenge to the *array* is governed by ss. 629 and 630.

The *order* of peremptory challenge is determined by s. 635.

Jurors who have been directed to stand by may be recalled under s. 641.

Section 642 governs where a full jury cannot be provided from the panel summoned for the sittings.

635. (1) Order of challenges — The accused shall be called on before the prosecutor is called on to declare whether the accused challenges the first juror, for cause or peremptorily, and thereafter the prosecutor and the accused shall be called on alternately, in respect of each of the remaining jurors, to first make such a declaration.

(2) Where there are joint trials — Subsection (1) applies where two or more accused are to be tried together, but all of the accused shall exercise the challenges of the defence in turn, in the order in which their names appear in the indictment or in any other order agreed on by them,

(a) in respect of the first juror, before the prosecutor; and

(b) in respect of each of the remaining jurors, either before or after the prosecutor, in accordance with subsection (1).

R.S., c. C-34, s. 564; repealed R.S. 1985, c. 2 (1st Supp.), ss. 1 and 3; enacted 1992, c. 41, s. 2.

Commentary: This provision regulates the *order* of challenges to individual jurors.

The *general rule* of s. 635(1) is that, in respect of the *first prospective juror*, D is required to declare, prior to P, whether he/she challenges the juror, for cause or peremptorily. Thereafter, in respect of the *second and all subsequent prospective jurors*, P and D alternate in declaring first whether the juror is being challenged, for cause or peremptorily.

Subsection 635(2) makes s. 635(1) applicable to *joint trials*. In respect of the *first prospective juror*, the accused declare first, in the order in which their names appear in the indictment, or in any other agreed upon order, thereafter P will declare. Subsequently, in respect of the *second and all further prospective jurors*, P and the accused alternate, as would be the case in the trial of an individual accused, except that the several accused remain as a group and exercise their rights in the order in which their names appear in the indictment or in any other agreed upon order.

Related Provisions: Prospective jurors may be challenged *for cause* under s. 638 in accordance with the procedure enacted by ss. 639 and 640. The presiding judge may *excuse* prospective jurors from service under s. 632 or direct that they *stand by* until the selection process is otherwise completed under s. 633. A challenge to the *array* is governed by ss. 629 and 630.

Section 634 authorizes *peremptory* challenges of prospective jurors, fixes their number and ensures their availability whether or not a juror has been challenged for cause under s. 638.

Jurors whom the presiding judge has directed to stand by may be recalled under s. 641. Section 642 governs where a full jury cannot be provided from the panel summoned for the sittings.

636. [Repealed 1992, c. 41, s. 2.]

637. [Repealed 1992, c. 41, s. 2.]

638. (1) Challenge for cause — A prosecutor or an accused is entitled to any number of challenges on the ground that

(a) the name of a juror does not appear on the panel, but no misnomer or misdescription is a ground of challenge where it appears to the court that the description given on the panel sufficiently designates the person referred to;

(b) a juror is not indifferent between the Queen and the accused;

(c) a juror has been convicted of an offence for which he was sentenced to death or to a term of imprisonment exceeding twelve months;

(d) a juror is an alien;

(e) a juror, even with the aid of technical, personal, interpretative or other support services provided to the juror under section 627, is physically unable to perform properly the duties of a juror; or

(f) a juror does not speak the official language of Canada that is the language of the accused or the official language of Canada in which the accused can best give testimony or both official languages of Canada, where the accused is required by reason of an order under section 530 to be tried before a judge and jury who speak the official language of Canada that is the language of the accused or the official language of Canada in which the accused can best give testimony or who speak both official languages of Canada, as the case may be.

(2) No other ground — No challenge for cause shall be allowed on a ground not mentioned in subsection (1).

(3) [Repealed 1997, c. 18, s. 74]

(4) [Repealed 1997, c. 18, s. 74]

R.S., c. C-34, s. 567; 1977–78, c. 36, ss. 5, 6;R.S. 1985, c. 27 (1st Supp.), s. 132; c. 31 (4th Supp.), s. 96; 1997, c. 18, s. 74.

S. 638(1)(f) has been proclaimed in force in the provinces of Manitoba, New Brunswick, Ontario and in Yukon Territory and Northwest Territories.

Commentary: The section authorizes the *challenge* of prospective jurors *for cause* and specifies the *grounds*. By s. 638(2) *no* other ground of challenge for cause is permitted.

Under s. 638(1), either P or D may challenge *any number* of prospective jurors for cause, upon any ground described in ss. 638(1)(a)–(f). The cause alleged in most cases is under s. 638(1)(b), lack of indifference. The cause described in s. 638(1)(f) is, in terms, limited to cases where an order has been made under s. 530 respecting the language of trial.

Case Law

Guidelines

R. v. Williams, 15 C.R. (5th) 227, 124 C.C.C. (3d) 481, [1998] 1 S.C.R. 1128; reversing (1996), 48 C.R. (4th) 97, 106 C.C.C. (3d) 215 (B.C. C.A.) — The presumption that prospective jurors are indifferent or impartial must be displaced before they can be challenged and questioned. As a general rule, the party wishing to challenge calls evidence to support the basis of the concern. Where the basis of the concern is widely-known and accepted, the judge may the take judicial notice of it.

A judge should exercise the wide discretion allowed under s. 638(1)(b) in accordance with *Charter* considerations, especially the rights to a fair trial by an impartial jury and to equality before and under the law.

R. v. Sherratt (1991), 63 C.C.C. (3d) 193 (S.C.C.) — A trial judge must *not*, in exercising his/her discretion of admitting grounds of challenge for cause and settling the questions, effectively curtail D's statutory right of challenge for cause. Although D has no right to a favourable jury, and the selection procedure cannot be used to thwart the representativeness essential to the jury's proper functioning, challenges for cause are properly used to rid the jury of prospective members who are *not* indifferent, or otherwise fall within s. 638(1). They must *not* be used, however, merely to over or under-represent a certain class of persons, or as a "fishing expedition" to obtain personal information about the juror.Although s. 638 imposes little, if any, burden on the challenger, the trial judge retains a reasonable degree of control and, accordingly, some burden is placed on the challenger to ensure that the jury selection proceeds in accordance with underlying principle, and that sufficient information is given to the trial judge so as to confine the trial of the challenge within permissible bounds. There must be an "air of reality" to the application, but it is *not* limited to extreme cases.

R. v. Hubbert (1975), 31 C.R.N.S. 27, 29 C.C.C. (2d) 279 (Ont. C.A.); affirmed (1977), 38 C.R.N.S. 381, 33 C.C.C. (2d) 207 (S.C.C.) — The purpose of challenge for cause is to eliminate from the jury those persons within the five categories of subsection (1) and, save as to a juror whose name is not on the panel, to require that the truth of the challenge be decided by two triers chosen from the peers of the prospective jurors. Challenge for cause is *not* for the purpose of finding out what kind of juror the person called is likely to be — his personality, beliefs, prejudices, likes or dislikes. The challenge must never be used as a means of indoctrinating the jury panel to the proposed defence or otherwise to influence the result of the eventual trial. The questioning of prospective jurors by counsel, without challenge for cause, and whether sworn or unsworn, is *not* permitted in Ontario. The challenge for cause should *not* be used deliberately, as an aid to counsel in deciding whether to exercise the right of peremptory challenge, although indirectly a proper challenge and the trial of its truth may have that effect. The right of peremptory challenge by either party remains, even if the ground of challenge is found not true as does the right of P to stand aside a prospective juror. No distinction need be made between "not indifferent" and "not impartial". The trial judge has a wide discretion and must be firmly in control of the challenge process. In this era of rapid dissemination of news, prior information about a case and even the holding of a tentative opinion about it, does not render partial a juror sworn to render a true verdict. Trial judges will excuse from the case prospective jurors they find to be of obvious partiality, through close connection with parties or witnesses. A challenge for cause need not be put in writing. Counsel may do so, to spare opprobrium to the juror. The judge may require it. The *Code* does *not* require that a challenge, oral or written, be particularized. Counsel may be prepared to tell the trial judge the reason for his challenge. The "other party" to the proceedings may "deny" the challenge or, by inference, "admit the challenge". Once the judge is satisfied there is some foundation to the challenges, he proceeds to

S. 638

Criminal Code

the trial of its truth, with a brief explanation to the triers. The party challenging may call the prospective juror as a witness, without first calling other evidence to establish a *prima facie* case. It is unhelpful to characterize the questioning of the juror as "examination in chief" or "cross examination". The "other party" may question the juror and call all other evidence. By leave of the trial judge, the challenging party may reply. The section neither provides for, nor prohibits, addresses by counsel to the triers. Usually there will be no need for it. It is in the trial judge's discretion. The "charge" to the triers should be brief.

R. v. Guérin (1984), 13 C.C.C. (3d) 231 (Que. C.A.) — Although the trial judge may ask a few preliminary questions to screen the prospective jurors for bias, he may not usurp the accused's right to challenge for cause.

Not Indifferent Between the Queen and the Accused: S. 638(1)(b)

R. v. Williams, 15 C.R. (5th) 227, 124 C.C.C. (3d) 481, [1998] 1 S.C.R. 1128; reversing (1996), 48 C.R. (4th) 97, 106 C.C.C. (3d) 215 (B.C. C.A.) — Section 638(1)(b) is intended to prevent persons who may not be able to act impartially from sitting as jurors. To required evidence that some jurors will be unable to set their prejudices aside is to set too high a standard. The appropriate evidentiary standard is a "realistic potential for partiality". Absent evidence to the contrary, demonstration of wide-spread national or provincial prejudice against D's race will permit an inference that similar prejudice is replicated in the community of trial. Less wide-spread prejudice may suffice in some cases.

A judge should permit challenges if there is a *realistic possibility* that the jury pool may contain people whose racial prejudice might incline them to favour P rather than D in deciding matters at trial.

The expectation that jurors usually follow their oath does *not* obviate the need to permit a challenge for cause where it is established that the community suffers from wide-spread prejudice against persons of D's race sufficient to create a *realistic potential* for *partiality*.

Evidence of wide-spread racial prejudice may, depending on the nature of the evidence and the circumstances of the case, support the conclusion that there is a realistic potential for partiality. The potential becomes irrefutable where the prejudice can be linked to specific aspects of D's trial, as for example, a pervasive belief that persons of D's race are more likely to commit the offence charged.

A trial has a wide discretion to determine whether wide-spread racial prejudice in the community, without specific "links" to the trial, is sufficient to give an air or reality to a particular challenge. Where there are specific "links" to the trial, a challenge for cause *must* be permitted.

Section 638(2) involves two inquires. The first, before the judge, is to determine whether a challenge for cause should be permitted. The *test* is whether there is a *realistic potential* or possibility for *partiality*. Where a challenge for cause is permitted, the second inquiry occurs on the challenge itself. D may question potential jurors

i.   whether the juror harbours prejudices against people of D's race and, if so,

ii.   whether the juror is able to set those prejudices aside and act impartially.

The triers must decide whether the juror will be able to act impartially.

R. v. Sherratt (1991), 63 C.C.C. (3d) 193 (S.C.C.) — Where pre-trial publicity is relied on to establish lack of indifference, there is a distinction between mere publication of the facts and misrepresentation of the evidence, wide publicity of previous discreditable conduct by D and speculation as to guilt or innocence. The threshold is *not* whether the ground of alleged partiality will create partiality in a juror, but whether it could create such partiality as would prevent a juror from being indifferent as to the result. There must be a *realistic potential* for the existence of such partiality, on a ground sufficiently articulated in the application, before the challenge may proceed.

R. v. Keegstra, [1991] 4 W.W.R. 136, 3 C.R. (4th) 153, 63 C.C.C. (3d) 110 (Alta. C.A.) — The test to be applied in determining whether prospective jurors may be challenged for cause under s. 638(1)(b) on account of *pre-trial publicity* is whether there is any reason to doubt, on such account, that the impartiality of any one of the jurors might have been affected irretrievably.

R. v. Makow (1974), 28 C.R.N.S. 87, 20 C.C.C. (2d) 513 (B.C. C.A.) — D does *not* have an unfettered right to challenge for cause and examine or cross-examine a juror. There must be a *prima facie* case that the juror is *not* indifferent.

R. v. Nielsen (1984), 16 C.C.C. (3d) 39 (Man. C.A.); reversed on other grounds (1988), 62 C.R. (3d) 313, 40 C.C.C. (3d) 1 (S.C.C.) — A proposed defence question as to whether prospective jurors could maintain their own opinions if in disagreement with the other jurors was disallowed on the ground that it was irrelevant to a determination of whether a potential juror was impartial and unbiased.

R. v. Alward (1976), 39 C.R.N.S. 281, 32 C.C.C. (2d) 416 (N.B. C.A.); affirmed (1978), 39 C.R.N.S. 281 at 306, 35 C.C.C. (2d) 392 (S.C.C.) — A challenge for cause is not a fishing expedition to discover if a juror is impartial. Counsel wishing to challenge a juror must make out a *prima facie* case that the juror is not indifferent by stating facts indicating partiality.

R. v. Koh (1998), 131 C.C.C. (3d) 257, 21 C.R. (5th) 188 (Ont. C.A.) — Without sustainable objection from P, a trial judge should allow a challenge for cause by a member of a visible racial minority *without* strict compliance with the requirement that D establish a realistic potential for the existence of partiality. The fact of racism against visible minorities is a notorious fact that has repeatedly received judicial notice.

There is no compelling reason why every member of a visible racial minority charged with an offence should *not* have the right to challenge prospective jurors for cause.

The fact of racism may well be amenable to judicial notice as a fact that is so notorious as *not* to be the subject of dispute among reasonable persons. In the alternative, D, a member of a visible minority, may be taken as having established a *prima facie* case by merely requesting the right to make the challenge in view of the successive authorities all of which have spoken about the existence of the evil of racism.

R. v. Betker (1997), 7 C.R. (5th) 238, 115 C.C.C. (3d) 421 (Ont. C.A.) — There is a principled distinction between a want of indifference towards D and want of indifference towards the nature of the crime with which D is charged. Strong attitudes about a particular crime, even if accompanied by intense feelings of hostility and resentment towards those who are alleged to have committed it, will rarely, if ever, translate into partiality against D sufficient to found a challenge for cause.

R. v. Ali (1996), 110 C.C.C. (3d) 283 (Ont. C.A.) — Any proposed extension of the principles in *R. v. Parks* should await a case in which an *adequate evidentiary foundation* has been laid to permit an informed decision whether the decision should to be extended to

i.   *other* instances of alleged *racial prejudice*; and

ii.   *prejudice* based on *sexual preference*.

R. v. Glasgow (1996), 110 C.C.C. (3d) 57 (Ont. C.A.) — Challenges for cause based upon

i.   anti-black bias; and

ii.   pre-trial publicity

ought to be kept separate, *not* merged into a single question or series of them. The threat to a fair trial posed by potential jurors who have an anti-black bias is generic. It need *not* be traced to something specific to D or the case to be tried.

R. v. Cameron (1995), 22 O.R. (3d) 65 (Ont. C.A.) — Before questions may be asked of prospective jurors on a challenge for cause, counsel must articulate sufficient particularity of the proposed ground to show the existence of a realistic *potential* for the existence of partiality against D.

R. v. Cameron (1995), 22 O.R. (3d) 65 (Ont. C.A.) — *R. v. Parks, infra*, does *not* authorize use of the challenge for cause to ask wide-ranging questions of prospective jurors. *R. v. Parks* was a particular case decided upon a specific issue where it appeared the articulated ground of challenge showed the existence of a realistic potential for partiality. It ought *not* be taken as a point of departure.

R. v. Parks (1993), 24 C.R. (4th) 81, 84 C.C.C. (3d) 353 (Ont. C.A.); leave to appeal refused (April 28, 1994) (S.C.C.) — Where there is a *realistic possibility* that one or more jurors will discriminate against D because of D's colour, a challenge for cause which seeks to determine whether a prospective juror would, because of racial prejudice, not be impartial as between P and D should be permitted.

R. v. Zundel (1987), 56 C.R. (3d) 1, 31 C.C.C. (3d) 97 (Ont. C.A.); leave to appeal refused (1987), 56 C.R. (3d) xxviii (S.C.C.) — General grounds such as race, religion, political belief or opinions, and membership in a minority group are not valid grounds for challenging a juror. However, defence counsel is entitled to challenge jurors for cause on the basis of pretrial publicity and the notoriety of the accused.

R. v. Pirozzi (1987), 34 C.C.C. (3d) 376 (Ont. C.A.) — The trial judge has a discretion, to be exercised judicially, whether and to what extent questioning of prospective jurors will be allowed on the *voir dire*.

R. v. Proulx (1992), 76 C.C.C. (3d) 316, 357–70 (Que. C.A.) — Where, due to pre-trial publicity, there is a *realistic potential* for the *existence of partiality*, D should be allowed to challenge prospective jurors for cause. A *trial judge* ought *not* undertake the questioning of individual jurors on the issue of impartiality.

Related Provisions: Under s. 639 the trial judge may require that a challenge for cause be put in writing in Form 41 for trial under s. 640.

Section 632 describes the circumstances under which a judge may order that any juror be excused from jury service. Section 633 authorizes a judge to direct a juror whose name has been called under s. 631(3) to stand by for reasons of personal hardship or any other reasonable cause.

An unsuccessful challenge for cause does *not* prevent D or P from challenging the prospective juror peremptorily.

It is not uncommon in cases where challenge for cause is permitted under s. 638(1)(b) for counsel to submit to the trial judge for approval of a list of questions to be put to each prospective juror.

639. (1) Challenge in writing — Where a challenge is made on a ground mentioned in section 638, the court may, in its discretion, require the party that challenges to put the challenge in writing.

(2) Form — A challenge may be in Form 41.

(3) Denial — A challenge may be denied by the other party to the proceedings on the ground that it is not true.

R.S., c. C-34, s. 568.

Commentary: Under this section where a challenge for cause is made under s. 638(1), the trial judge may require the challenge to be put in writing in Form 41. Under subsection (3), the responding party may deny the challenge on the ground that it is not true.

Related Provisions: The grounds upon which a challenge for cause may be made are set out in s. 638(1), the procedure for their trial in s. 640. No other causes are permitted by s. 638(2).

Form 41 does *not* require any specification of the particulars or evidentiary basis of the challenge, other than a repetition of the statutory ground of challenge under s. 638(1).

See also the corresponding note to s. 638, *supra*.

640. (1) Objection that name not on panel — Where the ground of a challenge is that the name of a juror does not appear on the panel, the issue shall be tried by the judge on the *voir dire* by the inspection of the panel, and such other evidence that the judge thinks fit to receive.

(2) Other grounds — Where the ground of a challenge is one not mentioned in subsection (1), the two jurors who were last sworn, or if no jurors have then been sworn, two persons present whom the court may appoint for the purpose, shall be sworn to determine whether the ground of challenge is true.

(3) If challenge not sustained, or if sustained — Where the finding, pursuant to subsection (1) or (2) is that the ground of challenge is not true, the juror shall be sworn, but if the finding is that the ground of challenge is true, the juror shall not be sworn.

(4) Disagreement of triers — Where, after what the court considers to be a reasonable time, the two persons who are sworn to determine whether the ground of challenge is true are unable to agree, the court may discharge them from giving a verdict and may direct two other persons to be sworn to determine whether the ground of challenge is true.

R.S., c. C-34, s. 569.

Commentary: The section provides the *procedure* for the trial of *challenges for cause.*

Where the challenge for cause is that the *name* of the juror does *not appear* on the *panel* (s. 638(1)(a)), the trial judge determines the issue under s. 640(1) on a *voir dire* by the inspection of the panel and on such other evidence as he/she thinks fit to receive.

In *any other* case of *challenge for cause*, the issue is determined under s. 640(2) by *two triers* who shall be the last two jurors sworn or, if none have been sworn, two persons, in court, sworn to try the issue. The issue to be tried is whether the ground of challenge is true. Where the triers' finding is that the ground of *challenge* is *true*, the prospective juror shall not be sworn. Where the finding is that the ground of *challenge* is *not true*, the prospective juror shall be sworn, subject to the rights of peremptory challenge being exercised. Under s. 640(4), where the triers are unable to determine the truth of the challenge within a reasonable time, they may be discharged and two new triers selected and sworn to determine the issue.

Case Law

Cloutier v. R. (1979), 12 C.R. (3d) 10, 48 C.C.C. (2d) 1 (S.C.C.) — After an unsuccessful challenge for cause, D may challenge peremptorily.

R. v. English (1993), 84 C.C.C. (3d) 511 (Nfld. C.A.) — There is *no* statutory requirement that the first two triers of a challenge for cause selected from the jury panel be themselves questioned concerning their own impartiality.

R. v. English (1993), 84 C.C.C. (3d) 511 (Nfld. C.A.) — Section 640 does *not* specifically provide the procedure to be followed with respect to the first two triers of a challenge for cause. A decision to keep the initial triers until two jurors have been selected, rather than replace a trier with the first juror selected, does *not* reflect error.

R. v. English (1993), 84 C.C.C. (3d) 511 (Nfld. C.A.) — Where a challenge for cause due to lack of impartiality is based on *pre-trial publicity*, it is preferable, though *not* statutorily required, that the jurors selected, except the triers, remain out of the court room while subsequent jurors are picked.

R. v. Sampson (1935), 63 C.C.C. 24 (N.S. C.A.); affirmed on other grounds (1935), 63 C.C.C. 384 (S.C.C.) — If two or more jurors have been sworn when a challenge for cause is made, s. 640(2) provides that the two jurors last sworn shall be sworn as triers, and that if no jurors have been sworn, "two persons present whom the court may appoint for that purpose" shall be sworn as triers. Under this provision, it is *not* necessary that the "two persons present" be selected from persons not on the jury panel; any two persons may be selected.

R. v. Brigham (1988), 44 C.C.C. (3d) 379 (Que. C.A.) — The two persons appointed to be triers are to remain until two jurors have been sworn and it is improper to replace one of them with the first juror sworn. Where the triers are unable to agree as to whether or not a prospective juror is impartial, both triers should be discharged from giving a verdict and two other persons sworn to determine the challenge.

R. v. Guérin (1984), 13 C.C.C. (3d) 231 (Que. C.A.) — Where the judge refused to permit counsel to question jurors, and decided to research the issue of impartiality by questioning the juror himself, it was held that although the judge had wide discretion in controlling challenge procedure, and might initially pose questions to prospective jurors, impartiality was to be determined by two sworn jurors under subsection (4). Although the impartiality of a prospective juror was a question of fact, not one of law, the improper procedure tainted the jury selection with illegality and amounted to a fundamental defect in the constitution of the tribunal.

Related Provisions: The grounds of challenge for cause appear in s. 638(1). No other ground is permitted by s. 638(2). Section 639 permits the trial judge to require a challenge for cause to be put in writing in Form 41.

In each challenge for cause under other than s. 638(1)(a), the triers are instructed by the trial judge as to the nature of their obligations and duties. It is not generally the practice to have them retire to determine the matter.

See the corresponding notes to ss. 638 and 639, *supra.*

641. (1) Calling jurors who have stood by — Where a full jury has not been sworn and no names remain to be called, the names of those who have been directed to stand by shall be called again in the order in which their names were drawn and they shall be sworn, unless excused by the judge or challenged by the accused or the prosecutor.

(2) Other jurors becoming available — Where, before a juror is sworn pursuant to subsection (1), other jurors in the panel become available, the prosecutor may require the names of those jurors to be put into and drawn from the box in accordance with section 631, and those jurors shall be challenged, directed to stand by, excused or sworn, as the case may be, before the names of the jurors who were originally directed to stand by are called again.

R.S., c. C-34, s. 570, 1992, c. 41, s. 3.

Commentary: The section describes the *procedure* to be followed when a full jury has not been sworn and no names remain to be called.

Under s. 641(1), in the circumstances described, it is the *general rule* that the names of those jurors whom the judge has directed to stand by will be called again in the order originally drawn. The persons stood by will then be sworn, unless excused by the trial judge or challenged by D or P.

Section 641(2) applies where other jurors in the panel become available *before a juror is sworn under s. 641*. P may require that the names of the newly-available jurors be put in the box and drawn in accordance with s. 631. The newly-available jurors shall then be challenged, directed to stand by, excused or sworn, as the case may be, before the names of the jurors originally directed to stand by are recalled.

Case Law [See s. 642 and 643]

Related Provisions: Under s. 642, the summoning of *talesmen*, is the next step in the selection process where s. 641 fails to fill the jury vacancies.

Section 643(3) provides that failure to comply with s. 641 does *not* affect the validity of the proceeding. Formal defects in the jury process are generally *not* fatal to the validity of the proceedings under ss. 670–672.

The procedural steps to be followed in empanelling a jury are described in ss. 631–635 and ss. 638–640.

642. (1) Summoning other jurors when panel exhausted — Where a full jury cannot be provided notwithstanding that the relevant provisions of this Part have been complied with, the court may, at the request of the prosecutor, order the sheriff or other proper officer forthwith to summon as many persons, whether qualified jurors or not, as the court directs for the purpose of providing a full jury.

(2) Orally — Jurors may be summoned under subsection (1) by word of mouth, if necessary.

(3) Adding names to panel — The names of the persons who are summoned under this section shall be added to the general panel for the purposes of the trial, and the same proceedings shall be taken with respect to calling and challenging those persons, excusing them and directing them to stand by as are provided in this Part with respect to the persons named in the original panel.

R.S., c. C-34, s. 571; 1992, c. 41, s. 4.

Commentary: The section describes what must be done where a full jury cannot be provided in accordance with the relevant provisions of the *Code*.

Under s. 642(2) the court, at the request of P, may order the sheriff or proper officer forthwith to summon, by word of mouth if necessary, as many persons, *whether qualified jurors or not*, as the court directs, to provide a full jury. The procedure is described as ordering a *tales*, the persons summoned, as *talesmen*.

Under s. 642(3), the names of the *talesmen* are added to the general panel for the purposes of the trial. Their selection as jurors is in accordance with the procedure followed for the original panel members.

Case Law

R. v. Ladouceur (1998), 124 C.C.C. (3d) 269 (Ont. C.A.) — Where the balance of the jury panel has been released, s. 642(1) permits resort to *talesmen* to replace a juror who has been excused prior to D being given in charge of the jury.

R. v. Rowbotham (1988), 63 C.R. (3d) 113, 41 C.C.C. (3d) 1 (Ont. C.A.) — Where a full jury cannot be provided, notwithstanding the relevant provisions of the *Code* have been complied with, this section sets out the exclusive procedure to be followed. The *talesmen* are summoned pursuant to this section and their names added to the general panel. The same proceedings be taken with respect to calling and challenging the *talesmen* and directing them to stand by as are prescribed with respect to persons named in the original panel. Where as a result of challenges and directions to stand by a full jury cannot be obtained, even with the addition of *talesmen*, the *talesmen* added to the panel and directed by P to stand by must be called again and sworn unless challenged by D or unless P challenges them either peremptorily or for cause. P cannot direct those persons to stand by a second time, and they must be dealt with as required by the *Code* before a second tales is ordered. If a full jury cannot be obtained even with the addition of *talesmen* first summoned, successive directions to summon *talesmen* may be made. However, each group of *talesmen*, including those directed to stand by, must be dealt with in accordance with the *Code* before a subsequent order for summoning *talesmen* is made.

Related Provisions: At common law, it was *not* permissible to have a jury composed wholly of *talesmen* prayed because of a complete absence of jurors who had been summoned. Such prospects would now seem, at least, unlikely, if not of questionable validity.

In most instances, jury selection is accomplished through the application of ss. 631–635 and 638–640, without recourse to either ss. 641 or 642.

The saving provision of s. 643(3) does *not* apply to failure to comply with the directions of this section, although ss. 670–672, which forgive certain formal defects in the jury process, apply.

643. (1) Who shall be jury — **The twelve jurors whose names are drawn and who are sworn in accordance with this Part shall be the jury to try the issues of the indictment, and the names of the jurors so drawn and sworn shall be kept apart until the jury gives its verdict or until it is discharged, whereupon the names shall be returned to the box as often as occasion arises, as long as an issue remains to be tried before a jury.**

(2) Same jury may try another issue by consent — **The court may try an issue with the same jury in whole or in part that previously tried or was drawn to try another issue, without the jurors being sworn again, but if the prosecutor or the accused objects to any of the jurors or the court excuses any of the jurors, the court shall order those persons to withdraw and shall direct that the required number of names to make up a full jury be drawn and, subject to the provisions of this Part relating to challenges, orders to excuse and directions to stand by, the persons whose names are drawn shall be sworn.**

(3) Sections directory — **Failure to comply with the directions of this section or section 631, 635 or 641 does not affect the validity of a proceeding.**

R.S., c. C-34, s. 572; 1992, c. 41, s. 5.

Commentary: In general, the full complement of jurors sworn is the jury which tries the issues of the indictment. The names of the jurors sworn are kept apart, until verdict or discharge, when they are returned to the box to be used, as required, so long as an issue remains to be tried by a jury.

Under s. 643(2), where P and D *consent*, the same jury, in whole or in part, may try more than one issue without the jurors being re-sworn. Upon objection by P or D, or where any of the jurors are excused, the jurors are ordered to withdraw and the selection process must be completed under the general rules of this Part.

Under s. 643(3), a *failure to comply* with the directions of s. 631 (selection of jurors from the panel), s. 635 (order of challenges), s. 641 (calling jurors who have stood by) and s. 643 (who shall be jury) does *not* affect the validity of a proceeding.

Case Law

R. v. Rowbotham (1988), 63 C.R. (3d) 113, 41 C.C.C. (3d) 1 (Ont. C.A.) — Subsection (3) applies only to irregularities and not where the error is such that D has been deprived of a statutory right, or where the error deprives D of the right to a trial by a jury lawfully constituted.

Related Provisions: Other curative provisions respecting formal defects in the jury process are found in ss. 670–672. Procedural irregularities may also fall within s. 686(1)(b)(iv).

The separation of jurors is permitted under s. 647, their discharge and replacement under s. 644. Section 652, describes when a jury may take a view and s. 653, what shall occur where they cannot agree on a verdict.

644. (1) Discharge of juror — Where in the course of a trial the judge is satisfied that a juror should not, by reason of illness or other reasonable cause, continue to act, the judge may discharge the juror.

(1.1) Replacement of juror — A judge may select another juror to take the place of a juror who by reason of illness or other reasonable cause cannot continue to act, if the jury has not yet begun to hear evidence, either by drawing a name from a panel of persons who were summoned to act as jurors and who are available at the court at the time of replacing the juror or by using the procedure referred to in section 642.

(2) Trial may continue — Where in the course of a trial a member of the jury dies or is discharged pursuant to subsection (1), the jury shall, unless the judge otherwise directs and if the number of jurors is not reduced below ten, be deemed to remain properly constituted for all purposes of the trial and the trial shall proceed and a verdict may be given accordingly.

R.S., c. C-34, s. 573; 1972, c. 13, s. 47; 1980–81–82–83, c. 47, s. 53,1992, c. 41, s. 6; 1997, c. 18, s. 75.

Commentary: The section describes the bases upon which a *juror* may be *discharged* and *replaced* and D's trial continued.

Section 644(1), applicable "in the course of the trial", permits the presiding judge to discharge a juror where the judge is satisfied that a juror should not, by reason of *illness* or *other reasonable cause*, continue to act.

Section 644(1.1) outlines the circumstances in which a juror who, because of illness or other reasonable cause, cannot continue to act. The juror may *only* be replaced *before* evidence is heard. The replacement may be made either by drawing a name from the panel of available jurors, or invoking s. 642.

Where, in the course of a trial, a juror dies or is discharged under s. 644(1), the jury remains, nonetheless, properly constituted for all purposes of the trial. Under s. 644(2), the trial will proceed and a verdict be given, provided the number of jurors is *not* reduced below ten.

Case Law

In The Course of a Trial: Ss. 644(1), (2)

Basarabas v. R. (1982), 31 C.R. (3d) 193, 2 C.C.C. (3d) 257 (S.C.C.) — *See also*: *R. v. Mohamed* (1991), 64 C.C.C. (3d) 1 (B.C. C.A.) — A jury trial commences only when D has been put in charge of the jury. A juror who is discharged after the jury has been empanelled, but before the accused has been put in charge of the jury and before any evidence has been called, is not discharged "in the course of a trial" and must be replaced so that the verdict is rendered by a complete jury of 12 members.

R. v. Emkeit (1971), 14 C.R.N.S. 290, 3 C.C.C. (2d) 309 (Alta. C.A.); affirmed on other grounds (1972), 17 C.R.N.S. 180, 6 C.C.C. (2d) 1 (S.C.C.) — The judge's power to discharge a juror "in the course of a trial" may be exercised after the trial has commenced, that is after D has been given in charge to the jury. A discharge, after this point and before P's opening to the jury, was valid.

R. v. Wellman (1996), 108 C.C.C. (3d) 372 (B.C. C.A.) — The authority to continue a trial with fewer than 12 jurors is only engaged *after* D has been given in charge of the jury. A trial cannot commence with fewer than 12 jurors.

R. v. Singh (1996), 108 C.C.C. (3d) 244 (B.C. C.A.) — A discharged juror may be replaced, even in the absence of consent, after D has been given in charge of the jury, but *no* evidence has been called. At all events, where juror substitution causes D no prejudice, any irregularity may be cured by the combined effect of ss. 670 and 686(1)(b)(iv).

R. v. Richardson (1987), 39 C.C.C. (3d) 262 (N.S. C.A.) — Where D was arraigned and entered a plea of not guilty, the jury was selected, sworn and polled and the proclamation giving D in charge of the jury was read, the trial judge acted within his jurisdiction when, after excusing one juror from service, he directed the trial to continue with an 11-person jury.

Nature of Hearing

R. v. Chambers (1990), 80 C.R. (3d) 235, 59 C.C.C. (3d) 321 (S.C.C.); reversing (1989), 47 C.C.C. (3d) 503 (B.C. C.A.) — Although D does *not* have an absolute right to be present at a hearing to consider the dismissal of a juror for reasons of health, it is preferable that the trial judge advise counsel in court in the presence of D of the nature of the health or hardship problem and hear submissions on the issue. A formal hearing, involving the calling of evidence, need *not* necessarily be held, *provided* the trial judge explains the problem and affords counsel the opportunity to make submissions.

R. v. Hanna (1993), 80 C.C.C. (3d) 289 (B.C. C.A.) — An inquiry concerning the ability of a juror to continue to act is *not* subject to the usual rules of the adversarial system. As a general rule, any inquiry ought to take place on the record and in open court. The juror need *not* be put under oath, nor subjected to cross-examination by counsel. The role of counsel is to suggest questions for the trial judge to ask the juror and to make submissions when all proper inquiry has been made.

Other Reasonable Cause: S. 644(1)

R. v. Holcomb (1973), 15 C.C.C. (2d) 239 (S.C.C.); affirming (1973), 12 C.C.C. (2d) 417 (N.B. C.A.) — The words "other reasonable cause" are read *ejusdem generis* with the word "illness". They include misconduct on the part of a juror or such interference with a juror as to suggest that he may have been interfered with, whether or not there was intentional wrongdoing.

R. v. Andrews (1984), 41 C.R. (3d) 82, 13 C.C.C. (3d) 207 (B.C. C.A.) — Impartiality is a valid ground for discharging a juror during the course of a trial. It is important not only that the jurors be impartial but that they be seen to be impartial. There is no prescribed procedure to be followed, but what must be done must not prejudice the fair trial of an accused.

R. v. Sophonow (No. 2) (1986), 50 C.R. (3d) 193, 25 C.C.C. (3d) 415 (Man. C.A.); leave to appeal refused (1986), 54 C.R. (3d) xxviin (S.C.C.) — D has a *prima facie* right to be convicted only on the verdict of 12 of his peers. Before a juror is discharged under this section on the basis of the unsworn statement of the foreman that the juror claims to have psychic powers, which statement the juror denies, D has a right to participate in the inquiry by cross-examination and representations.

R. v. Tsoumas (1973), 11 C.C.C. (2d) 344 (Ont. C.A.) — Subsection (1) empowers the trial judge to discharge a juror who is unable to act consistently with the principle that a juror must not only be impartial but manifestly be seen to be impartial.

R. v. Lessard (1992), 14 C.R. (4th) 330, 74 C.C.C. (3d) 552 (Que. C.A.) — D is *not* entitled to a mistrial as of right where a juror discloses that he/she has been bribed by a gang of which D is a member. The *test* to be applied is whether there is a real danger that D's position has been prejudiced in the circumstances. The decision of a trial judge whether to discharge a bribed juror should take into account the general atmosphere of the trial, the particular circumstances of the case, any observations made during the course of the trial and the reactions of other jurors to the trial judge's remarks concerning the incident. The decision of the trial judge ought only to be reversed where it is clearly mistaken and reflects an improper exercise of judicial discretion.

Charter Considerations

R. v. Genest (1990), 61 C.C.C. (3d) 251 (Que. C.A.); leave to appeal refused (1991), 62 C.C.C. (3d) vi (note) (S.C.C.) — *See also: R. v. Lessard* (1992), 14 C.R. (4th) 330, 74 C.C.C. (3d) 552 (Que. C.A.) — Section 644(2), which permits a jury trial to continue notwithstanding the discharge of up to two jurors, does *not* infringe *Charter* s. 11(f).

Related Provisions: The phrase "other reasonable cause" in s. 644(1), neither there nor elsewhere defined, *semble*, comprehends any cause which reasonably bears upon the apparent ability of a juror to discharge his/her functions in a competent and impartial manner. It also appears in ss. 632(c) and 633 as "any other reasonable cause", to describe a basis upon which a trial judge may excuse a prospective juror from service, or direct such a person to stand by whilst the selection procedure otherwise continues.

Where the death or discharge of jurors reduces their number to fewer than ten, a mis-trial will be declared.

The phrase "in the course of a trial" is also *not* defined in the section, nor elsewhere. It would appear that a jury trial commences when D is given in charge of the jury after arraignment.

Trial

645. (1) Trial continuous — **The trial of an accused shall proceed continuously subject to adjournment by the court.**

(2) Adjournment — **The judge may adjourn the trial from time to time in the same sittings.**

(3) Formal adjournment unnecessary — **No formal adjournment of trial or entry thereof is required.**

(4) Questions reserved for decision — **A judge, in any case tried without a jury, may reserve final decision on any question raised at the trial, or any matter raised further to a pre-hearing conference, and the decision, when given, shall be deemed to have been given at the trial.**

(5) Questions reserved for decision in a trial with a jury — **In any case to be tried with a jury, the judge before whom an accused is or is to be tried has jurisdiction, before any juror on a panel of jurors is called pursuant to subsection 631(3) and in the absence of any such juror, to deal with any matter that would ordinarily or necessarily be dealt with in the absence of the jury after it has been sworn.**

    R.S., c. C-34, s. 574; R.S. 1985, c. 27 (1st Supp.), s. 133; 1997, c. 18, s. 76.

Commentary: The section covers trial continuity and the determination of issues which arise, at trial.

In general, D's trial is to proceed continuously, subject to adjournment from time to time, in the same sittings of the court. No formal adjournment or entry thereof is required.

In trials by judge without a jury, s. 645(4) permits the judge to reserve final decision on any issue raised at trial. The decision, later given, is deemed to have been given at trial.

In jury cases, s. 645(5) authorizes the determination of certain issues prior to the formal commencement of trial proceedings. The determinations *must* be made by the judge before whom D is or is to be tried and *may* be made prior to the calling of any juror from the panel under s. 631(3), and in the absence of any such juror. *What* may be determined is any matter that would ordinarily or necessarily be decided in the absence of the jury after it has been sworn. In essence, the section permits pre-trial determination of any or all matters that, when raised at trial, would be dealt with and determined in the absence of the jury, as for example admissibility of evidence.

Case Law

Proceed Continuously

Franklin v. R. (1985), 45 C.R. (3d) 90, 18 C.C.C. (3d) 97 (S.C.C.) — There will be *no* loss of jurisdiction where a trial court, acting on an indictment, fails to proceed at the time set for trial, absent unconstitutional conduct.

Commencement of Trial [See also digests under s. 644(1), (2)]

Basarabas v. R. (1982), 31 C.R. (3d) 193, 2 C.C.C. (3d) 257 (S.C.C.); reversing (1981), 62 C.C.C. (2d) 13 (B.C. C.A.) — A jury trial commences only when D has been put in charge of the jury.

Adjournment: Ss. 645(2), (3)

Darville v. R. (1956), 25 C.R. 1, 116 C.C.C. 113 (S.C.C.) — "[The] conditions [that] must ordinarily be established by affidavit in order to entitle a party to an adjournment on the ground of the absence of witnesses ... [are] as follows: (a) that the absent witnesses are material witnesses in the case; (b) that the party applying has been guilty of no laches or neglect in omitting to endeavour to procure the attendance of these witnesses; (c) that there is a reasonable expectation that the witnesses can be procured at the future time to which it is sought to put off the trial".

R. v. Roebuck (1985), 36 Man. R. (2d) 270 (C.A.) — The trial judge has the discretion to grant or refuse an adjournment and this discretion is not to be interfered with unless an error has clearly been committed.

Masuzumi v. R., [1984] N.W.T.R. 285 (C.A.) — In the absence of a request for an adjournment at trial, D could not later complain concerning the calling of a witness whose name was not on the indictment.

R. v. Denda (1986), 17 O.A.C. 222 (C.A.) — An accused should be entitled to an adjournment to prepare for cross-examination where defence counsel is surprised by P calling the co-accused as a witness. An overnight adjournment was insufficient in these circumstances.

R. v. Kaipiainen (1954), 17 C.R. 388, 107 C.C.C. 377 (Ont. C.A.) — Refusal of an adjournment to obtain commission evidence in a foreign country may be a denial of justice where the evidence was material.

Exclusion of Witnesses

R. v. Grabowski (1983), 8 C.C.C. (3d) 78 (Que. C.A.); affirmed (1985), 22 C.C.C. (3d) 449 (S.C.C.) — The question of which witnesses, if any, are to be excluded during a trial are questions of practice within the discretion of the trial judge. As a result, where a trial judge grants a motion that all the witnesses are to be excluded, except a police officer, and the police officer is the last Crown witness to testify, no prejudice will occur if the trial judge gives sufficient warning to the jury concerning the weight to be attached to the officer's testimony.

R. v. Warren (1973), 24 C.R.N.S. 349, 14 C.C.C. (2d) 188 (N.S. C.A.); leave to appeal refused (1973), 14 C.C.C. (2d) 188n (S.C.C.) — A witness cannot be prevented from testifying even if he has intentionally disobeyed an order for exclusion.

R. v. Livingston (1985), 46 C.R. (3d) 50 (Sask. C.A.); leave to appeal refused (1985), 46 C.R. (3d) 50n (S.C.C.) — Where a witness remains in the courtroom despite an exclusion order, the correct procedure is for the trial judge to allow the evidence of that witness to be tendered but to instruct the jury to consider what weight to give to the testimony.

Pre-Trial Applications: S. 645(5)

R. v. Litchfield (1993), 25 C.R. (4th) 137, 86 C.C.C. (3d) 97 (S.C.C.) — An indictment is preferred only when it is lodged with the trial judge. It may be preferred, however, once the trial judge has been assigned. D may apply to the assigned trial judge to divide or sever the counts after the indictment has been preferred, but before the court has been constituted to begin hearing evidence. It is the trial judge who should hear such applications.

Voir Dire

R. v. Gauthier (1975), 33 C.R.N.S. 46, 27 C.C.C. (2d) 14 (S.C.C.) — In a trial by judge alone, the evidence on a *voir dire* does not become part of the evidence at trial unless both parties consent to have it used in the trial.

Note-taking by Jurors

R. v. Andrade (1985), 18 C.C.C. (3d) 41 (Ont. C.A.) — In the absence of objection by counsel, the trial judge may instruct the jury that they are entitled to take notes. The trial judge may also, in his discretion, permit questions to be put to a witness by a juror, except a question which, if answered, would elicit evidence that is inadmissible.

Procedure on Directed Verdict

R. v. Rowbotham (1994), 30 C.R. (4th) 141, 90 C.C.C. (3d) 449 (S.C.C.) — In a jury trial, where the trial judge rules that there is *no* evidence upon which a properly instructed jury may convict, the judge should withdraw the case from the jury and enter a verdict of acquittal.

Reasons

R. v. Morin (1992), 16 C.R. (4th) 291, 76 C.C.C. (3d) 193 (S.C.C.) — There is no obligation on a trial judge to record all or any specific part of the process of deliberation on the facts. The trial judge must consider all the evidence in relation to the ultimate issue, but unless the reasons show that this was not done, the failure to record it as having been done affords no basis for a conclusion of legal error in this respect.

MacDonald v. R. (1976), 29 C.C.C. (2d) 257 (S.C.C.) — Neither the *Code* nor the common law imposes an obligation upon a trial judge to give reasons and, although it is preferable that he do so, the absence of reasons does not raise a question of law. Nevertheless, the appellate court may review the record of the proceedings to determine whether the trial judge erred in a matter that could reasonably have affected his verdict.

R. v. Dupuis (1992), 12 C.R. (4th) 185 (Sask. C.A.) — Failure to give reasons does not, *per se*, constitute an error of law. An omission to deal with a relevant issue or an indication that the trial judge was unaware of or failed to appreciate material evidence may constitute reversible error. (Bayda C.J.S. and Sherstobitoff J.A.)

Related Provisions: Trial proceedings may also be adjourned under s. 474 where no jury panel has been summoned. In trials without jury, express authority to adjourn proceedings is given under s. 571.

The section does not define or describe when a jury trial commences. It would seem reasonable to conclude that it does so when the jurors have been sworn and D given in their charge.

Sections 669.1 and 669.2 furnish authority for various judges to act prior to plea and for the purpose of an adjournment, as well as the continuation of proceedings, where the presiding judicial officer is unable to act.

646. Taking evidence — On the trial of an accused for an indictable offence, the evidence of the witnesses for the prosecutor and the accused and the address of the prosecutor and the accused or counsel for the accused by way of summing up shall be taken in accordance with the provisions of Part XVIII relating to the taking of evidence at preliminary inquiries.

R.S., c. C-34, s. 575.

Commentary: Under this section, where D is tried for an indictable offence, the evidence of the witnesses and the addresses of counsel or the accused must be taken as under Part XVIII applicable to preliminary inquiries.

Case Law

R. v. Paul (1987), 79 N.S.R. (2d) 36 (C.A.) — Where the transcript failed to include D's cross-examination and re-examination, and a preliminary part of the judge's charge to the jury, there was held to be no miscarriage of justice. The trial judge had provided a resume of the missing portion of the jury charge and the evidence of three Crown witnesses established the elements of the offence, which was not necessarily affected by the accused's cross-examination.

R. v. Robillard, [1969] 4 C.C.C. 120 (Que. C.A.) — The provisions of this section are mandatory. The failure to record the addresses of counsel resulted in D being granted a new trial where the accused complained of Crown counsel's address.

R. v. Herman, [1986] 1 W.W.R. 725 (Sask. C.A.) — An accurate and complete record of the proceedings is essential when the liberty of D is at issue. Consequently, where the recording device at trial was faulty and the evidence of a principal witness was missing, D's conviction was quashed and an acquittal entered.

Related Provisions: The taking of evidence at a preliminary inquiry is governed by s. 540.

In general, evidence at a criminal trial is given *viva voce* and under oath or affirmation *in the proceedings*. Physical evidence is there produced and identified or otherwise authenticated by witnesses. In certain circumstances, evidence taken on commission (ss. 709–714) or given elsewhere, as for example at the preliminary inquiry (s. 715) may be admitted as evidence at trial. Section 655 authorizes the making of admissions of fact at a criminal trial.

647. (1) Separation of jurors — The judge may, at any time before the jury retires to consider its verdict, permit the members of the jury to separate.

(2) Keeping in charge — Where permission to separate under subsection (1) cannot be given or is not given, the jury shall be kept under the charge of an officer of the court as the judge directs, and that officer shall prevent the jurors from communicating with anyone other than himself or another member of the jury without leave of the judge.

(3) Non-compliance with subsection (2) — Failure to comply with subsection (2) does not affect the validity of the proceedings.

(4) Empanelling new jury in certain cases — Where the fact that there has been a failure to comply with this section or section 648 is discovered before the verdict of the jury is returned, the judge may, if he considers that the failure to comply might lead to a miscarriage of justice, discharge the jury and

(a) direct that the accused be tried with a new jury during the same session or sittings of the court; or

(b) postpone the trial on such terms as justice may require.

(5) Refreshment and accommodation — The judge shall direct the sheriff to provide the jurors who are sworn with suitable and sufficient refreshment, food and lodging while they are together until they have given their verdict.

R.S., c. C-34, s. 576; 1972, c. 13, s. 48.

Commentary: The section permits separation and *sequestration* of jurors in a criminal trial.

Under s. 647(1), jurors may be permitted to separate at any time before they retire to consider their verdict. Permission is routinely given at the outset of the trial and maintained absent reason to the contrary, until deliberations commence.

Where permission to separate under s. 647(1) is *not* given, the jurors are kept together under the charge of a designated court officer who must prevent any and all communication with persons other than fellow jurors or the designated officer.

In general, non-compliance with the conditions of sequestration imposed under s. 647(2) does *not* invalidate the proceedings, but where such failure, or breach of a non-publication order under s. 648, is discovered *prior* to verdict, the presiding judge may discharge the jury, if he/she considers the failure to comply might lead to a miscarriage of justice. Where the jury is discharged, under s. 647(4), a new jury may be empanelled and trial proceedings recommenced at the same sittings or the trial postponed on such terms as justice requires.

Under s. 647(5), jurors must be given suitable and sufficient refreshment, food and lodging while they are together, until they have given their verdict.

Case Law

Separation of Jurors

Demeter v. R. (1977), 38 C.R.N.S. 317, 34 C.C.C. (2d) 137 (S.C.C.) — The decision of the trial judge as to when to sequester the jury is a discretionary one. It is *not* a decision on a question of law.

Copy of Indictment

Manchuk v. R. (1938), 70 C.C.C. 161 (S.C.C.) — In circumstances where the indictment contains an endorsement of D's conviction on a previous trial, the jury should *not* be given the original indictment. A copy should be substituted.

Copy of Criminal Code

R. v. Wong (1978), 41 C.C.C. (2d) 196 (B.C. C.A.) — Giving juries written extracts from evidence or from a judge's charge, or memoranda of law or copies of a relevant statute is a dangerous procedure and should be adopted only in very special circumstances and with great care.

R. v. Vawryk (1979), 46 C.C.C. (2d) 290 (Man. C.A.) — Under stringent safeguards, it would *not* be improper, within the discretion of the trial judge, to give a jury typed extracts of specific sections of the *Code*.

R. v. Tuckey (1985), 46 C.R. (3d) 97 (Ont. C.A.) — The jury may have typewritten copies of the *Code* if the judge advises the jury to accept the law as given in the charge and *not* to engage in its own interpretation of the *Code* sections.

R. v. Stanford (1975), 27 C.C.C. (2d) 520 (Que. C.A.) — It is not only permissible but prudent to give a jury the text of the *Code*, rather than have them rely on their memories, which may be imprecise.

R. v. Crothers (1978), 43 C.C.C. (2d) 27 (Sask. C.A.) — Where a trial judge gave the jury copies of a relevant section of the *Code* with instructions to use it only to understand the judge's previous instructions, it was held that this did *not* eliminate the possibility that some jurors might place their own interpretation on the section so that the danger of such a practice out-weighed any benefit.

Instructions of Trial Judge

R. v. W. (D.) (1991), 63 C.C.C. (3d) 397 (S.C.C.) — On the issue of *credibility* the jury should be instructed that if they believe the evidence of D they must acquit; if they do *not* believe the evidence of D but are left in a reasonable doubt by it they must acquit; and even if they are *not* left in doubt by the evidence of D, they must ask whether on the basis of the evidence which they do accept, they are convinced beyond a reasonable doubt of D's guilt.

R. v. Morin (1988), 66 C.R. (3d) 1, 44 C.C.C. (3d) 193 (S.C.C.) — The jury is *not* to be instructed to apply the criminal standard in two stages of fact-finding and guilt. The jury should be told that the facts are not to be examined separately and in isolation with reference to the criminal standard. Where issues of credibility arise, the jury should also be instructed that it is not necessary for them to believe the defence evidence on a vital issue, but that they are to acquit if the defence evidence leaves them in a state of doubt after considering it in the context of the whole of the evidence.

Quebec (A.G.) v. Belmoral Mines Ltd. (1986), 55 C.R. (3d) 378 (Que. C.A.); affirmed (1989), 69 C.R. (3d) 37 (S.C.C.) — It is proper in a complex case for the judge to give *written* instructions to the jury.

R. v. Gaumont (1981), 63 C.C.C. (2d) 176 (Que. C.A.); leave to appeal refused (1983), 46 N.R. 625 (S.C.C.) — The trial judge has the right to recall the jury on his own initiative and give them further instructions.

Excerpts of Evidence

Olbey v. R. (1979), 14 C.R. (3d) 44, 50 C.C.C. (2d) 257 (S.C.C.) — The jury should *not* be allowed to hear or read back certain parts of the evidence without also hearing counterbalancing or qualifying portions.

Cathro v. R. (1956), 22 C.R. 231, 113 C.C.C. 225 (S.C.C.) — The jury should *not* be given, to take with them into the jury room, a transcript of only part of a trial judge's charge, particularly if that part of the charge contains important references to the evidence and contentions of P, and none to those of the defence.

R. v. Thomas (1987), 20 B.C.L.R. (2d) 241 (C.A.) — Where the jury asks for transcripts of the evidence, the trial judge ought to try to identify the precise segments of the evidence that are required. Having found that out, he should then provide whatever the jury reasonably requires, subject only to whatever safeguards, if any, are necessary to ensure a fair trial.

R. v. Kluke (1987), 22 O.A.C. 107 (C.A.) — A demonstration by a firearms expert was given a second time to the jury upon its request after it had retired to consider its verdict. This was held to have, in effect, allowed further evidence to be adduced after the jury had retired. Inferences possibly drawn by the jury from the demonstration could not properly be challenged by cross-examination, and, therefore, could have prejudiced D.

R. v. Corriveau (1985), 19 C.C.C. (3d) 238 (Ont. C.A.) — Having received the jury's request to review the testimony of four witnesses, the trial judge was obligated to assist the jury in its deliberations. Since transcripts were not available for review and hearing all the evidence would have taken over eight hours, the judge should have offered to review his notes of the evidence with regard to the four witnesses or asked the jury if they could limit the review to a specific part or parts of the evidence in question.

R. v. Andrade (1985), 18 C.C.C. (3d) 41 (Ont. C.A.) — The trial judge may properly refuse a request by the jury to have a transcript of the entire proceedings for their use during deliberations. The jury is, however, entitled to have the whole or a part of the evidence of a witness or witnesses read back to them at their request and, in the circumstances, it would have been preferable for the judge to have so reminded the jury.

Deliberations

R. v. Owen (1983), 4 C.C.C. (3d) 538 (N.S. C.A.) — Where a jury deliberated until early morning as there was no accommodation available for them, the accused's appeal against conviction was allowed on the basis that the unavailability of accommodation suggested the jury deliberated under pressure and without benefit of a review of the evidence so that their decision was unsafe and unsatisfactory.

R. v. Kulak (1979), 7 C.R. (3d) 304, 46 C.C.C. (2d) 30 (Ont. C.A.) — A jury should *not* be allowed to continue deliberating into the morning except in exceptional circumstances which should be set out in the record.

Charbonneau v. R. (1964), 44 C.R. 330, [1965] 3 C.C.C. 352 (Que. C.A.) — Where the jury was asked to deliberate again after having rendered one verdict for two offences, they did so in open court. A new trial was ordered on the ground that this violated the elementary principle of free discussion by jurors during their deliberations without any influence from the judge or the public.

Communication With Jurors: Ss. 647(2),(3) [See also s. 686(1)(iii)]

R. v. Chambers (1990), 80 C.R. (3d) 235, 59 C.C.C. (3d) 321 (S.C.C.) — See digest under s. 644 "Nature of Hearing", *supra*.

Koufis v. R. (1941), 76 C.C.C. 161 (S.C.C.) — Where there is no evidence that members of the jury had knowledge of inflammatory newspaper articles concerning the accused which were circulated in the district where the trial was to take place, or that the jury did not give a free unbiased verdict, there is no ground for setting aside a conviction.

R. v. Rosebush (1992), 77 C.C.C. (3d) 241 (Alta. C.A.) — D's right to be present at trial includes the right to direct knowledge of anything that transpires during the course of the trial which could involve D's vital interests, including any inquiry that might affect the fairness of the trial. A trial judge ought avoid individual juror interviews except with a court reporter present to ensure an accurate and complete record. In some cases, it would be sound practice to invite comment from counsel, perhaps in the absence of D and the jury, before finally deciding the steps to be taken.

R. v. Horne (1987), 35 C.C.C. (3d) 427 (Alta. C.A.); leave to appeal refused (1987), 86 N.R. 265n (S.C.C.) — Communication by a witness with a member of a jury will only result in a mistrial if there is real prejudice to D or P. Where the communication takes place after the jury has been sequestered, there is a presumption of prejudice. However, where the communication takes place prior to deliberations, the extent of the prejudice can be determined on a *voir dire* and, if there is no real prejudice, the trial can continue.

R. v. Gauthier (1996), 108 C.C.C. 231 (B.C. C.A.) — Use of a *verdict sheet* which requires the jury to set out the facts constituting the basis of the verdict violates the integrity of the jury room and the principle that a jury need only be unanimous with respect to their verdict, *not* the facts on which it is based.

R. v. Friesen (1964), 43 C.R. 42 (B.C. C.A.) — In cases where the jurors are permitted to separate, conversations between jurors and witnesses for the prosecution cannot be a sufficient ground of complaint unless they are shown to be related to the subject matter of the trial. Casual and social greetings between jurors and witnesses in crowded corridors, while undesirable, are unavoidable.

R. v. Cameron (1991), 64 C.C.C. (3d) 96, 2 O.R. (3d) 633 (C.A.) — Subsection 647(3) has *no* application to irregularities which occur after a jury has retired to consider its verdict. Actual prejudice need not be demonstrated in such cases. The appearance of unfairness produced when unsworn court constables, the court reporter, a sheriff's deputy, a sheriff's officer in charge of prisoner control and a uniformed police constable related to V dined with the jurors was sufficient to invoke s. 686(1)(a)(iii).

R. v. Hertrich (1982), 67 C.C.C. (2d) 510 (Ont. C.A.); leave to appeal refused (1982), 45 N.R. 629 (S.C.C.) — D is entitled to be present when a juror is examined concerning potentially prejudicial communications received by the juror during the course of the trial. Furthermore, when such an incident is brought to the attention of the trial judge, it is his duty to personally inquire into the matter, he may not delegate that function to another official, such as the sheriff.

R. v. Gilson (1965), 46 C.R. 368, [1965] 4 C.C.C. 61 (Ont. C.A.) — Where an irregularity is discovered *after* the verdict, such as the entering of the jury room by the sheriff to give a legal opinion as to the validity of a seach warrant, an appeal from the verdict will only be allowed if an actual miscarriage of justice is shown to have taken place.

Frisco v. R. (1970), 14 C.R.N.S. 194 (Que. C.A.) — An interview by the trial judge with a juror where he discussed not only the latter's health but also threats made against the juror and his family as well as the juror's opinion as to the D's guilt, was contrary to the principles regarding a fair trial as enunciated in s. 650.

Questions From the Jury

R. v. S. (W.D.) (1994), 93 C.C.C. (3d) 1 (S.C.C.) — Questions from the jury should be handled as follows:

i. All questions received from the jury must be considered to be of significance and importance.

ii. *Counsel* must be *advised* of the question and their submissions heard as to the nature and content of the response.

iii. The *answer* to the question must be *correct* and *comprehensive*. Even if the issue were covered in the original charge it must, in its essence, be repeated even if this seems to be repetitious.

iv. No precise formula need be used, but the response to the question must always be accurate and complete.

v. The longer the delay the more important it will be that the recharge be correct and comprehensive. As a general rule, an error in the recharge on the question presented will not be saved by a correct charge which was given earlier. The question indicates the concern or confusion of the jury. It is that concern or confusion which must be correctly addressed on the recharge.

R. v. Giuliano (1984), 14 C.C.C. (3d) 20 (Ont. C.A.) — *See also*: *Paquette v. R*, [1979] 2 S.C.R. 26 — Any inquiry from the jury, not of a purely administrative nature, must be read in open court and counsel given an opportunity to make submissions prior to the trial judge's response to the jury. A trial judge is not entitled to reject, off the record, an inquiry from the jury on the basis that it is not framed in the form of a question or other manner satisfactory to him.

R. v. Hay (1982), 30 C.R. (3d) 37, 70 C.C.C. (2d) 286 (Sask. C.A.) — The trial judge should disclose to counsel in open court questions received from the jury and give counsel an opportunity to make submissions before he attempts to answer them.

Related Provisions: Section 647(1), unlike its predecessors, is without exception. Until retirement for deliberation, separation is permissible in *all* criminal cases.

Section 648 restricts publication and broadcast of information regarding any portion of the trial at which the jury was not present, only where the jury has been permitted to separate. D has the right to be present during the whole of D's trial, unless exception is made (s. 650(2)) or D absconds (s. 475).

The basis upon which a jury may be discharged on account of their inability to agree upon a verdict is contained in s. 653. Under s. 654 a verdict may be taken on a Sunday and/or holiday.

648. (1) Restriction on publication — Where permission to separate is given to members of a jury under subsection 647(1), no information regarding any portion of the trial at which the jury is not present shall be published, after the permission is granted, in any newspaper or broadcast before the jury retires to consider its verdict.

(2) Offence — Every one who fails to comply with subsection (1) is guilty of an offence punishable on summary conviction.

(3) "newspaper" — In this section, "newspaper" has the same meaning as in section 297.

1972, c. 13, s. 49.

Commentary: Section 648(1) restricts newspaper *publication and broadcast* of information regarding any portion of the trial at which the jury is *not* present, whether or not any jurors have been sworn, in cases where the jury has been permitted to separate under s. 647(1), until the jury retires to consider its verdict. "Newspaper" is defined in s. 297.

Failure to comply with s. 648(1) is a summary conviction offence under subsection (2).

Case Law

Jurisdiction

Toronto Sun Publishing Corp. v. Alberta (A.G.), [1985] 6 W.W.R. 36 (Alta. C.A.) — A judge of a superior court has the jurisdiction to make an order which goes beyond the statutory ban in the course of controlling proceedings in his court. If the judge has the jurisdiction to make the order, he has the jurisdiction to vary or rescind it on the motion of an affected party even after the imposition of sentence.

R. v. Unnamed Person (1985), 22 C.C.C. (3d) 284 (Ont. C.A.) — The superior courts do *not* have inherent jurisdiction to issue non-publication orders respecting matters pending in inferior courts unless these other courts require assistance to fully and effectively administer justice.

Any Portion of the Trial

R. v. Dobson (1985), 19 C.C.C. (3d) 93 (Ont. C.A.); leave to appeal refused (1985), 9 O.A.C. 400 (S.C.C.) — An attempt by the father of V to attack D after the jury had left the court room was held *not* to have taken place during a portion of the trial within the meaning of this section.

Violation of Section — Effect on Verdict

R. v. Wilson (1993), 78 C.C.C. (3d) 568, 19 C.R. (4th) 132 (Man. C.A.); leave to appeal refused (May 19, 1993) (S.C.C.) — In an application for a declaration that a criminal conviction was improperly recorded because of improper interference during the deliberations of the jury, s. 649 bars repetition of any comments by jurors during the deliberation process and conversations which occurred in the jury room.

R. v. Demeter (1975), 25 C.C.C. (2d) 417 (Ont. C.A.); affirmed on other grounds (1978), 38 C.R.N.S. 317, 34 C.C.C. (2d) 137 (S.C.C.) — Violation of the provisions of this section does *not* warrant the setting aside of the verdict of the jury unless the violation has resulted in a miscarriage of justice. There should be no interference with the discretion of the trial judge in refusing to declare a mistrial unless he has acted on a wrong principle.

Related Provisions: Section 648(1) may attract *Charter* s. 2(b) scrutiny. The provisions do *not* apply where the proceedings in the absence of the jury take place after the jury has been sequestered.

Restrictions on newspaper publication and broadcast of evidence taken in criminal proceedings may also be imposed under ss. 539 (preliminary inquiries), 157 (judicial interim release hearings), and in respect of certain aspects of the testimony of youthful complainants of sexual offences, under ss. 486(3), (3.1) and (4).

The summary conviction offence of s. 648(2) is punished under s. 787(1).

---

649. Disclosure of jury proceedings — **Every member of a jury, and every person providing technical, personal, interpretative or other support services to a juror with a physical disability, who except for the purposes of**

> **(a) an investigation of an alleged offence under subsection 139(2) in relation to a juror, or**
>
> **(b) giving evidence in criminal proceedings in relation to such an offence, discloses any information relating to the proceedings of the jury when it was absent from the courtroom that was not subsequently disclosed in open court is guilty of an offence punishable on summary conviction.**

1972, c. 13, s. 49 1998, c. 9, s. 7.

Commentary: The section prohibits *disclosure by jury* members and support persons of any information relating to the proceedings of the jury when it was absent from the courtroom that was *not* subsequently disclosed in open court. The summary conviction offence created by the section is subject to exception, for the purposes of the *investigation* of an alleged offence under s. 139(2) in relation to a juror, and the *giving of evidence* in relation to such an offence. No other exception is made.

Case Law

R. v. Zacharias (1987), 39 C.C.C. (3d) 280 (B.C. C.A.) — It was improper for the Attorney General's office, while conducting an investigation following a report that the jury had received prejudicial information about D from third parties, to ask the jurors questions relating to their deliberations. However, the disclosures revealed information such that, in the circumstances, the guilty verdict could not stand.

R. v. Gumbly (1996), 112 C.C.C. (3d) 61 (N.S. C.A.) — Fresh evidence directed to challenge the integrity of the trial process must be *admissible* evidence.

R. v. Perras (No. 2) (1974), 18 C.C.C. (2d) 47 (Sask. C.A.) — The court of appeal cannot entertain an application for leave to examine the jurors for the purpose of impeaching their verdict. The principle precluding the court from accepting the evidence of a juror, either oral or by affidavit, as to what transpired in a jury room or jury box, is applicable to a third party.

Related Provisions: The section applies irrespective of whether the jurors were permitted to separate under s. 647(1) and is a general prohibition against disclosure of any information relating to the proceedings of the jury not later publicly disclosed, whether it occurred during deliberations or otherwise in the course of the trial.

The offence is punishable under s. 787(1).

650. (1) Accused to be present — Subject to subsections (1.1) and (2), an accused other than a corporation shall be present in court during the whole of the accused's trial.

(1.1) Video links — Where the court so orders, and where the prosecutor and the accused so agree, the accused may appear by counsel or by closed-circuit television or any other means that allow the court and the accused to engage in simultaneous visual and oral communication, for any part of the trial other than a part in which the evidence of a witness is taken.

(1.2) Video links — Where the court so orders, an accused who is confined in prison may appear by closed-circuit in prison television or any other means that allow the court and the accused to engage in simultaneous visual and oral communication, for any part of the trial other than a part in which the evidence of a witness is taken, if the accused is given the opportunity to communicate privately with counsel, in a case in which the accused is represented by counsel.

(2) Exceptions — The court may

    (a) cause the accused to be removed and to be kept out of court, where he misconducts himself by interrupting the proceedings so that to continue the proceedings in his presence would not be feasible;

    (b) permit the accused to be out of court during the whole or any part of his trial on such conditions as the court considers proper; or

    (c) cause the accused to be removed and to be kept out of court during the trial of an issue as to whether the accused is unfit to stand trial, where it is satisfied that failure to do so might have an adverse effect on the mental condition of the accused.

(3) To make defence — An accused is entitled, after the close of the case for the prosecution, to make full answer and defence personally or by counsel.

R.S., c. C-84, s. 577; 1972, c. 13, s. 50; 1991, c. 43, s. 9, Schedule, item 4; 1994, c. 44, s. 61; 1997, c. 18, s. 77(2).

Commentary: The section defines the scope of D's *right to be present* and make a defence at trial, and permits presence by electronic means in certain circumstances.

The *general rule* of s. 650(1) is that D, other than a corporation, shall be *present* in court during the whole of D's trial, subject to the three exceptions of s. 650(2). On consent, a court may order that D's presence be by counsel or electronic means. This option is *not* available when evidence is being taken. It also requires that D and the court be able to simultaneously engage in visual and oral communication.Under s. 650(1.2), where D is confined in prison and is represented by counsel and has the opportunity to privately communicate with counsel and no evidence is being taken, the court may order the accused to appear by closed-circuit television or similar means.

Under s. 650(2)(a), D may be *removed* for *misconduct*, but only where it is to such an extent that it interrupts the proceedings so that to continue them in D's presence would not be feasible. Under s. 650(2)(b), the trial judge may *permit* D to be out of court during all or any part of the trial, subject to terms. Section 650(2)(c) permits *removal* of D during a *fitness hearing* where the court is satisfied that failure to do so might have an adverse effect on D's mental condition.

Under s. 650(3), D is entitled, after the close of P's case, to make full answer and defence, personally or by counsel.

Case Law

Requirement of Presence [See also s. 686]

R. v. Rosebush (1992), 77 C.C.C. (3d) 241 (Alta. C.A.) — *See* digest under s. 647, *Communication with Jurors, supra.*

R. v. Howell (1995), 22 C.R. 263 (Ont. C.A.) — D must be present throughout the trial unless one of the exceptions of s. 650(2) applies. If the trial judge charges the jury in D's absence, and the case does *not* fall within any of the exceptions, the proceedings are invalid and a new trial must be ordered. Section 650(2)(b) only applies if there is a request, either express or implied, by D to be absent.

Meunier v. R. (1966), 48 C.R. 14 (Que. C.A.); affirmed (1967), 50 C.R. 75 (S.C.C.) — This section is imperative and its contravention vitiates proceedings without prejudice being shown.

Whole of the Trial: S. 650(1)

R. v. Chambers (1990), 80 C.R. (3d) 235, 59 C.C.C. (3d) 321 (S.C.C.); reversing (1989), 47 C.C.C. (3d) 503 (B.C. C.A.) — *See* digest under s. 647, *Communication with Jurors, supra.*

R. v. Barrow (1987), 61 C.R. (3d) 305, 38 C.C.C. (3d) 193 (S.C.C.) — For the purposes of subsection (1), jury selection should be considered part of the trial. Therefore, where the trial judge conferred with jurors during the jury selection process, out of earshot of D and his counsel, it was held that this section was violated. A new trial was ordered.

R. v. Côté (1986), 49 C.R. (3d) 351, 23 C.C.C. (3d) 481 (S.C.C.) — D has a right to be present during the examination of jurors by the trial judge where the issue possibly involves the accused's vital interests. If on the facts of a case it is uncertain whether D's vital interests are involved, the trial judge may, in the absence of D, investigate the matter. This would include questioning the jurors. But, as of the moment when it appears that those vital interests are in issue, the issue must be determined in the presence of D. Where a judge is being told by jurors that the integrity of other jurors is in doubt, D's vital interests are in issue, and the investigation and determination of that issue must be conducted in the presence of D.

Paquette v. R., [1979] 2 S.C.R. 26 (S.C.C.) — The jury is entitled to have its questions answered and dealt with in open court and D is entitled to be present.

R. v. Reale (1973), 13 C.C.C. (2d) 345 (Ont. C.A.); affirmed (1974), 22 C.C.C. (2d) 571 (S.C.C.) — Where D is deprived of the assistance of an interpreter during the trial judge's charge, D is *not* present for that part of the proceedings for the purpose of the section any more than if he were unconscious or had been physically removed from the court room.

Ginoux v. R. (1971), 15 C.R.N.S. 117 (Que. C.A.); affirmed without reasons (1971), 16 C.R.N.S. 256 (S.C.C.) — Where upon preparing to hear argument on the admissibility of a question put to D in examination-in-chief, the trial judge ordered the jury and D to withdraw, this section had been breached and a new trial was ordered.

R. v. Quick (1993), 82 C.C.C. (3d) 51 (B.C. C.A.) — Where counsel advise the trial judge, in chambers and in the absence of D, of decisions which they have made concerning the conduct of their cases and prospective problems which may arise, and the discussions have *no* bearing on D's guilt, there is *no*

S. 650   Criminal Code

infringement of D's right to be present under *Code* s. 650. At all events, a violation of s. 650 in such circumstances could be cured by s. 686(1)(b)(iv) where there is no suggestion of prejudice and counsel for D has indicated that D's presence is *not* required.

R. v. Fenton (1984), 11 C.C.C. (3d) 109 (B.C. C.A.) — A judge's action in interviewing a juror in chambers in the absence of either D or his counsel, and subsequently discharging the juror, constituted a violation of this section, notwithstanding that D's counsel had not objected to the process.

R. v. Giuliano (1984), 14 C.C.C. (3d) 20 (Ont. C.A.) — It is incumbent upon the judge to read a communication from the jury in open court, thereby giving counsel the right to make submissions, and answer questions for the jury in the presence of all parties.

R. v. Petrovic (1984), 41 C.R. (3d) 275, 13 C.C.C. (3d) 416 (Ont. C.A.); leave to appeal refused January 31, 1985 (S.C.C.) — Where a Crown witness acted as interpreter for D during a sentencing *voir dire*, and occasionally summarized the evidence rather than giving a simultaneous translation, it was held that the accidental contravention of D's right to be meaningfully present during sentencing proceedings did not vitiate his conviction where the trial was otherwise untainted with jurisdictional error. A review of his sentence under *Charter* s. 24(1) was an adequate remedy for the denial of his rights.

R. v. Hertrich (1982), 67 C.C.C. (2d) 510 (Ont. C.A.); leave to appeal refused (1982), 45 N.R. 629 (S.C.C.) — This section requires the presence of D during the "whole of his trial". D has a right to have direct knowledge of anything transpiring in the course of the trial that affects his vital interests. A judge's inquiry concerning the impartiality of certain jurors involves such a vital issue and therefore is part of the "trial".

R. v. Grimba (1980), 56 C.C.C. (2d) 570 (Ont. C.A.) — Where D was excluded from the courtroom during argument regarding the admissibility of certain evidence and when rulings were made, and the reasons for the exclusion did not fall properly within the exceptions of the section, the section was contravened. The fact that D or his counsel did not object could not be construed as a waiver of D's rights under the section.

R. v. Hay (1982), 30 C.R. (3d) 37, 70 C.C.C. (2d) 286 (Sask. C.A.) — The trial judge's failure to disclose to D the nature of questions from the jury is akin to conducting part of the trial in the absence of D, and should not be allowed.

Waiver of Right

R. v. Page, [1969] 1 C.C.C. 90 (B.C. C.A.) — Counsel may waive D's right to be present or request permission for D to be out of court during the whole or any part of the trial, but such a drastic interference with the rights of D may only be done with his approval. There is no implied authority of waiver, although approval may be inferred from what has occurred.

R. v. Dunbar (1982), 28 C.R. (3d) 324, 68 C.C.C. (2d) 13 (Ont. C.A.) — Where D was directed to leave the courtroom during examination and cross-examination while the court determined the propriety of questions sought to be asked, it was held that acquiescence by defence counsel in D's exclusion did not constitute a waiver of D's right to be present during the trial, and that the section had been contravened.

R. v. Dumont (1984), 37 C.R. (3d) 399 (Sask. C.A.) — Counsel cannot waive D's right to be present during the whole trial, including a redirection to the jury.

Motion for Non-Suit — Directed Verdict

R. v. Charemski (1998), 123 C.C.C. (3d) 225 (S.C.C.) — The *test* to determine whether a case should go to the jury is whether there is *any* evidence upon which a *reasonable* jury, *properly instructed, could* return a verdict of *guilty*. A motion for a directed verdict fails in every case where there is admissible evidence which *could*, if believed, result in a conviction.

P must adduce *some* evidence of culpability for every essential definitional element of the crime charged upon which P has the evidential burden in order to survive a motion for a directed verdict. Where P's evidence is entirely circumstantial, whether there is a rational explanation for it, other than D's guilt, is a jury question.

R. v. Monteleone (1987), 59 C.R. (3d) 97, 35 C.C.C. (3d) 193 (S.C.C.); affirming (1982), 67 C.C.C. (2d) 489 (Ont. C.A.) — Where there is any admissible evidence before a court, either direct or circumstantial, which, if believed by a properly charged jury, acting reasonably would justify a conviction, the trial judge is *not* justified in directing a verdict of acquittal.

R. v. Genser (1986), 27 C.C.C. (3d) 264 (Man. C.A.); affirmed (1987), 39 C.C.C. (3d) 576 (S.C.C.) — The proper test for considering whether to grant a motion for a non-suit is whether sufficient evidence exists upon which a properly instructed jury could convict if acting reasonably.

Mezzo v. R. (1986), 52 C.R. (3d) 113, 27 C.C.C. (3d) 97 (S.C.C.) — A trial judge is *not* entitled to direct a verdict of acquittal and thus withdraw the case from a jury where there is admissible evidence which could, if believed, result in conviction.

Vander-beek v. R. (1970), 12 C.R.N.S. 168, 2 C.C.C. (2d) 45 (S.C.C.) — Where at the close of P's case there is ample evidence upon which the trial judge can convict, there can be no basis for a directed verdict of acquittal at this stage of the trial.

R. v. Boissonneault (1986), 29 C.C.C. (3d) 345 (Ont. C.A.) — A trial judge is obliged to rule at once on a motion to acquit at the end of P's case on the ground that no *prima facie* case has been established. The trial judge is *not* entitled to postpone the decision pending D's election to call evidence.

R. v. Melo (1986), 29 C.C.C. (3d) 173 (Ont. C.A.) — There is *no* room for the application of the doctrine of reasonable doubt at the end of P's case. The test on a motion for a directed verdict is an objective one. There is no basis for forming an opinion with respect to the ultimate decision. The issue is not whether the trial judge would eventually have acquitted D, but whether evidence exists upon which a trier of fact properly instructed and acting reasonably could have convicted D.

Full Answer and Defence: S. 650(3)

R. v. Brouillard (1985), 44 C.R. (3d) 124, 17 C.C.C. (3d) 193 (S.C.C.) — Excessive questioning, interruption of witnesses and cross-examination of D may create a doubt as to a judge's impartiality. Greater prudence and judicial restraint are necessary when D is testifying.

Aucoin v. R., [1979] 1 S.C.R. 554 (S.C.C.) — D unrepresented at trial, is deprived of the right to make full answer and defence where he is *not* invited by the trial judge to make submissions at the close of P's evidence.

R. v. M. (S.H.), (December 2, 1987), Doc. Nos. Calgary Appeals 18987Y0, 18949Y0 (Alta. C.A.) — While trial judges have the right, and in some cases the duty, to interfere in a trial, the limits of the allowable conduct should be relative to the facts and circumstances of the particular case.

R. v. Simmons, [1923] 3 W.W.R. 749 (B.C. C.A.) — The right to make full answer and defence includes not only the right to call witnesses and present argument, but also a right to cross-examine P witnesses with the utmost freedom for the observation of the jury. Any interference by the trial judge with the right of cross-examination, for example, as to previous inconsistent statements made in writing by the witness, will constitute a miscarriage of justice, entitling D to a new trial.

R. v. Campbell (1981), 64 C.C.C. (2d) 54 (N.S. C.A.) — Where the trial judge intervened in cross-examination and in the summation by defence counsel, and at the conclusion of the trial chastised defence counsel, it was held, on appeal, that it was manifest that the trial judge had not been impartial and that the defence counsel had not been given every opportunity to make full answer and defence. A new trial was ordered.

R. v. B (L.C.) (1996), 46 C.R. (4th) 368, 104 C.C.C. (3d) 353 (Ont. C.A.) — Where D has retained counsel, D is entitled to the effective assistance of counsel. The right of effective assistance of counsel is a constitutionally protected right and an aspect of D's right to make full answer and defence and to have a fair trial. Ineffective representation by counsel may be cast as a *Charter* violation or the cause of a miscarriage of justice.

R. v. Joanisse (1995), 44 C.R. (4th) 364, 102 C.C.C. (3d) 35 (Ont. C.A.) — Where D claims *ineffective representation* by counsel at trial, D must establish,

i. the facts on which the claim of incompetence rests;

ii. that the representation was incompetent when adjudged against a standard of reasonableness in the circumstances of the case and at the time any impugned decisions were made; and,

iii. that the incompetent representation, either by rendering the verdict unreliable or process unfair, resulted in a miscarriage of justice and denial of the right to fair trial.

R. v. Silvini (1991), 9 C.R. (4th) 233, 68 C.C.C. (3d) 251 (Ont. C.A.) — D is entitled to receive the effective assistance of counsel in making full answer and defence to a charge. Such assistance entails provision of competent advice, unburdened by a conflict of interest. D's conviction may be set aside where it is shown that there is a reasonable probability that, but for the unprofessional error of counsel, the result would have been different.

R. v. Gronka (1979), 45 C.C.C. (2d) 573 (Ont. C.A.) — Where D is *not* represented by counsel at his trial, and after the evidence is taken he is not given the opportunity to make submissions, he is deprived of his right to make full answer and defence.

R. v. Torbiak (1974), 26 C.R.N.S. 108, 18 C.C.C. (2d) 229 (Ont. C.A.) — The trial judge may interject himself into the examination of a witness on account of the failure of counsel to ask questions which ought to be asked. The limits of allowable conduct are relevant to the facts and circumstances of each trial.

R. v. Laperrière (1995), 101 C.C.C. (3d) 462 (Que. C.A.), notice of appeal filed (September 29, 1995), Doc. 24889 (S.C.C.) — It is *not* sufficient for D to demonstrate the appearance of a conflict of interest. It must also be shown that the result of the proceedings would have been different.

R. v. Pilon (1973), 23 C.R.N.S. 392 (Que. C.A.) — D was held to have been denied the right of full answer and defence when the trial judge prevented his counsel from cross-examining fully P's principal witness.

Right to Counsel

Barrette v. R. (1976), 33 C.R.N.S. 377, 29 C.C.C. (2d) 189 (S.C.C.) — Where there is nothing that could have allowed the trial judge to conclude that the failure of defence counsel to appear was attributable to D, or that it was a planned manoeuvre of which D was aware, an adjournment should have been granted. It could not be said that D suffered no prejudice in having to proceed without the assistance of counsel and without an eye witness being present to testify. D cannot be made accountable for the delays caused by the failure of lawyers generally to proceed on the date set for trial.

Spataro v. R. (1972), 7 C.C.C. (2d) 1 (S.C.C.) — Where a trial judge decides that an application by D to discharge his counsel is not made in good faith but is really for the purpose of delaying the trial, the judge's decision not to permit D's application is not a miscarriage of justice. The right of the defence to discharge counsel is not a licence to obstruct the course of justice.

Vescio v. R. (1949), 6 C.R. 433, 92 C.C.C. 161 (S.C.C.) — An accused is entitled to have counsel and, generally, if he is unable to retain counsel, the court will appoint one. But there is no statutory necessity for defence by counsel.

R. v. Rain (1998), 130 C.C.C. (3d) 167 (Alta. C.A.); leave to appeal refused (April 1, 1999), Doc. 27041 (S.C.C.) — Where the assistance of counsel is *essential* to ensure a fair trial, the *Charter* requires the provision of funded counsel if D wishes counsel but cannot afford to pay a lawyer. When legal aid is refused and exceptional circumstances make it probable that the trial judge cannot discharge the duty to ensure a fair trial, the appointment of counsel becomes necessary.

There are two aspects to the test a trial judge must apply in deciding whether to appoint funded counsel for D:

i.   the circumstances of D; and,

ii.   the nature of the charge(s).

The first test requires consideration of whether D can *afford* to retain counsel and whether D has the *education, experience* and other *abilities* essential to conduct his/her own *defence*.

The second test requires examination of the *seriousness* of the offence(s), the *complexity* of the case and the *length* of the trial.

The central concern throughout is the fairness of the trial.

R. v. Valley (1986), 26 C.C.C. (3d) 207 (Ont. C.A.); leave to appeal refused (1986), 26 C.C.C. (3d) 207n (S.C.C.) — Comments made by a trial judge on the conduct of defence counsel, notwithstanding their severity and frequency, were held not to reflect unfairly on the integrity of the defence so as to destroy the appearance of a fair trial. Such comments must be judged as they would be by a reasonable person present throughout the whole trial, having regard to the whole conduct of the trial.

R. v. Cook (1980), 53 C.C.C. (2d) 217 (Ont. C.A.) — A new trial was ordered where defence counsel had been impaired by alcohol or drugs during significant parts of the trial and this circumstance had interfered with D's right to make full answer and defence.

R. v. DePatie (1970), 2 C.C.C. (2d) 339 (Ont. C.A.) — Where D alleged that the offence was committed by a second accused, and the same counsel represented both accused at their separate trials, it was held that there was a conflict of interest on the part of the counsel.

Reopening Case

R. v. Champagne (1969), 8 C.R.N.S. 245 (B.C. C.A.) — Where P has closed its case and the defence closed its case, after announcing its intention to call no evidence, the trial judge in exercising his discretion to reopen P's case should consider what is in the interests of justice and without unfair consequences to D.

Order of Addresses

R. v. Rose, [1998] 3 S.C.R. 262, 129 C.C.C. (3d) 449, 20 C.R. (5th) 246 — Defending against a criminal charge does *not* intrinsically imply a temporal order of speaking with D "answering" P's address with an address in reply. The right to address the jury last is *not* a fundamental advantage.

To remedy unfairness from an improper jury address, a trial judge may

i.   give a specific *correcting* reference in the charge; or,

ii.   where a curative instruction will *not* suffice, grant the prejudiced party a *limited right* of *reply*.

The right described in item ii may be given where

i.   P has added or *substituted* a *substantive* legal *theory* of *liability* that has so *dramatically* changed that D could not reasonably have been *expected* to *answer* it; or,

ii.   D has *actually* been misled by P about the *theory* that P intends to advance.

The reply is strictly confined to those issues improperly mentioned by P.

Charter Considerations

R. v. Rose, [1998] 3 S.C.R. 262, 129 C.C.C. (3d) 449, 20 C.R. (5th) 246 — Sections 651(3) and (4) do *not* infringe D's right to procedural fairness or the presumption of innocence under ss. 7 and 11(d) of the *Charter*.

R. v. St. Laurent (1984), 38 C.R. (3d) 94, 11 C.C.C. (3d) 74 (Que. C.A.) — Where P called defence counsel as a witness on a *voir dire* concerning a statement of D, this was held to have brought the administration of justice into disrepute within the meaning of *Charter* s. 24(2). Counsel should avoid calling his adversary, since the result, in this case, was that D thereafter was represented by different counsel new to the case. The procedure at trial had been totally unnecessary and had violated D's right to be represented by counsel of his choice.

Related Provisions: The trial may proceed in D's absence under s. 475, where D has absconded during the course of the trial. Similarly, D may be excluded from the courtroom and be required to watch, on closed-circuit television, the testimony of a youthful V or other witness in cases of sexual assault, interference or exploitation under section 715.1. Where V or another witness is under 14 years, he/she may be permitted to have a support person present while V testifies, under s. 486(1.2). D can be prevented from personally cross-examining V or another witness who is under 14 years, under circumstances set out in s. 486(2.3).

Section 650 plainly refers to the physical presence of D at trial, subject to the exceptions there contained and elsewhere made. Interpreters are frequently provided to ensure linguistic presence.

The entire criminal trial process must comport with the standards of fundamental justice in *Charter* s. 7.

The section is only applicable to individual accused. A corporate accused's appearance, plea and trial are regulated by ss. 620–623.

The right of an appellant who is in custody to attend on the hearing of his/her appeal is determined under s. 688.

650.1 Pre-charge conference — **A judge in a jury trial may, before the charge to the jury, confer with the accused or counsel for the accused and the prosecutor with respect to the matters that should be explained to the jury and with respect to the choice of instructions to the jury.**

1997, c. 18, s. 78.

S. 650.1   Criminal Code

Commentary: The section, which codifies existing practice, *permits* but does *not* require a pre-charge conference in a jury trial.

A pre-charge conference may be held at any time *before* the *charge* to the jury. It may include the judge, D or counsel for D, and the prosecutor, and discuss instructions to the jury.

Related Provisions: Pre-hearing conferences are governed by *Code*, s. 625.1 and may be the subject of court rules under s. 482(3)(c).

Pre-charge conferences affect the vital interests of D. They should be held in court, in D's presence, but the jury's absence, before counsel address the jury. Discussion by counsel of defences of liability for which there is no air of reality may be avoided when the conference precedes the addresses.

Section 650 governs the presence of D and the exceptions to the rule.

651. (1) **Summing up by prosecutor** — Where an accused, or any one of several accused being tried together, is defended by counsel, the counsel shall, at the end of the case for the prosecution, declare whether or not he intends to adduce evidence on behalf of the accused for whom he appears and if he does not announce his intention to adduce evidence, the prosecutor may address the jury by way of summing up.

(2) **Summing up by accused** — Counsel for the accused or the accused, where he is not defended by counsel, is entitled, if he thinks fit, to open the case for the defence, and after the conclusion of that opening to examine such witnesses as he thinks fit, and when all the evidence is concluded to sum up the evidence.

(3) **Accused's right of reply** — Where no witnesses are examined for an accused, he or his counsel is entitled to address the jury last, but otherwise counsel for the prosecution is entitled to address the jury last.

(4) **Prosecutor's right of reply where more than one accused** — Where two or more accused are tried jointly and witnesses are examined for any of them, all the accused or their respective counsel are required to address the jury before it is addressed by the prosecutor.

R.S., c. C-34, s. 578.

Commentary: The section authorizes the *addresses of counsel* and governs their *order*.

At the conclusion of P's case, under s. 651(1), defending counsel must declare (elect) whether evidence will be adduced on behalf of D. Where evidence will be adduced on behalf of D, defending counsel may open to the jury, prior to adducing evidence. Each accused in a joint trial has an equivalent right. Where D, or *any* of several accused jointly tried, adduces *evidence* in defence, defending counsel must address the jury *prior* to P. Where D or *all* accused elect to call *no* evidence, P must address the jury first in summing up, followed by defending counsel.

Section 651(3) has attracted scrutiny under *Charter* ss. 7 and 11(d).

Case Law
Obligation of Fairness on Crown [See s. 603 "Disclosure"]
Order of Defence Evidence
R. v. Smuk (1971), 15 C.R.N.S. 218, 3 C.C.C. (2d) 457 (B.C. C.A.) — The defence is entitled to call its witnesses in any order it sees fit; and the fact that D testifies after having heard all the evidence is only a factor which may be considered in determining D's credibility. D's testimony is not to be prejudged as carrying less weight merely because D had testified last.

R. v. Angelantoni (1975), 31 C.R.N.S. 342, 28 C.C.C. (2d) 179 (Ont. C.A.) — A trial judge cannot direct either the calling of D or the order in which D will testify.

R. v. Archer (1972), 26 C.R.N.S. 225 (Ont. C.A.) — Where D's sole defence is alibi, D should be the first witness called for the defence.

906

Address by Prosecutor

Pisani v. R. (1970), 1 C.C.C. (2d) 477 (S.C.C.) — Although P is obliged to be accurate, fair and dispassionate in conducting the prosecution and in addressing the jury, there is no unyielding general rule that an inflammatory or other improper address to the jury is *per se* conclusive of the fact that there has been an unfair trial. P put before the jury, as facts to be considered, matters of which there was no evidence and which bore so directly on the central issue in the case and which were so prejudicial to that issue that D was deprived of a fair trial.

R. v. Clarke (1981), 63 C.C.C. (2d) 224 (Alta. C.A.); leave to appeal refused (1981), 63 C.C.C. (2d) 224n (S.C.C.) — Although counsel may comment on nothing but admissible evidence during closing submissions, such comments should not be misleading by virtue of the absence of undisputed facts of which the jury is not aware due to trial safeguards.

R. v. Gordon (1983), 4 C.C.C. (3d) 492 (Ont. C.A.) — In his address P asked the jury at length whether they thought the prosecution was trying to frame D. By making his own honesty and integrity an integral part of his case, P had inevitably prejudiced D. The prejudice could have been cured by a proper caution by the trial judge, but had not been.

Address by Defence

R. v. Thomas (1976), 12 N.R. 310 (S.C.C.) — Where D is represented by counsel he/she is not entitled to address the jury personally. Only an unrepresented accused may exercise that right.

R. v. Morgentaler (1985), 48 C.R. (3d) 1, 22 C.C.C. (3d) 353 (Ont. C.A.); reversed on other grounds (1988), 62 C.R. (3d) 1, 37 C.C.C. (3d) 449 (S.C.C.) — Where defence counsel's address to the jury was a very serious misstatement of the jury's duty and right to carry out its oath, the error was not capable of correction by the trial judge.

Order of Addresses: Ss. 651(3), (4)

R. v. Coffin (1956), 23 C.R. 1, 114 C.C.C. 1 (S.C.C.) — There is no requirement in this section restricting the addresses to one for each side, so as to conflict with the practice long established in trial by a mixed jury in Quebec. Under this practice, one counsel for each side addressed the jury in one language and his/her associate addressed it in the other.

R. v. Hawke (1975), 29 C.R.N.S. 1, 22 C.C.C. (2d) 19 (Ont. C.A.) — Where the sole evidence for the defence was a witness whose testimony was ruled inadmissible on a *voir dire*, the defence was entitled to address the jury last.

Charter Considerations

R. v. Hutchinson (1995), 41 C.R. (4th) 120, 99 C.C.C. (3d) 88 (N.S. C.A.) — Section 651(3) does *not* violate *Charter* ss. 7 or 11(d).

R. v. Rowbotham (1988), 63 C.R. (3d) 113, 41 C.C.C. (3d) 1 (Ont. C.A.) — Where a trial judge finds that representation of D by counsel is essential to a fair trial, D has a constitutional right to be provided with counsel at the expense of the state if he/she lacks the means to employ counsel. A stay of proceedings until funded counsel is provided is an appropriate remedy under *Charter* s. 24(1) where the prosecution insists on proceeding with the trial in breach of D's *Charter* right to a fair trial.

R. v. Tzimopoulos (1986), 54 C.R. (3d) 1 (Ont. C.A.); leave to appeal refused (1987), 54 C.R. (3d) xxviin (S.C.C.) — The order of addresses as prescribed by subsection (3) is not so unfair as to be incompatible with the principles of fundamental justice.

Related Provisions: Under *C.E.A.* s. 4(6) neither P nor the trial judge may comment upon the failure of D or D's spouse to testify at trial. In some instances, of course, under *C.E.A.* ss. 4(2), (4) and (5), D's spouse is a competent and compellable witness for P without the consent of D.

The section does *not* regulate the order of addresses amongst defending counsel in a joint trial but it is the general practice to have counsel address the jury in the order in which D's name appears on the indictment. There is no right of reply.

652. (1) View — **The judge may, where it appears to be in the interests of justice, at any time after the jury has been sworn and before it give its verdict, direct the jury to have a view of any place, thing or person, and shall give directions respecting the man-**

ner in which, and the persons by whom, the place, thing or person shall be shown to the jury, and may for that purpose adjourn the trial.

(2) **Directions to prevent communication** — Where a view is ordered under subsection (1), the judge shall give any directions that he considers necessary for the purpose of preventing undue communication by any person with members of the jury, but failure to comply with any directions given under this subsection does not affect the validity of the proceedings.

(3) **Who shall attend** — Where a view is ordered under subsection (1) the accused and the judge shall attend.

R.S., c. C-34, s. 579.

Commentary: The section authorizes the taking of a *view by the jury* of any *place, thing* or *person* in certain circumstances, and provides for the procedure to be followed when a view is ordered.

Under s. 652(1), a view may be ordered at any time after the jury has been sworn and before it gives its verdict. The sole criterion to be applied is whether it is in the interests of justice to direct such a view. The view may be of any *place, thing or person* and must include directions as to the manner in which and the persons by whom the subject shall be shown to the jury. The trial may be adjourned to permit the jury to take a view. Under s. 652(3) both D and the judge must attend.

Under s. 652(2), a judge is authorized to give any directions considered necessary to prevent undue communication with jurors, *semble*, whilst taking a view. Failure to comply with the provision, however, does *not* invalidate the proceedings.

Case Law

R. v. Gavin (1983), 10 C.C.C. (3d) 92 (B.C. C.A.) — Before a new trial need be ordered because D has *not* been present during a part of his trial or at a view, it must be shown that something was done of a nature to advance the case in the absence of D. The presentation of submissions by defence counsel during the course of the view was something which occurred to advance the case. D was not present, at the time. A new trial was ordered.

R. v. Prentice (1965), 47 C.R. 231, [1965] 4 C.C.C. 118 (B.C. C.A) — A provincial court judge has the authority to take a view.

R. v. Predac (1983), 37 C.R. (3d) 94 (Ont. C.A.) — It is a defect going to jurisdiction for the jury to take a view of the scene of the crime when the judge, counsel, and D are not present. This must result in a mistrial even if the court arranges a second view with all present.

R. v. Auger (1982), 4 C.C.C. (3d) 282 (Que. C.A.); leave to appeal refused (1983), 4 C.C.C. (3d) 282n (S.C.C.) — A trial judge has the power to permit the absence of D from the view as from any other part of the trial. D who requested absence was unable to invoke his non-participation in viewing the site as a ground of appeal.

R. v. Tanguay (1971), 15 C.R.N.S. 21 (Que. C.A.) — This section also applies to a judge sitting alone. A judge is not entitled to visit a place in the absence of D and his lawyer. It is especially so where observations made are used as corroboration of evidence given.

Related Provisions: A view is directed to *assist* jurors in their *appreciation* of the evidence given, *not* as a supplement or alternative thereto, nor replacement therefor. The taking of a view is an integral part of the trial, hence, subject to ss. 475 and 650(2), D must be present.

The section would appear equally applicable to non-jury trials under s. 572 of Part XIX.

653. (1) **Disagreement of jury** — Where the judge is satisfied that the jury is unable to agree on its verdict and that further detention of the jury would be useless, he may in his discretion discharge that jury and direct a new jury to be empanelled during the sittings of the court, or may adjourn the trial on such terms as justice may require.

(2) Discretion not reviewable — A discretion that is exercised under subsection **(1) by a judge is not reviewable.**

R.S., c. C-34, s. 580.

Commentary: The section authorizes the trial judge to *discharge* the jury in certain circumstances and limits the reviewability of the decision.

Under s. 653(1), a trial judge is authorized to discharge a jury where the judge is satisfied that the jury is *unable to agree* on its verdict, *and* that *further detention* of the jury would be *useless*. Where *both* conditions have been satisfied, the trial judge has a discretion to discharge the jury and direct that a new jury be empanelled during the sittings of the court, or adjourn the trial on such terms as justice may require.

Section 653(2) exempts the exercise of discretion under s. 653(1) from review.

Case Law

Summing-up to Jury

R. v. Menard (1998), 125 C.C.C. (3d) 416 (S.C.C.) — While there may be a considerable benefit in instructing the jury about the criminal trial process and some fundamental evidentiary principles at the outset of trial proceedings, a trial judge should await the evidence before giving similar early instruction on matters of substantive law.

R. v. G. (R.M.) (1996), 110 C.C.C. (3d) 26 (S.C.C.) — In summing-up a trial judge should outline the defence position and refer the jury to its essential elements to ensure the jury's proper appreciation of the evidence.

R. v. K. (B.A.) (1998), 126 C.C.C. (3d) 481 (B.C. C.A.) — Where a jury requests a copy of the trial judge's charge, which is in illegible form, there are several options available to assist them, including:

i.   ascertain the *portion* of the instructions that are of concern and *recharge* on them;

ii.   have the court reporter *read back* the relevant portions; or

iii. have the court report *re-play* an audiotape of the charge.

(per Southin and Hinds JJ.A.)

R. v. D. (D.) (1998), 129 C.C.C. (3d) 506, 21 C.R. (5th) 124 (Ont. C.A.) — A trial judge must ensure that any evidence read back to the jury to answer a jury question is read back together with any other portions of the evidence that qualify or contextualize it.

Jury Instructions on Right to Disagree

R. v. Naglik (1993), 23 C.R. (4th) 335, 83 C.C.C. (3d) 526 (S.C.C.); reversing (1991), 65 C.C.C. (3d) 272 (Ont. C.A.) — A trial judge must *not* instruct a jury in such a way as to leave the impression that they *must* reach a verdict. The jury should clearly understand that they have the right to disagree.

Harrison v. R. (1974), 27 C.R.N.S. 294, 18 C.C.C. (2d) 129 (S.C.C.) — The trial judge is *not* obligated to tell the jury that they may disagree. A direction that whatever verdict is returned must be unanimous is *not* improper.

Latour v. R. (1951), 11 C.R. 1, 98 C.C.C. 258 (S.C.C.) — The jury must *not* be instructed in such a way as to exclude the possibility of a disagreement.

R. v. Misra (1985), 44 C.R. (3d) 179, 18 C.C.C. (3d) 134 (Sask. Q.B.); reversed on other grounds (1986), 54 C.R. (3d) 305, 32 C.C.C. (3d) 97 (Sask. C.A.) — This section is the sole available procedure where jurors are unable to agree on a verdict.

Jury Exhortations

R. v. G. (R.M.) (1996), 110 C.C.C. (3d) 26 (S.C.C.) — An *exhortation* to an apparently deadlocked jury must be delicately balanced, carefully crafted and encourage jurors to endeavour to reach a verdict by reasoning together. The *purpose* of an exhortation is to assist in the deliberation process, *not* to influence the content of the jurors' discussion. It is inappropriate in an exhortation to suggest that jurors be instructed to consider

i.   expense;

ii.   hardship; and

iii. inconvenience

to the participants associated with a new trial, or to consider carefully only the position of the majority, *not* that of the minority.

R. v. G. (R.M.) (1996), 110 C.C.C. (3d) 26 (S.C.C.) — The following priniciples apply to exhortations given to apparently deadlocked juries:

i.   by their oath, jurors must try to render a verdict based on the evidence at trial;

ii.   the strength and genius of the jury trial is that members of the community reason together to reach a verdict based on the evidence;

iii.   a jury must be permitted to deliberate without pressure being imposed on them;

iv.   any exhortation to an apparently deadlocked jury should avoid reference to extraneous and irrelevant factors and *not* encourage a juror, by reference to such factors, to abandon an honestly-held view of the evidence;

v.   a juror ought *not* be exhorted to change his/her mind solely for the purpose of confirmatory; and

vi   no deadline for reaching a verdict ought to be imposed, nor should a jury be rushed into returning a verdict.

R. v. Sims (1992), 15 C.R. (4th) 279, 75 C.C.C. (3d) 278 (S.C.C.); reversing (1991), 64 C.C.C. (3d) 403 (B.C. C.A.) — The dangers associated with a trial judge expressing his/her opinion on issues of fact during an exhortation to a deadlocked jury are of such potential detriment to D's fair trial interest that such comment ought *not* generally be made. Even in exceptional cases, for example where the jury *requests* the judge's view, or where it is apparent from the jury's questioning that they require further clarification, the opinion required ought be offered in a balanced and fair way which will *not* sway the jury's decision-making process to one side or the other.

R. v. Littlejohn (1978), 41 C.C.C. (2d) 161 (Ont. C.A.) — Where a jury is having difficulty reaching a unanimous verdict, any comment made to them by the trial judge should avoid language which is coercive and which interferes with the jury's right to deliberate in complete freedom. In determining whether the judge's remarks cross the line between exhortation and coercion, the entire sequence of events should be considered.

R. v. Neverson (1998), 124 C.C.C. (3d) 468 (Que. C.A.) — An exhortation which alerts the jury to the practical inconveniences of disagreement and the impact on V's father to have to testify again about witnessing his son's murder vitiates the verdict.

Polling of Jury

R. v. Head (1986), 55 C.R. (3d) 1, 30 C.C.C. (3d) 481 (S.C.C.) — The power or duty of the trial judge to intervene when a jury verdict is returned and to inquire as to the true nature of the verdict must be exercised prior to the jury's discharge. After a jury is discharged following a verdict of not guilty on the offence charged, the judge is *functus officio*. The jury cannot be recalled to deal with any included offences.

Laforet v. R. (1979), 50 C.C.C. (2d) 1 (S.C.C.) — The polling of the jury, after rendering its verdict is *not* a legal requirement. A request to poll is usually allowed where doubt as to unanimity appears to exist.

R. v. Logan (1944), 82 C.C.C. 234 (B.C. C.A.) — Where a jury, instead of bringing in simply a verdict of guilty, brings in a verdict of guilty with further words added, the verdict can be accepted and acted upon only if it is possible to be sure what the jury really meant. If it is *not* possible to be sure, the usual course is for the trial judge to ask the jury to reconsider their verdict, and make it clear what was meant.

R. v. Tuckey (1985), 46 C.R. (3d) 97 (Ont. C.A.) — *See also: R. v. Thatcher* (1987), 57 C.R. (3d) 97 (S.C.C.) — There is generally *no* justification in a criminal case to ask the jury to answer questions or to particularize the basis of their verdict. The jury are entitled to arrive at a unanimous verdict for different reasons and on separate evidential bases. They need *not* be unanimous in anything but the actual verdict. The trial judge is entitled to make up his own mind on disputed questions of fact which are relevant to sentence.

R. v. Thomas (1983), 5 C.C.C. (3d) 464 (Que. C.A.) — Where the trial judge properly exercised his discretion to permit the jury to be polled, with the result of the poll being that all jurors were in agreement with the guilty verdict, at that point the jury was *functus* and the judge erred in sending the jury back for further deliberations.

Charter Considerations

R. v. Misra (1985), 44 C.R. (3d) 179, 18 C.C.C. (3d) 134 (Sask. Q.B.); reversed on other grounds (1986), 54 C.R. (3d) 305, 32 C.C.C. (3d) 97 (Sask. C.A.) — The inability of a jury to agree on a verdict does *not* constitute an acquittal, hence, D may not invoke *Charter* s. 11(h).

Related Provisions: The section is *not* exhaustive of the circumstances under which a jury may be discharged prior to verdict. The reception of inadmissible evidence of such prejudice as to impair the fairness of the trial is another basis upon which a mistrial may be declared and the jury discharged.

In cases involving several accused and/or counts, each accused is arraigned, pleads and is given in charge of the jury in respect of each count. A verdict of the jury, even if it be only to record their inability to reach a verdict, is required in respect of each accused and/or count. It would seem permissible, accordingly, that disagreement may be reported and effect given thereto in respect of any accused and/or count.

Sections 660–663 contain special provisions relating to verdicts. Section 654 authorizes the taking of a jury verdict and any procedure incidental thereto on a Sunday or holiday.

654. Proceeding on Sunday, etc., not invalid — **The taking of the verdict of a jury and any proceeding incidental thereto is not invalid by reason only that it is done on Sunday or on a holiday.**

R.S., c. C-34, s. 581.

Commentary: The section authorizes the taking of a jury verdict and any proceedings incidental thereto on a Sunday or holiday.

Case Law

R. v. Baillie (1991), 66 C.C.C. (3d) 274 (B.C. C.A.) — The phrase "any proceeding incidental thereto" authorizes jury deliberations and the re-reading of evidence at their request by the trial judge on a Sunday.

Related Provisions: "Holiday" is defined in *I.A.* s. 35.

Section 20 permits the issuance and execution of certain process and forms of release on a holiday.

Evidence on Trial

655. Admissions at trial — **Where an accused is on trial for an indictable offence, he or his counsel may admit any fact alleged against him for the purpose of dispensing with proof thereof.**

R.S., c. C-34, s. 582.

Commentary: In trials of indictable offences, D or D's counsel may admit any *fact* alleged against him. The admission dispenses with proof by P of such fact by admissible evidence.

The section does *not* authorize P to make any formal admissions, nor permit admissions of matters involving issues of mixed fact and law or pure questions of law.

Case Law

Park v. R. (1981), 21 C.R. (3d) 182, 26 C.R. (3d) 164, 59 C.C.C. (2d) 385 (S.C.C.) — D may admit the *voluntariness* of a *statement*, thereby dispensing with the necessity of a *voir dire*. The waiver of a *voir dire* must be express; silence or mere lack of objection will not constitute a valid waiver.

Castellani v. R. (1969), 9 C.R.N.S. 111, [1970] 4 C.C.C. 287 (S.C.C.) — P is *not* obliged to accept an admission made by D. Where this section is invoked, it is for P, not D, to state which facts it alleges and in respect of which it seeks admissions. It is *not* open to D to frame P's allegations so as to conform to D's own purpose, then insist on admitting them.

R. v. Fong (1994), 92 C.C.C. (3d) 171 (Alta. C.A.) — Counsel may admit the *competency* of a child witness to give sworn testimony. A trial judge may rely on the s. 655 admission in deciding whether the statutory requirements of s. 16(1) *C.E.A.* have been met.

R. v. Coburn (1982), 27 C.R. (3d) 259, 66 C.C.C. (2d) 463 (Ont. C.A.) — When it becomes apparent on a trial that there is a conflict between D's evidence and the agreed statement of facts, the trial judge should require P to call evidence on the points in issue. A conviction may not be based on the trial judge's acceptance of a fact in the agreed statement of facts over D's *viva voce* evidence on the same issue.

Related Provisions: A plea of guilty is a form of admission, though *not* generally regarded as falling within s. 655. By the plea, D admits not only all of the essential elements of the offence, but further, that P may prove them beyond a reasonable doubt by admissible evidence, a form of proof which D waives.

The section is *not* exhaustive of the circumstances under which formal proof of an issue, whether of fact or law, may be obviated by the agreement of counsel or otherwise. In each case of agreement, however, the precise nature and scope of the agreement ought plainly to be stated on the record.

656. Presumption — valuable minerals — In any proceeding in relation to theft or possession of a valuable mineral that is unrefined, partly refined, uncut or otherwise unprocessed by any person actively engaged in or on a mine, if it is established that the person possesses the valuable mineral, the person is presumed, in the absence of evidence raising a reasonable doubt to the contrary, to have stolen or unlawfully possessed the valuable mineral.

R.S., c. C-34, s. 583; 1999, c. 5, s. 24.

Commentary: This section enacts a *rebuttable presumption* applicable in prosecutions for theft of ores or minerals.

The presumption requires that there be *evidence* that an operator, workman or labourer actively engaged in or on a mine was in unlawful possession of a specified ore or mineral. The section makes such evidence, in the *absence of any evidence to the contrary, proof* that the ore or mineral was *stolen* by the person in unlawful possession thereof.

The section may attract *Charter* ss. 7 and 11(d) scrutiny.

Related Provisions: Theft is defined in s. 322 and punished in s. 334. Under s. 333, it is *not* an offence to take a specimen of ore or mineral from land, for the purpose of exploration or scientific investigation, provided the land is not enclosed and neither occupied nor worked as a mine, quarry or digging.

Part X, "Fraudulent Transactions Relating to Contracts and Trade", prohibits certain fraudulent conduct relating to minerals (s. 394) and mines (s. 396). The terms of s. 656 would render it of doubtful application in such cases.

A warrant to search for and seize precious metals from any person, or in any place, may be issued under s. 395.

657. Use in evidence of statement by accused — A statement made by an accused under subsection 541(3) and purporting to be signed by the justice before whom it was made may be given in evidence against the accused at his or her trial without proof of the signature of the justice, unless it is proved that the justice by whom the statement purports to be signed did not sign it.

R.S., c. C-34, s. 584; 1994, c. 44, s. 62.

Commentary: The section authorizes the admission into evidence at trial of a *statement* made by D, not represented by counsel, *after caution* at the *preliminary inquiry* under s. 541(3) and signed by the presiding justice. No proof of the justice's signature is generally required, unless the contrary is established.

The provision may attract *Charter* s. 13 scrutiny.

Related Provisions: Under s. 541, after P's witnesses have testified at the preliminary inquiry, D is addressed, in the language of s. 541(1) or the like, and any response recorded, before D is afforded the opportunity to call witnesses.

The section does *not* affect the basis upon which P may adduce evidence of what is alleged to be D's remarks or statements to or a record of interview with persons in authority, whether upon arrest, detention, or otherwise.

Section 715 describes the basis upon which *evidence* given, *inter alia*, upon the preliminary inquiry into the charge may be admitted as evidence at trial.

657.1 (1) Proof of ownership and value of property — In any proceedings, an affidavit or a solemn declaration of a person who claims to be the lawful owner of, or the person lawfully entitled to possession of, property that was the subject-matter of the offence, or any other person who has specialized knowledge of the property or of that type of property, containing the statements referred to in subsection (2), shall be admissible in evidence and, in the absence of evidence to the contrary, is evidence of the statements contained in the affidavit or solemn declaration without proof of the signature of the person appearing to have signed the affidavit or solemn declaration.

(2) Statements to be made — For the purposes of subsection (1), a person shall state in an affidavit or a solemn declaration

(a) that the person is the lawful owner of, or is lawfully entitled to possession of, the property, or otherwise has specialized knowledge of the property or of property of the same type as that property;

(b) the value of the property;

(c) in the case of a person who is the lawful owner of or is lawfully entitled to possession of the property, that the person has been deprived of the property by fraudulent means or otherwise without the lawful consent of the person;

(c.1) in the case of proceedings in respect of an offence under section 342, that the credit card had been revoked or cancelled, is a false document within the meaning of section 321 or that no credit card that meets the exact description of that credit card was ever issued; and

(d) any facts within the personal knowledge of the person relied on to justify the statements referred to in paragraphs (a) to (c.1).

(3) Notice of intention to produce affidavit or solemn declaration — Unless the court orders otherwise, no affidavit or solemn declaration shall be received in evidence pursuant to subsection (1) unless the prosecutor has, before the trial or other proceeding, given to the accused a copy of the affidavit or solemn declaration and reasonable notice of intention to produce it in evidence.

(4) Attendance for examination — Notwithstanding subsection (1), the court may require the person who appears to have signed an affidavit or solemn declaration referred to in that subsection to appear before it for examination or cross-examination in respect of the issue of proof of any of the statements contained in the affidavit or solemn declaration.

R.S. 1985, c. 23 (4th Supp.), s. 3;1994, c. 44, s. 63; 1997, c. 18, s. 79.

Commentary: This section permits P to establish, by *affidavit* or *solemn declaration*, essential elements of its proof in proceedings for listed offences.

Under s. 657.1(1), *proof by affidavit or solemn declaration* is permissible in any proceedings. The affidavit or solemn declaration which may be received must be of a *person* who claims to be either the *lawful owner or person entitled to possession of the property* that is the subject-matter of the offence, or has specialized knowledge of the property or the type of property. The *content* of the affidavit or solemn declaration must meet the requirements of s. 657.1(2):

i.   *identify* the *deponent* as a person described in s. 657.1(1);

ii.   *specify* the *value* of the *property*;

iii. assert that the *deponent*, if the owner or person entitled to possession of the property, has been *deprived* of the property by fraudulent means or otherwise, without consent;

iv.   in the case of a credit card offence under s. 342, that the card was revoked, cancelled, a false document under s. 321 or never issued; and,

v.   disclose the facts *within the personal knowledge of the deponent* upon which reliance is placed to justify the statements in (a)–(c.1), *supra*.

The affidavit or solemn declaration may only be received in proceedings where the *notice and disclosure* requirements of subsection (3) have been met, absent an order otherwise by the court in which the proceedings are taken. P must, before the trial or other proceedings, give D a *copy* of the affidavit or solemn declaration and, further, *reasonable notice* of P's *intention to produce* it in evidence.

The *effect* of reception of the affidavit or solemn declaration into evidence is that, *in the absence of evidence to the contrary*, the affidavit or solemn declaration is *evidence* of the *statements contained therein*, without proof of the signature of the deponent. Subsection (4) permits the court which receives the affidavit or solemn declaration in evidence to require the deponent to appear for examination or cross-examination in respect of the issue of proof of any of the statements contained in the affidavit or solemn declaration.

Related Provisions: Under s. 655, in proceedings for indictable offences, D or D's counsel may admit any fact alleged against D for the purposes of dispensing with proof thereof.

Sections 348(2) and 350 aid P's proof of the essential elements of an offence under s. 348, and ss. 354(2), 359 and 360 assist in proof of an offence under s. 354. The NSF cheque presumption of s. 362(4) may be relied upon in proceedings under s. 362.

Sections 711 (commission evidence) and 715 (evidence previously taken) also permit the reception of evidence not given *viva voce* in the presence of the trier of fact. The absence of the witness is a matter upon which the trial judge is permitted to comment when instructing the jury on how to assess or weigh the evidence.

Proof of service of any document may be made under s. 4(6) by the affidavit or solemn declaration of the person claiming to have served it. Service of a *subpoena* (s. 701) and a summons (s. 509(3)), as well as the issue of an appearance notice (s. 501(5)) may be proven by the affidavit of the issuing or serving officer or by a statement in writing certifying service under s. 4(6)(b). Failures to appear in court or for *I.C.A.* purposes may be proven by certificate under s. 145(9).

657.2 (1) Theft and possession — Where an accused is charged with possession of any property obtained by the commission of an offence, evidence of the conviction or discharge of another person of theft of the property is admissible against the accused, and in the absence of evidence to the contrary is proof that the property was stolen.

(2) Accessory after the fact — Where an accused is charged with being an accessory after the fact to the commission of an offence, evidence of the conviction or discharge of another person of the offence is admissible against the accused, and in the absence of evidence to the contrary is proof that the offence was committed.

Commentary: The section enacts a rule of evidence which permits introduction of evidence of another's conviction or discharge of an offence on D's trial for a related offence.

Under s. 657.2(1), where D is charged with possession of property obtained by crime, the conviction or discharge of the thief is admissible at D's trial. In the absence of evidence to the contrary, it is proof that the property was stolen.

Section 657.2(2) applies where D is charged with being an *accessory after the fact* to the commission of an offence. To prove that the principal offence was committed, in the absence of evidence to the contrary, P may adduce evidence of the conviction or discharge of another person of the principal offence.

Related Provisions: Possession of property obtained by crime is an offence under s. 354. The underlying offence by which the property was obtained is *not* restricted to theft, unlike the evidentiary assistance offered by s. 657.2(1). Proof of D's knowledge of the spurious character of the property may be helped by ss. 359 and 360.

The essential elements of accessoryship after the fact are described in s. 23. An accessory may be convicted even if the principal cannot be found guilty under s. 23.1. The general punishment provision for accessoryship after the fact appears in s. 463.

657.3 (1) Expert testimony — In any proceedings, the evidence of a person as an expert may be given by means of a report accompanied by the affidavit or solemn declaration of the person, setting out, in particular, the qualifications of the person as an expert if

   (a) the court recognizes that person as an expert; and

   (b) the party intending to produce the report in evidence has, before the proceeding, given to the other party a copy of the affidavit or solemn declaration and the report and reasonable notice of the intention to produce it in evidence.

(2) Attendance for examination — Notwithstanding subsection (1), the court may require the person who appears to have signed an affidavit or solemn declaration referred to in that subsection to appear before it for examination or cross-examination in respect of the issue of proof of any of the statements contained in the affidavit or solemn declaration or report.

1997, c. 18, s. 80.

Commentary: This section permits *expert* evidence to be admitted by a *report* and accompanying affidavit or solemn declaration.

Section 657.3 applies to any "any proceeding", not merely the jury trial of indictable offences. It is permissive, *not* limitative. The affidavit or solemn declaration which accompanies the report must set out the qualifications of the expert. The report should contain the substance of the expert's opinion.

Under s. 657.3(1), the report of an expert may be received if the judge is satisfied of the qualifications of the expert and the notice and disclosure of s. 657.3(1)(b) have been provided to the opposite party. The notice must be reasonable. Disclosure includes copy of the affidavit or solemn declaration and the report.

Section 657.3(2) permits the court to require the affiant or declarant to appear personally for examination or cross-examination about any issue relating to proof of the contents of the affidavit, solemn declaration or report.

Related Provisions: Sections 755 and 756 govern reception of expert evidence and remand for observation in dangerous offender proceedings. *C.E.A.* s. 7 limits the number of expert witnesses who may be called by a party.

The admissibility of expert opinion evidence depends upon four criteria:

i.   *relevance*;

ii.   *necessity* in assisting the trier of fact;

iii. *absence* of any *exclusionary* rule; and,

iv.   a *properly-qualified* expert.

Section 657.3 does *not* alter the admissibility of criteria, nor make admissible what otherwise would be excluded. It relates to the *manner* in which expert evidence may be received at trial.

Children and Young Persons

658. (1) Testimony as to date of birth — In any proceedings to which this Act applies, the testimony of a person as to the date of his or her birth is admissible as evidence of that date.

(2) Testimony of parent — In any proceedings to which this Act applies, the testimony of a parent as to the age of a person of whom he or she is a parent is admissible as evidence of the age of that person.

(3) Proof of age — In any proceedings to which this act applies,

(a) a birth or baptismal certificate or a copy of such a certificate purporting to be certified under the hand of the person in whose custody the certificate is held is evidence of the age of that person; and

(b) an entry or record of an incorporated society or its officers who have had the control or care of a child or young person at or about the time the child or young person was brought to Canada is evidence of the age of the child or young person if the entry or record was made before the time when the offence is alleged to have been committed.

(4) Other evidence — In the absence of any certificate, copy, entry or record mentioned in subsection (3), or in corroboration of any such certificate, copy, entry or record, a jury, judge, justice or provincial court judge, as the case may be, may receive and act on any other information relating to age that they consider reliable.

(5) Inference from appearance — In the absence of other evidence, or by way of corroboration of other evidence, a jury, judge, justice or provincial court judge, as the case may be, may infer the age of a child or young person from his or her appearance.

R.S., c. C-34, s. 585; 1994, c. 44, s. 64.

Commentary: This section describes several means of proving a person's age in any proceedings to which the *Code* applies.

Proof of a person's age may be made by the *testimony* of the person or a parent. Under s. 658(1), a person may testify as to the date of his/her birth. Under s. 658(2), a parent may testify as to the age of his/her child. The testimony of each is admissible as evidence of the date of birth or age, as the case may be.

Proof of a person's age may also be made by introduction of a person's *birth or baptismal certificate* or a copy of it, and *entries or record* of an incorporated society, provided the requirements of s. 658(3) have been met. In the absence or corroboration of any certificate, copy, entry or record, the court may receive and act upon any other information relating to age that the court consider reliable.

Section 658(5) permits the court in any case to infer the age of a child or young person from his/her appearance, in the absence or corroboration of other evidence.

Related Provisions: Proof of age may also be made under provincial laws of evidence incorporated by *C.E.A.* s. 40. *Quaere* whether "any other information" in s. 658(4) enlarges the ambit of admissibility?

Age is determined under *I.A.* s. 30.

Corroboration

659. Children's evidence — Any requirement whereby it is mandatory for a court to give the jury a warning about convicting an accused on the evidence of a child is abrogated.

1993, c. 45, s. 9.

Commentary: This section abrogates any requirement that makes it mandatory to warn a jury about convicting D on the evidence of a child.

In terms the section is *not* limited to statutory provisions, nor to prosecutions involving certain offences. There is, further, no distinction based upon the form of the evidence (sworn or unsworn) or limitation to cases in which the child is also the complainant.

Related Provisions: A similar rule appears in s. 274 applicable to listed crimes irrespective of V's age and rules that it is unsafe to find D guilty in the absence of corroboration.

Sections 47(3) (treason and high treason), 133 (perjury) and 292(2) (procuring a feigned marriage) are the remaining *Code* provisions which require corroboration.

Section 659 would not appear to restrict the discretion of a trial judge in circumstances of the nature described in *R. v. Marquard* (1993), 85 C.C.C. (3d) 193, 25 C.R. (4th) 1 (S.C.C.)

660. Full offence charged, attempt proved — Where the complete commission of an offence charged is not proved but the evidence establishes an attempt to commit the offence, the accused may be convicted of the attempt.

R.S., c. C-34, s. 587.

Commentary: The section authorizes a conviction for an attempt to commit the offence charged, where an attempt is established on the evidence, but the offence charged is not proven.

Related Provisions: What constitutes an attempt is defined in s. 24. The general rules respecting punishment upon conviction for attempt are found in s. 463.

Section 661 describes the verdict to be rendered where an attempt is charged, but the full offence has been proven.

D may also be convicted of an attempt to commit an included offence under s. 662(1)(b), and, in particular, attempted murder on a count charging first degree murder under s. 662(2).

661. (1) Attempt charged, full offence proved — Where an attempt to commit an offence is charged but the evidence establishes the commission of the complete offence, the accused is not entitled to be acquitted, but the jury may convict him of the attempt unless the judge presiding at the trial, in his discretion, discharges the jury from giving a verdict and directs that the accused be indicted for the complete offence.

(2) Conviction a bar — An accused who is convicted under this section is not liable to be tried again for the offence that he was charged with attempting to commit.

R.S., c. C-34, s. 588.

Commentary: The section governs cases where P alleges an *attempt* to commit an offence, but *proves* the commission of the *complete* offence. Section 661(1) disentitles D to an acquittal. There are two alternatives. D may be convicted of the attempt, notwithstanding proof of the complete offence, or the trial judge may discharge the jury from giving the verdict on the count, and direct that D be indicted for the full offence. Section 661(2) prohibits a retrial of D for the attempt, if convicted, of the complete offence.

Case Law

R. v. Doiron (1960), 34 C.R. 188, 129 C.C.C. 283 (B.C. C.A.) — Where an attempt to commit an offence is charged, but the evidence establishes the commission of the completed offence, D is *not* entitled to an acquittal. D may be convicted of the attempt.

Related Provisions: The section abrogates the common law rule that barred conviction of the full offence, if a felony, upon indictment for an attempt that was always a misdemeanour.

It would appear that where the trial judge elects to continue the trial to verdict, and D is convicted of attempt on proof of the complete offence, a subsequent prosecution for the full offence would be barred by a special plea of *autrefois convict* under ss. 609 and 610(1).

662. (1) Offence charged, part only proved — A count in an indictment is divisible and where the commission of the offence charged, as described in the enactment creating it or as charged in the count, includes the commission of another offence, whether punishable by indictment or on summary conviction, the accused may be convicted

(a) of an offence so included that is proved, notwithstanding that the whole offence that is charged is not proved; or

(b) of an attempt to commit an offence so included.

(2) **First degree murder charged** — For greater certainty and without limiting the generality of subsection (1), where a count charges first degree murder and the evidence does not prove first degree murder but proves second degree murder or an attempt to commit second degree murder, the jury may find the accused not guilty of first degree murder but guilty of second degree murder or an attempt to commit second degree murder, as the case may be.

(3) **Conviction for infanticide or manslaughter on charge of murder** — Subject to subsection (4), where a count charges murder and the evidence proves manslaughter or infanticide but does not prove murder, the jury may find the accused not guilty of murder but guilty of manslaughter or infanticide, but shall not on that count find the accused guilty of any other offence.

(4) **Conviction for concealing body of child where murder or infanticide charged** — Where a count charges the murder of a child or infanticide and the evidence proves the commission of an offence under section 243 but does not prove murder or infanticide, the jury may find the accused not guilty of murder or infanticide, as the case may be, but guilty of an offence under section 243.

(5) **Conviction for dangerous driving where manslaughter charged** — For greater certainty, where a count charges an offence under section 220, 221 or 236 arising out of the operation of a motor vehicle or the navigation or operation of a vessel or aircraft, and the evidence does not prove such offence but does prove an offence under section 249, the accused may be convicted of an offence under section 249.

(6) **Conviction for break and enter with intent** — Where a count charges an offence under paragraph 348(1)(*b*) and the evidence does not prove such offence but does prove an offence under paragraph 348(1)(*a*), the accused may be convicted of an offence under paragraph 348(1)(*a*).

R.S., c. C-34, s. 589; 1973–74, c. 38, s. 6; 1974–75–76, c. 105, s. 11; R.S. 1985, c. 27 (1st Supp.), s. 134.

Commentary: The section enacts a general rule and several specific rules applicable where an offence is charged but only part thereof proven.

Section 662(1), having declared a count to be divisible, provides that, where the commission of the offence, as described in the statutory definition or as charged in the count, *includes* the commission of any other offence, whether punishable on indictment or on summary conviction, D may be convicted of the offence so included or an attempt to commit it, where the evidence proves its commission, but not that of the offence charged.

Sections 662(2)–(6) without detracting from the general provisions of s. 662(1), enact rules of specific application to counts charging listed offences and permit conviction of other specified offences upon proper proof.

Case Law

Application to Summary Conviction Proceedings

Rickard v. R. (1970), 12 C.R.N.S. 172, 1 C.C.C. (2d) 153 (S.C.C.) — This section applies to summary conviction proceedings.

Included Offences: S. 662(1)

Luckett v. R. (1980), 50 C.C.C. (2d) 489 (S.C.C.) — In order for D to be convicted of a lesser offence than the one charged, the lesser offence must be included in the offence charged as described in the enactment creating it. It is not necessary that the lesser offence be included in all the subsections of the enactment.

Smith v. R. (1978), 6 C.R. (3d) 216, 43 C.C.C. (2d) 417 (S.C.C.) — The trial judge has the duty to charge the jury on included offences unless the evidence with respect to the included offence is so tenuous as to justify a refusal to charge on it.

Fergusson v. R. (1961), 36 C.R. 271, 132 C.C.C. 112 (S.C.C.) — The expression "lesser offence" is a "part of an offence" which is charged. It must necessarily include some elements of the major offence, but be lacking in others, without which the major offence would be incomplete. A person charged with robbery, for example, may be found guilty of theft, but *not* of unlawful possession of stolen goods.

R. v. McDowell, [1977] 1 W.W.R. 97 (Alta. C.A.) — There are three ways in which one offence may be included in another: by a *description in the enactment* that includes the commission of another offence; by a *description* of the offence *in the count* that includes the commission of another offence; or, by *statutory enactment*.

R. v. Rinnie (1970), 9 C.R.N.S. 81, [1970] 3 C.C.C. 218 (Alta. C.A.) — Some offences are included offences as a matter of law, others are included by the addition of apt words of description in the indictment charging the principal offence. In the latter case, the test as to whether a lesser offence may be included is not whether the facts are the same but whether the offences are similar. An amendment to broaden the charge in an indictment to include an offence not included by law cannot be made after D has pleaded to the original charge and the trial commenced.

R. v. Longson (1976), 31 C.C.C. (2d) 421 (B.C. C.A.) — *See also*: *R. v. De Champlain* (1982), 68 C.C.C. (2d) 281 (Que. C.A.) — Where there is a count in the indictment which contains an included offence, and where there is evidence upon which a jury could convict of such included offence if not satisfied of D's guilt of the specific offence charged, the jury should be properly instructed on the law relating to the included offence. They should be told that if they are not satisfied as to the guilt of D on the specific offence, then they should consider the included offence and render a verdict on that.

R. v. Manuel (1960), 128 C.C.C. 383 (B.C. C.A.) — To be an included offence, the inclusion must form such an apparent and essential constituent of the offence charged that D, in reading the charge, will be fairly informed in every instance that he will have to meet not only the offence charged but also the specific offences to be included. Such apparent inclusion must appear from the enactment creating the offence or from the offence as charged in the count.

R. v. Morehouse (1982), 65 C.C.C. (2d) 231 (N.B. C.A.); leave to appeal refused (1982), 40 N.B.R. (2d) 90 (S.C.C.) — There are two principles regarding the meaning of "an included offence". An included offence is part of the offence charged. The offence charged must be sufficient to inform D of the included offences which must be met.

R. v. Foote (1974), 26 C.R.N.S. 304, 16 C.C.C. (2d) 44 (N.B. C.A.) — Extortion is *not* an included offence of robbery.

Simpson v. R. (1981), 20 C.R. (3d) 36 (Ont. C.A.) — *See also*: *R. v. Angevine* (1984), 61 N.S.R. (2d) 263 (C.A.) — To constitute an "included offence" within the meaning of subsection (1), the essential elements of the "included offence" must be contained in the offence charged, either as described in the enactment creating the offence or as charged in the count. Specific statutory provisions may permit conviction for certain offences which are not "included offences" within the meaning of subsection (1), but such enactments put D on notice that he must meet such offences. Absent apt words of description in an indictment charging attempted murder, the offences of causing bodily harm with intent to wound, assault causing bodily harm and unlawfully causing bodily harm are *not* "included offences".

R. v. Harmer (1976), 33 C.C.C. (2d) 17 (Ont. C.A.) — An offence which is *not* included in the charge of another offence *simpliciter* may become included by the addition of apt words of description to the original charge. Assault causing bodily harm may properly be made an included offence on a robbery charge by including in the charge an allegation of assault causing bodily harm.

R. v. Boisvert (1991), 68 C.C.C. (3d) 478 (Que. C.A.) — *See also*: *R. v. Colburne* (1991), 66 C.C.C. (3d) 235 at 247 (Que. C.A.) — On an indictment for robbery, particularized as an assault with intent to steal under s. 343(c), D may be convicted of attempted theft through s. 662(1)(b) where the evidence fails to prove an assault, but does prove attempted theft (and theft).

Included Offences — Murder and Attempted Murder: S. 662(2)

R. v. Chichak (1978), 38 C.C.C. (2d) 489 (Alta. C.A.) — Under s. 662(3), the only included offences of murder are manslaughter and infanticide. It in is in error to acquit D of second degree murder and of manslaughter but convict of assault causing bodily harm.

R. v. Angevine (1984), 61 N.S.R. (2d) 263 (C.A.) — *See also: Simpson v. R.* (1981), 20 C.R. (3d) 36 (Ont. C.A.) — Where an indictment charging attempted murder includes a description of the manner in which the offence was committed, the offence of causing bodily harm with intent to wound is an included offence.

Related Provisions: Under s. 662(1), where D is convicted of an included offence which is exclusively a summary conviction offence, the appeal will be to the "court of appeal" under Part XXI ("Appeals — Indictable Offences") since the conviction was recorded "in proceedings, by indictment", as described in s. 675(1). It is the nature of the proceedings, not the nature of the conviction, which is determinative of appellate rights.

Provisions similar to ss. 662(2) and (3) are found in ss. 610(2)–(4), which bar subsequent indictments for the same homicide charging it as murder, first degree murder or infanticide, as the case may be.

663. No acquittal unless act or omission not wilful — Where a female person is charged with infanticide and the evidence establishes that she caused the death of her child but does not establish that, at the time of the act or omission by which she caused the death of the child,

    (a) she was not fully recovered from the effects of giving birth to the child or from the effect of lactation consequent on the birth of the child, and

    (b) the balance of her mind was, at that time, disturbed by reason of the effect of giving birth to the child or of the effect of lactation consequent on the birth of the child,

she may be convicted unless the evidence establishes that the act or omission was not wilful.

R.S., c. C-34, s. 590.

Commentary: The section applies only where D is a female, charged with infanticide. In general, it permits a conviction of infanticide to be recorded where the evidence *establishes* that D caused P's death, but does *not* establish that, at such time, her condition was as described in either s. 663(a) or (b). The exception to the general rule of conviction in such circumstances occurs where the evidence establishes that D's act or omission was *not* wilful.

The use of "establishes", in the circumstances, may place an onus of proof on D and attract *Charter* ss. 7 and 11(d) scrutiny.

Related Provisions: Infanticide is defined in s. 233 and punished in s. 237. "Wilful" requires proof of an ulterior motive or purpose.

The effect of the subsection is to permit conviction of infanticide in all cases where D, a female person, has caused the death of her child, even without proof of s. 663(a) or (b), except where the act or omission causing death is *established* not to be wilful.

Previous Convictions

664. No reference to previous conviction — No indictment in respect of an offence for which, by reason of previous convictions, a greater punishment may be imposed shall contain any reference to previous convictions.

R.S., c. C-34, s. 591.

Commentary: The section bars reference to previous convictions in an indictment charging an offence, for which, by reason of previous convictions, a greater punishment may be imposed. It is a rule of criminal pleading, not a rule of evidence.

Related Provisions: Section 727 authorizes the introduction of evidence of previous convictions on the issue of sentence and s. 666 describes the circumstances under which such evidence may be adduced in response to evidence of D's good character. Previous convictions may be proven under s. 667. Examination of witnesses as to previous convictions is permitted under *C.E.A.* s. 12. A similar provision to s. 664, appears in s. 789(2) in respect of summary conviction proceedings.

665. [Repealed 1995, c. 22, s. 3]
Commentary: See s. 727.

666. Evidence of character — Where, at a trial, the accused adduces evidence of his good character, the prosecutor may, in answer thereto, before a verdict is returned, adduce evidence of the previous conviction of the accused for any offences, including any previous conviction by reason of which a greater punishment may be imposed.

R.S., c. C-34, s. 593.

Commentary: The section permits P to introduce evidence of D's previous conviction of any offence, where D has adduced evidence of good character. The evidence may be adduced in response at any time before verdict. The previous conviction may include an offence which may result in imposition of a greater punishment.

Case Law
Putting Character in Issue
R. v. Drysdale, [1969] 2 C.C.C. 141 (Man. C.A.) — Where D's statement of his good character was *not* made at trial, nor under oath, but was secured by the police in the course of their investigation and introduced by P as part of their case, evidence of D's previous conduct could *not* be properly adduced except for the limited purpose of showing D's intention.

R. v. McNamara (No. 1) (1981), 56 C.C.C. (2d) 193 (Ont. C.A.) — *See also*: *R. v. Tierney* (1982), 31 C.R. (3d) 66, 70 C.C.C. (2d) 481 (Ont. C.A.) — Although D does *not* put his character in issue by denying guilt, repudiating the allegations against him or by proferring an explanation of matters essential to his defence, he does so by expressly or impliedly asserting that he would not have done the act alleged to have been committed because he is a person of good character. D may put his character in issue as much by his *own testimony* as by adducing *general reputation evidence*. P's rebutting evidence may be extrinsic evidence of bad reputation or of similar acts as well as cross-examination of D or specific acts of previous disreputable conduct, although the trial judge may retain an exclusionary discretion in respect of other acts, remote in time, which did not result in a conviction and were gravely prejudicial.

R. v. Demyen (No. 2) (1976), 31 C.C.C. (2d) 383 (Sask. C.A.) — Where P's witness, in cross-examination, gave his opinion of D's relationship with V and D's attitude towards V, it was *not* evidence of good character, but merely the witness's personal view.

Character Evidence in Cases of Sexual Assault
R. v. Profit (1993), 24 C.R. (4th) 279, 85 C.C.C. (3d) 232 (S.C.C.); reversing (1992), 16 C.R. (4th) 332 (Ont. C.A.) — A trial judge is entitled to find, as a matter of weight, that the probative value of character evidence as to morality is diminished in cases of sexual assault upon children.

R. v. Kootenay (1994), 27 C.R. (4th) 376, 87 C.C.C. (3d) 109 (Alta. C.A.) — Evidence of D's good reputation is admissible in proof either that D is a credible witness or the sort of person who is unlikely to have committed the offence charged. A trial judge is *not* required in every case to direct the jury concerning the relevance of evidence of D's good character. In each case, the trial judge must decide what assistance a jury requires in weighing the evidence of any witness including D.

Scope of Rebutting Evidence When Character Put in Issue

Morris v. R. (1978), 6 C.R. (3d) 36, 43 C.C.C. (2d) 129 (S.C.C.) — Where D puts his character in issue, P is *not* restricted solely to proving prior convictions. The purpose of this section is to permit the admission of previous convictions which would otherwise, under the rules of evidence, be inadmissible on the basis that bad character cannot generally be proven by specific acts of misconduct.

R. v. Deyardin (1997), 119 C.C.C. (3d) 365 (Que. C.A.) — P may rebut evidence of good character by cross-examining D to demonstrate that D committed an offence and was granted a discharge for it. A limiting instruction is, however, required.

Subsequent Convictions

R. v. Close (1982), 68 C.C.C. (2d) 105 (Ont. C.A.) — Evidence of a previous conviction registered subsequent to the commission of the offence for which D is on trial may be admitted to establish the fact of specific criminal conduct at or near the time of the commission of the offence for which D is being tried. The subsequent previous conviction must relate to an offence which is so closely related in time to the offence for which D is being tried as to show his disposition at the time.

Related Provisions: The section constitutes an exception to the general rule prohibiting the introduction by P of evidence of D's bad character for the purpose of establishing complicity thereby. Proof of previous convictions, but for this statutory provision, constitutes a specific application of this general rule. Section 666 is *not* the only form of evidence that may be adduced in response to evidence of D's good character.

Section 727 prescribes the procedure followed where proof of previous convictions is adduced to seek an increased penalty, and s. 667 authorizes the manner in which proof may be made for those or present purposes.

667. (1) Proof of previous conviction — In any proceedings,

   (a) a certificate setting out with reasonable particularity the conviction, discharge under section 730 or the conviction and sentence in Canada of an offender signed by

      (i) the person who made the conviction or order for the discharge,

      (ii) the clerk of the court in which the conviction or order for the discharge was made, or

      (iii) a fingerprint examiner,

   is, on proof that the accused or defendant is the offender referred to in the certificate, evidence that the accused or defendant was so convicted, so discharged or so convicted and sentenced without proof of the signature or the official character of the person appearing to have signed the certificate;

   (b) evidence that the fingerprints of the accused or defendant are the same as the fingerprints of the offender whose fingerprints are reproduced in or attached to a certificate issued under subparagraph (*a*)(iii) is, in the absence of evidence to the contrary, proof that the accused or defendant is the offender referred to in that certificate;

   (c) a certificate of a fingerprint examiner stating that he has compared the fingerprints reproduced in or attached to that certificate with the fingerprints reproduced in or attached to a certificate issued under subparagraph (*a*)(iii) and that they are those of the same person is evidence of the statements contained in the certificate without proof of the signature or the official character of the person appearing to have signed the certificate; and

   (d) a certificate under subparagraph (*a*)(iii) may be in Form 44, and a certificate under paragraph (*c*) may be in Form 45.

(2) Idem — In any proceedings, a copy of the summary conviction or discharge under section 730 in Canada of an offender, signed by the person who made the conviction or order for the discharge or by the clerk of the court in which the conviction or order for the discharge was made, is, on proof that the accused or defendant is the offender referred to in the copy of the summary conviction, evidence of the conviction or discharge under section 730 of the accused or defendant, without proof of the signature or the official character of the person appearing to have signed it.

(2.1) Proof of identity — In any summary conviction proceedings, where the name of a defendant is similar to the name of an offender referred to in a certificate made under subparagraph (1)(*a*)(i) or (ii) in respect of a summary conviction or referred to in a copy of a summary conviction mentioned in subsection (2), that similarity of name is, in the absence of evidence to the contrary, evidence that the defendant is the offender referred to in the certificate or the copy of the summary conviction.

(3) Attendance and right to cross-examine — An accused against whom a certificate issued under subparagraph (1)(*a*)(iii) or paragraph (1)(*c*) is produced may, with leave of the court, require the attendance of the person who signed the certificate for the purposes of cross-examination.

(4) Notice of intention to produce certificate — No certificate issued under subparagraph (1)(*a*)(iii) or paragraph (1)(*c*) shall be received in evidence unless the party intending to produce it has given to the accused reasonable notice of his intention together with a copy of the certificate.

(5) "fingerprint examiner" — In this section "fingerprint examiner" means a person designated as such for the purposes of this section by the Solicitor General of Canada.

R.S., c. C-34, s. 594; 1972, c. 13, s. 51; R.S. 1985, c. 27 (1st Supp.), s. 136; 1995, c. 22, s. 10.

Commentary: The section describes a method of *proof of previous convictions.*

Proof of previous convictions, irrespective of their evidentiary purpose, in essence, involves proof of two elements. The first requires proof of the *conviction, discharge or conviction and sentence itself,* so that the trier knows that of which D has been found guilty. Second, it is necessary to prove the *identity of the person found guilty*; more accurately, that it was, in fact, D.

The conviction, discharge or conviction and sentence may be proven by *certificate* under s. 667(1)(a) or a *copy* of the summary conviction or discharge under s. 667(2). D's *identity* may be established, *inter alia*, by evidence of identical fingerprints under s. 667(1)(b), or upon the certificate of a fingerprint examiner under s. 667(1)(c) in prescribed form. Identity may also be established in other ways, as for example in summary conviction proceedings by similarity of name under s. 667(2.1), or, quite independently of the statute, as for example by *viva voce* testimony of a person present when the conviction was recorded.

In any case in which proof is proposed in part by the introduction of the certificate of a "fingerprint examiner" designated by the Solicitor General of Canada under s. 667(5), D must be given reasonable notice of the intention to adduce such evidence together with a copy of the certificate. The court may grant leave under s. 667(3) to require the attendance of the fingerprint examiner for the purposes of cross examination.

Case Law [See also, C.E.A. s. 12]

R. v. Albright (1987), 60 C.R. (3d) 97, 37 C.C.C. (3d) 105 (S.C.C.) — Nothing in this section indicates that proof of convictions may only be made as provided therein. The common law rules are still applicable. At common law all credible and trustworthy evidence is admissible at a sentence hearing, irrespective of the hearsay rule.

R. v. Gordon (1972), 8 C.C.C. (2d) 132 (B.C. C.A.) — This section provides for a convenient shortcut for P to prove certain necessary ingredients of its case. The provisions of the section must be strictly met.

R. v. Jonasson (1980), 56 C.C.C. (2d) 121 (Sask. C.A.); affirming (1980), 7 M.V.R. 19 (Sask. Dist. Ct.) — The *Code* provides a complete procedure by which a greater punishment may be sought by reason of a previous conviction. That being so, it is paramount and in no way subject to the *C.E.A.* provisions respecting proof of prior convictions and, therefore, a previous conviction may be proved in the manner prescribed by this section.

Charter Considerations

R. v. Albright (1987), 60 C.R. (3d) 97, 37 C.C.C. (3d) 105 (S.C.C.) — Failure by P to give advance notice of its intention to use a certificate to prove a previous conviction does *not* violate *Charter* s. 7.

Related Provisions: The evidence may be adduced, *inter alia*, for purposes described in s. 360 (knowledge of unlawful character of property), s. 727 (increased punishment), or s. 666 (rebuttal of evidence of D's good character). A separate provision relating to proof of previous convictions is found in *C.E.A.* s. 12(2).

"Clerk of the court" is defined in s. 2.

The certificates of the fingerprint examiner may be Form 44 or 45.

668. Accused found guilty may speak to sentence — Where a jury finds an accused guilty, or where an accused pleads guilty, the judge presiding at the trial shall ask the accused whether he has anything to say before sentence is passed upon him, but an omission to comply with this section does not affect the validity of the proceedings.

R.S., c. C-34, s. 595.

Commentary: The section imposes a duty upon the trial judge, where D has pleaded or has been found guilty by a jury, to ask D whether he has anything to say before sentence is passed. An omission to follow the section does not, however, vitiate the proceedings.

Related Provisions: Part XXIII contains general provisions relating to punishments, fines, forfeitures, costs and the restitution of property.

It is the general rule of s. 650(1) that D shall be present in court during the whole of his/her trial, subject to the exceptions of s. 650(2). Where D has absconded during the course of this trial, s. 475(1)(b)(i) authorizes the imposition of sentence upon him/her *in absentia*.

This section, the *allocutus*, originated at a time when D, incompetent on account of interest or crime, could neither give evidence nor call witnesses. It afforded D an opportunity, *inter alia*, to plead for clemency.

669. Sentence justified by any count — Where one sentence is passed on a verdict of guilty on two or more counts of an indictment, the sentence is good if any of the counts would have justified the sentence.

R.S., c. C-34, s. 596.

Commentary: As a general rule, sentence is passed in respect of each count upon which a finding of guilt has been made. The section does *not* invalidate a single sentence passed on D in respect of discrete findings of guilt, provided the sentence may be justified by any of the counts.

Case Law

R. v. Thorpe (1976), 32 C.C.C. (2d) 46 (Man. C.A.) — The preferred procedure where D is convicted of two offences is for D to be given concurrent sentences with the sentence for each imposed separately.

Related Provisions: Part XXIII contains general provisions relating to punishments, fines, forfeitures, costs and restitution of property.

Both D and P have right of appeal against the sentence imposed by a trial court under ss. 675(1)(b), (1.1) and (2) and ss. 676(1)(d), (1.1) and (4). The powers of the court of appeal on sentence appeals are defined by s. 687.

Jurisdiction

669.1 (1) Jurisdiction — Where any judge, court or provincial court judge by whom or which the plea of the accused or defendant to an offence was taken has not commenced to hear evidence, any judge, court or provincial court judge having jurisdiction to try the accused or defendant has jurisdiction for the purpose of the hearing and adjudication.

(2) Adjournment — Any court, judge or provincial court judge having jurisdiction to try an accused or a defendant, or any clerk or other proper officer of the court, or in the case of an offence punishable on summary conviction, any justice, may, at any time before or after the plea of the accused or defendant is taken, adjourn the proceedings.

R.S. 1985, c. 27 (1st Supp.), s. 137.

Commentary: The section provides for trial jurisdiction after plea and describes who may adjourn proceedings both before and after plea.

Under s. 669.1(1), any member of the trial court may hear and determine a case, notwithstanding that another member has recorded the plea, provided no evidence has been adduced. Section 669.1(2) authorizes any member of the trial court, clerk or other proper officer to adjourn proceedings both before or after plea.

The effect of s. 669.1(1) is to hold that the judicial officer who takes the plea of D does *not*, thereby, become seized of the trial. It is only the introduction of evidence after plea that has such effect. Prior to the introduction of evidence, the judicial officer who took the plea, as well as any other member of the court, may act as the trial judge.

In practical terms, judicial unavailability will *not* vitiate a trial under s. 669.1(2), since the proceedings may be adjourned by any member of the court to resume later before the trial judge.

Related Provisions: Section 669.2 describes the procedure followed where the trial judge dies or is, for any reason, unable to continue.

669.2 (1) Continuation of proceedings — Subject to this section, where an accused or a defendant is being tried by

    (a) a judge or provincial court judge,

    (b) a justice or other person who is, or is a member of, a summary conviction court, or

    (c) a court composed of a judge and jury,

as the case may be, and the judge, provincial court judge, justice or other person dies or is for any reason unable to continue, the proceedings may be continued before another judge, provincial court judge, justice or other person, as the case may be, who has jurisdiction to try the accused or defendant.

(2) Where adjudication is made — Where a verdict was rendered by a jury or an adjudication was made by a judge, provincial court judge, justice or other person before whom the trial was commenced, the judge, provincial court judge, justice or other person before whom the proceedings are continued shall, without further election by an accused, impose the punishment or make the order that is authorized by law in the circumstances.

(3) Where no adjudication is made — Subject to subsections (4) and (5), where the trial was commenced but no adjudication was made or verdict rendered, the judge, provincial court judge, justice or other person before whom the proceedings are continued shall, without further election by an accused, commence the trial again as if no evidence had been taken.

(4) Where no adjudication is made - jury trials — Where a trial that is before a court composed of a judge and a jury was commenced but no adjudication was made or verdict rendered, the judge before whom the proceedings are continued may, without further election by an accused,

   (a) continue the trial; or

   (b) commence the trial again as if no evidence had been taken.

(5) Where trial continued — Where a trial is continued under paragraph (4)(*a*), any evidence that was adduced before a judge referred to in paragraph (1)(*c*) is deemed to have been adduced before the judge before whom the trial is continued but, where the prosecutor and the accused so agree, any part of that evidence may be adduced again before the judge before whom the trial is continued.

R.S. 1985, c. 27 (1st Supp.), s. 137; 1994, c. 44, s. 65.

Commentary: The section defines the procedure where the *trial judge* dies or is, for any reason, *unable to continue* the trial proceedings. The general rule of s. 669.2(1) is that, subject to the section, another judge of the trial court may continue the proceedings commenced by a judge who has died or who is, for any reason, unable to continue.

Under s. 669.2(2), where a verdict was rendered by a jury or adjudication made by the original trial judge who has since died or is unable to continue, the substitute judge will sentence D.

Sections 669.2(3)–(5) should be considered together. Section 669.2(3) enacts a general rule that where a trial has commenced but no adjudication has been made or verdict rendered, the substitute judicial officer before whom the proceedings are continued is required to commence the trial again without further election by D, as if no evidence had been taken.

Sections 669.2(4) and (5) apply to jury trials, Under s. 669.2(4), the substitute judge, without further election by D, may continue the trial or commence the trial again, as if no evidence had been taken. Where the trial is continued, s. 669.2(5) deems the evidence given prior to judicial substitution to have been given thereafter, subject to the right of the parties to agree to adduce again before the substitute judge any part of the evidence already given.

Case Law

Ritcey v. R. (1980), 50 C.C.C. (2d) 481 (S.C.C.) — Where provincial legislation authorized a judge for eight weeks following his resignation to adjudicate on proceedings previously tried or heard before him, this did not extend to sentencing proceedings which, although they had come before the judge prior to his resignation, had been adjudicated before another judge who died prior to sentencing, in circumstances where further evidence and submissions with respect to the sentencing were heard after the judge's resignation.

Related Provisions: Section 669.1 provides for trial jurisdiction after plea and describes who may adjourn proceedings before, as well as after plea.

Provisions similar to s. 669.2 appear in s. 547.1 (preliminary inquiry). Section 669.2 is made applicable to "judge alone" trials under Part XIX by s. 572, and to summary conviction proceedings by s. 795.

Section 669.3 permits a judge or provincial court judge who is appointed to another court while conducting a trial to continue the trial until its completion.

669.3 Jurisdiction when appointment to another court — Where a court composed of a judge and a jury, a judge or a provincial court judge is conducting a trial and the judge or provincial court judge is appointed to another court, he or she continues to have jurisdiction in respect of the trial until its completion.

1994, c. 44, s. 66.

Commentary: Under this section, any judge or provincial court judge who is appointed to another court while conducting a trial continues to have jurisdiction in respect of the trial until its completion.

Related Provisions: The section is made applicable to Part XIX "Judge Alone" trials by s. 572 and to summary conviction proceedings by s. 795.

Other related provisions are described in the corresponding note to s. 669.2.

Formal Defects in Jury Process

670. Judgment not to be stayed on certain grounds — Judgment shall not be stayed or reversed after verdict on an indictment

(a) by reason of any irregularity in the summoning or empanelling of the jury; or

(b) for the reason that a person who served on the jury was not returned as a juror by a sheriff or other officer.

R.S., c. C-34, s. 598.

Commentary: The section provides that neither any irregularity in the summoning or empanelling of the jury, nor the fact that a person not returned as a juror served as a juror, shall be a basis upon which to stay or reverse the verdict of the jury.

Case Law

R. v. Singh (1996), 108 C.C.C. (3d) 244 (B.C. C.A.) — A discharged juror may be replaced, even in the absence of consent, after D has been given in charge of the jury, but no evidence has been called. At all events, where juror substitution causes D no prejudice, any irregularity may be cured by the combined effect of ss. 670 and 686(1)(b)(iv).

R. v. Butler (1984), 3 C.R. (4th) 174, 63 C.C.C. (3d) 243 (B.C. C.A.) — An illegality in the selection of the jury panel occurs when it is a fixed policy of the Sheriff deliberately to exclude Native people from the jury panel. A trial before a jury selected from such a panel is conducted without jurisdiction.

R. v. Rowbotham (1988), 63 C.R. (3d) 113, 41 C.C.C. (3d) 1 (Ont. C.A.) — Paragraph (a) applies only to irregularities and *not* where the error is such that D has been deprived of a statutory right, or where the error deprives D of the right to a trial by a jury lawfully constituted.

Related Provisions: A prospective juror may be challenged for cause under s. 638(1)(a) upon the grounds that his/her name does not appear on the panel. The challenge is tried by the judge under s. 640(1).

Similar curative or saving provisions in respect of juries may be found in ss. 643(3), 671 and 672. The substantive and procedural provisos which a court of appeal may apply on appeals by D from conviction are contained in ss. 686(1)(b)(iii) and (iv).

671. Directions respecting jury or jurors directory — No omission to observe the directions contained in any Act with respect to the qualification, selection, balloting or distribution of jurors, the preparation of the jurors' book, the selecting of jury lists or the drafting of panels from the jury lists is a ground for impeaching or quashing a verdict rendered in criminal proceedings.

R.S., c. C-34, s. 599.

Commentary: The section describes several matters relating to jury qualification and selection that afford no ground for impeaching or quashing a jury verdict.

Case Law

Re Alberta Jury Act (1946), 2 C.R. 94, 86 C.C.C. 296 (Alta. C.A.); affirmed (1947), 4 C.R. 1, 88 C.C.C. 48 (S.C.C.) — If the fact is discovered after verdict that a juror was *not* properly qualified, this will *not* be a ground for questioning the validity of the verdict.

R. v. Stewart (1932), 58 C.C.C. 358 (S.C.C.) — The effect of this section is to preclude an appeal after verdict on the ground of disqualification of a juror where no complaint was made at trial.

R. v. Butler (1984), 3 C.R. (4th) 174, 63 C.C.C. (3d) 243 (B.C. C.A.) — An illegality in the selection of the jury panel occurs when it is a fixed policy of the Sheriff deliberately to exclude Native people from the jury panel. A trial before a jury selected from such a panel is conducted without jurisdiction.

R. v. Rushton (1974), 28 C.R.N.S. 120, 20 C.C.C. (2d) 297 (Ont. C.A.) — The presence of a juror who is absolutely disqualified from jury duty on the jury is not a ground for interfering with a verdict otherwise legally rendered. Similarly the presence of an exempted juror will not invalidate an otherwise valid verdict.

Related Provisions: Under s. 626(1), the qualification and summoning of jurors to serve in criminal proceedings is governed by provincial legislation.

The section does *not* override the right to challenge the array in accordance with ss. 629 and 630.

Other curative or saving provisions in respect of juries appear in ss. 643(3), 670 and 672. A court of appeal may apply substantive and procedural provisos, *inter alia*, to preserve jury verdicts, under ss. 686(1)(b)(iii) and (iv).

672. Saving powers of court — **Nothing in this Act alters, abridges or affects any power or authority that a court or judge had immediately before April 1, 1955, or any practice or form that existed immediately before April 1, 1955, with respect to trials by jury, jury process, juries or jurors, except where the power or authority, practice or form is expressly altered by or is inconsistent with this Act.**

R.S., c. C-34. s. 600.

Commentary: The section incorporates all pre-April 1, 1955, authority of a judge, as well as then existing practices and forms relating to trial by jury, jury process, juries or jurors, except to the extent of express alteration by or inconsistency with the *Code*. The section, in other words, provides an additional source of authority in designated areas to fill *lacunae* of the *Code*, provided such authority is neither expressly altered by nor inconsistent with the *Code* itself.

Case Law

R. v. Jacobson (1988), 46 C.C.C. (3d) 50 (Sask. C.A.) — Where a verdict of guilty has been returned by a jury in respect of a non-existent offence, P having charged an offence not yet proclaimed in force, this section empowers the trial judge to arrest judgment and discharge D.

Related Provisions: Similar provisions in ss. 8(2) and (3) continue, to an equivalent degree the English criminal law in force in a province immediately prior to April 1, 1955, including any rule and principle that renders any circumstance a justification for an act or defence to a charge.

PART XX.1 — MENTAL DISORDER

Interpretation

672.1 Definitions — **In this Part,**

"accused" includes a defendant in summary conviction proceedings and an accused in respect of whom a verdict of not criminally responsible on account of mental disorder has been rendered;

"assessment" means an assessment by a medical practitioner of the mental condition of the accused pursuant to an assessment order made under section 672.11, and any incidental observation or examination of the accused;

"chairperson" includes any alternate that the chairperson of a Review Board may designate to act on the chairperson's behalf;

"court" includes a summary conviction court as defined in section 785, a judge, a justice and a judge of the court of appeal as defined in section 673;

"disposition" means an order made by a court or Review Board under section 672.54 or an order made by a court under section 672.58;

928

"dual status offender" means an offender who is subject to a sentence of imprisonment in respect of one offence and a custodial disposition under paragraph 672.54(c) in respect of another offence;

"hospital" means a place in a province that is designated by the Minister of Health for the province for the custody, treatment or assessment of an accused in respect of whom an assessment order, a disposition or a placement decision is made.

"medical practitioner" means a person who is entitled to practise medicine by the laws of a province;

"party", in relation to proceedings of a court or Review Board to make or review a disposition, means

    (a) the accused,

    (b) the person in charge of the hospital where the accused is detained or is to attend pursuant to an assessment order or a disposition,

    (c) an Attorney General designated by the court or Review Board under subsection 672.5(3),

    (d) any interested person designated by the court or Review Board under subsection 672.5(4), or

    (e) where the disposition is to be made by a court, the prosecutor of the charge against the accused;

"placement decision" means a decision by a Review Board under subsection 672.68(2) as to the place of custody of a dual status offender;

"prescribed" means prescribed by regulations made by the Governor in Council under section 672.95;

"Review Board" means the Review Board established or designated for a province pursuant to subsection 672.38(1);

"verdict of not criminally responsible on account of mental disorder" means a verdict that the accused committed the act or made the omission that formed the basis of the offence with which the accused is charged but is not criminally responsible on account of mental disorder,

1991, c. 43, s. 4.

Commentary: The section defines terms in Part XX.1.

Related Provisions: "Protected statement" is defined in and for the purpose of s. 672.21 by s. 672.21(1) and "application for federal employment" similarly in s. 672.37(1). "Disposition information" is defined in s. 672.51(1) for the purposes of the section, and "electro-convulsive therapy" and "psycho-surgery" for similar purposes in s. 672.61(2). "Designated offence" and "serious personal injury offence" are defined in s. 672.64(1) and 672.65(1) upon the same basis.

Other sources of definitional assistance are described in the corresponding note to s. 2.

Assessment Orders

672.11 Assessment order — A court having jurisdiction over an accused in respect of an offence may order an assessment of the mental condition of the accused, if it has reasonable grounds to believe that such evidence is necessary to determine

    (a) whether the accused is unfit to stand trial;

(b) whether the accused was, at the time of the commission of the alleged offence, suffering from a mental disorder so as to be exempt from criminal responsibility by virtue of subsection 16(1);

(c) whether the balance of the mind of the accused was disturbed at the time of commission of the alleged offence, where the accused is a female person charged with an offence arising out of the death of her newly-born child;

(d) the appropriate disposition to be made, where a verdict of not criminally responsible on account of mental disorder or unfit to stand trial has been rendered in respect of the accused; or

(e) whether an order should be made under subsection 747.1(1) to detain the accused in a treatment facility, where the accused has been convicted of the offence.

1991, c. 43, s. 4; 1995, c. 22, s. 10.

Commentary: This and several other sections (ss. 672.11–672.2) authorize *assessment orders*, set the *criteria* for their grant, specify their *terms* and regulate their execution.

Authority to make an assessment order rests with any "*court* having jurisdiction over an *accused* in respect of an offence". Section 672.1 defines both "court" and "accused". *What* is to be assessed is the *mental condition* of D.

An *assessment order* may *only* be made where the court has *reasonable grounds to believe* that such evidence, *viz.*, evidence obtained by the assessment, is necessary to determine *any* of the matters described in paragraphs 672.11(a)–(e). The section is silent concerning the nature of the foundation to be laid in support of the requisite finding of reasonably grounded belief. The section does *not* insist upon the *evidence* or report of a duly qualified medical practitioner or, indeed, upon any, let alone specific, sworn testimony. At all events, the basis for the belief should plainly appear in the record of proceedings. Where practicable, the evidence or a report of a duly qualified medical practitioner would furnish the requisite support. Observations of D's conduct at relevant times may also ground the required finding.

The *substance* of the reasonably grounded belief must be the *necessity* of *obtaining evidence* (through the assessment procedure) to determine any matter or issue described in paragraphs 672.11(a)–(e). No other purpose will suffice.

Case Law

R. v. Roussel (1996), 112 C.C.C. (3d) 538 (N.B. C.A.) — The *results* of a psychiatric report prepared under *Code* s. 672.11 may be *admitted* at a *sentencing* hearing, provided D is permitted to challenge the findings.

Related Provisions: "Accused", "assessment", "court", "disposition" and "verdict of not criminally responsible on account of mental disorder" are defined in s. 672.1. "Mental disorder" and "unfit to stand trial" are defined in s. 2.

Section 672.12(1) governs *when* an assessment order may be made and s. 672.12(2) and (3) impose limitations upon P's right to seek and the court to make the order. An assessment order may be in Form 48. Its contents are governed by s. 672.13(1), its duration by s. 672.14 and extensions thereof by s. 672.15. Section 672.16(1) enacts a *presumption* of out-of-custody assessments, except in cases in which s. 672.16(3) applies where the presumption is reversed. The orders may be varied under s. 672.18 and will take precedence over judicial interim release hearings because of s. 672.17. No treatment may be carried out during the period of assessment. Section 672.191 specifies the time within which D must appear in court after an assessment is complete.

Sections 672.2 and 672.21 govern the preparation of assessment reports and enact admissibility rules respecting "protected statements" and references thereto.

672.12 (1) Where court may order assessment — The court may make an assessment order at any stage of proceedings against the accused of its own motion, on application of the accused or, subject to subsections (2) and (3), on application of the prosecutor.

(2) Limitation on prosecutor's application for assessment of fitness —

Where the prosecutor applies for an assessment in order to determine whether the accused is unfit to stand trial for an offence that is prosecuted by way of summary conviction, the court may only order the assessment if

(a) the accused raised the issue of fitness; or

(b) the prosecutor satisfies the court that there are reasonable grounds to doubt that the accused is fit to stand trial.

(3) Limitation on prosecutor's application for assessment — Where the

prosecutor applies for an assessment in order to determine whether the accused was suffering from a mental disorder at the time of the offence so as to be exempt from criminal responsibility, the court may only order the assessment if

(a) the accused puts his or her mental capacity for criminal intent into issue; or

(b) the prosecutor satisfies the court that there are reasonable grounds to doubt that the accused is criminally responsible for the alleged offence, on account of mental disorder.

1991, c. 43, s. 4.

Commentary: This section describes *when* and *by whom* applications for assessment orders may be made.

By s. 672.12(1) an assessment order may be made *at any stage of the proceedings* against D. The application may be initiated by D, the court of its own motion or, subject to the limitations of s. 672.12(2) and (3), P.

P's right to seek an assessment order is limited in two instances. Where P seeks to obtain evidence to determine whether D *is unfit to stand trial* for an offence that *is* prosecuted by *summary conviction*, P must show that D raised the issue of fitness or, there are *reasonable grounds to doubt* that D is fit to stand trial. Where P seeks to obtain evidence to determine whether D may be *exempt from criminal responsibility* on account of *mental disorder*, P must show that: D put his/her capacity for criminal intent into issue or, there are *reasonable grounds to doubt* that D is criminally responsible on account of mental disorder.

Related Provisions: The basis upon which an assessment order may be granted is stated in s. 672.11. The order may be in Form 48 and must specify the matters described in s. 672.13.

An assessment order may require preparation of an assessment report under s. 672.2. Section 672.21 enacts a rule of admissibility which generally bars admission of "protected statements" contained in assessment reports, as well references thereto.

Other related provisions are discussed in the corresponding note to s. 672.11.

672.13 (1) Contents of assessment order — An assessment order must specify

(a) the service that or the person who is to make the assessment, or the hospital where it is to be made;

(b) whether the accused is to be detained in custody while the order is in force; and

(c) the period that the order is to be in force, including the time required for the assessment and for the accused to travel to and from the place where the assessment is to be made.

(2) Form — An assessment order may be in Form 48.

1991, c. 43, s. 4.

Commentary: The section describes the *contents* and prescribes the *form* of *assessment orders*.

The requirements of s. 672.13(1) are mandatory. The order *must* identify the service or person who is to conduct the assessment or the hospital where it is to be made, specify whether D is to be detained in custody during such time and designate the period or duration of the order, including the times required for assessment and travel. Under s. 672.13(2), the order may be in Form 48.

Related Provisions: "Assessment" and "hospital" are defined in s. 672.1. The period for which an assessment order is in force is governed by s. 672.14.

Other related provisions are discussed in the corresponding note to s. 672.11.

672.14 (1) General rule for period — An assessment order shall not be in force for more than thirty days.

(2) Exception in fitness cases — No assessment order to determine whether the accused is unfit to stand trial shall be in force for more than five days, excluding holidays and the time required for the accused to travel to and from the place where the assessment is to be made, unless the accused and the prosecutor agree to a longer period not exceeding thirty days.

(3) Exception for compelling circumstances — Notwithstanding subsections (1) and (2), a court may make an assessment order that remains in force for sixty days where the court is satisfied that compelling circumstances exist that warrant it.

1991, c. 43, s. 4.

Commentary: The section prescribes the *period* for which *assessment orders* remain in force.

In general, assessment orders must *not* remain in force for more than thirty days. There are two exceptions to the general rule. Under s. 672.14(2), absent agreement by D and P to a longer period not exceeding thirty days, an assessment order to determine D's *fitness* to stand trial must *not* be in force for more than five days, exclusive of holidays and travel time. Where compelling circumstances exist which warrant it, s. 672.14(3) permits *any* assessment order to be made to remain in force for sixty days. The provision is silent as to what constitutes "compelling circumstances", or how they may be made to appear.

Related Provisions: Extensions of assessment orders are governed by s. 672.15 and variations by s. 672.18.

Other related provisions are discussed in the corresponding note to s. 672.11.

672.15 (1) Extensions — Subject to subsection (2), a court may extend an assessment order, of its own motion or on the application of the accused or the prosecutor made during or after the period that the order is in force, for any further period that is required, in its opinion, to complete the assessment of the accused.

(2) Maximum duration of extensions — No extension of an assessment order shall exceed thirty days, and the period of the initial order together with all extensions shall not exceed sixty days.

1991, c. 43, s. 4.

Commentary: This provision authorizes *extensions* of assessment orders, prescribes their length and limits the maximum period for assessment.

In general, s. 672.15(1) permits extension of an assessment order on application by D, P or upon the court's own motion at any time during or after the period of the order. An extension may be for any further period required to complete the assessment, *provided*, under s. 672.15(2), that the extension does *not* itself exceed thirty days and the combined period of the initial order and extensions does *not* exceed sixty days.

Section 672.15(2), permits more than one extension to be given, *provided* the total assessment period does not exceed the statutory maximum. It does *not* describe the basis or material upon which such extensions are to be given, although it would appear necessary to show that a "further period ... is required ... to complete the assessment" of D.

Related Provisions: *Variations* in assessment orders are permitted by s. 672.18. Section 672.19 bars inclusion of a term directing treatment.

Other related provisions are discussed in the corresponding note to s. 672.11.

672.16 (1) Presumption against custody — Subject to subsection (3), an accused shall not be detained in custody pursuant to an assessment order unless

(a) the court is satisfied that on the evidence custody is necessary to assess the accused, or that on the evidence of a medical practitioner custody is desirable to assess the accused and the accused consents to custody;

(b) custody of the accused is required in respect of any other matter or by virtue of any other provision of this Act; or

(c) the prosecutor, having been given a reasonable opportunity to do so, shows that detention of the accused in custody is justified on either of the grounds set out in subsection 515(10).

(2) Report of medical practitioner — For the purposes of paragraph (1)(a), where the prosecutor and the accused agree, the evidence of a medical practitioner may be received in the form of a report in writing.

(3) Presumption of custody in certain circumstances — An accused who is charged with an offence described in any of paragraphs 515(6)(a) to (d) in the circumstances described in that paragraph, or an offence described in subsection 522(2), shall be detained in custody pursuant to an assessment order, unless the accused shows that custody is not justified under the terms of that paragraph or subsection.

1991, c. 43, s. 4.

Commentary: The section enacts a general rule that assessment orders *not* require D's detention, absent exceptional circumstances which appear grounded in public safety.

Under s. 672.16(1), it is the *general* rule that D *not* be detained in *custody* for assessment under an assessment order. There are, however, five *exceptions*:

i.   under s. 672.16(1)(a), where the court is satisfied that custody is *necessary for assessment*;

ii.   under s. 672.16(1)(a), where the court is satisfied on the *evidence* or, on consent, *report* in writing of a medical practitioner that custody is *desirable for assessment and* D *consents* to custody;

iii. under s. 672.16(1)(b), where D's *custody* is *required* in respect of *any other matter* or otherwise under the *Code*;

iv.   under s. 672.16(1)(c), where P *shows cause* why *detention* is *justified* under *Code* s. 515(10); or,

v.   under s. 672.16(3), where D is charged with an offence described in *any* of ss. 515(6)(a)–(d) or 522(2), is required to show cause that custody is not justified, and fails to do so.

Related Provisions: The offences described in ss. 515(6)(a)–(d) and 522(2) are crimes alleged to have been committed in circumstances in which D will bear the onus of showing cause why detention in custody is *not* justified. Detention in custody is justified only upon the grounds described in s. 515(10).

Other related provisions are discussed in the corresponding note to s. 672.11.

672.17 Assessment order takes precedence over bail hearing — During the period that an assessment order of an accused charged with an offence is in force, no order for the interim release or detention of the accused may be made by virtue of Part XVI or section 679 in respect of that offence or an included offence.

1991, c. 43, s. 4.

Commentary: The section ensures that, during its currency, an assessment order takes precedence over any judicial interim release or detention order made under Part XVI or, pending appeal, under s.

679, in respect of either the offence charged or an included offence. It does so by barring the making of any of the designated orders during the period of assessment.

Related Provisions: Section 523(1) enacts the general rule which defines the period for which a judicial interim release order remains in effect. Section 679 governs the release of an appellant pending determination of an appeal in proceedings by indictment. Section 627.17 contains no reference to priority in cases of release pending summary conviction appeal under ss. 816 and 831.

Section 523(1.1) ensures the application of an existing interim release or detention order where a new information charging the same or an included offence is laid. The language used in this section and s. 523(1.1) is less expansive than the phrases "the offence charged or any other indictable offence in respect of the same transaction" used in s. 548(1).

Other related provisions are described in the corresponding note to s. 672.11.

672.18 Application to vary assessment order — Where at any time while an assessment order made by a court is in force the prosecutor or an accused shows cause, the court may vary the terms of the order respecting the interim release or detention of the accused in such manner as it considers appropriate in the circumstances.

1991, c. 43, s. 4.

Commentary: The section authorizes a court to *vary* the *interim release* or *detention* terms of an assessment order at any time during its currency, *provided* P or D shows cause in support of the variance. The terms may be varied in such manner as the court considers appropriate in the circumstances.

Section 672.18 offers no assistance as to requirements of notice, the procedure to be followed on the hearing or the evidence which may there be given. It authorizes no variance in the other terms of the assessment order.

Related Provisions: The authority to vary the release or detention terms of an assessment order under this section would appear somewhat more expansive than the similar authority afforded in the case of judicial interim release by ss. 520, 521, 523(2) and 680.

Other related provisions are described in the corresponding note to s. 672.11.

672.19 No treatment order on assessment — No assessment order may direct that psychiatric or any other treatment of the accused be carried out, or direct the accused to submit to such treatment.

1991, c. 43, s. 4.

Commentary: The section makes it clear that an *assessment* order may *not* direct that any psychiatric or other *treatment* of D be carried out, or that D submit to such treatment.

Related Provisions: An assessment order must contain the requirements of s. 672.13(1) and may be in Form 48. Neither contains reference to treatment nor requires D's submission thereto.

Section 672.58 authorizes the Review Board to make a treatment disposition in respect of an unfit accused, subject to the limitations imposed by ss. 672.61 and 672.62.

Other related provisions are discussed in the corresponding note to s. 672.11.

672.191 When assessment completed — An accused in respect of whom an assessment order is made shall appear before the court that made the order as soon as is practicable after the assessment is completed and not later than the last day of the period that the order is to be in force.

1997, c. 18, s. 81.

Commentary: This section governs re-appearance of an accused after the completion of a court-ordered assessment. The general rule is that D is to appear before the court which ordered the assessment as soon as practicable after the assessment has been completed. In every event, D's re-appearance must not be later than the final day of the order.

Related Provisions: Assessment orders are governed by ss. 672.11-672.19. Their provisions are discussed in the *Commentary* which accompanies each section.

Assessment Reports

672.2 (1) Assessment reports — **An assessment order may require the person who makes the assessment to submit in writing an assessment report on the mental condition of the accused.**

(2) Assessment report to be filed with court — **An assessment report shall be filed with the court that ordered it, within the period fixed by the court.**

(3) Court to send assessment report to Review Board — **The court shall send to the Review Board without delay a copy of any report filed with it pursuant to subsection (2), to assist in determining the appropriate disposition to be made in respect of the accused.**

(4) Copies of reports to accused and prosecutor — **Subject to subsection 672.51(3), copies of any report filed with a court pursuant to subsection (2) shall be provided without delay to the prosecutor, the accused and any counsel representing the accused.**

1991, c. 43, s. 4.

Commentary: The section authorizes the completion, filing and distribution of a written *assessment report* prepared by the person who assessed D's mental condition on an assessment order.

By s. 672.2(1), an assessment order may include a term which requires the person who makes the assessment to complete a report on D's mental condition. The report must be filed with the ordering court under s. 672.2(2) within a time period fixed by it. Under s. 672.2(4), P, D and D's counsel are entitled to *copies* of the report, although s. 675.51(3) authorizes the court to withhold disclosure to D of some or all information likely to endanger the life or safety of another person, or which would seriously impair D's treatment or recovery. The ordering court is required by s. 672.2(3) to provide a *copy* of the report without delay to the *Review Board* to assist in their determination of an appropriate disposition for D.

Related Provisions: Section 672.21 enacts an admissibility rule which generally bars reception of any "protected statement" or reference to it without D's consent, unless certain exceptions are applicable.

At a disposition hearing under s. 672.5, the author of an assessment report may be cross-examined under s. 672.5(11).

Other related provisions are discussed in the corresponding note to s. 672.11.

Protected Statements

672.21 (1) Definition of "protected statement" — **In this section, "protected statement" means a statement made by the accused during the course and for the purposes of an assessment or treatment directed by a disposition, to the person specified in the assessment order or the disposition, or to anyone acting under that person's direction.**

(2) Protected statements not admissible against accused — **No protected statement or reference to a protected statement made by an accused is admissible in evidence, without the consent of the accused, in any proceeding before a court, tribunal, body or person with jurisdiction to compel the production of evidence.**

(3) Exceptions — Notwithstanding subsection (2), evidence of a protected statement is admissible for the purpose of

(a) determining whether the accused is unfit to stand trial;

(b) making a disposition or placement decision respecting the accused;

(c) finding whether the accused is a dangerous mentally disordered accused under section 672.65;

(d) determining whether the balance of the mind of the accused was disturbed at the time of commission of the alleged offence, where the accused is a female person charged with an offence arising out of the death of her newly-born child;

(e) determining whether the accused was, at the time of the commission of an alleged offence, suffering from automatism or a mental disorder so as to be exempt from criminal responsibility by virtue of subsection 16(1), if the accused puts his or her mental capacity for criminal intent into issue, or if the prosecutor raises the issue after verdict;

(f) challenging the credibility of an accused in any proceeding where the testimony of the accused is inconsistent in a material particular with a protected statement that the accused made previously; or

(g) establishing the perjury of an accused who is charged with perjury in respect of a statement made in any proceeding.

1991, c. 43, s. 4.

Commentary: This provision enacts a *rule of admissibility* which generally bars evidence of or references to "protected statements" as defined in the section, save in exceptional circumstances.

A "protected statement" is a statement made by D *during the course and for the purpose* of an *assessment* or *treatment* directed by a disposition. It must be made *to the person* specified in the assessment order or disposition or another acting under that person's direction. A "protected statement", in other words, involves elements of *time, purpose,* and a *designated recipient.* Statements made otherwise fall outside the scope of the admissibility rule enacted by the section and are admitted or not according to general principle.

The *general admissibility rule* enacted by s. 672.21(2) holds *inadmissible* both the protected statement and references thereto, *without D's consent,* in any proceeding where the production of evidence may be compelled. The rule would *not* appear to bar derivative evidence. *Quaere* whether identification of its source is barred?

The *exceptions* of s. 672.21(3) are inclusionary. *Evidence of a protected statement* is *admissible*:

i.   in *fitness* hearings;

ii.   in making a *disposition* or *placement decision* concerning D;

iii. in *applications* to have D declared a *dangerous mentally-disordered accused*;

iv.   in determining whether the balance of D's mind was disturbed at the time she committed an offence arising out of the death of her newly-born child;

v.   in deciding whether D suffered from *automatism* or a *mental disorder* exempting from criminal responsibility under s. 16(1), *if* D puts his/her *mental capacity for intent in issue,* or P raises the *issue after verdict*;

vi.   to *challenge* D's *credibility* in any proceeding, where his/her testimony is *inconsistent in a material particular* with a previous protected statement; or,

vii. to establish D's *perjury* in respect of a statement made in any proceeding.

Case Law

R. v. G. (B.) (1997), 10 C.R. (5th) 235, 119 C.C.C. (3d) 276 (Que. C.A.); application for leave to appeal filed , Doc. No. 26226 (S.C.C.) — Under s. 672.21(3)(f), an admission to a psychiatrist may be used to cross-examine D on the issue of credibility, provided the statement would be otherwise admissible.

Related Provisions: The authority to order an assessment report is given by s. 672.2(1).

The exception of s. 672.21(3)(f) appears more narrowly drawn than would result from the application of either *CEA*, s. 10 or 11, or under *R. v. Kuldip* (1990), 61 C.C.C. (3d) 385 (S.C.C.), neither of which insist upon inconsistency *in any material particular* to permit cross-examination.

Other related provisions are discussed in the corresponding note to s. 672.11.

Fitness to Stand Trial

672.22 Presumption of fitness — **An accused is presumed fit to stand trial unless the court is satisfied on the balance of probabilities that the accused is unfit to stand trial.**

1991, c. 43, s. 4.

Commentary: The section, the first of several (ss. 672.22–672.33) which govern *fitness to stand trial*, enacts a *presumption* of *fitness* and permits its *rebuttal* by evidence that satisfies the court on a *balance of probabilities* that D is unfit to stand trial. It would appear consistent with existing case law.

Related Provisions: "Unfit to stand trial" and "mental disorder" are defined in s. 2 of the *Code*. Unfitness refers to an inability, on account of *mental disorder*, to conduct a defence *at any stage of the proceedings* before a verdict is rendered, or to instruct counsel to do so. The definitions of "accused" and "court" in s. 672.1 also make it clear that the rule applies to summary conviction proceedings.

Section 672.23 describes the *basis* upon which the trial of a fitness issue may be directed and upon whom rests the onus of proof. The court is obliged to appoint counsel for an otherwise unrepresented D under s. 672.24.

Section 672.25 governs the *timing* of the trial of a fitness issue and describes the circumstances in which its trial must or may be postponed. Sections 672.26 and 672.27 direct by whom the issue shall be tried. Where D is acquitted or discharged before the issue is tried, no trial of the issue is to be held.

Where D is found *fit* to stand trial after trial of the issue, s. 672.28 directs that the proceedings continue. A *hospital order* may be made under s. 672.29 to ensure that D continues to be fit and does not decompensate during the trial proceedings.

Where D is found *unfit* to stand trial, a disposition hearing may be conducted and disposition made by the court under s. 672.45 or the Review Board, in accordance with ss. 672.47–672.49. Procedure at disposition hearings is governed by s. 672.5 and dispositions, whether by the court or the Board, by s. 672.54. A treatment disposition may be made under ss. 672.58–672.63. The *review* of dispositions by the Review Board is governed by ss. 672.81–672.85.

Under s. 672.32, a finding of unfitness does *not* bar subsequent trial, provided D has become and remains fit. Section 672.33 requires the court having jurisdiction in respect of the alleged offence to review the sufficiency of P's case at times specified and to acquit D where a *prima facie* case is *not* made out.

In proceedings upon indictment, a finding of unfitness may be appealed to the Court of Appeal by D under s. 675(3) and by P under s. 676(3). A similar right in summary conviction proceedings is conferred by ss. 813(a)(iii) and (b)(iii) and s. 830.

Appeals to the court of appeal from dispositions made after a mental disorder verdict are permitted and governed by ss. 672.72–672.8.

672.23 (1) Court may direct issue to be tried — **Where the court has reasonable grounds, at any state of the proceedings before a verdict is rendered, to believe that the accused is unfit to stand trial, the court may direct, of its own motion or on application of the accused or the prosecutor, that the issue of fitness of the accused be tried.**

(2) Burden of proof — **An accused or a prosecutor who makes an application under subsection (1) has the burden of proof that the accused is unfit to stand trial.**

1991, c. 43, s. 4.

Commentary: The section describes the basis upon which the *trial of* an *issue* of D's *fitness to stand trial* may be directed and assigns the burden of proof on the issue.

Under s. 672.23(1), the *trial* of a fitness issue may be directed at *any stage of the proceedings before* a *verdict* is rendered, provided the court has *reasonable grounds to believe* that D is *unfit* to stand trial. The section is silent as to what constitutes "reasonable grounds to believe", as well the nature of evidence which may sustain such a finding. The trial of the issue may be directed by the court of its own motion or upon the application of P or D.

Where D or P applies to have the issue of fitness tried, the *applicant* will bear the *burden of proof* under s. 672.23(2). The section says nothing of the incidence of the burden of proof where the issue is raised by the court *suo motu*.

Related Provisions: Section 672.22 enacts a *rebuttable* presumption of fitness and designates the quantum or standard of proof required in rebuttal as "on a balance of probabilities". Other related provisions are discussed in the corresponding note to s. 672.22.

"Mental disorder" within s. 2 at the time of an act or omission said to constitute an offence may exempt D from criminal responsibility under s. 16. The relevant related provisions are discussed in the corresponding note to the section and s. 672.34.

672.24 (1) Counsel — **Where the court has reasonable grounds to believe that an accused is unfit to stand trial and the accused is not represented by counsel, the court shall order that the accused be represented by counsel.**

(2) Counsel fees and disbursements — **Where counsel is assigned pursuant to subsection (1) and legal aid is not granted to the accused pursuant to a provincial legal aid program, the fees and disbursements of counsel shall be paid by the Attorney General to the extent that the accused is unable to pay them.**

(3) Taxation of fees and disbursements — **Where counsel and the Attorney General cannot agree on the fees or disbursements of counsel, the Attorney General or the counsel may apply to the registrar of the court and the registrar may tax the disputed fees and disbursements.**

1991, c. 43, s. 4; 1997, c. 18, s. 82.

Commentary: Under this section, the court must order that an unrepresented accused be *represented by counsel*, where it has *reasonable grounds* to believe D is *unfit* to stand trial. In other words, in each case where there is a basis to direct the trial of a fitness issue, D shall have counsel. Where D is denied legal aid for counsel so assigned, the Attorney General will pay counsel's fees to the extent that D is unable to do so and, where counsel and the Attorney General cannot agree on counsel's fees or disbursements, either may apply to the registrar of the court to tax the fees.

Related Provisions: "Counsel" is defined in s. 2. Under *Charter* s. 10(b), everyone has the right on arrest or detention to retain and instruct counsel without delay, and to be informed of that right.

Counsel may also be *assigned* to act on behalf of an accused who is a party to an appeal or to proceedings, preliminary or incidental to an appeal in indictable proceedings, under s. 684 (court of appeal), or s. 694.1 (Supreme Court of Canada). Section 839(2) incorporates s. 684 in summary conviction appeals to the court of appeal.

Other related provisions are canvassed in the corresponding note to s. 672.22.

672.25 (1) Postponing trial of issue — **The court shall postpone directing the trial of the issue of fitness of an accused in proceedings for an offence for which the accused may be prosecuted by indictment or that is punishable on summary conviction, until the prosecutor has elected to proceed by way of indictment or summary conviction.**

(2) Idem — The court may postpone directing the trial of the issue of fitness of an accused

 (a) where the issue arises before the close of the case for the prosecution at a preliminary inquiry, until a time that is not later than the time the accused is called on to answer to the charge; or

 (b) where the issue arises before the close of the case for the prosecution at trial, until a time not later than the opening of the case for the defence or, on motion of the accused, any later time that the court may direct.

1991, c. 43, s. 4.

Commentary: This section helps to establish the *time* within which the trial of an *issue* of *fitness* may be directed by requiring or permitting its postponement in certain cases until the mode of procedure or nature of P's case is disclosed.

The *mandatory* terms of s. 672.25(1) apply only to offences triable either way, and *require* postponement of the trial of a fitness issue *until P has elected mode of procedure*. The provision would appear designed to relieve against any unfairness which may ensue to D who may be found unfit prior to P's election of mode of procedure.

Section 672.25(2) is *discretionary*. At *preliminary inquiry*, s. 672.25(2)(a) authorizes postponement of trial of the issue which arises during the course of P's case until a time *not later than* the time D is called upon to *answer to the charge*. At *trial*, s. 672.25(2)(b) permits the court to postpone the trial of an issue of fitness arising during P's case until *not later than* the *opening* of *D's case* or, on motion by D, any later time the court may direct. The subsection clarifies the authority at preliminary inquiry not previously the subject of express provision, and substantially replicates existing law applicable to trials. The manifest purpose of each provision is to permit D to be discharged at the conclusion of P's case in the absence of an evidentiary basis sufficient to put him/her on trial or defence.

Related Provisions: Under s. 672.3, where D is discharged or acquitted at the conclusion of P's case, the issue of fitness will *not* be tried.

Other related provisions are discussed in the corresponding note to s. 672.22.

672.26 Trial of issue by judge and jury — Where an accused is tried or is to be tried before a court composed of a judge and jury,

 (a) if the judge directs that the issue of fitness of the accused be tried before the accused is given in charge to a jury for trial on the indictment, a jury composed of the number of jurors required in respect of the indictment in the province where the trial is to be held shall be sworn to try that issue and, with the consent of the accused, the issues to be tried on the indictment; and

 (b) if the judge directs that the issue of fitness of the accused be tried after the accused has been given in charge to a jury for trial on the indictment, the jury shall be sworn to try that issue in addition to the issues in respect of which it is already sworn.

1991, c. 43, s. 4.

Commentary: The section describes *who* shall try a fitness issue in *jury trials*. It substantially tracks former s. 615(5)(b).

Where an issue of fitness is directed in a jury trial, it will be tried by a jury. Where the issue is directed *before* D is *given in charge* of the jury for trial, s. 672.26(a) requires that a *jury*, equivalent in size to the trial jury, be empanelled for such purpose. With D's *consent* (in the event of a finding of fitness), the fitness jury may also try the issues to be tried on the indictment. Where the trial of the issue is directed *after* D has been *given in charge* of the jury for trial, the *trial jury* must be sworn to try the fitness issue, in addition to the issues to be tried on the indictment.

Related Provisions: Section 672.27 applies to the trial of fitness issues in cases other than those tried by judge and jury. The assignment of authority to try the issue co-incides with the division of responsibility between the trier of fact and the trier of law.

Other related provisions are discussed in the corresponding note to s. 672.22.

672.27 Trial of issue by court — The court shall try the issue of fitness of an accused and render a verdict where the issue arises

    (a) in respect of an accused who is tried or is to be tried before a court other than a court composed of a judge and jury; or

    (b) before a court at a preliminary inquiry or at any other stage of the proceedings.

1991, c. 43, s. 4.

Commentary: This provision governs the *trial of a fitness issue* in proceedings *other than* trials by *judge and jury*. In each case, it is the *court* which must try and determine the fitness issue. The section applies, not only to cases tried or to be tried otherwise than before a court composed of a judge and jury, but also to the preliminary inquiry and "at any other stage of the proceedings".

The section replicates former s. 615(5)(c) applicable to non-jury trials, and makes specific the incorporated reference to s. 615 contained in former s. 537(4) applicable to preliminary inquiries.

Related Provisions: "Accused" and "court" are defined in s. 672.1 and include a summary conviction court. In jury trials, s. 672.26 governs.

Discussion of other related provisions appears in the corresponding note to s. 672.22.

672.28 Proceeding continues where accused is fit — Where the verdict on trial of the issue is that an accused is fit to stand trial, the arraignment, preliminary inquiry, trial or other stage of the proceeding shall continue as if the issue of fitness of the accused had never arisen.

1991, c. 43, s. 4.

Commentary: The section duplicates former s. 615(6) and provides for the *continuation* of the proceedings, including arraignment, preliminary inquiry, trial or other proceeding, where D has been *found fit* by verdict after trial of the issue, as if the fitness issue had never arisen.

Related Provisions: Where D has been found *unfit* to stand trial after trial of the issue, s. 672.32 enacts that such a finding does *not* permanently bar subsequent proceedings. The adequacy of P's case is to be reviewed every two years under s. 672.33.

Other related provisions are discussed in the corresponding note to s. 672.22.

672.29 Where continued detention in custody — Where an accused is detained in custody on delivery of a verdict that the accused is fit to stand trial, the court may order the accused to be detained in a hospital until the completion of the trial, if the court has reasonable grounds to believe that the accused would become unfit to stand trial if released.

1991, c. 43, s. 4.

Commentary: This new provision permits D, found fit to stand trial, to be *detained in a hospital* pending the completion of the trial in certain circumstances.

The discretion provided for in the section only becomes engaged where D is *detained in custody* on delivery of the fitness verdict, *and* the court has *reasonable grounds* to believe that D *would become unfit* to stand trial *if released*. The court may then order D detained in a hospital until the completion of the trial, apparently to prevent deterioration of D's condition to a state of unfitness before the merits of the case may be tried.

The concluding phrase "if released" might have been more felicitously expressed "if returned to custody" if the provision was intended, as it appears to have been, to obviate deterioration *in custody* likely to give rise to constant re-visitation of fitness issues.

Related Provisions: Section 747.1, not yet in force, permits a sentencing court to make a *hospital order* as the initial part of a sentence of imprisonment in certain cases. The general rule of s. 742.2, not yet in force, is that D be detained in accordance with the order in a treatment facility recommended by the correctional authorities in whose custody D is or is to be confined.

An analogous authority to ss. 672.29 and 672.49, permits the Review Board or chairperson to require D's continued detention in a hospital pending court determination of a fitness issue.

Other related provisions are discussed in the corresponding note to s. 672.22.

672.30 Acquittal — Where the court has postponed directing the trial of the issue of fitness of an accused pursuant to subsection 672.25(2) and the accused is discharged or acquitted before the issue is tried, it shall not be tried.

1991, c. 43, s. 4.

Commentary: This section substantially duplicates former s. 615(8) except that it makes express reference to D being *discharged* so as to ensure its application to the preliminary inquiry. Like its predecessor, it bars the trial of an issue of fitness postponed under s. 672.25(2), where D is discharged or acquitted at the end of P's case, or before the issue is otherwise tried.

Related Provisions: The authority to *postpone* the *trial* of the *fitness issue* appears in s. 672.25(2). A finding of *unfitness* engages ss. 672.31 to 672.33.

Other related provisions are discussed in the corresponding note to s. 672.22.

672.31 Verdict of unfit to stand trial — Where the verdict on trial of the issue is that an accused is unfit to stand trial, any plea that has been made shall be set aside and any jury shall be discharged.

1991, c. 43, s. 4.

Commentary: The section substantially repeats former s. 615(7) without reference to the automatic custodial remand pending the pleasure of the Lieutenant Governor being made known.

The provision applies where D has been found *unfit* to stand trial after trial of the issue. Any *plea* entered by or on behalf of D is *set aside*, and any *jury*, whether empanelled to try fitness, the issues on the indictment or both, is *discharged*.

Related Provisions: Section 672.32 governs the taking of subsequent proceedings on an indictment after D has been found *unfit* to stand trial. Section 672.28, potentially s. 672.29, applies where D has been found *fit* to stand trial.

Other related provisions are discussed in the corresponding note to s. 672.22.

672.32 (1) Subsequent proceedings — A verdict of unfit to stand trial shall not prevent the accused from being tried subsequently where the accused becomes fit to stand trial.

(2) Burden of proof — The burden of proof that the accused has subsequently become fit to stand trial is on the party who asserts it, and is discharged by proof on the balance of probabilities.

1991, c. 43, s. 4.

Commentary: The section provides that a finding of unfitness does *not* bar subsequent proceedings and assigns the burden of proof in such cases.

Under s. 672.32(1) enacts that a finding of unfitness does *not* bar subsequent trial proceedings where D becomes fit to stand trial. By s. 672.32(2), the *onus* of displacing an earlier finding of unfitness rests upon the party who asserts it. The *standard* of proof required is proof (of fitness) on a *balance of probabilities*.

Related Provisions: The finding of unfitness displaces the presumption of fitness enacted by s. 672.22. The requirement of s. 672.32(2) that the party asserting fitness bear the evidential and persuasive burden of establishing it accords with general principle.

Other related provisions are discussed in the corresponding note to s. 672.22.

672.33 (1) Prima facie case to be made every two years — The court that has jurisdiction in respect of the offence charged against an accused who is found unfit to stand trial shall hold an inquiry, not later than two years after the verdict is rendered and every two years thereafter until the accused is acquitted pursuant to subsection (6) or tried, to decide whether sufficient evidence can be adduced at that time to put the accused on trial.

(2) Court may order inquiry to be held — On application of the accused, the court may order an inquiry under this section to be held at any time if it is satisfied, on the basis of the application and any written material submitted by the accused, that there is reason to doubt that there is a *prima facie* case against the accused.

(3) Burden of proof — At an inquiry under this section, the burden of proof that sufficient evidence can be adduced to put the accused on trial is on the prosecutor.

(4) Admissible evidence at an inquiry — In an inquiry under this section, the court shall admit as evidence

(a) any affidavit containing evidence that would be admissible if given by the person making the affidavit as a witness in court; or

(b) any certified copy of the oral testimony given at a previous inquiry or hearing held before a court in respect of the offence with which the accused is charged.

(5) Conduct of inquiry — The court may determine the manner in which an inquiry under this section is conducted and may follow the practices and procedures in respect of a preliminary inquiry under Part XVIII where it concludes that the interests of justice so require.

(6) Where prima facie case not made — Where, on the completion of an inquiry under this section, the court is satisfied that sufficient evidence cannot be adduced to put the accused on trial, the court shall acquit the accused.

1991, c. 43, s. 4.

Commentary: This section requires periodic judicial inquiry into the adequacy of P's case against D found unfit to stand trial, and regulates the conduct of the inquiry.

Under s. 672.33(1), the *initial inquiry* must be held not later than two years after the finding of unfitness has been made. Further inquiries must be held at least *every two years* thereafter until D is either acquitted under s. 672.33(6) or tried. The inquiry is to be conducted by "the court that has jurisdiction in respect of the offence" but, *semble*, not necessarily the judicial officer who presided in the earlier proceedings which resulted in the verdict. The issue on the inquiry is whether *sufficient evidence* can be adduced at the time of the inquiry *to put D on trial*. The standard applied would appear analogous to that which would authorize an order to stand trial at preliminary inquiry. Under s. 672.33(2), D may apply to the court to order an inquiry *at any time*. The order may be made *provided* the court is satisfied, on the basis of the application and any written material submitted by D, that there is *reason to doubt* that there is a *prima facie* case against D.

The *conduct of the inquiry* is governed by ss. 672.33(3)–(5). Under s. 672.33(3), P bears the burden of proving that sufficient evidence can be adduced to put D on trial. By s. 672.33(5), the court is left to determine the *manner* in which the inquiry is to be conducted. Where the court concludes that the interests of justice so require, the procedure at preliminary inquiry may be followed. Section 672.33(4) facilitates P's proof by requiring admission of *affidavits* containing evidence which would be admissible if given *viva voce*, as well certified copies of oral testimony previously given in proceedings in respect of the offence charged. The latter provision, s 672.33(4)(b), would appear to permit reception of evidence given at a judicial interim release hearing, where the rules of admissibility are somewhat less stringent.

Under s. 672.33(6), D is to be *acquitted* where the court is *satisfied* that sufficient evidence cannot be adduced to put him/her on trial.

Related Provisions: The standard of proof required of P is that demanded at preliminary inquiry to justify an order to stand trial under s. 548(1)(a), and applied by a trial judge in deciding whether there is "sufficient" evidence to warrant consideration of P's case by a jury.

The reference in s. 672.33(5) to "the practices and procedures in respect of a preliminary inquiry under Part XVIII..." would appear to include ss. 537–542.

Other related provisions are discussed in the corresponding note to s. 672.22.

Verdict of Not Criminally Responsible on Account of Mental Disorder

672.34 Verdict of not criminally responsible on account of mental disorder — Where the jury, or the judge or provincial court judge where there is no jury, finds that an accused committed the act or made the omission that formed the basis of the offence charged, but was at the time suffering from mental disorder so as to be exempt from criminal responsibility by virtue of subsection 16(1), the jury or the judge shall render a verdict that the accused committed the act or made the omission but is not criminally responsible on account of mental disorder.

1991, c. 43, s. 4.

Commentary: This section creates a *special verdict* of *not criminally responsible on account of mental disorder* and describes the findings of fact required before the verdict may be rendered.

To render a verdict of not criminally responsible on account of mental disorder, the trier of fact, jury, judge or provincial court judge, must find:

i.   that D committed the act or made the omission that formed the basis of the offence charged; and,

ii. that D, at the time of the act or omission, suffered from a *mental disorder* which rendered him/her *incapable of appreciating* the *nature and quality* of the act or omission *or* of *knowing* that it was *wrong*.

The verdict rendered acknowledges that D did the act or made the omission, but exempts from criminal responsibility due to the nature and extent of a then-existing mental disorder.

Related Provisions: "Mental disorder" is defined in s. 2 and the nature or extent required to exempt from criminal responsibility in s. 16(1). Apart from the deletion of the reference to "a state of natural imbecility" as a basis of incapacity, as well as the repeal of former s. 16(3) relating to specific delusions, the standard for criminal responsibility would appear little altered by the new s. 16(1).

Where a verdict of not criminally responsible on account of mental disorder is rendered in relation to D, the *trial court* may hold a *disposition hearing* and make a disposition under s. 672.45. Where the trial court *fails* to make a disposition, the Review Board has authority to do so under ss. 672.47 to 672.49. Procedure on disposition hearings is governed by ss. 672.5 to 672.52 and dispositions, whether by the court or by the Board, by s. 672.54. Treatment may *not* be a term or condition of disposition unless consented to by D under s. 672.55.

The *period* during which D may be subject to a disposition after a special verdict exempting from criminal responsibility is governed by the "capping" provisions of s. 672.64, unless P invokes the provisions of s. 672.65 to have D declared a DMDA and the disposition cap increased to life.

In *proceedings by indictment*, D may appeal to the court of appeal from the special verdict under s. 675(3). The right of the Attorney General to appeal to the court of appeal is found " within s. 676(1)(a). In *summary conviction proceedings*, both D and P have a right of appeal from the special verdict under ss. 813(a)(iii) and (b)(iii), as does any "party to the proceedings" under s. 830 on the grounds there stated.

Any *party* may appeal to the court of appeal against disposition made by a court or the Review Board under s. 672.72 and in accordance with ss. 672.73 to 672.78. Appeals in DMDA proceedings are governed by ss. 672.79 and 672.8.

Reviews of dispositions are governed by ss. 672.81 to 672.85.

The considerations which apply to the issue of fitness appear in ss. 672.22 to 672.33 and are described in the corresponding note to s. 672.22.

672.35 Effect of verdict of not criminally responsible on account of mental disorder — Where a verdict of not criminally responsible on account of mental disorder is rendered, the accused shall not be found guilty or convicted of the offence, but

(a) the accused may plead *autrefois acquit* in respect of any subsequent charge relating to that offence;

(b) any court may take the verdict into account in considering an application for judicial interim release or in considering what dispositions to make or sentence to impose for any other offence; and

(c) the National Parole Board or any provincial parole board may take the verdict into account in considering an application by the accused for parole or pardon in respect of any other offence.

1991, c. 43, s. 4.

Commentary: This provision, without an equivalent under the former scheme, describes the *legal effect of the special verdict* of not criminally responsible on account of mental disorder, as well its use in certain subsequent proceedings and applications.

The special verdict bars a finding of guilt and conviction of the offence in respect of which it has been given. It may be raised under a plea of *autrefois acquit* in answer to any subsequent charge relating to that offence. It can also be considered in determining whether judicial interim release ought to be granted, or the disposition to be made or sentence imposed for any other offence. Parole authorities, both federal and provincial, may take cognizance of the verdict in considering D's application for parole or pardon in respect of any other offence.

Related Provisions: Section 672.36 enacts that the special verdict is *not* a previous conviction for sentencing purposes in cases where greater punishment is provided by reason of prior convictions. Section 672.37 governs reference to the verdict on applications for federal employment.

The corresponding note to s. 672.34 discusses other related provisions.

672.36 Verdict not a previous conviction — A verdict of not criminally responsible on account of mental disorder is not a previous conviction for the purposes of any offence under any Act of Parliament for which a greater punishment is provided by reason of previous convictions.

1991, c. 43, s. 4.

Commentary: This entirely new provision bars use of a special verdict of not criminally responsible on account of mental disorder as a *previous conviction* for the purposes of any federal offence which attracts a greater punishment due to previous convictions.

Related Provisions: The legal effect of the special verdict, as well, permitted use thereof in subsequent proceedings, is described in s. 672.35. Its exclusion from applications for federal employment is governed by s. 672.37. The special verdict is authorized by s. 672.34 and the nature of the incapacity required described in s. 16(1) and the definition of "mental disorder" in s. 2.

Other related provisions are described in the corresponding note to ss. 16 and 672.34.

672.37 (1) Definition of "application for federal employment" — In this section, "application for federal employment" means an application form relating to

(a) employment in any department, as defined in section 2 of the *Financial Administration Act*;

(b) employment by any Crown corporation as defined in subsection 83(1) of the *Financial Administration Act*;

(c) enrolment in the Canadian Forces; or

(d) employment in connection with the operation of any work, undertaking or business that is within the legislative authority of Parliament.

(2) Application for federal employment — No application for federal employment shall contain any question that requires the applicant to disclose any charge or finding that the applicant committed an offence that resulted in a finding or a verdict of not criminally responsible on account of mental disorder if the applicant was discharged absolutely or is no longer subject to any disposition in respect of that offence.

(3) Punishment — Any person who uses or authorizes the use of an application for federal employment that contravenes subsection (2) is guilty of an offence punishable on summary conviction.

1991, c. 43, s. 4.

Commentary: This novel section forbids questions on applications for federal employment, as defined in s. 672.37(1), that require an applicant to disclose any charge or finding that resulted in a special verdict of not criminally responsible on account of mental disorder, if the applicant has been discharged absolutely or is no longer subject to any disposition in respect of the offence.

It is a summary conviction offence to use or authorize the use of an application for federal employment which contravenes s. 672.37(2).

Related Provisions: The effect of the special verdict is described in ss. 672.35 and 672.36. Other related provisions are described in the corresponding note to s. 672.34.

Review Boards

672.38 (1) Review boards to be established — A Review Board shall be established or designated for each province to make or review dispositions concerning any accused in respect of whom a verdict of not criminally responsible by reason of mental disorder or unfit to stand trial is rendered, and shall consist of not fewer than five members appointed by the lieutenant governor in council of the province.

(2) Treated as provincial board — A Review Board shall be treated as having been established under the laws of the province.

(3) Personal liability — No member of a Review Board is liable for any act done in good faith in the exercise of the member's powers or the performance of the member's duties and functions or for any default or neglect in good faith in the exercise of those powers or the performance of those duties and functions.

1991, c. 43, s. 4; 1997, c. 18, s. 83.

Commentary: The section requires the establishment or designation of Review Boards for each province, describes their purpose and makes general provision for their composition.

Under s. 672.38(1), the Review Board established or designated for each province, is obliged to make or review dispositions concerning any accused who is the subject of a mental disorder verdict. The Board must consist of not fewer than five members appointed by the Lieutenant-Governor-in-Council of the province.

Under s. 672.38(2), the Review Board is treated as having been established under provincial law. This provision would appear designed to deny access to the *Federal Court Act* as a means of reviewing Board decisions.

Under s. 672.38(3), no personal liability may attach to a member of the Board in respect of any exercise of powers or performance of duties or neglect of same provided the act or omission was a *good faith* one.

Related Provisions: "Review Board" is defined in s. 672.1 and its composition determined by s. 672.39. The qualifications of the chairperson of the Board are governed by s. 672.4. What constitutes a quorum of the Board is defined in s. 672.41. A majority vote is determinative under s. 672.42. Rules governing the practice and procedure before the Board may be passed under s. 672.44.

Where the trial court makes *no* disposition on a disposition hearing held under s. 672.45(1) after a mental disorder verdict, the Board must do so under s. 672.47. Section 672.48 describes the Board's role where D has been found *unfit* to stand trial. The *procedure* of the hearing is governed by s. 672.5 and the *terms* of the disposition, by ss. 672.54 to 672.63. The maximum period during which D will be subject to a disposition is governed by the "capping" provisions of s. 672.64.

The Review Board, under ss. 672.81 to 672.85, is required and authorized to review dispositions made after mental disorder verdicts. Its role in supervision of mentally-disordered offenders who have been transferred to other provinces is described in ss. 672.88 and 672.89.

Any party may appeal to the court of appeal against a disposition or placement decision made by the Review Board under s. 672.72(1). The hearing and disposition of these appeals are governed by ss. 672.73 to 672.78. The Board would appear to have no role in appeals taken from determinations made on DMDA applications.

672.39 Members of Review Board — A Review Board must have at least one member who is entitled under the laws of a province to practise psychiatry and, where only one member is so entitled, at least one other member must have training and experience in the field of mental health, and be entitled under the laws of a province to practise medicine or psychology.

1991, c. 43, s. 4.

Commentary: The section requires mental health professionals on a Review Board. At least one Board member must be entitled to practice psychiatry under provincial law. Where only one member is a psychiatrist, at least one other member must have training and experience in the field of mental health, and be a duly qualified medical practitioner or psychologist.

Related Provisions: See the corresponding note to s. 672.38.

672.4 (1) Chairperson of a Review Board — Subject to subsection (2), the chairperson of a Review Board shall be a judge of the Federal Court or of a superior, district or county court of a province, or a person who is qualified for appointment to, or has retired from, such a judicial office.

(2) Transitional — Where the chairperson of a Review Board that was established before the coming into force of subsection (1) is not a judge or other person referred to therein, the chairperson may continue to act until the expiration of his or her term of office if at least one other member of the Review Board is a judge or other person referred to in subsection (1) or is a member of the bar of the province.

1991, c. 43, s. 4.

Commentary: This section prescribes the qualifications of a chairperson of a Review Board.

Under s. 672.4(1), the chairperson must be a present or former judge of a designated court or a person qualified for appointment thereto. By s. 672.4(2), any chairperson of a Review Board established before s. 672.4(1) came into force continues to so act until the expiration of his/her term, provided at least one other Board member is a person described in s. 672.4(1) or a member of the provincial bar.

Related Provisions: Related provisions are described in the corresponding note to s. 672.38.

672.41 (1) Quorum of Review Board — **Subject to subsection (2), the quorum of a Review Board is constituted by the chairperson, a member who is entitled under the laws of a province to practise psychiatry, and any other member.**

(2) Transitional — **Where the chairperson of a Review Board that was established before the coming into force of this section is not a judge or other person referred to in subsection 672.4(1), the quorum of the Review Board is constituted by the chairperson, a member who is entitled under the laws of a province to practise psychiatry, and a member who is a person referred to in that subsection or a member of the bar of the province.**

1991, c. 43, s. 4.

Commentary: The section provides for what constitutes a *quorum* of a Review Board. In general, a quorum consists of the chairperson, and two members, one of whom is a duly qualified psychiatrist. In the case of a Review Board established *prior* to the coming into force of the section whose chairperson is not a judge or other person described in s. 672.4(1), the quorum comprises the chairperson, the psychiatrist member and another member who is either a person described in s. 672.4(1) or a member of the provincial bar.

Related Provisions: Related provisions are discussed in the corresponding note to s. 672.38.

672.42 Majority vote — **A decision of a majority of the members present and voting is the decision of a Review Board.**

1991, c. 43, s. 4.

Commentary: This new provision enacts that the decision of a Review Board is the decision of a *majority* of its members present and voting.

Related Provisions: See the corresponding note to s. 672.38 for a discussion of the relevant related provisions.

672.43 Powers of Review Boards — **At a hearing held by a Review Board to make a disposition or review a disposition in respect of an accused, the chairperson has all the powers that are conferred by sections 4 and 5 of the *Inquiries Act* on persons appointed as commissioners under Part I of that Act.**

1991, c. 43, s. 4.

Commentary: The section gives the chairperson of a Review Board all of the powers held by commissioners appointed under Part I of the *Inquiries Act* by ss. 4 and 5 of that *Act*.

Related Provisions: The corresponding note to s. 672.38 describes the relevant related provisions.

672.44 (1) Rules of Review Board — **A Review Board may, subject to the approval of the lieutenant governor in council of the province, make rules providing for the practice and procedure before the Review Board.**

(2) Application and publication of rules — **The rules made by a Review Board under subsection (1) apply to any proceeding within its jurisdiction, and shall be published in the *Canada Gazette*.**

(3) Regulations — **Notwithstanding anything in this section, the Governor in Council may make regulations to provide for the practice and procedure before Review Boards, in particular to make the rules of Review Boards uniform, and all regulations made under this subsection prevail over any rules made under subsection (1).**

1991, c. 43, s. 4.

Commentary: The section, permits rules to be made regulating Review Board practice and procedure.

Under s. 672.44(1), a Review Board may make rules providing for the practice and procedure before it. The rules are subject to the approval of the lieutenant-governor-in-council of the province and apply to any proceedings within the jurisdiction of the Board. They must be published in the *Canada Gazette*.

Under s. 672.44(3), the Governor-in-Council retains authority to provide for Review Board practice and procedure by regulation, in particular to ensure uniformity. Any regulations under s. 672.44(3) prevail over rules made under s. 672.44(1).

Related Provisions: The authority to make rules of court is conferred by s. 482(1) on a superior court of criminal jurisdiction and court of appeal. A similar authority is given to courts of criminal jurisdiction and appeal courts within s. 812 that are not also superior courts of criminal jurisdiction or courts of appeal under s. 482(2), but requires the approval of the lieutenant-governor-in-council of the province. Under s. 482(5), the Governor-in-Council has an overriding authority to make such provision as is considered proper to secure uniformity in the rules of court in criminal matters and the uniform rules prevail.

Other related provisions are discussed in the corresponding note to s. 672.38.

Disposition Hearings

672.45 (1) Hearing to be held by a court — Where a verdict of not criminally responsible on account of mental disorder or unfit to stand trial is rendered in respect of an accused, the court may of its own motion, and shall on application by the accused or the prosecutor, hold a disposition hearing.

(2) Disposition to be made — At a disposition hearing, the court shall make a disposition in respect of the accused, if it is satisfied that it can readily do so and that a disposition should be made without delay.

1991, c. 43, s. 4.

Commentary: This new provision *authorizes* a *court* to conduct a *disposition hearing* upon application therefor after a *mental disorder verdict*.

Under s. 672.45(1), there must first be the requisite *mental disorder verdict*. Where application is made therefor by either D or P, the court *must* hold a disposition hearing. It *may* do so *suo motu*.

Under s. 672.45(2), a disposition is *only* required where the court is satisfied that it can readily do so, *and* that a disposition should be made without delay. Absent such findings, *semble*, no disposition should be made, although the hearing is required to be held.

Related Provisions: "Disposition" is defined in s. 672.1. "Court" defined in the same section includes a summary conviction court, judge, justice or judge of the court of appeal. "Mental disorder" and "unfit to stand trial" are defined in s. 2.

The procedure at the disposition hearing is governed by s. 672.5. The terms which may be included in a disposition are described in ss. 672.54 to 672.63. The maximum period for which dispositions may be in force is determined by the "capping" provisions of s. 672.64, subject to P's application to have D declared a DMDA under s. 672.65. Sections 672.64 and 672.65 have not yet been proclaimed in force.

Where the trial court makes *no* disposition under s. 672.45 after a mental disorder verdict, the Review Board is required to do so under s. 672.47. It will follow the procedural mandate of s. 672.5, and impose a disposition in accordance with ss. 672.54 to 672.63 and within the caps of s. 672.64. DMDA proceedings may *not* be taken before the Board.

Sections 672.81 to 672.85 govern the authority of the Review Board to review dispositions made by the court or dispositions and placement decisions made by the Review Board itself.

Appeals to the court of appeal from dispositions made by a court or the Review Board may be taken under s. 672.72(1) in accordance with the provisions of ss. 672.72(2), (3) and 672.73 to 672.78.

Appeals from the mental disorder verdicts which underlie the dispositions made by the court or Review Board are discussed in the corresponding notes to ss. 672.22 and 672.34.

672.46 (1) Status quo pending Review Board hearing — Where the court does not make a disposition in respect of the accused at a disposition hearing, any order for the interim release or detention of the accused or any appearance notice, promise to appear, summons, undertaking or recognizance in respect of the accused that is in force at the time the verdict of not criminally responsible on account of mental disorder or unfit to stand trial is rendered continues in force, subject to its terms, until the Review Board makes a disposition.

(2) Variation of order — Notwithstanding subsection (1), a court may, on cause being shown, vacate any order, appearance notice, promise to appear, summons, undertaking or recognizance referred to in that subsection and make any other order for the interim release or detention of the accused that the court considers to be appropriate in the circumstances, including an order directing that the accused be detained in custody in a hospital pending a disposition by the Review Board in respect of the accused.

1991, c. 43, s. 4.

Commentary: This new section governs the question of D's liberty pending disposition by the Review Board, where the court has *not* made a disposition on a s. 672.45 disposition hearing.

Section 672.46(1) enacts the general rule. It maintains the *status quo*, whether release or detention, until the Review Board makes a disposition. Where cause is shown, s. 672.46(2) authorizes the court to *vacate* any then-existing form of release and make *any other order* for D's interim release or detention that the court *considers appropriate* in the circumstances, including a direction that D be detained in custody in a hospital pending disposition by the Review Board.

It may be observed that s. 672.46(2) neither contains its own nor incorporates by reference any other notice provisions. It is silent upon the material, if any, to be filed or criteria to be applied in determining the issue.

Related Provisions: A court is only authorized to make a disposition after mental disorder verdict, where it is satisfied that it can readily do so, and that a disposition should be made without delay. The disposition hearing may be initiated by the court of its own motion or upon application by P or D.

Other related provisions are discussed in the corresponding note to s. 672.45.

672.47 (1) Review board to make disposition where court does not — Where a verdict of not criminally responsible on account of mental disorder or unfit to stand trial is rendered and the court makes no disposition in respect of an accused, the Review Board shall, as soon as is practicable but not later than forty-five days after the verdict was rendered, hold a hearing and make a disposition.

(2) Extension of time for hearing — Where the court is satisfied that there are exceptional circumstances that warrant it, the court may extend the time for holding a hearing under subsection (1) to a maximum of ninety days after the verdict was rendered.

(3) Where disposition made by court — Where a court makes a disposition under section 672.54 other than an absolute discharge in respect of an accused, the Review Board shall hold a hearing on a day not later than the day on which the disposition ceases to be in force, and not later than ninety days after the disposition was made, and shall make a disposition in respect of the accused.

1991, c. 43, s. 4.

Commentary: This section enacts *time limits* within which *dispositions* are to be made by the *Review Board* after a mental disorder verdict.

Sections 672.47(1) and (2) apply where the *court* has made *no disposition* after verdict or finding. The Review Board, under s. 672.47(1), *must* hold a hearing and make a disposition as soon as it is practicable, and within 45 days of the verdict or finding, *unless* there are exceptional circumstances which warrant an extension of the time to a maximum of 90 days after verdict or finding.

Section 672.47(3) applies where a *court* has made a *disposition* under s. 672.54, other than an absolute discharge. The Review Board must then hold a hearing and make a disposition within 90 days of the court disposition.

Related Provisions: The authority for a court to hold a disposition hearing and make a disposition after a mental disorder verdict is provided by s. 672.45. Where the court makes no disposition and the Board is required to act under this provision, s. 672.46 preserves the *status quo* until it does so.

Further related provisions are discussed in the corresponding note to s. 672.45.

672.48 (1) Review board to determine fitness — Where a Review Board holds a hearing to make or review a disposition in respect of an accused who has been found unfit to stand trial, it shall determine whether in its opinion the accused is fit to stand trial at the time of the hearing.

(2) Review board shall send accused to court — If a Review Board determines that the accused is fit to stand trial, it shall order that the accused be sent back to court, and the court shall try the issue and render a verdict.

(3) Chairperson may send accused to court — The chairperson of a Review Board may, with the consent of the accused and the person in charge of the hospital where an accused is being detained, order that the accused be sent back to court for trial of the issue of whether the accused is unfit to stand trial, where the chairperson is of the opinion that

(a) the accused is fit to stand trial, and

(b) the Review Board will not hold a hearing to make or review a disposition in respect of the accused within a reasonable period.

1991, c. 43, s. 4.

Commentary: This new provision obliges the Review Board and authorizes its chairperson to *return* an *apparently fit accused* to court for re-trial of the fitness issue.

The obligations of the Review Board in respect of D found unfit to stand trial appear in ss. 672.48(1) and (2). Under s. 672.48(1), the Board, upon a disposition hearing or review, must determine whether, in its opinion, D is fit to stand trial *at the time of the hearing*. Where the *Board determines* that D is *fit* to stand trial, s. 672.48(2) requires it to order D to *return to court* where the court must try the fitness issue and render a verdict.

The *chairperson* has *exceptional authority* to return an apparently fit accused to court under s. (3). The authority may only be exercised with the *consent* of D and the person in charge of the hospital where D is detained, and where the chairperson is of the opinion that D is fit to stand trial and the Board disposition or review hearing will *not* be held within a reasonable period. D's return to court is for re-trial of the issue of fitness.

Related Provisions: The trial of an issue of fitness may be directed under s. 672.23 and counsel appointed under s. 672.24. The trial of the issue may be postponed under s. 672.25 and determined in accordance with ss. 672.26 and 672.27. Where D is found *fit*, the trial continues under s. 672.28. Where D is found *unfit*, a disposition must be made by the court under s. 672.45 or the Board under s. 672.47 and the present section.

Other related provisions are discussed in the corresponding note to s. 672.45.

672.49 (1) Continued detention in hospital — In a disposition made pursuant to section 672.47 the Review Board or chairperson may require the accused to continue to be detained in a hospital until the court determines whether the accused is fit to stand trial, if the Review Board or chairperson has reasonable grounds to believe that the accused would become unfit to stand trial if released.

(2) Copy of disposition to be sent to court — The Review Board or chairperson shall send a copy of a disposition made pursuant to section 672.47 without delay to the court having jurisdiction over the accused and to the Attorney General of the province where the accused is to be tried.

1991, c. 43, s. 4.

Commentary: This new provision *permits* the continued *detention* of D *in hospital pending court determination of fitness* to stand trial, and requires disclosure of s. 672.47 dispositions of the Board.

Under s. 672.49(1), the Review Board or chairperson, in a disposition under s. 672.47, may require D to remain detained in a hospital until court determination of the fitness issue. The order may only be made where the applicable authority has *reasonable grounds* to believe that D would become unfit if released. The order would appear to guard against relapses into unfitness.

Section 672.49(2) ensures timely communication to the court and prosecutorial authority of a copy of any s. 672.47 disposition made in relation to D. The obligation is that of the Board or chairperson.

Related Provisions: A similar authority appears in s. 672.29 to ensure D remains fit during the remainder of a trial after a finding of fitness.

Other related provisions are described in the corresponding note to s. 672.45.

672.5 (1) Procedure at disposition hearing — A hearing held by a court or Review Board to make or review a disposition in respect of an accused shall be held in accordance with this section.

(2) Hearing to be informal — The hearing may be conducted in as informal a manner as is appropriate in the circumstances.

(3) Attorneys general may be parties — On application, the court or Review Board shall designate as a party the Attorney General of the province where the disposition is to be made and, where an accused is transferred from another province, the Attorney General of the province from which the accused is transferred.

(4) Interested person may be a party — The court or Review Board may designate as a party any person who has a substantial interest in protecting the interests of the accused, if the court or Review Board is of the opinion that it is just to do so.

(5) Notice of hearing — Notice of the hearing shall be given to the parties, the Attorney General of the province where the disposition is to be made and, where the accused is transferred to another province, the Attorney General of the province from which the accused is transferred, within the time and in the manner prescribed, or within the time and in the manner fixed by the rules of the court or Review Board.

(6) Order excluding the public — Where the court or Review Board considers it to be in the best interests of the accused and not contrary to the public interest, the court or Review Board may order the public or any members of the public to be excluded from the hearing or any part of the hearing.

(7) Right to counsel — The accused or any other party has the right to be represented by counsel.

(8) Assigning counsel — The court or Review Board shall, if an accused is not represented by counsel, assign counsel to act for any accused

    (a) who has been found unfit to stand trial; or

    (b) wherever the interests of justice so require.

(8.1) Counsel fees and disbursements — Where counsel is assigned pursuant to subsection (8) and legal aid is not granted to the accused pursuant to a provincial legal aid program, the fees and disbursements of counsel shall be paid by the Attorney General to the extent that the accused is unable to pay them.

(8.2) Taxation of fees and disbursements — Where counsel and the Attorney General cannot agree on the fees or disbursements of counsel, the Attorney General or the counsel may apply to the registrar of the court and the registrar may tax the disputed fees and disbursements.

(9) Right of accused to be present — Subject to subsection (10), the accused has the right to be present during the whole of the hearing.

(10) Removal or absence of accused — The court or the chairperson of the Review Board may

    (a) permit the accused to be absent during the whole or any part of the hearing on such conditions as the court or chairperson considers proper; or

    (b) cause the accused to be removed and barred from re-entry for the whole or any part of the hearing

        (i) where the accused interrupts the hearing so that to continue in the presence of the accused would not be feasible,

        (ii) on being satisfied that failure to do so would likely endanger the life or safety of another person or would seriously impair the treatment or recovery of the accused, or

        (iii) in order to hear, in the absence of the accused, evidence, oral or written submissions, or the cross-examination of any witness concerning whether grounds exist for removing the accused pursuant to subparagraph (ii).

(11) Rights of parties at hearing — Any party may adduce evidence, make oral or written submissions, call witnesses and cross-examine any witness called by any other party and, on application, cross-examine any person who made an assessment report that was submitted to the court or Review Board in writing.

(12) Request to compel attendance of witnesses — A party may not compel the attendance of witnesses, but may request the court or the chairperson of the Review Board to do so.

(13) Video links — Where the accused so agrees, the court or the chairperson of the Review Board may permit the accused to appear by closed-circuit television or any other means that allow the court or Review Board and the accused to engage in simultaneous visual and oral communication, for any part of the hearing.

1991, c. 43, s. 4; 1997, c. 18, s. 84.

Commentary: This section, without equivalent under the former scheme, provides the *procedure* to be followed in *disposition hearings* and on *review* before courts and Review Boards.

Sections. 672.5(2) and (6) envisage a *public hearing* conducted in as *informal* a manner as is appropriate in the circumstances. Under s. 672.5(6), the court or Review Board may order that some or all members of the public be excluded from all or part of the hearing where it considers it to be in D's best interest and not contrary to the public interest to do so.

D has the right to be *present* during the entire hearing under s. 672.5(9), subject to the authority of the court or chairperson of the Board under s. 672.5(10) to *permit* D to be absent or *cause* D *to be removed* and barred from re-entry for the whole or any part of the hearing. Under s. 672.5(7), D also has the right to be represented by counsel. Where D is unrepresented, the court or Board must assign counsel where D has been found unfit or, in any case, where the interests of justice so require. Where D is denied legal aid for counsel so assigned, the Attorney General will pay counsel's fees to the extent that D is unable to do so and, where counsel and the Attorney General cannot agree on cunsel's fees or disbursements, either may apply to the registrar of the court to tax the fees.

The *parties* to the hearing, in addition to D, are determined by ss. 672.5(3) and (4). *On application*, the court or Board *must* designate as a party the Attorney General of the province where the disposition is to be made and, in the case of inter-provincial transfers, the Attorney General from the province from which D has been transferred. Under s. 672.5(4), the court or Board, if of the opinion that it is just to do so, *may* designate as a party *any person* who has a *substantial interest in protecting D's interest*. Under s. 672.5(5), *notice* must be given to all parties, as well the Attorney General (*semble* even where *not* a party) within the time and in the manner prescribed or fixed by the applicable rules. Under s. 672.5(7), each party has the right to be represented by counsel, but there is no authority in s. 672.5(8) or otherwise to appoint counsel for a party other than D.

Section 672.5(11) which describes the rights of the parties at the hearing. Each may adduce evidence, call witnesses and cross-examine witnesses called by any other party and, on application, cross-examine the author of any written assessment report. No party has the right to compel the attendance of any witness, but may ask the court or chairperson to do so.

Section 672.5(13) permits the court or Review Board, provided D consents, to allow D to appear by closed-circuit television or similar means that allow simultaneous oral and visual communication.

Case Law

Blackman v. British Columbia (Review Board) (1995), 95 C.C.C. (3d) 412 (B.C. C.A.) — Section 672.5(6) does *not* contravene *Charter* ss. 7 or 15(1).

Related Provisions: Disposition hearings may be held before a court under s. 672.45, or the Review Board under s. 672.47 after mental disorder verdict. Where the court makes *no* disposition under s. 672.45, the Board is required to do so under s. 672.47. The status quo is maintained by s. 672.46 pending the Board hearing.

Other related provisions are discussed in the corresponding note to s. 672.45.

672.51 (1) Definition of "disposition information" — In this section, "disposition information" means all or part of an assessment report submitted to the court or Review Board and any other written information before the court or Review Board about the accused that is relevant to making a disposition.

(2) Disposition information to be made available to parties — Subject to this section, all disposition information shall be made available for inspection by, and the court or Review Board shall provide a copy of it to, each party and any counsel representing the accused.

(3) Exception where disclosure dangerous to any person — The court or Review Board shall withhold some or all of the disposition information from an accused where it is satisfied, on the basis of that information and the evidence or report of the medical practitioner responsible for the assessment or treatment of the accused, that disclosure of the information would be likely to endanger the life or safety of another person or would seriously impair the treatment or recovery of the accused.

(4) Idem — Notwithstanding subsection (3), the court or Review Board may release some or all of the disposition information to an accused where the interests of justice make disclosure essential in its opinion.

(5) Exception where disclosure unnecessary or prejudicial — The court or Review Board shall withold disposition information from a party other than the accused or an Attorney General, where disclosure to that party, in the opinion of the court or Review Board, is not necessary to the proceeding and may be prejudicial to the accused.

(6) Exclusion of certain persons from hearing — A court or Review Board that withholds disposition information from the accused or any other party pursuant to subsection (3) or (5) shall exclude the accused or the other party, as the case may be, from the hearing during

(a) the oral presentation of that disposition information; or

(b) the questioning by the court or Review Board or the cross-examination of any person concerning that disposition information.

(7) Prohibition of disclosure in certain cases — No disposition information shall be made available for inspection or disclosed to any person who is not a party to the proceedings

(a) where the disposition information has been withheld from the accused or any other party pursuant to subsection (3) or (5); or

(b) where the court or Review Board is of the opinion that disclosure of the disposition information would be seriously prejudicial to the accused and that, in the circumstances, protection of the accused takes precedence over the public interest in disclosure.

(8) Idem — No part of the record of the proceedings in respect of which the accused was excluded pursuant to subparagraph 672.5(10)(*b*)(ii) or (iii) shall be made available for inspection to the accused or to any person who is not a party to the proceedings.

(9) Information to be made available to specified persons — Notwithstanding subsections (7) and (8), the court or Review Board may make any disposition information, or a copy of it, available on request to any person or member of a class of persons

(a) that has a valid interest in the information for research or statistical purposes, where the court or Review Board is satisfied that disclosure is in the public interest;

(b) that has a valid interest in the information for the purposes of the proper administration of justice; or

(c) that the accused requests or authorizes in writing to inspect it, where the court or Review Board is satisfied that the person will not disclose or give to the accused a copy of any disposition information withheld from the accused pursuant to subsection (3), or of any part of the record of proceedings referred to in subsection (8), or that the reasons for withholding that information from the accused no longer exist.

(10) Disclosure for research or statistical purposes — A person to whom the court or Review Board makes disposition information available under paragraph (9)(*a*) may disclose it for research or statistical purposes, but not in any form or manner that could reasonably be expected to identify any person to whom it relates.

(11) Prohibition on publication — No person shall publish in any newspaper within the meaning of section 297 or broadcast

(a) any disposition information that is prohibited from being disclosed pursuant to subsection (7); or

(b) any part of the record of the proceedings in respect of which the accused was excluded pursuant to subparagraph 672.5(10)(*b*)(ii) or (iii).

(12) Powers of courts not limited — Except as otherwise provided in this section, nothing in this section limits the powers that a court may exercise apart from this section.

1991, c. 43, s. 4; 1997, c. 18, s. 85.

Commentary: This section, without analogue under the old scheme, governs *disclosure* of "disposition information" as defined in its s. 672.51(1).

"Disposition information" comprises all or part of an *assessment report*, as well any other *written* information before the court or Review Board about D that is *relevant* to making a disposition. In general, all disposition information must be made available for inspection by and copies provided to each party and counsel for D.

Under ss. 672.51(3) and (4), some or all disposition information may be *withheld* from D, but only where the court or Board is satisfied, on the basis of the information *and* the evidence or report of the medical practitioner responsible for D's assessment or treatment that disclosure:

i. would be *likely to endanger* the life or safety of another person; or,

ii. would *seriously impair* the treatment or recovery of D.

Under s. 672.51(4), *disclosure* may nonetheless be made to D in whole or in part, where the court or Board concludes that it is essential in the interests of justice. Section 672.51(5) authorizes the court or Review Board to *withhold disclosure* of disposition information from a party other than D or the Attorney General where the court or Board is of the opinion that disclosure to the party is *not* necessary to the proceeding and may be prejudicial to D. To ensure that the disposition information withheld from disclosure under s. 672.51(3) or (5) does not come to the attention of D or the other party, s. 672.51(6) requires exclusion of D or the party from the hearing during disclosure of the information, and s. 672.51(8) bars disclosure to D of the hearing record to an equivalent extent.

Sections 672.51(7) to (11) govern *disclosure and publication* of disposition information to *persons not parties* to the proceedings. In general, where disclosure to D or another party has been withheld under s. 672.51(3) or (5), as well under s. 672.51(8) during exclusion from the hearing, disclosure to other non-parties is barred under s. 672.51(7)(a), as it is where s. 672.51(7)(b) obtains. It may nonetheless be made available under s. 672.51(9) or (10) for research or statistical purposes. The *prohibition on publication* in s. 672.51(11) is attracted by a s. 672.51(7) non-disclosure or a s. 672.5(10)(b)(ii) or (iii) exclusion order. By s. 672.51(12), the authority of a *court* apart from the section remains unimpaired.

Related Provisions: Section 672.2 authorizes the preparation and distribution of an *assessment report* on the mental condition of D. The general rule which bars admissibility of "protected statements" contained in the report, as well references thereto, in any proceedings where production of evidence may be compelled, does *not* apply to disposition hearings because of the exception of s. 672.21(3)(b).

Section 672.52 requires a record to be maintained of the disposition hearing and s. 672.5 describes the procedure to be followed on the hearing.

Other related provisions are discussed in the corresponding note to s. 672.45.

672.52 (1) Record of proceedings — The court or Review Board shall cause a record of the proceedings of its disposition hearings to be kept, and include in the record any assessment report submitted.

(2) Transmittal of transcript to Review Board — Where a court makes a disposition, it shall send without delay a transcript of the disposition hearing, any document or information relating thereto in the possession of the court, and all exhibits filed with the court or copies of those exhibits, to the Review Board that has jurisdiction in respect of the matter.

(3) Reasons for disposition and copies to be provided — The court or Review Board shall state its reasons for making a disposition in the record of the proceedings, and shall provide every party with a copy of the disposition and those reasons.

1991, c. 43, s. 4.

Commentary: This section requires that a *record* be kept of the proceedings of disposition hearings, including the reasons for making a disposition, and ensures its transmittal to the appropriate Review Board.

Section 672.52(1) that requires that a record be kept of the proceedings of disposition hearings. The record must include any *assessment report* and, by s. 672.52(3), the *reasons* for disposition. The disposition and reasons must be furnished to each party. These provisions would seem essential in consequence of the rights of appeal afforded by s. 672.72.

Section 672.52(2) is applicable where the disposition is made by a *court*. The transcript of proceedings, any documents or information relating thereto in the court's possession and all exhibits filed or copies thereof are to be forwarded to the relevant Review Board, *semble*, to facilitate its review of the court's disposition.

Related Provisions: Section 540 governs the manner in which evidence is taken at preliminary inquiry. The section also applies to non-jury (ss. 557, 572) and jury (s. 646) trials. It is *not* expressly incorporated into Part XX.1, but could easily be applied to complete the necessary record.

Other related provisions are discussed in the corresponding note to s. 672.45.

672.53 Proceedings not invalid — **Any procedural irregularity in relation to a disposition hearing does not affect the validity of the hearing unless it causes the accused substantial prejudice.**

1992, c. 43, s. 4.

Commentary: This new provision ensures that *procedural irregularities* in the conduct of the disposition hearing do *not* affect its validity, absent substantial prejudice to D.

Related Provisions: A similar provision appears in s. 686(1)(b)(iv) applicable in indictable appeals and incorporated by reference in summary conviction appeals under s. 813 by s. 822(1).

Other related provisions are discussed in the corresponding note to s. 672.45.

Dispositions by a Court or Review Board

Terms of Dispositions

672.54 Dispositions that may be made — Where a court or Review Board makes a disposition pursuant to subsection 672.45(2) or section 672.47, it shall, taking into consideration the need to protect the public from dangerous persons, the mental condition of the accused, the reintegration of the accused into society and the other needs of the accused, make one of the following dispositions that is the least onerous and least restrictive to the accused:

    (a) where a verdict of not criminally responsible on account of mental disorder has been rendered in respect of the accused and, in the opinion of the court or Review Board, the accused is not a significant threat to the safety of the public, by order, direct that the accused be discharged absolutely;

    (b) by order, direct that the accused be discharged subject to such conditions as the court or Review Board considers appropriate; or

    (c) by order, direct that the accused be detained in custody in a hospital, subject to such conditions as the court or Review Board considers appropriate.

1991, c. 43, s. 4.

Commentary: Sections 672.54–672.63 designate the types of *dispositions* which may be made by courts and Review Boards in disposition hearings held following mental disorder verdicts.

Section 672.54 enumerates the *factors* to be considered by the court or Review Board in determining which of three designated dispositions is to be made following a mental disorder verdict. The factors to be considered are:

i.   the *need* to *protect* the public from dangerous persons;

ii.   D's *mental* condition;

iii. D's *re-integration* into society; and,

iv.   D's other *needs*.

The disposition made must be the least onerous *and* least intrusive to D of:

i.   an *absolute discharge*, where D has been found not criminally responsible on account of mental disorder and the disposition authority is of opinion that D is *not* a significant threat to the public;

ii.   a *conditional discharge*; or,

iii. a *hospital detention order*, with such conditions as the court or Board considers appropriate.

Case Law

General Principles

Chambers v. British Columbia (Attorney General) (1997), 116 C.C.C. (3d) 406 (B.C. C.A.) — "Significant threat" refers to criminal conduct.

Winko v. British Columbia (Forensic Psychiatric Institute) (1996), 112 C.C.C. (3d) 31 (B.C. C.A.) — Proceedings before a review board are inquisitorial, *not* adversarial. *No* onus is imposed upon either party.

Davidson v. British Columbia (Attorney General) (1993), 87 C.C.C. (3d) 269 (B.C. C.A.) — Section 672.54 provides, in effect, that a review board must discharge absolutely D, who has been found not criminally responsible on account of mental disorder, if in the opinion of the board, D is *not a significant* threat to the safety of the public. Otherwise, the board is to direct that D be discharged subject to conditions, or detained in a hospital subject to conditions.

Davidson v. British Columbia (Attorney General) (1993), 87 C.C.C. (3d) 269 (B.C. C.A.) — Proceedings before the board are *not* adversarial nor penal in purpose or effect. The board's task is to balance the protection of society as against D's right to liberty unless deprived of it in accordance with the principles of fundamental justice. It must determine the likelihood of something happening in the future. There is no burden on P or the hospital to prove beyond a *reasonable doubt* that D is a significant threat to the public.

Orlowski v. British Columbia (Attorney General) (1992), 75 C.C.C. (3d) 138 (B.C. C.A.) — By s. 672.54, a review board must consider the listed factors and make the one of three dispositions which is the least onerous and restrictive to D. The board is to discharge D absolutely under s. 672.54(a) *only* where it is of opinion that D is *not a significant* threat to the safety of the public. If the board is *not* of such opinion, it need *not* order an absolute discharge.

Orlowski v. British Columbia (Attorney General) (1992), 75 C.C.C. (3d) 138 (B.C. C.A.) — The board, except in cases where an adverse finding under s. 672.54(a) can be necessarily inferred from the reasons for disposition, ought make an express finding whether it is of opinion that D is *not* a significant threat. Such a finding is necessary both on account of the structure of s. 672.54 and to facilitate appellate review.

Orlowski v. British Columbia (Attorney General) (1992), 75 C.C.C. (3d) 138 (B.C. C.A.) — "Threat" has a relative connotation. Where a board is concerned that D, with an appropriate history, is *not* presently and will *not* become a significant threat upon continuation of prescribed medication, but is also of opinion that D *may* be a significant threat upon failure to take medication, the board does *not* have an opinion that D is *not* a significant threat. An express finding should be made whether the board is of opinion that D is *not* a significant threat.

Orlowski v. British Columbia (Attorney General) (1992), 75 C.C.C. (3d) 138 (B.C. C.A.) — There is a distinction between a *threat* to the public safety and a "significant threat". D's right to an absolute discharge cannot be foreclosed simply because he/she may be a threat to public safety.

Peckham v. Ontario (Attorney General) (1994), 93 C.C.C. (3d) 443 (Ont. C.A.); leave to appeal refused (1995), 94 C.C.C. (3d) vi (S.C.C.) — In considering the "mental condition" of D under s. 672.54, the Board must consider D's mental condition at the time of the hearing. "Mental condition" in s. 672.54 is *not* restricted to a determination whether D continues to suffer from the "mental disorder" which led to the finding of unfit/not criminally responsible.

Charter Considerations

Winko v. British Columbia (Forensic Psychiatric Institute) (1996), 112 C.C.C. (3d) 31 (B.C. C.A.) — Section 672.54 does *not* contravene *Charter*, ss. 7, 9, 12 or 15.

R. v. LePage (1997), 119 C.C.C. (3d) 193 (Ont. C.A.) — Section 672.54 and related provisions dealing with disposition orders after a finding of N.C.R. do *not* offend *Charter* s. 15(1).

Related Provisions: "Hospital" is defined in s. 672.1, as are"court", "disposition" and "Review Board".

Dispositions may be made after mental disorder verdict by a court under s. 672.45(2), or the Review Board under s. 672.47. Section 672.55 enacts a general rule that a disposition must *not* direct *treatment* unless D consents, but s. 672.58 permits a *treatment disposition* where D has been found unfit and the court has not made a disposition under ss. 672.45(2) and 672.54. The *consent* of the treatment facility or person is required under s. 672.62 and the order may only be made upon compliance with ss. 672.59 and 672.6. It must *not* include the performance of any treatment that is prohibited by s. 672.61. Under s. 672.75, the filing of a notice of appeal suspends the application of a disposition made under s. 672.54(a) or 672.58.

Where the disposition made is a *conditional discharge* under s. 672.54(b) or *detention* in a *hospital* under s. 672.54(c), the Board may delegate its authority to vary restrictions on D's liberty to the person in charge of the hospital authority. The effective date and term of a disposition is governed by s. 672.63 and the "capping" provisions of s. 672.64. Where D is found a DMDA, on application under s. 672.65, the cap may be increased to life. Dispositions for dual status offenders are governed by ss. 672.67 to 672.71. *Please note: Sections 672.64 and 672.54 are not yet in force.*

The authority of the Review Board to *review* dispositions is provided for and governed by ss. 672.81 to 672.85. Interprovincial transfers for defined purposes are authorized by ss. 672.86 to 672.89.

Any party may *appeal* to the court of appeal against the disposition under s. 672.72(1). The conduct of appeals and their determination is provided for in ss. 672.72(2), (3) and 672.73 to 672.78.

672.55 (1) Treatment not a condition — No disposition made under section 672.54 shall direct that any psychiatric or other treatment of the accused be carried out or that the accused submit to such treatment except that the disposition may include a condition regarding psychiatric or other treatment where the accused has consented to the condition and the court or Review Board considers the condition to be reasonable and necessary in the interests of the accused.

(2) Effective period of disposition — No disposition made under paragraph 672.54(c) by a court shall continue in force for more than ninety days after the day that it is made.

1991, c. 43, s. 4; 1997, c. 18, s. 86.

Commentary: This new provision limits the *terms* and *duration* of a s. 672.54 disposition.

By s. 672.55(1), no s. 672.54 disposition may direct that D receive or submit to any psychiatric or other treatment unless D consents and the court or Review Board considers it reasonable and necessary in the interests of D. Under s. 672.55(2), hospital detention orders under s. 672.54(c) must *not* continue in force for more than ninety days after being made.

Related Provisions: A court may make a treatment disposition under s. 672.58, in accordance with the criteria and based upon the evidence described in s. 672.59 and upon notice to D under s. 672.6. The disposition must *not* include treatment prohibited under s. 672.61, and requires consent of the person in charge of the treatment facility or treatment, as the case may be, under s. 672.62.

Under s. 747.1, not yet in force, a sentencing court may order D to be detained in a treatment facility as the initial part of a sentence of imprisonment in accordance with ss. 742.2 to 747.8, not yet in force.

Other related provisions are discussed in the corresponding note to s. 672.54.

672.56 (1) Delegated authority to vary restrictions on liberty of accused — A Review Board that makes a disposition in respect of an accused under paragraph 672.54(*b*) or (*c*) may delegate to the person in charge of the hospital authority to direct that the restrictions on the liberty of the accused be increased or decreased within any limits and subject to any conditions set out in that disposition, and any direction so made is deemed for the purposes of this Act to be a disposition made by the Review Board.

(2) Notice to accused and Review Board of increase in restrictions — A person who increases the restrictions on the liberty of the accused significantly pursuant to authority delegated to the person by a Review Board shall

(a) make a record of the increased restrictions on the file of the accused; and

(b) give notice of the increase as soon as is practicable to the accused and, if the increased restrictions remain in force for a period exceeding seven days, to the Review Board.

1991, c. 43, s. 4.

Commentary: This new provision authorizes a Review Board to *delegate authority* to *vary restrictions* on D's liberty imposed in certain dispositions, as well to ensure that any increased restrictions are recorded and notice given to D and the Board.

Where the Review Board has ordered D discharged conditionally or has made a custodial hospital order with conditions, s. 672.56(1) empowers the Board to delegate its authority to vary (increase or decrease) the restrictions on D's liberty, within defined limits or conditions, to the person in charge of the hospital authority. Any direction is deemed a disposition of the Board.

Where there is a *significant increase* in the *restrictions* on D's liberty, s. 672.56(2) requires the delegated authority to *record* the restrictions on D's file and give *notice* thereof to D, as soon as practicable. Where the increased restrictions remain in force for a period exceeding seven days, the Board must also be notified.

Case Law

R. v. Pinet (1995), 40 C.R. (4th) 113, 100 C.C.C. (3d) 343 (Ont. C.A.) — A delegation of authority to transfer to a facility of a different security category is within s. 672.56(2) .

Related Provisions: Dispositions made by the Board, as is the effect of a variation made by the hospital authority under s. 672.56(1), may be reviewed by the Board under s. 672.82 and, *semble*, are subject to appeal under s. 672.72.

Other related provisions are described in the corresponding note to s. 672.54.

672.57 Warrant of committal — Where the court or Review Board makes a disposition under paragraph 672.54(*c*), it shall issue a warrant of committal of the accused, which may be in Form 49.

1991, c. 43, s. 4.

Commentary: The section requires a court or Review Board which makes a custodial hospital order under s. 672.54(c) to issue a *warrant* for D's committal which may be in Form 49.

Related Provisions: The general form for a warrant for committal is Form 8. Forms 20–27 are warrants of committal applicable in particular circumstances.

Other related provisions are discussed in the corresponding note to s. 672.54.

672.58 Treatment disposition — Where a verdict of unfit to stand trial is rendered and the court has not made a disposition under section 672.54 in respect of an accused, the court may, on application by the prosecutor, by order, direct that treatment of the accused be carried out for a specified period not exceeding sixty days, subject to such conditions as the court considers appropriate and, where the accused is not detained in

custody, direct that the accused submit to that treatment by the person or at the hospital specified.

1991, c. 43, s. 4.

Regulation: The following regulation prescribes the time within which and the manner in which a prosecutor is to notify an accused of an application to a court for an order directing treatment of the accused:

Regulations Prescribing the Time Within which and the Manner in which a Prosecutor is to Notify an Accused of an Application to a Court for an Order Directing Treatment of the Accused — SOR/92-665

Short Title

1. These Regulations may be cited as the *Notice of Application for Treatment Regulations*.

Interpretation

2. In these Regulations, Act means the *Criminal Code*.

Notice of Application for Treatment of an Accused

3. A prosecutor who files with the court an application for an order directing the treatment of an accused pursuant to section 672.58 of the Act shall notify the accused of the application forthwith by serving a copy of the application personally on the accused and on the accused's counsel.

Commentary: This section, without prior precedent, authorizes a *court* to make a *treatment order* in specified circumstances.

A treatment order may be made where D has been found *unfit* and the *court* makes *no disposition* under s. 672.54. The application must be initiated by P. The order must be for a period specified, *not* to exceed 60 days, and may be subject to such conditions as the court considers appropriate. Where D is out of custody, the order may direct that D submit to the specified treatment by a named person or at a specified hospital.

Related Provisions: A treatment disposition under s. 672.58 may only be made in accordance with the criteria and based upon the evidence described in s. 672.59. The disposition must *not* include any treatment prohibited under s. 672.61. The consent of the treatment facility or practitioner is required under s. 672.62. Notice of the application must be given by P to D under s. 672.6. D must be notified in writing and as soon as practicable of P's application.

Under s. 672.75, the filing of a notice of appeal against a s. 672.58 treatment disposition suspends its application pending determination of the appeal. On application by any party, however, a judge of the court of appeal, under s. 676(2)(a), may direct that the disposition be carried out pending the determination of the appeal.

Section 747.1, not yet in force permits a sentencing court to order D detained in a treatment facility as the initial part of a sentence of imprisonment in accordance with ss. 747.2 to 747.8.

Other related provisions are discussed in the corresponding note to s. 672.54.

672.59 (1) Criteria for disposition — No disposition may be made under section 672.58 unless the court is satisfied, on the basis of the testimony of a medical practitioner, that a specific treatment should be administered to the accused for the purpose of making the accused fit to stand trial.

(2) Evidence required — The testimony required by the court for the purposes of subsection (1) shall include a statement that the medical practitioner has made an assessment of the accused and is of the opinion, based on the grounds specified, that

(a) the accused, at the time of the assessment, was unfit to stand trial;

(b) the psychiatric treatment and any other related medical treatment specified by the medical practitioner will likely make the accused fit to stand trial within a period not exceeding sixty days and that without that treatment the accused is likely to remain unfit to stand trial;

(c) the risk of harm to the accused from the psychiatric and other related medical treatment specified is not disproportionate to the benefit anticipated to be derived from it; and

(d) the psychiatric and other related medical treatment specified is the least restrictive and least intrusive treatment that could, in the circumstances, be specified for the purpose referred to in subsection (1), considering the opinions referred to in paragraphs (b) and (c).

1991, c. 43, s. 4.

Commentary: This section sets out the *criteria* to be met and *evidence* to be given before a court may make a s. 672.58 *treatment disposition* in respect of an unfit accused. The object of the order is to render D fit to stand trial.

The conjoint operation of ss. 672.59(1) and (2) requires that the evidentiary basis of the order be the *testimony* of a *medical practitioner*. The practitioner must state:

i.   that a *specific treatment* should be administered to D *to render D fit* to stand trial;

ii. that the practitioner has *made an assessment* of D; and,

iii. that, on grounds specified, the practitioner holds the opinions described in s. 672.59(2)(a)–(d).

The court must be satisfied, on the basis of such testimony, that a specific treatment should be administered to render D fit to stand trial before a s. 672.58 order may be made.

Related Provisions: "Assessment" and "medical practitioner" are defined in s. 672.1.

Other related provisions are discussed in the corresponding note to ss. 672.54 and 672.58.

672.6 (1) Notice required — The court shall not make a disposition under section 672.58 unless the prosecutor notifies the accused, in writing and as soon as practicable, of the application.

(2) Challenge by accused — On receiving the notice referred to in subsection (1), the accused may challenge the application and adduce evidence for that purpose.

1991, c. 43, s. 4; 1997, c. 18, s. 87.

Commentary: D must be notified in writing and as soon as practicable of P's s. 672.58 application, and be permitted to contest it by the introduction of evidence.

Related Provisions: Related provisions are described in the corresponding note to s. 672.54.

672.61 (1) Exception — The court shall not direct, and no disposition made under section 672.58 shall include, the performance of psychosurgery or electro-convulsive therapy or any other prohibited treatment that is prescribed.

(2) Definitions — In this section,

"electro-convulsive therapy" means a procedure for the treatment of certain mental disorders that induces, by electrical stimulation of the brain, a series of generalized convulsions;

"psychosurgery" means any procedure that by direct or indirect access to the brain removes, destroys or interrupts the continuity of histologically normal brain tissue, or inserts indwelling electrodes for pulsed electrical stimulation for the purpose of altering behaviour or treating psychiatric illness, but does not include neurological procedures

used to diagnose or treat intractable physical pain, organic brain conditions, or epilepsy, where any of those conditions is clearly demonstrable.

1991, c. 43, s. 4.

Commentary: Under this new provision, a court is *prohibited* from directing or including in a s. 672.58 disposition the performance of psychosurgery or electro-convulsive therapy, as defined in s. 672.61(2), or any other form of prohibited treatment.

Related Provisions: It would appear that other forms of prohibited treatment may be included in regulations, thereby obviating the need to amend the *Code* for such purpose.

Other related provisions are discussed in the corresponding note to s. 672.54.

672.62 (1) Consent of hospital required for treatment — No court shall make a disposition under section 672.58 without the consent of

(a) the person in charge of the hospital where the accused is to be treated; or

(b) the person to whom responsibility for the treatment of the accused is assigned by the court.

(2) Consent of accused not required for treatment — The court may direct that treatment of an accused be carried out pursuant to a disposition made under section 672.58 without the consent of the accused or a person who, according to the laws of the province where the disposition is made, is authorized to consent for the accused.

1991, c. 43, s. 4.

Commentary: This section requires *consent* of the hospital or individual designated to treat D under a s. 672.58 order, but permits the court to direct that treatment be carried out without D's consent.

Under s. 672.62(1), it would appear that, *absent* consent of the person in charge of the hospital, or the individual to whom responsibility for D's treatment is assigned, the court is barred from making a s. 672.58 treatment order. It is made plain by s. 672.62(2), however, that the consent of D or his or her authorized representative is *not* a condition precedent to the making of a s. 672.58 order: the court may *direct* D's treatment under the order *without* such consent.

Related Provisions: No disposition under s. 672.58 may include the performance of treatment prohibited by s. 672.61. The effective date of a disposition is determined by s. 672.63.

Other related provisions are discussed in the corresponding note to s. 672.54.

672.63 Effective date of disposition — A disposition shall come into force on the day that it is made or on any later day that the court or Review Board specifies in it, and shall remain in force until the date of expiration that the disposition specifies or until the Review Board holds a hearing pursuant to section 672.47 or 672.81.

1991, c. 43, s. 4.

Commentary: The section sets out the *effective date* of a *disposition* made by a court or Review Board.

A disposition comes into force on the date made or any later date specified in the order. It remains in force until its specified expiration date, or until the Board holds a s. 672.47 or 672.81 hearing.

Related Provisions: Under s. 672.75, the filing of a notice of appeal against the disposition made under s. 672.54(a) or 672.58 suspends the application of the disposition pending determination of the appeal, unless otherwise ordered by a judge of a court of appeal under s. 672.6.

Other related provisions are described in the corresponding note to s. 672.54.

Capping of Dispositions

672.64 (1) Definitions — In this section, sections 672.65, 672.79 and 672.8,

"designated offence" means an offence included in the schedule to this Part, an offence under the *National Defence Act* referred to in subsection (2), or any conspiracy or attempt to commit, being an accessory after the fact in relation to, or any counselling in relation to, such an offence;

"cap" means the maximum period during which an accused is subject to one or more dispositions in respect of an offence, beginning at the time when the verdict is rendered.

(2) Additional designated offences under the national defence act — An offence contrary to any of the following sections of the *National Defence Act* is a designated offence if it is committed in the circumstances described:

(a) section 73 (offences by commanders when in action), where the accused person acted from cowardice;

(b) section 74 (offences by any person in presence of enemy), 75 (offences related to security) or 76 (offences related to prisoners of war), where the accused person acted otherwise than traitorously;

(c) section 77 (offences related to operations), where the accused person committed the offence on active service;

(d) section 107 (wrongful acts in relation to aircraft or aircraft material) or 127 (injurious or destructive handling of dangerous substances), where the accused person acted wilfully;

(e) section 130 (service trial of civil offences), where the civil offence is included in the schedule to this Part; and

(f) section 132 (offences under law applicable outside Canada), where a court martial determines that the offence is substantially similar to an offence included in the schedule to this Part.

(3) Cap for various offences — Where a verdict of not criminally responsible on account of mental disorder or unfit to stand trial is rendered in respect of an accused, the cap is

(a) life, where the offence is

(i) high treason under subsection 47(1) or first or second degree murder under section 229,

(ii) an offence under section 73 (offences by commanders when in action), section 74 (offences by any person in presence of enemy), section 75 (offences related to security) or section 76 (offences related to prisoners of war) of the *National Defence Act*, if the accused person acted traitorously, or first or second degree murder punishable under section 130 of that Act,

(iii) any other offence under any Act of Parliament for which a minimum punishment of imprisonment for life is provided by law;

(b) ten years, or the maximum period during which the accused is liable to imprisonment in respect of the offence, whichever is shorter, where the offence is a designated offence that is prosecuted by indictment; or

(c) two years, or the maximum period during which the accused is liable to imprisonment in respect of the offence, whichever is shorter, where the offence is an offence under this Act or any other Act of Parliament, other than an offence referred to in paragraph (*a*) or (*b*).

(4) Longest cap applies where two or more offences — Subject to subsection (5), where an accused is subject to a verdict in relation to two or more offences, even if they arise from the same transaction, the offence with the longest maximum period of imprisonment as a punishment shall be used to determine the cap that applies to the accused in respect of all the offences.

(5) Offence committed while subject to previous disposition — Where a verdict of not criminally responsible on account of mental disorder or unfit to stand trial is rendered in respect of an accused who is subject to a disposition other than an absolute discharge in respect of a previous offence, the court may order that any disposition that it makes in respect of the offence be consecutive to the previous disposition, even if the duration of all the dispositions exceeds the cap for the offences determined pursuant to subsections (3) and (4).

1991, c. 43, s. 4. Not in force at date of publication.

Commentary: The concept of "capping", is introduced and governed by this section. It appears based upon the principle that D's detention under a mental disorder verdict should *not* exceed the maximum sentence which *could* be imposed upon conviction.

The exhaustive definitions of "designated offence" and "cap" in s. 672.64(1) apply not only to this section, but also to applications to have D declared a dangerous mentally disordered accused (DMDA) and appeals from dispositions made in such cases. A "designated offence" is:

i.   an offence listed in the Schedule to Part XX.1;

ii.   an offence under the *National Defence Act* (*NDA*) described in s. 672.64(2); or,

iii.   a conspiracy, attempt, accessory after the fact or counselling in relation to an offence in i or ii, *supra*.

The substance of the "cap" is determined by s. 672.64(3) and varies depending upon the category of designated offence. The cap for offences described in s. 672.64(3)(a), those which carry a minimum of life imprisonment, is *life*. Under s. 672.64(3)(b), the cap is the *lesser* of ten years or the maximum period of imprisonment upon conviction, where the designated offence is prosecuted by indictment. For any other designated offences, s. 672.64(3)(c) fixes the cap at the *lesser* of two years or the maximum period of imprisonment upon conviction.

Sections 672.64(4) and 672.64(5) should be read together. Under s. 672.64(4), the cap for an accused who is subject to a mental disorder verdict in relation to two or more offences is determined for *all* offences by reference to the offence which carries the longest maximum period of imprisonment, even if the offences arise from the same transaction. Section 672.64(5) governs the case where D is already subject to a disposition (other than an absolute discharge) when a further mental disorder verdict is rendered. The most recent disposition may be made consecutive to any existing disposition even if the combined period exceeds the cap which ss. 672.64(3) and 672.64(4) would otherwise permit.

Related Provisions: Under s. 672.65, P may apply to have D, found not criminally responsible on account of mental disorder in relation to a "serious personal injury offence", declared a DMDA. The application precedes any disposition made in the usual course in respect of the offence and, if successful, permits the court to increase the "cap" to a maximum of life. Sections 754 to 758 of Part XXIV "Dangerous Offenders" apply to the DMDA application under s. 672.66(1).

Under s. 672.79, an accused found to be a DMDA may appeal to the court of appeal against the increase in the "cap". Section 672.8 permits an appeal by the Attorney General against the dismissal of a DMDA application.

The Schedule to Part XX.1 appears after s. 672.95, *infra*.

Proposed Addition — 672.65

Dangerous Mentally Disordered Accused

672.65 (1) Definition of "serious personal injury offence" — In this section, "serious personal injury offence" means

(a) an offence or attempt to commit an offence mentioned in section 271 (sexual assault), 272 (sexual assault with a weapon, threats to a third party or causing bodily harm) or 273 (aggravated sexual assault); or

(b) any designated offence prosecuted by indictment involving

(i) the use or attempted use of violence against another person, or

(ii) conduct endangering or likely to endanger the life or safety of another person or inflicting or likely to inflict severe psychological damage on another person,

and for which the accused is liable to imprisonment for ten years or more.

(2) Application for a finding that accused is a dangerous mentally disordered accused — Where a verdict of not criminally responsible on account of mental disorder is rendered in respect of an accused, the prosecutor may, before any disposition is made, apply to the court that rendered the verdict or to a superior court of criminal jurisdiction for a finding that the accused is a dangerous mentally disordered accused.

(3) Grounds for finding — On an application made under this section, the court may find the accused to be a dangerous mentally disordered accused where it is satisfied that

(a) the offence that resulted in the verdict is a serious personal injury offence described in paragraph (1)(b), and the accused constitutes a threat to the life, safety, physical or mental well-being of other persons on the basis of evidence establishing

(i) a pattern of repetitive behaviour by the accused, of which the offence that resulted in the verdict is a part, that shows a failure to exercise behavioural restraint and a likelihood that the accused will cause death or injury to other persons or inflict severe psychological damage on other persons, through failure in the future to exercise restraint,

(ii) a pattern of persistent aggressive behaviour by the accused, of which the offence that resulted in the verdict is a part, or

(iii) any behaviour by the accused, associated with the offence that resulted in the verdict, that is of such a brutal nature as to compel the conclusion that the behaviour of the accused in future is unlikely to be inhibited by normal standards of behavioural restraint; or

(b) the offence that resulted in the verdict is a serious personal injury offence described in paragraph (1)(a), and the accused, by conduct in any sexual matter including the conduct in the commission of the offence that resulted in the verdict, has shown a failure to control sexual impulses and a likelihood that the accused will cause injury, pain or other harm to other persons through failure in the future to control such impulses.

(4) Court may increase duration of disposition — Where the court finds the accused to be a dangerous mentally disordered accused under this section, it may increase the cap in respect of the offence to a maximum of life.

1991, c. 43, s. 4. Not in force at date of publication.

Commentary: With apparent borrowing from Part XXIV "Dangerous Offenders", this and the following section permit P to institute proceedings to have D, found not criminally responsible on account of mental disorder, declared a *dangerous mentally disordered accused* (DMDA) and made subject to a disposition cap of life, rather than that otherwise applicable under s. 672.64.

The provisions of this section may only be invoked where D has first been found not criminally responsible on account of mental disorder in respect of a "serious personal injury offence", as defined in s. 672.65(1). Under s. 672.65(2), P must apply to the trial court or superior court of criminal jurisdiction *before any disposition is made* for a finding that D is a DMDA. D may only be so found where the court is satisfied that the requirements of s. 672.65(3)(a) or (b) have been met. Under s. 672.65(4), the making of either finding entitles the court to increase the disposition cap in respect of the offence to a maximum of life.

Related Provisions: "Designated offence" and "cap" are defined in s. 672.64(1) and the "caps" for various offences described in s. 672.64(3).

Section 672.66 incorporates the provisions of ss. 754 to 758 of Part XXIV "Dangerous Offenders" into DMDA applications taken under this section. The incorporated provisions deal with the hearing of the application (s. 754), the evidence which must or may be given (ss. 755, 757) and the presence of D on the hearing of the application (s. 758).

Other related provisions are described in the corresponding note to s. 672.54.

Proposed Addition — 672.66

672.66 (1) Sections 754 to 758 apply — Sections 754 to 758 apply, with such modifications as the circumstances require, to an application under section 672.65 as if it were made under Part XXIV and the accused were an offender.

(2) Transmittal of transcript to Review Board — Where a court makes a finding that the accused is a dangerous mentally disordered accused, it shall send without delay to the Review Board that has jurisdiction in respect of the matter a transcript of the hearing of the application, any document or information relating to it in the possession of the court, and all exhibits filed with the court or copies of them.

1991, c. 43, s. 4. Not in force at date of publication.

Commentary: The *procedure* on DMDA applications and *transmittal of* the *record* thereof to the appropriate Review Board are governed by this section.

The incorporation of ss. 754 to 758 by s. 672.66(1) ensures that the procedure followed on DMDA applications tracks that required in dangerous offender applications under Part XXIV. The incorporated provisions include the requirement that the Attorney General of the province *consent* to the application, and that proper *notice* thereof be furnished to D. *Evidence* of D's *character and repute* would appear admissible on the issue of whether D is or is not a DMDA, and the evidence of nominated psychiatrists receivable by the incorporation of ss. 755 and 757.

Where D is found to be a DMDA, s. 672.66(2) requires the court to send without delay to the Review Board:

i)   a *transcript* of the DMDA hearing;

ii) any *document or information* relating to the hearing in the possession of the court; and,

iii) all *exhibits* filed with the court and copies thereof.

Dual Status Offenders

672.67 (1) Where court imposes a sentence — Where a court imposes a sentence of imprisonment on an offender who is, or thereby becomes, a dual status offender, that sentence takes precedence over any prior custodial disposition, pending any placement decision by the Review Board.

(2) Custodial disposition by court — Where a court imposes a custodial disposition on an accused who is, or thereby becomes, a dual status offender, the disposition takes precedence over any prior sentence of imprisonment except a hospital order, as defined in section 747, pending any placement decision by the Review Board.

1991, c. 43, s. 4;1995, c. 22, s. 10.

Commentary: Sections 672.67 to 672.71 govern those accused who are simultaneously subject to sentences of imprisonment and s. 672.54(c) custodial disposition(s) following a mental disorder verdict.

Section 672.67 describes the order of *priority* as between sentences of imprisonment and custodial dispositions. Under s. 672.67(1), *a sentence of imprisonment* imposed on an offender who is or thereby becomes a "dual status offender" (DSO) takes precedence *until* a placement decision is made by the Review Board. Under s. 672.67(2), a *custodial disposition* imposed upon D who is or thereby becomes a DSO takes precedence over any prior sentence of imprisonment *except* a hospital order within s. 736.1, *until* a placement decision by the Board.

The effect of the section is to accord *priority* to the *most recent order* made pending determination of D's placement by the Review Board.

Related Provisions: "Disposition", "dual status offender" and "placement decision" are defined in s. 672.1, "hospital order" in s. 736.1, not yet in force.

Section 672.68(2) authorizes the Review Board to make a placement decision in respect of a DSO, upon application by the Minister or of its own motion. The decision is to be made upon consideration of the factors listed in s. 672.68(3) within the time prescribed by s. 672.68(3). Reviews of placement decisions by the Board are governed by s. 672.69.

Section 672.7 requires both the Minister and Board to notify each other of the intended discharge of a DSO. Section 672.1 ensures that time spent in detention by a DSO, pursuant to a placement decision or custodial disposition, counts to an equivalent extent as service of the term of imprisonment.

Under s. 672.72(1), any party may appeal to the court of appeal against a placement decision made by the Review Board. The appeals are heard and determined in accordance with ss. 672.72(2), (3) and 672.73 to 672.78.

672.68 (1) Definition of "minister" — In this section and in sections 672.69 and 672.7, "Minister" means the Solicitor General of Canada or the Minister responsible for correctional services of the province to which a dual status offender may be sent pursuant to a sentence of imprisonment.

(2) Placement decision by Review Board — On application by the Minister or of its own motion, where the Review Board is of the opinion that the place of custody of a dual status offender pursuant to a sentence or custodial disposition made by the court is inappropriate to meet the mental health needs of the offender or to safeguard the well-being of other persons, the Review Board shall, after giving the offender and the Minister reasonable notice, decide whether to place the offender in custody in a hospital or in a prison.

(3) **Idem** — In making a placement decision, the Review Board shall take into consideration

   (a) the need to protect the public from dangerous persons;

   (b) the treatment needs of the offender and the availability of suitable treatment resources to address those needs;

   (c) whether the offender would consent to or is a suitable candidate for treatment;

   (d) any submissions made to the Review Board by the offender or any other party to the proceedings and any assessment report submitted in writing to the Review Board; and

   (e) any other factors that the Review Board considers relevant.

(4) **Time for making placement decision** — The Review Board shall make its placement decision as soon as practicable but not later than thirty days after receiving an application from, or giving notice to, the Minister under subsection (2), unless the Review Board and the Minister agree to a longer period not exceeding sixty days.

(5) **Effects of placement decision** — Where the offender is detained in a prison pursuant to the placement decision of the Review Board, the Minister is responsible for the supervision and control of the offender.

                                                                        1991, c. 43, s. 4.

Commentary: This section describes when and on what basis the Review Board may make a *placement decision* in respect of a DSO and who shall supervise and control such persons.

The procedure authorized by the section may be invoked by application of the Minister, as defined in s. 672.68(1), or the Board of its own motion. Where the Review Board is of the opinion that the place of custody of a DSO, whether under sentence or a court ordered custodial disposition, is *inappropriate* to meet D's mental health needs or safeguard the well-being of others, the Board must decide, on reasonable notice to D and the Minister, whether custody should be in a hospital or a prison.

In making its placement decision within the time limits described in s. 672.68(4), which must *not* exceed sixty days from receipt of the application from or giving of notice to the Minister, the Board must consider the factors enumerated in s. 672.68(2). Where the Board decides that D should be detained in prison, the Minister becomes responsible for D's supervision and control.

Related Provisions: "Placement decision" is defined in s. 672.1.

The Board's review of placement decisions is governed by s. 672.69.

Other related provisions are discussed in the corresponding note to s. 672.67.

672.69 (1) **Minister and Review Board entitled to access** — The Minister and the Review Board are entitled to have access to any dual status offender in respect of whom a placement decision has been made, for the purpose of conducting a review of the sentence or disposition imposed.

(2) **Review of placement decisions** — The Review Board shall hold a hearing as soon as is practicable to review a placement decision, on application by the Minister or the dual status offender who is the subject of the decision, where the Review Board is satisfied that a significant change in circumstances requires it.

(3) **Idem** — The Review Board may of its own motion hold a hearing to review a placement decision after giving the Minister and the dual status offender who is subject to it reasonable notice.

(4) **Minister shall be a party** — The Minister shall be a party in any proceedings relating to the placement of a dual status offender.

                                                                        1991, c. 43, s. 4.

Commentary: This section authorizes a *review* of a *placement decision* relating to a DSO, provides *access* to the offender for such purpose and ensures timely *notice* is given to the parties.

Under s. 672.69(2), the review process may be initiated by the Minister or the DSO. The Board is *required* to hold a hearing *as soon as practicable* to review the placement decision, where it is satisfied that a significant change in circumstances requires it. Under s. 672.69(1), both the Board and Minister have access to the DSO for the purpose of conducting a review of the sentence or disposition. The Minister is a party to any proceedings related to the placement of a DSO.

Under s. 672.69(3), the Board may itself initiate a review hearing after reasonable notice to the Minister and DSO. The form of notice is not expressly stated.

Related Provisions: Related provisions are discussed in the corresponding note to s. 672.67.

672.7 (1) Notice of discharge — Where the Minister or the Review Board intends to discharge a dual status offender from custody, each shall give written notice to the other indicating the time, place and conditions of the discharge.

(2) Warrant of committal — A Review Board that makes a placement decision shall issue a warrant of committal of the accused, which may be in Form 50.

1991, c. 43, s. 4.

Commentary: Section 672.7(1) ensures that both correctional authorities and the Review Board are aware of the impending release of a DSO by requiring the Minister and Board to notify each other in writing of the *time, place* and *conditions* of discharge from custody of any DSO whom either intends to discharge.

Section 672.7(2) requires the Review Board to issue a warrant of committal in respect of each placement decision. The warrant may be in Form 50.

Related Provisions: The form of written notice is not prescribed by the section, but could be the subject of rules passed by the Board under s. 672.44 or regulations of the Governor-in-Council under s. 672.95.

Other related provisions are described in the corresponding note to s. 672.67.

672.71 (1) Detention to count as service of term — Each day of detention of a dual status offender pursuant to a placement decision or a custodial disposition shall be treated as a day of service of the term of imprisonment, and the accused shall be deemed, for all purposes, to be lawfully confined in a prison.

(2) Disposition takes precedence over probation orders — When a dual status offender is convicted or discharged on the conditions set out in a probation order made under section 730 in respect of an offence but is not sentenced to a term of imprisonment, the custodial disposition in respect of the accused comes into force and, notwithstanding subsection 732.2(1), takes precedence over any probation order made in respect of the offence.

1991, c. 43, s. 4; 1995, c. 22, s. 10.

Commentary: The provisions of this section resolve difficulties which arise where placement decisions, custodial dispositions and probation orders *overlap* in the case of a DSO.

Under s. 672.71(1), a DSO detained pursuant to a placement decision or custodial disposition receives an equivalent credit against his/her term of imprisonment, and is deemed, for all purposes, to be lawfully confined in a prison. Under s. 672.71(2), where a DSO receives a conditional discharge under s. 736 or is convicted but not sentenced to a term of imprisonment for an offence, the custodial disposition comes into force and, s. 738(1) notwithstanding, takes precedence over the probation order.

Related Provisions: It would appear that any elopement from hospital custody under a placement decision may attract liability under s. 144(b) or 145(1)(a).

Other related provisions are discussed in the corresponding note to s. 672.67.

Appeals

672.72 (1) Grounds for appeal — Any party may appeal against a disposition made by a court or a Review Board, or a placement decision made by a Review Board, to the court of appeal of the province where the disposition or placement decision was made on any ground of appeal that raises a question of law or fact alone or of mixed law and fact.

(2) Limitation period for appeal — An appellant shall give notice of an appeal against a disposition or placement decision in the manner directed by the applicable rules of the court within fifteen days after the day on which the appellant receives a copy of the placement decision or disposition and the reasons for it or within any further time that the court of appeal, or a judge of that court, may direct.

(3) Appeal to be heard expeditiously — The court of appeal shall hear an appeal against a disposition or placement decision in or out of the regular sessions of the court, as soon as practicable after the day on which the notice of appeal is given, within any period that may be fixed by the court of appeal, a judge of the court of appeal, or the rules of that court.

1991, c. 43, s. 4; 1997, c. 18, s. 88.

Commentary: Sections 672.72 to 672.8 authorize and regulate *appeals* to the provincial court of appeal *from dispositions and placement decisions* made by a court or Review Board.

This section confers *rights of appeal*, prescribes the time within which notice of appeal must be given and accords priority in hearing to appeals taken under this section.

Under s. 672.72(1), each party to the proceedings may appeal to the provincial court of appeal against a disposition made by a Review Board or court or a placement decision made by a Review Board. The appeal may be based upon *any ground* that raises a question of *law* or *fact* alone or of *mixed law and fact*. Leave to appeal is *not* required and the rights of appeal of each party are the same.

The *time* within which *notice of appeal* must be given in accordance with the applicable rules is within *fifteen days* after the day on which the appellant is provided with a copy of the placement decision or disposition and the reasons therefor. Under s. 672.72(2), the time for giving notice of appeal may be extended by the court of appeal or a judge thereof.

Hearing priority is governed by s. 672.72(3). Appeals under this section are to be heard *as soon as practicable* after notice of appeal is given within any time period, in or out of the court's regular sittings, that may be fixed by the court, a judge of appeal, or the rules of the court.

Related Provisions: "Disposition" and "placement decisions", as well as "court" and "Review Board" are defined in s. 672.1. The inclusion of a summary conviction court in the definition of "court" would appear to permit an appeal to the court of appeal in summary conviction proceedings.

In general, an appeal under s. 672.72 must be based upon the *transcript* of proceedings before the court or Board. Subsection 672.73(1), however, confers on the court of appeal the same powers to receive further evidence as the court has in indictable appeals under ss. 683(1) and (2). The record of the Review Board or court is transmitted to the court of appeal under s. 672.74 after notice of appeal has been given. The authority of the court of appeal to determine the appeal is governed by s. 672.78.

Under s. 672.75, the filing of a notice of appeal against a disposition made under s. 672.54(a) or 672.58 suspends the application of the disposition pending determination of the appeal, subject to the authority of the judge of appeal to order otherwise under s. 672.76. The effect of a suspension of a disposition is described in s. 672.77.

Appeals may also be taken by D and the Attorney General after DMDA proceedings have been taken. Section 672.79 describes D's rights of appeal from an increase in the "cap" imposed in DMDA proceedings and s. 672.8 does likewise for the Attorney General where the application has been dismissed. Each section also describes the authority of the court of appeal to determine the appeals taken and s. 672.8(3) incorporates the indictable appeal procedure in both instances.

The review of dispositions by the Review Board is governed by ss. 672.81 to 672.85.

672.73 (1) Appeal on the transcript — An appeal against a disposition by a court or Review Board or placement decision by a Review Board shall be based on a transcript of the proceedings and any other evidence that the court of appeal finds necessary to admit in the interests of justice.

(2) Additional evidence — For the purpose of admitting additional evidence under this section, subsections 683(1) and (2) apply, with such modifications as the circumstances require.

1991, c. 43, s. 4.

Commentary: This section governs the *form* of s. 672.72 *appeals*.

Under s. 672.73(1), appeals are to be based on the *transcript* of the proceedings in which the disposition or placement decision was made and *any other evidence* that the court of appeal finds necessary to admit *in the interests of justice*. By s. 672.73(2), the additional evidence is to be admitted according to ss. 683(1) and (2), the provisions applicable on indictable appeals.

Related Provisions: The statutory standard applied by s. 683(1) to the admission of further evidence is "the interests of justice", the same language used in s. 672.73(1). The authority is more restrictive than is applicable to appeals against sentence under s. 687.

Other related provisions are described in the corresponding note to s. 672.72.

672.74 (1) Notice of appeal to be given to court or Review Board — The clerk of the court of appeal, on receiving notice of an appeal against a disposition or placement decision, shall notify the court or Review Board that made the disposition.

(2) Transmission of records to court of appeal — On receipt of notification under subsection (1), the court or Review Board shall transmit to the court of appeal, before the time that the appeal is to be heard or within any time that the court of appeal or a judge of that court may direct,

(a) a copy of the disposition or placement decision;

(b) all exhibits filed with the court or Review Board or a copy of them; and

(c) all other material in its possession respecting the hearing.

(3) Record to be kept by court of appeal — The clerk of the court of appeal shall keep the material referred to in subsection (2) with the records of the court of appeal.

(4) Appellant to provide transcript of evidence — Unless it is contrary to an order of the court of appeal or any applicable rules of court, the appellant shall provide the court of appeal and the respondent with a transcript of any evidence taken before a court or Review Board by a stenographer or a sound recording apparatus, certified by the stenographer or in accordance with subsection 540(6), as the case may be.

(5) Saving — An appeal shall not be dismissed by the court of appeal by reason only that a person other than the appellant failed to comply with this section.

1991, c. 43, s. 4.

Commentary: The section governs *completion* and *transmittal* of the *record* to the court of appeal in appeals against disposition or placement decisions.

Under s. 672.74(1), the clerk of the court of appeal must notify the court or Review Board that made the disposition or placement decision that an appeal has been taken. The court or Review Board is required to transmit to the court of appeal, within a time specified, the record described in s. 672.74(2) which will then be kept by the clerk with the court of appeal records. By s. 672.74(4), the *appellant* must *provide* the court of appeal and respondent with a *transcript* of the proceedings under review.

Section 672.74(5) is a saving clause enacted to ensure that want of compliance by a person *other than* the appellant does not *per se* entitle the court of appeal to dismiss the appeal.

Related Provisions: Related provisions are discussed in the corresponding note to s. 672.72.

672.75 Automatic suspension of certain dispositions — The filing of a notice of appeal against a disposition made under paragraph 672.54(*a*) or section 672.58 suspends the application of the disposition pending the determination of the appeal.

1991, c. 43, s. 4.

Commentary: Under this section, the *filing* of a *notice of appeal* automatically *suspends* the application of an absolute discharge (s. 672.54(a)) and hospital treatment orders (s. 672.58) pending the determination of an appeal to the court of appeal.

Related Provisions: Under s. 672.76, a judge of the court of appeal may make an order directing that a disposition made under s. 672.54(a) or 672.58 be carried out. The effect of suspension of disposition is described in s. 672.77.

Under s. 261, an appellate court may stay the operation of a driving prohibition. Under s. 683(5), payment of certain monetary penalties may be suspended by the court of appeal until the appeal has been determined. The court may also revoke the suspension of payment under s. 683(6).

Other related provisions are discussed in the corresponding note to s. 672.72, *supra*.

672.76 (1) Application respecting dispositions under appeal — Any party who gives notice to each of the other parties, within the time and in the manner prescribed, may apply to a judge of the court of appeal for an order under this section respecting a disposition or placement decision that is under appeal.

(2) Discretionary powers respecting suspension of dispositions — On receipt of an application made pursuant to subsection (1) a judge of the court of appeal may, if satisfied that the mental condition of the accused justifies it,

(a) by order, direct that a disposition made under paragraph 672.54(*a*) or section 672.58 be carried out pending the determination of the appeal, notwithstanding section 672.75;

(b) by order, direct that the application of a placement decision or a disposition made under paragraph 672.54(*b*) or (*c*) be suspended pending the determination of the appeal;

(c) where the application of a disposition is suspended pursuant to section 672.75 or paragraph (*b*), make any other disposition in respect of the accused that is appropriate in the circumstances, other than a disposition under paragraph 672.54(*a*) or section 672.58, pending the determination of the appeal;

(d) where the application of a placement decision is suspended pursuant to an order made under paragraph (*b*), make any other placement decision that is appropriate in the circumstances, pending the determination of the appeal; and

(e) give any directions that the judge considers necessary for expediting the appeal.

(3) Copy of order to parties — A judge of the court of appeal who makes an order under this section shall send a copy of the order to each of the parties without delay.

1991, c. 43, s. 4.

Commentary: This section permits a *judge* of the *court of appeal* to make orders *suspending* or *enforcing dispositions* or *placement decisions* pending an appeal to the court of appeal.

Under s. 672.76(1), an *application* for an order under the section may be commenced by *any party* upon timely *notice* in the prescribed manner to all other parties. The subsection *requires* the filing of no further material.

The authority of a judge of the court of appeal to suspend or enforce dispositions or placement decisions only becomes engaged when the judge is *satisfied* that the mental condition of D justifies it. In such cases, under s. 672.76(2), the judge may:

i.   direct that the disposition (ss. 672.54(a) and 672.58) whose operation is automatically suspended pending appeal by s. 672.75 be *carried out*;

ii. direct that the application of a placement decision or disposition under s. 672.54(b), (c) be *suspended* and make *any other* placement decision or disposition pending appeal that is *appropriate, other than* a disposition under s. 672.54(a) or 672.58; and,

iii. give any *directions* considered necessary *to expedite* the appeal.

Under s. 672.76(3), the judge of appeal is to send a copy of the order to each party without delay.

Related Provisions: The effect of s. 672.75 is automatically to suspend the application of dispositions under ss. 672.54(a) and 672.58 upon filing of a notice of appeal. The effect of suspension of a disposition is described in s. 672.77.

Other related provisions are discussed in the corresponding note to ss. 672.72 and 672.75.

672.77 Effect of suspension of disposition — Where the application of a disposition or placement decision appealed from is suspended, a disposition, or in the absence of a disposition any order for the interim release or detention of the accused, that was in effect immediately before the disposition or placement decision appealed from took effect, shall be in force pending the determination of the appeal, subject to any disposition made under paragraph 672.76(2)(c).

1991, c. 43, s. 4.

Commentary: Under this section, the suspension of a disposition or placement decision pending appeal will revive the application of a previous disposition or, in its absence, an order for D's interim release or detention. The preceding disposition or order will remain in force pending the determination of D's appeal, subject to any disposition made by a judge of the court of appeal under s. 672.76(2)(c).

Related Provisions: Under s. 672.75, the filing of a notice of appeal against a s. 672.54(a) or 672.58 disposition suspends the application of the disposition pending determination of the appeal. Section 672.76 authorizes a judge of the court of appeal to direct that these dispositions be carried out notwithstanding s. 672.75, or that the application of others be suspended pending determination of an appeal.

Other related provisions are described in the corresponding note to s. 672.72 and s. 672.75.

672.78 (1) Powers of court of appeal — The court of appeal may allow an appeal against a disposition or placement decision and set aside an order made by the court or Review Board, where the court of appeal is of the opinion that

(a) it is unreasonable or cannot be supported by the evidence;

(b) it is based on a wrong decision on a question of law; or

(c) there was a miscarriage of justice.

(2) Idem — The court of appeal may dismiss an appeal against a disposition or placement decision where the court is of the opinion

(a) that paragraphs (1)(a), (b) and (c) do not apply; or

(b) that paragraph (1)(b) may apply, but the court finds that no substantial wrong or miscarriage of justice has occurred.

(3) Orders that the court may make — Where the court of appeal allows an appeal against a disposition or placement decision, it may

(a) make any disposition under section 672.54 or any placement decision that the Review Board could have made;

(b) refer the matter back to the court or Review Board for rehearing, in whole or in part, in accordance with any directions that the court of appeal considers appropriate; or

(c) make any other order that justice requires.

1991, c. 43, s. 4; 1997, c. 18, s. 89.

Commentary: This section describes the *dispositive powers* of the *court of appeal* on appeals from dispositions and placement decisions.

The court of appeal may *allow* the appeal on any basis described in s. 672.78(1) and, under s. 672.78(3) may:

i.   make *any* s. 672.54 *disposition or placement decision* that the court or Board could have made;

ii.   *refer* the matter *back* to the Board or court for re-hearing, in whole or in part, *with* appropriate *directions*; or,

iii. make *any other order* that *justice requires.*

The basis upon which an appeal may be dismissed is described in s. 672.78(2).

Case Law

Peckham v. Ontario (Attorney General) (1994), 93 C.C.C. (3d) 443 (Ont. C.A.); leave to appeal refused (1995), 37 C.R. (4th) 399, 94 C.C.C. (3d) vi (S.C.C.) — In the application of s. 672.78(1)(a), an appellate court must recognize the advantages of the Board in assessing credibility and its expertise in determining an appropriate disposition. An appellate court will intervene, however, if, after due regard to the Board's advantaged position and expertise, the court considers the disposition is unreasonable.

Related Provisions: The provisions appear borrowed, in part, from *Code* ss. 686(1)(a) and (b), which govern the determination of appeals from conviction and mental disorder verdicts in proceedings by indictment.

Other related provisions are discussed in the corresponding note to s. 672.72.

672.79 (1) Appeal by dangerous mentally disordered accused — Where a court finds an accused to be a dangerous mentally disordered accused and increases the cap applicable to the accused pursuant to section 672.65, the accused may appeal to the court of appeal against the increase in the cap on any ground of law or fact or mixed law and fact.

(2) Disposition of appeal — On an appeal by an accused under subsection (1), the court of appeal may

(a) quash any increase in the cap and impose any other cap that might have been imposed in respect of the offence, or order a new hearing; or

(b) dismiss the appeal.

1991, c. 43, s. 4.

Commentary: This section confers *rights of appeal* where D is found a DMDA and the court has increased the disposition cap under s. 672.65. It also describes the dispositive powers of the court of appeal.

Under s. 672.79(1), D, found to be a DMDA and subject to an increased disposition cap, may appeal to the court of appeal against *the increase in the cap* on any ground of law, fact or mixed law and fact. On the appeal, the court of appeal under s. 672.79(2) may:

i.   *quash* any *increase* in the *cap* and *impose any other cap* which may have been imposed;

ii.   order a *new hearing*; or,

iii.   *dismiss* the appeal.

Related Provisions: Section 672.8(3) incorporates the Part XXI indictable appeal procedure into appeals under s. 672.79. The Attorney General's right of appeal and the authority of the court of appeal with respect thereto is found in s. 672.8. The incorporated provisions of Part XXI would appear to include the authority to receive further evidence under s. 683 and to assign counsel for D under s. 684.

Proceedings to have D found a DMDA are commenced under s. 672.65(2) in respect of a "serious personal injury offence" as defined in s. 672.65(1). Where D is found a DMDA under s. 672.65(3), the court may increase the disposition "cap" to life under s. 672.65(4). The procedural and evidentiary provisions of ss. 754 to 758 in Part XXIV apply under s. 672.66(1). Where D is *not* found to be a DMDA, the general rule of s. 672.64 applies with respect to disposition "caps".

672.8 (1) Appeal by Attorney General — The Attorney General may appeal against the dismissal of an application for a finding that the accused is a dangerous mentally disordered accused on any ground of law.

(2) Disposition of appeal — On an appeal by the Attorney General under subsection (1), the court of appeal may

(a) allow the appeal, designate the accused as a dangerous mentally disordered accused, and increase the cap in respect of the offence to a maximum of life, or order a new hearing; or

(b) dismiss the appeal.

(3) Part XXI applies to appeal — The provisions of Part XXI with respect to procedure on appeals apply, with such modifications as the circumstances require, to appeals under this section or section 672.79.

1991, c. 43, s. 4.

Commentary: This section authorizes and governs the disposition of *appeals by the Attorney General* against dismissal of DMDA applications.

Under s. 672.8(1), the Attorney General may appeal to the court of appeal from the *dismissal* of a DMDA application "on any ground of law". Under s. 672.8(2), the court of appeal may allow the appeal, designate D a "DMDA" and increase the disposition cap to a maximum of life, or order a new hearing. The court may also dismiss the Attorney General's appeal.

The procedural provisions of Part XXI "Appeals — Indictable Offences" apply by s. 672.8(3).

Related Provisions: D's appeal against an increase in the disposition "cap" in DMDA proceedings is governed by s. 672.79.

Other related provisions are described in the corresponding note to s. 672.79.

Review of Dispositions

672.81 (1) Mandatory review of dispositions — A Review Board shall hold a hearing not later than twelve months after making a disposition and every twelve months thereafter for as long as the disposition remains in force, to review any disposition that it has made in respect of an accused, other than an absolute discharge under paragraph s. 672.54(a).

(2) Additional mandatory reviews in custody cases — The Review Board shall hold a hearing to review any disposition made under paragraph 672.54(b) or (c) as soon as is practicable after receiving notice that the person in charge of the place where the accused is detained or directed to attend

(a) has increased the restrictions on the liberty of the accused significantly for a period exceeding seven days; or

(b) requests a review of the disposition.

(3) Idem — Where an accused is detained in custody pursuant to a disposition made under paragraph 672.54(*c*) and a sentence of imprisonment is subsequently imposed on the accused in respect of another offence, the Review Board shall hold a hearing to review the disposition as soon as is practicable after receiving notice of that sentence.

1991, c. 43, s. 4.

Commentary: Sections 672.81 to 672.85 create a system for first and subsequent *annual reviews* of *dispositions* and impose special duties on the Review Board concerning unfit accused.

The reviews under s. 672.81 are *mandatory*.

Under s. 672.81(1), the Board must hold a *hearing* not later than twelve months after making a disposition and every twelve months thereafter, so long as the disposition remains in force. The rule does *not* apply to an absolute discharge under s. 672.54(a).

Under s. 672.81(2), the Board must hold a hearing *as soon as practicable* after receiving *notice* that the *person in charge* of the place where D is detained or directed to attend under a s. 672.54(b) or (c) dispositions has *significantly increased* the restrictions on D's liberty for a *period exceeding seven days*, or *requests a review* of the disposition.

By s. 672.81(3), the Board must hold a hearing to review a s. 672.54(c) disposition *as soon as practicable* after it receives *notice* that D, under such disposition, has been sentenced subsequently to a term of imprisonment, thereby making him/her a DSO.

Case Law

Hutchinson v. British Columbia (Adult Forensic Psychiatric Services, Director) (1998), 130 C.C.C. (3d) 567 (B.C. C.A.) — When a dual status offender is incarcerated for the offences of which s/he has been found guilty, the review board ceases to have *primary* responsibility for his/her custody. There is *no* reason for rigid adherence to the usual schedule of review board hearings in such circumstances, since the offender is in the custody of the federal authorities. There is *no* loss of jurisdiction by the review board.

Pinet v. Ontario (1995), 40 C.R. (4th) 113, 100 C.C.C. (3d) 343 (Ont. C.A.) — Any disposition made under s. 672.81(1) must be made by applying the criteria and scheme of s. 672.54. Under s. 672.54 only three dispositions are possible. Consideration of the least-onerous and restrictive disposition is required *only* with respect to a determination whether D should be discharged absolutely, subject to conditions or detained in a hospital subject to conditions. Once that determination has been made, it is *not* necessary that the Board, in imposing conditions, consider whether the type of hospital or conditions comtemplated would be the least-onerous and restrictive.

Related Provisions: "Disposition" is defined in s. 672.1 as an order made by a court or Review Board under s. 672.54 or an order made by a court under s. 672.58. Dispositions are made at disposition hearings whose conduct is governed by s. 672.5. The *terms* of dispositions are described in ss. 672.54 to 672.63 and their "caps" fixed by s. 672.64, absent a finding on application duly made that D is a DMDA under s. 672.65.

Note: The capping and DMDA provisions are not yet in force.

Section 672.82 authorizes the Board, at the request of any party, to hold a review hearing at any time. The review procedure in all cases follows s. 672.5. D's attendance is compelled under s. 672.85. The authority of the Board on the hearing is governed by s. 672.83.

Section 672.72 permits any party to appeal to the court of appeal against a disposition made by a court or Review Board. The appeal is taken on the transcript, subject to the right of the court to receive further evidence under s. 672.73. The powers of the court of appeal are described in s. 672.78. Under s. 672.82(2), a request for a review of a disposition under s. 672.82(1) constitutes a deemed abandonment of any appeal taken under s. 672.72 against the disposition.

672.82 (1) Discretionary review on request — A Review Board may hold a hearing to review any of its dispositions at any time, at the request of the accused or any other party.

(2) Review cancels appeal — Where a party requests a review of a disposition under this section, the party is deemed to abandon any appeal against the disposition taken under section 672.72.

1991, c. 43, s. 4.

Commentary: This section permits the Review Board to conduct further *review hearings* and restricts *appellate rights* in such cases.

Under s. 672.82(1), a Review Board *may* conduct a hearing at any time to review *any* of its dispositions, at the request of D or another party. These reviews are *in addition to* those mandated by s. 672.81.

Under s. 672.82(2), a *request* for a discretionary review under s. 672.82(1) constitutes a *deemed abandonment* of *any* appeal against the disposition under s. 672.72. The provision endeavours to bar a multiplicity of proceedings to review the same disposition.

Case Law

Peckham v. Ontario (Attorney General) (1994), 93 C.C.C. (3d) 443 (Ont. C.A.); leave to appeal refused (1995), 94 C.C.C. (3d) vi (S.C.C.) — A s. 672.82 hearing is *not*, strictly speaking, an adversarial proceeding. It is more like an inquiry into the factors in s. 672.54 than a trial. The Board is required to consider the factors in s. 672.54, thereby to decide what is a fit disposition. If the Board decides that D is *not* a significant threat to the safety of the public, D must be discharged absolutely. If the Board is unable to conclude that D is *not* a significant threat to the safety of the public, it must consider the other available dispositions.

Peckham v. Ontario (Attorney General) (1994), 93 C.C.C. (3d) 443 (Ont. C.A.); leave to appeal refused (1995), 94 C.C.C. (3d) vin (S.C.C.) — On a hearing under s. 672.82, the proper test for the Board to apply in determining the disposition to be made is that of s. 672.54. Where the Board concludes that D is not a significant threat to the safety of the public, it must order that D be discharged absolutely. Otherwise, the Board may order that D be discharged subject to conditions, or detained in custody subject to such conditions as the Board considers appropriate.

Related Provisions: Section 672.82 enacts that certain reviews are mandatory. The procedure followed in all cases is provided by s. 672.84.

Other related provisions are described in the corresponding note to s. 672.81.

672.83 (1) Disposition by Review Board — At a hearing held pursuant to section 672.81 or 672.82, the Review Board shall, except where a determination is made under subsection 672.48(1) that the accused is fit to stand trial, review the disposition made in respect of the accused and make any other disposition that the Review Board considers to be appropriate in the circumstances.

(2) Certain provisions applicable — Subsection 672.52(3), and sections 672.64 and 672.71 to 672.82 apply to a disposition made under this section, with such modifications as the circumstances require.

1991, c. 43, s. 4; 1997, c. 18, s. 90.

Commentary: This section applies to ss. 672.81 and 672.82 review hearings.

Except where a determination is made under s. 672.48(1) that D is fit to stand trial, s. 672.83(1) requires the Board to review the applicable disposition and make any other disposition that it considers to be *appropriate in the circumstances*. Unlike under the preceding scheme, the decision is that of the Board, not the Lieutenant Governor.

Section 672.83(2) incorporates several other sections in the Part to dispositions made on review under this section. *Reasons* for a disposition must be stated in the record and *copies* of the disposition and reasons must be provided to every party. The *disposition caps* of s. 672.64 apply. Appeals are governed by ss. 672.72 to 672.8 and the review provisions of ss. 672.81 and 672.82 also apply.

977

Case Law

R. v. Pinet (1995), 40 C.R. (4th) 113, 100 C.C.C. (3d) 343 (Ont. C.A.) — *See* digest under s. 672.81, *supra.*

Peckham v. Ontario (Attorney General) (1994), 93 C.C.C. (3d) 443 (Ont. C.A.); leave to appeal refused (1995), 94 C.C.C. (3d) vi (S.C.C.) — *See* digest under s. 672.82, *supra.*

Related Provisions: The procedure followed at a disposition hearing under s. 672.5 applies on the review hearing under s. 672.84.

Other related provisions are described in the corresponding note to s. 672.81.

672.84 Procedure for review — The Review Board shall hold a hearing to review a disposition under section 672.81 or 672.82 in accordance with the procedures described in section 672.5.

1991, c. 43, s. 4.

Commentary: This section applies the disposition hearings procedures of s. 672.5 to review hearings under ss. 672.81 and 672.82.

Related Provisions: The procedure followed at a disposition hearing under s. 672.5 is described in the *Commentary* which accompanies the section. It applies equally to the mandatory review of s. 672.81 and the discretionary review of s. 672.82.

Other related provisions are discussed in the corresponding note to s. 672.81.

672.85 Bringing accused before Review Board — For the purpose of bringing the accused in respect of whom a hearing under section 672.81 is to be held before the Review Board, the chairperson

(a) shall order the person having custody of the accused to bring the accused to the hearing at the time and place fixed for it; or

(b) may issue a summons or warrant to compel the accused to appear at the time and place fixed for the hearing, if the accused is not in custody.

1991, c. 43, s. 4.

Commentary: These provisions empower the chairperson of the Review Board to make an order or issue process (summons or warrant) to ensure or compel D's attendance at a s. 672.81 (mandatory) hearing.

Related Provisions: Section 672.9 governs the execution of a warrant or service of process in relation to a disposition made in respect of an accused. Each may be done anywhere in Canada.

Other related provisions are discussed in the corresponding note to s. 672.81.

Interprovincial Transfers

672.86 (1) Interprovincial transfers — An accused who is detained in custody or directed to attend at a hospital pursuant to a disposition made by a court or Review Board under paragraph 672.54(c) or a court under section 672.58 may be transferred to any other place in Canada where

(a) the Review Board of the province where the accused is detained or directed to attend recommends a transfer for the purpose of the reintegration of the accused into society or the recovery, treatment or custody of the accused; and

(b) the Attorneys General of the provinces to and from which the accused is to be transferred give their consent.

(2) Transfer where accused in custody — Where an accused who is detained in custody is to be transferred, an officer authorized by the Attorney General of the prov-

ince where the accused is being detained shall sign a warrant specifying the place in Canada to which the accused is to be transferred.

(3) Transfer where accused not in custody — Where an accused who is not detained in custody is to be transferred, the Review Board of the province where the accused is directed to attend shall, by order,

(a) direct that the accused be taken into custody and transferred pursuant to a warrant described in subsection (2); or

(b) direct the accused to attend at a specified place in Canada, subject to any conditions that the Review Board considers appropriate.

1991, c. 43, s. 4.

Commentary: Sections 672.86 to 672.89 provide for and govern inter-provincial *transfers* of certain accused who are subject to mental disorder verdicts and certain types of dispositions. The authority to transfer is considerably enlarged from former s. 617(2).

Under s. 672.86(1), an accused, detained in custody or directed to attend at a hospital pursuant to a court or Board disposition under s. 672.54(c) or a court treatment disposition under s. 672.58, may be transferred elsewhere in Canada where the *Review Board* of the applicable province *recommends* a transfer for the purpose of D's re-integration into society, recovery, treatment or custody *and* the *Attorney General* of the transferring and recipient provinces *consents*.

The inter-provincial transfer of an accused detained in custody is accomplished under s. 672.86(2) by warrant, signed by an officer authorized by the Attorney General of the transferring province, which specifies the place of transfer. Out of custody inter-provincial transfers are achieved by order of the Review Board of the recipient province under s. 672.86(3).

Related Provisions: Section 478(3) describes the circumstances in which charges outstanding against D in one province may be transferred to another, to be concluded by guilty plea. Section 733 authorizes the transfer of probation orders to another territorial division for enforcement. Section 527(1) authorizes the issuance of a warrant to compel the attendance of a prisoner in court for a specified purpose. The prisoner may be transferred from another province for such purpose.

The authority provided by a warrant under s. 672.86(2) is described in s. 672.87. Section 672.88 determines which Review Board shall have jurisdiction over an accused transferred under s. 672.86 and 672.89 governs similar jurisdiction over other inter-provincial transfers. The review jurisdiction of the relevant Board is described in ss. 672.81 to 672.83 and the procedure followed that of s. 672.5.

The execution of a warrant or process issued with respect to a disposition or assessment order is governed by s. 672.9.

672.87 Delivery and detention of accused — A warrant described in subsection 672.86(2) is sufficient authority

(a) for any person who is responsible for the custody of an accused to have the accused taken into custody and conveyed to the person in charge of the place specified in the warrant; and

(b) for the person specified in the warrant to detain the accused in accordance with any disposition made in respect of the accused under paragraph 672.54(*c*).

1991, c. 43, s. 4.

Commentary: This section describes the extent of authority conferred by a s. 672.86(2) warrant to transfer a mentally disordered accused. In essence, the warrant provides authority to have D taken into custody, conveyed to the person in charge of the place of transfer and there detained in custody in accordance with any s. 672.54(c) disposition.

Related Provisions: Section 672.86 describes the circumstances in which an accused, detained in custody or directed to attend at a hospital pursuant to a s. 672.54(c) or s. 672.58 disposition, may be transferred to another province for recovery, treatment or custody purposes. Review Board jurisdiction over s. 672.86 transfers is governed by s. 672.88.

Other related provisions are discussed in the corresponding note to s. 672.86.

672.88 (1) Review board of receiving province has jurisdiction over transferee — The Review Board of the province to which an accused is transferred pursuant to section 672.86 has exclusive jurisdiction over the accused, and may exercise the powers and shall perform the duties mentioned in sections 672.5 and 672.81 to 672.83 as if that Review Board had made the disposition in respect of the accused.

(2) Agreement — Notwithstanding subsection (1), the Attorney General of the province to which an accused is transferred may enter into an agreement subject to this Act with the Attorney General of the province from which the accused is transferred, enabling the Review Board of that province to exercise the powers and perform the duties referred to in subsection (1) in respect of the accused, in the circumstances and subject to the terms and conditions set out in agreement.

1991, c. 43, s. 4.

Commentary: This section clarifies which Review Board has jurisdiction over mentally disordered accused transferred under s. 672.86.

In general, under s. 672.88(1), the Review Board of the province *to which* D is transferred under s. 672.86 exercises the powers and performs the duties described in ss. 672.5 and 672.81 to 672.83, as if it had made the disposition in respect of D. Subsection 672.88(2) permits the original Review Board to retain jurisdiction in accordance with an agreement between the Attorneys General of the affected provinces.

Related Provisions: "Review Board" is defined in s. 672.1, its composition, authority and procedure by ss. 672.38 to 672.44. The authority of the Board to make dispositions after mental disorder verdicts is found in s. 672.47, its right of review in ss. 672.81 to 672.85. Review Board jurisdiction over inter-provincial transfers otherwise than under s. 672.86 is governed by s. 672.89.

Other related provisions are discussed in the corresponding notes to ss. 672.38, 672.54, 672.81 and 672.86.

672.89 (1) Other interprovincial transfers — Where an accused who is detained in custody pursuant to a disposition made by a Review Board is transferred to another province otherwise than pursuant to section 672.86, the Review Board of the province from which the accused is transferred has exclusive jurisdiction over the accused and may continue to exercise the powers and shall continue to perform the duties mentioned in sections 672.5 and 672.81 to 672.83.

(2) Agreement — Notwithstanding subsection (1), the Attorneys General of the provinces to and from which the accused is to be transferred as described in that subsection may, after the transfer is made, enter into an agreement subject to this Act, enabling the Review Board of the province to which an accused is transferred to exercise the powers and perform the duties referred to in subsection (1) in respect of the accused, subject to the terms and conditions and in the circumstances set out in the agreement.

1991, c. 43, s. 4.

Commentary: This provision clarifies which Review Board has jurisdiction in respect of an accused detained in custody by a Review Board disposition who is transferred to another province *otherwise than pursuant to s. 672.86.*

Section 672.89(1) states the *general rule.* The Review Board of the province *from which* the transfer is made retains exclusive jurisdiction over D for the purposes of the powers and duties of ss. 672.5 and 672.81 to 672.83. Under s. 672.89(2), an *agreement* between the respective Attorneys General may permit the Review Board of the province *to which* D is transferred to exercise jurisdiction.

Related Provisions: Section 672.88 determines which Review Board shall have jurisdiction over inter-provincial transfers under s. 672.86.

Other related provisions are discussed in the corresponding note to s. 672.86.

Enforcement of Orders and Regulations

672.9 Execution of warrant anywhere in Canada — Any warrant or process issued in relation to an assessment order or disposition made in respect of an accused may be executed or served in any place in Canada outside the province where the order or disposition was made as if it had been issued in that province.

1991, c. 43, s. 4; 1997, c. 18, s. 91.

Commentary: Under this new section, any *warrant or process* issued in relation to an assessment order or disposition made in respect of an accused may be validly executed or served *anywhere in Canada*.

Related Provisions: Section 672.91 authorizes a peace officer to *arrest without warrant* anywhere in Canada an accused whom the officer has reasonable grounds to believe has contravened or wilfully failed to comply with a disposition or any condition of it or is about to do so. An accused, arrested without warrant under s. 672.91, must be brought before a justice in accordance with s. 672.92. Whether D ought to be released will be decided under s. 672.93. The jurisdiction of the Review Board to review such cases is governed by s. 672.94.

672.91 Arrest without warrant for contravention of disposition — A peace officer may arrest an accused without a warrant at any place in Canada if the peace officer has reasonable grounds to believe that the accused has contravened or wilfully failed to comply with the disposition or any condition of it, or is about to do so.

1991, c. 43, s. 4.

Commentary: This section authorizes a *peace officer* to *arrest* an accused *without warrant* anywhere in Canada where the officer has *reasonable grounds* to believe that the accused:

i.   has contravened or been about to contravene; or,

ii.   has wilfully failed or been about to fail to comply with a disposition or any condition of it.

Related Provisions: Under s. 672.9, a warrant or process issued in relation to an assessment order or disposition may be executed or served anywhere in Canada. A similar provision appears in respect of process issued out of the superior court of criminal jurisdiction (ss. 702(1), 703(1)), a court of appeal (s. 683(4)) and the Supreme Court of Canada (s. 695(1)).

Other related provisions are described in the corresponding note to s. 672.9.

672.92 (1) Accused to be brought before justice — An accused who is arrested pursuant to section 672.91 shall be taken before a justice having jurisdiction in the territorial division in which the accused is arrested, without unreasonable delay and in any event within twenty-four hours after the arrest.

(2) Idem — If a justice described in subsection (1) is not available within twenty-four hours after the arrest, the accused shall be taken before a justice as soon as is practicable.

1991, c. 43, s. 4.

Commentary: This section establishes the time periods within which an accused, arrested without warrant under s. 672.91, is to be brought before a justice.

In the usual course, D is to be taken before a justice in the territorial division of his/her arrest *without unreasonable delay and*, in any event, *within twenty-four hours* of arrest. Where a justice is *not* available within twenty-four hours, D must be taken before a justice under s. 672.92(2) *as soon as is practicable*.

Related Provisions: The arrest under s. 672.91 is made without warrant and may take place anywhere in Canada. The authority of the justice to release D is governed by s. 672.93.

Other related provisions are described in the corresponding note to s. 672.9.

672.93 (1) Where justice to release accused — A justice shall release an accused who is brought before the justice pursuant to section 672.92 unless the justice is satisfied that there are reasonable grounds to believe that the accused has contravened or failed to comply with a disposition.

(2) Order of justice pending decision of Review Board — If the justice is satisfied that there are reasonable grounds to believe that the accused has contravened or failed to comply with a disposition, the justice may make an order that is appropriate in the circumstances in relation to the accused, pending a hearing of the Review Board of the province where the disposition was made, and shall cause notice of that order to be given to that Review Board.

1991, c. 43, s. 4.

Commentary: This section describes the *authority* of the *justice* before whom D appears under s. 672.92 after arrest without warrant.

Under s. 672.93(1) a justice must *release* D, *unless satisfied* that there are *reasonable grounds* to believe that D *has contravened or failed to comply* with a disposition. In the event of either finding, the justice is authorized by s. 672.93(2) to make an order appropriate in the circumstances in relation to D, pending a hearing before the appropriate Review Board to whom *notice* must be given.

The section would appear silent concerning what is to be done in relation to D arrested without warrant for an anticipated contravention or failure to comply with a disposition or condition. *Quaere* whether in such cases D ought to be released unconditionally?

Related Provisions: The powers and duties of the Review Board on receipt of notice under s. 672.93(2) are described in s. 672.94.

See also the *Commentary* which accompanies s. 672.5 and ss. 672.81 to 672.83.

For analogous provisions in the context of judicial interim release, see s. 524 and ss. 525(5) to (8).

672.94 Powers of Review Board — Where a Review Board receives a notice given pursuant to subsection 672.93(2), it may exercise the powers and shall perform the duties mentioned in sections 672.5 and 672.81 to 672.83 as if the Review Board were reviewing a disposition.

1991, c. 43, s. 4.

Commentary: This section requires the Review Board to comply with ss. 672.5 and 672.81 to 672.83 upon receipt of a notice under s. 672.93(2), as if it were reviewing a disposition.

Related Provisions: The notice under s. 672.93(2) is given where a justice is satisfied that there are reasonable grounds to believe that D, arrested without warrant under s. 672.9, has contravened or failed to comply with the disposition and has made an interim order pending a hearing before the Board.

The procedure followed by the Board under s. 672.94 duplicates that followed on a disposition hearing under s. 672.5. The duties of the Board are described in ss. 672.81 to 672.83.

Other related provisions are discussed in the corresponding note to s. 672.9.

672.95 Regulations — The Governor in Council may make regulations

    (a) prescribing anything that may be prescribed under this Part; and

    (b) generally to carry out the purposes and provisions of this Part.

1991, c. 43, s. 4.

Commentary: Under this section, the Governor in Council may make regulations prescribing anything that may be prescribed under Part XX.1 and, generally, to carry out its purposes and provisions.

Related Provisions: Under s. 672.44(3), the Governor in Council may make regulations to provide for the practice and procedure before Review Boards, in particular to make the rules of Review Boards uniform. Any regulation made by the Governor in Council prevails over any rules made by the Board under s. 672.44(1). The *Notice of Application for Treatment Regulations* appear after s. 672.58, *supra*. An analogous overriding authority of the Governor in Council appears in s. 482(5), which permits the Governor in Council to make such provision as is considered proper to secure uniformity in the rules of court in criminal matters. The uniform rules prevail and have the same effect as if enacted by the court.

Schedule to Part XX.1 — Designated Offences - Criminal Code
(Subsection 672.64(1))

1. Section 49 — acts intended to alarm Her Majesty or break public peace
2. Section 50 — assisting alien enemy to leave Canada, or omitting to prevent treason
3. Section 51 — intimidating Parliament or legislature
4. Section 52 — sabotage
5. Section 53 — inciting to mutiny
6. Section 75 — piratical acts
7. Section 76 — hijacking
8. Section 77 — endangering safety of aircraft
9. Section 78 — offensive weapons and explosive substances
10. Section 80 — breach of duty (explosive substances)
11. Section 81 — using explosives
12. Section 82 — possession of explosives without lawful excuse
13. Subsection 85(1) — using firearm in commission of offence
13.1 Subsection 85(2) — using imitation firearm in commission of offence
14. Subsection 86(1) — careless use of firearm, etc.
15. Subsection 87(1) — pointing a firearm
16. Subsection 88(1) — possession of weapon for dangerous purpose
17. Section 151 — sexual interference
18. Section 152 — invitation to sexual touching
19. Section 153 — sexual exploitation
20. Section 155 — incest
21. Section 159 — anal intercourse
22. Subsection 160(2) — compelling commission of bestiality
23. Subsection 160(3) — bestiality in presence of child or inciting child to commit bestiality
24. Section 220 — causing death by criminal negligence
25. Section 221 — causing bodily harm by criminal negligence
26. Section 223 — causing injury to child before or during birth
27. Section 236 — manslaughter
28. Section 238 — killing unborn child in act of birth
29. Section 239 — attempt to commit murder
30. Section 241 — counselling or aiding suicide
31. Section 244 — causing bodily harm with intent

32. Paragraph 245(a) — administering noxious thing with intent to endanger life or cause bodily harm

33. Section 246 — overcoming resistance to commission of offence

34. Section 247 — setting traps likely to cause death or bodily harm

35. Section 248 — interfering with transportation facilities

36. Subsection 249(3) — dangerous operation of motor vehicles, vessels and aircraft causing bodily harm

37. Subsection 249(4) — dangerous operation of motor vehicles, vessels and aircraft causing death

38. Subsection 255(2) — impaired driving causing bodily harm

39. Subsection 255(3) — impaired driving causing death

40. Section 262 — impeding attempt to save life

41. Paragraph 265(1)(a) — assault

42. Section 267 — assault with a weapon or causing bodily harm

43. Section 268 — aggravated assault

44. Section 269 — unlawfully causing bodily harm

45. Subsection 269.1(1) — torture

46. Paragraph 271(1)(a) — sexual assault

47. Section 272 — sexual assault with a weapon, threats to a third party or causing bodily harm

48. Section 273 — aggravated sexual assault

49. Subsection 279(1) — kidnapping

50. Subsection 279(2) — forcible confinement

51. Section 279.1 — hostage taking

52. Section 280 — abduction of person under sixteen

53. Section 281 — abduction of person under fourteen

54. Paragraph 282(a) — abduction in contravention of custody order

55. Paragraph 283(1)(a) — abduction where no custody order

56. Section 344 — robbery

57. Section 345 — stopping mail with intent

58. Section 346 — extortion

59. Section 348 — breaking and entering with intent, committing offence or breaking out

60. Subsection 349(1) — being unlawfully in dwelling-house

61. Subsection 430(2) — mischief that causes actual danger to life

62. Section 431 — attack on premises, etc., of internationally protected person

63. Section 433 — arson (disregard for human life)

64. Section 434 — arson (damage to property)

65. Section 434.1 — arson (own property)

66. Section 435 — arson for fraudulent purpose

Atomic Energy Control Act

67. Section 20 — offence and punishment

Emergencies Act

68A. Subparagraph 8(1)(j)(ii) — contravention of public welfare emergency regulation

69. Subparagraph 19(1)(e)(ii) — contravention of public order emergency regulation

70. Subparagraph 30(1)(l)(ii) — contravention of international emergency regulation

71. Paragraph 40(3)(b) — contravention of war emergency regulation

Canadian Environmental Protection Act

72. Section 115 — damage to environment and death or harm to persons

Controlled Drugs and Substances Act

73. Subsections 4(3) and (4) — possession
74. Subsections 5(3) and (4) — trafficking
75. Subsection 6(3) — importing and exporting
76. Subsection 7(2) — production
77. Section 5 — importing and exporting

National Defence Act

78. Section 78 — offence of being spy

79. Section 79 — mutiny with violence

80. Section 80 — mutiny without violence

81. Section 81 — offences related to mutiny

82. Section 82 — advocating governmental change by force

83. Section 83 — disobedience of lawful command

84. Section 84 — striking or offering violence to a superior officer

85. Section 88 — desertion

86. Paragraph 98(c) — maiming or injuring self or another person

87. Section 105 — offences in relation to convoys

88. Section 106 — disobedience of captain's orders — ships

89. Section 110 — disobedience of captain's orders — aircraft

90. Section 128 — conspiracy

Official Secrets Act

91. Section 3 — spying

92. Section 4 — wrongful communication, etc., of information

93. Section 5 — unauthorized use of uniforms, falsification of reports, etc.

1995, c. 39, s. 154.

PART XXI — APPEALS — INDICTABLE OFFENCES

Interpretation

673. Definitions — In this Part,

"court of appeal" means the court of appeal, as defined by the definition "court of appeal" in section 2, for the province or territory in which the trial of a person by indictment is held;

"indictment" includes an information or charge in respect of which a person has been tried for an indictable offence under Part XIX;

"registrar" means the registrar or clerk of the court of appeal;

"sentence" includes

(a) a declaration made under subsection 199(3),

(b) an order made under subsection 100(1) or (2), section 161, subsection 194(1) or 259(1) or (2), section 261 or 462.37, subsection 491.1(2) or 730(1) or 25 section 737, 738, 739, 742.1, 742.3, 743.6, 745.4 or 745.5,

---

Proposed Amendment — Conditional Amendment — 673"sentence"

On the later of the day on which 1995, c. 22, s. 5(2) comes into force [Not in force at date of publication.] and 1995, c. 39, s. 155 comes into force [In force December 1, 1998], paragraph (b) in the definition of "sentence"in s. 673 is replaced by the following:

(b) an order made under subsection 109(1) or 110(1), section 161, subsection 194(1) or 259(1) or (2), section 261 or 462.37, subsection 491.1(2) or 730(1) or section 737, 738, 739, 742.3 or 745.2 or subsection 747.1(1), and

1995, c. 39, s. 190(b) [Not in force at date of publication.]

(c) a disposition made under section 731 or 732 or subsection 732.2(3) or (5), 742.4(3) or 742.6(9), and

(d) an order made under subsection 16(1) of the *Controlled Drugs and Substances Act;*

"trial court" means the court by which an accused was tried and includes a judge or a provincial court judge acting under Part XIX.

R.S., c. C-34, s. 601; 1972, c. 13, s. 52; 1973–74, c. 38, s. 6.1; c. 50, s. 3; 1974–75–76, c. 93, s. 72; 1976–77, c. 53, s. 4;R.S. 1985, c. 27 (1st Supp.), ss. 138, 203; c. 23 (4th Supp.), s. 4; c. 42 (4th Supp.), s. 4; 1992, c. 1, s. 58(1), Schedule 1; item 12; 1993, c. 45, ss. 10, 16, 19; 1995, c. 22, s. 5(1), 5(2); 1995, c. 39, s. 190(a); 1996, c. 19, s. 74(2); 1999, c. 5, ss. 25, 51.

Transitional Provision S.C. 1991, c. 43: 1991, c. 43, s. 10 provides as follows:

Proposed Transition Provision

10(8) Hospital Orders During Transitional Period — Where, before the coming into force of section 5 of this Act, a person has committed an offence but a sentence has not been imposed on that person for that offence, that person may be detained in accordance with section 736.11 of the *Criminal Code*, as enacted by section 6 of this Act. Not in force at date of publication.

Commentary: The section defines several terms for the purposes of Part XXI only.

Case Law

Sentence [See also s. 675]

R. v. Chiasson (1995), 41 C.R. (4th) 193, 99 C.C.C. (3d) 289 (S.C.C.) — The definition "sentence" in s. 673 is *not* exhaustive. It includes, *inter alia*, a s. 741.2 parole ineligibility order.

R. v. Pope (1980), 52 C.C.C. (2d) 538 (B.C. C.A.) — A refusal to order forfeiture under the *N.C.A.* is *not* a "sentence" within s. 673.

R. v. Pawlyk (1991), 4 C.R. (4th) 388, 65 C.C.C. (3d) 63 (Man. C.A.) — Refusal to make a forfeiture order under s. 462.37(1) is a "sentence" within s. 673.

Roberts v. Cour de Jurisdiction Criminelle (1980), 28 C.R. (3d) 257 (Que. C.A.) — An order requiring D to pay costs is an "order" within the definition of "sentence".

R. v. Brassard (1992), 78 C.C.C. (3d) 329 (Que. C.A.) — *See* disgest under s. 676 "Status to Appeal: Trial Court", *infra*.

Related Provisions: Other sections providing definitions are described in the corresponding note to s. 2.

Right of Appeal

674. Procedure abolished — **No proceedings other than those authorized by this Part and Part XXVI shall be taken by way of appeal in proceedings in respect of indictable offences.**

R.S., c. C-34, s. 602.

Commentary: The section, in effect, abolishes all rights and forms of appeal in proceedings in respect of indictable offences, other than those authorized by Parts XXI (Appeals — Indictable Offences) and XXVI (Extraordinary Remedies).

The right of appeal is an exceptional statutory right. The substantive and procedural provisions relating to it, accordingly, are generally regarded as exhaustive and exclusive.

Case Law

R. v. Keegstra (1995), 39 C.R. (4th) 205, 98 C.C.C. (3d) 1 (S.C.C.) — When the *constitutionality* of a law is challenged in the context of criminal proceedings, the determinations of culpability and constitutionality are two distinct rulings. Under *Supreme Court Act* s. 40, the Supreme Court of Canada has jurisdiction to hear applications for leave to appeal on any ground questioning the constitutionality of a *Code* provision. The limitations of *Code* s. 674 and *SCA* s. 40(3) are *not* aimed at rulings on constitutionality. Either party may seek leave to appeal rulings on constitutionality regardless of whether the ruling on culpability is appealed.When a constitutional issue is put before the Supreme Court of Canada on any appeal under the *Criminal Code*, leave need *not* be sought under *SCA* s. 40

Mills v. R. (1986), 52 C.R. (3d) 1, 26 C.C.C. (3d) 481 (S.C.C.) — The grant or denial of *Charter* relief is appealable as a question of law under the *Code*. Interlocutory appeals in respect of *Charter* remedies refused or granted under s. 24(1) are *not* authorized by the *Code*, hence, are unavailable.

R. v. La Chapelle (1988), 60 Alta. L.R. (2d) 210 (C.A.) — *See also*: *R. v. Paquette* (1987), 38 C.C.C. (3d) 353 (Alta. C.A.) — Jury selection forms part of the trial for the purpose of an attack on the constitutional validity of the selection process. Where rejected at trial, however, the attack must await the conclusion of trial proceedings and verdict.

R. v. Bird (1984), 12 C.C.C. (3d) 523 (Man. C.A.) — The court has jurisdiction to hear an appeal based on the constitutionality of *Code* provisions. *Charter* s. 24 is only one method of bringing *Charter* arguments before the court.

R. v. Morgentaler (1984), 41 C.R. (3d) 262, 16 C.C.C. (3d) 1 (Ont. C.A.) — The only rights of appeal to a court of appeal in respect of an indictable offence are described in this section. There is no inherent appeal jurisdiction in criminal cases. Neither *Charter* s. 24(1) nor s. 52(1) of the *Constitution Act* gives any right of appeal to a court of appeal, or jurisdiction in a court of appeal to hear an appeal, where there is a lower court of competent jurisdiction to which to apply for a *Charter* remedy.

Related Provisions: Appeals in summary conviction proceedings are governed by ss. 812–839 in Part XXVII "Summary Convictions".

Rights of appeal in proceedings by indictment are found in ss. 675 and 676, the procedure on appeals in ss. 678–685. The powers of a court of appeal are described in ss. 686–689. Appeals to the Supreme Court of Canada are governed by ss. 691–696.

The extraordinary remedies of Part XXVI are limited to jurisdictional error.

675. (1) **Right of appeal of person convicted** — A person who is convicted by a trial court in proceedings by indictment may appeal to the court of appeal

    (a) against his conviction

        (i) on any ground of appeal that involves a question of law alone,

        (ii) on any ground of appeal that involves a question of fact or a question of mixed law and fact, with leave of the court of appeal or a judge thereof or on the certificate of the trial judge that the case is a proper case for appeal, or

        (iii) on any ground of appeal not mentioned in subparagraph (i) or (ii) that appears to the court of appeal to be a sufficient ground of appeal, with leave of the court of appeal; or

    (b) against the sentence passed by the trial court, with leave of the court of appeal or a judge thereof unless that sentence is one fixed by law.

(1.1) **Summary conviction appeals** — A person may appeal, pursuant to subsection (1), with leave of the court of appeal or a judge of that court, to that court in respect of a summary conviction or a sentence passed with respect to a summary conviction as if the summary conviction had been a conviction in proceedings by indictment if

    (a) there has not been an appeal with respect to the summary conviction;

    (b) the summary conviction offence was tried with an indictable offence; and

    (c) there is an appeal in respect of the indictable offence.

(2) **Appeal against absolute term in excess of 10 years** — A person who has been convicted of second degree murder and sentenced to imprisonment for life without eligibility for parole for a specified number of years in excess of ten may appeal to the court of appeal against the number of years in excess of ten of his imprisonment without eligibility for parole.

(2.1) **Persons under eighteen** — A person who was under the age of eighteen at the time of the commission of the offence for which the person was convicted of first degree murder or second degree murder and sentenced to imprisonment for life without eligibility for parole until the person has served the period specified by the judge presiding at the trial may appeal to the court of appeal against the number of years in excess of the minimum number of years of imprisonment without eligibility for parole that are required to be served in respect of that person's case.

(2.1) **Appeal against s. 741.2 order** — A person against whom an order under section 741.2 has been made may appeal to the court of appeal against the order.

(3) **Appeals against verdicts based on mental disorder** — Where a verdict of not criminally responsible on account of mental disorder or unfit to stand trial is rendered in respect of a person, that person may appeal to the court of appeal against that verdict on any ground of appeal mentioned in subparagraph (1)(a)(i), (ii) or (iii) and subject to the conditions described therein.

(4) **Where application for leave to appeal refused by judge** — Where a judge of the court of appeal refuses leave to appeal under this section otherwise than under paragraph (1)(b), the appellant may, by filing notice in writing with the court of appeal within seven days after refusal, have the application for leave to appeal determined by the court of appeal.

R.S., c. C-34, s. 603; 1974–75–76, c. 105, s. 13; 1991, c. 43, s. 9, Schedule, item 5; 1995, c. 42, s. 73; 1997, c. 18, s. 92.

Note: S.C. 1997, c. 18, s. 92(2) amended s. 675 by adding a subsection "(2.1) Persons under eighteen". Unfortunately there already existed a s. 675(2.1), "(2.1) Appeal against s. 741.2 order". The two subsections are substantively different and should not be read together. It is an error that will have to be legislatively corrected.

Commentary: The section defines D's *rights of appeal* from dispositions made at trial in *proceedings by indictment* and summary convictions where the conditions of s. 675(1.1) are met.

Under ss. 675(1)(a) and (3), D may appeal against *conviction*, a verdict of *unfitness* or a verdict of *not criminally responsible* on account of mental disorder. The right of appeal is absolute, where the ground of appeal raises a question of law alone, but requires leave of the court of appeal, a judge thereof or the certificate of the trial judge in all other cases. In general, under s. 675(4), where a judge of the court of appeal refuses leave to appeal, D, by filing notice in writing with the court of appeal within seven days thereafter, may have the application for leave to appeal determined by the court.

Under s. 675(1)(b), D may appeal against the *sentence* imposed at trial, with leave of the court of appeal or a judge thereof, unless the sentence is one fixed by law. If leave to appeal is refused by a single judge, D may *not* apply to the court under s. 675(4) to determine the matter of leave to appeal. Under ss. 675(2) and (2.1), D may appeal, without leave, against an order increasing the period of parole ineligibility upon conviction of second degree murder or other offence and, for young offenders, of first or second degree murder.

Under s. 675(1.1), D may appeal against a summary conviction or the sentence arising from a summary conviction where there is *no* other appeal in respect of the summary conviction, the summary conviction was *tried with* an *indictable* offence and there is an *appeal* in respect of the *indictable* offence. Leave to appeal is required.

Case Law

Jurisdiction; Timing and Status

R. v. Druken, [1998] 1 S.C.R. 978, 126 C.C.C. (3d) 1 (S.C.C.) — The decision of a trial judge to remove counsel for D is to be reviewed after the trial through the usual appellate process.

R. v. Bird (1984), 12 C.C.C. (3d) 523 (Man. C.A.) — Rulings on evidence should *not* be appealed until the trial is over.

R. v. Koaches, [1968] 2 C.C.C. 148 (Ont. C.A.) — *See also*: *R. v. Louis* (1957), 26 C.R. 84, 117 C.C.C. 284 (Sask. C.A.) — There is *no* right of appeal in a third party affected by an order of forfeiture.

Against Conviction: S. 675(1)(a)

R. v. Foti (1994), 87 C.C.C. (3d) 187 (Man. C.A.) — D has *no* right of appeal from a finding of guilt which has been conditionally stayed on application of the rule against multiple convictions.

R. v. Yaworski (1959), 31 C.R. 55, 124 C.C.C. 151 (Man. C.A.) — Where D, charged with an indictable offence, is found guilty, of a summary conviction offence (whether rightly or wrongly), the indictable appeal procedure is to be followed. The *nature* of the *proceedings*, not the *nature* of the *conviction*, determines the forum of appeal.

R. v. Mol (1988), 70 Nfld. & P.E.I.R. 167 (P.E.I. C.A.), quashing (1987), 65 Nfld. & P.E.I.R. 17 (P.E.I.S.C.) — D's right of appeal does *not* arise unless and until a court has entered a conviction.

After Guilty Plea [See also ss. 606 and 686]

Brosseau v. R. (1968), 5 C.R.N.S. 331, [1969] 3 C.C.C. 129 (S.C.C.) — When a plea of guilty is offered and there is reason to doubt that D understands what he is doing, and the presiding judge fails to make due inquiry as to whether D fully appreciates the nature of the charge or the effect of his plea, D's conviction may be quashed.

R. v. Newman (1993), 79 C.C.C. (3d) 394 (Ont. C.A.) — A court of appeal may permit D to withdraw a plea of guilty, set aside the conviction and order a new trial where the court is satisfied that D was deprived of his/her right to effective counsel and that the plea of guilty embraced a factual foundation that D was not prepared to accept for the purposes of sentencing, so that D was deprived of a fair trial.

R. v. Ballegeer, [1969] 3 C.C.C. 353 (Man. C.A.) — *See also*: *Colligan v. R.* (1955), 21 C.R. 120 (Que. C.A.) — There is a heavy onus on D who, having pleaded guilty in court and been sentenced, seeks leave to change his plea to not guilty and to be given a new trial.

Against Sentence: S. 675(1)(b) [See also s. 673]

R. v. Fallofield (1973), 22 C.R.N.S. 342, 13 C.C.C. (2d) 450 (B.C. C.A.) — *See also*: *R. v. Christman* (1973), 22 C.R.N.S. 338, 11 C.C.C. (2d) 245n (Alta. C.A.); *R. v. McInnis* (1973), 23 C.R.N.S. 152, 13 C.C.C. (2d) 471 (Ont. C.A.) — The determination by the trial court whether it will order a discharge can be the subject matter of an appeal as to sentence. Under its power to vary a sentence, a court of appeal may substitute a discharge for a conviction.

R. v. Mahon, [1969] 2 C.C.C. 179 (B.C. C.A.) — The disposition of an application for leave to appeal against sentence is in the control of the court. The appellant's application to abandon his appeal was refused, and the court corrected a sentence which had *not* been warranted by law.

R. v. Olah (1997), 115 C.C.C. (3d) 389 (Ont. C.A.) — The phrase "fixed by law" in s. 675 does *not* bar appellate review of a sentence, including a period of parole ineligibility, where the lesser punishment provisions of *Charter* s. 11(i) and/or s. 44(e) of the *Interpretation Act* may be applicable.

R. v. Clifford, [1969] 2 C.C.C. 363 (Ont. C.A.) — Subject to the approval of the court, an appellant may withdraw his application for leave to appeal sentence at any time before the hearing commences.

Roberts v. Cour de Jurisdiction Criminelle (1980), 28 C.R. (3d) 257 (Que. C.A.) — A judgment requiring D to pay costs is a "sentence" from which D may appeal.

Setting Aside Dismissal of Appeal

R. v. Jacobs (1971), 2 C.C.C. (2d) 26 (S.C.C.) — The decision of a court of appeal to rescind a previous judgment dismissing an appeal, due to failure of counsel to appear, is a proper exercise by the court of its discretionary power relating to practice concerning the proper administration of justice in criminal matters.

R. v. Blaker (1983), 6 C.C.C. (3d) 385 (B.C. C.A.) — A court of appeal may vary or set aside an order disposing of an appeal where the disposition was not based on the merits and where the court finds that it is in the interest of justice to do so. An order dismissing for want of prosecution due to counsel's failure to file a complete transcript was set aside where the failure was the result of the court reporter having lost her notes.

R. v. H. (E.F.); R. v. Rhingo (1997), 115 C.C.C. (3d) 89 (Ont. C.A.) — The authority to re-open proceedings in the exercise of an appellate court's ancillary or inherent jurisdiction to control its own process does not permit re-opening cases heard and disposed of on their own merits.

R. v. D. (J.F.) (1988), 25 O.A.C. 78 (C.A.) — Only in exceptional circumstances will the court set aside the dismissal of an appeal due to the failure of D to surrender into custody.

R. v. Watson (1975), 23 C.C.C. (2d) 366 (Ont. C.A.) — The court of appeal may rescind a previous dismissal of an appeal where the appeal was dismissed as abandoned upon a notice of abandonment filed by D. Such a dismissal is not an adjudication upon the merits.

Stay Pending Appeal [See also ss. 683(5) and 261]

R. v. Trabulsey (1993), 84 C.C.C. (3d) 240 (Ont. Gen. Div.) — The filing of a notice of appeal does not operate to stay or suspend the operation of the terms of a probation order.

Related Provisions: "Court of appeal", "indictment", "sentence" and "trial court" are defined in s. 673.

In general, the *Code* confers *rights* of appeal and defines the *authority* of the *court* of appeal, both upon the hearing and in the determination or disposition of the appeal (ss. 686–687). Appellate procedure is generally governed by rules of court passed by a majority of the judges of the court of appeal under s. 482(1). The rules vary from one jurisdiction to another and should be consulted before undertaking appellate proceedings. The rights of appeal of the Attorney General from dispositions made in proceedings by indictment are described in ss. 676 and 696.

Rights of appeal in *dangerous offender* proceedings are conferred by s. 759 and, in respect of applications for the extraordinary remedies of *mandamus, habeas corpus, certiorari* and prohibition, by s. 784.

It is the *nature* of the *proceedings* in the trial court, *not* the nature of the *conviction* recorded or level of the trial court in the judicial hierarchy that determines appellate rights. In all cases in which proceedings must be or have been taken by indictment, whether the trial is before a provincial court judge or judge sitting alone under Part XIX, or a court composed of a judge and jury under Part XX, whether upon an information or indictment, Part XXI applies.

676. (1) **Right of Attorney General to appeal** — The Attorney General or counsel instructed by him for the purpose may appeal to the court of appeal

(a) against a judgment or verdict of acquittal or a verdict of not criminally responsible on account of mental disorder of a trial court in proceedings by indictment on any ground of appeal that involves a question of law alone;

(b) against an order of a superior court of criminal jurisdiction that quashes an indictment or in any manner refuses or fails to exercise jurisdiction on an indictment;

(c) against an order of a trial court that stays proceedings on an indictment or quashes an indictment; or

(d) with leave of the court of appeal or a judge thereof, against the sentence passed by a trial court in proceedings by indictment, unless that sentence is one fixed by law.

(1.1) **Summary conviction appeals** — The Attorney General or counsel instructed by the Attorney General may appeal, pursuant to subsection (1), with leave of the court of appeal or a judge of that court, to that court in respect of a summary conviction or a sentence passed with respect to a summary conviction or a sentence passed with respect to a summary conviction as if the summary conviction had been a conviction in proceedings by indictment if

(a) there has not been an appeal with respect to the summary conviction;

(b) the summary conviction offence was tried with an indictable offence; and

(c) there is an appeal in respect of the indictable offence.

(2) **Acquittal** — For the purposes of this section, a judgment or verdict of acquittal includes an acquittal in respect of an offence specifically charged where the accused has, on the trial thereof, been convicted or discharged under section 730 of any other offence.

(3) **Appeal against verdict of unfit** — The Attorney General or counsel instructed by the Attorney General for the purpose may appeal to the court of appeal against a verdict that an accused is unfit to stand trial, on any ground of appeal that involves a question of law alone.

(4) **Appeal against ineligible parole period** — The Attorney General or counsel instructed by him for the purpose may appeal to the court of appeal in respect of a conviction for second degree murder, against the number of years of imprisonment without eligibility for parole, being less than twenty-five, that has been imposed as a result of that conviction.

(5) **Appeal against decision not to make s. 741.2 order** — The Attorney General or counsel instructed by the Attorney General for the purpose may appeal to the court of appeal against the decision of the court not to make an order under section 741.2.

R.S., c. C-34, s. 605; 1974–75–76, c. 105, s. 15; R.S. 1985, c. 27 (1st Supp.), s. 139; 1991, c. 43, s. 9, Schedule, item 6; 1995, c. 22, s. 10; 1995, c. 42, s. 74; 1997, c. 18, s. 93.

Commentary: The section defines the *rights of appeal* of the Attorney General or counsel instructed by him/her for the purpose, in *proceedings by indictment* and summary convictions of s. 676(1.1) are met.

Under s. 676(1)(a), the Attorney General, or counsel instructed by him/her for such purpose, may appeal to the court of appeal against a judgment or a verdict of *acquittal* or *of not criminally responsible on account of mental disorder* of a trial court in proceedings by indictment, upon a *question of law alone.*

Leave to appeal is not required. Section 676(3) affords an equivalent right of appeal against a verdict of *unfit* to stand trial. Under s. 676(2), a judgment or verdict of acquittal includes an acquittal of the offence charged where D has, nonetheless, been found guilty of a lesser offence.

Under ss. 676(1)(b) and (c), the Attorney General, or counsel instructed by him/her for the purpose, may appeal to the court of appeal against an order of the superior court of criminal jurisdiction that *quashes an indictment* or in any manner *fails or refuses to exercise jurisdiction* upon it, or an *order* of any trial court *staying proceedings* on an indictment or quashing an indictment. The grounds upon which such appeals may be taken are *not* specified, hence are *not* limited, as under s. 676(1)(a), to questions of law alone.

Under s. 676(1)(d), the Attorney General or counsel instructed by him/her for the purpose may appeal against the *sentence* imposed at trial, with *leave* of the court of appeal or a judge thereof, unless the sentence is fixed by law. Under ss. 676(4) and (5), the Attorney General, or counsel instructed by him/her for such purpose, may appeal to the court of appeal against an order of parole ineligibility or a failure to make such an order. Leave to appeal is *not* required.

Under s. 676(1.1), the Attorney General, or counsel instructed by him/her, may appeal against a summary conviction or the sentence arising from a summary conviction where there is *no* other appeal in respect of the summary conviction, the summary conviction was tried with an indictable offence and there is an appeal in respect of the indictable offence. Leave to appeal is required.

Case Law
Status to Appeal

R. v. V. (E.) (1994), 30 C.R. (4th) 78, 90 C.C.C. (3d) 484 (Ont. C.A.) — P's right of appeal from an acquittal is an appellate remedy, *not* a licence to refer legal questions to the court of appeal for its consideration and advice.

R. v. Morgentaler (1985), 44 C.R. (3d) 189, 19 C.C.C. (3d) 573 (Ont. C.A.); reversed in part on other grounds (1988), 62 C.R. (3d) 1 (S.C.C.) — In a criminal proceeding P represents the public interest, and it alone is given the right to appeal from an acquittal. To permit a third party to intervene to raise an additional ground of appeal would enlarge the scope of a P appeal from an acquittal beyond that contemplated by Parliament.

Status to Appeal: "Trial Court"

R. v. Rowbotham (1994), 30 C.R. (4th) 141, 90 C.C.C. (3d) 449 (S.C.C.) — Where a trial judge withdraws a case from the jury and enters a verdict of acquittal, the "trial court" for the purposes of s. 676(1)(a) is the judge alone.

R. v. O'Leary (1991), 64 C.C.C. (3d) 573 (Nfld. C.A.) — Where D first appears in respect of an offence triable either way, and P has *not* elected the mode of procedure, a provincial court judge sits as a "justice" and *not* as "a trial court" within s. 676(1)(a). A provincial court judge only becomes "a trial court" in respect of offences triable either way, where P *elects* to proceed by indictment and D *elects* trial by provincial court judge.

R. v. B. (I.) (1994), 93 C.C.C. (3d) 121 (Ont. C.A.) — P may appeal an order of a youth court judge staying proceedings upon an information on account of abuse of process, notwithstanding that no evidence has been adduced. A youth court judge is "a trial court" within *Code* s. 676(1)(c).

R. v. Brassard (1992), 78 C.C.C. (3d) 329 (Que. C.A.) — P has a right of appeal under *Code* s. 676(1) from an order of a judge of the Court of Quebec staying proceedings against D, notwithstanding that the order is made prior to plea and preferment of the indictment. Although "trial court" is defined in s. 673 as the court by which D is tried, s. 676(1)(c) ought to be interpreted to provide for an appeal from a stay of proceedings ordered as a *Charter* remedy by a judge competent to try D.

"Counsel Instructed by Him for the Purpose"

R. v. Harrison (1976), 28 C.C.C. (2d) 279 (S.C.C.) — There is *implied authority* in the Attorney General to delegate the power to instruct counsel to a responsible subordinate. If the authority of counsel is questioned, it would normally be sufficient if counsel produces a letter which he/she can say he/she received and believes to be signed by the Attorney General, Deputy Attorney General, or an officer of the department whom counsel understands to have requisite authority to instruct criminal appeals.

R. v. Badall (1974), 17 C.C.C. (2d) 420 (S.C.C.) — A notice of appeal signed by an "Agent for the Attorney General of Canada" is valid.

R. v. Persaud (1989), 52 C.C.C. (3d) 464 (Ont. C.A.) — A provincial court judge who quashes an information after arraignment but prior to election by D does *not* constitute a trial court, hence P has *no* right of appeal under this section.

Judgment or Verdict of Acquittal: S. 676(1)(a)

Cheyenne Realty Ltd. v. Thompson (1974), 15 C.C.C. (2d) 49 (S.C.C.) — *See also: R. v. Kripps Pharmacy Ltd.* (1981), 60 C.C.C. (2d) 332 (B.C. C.A.); leave to appeal refused (1981), 60 C.C.C. (2d) 332n (S.C.C.) — The dismissal of a charge on the basis that the municipal by-law upon which the charge was founded is invalid amounts to a verdict of acquittal which is appealable.

R. v. Holliday (1973), 26 C.R.N.S. 279, 12 C.C.C. (2d) 56 (Alta. C.A.) — The declaration of a *mistrial* is *not* a judgment or *verdict* of acquittal. P has *no* right of appeal, but may proceed again in respect of the same offence.

R. v. Belecque, (September 23, 1988), Doc. No. CA008644 (B.C. C.A.) — Section 676(1)(c) is *not* limited in its scope to cases where quashing an indictment was tantamount to an acquittal.

R. v. Sanver (1973), 28 C.R.N.S. 10, 12 C.C.C. (2d) 105 (N.B. C.A.) — A judgment dismissing an information on the plea of *autrefois acquit* was appealable as being, in effect, an acquittal.

R. v. Ashini (1989), 52 C.C.C. (3d) 329 (Nfld. C.A.) — Where D charged in separate informations were jointly tried, the trial court was without jurisdiction and the acquittals were nullities against which P was entitled to appeal.

Not Criminally Responsible on Account of Mental Disorder [Cases decided under former s. 676(3)]

R. v. Sullivan (1995), 37 C.R. (4th) 333, 96 C.C.C. (3d) 135 (B.C. C.A.) — P may appeal from a verdict of not criminally responsible on account of mental disorder under s. 676(1)(a).

Question of Law Alone: S. 676(1)(a) [See also ss. 691 and 693]

R. v. Mara (1997), 115 C.C.C. (3d) 539 (S.C.C.) — Where the facts concerning a performance are undisputed, whether the performance is indecent is a question of law alone.

R. v. Morin (1992), 16 C.R. (4th) 291, 76 C.C.C. (3d) 193 (S.C.C.) — If a trial judge finds all the facts necessary to reach a conclusion in law, and in order to reach that conclusion the facts can simply be accepted as found, a court of appeal may disagree with the conclusion reached without trespassing on the fact-finding function of the trial judge. The disagreement concerns a question of law, *not* the facts nor inferences to be drawn therefrom. The same reasoning applies where the facts are accepted or not in dispute.

R. v. Morin (1992), 16 C.R. (4th) 291, 76 C.C.C. (3d) 193 (S.C.C.) — Failure to appreciate evidence only amounts to an error of law where it is based on a misapprehension of some legal principle.

R. v. Morin (1992), 16 C.R. (4th) 291, 76 C.C.C. (3d) 193 (S.C.C.) — There is *no* obligation on a trial judge to record all or any specific part of the process of deliberation on the facts. The trial judge must consider all the evidence in relation to the ultimate issue, but unless the reasons show that this was *not* done, the failure to record it as having been done affords no basis for a conclusion of legal error in this respect.

R. v. B. (G.) (1990), 77 C.R. (3d) 370, 56 C.C.C. (3d) 181 (S.C.C.); affirming (1988), 65 Sask. R. 134 (C.A.) — The admissibility of evidence, whether evidence is capable of constituting corroboration and the interpretation of a statute are questions of law. A question of law also arises where a finding that P has *not* proven guilt beyond a reasonable doubt is based on an erroneous approach to or treatment of evidence adduced at trial, self-misdirection with respect to relevant evidence or where there is error as to the legal effect, rather than the inferences to be drawn from, undisputed or found facts.

Schuldt v. R. (1985), 49 C.R. (3d) 136, 23 C.C.C. (3d) 225 (S.C.C.); reversing (1983), 23 Man. R. (2d) 75 (C.A.) — A finding as to intention D is a question of fact. The total absence of a foundation for a finding of fact, however, is an error of law. In the case of an acquittal this type of error will occur only if there has been a transfer by law to D of the burden of proof of a given fact. Without a shifting of the burden of proof upon D there is always some evidence upon which to make a finding of fact favourable to D, and such a finding, if in error, is an error of fact.

Fanjoy v. R. (1985), 48 C.R. (3d) 113, 21 C.C.C. (3d) 312 (S.C.C.) — The decision to exercise judicial discretion to intervene in cross-examination, or to refrain from intervention, involves a question of law and fact.

Johnson v. R. (1975), 23 C.R.N.S. 273, 13 C.C.C. (2d) 402 (S.C.C.) — Whether certain conduct constitutes an offence under the *Code* is a question of law. The true meaning to be attributed to the interrelation of two sections of the *Code* also raises a question of law alone.

Sunbeam Corp. v. R., [1969] 2 C.C.C. 189 (S.C.C.) — The question of *sufficiency* of evidence to support a conviction is a question of fact.

Lampard v. R. (1969), 6 C.R.N.S. 157, [1969] 3 C.C.C. 249 (S.C.C.) — Whether D's acts were done with a guilty state of mind, is a question of fact. If the trial judge errs in finding that the onus of proving that D's guilty intent had *not* been satisfied, this too is an error of fact, *not* an error of law.

R. v. Kipnes (1971), 2 C.C.C. (2d) 56 (Alta. C.A.) — It is a question of law where the trial judge applies misconceptions of the law as to what is necessary to be proved in order to establish the P's case.

R. v. Huot, [1969] 1 C.C.C. 256 (Man. C.A.) — *See also*: *R. v. Watterson* (1987), 21 O.A.C. 296 (C.A.) — The question of law alone in P's appeal must *not* be in the abstract but directly and concretely related to the acquittal. A finding that certain documents were not obscene was, at most, a question of mixed law and fact.

R. v. Sanver (1973), 28 C.R.N.S. 10, 12 C.C.C. (2d) 105 (N.B. C.A.) — The improper dismissal of a charge on the basis of *autrefois acquit* is a question of law alone.

R. v. Baig (1985), 46 C.R. (3d) 222, 20 C.C.C. (3d) 515 (Ont. C.A.); affirmed on other grounds (1987), 61 C.R. (3d) 97, 37 C.C.C. (3d) 181 (S.C.C.) — A total absence of evidence supporting the trial judge's conclusion raises a question of law.

R. v. Davis (1973), 14 C.C.C. (2d) 517 (Ont. C.A.); affirmed (sub nom. *Sokoloski v. R.)* 33 C.C.C. (2d) 496 — Where, on the evidence accepted by the trial judge, P has established the ingredients of the offence, it is error in law to acquit.

R. v. Richard, [1986] R.L. 12 (Que. C.A.) — The failure of the trial judge to consider conclusive evidence incriminating D constituted an error of law.

R. v. Dixon (1988), 64 C.R. (3d) 372, 42 C.C.C. (3d) 318 (Y.T. C.A.) — The interpretation of the term "bodily harm" is a question of law. Where the drawing of an inference from facts includes a legal element, the question of whether the legal element has been correctly defined and applied is a question of law.

Question of Fact

R. v. Kent (1994), 92 C.C.C. (3d) 344 (S.C.C.); reversing (1993), 122 N.S.R. (2d) 348 (N.S. C.A.) — On an appeal from acquittal, an appellate court has *no* jurisdiction to consider the reasonableness of a trial judge's verdict. The question whether the proper inference has been drawn from the facts established in evidence, also the sufficiency of evidence are questions of fact.

R. v. Roman (1987), 38 C.C.C. (3d) 385 (Nfld. C.A.) — *See also*: *Wild v. R.* (1970), 12 C.R.N.S. 306, [1970] 4 C.C.C. 40 (S.C.C.) — P may appeal an acquittal on a matter of fact where the trial judge has failed to appreciate or has disregarded the evidence. This is the case where the trial judge has founded the acquittal on conjectural possibility rather than reasonable doubt.

R. v. Whynot (Stafford) (1983), 37 C.R. (3d) 198, 9 C.C.C. (3d) 449 (N.S. C.A.) — P does *not* have a right to appeal an acquittal on the ground that the verdict of the jury was perverse on a question of fact. A finding of fact is only appealable by D.

R. v. Moreau (1986), 51 C.R. (3d) 209, 26 C.C.C. (3d) 359 (Ont. C.A.) — P has no right of appeal with respect to a question of fact, in the absence of a misdirection as to a governing principle or a disregard of relevant evidence.

R. v. Atlantic Sugar Refineries Co. (1978), 41 C.C.C. (2d) 209 (Que. C.A.) — Although the intention of D is a question of fact, a judge's misdirection concerning the intention required is an error of law.

Sentence: S. 676(1)(d) [See also "sentence" in s. 673]

Hunt v. R. (1979), 7 C.R. (3d) 38, 45 C.C.C. (2d) 257 (S.C.C.) — P may appeal the grant of a discharge, with leave, as a matter of sentence: or, as of right, on a question of law alone, the right of the court to grant the discharge.

R. v. Smith (1981), 25 C.R. (3d) 190 (Alta. C.A.) — A litigant before the appellate court may repudiate a position taken by counsel in the trial court where the public interest and the orderly administration of justice is outweighed by the gravity of the crime and the gross insufficiency of the sentence.

R. v. Irwin (1979), 10 C.R. (3d) S-33, 48 C.C.C. (2d) 423 (Alta. C.A.) — *See also*: *R. v. Hogan* (1979), 50 C.C.C. (2d) 439 (N.S. C.A.) — P should *not* be permitted to introduce new evidence on an appeal against sentence unless it is something that P counsel at trial could not reasonably be expected to have introduced, or perhaps in cases where D is a real danger to the public.

R. v. Wood (1976), 26 C.C.C. (2d) 100 (Alta. C.A.) — P's right of appeal against sentence should *not* be restricted by the position of counsel at trial, nor should the appellate court be bound by P's stated position. The position, however, may be taken into consideration.

R. v. Cooper (1997), 117 C.C.C. (3d) 249 (Nfld. C.A.) — The fact that P takes *no* specific position on sentence at trial does *not* preclude P from asserting on appeal that the sentence was not fit.

R. v. Dubien (1982), 27 C.R. (3d) 378, 67 C.C.C. (2d) 341 (Ont. C.A.) — Counsel for P at trial cannot take away the discretion vested in the Attorney General to determine whether an appeal should or should not be taken, or the obligation imposed on the appeal court to consider the fitness of the sentence when the matter is before it.

R. v. Richards (1979), 11 C.R. (3d) 193, 49 C.C.C. (2d) 517 (Ont. C.A.) — Where the terms of sentence have been substantially performed, the court of appeal will not vary the sentence unless the court is satisfied that the sentence was so manifestly wrong as to require court intervention in the interests of justice.

R. v. Agozzino (1968), 6 C.R.N.S. 147, [1970] 1 C.C.C. 380 (Ont. C.A.) — The court will *not* give effect, on P's appeal against sentence, to the repudiation by P of the position taken by its counsel at trial.

R. v. MacArthur (1978), 39 C.C.C. (2d) 158 (P.E.I. C.A.) — P will *not* be allowed to repudiate its position at trial unless it can be shown that the public interest in the orderly administration of justice is outweighed by the gravity of the crime and the gross insufficiency of the sentence.

Charter Considerations

R. v. Morgentaler (1985), 48 C.R. (3d) 1, 22 C.C.C. (3d) 353 (Ont. C.A.); reversed in part on other grounds (1988), 62 C.R. (3d) 1, 37 C.C.C. (3d) 449 (S.C.C.) — Section 676(1)(a) does *not* contravene *Charter* ss. 7, 11(d) or (h).

Related Provisions: Under s. 696, the Attorney General of Canada has equivalent rights of appeal in proceedings instituted at the instance of the Government of Canada and conducted by or on behalf of that government.

"Attorney General" is defined in s. 2 and, for the purposes of s. 676, includes his/her lawful deputy.

Other related provisions are described in the corresponding note to s. 675, *supra*.

676.1 Appeal re costs — A party who is ordered to pay costs may, with leave of the court of appeal or a judge of a court of appeal, appeal the order or the amount of costs ordered.

1997, c. 18, s. 94.

Commentary: The section creates a *qualified* right of appeal. A party who is ordered to pay costs may appeal to the court of appeal. Leave to appeal, granted by the court or a judge of it, is required. The appeal may be taken against the making or amount of the order.

Related Provisions: There is no general *Code* authority to award costs in indictable matters. Section 683(3) bars an award of costs on an appeal. Costs may be awarded, however, where an adjournment is required to cure prejudice to D because the indictment has been amended (s. 601(5)).

The rule is different in summary conviction proceedings. Costs may be awarded at trial (ss. 803(4) and 809) and on summary conviction appeal (ss. 826 and 827), as well as on further appeal to the court of appeal under s. 839(3).

Section 676.1 does *not* specify the basis upon which an appeal may be taken, nor does it define the disposition powers of the court.

677. Specifying grounds of dissent — Where a judge of the court of appeal expresses an opinion dissenting from the judgment of the court, the judgment of the court shall specify any grounds in law on which the dissent, in whole or in part, is based.

R.S., c. C-34, s. 606; 1994, c. 44, s. 67.

Commentary: The section appears somewhat incongruous, positioned in a group of sections that confer rights of appeal. It requires that the *formal judgment* of the court of appeal *specify* any *grounds* of law upon which the *dissent* of a judge of appeal, in whole or in part, is based.

Case Law

Warkentin v. R. (1976), 35 C.R.N.S. 21, 30 C.C.C. (2d) 1 (S.C.C.) — Where in the formal judgment of the court of appeal the grounds of dissent were *not* specified, such an irregularity was *not* fatal to the individual's right to appeal nor to the jurisdiction of the court to hear the appeal.

Related Provisions: A dissent on a question of law may found an appeal to the Supreme Court of Canada, as of right, under ss. 691(1)(a), 692(3)(a) and 693(1)(a).

Procedure on Appeals

678. (1) Notice of appeal — An appellant who proposes to appeal to the court of appeal or to obtain the leave of that court to appeal shall give notice of appeal or notice of his application for leave to appeal in such manner and within such period as may be directed by rules of court.

(2) Extension of time — The court of appeal or a judge thereof may at any time extend the time within which notice of appeal or notice of an application for leave to appeal may be given.

R.S., c. C-34, s. 607; 1972, c. 13, s. 53; 1974–75–76, c. 105, s. 16.

Commentary: The section requires that notice of appeal or notice of application for leave to appeal be given in the manner and within the time directed by rules of court. The court of appeal or a judge thereof, under s. 678(2), may, at any time, extend the time within which the notice may be given.

Case Law
Extension of Time Limit: S. 678(2)

R. v. O'Malley (1997), 119 C.C.C. (3d) 360 (B.C. C.A.) — The Court of Appeal has no jurisdiction to review the order of a single judge of the court refusing an extension of time within which to appeal.

R. v. Antoine (1972), 17 C.R.N.S. 313, 6 C.C.C. (2d) 162 (Man. C.A.) — Before an extension of time is granted, the applicant must show that a *bona fide* intention to appeal existed before the time limit expired, and that the judgment sought to be appealed from is arguably wrong.

R. v. Stokes (1966), 49 C.R. 97 (Man. C.A.) — The extension of time must be granted by "the court of appeal or a judge thereof" *not* by the registrar.

R. v. Hetsberger (1979), 47 C.C.C. (2d) 154 (Ont. C.A.) — In a case where the consequences of conviction were unexpectedly great and there was arguably no offence in law, an extension was granted in spite of there being no intent to appeal within the requisite time period.

R. v. Gruener (1979), 46 C.C.C. (2d) 88 (Ont. C.A.) — In considering whether it is arguable that the judgment appealed from is wrong, the appellate judge should *not* consider whether objections to the charge were made by counsel at trial.

R. v. Dunbrook (1978), 44 C.C.C. (2d) 264 (Ont. C.A.) — The day of an acquittal should *not* be included in calculating the time period for appeals without leave. An attempt by P to serve a notice of appeal on the last day of the requisite time period may show a *bona fide* intention to appeal.

R. v. Audy (No. 1) (1977), 34 C.C.C. (2d) 228 (Ont. C.A.) — The court of appeal has jurisdiction to rescind previous orders refusing extensions of time where the interests of justice so require.

R. v. Kelly (1976), 33 C.C.C. (2d) 248 (Ont. C.A.) — *See also: Charest v. R.* (1957), 26 C.R. 250, 119 C.C.C. 199 (Que. C.A.) — Where D has signed a waiver of right to appeal under the *Penitentiary Act,* the court of appeal may still allow an appeal to proceed, but only where there is much merit in the appeal. A waiver should not be treated lightly.

R. v. Scheller (No. 2) (1976), 37 C.R.N.S. 349, 32 C.C.C. (2d) 286 (Ont. C.A.) — Following a dismissal of charges against D, P's attempt to relay the charges was stayed as an abuse of process. An extension of time to appeal the original dismissal was denied since P's deliberate choice of relaying the charges displayed no *bona fide* intention to appeal within the time limit.

R. v. Grover (1967), 1 C.R.N.S. 129, [1967] 3 C.C.C. 387 (Ont. C.A.) — *See also*: *R. v. Sutton*, (January 14, 1988), Vancouver Doc. No. CA007567 (B.C. C.A.) — An extension of time was granted where P sought to appeal an unlawfully imposed suspended sentence three months after sentencing. The appeal court has jurisdiction to declare the illegality of the sentence and put the proceedings right.

R. v. Walker (1978), 46 C.C.C. (2d) 124 (Que. C.A.) — D's second application for an extension was granted where a special change in his circumstances arose following the original refusal.

Related Provisions: Under s. 482(1), the court of appeal may make rules respecting criminal appeals not inconsistent with the *Code*. Service of a notice of appeal or notice of application for leave to appeal may be made substitutionally on a respondent who cannot be found, after reasonable efforts, under s. 678.1.

Other related provisions are discussed in a corresponding note to s. 675, *supra*.

678.1 Service where respondent cannot be found — Where a respondent cannot be found after reasonable efforts have been made to serve him with a notice of appeal or notice of an application for leave to appeal, service of the notice of appeal or the notice of the application for leave to appeal may be effected substitutionally in the manner and within the period directed by a judge of the court of appeal.

R.S. 1985, c. 27 (1st Supp.), s. 140.

Commentary: The section authorizes *substitutional service*, in a *manner* and within a *period* directed by a judge of the court of appeal, of a notice of appeal or notice of application for leave to appeal upon a respondent who cannot be found, after reasonable efforts have been made to effect (personal) service.

Related Provisions: Any order for substitutional service should try to ensure the likelihood of the respondent receiving notification of the appellate proceedings and include disclosure of the time and date of hearing.

679. (1) Release pending determination of appeal — A judge of the court of appeal may, in accordance with this section, release an appellant from custody pending the determination of his appeal if,

(a) in the case of an appeal to the court of appeal against conviction, the appellant has given notice of appeal or, where leave is required, notice of his application for leave to appeal pursuant to section 678;

(b) in the case of an appeal to the court of appeal against sentence only, the appellant has been granted leave to appeal; or

(c) in the case of an appeal or an application for leave to appeal to the Supreme Court of Canada, the appellant has filed and served his notice of appeal or, where leave is required, his application for leave to appeal.

(2) Notice of application for release — Where an appellant applies to a judge of the court of appeal to be released pending the determination of his appeal, he shall give written notice of the application to the prosecutor or to such other person as a judge of the court of appeal directs.

(3) Circumstances in which appellant may be released — In the case of an appeal referred to in paragraph (1)(a) or (c), the judge of the court of appeal may order

that the appellant be released pending the determination of his appeal if the appellant establishes that

    (a) the appeal or application for leave to appeal is not frivolous,

    (b) he will surrender himself into custody in accordance with the terms of the order, and

    (c) his detention is not necessary in the public interest.

(4) **Idem** — In the case of an appeal referred to in paragraph (1)(*b*), the judge of the court of appeal may order that the appellant be released pending the determination of his appeal or until otherwise ordered by a judge of the court of appeal if the appellant establishes that

    (a) the appeal has sufficient merit that, in the circumstances, it would cause unnecessary hardship if he were detained in custody;

    (b) he will surrender himself into custody in accordance with the terms of the order; and

    (c) his detention is not necessary in the public interest.

(5) **Conditions of order** — Where the judge of the court of appeal does not refuse the application of the appellant, he shall order that the appellant be released

    (a) on his giving an undertaking to the judge, without conditions or with such conditions as the judge directs, to surrender himself into custody in accordance with the order, or

    (b) on his entering into a recognizance

        (i) with one or more sureties,

        (ii) with deposit of money or other valuable security,

        (iii) with both sureties and deposit, or

        (iv) with neither sureties nor deposit,

    in such amount, subject to such conditions, if any, and before such justice as the judge directs,

and the person having the custody of the appellant shall, where the appellant complies with the order, forthwith release the appellant.

(6) **Application of certain provisions of s. 525** — The provisions of subsections 525(5), (6) and (7) apply with such modification as the circumstances require in respect of a person who has been released from custody under subsection (5) of this section.

(7) **Release or detention pending hearing of reference** — Where, with respect to any person, the Minister of Justice gives a direction or makes a reference under section 690, this section applies to the release or detention of that person pending the hearing and determination of the reference as though that person were an appellant in an appeal described in paragraph (1)(a).

(7.1) **Release or detention pending new trial or new hearing** — Where, with respect to any person, the court of appeal or the Supreme Court of Canada orders a new trial, section 515 or 522, as the case may be, applies to the release or detention of that person pending the new trial or new hearing as though that person were charged with the offence for the first time, except that the powers of a justice under section 515 or of a judge under section 522 are exercised by a judge of the court of appeal.

(8) Application to appeals on summary conviction proceedings — This section applies to applications for leave to appeal and appeals to the Supreme Court of Canada in summary conviction proceedings.

(9) Form of undertaking or recognizance — An undertaking under this section may be in Form 12 and a recognizance under this section may be in Form 32.

(10) Directions for expediting appeal, new trial, etc. — A judge of the court of appeal, where on the application of an appellant he does not make an order under subsection (5) or where he cancels an order previously made under this section, or a judge of the Supreme Court of Canada on application by an appellant in the case of an appeal to that Court, may give such directions as he thinks necessary for expediting the hearing of the appellant's appeal or for expediting the new trial or new hearing or the hearing of the reference, as the case may be.

R.S., c. C-34, s. 608; c. 2 (2d Supp.), s. 12;R.S. 1985, c. 27 (1st Supp.), s. 141; 1997, c. 18, s. 95.

Commentary: The section authorizes the *release* of an *appellant* pending the determination of an *appeal* to the *court of appeal* or *Supreme Court of Canada*, or a *new trial* or hearing ordered by either court.

Where D appeals or applies for leave to appeal to the court of appeal against *conviction*, or *conviction and sentence*, or appeals or applies for leave to appeal to the Supreme Court of Canada, D must first give *notice* of appeal, or of application for leave to appeal or, in the case of the Supreme Court of Canada, file and serve the same documents under s. 679(1)(a) or (c). The appellant must then establish that the appeal or application for leave to appeal is *not frivolous*, that he/she will *surrender* into custody as the court requires, and that his/her detention is *not necessary in the public interest*. The "public interest" criterion, as it appears in s. 515(10)(b), has been held to be constitutionally invalid under *Charter* s. 11(e).

Where D appeals to the *court* of *appeal* against *sentence only*, under s. 679(1)(b) D must first obtain leave to appeal and thereafter establish, under s. 679(4), that the appeal has sufficient merit that, in the circumstances, it would cause unnecessary hardship if D were detained in custody. The requirements of surrender and detention not being necessary in the public interest must also be met. Sections 679(5) and (9) govern the form of release.

Where a new trial or hearing is ordered, or the Minister of Justice gives a direction or orders a reference under s. 690, release or detention is determined under s. 679(3). Section 679(8) makes the section, presumably s. 679(1)(c) and s. 679(3), applicable to applications for leave to appeal and appeals to the Supreme Court of Canada in summary conviction proceedings.

Where it is alleged that, after release pending appeal, an appellant has either contravened or been about to contravene the release order or has, since release, committed an indictable offence, s. 679(6) makes applicable ss. 525(5)–(7). D may be arrested, with or without warrant, and will be taken before a judge of the court of appeal to show cause why detention is not justified under s. 515(10).

Where D has been detained, either for failure to meet the onus to justify release or because of cancellation of a release order, a judge of the court of appeal or Supreme Court of Canada, as the case may be, may give such directions as he/she thinks necessary to *expedite* the appeal, new trial, hearing or reference.

Case Law

Jurisdiction

R. v. Parsons (1997), 124 C.C.C. (3d) 92 (Nfld. C.A.) — Where D is alleged to have breached a release order made by a judge of the court of appeal pending a new trial on a charge of murder, a *single* judge of the court of appeal may hear P's application to revoke the order under s. 524.

R. v. Johnson (1998), 31 C.C.C. (3d) 343, 21 C.R. (5th) 135 (N.S. C.A. [In Chambers]) — Where the Minister of Justice directs a reference under *Code* s. 690, which may involve the hearing of an appeal from conviction, the relevant factors to consider in deciding whether D should be released pending the hearing are set out in s. 679(3).

R. v. U. (F.J.) (1995), 95 C.C.C. (3d) 408 (Ont. C.A.) — The *Code* does *not* provide any authority for a judge of the court of appeal to *revoke* an order of another judge of the same court releasing an appellant pending the hearing of his/her appeal to the Supreme Court of Canada. The referential incorporation by s. 679(6) of ss. 525(5), (6) and (7), permits a judge of the court of appeal to issue a warrant for the arrest of the appellant where the requirements of s. 525(5) have been met.

R. v. Zundel (1990), 54 C.C.C. (3d) 400 (Ont. C.A.) — An applicant for leave to appeal to the Supreme Court of Canada has status to apply to a judge of a provincial court of appeal for judicial interim release pending the determination of his/her appeal to the Supreme Court of Canada, upon filing and service of the notice of application for leave to appeal setting out the grounds on which leave to appeal will be sought, notwithstanding that all documents required under Rule 23(1) of the *Rules of the Supreme Court of Canada* have not been filed and served.

R. v. Morris (1985), 21 C.C.C. (3d) 242 (Ont. C.A.) — A judge of the court of appeal has the power to grant release only from the custody to which D is subject pending the determination of D's appeal, and not from some future custody which may be imposed.

R. v. Smale (1979), 51 C.C.C. (2d) 126 (Ont. C.A.) — The court of appeal has jurisdiction to order release pending appeal prior to the imposition of sentence by the trial court, where D has been remanded into custody pending sentencing. This jurisdiction should only be exercised sparingly.

Successive Applications

R. v. D'Agostino (1998), 127 C.C.C. (3d) 209 (Alta. C.A. [In Chambers]) — An appellant, denied bail on an application under *Code* s. 679, may make a second application to a single judge of the court of appeal where there is a material change in circumstances. It is preferable but *not* essential that the same judge hear both applications.

R. v. Daniels (1997), 119 C.C.C. (3d) 413 (Ont. C.A.) — Section 680, which provides the only means by which the correctness of a decision under s. 679 may be challenged, does *not* foreclose a second application under s. 679 where the circumstances have changed. The right to bring a second application does *not* require express statutory application.

While it is usually preferable for the judge who heard the first s. 679 application to hear subsequent applications, there is *no* invariable rule.

Grounds For Release — Onus

R. v. Brent (No. 2), [1972] 4 W.W.R. 766 (B.C. C.A.) — Notwithstanding that by virtue of a new trial having been ordered D is to be presumed innocent of the offence, the *onus* is on the *applicant* to satisfy the court that he will surrender himself into custody in accordance with the terms of the order and that his detention is *not* necessary in the public interest.

R. v. Ponak (1969), 15 C.R.N.S. 105, [1970] 1 C.C.C. 250 (B.C. C.A.) — The applicant has the burden of proving to the reasonable satisfaction of the judge, on the balance of probabilities, that the conditions outlined in s. 679(3) have been met.

R. v. Matz (1988), 55 Man. R. (2d) 79 (C.A.) — At least one of the grounds for which leave is sought must have merit.

R. v. Babineau (1979), 28 N.B.R. (2d) 69 (C.A.) — On a hearing for release pending appeal from conviction, the onus is on the appellant to satisfy the court that the appeal is *not* frivolous, that there is some arguable point, and that detention is *not* necessary in the public interest. The appellant must put before the court some in-depth information about the circumstances giving rise to the grounds of appeal relied upon.

R. v. Davison (1974), 20 C.C.C. (2d) 424 (Ont. C.A.) — The onus is on the applicant to show that an appeal is *not* frivolous and that the grounds of appeal raise an arguable point, even in circumstances where the appeal has not proceeded due to a lengthy delay in the preparation of the transcripts.

R. v. Zarubin (1986), 54 Sask. R. 302 (C.A.) — Where no argument was presented on whether or not the appeal was frivolous, or whether the detention was necessary in the public interest, D's application for release was refused.

Public Interest [See also s. 515(10)]

R. v. S. (J.T.) (1996), 112 C.C.C. (3d) 184 (Alta. C.A.) — The "public interest" does *not* require that D demonstrate a ground of appeal which has a strong probability of success.

R. v. Nguyen (1997), 10 C.R. (5th) 325, 119 C.C.C. (3d) 269 (B.C. C.A. [In Chambers]) — Release should be granted unless some factor(s) would cause ordinary, reasonable, fair-minded members of society, or persons informed about the philosophy of the legislation, *Charter* values and the actual circumstances of the case, to believe that detention is required to maintain public confidence in the administration of justice. The relevant circumstances are those of the offence and offender.

R. v. Farinacci (1993), 25 C.R. (4th) 350, 86 C.C.C. (3d) 32 (Ont. C.A.) — *See also*: *R. v. Baltovich* (1992), 10 O.R. (3d) 737 (Ont. C.A.); *R. v. Pabani* (1991), 10 C.R. (4th) 381 (Ont. C.A.); *R. v. Branco* (1993), 25 C.R. (4th) 370, 87 C.C.C. (3d) 71 (B.C. C.A.) — The "public interest" requirement in s. 679(3)(c) is *not* unconstitutionally vague.

R. v. Pabani (1991), 10 C.R. (4th) 381 (Ont. C.A.) — "Public interest" in s. 679(3) does *not* relate solely to the prevention of further criminal acts. It involves a wider concept including matters of public perception of and confidence in the administration of justice. The unlikelihood of recidivism is *not* conclusive. Release of a person convicted of a serious crime involving violence to the person, in particular spousal abuse, is a matter of real public concern.

R. v. Demyen (1975), 26 C.C.C. (2d) 324 (Sask. C.A.) — The judge has a wide and unfettered discretion to determine what constitutes the public interest. Public interest has a comprehensive meaning and must be decided in the circumstances of each case. Any action which may detrimentally affect the public confidence and respect in courts would be contrary to the public interest. Further, the appellant must show something more than the fact that his appeal is not frivolous and that he will surrender himself into custody to establish that his detention is not necessary in the public interest.

Charter Considerations

R. v. Farinacci (1993), 25 C.R. (4th) 350, 86 C.C.C. (3d) 32 (Ont. C.A.) — *See also*: *R. v. Baltovich* (1992), 10 O.R. (3d) 737 (Ont. C.A.); *R. v. Pabani* (1991), 10 C.R. (4th) 381 (Ont. C.A.); *R. v. Branco* (1993), 25 C.R. (4th) 370, 87 C.C.C. (3d) 71 (B.C. C.A.) — *Charter* s. 11(e) does *not* apply to release pending appeal.

R. v. Sutherland (1994), 30 C.R. (4th) 265, 90 C.C.C. (3d) 376 (Sask. C.A.) — Section 679(7) is constitutionally invalid to the extent that it applies to a person who has been granted a new trial by the court of appeal. Such a person is in the same position as a person charged with an offence. Judicial interim release is determined under s. 515(10) and 522.

Related Provisions: Section 680 authorizes a review, of decisions made under s. 679.

An undertaking may be in Form 12, a recognizance in Form 32. It is common for the release order to contain terms, which require an appellant to surrender into custody on the day prior to the hearing of his/her appeal, or on a fixed date if it is not by then perfected, to remain within the province, to notify the registrar of any change of address, or similar conditions. Failure to surrender into custody under the order may result in the dismissal of D's appeal as abandoned.

Breach of a term of the release order including failure to surrender as required, may engage ss. 145(2) and (3).

680. (1) Review by court of appeal — A decision made by a judge under section 522 or subsection 524(4) or (5) or a decision made by a judge of the court of appeal under section 261 or 679 may, on the direction of the chief justice or acting chief justice of the court of appeal, be reviewed by that court and that court may, if it does not confirm the decision,

(a) vary the decision; or

(b) substitute such other decision as, in its opinion, should have been made.

(2) Single judge acting — On consent of the parties, the powers of the court of appeal under subsection (1) may be exercised by a judge of that court.

(3) Enforcement of decision — A decision as varied or substituted under this section shall have effect and may be enforced in all respects as though it were the decision originally made.

R.S., c. 2 (2d Supp.), s. 12; 1974–75–76, c. 93, s. 73;R.S. 1985, c. 27 (1st Supp.), s. 142; 1994, c. 44, s. 68.

Commentary: The section authorizes the *review* of decisions made by a *judge* of the *superior court* of criminal jurisdiction and of the *court of appeal* respecting the release or detention of D.

Section 680(1) governs decisions made by a judge of the superior court of criminal jurisdiction at a judicial interim release hearing (s. 522) or on a misconduct hearing (ss. 524(4), (5)), as well as determinations made by a judge of the court of appeal relating to stays of the operation of driving prohibitions (s. 261) or release of an appellant (s. 679) pending appeal. The procedure involves two steps. An *application* is made to the chief justice or acting chief justice of the court of appeal for a *direction* that the decision be reviewed by the court of appeal. If the direction is refused, no review will be held. Where a review is directed, the court of appeal, or under s. 680(2), with the consent of the parties, a single judge of the court of appeal, will review the order and either confirm, vary or substitute the decision that, in his/her opinion, should have been made. Under s. 680(3), an order made on review has the same effect and is as enforceable as if it had been made at first instance.

Case Law
Nature and Right of Review

R. v. Bukmeier (1996), 107 C.C.C. (3d) 272 (B.C. C.A.) — An order detaining D made by the trial judge under s. 523(2)(a) is *not* reviewable by a provincial appellate court, rather, only by the Supreme Court of Canada with leave under s. 40 of the *Supreme Court Act*.

Nature of Review

R. v. Desjarlais (1984), 14 C.C.C. (3d) 77 (Man. C.A.) — *See also*: *R. v. Perron* (1989), 73 C.R. (3d) 174, 51 C.C.C. (3d) 518 (Que. C.A.) — The court of appeal, on a review of an order by a judge of the court of appeal granting release pending appeal, may substitute its opinion for that of the single judge.

R. v. Smith (1973), 13 C.C.C. (2d) 374 (N.B. C.A.) — The duty of the court under this section is to examine the record judicially and to render the decision that the court thinks should have been made by the judge below, giving proper regard to his/her findings of fact and the inferences which he/she drew.

R. v. Benson (1992), 14 C.R. (4th) 245, 73 C.C.C. (3d) 303 (N.S. C.A.) — The nature of a *review* is the *correctness*, not the *reasonableness* of the decision at first instance. The court may also receive and consider additional evidence which bears upon the application, provided it is relevant and arose subsequent to the order under review. The court may substitute its opinion for that of the judge of appeal after consideration of the record, the governing principles and the findings and conclusion made at first instance.

R. v. Moore (1979), 49 C.C.C. (2d) 78 (N.S. C.A.) — A review under this section is a review of the record, not a consideration of the application *de novo*. An order for review under this section should be directed by the chief justice unless D would have no hope of success on the record.

R. v. West (1972), 20 C.R.N.S. 15, 9 C.C.C. (2d) 369 (Ont. C.A.) — A review of an order for interim release is an appeal, not a hearing *de novo*. Neither side has the *right* to submit additional material; however, the court of appeal may, as in an appeal, grant leave to a party, in the usual way and upon the usual grounds, to produce new evidence.

R. c. Quinton (1993), 24 C.R. (4th) 242 (Que. C.A.) — On review of a decision of a single judge of appeal, the court of appeal must make its own determination of the facts. The applicant need not establish that the decision of the single judge is unreasonable or reflects manifest error.

Public Interest [See also s. 515(10)]

R. v. Benson (1992), 14 C.R. (4th) 245, 73 C.C.C. (3d) 303 (N.S. C.A.) — The "public interest" consideration of s. 679(3)(c) is of equal weight and importance with the matters of s. 679(3)(a) and (b). In determining the "public interest", the factors to be considered include:

i.   the nature of the offence;

ii.   V's age;

iii. the circumstances surrounding the offence; and

iv.   the public attitude towards the offence.

R. c. Quinton (1993), 24 C.R. (4th) 242 (Que. C.A.) — The "public interest" criterion is addressed differently when release is sought pending appeal. The appellant has already been convicted and cannot invoke the presumption of innocence. Considerations should include:

i.   the type of crime;

ii. the personal situation of the appellant; and,

iii. public confidence in the criminal justice system.

Related Provisions: There are no express provisions whereby misconduct hearings may be held, as for example where an appellant, since release by the court or a judge thereof under this section, has contravened the terms of the release order. Misconduct may, at all events, attract liability under ss. 145(2) and (3).

There is no express incorporation of s. 679(10) (order expediting the hearing of an appeal). The words of s. 680(1)(b) *viz*, "substitute such other decision as, in its opinion, should have been made", may permit such an order.

681. [Repealed 1991, c. 43, s. 9, Schedule, item 7.]

682. (1) Report by judge — Where, under this Part, an appeal is taken or an application for leave to appeal is made, the judge or provincial court judge who presided at the trial shall, at the request of the court of appeal or a judge thereof, in accordance with rules of court, furnish it or him with a report on the case or on any matter relating to the case that is specified in the request.

(2) Transcript of evidence — A copy or transcript of

(a) the evidence taken at the trial,

(b) any charge to the jury and any objections that were made to a charge to the jury,

(c) the reasons for judgment, if any, and

(d) the addresses of the prosecutor and the accused, if a ground for the appeal is based on either of the addresses,

shall be furnished to the court of appeal, except in so far as it is dispensed with by order of a judge of that court.

(3) [Repealed 1997, c. 18, s. 96(2)]

(4) Copies to interested parties — A party to an appeal is entitled to receive, on payment of any charges that are fixed by rules of court, a copy or transcript of any material that is prepared under subsections (1) and (2).

(5) Copy for minister of justice — The Minister of Justice is entitled, on request, to receive a copy or transcript of any material that is prepared under subsection (1) and (2).

R.S., c. C-34, s. 609; 1972, c. 13, s. 55; 1974–75–76, c. 105, s. 17; R.S. 1985, c. 27 (1st Supp.), ss. 143, 203; 1997, c. 18, s. 96.

Commentary: The section describes the *materials* to be forwarded to the court of appeal for its *use on the hearing of an appeal* under this Part.

Under s. 682(1), the *trial judge* is obliged to provide, at the request of the court of appeal or of a judge thereof, in accordance with rules of court, a *report* on the case, or any matter relating thereto. It is only upon and to the extent of a request therefor that a report of a trial judge is required.

In general, a transcript or copy of the evidence, charge, objections to the charge and reasons for judgment must be furnished to the court of appeal under s. 682(2), *except* to the extent dispensed with by an order of a judge of the court. The addresses of counsel are included, *semble*, only where a ground of appeal is based thereon. Under s. 682(4), each party to the appeal is entitled to receive, on payment of any charges fixed by rules of court, a copy or transcript of all material prepared for the court (report and transcript) under ss. 682(1)–(2). The Minister of Justice has a similar entitlement, on request, under s. 682(5).

Case Law
Report of Trial Judge: S. 682(1)

R. v. E. (A.W.) (1993), 23 C.R. (4th) 357, 83 C.C.C. (3d) 462 (S.C.C.) — Section 682(1) is an historical anachronism. A report of the trial judge ought only be requested in rare situations where something occurred which is not reflected in the transcript and is not the subject of agreement between counsel. There ought to be no standing request from courts of appeal to trial judges routinely to make a report.

R. v. E. (A.W.) (1993), 83 C.C.C. (3d) 462 (S.C.C.) — In the rare case where a trial judge's report is sought, trial counsel probably ought be given the opportunity to appear before the trial judge to make submissions with respect to the report. Copies of the report ought to be provided to appellate counsel so that they may make submissions in respect of it.

Baron v. R. (1930), 53 C.C.C. 154 (S.C.C.) — This section does not enable the trial judge, after an appeal has been argued, to put before the court of appeal, by way of certificate or otherwise, his/her answer to the various points taken upon the appeal.

R. v. Hawke (1975), 29 C.R.N.S. 1, 22 C.C.C. (2d) 19 (Ont. C.A.) — Where the trial has been completed and rulings made, it is inappropriate to deliver supplementary reasons *only* by reason of an appeal. This situation is to be distinguished from a case where the trial judge indicates the result he has arrived at but announces that he intends to give reasons later.

R. v. Mathieu, [1967] 3 C.C.C. 237 (Que. C.A.) — The report contemplated by this section is not intended to give the trial judge an opportunity to explain his decision or to answer the grounds of appeal. The report should be limited to incidents of the trial or to the judge's views on the credibility of D and other witnesses.

Transcripts: S. 682(2)

R. v. Hayes (1989), 68 C.R. (3d) 245, 48 C.C.C. (3d) 161 (S.C.C.) — As a general rule, before a new trial will be ordered because of a gap in a transcript there must be a serious possibility that there was an error in the missing portion of the transcript, or that the omission deprived the appellant of a ground of appeal. The trial judge's notes as to his charge to the jury may be accepted as accurate. It is also significant that counsel did *not* object to the charge.

R. v. Johnston (1976), 35 C.R.N.S. 164, 28 C.C.C. (2d) 222 (N.B. C.A.) — The purpose of s. 682(3) is to furnish the trial judge with an opportunity to inform the court of appeal of any disagreement which he might have as to the accuracy of the transcript. Where there is no dispute as to the transcript's accuracy, the fact that the transcript has not been certified due to the death of the trial judge does not entitle D to have his conviction set aside.

R. v. Robillard, [1969] 4 C.C.C. 120 (Que. C.A.) — Failure to comply with the mandatory *Code* provisions requiring that a copy or transcript of the addresses of P and D be furnished to the court of appeal led to a new trial being ordered.

R. v. Trotchie (1982), 66 C.C.C. (2d) 396 (Sask. C.A.) — Section 682(2), which provides for an order dispensing with the usual transcript requirements, cannot be used to relieve against the duty to record the proceedings. Although an order may be made obviating the need to transcribe the proceedings, the proceedings must be recorded and the failure to do so is a valid ground for setting aside a conviction and ordering a new trial.

Related Provisions: In most cases the court of appeal will determine an appeal on the basis of a transcript and/or agreed statement of fact, including the charge to the jury or reasons for judgment, as well as any proceedings subsequent thereto. Where the evidence taken has not been transcribed for the court of appeal, the judge's notes and/or report may be of assistance, indeed required, but, *semble*, not otherwise.

683. (1) Powers of court of appeal — For the purposes of an appeal under this Part, the court of appeal may, where it considers it in the interests of justice,

(a) order the production of any writing, exhibit, or other thing connected with the proceedings;

(b) order any witness who could have been a compellable witness at the trial, whether or not he was called at the trial,

(i) to attend and be examined before the court of appeal, or

(ii) to be examined in the manner provided by rules of court before a judge of the court of appeal, or before any officer of the court of appeal or justice of the peace or other person appointed by the court of appeal for the purposes;

(c) admit, as evidence, an examination that is taken under subparagraph (b)(ii);

(d) receive the evidence, if tendered, of any witness, including the appellant, who is a competent but not compellable witness;

(e) order that any question arising on the appeal that

(i) involves prolonged examination of writings or accounts, or scientific or local investigation,

(ii) cannot in the opinion of the court of appeal conveniently be inquired into before the court of appeal,

be referred for inquiry and report, in the manner provided by rules of court, to a special commissioner appointed by the court of appeal; and

(f) act upon the report of a commissioner who is appointed under paragraph (e) in so far as the court of appeal thinks fit to do so;

(g) amend the indictment, unless it is of the opinion that the accused has been misled or prejudiced in his defence or appeal.

(2) Parties entitled to adduce evidence and be heard — In proceedings under this section, the parties or their counsel are entitled to examine or cross-examine witnesses and, in an inquiry under paragraph (1)(e), are entitled to be present during the inquiry, and to adduce evidence and to be heard.

(3) Other powers — A court of appeal may exercise in relation to proceedings in the court, any powers not mentioned in subsection (1) that may be exercised by the court on appeals in civil matters, and may issue any process that is necessary to enforce the orders or sentences of the court, but no costs shall be allowed to the appellant or respondent on the hearing and determination of an appeal or on any proceedings preliminary or incidental thereto.

(4) Execution of process — Any process that is issued by the court of appeal under this section may be executed anywhere in Canada.

(5) Power to order suspension — Where an appeal or an application for leave to appeal has been filed in the court of appeal, that court, or a judge of that court, may, where it considers it to be in the interests of justice, order that

(a) any obligation to pay a fine,

(b) any order of forfeiture or disposition of forfeited property,

(c) any order to make restitution under section 738 or 739,

(d) any order to pay a victim fine surcharge under section 737

(e) the conditions prescribed in a probation order under subsections 732.1(2) and (3)

be suspended until the appeal has been determined.

(6) Revocation of suspension order — The court of appeal may revoke any order it makes under subsection (5) where it considers the revocation to be in the interests of justice.

R.S., c. C-34, s. 610; R.S. 1985, c. 27 (1st Supp.), s. 144; c. 23 (4th Supp.), s. 5; 1995, c. 22, s. 10; 1997, c. 18, ss. 97, 141(b).

Commentary: The section confers a wide range of non-dispositive authority on a court of appeal.

Under ss. 683(1) and (2) the court of appeal may *receive evidence* in any manner described, where it considers it in the *interests of justice* to do so. Section 683(2) entitles the parties to examine or cross-examine witnesses in proceedings under the section and be present, be heard and adduce evidence at any inquiry under s. 683(1)(e). Any process issued by a court of appeal may be executed anywhere in Canada.

Section 683(3) is a residual power. It authorizes the court of appeal to exercise, in relation to proceedings in the court, any power, *not* specifically enumerated in s. 683(1), that it may exercise in relation to *civil matters*, including the issuance of process, but *excluding* the award of *costs*.

Sections 683(5) and (6) permit the court or a judge of the court under s. 683(5) to order or revoke a *stay* suspending the obligations specified. The order may be made, in the interests of justice, until the appeal has been determined.

Under s. 683(1)(g), the court of appeal is specifically authorized to *amend the indictment* upon which D has been tried, *unless* the court is of the opinion that D has been *misled or prejudiced* in D's defence or on appeal.

Case Law

New Evidence: Ss. 683(1), (2)

R. v. Warsing, [1998] 3 S.C.R. 579, 130 C.C.C. (3d) 259, 21 C.R. (5th) 75 — Due diligence is only one factor to be considered in deciding whether fresh evidence should be received on appeal. The absence of due diligence, especially in criminal cases, should be assessed in light of other circumstances. If the evidence is compelling and the interests of justice require its admission, the failure to meet the due diligence test should give way to permit its admission.

Stolar v. R. (1988), 62 C.R. (3d) 313, 40 C.C.C. (3d) 1 (S.C.C.) — The procedure which should be followed when an application is made to the court of appeal for the admission of fresh evidence is that the motion should be heard and, if not dismissed, judgment should be reserved and the appeal heard. If, having heard the appeal, the court is of the opinion that the evidence could not reasonably have affected the result, it should dismiss the application of the introduction of fresh evidence and proceed to a disposition of the appeal. On the other hand, if the court is of the view that the fresh evidence is of such nature and effect that, taken with the other evidence, it would be conclusive of the issues in the case, the court of appeal can dispose of the matter then and there. Where, however, the fresh evidence does not possess that decisive character which would allow an immediate disposition of the appeal, but nevertheless has sufficient weight or probative force that, if accepted by the trier of fact, when considered with the other evidence in the case, it might have altered the result at trial, the court of appeal should admit the proffered evidence and direct a new trial where the evidence could be heard and the issues determined by the trier of fact.

Palmer v. R. (1980), 14 C.R. (3d) 22, 50 C.C.C. (2d) 194 (S.C.C.) — Special grounds must be shown to justify the exercise of the appellate court's discretion to admit new evidence. The following principles have emerged from applications of this nature: (1) the evidence should generally not be admitted if, by due diligence, it could have been adduced at trial, provided that this principle will not be applied as strictly in criminal as in civil cases; (2) the evidence must be relevant and bear upon a decisive or potentially decisive issue in the trial; (3) the evidence must be reasonably capable of belief; and (4) it must be such that, if believed, it could reasonably, when taken with the other evidence adduced at trial, be expected to have affected the result.

R. v. O'Brien (1977), 38 C.R.N.S. 325, 35 C.C.C. (2d) 209 (S.C.C.) — The court of appeal may *only* admit fresh evidence which would have been *admissible* at trial.

McMartin v. R. (1964), 43 C.R. 403 (S.C.C.) — The fact that the proposed evidence is of sufficient strength that it might reasonably affect the verdict constitutes strong grounds. The evidence should *not* be excluded only because reasonable diligence was *not* exercised to obtain it at or before trial.

R. v. Sauve (1997), 13 C.R. (5th) 391, 121 C.C.C. (3d) 225 (B.C. C.A.) — Where fresh evidence is directed to issues which relate to the validity of the trial process, *not* the issue decided at trial, the traditional fresh evidence criteria do *not* apply. The interests of justice require that the court of appeal admit the evidence.

R. v. Creamer (1995), 39 C.R. (4th) 383, 97 C.C.C. (3d) 108 (B.C. C.A.) — The test to be applied where the fresh evidence relates to non-disclosure is whether the evidence P withheld *might* have affected the outcome. It is *not* necessary to show that the evidence *must* be expected to have affected the result.

R. v. Cheung (1990), 56 C.C.C. (3d) 381 (B.C. C.A.) — Where P, as respondent in an appeal from conviction, seeks to invoke ss. 683(1)(a) and (d) to tender further evidence on appeal to correct an error in the trial record, the evidence should only be received where it is absolutely clear that the course of the trial would not have been, in any respect, different had the error been discoverd and its rectification sought at trial.

R. v. Bonin (1989), 47 C.C.C. (3d) 230 (B.C. C.A.); leave to appeal refused (1989), 102 N.R. 400n (S.C.C.) — The court of appeal can take judicial notice of materials concerning social and economic facts, such as statistics of impaired driving and its consequences, where such materials were not submitted to the court below and do not fall within s. 683(1)(d).

R. v. Gumbly (1996), 112 C.C.C. (3d) 61 (N.S. C.A.) — Fresh evidence directed to challenge the integrity of the trial process must be *admissible* evidence.

R. v. Nickerson (1993), 21 C.R. (4th) 262, 81 C.C.C. (3d) 398 (N.S. C.A.) — *See also*: *R. v. R. (K.A.)* (1993), *(*sub nom. *R. v. R.)* 18 C.R. (4th) 122, 79 C.C.C. (3d) 253 (N.S. C.A.) — Section 683(1)(a) does *not* authorize either an order for production of a physician's file relating to V or discussions between the physician and counsel for a party to a criminal appeal. In appropriate cases, it authorizes production of documentary material *connected with the proceeding* or the examination of a witness before the court or a person appointed for such purpose.

R. v. Young (1970), 11 C.R.N.S. 104, [1970] 5 C.C.C. 142 (N.S. C.A.) — An affidavit filed in support of an application to admit fresh evidence should indicate the evidence desired to be used; set forth when and how the appellant came to be aware of its existence; show what efforts, if any, had been made to have it adduced at trial; and state that had it been adduced the verdict might have been different. Where the fresh evidence is not by its nature conclusive, but is of sufficient strength that it might reasonably affect a jury's verdict, a new trial should be ordered.

R. v. Rajaeefard (1996), 46 C.R. (4th) 111, 104 C.C.C. (3d) 225 (Ont. C.A.) — New evidence relevant to the validity of the trial process, rather than a finding made at trial, may be admitted *without* satisfaction of the traditional criteria for reception of fresh evidence.

R. v. Edwards; R. v. Levo (1996), 46 C.R. (4th) 319, 105 C.C.C. (3d) 21 (Ont. C.A.); application for leave to appeal refused (1996), 108 C.C.C. (3d) vi (S.C.C.) — The *Code* does *not* authorize different standards for the introduction of fresh evidence in conviction and sentence appeals.

R. v. W. (W.) (1995), 43 C.R. (4th) 26, 100 C.C.C. (3d) 225 (Ont. C.A.) — Where it is argued that trial counsel's conduct resulted in a miscarriage of justice, the interests of justice will generally require that the court receive otherwise admissible evidence relevant to that claim. The proposed evidence must provide a basis upon which the court could conclude that a miscarriage of justice has occurred. The opposing party must be given adequate notice of the material, an opportunity to challenge it by cross-examination and to offer additional material relevant to the issue.

R. v. Barbeau (1996), 110 C.C.C. (3d) 69 (Que. C.A.) — The traditional criteria for the admission of new evidence on appeal do *not* apply where the purpose of the evidence is to challenge the very validity of the trial process.

R. c. Patoine (1993), 27 C.R. (4th) 344 (C.A. Qué.) — Mere diligence is *not* a threshold criterion on a motion under s. 683(1)(b)(ii), rather only one of several factors to be considered by the court that hears the appeal in deciding whether fresh evidence ought be admitted. (Chamberland and Baudoin JJ.A.)

R. v. Ledinski (1995), 102 C.C.C. (3d) 445 (Sask. C.A.) — ere is no lower standard of admissibility of fresh evidence where *Charter* violations are raised on appeal.

Amending Indictment: S. 683(1)(g)

R. v. Irwin (1998), 123 C.C.C. (3d) 316 (Ont. C.A.) — The scope of the amendment authority in *Code* s. 683(1)(g) is no different than the authority to amend at trial under s. 601. The appellate authority to amend includes defects in substance or form, and variations between the evidence and the charge.

An amendment on appeal may cure a variance between the charge and the evidence, regardless of whether the amendment materially changes the charge, substitutes a new charge, or adds an additional charge.

The power of amendment may *only* be exercised if D will *not* be "mislead or prejudiced in his defence or appeal". The *nature* of the proposed amendment and the stage of proceedings at which it is sought are important factors to consider in deciding whether D has been mislead or prejudiced. The risk prejudice is especially great where the proposed amendment would *materially* amend the charge on appeal and affirm the conviction on the basis of the amendment.

R. v. St. Clair (1994), 88 C.C.C. (3d) 402 (Ont. C.A.) — In determining whether to amend an indictment on appeal, a court of appeal should consider

i.   the original *indictment*;

ii. the *evidence* at trial;

iii. the *positions* of the parties at trial;

iv. the *instructions* of the trial judge;

v.   the *verdict* of the jury; and,

vi. the *issues* raised on appeal.

R. v. Symes (1989), 49 C.C.C. (3d) 81 (Ont. C.A.) — It is open to the court of appeal to amend the indictment to particularize the offence charged in such a way that it encompasses an included offence and then to substitute a conviction for the included offence.

Residual Powers: S. 683(3)

Dobney Foundry v. R. (No. 3) (1986), 29 C.C.C. (3d) 285 (B.C. C.A.) — Although a formal order had been entered by the court of appeal quashing various search warrants without making provision for the disposition of the documents seized under the warrants, nevertheless, the court could, by virtue of s. 683(3), make a further order for the disposition of the documents.

R. v. H. (E.F.); R. v. Rhingo (1997), 115 C.C.C. (3d) 89 (Ont. C.A.) — The authority to re-open proceedings in the exercise of an appellate court's ancillary or inherent jurisdiction to control its own process does not permit re-opening cases heard and disposed of on their merits.

R. v. Church of Scientology (1986), 25 C.C.C. (3d) 149 (Ont. C.A.) — The court of appeal, *not* a single judge, has ancillary jurisdiction to make an order to prevent the frustration of an appeal.

Suspension of Fine Pending Appeal: Ss. 683(5), (6) [See also s. 261]

R. v. CHEK TV Ltd. (1986), 27 C.C.C. (3d) 380 (B.C. C.A.) — Suspension of a penalty is available where the "interests of justice" so require. The interests of justice include more than the merits of the appeal but also the public interest.

R. v. Martin (1988), 86 N.B.R. (2d) 258 (C.A.) — An application under s. 683(5) must be made to the full panel not a single judge of the court of appeal.

R. v. Metro News Ltd. (1985), 21 C.C.C. (3d) 492 (Ont. C.A.) — The court of appeal does *not* have the power to order a stay in the payment of a fine imposed upon a corporation pending appeal where P has *not* yet sought to enforce payment. (But see s. 683(5)(a)).

Stays Of Probation Order Pending Appeal [See also ss. 261 and 675]

R. v. Keating (1991), 66 C.C.C. (3d) 530 (N.S. C.A.) — A single judge of the Appeal Division may stay the operation of a probation order pursuant to Rule 65 of the *Nova Scotia Rules of Civil Procedure* which is made under s. 482 of the *Code*, and makes the *Civil Procedure Rules* and related rules and practice of the Supreme Court applicable, *mutatis mutandis*, to criminal appeals.

Related Provisions: This authority is exercised by the court, not a judge thereof, on the hearing of an appeal or, depending upon provincial practice, on a motion prior to such hearing. Section 687 authorizes the determination or disposition of the appeal on its merits.

Section 695(1) confers similar authority upon the Supreme Court of Canada in appeals to that court (ss. 691–694 and 696).

684. (1) **Legal assistance for appellant** — A court of appeal or a judge of that court may, at any time, assign counsel to act on behalf of an accused who is a party to an appeal or to proceedings preliminary or incidental to an appeal where, in the opinion of the court or judge, it appears desirable in the interests of justice that the accused should have legal assistance and where it appears that the accused has not sufficient means to obtain that assistance.

(2) **Counsel fees and disbursements** — Where counsel is assigned pursuant to subsection (1) and legal aid is not granted to the accused pursuant to a provincial legal aid program, the fees and disbursements of counsel shall be paid by the Attorney General who is the appellant or respondent, as the case may be, in the appeal.

(3) **Taxation of fees and disbursements** — Where subsection (2) applies and where counsel and the Attorney General cannot agree on fees or disbursements of counsel, the Attorney General or the counsel may apply to the registrar of the court of appeal and the registrar may tax the disputed fees and disbursements.

R.S., c. C-34, s. 611; R.S. 1985, c. 34 (3d Supp.), s. 9.

Commentary: Under this section *counsel* may be *assigned* to act on behalf of D, a party to an appeal or proceedings preliminary or incidental to an appeal in the court of appeal.

Under s. 684(1), it is the court of appeal or a judge thereof who may assign counsel to act on behalf of D. D need *not* be an appellant. D, for example, may be the respondent in an appeal by the Attorney General. The authority may be exercised where the court or judge is of the opinion that it appears *desirable in the interests of justice* that D have legal assistance but lacks sufficient means to obtain such aid.

Sections 684(2) and (3) are concerned with the payment of counsel assigned under s. 684(1). Where legal aid is not granted under a provincial legal aid program, the fees and disbursements of counsel must be paid by the Attorney General who is the appellant or respondent in the appeal to which D is a party. Disagreements between the Attorney General and assigned counsel as to fees and disbursements are determined upon application to the registrar who may tax the disputed amounts.

Case Law

R. v. Johal (1998), 127 C.C.C. (3d) 273 (B.C. C.A. [In Chambers]) — Section 684 only operates when D is *not* granted legal aid and cannot otherwise obtain legal assistance. The section provides *no* authority to direct that counsel be paid by the Attorney General, nor does it contemplate a judge assigning counsel after legal aid has been offered, but apparently rejected.

R. v. Bernardo (1997), 12 C.R. (5th) 310, 121 C.C.C. (3d) 123 (Ont. C.A.) — Under s. 684(1), a judge and the Court have concurrent jurisdiction. Where appropriate, the Court may exercise its jurisdiction, notwithstanding a single judge has refused the application.

The "interests of justice" in s. 684(1) must take into account the broad access to appellate review contemplated by *Code* s. 675 and the wide remedial powers of the Court under s. 686.

Counsel should be appointed where

i.   D cannot effectively present the appeal without a lawyer's help; and

ii.   the Court cannot properly decide the case without the help of counsel.

The Court should consider first whether the appeal is arguable. The next issue is whether D can effectively advance the grounds of appeal without counsel. The complexities of the arguments and D's ability to make them should be considered.

Complexity of argument is a product of

i.   the grounds of appeal;

ii. the length and content of the trial record;

iii. the relevant legal principles; and

iv. the application of the principles to the facts of the case.

D's ability to make arguments in support of the grounds of appeal is a function of D's ability to

i.   understand the written word;

ii. comprehend the applicable legal principles;

iii. relate the principles to the facts; and

iv. articulate the end product.

R. v. Robinson (1989), 73 C.R. (3d) 81, 51 C.C.C. (3d) 452 (Alta. C.A.) — There is no unconditional entitlement to appointment of counsel for an appeal. The discretionary nature of s. 684 does not offend *Charter* s. 7, 10(b), 11(d) or 15.

Related Provisions: Similar provision is made in s. 694.1 where D is a party to an appeal to the Supreme Court of Canada or to proceedings preliminary or incidental thereto. No corresponding provision applies at trial. Under s. 615(4), counsel may be assigned for an unrepresented D in respect of whom an issue of fitness is being directed.

Upon arrest or detention everyone has the right to retain and instruct counsel without delay and the right to be informed of such right under *Charter* s. 10(b).

685. Summary determination of frivolous appeals — Where it appears to the registrar that a notice of appeal, which purports to be on a ground of appeal that involves a question of law alone, does not show a substantial ground of appeal, the registrar may refer the appeal to the court of appeal for summary determination, and, where an appeal is referred under this section, the court of appeal may, if it considers that the appeal is frivolous or vexatious and can be determined without being adjourned for a full hearing, dismiss the appeal summarily, without calling on any person to attend the hearing or to appear for the respondent on the hearing.

R.S., c. C-34, s. 612.

Commentary: The section allows *summary determination of frivolous appeals* upon a reference by the registrar. The registrar must be of the view that the notice of appeal, purportedly based on a question of law alone, fails to disclose a substantial ground of appeal. Once the registrar has so concluded, he/she may refer the appeal to the court of appeal for summary determination. The court of appeal, upon the reference of the registrar, must examine the matter and determine whether the appeal is frivolous or vexatious, and can be determined without a full hearing. Where the court of appeal so determines, it may dismiss the appeal summarily, without attendance of D or counsel. Where the court of appeal does not so determine, the matter must be adjourned to a full hearing in accordance with rules of the court.

Case Law

Maltby v. Saskatchewan (A.G.) (1984), 13 C.C.C. (3d) 308 (Sask. C.A.) — It is the court's prerogative to refuse to hear an appeal where the issue is moot, except where the circumstances are of a demanding nature such as where a question of law of nation-wide importance is involved and the courts below are of differing opinions.

Related Provisions: The section does *not* expressly apply to appeals to the Supreme Court of Canada, unless it may be said to fall within the general incorporation of appellate authority under s. 695(1). By s. 822(1), the section applies to summary conviction appeals taken under s. 813.

Powers of the Court of Appeal

686. (1) Powers — On the hearing of an appeal against a conviction or against a verdict that the appellant is unfit to stand trial or not criminally responsible on account of mental disorder, the court of appeal

(a) may allow the appeal where it is of the opinion that

(i) the verdict should be set aside on the ground that it is unreasonable or cannot be supported by the evidence,

(ii) the judgment of the trial court should be set aside on the ground of a wrong decision on a question of law, or

(iii) on any ground there was a miscarriage of justice;

(b) may dismiss the appeal where

(i) the court is of the opinion that the appellant, although he was not properly convicted on a count or part of the indictment, was properly convicted on another count or part of the indictment,

(ii) the appeal is not decided in favour of the appellant on any ground mentioned in paragraph (*a*),

(iii) notwithstanding that the court is of the opinion that on any ground mentioned in subparagraph (*a*)(ii) the appeal might be decided in favour of the appellant, it is of the opinion that no substantial wrong or miscarriage of justice has occurred; or

(iv) notwithstanding any procedural irregularity at trial, the trial court had jurisdiction over the class of offence of which the appellant was convicted and the court of appeal is of the opinion that the appellant suffered no prejudice thereby;

(c) may refuse to allow the appeal where it is of the opinion that the trial court arrived at a wrong conclusion respecting the effect of a special verdict, may order the conclusion to be recorded that appears to the court to be required by the verdict, and may pass a sentence that is warranted in law in substitution for the sentence passed by the trial court; or

(d) may set aside a conviction and find the appellant unfit to stand trial or not criminally responsible on account of mental disorder and may exercise any of the powers of the trial court conferred by or referred to in section 672.45 in any manner deemed appropriate to the court of appeal in the circumstances.

(2) Order to be made — Where a court of appeal allows an appeal under paragraph (1)(*a*), it shall quash the conviction and

(a) direct a judgment or verdict of acquittal to be entered; or

(b) order a new trial.

(3) Substituting verdict — Where a court of appeal dismisses an appeal under subparagraph (1)(*b*)(i), it may substitute the verdict that in its opinion should have been found and

(a) affirm the sentence passed by the trial court; or

(b) impose a sentence that is warranted in law or remit the matter to the trial court and direct the trial court to impose a sentence that is warranted in law.

(4) **Appeal from acquittal** — If an appeal is from an acquittal or verdict that the appellant or respondent was unfit to stand trial or not criminally responsible on account of mental disorder, the court of appeal may

(a) dismiss the appeal; or

(b) allow the appeal, set aside the verdict and

(i) order a new trial, or

(ii) except where the verdict is that of a court composed of a judge and jury, enter a verdict of guilty with respect to the offence of which, in its opinion, the accused should have been found guilty but for the error in law, and pass a sentence that is warranted in law, or remit the matter to the trial court and direct the trial court to impose a sentence that is warranted in law.

(5) **New trial under Part XIX** — Subject to subsection (5.01), if an appeal is taken in respect of proceedings under Part XIX and the court of appeal orders a new trial under this Part, the following provisions apply:

(a) if the accused, in his notice of appeal or notice of application for leave to appeal, requested that the new trial, if ordered, should be held before a court composed of a judge and jury, the new trial shall be held accordingly;

(b) if the accused, in his notice of appeal or notice of application for leave to appeal, did not request that the new trial, if ordered, should be held before a court composed of a judge and jury, the new trial shall, without further election by the accused, be held before a judge or provincial court judge, as the case may be, acting under Part XIX, other than a judge or provincial court judge who tried the accused in the first instance, unless the court of appeal directs that the new trial be held before the judge or provincial court judge who tried the accused in the first instance;

(c) if the court of appeal orders that the new trial shall be held before a court composed of a judge and jury the new trial shall be commenced by an indictment in writing setting forth the offence in respect of which the new trial was ordered; and

(d) notwithstanding paragraph (*a*), if the conviction against which the accused appealed was for an offence mentioned in section 553 and was made by a provincial court judge, the new trial shall be held before a provincial court judge acting under Part XIX, other than the provincial court judge who tried the accused in the first instance, unless the court of appeal directs that the new trial be held before the provincial court judge who tried the accused in the first instance.

5.01 **New trial under Part XIX — Nunavut** — If an appeal is taken in respect of proceedings under Part XIX and the Court of Appeal of Nunavut orders a new trial under Part XXI, the following provisions apply:

(a) if the accused, in the notice of appeal or notice of application for leave to appeal, requested that the new trial, if ordered, should be held before a court composed of a judge and jury, the new trial shall be held accordingly;

(b) if the accused, in the notice of appeal or notice of application for leave to appeal, did not request that the new trial, if ordered, should be held before a court composed of a judge and jury, the new trial shall, without further election by the accused, and without a further preliminary inquiry, be held before a judge, acting under Part XIX, other than a judge who tried the accused in the first instance, unless the Court of Appeal of Nunavut directs that the new trial be held before the judge who tried the accused in the first instance;

(c) if the Court of Appeal of Nunavut orders that the new trial shall be held before a court composed of a judge and jury, the new trial shall be commenced by an indictment in writing setting forth the offence in respect of which the new trial was ordered; and

(d) despite paragraph (a), if the conviction against which the accused appealed was for an indictable offence mentioned in section 553, the new trial shall be held before a judge acting under Part XIX, other than the judge who tried the accused in the first instance, unless the Court of Appeal of Nunavut directs that the new trial be held before the judge who tried the accused in the first instance.

(5.1) Election if new trial a jury trial — Subject to subsection (5.2), if a new trial ordered by the court of appeal is to be held before a court composed of a judge and jury,

(a) the accused may, with the consent of the prosecutor, elect to have the trial heard before a judge without a jury or a provincial court judge;

(b) the election shall be deemed to be a re-election within the meaning of subsection 561(5); and

(c) subsection 561(5) applies, with such modifications as the circumstances require, to the election.

5.2 Election if new trial a jury trial — Nunavut — If a new trial ordered by the Court of Appeal of Nunavut is to be held before a court composed of a judge and jury, the accused may, with the consent of the prosecutor, elect to have the trial heard before a judge without a jury. The election shall be deemed to be a re-election within the meaning of subsection 561.1(1), and subsection 561.1(6) applies, with any modifications that the circumstances require, to the election.

(6) Where appeal allowed against verdict of unfit to stand trial — Where a court of appeal allows an appeal against a verdict that the accused is unfit to stand trial, it shall, subject to subsection (7), order a new trial.

(7) Appeal court may set aside verdict of unfit to stand trial — Where the verdict that the accused is unfit to stand trial was returned after the close of the case for the prosecution, the court of appeal may, notwithstanding that the verdict is proper, if it is of the opinion that the accused should have been acquitted at the close of the case for the prosecution, allow the appeal, set aside the verdict and direct a judgment or verdict of acquittal to be entered.

(8) Additional powers — Where a court of appeal exercises any of the powers conferred by subsection (2), (4), (6) or (7), it may make any order, in addition, that justice requires.

R.S., c. C-34, s. 613; 1974–75–76, c. 93, s. 75; R.S. 1985, c. 27 (1st Supp.), ss. 145, 203; 1991, c. 43, s. 9, Schedule, item 8; 1997, c. 18, s. 98; 1999, c. 3, s. 52; 1999, c. 5, s. 26.

Commentary: The section defines the authority of the court of appeal to *determine appeals* taken under ss. 675 and 676 *in proceedings on indictment, except* for appeals against *sentence* for which special provision is made in s. 687.

The principal dispositive authority in appeals by D against conviction, a verdict of unfit to stand trial, or not criminally responsible on account of mental disorder, is found in ss. 686(1)–(3).

Section 686(1)(a) defines the three discrete bases upon which an appeal by D may be *allowed: unreasonable or unsupportable verdict, error of law* and *miscarriage of justice*. Where an appeal by D is allowed under s. 686(1)(a), s. 686(2) requires the conviction be quashed and either an acquittal entered or new trial ordered. In appropriate cases, a verdict of not criminally responsible on account of mental disorder or unfit to stand trial may be substituted on appeal, under s. 686(1)(d). The authority of the court in successful appeals from a verdict of unfitness or not criminally responsible on account of mental disorder is described in ss. 686(6) and (7).

Section 686(1)(d) and, to a lesser extent, s. 686(1)(c), define the authority of the court of appeal to *dismiss* an appeal from conviction, a verdict of unfit to stand trial or of not criminally responsible on account of mental disorder. Section 686(1)(b)(i), together with s. 686(3), permits the dismissal of an appeal, the substitution of the appropriate verdict, and the affirmation or imposition of the appropriate sentence. The provisos of ss. 686(1)(b)(iii) and (iv) mark the limits of the authority of the court of appeal to sustain the verdict at trial, where substantive legal error or procedural irregularity has occurred. The authority of s. 686(1)(c), like the use of special verdicts, has fallen into desuetude.

The special provisions of s. 686(5) apply where the trial was conducted before a judge or provincial court judge under Part XIX. Where the new trial ordered is a jury trial, s. 686(5.1) provides for a *re-election* for trial before a judge alone. Section 686(8) authorizes the making of additional or incidental orders where the appeal has been determined under ss. 686(2), (4), (6) or (7).

In appeals from *acquittal*, the dispositive authority is s. 686(4). The section, in particular s. 686(4)(a), contains *no* express reference to nor incorporation of the substantive or procedural provisos of ss. 686(1)(b)(iii) and (iv). Under s. 686(4)(b)(ii), the court of appeal may *not* enter a finding of guilt or record a conviction where the acquittal at trial has been by a jury verdict. No express authority is given to determine appeals taken under ss. 676(1)(b) or (c). The provisions of ss. 686(6) and (7) would appear applicable to appeals by P from a verdict of unfitness. The additional powers conferred by s. 686(8) are also available on appeals by P.

Case Law

Stare Decisis

Sellars v. R. (1980), 20 C.R. (3d) 381, 52 C.C.C. (2d) 345 (S.C.C.) — An *obiter* opinion on a point of law expressed by the Supreme Court of Canada is binding one lower courts.

Wolf v. R. (1974), 27 C.R.N.S. 150, 17 C.C.C. (2d) 425 (S.C.C.) — A provincial appellate court is *not* obliged, as a matter of either law or practice, to follow a decision of an appellate court of another province unless it is persuaded that it should do so on its merits or for other independent reasons. The *only* required uniformity among provincial appellate courts is that which results from a decision of the Supreme Court of Canada.

R. v. Santeramo (1976), 36 C.R.N.S. 1, 32 C.C.C. (2d) 35 (Ont. C.A.) — Where the liberty of a subject is in issue, the court of appeal will refuse to follow one of its own judgments which it feels was wrongly decided.

Verdict Unreasonable or Not Supported by Evidence: S. 686(1)(a)(i)

R. v. Burke, [1996] 1 S.C.R. 474, 105 C.C.C. (3d) 205 (S.C.C.) — The standard of review under s. 686(1)(a)(i) is whether the verdict is one that a properly instructed jury, acting judicially, could reasonably have rendered. The section may *only* be invoked where the appellate court has

i.   considered all of the evidence before the trier of fact; and,

ii.   determined that a conviction cannot be reasonably supported by the evidence.

Conscious of the advantage enjoyed by the trier of fact, an appellate court may nonetheless invoke s. 686(1)(a)(i) where the "unreasonableness" rests on a question of credibility.

R. v. François (1994), 31 C.R. (4th) 201, 91 C.C.C. (3d) 289 (S.C.C.) — To determine whether a verdict is unreasonable requires a court of appeal to re-examine and, to some extent, to re-weigh and consider the effect of evidence. This approach applies where the objection to conviction is based on credibility.

R. v. François (1994), 31 C.R. (4th) 201, 91 C.C.C. (3d) 289 (S.C.C.) — Where a conviction is alleged to be unreasonable because the testimony is so *incredible* that a verdict found upon it must be unreasonable, special difficulties arise for a court of appeal, especially where the challenge to credibility is based on the witness' alleged lack of truthfulness and sincerity, rather than on other aspects of credibility. The determination of credibility in such cases turns not only on factors such as the significance of any alleged inconsistencies or motives for fabrication, but also the demeanour of the witness and the common sense of the jury which the court of appeal cannot assess. A jury may deal with inconsistencies and the motive to concoct in a variety of ways. A court of appeal may *not* infer from the mere presence of contradictory details or motives to concoct that a verdict is unreasonable. A court of appeal must also consider that a jury may bring to the difficult business of deciding where lies the truth special qualities which the reviewing court may *not* share.

R. v. Burns (1994), 29 C.R. (4th) 113, 89 C.C.C. (3d) 193 (S.C.C.); reversing (1992), 74 C.C.C. (3d) 124 (B.C. C.A.) — In a trial by judge alone, a failure by the judge to indicate expressly that all relevant considerations have been taken into account in reaching a verdict is *not* a basis upon which an appeal may be allowed under s. 686(1)(a)(i). It is *not* error, *per se*, for a trial judge *not* to give reasons for deciding a problematic point in a particular way. A trial judge is *not* required to demonstrate that s/he knows the law and has considered all aspects of the evidence. Nor is a trial judge required to explain why s/he has no reasonable doubt of D's guilt.

R. v. Burns (1994), 29 C.R. (4th) 113, 89 C.C.C. (3d) 193 (S.C.C.); reversing (1992), 74 C.C.C. (3d) 124 (B.C. C.A.) — Where a trial judge's brief reasons contain conclusions that are supported by the evidence, a court of appeal should *not* allow an appeal simply because the trial judge fails to discuss collateral issues that may arise in the case.

R. v. Burns (1994), 29 C.R. (4th) 113, 89 C.C.C. (3d) 193 (S.C.C.) — Under s. 686(1)(a)(i), a court of appeal is entitled to review the evidence, re-examining and re-weighing it *only* to determine whether it is *reasonably capable* of supporting the conclusion of the trial judge.

R. v. W. (R.) (1992), 13 C.R. (4th) 257, 74 C.C.C. (3d) 134 (S.C.C.) — *See also: R. v. Proulx* (1992), 76 C.C.C. (3d) 316 (Que. C.A.) — In determining whether to allow an appeal on the ground that the verdict is unreasonable or cannot be supported by the evidence, a court of appeal must re-examine and, to some extent, re-weigh and consider the effect of the evidence. The test is whether a trier of fact, properly instructed and acting reasonably, *could* have convicted. Great deference should be accorded to findings of credibility made at trial.

R. v. S. (P.L.) (1991), 5 C.R. (4th) 351, 64 C.C.C. (3d) 193 (S.C.C.) — The role of an appellate court under s. 686(1)(a)(i) is to determine whether, on the facts that were before it, a jury, properly instructed and acting reasonably, could convict. The exercise of the power is predicated upon D having had a proper trial on legally admissible evidence accompanied by legally-correct jury instructions. Where an appellate court finds legal error, hence that D has *not* had a legally-correct trial, D is entitled to a new trial or acquittal, as the case may be. The appellate court cannot substitute its opinion for that of the trial court that the evidence proves guilt beyond a reasonable doubt, except where the evidence is so overwhelming that a trier of fact would inevitably convict.

R. v. Yebes (1987), 59 C.R. (3d) 108, 36 C.C.C. (3d) 417 (S.C.C.) — *See also: R. v. Corbett* (1973), 14 C.C.C. (2d) 385 (S.C.C.) — The test of whether a verdict was reasonable is whether the verdict was one which a properly instructed jury acting judicially could reasonably have rendered.

R. v. Caouette (1972), 9 C.C.C. (2d) 449 (S.C.C.) — The issue of whether there is any evidence to support a conviction is a matter of law.

R. v. Guyatt (1997), 119 C.C.C. (3d) 304 (B.C. C.A.) — Under s. 686(1)(a)(i), the test is whether a properly instructed jury could reasonably have convicted. The court may not set aside a verdict, where there is evidence on which a jury could convict, on the basis that the verdict is unsafe.

R. v. Sanghi (1971), 6 C.C.C. (2d) 123 (N.S. C.A.) — The court of appeal has the power to quash a conviction where the trier of fact reached an illogical conclusion from the evidence or erred in appreciation of the evidence.

R. v. G. (A.) (1998), 133 C.C.C. (3d) 30, 21 C.R. (5th) 149 (Ont. C.A.)notice of appeal as of right filed (S.C.C. #26924) — It is *not* necessary to introduce terms such as "lurking doubt" to define a provincial appellate court's jurisdiction to review the reasonableness of a verdict under s. 686(1)(a). The court is *not* limited in its jurisdiction to matters of law and mixed law and fact, rather, has plenary powers over *all* questions of fact and may reverse trial judges in situations where they have demonstrated *no* error in their reasons for conviction.

R. v. Morrissey (1995), 38 C.R. (4th) 4, 97 C.C.C. (3d) 193 (Ont. C.A.) — Where a trial judge is mistaken as to the substance of *material* parts of the evidence, and D's errors played an essential part in the reasoning process which led to conviction, D's conviction is *not* based exclusively on the evidence, and therefore is *not* a true verdict.

R. v. Malcolm (1993), 21 C.R. (4th) 241, 81 C.C.C. (3d) 196 (Ont. C.A.) — Despite the limited scope of s. 686(1)(a)(i), an appellate court should *not* avoid its responsibility simply because it is faced with the decision of a trial judge that reflects no legal mis-direction and an appreciation of the difficulties inherent in P's case. The reaction of an appellate court as to when an injustice has been done is subjective. It must ask itself whether the verdict is unsafe or unsatisfactory.

R. v. Quercia (1990), 1 C.R. (4th) 385, 60 C.C.C. (3d) 380 (Ont. C.A.) — In determining whether to allow an appeal under s. 686(1)(a)(i), an appellate court must independently examine and assess the evidence adduced at trial, thereby to reach its own conclusion as to the reasonableness of the verdict. It must decide, with due deference to the advantages of the trier of fact in seeing and hearing the witnesses, whether the totality of the evidence, including evidence adduced on behalf of D, is such that the verdict is one that a properly instructed jury, acting judicially, could reasonably have rendered.

R. v. McLaughlin (1974), 25 C.R.N.S. 362, 15 C.C.C. (2d) 562 (Ont. C.A.) — In cases of inconsistent verdicts, the court of appeal will quash the conviction if the verdicts are violently at odds and the same ingredients are common to both charges. The conclusions of the jury must be shown to be unreasonable.

Wrong Decision on Question of Law: S. 686(1)(a)(ii)

R. v. Jacquard (1997), 4 C.R. (5th) 280, [1997] 2 S.C.R. 314, 113 C.C.C. (3d) 1 — Appellate courts ought adopt a *functional approach* to review of jury instructions. The purpose of appellate review is to ensure that juries are *properly, not perfectly* instructed.

A jury instruction is proper provided an appellate court, considering the instruction as a whole, concludes that the jury was left with a *sufficient understanding* of the facts as they relate to the relevant issues.

Fanjoy v. R. (1985), 48 C.R. (3d) 113, 21 C.C.C. (3d) 312 (S.C.C.) — The decision to exercise judicial discretion to intervene in cross-examination or to refrain from intervention is one involving consideration of both law and fact.

Imrich v. R. (1977), 39 C.R.N.S. 75, 34 C.C.C. (2d) 143 (S.C.C.) — The failure of counsel to object to the trial judge's charge to the jury does *not* preclude raising the error on appeal, where the error alleged was a failure to place essential matters before the jury.

R. v. Hunter (1985), 23 C.C.C. (3d) 331 (Alta. C.A.); leave to appeal refused (1986), 66 N.R. 319n (S.C.C.) — Failure to give reasons is not an error in law.

R. v. Arthur (1982), 63 C.C.C. (2d) 117 (B.C. C.A.); leave to appeal refused December 21, 1981 — The exclusion of evidence which is admissible and relevant is an error of law as is the application by an appellate judge of the wrong test in setting aside a verdict as unreasonable.

R. v. D. (D.) (1998), 126 C.C.C. (3d) 435 (Man. C.A.) — As a general rule, it is *not* acceptable for a trial judge simply to summarize all the evidence and the legal principles, then to expect the jury to piece together the theories for itself. On rare occasions, however, where the trial is very short, the evidence straight-forward and the closing addresses of counsel adequate, the trial judge *may* be under less of a duty to set out in detail the theories of the defence for which there is a basis in the evidence.

R. v. G. (M.) (1994), 93 C.C.C. (3d) 347 (Ont. C.A.); leave to appeal refused (March 23, 1995), Doc. No. 24484 (S.C.C.) — A trial judge is *not* required to discuss all aspects of a case in his/her reasons for judgment. Where the reasons demonstrate a failure to grasp an important point, however, an appellate court must examine the effect of such failure on the validity of the verdict.

R. v. Caron (1998), 16 C.R. (5th) 276, 126 C.C.C. (3d) 84 (Que. C.A.) — The duty of a trial judge to put all *alternative* defences to the jury that have a *factual* basis does *not* require submission of a defence that D has excluded as an alternative by eliminating any factual basis for it.

Miscarriage of Justice: S. 686(1)(a)(iii) [See also Code s. 650 Full Answer and Defence: s. 650(3) and Charter s. 7]

R. v. S. (R.D.) (1997), 10 C.R. (5th) 1, 118 C.C.C. (3d) 353 (S.C.C.) — *Impartiality* is a state of mind in which the adjudicator is disinterested in the conclusion and is open to persuasion by the evidence and submisssion.

Bias denotes a state of mind that is in some way predisposed to a particular result, or closed with regard to certain issues.

The *test* to be applied when it is alleged that a decision-maker is *not* impartial is whether the particular conduct gives rise to a reasonable apprehension of bias. Actual bias need *not* be shown. The test contains two objectives elements

i.   the *person* considering the alleged bias must be *reasonable*; and,

ii. the *apprehension* of bias must also be *reasonable* in the circumstances of the case.

The reasonable person must be

i.   informed;

ii. with knowledge of all relevant circumstances, including the traditions of integrity and impartiality that form part of the background;

iii. apprised of the fact that impartiality is one of the duties judges swear to uphold; and

iv. aware of the social reality that forms the background to a particular case, including an awareness and acknowledgement of the prevalence of racism or gender bias in a community.

Fanjoy v. R. (1985), 48 C.R. (3d) 113, 21 C.C.C. (3d) 312 (S.C.C.) — An unfairly prejudicial cross-examination of D is a miscarriage of justice.

R. v. Duke (1985), 22 C.C.C. (3d) 217 (Alta. C.A.) — *See also*: *R. v. Hertrich* (1982), 67 C.C.C. (2d) 510 (Ont. C.A.); *R. v. Masuda* (1953), 106 C.C.C. 122 (B.C. C.A.); *R. v. Cameron* (1991), 2 O.R. (3d) 633 (Ont. C.A.) — Where there is the appearance of an unfair process, there is a miscarriage of justice.

R. v. Brown (1982), 1 C.C.C. (3d) 107 (Alta. C.A.); affirmed (1985), 21 C.C.C. (3d) 477 (S.C.C.) — Permitting improper and irrelevant questions is not of itself a miscarriage of justice. Where there was no evidence indicating that the question operated prejudicially to D on a material issue, D's appeal should be dismissed.

R. v. Guyatt (1997), 119 C.C.C. (3d) 304 (B.C. C.A.) — Section 686(1)(a)(iii) is concerned with the impact of an error on trial proceedings which makes the trial unfair. Its focus is *not* the verdict, but, rather, the fairness of the process which produced the verdict.

R. v. Strauss (1995), 100 C.C.C. (3d) 303 (B.C. C.A.) — To establish that the performance of trial counsel was so deficient to deprive him/her of the right to make full answer and defence, and of a fair trial, D must show

i.   that trial counsel made errors so serious that he/she was *not* functioning as counsel; and

ii. that there was a *reasonable probability* that, *absent* the *errors*, the *result* would have been *different.*

R. v. Starr (1972), 7 C.C.C. (2d) 519 (N.B. C.A.) — In deciding whether a conviction gives rise to a miscarriage of justice, the court of appeal may quite properly consider the failure of D to testify or call evidence to rebut a strong inference of guilt.

R. v. B. (L.C.) (1996), 46 C.R. (4th) 368, 104 C.C.C. (3d) 353 (Ont. C.A.) — Where D asserts the denial of the *effective assistance* of *counsel*, D must establish a factual basis for the claim in the *performance* aspect of the issue. Fresh evidence will often be required to permit the court realistically to consider the competence of trial counsel when measured against a standard of reasonableness. Considerable deference should be accorded the tactical/strategic decisions of counsel. To obtain appellate relief on the basis of a denial of the effective assistance of counsel, D must establish

i   that counsel provided ineffective/incompetent representation; and,

ii   that, as a result, D suffered *prejudice* in that there is a *reasonable probability* that, with competent representation, the result would have been different

R. v. Peterson (1996), 47 C.R. (4th) 161, 106 C.C.C. (3d) 64 (Ont. C.A.); leave to appeal refused (1997), 109 C.C.C. (3d) vi (note) (S.C.C.) — Where a breach of P's *disclosure* obligations has been established on appeal, the court must consider the extent to which non-disclosure may have prejudiced D's right to make full answer and defence. The court is concerned with whether there has been a miscarriage of justice. Prejudice as a consequence of non-disclosure requires satisfaction of the court that there is a *reasonable probability* that, with proper disclosure, the result might have been different. A *"reasonable probability"* is a probability sufficient to undermine confidence in the outcome.

R. v. Wicksted (1996), 106 C.C.C. (3d) 385 (Ont. C.A.); affirmed (1997), 4 C.R. (5th) 196, [1997] 1 S.C.R. 307, 113 C.C.C. (3d) 318 (S.C.C.) — Where evidence is alleged to have been "lost" by P due to an investigator's failure to make notes or a record of all conversations with a prospective witness, there must be a *substantial* air of reality about the claim that the "lost" evidence would actually assist D in his/her defence.

R. v. W. (W.) (1995), 100 C.C.C. (3d) 225 (Ont. C.A.) — Where *conflict* of *interest* is raised on appeal, the issue is whether, on a review of the record supplemented by the fresh evidence, D have demonstrated that their *joint representation* resulted in a *miscarriage* of *justice*. D are required to show

i.   an *actual* conflict between the respective *interests* represented by counsel; and

ii.   some *impairment* of counsel's *ability* to *represent effectively* the interests of D as a result of that conflict.

D need *not* demonstrate that, but for the ineffective representation of counsel, the verdict could have been different.

R. v. W. (W.) (1995), 100 C.C.C. (3d) 225 (Ont. C.A.) — In the context of joint representation of co-accused, an actual conflict of interest exists where a course of conduct dictated by the best interests of one accused, if followed, would be inconsistent with the best interests of the co-accused. The issue is *not* whether the accused *could* have been more effectively represented by separate counsel, but whether their joint representation placed counsel in a conflict of interest such that the assistance provided to either or both was adversely affected.

R. v. Morrissey (1995), 38 C.R. (4th) 4, 97 C.C.C. (3d) 193 (Ont. C.A.) — Where misapprehension of the evidence is alleged on appeal from conviction, a court of appeal should first consider the reasonableness of the verdict under s. 686(1)(a)(i). If the verdict is unreasonable, D will be acquitted. If the verdict is *not* unreasonable, the court should determine whether the misapprehension of evidence occasioned a miscarriage of justice under s. 686(1)(a)(iii). If the misapprehension of the evidence has rendered D's trial unfair, the conviction must be quashed.

R. v. Barrett (1993), 23 C.R. (4th) 49, 82 C.C.C. (3d) 266 (Ont. C.A.) — An unreasonable conclusion as to voluntariness of an incriminatory statement to investigating officers, *viz.*, one that could not be supported by the evidence or is based on a palpable or overriding error of fact, which leads to an erroneous ruling of admissibility, constitutes an error of law which requires appellate intervention, subject to the curative proviso of s. 686(1)(b)(iii).

R. v. Barbeau (1996), 110 C.C.C. (3d) 69 (Que. C.A.) — To attack the validity of a trial based upon a *conflict* of *interest* because of the *joint representation* of two accused, D must demonstrate an *actual, not* an apparent or potential conflict of interest.

Substituted Verdict: S. 686(1)(b)(i), (3)

Wigman v. R. (1987), 56 C.R. (3d) 289, 33 C.C.C. (3d) 97 (S.C.C.) — Where D is convicted of attempted murder on the basis of a charge to the jury which is not in conformity with a subsequent Supreme Court of Canada decision regarding intent released prior to the hearing of D's appeal against his conviction, it may be appropriate to dismiss the appeal but to substitute a conviction for the included offence of causing bodily harm with intent to endanger life.

Lake v. R., [1969] 2 C.C.C. 224 (S.C.C.) — The Supreme Court of Canada and provincial appellate courts have the jurisdiction, when dismissing an appeal, to *amend* a conviction and *substitute* whatever verdict the court is of the opinion should have been found at first instance.

R. v. Terlecki (1983), 4 C.C.C. (3d) 522 (Alta. C.A.); affirmed (1985), 22 C.C.C. (3d) 224 (S.C.C.) — D was found guilty of impaired driving and a breathalyzer offence but a conviction was registered only for the breathalyzer offence because of the rule against multiple convictions for the same delict. D successfully appealed his breathalyzer conviction but this section gave the court of appeal power to substitute a conviction for impaired driving.

R. v. Letendre (1979), 7 C.R. (3d) 320, 46 C.C.C. (2d) 398 (B.C. C.A.) — While quashing a conviction and ordering a new trial, the court of appeal, acting on its own initiative, also set aside an acquittal which had been entered on an alternative count under the *Kienapple* principle. Both offences were capable of being retried.

R. v. Kent (1986), 27 C.C.C. (3d) 405 (Man. C.A.) — The court of appeal is empowered to substitute a verdict of guilty of a lesser but included offence where there has been misdirection of the jury as to whether D could be convicted of a lesser included offence.

R. v. McLeod (1983), 6 C.C.C. (3d) 29 (Ont. C.A.); affirmed (1986), 66 N.R. 308 (S.C.C.) — D was convicted of attempted murder and use of a firearm, but acquitted under the *Kienapple* rule of attempted robbery. In quashing the convictions, the appeal court ordered a new trial on all three charges.

R. v. Nantais (1966), 48 C.R. 186, [1966] 4 C.C.C. 108 (Ont. C.A.) — The court of appeal may dismiss an appeal and substitute a conviction for a lesser included offence where it finds that, upon the evidence, the conviction under the indictment was improper, and the verdict substituted is one that "should have been found".

No Substantial Wrong: S. 686(1)(b)(iii)

R. v. Haughton (1994), 20 O.R. (3d) 63 (S.C.C.) — The application of s. 686(1)(b)(iii) requires an appellate court to consider whether a properly instructed jury, acting reasonably, *could* have come to a different conclusion absent the error. In the application of this test, the findings of the jury may be a factor in determining what the hypothetical reasonable jury would have done, provided those findings are *not* tainted by error.

R. v. Tran (1994), 32 C.R. (4th) 34, 92 C.C.C. (3d) 218 (S.C.C.) — The curative provisos of s. 686(1)(b) do *not* apply when an infringement of *Charter* s. 14 is at issue.

R. v. Bevan (1993), 21 C.R. (4th) 277, 82 C.C.C. (3d) 310 (S.C.C.); reversing (1991), 4 C.R. (4th) 245, 63 C.C.C. (3d) 333 (Ont. C.A.) — In determining whether to apply s. 686(1)(b)(iii) to a trial judge's error, an appellate court must determine whether there is any *reasonable possibility* that the *verdict* would have been *different*, had the error not occurred.

R. v. Elshaw (1991), 7 C.R. (4th) 333, 67 C.C.C. (3d) 97 (S.C.C.) — Where evidence should have been excluded under *Charter* s. 24(2), its erroneous admission will generally amount to a substantial wrong or miscarriage of justice, thereby making s. 686(1)(b)(iii) inapplicable.

John v. R. (1985), 49 C.R. (3d) 57, 23 C.C.C. (3d) 326 (S.C.C.) — The appellate court cannot, with anything approaching reality, retry a case to assess the worth of residual evidence after improperly adduced evidence has been extracted. An appeal court does not have the advantage of seeing the witnesses and was never intended to replace the jury. Consequently, in such a situation s. 686(1)(b)(iii) should not be invoked, but rather a new trial ordered.

Fanjoy v. R. (1985), 48 C.R. (3d) 113, 21 C.C.C. (3d) 312 (S.C.C.) — Section 686(1)(b)(iii) may be applied *only* where the appeal court is of the opinion that on the ground of a wrong question of law an appeal might be decided in favour of the appellant but it is also of the opinion that no substantial wrong or miscarriage of justice has occurred. The failure of the trial judge to limit unfairly prejudicial cross-examination of D was *not* an error of law alone but one involving both law and fact.

Wildman v. R. (1984), 14 C.C.C. (3d) 321 (S.C.C.) — When evaluating the possible effect of improperly excluded exculpatory evidence for the purposes of determining whether there has been no substantial wrong, the benefit should go to D.

Alward v. R. (1977), 39 C.R.N.S. 281 at 306, 35 C.C.C. (2d) 392 (S.C.C.) — Where on a charge of murder arising from a killing during a robbery, P leads inadmissible similar fact evidence of two subsequent robberies committed by D, the curative provisions of s. 686(1)(b)(iii) are inapplicable since the inclusion of such inadmissible evidence represents a substantial miscarriage of justice.

Avon v. R. (1971), 4 C.C.C. (2d) 357 (S.C.C.) — Section 686(1)(b)(iii) may be applied in a situation in which the trial judge has breached *C.E.A.* s. 4(6) which prohibits comment on the failure of D to testify.

Colpitts v. R. (1965), 47 C.R. 175, [1966] 1 C.C.C. 146 (S.C.C.) — Once an error in law has been found to have occurred at trial, the onus is on P to satisfy the court that the verdict would necessarily have been the same if such error had not occurred. This is a condition precedent to the application of s. 686(1)(b)(iii). Even if the onus is discharged the court is not bound to apply the section.

R. v. Leaney (1987), 38 C.C.C. (3d) 263 (Alta. C.A.); affirmed in part (1989), 71 C.R. (3d) 325, 50 C.C.C. (3d) 289 (S.C.C.) — Where no reasonable jury, properly instructed and acting judicially, could have failed to convict D on the admissible evidence presented at trial, the fact that inadmissible evidence was incorrectly allowed by the judge did *not* result in a substantial wrong or miscarriage of justice.

R. v. B. (J.N.) (1989), 68 C.R. (3d) 145, 48 C.C.C. (3d) 71 (Man. C.A.) — *See also: R. v. Leaney* (1989), 71 C.R. (3d) 325, 50 C.C.C. (3d) 289 (S.C.C.) — Where there is evidence sufficient to inculpate D, the court of appeal may properly take into account D's failure to testify, without infringing *Charter* s. 11(c).

R. v. Silvini (1991), 9 C.R. (4th) 233, 68 C.C.C. (3d) 251 (Ont. C.A.) — A claim that D was prejudiced by deficient performance of counsel requires a showing of a reasonable probability that, but for counsel's unprofessional errors, the result would have been different. In such circumstances, s. 686(1)(b)(iii) will *not* save the conviction.

R. v. Adams (1989), 49 C.C.C. (3d) 100 (Ont. C.A.) — Where there has been misdirection with respect to the *mens rea* of an offence, it is not open to the court of appeal to apply the curative proviso. However, the court may substitute a conviction for an included offence which also had been put to the jury.

R. v. Morin (1987), 36 C.C.C. (3d) 50 (Ont. C.A.); affirmed (1988), 66 C.R. (3d) 1, 44 C.C.C. (3d) 193 (S.C.C.) — Where the trial judge made errors of such gravity in his charge to the jury that the court was satisfied that but for those errors the verdict would not necessarily have been the same, P's appeal was allowed and a new trial ordered.

R. v. Bordonaro (1986), 20 O.A.C. 239 (C.A.) — The trial judge's inadvertent failure to deal with a question submitted by the jury could not be cured by s. 686(1)(b)(iii).

R. v. Fischer (1987), 31 C.C.C. (3d) 303 (Sask. C.A.) — A failure of the trial judge to adequately and succinctly explain the position of the defence to the jury was a defect which could not be cured by s. 686(1)(b)(iii).

Suffered No Prejudice Thereby: S. 686(1)(b)(iv) [See also s. 591]

R. v. Tran (1994), 32 C.R. (4th) 34, 92 C.C.C. (3d) 218 (S.C.C.) — The curative provisos of s. 686(1)(b) do *not* apply when an infringement of *Charter* s. 14 is at issue.

R. v. Heidemann (1988), 87 A.R. 38 (C.A.) — Failure of P to make a formal application to apply the evidence adduced with respect to the trial of the first information to the trial of the second information was a procedural irregularity at trial which could be cured by the application of s. 686(1)(b)(iv).

R. v. Singh (1996), 108 C.C.C. (3d) 244 (B.C. C.A.) — A discharged juror may be replaced, even in the absence of consent, after D has been given in charge of the jury, but *no* evidence has been called. At all events, where juror substitution causes D no prejudice, any irregularity may be cured by the combined effect of ss. 670 and 686(1)(b)(iv).

R. v. Quick (1993), 82 C.C.C. (3d) 51 (B.C. C.A.) — Where counsel advise the trial judge, in chambers and in the absence of D, of decisions which they have made concerning the conduct of their cases and prospective problems which may arise, and the discussions have *no* bearing on D's guilt, there is *no* infringement of D's right to be present under *Code* s. 650. At all events, a violation of s. 650 in such circumstances could be cured by s. 686(1)(b)(iv) where there is no suggestion of prejudice and counsel for D has indicated that D's presence is *not* required.

R. v. Skin, (February 22, 1988), Doc. No. CA007364 (B.C. C.A.) — Section 686(1)(b)(iv) could properly be applied to cure the procedural irregularity which occurred when D's counsel re-elected trial by judge alone when D was *not* present in court. Since D had *not* stated before, during or after trial that he desired trial by any mode other than by judge alone, it was to be taken that he had waived what he desired as to mode and forum of trial.

R. v. Joinson (1986), 32 C.C.C. (3d) 542 (B.C. C.A.) — This subsection was used to cure the procedural irregularity that took place when the trial judge gave judgment convicting D on the erroneous assumption that D was in the courtroom. D had suffered no prejudice and the trial judge was careful to recognize D's rights by reading the transcript of the proceedings which took place in D's absence when D appeared voluntarily for sentencing.

R. v. Mitchell (1997), 121 C.C.C. (3d) 139 (Ont. C.A.) — The failure to arraign D is a procedural error which may be cured by s. 686(1)(b)(iv).

R. v. Peterson (1996), 47 C.R. (4th) 161, 106 C.C.C. (3d) 64 (Ont. C.A.); leave to appeal refused (1997), 109 C.C.C. (3d) vi (note) (S.C.C.) — Where an inquiry into a child witness' competence indicates a general acceptance of the duty to tell the truth, *semble* the absence of a specific commitment to tell the truth constitutes a procedural error curable under s. 686(1)(b)(iv).

R. v. Krack (1990), 56 C.C.C. (3d) 555 (Ont. C.A.) — The failure to conduct the mandatory inquiry of *C.E.A.* s. 16(1) may be a procedural irregularity which does *not* result in a loss of jurisdiction in the trial court. It may be remedied by the proviso of s. 686(1)(b)(iv), where D's right to a fair trial has not been prejudiced.

R. v. Pottinger (1990), 76 C.R. (3d) 393, 54 C.C.C. (3d) 246 (Ont. C.A.) — The trial together of separate informations against D, even with consent, is a jurisdictional defect, *not* a procedural irregularity curable under s. 686(1)(b)(iv).

R. v. Rowbotham (1988), 63 C.R. (3d) 113, 41 C.C.C. (3d) 1 (Ont. C.A.) — *See also*: *R. v. Bain* (1989), 68 C.R. (3d) 50 (Ont. C.A.) — Where a trial judge improperly applied provincial legislation to the jury selection procedure in trying to expand the original jury panel rather than resorting to the "stand-asides", the error required a new trial as D were deprived of their statutory right under s. 642 and that of trial by a jury lawfully constituted.

R. v. Cloutier (1988), 43 C.C.C. (3d) 35 (Ont. C.A.); leave to appeal refused 104 N.R. 160 (note), 37 O.A.C. 320 (note) (S.C.C.) — *See also: R. v. Hollwey* (1992), 71 C.C.C. (3d) 314 (Ont. C.A.); leave to appeal refused (1992), 75 C.C.C. (3d) vi (note) (S.C.C.); *R. v. Bourassa* (1991), 67 C.C.C. (3d) 143 (Que. C.A.); *R. v. Rosebush* (1992), 77 C.C.C. (3d) 241 (Alta. C.A.) — If the court of appeal is of the opinion that an appellant's exclusion from some stage of his trial did not affect the outcome of the trial adversely to the appellant, then the court may dismiss the appeal. It is the opinion of the court of appeal as to whether the appellant "suffered no prejudice thereby" that prevails, not the appellant's perception that he suffered prejudice.

Guilty Plea [See also ss. 606 and 675]

R. v. Melanson (1983), 59 N.S.R. (2d) 54 (C.A.) — An appeal court, in evaluating the grounds justifying a change of plea, should give great importance to whether D was represented by counsel when entering his plea. Where D was represented by counsel, the court should be able to rely on the fact that the charge had been fully explained to D and that D had fully understood the nature of the charge, the facts to which he was admitting and the effect of the plea.

R. v. Newman (1993), 79 C.C.C. (3d) 394 (Ont. C.A.) — A court of appeal may permit D to withdraw a plea of guilty, set aside the conviction and order a new trial where the court is satisfied that D was deprived of his/her right to effective counsel and that the plea of guilty embraced a factual foundation that D was not prepared to accept for the purposes of sentencing, so that D was deprived of a fair trial.

Lamoureux v. R. (1984), 40 C.R. (3d) 369, 13 C.C.C. (3d) 101 (Que. C.A.) — A plea of guilty must always be a free and voluntary act by D himself, untainted by any threats or promises. The integrity of the process requires that a change of plea be granted in cases where it is established that the guilty plea was the result of improper pressure from counsel.

Mental Disorder [Insanity] [Cases decided under former s. 686(1)(d)]

R. v. Warsing, [1998] 3 S.C.R. 579, 130 C.C.C. (3d) 259, 21 C.R. (5th) 75 — There are circumstances in which it is appropriate to permit D to raise a defence of NCRMD for the first time on appeal.

Where a defence of NCRMD is raised for the first time on appeal, a court of appeal may invoke s. 686(1)(d) to set aside the conviction and find D NCRMD. If the court of appeal concludes that it cannot determine the NCRMD issue, to avoid a miscarriage of justice, it may order a new trial under s. 686(1)(a)(iii) and (2)(b).

Where NCRMD is raised for the first time on appeal, but the court of appeal does *not* invoke s. 686(1)(d) to set aside the conviction and find D NCRMD, it may not be proper to limit the new trial to a determination of the NCRMD issue. A limited trial that restricts D's right to control his/her defence offends fundamental justice. Further, if the evidence of mental disorder were rejected as a basis for the special verdict of NCRMD, the evidence may nonetheless be relevant to the adequacy of P's proof of the necessary mental element.

R. v. Hendry (1985), 37 Man. R. (2d) 66 (C.A.) — The court has authority to set aside a conviction and substitute a finding of not guilty by reason of insanity on the basis of psychiatric evidence that comes to light after D's detention.

R. v. Mailloux (1986), 25 C.C.C. (3d) 171 (Ont. C.A.); affirmed (1988), 67 C.R. (3d) 75, 45 C.C.C. (3d) 193 (S.C.C.) — *See also: R. v. Scono* (1986), 13 O.A.C. 23 (C.A.) — A court of appeal does *not* have the power to come to its own conclusion on the issue of insanity and thereby disregard a jury's verdict unless the jury did not act judicially or was not properly instructed.

R. v. Irwin (1977), 36 C.C.C. (2d) 1 (Ont. C.A.) — In an appeal from D's conviction for murder of her child, the court, on its own motion, raised the issue of insanity for the first time. Psychiatric evidence indicating a personality disorder and post partum depression led to the setting aside of the conviction and a substituted verdict of not guilty by reason of insanity.

Fitness to Stand Trial: Ss. 686(6), (7)

R. v. Budic (No. 2) (1977), 35 C.C.C. (2d) 333 (Alta. C.A.) — Where the court of appeal finds that D is fit to stand trial, subject to s. 686(7), a new trial must be ordered. Where amendments to the *Code* intervene, a new indictment must be preferred and the charge laid and tried on the basis of the *Code* as amended. D must be allowed to amend his notice of appeal to request that the new trial be before a judge and jury.

Verdict of Acquittal: S. 686(2)(a)

R. v. Sophonow (1986), 50 C.R. (3d) 193, 25 C.C.C. (3d) 415 (Man. C.A.); leave to appeal refused (1986), 54 C.R. (3d) xxviin (S.C.C.) — A verdict of acquittal was directed where the errors of law required the guilty verdict to be set aside and as this was the third trial on the same charge the notoriety of the case impaired the chances that D would obtain a fair trial if a fourth one was ordered.

New Trial: S. 686(2)(b)

R. v. Guillemette (1986), 51 C.R. (3d) 273, 26 C.C.C. (3d) 1 (S.C.C.) — Where the appellant is convicted of an included offence, the court of appeal is without jurisdiction to order a new trial on the principal charge unless P had appealed the acquittal on that charge.

R. v. Gunn (1982), 27 C.R. (3d) 120, 66 C.C.C. (2d) 294 (S.C.C.) — A "new trial" means a full, new trial. There is no authority for the court of appeal to order a continuation of the original trial.

Savard v. R. (1945), 1 C.R. 105, 85 C.C.C. 254 (S.C.C.) — Where there was insufficient evidence to support a conviction on the hypothesis advanced by P at trial, a new trial cannot be ordered because P contends that a conviction might possibly be supported on a wholly different basis.

R. v. Rowbotham (1988), 63 C.R. (3d) 113, 41 C.C.C. (3d) 1 (Ont. C.A.) — Where D was convicted on only 1 of 4 counts and the court of appeal subsequently found that the jury had been improperly selected and ordered a new trial, the new trial was limited to the count on which D had been convicted. The jury selection ruling did not make the previous proceedings and acquittals a complete nullity.

Election: S. 686(5)

R. v. Budic (No. 2) (1977), 35 C.C.C. (2d) 333 (Alta. C.A.) — D may be allowed to amend the notice of appeal to request that the new trial ordered by the court of appeal be before a judge and jury, where intervening amendments to the *Code* necessitate the preferring of a new indictment and a trial on the basis of the *Code* as amended.

R. v. Sagliocco (1979), 10 C.R. (3d) 62, 45 C.C.C. (2d) 493 (B.C. S.C.); affirmed (1979), 51 C.C.C. (2d) 188 (B.C. C.A.) — In a new trial ordered by the court from an appeal from an acquittal, D does *not* have the right to re-elect.

Sentence: Sentence on Substituted Conviction: Ss. 686(1)(b)(i), (3)

R. v. Kjeldsen (1980), 53 C.C.C. (2d) 55 (Alta. C.A.) — Where on an appeal from a conviction for first degree murder, the court of appeal substitutes a conviction for second degree murder, the court has jurisdiction to set the period of parole non-eligibility without the benefit of a jury recommendation under s. 743.

Crown Appeal From Acquittal: S. 686(4)

R. v. Power (1994), 29 C.R. (4th) 1, 89 C.C.C. (3d) 1 (S.C.C.); reversing (1993), 81 C.C.C. (3d) 1 (Nfld. C.A.) — Section 686(4) confers *no* discretion upon a court of appeal other than the discretion to dismiss or allow an appeal. In particular, the court is *not* empowered to inquire into the exercise of prosecutorial discretion.

R. v. Tortone (1993), 23 C.R. (4th) 83, 84 C.C.C. (3d) 15 (S.C.C.) — On an appeal from acquittal, it is *not* open to an appellate court to interfere with inferences of fact drawn by the trial judge simply because the appellate court would draw different inferences. An appellate court may overturn a trial finding, however, where the judge has *not* directed his or her mind to an issue that requires determination in order to reach the verdict.

R. v. Mackenzie (1993), 78 C.C.C. (3d) 193 (S.C.C.) — On an appeal by P from acquittal, a requirement that P show that a jury verdict "might have been different", had it been properly instructed, is simply the converse of "would not necessarily have been the same", hence is consistent with the standard to be applied in such cases.

R. v. Cassidy (1989), 71 C.R. (3d) 351, 50 C.C.C. (3d) 193 (S.C.C.) — Where D was acquitted at trial, for the court of appeal to substitute a conviction, all the findings of fact necessary to support a verdict of guilty must have been made either explicitly by the trial judge or not be in issue.

Vezeau v. R. (1976), 34 C.R.N.S. 309, 28 C.C.C. (2d) 81 (S.C.C.) — *See also*: *R. v. Morin* (1987), 66 C.R. (3d) 1, 44 C.C.C. (3d) 193 (S.C.C.) — Where P appeals a jury acquittal, in order to obtain a new trial, the onus is on P to satisfy the appellate court that the verdict would not necessarily have been the same had the jury been properly directed.

Wexler v. R. (1939), 72 C.C.C. 1 (S.C.C.) — P will *not* be granted a new trial to advance a theory that was *not* advanced at the original trial.

R. v. E. (L.) (1994), 94 C.C.C. (3d) 228 (Ont. C.A.) — A court of appeal has the authority to enter a stay of proceedings where a new trial would constitute an abuse of process.

R. v. Varga (1994), 30 C.R. (4th) 78, 90 C.C.C. (3d) 484 (Ont. C.A.) — P's right of appeal from an acquittal is an appellate remedy, *not* a licence to refer legal questions to the court of appeal for its consideration and advice.

R. v. Varga (1994), 30 C.R. (4th) 78, 90 C.C.C. (3d) 484 (Ont. C.A.) — In some instances, a court of appeal will *not* consider the merits of a ground of appeal advanced by P notwithstanding that it alleges an error of law that is germane to an acquittal. P can *not* advance a new theory of liability on appeal, nor raise arguments that it chose not to advance at trial. An appeal by *P* can *not* be the means whereby P puts forward a different case than that advanced at trial.

R. v. Banas (1982), 65 C.C.C. (2d) 224 (Ont. C.A.) — *See also*: *R. v. Bailey* (1983), 32 C.R. (3d) 337, 4 C.C.C. (3d) 21 (Ont. C.A.); *R. v. Voykin* (1986), 29 C.C.C. (3d) 280 (Alta. C.A.) — P is *not* precluded from appealing a directed verdict because counsel at trial did not continue a trial considered to be fruitless and unlikely to result in a conviction due to the erroneous exclusion of critical evidence. Where P unreasonably declines to present substantial evidence in P's possession which would support a conviction merely to appeal an adverse ruling upon the admissibility of other evidence. P will be precluded from successfully appealing the acquittal.

R. v. Anthes Business Forms (1975), 26 C.C.C. (2d) 349 (Ont. C.A.) — A Crown appeal from acquittal must be limited to a question of law and will be allowed only if the court is satisfied that the judgment would not necessarily have been the same but for the error in law.

Additional Orders: S. 686(8)

R. v. Thomas, [1998] 3 S.C.R. 535, 130 C.C.C. (3d) 225, 21 C.R. (5th) 42 — Section 686(8) does *not* confer unlimited discretion on a court of appeal to issue ancillary orders. The court is constrained by what justice requires and should *not* issue an order that is at direct variance with the court's underlying judgment. Any order made under s. 686(8) must also be consistent with the section when read in its entirety.

In each case, a court of appeal must assess whether it has jurisdiction to issue a particular ancillary order under s. 686(8) having regard to

i.   the *basis* upon which the *appeal* is *determined*; and,

ii.   the *powers* of the court under s. 686 *generally*.

Orders limiting the scope of a new trial after allowing an appeal from a jury verdict do not accord with the powers granted to courts of appeal under s. 686. The words "new trial" in ss. 686(4)(b)(i) and 686(2)(b) mean a *full* new trial, at least after a jury verdict. As a matter of principle, courts of appeal should *not* restrict the scope of a jury's jurisdiction on a new trial by confining the scope of issues normally within its province.

R. v. Pearson, [1998] 3 S.C.R. 620, 130 C.C.C. (3d) 293, 21 C.R. (5th) 106 — The unique nature of entrapment permits use of s. 686(8) to limit a new trial to the issue of entrapment. Where s. 686(8) is used to make such an "additional order", D's *conviction* is *quashed*, the verdict of guilt affirmed and the new trial limited to the post-verdict entrapment motion.

R. v. Warsing, [1998] 3 S.C.R. 579, 130 C.C.C. (3d) 259, 21 C.R. (5th) 75 — Where NCRMD is raised for the first time on appeal, but the court of appeal does *not* invoke s. 686(1)(d) to set aside the conviction and find D NCRMD, it may *not* be proper to limit the new trial to a determination of the NCRMD issue. A limited trial that restricts D's right to control his/her defence offends fundamental justice. Further, if the evidence of mental disorder were rejected as a basis for the special verdict of NCRMD, the evidence may nonetheless be relevant to the adequacy of P's proof of the necessary mental element.

R. v. Sullivan (1991), 63 C.C.C. (3d) 97 (S.C.C.) — *See also*: *Rickard v. R.*, [1970] S.C.R. 1022; *R. v. Guillemette* (1986), 51 C.R. (3d) 273, 26 C.C.C. (3d) 1 (S.C.C.); *R. v. P. (D.W.)*, 70 C.R. (3d) 315, 49 C.C.C. (3d) 417 (S.C.C.) — As a general rule, a court of appeal has *no* jurisdiction to disturb an acquittal unless P has appealed from the acquittal. Where the *Kienapple* rule applies, however, s. 686(8) provides supplementary powers to the court of appeal to consider an acquittal at trial notwithstanding the absence of an appeal by P from it.

R. v. P. (D.W.) (1989), 70 C.R. (3d) 315, 49 C.C.C. (3d) 417 (S.C.C.) — Where the court of appeal quashes a conviction, it is open to the court to enter a conviction on a related offence of which D was acquitted at trial because of the rule against multiple convictions, even though there has been no Crown appeal. The preferable course is, however, to remit the case to the trial judge to enter a conviction.

R. v. Pringle (1989), 70 C.R. (3d) 305, 48 C.C.C. (3d) 449 (S.C.C.) — Where, on appeal, a conviction is quashed and an acquittal entered, the case may be remitted to the trial judge to determine whether convictions should be entered on charges previously stayed because of the rule against multiple convictions.

R. v. Gunn (1982), 27 C.R. (3d) 120, 66 C.C.C. (2d) 294 (S.C.C.) — In allowing P's appeal against acquittal, an appellate court cannot direct that the trial should be continued under an amended indictment with the defence to call evidence or close its case and proceed to final disposition. While the court has the power to order a full new trial to proceed on the amended indictment, it cannot force D to accept P's case without opportunity to cross-examine under the amended charge.

Elliott v. R. (No. 2) (1977), 40 C.R.N.S. 257, 38 C.C.C. (2d) 177 (S.C.C.) — The powers to "make any order, in addition, which justice requires" are *not* to be narrowly construed. An order for a new trial may be dependent upon an additional order allowing the amendment of an indictment to conform with the evidence.

R. v. Foti (1994), 87 C.C.C. (3d) 187 (Man. C.A.) — D has *no* right of appeal from a finding of guilt which has been conditionally stayed on application of the rule against multiple convictions. Where an appellate court makes an order under *Code* s. 686(2) on appeal from conviction, however, it may exercise its ancillary jurisdiction under *Code* s. 686(8) with respect to a charge that was conditionally stayed at trial, *provided* the successful ground of appeal against conviction also applies to the conditionally stayed charge.

R. v. Wade (1994), 29 C.R. (4th) 327, 89 C.C.C. (3d) 39 (Ont. C.A.); reversed in part (1995), 41 C.R. (4th) 108, 98 C.C.C. (3d) 97 (S.C.C.) — The broad ancillary jurisdiction of s. 686(8) should be given a generous construction consonant with its remedial purposes. In an appropriate case, a court of appeal may limit the issues to be determined at a new trial.

R. v. Cook (1979), 9 C.R. (3d) 85, 47 C.C.C. (2d) 186 (Ont. C.A.) — *See also*: *R. v. Ruptash* (1982), 68 C.C.C. (2d) 182 (Alta. C.A.) — By virtue of s. 686(8), the court of appeal has the jurisdiction to order that a new trial be held with respect to an included offence only.

R. v. Gorecki (No. 2) (1976), 32 C.C.C. (2d) 135 (Ont. C.A.) — Notwithstanding the general rule precluding reception on appeal of evidence available to be called at trial, the interests of justice required the reception of evidence of D's insanity. A new trial limited to the issue of insanity was required, as the fresh evidence might reasonably have affected the verdict of the jury.

Charter Considerations

R. v. Skalbania (1997), 120 C.C.C. (3d) 218 (S.C.C.) — Section 686(4)(b)(ii) does *not* violate *Charter* s. 7.

R. v. Switzer (1985), 22 C.C.C. (3d) 60 (B.C. S.C.) — The provisions of *Charter* s. 11(f) do *not* permit D to re-elect trial by judge and jury after the court of appeal has ordered a new trial in circumstances where D originally elected trial by provincial court judge.

Related Provisions: Section 687 provides authority to determine sentence appeals. The court of appeal is given plenary authority to annul or vary orders for compensation or restitution made at trial under s. 689(2).

Under s. 695(1), the Supreme Court of Canada may, on an appeal to that court, make any order that the court of appeal might have made on an appeal under Part XXI. Equivalent authority is conferred upon the summary conviction appeal court under s. 822(1) in respect of appeals under s. 812. The provisions of Part XXI also apply to appeals taken in respect of application for extraordinary remedies under Part XXVI, under s. 784(2) and, under s. 839(2), to appeals to the court of appeal from decisions in summary conviction proceedings under ss. 822 and 834.

Section 683 confers upon the court of appeal a wide range of authority to be exercised on the hearing of an appeal, but not determinative of it.

687. (1) Powers of court on appeal against sentence — Where an appeal is taken against sentence the court of appeal shall, unless the sentence is one fixed by law, consider the fitness of the sentence appealed against, and may on such evidence, if any, as it thinks fit to require or to receive,

    (a) vary the sentence within the limits prescribed by law for the offence of which the accused was convicted; or

    (b) dismiss the appeal.

(2) Effect of judgment — A judgment of a court of appeal that varies the sentence of an accused who was convicted has the same force and effect as if it were a sentence passed by the trial court.

R. S., c. C-34, s. 614.

Commentary: The section defines the *adjudicative authority* of the court of appeal on appeals against *sentence*. Unless the sentence is fixed by law, the court must consider the *fitness* of the sentence. Specific authority is given to require or receive *evidence* on the hearing of the appeal. The court, under s. 687(1) may then either *vary* the sentence within legal limits or *dismiss* the appeal, thereby affirming the sentence passed at trial. Under s. 687(2), any variation in the sentence imposed has the same force and effect as if it were a sentence passed by the trial court.

Case Law

General Principles

R. v. M. (C.A.), 46 C.R. (4th) 269, [1996] 1 S.C.R. 500, 105 C.C.C. (3d) 327 (S.C.C.) — There is no *a priori* ceiling on fixed term sentences under the *Code*.

Hill v. R. (No. 2) (1975), 25 C.C.C. (2d) 6 (S.C.C.) — Where D appeals the sentence, the court of appeal is not limited to a reduction in sentence but may increase the sentence, notwithstanding that there has not been a cross-appeal by P, as long as D is given reasonable notice by P that it will seek an increased penalty and D has been given an opportunity to be heard.

Lowry v. R. (1972), 19 C.R.N.S. 315, 6 C.C.C. (2d) 531 (S.C.C.) — The *Code* does *not* require that D be present when sentence is passed by a court of appeal. However, the court of appeal is bound to afford the convicted person an opportunity to make submissions or to have them made on his behalf before awarding sentence.

R. v. Christman (1973), 22 C.R.N.S. 338, 11 C.C.C. (2d) 245n (Alta. C.A.) — *See also: R. v. Fallofield* (1973), 22 C.R.N.S. 342, 13 C.C.C. (2d) 450 (B.C. C.A.); *R. v. McInnis* (1973), 23 C.R.N.S. 152, 13 C.C.C. (2d) 471 (Ont. C.A.) — On an appeal against sentence, the court of appeal may consider whether the trial court erred in *not* granting D a discharge and in a proper case may itself make such an order.

R. v. Warr (1987), 62 Nfld. & P.E.I.R. 158 (Nfld. C.A.) — The court is generally reluctant to increase a sentence on appeal where the sentence imposed at trial has already been served.

R. v. T. (J.C.) (1998), 124 C.C.C. (3d) 385 (Ont. C.A.) — An appellate court must treat a trial judge's decision to impose a conditional sentence with the same defence it accords to decision concerning the duration of a custodial sentence.

R. v. Glykis (1995), 41 C.R. (4th) 310, 100 C.C.C. (3d) 97 (Ont. C.A.) — A *Charter* breach should *not* be considered in imposing sentence unless it mitigated the seriousness of the offence or constituted a form of punishment or undue hardship.

R. v. H. (J.) (1998), (sub nom. *Protection de la jeunesse — 965)* 129 C.C.C. (3d) 219 (Que. C.A.) — It is *not* an error in principle to depart from a joint submission. (per Fish and Beauregard JJ. A.)

Fitness of Sentence

R. v. M. (C.A.), 46 C.R. (4th) 269, [1996] 1 S.C.R. 500, 105 C.C.C. (3d) 327 (S.C.C.) — In the absence of

   i.   error in principle;

   ii.   failure to consider a relevant factor; or,

   iii.   overemphasis of the appropriate factors

a court of appeal should only intervene to vary a sentence at trial if it is *demonstrably unfit*. A court of appeal should only intervene to minimize the disparity of sentences where the sentence is in *substantial and marked departure* from sentences customarily imposed for similar offenders committing similar crimes.

R. v. Shropshire (1995), 43 C.R. (4th) 269, 102 C.C.C. (3d) 193 (S.C.C.) — It is error for a court of appeal to reduce a period of parole ineligibility because the trial judge has not given specific reasons which, in the opinion of the court of appeal, justify the increase. A court of appeal may *not* modify a parole ineligibility order simply because its members feel that a different order ought to have been made. The order ought to be varied only if the court of appeal is convinced it is *not* fit, *i.e.*, it is clearly unreasonable.

R. v. Brown (1991), 66 C.C.C. (3d) 1, 6 C.R. (4th) 353 (S.C.C.) — The sentencing judge is bound by the express and implied factual implications of a jury verdict. Where, on counts of dangerous driving causing death and bodily harm, a jury finds guilt of dangerous driving *simpliciter*, they have negated the causal *nexus* required in the more serious charges. Since Parliament chose to make dangerous driving a consequence related crime, the consequence of death or bodily harm must be taken to be excluded under a finding of guilt of dangerous driving *simpliciter*.

R. v. Johnson (1996), 112 C.C.C. (3d) 225 (B.C. C.A.) — Absent error in principle, an appellate court should *only* disturb a sentence if it can be said to be *unreasonable* or *demonstrably unfit* as being clearly outside the range of sentence imposed for the type of offence and offender. Deference occupies a position of lesser importance where there is a demonstrated error in principle.

R. v. McNeil (1998), 16 C.R. (5th) 311, 125 C.C.C. (3d) 71 (N.S. C.A.) — A decision by a trial judge to impose consecutive rather than concurrent sentences is entitled to the same deference as a decision about the length of sentence.

R. v. Muise (1994), 94 C.C.C. (3d) 119 (N.S. C.A.) — A court of appeal will not interfere with a period of parole ineligibility fixed by the trial judge unless it is clearly excessive or inadequate. Where a trial judge

i.   applies the correct principles of sentence;

ii.   considers all of the relevant facts; and,

iii. imposes a sentence which is neither clearly excessive nor inadequate

the sentence imposed is fit.

R. v. Wood (1988), 43 C.C.C. (3d) 570 (Ont. C.A.) — Where Crown counsel overreaches, in attaching as a condition of acceptance of a plea to a lesser offence, a joint submission to a sentence far in excess of the usual range of sentence for such offences, the court of appeal will reduce the sentence despite the joint submission.

R. v. Simmons (1973), 13 C.C.C. (2d) 65 (Ont. C.A.) — On an appeal against sentence, the appellate court should only find the sentence *not* fit if it appears the trial judge erred in principle and/or the sentence is manifestly excessive or inadequate. It is the court's duty to re-examine both fact and principle and pass upon the fitness of the sentence imposed.

R. v. Dubuc (1998), 131 C.C.C. (3d) 250, 21 C.R. (5th) 292 (Que. C.A.) — Where a negotiated disposition results in a joint submission on sentence, contingent on a plea of guilty, the joint submission, which falls within the acceptable range of sentence, is entitled to particular weight and should *not* be disregarded or overlooked.

A trial judge who intends to reject a joint submission should make it clear from the outset so that the parties can include in the record materials essential for a meaningful appellate review.

R. v. H. (J.) (1998), (sub nom. *Protection de la jennesse — 965*) 129 C.C.C. (3d) 219 (Que. C.A.) — Unless a trial judge

i.   erred in principle;

ii.   ignored a material consideration; or,

iii. attributed inadequate or excessive importance to a relevant factor,

an appellate court may vary a sentence imposed only if it is demonstrably unfit. (per Fish and Beauregard JJ. A.)

R. v. Mikkelson (1973), 14 C.C.C. (2d) 255 (Sask. C.A.) — Where there is a marked departure in the sentence imposed from those usually imposed for such offences, the record should disclose justification for such disparity. In the absence of such record, it is incumbent on the appellate court to alter the sentence and impose a more appropriate one.

Sentencing Principles [See s. 717]

New Evidence

R. v. L. (R.M.) (1987), 77 N.S.R. (2d) 224 (C.A.) — To be received by a court of appeal under this section, proferred evidence must at least be credible and of so cogent a nature that, had it been adduced at the sentencing hearing, it might reasonably have induced that tribunal to impose a sentence less severe than it did.

R. v. Edwards; R. v. Levo (1996), 46 C.R. (4th) 319, 105 C.C.C. (3d) 21 (Ont. C.A.); leave to appeal refused (1997), 108 C.C.C. (3d) vi (S.C.C.) — The *Code* does *not* authorize different standards for the introduction of fresh evidence in conviction and sentence appeals.

Effect of Judgment

R. v. Crowe (1986), 55 Sask. R. 9 (C.A.) — *See also*: *R. v. Boyd* (1979), 47 C.C.C. (2d) 369 (Ont. C.A.) — By virtue of s. 687(2), the sentence began on the date that D was sentenced by the trial court.

Related Provisions: "Sentence" is defined in s. 673. Rights of appeal from sentence are conferred by ss. 675(1)(b) and 676(1)(d). Although discrete rights of appeal, without leave, are given in respect of a period of parole ineligibility upon conviction of second degree murder (ss. 675(2) and 676(4)), such an order is, nonetheless, a "sentence" under s. 673. Its fitness will be determined on appeal under s. 687. The court also has jurisdiction to deal with the appropriateness of orders of restitution under s. 689(2).

The specific authority of a court of appeal to receive further or "fresh" evidence on an appeal against sentence (s. 687(1)), obviates the more rigorous standards applicable under s. 683(1)(d).

688. (1) Right of appellant to attend — Subject to subsection (2), an appellant who is in custody is entitled, if he desires, to be present at the hearing of the appeal.

(2) Appellant represented by counsel — An appellant who is in custody and who is represented by counsel is not entitled to be present

    (a) at the hearing of the appeal, where the appeal is on a ground involving a question of law alone,

    (b) on an application for leave to appeal, or

    (c) on any proceedings that are preliminary or incidental to an appeal,

unless rules of court provide that he is entitled to be present or the court of appeal or a judge thereof gives him leave to be present.

(3) Argument may be oral or in writing — An appellant may present his case on appeal and his argument in writing instead of orally, and the court of appeal shall consider any case of argument so presented.

(4) Sentence in absence of appellant — A court of appeal may exercise its power to impose sentence notwithstanding that the appellant is not present.

R.S., c. C-34, s. 615.

Commentary: The section determines when an *appellant*, in *custody*, may be *present* at the hearing of an appeal to the court of appeal.

The general rule of s. 688(1) is that, subject to s. 688(2), an appellant confined to custody is entitled, if he/she desires, to be present at the hearing of an appeal. Under s. 688(2) an appellant, in custody and represented by counsel, is *not* entitled to be present at the hearing of an appeal based on questions of law alone, nor on an application for leave to appeal nor any proceedings preliminary or incidental to an appeal, unless the rules of court so provide or a judge of the court of appeal gives leave for the appellant to appear. Under s. 688(4), the jurisdiction of the court of appeal to impose sentence is unaffected by whether the appellant is present.

Section 688(3) permits an appellant to present his/her case on appeal and argument in writing rather than orally and obliges the court of appeal to consider any such argument.

Case Law

Lowry v. R. (1972), 19 C.R.N.S. 315, 6 C.C.C. (2d) 531 (S.C.C.) — The *Code* does not require that D be present when sentence is passed by a court of appeal, even where D is the respondent in the appeal. However, the court of appeal is bound to afford the convicted person an opportunity to make submissions or to have them made on his/her behalf before passing sentence.

Smith v. R. (1965), 47 C.R. 1, [1966] 1 C.C.C. 162 (S.C.C.) — The right to attend granted by this section is imperative. The court of appeal has *no* right to hear an appeal, but must adjourn it, when an appellant, who has expressed a desire to be present, is not present when the appeal comes on for hearing.

R. v. Elworthy (1983), 49 B.C.L.R. 188 (C.A.) — Where the appeal appeared to involve issues of mixed law and fact and not law alone, D was entitled to be present at the hearing and did not require the leave of the court for an order to release him for that purpose.

R. v. Morin (1993), 78 C.C.C. (3d) 559 (Ont. C.A.) — An application for judicial interim release pending appeal is a proceeding that is *incidental* to an appeal, hence a judge of the court of appeal may permit an appellant to be present on the hearing of the application.

R. v. Morin (1993), 78 C.C.C. (3d) 559 (Ont. C.A.) — An appellant must show cause why an order should be made under s. 688(2) permitting him to be present, *inter alia*, on a proceeding incidental to an appeal. The onus may be discharged in respect of an application for judicial interim release pending appeal when the appellant shows that attendance may be necessary

i.   for the appellant to *testify* during the hearing;

ii.   to *obtain instructions* from the appellant concerning a possible waiver of solicitor-client privilege; and,

iii.   in the event that certain *factual issues* become in dispute.

Related Provisions: A similar provision appears in s. 694.2 for appeals to the Supreme Court of Canada.

By s. 822(1) these provisions apply to s. 812 summary conviction appeals.

689. (1) Restitution or forfeiture of property — Where the trial court makes an order for compensation or for the restitution of property under section 738 or 739 or an order of forfeiture of property under subsection 462.37(1), the operation of the order is suspended

(a) until the expiration of the period prescribed by rules of court for the giving of notice of appeal or of notice of application for leave to appeal, unless the accused waives an appeal; and

(b) until the appeal or application for leave to appeal has been determined, where an appeal is taken or application for leave to appeal is made.

(2) Annulling or varying order — The court of appeal may by order annul or vary an order made by the trial court with respect to compensation or the restitution of property within the limits prescribed by the provision under which the order was made by the trial court, whether or not the conviction is quashed.

R.S., c. C-34, s. 616; c. 42 (4th Supp.), s. 5; 1995, c. 22, s. 10.

Commentary: The section defines the authority of the court of appeal to deal with orders for compensation, restitution and forfeiture of property under s. 462.37(1).

Under s. 689(1) the operation of an order for compensation, restitution or forfeiture is *suspended* until the *expiration* of the statutory appeal period or waiver thereof or, where an appeal has been taken, until the appeal is determined.

Under s. 689(2) the court of appeal may annul or vary an order of the trial court with respect to compensation or restitution of property within the limits of the enabling authority. The court may exercise this discretion, whether or not the conviction is quashed.

Related Provisions: Sections 738–741.2 authorize and limit the making of restitution orders.

The orders are also a "sentence" under s. 673 reviewable on an appeal against sentence under ss. 675(1)(b) and 676(1)(d).

Under s. 822(1), these provisions apply to s. 812 summary conviction appeals. *Semble*, the Supreme Court of Canada would have equivalent jurisdiction, provided the authority of s. 689 is not restricted to cases in which the fitness of sentence is an issue.

Powers of Minister of Justice

690. Powers of minister of justice — The Minister of Justice may, on an application for the mercy of the Crown by or on behalf of a person who has been convicted in proceedings by indictment or who has been sentenced to preventive detention under Part XXIV,

(a) direct, by order in writing, a new trial or, in the case of a person under sentence of preventive detention, a new hearing, before any court that he thinks proper, if after inquiry he is satisfied that in the circumstances a new trial or hearing, as the case may be, should be directed;

(b) refer the matter at any time to the court of appeal for hearing and determination by that court as if it were an appeal by the convicted person or the person under sentence of preventive detention, as the case may be; or

(c) refer to the court of appeal at any time, for its opinion, any question on which he desires the assistance of that court, and the court shall furnish its opinion accordingly.

R.S., c. C-34, s. 617.

Commentary: The section defines the authority of the Minister of Justice in applications for the *mercy* of the Crown.

Applications for the mercy of the Crown may be made by or on behalf of a person convicted in proceedings by indictment, or a person sentenced to preventive detention under Part XXIV. The authority of the Minister is threefold. Under s. 690(a), if he/she thinks it appropriate after inquiry, the Minister may *direct a new trial or hearing* before any court that he/she thinks proper. Under s. 690(b), the Minister may *refer the matter* to the court of appeal for hearing and determination by the court, as if it were an appeal by a convicted person or one under sentence of preventive detention, as the case may be. Finally, under s. 690(c), the Minister may refer to the court of appeal at any time, for its opinion, any question on which he/she desires its assistance. The court shall furnish its opinion accordingly.

Case Law

Declaratory Relief

Wilson v. Canada (Min. of Justice) (1985), 46 C.R. (3d) 91, 20 C.C.C. (3d) 206 (Fed. C.A.); leave to appeal refused (1985), 46 C.R. (3d) xxv (S.C.C.) — An action for declaratory relief is available against the Minister's refusal to intervene under this section. The basis of the application is *Charter* s. 7.

Release Pending Hearing

R. v. Johnson (1998), 131 C.C.C. (3d) 343, 21 C.R. (5th) 135 (N.S. C. A. [In Chambers]) — Where the Minister of Justice directs a reference under *Code* s. 690, which may involve the hearing of an appeal from conviction, the relevant factors to consider in deciding whether D should be released pending the hearing are set out in s. 679(3).

New Trial: S. 690(a)

R. v. Peel (1921), 36 C.C.C. 221 (N.S. C. A.) — Where a new trial is ordered by the Minister of Justice, after a conviction has been affirmed on appeal, there is no jurisdiction to grant bail pending the new trial.

Reference to Court of Appeal: Ss. 690(b); (c)

R. v. Coffin (1956), 116 C.C.C. 215 (S.C.C.) — The Minister of Justice may, if he so desires, refer a matter to the Supreme Court of Canada, either under the powers given to the Governor General by letters patent or under the *Supreme Court Act*, and if the Minister does so, the court has jurisdiction to hear the reference.

R. v. Gorecki (No. 2) (1976), 32 C.C.C. (2d) 135 (Ont. C.A.) — *See also: R. v. Marshall* (1983), 57 N.S.R. (2d) 286 (C.A.) — Where prior to a reference under this section there has already been an unsuccessful appeal, the court of appeal may only deal with the ground upon which the Minister referred the case. Although the court will only hear such new evidence as might be heard on a regular appeal, the rules with respect to fresh evidence are not to be applied as strictly. The court should consider each case on its merits.

Related Provisions: Sections 748–751 authorize the extension of the royal prerogative of mercy and permit the Governor in Council to grant a free or conditional pardon or order the remission, in whole or in part, of a particular penalty, fine or forfeiture.

The Governor in Council may also direct a reference to the Supreme Court of Canada under s. 53(2) of the *Supreme Court Act*, R.S. 1985, c. S-26.

Appeals to the Supreme Court of Canada

691. (1) Appeal from conviction — A person who is convicted of an indictable offence and whose conviction is affirmed by the court of appeal may appeal to the Supreme Court of Canada

    (a) on any question of law on which a judge of the court of appeal dissents; or

    (b) on any question of law, if leave to appeal is granted by the Supreme Court of Canada.

(2) Appeal where acquittal set aside — A person who is acquitted of an indictable offence other than by reason of a verdict of not criminally responsible on account of mental disorder and whose acquittal is set aside by the court of appeal may appeal to the Supreme Court of Canada

    (a) on any question of law on which a judge of the court of appeal dissents;

    (b) on any question of law, if the Court of Appeal enters a verdict of guilty against the person; or

    (c) on any question of law, if leave to appeal is granted by the Supreme Court of Canada.

R.S., c. C-34, s. 618; 1974-75-76, c. 105, s. 18;R.S. 1985, c. 34 (3d Supp.), s. 10; 1991, c. 43, s. 9, Schedule, item 9; 1997, c. 18, s. 99.

Commentary: The section describes the basis upon which appeals may be taken to the Supreme Court of Canada from decisions of the provincial courts of appeal affirming D's conviction of an indictable offence or setting aside the acquittal of D or a co-accused.

Section 691(1) applies where D's *conviction* of an indictable offence has been *affirmed* by the court of appeal. D has an appeal as of right, on any question of law on which a judge of the court of appeal dissents, on which the Supreme Court of Canada grants leave to appeal.

Section 691(2) applies where D's *acquittal* at trial, other than by the verdict of not criminally responsible on account of mental disorder, has been *set aside* by the court of appeal. D may appeal to the Supreme Court of Canada on any question of law on which a judge of the court of appeal dissents, on which the Supreme Court of Canada grants leave, or if the court of appeal enters a verdict of guilty.

Case Law

Question of Law [See also ss. 676 and 693]

R. v. Yebes (1987), 59 C.R. (3d) 108, 36 C.C.C. (3d) 417 (S.C.C.) — Since the question of whether a verdict was reasonable requires the court of appeal to give legal content to the concept of "unreasonable", the question is one of law such as to allow an appeal to the Supreme Court of Canada within s. 691(1)(a).

R. v. Wigman (1987), 56 C.R. (3d) 289, 33 C.C.C. (3d) 97 (S.C.C.) — Leave granted at large under s. 691(1)(b) relates to any question of law that goes to the validity of the verdict of acquittal. The appellant is entitled to raise a new issue of law and take advantage of changes in the law occurring subsequent to his/her conviction at trial, while he/she is still "in the system" — i.e., before final disposition of his/her case.

Mahoney v. R. (1981), 27 C.R. (3d) 97, 67 C.C.C. (2d) 197 (S.C.C.) — A question of law alone is involved in the application of the curative proviso in s. 686(1)(b)(iii) by a court of appeal. An appeal lies upon this basis to the Supreme Court of Canada.

Demenoff v. R. (1964), 41 C.R. 407 (S.C.C.) — For an appeal as of right under s. 691(1)(a) the ground of appeal must raise a question of law in the strict sense and it is insufficient that the question is one of mixed law and fact. Furthermore, the question involved must be one in respect of which there is a disagreement (express or implied) between the minority and the majority in the court of appeal.

R. v. Brown (1962), 37 C.R. 101 (S.C.C.) — A disagreement as to what verdict should have been entered by the court following the rendering of a special verdict by the jury is a disagreement on a question of law. Also, when one judge holds a passage in the charge to the jury to be material and fatally misleading and another judge finds the same passage to be irrelevant, this constitutes disagreement on a point of law.

Pearson v. R. (1959), 30 C.R. 14, 123 C.C.C. 271 (S.C.C.) — Where the dissenting judgment is based solely on the sufficiency of the evidence to support a conviction, there is no dissent on a ground of law.

Leave to Appeal: S. 691(1)(b)

R. v. Thomas (1990), 75 C.R. (3d) 352 (S.C.C.) — *See also: R. v. Wigman* (1987), 56 C.R. (3d) 289, 33 C.C.C. (3d) 97 (S.C.C.); reversing in part (1983), 6 C.C.C. (3d) 289 (B.C. C.A.) — Where an applicant for leave to appeal seeks to raise the invalidity of a law under which he/she was convicted, on grounds arising out of a decision of the Supreme Court of Canada given after trial and appeal to the provincial appellate court, the test is whether the applicant is still *in the judicial system*. An applicant will still be *in the judicial system* if *any* of the following apply:

(a)   an *appeal* has been taken to the Supreme Court of Canada;

(b)   a timely *application* for *leave* to appeal to the Supreme Court of Canada has been made; or,

(c)   an *application* for an *extension* of *time* has been granted under the normal criteria.

R. v. Chaulk (1989), 69 C.R. (3d) 217, 48 C.C.C. (3d) 65 (S.C.C.) — The Supreme Court of Canada has jurisdiction to determine an application for leave to appeal on the basis of written material and without according an oral hearing.

R. v. Wigman (1987), 56 C.R. (3d) 289, 33 C.C.C. (3d) 97 (S.C.C.) — Where the Supreme Court of Canada grants unrestricted leave to appeal, D is entitled to raise any question of law on appeal, including questions raised by a Supreme Court decision subsequent to the granting of leave to appeal.

Demeter v. R. (1977), 38 C.R.N.S. 317, 34 C.C.C. (2d) 137 (S.C.C.) — The fact that leave to appeal was granted with respect to an issue does *not* preclude the court from later deciding that the question was *not* one of law.

Hill v. R. (1976), 23 C.C.C. (2d) 321 (S.C.C.) — The Supreme Court of Canada will not as a rule entertain an appeal concerning the fitness of a sentence. It does have jurisdiction to grant leave to appeal on a question of law concerning the jurisdictional validity of the sentence imposed.

Accused Acquitted at Trial: S. 691(2)

R. v. Puskas (1998), 16 C.R. (5th) 324, 125 C.C.C. (3d) 433 (S.C.C.) — Under s. 44(c) of the *Interpretation Act*, an appeal taken as of right under former s. 691(2) of the *Criminal Code* as it stood before its repeal and substitution, should be quashed since the new enactment gives no appeal as of right from decisions of provincial appellate courts ordering a new trial after an acquittal.

R. v. Kalanj (1989), 70 C.R. (3d) 260, 48 C.C.C. (3d) 459 (S.C.C.) — A judicial stay of proceedings is tantamount to an acquittal.

R. v. Guillemette (1986), 51 C.R. (3d) 273, 26 C.C.C. (3d) 1 (S.C.C.) — Where the court of appeal set aside D's acquittal of murder and ordered a new murder trial, on an appeal by D against his conviction for manslaughter, D had an automatic right of appeal to the Supreme Court of Canada under s. 691(2). D was entitled to appeal for a restoration of his murder acquittal and an order that the new trial be on a charge of manslaughter, the Crown not having appealed the murder acquittal, and nothing more. D could *not* appeal the manslaughter conviction under s. 691(1) since the court of appeal had not affirmed that conviction.

Position of Respondent

R. v. Keegstra (1995), 39 C.R. (4th) 205, 98 C.C.C. (3d) 1 (S.C.C.) — In general, a respondent in a criminal appeal under *Code* ss. 691 or 693 may raise any argument which supports the order of the court below. However, if the respondent makes a new argument, which lacks a sufficient evidentiary record, the court may exercise its discretion to not hear it.

Related Provisions: Section 692 confers the similar rights of appeal to the Supreme Court of Canada from a special verdict of not criminally responsible on account of mental disorder or a verdict of unfit to stand trial.

The rights of appeal of the Attorney General are described in ss. 693 and 696.

The authority of the Supreme Court of Canada to determine appeals under Part XXI is equivalent to that of the provincial court of appeal. The authority is incorporated by reference in s. 695(1).

692. (1) Appeal against affirmation of special verdict of not criminally responsible on account of mental disorder — A person who has been found not criminally responsible on account of mental disorder and

(a) whose verdict is affirmed on that ground by the court of appeal, or

(b) against whom a verdict of guilty is entered by the court of appeal under sub-paragraph 686(4)(b)(ii),

may appeal to the Supreme Court of Canada.

(2) Appeal against affirmation of verdict of unfit to stand trial — A person who is found unfit to stand trial and against whom that verdict is affirmed by the court of appeal may appeal to the Supreme Court of Canada.

(3) Grounds of appeal — An appeal under subsection (1) or (2) may be

(a) on any question of law on which a judge of the court of appeal dissents; or

(b) on any question of law, if leave to appeal is granted by the Supreme Court of Canada.

R.S., c. C-34, s. 620; R.S. 1985, c. 34 (3d Supp.), s. 11; 1991, c. 43, s. 9, Schedule, item 10.

Commentary: The section defines the rights of appeal to the Supreme Court of Canada where D has been found not criminally responsible on account of mental disorder or unfit to stand trial.

Section 692(1) applies where a verdict of not criminally responsible on account of mental disorder has been affirmed by the court of appeal, or a verdict of guilty entered in substitution therefor under s. 686(4)(b)(ii). Section 692(2) applies where a trial finding that D was *unfit* to stand trial has been affirmed by the court of appeal. In either case, D may appeal to the Supreme Court of Canada, as of right, on any question of law on which a judge of the court of appeal dissents, or on any question of law on which the Supreme Court of Canada grants leave to appeal.

The section gives no right of appeal where a finding of unfitness has been set aside and a new trial ordered by the court of appeal.

Related Provisions: The "defence" of not criminally responsible on account of mental disorder is governed by ss. 16 and 672.34, the issue of unfitness by s. 672.22.

D's right of appeal to the court of appeal from a finding of unfitness or a verdict of not criminally responsible on account of mental disorder is described in s. 675(3). It is *not* limited to questions of law alone, although it is only in respect of such grounds that leave to appeal is not required. P's right of appeal to the court of appeal from similar findings is limited to questions of law alone under ss. 676(1)(a) and (3). The authority of the court of appeal to determine such appeals is described in ss. 686(1), (2), (4), (6) and (7). The Supreme Court of Canada has equivalent authority under s. 695(1).

693. (1) **Appeal by Attorney General** — **Where a judgment of a court of appeal sets aside a conviction pursuant to an appeal taken under section 675 or dismisses an appeal taken pursuant to paragraph 676(1)(a), (b) or (c) or subsection 676(3), the Attorney General may appeal to the Supreme Court of Canada**

(a) **on any question of law on which a judge of the court of appeal dissents, or**

(b) **on any question of law, if leave to appeal is granted by the Supreme Court of Canada.**

(2) **Terms** — **Where leave to appeal is granted under paragraph (1)(b), the Supreme Court of Canada may impose such terms as it sees fit.**

R.S., c. C-34, s. 621; R.S. 1985, c. 27 (1st Supp.), s. 146; c. 34 (3d Supp.), s. 12.

Commentary: The section defines the rights of the Attorney General to appeal to the Supreme Court of Canada from a decision of a provincial court of appeal setting aside a conviction in an appeal taken by D under s. 675 or dismissing an appeal by the Attorney General under ss. 676(1)(a), (b), (c) or (3). The appeals are as of right, on any question of law on which a judge of the court of appeal dissents, or, with leave of the Supreme Court of Canada, on any question of law.

Section 693(2) authorizes the Supreme Court of Canada to impose such terms as it sees fit upon granting the Attorney General leave to appeal. Frequently, the court requires the Attorney General to pay the costs of the respondent D.

Case Law

Question of Law [See also ss. 676, 691]

R. v. Wigman (1987), 56 C.R. (3d) 289, 33 C.C.C. (3d) 97 (S.C.C.) — *See also*: *R. v. Caouette* (1972), 9 C.C.C. (2d) 449 (S.C.C.) — Leave granted under s. 693(1)(b) relates to *any* question of law that goes to the validity of the verdict of acquittal.

R. v. Cotroni (1979), 7 C.R. (3d) 185, 45 C.C.C. (2d) 1 (S.C.C.) — The question of whether evidence of a conspiracy is evidence of the conspiracy alleged in the indictment is a question of law. A finding that there is no evidence to go to the jury also raises a question of law.

R. v. Olan (1978), 5 C.R. (3d) 1, 41 C.C.C. (2d) 145 (S.C.C.) — *See also*: *R. v. Caouette* (1972), 9 C.C.C. (2d) 449 (S.C.C.) — The question of whether there was any evidence to go to the jury is not one of sufficiency of evidence. It is a question of law.

Fergusson v. R. (1961), 36 C.R. 271, 132 C.C.C. 112 (S.C.C.) — Where the decision of the court below was based on placing a different weight on the evidence than that of the trial judge, this is a mixed question of law and fact.

Right of Appeal

R. v. Laba (1994), 94 C.C.C. (3d) 385, 34 C.R. (4th) 360 (S.C.C.); reversing in part (1992), 12 O.R. (3d) 239, 74 C.C.C. (3d) 538 (C.A.) — No appeal lies to the Supreme Court of Canada under *Code* s. 693(1)(b) from an order of a provincial court of appeal allowing an appeal by P from an order of a motions court judge staying proceedings on an indictment and, at least implicitly, lifting the stay.

R. v. Laba (1994), 94 C.C.C. (3d) 385, 34 C.R. (4th) 360 (S.C.C.); reversing in part (1992), 12 O.R. (3d) 239, 74 C.C.C. (3d) 538 (C.A.) — A "dual proceedings s. 40" analytical approach should be adopted for appeals against successful s. 52 *Constitution Act* challenges to the constitutionality of laws. An appeal against a ruling on the constitutionality of a law that cannot be piggybacked onto *Code* proceedings is a judgment of the highest court of final resort in a province in which judgment can be had for the purposes of s. 40(1) of the *Supreme Court Act.*

Position of Respondent

R. v. Keegstra (1995), 39 C.R. (4th) 205, 98 C.C.C. (3d) 1 (S.C.C.) — In general, a respondent in a criminal appeal under *Code* ss. 691 or 693 may raise any argument which supports the order of the court below. However, if the respondent makes a new argument, which lacks a sufficient evidentiary record, the court may exercise its discretion to not hear it.

Related Provisions: "Attorney General" is defined in s. 2. Under s. 696, the Attorney General of Canada has the same rights of appeal in proceedings instituted at the instance of the Government of Canada and conducted by or on behalf of that government as does the Attorney General of the province under Part XXII.

The authority of the Supreme Court of Canada to determine appeals by the Attorney General is found in s. 695(1) incorporating the dispositive authority of the court of appeal in such matters.

The procedure followed in appeals to the Supreme Court of Canada is set out in the *Supreme Court Act* and the rules passed thereunder.

694. Notice of appeal — No appeal lies to the Supreme Court of Canada unless notice of appeal in writing is served by the appellant on the respondent in accordance with the *Supreme Court Act.*

R.S., c. C-34, s. 622; R.S. 1985, c. 34 (3d Supp.), s. 13.

Commentary: Under this section there is no appeal to the Supreme Court of Canada unless a notice of appeal in writing is served by the appellant on the respondent, in accordance with the *Supreme Court Act.*

Related Provisions: A similar provision appears in s. 678 in relation to appeals to the provincial court of appeal.

The applicable rules respecting the notice of appeal, its service and filing, are found in the *Rules of the Supreme Court of Canada* passed pursuant to the *Supreme Court Act.*

694.1 (1) Legal assistance for accused — The Supreme Court of Canada or a judge thereof may, at any time, assign counsel to act on behalf of an accused who is a party to an appeal to the Court or to proceedings preliminary or incidental to an appeal to the Court where, in the opinion of the Court or judge, it appears desirable in the interests of justice that the accused should have legal assistance and where it appears that the accused has not sufficient means to obtain that assistance.

(2) Counsel fees and disbursements — Where counsel is assigned pursuant to subsection (1) and legal aid is not granted to the accused pursuant to a provincial legal aid program, the fees and disbursements of counsel shall be paid by the Attorney General who is the appellant or respondent, as the case may be, in the appeal.

(3) Taxation of fees and disbursements — Where subsection (2) applies and counsel and the Attorney General cannot agree on fees or disbursements of counsel, the Attorney General or the counsel may apply to the Registrar of the Supreme Court of Canada, and the Registrar may tax the disputed fees and disbursements.

R.S. 1985, c. 34 (3d Supp.), s. 13.

Commentary: The section duplicates the provisions of s. 684 applicable on appeals by D to the court of appeal.

Under s. 694.1(1), the Supreme Court of Canada, or a judge thereof, may assign counsel to act on behalf of D who is party to an appeal or to proceedings preliminary or incidental to an appeal to that court. It is *not* necessary that D be an appellant before the Supreme Court of Canada. D, for example, could be a respondent in an appeal by the Attorney General. The authority may be exercised where the court or a judge thereof is of the opinion that it appears desirable in the *interests of justice* that D have legal assistance and D has *not sufficient means* to obtain such aid.

Sections 694.1(2) and (3) are concerned with the payment of counsel assigned under s. 694.1(1). Where legal aid is not granted to D under a provincial legal aid program, the fees and disbursements of counsel must be paid by the Attorney General who is the appellant or respondent on the appeal to which D is a party. Disagreements between the Attorney General and assigned counsel as to fees or disbursements are determined upon application to the Registrar of the Supreme Court of Canada who may tax the disputed amounts.

Related Provisions: Similar provision is made in s. 684 in respect of accused who are parties to an appeal to the provincial court of appeal or proceedings preliminary or incidental to such an appeal. There is no corresponding provision applicable at trial, except s. 615(4), which requires the assignment of counsel for an unrepresented accused in respect of whom an issue of fitness is being directed.

694.2 (1) Right of appellant to attend — Subject to subsection (2), an appellant who is in custody and who desires to be present at the hearing of the appeal before the Supreme Court of Canada is entitled to be present at it.

(2) Appellant represented by counsel — An appellant who is in custody and who is represented by counsel is not entitled to be present before the Supreme Court of Canada

(a) on an application for leave to appeal,

(b) on any proceedings that are preliminary or incidental to an appeal, or

(c) at the hearing of the appeal,

unless rules of court provide that entitlement or the Supreme Court of Canada or a judge thereof gives the appellant leave to be present.

R.S. 1987, c. 34 (3d Supp.), s. 13.

Commentary: The section duplicates s. 688, applicable on appeals by D to the provincial court of appeal. The general rule of s. 694.2(1) is that, subject to s. 694.2(2), an appellant in custody is entitled, if he/she desires, to be present at the hearing of the appeal. Section 694.2(2) enacts a general rule that an appellant in custody and represented by counsel is not entitled to be present at the hearing of an appeal, an application for leave to appeal or in any proceedings preliminary or incidental to an appeal, unless rules of court provide that entitlement or the Supreme Court of Canada or a judge thereof gives the appellant leave to be present.

Related Provisions: The similar provision in s. 688 is described in its Commentary.

695. (1) Order of Supreme Court of Canada — The Supreme Court of Canada may, on an appeal under this Part, make any order that the court of appeal might have made and may make any rule or order that is necessary to give effect to its judgment.

(2) [Repealed 1999, c. 5, s. 27.]

R.S., c. C-34, s. 623; 1999, c. 5, s. 27.

Commentary: The section defines the authority of the Supreme Court of Canada to determine appeals brought under Part XXI.

Under s. 695(1), the Supreme Court of Canada may make *any order* on appeal that the *court of appeal* might have made and, further, any order or rule necessary to give effect to its judgment. The section is not, in terms, limited to the dispositive or adjudicative authority of s. 686 but, for example, would include the authority to receive further evidence under s. 683.

Section 695(2) *deems abandoned* appeals to the Supreme Court of Canada not *brought* on for hearing by the appellant at the session of the court during which the judgment under appeal was pronounced, or during the next session. An order of the court or a judge thereof may revivify the appeal and restore it to the list for hearing.

Case Law

R. v. Barnes (1991), 3 C.R. (4th) 1, 63 C.C.C. (3d) 1 (S.C.C.); affirming (1990), 54 C.C.C. (3d) 368 (B.C. C.A.) — Section 695(1) does *not* allow the Supreme Court of Canada, in all circumstances, to make a decision that, in its opinion, the court of appeal could and should have made. In the absence of an appeal by P, D cannot leave the Supreme Court of Canada with less than what the court of appeal ordered.

R. v. Morin (1988), 66 C.R. (3d) 1, 44 C.C.C. (3d) 193 (S.C.C.) — A party wishing to introduce fresh evidence on the argument of an appeal to the Supreme Court should apply by motion with an affidavit in support establishing the preconditions for reception for an order admitting the evidence. This procedure should be followed even where the court of appeal refused to admit the fresh evidence.

R. v. Yebes (1987), 59 C.R. (3d) 108, 36 C.C.C. (3d) 417 (S.C.C.) — In considering an appeal, the Supreme Court of Canada must put itself in the place of the court of appeal and consider the matter anew.

Perka v. R. (1984), 42 C.R. (3d) 113, 14 C.C.C. (3d) 385 (S.C.C.) — A respondent may advance any argument to sustain the judgment below, and is *not* limited to the appellant's points of law. However, a party cannot raise an entirely new argument which has not been raised below and in relation to which it might have been necessary to adduce evidence at trial.

R. v. Borg (1969), 7 C.R.N.S. 85, [1969] 4 C.C.C. 262 (S.C.C.); reversing (1968), 5 C.R.N.S. 222, [1969] 2 C.C.C. 114 (Alta. C.A.) — Where the court of appeal had set aside a conviction on one of D's grounds, without considering the other grounds the Supreme Court of Canada, in addition to reversing the conclusion of the court of appeal, can determine the remaining grounds adversely to D and restore the conviction.

Related Provisions: The procedure followed on appeal to the Supreme Court of Canada is governed by the *Supreme Court Act* and the rules of the court passed in accordance therewith.

The scope of the authority conferred by ss. 683, 686 and 689 are discussed in the notes which accompany each section.

Appeals by Attorney General of Canada

696. Right of Attorney General of Canada to appeal — The Attorney General of Canada has the same rights of appeal in proceedings instituted at the instance of the Government of Canada and conducted by or on behalf of that Government as the Attorney General of a province has under this Part.

R.S., c. C-34, s. 624.

Commentary: Under this section the Attorney General of Canada has the same rights of appeal in proceedings instituted at the instance of the Government of Canada and conducted by or on behalf of that government, as the Attorney General of the province has in indictable proceedings under Part XXI.

Case Law

R. v. Mullin (1968), 66 W.W.R. 367 (Alta. C.A.) — The Attorney General of Canada has the same right to have "counsel instructed by him" conduct his appeal as does the Attorney General of a province.

Related Provisions: "Attorney General" is defined in s. 2. The rights of the Attorney General to appeal in proceedings by indictment are governed by s. 676.

Under ss. 813, 820(4) and 839(5) the Attorney General of Canada has the same rights of appeal in summary conviction proceedings instituted at the instance of the Government of Canada and conducted by or on behalf of that government as the Attorney General of the province has in such proceedings under Part XXVII.

PART XXII — PROCURING ATTENDANCE

Application

697. Application — Except where section 527 applies, this Part applies where a person is required to attend to give evidence in a proceeding to which this Act applies.
R.S., c. C-34, s. 625; R.S. 1985, c. 27 (1st Supp.), s. 147.

Commentary: Except for inmate witnesses, Part XXII applies to procure the attendance of witnesses in any proceedings to which the *Code* applies.

Related Provisions: Section 527 describes how to procure the attendance of a prisoner, *inter alia*, to give evidence in any proceedings to which the *Code* applies.

The *issuance* of process to compel the attendance of a witness is governed by ss. 698–700. Execution or service of process must accord with ss. 701–703.2. The *procedure* followed in relation to defaulting or absconding witnesses is governed by ss. 704–708.

Part XXII also permits evidence taken or given elsewhere to be read in trials upon indictment. Evidence on commission is authorized under ss. 709–714, and that given upon a previous trial, preliminary inquiry or investigation of the charge received under s. 715. Videotaped evidence may be received under s. 715.1.

Process

698. (1) Subpoena — Where a person is likely to give material evidence in a proceeding to which this Act applies, a subpoena may be issued in accordance with this Part requiring that person to attend to give evidence.

(2) Warrant in form 17 — Where it is made to appear that a person who is likely to give material evidence

(a) will not attend in response to a subpoena if a subpoena is issued, or

(b) is evading service of a subpoena,

a court, justice or provincial court judge having power to issue a subpoena to require the attendance of that person to give evidence may issue a warrant in Form 17 to cause that person to be arrested and to be brought to give evidence.

(3) Subpoena issued first — Except where paragraph (2)(a) applies, a warrant in Form 17 shall not be issued unless a subpoena has first been issued.
R.S., c. C-34, s. 626; R.S. 1985, c. 27 (1st Supp.), s. 203.

Commentary: Under this section *process* may issue to *compel* the *attendance* of persons whom the parties require to give *material evidence* in proceedings to which the *Code* applies.

The effect of ss. 698(1) and (3) is that, as a general rule, the attendance of a person likely to give material evidence in criminal proceedings will be compelled, at first instance, by the issuance of a *subpoena*, in accordance with Part XXII. Section 698(2) constitutes an *exception* to the general rule: it permits the issuance of a *warrant*, in Form 17, to compel the attendance of a witness who will either *not* attend in response to a subpoena, if issued, or who is *evading* service thereof. Under s. 698(2)(a), the warrant is issued at first instance to compel the attendance of the witness. Under s. 698(2)(b), a subpoena is issued and service attempted so as to permit a conclusion of evasion before a warrant may issue.

Case Law

R. v. Scott (1990), 2 C.R. (4th) 153, 61 C.C.C. (3d) 300 (S.C.C.) — *See also*: *R. v. Kinzie* (1956), 25 C.R. 6 (Ont. C.A.) — Before issuing a warrant, a trial judge must be satisfied not only that *proper attempts* have been undertaken to *serve* the *proposed witness* with a subpoena, but also that the proposed witness is a *material* witness.

R. v. Gingras (1992), 11 C.R. (4th) 294, 71 C.C.C. (3d) 53 (Alta. C.A.) — A trial judge of the superior court of criminal jurisdiction of a province has jurisdiction to quash a subpoena issued by another judge of the same court. Where it is apparent that an applicant is unaware whether there is anything relevant in files sought to be obtained under subpoena, a subpoena should *not* be issued under s. 698.

R. v. French (1977), 37 C.C.C. (2d) 201 (Ont. C.A.); affirmed on other grounds (1979), 47 C.C.C. (2d) 411 (S.C.C.) — The routine securing and serving of a subpoena on a hospital to produce public hospital records did *not* conform with the *Public Hospitals Act*, which requires a process issued out of a court.

Related Provisions: A subpoena is issued under s. 699, its contents prescribed by s. 700. The service of a subpoena and execution of a warrant must accord with ss. 701–703.2.

The procedure to ensure the attendance of a *defaulting or absconding witness* is prescribed by ss. 704–708.

A warrant for a witness in Form 17 requires the peace officers to whom it is directed to arrest and bring the witness before a specified court. Under s. 706, the witness may be detained in custody or released on a recognizance in Form 32 to appear and give evidence when required.

Under s. 699(6), a subpoena may be in Form 16. A *subpoena ad testificandum* requires attendance to give evidence. A *subpoena duces tecum* requires not only that the witness give evidence but, further, bring anything in his/her possession or under his/her control that relates to the charge and, more particularly, the things specified in the subpoena.

699. **(1) Who may issue** — If a person is required to attend to give evidence before a superior court of criminal jurisdiction, a court of appeal, an appeal court or a court of criminal jurisdiction other than a provincial court judge acting under Part XIX, a subpoena directed to that person shall be issued out of the court before which the attendance of that person is required.

(2) Order of judge — If a person is required to attend to give evidence before a provincial court judge acting under Part XIX or a summary conviction court under Part XXVII or in proceedings over which a justice has jurisdiction, a subpoena directed to the person shall be issued

    (a) by a provincial court judge or a justice, where the person whose attendance is required is within the province in which the proceedings were instituted; or

    (b) by a provincial court judge or out of a superior court of criminal jurisdiction of the province in which the proceedings were instituted, where the person whose attendance is required is not within the province.

(3) Order of judge — A subpoena shall not be issued out of a superior court of criminal jurisdiction pursuant to paragraph (2)(*b*), except pursuant to an order of a judge of the court made on application by a party to the proceedings.

(4) Seal — A subpoena or warrant that is issued by a court under this Part shall be under the seal of the court and shall be signed by a judge of the court or by the clerk of the court.

(5) Signature — A subpoena or warrant that is issued by a justice or provincial court judge under this Part shall be signed by the justice or provincial court judge.

(5.1) Sexual offences — Notwithstanding anything in subsection (1) to (5), in the case of an offence referred to in subsection 278.2(1), a subpoena requiring a witness to bring to the court a record, the production of which is governed by sections 278.1 to 278.91, must be issued and signed by a judge.

(6) Form of subpoena — Subject to subsection (7), a subpoena issued under this Part may be in Form 16.

(7) Form of subpoena in sexual offences — In the case of an offence referred to in subsection 278.2(1), a subpoena requiring a witness to bring anything to the court shall be in Form 16.1

R.S., c. C-34, s. 627; R.S. 1985, c. 27 (1st Supp.), s. 203; 1994, c. 44, s. 69; 1997, c. 30, s. 2; 1999, c. 5, s. 28.

Commentary: The section describes the authority by whom a subpoena may be issued under this Part and its form. Section 700 prescribes the contents of a subpoena.

Where the witness is to give evidence before a superior court of criminal jurisdiction, a court of appeal, an appeal court or a court of criminal jurisdiction, other than a provincial court judge, s. 699(1) requires that the subpoena be issued out of the court before which the witness is to give evidence. The subpoena must, subject to s. 699(5.1) and s. 699(7), be in Form 16 and be under the seal of the court and signed by a judge or the clerk of the court.

Where the witness is to testify in summary conviction proceedings under Part XXVII, or in proceedings over which a justice has jurisdiction, under s. 699(2)(a) the subpoena must be issued by a justice, where the witness is within the province in which the proceedings were instituted. In similar circumstances, where the witness is *not* in the province in which the proceedings were instituted, the subpoena must be issued under s. 699(2)(b) by a provincial court judge or out of the superior court of criminal jurisdiction in that province. Under s. 699(3), a subpoena may only be issued under s. 699(2)(b) out of the superior court of criminal jurisdiction upon application by a party to the proceedings and pursuant to an order of a judge of the court.

Under s. 699(5.1), *a judge* must issue and sign a subpoena in respect of a record governed by ss. 278.1 to 278.91 in the case of an offence referred to in s. 278.2(1). The subpoena must be in Form 16.1.

Case Law

Medicine Hat Greenhouses Ltd. v. German (No. 2), (sub nom. *German v. R)* 34 C.C.C. (2d) 339 — An order for the issue of subpoenas by a superior court judge may be reviewed by the Appeal Division, as well as the Trial Division, not under any express *Code* provision, but in the inherent jurisdiction of the court to review its own process. *Semble* intervention is exceptional.

Saskatchewan (A.G.) v. Boychuk (1977), 38 C.R.N.S. 290, (sub nom. *R. v. McConnell)* 35 C.C.C. (2d) 435 — The duty to issue a subpoena under s. 699(2)(a) must be read and construed in light of s. 698(1). "The right to issue a subpoena is restricted to requiring a person to attend and give evidence who is likely to give material evidence."

Related Provisions: "Superior court of criminal jurisdiction", "court of appeal", "court of criminal jurisdiction", "provincial court judge" and "justice" are defined in s. 2. The definitions of "appeal court" in ss. 812 and 829 and "summary conviction court" in s. 785 are limited to Part XXVII or portions thereof and do not generally apply to other Parts of the *Code*, in particular, to Part XXII.

A subpoena issued under s. 699(2)(b), by s. 701(2), must be served personally on the witness. Other related provisions are described in the corresponding note to s. 698, *supra*.

700. (1) Contents of subpoena — A subpoena shall require the person to whom it is directed to attend, at a time and place to be stated in the subpoena, to give evidence and, if required, to bring with him anything that he has in his possession or under his control relating to the subject-matter of the proceedings.

(2) Witness to appear and remain — A person who is served with a subpoena issued under this Part shall attend and shall remain in attendance throughout the proceedings unless he is excused by the presiding judge, justice or provincial court judge.

R.S., c. C-34, s. 628; R.S. 1985, c. 27 (1st Supp.), ss. 148, 203.

Commentary: The section prescribes the *contents of a subpoena* and, further, the obligations of a witness thereunder.

Under s. 700(1), a subpoena will require the witness to *attend to give evidence* at a designated time and place. The witness may also be required to *bring* with him/her anything which he/she has in his/her possession, or under his/her control, relating to the subject-matter of the proceedings. Under s. 700(2), service of a subpoena compels the witness to attend and remain in attendance throughout the proceedings, unless excused by the presiding judge or justice.

Related Provisions: A subpoena which compels attendance to *give evidence*, without further requirement of the witness, is described as a *subpoena ad testificandum*. One which further requires the witness to *bring things relevant* to the subject-matter of the proceedings, as well as to testify, is known as a *subpoena duces tecum*. Form 16 is used for both types of subpoena.

The word "anything" used in s. 700(1) in relation to the requirement for a witness served with a *subpoena duces tecum* is a word of wide and comprehensive import. Form 16, in addition to the general requirement that the witness "bring with you anything ... that relates to said charge" may also enumerate specific documents, objects or other things that are required of the witness.

Other related provisions are described in the corresponding note to s. 698.

Execution or Service of Process

701. (1) Service — Subject to subsection (2), a subpoena shall be served in a province by a peace officer or any other person who is qualified in that province to serve civil process, in accordance with subsection 509(2), with such modifications as the circumstances require.

(2) Personal service — A subpoena that is issued pursuant to paragraph 699(2)(*b*) shall be served personally on the person to whom it is directed.

(3) Proof of service — Service of a subpoena may be proved by the affidavit of the person who effected service.

R.S., c. C-34, s. 629; 1972, c. 13, s. 56; 1994, c. 44, s. 70.

Commentary: The section describes the *manner* in which a *subpoena* is *served*.

Under s. 701(1), a subpoena must be served by a *peace officer* or anyone else who is qualified in the province of service. It must be delivered personally to the witness or, if the witness cannot conveniently be found, left for the witness at his/her last or usual place of abode with an inmate apparently at least 16 years of age.

A subpoena issued under s. 699(2)(b) to compel attendance of a person who is *not* within the province in summary conviction proceedings, or proceedings over which a justice has jurisdiction, must be served personally under s. 701(2). Under s. 701(3), service of the subpoena may be proven by the affidavit of the serving officer.

Related Provisions: "Peace officer" is defined in s. 2. Section 701.1 provides for service and proof of service notwithstanding s. 701, in respect of provincial offences.

Other related provisions are described in the corresponding note to s. 698, *supra*.

701.1 Service in accordance with provincial laws — Notwithstanding section 701, in any province service and proof of service of any subpoena, summons or other document may be made in accordance with the laws of the province relating to offences created by the laws of the province.

1997, c. 18, s. 100.

Commentary: This provision incorporates provincial laws relating to service and proof of service of subpoenas, summons and other documents. The section overrides the general rules relating to service of a subpoena contained in s. 701.

Related Provisions: The rules of s. 701 require personal service of a subpoena by a peace officer or duly qualified civil process server in accordance with s. 509(2). Proof of service may be made by oral or affidavit evidence under ss. 4(6) and (7), 509(3) and 701(3).

C.E.A. s. 40 contains a provision similar to s. 701.1, but it is subject to, not predominant over federal provisions.

702. (1) Subpoena effective throughout Canada — A subpoena that is issued by a provincial court judge or out of a superior court of criminal jurisdiction, a court of appeal, an appeal court or a court of criminal jurisdiction has effect anywhere in Canada according to its terms.

(2) Subpoena effective throughout province — A subpoena that is issued by a justice has effect anywhere in the province in which it is issued.

R.S., c. C-34, s. 630; R.S. 1985, c. 27 (1st Supp.), s. 203; 1994, c. 44, s. 71.

Commentary: The section describes the *territorial jurisdiction* within which a *subpoena* is *effective*. Under s. 702(1), a subpoena issued out of a superior court of criminal jurisdiction, a court of appeal, an appeal court or a court of criminal jurisdiction, has effect anywhere in Canada, according to its terms. Under s. 702(2), a subpoena issued by a justice only has effect within the province in which it is issued.

Related Provisions: A subpoena issued under s. 699(2)(b), must be served *personally* on the witness, under s. 701(2).

Sections 703 and 703.1 describe the territorial jurisdiction within which a warrant and summons, respectively, are effective.

Other related provisions are described in the corresponding notes to ss. 698 and 699, *supra*.

703. (1) Warrant effective throughout Canada — Notwithstanding any other provision of this Act, a warrant of arrest or committal that is issued out of a superior court of criminal jurisdiction, a court of appeal, an appeal court within the meaning of section 812 or a court of criminal jurisdiction other than a provincial court judge acting under Part XIX may be executed anywhere in Canada.

(2) Warrant effective in a province — Notwithstanding any other provision of this Act but subject to subsection 705(3), a warrant of arrest or committal that is issued by a justice or provincial court judge may be executed anywhere in the province in which it is issued.

R.S., c. C-34, s. 631; R.S. 1985, c. 27 (1st Supp.), s. 149.

Commentary: The section determines the *territorial jurisdiction* within which a *warrant of arrest or committal* may be executed.

Under s. 703(1), a warrant issued out of a superior court of criminal jurisdiction, a court of appeal, an appeal court as defined in s. 812 or a court of criminal jurisdiction, other than a provincial court judge under Part XIX, may be executed anywhere in Canada.

Under s. 703(2), a warrant issued by a justice or a provincial court judge may be executed anywhere in the province in which it is issued, *except* that a warrant issued for a witness who has failed to attend or remain in attendance when served with a subpoena or bound by a recognizance under ss. 705(1) or (2), may be executed, under s. 705(3), anywhere in Canada.

Related Provisions: Warrants of arrest or committal in respect of witnesses are in Forms 17–20.

Sections 704 and 705 describe the circumstances under which a warrant may be issued to compel the attendance of a defaulting or absconding witness, and ss. 706–708 define the procedure to be followed upon default.

703.1 Summons effective throughout Canada — A summons may be served anywhere in Canada and, if served, is effective notwithstanding the territorial jurisdiction of the authority that issued the summons.

R.S. 1985, c. 27 (1st Supp.), s. 149.

Commentary: The section provides that effective service of a summons may be made anywhere in Canada, notwithstanding the territorial jurisdiction of the issuing authority.

Related Provisions: The content of a summons and the manner in which it must be served are described in s. 509. Failure to appear in response to a summons may attract the issuance of a warrant of arrest under s. 510, as well as criminal liability under s. 145(4).

703.2 Service of process on a corporation — Where any summons, notice or other process is required to be or may be served on a corporation, and no other method of service is provided, service may be effected by delivery

(a) in the case of a municipal corporation, to the mayor, warden, reeve or other chief officer of the corporation, or to the secretary, treasurer or clerk of the corporation; and

(b) in the case of any other corporation, to the manager, secretary or other executive officer of the corporation or of a branch thereof.

R.S. 1985, c. 27 (1st Supp.), s. 149.

Commentary: The section provides for the *service of process on a corporation* where no other method of service is prescribed.

Service on a *municipal corporation* may be effected by a delivery of the process to the mayor, warden, reeve, other chief officer, secretary, treasurer or clerk of the corporation. Service on any *other corporation* is effective by delivery of the process to the manager, secretary or other executive officer of the corporation or of a branch thereof.

Related Provisions: Section 621 authorizes notice of an indictment to be served on a corporation but makes no provision for the method of service. The trial of a corporation for an indictable offence is governed by ss. 620, 622 and 623. In summary conviction proceedings, s. 800 applies.

Defaulting or Absconding Witness

704. (1) Warrant for absconding witness — Where a person is bound by recognizance to give evidence in any proceedings, a justice who is satisfied on information being made before him in writing and under oath that the person is about to abscond or has absconded may issue his warrant in Form 18 directing a peace officer to arrest that person and to bring him before the court, judge, justice or provincial court judge before whom he is bound to appear.

(2) Endorsement of warrant — Section 528 applies, with such modifications as the circumstances require, to a warrant issued under this section.

(3) Copy of information — A person who is arrested under this section is entitled, on request, to receive a copy of the information upon which the warrant for his arrest was issued.

R.S., c. C-34, s. 632; R.S. 1985, c. 27 (1st Supp.), s. 203.

Commentary: Under this section a *warrant* may issue for the *arrest* of one bound by a recognizance to give evidence in criminal proceedings.

Under s. 704(1), a *warrant* may be issued by a *justice* who is satisfied, by an information in writing and under oath, that a person, bound by a recognizance to give evidence, is about to abscond or has absconded. The warrant, in Form 18, directs peace officers to arrest the witness and to bring him/her before the court before whom he/she has been bound over to appear. Under s. 704(2), the warrant may be endorsed for execution in a territorial jurisdiction other than that of the issuing justice, upon compliance with s. 528. A copy of the information upon which the warrant was issued must be provided to the witness upon request.

Related Provisions: Under s. 500, a witness whose evidence is material may be required to enter into a recognizance at the conclusion of the preliminary inquiry to give evidence at trial. The procedure is often described as having the witness "bound over". A witness arrested with a warrant may also be released on a recognizance under s. 706, to appear and give evidence when required.

Section 704 applies where the witness has already been bound over by entering into a recognizance and has either absconded or been about to do so. Section 705 describes the procedure where the witness has defaulted in his/her appearance in accordance with a subpoena or a recognizance issued to compel such attendance.

The procedure followed where the witness has been arrested with warrant and brought before the court is described in s. 706. Detention thereafter is governed by s. 707.

Section 703 defines the territorial jurisdiction within which a warrant of arrest may be executed.

705. (1) Warrant when witness does not attend — Where a person who has been served with a subpoena to give evidence in a proceeding does not attend or remain in attendance, the court, judge, justice or provincial court judge before whom that person was required to attend may, if it is established

(a) that the subpoena has been served in accordance with this Part, and

(b) that the person is likely to give material evidence,

issue or cause to be issued a warrant in Form 17 for the arrest of that person.

(2) Warrant where witness bound by recognizance — Where a person who has been bound by a recognizance to attend to give evidence in any proceeding does not attend or does not remain in attendance, the court, judge, justice or provincial court judge before whom that person was bound to attend may issue or cause to be issued a warrant in Form 17 for the arrest of that person.

(3) Warrant effective throughout Canada — A warrant that is issued by a justice or provincial court judge pursuant to subsection (1) or (2) may be executed anywhere in Canada.

R.S., c. C-34, s. 633; R.S. 1985, c. 27 (1st Supp.), s. 203.

Commentary: The section sets out the procedure followed where a witness, served with a subpoena or bound by a recognizance, *fails to attend or remain in attendance* to give evidence in criminal proceedings.

Under s. 705(1), a Form 17 *warrant* may be issued for the *arrest* of the witness, provided it is further established that the subpoena has been properly served and the witness is likely to give material evidence.

Under s. 705(2), similar provision is made for the issuance of a warrant for the arrest of a witness who is bound by a recognizance to attend to give evidence and either fails to attend or remain in attendance to do so in accordance with the terms thereof.

A warrant issued by a justice or provincial court judge under s. 705(1) or (2) may be executed *anywhere in Canada*.

Related Provisions: Under s. 701(1) a subpoena is served in accordance with s. 509(2), except that a subpoena issued under s. 699(2)(b) must be served personally on the witness under s. 701(2). Proof of service of a subpoena may be made, *inter alia*, by the affidavit of the serving officer. In most instances, the requirement of s. 705(1)(b), namely, that the proposed witness is likely to give material evidence, will be acknowledged or appear from the evidence given at the preliminary inquiry or the statements of the witness. In jury trials the determination of whether to issue a warrant ought to be made in the absence of the jury.

Section 705(2) does *not*, in terms, require proof of the materiality of the evidence of the proposed witness, nor of the entering into of the recognizance, although each may be established with comparative facility in the absence of the jury, prior to the issuance of the warrant.

In general, an arrest warrant issued by a justice or provincial court judge may be executed only in the province of its issue under s. 703 (2). Section 705(3) is the sole exception to the rule.

Sections 706 and 707 provide the procedure to be followed when a witness has been arrested under warrant. Failure, without lawful excuse, to appear or remain in attendance to give evidence when required by law to do so, is punishable as contempt under s. 708.

Section 704 authorizes the issuance of a warrant for the arrest of an absconding witness in the circumstances there described.

706. Order where witness arrested under warrant — Where a person is brought before a court, judge, justice or provincial court judge under a warrant issued pursuant to subsection 698(2), or section 704 or 705, the court, judge, justice or provincial court judge may order that the person

(a) be detained in custody, or

(b) be released on recognizance in Form 32, with or without sureties, to appear and give evidence when required.

R.S., c. C-34, s. 634; R.S. 1985, c. 27 (1st Supp.), s. 203.

Commentary: The section describes the procedure to be followed where a witness, arrested under a warrant under s. 698(2), or s. 704 or 705, is brought before the court in accordance with the warrant. The court may either order that the witness be *detained* in custody or be *released* on a recognizance in Form 32, with or without sureties, to appear and give evidence in the proceedings when required.

Related Provisions: A warrant is executed under s. 514 in the territorial jurisdiction permitted by ss. 703 and 705(3). Failure to attend or remain in attendance in accordance with a recognizance may attract liability for contempt under s. 708 or, *semble*, for breach of recognizance under s. 145(2) or (3).

Section 707 provides the maximum period for which a witness may be detained *qua* witness under the *Code*.

707. (1) Maximum period for detention of witness — No person shall be detained in custody under the authority of any provision of this Act, for the purpose only of appearing and giving evidence when required as a witness, for any period exceeding thirty days unless prior to the expiration of those thirty days he has been brought before a judge of a superior court of criminal jurisdiction in the province in which he is being detained.

(2) Application by witness to judge — Where at any time prior to the expiration of the thirty days referred to in subsection (1), a witness being detained in custody as described in that subsection applies to be brought before a judge of a court described therein, the judge before whom the application is brought shall fix a time prior to the expiration of those thirty days for the hearing of the application and shall cause notice of the time so fixed to be given to the witness, the person having custody of the witness and such other persons as the judge may specify, and at the time so fixed for the hearing of the application the person having custody of the witness shall cause the witness to be brought before a judge of the court for that purpose.

(3) Review of detention — If the judge before whom a witness is brought under this section is not satisfied that the continued detention of the witness is justified, he shall order him to be discharged, or to be released on recognizance in Form 32, with or without sureties, to appear and to give evidence when required, but if the judge is satisfied that the continued detention of the witness is justified, he may order his continued detention until the witness does what is required of him pursuant to section 550 or the trial is concluded, or until the witness appears and gives evidence when required, as the case may be, except that the total period of detention of the witness from the time he was first detained in custody shall not in any case exceed ninety days.

R.S., c. C-34, s. 635.

Commentary: This section defines the *maximum period* during which a *witness* may be *detained* in custody, *qua* witness, in criminal proceedings and prescribes the *procedure* to be followed to *review* the necessity of *detention*.

In general, a witness must *not* be detained in custody, *qua* witness, for a period exceeding 30 days, absent justification therefor. In combination, ss. 707(1) and (2) require that, upon application by the witness prior to the expiration of 30 days of detention (*qua* witness), a judge of the superior court of criminal jurisdiction *shall* fix a date within such period for the hearing of the application. *Notice* is given to the witness, gaoler and such other persons as may be specified. The witness must be produced upon the hearing.

Under s. 707(3), the judge will inquire into the justification for the continued detention of the witness. Where the judge is *not* satisfied that the continued detention of the witness is justified, the witness must either be discharged, or released on a recognizance in Form 32, with or without sureties, to appear and give evidence when required. Where the judge is satisfied that the continued detention of the witness is justified, the witness is ordered detained until compliance is made with a recognizance under s. 550, the trial is concluded or the witness appears and gives evidence as required. No person may be detained, *qua* witness, for a period exceeding 90 days.

Related Provisions: The section does *not* define the criteria to determine whether the continued detention of a witness is justified. It would appear, however, that the crucial issue is whether detention is necessary to ensure attendance to give evidence or whether attendance may be insured by other, less coercive, means, namely, a recognizance with or without sureties. The section makes *no* express reference to the inclusion of terms in the recognizance, though it would appear that each will require the witness to attend and remain in attendance, as there described, to give evidence.

It is s. 706 that authorizes detention of a witness who has been arrested with warrant, due to the unlikelihood of a response to or evasion of service of a subpoena under s. 698(2), or as an absconding or defaulting witness under ss. 704 or 705.

The failure of a witness to attend to give evidence, or remain in attendance for such purpose, without lawful excuse, may attract liability for contempt under s. 708 or *semble*, breach of recognizance under ss. 145(2) or (3).

708. (1) Contempt — **A person who, being required by law to attend or remain in attendance for the purpose of giving evidence, fails, without lawful excuse, to attend or remain in attendance accordingly is guilty of contempt of court.**

(2) Punishment — **A court, judge, justice or provincial court judge may deal summarily with a person who is guilty of contempt of court under this section and that person is liable to a fine not exceeding one hundred dollars or to imprisonment for a term not exceeding ninety days or to both, and may be ordered to pay the costs that are incident to the service of any process under this Part and to his detention, if any.**

(3) Form — **A conviction under this section may be in Form 38 and a warrant of committal in respect of a conviction under this section may be in Form 25.**
R.S., c. C-34, s. 636; R.S. 1985, c. 27 (1st Supp.), s. 203.

Commentary: Under s. 708(1), it is contempt of court for a person, required by law to attend or remain in attendance to give evidence in proceedings, to fail, *without lawful excuse*, to do so. Under s. 708(2), the presiding judicial officer may deal summarily with the matter. The maximum penalty is a fine not exceeding $100, a term of imprisonment not exceeding 90 days, or both. Further the witness may be ordered to pay any costs incidental to the service of process and detention. A conviction may be recorded in Form 38 and a warrant of committal issued in Form 25.

Case Law

R. v. Stong (1975), 26 C.C.C. (2d) 330 (Ont. C.A.) — This section applies only to a person who is required to attend or remain in attendance as a witness. It does *not* apply to a solicitor who was to act as counsel at trial.

Related Provisions: Failure to comply with the terms of a recognizance may attract liability under ss. 145(2) and (3).

Sections 10(1) and (3) authorize appeals to the court of appeal under Part XXI from conviction and sentence of contempt committed in the face of the court.

Electronically Transmitted Copies

708.1 Electronically transmitted copies — A copy of a summons, warrant or subpoena transmitted by a means of telecommunication that produces a writing has the same probative force as the original for the purposes of this Act.

1997, c. 18, s. 101.

Commentary: This evidentiary provision equates the *probative value* of electronically-transmitted copies of summons, warrants and subpoenas with documentary originals.

Related Provisions: Related provisions are discussed in the corresponding notes to ss. 508.1 and 701.1.

Evidence on Commission

709. (1) Order appointing commissioner — A party to proceedings by way of indictment or summary conviction may apply for an order appointing a commissioner to take the evidence of a witness who

    (a) is, by reason of

        (i) physical disability arising out of illness, or

        (ii) any other good and sufficient cause,

    not likely to be able to attend at the time the trial is held; or

    (b) is out of Canada.

(2) Idem — A decision under subsection (1) is deemed to have been made at the trial held in relation to the proceedings mentioned in that subsection.

R.S., c. C-34, s. 637; R.S. 1985, c. 27 (1st Supp.), s. 150; 1994, c. 44, s. 72.

Commentary: Section 709(1) describes *who* may apply for an order appointing a commissioner to take the evidence of a witness and the circumstances in which an order may be made.

Application may be made by *any party* to proceedings upon indictment or summary conviction. "Party", left undefined, would at least include P and D. The witness whose evidence it is proposed to take on commission must *not* likely be able to attend at the time of trial, because of either physical disability arising out of illness, or some other good or sufficient cause. An order may also be made when the proposed witness is out of Canada.

Section 709(1) merely authorizes the making of an application and specifies the grounds on which it may be brought. It does *not* contain any criteria by which the merits of the application are determined, nor any description of the forum in which the application is to be made. Under s. 709(2), any decision made on an application under s. 709(1) is deemed to have been made at trial of the matter to which the application relates. *Semble* the decision is thereby subject to appellate review.

Case Law
Proceedings

R. v. Lester (1972), 6 C.C.C. (2d) 227 (Ont. C.A.) — An appeal is a "proceeding" within the meaning of this section and an order may be made for the taking of evidence on commission. On an appeal, however, the evidence to be taken must meet the test for the use of fresh evidence.

Discretion

R. v. Bulleyment (1979), 46 C.C.C. (2d) 429 (Ont. C.A.) — Where application is made during a trial, the judge is entitled to take into consideration such factors as whether the trial will be seriously disrupted by the taking of the evidence and the possible prejudice to the opposite party resulting thereupon, as well as the consequence that the tribunal of fact will not have the advantage of observing the demeanour of the witness.

Notice of Application

R. v. Pelletier (1985), 63 N.B.R. (2d) 200 (C.A.) — Although D has the right to be present when evidence is being taken, this does *not* include a right to notice of the application for an order appointing a commissioner to take the evidence.

R. v. Pawlowski (1993), 79 C.C.C. (3d) 353 (Ont. C.A.) — A superior court has the inherent jurisdiction to award *costs* against P in a criminal case. The jurisdiction may be exercised in cases of serious prosecutorial misconduct and *Charter* infringement. An order may be made where P unsuccessfully applies for an order to take evidence on commission. No appeal lies to the court of appeal from an order dismissing an application by P to have evidence taken on commission or awarding costs on the application. (per Galligan, Tarnopolsky JJ.A.)

Related Provisions: Section 710 describes the forum in which and the material upon which applications under s. 709(a) shall be made. Section 712(1) is to a similar effect in respect of a proposed witness who is out of Canada. The reception of evidence taken under ss. 709(a) and 710 is governed by s. 711, and that of a witness out of Canada by ss. 709(b) and 712(2).

Under s. 713(1), the order appointing a commissioner may provide for the presence of D or counsel. In general, the practice and procedure in *civil* matters in the superior court of the province is followed in connection with the appointment of commissioners, the taking of evidence, the certification and return thereof and its use in the proceedings, subject to the provisions of Part XXII and rules of court, as for example under s. 482(3)(a).

The difficulty of the trier of fact assigning weight to evidence taken upon commission and read as evidence in the proceedings may be obviated, in part, by videotaping the testimony for replay before the trier of fact.

710. (1) Application where witness is ill — An application under paragraph 709(1)(*a*) shall be made

 (a) to a judge of a superior court of the province in which the proceedings are taken,

 (b) to a judge of a county or district court in the territorial division in which the proceedings are taken, or

 (c) to a provincial court judge, where

  (i) at the time the application is made, the accused is before a provincial court judge presiding over a preliminary inquiry under Part XVIII, or

  (ii) the accused or defendant is to be tried by a provincial court judge acting under Part XIX or XXVII.

(2) Evidence of medical practitioner — An application under subparagraph 709(1)(*a*)(i) may be granted on the evidence of a registered medical practitioner.

    R.S., c. C-34, s. 638; R.S. 1985, c. 27 (1st Supp.), s. 151; 1994, c. 44, s. 73.

Commentary: The section describes the *forum* in which applications may be made to appoint a commissioner to take the evidence of a witness who is not likely to be able to attend at trial on account of physical disability arising out of illness or for some other good or sufficient cause.

Under s. 710(1), an application under s. 709(1)(a) must be made to a judge of the *superior* court of the province where the proceedings are taken, or a judge of the county or district court in the territorial division where the proceedings are taken. It would appear, on a plain reading, that any judge of either court may determine the matter, irrespective of whether the trial is to be held in that court. The application may only be made before a *provincial* court judge where D is before a provincial court judge conducting a preliminary inquiry, or is to be tried by a provincial court judge without a jury under Part XIX, or sitting as a summary conviction court under Part XXVII.

Section 710(2) permits an order appointing a commissioner to take the evidence of a witness who is disabled by illness, to be be made upon the evidence of a registered medical practitioner.

Related Provisions: Neither s. 709 nor, with the possible exception of s. 710(1)(c), s. 710 defines the *time* at which an application to appoint a commissioner may be made. The language of s. 709 would appear to permit applications both prior to and at trial. Section 710(1)(c)(i) appears to contemplate applications made during the preliminary inquiry and s. 710(1)(c)(ii) those in advance of trial.

Section 711 describes the circumstances under which the evidence of a witness taken under ss. 709(1)(a) and 710 may be admitted as evidence in the proceedings.

Other related provisions are described in the corresponding note to s. 709, *supra*.

711. Admitting evidence of witness who is ill — Where the evidence of a witness mentioned in paragraph 709(1)(a) is taken by a commissioner appointed under section 710, it may be admitted in evidence in the proceedings if

    (a) it is proved by oral evidence or by affidavit that the witness is unable to attend by reason of death or physical disability arising out of illness or some other good and sufficient cause,

    (b) the transcript of the evidence is signed by the commissioner by or before whom it purports to have been taken; and

    (c) it is proved to the satisfaction of the court that reasonable notice of the time for taking the evidence was given to the other party, and that the accused or his counsel, or the prosecutor or his counsel, as the case may be, had or might have had full opportunity to cross-examine the witness.

R.S., c. C-34, s. 639; R.S. 1985, c. 27 (1st Supp.), s. 152; 1994, c. 44, s. 74; 1997, c. 18, s. 102.

Commentary: The section lists the *conditions precedent* to be satisfied before the evidence of a witness described in s. 709(a), taken by a commissioner under s. 710, may be *admitted in evidence* in criminal proceedings.

There are three conditions precedent. The *witness* must be unable to attend by reason of death or physical disability arising out of illness or some other good and sufficient cause. Proof may be made by oral evidence or affidavit. The *transcript* of the evidence which it is proposed to admit must be signed by the commissioner by or before whom it purports to be taken. It must be satisfactorily proven that reasonable *notice* of the time for taking the evidence was given to the party opposite, P or D, who had or might have had full *opportunity* of cross-examination.

Related Provisions: Whether s. 711 has been met, thereby permitting reception of the evidence taken on commission, is a question to be determined by the trial judge, in the absence of the jury, prior to the evidence being admitted in the proceedings. The section does *not* purport to permit the reception of evidence which, if given *viva voce*, would not be receivable in the proceedings. The reception of the evidence in a form that does not permit the trier of fact to observe the demeanour of the witness whose evidence was taken is properly the subject of judicial comment.

The requirements of s. 711(a) may be met by the report and affidavit or solemn declaration provided for by s. 657.3.

Section 712(2) permits the evidence taken on commission of a witness who is out of Canada to be admitted in the proceedings, without satisfaction of further conditions precedent. The disparity may attract *Charter* ss. 7 and 15 scrutiny.

712. (1) Application for order when witness out of Canada — An application that is made under paragraph 709(1)(b)(1) shall be made

    (a) to a judge of a superior court of criminal jurisdiction or of a court of criminal jurisdiction before which the accused is to be tried; or

    (b) to a provincial court judge, where the accused or defendant is to be tried by a provincial court judge acting under Part XIX or XXVII.

(2) Admitting evidence of witness out of Canada — Where the evidence of a witness is taken by a commissioner appointed under this section, it may be admitted in evidence in the proceedings.

(3) [Repealed R.S. 1985, c. 27 (1st Supp.), s. 153.]
R.S., c. C-34, s. 640; R.S. 1985, c. 27 (1st Supp.), s. 153; 1994, c. 44, s. 75; 1997, c. 18, s. 103.

Commentary: The section describes the *forum* in which application may be made to appoint a commissioner to take the evidence of a *witness who is out of Canada*, and defines the circumstances under which the evidence may be admitted in evidence in subsequent proceedings.

Under s. 712(1), P or D must apply to a judge of the superior court of criminal jurisdiction or of a court of criminal jurisdiction before which D is to be tried, unless the matter is to be tried by a provincial court judge, either without a jury upon indictment under Part XIX, or in summary conviction proceedings under Part XXVII.

Section 712(2) permits the evidence taken by a commissioner under this section to be admitted in evidence in the proceedings.

Case Law

R. v. Bulleyment (1979), 46 C.C.C. (2d) 429 (Ont. C.A.) — "Before which the accused is to be tried", applies to the court before which the application is to be made, *not* to the time limit within which it is to be made. The trial judge does *not* have the discretion to exclude admissible evidence properly taken on commission and which is of a substantial probative value. The word "may" applies to the parties and either party may tender the evidence, but is not obliged to do so.

Related Provisions: The courts before which an application under s. 709(1)(a) may be made are defined in slightly different terms than in s. 712(1) in respect of applications under s. 709(1)(b), and more clearly relate the application to the forum of trial.

Unlike s. 710(1)(c)(i), s. 712 contains no reference to applications during a preliminary inquiry and, unlike s. 711, s. 712(2) contains no conditions precedent to the receipt of evidence taken upon commission under ss. 710(b) and 712(1).

This section, like s. 711, does not authorize reception of evidence which, if given otherwise, would not be receivable in the proceedings. In addition, the reception of evidence in a form which does not permit the trier of fact to observe the demeanour of the witness may attract judicial comment.

The disparity between ss. 711 and 712(2) may attract *Charter* ss. 7 and 15(1) scrutiny of the latter.

713. (1) Providing for presence of accused counsel — A judge or provincial court judge who appoints a commissioner may make provision in the order to enable an accused to be present or represented by counsel when the evidence is taken, but failure of the accused to be present or to be represented by counsel in accordance with the order does not prevent the admission of the evidence in the proceedings if the evidence has otherwise been taken in accordance with the order and with this Part.

(2) Return of evidence — An order for the taking of evidence by commission shall indicate the officer of the court to whom the evidence that is taken under the order shall be returned.
R.S., c. C-34, s. 641; R.S. 1985, c. 27 (1st Supp.), s. 203; 1997, c. 18, s. 104.

Commentary: Under s. 713(1) an order appointing a commissioner may include a term which enables D to be present or be represented by counsel when the evidence is taken. The failure of D or counsel to be present, however, does *not* prevent the admission of the evidence, where it has otherwise been taken in accordance with the order and Part XXII.

Section 713(2) requires the order for the taking of evidence by commission to designate the officer of the court to whom the return of the evidence shall be made.

Section 713(1) may attract *Charter* s. 7 scrutiny for its failure to require D's attendance on the taking of evidence.

Case Law

R. v. Neverson (1998), 124 C.C.C. (3d) 468 (Que. C.A.) — Where an order to take commission evidence includes a term that D be present if it can be arranged without undue risk that D would escape or fail to return to Canada, D's absence is *not* fatal to the admissibility of the evidence where it appears that Canadian authorities could *not* obtain sufficient guarantees that D would remain in prison in the foreign jurisdiction where the evidence was to be taken.

R. v. Branco (1988), 62 C.R. (3d) 371, 41 C.C.C. (3d) 248 (Ont. C.A.) — D had a right to be present where the evidence of his accomplice was taken in the United States on commission.

Charter Considerations

R. v. Beck (1996), 108 C.C.C. (3d) 385 (Alta. C.A.) — Section 713(2) does *not* offend *Charter* ss. 7 or 11(d).

Related Provisions: Section 714 adopts the practice and procedure in civil matters in the superior court of the province, *inter alia*, in the taking of evidence by commissioners, its verification and return, except where otherwise provided by Part XXII or rules of court, as for example, under ss. 482(1) and (3)(a).

The basis upon which a commissioner may be appointed to take the evidence of a witness who is unable or unlikely to attend at trial is described in ss. 709, 710 and 712.

713.1 Evidence not excluded — Evidence taken by a commissioner appointed under section 712 shall not be excluded by reason only that it would have been taken differently in Canada, provided that the process used to take the evidence is consistent with the law of the country where it was taken and that the process used to take the evidence was not contrary to the principles of fundamental justice.

1994, c. 44, s. 76.

Commentary: The section enacts a rule of *admissibility* relating to evidence taken on commission in a manner different than what would apply in Canada. The evidence is *not* to be *excluded provided* the process used to take it is

i.   consistent with the law of the country where the evidence is taken; and,

ii. *not* contrary to the principles of fundamental justice.

Related Provisions: The admissibility rule of s. 713.1 relates exclusively to the effect of the manner in which the evidence is taken in the foreign jurisdiction on its admissibility in the domestic proceeding. It does not purport to affect the operation of other admissibility rules which may require exclusion of some or all of the evidence.

Other related provisions are discussed in the corresponding notes to s. 709-712, *supra*.

714. Rules and practice same as in civil cases — Except where otherwise provided by this Part or by rules of court, the practice and procedure in connection with the appointment of commissioners under this Part, the taking of evidence by commissioners, the certifying and return thereof and the use of the evidence in the proceedings shall, as far as possible, be the same as those that govern like matters in civil proceedings in the superior court of the province in which the proceedings are taken.

R.S., c. C-34. s. 642.

Commentary: The section makes applicable to the taking of evidence on commission under Part XXII the *practice and procedure in civil matters* in the superior court of the province in connection with the appointment of commissioners, the taking of evidence on commission, its certification and return, as well as its use in the proceedings. The civil practice and procedure is applicable only to the extent that it is not otherwise provided in Part XXII, or by rules of court, as for example, under ss. 482(1) and (3)(a).

Case Law

R. v. Robertson (1982), 31 C.R. (3d) 383, 66 C.C.C. (2d) 210 (B.C. C.A.); leave to appeal refused (1982), 31 C.R. (3d) 383n (S.C.C.) — Where the assistance of a foreign court is required to compel attendance and testimony of an unwilling witness, appointment of a commissioner and his authority to conduct an examination stem from the order of the foreign court, not the local court. The foreign court is *not* bound to make an order precisely in the terms of the request, and the commissioner is bound to conduct the examination in accordance with the terms of the foreign order. Where foreign order gave the commissioner the power to prescribe the practice and procedure to be followed, it included rulings based on objections to relevancy. The admissibility of the evidence at trial, however, depends *not* on the commissioner's rulings but on the decisions of the trial court.

Related Provisions: The bases upon which a commissioner may be appointed under this Part are set out in ss. 709, 710 and 712. Provision may be made for the presence of the accused or counsel under s. 713.

The evidence taken upon commission may be admitted in the proceedings under ss. 711 and 712(2).

Evidence Previously Taken

715. (1) Evidence at preliminary inquiry may be read at trial in certain cases — Where, at the trial of an accused, a person whose evidence was given at a previous trial on the same charge, or whose evidence was taken in the investigation of the charge against the accused or on the preliminary inquiry into the charge, refuses to be sworn or to give evidence, or if facts are proved on oath from which it can be inferred reasonably that the person

(a) is dead,

(b) has since become and is insane,

(c) is so ill that he is unable to travel or testify, or

(d) is absent from Canada,

and where it is proved that the evidence was taken in the presence of the accused, it may be admitted as evidence in the proceedings without further proof, unless the accused proves that the accused did not have full opportunity to cross-examine the witness.

(2) Admission of evidence — Evidence that has been taken on the preliminary inquiry or other investigation of a charge against an accused may be admitted as evidence in the prosecution of the accused for any other offence on the same proof and in the same manner in all respects, as it might, according to law, be admitted as evidence in the prosecution of the offence with which the accused was charged when the evidence was taken.

(3) Absconding accused deemed present — For the purposes of this section, where evidence was taken at a previous trial or preliminary hearing or other proceeding in respect of an accused in the absence of the accused, who was absent by reason of having absconded, the accused is deemed to have been present during the taking of the evidence and to have had full opportunity to cross-examine the witness.

R.S., c. C-34, s. 643; 1974–75–76, c. 93, s. 76; 1994, c. 44, s. 77; 1997, c. 18, s. 105.

Commentary: The section describes the circumstances under which *evidence previously given* may be *admitted as evidence* in later trial proceedings.

Under s. 715(1) there are several conditions precedent. The evidence sought to be admitted must be evidence given by a witness at a previous trial, in the investigation, or on the preliminary inquiry on the charge being tried. Section 715(2) authorizes the reception of the evidence in a prosecution of an offence other than that in respect of which it had earlier been given. The witness must *refuse* to be sworn or to give evidence, or it must be reasonably inferred from the evidence given under oath that the witness is dead, insane, too ill to travel or testify, or absent from Canada. The witness, in other words, must be *unavailable* to testify, by reason of an enumerated cause. The evidence must have been taken in D's presence. Under s. 715(3), D is *deemed* to have been *present* and have had *full opportunity* to cross-examine, where evidence was taken at a previous trial, preliminary hearing or other proceeding in D's absence, because D absconded during the course of the proceeding. The evidence must be properly authenticated by the court.

Satisfaction of the conditions precedent permits the evidence earlier given to be admitted as evidence in the trial proceedings, without further proof. The evidence may *not*, however, be admitted where D proves that there was not a full opportunity for D to cross-examine the witnesses.

The section has been challenged under *Charter*. s. 7.

Case Law
Application of Section: S. 715(1)

R. v. Hawkins (1996), 111 C.C.C. (3d) 129 (S.C.C.) — A marriage between D and a witness for P entered into after preliminary inquiry but prior to trial does *not* constitute a refusal to give evidence at trial, hence permit recourse to *Code* s. 715 in respect of D's spouse.

R. v. Hawkins (1996), 111 C.C.C. (3d) 129 (S.C.C.) — Testimony at preliminary inquiry *not* rendered admissible by *Code* s. 715 may be received under a principled exception to the hearsay rule.*Necessity* is met where the witness is generally unavailable to testify at trial, as for example, because of a rule of competence, and there is *no* other means of presenting evidence of similar value at trial.*Reliability* is concerned with threshold, *not* ultimate reliability. The trial judge must decide whether the particular hearsay statement exhibits sufficient *indicia* of reliability to afford the trier of fact a satisfactory basis for evaluating its truth. There are generally sufficient guarantees of trustworthiness surrounding evidence given at preliminary inquiry to establish reliability. Internal contradictions in the evidence relate to ultimate, *not* threshold reliability.

R. v. Robillard (1978), 41 C.C.C. (2d) 1 (S.C.C.) — The trial judge has a discretion to permit P to reopen its case to correct an omission due to inadvertence, such as the failure to identify D as the person referred to in testimony given at the preliminary inquiry which was read in at trial pursuant to this section.

R. v. Cull, [1965] 3 C.C.C. 121 (Man. C.A.) — Consent of both counsel obviates the necessity of complying with the provisions of this section.

R. v. Menard (1996), 108 C.C.C. (3d) 424 (Ont. C.A.) — An out-of-court sworn examination and cross-examination, taken as part of a pilot project, introduced on consent at the preliminary inquiry in the absence of D, is doubtfully admissible at trial under *Code* s. 715. It may be admitted, however, under the principled approach to hearsay evidence where the witness is too ill to attend for trial.

R. v. Valence (1982), 5 C.C.C. (3d) 552 (Que. C.A.); leave to appeal granted (1983), 46 N.R. 628n (S.C.C.) — Where a witness has initially refused to testify, resulting in his evidence at the preliminary inquiry being read in pursuant to this section, but he then changes his mind and agrees to testify, it is proper that defence counsel be permitted to cross-examine the witness.

Lambert v. R. (1974), 28 C.R.N.S. 238 (Que. C.A.) — Although the witness had testified at the trial in question, his vague and hostile answers, and his refusal to answer proper questions, had the effect of making his attitude the equivalent of a refusal to testify within the meaning of the section.

R. v. R. (R.W.) (1987), 35 C.C.C. (3d) 50 (Sask. C.A.) — The witness need only have refused to testify or be absent from Canada for this section to apply. It need *not* be proved that the absence is permanent or that the absence or refusal to testify is unavoidable and unjustified.

Full Opportunity to Cross-examine: S. 715(1)

R. v. Potvin (1989), 68 C.R. (3d) 193 (S.C.C.) — D is *not* deprived of "full opportunity" to cross-examine a witness at the preliminary hearing merely because the defence counsel, for tactical reasons, has conducted the cross-examination of a witness differently than he would have at trial, provided that the presiding justice did not improperly restrict the cross-examination at the preliminary hearing.

R. v. Kaddoura (1987), 60 C.R. (3d) 393, 41 C.C.C. (3d) 371 (Alta. C.A.); leave to appeal refused (1988), 64 C.R. (2d) xxxn, 42 C.C.C. (3d) vin (S.C.C.) — The section should not be misused. If P is forewarned before the preliminary inquiry begins that the witness intends to permanently depart Canada after testifying, the defence should be promptly advised so that the future use of this section may be contemplated in the conduct of the defence.

Exclusion of Evidence

R. v. Potvin (1989), 68 C.R. (3d) 193 (S.C.C.) — The word "may" in s. 715(1) confers on the trial judge a *discretion* not to allow the previous testimony to be *admitted* in circumstances that would operate unfairly to D. The circumstances will be relatively rare. The discretion is *not* a blanket authority to undermine the object of the subsection. It may be exercised both where there was unfairness in the *manner* in which the evidence was *obtained*, and where the admission would affect the *fairness* of the *trial* itself — i.e., where it is highly prejudicial to D but only of marginal probative value.

R. v. Barembruch (1997), 119 C.C.C. (3d) 185 (B.C. C.A.) — Where P fails to disclose information which could have been used to impeach the credibility of V a preliminary inquiry, there may be a denial of the right to make full answer and defence, hence a bar to introduction of the evidence under s. 715.

R. v. Syliboy (1989), 51 C.C.C. (3d) 503 (N.B. C.A.) — The trial judge properly permitted counsel for D in the course of cross-examining the co-accused to read in the evidence of a witness who was put out of the country, even though P's application to do so had been denied.

Charter Considerations

R. v. Potvin (1989), 68 C.R. (3d) 193 (S.C.C.) — Section 715(1) does *not* contravene *Charter* s. 7 or 11(d).

Related Provisions: Sections 709–714 provide for the order and receipt of evidence taken upon commission.

Proof of the conditions precedent is made upon a *voir dire*. Where compliance is established, the evidence is then read in the presence of the jury. Proof of compliance with the conditions precedent does not require that all the evidence be received. It may appear, for example, that portions require exclusion under the adjectival law. Editing may be required. Especially in cases where editing must be done to exclude passages which are not receivable under the law of evidence, arguably in all cases, the transcript read as evidence under the section ought *not* to be filed as an exhibit.

The trial judge may comment on the manner in which the evidence read in should be weighed, in the absence of an opportunity of the trier of fact to observe the demeanour of the witness.

Videotaped Evidence

715.1 In any proceeding relating to an offence under section 151, 152, 153, 155 or 159, subsection 160(2) or (3), or section 163.1, 170, 171, 172, 173, 210, 211, 212, 213, 266, 267, 268, 271, 272, or 273, in which the complainant or other witness was under the age of eighteen years at the time the offence is alleged to have been committed, a videotape made within a reasonable time after the alleged offence, in which the complainant or witness describes the acts complained of, is admissible in evidence if the complainant or witness, while testifying, adopts the contents of the videotape.

R.S. 1985, c. 19 (3d Supp.), s. 16; 1997, c. 16, s. 7.

Commentary: The section authorizes limited reception of a *videotaped description of the acts complained of adopted* by the complainant or other witness in certain proceedings. There are several conditions precedent to admissibility.

The evidence must be proposed for admission in proceedings relating to an *enumerated offence*. It may only be received in such cases. The complainant or other witness must have been *under 18 years of age* at the time the *offence* is *alleged* to have been committed. The videotape must be made within a *reasonable time* after the alleged offence and must contain V's *description of the acts* of which complaint is made. The complainant or other witness must *adopt* the *contents* of the videotape *while testifying* in the proceedings in which it is tendered.

The section has been subject to challenge under *Charter* ss. 7 and 11(d).

Case Law
General Purpose of Section
R. v. F. (C.C.) (1997), 220 N.R. 362 (S.C.C.) — The primary goal of s. 715.1, a statutory exception to the hearsay rule, is to create a record of what is probably the best recollection of the event. It also helps prevent, or reduce materially the likelihood of inflicting further injury on V as a result of participation in court proceedings.

Acts Complained Of
R. v. Meddoui (1990), 61 C.C.C. (3d) 345 (Alta. C.A.) — "Acts complained of" includes a description of V's assailant.

R. v. Scott (1993), 27 C.R. (4th) 55, 87 C.C.C. (3d) 327 (Ont. C.A.) — The contents of the videotaped statement under s. 715.1 are limited to a description of "the acts complained of" which may include,

i.   the *events* which occurred from the time V met the assailant until the latter left after committing the offence;

ii.   V's *description* of the assailant's physical features or *name*, if known to V; and,

iii.   *statements made* by the assailant during the events which underlie the charge.

R. v. A. (J.F.) (1993), 82 C.C.C. (3d) 295 (Ont. C.A.) — Section 715.1 does *not* render admissible responses by persons other than V, nor the answers of V given in response to questions put by investigators. References to other sexual assaults not encompassed by the indictment, as well the aberrant sexual conduct of others, are not admissible under the section.

R. v. Toten (1993), 83 C.C.C. (3d) 5 (Ont. C.A.) — The videotaped statement must describe the "acts complained of". Reference to other offences or hearsay statements are *not* made admissible by s. 715.1. The trial judge may edit the tape as part of the inherent duty to control proceedings.

Police Questioning
R. v. F. (C.C.) (1997), 220 N.R. 362 (S.C.C.) — It is preferable, where reasonably possible, that police *not* conduct a pre-video interview of V. The ultimate reliability of the videotape is not an issue to be resolved on the *voir dire*. The fact that a pre-video interview was conducted goes to weight, not admissibility.

During the videotaped interview, police should ask simple, open-ended questions of V, although it may be necessary and appropriate, on occasion, to ask leading questions.

Adopts the Contents
R. v. F. (C.C.) (1997), 220 N.R. 362 (S.C.C.) — "Adopts"should be given a meaning consistent with the section's aim and purpose and "confirme"in the French text. The strict test used for adoption of prior inconsistent statements is not appropriate because of the section's guarantees of trustworthiness and reliability.

Where the trial judge decides that a statement has been *adopted*, the videotape becomes *evidence* of the events described as if V testified to a similar effect. The adopted statement, along with the *viva voce* evidence given at trial, constitutes the evidence in-chief of V.

R. v. Meddoui (1990), 61 C.C.C. (3d) 345 (Alta. C.A.) — A witness *adopts* a videotape, whether or not he/she recalls the events discussed, provided he/she believes them to be true, having recalled giving the statement and attempting then to be honest and truthful. The videotape is then admissible in proof of the truth of its contents. Its weight is for the trier of fact, having regard to all factors relevant to V's trustworthiness.

R. v. Toten (1993), 83 C.C.C. (3d) 5 (Ont. C.A.) — To *adopt* the contents, V must, from present recollection, recall making the statement and that it accurately describes the events which took place.

Necessity and Reliability
R. v. F. (C.C.) (1997), 220 N.R. 362 (S.C.C.) — A witness who cannot remember the events cannot be effectively cross-examined on the contents of his/her statement.

Several factors in s. 715.1 provide the requisite *reliability* of the videotaped statement, including:

i.   the requirement that the statement be made within a *reasonable time*;

ii. the fact that the trier of fact may watch the entire interview, hence can observe the demeanour and assess the personality and intelligence of V; and,

iii. the requirement that V *attest* that s/he was trying to be *truthful* when making the statement.

V may also be cross-examined at trial as to whether s/he was actually telling the truth when making the statement.

Necessity is established where V has *no* independent memory of the events.

The trier of fact should receive a special warning of the dangers of convicting D only on the basis of videotape.

Discretion to Exclude

R. v. F. (C.C.) (1997), 220 N.R. 362 (S.C.C.) — The context of a videotape should be reviewed on a *voir dire* to ensure that the contents conform to the rules of evidence. The tape may be excluded if its prejudicial effect exceeds its probative value, but the exclusionary discretion should not be used to determine issues of weight. Conflicts in evidence about the utility of the tape to provide an honest and complete account of V's story will not render the tape inadmissible unless the trial judge is satisfied that its introduction could interfere with the fact-finding process.

R. v. Scott (1993), 27 C.R. (4th) 55, 87 C.C.C. (3d) 327 (Ont. C.A.) — Evidence that meets the statutory criteria of s. 715.1 may be excluded where its prejudicial effect outweighs its probative value or where it is incapable of assisting the trier of fact to determine the validity of the allegations.

R. v. Toten (1993), 83 C.C.C. (3d) 5 (Ont. C.A.) — The trial judge has a discretion to exclude a videotaped statement which satisfies s. 715.1 if its admission would have a negative impact on the fact-finding function of the trial. Exclusion may be ordered where it is clear that the interview has been rehearsed and scripted. A judge should be very cautious, however, in excluding a videotape to avoid the undermining of the purpose of the section which is to *include* evidence which meets the statutory criteria.

R. v. Toten (1993), 83 C.C.C. (3d) 5 (Ont. C.A.) — The purpose of s. 715.1 is to assist the trier of fact in receiving a full and candid account of the facts concerning the alleged offence.

Factors Affecting Weight

R. v. F. (C.C.) (1997), 220 N.R. 362 (S.C.C.) — Questions concerning

i. the *circumstances* in which the videotape was made;

ii. the *necessity* of V's statement; and,

iii. the overall *reliability* of the evidence

are matters for the trier of fact to consider in assigning weight to the videotape.

Parts of the videotape contradicted in cross-examination are not rendered inadmissible, but may be of less weight in the final analysis. The fact of contradiction does not *per se* mean that the videotape is wrong or unreliable.

Jury Instructions

R. v. F. (C.C.) (1997), 220 N.R. 362 (S.C.C.) — It is not always appropriate to apply adult credibility assessment standards to determine the credibility of a child. Children have peculiar perspectives which can affect their recollection of events. Inconsistencies, especially in relation to peripheral matters, should be assessed in context.

Charter Considerations

R. v. L. (D.O.) (1993), 85 C.C.C. (3d) 289 (S.C.C.) — *See also*: *R. v. Toten* (1993), 83 C.C.C. (3d) 5 (Ont. C.A.) — Section 715.1 does not infringe *Charter* ss. 7 or 11 (d).

Related Provisions: There is no reference to the evidentiary value of the videotape, which would appear to be a previous statement adopted by V or another witness whilst giving evidence in the proceedings. In the usual course, the rules of evidence would *not* permit the reception of a prior *consistent* statement, absent an allegation of recent fabrication. The videotape at least permits the trier of fact to observe witness' demeanour on the earlier occasion.

Issues of tape authenticity and accuracy, *semble*, will be matters of fact for the jury.

The rules respecting recent complaint in cases to which the section applies are abrogated by s. 275 and, although what is held receivable under s. 715.1 need not qualify as a "recent complaint", the section, nonetheless, permits reception of a prior (videotaped) complaint. *Quaere* whether D is permitted to adduce evidence of an absence of complaint at the first reasonable opportunity?

The reception of evidence of complainants under 18 years of age in cases of sexual assault, interference and exploitation is governed by ss. 486(2.1)–(4). The manner in which the evidence of a witness under 14 years of age, or of diminished mental capacity, may be received, if at all, is described in *C.E.A.* s. 16. D's spouse is a competent and compellable witness for P without D's consent under *C.E.A.* s. 4(2) where D is charged with an offence listed in s. 715.1.

715.2 (1) Evidence of complainant — In any proceedings relating to an offence under section 151, 152, 153, 153.1, 155 or 159, subsection 160(2) or (3) or section 163.1, 170, 171, 172, 173, 210, 211, 212, 213, 266, 267, 268, 271, 272 or 273 in which the complainant or other witness is able to communicate evidence but may have difficulty doing so by reason of a mental or physical disability, a videotape, made within a reasonable time after the alleged offence, in which the complainant or witness describes the acts complained of is admissible in evidence if the complainant or witness adopts the contents of the videotape while testifying.

(2) Order prohibiting use — The presiding judge may prohibit any other use of a videotape referred to in subsection (1).

1998, c. 9, s. 8.

Commentary: This section permits reception of a videotape of a complainant or witness who has a *mental* or *physical disability* that makes it *difficult* to *communicate* evidence. There are several requirements contained in the section.

The *evidence* must be offered in proceedings relating to a *listed* offence. The complainant or other witness must be able to *communicate* his/her evidence but has *difficulty* doing so because of a *mental* or *physical* disability.

In addition to the requirements that relate to the witness, there are several restrictions that concern the videotape itself. The videotape must be made within a *reasonable time after* the *alleged offence*. The complainant or witness must *describe* on the videotape the *acts* of which s/he complains. The complainant or witness must *adopt* the *contents* of the videotape while *testifying*.

Under s. 7145.2(2), the presiding judge may prohibit any other use of the videotape described in s. 715.2(1)

Related Provisions: Section 715.2(1) is similar in form and content to s. 715.1. Under s. 715.2, however, the complainant or witness may be of *any* age, provided s/he suffers from a mental or physical disability of the extent described.

Section 715.2(1) applies to the new offence of section 153.1 (sexual exploitation of person with disability), but *not* s. 155 (incest). Otherwise, the offences listed in ss. 715.1 and 715.2 are identical. Section 715.2(2) is without equivalent in s. 715.1.

Under *C.E.A.* s. 16(3), a witness who does *not* understand the nature of an oath or solemn affirmation, but is able to communicate the evidence, may testify on promising to tell the truth.

PART XXIII — SENTENCING

Interpretation

716. Definitions — In this Part,

"accused" includes a defendant;

"alternative measures" means measures other than judicial proceedings under this Act used to deal with a person who is eighteen years of age or over and alleged to have committed an offence;

"court" means

(a) a superior court of criminal jurisdiction,

(b) a court of criminal jurisdiction,

(c) a justice or provincial court judge acting as a summary conviction court under Part XXVII, or

(d) a court that hears an appeal;

"fine" includes a pecuniary penalty or other sum of money, but does not include restitution.

1995, c. 22, s. 6; 1999, c. 5, s. 29.

Commentary: The section contains definitions applicable to Part XXIII only.

Related Provisions: Other definitions applicable to specific provisions in Part XXIII are set out in ss. 732.1, 734.8 and 742.

Alternative Measures

717. (1) When alternative measures may be used — Alternative measures may be used to deal with a person alleged to have committed an offence only if it is not inconsistent with the protection of society and the following conditions are met:

(a) the measures are part of a program of alternative measures authorized by the Attorney General or the Attorney General's delegate or authorized by a person, or a person within a class of persons, designated by the Lieutenant Governor in Council of a province;

(b) the person who is considering whether to use the measures is satisfied that they would be appropriate, having regard to the needs of the person alleged to have committed the offence and the interests of society and of the victim;

(c) the person, having been informed of the alternative measures, fully and freely consents to participate therein;

(d) the person has, before consenting to participate in the alternative measures, been advised of the right to be represented by counsel;

(e) the person accepts responsibility for the act or omission that forms the basis of the offence that the person is alleged to have committed;

(f) there is, in the opinion of the Attorney General or the Attorney General's agent, sufficient evidence to proceed with the prosecution of the offence; and

(g) the prosecution of the offence is not in any way barred at law.

(2) Restriction on use — Alternative measures shall not be used to deal with a person alleged to have committed an offence if the person

(a) denies participation or involvement in the commission of the offence; or

(b) expresses the wish to have any charge against the person dealt with by the court.

(3) Admissions not admissible in evidence — No admission, confession or statement accepting responsibility for a given act or omission made by a person alleged to have committed an offence as a condition of the person being dealt with by alternative measures is admissible in evidence against that person in any civil or criminal proceedings.

(4) No bar to proceedings — The use of alternative measures in respect of a person alleged to have committed an offence is not a bar to proceedings against the person under this Act, but, if a charge is laid against that person in respect of that offence,

(a) where the court is satisfied on a balance of probabilities that the person has totally complied with the terms and conditions of the alternative measures, the court shall dismiss the charge; and

(b) where the court is satisfied on a balance of probabilities that the person has partially complied with the terms and conditions of the alternative measures, the court may dismiss the charge if, in the opinion of the court, the prosecution of the charge would be unfair, having regard to the circumstances and that person's performance with respect to the alternative measures.

(5) Laying of information, etc. — Subject to subsection (4), nothing in this section shall be construed as preventing any person from laying an information, obtaining the issue or confirmation of any process, or proceeding with the prosecution of any offence, in accordance with law.

1995, c. 22, s. 6.

Note: 1997, c. 18, s. 106 was not in force at the date of publication. This section purported to amend s. 717 of the Criminal Code as it existed prior to the 1995, c. 22 amendments. The reference to s. 717 of the Code has been replaced by s. 718.3 in accordance with 1995, c. 22, s. 18 (Sch. IV).

Commentary: The section provides for a form of *diversion* in that it authorizes the court to dismiss a charge without a trial having taken place where D has completed or partially completed an "alternative measure". Acceptable kinds of alternative measures are *not* specified. Rather, it is sufficient that the measures are part of a program authorized by the province or territory.

Section 717(1) permits the use of alternative measures only if it is *not* inconsistent with the protection of society. It sets out a number of preconditions similar to those in *Y.O.A.* s. 4, except that the interests of V as well as those of society must be considered; and while D must be told of the right to be represented by counsel, there is *no* requirement of a reasonable opportunity to consult with counsel.

Section 717(2) prohibits the use of alternative measures where D denies involvement in the offence or wishes to have the charge dealt with in court.

Under s. 717(3) any expression of responsibility for the act/omission underlying the offence is not admissible in civil or criminal proceedings.

Related Provisions: *Y.O.A.* s. 4 authorizes alternative measures for young offenders. Sections 717.1, 717.2, 717.3 and 717.4 deal with the keeping, disclosure and use of records concerning D who receives alternative measures.

717.1 Records of persons dealt with — Sections 717.2 to 717.4 apply only in respect of persons who have been dealt with by alternative measures, regardless of the degree of their compliance with the terms and conditions of the alternative measures.

1995, c. 22, s. 6.

Commentary: The section specifies that special record keeping and disclosure provisions of ss. 717.2 and 717.4 apply to persons who have been dealt with by alternative measures. The degree of compliance with the terms of the alternative measures is *not* a factor.

Related Provisions: See the corresponding note to s. 717.1, *supra*.

717.2 (1) Police records — A record relating to any offence alleged to have been committed by a person, including the original or a copy of any fingerprints or photographs of the person, may be kept by any police force responsible for, or participating in, the investigation of the offence.

(2) Disclosure by peace officer — A peace officer may disclose to any person any information in a record kept pursuant to this section that it is necessary to disclose in the conduct of the investigation of an offence.

(3) Idem — A peace officer may disclose to an insurance company any information in a record kept pursuant to this section for the purpose of investigating any claim arising out of an offence committed or alleged to have been committed by the person to whom the record relates.

1995, c. 22, s. 6.

Commentary: Notwithstanding that D has been dealt with by alternative measures, s. 717.2(1) authorizes the police to keep records including D's fingerprints and photographs.

The information contained in the record may be disclosed by the police to any person pursuant to s. 717.2(2), where it is necessary to do so in the conduct of an investigation of an offence.

Section 717.2(3) authorizes the police to disclose the information contained in such a record about D to an insurance company investigating a claim arising out of an offence or alleged offence by D.

Related Provisions: See the corresponding note to s. 717.1, *supra*.

717.3 (1) Government records — A department or agency of any government in Canada may keep records containing information obtained by the department or agency

(a) for the purposes of an investigation of an offence alleged to have been committed by a person;

(b) for use in proceedings against a person under this Act; or

(c) as a result of the use of alternative measures to deal with a person.

(2) Private records — A person or organization may keep records containing information obtained by the person or organization as a result of the use of alternative measures to deal with a person alleged to have committed an offence.

1995, c. 22, s. 6.

Commentary: Section 717.3(1) authorizes the keeping of information by any department or agency at any level of government in Canada where it has obtained the information to investigate an alleged offence, to use in criminal proceedings, or because of the imposition of alternative measures.

Section 717.3(2) permits individuals and non-government organizations to keep records it obtains due to the use of alternative measures.

Related Provisions: See the corresponding note to s. 717.1, *supra*.

717.4 (1) Disclosure of records — Any record that is kept pursuant to section 717.2 or 717.3 may be made available to

(a) any judge or court for any purpose relating to proceedings relating to offences committed or alleged to have been committed by the person to whom the record relates;

(b) any peace officer

(i) for the purpose of investigating any offence that the person is suspected on reasonable grounds of having committed, or in respect of which the person has been arrested or charged, or

(ii) for any purpose related to administration of the case to which the record relates;

(c) any member of a department or agency of a government in Canada, or any agent thereof, that is

    (i) engaged in the administration of alternative measures in respect of the person, or

    (ii) preparing a report in respect of the person pursuant to this Act; or

(d) any other person who is deemed, or any person within a class of persons that is deemed, by a judge of a court to have a valid interest in the record, to the extent directed by the judge, if the judge is satisfied that the disclosure is

    (i) desirable in the public interest for research or statistical purposes, or

    (ii) desirable in the interest of the proper administration of justice.

(2) **Subsequent disclosure** — Where a record is made available for inspection to any person under subparagraph (1)(d)(i), that person may subsequently disclose information contained in the record, but may not disclose the information in any form that would reasonably be expected to identify the person to whom it relates.

(3) **Information, copies** — Any person to whom a record is authorized to be made available under this section may be given any information contained in the record and may be given a copy of any part of the record.

(4) **Evidence** — Nothing in this section authorizes the introduction into evidence of any part of a record that would not otherwise be admissible in evidence.

(5) **Idem** — A record kept pursuant to section 717.2 or 717.3 may not be introduced into evidence, except for the purposes set out in paragraph 721(3)(c), more than two years after the end of the period for which the person agreed to participate in the alternative measures.

1995, c. 22, s. 6.

Commentary: The section permits access to records kept by police and government agencies pursuant to ss. 717.2 and 717.3, for purposes of law enforcement and the administration of justice. Access is automatic for judges, peace officers and some government employees in the circumstances set out. Access may be granted to other persons upon application to a judge. In general, s. 717.4(5) provides that records kept pursuant to ss. 717.2 or 717.3 may *not* be introduced into evidence more than 2 years after the end of the alternative measures.

Related Provisions: See the corresponding note to s. 717.1, *supra*.

Purpose and Principles of Sentencing

718. Purpose — The fundamental purpose of sentencing is to contribute, along with crime prevention initiatives, to respect for the law and the maintenance of a just, peaceful and safe society by imposing just sanctions that have one or more of the following objectives:

    (a) to denounce unlawful conduct;

    (b) to deter the offender and other persons from committing offences;

    (c) to separate offenders from society, where necessary;

    (d) to assist in rehabilitating offenders;

    (e) to provide reparations for harm done to victims or to the community; and

    (f) to promote a sense of responsibility in offenders, and acknowledgment of the harm done to victims and to the community.

1995, c. 22, s. 6.

Commentary: The section enumerates the *objectives* of sentencing. They include principles recognized at common law, reparation to victims and the promotion of responsibility in offenders.

Related Provisions: Section 718.2 sets out *additional* principles to be considered in sentencing. The principle of proportionality is contained in s. 718.1.

718.1 **Fundamental principle** — **A sentence must be proportionate to the gravity of the offence and the degree of responsibility of the offender.**

1995, c. 22, s. 6.

Commentary: The section codifies the principle of proportionality.

Related Provisions: Section 718 sets out the objectives of sentencing. Additional principles are contained in s. 718.2

718.2 **Other sentencing principles** — **A court that imposes a sentence shall also take into consideration the following principles:**

(a) a sentence should be increased or reduced to account for any relevant aggravating or mitigating circumstances relating to the offence or the offender, and, without limiting the generality of the foregoing,

(i) evidence that the offence was motivated by bias, prejudice or hate based on race, national or ethnic origin, language, colour, religion, sex, age, mental or physical disability, sexual orientation, or any other similar factor, or

(ii) evidence that the offender, in committing the offence, abused the offender's spouse or child,

(iii) evidence that the offender, in committing the offence, abused a position of trust or authority in relation to the victim, or

(iv) evidence that the offence was committed for the benefit of, at the direction of or in association with a criminal organization

shall be deemed to be aggravating circumstances;

(b) a sentence should be similar to sentences imposed on similar offenders for similar offences committed in similar circumstances;

(c) where consecutive sentences are imposed, the combined sentence should not be unduly long or harsh;

(d) an offender should not be deprived of liberty, if less restrictive sanctions may be appropriate in the circumstances; and

(e) all available sanctions other than imprisonment that are reasonable in the circumstances should be considered for all offenders, with particular attention to the circumstances of aboriginal offenders.

1995, c. 22, s. 6; 1997, c. 23, s. 17.

Commentary: This provision requires the sentencing court to take into account specified principles. Section 718.2(a) provides for consideration of aggravating or mitigating circumstances, and specifies that breach of trust, motives of prejudice or hate and evidence that the offence was committed in the context of organized crime shall be aggravating factors. Section 718.2(b) recognizes the principle of consistency, and (c), totality of sentence. Under s. 718.2(d) incarceration is to be used as a last resort. Under s. 718.2(e) all non-custodial sanctions should be considered.

Related Provisions: Section 718 sets out the objectives of sentencing. The principle of proportionality is contained in s. 718.1.

Punishment Generally

718.3 (1) Degrees of punishment — Where an enactment prescribes different degrees or kinds of punishment in respect of an offence, the punishment to be imposed is, subject to the limitations prescribed in the enactment, in the discretion of the court that convicts a person who commits the offence.

(2) Discretion respecting punishment — Where an enactment prescribes a punishment in respect of an offence, the punishment to be imposed is, subject to the limitations prescribed in the enactment, in the discretion of the court that convicts a person who commits the offence, but no punishment is a minimum punishment unless it is declared to be a minimum punishment.

(3) Imprisonment in default where term not specified — Where an accused is convicted of an offence punishable with both fine and imprisonment and a term of imprisonment in default of payment of the fine is not specified in the enactment that prescribes the punishment to be imposed, the imprisonment that may be imposed in default of payment shall not exceed the term of imprisonment that is prescribed in respect of the offence.

(4) Cumulative punishments — Where an accused

(a) is sentenced while under sentence for an offence, and a term of imprisonment, whether in default of payment of a fine or otherwise, is imposed,

(b) is convicted of an offence punishable with both a fine and imprisonment and both are imposed, or

(c) is convicted of more offences than one, and

(i) more than one fine is imposed,

(ii) terms of imprisonment for the respective offences are imposed, or

(iii) a term of imprisonment is imposed in respect of one offence and a fine is imposed in respect of another offence,

the court that sentences the accused may direct that the terms of imprisonment that are imposed by the court or result from the operation of subsection 734(4) shall be served consecutively.

Proposed Amendment — 718.3

the court that sentences the accused may direct that the terms of imprisonment shall be served one after the other.

1997, c. 18, s. 106(3) [Not in force at date of publication.]

1995, c. 22, s. 6; 1997, c. 18, ss. 106, 141(c); 1999, c. 5, s. 30.

The following subsection was enacted by S.C. 1995, c. 22, s. 6:

(5) Idem — *Where an offender who is under a conditional sentence imposed under section 742.1 is convicted of a second offence that was committed while the offender was under the conditional sentence,*

(a) a sentence of imprisonment imposed for the second offence shall be served consecutively to the conditional sentence; and

(b) the offender shall be imprisoned until the expiration of the sentence imposed for the second offence, or for any longer period resulting from the operation of subparagraph 742.6(9)(c)(i) or paragraph 742.6(9)(d).

This subsection was never proclaimed in force and was later repealed by S.C. 1999, c. 5, s. 30.

Commentary: The section describes the degrees of punishment which may be imposed upon D, in the discretion of the court, and the circumstances under which cumulative punishments may be imposed. Sections. 718.3(1) and (2) underscore the discretionary nature of the imposition of punishment, subject to the limitations prescribed in the enactment. In general, where an enactment prescribes punishment of different degrees or kinds in respect of an offence, the punishment imposed, subject to statutory limitations, is in the discretion of the convicting court. Further, under s. 718.3(2), no punishment is a minimum punishment, unless it is described to be so in the enactment. Where a convicted person may be both fined and imprisoned upon conviction, and the enactment does not specify the term of the imprisonment in default of payment, under s. 718.3(3), the default term must not exceed the term prescribed in respect of the offence.

Section 718.3(4) defines the circumstances in which a convicting court may direct that terms of imprisonment may be served consecutively. The order must be made explicit, otherwise the terms will be served concurrently.

Section 718.3(5) directs a court to sentence D to a consecutive term upon conviction of a second offence where D was under a conditional sentence governed by s. 742.1 and is sentenced to a prison term for the second offence. Under s. 718.3(5)(b), D must be imprisoned until the expiration of the sentence for the second offence, or longer if subject to the provisions of ss. 742.6(9)(c)(i) or 742.6(9)(d).

Case Law
Consecutive Sentences: S. 718.3(4)

R. v. Senior (1997), 116 C.C.C. (3d) 152 (S.C.C.) — Consecutive sentences may be imposed when D is *convicted* on the date of sentencing on a second set of charges while under sentences of imprisonment on an earlier set of charges.

R. v. Clermont (1988), 45 C.C.C. (3d) 480 (S.C.C.) — Where D receives a suspended sentence and probation and is subsequently sentenced to five years for another offence during the probation period, the trial judge, upon revoking the probation order, only has jurisdiction to impose a sentence that could have been imposed had sentencing not been suspended. The trial judge has no power to impose a sentence consecutive to the subsequent five-year sentence, as D would *not* have been under sentence at the time of the suspension of sentence.

Paul v. R. (1982), 27 C.R. (3d) 193, 67 C.C.C. (2d) 97 (S.C.C.) — Under s. 717(4)(c) [now 718.3(4)], a judge may order that a sentence be served consecutively to another sentence he has previously imposed or is at the same time imposing. By s. 717(4)(a) [now 718.3(4)], however, he cannot order that a sentence be made consecutive to that imposed by another judge in another case unless that sentence has already been imposed by the other judge at the time of the conviction in the case in which he is sentencing. The application of s. 717(4)(a) [now s. 718.3(4)] is restricted to sentences imposed by different judges.

R. v. Munilla (1986), 38 Man. R. 79 (C.A.) — *See also*: *R. v. H. (E.R.)* (1987), 81 N.S.R. (2d) 156 (C.A.) — Where the charges against D arise out of separate and distinct transactions, consecutive sentences should be imposed.

R. v. Veniot (1985), 70 N.S.R. (2d) 62 (C.A.) — A sentence cannot be both consecutive and commence forthwith at the same time. If the sentence is to commence immediately it should be made concurrent.

R. v. Haines (1975), 29 C.R.N.S. 239 (Ont. C.A.) — The practice of imposing one long sentence and several short concurrent sentences is improper. Offences should be grouped into categories and concurrent sentences imposed for offences in the same category but consecutive to the sentence for offences in other categories.

R. v. Desmarest (1986), 2 Q.A.C. 151 (C.A.) — Concurrent sentences should be imposed where D is convicted of a number of offences arising out of the same transaction. Where offences arise out of separate transactions, consecutive sentences are appropriate. Offences arising from a single transaction can be categorized together and concurrent sentences imposed within each category. Between categories, however, sentences are to be served consecutively.

Consecutive to Life Imprisonment or Preventive Detention

R. v. Camphaug (1986), 28 C.C.C. (3d) 125 (B.C. C.A.) — *See also*: *R. v. Sinclair* (1972), 6 C.C.C. (2d) 523 (Ont. C.A.) — The court does *not* have the power to impose a sentence consecutive to a sentence of life imprisonment.

R. v. Robillard (1985), 22 C.C.C. (3d) 505 (Que. C.A.) — Sentences imposed on D serving a sentence of preventive detention cannot be made consecutive, only concurrent to the indeterminate sentence.

Burden of Proof [Aggravating Facts][See also, s. 724]

R. v. Brown (1991), 6 C.R. (4th) 353, 66 C.C.C. (3d) 1 (S.C.C.) — The sentencing judge is bound by the express and implied factual implications of a jury verdict

R. v. Gardiner (1982), 30 C.R. (3d) 289, 68 C.C.C. (2d) 477 (S.C.C.); affirming (1979), 52 C.C.C. (2d) 183 (Ont. C.A.) — P is required to prove aggravating facts with respect to sentencing beyond a reasonable doubt.

R. v. Gobin (1993), 85 C.C.C. (3d) 481 (Man. C.A.) — On a plea of guilty, absent firm agreement as to the facts of the offence, P may put forward P's understanding of the facts. It is open to counsel for D to make submissions based upon a different and less aggravating version of the facts, provided it is consistent with the allegations in the indictment. If P wishes to contest D's version, P must adduce evidence in support of the more aggravated circumstances. P's failure to call evidence will lead to the acceptance of D's version, absent some manifest reason that D's interpretation is contrived or erroneous. Similar principles apply after a jury verdict. (per Huband and Helper JJ.A.)

R. v. Desjarlais (1987), 50 Man. R. (2d) 1 (C.A.) — In sentencing, any facts in dispute *not* proved by P are to be disregarded. A plea of guilty is only an admission of the essential legal ingredients of the offence.

R. v. Holt (1983), 4 C.C.C. (3d) 32 (Ont. C.A.); leave to appeal refused (1983), 4 C.C.C. (3d) 32n (S.C.C.) — If P advances contested aggravating facts in a sentencing proceeding for the purpose of supporting a lengthier sentence, it must prove those aggravating circumstances beyond a reasonable doubt. However, it does *not* follow that all possible mitigating facts must be assumed in favour of D where there is no proof of such facts.

R. v. Poorman (1991), 6 C.R. (4th) 364, 66 C.C.C. (3d) 82 (Sask. C.A.) — When oral submissions made during an informal sentencing hearing give rise to a controversy on a material issue, the trial judge must either hold a formal evidentiary hearing during which P must prove the aggravating facts alleged beyond a reasonable doubt, or accept D's version of the facts so far as possible.

Sentencing Circles

R. v. Johnson (1994), 31 C.R. (4th) 262, 91 C.C.C. (3d) 21 (Y.T. C.A.) — Sentencing circles are *not* prescribed by the *Criminal Code*. Rules may be made and published under s. 482(2) to provide for sentencing circles to assist trial judges in imposing sentence in certain kinds of cases. The rules will inform those involved of the kinds of cases to which sentencing circles apply and what the parties may expect in such cases.

Related Provisions: Sections. 734-736 provide for the imposition and enforcement of fines. Section 736 permits resort to a fine option program. Section 737 imposes a victim fine surcharge in addition to any other punishment.

Sections. 743-745.5 provide for the place and manner in which a sentence of imprisonment may be served.

The conditional sentence of imprisonment is governed by ss. 742-742.7

Section 724 describes the information which may be accepted in determining sentence. Other offences may be taken into account under s. 725.

719. (1) Commencement of sentence — A sentence commences when it is imposed, except where a relevant enactment otherwise provides.

(2) Time at large excluded from term of imprisonment — Any time during which a convicted person is unlawfully at large or is lawfully at large on interim release granted pursuant to any provision of this Act does not count as part of any term of imprisonment imposed on the person.

(3) Determination of sentence — In determining the sentence to be imposed on a person convicted of an offence, a court may take into account any time spent in custody by the person as a result of the offence.

(4) When time begins to run — Notwithstanding subsection (1), a term of imprisonment, whether imposed by a trial court or the court appealed to, commences or shall be deemed to be resumed, as the case may be, on the day on which the convicted person is arrested and taken into custody under the sentence.

(5) When fine imposed — Notwithstanding subsection (1), where the sentence that is imposed is a fine with a term of imprisonment in default of payment, no time prior to the day of execution of the warrant of committal counts as part of the term of imprisonment.

(6) Application for leave to appeal — An application for leave to appeal is an appeal for the purposes of this section.

1995, c. 22, s. 6.

Commentary: The section determines the commencement date of the sentence imposed upon a person convicted of a criminal offence.

In general, under s. 719(1), a sentence commences when it is imposed, except where there is a statutory provision to the contrary. In determining the sentence to be imposed the sentencing court, under s. 719(3), may take into account any time spent in custody by D as a result of the offence but, under s. 719(2), any time during which D was unlawfully at large, or lawfully at large on interim release does not count as part of the term of imprisonment.

Both ss. 719(4) and (5) operate notwithstanding the general provisions of s. 719(1) that a sentence commences when imposed. Under s. 719(4), a sentence imposed by a trial or appeal court commences, or is deemed to be commenced, on the date on which D is arrested and taken into custody under the sentence. Where the sentence is a fine with a term of imprisonment in default, no time prior to the date of execution of the warrant of committal counts as part of the term of imprisonment.

Case Law

When Time Begins to Run: S. 719(1)

R. v. Goyette, [1982] 1 S.C.R. 688; affirming (1981), 45 N.R. 584 (Que. C.A.) — D's term of imprisonment for failure to pay a fine commenced on the date of the execution of the warrant of committal.

R. v. Fuller (1968), 5 C.R.N.S. 148, [1969] 3 C.C.C. 348 (Man. C.A.) — The trial judge does *not* have jurisdiction to withhold the warrant of committal. The "practice of coupling a sentence of imprisonment with a direction that the warrant be held to permit the prisoner to leave town" was held to be illegal.

R. v. MacFarlane (1986), 60 Nfld. & P.E.I.R. 63 (P.E.I. C.A.) — Sentences cannot be backdated.

Time Spent In Custody: S. 719(3)

R. v. Tallman (1989), 68 C.R. (3d) 367, 48 C.C.C. (3d) 81 (Alta. C.A.) — *See also*: *R. v. Meilleur* (1981), 22 C.R. (3d) 185 (Ont. C.A.) — There is *no* fixed formula for the credit to be given for time spent in pre-trial custody, but generally it should be somewhat more than the actual time spent.

R. v. Chiechie (1983), 21 M.V.R. 221 (Man. C.A.) — The court is *not* to create a formula by applying a multiplier to the period of time spent in custody prior to sentencing.

R. v. McDonald (1998), 17 C.R. (5th) 1, 127 C.C.C. (3d) 57 (Ont. C.A.) — Section 719(3) offers *no* fixed rule for calculating the amount of credit to be given for pre-sentence custody in determining what sentence to impose. There is *no* reason, however, to depart from the *general* rule of *double* credit, *where appropriate*, in cases of minimum punishment, even though the sentence imposed may be less than the statutory minimum. In every event, the sentencing judge must be satisfied that, when the proposed sentence and pre-sentence custody are combined, the "effective" punishment is the statutory minimum.

The language of s. 344(a), in particular the distinction between "punishment" and "sentence", permits a court to consider pre-sentence custody as directed by s. 719(3). It is the total *punishment* that must add up to at least four years imprisonment.

In calculating the total *punishment* and taking into account the *pre-sentence custody* as permitted by s. 719(3), a trial judge may deduct from the four years any period of the pre-sentence custody that s/he considers appropriate. The final number is the sentence that commences when imposed.

Temporary Absence Recommendations

R. v. Laycock (1989), 51 C.C.C. (3d) 65 (Ont. C.A.) — A sentencing judge cannot do more than recommend or refuse to recommend temporary absence and cannot order that such early release be denied.

Prohibition Orders

R. v. Neuberger (1997), 118 C.C.C. 348 (B.C. C.A.) — A prohibition order may *not* be made consecutive to another prohibition order.

Related Provisions: The authority of the court of appeal to determine sentence appeals is described in s.687. A sentence imposed by the court of appeal under s.686(1)(b)(i) and s. 719(3) may run from the date of its imposition by the court, or the date of the original sentence. If the original sentence in such a case is affirmed, it runs from the date of its imposition at trial.

Section 719(3) permits time spent in custody as a result of the offence to be considered in determining the sentence to be imposed. Upon conviction of high treason or murder, s. 746 requires certain periods of time spent in custody to be considered.

The location and manner in which a sentence of imprisonment will be served is determined by ss. 743-743.6.

The conditional sentence of imprisonment is governed by ss. 742-742.7.

Procedure and Evidence

720. Sentencing proceedings — A court shall, as soon as practicable after an offender has been found guilty, conduct proceedings to determine the appropriate sentence to be imposed.

1995, c. 22, s. 6.

Commentary: The section requires that sentencing take place expeditiously after a finding of guilt.

Related Provisions: Section 723 requires the court to give P and D an opportunity to make submissions before sentence is imposed. Section 724 sets out the procedure to be followed when facts are in dispute. Section 726 permits D to speak before sentence is imposed.

721. (1) Report by probation officer — Subject to regulations made under subsection (2), where an accused, other than a corporation, pleads guilty to or is found guilty of an offence, a probation officer shall, if required to do so by a court, prepare and file with the court a report in writing relating to the accused for the purpose of assisting the court in imposing a sentence or in determining whether the accused should be discharged pursuant to section 730.

(2) Provincial regulations — The Lieutenant Governor in Council of a province may make regulations respecting the types of offences for which a court may require a report, and respecting the content and form of the report.

(3) Content of report — Unless otherwise specified by the court, the report must, wherever possible, contain information on the following matters:

> **(a) the offender's age, maturity, character, behaviour, attitude and willingness to make amends;**

> **(b) the history of previous dispositions under the Young Offenders Act and of previous findings of guilt under this Act and any other Act of Parliament;**

> **(c) the history of any alternative measures used to deal with the offender, and the offender's response to those measures; and**

(d) any matter required, by any regulation made under subsection (2), to be included in the report.

(4) Idem — The report must also contain information on any other matter required by the court, after hearing argument from the prosecutor and the offender, to be included in the report, subject to any contrary regulation made under subsection (2).

1995, c. 22, s. 6.

Commentary: Section 721(1) requires a probation officer to prepare a pre- sentence report when ordered to do so by a court. Section 721(3) sets out the matters which the report should address, and s. 721(4) permits the court to require information on other matters. By s. 721(2), provinces may make regulations concerning the types of offences for which pre-sentence reports can be ordered, and their content.

Case Law
Pre-Sentence Report: Ss. 721(1), (2)

R. v. Roussel (1996), 112 C.C.C. (3d) 538 (N.B. C.A.) — *See also: R. v. Sparks* (1985), 66 N.S.R. (2d) 253 (C.A.) — A pre-sentence report should *not* refer to uncharged criminal conduct.

R. v. Bartkow (1978), 1 C.R. (3d) S-36 (N.S. C.A.) — The function of those who prepare pre-sentence reports is to "supply a picture of the accused as a person in society — background, family, education, employment record, physical and mental health, associates and social activities, and potentialities and motivations. Their function is *not* to supply evidence of criminal offences or details of a criminal record or tell the court what sentence should be imposed."

R. v. Rudyk (1975), 1 C.R. (3d) S-26 (N.S. C.A.) — A pre-sentence report should *not* contain the investigator's impressions of the facts relating to the offence charged, whether based on information received from D, the police or other witness no matter how favourable or unfavourable to D. If such information is contained in the report it should be disregarded by the trial judge.

R. v. Edwards (1986), 60 Nfld. & P.E.I.R. 36 (P.E.I. C.A.) — The sole *purpose* of a pre-sentence report is to provide the court with a social and psychological profile of D. The report is to have *no* other content except that specifically requested by the trial judge.

Evidentiary Effect of Pre-Sentence Report

R. v. Urbanovich (1985), 19 C.C.C. (3d) 43 (Man. C.A.) — A pre-sentence report is not evidence with respect to the charge. It is only information gathered to enable the Court to assess the character of D for sentencing. Any material in the report which relates to the offence charged is inadmissible and inappropriate.

Related Provisions: Section 722.1 requires that P and D receive copies of the pre-sentence report and victim impact statement after they are filed. Section 722 requires the court to consider a victim impact statement if one is prepared in accordance with that section.

722. (1) Victim impact statement — For the purpose of determining the sentence to be imposed on an offender or whether the offender should be discharged pursuant to section 730 in respect of any offence, the court shall consider any statement that may have been prepared in accordance with subsection (2) of a victim of the offence describing the harm done to, or loss suffered by, the victim arising from the commission of the offence.

(2) Procedure for victim impact statement — A statement referred to in subsection (1) must be

(a) prepared in writing in the form and in accordance with the procedures established by a program designated for that purpose by the Lieutenant Governor in Council of the province in which the court is exercising its jurisdiction; and

(b) filed with the court.

(3) Other evidence concerning victim admissible — A statement of a victim of an offence prepared and filed in accordance with subsection (2) does not prevent the court from considering any other evidence concerning any victim of the offence for the purpose of determining the sentence to be imposed on the offender or whether the offender should be discharged pursuant to section 730.

(4) Definition of "victim" — For the purposes of this section, "victim", in relation to an offence

(a) means the person to whom harm was done or who suffered physical or emotional loss as a result of the commission of the offence; and

(b) where the person described in paragraph (a) is dead, ill or otherwise incapable of making a statement referred to in subsection (1), includes the spouse or any relative of that person, anyone who is in law or fact the custody of that person or is responsible for the care or support of that person or any dependant of that person.

1995, c. 22, s. 6.

Commentary: The court is required by s. 722(1) to consider any statement prepared by a victim in accordance with that section. "Victim" is defined in s. 722(4). By virtue of s. 722(3) the court is not prevented from considering any other evidence concerning any victim of the offence even though a victim impact statement has been filed.

Related Provisions: Section 722.1 requires that P and D receive a copy of the victim impact statement once it is filed.

722.1 Copies of documents — The clerk of the court shall provide a copy of a document referred to in section 721 or subsection 722(1), as soon as practicable after filing, to the offender or counsel for the offender, as directed by the court, and to the prosecutor.

1995, c. 22, s. 6.

Commentary: The section codifies the entitlement of P and D to receive copies of the pre-sentence report and victim impact statement, once filed.

Related Provisions: Pre-sentence reports are governed by s. 721 and victim impact statements by s. 722.

723. (1) Submissions on facts — Before determining the sentence, a court shall give the prosecutor and the offender an opportunity to make submissions with respect to any facts relevant to the sentence to be imposed.

(2) Submission of evidence — The court shall hear any relevant evidence presented by the prosecutor or the offender.

(3) Production of evidence — The court may, on its own motion, after hearing argument from the prosecutor and the offender, require the production of evidence that would assist it in determining the appropriate sentence.

(4) Compel appearance — Where it is necessary in the interests of justice, the court may, after consulting the parties, compel the appearance of any person who is a compellable witness to assist the court in determining the appropriate sentence.

(5) Hearsay evidence — Hearsay evidence is admissible at sentencing proceedings, but the court may, if the court considers it to be in the interests of justice, compel a person to testify where the person

(a) has personal knowledge of the matter;

(b) is reasonably available; and

(c) is a compellable witness.

1995, c. 22, s. 6.

Commentary: The section codifies procedural aspects of the sentencing hearing. By s. 723(1) P and D are entitled to make *submissions*, and by s. 723(2) to call any relevant *evidence*, before the court passes sentence. The court is empowered by s. 723(3) to require the production of evidence on its own motion, after hearing argument from P and D. Similarly, by s. 723(4) after consulting the parties, the court can require the attendance of any compellable witness for its assistance. In general, hearsay evidence is admissible but s. 723(5) permits the court to compel viva voce testimony from any person who has personal knowledge of the matter, is reasonably available, and is a compellable witness, when it is in the interests of justice to do so.

Related Provisions: Section 726.1 directs the court to consider any relevant information. Section 726 entitles D to speak before sentence is passed. Sections 721 and 722 provide for the preparation of pre-sentence reports and victim impact statements. Section 724 governs the finding of facts by the court. Section 725 deals with other offences.

724. (1) Information accepted — In determining a sentence, a court may accept as proved any information disclosed at the trial or at the sentencing proceedings and any facts agreed on by the prosecutor and the offender.

(2) Jury — Where the court is composed of a judge and jury, the court

(a) shall accept as proven all facts, express or implied, that are essential to the jury's verdict of guilty; and

(b) may find any other relevant fact that was disclosed by evidence at the trial to be proven, or hear evidence presented by either party with respect to that fact.

(3) Disputed facts — Where there is a dispute with respect to any fact that is relevant to the determination of a sentence,

(a) the court shall request that evidence be adduced as to the existence of the fact unless the court is satisfied that sufficient evidence was adduced at the trial;

(b) the party wishing to rely on a relevant fact, including a fact contained in a presentence report, has the burden of proving it;

(c) either party may cross-examine any witness called by the other party;

(d) subject to paragraph (e), the court must be satisfied on a balance of probabilities of the existence of the disputed fact before relying on it in determining the sentence; and

(e) the prosecutor must establish, by proof beyond a reasonable doubt, the existence of any aggravating fact or any previous conviction by the offender.

1995, c. 22, s. 6.

Commentary: The section deals with the finding of facts for sentencing purposes. In general, by s. 724(1) the court may take as proved any information disclosed during the trial or sentencing hearing, or any facts agreed on by P and D. In the case of a jury trial s. 724(2) requires the court to accept all facts essential to the verdict, but permits additional findings to be made based on the evidence at trial or further evidence called by either party. Section 724(3) prescribes a procedure for resolving disputed facts, which requires the party seeking to rely on the facts to prove them on a balance of probabilities, except for aggravating facts relied on by P which must be proved beyond a reasonable doubt.

Case Law

Proof of Facts as Basis for Sentence

R. v. Gauthier (1996), 108 C.C.C. (3d) 231 (B.C. C.A.) — In determining a fit sentence upon conviction after a jury trial, a trial judge is obliged to reach his/her own conclusions as to the facts surrounding the offence from the conflicts in the evidence at trial left unresolved by the jury verdict. The trial judge is *not* required to give D the benefit of the most favourable view of the evidence.

R. v. Roussel (1996), 112 C.C.C. (3d) 538 (N.B. C.A.) — The results of a psychiatric report prepared under *Code* s. 672.11 may be admitted at a sentencing hearing, provided D is permitted to challenge the findings.

Related Provisions: See the corresponding note to s. 723, *supra*.

725. (1) Other offences — In determining the sentence, a court

(a) shall consider, if it is possible and appropriate to do so, any other offences of which the offender was found guilty by the same court, and shall determine the sentence to be imposed for each of those offences;

(b) shall consider, if the Attorney General and the offender consent, any outstanding charges against the offender to which the offender consents to plead guilty and pleads guilty, if the court has jurisdiction to try those charges, and shall determine the sentence to be imposed for each charge unless the court is of the opinion that a separate prosecution for the other offence is necessary in the public interest;

(b.1) shall consider any outstanding charges against the offender, unless the court is of the opinion that a separate prosecution for one or more of the other offences is necessary in the public interest, subject to the following conditions:

(i) the Attorney General and the offender consent,

(ii) the court has jurisdiction to try each charge,

(iii) each charge has been described in open court,

(iv) the offender has agreed with the facts asserted in the description of each charge, and

(v) the offender has acknowledged having committed the offence described in each charge; and

(c) may consider any facts forming part of the circumstances of the offence that could constitute the basis for a separate charge.

(1.1) Attorney General's consent — For the purpose of paragraphs (1)(b) and (b.1), the Attorney General shall take the public interest into account before consenting.

(2) No further proceedings — The court shall, on the information or indictment, note

(a) any outstanding charges considered in determining the sentence under paragraph (1)(b.1), and

(b) any facts considered in determining the sentence under paragraph (1)(c),

and no further proceedings may be taken with respect to any offence described in those charges or disclosed by those facts unless the conviction for the offence of which the offender has been found guilty is set aside or quashed on appeal.

1995, c. 22, s. 6; 1999, c. 5, s. 31.

Commentary: The section permits the sentencing court to consider other offences of which it has found D guilty, or with the consent of P and D any other offences to which D pleads guilty, and to pass sentence for those offences. The court may also consider any facts concerning the offence which could constitute a separate charge, but pursuant to s. 725(2) must note those facts on the charging document, as they cannot be the subject of further proceedings.

Related Provisions: See the corresponding notes to s. 723, *supra* and s. 726.1, *infra*.

726. Offender may speak to sentence — Before determining the sentence to be imposed, the court shall ask whether the offender, if present, has anything to say.

1995, c. 22, s. 6.

Commentary: The provision entitles D to address the court before sentence is passed.

Case Law

Effect of Non-compliance

R. v. Senek (1998), *(*sub nom. *R. v. S. (D.J.))* 130 C.C.C. (3d) 473 (Man. C.A.) — Failure to comply with s. 726 does *not pre se* invalidate a sentencing hearing.

R. v. Roussel (1996), 112 C.C.C. (3d) 538 (N.B. C.A.) — The results of a psychiatric report prepared under *Code* s. 672.11 may be admitted at a sentencing hearing, provided D is permitted to challenge the findings.

Related Provisions: See the corresponding notes to s. 723, *supra* and s. 726.1, *infra*.

726.1 Relevant information — In determining the sentence, a court shall consider any relevant information placed before it, including any representations or submissions made by or on behalf of the prosecutor or the offender.

1995, c. 22, s. 6.

Commentary: The sentencing court is required to consider any relevant information, including submissions by P or D.

Related Provisions: Sections 721 and 722 provide for the preparation of pre-sentence reports and victim impact statements. Section 723 permits the calling of evidence and the making of submissions. Section 724 governs the finding of facts by the court. Section 725 deals with other offences. Section 726 entitles D to speak before sentence is passed.

726.2 Reasons for sentence — When imposing a sentence, a court shall state the terms of the sentence imposed, and the reasons for it, and enter those terms and reasons into the record of the proceedings.

1995, c. 22, s. 6.

Commentary: The provision requires the court to state both the sentence and the reasons for it, and to enter them into the record.

Related Provisions: Section 730 deals with absolute and conditional discharges. Section 731 governs the making of a probation order. Section 734 empowers the court to impose a fine. Section 732 provides for intermittent sentences of imprisonment. Section 742.1 permits the imposition of a conditional sentence of imprisonment.

727. (1) Previous conviction — Subject to subsections (3) and (4), where an offender is convicted of an offence for which a greater punishment may be imposed by reason of previous convictions, no greater punishment shall be imposed on the offender by reason thereof unless the prosecutor satisfies the court that the offender, before making a plea, was notified that a greater punishment would be sought by reason thereof.

(2) Procedure — Where an offender is convicted of an offence for which a greater punishment may be imposed by reason of previous convictions, the court shall, on application by the prosecutor and on being satisfied that the offender was notified in accordance with subsection (1), ask whether the offender was previously convicted and, if the offender does not admit to any previous convictions, evidence of previous convictions may be adduced.

(3) Where hearing ex parte — Where a summary conviction court holds a trial pursuant to subsection 803(2) and convicts the offender, the court may, whether or not the offender was notified that a greater punishment would be sought by reason of a previous conviction, make inquiries and hear evidence with respect to previous convictions of the offender and, if any such conviction is proved, may impose a greater punishment by reason thereof.

(4) Corporations — Where, pursuant to section 623, the court proceeds with the trial of a corporation that has not appeared and pleaded and convicts the corporation, the court may, whether or not the corporation was notified that a greater punishment would be sought be reason of a previous conviction, make inquiries and hear evidence with respect to previous convictions of the corporation and, if any such conviction is proved, may impose a greater punishment by reason thereof.

(5) Section does not apply — This section does not apply to a person referred to in paragraph 745(b).

1995, c. 22, s. 6.

Commentary: The section permits the use of previous convictions on the issue of sentence after conviction of an offence for which a greater punishment may be imposed by reason of previous convictions.

Under s. 727(1), it is the general rule in cases where D is convicted of an offence for which a greater punishment may be imposed by reason of previous convictions, that no such punishment may be imposed, unless P satisfies the court that, prior to plea, D was notified that P would seek such increased punishment by reason thereof. There are three exceptions. Where an *ex parte* summary conviction trial has been held on account of D's failure to appear or trial, under s. 727(3) the court may make inquiries and hear evidence with respect to previous convictions and, upon proof, impose a greater punishment by reason thereof, irrespective of earlier notice. Section 727(4) makes similar provision for trials of a corporate accused which has neither appeared nor pleaded. Section 727(5) makes the section inapplicable to persons convicted of second degree murder under circumstances described in s. 745(b).

Section 727(2) describes the procedure followed where D is convicted of an offence for which a greater punishment may be imposed by reason of previous convictions and the requisite notice of s.727(1) has been proven. In such circumstances the trial court, on application by P, must ask D whether he/she was previously convicted and, absent admission, evidence of previous convictions may be adduced.

Case Law
Nature of Notice Required: S. 727(1)

R. v. Duncan (1983), 1 C.C.C. (3d) 444 (B.C. C.A.) — Whether D has received notice before plea that a greater punishment would be sought because of previous convictions is a question of fact. There are *no* legal requirements for the notice. The court must be satisfied, however, that notice was given.

R. v. Bohnet (1976), 31 C.C.C. (2d) 253 (N.W.T. C.A.) — It is the number of previous convictions that engage the applicable penalty provision *not* the number of times that P has sought a greater penalty on any prior conviction.

R. v. Monk (1981), 24 C.R. (3d) 183, 62 C.C.C. (2d) 6 (Ont. C.A.) — There is *no* requirement that the notice specify the number of previous convictions or the particulars thereof. The intent of the notice is to inform D that a greater penalty will be sought upon conviction.

R. v. Pidlubny (1973), 20 C.R.N.S. 310, 10 C.C.C. (2d) 178 (Ont. C.A.) — On a charge of impaired driving, notice served before plea stating that "a greater punishment will be sought by reason of a previous conviction or convictions" is sufficient. The prior conviction does *not* have to be identified.

R. v. Bear (1979), 47 C.C.C. (2d) 462 (Sask. C.A.) — The notice need *not* set out the nature or character of the greater punishment to be sought.

Means of Proof

R. v. Protz, [1984] 5 W.W.R. 263 (Sask. C.A.) — D's admission of a previous conviction during trial is admissible to establish a prior conviction.

R. v. Jonasson (1980), 56 C.C.C. (2d) 121 (Sask. C.A.) — *Code* s. 740 [now s. 727] is a complete code of procedure by which a greater punishment can be sought because of a previous conviction. This procedure is paramount and is not in any way subject to or affected by *C.E.A.* provisions.

Related Provisions: The section does not apply to cases in which the evidence of previous conviction is adduced for a purpose other than increased punishment, as for example, under s. 360 in proof of the element of knowledge of the unlawful character of the subject-matter of the proceedings, or under s. 666 in rebuttal of evidence of good character. Previous convictions may be proven under s. 667.

728. Sentence justified by any count — Where one sentence is passed on a verdict of guilty on two or more counts of an indictment, the sentence is good if any of the counts would have justified the sentence.

1995, c. 22, s. 6.

Commentary: As a general rule, sentence is passed in respect of each count upon which a finding of guilt has been made. The section does not invalidate a single sentence passed on D in respect of discrete findings of guilt, provided the sentence may be justified by any of the counts.

Case Law

R. v. Thorpe (1976), 32 C.C.C. (2d) 46 (Man. C.A.) — The preferred procedure where D is convicted of two offences is for D to be given concurrent sentences with the sentence for each imposed separately.

Related Provisions: Part XXIII contains general provisions relating to punishment, fines, forfeitures, costs and restitution of property.

Both D and P have right of appeal against the sentence imposed by a trial court under ss. 675(1)(b), (1.1) and (2) and ss. 676(1)(d), (1.1) and (4). The powers of the court of appeal on sentence appeals are defined by s. 687.

729. (1) Proof of certificate of analyst — In

  (a) a prosecution for failure to comply with a condition in a probation order that the accused not have in possession or use drugs,

or

  (b) a hearing to determine whether the offender breached a condition of a conditional sentence that the offender not have in possession or use drugs,

a certificate purporting to be signed by an analyst stating that the analyst has analyzed or examined a substance and stating the result of the analysis or examination is admissible in evidence and, in the absence of evidence to the contrary, is proof of the statements contained in the certificate without proof of the signature or official character of the person appearing to have signed the certificate.

(2) Definition of "analyst" — In this section, "analyst" means a person designated as an analyst under the *Food and Drugs Act* or under the *Narcotic Control Act*.

(3) Notice of intention to produce certificate — No certificate shall be admitted in evidence unless the party intending to produce it has, before the trial or hearing, as the case may be, given reasonable notice and a copy of the certificate to the party against whom it is to be produced.

(4) Proof of service — Service of any certificate referred to in subsection (1) may be proved by oral evidence given under oath by, or by the affidavit or solemn declaration of, the person claiming to have served it.

(5) Attendance for examination — Notwithstanding subsection (4), the court may require the person who appears to have signed an affidavit or solemn declaration referred to in that subsection to appear before it for examination or cross-examination in respect of the issue of proof of service.

(6) **Requiring attendance of analyst** — The party against whom a certificate of an analyst is produced may, with leave of the court, require the attendance of the analyst for cross-examination.

1995, c. 22, s. 6.

Commentary: The section permits the use of a *certificate* of analysis to prove *breach of probation* or breach of a *term* of a *conditional sentence* based on possession or use of drugs. Section 729(1) prescribes the content of the certificate of analysis. Section 729(2) defines "analyst". Reasonable notice of the intention to introduce the certificate must be given to the other party along with a copy of the certificate, under s. 729(3). Service may be by oral evidence or affidavit/solemn declaration under s. 729(4), subject to the court pursuant to s. 729(5) requiring *viva voce* evidence. Section 729(6) permits the other party, with leave of the court to require the analyst to attend for cross-examination.

Related Provisions: Section 732.1 sets out the compulsory and optional conditions of a probation order. Section 733.1 creates the offence of breach of probation.

Section 742.1 permits the imposition of a conditional sentence of imprisonment. Section 742.3 sets out the compulsory and optional conditions of the order. Section 742.6 sets out the procedure to be followed where a breach of the order is alleged.

Absolute and Conditional Discharges

730. (1) Conditional and absolute discharge — Where an accused, other than a corporation, pleads guilty to or is found guilty of an offence other than an offence for which a minimum, punishment is prescribed by law or an offence punishable by imprisonment for fourteen years or for life, the court before which the accused appears may, if it considers it to be in the best interests of the accused and not contrary to the public interest, instead of convicting the accused, by order direct that the accused be discharged absolutely or on the conditions prescribed in a probation order made under subsection 731(2).

(2) Period for which appearance notice, etc., continues in force — Subject to Part XVI, where an accused who has not been taken into custody or who has been released from custody under or by virtue of any provision of Part XVI pleads guilty of or is found guilty of an offence but is not convicted, the appearance notice, promise to appear, summons, undertaking or recognizance issued to or given or entered into by the accused continues in force, subject to its terms, until a disposition in respect of the accused is made under subsection (1) unless, at the time the accused pleads guilty or is found guilty, the court, judge or justice orders that the accused be taken into custody pending such a disposition.

(3) Effect of discharge — Where a court directs under subsection (1) that an offender be discharged of an offence, the offender shall be deemed not to have been convicted of the offence except that

(a) the offender may appeal from the determination of guilt as if it were a conviction in respect of the offence;

(b) the Attorney General and, in the case of summary conviction proceedings, the informant or the informant's agent may appeal from the decision of the court not to convict the offender of the offence as if that decision were a judgment or verdict of acquittal of the offence or a dismissal of the information against the offender; and

(c) the offender may plead autrefois convict in respect of any subsequent charge relating to the offence.

(4) **Where person bound by probation order convicted of offence** —

Where an offender who is bound by the conditions of a probation order made at a time when the offender was directed to be discharged under this section is convicted of an offence, including an offence under section 733.1, the court that made the probation order may, in addition to or in lieu of exercising its authority under subsection 732.2(5), at any time when it may take action under that subsection, revoke the discharge, convict the offender of the offence to which the discharge relates and impose any sentence that could have been imposed if the offender had been convicted at the time of discharge, and no appeal lies from a conviction under this subsection where an appeal was taken from the order directing that the offender be discharged.

1995, c. 22, s. 6; 1997, c. 18, ss. 107, 141(d).

Note: 1997, c. 18, s. 107 was not in force at the date of publication. This section purported to amend s. 736 of the Criminal Code as it existed prior to the 1995, c. 22 amendments. The reference to s. 736 of the Code has been replaced by s. 730 in accordance with 1995, c. 22, s. 18 (Sch. IV). If proclaimed in force, 1997, c. 18, s. 107 will amend s. 730(1) by deleting the words "made under s. 731(2)" from the last line.

Commentary: The section governs the availability, operation, effect and enforcement of absolute and conditional discharges including rights of appeal from each disposition.

Section 730(1) describes the circumstances under which an absolute or conditional discharge may be granted. D must *not* be a *corporation* and must plead or be found guilty of an offence which must *not* be one for which a *minimum punishment* is prescribed by law or one punishable by imprisonment for life or 14 years. D may only be awarded an absolute or conditional discharge where it is in D's best interests and *not* contrary to the public interest to do so. Where it is determined that a discharge shall be given, a finding of guilt is recorded. No conviction is entered. It is then directed that D be discharged. The discharge may be either absolute, or in accordance with the conditions prescribed in a probation order.

Under s. 730(2), D's release form continues in force, notwithstanding the finding of guilt, unless, at the time of entry of the plea or finding, the court orders D be taken into custody pending sentence.

Appellate rights in respect of discharges and applications therefore are governed by s. 730(3). D may appeal from the finding of guilt, as if it were a conviction, and P from the failure to convict, as if it were a judgment or verdict of acquittal or dismissal of the information. In summary conviction proceedings, the informant or informant's agent has rights of appeal equivalent to P. D may plead *autrefois convict* in respect of any subsequent charge relating to the offence.

Section 730(4) authorizes the *revocation* of a discharge where D, bound by the conditions of a probation order made upon discharge, is convicted of an offence. Upon conviction, the court which ordered the discharge may, in lieu of, but within the time period for revoking a probation order under s. 732.2(5), revoke the discharge, convict D of the offence for which the discharge was awarded, and impose any sentence that could have been imposed at first instance. No appeal may be taken from conviction where an appeal was taken from the order directing D's discharge.

Case Law

In The Proceedings Commenced Against Him: S. 730(1)

R. v. Sampson (1975), 23 C.C.C. (2d) 65 (Ont. C.A.) — This phrase relates only to those proceedings with respect to which D was found guilty. Where D is convicted of a lesser included offence, rather than the offence charged, a discharge is available if the offence of which D was convicted falls within the parameters of this section.

General Principles: S. 730(1)

R. v. Bram (1982), 30 C.R. (3d) 398 (Alta. C.A.) — Absolute discharges should be granted sparingly in the interests of preserving the principle of general deterrence. They should *not* be confined to cases of trivial or unintentional offences.

R. v. Tan (1975), 22 C.C.C. (2d) 184 (B.C. C.A.) — The court may consider whether D has been granted a discharge on a previous occasion in considering whether a further discharge is in the best interests of D and not contrary to the public interest.

R. v. Fallofield (1973), 22 C.R.N.S. 342, 13 C.C.C. (2d) 450 (B.C. C.A.) — The granting of a conditional or absolute discharge should *not* be restricted to cases of strict liability or where the offence committed was entirely unintentional or unavoidable. There is nothing which limits the use of the discharge to a technical or trivial violation. The section may be used in respect of any offence other than an offence for which a minimum punishment is prescribed by law, or the offence is punishable by imprisonment for 14 years or for life or by death. The commission of an offence is contemplated, and there is nothing in the language of the section that limits it to a technical or trivial violation. There are two conditions precedent to the exercise of the jurisdiction. The court must consider that it is in the *best interests* of D that D should be discharged either absolutely or upon condition. The court must consider whether a grant of discharge is contrary to the *public interest*. Generally, the first condition would presuppose that D is a person of good character, without previous conviction, that it is *not* necessary to enter a conviction against D in order to deter D from future offences or to rehabilitate D, and that the entry of a conviction against D may have significant repercussions. In the context of the second condition, the public interest in the deterrence of others, while it must be given due weight, does not preclude the judicious use of the discharge provisions. The powers given by the section should *not* be exercised as an alternative to probation or suspended sentence. The section should *not* be applied routinely to any particular offence.

R. v. Culley (1977), 36 C.C.C. (2d) 433 (Ont. C.A.) — The provisions empowering the court to grant a discharge are not primarily applicable to youthful offenders, as distinct from mature offenders.

R. v. McInnis (1973), 23 C.R.N.S. 152, 13 C.C.C. (2d) 471 (Ont. C.A.) — The purpose of the section is to make a disposition of the case which, in appropriate circumstances, will avoid ascribing a criminal record to D.

R. v. Sanchez-Pino (1973), 22 C.R.N.S. 350, 11 C.C.C. (2d) 53 (Ont. C.A.) — The requirement that the granting of a discharge be "in the best interests of the accused" means deterrence of the offender himself and rehabilitation through correctional or treatment centres is not a relevant consideration, except to the extent required by conditions in a probation order. Normally D will be a person of good character, or at least of such character that the entry of a conviction against him may have significant repercussions. One element brought in by the requirement that the discharge not be "contrary to the public interest", is the necessity or otherwise of a sentence which will be a deterrent to others.

Form of Discharge: Conditional or Absolute

R. v. Hébert, [1986] R.J.Q. 236 (C.A.) — A discharge must be either conditional or unconditional, but *not* both. Therefore a sentence which was conditional, but which was to become unconditional after a definite period if the conditions of probation were respected and an indemnity paid, was improper.

Immigration Status

Mason v. R. (1978), 6 C.R. (3d) 14 (Ont. C.A.) — *See also: R. v. Chiu* (1984), 31 Man. R. (2d) 15 (C.A.) — *Contra: R. v. Kerr* (1982), 43 A.R. 254 (C.A.) — The court will *not* grant a discharge solely on the basis that D's immigration status is in jeopardy. The status is a factor to be considered, however, in determining whether it is a proper case for a discharge.

Charter Considerations

R. v. Elendiuk (1986), 27 C.C.C. (3d) 94 (Alta. C.A.) — Where D has committed an offence while on probation, the revocation, by virtue of s. 736(4), of a conditional discharge and the subsequent conviction and sentencing of D on the original charge does not offend the guarantee against double jeopardy in *Charter* s. 11(h). A conditional discharge is *not* final punishment; the court has explicitly reserved the right to convict and sentence D during the conditional period.

Related Provisions: In proceedings by indictment D's rights of appeal from conviction are under s. 675(1)(a) and those of P, from acquittal or not criminally responsible on account of mental disorder, in s. 676(1)(a). In summary conviction proceedings, D's rights of appeal from conviction are under ss. 675(1.1), 813(a) and 830(1), those of the informant and P, under ss. 676(1.1), 813(b) and 831(1). A disposition under s. 730(1) is a "sentence" within ss. 673 and 785(1) for appellate purposes under Parts XXI and XXVII, respectively.

Section 732.1 describes the contents of a probation order and s. 732.2 when it comes into force. A probation order may be transferred under s. 733. Failure or refusal to comply with a probation order is made a summary conviction offence by s. 733.1

Probation

731. (1) Making of probation order — Where a person is convicted of an offence, a court may, having regard to the age and character of the offender, the nature of the offence and the circumstances surrounding its commission,

  (a) if no minimum punishment is prescribed by law, suspend the passing of sentence and direct that the offender be released on the conditions prescribed in a probation order; or

  (b) in addition to fining or sentencing the offender to imprisonment for a term not exceeding two years, direct that the offender comply with the conditions prescribed in a probation order.

(2) Idem — A court may also make a probation order where it discharges an accused under subsection 730(1).

1995, c. 22, s. 6.

Commentary: The section describes the circumstances under which a *probation* order may be made. Under s. 731(1), in determining whether to order a convicted offender to comply with the terms of a probation order, the sentencing court must have regard to D's *age* and *character*, as well as the *nature* of the offence and the *circumstances* surrounding its commission. A probation order may be made under the section *only* in circumstances which fall within ss. 731(1)(a) or (b). Under s. 731(1)(a), the passing of sentence is suspended and D ordered to comply with the terms of a probation order. No other punishment is imposed for the offence of which D has been convicted which must not be an offence which carries a minimum punishment. Under s. 731(1)(b), a probation order is imposed in addition to a fine or term of imprisonment for a term not exceeding two years. The sentence, in other words, combines a fine and probation or imprisonment and probation, though not a fine plus imprisonment plus probation. Section 731(2) empowers the court to make a probation order where D is discharged.

Case Law

Not Exceeding Two Years: S. 731(1)(b)

R. v. McLeren, (May 20, 1988), Doc. No. CA 08829 (B.C. C.A.) — *See also: R. v. Gauthier* (1991), 3 B.C.A.C. 239, 7 W.A.C. 239 (C.A.) — Where D is already serving a sentence or combination of sentences exceeding two years, a term of probation may *not* be imposed as part of a fresh sentence.

R. v. Hackett (1986), 30 C.C.C. (3d) 159 (B.C. C.A.) — Where concurrent sentences are imposed, the test is whether the longest of those sentences exceeds two years.

Young v. R. (1980), 27 C.R. (3d) 85 (B.C. C.A.) — *See also: R. v. Sutton,* (January 14, 1988), Doc. No. CA 007567 (B.C. C.A.) — It was contrary to the intent of the *Code* to contemplate imposing a period of probation following consecutive sentences which totalled more than two years, even if none of those sentences was in itself longer than two years.

R. v. Amaralik (1985), 16 C.C.C. (3d) 22 (N.W.T. C.A.) — Parliament intended that probation be imposed only when the sentence or total of sentences to be served did not exceed two years.

R. v. Miller (1987), 58 C.R. (3d) 396, 36 C.C.C. (3d) 100 (Ont. C.A.) — A term of probation imposed to follow concurrent sentences of two years less a day becomes illegal, in view of s. 737(1)(b), when subsequent consecutive prison sentences are imposed so that the total prison sentence being served is in excess of two years.

Imprisonment and Fine: S. 731(1)(b)

R. v. Blacquiere (1975), 24 C.C.C. (2d) 168 (Ont. C.A.) — *See also: R. v. Kelly* (1995), 104 C.C.C. (3d) 95 (Nfld. C.A.); *R. v. Lindsay* (1986), 76 N.S.R. (2d) 361 (C.A.) — A probation order may not be made if both a fine and imprisonment are imposed.

R. v. St. James (1981), 20 C.R. (3d) 389 (Que. C.A.) — Under s. 737(1)(a), the court cannot suspend D's sentence, impose probation and at the same time impose a fine. Nor can the court, under s. 737(1)(b), impose imprisonment, a fine and a probation order at the same time.

Related Provisions: A probation order comes into force under s. 732.2 and may be transferred to another territorial division under s.733. Failure or refusal to comply with a probation order is a summary conviction offence under s. 733.1. A disposition under s.731(1) is a "sentence" within ss. 673 and 785(1) for appellate purposes under Parts XXI and XXVII, respectively.

Section 732.2.(3)(d) permits the inclusion of a probationary term which requires D to abstain from owning, possessing or carrying a weapon. Section 100(1) requires and s. 100(2) permits orders prohibiting D from having in his/her possession any firearm, ammunition or explosive substance for a specified period, upon conviction of or discharge for certain offences. Sections 738-740 make separate provisions for restitution orders and an enforcement mechanism is provided by s. 741.

731.1 (1) Firearm, etc., prohibitions — Before making a probation order, the court shall consider whether section 100 is applicable.

(2) Idem — For greater certainty, a condition of a probation order referred to in paragraph 732.1(3)(d) does not affect the operation of section 100.

1995, c. 22, s. 6.

Commentary: A court must consider whether a firearms prohibition order is to be imposed. The inclusion in a probation order of a condition that D not own, possess or carry a weapon does not affect the applicability of the firearms prohibition provision.

Related Provisions: Firearms prohibition orders are authorized by s. 100. The circumstances in which a probation order may be made are set out in s. 731. The conditions that must or may be included are specified in s. 732.1.

732. (1) Intermittent sentence — Where the court imposes a sentence of imprisonment of ninety days or less on an offender convicted of an offence, whether in default of payment of a fine or otherwise, the court may, having regard to the age and character of the offender, the nature of the offence and the circumstances surrounding its commission, and the availability of appropriate accommodation to ensure compliance with the sentence, order

(a) that the sentence be served intermittently at such times as are specified in the order; and

(b) that the offender comply with the conditions prescribed in a probation order when not in confinement during the period that the sentence is being served and, if the court so orders, on release from prison after completing the intermittent sentence.

(2) Application to vary intermittent sentence — An offender who is ordered to serve a sentence of imprisonment intermittently may, on giving notice to the prosecutor, apply to the court that imposed the sentence to allow it to be served on consecutive days.

(3) Court may vary intermittent sentence if subsequent offence — Where a court imposes a sentence of imprisonment on a person who is subject to an intermittent sentence in respect of another offence, the unexpired portion of the intermittent sentence shall be served on consecutive days unless the court otherwise orders.

1995, c. 22, s. 6.

Commentary: A court may order that a sentence of 90 days or less be served intermittently. In addition to considering the character of D and the nature of his offence, the court may consider the availability of appropriate jail accommodation. Pursuant to s. 732(1)(b), a probation order may be imposed with respect to the period when D is not in custody while under sentence, and also on the expiry of the intermittent sentence. Under s. 732(2) D may apply to serve the intermittent sentence on consecutive days. If D is sentenced for another offence, by virtue of s. 732(3) the remaining portion of the intermittent sentence is to be served on consecutive days unless the court orders otherwise.

Case Law

Intermittent Sentence: S. 732(1)

R. v. Fletcher (1982), 2 C.C.C. (3d) 221 (Ont. C.A.) — *See also*: *R. v. Aubin* (1992), 72 C.C.C. (3d) 189 (Que. C.A.); *R. v. Drost* (1996), 104 C.C.C. (3d) 389 (N.B C.A.) — A sentence of two consecutive terms of 90 days to be served intermittently is deemed by the *Parole Act* to be a single sentence of 180 days intermittent. An intermittent sentence is not authorized by the *Code* because it is over 90 days.

R. v. Weber (1980), 52 C.C.C. (2d) 468 (Ont. C.A.) — *See also*: *Demedeiros v. R.* (1979), 12 C.R. (3d) 113 (B.C. C.A.) — A period of probation imposed under s. 732.2(1)(c) should *not* exceed that required to serve the sentence of imprisonment intermittently. However, it is open to the court to direct under s. 732.2(1)(b) a period of probation commencing upon the expiration of the intermittent sentence. Section 732.2(1)(b) need *not* be construed so as to make it an exclusive alternative to s. 732.2(1)(c).

Related Provisions: Conditions which must and may be imposed in a probation order are set out in s.732.1.

732.1 (1) Definitions — In this section and section 732.2,

"change", in relation to optional conditions, includes deletions and additions;

"optional conditions" means the conditions referred to in subsection (3).

(2) Compulsory conditions of probation order — The court shall prescribe, as conditions of a probation order, that the offender do all of the following:

(a) keep the peace and be of good behaviour;

(b) appear before the court when required to do so by the court; and

(c) notify the court or the probation officer in advance of any change of name or address, and promptly notify the court or the probation officer of any change of employment or occupation.

(3) Optional conditions of probation order — The court may prescribe, as additional conditions of a probation order, that the offender do one or more of the following:

(a) report to a probation officer

(i) within two working days, or such longer period as the court directs, after the making of the probation order, and

(ii) thereafter, when required by the probation officer and in the manner directed by the probation officer;

(b) remain within the jurisdiction of the court unless written permission to go outside that jurisdiction is obtained from the court or the probation officer;

(c) abstain from

(i) the consumption of alcohol or other intoxicating substances, or

(ii) the consumption of drugs except in accordance with a medical prescription;

(d) abstain from owning, possessing or carrying a weapon;

(e) provide for the support or care of dependants;

(f) perform up to 240 hours of community service over a period not exceeding eighteen months;

(g) if the offender agrees, and the subject to the program director's acceptance of the offender, participate actively in a treatment program approved by the province; and

(h) comply with such other reasonable conditions as the court considers desirable, subject to any regulations made under subsection 738(2), for protecting society and for facilitating the offender's successful reintegration into the community.

(4) Form and period of order — A probation order may be in Form 46, and the court that makes the probation order shall specify therein the period for which it is to remain in force.

(5) Proceedings on making order — A court that makes a probation order shall

(a) cause to be given to the offender

   (i) a copy of the order,

   (ii) an explanation of the substance of subsections 732.2(3) and (5) and section 733.1, and

   (iii) an explanation of the procedure for applying under subsection 732.2(3) for a change to the optional conditions; and

(b) take reasonable measures to ensure that the offender understands the order and the explanations given to the offender under paragraph (a).

1995, c. 22, s. 6.

Commentary: The conditions of a probation order set out in s. 732.1(2) are mandatory. Additional optional conditions are set out in s.732.1(3). The order must specify the period for which it is in force. Compliance with s. 732.1(5) ensures that D is made aware of the terms of the order, the consequences of conviction and failure to comply while on probation, and the procedure for seeking a change in optional conditions or duration of the order.

Case Law
Conditions: S. 732.1(2), (3)

R. v. L. (1986), 50 C.R. (3d) 398 (Alta. C.A.) — The court may *not* impose a custodial term as a condition of a probation order.

R. v. M. (D.E.S.) (1993), 21 C.R. (4th) 55, 80 C.C.C. (3d) 371 (B.C. C.A.) — In appropriate circumstances, a probation order may require D to be strictly confined to his home and home property, except for such absences for employment or otherwise as may be approved by his probation officer.

R. v. Debaat (1992), 15 C.R. (4th) 226 (B.C. C.A.) — *See also*: *R. v. Dashner* (1974), 25 C.R.N.S. 240, 15 C.C.C. (2d) 139 (B.C. C.A.) — Inclusion of a restitution or reparation term in a probation order under s. 732.1(3)(e) should only be made on *evidence* which shows that the amount ordered is for actual loss or damage sustained by the person aggrieved or injured, and that D has the means to pay for it.

R. v. Rogers (1990), 2 C.R. (4th) 192, 61 C.C.C. (3d) 481 (B.C. C.A.) — A probation order which compels D to take psychiatric treatment or medication infringes *Charter* s. 7 and will only be exceptionally saved by s. 1. No particular form of order is appropriate for all cases. Conditions should be designed to ensure the protection of the public, but not by compelling D to undergo medical treatment, including the compulsory taking of medication.

R. v. Shaw (1977), 36 C.R.N.S. 358 (Ont. C.A.) — Section 732.1(3)(h) authorizes the imposition of a community service order as a term of probation. In appropriate cases it should be more extensively used.

R. v. Ziatas (1973), 13 C.C.C. (2d) 287 (Ont. C.A.) — The terms of the probation order are not to be imposed as additional punishment but rather with a desire to secure the good conduct of D and to prevent the repetition by him of the same offence or the commission of other offences.

R. v. Taylor (1997), 122 C.C.C. (3d) 376 (Sask. C.A.) — In an appropriate case, banishment may be included as a term of a probation order under s. 732.1(3)(h).

R. v. Kieling (1991), 64 C.C.C. (3d) 124 (Sask. C.A.) — Section 732.1(3)(h) does *not* permit the court to impose a term *requiring* D to take medication.

Privilege

R. v. Walker (1992), 74 C.C.C. (3d) 97 (B.C. C.A.) — There is no privilege based upon a duty of confidentiality owed by a probation officer to a probationer.

Proceedings on Making of Order: S. 737(5)

R. v. Sterner (1982), 64 C.C.C. (2d) 160 (S.C.C.); affirming (1981), 60 C.C.C. (2d) 68 (Sask. C.A.) — The administrative provisions of s. 732.1(5) are delegable to a court official. It is not necessary that the judge personally inform D of the consequences of a breach of the probation order.

Related Provisions: The making of a probation order is authorized by s. 731. Its coming into force is governed by s. 732.2. The consequences of a breach of probation are set out in s. 733.1, and of conviction of another offence while on probation in s. 732.2(5). Under s. 732.2(3) D may apply to change the optional conditions and/or the duration of the order.

732.2 (1) Coming into force of order — A probation order comes into force

(a) on the date on which the order is made;

(b) where the offender is sentenced to imprisonment under paragraph 731(1)(b) or was previously sentenced to imprisonment for another offence, as soon as the offender is released from prison or, if released from prison on conditional release, at the expiration of the sentence of imprisonment; or

(c) where the offender is under a conditional sentence, at the expiration of the conditional sentence.

(2) Duration of order and limit on term of order — Subject to subsection (5),

(a) where an offender who is bound by a probation order is convicted of an offence, including an offence under section 733.1, or is imprisoned under paragraph 731(1)(b) in default of payment of a fine, the order continues in force except in so far as the sentence renders it impossible for the offender for the time being to comply with the order; and

(b) no probation order shall continue in force for which more than three years after the date on which the order came into force.

(3) Changes to probation order — A court that makes a probation order may at any time, on application by the offender, the probation officer or the prosecutor, require the offender to appear before it and, after hearing the offender and one or both of the probation officer and the prosecutor,

(a) make any changes to the optional conditions that in the opinion of the court are rendered desirable by a change in the circumstances since those conditions were prescribed,

(b) relieve the offender, either absolutely or on such terms or for such period as the court deems desirable, of compliance with any optional condition, or

(c) decrease the period for which the probation order is to remain in force,

and the court shall thereupon endorse the probation order accordingly and, if it changes the optional conditions, inform the offender of its action and give the offender a copy of the order so endorsed.

(4) Judge may act in chambers — All the functions of the court under subsection (3) may be exercised in chambers.

(5) Where person convicted of offence — Where an offender who is bound by a probation order is convicted of an offence, including an offence under section 733.1, and

(a) the time within which an appeal may be taken against that conviction has expired and the offender has not taken an appeal,

(b) the offender has taken an appeal against that conviction and the appeal has been dismissed, or

(c) the offender has given written notice to the court that convicted the offender that the offender elects not to appeal the conviction or has abandoned the appeal, as the case may be,

in addition to any punishment that may be imposed for that offence, the court that made the probation order may, on application by the prosecutor, require the offender to appear before it and, after hearing the prosecutor and the offender,

(d) where the probation order was made under paragraph 731(1)(a), revoke the order and impose any sentence that could have been imposed if the passing of sentence had not been suspended, or

(e) make such changes to the optional conditions as the court deems desirable, or extend the period for which the order is to remain in force for such period, not exceeding one year, as the court deems desirable,

and the court shall thereupon endorse the probation order accordingly and, if it changes the optional conditions or extends the period for which the order is to remain in force, inform the offender of its action and give the offender a copy of the order so endorsed.

(6) Compelling appearance of person bound — The provisions of Parts XVI and XVIII with respect to compelling the appearance of an accused before a justice apply, with such modifications as the circumstances require, to proceedings under subsections (3) and (5).

1995, c. 22, s. 6.

Commentary: The section defines the commencement and duration of a probation order and the circumstances under which it may be varied or revoked.

Under s. 732.2(1) a probation order comes into force on the date on which it is made or, where D is sentenced to a term of imprisonment under s. 731(1)(b), upon the expiration of the sentence. The order must not continue in force for more than three years from the date of its commencement, subject to a revocation hearing under s. 732.2(5). It continues to apply notwithstanding D is convicted during its term of an offence, including breach of probation, except to the extent that D's incarceration makes compliance with some terms impossible.

A probation order may be varied under s. 732.2(3) by the sentencing court upon application by D or P or the probation officer. D's attendance may be compelled upon the application by means authorized in Parts XVI and XVIII. D and P and/or the probation officer are heard on the application. The variations which may be made upon the application include changes in or additions to the optional conditions rendered desirable by a change in circumstances, relief, absolutely or on terms, from compliance with any condition, and a decrease in the term of the order.

Revocation proceedings, authorized and regulated by s. 732.2(5) are engaged by D's conviction, during the currency of the probationary term, of an offence, including breach of probation. Where appellate proceedings in respect of the subsequent conviction have not been taken in time or at all, have been abandoned, or have been taken and the conviction affirmed, P may apply to the court which made the probation order to have the order revoked. D's attendance on the hearing may be compelled under Parts XVI and XVIII. A hearing is conducted. In addition to any punishment imposed for the subsequent offence, the court may revoke the order suspending the passing of the original sentence and impose any sentence that could have been imposed at first instance. In any other case, that is to say, where probation has been imposed in addition to a custodial or pecuniary penalty, the court may vary the order, including extending its term for a period not exceeding one year. Any disposition made on the revocation hearing must be endorsed on the probation order and, where any changes thereto are made, D given a copy of the order.

Case Law

Multiple Probation Orders

R. v. Hunt (1982), 2 C.C.C. (3d) 126 (N.S. C.A.) — *See also*: *R. v. L. (T.S.)* (1988), 46 C.C.C. (3d) 126 (N.S. C.A.) — Multiple probation orders may *not* be ordered to operate consecutively.

Modification of Orders

R. v. H. (1983), 6 C.C.C. (3d) 382 (Alta. C.A.) — The court of appeal has jurisdiction to amend probation orders made previously at the court of appeal level. The panel that amends the order need not be the same one that originally imposed the order. A single judge of the court of appeal does *not* have jurisdiction under the Alberta Rules of Court to amend a previously imposed probation order. However, a judge of the original sentencing court has jurisdiction to amend an order imposed by the court of appeal if a change in circumstances makes such an order desirable.

Stay of Probation Order (See now s. 683(5)(e); (6))

R. v. Trabulsey (1993), 84 C.C.C. (3d) 240 (Ont. Gen. Div.) — The filing of a notice of appeal does *not* operate to stay or suspend the operation of the terms of a probation order.

Re-sentencing — Jurisdiction: S. 732.2(5)

R. v. Clermont (1988), 45 C.C.C. (3d) 480 (S.C.C.) — Upon the revocation of a probation order, the judge may only impose a sentence that could have been imposed had sentencing not been suspended. Therefore, where D was not under sentence at the time of the suspension of sentence, to which a subsequent sentence could be made consecutive, upon re-sentencing the court could not order a consecutive sentence even though at the time of re-sentencing D was now serving a sentence for manslaughter.

R. v. Tuckey (1977), 34 C.C.C. (2d) 572 (Ont. C.A.) — In a proceeding under s. 738(4), the basic principles of natural justice must prevail. Although there is no requirement for an information on oath, the minimum requirement is that D should be given reasonable notice in writing of P's intention to take such proceedings. The notice should clearly articulate the nature of the proceedings, the grounds upon which P intends to rely in support of the application, the nature of the order sought, and the hearing date. The trial judge must impose a sentence proportionate to the offence which D had committed. At the time of suspending sentence, the trial judge should not indicate the precise sentence that will be imposed if D breaches probation.

R. v. Graham (1975), 27 C.C.C. (2d) 475 (Ont. C.A.) — Only the judge who convicted D and suspended sentence has jurisdiction to revoke the probation order and impose the sentence that could have been imposed if the sentence had not been suspended, unless a proper transfer order is made under s. 739(1) or, the judge being unable to act, another judge invokes the jurisdiction provided by s. 739(2).

Re-sentencing — Charter Considerations

R. v. Elendiuk (No. 2) (1986), 67 A.R. 221 (C.A.) — *Charter* s. 11(h) is only triggered when D is finally punished, as well as finally tried. A probation order is not final punishment. The court has explicitly reserved the right to modify or revoke the order and impose sentence.

R. v. Linklater (1983), 9 C.C.C. (3d) 217 (Y.T. C.A.) — Re-sentencing pursuant to this section does *not* violate the right against double punishment in *Charter* s. 11(b), where the probation order was rehabilitative in effect and not punitive. In any event, if such a prohibition order does violate s. 11(b), it is cured by *Charter* s. 1.

Related Provisions: Dispositions under ss. 732.2(3) and (5) are a "sentence" in ss.673 and 785(1) for appellate purposes under Parts XXI and XXVII, respectively.

It would seem preferable, in light of *Charter* s.7, that D be present at the variation and revocation hearings, as what there transpires may well affect D's liberty.

It would appear that the procedure of s. 732.2(3) (variation) is designed to be somewhat informal. Neither s.732.2 nor s. 732.2(5) contains any formal commencement or notice requirements. Little assistance is afforded by s.738(5) as to the basis upon which the application is to be determined.

Charter s.11(i) guarantees to D the benefit of lesser punishment where the punishment for the offence has been varied between the time of commission and sentencing, as for example where such a variation occurred in the context of a revocation hearing under s. 732.2(5)(d).

733. (1) Transfer of order — Where an offender who is bound by a probation order becomes a resident of, or is convicted or discharged under section 730 of an offence including an offence under section 733.1 in, a territorial division other than the territorial division where the order was made, on the application of a probation officer, the court that made the order may, subject to subsection (1.1), transfer the order to a court in that other territorial division that would, having regard to the mode of trial of the offender, have had jurisdiciton to make the order in that other territorial division if the offender had been tried and convicted there of the offence in respect of which the order was made, and the order may thereafter be dealt with and enforced by the court to which it is so transferred in all respects as if that court had made the order.

(1.1) Attorney General's consent — The transfer may be granted only with

(a) the consent of the Attorney General of the province in which the probation order was made, if the two territorial divisions are not in the same province; or

(b) the consent of the Attorney General of Canada, if the proceedings that led to the issuance of the probation order were instituted by or on behalf of the Attorney General of Canada.

(2) Where court unable to act — Where a court that has made a probation order or to which a probation order has been transferred pursuant to subsection (1) is for any reason unable to act, the powers of that court in relation to the probation order may be exercised by any other court that has equivalent jurisdiction in the same province.

1995, c. 22, s. 6; 1999, c. 5, s. 32.

Commentary: A probation order may be transferred for enforcement purposes to a territorial division other than where it was made.

The transfer mechanism begins by application of the probation officer. It is available where the probationer becomes a resident of, or is convicted or discharged in respect of any offence, including breach of probation, in a territorial division other than where the probation order was made. The application is made to the sentencing court, or, in circumstances of incapacity under s. 733(2), to another court of equivalent jurisdiction in the same province. Consent to transfer proceedings is only required where the territorial division of the original and transfer jurisdiction are not in the same province. It must be given by the Attorney General of the province of the original order. The effect of a transfer is to authorize a court of equivalent jurisdiction in the territorial division to which the order is transferred to enforce the order as if it were the sentencing court. In the event of incapacity of the sentencing court, under s. 733(2), another member of the court to which jurisdiction has been transferred has equivalent authority.

Related Provisions: Variation and revocation proceedings may be taken before the substitute court (court of transfer) under ss. 732.2(3) and (5).

Other related provisions are described in the corresponding note to s. 732.2. "Attorney General" is defined in s. 2.

733.1 (1) Failure to comply with probation order — An offender who is bound by a probation order and who, without reasonable excuse, fails or refuses to comply with that order is guilty of

(a) an indictable offence and is liable to imprisonment for a term not exceeding two years; or

(b) an offence punishable on summary conviction and is liable to imprisonment for a term not exceeding eighteen months, or to a fine not exceeding two thousand dollars, or both.

(2) Where accused may be tried and punished — An accused who is charged with an offence under subsection (1) may be tried and punished by any court having jurisdiction to try that offence in the place where the offence is alleged to have been committed or in the place where the accused is found, is arrested or is in custody, but where the place where the accused is found, is arrested or is in custody is outside the province in which the offence is alleged to have been committed, no proceedings in respect of that offence shall be instituted in that place without the consent of the Attorney General of that province.

1995, c. 22, s. 6.

Commentary: The section creates a hybrid offence of failure or refusal to comply with a probation order and authorizes its trial in various territorial jurisdictions. An 18 month maximum term of imprisonment applies if P proceeds summarily.

The section punishes failure or refusal of a probationer to comply with an order which is without reasonable excuse. Under s. 733.1(2) D maybe tried where the offence is alleged to have been committed, or where D is found, arrested or in custody. Where D is found, arrested or in custody in a province other than that in which the offence is alleged to have been committed, he may be prosecuted only with the consent of the Attorney General of that province.

The predecessor of this section has been the subject of *Charter* s.11 (h) challenge.

Case Law
Res Judicata

R. v. Pinkerton (1979), 7 C.R. (3d) 39, 46 C.C.C. (2d) 284 (B.C. C.A.) — The rule against multiple convictions does *not* apply to a charge of breach of probation arising from the commission of an offence while on probation. Although the two charges arose out of the same incident, they do not have the same or substantially the same elements, nor can they be viewed reasonably as alternative charges. In any event, Parliament has clearly indicated that multiple convictions are envisaged. It was the intention of Parliament that if the conduct of a person constitutes an offence as well as constituting a breach of a probation order, he should be liable to punishment for that offence as well as punishment for breach of the probation order.

R. v. Furlong (1993), 22 C.R. (4th) 193, 81 C.C.C. (3d) 449 (Nfld. C.A.) — Breach of probation and breach of recognizance entail elements which are additional and distinct from one another and relate to the respective culpability of each offence. The respective breaches of the orders, even if both are grounded upon the same act, must be treated as arising from entirely different causes, matters or delicts. (Mahoney and Marshall JJ.A.)

Related Provisions: The section may apply even where the probation order has not been formally transferred under s. 733 to the province where D is found, arrested or in custody.

Under s. 732.1(5), where a court makes a probation order, it must inform D of the provision of this section as well as s. 732.2(5). A conviction under this section may result in an application by P under s. 732.2(5) to revoke the probation order and impose a sentence upon D for the original offence or vary the terms of the order, as the case may be.

The section is an exception to s. 478(1) in that it permits the courts of one province to try offences committed entirely in another province.

Fines and Forfeiture

734. (1) Power of court to impose fine — Subject to subsection (2), a court that convicts a person, other than a corporation, of an offence may fine the offender by making an order under section 734.1

(a) if the punishment for the offence does not include a minimum term of imprisonment, in addition to or in lieu of any other sanction that the court is authorized to impose; or

(b) if the punishment for the offence includes a minimum term of imprisonment, in addition to any other sanction that the court is required or authorized to impose.

(2) Offender's ability to pay — Except when the punishment for an offence includes a minimum fine or a fine is imposed in lieu of a forfeiture order, a court may fine an offender under this section only if the court is satisfied that the offender is able to pay the fine or discharge it under section 736.

(3) Meaning of default of payment — For the purposes of this section and sections 734.1 to 737, a person is in default of payment of a fine if the fine has not been paid in full by the time set out in the order made under section 734.1.

(4) Imprisonment in default of payment — Where an offender is fined under this section, a term of imprisonment, determined in accordance with subsection (5), shall be deemed to be imposed in default of payment of the fine.

(5) Determination of term — The length, in days, of the term of imprisonment referred to in subsection (4) is the lesser of

(a) a fraction, rounded down to the nearest whole number, of which

(i) the numerator is the unpaid amount of the fine plus the costs and charges of committing and conveying the defaulter to prison, calculated in accordance with regulations made under subsection (7), and

(ii) the denominator is equal to eight times the provincial minimum hourly wage, at the time of default, in the province in which the fine was imposed, and

(b) the maximum term of imprisonment, expressed in days, that the court could itself impose on conviction.

(6) Moneys found on offender — All or any part of a fine imposed under this section may be taken out of moneys found in the possession of the offender at the time of the arrest of the offender if the court making the order, on being satisfied that ownership of or right to possession of those moneys is not disputed by claimants other than the offender, so directs.

(7) Provincial regulations — The lieutenant governor in council of a province may make regulations repecting the calculation of the costs and charges referred to in subparagraph (5)(a)(i) and in paragraph 734.8(1)(b).

(8) Application to other law — This section and sections 734.1 to 734.8 and 736 apply to a fine imposed under any Act of Parliament, except that subsections (4) and (5) do not apply if the term of imprisonment in default of payment of the fine provided for in that Act or regulation is

(a) calculated by a different method; or

(b) specified, either as a minimum or a maximum.

1995, c. 22, s. 6; 1999, c. 5, s. 33.

Commentary: Section 734(1) authorizes the imposition of a fine on D who is *not* a corporation, for any offence other than one for which there is a minimum term of imprisonment. The fine may be in addition to or in lieu of any other sanction. The court must be satisfied under s.734(2) that D is able to pay or discharge the fine. A term of imprisonment in default of payment, calculated by formula under s.734(5), is deemed to apply. D is in *default* if the fine has *not* been paid in full by the time specified in the order made under s.734.1. The fine may be taken out of money found in D's possession on his/her arrest, pursuant to s.734(6).

Case Law

Jurisdiction

R. v. Ward (1980), 56 C.C.C. (2d) 15 (Ont. C.A.) — The court has *no* jurisdiction to impose one concurrent fine in respect of separate offences. A separate fine must be imposed on each count for which it is intended that a fine be imposed. Furthermore, a fine so large that it cannot be paid within a reasonable time by the offender should not be imposed in lieu of a jail sentence.

Forthwith

R. v. Arsenault (1984), 55 N.B.R. (2d) 179 (C.A.) — *See also*: *R. v. Brooks* (March 8, 1988), Doc. 01779 (N.S. C.A.) — The imposition of a fine without an investigation of D's ability to pay is an error in principle.

Related Provisions: Under s. 736 a fine may b e discharged, in whole or in part, by an individual accused under a fine option program. A default term may be reduced on partial payment of the fine under s. 734.8. The disposition of fines is governed by s. 734.4 and civil enforcement of fines by s. 734.6. Non-renewal of licences as a consequence of default is authorized by s. 734.5.

The imposition and enforcement of fines on corporate accused is governed by s. 735.

Under s. 683(5), the court of appeal may order, *inter alia*, that any obligation to pay a fine be suspended until an appeal has been determined. The provisions also apply to summary conviction appeals under s. 813, pursuant to s.822(1).

"Court" and "accused" are defined in s. 716.

734.1 Terms of order imposing fine — A court that fines an offender under section 734 shall do so by making an order that clearly sets out

(a) the amount of the fine;

(b) the manner in which the fine is to be paid;

(c) the time or times by which the fine, or any portion thereof, must be paid; and

(d) such other terms respecting the payment of the fine as the court deems appropriate.

1995, c. 22, s. 6.

Commentary: By virtue of s. 734.1 the sentencing court must make an order which clearly specifies various aspects, including the amount of the fine, the manner of its payment, and the time(s) by which it or any portion must be paid.

Related Provisions: The *general* power to impose a fine is set out in s. 734. Under s. 736 a fine may be discharged in whole or in part, by an individual accused under a fine option program. A default term may be reduced on partial payment. The disposition of fines is governed by s. 734.4 and civil enforcement of fines by s. 734.6. Non-renewal of licences as a consequence of default is authorized by s. 734.5.

The imposition and enforcement of fines on corporate accused is governed by s. 735.

Under s. 683(5), the court of appeal may order, *inter alia* that any obligation to pay a fine be suspended until an appeal has been determined. The provisions also apply to summary conviction appeals under s. 813, pursuant to s.822(1).

"Court" and "accused" are defined in s. 716.

734.2 Proceedings on making order — A court that makes an order under section 734.1 shall

(a) cause to be given to the offender

(i) a copy of the order,

(ii) an explanation of the substance of sections 734 to 734.8 and 736,

(iii) an explanation of available programs referred to in section 736 and of the procedure for applying for admission to such programs, and

(iv) an explanation of the procedure for applying under section 734.3 for a change in the terms of the order; and

(b) take reasonable measures to ensure that the offender understands the order and the explanations given to the offender under paragraph (a).

1995, c. 22, s. 6.

Commentary: When a court imposes a fine, pursuant to s. 734.2(a) D must be given a copy of the order and advised of its terms, the consequences of default of payment, the availability of a fine option program, and the procedure for applying for a change in the terms of the order. Under s. 734.2(b) the court must take reasonable measures to ensure that D understands this information.

Related Provisions: The *general* power to impose a fine is set out in s. 734 and the contents of the order in s. 734.1. Application to change an order may be made under s. 734.3. Civil enforcement of fines is governed by s. 734.6 and non-renewal of licences as a consequence of default by s. 734.5. Fine option programs are authorized by s. 736.

734.3 Change in terms of order — A court that makes an order under section 734.1, or a person designated, either by name or by title of office, by that court, may, on application by or on behalf of the offender, subject to any rules made by the court under section 482, change any term of the order except the amount of the fine, and any reference in this section and sections 734, 734.1, 734.2 and 734.6 to an order shall be read as including a reference to the order as changed pursuant to this section.

1995, c. 22, s. 6.

Commentary: Section 734.3 authorizes D to apply to the sentencing court or a person designated by it to change any term of the fine order *except* the amount.

Related Provisions: The general power to impose a fine is set out in s. 734. The making of a fine order is required by s. 734.1, and the proceedings on making such an order are set out in s. 734.2.

734.4 (1) Proceeds to go to provincial treasurer — Where a fine or forfeiture is imposed or a recognizance is forfeited and no provision, other than this section, is made by law for the application of the proceeds thereof, the proceeds belong to Her Majesty in right of the province in which the fine or forfeiture was imposed or the recognizance was forfeited, and shall be paid by the person who receives them to the treasurer of that province.

(2) Proceeds to go to receiver general for Canada — Where

(a) a fine or forfeiture is imposed

(i) in respect of a contravention of a revenue law of Canada,

(ii) in respect of a breach of duty or malfeasance in office by an officer or employee of the Government of Canada, or

(iii) in respect of any proceedings instituted at the instance of the Government of Canada in which that government bears the costs of prosecution, or

(b) a recognizance in connection with proceedings mentioned in paragraph (a) is forfeited, the proceeds of the fine, forfeiture or recognizance belong to Her Majesty in right of Canada and shall be paid by the person who receives them to the Receiver General.

(3) Direction for payment to municipality — Where a provincial, municipal or local authority bears, in whole or in part, the expense of administering the law under which a fine or forfeiture is imposed or under which proceedings are taken in which a recognizance is forfeited,

(a) the Lieutenant Governor in Council of a province may direct that the proceeds of a fine, forfeiture or recognizance that belongs to Her Majesty in right of the province shall be paid to that authority; and

(b) the Governor in Council may direct that the proceeds of a fine, forfeiture or recognizance that belongs to Her Majesty in right of Canada shall be paid to that authority.

Commentary: The section determines who shall receive the proceeds of fines or forfeitures, where there is no other applicable provision.

The general rule of s. 734.4(1) is that the proceeds of fines, penalties or forfeitures belong to Her Majesty in right of the province in which the order was made, and must be paid over to the Provincial Treasurer. Sections 734.4(2) and (3) describe the circumstances under which the proceeds belong to or must be shared with other governmental authorities. Under s. 734.4(2), in the circumstances there described, the proceeds belong to Her Majesty in right of Canada and must be paid to the Receiver General. Under s. 734.4(3) there is provision for sharing, as amongst the various levels of authority, of the proceeds of a fine, penalty or forfeiture where a provincial, municipal or local authority bears, in whole or in part, the expense of administering the law under which the proceeds were collected. The authority to whom the proceeds would normally be payable under s. 734.4(1) or (2) directs payment to the relevant provincial, municipal or local administering authority.

Related Provisions: The general rule of s. 734.4(1) applies only where no other provision is made by law for the application for the proceeds of a fine, penalty or forfeiture. In general, the scheme of 734.4(1) and (2) ensures that the proceeds follow prosecutorial responsibility. Section 734.4(3) endeavours to ensure that other levels of government, charged with the responsibility of administering the laws under which fines, penalties or forfeitures are imposed, recoup part of their administrative costs by receipt of the proceeds of penalties imposed thereunder.

The general rule for civil enforcement of fines and forfeitures is found in s. 734.6.

734.5 Licences, permits, etc. — If an offender is in default of payment of a fine,

(a) where the proceeds of the fine belong to Her Mafesty in right of a province by virtue of subsection 734.4(1), the person responsble, by or under an Act of the legislature of the province, for issuing, renewing or suspending a licence, permit or other similar instrument in relation to the offender may refuse to issue or renew or may suspend the licence, permit or other instrument until the fine is paid in full, proof of which lies on the offender; or

(b) where the proceeds of the fine belong to Her Majesty in right of Canada by virtue of subsection 734.4(2), the person responsible, by or under an Act of Parliament, for issuing or renewing a licence, permit or other similar instrument in relation to the offender may refuse to issue or renew or may suspend the licence, permit or other instrument until the fine is paid in full, proof of which lies on the offender.

1995, c. 22, s. 6; 1999, c . 5, s. 34.

Commentary: Where D is in default of payment of a fine the section authorizes the province to which the proceeds of a fine belongs, or the federal government where the proceeds belong to it, to refuse to renew a licence, permit or other instrument until the fine is paid.

Related Provisions: The general power to impose a fine and the calculation of a term of imprisonment in default is set out in s.734. Civil enforcement of fines is governed by s. 734.6.

734.6 (1) Civil enforcement of fines, forfeiture — Where

    (a) an offender is in default of payment of a fine, or

    (b) a forfeiture imposed by law is not paid as required by the order imposing it,

then, in addition to any other method provided by law for recovering the fine or forfeiture,

    (c) the Attorney General of the province to whom the proceeds of the fine or forfeiture belong, or

    (d) the Attorney General of Canada, where the proceeds of the fine or forfeiture belong to Her Majesty in right of Canada,

may, by filing the order, enter as a judgment the amount of the fine or forfeiture, and costs, if any, in any civil court in Canada that has jurisdiction to enter a judgment for that amount.

(2) Effect of filing order — An order that is entered as a judgment under this section is enforceable in the same manner as if it were a judgment obtained by the Attorney General of the province or the Attorney General of Canada, as the case may be, in civil proceedings.

1995, c. 22, s. 6.

Commentary: Where D is in default of payment of a fine or a forfeiture has not been paid, the order may be filed, and entered and enforced as a judgment in any civil court in Canada with jurisdiction over that amount. Section 734.6(1) stipulates that this is in addition to any other method provided by law for recovery.

Related Provisions: The power to impose a fine is contained in s. 734. The terms of an order imposing a fine are set out in s.734.1. Refusal to issue permits or licences to D who is in default of payment is authorized by s. 734.5.

734.7 (1) Warrant of committal — Where time has been allowed for payment of a fine, the court shall not issue a warrant of committal in default of payment of the fine

    (a) until the expiration of the time allowed for payment of the fine in full; and

    (b) unless the court is satisfied

        (i) that the mechanisms provided by sections 734.5 and 734.6 are not appropriate in the circumstances, or

        (ii) that the offender has, without reasonable excuse, refused to pay the fine or discharge it under section 736.

(2) Reasons for committal — Where no time has been allowed for payment of a fine and a warrant committing the offender to prison for default of payment of the fine is issued, the court shall state in the warrant the reason for immediate committal.

(2.1) Period of imprisonment — The period of imprisonment in default of payment of the fine shall be specified in a warrant of committal referred to in subsection (1) or (2).

(3) Compelling appearance of person bound — The provisions of Parts XVI and XVIII with respect to compelling the appearance of an accused before a justice apply, with such modifications as the circumstances require, to proceedings under paragraph (1)(b).

(4) Effect of imprisonment — The imprisonment of an offender for default of payment of a fine terminates the operation of sections 734.5 and 734.6 in relation to that fine.

1995, c. 22, s. 6; 1999, c. 5, s. 35.

Commentary: Pursuant to s. 734.7(1) a warrant of committal may not issue until the time allowed for payment of the fine in full has expired, and the court is satisfied that refusal to issue a permit or licence and civil enforcement of the fine are not appropriate, or D has refused to pay the fine without reasonable excuse. If no time was allowed for payment, s. 734.7(2) requires the court issuing the warrant of committal to state the reason for immediate committal. D's appearance in court may be compelled under Parts XVI and XVIII. Section 734.7(4) provides that if D is imprisoned for default, payment of the fine may not be enforced civilly, nor may a licence or permit be refused D.

Related Provisions: Section 734.1 governs the terms of orders imposing fines, including time for payment. Refusal to issue permits or licences to D who is in default of payment is authorized in s. 734.5. Section 734.6 provides that fines may be enforced as civil judgments.

734.8 (1) Definition of "penalty" — In this section, "penalty" means the aggregate of

(a) the fine, and

(b) the costs and charges of committing and conveying the defaulter to prison, calculated in accordance with regulations made under subsection 734(7).

(2) Reduction of imprisonment on part payment — The term of imprisonment in default of payment of a fine shall, on payment of a part of the penalty, whether the payment was made before or after the execution of a warrant of committal, be reduced by the number of days that bears the same proportion to the number of days in the term as the part paid bears to the total penalty.

(3) Minimum that can be accepted — No amount offered in part payment of a penalty shall be accepted after the execution of a warrant of committal unless it is sufficient to secure a reduction of sentence of one day, or a whole number multiple of one day, and no part payment shall be accepted until any fee that is payable in respect of the warrant or its execution has been paid.

(4) To whom payment made — Payment may be made under this section to the person that the Attorney General directs or, if the offender is imprisoned, to the person who has lawful custody of the prisoner or to any other person that the Attorney General directs.

(5) Application of money paid — A payment under this section shall be applied firstly to the payment in full of costs and charges, secondly to the payment in full of any victim fine surcharge imposed under subsection 737(1), and thereafter to payment of any part of the fine that remains unpaid.

1995, c. 22, s. 6; 1999, c. 5, s. 36.

Commentary: "Penalty" is defined by s. 734.8(1) as the total of the fine plus the costs of committing and conveying to prison D who has defaulted in payment. Section s. 734.8(1) provides for a pro rata deduction in the number of days in jail, where only partial payment of the penalty is made, and s. 734.8(3) requires that the part payment must be enough to reduce the jail term by one day or a multiple thereof. Under s. 734.8(4) payment may be made to the jailer. Section 734.8(5) requires that the payment be applied first to costs and charges, then to any victim fine surcharge, and lastly to the unpaid portion of the fine.

Related Provisions: A warrant of committal in default of payment may be obtained pursuant to s. 734.7. Victim fine surcharges are authorized by s. 737.

735. (1) Fines on corporations — A corporation that is convicted of an offence is liable, in lieu of any imprisonment that is prescribed as punishment for that offence, to be fined in an amount, except where otherwise provided by law,

    (a) that is in the discretion of the court, where the offence is an indictable offence; or

    (b) not exceeding twenty-five thousand dollars, where the offence is a summary conviction offence.

(1.1) Application of certain provisions — fines — A court that imposes a fine under subsection (1) or under any other Act of Parliament shall make an order that clearly sets out

    (a) the amount of the fine;

    (b) the manner in which the fine is to be paid;

    (c) the time or times by which the fine, or any portion of it, must be paid; and

    (d) any other terms respecting the payment of the fine that the court deems appropriate.

(2) Effect of filing order — Section 734.6 applies, with any modifications that are required, when a corporate offender fails to pay the fine in accordance with the terms of the order.

1995, c. 22, s. 6; 1999, c. 5, s. 37.

Commentary: The section enacts the general punishment provision applicable to corporate accused, but subject to other express enactment. In lieu of imprisonment, a corporate accused convicted of an indictable offence may be fined an amount that is in the discretion of the court. No minimum or maximum is provided. A corporate accused convicted of a summary conviction offence may be fined in a amount not exceeding $25,000. No minimum fine is provided. Fines on corporations may be enforced as civil judgments pursuant to s. 734.6.

Related Provisions: Both this provision and s. 787(1) applicable to summary conviction offences only apply "except where otherwise provided by law".

"Corporation" is not defined in the *Code* but is defined in *I.A.* s. 35(1) so as to exclude partnerships that are considered separate legal entities under provincial law.

736. (1) Fine option program — An offender who is fined under section 734 may, whether or not the offender is serving a term of imprisonment imposed in default of payment of the fine, discharge the fine in whole or in part by earning credits for work performed during a period not greater than two years in a program established for that purpose by the Lieutenant Governor in Council

    (a) of the province in which the fine was imposed, or

    (b) of the province in which the offender resides, where an appropriate agreement is in effect between the government of that province and the government of the province in which the fine was imposed,

if the offender is admissible to such a program.

(2) Credits and other matters — A program referred to in subsection (1) shall determine the rate at which credits are earned and may provide for the manner of crediting any amounts earned against the fine and any other matters necessary for or incidental to carrying out the program.

(3) Deemed payment — Credits earned for work performed as provided by subsection (1) shall, for the purposes of this Act, be deemed to be payment in respect of a fine.

(4) Federal-provincial agreement — Where, by virtue of subsection 734.4(2), the proceeds of a fine belong to Her Majesty in right of Canada, an offender may discharge the fine in whole or in part in a fine option program of a province pursuant to subsection (1), where an appropriate agreement is in effect between the government of the province and the Government of Canada.

1995, c. 22, s. 6.

Note: 1997, c. 18, s. 107 was not in force at the date of publication. This section purported to amend s. 736 of the Criminal Code as it existed prior to the 1995, c. 22 amendments. The reference to s. 736 of the Code has been replaced by s. 730 in accordance with 1995, c. 22, s. 18 (Sch. IV)

Commentary: Section 736(1) permits the discharge of a fine by an individual accused, in whole or in part, by earning credits for work performed during a period of not more than two years in a fine option program, approved by the Lieutenant Governor in Council of the province where the fine was imposed or, in the event of a reciprocal enforcement agreement, in the province where D resides. The program must determine the rate at which credits are earned and, under s. 736(3) they are deemed to be payment in respect of the fine.

Section 736(4) permits the whole or partial discharge of a fine, the proceeds of which under s.734.4(2) belong to Her Majesty in right of Canada, in a fine option program of a province, where the requisite agreement between the Government of Canada and the province is in effect.

Related Provisions: Section 734.4. provides for the destination of the proceeds of, *inter alia*, fines and s.734.6 for their enforcement by way of civil judgments.

Section 735 authorizes the imposition of fines on corporations and their enforcement. The fine option program is not available to corporate accused.

737. (1) Victim fine surcharge — Subject to subsection (2), where an offender is convicted or discharged under section 730 of an offence under this Act or Part III or IV of the *Food and Drugs Act* or the *Narcotic Control Act*, the court imposing sentence on or discharging the offender shall, in addition to any other punishment imposed on the offender, order the offender to pay a victim fine surcharge in an amount not exceeding

(a) fifteen per cent of any fine that is imposed on the offender for that offence or, where no fine is imposed on the offender for that offence, ten thousand dollars, or

(b) such lesser amount as may be prescribed by, or calculated in the manner prescribed by, regulations made by the Governor in Council under subsection (5),

subject to such terms and conditions as may be prescribed by those regulations.

(2) Exception — Where the offender establishes to the satisfaction of the court that undue hardship to the offender or the dependants of the offender would result from the making of an order under subsection (1), the court is not required to make the order.

(3) Written reasons for not making order — Where the court does not make an order under subsection (1), the court shall

(a) provide the reasons why the order is not being made; and

(b) enter the reasons in the record of the proceedings or, where the proceedings are not recorded, provide written reasons.

(4) Amounts applied to aid victims — A victim fine surcharge imposed under subsection (1) shall be applied for the purposes of providing such assistance to victims of offences as the Lieutenant Governor in Council of the province in which the surcharge is imposed may direct from time to time.

(5) Regulations — The Governor in Council may, for the purposes of subsection (1), make regulations prescribing the maximum amount or the manner of calculating the maximum amount of a victim fine surcharge to be imposed under that subsection, not exceeding the amount referred to in paragraph (1)(a), and any terms and conditions subject to which the victim fine surcharge is to be imposed.

(6) Enforcement — Subsections 734(2) to (5) and sections 734.1, 734.3, 734.5 and 734.7 apply, and section 736 does not apply, in respect of a victim fine surcharge imposed under subsection (1).

1995, c. 22, s. 6; 1999, c. 5, s. 38.

Commentary: The section authorizes the order of a VFS upon conviction or discharge under certain federal statutes. The order is in addition to any other punishment which may be imposed on D upon conviction or discharge.

The conjoint effect of ss. 737(1) and (2) makes a VFS mandatory where D has been convicted or found guilty of an offence under the *Code* or under Part III or IV of the *FDA* or *NCA* The sentencing court, in addition to any other punishment, must order a VFS in the amount authorized by s. 737(1) unless D satisfies the court under s. 737(2) that undue hardship to D or D's dependents would result from such an order. Where no VFS order is made, reasons must be given in written or recorded form.

A VFS is applied to provide assistance to victims of offences in accordance with the directions given from time to time by the Lieutenant Governor in Council of the province where it is imposed.

Under s. 737(5), the Governor in Council may make regulations prescribing the maximum amount of VFS, or the manner of its calculation, not exceeding the amount in s. 737(1)(a), as well as any terms and conditions subject to which the VFS is to be imposed.

The provisions concerning ability to pay, default in payment of fines, orders imposing fines, changes in terms of an order and warrants of committal in default of payment apply to a VFS. The fine option program of s. 736 is inapplicable.

The section may be constitutionally vulnerable upon a division-of- powers basis.

Case Law
Constitutionality of VFS

R. v. Crowell (1992), 16 C.R. (4th) 249, 76 C.C.C. (3d) 413 (N.S. C.A.) — While the VFS shares some characteristics of a tax, it is *not* a tax, rather a penalty in the nature of a general kind of restitution. It is structurally different than a tax since it is *not* compulsory. The VFS is penal in its pith and substance, thereby properly a matter for Parliament under s. 91(27) of the *Constitution Act, 1867*.

Related Provisions: A VFS is a "sentence" under s. 673 for the purposes of appeals in indictable matters. It is not included in the expansive definition of "sentence", however, in s. 785 of Part XXVII. Under s. 683(5), upon the filing of a notice of appeal or notice of application for leave to appeal, the court of appeal may order that payment of a VFS be suspended until the appeal has been determined. A VFS is not governed by the stay provisions of s. 689.

Restitution

738. (1) Restitution to victims of offences — Where an offender is convicted or discharged under section 730 of an offence, the court imposing sentence on or discharging the offender may, on application of the Attorney General or on its own motion, in addition to any other measure imposed on the offender, order that that offender make restitution to another person as follows:

(a) in the case of damage to, or the loss or destruction of, the property of any person as a result of the commission of the offence or the arrest or attempted arrest of the offender, by paying to the person an amount not exceeding the replacement value of the property as of the date the order is imposed, less the value of any part of the property that is returned to that person as of the date it is returned, where the amount is readily ascertainable;

(b) in the case of bodily harm to any person as a result of the commission of the offence or the arrest or attempted arrest of the offender, by paying to the person an amount not exceeding all pecuniary damages, including loss of income or support, incurred as a result of the bodily harm, where the amount is readily ascertainable; and

(c) in the case of bodily harm or threat of bodily harm to the offender's spouse or child, or any other person, as a result of the commission of the offence or the arrest or attempted arrest of the offender, where the spouse, child or other person was a member of the offender's household at the relevant time, by paying to the person in question, independently of any amount ordered to be paid under paragraphs (a) and (b), an amount not exceeding actual and reasonable expenses incurred by that person, as a result of moving out of the offender's household, for temporary housing, food, child care and transportation, where the amount is readily ascertainable.

(2) Regulations — The Lieutenant Governor in Council of a province may make regulations precluding the inclusion of provisions on enforcement of restitution orders as an optional condition of a probation order or of a conditional sentence order.

1995, c. 22, s. 6.

Commentary: The section provides that D who is convicted or discharged may be ordered to make restitution to another person for the cost of property damage, pecuniary damages including loss of income in the case of bodily harm, and reasonable living expenses in the case of bodily harm or threat of it. Section 738(1) permits the order to be made on application by the Attorney General or on the court's own motion. It may be imposed in addition to any other measure.

Related Provisions: Restitution to persons acting in good faith is provided for by s. 739. Section 740 gives restitution orders priority over fines and forfeitures. Section 741 permits restitution orders to be enforced as civil judgments.

739. Restitution to persons acting in good faith — Where an offender is convicted or discharged under section 730 of an offence and

(a) any property obtained as a result of the commission of the offence has been conveyed or transferred for valuable consideration to a person acting in good faith and without notice, or

(b) the offender has borrowed money on the security of that property from a person acting in good faith and without notice,

the court may, where that property has been returned to the lawful owner or the person who had lawful possession of that property at the time the offence was committed, order the offender to pay as restitution to the person referred to in paragraph (a) or (b) an amount not exceeding the amount of consideration for that property or the total amount outstanding in respect of the loan, as the case may be.

1995, c. 22, s. 6.

Commentary: The section provides that where property obtained by D's offence has been conveyed to a person acting in good faith, or D has borrowed money from a third person on the security of that property and the property has been returned to the lawful owner or possessor, D may be ordered to pay restitution to the third person.

Related Provisions: The general authority to order restitution is contained in s. 738. Section 740 gives restitution orders priority over fines. Section 741 permits restitution orders to be enforced as civil judgments.

740. Priority to restitution — Where the court finds it applicable and appropriate in the circumstances of a case to make, in relation to an offender, an order of restitution under section 738 or 739, and

   (a) an order of forfeiture under this or any other Act of Parliament may be made in respect of property that is the same as property in respect of which the order of restitution may be made, or

   (b) the court is considering ordering the offender to pay a fine and it appears to the court that the offender would not have the means or ability to comply with both the order of restitution and the order to pay the fine,

the court shall first make the order of restitution and shall then consider whether and to what extent an order of forfeiture or an order to pay a fine is appropriate in the circumstances.

1995, c. 22, s. 6.

Commentary: The section requires the sentencing court to first make an order of restitution before imposing an order of forfeiture in respect of the same property, or imposing a fine if D is unable to pay both a fine and restitution.

Related Provisions: The general authority to order restitution is contained in s. 738 and restitution to persons acting in good faith is provided for by s. 739. Section 741 permits restitution orders to be enforced as civil judgments.

741. (1) Enforcing restitution order — Where an amount that is ordered to be paid under section 738 or 739 is not paid forthwith, the person to whom the amount was ordered to be paid may, by filing the order, enter as a judgment the amount ordered to be paid in any civil court in Canada that has jurisdiction to enter a judgment for that amount, and that judgment is enforceable against the offender in the same manner as if it were a judgment rendered against the offender in that court in civil proceedings.

(2) Moneys found on offender — All or any part of an amount that is ordered to be paid under section 738 or 739 may be taken out of moneys found in the possession of the offender at the time of the arrest of the offender if the court making the order, on being satisfied that ownership of or right to possession of those moneys is not disputed by claimants other than the offender, so directs.

1995, c. 22, s. 6.

Commentary: Section 741(1) permits unpaid restitution orders to be entered as civil judgments. Under s.741(2), money found on D on arrest may be applied in payment of a restitution order.

Related Provisions: The general authority to order restitution is contained in s. 738 and restitution to persons acting in good faith is provided for by s. 739.

741.1 Notice of orders of restitution — Where a court makes an order of restitution under section 738 or 739, it shall cause notice of the content of the order, or a copy of the order, to be given to the person to whom the restitution is ordered to be paid.

1995, c. 22, s. 6.

Commentary: The sentencing court must provide a copy of the restitution order or to give notice of it to V who is to receive the restitution.

Related Provisions: The general power to order restitution is set out in ss. 738 and 739.

741.2 Civil remedy not affected — A civil remedy for an act or omission is not affected by reason only that an order for restitution under section 738 or 739 has been made in respect of that act or omission.

1995, c. 22, s. 6.

Commentary: A restitution order does *not* affect any civil remedy for the underlying conduct.

Related Provisions: The general power to order restitution is contained in ss. 738 and 739.

Conditional Sentence of Imprisonment

742. Definitions — In sections 742.1 to 742.7,

"change", in relation to optional conditions, includes deletions and additions;

"optional conditions" means the conditions referred to in subsection 742.3(2);

"supervisor" means a person designated by the Attorney General, either by name or by title of office, as a supervisor for the purposes of sections 742.1 to 742.7.

1995, c. 22, s. 6.

Commentary: The section provides definitions of the words "change", "optional conditions" and "supervisor" that apply to all *Code* sections respecting conditional sentences of imprisonment.

Related Provisions: Section 742.1 authorizes the imposition of a conditional sentence of imprisonment and s. 742.3 specifies those conditions that must be included in the order, as well as those that are optional. The procedure for changing conditions is set out in s. 742.4 and for transferring the order to another territorial division in s. 742.5. The procedure in the event of breach of a condition is contained in s. 742.6

742.1 Imposing of conditional sentence — Where a person is convicted of an offence, except an offence that is punishable by a minimum term of imprisonment, and the court

 (a) imposes a sentence of imprisonment of less than two years, and

 (b) is satisfied that serving the sentence in the community would not endanger the safety of the community and would be consistent with the fundamental purpose and principles of sentencing set out in sections 718 to 718.2,

the court may, for the purposes of supervising the offender's behaviour in the community, order that the offender serve the sentence in the community, subject to the offender's complying with the conditions of a conditional sentence order made under section 742.3.

1995, c. 22, s. 6; 1997, c. 18, s. 107.1.

Commentary: Under this section, D may serve his/her sentence in the community where s/he is convicted of an offence. The offence must *not* be punishable by a *minimum* term of imprisonment, and the sentence must be *less* than two years. The court must also be satisfied that the safety of the community would *not* be endangered. D must comply with the terms of a conditional sentence order.

Case Law

General Principles

R. v. Sidhu (1998), 129 C.C.C. (3d) 26, 19 C.R. (5th) 334 (B.C. C.A.) — Section 742.1(b), as amended, merely clarifies the previous version of the section. Sentencing judges should give effect to the amended section when sentencing individuals, even if the offences occurred before the present section came into effect.

R. v. Stevens (1997), 121 C.C.C. (3d) 193 (B.C. C.A.) — Section 742.1 applies to all crimes that do not carry a minimum term of imprisonment where the sentence imposed is less than two years. Offences should *not* be classified for sentencing purposes.

R. v. Stevens (1997), 115 C.C.C. (3d) 372 (Man. C.A.) — As a result of the recent emphasis on remedial sentences, a trial judge ought be reluctant to incarcerate a person who is a good candidate for rehabilitation. Denunciation and general deterrence may both be achieved by a conditional sentence.

R. v. W. (L.F.) (1997), 119 C.C.C. (3d) 97 (Nfld. C.A.) — The courts may not exempt certain categories of offences from the conditional sentence scheme, nor impose more rigorous standards for its application to them. The process defined by s. 742.1(b) provides adequate scope to give due weight to deterrence, denunciation and other relevant considerations.

R. v. Alfred (1998), 122 C.C.C. (3d) 213 (Ont. C.A.) — A trial judge cannot, in effect, impose a penitentiary sentence, part of which is to be served as a conditional sentence.

R. v. Ly (1997), 5 C.R. (5th) 163, 114 C.C.C. (3d) 279 (Ont. C.A.) — It is only rarely that s. 742.1 will be applicable to charges of trafficking in narcotics.

R. v. Pierce (1997), 5 C.R. (5th) 171, 114 C.C.C. (3d) 23 (Ont. C.A.) — In the context of crimes of dishonesty, especially those which involve a breach of trust, in order to resolve the issue whether community service of the sentence would endanger the safety of the community, the risk of endangering the safety of the community must be assessed by reference to

i.   the danger that the particular offender may pose; and,

ii.   the danger that others may pose,

if the offender is permitted to serve the sentence in the community.

A judge should decide first whether the circumstances of offence and offender call for a penitentiary sentence, as opposed to a reformatory sentence.

Where a penitentiary sentence is apt, a conditional sentence is *not* available.

Where a reformatory sentence is appropriate, the full panoply of sentencing guidelines ought be considered to determine the length and method of service of the sentence. The approach should be global and consider all relevant *Code* guidelines. The ultimate duty of the trial is the imposition of a fit sentence which should

i.   be responsive to all the *Code* sentencing guidelines; and

ii.   reflect, where possible, the new sentencing direction in s. 742.1.

R. v. Wismayer (1997), 5 C.R. (5th) 248, 115 C.C.C. (3d) 18 (Ont. C.A.) — There is *no* absolute entitlement to a conditional sentence. The sentencing judge must decide whether it is appropriate in all of the circumstances.

The principles and objectives of sentencing are *not* wholly exhausted when a judge decides to impose a term of imprisonment of less than two years. They must also be considered in deciding whether to impose a conditional sentence.

Section 742.1 is *not* restricted to any particular kind of offence and is available even where, absent appropriate controls, there may be some risk of D re-offending. The issue is not simply whether D will endanger the community if not in custody, rather, whether the community will be endangered if D is required to serve the sentence of imprisonment in the community, subject to the terms of a conditional sentence order.

In determining the length of a conditional sentence, the trial judge should bear in mind

i.   that D may end up serving the sentence in prison; and

ii.   that the community service portion of the sentence is not subject to reduction through parole.

The primary consideration in determining whether to impose a conditional sentence is the express statutory factor of danger to the community.

R. v. Jean (1997), 116 C.C.C. (3d) 565 (Que. C.A.) — Where the sentence a trial judge decides to impose does not exceed two years, s/he should decide

i.   whether having D serve the sentence in the community would not endanger the safety of the community; and,

ii. whether in light of all the principles and objectives of sentencing, community service is appropriate.

The assessment of danger for the safety of the community is to be made in light of the possibility of any threat to

i. physical;

ii. material; and

iii. at times, moral or psychological

safety to which D's presence in the community may give rise. The assessment must consider the points of view of both D and his/her community.

R. v. Maheu (1997), 116 C.C.C. (3d) 361 (Que. C.A.) — The public safety component of s. 742.1 includes the risk of recidivism. If the safety of the public will be endangered by community service, a conditional sentence may not be imposed.

R. v. Horvath (1997), 117 C.C.C. (3d) 110 (Sask. C.A.) — Section 742.1 requires three separate and distinct basic decisions.

A judge should decide first whether a sentence of imprisonment ought be imposed and, if so, its length. This foundation decision should be made as if s. 742.1 did not exist.

Where there is no minimum sentence or the sentence imposed is less than two years, the judge must decide whether community service of the sentence would endanger the safety of the community.

Where community service of the sentence would not endanger the community safety, the final decision is whether the sentence should, in fact, be served in the community.

Variation of Sentence

R. v. S. (R.N.) (1997), 121 C.C.C. (3d) 426 (B.C. C.A.); application for leave to appeal (February 3, 1998), Doc. 26462 (S.C.C.) — Where D has been sentenced *prior* to the proclamation of the conditional sentence provisions, s. 44(e) *I.A.* permits the court of appeal to consider the appropriatensess of a conditional sentence on an appeal heard after proclamation.

R. v. R. (R.A.) (1997), 125 C.C.C. (3d) 558 (Man. C.A.); leave to appeal granted (1997), 227 N.R. 297n (S.C.C.) — *See also: R. v. Bunn* (1997), 125 C.C.C. (3d) 570 (Man. C.A.); leave to appeal granted (1998), 227 N.R. 297n (S.C.C.)Where conditional sentencing provisions, *not* in force at the *time* of *sentencing*, are in force at the *time* of the determination of a sentence *appeal*, the court of appeal may impose a conditional sentence in accordance with the law then in force.

R. v. Dowd (1997), 120 C.C.C. (3d) 360 (N.B. C.A.) — As a result of *Charter* s. 11(i), a court of appeal may vary a sentence of imprisonment prior to proclamation of s. 742.1 to a conditional sentence.

R. v. Fleet (1997), 120 C.C.C. (3d) 457 (Ont. C.A.) — Where a court of appeal is asked to impose a sentencing option not available at trial, for example, a conditional sentence, as much information as possible about D's current circumstances should be provided. The material should also indicate

i. the suitability of D for a conditional sentence;

ii. the conditions proposed to protect the community; and

iii. how the proposed sentence meets the other principles and objectives of sentencing.

Related Provisions: The compulsory and optional terms of a conditional sentence order are set out in s. 742.3. The procedure for changing conditions is set out in s. 742.4 and for transferring the order to another territorial division in s. 742.5. The procedure for breach of a condition is contained in s. 742.6

742.2 (1) Firearm, etc., prohibitions — Before imposing a conditional sentence under section 742.1, the court shall consider whether section 100 is applicable.

(2) Idem — For greater certainty, a condition of a conditional sentence referred to in paragraph 742.3(2)(b) does not affect the operation of section 100.

1995, c. 22, s. 6.

Commentary: By virtue of s. 742.1(1), before the court imposes a conditional sentence, it must consider the applicability of a firearms prohibition order. A provision of the conditional sentence order which requires D to abstain from owning, possessing or carrying a weapon does *not* interfere with the operation of a s. 100 order.

Related Provisions: The compulsory and optional conditions of a conditional sentence order are set out in s. 742.3. Firearms prohibition orders are governed by s. 100.

742.3 (1) Compulsory conditions of conditional sentence order — The court shall prescribe, as conditions of a conditional sentence order, that the offender do all of the following:

(a) keep the peace and be of good behaviour;

(b) appear before the court when required to do so by the court;

(c) report to a supervisor

(i) within two working days, or such longer period as the court directs, after the making of the conditional sentence order, and

(ii) thereafter, when required by the supervisor and in the manner directed by the supervisor;

(d) remain within the jurisdiction of the court unless written permission to go outside that jurisdiction is obtained from the court or the supervisor; and

(e) notify the court or the supervisor in advance of any change of name or address, and promptly notify the court or the supervisor of any change of employment or occupation.

(2) **Optional conditions of conditional sentence order** — The court may prescribe, as additional conditions of a conditional sentence order, that the offender do one or more of the following:

(a) abstain from

(i) the consumption of alcohol or other intoxicating substances, or

(ii) the consumption of drugs except in accordance with a medical prescription;

(b) abstain from owning, possessing or carrying a weapon;

(c) provide for the support or care of dependants;

(d) perform up to 240 hours of community service over a period not exceeding eighteen months;

(e) attend a treatment program approved by the province; and

(f) comply with such other reasonable conditions as the court considers desirable, subject to any regulations made under subsection 738(2), for securing the good conduct of the offender and for preventing a repetition by the offender of the same offence or the commission of other offences.

(3) **Proceedings on making order** — A court that makes an order under this section shall

(a) cause to be given to the offender

(i) a copy of the order,

(ii) an explanation of the substance of sections 742.4 and 742.6, and

(iii) an explanation of the procedure for applying under section 742.4 for a change to the optional conditions; and

(b) take reasonable measures to ensure that the offender understands the order and the explanations given to the offender under paragraph (a).

1995, c. 22, s. 6.

Commentary: Section 742.3(1) sets out those conditions of a conditional sentence order which are compulsory. Optional conditions are contained in s. 742.3(2). Section 742.3(3) requires the court to ensure that D receives and understands a copy of the conditional sentence order, an explanation of any firearms prohibition order, the procedure upon breach of a condition, and the procedure for applying for a change to the conditions of the order.

Case Law

Other Reasonable Conditions: S. 742.3(2)(f)

R. v. Sidhn (1998), 129 C.C.C. (3d) 26, 19 C.R. (5th) 334 (B.C. C.A.) — A condition of *house arrest* may be imposed under s. 742.3(2)(f) for the purposes of rehabilitation and maintenance of rehabilitation of D.

Related Provisions: See the corresponding note to ss. 742 and 742.1, *supra*.

742.4 (1) Supervisor may propose changes to optional conditions —

Where an offender's supervisor is of the opinion that a change in cirumstances makes a change to the optional conditions desirable, the supervisor shall give written notification of the proposed change, and the reasons for it, to the offender, to the prosecutor and to the court.

(2) Hearing — Within seven days after receiving a notification referred to in subsection (1),

(a) the offender or the prosecutor may request the court to hold a hearing to consider the proposed change, or

(b) the court may, of its own initiative, order that a hearing be held to consider the proposed change,

and a hearing so requested or ordered shall be held within thirty days after the receipt by the court of the notification referred to in subsection (1).

(3) Decision at hearing — At a hearing held pursuant to subsection (2), the court

(a) shall approve or refuse to approve the proposed change; and

(b) may make any other change to the optional conditions that the court deems appropriate.

(4) Where no hearing requested or ordered — Where no request or order for a hearing is made within the time period stipulated in subsection (2), the proposed change takes effect fourteen days after the receipt by the court of the notification referred to in subsection (1), and the supervisor shall so notify the offender and file proof of that notification with the court.

(5) Changes proposed by offender or prosecutor — Subsections (1) and (3) apply, with such modifications as the circumstances require, in respect of a change proposed by the offender or the prosecutor to the optional conditions, and in all such cases a hearing must be held, and must be held within thirty days after the receipt by the court of the notification referred to in subsection (1).

(6) Judge may act in chambers — All the functions of the court under this section may be exercised in chambers.

1995, c. 22, s. 6; 1999, c. 5, s. 39.

Commentary: The section permits D's supervisor to initiate a change in the optional conditions of a conditional sentence order, by notifying D, P and the court in writing. By virtue of s. 742.4(4), where there is no request for a hearing, the proposed change takes effect 14 days after the court receives notification. The supervisor notifies D of this. Sections 742.4.(2) and (3) provide for a hearing where D or P request it or the court requires it, at which time the court can refuse or approve the change, or make changes to any other optional conditions.

Under s. 742.4(5), D or P can initiate a change in the optional conditions but in such cases a hearing must be held. Section 742.4(6) permits hearings to take place in chambers.

Related Provisions: See the corresponding note to ss. 742 and 742.1, *supra*.

742.5 (1) Transfer of order — Where an offender who is bound by a conditional sentence order becomes a resident of a territorial division, other than the territorial division where the order was made, on the application of a supervisor, the court that made the order may, subject to subsection (1.1), transfer the order to a court in that other territorial division that would, having regard to the mode of trial of the offender, have had jurisdiction to make the order in that other territorial division if the offender had been tried and convicted there of the offence in respect of which the order was made, and the order may thereafter be dealt with and enforced by the court to which it is so transferred in all respects as if that court had made the order.

(1.1) Attorney General's consent — The transfer may be granted only with

(a) the consent of the Attorney General of the province in which the conditional sentence order was made, if the two territorial divisions are not in the same province; or

(b) the consent of the Attorney General of Canada, if the proceedings that led to the issuance of the conditional sentence order were instituted by or on behalf of the Attorney General of Canada.

(2) Where court unable to act — Where a court that has made a conditional sentence order or to which a conditional sentence order has been transferred pursuant to subsection (1) is for any reason unable to act, the powers of that court in relation to the conditional sentence order may be exercised by any other court that has equivalent jurisdiction in the same province.

1995, c. 22, s. 6; 1999, c. 5, s. 40.

Commentary: The section permits the transfer of a conditional sentence order where D moves from one territorial division to another. On application from the supervisor, and where the territorial divisions are not in the same province, on the consent of the Attorney General of the original province, the original court transfers the order to a court of concurrent jurisdiction in the new territorial division pursuant to s. 742.5(1).

Under s. 742.5(1), where the judge who made the original order or the new judge is unable to act, his/her powers may be exercised by another judge of equivalent jurisdiction in the same province.

Related Provisions: See the corresponding note to ss. 742 and 742.1, *supra*.

742.6 (1) Procedure on breach of condition — For the purpose of proceedings under this section,

(a) the provisions of Parts XVI and XVIII with respect to compelling the appearance of an accused before a justice apply, with any modifications that the circumstances require, and any reference in those Parts to committing an offence shall be read as a reference to breaching a condition of a conditional sentence order;

(b) the powers of arrest for breach of a condition are those that apply to an indictable offence, with any modifications that the circumstances require, and subsection 495(2) does not apply;

(c) despite paragraph (a), if an allegation of breach of condition is made, the proceeding is commenced by

(i) the issuance of a warrant for the arrest of the offender for the alleged breach,

(ii) the arrest without warrant of the offender for the alleged breach, or

(iii) the compelling of the offender's appearance in accordance with paragraph (d);

(d) if the offender is already detained or before a court, the offender's appearance may be compelled under the provisions referred to in paragraph (a);

(e) if an offender is arrested for the alleged breach, the peace officer who makes the arrest, the officer in charge or a judge or justice may release the offender and the offender's appearance may be compelled under the provisions referred to in paragraph (a); and

(f) any judge of a superior court of criminal jurisdiction or of a court of criminal jurisdiction or any justice of the peace may issue a warrant to arrest no matter which court, judge or justice sentenced the offender, and the provisions that apply to the issuance of telewarrants apply, with any modifications that the circumstances require, as if a breach of condition were an indictable offence.

(2) **Interim release** — For the purpose of the application of section 515, the release from custody of an offender who is detained on the basis of an alleged breach of a condition of a conditional sentence order shall be governed by subsection 515(6).

(3) **Hearing** — The hearing of an allegation of a breach of condition shall be commenced within thirty days, or as soon thereafter as is practicable, after

(a) the offender's arrest; or

(b) the compelling of the offender's appearance in accordance with paragraph (1)(d).

(3.1) **Place** — The allegation may be heard by any court having jurisdiction to hear that allegation in the place where the breach is alleged to have been committed or the offender is found, arrested or in custody.

(3.2) **Attorney General's consent** — If the place where the offender is found, arrested or in custody is outside the province in which the breach is alleged to have been committed, no proceedings in respect of that breach shall be instituted in that place without

(a) the consent of the Attorney General of the province in which the breach is alleged to have been committed; or

(b) the consent of the Attorney General of Canada, if the proceedings that led to the issuance of the conditional sentence order were instituted by or on behalf of the Attorney General of Canada.

(3.3) **Adjournment** — A judge may, at any time during a hearing of an allegation of breach of condition, adjourn the hearing for a reasonable period.

(4) **Report of supervisor** — An allegation of a breach of condition must be supported by a written report of the supervisor, which report must include, where appropriate, signed statements of witnesses.

(5) **Admission of report on notice of intent** — The report is admissible in evidence if the party intending to produce it has, before the hearing, given the offender reasonable notice and a copy of the report.

(6) **Proof of service** — Service of any report referred to in subsection (4) may be proved by oral evidence given under oath by, or by the affidavit or solemn declaration of, the person claiming to have served it.

(7) **Attendance for examination** — Notwithstanding subsection (6), the court may require the person who appears to have signed an affidavit or solemn declaration referred to in that subsection to appear before it for examination or cross-examination in respect of the issue of proof of service.

(8) **Requiring attendance of supervisor or witness** — The offender may, with leave of the court, require the attendance, for cross-examination, of the supervisor or of any witness whose signed statement is included in the report.

(9) **Powers of court** — Where the court is satisfied, on a balance of probabilities, that the offender has without reasonable excuse, the proof of which lies on the offender, breached a condition of the conditional sentence order, the court may

    (a) take no action;

    (b) change the optional conditions;

    (c) suspend the conditional sentence order and direct

        (i) that the offender serve in custody a portion of the unexpired sentence, and

        (ii) that the conditional sentence order resume on the offender's release from custody, either with or without changes to the optional conditions; or

    (d) terminate the conditional sentence order and direct that the offender be committed to custody until the expiration of the sentence.

(10) **Warrant or arrest — suspension of running of conditional sentence** — The running of a conditional sentence imposed on an offender is suspended during the period that ends with the determination of whether a breach of condition had occurred and begins with the earliest of

    (a) the issuance of a warrant for the arrest of the offender for the alleged breach,

    (b) the arrest without warrant of the offender for the alleged breach, and

    (c) the compelling of the offender's appearance in accordance with paragraph (1)(d).

(11) **Conditions continue** — If the offender is not detained in custody during any period referred to in subsection (10), the conditions of the order continue to apply, with any changes made to them under section 742.4, and any subsequent breach of those conditions may be dealt with in accordance with this section.

(12) **Detention under s. 515(6)** — A conditional sentence referred to in subsection (10) starts running again on the making of an order to detain the offender in custody under subsection 515(6) and, unless section 742.7 applies, continues running while the offender is detained under the order.

(13) **Earned remission does not apply** — Section 6 of the *Prisons and Reformatories Act* does not apply to the period of detention in custody under subsection 515(6).

(14) Unreasonable delay in execution — Despite subsection (10), if there was unreasonable delay in the execution of a warrant, the court may, at any time, order that any period between the issuance and execution of the warrant that it considers appropriate in the interest of justice is deemed to be time served under the conditional sentence unless the period has been so deemed under subsection (15).

(15) Allegation dismissed or reasonable excuse — If the allegation is withdrawn or dismissed or the offender is found to have had a reasonable excuse for the breach, the sum of the following periods is deemed to be time served under the conditional sentence:

(a) any period for which the running of the conditional sentence was suspended; and

(b) if subsection (12) applies, a period equal to one half of the period that the conditional sentence runs while the offender is detained under an order referred to in that subsection.

(16) Powers of court — If a court is satisfied, on a balance of probabilities, that the offender has without reasonable excuse, the proof of which lies on the offender, breached a condition of the conditional sentence order, the court may, in exceptional cases and in the interests of justice, order that some or all of the period of suspension referred to in subsection (10) is deemed to be time served under the conditional sentence.

(17) Considerations — In exercising its discretion under subsection (16), a court shall consider

(a) the circumstances and seriousness of the breach;

(b) whether not making the order would cause the offender undue hardship based on the offender's individual circumstances; and

(c) the period for which the offender was subject to conditions while the running of the conditional sentence was suspended and whether the offender complied with those conditions during that period.

1995, c. 22, s. 6; 1999, c. 5, s. 41.

Commentary: The section sets out the procedure to be followed where a breach of condition is alleged. D may be compelled to appear before a justice by way of Parts XVI and XVIII. Pursuant to s. 742.6(3) a hearing will be held within 30 days of D's arrest, either in the place where s/he has been found, or in the place where s/he allegedly committed the breach. Under ss. 742.6(4) and (5) a written report must be prepared by the supervisor which is admissible only if D has been given reasonable notice and a copy of it. The supervisor may be required to attend in court for cross-examination under s. 742.6(8). Where the court is satisfied on a balance of probabilities that D has breached a condition without reasonable excuse, the court pursuant to s. 742.6(9) can change the optional conditions, suspend the order and require D to serve a portion of the unexpired sentence in custody, terminate the order so that D serves the remainder of the sentence in custody, or do nothing.

Related Provisions: See the corresponding note to ss. 742 and 742.1, *supra*.

742.7 (1) If person imprisoned for new offence — If an offender who is subject to a conditional sentence is imprisoned as a result of a sentence imposed for another offence, whenever committed, the running of the conditional sentence is suspended during the period of imprisonment for that other offence.

(2) Breach of condition — If an order is made under paragraph 742.6(9)(c) or (d) to commit an offender to custody, the custodial period ordered shall, unless the court

1105

considers that it would not be in the interests of justice, be served consecutively to any other period of imprisonmnent that the offender is serving when that order is made.

(3) Multiple sentences — If an offender is serving both a custodial period referred to in subsection (2) and any other period of imprisonment, the periods shall, for the purpose of section 743.1 and section 139 of the *Corrections and Conditional Release Act*, be deemed to constitute one sentence of imprisonment.

(4) Conditional sentence resumes — The running of any period of the conditional sentence that is to be served in the community resumes upon the release of the offender from prison on parole, on statutory release, on earned remission, or at the expiration of the sentence.

1995, c. 22, s. 6; 1999, c. 5, s. 42.

Commentary: Under this section, where D has been sentenced to imprisonment while at large under a conditional sentence, the conditional sentence is suspended, unless the court orders otherwise.

Related Provisions: See the corresponding note to ss. 742 and 742.1, *supra*.

Imprisonment

743. Imprisonment when no other provision — Every one who is convicted of an indictable offence for which no punishment is specially provided is liable to imprisonment for a term not exceeding five years.

1995, c. 22, s. 6.

Commentary: The section enacts a general punishment provision upon conviction of an indictable offence. It applies only where no punishment is specifically provided for the offence.

Related Provisions: *Charter* s. 11(f) guarantees D the benefit of trial by jury where the maximum punishment for the offence is imprisonment for five years or a more severe punishment.

Sections 126 and 127 enact general punishment provisions for disobeying a statute or a lawful order of a court of justice or person or body of persons authorized to make or give an order, other than an order for the payment of money. In each case, where no other provision is made therefor, the maximum punishment is imprisonment for a term not exceeding two years.

743.1 (1) Imprisonment for life or more than two years — Except where otherwise provided, a person who is sentenced to imprisonment for

    (a) life,

    (b) a term of two years or more, or

    (c) two or more terms of less than two years each that are to be served one after the other and that, in the aggregate, amount to two years or more,

shall be sentenced to imprisonment in a penitentiary.

(2) Subsequent term less than two years — Where a person who is sentenced to imprisonment in a penitentiary is, before the expiration of that sentence, sentenced to imprisonment for a term of less than two years, the person shall serve that term in a penitentiary, but if the previous sentence of imprisonment in a penitentiary is set aside, that person shall serve that term in accordance with subsection (3).

(3) Imprisonment for term less than two years — A person who is sentenced to imprisonment and who is not required to be sentenced as provided in subsection (1) or (2) shall, unless a special prison is prescribed by law, be sentenced to imprisonment in a prison or other place of confinement, other than a penitentiary, within the province in which the person is convicted, in which the sentence of imprisonment may be lawfully executed.

(3.1) Long-term supervision — Notwithstanding subsection (3), an offender who is required to be supervised by an order made under paragraph 753.1(3)(b) and who is sentenced for another offence during the period of the supervision shall be sentenced to imprisonment in a penitentiary.

(4) Sentence to penitentiary of person serving sentence elsewhere — Where a person is sentenced to imprisonment in a penitentiary while the person is lawfully imprisoned in a place other than a penitentiary, that person shall, except where otherwise provided, be sent immediately to the penitentiary, and shall serve in the penitentiary the unexpired portion of the term of imprisonment that the person was serving when sentenced to the penitentiary as well as the term of imprisonment for which that person was sentenced to the penitentiary.

(5) Transfer to penitentiary — Where, at any time, a person who is imprisoned in a prison or place of confinement other than a penitentiary is subject to two or more terms of imprisonment, each of which is for less than two years, that are to be served one after the other, and the aggregate of the unexpired portions of those terms at that time amounts to two years or more, the person shall be transferred to a penitentiary to serve those terms, but if any one or more of such terms is set aside or reduced and the unexpired portions of the remaining term or terms on the day on which that person was transferred under this section amounted to less than two years, that person shall serve that term or terms in accordance with subsection (3).

(6) Newfoundland — For the purposes of subsection (3), "penitentiary" does not, until a day to be fixed by order of the Governor in Council, include the facility mentioned in subsection 15(2) of the *Corrections and Conditional Release Act*.

1995, c. 22, s. 6; 1997, c. 17, s. 1.

Commentary: Where D's sentence consists, in whole or in part, of a term of imprisonment, this section generally determines the place of imprisonment.

Under s. 743.1(1), and except where otherwise provided, D, sentenced to imprisonment for a term of two years or more, whether as an individual or aggregate of two or more terms, and including imprisonment for life, must be sentenced to imprisonment in a penitentiary. Under s. 743.1(2) penitentiary inmates, who, whilst there confined, are sentenced to a further term of imprisonment of less than two years, must serve the later imposed sentence in a penitentiary, unless the earlier penitentiary sentence is set aside, in which case they shall serve that term in accordance with s. 743.1(3). Under s. 743.1(3), persons sentenced to a term of imprisonment that neither s. 743.1(1) or (2) requires to be served in a penitentiary, must be sentenced to imprisonment in a prison or other place of confinement in a province other than a penitentiary.

Sections 743.1(4) and (5) provide for the transfer of non- penitentiary inmates in other institutions to the penitentiary when further sentences of imprisonment are imposed. Under s. 743.1(4), the imposition of a penitentiary term on a non-penitentiary inmate requires immediate transfer of the inmate to the penitentiary to serve the unexpired portion of the non-penitentiary sentence, as well as the penitentiary sentence, except where otherwise provided. Under s. 743.1(5) where D, a non-penitentiary inmate, is subject to consecutive sentences that aggregate two years or more, those sentences will be served in a penitentiary, unless any one or more of them are set aside and varied to an aggregate of less than two years on the date of transfer, in which case the sentence will be served in a provincial institution under s. 743.1(3).

Case Law

Subsequent Term Less Than Two Years

Olson v. R. (1980), 50 C.C.C. (2d) 275 (S.C.C.) — Where D is imprisoned in a penitentiary at the time sentence is imposed for offences committed while on mandatory supervision, the sentence is properly served in a penitentiary even though it is a term of less than two years.

Dinardo v. R. (1982), 67 C.C.C. (2d) 505 (Ont. C.A.) — A prisoner who is convicted and sentenced to a term of less than two years while on mandatory supervision is required to serve the sentence in a federal penitentiary.

Place of Imprisonment

R. v. Deans (1977), 39 C.R.N.S. 338, 37 C.C.C. (2d) 221 (Ont. C.A.) — *See also*: *R. v. McCullough* (1983), 3 C.C.C. (3d) 432 (Alta. C.A.) — Where D is sentenced to a term of two years or more, he must be sentenced to imprisonment in a penitentiary. If the court wishes D to receive treatment at a mental health centre or other psychiatric facility, such objective can only be achieved by a *recommendation* to the appropriate authority that D serve his sentence at such facility in order to receive the appropriate treatment. The recommendation should not be made absent satisfactory evidence that the centre is willing to accept D who is willing to accept treatment.

Related Provisions: "Prison" is defined in s. 2 and prison breach made an indictable offence under s. 144. Other escape offences are found in ss. 145(1), 146 and 147. Section 149 describes the manner in which sentences for escapes committed whilst undergoing imprisonment shall be served.

Upon sentence to a term of imprisonment, a warrant of committal is issued, executed and D delivered to the keeper of a prison under s. 744. The actual institution and manner in which the sentence is served is determined by the applicable correctional statute and regulations under s. 743.3 and the authorities in charge of such institutions.

743.2 Report by court to correctional service — **A court that sentences or commits a person to penitentiary shall forward to the Correctional Service of Canada its reasons and recommendation relating to the sentence or committal, any relevant reports that were submitted to the court, and any other information relevant to administering the sentence or committal.**

1995, c. 22, s. 6.

Commentary: The section requires a court which sentences or commits a person to penitentiary to forward to the Correctional Services of Canada:

i.   the *reasons* and *recommendations* relating to the sentence or committal;

ii.   any relevant *reports* submitted to the court; and

iii. any other *information* relevant to the administration of the sentence or committal.

Related Provisions: "Court" is defined in s. 716 to include all levels of trial court and "a court that hears an appeal". "Penitentiary" is defined in s. 2(1) of the *Correctional and Conditional Release Act* (C.C.R.A.) for the purposes of Part I of the Act.

Under s. 760, a court which finds D to be a dangerous offender and imposes a sentence of detention in a penitentiary for an indeterminate period is required to order that a copy of specified materials, including a transcript of trial proceedings, be furnished to the Solicitor General of Canada for his or her information.

743.3 Sentence served according to regulations — **A sentence of imprisonment shall be served in accordance with the enactments and rules that govern the institution to which the prisoner is sentenced.**

1995, c. 22, s. 6.

Commentary: The section requires service of a sentence of imprisonment in accordance with the enactments and rules of the institution to which D is sentenced.

Case Law

R. v. Moore (1983), 33 C.R. (3d) 97 (S.C.C.); affirming (1983), 41 O.R. (2d) 271 (C.A.) — The National Parole Board was *not* entitled to forfeit the period of earned remission immediately upon the release of an inmate who was entitled to be released under mandatory supervision by a procedure colloquially called "gating". Mandatory supervision could only be revoked by reason of the post-release conduct of the inmate while at large, as if he were a paroled inmate and on parole.

Related Provisions: In general, s. 743.1 determines whether the sentence imposed shall be served in a federal penitentiary or a provincial correctional institution.

Other related provisions are described in the corresponding note to s. 743.1, *supra*.

743.4 (1) Transfer of young person to place of custody — Where a young person is sentenced to imprisonment under this or any other Act of Parliament, the young person may, with the consent of the provincial director, be transferred to a place of custody for any portion of the young person's term of imprisonment, but in no case shall that young person be kept in a place of custody under this section after that young person attains the age of twenty years.

(2) Removal of young person from place of custody — Where the provincial director certifies that a young person transferred to a place of custody under subsection (1) can no longer be held therein without significant danger of escape or of detrimentally affecting the rehabilitation or reformation of other young persons held therein, the young person may be imprisoned during the remainder of his term of imprisonment in any place where that young person might, but for subsection (1), have been imprisoned.

(3) Words and expressions — For the purposes of this section, the expressions "provincial director" and "young person" have the meanings assigned by subsection 2(1) of the *Young Offenders Act*, and the expression "place of custody" means "open custody" or "secure custody" within the meaning assigned by subsection 24.1(1) of that Act.

1995, c. 22, s. 6.

Commentary: The section authorizes the transfer of young offenders to different places of custody, during a term of imprisonment. "Adult", "provincial director" and "young person" have the meanings assigned by *Y.O.A.* s. 2(1), and "place of custody" as used in the section means "open custody" or "secure custody" as defined in *Y.O.A.* s. 24.1(1).

Section 734.4(1) authorizes the transfer of a young person sentenced to a term of imprisonment under any Federal enactment, with the consent of the provincial director, to a place of custody for any portion of the term of imprisonment. The young person must not be kept in custody after he/she attains the age of 20 years. Where a young person transferred under s. 734.4(1) can no longer be held in the place of custody without significant danger of escape or of detrimentally affecting the rehabilitation or reformation of other young persons there confined, the provincial director may so certify and D will be imprisoned in any place where he/she might have been imprisoned without the s. 734.4(1) transfer.

Related Provisions: A "young person" under s. 2(1) of the *Y.O.A.* means a person who is or, in the absence of evidence to the contrary, appears to be 12 years of age or more, but under 18 years of age. A "child" is one who is or, in the absence of evidence to the contrary, appears to be under the age of 12 years. An "adult" is a person who is neither a "young person" nor "child". Age is determined by I.A. s. 30.

743.5 (1) Transfer of jurisdiction — Where a person is or has been sentenced for an offence while subject to a disposition made under paragraph 20(1)(j), (k) or (k.1) of the *Young Offenders Act*, on the application of the Attorney General or the Attorney General's agent, a court of criminal jurisdiction may, unless to so order would bring the administration of justice into disrepute, order that the remaining portion of the disposition made under that Act be dealt with, for all purposes under this Act or any other Act of Parliament, as if it had been a sentence imposed under this Act.

(2) **Whether sentence to be served concurrently or consecutively** — Where an order is made under subsection (1), in respect of a disposition made under paragraph 20(1)(k) or (k.1) of the *Young Offenders Act*, the remaining portion of the disposition to be served pursuant to the order shall be served concurrently with the sentence referred to in subsection (1), where it is a term of imprisonment, unless the court making the order orders that it be served consecutively.

(3) **Remaining portion deemed to constitute one sentence** — For greater certainty, the remaining portion of the disposition referred to in subsection (2) shall, for the purposes of section 139 of the *Corrections and Conditional Release Act* and section 743.1 of this Act, be deemed to constitute one sentence of imprisonment.

1995, c. 22, s. 6, s. 19(b), s. 20(b).

Commentary: The section authorizes, in certain circumstances, the combination of *Y.O.A.* and *Code* sentences.

Section 743.5(1) applies to persons sentenced under the *Code*, who, at the time of sentencing, are subject to a probation or custody order under *Y.O.A.* s. 20(1)(j), (k) or (k.1). Upon application of the Attorney General or an agent thereof, the *Code* sentencing court may order that the remaining portion of the *Y.O.A.* disposition be dealt with under the *Code* or other federal enactment, as if it had been imposed under the *Code*, unless to do so would bring the administration of justice into disrepute. Where the *Y.O.A.* disposition is a term of custody under s. 20(1)(k) or (k.1), the remaining portion thereof is to be served concurrently to the sentence imposed under 743.5(1) where it is a term of imprisonment, unless the court orders, under s. 743.5(2) that it be served consecutively.

Related Provisions: *Y.O.A.* s. 20(1)(j) permits the youth court to place a young person on probation under s. 23 for a specified period not exceeding two years. *Y.O.A.* s. 20(1)(k) permits custody orders for a specified period not exceeding two years from the date of committal, or three years if the offence committed is punishable under the *Code* or other federal enactment by imprisonment for life. *Y.O.A.* s. 20(1)(k.1) permits the youth court to order a young person to serve a disposition not exceeding five years less a day, comprised of custodial and community supervision components. "Attorney General" is defined in s. 2.

The phrase "would bring the administration of justice into disrepute" also appears in the English version of *Charter* s. 24(2).

Eligibility for Parole

743.6 (1) Power of court to delay parole — Notwithstanding subsection 120(1) of the *Corrections and Conditional Release Act*, where an offender is sentenced, after the coming into force of this section, to a term of imprisonment of two years or more, including a sentence of imprisonment for life imposed otherwise than as a minimum punishment, on conviction for an offence set out in Schedule I or II to that Act that were prosecuted by way of indictment, the court may, if satisfied, having regard to the circumstances of the commission of the offence and the character and circumstances of the offender, that the expression of society's denunciation of the offences or the objective of specific or general deterrence so requires, order that the portion of the sentence that must be served before the offender may be released on full parole is one half of the sentence or ten years, whichever is less.

(1.1) Power of court to delay parole — Notwithstanding subsection 120(1) of the *Corrections and Conditional Release Act*, where an offender receives a sentence of imprisonment of two years or more, including a sentence of imprisonment for life imposed otherwise than as a minimum punishment, on conviction for a criminal organization offence, the court may order that the portion of the sentence that must be served before the offender may be released on full parole is one half of the sentence or ten years, whichever is less.

(2) **Principles that are to guide the court** — For greater certainty, the paramount principles that are to guide the court under this section are denunciation and specific or general deterrence, with rehabilitation of the offender, in all cases, being subordinate to those paramount principles.

1995, c. 22, s. 6; c. 42, s. 86(b); 1997, c. 23, s. 18.

Commentary: Section 743.6(1) operates notwithstanding s. 120(1) of the *Corrections and Conditional Release Act (C.C.R.A.)* which enacts the general rule of eligibility for release on full parole. The section is engaged where D is sentenced, after the coming into force of the section, to a term of imprisonment of two years or more upon conviction of one or more offences listed in *Schedules I and II* to the C.C.R.A. which have been prosecuted by indictment. The sentencing court must consider

(a)   the *circumstances* of the *commission* of the *offences*;

(b)   the *character* of D; and,

(c)   the *circumstances* of D.

Where the court is satisfied that the expression of society's *denunciation* of the offences or the objective of specific or general *deterrence* so requires, it may order that the portion of the sentence that must be served before D may be released on full parole be

(a)   one-half of the sentence; or,

(b)   ten (10) years, whichever is less.

Section 743.6(1.1) also operates notwithstanding s. 120 *C.C.R.A.* The court may order that D serve one-half his sentence or ten years, whichever is less, before release on full parole where D was sentenced to a term of imprisonment of two years or more, other than a life sentence imposed as a minimum punishment, on conviction for a *criminal organization offence*.

Under s. 743.6(2) denunciation, as well specific and general deterrence are the paramount principles to be applied under the section. Rehabilitation is to occupy a subordinate place.

Case Law [Cases decided prior to amendment under former s. 741.2]

R. v. Garoufalis (1998), 131 C.C.C. (3d) 242 (Man. C.A.) — An *increased* period of parole ineligibility should *only* be imposed where the trial judge finds that a fit term of imprisonment is insufficient to satisfy denunciation or deterrence.

R. v. Shorting (1995), 102 C.C.C. (3d) 385 (Man C.A.); varied (1996), 110 C.C.C. (3d) 383 (S.C.C.) — Section 741.2 applies to *all* offences listed in Schedule I and II of the *CCRA* whether a fixed term or non-mandatory life term is in issue. (per Helper and Kroft JJ.A.)

R. v. Chaisson (1995), 102 C.C.C. (3d) 564 (N.B. C.A.) — Failure to give reasons for imposing a s. 741.2 order which was *not* requested by P is *not* fatal to the validity of the order. It may be a factor to consider, however, where the reasons given for the sentence imposed are inadequate. Orders for parole ineligibility are *not* restricted to serious cases.

R. v. Nichol (1995), 102 C.C.C. (3d) 441 (Ont. C.A.) — A parole ineligibility order may only be made in respect of a listed offence. Break, enter and commit an indictable offence is *not* a listed offence. It does not become so where the offence committed upon break and entry is itself one listed in s. 741.2.

R. v. Goulet (1995), 37 C.R. (4th) 373, 97 C.C.C. (3d) 61 (Ont. C.A.) — *See also*: *R. v. Matwiy* (1996), 105 C.C.C. (3d) 251 (Alta. C.A.) — A sentencing judge should first decide what is a fit sentence having regard to accepted sentencing principles, including rehabilitation. The judge should next consider whether the particular circumstances of the offence, or the character or circumstances of the offender require that the normal statutory powers of the parole board be circumscribed by a s. 741.2 order.

R. v. Goulet (1995), 37 C.R. (4th) 373, 97 C.C.C. (3d) 61 (Ont. C.A.) — A s. 741.2 order ought not be made routinely upon conviction of a scheduled offence. It ought only be invoked as an exceptional measure where P has established on clear evidence that an increase in the period of parole ineligibility is required. Clear and specific reasons should be given for the order.

R. v. Goulet (1995), 37 C.R. (4th) 373, 97 C.C.C. (3d) 61 (Ont. C.A.) — Factors which a sentencing judge may consider in determining whether to make a s. 741.2 order include

i. whether the offence involved any unusual violence, brutality or degradation;

ii. whether the offender is likely to be deterred or rehabilitated within the normal period of parole ineligibility;

iii. whether the offender has a history of prior parole violations, or violations of other forms of conditional release; and,

iv. whether significant prior custodial sentences have had any impact on the offender.

General concerns not specific to the particular offence, for example the frequency of the commission of the type of offence in the community, are not a basis upon which to found a s. 741.2 order.

R. v. Dankyi (1993), 25 C.R. (4th) 395, 86 C.C.C. (3d) 368 (Que. C.A.) — A trial judge should clearly enunciate the reasons for increasing a period of parole ineligibility.

R. v. Warren (1994), 95 C.C.C. (3d) 86 (Sask. C.A.) — Section 741.2 does *not* contravene *Charter* s. 7.

Related Provisions: "Criminal organization offence" is defined in s. 2. Under s. 120(1) *C.C.R.A.*, the portion of a sentence of imprisonment which must generally be served before D may be released on full parole is the lesser of one-third of the sentence and seven years. The provision is expressly made subject to *Code* ss. 746.1, 761 and any order made under s. 743.6.

Parole ineligibility in cases of first and second degree murder is governed by ss. 745-745.5 and, in the case of dangerous offenders by s. 761.

Section 743.2 requires a court which sentences D to a penitentiary term to forward to the Correctional Services of Canada its reasons and recommendations relating to sentence, any relevant reports submitted to the court and any other information relevant to administering the sentence.

Schedules I and II to the C.C.R.A. are as follows:

Schedule I — (Subsections 107(1), 125(1) and 126(1) and sections 129 and 130)

1. An offence under any of the following provisions of the *Criminal Code*, that was prosecuted by way of indictment:

(a) paragraph 81(2)(a) (causing injury with intent);

(b) section 85 (use of firearm during commission of offence);

(c) subsection 86(1) (pointing a firearm);

(d) section 144 (prison breach);

(e) section 151 (sexual interference);

(f) section 152 (invitation to sexual touching);

(g) section 153 (sexual exploitation);

(h) section 155 (incest);

(i) section 159 (anal intercourse);

(j) section 160 (bestiality, compelling, in presence of or by child);

(k) section 170 (parent or guardian procuring sexual activity by child);

(l) section 171 (householder permitting sexual activity by or in presence of child);

(m) section 172 (corrupting children);

(n) subsection 212(2) (living off the avails of prostitution by a child);

(o) subsection 212(4) (obtaining sexual services of a child);

(o.1) section 220 (causing death by criminal negligence);

(o.2) section 221 (causing bodily harm by criminal negligence);

(p) section 236 (manslaughter);

(q) section 239 (attempt to commit murder);

(s) section 246 (overcoming resistance to commission of offence);

(s.1) subsections 249(3) and (4) (dangerous operation causing bodily harm and dangerous operation causing death);

(s.2) subsections 255(2) and (3) (impaired driving causing bodily harm and impaired driving causing death);

(s.3) section 264 (criminal harassment);

(t) section 266 (assault);

(u) section 267 (assault with a weapon or causing bodily harm);

(v) section 268 (aggravated assault);

(w) section 269 (unlawfully causing bodily harm);

(x) section 270 (assaulting a peace officer);

(y) section 271 (sexual assault);

(z) section 272 (sexual assault with a weapon, threats to a third party or causing bodily harm);

(z.1) section 273 (aggravated sexual assault);

(z.2) section 279 (kidnapping);

(z.3) section 344 (robbery);

(z.4) section 433 (arson — disregard for human life);

(z.5) section 434.1 (arson — own property);

(z.6) section 436 (arson by negligence); and

(z.7) paragraph 465(1)(a) (conspiracy to commit murder).

2. An offence under any of the following provisions of the *Criminal Code*, as they read immediately before July 1, 1990, that was prosecuted by way of indictment:

(a) section 433 (arson);

(b) section 434 (setting fire to other substance); and

(c) section 436 (setting fire by negligence).

3. An offence under any of the following provisions of the *Criminal Code*, chapter C-34 of the Revised Statutes of Canada, 1970, as they read immediately before January 4, 1983, that was prosecuted by way of indictment:

(a) section 144 (rape);

(b) section 145 (attempt to commit rape);

(c) section 149 (indecent assault on female);

(d) section 156 (indecent assault on male);

(e) section 245 (common assault); and

(f) section 246 (assault with intent).

4. An offence under any of the following provisions of the *Criminal Code*, chapter C-34 of the Revised Statutes of Canada, 1970, as they read immediately before January 1, 1988, that was prosecuted by way of indictment:

(a) section 146 (sexual intercourse with a female under 14);

(b) section 151 (seduction of a female between 16 and 18);

(c) section 153 (sexual intercourse with step-daughter);

(d) section 155 (buggery or bestiality);

(e) section 157 (gross indecency);

(f) section 166 (parent or guardian procuring defilement); and

(g) section 167 (householder permitting defilement).

5. The offence of breaking and entering a place and committing an indictable offence therein, as provided for by paragraph 348(1)(b) of the *Criminal Code*, where the indictable offence is an offence set out in sections 1 to 4 of this Schedule and its commission

(a) is specified in the warrant of committal;

(b) is specified in the Summons, Information or Indictment on which the conviction has been registered;

(c) is found in the reasons for judgment of the trial judge; or

(d) is found in a statement of facts admitted into evidence pursuant to section 655 of the *Criminal Code*.

Schedule II — (Subsections 107(1) and 125(1) and sections 129, 130 and 132)

1. An offence under any of the following provisions of the *Narcotic Control Act* that was prosecuted by way of indictment:

(a) section 4 (trafficking);

(b) section 5 (importing and exporting);

(c) section 6 (cultivation);

(d) section 19.1 (possession of property obtained by certain offences); and

(e) section 19.2 (laundering proceeds of certain offences).

2. An offence under any of the following provisions of the *Food and Drugs Act* that was prosecuted by way of indictment:

(a) section 39 (trafficking in controlled drug);

(b) section 44.2 (possession of property obtained by trafficking in controlled drug);

(c) section 44.3 (laundering proceeds of trafficking in controlled drug);

(d) section 48 (trafficking in restricted drug);

(e) section 50.2 (possession of property obtained by trafficking in restricted drug); and

(f) section 50.3 (laundering proceeds of trafficking in restricted drug).

3. The offence of conspiring, as provided by paragraph 465(1)(c) of the *Criminal Code*, to commit any of the offences referred to in section 1 or 2 of this Schedule, that was prosecuted by way of indictment.

Delivery of Offender to Keeper of Prison

744. Execution of warrant of committal — **A peace officer or other person to whom a warrant of committal authorized by this or any other Act of Parliament is directed shall arrest the person named or described therein, if it is necessary to do so in order to take that person into custody, convey that person to the prison mentioned in the warrant and deliver that person, together with the warrant, to the keeper of the prison who shall thereupon give to the peace officer or other person who delivers the prisoner a receipt in Form 43 setting out the state and condition of the prisoner when delivered into custody.**

1995, c. 22, s. 6.

Commentary: The section describes what must be done to confine D who has been sentenced to a term of imprisonment or otherwise ordered confined to a prison.

Where D is ordered confined to a prison, under sentence of imprisonment or otherwise, a *warrant of committal* directed to peace officers is prepared. D may be arrested, if necessary, to be taken into custody. A peace officer must then *convey* D to the designated prison and *deliver* D, together with the *warrant of committal*, to the keeper of the prison. The *keeper receives* D and issues to the delivering officer a receipt in Form 43, recording the state and condition of D when delivered.

Related Provisions: A warrant of committal may be in Form 8 or Forms 19–27, as the case may be.

Sections 25–31 protect persons administering and enforcing the law.

Imprisonment for Life

745. Sentence of life imprisonment — Subject to section 745.1, the sentence to be pronounced against a person who is to be sentenced to imprisonment for life shall be

(a) in respect of a person who has been convicted of high treason or first degree murder, that the person be sentenced to imprisonment for life without eligibility for parole until the person has served twenty-five years of the sentence;

(b) in respect of a person who has been convicted of second degree murder where that person has previously been convicted of culpable homicide that is murder, however described in this Act, that the person be sentenced to imprisonment for life without eligibility for parole until the person has served twenty-five years of the sentence;

(c) in respect of a person who has been convicted of second degree murder, that the person be sentenced to imprisonment for life without eligibility for parole until the person has served at least ten years of the sentence or such greater number of years, not being more than twenty-five years, as has been substituted therefor pursuant to section 745.4; and

(d) in respect of a person who has been convicted of any other offence, that the person be sentenced to imprisonment for life with normal eligibility for parole.

1995, c. 22, s. 6.

Commentary: The section prescribes the sentence to be pronounced against a person to be sentenced to imprisonment for life except where D, under the age of eighteen years at the time of the commission of the offence, has been convicted of first or second degree murder.

Under s. 745(a), the sentence upon conviction of high treason or first degree murder is imprisonment for life without eligibility for parole until D has served twenty-five years of the sentence. Section 745(b) requires that the same sentence be imposed where D, previously convicted of culpable homicide, that is murder, however described under the Code, is convicted of second degree murder. Where D, under the age of eighteen years at the time the offence was committed, is convicted of first degree murder, the sentence imposed is in accordance with s. 745.1.

Under s. 745(c) where D has been convicted of second degree murder, D must be sentenced to imprisonment for life without eligibility for parole until D has served at least ten years of the sentence, or such greater number of years, in excess of ten but not more than twenty-five, as is substituted under s. 745.4. Where D, under the age of eighteen years at the time the offence was committed, is convicted of second degree murder, the sentence imposed is in accordance with s. 745.1.

In all other cases, D is sentenced under 745(d) to imprisonment for life with normal eligibility for parole.

Case Law

Charter Considerations

R. v. Luxton (1990), 79 C.R. (3d) 193, 58 C.C.C. (3d) 449 (S.C.C.) — The combined effect of ss. 231(5)(e) and 745(a) accords with the principles of fundamental justice, does not demonstrate arbitrariness in violation of s. 9 and does not constitute cruel and unusual punishment under *Charter* s. 12.

R. v. Mitchell (1987), 39 C.C.C. (3d) 141 (N.S. C.A.) — *See also*: *R. v. Bowen* (1988), 63 Alta. L.R. (2d) 311 (Q.B.); *R. v. Cairns* (1989), 51 C.C.C. (3d) 90 (B.C. C.A.) — The mandatory minimum sentence under this section does *not* infringe *Charter* s. 7, 9 or 12.

R. v. Harris (1993), 25 C.R. (4th) 389, 86 C.C.C. (3d) 284 (Que. C.A.) — Section 745(b) applies only to cases of a second murder committed after conviction of the first murder.

R. v. Lefebvre (1992), 72 C.C.C. (3d) 162 (Que. C.A.); leave to appeal refused (1992), 72 C.C.C. (3d) vi (S.C.C.) — The conjoint operation of ss. 231(4)(a), 235 and 745 [*sic*] does *not* infringe *Charter* s. 7, 9 or 12.

Related Provisions: High treason is defined in s.46(1) and punished under s.47(1). Murder is defined in ss.229 and classified for sentencing purposes, as first and second degree murder, under s.231.

In jury trials in which D is convicted of second degree murder, s. 745.2 requires the submission of a statutory question for the jury to obtain their recommendation, if any, on parole ineligibility. The parole ineligibility term is then fixed in accordance with s. 745. Where D was under the age of eighteen years at the time of the commission of what is found by a jury to have been first or second degree murder, the period of parole ineligibility is fixed in accordance with s. 745.1. The statutory question to the jury where D was under the age of sixteen years is set out in s. 745.3.

In any case, where D's parole ineligibility period is fixed at some number of years in excess of 15, the provisions of s. 745.6-745.64 may become engaged upon application by D for judicial review of the periods of parole ineligibility.

The period of imprisonment served for the purposes of ss. 745.1, 745.4, 745.5 and 745.6 includes time spent in custody prior to sentence under s. 746.

Section 746.1 restricts the jurisdiction of parole authorities during periods of fixed parole ineligibility.

745.1 Persons under eighteen — The sentence to be pronounced against a person who was under the age of eighteen at the time of the commission of the offence for which the person was convicted of first degree murder or second degree murder and who is to be sentenced to imprisonment for life shall be that the person be sentenced to imprisonment for life without eligibility for parole until the person has served

    (a) such period between five and seven years of the sentence as is specified by the judge presiding at the trial, or if no period is specified by the judge presiding at the trial, five years, in the case of a person who was under the age of sixteen at the time of the commission of the offence;

    (b) ten years, in the case of a person convicted of first degree murder who was sixteen or seventeen years of age at the time of the commission of the offence; and

    (c) seven years, in the case of a person convicted of second degree murder who was sixteen or seventeen years of age at the time of the commission of the offence.

                                                                               1995, c. 22, s. 6, s. 21(b).

Commentary: The section prescribes the *sentence* to be pronounced against D who was *under the age of eighteen* at the time of the commission of the offence for which he/she was convicted of *first degree murder* or *second degree murder*.

In all cases, D will be sentenced to imprisonment for life. Where D was *under sixteen* at the time of the commission of either first or second degree murder, the parole ineligibility period may be fixed by the trial judge at between five (5) and seven (7) years. Absent such an order the period will be five (5) years. Where D was sixteen (16) or seventeen (17) years of age at the time of commission, the parole ineligibility period is fixed at ten (10) or seven (7) years depending upon the classification of the offence as first degree (10 years) or second degree (7 years) murder.

Related Provisions: The rule of s. 745.1 is exceptional. The general rule in such cases is found in s. 745(a), (b), and (c).

The parole ineligibility question put to the jury in cases to which s. 745.1 applies is found in s. 745.3. The factors to be considered in fixing the period of parole ineligibility are listed in s. 745.5 and are similar to those of s. 745.4.

Section 746, which includes the time spent in custody prior to sentence for the purposes of parole ineligibility calculations, includes reference to ss. 745.1 and 745.5.

Section 746.1 circumscribes the jurisdiction of parole authorities during periods of parole ineligibility fixed under s. 745.1.

745.2 Recommendation by jury — Subject to section 745.3, where a jury finds an accused guilty of second degree murder, the judge presiding at the trial shall, before discharging the jury, put to them the following question:

You have found the accused guilty of second degree murder and the law requires that I now pronounce a sentence of imprisonment for life against the accused. Do you wish to make any recommendation with respect to the number of years that the accused must serve before the accused is eligible for release on parole? You are not required to make any recommendation but if you do, your recommendation will be considered by me when I am determining whether I should substitute for the ten year period, which the law would otherwise require the accused to serve before the accused is eligible to be considered for release on parole, a number of years that is more than ten but not more than twenty-five.

1995, c. 22, s. 6.

Commentary: The section, applicable only where a jury finds D guilty of second degree murder, requires submission to the jury, before their discharge, of the statutory question concerning parole ineligibility. The form of the question makes it clear that no recommendation need be made, but that if made, it may be for a number of years which is more than 10 but not more than 25. The section does *not* apply to an accused who was under 18 years of age at the time of the commission of the offence for which he/she was convicted of second degree murder.

The section does *not* describe the procedure to be followed, nor enumerate the factors to be considered by the jury in determining whether or what to recommend on the issue. No reference is made, for example, to whether counsel are permitted to adduce evidence or address the jury on the issue or, if so, in what order and subject to what limitations.

Case Law
Jury Recommendation

R. v. Nepoose (1988), 69 C.R. (3d) 59, 46 C.C.C. (3d) 421 (Alta. C.A.) — A jury's recommendation as to parole ineligibility should be based solely on the evidence leading to conviction. Separate submissions by counsel to the jury on the issue should *not* be allowed.

R. v. Cruz (1998), 16 C.R. (5th) 136, 124 C.C.C. (3d) 157 (B.C. C.A.) — Section 745.2 is *not* designed to bring the jury any further into the sentencing process than permitting them to make or not make a recommendation concerning parole eligibility. The facts to which s. 754.4 refers are for the trial judge, *not* the jury to consider. *Semble*, counsel need *not* be given the opportunity to address the jury under s. 745.2. (per Hollinrake and Ryan JJ.A.).

R. v. Joseph (1984), 15 C.C.C. (3d) 314 (B.C. C.A.) — The jury's recommendation is only one factor to be considered in determining parole eligibility.

R. v. Jordan (1983), 7 C.C.C. (3d) 143 (B.C. C.A.) — The fact that the jury makes no recommendation is only a factor to be taken into account. The trial judge has the ultimate responsibility of imposing the sentence which is most fit given all the circumstances.

R. v. Ly (1992), 72 C.C.C. (3d) 57 (Man. C.A.) — A trial judge should be slow to disregard a jury recommendation of leniency, especially in the case of a youthful offender (per Scott C.J.M., Twaddle J.A.).

R. v. Okkuatsiak (1993), 20 C.R. (4th) 400, 80 C.C.C. (3d) 251 (Nfld. C.A.) — The *Code* does *not* provide for a sentence hearing before the jury concerning their parole ineligibility recommendation to the trial judge. The jury need *not* be unanimous in their recommendation.

R. v. Larter (1982), 2 C.C.C. (3d) 240 (P.E.I. C.A.); reversing (1981), 33 Nfld. & P.E.I.R. 245 (P.E.I. S.C.) — A jury should *only* be asked for a recommendation when they "find" D guilty after having heard all the evidence. Where the court accepted D's guilty pleas before the completion of P's case, the jury did *not* find them guilty in the sense contemplated by the section.

Charter Considerations

R. v. Okkuatsiak (1993), 20 C.R. (4th) 400, 80 C.C.C. (3d) 251 (Nfld. C.A.) — *Contra*: *R. v. Atsiqtaq*, [1988] N.W.T.R. 315 (S.C.) — The section does *not* contravene *Charter* s. 7, even though it does *not* require that D be permitted to address the jury on the parole ineligibility issue.

Related Provisions: The jury recommendation, if any, is one of the factors which the trial judge must consider in fixing the parole ineligibility period under s. 745.4. The comparable provision in the case of young offenders is s. 745.3. Where the period of parole ineligibility is fixed at more than 15 years, the judicial review mechanism of s. 745.6 may become engaged after D has served 15 years of the sentence as calculated under s. 746.

Section 746.1 delineates the restrictions on parole during a fixed parole ineligibility period.

745.3 Persons under sixteen — Where a jury finds an accused guilty of first degree murder or second degree murder and the accused was under the age of sixteen at the time of the commission of the offence, the judge presiding at the trial shall, before discharging the jury, put to them the following question:

You have found the accused guilty of first degree murder (or second degree murder) and the law requires that I now pronounce a sentence of imprisonment for life against the accused. Do you wish to make any recommendation with respect to the period of imprisonment that the accused must serve before the accused is eligible for release on parole? You are not required to make any recommendation but if you do, your recommendation will be considered by me when I am determining the period of imprisonment that is between five years and seven years that the law would require the accused to serve before the accused is eligible to be considered for release on parole.

1995, c. 22, s. 6, s. 22(b).

Commentary: This section applies to an accused found guilty by a jury of either first or second degree murder in respect of an offence committed whilst D was under sixteen years of age. It requires submission to the jury, prior to discharge, of the statutory question concerning parole ineligibility. It is clear from the question that no recommendation need be made. Any recommendation made may be for a period of imprisonment that is between five and seven years.

Related Provisions: Like s. 745.2, s. 745.3 does not describe the procedure to be followed, nor enumerate the factors to be considered by the jury in determining whether or what to recommend on the issue. No reference is made, for example, to whether counsel is permitted to adduce evidence or address the jury on the issue or, if so, in what order and subject to what limitations.

The language of the question in this section "the period of imprisonment" is slightly different than s. 745.2, "the number of years. . .", thereby not appearing to restrict the period of recommendation to a "years" calculation. Similar language appears in ss. 745.5 (ineligibility for parole) and 745.1 (sentence of life imprisonment).

The jury recommendation is one of the factors listed in s. 745.5. that the trial judge must consider in fixing the period of parole ineligibility under that section. The sentence to be imposed is described in s. 745.1.

745.4 Ineligibility for parole — Subject to section 745.5, at the time of the sentencing under section 745 of an offender who is convicted of second degree murder, the judge who presided at the trial of the offender or, if that judge is unable to do so, any judge of the same court may, having regard to the character of the offender, the nature of the offence and the circumstances surrounding its commission, and to the recommendation, if any, made pursuant to section 745.2, by order, substitute for ten years a number of years of imprisonment (being more than ten but nor more than twenty-five) without eligibility for parole, as the judge deems fit in the circumstances.

1995, c. 22, s. 6.

Commentary: The section defines the *factors* to be considered by a judge in fixing a period of *parole ineligibility* upon conviction of second degree murder and prescribes the limits within which such period may be fixed. It has *no* application to cases of first or second degree murder where the person convicted was under the age of 18 at the time of the commission of the offence.

The period of parole ineligibility is generally fixed by the judge who presided at D's trial. Another judge of the same court may do so, if the trial judge is unable to act. The *factors* which must be considered in fixing the parole ineligibility period are the *character* of the *offender*, the *nature* of the *offence*, the *circumstances* surrounding the *commission* of the *offence* and the *recommendation*, if any, of the jury.

The period of parole ineligibility fixed must *not* be less than 10 nor more than 25 years.

Case Law

General Principles

R. v. Shropshire (1995), 43 C.R. (4th) 269, 102 C.C.C. (3d) 193 (S.C.C.) — To justify a s. 744 order, an assessment of future dangerousness and denunciation, as well as deterrence, are relevant. The general rule of a period of parole ineligibility of ten years may be ousted by a determination by the trial judge that, according to the s. 744 criteria, D ought to wait a longer period before suitability for release into the general public is assessed.

R. v. Brown (1993), 83 C.C.C. (3d) 394 (B.C. C.A.) — The period of parole ineligibility ought *not* to be increased except in unusual circumstances. It ought *not* to be increased so as to reject implicitly the finding of the jury that first degree murder had not been proven.Denunciation is a factor to be considered to ensure that the sentence is commensurate with the gravity of the offence. It cannot justify, however, the imposition of a sentence which is longer or more severe than one commensurate with the gravity of the offence.

R. v. Gourgon (1981), 21 C.R. (3d) 384 (B.C. C.A.) — The following factors should be considered in fixing the eligibility period for parole: (1) the minimum period of ineligibility should not be extended beyond the minimum of ten years except in unusual circumstances; (2) the imposed sentence should not impliedly reject the finding of the jury that the killing was not planned and deliberate and not one of the offences in s. 214(5); (3) the recommendation of the jury; (4) the cases where D cannot be released upon parole until 25 years have elapsed; (5) the character of D; (6) the nature of the offence and the circumstances surrounding it; (7) any ameliorating or mitigating circumstances; (8) public confidence in the administration of justice; (9) deterrence to others; (10) denunciation of the crime itself; (11) sentences in like cases; and (12) protection of society.

R. v. Ly (1992), 72 C.C.C. (3d) 57 (Man. C.A.) — The parole ineligibility period should *not* be set on the basis that a longer period is required to protect the public from the danger of D committing a further violent crime. The minimum sentence is imprisonment for life. It should be assumed that the parole board will do its job and *not* release a dangerous offender.In general, parole ineligibility should be fixed at ten years. It should be increased only in exceptional cases, as for example, where the murder is committed in the course of another crime, particularly a crime of violence. The youth of D is an important consideration in fixing the period of parole ineligibility. Parliament's purpose in allowing an increase in the parole ineligibility period was to permit the court to deter and denounce the crime (per Scott C.J.M., Twaddle J.A.).

R. v. Olsen (1999), 131 C.C.C. (3d) 355 (Ont. C.A.) — A trial judge must consider a jury's recommendation or lack of recommendation in determining the period of parole ineligibility, but is entitled to give it little or no weight when the recommendation is unreasonable or irrational.

R. v. Wenarchuk (1982), 67 C.C.C. (2d) 169 (Sask. C.A.) — An order under this section is a two-step process. The trial judge should first consider whether to exercise his discretion under this section, and then should consider the number of years to be served. For each stage of the decision he should consider the character of D, the nature of the offence and the circumstances surrounding its commission, and the recommendations of the jury.Rehabilitation is not a consideration; rather, the emphasis should be on society's repudiation of the crime by the particular accused combined with individual and general deterrence.

Jurisdiction Where No Jury

R. v. Kjeldsen (1980), 53 C.C.C. (2d) 55 (Alta. C.A.) — Notwithstanding the fact that the court did not have the benefit of a recommendation by a jury, the court of appeal, when substituting a verdict of second degree murder, had the power to increase the ineligibility for parole period beyond 10 years.

R. v. O'Brien (1982), 28 C.R. (3d) 287, 26 C.C.C. (2d) 374 (B.C. C.A.) — The period of parole ineligibility may be increased on a guilty plea.

Appeals [See also ss. 675(2) and 676(4)]

R. v. Shropshire (1995), 43 C.R. (4th) 269, 102 C.C.C. (3d) 193 (S.C.C.) — It is error for a court of appeal to reduce a period of parole ineligibility because the trial judge has not given specific reasons which, in the opinion of the court of appeal, justify the increase. A court of appeal may *not* modify a parole ineligibility order simply because its members feel that a different order ought to have been made. The order ought to be varied only if the court of appeal is convinced it is *not* fit, *i.e.*, it is clearly unreasonable.

Evidence

R. v. Ly (1992), 72 C.C.C. (3d) 57 (Man. C.A.) — In determining the period of parole ineligibility, a trial judge must *not* use a statement of a co-accused to any greater extent than could the trier of fact when it is admitted as evidence at trial.

Related Provisions: The jury recommendation, if any, is made in response to the statutory question of s. 745.2.

Other related provisions are discussed in the corresponding notes to ss. 745 and 745.2, supra.

The applicable provisions in respect of accused convicted of either first degree murder or second degree murder who committed the offence when under the age of eighteen are s. 742.1 (sentence of life imprisonment), s. 745.3 (recommendation by jury) and s. 745.5 (ineligibility for parole).

745.5 Idem — **At the time of the sentencing under section 745.1 of an offender who is convicted of first degree murder or second degree murder and who was under the age of sixteen at the time of the commission of the offence, the judge who presided at the trial of the offender or, if that judge is unable to do so, any judge of the same court, may, having regard to the age and character of the offender, the nature of the offence and the circumstances surrounding its commission, and to the recommendation, if any, made pursuant to section 745.3, by order, decide the period of imprisonment the offender is to serve that is between five years and seven years without eligibility for parole, as the judge deems fit in the circumstances.**

1995, c. 22, s. 6, 23(b).

Commentary: This section lists the *factors* to be considered by the judge who fixes the period of *parole ineligibility* in the case of an *accused* convicted of *first or second degree murder* in respect of an *offence committed* whilst D was *under* the age of *sixteen*.

The period of parole ineligibility is generally fixed by the judge who presided at D's trial. Another judge of the same court may do so, if the trial judge is unable to act. The *factors* which must be considered in fixing the parole ineligibility period are the *age* and *character* of the offender, the *nature* of the *offence*, the *circumstances* surrounding the *commission* of the offence and the *recommendation*, if any, of the jury.

The period of imprisonment to be served before parole ineligibility is to be fixed "between five and seven years".

Related Provisions: Section 745.5 adds D's age to the list of factors to be considered under s. 745.4 in determining the period of parole ineligibility. The period fixed under s. 745.5 is "the period of imprisonment", whereas s. 745.4 refers to "a number of years of imprisonment".

Other related provisions are discussed in the corresponding note to ss. 745.1 and 745.3.

745.6 (1) Application for judicial review — Subject to subsection (2), a person may apply, in writing, to the appropriate Chief Justice in the province in which their conviction took place for a reduction in the number of years of imprisonment without eligibility for parole if the person

(a) has been convicted of murder or high treason;

(b) has been sentenced to imprisonment for life without eligibility for parole until more than fifteen years of their sentence has been served; and

(c) has served at least fifteen years of their sentence.

(2) **Exception — multiple murderers** — A person who has been convicted of more than one murder may not make an application under subsection (1), whether or not proceedings were commenced in respect of any of the murders before another murder was committed.

(3) **Definition of "appropriate chief justice"** — For the purposes of this section and sections 745.61 to 745.64, the "appropriate Chief Justice" is

(a) in relation to the Province of Ontario, the Chief Justice of the Ontario Court;

(b) in relation to the Province of Quebec, the Chief Justice of the Superior Court;

(c) in relation to the Provinces of Prince Edward Island and Newfoundland, the Chief Justice of the Supreme Court, Trial Division;

(d) in relation to the Provinces of New Brunswick, Manitoba, Saskatchewan and Alberta, the Chief Justice of the Court of Queen's Bench;

(e) in relation to the Provinces of Nova Scotia and British Columbia, the Chief Justice of the Supreme Court; and

(f) in relation to the Yukon Territory, the Northwest Territories and Nunavut, the Chief Justice of the Court of Appeal thereof.

1995, c. 22, s. 6; 1996, c. 34, s. 2(2); 1998, c. 15, s. 20.

Commentary: The section authorizes judicial review of parole ineligibility periods for murder or high treason that are fixed at more than 15 years by operation of law or judicial order. D must have served at least 15 years of the sentence before applying. Section 745.6(1) requires that D apply in writing to the Chief Justice of the province in which the conviction took place. "Chief Justice" is defined in s. 745.6(3). Section 745.6(1) does *not* apply to multiple murders (unless at least one of the murders for which the person was convicted was committed after January 9, 1997).

Case Law

Jurisdiction: Time of Application

R. v. Frederick (1989), 52 C.C.C. (3d) 433 (Ont. H.C.) — The application for judicial review may *not* be brought earlier than 15 years.

Related Provisions: Section 745.61 provides for initial judicial screening of the application, to determine whether D has shown it has a reasonable prospect of success. Only if D meets the onus on him/her will a jury be empanelled to hear the application, in accordance with the procedure outlined in s. 745.63. Section 745.62 permits either D or the Attorney General to appeal from a decision made under s. 745.61. Pursuant to s. 745.64, the Chief Justice of each province may make rules pertaining to judicial review applications.

745.61 (1) On receipt of an application under subsection 745.6(1), the appropriate Chief Justice shall determine, or shall designate a judge of the superior court of criminal jurisdiction to determine, on the basis of the following written material, whether the applicant has shown, on a balance of probabilities, that there is a reasonable prospect that the application will succeed:

(a) the application;

(b) any report provided by the Correctional Service of Canada or other correctional authorities; and

(c) any other written evidence presented to the Chief Justice or judge by the applicant or the Attorney General.

(2) Criteria — In determining whether the applicant has shown that there is a reasonable prospect that the application will succeed, the Chief Justice or judge shall consider the criteria set out in paragraphs 746.63(1)(*a*) to (*e*), with such modifications as the circumstances require.

(3) Decision re new application — If the Chief Justice or judge determines that the applicant has not shown that there is a reasonable prospect that the application will succeed, the Chief Justice or judge may

(a) set a time, not earlier than two years after the date of the determination, at or after which another application may be made by the applicant under subsection 745.6(1); or

(b) decide that the applicant may not make another application under that subsection.

(4) Where no decision re new application — If the Chief Justice or judge determines that the applicant has not shown that there is a reasonable prospect that the application will succeed but does not set a time for another application or decide that such an application may not be made, the applicant may make another application no earlier than two years after the date of the determination.

(5) Designation of judge to empanel jury — If the Chief Justice or judge determines that the applicant has shown that there is a reasonable prospect that the application will succeed, the Chief Justice shall designate a judge of the superior court of criminal jurisdiction to empanel a jury to hear the application.

1996, c. 34, s. 2(2).

Editor's Note: Section 745.61 of the Criminal Code applies in respect of applications for judicial review made after January 9, 1997 in respect of crimes committed before or after that date, unless the applicant has, before that date, made an application under s. 745.6(1) of the Code as it read immediately before that date and the application had not yet been disposed of before that date: see 1996, c. 34, s. 7.

Commentary: The Chief Justice, under s. 745.61(1), must designate a judge of the superior court of criminal jurisdiction to determine, or must him/herself determine, whether D has shown on a balance of probabilities that the application has a reasonable prospect of success. That judge is to consider the application, any report from the correctional authorities, and any other written evidence from D or the Attorney General. Under s. 745.61(2), the determination is to be made having regard to the criteria specified in s. 745.63(1). If D does not satisfy the onus on him/her, ss. 745.61(3) and (4) prohibit D from making a new application until at least two years from the date of the initial determination, or such later time as the reviewing judge specifies. Alternatively, the reviewing judge may prohibit D from making any new application. If D satisfies the onus on him/her, s. 745.61(5) requires the Chief Justice to designate a judge of the superior court of criminal jurisdiction to empanel a jury to hear the application.

Related Provisions: Section 745.6 authorizes written application for judicial review of parole ineligibility periods longer than 15 years imposed in murder cases. The procedure for the hearing by a jury of such application is set out in s. 745.63.

Section 745.62 permits either D or the Attorney General to appeal from a decision made under s. 745.61. Pursuant to s. 745.64, the Chief Justice of each province may make rules pertaining to judicial review applications.

745.62 (1) Appeal — The applicant or the Attorney General may appeal to the Court of Appeal from a determination or a decision made under section 745.61 on any question of law or fact or mixed law and fact.

(2) Documents to be considered — The appeal shall be determined on the basis of the documents presented to the Chief Justice or judge who made the determination or decision, any reasons for the determination or decision and any other documents that the Court of Appeal requires.

(3) Sections to apply — Sections 673 to 696 apply, with such modifications as the circumstances require.

1996, c. 34, s. 2(2).

Editor's Note: Section 745.62 of the Criminal Code applies in respect of applications for judicial review made after January 9, 1997, in respect of crimes committed before or after that date, unless the applicant has, before that date, made an application under s. 745.61(1) of the Code as it read immediately before that date and the application had not yet been disposed of before that date: see 1996, c. 34, s. 7.

Commentary: Section 745.62(1) provides for appellate review by the Court of Appeal of a determination or decision made under s. 745.61. Both D and the Attorney General have a right of appeal, on any question of law or fact or mixed law and fact. Under s. 745.62(2) the Court of Appeal may consider not only any documents that were before the reviewing judge or Chief Justice and the reasons for the determination or decision, but also any other documents that it requires. Section 745.62(3) makes applicable the procedure governing indictable appeals.

Related Provisions: Section 745.6 authorizes written application for judicial review of parole ineligibility periods longer than 15 years imposed in murder cases. Section 745.61 provides for judicial screening of the application to determine whether D has shown it has a reasonable prospect of success. The procedure for the hearing by jury of such application is set out in s. 745.63. Section 745.64 empowers the Chief Justice of each province to make rules pertaining to judicial review applications.

The procedure governing appeals in respect of indictable offences is contained in ss.673-696.

745.63 (1) Hearing of application — The jury empaneled under subsection 745.61(5) to hear the application shall consider the following criteria and determine whether the applicant's number of years of imprisonment without eligibility for parole ought to be reduced:

    (a) the character of the applicant;

    (b) the applicant's conduct while serving the sentence;

    (c) the nature of the offence for which the applicant was convicted;

    (d) any information provided by a victim at the time of the imposition of the sentence or at the time of the hearing under this section; and

    (e) any other matters that the judge considers relevant in the circumstances.

(2) Definition of "victim" — In paragraph (1)(d), "victim" has the same meaning as in subsection 722(4).

(3) Reduction — The jury hearing an application under subsection (1) may determine that the applicant's number of years of imprisonment without eligibility for parole ought to be reduced. The determination to reduce the number of years must be by unanimous vote.

(4) No reduction — The applicant's number of years of imprisonment without eligibility for parole is not reduced if

(a) the jury hearing an application under subsection (1) determines that the number of years ought not to be reduced;

(b) the jury hearing an application under subsection (1) concludes that it cannot unanimously determine that the number of years ought to be reduced; or

(c) the presiding judge, after the jury has deliberated for a reasonable period, concludes that the jury is unable to unanimously determine that the number of years ought to be reduced.

(5) Where determination to reduce number of years — If the jury determines that the number of years of imprisonment without eligibility for parole ought to be reduced, the jury may, by a vote of not less than two thirds of the members of the jury,

(a) substitute a lesser number of years of imprisonment without eligibility for parole than that then applicable; or

(b) terminate the ineligibility for parole.

(6) Decision re new application — If the applicant's number of years of imprisonment without eligibility for parole is not reduced, the jury may

(a) set a time, not earlier than two years after the date of the determination or conclusion under subsection (4), at or after which another application may be made by the applicant under subsection 745.6(1); or

(b) decide that the applicant may not make another application under that subsection.

(7) Two-thirds decision — The decision of the jury under paragraph (6)(*a*) or (*b*) must be made by not less than two thirds of its members.

(8) If no decision re new application — If the jury does not set a date at or after which another application may be made or decide that such an application may not be made, the applicant may make another application no earlier than two years after the date of the determination or conclusion under subsection (4).

1996, c. 34, s. 2(2).

Editor's Note: Section 745.63 of the Criminal Code, other than paragraph 745.63(1)(d), applies in respect of applications for judicial review made after January 9, 1997, in respect of crimes committed before or after that date, unless the applicant has, before that date, made an application under s. 745.6(1) of the Code as it read immediately before that date and the application had not yet been disposed of before that date. Paragraph 745.63(1)(d) applies in respect of hearings held after January 9, 1997, with respect to applications for judicial review in respect of crimes committed before or after that date: see 1996, c. 34, ss. 7, 8 (as amended by 1997, c. 18, s. 139.1).

Commentary: The procedure on the hearing of the application by a jury is set out in s. 745.63. The jury must consider the criteria set out in s. 745.63(1): D's character, D's conduct while serving the sentence, the nature of D's offence, any information provided by a victim either at the hearing or at the original sentencing, and any other matters the presiding judge deems relevant. Under s. 745.63(2), "victim" is given an expanded definition, to include relatives of the deceased. Sections. 745.63(3) and (4) require that the jury be unanimous in its decision as to whether the number of years of parole ineligibility ought to be reduced. If the presiding judge concludes that the jury is unable to reach a unanimous determination the application is defeated. Where the jury determines that the parole ineligibility period should be reduced, under s. 745.63(5) it may by a two-thirds vote substitute a lesser number of years, or terminate the parole ineligibility. Where the parole ineligibility period is not reduced, the jury may under ss. 745.63(6) and (7) by two-thirds vote decide that D may not make another application, or set a date at least two years into the future after which time D may make a new application. If no decision is made about the making of a new application, s. 745.63(8) provides that D must wait a minimum of two years before doing so.

Case Law

Nature of Hearing

R. v. Swietlinski (1994), 92 C.C.C. (3d) 449, 33 C.R. (4th) 295, 24 C.R.R. (2d) 71, [1994] 3 S.C.R. 481 — The s. 745 [now s. 745.63] re-assessment procedure is to re-examine the sentence in light of new information or factors which could not have been known initially, and call attention to changes in the applicant's situation which might justify imposing a less harsh penalty.

R. v. Swietlinski (1994), 92 C.C.C. (3d) 449, 33 C.R. (4th) 295, 24 C.R.R. (2d) 71, [1994] 3 S.C.R. 481 — Under s. 745 [now 745.63], a jury has a broad discretionary power which requires that jurors follow a different analytical approach than that followed at trial. The listed factors are to be weighed as a whole.

Character of the Applicant

R. v. Swietlinski (1994), 92 C.C.C. (3d) 449, 33 C.R. (4th) 295, 24 C.R.R. (2d) 71, [1994] 3 S.C.R. 481 — The character of the applicant at the time of the offence, as well at the time of the hearing, is relevant on the s. 745 [now 745.63] hearing.

Hearing Procedure

Poulin v. Quebec (Attorney General) (1991), 68 C.C.C. (3d) 472 (Que. S.C.) — At the hearing, P may invite the jury to consider the applicant's silence there, in assessing the evidence called in support of the application.

Charter Considerations

R. v. Vaillancourt (1988), 66 C.R. (3d) 66, 43 C.C.C. (3d) 238 (Ont. H.C.) — Rules promulgated under s. 745(5) [now s. 745.63], which require the applicant to disclose the nature of the evidence to be called and to lead evidence first and address the jury before P, do not infringe the principles of fundamental justice. As the applicant is no longer a person charged with an offence, the presumption of innocence and the right not to be compelled to testify in *Charter* ss. 11(c) and (d), do not apply.

Related Provisions: Section 745.6 authorizes written application for judicial review of parole ineligibility periods longer than 15 years imposed in murder cases. Section 745.61 provides for judicial screening of the application to determine whether D has shown it has a reasonable prospect of success, and s. 745.62 for appeal of that determination.

The procedure for the hearing by the jury of such application is set out in s. 745.63. "Victim" is defined for the purpose of the hearing in s. 722(4). Section 745.64 empowers the Chief Justice of each province to make rules pertaining to judicial review applications.

745.64 (1) Rules — The appropriate Chief Justice in each province or territory may make such rules as are required for the purposes of sections 745.6 to 745.63.

(2) Territories — When the appropriate Chief Justice is designating a judge of the superior court of criminal jurisdiction, for the purpose of a judicial screening under subsection 745.61(1) or to empanel a jury to hear an application under subsection 745.61(5), in respect of a conviction that took place in the Yukon Territory, the Northwest Territories or Nunavut, the appropriate Chief Justice may designate the judge from the Court of Appeal of the Yukon Territory, the Northwest Territories or Nunavut, or the Supreme Court of the Yukon Territory or the Northwest Territories or the Nunavut Court of Justice, as the case may be.

1996, c. 34, s. 2(2); 1998, c. 15, s. 20 [Repealed 1999, c. 3, (Sched., item 9).]; 1999, c. 3, s. 53.

Commentary: The section permits each Chief Justice to make rules for the hearing of parole ineligibility applications. Section 745.64(2) allows in the case of convictions that took place in the Yukon, Nunavut or Northwest Territories the designation of a judge from the Court of Appeal or the Supreme Court of the respective Territory.

Related Provisions: Section 745.6 authorizes written application for judicial review of parole ineligibility periods longer than 15 years imposed in murder cases. Section 745.61 provides for judicial screening of the application to determine whether D has shown it has a reasonable prospect of success, and s. 745.62 for appeal of that determination.

The procedure for the hearing by the jury of such application is set out s. 745.63.

746. Time spent in custody — In calculating the period of imprisonment served for the purposes of section 745, 745.1, 745.4 745.5 or 745.6, there shall be included any time spent in custody between,

> **(a)** in the case of a sentence of imprisonment for life imposed after July 25, 1976, the day on which the person was arrested and taken into custody in respect of the offence for which that person was sentenced to imprisonment for life and the day the sentence was imposed; or

> **(b)** in the case of a sentence of death that has been or is deemed to have been commuted to a sentence of imprisonment for life, the day on which the person was arrested and taken into custody in respect of the offence for which that person was sentenced to death and the day the sentence was commuted or deemed to have been commuted to a sentence of imprisonment for life.

1995, c. 22, s. 6, s. 24(b).

Commentary: The section requires that there be included in calculating the period of imprisonment served for the purposes of ss. 745 and 745.1 (sentence of life imprisonment), 745.4 and 745.5 (parole ineligibility) and 745.6 (judicial review of parole ineligibility), any time spent in custody, from the date of arrest and custody in respect of the offence to the date upon which the sentence of imprisonment for life was passed or sentence of death deemed or actually commuted.

Related Provisions: In practical terms, the effect of the section is to start the period of parole ineligibility running from the date of arrest and custody on the charge. Pre-sentence custody may be considered by a sentencing judge under s. 719(3) but there is *not*, as here, any mandatory rule.

Other related provisions described in the corresponding notes to ss. 745, 745.1, 745.4, 745.5 and 745.6, *supra*.

746.1 (1) Parole prohibited — Unless Parliament otherwise provides by an enactment making express reference to this section, a person who has been sentenced to imprisonment for life without eligibility for parole for a specified number of years pursuant to this Act shall not be considered for parole or released pursuant to a grant of parole under the *Corrections and Conditional Release Act* or any other Act of Parliament until the expiration or termination of the specified number of years of imprisonment.

(2) Absences with or without escort and day parole — Subject to subsection (3), in respect of a person sentenced to imprisonment for life without eligibility for parole for a specified number of years pursuant to this Act, until the expiration of all but three years of the specified number of years of imprisonment,

> **(a)** no day parole may be granted under the *Corrections and Conditional Release Act*;

> **(b)** no absence without escort may be authorized under that Act or the *Prisons and Reformatories Act*; and

> **(c)** except with the approval of the National Parole Board, no absence with escort otherwise than for medical reasons or in order to attend judicial proceedings or a coroner's inquest may be authorized under either of those Acts.

(3) Young offenders — In the case of any person convicted of first degree murder or second degree murder who was under the age of eighteen at the time of the commission of the offence and who is sentenced to imprisonment for life without eligibility for parole for a specified number of years pursuant to this Act, until the expiration of all but one fifth of the period of imprisonment the person is to serve without eligibility for parole,

(a) no day parole may be granted under the *Corrections and Conditional Release Act*;

(b) no absence without escort may be authorized under that Act or the *Prisons and Reformatories Act*; and

(c) except with the approval of the National Parole Board, no absence with escort otherwise than for medical reasons or in order to attend judicial proceedings or a coroner's inquest may be authorized under either of those Acts.

1995, c. 22, s. 6; 1995, c. 42, s. 87(b); 1997, c. 17, s. 8

Commentary: This section defines the scope of a parole ineligibility order, in particular, limiting the granting of conditional liberty by the National Parole Board during such period.

Under s. 746.1(1) absent any federal enactment that expressly overrides the subsection, no consideration may be given for parole or release pursuant to the terms of a grant of parole under Part II of the *Corrections and Conditional Release Act* or other Federal enactment, until the termination of the parole ineligibility period.

Under s. 746.1(2) a person sentenced to imprisonment for life without eligibility for parole for a specified number of years under the *Code*, other than one convicted of first or second degree murder who was under 18 at the time of the commission of the offence, may not be granted day parole, absence without escort or absence with escort otherwise than for specified reasons (except with the approval of the National Parole Board), until the expiration of all but three of the specified number of years of imprisonment. Section 746.1(3) makes similar provision for offenders convicted of first or second degree murder who were under 18 at the time of commission of the offence except that the proscribed period is all but one fifth of the parole ineligibility period.

Related Provisions: The provisions of s. 746, which include pre-sentence custody in calculations of the period of imprisonment under ss. 745, 745.1, 745.4, 745.5 and 745.6 do not apply to s. 746.1. *Quaere* whether the parole ineligibility period of s. 746 includes such time spent in custody?

In practical terms, the section ousts the jurisdiction of the parole authorities, *a fortiori*, a grant of conditional liberty during the prescribed period.

An initial period of parole ineligibility which exceeds fifteen years may be varied upon judicial review under s. 745.6. There is *no* equivalent provision in respect of offenders sentenced for murders committed whilst under eighteen.

Proposed Addition — 747 to 747.8

Hospital Orders

747. Definitions — In this section and sections 747.1 to 747.8,

"assessment report" means a written report made pursuant to an assessment order made under section 672.11 by a psychiatrist who is entitled under the laws of a province to practise psychiatry or, where a psychiatrist is not practicably available, by a medical practitioner;

"hospital order" means an order by a court under section 747.1 that an offender be detained in a treatment facility;

"medical practitioner" means a person who is entitled to practise medicine by the laws of a province;

"treatment facility" means any hospital or place for treatment of the mental disorder of an offender, or a place within a class of such places, designated by the Governor in Council, the Lieutenant Governor in Council of the province in which the offender is sentenced or a person to whom authority has been delegated in writing for that purpose by the Governor in Council or that Lieutenant Governor in Council.

1995, c. 22, s. 6.

747.1 (1) Court may make a hospital order — A court may order that an offender be detained in a treatment facility as the initial part of a sentence of imprisonment where it finds, at the time of sentencing, that the offender is suffering from a mental disorder in an acute phase and the court is satisfied, on the basis of an assessment report and any other evidence, that immediate treatment of the mental disorder is urgently required to prevent further significant deterioration of the mental or physical health of the offender, or to prevent the offender from causing serious bodily harm to any person.

(2) Limitation on hospital order — A hospital order shall be for a single period of treatment not exceeding sixty days, subject to any terms and conditions that the court considers appropriate.

(3) Form — A hospital order may be in Form 51.

(4) Warrant of committal — A court that makes a hospital order shall issue a warrant for committal of the offender, which may be in Form 8.

1995, c. 22, s. 6.

747.2 (1) Recommended treatment facility — In a hospital order, the court shall specify that the offender be detained in a particular treatment facility recommended by the central administration of any penitentiary, prison or other institution to which the offender has been sentenced to imprisonment, unless the court is satisfied, on the evidence of a medical practitioner, that serious harm to the mental or physical health of the offender would result from travelling to that treatment facility or from that delay occasioned in travelling there.

(2) Court chooses treatment facility — Where the court does not follow a recommendation referred to in subsection (1), it shall order that the offender be detained in a treatment facility that is reasonably accessible to the place where the accused is detained when the hospital order is made or to the place where the court is located.

1995, c. 22, s. 6.

747.3 Condition — No hospital order may be made unless the offender and the person in charge of the treatment facility where the offender is to be detained consent to the order and its terms and conditions, but nothing in this section shall be construed as making unnecessary the obtaining of any authorization or consent to treatment from any other person that is or may be required otherwise than under this Act.

1995, c. 22, s. 6.

747.4 Exception — No hospital order may be made in respect of an offender

(a) who is convicted of or is serving a sentence imposed in respect of a conviction for an offence for which a minimum punishment of imprisonment for life is prescribed by law;

(b) who has been found to be a dangerous offender pursuant to section 753;

(c) where the term of imprisonment to be served by the offender does not exceed sixty days;

(d) where the term of imprisonment is imposed on the offender in default of payment of a fine or of a victim fine surcharge imposed under subsection 737(1); or

(e) where the sentence of imprisonment imposed on the offender is ordered under paragraph 732(1)(a) to be served intermittently.

1995, c. 22, s. 6.

747.5 (1) Offender to serve remainder of sentence — An offender shall be sent or returned to a prison to serve the portion of the offender's sentence that remains unexpired where

(a) the hospital order expires before the expiration of the sentence; or

(b) the consent to the detention of the offender in the treatment facility pursuant to the hospital order is withdrawn either by the offender or by the person in charge of the treatment facility.

(2) Transfer from one treatment facility to another — Before the expiration of a hospital order in respect of an offender, the offender may be transferred from the treatment facility specified in the hospital order to another treatment facility where treatment of the offender's mental disorder is available, if the court authorizes the transfer in writing and the person in charge of the treatment facility consents.

1995, c. 22, s. 6.

747.6 Detention to count as service of term — Each day that an offender is detained under a hospital order shall be treated as a day of service of the term of imprisonment of the offender, and the offender shall be deemed, for all purposes, to be lawfully confined in a prison during that detention.

1995, c. 22, s. 6.

747.7 Application of section 12 of *Corrections and Conditional Release Act* — Notwithstanding section 12 of the *Corrections and Conditional Release Act*, an offender in respect of whom a hospital order is made and who is sentenced or committed to a penitentiary may, during the period for which that order is in force, be received in a penitentiary before the expiration of the time limited by law for an appeal and shall be detained in the treatment facility specified in the order during that period.

1995, c. 22, s. 6.

747.8 Copy of warrant and order given to prison and hospital — Where a court makes a hospital order in respect of an offender, the court shall cause a copy of the order and of the warrant of committal issued pursuant to subsection 747.1 to be sent to the central administration of the penitentiary, prison or other institution where the term of imprisonment imposed on the offender is to be served and to the treatment facility where the offender is to be detained for treatment.

1995, c. 22, s. 6.

Pardons and Remissions

748. (1) To whom pardon may be granted — Her Majesty may extend the royal mercy to a person who is sentenced to imprisonment under the authority of an Act of Parliament, even if the person is imprisoned for failure to pay money to another person.

(2) Free or conditional pardon — The Governor in Council may grant a free pardon or a conditional pardon to any person who has been convicted of an offence.

(3) Effect of free pardon — Where the Governor in Council grants a free pardon to a person, that person shall be deemed thereafter never to have committed the offence in respect of which the pardon is granted.

(4) Punishment for subsequent offence not affected — No free pardon or conditional pardon prevents or mitigates the punishment to which the person might otherwise be lawfully sentenced on a subsequent conviction for an offence other than that for which the pardon was granted.

1995, c. 22, s. 6.

Commentary: The section authorizes the extension of the royal mercy and the grant of pardons by the Governor in Council.

Under s. 748(1), Her Majesty may extend the royal mercy to any person sentenced to imprisonment under Federal enactment, even though the imprisonment may only be in default of payment of money to another.

Under ss. 748(2)-(4), the Governor in Council may grant pardons to any person convicted of a criminal offence. Where a free pardon has been granted, D is deemed never to have committed the offence in respect of which the pardon has been granted. A pardon may also be conditional. Pardons neither prevent nor mitigate the punishment to which D might otherwise lawfully be sentenced on a subsequent offence, other than that for which the pardon was granted.

Case Law

R. v. Peterson (1998), 122 C.C.C. (3d) 254 (B.C. C.A.) — The combined operation of *Code* s. 748(3) and s. 5 of the *Criminal Records Act* bars cross-examination on prior convictions for which a witness has received a free pardon.

R. v. Spring (1977), 35 C.C.C. (2d) 308 (Ont. C.A.) — Where D has been previously pardoned, he may be treated as a first offender with respect to sentencing for a subsequent offence.

Related Provisions: A pardon may be obtained under ss.3 and 4 and revoked under s. 7 of the *Criminal Records Act*. Section 5 of the Act describes the effect of the grant of a pardon.

Section 749 makes it clear that nothing in the *Code* in any manner limits or affects Her Majesty's royal prerogative of mercy.

The Governor in Council may also order the entire remission of a pecuniary penalty, fine or forfeiture under s. 748.1.

Under s.690, where an application is made for the mercy of the Crown, the Minister of Justice may order a new trial, hearing or direct a reference in the case of D convicted in proceedings by indictment or sentenced to a term of preventive detention under Part XXIV.

748.1 (1) Remission by Governor in Council — The Governor in Council may order the remission, in whole or in part, of a fine or forfeiture imposed under an Act of

Parliament, whoever the person may be to whom it is payable or however it may be recoverable.

(2) Terms of remission — An order for remission under subsection (1) may include the remission of costs incurred in the proceedings, but no costs to which a private prosecutor is entitled shall be remitted.

1995, c. 22, s. 6.

Commentary: The section permits the Governor in Council to order entire or partial remission of the pecuniary penalty, fine or forfeiture imposed under Federal enactment. It matters not to whom the pecuniary penalty, fine or forfeiture is payable, nor the manner of its recovery. Costs may be ordered remitted, except those payable to a private prosecutor.

Related Provisions: The Governor in Council may also grant pardons under ss. 748(2)-(4). Pardons may be obtained under ss.3 and 4 and revoked under s. 7 of the *Criminal Records Act*. Their effect is described in s.5 of the Act. A form of pardon is prescribed in its Schedule.

The royal mercy may be extended under s. 748.1(1) to any person sentenced to imprisonment under Federal enactment, whether in default of payment of a pecuniary penalty or otherwise. The *Code* provisions do not, in any manner, limit or affect Her Majesty's royal prerogative.

Under s.690, where an application is made for the mercy of the Crown, the Minister of Justice may order a new trial, hearing or direct a reference in the case of any accused convicted in proceedings by indictment or sentenced to a term of preventive detention under Part XXIV.

749. Royal prerogative — Nothing in this Act in any manner limits or affects Her Majesty's royal prerogative of mercy.

Commentary: The section ensures that Her Majesty's royal prerogative of mercy remains unaffected and not limited by any *Code* provision.

Related Provisions: Section 748(1) permits the extension of the royal mercy to anyone sentenced to imprisonment under Federal enactment.

The Governor in Council may also grant pardons under ss. 748(2)-(4). Pardons may be obtained under ss.3 and 4 and revoked under s. 7 of the *Criminal Records Act*. Their effect is described in s. 7 of the Act and a form of pardon in its Schedule.

The Governor in Council may also order the entire or partial remission of a pecuniary penalty, fine or forfeiture under s. 748.1.

Disabilities

750. (1) Public office vacated for conviction — Where a person is convicted of an indictable offence for which the person is sentenced to imprisonment for two years or more and holds, at the time that person is convicted, an office under the Crown or other public employment, the office or employment forthwith becomes vacant.

(2) When disability ceases — A person to whom subsection (1) applies is, until undergoing the punishment imposed on the person or the punishment substituted therefor by competent authority or receives a free pardon from Her Majesty, incapable of holding any office under the Crown or other public employment, or of being elected or sitting or voting as a member of Parliament or of a legislature or of exercising any right of suffrage.

(3) Disability to contract — No person who is convicted of an offence under section 121, 124 or 418 has, after that conviction, capacity to contract with Her Majesty or to receive any benefit under a contract between Her Majesty and any other person or to hold office under Her Majesty.

(4) **Application for restoration of privileges** — A person to whom subsection (3) applies may, at any time before a pardon is granted to the person under section 4.1 of the *Criminal Records Act*, apply to the Governor in Council for the restoration of one or more of the capacities lost by the person by virtue of that subsection.

(5) **Order of restoration** — Where an application is made under subsection (4), the Governor in council may order that the capacities lost by the applicant by virtue of subsection (3) be restored to that applicant in whole or in part and subject to such conditions as the Governor in Council considers desirable in the public interest.

(6) **Removal of disability** — Where a conviction is set aside by competent authority, any disability imposed by this section is removed.

1995, c. 22, s. 6.

Commentary: The section prescribes the disabilities which ensue upon conviction of certain indictable offences.

Section 750(1) and (2) detail the disabilities which ensue when D, who holds office under the Crown or other public employment, is convicted of an indictable offence and sentenced to imprisonment for a term of two years or more. Upon conviction and sentence, D's office or employment forthwith becomes vacant. Further, until D serves or otherwise discharges the punishment imposed or receives a free pardon from Her Majesty, D is incapable of holding any office under the Crown or public employment, of being elected, sitting or voting as a member of Parliament or a legislature or of exercising any right of suffrage. To the extent at least that D is denied the right to vote, the subsection may attract scrutiny under *Charter* ss.3 and 15(1).

Sections. 750(3) - (5) prescribe the disabilities associated with conviction of certain offences. Under s. 750 (3), where D has been convicted of an offence under ss.121 (frauds upon the government), 124 (selling or purchasing office) or 418 (selling defective stores to Her Majesty), D lacks capacity to contract with or hold office under Her Majesty and to receive any benefit under a contract between Her Majesty and any other person. D may, however, at any time before a pardon is granted under s.4 of the *Criminal Records Act*, apply to the Governor in Council for a restoration of one or more of the capacities lost upon conviction. Under s. 750(5), any order given by the Governor in Council may restore the capacities in whole or in part and subject to such conditions as are considered advisable in the public interest.

Where any conviction upon which a disability or incapacity is founded is set aside, the disability is also removed by s. 750(6).

Related Provisions: The royal mercy may be extended by Her Majesty and there is nothing in the *Code* which in any manner limits or affects Her Majesty in its exercise. The Governor in Council may grant pardons under s. 748 and order the entire or partial remission of any pecuniary penalty, fine or forfeiture under 748.1.

Miscellaneous Provisions

751. Costs to successful party in case of libel — The person in whose favour judgment is given in proceedings by indictment for defamatory libel is entitled to recover from the opposite party costs in a reasonable amount to be fixed by order of the court.

1995, c. 22, s. 6.

Commentary: The section authorizes the award of *costs* to the successful party in proceedings by indictment for *defamatory libel*. The costs, recoverable from the opposite party, are in a reasonable amount fixed by the court.

Related Provisions: Defamatory libel is governed by ss.297-317.

There is no general authority to award costs either for or against a party in proceedings upon indictment. Some specific provisions, however, do authorize costs, for example, as a condition of a change of venue on application by P under s.599(3), or upon an adjournment under s.601(5). None are allowable on appeal in indictable proceedings under s.683(3), except in respect of legal assistance under ss.684 and 694.1.

Costs may be awarded in summary conviction proceedings at trial (s.809) and on appeal (ss.826, 834(1) and 839(3)).

The recovery of costs under 751 is governed by s. 751.1. A costs award under s. 751 is not expressly contained within the definition of "sentence" in s.673.

751.1 How recovered — Where costs that are fixed under section 751 are not paid forthwith, the party in whose favour judgment is given may enter judgment for the amount of the costs by filing the order in any civil court of the province in which the trial was held that has jurisdiction to enter a judgment for that amount, and that judgment is enforceable against the opposite party in the same manner as if it were a judgment rendered against that opposite party in that court in civil proceedings.

1995, c. 22, s. 6.

Commentary: The section authorizes the recovery of costs awarded in a case of defamatory libel but not paid forthwith. Recovery is made by filing the order for costs in the civil court that has jurisdiction in respect of that amount, thus entering judgment in favour of the successful party in the amount thereof which is enforceable as if a judgment in civil proceedings.

Related Provisions: The recovery or enforcement mechanism is common with fines (s. 734.6), restitution orders (s. 741) and other pecuniary penalties.

The award of costs in defamatory libel cases permitted by s. 751 is not expressly included in the expansive definition of "sentence" in s.673.

PART XXIV — DANGEROUS OFFENDERS AND LONG-TERM OFFENDERS

Interpretation

752. Definitions — In this Part,

"court" means the court by which an offender in relation to whom an application under this Part is made was convicted, or a superior court of criminal jurisdiction;

"serious personal injury offence" means

> **(a) an indictable offence, other than high treason, treason, first degree murder or second degree murder, involving**
>
> > **(i) the use or attempted use of violence against another person, or**
> >
> > **(ii) conduct endangering or likely to endanger the life or safety of another person or inflicting or likely to inflict severe psychological damage upon another person,**
>
> **and for which the offender may be sentenced to imprisonment for ten years or more, or**
>
> **(b) an offence or attempt to commit an offence mentioned in section 271 (sexual assault), 272 (sexual assault with a weapon, threats to a third party or causing bodily harm) or 273 (aggravated sexual assault).**

R.S., c. C-34, s. 687; 1976–77, c. 53, s. 14; 180–81–82–83, c. 125, s. 26.

Commentary: This section exhaustively defines "court" and "serious personal injury offence".

"Court" refers to the court in which the conviction for the underlying or predicate offence was recorded, or the superior court of criminal jurisdiction. It represents, in other words, the court in which dangerous offender proceedings are taken.

"Serious personal injury offence" defines the two categories of offence which may serve as an offence predicate to initiate dangerous offender applications. Under s. 752(a), the offence must be an *indictable* offence, other than treason, high treason or murder, for which D may be sentenced to imprisonment for 10 years or more. The offence must also involve the actual or attempted use of *violence* against another, or *conduct* endangering or likely to endanger the life or safety of another, or inflicting or likely to inflict severe psychological damage upon another. A "serious personal injury offence" uner s. 752(b) is an offence or an attempt to commit an offence contrary to s. 271 (sexual assault), 272 (sexual assault with a weapon, threats to a third party, causing bodily harm, or sexual assault by multiple accused) or 273 (aggravated sexual assault).

Case Law

General Principles

R. v. Milne (1987), 61 C.R. (3d) 55, (sub nom. *Milne v. Canada)* 38 C.C.C. (3d) 502 — D was found to be a dangerous offender prior to amendments to this section which deleted "gross indecency" as a "serious personal injury offence". D's continuing detention did *not* infringe *Charter* ss. 9 or 12.

Serious Personal Injury Offence

R. v. Yanoshewski (1996), 104 C.C.C. (3d) 512 (Sask. C.A.) — Sexual assault may constitute a "serious personal injury offence" under either paragraph (a) or (b) of the definition in s. 752.

Related Provisions: "Superior court of criminal jurisdiction" is defined in s. 2.

Dangerous Offenders and Long-Term Offenders

752.1 (1) Application for remand for assessment — Where an offender is convicted of a serious personal injury offence or an offence referred to in paragraph 753.1(2)(a) and, before sentence is imposed on the offender, on application by the prosecution, the court is of the opinion that there are reasonable grounds to believe that the offender might be found to be a dangerous offender under section 753 or a long-term offender under section 753.1, the court may, by order in writing remand the offender, for a period not exceeding sixty days, to the custody of the person that the court directs and who can perform an assessment, or can have an assessment performed by experts. The assessment is to be used as evidence in an application under section 753 or 753.1.

(2) Report — The person to whom the offender is remanded shall file a report of the assessment with the court not later than fifteen days after the end of the assessment period and make copies of it available to the prosecutor and counsel for the offender.

1997, c. 17, s. 4

Commentary: This section authorizes assessment of persons who may become the subject of dangerous or long-term offender proceedings.

Where D has been convicted of a serious personal injury offence as defined in s. 752, or an offence described in s. 753.1(2)(a), P may apply before sentence is passed for an assessment order under s. 752.1(1). If the court concludes that there are reasonable grounds to believe that D might be found to be a dangerous or long-term offender, the court may remand D, by order in writing, for a period of not more than sixty (60) days for expert assessment. In dangerous and long-term offender applications, the assessment may be used as evidence.

Within fifteen (15) days of the end of the assessment period, the person to whom D was remanded must file a report of the assessment with the court. P and D are entitled to copies.

Related Provisions: "Serious personal injury offence" is defined in s. 752.

Applications to have D declared a dangerous offender are governed by ss. 753 and 754. Section 757 permits the introduction of evidence of D's character on the hearing. Section 758 requires that D be present, subject to certain exceptions.

Long-term offender applications are controlled by ss. 753.1 and 754. Long-term supervision is governed by s. 753.2. Sections 753.3 and 753.4 apply to breaches of long-term supervision orders and new offences committed during supervision.

The report which s. 752.1(2) requires is to be completed by the person to whom the prospective dangerous or long-term offender has been remanded. The reporter is not necessarily the expert who conducted the assessment.

Expert testimony may be given by report and accompanying affidavit or solemn declaration under s. 657.3.

753. (1) **Application for finding that an offender is a dangerous offender** — The court may, on application made under this Part following the filing of an assessment report under subsection 752.1(2), find the offender to be a dangerous offender if it is satisfied

(a) that the offence for which the offender has been convicted is a serious personal injury offence described in paragraph (*a*) of the definition of that expression in section 752 and the offender constitutes a threat to the life, safety or physical or mental well-being of other persons on the basis of evidence establishing

(i) a pattern of behaviour by the offender, of which the offence for which he or she has been convicted forms a part, showing a failure to restrain his or her behaviour and likelihood of causing death or injury to other persons, or inflicting severe psychological damage on other persons, through failure in the future to restrain his or her behaviour,

(ii) a pattern of persistent aggressive behaviour by the offender, of which the offence for which he or she has been convicted forms a part, showing a substantial degree of indifference on the part of the offender respecting the reasonably foreseeable consequences to other persons of his or her behaviour, or

(iii) any behaviour by the offender, associated with the offence for which he or she has been convicted, that is of such a brutal nature as to compel the conclusion that the offender's behaviour in the future is unlikely to be inhibited by normal standards of behaviourial restraint; or

(b) that the offence for which the offender has been convicted is a serious personal injury offence described in paragraph (*b*) of the definition of that expression in section 752 and the offender, by his or her conduct in any sexual matter including that involved in the commission of the offence for which he or she has been convicted, has shown a failure to control his or her sexual impulses and a likelihood of causing injury, pain or other evil to other persons through failure in the future to control his or her sexual impulses.

(2) **Time for making application** — An application under subsection (1) must be made before sentence is imposed on the offender unless

(a) before the imposition of sentence, the prosecution gives notice to the offender of a possible intention to make an application under section 752.1 and an application under subsection (1) not later than six months after that imposition; and

(b) at the time of the application under subsection (1) that is not later than six months after imposition of sentence, it is shown that relevant evidence that was not reasonably available to the prosecution at the time of the imposition of sentence became available in the interim.

(3) **Application for remand for assessment after imposition of sentence** — Notwithstanding subsection 752.1(1), an application under that subsection may be made after the imposition of sentence or after an offender begins to serve the sentence in a case to which paragraphs (2)(*a*) and (*b*) apply.

(4) If offender found to be dangerous offender — If the court finds an offender to be a dangerous offender, it shall impose a sentence of detention in a penitentiary for an indeterminate period.

(4.1) If application made after sentencing — If the application was made after
the offender begins to serve the sentence in a case to which paragraphs (2)(*a*) and (*b*)
apply, the sentence of detention in a penitentiary for an indeterminate period referred
to in subsection (4) replaces the sentence that was imposed for the offence for which the
offender was convicted.

(5) If offender not found to be dangerous offender — If the court does not
find an offender to be a dangerous offender,

> (a) the court may treat the application as an application to find the offender to be
> a long-term offender, section 753.1 applies to the application and the court may
> either find that the offender is a long-term offender or hold another hearing for
> that purpose; or

> (b) the court may impose sentence for the offence for which the offender has been
> convicted.

(6) Victim evidence — Any evidence given during the hearing of an application
made under subsection (1) by victim of an offence for which the offender was convicted
is deemed also to have been given during any hearing under paragraph (5)(*a*) held with
respect to the offender.

R.S., c. C-34, s. 688; 1976–77, c. 53, s. 14;1997, c. 17, s. 4

Commentary: This section authorizes and governs applications to have an accused declared a dangerous offender.

As a general rule, dangerous offender applications follow conviction of a serious personal injury offence, and the filing of an assessment report, but precede sentence. The basis upon which D may be
found a dangerous offender are described in ss. 753(1)(a) and (b). Each requires proof of more than the
underlying conviction of a serious personal injury offence. The requirements of ss. 753(1)(a) and (b) are
alternatives, not cumulative. Where D is found to be a dangerous offender, s. 753(4) requires the judge
to impose a sentence of detention in a penitentiary for an indeterminate period.

Where the dangerous offender application fails, s. 753(5) permits it to be converted to an application to
find D to be a long-term offender. A finding may be made or a separate hearing held. The court may also
impose sentence on D for the underlying offence. By s. 753(6), any evidence given by V on the dangerous offender application is deemed to have been given during any long-term offender hearing held under
s. 753(5).

Section 753(2) describes the circumstances in which a dangerous offender application may be made
after D has been sentenced for the predicate offence. The requirements involve pre-sentence notice of a
"possible intention" to apply for a remand for assessment, an application to have D declared a dangerous
offender withing six (6) months of the imposition of sentence and proof that relevant evidence, not
reasonably available at the time sentence was imposed, has since become available. An application for a
remand for assessment may be made under s. 753(3). Where D is found to be a dangerous offender, the
mandatory sentence replaces what was imposed earlier under s. 753(4.1).

Case Law
Burden of Proof
R. v. Jackson (1981), 23 C.R. (3d) 4, 61 C.C.C. (2d) 540 (N.S. C.A.) — The onus is on P to establish
beyond a reasonable doubt all the necessary elements to constitute D a dangerous offender.

General Principles (Dangerous Offender)
R. v. Currie (1997), 7 C.R. (5th) 74, [1997] 2 S.C.R. 260, 115 C.C.C. (3d) 205 — Under s. 753(b), P
must prove beyond a reasonable doubt

i.   that D has been convicted of a "serious personal injury offence" as described in s. 752(b); and

ii.   that there is a "likelihood" that D will cause "injury, pain or other evil to other persons through failure in the future to control his sexual impulses".

R. v. Carleton (1983), 36 C.R. (3d) 393, 6 C.C.C. (3d) 480 (S.C.C.); affirming (1981), 23 C.R. (3d) 129, 69 C.C.C. (2d) 1 (Alta. C.A.) — *See also: R. v. Poutsoungas* (1989), 49 C.C.C. (3d) 388 (Ont. C.A.) — The probability of a cure is *not* relevant to the question whether D was a dangerous offender since that determination is to be based on past conduct; however, it is relevant in deciding whether a sentence of indeterminate detention is required.

R. v. Currie (1995), 103 C.C.C. (3d) 281 (Ont. C.A.); reversed (1997), 7 C.R. (5th) 74, [1997] 2 S.C.R. 260, 115 C.C.C. (3d) 205 — In deciding whether D is a dangerous offender, a judge is required to consider

i.   the *facts* constituting the *predicate offences*;

ii.   D's *criminal record;* and,

iii.   the *expert testimony* of psychiatrists

but *not* the other checks and balances in the penal system.

R. v. Lewis (1984), 12 C.C.C. (3d) 353 (Ont. C.A.); appeal abated on death of appellant (1985), 25 C.C.C. (3d) 288n (S.C.C.) — D may be found to be a dangerous offender if the evidence establishes any one of the three tests set out in s. 753(a).

R. v. Yanoshewski (1996), 104 C.C.C. (3d) 512 (Sask. C.A.) — D may *not* be found a dangerous offender upon the basis of conviction of an offence which occurred prior to enactment of dangerous offender legislation.

Pattern of Repetitive Behaviour: S. 753(1)(a)(i)

R. v. Langevin (1984), 39 C.R. (3d) 333, 11 C.C.C. (3d) 336 (Ont. C.A.) — The existence of a "pattern of repetitive behaviour" within the meaning of s. 753(a)(i) is *not* determined only by the number of offences. The elements of similarity in D's behaviour are also relevant.

Pattern of Persistent Agressive Behaviour: S. 753(1)(a)(ii)

R. v. George (1998), 126 C.C.C. (3d) 384 (B.C. C.A.) — In determining what constitutes a *pattern* of persistent aggressive behaviour under s. 753(1)(a)(ii), a judge should distinguish between childhood aggression and adult criminality. The former, which may reflect the background and circumstances of may disadvantaged children, is *not* necessarily indicative of dangerousness.

Brutal Nature: S. 753(1)(a)(iii)

R. v. Langevin (1984), 39 C.R. (3d) 333, 11 C.C.C. (3d) 336 (Ont. C.A.) — The brutal nature of the conduct which must be established does *not* demand a situation of stark horror. Conduct which is coarse, savage and cruel and which is capable of inflicting severe psychological damage on V is sufficiently brutal to meet the test.

Failure to Control Sexual Impulses: S. 753(1)(b)

R. v. Currie (1997), 7 C.R. (5th) 74, [1997] 2 S.C.R. 260, 115 C.C.C. (3d) 205 (S.C.C.) — The prospective dangerousness of the offender in s. 753(b) is measured by reference to his/her "conduct in any sexual matter, including that involved in the commission of the offence for which he has been convicted". There need not be a focus upon the objective seriousness of the predicate offence to determine the application. "Any sexual matter" may, but need not refer to the predicate offence. Provided D's past conduct in any sexual matter demonstrates a present likelihood of inflicting future harm upon others, the designation "dangerous offender" if justified.

R. v. Dawson (1969), 8 C.R.N.S. 395, [1970] 3 C.C.C. 212 (B.C. C.A.) — Mere proof of a conviction may be supplemented with evidence of the circumstances to establish a failure to control sexual impulses and conversely D may adduce evidence to show that the conviction was not in a sexual matter or that it did not show a failure to control his sexual impulses.

R. v. Kanester, [1968] 1 C.C.C. 351 (B.C. C.A.) — A sexual offence for which D was *not* convicted may be evidence that D has shown a failure to control his sexual impulses.

Injury, Pain or Other Evil: S. 753(1)(b)

R. v. Dwyer (1977), 34 C.C.C. (2d) 293 (Alta. C.A.); leave to appeal refused (1977), 34 C.C.C. (2d) 293n (S.C.C.) — "Evil" under the former provisions need *not* be construed *ejusdem generis* with "injury" and "pain", hence is not restricted to violence or some type of physical injury.

Charter Considerations

R. v. Lyons (1988), 61 C.R. (3d) 1, 37 C.C.C. (3d) 1 (S.C.C.); affirming (1984), 15 C.C.C. (3d) 129 (N.S. C.A.), which affirmed (1984), 62 N.S.R. 383 (N.S. Co. Ct.) — The provisions of this part concerning a finding of dangerous offender status do *not* offend *Charter* ss. 7, 9 or 12.

Related Provisions: Section 752 defines "court" and "serious personal injury offence" for the purposes of Part XXIV.

Section 754 sets out several requirements which must be satisfied before a dangerous offender application may be heard. It also enacts procedural and evidentiary rules which govern the hearing. Section 758 provides for the presence of the accused. Evidence of the offender's character may be adduced under s. 757. Appellate rights and remedies are contained in s. 759.

Long-term offender applications are commenced in accordance with s. 753.1. The requirements of s. 754 would also appear to apply. Long-term supervision is governed by s. 753.2. Section 753.3 provides a mechanism to deal with breaches of orders of long-term supervision. Section 753.4 applies where D is convicted of another offence whilst under a long-term supervision order. Appellate rights and remedies are also contained in s. 759.

753.1 (1) Application for finding that an offender is a long-term offender

— The court may, on application made under this Part following the filing of an assessment report under subsection 752.1(2), find an offender to be a long-term offender if it is satisfied that

(a) it would be appropriate to impose a sentence of imprisonment of two years or more for the offence for which the offender has been convicted;

(b) there is a substantial risk that the offender will reoffend; and

(c) there is a reasonable possibility of eventual control of the risk in the community.

(2) Substantial risk — The court shall be satisfied that there is a substantial risk that the offender will reoffend if

(a) the offender has been convicted of an offence under section 151 (sexual interference), 152 (invitation to sexual touching) or 153 (sexual exploitation), subsection 173(2) (exposure) or section 271 (sexual assault), 272 (sexual assault with a weapon) or 273 (aggravated sexual assault), or has engaged in serious conduct of a sexual nature in the commission of another offence of which the offender has been convicted; and

(b) the offender

(i) has shown a pattern of repetitive behaviour, of which the offence for which he or she has been convicted forms a part, that shows a likelihood of the offender's causing death or injury to other persons or inflicting severe psychological damage on other persons, or

(ii) by conduct in any sexual matter including that involved in the commission of the offence for which the offender has been convicted, has shown a likelihood of causing injury, pain or other evil to other persons in the future through similar offence.

(3) If offender found to be long-term offender — Subject to subsection (3.1), (4) and (5), if the court finds an offender to be a long-term offender, it shall

(a) impose a sentence for the offence for which the offender has been convicted, which sentence must be a minimum punishment of imprisonment for a term of two years; and

(b) order the offender to be supervised in the community, for a period not exceeding ten years, in accordance with section 753.2 and the *Corrections and Conditional Release Act.*

(3.1) Exception – if application made after sentencing — The court may not impose a sentence under paragraph (3)(*a*) and the sentence that was imposed for the offence for which the offender was convicted stands despite the offender's being found to be a long-term offender, if the application was one that

(a) was made after the offender begins to serve the sentence in a case to which paragraphs 753(2)(*a*) and (*b*) apply; and

(b) was treated as an application under this section further to the court deciding to do so under paragraph 753(5)(*a*).

(4) Exception-life sentence — The court shall not make an order under paragraph (3)(*b*) if the offender has been sentenced to life imprisonment.

(5) Exception to length of supervision where new declaration — If the offender commits another offence while required to be supervised by an order made under paragraph (3)(*b*), and is thereby found to be a long-term offender, the periods of supervision to which the offender is subject at any particular time must not total more than ten years.

(6) If offender not found to be long-term offender — If the court does not find an offender to be a long-term offender, the court shall impose sentence for the offence for which the offender has been convicted.

1997, c. 17, s. 4

Commentary: This section defines the basis upon which D may be declared a long-term offender. It also describes the disposition which is to be made as a result of the finding.

Sections 753.1(1) and (2) describe the test to be applied. The court must be satisfied that

i.   the predicate offence warrants a sentence of imprisonment of two years or more;

ii.   there is a substantial risk that D will re-offend;

iii. there is a reasonable possibility of eventual control of the risk in the community.

The substantial risk requirement of item ii is met where the provisions of s. 753.1(2) have been satisfied. What is involved is conviction of a listed predicate offence, or proof of serious conduct of a sexual nature in the commission of another offence of which D has been convicted, and satisfaction of either requirement of s. 753.1(2)(b).

Where D is found to be a long-term offender, s. 753.1(3) describes the constituents of the sentence to be imposed. As a general rule, there must be a term of imprisonment of at least two years. It must be followed by a period of community supervision governed by *Code* s. 753.2 and *C.C.R.A.*, which must not exceed ten years.

The general rule is subject to three exceptions in ss. 753.1(3.1), (4) and (5). The minimum custodial sentence requirement of s. 753.1(3)(a) does not apply where the long-term offender application was made after D had begun to serve the sentence for the predicate offence and was converted from a dangerous offender application under s. 753(5)(a). The community supervision provision also does not apply where D has been sentenced to life imprisonment for the predicate offence. Under s. 753.1(5), offenders who commit other offences during community supervision, resulting in long-term offender applications, must not be subject to community supervision orders at any time exceeding ten years.

Where the long-term offender application fails, s. 753.1(6) requires that D be sentenced for the predicate offence.

Related Provisions: After D has been convicted of an offence which may give rise to a long-term offender application, a *remand* for assessment may be ordered under s. 752.1. The *filing* of the assessment report is required before D may be found a long-term offender.

The procedural requirements of a s. 754 apply to the hearing of the application. Notice and the consent of the Attorney General are required. The presence of D is governed by s. 758. *C.C.R.A.* describes the manner in which long-term supervision is carried out. Sections 753.2(3) and (4) permit applications to reduce or terminate long-term supervision, on notice to the Attorney General. Section 753.3 applies where D is alleged to have breached a long-term supervision order. Section 753.4 dictates what happens when D is convicted of another offence during long-term supervision and a sentence of imprisonment is imposed.

Under s. 759(1.1), D may appeal from a *finding* that s/he is a long-term offender, and from the *length* of the period of long-term supervision. The dispositive authority of the court is found in ss. 759(3.1) and (3.2). The Attorney General may appeal from the *dismissal* of an application, or from the *length* of the *period* of long-term supervision, but only on a question of law. Sections 759(4.1) and (4.2) describe the dispositive authority of the court.

Other provisions relating to dangerous offender applications are discussed in the corresponding note to s. 753.

753.2 (1) Long-term supervision — Subject to subsection (2), an offender who is required to be supervised by an order made under paragraph 753.1(3)(*b*) shall be supervised in accordance with the *Corrections and Conditional Release Act* when the offender has finished serving

(a) the sentence for the offence for which the offender has been convicted; and

(b) all other sentences for offences for which the offender is convicted and for which sentence of a term of imprisonment is imposed on the offender, either before or after the conviction for the offence referred to in paragraph (*a*).

(2) Non-carceral sentences — A sentence imposed on an offender referred to in subsection (1), other than a sentence that requires imprisonment of the offender, is to be served concurrently with the long-term supervision ordered under paragraph 753.1(3)(*b*).

(3) Application for reduction in period of long- term supervision — An offender who is required to be supervised, a member of the National Parole Board, or, on approval of that Board, the parole supervisor, as that expression is defined in subsection 134.2(2) of the *Corrections and Conditional Release Act*, of the offender, may apply to a superior court of criminal jurisdiction for an order reducing the period of long-term supervision or terminating it on the ground that the offender no longer presents a substantial risk of reoffending and thereby being a danger to the community. The onus of proving that ground is on the applicant.

(4) Notice to Attorney General — The applicant must give notice of an application under subsection (3) to the Attorney General at the time the application is made.

1997, c. 17, s. 4

Commentary: This section provides for the manner in which the community supervision portion of a sentence imposed on long-term offenders will be carried out.

Under s. 753.2(1), supervision is carried out in accordance with *C.C.R.A.* after the custodial sentence and any other sentences of imprisonment have been completed. Any non-carceral sentences are to be served concurrently with the period of long-term supervision.

Sections 753.2(3) and (4) permit *reduction* or *termination* of periods of long-term supervision. Application may be made by D, a member of the National Parole Board or, with Board approval, D's parole supervisor. Where D demonstrates that s/he no longer represents a substantial risk of re-offending, thereby a danger to the community, the period may be terminated or reduced. Section 753.2(4) entitles the Attorney General to notice of the application.

Related Provisions: Failure or refusal to comply with a long-term supervision order is an indictable offence under s. 753.3. Where a long-term offender is convicted of an offence and sentenced to a term of imprisonment, the period of long-term supervision is interrupted until the sentence has been served under s. 753.4(1). Unless the period is terminated or reduced under s. 753.4(2), it will resume at the end of the term of imprisonment.

Other related provisions are discussed in the corresponding note to s. 753.1.

753.3 (1) **Breach of order of long-term supervision** — An offender who is required to be supervised by an order made under paragraph 753.1(3)(*b*) and who, without reasonable excuse, fails or refuses to comply with that order is guilty of an indictable offence and liable to imprisonment for a term not exceeding ten years.

(2) **Where accused may be tried and punished** — An accused who is charged with an offence under subsection (1) may be tried and punished by any court having jurisdiction to try that offence in the place where the offence is alleged to have been committed or in the place where the accused is found, is arrested or is in custody, but if the place where the accused is found, is arrested or is in custody is outside the province in which the offence is alleged to have been committed, no proceedings in respect of that offence shall be instituted in that place without the consent of the Attorney General of that province.

1997, c. 17, s. 4

Commentary: This section creates an indictable offence for *failure* or *refusal* to *comply* with an order of long-term supervision. It also contains expanded trial jurisdiction provisions.

Section 753.3(1) is the offence-creating section. The *external circumstances* include the absence of reasonable excuse and a failure or refusal to comply with an order of long-term supervision. No ulterior *mental element* need be proven.

Under s. 753.3(2), the offence may be tried by a court of competent offence jurisdiction where the offence occurred or where D is found, arrested or in custody. D may also be tried if found, arrested or in custody in a province other than where the offence was committed with the consent of the Attorney General of the province where the offence was committed.

Related Provisions: Community supervision, as part of the sentence imposed on long-term offenders, is required by s. 753.1(3)(b) and regulated by s. 753.2 and *C.C.R.A.*

A long-term offender convicted of an offence when subject to an order of long-term supervision and sentenced to a term of imprisonment must serve the custodial sentence in accordance with s. 753.4. A similar provision appears in s. 742.7 for conditional sentences.

The provisions of s. 753 are similar to those of s. 733.1, which applies to probation orders, and s. 742.6(3) which relates to conditional sentences.

Other related provisions are discussed in the corresponding note to s. 753.1.

753.4 (1) **Where new offence** — Where an offender who is required to be supervised by an order made under paragraph 753.1(3)(*b*) commits one or more offences under this or any other Act and a court imposes a sentence of imprisonment for the offence or offence, the long-term supervision is interrupted until the offender has finished serving all the sentences, unless the court orders its termination.

(2) **Reduction in term of long-term supervision** — A court that imposes a sentence of imprisonment under subsection (1) may order a reduction in the length of the period of the offender's long-term supervision.

1997, c. 17, s. 4

Commentary: Section 753.4 sets out what happens when D, under a long-term supervision order, is convicted of an offence and sentenced to a term of imprisonment.

Under s. 753.4(1), the long-term supervision is interrupted until the sentence of imprisonment has been served, unless the convicting court terminates the supervision order. The length of the order may also be reduced under s. 753.4(2).

Related Provisions: Failure or refusal to comply with a long-term supervision order is an indictable offence under s. 753.3.

Other related provisions are discussed in the corresponding note to s. 753.1.

754. (1) Hearing of application — **Where an application under this Part has been made, the court shall hear and determine the application except that no such application shall be heard unless**

   (a) the Attorney General of the province in which the offender was tried has, either before or after the making of the application, consented to the application;

   (b) at least seven days notice has been given to the offender by the prosecutor, following the making of the application, outlining the basis on which it is intended to found the application; and

   (c) a copy of the notice has been filed with the clerk of the court or the provincial court judge, as the case may be.

(2) By court alone — **An application under this Part shall be heard and determined by the court without a jury.**

(3) When proof unnecessary — **For the purposes of an application under this Part, where an offender admits any allegations contained in the notice referred to in paragraph (1)(*b*), no proof of those allegations is required.**

(4) Proof of consent — **The production of a document purporting to contain any nomination or consent that may be made or given by the Attorney General under this Part and purporting to be signed by the Attorney General is, in the absence of any evidence to the contrary, proof of that nomination or consent without proof of the signature or the official character of the person appearing to have signed the document.**
                    R.S., c. C-34, s. 689; 1976–77, c. 53, s. 14;R.S. 1985, c. 27 (1st Supp.), s. 203.

Commentary: The section describes the conditions precedent to the hearing and determination of a dangerous and long-term offender applications and, to some extent at least, the procedure to be followed upon the hearing.

Applications are heard and determined by a convicting court or a judge of the superior court of criminal jurisdiction, in all cases without a jury. The Attorney General of the province must *consent* to the bringing of the application, either before or after the application has been made. The consent of the Attorney General may be proven under s. 754(4) by production of a document containing such consent, purporting to be signed by the Attorney General. In the *absence* of *any evidence* to the *contrary*, the document is *proof* of the *consent*, without proof of the signature or the official character of the signing authority. Under s. 754(1)(b), P must give to D at least seven days' *notice* after the making of the application outlining the basis therefor. Under s. 754(3), D may *admit* any allegation contained in the notice, thereby obviating the necessity for its proof on the hearing. A copy of the notice must be filed with the clerk of the court or provincial court judge who is to determine the application.

Case Law

Notice of Application

R. v. Van Boeyen (1996), 107 C.C.C. (3d) 135 (B.C. C.A.) — Notice of application need *not* be served personally upon D. Service on counsel for D is sufficient.

R. v. Corbiere (1995), 80 O.A.C. 222 (C.A.) — In deciding whether written notice has been given under s. 754(1)(b), a court should consider the cumulative effect of documents served in the context of the evidentiary disclosure provided to D.

R. v. Currie (1984), 12 C.C.C. (3d) 28 (Ont. C.A.) — There is *no* minimum time period for giving notice of the making of an application for an order under this Part, nor need the application be made in writing. The application need only be made to the court in the presence of D. Following the making of the application D is to be given seven days notice of the basis on which the application is to be founded. This notice must be in writing. In order to give effect to the provisions of this section, it is incumbent upon the court, at the time the application is made, that it adjourn the application for hearing to a date at least seven days hence.

Charter Considerations

R. v. Lyons (1987), 61 C.R. (3d) 1, 37 C.C.C. (3d) 1 (S.C.C.) — The failure of P to inform D prior to his election or plea that it intends to bring a dangerous offender application does *not* offend *Charter*, s. 7.

Related Provisions: As a general rule, subject to limited exceptions, D must be present on the hearing of an application. The *evidence* which may be adduced includes character evidence under s. 757, as well as any admissions under s. 754(3). The provisions do not restrict the reception of any other evidence relevant to the issues on the application otherwise properly receivable. The s. 752.1 assessment is used as evidence on the hearing.

The relevant standards to be applied in deciding whether D is a dangerous or long-term offender are described in ss. 753 and 753.1.

Section 759 confers rights of appeal from a sentence of detention in a penitentiary for an indeterminate period, as well as from the dismissal of an application for an order under this Part.

755. [Repealed 1997, c. 17, s. 5.]

756. [Repealed 1997, c. 17, s. 5.]

757. Evidence of character — Without prejudice to the right of the offender to tender evidence as to his or her character and repute, evidence of character and repute may, if the court thinks fit, be admitted on the question of whether the offender is or is not a dangerous offender or a long-term offender.

R.S., c. C-34, s. 692; 1976–77, c. 53, s. 14;1997, c. 17, s. 5

Commentary: This section expressly permits the reception of *evidence* of D's *character and repute* in dangerous offender proceedings, upon the question of whether D is a dangerous offender. The provision operates without prejudice to D's right to tender evidence of character and repute.

The reception of evidence of D's character and repute is *not* dependent upon D putting character in issue in the proceedings. The evidence contemplated by the section would appear admissible as part of P's case, provided the court thinks fit to receive it.

Related Provisions: The general rule relating to the reception of evidence in dangerous offender applications, as in criminal proceedings generally, is relevance. Section 755(1) holds expert evidence receivable and s. 754(3) permits admissions to be made of allegations contained in the notice required under s. 754(1)(b). Evidence may also be obtained as a result of observations made under s. 756.

Other related provisions are described in the corresponding notes to ss. 752 and 754, *supra*.

758. (1) Presence of accused at hearing of application — The offender shall be present at the hearing of the application under this Part and if at the time the application is to be heard

(a) he is confined in a prison, the court may order, in writing, the person having the custody of the accused to bring him before the court; or

(b) he is not confined in a prison, the court shall issue a summons or a warrant to compel the accused to attend before the court and the provisions of Part XVI relating to summons and warrant are applicable with such modifications as the circumstances require.

(2) Exception — Notwithstanding subsection (1), the court may

(a) cause the offender to be removed and to be kept out of court, where he misconducts himself by interrupting the proceedings so that to continue the proceedings in his presence would not be feasible; or

(b) permit the offender to be out of court during the whole or any part of the hearing on such conditions as the court considers proper.

R.S., c. C-34, s. 693; 1976–77, c. 53, s. 14.

Commentary: The section requires, with limited exceptions, that D be *present at the hearing* of a dangerous offender application.

Section 758(1) establishes the general rule that D must be present at the hearing and makes provision to ensure such presence by authorizing transfer from a place of custody, or the issuance of process to compel attendance, where D is not already in custody.

Section 758(2) enacts two exceptions to the general rule: D may be *removed* under s. 758(2)(a) on account of *misconduct*, or, under s. 758(2)(b), *permitted* to be out of court, during the whole or any part of the hearing, on such terms as the court considers *appropriate*.

Related Provisions: As a general rule, D must be present at trial under s. 650. Exceptions are provided for in s. 650(1.1), (1.2) and (2). Proceedings, in some instances, may be continued where D absconds during the course of trial (ss. 475 and 598), or during the preliminary inquiry (s. 544).

Other related provisions are described in the corresponding notes to ss. 753 and 753.1, *supra*.

759. (1) Appeal – dangerous offender — An offender who is found to be a dangerous offender under this Part may appeal to the court of appeal against that finding on any ground of law or fact or mixed law and fact.

(1.1) Appeal – long-term offender — An offender who is found to be a long-term offender under this Part may appeal to the court of appeal against that finding or against the length of the period of long-term supervision ordered, on any ground of law or fact or mixed law and fact.

(2) Appeal by Attorney General — The Attorney General may appeal to the court of appeal against the dismissal of an application for an order under this Part, or against the length of the period of long-term supervision of a long-term offender, on any ground of law.

(3) Disposition of appeal – dangerous offender — On an appeal against a finding that an offender is a dangerous offender, the court of appeal may

(a) allow the appeal and

(i) find that the offender is not a dangerous offender, find that the offender is a long-term offender, impose a minimum sentence of imprisonment for two years, for the offence for which the offender has been convicted, and order the offender to be supervised in the community, for a period that does not, subject to subsection 753.1(5), exceed ten years, in accordance with section 753.2 and the *Corrections and Conditional Release Act*,

(ii) find that the offender is not a dangerous offender and impose sentence for the offence for which the offender has been convicted, or

(iii) order a new hearing; or

(b) dismiss the appeal.

(3.1) Disposition of appeal – long-term offender — On an appeal against a finding that an offender is a long-term offender, the court of appeal may

   (a) allow the appeal and

      (i) **find that the offender is not a long-term offender and quash the order for long-term supervision, or**

      (ii) **order a new hearing; or**

   (b) dismiss the appeal,

(3.2) Disposition of appeal – long-term offender — On an appeal by a long-term offender against the length of a period of long-term supervision of the long-term offender, the court of appeal may

   (a) allow the appeal and change the length of the period; or

   (b) dismiss the appeal.

(4) Disposition of appeal by Attorney General — On an appeal against the dismissal of an application for an order that an offender is a dangerous offender under this Part, the court of appeal may

   (a) allow the appeal and

      (i) find that the offender is a dangerous offender,

      (ii) find that the offender is not a dangerous offender, find that the offender is a long-term offender, impose a minimum sentence of imprisonment for two years, for the offence for which the offender has been convicted, and order the offender to be supervised in the community, for a period that does not, subject to subsection 753.1(5), exceed ten years, in accordance with section 753.2 and the *Corrections and Conditional Release Act*, or

      (iii) order a new hearing; or

   (b) dismiss the appeal.

(4.1) Disposition of appeal by Attorney General — On an appeal by the Attorney General against the length of a period of long-term supervision of a long-term offender, the court of appeal may

   (a) allow the appeal and change the length of the period; or

   (b) dismiss the appeal.

(4.2) Disposition of appeal by Attorney General — On an appeal against the dismissal of an application for a finding that an offender is a long-term offender under this Part, the court of appeal may

   (a) allow the appeal and

      (i) find that the offender is a long-term offender, impose a minimum sentence of imprisonment for two years, for the offence for which the offender has been convicted, and order the offender to be supervised in the community, for a period that does not, subject to subsection 753.1(5), exceed ten years, in accordance with section 753.2 and the *Corrections and Conditional Release Act*, or

      (ii) order a new hearing; or

   (b) dismiss the appeal.

(5) Effect of judgment — A judgment of the court of appeal finding that an offender is or is not a dangerous offender or a long-term offender, or changing the length of the period of long-term supervision ordered, has the same force and effect as if it were a finding by or judgment of the trial court.

(6) **Commencement of sentence** — Notwithstanding subsection 719(1), a sentence imposed on an offender by the court of appeal pursuant to this section shall be deemed to have commenced when the offender was sentenced by the court by which he was convicted.

(7) **Part XXI applies re appeals** — The provisions of Part XXI with respect to procedure on appeals apply, with such modifications as the circumstances require, to appeals under this section.

R.S., c. C-34, s. 694; 1976–77, c. 53, s. 14;1995, c. 22, s. 10; 1997, c. 17, s. 6

Commentary: This section creates appellate rights and remedies in dangerous and long-term offender proceedings. The procedure followed on appeals is that of Part XXI.

In dangerous offender proceedings, D may appeal to the court of appeal against the finding that s/he is a dangerous offender. Leave to appeal is not required. The appeal may be based on grounds of law, fact or mixed law and fact. The powers of the court of appeal, defined in s. 759(3), include, but are not limited to substitution of a finding that D is not a dangerous offender, but rather, a long-term offender and imposition of the appropriate sentence. The Attorney General may appeal from the dismissal of a dangerous offender application, but only on a question of law alone under s. 759(2). The dispositive powers of the court in s. 759(4) include the authority to find D a dangerous offender or to find that D is not a dangerous offender, but rather, a long-term offender and impose the proper sentence.

In long-term offender proceedings, D may appeal from a finding or the length of the period of long-term supervision on any ground of law, fact of mixed law and fact. The dispositive powers of the court are contained in s. 759(3.1) (finding) and (3.2) (period). Under s. 759(2), the Attorney General may appeal against the dismissal of the application, or the period of long-term supervision ordered, but only on a question of law. The dispositive authority of the court is found in s. 759(4.2) (dismissal) and (4.1) (period).

Sections 759(5) and (6) describe the effect of a judgment of the court of appeal on an appeal under this section. A sentence imposed by the court of appeal has the same force and effect as if it had been passed by the trial court, and is deemed to have commenced when D was sentenced by the convicting court, notwithstanding the provisions of s. 719(2).

Case Law

Appeal Against Finding: S. 759(1)

R. v. Oliver (1997), 114 C.C.C. (3d) 50 (Alta. C.A.) — D's right of appeal against a finding that s/he is a dangerous offender is contained in *Code* s. 759(1), the disposition power of the court in s. 759(7) [now s. 759(4)].

Appeal Against Dismissal of Application: S. 759(2)

R. v. Galbraith (1972), 5 C.C.C. (2d) 37 (B.C. C.A.); leave to appeal refused (1972), 6 C.C.C. (2d) 188n (S.C.C.) — Under former provisions it was held that a judgment that an application is defective in form was a dismissal of the application against which P had a right of appeal.

R. v. Currie (1984), 12 C.C.C. (3d) 28 (Ont. C.A.) — Where P was *not* in a position to make the dangerous offender application because it could not comply with the notice requirements and the trial judge had refused P a further adjournment, there had *not* been a dismissal of the application against which P could appeal. The proper course was to apply for *certiorari*.

Disposition of Appeal

R. v. George (1998), 126 C.C.C. (3d) 384 (B.C. C.A.) — Under s. 759(3)(a)(iii), where a court of appeal allows an appeal against the *finding* that D is a dangerous offender, it may order a new hearing for sentence on the predicate offence.

Related Provisions: The section gives no further right of appeal to the Supreme Court of Canada as is given, for example, under ss. 691–696 of Part XXI, in indictable matters. Appeals to the Supreme Court of Canada would appear governed by s. 41 of the *Supreme Court Act*.

Section 759(6) is an exception to the general rule of s. 719(1) that a sentence commences when it is imposed.

"Court of appeal" is defined in s. 2.

It would appear that the rights of appeal given under ss. 759(1) and (2) are unqualified. No leave of the court or a judge is required. *Cf.* ss. 675(1)(a)(ii) and (iii) and ss. 675(1)(b) and 676(1)(d).

Quaere whether an appeal against the custodial portion of a long-term offender sentence must be undertaken separately under ss. 675(1)(b) (D) or s. 676(1)(d) (Attorney Generay), as the case may be?

760. **Disclosure to Correctional Service of Canada** — Where a court finds an offender to be a dangerous offender or a long-term offender, the court shall order that a copy of all reports and testimony given by psychiatrists, psychologists, criminologists and other experts and any observations of the court with respect to the reasons for the finding, together with a transcript of the trial of the offender, be forwarded to the Correctional Service of Canada for information.

R.S., c. C-34, s. 695; 1976–77, c. 53, s. 14.; 1997, c. 17, s. 7

Commentary: The section imposes a statutory obligation upon a court which has found D a dangerous or long-term offender. The court is required to order that a *copy* of the *reports* or *testimony* given by psychiatrists, psychologists or criminologists, any observations of the court with respect to the reasons for sentence, and a *transcript* of trial proceedings be forwarded to the Solicitor General of Canada for his/her information.

Related Provisions: The section describes no specific use which the Solicitor General may make of the disclosure made under this section.

Parole review is determined under s. 761.

761. (1) **Review for parole** — Subject to subsection (2), where a person is in custody under a sentence of detention in a penitentiary for an indeterminate period, the National Parole Board shall, as soon as possible after the expiration of seven years from the day on which that person was taken into custody and not later than every two years after the previous review, review the condition, history and circumstances of that person for the purposes of determining whether he or she should be granted parole under Part II of the *Corrections and Conditional Release Act* and, if so, on what conditions.

(2) **Idem** — Where a person is in custody under a sentence of detention in a penitentiary for an indeterminate period that was imposed before October 15, 1977, the National Parole Board shall, at least once in every year, review the condition, history and circumstances of that person for the purpose of determining whether he should be granted parole under Part II of the *Corrections and Conditional Release Act* and, if so, on what conditions.

1976–77, c. 53, s. 14; 1992, c. 20, s. 215(1)(a); 1997, c. 17, s. 8.

Commentary: The section determines when the case of a dangerous offender sentenced to detention in a penitentiary for an indeterminate period shall be reviewed by the National Parole Board.

Section 761(1) applies in respect of sentences of detention in a penitentiary for an indeterminate period imposed after October 15, 1977, when the present scheme came into force. The initial review to determine whether the offender to determine whether the offender ought to be granted parole under Part II of the C.C.R.A. and, if so, on what conditions, must take place as soon as possible after the expiration of three years from the date on which D was taken into custody. Subsequent reviews must take place every two years.

Under s. 761(2), applicable to cases where D has been sentenced to detention in a penitentiary for an indeterminate period prior to October 15, 1977, the review takes place annually.

Related Provisions: Section 743.6 defines the circumstances in which a sentencing court may fix a period within which D will *not* be eligible to be released on full parole. Parole ineligibility periods in cases of high treason, treason and murder are fixed in accordance with ss. 745–745.4, 746 and 746.1 and, if in excess of 15 years, may be reviewed under s. 745.6.

PART XXV — EFFECT AND ENFORCEMENT OF RECOGNIZANCES

762. (1) Applications for forfeiture of recognizances — Applications for the forfeiture of recognizances shall be made to the courts, designated in column II of the schedule, of the respective provinces designated in column I of the schedule.

(2) Definitions — In this Part

"**clerk of the court**" means the officer designated in column III of the schedule in respect of the court designated in column II of the schedule;

"**schedule**" means the schedule to this Part.

R.S., c. C-34, s. 696.

Commentary: The section designates the courts in which *applications* for the *forfeiture* of *recognizances* shall be made and defines terms used in the Part.

Applications for the forfeiture of recognizances must be made in the courts designated in column II of the schedule in respect of the provinces shown in column I. The schedule follows s. 773 and includes, in column III, the clerk of the court in which forfeiture proceedings are to take place.

Related Provisions: In addition to applications under this Part to forfeit a recognizance for want of compliance, liability may be attracted under s. 145(2) or (3) and a warrant issued for D's arrest.

Sections 766–769 describe the rights of a surety to render a person bound by a recognizance into custody. Section 769 makes applicable the judicial interim release provisions in Parts XVI, XXI and XXVII in such cases.

Sections 770–773 describe the procedure to enforce a recognizance upon default.

763. Recognizance binding — Where a person is bound by recognizance to appear before a court, justice or provincial court judge for any purpose and the session or sittings of that court or the proceedings are adjourned or an order is made changing the place of trial, that person and his sureties continue to be bound by the recognizance in like manner as if it had been entered into with relation to the resumed proceedings or the trial at the time and place at which the proceedings are ordered to be resumed or the trial is ordered to be held.

R.S., c. C-34, s. 697; R.S. 1985, c. 27 (1st Supp.), s. 203.

Commentary: The section continues the binding effect of recognizances in respect of the persons named therein and the sureties, notwithstanding the adjournment of the proceedings at which the person bound thereby was to appear, or a change in the venue of the trial. A fresh recognizance is, accordingly, unnecessary each time the matter is adjourned or when a change of venue has been ordered.

Related Provisions: The period for which recognizances continue in force is governed by s. 523. A Form 32 recognizance requires the person bound thereby to attend court at a specified time and location or "at the time and place fixed by the court" and attend "... thereafter as required by the court in order to be dealt with according to law".

764. (1) Responsibility of sureties — Where an accused is bound by recognizance to appear for trial, his arraignment or conviction does not discharge the recognizance, but it continues to bind him and his sureties, if any, for his appearance until he is discharged or sentenced, as the case may be.

(2) Committal or new sureties — Notwithstanding subsection (1), the court, justice or provincial court judge may commit an accused to prison or may require him to furnish new or additional sureties for his appearance until he is discharged or sentenced, as the case may be.

(3) Effect of committal — The sureties of the accused who is bound by recognizance to appear for trial are discharged if he is committed to prison pursuant to subsection (2).

(4) Endorsement on recognizance — The provisions of section 763 and subsections (1) to (3) of this section shall be endorsed on any recognizance entered into pursuant to this Act.

R.S., c. C-34, s. 698; R.S. 1985, c. 27 (1st Supp.), s. 203.

Commentary: The section describes the *period* of responsibility for D and any sureties under a recognizance, and the circumstances under which the sureties may be relieved on D's committal.

As a general rule, neither the arraignment nor conviction of D discharges a recognizance which continues to bind both D and the sureties, until sentencing or discharge under s. 736.

Under s. 764(2), the presiding judge may, however, commit D to prison, or require new or additional sureties for D's appearance, until discharge or sentence, as the case may be. Such an order discharges D's sureties on the original recognizance under s. 764(3).

Under s. 764(4) the provisions of ss. 763 and 764(1)–(3) must be endorsed on each recognizance, to apprise the sureties of the duration of their responsibilities thereunder.

Related Provisions: Section 523 describes the period during which a recognizance continues in force.

Section 765 describes the effect of D's arrest on another charge upon any existing recognizances. Sections 766–768 authorize a surety to render into custody a person bound by a recognizance, and s. 769 makes applicable the judicial interim release provisions of Parts XVI, XXI and XXVII in such cases.

The *enforcement* of a recognizance upon which there has been default is governed by ss. 770–773.

765. Effect of subsequent arrest — Where an accused is bound by recognizance to appear for trial, his arrest on another charge does not vacate the recognizance, but it continues to bind him and his sureties, if any, for his appearance until he is discharged or sentenced, as the case may be, in respect of the offence to which the recognizance relates.

R.S., c. C-34, s. 699.

Commentary: Under this section where D, already bound by a recognizance, is arrested on another charge, the original recognizance is *not* thereby vacated, but rather continues to bind both D and the sureties for D's appearance, until D is sentenced or discharged in respect of the offence to which the recognizance relates. In other words, arrest upon another charge does *not, per se,* relieve D or the sureties of any obligations under an existing recognizance.

Related Provisions: Where D is arrested on another charge whilst already at liberty on a recognizance, D must establish why he/she ought not to be detained in custody pending trial on the later charge under s. 515(6)(a) or (c) and s. 522(2). Section 524 describes the circumstances under which D may be arrested for alleged misconduct whilst on judicial interim release, notwithstanding that no further charge may be laid, and the procedure to be followed thereafter. At a hearing under s. 524(4) or (8), the judge or justice shall *cancel* the recognizance, unless D shows cause why detention is not justified under s. 515(10).

Other related provisions are described in the corresponding note to s. 762, *supra.*

766. (1) Render of accused by sureties — A surety for a person who is bound by recognizance to appear may, by an application in writing to a court, justice or provincial court judge, apply to be relieved of his obligation under the recognizance, and the court, justice or provincial court judge shall thereupon issue an order in writing for committal of that person to the prison nearest to the place where he was, under the recognizance, bound to appear.

(2) Arrest — An order under subsection (1) shall be given to the surety and upon receipt thereof he or any peace officer may arrest the person named in the order and deliver that person with the order to the keeper of the prison named herein, and the keeper shall receive and imprison that person until he is discharged according to law.

(3) Certificate and entry of render — Where a court, justice or provincial court judge issues an order under subsection (1) and receives from the sheriff a certificate that the person named in the order has been committed to prison pursuant to subsection (2), the court, justice or provincial court judge shall order an entry of the committal to be endorsed on the recognizance.

(4) Discharge of sureties — An endorsement under subsection (3) vacates the recognizance and discharges the sureties.

R.S., c. C-34, s. 700; R.S. 1985, c. 27 (1st Supp.), s. 203.

Commentary: The section provides a *procedure* whereby a *surety* for a person bound by a recognizance may *render* that person *into custody* and be relieved of any subsequent obligations under the recognizance.

Under s. 766(1), a surety initiates the procedure by making an *application* to a court, justice or provincial court judge to be relieved of his/her obligation under the recognizance. Upon receipt of the written application, the court, justice or provincial court judge must thereupon issue an *order in writing for* the *committal* of the person bound to appear. The committal is to the prison nearest the place of the scheduled court appearance. Under s. 766(2), the order for committal is given to the surety, and may be executed by the surety or any peace officer. Upon arrest, the person bound by the recognizance must be delivered, with the order, to the designated prison and there confined until discharged according to law.

Sections 766(3) and (4) describe what shall be done upon committal and the effect thereof on the obligations of the sureties. Under s. 766(3), the sheriff will provide a certificate of committal to the court, justice or provincial court judge who issued the order. He/she shall, in turn, order that the committal be endorsed on the recognizance. The endorsement vacates the recognizance and discharges the sureties.

Related Provisions: Under s. 769, the judicial interim release provisions of Parts XVI, XXI and XXVII apply to a person who has been rendered into custody by a surety and committed to prison. A surety may also render a person bound by a recognizance by bringing the person and giving him/her into the custody of the court under s. 767.

Section 767.1 authorizes the *substitution* of another surety for the one who has applied under s. 766(1) to be relieved of obligations under a recognizance, without committal of the person bound by the recognizance.

Default proceedings are taken under ss. 770–773.

767. Render of accused in court by sureties — A surety for a person who is bound by recognizance to appear may bring that person into the court at which he is required to appear at any time during the sittings thereof and before his trial and the surety may discharge his obligation under the recognizance by giving that person into the custody of the court, and the court shall thereupon commit that person to prison until he is discharged according to law.

R.S., c. C-34, s. 701.

Commentary: The section provides another means whereby a *surety* may *render* a person bound by a recognizance *into custody* and be relieved of his/her obligations under the recognizance.

The procedure is commenced by the surety bringing the person bound by the recognizance into the court in which he/she is required to appear. The return may be made at any time during the sittings of the court and prior to trial. The surety discharges his/her obligation under the recognizance by giving the person bound by the recognizance into the custody of the court. The person bound by the recognizance is thereupon committed to prison, until discharged according to law.

Related Provisions: The surety substitute procedure of s. 767.1 is also available where s. 767 is engaged to render the person bound by a recognizance into custody. A surety may also invoke the provisions of s. 766 to render a person bound by a recognizance into custody.

The judicial interim release provisions of Parts XVI, XXI and XXVII are made applicable to proceedings under s. 767 by s. 769.

Default proceedings may be taken under ss. 770–773.

767.1 (1) Substitution of surety — **Notwithstanding subsection 766(1) and section 767, where a surety for a person who is bound by a recognizance has rendered the person into the custody of a court pursuant to section 767 or applies to be relieved of his obligation under the recognizance pursuant to subsection 766(1), the court, justice or provincial court judge, as the case may be, may, instead of committing or issuing an order for the committal of the person to prison, substitute any other suitable person for the surety under the recognizance.**

(2) Signing of recognizance by new sureties — **Where a person substituted for a surety under a recognizance pursuant to subsection (1) signs the recognizance, the original surety is discharged, but the recognizance and the order for judicial interim release pursuant to which the recognizance was entered into are not otherwise affected.**

R.S. 1985, c. 27 (1st Supp.), s. 167.

Commentary: The section authorizes the *substitution* of one *surety* for another who has rendered a person bound by a recognizance into the custody of the court under s. 767, or has applied to be relieved of the obligation of the surety under s. 766(1). Under s. 767.1(1) a substitution order may be made as an alternative to committing or issuing an order for the committal of the person bound by the recognizance to prison. "Any other suitable person" may be substituted for the surety under the recognizance.

Under s. 767.1(2), where the substitute surety signs the recognizance, the original surety is discharged. The recognizance and order for judicial interim release under which it was authorized are otherwise unaffected.

Related Provisions: Under s. 515(2.1), the justice, judge or court who orders D released may name particular persons as sureties. There is no express authority given in the review procedure of ss. 520(7)(e), 521(8)(e), 680(1)(b) or 523(2) to substitute sureties, although the language is perhaps sufficiently expansive to permit it to be done, quite independently of the procedure under ss. 766(1) and 767.

Other related provisions are discussed in the corresponding note to s. 762, *supra*.

768. Rights of surety preserved — **Nothing in this Part limits or restricts any right that a surety has of taking and giving into custody any person for whom, under a recognizance, he is a surety.**

R.S., c. C-34, s. 702.

Commentary: The section preserves the rights of a surety to take and give into custody any person for whom he/she is a surety under a recognizance. The rights remain unaffected by the provisions of Part XXV.

Related Provisions: In this Part, ss. 766 and 767 permit sureties to apply to be relieved of obligations under a recognizance (s. 766(1)), as well as to render such a person into the custody of the court for a similar purpose (s. 767). Sureties may be substituted under s. 767.1.

769. Application of judicial interim release provisions — **Where a surety for a person has rendered him into custody and that person has been committed to prison, the provisions of Parts XVI, XXI and XXVII relating to judicial interim release apply, with such modifications as the circumstances require, in respect of him and he shall**

forthwith be taken before a justice or judge as an accused charged with an offence or as an appellant, as the case may be, for the purposes of those provisions.

R.S., c. C-34, s. 703; c. 2 (2d Supp.), s. 14.

Commentary: The section makes the *judicial interim release* provisions of Parts XVI, XXI and XXVII applicable to persons bound by a recognizance, who have been rendered into custody by their sureties. The person rendered into custody must be taken forthwith before a justice or judge as a person charged with an offence, or an appellant, as the case may be.

Related Provisions: The release of persons charged with an indictable offence is governed by s. 515, where the offence charged is *not* listed in *Code* s. 469, and s. 522 where the offence is so listed. On appeal, the applicable provision is s. 679.

Section 795 incorporates the provisions of Parts XVI and XVIII with respect to compelling D's appearance before a justice, with such modifications as the circumstances require, to summary conviction proceedings. On appeal, the applicable provisions are found in ss. 816–818, 831 and 832.

770. (1) Default to be endorsed — **Where, in proceedings to which this Act applies, a person who is bound by recognizance does not comply with a condition of the recognizance, a court, justice or provincial court judge having knowledge of the facts shall endorse or cause to be endorsed on the recognizance a certificate in Form 33 setting out**

(a) **the nature of the default,**

(b) **the reason for the default, if it is known,**

(c) **whether the ends of justice have been defeated or delayed by reason of the default, and**

(d) **the names and addresses of the principal and sureties.**

(2) Transmission to clerk of court — **A recognizance that has been endorsed pursuant to subsection (1) shall be sent to the clerk of the court and shall be kept by him with the records of the court.**

(3) Certificate is evidence — **A certificate that has been endorsed on a recognizance pursuant to subsection (1) is evidence of the default to which it relates.**

(4) Transmission of deposit — **Where, in proceedings to which this section applies, the principal or surety has deposited money as security for the performance of a condition of a recognizance, that money shall be sent to the clerk of the court with the defaulted recognizance, to be dealt with in accordance with this Part.**

R.S., c. C-34, s. 704; R.S. 1985, c. 27 (1st Supp.), s. 203; 1997, c. 18, s. 108.

Commentary: The section describes the initial steps to be taken to *enforce* a *recognizance* upon which there has been a *default*.

Under s. 770(1), upon non-compliance with a condition of the recognizance by a person bound thereby, a court, justice or provincial court judge, having knowledge thereof, must *endorse* or cause to be endorsed a Form 33 certificate on the recognizance. The *certificate* must set out the matters described in ss. 770(1)(a)-(d), and be forwarded to the clerk of the court as defined in s. 762(2) and the schedule to s. 773. Any money which has been deposited as security under the recognizance must also be forwarded to the clerk of the court under s. 770(4).

Under s. 770(3), the Form 33 certificate is *evidence* of the default to which it relates.

Case Law

Purves v. Canada (A.G.) (1990), 54 C.C.C. (3d) 355 (B.C. C.A.); reversing (1988), 45 C.C.C. (3d) 444 (B.C. S.C.); leave to appeal refused (November 22, 1990), Doc. No. 21952 (S.C.C.) — A provincial court has jurisdiction under s. 770 to consider an application to endorse D's default on a recognizance, notwithstanding that proceedings upon the underlying information have been stayed under s. 579. Where proceedings to endorse default on a recognizance are taken after the return of any deposited monies or the removal of any *caveat* on title, a hearing must be held under s. 771 before any forfeiture may be ordered.

Related Provisions: In addition to the proceedings which may be taken against the principal and sureties upon default under a recognizance under ss. 771–773, the principal may be liable under s. 145(2) or (3).

771. (1) **Proceedings in case of default** — Where a recognizance has been endorsed with a certificate pursuant to section 770 and has been received by the clerk of the court pursuant to that section,

(a) a judge of the court shall, on the request of the clerk of the court or the Attorney General or counsel acting on his behalf, fix a time and place for the hearing of an application for the forfeiture of the recognizance; and

(b) the clerk of the court shall, not less than ten days before the time fixed under paragraph (*a*) for the hearing, send by registered mail, or have served in the manner directed by the court or prescribed by the rules of court, to each principal and surety named in the recognizance, directed to the principal or surety at the address set out in the certificate, a notice requiring the person to appear at the time and place fixed by the judge to show cause why the recognizance should not be forfeited.

(2) **Order of judge** — Where subsection (1) has been complied with, the judge may, after giving the parties an opportunity to be heard, in his discretion grant or refuse the application and make any order with respect to the forfeiture of the recognizance that he considers proper.

(3) **Judgment debtors of the crown** — Where, pursuant to subsection (2), a judge orders forfeiture of a recognizance, the principal and his sureties become judgment debtors of the Crown, each in the amount that the judge orders him to pay.

(3.1) **Order may be filed** — An order made under subsection (2) may be filed with the clerk of the superior court and if an order is filed, the clerk shall issue a writ of *fieri facias* in Form 34 and deliver it to the sheriff of each of the territorial divisions in which the principal or any surety resides, carries on business or has property.

(4) **Transfer of deposit** — Where a deposit has been made by a person against whom an order for forfeiture of a recognizance has been made, no writ of *fieri facias* shall issue, but the amount of the deposit shall be transferred by the person who has custody of it to the person who is entitled by law to receive it.

R.S., c. C-34, s. 705; 1972, c. 13, s. 60; R.S. 1985, c. 27 (1st Supp.), s. 168; 1994, c. 44, s. 78; 1999, c. 5, s. 43.

Commentary: The section authorizes the conduct of a *hearing* to determine whether, or to what extent, *forfeiture* shall be ordered under a recognizance upon which there has been default.

Under s. 771(1), where a recognizance, endorsed with a certificate of default in Form 33, has been received by the clerk of the court, a time and place are fixed for the hearing of an application for forfeiture of the recognizance. The proceedings may be initiated by a request of the clerk of the court, or the Attorney General or counsel acting on his/her behalf. A *notice* of the hearing must be sent by the clerk of the court by registered mail, or served in a manner directed by the court or prescribed by the rules of court, not less than 10 days before the hearing, to each principal and surety named in the recognizance. The notice requires the principal and each surety to appear at the designated time and place to show cause why the recognizance should not be forfeited.

At the hearing under s. 771(2), the parties have an opportunity to be heard. The presiding judge has a wide discretion to grant or refuse the application for forfeiture, and make any order in respect to forfeiture that he/she considers proper.

Sections 771(3) and (4) describe the effect of an order of forfeiture. The principal and sureties become judgment debtors of P, each in the amount that the judge orders him/her to pay. Any amount deposited under the recognizance is transferred to the person lawfully entitled thereto under the order of forfeiture. Section 771(3.1) permits the filing of an order of forfeiture with the clerk of the superior court or, in Quebec, the prothonotary. Upon the filing of an order, a writ of *fieri facias*, in Form 34, will issue for delivery to the sheriff of each of the territorial divisions where the principal or surety resides, carries on business or has property.

Case Law

Purves v. Canada (A.G.) (1990), 54 C.C.C. (3d) 355 (B.C. C.A.); reversing (1988), 45 C.C.C. (3d) 444 (B.C. S.C.); leave to appeal refused (1990), 59 C.C.C. (3d) vi (note) (S.C.C.) — See digest under s. 770, *supra*.

R. v. Coles (1982), 2 C.C.C. (3d) 65 (B.C. C.A.) — There is *no* right of appeal under Part XXVII from an order forfeiting a recognizance, notwithstanding that the order was made by a provincial judge.

R. v. Huang (1998), 127 C.C.C. (3d) 397 (Ont. C.A.) — In deciding whether to order forfeiture of a recognizance because of failure to appear, the extent to which the *surety* is at *fault* is *relevant*.

Where a surety connived at, aided or abetted the disappearance, the whole sum should be forfeited. Where a surety failed to exercise due diligence to secure appearance, forfeiture of all or a substantial part of the sum may be appropriate. Where a surety did *not* fail to exercise due diligence and used every effort to secure D's attendance, the entire sum may be remitted.

R. v. Martin (No. 2) (1980), 57 C.C.C. (2d) 31 (Ont. C.A.) — A surety, whose only property is real or immovable property situate in another province, is not "put at risk" of having his property taken in execution in the event of a default, hence is *not* be a "sufficient surety".

Related Provisions: Execution of a writ of *fieri facias* follows s. 772. Committal may follow under s. 773, where there are insufficient goods and chattels, lands and tenements found to satisfy the writ.

772. (1) Levy under writ — Where a writ of *fieri facias* is issued pursuant to section 771, the sheriff to whom it is delivered shall execute the writ and deal with the proceeds thereof in the same manner in which he is authorized to execute and deal with the proceeds of writs of *fieri facias* issued out of superior courts in the province in civil proceedings.

(2) Costs — Where this section applies, the Crown is entitled to the costs of execution and of proceedings incidental thereto that are fixed, in the Province of Quebec, by any tariff applicable in the Superior Court in civil proceedings, and in any other province, by any tariff applicable in the superior court of the province in civil proceedings, as the judge may direct.

R.S., c. C-34, s. 706.

Commentary: The section adopts the procedure applicable to writs of *fieri facias* issued out of the superior court of the province in civil proceedings to the execution of such writs and disposition of proceeds thereof under Part XXV. P is entitled to the costs of execution and incidental proceedings fixed by the applicable tariff.

Related Provisions: Committal may be ordered under s. 773 when a writ of *fieri facias* is not satisfied.

773. (1) Committal when writ not satisfied — Where a writ of *fieri facias* has been issued under this Part and it appears from a certificate in a return made by the sheriff that sufficient goods and chattels, lands and tenements cannot be found to satisfy the writ, or that the proceeds of the execution of the writ are not sufficient to satisfy it, a judge of the court may, upon the application of the Attorney General or counsel acting on his behalf, fix a time and place for the sureties to show cause why a warrant of committal should not be issued in respect of them.

(2) **Notice** — Seven clear days notice of the time and place fixed for the hearing pursuant to subsection (1) shall be given to the sureties.

(3) **Hearing** — The judge shall, at the hearing held pursuant to subsection (1), inquire into the circumstances of the case and may in his discretion

(a) order the discharge of the amount for which the surety is liable; or

(b) make any order with respect to the surety and to his imprisonment that he considers proper in the circumstances and issue a warrant of committal in Form 27.

(4) **Warrant to committal** — A warrant of committal issued pursuant to this section authorizes the sheriff to take into custody the person in respect of whom the warrant was issued and to confine him in a prison in the territorial division in which the writ was issued or in the prison nearest to the court, until satisfaction is made or until the period of imprisonment fixed by the judge has expired.

(5) **Definition of "Attorney General"** — In this section and in section 771, "Attorney General" means, where subsection 734.4(2) applies, the Attorney General of Canada.

R.S., c. C-34, s. 707; 1995, c.22, s. 10.

Schedule — Part XXV
(Section 762)

Column I.	Column II.	Column III.
Ontario	A judge of the Court of Appeal in respect of a recognizance for the appearance of a person before the Court.	The Registrar of the Court of Appeal.
	The Superior Court of Justice in respect of all other recognizances.	A Registrar of the Superior Court of Justice.
Quebec	The Court of Quebec, Criminal and Penal Division.	The Clerk of the Court.
Nova Scotia	The Supreme Court.	A Prothonotary of the Supreme Court.
New Brunswick	The Court of Queen's Bench.	The Registrar of the Court of Queen's Bench.

British Columbia	**The Supreme Court in respect of a recognizance for the appearance of a person before that court or the Court of Appeal.**	**The District Registrar of the Supreme Court.**
Prince Edward Island	**The Supreme Court, Trial Division.**	**The Prothonotary.**
Manitoba	**The Court of Queen's Bench.**	**The Registrar or a Deputy Registrar of the Court of Queen's Bench.**
Saskatchewan	**The Court of Queen's Bench.**	**The Local Registrar of the of Queen's Bench.**
Alberta	**The Court of Queen's Bench.**	**The Clerk of the Court of Queen's Bench.**
Newfoundland	**The Supreme Court.**	**The Registrar of the Supreme Court.**
Yukon Territory	**The Supreme Court.**	**The Clerk of the Supreme Court.**
Northwest Territories	**The Supreme Court.**	**The Clerk of the Supreme Court.**
Nunavut	**The Nunavut Court of Justice**	**The Clerk of the Nunavut Court of Justice**

R.S., c. C-34, Schedule to Part XXII; 1972, c. 17, s. 3; 1974–75–76, c. 93, s. 84; 1978–79, c. 11, s. 10;R.S. 1985, c. 11 (1st Supp.), s. 2; c. 27 (2d Supp.), (Sched., item 6); 1992, c. 1, s. 58(1), (Sched. I, item 15); 1992, c. 51, ss. 40–42; 1993, c. 28, s. 78 (Sched. III, item 35) [Amended 1998, c. 15, s. 20; Repealed 1999, c. 3, (Sched., item 9).]; 1998, c. 30, s. 14(d); 1999, c. 3. s. 54; 1999, c. 5, s. 44.

Commentary: The section authorizes *committal* where a writ of *fieri facias* has been issued and the sheriff certifies in his/her return that sufficient goods and chattels, lands and tenements cannot be found to satisfy the writ, or the proceedings on the execution of the writ are not sufficient to satisfy it.

Under s. 773(1), upon receipt of the sheriff's certificate of non-satisfaction of the writ, the Attorney General, or counsel on his/her behalf, may apply to a judge of the court shown in the schedule to fix a time and a place for a *hearing* for the sureties to show cause why a warrant of committal should not be issued in respect of them. Under s. 773(2), the sureties must be given seven clear days notice of the time and place fixed for the hearing.

On the show cause hearing, the judge will inquire into the circumstances of the case and may order the discharge of the amount for which the surety is liable, or make any order with respect to the surety and to his/her imprisonment that the judge considers proper in the circumstances. In the event of committal, a warrant will issue in Form 27. Under the warrant of committal the sheriff will take the surety into custody, where he/she will be confined until satisfaction is made under the writ, or the period of imprisonment fixed by the judge on the show cause hearing has expired.

Related Provisions: The Schedule to the section, in particular Column II, describes the court in which the show cause hearing shall be held.

PART XXVI — EXTRAORDINARY REMEDIES

774. Application of Part — This Part applies to proceedings in criminal matters by way of *certiorari, habeas corpus, mandamus, procedendo* and **prohibition.**

R.S., c. C-34, s. 708; R.S. 1985, c. 27 (1st Supp.), s. 169.

Commentary: The section describes the application of the *Part.*

Case Law

General Principles

R. v. W. (A.G.) (1992), 146 N.R. 141 (S.C.C.) — *See also: R. v. Moore* (1988), 65 C.R. (3d) 1, [1988] 1 S.C.R. 1097, 41 C.C.C. (3d) 289 (S.C.C.) — A provincial court judge conducting a preliminary inquiry has jurisdiction under *Code* s. 601 to determine the validity of an information. The correctness of his/her ruling in that regard cannot generally be challenged by *certiorari.*

R. v. Jones (Nos. 1 and 2) (1974), 16 C.C.C. (2d) 338 (Ont. C.A.); leave to appeal refused (1974), 16 C.C.C. (2d) 338n (S.C.C.) — An application for extraordinary relief must not be used as a substitution for an appeal. The trial judge's interpretation of *Code* sections on jury selection does not raise a jurisdictional issue. The matters may be raised on appeal.

Certiorari [Motion to Quash]

R. v. Jobin, [1995] 2 S.C.R. 78, 38 C.R. (4th) 176, 97 C.C.C. (3d) 97 (S.C.C.) — Where third parties in criminal proceedings seek to quash *subpoenae* issued to them, they ought to apply to the superior court of criminal jurisdiction for *certiorari.* An appeal may be taken to the court of appeal under *Code* s. 784(1) from a decision given on application for *certiorari*, thereafter with leave to the Supreme Court of Canada.

Dubois v. R. (1986), 51 C.R. (3d) 193, 25 C.C.C. (3d) 221 (S.C.C.) — The only ground upon which to review a discharge or committal for trial is lack of jurisdiction. Where a discharge is based on reasonable doubt, there is jurisdictional error. There is an assumption of the function of the ultimate trier of fact.

Forsythe v. R. (1980), 15 C.R. (3d) 280, 53 C.C.C. (2d) 225 (S.C.C.) — Lack of jurisdiction includes not only lack of initial jurisdiction but also loss of jurisdiction. Jurisdiction will be lost if a justice fails to observe mandatory *Code* provisions. A denial of natural justice goes to jurisdiction, but in the case of a preliminary inquiry arises only by a complete denial to D of the right to cross-examine or to call witnesses. The refusal of the justice to allow cross-examination on the police officer's notes, even if wrong, does *not* result in a loss of jurisdiction.

Quebec (A.G.) v. Cohen (1979), 13 C.R. (3d) 36 (S.C.C.) — A decision concerning the admissibility of evidence, even if erroneous, does not affect jurisdiction.

Patterson v. R. (1970), 10 C.R.N.S. 55, 2 C.C.C. (2d) 227 (S.C.C.) — The refusal of a justice conducting a preliminary inquiry to order production of a statement made by a P witness does not go to jurisdiction and, thus, is not reviewable by *certiorari.*

R. v. Parsons (1992), 13 C.R. (4th) 248, 72 C.C.C. (3d) 137 (Nfld. C.A.) — Judicial review by *certiorari* of a decision of a justice at preliminary inquiry only lies where it is alleged that the justice acted *in excess of* his/her assigned *jurisdiction*, or in *breach of the principles of natural justice.* The superior court is *not* entitled to quash a justice's decision made within his/her jurisdiction on the ground of error of law or because the decision of the justice differs from that which the superior court might have made.

R. v. Pike (1992), 77 C.C.C. (3d) 155 (Nfld. C.A.) — When a bill of indictment is filed with the trial court, D arraigned and a plea taken, the indictment supersedes the information and becomes the operative document. D may no longer impeach the order to stand trial by *certiorari* since the indictment constitutes a new jurisdictional starting point.

Martin v. R. (1977), 41 C.C.C. (2d) 308 (Ont. C.A.); affirmed (1978), 41 C.C.C. (2d) 342 (S.C.C.) — A provincial court judge conducting a preliminary inquiry acts in excess of his jurisdiction only if he commits D without any evidence at all, in the sense of an entire absence of proper material as a basis for the formation of a judicial opinion that the evidence was sufficient to put D on trial.

Habeas Corpus [See also Charter s. 10]

Idziak v. Canada (Minister of Justice) (1992), 77 C.C.C. (3d) 65 (S.C.C.) — *Habeas corpus* is available to challenge the validity of a warrant of surrender issued by the Minister of Justice in extradition proceedings notwithstanding that the warrant had yet to be executed and the fugitive was being held on the warrant of committal. *Habeas corpus* is available to challenge secondary forms of detention. A fugitive was *not* bound to apply to the Federal Court to review the Minister's decision. The executive decision of the Minister to surrender the fugitive is subject to s. 7 *Charter* review in provincial superior courts.

R. v. Pearson (1992), 17 C.R. (4th) 1, 77 C.C.C. (3d) 124 (S.C.C.) — *Habeas corpus* is available as a remedy against denial of judicial interim release where D claims that the reverse onus provisions of s. 515(6)(d) are unconstitutional and seeks a new hearing in accordance with constitutionally valid criteria. In most instances, however, *habeas corpus* is *not* a remedy against refusal to grant judicial interim release.

R. v. Miller (1985), 49 C.R. (3d) 1, 23 C.C.C. (3d) 97 (S.C.C.); affirming (1982), 29 C.R. (3d) 153, 70 C.C.C. (2d) 129 (Ont. C.A.) — On an application for *habeas corpus* even without *certiorari* in aid, a court can consider affidavit or other extrinsic evidence to determine whether there has been an absence or an excess of jurisdiction. Extrinsic evidence must not be permitted, however, to convert an application for *habeas corpus* into an appeal on the merits. The record of a superior court or court of general common law jurisdiction is conclusive as to the facts on which the court's jurisdiction depends and cannot be controverted by extrinsic evidence.

Goldhar v. R. (1960), 126 C.C.C. 337 (S.C.C.) — The conviction and sentence of a competent court, regular on its face, is legal justification for imprisoning D and an application for a writ of *habeas corpus* will not be entertained. The appropriate route is by way of an appeal.

R. v. Fern (1983), (sub nom. *Illinois v. Fern*) 23 Alta. L.R. (2d) 369 (C.A.) — Provincial superior courts retain their jurisdiction to grant *habeas corpus* in extradition proceedings despite review procedures established under the *Federal Court Act*.

Meier v. R. (1983), 6 C.C.C. (3d) 165 (B.C. S.C.); affirmed (1983), 8 C.C.C. (3d) 210 (B.C. C.A.); leave to appeal refused (1983), 3 D.L.R. (4th) 567n (S.C.C.) — While a superior court judge has jurisdiction on a *habeas corpus* application to review a detention order made by a superior court judge sitting as an extradition judge, the judicial review is limited to consideration as to whether evidence existed to justify the detention, and does not extend to an assessment of the sufficiency of the evidence.

Cardinal v. R. (1982), (sub nom. *Cardinal v. Kent Institution*) 67 C.C.C. (2d) 252 (B.C. C.A.); reversed on other grounds (1986), 49 C.R. (3d) 35, 23 C.C.C. (3d) 118 (S.C.C.) — On an application for a writ of *habeas corpus*, a jurisdictional error is properly determined on the basis of affidavit evidence.

Habeas Corpus with Certiorari in Aid

R. v. Miller (1985), 49 C.R. (3d) 1, 23 C.C.C. (3d) 97 (S.C.C.); affirming (1982), 29 C.R. (3d) 153, 70 C.C.C. (2d) 129 (Ont. C.A.) — *See also*: *Cardinal v. R.* (1982), (sub nom. *Cardinal v. Kent Institution*) 67 C.C.C. (2d) 252 (B.C. C.A.); reversed on other grounds (1986), 49 C.R. (3d) 35, 23 C.C.C. (3d) 118 (S.C.C.) — A decision to subject a prisoner to a more severe form of restriction is open to challenge by way of *habeas corpus*. The exclusive jurisdiction possessed by the Federal Court to order *certiorari* to quash decisions of federal boards does *not* preclude a provincial superior court from issuing *certiorari* in aid on a *habeas corpus* application.

Gallichon v. Canada (Commissioner of Corrections) (1995), 43 C.R. (4th) 187, 101 C.C.C. (3d) 414 (Ont. C.A.) — A serving prisoner who alleges the continuation of a sentence to be unconstitutional ought commence an action or bring *habeas corpus* with *certiorari* in aid coupled with an application for *Charter* relief.

Mandamus

Cheyenne Realty Ltd. v. Thompson (1974), 15 C.C.C. (2d) 49 (S.C.C.) — *Mandamus* will *not* ordinarily issue when an appeal remedy is available.

Forest v. Registrar of Manitoba Court of Appeal (1977), 35 C.C.C. (2d) 497 (Man. C.A.) — An application for *mandamus* may be brought first in the court of appeal, but this original jurisdiction should only be exercised sparingly by the appellate court in exceptional cases. It is more appropriate that an application for *mandamus* be first taken to the Court of Queen's Bench.

R. v. Beason (1983), 36 C.R. (3d) 73, 7 C.C.C. (3d) 20 (Ont. C.A.) — The rule that *mandamus* is not available where there is an appeal is not an inflexible rule of law, but a rule regulating the discretion of the courts in granting *mandamus*. *Mandamus* is available to P against an order quashing an indictment on the basis that D's right under the *Charter* to be tried within a reasonable time had been violated. However, an appeal would be the preferable remedy.

Prohibition

Kendall v. R. (1982), 2 C.C.C. (3d) 224 (Alta. C.A.) — Prohibition will *not* be granted where the matter has *not* yet been tried on the merits, unless there are special circumstances. The applicants have the normal appellate remedy if, after trial, the issue is not academic.

R. v. Turkiewicz (1979), 10 C.R. (3d) 352, 50 C.C.C. (2d) 406 (Ont. C.A.) — Where application is for prohibition only, the record remains in the inferior court. Only judicial dignity requires that the court refrain from resuming proceedings.

Stewart v. R. (1977), 36 C.C.C. (2d) 5 (Ont. C.A.) — Prohibition does *not* lie to review a decision of the trial judge as to whether to grant a mistrial.

Charter Relief [See Court of Competent Jurisdiction, Charter, s. 24]

Related Provisions: The Part is concerned, principally, with the availability of and limitations upon the extraordinary remedies of *habeas corpus* and *certiorari*. With the exception of s. 784(1), there is no reference to *mandamus* or prohibition. Section 774 contains the only reference to *procedendo*.

Extraordinary remedies lie only in respect of jurisdictional error. *Certiorari* lies to quash an order made in excess of jurisdiction and prohibition to prevent proceedings or their continuance in similar circumstances. *Mandamus* will compel a tribunal of limited jurisdiction to exercise it (though not in a particular way) and *procedendo* is to a similar effect. *Habeas corpus* questions the authority or jurisdiction by which a person is detained.

775. Detention on inquiry to determine legality of imprisonment — Where proceedings to which this Part applies have been instituted before a judge or court having jurisdiction, by or in respect of a person who is in custody by reason that he is charged with or has been convicted of an offence, to have the legality of his imprisonment determined, the judge or court may, without determining the question, make an order for the further detention of that person and direct the judge, justice or provincial court judge under whose warrant he is in custody, or any other judge, justice or provincial court judge to take any proceedings, hear such evidence or do any other thing that, in the opinion of the judge or court, will best further the ends of justice.

R.S., c. C-34, s. 709; R.S. 1985, c. 27 (1st Supp.), s. 203.

Commentary: The section applies where proceedings have been commenced under this Part to determine the *legality* of imprisonment. Without determining the legality of the custody, the applicant may be ordered further detained, and the judicial officer under whose warrant he/she is in custody or other judicial officer ordered to take such proceedings, directed to hear such evidence, or do any other thing that the judge to whom the application has been made finds will best further the ends of justice.

The provision may be subject to *Charter* s. 7 scrutiny.

Case Law

Ferreira v. R. (1981), 58 C.C.C. (2d) 147 (B.C. C.A.) — Even where the court has determined that D's detention was unlawful, it may, nevertheless, make an order under this section for further detention.

Re Demerais (1978), 5 C.R. (3d) 229, 42 C.C.C. (2d) 287 (Ont. C.A.) — Where there was no evidence to support a committal on the offence of first degree murder with which D was charged but where there was evidence to support the serious, although lesser, included offence of second degree murder, the interests of society required that D be detained. The court quashed the committal for first degree murder, ordered that D be detained and that the matter be remitted to the provincial judge to permit P to call further evidence, if any, relating to first degree murder.

Related Provisions: Section 776 describes the circumstances under which a conviction or order is not removable by *certiorari*. Sections 777 and 778 give the superior court of criminal jurisdiction authority to remedy certain procedural defects made at first instance. Under ss. 781 and 782, other defects are held not to vitiate proceedings.

776. **Where conviction of order not reviewable** — No conviction or order shall be removed by *certiorari*

(a) **where an appeal was taken, whether or not the appeal has been carried to a conclusion; or**

(b) **where the defendant appeared and pleaded and the merits were tried, and an appeal might have been taken, but the defendant did not appeal.**

R.S., c. C-34, s. 710.

Commentary: This privative clause bars access to *certiorari* in two instances. Under s. 776(a), a conviction or order may *not* be removed by *certiorari* where an *appeal* was *taken*. It matters not whether the appeal has been determined on its merits. Under s. 776(b), *certiorari* is unavailable to remove a conviction or order where D *appeared* and *pleaded*, the *merits* were *tried* and an appeal may have been taken, but D did *not appeal*.

Case Law

Sanders v. R. (1969), 8 C.R.N.S. 345, [1970] 2 C.C.C. 57 (S.C.C.) — Section 776(b) compels resort to appeal procedures where available. The application of this section is not restricted to cases in which proceedings are attacked for error of law on the face of the record. If D's argument that the merits are only tried in a case where the court had jurisdiction was given effect to, then the section would cease to have any real meaning. The section is intended to apply in cases where *certiorari* would otherwise have been available. Trial decisions in which courts have granted *certiorari* in "exceptional circumstances", notwithstanding this section, constituted a refusal by the courts to apply the section.

Carleton v. R. (1982), 2 C.C.C. (3d) 310 (B.C. C.A.) — Section 776(b) is *not* a bar to removing a warrant of committal by *certiorari* to correct an illegal sentence apparent on the face of the warrant. A warrant of committal is *not* a "conviction or order" as contemplated by the section.

Gallicano v. R. (1978), 42 C.C.C. (2d) 113 (B.C. C.A.) — Where a plea of guilty is taken, the merits of the case have been tried and this section precludes proceedings by way of *certiorari*.

R. v. Eross, [1970] 5 C.C.C. 169 (B.C. C.A.) — *See also*: *R. v. Conley* (1979), 47 C.C.C. (2d) 359 (Alta. C.A.) — This section is *not* intended to apply to P.

Beaupré v. R. (1981), 61 C.C.C. (2d) 92 (Man. C.A.) — *Certiorari* is not available to quash the conviction of D where the section of the *Code* under which D was convicted was subsequently ruled *ultra vires* by the Supreme Court of Canada in other proceedings.

Roberts v. Cour de Jurisdiction Criminelle (1980), 28 C.R. (3d) 257 (Que. C.A.) — A judgment requiring D to pay costs was a "sentence" which D could have appealed but failed to do so. *Certiorari* to quash the order was barred by this section.

Related Provisions: Sections 777 and 778 describe the circumstances under which a conviction or order is remediable. Sections 781 and 782 provide that certain defects do not vitiate the order, warrant, conviction or other proceeding.

777. (1) **Conviction or order remediable, when** — No conviction, order or warrant for enforcing a conviction or order shall, on being removed by *certiorari*, be held to be invalid by reason of any irregularity, informality or insufficiency therein, where the court before which or the judge before whom the question is raised, on perusal of the evidence, is satisfied

(a) **that an offence of the nature described in the conviction, order or warrant, as the case may be, was committed,**

(b) **that there was jurisdiction to make the conviction or order or issue the warrant, as the case may be, and**

(c) that the punishment imposed, if any, was not in excess of the punishment that might lawfully have been imposed,

but the court or judge has the same powers to deal with the proceedings in the manner that the court or judge considers proper that are conferred on a court to which an appeal might have been taken.

(2) Correcting punishment — Where, in proceedings to which subsection (1) applies, the court or judge is satisfied that a person was properly convicted of an offence but the punishment that was imposed is greater than the punishment that might lawfully have been imposed, the court or judge

(a) shall correct the sentence,

(i) where the punishment is a fine, by imposing a fine that does not exceed the maximum fine that might lawfully have been imposed,

(ii) where the punishment is imprisonment, and the person has not served a term of imprisonment under the sentence that is equal to or greater than the term of imprisonment that might lawfully have been imposed, by imposing a term of imprisonment that does not exceed the maximum term of imprisonment that might lawfully have been imposed, or

(iii) where the punishment is a fine and imprisonment, by imposing a punishment in accordance with subparagraph (i) or (ii), as the case requires; or

(b) shall remit the matter to the convicting judge, justice or provincial court judge and direct him to impose a punishment that is not greater than the punishment that may be lawfully imposed.

(3) Amendment — Where an adjudication is varied pursuant to subsection (1) or (2), the conviction and warrant of committal, if any, shall be amended to conform with the adjudication as varied.

(4) Sufficiency of statement — Any statement that appears in a conviction and is sufficient for the purpose of the conviction is sufficient for the purposes of an information, summons, order or warrant in which it appears in the proceedings.

R.S., c. C-34, s. 711; R.S. 1985, c. 27 (1st Supp.), s. 203.

Commentary: The section describes the circumstances under which *irregularities, informalities* and *insufficiencies* will *not* vitiate earlier proceedings or process, and expressly permits the correction of certain sentences.

Under s. 777(1), a conviction, order or warrant of enforcement shall *not* be held invalid, on removal by *certiorari*, on account of any irregularity, informality or insufficiency, where the reviewing court is satisfied that the circumstances of ss. 777(1)(a)-(c), obtain. It is necessary that an offence of the nature described in the conviction, order or warrant was committed. The conviction, order or warrant must have been made within the jurisdiction of the tribunal. The punishment imposed must *not* exceed the lawful limits. The reviewing court may then deal with the matter, as it considers proper, in the same manner as an appellate court on an appeal.

Under s. 777(2), a punishment, greater than what might lawfully be imposed, may be corrected to a lawful penalty by the reviewing court, or by the court of first instance, provided the reviewing court is satisfied of the propriety of the conviction.

Any *variation* in an adjudication must be endorsed on the conviction and warrant of committal. Section 777(4) declares any statement sufficient for the purpose of conviction to be sufficient for the purposes of an information, summons, order or warrant.

Case Law

Carleton v. R. (1982), 2 C.C.C. (3d) 310 (B.C. C.A.) — The court has the power under this section, on a *certiorari* application, to correct consecutive sentences which have been imposed illegally, or remit the matter back to the trial judge for correction.

Related Provisions: The section is *deemed* to apply in the circumstances described in s. 778.

Sections 781 and 782 describe further matters which do not invalidate an order, conviction, warrant or other proceeding.

778. Irregularities within section 777 — Without restricting the generality of section 777, that section shall be deemed to apply where

(a) the statement of the adjudication or of any other matter or thing is in the past tense instead of in the present tense;

(b) the punishment imposed is less than the punishment that might by law have been imposed for the offence that appears by the evidence to have been committed; or

(c) there has been an omission to negative circumstances, the existence of which would make the act complained of lawful, whether those circumstances are stated by way of exception or otherwise in the provision under which the offence is charged or are stated in another provision.

R.S., c. C-34, s. 712.

Commentary: The section describes three irregularities to which the remedial provisions of s. 777 are *deemed* to apply. No conviction, order or warrant of enforcement is invalidated thereby.

Related Provisions: Related provisions are described in corresponding note to s. 777, *supra*.

779. (1) General order for security by recognizance — A court that has authority to quash a conviction, order or other proceeding on *certiorari* may prescribe by general order that no motion to quash any such conviction, order or other proceeding removed to the court by *certiorari*, shall be heard unless the defendant has entered into a recognizance with one or more sufficient sureties, before one or more justices of the territorial division in which the conviction or order was made or before a judge or other officer, or has made a deposit to be prescribed with a condition that the defendant will prosecute the writ of *certiorari* at his own expense, without wilful delay, and, if ordered, will pay to the person in whose favour the conviction, order or other proceeding is affirmed his full costs and charges to be taxed according to the practice of the court where the conviction, order or proceeding is affirmed.

(2) Provisions of Part XXV — The provisions of Part XXV relating to forfeiture of recognizances apply to a recognizance entered into under this section.

R.S., c. C-34, s. 713.

Commentary: Section 779(1) authorizes the superior court of criminal jurisdiction to prescribe, by general order, that proceedings on *certiorari* shall *not* be heard, unless D has entered into a recognizance with sureties, or made a deposit with a condition that the matter will be prosecuted at D's expense without wilful delay. D may also be ordered to pay the party, in whose favour the adjudication is affirmed, his/her full costs and charges, as taxed according to the practice of the court.

Where D has entered into a recognizance under s. 779(1), the forfeiture of the recognizance follows Part XXV.

Related Provisions: Sections 482(1) and (3)(c) expressly authorize the superior court of criminal jurisdiction and the court of appeal to make rules regulating, *inter alia*, proceedings with respect to *mandamus, certiorari, habeas corpus, procedendo* and prohibition.

Sections 770–773 govern the forfeiture of recognizances.

780. Effect of order dismissing application to quash — Where a motion to quash a conviction, order or other proceeding is refused, the order of the court refusing the application is sufficient authority for the clerk of the court forthwith to return the conviction, order or proceeding to the court from which or the person from whom it was removed, and for proceedings to be taken with respect thereto for the enforcement thereof.

R.S., c. C-34, s. 714.

Commentary: Under this section, the order of a court refusing to quash a conviction, order or other proceeding is sufficient authority for the clerk of the court to return the conviction, order or other proceeding to the court of origin. Proceedings may then be taken to enforce the adjudication.

Case Law

Batchelor v. R. (1977), 38 C.C.C. (2d) 113 (S.C.C.) — Once the application is disposed of by the Supreme Court, this section automatically returns jurisdiction to proceed to the provincial court without invoking the old procedure of *procedendo*.

Related Provisions: The section is similar in effect to, but obviates the need to invoke, the extraordinary remedy of *procedendo*. Section 507(8) permits the issuance of process to compel re-attendance.

Section 776 describes the circumstances under which a conviction or order is removable by *certiorari*, and ss. 777 and 778 define when a conviction, order, sentence or warrant of enforcement may be remedied, on being removed by *certiorari*.

781. (1) Want of proof of order in council — No order, conviction or other proceeding shall be quashed or set aside, and no defendant shall be discharged, by reason only that evidence has not been given

(a) of a proclamation or order of the Governor in Council or the lieutenant governor in council;

(b) of rules, regulations or by-laws made by the Governor in Council under an Act of Parliament or by the lieutenant governor in council under an Act of the legislature of the province; or

(c) of the publication of a proclamation, order, rule, regulation or by-law in the *Canada Gazette* or in the official gazette for the province.

(2) Judicial notice — Proclamations, orders, rules, regulations and by-laws mentioned in subsection (1) and the publication thereof shall be judicially noticed.

R.S., c. C-34, s. 715.

Commentary: Section 781(1) declares that no order, conviction or other proceedings shall be quashed or set aside, nor defendant discharged, by reason *only* that evidence has not been given of a matter which must be judicially noticed under s. 781(2). Proclamations or orders of the Governor in Council, or the lieutenant governor in council of a province, as well as rules, regulations or by-laws made by either under enabling Federal or Provincial enactment, must be judicially noticed as must their publication in the Canada or official provincial Gazette.

Related Provisions: Judicial notice under s. 781 operates as a substitute or replacement for formal proof, by witness or exhibit.

Under *C.E.A.* ss. 17 and 18, *judicial notice* must be taken of all Acts of the Imperial Parliament and Parliament of Canada. Formal proof thereof is not necessary. Sections 20–22 and *C.E.A.* s. 24 permit documentary proof of certain types of proclamation, order, regulation and appointment made under federal or provincial enabling legislation.

Section 782 enacts that formal defects in a warrant of committal do not vitiate the warrant. Sections 777 and 778 describe when a conviction, order, sentence or warrant of committal are remediable on removal by *certiorari*.

782. Defect in form — No warrant of committal shall, on *certiorari* or *habeas corpus*, be held to be void by reason only of any defect therein, where

    (a) it is alleged in the warrant that the defendant was convicted; and

    (b) there is a valid conviction to sustain the warrant.

R.S., c. C-34, s. 716.

Commentary: Under this section, certain formal defects will *not* invalidate a warrant of committal in proceedings on *certiorari* and *habeas corpus*. The saving provisions of this section apply where the warrant alleges D's conviction and a valid conviction sustains the warrant.

Case Law

Ex parte Le Clerc (1975), 21 C.C.C. (2d) 16 (Que. C.A.); affirmed (1975), 21 C.C.C. (2d) 16n (S.C.C.) — This section applied where a warrant of committal was in the form of a minute of conviction, rather than in the form of a warrant of committal, but contained all the essential elements of a warrant of committal.

Related Provisions: Under s. 781, no order, conviction or other proceeding shall be quashed nor defendant discharged, by reason only that evidence has not been given of a matter of which judicial notice must be taken under the section.

Other related provisions are described in the corresponding note to s. 781, *supra*.

783. No action against official when conviction, etc., quashed — Where an application is made to quash a conviction, order or other proceeding made or held by a provincial court judge acting under Part XIX or a justice on the ground that he exceeded his jurisdiction, the court to which or the judge to whom the application is made may, in quashing the conviction, order or other proceeding, order that no civil proceedings shall be taken against the justice or provincial court judge or against any officer who acted under the conviction, order or other proceeding or under any warrant issued to enforce it.

R.S., c. C-34, s. 717.

Commentary: The section authorizes the making of a consequential order where a conviction, order, or other proceeding is quashed on the ground that a provincial court judge acting under Part XIX (Indictable Offences — Trial Without Jury), or a justice, exceeded his jurisdiction. The order saves harmless against civil proceedings the provincial court judge or justice and any officer acting under the conviction, order or other proceeding or warrant of enforcement.

Case Law

Mayrand v. Cronier (1981), 23 C.R. (3d) 114, 63 C.C.C. (2d) 561 (Que. C.A.) — The granting of the immunity provided by this section, although discretionary, should be the rule and should only be refused where there are serious reasons such as dishonest or malicious conduct.

Related Provisions: Sections 25–31, afford general protection to persons who administer or enforce the law.

784. (1) Appeal in mandamus etc. — An appeal lies to the court of appeal from a decision granting or refusing the relief sought in proceedings by way of *mandamus, certiorari* or prohibition.

(2) Application of Part XXI — Except as provided in this section, Part XXI applies, with such modifications as the circumstances require, to appeals under this section.

(3) Refusal of application, and appeal — Where an application for a writ of *habeas corpus ad subjiciendum* is refused by a judge of a court having jurisdiction therein, no application may again be made on the same grounds, whether to the same or to another court or judge, unless fresh evidence is adduced, but an appeal from that refusal shall lie to the court of appeal, and where on the appeal the application is refused a further appeal shall lie to the Supreme Court of Canada, with leave of that Court.

(4) Where writ granted — Where a writ of *habeas corpus ad subjiciendum* is granted by any judge, no appeal therefrom shall lie at the instance of any party including the Attorney General of the province concerned or the Attorney General of Canada.

(5) Appeal from judgment on return of writ — Where a judgment is issued on the return of a writ of *habeas corpus ad subjiciendum*, an appeal therefrom lies to the court of appeal, and from a judgment of the court of appeal to the Supreme Court of Canada, with the leave of that court, at the instance of the applicant or the Attorney General of the province concerned or the Attorney General of Canada, but not at the instance of any other party.

(6) Hearing of appeal — An appeal in *habeas corpus* matters shall be heard by the court to which the appeal is directed at an early date, whether in or out of the prescribed sessions of the court.

R.S., c. C-34, s. 719; 1997, c. 18, s. 109.

Commentary: The section defines the *rights of appeal* to the court of appeal from decisions relating to the extraordinary remedies of *mandamus, certiorari*, prohibition and *habeas corpus*.

Under s. 784(1), an *appeal* lies to the court of appeal from a decision granting or refusing the relief sought in proceedings by way of *mandamus, certiorari* and prohibition. The appeals are determined in accordance with Part XXI (Appeals — Indictable Offences), except as provided in the section.

Sections 784(3)–(6) govern appeals in *habeas corpus* proceedings. Where a writ of *habeas corpus ad subjiciendum* is refused by one judge, s. 784(3) bars further applications therefor, absent fresh evidence, but permits an appeal to the court of appeal and, thereafter, with leave of that court, to the Supreme Court of Canada, where the application is refused. Where a writ of *habeas corpus ad subjiciendum* is granted, s. 784(4) bars *all* appeals, including those of the Attorney General. Under s. 784(5), where a judgment is issued on the return of a writ of *habeas corpus ad subjiciendum*, there is a right of appeal, by applicant and the Attorney General to the court of appeal and, with leave, to the Supreme Court of Canada. Section 784(6) requires appeals in *habeas corpus* matters to be heard at an early date.

Case Law
Jurisdiction

United States of America v. Desfossés (1997), 7 C.R. (5th) 233, 115 C.C.C. (3d) 257 (S.C.C.) — There is no refusal of a writ of *habeas corpus* where D's application for it has been dismissed after a hearing on the merits in accordance with a consent procedure which treats the writ as having been issued. D, accordingly has *no* right of appeal to the Supreme Court of Canada.

R. v. Sagutch (1991), 63 C.C.C. (3d) 569 (B.C. C.A.) — The incorporation of Part XXI by s. 784(2) makes s. 686, including s. 686(1)(b)(iv), applicable to appeals in extraordinary remedies cases.

Meier v. R. (1983), 8 C.C.C. (3d) 210 (B.C. C.A.); affirming (1983), 6 C.C.C. (3d) 165 (B.C. S.C.); leave to appeal refused (1983), 3 D.L.R. (4th) 567n (S.C.C.) — An appeal from dismissal of a petition for *habeas corpus* in extradition proceedings lies to the court of appeal.

Quebec (P.G.) v. Mathieu (1986), 50 C.R. (3d) 156 (Que. C.A.) — The grounds for an appeal by P from a decision granting *certiorari* are *not* limited to questions of law alone.

Bank of Nova Scotia v. R. (1983), 7 C.C.C. (3d) 165 (Sask. C.A.); reversing (1983), 24 Sask. R. 312 (Q.B.) — This section does *not* confer jurisdiction to hear an appeal from an order in a pending application. Appeal rights are statutory only. An order to allow cross-examination of the deponents of affidavits is *not* a *decision* within the meaning of s. 784(1).

Notice of Appeal

Kipnes v. Alberta (A.G.), [1966] 4 C.C.C. 387 (Alta. C.A.) — The rules with respect to appeals from acquittal, conviction, or sentence do *not* apply to appeals from *certiorari* proceedings. In the absence of a special rule dealing with these matters, the civil rules respecting service of notice of appeal apply.

Stay Pending Appeal [See also ss. 261, 683(5)(6)]

R. v. Boutin (1990), 58 C.C.C. (3d) 237 (Que. C.A.); leave to appeal refused (1990), 59 C.C.C. (3d) vi (note) (S.C.C.) — To obtain a stay of trial proceedings pending determination of an appeal from a decision refusing *certiorari* to quash an order to stand trial, an applicant must first establish a *prima facie* case that the appeal raises a *serious question*. The applicant must next show that, absent a stay, he/she would suffer *irreparable harm*. Finally, the *balance of convenience*, to be decided by determining which party would suffer the greater harm if the stay were granted or refused, must favour the entry of a stay.

Charter Remedies

R. v. Corbeil (1986), 27 C.C.C. (3d) 245 (Ont. C.A.) — "[W]here the inferior court is a court of competent jurisdiction to try the case, there is no automatic loss of jurisdiction by that court in ruling adversely to D on a *Charter* issue unless the ruling is manifestly and palpably wrong ... [E]xtraordinary relief should only be invoked where a palpable infringement of a constitutional right has taken place or is clearly threatened ... [O]nly in special and exceptional circumstances can it be said that the denial of a constitutional right has resulted in a loss of jurisdiction so as to justify the extraordinary remedies of *certiorari* and prohibition."

Related Provisions: Sections 675 and 676 grant rights of appeal in proceedings upon indictment.

PART XXVII — SUMMARY CONVICTIONS

Interpretation

785. (1) Definitions — In this Part

"clerk of the appeal court" includes a local clerk of the appeal court;

"informant" means a person who lays an information;

"information" includes

(a) a count in an information, and

(b) a complaint in respect of which a justice is authorized by an Act of Parliament or an enactment made thereunder to make an order;

"order" means any order, including an order for the payment of money;

"proceedings" means

(a) proceedings in respect of offences that are declared by an Act of Parliament or an enactment made thereunder to be punishable on summary conviction, and

(b) proceedings where a justice is authorized by an Act of Parliament or an enactment made thereunder to make an order;

"prosecutor" means the Attorney General or where the Attorney General does not intervene, the informant, and includes counsel or an agent acting on behalf of either of them;

"sentence" includes

(a) a declaration made under subsection 199(3),

Proposed Amendment — 785 "sentence"(b)

On the coming into force of section 747.1 of the *Criminal Code*, as enacted by section 6 of 1995, c. 22, paragraph (b) of the definition "sentence" in section 785 of the *Criminal Code* is replaced by the following:

(b) an order made under subsection 100(2) or 259(1) or (2), section 261, subsection 730(1), section 737, 738, 739 or 742.3 or subsection 747.1(1) and

1995, c. 22, s. 7(2). Not in force at date of publication.

(b) an order made under subsection 110(1) or 259(1) or (2), section 261 or subsection 736(1), and

(c) a disposition made under section 731 or 732 or subsection 732.2(3) or (5), 742.4(3) or 742.6(9);

(d) an order made under subsection 16(1) of the *Controlled Drugs and Substances Act*;

"summary conviction court" means a person who has jurisdiction in the territorial division where the subject-matter of the proceedings is alleged to have arisen and who

(a) is given jurisdiction over the proceedings by the enactment under which the proceedings are taken,

(b) is a justice or provincial court judge, where the enactment under which the proceedings are taken does not expressly give jurisdiction to any person or class of persons, or

(c) is a provincial court judge, where the enactment under which the proceedings are taken gives jurisdiction in respect thereof to two or more justices;

"trial" includes the hearing of a complaint.

R.S., c. C-34, s. 720; 1972, c. 13, s. 61; 1974–75–76, c. 93, s. 85; 1976–77, c. 53, s. 4;R.S. 1985, c. 27 (1st Supp.), ss. 170, 203; 1992, c. 1, s. 58(1), Schedule 1, item 16; 1995, c. 22, s. 7; 1995, c. 39, s. 156; 1996, c. 19, s. 76.

Commentary: The section defines terms used in Part XXVII.

Case Law

Prosecutor

Edmunds v. R. (1981), 21 C.R. (3d) 168, 58 C.C.C. (2d) 485 (S.C.C.) — Where D, charged with a strictly indictable offence, elects trial by provincial court judge, Part XXVII and its definition of "prosecutor" does not apply. This Part only applies to a dual procedure offence where P has elected to proceed by summary conviction.

R. v. Thomas (1979), 53 C.C.C. (2d) 472 (B.C. C.A.) — A prosecutor may *not* act for both the Attorney General of Canada and of the province at the same time, but may be the authorized agent for both to avoid any dispute as to his/her authority to prosecute a case.

R. v. Maher (1986), 27 C.C.C. (3d) 476 (Nfld. C.A.) — The Attorney General has the right to appoint police officers as prosecutors in summary conviction matters. A judge does not have the discretion to refuse to hear a person properly appointed under statutory authority to act as a prosecutor.

Bradley v. R. (1975), 35 C.R.N.S. 192, 24 C.C.C. (2d) 482 (Ont. C.A.) — The Attorney General and his agent, P, represent the Sovereign in the prosecution of crimes. The role of the private prosecutor, permitted by statute, is parallel to, but not in substitution for, the role of the Attorney General. Where the two roles come into conflict, the role of P is paramount and if in P's opinion the interests of justice require, P may intervene and take over the private prosecution.

Summary Conviction Court

R. v. Fields (1986), 53 C.R. (3d) 260, 28 C.C.C. (3d) 353 (Ont. C.A.) — A summary conviction court under this Part is a court of record with the power to punish for contempt *in facie curiae*.

Charter Considerations — Prosecution by Agents

R. v. Blundon (1987), 63 Nfld. & P.E.I.R. 253 (Nfld. T.D.); affirmed (1988), 71 Nfld. & P.E.I.R. 152 (Nfld. C.A.) — The prosecution of offences by police officers properly designated as agents under this section does *not* violate D's rights under *Charter* ss. 7, 11(d) or 15(1). A provincial court judge does not have the inherent jurisdiction to refuse to hear such an agent.

Related Provisions: Sections which describe or punish an offence also indicate whether it must be prosecuted by indictment, upon summary conviction or may be tried either way. P elects mode of procedure. Under *I.A.* s. 34(1)(a), offences triable either way are *deemed* to be indictable offences, unless and until P elects to proceed by summary conviction. Part XXVII governs trial and appeal proceedings in summary conviction matters.

786. (1) Application of Part — Except where otherwise provided by law, this Part applies to proceedings as defined in this Part.

(2) Limitation — No proceedings shall be instituted more than six months after the time when the subject-matter of the proceedings arose, unless the prosecutor and the defendant so agree.

R.S., c. C-34, s. 721.; 1997, c. 18, s. 110.

Commentary: By s. 786(1) Part XXVII applies to summary conviction proceedings, *except where otherwise provided by law*. In other words the Part enacts the *general rules* applicable to summary conviction trials and appeals. The general rule of s. 786(2) is that no proceedings shall be instituted more than six months after the time when the subject-matter of the proceedings arose unless D and P agree, "except where otherwise provided by law".

Case Law

Crown Election as to Mode of Procedure

R. v. Petersen (1982), 30 C.R. (3d) 165, 69 C.C.C. (3d) 385 (S.C.C.); reversing (1980), 8 M.V.R. 139 (Sask. C.A.) — Where the trial judge dismissed the charges against D on the basis of lack of jurisdiction, P, which had previously elected to proceed summarily, then proceeded by indictment. It was held that once a court dismisses charges in the erroneous belief that it lacks jurisdiction, further proceedings on the same charge are barred, whether taken summarily or by indictment. P's remedy in the face of such judicial error, is to appeal or apply for a prerogative writ.

Edmunds v. R. (1981), 21 C.R. (3d) 168, 58 C.C.C. (2d) 485 (S.C.C.) — Although D, charged with an indictable offence, elects a summary form of trial before a provincial judge, the offence remains an indictable offence and the provisions with respect to summary conviction offences do not apply.

R. v. Burke (1992), 78 C.C.C. (3d) 163 (Nfld. C.A.) — In the case of hybrid offences, a reference to a section of the *Criminal Code* which describes an offence or provides the punishment imposed on summary conviction does *not* constitute P's election to proceed in that manner. P is *not* barred from later electing to proceed by indictment.

R. v. Laws (1998), 18 C.R. (5th) 257, 128 C.C.C. (3d) 516 (Ont. C.A.) — The Crown's *discretion* to choose the mode of procedure, a cornerstone of the administration of justice, is constitutionally sound.

R. v. Kalkhorany (1994), 17 O.R. (3d) 783 (Ont. C.A.) — Where P has elected to proceed by summary conviction, a plea has been taken and evidence given, it is *not* open to P to "re-elect" to proceed by indictment upon the information.

R. v. Phelps (1993), 79 C.C.C. (3d) 550 (Ont. C.A.) — P's election to proceed summarily in respect of an offence triable either way, made outside the six-month limitation period, is a nullity, as are any proceedings subsequent to the election.

R. v. Gougeon (1980), 55 C.C.C. (2d) 218 (Ont. C.A.) — P is *not* obliged to elect its manner of proceeding at D's first appearance before the court.

R. v. Wardley (1978), 11 C.R. (3d) 282, 43 C.C.C. (2d) 345 (Ont. C.A.) — If D, charged with the indictable offence of trafficking, elects trial by provincial court judge and pleads not guilty to the offence as charged but guilty to possession, a hybrid offence, then D is deemed to plead guilty to the indictable offence of possession. There is no provision for P to elect to proceed by summary conviction after plea and the judge cannot sentence D as if P had proceeded summarily.

R. v. Robert (1973), 13 C.C.C. (2d) 43 (Ont. C.A.) — *See also*: *R. v. Hawryluk* (1975), 29 C.C.C. (2d) 41 (N.B. C.A.) — Where P fails to elect a mode of procedure for a hybrid offence, and the case proceeds in a summary conviction court, P is *deemed* to have elected to proceed by summary conviction.

Limitation Periods

Dressler v. Tallman Gravel & Sand Supply Ltd. (No. 2) (1962), 39 C.R. 180, [1963] 2 C.C.C. 25 (Man. C.A.) — Where an information alleges a continuing offence, it may be amended to delete a part of the charge which refers to an offence committed outside the limitation period. This type of amendment is not the same as laying a new charge.

R. v. Kelly (1998), 128 C.C.C. (3d) 206 (Ont. C.A.) — An election by P to proceed summarily on an information sworn more than six months after the time when the subject-matter of the proceedings arose, and any proceedings that follow, are null and void.

R. v. Belair (1988), 64 C.R. (3d) 179, 41 C.C.C. (3d) 329 (Ont. C.A.) — Where P elected to proceed by summary conviction, but the information was quashed prior to plea as barred by the limitation period, P was entitled to lay a new information and proceed by way of indictment.

R. v. Parkin (1986), 28 C.C.C. (3d) 252 (Ont. C.A.); leave to appeal refused (1986), 17 O.A.C. 377n (S.C.C.) — It was held to be an abuse of process for P, after the commencement of the trial by summary conviction, to withdraw the charge in order to present a second information and proceed by way of indictment upon discovering that the offence occurred outside the six-month period.

R. v. Bobcaygeon (1974), 17 C.C.C. (2d) 236 (Ont. C.A.) — The lack of a date in the jurat of an information which thus fails to disclose that it was laid within the six-month limitation period applicable to summary conviction proceedings renders the information a nullity.

R. v. Southwick (1967), 2 C.R.N.S. 46, [1968] 1 C.C.C. 356 (Ont. C.A.) — As long as the information is laid within the six-month limitation period, a summons issued as a result of that information is valid, even if issued outside of the six-month period.

R. v. Chaussé (1986), 51 C.R. (3d) 332, 28 C.C.C. (3d) 412 (Que. C.A.) — The limitation period for summary conviction proceedings prevents conviction for a summary conviction offence included in an indictable offence where the information was laid more than six months after the fact.

Charter Considerations

R. v. Quinn (1989), 73 C.R. (3d) 77, 54 C.C.C. (3d) 157 (Que. C.A.) — Where P initially intended to proceed summarily, but could not because the limitation period had expired by the time it received the certificate of drug analysis, and so decided to proceed by indictment, *Charter* s. 7 had been infringed. The proceedings were stayed.

Related Provisions: There is no general limitation period applicable to proceedings on indictment. Some offences, for example treason under ss. 46(2)(a) and 48(1), have their own limitation period.

Charter s. 11(b) guarantees anyone charged with an offence the right to be tried within a reasonable time. Delays in the prosecutorial process may also be relevant to a determination whether a stay of proceedings should be entered for a breach of *Charter* s. 7 or due to an abuse of process.

Under s. 788(1), proceedings are commenced by laying an information in Form 2. The formalities of the information are described in s. 789. The issuance of process to compel D's appearance, or the confirmation of process earlier issued, institutes proceedings against D.

Punishment

787. (1) General penalty — Except where otherwise provided by law, every one who is convicted of an offence punishable on summary conviction is liable to a fine of not more than two thousand dollars or to imprisonment for six months or to both.

(2) Imprisonment in default where not otherwise specified — Where the imposition of a fine or the making of an order for the payment of money is authorized by law, but the law does not provide that imprisonment may be imposed in default of payment of the fine or compliance with the order, the court may order that in default of payment of the fine or compliance with the order, as the case may be, the defendant shall be imprisoned for a term not exceeding six months.

(3) to (11) [Repealed R.S. 1985, c. 27 (1st Supp.), s. 171.]

R.S., c. C-34, s. 722; R.S. 1985, c. 27 (1st Supp.), s. 171.

Commentary: The section enacts *general punishment* provisions for summary conviction proceedings and prescribes the *maximum term of imprisonment in default* of payment of a pecuniary penalty.

Under s. 787(1), *except where otherwise provided by law*, the *maximum* punishment upon summary conviction is a fine of *not* more than $2,000, imprisonment for *not* more than *six* months, or both. The general rule is subject to exception in the enactment which creates or punishes the offence.

Section 787(2) applies where the imposition of a fine or the making of an order for the payment of money is authorized by law, but no provision is made for the imposition of imprisonment in default of payment. The default term in such cases may *not* exceed imprisonment for six months.

Case Law

R. v. Natrall (1973), 20 C.R.N.S. 265, 9 C.C.C. (2d) 390 (B.C. C.A.) — The power to fine rather than imprison and to order *imprisonment* in default of payment of the fine is permissive and discretionary, *not* mandatory. The court can impose a fine without ordering imprisonment in default.

Related Provisions: Under s. 718.3(3), a default term must not exceed the term of imprisonment that is prescribed for the offence. Default terms for indictable offences are governed by s. 734(4) and (5).

Fines of corporate accused convicted of summary conviction offences are governed by s. 735(1)(b). The maximum fine must not exceed $25,000, except where otherwise provided by law.

An individual accused may discharge a fine, in whole or in part, in accordance with a fine option program under s. 736.

The destination of fines is in accordance with s. 734.4. They may be recovered in civil proceedings under s. 734.6. Restitution orders are made under ss. 738-741.2.

Information

788. (1) Commencement of proceedings — **Proceedings under this Part shall be commenced by laying an information in Form 2.**

(2) One justice may act before the trial — **Notwithstanding any other law that requires an information to be laid before or to be tried by two or more justices, one justice may**

(a) **receive the information;**

(b) **issue a summons or warrant with respect to the information; and**

(c) **do all other things preliminary to the trial.**

R.S., c. C-34, s. 723.

Commentary: Under this section, summary conviction proceedings must be *commenced* by laying an information in Form 2 before a justice of the peace. A single justice of the peace may receive the information, issue process and do all things preliminary to the trial.

Case Law

R. v. Stevenson (1983), 50 N.B.R. (2d) 387 (S.C.C.); affirming (1979), 28 N.B.R. (2d) 306 (C.A.) — In the absence of a statutory restriction, anyone is entitled to lay an information.

Related Provisions: Under s. 786(2), proceedings must not be instituted more than six months after the time when the subject-matter of the proceedings arose, unless P and D agree.

An information in Form 2 is in writing and under oath. It may charge more than one offence, or relate to more than one matter of complaint, provided each offence or matter of complaint, is set out in a separate count. The rules of criminal pleading in ss. 581–593 and s. 601 of Part XX apply, with such modifications as the circumstances require, to summary conviction proceedings under s. 795. Section 794 provides that there is no need to set out or negative any exception, exemption, proviso, excuse or qualification in an information in summary conviction proceedings.

789. (1) Formalities of information — In proceedings to which this Part applies, an information

(a) shall be in writing and under oath; and

(b) may charge more than one offence or relate to more than one matter of complaint, but where more than one offence is charged or the information relates to more than one matter of complaint, each offence or matter of complaint, as the case may be, shall be set out in a separate count.

(2) **No reference to previous convictions** — No information in respect of an offence for which, by reason of previous convictions, a greater punishment may be imposed shall contain any reference to previous convictions.

R.S., c. C-34, s. 724.

Commentary: The section complements s. 788 in describing the formalities of an information laid before a justice to initiate summary conviction proceedings.

Under s. 789(1), an information must be *in writing* and *under oath*. It may charge more than one offence or relate to more than one matter of complaint, but each offence or matter of complaint must be set out in a separate count. Section 789(2) forbids any reference to previous convictions in an information where a greater punishment may be imposed by reason of previous conviction.

Case Law
Duplicity: S. 789(1)(b)
R. v. City of Sault Ste. Marie (1978), 3 C.R. (3d) 30, 40 C.C.C. (2d) 353 (S.C.C.); affirming (1976), 30 C.C.C. (2d) 257 (Ont. C.A.) — The primary test for duplicity is: does D know what case is to be met, or is D prejudiced in the preparation of his defence by ambiguity in the charge? A duplicitous information can be amended by the summary conviction court or the appeal court exercising the powers of the summary conviction court.

Joint Trial of Counts
R. v. Grant (1992), 52 O.A.C. 244 (C.A.) — The joint trial of indictable and summary conviction offences is *not* authorized by law. It is a procedural irregularity which may be subject to the application of either s. 686(1)(b)(iii) or s. 686(1)(b)(iv), where D has suffered no prejudice.

Validity of Information
R. v. Schille (1976), 28 C.C.C. (2d) 230 (B.C. C.A.) — An information which sets out the time and place of the alleged offences in the preface, rather than in the counts themselves is valid. The preface is to be taken as part of and included in the counts.

R. v. Welsford (1967), 2 C.R.N.S. 5, [1968] 1 C.C.C. 1 (Ont. C.A.); affirmed (1969), 6 C.R.N.S. 90, [1969] 4 C.C.C. 1 (S.C.C.) — While the informant might sign his name by rubber stamp, a justice of the peace must place his signature in the jurat in his own handwriting. A stamped signature is valid only if the act is procedural in nature and not judicial in character.

Presence of Information
R. v. Veltri Stamping Co. (1986), 17 O.A.C. 81 (C.A.) — *See also*: *Perrault v. R.* (1982), 65 C.C.C. (2d) 279 (Sask. C.A.) — The information need *not* be physically present in the courtroom to confer jurisdiction upon the judge. It is sufficient that there is an information in existence.

Related Provisions: The rules of criminal pleading and joinder contained in ss. 581–593 and s. 601 of Part XX apply to summary conviction proceedings, with such modifications as the circumstances require, by s. 795. Exceptions, excuses, exemptions, provisos and qualifications need not be set out nor negatived in the information or count under s. 794.

A provision similar to s. 789(2) appears in s. 664. Evidence of previous convictions may be introduced under ss. 666–667 and 727, made applicable by s. 795, as well as under *C.E.A.* s. 12.

790. (1) Any justice may act before and after trial — Nothing in this Act or any other law shall be deemed to require a justice before whom proceedings are commenced or who issues process before or after the trial to be the justice or one of the justices before whom the trial is held.

(2) Two or more justices — Where two or more justices have jurisdiction with respect to proceedings, they shall be present and act together at the trial, but one justice may thereafter do anything that is required or is authorized to be done in connection with the proceedings.

(3) and (4) [Repealed R.S. 1985, c. 27 (1st Supp.), s. 172.]
R.S., c. C-34, s. 725; 1974–75–76, c. 93, s. 86; R.S. 1985, c. 27 (1st Supp.), s. 172.

Commentary: The section authorizes any justice to act prior to trial. Under s. 790(1), the justice before whom summary conviction proceedings are commenced by the laying of an information in Form 2, or who issues process before or after the trial, need *not* be the summary conviction court before whom D's trial is held. Section 790(2) is an anachronism.

Related Provisions: The practical effect of s. 790(1) is to permit different justices to receive the information, to issue process and to adjourn the matter from time to time until trial, when the provisions of ss. 798–803 apply. Summary conviction proceedings may be continued by another summary conviction court under ss. 669.1 and 669.2, made applicable by s. 795.

791. [Repealed R.S. 1985, c. 27 (1st Supp.), s. 173.]

792. [Repealed R.S. 1985, c. 27 (1st Supp.), s. 174.]

793. [Repealed R.S. 1985, c. 27 (1st Supp.), s. 175.]

794. (1) No need to negative exception, etc. — No exception, exemption, proviso, excuse or qualification prescribed by law is required to be set out or negatived, as the case may be, in an information.

(2) Burden of proving exception, etc. — The burden of proving that an exception, exemption, proviso, excuse or qualification prescribed by law operates in favour of the defendant is on the defendant, and the prosecutor is not required, except by way of rebuttal, to prove that the exception, exemption, proviso, excuse or qualification does not operate in favour of the defendant, whether or not it is set out in the information.
R.S., c. C-34, s. 730.

Commentary: The section enacts a further rule of pleading applicable to informations in summary conviction proceedings, as well as a related rule of proof.

Under s. 794(1), it is *not* necessary for a valid information or count that it set out or negative any exception, exemption, proviso, excuse or qualification prescribed by law. Under s. 794(2), the burden of proving that any such exception, exemption, proviso, excuse or qualification operates in favour of D rests on D. P is *not* required to prove the negative, except by way of rebuttal.

The shift in onus of proof may attract *Charter* ss. 7 and 11(d) scrutiny.

Case Law

Hundt v. R. (1971), 3 C.C.C. (2d) 279 (Alta. C.A.) — It is unnecessary for the charge to set out anything other than that D committed the offence, as set out in the statute. The inclusion of statements negativing the qualification of D to seek exemption under the statute is unnecessary and redundant.

Charter Considerations

R. v. Lee's Poultry Ltd. (1985), 43 C.R. (3d) 289, 17 C.C.C. (3d) 539 (Ont. C.A.) — An identical provision to this section, contained in the *Ontario Provincial Offences Act*, does *not* offend *Charter* s. 11(d).

Related Provisions: No comparable provision applies in indictable proceedings.

Under s. 795, the rules of criminal pleading and joinder of ss. 581-593 and s. 601 in Part XX apply to summary conviction proceedings, with such modifications as the circumstances require.

Application

795. Application of Parts XVI, XVIII, and XX.1 — The provisions of Parts XVI and XVIII with respect to compelling the appearance of an accused before a justice, and the provisions of Parts XX and XX.1, in so far as they are not inconsistent with this Part, apply, with such modifications as the circumstances require, to proceedings under this Part.

R.S., c. C-34, s. 731; R.S. 1985, c. 27 (1st Supp.), s. 176; 1991, c. 43, s. 7.

Commentary: The section makes applicable to summary conviction proceedings, insofar as they are *not* inconsistent with Part XXVII, and with such modifications as the circumstances require, the provisions of Part XVI (Compelling Appearance of D Before a Justice, and Interim Release), XVIII (Procedure on Preliminary Inquiry) with respect to compelling the appearance of D before a justice, Part XX (Procedure in Jury Trials and General Provisions) and Part XX.1 (Mental Disorder). In the result, as a general rule, the procedure to compel D's appearance and at trial is the same in indictable as in summary conviction proceedings. Further, there is little, if any, disparity, in the rules of criminal pleading.

Case Law

R. v. Grant (1992), 52 O.A.C. 244 (C.A.) — See digest under s. 789, *supra*.

Related Provisions: The incorporated provisions of Part XX include the rules of pleading and joinder, in ss. 581–593 and s. 601, as supplemented by s. 794, and the provisions of ss. 606–610 and s. 613 relating to pleas.

796. [Repealed R.S. 1985, c. 27 (1st Supp.), s. 176.]

797.]Repealed R.S. 1985, c. 27 (1st Supp.), s. 176.]

798. Jurisdiction — Every summary conviction court has jurisdiction to try, determine and adjudge proceedings to which this Part applies in the territorial division over which the person who constitutes that court has jurisdiction.

R.S., c. C-34, s. 733.

Commentary: Under this section, every summary conviction court, as defined in s. 785, has jurisdiction to try, determine and adjudge summary conviction proceedings in the territorial division in which the court has jurisdiction.

Case Law

Contempt Authority

R. v. Fields (1986), 53 C.R. (3d) 260, 28 C.C.C. (3d) 353 (Ont. C.A.) — A judge presiding in a summary conviction court has the inherent jurisdiction to register a conviction for contempt in the face of the court and to fine and imprison a person found guilty of such contempt.

Mistrial

R. v. Bertucci (1984), 11 C.C.C. (3d) 83 (Sask. C.A.) — A trial judge has jurisdiction to declare a mistrial after an adjudication of guilt and before the imposition of sentence. The power to disqualify himself for good and sufficient reason and declare a mistrial exists apart from the express provisions of the *Code*. An adjudication of guilt does not affect that power.

Joint Trials on Separate Informations [See also s. 591]

R. v. Clunas (1992), 70 C.C.C. (3d) 115 (S.C.C.) — The court may order two or more indictments or informations to be tried together where it is in the *interests of justice* and D or the offences could have been jointly charged. The court should seek the *consent* of both D and P. Where consent is withheld, the court should explore the reasons, but it can order joinder whether or not D consents, providing the foregoing criteria for joinder are met. Summary conviction offences should be joined with indictable offences only where the trial on the indictable offence is to take place in provincial court. In the event of any conflict as to the applicable procedure, indictable procedures should apply.

Related Provisions: The territorial division in which a summary conviction court has jurisdiction is determined by the terms of the appointment of the court.

In general, a summary conviction court has jurisdiction to try any *Code* summary conviction offence alleged to have been committed within the territorial jurisdiction of the court, namely, the territorial division in which the court is sitting. The *Code*, however, contains a number of provisions extending territorial jurisdiction, as for example in ss. 7 and 476–481.

799. Non-appearance of prosecutor — Where, in proceedings to which this Part applies, the defendant appears for the trial and the prosecutor, having had due notice, does not appear, the summary conviction court may dismiss the information or may adjourn the trial to some other time on such terms as it considers proper.

R.S., c. C-34, s. 734.

Commentary: The section describes the authority of a summary conviction court, where D appears for trial but P, with due notice, fails to attend. The court may either *dismiss* the information, or *adjourn* the trial to another time, upon such terms as it considers proper.

Case Law

R. v. Hayward (1981), 59 C.C.C. (2d) 134 (Nfld. C.A.) — There is *no* authority to dismiss any case for lack of prosecution because P or counsel becomes a witness in the case.

Related Provisions: The general authority to *adjourn* summary conviction proceedings is contained in s. 803. Section 809 empowers a summary conviction court to award and order such costs as it considers reasonable, and *not* inconsistent with the scale of fees established by s. 840.

Under s. 813(b)(i), the informant, the Attorney General or his/her agent may appeal to the appeal court, as defined in s. 812, from an order dismissing an information.

800. (1) When both parties appear — Where the prosecutor and defendant appear for the trial, the summary conviction court shall proceed to hold the trial.

(2) Counsel or agent — A defendant may appear personally or by counsel or agent, but the summary conviction court may require the defendant to appear personally and may, if it thinks fit, issue a warrant in Form 7 for the arrest of the defendant and adjourn the trial to await his appearance pursuant thereto.

(2.1) Video links — Where the court so orders and the defendant agrees, the defendant who is confined in prison may appear by closed-circuit television or any other means that allow the court and the defendant to engage in simultaneous visual and oral communication, if the defendant is given the opportunity to communicate privately with counsel, in a case in which the defendant is represented by counsel.

(3) Appearance by corporation — Where the defendant is a corporation, it shall appear by counsel or agent, and if it does not appear, the summary conviction court may, on proof of service of the summons, proceed *ex parte* to hold the trial.

R.S., c. C-34, s. 735; 1997, c. 18, s. 111.

Commentary: The section describes the *manner* in which *individual* and *corporate accused* may *appear* for trial on summary conviction matters.

Under s. 800(2), an *individual accused* may appear *personally* or by *counsel* or *agent*. The summary conviction court may, however, require D to appear personally and issue a warrant in Form 7 for D's arrest. The proceedings may then be adjourned to await D's appearance under the warrant.

Under s. 800(2.1), D may appear by closed-circuit television or similar means where conditions precedent of the subsection have been met.

Under s. 800(3), a *corporate accused* must appear by *counsel* or *agent*. Where a corporate accused fails to appear in either manner, and it is proven that service has been made of the summons, the summary conviction court may proceed with an *ex parte* trial.

Where both P and D appear for trial, the summary conviction court will hold the trial under s. 800(1).

Case Law

Appearance

R. v. Westmin Resources Ltd., [1985] 1 W.W.R. 30 (B.C. C.A.); leave to appeal refused (1985), 56 N.R. 240 (S.C.C.) — Personal appearance obviates the need for a summons. Once counsel appeared on behalf of a correctly identified offender and entered a plea, it could no longer be argued that D company had not been served with the summons.

R. v. Okanee (1981), 59 C.C.C. (2d) 149 (Sask. C.A.) — An accused who appears by counsel in a summary conviction court has complied with his undertaking to appear and may *not* be charged with failing to attend court. Furthermore, although this section gives the court the power to compel D to appear personally, it is improper in such circumstances to issue a bench warrant.

Identity of Accused

R. v. Fedoruk, [1966] 3 C.C.C. 118 (Sask. C.A.) — Where counsel appears for a person bearing the same name as a person named as D in an information and wishes to argue that his client is *not* the person named in the information, or that the person so named has not been served, the proper procedure is to raise the point without plea so that the court may cause D to appear personally.

Related Provisions: The procedure followed in a summary conviction trial combines ss. 801–803, and Part XX, which is incorporated in summary conviction proceedings by s. 795, insofar as it is not inconsistent with Part XXVII.

In summary conviction proceedings, the trial of both an individual and corporate accused may be held *ex parte*, but only where each has been properly served and fails to appear or remain in attendance as required.

The *adjudicative* authority of a summary conviction court is described in ss. 804–809. There are two modes of appeal under ss. 812–838.

801. (1) Arraignment — Where the defendant appears for the trial, the substance of the information laid against him shall be stated to him, and he shall be asked,

(a) whether he pleads guilty or not guilty to the information, where the proceedings are in respect of an offence that is punishable on summary conviction; or

(b) whether he has cause to show why an order should not be made against him, in proceedings where a justice is authorized by law to make an order.

(2) Finding of guilt, conviction or order if charge admitted — Where the defendant pleads guilty or does not show sufficient cause why an order should not be made against him, as the case may be, the summary conviction court shall convict the defendant, discharge the defendant under section 730 or make an order against the defendant accordingly.

(3) Procedure if charge not admitted — Where the defendant pleads not guilty or states that he has cause to show why an order should not be made against him, as the case may be, the summary conviction court shall proceed with the trial, and shall take the evidence of witnesses for the prosecutor and the defendant in accordance with the provisions of Part XVIII relating to preliminary inquiries.

(4) and (5) [Repealed R.S. 1985, c. 27 (1st Supp.), s. 177(2).]

R.S., c. C-34, s. 736; R.S. 1985, c. 27 (1st Supp.), s. 177; 1995, c. 22, s. 10.

Commentary: The section describes what is to occur on arraignment in summary conviction proceedings.

Where D appears for trial, s. 801(1) requires that the *substance* of the information be stated to D. It is perhaps *not* necessary, but nonetheless advisable, to have the information read as laid. D must be asked whether he/she pleads guilty or not guilty in respect of the summary conviction offence alleged, or whether he/she has cause to show why an order should not be made against him/her, as for example under s. 810, as the case may be. D's plea should then be recorded.

Under s. 801(2), where D pleads guilty, or does not show sufficient cause why an order should not be made against him/her, the court will record a finding of guilt and either enter a conviction or discharge D under s. 730, or make an order against him/her accordingly.

Under s. 801(3), where D pleads not guilty or states he/she has cause to show, as the case may be, a trial must be held. The evidence of witnesses for P and D is taken in accordance with Part XVIII.

Case Law

Commencement of Trial

R. v. Petersen (1982), 30 C.R. (3d) 165 (S.C.C.); reversing (1980), 8 M.V.R. 139 (Sask. C.A.) — Once a plea is entered before a court, the trial commences and D is in jeopardy.

Withdrawal of Information

R. v. Anthony (1982), 69 C.C.C. (2d) 424 (N.S. C.A.); affirming (1981), 14 M.V.R. 142 (N.S. Co. Ct.) — The trial judge has discretion to allow P to withdraw an information after D's arraignment and plea.

Special Pleas

R. v. Riddle (1980), 48 C.C.C. (2d) 365 (S.C.C.); affirming (1977), 36 C.C.C. (2d) 391 (Alta. C.A.) — The plea of *autrefois acquit* is available in summary conviction proceedings. The fact that D did *not* request a certificate of dismissal is *not* a bar to the raising of the defence.

Proceed with the Trial: S. 801(3)

Boylan v. R. (1979), 8 C.R. (3d) 36, 46 C.C.C. (2d) 415 (Sask. C.A.) — The requirement of s. 540(1) that a record of the evidence be taken at a preliminary hearing is mandatory not directory. By s. 801(3), those purposes include summary conviction proceedings.

Related Provisions: The special pleas of ss. 607–610 in Part XX are incorporated in summary conviction proceedings by s. 795(1). For similar reasons, the procedure followed in summary conviction trials is substantially the same as under Part XX (Procedure in Jury Trials and General Provisions), subject to the specific provisions of Part XXVII.

Applications under s. 810 exemplify proceedings to which s. 801(1)(b) applies.

The section does *not* authorize the trial of separate informations together, nor permit the joint trial of summary conviction and indictable offences before a provincial court judge sitting at one and the same time under Parts XIX and XXVII. The trial of separate informations together is permissible under *R. v. Clunas* (1992), 11 C.R. (4th) 238, 70 C.C.C. (3d) 115, [1992] 1 S.C.R. 595. The joint trial of indictable and summary conviction offences is a *procedural irregularity* which may be saved under *Code* s. 686(1)(b)(iii) or (iv) in the absence of prejudice to D. See, *R. v. Grant* (1992), 52 O.A.C. 244 (C.A.).

In cases in which the offence charged is triable either way, P should first elect mode of procedure. Where P elects to proceed by summary conviction, the offence will be tried under Part XXVII.

802. (1) Right to make full answer and defence — The prosecutor is entitled personally to conduct his case and the defendant is entitled to make his full answer and defence.

(2) Examination of witnesses — The prosecutor or defendant, as the case may be, may examine and cross-examine witnesses personally or by counsel or agent.

(3) On oath — Every witness at a trial in proceedings to which this Part applies shall be examined under oath.

R.S., c. C-34, s. 737.

Commentary: The section describes the manner in which the parties in summary conviction proceedings may conduct the trial. P is entitled personally to conduct his/her case and in so doing may examine or cross-examine witnesses personally, or by counsel or agent. D is entitled to make full answer and defence by examining or cross-examining witnesses personally, or by counsel or agent. Under s. 802(3) each witness must be examined under oath.

Case Law

Prosecutor Entitled Personally to Conduct Case: S. 802(1)

Bradley v. R. (1975), 35 C.R.N.S. 192, 24 C.C.C. (2d) 482 (Ont. C.A.) — This section which gives P the right to personally conduct his case is not inconsistent with the right of the Attorney General to intervene where in his opinion the interests of justice require that a Crown prosecutor take over the private prosecution.

Full Answer and Defence: S. 802(1) [See also s. 650]

R. v. Field (1983), 6 C.C.C. (3d) 182 (N.S. C.A.) — The inability to make full answer and defence is a substantive defence but, where a charge is laid within the six-month limitation period, D is precluded from arguing delay in laying the charge as the basis of such defence.

R. v. Dresen, [1988] N.W.T.R. 194 (C.A.) — Where D chose to proceed to trial without counsel, but was unsure of his role in making submissions, the trial judge should not have pronounced sentence immediately after P's submissions but should have given D the opportunity to reply to P's summation and submissions.

Related Provisions: The section makes no reference to the order in which the evidence is to be adduced, but the general order of trials on indictment is followed. Admissions may also be made in summary conviction proceedings, due to the incorporation by s. 795 of s. 655 applicable in trials upon indictment.

The reference to "under oath" in s. 802(3) does not foreclose receipt of evidence given by affirmation under *C.E.A.* s. 14.

Part XXVII contains no evidentiary rules unique to summary conviction proceedings. The general rules of evidence apply, including any evidentiary provisions that may be contained in Part XX, incorporated by s. 795.

"Prosecutor" is defined in s. 785 to mean the Attorney General or, where the Attorney General does *not* intervene, the informant, and includes counsel or an agent acting on behalf of either of them.

The *evidence* given at trial, under s. 801(3) is taken in accordance with Part XVIII relating to preliminary inquiries.

803. (1) Adjournment — The summary conviction court may, in its discretion, before or during the trial, adjourn the trial to a time and place to be appointed and stated in the presence of the parties or their counsel or agents.

(2) Non-appearance of defendant — Where a defendant does not appear at the time and place appointed for the trial after having been notified of that time and place, or where a defendant does not appear for the resumption of a trial that has been adjourned in accordance with subsection (1), the summary conviction court

    (a) may proceed *ex parte* to hear and determine the proceedings in the absence of the defendant as fully and effectually as if the defendant had appeared; or

    (b) may, if it thinks fit, issue a warrant in Form 7 for the arrest of the defendant and adjourn the trial to await his appearance pursuant thereto.

(3) Consent of Attorney General required — Where, at the trial of a defendant, the summary conviction court proceeds in the manner described in paragraph (2)(*a*), no proceedings under section 145 arising out of the failure of the defendant to appear at the time and place appointed for the trial or for the resumption of the trial shall be instituted or if instituted shall be proceeded with, except with the consent of the Attorney General.

(4) Non-appearance of prosecutor — Where the prosecutor does not appear at the time and place appointed for the resumption of an adjourned trial, the summary conviction court may dismiss the information with or without costs.

(5)–(8) [Repealed 1991, c. 43, s. 9, Schedule, item 11.]

R.S., c. C-34, s. 738; c. 2 (2d Supp.), s. 15; 1972, c. 13, s. 63; 1974–75–76, c. 93, s. 87; 1991, c. 43, s. 9, Schedule, item 11; 1994, c. 44, s. 79; 1997, c. 18, s. 112.

Commentary: The section contains several provisions relating to the trial of summary conviction matters.

Under s. 803(1), a summary conviction court has the *general authority*, before or during trial, to *adjourn* the trial to a time and place specified, in the presence of P and D, their counsel or agents.

Sections 803(2)–(4) apply where one of the parties, P or D, *fails to appear* at the trial proceedings when required to do so. Under s. 803(2), where it is shown that D, after having been notified of the time and place, fails to appear for trial or the resumption thereof pursuant to an adjournment, the summary conviction court may either *proceed* with an *ex parte* trial, or *issue a warrant* in Form 7 for D's arrest and *adjourn* the trial to await D's re-appearance. Where the trial proceedings are continued *ex parte*, s. 803(3) restricts the circumstances in which D may be prosecuted for failure to appear. No proceedings may be instituted under s. 145 or, if instituted, shall proceed, except with the consent of the Attorney General. There is no such requirement of consent where a warrant is issued for D's arrest and the trial proceedings adjourned accordingly. The failure of P to appear on the resumption of trial permits the court, under s. 803(4), to dismiss the information with or without costs.

Case Law

Adjournments

Batchelor v. R. (1978), 38 C.C.C. (2d) 113 (S.C.C.) — Where D refuses to agree to the trial date suggested by P, the proper procedure is for the trial judge to set the trial date and then adjourn the proceedings from time to time for periods not exceeding eight days until the trial date is reached.

R. v. Szoboszloi, [1970] 5 C.C.C. 366 (Ont. C.A.); leave to appeal refused [1970] 5 C.C.C. 367n (S.C.C.) — Where D who has been personally served with a summons fails to appear, the court may adjourn the proceedings without issuing a bench warrant.

Ex Parte Proceedings

R. v. Tarrant (1984), 13 C.C.C. (3d) 219 (B.C. C.A.) — The issuance of a bench warrant for the arrest of D did *not* prevent the court from reconvening and proceeding *ex parte*.

R. v. Okanee (1981), 59 C.C.C. (2d) 149 (Sask. C.A.) — The provisions with respect to *ex parte* proceedings apply not only where D has been issued with an appearance notice or served with a summons but also where D has been released on an undertaking and fails to appear either personally or by counsel or agent.

Charter Considerations

R. v. Tarrant (1984), 13 C.C.C. (3d) 219 (B.C. C.A.) — *See also*: *R. v. Rogers*, [1984] 6 W.W.R. 89 (Sask. C.A.) — Section 803(2)(a) does *not* violate *Charter* s. 7 or 11(d).

Related Provisions: An appearance notice issued by a peace officer, is confirmed by the laying of an information under s. 505 and the conduct of a hearing under s. 508.

The failure of D to appear or re-attend a trial in response to a confirmed appearance notice or a summons may attract liability under ss. 145(2), (4) or (5), as well as the issuance of a warrant of arrest under s. 803(2)(b).

The general authority to proceed with a trial, where D *absconds* during the course of trial is found in s. 475, *not* made applicable to summary conviction proceedings under s. 795. A similar provision exists in respect of preliminary inquiries under s. 544.

Where P fails to appear for trial, s. 799 permits the summary conviction court to dismiss the information or adjourn the trial to some other time, upon such terms as it considers proper.

Adjudication

804. Finding of guilt, conviction, order or dismissal — When the summary conviction court has heard the prosecutor, defendant and witnesses, it shall, after considering the matter, convict the defendant, discharge the defendant under section 730, make an order against the defendant or dismiss the information, as the case may be.
R.S., c. C-34, s. 739; R.S. 1985, c. 27 (1st Supp.), s. 178; 1995, c. 22, s. 10.

Commentary: The section describes the determinations which may be made by the summary conviction court after P, D and the various witnesses have been heard. After considering the matter, the summary conviction court may convict D, discharge him/her absolutely or upon conditions under s. 730, make an order against him/her, or dismiss the information.

Case Law

Motion for Dismissal — Non-Suit [See also s. 645, "Motion for Non-Suit"]

R. v. Kennedy (1973), 21 C.R.N.S. 251, 11 C.C.C. (2d) 263 (Ont. C.A.) — The trial judge, before requiring D to adduce evidence in his defence, must satisfy himself that the evidence then before the court raises a *prima facie* case which D is called upon to meet. If the evidence does make out such a *prima facie* case, the judge should so rule before calling upon D to elect as to whether he wishes to put in evidence in his defence.

Stay of Proceedings [See also s. 8, "Abuse of Process"]

R. v. Cutforth (1988), 61 C.R. (3d) 187, 40 C.C.C. (3d) 253 (Alta. C.A.) — A stay of proceedings is a discretionary remedy available to a summary conviction court. Although the remedy is *not* specifically provided for in this section, it is inferentially included in the remedies provided by the section and is available under *Charter* s. 24(1) to remedy a *Charter* breach.

Related Provisions: Where a conviction is recorded or an order made in relation to D, a minute or memorandum of the order must be made by the summary conviction court under s. 806. An order of dismissal may be drawn up at D's request under s. 808. Costs may be awarded under s. 809.

Rights of appeal in summary conviction matters are provided in ss. 813 and 830.

805. [Repealed R.S. 1985, c. 27 (1st Supp.), s. 179.]

806. (1) Memo of conviction or order — Where a defendant is convicted or an order is made in relation to the defendant, a minute or memorandum of the conviction or order shall be made by the summary conviction court indicating that the matter was dealt with under this Part and, on request by the defendant, the prosecutor or any other person, the court shall cause a conviction or order in Form 35 or 36, as the case may be, and a certified copy of the conviction or order to be drawn up and shall deliver the certified copy to the person making the request.

(2) Warrant of committal — Where a defendant is convicted or an order is made against him, the summary conviction court shall issue a warrant of committal in Form 21 or 22, and section 528 applies in respect of a warrant of committal issued under this subsection.

(3) Admissibility of certified copy — Where a warrant of committal in Form 21 is issued by a clerk of a court, a copy of the warrant of committal, certified by the clerk, is admissible in evidence in any proceeding.
R.S., c. C-34, s. 741; 1972, c. 13, s. 64; 1994, c. 44, s. 80.

Commentary: The section describes the *records* to be made of convictions or orders made in relation to defendants in summary conviction proceedings.

Under s. 806(1), where D is convicted or an order made against him/her in summary conviction proceedings, a *minute or memorandum* of the conviction or order must be made by the summary conviction court. At the request of D, P, or any other person, the court must have a conviction or order in Form 35 or 36 and a certified copy thereof drawn up for delivery to the requesting party.

Upon conviction or order made against D, the summary conviction court must also, under s. 806(2), issue a warrant of committal in Form 21 or 22. The warrant may be endorsed in Form 28 under s. 528 to permit its execution outside the territorial jurisdiction of the summary conviction court. Under s. 806(3), a certified copy of a Form 21 warrant of committal issued by a clerk of the court is admissible in evidence in any proceeding.

Related Provisions: A warrant of committal is executed in accordance with s. 744 and D delivered, together with the warrant, to the keeper of the prison named therein. A receipt in Form 43 is given to the delivering officer disclosing D's state and condition upon delivery. Section 808 authorizes the drawing up of an order of dismissal upon request therefor by D.

Costs may be awarded at trial in accordance with the general provisions of s. 809.

Other related provisions are discussed in the corresponding note to s. 804, *supra*.

---

807. Disposal of penalties when joint offenders — Where several persons join in committing the same offence and upon conviction each is adjudged to pay an amount to a person aggrieved, no more shall be paid to that person than an amount equal to the value of the property destroyed or injured or the amount of the injury done, together with costs, if any, and the residue of the amount adjudged to be paid shall be applied in the manner in which other penalties imposed by law are directed to be applied.

R.S., c. C-34, s. 742.

Commentary: The section provides for the *disposal of penalties* when each of several joint offenders is adjudged to pay an amount to a person aggrieved. It ensures that a person aggrieved does *not* receive more than full recovery.

The section only applies where several persons join in and are convicted of the same offence and each is required to pay an amount to a person aggrieved. The amount paid must *not* exceed the value of the property destroyed or injured or the amount of injury done, together with costs. Any residue is applied in the same manner in which pecuniary penalties are applied.

Related Provisions: Payment to a person aggrieved may be made by an order of restitution under ss. 738–741.2 or as the term of a probation order under s. 732.1(3)(h).

The manner in which monetary penalties are applied is described in ss. 734.8(4), *734.8(5)*. It would *not* appear that a VFS under s. 737 falls within s. 807, as it is *not* an amount paid to a person aggrieved, but rather to a fund to provide such assistance to victims of offences as the Lieutenant Governor in Council of the province may direct from time to time.

---

808. (1) Order of dismissal — Where the summary conviction court dismisses an information, it may, if requested by the defendant, draw up an order of dismissal, and shall give to the defendant a certified copy of the order of dismissal.

(2) Effect of certificate — A copy of an order of dismissal, certified in accordance with subsection (1) is, without further proof, a bar to any subsequent proceedings against the defendant in respect of the same cause.

R.S., c. C-34, s. 743.

Commentary: The section authorizes the drawing up of an *order of dismissal* upon request by D and providing him/her with a certified copy thereof. Under s. 808(2), a certified copy of the order bars subsequent proceedings against D in respect of the same cause.

Case Law

Order of Dismissal (Certificate): S. 808(1)

R. v. Walsh (1996), 47 C.R. (4th) 184, 106 C.C.C. (3d) 462 (N.S. C.A.) — "Proceedings" in s. 808(2) has the meaning assigned to it in s. 785. *Semble*, it does *not* apply to proceedings on indictment or in respect of indictable offences.

R. v. Canadian Pacific (1976), 32 C.C.C. (2d) 14 (Alta. C.A.) — An order dismissing an information includes an acquittal or a disposition which is tantamount to an acquittal. A disposition which is tantamount to an acquittal is one which deals with the issue raised in the information on the merits in law or on the facts, as distinguished from one which deals with procedural or technical defects in the information. Where no evidence is offered after refusal of a request for adjournment, a certificate may be requested under the section.

R. v. Anthony (1982), 69 C.C.C. (2d) 424 (N.S. C.A.); affirming (1981), 14 M.V.R. 142 (N.S. Co. Ct.) — A certificate of dismissal is only to be granted where D was in jeopardy. Where there was no intention to try D on the merits of the offence as charged, a certificate of dismissal should not issue.

R. v. Pirri (1978), 41 C.C.C. (2d) 499 (N.S. C.A.) — Where the charge was dismissed after P offered no evidence, having been refused an amendment of the reference to the section number in the charge, an order of dismissal was properly issued under this section.

Autrefois Acquit

R. v. Riddle (1980), 48 C.C.C. (2d) 365 (S.C.C.); affirming (1977), 36 C.C.C. (2d) 391 (Alta. C.A.) — The plea of *autrefois acquit* is available in summary conviction proceedings. The fact that D does not request a certificate of dismissal is not a bar to raising the defence. D is in jeopardy from the moment issue is joined before a judge having jurisdiction until the final determination when a verdict is rendered. The plea is available where P offers no evidence after a plea of not guilty.

Logan v. R. (1981), 25 C.R. (3d) 35, 64 C.C.C. (2d) 238 (N.S. C.A.) — A plea of *autrefois acquit* will not succeed in a subsequent provincial prosecution if the charge has been dismissed in the first instance only because the offence is *ultra vires* Parliament.

Related Provisions: Records of conviction, acquittal and other orders in trials without a jury are made under s. 570.

The special pleas of ss. 607–610 apply in summary conviction proceedings under s. 795. The provisions of s. 808(2) comport with the constitutional guarantee of *Charter* s. 11(h).

Sections 813(b) and 830(1) describe the rights of appeal which may be invoked by the informant, Attorney General or his/her agent.

Costs may be awarded under s. 809.

809. (1) Costs — The summary conviction court may in its discretion award and order such costs as it considers reasonable and not inconsistent with such of the fees established by section 840 as may be taken or allowed in proceedings before that summary conviction court, to be paid

(a) to the informant by the defendant, where the summary conviction court convicts or makes an order against the defendant; or

(b) to the defendant by the informant, where the summary conviction court dismisses an information.

(2) Order set out — An order under subsection (1) shall be set out in the conviction, order or order of dismissal, as the case may be.

(3) Costs are part of fine — Where a fine or sum of money or both are adjudged to be paid by a defendant and a term of imprisonment in default of payment is imposed, the defendant is, in default of payment, liable to serve the term of imprisonment imposed, and for the purposes of this subsection, any costs that are awarded against the defendant shall be deemed to be part of the fine or sum of money adjudged to be paid.

(4) Where no fine imposed — Where no fine or sum of money is adjudged to be paid by a defendant, but costs are awarded against the defendant or informant, the person who is liable to pay them is, in default of payment, liable to imprisonment for one month.

(5) Definition of "costs" — In this section, "costs" includes the costs and charges, after they have been ascertained, of committing and conveying to prison the person against whom costs have been awarded.

R.S., c. C-34, s. 744.

Commentary: The section permits *costs* to be awarded in summary conviction proceedings.

Under s. 809(1), a summary conviction court may award and order such costs as it considers reasonable and *not* inconsistent with such of the fees established by s. 840 as may be applicable in summary conviction proceedings. "Costs", defined in s. 809(5), may be ordered paid to the informant by D, where D is convicted or has an order made against him/her, or may be ordered paid to D by the informant, where the court dismisses an information. There is no provision which permits the court to penalize the successful party by awarding costs against him/her. The costs order, under s. 809(2), must be set out in the conviction, dismissal or order.

In cases in which D is ordered to pay a fine or sum of money, and a term of imprisonment is imposed in default, D must serve the default term. Any award of costs against him/her is *deemed* to be part of the fine or other amount of money to be paid. Under s. 809(4), where there has been no fine or other pecuniary penalty imposed, any costs awarded and unpaid attract a default term of imprisonment of one month.

Related Provisions: Costs may also be awarded on appeals in summary conviction proceedings under ss. 826, 834(1) and 839(3). There is no general statutory power to award costs in indictable matters, either at trial or on appeal (s. 683(3)), although specific provision is sometimes made, as for example in cases of change of venue granted at P's request (s. 599(3)), defamatory libel (ss. 751 and 751.1) or on an adjournment granted because D was misled by the form of the indictment (s. 601(5) and (6)).

Sureties to Keep the Peace

810. (1) Where injury or damage feared — An information may be laid before a justice by or on behalf of any person who fears on reasonable grounds that another person will cause personal injury to him or her or to his or her spouse or child or will damage his or her property.

(2) Duty of justice — A justice who receives an information under subsection (1) shall cause the parties to appear before him or before a summary conviction court having jurisdiction in the same territorial division.

(3) Adjudication — The justice or the summary conviction court before which the parties appear may, if satisfied by the evidence adduced that the person on whose behalf the information was laid has reasonable grounds for his or her fears,

(a) order that the defendant enter into a recognizance, with or without sureties, to keep the peace and be of good behaviour for any period that does not exceed twelve months, and comply with such other reasonable conditions prescribed in the recognizance, including the conditions set out in subsections (3.1) and (3.2), as the court considers desirable for securing the good conduct of the defendant; or

(b) commit the defendant to prison for a term not exceeding twelve months if he or she fails or refuses to enter into the recognizance.

(3.1) Conditions — Before making an order under subsection (3), the justice or the summary conviction court shall consider whether it is desirable, in the interests of the safety of the defendant or any other person, to include as a condition of the recognizance that the defendant be prohibited from possessing any firearm, crossbow, prohibited weapon, restricted weapon, prohibited device, ammunition, prohibited ammunition or explosive substance, or all such things, for any period specified in the recognizance and, where the justice or summary conviction court decides that it is so desirable, the justice or summary conviction court shall add such a condition to the recognizance.

(3.11) Where the justice or summary conviction court adds a condition described in subsection (3.1) to a recognizance order, the justice or summary conviction court shall specify in the order the manner and method by which

(a) the things referred to in that subsection that are in the possession of the accused shall be surrendered, disposed of, detained, stored or dealt with; and

(b) the authorizations, licences and registration certificates held by the person shall be surrendered.

(3.12) Where the justice or summary conviction court does not add a condition described in subsection (3.1) to a recognizance order, the justice or summary conviction court shall include in the record a statement of the reasons for not adding the condition.

(3.2) **Idem** — Before making an order under subsection (3), the justice or the summary conviction court shall consider whether it is desirable, in the interests of the safety of the informant, of the person on whose behalf the information was laid or of that person's spouse or child, as the case may be, to add either or both of the following conditions to the recognizance, namely, a condition

(a) prohibiting the defendant from being at, or within a distance specified in the recognizance from, a place specified in the recognizance where the person on whose behalf the information was laid or that person's spouse or child, as the case may be, is regularly found; and

(b) prohibiting the defendant from communicating, in whole or in part, directly or indirectly, with the person on whose behalf the information was laid or that person's spouse or child, as the case may be.

(4) **Forms** — A recognizance and committal to prison in default of recognizance under subsection (3) may be in Forms 32 and 23, respectively.

(4.1) **Modification of recognizance** — The justice or the summary conviction court may, on application of the informant or the defendant, vary the conditions fixed in the recognizance.

(5) **Procedure** — The provisions of this Part apply, with such modifications as the circumstances require, to proceedings under this section.

R.S., c. C-34, s. 745; 1974–75–76, c. 93, s. 88; 1980–81–82–83, c. 125, s. 28; 1991, c. 40, s. 33; 1994, c. 44, s. 81; 1995, c. 22, s. 8; 1995, c. 39, s. 157

Commentary: This section provides a statutory procedure to obtain an order which requires a person to keep the peace and be of good behaviour, notwithstanding the absence of a formal criminal prosecution.

The procedure is commenced by the laying of an information before a justice. The informant must be a person who fears on *reasonable grounds* that another person will

i.   cause *personal injury* to him/her, or to his/her child/spouse; or,

ii. *damage* his/her *property*.

or anyone on behalf of such a person.

Under s. 810(2), the justice who receives the information must cause the parties, the informant and the person feared, to attend before him/her or a summary conviction court having jurisdiction in the same territorial division.

A hearing is conducted by the justice or summary conviction court under s. 810(3) in accordance with Part XXVII. If the justice or court is satisfied that the informant has *reasonable grounds* for his/her fears, D may be required to enter into a recognizance in Form 32, with or without sureties, to keep the peace and and be of good behaviour for a period not exceeding 12 months. Additional reasonable conditions may be prescribed to secure good conduct of the respondent. Under s. 810(3.1), D may be prohibited from possessing any firearm, ammunition or explosive substance or required to surrender any *f.a.c.* as a condition of the recognizance. If the respondent fails or refuses to enter into a recognizance, he/she may be committed to prison by an order in Form 23, for not more than 12 months. Section 810(3.2) authorizes inclusion of additional conditions which prohibit attendance at or near a specified location and communication, in whole or in part, directly or indirectly, with the person on whose behalf the information was laid, or that person's spouse/child, as the case may be.

The section provides a special preventative remedy which does not involve the laying of a formal charge, nor engage the full scope of the criminal process. It may attract *Charter* s. 7 scrutiny.

Case Law

R. v. Allen (1985), 18 C.C.C. (3d) 155 (Ont. C.A.) — Although this section does *not* create an offence, a warrant for arrest issued under this section is valid.

R. v. Wakelin (1992), 71 C.C.C. (3d) 115 (Sask. C.A.) — *See also*: *R. v. Allen* (1985), 18 C.C.C. (3d) 155 (Ont. C.A.) — *Contra*: *MacAusland v. Pyke* (1995), 37 C.R. (4th) 321, 96 C.C.C. (3d) 373 (N.S. S.C.) — A person against whom an information has been laid under s. 810 may be subject to the judicial interim release provisions of s. 515 pending the determination of the s. 810 proceedings.

Related Provisions: A similar procedure, without the laying of an information, initiates a misconduct hearing under s. 524. The inquiry of s. 810 is not to determine whether D is "guilty" or "not guilty", but only to determine whether, on the evidence adduced, the informant had *reasonable* grounds for his/her fears. No plea is entered. Committal would appear to be for failure or refusal to enter into the recognizance, not to secure the good conduct of the respondent.

Under s. 811, a breach of the recognizance is a summary conviction offence.

Section 813(a) permits D, in proceedings under Part XXVII, to appeal from an order made against him/her, and s. 830(1) authorizes a party to proceedings to which Part XXVII applies to appeal against a determination of a summary conviction court, on specified grounds.

810.01 (1) When fear of criminal organization offence — A person who fears on reasonable grounds that another person will commit a criminal organization offence may, with the consent of the Attorney General, lay an information before a provincial court judge.

(2) Appearances — A provincial court judge who receives an information under subsection (1) may cause the parties to appear before the provincial court judge.

(3) Adjudication — The provincial court judge before whom the parties appear may, if satisfied by the evidence adduced that the informant has reasonable grounds for the fear, order that the defendant enter into a recognizance to keep the peace and be of good behaviour for any period that does not exceed twelve months and to comply with any other reasonable conditions prescribed in the recognizance, including the conditions set out in subsection (5), that the provincial court judge considers desirable for preventing the commission of a criminal organization offence.

(4) Refusal to enter into recognizance — The provincial court judge may commit the defendant to prison for a term not exceeding twelve months if the defendant fails or refuses to enter into the recognizance.

(5) Conditions-firearms — Before making an order under subsection (3), the provincial court judge shall consider whether it is desirable, in the interests of the safety of the defendant or of any other person, to include as a condition of the recognizance that the defendant be prohibited from possessing any firearm, cross-bow, prohibited weapon, restricted weapon, prohibited device, ammunition, prohibited ammunition or explosive substance, or all of those things, for any period specified in the recognizance, and where the provincial court judge decides that it is so desirable, the provincial court judge shall add such a condition to the recognizance.

(5.1) Surrender, etc. — Where the provincial court judge adds a condition described in subsection (5) to a recognizance, the provincial court judge shall specify in the recognizance the manner and method by which

(a) the things referred to in that subsection that are in the possession of the defendant shall be surrendered, disposed of, detained, stored or dealt with; and

(b) the authorizations, licences and registration certificates held by the defendant shall be surrendered.

(5.2) Reasons — Where the provincial court judge does not add a condition described in subsection (5) to a recognizance, the provincial court judge shall include in the record a statement of the reasons for not adding the condition.

(6) Variance of conditions — The provincial court judge may, on application of the informant, the Attorney General or the defendant, vary the conditions fixed in the recognizance.

(7) Other provisions to apply — Subsections 810(4) and (5) apply, with any modifications that the circumstances require, to recognizance made under this section.

1997, c. 23, s. 19, 26.

Commentary: This section adapts the sureties to keep the peace scheme of s. 810 to criminal organization offences, but leaves a supervisory role for the Attorney General.

Anyone who has a reasonably grounded fear that another person will commit a criminal organization offence may lay an information before a provincial court judge, with the consent of the Attorney General, to compel the attendance of the parties before the judge.

When the parties appear, the judge conducts a hearing in accordance with Part XXVII, to determine whether the informant has reasonable grounds for the articulated fear. If satisfied that the fear is reasonably grounded, the provincial court judge may order the defendant to enter into a recognizance to keep the peace and be of good behaviour for not more than twelve months. The defendant may also be required to comply with any other reasonable conditions that the judge considers desirable for preventing commission of a criminal organization offence. The further conditions may include, but are not limited to the firearms prohibition and surrender terms of s. 810.01(5). The recognizance may be in Form 32.

Under s. 810.01(4), a defendant who fails or refuses to enter into a recognizance may be imprisoned for not more than twelve months. The committal order may be in Form 23.

The conditions of a recognizance may be varied on application by the informant, Attorney General or defendant.

Related Provisions: "Criminal organization offence" and "provincial court judge" are defined in s. 2. Prosecutorial responsibility for criminal organization offences is governed by s. 467.2 and the definition of "attorney general" in s. 2.

The procedure followed under s. 810.01 tracks what is done under s. 810 (fear of personal injury or property damage) and 810.1 (fear of sexual offence).

Breach of recognizance is an offence triable either way under s. 811.

810.1 (1) Where fear of sexual offence — Any person who fears on reasonable grounds that another person will commit an offence under section 151, 152, 155 or 159, subsection 160(2) or (3), section 170 or 171, subsection 173(2) or section 271, 272 or 273, in respect of one or more persons who are under the age of fourteen years, may lay an information before a provincial court judge, whether or not the person or persons in respect of whom it is feared that the offence will be committed are named.

(2) Duty of provincial court judge — A provincial court judge who receives an information under subsection (1) shall cause the parties to appear before the provincial court judge.

(3) Adjudication — The provincial court judge before whom the parties appear may, if satisfied by the evidence adduced that the informant has reasonable grounds for the fear, order the defendant to enter into a recognizance and comply with the conditions fixed by the provincial court judge, including a condition prohibiting the defendant from engaging in any activity that involves contact with persons under the age of fourteen years and prohibiting the defendant from attending a public park or public swimming area where persons under the age of fourteen years are present or can reasonably be expected to be present, or a daycare centre, schoolground, playground or community centre, for any period fixed by the provincial court judge that does not exceed twelve months.

(3.1) Refusal to enter into recognizance — The provincial court judge may commit the defendant to prison for a term not exceeding twelve months if the defendant fails or refuses to enter into the recognizance.

(4) Judge may vary recognizance — The provincial court judge may, on application of the informant or the defendant, vary the conditions fixed in the recognizance.

(5) Other provisions to apply — Subsections 810(4) and (5) apply, with such modifications as the circumstances require, to recognizances made under this section.

1993, c. 45, s. 11; 1997, c. 18, s. 113(2).

Commentary: Under this section, a person, who causes in another a reasonably grounded fear of a listed *sexual offence* in respect of one or more persons under 14 years of age, may be required to enter into a recognizance.

Under s. 810.1(1), proceedings are *commenced* by the laying of an information before a provincial court judge. The informant may be anyone who can depose to the requisite state of mind. The informant must disclose a reasonably grounded fear that another person (the defendant) will commit a listed sexual offence in respect of one or more persons under 14 years of age. The prospective victim of the apprehended sexual offence need not be named in the information.

The provincial court judge who receives the information must cause the parties to appear before him or her under s. 810.1(2). A hearing is conducted to determine whether the informant had reasonable grounds for the fear asserted. If the provincial court judge is satisfied that the informant had the requisite reasonably grounded fear, the defendant may be ordered to enter into a recognizance in Form 32 and comply with specified conditions. Under s. 810.1(3), the conditions imposed may include prohibitions against the defendant engaging in any activity or attending at premises or places where there is or is likely to be contact with persons under 14 years of age. Under s. 810.1(3.1), if D fails or refuses to enter into a recognizance, he may be imprisoned by a provincial court judge for a term of up to twelve months. The period of the recognizance must *not* exceed 12 months.

Under s. 810.1(4), the informant or defendant may apply to the provincial court judge to vary the conditions of the recognizance. Part XXVII applies to recognizances made under s. 810.1.

Related Provisions: The procedure followed under s. 810.1 is similar to that of s. 810 which is described in the *Commentary* which accompanies the section.

Breach of a s. 810.1 recognizance is a summary conviction offence under s. 811 punishable in accordance with s. 787(1). Where D is convicted or conditionally discharged of an offence listed in s. 161, a prohibition order may be made containing terms that are similar to those which may be included in a recognizance under s. 810.1. The offences listed in s. 161, with the addition of s. 281 (abduction of person under fourteen) include those listed in s. 810.1, other than a breach of s. 173(2) (exposure).

Rights of appeal from dispositions made on applications under s. 810.1 are governed by s. 813(a)(i) (defendant), 813(b)(i) (informant and agent of the Attorney General) and s. 830(1) ("a party to proceedings").

810.2 (1) Where fear of serious personal injury offence — Any person who fears on reasonable grounds that another person will commit a serious personal injury offence, as that expression is defined in section 752, may, with the consent of the Attorney General, lay an information before a provincial court judge, whether or not the person or persons in respect of whom it is feared that the offence will be committed are named.

(2) Duty of provincial court judge — A provincial court judge who receives an information under subsection (1) may cause the parties to appear before the provincial court judge.

(3) Adjudication — The provincial court judge before whom the parties appear may, if satisfied by the evidence adduced that the informant has reasonable grounds for the fear, order that the defendant enter into a recognizance to keep the peace and be of good behaviour for any period that does not exceed twelve months and to comply with any other reasonable conditions prescribed in the recognizance, including the conditions set out in subsection (5) and (6), that the provincial court judge considers desirable for securing the good conduct of the defendant.

(4) Refusal to enter into recognizance — The provincial court judge may commit the defendant to prison for a term not exceeding twelve months if the defendant fails or refuses to enter into the recognizance.

(5) Conditions — firearms — Before making an order under subsection (3), the provincial court judge shall consider whether it is desirable, in the interests of the safety of the defendant or of any other person, to include as a condition of the recognizance that the defendant be prohibited from possessing any firearm or any ammunition or explosive substance for any period of time specified in the recognizance and that the defendant surrender any firearms acquisition certificate that the defendant possesses, and where the provincial court judge decides that it is not desirable, in the interests of the safety of the defendant or any other person, for the defendant to possess any of those things, the provincial court judge may add the appropriate condition to the recognizance.

Proposed Amendment — Conditional Amendment — 810.2(5), (5.1), (5.2)

On the later of the coming into force of s. 810.2(5) of the *Code* as enacted by 1997, c. 17, s. 9 and ss. 810(3.1) - (3.12) of the *Code* as enacted by 1995, c. 39, s. 157, s. 810.2(5) is replaced by the following:

(5) Conditions — firearms — Before making an order under subsection (3), the provincial court judge shall consider whether it is desirable, in the interests of the safety of the defendant or of any other person, to include as a condition of the recognizance that the defendant be prohibited from possessing any firearm, cross-bow, prohibited weapon, restricted weapon, prohibited device, ammunition, prohibited ammunition or explosive substance, or all such things, for any period specified in the

recognizance, and where the provincial court judge decides that it is so desirable, the provincial court judge shall add such a condition to the recognizance.

(5.1) Surrender, etc. — Where the provincial court judge adds a condition described in subsection (5) to a recognizance order, the provincial court judge shall specify in the order the manner and method by which

(a) the things referred to in that subsection that are in the possession of the defendant shall be surrendered, disposed of, detained, stored or dealt with; and

(b) the authorization, licences and registration certificates held by the defendant shall be surrendered.

(5.2) Reasons — Where the provincial court judge does not add a condition described in subsection (5) to a recognizance order, the provincial court judge shall include in the record a statement of the reasons for not adding the condition.

1997, c. 17, s. 9(2). Not in force at date of publication.

(6) Conditions — reporting and monitoring — Before making an order under subsection (3), the provincial court judge shall consider whether it is desirable to include as a condition of the recognizance that the defendant report to the correctional authority of a province or to an appropriate police authority, and where the provincial court judge decides that it is desirable for the defendant to so report, the provincial court judge may add the appropriate condition to the recognizance.

(7) Variance of conditions — The provincial court judge may, on application of the informant, of the Attorney General or of the defendant, vary the conditions fixed in the recognizance.

(8) Other provisions to apply — Subsections 810(4) and (5) apply, with such modifications as the circumstances require, to recognizance made under this section.

1997, c. 17, s. 9(1)

Commentary: This section adapts the sureties to keep the peace scheme of s. 810 to reasonably apprehended *serious personal injury* offences, but assigns a supervisory role to the Attorney General.

Under s. 810.2(1), anyone who has a *reasonably-grounded* fear that someone else will commit a *serious personal injury offence* within s. 752 may lay an information before a provincial court judge, with the *consent* of the Attorney Genera. It doesn't matter whether the prospective victim is named in the information.

The provincial court judge who receives the information is required to have the parties appear before him/her under s. 810.2(2).

When the parties appear, the judge conducts a *hearing* in accordance with Part XXVII, to determine whether the informant has *reasonable* grounds for the articulated fear. If satisfied that the fear is reasonably grounded, the provincial court judge may order the defendant to enter into a *recognizance* to keep the peace and be of good behaviour for not more than twelve months. The defendant may also be required to comply with any other reasonable conditions that the judge considers desirable for securing the good conduct of the defendant. The further conditions may include, but are *not* limited to a *prohibition* against possession of firearms and other regulated items and *surrender* of such items then in the possession of the defendant and the documentation that permits it. Reasons are required under s. 810.2(5.2) where these orders are *not* made. A reporting and monitoring condition may also be included under s. 810.2(6). The recognizance may be in Form 32.

Under s. 810.2(4), a defendant who fails or refuses to enter into a recognizance may be imprisoned for not more than twelve months. The committal order may be in Form 23.

The conditions of a recognizance may be varied on application by the informant, Attorney General or defendant.

Related Provisions: "Serious personal injury offence" is defined in s. 752. "Provincial court judge" and "Attorney General" are defined in s. 2.

Other related provisions are described in the *Commentary* to ss. 810, 810.1, and 810.1, *supra*.

811. Breach of recognizance — A person bound by a recognizance under section 810, 810.01, 810.1 or 810.2 who commits a breach of the recognizance is guilty of

(a) an indictable offence and liable to imprisonment for a term not exceeding two years; or

(b) an offence punishable on summary conviction.

1993, c. 45, s. 11; 1994, c. 44, s. 82; 1997, c. 17, s. 10; c. 23, ss. 20, 27.

Commentary: The section creates a dual procedure offence of breach of a recognizance entered into under ss. 810, 810.01, 810.1 and 810.2. The *external circumstances* consist of any act or omission which is in breach of the recognizance. The *mental element* requires proof of the intention to cause the external circumstances of the offence.

Case Law

R. v. Simanek (1993), 82 C.C.C. (3d) 576 (Ont. C.A.) — The procedure of s. 811 is to be followed where it is alleged that there has been a breach of a recognizance entered into under s. 810. Section 145(3) does *not* apply in such cases.

Related Provisions: Breach of a recognizance under s. 810(3)(a), attracts a lesser maximum punishment under s. 811 than does a failure or refusal to enter into the recognizance under s. 810(3)(b).

A breach of a recognizance in accordance with which D has been released prior to trial may attract liability under ss. 145(2), (3) and (5). Under s. 145, the breach of a recognizance must be "without lawful excuse, proof of which lies on D". No such requirement appears in s. 811.

Under s. 732.1(2)(a), a probation order must include terms which require D to keep the peace and be of good behaviour. A breach of the order may attract liability under s. 733.1(1)(b), for failure or refusal to comply, re-sentencing on the original offence under ss. 731(1)(a) and 732.2(5)(d), or variation of the terms of the order under ss. 732.2(3) and (5)(e).

Appeal

812. (1) Definition of "appeal court" — For the purposes of sections 813 to 828 "appeal court" means

(a) in the Province of Ontario, the Superior Court of Justice sitting in the region, district or county or group of counties where the adjudication was made;

(b) in the Province of Quebec, the Superior Court;

(c) in the Provinces of Nova Scotia and British Columbia, the Supreme Court;

(d) in the Provinces of New Brunswick, Manitoba, Saskatchewan and Alberta, the Court of Queen's Bench;

(e) [Repealed 1992, c. 51, s. 43(2).];

(f) in the Province of Prince Edward Island, the Trial Division of the Supreme Court;

(g) in the Province of Newfoundland, the Trial Division of the Supreme Court; and

(h) in the Yukon Territory and Northwest Territories, a judge of the Supreme Court of the territory; and

(i) in Nunavut, a judge of the Nunavut Court of Justice.

(2) When appeal court is Court of Appeal of Nunavut — A judge of the Court of Appeal of Nunavut is the appeal court for the purposes of sections 813 to 828 if the appeal is from a conviction, order, sentence or verdict of a summary conviction court consisting of a judge of the Nunavut Court of Justice.

R.S., c. C-34, s. 747; 1972, c. 13, s. 65; c. 17, s. 2; 1974–75–76, c. 19, s. 1; 1978–79, c. 11, s. 10; R.S. 1985, c. 11 (1st Supp.), s. 2; c. 27 (2d Supp.) (Sched., item 6); 1990, c. 16, s. 7; 1990, c. 17, s. 15; 1992, c. 51, s. 43; 1993, c. 28, s. 78 (Sched. III, item 36) [Repealed 1999, c. 3, (Sched., item 9).]; 1998, c. 30, s. 14(d); 1999, c. 3, s. 55.

Commentary: The section defines "appeal court" for the purposes of appeals under ss. 813–828.

The definition applicable in Ontario imposes a geographical limitation upon the appeal court. No such restriction is imposed elsewhere. The appeal court is also the superior court of criminal jurisdiction.

Case Law

Ritcey v. R. (1980), 50 C.C.C. (2d) 481 (S.C.C.) — A summary conviction appeal court judge may, after his resignation, render judgment with respect to appeals heard prior to his resignation, if provincial legislation so prescribes.

Related Provisions: Rights of appeal are conferred by s. 813 and are engaged by filing a notice of appeal under s. 815. Appellate procedure is governed largely by rules enacted under s. 482(2), as well as the provisions of ss. 821–828.

The judicial interim release of an appellant who was a defendant in the summary conviction court is authorized by ss. 816 and 819. An appeal by the prosecutor, other than the Attorney General or counsel acting on his/her behalf, requires compliance with ss. 817 and 818.

As a general rule, appeals under s. 813 are heard and determined on the record in accordance with the provisions of ss. 683–689, except for ss. 683(3) and 686(5), made applicable to summary conviction appeals by s. 822(1). In some cases, however, the appeal may be determined by holding a trial *de novo* under ss. 822(4)–(7). A further appeal may be taken to the court of appeal under s. 839(1)(a), with leave of the court of appeal or a judge thereof, on a question of law alone.

813. Appeal by defendant, informant or Attorney General — Except where otherwise provided by law,

(a) the defendant in proceedings under this Part may appeal to the appeal court

(i) from a conviction or order made against him;

(ii) against a sentence passed on him; or

(iii) against a verdict of unfit to stand trial or not criminally responsible on account of mental disorder; and

(b) the informant, the Attorney General or his agent in proceedings under this Part may appeal to the appeal court

(i) from an order that stays proceedings on an information or dismisses an information,

(ii) against a sentence passed upon a defendant; or

(iii) against a verdict of not criminally responsible on account of mental disorder or unfit to stand trial,

and the Attorney General of Canada or his agent has the same rights of appeal in proceedings instituted at the instance of the Government of Canada and conducted by or on behalf of that government as the Attorney General of a province or his agent has under this paragraph.

R.S., c. C-34, s. 748; R.S. 1985, c. 27 (1st Supp.), s. 180; 1991, c. 43, s. 9, Schedule, item 12.

Commentary: The section confers *rights of appeal* from adjudications made in summary conviction proceedings.

Under s. 813(a), D may appeal to the appeal court from a *conviction* or *order* made against or *sentence* imposed upon him/her, or against a verdict of unfit to stand trial or not criminally responsible on account of mental disorder. Leave to appeal is *not* required in any case nor is any restriction placed upon the nature of the grounds which may be raised.

Under s. 813(b), the *informant, Attorney General* or his/her *agent* may appeal to the appeal court from an *order staying proceedings* on an information, or *dismissing an information*, as well as against a *sentence* imposed upon D, or against a verdict of not criminally responsible on account of mental disorder or unfit to stand trial. The Attorney General of Canada has equivalent rights of appeal in proceedings instituted at the instance of and conducted by or on behalf of the Government of Canada. Leave to appeal is *not* required. No restriction is placed upon the nature of the grounds which may be raised.

Case Law

Appeal From Conviction or Order: S. 813(a)(i)

R. v. Praisley (1964), 44 C.R. 296, [1965] 1 C.C.C. 316 (B.C. C.A.) — *See also: R. v. Ferencsik* (1970), 10 C.R.N.S. 273, [1970] 4 C.C.C. 166 (Ont. C.A.) — Appeals from conviction and sentence are two distinct and separate steps. After a trial *de novo* on an appeal against conviction only, there is no jurisdiction to vary the sentence imposed by the lower court, where the conviction is affirmed.

R. v. Smith (1984), 57 N.B.R. (2d) 78 (C.A.) — D was convicted of the summary conviction offence of breach of probation based on an indictable conviction for theft. Although the theft conviction was quashed on appeal to the court of appeal, the court had no jurisdiction to hear the appeal relating to the summary conviction offence.

R. v. Wacker (1958), 28 C.R. 214, 121 C.C.C. 185 (Ont. C.A.) — A trial only begins after plea. If a court rules it has no jurisdiction prior to plea being taken, no appeal against that ruling lies under this section.

Appeal From Dismissal of Information: S. 813(b)(i)

R. v. Aleksich (1979), 50 C.C.C. (2d) 62 (B.C. C.A.) — *See also: R. v. Croquet* (1973), 23 C.R.N.S. 374, 12 C.C.C. (2d) 331 (B.C. C.A.); and *R. v. Davis* (1977), 37 C.R.N.S. 302, 34 C.C.C. (3d) 388 (Ont. C.A.) — Where a ruling is made during the course of a trial which in effect makes it futile for P to proceed further with the calling of evidence because the issue was fundamental to its case, P can elect not to adduce all the evidence it might otherwise have done and, upon dismissal of the charge, proceed immediately to appeal to resolve the issue. If P is successful, it is entitled to a new trial.

R. v. Multitech Warehouse (Manitoba) Direct Inc. (1995), 100 C.C.C. (3d) 153 (Man. C.A.) — On an appeal by the Attorney General under *Code* s. 813(b)(i), a summary conviction appeal court, has jurisdiction to reverse a finding of fact made by a summary conviction court, having paid due heed to the indisputable advantage given the trial judge who saw and heard the witnesses.

R. v. Yaworski (1959), 31 C.R. 55, 124 C.C.C. 151 (Man. C.A.) — Where D charged with an indictable offence is found guilty of a summary conviction offence (whether rightly or wrongly), the proper appeal procedure to follow is that of an appeal from an indictable offence. The nature of the proceedings *not* the nature of the conviction determines the forum of appeal.

R. v. Crocker (1986), 73 N.S.R. (2d) 151 (C.A.) — *See also: R. v. Sall* (1990), 54 C.C.C. (3d) 48 (Nfld. C.A.); *R. v. Giles* (1990), 54 C.C.C. (3d) 66 (Nfld. C.A.); reversing (1988), 68 Nfld. & P.E.I.R. 117 (Nfld. T.D.) — P has a right of appeal under this section on issues of fact. An acquittal may only be set aside where the verdict is unreasonable or not supported by the evidence.

R. v. Moore (1987), 38 C.C.C. (3d) 471 (Ont. C.A.) — An order quashing an information as lacking in sufficient detail is *not* an order dismissing an information within the meaning of this section. The proper appeal route for P is an appeal by transcript under s. 830.

R. v. Yanke (1983), 4 C.C.C. (3d) 26 (Sask. C.A.) — The dismissal of an information for want of prosecution is an order dismissing an information.

Related Provisions: "Appeal court", "informant" and "proceedings" are defined in s. 812, "Attorney General" in s. 2. The term "prosecutor", used throughout Part XXVII, is *not* used in s. 813.

The corresponding rights of appeal in proceedings by indictment are found in ss. 675 and 676 (Attorney General).

Other related provisions are described in the corresponding note to s. 812, *supra*.

814. (1) **Manitoba and Alberta** — In the Provinces of Manitoba and Alberta, an appeal under section 813 shall be heard at the sittings of the appeal court that is held nearest to the place where the cause of the proceedings arose, but the judge of the appeal court may, on the application of one of the parties, appoint another place for the hearing of the appeal.

(2) **Saskatchewan** — In the Province of Saskatchewan, an appeal under section 813 shall be heard at the sittings of the appeal court at the judicial centre nearest to the place where the adjudication was made, but the judge of the appeal court may, on the application of one of the parties, appoint another place for the hearing of the appeal.

(3) **British Columbia** — In the Province of British Columbia, an appeal under section 813 shall be heard at the sittings of the appeal court that is held nearest to the place where the adjudication was made, but the judge of the appeal court may, on the application of one of the parties, appoint another place for the hearing of the appeal.

(4) **Territories** — In the Yukon Territory, the Northwest Territories and Nunavut, an appeal under section 813 shall be heard at the place where the cause of the proceedings arose or at the place nearest thereto where a court is appointed to be held.

R.S., c. C-34, s. 749; 1984, c. 41, s. 2; 1993, c. 28, s. 78 (Sched. III, item 37).

Commentary: The section designates the *place* at which appeals under s. 813 shall be heard in certain provinces and the territories.

In Manitoba, Alberta, and British Columbia the appeal is to be heard at the sittings of the appeal court nearest to the place where the cause of proceedings arose (Manitoba and Alberta) or where the adjudication was made (British Columbia). A similar provision applies in Saskatchewan, except that it is the sittings of the appeal court at the judicial center nearest the place where the adjudication was made. In the Yukon Territory and the Northwest Territories, the hearing takes place where the cause of proceedings arose. In each case, however, a judge of the appeal court may appoint another place for the hearing of the appeal.

Related Provisions: Geographical proximity to the place in which the adjudication was made or proceedings arose is of value in view of ss. 822(4)–(7) which permits the appeal to be heard and determined as a trial *de novo*.

Other related provisions are described in the corresponding note to s. 812, *supra*.

815. (1) **Notice of appeal** — An appellant who proposes to appeal to the appeal court shall give notice of appeal in such manner and within such period as may be directed by rules of court.

(2) **Extension of time** — The appeal court or a judge thereof may extend the time within which notice of appeal may be given.

R.S., c. C-34, s. 750; 1972, c. 13, s. 66; 1974–75–76, c. 93, s. 89.

Commentary: The section requires that an *appeal* be *commenced* by *giving notice of appeal* in such manner and within such period as may be directed by rules of court. Under s. 815(2), the appeal court or a judge thereof may, at any time, extend the time within which notice of appeal may be given.

Case Law

Rescinding Notice of Abandonment

R. v. Robertson (1978), 45 C.C.C. (2d) 344 (Ont. C.A.) — A summary conviction appeal court has the jurisdiction to entertain an application to rescind a notice of abandonment filed by the appellant. The jurisdiction must be exercised on the basis of judicial discretion. The test is whether such a remedy is required to avoid a miscarriage of justice.

Extension of Time: S. 815(2)

Neal v. Saskatchewan (A.G.) (1977), 56 C.C.C. (2d) 128 (S.C.C.) — An extension of time after the expiration of the appeal period cannot be granted *ex parte*.

R. v. Ruffo (1982), 1 C.C.C. (3d) 358 (Ont. C.A.) — As a general rule, notice of an application to extend the time for service and filing of the notice of appeal must be given to the respondent. However, where it is impossible to serve notice of the application to extend the time for service because the respondent cannot be found, an *ex parte* order can be made. The granting of an application to extend the time for appealing without notice to the opposite party is exceptional and the onus lies on the party seeking an *ex parte* order to bring himself within an exception.

R. v. Holmes (1982), 2 C.C.C. (3d) 471 (Ont. C.A.) — A judge extending the time for service cannot validate the prior service of a notice of appeal made out of time. Consequently, where service of the notice is made out of time and thereafter an order is made extending the time, the notice of appeal must be re-served within the extended time.

Related Provisions: Under s. 482(2), the appeal court may pass rules, not inconsistent with the *Code* or other federal enactment, governing the procedure on appeals under s. 813. Those rules should be consulted to determine the form of the notice of appeal, as well as the time within which it must be filed, and the requirements of service on the respondent.

Under s. 820(2) an appellant must appeal a conviction, order or sentence in order to place its validity in issue. A conviction, order or sentence is deemed *not* to have been appealed against until the contrary is shown.

Payment of a fine does *not* waive D's right of appeal under s. 813. The incorporation, *inter alia*, of s. 683(5), by s. 822(1), authorizes the appeal court to order that any obligation to pay a fine or similar pecuniary penalty be suspended until the appeal has been determined. The general stay authority of s. 689 in respect of restitution orders is also applicable to summary conviction appeals under s. 822(1).

Interim Release of Appellant

816. (1) Undertaking or recognizance of appellant — A person who was the defendant in proceedings before a summary conviction court and by whom an appeal is taken under section 813 shall, if he is in custody, remain in custody unless the appeal court at which the appeal is to be heard orders that the appellant be released

(a) on his giving an undertaking to the appeal court, without conditions or with such conditions as the appeal court directs, to surrender himself into custody in accordance with the order,

(b) on his entering into a recognizance without sureties in such amount, with such conditions, if any, as the appeal court directs, but without deposit of money or other valuable security, or

(c) on his entering into a recognizance with or without sureties in such amount, with such conditions, if any, as the appeal court directs, and on his depositing with that appeal court such sum of money or other valuable security as the appeal court directs,

and the person having the custody of the appellant shall, where the appellant complies with the order, forthwith release the appellant.

(2) Application of certain provisions of section 525 — The provisions of subsections 525(5), (6) and (7) apply with such modifications as the circumstances require in respect of a person who has been released from custody under subsection (1).

R.S., c. C-34, s. 752; c. 2 (2d Supp.), s. 16; 1974–75–76, c. 39, s. 91; R.S. 1985, c. 27 (1st Supp.), s. 181.

Commentary: The section governs the *release* of an *appellant*, who was a *defendant* at trial, pending the determination of an appeal under s. 813. The general rule of s. 816(1) is that, where an appellant who was a defendant at trial is in custody, he/she shall remain there pending the determination of the appeal. The appellant may, however, be released by the appeal court under s. 816(1), on giving an undertaking or entering into a recognizance in accordance with ss. 816(1)(a)-(c). It would appear that the *onus* is on the appellant to justify release, but the section contains no express provision to that effect, nor a statement of the criteria to be applied in determining the issue. Where the appellant complies with the release order, he/she is forthwith released from custody.

Section 816(2) applies where the appellant has been released from custody pending appeal and is alleged, thereafter, to have contravened or been about to contravene the undertaking or recognizance or to have committed an indictable offence. The procedure followed in such cases is as described in ss. 525(5)–(7), modified as to the circumstances.

Related Provisions: There is *no* statutory right of review of an order made by the appeal court under s. 816, although s. 819 permits the hearing of the appeal to be expedited, if it has not been commenced within 30 days from the day on which notice of appeal was given. Neither would there appear to be a right of review of an order made under s. 816(2) in the application of the provisions of s. 525(7).

In *indictable appeal* proceedings, judicial interim release is determined under ss. 679(3) and (4) and, where ordered, governed by s. 679(5). A decision of a judge of appeal under s. 679 may be reviewed by the court of appeal, or, on consent, a single judge thereof, by direction of the chief justice or acting chief justice under s. 680.

Section 817 requires a *private prosecutor* who is an *appellant* under s. 813 to give an undertaking or enter into a recognizance to appear personally or by counsel at the sittings of the appeal court at which the appeal is to be heard. An order made by a justice under s. 817 may be reviewed by the appeal court under s. 818.

817. (1) Undertaking or recognizance of prosecutor — The prosecutor in proceedings before a summary conviction court by whom an appeal is taken under section 813 shall, forthwith after filing the notice of appeal and proof of service thereof in accordance with section 815, appear before a justice, and the justice shall, after giving the prosecutor and the respondent a reasonable opportunity to be heard, order that the prosecutor

(a) give an undertaking as prescribed in this section; or

(b) enter into a recognizance in such amount, with or without sureties and with or without deposit of money or other valuable security, as the justice directs.

(2) Condition — The condition of an undertaking or recognizance given or entered into under this section is that the prosecutor will appear personally or by counsel at the sittings of the appeal court at which the appeal is to be heard.

(3) Appeals by Attorney General — This section does not apply in respect of an appeal taken by the Attorney General or by counsel acting on behalf of the Attorney General.

(4) Form of undertaking or recognizance — An undertaking under this section may be in Form 14 and a recognizance under this section may be in Form 32.

R.S., c. 2 (2d Supp.), s. 16.

Commentary: The section requires a *private prosecutor* who is an *appellant* under s. 813 to give an *undertaking* or enter into a *recognizance* with a statutory condition that he/she will appear personally or by counsel at the sittings of the appeal court at which the appeal is to be heard.

Under s. 817(1), it is the obligation of P, forthwith after filing the notice of appeal and proof of service under s. 815, to appear before a justice. Both P and D are given a *reasonable* opportunity to be heard. P will then be ordered to give an undertaking (Form 14) or enter into a recognizance (Form 32) with the statutory condition of s. 817(2). The recognizance may be with or without sureties and/or deposit.

The requirements of the section do *not* apply in respect of appeals taken by the Attorney General or counsel acting on his/her behalf.

Case Law

Broadfoot v. R. (1977), 35 C.C.C. (2d) 493 (Ont. C.A.) — This section is mandatory. The fact that counsel for the informant was an Assistant Crown Attorney did not necessarily mean that he was acting as agent for the Attorney General. The informant was required to comply with this section.

Related Provisions: A determination by the justice may be reviewed by the appeal court under s. 818.

"Prosecutor", "proceedings" and "summary conviction court" are defined in s. 785 for the purposes of Part XXVII.

Section 816 governs judicial interim release where D is the appellant.

Other related provisions are discussed in the corresponding note to s. 816, *supra*.

818. (1) **Application to appeal court for review** — Where a justice makes an order under section 817, either the appellant or the respondent may, before or at any time during the hearing of the appeal, apply to the appeal court for a review of the order made by the justice.

(2) **Disposition of application by appeal court** — On the hearing of an application under this section, the appeal court, after giving the appellant and the respondent a reasonable opportunity to be heard, shall

(a) dismiss the application; or

(b) if the person applying for the review shows cause, allow the application, vacate the order made by the justice and make the order that in the opinion of the appeal court should have been made.

(3) **Effect of order** — An order made under this section shall have the same force and effect as if it had been made by the justice.

R.S., c. 2 (2d Supp.), s. 16; 1974-75-76, c. 93, s. 91.1.

Commentary: The section authorizes applications to the *appeal court* to *review* the *order* of a *justice* under s. 817.

Under s. 818(1), either the appellant (P) or respondent (D) may apply to the appeal court for a review of the order made by a justice under s. 817. The application may be made before or at any time during the hearing of the appeal.

Under s. 818(2), the appeal court must afford both parties a reasonable opportunity to be heard. The court may then dismiss the application or, if the applicant *shows cause*, allow the application, vacate the order made by the justice, and substitute therefor the order that, in the opinion of the appeal court, should have been made. Under s. 818(3), the order shall have the same effect as if it had been made by the justice at first instance.

Related Provisions: There is no comparable right of review where a judicial interim release order has been made or refused in respect of D who is an appellant under s. 813. The only remedy would appear to be to expedite the hearing of an appeal under s. 819.

Other related provisions are discussed in the corresponding note to s. 816, *supra*.

819. (1) **Application to fix date for hearing of appeal** — Where, in the case of an appellant who has been convicted by a summary conviction court and who is in custody pending the hearing of his appeal, the hearing of his appeal has not commenced within thirty days from the day on which notice of his appeal was given in accordance with the rules referred to in section 815, the person having the custody of the appellant shall, forthwith on the expiration of those thirty days, apply to the appeal court to fix a date for the hearing of the appeal.

(2) Order fixing date — On receiving an application under subsection (1), the appeal court shall, after giving the prosecutor a reasonable opportunity to be heard, fix a date for the hearing of the appeal and give such directions as it thinks necessary for expediting the hearing of the appeal.

R.S., c. 2 (2d Supp.), s. 16; 1974–75–76, c. 93, s. 92.

Commentary: The section authorizes an application to the appeal court to fix a *date for* the *hearing* of D's appeal when D is in custody and the appeal has not been heard within a statutorily defined period.

Under s. 819(1), the onus rests upon the gaoler in whose custody defendant/appellant is detained, forthwith after the expiration of 30 days after notice of appeal was given, to apply to the appeal court to fix a date for the hearing of the appeal. No application need be initiated by the defendant/appellant.

Under s. 819(2) the appeal court must give P a reasonable opportunity to be heard, fix a date for the hearing of the appeal, and give the necessary directions to expedite the hearing.

Related Provisions: A similar provision appears in s. 525 in respect of delays in trial proceedings where D is in custody charged with a non-s. 469 offence. There is, in s. 526, a general authority to give directions to expedite proceedings whenever D appears before a court under Part XVI. A more restrictive authority is conferred on a judge of the court of appeal in indictable matters under s. 679(10).

820. (1) Payment of fine not a waiver of appeal — A person does not waive his right of appeal under section 813 by reason only that he pays the fine imposed on conviction, without in any way indicating an intention to appeal or reserving the right to appeal.

(2) Presumption — A conviction, order or sentence shall be deemed not to have been appealed against until the contrary is shown.

R.S., c. C-34, s. 753.

Commentary: Under s. 820(1), the right of appeal is *not* waived solely by payment of a fine. It matters not whether, on payment, there was given any indication of an intention to appeal or a reservation of such right.

Section 820(2) provides that nothing is appealed until notice of appeal with respect thereto has been given. It is otherwise presumed that no appeal has been taken.

Related Provisions: In indictable matters under s. 683(5) the court of appeal may suspend the obligation to pay pecuniary penalties until the appeal has been determined. Under s. 689, the operation of a restitution order (ss. 738–741.2), is suspended pending appeal, subject to contrary order by the court. Under s. 822(1), the appeal court, as defined in s. 812, has equivalent authority in summary conviction appeals under s. 813.

Procedure on Appeal

821. (1) Notification and transmission of conviction, etc. — Where a notice of appeal has been given in accordance with the rules referred to in section 815, the clerk of the appeal court shall notify the summary conviction court that made the conviction or order appealed from or imposed the sentence appealed against of the appeal and on receipt of the notification that summary conviction court shall transmit the conviction, order or order of dismissal and all other material in its possession in connection with the proceedings to the appeal court before the time when the appeal is to be heard, or within such further time as the appeal court may direct, and the material shall be kept by the clerk of the appeal court with the records of the appeal court.

(2) Saving — An appeal shall not be dismissed by the appeal court by reason only that a person other than the appellant failed to comply with the provisions of this Part relating to appeals.

(3) Appellant to furnish transcript of evidence — Where the evidence on a trial before a summary conviction court has been taken by a stenographer duly sworn or by a sound recording apparatus, the appellant shall, unless the appeal court otherwise orders or the rules referred to in section 815 otherwise provide, cause a transcript thereof, certified by the stenographer or in accordance with subsection 540(6), as the case may be, to be furnished to the appeal court and the respondent for use on the appeal.

R.S., c. C-34, s. 754; 1972, c. 13, s. 67; 1974–75–76, c. 93, s. 93.

Commentary: The section describes what must be provided to the appeal court in appeals under s. 813.

Under s. 821(1), the clerk of the appeal court must *notify* the summary conviction court, from which the appeal has been taken, of the appeal. The summary conviction court, upon receipt of notification, must *transmit* the conviction, order, or order of dismissal and all other material in its possession in relation to the proceedings to the appeal court before the hearing of the appeal. The material remains with the records of the appeal court. Under s. 821(3), the appellant must, unless the appeal court otherwise orders or the rules otherwise provide, furnish a proper *transcript* of the trial proceedings to the appeal court and respondent for use on the appeal.

Under s. 821(2), an appeal shall *not* be dismissed by reason only of a failure of someone other than the appellant to comply with the provisions of Part XXVII, as for example, a failure of the summary conviction court to transmit the record under s. 821(1).

Related Provisions: Under s. 801(3), the evidence of witnesses for P and D in summary conviction proceedings is taken in accordance with the provisions of Part XVIII relating to preliminary inquiries.

Several other provisions require transmission of the record from one court to another for the purpose of further judicial proceedings. Under s. 543(2), the transcript of any evidence taken and all documents relevant to the inquiry are transmitted to the territorial division in which a preliminary inquiry shall be continued after having been commenced in another territorial division. Section 551 requires the transmission of the record of the preliminary inquiry to the trial court. The record is also transmitted under ss. 599(4) and (5) where a change of venue has been ordered. Section 682(2) describes the record transmitted to the court of appeal in indictable matters.

Section 822 defines the *adjudicative* authority of the appeal court in appeals under s. 813. In general, an appeal is determined on the record of the trial court but, on occasion, it may be necessary to hear the matter de novo under ss. 822(4)-(7). Section 825 empowers an appeal court to dismiss an appeal on account of appellant's failure to comply with orders made under s. 816 or 817, as well as a failure to prosecute the appeal. Costs may be awarded and enforced under ss. 826-828.

822. (1) Certain sections applicable to appeals — Where an appeal is taken under section 813 in respect of any conviction, acquittal, sentence, verdict or order, sections 683 to 689, with the exception of subsections 683(3) and 686(5), apply, with such modifications as the circumstances require.

(2) New trial — Where an appeal court orders a new trial, it shall be held before a summary conviction court other than the court that tried the defendant in the first instance, unless the appeal court directs that the new trial be held before the summary conviction court that tried the defendant in the first instance.

(3) Order of detention or release — Where an appeal court orders a new trial, it may make such order for the release or detention of the appellant pending the trial as may be made by a justice pursuant to section 515 and the order may be enforced in the same manner as if it had been made by a justice under that section, and the provisions of Part XVI apply with such modifications as the circumstances require to the order.

(4) Trial de novo — Notwithstanding subsections (1) to (3), where an appeal is taken under section 813 and where, because of the condition of the record of the trial in the summary conviction court or for any other reason, the appeal court, upon application of the defendant, the informant, the Attorney General or his agent, is of the opinion that the interests of justice would be better served by hearing and determining the appeal by holding a trial *de novo*, the appeal court may order that the appeal shall be heard by way of trial *de novo* in accordance with such rules as may be made under section 482 and for this purpose the provisions of sections 793 to 809 apply with such modifications as the circumstances require.

(5) **Former evidence** — The appeal court may, for the purpose of hearing and determining an appeal under subsection (4), permit the evidence of any witness taken before the summary conviction court to be read if that evidence has been authenticated in accordance with section 540 and if

(a) the appellant and respondent consent,

(b) the appeal court is satisfied that the attendance of the witness cannot reasonably be obtained, or

(c) by reason of the formal nature of the evidence or otherwise the court is satisfied that the opposite party will not be prejudiced, and any evidence that is read under the authority of this subsection has the same force and effect as if the witness had given the evidence before the appeal court.

(6) **Appeal against sentence** — Where an appeal is taken under subsection (4) against sentence, the appeal court shall, unless the sentence is one fixed by law, consider the fitness of the sentence appealed against and may, on such evidence, if any, as it thinks fit to require or receive, by order,

(a) dismiss the appeal, or

(b) vary the sentence within the limits prescribed by law for the offence of which the defendant was convicted;

and in making any order under paragraph (*b*) the appeal court may take into account any time spent in custody by the defendant as a result of the offence.

(7) **General provisions re appeals** — The following provisions apply in respect of appeals under subsection (4):

(a) where an appeal is based on an objection to an information or any process, judgment shall not be given in favour of the appellant

(i) for any alleged defect therein in substance or in form, or

(ii) for any variance between the information or process and the evidence adduced at the trial,

unless it is shown

(iii) that the objection was taken at the trial, and

(iv) that an adjournment of the trial was refused notwithstanding that the variance referred to in subparagraph (ii) had deceived or misled the appellant; and

(b) where an appeal is based on a defect in a conviction or an order, judgment shall not be given in favour of the appellant, but the court shall make an order curing the defect.

R.S., c. C-34, s. 755; c. 2 (2d Supp.), s. 17; 1974–75–76, c. 93, s. 94; 1984, c. 40, s. 20;1991, c. 43, s. 9, Schedule, item 13.

Commentary: This section defines the *adjudicative authority* of the appeal court in appeals under s. 813. Sections 822(1)–(3) apply where the appeal is heard on the record of the summary conviction court, whereas ss. 822(4)–(8) govern appeals heard as trials *de novo* under s. 822(4).

Under s. 822(1), applicable to *appeals on the record* against conviction, acquittal, sentence, verdict or order, the appeal court has the *same powers* as the *court of appeal* in *indictable matters* under ss. 683–689, except ss. 683(3) and 686(5). Section 683(3) empowers the court of appeal to exercise, as a residual authority, any power that it may exercise in civil matters. Section 686(5) refers to the consequential orders that may be made where the court of appeal in indictable matters orders a new trial in proceedings in which D was tried by a judge without a jury under Part XIX. Neither authority is of any practical value in appeals under s. 813. Sections 822(2) and (3), apply where new trials are ordered. Section 822(2) permits the appeal court, in appropriate cases, to *remit* the matter to the summary conviction court that held the first trial, rather than in accordance with the general rule that the re-trial be before another summary conviction court. Under s. 822(3), the appeal court may make any order contemplated by s. 515 relating to the release or detention of the appellant pending the new trial.

Section 822(4) describes the circumstances under which an appeal taken under s. 813 may be heard by way of trial *de novo*, rather than on the record of trial proceedings. Application may be made by D, the informant, Attorney General or his/her agent to the appeal court for an order that the appeal be heard as a trial *de novo*. The application may be based on the condition of the record in the summary conviction court or any other reason. The appeal court must determine whether the interests of justice would be better served by hearing and determining the appeal by holding a trial *de novo*. Where a trial *de novo* is ordered, it is held in accordance with the rules passed under s. 482 and the provisions of ss. 793–809. Section 822(5) permits the evidence of any witness taken before the summary conviction court upon the first trial to be read as evidence on the trial *de novo*, if properly authenicated under s. 740, and if *any* of the conditions of ss. 822(5)(a)–(c), are satisfied. The evidence, when read, has the same force and effect as if given *viva voce* at the trial *de novo*.

Sections 822(6) and (7) define the authority of the appeal court to determine appeals heard by trial *de novo*. Section 822(6), applicable only to appeals against sentence, essentially duplicates the authority of the court of appeal in indictable matters under s. 687, except that the appeal court is expressly authorized, in varying a sentence, to take into account any time spent in custody by D as a result of the offence. Section 822(7) relates to appeals based upon objections to an information, conviction, order or other process or variances between such process and the evidence adduced at trial.

Case Law

Jurisdiction

R. v. Bursey (1982), 53 N.S.R. (2d) 353 (C.A.) — The appeal court should *not* substitute its view of the facts for that of the trial judge.

R. v. MacNeil (1979), 46 C.C.C. (2d) 383 (Ont. C.A.) — *See also*: *R. v. Benson* (1978), 40 C.C.C. (2d) 271 (B.C. C.A.) — D is entitled to appeal against conviction, notwithstanding that sentence has *not* yet been imposed. The appeal court may exercise its discretion to adjourn the hearing of the appeal pending the imposition of sentence.

Crown Appeals

R. v. Medicine Hat Greenhouses Ltd. (1981), 59 C.C.C. (2d) 257 (Alta. C.A.); leave to appeal refused (1981), 38 N.R. 180n (S.C.C.) — *See also*: *Billard v. R.* (1984), 27 M.V.R. 101 (N.S. C.A.); affirming (1983), 60 N.S.R. (2d) 431 (Co. Ct.) — On an appeal on a question of fact alone, it may be that the summary conviction appeal court is restricted to ordering a new trial. Whether Parliament intended to allow the substitution of a finding of guilt only where there was an error of law was left open for future argument.

R. v. Antonelli (1977), 38 C.C.C. (2d) 206 (B.C. C.A.) — *See also*: *R. v. Purves* (1980), 12 C.R. (3d) 362, 50 C.C.C. (2d) 211 (Man. C.A.); *R. v. Wilke* (1980), 56 C.C.C. (2d) 61 (Ont. C.A.); *R. v. Nelson*, [1979] 3 W.W.R. 97 (Sask. C.A.) — Notwithstanding that the primary procedure automatically invoked by the launching of an appeal is an appeal on the record, P may appeal on a question of fact alone an order dismissing an information.

Unreasonable Verdict [See also s. 686(1)(a)(i)]

R. v. Arthur (1981), 63 C.C.C. (2d) 117 (B.C. C.A.); leave to appeal refused December 21, 1981 (S.C.C.) — *See also: R. v. Colbeck* (1978), 42 C.C.C. (2d) 117 (Ont. C.A.) — The function of the appeal court is to determine whether the evidence was such that a properly instructed jury acting judicially could have reached the same conclusion as the trial court.

Billard v. R. (1984), 27 M.V.R. 101 (N.S. C.A.); affirming (1983), 60 N.S.R. (2d) 431 (Co. Ct.) — The power to enter a conviction on a summary conviction appeal exists on an appeal against an acquittal based on the ground that it was "unreasonable or cannot be supported by the evidence". It is *not* restricted to appeals that involve an error of law alone.

R. v. Backman (1982), 53 N.S.R. (2d) 39 (C.A.) — An appeal court has no jurisdiction to retry the case and cannot substitute its interpretation of the facts for that of the trial judge. A trial verdict is "unreasonable" only if it is so illogical that no reasonable jury acting judicially could have reached it.

R. v. Wright (1984), 3 O.A.C. 293 (C.A.) — The appeal court had no jurisdiction to substitute its own assessment of the evidence. If the court found the trial judge's reasons to be unsatisfactory, then the proper disposition was to set aside the conviction and order a new trial.

R. v. Saikaley (1979), 52 C.C.C. (2d) 191 (Ont. C.A.) — A court hearing an appeal from a summary conviction may decline to convict where the conviction turns on matters of credibility if the court is satisfied that the basis for the finding of credibility is so tenuous that it would be unreasonable to base a conviction upon such a finding.

Sentence Appeals

R. v. Sproule (1978), 39 C.C.C. (2d) 430 (Ont. C.A.) — Where P does *not* appeal from sentence nor give notice of an intention to ask for an increase in sentence, it is an error in principle for the court hearing D's appeal against sentence to increase the sentence.

Trial De Novo: Ss. 822(4)–(7)

R. v. Winters (1981), 21 C.R. (3d) 230, 59 C.C.C. (2d) 454 (B.C. C.A.) — The summary conviction appeal court has a very broad discretion as to whether to order a trial *de novo* or whether to admit fresh evidence on appeal which D could have given at trial where the interests of justice so require. An attempt by D to alter his tactics from his trial position is a matter to be considered when the appeal court exercises its discretion.

R. v. Steinmiller (1979), 47 C.C.C. (2d) 151 (Ont. C.A.) — The judge on a application for a trial *de novo* does not have the jurisdiction to dispose of the appeal and order a new trial.

R. v. Duggan (1976), 31 C.C.C. (2d) 167 (Ont. C.A.) — D may not be represented by an agent who is not a barrister or solicitor at an appeal by way of trial *de novo*.

Charter Considerations

R. v. Century 21 Ramos Inc. (1987), 56 C.R. (3d) 150, 32 C.C.C. (3d) 353 (Ont. C.A.) — The different appeal procedures provided by the *Code* with respect to indictable and summary conviction offences, in particular, the fact that where P proceeds by way of summary conviction, as opposed to indictment, it is not restricted to an appeal on a question of law alone, do not violate the right to equality before the law as guaranteed by *Charter* s. 15.

Related Provisions: The authority of the appeal court to make rules relating to appeals under s. 813 appears in s. 482(2). Approval of the Lieutenant Governor in Council is no longer required since all appeal courts are also superior courts of criminal jurisdiction. The rules must *not* be inconsistent with the *Code* or other Federal enactment. The rules passed under the subsection, in large measure, determine the procedure to be followed in such cases.

The procedure on a trial *de novo* duplicates that followed in trial proceedings before a summary conviction court. By s. 795, it includes the provisions of Parts XVI and XVIII with respect to compelling D's appearance before a justice and Part XX, except s. 617, insofar as they are not inconsistent with Part XXVII.

The appeal court may award costs under s. 826. An appeal may be dismissed for failure to appear or want of prosecution under s. 825.

823. [Repealed 1991, c. 43, s. 9, Schedule, item 14.]

824. Adjournment — The appeal court may adjourn the hearing of an appeal from time to time as may be necessary.

R.S., c. C-34, s. 756.

Commentary: The section confers upon the appeal court a general power of adjournment.

Related Provisions: Under s. 819(2), the hearing of an appeal may be ordered expedited where D is in custody and the appeal has not been commenced within 30 days from the giving of notice of appeal. An appeal may also be dismissed under s. 825 for failure to appear or want of prosecution.

825. Dismissal for failure to appear or want of prosecution — The appeal court may, on proof that notice of an appeal has been given and that

(a) the appellant has failed to comply with any order made under section 816 or 817 or with the conditions of any undertaking or recognizance given or entered into as prescribed in either of those sections, or

(b) the appeal has not been proceeded with or has been abandoned, order that the appeal be dismissed.

R.S., c. C-34, s. 757; c. 2 (2d Supp.), s. 18.

Commentary: The section describes the circumstances in which the appeal court may dismiss an appeal taken under s. 813 without a hearing. Under s. 825(a), an appeal may be dismissed where the appellant has failed to comply with any order of judicial interim release under s. 816, an undertaking given or recognizance entered into under s. 817 by a private prosecutor who is an appellant, or the conditions contained in any such order. Under s. 825(b), an appeal may be dismissed where it has not been proceeded with or has been abandoned. In each case, it must also be shown that notice of appeal has been given.

Case Law

R. v. Clarke (1981), 62 C.C.C. (2d) 442 (Alta. C.A.) — Under this section, a judge of the appeal court may dismiss an appeal for want of compliance with the Rules.

Related Provisions: The section does *not* expressly state whether the order contemplated therein may be made on summary application or only upon the hearing of the appeal.

Section 795 also authorizes the appeal court to summarily determine frivolous appeals, as may be done in indictable matters by the court of appeal under s. 685. The additional authority of s. 825 is not expressly given to the court of appeal in indictable matters, although such orders are not infrequently there made and, in many cases, expressly authorized by the conditions of D's release order.

Provision is generally made in the applicable rules passed under s. 482(2) for abandonment by formal notice. Whether an appeal has not been proceeded with is, in every event, a question of fact.

826. Costs — Where an appeal is heard and determined or is abandoned or is dismissed for want of prosecution, the appeal court may make any order with respect to costs that it considers just and reasonable.

R.S., c. C-34, s. 758.

Commentary: The section constitutes general authority for the appeal court to make *any order with respect to costs* that it considers *just and reasonable*, where an appeal is heard and determined or is abandoned or dismissed for want of prosecution.

Case Law

Discretionary Nature of Order

R. v. Duguay (1990), 57 C.C.C. (3d) 309 (Que. C.A.) — A summary conviction appeal court which has dismissed an appeal from conviction with costs may order the imprisonment of the appellant in default of payment of the costs.

R. v. Trask (1987), 59 C.R. (3d) 179, 37 C.C.C. (3d) 92 (S.C.C.) — The court should *not* fetter its discretion by adopting the position that costs be allowed to all successful D appellants. While P might often be required to pay costs when it appeals a summary conviction matter, it does *not* follow that D who successfully appeals, should invariably have his/her costs. When P appeals a matter in order to settle a point of law, the public benefits. An individual should not be put to substantial expense because of P's initiative in seeking to effect a valid social purpose.

Costs Against Prosecution

R. v. Ouellette (1980), 15 C.R. (3d) 372, 52 C.C.C. (2d) 336 (S.C.C.); affirming (1979), 50 C.C.C. (2d) 346 (Que. C.A.) — P can be ordered to pay costs. The amount of costs is discretionary, but it must be just and reasonable.

Right of Appeal from Order of Costs

R. v. Masurak (1961), 37 C.R. 5, 132 C.C.C. 279 (Sask. C.A.) — Whether an order is made as to costs in a summary conviction appeal is a matter of discretion and not a question of law which gives a right of appeal to the court of appeal.

Related Provisions: Section 827 describes to whom costs may be payable and what may be done in a case of non-payment.

In summary conviction trial proceedings, costs may be awarded under s. 809 provided, *inter alia*, they are not inconsistent with the applicable fees established by s. 840. There is no such limitation imposed under s. 826.

Where a further appeal is taken to the court of appeal under s. 839(1)(a), costs may be awarded under s. 839(3).

827. (1) To whom costs payable, and when — Where the appeal court orders the appellant or respondent to pay costs, the order shall direct that the costs be paid to the clerk of the court, to be paid by him to the person entitled to them, and shall fix the period within which the costs shall be paid.

(2) Certificate of non-payment of costs — Where costs are not paid in full within the period fixed for payment and the person who has been ordered to pay them has not been bound by a recognizance to pay them, the clerk of the court shall, on application by the person entitled to the costs, or by any person on his behalf, and on payment of any fee to which the clerk of the court is entitled, issue a certificate in Form 42 certifying that the costs or a part thereof, as the case may be, have not been paid.

(3) Committal — A justice having jurisdiction in the territorial division in which a certificate has been issued under subsection (2) may, upon production of the certificate, by warrant in Form 26, commit the defaulter to imprisonment for a term not exceeding one month, unless the amount of the costs and, where the justice thinks fit so to order, the costs of the committal and of conveying the defaulter to prison are sooner paid.

R.S., c. C-34, s. 759.

Commentary: The section provides for the making of an award of *costs* and its *enforcement* in cases of *default*.

Under s. 827(1), an order of costs must direct that they be paid to the clerk of the court for re-payment to the party entitled thereto. The order must also fix the period for their payment.

Sections 827(2) and (3) apply where there has been default of payment of costs under an order under ss. 826 and 827(1). Section 827(2) applies where costs have *not* been paid in full, as required by the order, and the defaulting party is not bound by a recognizance to make such payment. The person entitled to the costs, or anyone on his/her behalf, may apply to the clerk of the court for a certificate in Form 42 certifying the fact and extent of non-payment. Under s. 827(3), where the certificate is produced to a justice in the territorial division in which it was issued, a warrant in Form 26 may be issued committing the defaulter to imprisonment for a term not exceeding one month, failing payment of the costs and, where ordered, the additional costs of committal and conveying the defaulter to prison.

Related Provisions: An award of costs at a summary conviction trial is made and enforced under s. 809.

Section 826 permits an award of costs on an appeal under s. 813 and s. 834(1) does likewise in appeals under s. 830. Section 839(3) applies to further summary conviction appeals to the court of appeal.

828. (1) Enforcement of conviction or order by court of appeal — A conviction or order made by the appeal court may be enforced

    (a) in the same manner as if it had been made by the summary conviction court; or

    (b) by process of the appeal court.

(2) Enforcement by justice — Where an appeal taken against a conviction or order adjudging payment of a sum of money is dismissed, the summary conviction court that made the conviction or order or a justice for the same territorial division may issue a warrant of committal as if no appeal had been taken.

(3) Duty of clerk of court — Where a conviction or order that has been made by an appeal court is to be enforced by a justice, the clerk of the appeal court shall send to the justice the conviction or order and all writings relating thereto, except the notice of intention to appeal and any recognizance.

R.S., c. C-34, s. 760.

Commentary: The section provides for the *enforcement* of convictions or orders made by the appeal court.

Section 828(1) authorizes two methods of enforcement: in the same manner as the summary conviction court or by the process of the appeal court.

Under s. 828(2), a *warrant of committal* may be issued where an appeal taken against conviction or an order adjudging payment of a sum of money is dismissed by the appeal court. The warrant may be issued by the summary conviction court that made the conviction or order or a justice for the same territorial division.

The clerk of the appeal court under s. 828(3) must send to a justice the conviction, order and related writings, except the notice of appeal and recognizance, where the conviction or order of the appeal court is to be enforced by a justice.

Case Law

Costs

R. v. Duguay (1990), 57 C.C.C. (3d) 309 (Que. C.A.) — Sections 828(1)(a) and 809(3) empower the appeal court, *inter alia*, to order imprisonment for non-payment of costs.

Related Provisions: Part XXII "Procuring Attendance", in particular ss. 701–708 provides for the service and execution of process to compel the attendance of witnesses. Part XXV, "Effect and Enforcement of Recognizances", describes how recognizances may be enforced. Part XXIII "Punishments, Fines, Forfeitures, Costs and Restitution of Property", *inter alia*, defines the manner in which the various forms of sentence may be enforced. It is of general application and applies without the need for express incorporation in proceedings under Part XXVII.

The decision of the court of appeal on further appeal under s. 839(1) is also enforceable under s. 839(4), in the same manner as if it had been made at trial in summary conviction proceedings. A similar provision appears in s. 835 in respect of appeals taken under s. 830.

Summary Appeal on Transcript or Agreed Statement of Facts

829. (1) Definition of "appeal court" — Subject to subsection (2), for the purposes of sections 830 to 838, "appeal court" means, in any province, the superior court of criminal jurisdiction for the province.

(2) Nunavut — If the appeal is from a conviction, judgment, verdict or other final order or determination of a summary conviction court consisting of a judge of the

Nunavut Court of Justice, "appeal court" means a judge of the Court of Appeal of Nunavut.

R.S., c. C-34, s. 761; R.S. 1985, c. 27 (1st Supp.), s. 182; 1999, c. 3, s. 56.

Commentary: The section defines "appeal court" for the purposes of ss. 830–838.

Related Provisions: The definition of "appeal court" for the purposes of ss. 813–828, is found in s. 812. It contains territorial limitations in respect of the province of Ontario. No such limitation appears under s. 829.

The rights of appeal to the appeal court, as well as the form and manner in which the appeals are commenced, heard and determined, are described in s. 830.

Under s. 836, an appeal under s. 830 bars an appeal from the same determination under s. 813. Where no appeal is provided by law from a conviction or order, s. 830 may not be engaged to create a right of appeal.

The judicial interim release of an appellant who was a defendant at trial is governed by ss. 816 and 819, made applicable by s. 831. An appeal by a private prosecutor requires compliance with s. 817 under ss. 831 and 832.

The authority of the appeal court to determine an appeal under s. 830 is defined in s. 834. Its decisions may be enforced under s. 835.

830. (1) Appeals — A party to proceedings to which this Part applies or the Attorney General may appeal against a conviction, judgment, verdict of acquittal or verdict of not criminally responsible on account of mental disorder or of unfit to stand trial or other final order or determination of a summary conviction court on the ground that

(a) it is erroneous in point of law;

(b) it is in excess of jurisdiction; or

(c) it constitutes a refusal or failure to exercise jurisdiction.

(2) Form of appeal — An appeal under this section shall be based on a transcript of the proceedings appealed from unless the appellant files with the appeal court, within fifteen days of the filing of the notice of appeal, a statement of facts agreed to in writing by the respondent.

(3) Rules for appeals — An appeal under this section shall be made within the period and in the manner directed by any applicable rules of court and where there are no such rules otherwise providing, a notice of appeal in writing shall be served on the respondent and a copy thereof, together with proof of service, shall be filed with the appeal court within thirty days after the date of the conviction, judgment or verdict of acquittal or other final order or determination that is the subject of the appeal.

(4) Rights of Attorney General of Canada — The Attorney General of Canada has the same rights of appeal in proceedings instituted at the instance of the Government of Canada and conducted by or on behalf of that Government as the Attorney General of a province has under this section.

R.S., c. C-34, s. 762; R.S. 1985, c. 27 (1st Supp.), s. 182; 1991, c. 43, s. 9, Schedule, item 15.

Commentary: The section defines *rights of appeal* and the procedure followed in the commencement and hearing of the appeal.

Under s. 830(1), any *party* to summary conviction proceedings, as well as the *Attorney General*, may appeal against a *conviction, judgment, verdict of acquittal, verdict of not criminally responsible* on account of mental disorder or of *unfit to stand* trial, or other *final* order or determination of a summary conviction court. There are not, in other words, any appeals *in limine litis*. Under s. 830(4), the Attorney General of Canada has the same rights of appeal as the Attorney General of the province in proceedings instituted at the instance of and conducted by or on behalf of the Government of Canada. The appeal may only be taken upon the ground that the adjudication is erroneous in *law*, or in excess of or constitutes a refusal or failure of the summary conviction court to exercise *jurisdiction*. Briefly put, appeals under this section are limited to legal and jurisdictional error.

Under s. 830(3), an appeal under this section must be taken within the period and in the manner directed by the applicable rules of court under s. 482(1). In the absence of any such rules, the appellant must serve a notice of appeal in writing on the respondent and file a copy and proof of service thereof with the appeal court within 30 days after the date of the adjudication or determination under appeal.

In accordance with s. 830(2), appeals under this section, as a general rule, are based on a transcript of trial proceedings. The appeal may be based upon a statement of facts filed by the appellant and agreed to in writing by the respondent within 15 days of the filing of the notice of appeal.

Case Law

Quashing of Information

R. v. Moore (1987), 38 C.C.C. (3d) 471 (Ont. C.A.) — This section is the proper appeal route where the trial judge quashes the information as lacking in sufficient detail.

Related Provisions: The "Attorney General", as defined in s. 2, would appear to have a right of appeal under s. 830(1), notwithstanding that he/she did not intervene at the trial and thereby become the "prosecutor", hence a party to the trial proceedings.

Other related provisions are described in the corresponding note to s. 829, *supra*.

831. Application — The provisions of sections 816, 817, 819 and 825 apply, with such modifications as the circumstances require, in respect of an appeal under section 830, except that on receiving an application by the person having the custody of an appellant described in section 819 to appoint a date for the hearing of the appeal, the appeal court shall, after giving the prosecutor a reasonable opportunity to be heard, give such directions as it thinks necessary for expediting the hearing of the appeal.

R.S., c. C-34, s. 763; R.S. 1985, c. 27 (1st Supp.), s. 182.

Commentary: The section authorizes the *judicial interim release* of an appellant who was a *defendant* in proceedings before a summary conviction court and requires a *private prosecutor* to give an *undertaking* or enter into a *recognizance* prior to the hearing of an appeal under s. 830.

The basis upon which an *appellant/defendant* may be released pending appeal under s. 830 is described in s. 816. There are no rights of review, although under s. 819, as modified by this section, an appeal court shall give such directions as it thinks necessary to expedite the hearing of the appeal where the appellant remains in custody and the hearing of the appeal has not commenced within 30 days of the filing of the notice of appeal.

A *private prosecutor* is required to give an *undertaking* or enter into a *recognizance* to appear personally or by counsel at the sittings of the appeal court at which the appeal is to be heard under s. 817. Under s. 831, there is no incorporation of s. 818, hence *no review* of the order made in respect of a private prosecutor.

The incorporation of s. 825 into appeals under s. 830 by s. 831 empowers the appeal court to dismiss appeals for failure of the appellant to appear or comply with an order under ss. 816 or 817, or where the appeal has not been proceeded with or has been abandoned.

Related Provisions: The provisions should be read together with s. 832, *infra*, which, *inter alia*, permits the appeal court to order the appellant to appear before a justice to give an undertaking or enter into a recognizance under s. 816 or 817.

Other related provisions are described in the corresponding notes that accompany ss. 816, 817, 819, 825 and 829, *supra*.

832. (1) Undertaking or recognizance — When a notice of appeal is filed pursuant to section 830, the appeal court may order that the appellant appear before a justice and give an undertaking or enter into a recognizance as provided in section 816 where the defendant is the appellant, or as provided in section 817, in any other case.

(2) Attorney General — Subsection (1) does not apply where the appellant is the Attorney General or counsel acting on behalf of the Attorney General.

R.S., c. C-34, s. 764; R.S. 1985, c. 27 (1st Supp.), s. 182.

Commentary: Section 832(1) applies when a notice of appeal is filed pursuant to s. 830 and permits an appeal court to order the appellant to appear before a justice and undertake or enter into a recognizance, as required by s. 816 or 817, as the case may be. The subsection has *no* application where the Attorney General or counsel acting on behalf of the Attorney General is the appellant. It applies only to private prosecutors.

Related Provisions: Section 831 incorporates, *inter alia*, the provisions of ss. 816 and 817 to appeals under s. 830. The present section modifies the procedure somewhat, although the basic principles would appear common to both forms of appeal.

Other related provisions are described in the notes to ss. 816, 817, 819, 825 and 829, *supra*.

833. No writ required — No writ of *certiorari* or other writ is required to remove any conviction, judgment, verdict or other final order or determination of a summary conviction court for the purpose of obtaining the judgment, determination or opinion of the appeal court.

R.S., c. C-34, s. 765; R.S. 1985, c. 27 (1st Supp.), s. 182; 1991, c. 43, s. 9, Schedule, item 16.

Commentary: The section enacts that no writ of *certiorari* or other writ is required to remove the adjudication or determination from which an appeal is taken to obtain the judgment, determination or opinion of the appeal court.

Related Provisions: Appeals under s. 830 are described as a "summary appeal on transcript or agreed statement of facts". There is provision, comparable to s. 821 applicable to appeals under s. 825, requiring the summary conviction court to transmit the record to the "appeal court" under s. 829.

Certiorari and the other extraordinary remedies of *habeas corpus, mandamus, procedendo* and prohibition are governed by Part XXVI "Extraordinary Remedies".

834. (1) Powers of appeal court — When a notice of appeal is filed pursuant to section 830, the appeal court shall hear and determine the grounds of appeal and may

(a) affirm, reverse or modify the conviction, judgment or verdict or other final order or determination, or

(b) remit the matter to the summary conviction court with the opinion of the appeal court,

and may make any other order in relation to the matter or with respect to costs that it considers proper.

(2) Authority of judge — Where the authority and jurisdiction of the appeal court may be exercised by a judge of that court, the authority and jurisdiction may, subject to any applicable rules of court, be exercised by a judge of the court sitting in chambers as well in vacation as in term time.

R.S., c. C-34, s. 766; R.S. 1985, c. 27 (1st Supp.), s. 182; 1991, c. 43, s. 9, Schedule, item 17.

Commentary: The section defines the *powers of the appeal court to determine appeals* under s. 830 and to make consequential orders in such cases.

Under s. 834(1), the dispositive authority of the appeal court is to affirm, reverse or modify the adjudication or determination of the summary conviction court, or to remit the matter to the summary conviction court with the opinion of the appeal court. The appeal court may also make any other order in relation to the matter, or with respect to costs, that it considers proper.

Section 834(2) enables a judge of the appeal court to exercise the authority given to a judge of the appeal court, subject to any applicable rules of court, at any sittings of the court.

Related Provisions: The authority of the "appeal court" on appeals under s. 830 is not nearly so expansive as that given the "appeal court" on appeals under s. 813 by s. 822(1). In particular, none of the dispositive or ancillary powers of the court of appeal in indictable matters are incorporated under s. 834. The decision of an appeal court in an appeal under s. 830 may be enforced under s. 835.

835. (1) Enforcement — Where the appeal court renders its decision on an appeal, the summary conviction court from which the appeal was taken or a justice exercising the same jurisdiction has the same authority to enforce a conviction, order or determination that has been affirmed, modified or made by the appeal court as the summary conviction court would have had if no appeal had been taken.

(2) Idem — An order of the appeal court may be enforced by its own process.
R.S., c. C-34, s. 767; R.S. 1985, c. 27 (1st Supp.), s. 182.

Commentary: The section authorizes two methods by which a decision of the appeal court on an appeal under s. 830 may be enforced: by the summary conviction court from which the appeal was taken, or by the process of the appeal court.

Related Provisions: A similar provision appears in s. 828(1), applicable to appeals under s. 813. Other related provisions are described in the corresponding note to s. 828, *supra*.

836. Appeal under section 830 — Every person who appeals under section 830 from any conviction, judgment, verdict or other final order or determination in respect of which that person is entitled to an appeal under section 813 shall be taken to have abandoned all the person's rights of appeal under section 813.
R.S., c. C-34, s. 768; 1985, c. 27 (1st Supp.), s. 182; 1991, c. 43, s. 9, Schedule, item 18.

Commentary: Under this section, an appeal taken under s. 830 against a conviction, judgment, verdict, or other final order or determination in respect of which an appeal could be taken under s. 813 is *deemed* to be an *abandonment* of all rights of appeal under s. 813. Put shortly the appellate rights of Part XXVII are mutually exclusive, not cumulative.

Related Provisions: The rights of appeal given under s. 813 permit appeals to be taken from a conviction or order made against D, or an order staying proceedings on or dismissing an information, as well as against sentence, or against a verdict of unfit to stand trial or not criminally responsible on account of mental disorder. The grounds of appeal are unrestricted. Under s. 830, an appeal may be taken against a conviction, judgment, verdict of acquittal, verdict of not criminally responsible on account of mental disorder or of unfit to stand trial, or other final order or determination, but only upon questions of law or allegations of jurisdictional error.

837. Appeal barred — Where it is provided by law that no appeal lies from a conviction or order, no appeal under section 830 lies from such a conviction or order.
R.S., c. C-34, s. 769; R.S. 1985, c. 27 (1st Supp.), s. 182.

Commentary: Under this section, any law that enacts that no appeal lies from a conviction or order bars an appeal under s. 830 from that order.

Related Provisions: No similar provision is enacted in relation to appeals under s. 813.

838. Extension of time — The appeal court or a judge thereof may at any time extend any time period referred to in section 830, 831 or 832.
R.S., c. C-34, s. 770; R.S. 1985, c. 27 (1st Supp.), s. 182.

Commentary: The section permits the appeal court or a judge thereof, at any time, to *extend* any *time* period mentioned in ss. 830–832. The provision would appear to permit extensions of time to be given both before and after the expiration of the relevant time period.

Related Provisions: The section does *not* describe the criteria to be applied in determining whether to order an extension of time. Rules of court passed under s. 482(1) may supplement the statutory provision. Section 815(2) permits a judge of the appeal court as defined in s. 812, at any time, to extend the time within which notice of appeal may be given.

Section 830 confers rights of appeal to the "appeal court" as defined in s. 829 and imposes time limits for the service and filing of the notice of appeal and agreed statement of facts. The time limit for filing and serving the notice of appeal only applies where there are no applicable rules of court which provide otherwise. Sections 831 and 832 relate to interim release of D who is an appellant under s. 830 and the obligation on a private prosecutor to give an undertaking or enter into a recognizance to prosecute an appeal in which he/she is the appellant.

Appeals to Court of Appeal

839. (1) Appeal on question of law — Subject to subsection (1.1), an appeal to the court of appeal, as defined in section 673 may, with leave of that court or a judge thereof, be taken on any ground that involves a question of law alone, against

(a) a decision of a court in respect of an appeal under section 822; or

(b) a decision of an appeal court under section 834, except where that court is the court of appeal.

(1.1) Nunavut — An appeal to the Court of Appeal of Nunavut may, with leave of that court or a judge of that court, be taken on any ground that involves a question of law alone, against a decision of a judge of the Court of Appeal of Nunavut acting as an appeal court under susection 812(2) or 829(2).

(2) Sections applicable — Sections 673 to 689 apply with such modifications as the circumstances require to an appeal under this section.

(3) Costs — Notwithstanding subsection (2), the court of appeal may make any order with respect to costs that it considers proper in relation to an appeal under this section.

(4) Enforcement of decision — The decision of the court of appeal may be enforced in the same manner as if it had been made by the summary conviction court before which the proceedings were originally heard and determined.

(5) Right of Attorney General of Canada to appeal — The Attorney General of Canada has the same rights of appeal in proceedings instituted at the instance of the Government of Canada and conducted by or on behalf of that Government as the Attorney General of a province has under this Part.

R.S., c. C-34, s. 771; R.S. 1985, c. 27 (1st Supp.), s. 183.

Commentary: The section authorizes further *appeals to the court of appeal* in summary conviction matters, and defines the authority of the court to hear and determine such appeals, as well as to enforce its judgment.

In combination, ss. 839(1) and (2) authorize appeals to be taken to the court of appeal, with *leave* of the *court or a judge* thereof, on *questions of law alone*, from decisions of the appeal court under s. 822 (s. 813 appeals) and, except where the appeal court is also the court of appeal under s. 834 (s. 830 appeals). The appeal is taken, heard and determined in accordance with ss. 673–689, applicable in appeals from proceedings on indictment, modified accordingly. Under s. 839(5), the Attorney General of Canada has the same rights of appeal in proceedings initiated at the instance of and conducted by or on behalf of the Government of Canada as the Attorney General of the province under Part XVII.

Under s. 839(1), the court of appeal is expressly authorized to make any order with respect to *costs* that it considers proper in relation to an appeal under this section. The decision of the court of appeal is enforceable in the same manner as if it had been made at trial.

Case Law

Jurisdiction

R. v. Dennis (1960), 32 C.R. 210, 125 C.C.C. 329 (S.C.C.) — D has a right of appeal to the court of appeal from a dismissal of his appeal in the court below on the basis of preliminary objections entered by P.

R. v. Canadian Pacific Ltd. (1976), 32 C.C.C. (2d) 14 (Alta. C.A.) — An appeal lies under this section to the court of appeal only after the appeal in the court below has been finally determined. There is no right of appeal from an order setting down an appeal for hearing.

R. v. Gillispie (1997), 115 C.C.C. (3d) 461 (Man. C.A.) — Where a judge or the court has refused leave to appeal, the jurisdiction of the court or a judge of it is exhausted. A demonstrable and decisive error by a judge exercising jurisdiction under s. 839(1), however, may give rise to a right of review.

R. v. Giftwares Wholesale Co. (No. 2) (1980), 53 C.C.C. (2d) 380 (Man. C.A.) — *See also: R. v. Mellquist* (1988), 42 C.C.C. (3d) 231 (Sask. C.A.) — The court of appeal may refuse leave to appeal on a question of law alone if it is *not* persuaded that the question of law is one of importance.

R. v. Church of Scientology of Toronto (1991), 63 C.C.C. (3d) 328 (Ont. C.A.); leave to appeal refused (1991), 5 C.R.R. (2d) 384 (note) (S.C.C.) — The decision of a judge of the appeal court under s. 490(17) is a "a decision of a court in respect of an appeal under section 822" for the purpose of s. 839(1)(a).

R. v. Culley (1977), 36 C.C.C. (2d) 433 (Ont. C.A.) — *See also, R. v. Paterson* (1962), 39 C.R. 156, [1962] 2 C.C.C. 369 (B.C. C.A.) — The holding by a lower court that the discharge provisions of the *Code* are primarily applicable to young offenders constitutes an error of law. Although the court of appeal may not review the fitness of sentence, but is restricted to reviewing errors of law, the sentence imposed by the court would have been inextricably bound up with the misdirection on a question of law and the appeal may properly be considered to involve a question of law alone. Thus, the court may grant leave to appeal and review the fitness of the sentence.

Standing

Scullion v. Canadian Breweries (1956), 24 C.R. 223, 114 C.C.C. 337 (S.C.C.) — Where the parties to an appeal are the informant and D, the informant as well as D has a further right of appeal to the court of appeal.

Question of Law Alone [See also ss. 676; 691; 693]

Ogg-Moss v. R. (1984), 41 C.R. (3d) 297, 14 C.C.C. (3d) 116 (S.C.C.); affirming (1981), 24 C.R. (3d) 264, 60 C.C.C. (2d) 127 (Ont. C.A.) — The definition and meaning of the various terms in a section of the *Code* and the question of whether there was any evidence capable of sustaining the applicability of the section are questions of law.

R. v. Loughery (1992), 73 C.C.C. (3d) 411 (Alta. C.A.) — Fitness of sentence is *not* a question of law alone (Foisy J.A. and Prowse J. (*ad hoc*); Major J.A. dissenting).

R. v. Good (1983), 6 C.C.C. (3d) 105 (Alta. C.A.) — Although reasonableness of notice is a question of fact, the meaning of "reasonable notice" in the *Code* is a question of law alone.

R. v. Thomas (No. 2) (1980), 53 C.C.C. (2d) 285 (B.C. C.A.) — *See also: R. v. Guida* (1989), 51 C.C.C. (3d) 305 (Que. C.A.) — The fitness or appropriateness of the sentence is not a question of law alone, unless the sentence imposed was an illegal one.

R. v. Dunnett (1990), 62 C.C.C. (3d) 14, 26 M.V.R. (2d) 194 (N.B. C.A.); leave to appeal refused (1991), 62 C.C.C. (3d) vi (note), 29 M.V.R. (2d) 87 (note) (S.C.C.) — The determination as to whether a person's constitutional rights have been violated is a question of law. The issue of the reasonableness of the opportunity for D to exercise his right to counsel is also a question of law.

R. v. Waite (1964), 46 C.R. 23, [1965] 1 C.C.C. 301 (N.B. C.A.) — Whether there is *any* evidence to support a conviction is a question of law. The *sufficiency* of evidence is a question of fact. The examining and weighing of conflicting evidence on a controversial issue does *not* involve a question of law alone.

R. v. McCullagh (1990), 53 C.C.C. (3d) 130 (Ont. C.A.) — Misinterpretation of the trial judge's reasons on an issue of law is an error of law.

R. v. Marshall (1989), 52 C.C.C. (3d) 130 (Ont. C.A.) — The interpretation of uncontested facts is a question of fact and *not* one of law.

R. v. Hook (1955), 22 C.R. 378, 113 C.C.C. 248 (Ont. C.A.) — The question of whether the *proper inference* has been drawn by the trial judge from facts established in evidence is purely a "question of fact".

R. v. Moreau (1992), 76 C.C.C. (3d) 181 (Que. C.A.) — The application of too restrictive a test as to the availability of a discharge is an error of law.

R. v. Farmer's Fruit Store Ltd. (1984), 37 Sask. R. 241 (C.A.); reversing (1983), 30 Sask. R. 128 (Q.B.) — The proper construction of a by-law was a question of law.

Procedural Considerations

R. v. Mallen (1992), 70 C.C.C. (3d) 561 (B.C. C.A.) — Where the summary conviction appeal court finds error in one respect, but upholds an appellant's conviction on another basis, the respondent P may rely on any basis to support the decisions upon further appeal to the court of appeal. No "cross-appeal" is available to P.

R. v. Emery (1981), 61 C.C.C. (2d) 84 (B.C. C.A.); leave to appeal refused (1981), 40 N.R. 358n (S.C.C.) — An appeal to the court of appeal is an appeal from the decision of the summary conviction appeal court, not an appeal from the decision of the summary conviction court, although that decision may be of importance in determining the outcome of the appeal.

R. v. Broda (1983), 7 C.C.C. (3d) 161 (Sask. C.A.) — D appealed both her conviction and sentence to the summary conviction appeal court. The conviction was overturned by that court making it unnecessary to deal with the issue of sentence. The court of appeal restored the conviction but remitted the matter of sentence to the summary conviction appeal court to dispose of the original appeal against sentence.

Costs [See also s. 809]

Trask v. R. (1987), 59 C.R. (3d) 179, 37 C.C.C. (3d) 92 (S.C.C.) — The court should not fetter its discretion by adopting the proposition that costs be allowed to all successful D appellants. While P might often be required to pay costs when it appeals a summary conviction matter it does not follow that D who successfully appeals should invariably have his costs. When P appeals a matter in order to settle a point of law, the public benefits. An individual should not be put to substantial expense because of P's initiative in seeking to effect a valid social purpose.

R. v. Ouellette (1980), 15 C.R. (3d) 372, 52 C.C.C. (2d) 336 (S.C.C.); affirming (1979), 50 C.C.C. (2d) 346 (Que. C.A.) — Section 839(3) binds P, who can be ordered to pay costs.

R. v. King (1986), 26 C.C.C. (3d) 349 (B.C. C.A.) — Due to public interest, costs are to be awarded to D in criminal proceedings only where a prosecution is frivolous, it is conducted for an oblique motive, or P is pursuing the action as a test case.

Related Provisions: Appeals to the Supreme Court of Canada in summary conviction matters are governed by s. 40 of the *Supreme Court Act*.

The provisions of ss. 673–689, incorporated by s. 839(2), are discussed in the notes to each of those sections.

Fees and Allowances

840. (1) Fees and allowances — Subject to subsection (2), the fees and allowances mentioned in the schedule to this Part are the fees and allowances that may be taken or allowed in proceedings before summary conviction courts and justices under this Part.

(2) Order of lieutenant governor in council — The lieutenant governor in council of a province may order that all or any of the fees and allowances mentioned in the schedule to this Part shall not be taken or allowed in proceedings before summary conviction courts and justices under this Part in that province and, when the lieutenant governor in council so orders, he or she may fix any other fees and allowances for any items similar to those mentioned in the schedule, or any other items, to be taken or allowed instead.

R.S., c. C-34, s. 772; 1994, c. 44, s. 83; 1997, c. 18, s. 114.

Schedule

(Section 840)

FEES AND ALLOWANCES THAT MAY BE CHARGED BY
SUMMARY CONVICTION COURTS AND JUSTICES

1.	Information	$1.00
2.	Summons or warrant	0.50
3.	Warrant where summons issued in first instance	0.30
4.	Each necessary copy of summons or warrant	0.30
5.	Each subpoena or warrant to or for witnesses	0.30

(A subpoena may contain any number of names. Only one subpoena may be issued on behalf of a party in any proceeding, unless the summary conviction court or the justice considers it necessary or desirable that more than one subpoena be issued.)

6.	Information for warrant for witness and warrant for witness ...	1.00
7.	Each necessary copy of subpoena to or warrant for witness	$0.20
8.	Each recognizance	1.00
9.	Hearing and determining proceeding	1.00
10.	Where hearing lasts more than two hours	2.00
11.	Where two or more justices hear and determine a proceeding, each is entitled to the fee authorized by item 9.	
12.	Each warrant of committal	0.50
13.	Making up record of conviction or order on request of a party to the proceedings	1.00
14.	Copy of a writing other than a conviction or order, on request of a party to the proceedings; for each folio of one hundred words	0.10
15.	Bill of costs, when made out in detail on request of a party to the proceedings	0.20

(Items 14 and 15 may be charged only where there has been an adjudication.)

16.	Attending to remand prisoner	1.00
17.	Attending to take recognizance of bail	1.00
18.	Arresting a person on a warrant or without a warrant	1.50
19.	Serving summons or subpoena	0.50
20.	Mileage to serve summons or subpoena or to make an arrest, both ways, for each mile	0.10

(Where a public conveyance is not used, reasonable costs of transportation may be allowed.)

21.	Mileage where service cannot be effected on proof of a diligent ,attempt to effect service, each way, for each mile............	0.10
22.	Returning with prisoner after arrest to take him before a summary conviction court or justice at a place different from the place where the peace officer received the warrant to arrest, if the journey is of necessity over a route different from that taken by the peace officer to make the arrest, each way, for each mile	0.10

23.	Taking a prisoner to prison on remand or committal, each way, for each mile	0.10
	(Where a public conveyance is not used, reasonable costs of may be allowed. No charge may be made under this item in respect of a service for which a charge is made under item 22.)	
24.	Attending summary conviction court or justice on summary conviction proceedings, for each day necessarily employed	2.00

(No more than $2.00 may be charged under this item in respect of any day notwithstanding the number of proceedings that the peace officer attended on that day before that summary conviction court or justice.)

FEES AND ALLOWANCES THAT MAY BE ALLOWED TO WITNESSES

25.	Each day attending trial	$4.00
26.	Mileage travelled to attend trial, each way, for each mile	0.10

FEES AND ALLOWANCES THAT MAY BE ALLOWED TO INTERPRETERS

27.	Each half day attending trial	$2.50
28.	Actual living expenses when away from ordinary place of residence, not to exceed per day	10.00
29.	Mileage travelled to attend trial, each way, for each mile	0.10

R.S., c. C-34, Schedule to Part XXIV.

Commentary: The section prescribes the fees and allowances that may be taken or allowed in summary conviction proceedings, subject to an order of the Lieutenant Governor in Council of a province that such fees or allowances shall not be taken or allowed in that province. Other fees and allowances may be fixed for similar itemsor any other items.

Related Provisions: Sections 809, 826, 830(1) and 839(3) authorize the award of costs in summary conviction trial and appellate proceedings.

PART XXVIII — FORMS

841. (1) Forms — The forms set out in this Part varied to suit the case or forms to the like effect shall be deemed to be good, valid and sufficient in the circumstances for which, respectively, they are provided.

(2) Seal not required — No justice is required to attach or affix a seal to any writing or process that he is authorized to issue and in respect of which a form is provided by this Part.

(3) Official languages — Any pre-printed portions of a form set out in this Part varied to suit the case or of a form to the like effect shall be printed in both official languages.

Commentary: The section *deems* the statutory forms, varied to suit the case or forms to the like effect, to be good, valid and sufficient in the applicable circumstances. No seal need be attached by a justice to a statutory form.

Case Law

R. v. Goodine (1992), 71 C.C.C. (3d) 146 (N.S. C.A.) — *See also*: *R. v. Sorensen* (1990), 59 C.C.C. (3d) 211 (Ont. Gen. Div.) — Failure to comply with s. 841(3) does *not* render an information a nullity. An information must be sworn and in writing. If the writing is deficient, it may be amended under s. 601. Under *I.A.* s. 32, deviations from prescribed form, *not* affecting substance or calculated to mislead, do *not* invalidate the form used. An information with an English text only is defective in form only, hence need *not* be amended.

Related Provisions: Section 32 *I.A.* provides that deviations from prepared forms that do *not* affect the substance and are *not* calculated to mislead, do *not* invalidate the form.

In cases in which there is a variance between the enactment and a prescribed form that *may* be used thereunder, it is a prudent course to follow the enactment in preference to the non-compliant form.

[Forms]

Form 1 — Information To Obtain A Search Warrant
(Section 487)

Canada,

      Province of ....,
      (territorial division).

This is the information of A.B., of ...., in the said *(territorial division)*, *(occupation)*, hereinafter called the informant, taken before me.

The informant says that *(describe things to be searched for and offence in respect of which search is to be made)*, and that he believes on reasonable grounds that the said things, or some part of them, are in the *(dwelling-house, etc.)* of C.D., of ...., in the said *(territorial division)*. *(Here add the grounds of belief, whatever they may be)*.

Wherefore the informant prays that a search warrant may be granted to search the said *(dwelling-house, etc.)* for the said things.

Sworn before me
this .... day of
.........., A.D. ....,
at ....

....
(Signature of Informant)

....
A Justice of the Peace in and for

Form 2 — Information
(Section 506 and 788)

Canada,

      Province of ....,
      (territorial division).

This is the information of C.D., of ...., *(occupation)*, hereinafter called the informant.

The informant says that (*if the informant has no personal knowledge state that he believes on reasonable grounds and state the offence*).

Sworn before me

this .... day of

.........., A.D. ....,

at ....

....   (*Signature of Informant*)

A Justice of the Peace in and for

Note: The date of birth of the accused may be mentioned on the information or indictment.

Form 3

Repealed R.S., c. 27 (1st Supp.), s. 184(2).

Form 4 — Heading of Indictment
(Sections 566, 566.1, 580 and 591)

Canada,

                    Province of ....,
                    (*territorial division*).

In the (*set out name of the court*) —

Her Majesty the Queen —

against —

(*name of accused*)

(*Name of accused*) stands charged

    1. That he (*state offence*).

    2. That he (*state offence*).

Dated this .... day of .... A.D. ...., at ....

          . . . .

          (*Signature of signing officer, Agent of Attorney General, etc., as the case may be*)

1999, c. 3, s. 58.

Note: The date of birth of the accused may be mentioned on the information or indictment.

Form 5 — Warrant to Search
(Section 487)

Canada,

                    Province of ....,
                    (*territorial division*).

To the peace officers in the said (*territorial division*) or to the (*named public officers*):

Whereas it appears on the oath of A.B., of .... that there are reasonable grounds for believing that (*describe things to be searched for and offence in respect of which search is to be made*) are in .... at.......... , hereinafter called the premises;

This is, therefore, to authorize and require you between the hours of (*as the justice may direct*) to enter into the said premises and to search for the said things and to bring them before me or some other justice.

Dated this .... day of .... A.D. ...., at ....

....

A Justice of the Peace in and for

....

1999, c. 5, s. 45.

Proposed Addition — Form 5.01

Form 5.01 — Information to Obtain a Warrant to take Bodily Substances for Forensic DNA Analysis

(Subsection 487.05(1))

Canada,

Province of ....,

(*territorial division*).

This is the information of (*name of peace officer*), (*occupation*), of .... in the said (*territorial division*), hereinafter called the informant, taken before me.

The informant says that he or she has reasonable grounds to believe

(a) that (*offence*), a designated offence within the meaning of section 487.04 of the *Criminal Code*, has been committed;

(b) that a bodily substance has been found

(i) at the place where the offence was committed,

(ii) on or within the body of the victim of the offence,

(iii) on anything worn or carried by the victim at the time when the offence was committed, or

(iv) on or within the body of any person or thing or at any place associated with the commission of the offence;

(c) that (*name of person*) was a party to the offence; and

(d) that forensic DNA analysis of a bodily substance from (*name of person*) will provide evidence about whether the bodily substance referred to in paragraph (b) was from that person.

The reasonable grounds are:

The informant therefore requests that a warrant be issued authorizing the taking from (*name of person*) of the number of samples of bodily substances that are reasonably required for forensic DNA analysis, provided that the person taking the samples is able by virtue of training or experience to take them by means of the investigative procedures described in subsection 487.06(1) of the *Criminal Code* and provided that, if the person taking the samples is not a peace officer, he or she take the samples under the direction of a peace officer.

Sworn to before me

this ....day of.........,

A.D. ...., at ....

....

(Signature of informant)

....

(Signature of provincial court judge)

1998, c. 37, s. 24 [Not in force at date of publication.]

Proposed Addition — Form 5.02

Form 5.02 — Warrant Authorizing the Taking of Bodily Substances for Forensic DNA Analysis
(Subsection 487.05(1))

Canada,

Province of ....,

(territorial division).

To the peace officers in *(territorial division)*:

Whereas it appears on the oath of *(name of peace officer)* of .... in the said *(territorial division)*, that there are reasonable grounds to believe

(a) that *(offence)*, a designated offence within the meaning of section 487.04 of the *Criminal Code*, has been committed;

(b) that a bodily substance has been found

(i) at the place where the offence was committed,

(ii) on or within the body of the victim of the offence,

(iii) on anything worn or carried by the victim at the time when the offence was committed, or

(iv) on or within the body of any person or thing or at any place associated with the commission of the offence;

(c) that *(name of person)* was a party to the offence; and

(d) that forensic DNA analysis of a bodily substance from *(name of person)* will provide evidence about whether the bodily substance referred to in paragraph (b) was from that person.

And whereas I am satisfied that it is in the best interests of the administration of justice to issue this warrant.

This is therefore to authorize and require you to take from *(name of person)* or cause to be taken by a person acting under your direction, the number of samples of bodily substances that are reasonably required for forensic DNA analysis, provided that the person taking the samples is able by virtue of training or experience to take them by means of the investigative procedures described in subsection 487.06(1) of the *Criminal Code* and provided that, if the person taking the samples is not a peace officer, he or she take the samples under the direction of a peace officer. This warrant is subject to the following terms and conditions that I consider advisable to ensure that the taking of the samples is reasonable in the circumstances:

Dated this ...... day of ....

A.D. ...., at ....

....

(*Signature of provincial court judge*)

1998, c. 37, s. 24 [Not in force at date of publication.]

Proposed Addition — Form 5.03

Form 5.03 — Order Authorizing the Taking of Bodily Substances for Forensic DNA Analysis
(Paragraph 487.05(1)(a))

Canada,
Province of ....,
(*territorial division*).

To the peace officers in (*territorial division*):

Whereas (*name of offender*) has been convicted, discharged under section 730 of the *Criminal Code* or, in the case of a young person, found guilty under the *Young Offenders Act* of (*offence*), an offence that is a primary designated offence within the meaning of section 487.04 of the *Criminal Code*.

Therefore, you are authorized to take from (*name of offender*) or cause to be taken by a person acting under your direction, the number of samples of bodily substances that are reasonably required for forensic DNA analysis, provided that the person taking the samples is able by virtue of training or experience to take them by means of the investigative procedures described in subsection 487.06(1) of the *Criminal Code* and provided that, if the person taking the samples is not a peace officer, he or she take the samples under the direction of a peace officer.

This order is subject to the following terms and conditions that I consider advisable to ensure that the taking of the samples is reasonable in the circumstances:

Dated this ...... day of ....

A.D. ...., at ....

....

(*Signature of judge of the court*)

1998, c. 37, s. 24 [Not in force at date of publication.]

Proposed Addition — Form 5.04

Form 5.04 — Order Authorizing the Taking of Bodily Substances for Forensic DNA Analysis
(Paragraph 487.05(1)(b) and subsection 487.052(1))

Canada,
Province of ....,
(*territorial division*).

To the peace officers in (*territorial division*):

Whereas (*name of offender*), in this order called the "offender", has been convicted, discharged under section 730 of the *Criminal Code* or, in the case of young person, found guilty under the *Young Offenders Act* of (*offence*), an offence that is

    (a) a secondary designated offence within the meaning of section 487.04 of the *Criminal Code*, or

    (b) a designated offence within the meaning of section 487.04 of the *Criminal Code* committed before subsection 5(1) of the *DNA Identification Act* came into force;

Whereas I have considered the offender's criminal record, the nature of the offence and the circumstances surrounding its commission and the impact that this order would have on the offender's privacy and security of the person;

And whereas I am satisfied that it is in the best interests of the administration of justice to make this order;

Therefore, you are authorized to take from (*name of offender*) or cause to be taken by a person acting under your direction, the number of samples of bodily substances that are reasonably required for forensic DNA analysis, provided that the person taking the samples is able by virtue of training or experience to take them by means of the investigative procedures described in subsection 487.06(1) of the *Criminal Code* and provided that, if the person taking the samples is not a peace officer, he or she take the samples under the direction of a peace officer.

This order is subject to the following terms and conditions that I consider advisable to ensure that the taking of the samples is reasonable in the circumstances:

Dated this ...... day of ....

A.D. ...., at ....

....

(*Signature of judge of the court*)

1998, c. 37, s. 24 [Not in force at date of publication.]

Proposed Addition — Form 5.05

Form 5.05 — Application for an Authorization to take Bodily Substances for Forensic DNA Analysis
(Subsection 487.055(1))

Canada,

Province of ....,

(*territorial division*).

I, (*name of peace officer*), (*occupation*), of .... in the said (*territorial division*), apply for an authorization to take bodily substances for forensic DNA analysis. A certificate referred to in paragraph 667(1)(a) of the *Criminal Code* is filed with this application.

Whereas (*name of offender*)

    (a) before subsection 487.055(1) of the *Criminal Code* came into force, had been declared a dangerous offender under Part XXIV of that Act,

(b) before subsection 487.55(1) of the *Criminal Code* came into force, had been convicted of more than one murder committed at different times, or

(c) before subsection 476.55(1) of the *Criminal Code* came into force, had been convicted of more than one sexual offence within the meaning of subsection 487.055(3) of the *Criminal Code* and is currently serving a sentence of at least two years imprisonment for one or more of those offences;

And whereas I have considered the offender's criminal record, the nature of the offence and the circumstances surrounding its commission and the impact that this authorization would have on the offender's privacy and security of the person;

Therefore, I request that an authorization be granted under subsection 487.55(1) of the *Criminal Code* to take from (*name of offender*) the number of samples of bodily substances that is reasonably required for forensic DNA analysis, provided that the person taking the samples is able by virtue of training or experience to take them by means of the investigative procedures described in subsection 487.06(1) of the *Criminal Code* and provided that, if the person taking the samples is not a peace officer, he or she take the samples under the direction of a peace officer.

Dated this ...... day of ....

A.D. ...., at ....

....

(*Signature of applicant*)

1998, c. 37, s. 24 [Not in force at date of publication.]

Proposed Addition — Form 5.06

Form 5.06 — Authorization for the Taking of Bodily Substances for Forensic DNA Analysis

(Subsection 487.055(1))

Canada,

Province of ....,

(*territorial division*).

To the

peace officers in (*territorial division*):

Whereas (*name of offender*)

(a) before subsection 487.055(1) of the *Criminal Code* came into force, had been declared a dangerous offender under Part XXIV of that Act,

(b) before subsection 487.55(1) of the *Criminal Code* came into force, had been convicted of more than one murder committed at different times, or

(c) before subsection 476.55(1) of the *Criminal Code* came into force, had been convicted of more than one sexual offence within the meaning of subsection 487.055(3) of the *Criminal Code* and is currently serving a sentence of at least two years imprisonment for one or more of those offences;

Whear as (*name of peace officer*), a peace officer of the said territorial division, has applied for an authorization for the taking of the number of samples of bodily substances from (*name of offender*) that is reasonably required for forensic DNA analysis by means of the investigative procedures described in subsection 487.06(1) of that Act;

And whereas I have considered the offender's criminal record, the nature of the offence and the circumstances surrounding its commission and the impact that this authorization would have on the offender's privacy and security of the person;

Therefore, the peace officers of the said territorial division, are authorized to take from (*name of offender*) or cause to be taken by a person acting under their direction those samples, provided that the person taking the samples is able by virtue of training or experience to take them by means of the investigative procedures described in subsection 487.06(1) of the *Criminal Code* and provided that, if the person taking the samples is not a peace officer, he or she take the samples under the direction of a peace officer.

This authorization is subject to the following terms and conditions that I consider advisable to ensure that the taking of the samples is reasonable in the circumstances:

Dated this ...... day of ....

A.D. ...., at ....

....

(*Signature of provincial court judge*)

1998, c. 37, s. 24 [Not in force at date of publication.]

Proposed Addition — Form 5.07

Form 5.07 — Report to a Provincial Court Judge or the Court
(Subsection 487.057(1))

Canada,

Province of ....,

(*territorial division*).

❏ To (*name of judge*), a judge of the provincial court who issued a warrant under section 487.05 or granted an authorization under section 487.055 or 487.091 of the *Criminal Code* or to another judge of that court:

❏ To the court from which an order under section 487.051 or 487.052 of the *Criminal Code* was made:

I, (*name of peace officer*), have (*state here whether you have acted in execution of a warrant under section 487.05 or an order under section 487.051 or 487.052, or under an authorization under section 487.052, or under an authorization under section 487.055 or 487.091*) of the *Criminal Code*.

I have (*state here whether you have taken the samples yourself or caused them to be taken under your direction*) from (*name of offender*) the number of samples of bodily substances that I believe are reasonably required for forensic DNA analysis, in accordance with (*state whether the taking of the samples was under the warrant issued or an authorization granted by the judge or another judge of the court or an order made by the court.*)

The samples were taken at .... a.m./p.m. on the .... day of .... A.D. ......

I (*or state the name of the person who took the samples*) was able by virtue of training or experience to take the following samples from (*name of offender*) in accordance with subsection 487.06(1) of the *Criminal Code* and did so take them:

❏ Individual hairs, including the root sheath

❏ epithelial cells taken by swabbing the lips, tongue or inside cheeks of the mouth

❏ blood taken by pricking the skin surface with a sterile lancet

Any terms or conditions in the (*warrant, order or authorization*) have been complied with.

Dated this ...... day of ....

A.D. ...., at ....

....

(*Signature of peace officer*)

1998, c. 37, s. 24 [Not in force at date of publication.]

Proposed Addition — Form 5.08

Form 5.08 — Application for an Authorization for Taking Additional Samples of Bodily Substances for Forensic DNA Analysis

(Subsection 487.091(1))

Canada,

Province of ....,

(*territorial division*).

I, (*name of peace officer*), (*occupation*), of .... in the said (*territorial division*), apply for an authorization to take additional samples of bodily substances for forensic DNA analysis.

Whereas samples of bodily substances were taken from (*name of offender*) for the purpose of forensic DNA analysis, in execution of an order made under section 487.051 or 487.052 of the *Criminal Code* or an authorization granted under section 487.055 of the *Criminal Code* (*attach a copy of the order or authorization*);

And whereas on (*day/month/year*) it was determined that a DNA profile could not be derived from the samples for the following reasons:

Therefore, I request that an authorization be granted under subsection 487.091(1) of the *Criminal Code* to take from (*name of offender*) the number of additional samples of bodily substances that is reasonably required for forensic DNA analysis, provided that the person taking the samples is able by virtue of training or experience to take them by means of the investigative procedures described in subsection 487.06(1) of the *Criminal Code* and provided that, if the person taking the samples is not a peace officer, he or she take the samples under the direction of a peace officer.

Dated this ...... day of ....

A.D. ...., at ....

....

(*Signature of applicant*)

1998, c. 37, s. 24 [Not in force at date of publication.]

Proposed Addition — Form 5.09

Form 5.09 — Authorization for the Taking of Additional Samples of Bodily Substances for Forensic DNA Analysis
(Subsection 487.091(1))

Canada,

Province of ....,

(territorial division).

To the peace officers in *(territorial division)*:

Whereas samples of bodily substances were taken from *(name of offender)* for the purpose of forensic DNA analysis, in execution of an order made under section 487.051 or 487.052 of the *Criminal Code* or an authorization granted under section 487.055 of the *Criminal Code*;

Whereas on *(day/month/year)* it was determined that a DNA profile could not be derived from the samples for the following reasons:

And whereas *(name of peace officer)*, a peace officer of the said territorial division, has applied for an authorization for the taking of the number of samples of additional samples of bodily substances from *(name of offender)* that is reasonably required for forensic DNA analysis by means of the investigative procedures described in subsection 487.06(1) of that Act;

Therefore, the peace officers of the said territorial division, are authorized to take from *(name of offender)* or cause to be taken by a person acting under their direction those additional samples, provided that the person taking the samples is able by virtue of training or experience to take them by means of the investigative procedures described in subsection 487.06(1) of the *Criminal Code* and provided that, if the person taking the samples is not a peace officer, he or she take the samples under the direction of a peace officer.

This authorization is subject to the following terms and conditions that I consider advisable to ensure that the taking of the samples is reasonable in the circumstances:

Dated this ...... day of ....

A.D. ...., at ....

....

(Signature of provincial court judge)

1998, c. 37, s. 24 [Not in force at date of publication.]

Form 5.1 — Warrant To Search
(Section 487.1)

Canada,

Province of ....,

(territorial division).

To A.B. and other peace officers in the *(territorial division in which the warrant is intended for execution)*:

Whereas it appears on the oath of A.B., a peace officer in the *(territorial division in which the warrant is intended for execution)*, that there are reasonable grounds for dispensing with an information presented personally and in writing; and that there are reasonable grounds for believing that the following things

(*describe things to be searched for*)

relevant to the investigation of the following indictable offence

(*describe offence in respect of which search is to be made*)

are to be found in the following place or premises

(*describe place or premises to be searched*):

This is, therefore, to authorize you to enter the said place or premises between the hours of (*as the justice may direct*) and to search for and seize the said things and to report thereon as soon as practicable but within a period not exceeding seven days after the execution of the warrant to the clerk of the court for the (*territorial division in which the warrant is intended for execution*).

Issued at (*time*) on the (*day*) of (*month*) A.D. (*year*), at (*place*).

....

A Judge of the Provincial Court in and for the Province of (*specify province*).

To the Occupant: This search warrant was issued by telephone or other means of telecommunication. If you wish to know the basis on which this warrant was issued, you may apply to the clerk of the court for the territorial division in which the warrant was executed, at *address*, to obtain a copy of the information on oath.

You may obtain from the clerk of the court a copy of the report filed by the peace officer who executed this warrant. That report will indicate the things, if any, that were seized and the location where they are being held.

Form 5.2 — Report To A Justice
Section 489.1

Canada

       Province of ....,
       (*territorial division*)

.

To the justice who issued a warrant to the undersigned pursuant to section 256, 487 or 487.1 of the *Criminal Code* (*or another justice for the same territorial division or, if no warrant was issued, any justice having jurisdiction in respect of the matter*).

I, (*name of the peace officer or other person*) have (*state here whether you have acted under a warrant issued pursuant to section 256, 487 or 487.1 of the Criminal Code or under section 489 of the Code or otherwise in the execution of duties under the Criminal Code or another Act of Parliament to be specified*)

1. searched the premises situated at ....; and

2. seized the following things and dealt with them as follows:

Property
Seized   Disposition
(*describe   (*state, in respect of each thing
(*each thing   (*seized, whether
(*seized*)

Form 5.2   Criminal Code, Part XXVIII

> *(a) it was returned to the person lawfully entitled to its possession, in which case the receipt therefor shall be attached hereto, or*
>
> *(b) it is being detained to be dealt with according to law, and the location and manne in which, or where applicable, the person by whom it is being detained).*

1. ....
2. ....
3. ....
4. ....

In the case of a warrant issued by telephone or other means of telecommunication, the statements referred to in subsection 487.1(9) of the *Criminal Code* shall be specified in the report.

Dated this .... day of .... A.D. ...., at ....

....
Signature of peace
officer or other
person
R.S. 1985, c.27(1st Supp.), s.184(3).

Form 5.3 — Report To A Judge of Property Seized
(Section 462.32)

Canada
   Province of ....,
   (territorial division)

To a judge of the court from which the warrant was issued *(specify court)*:

I, *(name of the peace officer or other person)* have acted under a warrant issued under section 462.32 of the *Criminal Code* and have

   1. searched the premises situated at ....; and

   2. seized the following property:

Property Seized *(describe each item of property seized)*	**Location** *(state, in respect of each item of property seized, the location where it is being detained).*
1.	
2.	
3.	
4.	

Dated this .... day of .... A.D. .... **at**
....

. . . .
**Signature of peace
officer or other
person
R.S. 1985, c. 42(4th Supp.), s. 6.**

Form 6 — Summons to a Person Charged With an Offence
(Sections 493, 508 and 512)

Canada,

Province of ....,
(territorial division).

To A.B., of ...., *(occupation)*:

Whereas you have this day been charged before me that *(set out briefly the offence in respect of which the accused is charged)*;

This is therefore to command you, in Her Majesty's name:

(a) to attend court on ...., the .... day of .... A.D. ...., at .... o'clock in the .... noon, at .... or before any justice for the said *(territorial division)* who is there, and to attend thereafter as required by the court, in order to be dealt with according to law; and

(b) to appear on ...., the .... day of .... A.D..........., at .... o'clock in the .... noon, at ...., for the purposes of the *Identification of Criminals Act. (Ignore, if not filled in).*

You are warned that failure without lawful excuse to attend court in accordance with this summons is an offence under subsection 145(4) of the *Criminal Code.*

Section 145(4) of the *Criminal Code* states as follows:

(4) Every one who is served with a summons and who fails, without lawful excuse, the proof of which lies on him, to appear at a time and place stated therein, if any, for the purposes of the *Identification of Criminals Act* or to attend court in accordance therewith, is guilty of

(a) an indictable offence and is liable to imprisonment for a term not exceeding two years; or

(b) an offence punishable on summary conviction.

Section 510 of the *Criminal Code* states as follows:

510. Where an accused who is required by a summons to appear at a time and place stated therein for the purposes of the *Identification of Criminals Act* does not appear at that time and place, a justice may issue a warrant for the arrest of the accused for the offence with which he is charged.

Dated this .... day of .... A.D. ...., at ....

. . . .
**A Justice of the Peace in
and for .... *or* Judge
R.S. 1985, c. 27(1st Supp.), s. 184(4).**

Form 7 — Warrant for Arrest
(Sections 475, 493, 597, 800 and 803)

Canada,

> Province of ....,
> (*territorial division*).

To the peace officers in the said (*territorial division*):

This warrant is issued for the arrest of A.B., of ...., (*occupation*), hereinafter called the accused.

Whereas the accused has been charged that (*set out briefly the offence in respect of which the accused is charged*);

And whereas:*

(a) there are reasonable grounds to believe that it is necessary in the public interest to issue this warrant for the arrest of the accused [507(4), 512(1)];

(b) the accused failed to attend court in accordance with the summons served on him [512(2)];

(c) (an appearance notice *or* a promise to appear *or* a recognizance entered into before an officer in charge) was confirmed and the accused failed to attend court in accordance therewith [512(2)];

(d) it appears that a summons cannot be served because the accused is evading service [512(2)];

(e) the accused was ordered to be present at the hearing of an application for a review of an order made by a justice and did not attend the hearing [520(5), 521(5)];

(f) there are reasonable grounds to believe that the accused has contravened or is about to contravene the (promise to appear *or* undertaking *or* recognizance) on which he was released [524(1), 525(5), 679(6)];

(g) there are reasonable grounds to believe that the accused has since his release from custody on (a promise to appear *or* an undertaking *or* a recognizance) committed an indictable offence [524(1), 525(5), 679(6)];

(h) the accused was required by (an appearance notice *or* a promise to appear *or* a recognizance entered into before an officer in charge *or* a summons) to attend at a time and place stated therein for the purposes of the *Identification of Criminals Act* and did not appear at that time and place [502, 510];

(i) an indictment has been found against the accused and the accused has not appeared or remained in attendance before the court for his trial [597];

(j)**

This is, therefore, to command you, in Her Majesty's name, forthwith to arrest the said accused and to bring him before (*state court, judge or justice*), to be dealt with according to law.

(*Add where applicable*) Whereas there are reasonable grounds to believe that the accused is or will be present in (*here describe dwelling-house*);

This warrant is also issued to authorize you to enter the dwelling-house for the purpose of arresting or apprehending the accused, subject to the condition that you may not enter the dwelling-house unless you have, immediately before entering the dwelling-house, reasonable grounds to believe that the person to be arrested or apprehended is present in the dwelling-house.

Dated this .... day of .... A.D. ...., at ....

. . . .

Judge, Clerk of the Court,
Provincial Court Judge *or* Justice

---

*Initial applicable recital.

**For any case not covered by recitals (a) to (i), insert recital in the words of the statute authorizing the warrant.*

1999, c. 5, s. 46.

Form 7.1 — Warrant to Enter Dwelling-House
(Section 529.1)

Canada,

Province of ....,
(*territorial division*).

To the peace officers in the said (*territorial division*):

This warrant is issued in respect of the arrest of A.B., or a person with the following description ( ), of ...., (*occupation*).

Whereas there are reasonable grounds to believe:*

(a) a warrant referred to in this or any other Act of Parliament to arrest or apprehend the person is in force anywhere in Canada;

(b) grounds exist to arrest the person without warrant under paragraph 495(1)(a) or (b) of the *Criminal Code*; or

(c) grounds exist to arrest or apprehend without warrant the person under an Act of Parliament, other than this Act;

And whereas there are reasonable grounds to believe that the person is or will be present in (*here describe dwelling-house*);

This warrant is issued to authorize you to enter the dwelling-house for the purpose of arresting or apprehending the person.

Dated this .... day of .... A.D. ...., at ....

. . . .

Judge, Clerk of the Court,
Provincial Court Judge or Justice

---

*Initial applicable recital.

1997, c. 39, s. 3.

Form 8 — Warrant for Committal
(Sections 493 and 515)

Canada,
> **Province of** ....,
> (*territorial division*).

To the peace officers in the said (*territorial division*) and to the keeper of the (*prison*) at ....:

This warrant is issued for the committal of A.B., of ...., (*occupation*), hereinafter called the accused.

Whereas the accused has been charged that (*set out briefly the offence in respect of which the accused is charged*);

And whereas:[*]

(a) the prosecutor has shown cause why the detention of the accused in custody is justified [515(5)];

(b) an order has been made that the accused be released on (giving an undertaking *or* entering into a recognizance) but the accused has not yet complied with the order [519(1), 520(9), 524(12), 525(8)];[**]

(c) the application by the prosecutor for a review of the order of a justice in respect of the interim release of the accused has been allowed and that order has been vacated, and the prosecutor has shown cause why the detention of the accused in custody is justified [521];

(d) the accused has contravened or was about to contravene his (promise to appear *or* undertaking *or* recognizance) and the same was cancelled, and the detention of the accused in custody is justified or seems proper in the circumstances [524(4), 524(8)];

(e) there are reasonable and probable grounds to believe that the accused has after his release from custody on (a promise to appear *or* an undertaking *or* a recognizance) committed an indictable offence and the detention of the accused in custody is justified or seems proper in the circumstances [524(4), 524(8)];

(f) the accused has contravened or was about to contravene the (undertaking *or* recognizance) on which he was released and the detention of the accused in custody seems proper in the circumstances [525(7), 679(6)];

(g) there are reasonable grounds to believe that the accused has after his release from custody on (an undertaking *or* a recognizance) committed an indictable offence and the detention of the accused in custody seems proper in the circumstances [525(7), 679(6)];

(h)[***]

This is, therefore, to command you, in Her Majesty's name, to arrest, if necessary, and take the accused and convey him safely to the (*prison*) at ...., and there deliver him to the keeper thereof, with the following precept:

I do hereby command you the said keeper to receive the accused in your custody in the said prison and keep him safely there until he is delivered by due course of law.

Form 9 — Appearance Notice   **Form 9**

Dated this .... day of .... A.D. ...., at ....

....

Judge, Clerk of the Court,
Provincial Court Judge *or* Justice

---

*Initial applicable recital.

**If the person having custody of the accused is authorized under paragraph 519(1)(b) to release him upon his complying with an order, endorse the authorization on this warrant and attach a copy of the order.*

***For any case not covered by recitals (a) to (g), insert recital in the words of the statute authorizing the warrant.*

Form 9 — Appearance Notice Issued By a Peace Officer to a Person Not Yet Charged With an Offence

(Section 493)

Canada,

               Province of ....,

               (*territorial division*).

To A.B., of ...., (*occupation*):

You are alleged to have committed (*set out substance of offence*).

1. You are required to attend court on .... day, the .... day of .... A.D. ...., at .... o'clock in the .... noon, in courtroom No. ...., at .... court, in the municipality of.......... , and to attend thereafter as required by the court, in order to be dealt with according to law.

2. You are also required to appear on .... day, the .... day of.......... A.D. ...., at .... o'clock in the .... noon, at (*police station*), (*address*), for the purposes of the *Identification of Criminals Act*. (*Ignore, if not filled in*).

You are warned that failure to attend court in accordance with this appearance notice is an offence under subsection 145(5) of the *Criminal Code*.

Section 145(5) and (6) of the *Criminal Code* state as follows:
"

    (5) Every person who is named in an appearance notice or promise to appear, or in a recognizance entered into before an officer in charge, that has been confirmed by a justice under section 508 and who fails, without lawful excuse, the proof of which lies on the person, to appear at a time and place stated therein, if any, for the purposes of the *Identification of Criminals Act* or to attend court in accordance therewith, is guilty of

        (a) an indictable offence and is liable to imprisonment for a term not exceeding two years; or

        (b) an offence punishable on summary conviction.

    (6) For the purposes of subsection (5), it is not a lawful excuse that an appearance notice, promise to appear or recognizance states defectively the substance of the alleged offence."

Section 502 of the *Criminal Code* states as follows:
"

    502. Where an accused who is required by an appearance notice or promise to appear or by a recognizance entered into before an officer in charge or another peace officer to

appear at a time and place stated therein for the purposes of the *Identification of Criminals Act* does not appear at that time and place, a justice may, where the appearance notice, promise to appear or recognizance has been confirmed by a justice under section 508, issue a warrant for the arrest of the accused for the offence with which the accused is charged."

Issued at .... a.m./p.m. this .... day of .... A.D............ , at ....

. . . .
(Signature of peace officer)

. . . .
(Signature of accused)

1997, c. 18, s. 115.

Form 10 — Promise to Appear
(Section 493)

Canada,

> Province of ....,
> *(territorial division)*.

I, A.B., of ...., *(occupation)*, understand that it is alleged that I have committed (*set out substance of offence*).

In order that I may be released from custody,

1. I promise to attend court on .... day, the .... day of.......... A.D. ...., at .... o'clock in the .... noon, in courtroom No. ...., at court, in the municipality of ...., and to attend thereafter as required by the court, in order to be dealt with according to law.

2. I also promise to appear on .... day, the .... day of.......... A.D. ...., at .... o'clock in the .... noon, at *(police station)*, *(address)*, for the purposes of the *Identification of Criminals Act*. (*Ignore if not filled in*).

I understand that failure without lawful excuse to attend court in accordance with this promise to appear is an offence under subsection 145(5) of the *Criminal Code*.

Subsections 145(5) and (6) of the *Criminal Code* state as follows:

"

> (5) Every one who is named in an appearance notice or promise to appear, or in a recognizance entered into before an officer in charge, or another peace officer, that has been confirmed by a justice under section 508 and who fails, without lawful excuse, the proof of which lies on the person, to appear at a time and place stated therein, if any, for the purposes of the *Identification of Criminals Act* or to attend court in accordance therewith, is guilty of
>
> > (a) an indictable offence and is liable to imprisonment for a term not exceeding two years; or
> >
> > (b) an offence punishable on summary conviction.
>
> (6) For the purposes of subsection (5), it is not a lawful excuse that an appearance notice, promise to appear or recognizance states defectively the substance of the alleged offence."

Section 502 of the *Criminal Code* states as follows:

"

> 502. Where an accused who is required by an appearance notice or promise to appear or by a recognizance entered into before an officer in charge or another peace officer to

appear at a time and place stated therein for the purposes of the *Identification of Criminals Act* does not appear at that time and place, a justice may, where the appearance notice, promise to appear or recognizance has been confirmed by a justice under section 508, issue a warrant for the arrest of the accused for the offence with which the accused is charged."

Dated this .... day of .... A.D. ...., at ....

....

(Signature of accused)

1997, c. 18, s. 115.

Form 11 — Recognizance Entered Into Before an Officer in Charge or Other Peace Officer
(Section 493)

Canada,

Province of ....,
(territorial division).

I, A.B., of ...., *(occupation)*, understand that it is alleged that I have committed *(set out substance of offence)*.

In order that I may be released from custody, I hereby acknowledge that I owe $ *(not exceeding $500)* to Her Majesty the Queen to be levied on my real and personal property if I fail to attend court as hereinafter required. *(or, for a person not ordinarily resident in the province in which the person is in custody or within two hundred kilometers of the place in which the person is in custody)*

In order that I may be released from custody, I hereby acknowledge that I owe $ *(not exceeding $500)* to Her Majesty the Queen and deposit herewith *(money or other valuable security not exceeding in amount or value $500)* to be forfeited if I fail to attend court as hereinafter required.

1. I acknowledge that I am required to attend court on .... day, the.......... day of .... A.D. ...., at .... o'clock in the.......... noon, in courtroom No. ...., at .... court, in the municipality of ...., and to attend thereafter as required by the court, in order to be dealt with according to law.

2. I acknowledge that I am also required to appear on .... day, the.......... day of .... A.D. ...., at .... o'clock in the.......... noon, at *(police station)*, *(address)*, for the purposes of the *Identification of Criminals Act*. *(Ignore if not filled in)*.

I understand that failure without lawful excuse to attend court in accordance with this recognizance to appear is an offence under subsection 145(5) of the *Criminal Code*.

Section 145(5) and (6) of the *Criminal Code* state as follows:
"

(5) Every person who is named in an appearance notice or promise to appear, or in a recognizance entered into before an officer in charge or another peace officer, that has been confirmed by a justice under section 508 and who fails, without lawful excuse, the proof of which lies on the person, to appear at a time and place stated therein, if any, for the purposes of the *Identification of Criminals Act* or to attend court in accordance therewith, is guilty of

(a) an indictable offence and is liable to imprisonment for a term not exceeding two years; or

(b) an offence punishable on summary conviction.

(6) For the purposes of subsection (5), it is not a lawful excuse that an appearance notice, promise to appear or recognizance states defectively the substance of the alleged offence."

Section 502 of the *Criminal Code* states as follows:

"

502. Where an accused who is required by an appearance notice or promise to appear or by a recognizance entered into before an officer in charge or another peace officer to appear at a time and place stated therein for the purposes of the *Identification of Criminals Act* does not appear at that time and place, a justice may, where the appearance notice, promise to appear or recognizance has been confirmed by a justice under section 508, issue a warrant for the arrest of the accused for the offence with which he is charged."

Dated this .... day of .... A.D. ...., at ....

. . . .

(Signature of accused)

1997, c. 18, s. 115.

Form 11.1 — Undertaking Given to a Peace Officer or an Officer in Charge
(Sections 493, 499 and 503)

Canada,

Province of ....,

(territorial division).

I, A.B., of ...., *(occupation)*, understand that it is alleged that I have committed *(set out substance of the offence)*.

In order that I may be released from custody by way of (a promise to appear *or* a recognizance entered into before an officer in charge), I undertake to *(insert any conditions that are directed)*:

(a) remain within *(designated territorial jurisdiction)*;

(b) notify *(name of peace officer or other person designated)* of any change in my address, employment or occupation;

(c) abstain from communicating with *(name of witness or other person)* or from going to *(name or description of place)* except in accordance with the following conditions: *(as the peace officer or other person designated specifies)*;

(d) deposit my passport with *(name of peace officer or other person designated)*;

(e) to abstain from possession a firearm and to surrender to *(name of peace officer or other person designated)* any firearm in my possession and any authorization, license or registration certificate or other document enabling the acquisition or possession of a firearm;

(f) report at *(state times)* to *(name of peace officer or other person designated)*; and

(g) to abstain from

(i) the consumption of alcohol or other intoxicating substances, or

(ii) the consumption of drugs except in accordance with a medical prescription.

I understand that I am not required to give an undertaking to abide by the conditions specified above, but that if I do not, I may be kept in custody and brought before a justice so that the prosecutor may be given a reasonable opportunity to show cause why I should not be released on giving an undertaking without conditions.

I understand that if I give an undertaking to abide by the conditions specified above, then I may apply, at any time before I appear, or when I appear, before a justice pursuant to (a promise to appear *or* a recognizance entered into before an officer in charge or another peace officer), to have this undertaking vacated or varied and that my application will be considered as if I were before a justice pursuant to section 515 of the *Criminal Code*.

I also understand that this undertaking remains in effect until it is vacated or varied.

I also understand that failure without lawful excuse to abide by any of the conditions specified above is an offence under subsection 145(5.1) of the *Criminal Code*.

"

(5.1) Every person who, without lawful excuse, the proof of which lies on the person, fails to comply with any condition of an undertaking entered into pursuant to subsection 499(2) or 503(2.1)

(a) is guilty of an indictable offence and is liable to imprisonment for a term not exceeding two years; or

(b) is guilty of an offence punishable on summary conviction."

Dated this .... day of .... A.D. ...., at ....

. . . .
(Signature of accused)

1997, c. 18, s. 115.

Form 12 — Undertaking Given to a Justice or a Judge
(Sections 493 and 679)

Canada,

         Province of ....,
         (territorial division).

I, A.B., of ...., *(occupation)*, understand that I have been charged that *(set out briefly the offence in respect of which accused is charged)*.

In order that I may be released from custody, I undertake to attend court on .... day, the .... day of .... A.D. ...., and to attend thereafter as required by the court in order to be dealt with according to law *(or, where date and place of appearance before court are not known at the time undertaking is given, to attend at the time and place fixed by the court and thereafter as required by the court in order to be dealt with according to law)*. *(and where applicable)*

I also undertake to *(insert any conditions that are directed)*

(a) report at *(state times)* to *(name of peace officer or other person designated)*;

(b) remain within *(designated territorial jurisdiction)*;

(c) notify *(name of peace officer or other person designated)* of any change in my address, employment or occupation;

(d) abstain from communication with *(name of witness or other person)* except in accordance with the following conditions: *(as the justice or judge specifies)*;

(e) **deposit my passport** (*as the justice or judge directs*); **and**

(f) (*any other reasonable conditions*).

I understand that failure without lawful excuse to attend court in accordance with this undertaking is an offence under subsection 145(2) of the *Criminal Code*.

Subsection 145(2) and (3) of the *Criminal Code* state as follows:

(2) Every one who,

(a) being at large on his undertaking or recognizance given to or entered into before a justice or judge, fails, without lawful excuse, the proof of which lies on him, to attend court in accordance with the undertaking or recognizance, or

(b) having appeared before a court, justice or judge, fails, without lawful excuse, the proof of which lies on him, to attend court as thereafter required by the court, justice or judge,

or to surrender himself in accordance with an order of the court, justice or judge, as the case may be, is guilty of an indictable offence and liable to imprisonment for a term not exceeding two years or is guilty of an offence punishable on summary conviction.

(3) Every person who is at large on an undertaking or recognizance given to or entered into before a justice or judge and is bound to comply with a condition of that undertaking or recognizance directed by a justice or judge, and every person who is bound to comply with a direction ordered under subsection 515(12) or 522(2.1), and who fails, without lawful excuse, the proof of which lies on that person, to comply with that condition or direction, is guilty of

(a) an indictable offence and is liable to imprisonment for a term not exceeding two years; or

(b) an offence punishable on summary conviction.

Dated this .... day of .... A.D. ...., at ....)

. . . .
(Signature of appellant)

Form 13 — Undertaking By Appellant (Defendant)
(Sections 816, 832 and 834)

Canada,

Province of ....,

(territorial division).

I, A.B., of ...., (*occupation*), being the appellant against conviction (*or* against sentence *or* against an order *or* by way of stated case) in respect of the following matter (*set out the offence, subject-matter of order or question of law*) undertake to appear personally at the sittings of the appeal court at which the appeal is to be heard. (*and where applicable*)

I also undertake to (*insert any conditions that are directed*)

(a) report at (*state times*) to (*name of peace officer or other person designated*);

(b) remain within (*designated territorial jurisdiction*);

(c) notify (*name of peace officer or other person designated*) of any change in my address, employment or occupation;

(d) abstain from communicating with (*name of witness or other person*) except in accordance with the following conditions: (*as the justice or judge specifies*);

(e) deposit my passport (*as the justice or judge directs*); and

(f) (*any other reasonable conditions*).

Dated this .... day of .... A.D ...., at ....

. . . .

(Signature of appellant)

Form 14 — Undertaking by Appellant (Prosecutor)
(Section 817)

Canada,

Province of ....,

(*territorial division*).

I, A.B., of ...., (*occupation*), being the appellant against an order of dismissal (*or against sentence*) in respect of the following charge (*set out the name of the defendant and the offence, subject-matter of order or question of law*) undertake to appear personally or by counsel at the sittings of the appeal court at which the appeal is to be heard.

Dated this .... day of .... A.D ...., at ....

....

(Signature of appellant)

Form 15 — Warrant to Convey Accused Before Justice Of Another Territorial Division
(Section 543)

Canada,

Province of ....,

(*territorial division*).

To the peace officers in the said (*territorial division*):

Whereas A.B., of .... hereinafter called the accused, has been charged that (*state place of offence and charge*);

And Whereas I have taken the deposition of X.Y. in respect of the said charge;

And Whereas the charge is for an offence committted in the (*territorial division*);

This is to command you, in Her Majesty's name, to convey the said A.B., before a justice of the (*last mentioned territorial division*).

Dated this .... day of .... A.D. ...., at ....

. . . .

A Justice of the Peace in and for

. . . .

Form 16 — Subpoena to a Witness
(Section 699)

Canada,

Province of ....,

(*territorial division*).

To E.F., of ...., (*occupation*);

Whereas A.B. has been charged that (*state offence as in the information*), and it has been made to appear that you are likely to give material evidence for (the prosecution *or* the defence);

This is therefore to command you to attend before (*set out court or justice*), on .... the .... day of .... A.D. ...., at.......... o'clock in the .... noon at .... to give evidence concerning the said charge.*

*Where a witness is required to produce anything, add the following:

> and to bring with you anything in your possession or under your control that relates to the said charge, and more particularly the following: (*specify any documents, objects or other things required*).

Dated this .... day of .... A.D. ...., at ....

....

A Judge, Justice *or* Clerk of the court

(*Seal if required*) ....

1999, c. 5, s. 47.

Form 16.1 — Subpoena to a witness in the case of proceedings in respect of an offence referred to in s. 278.2(1) of the Criminal Code

(Subsections 278.3(5) and 699(7))

Canada,

Province of ....,

(*territorial division*).

To E.F., of ...., (*occupation*);

Whereas A.B. has been charged that (*state offence as in the information*), and it has been made to appear that you are likely to give material evidence for (the prosecution *or* the defence);

This is therefore to command you to attend before (*set out court or justice*), on .... the .... day of .... A.D. ...., at.......... o'clock in the .... noon at .... to give evidence concerning the said charge, and to bring with you anything in your possession or under your control that relates to the said charge, and more particularly the following: (*specify any documents, objects or other things required*).

Dated this .... day of .... A.D. ...., at ....

Take Note

You are only required to bring the things specified above to the court on the date and at the time indicated, and you are not required to provide the things specified to any person or to discuss their contents with any person unless and until ordered by the court to do so.

If anything specified above is a "record" as defined in section 278.1 of the *Criminal Code*, it may be subject to a determination by the court in accordance with sections 278.1 to 278.91 of the *Criminal Code* as to whether and to what extent it should be produced.

If anything specified above is a "record" as defined in section 278.1 of the *Criminal Code*, the production of which is governed by sections 278.1 to 278.91 of the *Criminal Code*, this subpoena must be accompanied by a copy of an application for the production of the record made pursuant to section 278.3 of the *Criminal Code*, and you will have an opportunity to make submissions to the court concerning the production of the record.

If anything specified above is a "record" as defined in section 278.1 of the *Criminal Code*, the production of which is governed by sections 278.1 to 278.91 of the *Criminal Code*, you are not required to bring it with you until a determination is made in accordance with those sections as to whether and to what extent it should be produced.

As defined in section 278.1 of the *Criminal Code*, "record" means any form of record that contains personal information for which there is a reasonable expectation of privacy and includes, without limiting the generality of the foregoing, medical, psychiatric, therapeutic, counselling, education, employment, child welfare, adoption and social services records, personal journals and diaries, and records containing personal information the production or disclosure of which is protected by any other Act of Parliament or a provincial legislature, but does not include records made by persons responsible for the investigation or prosecution of the offence.

....
Judge, Clerk of the Court
Provincial Court Judge *or* **Justice**
(Seal if required)   ....

3.1 (1) Review after three years — On the expiration of three years after the coming into force of this Act, the provisions contained herein shall be referred to such committee of the House of Commons, of the Senate or of both Houses of Parliament as may be designated or established by Parliament for that purpose.

(2) Report — The committee designated or established by Parliament for the purpose of subsection (1) shall, as soon as practicable, undertake a comprehensive review of the provisions and operation of this Act and shall, within one year after the review is undertaken or within such further time as the House of Commons may authorize, submit a report to Parliament thereon including such recommendations pertaining to the continuation of those sections and changes required therein as the committee may wish to make.

1997, c. 30, s. 3.

Form 17 — Warrant for Witness
(Sections 698 and 705)

Canada,

     Province of ....,
     (territorial division).

To the peace officers in the *(territorial division)*:

Whereas A.B. of ...., has been charged that *(state offence as in the information)*;

And Whereas it has been made to appear that E.F. of .... hereinafter called the witness, is likely to give material evidence for (the prosecution *or* the defence) and that*

*Insert whichever of the following is appropriate:

(a) the said E.F. will not attend unless compelled to do so;

(b) the said E.F. is evading service of a subpoena;

(c) the said E.F. was duly served with a subpoena and has neglected (to attend at the time and place appointed therein *or* to remain in attendance);

(d) the said E.F. was bound by a recognizance to attend and give evidence and has neglected (to attend *or* to remain in attendance).

This is therefore to command you, in Her Majesty's name, to arrest and bring the witness forthwith before (*set out court or justice*) to be dealt with in accordance with section 706 of the *Criminal Code*.

Dated this .... day of .... A.D. ...., at ....

....

A Justice*or* Clerk of the Court

Form 18 — Warrant to Arrest an Absconding Witness
(Section 704)

Canada,

            Province of ....,
            (*territorial division*).

To the peace officers in the (*territorial division*):

Whereas A.B., of .... has been charged that (*state offence as in the information*);

And Whereas I am satisfied by information in writing and under oath that C.D., of ...., hereinafter called the witness, is bound by recognizance to give evidence on the trial of the accused on the said charge, and that the witness (has absconded *or* is about to abscond):

This is therefore to command you, in Her Majesty's name, to arrest the witness and bring him forthwith before (*the court, judge, justice or provincial court judge before whom the witness is bound to appear*) to be dealt with in accordance with section 706 of the *Criminal Code*.

Dated this .... day of .... A.D. ...., at ....

....

A Justice of the Peace in and for

....
....

A Justice of the Peace in and for

....

R.S. 1985, c. 27(1st Supp.), s. 184(9).

Form 19 — Warrant Remanding a Prisoner
(Sections 516 and 537)

Canada,

            Province of ....,
            (*territorial division*).

To the peace officers in the (*territorial division*):

You are hereby commanded forthwith to arrest, if necessary, and convey to the (*prison*) at .... the persons named in the following schedule each of whom has been remanded to the time mentioned in the schedule:

Person charged	Offence	Remanded to

And I hereby command you, the keeper of the said prison, to receive each of the said persons into your custody in the prison and keep him safely until the day when his remand expires and then to have him before me or any other justice at .... at .... o'clock in the .... noon of the said day, there to answer to the charge and to be dealt with according to law, unless you are otherwise ordered before that time.

Dated this .... day of .... A.D. ...., at ....

....
A Justice of the Peace in and for

....
R.S. 1985, c. 27(1st Supp.), s. 184(9).

Form 20 — Warrant of Committal of Witness for Refusing to be Sworn or to Give Evidence
(Section 545)

Canada,

Province of ....,
(*territorial division*).

To the peace officers in the (*territorial division*):

Whereas A.B. of .... , hereinafter called the accused, has been charged that (*set out offence as in the information*);

And Whereas E.F. .... , hereinafter called the witness, attending before me to give evidence for (the prosecution *or* the defence) concerning the charge against the accused (refused to be sworn *or* being duly sworn as a witness refused to answer certain questions concerning the charge that were put to him *or* refused or neglected to produce the following writings, namely .... *or* refused to sign his deposition) having been ordered to do so, without offering any just excuse for such refusal or neglect;

This is therefore to command you, in Her Majesty's name, to arrest, if necessary, and take the witness and convey him safely to the prison at.......... , and there deliver him to the keeper thereof, together with the following precept:

I do hereby command you, the said keeper, to receive the said witness into your custody in the said prison and safely keep him there for the term of .... days, unless he sooner consents to do what was required of him, and for so doing this is a sufficient warrant.

Dated this .... day of .... A.D. ...., at ....

....
A Justice of the Peace in and for

....
R.S. 1985, c. 27(1st Supp.), s. 184(19).

Form 21 — Warrant of Committal on Conviction
(Sections 570 and 806)

Canada
Province of ....,

(territorial division).

To the peace officers in the territorial division of *(name)* and to the keeper of a federal penitentiary (or provincial correctional institution for the province of ...., as the case may be)

Whereas *(name)*, hereinafter called the offender was on the.......... day of .... 19..........., convicted by (name of judge and court) of having committed the following offence(s) and it was adjudged that the offender be sentenced as follows:

Offence	*Sentence*	*Remarks*
(state offence of which offender was convicted)	*(state term of imprisonment for the offence and, in case of imprisonment for default of payment of fine, so indicate together with the amount thereof and costs applicable and whether payable forthwith or within a timed fixed)*	*(state whether the sentence is consecutive or concurrent, and specify consecutive or concurrent to/with what other sentence)*

1. ....
2. ....
3. ....
4. ....

You are hereby commanded, in Her Majesty's name, to arrest the offender if it is necessary to do so in order to take the offender into custody, and to take and convey him safely to a federal penitentiary (or provincial correctional institution for the province of ...., as the case may be) and deliver him to the keeper thereof, who is hereby commanded to receive the accused into custody and to imprison him there for the term(s) of his sentence, unless, where a term of imprisonment was imposed only in default of payment of a fine or costs, the said amounts and the costs and charges of the committal and of conveying the offender to the said prison are sooner paid, and this is a sufficient warrant for so doing.

Dated this .... day of .... A.D. ...., at ....

....

Clerk of the Court,
Justice, Judge or
Provincial Court Judge
R.S. 1985, c. 27(1st Supp.), s. 184(10);
1995, c. 22, s. 9.

Form 22 — Warrant of Committal on an Order For the Payment of Money
(Section 806)

Canada,

        Province of ....,
        (territorial division).

To the peace officers in the (*territorial division*) and to the keeper of the (*prison*) at
..........:

Whereas A.B., hereinafter called the defendant, was tried on an information alleging that (*set out matter of complaint*), and it was ordered that (*set out the order made*), and in default that the defendant be imprisoned in the (*prison*) at .... for a term of.......... ;

I hereby command you, in Her Majesty's name, to arrest, if necessary, and take the defendant and convey him safely to the (*prison*) at ...., and deliver him to the keeper thereof, together with the following precept:

I hereby command you, the keeper of the said prison, to receive the defendant into your custody in the said prison and imprison him there for the term of ...., unless the said amounts and the costs and charges of the committal and of conveying the defendant to the said prison are sooner paid, and for so doing this is a sufficient warrant.

Dated this .... day of .... A.D. ...., at ....

....

A Justice of the Peace in and for

....

R.S. 1985, c. 27(1st Supp.), s. 184(19).

Form 23 — Warrant of Committal for Failure to Furnish Recognizance to Keep the Peace
(Sections 810 and 810.1)

Canada,

Province of ....,

(*territorial division*).

To the peace officers in the (*territorial division*) and to the keeper of the (*prison*) at
..........:

Whereas A.B., hereinafter called the accused, has been ordered to enter into a recognizance to keep the peace and be of good behaviour, and has (refused *or* failed) to enter into a recognizance accordingly;

You are hereby commanded, in Her Majesty's name, to arrest, if necessary, and take the accused and convey him safely to the (*prison*) at.......... and deliver him to the keeper thereof, together with the following precept:

You, the said keeper, are hereby commanded to receive the accused into your custody in the said prison and imprison him there until he enters into a recognizance as aforesaid or until he is discharged in due course of law.

Dated this .... day of .... A.D. ...., at ....

....

Clerk of the Court, Justice
or Provincial Court Judge

R.S. 1985, c. 27(1st Supp.), ss. 184(19), 206; 1993, c. 45, s. 12.

(*Seal, if required*)

Form 24 — Warrant of Committal of Witness for Failure to Enter into Recognizance
(Section 550)

Canada,

        Province of ....,
        (*territorial division*).

To the peace officers in the (*territorial division*) and to the keeper of the (*prison*) at ....:

Whereas A.B., hereinafter called the accused, was committed for trial on a charge that (*state offence as in the information*);

And Whereas E.F., hereinafter called the witness, having appeared as a witness on the preliminary inquiry into the said charge, and being required to enter into a recognizance to appear as a witness on the trial of the accused on the said charge, has (failed *or* refused) to do so;

This is therefore to command you, in Her Majesty's name, to arrest, if necessary, and take and safely convey the said witness to the (*prison*) at .... and there deliver him to the keeper thereof, together with the following precept:

I do hereby command you, the said keeper, to receive the witness into your custody in the said prison and keep him there safely until the trial of the accused on the said charge, unless before that time the witness enters into the said recognizance.

Dated this .... day of .... A.D. ...., at ....

      . . . .
      A Justice of the Peace in and for
      . . . .
      R.S. 1985, c. 27(1st Supp.), s. 184(19).

Form 25 — Warrant of Committal for Contempt
(Section 708)

Canada,

        Province of ....,
        (*territorial division*).

To the peace officers in the said (*territorial division*) and to the keeper of the (*prison*) at ....:

Whereas E.F. of ...., hereinafter called the defaulter, was on the......... day of .... A.D. ...., at ...., convicted before......... for contempt in that he did not attend before .... to give evidence on the trial of a charge that (*state offence as in the information*) against A.B. of ...., although (duly subpoenaed *or* bound by recognizance to appear and give evidence in that behalf, *as the case may be*) and did not show any sufficient excuse for his default;

And Whereas in and by the said conviction it was adjudged that the defaulter (*set out punishment adjudged*);

And Whereas the defaulter has not paid the amounts adjudged to be paid; (*delete if not applicable*)

This is therefore to command you, in Her Majesty's name, to arrest, if necessary, and take the defaulter and convey him safely to the prison at.......... and there deliver him to the keeper thereof, together with the following precept:

I do hereby command you, the said keeper, to receive the defaulter into your custody in the said prison and imprison him there* and for so doing this is a sufficient warrant.

*Insert whichever of the following is applicable:

    (a) for the term of ....;

    (b) for the term of .... unless the said sums and the costs and charges of the committal and of conveying the defaulter to the said prison are sooner paid; or

    (c) for the term of .... and for the term of (if consecutive so state) unless the said sums and costs and charges of the committal and of conveying the defaulter to the said prison are sooner paid.

Dated this .... day of .... A.D. ...., at ....

       . . . .

       A Justice or Clerk of
       the Court

(Seal, if required)

Form 26 — Warrant of Committal in Default of Payment of Costs of an Appeal
(Section 827)

Canada,

       Province of ....,
       (territorial division).

To the peace officers of (territorial division) and to the keeper of the (prison) at ....:

Whereas it appears that on the hearing of an appeal before the (set out court), it was adjudged that A.B., of ...., hereinafter called the defaulter, should pay to the Clerk of the Court the sum of .... dollars in respect of costs;

And Whereas the Clerk of the Court has certified that the defaulter has not paid the sum within the time limited therefor;

I do hereby command you, the said peace officers, in Her Majesty's name, to take the defaulter and safely convey him to the (prison) at.......... and deliver him to the keeper thereof, together with the following precept:

I do hereby command you, the said keeper, to receive the defaulter into your custody in the said prison and imprison him for the term of ...., unless the said sum and the costs and charges of the committal and of conveying the defaulter to the said prison are sooner paid, and for so doing this is a sufficient warrant.

Dated this .... day of .... A.D. ...., at ....

       . . . .

       A Justice of the Peace in and for

       . . . .

Form 27 — Warrant of Committal on Forfeiture of a Recognizance

(Section 773)

Canada,

Province of ....,

(*territorial division*).

To the sheriff of (*territorial division*) and to the keeper of the (*prison*) at ....:

You are hereby commanded to arrest, if necessary, and take (A.B. and C.D. *as the case may be*) hereinafter called the defaulters, and to convey them safely to the (*prison*) at .... and deliver them to the keeper thereof, together with the following precept:

You, the said keeper, are hereby commanded to receive the defaulters into your custody in the said prison and imprison them for a period of .... or until satisfaction is made of a judgment debt of .... dollars due to Her Majesty the Queen in respect of the forfeiture of a recognizance entered into by .... on the .... day of .... A.D. ....

Dated this .... day of .... A.D. ...., at ....

. . . .

A Justice of the Peace in and for

. . . .

A Justice of the Peace in and for

. . . .

Form 28 — Endorsement of Warrant

(Sections 487 and 528)

Canada,

Province of ....,

(*territorial division*).

Pursuant to application this day made to me, I hereby authorize the arrest of the accused (*or* defendant) (*or* execution of this warrant, in the case of a warrant issued pursuant to section 487), within the said (*territorial division*).

Dated this .... day of .... A.D. ...., at ....

. . . .

A Justice of the Peace in and for

. . . .

R.S. 1985, c. 27(1st Supp.), s. 184(12).

Form 29 — Endorsement of Warrant
(Section 507)

Canada,

        Province of ....,
        (*territorial division*).

Whereas this warrant is issued under section 507, 508 or 512 of the *Criminal Code* in respect of an offence other than an offence mentioned in section 522 of the *Criminal Code*, I hereby authorize the release of the accused pursuant to section 499 of that Act.

Dated this .... day of .... A.D. ...., at ....

               ....

               A Justice of the Peace in and for

               ....

Form 30 — Order for Accused to be Brought Before Justice Prior to Expiration of Period of Remand
(Section 537)

Canada,

        Province of ....,
        (*territorial division*).

To the keeper of the (*prison*) at ....:

Whereas by warrant dated the .... day of .... A.D. ...., I committed A.B., hereinafter called the accused, to your custody and required you safely to keep [him] until the .... day of .... A.D. ...., and then to have him before me or any other justice at .... at .... o'clock in the .... noon to answer to the charge against him and to be dealt with according to law unless you should be ordered otherwise before that time;

Now, therefore, I order and direct you to have the accused before.......... at .... at .... o'clock in the .... noon to answer to the charge against him and to be dealt with according to law.

Dated this .... day of .... A.D. ...., at ....

               ....

               A Justice of the Peace in and for

               ....

Form 31 — Deposition of a Witness
(Section 540)

Canada,

        Province of ....,
        (*territorial division*).

These are the depositions of X.Y., of ...., and M.N., of ...., taken before me, this .... day of .... A.D., ... at.........., in the presence and hearing of A.B., hereinafter called the accused, who stands charged (*state offence as in the information*).

X.Y., having been duly sworn, deposes as follows: (*insert deposition as nearly as possible in words of witness*).

M.N., having been duly sworn, deposes as follows:

I certify that the depositions of X.Y., and M.N., written on the several sheets of paper hereto annexed to which my signature is affixed, were taken in the presence and hearing of the accused (and signed by them respectively, in is presence, *where they are required to be signed by witness*). In witness whereof I have hereto signed my name.

. . . .

A Justice of the Peace in and for

. . . .

Form 32 — Recognizance
(Sections 493, 550, 679, 706, 707, 810, 810.1 and 817)

Canada,

Province of ....,

(*territorial division*).

Be it remembered that on this day the persons named in the following schedule personally came before me and severally acknowledged themselves to owe to Her Majesty the Queen the several amounts set opposite their respective names, namely,

Name	Address	Occupation	Amount
A.B.			
C.D.			
E.F.			

to be made and levied of their several goods and chattels, lands and tenements, respectively, to the use of Her Majesty the Queen, if the said A.B. fails in any of the conditions hereunder written.

Taken and acknowledged before me on the .... day of .... A.D............ , at ....

. . . .

Judge, Clerk of the Court,

Provincial Court Judge *or* Justice

1. Whereas the said ...., hereinafter called the accused, has been charged that (*set out the offence in respect of which the accused has been charged*);

Now, therefore, the condition of this recognizance is that if the accused attends court on .... day, the .... day of .... A.D............ , at .... o'clock in the .... noon and attends thereafter as required by the court in order to be dealt with according to law (*or, where date and place of appearance before court are not known at the time recognizance is entered into if the accused attends at the time and place fixed by the court and attends thereafter as required by the court in order to be dealt with according to law*) [515, 520, 521, 522, 523, 524, 525, 680];

And further, if the accused (*insert in Schedule of Conditions any additional conditions that are directed*), the said recognizance is void, otherwise it stands in full force and effect.

2. Whereas the said ...., hereinafter called the appellant, is an appellant against his conviction (*or against his sentence*) in respect of the following charge (*set out the offence for which the appellant was convicted*) [679, 680];

Now, therefore, the condition of this recognizance is that if the appellant attends as required by the court in order to be dealt with according to law;

And further, if the appellant (*insert in Schedule of Conditions any additional conditions that are directed*), the said recognizance is void, otherwise it stands in full force and effect.

3. Whereas the said ...., hereinafter called the appellant, is an appellant against his conviction (*or against his sentence or against an order or by way of stated case*) in respect of the following matter (*set out offence, subject-matter of order or question of law*) [816, 831, 832, 834];

Now, therefore, the condition of this recognizance is that if the appellant appears personally at the sittings of the appeal court at which the appeal is to be heard;

And further, if the appellant (*insert in Schedule of Conditions any additional conditions that are directed*), the said recognizance is void, otherwise it stands in full force and effect.

4. Whereas the said ...., hereinafter called the appellant, is an appellant against an order of dismissal (*or against sentence*) in respect of the following charge (*set out the name of the accused and the offence, subject-matter of order or question of law*) [817, 831, 832, 834];

Now, therefore, the condition of this recognizance is that if the appellant appears personally or by counsel at the sittings of the appeal court at which the appeal is to be heard the said recognizance is void, otherwise it stands in full force and effect.

5. Whereas the said ...., hereinafter called the accused, was ordered to stand trial on a charge that (*set out the offence in respect of which the accused has been charged*);

And whereas A.B. appeared as a witness on the preliminary inquiry into the said charge [550, 706, 707];

Now, therefore, the condition of this recognizance is that if the said A.B. appears at the time and place fixed for the trial of the accused to give evidence on the indictment that is found against the accused, the said recognizance is void, otherwise it stands in full force and effect.

6. The condition of the above written recognizance is that if A.B. keeps the peace and is of good behaviour for the term of .... commencing on.........., the said recognizance is void, otherwise it stands in full force and effect [810 and 810.1].

7. Whereas a warrant was issued under section 462.32 or a restraint order was made under subsection 462.33(3) of the *Criminal Code* in relation to any property (*set out a description of the property and its location*);

Now, therefore, the condition of this recognizance is that A.B. shall not do or cause anything to be done that would result, directly or indirectly, in the disappearance, dissipaton or reduction in value of the property or otherwise affect the property so that all or a part thereof could not be subject to an order of forfeiture under section 462.37 or 462.38 of the *Criminal Code* or any other provision of the *Criminal Code* or any other Act of Parliament [462.34].

Schedule of Conditions

(a) reports at (*state times*) to (*name of peace officer or other person designated*),

(b) remains within (*designated territorial jurisdiction*),

(c) notifies (*name of peace officer or other person designated*) of any change in his address, employment or occupation,

(d) abstains from communicating with (*name of witness of other person*) except in accordance with the following conditions: (*as the justice or judge specifies*),

(e) deposits his passport (*as the justice or judge directs*), and

(f) (*any other reasonable conditions*).

Note: Section 763 and subsections 764(1) to (3) of the Criminal Code state as follows:

763. Where a person is bound by recognizance to appear before a court, justice or provincial court judge for any purpose and the session or sittings of that court or the proceedings are adjourned or an order is made changing the place of trial, that person and his sureties continue to be bound by the recognizance in like manner as if it had been entered into with relation to the resumed proceedings or the trial at the time and place at which the proceedings are ordered to be resumed or the trial is ordered to be held.

764. (1) Where an accused is bound by recognizance to appear for trial, his arraignment or conviction does not discharge the recognizance, but it continues to bind him and his sureties, if any, for his appearance until he is discharged or sentenced, as the case may be.

(2) Notwithstanding subsection (1), the court, justice or provincial court judge may commit an accused to prison or may require him to furnish new or additional sureties for his appearance until he is discharged or sentenced, as the case may be.

(3) The sureties of an accused who is bound by recognizance to appear for trial are discharged if he is committed to prison pursuant to subsection (2).

Form 33 — Certificate of Default to be Endorsed on Recognizance
(Section 770)

I hereby certify that A.B. (has not appeared as required by this recognizance *or* has not complied with a condition of this recognizance) and that by reason thereof the ends of justice have been (defeated *or* delayed, *as the case may be*).

The nature of the default is .... and the reason for the default is..........
(*state reason if known*).

The names and addresses of the principal and sureties are as follows:

Dated this .... day of .... A.D. ...., at ....

....

Clerk of the Court, Judge,
Justice *or* Provincial Court Judge

(*Seal, if required*)

Form 34 — Writ of Fieri Facias
(Section 771)

Elizabeth II by the Grace of God, etc.

To the sheriff of (*territorial division*), *Greeting*.

You are hereby commanded to levy of the goods and chattels, lands and tenements of each of the following persons the amount set opposite the name of each:

Name   Address   Occupation   Amount

And you are further commanded to make a return of what you have done in execution of this writ.

Dated this .... day of .... A.D. ...., at ....

....

Clerk of the ....

(Seal)

Form 35 — Conviction
(Sections 570 and 806)

Canada,

Province of ....,

(territorial division).

Be it remembered that on the .... **day of** .... **at** ...., **A.B.,** *(date of birth)* **hereinafter called the accused, was tried under Part (XIX** *or* **XXVII) of the** *Criminal Code* **on the charge that** *(state fully the offence of which accused was convicted)*, **was convicted of the said offence and the following punishment was imposed on him, namely,**[*]

[*]*Use whichever of the following forms of sentence is applicable*:

(a) That the said accused be imprisoned in the *(prison)* at .... for the term of ....;

(b) That the said accused forfeit and pay the sum of .... dollars to be applied according to law and also pay to .... the sum of.......... dollars in respect of costs and in default of payment of the said sums (forthwith *or within a time fixed, if any*) to be imprisoned in the *(prison)* at .... for the term of .... unless the said sums and costs and charges of the committal and of conveying the accused to the said prison are sooner paid;

(c) That the said accused be imprisoned in the *(prison)* at.......... for the term of .... and in addition forfeit and pay the sum of .... dollars to be applied according to law and also pay to .... the sum of .... dollars in respect of costs and in default of payment of the said sums (forthwith *or within a time fixed, if any*), to be imprisoned in the *(prison)* at .... for the term of .... *(if sentence to be consecutive, state accordingly)* unless the said sums and costs and charges of the committal and of conveying the accused to the said prison are sooner paid.

Dated this .... day of .... A.D. ...., at ....

....

Clerk of the Court, Justice
or Provincial Court Judge

(Seal, if required)

Form 36 — Order Against an Offender
(Sections 570 and 806)

Canada,

Province of ....,

(territorial division).

Be it remembered that on the .... **day of** .... **A.D.** ...., **at** ...., **A.B.,** *(date of birth)* **of** ...., **was tried on an information** *(indictment)* **alleging that** *(set out matter of complaint or alleged offence)*, **and it was ordered and adjudged that** *(set out the order made)*.

Dated this .... day of .... A.D. ...., at ....

. . . .

Justice *or* **Clerk**
of the Court
R.S. 1985, c. 27 (1st Supp.), s. 184(15).

Form 37 — Order Acquitting Accused
(Section 570)

Canada,

         Province of ....,
         (territorial division).

Be it remembered that on the .... day of .... A.D. ...., at ...., A.B., of ...., *(occupation), (date of birth)* **was tried on the charge that** *(state fully the offence of which the accused was acquitted)* **and was found not guilty of the said offence.**

Dated this .... day of .... A.D. ...., at ....

. . . .

         Provincial Court Judge *or* **Clerk of the Court**

(Seal, if required)

         R.S. 1985, c. 27(1st Supp.), ss.184(16), 203, 206.

Form 38 — Conviction for Contempt
(Section 708)

Canada,

         Province of ....,
         (territorial division).

Be it remembered that on the .... day of .... A.D. ...., at .... in the *(territorial division),* **E.F. of ...., hereinafter called the defaulter, is convicted by me for contempt in that he did not attend before** *(set out court or justice) to give evidence on the trial of a charge that (state fully offence with which accused was charged),* **although (duly subpoenaed** *or* **bound by recognizance to attend to give evidence,** *as the case may be)* **and has not shown before me any sufficient excuse for his default;**

Wherefore I adjudge the defaulter for his said default, *(set out punishment as authorized and determined in accordance with section 708 of the Criminal Code).*

Dated this .... day of .... A.D. ...., at ....

. . . .

         A Justice *or* **Clerk of the**
         Court

(Seal, if required)

Form 39 — Order for Discharge of a Person in Custody
(Sections 519 and 550)

Canada,

> Province of ....,
> (*territorial division*).

To the keeper of the (*prison*) at ....:

I hereby direct you to release E.F., detained by you under a (warrant of committal *or* order) dated the .... day of .... A.D........... , if the said E.F. is detained by you for no other cause.

> ....
> A Judge, Justice *or* Clerk
> of the Court

(*Seal, if required*)

Form 40 — Challenge to Array
(Section 629)

Canada,

> Province of ....
> (*territorial division*).

The Queen —

v. —

C.D.

The (prosecutor *or* accused) challenges the array of the panel on the ground that X.Y., (sheriff *or* deputy sheriff), who returned the panel, was guilty of (partiality *or* fraud *or* wilful misconduct) on returning it.

Dated this .... day of .... A.D. ...., at ....

> ....
> Counsel for (prosecutor
> *or*accused)

Form 41 — Challenge for Cause
(Section 639)

Canada,

> Province of ....
> (*territorial division*).

> ....
> Counsel for (prosecutor
> *or* accused)

The Queen —

v. —

1251

Form 41   Criminal Code, Part XXVIII

C.D.

The (prosecutor *or* accused) challenges G.H. on the ground that (*set out ground of challenge in accordance with s. 638(1) of the Criminal Code*).

....

Counsel for (prosecutor *or* accused)

Form 42 — Certificate of Non-Payment of Costs of Appeal
(Section 827)

In the Court of ....

(*Style of Cause*)

I hereby certify that A.B. (the appellant *or* respondent, *as the case may be*) in this appeal, having been ordered to pay costs in the sum of .... dollars, has failed to pay the said costs within the time limited for the payment thereof.

Dated this .... day of .... A.D. ...., at ....

....

....

Clerk of the Court of

....

(*Seal*)

Form 43 — Jailer's Receipt to Peace Officer for Prisoner
(Section 734)

I hereby certify that I have received from X.Y., a peace officer for (*territorial division*), one A.B., together with a (warrant *or* order) issued by (*set out court or justice, as the case may be*).*

*Add a statement of the condition of the prisoner

Dated this .... day of .... A.D. ...., at ....

....

Keeper of (*prison*)

Form 44 — Fingerprint Examiner's Certificate
(Section 667)

I, (*name*), a fingerprint examiner designated as such for the purposes of section 667 of the *Criminal Code* by the Solicitor General of Canada, do hereby certify that (*name*) also known as (*aliases if any*), FPS Number ...., whose fingerprints are shown reproduced below (*reproduction of fingerprints*) or attached hereto, has been convicted, discharged under section 736 of the *Criminal Code* or convicted and sentenced in Canada as follows:

(*record*)

Dated this .... day of .... A.D. ...., at ....

....

Fingerprint Examiner

R.S. 1985, c. 27(1st Supp.), s. 184(17).

Form 45 — Fingerprint Examiner's Certificate
(Section 667)

I, (*name*), a fingerprint examiner designated as such for the purposes of section 667 of the *Criminal Code* by the Solicitor General of Canada, do hereby certify that I have compared the fingerprints reproduced in or attached to exhibit A with the fingerprints reproduced in or attached to the certificate in Form 44 attached marked exhibit B and that they are those of the same person.

Dated this .... day of .... A.D. ...., at ....

....

Fingerprint Examiner

R.S. 1985, c. 27(1st Supp.), s. 184(18).

Form 46 — Probation Order
(Section 732.1)

Canada,

     Province of ....

     (*territorial division*).

Whereas on the .... day of .... at ...., A.B., hereinafter called the accused, (pleaded guilty to or was tried under (*here insert Part XIX, XX or XXVII, as the case may be*) of the *Criminal Code* and was (*here insert convicted or found guilty, as the case may be*) on the charge that (*here state the offence to which the accused pleaded guilty or for which the accused was convicted or found guilty, as the case may be*));

And whereas on the .... day of .... the court adjudged*

Use whichever of the following forms of disposition is applicable:

     (a) that the accused be discharged on the conditions hereinafter prescribed:

     (b) that the passing of sentence on the accused be suspended and that the said the accused be released on the conditions hereinafter prescribed:

     (c) that the accused forfeit and pay the sum of .... dollars to be applied according to law and in default of payment of the said sum forthwith (*or within a time fixed, if any*), be imprisoned in the (*prison*) at .... for the term of .... unless the said sum and charges of the committal and of conveying the said accused to the said prison are sooner paid, and in addition thereto, that the said accused comply with the conditions hereinafter prescribed:

     (d) that the accused be imprisoned in the (*prison*) at .... for the term of .... and, in addition thereto, that the said accused comply with the conditions hereinafter prescribed:

Now therefore the said accused shall, for the period of .... from the date of this order (*or, where paragraph (d) is applicable* the date of expiration of his sentence of imprisonment) comply with the following conditions, namely, that the said accused shall keep the peace and be of good behaviour and appear before the court when required to do so by the court, and, in addition,

Form 46   Criminal Code, Part XXVIII

(here state any additional conditions prescribed pursuant to subsection 732.1(3) of the Criminal Code).

Dated this .... day of .... A.D. ...., at ....

. . . .

Clerk of the Court, Justice
or Provincial Court Judge
R.S. 1985, c. 27(1st Supp.), s. 206; 1995, c. 22, s. 10 (Sch. I, item 35).

Form 47 — Order To Disclose Income Tax Information
(Section 462.48)

Canada,

Province of . . .
. . . . ,

(territorial division).

To A.B., of ...., *(office or occupation)*:

Whereas, it appears on the oath of C.D., of ...., that there are reasonable grounds for believing that E.F., of ...., has committed or benefited from the commission of the offence of .... and that the information or documents *(describe information or documents)* are likely to be of substantial value to an investigation of that offence or a related matter; and

Whereas there are reasonable grounds for believing that it is in the public interest to allow access to the information or documents, having regard to the benefit likely to accrue to the investigation if the access is obtained;

This is, therefore, to authorize and require you between the hours of *(as the judge may direct)*, during the period commencing on .... and ending on ...., to produce all the above-mentioned information and documents to one of the following police officers, namely, *(here name police officers)* and allow the police officer to remove the information or documents, *or* to allow the police officer access to the above-mentioned information and documents and to examine them, *as the judge directs*, subject to the following conditions *(state conditions)*: ....

Dated this .... day of .... A.D. ...., at ....

. . . .

Signature of
Judge
R.S. 1985, c. 42(4th Supp.), s. 8.

Form 48 — Assessment Order
(Section 672.13)

Canada,
Province of
(territorial division)

Whereas, I have reasonable grounds to believe that evidence of the mental condition of *(name of accused*, who has been charged with .... may be necessary to determine*

1254

❏ whether the accused is unfit to stand trial

❏ whether the accused suffered from a mental disorder so as to exempt the accused from criminal responsibility by virtue of subsection 16(1) of the *Criminal Code* at the time of the act or omission charged against the accused

❏ whether the accused is a dangerous mentally disordered accused under section 672.65 of the *Criminal Code*

❏ whether the balance of the mind of the accused was disturbed at the time of commission of the alleged offence, where the accused is a female person charged with an offence arising out of the death of her newly-born child

❏ where a verdict of unfit to stand trial or a verdict of not criminally responsible on account of mental disorder has been rendered in respect of the accused, the appropriate disposition to be made in respect of the accused pursuant to section 672.54 or 672.58 of the *Criminal Code*

❏ where the accused has been convicted of the offence, whether an order under subsection 747.1(1) of the *Criminal Code* should be made in respect of the accused

I hereby order an assessment of the mental condition of (*name of accused*) to be conducted by/at (*name of person or service by whom or place where assessment is to be made*) for a period of ....days

This order is to be in force for a total of .... days, including travelling time, during which time the accused is to remain*

❏ in custody at (*place where accused is to be detained*)

❏ out of custody, on the following conditions:
  set out conditions, where applicable)

*Check applicable option.

Dated this .... day of .... A.D. ...., at ....

....
(Signature of justice or judge or clerk of the court, as the case may be)
1995, c. 22, s. 10 (Sch. I, item 36).

Form 49 — Warrant of Committal Disposition of Detention
(Section 672.57)

Canada,
Province of
(*territorial division*)

To the peace officers, in the said (*territorial division*) and to the keeper (*administrator, warden*) of the (*prison, hospital or other appropriate place where the accused is detained*).

This warrant is issued for the committal of A.B., of .... (*occupation*), hereinafter called the accused.

Whereas the accused has been charged that (*set out briefly the offence in respect of which the accused was charged*);

And whereas the accused was found*

❏ unfit to stand trial

❏   not criminally responsible on account of mental disorder

This is, therefore, to command you, in Her Majesty's name, to take the accused in custody and convey the accused safely to the (*prison, hospital or other appropriate place*) at .... and there deliver the accused to the keeper (*administrator, warden*) with the following precept:

I do therefore command you the said keeper (*administrator, warden*) to receive the accused in your custody in the said (*prison, hospital or other appropriate place*) and to keep the accused safely there until the accused is delivered by due course of law.

The following are the conditions to which the accused shall be subject while in your (*prison, hospital or other appropriate place*):

The following are the powers regarding the restrictions (*and the limits and conditions on these restrictions*) on the liberty of the accused that are hereby delegated to you the said keeper (*administrator, warden*) of the said (*prison, hospital or other appropriate place*):

*Check applicable option.

Dated this .... day of .... A.D. ...., at ....

....
(Signature of judge, clerk of the court, provincial court judge or chairperson of the Review Board)

Form 50 — Warrant of Committal Placement Decision
(Section 672.7(2))

Canada,
Province of
(*territorial division*)

To the peace officers, in the said (*territorial division*) and to the keeper (*administrator, warden*) of the (*prison, hospital or other appropriate place where the accused is detained*).

This warrant is issues for the committal of A.B., of .... (*occupation*), hereinafter called the accused.

Whereas the accused has been charged that (*set out briefly the offence in respect of which the accused was charged*);

And whereas the accused was found*

❏   unfit to stand trial

❏   not criminally responsible on account of mental disorder

And whereas the Review Board has held a hearing and decided that the accused shall be detained in custody;

And whereas the accused is required to be detained in custody pursuant to a warrant of committal issued by (*set out the name of the Judge, Clerk of the Court, Provincial Court Judge or Justice as well as the name of the court and territorial division*), dated the .... day of .... in respect of the offence that (*set out briefly the offence in respect of which the accused was charged or convicted*);

This is, therefore to command you, in Her Majesty's name, to*

❏   execute the warrant of committal issued by the court, according to its terms

❏   execute the warrant of committal issued herewith by the Review Board

*Check the applicable option.

Dated this .... day of .... A.D. ...., at ....

....
(Signature of chairperson of the Review Board)

Form 51

Form 51 — Hospital Order

(Section 747.1(3))

Canada,

Province of

(territorial division)

Whereas *(name of offender)*, who has been convicted of *(offence)* and sentenced to a term of imprisonment of *(length of term of imprisonment)*, is suffering from a mental disorder in an acute phase and immediate treatment of the mental disorder is urgently required to prevent significant deterioration of the mental or physical health of the offender or to prevent the offender from causing serious bodily harm to any person;

And whereas *(name of offender)* and *(name of treatment facility)* have consented to this order and its terms and conditions;

I hereby order that *(name of offender)* be detained for treatment at *(name of treatment facility)* for a period not to exceed *(length of period not to exceed sixty days)* subject to the following terms and conditions:

(set out terms and conditions, where applicable)

Dated this .... day of .... A.D. ...., at ....

....
(Signature of justice or judge or clerk of the court, as the case may be)
1995, c. 22, s. 10 (Sch. I, item 37).

CANADA EVIDENCE ACT

An Act respecting Witnesses and Evidence

R.S.C. 1985, c. C-5, as am. R.S.C. 1985, c. 19 (3d Supp.), ss. 17, 18; 1992, c. 1, s. 142 (Sched. V, items 9(1) and 9(2)); 1992, c. 47, s. 66; 1993, c. 28, s. 78 (Sched. III, item 8); 1993, c. 34, s. 15; 1994, c. 44, ss. 85–93; 1995, c. 28, s. 47; 1997, c. 18, ss. 116-118; 1998, c. 9, s. 1 [Sections 37 and 38 reproduced.].

See Table of Amendments for coming into force.

Short Title

1. Short title — This Act may be cited as the *Canada Evidence Act.*

R.S., c. E-10, s. 1.

PART I — APPLICATION

2. Application — This Part applies to all criminal proceedings and to all civil proceedings and other matters whatever respecting which Parliament has jurisdiction.

R.S., c. E-10, s. 2.

Witnesses

3. Interest or crime — A person is not incompetent to give evidence by reason of interest or crime.

R.S., c. E-10, s. 3.

4. (1) Accused and spouse — Every person charged with an offence, and, except as otherwise provided in this section, the wife or husband, as the case may be, of the person so charged, is a competent witness for the defence whether the person so charged is charged solely or jointly with any other person.

(2) Idem — The wife or husband of a person charged with an offence against subsection 50(1) of the *Young Offenders Act* or with an offence against any of sections 151, 152, 153, 155 or 159, subsection 160(2) or (3), or sections 170 to 173, 179, 212, 215, 218, 271 to 273, 280 to 283, 291 to 294 or 329 of the *Criminal Code*, or an attempt to commit any such offence, is a competent and compellable witness for the prosecution without the consent of the person charged.

(3) Communications during marriage — No husband is compellable to disclose any communication made to him by his wife during their marriage, and no wife is compellable to disclose any communication made to her by her husband during their marriage.

(4) Offences against young persons — The wife or husband of a person charged with an offence against any of sections 220, 221, 235, 236, 237, 239, 240, 266, 267, 268 or 269 of the *Criminal Code* where the complainant or victim is under the age of fourteen years is a competent and compellable witness for the prosecution without the consent of the person charged.

(5) Saving — Nothing in this section affects a case where the wife or husband of a person charged with an offence may at common law be called as a witness without the consent of that person.

(6) Failure to testify — The failure of the person charged, or of the wife or husband of such person, to testify shall not be made the subject of comment by the judge or by counsel for the prosecution.

R.S., c. E-10, s. 4; 1980–81–82–83, c. 110, s. 71; c. 125, s. 29; 1984, c. 40, s. 27; R.S. 1985, c. 19 (3d Supp.), s. 17.

Case Law

"Person Charged" [See also Charter ss. 11(c) and 13]

R. v. Hawkins (1996), 2 C.R. (5th) 245, 111 C.C.C. (3d) 129 (S.C.C.) — The *common law rule* that D's *spouse* is an *incompetent* witness in proceedings where D is charged, except where the charge involves the person, liberty or health of the witness spouse, has been *modified* by

i.   C.E.A. s. 4(1), which renders the spouse *competent* to testify on behalf of D spouse; and

ii.   C.E.A. s. 4(2), which renders the spouse *competent* and *compellable* for P in respect of certain offences which tend generally to implicate the health and security of the witness spouse.

R. v. Jobin, [1995] 2 S.C.R. 78, 38 C.R. (4th) 176, 97 C.C.C. (3d) 97 (S.C.C.) — Persons who are separately charged accused, suspects or unindicted co-conspirators are compellable witnesses for P at another separately charged accused's preliminary inquiry. The focus of *Charter* protection is on the purpose/character of the proceedings. Absent evidence to suggest that the *subpoenae* issued could be regarded as a form of pre-trial interrogation or were otherwise objectionable, there was no *Charter* infringement

R. v. Primeau (1995), 38 C.R. (4th) 189, 97 C.C.C. (3d) 1 (S.C.C.) — Even if a person is separately charged as an accused, a witness appearing at another person's criminal trial will ordinarily be compellable there unless it is established that the predominant purpose in compelling the testimony is incrimination of the witness. A similar test is followed when the evidence is sought at a preliminary inquiry.

R. v. Amway Corp. (1989), 68 C.R. (3d) 97 (S.C.C.) — A corporation may be a person charged with an offence, but cannot be a witness. It therefore cannot come within *Charter* s. 11(c) and its officers can be compelled to testify.

R. v. N.M. Paterson & Sons Ltd. (1980), 19 C.R. (3d) 164, 55 C.C.C. (2d) 289 (S.C.C.) — An officer or employee who is the directing mind of an accused corporation is compellable as a witness on behalf of the prosecution.

Crooks v. R. (1982), 2 C.C.C. (3d) 57 (Ont. H.C.); affirmed (1982), 2 C.C.C. (3d) 64 (Ont. C.A.) — Where co-accused are charged separately, they are competent and compellable witnesses at one another's preliminary hearing and trial.

"Husband" or "Wife"

R. v. Salituro (1991), 68 C.C.C. (3d) 289 (S.C.C.); affirming (1990), 78 C.R. (3d) 68, 56 C.C.C. (2d) 350 (Ont. C.A.) — Irreconcilably separated spouses are *competent* to testify against each other in criminal proceedings.

R. v. Jeffrey (1993), 25 C.R. (4th) 104, 84 C.C.C. (3d) 31 (Alta. C.A.) — Proof of irreconcilable separation is to be made on a balance of probabilities.

R. v. Lonsdale (1973), 24 C.R.N.S. 225, 15 C.C.C. (2d) 201 (Alta. C.A.) — A person is D's husband or wife for the purposes of s. 4 even though the marriage took place after the incident giving rise to the charge but before the trial was held.

R. v. Jackson (1981), 23 C.R. (3d) 4, 61 C.C.C. (2d) 540 (N.S. C.A.) — Section 4 does *not* render a common law spouse incompetent to testify for P.

R. v. Marchand (1980), 55 C.C.C. (2d) 77 (N.S. C.A.) — *See also: R. v. Bailey* (1983), 32 C.R. (3d) 337, 4 C.C.C. (3d) 21 (N.S. C.A.) — Divorced spouses do *not* come within the terms "husband" or "wife".

R. v. Clark (1983), 35 C.R. (3d) 357, 7 C.C.C. (3d) 46 (Ont. C.A.); leave to appeal refused (1983), 7 C.C.C. (3d) 46n (S.C.C.) — An objection to the competency of a witness to testify must be taken at the first reasonable opportunity and where no objection was taken at trial, there was no need for the court on appeal to decide whether the trial judge should have inquired into the validity of annulment proceedings.

Ex parte Cote (1971), 5 C.C.C. (2d) 49 (Sask. C.A.) — Unless the provisions of the provincial *Marriage Act* or the requirements for a valid marriage at common law have been satisfied, a person does not have the status of husband or wife.

Communication Privilege: S. 4(3)

R. v. Zylstra (1995), 41 C.R. (4th) 130, 99 C.C.C. (3d) 477 (Ont. C.A.) — Where s. 4(3) CEA *privilege* is asserted it must be done in the *presence of the jury*. A special instruction is required. It is *not* barred by s. 4(6) which does *not* apply to a spouse who has testified. At a minimum the jury should be instructed

i.   that the *privilege* of s. 4(3) is a *statutory* one which all legally married witnesses are entitled to assert at trial; and

ii.   that the privilege, as well the decision whether to assert/waive it, *rests with the witness, not* D.

R. v. Zylstra (1995), 41 C.R. (4th) 130, 99 C.C.C. (3d) 477 (Ont. C.A.) — Section 4(3) is unambiguous. It provides that, where a wife/husband is otherwise compellable/competent to give evidence, there is *no* compulsion to divulge communications with a spouse.

Lloyd v. R. (1981), 31 C.R. (3d) 157, 64 C.C.C. (2d) 169 (S.C.C.) — *See also: R. v. Jean* (1979), 7 C.R. (3d) 338, 46 C.C.C. (2d) 176 (Alta. C.A.); affirmed (1980), 16 C.R. (3d) 193, 51 C.C.C. (2d) 192 (S.C.C.); *R. v. Conroy* (1980), 57 C.C.C. (2d) 446 at 449 (Ont. C.A.) — The combined effect of s. 4(3) and s. 189(6) of the *Criminal Code* is that intercepted communications between a husband and wife are privileged and inadmissible at the instance of P, where the recipient spouse does *not* wish to reveal them.

R. v. Jean (1979), 7 C.R. (3d) 338, 46 C.C.C. (2d) 176 (Alta. C.A.), affirmed (1980), 16 C.R. (3d) 193, 51 C.C.C. (2d) 192 (S.C.C.) — *See also: Mailloux v. R.* (1980), 30 C.R. (3d) 121, 55 C.C.C. (2d) 193 at 196 (Ont. C.A.) — *Contra: R. v. St-Jean* (1976), 34 C.R.N.S. 378, 32 C.C.C. (2d) 438 (Que. C.A.) — Even where the spouse is a *compellable* witness on behalf of P under s. 4(2), s. 4(3) still limits the extent of the compulsion so that the spouse need not disclose any communication made during the marriage.

R. v. Kotapski (1981), 66 C.C.C. (2d) 78 (Que. S.C.); affirmed (1984), 13 C.C.C. (3d) 185 (Que. C.A.); leave to appeal refused (1984), 57 N.R. 318 (S.C.C.) — The privilege in s. 4(3) applies only to the recipient spouse, if he/she testifies, and does not apply to render inadmissible documents sent by a husband to his wife which come into the possession of a third party.

Competent and Compellable for Crown: S. 4(4)

R. v. Salituro (1991), 68 C.C.C. (3d) 289 (S.C.C.); affirming (1990), 78 C.R. (3d) 68, 56 C.C.C. (3d) 350 (Ont. C.A.) — *See also: R. v. Jeffrey* (1993), 25 C.R. (4th) 104, 84 C.C.C. (3d) 31 (Alta. C.A.) — Where, at the time of trial, the spouses are *irreconcilably separated*, one spouse is competent to testify against the other even though the charge does *not* fall within the common law exceptions or the exceptions in subsection (4).

Wildman v. R. (1984), 14 C.C.C. (3d) 321 (S.C.C.) — Section 4(4) is a procedural amendment and has retrospective application where the trial occurs after the amendment has come into force, even though the charge was laid prior to that time.

Gosselin v. R. (1903), 7 C.C.C. 139 (S.C.C.) — Where an earlier version of the statute made the spouse of a person charged a competent witness in certain circumstances, he or she could be compelled to testify.

R. v. Jeffrey (1993), 25 C.R. (4th) 104, 84 C.C.C. (3d) 31 (Alta. C.A.) — The time for determining whether there is an irreconcilable separation is the time of trial. P is required to prove such a separation between D and his or her spouse on a balance of probabilities.

R. v. Lonsdale (1973), 24 C.R.N.S. 225, 15 C.C.C. (2d) 201 (Alta. C.A.) — Where D is charged with attempting to murder his wife, the latter is both a competent and compellable witness for P as the offence is one involving personal violence to the wife and it does not matter that there was no actual injury to her.

R. v. Sillars (1978), 12 C.R. (3d) 202, 45 C.C.C. (2d) 283 (B.C. C.A.) — *See also*: *R. v. Czipps* (1979), 12 C.R. (3d) 193, 48 C.C.C. (2d) 166 (Ont. C.A.) — Pursuant to s. 4(4) a spouse is a competent witness for P where the threat to her person, liberty or health is apparent from the wording of the charge and also where the threat is apparent from evidence of the surrounding circumstances. If a spouse is competent, she is also compellable.

R. v. Singh, [1970] 1 C.C.C. 299 (B.C. C.A.) — On a charge of conspiracy where D's wife is an incompetent witness for P in respect of her husband, she is also incompetent for P in respect of his alleged co-conspirator.The offences covered by s. 4(4) include those alleged by the spouse to affect her person, health or liberty.

R. v. McGinty (1986), 52 C.R. (3d) 161, 27 C.C.C. (3d) 36 (Y.T. C.A.) — Under s. 4(4) in cases involving violence against them, spouses are competent and compellable witnesses against their accused spouses.

Common Law Exceptions: S. 4(5)

R. v. Salituro (1991), 68 C.C.C. (3d) 289 (S.C.C.); affirming (1990), 78 C.R. (3d) 68, 56 C.C.C. (3d) 350 (Ont. C.A.) — The courts have authority to extend the exception to the common law rule of spousal testimonial incompetency at the instance of P and should do so in the case of permanently and irreconcilably separated spouses.

Other Privileges

R. v. Fosty (1991), 8 C.R. (4th) 368, (sub nom. *R. v. Gruenke*) 67 C.C.C. (3d) 289 — To come within a case-by-case privilege, communications for which there is a *prima facie* presumption against privilege must meet four criteria:

i.   they must originate in *confidence* that they will not be disclosed;

ii.   the *element* of *confidentiality* must be *essential* to the maintenance of relations between the parties;

iii. the *relation* must be one which, in the opinion of the community, is to be *sedulously fostered*; and,

iv.   the injury that would result from disclosure must be *greater* than the *benefit* thereby gained.

There is neither at common law nor under the *Charter* a *prima facie* privilege for religious communications, but they may be subject to privilege on a case-by-case basis, if the criteria *supra* are met.

R. v. Ryan (1991), 69 C.C.C. (3d) 226 (N.S. C.A.) — No privilege attached to the files of child protection agencies which had been involved with V. The files could be subpoenaed by D.

Comment on Failure to Testify: S. 4(6)

R. v. Noble (1997), 6 C.R. (5th) 1, [1997] 1 S.C.R. 874, 114 C.C.C. (3d) 385 (S.C.C.) — Where the case against D does *not* otherwise prove guilt beyond a reasonable doubt, the trier of fact may *not* infer guilt from failure to testify. D's silence at trial may *not* constitute evidence of guilt without shifting the burden of proof to D. Silence is neither inculpatory, nor exculpatory evidence.

The silence of D may be used by the trier of fact in a very limited sense, *viz.*, to indicate

i.   that there is *no* evidence to support speculative explanations of P's case; or

ii.   that D has advanced *no* evidence that requires P to negate an affirmative defence.

D's silence may not be used to negate a rational explanation consistent with innocence and capable of raising a reasonable doubt concerning guilt.

There is no practical way to prevent a jury from drawing an improper inference from D's silence.

The significance of the failure to testify in the context of a defence of alibi is an exception to the general rule that D's silence is not an item of evidence in the case against D. Where an alibi is asserted, the trier of fact may draw an adverse inference against D from failure to testify.

R. v. François (1994), 31 C.R. (4th) 201, 91 C.C.C. (3d) 289 (S.C.C.) — *See also*: *R. v. Johnson* (1993), 21 C.R. (4th) 336, 79 C.C.C. (3d) 42 (Ont. C.A.); leave to appeal refused (1993),25 C.R. (4th) 68n, 84 C.C.C. (3d) vi (note) S.C.C. — Subject to the *caveat* that failure to testify cannot be used to shore up P's case which does *not* otherwise establish guilt beyond a reasonable doubt, a jury is permitted to draw an adverse inference from D's failure to testify.

R. v. Potvin (1989), 68 C.R. (3d) 193, 47 C.C.C. (3d) 289 (S.C.C.) — An offhand remark that no defence was called does *not* violate s. 4(6).

R. v. Newton (1976), 34 C.R.N.S. 161, 28 C.C.C. (2d) 286 (S.C.C.) — A comment on the inference arising from the unexplained possession of goods recently stolen does not constitute a comment prohibited by s. 4(6).

Vezeau v. R. (1976), 34 C.R.N.S. 309, 28 C.C.C. (2d) 81 (S.C.C.) — Section 4(6) does *not* authorize a trial judge to direct the jury that no adverse inference could be drawn from the fact D failed to testify. It is open to the jury to draw such an inference.

McConnell v. R. (1968), 4 C.R.N.S. 269, [1968] 4 C.C.C. 257 (S.C.C.) — An instruction to the jury that they were not to be influenced in their decision by D not testifying was not a comment in violation of s. 4(6) but rather a comment on the right of D to refrain from testifying.

R. v. Gray (1986), 25 C.C.C. (3d) 145 (B.C. C.A.) — Where D testified that he was at home at the time of the offence, a statement by Crown counsel that the jury had not heard from D's wife did not constitute a comment prohibited by s. 4(6).

R. v. Sherman (1979), 47 C.C.C. (2d) 521 (B.C. C.A.) — *See also*: *R. v. Agawa* (1975), 31 C.R.N.S. 293, 28 C.C.C. (2d) 379 (Ont. C.A.) — An instruction to the jury at the opening of the trial that following the case for P the defence "may" open and outline its evidence does not constitute a comment on the failure of D to testify.

R. v. Marciniec (1963), 40 C.R. 182, [1963] 2 C.C.C. 212 (Man. C.A.) — An instruction to the jury that D's statements to the police were not under oath and he was not subject to cross-examination did *not* constitute a comment upon his failure to testify.

R. v. Cuff (1989), 49 C.C.C. (3d) 65 (Nfld. C.A.) — This subsection does not prevent counsel for one accused from commenting on the failure of a co-accused to testify.

R. v. C. (R.C.) (1996), 107 C.C.C. (3d) 362 (N.S. C.A.) — Section 4(6) was enacted to prevent a trial judge from telling a jury, directly or in effect, that they may draw an *adverse inference* from D's failure to testify.

R. v. D. (D.E.) (1987), 57 C.R. (3d) 163 (N.S. C.A.) — Reference to the complainant's evidence being uncontradicted did not violate s. 4(6) nor was it an infringement of *Charter* s. 11(c).

R. v. Shermetta (1986), 32 C.C.C. (3d) 215 (N.S. C.A.) — In a conspiracy trial where one of two accused testified, a comment by the trial judge that one of D "at least" gave an explanation was a comment on the failure of the co-accused to testify.

R. v. Miller (1983), 21 C.R. (5th) 178, 131 C.C.C. (3d) 141 (Ont. C.A.) — Section 4(6) is entirely separate and distinct from the question of when a trier of fact may draw an adverse inference from D's failure to testify. The section assures D that no *greater* weight will be placed on the failure to testify because of a *comment* by P or the trial judge.

R. v. Milec (1996), 110 C.C.C. (3d) 439 (Ont. C.A.) — The failure of D to testify cannot constitute evidence of an essential element of the offence charged.

R. v. Creighton (1993), 20 C.R. (4th) 331, 80 C.C.C. (3d) 421 (Ont. C.A.); reversed on other grounds (1995), 37 C.R. (4th) 197, (sub nom. *R. v. Crawford)* 96 C.C.C. (3d) 481 — *See also*: *R. v. Naglik* (1991), 65 C.C.C. (3d) 272 (Ont. C.A.); reversed (1993), 23 C.R. (4th) 335, 83 C.C.C. (3d) 526 (S.C.C.); *R. v. Silvini* (1991), 9 C.R. (4th) 233, 68 C.C.C. (3d) 257 (Ont. C.A.) — On the joint trial of two accused, counsel for one accused is *not* prohibited from commenting on the failure of the co-accused to testify, nor from eliciting evidence that the co-accused had not made a statement to the police. Where one accused, as part of his or her defence, makes an attack on a co-accused being jointly tried, the trial judge is required *not* to limit such an attack. Where the attack by one infringes a constitutionally-protected right of another co-accused, the remedy of the latter is to seek severance.

R. v. Boss (1988), 68 C.R. (3d) 123, 46 C.C.C. (3d) 523 (Ont. C.A.) — *See also*: *R. v. Cuff* (1989), 49 C.C.C. (3d) 65 (Nfld. C.A.) — While the section prohibits both the trial judge and P from commenting on D's failure to testify, counsel for D is entitled to comment on the issue. The section does *not* offend *Charter* s. 7, 11(c) or 11(d).

R. v. Wildman (1981), 60 C.C.C. (2d) 289 (Ont. C.A.); reversed on other grounds (1984), 14 C.C.C. (3d) 321 (S.C.C.) — A comment by P in his closing address that P was prohibited by law from calling D's wife to testify did not come within s. 4(6).

Pratte v. Maher (1963), 43 C.R. 214, [1965] 1 C.C.C. 77 (Que. C.A.) — *See also*: *R. v. Binder* (1948), 6 C.R. 83, 92 C.C.C. 20 (Ont. C.A.) — Section 4(6) does not apply to a trial by judge alone. The judge is *not* prohibited from remarking on the silence of D and drawing from it necessary conclusions.

Charter Considerations

R. v. Amway Corp. (1989), 68 C.R. (3d) 97 (S.C.C.) — As a corporation cannot be a witness it cannot come within *Charter* s. 11(c) and its officers are compellable at examinations for discovery in forfeiture proceedings under the *Customs Act*.

R. v. S.(R.J.) (1995), 36 C.R. (4th) 1, 96 C.C.C. (3d) 1 (S.C.C.) — A person charged with an offence can be compelled to give evidence against another person being separately tried for the same offence without an infringement of the right to silence in *Charter* s.7.

R. v. Thompson (1994), 32 C.R. (4th) 143, 90 C.C.C. (3d) 519 (Alta. C.A.) — The failure to extend the non-compellability of *C.E.A.* s. 4 to common-law spouses does *not* offend *Charter* s. 15.

R. v. Creighton (1993), 20 C.R. (4th) 331, 80 C.C.C. (3d) 421 (Ont. C.A.); reversed on other grounds (1995), 37 C.R. (4th) 197, (sub nom. *R. v. Crawford*) 96 C.C.C. (3d) 481 — *See also*: *R. v. Naglik* (1991), 65 C.C.C. (3d) 272 (Ont. C.A.); reversed (1993), 23 C.R. (4th) 335, 83 C.C.C. (3d) 526 (S.C.C.); *R. v. Silvini* (1991), 68 C.C.C. (3d) 251, 9 C.R. (4th) 233 (C.A.) — *Charter* s. 11(c) does *not* prohibit counsel for a co-accused commenting on the failure of another accused to testify in a joint trial.

5. (1) Incriminating questions — **No witness shall be excused from answering any question on the ground that the answer to the question may tend to criminate him, or may tend to establish his liability to a civil proceeding at the instance of the Crown or of any person.**

(2) Answer not admissible against witness — **Where with respect to any question a witness objects to answer on the ground that his answer may tend to criminate him, or may tend to establish his liability to a civil proceeding at the instance of the Crown or of any person, and if but for this Act, or the Act of any provincial legislature, the witness would therefore have been excused from answering the question, then although the witness is by reason of this Act or the provincial Act compelled to answer, the answer so given shall not be used or admissible in evidence against him in any criminal trial or other criminal proceeding against him thereafter taking place, other than a prosecutor for perjury in the giving of that evidence or for the giving of contradictory evidence.**

R.S., c. E-10, s. 5; 1997, c. 18, s. 116.

Case Law

Privilege Against Self-Incrimination: S. 5(1)[See also Charter ss. 11(c) and 13]

Marcoux v. R. (1975), 29 C.R.N.S. 211, 24 C.C.C. (2d) 1 (S.C.C.) — The privilege is testimonial only and extends to D *qua* witness and not *qua* accused. Depending on the circumstances of the case, evidence of the offer to, and refusal of, a line-up by D may be admissible.

Summa Corp. v. Meier (1981), 127 D.L.R. (3d) 238 (B.C. C.A.); leave to appeal refused (1981), 39 N.R. 538 (S.C.C.) — This section has abolished the common law privilege against self-incrimination, including where an individual who has criminal proceedings pending in a foreign jurisdiction is to be examined in Canada.

R. v. Sweeney (No. 2) (1977), 40 C.R.N.S. 37, 35 C.C.C. (3d) 245 (Ont. C.A.) — *See also*: *R. v. Malcolm* (1989), 71 C.R. (3d) 238, 50 C.C.C. (3d) 172 (Man. C.A.); *R. v. Stevenson* (1990), 58 C.C.C. (3d) 464 (Ont. C.A.) — In its modern form, the privilege against self-incrimination means only the right of a witness, as qualified by s. 5, to refuse to answer certain questions if the answers will tend to incriminate him/her and the absolute right of D not to go into the witness box. P is not prohibited from leading evidence of D's refusal to be examined by a Crown psychiatrist where D made sanity an issue.

Objection to Answer: S. 5(2) [See also case digests to Charter ss. 11(c) and 13]

Marcoux v. R. (1975), 29 C.R.N.S. 211, 24 C.C.C. (2d) 1 (S.C.C.) — The privilege must be expressly claimed by the witness when the question is put to him/her in the witness box.

R. v. Chaperon (1979), 52 C.C.C. (2d) 85 (Ont. C.A.) — *Contra*: *R. v. Mottola* (1959), 31 C.R. 4, 124 C.C.C. 288 (Ont. C.A.) — A witness is entitled to the protection of s. 5 even though it is sought by a counsel before the witness is sworn, rather than as an objection by the witness to each question asked.

R. v. Vigeant (1982), 3 C.C.C. (3d) 445 (Que. C.A.); leave to appeal refused (1982), 3 C.C.C. (3d) 445n (S.C.C.) — An objection made pursuant to s. 5(2) may not have a retroactive effect to cover questions already asked and answers already given.

R. v. Cote (1979), 8 C.R. (3d) 171, 50 C.C.C. (2d) 564 (Que. C.A.); leave to appeal refused (1979), 50 C.C.C. (2d) 564n (S.C.C.) — The witness need not object after each question but may object to a series of questions when it appears that all such questions will entail incriminating answers.

Scope of Section [See also Charter s. 13]

Di Iorio v. Montreal Jail Warden (1976), 35 C.R.N.S. 57, 33 C.C.C. (2d) 289 (S.C.C.) — The protection may be claimed by a person testifying at a provincial inquiry.

R. v. Coughlin (1982), 3 C.C.C. (3d) 259 (Ont. C.A.) — Where D's statement is ruled inadmissible, D may not be cross-examined on the trial proper with respect to the evidence given on the voir dire, whether or not s. 5(2) would preclude such cross-examination.

R. v. Chaperon (1979), 52 C.C.C. (2d) 85 (Ont. C.A.) — The only exception to s. 5(2) is a prosecution for perjury. A prosecution for giving contradictory evidence is not within that exception.

Charter Considerations [See also Charter ss. 11(c) and 13]

R. v. S. (R.J.) (1995), 36 C.R. (4th) 1, 96 C.C.C. (3d) 1 (S.C.C.) — There is no breach of *Charter* s. 7 where P compels a person separately charged with the same offence to testify as a prosecution witness on the trial of another.

R. v. Yakeleya (1985), 46 C.R. (3d) 282, 20 C.C.C. (3d) 193 (Ont. C.A.) — A trial does not constitute "other proceedings" in relation to the preliminary hearing on the same charge, but rather the two are part of the same proceedings.

6. (1) Evidence of person with physical disability — If a witness has difficulty communicating by reason of a physical disability, the court may order that the witness be permitted to give evidence by any means that enables the evidence to intelligible.

(2) Evidence of person with mental disability — If a witness with a mental disability is determined under section 16 to have the capacity to give evidence and difficulty communicating by reason of disability, the court may order that the witness be permitted to give evidence by any means that enables the evidence to be intelligible.

(3) Inquiry — The court may conduct an inquiry to determine if the means by which a witness may be permitted to give evidence under subsection (1) or (2) is necessary and reliable.

R.S., c. E-10, s. 6; 1998, c. 9, s. 1.

6.1 Identification of accused — For greater certainty, a witness may give evidence as to the identity of an accused whom the witness is able to identify visually or in any other sensory manner.

1998, c. 9, s. 1.

7. Expert witnesses — Where, in any trial or other proceeding, criminal or civil, it is intended by the prosecution or the defence, or by any party, to examine as witnesses professional or other experts entitled according to the law or practice to give opinion evidence, not more than five of such witnesses may be called on either side without the leave of the court or judge or person presiding.

R.S., c. E-10, s. 7.

Case Law

Number of Witnesses

R. v. Vincent (1963), 40 C.R. 365 (Man C.A.) — The fact P had called more than five expert witnesses without leave did not cause a miscarriage of justice where the opinion evidence played an insignificant part in the case.

Admissibility [See also Code s. 271]

R. v. Mohan (1994), 29 C.R. (4th) 243, 89 C.C.C. (3d) 402 (S.C.C.); reversing (1992), 13 C.R. (4th) 292, 71 C.C.C. (3d) 321 (Ont. C.A.) — Admission of expert evidence depends upon the application of four criteria:

i.   *relevance*;

ii.   *necessity* in *assisting* the trier of fact;

iii. *absence* of any *exclusionary* rule; and

iv. a properly-qualified *expert*.

Relevance, a threshold requirement, is decided by the trial judge as a question of law. Logically, relevant evidence may be excluded if,

i.   its probative value is overborne by its prejudicial effect;

ii.   the time required to receive it is not *commensurate* with its value; or,

iii. it can influence the trier of fact out of proportion to its reliability.

The reliability/effect factor (item iii) is of particular significance in deciding the admissibility of expert evidence: it ought be excluded where there is a danger it will be misused, distort the fact-finding process or confuse the jury.*Necessity* ought *not* be judged by too strict a standard. To be necessary, expert evidence must likely be outside the experience and knowledge of a trier of fact and be assessed in light of its potential to distort the fact-finding process. Proper instructions may offset the possibility that expert evidence will overwhelm or distract the jury. Experts, however, must *not* be allowed to usurp the functions of the trier of fact, thereby causing the trial to degenerate into a contest of experts.Expert evidence may be excluded if it offends an exclusionary rule other than the opinion rule.The expert must be one who is shown to have acquired special or peculiar knowledge through study or experience in respect of the matters upon which he or she undertakes to testify.

R. v. Mohan (1994), 29 C.R. (4th) 243, 89 C.C.C. (3d) 402 (S.C.C.); reversing (1992), 13 C.R. (4th) 292, 71 C.C.C. (3d) 321 (Ont. C.A.) — Expert evidence which advances a *novel scientific theory* or technique must be closely examined to determine whether,

i.   it meets a basic-threshold of *reliability*; and,

ii.   it is *essential* in that the trier of fact will be unable to reach a satisfactory conclusion without expert assistance.

The closer the evidence approaches an opinion on the ultimate issue, the stricter the application of the principle.

R. v. Marquard (1993), 25 C.R. (4th) 1, 85 C.C.C. (3d) 93 (S.C.C.) — The only requirement for admission of expert opinion is that the expert witness possess special knowledge and experience going beyond that of the trier of fact. Deficiencies in the expertise go to weight, not admissibility. Counsel who presents the expert ought to qualify the witness in the areas in which the expert is to give opinion evidence.

R. v. Marquard (1993), 25 C.R. (4th) 1, 85 C.C.C. (3d) 193 (S.C.C.) — While expert evidence on the ultimate credibility of a witness is *not* admissible, expert evidence on human conduct, as well as the psychological and physical factors which may lead to certain behaviour relevant to credibility, is admissible, provided it goes beyond the ordinary experience of the trier of fact. It is especially so in respect of the evidence of children.

R. v. Lavallee (1990), 76 C.R. (3d) 329, 55 C.C.C. (3d) 97 (S.C.C.); reversing (1988), 65 C.R. (3d) 387, 44 C.C.C. (3d) 113 (Man. C.A.) — *See also*: *R. v. Abbey* (1982), 29 C.R. (3d) 193, 68 C.C.C. (2d) 394 (S.C.C.); *R. v. Scardino* (1991), 6 C.R. (4th) 146 (Ont. C.A.) — Expert testimony is admissible to assist the fact-finder in drawing inferences in areas where the expert has relevant knowledge and/or experience beyond that of a lay person. It can, for example, assist the jury in dispelling the myths associated with the battered wife syndrome which lays at the basis of an assertion of self-defence under *Code* s. 34(2). As long as there is some admissible evidence to establish the foundation for the expert's opinion, the jury must not be instructed to ignore the testimony. A warning should, however, be given that, the greater the reliance of the expert upon facts not proved in evidence, the less weight may be attached to the opinion.

R. v. Conroy (1993), 84 C.C.C. (3d) 320 (Ont. C.A.) — A trial judge should expressly instruct the jury that opinions expressed in texts, *not* adopted by an expert in cross-examination, are *not* admissible in proof of the facts stated.

Conflicting Expert Evidence

R. v. Molnar (1990), 76 C.R. (3d) 125, 55 C.C.C. (3d) 446 (Ont. C.A.) — *See also*: *R. v. Parnell* (1983), 9 C.C.C. (3d) 353 (Ont. C.A.); leave to appeal refused (1984), 9 C.C.C. (3d) 353n (S.C.C.); *R. v. Platt*, [1981] Crim. L.R. 322 (C.A.) — In cases of conflicting expert evidence, the jury should *not* be told to decide which evidence they prefer. The jury should be instructed that, before they accept the opinion evidence of P's expert, they must feel sure he/she is correct.

8. Handwriting comparison — **Comparison of a disputed writing with any writing proved to the satisfaction of the court to be genuine shall be permitted to be made by witnesses, and such writings, and the evidence of witnesses respecting those writings, may be submitted to the court and jury as proof of the genuineness or otherwise of the writing in dispute.**

R.S., c. E-10, s. 8.

Case Law

Pitre v. R. (1932), 59 C.C.C. 148 (S.C.C.) — A witness who has carried on a regular correspondence with a person or has frequently seen a person's handwriting may be competent to prove the handwriting.

R. v. Abdi (1997), 116 C.C.C. (3d) 385 (Ont. C.A.) — A common law, the trier of fact could compare handwriting without expert assistance, provided that a properly proven or admitted standard used for comparison with a disputed writing has been admitted in evidence for other purposes.

C.E.A. s. 8 does *not* oust the operation of the common law rules concerning trier of fact comparison or handwriting. It permits a lay or expert witness to give opinion evidence of handwriting by comparison of disputed with known handwriting admitted for comparison purposes. It also does not preclude the trier of fact from making comparisons, in the absence of witness testimony, concerning the genuiness or otherwise of disputed writing.

Where a jury may make unassisted comparisons to determine authorship of disputed handwriting, they should be instructed

i.   of the absence of expert or other assistance and the need for care in making comparisons;

ii.   concerning the difficulties of the comparison in the circumstances;

iii. concerning the quality of the handwriting exemplar; and

iv.   on all other matters which may bear on the weight to be assigned to a comparison.

9. (1) Adverse witnesses — **A party producing a witness shall not be allowed to impeach his credit by general evidence of bad character, but if the witness, in the opinion of the court, proves adverse, the party may contradict him by other evidence, or, by leave of the court, may prove that the witness made at other times a statement inconsistent with his present testimony, but before the last mentioned proof can be given the circumstances of the supposed statement, sufficient to designate the particular occasion, shall be mentioned to the witness, and he shall be asked whether or not he did make the statement.**

(2) Previous statements in writing by witness not proved adverse — **Where the party producing a witness alleges that the witness made at other times a statement in writing, reduced to writing, or recorded on audio tape or video tape or**

otherwise, inconsistent with the witness' present testimony, the court may, without proof that the witness is adverse, grant leave to that party to cross-examine the witness as to the statement and the court may consider the cross-examination in determining whether in the opinion of the court the witness is adverse.

R.S., c. E-10, s. 9; 1994, c. 44, s. 85.

Case Law
Meaning of "Adverse": S. 9(1)

Wawanesa Mutual Ins. Co. v. Hanes, [1963] 1 C.C.C. 176 (Ont. C.A.); reversed [1963] 1 C.C.C. 321 (S.C.C.) — *See also*: *R. v. Cassibo* (1982), 70 C.C.C. (2d) 498 (Ont. C.A.) — The word "adverse" in s. 23 of the *Ontario Evidence Act*, in effect the same as s. 9(1), has a more comprehensive meaning than hostile. It includes not only *hostility of mind*, but also *opposed in interest* or *unfavourable* in the sense of *opposite in position* to that of the party calling the witness.

R. v. Wyman (1958), 28 C.R. 371, 122 C.C.C. 65 (N.B. C.A.) — *See also*: *R. v. McIntyre* (1963), 43 C.R. 262, [1963] 2 C.C.C. 380 (N.S. C.A.) — "Adverse" means hostile, not simply unfavourable.

Determination of Adverse: S. 9(1)

R. v. Coffin (1956), 23 C.R. 1, 114 C.C.C. 1 (S.C.C.) — *See also*: *R. v. Stewart* (1976), 31 C.C.C. (2d) 497 (S.C.C.) — Section 9(1) does not prohibit a witness from refreshing her memory by means of her previous statements. It is only where the object is to discredit or contradict one's own witness that s. 9 applies. Further, the trial judge has a discretion to permit leading questions to be put in examination-in-chief when it is considered necessary in the interests of justice.

R. v. Williams (1985), 44 C.R. (3d) 351, 18 C.C.C. (3d) 356 (Ont. C.A.); leave to appeal refused (1985), 44 C.R. (3d) 351n, 18 C.C.C. (3d) 356n (S.C.C.) — Where the finding of adversity can be made only on the basis of a prior inconsistent statement, the judge must be satisfied that the statement was made and it is not enough that there is some evidence upon which the jury could find it was made.

R. v. Cassibo (1982), 70 C.C.C. (2d) 498 (Ont. C.A.) — On a *voir dire* to determine whether a witness is adverse within the meaning of s. 9(1), the trial judge may receive evidence of the making of previous inconsistent statements, both oral and written. However, while the judge may consider on a s. 9(1) *voir dire*, cross-examination on a written statement which has taken place pursuant to s. 9(2), he/she should not permit cross-examination with respect to an oral statement. If he/she finds that the oral statement was made, and it is substantially inconsistent with the witness' testimony, the witness may be declared adverse, but inconsistency does not in every case justify a finding of adversity.

Effect of Cross-Examination Under S. 9(1)

R. v. B. (K.G.) (1993), 19 C.R. (4th) 1, 179 C.C.C. (3d) 257 (S.C.C.) — Evidence of prior inconsistent statements of a witness other than D may be *substantively admissible* where the criteria of *necessity* and *reliability* are satisfied. They will only be substantively admissible, however, if they would have been so when given by the witness at trial. The criterion of *reliability* will be met and allow the trier of fact to make a substantive use of the prior inconsistent statement if:

i.   the statement is made under *oath, solemn affirmation* or *solemn declaration* following an explicit warning to the witness as to the existence of severe criminal sanctions for the making of a false statement;

ii.   the statement is *video-taped* in its entirety; and

iii.   the *opposing party*, whether P or D, has a *full opportunity* to *cross-examine* the witness at *trial* respecting the statement.

Other circumstantial guarantees of reliability may also suffice to render prior inconsistent statements substantively admissible, provided that the presiding judge is satisfied that the circumstances furnish adequate assurances of reliability in place of those which the hearsay rule traditionally requires. The criterion of *necessity* should be given a flexible definition capable of encompassing diverse situations, including those in which evidence of the same value cannot be expected from the recanting witness or other sources. Where a sufficient degree of reliability is established, the trier of fact ought to be permitted to weigh both statements in light of the witness' explanation for the change. Where a party has adequately established the constituent elements necessary to render the prior inconsistent statement substantively admissible, the trial judge need *not* give the standard limiting instructions to the trier of fact, but may instead tell the jury or instruct him or herself that the prior inconsistent statement may be taken as evidence of its contents and given the weight appropriate in all of the circumstances. The trier of fact should be instructed to consider carefully the circumstances surrounding the making of the statement in assessing the credibility of the prior inconsistent statement relative to the witness's trial testimony.Where the prior inconsistent statement *lacks* the necessary circumstantial guarantees of *reliability*, and hence cannot pass the threshold test on the *voir dire* to be admitted as substantive evidence, but the party tendering the statement otherwise meets the requirements of *C.E.A.* ss. 9(1) or (2), the statement may nonetheless be tendered into evidence, but is subject to the *standard limiting instruction* that it is not evidence of its content and bears only on the credibility of the witness' evidence at trial.

R. v. C. (J.R.) (1996), 110 C.C.C. (3d) 373 (Sask. C.A.) — CEA s. 9 permits a party to cross-examine his/her own witness in certain circumstances to *impeach* the witness, *not* to *bolster* the credibility of *part* of the witness' evidence when contradicted otherwise by the witness.

Statement in or Reduced to Writing: S. 9(2) [See now s. 9(2)]

R. v. Handy (1978), 5 C.R. (3d) 97, 45 C.C.C. (2d) 232 (B.C. C.A.) — Notes made by a police officer of a conversation with the witness do not constitute a statement in writing or reduced to writing and cannot form the basis for invoking s. 9(2).

R. v. Carpenter (No. 2) (1982), 31 C.R. (3d) 261, 1 C.C.C. (3d) 149 (Ont. C.A.) — Although "statement" in s. 9(1) includes an oral statement, s. 9(2) requires a statement in writing or reduced to writing. Such a statement need not be formally signed or acknowledged and a verbatim written record of the questions asked and answers made, translated from French to English, comes within the subsection. The test on the application to cross-examine under s. 9(2) is whether the *ends of justice* would be best attained by permitting it.

Cross-Examination on Statement: S. 9(2)

R. v. B. (K.G.) (1993), 19 C.R. (4th) 1, 79 C.C.C. (3d) 257 (S.C.C.) — Where a party who has called a witness seeks to make substantive use of the witness's prior inconsistent statement, the party should give *notice* to such effect. On the *voir dire* under *C.E.A.* s. 9, the trial judge must first be satisfied that the necessary *indicia* of *reliability* have been established as present and genuine. The judge must then examine the circumstances under which the statement was made and be satisfied that the statement supported by the *indicia* of reliability was made voluntarily, if to a person in authority, and, further, that there are no other factors which would tend to bring the administration of justice into disrepute if the prior statement were admitted as substantive evidence. In most cases, the party seeking admission will be required to establish the conditions precedent to substantive admissibility on a balance of probabilities. The decision whether the prior inconsistent statement is true, or more reliable than the witness's testimony, is for the trier of fact on the trial not the trial judge on the *voir dire.*Where a party had adequately established the constituent elements necessary to render the prior inconsistent statements substantively admissible, the trial judge need *not* give the *standard limiting instructions* to the trier of fact, but may instead tell the jury or instruct him or herself that the prior inconsistent statement may be taken as evidence of its content and given the weight appropriate in all of the circumstances. The trier of fact should be instructed to consider carefully the circumstances surrounding the making of the statement in assessing the credibility of the prior inconsistent statement relative to the witness's trial testimony.Where the prior inconsistent statement *lacks* the necessary circumstantial guarantees of *reliability*, and hence cannot pass the threshold test on the *voir dire* to be admitted as substantive evidence, but the party tendering the statement otherwise meets the requirements of *C.E.A.* ss. 9(1) and (2), the statement may nonetheless be tendered into evidence, but is subject to the *standard limiting instruction* that it is not evidence of its content and bears only on the credibility of the witness' evidence at trial.

McInroy v. R. (1978), 5 C.R. (3d) 125, 42 C.C.C. (2d) 481 (S.C.C.) — There is no requirement that the witness be proved adverse before cross-examination may be permitted under s. 9(2). It is open to the trial judge to conclude a witness is lying when she testifies that she has no recollection of an event and to therefore conclude that her evidence at trial is inconsistent with her statement to police which contains a detailed account of the event.

Stewart v. R. (1976), 31 C.C.C. (2d) 497 (S.C.C.) — Where P applies under s. 9(2) to cross-examine on a statement, the judge may require P to examine the witness in a particular way before giving leave to cross-examine as to the statement, for example by requiring P to attempt to refresh the witness' memory as to the making of the statement and to permit the witness to read the statement.

R. v. Fraser (1990), 55 C.C.C. (3d) 551 (B.C. C.A.) — A trial judge has a discretion as to the manner in which cross-examination of a witness on a prior inconsistent statement may be conducted. The discretion should be exercised to minimize prejudice to D through such cross-examination.

R. v. Booth (1984), 15 C.C.C. (3d) 237 (B.C. C.A) — Before a witness can be declared adverse under s. 9(1), the procedure set out in *R. v. Milgaard, infra,* must be followed.

R. v. Moore (1984), 15 C.C.C. (3d) 541 (Ont. C.A.); leave to appeal refused (1985), 15 C.C.C. (3d) 541n (S.C.C.) — A trial judge may grant leave to counsel to cross-examine his own witness on a prior inconsistent statement in re-examination, where the witness in cross-examination has given evidence on a material matter which is contrary to a prior statement.

R. v. Aubin (1994), 94 C.C.C. (3d) 89 (Que. C.A.); leave to appeal refused (1995), 94 C.C.C. (3d) 89n, 94 C.C.C. (3d) vin (S.C.C.) — A witness' lack of memory of having made a prior statement may constitute a basis upon which to cross-examine a witness under *C.E.A.,* s. 9(2).

R. v. Milgaard (1971), 14 C.R.N.S. 34, 2 C.C.C. (2d) 206 (Sask. C.A.); leave to appeal refused (1971), 4 C.C.C. (2d) 566n (S.C.C.) — *See also: McInroy v. R.* (1978), 5 C.R. (3d) 125, 42 C.C.C. (2d) 481 (S.C.C.) — The right to cross-examine pursuant to s. 9(2) is within the discretion of the trial judge. The procedure to be followed is:

(1) Counsel should advise the court that s/he desires to make an application under *C.E.A.* s. 9(2).

(2) When the court is so advised, the court should direct the jury to retire.

(3) Upon retirement of the jury, counsel should advise the trial judge of the particulars of the application and produce for her/him the alleged statement in writing, or the writing to which the statement has been reduced.

(4) The trial judge should read the statement, or writing, and determine whether, in fact, there is an inconsistency between such statement or writing and the evidence the witness has given in court. If the trial judge decides there is *no* inconsistency, then that ends the matter. If s/he finds there is an inconsistency, s/he should call upon counsel to prove the statement or writing.

(5) Counsel should then prove the statement or writing. This may be done by producing the statement or writing to the witness. If the witness admits the statement, or the statement reduced to writing, such proof would be sufficient. If the witness does *not* so admit, counsel then could provide the necessary proof by other evidence.

(6) If the witness admits making the statement, counsel for the opposing party should have the right to cross-examine as to the circumstances under which the statement was made. A similar right to cross-examine should be granted if the statement is proved by other witnesses. It may be that s/he will be able to establish that there were circumstances which would render it improper for the trial judge to permit the cross-examination, notwithstanding the apparent inconsistencies. The opposing counsel, too, should have the right to call evidence as to factors relevant to obtaining the statement, for the purpose of attempting to show that cross-examination should not be permitted.

(7) The trial judge should then decide whether or not s/he will permit the cross-examination. If so, the jury should be recalled and the cross-examination conducted in their presence.

Evidentiary Value of Prior Statement

R. v. U. (F.J.) (1995), 42 C.R. (4th) 133, 101 C.C.C. (3d) 97 (S.C.C.); affirming (1994), 32 C.R. (4th) 378, 90 C.C.C. (3d) 541 (Ont . C.A.) — Necessity and reliability must be interpreted flexibly having regard to the circumstances of the case. When they have been met, prior inconsistent statements of witnesses other than D are substantively admissible, provided that they would have been admissible as the witness' sole testimony .

R. v. U. (F.J.) (1995), 42 C.R. (4th) 133, 101 C.C.C. (3d) 97 (S.C.C.); affirming (1994), 32 C.R. (4th) 378, 90 C.C.C. (3d) 541 (Ont. C.A.) — The gravest danger associated with hearsay evidence, the absence of contemporaneous cross-examination, does *not* exist in cases of prior inconsistent statements since the witness is available for cross-examination. Absence of an oath and demeanour evidence may be met through appropriate police procedures. Appropriate substitutes may be found. A prior statement is necessary evidence when a witness recants.

R. v. U (F.J.) (1995), 42 C.R. (4th) 133, 101 C.C.C. (3d) 97 (S.C.C.); affirming (1994), 32 C.R. (4th) 378, 90 C.C.C. (3d) 541 (Ont. C.A.) — A threshold of *reliability* may be established, where a witness is available for cross-examination, by a *striking similarity* between two statements. To eliminate or substantially reduce the likelihood of similarity between two statements arising through coincidence, the similar factual assertion must be so striking that it is highly unlikely that two people, independently, would have fabricated it. The necessary degree of similarity may result from

i.   the unique nature of the particular factual assertions in both statements; or

ii.   the cumulative combination of similar points which renders the overall similarity sufficiently distinctive to render coincidence unlikely.

R. v. U (F.J.) (1995), 42 C.R. (4th) 133, 101 C.C.C. (3d) 97 (S.C.C.); affirming (1994), 32 C.R. (4th) 378, 90 C.C.C. (3d) 541 (Ont. C.A.) — Where s. 9 *CEA* is invoked, the calling party must state its objectives in tendering the prior statement. Where the statement is used for *impeachment* purposes only, the inquiry terminates. Where the calling party seeks to make *substantive* use of the statement, the *voir dire* must consinue so that the trial judge can assess whether the threshold of reliability has been met. In rare cases, where the reliability criterion is to be met by the striking similarity between the statement being assessed and another statement which is clearly substantively admissible, the trial judge must be satisfied, on a balance of probabilities,

i.   that there are *striking similarities* between the two statements;

ii.   that there was neither reason nor opportunity for the declarants to collude; and

iii.   that there was *no* improper influence by interrogators or third parties.

Necessity is established whenever a witness recants. The prior statement must also relate evidence that would be admissible as the witness' sole testimony.

R. v. U. (F.J.), 1995, 42 C.R. (4th) 133, 101 C.C.C. (3d) 97 (S.C.C.); affirming (1994), 32 C.R. (4th) 378, 90 C.C.C. (3d) 541 (Ont. C.A.) — Where a prior statement is substantively admissible *inter alia* on the basis of its striking similarity with another statement, the trier of fact should be instructed to follow a two-step process to evaluate the evidence. The trier of fact must first be certain that the *statement* used as a reliability referrent was *made*, without considering the prior inconsistent statement. If satisfied that the other statement was made, the trier of fact may *compare* the *similarities* between the statements and, if they are sufficiently striking that it is unlikely two people would have fabricated them independently, the trier of fact may draw conclusions from that comparision about their truth.

R. v. B. (K.G.) (1993), 19 C.R. (4th) 1, 79 C.C.C. (3d) 257 (S.C.C.) — See digest under *Effect of Cross-Examination Under S. 9(1), supra.*

McInroy v. R. (1978), 5 C.R. (3d) 125, 42 C.C.C. (2d) 481 (S.C.C.) — *See also: R. v. Lunan* (1982), 2 C.C.C. (3d) 193 (Ont. C.A.) — Where a witness is cross-examined under s. 9(2), those portions of her prior statement which she rejected, in the sense of saying she could *not* remember the questions and answers, do *not* constitute evidence on the trial because she has not accepted what was said earlier. They go only to her credibility.

R. v. Thurston (1993), 63 O.A.C. 99 (Ont. C.A.) — Where a statement is *not* admissible as substantive evidence under *R. v. B. (K.G.)* (1993), 19 C.R. (4th) 1, 79 C.C.C. (3d) 257 (S.C.C.), it is only admissible in proof of the truth of its contents to the extent it is adopted by the witness at trial. Absent adoption, the statement is only admissible to test the credibility of its maker.

R. v. Atikian (1990), 3 C.R. (4th) 77, 62 C.C.C. (3d) 357 (Ont. C.A.) — It is only where a witness has acknowledged having made a prior statement and that it was true, in whole or in part, that there is any evidence upon which the trier of fact may find the witness has adopted his or her statement, thereby making it evidence in the proceedings.

Charter Considerations

R. v. Williams (1985), 44 C.R. (3d) 351, 18 C.C.C (3d) 356 (Ont. C.A.) — A mechanical application of the adverse witness requirement which precludes D from cross-examining a witness he has called as to that witness' prior confession to the crime alleged against D may violate *Charter* s. 7. A court has a residual discretion in favour of D to relax a strict rule of evidence where it is necessary to prevent a miscarriage of justice.

10. (1) Cross-examination as to previous statements — On any trial a witness may be cross-examined as to previous statements that the witness made in writing, or that have been reduced to writing, or recorded on audio tape or video tape or otherwise, relative to the subject-matter of the case, without the writing being shown to the witness or the witness being given the opportunity to listen to the audio tape or view the video tape or otherwise take cognizance of the statements, but, if it is intended to contradict the witness, the witness' attention must, before the contradictory proof can be given, be called to those parts of the statement that are to be used for the purpose of so contradicting the witness, and the judge, at any time during the trial, may require the production of the writing or tape or other medium for inspection, and thereupon make such use of it for the purposes of the trial as the judge thinks fit.

(2) Deposition of witness in criminal investigation — A deposition of a witness, purporting to have been taken before a justice on the investigation of a criminal charge and to be signed by the witness and the justice, returned to and produced from the custody of the proper officer shall be presumed, in the absence of evidence to the contrary, to have been signed by the witness.

R.S., c. E-10, s. 10; 1994, c. 44, s. 86.

Case Law
Previous Statement in Writing or Reduced to Writing [See now s. 10(1)]

R. v. Cherpak (1978), 42 C.C.C (2d) 166 (Alta. C.A.); leave to appeal refused (1978), 42 C.C.C (2d) 166n (S.C.C.) — *See also: R. v. Handy* (1978), 5 C.R. (3d) 97, 45 C.C.C. (2d) 232 (B.C. C.A.) — A report made by a police officer from his notes of an interview with a witness is not a statement of the witness within the meaning of this section.

R. v. Peebles (1989), 49 C.C.C. (3d) 168 (B.C. C.A.) — A witness, including D, cannot be cross-examined on previous oral or written statements made by counsel or an agent.

R. v. Morgan (1993), 80 C.C.C. (3d) 16 at 20 (Ont. C.A.) — Where a "will say" statement is an accurate transcript of the things said by the witness during interview, it is the witness' statement *reduced to writing* for the purposes of *C.E.A.* s. 10 and he/she is liable to cross-examination on it under the section.

Production

Patterson v. R. (1970), 10 C.R.N.S. 55, 2 C.C.C. (2d) 227 (S.C.C.) — The power to order production of a witness' written statement exists only at trial and does *not* extend to a judge presiding at a preliminary inquiry.

R. v. Cherpak (1978), 42 C.C.C. (2d) 166 (Alta. C.A.); leave to appeal refused (1978), 42 C.C.C. (2d) 166 (S.C.C.) — The section gives the trial judge power to order production of the statement for his/her own inspection, but counsel is *not* entitled to it in law or as of right.

R. v. Tousigant (1962), 38 C.R. 319, 133 C.C.C. 270 (B.C. C.A.) — *See also: R. v. Smith* (1983), 35 C.R. (3d) 86 (B.C. C.A.) — A prior statement within this section is not admissible to prove the facts set out in it, but only to test credibility.

R. v. Kerenko (1964), 45 C.R. 291, [1965] 3 C.C.C. 52 (Man. C.A.) — It is only when a witness requires his notes to refresh his memory at trial that he may be called upon to produce them. Section 10 has no bearing on this point.

R. v. Doiron (1985), 19 C.C.C. (3d) 350 (N.S. C.A.) — *See also: R. v. Savion* (1980), 13 C.R. (3d) 259, 52 C.C.C. (2d) 276 (Ont. C.A.) — There is a power to require production under s. 10(1). Where it is established that a statement within the meaning of the section has been made, generally the defence is entitled to a copy of it. It is improper for the trial judge to examine the statement himself and disclose it to the defence only where he determines there is a contradiction between the statement and the testimony given. Apart from s. 10, a trial judge has a general power to order production of statements to ensure a fair trial.

R. v. Wood (1989), 51 C.C.C. (3d) 201 (Ont. C.A.) — The rule against adducing prior consistent statements of a witness applies to cross-examination as well as to examination-in-chief.

R. v. Valley (1986), 26 C.C.C. (3d) 207 (Ont. C.A.); leave to appeal refused (1986), 26 C.C.C. (3d) 207n (S.C.C.) — Where it is not intended to contradict the witness by proof of the statement, defence counsel is entitled to cross-examine on the statement without showing it to the witness.

R. v. Peruta; R. v. Brouillette (1992), 78 C.C.C. (3d) 350 (Que. C.A.) — While *C.E.A.* s. 10 gives counsel the right to cross-examine a witness called by the adverse party on a previous statement, it does *not* give counsel the right to obtain the statement in the possession of the other party. There is no duty of disclosure on the defence which corresponds to the common law duty on P to disclose to the defence copies of all statements in its possession. (per Tyndale J.A., Moisan J.A. concurring)*C.E.A.* ss. 10 and 11 govern the procedure for cross-examination on prior statements, but do *not* give the adverse party the right to obtain the prior statement of the witness to be cross-examined. The discovery of evidence in P's possession is a constitutional right for D. There is *no* corresponding duty on D to divulge evidence in favour of P. (per Proulx J.A., Moisan J.A. concurring)

Privilege

R. v. Peruta; R. v. Brouillette (1992), 78 C.C.C. (3d) 350 — Statements made to an investigator retained by the defence are privileged and are *not* subject to disclosure to P.

Right to Cross-Examine

R. v. Keegstra (1994), 92 C.C.C. (3d) 505, 23 Alta. L.R. (3d) 4 (C.A.) — There is no requirement that a trial judge make an advance ruling on inconsistency before permitting cross-examination on a statement under *C.E.A.*, s. 10(1).

R. v. Logan (1988), 68 C.R. (3d) 1, 46 C.C.C. (3d) 354 (Ont. C.A.) — *See also*: *R. v. Ma* (1978), 6 C.R. (3d) 325, 44 C.C.C. (2d) 537 (B.C. C.A.) — Defence counsel may cross-examine a co-accused on a prior inconsistent statement to the police even though the statement has not been proved voluntary.

Cormier v. R. (1973), 25 C.R.N.S. 94 (Que. C.A.) — *See also*: *R. v. Savion* (1980), 13 C.R. (3d) 259, 52 C.C.C. (2d) 276 (Ont. C.A.) — Counsel is not required to satisfy the trial judge that there are contradictions between the witness' statement and his testimony, before cross-examining on the statement. The rules with respect to s. 9 are not applicable to s. 10.

Statement as Exhibit

R. v. Campbell (1990), 57 C.C.C. (3d) 200 (Alta. C.A.) — Where a prior statement of a witness has been the subject of extensive examination-in-chief and cross-examination, the statement may be marked as an exhibit to assist the jury in its determination of the consistency or otherwise of the witness' testimony.

R. v. Rodney (1988), 46 C.C.C. (3d) 323 (B.C. C.A.) — *See also*: *R. v. Larue* (1991), 65 C.C.C. (3d) 1 (B.C.C.A.); *R. v. Smith* (1983), 35 C.R. (3d) 86 (B.C. C.A.); *R. v. Newall* (1983), 9 C.C.C. (3d) 519 (B.C. C.A.) — A trial judge has discretion to permit all, part, or an edited portion of a statement on which there has been cross-examination to be marked as an exhibit. In exercising the discretion, the trial judge should consider the extent to which there has been cross-examination on the statement.

R. v. Rowbotham (1988), 63 C.R. (3d) 113, 41 C.C.C. (3d) 1 (Ont. C.A.) — The witness's prior statement, on which he was cross-examined, should not have been made an exhibit which went to the jury room.

Evidentiary Value of Statement as Exhibit [See also C.E.A. s. 9]

R. v. Campbell (1977), 1 C.R. (3d) 309, 38 C.C.C. (2d) 6 (Ont. C.A.) — *See also*: *R. v. Smith* (1983), 35 C.R. (3d) 86 (B.C. C.A.) — Where the statement is produced and marked as an exhibit, it does not become evidence of the truth of its contents.

11. Cross-examination as to previous oral statements — Where a witness, on cross-examination as to a former statement made by him relative to the subject-matter of the case and inconsistent with his present testimony, does not distinctly admit that he did make the statement, proof may be given that he did in fact make it, but before the proof can be given the circumstances of the supposed statement, sufficient to designate the particular occasion, shall be mentioned to the witness, and he shall be asked whether or not he did make the statement.

R. S., c. E-10, s. 11.

Case Law

[See also C.E.A. s. 9]

R. v. Krause (1984), 12 C.C.C. (3d) 392 (B.C. C.A.); reversed on other grounds (1986), 54 C.R. (3d) 294, 29 C.C.C. (3d) 385 (S.C.C.) — Section 11 does not apply to permit P to adduce in rebuttal evidence of a statement made by D, where there is no inconsistency between D's testimony and his statement.

R. v. Grant (1989), 71 C.R. (3d) 231, 49 C.C.C. (3d) 410 (Man. C.A.) — Where a prior inconsistent statement constitutes an admission by V in the position of a party, it is not necessary to put to the witness the circumstances of the statement.

R. v. Varga (1994), 30 C.R. (4th) 78, 90 C.C.C. (3d) 484 (Ont. C.A.) — Evidence of V's psychiatrist as to statements made by V may be introduced to contradict V's evidence concerning the content of the statements, hence undermine V's credibility. To be admissible under *C.E.A.* s. 11, the statements made by V to the psychiatrist must be

i.   oral;

ii.   inconsistent with V's evidence; and,

iii. relative to the subject-matter of the case.

Counsel for D may *not* elicit from the recipient evidence of prior inconsistent oral statements made by V which V acknowledged making during cross-examination or which relate only to a collateral matter.

R. v. Blunden (1976), 30 C.C.C. (2d) 122 (Ont. C.A.) — The jury should be told that if they find contradictions between the witness' previous statement and his evidence at trial, they can not use them to prove the truth of what was said in the statement. They can use them only in assessing credibility.

12. (1) Examination as to previous convictions — A witness may be questioned as to whether the witness has been convicted of any offence, excluding any offence designated as a contravention under the Contraventions Act, but including such an offence where the conviction was entered after a trial on an indictment.

(1.1) Proof of previous convictions — If the witness either denies the fact or refuses to answer, the opposite party may prove the conviction.

(2) How conviction proved — A conviction may be proved by producing

(a) a certificate containing the substance and effect only, omitting the formal part, of the indictment and conviction, if it is for an indictable offence, or a copy of the summary conviction, if it is for an offence punishable on summary conviction, purporting to be signed by the clerk of the court or other officer having the custody of the records of the court in which the conviction, if on indictment, was had, or to which the conviction, if summary, was returned; and

(b) proof of identity.

R.S., c. E-10, s. 12; 1992, c. 47, s. 66.

Case Law

"May be Questioned"

R. v. Underwood, [1998] 1 S.C.R. 77, 12 C.R. (5th) 241, 121 C.C.C. (3d) 117 — A *Corbett* application should be made and decided immediately after the close of P's case.If necessary, a *voir dire* should be held in which D discloses the evidence to be led in defence.

Evidence not disclosed by D on the *voir dire* may be adduced, but may require modification of the *Corbett* ruling if there is a significant departure from what was disclosed on the *voir dire*.

Corbett v. R. (1988), 64 C.R. (3d) 1, 41 C.C.C. (3d) 385 (S.C.C.) — The trial judge has a discretion under s. 12 to exclude prejudicial evidence of prior convictions in an appropriate case.

R. v. Charland (1996), 110 C.C.C. (3d) 300 (Alta. C.A.); aff'd (1997), 120 C.C.C. (3d) 481 (S.C.C.) — On an application to exclude/edit previous convictions of D, the trial judge must decide whether the permissible *probative value* of the evidence of prior convictions exceeds the risk of prejudice through improper jury use. The trial judge may consider the effectiveness of limiting instructions concerning jury use of evidence of previous convictions. While convictions of violent crime may not directly reflect on honesty and truthfulness, hence be of limited value on credibility, a lengthy record of such offences may reflect a disregard for societal rules, hence a likelihood of lying.

R. v. Halliday (1992), 77 C.C.C. (3d) 481 (Man. C.A.) — In the absence of a clear error in principle in the exercise of the discretion under s. 12, an appellate court ought be slow to substitute its view for that of the trial judge.

R. v. Brand (1995), 40 C.R. (4th) 137, 98 C.C.C. (3d) 477 (Ont. C.A.) — In determining whether to prohibit cross-examination of D on previous convictions under *CEA*, s. 12, the trial judge must weigh the risks for and against exclusion, bearing in mind the evidentiary value of the prior convictions on the issue of credibility and the fair trial of D.

R. v. Saroya (1994), 36 C.R. (4th) 253 (Ont. C.A.) — The balancing of interests required under is a balancing of probative value against prejudicial effect. The right to a fair trial is the context in which the balancing must be effected. The outcome of the exercise is the preservation of the right to a fair trial.

R. v. P. (G.F.) (1994), 29 C.R. (4th) 315, 89 C.C.C. (3d) 176 (Ont. C.A.) — In determining whether to prohibit cross-examination of D on prior convictions, a trial judge is obliged to weigh and balance the risks for and against exclusion. Exclusion is *not* only granted "as a last resort".

"Conviction"

Morris v. R. (1978), 6 C.R. (3d) 36, 43 C.C.C. (2d) 129 (S.C.C.) — *See also: R. v. Boyko* (1975), 28 C.C.C. (2d) 193 (B.C. C.A.) — This section permits cross-examination on a record under the *Juvenile Delinquents Act.*

Hewson v. R. (1978), 5 C.R. (3d) 155, 42 C.C.C. (2d) 507 (S.C.C.) — Evidence of a previous conviction may be adduced under *Code* s. 360 even though the conviction is under appeal.

R. v. Paterson (1998), 122 C.C.C. (3d) 254 (B.C. C.A.) — The combined operation of *Code* s. 748(3) and s. 5 of the *Criminal Records Act* bars cross-examination on prior convictions for which a witness has received a free pardon.

R. v. Geddes (1979), 52 C.C.C. (2d) 230 (Man. C.A.) — While D may be cross-examined as to his previous convictions, he may not be asked whether he testified at the trials leading to those convictions. Questioning under s. 12 should be confined to what is specifically allowable.

R. v. Miller (1998), 21 C.R. (5th) 178, 131 C.C.C. (3d) 141 (Ont. C.A.) — Section 12 is permissive, *not* restrictive. It does *not* limit defence cross-examination of P's witnesses *only* on the particulars of convictions. Subject to the trial judge's general discretion to limit cross-examination to what is relevant and proper, there is *no* reason to limit defence cross-examination of a non-accused witness where conduct has resulted in a criminal conviction.

R. v. R. (S.A.S.) (1996), 111 C.C.C. (3d) 305 (Ont. C.A.) — Cross-examination of D on previous criminal convictions ougt *not* include reference to the *name* of V. The identity of V is *irrelevant* to the assessment of D's credibility and capable of causing significant prejudice.

R. v. Menard (1996), 108 C.C.C. (3d) 424 (Ont. C.A.); aff'd (1998), 125 C.C.C. (3d) 416 (S.C.C.) — *Semble* it is not permissible for P to cross-examine D on details of D's prior criminal convictions.

R. v. Bricker (1994), 90 C.C.C. (3d) 268 (Ont. C.A.); leave to appeal refused (November 3, 1994), Doc. 24264 (S.C.C.). — Under s. 12, P may ask D for

i.   the *name* of the *crime*;

ii.   the *substance* and effect of the *indictment*;

iii. the *place* of *conviction*; and,

iv.   the *sentence* imposed

but may *not* cross-examine concerning the *details* of the offences of which D has been convicted.

R. v. Watkins (1992), 70 C.C.C. (3d) 341 (Ont. C.A.) — Section 12(1) permits cross-examination on convictions for offences under all federal statutes, subject to the discretion of *Corbett, supra.*

R. v. Danson (1982), 66 C.C.C. (2d) 369 (Ont. C.A.) — *See also: R. v. Dodge* (1993), 81 C.C.C. (3d) 433 (Que. C.A.) — An adjudication of guilt followed by the granting of a discharge is *not* a conviction within s. 12. D, unlike an ordinary witness, may not be cross-examined as to a discharge.

R. v. Stratton (1978), 3 C.R. (3d) 289, 42 C.C.C. (2d) 449 (Ont. C.A.) — Section 12 applies to foreign convictions, where the process of adjudication of guilt was of a character which would constitute a conviction under Canadian law.

R. v. Boyce (1975), 28 C.R.N.S. 336, 23 C.C.C. (2d) 16 (Ont. C.A.) — "Conviction" in s. 12 means the adjudication of guilt plus the sentence. D may be cross-examined as to the penalties imposed upon prior convictions.

Other Discreditable Conduct

R. v. Cullen (1989), 52 C.C.C. (3d) 459 (Ont. C.A.) — *See also*: *R. v. Titus* (1983), 2 C.C.C. (3d) 321 (S.C.C.); *R. v. Hoilett* (1991), 4 C.R. (4th) 372 (Ont. C.A.) — The limitations upon cross-examination of D on his criminal record do not apply on cross-examination of a witness. A witness may be cross-examined as to discreditable conduct including the circumstances of a charge for which the witness received a discharge, or an outstanding charge.

R. v. Davison (1974), 20 C.C.C. (2d) 424 (Ont. C.A.); leave to appeal refused (1974), 20 C.C.C. (2d) 424n (S.C.C.) — Generally, D can not be cross-examined as to his misconduct or discreditable associations which have not led to conviction, except where it is directly relevant to show the falsity of his evidence.

Cross-Examination on Outstanding Charges

R. v. Titus, [1983] 1 S.C.R. 259, 33 C.R. (3d) 17, 2 C.C.C. (3d) 321 — *See also*: *R. v. Gonzague* (1983), 34 C.R. (3d) 169, 179, 4 C.C.C. (3d) 505 (Ont. C.A.) — A witness *for P* may be cross-examined on the *fact* that (s)he is facing outstanding charges, as well as the *facts which underlie such charges*. Such cross-examination may disclose a bias, interest or motive to lie in return for favourable disposition of the charges by P.

R. v. Hoilett (1991), 4 C.R. (4th) 372 (Ont. C.A.) — Defence witnesses may *not* be cross-examined concerning the existence of outstanding charges which have *not* resulted in convictions.

Evidence of Previous Acquittals

R. v. Camacho (1998), 129 C.C.C. (3d) 94 (Ont. C.A.) — *See also*: *R. v. Martin* (1980), 53 C.C.C. (2d) 425 (Ont. C.A.) — As a general rule, evidence of a witness' *acquittal* on the charge(s) for which D is being tried is *irrelevant* to D's guilt or innocence and *inadmissible* at D's trial. There is an *exception* to the general rule, however, which permits admission of evidence of the witness' acquittal for the *limited purpose* of demonstrating that the witness has *no personal interest* in the outcome of the case.

Procedure

R. v. Clark (1977), 1 C.R. (3d) 368, 41 C.C.C. (2d) 561 (B.C. C.A.) — It is permissible to ask the witness a general question, such as "Were you convicted of any offence while in the United States", without reference to a specific conviction.

R. v. Boyko (1975), 28 C.C.C. (2d) 193 (B.C. C.A.) — *See also*: *R. v. St. Pierre* (1974), 17 C.C.C. (2d) 489 (Ont. C.A.) — The criminal record of a Crown witness or D may be adduced in examination-in-chief.

Effect/Evidentiary Value

R. v. Arcangioli (1994), 27 C.R. (4th) 1, 87 C.C.C. (3d) 289 (S.C.C.) — Evidence of a prosecution witness' prior conviction, including the circumstances which underlie it, may be admissible to support a defence that it was the witness, not D, who committed the offence charged. Evidence of a third party's character or violent disposition is admissible in D's defence even if it refers to only one event.

R. v. McIlvride (1979), 10 C.R. (3d) 95 (B.C. C.A.) — It is reversible error to charge the jury that D's prior criminal record brands him as an unreliable person to give evidence under oath.

R. v. Brooks (1998), 20 C.R. (5th) 116, 129 C.C.C. (3d) 227 (Ont. C.A.); notice of appeal as of right filed , Doc. 26948 (S.C.C.) — Convictions for acts of violence, such as assault, have less bearing on a person's credibility than do acts of dishonesty, like theft or fraud.

A court should be wary of admitting evidence of D's conviction for a *similar* crime to avoid the possibility of conviction based on D's disposition.

R. v. Brown (1978), 38 C.C.C. (2d) 339 (Ont. C.A.) — The probative value of previous convictions will vary and in the exercise of his discretion, the trial judge may direct the jury that a conviction for an offence committed many years before is of little value. There is no rule of law or practice that a witness with a single prior conviction automatically comes within a category of witnesses whose evidence must be carefully examined.

Proof: S. 12(2)

R. v. Howard (1983), 3 C.C.C. (3d) 399 (Ont. C.A.) — Where D testifies he can not recall a prior conviction, it is improper to cross-examine him as to the circumstances of the offence to "refresh" his memory. The conviction should be proved by producing a certificate pursuant to s. 12(2).

R. v. Stratton (1978), 3 C.R. (3d) 289, 42 C.C.C. (2d) 449 (Ont. C.A.) — Section 12(2) does *not* provide an exclusive method of proving previous convictions. A foreign conviction may be proved under s. 23.

Oaths and Solemn Affirmations

13. Who may administer oaths — Every court and judge, and every person having, by law or consent of parties, authority to hear and receive evidence, has power to administer an oath to every witness who is legally called to give evidence before that court, judge or person.

R.S., c. E-10, s. 13.

14. (1) Solemn affirmation by witness instead of oath — A person may, instead of taking an oath, make the following solemn affirmation:

I solemnly affirm that the evidence to be given by me shall be the truth, the whole truth and nothing but the truth.

(2) Effect — Where a person makes a solemn affirmation in accordance with subsection (1), his evidence shall be taken and have the same effect as if taken under oath.

R.S., c. E-10, s. 14; 1994, c. 44, s. 87.

Case Law

Incompetent

R. v. Hanna (1993), 80 C.C.C. (3d) 289 (B.C. C.A.) — Section 14 applies where the witness him/herself objects to taking the oath, or is objected to as incompetent to take an oath. The objection, by whomever taken, must be based on the witness' lack of religious belief.

R. v. Walsh (1978), 45 C.C.C. (2d) 199 (Ont. C.A.) — The phrase "incompetent to take an oath" does *not* refer to mental incompetency but to incompetency to take an oath because it would *not* bind the conscience of the witness due to an absence of religious belief. Neither moral depravity nor a disposition to lie disqualifies a person from testifying.

R. v. Hawke (1975), 29 C.R.N.S. 1, 22 C.C.C. (2d) 19 (Ont. C.A.) — When an objection is taken that a witness is incompetent to take an oath, the trial judge must determine that issue by examination of the witness and such other evidence as he or she deems appropriate. The determination that a witness may affirm does not flow automatically from a determination that he or she should not be sworn. Before a witness may affirm, a further inquiry is necessary to determine whether he or she appreciates the duty of speaking the truth.

15. (1) Solemn affirmation by deponent — Where a person who is required or who desires to make an affidavit or deposition in a proceeding or on an occasion on which or concerning a matter respecting which an oath is required or is lawful, whether on the taking of office or otherwise, does not wish to take an oath, the court or judge, or other officer or person qualified to take affidavits or depositions, shall permit the person to make a solemn affirmation in the words following, namely, "I, ..., do solemnly affirm, etc.", and that solemn affirmation has the same force and effect as if that person had taken an oath.

(2) Effect — Any witness whose evidence is admitted or who makes a solemn affirmation under this section or section 14 is liable to indictment and punishment for perjury in all respects as if he had been sworn.

R.S., c. E-10, s. 15; 1994, c. 44, s. 88.

16. (1) Witness whose capacity is in question — Where a proposed witness is a person under fourteen years of age or a person whose mental capacity is challenged, the court shall, before permitting the person to give evidence, conduct an inquiry to determine

(a) whether the person understands the nature of an oath or a solemn affirmation; and

(b) whether the person is able to communicate the evidence.

(2) Testimony under oath or solemn affirmation — A person referred to in subsection (1) who understands the nature of an oath or a solemn affirmation and is able to communicate the evidence shall testify under oath or solemn affirmation.

(3) Testimony on promise to tell truth — A person referred to in subsection (1) who does not understand the nature of an oath or a solemn affirmation but is able to communicate the evidence may, notwithstanding any provision of any Act requiring an oath or a solemn affirmation, testify on promising to tell the truth.

(4) Inability to testify — A person referred to in subsection (1) who neither understands the nature of an oath or a solemn affirmation nor is able to communicate the evidence shall not testify.

(5) Burden as to capacity of witness — A party who challenges the mental capacity of a proposed witness of fourteen years of age or more has the burden of satisfying the court that there is an issue as to the capacity of the proposed witness to testify under an oath or a solemn affirmation.

R.S., c. E-10, s. 16; R.S. 1985, c. 19 (3d Supp.), s. 18; 1994, c. 44, s. 89.

Case Law
Nature and Procedure of Inquiry

R. v. Marquard (1993), 25 C.R. (4th) 1, 85 C.C.C. (3d) 193 (S.C.C.) — Testimonial competence comprehends

i.   the capacity to *observe*, including interpretation;

ii.   the capacity to *recollect*, and,

iii. the capacity to *communicate*.

The *object* of any inquiry into testimonial competence is *not* to ensure that the evidence is credible, only to assure that it meets the minimum threshold of being receivable. The inquiry is into the *capacity* to perceive, recollect and communicate, not actual perception, recollection and communication. The test merely outlines the basic abilities that individuals whose competence is challenged need have if they are to testify.

R. v. Fong (1994), 92 C.C.C. (3d) 171 (Alta. C.A.) — Counsel may admit the competency of a child witness to give sworn testimony. Under s. 655 of the *Code*, a trial judge may rely on the admission in deciding whether the statutory requirements of s. 16(1) CEA have been met.

R. v. Ferguson (1996), 112 C.C.C. (3d) 342 (B.C. C.A.) — The s. 16(1) CEA inquiry in connection with a *child* witness may be conducted in the *presence* of the jury. The evidence given by the prospective witness may assist the trier of fact in assessing the weight, if any, to be assigned to the child's evidence. The issues of competence, to be decided by the trial judge, and credibility, to be determined by the jury, are tightly entwined. The possibility of prejudice to D if the witness is found incompetent ought be discussed with the trial judge, in the absence of the jury, prior to commencement of the s. 16(1) CEA inquiry.

R. v. Ferguson (1996), 112 C.C.C. (3d) 342 (B.C. C.A.) — A trial judge has a *discretion* to allow counsel to ask questions of a prospective child witness on a s. 16(1) CEA inquiry.

R. v. Ferguson (1996), 112 C.C.C. (3d) 342 (B.C. C.A.) — The *standard* of proof required on the competence issue is the civil standard of *balance of probabilities*, irrespective of which party tenders the witness.

R. v. G. (C.W.) (1994), 88 C.C.C. (3d) 240 (B.C. C.A.) — A trial judge must be satisfied by some acknowledgement from the witness which can be characterized as a promise that the proposed witness understands the difference between truth and falsehood and is committed to telling the truth. The promise to tell the truth is to get at the conscience of the witness in a manner intelligible to the witness. This purpose exists notwithstanding that a child under 12 is immune from prosecution for perjury. (per Southin and Goldie JJ.A.).

R. v. Farley (1995), 40 C.R. (4th) 190, 99 C.C.C. (3d) 76 (Ont. C.A.) — To "perceive" is to demonstrate an ability to perceive events as they occur, as well as an ability to differentiate between what was actually perceived from what one may have imagined, been informed of by others, or otherwise have come to believe. The capacity to remember refers to an individual's capacity to maintain a recollection of his/her actual perceptions of a prior event and the ability to distinguish the retained perceptions from information provided by other sources. A capacity to communicate includes the ability to understand questions and formulate intelligible responses.

R. v. Caron (1994), 19 O.R. (3d) 323 (Ont. C.A.) — To be "able to communicate the evidence", a witness must demonstrate some ability, not only to distinguish fact from fiction, but also a capacity and willingness, however limited, to relate to the court the essence of what happened. There must be some evidence that the proposed witness has the capacity to relate the contentious parts of his or her evidence with some independence and not entirely in response to suggestive questions.

R. v. Donovan (1991), 65 C.C.C. (3d) 511 at 518-519 (Ont. C.A.) — In determining the testimonial *competence* of a child under fourteen, a trial judge has no duty to inquire into the competency of the child at the time of the alleged occurrence before permitting him/her to give sworn evidence. The age of the child at the time of the relevant events and also the length of time between the events and testimony are important factors on the issue of credibility and weight, but *not* competence.

R. v. Khan (1990), 79 C.R. (3d) 1, 89 C.C.C. (3d) 92 (Ont. C.A.); affirming (1988), 64 C.R. (3d) 281, 42 C.C.C. (3d) 197 (Ont. Dist. Ct.) — Before a proposed witness can give evidence under oath, it must be established that the oath, in some way, gets a hold on the conscience of the witness, i.e., that he/she appreciates the significance of testifying in court under oath.

R. v. Leonard (1990), 54 C.C.C. (3d) 225 (Ont. C.A.) — An understanding of the nature of an oath requires that a child witness appreciate the solemnity of the occasion and understand the added responsibility to tell the truth over and above such duty as part of normal social conduct. To be sworn, a witness must also understand what it means to tell the truth in court and appreciate what happens in both a practical and moral sense when a lie is told in court.

R. v. Fletcher (1982), 1 C.C.C. (3d) 370 (Ont. C.A.); leave to appeal refused (1983), 48 N.R. 319 (S.C.C.) — *See also*: *R. v. G. (K.A.)* (1986), 40 C.C.C. (3d) 333 (Man. C.A.), reversed (1988), 62 C.R. (3d) 398, 40 C.C.C. (3d) 333 (S.C.C.); *R. v. Conners*, [1986] 5 W.W.R. 94 (Alta. C.A.) [This case was decided under the former s. 16] — In determining whether a child should be sworn, the judge must determine whether the child has a sufficient appreciation of the solemnity of the occasion and the added responsibility to tell the truth, which is involved in taking an oath, over and above the duty to tell the truth which is an ordinary duty of normal social conduct.

R. v. D. (R.R.) (1989), 69 C.R. (3d) 267, 47 C.C.C. (3d) 97 (Sask. C.A.) — *See also*: *R. v. R. (M.E.)* (1989), 71 C.R. (3d) 113, 49 C.C.C. (3d) 475 (N.S.C.A.); *R. v. Krack* (1990), 56 C.C.C. (3d) 555 (Ont. C.A.) — The *procedure* set out in s. 16(1) is *mandatory*. It requires the trial judge to determine whether the child understands the nature of an oath or a solemn affirmation, as well as whether the child has the ability to communicate the evidence. If the child does not understand the nature of an oath or a solemn affirmation but can communicate the evidence, the child cannot testify without first promising to tell the truth.

Evidence on Promise to Tell the Truth

R. v. Marquard (1993), 25 C.R. (4th) 1, 85 C.C.C. (3d) 193 (S.C.C.) — To "communicate the evidence" involves more than mere verbal ability. "The evidence" indicates the ability to testify about the matters before the court. The judge should to explore, in a general way, whether the witness is capable of perceiving and remembering events and communicating them to the court. Satisfaction of these requirements will then permit reception of the child's evidence, after the child has promised to tell the truth. It is unnecessary to determine in advance that the child perceived and recollects the very events at issue in the trial as a condition of a ruling that the child's evidence be received.

R. v. Ferguson (1996), 112 C.C.C. (3d) 342 (B.C. C.A.) — A promise to tell the truth implies an understanding of

i.   the *difference* between telling the *truth* and telling a *lie*; and

ii.   the *nature* of a *promise*.

A child witness who does *not* understand the *nature* of an oath or solemn affirmation may *only* testify under CEA s. 16(3) if s/he

i.   *promises* to tell the *truth*;

ii.   understands the *difference* between *truth* and *falsehoods*; and

iii.   understands the *duty* to tell the *truth* concerning his/her observations.

R. v. G. (C.W.) (1994), 88 C.C.C. (3d) 240 (B.C. C.A.) — A trial judge must be satisfied by some acknowledgement from the witness which can be characterized as a promise that the proposed witness understands the difference between truth and falsehood and is committed to telling the truth. The promise to tell the truth is to get at the conscience of the witness in a manner intelligible to the witness. This purpose exists notwithstanding that a child under 12 is immune from prosecution for perjury. (per Southin and Goldie JJ.A.).

R. v. McGovern (1993), 22 C.R. (4th) 359, 82 C.C.C. (3d) 301 (Man. C.A.); leave to appeal refused (November 18, 1993), Doc. 23733 (S.C.C.) — In permitting a witness to give evidence on promising to tell the truth, s. 16(3) *C.E.A.* implicitly requires that the witness understand what a promise is and the importance of keeping it. The determination whether a witness has the capacity to communicate the evidence is made by the trial judge in the course of the inquiry into competency.

R. v. McGovern (1993), 22 C.R. (4th) 359, 82 C.C.C. (3d) 301 (Man. C.A.); leave to appeal refused (November 18, 1993), Doc. 23733 (S.C.C.) — *See also*: *R. v. D. (R.R.)* (1989), 69 C.R. (3d) 267, 47 C.C.C. (3d) 97 (Sask. C.A.) — The mere fact that a witness testifies on a promise to tell the truth, rather than under oath, does *not* mean the testimony ought to be afforded less weight.

R. v. Wilson (1995), 38 C.R. (4th) 209 (N.S. C.A.) — Where a judge is satisfied that a witness under 14 years of age may testify on a promise to tell the truth, the witness must promise to tell the truth or give an undertaking tantamount to such a promise before his/her evidence may be received. (per Freeman and Pugsley JJ.A.)

R. v. Farley (1995), 40 C.R. (4th) 190, 99 C.C.C. (3d) 76 (Ont. C.A.). — There is a close relationship between an understanding of the duty to speak the truth and the making of a meaningful promise to tell the truth. The latter assumes the existence of the former.

General Caution Concerning Evidence of Children

R. v. Marquard (1993), 25 C.R. (4th) 1, 85 C.C.C. (3d) 193 (S.C.C.) — There is no fixed and precise formula to be followed in warning a jury about potential problems with the evidence of a witness, whether adult or child. Negative stereotypes ought not be applied, however, to the evidence of children.

R. v. W. (R.) (1992), 13 C.R. (4th) 257, 74 C.C.C. (3d) 134 (S.C.C.) — In recent years it has become recognized that the notion, found at common law and codified in legislation, that the evidence of children was inherently unreliable and, accordingly, should be treated with special caution, has been eliminated. There is also an appreciation that it may be wrong to apply adult tests for credibility to the evidence of children. Their evidence should be approached on a common sense basis, taking into account its strengths and weaknesses *in the particular case*.

R. v. K. (V.) (1991), 4 C.R. (4th) 338, 68 C.C.C. (3d) 18 (B.C. C.A.) — There is *no* statutory requirement nor rule of practice that a judge caution him/herself against the risks associated with relying solely upon the unsupported evidence of a *child* witness. Further, there is no rule of practice which requires such caution in the case of *sexual offences*, due to the nature of the offence alleged. Cautions, matters within the discretion of the trial judge, are dependent upon the circumstances of individual cases.

R. v. Donovan (1991), 65 C.C.C. (3d) 511 at 519 (Ont. C.A.) — The *age* of the child at the time of the relevant events and also the *length of time* between the events and testimony at trial are important factors on the issue of credibility and weight.

R. v. Tennant (1975), 31 C.R.N.S. 1, 23 C.C.C. (2d) 80 (Ont. C.A.) — Where the sworn evidence of the child witnesses was in direct conflict with that of D and with each other, it was misdirection not to caution the jury as to the frailties of the evidence of children.

Hearsay Evidence of Children's Statements

R. v. Khan (1990), 79 C.R. (3d) 1, 59 C.C.C. (3d) 92 (S.C.C.); affirming (1988), 64 C.R. (3d) 281, 42 C.C.C. (3d) 197 (Ont. C.A.) — Despite the need for caution, hearsay evidence of a child's statement alleging crimes against the child may be received where the general requirements of *necessity* and *reliability* are met. *Necessity* may be established where the child's evidence is itself inadmissible or expert evidence demonstrates that giving evidence might be traumatic for or harmful to the child. Factors relevant to establish *reliability* may include, but are not limited to, the timing of the statement, the demeanour, personality, intelligence and understanding of the child and the absence of reason for fabrication.

R. v. Hanna (1993), 80 C.C.C. (3d) 289 (B.C. C.A.) — Testimony at a prior trial may be admitted as an exception to the hearsay rule at a subsequent trial where the witness again testifies, provided the criteria of necessity and reliability are met. Where much of the witness' recollection of events had been lost by the passage of time between the events and the second trial, as well the subconscious desire to forget the horrifying and traumatic events experienced at age six, resorting to the evidence given at the first trial was the only way of getting the crucial evidence before the jury. The reliability requirement was met in that the evidence had been given on solemn affirmation and was subject to cross-examination.

R. v. A. (S.) (1992), 17 C.R. (4th) 233, 76 C.C.C. (3d) 522 (Ont. C.A.) — Where a child's out-of-court statement alleging criminal conduct against D is received and the child does *not* testify, a trial judge must alert the jury to the dangers inherent in relying upon such statements. The jury should be instructed that it must first determine whether the statement alleged was made and, if so, its content. In this respect, the jury should be told to consider the credibility of the witness who testifies as to the making of the statement, as well as the reliability of its evidence, especially as it relates to the making of the statement. The trial judge should apprise the jury of the positions of the parties on the issue and the evidence relied upon by each in support. The jury ought to be instructed that if, upon consideration of all the relevant evidence, it is *not* satisfied the statement was made, the contents cannot be relied on in determining whether P has proven D's guilt. Even if the jury is satisfied that the statement was made, the statement cannot be placed on the same footing as *viva voce* testimony. Out-of-court statements by persons who are not witnesses are subject to certain frailties which warrant a cautious approach by the jury. The frailties which include:

i.   that the statement was *not* made under oath or upon a promise to tell the truth;

ii. that the jury has *no* opportunity to see and hear V testify; and,

iii. that V is *not* subject to cross-examination

ought to be brought to the attention of the jury in language apt for the case. The jury should also be instructed to look to the other evidence when considering the *reliability* of V's out-of-court statements. The more salient features of that evidence ought be drawn to the jury's attention.

R. v. Aguilar (1992), 15 C.R. (4th) 157, 77 C.C.C. (3d) 462 (Ont. C.A.) — The fact that the child testifies bears on the *necessity* requirement. Necessity, however, cannot be equated with unavailability. Necessary means "reasonably necessary". A determination whether the admission of a child's out-of-court statement is necessary where the child testifies is an *ad hoc* one.

Khan v. College of Physicians & Surgeons of Ontario (1992), 76 C.C.C. (3d) 10 (Ont. C.A.) — The hearsay statement of a child is admissible if *reasonably* necessary and if *indicia* of reliability are present. Where the child testifies, *reasonable necessity* refers to the need to obtain an accurate and frank rendition of the child's version of events concerning the alleged assault. The child's oral evidence must usually be heard in such cases before it may be determined whether the hearsay statement is reasonably necessary.

Unsworn Evidence at Preliminary

R. v. Greenwood (1992), 70 C.C.C. (3d) 260 (Ont. C.A.) — *See also: R. v. Gray* (1991), 68 C.C.C. (3d) 193 (Ont. Gen. Div.) — Section 540(1)(a) does *not* deprive a justice of the authority to receive and order D to stand trial upon the basis of the unsworn evidence of a child under fourteen years of age. *C.E.A.*, s. 16(3) creates an exception to the general rule of s. 540(1)(a), and permits the reception of unsworn evidence at a preliminary hearing.

Charter Considerations

R. v. Bickford (1989), 51 C.C.C. (3d) 181 (Ont. C.A.) — *See also: R. v. Jack* (1989), 51 C.C.C. (3d) 255 (N.S. C.A.) — The repeal of the requirement that unsworn evidence of a child be corroborated does *not* violate *Charter* s. 7. The repeal is procedural in nature and operates retrospectively.

Judicial Notice

17. Imperial Acts, etc — Judicial notice shall be taken of all Acts of the Imperial Parliament, of all ordinances made by the Governor in Council, or the lieutenant governor in council of any province or colony that, or some portion of which, now forms or hereafter may form part of Canada, and of all the Acts of the legislature of any such province or colony, whether enacted before or after the passing of the *Constitution Act, 1867.*

R.S, c. E-10, s. 17.

Case Law

R. v. Whalen (1971), 15 C.R.N.S. 187, 4 C.C.C. (2d) 560 (N.B. C.A.) — An Order in Council adding a substance to the schedules to the *Food and Drugs Act* is an ordinance within s. 17.

R. v. Markin (1969), 7 C.R.N.S. 135, [1970] 1 C.C.C. 14 (B.C. C.A.) — Ordinance as used in s. 17 does not include a Lieutenant Governor's proclamation.

18. Acts of Canada — Judicial notice shall be taken of all Acts of Parliament, public or private, without being specially pleaded.

R.S., c. E-10, s. 18.

Documentary Evidence

19. Copies by Queen's Printer — Every copy of any Act of Parliament, public or private, printed by the Queen's Printer, is evidence of that Act and of its contents and every copy purporting to be printed by the Queen's Printer shall be deemed to be so printed, unless the contrary is shown.

R.S., c. E-10, s. 19.

Case Law

R. v. Welsh, (No. 6) (1977), 32 C.C.C. (2d) 363 (Ont. C.A.) — Where there is a discrepancy between an Act of Parliament as certified by the Clerk of the Parliaments and the version published by the Queen's Printer, the former is to be preferred.

20. Imperial proclamations, etc — Imperial proclamations, orders in council, treaties, orders, warrants, licences, certificates, rules, regulations, or other Imperial official records, Acts or documents may be proved

(a) in the same manner as they may from time to time be provable in any court in England;

(b) by the production of a copy of the *Canada Gazette*, or a volume of the Acts of Parliament purporting to contain a copy of the same or a notice thereof; or

(c) by the production of a copy thereof purporting to be printed by the Queen's Printer.

R.S., c. E-10, s. 20.

21. Proclamations, etc., of Governor General — Evidence of any proclamation, order, regulation or appointment, made or issued by the Governor General or by the Governor in Council, or by or under the authority of any minister or head of any department of the Government of Canada and evidence of a treaty to which Canada is a party, may be given in all or any of the following ways:

(a) by the production of a copy of the *Canada Gazette*, or a volume of the Acts of Parliament purporting to contain a copy of the treaty, proclamation, order, regulation or appointment or a notice thereof;

(b) by the production of a copy of the proclamation, order, regulation or appointment, purporting to be printed by the Queen's Printer;

(c) by the production of a copy of the treaty purporting to be printed by the Queen's Printer;

(d) by the production, in the case of any proclamation, order, regulation or appointment made or issued by the Governor General or by the Governor in Council, of a copy or extract purporting to be certified to be true by the clerk or assistant or acting clerk of the Queen's Privy Council for Canada; and

(e) by the production, in the case of any order, regulation or appointment made or issued by or under the authority of any minister or head of a department of the Government of Canada, of a copy or extract purporting to be certified to be true by the minister, by his deputy or acting deputy, or by the secretary or acting secretary of the department over which he presides.

R.S., c. E-10, s. 21; 1976–77, c. 28, s. 14.

Case Law

R. v. The "Evgenia Chandris" (1976), 27 C.C.C. (2d) 241 (S.C.C.) — Under the *Statutory Instruments Act*, instruments published in the *Canada Gazette* must be judicially noticed and the fact of publication needs *no* proof. The court can rely on the contents as printed by the Queen's Printer.

22. (1) Proclamations, etc., of Lieutenant Governor — Evidence of any proclamation, order, regulation or appointment made or issued by a lieutenant governor or lieutenant governor in council of any province, or by or under the authority of any member of the executive council, being the head of any department of the government of the province, may be given in all or any of the following ways:

(a) by the production of a copy of the official gazette for the province, purporting to contain a copy of the proclamation, order, regulation or appointment, or a notice thereof;

(b) by the production of a copy of the proclamation, order, regulation or appointment purporting to be printed by the government or Queen's Printer for the province; and

(c) by the production of a copy or extract of the proclamation, order, regulation or appointment purporting to be certified to be true by the clerk or assistant or acting clerk of the executive council, by the head of any department of the government of a province, or by his deputy or acting deputy, as the case may be.

(2) In the case of the territories — Evidence of any proclamation, order, regulation or appointment made by the Lieutenant Governor or Lieutenant Governor in

Council of the Northwest Territories, as constituted prior to September 1, 1905, or by the Commissioner in Council of the Yukon Territory, the Commissioner in Council of the Northwest Territories or the Legislature for Nunavut, may be given by the production of a copy of the *Canada Gazette* purporting to contain a copy of the proclamation, order, regulation or appointment, or a notice thereof.

R.S., c. E-10, s. 22; 1993, c. 28, s. 78 (Sched. III, item 8).

23. (1) Evidence of judicial proceedings, etc. — Evidence of any proceeding or record whatever of, in or before any court in Great Britain, the Supreme Court, Federal Court or Tax Court of Canada, any court in any province, any court in any British colony or possession or any court of record of the United States, of any state of the United States or of any other foreign country, or before any justice of the peace or coroner in any province, may be given in any action or proceeding by an exemplification or certified copy of the proceeding or record, purporting to be under the seal of the court or under the hand or seal of the justice or coroner or court stenographer, as the case may be, without any proof of the authenticity of the seal or of the signature of the justice or coroner or court stenographer or other proof whatever.

(2) Certificate where court has no seal — Where any court, justice or coroner or court stenographer referred to in subsection (1) has no seal, or so certifies, the evidence may be given by a copy purporting to be certified under the signature of a judge or presiding provincial court judge or of the justice or coroner or court stenographer, without any proof of the authenticity of the signature or other proof whatever.

R.S., c. E-10, s. 23; c. 10 (2d Supp.), s. 64; 1993, c. 34, s. 15; 1997, c. 18, s. 117.

Case Law

Cordes v. R. (1979), 10 C.R. (3d) 186, 47 C.C.C. (2d) 46 (S.C.C.) — A judge granting an authorization to intercept private communications does so as a judge and *not* as *persona designata*. The authorization may be proved under this section by filing a certified copy of it.

Re Wong Shue Teen (1975), 24 C.C.C. (2d) 501 (Fed. C.A.) — Section 23 is a rule concerning the proof of documents and does not relate to authentication. The certification by an American court official merely establishes that the certified copy is a faithful reproduction of the original document. It does not establish the genuineness of the original.

R. v. Duong (1998), 15 C.R. (5th) 209, 124 C.C.C. (3d) 392 (Ont. C.A.) — The prior conviction of a principal may be proven under *C.E.A.*, s. 23 by introduction of a certified copy of the indictment endorsed by the trial judge.

24. Certified copies — In every case in which the original record could be admitted in evidence,

(a) a copy of any official or public document of Canada or of any province, purporting to be certified under the hand of the proper officer or person in whose custody the official or public document is placed, or

(b) a copy of a document, by-law, rule, regulation or proceeding, or a copy of any entry in any register or other book of any municipal or other corporation, created by charter or Act of Parliament or the legislature of any province, purporting to be certified under the seal of the corporation, and the hand of the presiding officer, clerk or secretary thereof,

is admissible in evidence without proof of the seal of the corporation, or of the signature or official character of the person or persons appearing to have signed it, and without further proof thereof.

R.S., c. E-10, s. 24.

Case Law

[See also s. 40]

R. v. John and Murray Motors Ltd. (1979), 8 C.R. (3d) 80, 47 C.C.C. (2d) 49 (B.C. C.A.) — Section 24 does *not* preclude the use of methods provided by provincial legislation for proving a record. A certificate of incorporation was a public document and copies were admissible when certified in accordance with the provincial *Companies Act*.

25. Books and documents — Where a book or other document is of so public a nature as to be admissible in evidence on its mere production from the proper custody, and no other Act exists that renders its contents provable by means of a copy, a copy thereof or extract therefrom is admissible in evidence in any court of justice or before a person having, by law or by consent of parties, authority to hear, receive and examine evidence, if it is proved that it is a copy or extract purporting to be certified to be true by the officer to whose custody the original has been entrusted.

R.S., c. E-10, s. 25.

26. (1) Books kept in offices under government of Canada — A copy of any entry in any book kept in any office or department of the Government of Canada, or in any commission, board or other branch of the public service of Canada, shall be admitted as evidence of that entry, and of the matters, transactions and accounts therein recorded, if it is proved by the oath or affidavit of an officer of the office or department, commission, board or other branch of the public service of Canada that the book was, at the time of the making of the entry, one of the ordinary books kept in the office, department, commission, board or other branch of the public service of Canada, that the entry was made in the usual and ordinary course of business of the office, department, commission, board or other branch of the public service of Canada and that the copy is a true copy thereof.

(2) Proof of non-issue of licence or document — Where by any Act of Parliament or regulation made thereunder provision is made for the issue by a department, commission, board or other branch of the public service of Canada of a licence requisite to the doing or having of any act or thing or for the issue of any other document, an affidavit of an officer of the department, commission, board or other branch of the public service, sworn before any commissioner or other person authorized to take affidavits, setting out that he has charge of the appropriate records and that after careful examination and search of those records he has been unable to find in any given case that any such licence or other document has been issued, shall be admitted in evidence as proof, in the absence of evidence to the contrary, that in that case no licence or other document has been issued.

(3) Proof of mailing departmental matter — Where by any Act of Parliament or regulation made thereunder provision is made for sending by mail any request for information, notice or demand by a department or other branch of the public service of Canada, an affidavit of an officer of the department or other branch of the public service, sworn before any commissioner or other person authorized to take affidavits, setting out that he has charge of the appropriate records, that he has a knowledge of the facts in the particular case, that the request, notice or demand was sent by registered letter on a named date to the person or firm to whom it was addressed (including that address) and that he identifies as exhibits attached to the affidavit the post office certificate of registration of the letter and a true copy of the request, notice or demand, shall, on production and proof of the post office receipt for the delivery of the registered letter to the addressee, be admitted in evidence as proof, in the absence of evidence to the contrary, of the sending and of the request, notice or demand.

(4) Proof of official character — Where proof is offered by affidavit pursuant to this section it is not necessary to prove the official character of the person making the affidavit if that information is set out in the body of the affidavit.

R.S., c. E-10, s. 26.

27. Notarial acts in Quebec — Any document purporting to be a copy of a notarial act or instrument made, filed or registered in the Province of Quebec, and to be certified by a notary or prothonotary to be a true copy of the original in his possession as such notary or prothonotary, shall be admitted in evidence in the place and stead of the original and has the same force and effect as the original would have if produced and proved, but it may be proved in rebuttal that there is no original, that the copy is not a true copy of the original in some material particular or that the original is not an instrument of such nature as may, by the law of the Province of Quebec, be taken before a notary or be filed, enrolled or registered by a notary in that Province.

R.S., c. E-10, s. 27.

28. (1) Notice of production of book or document — No copy of any book or other document shall be admitted in evidence, under the authority of section 23, 24, 25, 26 or 27, on any trial, unless the party intending to produce the copy has before the trial given to the party against whom it is intended to be produced reasonable notice of that intention.

(2) Not less than 7 days — The reasonableness of the notice referred to in subsection (1) shall be determined by the court, judge or other person presiding, but the notice shall not in any case be less than seven days.

R.S., c. E-10, s. 28.

Case Law

R. v. Yerxa (1978), 42 C.C.C. (2d) 177 (N.B. C.A.) — The requirement of notice is limited to books and documents introduced under certain *C.E.A.* provisions. Where a document is tendered under another statute it is *not* necessary to comply with s. 28.

29. (1) Copies of entries — Subject to this section, a copy of any entry in any book or record kept in any financial institution shall in all legal proceedings be admitted in evidence as proof, in the absence of evidence to the contrary, of the entry and of the matters, transactions and accounts therein recorded.

(2) Admission in evidence — A copy of an entry in the book or record described in subsection (1) shall not be admitted in evidence under this section unless it is first proved that the book or record was, at the time of the making of the entry, one of the ordinary books or records of the financial institution, that the entry was made in the usual and ordinary course of business, that the book or record is in the custody or control of the financial institution and that the copy is a true copy of it, and such proof may be given by any person employed by the financial institution who has knowledge of the book or record or the manager or accountant of the financial institution, and may be given orally or by affidavit sworn before any commissioner or other person authorized to take affidavits.

(3) Cheques, proof of "no account" — Where a cheque has been drawn on any financial institution or branch thereof by any person, an affidavit of the manager or accountant of the financial institution or branch, sworn before any commissioner or other person authorized to take affidavits, setting out that he is the manager or accountant, that he has made a careful examination and search of the books and records for the purpose of ascertaining whether or not that person has an account with the financial institution or branch and that he has been unable to find such an account, shall be admitted in evidence as proof, in the absence of evidence to the contrary, that that person has no account in the financial institution or branch.

(4) Proof of official character — Where evidence is offered by affidavit pursuant to this section, it is not necessary to prove the signature or official character of the person making the affidavit if the official character of that person is set out in the body of the affidavit.

(5) Compulsion of production or appearance — A financial institution or officer of a financial institution is not in any legal proceedings to which the financial institution is not a party compellable to produce any book or record, the contents of which can be proved under this section, or to appear as a witness to prove the matters, transactions and accounts therein recorded unless by order of the court made for special cause.

(6) Order to inspect and copy — On the application of any party to a legal proceeding, the court may order that that party be at liberty to inspect and take copies of any entries in the books or records of a financial institution for the purposes of the legal proceeding, and the person whose account is to be inspected shall be notified of the application at least two clear days before the hearing thereof, and if it is shown to the satisfaction of the court that he cannot be notified personally, the notice may be given by addressing it to the financial institution.

(7) Warrants to search — Nothing in this section shall be construed as prohibiting any search of the premises of a financial institution under the authority of a warrant to search issued under any other Act of Parliament, but unless the warrant is expressly endorsed by the person under whose hand it is issued as not being limited by this section, the authority conferred by any such warrant to search the premises of a financial institution and to seize and take away anything in it shall, with respect to the books or records of the institution, be construed as limited to the searching of those premises for the purpose of inspecting and taking copies of entries in those books or records, and section 490 of the *Criminal Code* does not apply in respect of the copies of those books or records obtained under a warrant referred to in this section.

(8) Computation of time — Holidays shall be excluded from the computation of time under this section.

(9) Definitions — In this section,

"court" means the court, judge, arbitrator or person before whom a legal proceeding is held or taken;

"financial institution" means the Bank of Canada, the Business Development Bank of Canada and any institution incorporated in Canada that accepts deposits of money from its members or the public, and includes a branch, agency or office of any such Bank or institution;

"legal proceeding" means any civil or criminal proceeding or inquiry in which evidence is or may be given, and includes an arbitration.
R.S., c. E-10, s. 29; 1974–75–76, c. 14, s. 57; 1994, c. 44, s. 90; 1995, c. 28, s. 47(a).

Case Law
General: Relationship Between ss. 29, 30

R. v. Best (1978), 43 C.C.C. (2d) 236 (B.C. C.A.) — Sections 29 and 30 are independent of each other. The notice provisions of s. 30(7) do not apply to records adduced pursuant to s. 29.

Copy of Any Entry in Any Book or Record: S. 29(1)

R. v. Bell (1982), 26 C.R. (3d) 336, 65 C.C.C. (2d) 377 (Ont. C.A.) — The following propositions apply in determining whether recorded information is a "record kept in any financial institution": (1) A record may be in any, even an illegible form; (2) The form in which information is recorded may change from time to time, and the new form is equally a "record" of that kind of information; (3) A record may be a compilation or collation of other records; (4) It must have been produced for the bank's purposes as a reference source, or as part of its internal audit system and, at the relevant time must be kept for that purpose.Where the bank's only record of account transaction was a copy of the monthly statement produced by its computer, that was a "record" within the meaning of s. 29.

L.T.L. Industries Ltd. v. Winterbottom (1980), 27 O.R. (2d) 496, 106 D.L.R. (3d) 577 (Ont. C.A.) — "Entry" in this section means an ordinary financial or bookkeeping entry and does *not* cover items such as interoffice memos or written reports, although they may be covered by s. 30.

R. v. McMullen (1979), 47 C.C.C. (2d) 499 (Ont. C.A.) — A computer print-out of entries stored in a bank's computer is a "copy of any entry in any book or record kept in any financial institution" within the meaning of s. 29(1).

R. v. McGrayne (1979), 46 C.C.C. (2d) 63 (Ont. C.A.) — Proof of the matters set out in s. 29(2) may be given by the bank manager or accountant or by the person responsible for the records.

30. (1) Business records to be admitted in evidence — Where oral evidence in respect of a matter would be admissible in a legal proceeding, a record made in the usual and ordinary course of business that contains information in respect of that matter is admissible in evidence under this section in the legal proceeding on production of the record.

(2) Inference where information not in business record — Where a record made in the usual and ordinary course of business does not contain information in respect of a matter the occurrence or existence of which might reasonably be expected to be recorded in that record, the court may on production of the record admit the record for the purpose of establishing that fact and may draw the inference that the matter did not occur or exist.

(3) Copy of records — Where it is not possible or reasonably practicable to produce any record described in subsection (1) or (2), a copy of the record accompanied by two documents, one that is made by a person who states why it is not possible or reasonably practicable to produce the record and one that sets out the source from which the copy was made, that attests to the copy's authenticity and that is made by the person who made the copy, is admissible in evidence under this section in the same manner as if it were the original of the record if each document is

(a) an affidavit of each of those persons sworn before a commissioner or other person authorized to take affidavits; or

(b) a certificate or other statement pertaining to the record in which the person attests that the certificate or statement is made in conformity with the laws of a foreign state, whether or not the certificate or statement is in the form of an affidavit attested to before an official of the foreign state.

(4) Where record kept in form requiring explanation — Where production of any record or of a copy of any record described in subsection (1) or (2) would not convey to the court the information contained in the record by reason of its having been kept in a form that requires explanation, a transcript of the explanation of the record or copy prepared by a person qualified to make the explanation is admissible in evidence under this section in the same manner as if it were the original of the record if it is accompanied by a document that sets out the person's qualifications to make the explanation, attests to the accuracy of the explanation, and is

(a) an affidavit of that person sworn before a commissioner or other person authorized to take affidavits; or

(b) a certificate or other statement pertaining to the record in which the person attests that the certificate or statement is made in conformity with the laws of a foreign state, whether or not the certificate or statement is in the form of an affidavit attested to before an official of the foreign state.

(5) **Court may order other part of record to be produced** — Where part only of a record is produced under this section by any party, the court may examine any other part of the record and direct that, together with the part of the record previously so produced, the whole or any part of the other part thereof be produced by that party as the record produced by him.

(6) **Court may examine record and hear evidence** — For the purpose of determining whether any provision of this section applies, or for the purpose of determining the probative value, if any, to be given to information contained in any record admitted in evidence under this section, the court may, on production of any record, examine the record, admit any evidence in respect thereof given orally or by affidavit including evidence as to the circumstances in which the information contained in the record was written, recorded, stored or reproduced, and draw any reasonable inference from the form or content of the record.

(7) **Notice of intention to produce record or affidavit** — Unless the court orders otherwise, no record or affidavit shall be admitted in evidence under this section unless the party producing the record or affidavit has, at least seven days before its production, given notice of his intention to produce it to each other party to the legal proceeding and has, within five days after receiving any notice in that behalf given by any such party, produced it for inspection by that party.

(8) **Not necessary to prove signature and official character** — Where evidence is offered by affidavit under this section, it is not necessary to prove the signature or official character of the person making the affidavit if the official character of that person is set out in the body of the affidavit.

(9) **Examination on record with leave of court** — Subject to section 4, any person who has or may reasonably be expected to have knowledge of the making or contents of any record produced or received in evidence under this section may, with leave of the court, be examined or cross-examined thereon by any party to the legal proceeding.

(10) **Evidence inadmissible under this section** — Nothing in this section renders admissible in evidence in any legal proceeding

(a) such part of any record as is proved to be

(i) a record made in the course of an investigation or inquiry,

(ii) a record made in the course of obtaining or giving legal advice or in contemplation of a legal proceeding.

(iii) a record in respect of the production of which any privilege exists and is claimed, or

(iv) a record of or alluding to a statement made by a person who is not, or if he were living and of sound mind would not be, competent and compellable to disclose in the legal proceeding a matter disclosed in the record;

(b) any record the production of which would be contrary to public policy; or

(c) any transcript or recording of evidence taken in the course of another legal proceeding.

(11) Construction of this section — The provisions of this section shall be deemed to be in addition to and not in derogation of

(a) any other provision of this or any other Act of Parliament respecting the admissibility in evidence of any record or the proof of any matter; or

(b) any existing rule of law under which any record is admissible in evidence or any matter may be proved.

(12) Definitions — In this section,

"business" means any business, profession, trade, calling, manufacture or undertaking of any kind carried on in Canada or elsewhere whether for profit or otherwise, including any activity or operation carried on or performed in Canada or elsewhere by any government, by any department, branch, board, commission or agency of any government, by any court or other tribunal or by any other body or authority performing a function of government;

"copy" in relation to any record, includes a print, whether enlarged or not, from a photographic film of the record, and "photographic film" includes a photographic plate, microphotographic film or photostatic negative;

"court" means the court, judge, arbitrator or person before whom a legal proceeding is held or taken;

"legal proceeding" means any civil or criminal proceeding or inquiry in which evidence is or may be given, and includes an arbitration;

"record" includes the whole or any part of any book, document, paper, card, tape or other thing on or in which information is written, recorded, stored or reproduced, and, except for the purposes of subsections (3) and (4), any copy or transcript admitted in evidence under this section pursuant to subsection (3) or (4).

R.S., c. E-10, s. 30; 1994, c. 44, s. 91.

Case Law

Record Made in Usual and Ordinary Course of Business: Ss. 30(1), (2)

Cloutier v. R. (1979), 12 C.R. (3d) 10, 48 C.C.C. (3d) 1 (S.C.C.) — An air way-bill is a record made in the usual and ordinary course of business, but where what is sought to be introduced was *not* one of the three original copies specified by the *Carriage By Air Act* but a copy intended as a delivery receipt, it could *not* be admitted unless accompanied by an affidavit under subsection (3).

R. v. Penno (1977), 37 C.R.N.S. 391, 35 C.C.C. (2d) 266 (B.C. C.A.) — An inventory sheet made by employees in the usual and ordinary course of business was admissible under s. 30, or alternatively through the employees who made it.

R. v. Scheel (1978), 3 C.R. (3d) 359, 42 C.C.C. (2d) 31 (Ont. C.A.) — Summaries prepared by an accountant from exhibits and testimony given in the proceedings were admissible through the accountant, without resort to s. 30.

Affidavit: S. 30(3)

R. v. Parker (1984), 16 C.C.C. (3d) 478 (Ont. C.A.) — Affidavit evidence is admissible to prove the original record was made in the *usual* and *ordinary* course of business, as well as to establish the *authenticity* of the copy of the record and that it is not reasonably practicable to produce the original. Unless the affidavit sets out that the deponent made the copy, the copy is inadmissible.

Notice: S. 30(7)

R. v. Voykin (1986), 29 C.C.C. (3d) 280 (Alta. C.A.) — *See also*: *R. v. Penno* (1977), 37 C.R.N.S. 391, 35 C.C.C. (2d) 266 (B.C. C.A.) — Introduction of business records as exhibits at the preliminary hearing constitutes notice under subsection (7) as well as production for inspection.

Canada (Attorney General) v. Jarry (1991), 3 C.R. (4th) 369, 65 C.C.C. (3d) 566 (Que. C.A.) — The section only applies to documents tendered pursuant to s. 30 and *not* to those tendered for admission under another Act, as for example, s. 102 of the *Unemployment Insurance Act.*

Records Not Admissible: S. 30(10)

R. v. Baker (1977), 35 C.C.C. (2d) 314 (B.C. C.A.) — An authorization to intercept private communications is a record made in contemplation of legal proceedings and is *not* admissible under s. 30.

R. v. Laverty (No. 2) (1979), 9 C.R. (3d) 288, 47 C.C.C. (2d) 60 (Ont. C.A.) — Notes made by a fire marshall are a record made in the course of an investigation or inquiry and may not be used to cross-examine another expert witness.

31. (1) Definitions — In this section,

"corporation" means any bank, including the Bank of Canada and the Federal Business Development Bank, and each of the following carrying on business in Canada, namely, every railway, express, telegraph and telephone company (except a street railway and tramway company), insurance company or society, trust company and loan company;

"government" means the government of Canada or of any province and includes any department, commission, board or branch of any such government; and

"photographic film" includes any photographic plate, microphotographic film and photostatic negative.

(2) When print admissible in evidence — A print, whether enlarged or not, from any photographic film of

(a) an entry in any book or record kept by any government or corporation and destroyed, lost or delivered to a customer after the film was taken,

(b) any bill of exchange, promissory note, cheque, receipt, instrument or document held by any government or corporation and destroyed, lost or delivered to a customer after the film was taken, or

(c) any record, document, plan, book or paper belonging to or deposited with any government or corporation,

is admissible in evidence in all cases in which and for all purposes for which the object photographed would have been admitted on proof that

(d) while the book, record, bill of exchange, promissory note, cheque, receipt, instrument or document, plan, book or paper was in the custody or control of the government or corporation, the photographic film was taken thereof in order to keep a permanent record thereof, and

(e) the object photographed was subsequently destroyed by or in the presence of one or more of the employees of the government or corporation, or was lost or was delivered to a customer.

(3) Evidence of compliance with conditions — Evidence of compliance with the conditions prescribed by this section may be given by any one or more of the employees of the government or corporation, having knowledge of the taking of the photographic film, of the destruction, loss or delivery to a customer, or of the making of the print, as the case may be, either orally or by affidavit sworn in any part of Canada before any notary public or commissioner for oaths.

(4) Proof by notarial copy — Unless the court otherwise orders, a notarial copy of an affidavit under subsection (3) is admissible in evidence in lieu of the original affidavit.

R.S., c. E-10, s. 31; 1974–75–76, c. 14, s. 57; 1992, c. 1, s. 142 (Sch. V. items 9(1) and 9(2))

Case Law

R. v. Sanghi (1971), 6 C.C.C. (2d) 123 (N.S. C.A.) — A corporation that is an agent of P and subject to the control of the Governor in Council comes within the definition of "government" in this section.

32. (1) Order signed by Secretary of State — An order signed by the Secretary of State of Canada and purporting to be written by command of the Governor General shall be admitted in evidence as the order of the Governor General.

(2) Copies printed in Canada Gazette — All copies of official and other notices, advertisements and documents printed in the *Canada Gazette* are admissible in evidence as proof, in the absence of evidence to the contrary, of the originals and of the contents thereof.

R.S., c. E-10, s. 32.

33. (1) Proof of handwriting of person certifying — No proof shall be required of the handwriting or official position of any person certifying, in pursuance of this Act, to the truth of any copy of or extract from any proclamation, order, regulation, appointment, book or other document.

(2) Printed or written — Any copy or extract referred to in subsection (1) may be in print or in writing, or partly in print and partly in writing.

R.S., c. E-10, s. 33.

34. (1) Attesting witness — It is not necessary to prove by the attesting witness any instrument to the validity of which attestation is not requisite.

(2) Instrument, how proved — Any instrument referred to in subsection (1) may be proved by admission or otherwise as if there had been no attesting witness thereto.

R.S., c. E-10, s. 34.

35. Impounding of forged instrument — Where any instrument that has been forged or fraudulently altered is admitted in evidence, the court or the judge or person who admits the instrument may, at the request of any person against whom it is admitted in evidence, direct that the instrument shall be impounded and be kept in the custody of an officer of the court or other proper person for such period and subject to such conditions as to the court, judge or person admitting the instrument seem meet.

R.S., c. E-10, s. 35.

36. Construction — This Part shall be deemed to be in addition to and not in derogation of any powers of proving documents given by any existing Act or existing at law.

R.S., c. E-10, s. 36.

Case Law

R. v. Tatomir (1989), 51 C.C.C. (3d) 321 (Alta. C.A.); leave to appeal refused (1990), 70 Alta. L.R. (2d) liiin (S.C.C.) — P is entitled at common law to tender without notice an exemplification under the seal of the court, such as the official order of driving prohibition against D.

Disclosure of Government Information

37. (1) Objection to disclosure of information — A minister of the Crown in right of Canada or other person interested may object to the disclosure of information before a court, person or body with jurisdiction to compel the production of information by certifying orally or in writing to the court, person or body that the information should not be disclosed on the grounds of a specified public interest.

(2) Where objection made to superior court — Subject to sections 38 and 39, where an objection to the disclosure of information is made under subsection (1) before a superior court, that court may examine or hear the information and order its disclosure, subject to such restrictions or conditions as it deems appropriate, if it concludes that, in the circumstances of the case, the public interest in disclosure outweighs in importance the specified public interest.

(3) Where objection not made to superior court — Subject to sections 38 and 39, where an objection to the disclosure of information is made under subsection (1) before a court, person or body other than a superior court, the objection may be determined, on application, in accordance with subsection (2) by

(a) the Federal Court-Trial Division, in the case of a person or body vested with power to compel production by or pursuant to an Act of Parliament if the person or body is not a court established under a law of a province; or

(b) the trial division or trial court of the superior court of the province within which the court, person or body exercises its jurisdiction, in any other case.

(4) Limitation period — An application pursuant to subsection (3) shall be made within ten days after the objection is made or within such further or lesser time as the court having jurisdiction to hear the application considers appropriate in the circumstances.

(5) Appeal to Court of Appeal — An appeal lies from a determination under subsection (2) or (3)

(a) to the Federal Court of Appeal from a determination of the Federal Court-Trial Division; or

(b) to the court of appeal of a province from a determination of a trial division or trial court of a superior court of a province.

(6) Limitation period for appeal under subsection (5) — An appeal under subsection (5) shall be brought within ten days from the date of the determination appealed from or within such further time as the court having jurisdiction to hear the appeal considers appropriate in the circumstances.

(7) Limitation periods for appeals to Supreme Court of Canada — Notwithstanding any other Act of Parliament,

(a) an application for leave to appeal to the Supreme Court of Canada from a judgment made pursuant to subsection (5) shall be made within ten days from the date of the judgment appealed from or within such further time as the court having jurisdiction to grant leave to appeal considers appropriate in the circumstances; and

(b) where leave to appeal is granted, the appeal shall be brought in the manner set out in subsection 60(1) of the *Supreme Court Act* but within such time as the court that grants leave specifies.

1980–81–82–83, c. 111, s. 4.

Case Law

R. v. Meuckon (1990), 78 C.R. (3d) 196, 57 C.C.C. (3d) 193 (B.C. C.A.) — P can object to the disclosure of information under s. 37 by certifying *orally* that the information should *not* be disclosed on the ground of a public interest, which must be specified. The trial judge must decide whether the information might affect the outcome of the trial. If it would not, the privilege claim should be upheld. Where it would, the judge should consider whether upholding the claim would prevent D from making full answer and defence. If he or she concludes it would have that effect, the proceedings should be stayed.

R. v. Lines (1986), 27 C.C.C. (3d) 377 (N.W.T. C.A.) — This section contemplates an objection by a Minister of P or some person with an official status with respect to the public interest. D is *not* an "other person interested".

Charter Considerations

R. v. Archer (1989), 47 C.C.C. (3d) 567 (Alta. C.A.) — *Charter* s. 7 has *not* altered the rules of evidence protecting the identity of informers from disclosure.

Canada (Attorney General) v. Sander (1994), 90 C.C.C. (3d) 41 (B.C. C.A.) — Section 37(1) is *not* unconstitutionally vague, nor is it inoperative because it purports to derogate from the authority of the Provincial Court to invoke the *Charter*.

R. v. Richards (1997), 115 C.C.C. (3d) 377 (Ont. C.A.) — *C.E.A.* s. 37 does not oust the jurisdiction of a judge at preliminary inquiry to make evidentiary rulings. The section creates a separate means whereby P may assert a public interest privilege when faced with a ruling at preliminary inquiry which requires disclosure.

Where P asserts a claim of public interest immunity at preliminary inquiry

i.   a ruling on the issue should be sought from the presiding judge; and,

ii.   depending upon the result, application made under *C.E.A.* s. 37.

38. (1) Objection relating to international relations or national defence or security — Where an objection to the disclosure of information is made under subsection 37(1) on grounds that the disclosure would be injurious to international relations or national defence or security, the objection may be determined, on application, in accordance with subsection 37(2) only by the Chief Justice of the Federal Court, or such other judge of that court as the Chief Justice may designate to hear such applications.

(2) Limitation period — An application under subsection (1) shall be made within ten days after the objection is made or within such further or lesser time as the Chief Justice of the Federal Court, or such other judge of that court as the Chief Justice may designate to hear such applications, considers appropriate.

(3) Appeal to Federal Court of Appeal — An appeal lies from a determination under subsection (1) to the Federal Court of Appeal.

(4) Subsections 37(6) and (7) apply — Subsection 37(6) applies in respect of appeals under subsection (3), and subsection 37(7) applies in respect of appeals from judgments made pursuant to subsection (3), with such modifications as the circumstances require.

(5) Special rules for hearings — An application under subsection (1) or an appeal brought in respect of the application shall

(a) be heard *in camera*; and

(b) on the request of the person objecting to the disclosure of information, be heard and determined in the National Capital Region described in the schedule to the *National Capital Act*.

(6) Ex parte representations — During the hearing of an application under subsection (1) or an appeal brought in respect of the application, the person who made the objection in respect of which the application was made or the appeal was brought shall, on the request of that person, be given the opportunity to make representations *ex parte*.

1980–81–82–83, c. 111, s. 4.

Case Law

Goguen v. Gibson (1984), 10 C.C.C. (3d) 492 (Fed. C.A.) — Where disclosure is objected to on the grounds set out in subsection (1), the court has discretion to examine the documents involved. Examination should only be undertaken if it appears necessary to determine whether disclosure should be ordered. In deciding whether to examine, the court may consider the apparent balance of the competing public interests and the likelihood that examination could alter the view of that balance and the impression as to whether disclosure should be ordered. The court may order disclosure of some of the information under conditions.

39. (1) Objection relating to a confidence of the Queen's Privy Council — Where a minister of the Crown or the Clerk of the Privy Council objects to the disclosure of information before a court, person or body with jurisdiction to compel the production of information by certifying in writing that the information constitutes a confidence of the Queen's Privy Council for Canada, disclosure of the information shall be refused without examination or hearing of the information by the court, person or body.

(2) Definition — For the purpose of subsection (1), "a confidence of the Queen's Privy Council for Canada" includes, without restricting the generality thereof, information contained in

(a) a memorandum the purpose of which is to present proposals or recommendations to Council;

(b) a discussion paper the purpose of which is to present background explanations, analyses of problems or policy options to Council for consideration by Council in making decisions;

(c) an agendum of Council or a record recording deliberations or decisions of Council;

(d) a record used for or reflecting communications or discussions between ministers of the Crown on matters relating to the making of government decisions or the formulation of government policy;

(e) a record the purpose of which is to brief ministers of the Crown in relation to matters that are brought before, or are proposed to be brought before, Council or that are the subject of communications or discussions referred to in paragraph (d); and

(f) draft legislation.

(3) Definition of "council" — For the purposes of subsection (2), "Council" means the Queen's Privy Council for Canada, committees of the Queen's Privy Council for Canada, Cabinet and committees of Cabinet.

(4) Exception — Subsection (1) does not apply in respect of

(a) a confidence of the Queen's Privy Council for Canada that has been in existence for more than twenty years; or

(b) a discussion paper described in paragraph (2)(*b*)

(i) if the decisions to which the discussion paper relates have been made public, or

(ii) where the decisions have not been made public, if four years have passed since the decisions were made.

1980–81–82–83, c. 111, s. 4.

Case Law

MacKeigan v. Hickman (1989), 72 C.R. (3d) 129, 50 C.C.C. (2d) 449 (S.C.C.) — Judges are immune from testifying as to how and why they arrived at a particular judicial decision and cannot be compelled to testify at a provincial Royal Commission inquiry.

Carey v. R. (1986), 30 C.C.C. (3d) 498 (S.C.C.) — Cabinet documents, like other evidence, must be disclosed unless such disclosure would interfere with the public interest. However, because they concern the decision-making process at its highest level, courts must proceed with caution in having them produced.

Provincial Laws of Evidence

40. How applicable — In all proceedings over which Parliament has legislative authority, the laws of evidence in force in the province in which those proceedings are taken, including the laws of proof of service of any warrant, summons, subpoena or other document, subject to this Act and other Acts of Parliament, apply to those proceedings.

R.S., c. E-10, s. 37.

Case Law

R. v. Albright (1987), 60 C.R. (3d) 97, 37 C.C.C. (3d) 105 (S.C.C.) — Section 40 must be given a narrow scope, to avoid unacceptable differences from province to province on fundamental matters of criminal evidence. It should be restricted to the proof of matters within provincial competence. It does *not* incorporate provincial legislation with respect to proving prior convictions.

Bisaillon v. Keable (1983), 37 C.R. (3d) 289, 7 C.C.C. (3d) 385 (S.C.C.) — The combined effect of *Code* s. 8(2) and *C.E.A.* s. 40 is to incorporate in the criminal law the common law in effect in a province immediately before April 1, 1955, including the secrecy rule regarding police informers. A provincial statute cannot affect this rule.

Marshall v. R. (1960), 34 C.R. 216, 129 C.C.C. 232 (S.C.C.) — Provincial legislation making statements concerning motor vehicles inadmissible in *any* trial does *not* apply to a trial under the *Criminal Code* provisions.

R. v. Richardson (1980), 57 C.C.C. (2d) 403 (Alta. C.A.) — Where a provincial statute conflicts with *Code* s. 8 which preserves the common law in criminal proceedings, the latter prevails by virtue of s. 40.

R. v. Ward (1977), 38 C.C.C. (2d) 353 (Alta. C.A.); reversed (1979), 7 C.R. (3d) 153, 44 C.C.C. (2d) 498 (S.C.C.) — Where a provincial statute compels the driver of a car to make an accident report and provides that such report is admissible in evidence at a trial to prove the identity of the driver, the report can *not* be admitted at a trial on *Code* charges unless it meets the test of voluntariness.

*R. v. Murphy, (*sub nom. *Ex parte Belisle and Moreau) 5 C.R.N.S. 68, [1968] 4 C.C.C. 229 — A provision concerning the use of language in court was a law respecting procedure, *not* evidence, hence s. 40 did not apply.

Statutory Declarations

41. Solemn declaration — Any judge, notary public, justice of the peace, police or provincial court judge, recorder, mayor or commissioner authorized to take affidavits to be used either in the provincial or federal courts, or any other functionary authorized by law to administer an oath in any matter, may receive the solemn declaration of any person voluntarily making the declaration before him, in the following form, in attestation of the execution of any writing, deed or instrument, or of the truth of any fact, or of any account rendered in writing:

I, ..., solemnly declare that (*state the fact or facts declared to*), and I make this solemn declaration conscientiously believing it to be true, and knowing that it is of the same force and effect as if made under oath.

Declared before me ..... at ..... this ..... day of ..... 19 ...

R.S., c. E-10, s. 38.

Insurance Proofs

42. Affidavits, etc — Any affidavit, solemn affirmation or declaration required by any insurance company authorized by law to do business in Canada, in regard to any loss of or injury to person, property or life insured or assured therein, may be taken before any commissioner or other person authorized to take affidavits, before any justice of the peace or before any notary public for any province, and the commissioner, person, justice of the peace or notary public is required to take the affidavit, solemn affirmation or declaration.

R.S., c. E-10, s. 39.

PART II

Application

43. Foreign courts — This Part applies to the taking of evidence relating to proceedings in courts out of Canada.

R.S., c. E-10, s. 40.

Interpretation

44. Definitions — In this Part,

"cause" includes a proceeding against a criminal;

"court" means any superior court in any province;

"judge" means any judge of any superior court in any province;

"oath" includes a solemn affirmation in cases in which, by the law of Canada, or of a province, as the case may be, a solemn affirmation is allowed instead of an oath.

R.S., c. E-10, s. 41; 1984, c. 40, s. 27.

45. Construction — **This Part shall not be so construed as to interfere with the right of legislation of the legislature of any province requisite or desirable for the carrying out of the objects hereof.**

R.S., c. E-10, s. 42.

Procedure

46. Order for examination of witness in Canada — **Where, on an application for that purpose, it is made to appear to any court or judge that any court or tribunal of competent jurisdiction in the Commonwealth and Dependent Territories or in any foreign country, before which any civil, commercial or criminal matter is pending, is desirous of obtaining the testimony in relation to that matter of a party or witness within the jurisdiction of the first mentioned court, of the court to which the judge belongs or of the judge, the court or judge may, in its or his discretion, order the examination on oath on interrogatories, or otherwise, before any person or persons named in the order, of that party or witness accordingly, and by the same or any subsequent order may command the attendance of such party or witness for the purpose of being examined, and for the production of any writings or other documents mentioned in the order, and of any other writings or documents relating to the matter in question that are in the possession or power of that party or witness.**

R.S., c. E-10, s. 43.

Case Law
General Principles

United States District Court v. Royal American Shows Inc. (1982), 27 C.R. (3d) 1, 66 C.C.C. (2d) 125 (S.C.C.) — In the interests of comity, a liberal approach should be taken to requests for judicial assistance. Section 46 provides concurrently or separately for *viva voce* testimony and for documentary evidence, and supports a request for production of documents alone.

Zingre v. R. (1981), 61 C.C.C. (2d) 465 (S.C.C.) — In general, Canadian courts will only order an examination for the purpose of gathering evidence to be used at a trial, but that does not mean an order will never be made at the pre-trial stage. Section 46 does not distinguish between pre-trial and trial proceedings and an order may be made even if the evidence is to be used for pre-trial proceedings.

Re Request for International Judicial Assistance (1979), 49 C.C.C. (2d) 276 (Alta. Q.B.); reversed (1981), 58 C.C.C. (2d) 274 (Alta. C.A.); reversed (1982), 27 C.R. (3d) 1, 66 C.C.C. (2d) 125 (S.C.C.) — Letters rogatory may be enforced by the courts of one province with respect to documents held in another province by an employee of a federal department.

Prerequisites of Order

France (Republic) v. De Havilland Aircraft of Canada Ltd. (1991), 65 C.C.C. (3d) 449 (Ont. C.A.) — The taking of evidence on commission *may* be ordered if it appears that:

a.   a foreign court is desirous of obtaining the evidence;

b.   the witness whose evidence is sought is within the jurisdiction of the requested court;

c.   the evidence is in relation to a civil, commercial or criminal matter pending before the foreign court; and,

d.   the foreign court is a court of competent jurisdiction.

Judicial reciprocity is *not* an element of the requesting court's jurisdictional competence, but is a relevant consideration because it is a manifestation of the international comity between Canada and the requesting state. Provided there is a mechanism in place in the requesting jurisdiction which could respond favourably to a Canadian request by letters rogatory, it need *not* be the requesting court or tribunal.

47. Enforcement of the order — **On the service on the party or witness of an order referred to in section 46, and of an appointment of a time and place for the exami-**

nation of the party or witness signed by the person named in the order for taking the examination, or, if more than one person is named, by one of the persons named, and on payment or tender of the like conduct money as is properly payable on attendance at a trial, the order may be enforced in like manner as an order made by the court or judge in a cause pending in that court or before that judge.

R.S., c. E-10, s. 44.

48. Expenses and conduct money — Every person whose attendance is required in manner described in section 47 is entitled to the like conduct money and payment for expenses and loss of time as on attendance at a trial.

R.S., c. E-10, s. 45.

49. Administering oath — On any examination of parties or witnesses, under the authority of any order made in pursuance of this Part, the oath shall be administered by the person authorized to take the examination, or, if more than one person is authorized, by one of those persons.

R.S., c. E-10, s. 46.

50. (1) Right of refusal to answer or produce document — Any person examined under any order made under this Part has the like right to refuse to answer questions tending to criminate himself, or other questions, as a party or witness, as the case may be, would have in any cause pending in the court by which, or by a judge whereof, the order is made.

(2) Nature of right — No person shall be compelled to produce, under any order referred to in subsection (1), any writing or other document that he could not be compelled to produce at a trial of such a cause.

R.S., c. E-10, s. 47.

51. (1) Rules of court — The court may frame rules and orders in relation to procedure and to the evidence to be produced in support of the application for an order for examination of parties and witnesses under this Part, and generally for carrying this Part into effect.

(2) Letters rogatory — In the absence of any order in relation to the evidence to be produced in support of the application referred to in subsection (1), letters rogatory from any court of justice in the Commonwealth and Dependent Territories, or from any foreign tribunal, in which the civil, commercial or criminal matter is pending, shall be deemed and taken to be sufficient evidence in support of the application.

R.S., c. E-10, s. 48.

PART III

Application

52. Application of this Part — This Part extends to the following classes of persons:

(a) officers of any of Her Majesty's diplomatic or consular services while performing their functions in any foreign country, including ambassadors, envoys, ministers, charges d'affaires, counsellors, secretaries, attaches, consuls general, consuls, vice-consuls, pro-consuls, consular agents, acting consuls general, acting consuls, acting vice-consuls and acting consular agents;

(b) officers of the Canadian diplomatic, consular and representative services while performing their functions in any foreign country or in any part of the Commonwealth and Dependent Territories other than Canada, including, in addition to the diplomatic and consular officers mentioned in paragraph (*a*), high commissioners, permanent delegates, acting high commissioners, acting permanent delegates, counsellors and secretaries;

(c) Canadian Government Trade Commissioners and Assistant Canadian Government Trade Commissioners while performing their functions in any foreign country or in any part of the Commonwealth and Dependent Territories other than Canada;

(d) honorary consular officers of Canada while performing their functions in any foreign country or in any part of the Commonwealth and Dependent Territories other than Canada;

(e) judicial officials in a foreign country in respect of oaths, affidavits, solemn affirmations, declarations or similar documents that the official is authorized to administer, take or receive; and

(f) persons locally engaged and designated by the Deputy Minister of Foreign Affairs or any other persons authorized by that Deputy Minister while performing their functions in any foreign country or in any part of the Commonwealth and Dependent Territories other than Canada.

R.S., c. E-10, s. 49; 1984, c. 40, s. 27(3); 1994, c. 44, s. 92; 1997, c. 18, s. 118.

Oaths and Solemn Affirmations

53. Oaths taken abroad — Oaths, affidavits, solemn affirmations or declarations administered, taken or received outside Canada by any person mentioned in section 52, are as valid and effectual and are of the like force and effect to all intents and purposes as if they had been administered, taken or received in Canada by a person authorized to administer, take or receive oaths, affidavits, solemn affirmations or declarations therein that are valid and effectual under this Act.

R.S., c. E-10, s. 50.

Documentary Evidence

54. (1) Documents to be admitted in evidence — Any document that purports to have affixed, impressed or subscribed on it or to it the signature of any person authorized by any of paragraphs 52 (*a*) to (*d*) to administer, take or receive oaths, affidavits, solemn affirmations or declarations, together with their seal or with the seal or stamp of their office, or the office to which the person is attached, in testimony of any oath, affidavit, solemn affirmation or declaration being administered, taken or received by the person, shall be admitted in evidence, without proof of the seal or stamp or of the person's signature or official character.

(2) Status of statements — An affidavit, solemn affirmation, declaration or other similar statement taken or received in a foreign country by an official referred to in paragraph 52(*e*) shall be admitted in evidence without proof of the signature or official character of the official appearing to have signed the affidavit, solemn affirmation, declaration or other statement.

R.S., c. E-10, s. 51; 1994, c. 44, s. 93.

CONSTITUTION ACT, 1982

R.S.C. 1985, Appendix II, No. 44

En. Canada Act 1982 (U.K.), c. 11 Am. Constitution Amendment Proclamation, 1983, SI/84-102, Schedule.

· · · · ·

PART VII — GENERAL

52. (1) Primacy of Constitution of Canada — The Constitution of Canada is the supreme law of Canada, and any law that is inconsistent with the provisions of the Constitution is, to the extent of the inconsistency, of no force or effect.

(2) Constitution of Canada — The Constitution of Canada includes

(a) the *Canada Act 1982*, including this Act;

(b) the Acts and orders referred to in the schedule; and

(c) any amendment to any Act or order referred to in paragraph (a) or (b).

(3) Amendments to the Constitution of Canada — Amendments to the Constitution of Canada shall be made only in accordance with the authority contained in the Constitution of Canada.

Case Law

Factual Foundation for Challenge

Danson v. Ontario (A.G.) (1990), 43 C.P.C. (2d) 165 (S.C.C.); affirming (1987), 19 C.P.C. (2d) 249 (Ont. C.A.); reversing (1986), 9 C.P.C. (2d) 1 (Ont. Div. Ct.) — A proper factual foundation must exist before measuring legislation against the provisions of the *Charter*, especially where *effects* of the legislation are impeached. In constitutional litigation "adjudicative facts" must be distinguished from "legislative facts". *Adjudicative facts*, those which concern the immediate parties, are specific and must be proven by admissible evidence. *Legislative facts*, those which establish the purpose and background of legislation, including its social, economic and cultural context, are of a more general nature and are subject to less stringent admissibility requirements.

Status to Challenge [See also individual sections and s. 24 "Status of Applicant", infra]

CEMA v. Richardson, [1998] 3 S.C.R. 157 — As a general rule, a *Charter* provision may *only* be invoked by those who enjoy its protection. Under the *Big M Drug Mart* exception, however, standing is granted as of right to an accused charged under legislation that is alleged to be unconstitutional. The exception should be extended to permit corporations to invoke the *Charter* as *defendants* in *civil* proceedings instigated by the state or a state organ under a regulatory scheme.

The Supreme Court of Canada may hear arguments from parties who would *not* usually have standing to invoke the *Charter*. The court has a residuary discretion if the question involved is one of public importance.

Hy and Zel's Inc. v. Ontario (Attorney General), (sub nom. *Paul Magder Furs Ltd. v. Ontario (Attorney General)*) [1993] 3 S.C.R. 675 — In order for the court to exercise its discretion to grant standing in a civil case, where a party does not claim a breach of its own *Charter* rights but those of others

i.   a serious issue must be raised as to the constitutional validity of the relevant act;

ii.   the appellant must be directly affected by the act or have a genuine interest in its validity; and,

iii.   there exists no other reasonable and effective way to bring the act's validity before the court.

R. v. Wholesale Travel Group Inc. (1991), 8 C.R. (4th) 145, 67 C.C.C. (3d) 193 (S.C.C.) — See digest under s. 7 *General Principles.*

Borowski v. Canada (A.G.) (1989), 47 C.C.C. (3d) 1 (S.C.C.) — A challenge based on s. 52(1) is restricted to litigants who challenge a law or governmental action pursuant to a power granted by law. The court will not hear a private reference to provide a naked interpretation of two provisions of the *Charter.*

Basic Principles

CEMA v. Richardson, [1998] 3 S.C.R. 157 — The legal and practical effects of a legislative scheme must also be examined to determine constitutional validity. Over time, the effects might acquire such significance that they become the dominant feature of the legislation, thereby displacing the original purpose.

Eaton v. Brant County Board of Education (1996), 31 O.R. (3d) 574 (S.C.C.) — The authority to delare laws invalid for constitutional infringement ought *only* be exercised after according the enacting government the fullest opportunity to support the law's validity. To strike down a law by default works a serious injustice to the elected representatives who enacted the law, as well their constituency governed by it.

R. v. Big M Drug Mart Ltd. (1985), 18 C.C.C. (3d) 385 (S.C.C.) — Section 52 sets out the fundamental principle of constitutional law that the Constitution is supreme. The undoubted corollary to be drawn from this principle is that no one can be convicted of an offence under an unconstitutional law. Any accused, whether corporate or individual, may defend a criminal charge by arguing that the law under which the charge is brought is constitutionally invalid. Both the purpose and effects of legislation are relevant in assessing its constitutionality, and either an unconstitutional purpose or an unconstitutional effect can invalidate the legislation. A court not only has the power, but the duty, to regard legislation found to be inconsistent with the *Charter,* to the extent of the inconsistency, as being no longer "of force or effect".

Hunter v. Southam Inc. (1984), 41 C.R. (3d) 97, 14 C.C.C. (3d) 97 (S.C.C.) — It is the legislature's responsibility to enact legislation that embodies appropriate safeguards, and it should not fall to the courts to fill in the details that will render legislative lacunae constitutional.

Right of Appeal

R. v. Laba (1994), 94 C.C.C. (3d) 385, 34 C.R. (4th) 360 (S.C.C.); reversing in part (1992), 15 C.R. (4th) 198, 74 C.C.C. (3d) 538 (Ont. C.A.) — A "dual proceedings s. 40" analytical approach should be adopted for appeals against successful s. 52 *C.A.* challenges to the constitutionality of laws. An appeal against a ruling on the constitutionality of a law that cannot be piggybacked onto *Code* proceedings is a judgment of the highest court of final resort in a province in which judgment can be had for the purposes of s. 40(1) of the *Supreme Court Act.*

PART I — CANADIAN CHARTER OF RIGHTS AND FREEDOMS

Whereas Canada is founded upon principles that recognize the supremacy of God and the rule of law:

Guarantee of Rights and Freedoms

1. Rights and freedoms in Canada — The *Canadian Charter of Rights and Freedoms* **guarantees the rights and freedoms set out in it subject only to such reasonable limits prescribed by law as can be demonstrably justified in a free and democratic society.**

Case Law

Interpretation of *Charter* Guarantees

R. v. Therens (1985), 45 C.R. (3d) 97, 18 C.C.C. (3d) 481 (S.C.C.) — [Per Le Dain J.] — The *Charter,* because of its constitutional character, must be regarded by the courts as a new affirmation of rights and freedoms and of judicial power and responsibility in relation to their protection, unlike the *Canadian Bill of Rights*. By its very nature a constitutional charter of rights and freedoms must use general language which is capable of development and adaptation by the courts. Words used in the *Charter* should not be presumed to have the same meaning as similar words subject to judicial interpretation at the time the *Charter* was enacted.

R. v. Big M Drug Mart Ltd. (1985), 18 C.C.C. (3d) 385 (S.C.C.) — The meaning of a right or freedom guaranteed by the *Charter* is to be understood in the light of the interests it was meant to protect. This analysis is to be undertaken, and purpose of the right or freedom in question to be sought, by reference to the larger objects of the *Charter* itself, to the language chosen to articulate the specific right or freedom, to the historical origins of the concepts enshrined, and where applicable, to the meaning and purpose of other specific rights and freedoms with which it is associated within the text of the *Charter*. The interpretation should be a generous one rather than a legalistic one, aimed at fulfilling the purpose of the guarantee and securing for individuals the full benefit of the *Charter's* protection. The court must not overshoot the actual purpose of the right or freedom in question. It must place the *Charter* in its proper linguistic, philosophic and historical contexts. One of the major purposes of the *Charter* is to protect within reason from compulsion or restraint, and freedom in a broad sense embraces both the absence of coercion and restraint, and the right to manifest beliefs and practices. Subject to such limitations as are necessary to protect public safety, order, health, or morals or the fundamental rights and freedoms of others, no one is to be forced to act in a way contrary to his beliefs or his conscience.

Hunter v. Southam Inc. (1984), 41 C.R. (3d) 97, 14 C.C.C. (3d) 97 (S.C.C.) — The *Charter* is a purposive document, and the proper approach to its interpretation is a purposive one. The *Charter's* purpose is to guarantee and to protect, within the limits of reason, the enjoyment of the rights and freedoms it enshrines. It is intended to constrain government action inconsistent with those rights and freedoms, but is not itself an authorization for government action.

Criteria for Justifying Limitations

R.J.R. MacDonald Inc. v. Canada (Attorney General) (1995), 100 C.C.C. (3d) 449 (S.C.C.) — While context, deference and a flexible and realistic standard of proof are essential aspects of a s. 1 *Charter* analysis, they ought *not* be attenuated to such an extent to relieve the state of the burden of *Charter* s. 1 justification. Care ought to be taken in the first step of a s. 1 analysis *not* to overstate the objective of the infringing measures. (per McLachlin, Sopinka and Major J.J.)The requirements of s. 1 ought be applied flexibly in light of the specific factual and social context of each case. An overly-formalistic approach ought to be avoided. The evidentiary requirements under s. 1 will vary substantially, depending upon the nature of the legislation and of the right infringed. (per La Forest, L'Heureux-Dubé, Gonthier and Cory JJ.)

R. v. Oakes (1986), 50 C.R. (3d) 1, 24 C.C.C. (3d) 321 (S.C.C.) — Section 1 both guarantees the rights and freedoms set out in the provisions which follow it and states explicitly the exclusive justificatory criteria (outside of s. 33) against which limitations on those rights and freedoms may be measured. The onus of proving that a limitation on any *Charter* right is reasonable and demonstrably justified in a free and democratic society rests upon the party seeking to uphold the limitation on the preponderance of probabilities based on the following criteria: (1) the objective to be served by the measures limiting a *Charter* right must be sufficiently important, at least relating to societal concerns which are pressing and substantial in a free and democratic society, to warrant overriding a constitutionally-protected right or freedom; and (2) the means must be reasonable and demonstrably justified, in proportion to the importance of the objective. The proportionality test involves three components:

i.   the measures must be fair and not arbitrary, carefully designed to achieve the objective in question, and rationally connected to that objective;

ii.   the means should impair the *Charter* right as little as possible; and

iii. there must be a proportionality between the effects of the limiting measure and the objective.

R. v. Big M Drug Mart Ltd. (1985), 18 C.C.C. (3d) 385 (S.C.C.) — Not every interest or policy objective is entitled to s. 1 consideration. Parliament cannot rely upon an *ultra vires* purpose under s. 1.

"Prescribed By Law"

Canada v. Pharmaceutical Society (Nova Scotia) (1992), 15 C.R. (4th) 1, 74 C.C.C. (3d) 289 (S.C.C.) — The *doctrine of vagueness*, a principle of fundamental justice, is as well a part of a s. 1 analysis, since a law may be so vague that it fails to meet the "prescribed by law" requirement of s. 1.

Fundamental Freedoms

2. Fundamental freedoms — Everyone has the following fundamental freedoms:

    (a) freedom of conscience and religion;

    (b) freedom of thought, belief, opinion and expression, including freedom of the press and other media of communication;

    (c) freedom of peaceful assembly; and

    (d) freedom of association.

Case Law

Freedom of Conscience and Religion: S. 2(a)

R. v. Fosty (1991), 8 C.R. (4th) 368, (sub nom. *R. v. Gruenke)* 67 C.C.C. (3d) 289 — An individual's freedom of religion may be infringed by the admission of religious communications in a particular case, but s. 2(a) does *not* create a *prima facie* privilege.

Jones v. R. (1986), 28 C.C.C. (3d) 513 (S.C.C.) — Legislation or administrative action whose effect on religion is trivial or insubstantial does *not* violate s. 2(a).

R. v. Big M Drug Mart Ltd. (1985), 18 C.C.C. (3d) 385 (S.C.C.) — *See also: R. v. Videoflicks Ltd.* (1986), 55 C.R. (3d) 193; *R. v. Edwards Books & Art Ltd.*, 30 C.C.C. (3d) 385 (S.C.C.) — The essence of the concept of freedom of religion is the right to entertain such religious beliefs as a person chooses, the right to declare religious beliefs openly and without fear of hindrance and reprisal, and the right to manifest religious belief by worship and practice or by teaching and dissemination. Freedom of conscience and religion must at the very least mean that government may not coerce individuals to affirm a specific religious belief or to manifest a specific religious practice for a sectarian purpose. The *Charter* safeguards religious minorities from the threat of "the tyranny of the majority".

Freedom of Expression: S. 2(b)

Thomson Newspapers Co. v. Canada (Attorney General), [1998] 1 S.C.R. 877 — The publication of opinion survey results is an activity that conveys meaning, hence falls within the scope of *Charter*, s. 2(b).

Libman v. Quebec (Attorney General) (1997), 151 D.L.R. (4th) 385 (S.C.C.) — Freedom of expression in s. 2(b) must be interpreted broadly. Any activity or communication that conveys or attempts to convey meaning is included in s. 2(b), unless the expression is communicated in a manner that excludes the protection, as for example, violence.

C.B.C. v. New Brunswick (Attorney General), 2 C.R. (5th) 1, 110 C.C.C. (3d) 193, [1996] 3 S.C.R. 480 (S.C.C.) — The open court principle is inextricable tied to *Charter* s. 2(b) rights. The freedom to express ideas and opinions about the operation of the courts and the right of the public to obtain information about them fall within s. 2(b) which also protects the freedom of the press to gather and disseminate this information.

Measures that prevent the media from gathering information disclosed in court proceedings and disseminating it to the public restrict freedom of the press guaranteed by *Charter* s. 2(b). To the extent that measures prohibit public access to

  i.   the courts; and

  ii.   information about the courts

they may also restrict freedom of expression to the extent it encompasses the freedom of listeners to obtain information that fosters public criticism of the courts.

R.J.R. MacDonald Inc. v. Canada (Attorney General) (1995), 100 C.C.C. (3d) 449 (S.C.C.) — Freedom of expression entails the right to say nothing (per McLachlin, Sopinka and Major JJ.

Dagenais v. Canadian Broadcasting Corp. (1994), 34 C.R. (4th) 269, 94 C.C.C. (3d) 289 (S.C.C.) — The *common law rule* authorizing publication bans must be modified to give effect to the equal status of the freedom of expression under *Charter* s. 2(b) and the right to a fair trial under s. 11(d). A publication ban should only be ordered when

i.   it is necessary to prevent a real and substantial risk to the fairness of the trial, because reasonably available alternatives will not prevent the risk; and,

ii. the salutary effects of the ban outweigh the deleterious.

The *Charter* does not require that all conceivable steps be taken to remove even the most speculative risks to a fair trial.

NWAC v. Canada (1994), 173 N.R. 241, 119 D.L.R. (4th) 224, [1994] 3 S.C.R. 267, 84 F.T.R. 240n, [1995] 1 C.N.L.R. 47, 24 C.R.R. (2d) 233 — Section 2(b) does *not* guarantee any particular means of expression or place a positive obligation upon the government to fund or consult anyone.

R. v. Zundel (1992), 16 C.R. (4th) 1, 75 C.C.C. (3d) 449 (S.C.C.); reversing on constitutional grounds (sub nom. *R. v. Zundel (No. 2))* 53 C.C.C. (3d) 161 — Section 2(b) is to be given a broad, purposive interpretation. The guarantee's purpose is to permit free expression to promote truth, political or social participation, and self-fulfillment. It serves to protect the right of the minority to express his views, no matter how unpopular. All communications which convey or attempt to convey meaning are protected by s. 2(b), unless the physical form by which they are expressed, as for example a violent act, excludes protection. The *content* of the communication should *not* be considered in order to ensure that unpopular statements are given protection. Hate propaganda is, accordingly, protected by s. 2(b). The *falsity* of a publication does *not* remove it from the scope of s. 2(b) protection. A deliberate lie is *not* an illegitimate form of expression. While a deliberate lie does *not* serve to promote any of the values which underlie s. 2(b), neither can it be said that all deliberate lies have no value. In some cases, exaggeration, even clear falsification, may serve some useful social purpose or foster political participation or self-fulfillment. It cannot be assumed that falsity can be identified with sufficient accuracy to make it a fair criterion for the denial of constitutional protection. It is preferable to leave arguments relating the value of deliberate falsehood or its prejudicial effect to be dealt with under s. 1.A violent act is excluded from s. 2(b) protection because of the physical form in which it is communicated, *not* its content.

R. v. Butler (1992), 70 C.C.C. (3d) 129 (S.C.C.) — *Code* s. 163(8) violates *Charter* s. 2(b) in that it seeks to prohibit certain types of expressive activity. Activities cannot be excluded from the scope of s. 2(b) on the basis of the content or meaning being conveyed. The infringement is justifiable under s. 1. In light of judicial interpretation, s. 163(8) prescribes an intelligible standard. Its overriding objective is the avoidance of harm to society, and this is a sufficiently pressing and substantial concern to warrant a restriction on freedom of expression. There is a rational connection between the criminal sanction and the objective; the impairment of freedom of expression is minimal in light of the imposition of a standard of undue exploitation; and there is no equal alternative given the gravity of the harm.

Osborne v. Canada (Treasury Board), [1991] 2 S.C.R. 70, 37 C.C.E.L. 135 (S.C.C.) — Where opposing values call for a restriction on the freedom of speech, exceptional cases aside, the limits on the freedom are to be dealt with under the balancing test of s. 1, not by circumscription of the guarantee at the outset.

R. v. Keegstra (1990), 1 C.R. (4th) 129, 61 C.C.C. (3d) 1 (S.C.C.); reversing (1988), 65 C.R. (3d) 289, 43 C.C.C. (3d) 150 (Alta. C.A.) — *See also*: *R. v. Andrews* (1990), 1 C.R. (4th) 266, 61 C.C.C. (3d) 490 (S.C.C.); affirming (1988), 65 C.R. (3d) 320, 43 C.C.C. (3d) 193 (Ont C.A.) — "Expression" in s. 2(b) embraces all content of expression, irrespective of the meaning or message sought to be conveyed. It is irrelevant whether the expression is invidious and obnoxious, promotes hatred of an identifiable group, or threatens violence. If the purpose of government action is to restrict freedom of expression, s. 2(b) is infringed. Where it is only the effect of such action which restricts an activity, s. 2(b) only applies where it can be demonstrated by the party alleging infringement that the activity supports rather than undermines the principles which underlie freedom of expression.

Rocket v. Royal College of Dental Surgeons (Ontario), [1990] 2 S.C.R. 232 (S.C.C.); affirming (1988), 27 O.A.C. 52 (C.A.) — The freedom of expression protected by s. 2(b) includes commercial speech such as advertising, even though the *Charter* was not intended to protect economic interests, because advertising aims to convey a meaning, hence involves more than economics.

R. v. Skinner (1990), 77 C.R. (3d) 84, 56 C.C.C. (3d) 1 (S.C.C.); reversing (1987), 58 C.R. (3d) 137, 35 C.C.C. (3d) 203 (N.S. C.A.) — *See also*: *R. v. Stagnitta* (1990), 56 C.C.C. (3d) 17 (S.C.C.); affirming (1987), 58 C.R. (3d) 164, 36 C.C.C. (3d) 105 (Alta. C.A.); *Reference re ss. 193 & 195.1(1)(c) of the Criminal Code* (1990), 77 C.R. (3d) 1, 56 C.C.C. (3d) 65 (S.C.C.); affirming (1987), 60 C.R. (3d) 216, 38 C.C.C. (3d) 408 (Man. C.A.) — The scope of freedom of expression extends to the activity of communication for the purposes of engaging in prostitution. The s. 2(b) infringement is, however, justifiable under s. 1.

Freedom of the Press: S. 2(b)

Canadian Broadcasting Corp. v. New Brunswick (Attorney General) (1991), 67 C.C.C. (3d) 554, 85 D.L.R. (4th) 57 (S.C.C.) — *See also*: *Canadian Broadcasting Corp. v. Lessard* (1991), 67 C.C.C. (3d) 517 (S.C.C.) — Even where all the statutory prerequisites to the issuance of a search warrant have been met, the justice of the peace has a discretion to issue a warrant in all of the circumstances. The justice should strike a balance between the interest of the state in investigating and prosecuting crime, and the right of the media to privacy in gathering and disseminating news. The affidavit in support of the application should ordinarily disclose whether there are alternative sources of the information and whether they have been exhausted. If the information sought already has been disseminated by the media, this will weigh in favour of issuing the warrant. Consideration should be given to attaching conditions to the warrant so that the media are not unduly impeded.

Canadian Broadcasting Corp. v. Lessard (1991), 67 C.C.C. (3d) 517 (S.C.C.) — The media are entitled to careful consideration regarding the issuance of a search warrant and the conditions to be attached, so that the gathering and dissemination of news is disrupted as little as possible. Where the police fail to state there is no alternative source of the information, issuance of a warrant may be refused. Once the information has been published or broadcast, it passes into the public domain and a search does not interfere with the operation of the media. It then is appropriate to issue a search warrant even though the police have failed to specify there is no alternative source of the information.

R. v. Cdn. Newspapers Ltd. (1988), 65 C.R. (3d) 50, 43 C.C.C. (3d) 24 (S.C.C.) — A *Criminal Code* provision allowing the complainant in a sexual assault case to apply for a mandatory order prohibiting publication of the complainant's name or any information that could disclose it infringes on the freedom of the press under the *Charter*. However, the section imposes a reasonable limitation on the freedom of the press under the *Charter*, given the fact that sexual assault is one of the most unreported by its victims of the serious crimes largely because of the fear of publicity. The victim's need for certainty regarding the order renders inappropriate the granting of a discretion to the trial judge as to whether to grant the order.

Freedom of Association: S. 2(d)

CEMA v. Richardson, [1998] 3 S.C.R. 157 — Freedom of association protects *only* the *associational* aspect of activities, *not* the *activity* itself. An activity is *not* protected *only* because it is a foundational or essential purpose of an association.

Section 2(d) does not create a right to do in association what it is *unlawful* for an *individual* to do.

Libman v. Quebec (Attorney General) (1997), 151 D.L.R. (4th) 385 (S.C.C.) — Section 2(d) includes the exercise in association of the constitutional rights and freedoms of individuals.

Lavigne v. O.P.S.E.U. (1990), 3 O.R. (3d) 511 (note), [1991] 2 S.C.R. 211 (S.C.C.) — The essence of the s. 2(d) guarantee is protection of the individual's interest in self-actualization and fulfillment that can be realized only through association with others. The protection of this interest, as well the community interest in sustaining democracy, requires that freedom from compelled association be recognized under s. 2(d). Freedom from forced association and freedom to associate are but two sides of a bi-lateral freedom which has as its unifying purpose the advancement of individual aspirations. Section 2(d), however, does not provide protection from all forms of involuntary association: it was not intended to protect against such association with others as is a necessary and inevitable part of membership in a modern democratic community.

R. v. Skinner (1990), 77 C.R. (3d) 84, 56 C.C.C. (3d) 1 (S.C.C.); reversing (1987), 58 C.R. (3d) 137, 35 C.C.C. (3d) 203 (N.S. C.A.) — *See also*: *R. v. Stagnitta* (1990), 56 C.C.C. (3d) 17 (S.C.C.); affirming (1987), 58 C.R. (3d) 164, 36 C.C.C. (3d) 105 (Alta. C.A.); *References re ss. 193 & 195.1(1)(c) of the Criminal Code* (1990), 77 C.R. (3d) 1, 56 C.C.C. (3d) 65 (S.C.C.); affirming (1987), 60 C.R. (3d) 216, 38 C.C.C. (3d) 408 (Man. C.A.) — Communicating in a public place for the purpose of engaging in prostitution is the nature of the activity to which s. 213(1)(c) is directed. Its target is expressive conduct, not conduct of an associational nature. The mere fact that it limits the possibility of commercial activities or agreements is not sufficient to show a *prima facie* interference with *Charter* s. 2(d). The subsection does, however, infringe the freedom of expression guarantee in s. 2(b), but is justifiable under s. 1.

Democratic Rights

3. Democratic rights of citizens — Every citizen of Canada has the right to vote in an election of members of the House of Commons or of a legislative assembly and to be qualified for membership therein.

Case Law

Saskatchewan (Attorney General) v. Carter (1991), 5 C.R.R. (2d) 1 (S.C.C.) — The content of s. 3 is to be determined in a broad and purposive way, having regard to historical and social context. The broader philosophy underlying the historical development of the right to vote should be sought and practical considerations, such as social and physical geography, must be borne in mind. The court, most importantly, must be guided by the ideal of a "free and democratic society" upon which the *Charter* is founded.The purpose of the right to vote in s. 3 is not equality of voting power, *per se*, but the right to "effective representation" of which relative parity of voting power is a prime condition. Equity is but one of the factors which comprises the right to vote. Section 3 does not guarantee equality of voting power. Factors such as geography, community history, community interests and minority representation may require consideration to ensure that legislative assemblies effectively represent the diversity of our social mosaic.

Belczowski v. R. (1992), 12 C.R. (4th) 219 (Fed. C.A.) — *See also: Sauvé v. Canada (Attorney General)* (1992), 7 O.R. (3d) 481 (C.A.); affirmed (1993), [1993] 2 S.C.R. 438 (S.C.C.) — The s. 51(e) *Canada Elections Act* prohibition against prisoners voting infringes *Charter* s. 3 and cannot be justified under s. 1.

4. (1) Maximum duration of legislative bodies — No House of Commons and no legislative assembly shall continue for longer than five years from the date fixed for the return of the writs at a general election of its members.

(2) Continuation in special circumstances — In time of real or apprehended war, invasion or insurrection, a House of Commons may be continued by Parliament and a legislative assembly may be continued by the legislature beyond five years if such continuation is not opposed by the votes of more than one-third of the members of the House of Commons or the legislative assembly, as the case may be.

5. Annual sitting of legislative bodies — There shall be a sitting of Parliament and of each legislature at least once every twelve months.

Mobility Rights

6. (1) Mobility of citizens — Every citizen of Canada has the right to enter, remain in and leave Canada.

(2) Rights to move and gain livelihood — Every citizen of Canada and every person who has the status of a permanent resident of Canada has the right

    (a) to move to and take up residence in any province; and

    (b) to pursue the gaining of a livelihood in any province.

(3) **Limitation** — The rights specified in subsection (2) are subject to

    (a) any laws or practices of general application in force in a province other than those that discriminate among persons primarily on the basis of province of present or previous residence; and

    (b) any laws providing for reasonable residency requirements as a qualification for the receipt of publicly provided social services.

(4) **Affirmative action programs** — Subsections (2) and (3) do not preclude any law, program or activity that has as its object the amelioration in a province of conditions of individuals in that province who are socially or economically disadvantaged if the rate of employment in that province is below the rate of employment in Canada.

Case Law

CEMA v. Richardson, [1998] 3 S.C.R. 157 — The scope of s. 6 must reflect the fundamental purpose that underlies it. The hallmark of mobility required by s. 6 is *not* physical movement to another province. It is, rather, any attempt to *create wealth*, whether by *production, marketing*, or *performance* in another province.

Section 6 relates to an essential element of personhood. It guarantees that mobility in the pursuit of a livelihood will *not* be prevented through unequal treatment based on residence by the laws in force in the jurisdiction where the livelihood is pursued. The focus of the s. 6 analysis is *not* the *type* of economic *activity* involved, but rather, the *purpose* and *effect* of the legislation, and whether that *purpose* and *effect* infringe the right to be free from discrimination based on residence in the pursuit of a livelihood.

Sections 6(2)(b) and 6(3)(a) should be read together as defining a single right, *not* one right that is externally "saved" by another.

Section 6(3)(a) is *not* a "saving" provision, like ss. 6(3)(b), 6(4) or 1, none of which is essential to defining the purpose of the sections that they limit. The interdependence of ss. 6(2)(b) and 3(c) should be given full effect by determining the purpose and scope of the two provisions together without leaving room for a second application of s. 6(3)(a).

Whether legislation discriminates "among persons *primarily* on the basis of province of present . . . residence" under s. 6(3)(a) requires a comparison of residents of the origin province who *try* to make their *livelihood* in the *destination* province *with* residents of the *destination* province who also make their *livelihood* in the *destination* province. The appropriate comparison group will depend on the nature of the livelihood that is restricted.

"Primarily" in s. 6(3)(a) suggests that *other purposes* and *effects* must be weighed to determine whether the *residential* aspect of discrimination is *primary*.

United States of America v. Cotroni (1989), 48 C.C.C. (3d) 193 (S.C.C.) — The *Extradition Act* is a reasonable limit on the rights guaranteed by *Charter* s. 6(1).

Legal Rights

7. Life, liberty and security of person — Everyone has the right to life, liberty and security of the person and the right not to be deprived thereof except in accordance with the principles of fundamental justice.

Case Law

General Principles

R. v. Rose, [1998] 3 S.C.R. 262, 20 C.R. (5th) 246, 129 C.C.C. (3d) 449 — The right to make full answer and defence, a principle of fundamental justice, does *not* imply an entitlement to those rules and procedures most likely to result in a finding of innocence. D is entitled, however, to rules and procedures that are *fair* in the manner in which they *enable* D to *defend* against and *answer* P's case.

There are two discrete aspects to the right to make full answer and defence:

i.   the right to have P's full "case to meet" before being required to answer by adducing evidence; and,

ii. the right to self-defend against all of the state's efforts to achieve a conviction.

P may *not* engage in activities aimed at convicting D unless D is allowed to self-defend against the state and against the state's acts. The right to self-defend does *not* always imply answering words already spoken or deeds already done by P.

A finding that either s. 7 or 11(d) has been infringed necessarily entails that the other section has also been infringed.

Godbout v. Longueuil (City) (1997), 219 N.R. 1 (S.C.C.) — The liberty interest in s. 7 extends beyond the notion of mere freedom from physical constraint. It protects within its scope a narrow sphere of personal autonomy in which individuals may make inherently private choices free from state interference. It includes only those matters that can properly be characterized as fundamentally or inherently personal such tha, by their very nature, they implicate basic choices which go to the core of what it means to enjoy individual dignity and independence. Included, is the right to choose where to establish one's home.

R. v. Stillman (1997), 5 C.R. (5th) 1, [1997] 1 S.C.R. 607, 113 C.C.C. (3d) 321 (S.C.C.); reversing (1995), 97 C.C.C. (3d) 164 (N.B. C.A.) — Police conduct, *without* D's *consent* or *authority*, which intrudes upon D's body in more than minimal fashion, violates *Charter* s. 7.

R. v. Canadian Pacific Ltd. (1995), 41 C.R. (4th) 147 at 153, 99 C.C.C. (3d) 97 at 103 (S.C.C.) — The principles of fundamental justice require that laws provide the basis for coherent judicial interpretation and sufficiently delineate an area of risk. (per Gonthier, La Forest, L'Heureux-Dubé, McLachlin, Iacobucci and Major JJ.)

A law is unconstitutionally vague if it is so lacking in precision it does *not* give sufficient guidance for legal debate. Vagueness is *not* considered in the abstract, rather, assessed within the larger interpretative context developed through an analysis of considerations which include the

i.   purpose;

ii.   subject-matter;

iii. nature; and

iv.   prior judicial interpretation of the impugned provision, as well as

v.   societal values; and

vi.   related legislative provisions.

It is only after exhaustion of its interpretative role that a court is in a position to decide whether the provision affords sufficient guidance for legal debate. (per Gonthier, La Forest, L'Heureux-Dubé, McLachlin, Iacobucci and Major JJ.

The principles of fundamental justice do *not* prevent legislative use of broad and general terms which require courts, in a mediating role, to determine their application in particular circumstances. The courts must take a deferential approach in relation to legislative enactments with legitimate social policy objectives so as to avoid impeding the state's ability to pursue and promote these objectives. (per Gonthier, La Forest, L'Heureux-Dubé, McLachlin, Iacobucci and Major JJ.

It is open to D to argue that a statute is unconstitutionally vague, notwithstanding that D's conduct plainly falls within the core of the prohibition. Reasonable hypotheticals, however, have no place in the s. 7 vagueness analysis. The focus of any vagueness analysis is on the terms of the impugned law. If judicial interpretation of the provision is possible, the law is *not* unconstitutionally vague. (per Gonthier, La Forest, L'Heureux-Dubé, McLachlin, Iacobucci and Major JJ.

An allegation of overbreadth requres a proportionality analysis which involves the use of reasonable hypotheticals. The first step in the analysis requires the court to exhaust its interpretive function, not to proceed merely on the basis of the literal meaning of the provision (per Gonthier, La Forest, L'Heureux-Dubé, McLachlin, Iacobucci and Major JJ.

R. v. S. (R.J.) (1995), 21 O.R. (3d) 797n (S.C.C.); affirming (1993), 80 C.C.C. (3d) 397, 21 C.R. (4th) 47 (Ont. C.A.) — An accused who has been charged in a separate information and acquitted is a compellable witness for P at D's trial on a separate information. While a statutory compulsion to testify engages the liberty interest of *Charter* s. 7, it is affected in accordance with the principles of fundamental justice. The fundamental justice requirement is satisfied because neither the former accused's testimony, nor a limited class of evidence derived from that testimony, can later be used to incriminate him/her in other proceedings, except prosecutions for perjury or the giving of contradictory evidence. There is no breach of *Charter* s. 7 where P compels a person separately charged with the same offence to testify as a prosecution witness at the trial of another.

R. v. Heywood (1994), 34 C.R. (4th) 133, 94 C.C.C. (3d) 481, 24 C.R.R. (2d) 189 (S.C.C.); affirming (1992), 18 C.R. (4th) 63, 77 C.C.C. (3d) 502 (B.C. C.A.) — *Overbreadth* and *vagueness* are different concepts but are related in some cases. Both are the result of a lack of sufficient precision by a legislature in the *means* used to accomplish an objective. In cases of *vagueness*, the means are not clearly defined. In cases of *overbreadth*, the means are too sweeping in relation to the objective.

Overbreadth analysis considers the means chosen by the state in relation to its purpose. The court must consider whether the means used are necessary to achieve the state objective. The principles of fundamental justice are violated where the state, pursuing a legitimate objective, uses means which are broader than necessary to accomplish that objective. The effect of overbreadth is that, in some applications, the law is arbitrary or disproportionate.

R. v. L. (D.O.) (1994), 25 C.R. (4th) 285, 85 C.C.C. (3d) 289 (S.C.C.) — There is no constitutionally protected requirement that cross-examination be contemporaneous with the giving of evidence.

R. v. Creighton (1993), 23 C.R. (4th) 189, 83 C.C.C. (3d) 346 (S.C.C.) — As a general rule, the *mens rea* of an offence ought to relate to the consequences prohibited by the offence. There is no principle of fundamental justice, however, which requires an exact symmetry between the fault element and the consequences of the offence. No person may be imprisoned without proof of *mens rea*. The seriousness of an offence must not be disproportionate to the degree of moral fault. The principles of fundamental justice are satisfied provided an element of mental fault or moral culpability proportionate to the seriousness and consequences of the offence is present.

Cunningham v. Canada (1993), 80 C.C.C. (3d) 492 (S.C.C.) — The principles of fundamental justice are concerned not only with the interests of the person who claims that his/her liberty has been limited, but also with the protection of society. Fundamental justice requires that a fair balance be struck between these interests, both substantively and procedurally.

R. v. DeSousa (1992), 15 C.R. (4th) 66, 76 C.C.C. (3d) 124 (S.C.C.) — There is *no* constitutional requirement of subjective foresight of all consequences which comprise part of the *actus reus* (external circumstances) of an offence. Provided there is an *actus reus* to which a comparable mental state is attached, there is *no* further constitutional requirement that any other element of the *actus reus* (external circumstances) be linked to this or a further culpable mental state. No principle of fundamental justice bars Parliament from treating crimes with certain consequences as more serious than others which lack such consequences. Neither basic principles of criminal law nor fundamental justice require, by necessity, intention in relation to the consequences of an otherwise blameworthy act.

Canada v. Pharmaceutical Society (Nova Scotia) (1992), 15 C.R. (4th) 1, 74 C.C.C. (3d) 289 (S.C.C.) — The *doctrine of vagueness*, as a principle of fundamental justice, is based upon the requirements of *fair notice* to the citizen and *limitation of law enforcement discretion. Fair notice* includes a formal aspect *viz.*, acquaintance with the actual text of the law, as well a substantive content *viz.*, an understanding that certain conduct is the subject of legal restrictions. *Limitation of law enforcement discretion* is founded on the principle that a law must *not* be so devoid of precision in its content that a conviction will automatically flow from the decision to prosecute. A law will be unconstitutionally vague where it fails to provide an adequate basis for legal debate *i.e.*, for ascertaining its meaning by reasoned analysis applying legal criteria. Where it fails sufficiently to delineate any area of risk, it can provide neither fair notice to a citizen nor a limitation upon enforcement discretion.

Canada v. Pharmaceutical Society (Nova Scotia) (1992), 15 C.R. (4th) 1, 74 C.C.C. (3d) 289 (S.C.C.) — Overbreadth, whether it derives from the vagueness of a law or from another source, is no more than an analytical tool to establish a violation of a *Charter* right. It has no independent existence. Claims of overbreadth cannot be used to masquerade an absence of a constitutional foundation.

R. v. Wholesale Travel Group Inc. (1991), 8 C.R. (4th) 145, 67 C.C.C. (3d) 193 (S.C.C.) — The rights of s. 7 can only be enjoyed by human beings. A corporate accused is unable to seek a declaration that statutory provisions infringe s. 7. Where penal proceedings are pending in a case, however, a corporation may challenge their validity on the basis that they infringe the rights of an individual accused. The corporation may take the benefit from a finding that the provisions violate a human being's constitutional rights. The appropriate remedy under s. 52(1) in such cases is that the provision is of no force and effect, hence that it cannot apply to any accused, corporate or individual.

R. v. Seaboyer, (sub nom. R. v. Gayme) 7 C.R. (4th) 117, 66 C.C.C. (3d) 321 — The principles of fundamental justice reflect a spectrum of interests from the rights of D to broader societal concerns. Section 7 is to be construed as having regard to those interests and against the applicable principles and policies that have animated legislative and judicial practice in the field. The ultimate issue is whether the legislation, regarded purposively, conforms to the fundamental precepts which underlie our system of justice. A provision which denies D the right to present a full and fair defence would violate s. 7.

R. v. L. (W.K.) (1991), 6 C.R. (4th) 1, 64 C.C.C. (3d) 321 (S.C.C.) — The *Charter* does not insulate D from prosecution solely on the basis of the effluxion of time between the commission of the offence and the laying of the charge. The fair trial guarantees of *Charter* ss. 7 and 11(d) are not automatically undermined by reason of a lengthy pre-trial delay. What must be determined in each case is whether the delay has affected the fairness of the trial.

R. v. Hess (1990), (sub nom. *R. v. Nguyen)* 79 C.R. (3d) 332, 59 C.C.C. (3d) 161 (S.C.C.); reversing [1989] 3 W.W.R. 646 (Man. C.A.) — It is a principle of fundamental justice that a criminal offence punishable by imprisonment must have a *mens rea* component. Any such offence that denies D a due diligence defence infringes the right to liberty guaranteed in s. 7.

R. v. Logan (1990), 79 C.R. (3d) 169, 58 C.C.C. (3d) 391 (S.C.C.); affirming (1988), 68 C.R. (3d) 1, 46 C.C.C. (3d) 354 (Ont. C.A.) — It is *not* a principle of fundamental justice that, in all cases, the level of *mens rea* required to prove the guilt of a principal is also required in respect of a party. For certain offences, however, the objective ("... ought to have known ...") component of s. 21(2) will operate to restrict D's rights under *Charter* s. 7. Where the offence is one of the few for which s. 7 requires a minimum degree of *mens rea*, a party may not be convicted on the basis of a degree of *mens rea* below the constitutionally required minimum. In each case, it must first be determined whether fundamental justice requires a minimum degree of *mens rea* before D may be convicted as a principal in the offence. Where a minimum degree of *mens rea* is required to convict a principal, an equivalent minimum degree is required to convict a party. The words "or ought to have known" are inoperative when considering under s. 21(2) whether D is a party to any offence which constitutionally requires that foresight of the consequences be subjective.

R. v. Beare (1988), 66 C.R. (3d) 97, 45 C.C.C. (3d) 57 (S.C.C.) — The analysis of *Charter* s. 7 involves two steps: first, the triggering of its operation by a finding by the court that there has been a deprivation of the right to "life, liberty and security of the person", and second, a finding that the deprivation is contrary to the principles of fundamental justice. The common law, while not determinative in assessing whether a particular practice violates a principle of justice, is one of the major repositories of the basic tenets of the legal system. Legislation authorizing the fingerprinting of persons arrested but not yet convicted of an indictable offence, infringe the rights guaranteed by s. 7, but do not violate the principles of fundamental justice.

R. v. Vaillancourt (1987), 60 C.R. (3d) 289, 39 C.C.C. (3d) 118 (S.C.C.) — Before an accused can be convicted of an offence, the trier of fact must be satisfied beyond a reasonable doubt of the existence of all the essential elements of the offence. These essential elements include not only those set out in the section creating the offence, but also those required by *Charter* s. 7. Any provision creating an offence which allows for the conviction of the accused notwithstanding the existence of a reasonable doubt on any essential element, or which does not include an element required under s. 7, infringes on ss. 7 and 11(d). Where the legislature substitutes proof of a different element rather than simply eliminating any need to prove the essential element, the provision will only be valid if upon proof beyond a reasonable doubt of the substituted element it would be unreasonable for the trier of fact not to be satisfied beyond a reasonable doubt of the existence of the essential element.

Reference re Section 94(2) of the Motor Vehicle Act (1985), 48 C.R. (3d) 289, 23 C.C.C. (3d) 289 (S.C.C.) — A provision creating an absolute liability offence for driving while under a licence suspension coupled with a minimum seven-day jail term was unconstitutional. A law that has the potential to convict a person who has not really done anything wrong offends the principles of fundamental justice and, if imprisonment is available as a penalty, let alone mandatory, such a law then violates a person's right to liberty under s. 7. The principles of fundamental justice are not a protected interest, but rather a qualifier serving to establish the parameters of the protected rights of life, liberty and security of the person, and cannot be interpreted so narrowly as to frustrate or stultify those interests. It cannot be narrowly interpreted as being synonymous with natural justice since to do so would strip the protected interests of much, if not most, of their content. The principles of fundamental justice are to be found in the basic tenets of our legal system, and their limits are for the courts to develop within the acceptable sphere of judicial activity.

Operation Dismantle Inc. v. R., [1985] 1 S.C.R. 441 (S.C.C.) — Section 7 does not impose a duty on the government to refrain from those acts which might lead to consequences that deprive or threaten to deprive individuals of their life and security of the person. Remedial action by the courts is not justified where the link between the action and any alleged future harm is not capable of proof; there must be a cognizable threat to a legal interest before the courts will entertain the use of its process as a preventive measure.

General Defences and Fundamental Justice

R. v. Robinson, 46 C.R. (4th) 1, 105 C.C.C. (3d) 97, [1996] 1 S.C.R. 683 (S.C.C.); affirming (1984), 92 C.C.C. (3d) 193 (B.C. C.A.) — *See also*: *R. v. McMaster*, 46 C.R. (4th) 41, 105 C.C.C. (3d) 193, [1996] 1 S.C.R. 740 (S.C.C.) — The rules of *D.P.P. v. Beard*, namely,

i.   that intoxication only becomes relevant for the trier of fact to consider where it removes D's *capacity* to form the requisite intent; and,

ii.   that the *presumption* that a person intends the natural consequences of his/her acts cannot be rebutted by evidence falling short of incapacity

should be overruled. The rules infringe *Charter* ss. 7 and 11(d) and are not saved by s. 1. Rule ii, *supra*, at all events, is only a common sense *inference*, not a presumption.

R. v. Daviault (1994), 33 C.R. (4th) 165, 93 C.C.C. (3d) 21 (S.C.C.) — The *Leary* rule that the *mens rea* of a general intent offence cannot be negated by intoxication offends *Charter* s. 7 and 11(d).

R. v. Hess (1990), (sub nom. *R. v. Nguyen*) 79 C.R. (3d) 332, 59 C.C.C. (3d) 161 (S.C.C.); reversing [1989] 3 W.W.R. 646 (Man. C.A.) — It is a principle of fundamental justice that a criminal offence punishable by imprisonment must have a *mens rea* component. Any such offence that denies D a due diligence defence infringes the right to liberty guaranteed in s. 7.

R. v. Stevens (1988), 64 C.R. (3d) 297, 41 C.C.C. (3d) 193 (S.C.C.) — Section 7 is not applicable to render unconstitutional the statutory denial of the defence of honest belief to a charge of having sexual intercourse with a female under 14 years where the conduct took place before the *Charter* was in force, although the *Charter* was in force at the time of trial. Criminal liability for the offence is attached at the time the offence was committed, and it would be giving retrospective application to s. 7 to apply it to the offence merely because the liability imposed by the offence continued after the *Charter* came into force.

Evidentiary Rules and Fundamental Justice

Mooring v. Canada (National Parole Board), [1996] 3 W.W.R. 305, 192 N.R. 1 (S.C.C.) — The National Parole Board, as a statutory tribunal, is subject to the dictates of *Charter* s. 7 and must comply with the principles of fundamental justice in its conduct of proceedings. It does *not* follow, however, that the Board must possess or exercise a power to exclude evidence obtained by *Charter* infringement.

R. v. Potvin (1989), 68 C.R. (3d) 193, 47 C.C.C. (3d) 289 (S.C.C.) — A *Code* provision allowing the admission of previously-obtained testimony as evidence in a trial where the witness is unavailable does not contravene the accused's right to a fair trial, in the absence of circumstances which negated or minimized the accused's opportunity to cross-examine the witness when the previous testimony was given. The right to confront unavailable witnesses at trial is neither an established nor a basic principle of fundamental justice. However, the accused would have a constitutional right to have the evidence of prior testimony excluded where it was obtained in the absence of a full opportunity to cross-examine the witness.

Pre-Charter Conduct, Subsequent Detention and Fundamental Justice

Gamble v. R. (1988), 66 C.R. (3d) 193, 45 C.C.C. (3d) 204 (S.C.C.) — The *Criminal Law Amendment Act (No. 2), 1976* provided for a mandatory sentence on a conviction for first degree murder of life without parole eligibility for 25 years. The transitional provision under the Act, which required persons who were convicted at a trial ordered or held subsequent to the coming into force of the amending Act to be punished pursuant to the new provisions, contravened *Charter* s. 7 where the impugned conduct preceded the coming into force of the amending Act. The use of s. 7 to review a sentence handed down prior to the coming into force of the *Charter* did not necessarily give retrospective application to the section. Pre-*Charter* events may be taken into account to determine whether there is a continuing current violation of the liberty interest of the subject.

R. v. Stevens (1988), 64 C.R. (3d) 297, 41 C.C.C. (3d) 193 (S.C.C.) — Section 7 is not applicable to render unconstitutional the statutory denial of the defence of honest belief to a charge of having sexual intercourse with a female under 14 years where the conduct took place before the *Charter* was in force, although the *Charter* was in force at the time of trial. Criminal liability for the offence is attached at the time the offence was committed, and it would be giving retrospective application to s. 7 to apply it to the offence merely because the liability imposed by the offence continued after the *Charter* came into force.

Disclosure Issues and Fundamental Justice

R. v. W. (D.D.), [1998] 2 S.C.R. 681, 129 C.C.C. (3d) 226; affirming (1997), 114 C.C.C. (3d) 506 (B.C. C.A.) — Where adoption records sought by D are in the custody of a provincial government agency *not* involved in the investigation or prosecution of D, and are subject to a statutory requirement that generally prohibits disclosure, there is *no* error in refusing to order their production.

R. v. Dixon (1998), 122 C.C.C. (3d) 1 (S.C.C.) — The right to full disclosure is only one component of the right to make full answer and defence. The *Charter* right to make full answer and defence is not necessarily impaired solely because the right to disclosure was violated.

To determine whether the right to make full answer and defence was impaired by P's failure to disclose, there are two steps to be followed. The reliability of the result must be assessed first. The undisclosed information should be examined to determine its impact on the decision to convict. If an appellate court is satisfied that there is a reasonable possibility that, on its face, the undisclosed information affects the reliability of the conviction, a new trial should be ordered.

The effect of non-disclosure on the overall fairness of the trial process should be considered, even if undisclosed information does not affect the reliability of the trial result. What is assessed, on the basis of reasonable possibility, are the lines of inquiry with witnesses and the opportunities to garner additional evidence that could have been available to D if the relevant information had been disclosed. The diligence of defence counsel in pursuing disclosure from P is a factor to be considered.

Where D demonstrates a reasonable possibility that undisclosed information could have been used in

i.   meeting P's case;

ii.   advancing a defence; or,

iii.   making a decision which could have affected the conduct of the defence,

D has established that his/her *Charter* right to disclosure has been impaired.

In cases of incomplete disclosure by P, D is required to demonstrate on appeal from conviction

i.   that it is reasonably possible that the non-disclosed material affected the reliability of D's conviction; or,

ii.   that it is reasonably possible that the non-disclosed material affected the overall fairness of the trial

in order to obtain a new trial.

R. v. La (1997), 116 C.C.C. (3d) 97 (S.C.C.) — D need *not* establish an abuse of process for P to have failed to meet its disclosure obligations under *Charter* s. 7.

To establish a s. 7 *Charter* breach on the ground of lost or destroyed evidence, P must establish *actual prejudice* to the right to make full answer and defence.

The appropriateness of a stay of proceedings as a remedy for *Charter* infringement depends on the *effect* of the conduct amounting to an abuse of process or other prejudice on the *fairness* of the trial. It is often best assessed in the context of the trial as it unfolds.

The duty of P and the police to preserve the fruits of an investigation imposes an obligation on P to explain the loss of evidence. Where the explanation offered satisfies the trial judge that the evidence has not been destroyed or lost due to unacceptable negligence, there is no breach of the duty to disclose. Where the explanation offered fails to satisfy the judge, however, P has failed to meet its disclosure obligations and *Charter* s. 7 has been breached.

To determine whether P's explanation for the loss or destruction of evidence is satisfactory, the main consideration for a judge who is required to examine all of the circumstances is whether P or the police took reasonable steps in the circumstances to preserve the evidence for disclosure. The relevance that the evidence appeared to have at the time is also of significance. The loss or destruction of relevant evidence does not breach the duty to disclose if the conduct of the police was reasonable. An increase in the relevance of the evidence enhances the degree of care required of the police to ensure its preservation.

Conduct arising from a failure to disclose may amount to an abuse of process where it violates those fundamental principles that underlie the community's sense of decency and fair play. An abuse of process includes, but is not limited to deliberate destruction of evidence to avoid disclosure obligations and other conduct which proceeds from an improper motive. A stay of proceedings may be an appropriate remedy if it is one of those rarest of cases in which a stay may be imposed.

The content of the right to make full answer and defence in *Charter* s. 7 is not exhausted by P's obligation to disclose. Full disclosure by P and a satisfactory explanation of missing evidence does not disentitle D to rely on the right to make full answer and defence within *Charter* s. 7. In exceptional circumstances, the loss of a document may be so prejudicial that it impairs D's right to a fair trial.

To establish a breach of *Charter* s. 7 on the ground of lost evidence, where P has satisfied its disclosure obligations, D must establish actual prejudice to the right to make full answer and defence.

R. v. O'Connor (1995), 44 C.R. (4th) 1, 103 C.C.C. (3d) 1 (S.C.C.) — Disclosure issues normally engage ss. 7 and 11(d) *Charter* concerns. Challenges based on non-disclosure generally require proof of *actual prejudice* to D's ability to make full answer and defence. D must establish, on a balance of probabilities, that the non-disclosure prejudiced or had an adverse effect on D's ability to make full answer and defence. There must be a reasonable inquiry into the *materiality* of the non-disclosed information. The focus is primarily upon the *effect* of P's actions on the fairness of D's trial.

In determining what remedy is appropriate and just for *Charter* infringement based on non-disclosure, a court should consider whether P's breach of disclosure obligations has violated the fundamental principles which underpin the community's sense of decency and fair play, hence cause prejudice to the integrity of the judicial system. P's conduct and intention are very relevant for those purposes. *Males fidesis not* a prerequisite to a finding of flagrant and intentional misconduct required for a stay of proceedings.

R. v. O'Connor (1995), 44 C.R. (4th) 1, 103 C.C.C. (3d) 1 (S.C.C.) — A remedy for *Charter* infringement due to non-disclosure is typically a disclosure order and adjournment. In extreme cases, where prejudice to D's ability to make full answer and defence, or to the integrity of the justice system is irremediable, a stay of proceedings is appropriate. Other remedies include

i.   permitting D to recall witnesses for examination or cross-examination;

ii.   adjournments to permit D to subpoena additional witnesses; or,

iii.   in extreme cases, declaration of a mistrial.

Specific Applications

R. v. O'Connor (1995), 44 C.R. (4th) 1, 103 C.C.C. (3d) 1 (S.C.C.) — In general, there is no utility in maintaining two distinct approaches to abusive conduct by P. The principles of fundamental justice both reflect and accommodate the common law doctrine of abuse of process.

Conway v. Canada (A.G.) (1993), 23 C.R. (4th) 1, 83 C.C.C. (3d) 1 (S.C.C.) — There is a substantially-reduced level of privacy in a prison where cells are expected to be exposed and require observation. A prisoner cannot hold a reasonable expectation of privacy with respect to the common prison practices of frisk search, the count and the wind since imprisonment entails surveillance, searching and scrutiny. The absence of a reasonable expectation of privacy remains even where the prisoner is male and the guard female. The practices do *not* breach *Charter* s. 7.

R. v. Creighton (1993), 23 C.R. (4th) 189, 83 C.C.C. (3d) 346 (S.C.C.) — In unlawful act manslaughter under s. 222(5)(a), the *mens rea* comprises

i.   the *mens rea* of the underlying offence; and

ii.   objective foreseeability of the risk of bodily harm which is neither trivial nor transitory, in the context of the dangerous act.

Foreseeability of death is not required. There is no contravention of *Charter* s. 7. (per McLachlin, La Forest, L'Heureux-Dubé, Gonthier and Cory JJ.A.)

R. v. Potvin (1993), 23 C.R. (4th) 10, 83 C.C.C. (3d) 97 (S.C.C.) — *See also*: *R. v. Gallagher* (1993), 83 C.C.C. (3d) 122 (S.C.C.); *R. v. Frazer* (1993), 83 C.C.C. (3d) 126 (S.C.C.) — The appropriate forum for a s. 7 remedy with respect to appellate delay is the appellate court since it is in the best position to assess the consequences of the delay.

R. v. Potvin (1993), 23 C.R. (4th) 10, 83 C.C.C. (3d) 97 (S.C.C.) — *See also*: *R. v. Gallagher* (1993), 83 C.C.C. (3d) 122 (S.C.C.); *R. v. Frazer* (1993), 83 C.C.C. (3d) 126 (S.C.C.) — As a general rule, "any person charged" in *Charter* s. 11 does *not* include an accused who is a party to an appeal. Section 11(b) does *not* apply to delay in respect of an appeal by D from conviction or by P from acquittal or a stay of proceedings. When appellate delay affects the fairness of a trial, D may seek a remedy under *Charter* s. 7 by invoking the court's power to remedy an abuse of process which is now a principle of fundamental justice within *Charter* s. 7.

R. v. Stinchcombe (1991), 8 C.R. (4th) 277, 68 C.C.C. (3d) 1 (S.C.C.) — D's right to make full answer and defence, which is one of the principles of fundamental justice, imposes on P a duty in the context of indictable offences, to disclose all relevant material to the defence whether the material is inculpatory or exculpatory and whether or not P intends to introduce it at trial. The obligation is triggered by a request by D. Initial disclosure should occur before D is called upon to elect or plead, but there is a continuing obligation to disclose when additional material is received. P has a discretion to withhold or delay disclosure in some circumstances, for example to protect the identity of informers, but that discretion is reviewable by the trial judge.

R. v. L. (W.K.) (1991), 6 C.R. (4th) 1, 64 C.C.C. (3d) 321 (S.C.C.) — The delay between the commission of an offence and the laying of a charge will *not per se* justify a stay of proceedings as an abuse of process or a breach of *Charter* s. 7 or 11(d). To stay proceedings based merely on the passage of time would be to impose a judicially-created limitation period for crimes. Pre-charge delay is relevant only insofar as it bears upon the fairness of the trial, hence a potential breach of *Charter* ss. 7 and 11(d). The particular circumstances of the case must be considered and findings of fact made upon proper foundation.

R. v. S. (G.) (1990), 77 C.R. (3d) 303, 57 C.C.C. (3d) 92 (S.C.C.); affirming (1988), 46 C.C.C. (3d) 332 (Ont. C.A.) — *See also*: *R. v. P. (J.)* (1990), 57 C.C.C. (3d) 190 (S.C.C.); reversing (1988), 31 O.A.C. 231, reversing (August 23, 1988), Doc. No. Toronto 80507 (Ont. Fam. Ct.); *R. v. T. (A.)* (1990), 57 C.C.C. (3d) 255 (S.C.C.) — As the implementation by the province of a programme of alternative measures for young offenders is optional, neither *Charter* s. 7 nor s. 15(1) are offended by the designation of admission criteria for such programme.

Morgentaler v. R. (1988), 62 C.R. (3d) 1, 37 C.C.C. (3d) 449 (S.C.C.) — The *Criminal Code* provision prohibiting the procuring of a miscarriage except in accordance with specific procedures, infringes the right to security of the person. As such mandatory procedures were often unavailable, or only available at substantial expense and inconvenience to women, or significantly delayed the performing of the abortion, they were not in accord with the principles of fundamental justice. The section could not be justified as a reasonable limitation of women's right to security of the person under s. 7. The procedures and administrative structures established by the *Code* failed to satisfy the proportionality test.

R. v. Lyons (1987), 61 C.R. (3d) 1, (sub nom. *Lyons v. R.*) 37 C.C.C. (3d) 1 — Imposition of indeterminate detention under the *Criminal Code* provisions respecting "dangerous offenders" does not involve a deprivation of liberty that violates the principles of fundamental justice, since it is in accord with the fundamental purpose of the criminal law generally and of sentencing in particular, namely, the protection of society. Part XXI is in accord with the basic principles of penal policy that have animated legislative and judicial practice in Canada and other common law jurisdictions. The existence of a prosecutorial discretion does not violate the principles of fundamental justice.

Right to Silence and Fundamental Justice

R. v. Crawford, 37 C.R. (4th) 197, 96 C.C.C. (3d) 481, [1995] 1 S.C.R. 858 (S.C.C.); reversing (1993), 80 C.C.C. (3d) 421, 20 C.R. (4th) 331 (Ont. C.A.) — The right to pre-trial silence is not absolute. Application of *Charter* values must take into account other interests, in particular other *Charter* values which may conflict with the unrestricted and literal enforcement.

R. v. Crawford, 37 C.R. (4th) 197, 96 C.C.C. (3d) 481, [1995] 1 S.C.R. 858 (S.C.C.); reversing (1993), 80 C.C.C. (3d) 421, 20 C.R. (4th) 331 (Ont. C.A.) — An accused who testifies against a co-accused cannot rely on the right to silence to deprive the co-accused of the right to challenge that testimony by a full attack on the former's credibility, including reference to his/her pre-trial silence. The co-accused may thus dispel the evidence which implicates him/her emanating from his co-accused. He/she cannot, however, go further and ask the trier of fact to consider the evidence of his/her co-accused's silence as positive evidence of guilt on which P can rely to convict.

R. v. Crawford, 37 C.R. (4th) 197, 96 C.C.C. (3d) 481, [1995] 1 S.C.R. 858 (S.C.C.); reversing (1993), 80 C.C.C. (3d) 421, 20 C.R. (4th) 331 (Ont. C.A.) — The limited use which a jury may make of evidence elicited by one co-accused that another co-accused on a joint trial exercised the right to pre-trial silence should be the subject of a limiting instruction as follows:

i.   that the co-accused who has testified against the accused had the right to pre-trial silence and not to have the exercise of that right used as evidence as to innocence or guilt;

ii.   that the accused implicated by the evidence of the co-accused has the right to make full answer and defence, including the right to attack the credibility of the co-accused;

iii.   that the accused implicated by the evidence of the co-accused had the right, therefore, to attack the credibility of the co-accused by reference to the latter's failure to disclose the evidence to investigating authorities;

iv.   that this evidence is not to be used as positive evidence on the issue of innocence or guilt to draw an inference of consciousness of guilt or otherwise; and,

v.   that the evidence could be used as one factor in determining whether the evidence of the co-accused is to be believed.

R. v. Crawford, 37 C.R. (4th) 197, 96 C.C.C. (3d) 481, [1995] 1 S.C.R. 858 (S.C.C.); reversing (1993), 80 C.C.C. (3d) 421, 20 C.R. (4th) 331 (Ont. C.A.) — The fact that D exercised the right to choose to remain silent during the pre-trial investigation may not be used against D at a subsequent trial arising out of the investigation. No inference may be drawn against D because of the exercise of the right.

R. v. Whittle (1994), 32 C.R. (4th) 1, 92 C.C.C. (3d) 11 (S.C.C.); affirming (1992), 78 C.C.C. (3d) 49 (Ont. C.A.) — The "operating mind" standard applies with respect to the right to silence in deciding whether D has the mental capacity to make an active choice.

R. v. Broyles (1991), 9 C.R. (4th) 1, 68 C.C.C. (3d) 308 (S.C.C.) — The right to silence guaranteed by s. 7, which includes the right to choose whether to make a statement to the authorities, may be violated by the conduct of *any* agent of the state, not merely an undercover police officer.To determine whether D's friend is an agent of the state requires an examination of the *effect* of the relationship between the informer and authorities and of the particular exchange or contact with D. The test applied is whether the exchange between D and the informer would have taken place, in the form and manner in which it did, but for the intervention of the state or its agents.The acquisition of evidence by a state agent only violates s. 7 if the manner of the acquisition infringed D's right to choose to remain silent. In each case, it must be determined whether there is a causal link between the conduct of the state agent and the making of the statement by D. Factors to be considered include the *nature* of the *exchange* and the *relationship* between D and the state agent.

R. v. Hebert (1990), 77 C.R. (3d) 145, 57 C.C.C. (3d) 1 (S.C.C.); reversing (1988), 43 C.C.C. (3d) 56 (Y.T. C.A.) — Section 7 accords a detained person a pre-trial right to remain silent, a right which extends beyond the narrow formulation of the confessions rule and is based upon the fundamental concept of a suspect's right to freely choose whether to speak to the authorities or remain silent. An approach to pre-trial interrogation must emphasize the right of the detainee to make a meaningful choice and permit the rejection of statements obtained unfairly in circumstances that violate the right of choice. The test to determine whether a suspect's choice has been violated is essentially objective and the focus of the inquiry on the authorities' conduct*vis-à-vis* the suspect.The right to remain silent, however, is neither absolute, nor does it extend to prohibit police from obtaining confessions in all circumstances. The right must be qualified by considerations of the state interest and the repute of the judicial system. The *Clarkson* standard relating to waiver of a *Charter* right does not apply to the right to silence.An objective approach to the confessions rule should be retained and would permit the rule to be subject to certain limits. The right applies only after detention, but does not prohibit police questioning an accused or suspect in the absence of counsel earlier retained. Police persuasion which neither denies the suspect the right to choose, nor deprives him or her of an operating mind, does not breach the right to silence. The right does not affect voluntary statements made to fellow cell-mates but is only implicated when P acts to subvert the suspect's constitutional right to choose not to make a statement to the authorities. There is, accordingly, a distinction between the use of undercover agents to observe a suspect and their use to actively elicit information in violation of the suspect's choice to remain silent. It may also be appropriate, in certain cases, to receive the evidence, even where a violation of a suspect's right has been established. It is unlikely that statements will be inadmissible where police have acted with due care for a suspect's right. Exclusion will only result where the court is satisfied that the reception would be likely to bring the administration of justice into disrepute. (Per Dickson C.J.C., Lamer, La Forest, L'Heureux-Dubé, Gonthier, Cory and McLachlin, JJ.)

Fair Trial and Fundamental Justice

R. c. Khela (1995), 43 C.R. (4th) 368, 102 C.C.C. (3d) 1 (S.C.C.) — Failure by P to comply with a disclosure obligation may impair D's right to make full answer and defence, thereby infringing *Charter* s. 7.

R. v. Crawford, 37 C.R. (4th) 197, 96 C.C.C. (3d) 481, [1995] 1 S.C.R. 858 (S.C.C.); reversing (1993), 80 C.C.C. (3d) 421, 20 C.R. (4th) 331 (Ont. C.A.) — Co-accused have the right to cross-examine each other in making full answer and defence. Restrictions that apply to P may not apply to restrict this right of a co-accused.The right to make full answer and defence is not absolute. Assertion of the right in a joint trial requires regard for the effect of the public interest in joint trials with respect to charges arising out of a common enterprise. The discretion to order separate trials must be exercised on the basis of legal principle, including the principle that severance ought not be ordered unless it is established that a joint trial will work an injustice to the accused. Their mere assertion of a "cut-throat" defence is not sufficient to warrant separate trials.

R. v. L. (W.K.) (1991), 6 C.R. (4th) 1, 64 C.C.C. (3d) 321 (S.C.C.) — The delay in charging and prosecuting D does not, *per se*, infringe D's rights to a fair trial under ss. 7 and 11(d). The fairness of a particular trial may only be assessed by having regard to all of its circumstances.

Self-Incrimination and Fundamental Justice

R. v. Fitzpatrick (1995), 43 C.R. (4th) 343, 102 C.C.C. (3d) 144, (S.C.C.); affirming (1994), 32 C.R. (4th) 343, 90 C.C.C. (3d) 161 (B.C. C.A) — The privilege against self-incrimination under *Charter* s. 7 is *not* absolute, rather it ought to be considered in the context in which the claim for its application arises.

It is *not* contrary to fundamental justice for an individual to be convicted of a regulatory offence on the basis of a record or return which D is required to submit as a term and condition or participation in the regulatory sphere.

Semble, the *rationalia* which underlie the principle against self-incrimination are to protect against

i.   unrelialble confessions; and

ii. abuse of power by the state.

British Columbia Securities Commission v. Branch, [1995] 2 S.C.R. 3, 38 C.R. (4th) 133, 97 C.C.C. (3d) 505 (S.C.C.) — The privilege against self-incrimination requires that persons compelled to testify in any subsequent proceedings, which either engage *Charter* s. 7 or subjection to penal sanction, be provided with subsequent

i   "derivative use immunity"; and

ii   "use immunity" as guaranteed by *Charter* s. 13.

In some circumstances, exemptions from compulsion to testify may be granted.

R. v. S. (R.J.) (1995), 21 O.R. (3d) 797n (S.C.C.); affirming (1993), 80 C.C.C. (3d) 397, 21 C.R. (4th) 47 (Ont. C.A.) — The principle against self-incrimination, a part of fundamental justice, rests upon the idea that P must establish a "case to meet". The principle is not absolute. It may reflect different rules in different contexts and has the capacity to introduce new rules to benefit the overall system.

Disclosure

R. v. Stinchcombe (1995), 96 C.C.C. (3d) 318, [1995] 1 S.C.R. 754 — P can only produce what is in his/her possession/control. D has no absolute right to have original material produced. If P has the originals of documents which ought be produced, P should either produce the originals or allow their inspection. If the originals which had been in P's possession are not available, P should explain their absence. Where satisfactory explanation is given, P has discharged this obligation unless the conduct which resulted in absence/loss of the original is itself unconstitutional conduct.

8. Search or seizure — Everyone has the right to be secure against unreasonable search or seizure.

Case Law

General Principles

R. v. M. (M.R.), [1998] 3 S.C.R. 393, 20 C.R. (5th) 197, 129 C.C.C. (3d) 361 — To establish a s. 8 violation, D must establish a *reasonable expectation* of *privacy* with respect to the relevant *place*.

A *subjective* expectation of privacy with respect to one's *person* has been historically recognized and is reasonable. It does *not* become unreasonable simply by D's presence at school.

A *reasonable* expectation of privacy may be *diminished* in certain circumstances. It is *lessened* for students attending school. Students know that school teachers and authorities have to provide a safe school environment and maintain order and discipline there. Students also know that, sometimes, searches of students and their personal effects and seizure of prohibited items may be required.

Searches on school property by school officials are governed by *Charter* s. 8.

R. v. Lauda, [1998] 2 S.C.R. 683, 20 C.R. (5th) 316, 129 C.C.C. (3d) 225; affirming (1998), 13 C.R. (5th) 20, 122 C.C.C. (3d) 74 (Ont. C.A.) — A person who cultivates marijuahana on a farm on which he is a trespasser has *no* reasonable expectation of privacy. *Charter* s. 8 is *not* implicated.

R. v. Caslake (1998), 121 C.C.C. (3d) 97 (S.C.C.) — To be reasonable under *Charter* s. 8, a search must be authorized by law, the law itself must be reasonable and the search must be conducted in a reasonable manner.

To be "authorized by law", a search or seizure must

i. be authorized by a specific statutory or common law rule;

ii. be carried out in accordance with the procedural and substantive requirements of the law; and,

iii. not exceed its scope as to area and objects of search under the law.

A search or seizure is not "authorized by law" if any of items i-iii, *supra*, is not met.

Where D demonstrates that a search was warrantless, P must show, on a balance of probabilities, that the search was reasonable.

R. v. Belnavis (1997), 118 C.C.C. (3d) 405 (S.C.C.) — All of the relevant facts surrounding a passenger's presence in a motor vehicle should be considered to determine whether the passenger has a reasonable expectation of privacy.

R. v. Feeney (1997), 7 C.R. (5th) 101, [1997] 2 S.C.R. 13, 115 C.C.C. (3d) 129 (S.C.C.) — Procedures taken *incidental* to and *following* an unlawful arrest which impinge on D's *reasonable expectation* of *privacy* infringe *Charter* s. 8.

R. v. Stillman (1997), 5 C.R. (5th) 1, [1997] 1 S.C.R. 607, 113 C.C.C. (3d) 321 (S.C.C.); reversing (1995), 97 C.C.C. (3d) 164 (N.B. C.A.) — Where D, *not in custody*, discards something which offers potentially valuable DNA evidence, the police may ordinarily collect and test the item without any concern about D's consent. Where D has *abandoned* the item whilst in custody, the issue whether there has been relinquishment of nay privacy interest in it is determined on the particular facts of each case. The privacy expectation of those in custody ought *not* be reduced to such an extent so as to justify seizure of bodily samples without consent, especially where D is presumed to be innocent.

R. v. Edwards (1996), 26 O.R. (3d) 736 (note), 192 N.R. 81 (S.C.C.) — Section 8 is a personal right which protects people, *not* places.

R. v. Edwards (1996), 26 O.R. (3d) 736, 192 N.R. 81 (S.C.C.) — The right to challenge the legality of a search depends upon whether

i. D had a reasonable expectation of privacy; and, if so,

ii. the search was conducted reasonably.

Whether D has a *reasonable expectation of privacy* is decided on the basis of the totality of the circumstances which may include

i. presence at the time of the search;

ii. possession or control of the property or place searched;

iii.   ownership of the property or place;

iv.   historical use of the property or item;

v.   ability to regulate accesss;

vi.   existence of a subjective expectation of privacy; and

vii.   objective reasonableness of the expectation.

Where D establishes a reasonable expectation of privacy, the inquiry proceeds to the second stage to determine whether the search was conducted in a reasonable manner.

R. v. Evans (1996), 104 C.C.C. (3d) 23 (S.C.C.) — Individuals have a reasonable expectation of privacy in the approach to their home which is waived for the purpose of facilitating communication with the public. Members of the public, including police, who approach the door for some unauthorized purpose, exceed the terms of the implied invitation to knock and are intruders. Police who approach a residential dwelling to secure evidence against the occupant are engaged in a "search" of the occupant's home. To be constitutional, the search must be reasonable.

R. v. Evans (1996), 104 C.C.C. (3d) 23 (S.C.C.) — A warrantless search is presumed unreasonable unless the party seeking to justify it can rebut the presumption.

R. v. Bernshaw (1994), 95 C.C.C. (3d) 193, 35 C.R. (4th) 201, 176 N.R. 81, [1995] 3 W.W.R. 457, reversing (1993), 85 C.C.C. (3d) 404, 48 M.V.R. (2d) 246 (B.C. C.A.) — The requirement of s. 254(3) that reasonable and probable grounds exist is both a statutory and constitutional requirement under *Charter* s. 8.

R. v. Boersma (1994), 31 C.R. (4th) 386 (S.C.C.); affirming (1993), 38 B.C.A.C. 310 (B.C. C.A.) — There is *no* reasonable expectation of privacy where D cultivated marijuana on Crown land in plain sight from a private road.

143471 Canada Inc. c. Québec (Procureur général) (1994), 31 C.R. (4th) 120, 90 C.C.C. (3d) 1 (S.C.C.) — The expectation of privacy in business records is necessarily low since they do *not* ordinarily contain personal information. There is, however, a measure of privacy in commercial documents since they may contain confidential or sensitive material which the business would *not* want known publicly.

143471 Canada Inc. c. Québec (Procureur général) (1994), 31 C.R. (4th) 120, 90 C.C.C. (3d) 1 (S.C.C.) — Whether a search is regulatory or criminal in nature, a court must consider the extent of the intrusion. A greater intrusion requires that greater weight be attached to *Charter* s. 8. The privacy interest in business documents in a regulated field is relatively low. There is, however, a very real and significant privacy interest in maintaining the inviolability of residential premises, to a lesser extent business premises.

R. v. Potash (1994), 91 C.C.C. (3d) 315 (S.C.C.) — The scope of the constitutional guarantee varies with the context. Employers, subject to strict regulation concerning taxation, social affairs, health, safety and labour standards, may have considerably reduced expectations of privacy in relation to documents whose content is provided for in a governing statute and in premises where an activity subject to specific standards is conducted.

R. v. Colarusso (1994), 26 C.R. (4th) 289, 87 C.C.C. (3d) 193 (S.C.C.) — Constitutional requirements cannot be avoided by employing one state agent for which the prerequisites for a search may be less demanding, then permitting the law enforcement apparatus to claim the fruits of that search for criminal investigation purposes without complying with ordinarily stringent search requirements. Section 8 protects the rights of individuals against governmental encroachment.

R. v. Grant (1993), 24 C.R. (4th) 1, 84 C.C.C. (3d) 173 (S.C.C.) — In general, *exigent circumstances* exist if there is an imminent danger of the loss, removal, destruction or disappearance of the evidence if the search or seizure is delayed. The fact that the evidence sought is in a motor vehicle or other conveyance will often create such exigent circumstances, but there is no blanket exception for such conveyances.

R. v. Plant (1993), 24 C.R. (4th) 47, 84 C.C.C. (3d) 203 (S.C.C.) — Accessing computerized records of a city utilities commission does not violate *Charter* s. 8. While *Charter* s. 8 may be engaged in the absence of any proprietary interest, to extend s. 8 protection to commercial records requires that the information seized be of a personal and confidential nature.

R. v. Plant (1993), 24 C.R. (4th) 47, 84 C.C.C. (3d) 203 (S.C.C.) — Section 8 should seek to protect a biographical core of personal information which individuals in a free and democratic society would wish to maintain and control from dissemination to the state. Included within the protection is information which tends to reveal intimate details of the lifestyle and personal choices of the individual.

Conway v. Canada (A.G.) (1993), 23 C.R. (4th) 1, 83 C.C.C. (3d) 1 (S.C.C.) — There is a substantially-reduced level of privacy in a prison where cells are expected to be exposed and require observation. A prisoner cannot hold a reasonable expectation of privacy with respect to the common prison practices of frisk search, the count and the wind since imprisonment entails surveillance, searching and scrutiny. The absence of a reasonable expectation of privacy remains even where the prisoner is male and the guard female. The practices do *not* infringe *Charter* s. 8.

Baron v. Canada (1993), 78 C.C.C. (3d) 510 (S.C.C.) — The standard required by *Charter* s. 8 is one of credibly-based probability. "Reasonable grounds" imports the same standard as "reasonable and probable grounds" and is constitutionally sufficient. "Reasonable" comprehends a requirement of probability. A statute, as in s. 231.3(3)(b) of the *I.T.A.*, which requires the authorizing judge to be satisfied that a document or thing which "may afford evidence" is "likely to be found" in the place to be searched, does *not* dilute the minimum constitutional standard for the probability that the search will unearth evidence.

Baron v. Canada (1993), 78 C.C.C. (3d) 510 (S.C.C.) — A *residual discretion* in the judiciary to refuse to issue a search warrant in appropriate circumstances, notwithstanding compliance with statutory criteria for its issuance, is required by *Charter* s. 8. The judicial officer must be permitted to weigh *all* the surrounding circumstances to determine in each case whether the interest of the state to intrude on the privacy of the individual for the purposes of law enforcement is superior to the interest of the individual to be free of state intrusion.The use of the imperative "shall" in s. 231.3(3) of the *Income Tax Act* denies the issuing judge the discretion to refuse to issue a warrant where, in all of the circumstances, a search or seizure would be unreasonable. The subsection denies the judge the ability to weigh *all* the surrounding circumstances to determine whether in each case the interests of the state are superior to the individual's right to privacy. The subsection, accordingly, offends *Charter* s. 8.

R. v. Mellenthin (1992), 16 C.R. (4th) 273, 76 C.C.C. (3d) 481, [1993] 1 W.W.R. 193 (S.C.C.) — A check stop does *not* and cannot constitute a general warrant to search every vehicle, driver and passenger that is pulled over. The aim of check stops is to check for sobriety, licences, ownership, insurance and the mechanical fitness of vehicles. Police use of check stops ought not be extended beyond these aims. Absent reasonable and probable grounds for conducting a search, or where the presence of drugs, alcohol or weapons are in plain view, evidence flowing from such a search which includes police questions concerning the article searched, the search of an article or container in the vehicle and of the vehicle, ought not be admitted on account of a breach of *Charter* s. 8.

R. v. Wong (1990), 1 C.R. (4th) 1, 60 C.C.C. (3d) 460 (S.C.C.); reversing (1987), 56 C.R. (3d) 352, 34 C.C.C. (3d) 51 (Ont. Prov. Ct.) — Section 8 protects persons who have a reasonable expectation of privacy against unauthorized electronic search. Whether the object of an electronic search has a reasonable expectation of privacy does not depend on whether such person is engaged in illegal activities at the time of search. The occupant of an hotel room has a reasonable expectation of privacy, hence a warrantless video search of such premises constitutes a breach of s. 8.

R. v. Greffe (1990), 75 C.R. (3d) 257, 55 C.C.C. (3d) 161 (S.C.C.); reversing (1988), 62 C.R. (3d) 272, 41 C.C.C. (3d) 257 (Alta. C.A.) — Although confidential information supplied by a reliable informer may provide "reasonable and probable grounds" for a search or seizure, an informer's mere conclusory statement to a police officer does not constitute reasonable grounds. Relevant factors include the degree of detail provided, disclosure of the informer's source or means of knowledge and *indicia* of the informer's reliability. A conclusion that reasonable and probable grounds existed cannot be based wholly on the results of the search or seizure.The gravity of a breach of s. 8 may be increased when accompanied by a closely-related breach of s. 10. The intrusive nature of a search, as for example a rectal search, and consideration of human dignity and bodily integrity demand a high standard of justification to establish reasonableness. The absence of urgency or immediate necessity to conduct the search and the number of *Charter* breaches are also factors in assessing the gravity of the violation.

Cloutier v. Langlois (1990), 74 C.R. (3d) 316, 53 C.C.C. (3d) 257 (S.C.C.) — A frisk search incidental to a lawful arrest does not require the existence of reasonable and probable grounds as a prerequisite, but the search must be for a valid criminal justice objective and it must not be conducted in an abusive fashion, otherwise it is unreasonable.

R. v. Debot (1989), 73 C.R. (3d) 129, 52 C.C.C. (3d) 193 (S.C.C.) — The subject of a body search incident to arrest is detained and entitled to be informed of his s. 10(b) right. However, police conducting a body search incident to arrest are not obligated to suspend the search until the detainee has had the opportunity to retain and instruct counsel, except in limited circumstances. Denial of a right to counsel will rarely be a factor when determining the reasonableness of a search within the meaning of s. 8.Where a warrantless search is authorized by law, as for example by *F.D.A.* s. 37, information supplied by a reliable informer and corroborated by police investigation may meet the standard of reasonable grounds for the search.

Simmons v. R. (1988), 66 C.R. (3d) 297, 45 C.C.C. (3d) 296 (S.C.C.) — The personal search provisions of the *Customs Act*, providing for routine questioning by customs officers, searches of luggage, frisk or pat searches, and the requirement to remove in private such articles of clothing as will permit investigation of suspicious bodily bulges, do not violate *Charter* s. 8, given the existing problems in controlling illicit narcotics trafficking and the important government interest in enforcing customs laws, and the lower expectation of privacy one has at any border crossing.

Hunter v. Southam Inc. (1984), 41 C.R. (3d) 97, 14 C.C.C. (3d) 97 (S.C.C.) — In order to guarantee the individual's right to be secure against unreasonable search or seizure, s. 8 requires that an assessment be made in each case as to whether the public's interest in being left alone by government must give way to the government's interest in intruding on the individual's privacy in order to advance its goals, notably those of law enforcement. The *Charter* gives preference to the right of the individual to be free from state intervention over the interests of the State in advancing its purposes through such interference. As a means of preventing unjustified searches, a requirement of prior authorization, such as a valid warrant, is a pre-condition for a valid search or seizure, where it is feasible to obtain one.

Review of Warrant

R. v. Evans (1996), 104 C.C.C. (3d) 23 (S.C.C.) — Warrants issued solely on information obtained in violation of the *Charter* are invalid. Where a warrant has been issued *partially* on the basis of tainted evidence and partially on the basis of properly-obtained evidence, the court must decide whether the warrant would have been issued without the improperly-obtained evidence.

R. v. Wiley (1993), 24 C.R. (4th) 34, 84 C.C.C. (3d) 161 (S.C.C.) — Police may not rely upon facts obtained by *Charter* breach to obtain a search warrant. To determine the validity of a search warrant obtained, in part, by information acquired by *Charter* breach, the information to obtain the warrant must be considered absent the facts obtained during the constitutionally flawed search.

R. v. Grant (1993), 24 C.R. (4th) 1, 84 C.C.C. (3d) 173 (S.C.C.) — Where an information to obtain a search warrant contains facts in addition to those obtained by *Charter* breach, a reviewing court must consider whether the warrant would have been issued had the improperly-obtained facts been excised from the supportive information. Fraud, non-disclosure, misleading and new evidence are all relevant to a determination whether an information expunged of offending material could properly result in the issuance of a search warrant.

Search

Schreiber v. Canada (Attorney General), [1998] 1 S.C.R. 841, 16 C.R. (5th) 1, 124 C.C.C. (3d) 129 — A letter of request, authorized and sent by the Government of Canada to a foreign state, does *not*, by itself, engaged *Charter* s. 8, even where it asks that a search and seizure be conducted. (per L'Heureux-Dubé, McLachlin, Bastarache and Binnie JJ.)

R. v. Borden (1994), 33 C.R. (4th) 147, 92 C.C.C. (3d) 404, 171 N.R. 1, [1994] 3 S.C.R. 145, 24 C.R.R. (2d) 51, 119 D.L.R. (4th) 74, 134 N.S.R. (2d) 321, affirming (1993), 24 C.R. (4th) 184, 84 C.C.C. (3d) 380 (N.S. C.A.) — In general, a lawful search of the person need *not* be suspended pending exercise of the detainee's right to counsel. An exception exists, however, where the search requires the detainee's consent.

R. v. Potash (1994), 91 C.C.C. (3d) 315 (S.C.C.) — The power to make copies of documents under s. 22(e) of an *Act Respecting Collective Agreement Decrees* authorizes a *seizure* within s. 8. Other inspection powers are properly characterized as a *search* within the section.

R. v. Dersch (1993), 25 C.R. (4th) 88, 85 C.C.C. (3d) 1 (S.C.C.) — It is improper for a physician to take blood samples notwithstanding D's unequivocal instructions to the contrary. Provision of specific medical information about D without D's consent violates a doctor's common law duty of confidentiality to D. Since D had a reasonable expectation of privacy in respect of the information revealed, the obtaining of the information by the police in the circumstances is analogous to a search or seizure within *Charter* s. 8. The absence of a warrant in the circumstances renders the search, *prima facie*, unreasonable.

R. v. Mellenthin (1992), 16 C.R. (4th) 273, 76 C.C.C. (3d) 481, [1993] 1 W.W.R. 193 (S.C.C.) — A person detained at a check stop could reasonably be expected to feel compelled to respond to police questions. A detained person can consent to answer police questions, but the consent must be an informed one given at a time when the individual is fully aware of his/her rights.Police questions concerning an item to be searched, the search of the item and of the vehicle in which it is transported are all elements of a search under *Charter* s. 8.

R. v. Wise (1992), 70 C.C.C. (3d) 193 (S.C.C.) — The installation of an electronic tracking device in D's car and the subsequent monitoring of the car's movements constituted a search which, in the absence of prior authorization violated *Charter* s. 8. However, evidence obtained thereby should not be excluded under s. 24(2). The search was only minimally intrusive, given the lesser expectation of privacy in a car, the unsophisticated nature of the device, and the fact that the device was an extension of physical surveillance rather than a means of surreptitiously intercepting private communications. The evidence was real, not conscripted. The police acted in good faith, having reasonable and probable grounds and believing the installation of the device to be pursuant to a warrant to search the car, and in light of the threat of violence and sense of urgency.

Hufsky v. R. (1988), 63 C.R. (3d) 14, 40 C.C.C. (3d) 398 (S.C.C.) — Provincial legislation requiring the production for inspection of a driver's licence and insurance card does not contemplate a "search" within the meaning of s. 8 because it did not constitute an intrusion on a reasonable expectation of privacy. There is no such intrusion where a person is required to produce a licence or permit or other documentary evidence of a status or compliance with some legal requirement that is a lawful condition of the exercise of a right or privilege. The legislation imposed a reasonable limit on the *Charter* freedom against arbitrary detention, given the public importance of uncovering unlicensed or uninsured drivers. The existence of the spot check program was well-publicized.

Search Incident to Arrest

R. v. Caslake, [1998] 1 S.C.R. 51, 13 C.R. (5th) 1, 121 C.C.C. (3d) 97 — Police must act in accordance with the rule of law in conducting a search. They must objectively search within the permissible scope of the search power. They must also turn their minds to the permissible scope and satisfy themselves before searching that there is a valid purpose for it.

The most important limit on the common law power of search incident to arrest is that the search must be truly incidental to the arrest. Police must be able to explain why the search was conducted. The purpose must be

i.   to protect the police;

ii.   to protect the evidence;

iii.   to discover the evidence; or,

iv.   some other valid purpose.

Discrete reasonable and probable grounds for the search are not required, but police must have had

i.   subjectively some reason related to the arrest for conducting the search when it was carried out; and,

ii.   the reason must be objectively reasonable.

R. v. Stillman (1997), 5 C.R. (5th) 1, [1997] 1 S.C.R. 607, 113 C.C.C. (3d) 321 (S.C.C.); reversing (1995), 97 C.C.C. (3d) 164 (N.B. C.A.) — The common law power of *search incident to arrest* does *not* extend *beyond* the purposes of

i.   *protecting* the arresting officer from armed or dangerous suspects; or,

ii.   *preserving evidence* that may go out of existence or be otherwise lost.

Cloutier v. Langlois (1990), 74 C.R. (3d) 316, 53 C.C.C. (3d) 257 (S.C.C.) — A frisk search incidental to a lawful arrest does not require the existence of reasonable and probable grounds as a prerequisite, but the search must be for a valid criminal justice objective and it must not be conducted in an abusive fashion, otherwise it is unreasonable.

R. v. Debot (1989), 73 C.R. (3d) 129, 52 C.C.C. (3d) 193 (S.C.C.) — The subject of a body search incident to arrest is detained and entitled to be informed of his s. 10(b) right. However, police conducting a body search incident to arrest are not obligated to suspend the search until the detainee has had the opportunity to retain and instruct counsel, except in limited circumstances. Denial of a right to counsel will rarely be a factor when determining the reasonableness of a search within the meaning of s. 8.Where a warrantless search is authorized by law, as for example by *F.D.A.* s. 37 information supplied by a reliable informer and corroborated by police investigation may meet the standard of reasonable grounds for the search.

Searches on School Property

R. v. M. (M.R.), [1998] 3 S.C.R. 393, 20 C.R. (5th) 197, 129 C.C.C. (3d) 361 — Any search conducted by school authorities must be reasonable. It must be *authorized* by *statute* and *appropriate* in light of the *circumstances* presented and the nature of the suspected breach of school regulations. The *factors* to consider in deciding whether a *search* conducted by teachers or principals in response to information received was *reasonable* may be summarized in this way:

i.   The first step is to determine whether it can be *inferred* from the provisions of the relevant *Education Act* that *teachers* and *principals* are *authorized* to *conduct searches* of their students in appropriate circumstances. In the school environment, such a statutory authorization would be reasonable.

ii. The *search* itself must be carried out in a *reasonable* manner. It should be conducted in a sensitive manner and be minimally intrusive.

iii. In order to determine whether a search was reasonable, all the surrounding circumstances will have to be considered.

The approach to be taken in considering searches by teachers may be summarized in this manner:

i.   A warrant is *not* essential in order to conduct a search of a student by a school authority.

ii. The school authority must have *reasonable* grounds to believe that there has been a *breach* of school regulations or discipline and that a *search* of a student *would reveal evidence* of that breach.

iii. School authorities will be in the best position to assess information given to them and relate it to the situation existing in their school. Courts should recognize the preferred position of school authorities to determine if reasonable grounds existed for the search.

iv. The following may constitute reasonable grounds in this context: information received from one student considered to be credible, information received from more than one student, a teacher's or principal's own observations, or any combination of these pieces of information which the relevant authority considers to be credible. The compelling nature of the information and the credibility of these or other sources must be assessed by the school authority in the context of the circumstances existing at the particular school.

The modified standard for reasonable searches applies to searches of students

i.   on school property; and,

ii. conducted by teachers or school officials within the scope of their responsibility and authority to maintain order, discipline and safety within the school.

The standard does *not* apply

i.   to actions taken *beyond* the scope of the teachers' or principals' authority; or,

ii. if the school authorities are acting as *agents* of the *police*.

Seizure

R. v. Potash (1994), 91 C.C.C. (3d) 315 (S.C.C.) — The power to make copies of documents under s. 22(e) of an *Act Respecting Collective Agreement Decrees* authorizes a *seizure* within s. 8. Other inspection powers are properly characterized as a *search* within the section.

R. v. Colarusso (1994), 26 C.R. (4th) 289, 87 C.C.C. (3d) 193 (S.C.C.) — The essence of a seizure is the taking of something from a person by a public authority without consent. Absent exigent circumstances, prior authorization by a judicial officer is required to make a seizure valid for criminal law purposes.

R. v. Dyment (1988), 66 C.R. (3d) 348, 45 C.C.C. (3d) 244 (S.C.C.) — The essence of a seizure under s. 8 is the taking of a thing from a person by a public authority without that person's consent. The protection of the *Charter* extends to prevent a police officer, an agent of the state, from taking a substance as intimately personal as a person's blood from a person who holds it subject to a duty to respect the dignity and privacy of that person. Where a doctor takes a blood sample from an unconscious accused brought to a hospital for medical treatment and provides it upon request to a police officer, no consent can be implied and the receiving of the sample by the officer qualifies as a "seizure". The seizure was unreasonable and evidence obtained thereby should be excluded under s. 24(2).[Per Lamer J., and Beetz and Wilson JJ.] — The fact that a seizure is unlawful means that it is unreasonable under s. 8.[Per La Forest J. and Dickson C.J.C.] — Whether or not such a seizure is illegal, it is not reasonable. To use an individual's blood or other bodily substances confided to others for medical purposes for other purposes seriously violates the personal autonomy of the individual. There is no justification in the circumstances for police to fail to obtain a warrant.

Pohoretsky v. R. (1987), 58 C.R. (3d) 113, 33 C.C.C. (3d) 398 (S.C.C.) — The taking of a blood sample from an unconscious driver, without consent, without a warrant, and without any statutory authority is an unreasonable seizure and a serious violation of the sanctity of a person's body. The admission of the blood sample as evidence is likely to bring the administration of justice into disrepute.

Consent Searches and Seizures

R. v. Arp, [1998] 3 S.C.R. 339, 20 C.R. (5th) 1, 129 C.C.C. (3d) 321; affirming (1997), 116 C.C.C. (3d) 168 (B.C. C.A.) — To be valid, consent to the provision of bodily samples must be an *informed consent*. Where neither the police nor the consenting person *limit* the use that may be made of the evidence, however, as a general rule, *no* limitation or restriction should be imposed on its use.

The obligation on the police in obtaining a valid consent for the provision of bodily samples extends *only* to the disclosure of those anticipated purposes known to the police at the time the consent was given.

R. v. Borden (1994), 33 C.R. (4th) 147, 92 C.C.C. (3d) 404, 171 N.R. 1, [1994] 3 S.C.R. 145, 24 C.R.R. (2d) 51, 119 D.L.R. (4th) 74, 134 N.S.R. (2d) 321, affirming (1993), 24 C.R. (4th) 184, 84 C.C.C. (3d) 380 (N.S. C.A.) — The proper test to determine whether a person has consented to the taking of an item by the state is *not* mere voluntariness, but rather whether the person has sufficient information to truly relinquish the right to be secure from unreasonable seizure.

R. v. Borden (1994), 33 C.R. (4th) 147, 92 C.C.C. (3d) 404, 171 N.R. 1, [1994] 3 S.C.R. 145, 24 C.R.R. (2d) 51, 119 D.L.R. (4th) 74, 134 N.S.R. (2d) 321, affirming (1993), 24 C.R. (4th) 184, 84 C.C.C. (3d) 380 (N.S. C.A.) — A *consent* to the taking of blood may be *limited* to certain purposes. There is a *nexus* between the scope of a valid consent and the scope of D's knowledge in relation to the consequences of that consent.

Additional Factors

Baron v. Canada (1993), 78 C.C.C. (3d) 510 (S.C.C.) — The classification of a statute as "regulatory" may affect the exercise of discretion by the authorizing judge, but is *not* a basis for reading the requirement of a residual discretion out of s. 8.

R. v. Greffe (1990), 75 C.R. (3d) 257, 55 C.C.C. (3d) 161 (S.C.C.); reversing (1988), 62 C.R. (3d) 272, 41 C.C.C. (3d) 257 (Alta. C.A.) — Although confidential information supplied by a reliable informer may provide "reasonable and probable grounds" for a search or seizure, an informer's mere conclusory statement to a police officer does not constitute reasonable grounds. Relevant factors include the degree of detail provided, disclosure of the informer's source or means of knowledge and *indicia* of the informer's reliability. A conclusion that reasonable and probable grounds existed cannot be based wholly on the results of the search or seizure. The gravity of a breach of s. 8 may be increased when accompanied by a closely-related breach of s. 10. The intrusive nature of a search, as for example a rectal search, and consideration of human dignity and bodily integrity demand a high standard of justification to establish reasonableness. The absence of urgency or immediate necessity to conduct the search and the number of *Charter* breaches are also factors in assessing the gravity of the violation.

Strachan v. R. (1988), 67 C.R. (3d) 87, 46 C.C.C. (3d) 479 (S.C.C.) — Even where a substitution of police officers named to carry out a search warrant is not authorized by statute, the issuance and execution of the warrant does not violate the *Charter* if the officers showed respect for the spirit of s. 8 and awareness of the limitations on police search powers.

Kouretessis v. M.N.R. (1993), 81 C.C.C. (3d) 286 (S.C.C.) — Several pre-trial remedies are available to a person who has been the subject of a search. The *Code* provides for a speedy application for the return of seized items. At trial, D may attack the relevant warrant and seek exclusion of the evidence obtained thereby, as for example, on account of *Charter* s. 8 infringement. If the case does not proceed to trial, a party may seek civil damages for compensation.

9. Detention or imprisonment — Everyone has the right not to be arbitrarily detained or imprisoned.

Case Law

Random Vehicle Stops

R. v. Wilson (1990), 77 C.R. (3d) 137, 56 C.C.C. (3d) 142 (S.C.C.); affirming (1987), 76 A.R. 315 (C.A.) — Although s. 119 of the *Highway Traffic Act*, R.S.A. 1980, c. H-7 imposes a duty upon motorists to stop and furnish information when signalled or requested by a police officer, rather than conferring powers on the police, the section's language is broad enough to authorize random stops of motorists by a police officer. A random stop under the section constitutes an arbitrary detention under *Charter* s. 9 but is justified under s. 1. Where, however, a police officer has grounds for stopping a motorist that are reasonable and can be clearly expressed, the stop should not be regarded as random. In such circumstances, the stop, although a detention, is not arbitrary, hence not a violation of s. 9.

R. v. Ladouceur (1990), 77 C.R. (3d) 110, 56 C.C.C. (3d) 22 (S.C.C.); affirming (1987), 57 C.R. (3d) 45, 35 C.C.C. (3d) 240 (Ont. C.A.) — The random stop of a motorist under provincial highway traffic legislation for the purposes of a spot check violates *Charter* s. 9. The detention is arbitrary since the decision whether to stop a motorist rests in the absolute discretion of a police officer. This random routine check, however, is justifiable under s. 1 in that the legislation deals with a pressing and substantial concern and meets the proportionality test of s. 1.

Hufsky v. R. (1988), 63 C.R. (3d) 14, 40 C.C.C. (3d) 398 (S.C.C.) — Provincial legislation giving a police officer power to require the driver of a motor vehicle to stop and produce a driver's licence and proof of insurance constitutes arbitrary detention where it does not specify that there had to be some grounds or cause for stopping a particular driver, and leaves the choice of the drivers to the absolute discretion of the officer. A discretion is arbitrary if there are no criteria, express or implied, which govern its exercise.

Dangerous Offender Proceedings

R. v. Lyons (1987), 61 C.R. (3d) 1, (sub nom. *Lyons v. R.*) 37 C.C.C. (3d) 1 — The successful invocation of the dangerous offender provisions under the *Criminal Code* against an accused is not "arbitrary". Prosecutors have always had a discretion in prosecuting criminals to the full extent of the law. The provisions cannot be said to have been abused by prosecutors. The absence of prosecutorial discretion would in many cases render the application of the law arbitrary.

10. Arrest or detention — Everyone has the right on arrest or detention

   (a) to be informed promptly of the reasons therefor;

   (b) to retain and instruct counsel without delay and to be informed of that right; and

   (c) to have the validity of the detention determined by way of *habeas corpus* and to be released if the detention is not lawful.

Case Law

Detention

R. v. M. (M.R.), [1998] 3 S.C.R. 393, 20 C.R. (5th) 197, 129 C.C.C. (3d) 361 — The compelled attendance of a student at a principal's office, or some other form of restraint by a school authority, is *not* a "detention" for s. 10(b) purposes.

Dehghani v. Canada (Minister of Employment & Immigration) (1993), 20 C.R. (4th) 34 (S.C.C.) — A secondary examination by an immigration officer at a port of entry does *not* constitute a "detention" within *Charter* s. 10(b), since the element of state compulsion is insufficient.

Simmons v. R. (1988), 66 C.R. (3d) 297, 45 C.C.C. (3d) 296 (S.C.C.) — *See also*: *Jacoy v. R.* (1988), 66 C.R. (3d) 336, 45 C.C.C. (3d) 46 (S.C.C.) — A person coming into Canada required to undergo a strip-search by customs officials is "detained" within the meaning of s. 10(b) upon entering the search-room, in that the officer has assumed control over the person's movements by a demand which has significant legal consequences. The person must therefore be informed of his right to counsel prior to the search.

Thomsen v. R. (1988), 63 C.R. (3d) 1, 40 C.C.C. (3d) 411 (S.C.C.) — A demand for a breath sample into a roadside screening device constitutes a "detention" under s. 10(b). The restriction of the right to counsel contemplated until the breathalyzer stage is reasonable, given the need to administer the roadside test as quickly as possible to permit the use of a breathalyzer within two hours, and the importance of the role played by roadside testing in law enforcement.

Rahn v. R. (1985), 45 C.R. (3d) 134, 18 C.C.C. (3d) 516 (S.C.C.) — A demand to accompany a police officer to a police station and to submit to a breathalyzer test constitutes a detention within the meaning of s. 10, and anyone detained in those circumstances is entitled to be informed of the right to retain and instruct counsel without delay. Infringement of this right requires that the evidence of the breathalyzer test be excluded because its admission would bring the administration of justice into disrepute.

R. v. Therens (1985), 45 C.R. (3d) 97, 18 C.C.C. (3d) 481 (S.C.C.) — *See also: Trask v. R.* (1985), 45 C.R. (3d) 137, 18 C.C.C. (3d) 514 (S.C.C.) — A person subject to a demand for a breathalyzer test under the *Criminal Code* is "detained", and has a right to counsel without delay under s. 10(b).[Per Le Dain J., and Dickson C.J.C., McIntyre and Lamer JJ.] — *Charter* s. 10 must necessarily refer to a great variety of detentions of varying duration, in many of which it will not be possible to make effective use of *habeas corpus* because the detention will have ceased before an application can be made and determined. The purpose of s. 10 is to ensure that in certain situations a person is made aware of the right to counsel and is permitted to retain and instruct counsel without delay. Detention within s. 10 applies both to a deprivation of liberty by physical constraint other than arrest in which a person may reasonably require the assistance of counsel, and when a police officer or other agent of the state assumes control over the movement of a person by a demand or direction which may have significant legal consequence and which prevents or impedes access to counsel.

Reasons for Arrest/Detention: S. 10(a)

R. v. Borden (1994), 33 C.R. (4th) 147, 92 C.C.C. (3d) 404 (S.C.C.); affirming (1993), 84 C.C.C. (3d) 380 (N.S. C.A.) — Where a person is detained in relation to two offences, he or she has the right to be informed of the dual investigative intention.

R. v. Black (1989), 70 C.R. (3d) 97, 50 C.C.C. (3d) 1 (S.C.C.) — Section 10(b) must be interpreted in a purposive way and in light of s. 10(a), which requires the police to advise a person under arrest or detention of the reasons for it. A person can only exercise the s. 10(b) right in a meaningful way if he/she knows the extent of his/her jeopardy. Where after D has consulted counsel, police change the charge, D has not exhausted her right to counsel and is entitled to a reasonable opportunity to contact counsel again.

Relationship of S. 10(a) and (b)

R. v. Borden (1994), 33 C.R. (4th) 147, 92 C.C.C. (3d) 404 (S.C.C.); affirming (1993), 84 C.C.C. (3d) 380 (N.S. C.A.). — The rights of s. 10(a) and (b) are linked. A detainee must be informed of the reasons for the detention so he or she may make an informed choice whether to exercise the right to counsel and, if so, to obtain sound advice based on an understanding of the extent of his or her jeopardy.

Retain and Instruct Counsel Without Delay: S. 10(b)

R. v. Burlingham (1995), 38 C.R. (4th) 265, 97 C.C.C. (3d) 385 (S.C.C.); reversing (1993), 85 C.C.C. (3d) 343 (B.C. C.A.) — The right to counsel may be denied where police

i.   refuse to hold off and continue to question an arrested person despite repeated statements that he/she will say nothing without consulting his/her lawyer;

ii.   belittle D's lawyer with the express goal/effect of undermining D's relationship with a lawyer; and

iii.   pressure D to accept a "deal" without first affording D the choice to consult with his/her lawyer.

It is not sufficient, in a serious case where trickery has been used, to allow D to consult a lawyer chosen at random.

R. v. Prosper (1994), 33 C.R. (4th) 85, 92 C.C.C. (3d) 353 (S.C.C.); reversing (1992), 75 C.C.C. (3d) 1, 38 M.V.R. (2d) 268 (N.S. C.A.) — Section 10(b) imposes no substantive constitutional obligation on governments to ensure that duty counsel is available on arrest or detention to provide free and immediate temporary legal advice upon request.

R. v. Matheson (1994), 33 C.R. (4th) 136, 92 C.C.C. (3d) 434 (S.C.C.); reversing (1992), 78 C.C.C. (3d) 70 (P.E.I. S.C.) — *See also: R. v. Prosper* (1994), 33 C.R. (4th) 85, 92 C.C.C. (3d) 353 (S.C.C.); reversing (1992), 75 C.C.C. (3d) 1, 38 M.V.R. (2d) 268 (N.S. C.A.) — Section 10(b) imposes *no* positive obligation on governments to provide a system of "*Brydges* duty counsel" or otherwise afford all detainees a corresponding right to free, 24-hour preliminary legal advice.

R. v. Borden (1994), 33 C.R. (4th) 147, 92 C.C.C. (3d) 404 (S.C.C.); affirming (1993), 84 C.C.C. (3d) 380 (N.S. C.A.) — In general, a lawful search of the person need *not* be suspended pending exercise of the detainee's right to counsel. An exception exists, however, where the search requires the detainee's consent.

R. v. Prosper (1994), 33 C.R. (4th) 85, 92 C.C.C. (3d) 353 (S.C.C.); reversing (1992), 75 C.C.C. (3d) 1, 38 M.V.R. (2d) 268 (N.S. C.A.) — Where compelling and urgent circumstances exist, police need *not* hold off in their attempts to elicit incriminating evidence. Urgency is *not* created, however, by mere investigatory and evidentiary expediency.

R. v. Prosper (1994), 33 C.R. (4th) 85, 92 C.C.C. (3d) 353 (S.C.C.); reversing (1992), 75 C.C.C. (3d) 1, 38 M.V.R. (2d) 268 (N.S. C.A.) — Once a detainee has indicated a desire to exercise the right to counsel, the state must provide the detainee with a *reasonable opportunity* to consult with counsel. Agents of the state may *not* elicit incriminating evidence from the detainee until the opportunity has been provided. What constitutes a reasonable opportunity depends on the circumstances, including the availability of duty counsel services in the jurisdiction.

R. v. Whittle (1994), 32 C.R. (4th) 1, 92 C.C.C. (3d) 11 (S.C.C.); affirming (1992), 78 C.C.C. (3d) 49 (Ont. C.A.) — In exercising or waiving the right to counsel, D must possess the limited cognitive capacity that is required for fitness to stand trial. D must be *capable* of communicating with counsel to instruct counsel, *understand* the function of counsel and that he or she may dispense with counsel even if it is not in D's best interests. D need *not* have analytical ability, rather the mental capacity of an "operating mind".

R. v. Brydges (1990), 74 C.R. (3d) 129, 53 C.C.C. (3d) 330 (S.C.C.) — Where an accused in effect requests the assistance of counsel, a police officer is under a duty to facilitate contact with counsel by giving D a reasonable opportunity to exercise his/her right to counsel. Further, where D expresses a concern that his/her ability to afford a lawyer is an impediment to the exercise of such right, the officer has a duty to inform D of the existence of duty counsel and the availability of Legal Aid.

R. v. Leclair (1989), 67 C.R. (3d) 209, (sub nom. *R. v. Ross*) 46 C.C.C. (3d) 129 — Accused or detained persons have a right to choose their counsel and it is only if the lawyer chosen cannot be available within a reasonable time that the detainee or accused person should be expected to exercise the right to counsel by calling another lawyer. Reasonable diligence in the exercise of the right to choose one's counsel depends on the context facing the accused or detained person. Where the evidence reveals that the detainee or accused person has asserted a right to counsel, the burden of establishing an unequivocal waiver is on the Crown. The right to counsel also means that, once an accused or detained person has asserted that right, the police cannot in any way compel him/her to make a decision or participate in a process which could ultimately have an adverse effect in the conduct of an eventual trial until that person has had a reasonable opportunity to exercise that right. Since there is no legal obligation for a person to participate in a police line-up, counsel clearly have an important role in advising a client about participating voluntarily in the process. Detainees or accused persons can not be said to have waived their rights to counsel by participating in a line-up.

Strachan v. R. (1988), 67 C.R. (3d) 87, 46 C.C.C. (3d) 479 (S.C.C.) — Section 10(b) is not necessarily violated the moment D's request to contact counsel is refused. Police officers making arrests in a potentially volatile situation may be justified in preventing any new factors from entering the situation until some of the unknowns have been clarified. But once the police are clearly in control of the situation, they are required to allow D to contact a lawyer.

Tremblay v. R. (1987), 60 C.R. (3d) 59, 37 C.C.C. (3d) 565 (S.C.C.) — *See also: R. v. Smith* (1989), 71 C.R. (3d) 129, 50 C.C.C. (3d) 308 (S.C.C.) — If a detainee or accused person is not being reasonably diligent in the exercise of his right to counsel, the correlative duties imposed on the police in a situation where the accused has requested the assistance of counsel are suspended and are not a bar to the police continuing the investigation and demanding a breath sample.

R. v. Manninen (1987), 58 C.R. (3d) 97, 34 C.C.C. (3d) 385 (S.C.C.) — In addition to the duty to inform a detainee of his rights, s. 10(b) mandates that the police provide the detainee with a reasonable opportunity to exercise the right to retain and instruct counsel without delay. It is not necessary for an accused to make an express request to use the telephone: the duty to facilitate contact with counsel includes the duty to offer use of the telephone. Section 10(b) further imposes on the police the duty to cease questioning or otherwise attempting to elicit evidence from the detainee until he/she has had a reasonable opportunity to obtain advice from counsel as to how to exercise his/her rights.

Informed of Right to Retain and Instruct Counsel: S. 10(b)

R. v. Latimer (1997), 4 C.R. (5th) 1, 112 C.C.C. (3d) 193 (S.C.C.) — D has the right to be informed of the means to access duty counsel services available at the time of arrest. Where D is detained during regular business hours, and when legal assistance is available through a local telephone number easily ascertainable by D, there is *no* breach of *information component* of s. 10(b) by *not* providing D with the local telephone number.

R. v. Prosper (1994), 33 C.R. (4th) 85, 92 C.C.C. (3d) 353 (S.C.C.); reversing (1992), 75 C.C.C. (3d) 1, 38 M.V.R. (2d) 268 (N.S. C.A.) — It is constitutionally inadequate for law enforcement officials simply to repeat the words of s. 10(b) by cautioning detainees of their "right to retain and instruct counsel without delay".The *information* component of s. 10(b) requires that detainees be provided

i.   *information* about access to *counsel* free of charge where an accused meets the prescribed financial criteria of the applicable legal aid scheme; and,

ii.   *information* about access to *duty counsel* (staff lawyers or private practitioners) who provide immediate, although temporary legal advice irrespective of financial status

in relation to services actually available in the jurisdiction

R. v. Bartle (1994), 92 C.C.C. (3d) 289 (S.C.C.); reversing (1993), 22 C.R. (4th) 1, 81 C.C.C. (3d) 353 (Ont. C.A.) — The *information* component of s. 10(b), the right to be informed of the right to counsel, also requires that a detainee be given information about access to Legal Aid and to duty counsel. It must be comprehensive in scope and be presented in timely and comprehensible manner. Basic information about how to access available services which provide free, preliminary legal advice should be included in the standard s. 10(b) caution. Failure to provide such information is a breach of s. 10(b).

R. v. Pozniak (1994), 33 C.R. (4th) 49, 92 C.C.C. (3d) 472, 19 O.R. (3d) 802 (note) (S.C.C.); reversing (1993), 22 C.R. (4th) 1, 81 C.C.C. (3d) 353 (Ont. C.A.) — *See also*: *R. v. Harper* (1994), 33 C.R. (4th) 61, 92 C.C.C. (3d) 423 (S.C.C.); affirming (1992), 78 Man. R. (2d) 227 (Man. C.A.) — As part of the information component of s. 10(b), a detainee must be advised of whatever system for free and immediate legal advice exists in the jurisdiction at the time of detention and of how such advice may be accessed.

R. v. Bartle (1994), 92 C.C.C. (3d) 289 (S.C.C.); reversing (1993), 22 C.R. (4th) 1, 81 C.C.C. (3d) 353 (Ont. C.A.) — A breach of s. 10(b) is complete, except in cases of waiver or urgency, where state authorities fail to inform a detainee properly of his or her right to counsel and until correction of the failure.

R. v. Elshaw (1991), 7 C.R. (4th) 333, 67 C.C.C. (3d) 97 (S.C.C.) — Under s. 10(b), the significant fact is that the police obtained evidence from a detained person prior to fulfilling their responsibilities under the section, *not* the relatively short period of detention. The urgency or necessity of detention may mitigate the seriousness of a *Charter* violation, but only if it goes to the need to acquire information immediately, prior to advising the detainee of her/his s. 10(b) rights, rather than the right to restrict the suspect's movements by detention or arrest.

R. v. Schmautz (1990), 75 C.R. (3d) 129, 53 C.C.C. (2d) 556 (S.C.C.) — Where D was given his right to counsel at the outset of an interview about a hit and run incident, that warning was sufficient compliance with the *Charter* to permit the making of a breathalyzer demand at the conclusion of the interview, without a further s. 10(b) warning being given, because the demand was part of a single incident.

R. v. Brydges (1990), 74 C.R. (3d) 129, 53 C.C.C. (3d) 330 (S.C.C.) — [Per Lamer, Wilson, Gonthier and Cory JJ.] — As part of the information component of s. 10(b), each detainee must be informed, as a matter of routine, of the existence and availability of the applicable duty counsel and Legal Aid systems, so that D has a full understanding of the right to retain and instruct counsel.

R. v. Black (1989), 70 C.R. (3d) 97, 50 C.C.C. (3d) 1 (S.C.C.) — Section 10(b) must be interpreted in a purposive way and in light of s. 10(a), which requires the police to advise a person under arrest or detention of the reasons for it. A person can only exercise his s. 10(b) right in a meaningful way if he knows the extent of his jeopardy. Where after D has consulted counsel, police change the charge, D has not exhausted his right to counsel and is entitled to a reasonable opportunity to contact counsel again.

Baig v. R. (1987), 61 C.R. (3d) 97, 37 C.C.C. (3d) 181 (S.C.C.) — Absent proof of circumstances indicating that the accused did not understand his right to obtain counsel when he was informed of it, the onus has to be on him to prove that he asked for the right but it was denied or he was denied any opportunity to even ask for it. Once the police have complied with s. 10(b), by advising the accused without delay of his right to counsel without delay, there are no correlative duties triggered and cast upon them until the accused, if he so chooses, has indicated his desire to exercise his right to counsel.

Waiver

R. v. Prosper (1994), 33 C.R. (4th) 85, 92 C.C.C. (3d) 353 (S.C.C.); reversing (1992), 75 C.C.C. (3d) 1, 38 M.V.R. (2d) 268 (N.S. C.A.) — The burden of establishing unequivocal waiver is on P. The waiver must be *free* and *voluntary*. It must *not* be the product of either direct or indirect compulsion. A person who waives a right must *know* what is being given up for the waiver to be valid. The standard required for an effective waiver of the right to counsel is very high.

R. v. Borden (1994), 33 C.R. (4th) 147, 92 C.C.C. (3d) 404 (S.C.C.); affirming (1993), 84 C.C.C. (3d) 380 (N.S. C.A.) — The degree of D's awareness of the consequences of waiving the right to be secure from unreasonable seizure depends on the particular facts of the case. While D need *not* have a detailed comprehension of every possible outcome of giving consent, D should understand, where applicable, that the police are also planning to use the product of the seizure in an investigation different from the one for which D has been detained.

R. v. Prosper (1994), 33 C.R. (4th) 85, 92 C.C.C. (3d) 353 (S.C.C.); reversing (1992), 75 C.C.C. (3d) 1, 38 M.V.R. (2d) 268 (N.S. C.A.) — The right to counsel is *not* easily waived. Where a detainee who has previously asserted his or her s. 10(b) rights, indicates a change of mind and no longer wants legal advice, an additional information obligation must be met. The police must advise the detainee of

i.   the right to a *reasonable opportunity* to contact counsel; and,

ii.   the obligation of the police to hold off from trying to elicit incriminating evidence from the detainee during the period.

Indications of change of mind must be clear.

R. v. Bartle (1994), 92 C.C.C. (3d) 289 (S.C.C.); reversing (1993), 22 C.R. (4th) 1, 81 C.C.C. (3d) 353 (Ont. C.A.) — Section 10(b) rights may be waived by a detainee. The standard for waiver is high, especially where it is alleged to be implicit. Waiver must be *clear* and *unequivocal* and made with *full knowledge* of a detainee's s. 10(b) rights. An effective waiver of s. 10(b) rights requires that the detainee be fully apprised of the information that the detainee has the right to receive. The mere fact that a detainee indicates that he or she does *not* wish to hear the information conveyed by the standard s. 10(b) advice does not, *per se*, constitute a valid waiver of the information component. The waiver is only valid where it is clear that the detainee

i.   *fully* understands his or her s. 10(b) rights;

ii.   *fully* understands the means by which s. 10(b) rights may be exercised; and,

iii.   adverts to those rights.

R. v. Smith (1991), 63 C.C.C. (3d) 313 (S.C.C.); affirming (1990), 53 C.C.C. (3d) 97 (N.S. C.A.) — To establish a valid waiver of the right to counsel the trial judge must be satisfied that in all the circumstances revealed by the evidence D generally understood the sort of jeopardy he faced. When he made the decision to dispense with counsel, D need not have been aware of the precise charge faced or all of the factual details, but he must have had sufficient information to allow him to make an informed and appropriate decision as to whether or not to speak to a lawyer.

Clarkson v. R. (1986), 50 C.R. (3d) 289, 25 C.C.C. (3d) 207 (S.C.C.) — The purpose of s. 10(b) is to ensure that an accused is treated fairly in the criminal process. While this constitutional guarantee cannot be forced upon an unwilling accused, any voluntary waiver in order to be valid and effective must be premised on a true appreciation of the consequences of giving up the right. A waiver of the s. 10(b) right by an intoxicated accused must pass some form of "awareness of the consequences" test. Any waiver's effectiveness is dependent upon it being clear and unequivocal that the person is waiving the procedural safeguard and is doing so with full knowledge of the rights the procedure was enacted to protect and of the effect the waiver will have on those rights in the process.

Duties on Authorities: S. 10(b)

R. v. Burlingham (1995), 38 C.R. (4th) 265, 97 C.C.C. (3d) 385 (S.C.C.); reversing (1993), 85 C.C.C. (3d) 343 (B.C. C.A.) — Section 10(b) requires P or the police, when offering a plea bargain, to tender the offer to D's counsel or to D in the presence of his/her counsel, absent express waiver by D of the right to counsel. It offends s. 10(b) for P or the police to offer a plea bargain directly to D, especially when it is coercively left open only for a short period of time when D's counsel is known to be unavailable. Mere expediency, efficiency or facilitating the investigatory process do not create an urgency sufficient to permit a s. 10(b)*Charter* breach.

R. v. Bartle (1994), 92 C.C.C. (3d) 289 (S.C.C.); reversing (1993), 22 C.R. (4th) 1, 81 C.C.C. (3d) 353 (Ont. C.A.) — Under s. 10(b), state authorities must advise a detainee of:

i.   the right to be informed of the right to counsel;

ii.   the right to a reasonable opportunity to exercise the right; and,

iii   the right to have questioning curtailed until the reasonable opportunity has ceased.

Duty i is information. Duties ii and iii are implementation duties triggered only where a detainee expresses the wish to exercise the right to counsel.

R. v. Bartle (1994), 92 C.C.C. (3d) 289 (S.C.C.); reversing (1993), 22 C.R. (4th) 1, 81 C.C.C. (3d) 353 (Ont. C.A.) — Section 10(b) rights are not absolute. Unless a detainee invokes the right, and is reasonably diligent in exercising it, the correlative duty on the police to provide a reasonable opportunity and to refrain from eliciting evidence will either not arise or be suspended.

11. Proceedings in criminal and penal matters — Any person charged with an offence has the right

(a) to be informed without unreasonable delay of the specific offence;

(b) to be tried within a reasonable time;

(c) not to be compelled to be a witness in proceedings against that person in respect of the offence;

(d) to be presumed innocent until proven guilty according to law in a fair and public hearing by an independent and impartial tribunal;

(e) not to be denied reasonable bail without just cause;

(f) except in the case of an offence under military law tried before a military tribunal, to the benefit of trial by jury where the maximum punishment for the offence is imprisonment for five years or a more severe punishment;

(g) not to be found guilty on account of any act or omission unless, at the time of the act or omission, it constituted an offence under Canadian or international law or was criminal according to the general principles of law recognized by the community of nations;

(h) if finally acquitted of the offence, not to be tried for it again and, if finally found guilty and punished for the offence, not to be tried or punished for it again; and

(i) if found guilty of the offence and if the punishment for the offence has been varied between the time of commission and the time of sentencing, to the benefit of the lesser punishment.

Case Law
"Any Person Charged"

R. v. MacDougall, [1998] 3 S.C.R. 45, 19 C.R. (5th) 275, 128 C.C.C. (3d) 483 — *See also*: *R. v. Gallant*, [1998] 3 S.C.R. 80, 19 C.R. (5th) 302, 128 C.C.C. (3d) 509 — While s. 11 *Charter* protection is triggered when a person is "charged with an offence", the specific rights of the section vary with the stage of the proceedings. "Charged with an offence" is *not* restricted to a particular phase of the proceedings. Both a *textual* and *purposive* reading of "charged with an offence" includes both pre-conviction and post-conviction sentencing stages of the process.

R. v. Potvin (1993), 23 C.R. (4th) 10, 83 C.C.C. (3d) 97 (S.C.C.) — *See also*: *R. v. Gallagher* (1993), 83 C.C.C. (3d) 122 (S.C.C.); *R. v. Frazer* (1993), 83 C.C.C. (3d) 126 (S.C.C.) — As a general rule, "any person charged" in *Charter* s. 11 does *not* include an accused who is a party to an appeal. Section 11(b) does *not* apply to delay in respect of an appeal by D from conviction or by P from acquittal or a stay of proceedings. When appellate delay affects the fairness of a trial, D may seek a remedy under *Charter* s. 7 by invoking the court's power to remedy an abuse of process which is now a principle of fundamental justice within *Charter* s. 7.

R. v. C.I.P. Inc. (1992), 12 C.R. (4th) 237, 71 C.C.C. (3d) 129 (S.C.C.) — A corporate accused may invoke s. 11(b). The availability of witnesses and the reliability of their evidence could have a significant impact upon a corporate accused's ability to advance a defence such as due diligence. The right to a fair trial is fundamental to the adversarial system. There is no reason not to extend such protection to all accused. The societal interest in expedited trials applies as much to corporate as individual accused.

Trial Within a Reasonable Time: S. 11(b)

R. v. MacDougall, [1998] 3 S.C.R. 45, 19 C.R. (5th) 275, 128 C.C.C. (3d) 483 — *See also*: *R. v. Gallant*, [1998] 3 S.C.R. 80, 19 C.R. (5th) 302, 128 C.C.C. (3d) 509 — The right to be *tried* within a reasonable time under *Charter* s. 11(b) includes the right to be *sentenced* within a reasonable time.

Whether a *delay* in *sentencing* offends *Charter* s. 11(b) depends on whether the delay was unreasonable considering:

i.   the *length* of the delay;

ii. the *reasons* for the delay;

iii. the *effect* of any *waivers* of delay; and,

iv. the *prejudice* suffered by D.

Delay that is related to judicial illness may be

i.   *inherent* delay;

ii. *Crown* delay; or,

iii. *systemic* delay.

Inherent delay is delay related to judicial illness that takes place in the period *before* it is *reasonable* for P to apply to have the judge removed and replaced. This delay does *not* count against P.

Crown delay is delay that occurs *after* the time when it is *reasonable* for P to apply to have the judge removed and replaced.

Institutional or *systemic* delay occurs when the *delay* in *replacing* a judge after the time when it is reasonable for P to apply for removal is due to *lack* of judicial *resources*. If this delay is itself unreasonable, having regard to the pressures on the court system, it, like Crown delay, counts against P.

Where the trial judge becomes ill after conviction and prior to sentence, but is expected to return, P must balance

i.   the need to proceed with the utmost care and caution when considering removal of a judge seized with a case in order to protect judicial independence and fairness to D; and,

ii. the need to protect D's s. 11(b) *Charter* rights and prevent undue prejudice to D.

P must determine whether apprehension of a s. 11(b) *Charter* violation has reached the stage where it outweighs the general rule that the judge seized of a case should conclude it. Where the apprehension of a s. 11(b) violation outweighs the general rule, P has a duty to apply to remove and replace the seized judge.

R. v. Collins (1995), 40 C.R. (4th) 273, 99 C.C.C. (3d) 385 (S.C.C.) — *See also*: *R. v. Pelfrey* — A request by P for a lengthy adjournment with respect to a case in which D are in custody and have been pressing for an early trial date should be based on solid grounds.

R. v. Potvin (1993), 23 C.R. (4th) 10, 83 C.C.C. (3d) 97 (S.C.C.) — *See also*: *R. v. Gallagher* (1993), 83 C.C.C. (3d) 122 (S.C.C.); *R. v. Frazer* (1993), 83 C.C.C. (3d) 126 (S.C.C.) — Section 11(b) does *not* apply to delay in respect of an appeal by D from conviction or by P from acquittal or a stay of proceedings. When appellate delay affects the fairness of a trial, D may seek a remedy under *Charter* s. 7 by invoking the court's power to remedy an abuse of process which is now a principle of fundamental justice within *Charter* s. 7.

R. v. Morin (1992), 12 C.R. (4th) 1, 71 C.C.C. (3d) 1 (S.C.C.) — *See also*: *R. v. Sharma* (1992), 12 C.R. (4th) 45, 71 C.C.C. (3d) 184 (S.C.C.) — The primary purpose of *Charter* s. 11(b) is the protection of the individual rights of an accused. There is also, however, a well-recognized secondary interest of society as a whole in the expeditious trial of allegations of crime. A determination whether D's s. 11(b) rights have been denied involves a judicial determination, which balances the interests the section is designed to protect against factors which either inevitably lead to or otherwise cause delay, not the application of any mere administrative formula. The factors to be considered in analyzing how long is too long are as follows:

i.   the *length* of the delay;

ii.   the *waiver* of time periods;

iii.   the *reasons* for the delay, including

    (a)   inherent time requirements of the case;

    (b)   actions of D;

    (c)   actions of P;

    (d)   limitations on institutional resources; and,

    (e)   other reasons for delay; and,

iv.   *prejudice* to the accused.

R. v. Morin (1991), 71 C.C.C. (3d) 1 (S.C.C.); affirming (1990), 76 C.R. (3d) 37, 55 C.C.C. (3d) 209 (Ont. C.A.) — *See also*: *R. v. Sharma* (1992), 134 N.R. 368 (S.C.C.) — An inquiry into unreasonable delay should only be undertaken if the period is of sufficient length to raise an issue as to its reasonableness. A shorter period of delay will raise the issue if D shows prejudice. While prejudice may be inferred from the length of the delay, where it is not inferred and is not proved, the basis for D's application is seriously undermined. An investigation of unreasonable delay must take into account all reasons for the delay. An administrative guideline, which is neither a limitation period nor a fixed ceiling on delay, may be used to determine the acceptable delay attributable to resource limitations. In the Provincial Court a guideline of 8 to 10 months for institutional delay is suggested and after committal for trial, an additional 6 to 8 months. These guidelines require adjustment by trial courts to take into account local conditions and changing circumstances over time.

R. v. Askov (1990), 79 C.R. (3d) 273, 59 C.C.C. (3d) 449 (S.C.C.); reversing (1987), 60 C.R. (3d) 277, 37 C.C.C. (3d) 289 (Ont. C.A.) — Like other s. 11 guarantees, s. 11(b) is primarily concerned with an aspect of fundamental justice under s. 7. Its primary aim is to protect the individual's rights and ensure fundamental justice for D. There is also a community or societal interest implicit in the section, in that it ensures that lawbreakers are brought to trial, dealt with according to the law and, at trial, are treated fairly and justly. There are important practical benefits to a quick resolution of criminal charges for witnesses and victims. The community at large is also entitled to see that the justice system works fairly, efficiently and with reasonable dispatch. Four factors must be considered in determining whether a delay has been unreasonable:

    (a)   the length of the delay;

    (b)   the explanation for the delay;

    (c)   waiver; and

(d) prejudice to D.

Longer delays are more difficult to excuse. Very lengthy delays may not be justifiable. Delays attributable to P will weigh in favour of D, although the complexity of a case may justify more lengthy delay than would be tolerated in simple cases.*Systemic or institutional delays* also weigh against P. How long a delay occasioned by inadequate institutional resources is too long may be resolved by comparing the questioned jurisdiction with the better similar, hence comparable, districts in the country. The comparison need not be too precise nor exact but should look to the appropriate range of delay to determine what is a reasonable limit. The onus of justification rests with P. Delays may be justified, however, on account of D's conduct, as for example, by an informed, unequivocal and freely-given waiver of the delay.

R. v. Smith (1989), 73 C.R. (3d) 1, 52 C.C.C. (3d) 97 (S.C.C.) — In determining whether there has been a violation of s. 11(b), the court must balance the length of the delay, the reason for the delay including limits on institutional resources and the inherent time requirements of the case, waiver of time periods and prejudice to D. Although it is preferable that trial judges deal with s. 11(b) arguments, in this case the superior court judge properly heard the application where the preliminary inquiry was not scheduled to begin for several months, the preliminary inquiry judge would not have jurisdiction to hear the application and requiring the appellant to wait until trial would further delay his opportunity to assert his right.

R. v. Kalanj (1989), 70 C.R. (3d) 260, 48 C.C.C. (3d) 459 (S.C.C.) — The reckoning of time in determining whether a person has been accorded a trial within a reasonable time commences when an information is sworn, or where a direct indictment is laid when no information is sworn. Pre-information delay is not to be considered under s. 11(b).

Argentina (Republic) v. Mellino (1987), 33 C.C.C. (3d) 334 (S.C.C.) — Section 11(b) gives a *Charter* remedy for delay when a prosecution has been initiated; no fixed time is involved as in a statute of limitations. Rather one must take into account such matters as whether the delay is unreasonable having regard to the time particular procedures ordinarily take. Section 11 has no application to extradition hearings.

Rahey v. R. (1987), 57 C.R. (3d) 289, 33 C.C.C. (3d) 289 (S.C.C.) — *See also: R. v. Conway* (1989), 70 C.R. (3d) 209, 49 C.C.C. (3d) 289 (S.C.C.) — The factors to be considered and weighed in determining where a s. 11(b) right has been infringed are: the inherent time requirements of a particular case, the prejudice to the accused caused by the delay, and the acquiescence or consent of the accused to any waiver of time-periods. The appropriate remedy for a violation of s. 11(b) rights is a stay of proceedings.

Carter v. R. (1986), 52 C.R. (3d) 100, 26 C.C.C. (3d) 572 (S.C.C.) — While a delay between the commission of an offence and the laying of charges may result in deprivation of a fair hearing guaranteed by s. 11(d), pre-charge delay is irrelevant to determining whether there has been unreasonable delay under s. 11(b), except in exceptional circumstances as where one charge is withdrawn and a new charge substituted for the same delict.

Not Compellable as a Witness: S. 11(c) [See also Charter s. 13 and C.E.A. s. 5]

Vidéotron Ltée v. Industries Microlec produits électroniques Inc. (1992), 76 C.C.C. (3d) 289 (S.C.C.) — A respondent in contempt proceedings under the *Code of Civil Procedure* is *not* a compellable witness in such proceedings (per Gonthier J., Lamer C.J. and La Forest J. concurring).A respondent in contempt proceedings under the *Code of Civil Procedure* is a person "charged with an offence" under *Charter* s. 11, hence not compellable under s. 11(c) (per Lamer C.J.).

R. v. Clunas (1992), 70 C.C.C. (3d) 115 (S.C.C.) — When two or more accused are charged in separate informations or indictments with the same or different offences, and are proceeded against jointly, they will *not* be compellable one against the other.

R. v. Amway of Can. Ltd. (1989), 68 C.R. (3d) 97 (S.C.C.) — Section 11(c) was intended to protect the individual against the affront to dignity and privacy inherent in a practice which enables the prosecution to force the person charged to supply evidence out of his or her own mouth. A corporation *per se* cannot be a "witness", and therefore cannot come within s. 11(c). Corporate officers are therefore compellable to testify in criminal proceedings against the corporation.

Dubois v. R. (1985), 48 C.R. (3d) 193, 22 C.C.C. (3d) 513 (S.C.C.) — Under ss. 11(c) and 13, D enjoys the initial benefit of a right of silence and its corollary, a protection against self-incrimination. The underlying principle is that the Crown must first present a "case to meet".

R. v. S. (R.J.) (1993), 21 C.R. (4th) 47, 80 C.C.C. (3d) 397 (Ont. C.A.) — There is no breach of *Charter* s. 7 where P compels a person separately charged with the same offence to testify as a prosecution witness on the trial of another.

Presumption of Innocence: S. 11(d)

R. v. Rose, [1998] 3 S.C.R. 262, 20 C.R. (5th) 246, 129 C.C.C. (3d) 449 — A finding that either s. 7 or 11(d) has been infringed necessarily entails that the other section has also been infringed.

R. v. Richard, [1996] 3 S.C.R. 525, 3 C.R. (5th) 1, 110 C.C.C. (3d) 385 — For regulatory offences where imprisonment is *not* a possibility, *Charter* s. 11(d) does not prevent a provincial legislature from inferring from D's failure to act that D waives the right

i.   to be presumed innocent; and,

ii.   to a fair and public hearing by an independent and impartial tribunal

provided he/she is fully aware of the consequences of the failure to act and that the relevant procedural scheme provides adequate safeguards to ensure that D's conduct was *not* due to events over which D had no control.

R. v. Pearson (1992), 17 C.R. (4th) 1, 77 C.C.C. (3d) 124 (S.C.C.) — The effect of s. 11(d) is to create a procedural and evidentiary rule *at trial* that P must prove guilt beyond a reasonable doubt. The rule, accordingly, does *not* apply at the judicial interim release stage of the criminal process where there is no determination of guilt or innocence nor imposition of punishment.

R. v. Downey (1992), 13 C.R. (4th) 129, 72 C.C.C. (3d) 1 (S.C.C.) — It is *only* if proof of the *basic fact* contained in a presumption leads *inexorably* to proof of the *presumed fact* that a statutory presumption will *not* infringe *Charter* s. 11(d).

R. v. Chaulk (1990), 2 C.R. (4th) 1 (S.C.C.); reversing (1988), 53 Man. L.R. (2d) 297 (C.A.) — The real concern under s. 11(d) is not whether D must disprove an element of an offence or prove an excuse, but rather, whether D may nonetheless be convicted, where a reasonable doubt exists. It is the final effect of a provision on the verdict that is decisive. The presumption of innocence has been infringed when a possibility exists that D may be convicted, while a reasonable doubt exists. (Per Dickson C.J. and Lamer C.J., La Forest, Sopinka and Cory JJ.)

R. v. Keegstra (1990), 1 C.R. (4th) 129, 61 C.C.C. (3d) 1 (S.C.C.); reversing (1988), 65 C.R. (3d) 289, 43 C.C.C. (3d) 150 (Alta. C.A.) — *See also*: *R. v. Andrews* (1990), 1 C.R. (4th) 266, 61 C.C.C. (3d) 490 (S.C.C.); affirming (1988), 65 C.R. (3d) 320, 43 C.C.C. (3d) 193 (Ont. C.A.) — The presumption of innocence guarantee of s. 11(d) is infringed when D is liable to conviction despite the existence of a reasonable doubt as to guilt by the trier of fact.

R. v. Potvin (1989), 68 C.R. (3d) 193, 47 C.C.C. (3d) 289 (S.C.C.) — A requirement that D bear the burden of proving that he did not have a full opportunity to cross-examine the witness at the time previous testimony sought to be adduced at a trial was given does not violate *Charter* s. 11(d) in the absence of exceptional circumstances.

Schwartz v. R. (1988), 66 C.R. (3d) 251, 45 C.C.C. (3d) 97 (S.C.C.) — Where a statutory provision prohibits a person from committing an act without possessing a licence, another provision that places an onus on D to prove that that person was the holder of a licence does not constitute a reverse onus provision and is not invalidated by s. 11(d). Although D must establish that he falls within the exemption, D could not possibly be convicted despite the existence of a reasonable doubt as to his guilt because production of the licence resolves all doubts in favour of D, and in the absence of the licence, no defence is possible once commission of the act has been shown. The theory behind any licensing system is that when an issue arises as to possession of the licence, it is D who is in the best position to resolve the issue.

R. v. Cdn. Newspapers Ltd. (1988), 65 C.R. (3d) 50, 43 C.C.C. (3d) 24 (S.C.C.) — A *Criminal Code* provision providing for a mandatory order prohibiting publication of the complainant's name or any information that could disclose it on the application of a complainant in a sexual assault case does *not* violate D's right to a fair and public hearing. The public or the press are not restricted from attending trial proceedings.

Whyte v. R. (1988), 64 C.R. (3d) 123, 42 C.C.C. (3d) 97 (S.C.C.) — The exact characterization of a factor as an essential element, a collateral factor, an excuse, or a defence should not affect the analysis of the presumption of innocence. It is the final effect of a provision on the verdict that is decisive. If D is required to prove the factor on the balance of probabilities to avoid conviction, the provision violates the presumption of innocence. The trial of D cannot be divided neatly into stages, with the onus of proof on D at an intermediate stage and the ultimate onus on P. Where the provision substitutes proof of one element for proof of an essential element, the statutory presumption will only be valid where the existence of the substituted fact leads inexorably to the conclusion that the essential element exists, with no other reasonable possibilities.

Holmes v. R. (1988), 64 C.R. (3d) 97, 41 C.C.C. (3d) 497 (S.C.C.) — An offence that prohibits a person from committing a certain act "without lawful excuse, the proof of which lies upon him," does *not* violate the presumption of innocence, where, before it can have any effect, P must place before the court a complete case for conviction. The words "without lawful excuse" do not encompass excuses or justifications that would exist if the words were omitted from the provision, and thus require proof by D. Therefore, such common law defences need not be proved on a balance of probabilities, as they are not affected by the words "the proof of which lies upon him". Where an offence is proved beyond a reasonable doubt, according to law, without the aid of a statutory presumption, the accused cannot be said to be denied the benefit of the presumption of innocence only because his excuse for the commission of the offence is not accepted.

R. v. Vaillancourt (1987), 60 C.R. (3d) 289, 39 C.C.C. (3d) 118 (S.C.C.) — Before D can be convicted of an offence, the trier of fact must be satisfied beyond a reasonable doubt of the existence of all the essential elements of the offence. These essential elements include not only those set out in the section creating the offence, but also those required by *Charter* s. 7. Any provision creating an offence which allows for the conviction of D notwithstanding the existence of a reasonable doubt on any essential element, or which does not include an element required under s. 7, infringes on ss. 7 and 11(d). Where the legislature substitutes proof of a different element rather than simply eliminating any need to prove the essential element, the provision will only be valid if upon proof beyond a reasonable doubt of the substituted element it would be unreasonable for the trier of fact not to be satisfied beyond a reasonable doubt of the existence of the essential element.

R. v. Oakes (1986), 50 C.R. (3d) 1, 24 C.C.C. (3d) 321 (S.C.C.) — In general, a provision which requires an accused to disprove on a balance of probabilities the existence of a presumed fact, which is an important element of the offence in question, violates the presumption of innocence under s. 11(d). At a minimum, the presumption of innocence has three components: (i) an individual must be proven guilty beyond a reasonable doubt; (ii) it is P which must bear the burden of proof; and (iii) criminal prosecutions must be carried out in accordance with lawful procedures and principles of fairness. *N.C.A.* s. 8, which mandated a presumption of possession of a narcotic for the purpose of trafficking where possession was proved, was not a reasonable limitation of the accused's right under s. 11(d). There was no rational connection between the basic fact of possession and the statutory presumption.

Dubois v. R. (1985), 48 C.R. (3d) 193, 22 C.C.C. (3d) 513 (S.C.C.) — Section 11(d) imposes on P the burden of proving D's guilt beyond a reasonable doubt, as well as a burden of making out a case against an accused before he/she need respond, either by testifying or by calling other evidence.

R. v. Brown (1995), 35 C.R. (4th) 318, 26 C.R.R. (2d) 325 (Ct. Martial App. Ct.); leave to appeal refused (1995), 39 C.R. (4th) 361(note) (S.C.C.) — The possibility that a General Court Martial could reach its verdict by a simple majority does *not* breach the s. 11(d) presumption of innocence guarantee.

Fair Hearing: S. 11(d)

R. v. Leipert (1997), 4 C.R. (5th) 259, 112 C.C.C. (3d) 385 (S.C.C.) — The common law informer privilege rule does not offend the fair trial guarantee of *Charter* s. 11(d).

Dagenais v. Canadian Broadcasting Corp. (1994), 34 C.R. (4th) 269, 94 C.C.C. (3d) 289 (S.C.C.) — The common law rule authorizing publication bans must be modified to give effect to the equal status of the freedom of expression under *Charter* s. 2(b) and the right to a fair trial under *Charter* s. 11(d). A publication ban should only be ordered when

i.   it is necessary to prevent a real and substantial risk to the fairness of the trial, because reasonably available alternatives will not prevent the risk; and,

ii.   the salutary effects of the ban outweigh the deleterious.

The *Charter* does not require that all conceivable steps be taken to remove even the most speculative risks to a fair trial.

R. v. Pearson (1992), 17 C.R. (4th) 1, 77 C.C.C. (3d) 124 (S.C.C.) — The effect of s. 11(d) is to create a procedural and evidentiary rule *at trial* that P must prove guilt beyond a reasonable doubt. The rule, accordingly, does *not* apply at the judicial interim release stage of the criminal process where there is no determination of guilt or innocence nor imposition of punishment.

R. v. L. (W.K.) (1991), 6 C.R. (4th) 1, 64 C.C.C. (3d) 321 (S.C.C.) — The delay between the commission of an offence and the laying of a charge will *not per se* justify a stay of proceedings as an abuse of process or a breach of *Charter* s. 7 or 11(d). To stay proceedings based merely on the passage of time would be to impose a judicially-created limitation period for crimes. Pre-charge delay is relevant only insofar as it bears upon the fairness of the trial, hence a potential breach of *Charter* ss. 7 and 11(d). The particular circumstances of the case must be considered and findings of fact made upon proper foundation.

Independent and Impartial Tribunal: S. 11(d)

R. v. Généreux (1992), 70 C.C.C. (3d) 1 (S.C.C.) — *See also: R. v. Forster* (1992), 70 C.C.C. (3d) 59 (S.C.C.) — The s. 11(d) guarantee to a fair and public trial by an independent and impartial tribunal applies to proceedings of the General Court Martial.

R. v. Généreux (1992), 70 C.C.C. (3d) 1 (S.C.C.) — *See also: R. v. Forster* (1992), 70 C.C.C. (3d) 59 (S.C.C.) — To be "independent", a tribunal must have security of tenure, financial security and institutional independence with respect to matters of administration that relate directly to the exercise of the tribunal's judicial function.

R. v. Lippé (1990), 61 C.C.C. (3d) 127, 64 C.C.C. (3d) 513 (S.C.C.); reversing (1990), 80 C.R. (3d) 1, 60 C.C.C. (3d) 34 (Que. C.A.) — The use of part-time municipal court judges who are otherwise allowed to practise law does not infringe the judicial impartiality guarantee of s. 11(d). An independent tribunal within *Charter* s. 11(d) must be independent both from government and the parties. The fact that judges are part-time does not, *per se*, raise a reasonable apprehension of bias on an institutional level. Certain activities in which judges engage, however, as for example practising law, are incompatible with their duties as judges since they give rise to a reasonable apprehension of bias in the mind of a fully-informed person in a number of cases. The apprehension is, however, alleviated by judicial immunity, the oath taken by judges, the Code of ethics and the provisions of provincial legislation.

Valente v. R. (1985), 49 C.R. (3d) 97, 23 C.C.C. (3d) 193 (S.C.C.) — Although judicial independence is a status or relationship resting on objective conditions or guarantees, as well as a state of mind or attitude in the actual exercise of judicial functions, the test for independence and impartiality is whether the tribunal may be reasonably perceived as independent. The three essential conditions of judicial independence are: (i) security of tenure, up to the age of retirement such that judges may be removed only for cause related to the capacity to perform judicial functions; (ii) financial security, so that the right to salary and pension is established by law and is not subject to arbitrary interference by the executive; and (iii) the institutional independence of the tribunal with respect to matters of administration bearing directly and immediately on the exercise of its judicial function.

"Reasonable Bail": S. 11(e)

R. v. Pearson (1992), 17 C.R. (4th) 1, 77 C.C.C. (3d) 124 (S.C.C.) — Section 11(e) guarantees to any person charged with an offence the right "not to be denied reasonable bail without just cause". "Bail" refers to all forms of judicial interim release. "Reasonable bail" refers to the terms of the bail and requires that the quantum of bail and the restrictions imposed on D's liberty whilst on bail be *reasonable*. "Just cause" refers to the right to obtain bail and imposes constitutional standards on the grounds under which bail is granted or refused.

R. v. Morales (1992), 17 C.R. (4th) 74, 77 C.C.C. (3d) 91 (S.C.C.) — There is "just cause" within *Charter* s. 11(e) if the denial of bail can occur only in a narrow set of circumstances and if the denial is necessary to promote the proper functioning of the bail system.

Trial by Jury: S. 11(f)

R. v. Turpin (1989), 69 C.R. (3d) 97 (S.C.C.) — Section 11(f) is designed to protect the interests of those charged with criminal offences and to place corresponding duties on the state to respect such interests. It confers a "benefit" of a jury trial on D where a jury trial is in fact, from his/her perspective, a benefit which can be waived by D if it seems to be in his/her best interests to do so. However, the section does not confer on D a constitutional right to elect his/her mode of trial or to be tried by judge alone.

R. v. Mack (1988), 67 C.R. (3d) 1, 44 C.C.C. (3d) 513 (S.C.C.) — The issue of entrapment should be decided by the trial judge without a jury for policy reasons. Section 11(f) is not violated by this rule because the guilt or innocence of D is not in issue at the time an entrapment claim is to be decided.

R. v. Brown (1995), 35 C.R. (4th) 318, 26 C.R.R. (2d) 325 (Ct. Martial App. Ct.); leave to appeal refused (1995), 39 C.R. (4th) 361 (note) (S.C.C.) — Trial by General Court Martial for crimes which constitute *Criminal Code* offences, and which could have been tried by a civil court in Canada, does not violate *Charter* s. 11(f). The exception to the s. 11(f) *Charter* right to a jury trial is triggered by a military nexus with the crime charged. The offence must be so connected with the service in its nature and in the circumstances of its commission that it would tend to affect the general standard of discipline and efficiency of the service.

Double Jeopardy: S. 11(h)

R. v. Van Rassel (1990), 75 C.R. (3d) 150, 53 C.C.C. (3d) 353 (S.C.C.) — Where D was tried in the United States and then in Canada, s. 11(h) was not applicable because the offences were based on duties of a different nature. Section 11(h) only applies where the two offences are the same.

R. v. Shubley (1989), 74 C.R. (3d) 1, 52 C.C.C. (3d) 481 (S.C.C.) — Section 11(h) applies only to criminal proceedings or proceedings giving rise to true penal consequences. Prison disciplinary proceedings are not of that nature and s. 11(h) does not apply where D was previously found guilty of a prison disciplinary offence.

Thibault v. Corp. Professionnelle des Médecins du Québec (1988), 63 C.R. (3d) 273, 42 C.C.C. (3d) 1 (S.C.C.) — To the extent that provincial summary convictions legislation permits a prosecutor to appeal an acquittal by way of trial de novo, as of right and without having to allege errors committed by the justice in the original proceeding, it is inconsistent with s. 11(h) and of no force or effect. An accused who is acquitted by a judgment containing no error is "finally acquitted" within the meaning of s. 11(h). A corollary provision giving the accused the same right following a conviction is valid in its entirety. Although the *Charter* did not apply at the time of the original proceedings, s. 11(h) could be invoked where it applied at the time when a court had to decide whether to order the holding of a subsequent trial.

Wigglesworth v. R. (1987), 60 C.R. (3d) 193, 37 C.C.C. (3d) 385 (S.C.C.) — Where an R.C.M.P. officer assaulted a prisoner and was found guilty of a major service offence by an internal disciplinary tribunal and fined, s. 11(h) did not act to prevent a charge of assault under the *Criminal Code* from being laid, since he was not being tried and punished for the same offence. His conduct had a double aspect as a member of the R.C.M.P. and as a member of the public at large such that, while there was only one act of assault there were two distinct delicts, causes or matters which would sustain separate convictions.

Schmidt v. R. (1987), 58 C.R. (3d) 1, 33 C.C.C. (3d) 193 (S.C.C.) — The right protected by s. 11(h) is that of a person charged with an offence not to be tried for the offence again if he/she has already been finally acquitted of the offence. Section 11(h) does not apply to an extradition hearing as it is not intended to be given extraterritorial application so as to govern criminal processes in another country; rather it is intended to govern trials conducted by the governments of Canada mentioned in s. 32.

12. Treatment or punishment — Everyone has the right not to be subjected to any cruel and unusual treatment or punishment.

Case Law

R. v. M. (C.A.), 46 C.R. (4th) 269, 105 C.C.C. (3d) 327, [1996] 1 S.C.R. 500 (S.C.C.) — A legislative or judicial sentence that is grossly disproportionate, being so excessive as to outrage standards of decency, will violate *Charter* s. 12.

R. v. Brown (1994), 93 C.C.C. (3d) 97 (S.C.C.); reversing (1993), 19 C.R. (4th) 140, 80 C.C.C. (3d) 275 (Man. C.A.) — Where armed robbery is the underlying offence, s. 85(2) does *not* offend *Charter* s. 12.

R. v. Goltz (1991), 8 C.R. (4th) 82, 67 C.C.C. (3d) 481 (S.C.C.) — In determining whether the punishment is grossly disproportionate to the offence, the court should consider whether the punishment is *necessary* to achieve a valid penal purpose, whether there are valid *alternatives* to the punishment, and whether other punishments for other crimes in the same jurisdiction reveal great disproportion. An arbitrarily imposed sentence does *not* necessarily violate s. 12, which is concerned primarily with the effect of a punishment. A minimum seven-day sentence under a provincial motor vehicle statute for driving while prohibited was based on legislative concern to isolate bad drivers for the protection of the public and did not offend s. 12.

United States of America v. Cotroni (1989), 48 C.C.C. (3d) 196 (S.C.C.) — It is not for Canadian courts to rule upon the validity of laws of other countries, although they may consider whether a penalty would constitute cruel and unusual punishment for a particular accused.

R. v. Lyons (1987), 61 C.R. (3d) 1, (sub nom. *Lyons v. R.)* 37 C.C.C. (3d) 1 — Section 12 is concerned with the relation between the effects of and the reasons for punishment. These effects are first to be balanced against the particular circumstances of the offence, the characteristics of the offender and the particular purposes sought to be accomplished in sentencing that person in the manner challenged. If the punishment is found to be grossly disproportionate, a remedy must be afforded the offender in the absence of social objectives that transcend the circumstances of the particular case and are capable of justifying the punishment under *Charter* s. 1. The parole process ensures that the dangerous offender provisions of the *Criminal Code* do not violate *Charter* s. 12 in that they ensure that incarceration is imposed for only as long as the circumstances in the individual case require.

Smith v. R. (1987), 58 C.R. (3d) 193, 34 C.C.C. (3d) 97 (S.C.C.) — Punishment is "cruel and unusual" where it is so excessive as to outrage standards of decency or is grossly disproportionate to the offence or is arbitrarily imposed. In assessing whether a sentence is grossly disproportionate, the court must first consider the gravity of the offence, the personal characteristics of the offender and the particular circumstances of the case in order to determine what range of sentences would have been appropriate to punish, rehabilitate or deter this particular offender or to protect the public from this particular offender. The effect of the sentence actually imposed must be measured. Such effect is not limited to the quantum or duration of the sentence but includes its nature and the conditions under which it is applied. The numerous criteria under s. 2(b) of the *Bill of Rights* and the Eighth Amendment of the *U.S. Constitution* are useful as factors to determine whether a violation of s. 12 has occurred. *Charter* s. 1 permits the right of individual offenders not to receive grossly disproportionate punishments to be overridden to achieve some important societal objective.

13. Self-crimination — A witness who testifies in any proceedings has the right not to have any incriminating evidence so given used to incriminate that witness in any other proceedings, except in a prosecution for perjury or for the giving of contradictory evidence.

Case Law

[See also C.E.A. s. 5 and Charter s. 11(c)]

R. v. Calder, 46 C.R. (4th) 133, 105 C.C.C. (3d) 1, [1996] 1 S.C.R. 680 (S.C.C.) — Where P considers restricting use of a statement to cross-examination of D will lighten its task in having the evidence admitted for such purposes under *Charter*s. 24(2), P may seek a ruling to such effect either during its case or before cross-examining D. On a *voir dire*, the trial judge will consider admissibility of the statement for the limited purpose proposed.

R. v. S. (R.J.) (1995), 21 O.R. (3d) 797n (S.C.C.); affirming (1993), 80 C.C.C. (3d) 397, 21 C.R. (4th) 47 (Ont. C.A.) — The principle against self-incrimination, a part of fundamental justice, rests upon the idea that P must establish a "case to meet". The principle is not absolute. It may reflect different rules in different contexts and has the capacity to introduce new rules to benefit the overall system.

R. v. S. (R.J.) (1995), 21 O.R. (3d) 797n (S.C.C.); affirming (1993), 80 C.C.C. (3d) 397, 21 C.R. (4th) 47 (Ont. C.A.) — Section 13 does not exclusively define the scope of the available evidentiary immunity. The principle against self-incrimination is also recognized under *Charter* s. 24(2).

R. v. S. (R.J.) (1995), 21 O.R. (3d) 797n (S.C.C.); affirming (1993), 80 C.C.C. (3d) 397, 21 C.R. (4th) 47 (Ont. C.A.) — The principle against self-incrimination is recognized under *Charter* s. 24(2). Derivative evidence which could not have been obtained, or the significance of which could not have been appreciated, but for the testimony of a witness, ought generally to be excluded under s. 7 in the interests of trial fairness. This evidence, though not created by D and thus not self-incriminatory by definition, is self-incriminatory nonetheless because the evidence could not otherwise have become part of P's case. To this extent the witness must be protected against assisting P in creating a case to meet.

R. v. Kuldip (1990), 1 C.R. (4th) 285, 61 C.C.C. (3d) 385 (S.C.C.); reversing (1988), 62 C.R. (3d) 336, 40 C.C.C. (3d) 11 (Ont. C.A.) — There is a distinction between cross-examination for the purpose of impeaching credibility, and cross-examination made to incriminate or establish the guilt of D. Cross-examination on a prior inconsistent statement in order to impugn the credibility of D does *not* incriminate him/her, but rather is made to unveil a contradiction between what D is saying now and what D said on a previous occasion. If D chooses to testify, he/she is implicitly vouching for his credibility and, like any other witness, has opened the door to having the trustworthiness of his evidence challenged. Cross-examination of D at his/her second trial on testimony given by him/her at a previous trial on the same information, which is clearly for the purpose of undermining his/her credibility, does not violate s. 13.An objection made by D under *C.E.A.* s. 5(2) only prevents P from using that testimony to incriminate D at a later proceeding. It does *not* prohibit P from ever using the testimony in cross-examining D to challenge his/her credibility at a later proceeding.*C.E.A.* s. 5(2) and *Charter* s. 13 offer virtually identical protection. The difference between them is that s. 5(2) requires an objection at the first proceedings, while s. 13 does not. Neither prevents P from using the earlier testimony at a later proceeding for the purpose of determining credibility.

R. v. Amway of Can. Ltd. (1989), 68 C.R. (3d) 97 (S.C.C.) — Section 11(c) was intended to protect the individual against the affront to dignity and privacy inherent in a practice which enables the prosecution to force the person charged to supply evidence out of his/her own mouth. A corporation *per se* cannot be a "witness", and therefore cannot come within s. 11(c). Corporate officers are therefore compellable to testify in criminal proceedings against the corporation.

R. v. Mannion (1986), 53 C.R. (3d) 193, 28 C.C.C. (3d) 544 (S.C.C.) — The cross-examination of D on testimony given at his/her first trial which was inconsistent with his/her evidence at a second trial is a violation of s. 13 since the purpose of the cross-examination clearly was to incriminate the accused.

Dubois v. R. (1985), 48 C.R. (3d) 193, 22 C.C.C. (3d) 513 (S.C.C.) — The purpose of s. 13 is to protect individuals from being indirectly compelled to incriminate themselves and, unlike the similar provision in *C.E.A.* s. 5, does *not* depend on an objection on the part of the person giving testimony. It applies as much to testimony voluntarily given by D as to testimony given by a witness under compulsion. A retrial for the same or an included offence following an appeal is "any other proceeding[s]" within the meaning of s. 13. The evidence from the first proceedings need not be of an incriminating character. Any evidence P tenders as part of its case against an accused is incriminating evidence for the purposes of s. 13.

14. Interpreter — A party or witness in any proceedings who does not understand or speak the language in which the proceedings are conducted or who is deaf has the right to the assistance of an interpreter.

Case Law

R. v. Tran (1994), 32 C.R. (4th) 34, 92 C.C.C. (3d) 218 (S.C.C.) — The principle of linguistic understanding underlies s. 14.

R. v. Tran (1994), 32 C.R. (4th) 34, 92 C.C.C. (3d) 218 (S.C.C.) — To be sufficient, interpretation must be continuous, precise, impartial, competent and contemporaneous.

R. v. Tran (1994), 32 C.R. (4th) 34, 92 C.C.C. (3d) 218 (S.C.C.) — To determine whether there has been a breach of s. 14, it must be clear that D did *not* understand or speak the language of trial, hence required the assistance of an interpreter. What must be determined is whether there is a possibility that D may not have understood part of the proceedings due to D's difficulty with the language used in the proceedings.

R. v. Tran (1994), 32 C.R. (4th) 34, 92 C.C.C. (3d) 218 (S.C.C.) — To constitute a violation of *Charter* s. 14, a claimant must prove that the lapse in interpretation was in respect of the proceedings themselves, thereby involving V's vital interests, and was not merely in respect of some collateral or extrinsic matter. What must be considered is whether there was an unfolding or development in the proceeding with respect to a point of procedure, evidence and/or law.

R. v. Tran (1994), 32 C.R. (4th) 34, 92 C.C.C. (3d) 218 (S.C.C.) — To establish waiver, P must not only show that the waiver was clear, unequivocal and made with a knowledge and understanding of the right, but also that it was made personally by D or with counsel's assurance that the right and the effect on that right of waiving it were explained to D in a language in which D was fully conversant.

Equality Rights

15. (1) Equality before and under law and equal protection and benefit of law — Every individual is equal before and under the law and has the right to the equal protection and equal benefit of the law without discrimination and, in particular, without discrimination based on race, national or ethnic origin, colour, religion, sex, age or mental or physical disability.

(2) **Affirmative action programs** — Subsection (1) does not preclude any law, program or activity that has as its object the amelioration of conditions of disadvantaged individuals or groups including those that are disadvantaged because of race, national or ethnic origin, colour, religion, sex, age or mental or physical disability.

Case Law

Vriend v. Alberta (1998), 224 N.R. 1 (S.C.C.) — The essential requirements of a s. 15(1) analysis are satisfied by two inquiries:

i.　　whether there is a *distinction* which results in the *denial* of *equality* before or under the law, or of equal protection or benefit of the law; and

ii.　　whether the *denial* constitutes *discrimination* on the basis of an enumerated or analogous ground.

Benner v. Canada (Secretary of State), [1997] 1 S.C.R. 358 (S.C.C.) — When s. 15 is applied to questions of *status*, the critical time is not when the individual acquires the status, but when the status is held against the person or disentitles the person to a benefit.

Eaton v. Brant County Board of Education, [1997] 1 S.C.R. 241 — To make out a s. 15 *Charter* violation, a claimant must establish that the impugned provision creates a distinction on a prohibited or analogous ground which withholds an advantage or benefit from, or imposes a disadvantage or burden on the claimant. *Not every distinction* on a prohibited gound will constitute discrimination. In general distinctions based on *presumed*, rather than actual characteristics, are the hallmarks of discrimination.

Disability, as a prohibited ground, differs from other enumerated grounds which lack individual variations. Disability means vastly different things, however, depending on the individual and context. In the result, there is a "difference dilemma", wherby segregation can protect, as well as violate equality, depending upon the person and the state of disability.

Egan v. Canada, [1995] 2 S.C.R. 513 — There are three steps involved in s. 15 *Charter* analysis. Step one looks to whether the law has drawn a *distinction* between the claimant and others. Step two questions whether the distinction results in a *disadvantage* and examines whether the legislation imposes a burden, obligation or disadvantage on a group of persons to which the claimant belongs which is not imposed on others, or does not provide them with a benefit that it grants others. Step three assesses whether the distinction is based on an irrelevant personal characteristic enumerated in *Charter* s. 15(1) or one analogous thereto (per Lamer C.J.C., La Forest, gonthier and Major JJ.)

Miron v. Trudel, [1995] 2 S.C.R. 418 — Section 15(1) *Charter* analysis involves two steps. A claimant must first show a denial of "equal protection or equal benefit of the law" as compared with some other person. A claimant must next show that the denial constitutes discrimination. To establish discrimination, the claimant must show:

i.　　that the denial of equal protection/benefit rests upon a ground enumerated in s. 15(1) or an analogous ground; and

ii.　　that the unequal treatment is based upon the stereotypical application of presumed group or personal characteristics.

Where a s. 15(1) violation is established, the onus shifts to the party seeking to uphold the law to justify the discrimination under *Charter* s. 1 (per Sopinka, Cory, McLachlin and Iacobucci JJ.)There are three steps involved in s. 15 *Charter* analysis. Step one looks to whether the law has drawn a distinction between the claimant and others. Step two questions whether the distinction results in a disadvantage and examines whether the legislation imposes a burden, obligation or disadvantage on a group of person to which the claimant belongs which is not imposed on others, or does not provide them with a benefit that it grants others. Step three assesses whether the distinction is based on an irrelevant personal characteristic enumerated in *Charter* s. 15(1) or one analogous thereto. (per Lamer C.J. La Forest, Gonthier and Major JJ.)

R. v. S. (S.) (1990), 77 C.R. (3d) 273, 57 C.C.C. (3d) 115 (S.C.C.); reversing (1988), 63 C.R. (3d) 64, 42 C.C.C. (3d) 41 (Ont. C.A.) — *Y.O.A.* s. 4(1) is validly enacted pursuant to Parliament's power over criminal law and is not *ultra vires* Parliament. The decision of the Attorney-General of Ontario not to authorize a programme of alternative measures does not contravene *Charter* s. 15(1). The decision is in accordance with the permissive terms of s. 4. Furthermore, in this case a distinction based upon province of residence is not a distinction based upon a personal characteristic and so it does not give rise to a violation of s. 15(1).

R. v. S. (G.) (1990), 77 C.R. (3d) 303, 57 C.C.C. (3d) 92 (S.C.C.); affirming (1988), 46 C.C.C. (3d) 332 (Ont. C.A.) — *See also*: *R. v. P. (J.)* (1990), 57 C.C.C. (3d) 190 (S.C.C.); reversing (1988), 31 O.A.C. 231, reversing (August 23, 1988), Doc. No. Toronto 805070 (Ont. Fam. Ct.); *R. v. T. (A.)* (1990), 57 C.C.C. (3d) 255 (S.C.C.) — As the implementation by the province of a programme of alternative measures for young offenders is optional, neither *Charter* s. 7 nor s. 15(1) are offended by the designation of admission criteria for such programme.

R. v. Turpin (1989), 69 C.R. (3d) 97 (S.C.C.) — In defining the scope of the four basic equality rights, it is important to ensure that each right be given its full independent content, divorced from any justificatory factors applicable under *Charter* s. 1. Section 15 must be interpreted in a *Charter* context, which may involve entirely different considerations from the comparable provision in the *Canadian Bill of Rights*. The guarantee of equality before the law is designed to advance the value that all persons be subject to the equal demands and burdens of the law and not suffer any greater disability in the substance and application of the law than others. The internal qualification in s. 15 that the differential treatment be "without discrimination" is determinative of whether or not there has been a violation of the section. In determining whether there has been discrimination on grounds relating to the personal characteristics of the individual or group, the larger social, political and legal context must be examined as well as the impugned legislation. The application of s. 15 must advance its purpose in remedying or preventing discrimination against groups suffering social, political or legal disadvantage in our society. It is not a fundamental principle under s. 15 that the criminal law apply equally throughout the country, and such issues should be decided on a case-by-case basis.

Andrews v. Law Society of B.C., [1989] 1 S.C.R. 143 (S.C.C.) — A complainant under s. 15(1) must show not only that he is not receiving equal treatment before or under the law or that the law has a differential impact on him in the protection or benefit accorded by law, but, in addition, must show that the legislative impact of the law is discriminatory. Section 15(1) is not a general guarantee of equality, but is concerned with the application of the law. To approach the ideal of full equality before and under the law, the main consideration must be the impact of the law on the individual or group concerned, so that a law expressed to bind all should not have a more burdensome or less beneficial impact on one than another because of irrelevant personal differences. The purpose of s. 15 is to ensure equality in the formulation and application of the law. The analysis of discrimination must take place within the context of the enumerated grounds in s. 15(1) and thus analogous to them. However, the effect of the impugned distinction or classification on the complainant must also be considered.

Official Languages of Canada

16. (1) Official languages of Canada — English and French are the official languages of Canada and have equality of status and equal rights and privileges as to their use in all institutions of the Parliament and government of Canada.

(2) Official languages of New Brunswick — English and French are the official languages of New Brunswick and have equality of status and equal rights and privileges as to their use in all institutions of the legislature and government of New Brunswick.

(3) Advancement of status and use — Nothing in this Charter limits the authority of Parliament or a legislature to advance the equality of status or use of English and French.

17. (1) Proceedings of Parliament — Everyone has the right to use English or French in any debates and other proceedings of Parliament.

(2) Proceedings of New Brunswick legislature — Everyone has the right to use English or French in any debates and other proceedings of the legislature of New Brunswick.

18. (1) Parliamentary statutes and records — The statutes, records and journals of Parliament shall be printed and published in English and French and both language versions are equally authoritative.

(2) New brunswick statutes and records — The statutes, records and journals of the legislature of New Brunswick shall be printed and published in English and French and both language versions are equally authoritative.

19. (1) Proceedings in courts established by Parliament — Either English or French may be used by any person in, or in any pleading in or process issuing from, any court established by Parliament.

(2) Proceedings in New Brunswick courts — Either English or French may be used by any person in, or in any pleading in or process issuing from, any court of New Brunswick.

20. (1) Communications by public with federal institutions — Any member of the public in Canada has the right to communicate with, and to receive available services from, any head or central office of an institution of the Parliament or government of Canada in English or French, and has the same right with respect to any other office of any such institution where

   (a) there is a significant demand for communications with and services from that office in such language; or

   (b) due to the nature of the office, it is reasonable that communications with and services from that office be available in both English and French.

(2) Communications by public with New Brunswick institutions — Any member of the public in New Brunswick has the right to communicate with, and to receive available services from, any office of an institution of the legislature or government of New Brunswick in English or French.

21. Continuation of existing Constitutional provisions — Nothing in sections 16 to 20 abrogates or derogates from any right, privilege or obligation with respect to the English and French languages, or either of them, that exists or is continued by virtue of any other provision of the Constitution of Canada.

22. Rights and privileges preserved — Nothing in sections 16 to 20 abrogates or derogates from any legal or customary right or privilege acquired or enjoyed either before or after the coming into force of this Charter with respect to any language that is not English or French.

Minority Language Educational Rights

23. (1) **Language of instruction** — Citizens of Canada

(a) whose first language learned and still understood is that of the English or French linguistic minority population of the province in which they reside, or

(b) who have received their primary school instruction in Canada in English or French and reside in a province where the language in which they received that instruction is the language of the English or French linguistic minority population of the province,

have the right to have their children receive primary and secondary school instruction in that language in that province.

(2) **Continuity of language instruction** — Citizens of Canada of whom any child has received or is receiving primary or secondary school instruction in English or French in Canada, have the right to have all their children receive primary and secondary school instruction in the same language.

(3) **Application where numbers warrant** — The right of citizens of Canada under subsections (1) and (2) to have their children receive primary and secondary school instruction in the language of the English or French linguistic minority population of a province

(a) applies wherever in the province the number of children of citizens who have such a right is sufficient to warrant the provision to them out of public funds of minority language instruction; and

(b) includes, where the number of those children so warrants, the right to have them receive that instruction in minority language educational facilities provided out of public funds.

Case Law

Reference re s. 79(3), (4) & (7) of the Public Schools Act (Man.), [1993] 1 S.C.R. 839 — *See also: Mahe v. Alberta*, [1990] 1 S.C.R. 342 — The general right of instruction conferred by *Charter* s. 23, read in the context of the section as a whole, necessarily requires that the educational facilities be of or belong to the linguistic minority group and includes the right to a distinct physical setting and facilities. Section 23 confers upon minority language parents a right to manage and control the educational facilities where their children are taught. Under the "sliding scale" approach, the degree of management and control depends on the number of actual or potential children who will eventually take advantage of the contemplated program or facility. Governments, however, should have the widest possible discretion in selecting the means whereby their s. 23 obligations are met.

Enforcement

24. (1) **Enforcement of guaranteed rights and freedoms** — Anyone whose rights or freedoms, as guaranteed by this Charter, have been infringed or denied may apply to a court of competent jurisdiction to obtain such remedy as the court considers appropriate and just in the circumstances.

(2) **Exclusion of evidence bringing administration of justice into disrepute** — Where, in proceedings under subsection (1), a court concludes that evidence was obtained in a manner that infringed or denied any rights or freedoms guaranteed by this Charter, the evidence shall be excluded if it is established that, having regard to all the circumstances, the admission of it in the proceedings would bring the administration of justice into disrepute.

Case Law
Status of Applicant: S. 24(1)

CEMA v. Richardson, [1998] 3 S.C.R. 157 — As a general rule, a *Charter* provision may *only* be invoked by those who enjoy its protection. Under the *Big M Drug* Mart exception, however, standing is granted as of right to an accused charged under legislation that is alleged to be unconstitutional. The exception should be extended to permit corporations to invoke the *Charter* as *defendants* in *civil* proceedings instigated by the state or a state organ under a regulatory scheme.

The Supreme Court of Canada may hear arguments from parties who would *not* usually have standing to invoke the *Charter*. The court has a residuary discretion if the question involved is one of public importance.

Hy and Zel's Inc. v. Ontario (Attorney General), (sub nom. *Paul Magder Furs Ltd. v. Ontario (Attorney General))* [1993] 3 S.C.R. 675 — In order for the court to exercise its discretion to grant standing in a civil case, where a party does not claim a breach of its own *Charter* rights but those of others

i.   a serious issue must be raised as to the constitutional validity of the relevant act;

ii.   the appellant must be directly affected by the act or have a genuine interest in its validity; and,

iii.   there exists no other reasonable and effective way to bring the act's validity before the court.

R. v. C.I.P. Inc. (1992), 12 C.R. (4th) 237, 71 C.C.C. (3d) 129 (S.C.C.) — A corporate accused cannot invoke all *Charter* rights. A *Charter* right may be invoked, however, where a corporate accused can establish that it has an interest falling within the scope of a guarantee and one which accords with the guarantee's purpose.

Borowski v. Canada (A.G.) (1989), 47 C.C.C. (3d) 1 (S.C.C.) — For an applicant to have standing, s. 24(1) clearly requires an infringement or denial of a *Charter*-based right. The allegation by an applicant that the rights of a foetus, not his own rights, are infringed does not give the applicant standing.

Court of Competent Jurisdiction: S. 24(1)

Mooring v. Canada, [1996] 3 W.W.R. 305, 192 N.R. 161 (S.C.C.) — A court/tribunal is only "a court of competent jurisdiction" under *Charter* s. 24(1) where it has jurisdiction over

i.   the parties;

ii.   the subject matter; and

iii.   the remedy sought.

R. v. Seaboyer, (sub nom. *R. v. Gayme)* 7 C.R. (4th) 117, 66 C.C.C. (3d) 321 — *See also*: *R. v. Moore* (1992), 70 C.C.C. (3d) 127 (S.C.C.); affirming (1990), 60 C.C.C. (3d) 286 (P.E.I. C.A.) — The *Code* provides no authority for a justice presiding at a preliminary inquiry to hear and determine the constitutionality of an evidentiary provision of the *Code*.

Gamble v. R. (1988), 66 C.R. (3d) 193, 45 C.C.C. (3d) 204 (S.C.C.) — The superior court of a province has jurisdiction to hear an application for *habeas corpus* and for relief under *Charter* s. 24(1) by a person being incarcerated in the province, for the purpose of reviewing the legality of such detention or confinement, although the person had originally been convicted and sentenced by the court of another province. A purposive approach should be applied to the administration of the *Charter* remedies, particularly where *habeas corpus* is requested. *Habeas corpus* is available as a remedy under s. 24(1) to review the significant deprivation of liberty inherent in the operation of parole ineligibility provisions. Such a review does not circumvent the appeal process or constitute a *de facto* appeal on the merits.

Mills v. R. (1986), 52 C.R. (3d) 1, 26 C.C.C. (3d) 481 (S.C.C.) — A provincial court judge presiding at a preliminary hearing is not a court of competent jurisdiction under this section and has no jurisdiction to exclude evidence under s. 24(2). Courts exercising criminal jurisdiction, including a provincial court judge acting under Part XIX or Part XXVII of the *Code*, are courts of competent jurisdiction where jurisdiction over the offences and persons and power to make the orders sought is conferred by statute. The provincial superior court is a court of competent jurisdiction both when acting at first instance and as a reviewing court where prerogative relief is sought.

Procedure on Applications: S. 24(1)

R. v. L. (W.K.) (1991), 6 C.R. (4th) 1, 64 C.C.C. (3d) 321 (S.C.C.) — No particular procedure need be employed in applications under s. 24(1). The parties, in appropriate cases, may proceed on an agreed statement of facts or by way of affidavit. It is essential, however, that a judge's critical findings of fact on the application be supported by an adequate evidentiary basis. Issues of credibility, *semble*, should be resolved on the basis of *viva voce* testimony.

Timing of Application: S. 24(1)

R. v. DeSousa (1992), 15 C.R. (4th) 66, 76 C.C.C. (3d) 124 (S.C.C.) — A trial judge has the discretion to decide whether to hear an application to declare a *Code* section unconstitutional at the outset of a trial or to reserve decision until the end of the case. Two policy considerations, namely,

a.   that criminal proceedings should not be fragmented by interlocutory proceedings; and

b.   that the adjudication of constitutional issues ought to be discouraged absent factual foundation

generally favour disposition at the end of the case. There should be no departure from these policies, absent strong reason, as for example, where there is an apparently meritorious challenge to the law under which D is charged which is *not* dependent upon facts elicited at trial for adjudication.

R. v. Loveman (1992), 12 C.R. (4th) 167, 71 C.C.C. (3d) 123 (Ont. C.A.) — *See also*: *R. v. Kutynec* (1992), 12 C.R. (4th) 152, 70 C.C.C. (3d) 289 (Ont. C.A.) — Where there is no statutory requirement or practice direction that D give notice of an intention to assert a *Charter* challenge, a trial judge, able to control trial proceedings to ensure fairness to all and to preserve the integrity of the trial process, *may* refuse to entertain such an application upon no or inadequate notice. A trial judge should be somewhat reluctant to foreclose inquiry into an alleged *Charter* violation. In determining whether to permit such a challenge, a trial judge may consider:

i.   the absence of any statutory rule or practice direction requiring notice;

ii.   the point of the trial when counsel first indicates such an intention;

iii.   the extent to which P has been prejudiced by the absence of prior notice;

iv.   the nature of the argument to be advanced; and,

v.   the impact of the application on the course of the trial.

R. v. Vermette (1988), 64 C.R. (3d) 82, 41 C.C.C. (3d) 523 (S.C.C.) — It is premature for the trial judge to grant a stay of proceedings under s. 24(1) in advance of the jury selection process on the grounds that the public discussion of evidence to be adduced at trial prevents the selection of an impartial jury. It should not be assumed that a person subjected to such publicity will necessarily be biased.

Mills v. R. (1986), 52 C.R. (3d) 1, 26 C.C.C. (3d) 1 (S.C.C.) — A justice at a preliminary hearing cannot exclude evidence pursuant to s. 24(2) by reason of a *Charter* violation in the obtaining of that evidence.

Retrospective Operation

Benner v. Canada (Secretary of State), (February 27, 1997), Doc. No. 23811 (S.C.C.) — The *Charter* does *not* operate retroactively. There is no rigid test for deciding when a particular application of the *Charter* would be retrospective. Each case is decided on its own merits.It is *not* every instance which involves pre-*Charter* events that will involve retrospective application of the *Charter*. Where the fact situation is a *status* or a *characteristic*, the enactment is given no retrospective effect when applied to persons or things that acquired the status before the enactment, but continue with it at the relevant time. Where the fact is an *event*, retrospective effect would be given if it is applied to affix a new *duty*, penalty, or disability to a pre-*Charter* event.

Benner v. Canada (Secretary of State), (February 27, 1997), Doc. No. 23811 (S.C.C.) — When an issue of retrospective effect arises, the question is one of characterization: "Is the situation one of going back to *redress* an old event which took place prior to the *Charter*, but prior to the *Charter* creating the right, or simply an assessment of the contemporary application of a law which happened to be passed before the *Charter* came into effect?

Remedies: S. 24(1)

R. v. O'Connor (1995), 44 C.R. (4th) 1, 103 C.C.C. (3d) 1 (S.C.C.) — In determining what remedy is appropriate and just for *Charter* infringement based on non-disclosure, a court should consider whether P's breach of disclosure obligation has violated the fundamental principles which underpin the community's sense of decency and fair play, hence cause prejudice to the intergrity of the judicial system. P's conduct and intention are very relevant for those purposes. *Male fides* is *not* a prerequisite to a finding of flagrant and intentional misconduct required for a stay of proceedings.

R. v. O'Connor (1995), 44 C.R. (4th) 1, 103 C.C.C. (3d) 1 (S.C.C.) — A remedy for *Charter* infringement due to non-disclosure is typically a disclosure order and adjournment. In extreme cases, where prejudice to D's ability to make full answer and defence, or to the integrity of the justice system is irremediable, a stay of proceedings is appropriate. Other remedies include

i.   permitting D to recall witnesses for examination or cross-examination;

ii.   adjournments to permit D to subpoena additional witnesses; or,

iii.   in extreme cases, declaration of a mistrial.

R. v. C.I.P. Inc. (1992), 12 C.R. (4th) 237, 71 C.C.C. (3d) 129 (S.C.C.) — The imposition of a stay of proceedings is, for all intents and purposes, an acquittal. It should only be invoked where the court is satisfied that a particular right has been infringed.

Osborne v. Canada (Treasury Board), [1991] 2 S.C.R. 70, 37 C.C.E.L. 135 (S.C.C.) — In its selection of a just and appropriate remedy under s. 24(1), a court's primary concern must be to apply the measures that will best vindicate the values expressed in the *Charter* and to provide the form of remedy to those whose rights have been violated that best achieves that objective. Remedies include, but are not restricted to, a declaration that a law is of no force or effect under s. 52(1) of the *Constitution Act*, reading the law down or conferring a constitutional exemption.

Evidence Obtained in a Manner . . .: S. 24(2)

R. v. Goldhart (1996), 48 C.R. (4th) 297, 107 C.C.C. (3d) 481 (S.C.C.) — The concepts of proximate cause and remoteness were developed to restrain the potential reach of causation, a concept that has *not* been discarded entirely. A temporal link will often suffice, but is not dispositive in all cases, as for example, where the connection between the securing of the evidence and the breach is remote.The whole of the relationship between the breach and the evidence must be examined. Remoteness relates to both the temporal and causal connection. Where both connections are tenuous, the evidence may not have been obtained in a manner that infringes/denies *Charter* rights. A temporal connection may be so strong that the *Charter* breach is part of a single transaction, rendering of little importance a wak or non-existent causal connection.The applicability of *Charter* s. 24(2) is decided on a case-by-case basis.

R. v. Goldhart (1996), 48 C.R. (4th) 297, 107 C.C.C. (3d) 481 (S.C.C.) — Where testimony of a person arrested and charged as a result of evidence obtained by *Charter* infringement is a result of the person's own decision to co-operate, plead guilty and testify, there is *no* nexus established sufficient to implicate *Charter* S. 24(2).

R. v. Harper (1994), 33 C.R. (4th) 61, 92 C.C.C. (3d) 423 (S.C.C.); affirming (1992), 78 Man. R. (2d) 227 (Man. C.A.) — A statement made as part of a "chain of events" in which a *Charter* violation occurred is evidence"...obtained in a manner that infringed or denied ... rights ... guaranteed" by the *Charter* for the purposes of s. 24(2).

R. v. Kokesch (1990), 1 C.R. (4th) 62, 61 C.C.C. (3d) 207 (S.C.C.); reversing (1988), 46 C.C.C. (3d) 194 (B.C. C.A.) — Where observations made by police during an unlawful search of the perimeter of a dwellinghouse form the foundation for a warrant to search the premises, there is a sufficient *nexus* between the unconstitutional search and the subsequent discovery of the evidence to conclude that the evidence was "obtained in a manner that infringed" s. 8.

R. v. Brydges (1990), 74 C.R. (3d) 129, 53 C.C.C. (3d) 330 (S.C.C.) — A requirement of strict causation between the *Charter* infringement and the evidence obtained thereby is not appropriate under s. 24(2). Section 24(2) is implicated as long as a *Charter* violation occurred in the course of obtaining the evidence.

Strachan v. R. (1988), 67 C.R. (3d) 87, 46 C.C.C. (3d) 479 (S.C.C.) — The phrase "obtained in a manner" does not impose a causation requirement between the *Charter* violation and the obtaining of evidence. The approach used by courts should focus on the entire chain of events during which the *Charter* violation occurred and the evidence was obtained. Accordingly, the first inquiry under s. 24(2) would be to determine whether a *Charter* violation occurred in the course of obtaining the evidence. A temporal link is important but not determinative, as there may be situations where evidence will be too remote from the violation to have been "obtained in a manner" that infringed the *Charter*.

R. v. Therens (1985), 45 C.R. (3d) 97, 18 C.C.C. (3d) 481 (S.C.C.) — Section 24(2) is the sole basis for the exclusion of evidence because of an infringement or denial of a right or freedom guaranteed by the *Charter*. Evidence obtained directly by a violation of the right to counsel must be excluded even if the violation was in good faith.

Exclusion of Evidence (General Principles)

R. v. Cook (1998), 128 C.C.C. (3d) 1 (S.C.C.) — The distinction between incriminating and exculpatory statements is *not* a factor that should influence analysis under s. 24(2). The content does *not* change characterization of a statement as conscriptive evidence. Neither does the fact that P seeks to use the statement only in cross-examination influence the decision under s. 24(2).

R. v. Belnavis (1997), 118 C.C.C. (3d) 405 (S.C.C.) — The reasonable and probable grounds for a search must inform the assessment of the seriousness of the *Charter* breach when considering *Charter* s. 24(2).

R. v. Feeney (1997), 7 C.R. (5th) 101, [1997] 2 S.C.R. 13, 115 C.C.C. (3d) 129 (S.C.C.) — The *trial fairness* analysis begins with a characterization of the evidence as

i.   conscriptive; or,

ii.   non-conscriptive.

Evidence of conscriptive when D, in violation of his/her *Charter* rights is compelled to incriminate him/herself at the behest of the state by means of

i.   a *statement*;

ii.   the *use* of the *body*; or

iii. the *production* of *bodily samples*.

The absence of lawful authority for a *Charter* violation is one indication of bad faith.

There is a distinction between the tests for

i.   characterizing evidence as conscriptive derivative evidence; and,

ii.   determining whether conscriptive evidence is discoverable.

The derivative evidence inquiry is directed at a determination whether a piece of evidence ought be viewed as having a conscriptive nature because of its intimate relationship with other conscriptive evidence. Evidence is derivative if it would not have been obtained but for the conscriptive evidence. The inquiry is directed at whether evidence should be treated as a product of D's mind or body for s. 24(2) purposes, a matter not dependent on the constitutionality of alternative means of discovery.

Discoverability is concerned with whether a Charter breach was necessary to the discovery of and obtaining conscriptive evidence. If conscriptive evidence would have been obtained even if the Charter had not been breached, the evidence is discoverable and its admission, the conscription of D notwithstanding, would not affect trial fairness. In determining discoverability, the alternative means to obtain the evidence must be compliant with the Charter.

R. v. Stillman (1997), 5 C.R. (5th) 1, [1997] 1 S.C.R. 607, 113 C.C.C. (3d) 321 (S.C.C.); reversing (1995), 97 C.C.C. (3d) 164 (N.B. C.A.) — The primary aim and purpose of the *trial fairness* factor in s. 24(2) *Charter* analysis is to prevent D, whose *Charter* analysis is to prevent D, whose *Charter* rights have been infringed, from being forced or conscripted to provide evidence of

i.   confessions;

ii.   statements; or,

iii. bodily samples

for the benefit of the state. Consideration of the *trial fairness* factor requires classification of the evidence as

i.   *conscriptive*;

ii.   *non-conscriptive*.

Evidence is non-conscriptive where D was not compelled to participate in the creation or discovery of the evidence. Admission on non-conscriptive evidence will not render the trial unfair. Exclusion/admission will be dependent upon

i.   the seriousness of the *Charter* breach; and,

ii.   the effect of exclusion on the repute of the administration of justice.

Evidence is conscriptive where D has been compelled to incriminate him/herself

i.   by a statement; or

ii.   by use as evidence of D's body or bodily substances.

Derivative evidence obtained from statements which are conscriptive evidence is also conscriptive evidence.

Where P demonstrates, on a balance of probabilities, that conscriptive evidence would have been discovered by alternative non-conscriptive means, for example, through an independent source or by inevitable discovery, then its admission will not render the trial unfair and it will be necessary to consider the seriousness of the *Charter* breach and the effect of evidentiary exclusion to determine whether the evidence ought be received.Where P fails to demonstrate, on a balance of probabilities, that the evidence would have been discovered, by alternative non-conscriptive means, its admission will render the trial unfair and it will generally be excluded without considering the seriousness of the *Charter* breach or the effect of exclusion on the administration of justice.

R. v. Calder (1996), 46 C.R. (4th) 133, 105 C.C.C. (3d) 1 (S.C.C.) — *Charter* s. 24(2) is preoccupied with the *effect* that the admission of constitutionally-tainted evidence will have on the *repute* of the administration of justice. The effect on trial fairness of destroying D's credibility by cross-examining on a constitutionally-tainted statement is usually the same as use of the same evidence in P's case-in-chief to incriminate D. The arbiter of the effect of the admission of evidence on the administration of justice is the well-informed member of the community, not the carefully-instructed juror who has been apprised of the distinction between use for the purposes of incrimination and impeachment of credibility.

R. v. Calder (1996), 46 C.R. (4th) 133, 105 C.C.C. (3d) 1 (S.C.C.) — Use of evidence for the limited purpose of cross-examination as to credibility is an "admission" of the evidence under *Charter* s. 24(2).

R. v. Calder (1996), 46 C.R. (4th) 133, 195 C.C.C. (3d) 1 (S.C.C.) — Where evidence has been ordered excluded due to *Charter* infringement, P must establish a change in circumstances due to the limited use of the evidence to cross-examine D as to credit justifies varying the original decision to exclude. The order first made may be varied or revoked in the event of a change in circumstances. The distinction between the use of evidence for purpose of incrimination and its use for the purpose of cross-examination as to credibility has some relevance, but it will only be in very limited circumstances that a change in use will qualify as a material change to warrant re-opening of the admissibility issue.

R. v. Goldhart (1996), 48 C.R. (4th) 297, 107 C.C.C. (3d) 481 (S.C.C.) — There is a distinction between discovery of a person who is arrested and charged with an offence, and the evidence subsequently volunteered by such person. Discovery of a person is not the equivalent of evidence from that person favourable to P. Testimony cannot be treated in the same manner as an inanimate object.

R. v. Edwards (1996), 26 O.R. (3d) 736n (S.C.C.) — A claim for s. 24(2) *Charter* exclusion of evidence for a s. 8 *Charter* breach may only be made by the person whose *Charter* rights have been infringed.

R. v. Edwards (1996), 26 O.R. (3d) 736n (S.C.C.) — The right to challenge the legality of a search depends upon whether

i.   D had a reasonable expectation of privacy; and, if so,

ii.   the search was conducted reasonably.

Whether D has a *reasonable expectation* of *privacy* is decided on the basis of the totality of the circumstances which may include

i.   presence at the time of the search;

ii.   possession or control of the property or place searched;

iii.   ownership of the property or place;

iv.   historical use of the property or item;

v.   ability to regulate access;

vi.   existence of a subjective expectation of privacy; and

vii.   objective reasonableness of the expectation.

Where D establishes a reasonable expectation of privacy, the inquiry proceeds to the second stage to determine whether the search was conducted in a reasonable manner.

R. v. Harrer (1995), 42 C.R. (4th) 269, 101 C.C.C. (3d) 193 (S.C.C.); affirming (1994), 89 C.C.C. (3d) 276 (B.C. C.A.) — The *Charter* has no direct application to interrogations in the United States where U.S. authorities are not acting on behalf of any Canadian government. Absent a complaint against Canading police, D may argue that the admission of the evidence would violate D's liberty interests in a manner that is contrary to the principles of fundamental justice, or violate the fair trial guarantee of *Charter* s. 11(d).*Semble*, the situation would be different where the interrogation about a Canadian offence was conducted

i.   by Canadian police officers in the United States; or

ii.   by U.S. authorities acting as agents of Canadian police

in circumstances which would constitute a *Charter* breach if the interrogation had taken place in Canada.

R. v. Harrer (1995), 42 C.R. (4th) 269, 101 C.C.C. (3d) 193 (S.C.C.); affirming (1994), 89 C.C.C. (3d) 276 (B.C. C.A.) — It cannot be assumed that evidence was unfairly obtained or admitted because it was obtained in another country in a manner that would violate a *Charter* guarantee in Canada. Different balances may be struck in various countries between the interests of the state and of the individual. All these balances *may* be fair. D is entitled to a fair hearing, *not* one with the most favourable procedures imaginable.

R. v. Harrer (1995), 42 C.R. (4th) 269, 101 C.C.C. (3d) 193 (S.C.C.); affirming (1994), 89 C.C.C. (3d) 276 (B.C. C.A.) — The fact that evidence has been obtained lawfully in another country may be a factor in assessing trial fairness, but is *not* dispositive.

R. v. S. (R.J.) (1995), 21 O.R. (3d) 797n (S.C.C.); affirming (1993), 80 C.C.C. (3d) 397, 21 C.R. (4th) 47 (Ont. C.A.) — The test for exclusion of derivative evidence involves the question whether the evidence could have been obtained but for the witness' testimony. It requires an inquiry into logical probabilities, not mere possibilities. The important consideration is whether the evidence, practically speaking, could have been located. Logic must be applied to the facts of each case, not to the mere fact of independent evidence. There should be no automatic rule of exclusion in respect of any derivative evidence. Its exclusion is governed by the trial judge's discretion. The exercise of this discretion will depend upon the probative value of the evidence balanced against the prejudice caused to D by its admission. The burden is on D to demonstrate that the proposed evidence is derivative evidence deserving of a limited immunity protection.

R. v. S. (R.J.) (1995), 21 O.R. (3d) 797n (S.C.C.); affirming (1993), 80 C.C.C. (3d) 397, 21 C.R. (4th) 47 (Ont. C.A.) — The principle against self-incrimination is recognized under *Charter* s. 24(2). Derivative evidence which could not have been obtained, or the significance of which could not have been appreciated, but for the testimony of a witness, ought generally to be excluded under s. 7 in the interests of trial fairness. This evidence, though not created by D and thus not self-incriminatory by definition, is self-incriminatory nonetheless because the evidence could not otherwise have become part of P's case. To this extent the witness must be protected against assisting P in creating a case to meet.

R. v. Harper (1994), 33 C.R. (4th) 61, 92 C.C.C. (3d) 423 (S.C.C.); affirming (1992), 78 Man. R. (2d) 227 (Man. C.A.) — An applicant who seeks exclusion under s. 24(2) bears the ultimate burden or persuasion of satisfying the court, on a balance of probabilities, that admission of the proposed evidence could bring the administration of justice into disrepute. The burden on particular contested issues, however, may shift to P. Where P asserts that a detainee would *not* have acted any differently absent a *Charter* violation, P bears the burden of proof on the issue.

R. v. Bartle (1994), 92 C.C.C. (3d) 289 (S.C.C.); reversing (1993), 22 C.R. (4th) 1, 81 C.C.C. (3d) 353 (Ont. C.A.) — To exclude evidence under s. 24(2), the trial judge must find

i.   that a *Charter* violation occurred in the course of obtaining the evidence; and,

ii.   that, having regard to all the circumstances, admission of the evidence could bring the administration of justice into disrepute.

Under s. 24(2), D bears the burden of persuasion. In some instances, however, the onus shifts to P.Where P claims that there is no causal link between the *Charter* breach and obtaining the proffered evidence, P bears the burden of proving this assertion.Where an issue arises whether D would have acted any differently absent a s. 10(b) violation, the burden of persuasion rests on P. Where conscripted evidence is involved, the conclusion must be drawn that trial fairness has been adversely affected because the evidence might not have been obtained absent the breach.

R. v. Grant (1993), 24 C.R. (4th) 1, 84 C.C.C. (3d) 173 (S.C.C.) — Even though a search warrant is valid, an infringement of D's s. 8 *Charter* rights by warrantless perimeter search during the investigation requires the court to consider whether evidence ultimately obtained by execution of the warrant ought to be excluded under s. 24(2).

R. v. Broyles (1991), 9 C.R. (4th) 1, 68 C.C.C. (3d) 308 (S.C.C.) — The admission of self-incriminatory evidence obtained by *Charter* breach will generally render D's trial unfair, notwithstanding that there may be other admissible evidence which incriminates D. The seriousness of a *Charter* violation favours exclusion of tainted evidence, and is not attenuated by an assertion of investigative good faith. The seriousness of the offence is no *per se* justification for admission. The admission of other incriminatory evidence may reduce the effect on the reputation of the administration of justice of excluding the tainted evidence.

R. v. Elshaw (1991), 7 C.R. (4th) 333, 67 C.C.C. (3d) 97 (S.C.C.) — Police bad faith may strengthen the case for exclusion. Police good faith, however, will *not* strengthen the case for admission to cure an unfair trial as a result of the admission of self-incriminating evidence generated by *Charter* breach.

R. v. Greffe (1990), 75 C.R. (3d) 257, 55 C.C.C. (3d) 161 (S.C.C.); reversing (1988), 62 C.R. (3d) 272, 41 C.C.C. (3d) 257 (Alta. C.A.) — The purpose of the exclusionary rule of s. 24(2) is to prevent having the administration of justice brought into further disrepute by the admission, in the proceedings, of evidence obtained in a constitutionally impermissible manner. While the first set of factors in *Collins* bears on the fairness of the trial and the second, the seriousness of the *Charter* violation, the third set (of factors) recognizes the possibility that the administration of justice could be brought into disrepute by excluding evidence, notwithstanding it was obtained by *Charter* infringement.

Collins v. R. (1987), 56 C.R. (3d) 193, 33 C.C.C. (3d) 1 (S.C.C.) — *See also*: *Jacoy v. R.* (1988), 66 C.R. (3d) 336, 45 C.C.C. (3d) 46 (S.C.C.); *R. v. Genest* (1989), 67 C.R. (3d) 224, 45 C.C.C. (3d) 385 (S.C.C.) — The onus is on the applicant to establish on the balance of probabilities that admission of the evidence would bring the administration of justice into disrepute. The purpose of s. 24(2) is not to remedy police misconduct, but to prevent having the administration of justice brought into further disrepute by the admission of the evidence in the proceedings. Even though the inquiry under s. 24(2) will necessarily focus on the specific prosecution, it is the long-term consequences of regular admission or exclusion of such evidence on the repute of the administration of justice which must be considered. The relevant question is, would the admission of the evidence bring the administration of justice into disrepute in the eyes of a reasonable man, dispassionate and fully apprised of the circumstances of the case? The reasonable person is usually the average person in the community, but only when that community's current mood is reasonable. Three groups of factors should be considered. First, the effect of the admission of the evidence on the fairness of the trial should be considered with reference to the nature of the evidence obtained and the nature of the right violated. Real evidence obtained which existed irrespective of the violation of the *Charter* does not render a trial unfair by its admission. Second, the seriousness of the *Charter* violation bears on the disrepute that will result from judicial acceptance of evidence thereby obtained. Good faith on the part of the officials is relevant, and if alternate means of obtaining the evidence without violating the *Charter* were available, the violation is more serious. Third, evidence should not be excluded if the effect of such exclusion would bring the administration of justice into further disrepute than its admission. The availability of other remedies than s. 24(2) is not a relevant consideration.

Mills v. R. (1986), 52 C.R. (3d) 1, 26 C.C.C. (3d) 481 (S.C.C.) — A provincial court judge presiding at a preliminary hearing is not a court of competent jurisdiction under this section and has no jurisdiction to exclude evidence under s. 24(2). Courts exercising criminal jurisdiction, including a provincial court judge acting under *Code* Part XIX or XXVII, are courts of competent jurisdiction where jurisdiction over the offences and persons and power to make the orders sought is conferred by statute. The provincial superior court is a court of competent jurisdiction both when acting at first instance and as a reviewing court where prerogative relief is sought.

R. v. Therens (1985), 45 C.R. (3d) 97, 18 C.C.C. (3d) 481 (S.C.C.) — Section 24(2) is the sole basis for the exclusion of evidence because of an infringement or denial of a right or freedom guaranteed by the

Charter. Evidence obtained directly by a violation of the right to counsel must be excluded even if the violation was in good faith.

Exclusion of Evidence (Real Evidence): S. 24(2)

R. v. Mellenthin (1992), 16 C.R. (4th) 273, 76 C.C.C. (3d) 481, 489–91 (S.C.C.) — *See also*: *Thomson Newspapers Ltd. v. Canada (Director of Investigation & Research)* (1990), 76 C.R. (3d) 129, 54 C.C.C. (3d) 417, 511–4 (S.C.C.) — When considering the effect of the admission of *real evidence* on the *fairness of the trial*, a distinction is to be drawn between real evidence which D has been forced to *create* by constitutional infringement and real evidence which D has been forced merely to *locate* or *identify* by constitutional infringement. Independently-existing evidence that *could* have been found without compelled testimony is to be distinguished from independently-existing evidence that *would* have been found without compelled testimony.The fairness of a trial would be affected were checkstops accepted as a basis for warrantless searches and evidence derived therefrom automatically admitted. To admit evidence obtained in an unreasonable and unjustified search carried out while a motorist was detained in a checkstop would adversely and unfairly affect the trial process and bring the administration of justice into disrepute.

R. v. Black (1989), 70 C.R. (3d) 97, 50 C.C.C. (3d) 1 (S.C.C.) — The admission of physical evidence obtained as a direct result of a statement taken in violation of D's s. 10(b) right would not bring the administration of justice into disrepute where the evidence would have been uncovered by the police in any event.

Simmons v. R. (1988), 66 C.R. (3d) 297, 45 C.C.C. (3d) 296 (S.C.C.) — The admission of evidence obtained as a result of an unreasonable strip-search by customs officials at a border crossing, involving the violation of the accused's rights under *Charter* ss. 8 and 10(b), did not bring the administration of justice into disrepute, where the evidence was real evidence existing irrespective of the *Charter* violations, the officials acted in good faith based on accepted customs procedures and existing statutory requirements, and the breaches occurred years before the handing down of determinative judicial pronouncements on the meaning of "detention" under *Charter* s. 10(b).

Tremblay v. R. (1987), 60 C.R. (3d) 59, 37 C.C.C. (3d) 565 (S.C.C.) — Where the undue haste of the police officers in making a demand for a breath sample, in violation of the accused's right to counsel, was provoked by the actively obstructionist tactics of the accused in an attempt to stall for time, the reasons for the breach made it understandable and were relevant to the finding that the admission of the breathalyzer evidence would not bring the administration of justice into repute.

Sieben v. R. (1987), 56 C.R. (3d) 225, 32 C.C.C. (3d) 574 (S.C.C.) — *See also*: *Hamill v. R.* (1987), 56 C.R. (3d) 220, 33 C.C.C. (3d) 110 (S.C.C.) — Assuming that the writs of assistance formerly authorized under the *Narcotic Control Act* are constitutionally inadequate, a search made pursuant to such a writ must be considered warrantless and *prima facie* unreasonable. The admission into evidence of the results of that search would not, however, bring the administration of justice into disrepute because (i) its admission would in no way cause the trial to be unfair; (ii) the police officers had reasonable grounds to enter and search the premises; and (iii) the only reason a search warrant was not obtained was a good faith reliance on the sufficiency of writs of assistance prior to any *Charter* challenges as to their fundamental constitutionality.

Exclusion of Evidence (Self-Incriminatory Evidence): S. 24(2)

R. v. Cobham (1994), 6 M.V.R. (3d) 88, 33 C.R. (4th) 73, 92 C.C.C. (3d) 333 (S.C.C.) — The direct connection between the incriminating refusal evidence and the offence of refusing to "blow" creates a strong presumption that its admission would render the trial unfair.

R. v. Pozniak (1994), 33 C.R. (4th) 49, 92 C.C.C. (3d) 472, 19 O.R. (3d) 802 (note) (S.C.C.); reversing (1993), 22 C.R. (4th) 1, 81 C.C.C. (3d) 353 (Ont. C.A.) — *See also*: *R. v. Harper* (1994), 33 C.R. (4th) 61, 92 C.C.C. (3d) 423 (S.C.C.); affirming (1992), 78 Man. R. (2d) 227 (Man. C.A.) — Breath samples obtained after failure to advise a detainee of available free and immediate, preliminary legal advice are in the nature of conscripted evidence whose admission would impact negatively on trial fairness.

R. v. Prosper (1994), 33 C.R. (4th) 85, 92 C.C.C. (3d) 353 (S.C.C.); reversing (1992), 75 C.C.C. (3d) 1, 38 M.V.R. (2d) 268 (N.S. C.A.) — Breath samples obtained in breach of the informational and implementational aspects of *Charter* s. 10(b) are conscripted evidence upon charges of "over 80" and "impaired". Where they might *not* have been obtained absent infringement, they ought to be excluded on account of their effect on trial fairness.

R. v. Bartle (1994), 92 C.C.C. (3d) 289 (S.C.C.); reversing (1993), 22 C.R. (4th) 1, 81 C.C.C. (3d) 353 (Ont. C.A.) — Where P claims that there is no causal link between the *Charter* breach and obtaining the proffered evidence, P bears the burden of proving this assertion.Where an issue arises whether D would have acted any differently absent a s. 10(b) violation, the burden of persuasion rests on P. Where conscripted evidence is involved, the conclusion must be drawn that trial fairness has been adversely affected because the evidence might not have been obtained absent the breach.

R. v. Broyles (1991), 9 C.R. (4th) 1, 68 C.C.C. (3d) 308 (S.C.C.) — The admission of self-incriminatory evidence obtained by *Charter* breach will generally render D's trial unfair, notwithstanding that there may be other admissible evidence which incriminates D. The seriousness of a *Charter* violation favours exclusion of tainted evidence, and is not attenuated by an assertion of investigative good faith. The seriousness of the offence is no *per se* justification for admission. The admission of other incriminatory evidence may reduce the effect on the reputation of the administration of justice of excluding the tainted evidence.

R. v. Elshaw (1991), 7 C.R. (4th) 333, 67 C.C.C. (3d) 97 (S.C.C.) — Police bad faith may strengthen the case for exclusion. Police good faith, however, will *not* strengthen the case for admission to cure an unfair trial as a result of the admission of self-incriminating evidence generated by *Charter* breach.

R. v. Smith (1991), 63 C.C.C. (3d) 313 (S.C.C.); affirming (1990), 53 C.C.C. (3d) 97 (N.S. C.A.) — Where there is ample independent evidence of the offence such that D's statement to the police is not essential to substantiate the charge, the admission into evidence of the statement does not render the trial unfair, even though the statement might not have been made but for the *Charter* violation.

R. v. Leclair (1989), 67 C.R. (3d) 209, 46 C.C.C. (3d) 129 (S.C.C.) — Although a person's identity constitutes pre-existing "real evidence", the identification evidence obtained through a line-up is not simply pre-existing "real evidence" in this sense. Line-up evidence is evidence that could not have been obtained but for the participation of the accused in the construction of the evidence for the purposes of the trial, and the use of such evidence goes to the fairness of the trial process. The violation of the right to counsel of the accused prior to the line-up, in the absence of any mitigating factors, renders such evidence inadmissible.

Upston v. R. (1988), 63 C.R. (3d) 299, 42 C.C.C. (3d) 560 at 564 (S.C.C.) — Where the accused was not informed of his right to counsel when he was initially detained, evidence subsequently obtained in a completely voluntary way after he was informed of his right to counsel is not obtained as a result of the original breach of s. 10(b) and should not be excluded from evidence under s. 24.

Exclusion of Evidence (Review of Findings): S. 24(2)

R. v. Mellenthin (1992), 16 C.R. (4th) 273, 76 C.C.C. (3d) 481, 488 (S.C.C.) — *See also*: *R. v. Collins* (1987), 56 C.R. (3d) 193, 33 C.C.C. (3d) 1, 18 (S.C.C.) — A provincial appellate court ought *not* too readily interfere with the decision of a trial judge under s. 24(2), in particular in the absence of an unreasonable finding of fact or error of law.

R. v. Duguay (1989), 67 C.R. (3d) 252, 46 C.C.C. (3d) 1 (S.C.C.) — *See also*: *R. v. Kokesch* (1990), 1 C.R. (4th) 62, 61 C.C.C. (3d) 207 (S.C.C.); reversing (1988), 46 C.C.C. (3d) 194 (B.C. C.A.); *R. v. Greffe* (1990), 75 C.R. (3d) 257, 55 C.C.C. (3d) 161, 182 (S.C.C.); *R. v. Wise* (1992), 11 C.R. (4th) 253, 70 C.C.C. (3d) 193 (S.C.C.) — It is not the proper function of the Supreme Court of Canada to review findings of the courts below under s. 24(2) though it has jurisdiction to do so, absent some apparent error as to the applicable principles or rules of law, or absent a finding that is unreasonable.

25. Aboriginal rights and freedoms not affected by Charter — The guarantee in this Charter of certain rights and freedoms shall not be construed so as to abrogate or derogate from any aboriginal treaty or other rights or freedoms that pertain to the aboriginal peoples of Canada including

(a) any rights or freedoms that have been recognized by the Royal Proclamation of October 7, 1763; and

(b) any rights or freedoms that now exist by way of land claims agreements or may be so acquired.

SI/84–102, Schedule.

26. Other rights and freedoms not affected by Charter — The guarantee in this Charter of certain rights and freedoms shall not be construed as denying the existence of any other rights or freedoms that exist in Canada.

27. Multicultural heritage — This Charter shall be interpreted in a manner consistent with the preservation and enhancement of the multicultural heritage of Canadians.

28. Rights guaranteed equally to both sexes — Notwithstanding anything in this Charter, the rights and freedoms referred to in it are guaranteed equally to male and female persons.

Case Law

R. v. Hess (1990), (sub nom. *R. v. Nguyen*) 79 C.R. (3d) 332, 59 C.C.C. (3d) 161 (S.C.C.); reversing [1989] 3 W.W.R. 646 (Man. C.A.) — [Per Lamer C.J., Wilson, La Forest and L'Heureux-Dubé JJ.] — The section does *not* prevent Parliament from creating an offence, as in former *Code* s. 146(1), where an accused principal must be male and the complainant female, that, as a biological fact, can only be committed by one sex.

29. Rights respecting certain schools preserved — Nothing in this Charter abrogates or derogates from any rights or privileges guaranteed by or under the Constitution of Canada in respect of denominational, separate or dissentient schools.

30. Application to Territories and territorial authorities — A reference in this Charter to a province or to the legislative assembly or legislature of a province shall be deemed to include a reference to the Yukon Territory and the Northwest Territories, or to the appropriate legislative authority thereof, as the case may be.

31. Legislative powers not extended — Nothing in this Charter extends the legislative powers of any body or authority.

Application of Charter

32. (1) Application of Charter — This Charter applies

    (a) to the Parliament and government of Canada in respect of all matters within the authority of Parliament including all matters relating to the Yukon Territory and Northwest Territories; and

    (b) to the legislature and government of each province in respect of all matters within the authority of the legislature of each province.

(2) Exception — Notwithstanding subsection (1), section 15 shall not have effect until three years after this section comes into force.

Case Law

Vriend v. Alberta (1998), 224 N.R. 1 (S.C.C.) — The language of s. 32 does *not* limit the application of the *Charter* to *positive* actions encroaching on rights or excessive exercise of authority. Where the challenge involves a provincial Act that is said to be under inclusive by omission, s. 32 does not preclude the application of the *Charter*.

R. v. Cook (1998), 128 C.C.C. (3d) 1 (S.C.C.) — The application of the *Charter* abroad cannot be determined merely by reference to s. 32(1). There are limited circumstances in which the *Charter* can apply beyond Canada's territorial boundaries. The reach of domestic law is *not* always determined solely on the basis of territoriality.

Under international law, a state may invoke the *nationality* of the person subject to the domestic law as a valid basis of jurisdiction authority. Nationality is much broader than citizenship. It refers to a person who may not have full political and civil rights of citizenship, but nevertheless has a right of protection of the state and, in turn, owes allegiance to it. Although an objectionable extraterritorial effect would result from applying the *Charter* to foreign officers, even if they may be described as agents of Canadian authorities, to require Canadian authorities abroad to comply with *Charter* standards abroad may *not*, depending on the circumstances, interfere with the foreign state's sovereign authority and integrity.

The *Charter* applies to Canadian police officers conducting, in the United States, the investigation of a crime alleged to have been committed in Canada.

Where an investigation is conducted in the United States by Canadian officers in accordance with their powers of investigation that are derived from Canadian law, their conduct falls within s. 32(1) of the *Charter*. Further, the application of the *Charter* in the circumstances does *not* interfere with the territorial jurisdiction of the foreign state.

Schreiber v. Canada (Attorney General), [1998] 1 S.C.R. 841, 16 C.R. (5th) 1, 124 C.C.C. (3d) 129 (S.C.C.) — *Charter* rights and freedoms are guaranteed *only* against interference from actions taken by Parliament and the Government of Canada, or provincial legislatures and governments. Where there is no *action* by any of these entities that infringes a guaranteed *Charter* right or freedom, there is *no Charter* violation. (per L'Heureux-Dubé, McLachlin, Bastarache and Binnie JJ.)

Co-operation between states is a necessary reality of international criminal investigation and procedure. The fact that the Government of Canada may play a part in international investigations and proceedings, which might have implications for individual rights and freedoms, such as those in the *Charter*, does *not*, by itself, mean that the *Charter* is engaged. (per L'Heureux-Dubé, McLachlin, Bastarache and Binnie JJ.)

Godbout v. Longueuil (City) (1997), 219 N.R. 1 (S.C.C.) — The *Charter* applies to all entities that are essentially governmental in nature, not merely those that are formally part of the structure of federal or provincial governments. Under s. 32, entities are subject to *Charter* scrutiny in respect of certain governmental activities which they perform, even if the entities are not "governmental per se. Municipalities are subject to the *Charter*.

Eldridge v. British Columbia (Attorney General) (1997), 151 D.L.R. (4th) 577 (S.C.C.) — There are two ways in which the *Charter* may apply to provincial legislation:

i.   the legislation may be unconstitutional on its face because it violates a *Charter* right and is not saved by s. 1; or,

ii. the actions of a delegated decision-maker applying the legislation may infringe the *Charter*.

In cases which fall under item ii, supra, the legislation remains valid, but unconstitutional action is remedied under *Charter* s. 24(1).

The mere fact that an entity performs a "public function", or that an activity may be described as "public" in nature, is not enough to bring it within "government" for s. 32 *Charter* purposes. For the *Charter* to apply to a private entity, it must be found to be implementing a specific government policy or program.

The *Charter* may apply to a private entity because: i. the entity itself is "government"; or, ii. the activity in which the entity is engaged may be ascribed to "government" within *Charter* s. 32

An entity may be "government" under item i, *supra*, by its very nature or because of the degree of government control exercise over it. All of the activities of such an entity are subject to *Charter* scrutiny.

An entity may be "government" under item ii, *supra*, not, because of the nature of the entity, but because of the nature of the activity.

R. v. Harrer (1995), 42 C.R. (4th) 269, 101 C.C.C. (3d) 193 (S.C.C.); affirming (1994), 89 C.C.C. (3d) 276 (B.C. C.A.) — The *Charter* has no direct application to interrogation in the United States where U.S. authorities are *not* acting on behalf of any Canadian government. Absent a complaint against Canadian police, D may argue that the admission of evidence would violate D's liberty interests in a manner contrary to the principles of fundamental justice or the fair trial guarantee of *Charter* s. 11(d). *Semble*, the situation would be different where the interrogation about a Canadian offence was conducted

i.   by Canadian police officers in the United States; or

ii.   by U.S. authorities acting as agents of Canadian police

in circumstances which would constitute a *Charter* breach if the interrogation had taken place in Canada.

R. v. Dersch (1993), 25 C.R. (4th) 88, 85 C.C.C. (3d) 1 (S.C.C.) — A physician who participates in emergency treatment of D, which includes taking blood samples for medical purposes, does not thereby become an agent of government for s. 32 *Charter* purposes.

New Brunswick Broadcasting Co. v. Nova Scotia (Speaker of the House of Assembly), [1993] 1 S.C.R. 319 — A textual and purposive approach to *Charter* s. 32(1) does *not* support the conclusion that a legislative assembly can never be subject to the *Charter*. The tradition of curial deference does *not* extend to everything a legislative assembly might do, but is firmly attached to certain specific activities, *viz*, the privileges of legislative assemblies. (L'Heureux-Dubé, Gonthier, McLachlin and Iacobucci JJ.)The *Charter* does *not* apply to the members of the Nova Scotia House of Assembly when they exercise their inherent privileges. The inherent privileges of a legislative body such as the Nova Scotia House of Assembly enjoy constitutional status.

B.C.G.E.U. v. British Columbia (A.G.) (1988), 44 C.C.C. (3d) 289 (S.C.C.) — A common law breach of the criminal law, such as picketing of a court house which constitutes criminal contempt, is subject to *Charter* scrutiny.

33. (1) Exception where express declaration — Parliament or the legislature of a province may expressly declare in an Act of Parliament or of the legislature, as the case may be, that the Act or a provision thereof shall operate notwithstanding a provision included in section 2 or sections 7 to 15 of this Charter.

(2) Operation of exception — An Act or a provision of an Act in respect of which a declaration made under this section is in effect shall have such operation as it would have but for the provision of this Charter referred to in the declaration.

(3) Five year limitation — A declaration made under subsection (1) shall cease to have effect five years after it comes into force or on such earlier date as may be specified in the declaration.

(4) Re-enactment — Parliament or a legislature of a province may re-enact a declaration made under subsection (1).

(5) Five year limitation — Subsection (3) applies in respect of a re-enactment made under subsection (4).

Citation

34. Citation — This Part may be cited as the *Canadian Charter of Rights and Freedoms*.

CONTROLLED DRUGS AND SUBSTANCES ACT

S.C. 1996, c. 19, as am   S.C. 1996, c. 8, s. 35(a); 1997, c. 18, s. 140; SOR/97-230; SOR/98-157; SOR/98-173; 1999, c. 5, ss. 48, 49.

An Act respecting the control of certain drugs, their precursors and other substances and to amend certain other Acts and repeal the Narcotic Control Act in consequence thereof.

The Narcotic Control Act, *R.S.C. 1985, c. N-1, is no longer in force. It was repealed by the* Controlled Drugs and Substances Act, *S.C. 1996, c. 19 on May 14, 1997. We have, however, retained the* Narcotic Control Act, *because the Act remains of relevance to offences occurring before its repeal. It will therefore continue to be of great practical importance for some time to come. The* Narcotic Control Act *appears immediately following the* Controlled Drugs and Substances Act. *The* Narcotic Control Act *is replaced by the following:*

Short Title

1. Short title — This Act my be cited as the *Controlled Drugs and Substances Act.*

Interpretation

2. (1) Definitions — In this Act,

"adjudicator" means a person appointed or employed under the *Public Service Employment Act* who performs the duties and functions of an adjudicator under this Act and the regulations;

"analogue" means a substance that, in relation to a controlled substance, has a substantially similar chemical structure;

"analyst" means a person who is designated as an analyst under section 44;

"Attorney General" means

(a) the Attorney General of Canada, and includes their lawful deputy, or

(b) with respect to proceedings commenced at the instance of the government of a province and conducted by or on behalf of that government, the Attorney General of that province, and includes their lawful deputy;

"controlled substance" means a substance included in Schedule I, II, III, IV or V;

"designated substance offence" means

(a) an offence under Part I, except subsection 4(1), or

(b) a conspiracy or an attempt to commit, being an accessory after the fact in relation to, or any counselling in relation to, an offence referred to in paragraph (a);

"inspector" means a person who is designated as an inspector under section 30;

"**judge**" means a judge as defined in section 552 of the *Criminal Code* or a judge of a superior court of criminal jurisdiction;

"**justice**" has the same meaning as in section 2 of the *Criminal Code*;

"**Minister**" means the Minister of Health;

"**offence-related property**" means any property, within or outside Canada,

> (a) by means of or in respect of which a designated substance offence is committed,
>
> (b) that is used in any manner in connection with the commission of a designated substance offence, or
>
> (c) that is intended for use for the purpose of committing a designated substance offence,

but does not include a controlled substance or real property, other than real property built or significantly modified for the purpose of facilitating the commission of a designated substance offence;

"**possession**" means possession within the meaning of subsection 4(3) of the *Criminal Code*;

"**practitioner**" means a person who is registered and entitled under the laws of a province to practise in that province the profession of medicine, dentistry or veterinary medicine, and includes any other person or class or persons prescribed as a practitioner;

"**precursor**" means a substance included in Schedule VI;

"**prescribed**" means prescribed by the regulations;

"**produce**" means, in respect of a substance included in any of Schedules I to IV, to obtain the substance by any method or process including

> (a) manufacturing, synthesizing or using any means of altering the chemical or physical properties of the substance, or
>
> (b) cultivating, propagating or harvesting the substance or any living thing from which the substance may be extracted or otherwise obtained,

and includes offer to produce;

"**provide**" means to give, transfer or otherwise make available in any manner, whether directly or indirectly and whether or not for consideration;

"**sell**" includes offer for sale, expose for sale, have in possession for sale and distribute, whether or not the distribution is made for consideration;

"**traffic**" means, in respect of a substance included in any of Schedules I to IV,

> (a) to sell, administer, give, transfer, transport, send or deliver the substance,
>
> (b) to sell an authorization to obtain the substance, or
>
> (c) to offer to do anything mentioned in paragraph (a) or (b),

otherwise than under the authority of the regulations.

(2) **Interpretation** — For the purposes of this Act,

> (a) a reference to a controlled substance includes a reference to any substance that contains a controlled substance; and

(b) a reference to a controlled substance includes a reference to

    (i) all synthetic and natural forms of the substance, and

    (ii) any thing that contains or has on it a controlled substance and that is used or intended or designed for use

        (A) in producing the substance, or

        (B) in introducing the substance into a human body.

(3) Idem — For the purposes of this Act, where a substance is expressly named in any of Schedules I to VI, it shall be deemed not to be included in any other of those Schedules.

1996, c. 8, s. 35(a)

3. (1) Interpretaton — Every power or duty imposed under this Act that may be exercised or performed in respect of an offence under this Act may be exercised or performed in respect of a conspiracy, or an attempt to commit, being an accessory after the fact in relation to, or any counselling in relation to, an offence under this Act.

(2) Idem — For the purposes of sections 16 and 20, a reference to a person who is or was convicted of a designated substance offence includes a reference to an offender who is discharged under section 730 of the *Criminal Code*.

1995, c. 22, s. 18 (Sched. IV, item 26)

PART I — OFFENCES AND PUNISHMENT

Particular Offences

4. (1) Possession of substance — Except as authorized under the regulations, no person shall possess a substance included in Schedule I, II or III.

(2) Obtaining substance — No person shall seek or obtain

    (a) a substance included in Schedule I, II, III or IV, or

    (b) an authorization to obtain a substance included in Schedule I, II, III or IV

from a practitioner, unless the person discloses to the practitioner particulars relating to the acquisition by the person of every substance in those Schedules, and of every authorization to obtain such substances, from any other practitioner within the preceding thirty days.

(3) Punishment — Every person who contravenes subsection (1) where the subject-matter of the offence is a substance included in Schedule I

    (a) is guilty of an indictable offence and liable to imprisonment for a term not exceeding seven years; or

    (b) is guilty of an offence punishable on summary conviction and liable

        (i) for a first offence, to a fine not exceeding one thousand dollars or to imprisonment for a term not exceeding six months, or to both, and

        (ii) for a subsequent offence, to a fine not exceeding two thousand dollars or to imprisonment for a term not exceeding one year, or to both.

(4) Punishment — Subject to subsection (5), every person who contravenes subsection (1) where the subject-matter of the offence is a substance included in Schedule II

(a) is guilty of an indictable offence and liable to imprisonment for a term not exceeding five years less a day; or

(b) is guilty of an offence punishable on summary conviction and liable

(i) for a first offence, to a fine not exceeding one thousand dollars or to imprisonment for a term not exceeding six months, or to both, and

(ii) for a subsequent offence, to a fine not exceeding two thousand dollars or to imprisonment for a term not exceeding one year, or to both.

(5) Punishment — Every person who contravenes subsection (1) where the subject-matter of the offence is a substance included in Schedule II in an amount that does not exceed the amount set out for that substance in Schedule VIII is guilty of an offence punishable on summary conviction and liable to a fine not exceeding one thousand dollars or to imprisonment for a term not exceeding six months, or to both.

(6) Punishment — Every person who contravenes subsection (1) where the subject-matter of the offence is a substance included in Schedule III

(a) is guilty of an indictable offence and liable to imprisonment for a term not exceeding three years; or

(b) is guilty of an offence punishable on summary conviction and liable

(i) for a first offence, to a fine not exceeding one thousand dollars or to imprisonment for a term not exceeding six months, or to both, and

(ii) for a subsequent offence, to a fine not exceeding two thousand dollars or to imprisonment for a term not exceeding one year, or to both.

(7) Punishment — Every person who contravenes subsection (2)

(a) is guilty of an indictable offence and liable

(i) to imprisonment for a term not exceeding seven years, where the subject-matter of the offence is a substance included in Schedule I,

(ii) to imprisonment for a term not exceeding five years less a day, where the subject-matter of the offence is a substance included in Schedule II,

(iii) to imprisonment for a term not exceeding three years, where the subject-matter of the offence is a substance included in Schedule III, or

(iv) to imprisonment for a term not exceeding eighteen months, where the subject-matter of the offence is a substance included in Schedule IV; or

(b) is guilty of an offence punishable on summary conviction and liable

(i) for a first offence, to a fine not exceeding one thousand dollars or to imprisonment for a term not exceeding six months, or to both, and

(ii) for a subsequent offence, to a fine not exceeding two thousand dollars or to imprisonment for a term not exceeding one year, or to both.

(8) Determination of amount — For the purposes of subsection (5) and Schedule VIII, the amount of the substance means the entire amount of any mixture or substance, or the whole of any plant, that contains a detectable amount of the substance.

5. (1) Trafficking in substance — No person shall traffic in a substance included in Schedule I, II, III or IV or in any substance represented or held out by that person to be such a substance.

(2) **Possession for purpose of trafficking** — No person shall, for the purposes of trafficking, possess a substance included in Schedule I, II, III or IV.

(3) **Punishment** — Every person who contravenes subsection (1) or (2)

(a) subject to subsection (4), where the subject-matter of the offence is a substance included in Schedule I or II, is guilty of an indictable offence and liable to imprisonment for life;

(b) where the subject-matter of the offence is a substance included in Schedule III,

(i) is guilty of an indictable offence and liable to imprisonment for a term not exceeding ten years, or

(ii) is guilty of an offence punishable on summary conviction and liable to imprisonment for a term not exceeding eighteen months; and

(c) where the subject-matter of the offence is a substance included in Schedule IV,

(i) is guilty of an indictable offence and liable to imprisonment for a term not exceeding three years, or

(ii) is guilty of an offence punishable an summary conviction and liable to imprisonment for a term not exceeding one year.

(4) **Punishment in repect of specified substance** — Every person who contravenes subsection (1) or (2), where the subject-matter of the offence is a substance included in Schedule II in an amount that does not exceed the amount set out for that substance in Schedule VII, is guilty of an indictable offence and liable to imprisonment for a term not exceeding five years less a day.

(5) **Interpretation** — For the purposes of applying subsection (3) or (4) in respect or an offence under subsection (1), a reference to a substance included in Schedule I, II, III or IV include a reference to any substance represented or held out to be a substance included in that Schedule.

(6) **Interpretation** — For the purposes of subsection (4) and Schedule VII, the amount of the substance means the entire amount of any mixture or substance, or the whole of any plant, that contains a detectable amount of the substance.

6. (1) **Importing and exporting** — Except as authorized under the regulations, no person shall import into Canada or export from Canada a substance included in Schedule I, II, III, IV, V or VI.

(2) **Possession for the purpose of exporting** — Except as authorized under the regulations, no person shall possess a substance included in Schedule I, II, III, IV, V or VI for the purpose of exporting it from Canada.

(3) **Punishment** — Every person who contravenes subsection (1) or (2)

(a) where the subject-matter of the offence is a substance included in Schedule I or II, is guilty of an indictable offence and liable to imprisonment for life;

(b) where the subject-matter of the offence is a substance included in Schedule III or VI,

(i) is guilty of an indictable offence and liable to imprisonment for a term not exceeding ten years, or

(ii) is guilty of an offence punishable on summary conviction and liable to imprisonment for a term not exceeding eighteen months; and

(c) **where the subject-matter of the offence is a substance included in Schedule IV or V,**

(i) **is guilty of an indictable offence and liable to imprisonment for a term not exceeding three years, or**

(ii) **is guilty of an offence punishable on summary conviction and liable to imprisonment for a term not exceeding one year.**

7. (1) Production of substance — Except as authorized under the regulations, no person shall produce a substance included in Schedule I, II, III or IV.

(2) Punishment — Every person who contravenes subsection (1)

(a) **where the subject-matter of the offence is a substance included in Schedule I or II, other than cannabis (marihuana), is guilty of an indictable offence and liable to imprisonment for life.**

(b) **where the subject-matter of the offence is cannabis (marihuana), is guilty of an indictable offence and liable to imprisonment for a term not exceeding seven years;**

(c) **where the subject-matter of the offence is a substance included in Schedule III,**

(i) **is guilty of an indictable offence and liable to imprisonment for a term not exceeding ten years, or**

(ii) **is guilty of an offence punishable on summary conviction and liable to imprisonment for a term not exceeding eighteen months; and**

(d) **where the subject-matter of the offence is a substance included in Schedule IV,**

(i) **is guilty of an indictable offence and liable to imprisonment for a term not exceeding three years, or**

(ii) **is guilty of an offence punishable on summary conviction and liable to imprisonment for a term not exceeding one year.**

8. (1) Possession of property obtained by certain offences — No person shall possess any property or any proceeds of any property knowing that all or part of the property or proceeds was obtained or derived directly or indirectly as a result of

(a) **the commission in Canada of an offence under this Part except subsection 4(1) and this subsection;**

(b) **an act or omission anywhere that, if it had occurred in Canada, would have constituted an offence referred to in paragraph (a); or**

(c) **a conspiracy or an attempt to commit, being an accessory after the fact in relation to, or any counselling in relation to, an offence referred to in paragraph (a) or an act or omission referred to in paragraph (b).**

(2) Punishment — Every person who contravenes subsection (1)

(a) **is guilty of an indictable offence and liable to imprisonment for a term not exceeding ten years, where the value of the property or the proceeds exceeds one thousand dollars; or**

(b) **is guilty**

(i) **of an indictable offence and liable to imprisonment for a term not exceeding two years, or**

(ii) of an offence punishable on summary conviction and liable to a fine not exceeding two thousand dollars or to imprisonment for a term not exceeding six months, or to both,

where the value of the property or the proceeds does not exceed one thousand dollars.

(3) Exception — A peace officer or a person acting under the direction of a peace officer is not guilty of an offence under this section by reason only that the peace officer or person possesses property or the proceeds of property mentioned in subsection (1) for the purposes of an investigation or otherwise in the execution of the peace officer's duties.

1997, c. 18, s. 140(b)

Case Law
Multiple Convictions

R. v. Garoufalis (1998), 131 C.C.C. (3d) 242 (Man. C.A.) — The offence of possession of proceeds of crime has different legal elements than the offence of trafficking.

9. (1) Laundering proceeds of certain offences — No person shall use, transfer the possession of, send or deliver to any person or place, transport, transmit, alter, dispose of or otherwise deal with, in any manner or by any means, any property or any proceeds of any property with intent to conceal or convert that property or those proceeds and knowing or believing that all or a part of that property or of those proceeds was obtained or derived directly or indirectly as a result of

(a) the commission in Canada of an offence under this Part except subsection 4(1);

(b) an act or omission anywhere that, if it had occured in Canada, would have constituted an offence referred to in paragraph (a); or

(c) a conspiracy or an attempt to commit, being an accessory after the fact in relation to, or any counselling in relation to, an offence referred to in paragraph (a) or an act or ommission referred to in paragraph (b).

(2) Punishment — Every person who contravenes subsection (1)

(a) is guilty of an indictable offence and liable to imprisonment for a term not exceeding ten years; or

(b) is guilty of an offence punishable on summary conviction and liable to a fine not exceeding two thousand dollars or to imprisonment for a term not exceeding six months, or to both.

(3) Exception — A peace officer or a person acting under the direction of a peace officer is not guilty of an offence under subsection (2) if the peace officer or person does anything mentioned in subsection (1) for the purposes of an investigation or otherwise in the execution of their duties.

1997, c. 18, s. 140(c)(i), (ii); 1999, c. 5, s. 48

Sentencing

10. (1) Purpose of sentencing — Without restricting the generality of the *Criminal Code*, the fundamental purpose of any sentence for an offence under this Part is to contribute to the respect for the law and the maintenance of a just, peaceful and safe society while encouraging rehabilitation, and treatment in appropriate circumstances, of offenders and acknowledging the harm done to victims and to the community.

(2) Circumstances to take into consideration — If a person is convicted of a designated substance offence, the court imposing sentence on the person shall consider any relevant aggravating factors including that the person

(a) in relation to the commission of the offence,

(i) carried, used or threatened to use a weapon,

(ii) used or threatened to use violence,

(iii) trafficked in a substance included in Schedule I, II, III or IV or possessed such a substance for the purpose of trafficking, in or near a school, on or near school grounds or in or near any other public place usually frequented by persons under the age of eighteen years, or

(iv) trafficked in a substance included in Schedule I, II, III or IV, or possessed such a substance for the purpose of trafficking, to a person under the age of eighteen years;

(b) was previously convicted of a designated substance offence; or

(c) used the services of a person under the age of eighteen years to commit, or involved such a person in the commission of, a designated substance offence.

(3) Reasons — If, under subsection (1), the court is satisfied of the existence of one or more of the aggravating factors enumerated in paragraphs (2)(a) to (c), but decides not to sentence the person to imprisonment, the court shall give reasons for that decision.

1999, c. 5, s. 49

PART II — ENFORCEMENT
Search, Seizure and Detention

11. (1) Information for search warrant — A justice who, on *ex parte* application, is satisfied by information on oath that there are reasonable grounds to believe that

(a) a controlled substance or precursor in respect of which this Act has been contravened,

(b) any thing in which a controlled substance or precursor referred to in paragraph (a) is contained or concealed,

(c) offence-related property, or

(d) any thing that will afford evidence in respect of an offence under this Act

is in a place may, at any time, issue a warrant authorizing a peace officer, at any time, to search the place for any such controlled substance, precursor, property or thing and to seize it.

(2) Application of s. 487.1 of the Criminal Code — For the purposes of subsection (1), an information may be submitted by telephone or other means of telecommunication in accordance with section 487.1 of the *Criminal Code*, with such modifications as the circumstances require.

(3) Execution in another province — A justice may, where a place referred to in subsection (1) is in a province other than that in which the justice has jurisdiction, issue the warrant referred to in that subsection and the warrant may be executed in the other province after it has been endorsed by a justice having jurisdiction in that other province.

(4) Effect of endorsement — An endorsement that is made on a warrant as provided for in subsection (3) is sufficient authority to any peace officer to whom it was originally directed and to all peace officers within the jurisdiction of the justice by whom it is endorsed to execute the warrant and to deal with the things seized in accordance with the law.

(5) Search of person and seizure — Where a peace officer who executes a warrant issued under subsection (1) has reasonable grounds to believe that any person found in the place set out in the warrant has on their person any controlled substance, precursor, property or thing set out in the warrant, the peace officer may search the person for the controlled substance, precursor, property or thing and seize it.

(6) Seizure of things not specified — A peace officer who executes a warrant issued under subsection (1) may seize, in addition to the things mentioned in the warrant,

   (a) any controlled substance or precursor in respect of which the peace officer believes on reasonable grounds that this Act has been contravened;

   (b) any thing that the peace officer believes on reasonable grounds to contain or conceal a controlled substance or precursor referred to in paragraph (a);

   (c) any thing that the peace officer believes on reasonable grounds is offence-related property; or

   (d) any thing that the peace officer believes on reasonable grounds will afford evidence in respect of an offence under this Act.

(7) Where warrant not necessary — A peace officer may exercise any of the powers described in subsection (1), (5) or (6) without a warrant if the conditions for obtaining a warrant exist but by reason of exigent circumstances it would be impracticable to obtain one.

(8) Seizure of additional things — A peace officer who executes a warrant issued under subsection (1) or exercises powers under subsection (5) or (7) may seize, in addition to the things mentioned in the warrant and in subsection (6), any thing that the peace officer believes on reasonble grounds has been obtained by or used in the commission of an offence or that will afford evidence in respect of an offence.

12. Assistance and use of force — For the purpose of exercising any of the powers described in section 11, a peace officer may

   (a) enlist such assistance as the officer deems necessary; and

   (b) use as much force as is necessary in the circumstances.

13. (1) Sections 489.1 and 490 of the Criminal Code applicable — Subject to subsections (2) and (3), sections 489.1 and 490 of the *Criminal Code* apply to any thing seized under this Act.

(2) Sections 489.1 and 490 of the Criminal Code applicable — Where a thing seized under this Act is offence-related property, sections 489.1 and 490 of the *Criminal Code* apply subject to sections 16 to 22 of this Act.

(3) Provisions of this Act applicable — Where a controlled substance is seized under this Act or any other Act of Parliament or pursuant to a power of seizure at common law, this Act and the regulations apply in respect of that substance.

(4) Report to justice — Subject to the regulations, every peace officer who, pursuant to section 11, seizes a controlled substance shall, as soon as is reasonable in the circumstances after the seizure,

(a) prepare a report identifying the place searched, the controlled substance and the location where it is being detained;

(b) cause the report to be filed with the justice who issued the warrant or another justice for the same territorial division or, where by reason of exigent circumstances a warrant was not issued, a justice who would have had jurisdiction to issue a warrant; and

(c) cause a copy of the report to be sent to the Minister.

(5) Report to justice — A report in Form 5.2 of the *Criminal Code* may be filed as a report for the purposes of subsection (4).

(6) Recognizance — Where, pursuant to this section, an order is made under paragraph 490(9)(c) of the *Criminal Code* for the return of any offence-related property seized under this Act, the judge or justice making the order may require the applicant for the order to enter into a recognizance before the judge or justice, with or without sureties, in such amount and with such conditions, if any, as the judge of justice directs and, where the judge or justice considers it appropriate, require the applicant to deposit with the judge or justice such sum of money or other valuable security as the judge or justice directs.

Restraint Orders

14. (1) Application for restraint order — The Attorney General may make an application in accordance with this section for a restraint order under this section in respect of any offence-related property.

(2) Procedure — An application made under subsection (1) for a restraint order in respect of any offence-related property may be made *ex parte* and shall be made in writing to a judge and be accompanied by an affidavit sworn on the information and belief of the Attorney General or any other person deposing to the following matters:

(a) the offence against this Act to which the offence-related property relates;

(b) the person who is believed to be in possession of the offence-related property; and

(c) a description of the offence-related property.

(3) Restraint order — Where an application for a restraint order is made to a judge under subsection (1), the judge may, if satisfied that there are reasonable grounds to believe that the property is offence-related property, make a restraint order

(a) prohibiting any person from disposing of, or otherwise dealing with any interest in, the offence-related property specified in the order otherwise than in such manner as may be specified in the order; and

(b) at the request of the Attorney General, where the judge is of the opinion that the circumstances so require,

(i) appointing a person to take control of and to manage or otherwise deal with all or part of that property in accordance with the directions of the judge, and

(ii) requiring any person having possession of that property to give possession of the property to the person appointed under subparagraph (i).

(4) Minister of Supply and Services — Where the Attorney General so requests, a judge appointing a person under subparagraph (3)(b)(i) shall appoint the Minister of Supply and Services.

(5) Conditions — A restraint order made by a judge under this section may be subject to such reasonable conditions as the judge thinks fit.

(6) Order in writing — A restraint order made under this section shall be made in writing.

(7) Service of order — A copy of a restraint order made under this section shall be served on the person to whom the order is addressed in such manner as the judge making the order directs or in accordance with the rules of the court.

(8) Registration of order — A copy of a restraint order made under this section shall be registered against any property in accordance with the laws of the province in which the property is situated.

(9) Order continues in force — A restraint order made under this section remains in effect until

(a) an order is made under subsection 490(9) or (11) of the *Criminal Code* in relation to the property; or

(b) an order of forfeiture of the property is made under subsection 16(1) or 17(2) of this Act or section 490 of the *Criminal Code*.

(10) Offence — Any person on whom a restraint order made under this section is served in accordance with this section and who, while the order is in force, acts in contravention of or fails to comply with the order is guilty of an indictable offence or an offence punishable on summary conviction.

15. (1) Sections 489.1 and 490 of the Criminal Code applicable — Subject to sections 16 to 22, sections 489.1 and 490 of the *Criminal Code* apply, with such modifications as the circumstances require, to any offence-related property that is the subject-matter of a restraint order made under section 14.

(2) Recognizance — Where, pursuant to subsection (1), an order is made under paragraph 490(9)(c) of the *Criminal Code* for the return of any offence-related property that is the subject of a restraint order under section 14, the judge or justice making the order may require the applicant for the order to enter into a recognizance before the judge or justice, with or without sureties, in such amount and with such conditions, if any, as the judge or justice directs and, where the judge or justice considers it appropriate, require the applicant to deposit with the judge or justice such sum of money or other valuable security as the judge or justice directs.

Forfeiture of Offence-related Property

16. (1) Order of forfeiture of property on conviction — Subject to sections 18 and 19, where a person is convicted of a designated substance offence and, on application of the Attorney General, the court is satisfied, on a balance of probabilities, that any property is offence-related property and that the offence was committed in relation to that property, the court shall

(a) in the case of a substance included in Schedule VI, order that the substance be forfeited to Her Majesty in right of Canada and disposed of by the Minister as the Minister thinks fit; and

(b) in the case of any other offence-related property,

(i) where the prosecution of the offence was commenced at the instance of the government of a province and conducted by or on behalf of that government, order that the property be forfeited to Her Majesty in right of that province and disposed of by the Attorney General or Solicitor General of that province in accordance with the law, and

(ii) in any other case, order that the property be forfeited to Her Majesty in right of Canada and disposed of by such member of the Queen's Privy Council for Canada as may be designated for the purposes of this subparagraph in accordance with the law.

(2) **Property related to other offences** — Where the evidence does not establish to the satisfaction of the court that the designated substance offence of which a person has been convicted was committed in relation to property in respect of which an order of forfeiture would otherwise be made under subsection (1) but the court is satisfied, beyond a reasonable doubt, that that property is offence-related property, the court may make an order of forfeiture under subsection (1) in relation to that property.

(3) **Appeal** — A person who has been convicted of a designated substance offence or the Attorney General may appeal to the court of appeal from an order or a failure to make an order under subsection (1) as if the appeal were an appeal against the sentence imposed on the person in respect of the offence.

17. (1) Application for *in rem* forfeiture — Where an information has been laid in respect of a designated substance offence, the Attorney General may make an application to a judge for an order of forfeiture under subsection (2).

(2) **Order of forfeiture of property** — Subject to sections 18 and 19, where an application is made to a judge under subsection (1) and the judge is satisfied

(a) beyond a reasonable doubt that any property is offence-related property.

(b) that proceedings in respect of a designated substance offence in relation to the property referred to in paragraph (a) were commenced, and

(c) that the accused charged with the designated substance offence has died or absconded,

the judge shall order that the property be forfeited and disposed of in accordance with subsection (4).

(3) **Accused deemed absconded** — For the purposes of subsection (2), an accused shall be deemed to have absconded in connection with a designated substance offence if

(a) an information has been laid alleging the commission of the offence by the accused,

(b) a warrant for the arrest of the accused has been issued in relation to that information, and

(c) reasonable attempts to arrest the accused pursuant to the warrant have been unsuccessful during a period of six months beginning on the day on which the warrant was issued,

and the accused shall be deemed to have so absconded on the last day of that six month period.

(4) **Who may dispose of forfeited property** — For the purposes of subsection (2),

(a) in the case of a substance included in Schedule VI, the judge shall order that the substance be forfeited to Her Majesty in right of Canada and disposed of by the Minister as the Minister thinks fit; and

(b) in the case of any other offence-related property,

(i) where the proceedings referred to in paragraph (2)(b) were commenced at the instance of the government of a province, the judge shall order that the property be forfeited to Her Majesty in right of that province and disposed of by the Attorney General or Solicitor General of that province in accordance with the law, and

(ii) in any other case, the judge shall order that the property be forfeited to Her Majesty in right of Canada and disposed of by such member of the Queen's Privy Council for Canada as may be designated for the purposes of this subparagraph in accordance with the law.

18. **Voidable transfers** — A court may, before ordering that offence-related property be forfeited under subsection 16(1) or 17(2), set aside any conveyance or transfer of the property that occurred after the seizure of the property, or the making of a restraint order in respect of the property, unless the conveyance or transfer was for valuable consideration to a person acting in good faith.

19. (1) **Notice** — Before making an order under subsection 16(1) or 17(2) in relation to any property, a court shall require notice in accordance with subsection (2) to be given to, and may hear, any person who, in the opinion of the court, appears to have a valid interest in the property.

(2) **Manner of giving notice** — A notice given under subsection (1) shall

(a) be given or served in such manner as the court directs or as may be specified in the rules of the court;

(b) be of such duration as the court considers reasonable or as may be specified in the rules of the court; and

(c) set out the designated substance offence charged and a description of the property.

(3) **Order of restoration of property** — Where a court is satisfied that any person, other than

(a) a person who was charged with a designated substance offence, or

(b) a person who acquired title to or a right of possession of the property from a person referred to in paragraph (a) under circumstances that give rise to a reasonable inference that the title or right was transferred for the purpose of voiding the forfeiture of the property,

is the lawful owner or is lawfully entitled to possession of any property or any part of any property that would otherwise be forfeited pursuant to an order made under subsection 16(1) or 17(2) and that the person appears innocent of any complicity in an offence referred to in paragraph (a) or of any collusion in relation to such an offence, the court may order that the property or part be returned to that person.

20. (1) **Application** — Where any offence-related property is forfeited to Her Majesty pursuant to an order made under subsection 16(1) or 17(2), any person who claims an interest in the property, other than

(a) in the case of property forfeited pursuant to an order made under subsection 16(1), a person who was convicted of the designated substance offence in relation to which the property was forfeited,

(b) in the case of property forfeited pursuant to an order made under subsection 17(2), a person who was charged with the designated substance offence in relation to which the property was forfeited, or

(c) a person who acquired title to or a right of possession of the property from a person referred to in paragraph (a) or (b) under circumstances that give rise to a reasonable inference that the title or right was transferred from that person for the purpose of avoiding the forfeiture of the property,

may, within thirty days after the forfeiture, apply by notice in writing to a judge for an order under subsection (4).

(2) **Fixing day for hearing** — The judge to whom an application is made under subsection (1) shall fix a day not less than thirty days after the date of the filing of the application for the hearing of the application.

(3) **Notice** — An applicant shall serve a notice of the application made under subsection (1) and of the hearing of it on the Attorney General at least fifteen days before the day fixed for the hearing.

(4) **Order declaring interest not affected by forfeiture** — Where, on the hearing of an application made under subsection (1), the judge is satisfied that the applicant

(a) is not a person referred to in paragraph (1)(a), (b) or (c) and appears innocent of any complicity in any designated substance offence that resulted in the forfeiture of the property or of any collusion in relation to such an offence, and

(b) exercised all reasonable care to be satisfied that the property was not likely to have been used in connection with the commission of an unlawful act by the person who was permitted by the applicant to obtain possession of the property or from whom the applicant obtained possession or, where the applicant is a mortgagee or lienholder, by the mortgagor or lien-giver,

the judge may make an order declaring that the interest of the applicant is not affected by the forfeiture and declaring the nature and the extent or value of the interest.

(5) **Appeal from order made under subsection (4)** — An applicant or the Attorney General may appeal to the court of appeal from an order made under subsection (4), and the provisions of Part XXI of the *Criminal Code* with respect to procedure on appeals apply, with such modifications as the circumstances require, in respect of appeals under this subsection.

(6) **Return of property** — The Minister shall, on application made to the Minister by any person in respect of whom a judge has made an order under subsection (4), and where the periods with respect to the taking of appeals from that order have expired

and any appeal from that order taken under subsection (5) has been determined, direct that

(a) the property, or the part of it to which the interest of the applicant relates, be returned to the applicant; or

(b) an amount equal to the value of the interest of the applicant, as declared in the order, be paid to the applicant.

21. Appeals from orders under subsection 17(2) — Any person who, in their opinion, is aggrieved by an order made under subsection 17(2) may appeal from the order as if the order were an appeal against conviction or against a judgment or verdict of acquittal, as the case may be, under Part XXI of the *Criminal Code*, and that Part applies, with such modifications as the circumstances require, in respect of such an appeal.

22. Suspension of order pending appeal — Notwithstanding anything in this Act, operation of an order made in respect of property under subsection 16(1), 17(2) or 20(4) is suspended pending

(a) any application made in respect of the property under any of those provisions or any other provision of this or any other Act of Parliament that provides for restoration or forfeiture of the property, or

(b) any appeal taken from an order of forfeiture or restoration in respect of the property,

and the property shall not be disposed of or otherwise dealt with until thirty days have expired after an order is made under any of those provisions.

Forfeiture of Proceeds of Crime

23. (1) Application of sections 462.3 and 462.32 to 462.5 of the Criminal Code respecting proceeds — Sections 462.3 and 462.32 to 462.5 of the *Criminal Code* apply, with such modifications as the circumstances require, in respect of proceedings for a designated substance offence.

(2) Application of sections 462.3 and 462.32 to 462.5 of the Criminal Code respecting proceeds — For the purposes of subsection (1),

(a) a reference in section 462.37 or 462.38 or subsection 462.41(2) of the *Criminal Code* to an enterprise crime offence shall be deemed to be a reference to a designated substance offence;

(b) a reference in subsection 462.37(1) or 462.42(6), paragraph 462.43(c) or section 462.5 of the *Criminal Code* to the Attorney General in relation to the manner in which forfeited property is to be disposed of or otherwise dealt with shall be deemed to be a reference to

(i) where the prosecution of the offence in respect of which the property was forfeited was commenced at the instance of the government of a province and conducted by or on behalf of that government, the Attorney General or Solicitor General of that province, and

(ii) in any other case, such member of the Queen's Privy Council for Canada as may be designated for the purposes of this subparagraph; and

(c) a reference in subsection 462.38(2) of the *Criminal Code* to the Attorney General in relation to the manner in which forfeited property is to be disposed of or otherwise dealt with shall be deemed to be a reference to

(i) where the prosecution of the offence in respect of which the property was forfeited was commenced at the instance of the government of a province, the Attorney General or Solicitor General of that province, and

(ii) in any other case, such member of the Queen's Privy Council for Canada as may be designated for the purposes of this subparagraph.

PART III — DISPOSAL OF CONTROLLED SUBSTANCES

24. (1) Application for return of substance — Where a controlled substance has been seized, found or otherwise acquired by a peace officer or an inspector, any person may, within sixty days after the date of the seizure, finding or acquisition, on prior notification being given to the Attorney General in the prescribed manner, apply, by notice in writing to a justice in the jurisdiction in which the substance is being detained, for an order to return that substance to the person.

(2) Order to return substance forthwith — Where, on the hearing of an application made under subsection (1), a justice is satisfied that an applicant is the lawful owner or is lawfully entitled to possession of the controlled substance and the Attorney General does not indicate that the substance or a portion of it may be required for the purposes of a preliminary inquiry, trial or other proceeding under this or any other Act of Parliament, the justice shall, subject to subsection (5), order that the substance or the portion not required for the purposes of the proceeding be returned forthwith to the applicant.

(3) Order to return substance at specified time — Where, on the hearing of an application made under subsection (1), a justice is satisfied that an applicant is the lawful owner or is lawfully entitled to possession of the controlled substance but the Attorney General indicates that the substance or a portion of it may be required for the purposes of a preliminary inquiry, trial or other proceeding under this or any other Act of Parliament, the justice shall, subject to subsection (5), order that the substance or the portion required for the purposes of the proceeding be returned to the applicant.

(a) on the expiration of one hundred and eighty days after the application was made, if no proceeding in relation to the substance has been commenced before that time; or

(b) on the final conclusion of the proceeding or any other proceeding in relation to the substance, where the applicant is not found guilty in those proceedings of an offence committed in relation to the substance.

(4) Order to return substance refused — Where, on the hearing of an application made under subsection (1), a justice is not satisfied that an applicant is the lawful owner or is lawfully entitled to possession of the controlled substance, the justice shall order that the substance or the portion not required for the purposes of a preliminary inquiry, trial or other proceeding under this or any other Act of Parliament be forfeited to Her Majesty to be disposed of or otherwise dealt with in accordance with the regulations or, if there are no applicable regulations, in such manner as the Minister directs.

(5) Payment of compensation in lieu — Where, on the hearing of an application made under subsection (1), a justice is satisfied that an applicant is the lawful owner or is lawfully entitled to possession of a controlled substance, but an order has been made under subsection 26(2) in respect of the substance, the justice shall make an order that an amount equal to the value of the substance be paid to the applicant.

25. Disposal by Minister where no application — Where no application for the return of a controlled substance has been made under subsection 24(1) within sixty days after the date of the seizure, finding or acquisition by a peace officer or inspector and the substance or a portion of it is not required for the purposes of any preliminary inquiry, trial or other proceeding under this Act or any other Act of Parliament, the substance or the portion not required for the purposes of the proceeding shall be delivered to the Minister to be disposed of or otherwise dealt with in accordance with the regulations or, if there are no applicable regulations, in such manner as the Minister directs.

26. (1) Security, health or safety hazard — Where the Minister has reasonable grounds to believe that a controlled substance that has been seized, found or otherwise acquired by a peace officer or inspector constitutes a potential security, public health or safety hazard, the Minister may, on prior notification being given to the Attorney General in the prescribed manner, at any time, make an application, *ex parte*, to a justice for an order that the substance or a portion of it be forfeited to Her Majesty to be disposed of or otherwise dealt with in accordance with the regulations or, if there are no applicable regulations, in such manner as the Minister directs.

(2) Security, health or safety hazard — Where, on the hearing of an application made under subsection (1), a justice is satisfied that there are reasonable grounds to believe that the controlled substance constitutes a potential security, public health or safety hazard, the justice shall order that the substance or any portion not required for the purposes of a preliminary inquiry, trial or other proceeding under this or any other Act of Parliament be forfeited to Her Majesty to be disposed of or otherwise dealt with in accordance with the regulations or, if there are no applicable regulations, in such manner as the Minister directs.

27. Disposal following proceedings — Subject to section 24, where, pursuant to a preliminary inquiry, trial or other proceeding under this or any other Act of Parliament, the court before which the proceedings have been brought is satisfied that any controlled substance that is the subject of proceedings before the court is no longer required by that court or any other court, the court

(a) shall

(i) where it is satisfied that the person from whom the substance was seized came into possession of the substance in accordance with the regulations and continued to deal with it in accordance with the regulations, order that the substance be returned to the person, or

(ii) where it is satisfied that possession of the substance by the person from whom it was seized is unlawful and the person who is lawfully entitled to its possession is known, order that the substance be returned to the person who is the lawful owner or is lawfully entitled to its possession; and

(b) may, where it is not satisfied that the substance should be returned pursuant to subparagraph (i) or (ii) or where possession of the substance by the person from whom it was seized is unlawful and the person who is the lawful owner or is lawfully entitled to its possession is not known, order that the substance be forfeited to Her Majesty to be disposed of or otherwise dealt with in accordance with the regulations or, if there are no applicable regulations, in such manner as the Minister directs.

28. Disposal with consent — Where a controlled substance has been seized, found or otherwise acquired by a peace officer or inspector under this Act or the regulations and the substance or a portion of it is not required for the purposes of a preliminary inquiry, trial or other proceeding under this or any other Act of Parliament, the person who is the lawful owner or is lawfully entitled to its possession may consent to its disposal, and on such consent being given the substance or portion is thereupon forfeited to Her Majesty and may be disposed of or otherwise otherwise dealt with in accordance with the regulations or, if there are no applicable regulations, in such manner as the Minister directs.

29. Destruction of plant — The Minister may, on prior notification being given to the Attorney General, cause to be destroyed any plant from which a substance included in Schedule I, II III or IV may be extracted that is being produced otherwise than under the authority of and in accordance with a licence issued under the regulations.

PART IV — ADMINISTRATION AND COMPLIANCE

Inspectors

30. (1) Designation of inspectors — The Minister may designate, in accordance with the regulations made pursuant to paragraph 55(1)(n), any person as an inspector for the purposes of this Act and the regulations.

(2) Certificate of designation — An inspector shall be furnished with a prescribed certificate of designation, and on entering any place pursuant to subsection 31(1) shall, on request, produce the certificate to the person in charge of the place.

31. (1) Powers of inspector — Subject to subsection (2), an inspector may, to ensure compliance with the regulations, at any reasonable time enter any place the inspector believes on reasonable grounds is used for the purpose of conducting the business or professional practice of any person licensed or otherwise authorized under the regulations to deal in a controlled substance or a precursor and may for that purpose

(a) open and examine any receptacle or package found in that place in which a controlled substance or a precursor may be found;

(b) examine any thing found in that place that is used or may be capable of being used for the production, preservation, packaging or storage of a controlled substance or a precursor;

(c) examine any labels or advertising material or records, books, electronic data or other documents found in that place with respect to any controlled substance or precursor, other than the records of the medical condition of persons, and make copies thereof or take extracts therefrom;

(d) use or cause to be used any computer system at that place to examine any electronic data referred to in paragraph (c);

(e) reproduce any document from any electronic data referred to in paragraph (c) or cause it to be reproduced, in the form of a printout or other output;

(f) take the labels or advertising material or records, books or other documents referred to in paragraph (c) or the printout or other output referred to in paragraph (e) for examination or copying;

(g) use or cause to be used any copying equipment at that place to make copies of any document;

(h) examine any substance found in that place and take, for the purpose of analysis, such samples thereof as are reasonably required; and

(i) seize and detain in accordance with this Part, any controlled substance or precursor the seizure and detention of which the inspector believes on reasonable grounds is necessary.

(2) **Warrant required to enter dwelling-place** — Where a place referred to in subsection (1) is a dwelling-place, an inspector may not enter the dwelling-place without the consent of an occupant thereof except under the authority of a warrant issued under subsection (3).

(3) **Authority to issue warrant** — Where, on *ex parte* application, a justice is satisfied by information on oath that

(a) a place referred to in subsection (1) is a dwelling-place but otherwise meets the conditions for entry described in that subsection,

(b) entry to the dwelling-place is necessary for the purpose of ensuring compliance with the regulations, and

(c) entry to the dwelling-place has been refused or there are reasonable grounds to believe that entry will be refused,

the justice may issue a warrant authorizing the inspector named in it to enter that dwelling-place and exercise any of the powers mentioned in paragraphs (1)(a) to (i), subject to such conditions as may be specified in the warrant.

(4) **Use of force** — In executing a warrant issued under subsection (3), an inspector shall not use force unless the inspector is accompanied by a peace officer and the use of force is specifically authorized in the warrant.

(5) **Assistance to inspector** — The owner or other person in charge of a place entered by an inspector under subsection (1) and every person found there shall give the inspector all reasonable assistance in the power of that person and furnish the inspector with such information as the inspector may reasonably require.

(6) **Storage of substances seized** — Where an inspector seizes and detains a controlled substance or a precursor, the substance or precursor may, at the discretion of the inspector, be kept or stored at the place where it was seized or, at the direction of the inspector, be removed to any other proper place.

(7) **Notice** — An inspector who seizes a controlled substance or a precursor shall take such measures as are reasonable in the circumstances to give to the owner or other person in charge of the place where the seizure occurred notice of the seizure and of the location where the controlled substance or precursor is being kept or stored.

(8) **Return by inspector** — Where an inspector determines that to ensure compliance with the regulations it is no longer necessary to detain a controlled substance or a precursor seized by the inspector under paragraph (1)(i), the inspector shall notify in writing the owner or other person in charge of the place where the seizure occurred of that determination and, on being issued a receipt for it, shall return the controlled substance or precursor to that person.

(9) Return or disposal by Minister — Notwithstanding sections 24, 25 and 27, where a period of one hundred and twenty days has elapsed after the date of a seizure under paragraph (1)(i) and the controlled substance or precursor has not been returned in accordance with subsection (8), the controlled substance or precursor shall be returned, disposed of or otherwise dealt with in such manner as the Minister directs, in accordance with any applicable regulations.

32. (1) Obstructing inspector — No person shall, by act or omission, obstruct an inspector who is engaged in the performance of duties under this Act or the regulations.

(2) False statements — No person shall knowingly make any false or misleading statement verbally or in writing to an inspector who is engaged in the performance of duties under this Act or the regulations.

(3) Interference — No person shall, without the authority of an inspector, remove, alter or interfere in any way with anything seized, detained or taken under section 31.

PART V — ADMINISTRATIVE ORDERS FOR CONTRAVENTIONS OF DESIGNATED REGULATIONS

33. Designation of regulations — The Governor in Council may, by regulation, designate any regulation made under this Act (in this Part referred to as a "designated regulation") as a regulation the contravention of which shall be dealt with under this Part.

34. Contravention of designated regulation — Where the Minister has reasonable grounds to believe that a person has contravened a designated regulation, the Minister shall

(a) in the prescribed manner, serve a notice to appear on the person; and

(b) send a copy of the notice to appear to an adjudicator and direct the adjudicator to conduct a hearing to determine whether the contravention has occurred and to notify the Minister of the adjudicator's determination.

35. (1) Interim order — Where the Minister has reasonable grounds to believe that a person has contravened a designated regulation and the Minister is of the opinion that, as a result of that contravention, there is a substantial risk of immediate danger to the health or safety of any person, the Minister may, without giving prior notice to the person believed to have contravened the designated regulation, make an interim order in respect of the person

(a) prohibiting the person from doing anything that the person would otherwise be permitted to do under their licence, permit or authorization, or

(b) subjecting the doing of anything under the designated regulation by the person to the terms and conditions specified in the interim order,

and may, for that purpose, suspend, cancel or amend the licence, permit or authorization issued or granted to the person or take any other measures set out in the regulations.

(2) **Idem** — Where the Minister makes an interim order under subsection (1), the Minister shall forthwith

(a) in the prescribed manner, serve the interim order on the person;

(b) in the prescribed manner, serve a notice to appear on the person; and

(c) send a copy of the interim order and the notice to appear to an adjudicator and direct the adjudicator to conduct a hearing to determine whether the contravention has occurred and to notify the Minister of the adjudicator's determination.

36. (1) **Hearing by adjudicator** — Where an adjudicator receives from the Minister a copy of a notice to appear under paragraph 34(b) or 35(2)(c), the adjudicator shall conduct a hearing on a date to be fixed by the adjudicator at the request of the person on whom the notice was served, on two days notice being given to the adjudicator, which hearing date may not

(a) in the case of a notice served under paragraph 34(a), be less than thirty days, or more than forty-five days, after the day of service of the notice; or

(b) in the case of a notice served under paragraph 35(2)(b), be less than three days, or more than forty-five days, after the day of service of the notice.

(2) **Change of hearing date** — Where the adjudicator is unable to conduct a hearing on the date referred to in subsection (1), the adjudicator shall forthwith notify the person and fix, for the purpose of holding the hearing, the earliest possible date to which the adjudicator and the person agree.

(3) **Proceedings on default** — Where an adjudicator has received a copy of a notice to appear referred to in subsection (1) and where the person on whom the notice is served has not requested a date for a hearing within forty-five days after the notice was served on that person, or where the person, having requested a hearing, fails to appear for the hearing, the adjudicator shall proceed to make a determination in the absence of the person.

(4) **Time and place** — An adjudicator may, subject to the regulations, determine the time and place of any hearing or other proceeding under this Part.

37. Notice to appear — A notice to appear served on a person under paragraph 34(a) or 35(2)(b) shall

(a) specify the designated regulation that the Minister believes the person has contravened;

(b) state the grounds on which the Minister believes the contravention has occurred;

(c) state that the matter has been referred to an adjudicator for a hearing to be conducted on a date within the applicable period described in paragraph 36(1)(a) or (b); and

(d) set out such other information as is prescribed.

38. Proof of service — Proof of service of any notice, order or interim order under this Part shall be given in the prescribed manner.

39. Powers of adjudicator — For the purposes of this Act, an adjudicator has and may exercise the powers of a person appointed as a commissioner under Part I of the *Inquiries Act*.

40. Hearing procedure — An adjudicator shall deal with all matters as informally and expeditiously as the circumstances and considerations of fairness and natural justice permit.

41. (1) Determination by adjudicator — An adjudicator shall, after the conclusion of a hearing referred to in subsection 36(1) or a proceeding referred to in subsection 36(3), within the prescribed time, make a determination that the person who is the subject of the hearing or proceeding contravened or did not contravene the designated regulation.

(2) Notice of determination — Where an adjudicator has made a determination under subsection (1), the adjudicator shall

(a) forthwith notify the person and the Minister of the adjudicator's determination and the reasons; and

(b) where the adjudicator has determined that the person has contravened the designated regulation, notify the person of the opportunity to make representations to the Minister in writing in accordance with the regulations and within the prescribed time.

(3) Ministerial orders — Where an adjudicator has made a determination referred to in paragraph (2)(b) and the Minister has considered the determination and any representations referred to in that paragraph, the Minister shall forthwith make an order

(a) prohibiting the person from doing anything that they would, if they were in compliance with the designated regulation, be permitted to do, or

(b) subjecting the doing of anything under the designated regulation by the person to the terms and conditions specified in the order,

and may, for that purpose, suspend, cancel or amend any licence, permit or authorization issued or granted to the person under the regulations or take any other measures set out in the regulations.

(4) Ministerial orders — An order made under subsection (3) shall be served on the person to whom it is directed in the prescribed manner.

42. (1) Effect of order — An interim order made under subsection 35(1) and an order made under subsection 41(3) have effect from the time that they are served on the person to whom they are directed.

(2) Cessation of effect — An interim order that was made in respect of a person believed to have contravened a designated regulation ceases to have effect

(a) where the Minister makes an order under subsection 41(3), at the time the order is served on the person; and

(b) where an adjudicator has determined that the person did not contravene the designated regulation, at the time the adjudicator makes the determination.

(3) Application to revoke order — A person in respect of whom an order was made under subsection 41(3) may make an application in writing to the Minister in accordance with the regulations to revoke the order.

(4) Revocation of order — The Minister may, in the prescribed circumstances, revoke, in whole or in part, any order made under subsection 41(3).

43. Offence for contravenation of order — Every person commits an offence who contravenes an order or an interim order made under this Part.

PART VI — GENERAL

Analysis

44. Designation of Analysts — The Minister may designate, in accordance with the regulations made pursuant to paragraph 55(1)(o), any person as an analyst for the purposes of this Act and the regulations.

45. (1) Analysis — An inspector or peace officer may submit to an analyst for analysis or examination any substance or sample thereof taken by the inspector or peace officer.

(2) Report — An analyst who has made an analysis or examination under subsection (1) may prepare a certificate or report stating that the analyst has analysed or examined a substance or a sample thereof and setting out the results of the analysis or examination.

Offence and Punishment

46. Penalty — Every person who contravenes a provision of this Act for which punishment is not otherwise provided or a regulation, other than a designated regulation within the meaning of Part V,

(a) is guilty of an indictable offence and liable to a fine not exceeding five thousand dollars or to imprisonment for a term not exceeding three years, or to both; or

(b) is guilty of an offence punishable on summary conviction and liable to a fine not exceeding one thousand dollars or to imprisonment for a term not exceeding six months, or to both.

Evidence and Procedure

47. (1) Limitation — No summary conviction proceedings in respect of an offence under subsection 4(2) or 32(2), section 43 or the regulations shall be commenced after the expiration of one year after the time when the subject-matter of the proceedings arose.

(2) Venue — Proceedings in respect of a contravention of any provision of this Act or the regulations may be held in the place where the offence was committed or where the subject-matter of the proceedings arose or in any place where the accused is apprehended or happens to be located.

48. (1) Burden of proving exception, etc. — No exception, exemption, excuse or qualification prescribed by law is required to be set out or negatived, as the case may be, in an information or indictment for an offence under this Act or the regulations or under section 463, 464 or 465 of the *Criminal Code* in respect of such an offence.

(2) Burden of proving exception, etc. — In any prosecution under this Act, the prosecutor is not required, except by way of rebuttal, to prove that a certificate, licence, permit or other qualification does not operate in favour of the accused, whether or not the qualification is set out in the information or indictment.

49. (1) Copies of documents — A copy of any document filed with a department, ministry, agency, municipality or other body established by or pursuant to a law of a province, or of any statement containing information from the records kept by any such department, ministry, agency, municipality or body, purporting to be certified by any official having custody of that document or those records, is admissible in evidence in any prosecution for an offence referred to in subsection 48(1) and, in the absence of evidence to the contrary, is proof of the facts contained in that document or statement, without proof of the signature or official character of the person purporting to have certified it.

(2) Authentication — For the purposes of subsection (1), an engraved, lithographed, photocopied, photographed, printed or otherwise electronically or mechanically reproduced facsimile signature of an official referred to in that subsection is sufficient authentication of any copy referred to in that subsection.

(3) Evidence inadmissible under this section — Nothing in subsection (1) renders admissible in evidence in any legal proceeding such part of any record as is proved to be a record made in the course of an investigation or inquiry.

50. (1) Certificate issued pursuant to regulations — Subject to subsection (2), any certificate or other document issued pursuant to regulations made under paragraph 55(2)(c) is admissible in evidence in a preliminary inquiry, trial or other proceeding under this or any other Act of Parliament and, in the absence of evidence to the contrary, is proof that the certificate or other document was validly issued and of the facts contained in it, without proof of the signature or official character of the person purporting to have certified it.

(2) Certificate issued pursuant to regulations — The defence may, with leave of the court, require that the person who issued the certificate or other document

(a) produce an affidavit or solemn declaration attesting to any of the matters deemed to be proved under subsection (1); or

(b) appear before the court for examination or cross-examination in respect of the issuance of the certificate or other document.

51. (1) Certificate of analyst — Subject to this section, a certificate or report prepared by an analyst under subsection 45(2) is admissible in evidence in any prosecution for an offence under this Act or the regulations or any other Act of Parliament and, in the absence of evidence to the contrary, is proof of the statements set out in the certificate or report, without proof of the signature or official character of the person appearing to have signed it.

(2) Attendance of analyst — The party against whom a certificate or report of an analyst is produced under subsection (1) may, with leave of the court, require the attendance of the analyst for the purpose of cross-examination.

(3) Notice — Unless the court otherwise orders, no certificate or report shall be received in evidence under subsection (1) unless the party intending to produce it has, before its production at trial, given to the party against whom it is intended to be produced reasonable notice of that intention, together with a copy of the certificate or report.

52. (1) **Proof of notice** — For the purposes of this Act and the regulations, the giving of any notice, whether orally or in writing, or the service of any document may be proved by the oral evidence of, or by the affidavit or solemn declaration of, the person claiming to have given that notice or served that document.

(2) **Proof of notice** — Notwithstanding subsection (1), the court may require the affiant or declarant to appear before it for examination or cross-examination in respect of the giving of notice or proof of service.

53. (1) **Continuity of possession** — In any proceeding under this Act or the regulations, continuity of possession of any exhibit tendered as evidence in that proceeding may be proved by the testimony of, or the affidavit or solemn declaration of, the person claiming to have had it in their possession.

(2) **Alternative method of proof** — Where an affidavit or solemn declaration is offered in proof of continuity of possession under subsection (1), the court may require the affiant or declarant to appear before it for examination or cross-examination in respect of the issue of continuity of possession.

54. Copies of records, books or documents — Where any record, book, electronic data or other document is examined or seized under this Act or the regulations, the Minister, or the officer by whom the record, book, electronic data or other document is examined or seized, may make or cause to be made one or more copies thereof, and a copy of any such record, book, electronic data or other document purporting to be certified by the Minister or a person authorized by the Minister is admissible in evidence and, in the absence of evidence to the contrary, has the same probative force as the original record, book, electronic data or other document would have had if it had been proved in the ordinary way.

Regulations, Exemptions and Disqualifications

55. (1) **Regulations** — The Governor in Council may make regulations for carrying out the purposes and provisions of this Act, including the regulation of the medical, scientific and industrial uses and distribution of controlled substances and precursors and the enforcement of this Act and, without restricting the generality of the foregoing, may make regulations

(a) governing, controlling, limiting, authorizing the importation into Canada, exportation from Canada, production, packaging, sending, transportation, delivery, sale, provision, administration, possession or obtaining of or other dealing in any controlled substances or precursor or any class thereof;

(b) respecting the circumstances in which, the conditions subject to which and the persons or classes of persons by whom any controlled substances or precursor or any class thereof may be imported into Canada, exported from Canada, produced, packaged, sent, transported, delivered, sold, provided, administered, possessed, obtained or otherwise dealt in, as well as the means by which and the persons or classes of persons by whom such activities may be authorized;

(c) respecting the issuance, suspension, cancellation, duration and terms and conditions of any class of licence for the importation into Canada, exportation from Canada, production, packaging, sale, provision or administration of any substance included in Schedule I, II, III, IV, V or VI or any class thereof;

(d) respecting the issuance, suspension, cancellation, duration and terms and conditions of any permit for the importation into Canada, exportation from Canada or production of a specified quantity of a substance included in Schedule I, II, III, IV, V or VI or any class thereof;

(e) prescribing the fees payable on application for any of the licences or permits provided for in paragraphs (c) and (d);

(f) respecting the method of production, preservation, testing, packaging or storage of any controlled substance or precursor or any class thereof;

(g) respecting the premises, processes or conditions for the production or sale of any controlled substance or any class thereof, and deeming such premises, processes or conditions to be or not to be suitable for the purposes of the regulations;

(h) respecting the qualifications of persons who are engaged in the production, preservation, testing, packaging, storage, selling, providing or otherwise dealing in any controlled substance or precursor or any class thereof and who do so under the supervision of a person licensed under the regulations to do any such thing;

(i) prescribing standards of composition, strength, concentration, potency, purity or quality or any other property of any controlled substance or precursor;

(j) respecting the labelling, packaging, size, dimensions, fill and other specifications of packages used for the importation into Canada, exportation from Canada, sending, transportation, delivery, sale or provision of or other dealing in any substance included in Schedule I, II, III, IV, V or VI or any class thereof;

(k) respecting the distribution of samples of any substance included in Schedule I, II, III, IV, V or VI or any class thereof;

(l) controlling and limiting the advertising for sale of any controlled substance or precursor or any class thereof;

(m) respecting the records, books, electronic data or other documents in respect of controlled substances and precursors that are required to be kept and provided by any person or class of persons who imports into Canada, exports from Canada, produces, packages, sends, transports, delivers, sells, provides, administers, possesses, obtains or otherwise deals in any controlled substance or precursor or any class thereof;

(n) respecting the qualifications for inspectors and their powers and duties in relation to the enforcement of, and compliance with, the regulations;

(o) respecting the qualifications for analysts and their powers and duties;

(p) respecting the detention and disposal of or otherwise dealing with any controlled substance;

(q) respecting the disposal of or otherwise dealing with any precursor;

(r) respecting the taking of samples of substances under paragraph 31(1)(h);

(s) respecting the communication of any information obtained under this Act or the regulations from or relating to any person or class of persons who is or may be authorized to import into Canada, export from Canada, produce, package, send, transport, deliver, sell, provide, administer, possess, obtain or otherwise deal in any controlled substance or precursor or any class thereof

    (i) to any provincial professional licensing authority, or

(ii) to any person or class of persons where, in the opinion of the Governor in Council, it is necessary to communicate that information for the proper administration or enforcement of this Act or the regulations;

(t) respecting the making, serving, filing and manner of proving service of any notice, order, report or other document required or authorized under this Act or the regulations;

(u) prescribing the circumstances in which an order made under subsection 41(3) may be revoked by the Minister pursuant to subsection 42(4);

(v) prescribing forms for the purposes of this Act or the regulations;

(w) establishing classes or groups of controlled substances or precursors;

(x) conferring powers or imposing duties and functions on adjudicators in relation to hearings conducted and determinations made by them under Part V;

(y) governing the practice and procedure of hearings conducted and determinations made by adjudicators under Part V;

(z) exempting, on such terms and conditions as may be specified in the regulations, any person or class of persons or any controlled substance or precursor or any class thereof from the application of this Act or regulations; and

(z.1) prescribing anything that, by this Act, is to be or may be prescribed.

(2) Regulations pertaining to law enforcement — The Governor in Council, on the recommendation of the Solicitor General of Canada, may make regulations that pertain to investigations and other law enforcement activities conducted under this Act by a member of a police force and other persons acting under the direction and control of a member and, without restricting the generality of the foregoing, may make regulations

(a) authorizing the Solicitor General of Canada, or the provincial minister responsible for policing in a province, to designate a police force within the Solicitor General's jurisdiction or the minister's jurisdiction, as the case may be, for the purposes of this subsection;

(b) exempting, on such terms and conditions as may be specified in the regulations, a member of a police force that has been designated pursuant to paragraph (a) and other persons acting under the direction and control of the member from the application of any provision of Part I or the regulations;

(c) respecting the issuance, suspension, cancellation, duration and terms and conditions of a certificate, other document or, in exigent circumstances, an approval to obtain a certificate or other document, that is issued to a member of a police force that has been designated pursuant to paragraph (a) for the purpose of exempting the member from the application of this Act or the regulations;

(d) respecting the detention, storage, disposal or otherwise dealing with any controlled substance or precursor;

(e) respecting records, reports, electronic data or other documents in respect of a controlled substance or precursor that are required to be kept and provided by any person or class of persons; and

(f) prescribing forms for the purposes of the regulations.

(3) Incorporation by reference — Any regulations made under this Act incorporating by reference a classification, standard, procedure or other specification may incorporate the classification, standard, procedure or specification as amended from time to time, and, in such a case, the reference shall be read accordingly.

56. Exemption by Minister — The Minister may, on such terms and conditions as the Minister deems necessary, exempt any person or class of persons or any controlled substance or precursor or any class thereof from the application of all or any of the provisions of this Act or the regulations if, in the opinion of the Minister, the exemption is necessary for a medical or scientific purpose or is otherwise in the public interest.

57. Powers, duties and functions of Minister or Solicitor General of Canada — Any power, duty or function of

    (a) the Minister under this Act or the regulations, or

    (b) the Solicitor General of Canada under the regulations

may be exercised or performed by any person designated, or any person occupying a position designated, by the Minister or the Solicitor General, as the case may be, for that purpose.

58. Paramountcy of this Act and the regulations — In the case of any inconsistency or conflict between this Act or the regulations made under it, and the *Food and Drugs Act* or the regulations made under that Act, this Act and the regulations made under it prevail to the extent of the inconsistency or conflict.

59. Offence of making false or deceptive statements — No person shall knowingly make, or participate in, assent to or acquiesce in the making of, a false or misleading statement in any book, record, return or other document however recorded, required to be maintained, made or furnished pursuant to this Act or the regulations.

Amendments to Schedules

60. Schedules — The Governor in Council may, by order, amend any of Schedules I to VIII by adding to them or deleting from them any item or portion of an item, where the Governor in Council deems the amendment to be necessary in the public interest.

PART VII — TRANSITIONAL PROVISIONS, CONSEQUENTIAL AMENDMENTS, REPEAL AND COMING INTO FORCE

Transitional Provisions

61. References to prior enactments — Any reference in a designation by the Solicitor General of Canada under Part VI of the *Criminal Code* to an offence contrary to the *Narcotic Control Act* or Part III or IV of the *Food and Drugs Act* or any conspiracy or attempt to commit or being an accessory after the fact or any counselling in relation to such an offence shall be deemed to be a reference to an offence contrary to section 5 (trafficking), 6 (importing and exporting), 7 (production), 8 (possession of property obtained by certain offences) or 9 (laundering proceeds of certain offences) of this Act, as the case may be, or a conspiracy or attempt to commit or being an accessory after the fact or any counselling in relation to such an offence.

62. (1) Sentences for prior offences — Subject to subsection (2), where, before the coming into force of this Act, a person has committed an offence under the *Narcotic Control Act* or Part III or IV of the *Food and Drugs Act* but a sentence has not been imposed on the person for that offence, a sentence shall be imposed on the person in accordance with this Act.

(2) **Application of increased punishment** — Where any penalty, forfeiture or punishment provided by the *Narcotic Control Act* or section 31 or Part III or IV of the *Food and Drugs Act*, as those Acts read immediately before the coming into force of sections 4 to 9 of this Act, is varied by this Act, the lesser penalty, forfeiture or punishment applies in respect of any offence that was committed before the coming into force of those sections.

63. **Validation** — Every authorization issued by the Minister under subsection G.06.001(1) or J.01.033(1) of the *Food and Drug Regulations* or subsection 68(1) of the *Narcotic Control Regulations* before the coming into force of sections 78 and 90 of this Act is hereby declared to have been validly issued and every such authorization that is in force on the coming into force of sections 78 and 90 of this Act shall continue in force under this Act until it is revoked, as if it were an exemption made under section 56 of this Act.

. . . . .

Repeal

Narcotic Control Act

94. **Repeal of R.S., c. N-1** — The *Narcotic Control Act* is repealed.

Coming into Force

95. **Coming into force** — This Act or any of its provisions comes into force on a day or days to be fixed by order of the Governor in Council.

Schedule I
(Sections 2 to 7, 29, 55 and 60)

1. Opium Poppy (Papaver somniferum), its preparations, derivatives, alkaloids and salts, including:

(1) Opium

(2) Codeine (methylmorphine)

(3) Morphine (7,8-didehydro-4,5-epoxy-17-methylmorphinan -3,6-diol)

(4) Thebaine (paramorphine),

and the salts, derivatives and salts of derivatives of substances set out in subitems (1) to (4), including:

(5) Acetorphine (acetyletorphine)

(6) Acetyldihydrocodeine (4,5-epoxy-3-methoxy-17-methylmorphinan-6 -ol acetate)

(7) Benzylmorphine (7,8-didehydro-4,5-epoxy-17-methyl-3 -(phenylmethoxy) morphinan-6-ol)

(8) codoxime (dihydrocodeinone O-(carboxymethyl) oxime)

(9) Desomorphine (dihydrodeoxymorphine)

(10) Diacetylmorphine (heroin)

(11) Dihydrocodeine (4,5-epoxy-3-methoxy-17-methylmorphinan-6 -ol)

(12) Dihydromorphine (4,5-epoxy-17-methylmorphinan-3,6-diol)

(13) Ethylmorphine (7,8-didehydro-4,5-epoxy-3-ethoxy-17 -methylmorphinan-6-ol)

(14) Etorphine (tetrahydro-7α-(1-hydroxy-1-methylbutyl) -6,14-endo-ethenooripavine)

(15) Hydrocodone (dihydrocodeinone)

(16) Hydromorphinol (dihydro-14-hydroxymorphine)

(17) Hydromorphone (dihydromorphinone)

(18) Methyldesorphine (δ6-deoxy-6-methylmorphine)

(19) Methyldihydromorphine (dihydro-6-methylmorphine)

(20) Metopon (dihydromethylmorphinone)

(21) Morphine-N-oxide (morphine oxide)

(22) Myrophine (benzylmorphine myristate)

(23) Nalorphine (N-allylnormorphine)

(24) Nicocodine (6-nicotinylcodeine)

(25) Nicomorphine (dinicotinylmorphine)

(26) Norcodeine (N-desmethylcodeine)

(27) Normorphine (N-desmethylmorphine)

(28) Oxycodone (dihydrohydroxycodeinone)

(29) Oxymorphone (dihydrohydroxymorphinone)

(30) Pholcodine (3-[2-(4-morphonlinyl)ethylmorphine)

(31) Thebacon (acetyldihydrocodeinone)
but not including:

(32) Apomorphine (5,6,6a,7-tetrahydro-6-methyl-4H-dibenzo[de,g] quinoline-10,11-diol)

(33) Cyprenorphine (N-(cyclopropylmethyl)-6,7,8,14-tetrahydro-7α -(1-hydroxy-1-methylethyl)-6,14-endo -ethenonororipavine)

(34) Naloxone (4,5α-epoxy-3,14-dihydroxy-17-(2-pr openyl)morphinan-6-one)

(34.1) Naltrexone (17-(cycloproplmethyl)-4,5α-epoxy-3,14-dihydroxymorphinan-6-one)

(35) Narcotine (6,7-dimethoxy-3-(5,6,7,8-tetrahydro-4-me thoxy-6-methyl-1,3-dioxolos [4,5-g]isoquinolin-5-yl)-1(3H)-isobenzofuranone)

(36) Papaverine (1-[(3,4-dimethoxyphenyl)methyl]-6,7-dimethoxyisoquinoline)

(37) Poppy seed

SOR/97-230

2. Coca (Erythroxylon), its preparations, derivatives, alkaloids and salts, including:

(1) Coca leaves

(2) Cocaine (benzoylmethylecgonine)

(3) Ecgonine (3-hydroxy-2-tropane carboxylic acid)

3. Phenylpiperidines, their intermediates, salts, derivatives and analogues and salts of intermediates, derivatives and analogues, including:

(1) Allylprodine (3-allyl-1-methyl-4-phenyl-4-piperidinol propionate)

(2) Alphameprodine (α-3-ethyl-1-methyl-4-phenyl- 4-piperidinol propionate)

(3) Alphaprodine (α-1,3-dimethyl-4-phenyl-4-piperidi nolpropionate)

(4) Anileridine (ethyl 1-[2-(p-aminophenyl)ethyl]-4-phenylpiperidine -4-carboxylate)

(5) Betameprodine (β-3-ethyl-1-methyl-4-phenyl-4-piperidinol propionate)

(6) Betaprodine (β-1,3-dimethyl-4-phenyl-4-piperidinol propionate)

(7) Benzethidine (ethyl 1-(2-benzyloxyethyl)-4-phenyl-piperidine- 4-carboxylate)

(8) Diphenoxylate (ethyl 1-(3-cyano-3,3-diphenyl-propyl)-4-p henylpiperidine-4-carboxylate)

(9) Difenoxin (1-(3-cyno-3,3-diphenylpropyl)-4-phenylpiperidine-4-carboxylate)

(10) Etoxeridine (ethyl 1-[2-(2-hydroxyethoxy) ethyl]-4-phenylpiperidine-4-carboxylate)

(11) Farethidine (ethyl 1-(2-tetrahydrofurfury loxyethyl)-4-phenylpiperidine-4-carboxylate)

(12) Hydroxypethidine (ethyl 4-(m-hydroxyphenyl)-1-methylpiperidine-4- carboxylate)

(13) Ketobemidone (1-[4-(m-hydroxyphenyl)-1-methyl-4- piperidyl]-1-propanone)

(14) Methylphenylisonipecotonitrile (4-cyano-1-methyl-4-phenylpiperidine)

(15) Morpheridine (ethyl 1-(2-morpholinoethyl)-4-phenylpiperidine-4 -carboxylate)

(16) Norpethidine (ethyl 4-phenylpiperidine-4-carboxylate)

(17) Pethidine (ethyl 1-methyl-4-phenylpiperidine-4-carboxylate)

(18) Phenoperidine (ethyl 1-(3-hydroxy-3-phenylpropyl)-4-phenylpipe ridine-4-carboxylate)

(19) Piminodine (ethyl 1-[3-(phenylamino)propyl]-4-phenylpiperidine-4 -carboxylate)

(20) Properidine (isopropyl 1-methyl-4-phenylpiperidine-4-carboxylate)

(21) Trimeperidine (1,2,5-trimethyl-4-phenyl-4-piperidinol propionate)

(22) Pethidine Intermediate C (1-methyl-4-phenylpiperidine-4-4-carboxylate)
but not including

(23) Carbomethidine (ethyl 1-(2-carbamylethyl-4-phen ylpiperidine-4-carboxylate)

(24) Oxpheneridine (ethyl 1-(2-hydroxy-2-phenyl ethyl)-4-phenylpiperidine-4-carboxylate)

SOR/97-230

4. Phenazepines, their salts, derivatives and salts of derivatives including:

(1) Proheptazine (hexahydro-1,3-dimethyl-4-phenyl-1H-azepi n-4-ol propionate)
but not including

(2) Ethoheptazine (ethyl hexahydro-1-methyl-4-phenyl-azepine-4 -carboxylate)

(3) Metethoheptazine (ethyl hexahydro-1,3-dimethyl-4-phenylazepine-4- carboxylate)

(4) Metheptazine (ethyl hexahydro-1,2-dimethyl-4-phenylazepine-4- carboxylate)

SOR/97-230

5. Amidones, their intermediates, salts, derivatives and salts of intermediates and derivatives including:

(1) Dimethylaminodiphenylbutanonitrile (4-cyano-2-dimethylamino-4,4-4-diphenylbu tane)

(2) Dipipanone (4,4-diphenyl-6-piperidino-3-heptanone)

(3) Isomethadone (6-dimethylamino-5-methyl-4,4-diphenyl-3 -hexanone)

(4) Methadone (6-dimethylamino-4,4-diphenyl-3-heptanone)

(5) Normethadone (6-dimethylamino-4,4-diphenyl-3-hexanone)

(6) Norpipanone (4,4-diphenyl-6-piperidino-3-hexanone)

(7) Phenadoxone (6-morpholino-4,4-diphenyl-3-heptanone)

6. Methadols, their salts, derivatives and salts of derivatives including:

(1) Acetylmethadol (6-dimethylamino-4,4-diphenyl-3-heptanyl acetate)

(2) Alphacetylmethadol (α-6-dimethylamino-4,4-diphenyl-3-heptanol acetate)

(3) Alphamethadol (α-6-dimethylamino-4,4-diphenyl-3-h eptanol)

(4) Betacetylmethadol (β-6-dimethylamino-4,4-diphenyl-3-he ptanol acetate)

(5) Betamethadol (β-6-dimethylamino-4,4-diphenyl-3-he ptanol)

(6) Dimepheptanol (6-dimethylamino-4,4-diphenyl-3-heptanol)

(7) Noracymethadol (α-6-methylamino-4,4-diphenyl-3-hep tanol acetate)

SOR/97-230

7. Phenalkoxams, their salts, derivatives and salts of derivatives including:

(1) Dimenoxadol (dimethylaminoethyl 1-ethoxy-1,1-diphenylacetate)

(2) Dioxaphetyl butyrate (ethyl 2,2-diphenyl-4-morpholinobutyrate)

(3) Dextropropoxyphene ([S-(R*,S*)]-α-[2-(di-methylamino)- 1-methylethyl]-α-phenylbenzeneethanol, propanoate ester)

SOR/97-230

8. Thiambutenes, their salts, derivatives and salts of derivatives including:

(1) Diethylthiambutene (N,N-diethyl-1-methyl-3,3-di-2-thienylallylamine)

(2) Dimethylthiambutene (N,N,1-trimethyl-3,3-di-2-thienylallylamine)

(3) Ethylmethylthiambutene (N-ethyl-N,1-dimethyl-3,3-di-2-thie nylallylamine)

9. Moramides, their intermediates, salts, derivatives and salts of intermediates and derivatives including:

(1) Dextromoramide (d-1-(3-methyl-4-morpholino-2,2-diphenylbutyryl)pyrrolidine)

(2) Diphenylmorpholinoisovaleric acid (2-methyl-3-morpholino-1,1-diphenylpropionic acid)

(3) Levomoramide (1-1-(3-methyl-4-morpholino-2,2-diphenylbutyryl)pyrrolidine)

(4) Racemoramide (d,1-1-(3-methyl-4-morpholino-2,2-diphenylbutyryl) pyrrolidine)

10. Morphinans, their salts, derivatives and salts of derivatives including:

(1) Buprenorphine (17-(cyclopropylmethyl)-α-(1,1-dimethylethyl) -4,5-epoxy-18,19-dihydro-3-hydroxy- 6-methoxy-α-methyl-6,14-ethenomorphinan -7-methanol)

(2) Drotebanol (6β,14-dihydroxy-3,4-dimethoxy-17-methylmo rphinan)

(3) Levomethorphan (1-3-methoxy-17-methylmorphinan)

(4) Levorphanol (1-3-hydroxy-17-methylmorphinan)

(5) Levophenacylmorphan (1-3-hydroxy-17-phenacylmorphinan

(6) Norlevorphanol (1-3-hydroxymorphinan)

(7) Phenomorphan (3-hydroxy-17-(2-phenylethyl) morphinan)

(8) Racemethorphan (d,1-3-methoxy-17-methylmorphinan)

(9) Racemorphan (d,l-3-hydroxy-N-methylmorphinan)

(10) Dextromethorphan (d-1,2,3,9,10,10a-hexahydro-6-methoxy-11- methyl-4H-10,4a-iminoethano-phenanthren)

(11) Dextrorphan (d-1,2,3,9,10,10a-hexahydro-11-methyl-4H- 10,4a-iminoethanophenanthren-6-ol)

(12) Levallorphan (1-11-allyl-1,2,3,9,10,10a-hexahydro-4H-10,4a-iminoethanophenanthren-6-ol)

(13) Levangorphan (1-11-propargyl-1,2,3,9,10,10a-hexahydro-4H -10,4a-iminoethanophenanthren-6-ol)

(14) Butorphanol (17-(cyclobutylmethyl)morphinan-3,14-diol)

(15) Nalbuphine (17-(cyclobutylmethyl)-4,5α-epoxy-morphinan -3,6α, 14-triol)

SOR/97-230

11. Benzazocines, their salts, derivatives and salts of derivatives including:

(1) Phenazocine (1,2,3,4,5,6-hexahydro-6,11-dimethyl-3-phenethyl-2,6-methano-3-benzazocin-8-ol)

(2) Metazocine (1,2,3,4,5,6-hexahydro-3,6,11-trimethyl-2,6-methano-3-benzazocin-8-ol)

(3) Pentazocine (1,2,3,4,5,6-hexahydro-6,11-dimethyl-3-(3 -methyl-2-butenyl)-2,6-methano-3-be nzazocin-8-ol)

but not including

(4) Cyclazocine (1,2,3,4,5,6-hexahydro-6,11-dimethyl-3-(cyclopropylmethyl)-2, 6-methano-3-benzazocin-8-ol)

12. Ampromides, their salts, derivatives and salts of derivatives including:

(1) Diampromide (N-[2-(methylphenethylamino) propyl] propionanilide)

(2) Phenampromide (N-(1-methyl-2-piperidino) ethyl) propionanilide)

(3) Propiram (N-(1-methyl-2-piperidinoethyl)-N-2 -pyridylpropionamide)

13. Benzimidazoles, their salts, derivatives and salts of derivatives including:

(1) Clonitazene (2-(p-chlorobenzyl)-1-diethylaminoethyl-5 -nitrobenzimidazole)

(2) Etonitazene (2-(p-ethoxybenzyl)-1-diethylaminoethyl-5 -nitrobenzimidazole)

(3) Bezitramide (1-(3-cyano-3,3-diphenylpropyl)-4-(2 -oxo-3-propionyl-1-benzimidazolinyl)-pipe ridine)

14. Phencyclidine (1-(1-phenylcyclohexyl)piperidine), its salts, derivatives and analogues and salts of derivatives and analogues

15. Piritramide (1-(3-cyano-3,3-diphenylpropyl)-4-(1 -piperidino)piperidine-4-carboxylic acid amide), its salts, derivatives and salts of derivatives

16. Fentanyls, their salts, derivatives, and analogues and salts of derivatives and analogues, including:

(1) Acetyl-α-methylfentanyl (N-[1-(α-methylphenethyl)-4-piperidyl] acetanilide)

(2) Alfentanil (N-[1-[2-(4-ethyl-4,5-dihydro-5 -oxo-1H-tetrazol-1-yl)ethyl]-4-(methoxymethyl)-4-piperidyl]propionanilide)

(3) Carfentanil (methyl 4-[(1-oxopropyl)phenylamino]-1-(2-phenethyl) -4-piperidinecarboxylate)

(4) p-Fluorofentanyl (4'fluoro-N-(1-phenethyl-4-piperidyl) propionanilide)

(5) Fentanyl (N-(1-phenethyl-4-piperidyl) propionanilide)

(6) β-Hydroxyfentanyl (N-[1-(β-hydroxyphenethyl)-4-piperidyl] propionanilide)

(7) β-Hydroxy-3-methylfentanyl (N-[1-(β-hydroxyphenethyl)-3-methyl- 4-piperidyl] propionanilide)

(8) α-Methylfentanyl (N-[1-(α-methylphenethyl)-4-piperidyl] propionanilide)

(9) α-Methylthiofentanyl (N-[1-[1-methyl-2-(2-thienyl) ethyl]-4-piperidyl] propionanilide)

(10) 3-Methylfentanyl (N-(3-methyl-1-phenethyl-4-piperidyl) propionanilide)

(11)   3-Methylthiofentanyl   (N-[3-methyl-1-[2-(2-thienyl)   ethyl]-4-piperidyl] propionanilide)

(12)   Sufentanil   (N-[4-(methoxymethyl)-1-[2-(2-thienyl)ethyl]-4-piperidyl] propionanilide)

(13) Thiofentanyl (N-[1-[2-(2-thienyl)ethyl]-4-piperidyl]propionilide)

17. Tilidine (ethyl2-(dimethylamino)-1-phenyl-3-cyclohexene -1-carboxylate), its salts, derivatives and salts of derivatives

Schedule II
(Sections 2, 3, 4 to 7, 10, 29, 55 and 60)

1. Cannabis, its preparations, derivatives and similar synthetic preparations, including:

(1) Cannabis resin

(2) Cannabis (marihuana)

(3)   Cannabidiol   (2-[3-methyl-6-(1-methylethenyl)-2-cyclohexen-1-yl]-5-pentyl-1,3-benzenediol)

(4) Cannabinol(3-n-amyl-6,6,9-trimethyl-6-dibenzopyran-1-ol)

(5)   Nabilone   ((±)-trans-3-(1,1-dimethylheptyl)-6,6a,7,8,10,10a-hexahydro-1-hydroxy-6,6-dimethyl-9H-dibenzo[b,d]pyran-9-one)

(6) Pyrahexyl(3-n-hexyl-6,6,9-trimethyl-7,8,9,10-tetrahydro-6-dibenzopyran-1-ol)

(7)   Tetrahydrocannabinol(tetrahydro-6,6,9-trimethyl-3-pentyl-6H-dibenzo[b,d]pyran-1-ol)

but not including

(8) Non-viable Cannabis seed, with the exception of its derivatives

SOR/98-157, s. 1

Schedule III
(Sections 2 to 7, 29, 55 and 60)

1. Amphetamines, their salts, derivatives, isomers and analogues and salts of derivatives, isomers and analogues including:

(1) amphetamine (α-methylbenzeneethanamine)

(2) methamphetamine (N,α-dimethylbenzeneethanamine)

(3) N-ethylamphetamine (N-ethyl-α-methylbenzeneethanamine)

(4)   4-methyl-2,5-dimethoxyamphetamine   (STP)   (2,5-dimenthoxy-4,α-dimethylbenzeneethanamine)

(5)   3,4-methylenedioxyamphetamine   (MDA)   (α-methyl-1,3-benzodioxide-5-ethanamine)

(6) 2,5-dimethoxyamphetamine (2,5-dimethoxy-α-methylbenzeneethanamine)

(7) 4-methoxyamphetamine (4-methoxy-α-methylbenzeneethanamine)

(8) 2,4,5-trimethoxyamphetamine (2,4,5-trimethoxy-α-methylbenzeneethanamine)

(9) N-methyl-3,4-methylenedioxyamphetamine (N,α-dimethyl-1,3-benzodioxole-5-ethanamine)

(10) 4-ethoxy-2,5-dimethoxyamphetamine(4-ethoxy-2,5-dimethoxy-α-methylbenzeneethanamine)

(11) 5-methoxy-3,4-methylenedioxyamphetamine (7-methoxy-α-methyl-1,3-benzodioxole-5-ethanamine)

(12) N,N-dimethyl-3,4-methylenedioxyamphetamine (N,N,α-trimethyl-1,3-benzodioxole-5-ethanamine)

(13) N-ethyl-3,4-methylenedioxyamphetamine (N-ethyl-α-methyl-1,3-benzodioxole-5-ethanamine)

(14) 4-ethyl-2,5-dimethoxyamphetamine (DOET)(4-ethyl-2,5-dimethoxy-α-methylbenzeneethanamine)

(15) 4-bromo-2,5-dimethoxyamphetamine (4-bromo-2,5-dimethoxy-α-methylbenzeneethanamine)

(16) 4-chloro-2,5-dimethoxyamphetamine (4-chloro-2,5-dimethoxy-α-methylbenzeneethanamine)

(17) 4-ethoxyamphetamine (4-ethoxy-α-methyl-benzeneethanamine)

(18) Benzphetamine (N-benzyl-N,α-dimethylbenzeneethanamine)

(19) N-Propyl-3,4-methylenedioxyamphetamine (α-methyl-N-propyl-1,3-benzodioxole-5-ethanamine

(20) N-(2-Hydroxyethyl)-α-methylbenzeneethanamine

SOR/97-230

2. Methylphenidate (α-phenyl-2-piperidineacetic acid methyl ester) and any salt thereof

SOR/97-230

3. Methaqualone (2-methyl-3-(2-methylphenyl)-4(3H)-quinazolinone) and any salt thereof

4. Mecloqualone (2-methyl-3-(2-chlorophenyl)-4(3H)-quinazolinone) and any salt thereof

5. Lysergic acid diethylamide (LSD) (N,N-diethyllysergamide) and any salt thereof

6. N,N-Diethyltryptamine (DET) (3-[(2-diethylamino) ethyl]indole) and any salt thereof

7. N,N-Dimethyltryptamine (DMT) (3-[(2-dimethylamino)ethyl]indole) and any salt thereof

8. N-Methyl-3-piperidyl benzilate (LBJ) (3-[(hydroxydiphenylacetyl)oxy]-1-methylpiperidine) and any salt thereof

9. Harmaline (4,9-dihydro-7-methoxy-1-methyl-3H- pyrido(3,4-b)indole) and any salt thereof

10. Harmalol (4,9-dihydro-1-methyl-3H-pyrido (3,4-b)indol-7-ol) and any salt thereof

11. Psilocin (3-[2-(dimethylamino)ethyl]-4-hydroxyindole) and any salt thereof

12. Psilocybin (3-[2-(dimethylamino)ethyl]-4-phosphoryloxyindole) and any salt thereof

13. N-(1-phenylcyclohexyl)ethylamine (PCE) and any salt thereof

14. 1-[1-(2-Thienyl) cyclohexyl]piperidine (TCP) and any salt thereof

15. 1-Phenyl-N-propylcyclohexanamine and any salt thereof

16. 1-(1-Phenylcyclohexyl)pyrrolidine and any salt thereof

17. Mescaline (3,4,5-trimethoxybenzeneethanamine) and any salt thereof, but not peyote (lophophora)

18. 4-Methylaminorex (4,5-dihydro-4-methyl-5-phenyl-2-oxazolamine) and any salt thereof

19. Cathinone ((-)-α-aminopropiophenome) and any salt thereof

20. Fenetylline (d,1-3,7-dihydro-1,3-dimethyl-7-(2- [(1-methyl-2-phenethyl)amino]ethyl)-1H-purine -2, 6-dione) and any salt thereof

21. 2-Methylamino-1-phenyl-1-propanone and any salt thereof

22. 1-[1-(Phenylmethyl)cyclohexyl]piperidine and any salt thereof

23. 1-[1-(4-Methylphenyl)cyclohexyl]piperidine and any salt thereof

24. 4-bromo-2,5-dimethoxybenezeneethanamine and any salt, isomer or salt of isomer therof

SOR/97-230

25. Flunitrazepam (5-(o-fluorophenyl)-1,3-dihydro-1-methyl-7-nitro-2H-1,4-benzodiazepin-2-one)

SOR/98-173

26. 4-hydroxybutanoic acit (GHB) and any salf thereof

SOR/98-173

Schedule IV

(Sections 2 to 4, 5 to 7, 29, 55 and 60)

1. Barbiturates, their salts and derivatives including

(1) Allobarbital (5,5-diallylbarbituric acid)

(2) Alphenal (5-allyl-5-phenylbarbituric acid)

(3) Amobarital (5-ethyl-5-(3-methylbutyl) barbituric acid)

(4) Aprobarbital (5-allyl-5-isopropylbarbituric acid)

(5) Barbital (5,5-diethylbarbituric acid)

(6) Barbituric Acid (2,4,6(1H,3H,5H)-pyrimidinetrione)

(7) Butabarbital (5-sec-butyl-5-ethylbarbituric acid)

(8) Butalbital (5-allyl-5-isobutylbarbituric acid)

(9) Butallylonal (5-(2-bromoallyl)-5-sec-butylbarbituric acid)

(10) Butethal (5-butyl-5-ethylbarbituric acid)

(11) Cyclobarbital (5-(1-cyclohexen-1-yl)-5-ethylbarbituric acid)

(12) Cyclopal (5-allyl-5-(2-cyclopenten-1-yl)barbituric acid

(13) Heptabarbital (5-(1-cyclohepten-1-yl)-5-ethylbarbituric acid)

(14) Hexethal (5-ethyl-5-hexylbarbituric acid)

(15) Hexobarbital (5-(1-cyclohexen-1-yl)-1,5-dimethylbarbituric acid)

(16) Mephobarbital (5-ethyl-1-methyl-5-phenylbarbituric acid)

(17) Methabarbital (5,5-diethyl-1-methylbarbituric acid)

(18) Methylphenobarbital (5-ethyl-1-methyl-5-phenylbarbituric acid)

(19) Propallylonal(5-(2-bromoally)-5-isopropylbarbituric acid)

(20) Pentobarbital (5-ethyl-5-(1-methylbutyl)barbituric acid)

(21) Phenobarbital (5-ethyl-5-phenylbarbituric acid)

(22) Probarbital (5-ethyl-5-isopropylbarbituric acid)

(23) Phenylmethylbarbituric Acid (5-methyl-5-phenylbarbituric acid)

(24) Secobarbital (5-allyl-5-(1-methylbutyl)barbituric acid)

(25) Sigmodal (5-(2-bromoallyl)-5-(1-methylbutyl)barbituric acid)

(26) Talbutal (5-allyl-5-sec-butylbarbituric acid)

(27) Vinbarbital (5-ethyl-5-(1-methy-1-butenyl)barbituric acid)

(28) Vinylbital (5-(1-methylbutyl)-5-vinylbarbituric acid)

2. Thiobarbiturates, their salts and derivatives including:

(1) Thialbarbital (5-allyl-5-(2-cyclohexen-1-yl)-2-thiobarbituric acid)

(2) Thiamylal (5-allyl-5-(1-methylbutyl)-2-thiobarbituric acid)

(3) Thiobarbituric Acid (2-thiobarbituric acid)

(4) Thiopental (5-ethyl-5-(1-methylbutyl)-2-thiobarbituric acid)

3. Chlorphentermine (1-(p-chlorophenyl)-2-methyl-2-aminopropane) and any salt thereof

4. Diethylpropion (2-(diethylamino)propiophenone) and any salt thereof

5. Phendimetrazine (d-3,4-dimethyl-2-phenylmorpholine) and any salt thereof

6. Phenmetrazine (3-methyl-2-phenylmorpholine) and any salt thereof

7. Pipradol (α,α-diphenyl-2-piperidinemethanol) and any salt thereof

8. Phentermine (α,α-dimethylbenzeneethanamine) and any salt thereof

9. Butorphanol (1-N-cyclobutylmethyl-3,14-dihydroxymorphinan) and any salt thereof

10. Nalbuphine (N-cyclobutylmethyl-4,5-epoxy-morphinan-3,6,14-triol) and any salt thereof

11. Glutethiamide (2-ethyl-2-phenylglutarimide)

12. Clotiazepam (5-(o-chlorophenyl)-7-ethyl-1,3-dihydro-1-methyl-2H-thieno[2,3-e]-1,4-diazepin-2-one) and any salt thereof

SOR/97-230

13. Ethchlorvynol (ethyl-2-chlorovinyl ethynyl carbinol)

14. Ethinamate (1-ethynylcyclohexanol carbamate)

15. Mazindol (5-(p-chlorophenyl)-2,5-dihydro-3H-imidazo[2,1-a]isoindol-5-ol)

16. Meprobamate (2-methyl-2-propyl-1,3-propanediol dicarbonate)

17. Methyprylon (3,3-diethyl-5-methyl-2,4-piperidinedione)

18. Benzodiazepines, their salts and derivatives, including:

(1) Alprazolam (8-chloro-1-methyl-6-phenyl-4H-s-triazolo[4,3-a][1,4] benzodiazepine)

(2) Bromazepam (7-bromo-1,3-dihydro-5-(2-pyridyl)- 2H-1, 4-benzodiazepin-2-one)

(3) Camazepam (7-chloro-1,3-dihydro-3-(N,N-dime=thylcarbamoyl)-1-methyl-5-phenyl-2H-1,4-ben=zodiazepin-2-one)

(4) Chlodiazepoxide(7-chloro-2-(methylamino)-5-phenyl-3H-1,4-benzodiazepine-4-oxide)

(5) Clobazam(7-chloro-1-methyl-5-phenyl-1H-1,5-benzodiazepine-2,4(3H,5H)-dione)

(6) Clonazepam(5-(o-chlorophenyl)-1,3-dihydro-7-nitro-2H-1,4-benzodiazepin-2-one)

(7) Clorazepate(7-chloro-2,3-dihydro-2,2-dihydroxy-5 -phenyl-1H-1,4-benzodiazepine-3-carboxylic acid)

(8) Cloxazolam(10-chloro-11b-(o-chlorophenyl)-2,3,7,11b-tetrahydrooxazolo[3,2-d][1,4]benzodiazepin=6-(5H)-one)

(9) Delorazepam (7-chloro-5-(o-chlorophenyl)-1,3-dihydro-2H-1,4=benzodiazepin-2-one)

(10) Diazepam (7-chloro-1,3-dihydro-1-methyl-5-phenyl-2H-1,4-benzodiazepin-2-one)

(11) Estazolam (8-chloro-6-phenyl-4H-s-triazolo[4,3-a][1,4]benzodiazepine)

(12) Ethyl Loflazepate (ethyl7-chloro-5-(o-flourophenyl)-2,3-dihydro-2-oxo-1H-1,4-benzodiazepine-3-carboxylate)

(13) Fludiazepam(7-chloro-5-(o-flourophenyl)-1,3-dihydro-1-methyl-2H-1,4-benzodiazepin-2-one)

(14) [Repealed SOR/98-173]

(15) Flurazepam(7-chloro-1-[2-(diethylamino)ethyl]-5-(o-flourophenyl)-1,3-dihydro-2H-1,4-benzodiazepin-2-one)

(16) Halazepam(7-chloro-1,3-dihydro-5=phenyl-1-(2,2,2-triflouroethyl)-2H-1,4-benzodiazepin-2-one)

(17) Haloxazolam(10-bromo-11b-(o-flourophenyl)-2,3,7,11b-tetrahydrooxazolo[3,2-d][1,4] benzodiazepin-6(5H)-one)

(18) Ketazolam (11-chloro-8,12b-dihydro-2,8-dimethyl-12b -phenyl-4H-[1,3]-oxazino-[3,2-d][1,4] benzo=diazepine-4,7(6H)-dione)

(19) Loprazolam (6-(o-chlorophenyl)-2,4-dihydro-2-[(4 -methyl-1-piper-azinyl)methylene]-8-nitro- 1H-imidazo[1,2-a][1,4]benzodiazepin-1-one)

(20) Lorazepam (7-chloro-5-(o-chlorophenyl)-1,3-dihydro -3-hydroxy-2H-1,4-benzodiazepin-2-o ne)

(21) Lormetazepam (7-chloro-5(o-chlorophenyl)-1,3-dihydro-3 -hydroxy-1-methyl-2H-1,4-benzodiazepin -2-one)

(22) Medazepam (7-chloro-2,3-dihydro-1-methyl-5-ph enyl-1H-1,4-benzodiazepine)

(23) Nimetazepam (1,3-dihydro-1-methyl-7-nitro-5-phe nyl-2H-1,4-benzodiazepin-2-one)

(24) Nitrazepam (1,3-dihydro-7-nitro-5-phenyl-2H-1, 4-benzodiazepin-2-one)

(25) Nordazepam (7-chloro-1,3-dihydro-5-phenyl-(2H-1,4-benzodiazepin-2-one)

(26) Oxazepam (7-chloro-1,3-dihydro-3-hydroxy-5-p henyl-2H-1,4-benzodiazepin-2-one)

(27) Oxazolam (10-chloro-2,3,7,11b-tetrahydro-2-methyl- 11b-phenyloxazolo[3,2-d][1,4]benzodiazepin-6(5H)-one)

(28) Pinazepam (7-chloro-1,3-dihydro-5-phenyl-1-(2 -propynyl)-2H-1, 4-benzodiazepin-2-one)

(29) Prazepam (7-chloro-1-(cyclopropylmethyl)-1,3-dihydro -5-phenyl-2H-1,4-benzodiazepin-2-one)

(30) Temazepam (7-chloro-1,3-dihydro-3-hydroxy-1-methyl-5-phenyl-2H-1,4-benzodiazepin-2=one

(31) Tetrazepam (7-chloro-5-(cyclohexen-1-yl)-1,3-dihdyro-1-methyl-2H-1,4-benzodiazepin-2-one)

(32) Triazolam (8-chloro-6-(o-chlorophenyl)-1-methyl -4H-s-triazolo[4,3-a][1,4]benzodiazepine)

(33)   Flunitrazepam   (5-(o-flurophenyl)-1,3-dihydro-1-methyl-7-nitro-2H-1,4-
benzodiazepin-2-one)

SOR/97-230; 98-173

19. Catha edulis Forsk., its preparations, derivatives, alkaloids and salts, including:

(1) Cathine (d-threo-2-amino-1-hydroxy-1-phenylpropane)

20. Fencamfamin (d,1-N-ethyl-3-phenylbicyclo[2,2,1] heptan-2-amine) and any salt thereof

21. Fenproporex (d,1-3-[(α-methylphenethyl)amino] propionitrile) and my salt thereof

22. Mefenorex (d,1-N-(3-chloropropyl)-α-methylbenzeneethanamine) and any salt thereof

23. Anabolic steroids and their derivatives including:

(1) Androisoxazole (17β-hydroxy-17α-methylandrostano [3,2-c]isoxazole)

(2) Androstanolone (17β-hydroxy-5α-androstan-3-one)

(3) Androstenediol (androst-5-ene-3β,17β-diol)

(4) Bolandiol (estr-4-ene-3β,17β-diol)

(5) Bolasterone (17β-hydroxy-7α,17-dimethylandrost-4 -en-3-one)

(6) Bolazine (17β-hydroxy-2α-methyl-5α-androstan-3-one azine)

(7) Boldenone (17β-hydroxyandrosta-1,4-dien-3-one)

(8) Bolenol (19-nor-17α-pregn-5-en-17-ol)

(9) Calusterone (17β-hydroxy-7β,17-dimethylandrost-4- en-3-one)

(10) Clostebol (4-chloro-17β-hydroxyandrost-4-en-3 -one)

(11) Drostanolone (17β-hydroxy-2α-methyl-5α-androstan-3-one)

(12) Enestebol (4,17β-dihydroxy-17-methylandrosta-1,4-dien-3-one)

(13) Epitiostanol (2α, 3α-epithio-5α-androstan-17β-ol)

(14) Ethylestrenol (19-nor-17α-pregn-4-en-17-ol)

(15) 4-Hydroxy-19-nor testosterone

(16) Fluoxymesterone (9-fluoro-11β,17β-dihydroxy-17-methylandrost-4-en-3-one)

(17)   Formebolone   (11α,17β-dihydroxy-17-methyl-3-oxoandrosta-1,4   dien-2-
carboxaldehyde)

(18) Furazabol (17-methyl-5α-androstano[2,3-c] furazan-17β-ol)

(19) Mebolazine (17β-hydroxy-2α,17-dimethyl-5α -androstan-3-one azine)

(20) Mesabolone (17β1/n[(1-methoxycyclohexyl)oxy]-5α-androst- 1-en-3-one)

(21) Mesterolone (17β-hydroxy-1α-methyl-5α-androstan-3-one)

(22) Metandienone (17β-hydroxy-17-methylandrosta-1,4-dien -3-one)

(23) Metenolone (17β-hydroxy-1-methyl-5α-androst -1-en-3-one)

(24) Methandriol (17α-methylandrost-5-ene-3β,17β -diol)

(25) Methyltestosterone (17β-hydroxy-17-methylandrost-4-en-3 -one)

(26) Metribolone (17β-hydroxy-17-methylestra-4,9,11-trien -3-one)

(27) Mibolerone (17β-hydroxy-7α,17-dimethylestr-4-en -3-one)

(28) Nandrolone (17β-hydroxyestr-4-en-3-one)

(29) Norboletone (13-ethyl-17β-hydroxy-18,19-dinorpregn -4-en-3-one)

(30) Norclostebol (4-chloro-17β-hydroxyestr-4-en-3 -one)

(31) Norethandrolone (17α-ethyl-17β-hydroxyestr-4-en -3-one)

(32) Oxabolone (4,17β-dihydroxyestr-4-en-3-one)

(33) Oxandrolone (17β-hydroxy-17-methyl-2-oxa-5 α-androstan-3-one)

(34) Oxymesterone (4,17β-dihydroxy-17-methylandrost-4-en -3-one)

(35) Oxymetholone (17β-hydroxy-2-(hydroxymethylene)-17-methyl-5α-androstan-3-one)

(36) Prasterone (3β-hydroxyandrost-5-en-17-one)

(37) Quinbolone (17β-(1-cyclopenten-1-yloxy) androsta-1,4-dien-3-one)

(38) Stanozolol (17β-hydroxy-17-methyl-5α-androstano [3,2-c]pyrazole)

(39) Stenbolone (17β-hydroxy-2-methyl-5α-androst -1-en-3-one)

(40) Testosterone (17β-hydroxyandrost-4-en-3-one)

(41) Tibolone ((7α, 17α)-17-hydroxy-7-methyl-19-norpregn-5 (10)en-20-yn-3-one)

(42) Tiomesterone (1α,7α-bis(acetylthio)-17β-hydroxy-17-methylandrost-4-en-3-one)

(43) Trenbolone (17β-hydroxyestra-4,9,11-trien-3-one)

SOR/97-230

24. Zeranol (3,4,5,6,7,8,9,10,11,12-decahydro-7,14,16- trihydroxy-3-methyl-1H-2-benzoxacyclotetradecin -1- one)

Schedule V
(Sections 2, 4, 6, 55 and 60)

1. Phenylpropanolamine (2-amino-1-phenyl-1-propanol) and any salt thereof

2. Propylhexedrine (1-cyclohexyl-2-methylaminopropane) and any salt thereof

3. Pyrovalerone (1-(1-pyrrolidinyl))butyl p-tolyl ketone and any salt thereof

Schedule VI
(Section 2, 6, 55, and 60)

1. Benzyl methyl ketone (P2P) (1-phenyl-2-propanone)

2. Ephedrine (1-erythro-2-(methylamino)-1-phenylpropan-1-ol)

3. Ergometrine (9,10-didehydro-N-(2-hydroxy-1-methylethy l)-6-methylergoline-8-carboxamide)

4. Ergotamine (12'-hydroxy-2'-methyl-5'-(phenylmethyl) ergotaman-3',6', 18-trione)

5. Lysergic acid (9,10-didehydro-6-methylergoline-8-carboxylic acid)

6. Pseudoephedrine (d-threo-2-(methylamino)-1-phenylpropan-1 -ol)

Schedule VII
(Sections 5 and 60)

1. *Substance*: cannabis resin
Amount: 3kg

2. *Substance*: cannabis (marihuana)
Amount: 3kg

Schedule VIII
(Sections 4 and 60)

1. *Substance*: cannabis resin
Amount: 1g

2. *Substance*: cannabis (marihuana)
Amount: 30g

NARCOTIC CONTROL ACT

An Act to provide for the control of narcotic drugs

R.S.C. 1985, c. N-1, Am. R.S. 1985, c. 27 (1st Supp.), ss. 196–200, 203, 208; c. 27 (2d Supp.), s. 10; c. 42 (4th Supp.), s. 12; 1990, c. 16, s. 18; 1990, c. 17, s. 36; 1992, c. 1, s. 98; 1992, c. 20, ss. 215, 216; 1992, c. 51, s. 59; 1993, c. 28, s. 78 (Sch. III, item 113); 1993, c. 37, ss. 25–29; 1996, c. 8, ss. 32, 35; 1996, c. 16, ss. 60, 62, Repealed 1996, c. 19, s. 94.

[Note: The Narcotic Control Act *is no longer in force. It was repealed by the* Controlled Drugs and Substances Act, *S.C. 1996, c. 19, on May 14, 1997. We have, however, retained the* Narcotic Control Act *because the Act remains of relevance to offences occurring before its repeal (see sections 61 and 62 of the* Controlled Drugs and Substances Act. *It will therefore continue to be of great practical importance for some time to come.]*

See Table of Amendments for coming into force.

Short Title

1. Short title — This Act may be cited as the *Narcotic Control Act.*

R.S., c. N-1, s. 1. repealed 1996, c. 19, s. 94.

Interpretation

2. Definitions — In this Act,

"analyst" means a person designated as an analyst under the *Food and Drugs Act* or this Act;

"conveyance" includes any aircraft, vessel, motor vehicle or other conveyance of any description whatever;

"marihuana" means *Cannabis sativa* L.;

"minister" means

(a) with respect to Part I, the Minister of Health, and

(b) with respect to Part II, the Minister of Justice;

"narcotic" means any substance included in the schedule or anything that contains any substance included in the schedule;

"narcotic addict" means a person who through the use of narcotics,

(a) has developed a desire or need to continue to take a narcotic, or

(b) has developed a psychological or physical dependence upon the effect of a narcotic;

"opium poppy" means *Papaver somniferum* L.;

"possession" means possession as defined in the *Criminal Code*;

"practitioner" means a person who is registered and entitled under the laws of a province to practise in that province the profession of medicine, dentistry or veterinary medicine;

"prescription" means, in respect of a narcotic, an authorization given by a practitioner that a stated amount of the narcotic be dispensed for the person named therein;

"traffic" means

    (a) to manufacture, sell, give, administer, transport, send, deliver or distribute, or

    (b) to offer to do anything referred to in paragraph (*a*)

otherwise than under the authority of this Act or the regulations.

    R.S., c. N-1, s. 2; R.S. 1985, c. 27 (1st Supp.), s. 196; 1996, c. 8, s. 32(1)(j); repealed 1996, c. 19, s. 94.

Case Law

"Marihuana"

Perka v. R. (1984), 42 C.R. (3d) 113, 14 C.C.C. (3d) 385 (S.C.C.); affirming (1982), 69 C.C.C. (2d) 405 (B.C. C.A.) — Where a statutory term does not comprehend a broad category but consists of a scientific or technical word deliberately chosen by the legislature, such as "Cannabis sativa L.", its meaning should be confined to the meaning held by a consensus of the scientific community when the statutory provision was introduced, which in this case was in 1961. The scientific community thought then that there was just one species of cannabis marihuana. Therefore, the term covers all cannabis marihuana and *not* merely that which the scientific community now describes as the species "Cannabis sativa L."

"Narcotic"

R. v. Maskell (1981), 58 C.C.C. (2d) 408 (Alta. C.A.) — The *N.C.A.* does not say that cocaine must come from the coca plant. It makes it an offence to have in one's possession anything that contains any substance included in the schedule and cocaine is included in the schedule.

R. v. Rourke (1980), 54 C.C.C. (2d) 225 (B.C. C.A.) — The scope of s. 4(1) of the Act prohibits trafficking in heroin including synthetically produced heroin derived from synthetically produced morphine.

R. v. Verma (1996), 112 C.C.C. (3d) 155 (Ont. C.A.) — The definition of "narcotic" in s. 2 is exhaustive. It does *not* include a prescription.

Possession [See also Code s. 4]

R. v. Brett (1986), 53 C.R. (3d) 189, 41 C.C.C. (3d) 190 (B.C. C.A.) — Where P has proved possession on the basis of D's statement admitting knowledge and control of the prohibited drug, P does not have to also prove that the quantity of the drug was usable.

"Traffic"

R. v. Eccleston (1975), 24 C.C.C. (2d) 564 (B.C. C.A) — Where D-1 held a knife enabling D-2 to inhale a drug, and they then reversed their positions, both were guilty of administering a drug.

R. v. Taylor (1974), 17 C.C.C. (2d) 36 (B.C. C.A.) — *See also*: *R. v. O'Connor* (1975), 29 C.R.N.S. 100 (B.C. C.A.) — One can "give", "deliver" or "distribute" an object to another regardless of whether that object is owned by the one, another or other or all or none of them. "Distribute" means to deal out, apportion, allot or spread among many.

R. v. Chernecki (1971), 16 C.R.N.S. 230, 4 C.C.C. (2d) 556 (B.C. C.A.) — Where the accused offered to physically procure the narcotic, bring it back and deliver it to another, he had therefore offered to "transport" or "deliver" a narcotic which action constituted trafficking in a narcotic contrary to s. 4(1).

R. v. MacDonald (1963), 41 C.R. 75, (sub nom. *R. v. Harrington*) [1964] 1 C.C.C. 189 — *See also*: *R. v. Young* (1971), 14 C.R.N.S. 372, 2 C.C.C. (2d) 560 (B.C.C.A.); *R. v. Greene* (1976), 33 C.C.C. (2d) 251 (Nfld. C.A.); *R. v. Pappin* (1970), 12 C.R.N.S. 287 (Ont. C.A.); *R. v. Binkley* (1982), 69 C.C.C. (2d) 169 (Sask. C.A.) — The word "transport" is *not* meant in the sense of conveying or carrying or moving a narcotic from one place to another incidental to one's own use, but in the sense of doing so to promote its distribution to another.

R. v. Hurdus (1958), 28 C.R. 18, 120 C.C.C. 392 (B.C. C.A.) — Section 2 refers to an *offer* to do one of the prohibited acts specifically set out in the section, which if done constitutes trafficking. Purchasing is not one of them.

R. v. Christiansen (1973), 23 C.R.N.S. 229, 13 C.C.C. (2d) 504 (N.B. C.A.) — There was no distribution of a narcotic where it was given to one person only for his own use. Distribution means the allocation to a number of persons.

R. v. Verma (1996), 112 C.C.C. (3d) 155 (Ont. C.A.) — A person does *not* "administer" a substance within the definition of "traffic" by giving a person the means to obtain the substance from a third party, as for example, by writing a prescription.

R. v. Rowbotham (1992), 76 C.C.C. (3d) 542 (Ont. C.A.) — An offer or agreement to sell drugs to a police agent comes within the definition of "traffic".

R. v. Daniel (1982), 1 C.C.C. (3d) 101 (Ont. C.A.) — Where D had distilled *cannabis resin* from *cannabis marihuana* for his own use, his conviction for possession for the purpose of trafficking was upheld, for by giving *cannabis marihuana* a new formD was manufacturing, within the definition of trafficking. The fact that the manufacturing was for his own use did not constitute a defence because the *Act* intended to prohibit the creation of a narcotic.

R. v. Rousseau (1991), 70 C.C.C. (3d) 445 (Que. C.A.); leave to appeal refused (1992), 70 C.C.C. (3d) vi (note) (S.C.C.) — "Administer" in s. 2 includes the sale of a prescription by a physician which would permit another to obtain a narcotic for the purpose of making a profit. Such conduct would also amount to "sell" within the section. (per Dubé J.A.)A physician who personally procures a narcotic for another traffics in the narcotic and does not cease to do so if he procures the narcotic for another through the intermediary of an accomplice, an employee or agent, such as a pharmacist. (per Beauregard J.A.)The definition of "traffic" in s. 2 does *not* include "to make available". It specifies certain acts which constitute trafficking. A prescription issued by a physician is merely an authorization, *not* a direction, hence a prescribing physician does *not* traffic in the narcotic prescribed. The pharmacist is *not* the physician's agent. (per McCarthy J.A. dissenting)

R. v. Mancuso (1989), 51 C.C.C. (3d) 380 (Que. C.A.) — An accused who offers to sell narcotics intending to defraud the prospective purchaser commits the offence of trafficking where he intends the offer to be taken seriously.

R. v. Tan (1984), 42 C.R. (3d) 252, 15 C.C.C. (3d) 303 (Sask. C.A.) — The meaning to be given to the word "administer" in s. 2 is the more limited meaning of to apply, as a medicine, or to give remedially, rather than to make drugs available by giving a prescription.

PART I — OFFENCES AND ENFORCEMENT

Particular Offences

3. (1) Possession of narcotic — **Except as authorized by this Act or the regulations, no person shall have a narcotic in his possession.**

(2) Offence and punishment — **Every person who contravenes subsection (1) is guilty of an offence and liable**

> **(a) on summary conviction for a first offence, to a fine not exceeding one thousand dollars or to imprisonment for a term not exceeding six months or to both and, for a subsequent offence, to a fine not exceeding two thousand dollars or to imprisonment for a term not exceeding one year or to both; or**

> **(b) on conviction on indictment, to imprisonment for a term not exceeding seven years.**

R.S., c. N-1, s. 3; 1984, c. 40, s. 79.repealed 1996, c. 19, s. 94.

Case Law

General Principles [See also Code s. 4]

R. v. Land (1981), 22 C.R. (3d) 322, 60 C.C.C. (2d) 118 (B.C. C.A.) — *Cannabis sativa* is defined in the *N.C.A.* as including six substances, each one of which is a narcotic. It is the intention of the Act that unlawful possession of any one of these substances constitutes an offence and unlawful possession of two or more of these substances constitutes two or more separate offences.

R. v. Guiney (1961), 35 C.R. 316, 130 C.C.C. 406 (B.C. C.A.) — Actual physical possession, even though it is only momentary, is sufficient to constitute possession under the Act.

R. v. Hess (No. 1) (1948), 8 C.R. 42, 94 C.C.C. 48 (B.C. C.A.) — To constitute "possession" as regards the criminal law there must be manual handling of the thing co-existent with knowledge of what the thing is and some act of control over the thing (outside of public duty).

R. v. Fudge (1979), 49 C.C.C. (2d) 63 (Nfld. C.A.) — Where D was charged with an indictable offence of possession for the purpose of trafficking and not merely with "simple possession", a finding that D was in possession of a narcotic contrary to s. 3 of the Act is in fact a finding that he was guilty of an indictable offence under s. 3(2)(b).

R. v. Wardley (1978), 11 C.R. (3d) 282, 43 C.C.C. (2d) 345 (Ont. C.A.) — Where D, charged with possession of a narcotic for the purpose of trafficking pleads not guilty to that charge but pleads guilty to the included offence of simple possession, this guilty plea is to the indictable offence of possession. P does not have to elect at this stage whether to proceed summarily or by indictment.

R. v. Rawlyk (1972), 20 C.R.N.S. 188 (Sask. C.A.) — The schedule to the Act distinguishes between cannabis and cannabis resin so that the illegal possession of either of these is a separate and distinct offence.

Constructive Possession [See also Code s. 4]

R. v. Caldwell (1972), 19 C.R.N.S. 293, 7 C.C.C. (2d) 285 (Alta. C.A.) — Where the thing in question is *not* in D's physical possession, to constitute constructive possession D's *knowledge* of the possession by another must extend beyond quiescent knowledge and include some measure of *control* or right of control over the thing. "Consent" within the meaning of the *Code* definition of possession must necessarily mean active concurrence of D in the possession by another, and *not* merely passive acquiescence. An accused to whom *Code* s. 4(3)(b) applies is deemed to be in possession of a thing, even though possession by him as judicially defined (requiring some measure of control over the thing) does not exist.

R. v. Colvin (1942), 78 C.C.C. 282 (B.C. C.A.) — "*Knowledge* and *consent*" in *Code* s. 4(3)(b) cannot exist without the co-existence of some measure of control over the subject matter.

R. v. Fraser (1985), 70 N.S.R. (2d) 82 (C.A.) — Constructive possession requires three basic elements: *knowledge, consent* and *control*.

R. v. Chambers (1985), 9 O.A.C. 228 (C.A.) — Merely consorting with a person in possession of a drug is not by itself knowledge and consent sufficient to constitute joint possession, but would only be sufficient evidence to commit for trial.

Control

R. v. Coull (1986), 33 C.C.C. (3d) 186 (B.C. C.A.) — Possession must include both knowledge and some measure of control.

R. v. Hall (1959), 124 C.C.C. 238 (B.C. C.A.) — Control excludes a casual or hasty manual handling of the substance where the evidence is inconsistent with the handler's use of the substance for his own purposes.

R. v. Martin (1948), 7 C.R. 44, 92 C.C.C. 257 (Ont. C.A.) — Possession necessarily entails a degree of control over the drug. Where an accused had a list of places, at some of which places narcotics were subsequently located, but there was no evidence that he had power over either the narcotics or the places where they were found, D did not have control over them as contemplated by the *Code*.

Knowledge

R. v. Aiello (1978), 38 C.C.C. (2d) 485 (Ont. C.A.); affirmed (1979), 46 C.C.C. (2d) 128 (S.C.C.) — The *knowledge* necessary to constitute the offence of possession is established if it is proved beyond a reasonable doubt that D assumed *control* of a package *knowing* that it contained a *drug*, the trafficking in which was prohibited, or was *wilfully blind* to it being, or *reckless* as to whether it was such a drug.

Knowledge on the part of D need *not* be proved by direct evidence, but may be inferred from the surrounding circumstances.

R. v. Blondin (1970), 2 C.C.C. (2d) 118 (B.C. C.A.); affirmed (1971), 4 C.C.C. (2d) 566n (S.C.C.) — P must prove beyond a reasonable doubt that D *knew* the substance in his/her possession was a narcotic, although not necessarily that he/she knew it was cannabis resin.

Beaver v. R. (1957), 26 C.R. 193, 118 C.C.C. 129 (S.C.C.) — There is in law no possession of a forbidden substance without *knowledge* of the character of the forbidden substance.

R. v. Kelly (1966), 49 C.R. 216, [1967] 1 C.C.C. 215 (B.C. C.A.) — *See also*: *R. v. Larier* (1960), 35 C.R. 61, 129 C.C.C. 297 (Sask. C.A.) — Knowledge, being a state of mind, must be found to exist in the same way as intent, by proper inferences from facts proved.

R. v. Burgess, [1969] 3 C.C.C. 268 (Ont. C.A.) — Where D knew the substance in his possession was a drug, the possession of which was contrary to the statute, the fact that he believed it to be one drug and not another is immaterial.

Quantity

R. v. Quigley (1954), 20 C.R. 152, 111 C.C.C. 81 (Alta. S.C.) — Section 3 does *not* require a certain minimum of the prohibited drug to be found in D's possession.

R. v. McBurney (1974), 26 C.R.N.S. 114, 15 C.C.C. (2d) 361 (B.C. S.C.); affirmed (1975), 24 C.C.C. (2d) 44 (B.C. C.A.) — The possession of a pipe that on an earlier date, but not within the period of the charge, had been used for smoking hashish and contained a minute trace of cannabis resin, did *not* establish present possession.

R. v. Babiak (1974), 21 C.C.C. (2d) 464 (Man. C.A.) — Where there is enough of a drug remaining in a spoon for an analyst to identify it as heroin, that is all the law requires to justify a finding that there is heroin in the spoon.

Evidentiary Issues

R. v. LePage (1995), 36 C.R. (4th) 145 (S.C.C.); reversing (1993), 87 C.C.C. (3d) 43 (Ont. C.A.) — Whether an inference of possession can be drawn from the presence of fingerprints is a question of fact which depends on all the circumstances of the case as revealed by the evidence. A trial judge is entitled to draw an adverse inference from D's failure to offer an explanation for the presence of fingerprints once P has proven a *prima facie* case.

R. v. Risby (1976), 32 C.C.C. (2d) 242 (B.C. C.A.); affirmed (1978), 39 C.C.C. (2d) 567n (S.C.C.) — A statement made by D when he is first found in possession of material relevant to a criminal charge is admissible as part of the *res gestae* and may be introduced by D through cross-examination of the officer to whom it was made.

R. v. Graham (1972), 19 C.R.N.S. 117, 7 C.C.C. (2d) 93 (S.C.C.) — Explanatory statements made by D upon first being found "in possession" constitute a part of the *res gestae* and are necessarily admissible in any description of the circumstances under which the crime was committed.

3.1 (1) Failure to disclose previous prescriptions — No person shall, at any time, seek or obtain a narcotic or a prescription for a narcotic from a practitioner unless that person discloses to the practitioner particulars of every narcotic or prescription for a narcotic issued to that person by a different practitioner within the preceding thirty days.

(2) Offence and punishment — Every person who contravenes subsection (1)

(a) is guilty of an indictable offence and liable to imprisonment for a term not exceeding seven years; or

(b) is guilty of an offence punishable on summary conviction and liable

(i) for a first offence, to a fine not exceeding one thousand dollars or to imprisonment for a term not exceeding six months, and

(ii) for a subsequent offence, to a fine not exceeding two thousand dollars or to imprisonment for a term not exceeding one year.

(3) Limitation period — Summary conviction proceedings in respect of an offence under this section may be instituted at any time within but not later than one year from the time when the subject-matter of the proceedings arose.

R.S. 1985, c. 27 (1st Supp.), s. 197; repealed 1996, c. 19, s. 94.

4. (1) Trafficking — No person shall traffic in a narcotic or any substance represented or held out by the person to be a narcotic.

(2) Possession for purpose of trafficking — No person shall have in his possession any narcotic for the purpose of trafficking.

(3) Offence and punishment — Every person who contravenes subsection (1) or (2) is guilty of an indictable offence and liable to imprisonment for life.

R.S., c. N-1, s. 4.repealed 1996, c. 19, s. 94.

Case Law

Trafficking: S. 4 — Nature and Elements of Offence [See also N.C.A. s. 2]

R. v. Schartner (1977), 38 C.C.C. (2d) 89 (B.C. C.A.) — The aid that is required to constitute aiding in the offence of trafficking is aid to the seller of the narcotic, for the purpose of aiding the seller to sell.

R. v. Sherman (1977), 39 C.R.N.S. 255, 36 C.C.C. (2d) 207 (B.C. C.A.) — Where D is charged with offering to sell and deliver a narcotic to another, the *actus reus* is the making of the offer. The *mens rea* is the intention to make the offer. The fact that D did not intend to go through with the offer is not relevant.

R. v. O'Connor (1975), 29 C.R.N.S. 100, 23 C.C.C. (2d) 110 (B.C. C.A.), application for leave to appeal dismissed (1975), 23 C.C.C. (2d) 110n (S.C.C.) — D who purchases narcotics and transports them from home for use by himself and his spouse is transporting them for use by a second person and is therefore guilty of trafficking and cannot raise the doctrine of conjugal unity as a defence.

R. v. Larson (1972), 18 C.R.N.S. 149, 6 C.C.C. (2d) 145 (B.C. C.A.) — Once D is found to have given or delivered the drug to the police officer, the offence of trafficking is made out.

R. v. MacDonald (1963), 41 C.R. 75, (sub nom. *R. v. Harrington)* [1964] 1 C.C.C. 189 — There must be something more extensive than mere conveying, or carrying or moving incidental to one's own use of the drug to warrant a conviction under s. 4(1) for trafficking.

R. v. Wells, [1963] 2 C.C.C. 279 (B.C. C.A.) — D by preparing a list and checking off each buyer of the narcotics, participated in their distribution and did "distribute" within the meaning of "trafficking" in the Act.

R. v. Jordison (1957), 26 C.R. 267 (B.C. C.A.) — Trafficking may be established by proof of a single sale. It is not restricted to a course of conduct.

R. v. Verma (1996), 112 C.C.C. (3d) 155 (Ont. C.A.) — Non-compliance with the *Narcotic Control Regulations* does *not per se* constitute a breach of the Act.

R. v. Bollers (1979), 52 C.C.C. (2d) 62 (Ont. C.A.) — Where D represented a substance to be a narcotic when it was not, P had the onus of proving the substance to be the narcotic alleged.

R. v. Masters (1974), 15 C.C.C. (2d) 142 (Ont. C.A.); varying (1973), 12 C.C.C. (2d) 573 (Ont. Co. Ct.) — If the trafficking alleged is in a substance held out or represented to be a narcotic, it does not matter what the substance was. It was the proof of the representing or holding out that is the essential element of P's case and it need not prove what in fact the substance was.

R. v. Petrie, [1947] O.W.N. 601 (C.A.) — Where D made an offer to sell narcotics, P does not need to establish that D had narcotics in his possession or that he was able to carry out the offer that he made.

R. v. C. (N.) (1991), 64 C.C.C. (3d) 45 (Que. C.A.) — Where P alleges that D trafficked in a specified narcotic, it must prove that the designated narcotic, *not* a substance held out to be the narcotic, was the subject of trafficking.

R. v. Lauze (1980), 17 C.R. (3d) 90, 60 C.C.C. (2d) 468 (Que. C.A.) — Given the definition of "traffic" in the Act, once it is established that D gave a narcotic to another, even where it was for D's own use and he gave it merely to prevent the police from finding it, he is nevertheless guilty of trafficking.

R. v. Nittolo (1978), 44 C.C.C. (2d) 56 (Que. C.A.) — Where D gave narcotics to a woman with whom he shared a residence, for safe keeping by her while he went out, it was held that he had "given" the narcotic for the purposes of a charge of trafficking under s. 4 of the Act.

Trafficking: S. 4 — Mental Element

R. v. McGeough (1983), 36 C.R. (3d) 390 (Alta. C.A.) — Where D participates in a sale of a substance represented to the buyer by the co-accused to be cocaine, there arises a rebuttable presumption of fact that D believed the substance to be cocaine. If D does *not* adduce evidence to rebut this presumption, he can be convicted of trafficking despite there being no evidence of actual knowledge on his part.

R. v. Merritt (1975), 27 C.C.C. (2d) 156 (N.B. C.A.) — The *mens rea* is the holding out or representation by D that the substance is a narcotic, and not the honesty or dishonesty attending the representation or holding out. Moreover, it is not necessary to prove that the purchaser believed the substance was a narcotic.

R. v. Mamchur, [1978] 4 W.W.R. 481 (Sask. C.A.) — In proving the offence of trafficking based upon an offer to sell, there is no need to prove the intent to carry out the offer, but merely the intent to make it.

Trafficking: S. 4 — Purchaser: Agent of Purchaser

R. v. Greyeyes (1997), 116 C.C.C. (3d) 334 (S.C.C.) — A purchaser of narcotics, by purchase alone, does not aid or abet the offence of trafficking. A person who incidentally assists the purchaser should be considered a purchaser, not a trafficker. These persons aid or abet possession, not trafficking. (per L'Heureux-Dubé, La Forest, Sopinka and Gonthier JJ.)

A purchaser of a narcotic is not a trafficker, nor *per se* an aider or abettor of a trafficker. (per Cory, McLachlin and Major JJ.)

An agent for the purchaser who assists the purchaser in buying drugs is a party to the vendor's trafficking under s. 21(1)(b) or (c). (per Cory, McLachlin and Major JJ.)

Poitras v. R. (1973), 24 C.R.N.S. 159, 12 C.C.C. (2d) 337 (S.C.C.) — The civil law of "agency" does not serve to make non-criminal an act that would otherwise be criminal. Where D is found to have delivered, sold or traded in narcotics or offered to do so, the fact that he acted as agent for the purchaser is no defence to a charge of trafficking.

R. v. Dyer (1971), 17 C.R.N.S. 207, 5 C.C.C. (2d) 376 (B.C. C.A.); leave to appeal refused (1972), 17 C.R.N.S. 233n (S.C.C.) — The purchaser of a narcotic is not an accomplice of the vendor on a charge of trafficking, based on the sale to the purchaser.

R. v. Vinette, [1969] 3 C.C.C. 172 (B.C. C.A.) — Where D provided a customer for the seller of the drug and remained with the customer and seller during the sale, joining in their discussion, his activities constituted aiding and abetting the seller in the offence of trafficking.

R. v. Chlow (1982), 70 C.C.C. (2d) 205 (N.B. C.A.) — Where D's principal purpose in bringing about a sale and purchase of a narcotic is to assist the buyer and not the seller, his actions do not constitute trafficking.

R. v. Malally (1982), 52 N.S.R. (2d) 179 (C.A.) — D who introduced police officers to his friend for the purpose of the officers buying drugs from the friend was convicted of aiding and abetting in the trafficking of narcotics as he had acted to aid the seller of drugs.

R. v. Rowbotham (1988), 63 C.R. (3d) 113, 41 C.C.C. (3d) 1 (Ont. C.A.) — There is no policy which requires the law of conspiracy to be interpreted so broadly as to automatically make the mere purchaser of an illicit drug a party to an overall conspiracy to distribute that drug.

R. v. Greenlaw (1981), 60 C.C.C. (2d) 178 (Ont. C.A.) — Being an agent for the purchaser of a narcotic is no defence to a charge of trafficking if D engaged in one of the acts specified in the statutory definition of trafficking.

R. v. Meston (1975), 34 C.R.N.S. 323, 28 C.C.C. (2d) 497 (Ont. C.A.) — The purchaser of a narcotic does *not*, by virtue of the definition of "traffic" in s. 2, commit the offence of trafficking, but this does not preclude him from being considered an accomplice.

R. v. Pearson (1994), 89 C.C.C. (3d) 535 (Que. C.A.); leave to appeal refused (1994), 90 C.C.C. (3d) vi (note), 91 C.C.C. (3d) vi (note) (S.C.C.) — Even if D acts only as an agent for a purchaser, D may be convicted of trafficking where D's acts amount to trafficking under s. 2 *N.C.A.*

Trafficking: S. 4 — Included Offences [See also Code s. 662]

R. v. Shewfelt (1972), 18 C.R.N.S. 185, 6 C.C.C. (2d) 304 (B.C. C.A.) — *See also: R. v. Drysdelle* (1978), 41 C.C.C. (2d) 238 (N.B. C.A.); *R. v. Whynot* (1978), 16 Nfld. & P.E.I.R. 14 (Nfld. C.A.) — It is not what is disclosed in the evidence that makes an offence an included one to the other, but what is charged in the count. The offence of trafficking does not include the offence of possession.

Trafficking: S. 4 — Procedural Considerations

R. v. Peebles (1975), 24 C.C.C. (2d) 144 (B.C. C.A.) — It is not necessary to include in the charge the particular method of trafficking alleged.

R. v. Vickers (1963), 41 C.R. 235 (B.C. C.A.) — Where the evidence establishes separate and distinct acts, the first being mere possession of the drug and the second the transport and distribution of it, D may be charged and convicted of both possession and trafficking.

R. v. Kozodoy (1957), 117 C.C.C. 315 (Ont. C.A.) — On a charge of trafficking, failure to name the persons to whom it is alleged that the drug was distributed does not vitiate the count.

Hogan v. R. (1979), 8 C.R. (3d) 380 (Que. C.A.) — In view of the offence under s. 4(1) of the Act and the definition of the words "traffic" and "narcotic", it appears that a person who in the same transaction sells or delivers more than one substance mentioned in the schedule to the Act commits as many crimes as there are substances sold or delivered.

R. v. Khouri (1995), 97 C.C.C. (3d) 223 (Sask. C.A.) — D may be convicted of both trafficking (by selling) and possession of the proceeds of crime under *NCA* s. 19.1 in respect of the same transaction. (Per Tallis and Gerwing JJ.A.)

Possession for the Purpose of Trafficking: S. 4(2) — Nature and Elements of Offence

Beaver v. R. (1957), 26 C.R. 193, 118 C.C.C. 129 (S.C.C.) — In a sale of a narcotic, made without lawful authority, the accuracy or inaccuracy of the representation made by the seller to the buyer as to the nature of the substance sold and the honesty or dishonesty attending the representation, if inaccurate, are quite immaterial if the substance sold is represented or held out to be a drug by the seller to the buyer.

R. v. Roan (1985), 17 C.C.C. (3d) 534 (Alta. C.A.) — Where D loaned a co-accused the money for the purchase of narcotics on the basis that D would be repaid and would share in the proceeds from the resale of the narcotics, she was guilty of possession for the purpose of trafficking despite the fact that she was not in possession of the narcotics. Her conduct had aided the co-accused in the commission of the offence and therefore she was a party to the offence.

R. v. Taylor (1974), 17 C.C.C. (2d) 36 (B.C. C.A.) — The gravamen of the charge of possession for the purpose of trafficking is possession plus the intent or purpose of physically making the narcotic available to others, even if they are owners in common with the accused.

R. v. Podkydailo (1959), 32 C.R. 56, 125 C.C.C. 313 (B.C. C.A.) — Proof of transportation by itself is *not* conclusive proof of the purpose for which D had possession but is an important element in determining the purpose.

R. v. Gardiner (1987), 35 C.C.C. (3d) 461 (Ont. C.A.) — Where D, who was a passenger in a car stopped by the police, was found in possession of a quantity of cocaine which the trial judge accepted was for the use of D and the two other persons in the car, the facts were held not to support a charge of possession for the purpose of trafficking, but did support a charge of joint possession by all three persons in the vehicle.

R. v. Daniel (1982), 1 C.C.C. (3d) 101 (Ont. C.A.) — Where D had distilled cannabis resin from cannabis marihuana for his own use, his conviction for possession for the purpose of trafficking was upheld, for by giving cannabis marihuana a new form, D was manufacturing, thus coming within the definition of trafficking in s. 2 of the Act. The fact that the manufacturing was for his own use did *not* constitute a defence because the Act intended to prohibit the creation of a narcotic.

R. v. Jackson (1977), 35 C.C.C. (3d) 331 (Ont. C.A.) — Where D assisted a drug trafficker by hiding the trafficker's marihuana in D's apartment, D was guilty of aiding and abetting the offence of possession for the purpose of trafficking and not merely of simple possession.

R. v. Perry (1974), 30 C.R.N.S. 291, 18 C.C.C. (2d) 366 (P.E.I. C.A.) — The purchaser of a narcotic is *not* guilty of an offence in purchasing it, although once he has possession of it he becomes chargeable with the offence of possession.

Possession for the Purpose of Trafficking: S. 4(2) — Mental Element

R. v. Whalen (1974), 17 C.C.C. (2d) 162 (Nfld. C.A.) — In a charge under s. 4(2) the intention to traffic could be formed at any time after the purchase of the narcotic up to the time the charge was laid.

R. v. Ryckman (1981), 64 C.C.C. (2d) 192 (Ont. C.A.) — Where D was hired by the principal to pick marihuana and D knew the principal intended to traffic, the fact that D was *not* privy to any scheme of distribution and did not receive any money therefrom was not a defence to a charge of aiding and abetting the principal in an offence under s. 4(2).

R. v. Couture (1976), 33 C.C.C. (2d) 74 (Ont. C.A.) — The defence of mistake of fact as to the true identity of the drug seized on a charge under s. 4 must be based on an *honest* belief on the part of D. The reasonableness of D's belief is merely relevant evidence to be considered. Furthermore, D's mistaken belief must be innocent, so that where he thinks he has mescaline for sale when it is in fact phencyclidine, the defence of mistake of fact will fail. Possession of mescaline for sale is an offence, hence its possession is not innocent.

R. v. Weiler (1975), 23 C.C.C. (2d) 556 (Ont. C.A.) — The fact that D and a friend had joint possession of an amount of marihuana, and D acquiesced in the friends trafficking in the drug, does *not* mean that D could not have had the intention to use the portion of the drug for his own use.

Possession for the Purpose of Trafficking: S. 4(2) — Evidentiary Issues

R. v. Cripps (1969), 68 W.W.R. 456 (B.C. C.A.) — Evidence that D, charged under s. 4(2) of the Act, was in possession of plastic bags, a large amount of cash, and the prices of narcotics in the illegal market, was evidence relevant to the question of the *purpose* for which D had possession of the narcotic and was therefore admissible.

R. v. Wilson (1954), 11 W.W.R. 282 (B.C. C.A.) — Where an addict is found in possession of an amount of drugs larger than is needed for his own immediate use, courts will draw the inference that he had the drugs for sale or distribution.

R. v. Douglas (1977), 1 C.R. (3d) 238, 33 C.C.C. (2d) 395 (Ont. C.A.) — The fact that people who either use drugs or are addicted to them seek out or associate with D charged under s. 4(2) of the Act can lead to the rational inference that the subject of the visits were in some way involved with drugs.

Possession for the Purpose of Trafficking: S. 4(2) — Procedural Considerations

Morozuk v. R. (1986), 50 C.R. (3d) 179, 24 C.C.C. (3d) 257 (S.C.C.) — Where P charges the offence of possession of a narcotic for the purpose of trafficking and particularizes the narcotic as cannabis marihuana but it is proved to be cannabis resin, it is still the same offence, the gravamen of which is possession of a narcotic for the purpose of trafficking. In the absence of irreparable prejudice to D, the charge may be amended to comply with the evidence.

R. v. Barrett (1980), 15 C.R. (3d) 361, 54 C.C.C. (2d) 75 (Alta. C.A.) — Where D was charged with the possession of cannabis resin for the purpose of trafficking, when in fact the substance was cannabis, it was held that the word "resin" was superfluous on the information.

R. v. Dalzell (1979), 46 C.C.C. (2d) 193 (Alta. C.A.) — Where an indictment charges the accused jointly and severally with an offence, but it later appears that the admissible evidence will not support a joint charge against them all, the trial judge is entitled to proceed with the trial against each accused.

R. v. Doig (1980), 54 C.C.C. (2d) 461 (B.C. C.A.) — *See also*: *R. v. Dumais* (1979), 51 C.C.C. (2d) 106 (Ont. C.A.) — Where D and one of his employees were jointly charged with possession of a narcotic for the purpose of trafficking in circumstances where containers of marihuana were delivered to D's warehouse when the employee was present, it was open to the jury to convict D and acquit the employee even though they were jointly charged.

R. v. Maxwell (1978), 39 C.C.C. (2d) 439 (B.C. C.A.) — Where the indictment charged the accused with "being then and there together, did have in their possession a narcotic ... for the purpose of trafficking" it was held to charge the three accused jointly with one offence. It did not support a finding of possession by each accused.

Taylor v. Gotfried (1964), 43 C.R. 307, (sub nom. *R. v. Gotfried*) [1964] 2 C.C.C. 382 — Where an information failed to name the person who purchased the drugs or the price of the goods, the defect is not one that ought to be dealt with by the furnishing of particulars. The information fails to comply with *Code* s. 510(3).

R. v. Baumet (1986), 54 C.R. (3d) 176 (Sask. C.A.) — On a charge under s. 4(2) there is no requirement that the issues of intention and possession be decided separately.

5. (1) Importing and exporting — Except as authorized by this Act or the regulations, no person shall import into Canada or export from Canada any narcotic.

(2) Offence and punishment — Every person who contravenes subsection (1) is guilty of an indictable offence and liable to imprisonment for life but not less than seven years.

R.S., c. N-1, s. 5.repealed 1996, c. 19, s. 94.

Case Law

Importing and Exporting — Nature and Elements of Offence

R. v. Saunders (1987), 58 C.R. (3d) 83, 35 C.C.C. (3d) 385 (B.C. C.A.); affirmed (1990), 77 C.R. (3d) 397, 56 C.C.C. (3d) 220 (S.C.C.) — Where P charged D with conspiracy to import cocaine, when in reality D had imported heroin, D's appeal against conviction was allowed on the ground that P must prove the agreement charged in the indictment.

Bell v. R. (1983), 36 C.R. (3d) 289, 8 C.C.C. (3d) 97 (S.C.C.) — The word "import" means to bring into the country or cause to be brought into the country and the offence is complete when the goods enter the country. Accordingly, it is misconceived to characterize the offence of importing as a continuing offence that is only complete when D takes delivery. Nor is it necessary, in order to convict of importing, to show that D actually carried the goods into the country or was present at the point of entry. Furthermore, the offence may occur in whole or in part at more than one location in Canada, for example, in the province where the goods actually entered the country and in the province where the arrangements leading to the importation were made, and the courts in either jurisdiction could deal with the case.

R. v. Randall (1983), 7 C.C.C. (3d) 363 (N.S. C.A.) — Mere knowledge of, discussion of, or passive acquiescence in a plan of criminal conduct is not sufficient to prove that one is a member of the conspiracy. Therefore, where P proved that a conspiracy to import marihuana existed, and proved that D was a trafficker who had bought from the importer, this was not sufficient to prove D part of the conspiracy.

R. v. Salvador (1981), 21 C.R. (3d) 1, 59 C.C.C. (2d) 521 (N.S. C.A.) — D sought to raise the defence of necessity on a charge under s. 5(1) when his boat containing 8,300 pounds of cannabis resin crossed into Canadian waters due to adverse weather conditions. The defence failed. The boat did *not* break down and drift helplessly into Canadian waters, but sailed there deliberately to avoid the storm. In any event, as D was actively engaged in a joint criminal venture when the circumstances arose whereby they entered Canadian waters, it is unlikely that the defence of necessity had any application.

R. v. Williams (1998), 17 C.R. (5th) 75, 125 C.C.C. (3d) 552 (Ont. C.A.) — Where there is evidence that D was merely a passenger in a motor vehicle in which drugs were transported, the trial judge should instruct the jury expressly that passive acquiescence to the transportation of drugs is insufficient to support a conviction of importing.

R. v. Tan (1990), 44 O.A.C. 324 (C.A.) — Where heroin, secreted in baggage destined for Toronto where it was to be delivered to a purchaser, is held in bond at airport customs in Vancouver to await the continuation of its courier's flight to Toronto from Hong Kong, the courts of Ontario have jurisdiction to try the offence of importing heroin into Canada.

R. v. Tanney (1976), 31 C.C.C. (2d) 445 (Ont. C.A.) — D's conduct did not constitute importing when he only became involved with the drugs after they were in bond in Canada when he ordered their transhipment to New York. He did not exercise sufficient control over the drugs to be liable for the offence of importing, his acts at most constituting an attempt at exporting the drugs.

R. v. Hijazi (1974), 20 C.C.C. (2d) 183 (Ont. C.A.); leave to appeal refused (1974), 20 C.C.C. (2d) 183n (S.C.C.) — The act of importing is not completed at the moment the goods first physically enter Canada.

It extends to the point where delivery is taken from the bonded warehouse by or on behalf of the person claiming the goods.

R. v. Bell (1982), 66 C.C.C. (2d) 317 (Que. C.A.) — Where the R.C.M.P. removed goods containing a narcotic from the airport customs warehouse and subsequently returned them and D claimed them, the removal of the goods by the R.C.M.P. did not constitute an end to the importation which was a continuing offence and not completed until D took delivery.

Importing and Exporting — Mental Element

R. v. Blondin (1970), 2 C.C.C. (2d) 118 (B.C. C.A.); affirmed (1972), 4 C.C.C. (2d) 566n (S.C.C.) — In a charge under s. 5(1) the onus is on P to prove beyond a reasonable doubt that D knew the substance being imported was a narcotic, although not necessarily which narcotic, and the existence of this guilty knowledge may be inferred as a fact if it is established that D recklessly or wilfully shut his eyes or refrained from inquiring as to the nature of the substance.

R. v. Miller (1984), 12 C.C.C. (3d) 54 (B.C. C.A) — Where D helped to unload a cargo of marihuana from a ship in a remote area, the fact that D joined in the unloading knowing the nature and origin of the cargo made them party to a conspiracy to import. The fact that government agents provided the vessel, captain, pilot, fuel, repairs and provisions did *not* constitute entrapment.

R. v. Sandhu (1989), 73 C.R. (3d) 162, 50 C.C.C. (3d) 492 (Ont. C.A.) — The offence requires proof of actual knowledge or wilful blindness. Recklessness is distinct from wilful blindness and is not sufficient.

R. v. Duffy (1973), 11 C.C.C. (2d) 519 (Ont. C.A.) — P must prove beyond a reasonable doubt that D had actual knowledge that the substance he was importing was a substance the importation of which was prohibited by the *N.C.A.* It is not sufficient to prove that he "ought to have known" or that he "must have known" that fact.

R. v. Levac (1975), 32 C.C.C. (2d) 357 (Que. C.A.) — Evidence that D charged under s. 5(1) was himself a user of marihuana was evidence relevant to his guilty knowledge in connection with the actual importation of the cylinders containing the drug.

Importing and Exporting — Included Offences

R. v. Jarque, [1980] 1 W.W.R. 183 (Sask. C.A.) — Trafficking is not an included offence in a charge of unlawfully importing a narcotic into Canada. Where at trial D was charged with importing a narcotic contrary to s. 5(1) but convicted of trafficking contrary to s. 4(1) as an included offence, the finding of the appellate court in overturning the conviction that trafficking was not an included offence in a charge of importing did not entitle D to a plea of autrefois acquit to a subsequent charge under s. 4(1) based on the same facts.

Importing and Exporting — Punishment

R. v. Smith (1987), 58 C.R. (3d) 193, 34 C.C.C. (3d) 97 (S.C.C.) — The mandatory minimum sentence of seven years imprisonment imposed by subsection (2) is cruel and unusual punishment in violation of *Charter* s. 12 and is of no force and effect.

R. v. Saulnier (1987), 21 B.C.L.R. (2d) 232 (C.A.) — *See also*: *R. v. Cirone* (1988), 43 C.C.C. 228 (Alta. C.A.) — Sentences for importing, after the seven-year minimum sentence in s. 5(2) of the Act has been declared unconstitutional, should vary depending on the particular narcotic imported, the quantity of it imported, the degree of harm done by it, and whether D is a professional criminal. Also, guilty pleas, co-operation with the police and providing Crown evidence may lead to lesser sentences although long sentences are justified as a deterrent especially in areas where there is a severe drug abuse problem.

6. (1) Cultivation of opium poppy or marihuana — No person shall cultivate opium poppy or marihuana except under the authority of, and in accordance with, a licence issued to the person under the regulations.

(2) Offence and punishment — Every person who contravenes subsection (1) is guilty of an indictable offence and liable to imprisonment for a term not exceeding seven years.

(3) Destruction of plant — The Minister may cause to be destroyed any growing plant of opium poppy or marihuana cultivated otherwise than under authority of and in accordance with a licence issued under the regulations.

R.S., c. N-1, s. 6.repealed 1996, c. 19, s. 94.

Case Law

R. v. Arnold (1990), 74 C.R. (3d) 394 (B.C. C.A.) — "Cultivation" is a continuing offence which commences when seeding takes place and continues until the plants are harvested or die. Where D takes on the task of raising plants, "cultivation" continues until abandonment of the task, or maturity of the crop. One who undertakes to raise a crop to maturity does not cease to "cultivate" during periods of deliberate inactivity from labour and attention.

R. v. Powell (1983), 36 C.R. (3d) 396, 9 C.C.C. (3d) 442 (B.C. C.A.) — Possession of marihuana is not an included offence on a charge of cultivation of marihuana. The gravamen of the offence of cultivation is the active participation in growing the plants and does not necessarily involve possession.

R. v. Fahlman (1968), 5 C.R.N.S. 192 (B.C. Co. Ct.); affirmed on other grounds *(*sub nom. *R. v. Champagne)* 8 C.R.N.S. 245 — Where D dug the land, turned it over, levelled it and planted seeds that were Cannabis sativa L., D has unlawfully cultivated marihuana.

R. v. Gauvreau (1982), 26 C.R. (3d) 272, 65 C.C.C. (2d) 316 (Ont. C.A.) — The word "cultivate" in *N.C.A.* s. 6(1) does *not* include the processing of the opium poppy or marihuana plant after harvest.

David v. R. (1979), 9 C.R. (3d) 189, 50 C.C.C. (2d) 558 (Que. C.A.) — Where D had published a book entitled "The Cultivator's Handbook of Marijuana" a conviction for counselling another person to cultivate marihuana without a licence was upheld.

R. v. Flicek (1987), 56 Sask. R. 75 (C.A.) — Where D was seen leaving a hayfield in which there were marihuana plants growing as well as evidence of weeding, and D had green stains on his hands, it was held that there was insufficient evidence to show that he had bestowed labour and attention on the plant amounting to cultivation within the meaning of s. 6(1).

R. v. Busby (1972), 7 C.C.C. (2d) 234 (Y.T. C.A.) — Where marihuana plants were found growing in various stages in a basement where there were also marihuana seeds found, and marihuana plant material was found in a bedroom of the house, D was cultivating marihuana for the purposes of a charge under s. 6(1) of the Act. Cultivation requires that labour and attention be bestowed on the plants to assist them to grow.

Prosecutions

7. (1) Setting out or negativing exception, etc. not required — No exception, exemption, excuse or qualification prescribed by law is required to be set out or negatived, as the case may be, in an information or indictment for an offence under this Act or under section 463, 464 or 465 of the *Criminal Code* in respect of an offence under this Act.

(2) Burden of proving exception, etc — In any prosecution under this Act the burden of proving that an exception, exemption, excuse or qualification prescribed by law operates in favour of the accused is on the accused, and the prosecutor is not required, except by way of rebuttal, to prove that the exception, exemption, excuse or qualification does not operate in favour of the accused, whether or not it is set out in the information or indictment.

R.S., c. N-1, s. 7.repealed 1996, c. 19, s. 94.

8. (1) Procedure in prosecution for trafficking — In any prosecution for a contravention of subsection 4(2), if the accused does not plead guilty, the trial shall proceed as if it were a prosecution for an offence under section 3.

(2) **Idem** — After the close of the case for the prosecution pursuant to subsection (1) and after the accused has had an opportunity to make full answer and defence, the court shall make a finding as to whether or not the accused contravened subsection 3(1) and, if the court finds that the accused did not contravene subsection 3(1), the accused shall be acquitted but, if the court finds that the accused contravened subsection 3(1), the accused shall be given an opportunity of establishing that he was not in possession of the narcotic for the purpose of trafficking and, thereafter, the prosecutor shall be given an opportunity of adducing evidence to establish the contrary.

(3) **Conviction of possession or conviction of trafficking** — After compliance with subsection (2), in the case of finding a contravention by the accused of subsection 3(1),

> (a) if the accused establishes that he was not in possession of the narcotic for the purpose of trafficking, the accused shall be acquitted of the offence as charged but shall be convicted of an offence under section 3 and sentenced accordingly; or

> (b) if the accused fails to establish that he was not in possession of the narcotic for the purpose of trafficking, the accused shall be convicted of the offence as charged and sentenced accordingly.

R.S., c. N-1, s. 8.repealed 1996, c. 19, s. 94

Case Law

R. v. Oakes (1986), 50 C.R. (3d) 1, 24 C.C.C. (3d) 321 (S.C.C.); affirming (1983), 32 C.R. (3d) 193, 2 C.C.C. (3d) 339 (Ont. C.A.) — *See also*: *R. v. Baumet* (1986), 54 C.R. (3d) 176 (Sask. C.A.) — The right to be presumed innocent as guaranteed by *Charter* s. 11(d) renders the reverse onus in *N.C.A.* s. 8 inoperative.

9. (1) Certificate of analyst — Subject to this section, a certificate purporting to be signed by an analyst stating that the analyst has analyzed or examined a substance and stating the result of the analysis or examination is admissible in evidence in any prosecution for an offence referred to in subsection 7(1), and, in the absence of evidence to the contrary, is proof of the statements contained in the certificate without proof of the signature or official character of the person appearing to have signed the certificate.

(2) **Requiring attendance of analyst** — The party against whom a certificate of an analyst is produced pursuant to subsection (1) may, with leave of the court, require the attendance of the analyst for the purposes of cross-examination.

(3) **Notice of intention to produce certificate** — No certificate shall be admitted in evidence pursuant to subsection (1) unless the party intending to produce it has, before the trial, given to the party against whom it is intended to be produced reasonable notice of that intention together with a copy of the certificate.

(4) **Proof of service** — For the purposes of this Act, service of any certificate referred to in subsection (1) may be proved by oral evidence given under oath by, or by the affidavit or solemn declaration of, the person claiming to have served it.

(5) **Attendance for examination** — Notwithstanding subsection (4), the court may require the person who appears to have signed an affidavit or solemn declaration referred to in that subsection to appear before it for examination or cross-examination in respect of the issue of proof of service.

R.S., c. N-1, s. 9; R.S. 1985, c. 27 (1st Supp.), s. 198; repealed 1996, c. 19, s. 94.

Case Law
Certificate of Analyst: S. 9(1)

R. v. St. Pierre, [1984] C.A. 411 (Que. C.A.); affirmed [1987] 2 S.C.R. 690 (S.C.C.) — A certificate of analysis constitutes *prima facie* evidence as to the nature of the substance analyzed. P may adduce additional evidence to augment evidence provided by certificate.

Oliver v. R. (1981), 24 C.R. (3d) 1, 62 C.C.C. (2d) 97 (S.C.C.) — "Evidence to the contrary" is any evidence which tends to put in doubt the probative value Parliament has legislatively conferred upon the statements contained in a s. 9 certificate. This evidence may be in regard to the analyst himself, his qualifications, integrity, or regarding the procedures he followed to draw his conclusion — in fact, any evidence which could, as a matter of law, cause the trier of fact to have a reasonable doubt as to the analyst's conclusions had he testified as an expert witness in court.

R. v. Miller (1968), 65 W.W.R. 96 (B.C. C.A.); affirmed (1969), 67 W.W.R. 221 (S.C.C.) — The object of s. 9 is to permit proof being given by certificate that a substance contained a narcotic without having to call the analyst to give *viva voce* evidence. It is therefore implicit in the section that the analyst be permitted in his certificate to describe and identify the substance he analyzes.

R. v. Jordan (1984), 39 C.R. (3d) 50, 11 C.C.C. (3d) 565 (B.C. C.A.) — An analyst, in determining the nature of a substance for the purpose of s. 9, may rely, in reaching his conclusions, on tests done by others and on standard graphs produced by other laboratories.

R. v. Assu (1981), 64 C.C.C. (2d) 94 (B.C. C.A.) — Where a trial judge allowed P to re-open its case, on a charge of possessing a narcotic, for the purpose of proving that the substance was a narcotic, he erred in restricting P to proving compliance with the notice provisions in s. 9(3). He should have permitted P to prove the nature of the substance in any other manner.

R. v. Watkins, [1976] 4 W.W.R. 198 (B.C. C.A.) — Where defence counsel cross-examined the analyst who signed the certificate of analysis under s. 9 of the Act, attempting to show that the analyst had omitted an essential step in making the analysis, the trial judge usurped the function of the jury by then instructing them that there was no evidence to the contrary that the analysis had been properly made.

R. v. O'Quinn (1976), 36 C.C.C. (2d) 364 (B.C. C.A.) — Where the entire sample of a drug was destroyed by government analysis, the court refused to accept D's argument that as he was therefore prevented from applying under *Code* s. 533 to make his own analysis, he was denied the right to make full answer and defence. P was allowed by *N.C.A.* s. 9 to rely on the certificate of the analyst, so that the sample was not part of its case. The destruction of the entire sample does not render the certificate inadmissible.

R. v. Hardy (Nickerson) (1983), 45 N.B.R. (2d) 212 (Q.B.); reversed in part on other grounds (1984), 14 C.C.C. (3d) 201 (N.B. C.A.) — A certificate of analysis is not proof that a substance is a narcotic unless the substance named in the certificate is one named in the Act as a narcotic.

Requiring Attendance: S. 9(2)

Klippenstein v. R. (1975), 28 C.C.C. (2d) 235 (Man. C.A.) — Where a trial judge refuses to give leave to D to require the attendance of the analyst for cross-examination pursuant to s. 9(2) of the Act, the judge's ruling is a discretionary one with which the appeal court will be loathe to interfere. To avoid an awkward interruption of the trial, the better procedure under s. 9(2) of the Act would be for D to request production of the analyst before the trial opens.

Notice of Intention: S. 9(3)

Ebner v. R. (1979), 47 C.C.C. (2d) 293 (S.C.C.) — The fact that a certificate bore one date and a police officer, in his evidence, gave a different date, was not relevant to the issue of reasonableness of notice. D had been given four months notice and made fully aware of the contents of the certificate to be produced at trial.

R. v. Hamm (1976), 33 C.R.N.S. 339, 28 C.C.C. (2d) 257 (S.C.C.) — The fact that D was intoxicated when served with notice did *not* prevent proper service.

R. v. Jahns (1986), 70 A.R. 247 (C.A.) — Section 9(3) is *not* designed to blunt the possible use of certificates in every case of late service. The definition of reasonable notice depends on the circumstances.

Stauffer v. R. (1981), 22 C.R. (3d) 336, 62 C.C.C. (2d) 44 (Alta. C.A.); leave to appeal refused (1981), 39 N.R. 539 (S.C.C.) — A certificate of analysis prepared in only one official language is *not* rendered inadmissible by virtue of s. 3 of the *Official Languages Act.*

R. v. Chang (1996), 106 C.C.C. (3d) 87 (B.C. C.A.) — The introduction of certificates of analysis at preliminary inquiry satisfies the notice of requirement of NCA s. 9.

R. v. Finlay (1991), 65 C.C.C. (3d) 225 (B.C. C.A.) — In determining whether D has received reasonable notice under s. 9(3), all the circumstances must be considered.

R. v. Giesbrecht (1976), 60 C.C.C. (2d) 135 (B.C. C.A.) — A notice of intention to produce a certificate of analysis does not relate to a specific charge, so that when a certificate and notice to produce is given, the certificate can be tendered in evidence at the trial of any charge to which it relates.

Wong v. R. (1973), 14 C.C.C. (2d) 117 (B.C. S.C.) — *See also: R. v. Atkinson* (1976), 36 C.R.N.S. 255, 32 C.C.C. (2d) 361 (Man. C.A.); reversed on other grounds (1978), 1 C.R. (3d) 186, 37 C.C.C. (2d) 416n (S.C.C.); *Re Harrigan* (1977), 17 N.B.R. (2d) 478 (C.A.) — Certificates of analysis may be introduced into evidence at a preliminary inquiry without previous notice having been given. Section 9(3) requires notice to be given "before the trial". A preliminary inquiry is not a trial.

R. v. Henri (1972), 9 C.C.C. (2d) 52 (B.C. C.A.) — *See also: R. v. Pratt* (1974), 15 C.C.C. (2d) 119 (B.C. C.A.) — A notice as required by s. 9(3) of the Act must be, at the very least, precise and accurate and reasonably certain so that D is alerted with certainty and in a timely manner as to the procedure to be invoked. For P to avail itself of this section it must strictly comply with the provisions.

R. v. Flett (1970), 73 W.W.R. 699 (B.C. C.A.) — *See also: R. v. Meyer* (1973), 29 C.C.C. (2d) 165 (B.C. C.A.) — There is nothing in s. 9(3) that requires the notice to be served on D. It is sufficient if it is served on D's counsel, if there is one. Whether the notice is reasonable is a matter of fact.

R. v. Slaney (1983), 40 Nfld. & P.E.I.R. 420 (Nfld. C.A.) — As long as the notice required by s. 9(3) is not prejudicial or misleading to D, the certificates of analysis will be excluded only if service is not effected in sufficient time prior to trial.

R. v. Kennedy (1978), 17 Nfld. & P.E.I.R. 62 (Nfld. C.A.) — Under s. 9(3) of the Act P is *not* required to prove that the notice given was reasonable notice. If objection is taken by D, it is for the court to decide, in light of all the circumstances of the case, whether the notice was reasonable.

R. v. Morrison (1982), 70 C.C.C. (2d) 193 (N.B. C.A.) — The notice as required by s. 9(3) of the Act should be such as to bring home clearly to D that an analyst's certificate would be used to establish the nature of the substance involved in the charge. If the notice is reasonable as to time and substance, and not misleading, confusing or otherwise prejudicial to D, technical objections will not avail to invalidate it.

R. v. Breen (1975), 30 C.C.C. (2d) 229 (N.B. C.A.) — A notice under s. 9(3) is ineffective if it would leave D in doubt as to the intention of P. What is reasonable notice for the purpose of s. 9(3) of the Act is a question of fact to be determined in each case by the trial judge. The mere fact that notice is given just before trial does not mean it is *ipso facto* unreasonable in law.

R. v. Levesque (1973), 6 N.B.R. (2d) 762 (C.A.) — A trial begins when the first witness is called to the stand and the merits of P's case are first placed before the court. The arrest, arraignment, election of D and the plea are all matters preliminary to the trial.

R. v. Wood (1977), 20 N.S.R. (2d) 176 (C.A.) — Where a notice pursuant to s. 9(3) of the Act failed to show part of the laboratory number of the certificate, the omission did not constitute a significant error so as to prevent the notice from being reasonable notice.

R. v. Taylor (1983), 5 C.C.C. (3d) 260 (Ont. C.A.) — Where a notice under s. 9(3) stated that it was given "pursuant to the *Criminal Code*", the error was held not to cause confusion or prejudice. The *N.C.A.* does not command reference to itself in such a notice, nor does it particularize the form such notice should take.

R. v. Labine (1975), 23 C.C.C. (2d) 567 (Ont. C.A.) — *See also: R. v. Van Esch* (1975), 24 C.C.C. (2d) 523 (Ont. C.A.) — A court is entitled to find that a substance is a particular narcotic even where there is no certificate of analysis, if there is sufficient circumstantial evidence the cumulative effect of which leads to that conclusion.

R. v. Woodward (1975), 23 C.C.C. (2d) 508 (Ont. C.A.) — Where a notice of intention referred to a charge under s. 4(1), when in fact D was charged under s. 4(2), the notice was reasonable as D was not misled or prejudiced by it. A police officer's opinion evidence that the contents of certain plastic bags were marihuana based on the colour and odour of the substance was some, though not substantial, evidence of that fact and was properly admitted.

R. v. Bowles (1974), 16 C.C.C. (2d) 425 (Ont. C.A.) — Proof of service of a notice of intention under s. 9(3) of the Act is not a mere formality. A certificate of analysis goes to establish one of the essential elements of P's case. Proof of service must be made in the same manner as proof of any other essential element of P's case. The purpose of s. 9 is to avoid unnecessary use of the expensive time of the court and the expert witness, while at the same time, preserving all the essential rights of D.

R. v. Lewis (1972), 6 C.C.C. (2d) 516 (Ont. C.A.) — Even though no objection was taken in circumstances where the certificate of analysis was served on D's mother, and the trial judge admitted it in evidence, P was required to comply with s. 9(3). The service did not comply with s. 9(3).

R. v. McKenna (1979), 23 Nfld. & P.E.I.R. 127 (P.E.I. C.A.) — The fact that the certificate of analysis was not stapled, clipped or by other device attached to the notice, in circumstances where the documents were served by an officer accompanied by his verbal explanation, did not deprive D of reasonable notice as required by s. 9(3).

R. v. Devincentis, [1981] C.S.P. 1033, affirmed (1982), 5 C.C.C. (3d) 562 (Que. C.A.) — Where an analyst's certificate was entered as an exhibit at the preliminary inquiry and at trial, but no notice of intention was filed, there is no reasonable notice.

R. v. Marcil (1976), 31 C.C.C. (2d) 172 (Sask. C.A.) — Compliance with subsection (3) is a condition precedent to the admission of the certificate of the analyst pursuant to subsection (1), so that if a trial judge admits the certificate as evidence, it must be presumed as a finding of fact, that there was compliance with subsection (3). Where the judge then reverses this finding of fact in his judgment, there is an error in law, and the Crown should be granted the opportunity to reopen its case and call *viva voce* evidence to prove the nature of the substance.

Search, Seizure and Forfeiture

10. Entry and search — A peace officer may, at any time, without a warrant enter and search any place other than a dwelling-house, and under the authority of a warrant issued under section 12, enter and search any dwelling-house in which the peace officer believes on reasonable grounds there is a narcotic by means of or in respect of which an offence under this Act has been committed.

         R.S., c. N-1, s. 10; R.S. 1985, c. 27 (1st Supp.), s. 199; repealed 1996, c. 19, s. 94.

Case Law

R. v. Wiley (1993), 24 C.R. (4th) 34, 84 C.C.C. (3d) 161 (S.C.C.) — *See also*: *R. v. Grant* (1993), 24 C.R. (4th) 1, 84 C.C.C. (3d) 173 (S.C.C.) — Section 10 is only constitutionally applicable to warrantless searches where exigent circumstances render it impracticable to obtain prior judicial authorization.

R. v. Grant (1993), 24 C.R. (4th) 1, 84 C.C.C. (3d) 173 (S.C.C.) — A s. 487 warrant may be used to search for narcotics, even in a dwelling-house. The warrant need only comply with s. 487, *not* the special requirements of an *N.C.A.* warrant. It does not, however, give the executing officer the special search powers provided by the *N.C.A.*

R. v. Kokesch (1990), 1 C.R. (4th) 62, 61 C.C.C. (3d) 207 (S.C.C.); reversing (1988), 46 C.C.C. (3d) 194 (B.C. C.A.) — The perimeter of a dwelling-house is a "place" under subsection (1). Where police officers had no reasonable and probable grounds to believe that such a "place" contained a narcotic, hence did not comply with subsection (1), and, further, had no common law authority to trespass on the property to conduct a perimeter search, the search was unreasonable.

R. v. Arason (1992), 78 C.C.C. (3d) 1 (B.C. C.A.) — Section 10 *N.C.A.* authorizes warrantless searches of places other than dwelling-houses based on reasonable belief in the presence of narcotics. Section 12 *N.C.A.* permits a warrant to issue only where the place to be searched is a dwelling-house. For other locations, a search warrant should be obtained under *Code* s. 487.

R. v. Arason (1992), 78 C.C.C. (3d) 1 (B.C. C.A.) — There is *no N.C.A.* provision equivalent to *Code* s. 487(1)(e) which is itself "subject to any other Act of Parliament". There is, accordingly, no *N.C.A.* requirement to make a return as in s. 487(1)(e) of the *Code*.

R. v. Zastowny (1992), 76 C.C.C. (3d) 492 (B.C. C.A.) — An automobile is a "place" within s. 10, hence may be searched without warrant provided there are reasonable grounds for the search.

R. v. Nicholson (1990), 53 C.C.C. (3d) 403 (B.C. C.A.) — A garage does *not* fall within the expression "dwelling house".

R. v. Esau (1983), 4 C.C.C. (3d) 530 (Man. C.A.) — Under s. 10 a police officer in entering and searching a place other than a dwelling-house, must reasonably believe that there is a narcotic in such place by means of or in respect of which an offence under the Act has been committed.

R. v. Sunila (1986), 49 C.R. (3d) 272, 26 C.C.C. (3d) 177 (N.S. C.A.) — Where D's ship had briefly entered Canadian waters to transfer narcotics to a second ship, and was then pursued into international waters where, after the second ship had completed the importation of the narcotics, D's ship was stopped, searched and D arrested on a charge of conspiracy to import narcotics, it was held that there was no breach of any provisions of the *Charter*. The offence had been committed within the territorial waters of Canada and the ship was properly pursued under the principles of international law.

R. v. Debot (1986), 54 C.R. (3d) 120, 30 C.C.C. (3d) 207 (Ont. C.A.); affirmed on other grounds (1989), 73 C.R. (3d) 129, 52 C.C.C. (3d) 193 (S.C.C.) — Under *Charter* s. 8 a search of a vehicle pursuant to s. 10 will be reasonable in circumstances where there are reasonable grounds for believing the vehicle contains drugs and the vehicle is pulling away from the place where the alleged drug transaction took place.

R. v. Rao (1984), 40 C.R. (3d) 1, 12 C.C.C. (3d) 97 (Ont. C.A.) — Under s. 10 the search of a place other than a dwelling-house without a warrant, where obtaining a warrant is practicable, is unreasonable and in violation of *Charter* s. 8. If, however, obtaining a warrant is not practicable, a warrantless search may be reasonable, particularly in the case of vehicles, vessels or aircraft which may move quickly away, provided that there are reasonable grounds for believing they contain a narcotic.

R. v. Asencios (1987), 56 C.R. (3d) 344, 34 C.C.C. (3d) 168 (Que. C.A.) — Section 10 does not permit the police to enter premises owned by D, and in which the police had previously detected narcotics, to install a video camera.

R. v. Baylis (1988), 65 C.R. (3d) 62, 43 C.C.C. (3d) 514 (Sask. C.A.) — Where a justice worked at an airport, and was required to report to the police detachment which had a contract to provide security at theairport, there existed a reasonable apprehension of bias, thereby rendering illegal a search warrant issued by the justice under *N.C.A.* s. 10(2).

11. Search of person and seizure — A peace officer may search any person found in a place entered pursuant to section 10 and may seize and, from a place so entered, take away any narcotic found therein, anything therein in which the peace officer reasonably suspects a narcotic is contained or concealed, or any other thing by means of or in respect of which that officer believes on reasonable grounds an offence under this Act has been committed or that may be evidence of the commission of such an offence.

R.S., c. N-1, s. 10.repealed 1996, c. 19, s. 94.

12. Warrant to search dwelling-house — A justice who is satisfied by information on oath that there are reasonable grounds for believing that there is a narcotic, by means of or in respect of which an offence under this Act has been committed, in any dwelling-house may issue a warrant, under the hand of the justice, authorizing a peace officer named therein at any time to enter the dwelling-house and search for narcotics.

R.S., c. N-1, s. 10; repealed 1996, c. 19, s. 94.

Case Law

R. v. Grant (1993), 24 C.R. (4th) 1, 84 C.C.C. (3d) 173 (S.C.C.) — A s. 487 warrant may be used to search for narcotics, even in a dwelling-house. The warrant need only comply with s. 487, *not* the special requirements of an *N.C.A.* warrant. It does not, however, give the executing officer the special search powers provided by the *N.C.A.*

R. v. Strachan (1986), 49 C.R. (3d) 289, 24 C.C.C. (3d) 205 (B.C. C.A.) — A search warrant is not invalidated by the fact that the search is carried out by two officers named in the warrant and two who were not so named but were enrolled for the purpose of assisting with the search.

R. v. Cameron (1984), 16 C.C.C. (3d) 240 (B.C. C.A.) — Under s. 10 a search warrant may not be authorized unless the narcotics are present on the premises which are to be searched at the time the application for the warrant is made.

R. v. Gray (1993), 22 C.R. (4th) 114, 81 C.C.C. (3d) 174 (Man. C.A.) — The practice of the issuing justice assisting police with the preparation of an information to obtain a search warrant violates *Charter* s. 8. It is *not* proper for police to present a judicial officer with an unsigned or incomplete information to obtain a search warrant and, having received inappropriate direction with respect to both its technical language and content, to swear it in its altered form before the justice.

R. v. Komadowski (1986), 27 C.C.C. (3d) 319 (Man. C.A.); leave to appeal refused (1986), 27 C.C.C. (3d) 319n (S.C.C.) — A search warrant which is valid on its face is not open to collateral attack at the trial of the accused, but may only be impeached by direct attack by appeal, by action to set aside, or by one of the prerogative writs.

R. v. Zevallos (1987), 59 C.R. (3d) 153, 37 C.C.C. (3d) 79 (Ont. C.A.) — If the only issue sought to be resolved is one of admissibility at trial of the evidence of seizure, then it is preferable that the trial judge decide all aspects of the question of admissibility rather than to have them decided by different judges.

R. v. Haley (1986), 51 C.R. (3d) 363, 27 C.C.C. (3d) 454 (Ont. C.A.) — Where the offence charged is conspiracy to traffic in a narcotic contrary to *Code* s. 423(1)(d), the warrant issued for search and seizure is issued under the *Criminal Code* and therefore does not require that the police officers to whom it is directed be named specifically.

R. v. Fekete (1984), 11 C.C.C. (3d) 478 (Ont. H.C.); affirmed (1985), 44 C.R. (3d) 92, 17 C.C.C. (3d) 188 (Ont. C.A.) — All those participating in a search and seizure need not be named in a warrant. It is sufficient if just one officer is named.

R. v. Goodbaum (1977), 1 C.R. (3d) 152, 38 C.C.C. (2d) 473 (Ont. C.A.) — A warrant for the purpose of search and seizure of narcotics can only be issued under the provisions of the *N.C.A.* and one that is issued under *Code* s. 443 is invalid. The section protects the citizen by limiting the use of the powers of search and seizure in [now] ss. 10 and 11 to those police officers named in the warrant, so that a warrant issued to peace officers generally is invalid.

R. v. Kellett (1973), 14 C.C.C. (2d) 4 (Ont. C.A.) — The issuing of a warrant to search for "drugs" is not a proper exercise of the authority given in s. 10(2) [now s. 12] and such a warrant is therefore invalid.

R. v. Jamieson (1989), 48 C.C.C. (3d) 287 (N.S. C.A.) — An amendment could not be made to a previously issued search warrant where there was no further sworn information furnished to the justice of the peace and the warrant had expired.

R. v. MacFarlane (1992), 76 C.C.C. (3d) 54 (P.E.I. C.A.) — Sections 11 and 12 *N.C.A.* do *not* infringe *Charter* s. 8 because no provision is made for the executing officer tomake a return before the issuing justice as required for *Code* warrants.

13. [Repealed R.S. 1985, c. 27 (1st Supp.), s. 200.]

R.S. 1985, c. 27 (1st Supp.), s. 208 states:

> Nothing in sections 190, 195, 199 and 200 of this Act [Criminal Law Amendment Act, 1985] shall be construed as rendering invalid or inadmissible in any proceedings any evidence obtained by the exercise of a writ of assistance prior to the coming into force of those sections.

14. Powers of peace officer — For the purpose of exercising authority pursuant to any of sections 10 to 13, a peace officer may, with such assistance as that officer deems

necessary, break open any door, window, lock, fastener, floor, wall, ceiling, compartment, plumbing fixture, box, container or any other thing.

R.S., c. N-1, s. 10.repealed 1996, c. 19, s. 94.

Case Law

R. v. Gimson (1990), 77 C.R. (3d) 307, 54 C.C.C. (3d) 232 (Ont. C.A.); affirmed (1991), 69 C.C.C. (3d) 552 (S.C.C.) — *N.C.A.* ss. 10–12 and 14 provide a comprehensive set of special search powers which replace the common law rules, in particular, the requirement of announcement before entry. The powers of the police in executing an *N.C.A.* warrant are not, however, unrestricted and, in some circumstances, announcement may be required to comply with *Charter* s. 8. In each case, the facts will determine whether the search was conducted in a reasonable manner.

15. (1) Application for restoration — Where a narcotic or other thing has been seized under section 11, any person may, within two months after the date of the seizure, on prior notification being given to the Crown in the manner prescribed by the regulations, apply to a provincial court judge within whose territorial jurisdiction the seizure was made for an order of restoration under this section.

(2) Order of immediate restoration — Subject to section 16, where on the hearing of an application made under subsection (1) the provincial court judge is satisfied that the applicant is entitled to possession of the narcotic or other thing seized and that the thing seized is not or will not be required as evidence in any proceedings in respect of an offence under this Act, the provincial court judge shall order that the thing seized be restored forthwith to the applicant.

(3) Order of restoration at specified time — Where on the hearing of an application made under subsection (1) the provincial court judge is satisfied that the applicant is entitled to possession of the thing seized but is not satisfied that the thing is not or will not be required as evidence in any proceedings in respect of an offence under this Act, the provincial court judge shall order that the thing seized be restored to the applicant.

(a) on the expiration of four months after the date of the seizure, if no proceedings in respect of an offence under this Act have been commenced before that time; or

(b) on the final conclusion of any such proceedings, in any other case.

(4) Where application not made or order refused — Where no application has been made for the return of any narcotic or other thing seized under section 11 within two months after the date of the seizure, or an application therefor has been made but, on the hearing of the application, no order of restoration is made, the thing seized shall be delivered

(a) in the case of a narcotic, to the Minister, who may make such disposition thereof as the Minister thinks fit; and

(b) in the case of any other thing,

(i) where the proseuction of the offence in respect of which the thing was seized was commenced at the instance of the government of a province and conducted by or on behalf of that government, to the Attorney General or Solicitor General of that province, and

(ii) in any other case, to the Minister of Public Works and Government Services,

who may dispose of the thing in accordance with the law.

R.S., c. N-1, s. 10; R.S. 1985, c. 27 (1st Supp.), s. 203; 1993, c. 37, s. 25; 1996, c. 16, s. 60(1)(n); repealed 1996, c. 19, s. 94.

Case Law
Application: S. 15(1)

Aimonetti v. R. (1985), 19 C.C.C. (3d) 481 (Fed. C.A.) — Where an application for restoration is brought under s. 15(1) and dismissed, D is then estopped from recovering the goods in a subsequent civil action. The refusal of the restoration order determines conclusively the issue of the right to possession of the goods.

R. v. Martint (1977), 35 C.C.C. (2d) 366 (Alta. C.A.) — On an application for the return of items allegedly seized during a narcotics raid, the court must give P an opportunity to prove that the seizure was under s. 10 [now s. 15]. If this section does apply and is complied with, the court has jurisdiction to return or to refuse to return the money seized.

Aimonetti v. R. (1981), 58 C.C.C. (2d) 164 (Man. C.A.); leave to appeal refused (1981), 37 N.R. 290 (S.C.C.) — The scheme of the Act allows police authority to seize property related to the illicit trade in drugs, possession of which is then turned over to the Minister unless the applicant makes out a case for restoration. The procedures under the Act do not make the Minister owner of the property and D or anyone else can advance a civil claim to recover it from him. The section puts the onus on the applicant to show on a balance of probabilities that he is entitled to restoration of the thing seized.

Order of Immediate Restoration: Ss. 15(2), (3)

R. v. Fleming (1986), 51 C.R. (3d) 337, 25 C.C.C. (3d) 297 (S.C.C.) — In order to satisfy the court at a restoration hearing on the question of entitlement, a claimant must show on a balance of probabilities that he was in possession of the thing seized at the time of seizure. The burden is then on P to establish that the claimant is not entitled to the goods on the basis that a person should not profit from his wrongdoing, which requires a prior conviction, and P may fill the evidentiary gap by proving taint on the reasonable doubt standard at the restoration hearing. If there has been a prior conviction, the fact that the claimant is the innocent representative of the deceased owner would not entitle the claimant to restoration. However, where the owner of the goods died before conviction, then his innocent representative is entitled to the goods as long as the goods were not required as evidence and there was sufficient evidence of the deceased's possession of the goods at the time of seizure.

Collins v. R., [1980] 1 F.C. 146 (C.A.) — Where a judge of the Court of Sessions of the Peace in Quebec dismissed an application for restoration, his decision not being a decision of a "federal board, commission, or other tribunal", was not reviewable by the Federal Court.

R. v. Lewis (1979), 21 A.R. 236 (C.A.) — Once a thing seized has been made an exhibit, the provincial court judge's jurisdiction under subsections (2) and (3) is at an end since the exercise of his judgment has been foreclosed. Nor do the subsections continue to operate after conviction. The thing seized is then subject to the operation of s. 16(1) and to absolute forfeiture.

R. v. Hicks (1977), 38 C.R.N.S. 223, 36 C.C.C. (2d) 91 (Man. C.A.) — The section is not subservient to s. 16. It was not the intention of Parliament to forestall restoration of seized property until proceedings of forfeiture have been exhausted.

Collins v. R. (1983), 7 C.C.C. (3d) 377 (Que. C.A.) — Where D who had been acquitted on a charge of conspiracy to traffic, applied for the return of money seized during the drug raid, it was held that D was "entitled to possession" of the seized money without the judge having to examine in detail the circumstances of its acquisition.

Disposition by Minister: S. 15(4)

R. v. Pasta (1974), 6 N.R. 238 (Fed. C.A.) — A direction of the Minister under subsection (4) is not a decision that is required by law to be made on a judicial or quasi-judicial basis, hence is not reviewable under s. 28 of the *Federal Court Act*. The Minister's power under subsection (4) and s. 16(1) is merely custodial.

Spencer v. R. (1974), 26 C.R.N.S. 231 (N.S. C.A.) — Where D did not make any application within two months of seizure for the return of money seized by police, the money could not subsequently be returned to him by either a magistrate or the appeal court but must be delivered to the Minister to dispose of as he/she sees fit.

16. (1) Forfeiture on conviction — Where a person has been convicted of an offence under section 3, 4 or 5, any narcotic seized under section 11 by means of or in respect of which the offence was committed and any hypodermic needle, syringe, capping machine or other apparatus so seized that was used in any manner in connection with the offence, is forfeited to Her Majesty and shall be disposed of as the Minister directs.

(1.1) Idem — Where a person has been convicted of an offence under section 3, 4 or 5, any money seized under section 11 that was used for the purchase of the narcotic by means of or in respect of which the offence was committed is,

> **(a)** where the prosecution of the offence was commenced at the instance of the government of a province and conducted by or on behalf of that government, forfeited to Her Majesty in right of that province and shall be disposed of by the Attorney General or the Solicitor General of the province in accordance with the law; and

> **(b)** in any other case, forfeited to Her Majesty in right of Canada and shall be disposed of by the Minister of Public Works and Government Services in accordance with the law.

(2) Forfeiture of conveyance on application — Where a person has been convicted of an offence under section 4 or 5, the court may, on application by counsel for the Crown, order that any conveyance seized under section 11 that has been proved to have been used in any manner in connection with the offence be forfeited

> **(a)** where the prosecution of the offence was commenced at the instance of the government of a province and conducted by or on behalf of that government, to Her Majesty in right of that province, and

> **(b)** in any other case, to Her Majesty in right of Canada,

and, on the making of that order, the conveyance, except as provided in sections 17 to 19, shall, on the expiration of thirty days after the date of the forfeiture, be disposed of by the Attorney General or the Solicitor General of the province, or by the Minister of Public Works and Government Services, as the case may be, in accordance with the law.

R.S., c. N-1, s. 10; R.S. 1985, c. 27 (1st Supp.), s. 203; 1993, c. 37, s. 26; 1996, c. 16, s. 60(1)(n); repealed 1996, c. 19, s. 94.

Case Law

Application of Section

R. v. DeFrancesca (1995), 104 C.C.C. (3d) 189 (Ont. C.A.) — The NCA forfeiture provisions do *not* apply to D convicted under *Code* s. 465 of conspiracy to import/traffic in narcotics.

Conviction

Industrial Acceptance Corp. v. R. (1953), 107 C.C.C. 1 (S.C.C.) — "Convicted" means found guilty. A plea of guilty is also a conviction.

Timing of Application

R. v. Smith (1978), 2 C.R. (3d) 35 (Nfld. C.A.) — Although subsection (1) makes no reference to whether a forfeiture application should be made before or after sentence, it is preferable that it be made before sentencing.

Forfeiture of Conveyance

R. v. Breckner (1983), 6 C.C.C. (3d) 42 (B.C. C.A.) — A judge who makes a forfeiture order under s. 16(2) has the jurisdiction to set the order aside.

R. v. Pope (1980), 52 C.C.C. (2d) 538 (B.C. C.A.) — An order for forfeiture is not part of the sentence as that phrase is defined in *Code* s. 673. Therefore, a decision with respect to forfeiture under the *N.C.A.* cannot be the subject of an appeal.

Hicks v. R. (1977), 36 C.C.C. (2d) 91 (Man. C.A.) — Where D applies for restoration under s. 15(2), the judge is required to restore the property to her provided D has satisfied the requirements of s. 16. The forfeiture provision in s. 16(2) simply provides that where a person is convicted of an offence the court may, on the application of P, order that the conveyance used in connection with the offence be forfeited. It does *not* say that the conveyance shall have remained seized or that no order of restoration shall have been made.

R. v. Smith (1978), 2 C.R. (3d) 35 (Nfld. C.A.) — Although a magistrate who ordered forfeiture of a vehicle rather than imposing a fine against D convicted under s. 4(2), erred in considering the forfeiture as part of the sentence, this did not mean that on sentencing he could not take into consideration a prior forfeiture order, or take into consideration a sentence already imposed when determining the question of forfeiture after sentence.

17. (1) Application by person claiming interest in forfeited conveyance — Where any conveyance is forfeited to Her Majesty under subsection 16(2), any person (other than a person convicted of the offence that resulted in the forfeiture or a person in whose possession the conveyance was when seized) who claims an interest therein as owner, mortgagee, lienholder or holder of any like interest may, within thirty days after the forfeiture, apply by notice in writing to a judge for an order under subsection (4).

(2) Date of hearing — The judge to whom an application is made under subsection (1) shall fix a day not less than thirty days after the date of filing of the application for the hearing thereof.

(3) Notice to Minister or Attorney General of a province — The applicant for an order under subsection (4) shall, at least fifteen days before the day fixed for the hearing, serve a notice of the application and of the hearing on

(a) where the prosecution of the offence was commenced at the instance of the government of a province and conducted by or on behalf of that government, the Attorney General or the Solicitor General of the province, as the case may be; and

(b) in any other case, the Minister of Public Works and Government Services.

(4) Order by judge — Where, on the hearing of an application made under subsection (1), it is made to appear to the satisfaction of the judge

(a) that the applicant is innocent of any complicity in the offence that resulted in the forfeiture and of any collusion in relation to that offence with the person who was convicted thereof, and

(b) that the applicant exercised, with respect to the person permitted to obtain possession of the conveyance, all reasonable care that the conveyance was not likely to be used in connection with the commission of an unlawful act or, in the case of a mortgagee or lienholder, that the applicant exercised, with respect to the mortgagor or lien-giver, all reasonable care in order to be so satisfied,

the applicant is entitled to an order declaring that the interest of the applicant is not affected by the forfeiture and declaring the nature and extent of the interest.

(5) Appeal — The applicant, the Attorney General or the Solicitor General of the province or the Minister of Public Works and Government Services, as the case may be, may appeal to the court of appeal from an order made under subsection (4) and the appeal shall be asserted, heard and decided according to the ordinary procedure governing appeals to the court of appeal from orders or judgments of a judge.

R.S., c. N-1, s. 11; 1993, c. 37, s. 27; 1996, c. 16, s. 60(1)(n); repealed 1996, c. 19, s. 94.

18. Definitions — In section 17,

"court of appeal" means, in the province in which an order under section 17 is made, the court of appeal for that province as defined in the definition "court of appeal" in section 2 of the *Criminal Code*;

"judge" means

(a) in the Province of Ontario, a judge of the Ontario Court (General Division),

(b) in the Province of Quebec, a judge of the Superior Court for the district in which the conveyance, in respect of which an application for an order under section 17 is made, was seized,

(c) [Repealed 1992, c. 51, s. 59(1).]

(d) in the Provinces of New Brunswick, Manitoba, Saskatchewan and Alberta, a judge of the Court of Queen's Bench,

(e) in the Provinces of Nova Scotia and British Columbia, the Yukon Territory and the Northwest Territories, a judge of the Supreme Court, and

(f) in the Provinces of Prince Edward Island and Newfoundland, a judge of the Trial Division of the Supreme Court.

R.S., c. N-1, s. 11; 1972, c. 17, s. 2; 1974–75–76, c. 48, s. 25; 1978–79, c. 11, s. 10; R.S. 1985, c. 27 (2d Supp.), s. 10; 1990, c. 16, s. 18; 1990, c. 17, s. 36; 1992, c, 1, s. 98; 1992, c. 51, s. 59; repealed 1996, c. 19, s. 94.

19. Direction for restoration or payment — The Minister of Public Works and Government Services or the Attorney General or the Solicitor General of the province, as the case may be, shall, on application made to that Minister or to the Attorney General or the Solicitor General of the province by any person who has obtained a final order under section 17, direct that the conveyance to which the interest of the applicant relates be returned to the applicant or that an amount equal to the value of that interest, as declared in the order, be paid to the applicant.

R.S., c. N-1, s. 11; 1993, c. 37, s. 28; 1996, c. 16, s. 60(1)(n); repealed 1996, c. 19, s. 94.

Proceeds of Crime

19.1 (1) Possession of property obtained by certain offences — No person shall possess any property or any proceeds of any property knowing that all or part of the property or of those proceeds was obtained or derived directly or indirectly as a result of

(a) the commission in Canada of an offence under section 4, 5 or 6; or

(b) an act or omission anywhere that, if it had occurred in Canada, would have constituted an offence under section 4, 5 or 6.

(2) Punishment — Every person who contravenes subsection (1)

(a) is guilty of an indictable offence and is liable to imprisonment for a term not exceeding ten years, where the value of the subject-matter of the offence exceeds one thousand dollars; or

(b) is guilty

(i) of an indictable offence and is liable to imprisonment for a term not exceeding two years, or

(ii) of an offence punishable on summary conviction,

where the value of the subject-matter of the offence does not exceed one thousand dollars.

R.S. 1985, c. 42 (4th Supp.), s. 12; repealed 1996, c. 19, s. 94.

Case Law

R. v. Hayes (1995), 45 C.R. (4th) 41, 104 C.C.C. (3d) 316 (Que. C.A.) — Under NCA ss. 19.1 and 19.2, P must show that D had *specific knowledge* of the origin of the property as being a listed NCA offence. Wilful blindness is actual knowledge where D had suspicions concerning the origin and refused to eliminate the suspicions, *preferring* to remain in ignorance.

R. v. Khouri (1995), 97 C.C.C. (3d) 223 (Sask. C.A.) — D may be convicted of both trafficking (by selling) and possession of the proceeds of crime under *NCA* s. 19.1 in respect of the same transaction. (Per Tallis and Gerwing JJ.A.)

19.2 (1) Laundering proceeds of certain offences — No person shall use, transfer the possession of, send or deliver to any person or place, transport, transmit, alter, dispose of or otherwise deal with, in any manner and by any means, any property or any proceeds of any property with intent to conceal or convert that property or those proceeds and knowing that all or a part of that property or of those proceeds was obtained by or derived directly or indirectly as a result of

(a) the commission in Canada of an offence under section 4, 5 or 6; or

(b) an act or omission anywhere that, if it had occurred in Canada, would have constituted an offence under section 4, 5 or 6.

(2) Punishment — Every person who contravenes subsection (1)

(a) is guilty of an indictable offence and is liable to imprisonment for a term not exceeding ten years; or

(b) is guilty of an offence punishable on summary conviction.

R.S. 1985, c. 42 (4th Supp.), s. 12; repealed 1996, c. 19, s. 94.

19.3 (1) Part XII.2 of the Criminal Code applicable — Sections 462.3 and 462.32 to 462.5 of the *Criminal Code* apply, with such modifications as the circumstances require, in respect of proceedings for

(a) an offence under section 4, 5, 6, 19.1 or 19.2; or

(b) a conspiracy or an attempt to commit, being an accessory after the fact in relation to, or any counselling in relation to an offence referred to in paragraph (a).

(2) Idem — For the purposes of subsection (1),

(a) a reference in section 462.37 or 462.38 or subsection 462.41(2) of the *Criminal Code* to an enterprise crime offence shall be deemed to be a reference to an offence mentioned in paragraph (1)(a) or (b); and

(b) a reference, in relation to the manner in which forfeited property is to be disposed of, in subsection 462.37(1) or 462.38(2), paragraph 462.43(c) or section 462.5 of the *Criminal Code*, to the Attorney General shall be deemed to be a reference to

(i) where the prosecution of the offence in respect of which the thing was forfeited was commenced at the instance of the government of a province and conducted by or on behalf of that government, the Attorney General or Solicitor General of that province, and

1426

(ii) in any other case, the Minister of Public Works and Government Services.

R.S. 1985, c. 42 (4th Supp.), s. 12; 1993, c. 37, s. 29; 1996, c. 16, s. 60(1)(n); repealed 1996, c. 19, s. 94.

General

20. Regulations — The Governor in Council may make regulations

(a) providing for the issue of licences for the importation, export, sale, manufacture, production or distribution of narcotics and for the cultivation of opium poppy or marihuana;

(b) prescribing the form, duration and terms and conditions of any licence described in paragraph (a) and the fees payable therefor, and providing for the cancellation and suspension of licences described in that paragraph;

(c) authorizing the sale or possession of or other dealing in narcotics and prescribing the circumstances and conditions under which, and the persons by whom, narcotics may be sold, had in possession or otherwise dealt in;

(d) requiring physicians, dentists, veterinarians, pharmacists and other persons who deal in narcotics as authorized by this Act or the regulations to keep records and make returns;

(e) authorizing the communication of any information obtained under this Act or the regulations to provincial professional licensing authorities;

(f) prescribing the punishment by a fine not exceeding five hundred dollars or imprisonment for a term not exceeding six months, or both, to be imposed upon summary conviction for breach of any regulation; and

(g) generally, for carrying out the purposes and provisions of this Act.

R.S., c. N-1, s. 12.repealed 1996, c. 19, s. 94

21. Designation of analyst — The Minister may designate any person as an analyst for the purpose of this Act.

R.S., c. N-1, s. 13; 1984, c. 40, s. 45.repealed 1996, c. 19, s. 94.

22. Amendment of schedule — The Governor in Council may amend the schedule by adding thereto or deleting therefrom any substance, the inclusion or exclusion of which, as the case may be, is deemed necessary by the Governor in Council in the public interest.

R.S., c. N-1, s. 14.repealed 1996, c. 19, s. 94.

[Note: Part II as enacted by 1992, c. 20 was never proclaimed into force and as such has been omitted from the text of the Narcotic Control Act.]

Coming into Force

28. Coming into force — Part II or any provision thereof shall come into force on a day or days to be fixed by proclamation of the Governor in Council.

Repealed 1996, c. 19, s. 94.

Schedule

(Sections 2 and 22)

1. Opium Poppy (*Papaver somniferum*) its preparations, derivatives, alkaloids and salts, including:

(1) Opium,

(2) Codeine (Methylmorphine),

(3) Morphine,

(4) Thebaine,

and their preparations, derivatives and salts, including:

(5) Acetorphine,

(6) Acetyldihydrocodeine,

(7) Benzylmorphine,

(7.1) Buprenorphine,

(8) Codoxime,

(9) Desomorphine (dihydrodeoxymorphine),

(10) Diacetylmorphine (heroin),

(11) Dihydrocodeine

(12) Dihydromorphine,

(13) Ethylmorphine,

(14) Etorphine,

(15) Hydrocodone (dihydrocodeinone),

(16) Hydromorphone (dihydromorphinone),

(17) Hydromorphinol (dihydro-14-hydroxymorphine),

(18) Methyldesorphine (δ^6-deoxy-6-methylmorphine),

(19) Methyldihydromorphine (dihydro-6-methylmorphine),

(20) Metopon (dihydromethylmorphinone),

(21) Morphine-N-oxide (morphine-N-oxide),

(22) Myrophine (benzylmorphine myristate),

(23) Nalorphine (N-allylnormorphine),

(24) Nicocodine (6-nicotinylcodeine),

(25) Nicomorphine (dinicotinylmorphine),

(26) Norcodeine,

(27) Normorphine,

(28) Oxycodone (dihydrohydroxycodeinone),

(29) Oxymorphone (dihydrohydroxymorphinone),

(30) Pholcodine (β-4-morpholinoethylmorphine), and

(31) Thebacon (acetyldihydrocodeinone),
but not including:

(32) Apomorphine,

(33) Cyprenorphine,

(34) Naloxone,

(34.1) Naltrexone,

(35) Narcotine,

(36) Papaverine, and

(37) Poppy seed.

2. Coca (*Erythroxylon*), its preparations, derivatives, alkaloids and salts, including:

(1) Coca leaves,

(2) Cocaine, and

(3) Ecgonine (3-hydroxy-2-tropane carboxylic acid).

3. *Cannabis sativa*, its preparation, derivatives and similar synthetic preparations, including:

(1) Cannabis resin,

(2) Cannabis (marihuana),

(3) Cannabidiol,

(4) Cannabinol (3-n-amyl-6,6,9-trimethyl-6-dibenzopyran-1-ol),

(4.1) Nabilone (($\pm$)-trans-3 (1,1-dimethylheptyl)-6, 6a, 7, 8, 10, 10a-hexahydro-1-hydroxy-6,6- dimethyl-9H-dibenzo[b,d] phyran-9-one),

(5) Pyrahexyl (3-n-hexyl-6,6,9-trimethyl-7,8,9,10-tetrahydro-6-dibenzopyran-1-ol), and

(6) Tetrahydrocannabinol,
but not including:

(7) non-viable Cannabis seed.

4. Phenylpiperidines, their preparations, intermediates, derivatives and salts, including:

(1) Allyprodine (3-allyl-1-methyl-4-phenyl-4-phenyl-4-piperidyl propionate),

(2) Alphameprodine (α-3-ethyl-1-methyl-4-phenyl-4-piperidyl propionate),

(3) Alphaprodine (α-1-,3-dimethyl-4-phenyl-4-piperidyl propionate),

(4) Anileridine (ethyl 1-[2-p-aminophenyl) ethyl]-4-phenylpiperidine-4-carboxylate),

(5) Betameprodine (β-3-ethyl-1-methyl-4-phenyl-4-piperidyl propionate),

(6) Betaprodine (β-1,3-dimethyl-4-phenyl-4-piperidyl propionate),

(7) Benzethidine (ethyl (1-(2-benzyloxyethyl)-4-phenylpiperidine-4-carboxylate),

(8) Diphenoxylate (ethyl 1-(3-cyano-3,3-diphenylpropyl)-4-phenylpiperidine-4-carboxylate),

(9) Etoxeridine (ethyl 1-[2-(2-hydroxyethoxy) ethyl]-4-phenylpiperidine-4-carboxylate),

(10) Furethidine (ethyl 1-(2-tetrahydrofurfuryloxyethyl)-4-phenylpiperidine-4-carboxylate),

(11) Hydroxypethidine (ethyl 4-(m-hydroxyphenyl)-1-methyl-4-phenylpiperidine-4-carboxylate),

(12) Ketobemidone (1-[4-(m-hydroxyphenyl)-1-methyl-4-piperidyl]-1-propanone),

(13) Methylphenylisonipecotonitrile (4-cyano-1-methyl-4-phenylpiperidine),

(14) Morpheridine (ethyl 1-(2-morpholinoethyl)-4-phenylpiperidine-4-carboxylate),

(15) Norpethidine (ethyl 4-phenylpiperidine-4-carboxylate),

(16) Pethidine (ethyl 1-methyl-4-phenylpiperidine-4-carboxylate),

(17) Phenoperidine (ethyl 1-(3-hydroxy-3-phenylpropyl)-4-phenylpiperidine-4-carboxylate),

(18) Piminodine (ethyl 1-[3-(phenylamino) propyl]-4-phenylpiperidine-4-carboxylate),

(19) Properidine (isopropyl 1-methyl-4-phenyl-piperidine-4-carboxylate), and

(20) Trimeperidine (1,2,5-trimethyl-4-phenyl-4-piperidyl propionate), and not including:

(21) Carbamethidine (ethyl 1-(2-carbamylethyl)-4-phenylpiperidine-4-carboxylate), and

(22) Oxpheneridine (ethyl 1-(2-hydroxy-2-phenylethyl)-4-phenylpiperidine-4-carboxylate).

5. Phenazepines, their preparations, derivatives and salts, inlcuding:

(1) Proheptazine (hexahydro-1,3-dimethyl-4-phenyl-4-azepinyl propionate), but not including:

(2) Ethoheptazine (ethyl hexahydro-1-methyl-4-phenylazepine-4-carboxylate),

(3) Metethoheptazine (ethyl hexahydro-1,3-dimethyl-4-phenylazepine-4-carboxylate), and

(4) Metheptazine (ethyl hexahydro-1,2-dimethyl-4-phenylazepine-4-carboxylate).

6. Amidones, their preparations, intermediates, derivatives and salts, including:

(1) Dimethylaminodiphenylbutanonitrile (4-cyano-2-dimethylamino-4,4-diphenyl butane),

(2) Dipipanone (4,4-diphenyl-6-piperidino-3-heptanone),

(3) Isomethadone (6-dimethylamino-5-methyl-4,4-diphenyl-3-hexanone),

(4) Methadone (6-dimethylamino-4,4-diphenyl-3-heptanone),

(5) Normethadone (6-dimethylamino-4,4-diphenyl-3-hexanone), and

(6) Phenadoxone (6-morpholino-4,4-diphenyl-3-heptanone).

7. Methadols, their preparations, derivatives and salts, including:

(1) Acetylmethadol (6-dimethylamino-4,4-diphenyl-3-heptanyl acetate),

(2) Alphacetylmethadol (α-6-dimethylamino-4,4-diphenyl-3-heptanyl acetate),

(3) Alphamethadol (α-6-dimethylamino-4,4-diphenyl-3-heptanol),

(4) Betacetylmethadol (β-6-dimethylamino-4,4-diphenyl-3-heptanyl acetate),

(5) Betamethadol (β-6-dimethylamino-4,4-diphenyl-3-heptanol),

(6) Dimepheptanol (6-dimethylamino-4,4-diphenyl-3-heptanol), and

(7) Noracymethadol (α-6-methylamino-4,4-diphenyl-3-heptanyl acetate).

8. Phenalkoxams, their preparations, derivatives and salts, including:

(1) Dimenoxadol (dimethylaminoethyl 1-ethoxy-1,1-diphenylacetate),

(2) Dioxaphetylbutyrate (ethyl 2,2-diphenyl-4-morpholino butyrate), and

(3) Dextropropoxyphene ([[S-(R*,S*)]-α-[2-(dimethylamino)-1-methylethyl]- α-phenylbenzeneethanol, propanoate ester)

9. Thiambutenes, their preparations, derivatives and salts, including:

(1) Diethylthiambutene (N,N-diethyl-1-methyl-3,3-di-2-thienylallylamine),

(2) Dimethylthiambutene (N,N,1-trimethyl-3,3-di-2-thienylallylamine), and

(3) Ethylmethylthiambutene (N-ethyl-N,1-dimethyl-3,3-di-2-thienylallylamine).

10. Moramides, their preparations, intermediates, derivatives and salts, including:

(1) Dextromoramide (*d*-1-(3-methyl-4-morpholino-2,2-di-phenylbutyryl) pyrrolidine),

(2) Diphenylmorpholinoisovaleric acid (2-methyl-3-morpholino-1,1-diphenylpropionic acid),

(3) Levomoramide (*l*-1-(3-methyl-4-morpholino-2,2-diphenylbutyryl) pyrrolidine), and

(4) Racemoramide (*d,l*-1-(3-methyl-4-morpholino-2,2-diphenylbutyryl) pyrrolidine).

11. Morphinans, their preparations, derivatives and salts, including:

(1) Levomethorphan (*l*-1,2,3,9,10,10a-hexahydro-6-methoxy-11-methyl-4H-10, 4a-iminoethanophenanthrene),

(2) Levorphanol (*l*-1,2,3,9,10,10a-hexahydro-11-methyl-4H-10, 4a-iminoethanophenanthren-6-ol),

(3) Levophenacylmorphan (*l*-1,2,3,9,10,10a-hexahydro-11-phenacyl-4H-10, 4a-iminoethanophenanthren-6-ol),

(4) Norlevorphanol (*l*-1,2,3,9,10,10a-hexahydro-4H-10, 4a-iminoethanophenanthren-6-ol),

(5) Phenomorphan (*d,l*-1,2,3,9,10,10a-hexahydro-11-phenethyl-4H-10, 4a-iminoethanophenanthren-6-ol),

(6) Racemethorphan (*d,l*-1,2,3,9,10,10a-hexahydro-6-methoxy-11-methyl-4H-10,4a-iminoethano phenanthrene), and

(7) Racemorphan (*d,l*-1,2,3,9,10,10a-hexahydro-11-methyl-4H-10, 4a-iminoethanophenanthren-6-ol),

but not including:

(8) Dextromethorphan (*d,*-1,2,3,9,10,10a-hexahydro-6-methoxy-11-methyl-4H-10, 4a-iminoethanophenanthrene),

(9) Dextrorphan (*d,*1,2,3,9,10,10-hexahydro-11-methyl-4H-10, 4a-iminoethanophenanthren-6-ol),

(10) Levallorphan (*l*-11-allyl-1,2,3,9,10,10a-hexahydro-4H-10, 4a-iminoethanophenanthren-6-ol),

(11) Levargorphan (*l*-11-propargyl-1,2,3,9,10,10a-hexahydro-4H-10, 4a-iminoethanophenanthren-6-ol),

(12) Butorphanol and its salts, and

(13) Nalbuphine (17-(cyclobutylmethyl)-4,5α-epoxymorphinan-3,6α,14-triol).

12. Benzazocines, their preparations, derivatives and salts, including:

(1) Phenazocine (1,2,3,4,5,6-hexahydro-6,11-dimethyl-3-phenethyl-2,6-methano-3-benzazocin-8-o l),

(2) Metazocine (1,2,3,4,5,6-hexahydro-3,6,11-trimethyl-2,6-methano-3-benzazocin-8-ol), and

(3) Pentazocine (1,2,3,4,5,6-hexahydro-6,11-dimethyl-3-(3-methyl-2-butenyl)-2,6-methano-3-ben zazocin-8-ol),

but not including:

(4) Cyclazocine (1,2,3,4,5,6-hexahydro-6-11-dimethyl-3-(cyclopropylmethyl)-2,6-methano-3-benz azocin-8-ol).

13. Ampromides, their preparations, derivatives and salts, including:

(1) Diampromide (N-[2-(methylphenethylamino)-propyl]-propionanilide),

(2) Phenampromide (N-[2-(1-methyl-2-piperidyl)-ethyl]-propionanilide), and

(3) Propiram (N- (1-methyl-2-piperidinoethyl)-N-2-pyridylpropionamide).

14. Benzimidazoles, their preparations, derivatives and salts, including:

(1) Clonitazene (2-(p-chlorobenzyl)-1-diethylaminoethyl-5-nitrobenzimidazole), and

(2) Etonitazene (2-(p-ethoxybenzyl)-1-diethylaminoethyl-5-nitrobenzimidazole).

15. Phencyclidine, its salts and derivatives.

16. Fentanyl (1-phenylethyl-4-(phenylpropionylamino)-piperidine), its salts and derivatives.

17. Sufentanil (N-[4-(methoxymethyl)-1-[2-(2-thienyl) ethyl]-4-piperidinyl]-N-phenyl-propanamide), its salts and derivatives.

18. Tilidine (3-cyclohexene-1-carboxylic acid, 2-(dimethylamino)-1-phenylethyl ester, trans (±)), its preparations, derivatives and salts.

19. Carfentanil (methyl 4-[1-oxoprophyl)phenylamino]-1-(2-phenylethyl)-4-piperidine-carboxylate), its salts and derivatives.

20. Alfentanil (N-[1-[2-(4-ethyl-4,5-dihydro-5-oxo-1H-tetrazol-1-yl)ethyl]-4-(methoxymethyl) -4-piperidinyl]-N-phenylpropanamide), its salts and derivatives.

R.S., c. N-1, Schedule; SOR/71-359; SI/73-48; SI/77-113; SI/81-14, 150; SI/82-114, 241; SI/84-67; SI/86-6; SOR/87-517.repealed 1996, c. 19, s. 94.

FOOD AND DRUGS ACT

An Act respecting food, drugs, cosmetics and therapeutic devices

R.S.C. 1985, c. F-27,
Am. R.S. 1985, c. 27 (1st Supp.), ss. 191–195; c. 31 (1st Supp.), s. 11; c. 27 (3d Supp.), s. 1; c. 42 (4th Supp.), ss. 9–11; 1992, c. 1; 1993, c. 34, ss. 71, 73; 1993, c. 37, ss. 22–24; 1993, c. 44, s. 158; 1994, c. 38, ss. 18, 19; 1995, c.1, ss. 62, 63; 1996, c. 8, ss. 23.1, 23.2, 32; 1996, c. 16, ss. 60, 62, c. 19, ss. 77-82; 1997, c. 6, s. 62-66, 91.

See Table of Amendments for coming into force.

Short Title

1. Short title — This Act may be cited as the *Food and Drugs Act.*

R.S., c. F-27, s. 1.

Interpretation

2. Definitions — In this Act,

"advertisement" includes any representation by any means whatever for the purpose of promoting directly or indirectly the sale or disposal of any food, drug, cosmetic or device;

"analyst" means a person designated as an analyst for the purpose of the enforcement of this Act under section 28 or under section 13 of the *Canadian Food Inspection Agency Act*;

"contraceptive device" means any instrument, apparatus, contrivance or any substance other than a drug, that is manufactured, sold or represented for use in the prevention of conception;

"cosmetic" includes any substance or mixture of substances manufactured, sold or represented for use in cleansing, improving or altering the complexion, skin, hair or teeth, and includes deodorants and perfumes;

"Department" means the Department of National Health and Welfare;

"device" means any article, instrument, apparatus or contrivance, including any component, part or accessory thereof, manufactured, sold or represented for use in

(a) the diagnosis, treatment, mitigation or prevention of a disease, disorder or abnormal physical state, or its symptoms, in human beings or animals,

(b) restoring, correcting or modifying a body function or the body structure of human beings or animals,

(c) the diagnosis of pregnancy in human beings or animals, or

(d) the care of human beings or animals during pregnancy and at and after birth of the offspring, including care of the offspring,

and includes a contraceptive device but does not include a drug;

"drug" includes any substance or mixture of substances manufactured, sold or represented for use in

(a) the diagnosis, treatment, mitigation or prevention of a disease, disorder or abnormal physical state, or its symptoms, in human beings or animals,

(b) restoring, correcting or modifying organic functions in human beings or animals, or

(c) disinfection in premises in which food is manufactured, prepared or kept;

"food" includes any article manufactured, sold or represented for use as food or drink for human beings, chewing gum, and any ingredient that may be mixed with food for any purpose whatever;

"inspector" means any person designated as an inspector for the purpose of the enforcement of this Act under subsection 22(1) or under section 13 of the *Canadian Food Inspection Agency Act*;

"label" includes any legend, word or mark attached to, included in, belonging to or accompanying any food, drug, cosmetic, device or package;

"Minister" means the Minister of Health;

"package" includes any thing in which any food, drug, cosmetic or device is wholly or partly contained, placed or packed;

"prescribed" means prescribed by the regulations;

"sell" includes offer for sale, expose for sale, have in possession for sale and distribute, whether or not the distribution is made for consideration;

"unsanitary conditions" means such conditions or circumstances as might contaminate a food, drug or cosmetic with dirt or filth, or render injurious to health a food, drug or cosmetic.

R.S., c. F-27, s. 2; 1980–81–82–83, c. 47, s. 19;R.S. 1985, c. 27 (1st Supp.), s. 191; 1993, c. 34, s. 71; 1994, c. 38, s. 18; 1995, c. 1, s. 63; 1996, c. 8, ss. 23.1, 32(1)(g); 1997, c. 6, s. 62.

PART I — FOODS, DRUGS, COSMETICS AND DEVICES

General

3. (1) Prohibited advertising — No person shall advertise any food, drug, cosmetic or device to the general public as a treatment, preventative or cure for any of the diseases, disorders or abnormal physical states referred to in Schedule A.

(2) Prohibited label or advertisement where sale made — No person shall sell any food, drug, cosmetic or device

(a) that is represented by label, or

(b) that the person advertises to the general public

as a treatment, preventative or cure for any of the diseases, disorders or abnormal physical states referred to in Schedule A.

(3) Unauthorized advertising of contraceptive device prohibited — Except as authorized by regulation, no person shall advertise to the general public any contraceptive device or any drug manufactured, sold or represented for use in the prevention of conception.

R.S., c. F-27, s. 3.

Food

4. Prohibited sales of food — No person shall sell an article of food that

(a) has in or on it any poisonous or harmful substance;

(b) is unfit for human consumption;

(c) consists in whole or in part of any filthy, putrid, disgusting, rotten, decomposed or diseased animal or vegetable substance;

(d) is adulterated; or

(e) was manufactured, prepared, preserved, packaged or stored under unsanitary conditions.

R.S., c. F-27, s. 4.

5. (1) Deception, etc., regarding food — No person shall label, package, treat, process, sell or advertise any food in a manner that is false, misleading or deceptive or is likely to create an erroneous impression regarding its character, value, quantity, composition, merit or safety.

(2) Food labelled or packaged in contravention of regulations — An article of food that is not labelled or packaged as required by, or is labelled or packaged contrary to, the regulations shall be deemed to be labelled or packaged contrary to subsection (1).

R.S., c. F-27, s. 5.

Case Law
Elements of Offence

R. v. Rube (1992), 75 C.C.C. (3d) 575, [1993] 1 W.W.R. 385 (S.C.C.) — Section 5(1) creates an offence of strict liability in answer to which D may raise a defence of due diligence.

6. (1) Importation and interprovincial movement of food — Where a standard for a food has been prescribed, no person shall

(a) import into Canada,

(b) send, convey or receive for conveyance from one province to another, or

(c) have in possession for the purpose of sending or conveying from one province to another

any article that is intended for sale and that is likely to be mistaken for such food unless the article complies with the prescribed standard.

(2) Not applicable to carriers — Paragraphs (1)(*b*) and (*c*) do not apply to an operator of a conveyance that is used to carry an article or to a carrier of an article whose sole concern, in respect of the article, is the conveyance of the article unless the operator or carrier could, with reasonable diligence, have ascertained that the conveying or receiving for conveyance of the article or the possession of the article for the purpose of conveyance would be in violation of subsection (1).

(3) Labelling, etc., of food that is imported or moved interprovincially — Where a standard for a food has been prescribed, no person shall label, package, sell or advertise any article that

(a) has been imported into Canada,

(b) has been sent or conveyed from one province to another, or

(c) is intended to be sent or conveyed from one province to another

in such a manner that it is likely to be mistaken for such food unless the article complies with the prescribed standard.

R.S., c. F-27, s. 6; R.S. 1985, c. 27 (3d Supp.), s. 1.

6.1 (1) Governor in Council may identify standard or portion thereof — The Governor in Council may, by regulation, identify a standard or any portion of a standard prescribed for a food as being necessary to prevent injury to the health of the consumer or purchaser of the food.

(2) Where standard or portion thereof is identified — Where a standard or any portion of a standard prescribed for a food is identified by the Governor in Council pursuant to subsection (1), no person shall label, package, sell or advertise any article in such a manner that it is likely to be mistaken for such food unless the article complies with the standard or portion of a standard so identified.

R.S. 1985, c. 27 (3d Supp.), s. 1.

7. Unsanitary manufacture, etc., of food — No person shall manufacture, prepare, preserve, package or store for sale any food under unsanitary conditions.

R.S., c. F-27, s. 7.

Drugs

8. Prohibited sales of drugs — No person shall sell any drug that

(a) was manufactured, prepared, preserved, packaged or stored under unsanitary conditions; or

(b) is adulterated.

R.S., c. F-27, s. 8.

9. (1) Deception, etc., regarding drugs — No person shall label, package, treat, process, sell or advertise any drug in a manner that is false, misleading or deceptive or is likely to create an erroneous impression regarding its character, value, quantity, composition, merit or safety.

(2) Drugs labelled or packaged in contravention of regulations — A drug that is not labelled or packaged as required by, or is labelled or packaged contrary to, the regulations shall be deemed to be labelled or packaged contrary to subsection (1).

R.S., c. F-27, s. 9.

10. (1) Where standard prescribed for drug — Where a standard has been prescribed for a drug, no person shall label, package, sell or advertise any substance in such a manner that it is likely to be mistaken for that drug, unless the substance complies with the prescribed standard.

(2) Trade standards — Where a standard has not been prescribed for a drug, but a standard for the drug is contained in any publication referred to in Schedule B, no person shall label, package, sell or advertise any substance in such a manner that it is likely to be mistaken for that drug, unless the substance complies with the standard.

(3) Where no prescribed or trade standard — Where a standard for a drug has not been prescribed and no standard for the drug is contained in any publication referred to in Schedule B, no person shall sell the drug unless

(a) it is in accordance with the professed standard under which it is sold; and

(b) it does not resemble, in a manner likely to deceive, any drug for which a standard has been prescribed or is contained in any publication referred to in Schedule B.

R.S., c. F-27, s. 10.

11. Unsanitary manufacture, etc., of drug — No person shall manufacture, prepare, preserve, package or store for sale any drug under unsanitary conditions.

R.S., c. F-27, s. 11.

12. Drugs not to be sold unless safe manufacture indicated — No person shall sell any drug described in Schedule C or D unless the Minister has, in prescribed form and manner, indicated that the premises in which the drug was manufactured and the process and conditions of manufacture therein are suitable to ensure that the drug will not be unsafe for use.

R.S., c. F-27, s. 12.

13. Drugs not to be sold unless safe batch indicated — No person shall sell any drug described in Schedule E unless the Minister has, in prescribed form and manner, indicated that the batch from which the drug was taken is not unsafe for use.

R.S., c. F-27, s. 13.

14. (1) Samples — No person shall distribute or cause to be distributed any drug as a sample.

(2) Exception — Subsection (1) does not apply to the distribution, under prescribed conditions, of samples of drugs to physicians, dentists, veterinary surgeons or pharmacists.

R.S., c. F-27, s. 14.

15. Schedule f drugs not to be sold — No person shall sell any drug described in Schedule F.

R.S., c. F-27, s. 15.

Cosmetics

16. Prohibited sales of cosmetics — No person shall sell any cosmetic that

(a) has in or on it any substance that may cause injury to the health of the user when the cosmetic is used,

(i) according to the directions on the label or accompanying the cosmetic, or

(ii) for such purposes and by such methods of use as are customary or usual therefor;

(b) consists in whole or in part of any filthy or decomposed substance or of any foreign matter; or

(c) was manufactured, prepared, preserved, packaged or stored under unsanitary conditions.

R.S., c. F-27, s. 16.

17. Where standard prescribed for cosmetic — Where a standard has been prescribed for a cosmetic, no person shall label, package, sell or advertise any article in such a manner that it is likely to be mistaken for that cosmetic, unless the article complies with the prescribed standard.

R.S., c. F-27, s. 17.

18. Unsanitary conditions — No person shall manufacture, prepare, preserve, package or store for sale any cosmetic under unsanitary conditions.

R.S., c. F-27, s. 18.

Devices

19. Prohibited sales of devices — No person shall sell any device that, when used according to directions or under such conditions as are customary or usual, may cause injury to the health of the purchaser or user thereof.

R.S., c. F-27, s. 19.

20. (1) Deception, etc., regarding devices — No person shall label, package, treat, process, sell or advertise any device in a manner that is false, misleading or deceptive or is likely to create an erroneous impression regarding its design, construction, performance, intended use, quantity, character, value, composition, merit or safety.

(2) Devices labelled or packaged in contravention of regulations — A device that is not labelled or packaged as required by, or is labelled or packaged contrary to, the regulations shall be deemed to be labelled or packaged contrary to subsection (1).

R.S., c. F-27, s. 20; 1976–77, c. 28, s. 16.

21. Where standard prescribed for device — Where a standard has been prescribed for a device, no person shall label, package, sell or advertise any article in such a manner that is likely to be mistaken for such device, unless the article complies with the prescribed standard.

R.S., c. F-27, s. 21.

PART II

Administration and Enforcement

Inspection, Seizure and Forfeiture

22. (1) Inspectors — The Minister may designate any person as an inspector for the purpose of the enforcement of this Act.

(2) Certificate to be produced — An inspector shall be given a certificate in a form established by the Minister or the President of the Canadian Food Inspection Agency attesting to the inspector's designation and, on entering any place pursuant to subsection 23(1), an inspector shall, if so required, produce the certificate to the person in charge of that place.

R.S., c. F-27, s. 22; 1980–81–82–83, c. 47, s. 19; 1997, c. 6, s. 63.

23. (1) Powers of inspectors — Subject to subsection (1.1), an inspector may at any reasonable time enter any place where the inspector believes on reasonable grounds any article to which this Act or the regulations apply is manufactured, prepared, preserved, packaged or stored, and may

(a) examine any such article and take samples thereof, and examine anything that the inspector believes on reasonable grounds is used or capable of being used for that manufacture, preparation, preservation, packaging or storing;

(a.1) enter any conveyance that the inspector believes on reasonable grounds is used to carry any article to which section 6 or 6.1 applies and examine any such article found therein and take samples thereof;

(b) open and examine any receptacle or package that the inspector believes on reasonable grounds contains any article to which this Act or the regulations apply;

(c) examine and make copies of, or extracts from, any books, documents or other records found in any place referred to in this subsection that the inspector believes on reasonable grounds contain any information relevant to the enforcement of this Act with respect to any article to which this Act or the regulations apply and

(d) seize and detain for such time as may be necessary any article by means of or in relation to which the inspector believes on reasonable grounds any provision of this Act or the regulations has been contravened.

(1.1) Warrant required to enter dwelling-house — Where any place mentioned in subsection (1) is a dwelling-house, an inspector may not enter that dwelling-house without the consent of the occupant except under the authority of a warrant issued under subsection (1.2).

(1.2) Authority to issue warrant — Where on *ex parte* application a justice of the peace is satisfied by information on oath

(a) that the conditions for entry described in subsection (1) exist in relation to a dwelling-house,

(b) that entry to the dwelling-house is necessary for any purpose relating to the administration or enforcement of this Act, and

(c) that entry to the dwelling-house has been refused or that there are reasonable grounds for believing that entry thereto will be refused,

the justice of the peace may issue a warrant under his hand authorizing the inspector named therein to enter that dwelling-house subject to such conditions as may be specified in the warrant.

(1.3) Use of force — In executing a warrant issued under subsection (1.2), the inspector named therein shall not use force unless the inspector is accompanied by a peace officer and the use of force has been specifically authorized in the warrant.

(2) Definition of "article to which this Act or the regulations apply" — In subsection (1), "article to which this Act or the regulations apply" includes

(a) any food, drug, cosmetic or device;

(b) anything used for the manufacture, preparation, preservation, packaging or storing thereof; and

(c) any labelling or advertising material.

(3) **Assistance and information to be given inspector** — The owner or person in charge of a place entered by an inspector pursuant to subsection (1) and every person found therein shall give the inspector all reasonable assistance and furnish the inspector with any information he may reasonably require.

R.S., c. F-27, s. 22; R.S. 1985, c. 31 (1st Supp.), s. 11; c. 27 (3d Supp.), s. 2.

24. (1) **Obstruction and false statements** — No person shall obstruct or hinder, or knowingly make any false or misleading statement either orally or in writing to, an inspector while the inspector is engaged in carrying out his duties or functions under this Act or the regulations.

(2) **Interference** — Except with the authority of an inspector, no person shall remove, alter or interfere in any way with anything seized under this Part.

R.S., c. F-27, ss. 22, 37.

25. **Storage and removal** — Any article seized under this Act may, at the option of an inspector, be kept or stored in the building or place where it was seized or, at the direction of an inspector, the article may be removed to any other proper place.

R.S., c. F-27, ss. 22, 37.

26. **Release of seized articles** — An inspector who has seized any article under this Part shall release it when he is satisfied that all the provisions of this Act and the regulations with respect thereto have been complied with.

R.S., c. F-27, ss. 23, 37.

27. (1) **Destruction with consent** — Where an inspector has seized an article under this Part and its owner or the person in whose possession the article was at the time of seizure consents to its destruction, the article is thereupon forfeited to Her Majesty and may be destroyed or otherwise disposed of as the Minister or the Minister of Agriculture and Agri-Food may direct.

(2) **Forfeiture** — Where a person has been convicted of a contravention of this Act or the regulations, the court or judge may order that any article by means of or in relation to which the offence was committed, and any thing of a similar nature belonging to or in relation to which the offence was committed, and any thing of a similar nature belonging to or in the possession of the person or found with the article, be forfeited. On the making of the order, the article and thing are forfeited to Her Majesty and may be disposed of as the Minister or the Minister of Agriculture and Agri-Food may direct.

(3) **Order for forfeiture on application of inspector** — Without prejudice to subsection (2), a judge of a superior court of the province in which any article is seized under this Part may, on the application of an inspector and on such notice to such persons as the judge directs, order that the article and any thing of a similar nature found with it be forfeited to Her Majesty, if the judge finds, after making such inquiry as the judge considers necessary, that the article is one by means of or in relation to which any of the provisions of this Act or the regulations have been contravened. On the making of the order, the article or thing may be disposed of as the Minister or the Minister of Agriculture and Agri-Food may direct.

R.S., c. F-27, ss. 23, 37;1994, c. 38, s. 19;1995, c. 1, s. 62; 1994, c. 38, s. 19; 1995, c. 1, s. 62; 1996, c. 8, s. 23.2; 1997, c. 6, s. 64.

Analysis

28. Analysts — The Minister may designate any person as an analyst for the purpose of the enforcement of this Act.

1980–81–82–83, c. 47, s. 19.

29. (1) Analysis and examination — An inspector may submit to an analyst for analysis or examination, any article seized by the inspector, any sample therefrom or any sample taken by the inspector.

(2) Certificate or report — An analyst who has made an analysis or examination may issue a certificate or report setting out the results of the examination or analysis.

R.S., c. F-27, s. 24.

Regulations

30. (1) Regulations — The Governor in Council may make regulations for carrying the purposes and provisions of this Act into effect, and, in particular, but without restricting the generality of the foregoing, may make regulations

(a) declaring that any food or drug or class of food or drugs is adulterated if any prescribed substance or class of substances is present therein or has been added thereto or extracted or omitted therefrom;

(b) respecting

(i) the labelling and packaging and the offering, exposing and advertising for sale of food, drugs, cosmetics and devices,

(ii) the size, dimensions, fill and other specifications of packages of food, drugs, cosmetics and devices,

(iii) the sale or the conditions of sale of any food, drug, cosmetic or device, and

(iv) the use of any substance as an ingredient in any food, drug, cosmetic or device,

to prevent the purchaser or consumer thereof from being deceived or misled in respect of the design, construction, performance, intended use, quantity, character, value, composition, merit or safety thereof, or to prevent injury to the health of the purchaser or consumer;

(c) prescribing standards of composition, strength, potency, purity, quality or other property of any article of food, drug, cosmetic or device;

(d) respecting the importation of foods, drugs, cosmetics and devices in order to ensure compliance with this Act and the regulations;

(e) respecting the method of manufacture, preparation, preserving, packing, storing and testing of any food, drug, cosmetic or device in the interest of, or for the prevention of injury to, the health of the purchaser or consumer;

(f) requiring persons who sell food, drugs, cosmetics or devices to maintain such books and records as the Governor in Council considers necessary for the proper enforcement and administration of this Act and the regulations;

(g) respecting the form and manner of the Minister's indication under section 12, including the fees payable therefor, and prescribing what premises or what processes or conditions of manufacture, including qualifications of technical staff, shall or shall not be deemed to be suitable for the purposes of that section;

(h) requiring manufacturers of any drugs described in Schedule E to submit test portions of any batch of those drugs and respecting the form and manner of the Minister's indication under section 13, including the fees payable therefor;

(i) respecting the powers and duties of inspectors and analysts and the taking of samples and the seizure, detention, forfeiture and disposition of articles;

(j) exempting any food, drug, cosmetic or device from all or any of the provisions of this Act and prescribing the conditions of the exemption;

(k) prescribing forms for the purposes of this Act and the regulations;

(l) providing for the analysis of food, drugs or cosmetics other than for the purposes of this Act and prescribing a tariff of fees to be paid for that analysis;

(m) adding anything to any of the schedules, in the interest of, or for the prevention of injury to, the health of the purchaser or consumer, or deleting anything therefrom;

(n) respecting the distribution or the conditions of distribution of samples of any drug;

(o) respecting

(i) the method of manufacture, preparation, preserving, packing, labelling, storing and testing of any new drug, and

(ii) the sale or the conditions of sale of any new drug,

and defining for the purposes of this Act the expression "new drug"; and

(p) authorizing the advertising to the general public of contraceptive devices and drugs manufactured, sold or represented for use in the prevention of conception and prescribing the circumstances and conditions under which, and the persons by whom, those devices and drugs may be so advertised.

(2) **Regulations respecting drugs manufactured outside Canada** — Without limiting or restricting the authority conferred by any other provisions of this Act or any Part thereof for carrying into effect the purposes and provisions of this Act or any Part thereof, the Governor in Council may make such regulations governing, regulating or prohibiting

(a) the importation into Canada of any drug or class of drugs manufactured outside Canada, or

(b) the distribution or sale in Canada, or the offering, exposing or having in possession for sale in Canada, of any drug or class of drugs manufactured outside Canada,

as the Governor in Council deems necessary for the protection of the public in relation to the safety and quality of any such drug or class of drugs.

(3) **Regulations re the North American Free Trade Agreement** — Without limiting or restricting the authority conferred by any other provisions of this Act or any Part thereof for carrying into effect the purposes and provisions of this Act or any Part thereof, the Governor in Council may, for the purpose of implementing Article 1711 of the North American Free Trade Agreement, make regulations respecting the extent to which, if any, a person may, in seeking to establish the safety or effectiveness

of a new drug for the purposes of any regulations made under subsection (1) or (2), rely on test or other data submitted by any other person to the Minister in accordance with such regulations.

(4) **Definition** — In subsection (3), "North American Free Trade Agreement" has the meaning given to the word "Agreement" by subsection 2(1) of the *North American Free Trade Agreement Implementation Act.*

R.S., c. F-27, s. 25; 1976–77, c. 28, s. 16; 1980–81–82–83, c. 47, s. 19; 1993, c. 44, s. 158.

Offences and Punishment

31. Contravention of Act and regulations — Subject to section 31.1, every person who contravenes any of the provisions of this Act or of the regulations made under this Part is guilty of an offence and liable

(a) on summary conviction for a first offence to a fine not exceeding five hundred dollars or to imprisonment for a term not exceeding three months or to both and, for a subsequent offence to a fine not exceeding one thousand dollars or to imprisonment for a term not exceeding six months or to both; and

(b) on conviction on indictment to a fine not exceeding five thousand dollars or to imprisonment for a term not exceeding three years or to both.

R.S., c. F-27, ss. 26, 39, 46; 1996, c. 19, s. 77; 1997, c. 6, s. 65, 91.

31.1 Offences relating to food — Every person who contravenes any provision of this Act or the regulations, as it relates to food, is guilty of an offence and liable

(a) on summary conviction, to a fine not exceeding $50,000 or to imprisonment for a term not exceeding six months or to both; or

(b) on conviction by indictment, to a fine not exceeding $250,000 or to imprisonment for a term not exceeding three years or to both.

1997, c. 6, s. 66(1).

32. (1) Limitation period — A prosecution for a summary conviction offence under this Act may be instituted at any time within two years after the time the subject-matter of the prosecution becomes known to the Minsiter or, in the case of a contravention of a provision of the Act that relates to food, to the Minister of Agriculture and Agri-Food.

(2) **Minister's certificate** — A document purporting to have been issued by the Minister referred to in subsection (1), certifying the day on which the subject-matter of any prosecution became known to the Minister, is admissible in evidence without proof of the signature or official character of the person appearing to have signed the document and is evidence of the matters asserted in it.

R.S., c. F-27, s. 27; 1997, c. 6, s. 66(1), (2).

1997, c. 6, s. 66(2) states: for greater certainty, the two year limitation period provided for in subsection 32(1) of the Food and Drugs Act, as amended by 1997, c. 6, s. 66(1), only applies in respect of offences committed after the coming into force of that subsection.

33. Venue — A prosecution for a contravention of this Act or the regulations may be instituted, heard, tried or determined in the place in which the offence was committed or the subject-matter of the prosecution arose or in any place in which the accused is apprehended or happens to be.

R.S., c. F-27, s. 28.

34. (1) Want of knowledge — Subject to subsection (2), in a prosecution for the sale of any article in contravention of this Act, except Parts III and IV, or of the regulations made under this Part, if the accused proves to the satisfaction of the court or judge that

(a) the accused purchased the article from another person in packaged form and sold it in the same package and in the same condition the article was in at the time it was so purchased, and

(b) that the accused could not with reasonable diligence have ascertained that the sale of the article would be in contravention of this Act or the regulations,

the accused shall be acquitted.

(2) Notice of reliance on want of knowledge — Subsection (1) does not apply in any prosecution unless the accused, at least ten days before the day fixed for the trial, has given to the prosecutor notice in writing that the accused intends to avail himself of the provisions of subsection (1) and has disclosed to the prosecutor the name and address of the person from whom the accused purchased the article and the date of purchase.

R.S., c. F-27, ss. 29, 39, 46.

35. (1) Certificate of analyst — Subject to this section, in any prosecution for an offence under section 31, a certificate purporting to be signed by an analyst and stating that an article, sample or substance has been submitted to, and analysed or examined by, the analyst and stating the results of the analysis or examination is admissible in evidence and, in the absence of evidence to the contrary, is proof of the statements contained in the certificate without proof of the signature or official character of the person appearing to have signed it.

(2) Requiring attendance of analyst — The party against whom a certificate of an analyst is produced pursuant to subsection (1) may, with leave of the court, require the attendance of the analyst for the purposes of cross-examination.

(3) Notice of intention to produce certificate — No certificate shall be admitted in evidence pursuant to subsection (1) unless, before the trial, the party intending to produce the certificate has given reasonable notice of that intention, together with a copy of the certificate, to the party against whom it is intended to be produced.

(4) Proof of service — For the purposes of this Act, service of any certificate referred to in subsection (1) may be proved by oral evidence given under oath by, or by the affidavit or solemn declaration of, the person claiming to have served it.

(5) Attendance for examination — Notwithstanding subsection (4), the court may require the person who appears to have signed an affidavit or solemn declaration referred to in that subsection to appear before it for examination or cross-examination in respect of the issue of proof of service.

R.S., c. F-27, s. 30; R.S. 1985, c. 27 (1st Supp.), s. 192; 1996, c. 19, s. 78.

36. (1) Proof as to manufacturer or packager — In a prosecution for a contravention of this Act or of the regulations made under this Part, proof that a package containing any article to which this Act or the regulations apply bore a name or address purporting to be the name or address of the person by whom it was manufactured or packaged is, in the absence of evidence to the contrary, proof that the article was manufactured or packaged, as the case may be, by the person whose name or address appeared on the package.

(2) **Offence by employee or agent** — In a prosecution for a contravention described in subsection (1), it is sufficient proof of the offence to establish that it was committed by an employee or agent of the accused whether or not the employee or agent is identified or has been prosecuted for the offence.

(3) **Certified copies and extracts** — In a prosecution for a contravention described in subsection (1), a copy of a record or an extract therefrom certified to be a true copy by the inspector who made it pursuant to paragraph 23(1)(c) is admissible in evidence and is, in the absence of evidence to the contrary, proof of its contents.

(4) **Where accused had adulterating substances** — Where a person is prosecuted under this Part for having manufactured an adulterated food or drug for sale, and it is established that the person had in his possession or on his premises any substance the addition of which to that food or drug has been declared by regulation to cause the adulteration of the food or drug, the onus of proving that the food or drug was not adulterated by the addition of that substance lies on the accused.

R.S., c. F-27, ss. 31, 39, 46; 1996, c. 19, s. 79.

Exports

37. (1) **Conditions under which exports exempt** — This Act does not apply to any packaged food, drug, cosmetic or device, not manufactured for consumption in Canada and not sold for consumption in Canada, if the package is marked in distinct overprinting with the word "Export" or "Exportation" and a certificate that the package and its contents do not contravene any known requirement of the law of the country to which it is or is about to be consigned has been issued in respect of the package and its contents in prescribed form and manner.

(2) [Repealed 1996, c. 19, s. 80]

R.S., c. F-27, s. 32; 1993, c. 34, s. 73; 1996, c. 19, s. 80.

PART III — CONTROLLED DRUGS

[Note: Part III of the Food and Drugs Act *repealed 1996, c. 19, s. 81. Please note Part III of the Act was repealed by the* Controlled Drugs and Substances Act *on May 14, 1997. We have, however, retained the text of Part III as it remains of relevance to offences occurring before its repeal and will therefore continue to be of great practical importance for some time to come.]*

Controlled Drugs

38. **Definitions** — In this Part,

"controlled drug" means any drug or other substance included in Schedule G;

"possession" means possession within the meaning of subsection 4(3) of the *Criminal Code*;

"practitioner" means a person who is registered and entitled under the laws of a province to practise in that province the profession of medicine, dentistry or veterinary medicine;

"prescription" means, in respect of a controlled drug, an authorization given by a practitioner that a stated amount of the controlled drug be dispensed for the person named therein;

"traffic" means to manufacture, sell, export from or import into Canada, transport or deliver, otherwise than under the authority of this Part or the regulations.

R.S., c. F-27, s. 33; R.S. 1985, c. 27 (1st Supp.), s. 193; repealed 1996, c. 19, s. 81.

38.1 (1) Failure to disclose previous prescriptions — No person shall, at any time, seek or obtain a controlled drug or a prescription for a controlled drug from a practitioner unless that person discloses to the practitioner particulars of every controlled drug or prescription for a controlled drug issued to that person by a different practitioner within the preceding thirty days.

(2) Offence and punishment — Every person who contravenes subsection (1)

   (a) is guilty of an indictable offence and is liable to a fine not exceeding five thousand dollars or to imprisonment for a term not exceeding three years; or

   (b) is guilty of an offence punishable on summary conviction and is liable

      (i) for a first offence, to a fine not exceeding one thousand dollars or to imprisonment for a term not exceeding six months, and

      (ii) for a subsequent offence, to a fine not exceeding two thousand dollars or to imprisonment for a term not exceeding one year.

(3) Limitation period — Summary conviction proceedings in respect of an offence under this section may be instituted at any time within but not later than one year from the time when the subject-matter of the proceedings arose.

R.S. 1985, c. 27 (1st Supp), s. 194; repealed 1996, c. 19, s. 81.

39. (1) Trafficking in controlled drug — No person shall traffic in a controlled drug or any substance represented or held out by the person to be a controlled drug.

(2) Possession for trafficking — No person shall have in possession any controlled drug for the purpose of trafficking.

(3) Offence and punishment — Every person who contravenes subsection (1) or (2) is guilty of an offence and liable

   (a) on summary conviction, to imprisonment for a term not exceeding eighteen months; or

   (b) on conviction on indictment, to imprisonment for a term not exceeding ten years.

R.S., c. F-27, s. 34; repealed 1996, c. 19, s. 81.

40. (1) Procedure in prosecution for possession for trafficking — In any prosecution for a contravention of subsection 39(2), if the accused does not plead guilty, the trial shall proceed as if the issue to be tried is whether the accused was in possession of a controlled drug.

(2) Procedure on finding in respect of possession — If, pursuant to subsection (1), the court finds that the accused was not in possession of a controlled drug, the accused shall be acquitted but, if the court finds that the accused was in possession of a controlled drug, the accused shall be given an opportunity of establishing that he was not in possession of the controlled drug for the purpose of trafficking and, thereafter, the prosecutor shall be given an opportunity of adducing evidence to the contrary.

(3) Acquittal on conviction — If the accused establishes, pursuant to subsection (2), that he was not in possession of the controlled drug for the purpose of trafficking, the accused shall be acquitted of the offence as charged and, if the accused fails to so establish, the accused shall be convicted of the offence as charged and sentenced accordingly.

R.S., c. F-27, s. 35; repealed 1996, c. 19, s. 81.

41. **(1) Setting out or negativing exception, etc., not required** — No exception, exemption, excuse or qualification prescribed by law is required to be set out or negatived, as the case may be, in an information or indictment for an offence under section 39 or under section 463, 464 or 465 of the *Criminal Code* in respect of an offence under section 39.

(2) Burden of proving exception, etc — In any prosecution under this Part, the burden of proving that an exception, exemption, excuse or qualification prescribed by law operates in favour of the accused is on the accused, and the prosecutor is not required, except by way of rebuttal, to prove that the exception, exemption, excuse or qualification does not operate in favour of the accused, whether or not it is set out in the information or indictment.

R.S., c. F-27, s. 36; repealed 1996, c. 19, s. 81.

42. **(1) Entry and search** — A peace officer may, at any time, without a warrant enter and search any place other than a dwelling-house, and under the authority of a warrant issued under subsection (3), enter and search any dwelling-house in which the peace officer believes on reasonable grounds there is a controlled drug by means of or in respect of which an offence under this Part has been committed.

(2) Search of person and seizure — A peace officer may search any person found in a place entered pursuant to subsection (1) and may seize and take away any controlled drug found in that place and any other thing that may be evidence that an offence under this Part has been committed.

(3) Warrant to search dwelling-house — A justice who is satisfied by information on oath that there are reasonable grounds for believing that there is a controlled drug, by means of or in respect of which an offence under this Part has been committed, in any dwelling-house may issue a warrant under his hand authorizing a peace officer named therein at any time to enter the dwelling-house and search for controlled drugs.

(4) [Repealed R.S. 1985, c. 27 (1st Supp.), s. 195(2).]

(5) Powers of peace officer — For the purpose of exercising authority under this section, a peace officer may, with such assistance as that officer deems necessary, break open any door, window, lock, fastener, floor, wall, ceiling, compartment, plumbing fixture, box, container or any other thing.

R.S., c. F-27, s. 37; c. 10 (2d Supp.), s. 64; R.S. 1985, c. 27 (1st Supp.), s. 195; repealed 1996, c. 19, s. 81.

43. **(1) Application for restoration** — Where a controlled drug or other thing has been seized under this section, any person may, within two months after the date of the seizure, where prior notification has been given to the Crown in the manner prescribed by the regulations, apply to a provincial court judge within whose territorial jurisdiction the seizure was made for an order of restoration under subsection (2).

(2) Order of immediate restoration — Subject to section 44, where, on the hearing of an application made under subsection (1), the provincial court judge is satisfied that the applicant is entitled to possession of the controlled drug or other thing seized, and that the thing seized is not or will not be required as evidence in any proceedings in respect of an offence under this Part, he shall order that the thing seized be restored forthwith to the applicant.

(3) Order of restoration at later time — Where on the hearing of an application made under subsection (1) the provincial court judge is satisfied that the applicant is entitled to possession of the thing seized but is not satisfied that the thing is not or will not be required as evidence in any proceedings in respect of an offence under this Part, he shall order that the thing seized be restored to the applicant

> (a) on the expiration of four months after the date of seizure, if no proceedings in respect of an offence under this Part have been commenced before that time; or

> (b) on the final conclusion of any such proceedings, in any other case.

(4) Where application not made or order refused — Where no application has been made for the return of any controlled drug or other thing seized pursuant to subsection 42(2) within two months after the date of the seizure, or an application therefor has been made but, on the hearing of the application, no order of restoration is made, the thing seized shall be delivered

> (a) in the case of a controlled drug, to the Minister, who may make such disposition thereof as the Minister thinks fit; and

> (b) in the case of any other thing,

>> (i) where the prosecution of the offence in respect of which the thing was seized was commenced at the instance of the government of a province and conducted by or on behalf of that government, to the Attorney General or Solicitor General of that province, and

>> (ii) in any other case, to the Minister of Public Works and Government Services,

> who may dispose of the thing in accordance with the law.
> R.S., c. F-27, s. 37; R.S. 1985, c. 27 (1st Supp.), s. 203; 1993, c. 37, s. 22; 1996, c. 16, s. 60(1)(i); repealed 1996, c. 19, s. 81.

44. Forfeiture on conviction — Where a person has been convicted of an offence under this Part,

> (a) any controlled drug seized pursuant to subsection 42(2) by means of or in respect of which the offence was committed is forfeited to Her Majesty in right of Canada and shall be disposed of by the Minister as the Minister thinks fit, and

> (b) any money so seized that was used for the purchase of that controlled drug is,

>> (i) where the prosecution of the offence in respect of which the money was seized was commenced at the instance of the government of a province and conducted by or on behalf of that government, forfeited to Her Majesty in right of that province and shall be disposed of by the Attorney General or Solicitor General of that province in accordance with the law, and

>> (ii) in any other case, forfeited to Her Majesty in right of Canada and shall be disposed of by the Minister of Public Works and Government Services in accordance with the law.
> R.S., c. F-27, s. 37; 1993, c. 37, s. 23; 1996, c. 16, s. 60(1)(i); repealed 1996, c. 19, s. 81.

44.1 Interpretation — For the purposes of sections 44.2 to 44.4, a reference therein to an offence under section 39, 44.2 or 44.3 shall be deemed to include a reference to a conspiracy or an attempt to commit, being an accessory after the fact in relation to, or any counselling in relation to, such an offence.

R.S. 1985, c. 42 (4th Supp.), s. 9; repealed 1996, c. 19, s. 81.

44.2 (1) Possession of property obtained by trafficking in controlled drugs — No person shall possess any property or any proceeds of any property knowing that all or part of the property or of those proceeds was obtained or derived directly or indirectly as a result of

(a) the commission in Canada of an offence under section 39; or

(b) an act or omission anywhere that, if it had occurred in Canada, would have constituted an offence under section 39.

(2) Punishment — Every person who contravenes subsection (1)

(a) is guilty of an indictable offence and liable to imprisonment for a term not exceeding ten years, where the value of the subject-matter of the offence exceeds one thousand dollars; or

(b) is guilty

(i) of an indictable offence and liable to imprisonment for a term not exceeding two years, or

(ii) of an offence punishable on summary conviction, where the value of the subject-matter of the offence does not exceed one thousand dollars.

R.S. 1985, c. 42 (4th Supp.), s. 9; repealed 1996, c. 19, s. 81.

44.3 (1) Laundering proceeds of trafficking in controlled drugs — No person shall use, transfer the possession of, send or deliver to any person or place, transport, transmit, alter, dispose of or otherwise deal with, in any manner or by any means, any property or any proceeds of any property with intent to conceal or convert that property or those proceeds and knowing that all or a part of that property or of those proceeds was obtained or derived directly or indirectly as a result of

(a) the commission in Canada of an offence under section 39; or

(b) an act or omission anywhere that, if it had occurred in Canada, would have constituted an offence under section 39.

(2) Punishment — Every person who contravenes subsection (1)

(a) is guilty of an indictable offence and liable to imprisonment for a term not exceeding ten years; or

(b) is guilty of an offence punishable on summary conviction.

R.S. 1985, c. 42 (4th Supp.), s. 9; repealed 1996, c. 19, s. 81.

44.4 (1) Part XII.2 of the Criminal Code applicable — Sections 462.3 and 462.32 to 462.5 of the *Criminal Code* apply, with such modifications as the circumstances require, in respect of proceedings for an offence under section 39, 44.2 or 44.3.

(2) Idem — For the purposes of subsection (1),

(a) a reference in section 462.37 or 462.38 or subsection 462.41(2) of the *Criminal Code* to an enterprise crime offence shall be deemed to be a reference to an offence under section 39, 44.2 or 44.3; and

(b) a reference, in relation to the manner in which forfeited property is to be disposed of, in subsection 462.37(1) or 462.38(2), paragraph 462.43(c) or section

1451

462.5 of the *Criminal Code*, to the Attorney General shall be deemed to be a reference to

(i) where the prosecution of the offence in respect of which the thing was forfeited was commenced at the instance of the government of a province and conducted by or on behalf of that government, the Attorney General or Solicitor General of that province, and

(ii) in any other case, the Minister of Public Works and Government Services.

R.S. 1985, c. 42 (4th Supp.), s. 9; 1993, c. 37, s. 24; 1996, c. 16, s. 60(1)(i); repealed 1996, c. 19, s. 81.

45. (1) Regulations respecting controlled drugs — The Governor in Council may make regulations for carrying out the purposes and provisions of this Part, and, in particular, but without restricting the generality of the foregoing, may make regulations

(a) authorizing the manufacture, sale, importation, transportation, delivery or other dealing in controlled drugs and prescribing the circumstances and conditions under which, and the persons by whom, controlled drugs may be manufactured, sold, imported, transported, delivered, or otherwise dealt in;

(b) providing for the issue of licences for the importation, manufacture or sale of controlled drugs;

(c) prescribing the form, duration and terms and conditions of any licence described in paragraph (b) and the fees payable therefor, and providing for the cancellation and suspension of those licences;

(d) requiring persons who import, manufacture, sell, administer or deal in controlled drugs to maintain such books and records as the Governor in Council considers necessary for the proper administration and enforcement of this Part and the regulations made under this Part and to make such returns and furnish such information relating to the said controlled drugs as the Governor in Council may require;

(e) authorizing the communication of any information obtained under this Part or the regulations to provincial professional licensing authorities; and

(f) prescribing a fine not exceeding five hundred dollars or a term of imprisonment not exceeding six months, or both, to be imposed on summary conviction, as punishment for the contravention of any regulation.

(2) Amendment of schedule g — The Governor in Council may amend Schedule G by adding thereto or deleting therefrom any substance, the inclusion or exclusion of which, as the case may be, is deemed necessary by the Governor in Council in the public interest.

R.S., c. F-27, s. 38; repealed 1996, c. 19, s. 81

PART IV — RESTRICTED DRUGS

[Note: Part IV of the Food and Drugs Act *repealed 1996, c. 19, s. 81. Please note Part IV of the Act was repealed by the* Controlled Drugs and Substances Act *on May 14, 1997. We have, however, retained the text of Part IV as it remains of relevance to offences occurring*

before its repeal and will therefore continue to be of great practical importance for some time to come.]

Restricted Drugs

46. Definitions — In this Part,

"possession" means possession within the meaning of subsection 4(3) of the *Criminal Code;*

"regulations" means regulations made as provided for by or under section 51;

"restricted drug" means any drug or other substance included in Schedule H;

"traffic" means to manufacture, sell, export from or import into Canada, transport or deliver, otherwise than under the authority of this Part or the regulations.

R.S., c. F-27, s. 40.repealed 1996, c. 19, s. 81.

Case Law

"Traffic"

R. v. Faulkner (1997), 120 C.C.C. (3d) 377 (Ont. C.A.) — Giving a tab of LSD to a single individual does not come within the definition "traffic" in s. 46 *F.D.A.*, either by reference to "sell" or "deliver".

47. (1) Possession of restricted drug — Except as authorized by this Part or the regulations, no person shall have a restricted drug in his possession.

(2) Offence — Every person who contravenes subsection (1) is guilty of an offence and liable

(a) on summary conviction for a first offence, to a fine not exceeding one thousand dollars or to imprisonment for a term not exceeding six months, or to both and, for a subsequent offence, to a fine not exceeding two thousand dollars or to imprisonment for a term not exceeding one year or to both; or

(b) on conviction on indictment, to a fine not exceeding five thousand dollars or imprisonment for a term not exceeding three years or to both.

R.S., c. F-27, s. 41. repealed 1996, c. 19, s. 81.

48. (1) Trafficking in restricted drug — No person shall traffic in a restricted drug or any substance represented or held out by the person to be a restricted drug.

(2) Possession for trafficking — No person shall have in possession any restricted drug for the purpose of trafficking.

(3) Offence — Every person who contravenes subsection (1) or (2) is guilty of an of- fence and liable

(a) on summary conviction, to imprisonment for a term not exceeding eighteen months; or

(b) on conviction on indictment, to imprisonment for a term not exceeding ten years.

R.S., c. F-27, s. 42. repealed 1996, c. 19, s. 81.

49. (1) Procedure in prosecution for possession for trafficking — In any prosecution for a contravention of subsection 48(2), if the accused does not plead guilty, the trial shall proceed as if the issue to be tried is whether the accused was in possession of a restricted drug contrary to subsection 47(1).

(2) Procedure on finding in respect of possession — If, pursuant to subsection (1), the court finds that the accused was not in possession of a restricted drug contrary to subsection 47(1), the accused shall be acquitted but, if the court finds that the accused was in possession of a restricted drug contrary to subsection 47(1), the accused shall be given an opportunity of establishing that he was not in possession of the restricted drug for the purpose of trafficking, and thereafter, the prosecutor shall be given an opportunity of adducing evidence to the contrary.

(3) Acquittal and conviction — If the accused establishes, pursuant to subsection (2), that he was not in possession of the restricted drug for the purpose of trafficking, the accused shall be acquitted of the offence as charged but shall be convicted of an offence under subsection 47(1) and sentenced accordingly, and if the accused fails to so establish, the accused shall be convicted of the offence as charged and sentenced accordingly.

R.S., c. F-27, s. 43.repealed 1996, c. 19, s. 81.

50. (1) Setting out or negativing exception, etc., not required — No exception, exemption, excuse or qualification prescribed by law is required to be set out or negatived, as the case may be, in an information or indictment for an offence under this Part or under section 463, 464 or 465 of the *Criminal Code* in respect of an offence under this Part.

(2) Burden of proving exception, etc — In any prosecution under this Part, the burden of proving that an exception, exemption, excuse or qualification prescribed by law operates in favour of the accused is on the accused, and the prosecutor is not required, except by way of rebuttal, to prove that the exception, exemption, excuse or qualification does not operate in favour of the accused, whether or not it is set out in the information or indictment.

R.S., c. F-27, s. 44.repealed 1996, c. 19, s. 81.

50.1 Interpretation — For the purposes of section 44.4, as that section is applicable in respect of this Part by virtue of section 51, and sections 50.2 to 51, a reference therein to an offence under section 48, 50.2 or 50.3 shall be deemed to include a reference to a conspiracy or an attempt to commit, being an accessory after the fact in relation to, or any counselling in relation to, such an offence.

R.S. 1985, c. 42 (4th Supp.), s. 10; repealed 1996, c. 19, s. 81.

50.2 (1) Possession of property obtained by trafficking in restricted drugs — No person shall possess any property or any proceeds of any property knowing that all or part of the property or of those proceeds was obtained or derived directly or indirectly as a result of

(a) the commission in Canada of an offence under section 48; or

(b) an act or omission anywhere that, if it had occurred in Canada, would have constituted an offence under section 48.

(2) Punishment — Every person who contravenes subsection (1)

(a) is guilty of an indictable offence and is liable to imprisonment for a term not exceeding ten years, where the value of the subject-matter of the offence exceeds one thousand dollars; or

(b) is guilty

(i) of an indictable offence and is liable to imprisonment for a term not exceeding two years, or

(ii) of an offence punishable on summary conviction,

where the value of the subject-matter of the offence does not exceed one thousand dollars.

R.S. 1985, c. 42 (4th Supp.), s. 10; repealed 1996, c. 19, s. 81.

50.3 (1) Laundering proceeds of trafficking in restricted drugs — No person shall use, transfer the possession of, send or deliver to any person or place, transport, transmit, alter, dispose of or otherwise deal with, in any manner or by any means, any property or any proceeds of any property with intent to conceal or convert that property or those proceeds and knowing that all or a part of that property or of those proceeds was obtained or derived directly or indirectly as a result of

(a) the commission in Canada of an offence under section 48; or

(b) an act or omission anywhere that, if it had occurred in Canada, would have constituted an offence under section 48.

(2) Punishment — Every person who contravenes subsection (1)

(a) is guilty of an indictable offence and is liable to imprisonment for a term not exceeding ten years; or

(b) is guilty of an offence punishable on summary conviction.

R.S. 1985, c. 42 (4th Supp.), s. 10; repealed 1996, c. 19, s. 81.

51. (1) Application of certain provisions of Part III — Sections 42 to 45 apply in respect of this Part.

(2) Modification for purpose of application — For the purposes of subsection (1),

(a) there shall be substituted for the expression "controlled drug", wherever it appears in any of the sections referred to in that subsection, the expression "restricted drug";

(b) a reference in any of those sections

(i) to "Schedule G" shall be deemed to be a reference to Schedule H, and

(ii) to "this Part" shall be deemed to be a reference to Part IV; and

(c) a reference in section 44.4 or in a provision of the *Criminal Code* mentioned therein

(i) to "an offence under section 39, 44.2 or 44.3" shall be deemed to be a reference under section 48, 50.2 or 50.3, and

(ii) to "this Part" shall be deemed to be a reference to Part IV.

(3) Additional regulations — In addition to the regulations provided for by subsection (1), the Governor in Council may make regulations authorizing the possession or export of restricted drugs and prescribing the circumstances and conditions under which, and the persons by whom restricted drugs may be had in possession or exported.

R.S., c. F-27, s. 45; R.S. 1985, c. 42 (4th Supp.), s. 11; repealed 1996, c. 19, s. 81.

SCHEDULE G

[Note: Schedule G of the Food and Drugs Act *repealed 1996, c. 19, s. 82. Please note Schedule G of the Act was repealed by the* Controlled Drugs and Substances Act *on May 14, 1997. We have, however, retained the text of Schedule G as it remains of relevance to offences occurring before its repeal and will therefore continue to be of great practical importance for some time to come.]*

(Sections 30, 38, 45 and 51)

Amphetamine and its salts

Androisoxazole

Androstanolone

Androstenediol and its derivatives

Barbituric acid and its salts and derivatives

Benzphetamine and its salts

Bolandiol and its derivatives

Bolasterone

Bolazine

Boldenone and its derivatives

Bolenol

Butorphanol and its salts

Chlorphentermine and its salts

Calusterone

Clostebol and its derivatives

Diethylpropion and its salts

Drostanolone and its derivatives

Enestebol

Epitiostanol

Ethylestrenol

Fluoxymesterone

Formebolone

Furazabol

4-Hydroxy-19-nortestosterone and its derivatives

Mebolazine

Mesabolone

Mesterolone

Metandienone

Metenolone and its derivatives

Methamphetamine and its salts

Methandriol

Methaqualone and its salts

Methylphenidate and its salts

Methyltestosterone and its derivatives
Metribolone
Mibolerone
Nalbuphine and its salts
Nandrolone and its derivatives
Norboletone
Norclostebol and its derivatives
Norethandrolone
Oxabolone and its derivatives
Oxandrolone
Oxymesterone
Oxymetholone
Phendimetrazine and its salts
Phenmetrazine and its salts
Phentermine and its salts
Prasterone
Quinbolone
Stanozolol
Stenbolone and its derivatives
Testosterone and its derivatives
Thiobarbituric acid and its salts and derivatives
Tibolone
Tiomesterone
Trembolone and its derivatives
Zeranol
R.S., c. F-27, Schedule G; SOR/71–357, 460; SI/73–47; SI/77–112; SOR/77–824, SOR/78–426; SOR/79–756; SOR/81–85; SI/84–66; SOR/92–387. repealed 1996, c. 19, s. 82.

SCHEDULE H

[Note: Schedule H of the Food and Drugs Act *repealed 1996, c. 19, s. 82. Please note Schedule H of the Act was repealed by the* Controlled Drugs and Substances Act *on May 14, 1997. We have, however, retained the text of Schedule H as it remains of relevance to offences occurring before its repeal and will therefore continue to be of great practical importance for some time to come.]*

(Sections 30, 46 and 51)

Lysergic acid diethylamide (LSD) or any salt thereof
N,N-Diethyltryptamine (DET) or any salt thereof
N,N-Dimethyltryptamine (DMT) or any salt thereof
4-Methyl-2,5-dimethoxyamphetamine (STP(DOM)) or any salt thereof
3,4-methylenedioxyamphetamine (MDA) or any salt thereof
N-methyl-3-piperidyl benzilate (LBJ) or any salt thereof
2,3-dimethoxyamphetamine or any salt thereof

2,4-dimethoxyamphetamine or any salt thereof

2,5-dimethoxyamphetamine or any salt thereof

2,6-dimethoxyamphetamine or any salt thereof

3,4-dimethoxyamphetamine or any salt thereof

3,5-dimethoxyamphetamine or any salt thereof

4,9-dihydro-7-methoxy-1-methyl-3H-pyrido (3,4-b) indole (Harmaline) and any salt thereof

4,9-dihydro-1-methyl-3H-pyrido (3,4-b) indol-7-ol (Harmalol) and any salt thereof

4-methoxyamphetamine or any salt thereof

3-[2-(Dimethylamino) ethyl]-4-hydroxyindole (Psilocin) or any salt thereof

3-[2-(Dimethylamino) ethyl]-4-phosphoryloxyindole (Psilocybin) or any salt thereof

2,4,5-Trimethoxyamphetamine or any salt, isomer, or salt of isomer, thereof

3,4-methylenedioxy-N-methylamphetamine or any salt thereof

N-(1-phenycyclohexyl) ethylamine or any salt thereof

4-bromo-2, 5-dimethoxyamphetamine or any salt thereof

1-[1-(2-thienyl) cyclohexyl] piperidine and its salts

1-phenyl-N-propylcyclohexanamine or any salt thereof

3,4,5-trimethoxybenzeneethanamine (Mescaline) or any salt thereof but not including peyote (lophophora)

4-ethoxy-2, 5-dimethoxy-α-methylbenzeneethanamine or any salt, isomer, or salt of isomer, thereof

7-methoxy-α-methyl-1,3-benzodioxole-ethanamine (MMDA) or any salt, isomer or salt of isomer thereof

N,N,-α-trimethyl-1,3-benzodioxole-5-ethanamine or any salt, isomer or salt of isomer thereof

N-ethyl-α-methyl-1,3-benzodioxole-5-ethanamine or any salt, isomer or salt of isomer thereof

4-ethyl-2,5-dimethoxy-α-methylbenzeneethanamime (DOET) or any salt, isomer or salt of isomer thereof

4-ethoxy-α-methylbenzeneethanamine or any salt, isomer or salt of isomer thereof

4-chloro-2,5-dimethoxy-α-methylbenzeneethanamime or any salt, isomer or salt of isomer thereof

4,5-dihydro-4-methyl-5-phenyl-2-oxazolamine (4-methylaminorex) or any salt thereof

N-ethyl-α-methylbenzeneethanamine or any salt thereof

α-methyl-N-propyl-1, 3-benzodioxole-5-ethanamime or any salt, isomer or salt or isomer thereof

1-[1-(phenylmethyl)cyclohexyl]piperidine or any salt, isomer or salt or isomer thereof

1-[1-(4-methylphenyl)cyclohexyl]piperidine or any salt, isomer or salt of isomer thereof

2-methylamino-1-phenyl-1-propanone or any salt thereof

4-bromo-2,5-dimethoxybenzeneethanamine or any salt, isomer or salt of isomer thereof

N-(2-hydroxyethyl)-β-methylbenzeneethanamine or any salt, isomer or salt of isomer thereof

4-bromo-2,5-dimethoxybenzeneethanamine or any salt, isomer or salt of isomer thereof

N-(2-hydroxyethyl)-α-methylbenzeneethanamine or any salt, isomer or salt of isomer thereof

R.S., c. F-27, Schedule H; SOR/71–357, 564; SI/73–36; SOR/74–198, 611, 670; SOR/76–368; SOR/77–824; SOR/78–425, 650; SOR/79–938; SOR/86–90, 833; SOR/87–76, 406, 485, 574, 653; SOR/89–410; SOR/90–156; SOR/95-79. repealed 1996, c. 19, s. 82.

FIREARMS ACT

An Act respecting firearms and other weapons

S.C. 1995, c. 39, as am. 1996, c. 19, s. 76.1; 1999, c. 3, s. 64.

Short Title

1. Short title — This Act may be cited as the *Firearms Act.*

Case Law

Constitutional Considerations

Reference Re Firearms Act (Canada) (1998), 128 C.C.C. (3d) 225 (Alta. C.A.) — The *Firearms Act* is a valid exercise of the federal criminal law power.

Interpretation

2. (1) Definitions — In this Act,

"authorization to carry" means an authorization described in section 20;

"authorization to export" means an authorization referred to in section 44;

"authorization to import" means an authorization referred to in section 46;

"authorization to transport" means an authorization described in section 18 or 19;

"business" means a person who carries on a business that includes

(a) the manufacture, assembly, possession, purchase, sale, importation, exportation, display, repair, restoration, maintenance, storage, alteration, taking in pawn, transportation, shipping, distribution or delivery of firearms, prohibited weapons, restricted weapons, prohibited devices or prohibited ammunition,

(b) the possession, purchase or sale of ammunition, or

(c) the purchase of cross-bows

and includes a museum;

"carrier" means a person who carries on a transportation business that includes the transportation of firearms, prohibited weapons, restricted weapons, prohibited devices, ammunition or prohibited ammunition;

"chief firearms officer" means

(a) in respect of a province, the individual who is designated in writing as the chief firearms officer for the province by the provincial minister of that province,

(b) in respect of a territory, the individual who is designated in writing as the chief firearms officer for the territory by the federal Minister, or

(c) in respect of any matter for which there is no chief firearms officer under paragraph (a) or (b), the individual who is designated in writing as the chief firearms officer for the matter by the federal Minister, "commencement day", in respect of a provision of this Act or the expression "former Act" in a provision of this Act, means the day on which the provision comes into force;

"customs office" has the meaning assigned by subsection 2(1) of the *Customs Act*;

"customs officer" has the meaning assigned to the word "officer" by subsection 2(1) of the *Customs Act*;

"federal Minister" means the Minister of Justice;

"firearms officer" means

(a) in respect of a province, an individual who is designated in writing as a firearms officer for the province by the provincial minister of that province,

(b) in respect of a territory, an individual who is designated in writing as a firearms officer for the territory by the federal Minister, or

(c) in respect of any matter for which there is no firearms officer under paragraph (a) or (b), an individual who is designated in writing as a firearms officer for the matter by the federal Minister;

"former Act" means Part III of the *Criminal Code*, as it read from time to time before the commencement day;

"museum" means a person who operates a museum

(a) in which firearms, prohibited weapons, restricted weapons, prohibited devices or prohibited ammunition are possessed, bought, displayed, repaired, restored, maintained, stored or altered, or

(b) in which ammunition is possessed or bought;

"non-resident" means an individual who ordinarily resides outside Canada;

"prescribed" means

(a) in the case of a form or the information to be included on a form, prescribed by the federal Minister, and

(b) in any other case, prescribed by the regulations;

"provincial minister" means

(a) in respect of a province, the member of the executive council of the province who is designated by the lieutenant governor in council of the province as the provincial minister,

(b) in respect of a territory, the federal Minister, or

(c) in respect of any matter for which there is no provincial minister under paragraph (a) or (b), the federal Minister;

"regulations" means regulations made by the Governor in Council under section 117.

(2) **To be interpreted with Criminal Code** — For greater certainty, unless otherwise provided, words and expressions used in this Act have the meanings assigned to them by section 2 or 84 of the *Criminal Code*.

(3) **Aboriginal and treaty rights** — For greater certainty, nothing in this Act shall be construed so as to abrogate or derogate from any existing aboriginal or treaty rights of the aboriginal peoples of Canada under section 35 of the *Constitution Act, 1982*.

Her Majesty

3. (1) Binding on Her Majesty — This Act is binding on Her Majesty in right of Canada or a province.

(2) Canadian Forces — Notwithstanding subsection (1), this Act does not apply in respect of the Canadian Forces.

Purpose

4. Purpose — The purpose of this Act is

(a) to provide, notably by sections 5 to 16 and 54 to 73, for the issuance of

(i) licences, registration certificates and authorizations under which persons may possess firearms in circumstances that would otherwise constitute an offence under subsection 91(1), 92(1), 93(1) or 95(1) of the *Criminal Code*,

(ii) licences and authorizations under which persons may possess prohibited weapons, restricted weapons, prohibited devices and prohibited ammunition in circumstances that would otherwise constitute an offence under subsection 91(2), 92(2) or 93(1) of the *Criminal Code*, and

(iii) licences under which persons may sell, barter or give cross-bows in circumstances that would otherwise constitute an offence under subsection 97(1) of the *Criminal Code*;

(b) to authorize,

(i) notably by sections 5 to 12 and 54 to 73, the manufacture of or offer to manufacture, and

(ii) notably by sections 21 to 34 and 54 to 73, the transfer of or offer to transfer,

firearms, prohibited weapons, restricted weapons, prohibited devices, ammunition and prohibited ammunition in circumstances that would otherwise constitute an offence under subsection 99(1), 100(1) or 101(1) of the *Criminal Code*; and

(c) to authorize, notably by sections 35 to 73, the importation or exportation of firearms, prohibited weapons, restricted weapons, prohibited devices, ammunition, prohibited ammunition and components and parts designed exclusively for use in the manufacture of or assembly into automatic firearms in circumstances that would otherwise constitute an offence under subsection 103(1) or 104(1) of the *Criminal Code*.

Authorized Possession

Eligibility to Hold Licences

General Rules

5. (1) Public safety — A person is not eligible to hold a licence if it is desirable, in the interests of the safety of that or any other person, that the person not possess a firearm, a cross-bow, a prohibited weapon, a restricted weapon, a prohibited device, ammunition or prohibited ammunition.

(2) Criteria — In determining whether a person is eligible to hold a licence under subsection (1), a chief firearms officer or, on a reference under section 74, a provincial court judge shall have regard to whether the person, within the previous five years,

  (a) has been convicted or discharged under section 736 of the *Criminal Code* of

   (i) an offence in the commission of which violence against another person was used, threatened or attempted,

   (ii) an offence under this Act or Part III of the *Criminal Code*,

   (iii) an offence under section 264 of the *Criminal Code* (criminal harassment), or

   (iv) an offence relating to the contravention of subsection 5(3) or (4), 6(3) or 7(2) of the *Controlled Drugs and Substances Act*;

  (b) has been treated for a mental illness, whether in a hospital, mental institute, psychiatric clinic or otherwise and whether or not the person was confined to such a hospital, institute or clinic, that was associated with violence or threatened or attempted violence on the part of the person against any person; or

  (c) has a history of behaviour that includes violence or threatened or attempted violence on the part of the person against any person.

Unproclaimed subsection — 5(3)

(3) Exception — Notwithstanding subsection (2), in determining whether a non-resident who is eighteen years old or older and by or on behalf of whom an application is made for a sixty-day licence authorizing the non-resident to possess firearms that are neither prohibited firearms nor restricted firearms is eligible to hold a licence under subsection (1), a chief firearms officer or, on a reference under section 74, a provincial court judge may but need not have regard to the criteria described in subsection (2).

1996, c. 19, s. 76.1

6. (1) Court orders — A person is eligible to hold a licence only if the person is not prohibited by a prohibition order from possessing any firearm, cross-bow, prohibited weapon, restricted weapon, prohibited device or prohibited ammunition.

(2) Exception — Subsection (1) is subject to any order made under section 113 of the *Criminal Code* (lifting of prohibition order for sustenance or employment).

7. (1) Successful completion of safety course — An individual is eligible to hold a licence only if the individual

  (a) successfully completes the Canadian Firearms Safety Course, as given by an instructor who is designated by a chief firearms officer, and passes the tests, as administered by an instructor who is designated by a chief firearms officer, that form part of that Course;

  (b) except in the case of an individual who is less than eighteen years old, passes the tests, as administered by an instructor who is designated by a chief firearms officer, that form part of that Course;

  (c) successfully completed, before January 1, 1995, a course that the attorney general of the province in which the course was given had, during the period beginning on January 1, 1993 and ending on December 31, 1994, approved for the purposes of section 106 of the former Act; or

(d) passed, before January 1, 1995, a test that the attorney general of the province in which the test was administered had, during the period beginning on January 1, 1993 and ending on December 31, 1994, approved for the purposes of section 106 of the former Act.

(2) **Restricted firearms safety course** — An individual is eligible to hold a licence authorizing the individual to possess restricted firearms only if the individual

(a) successfully completes a restricted firearms safety course that is approved by the federal Minister, as given by an instructor who is designated by a chief firearms officer, and passes any tests, as administered by an instructor who is designated by a chief firearms officer, that form part of that course; or

(b) passes a restricted firearms safety test, as administered by an instructor who is designated by a chief firearms officer, that is approved by the federal Minister.

(3) **After expiration of prohibition order** — An individual against whom a prohibition order was made

(a) is eligible to hold a licence only if the individual has, after the expiration of the prohibition order,

(i) successfully completed the Canadian Firearms Safety Course, as given by an instructor who is designated by a chief firearms officer, and

(ii) passed the tests, as administered by an instructor who is designated by a chief firearms officer, that form part of that Course; and

(b) is eligible to hold a licence authorizing the individual to possess restricted firearms only if the individual has, after the expiration of the prohibition order,

(i) successfully completed a restricted firearms safety course that is approved by the federal Minister, as given by an instructor who is designated by a chief firearms officer, and

(ii) passed any tests, as administered by an instructor who is designated by a chief firearms officer, that form part of that course.

(4) **Exceptions** — Subsections (1) and (2) do not apply to an individual who

(a) in the prescribed circumstances, has been certified by a chief firearms officer as meeting the prescribed criteria relating to the safe handling and use of firearms and the laws relating to firearms;

(b) is less than eighteen years old and requires a firearm to hunt or trap in order to sustain himself of herself or his or her family;

(c) on the commencement day, possessed one or more firearms and does not require a licence to acquire other firearms;

(d) requires a licence merely to acquire cross-bows; or

paragraph — 7(4)(e)

(e) is a non-resident who is eighteen years old or older and by or on behalf of whom an application is made for a sixty-day licence authorizing the non-resident to possess firearms that are neither prohibited firearms nor restricted firearms.

(5) **Further exception** — Subsection (3) does not apply to an individual in respect of whom an order is made under section 113 of the *Criminal Code* (lifting of prohibition order for sustenance or employment) and who is exempted by a chief firearms officer from the application of that subsection.

Special Cases — Persons

8. (1) Minors — An individual who is less than eighteen years old and who is otherwise eligible to hold a licence is not eligible to hold a licence except as provided in this section.

(2) Minors hunting as a way of life — An individual who is less than eighteen years old and who hunts or traps as a way of life is eligible to hold a licence if the individual needs to hunt or trap in order to sustain himself or herself or his or her family.

(3) Hunting, etc. — An individual who is twelve years old or older but less than eighteen years old is eligible to hold a licence authorizing the individual to possess, in accordance with the conditions attached to the licence, a firearm for the purpose of target practice, hunting or instruction in the use of firearms or for the purpose of taking part in an organized competition.

(4) No prohibited or restricted firearms — An individual who is less than eighteen years old is not eligible to hold a licence authorizing the individual to possess prohibited firearms or restricted firearms or to acquire firearms or cross-bows.

(5) Consent of parent or guardian — An individual who is less than eighteen years old is eligible to hold a licence only if a parent or person who has custody of the individual has consented, in writing or in any other manner that is satisfactory to the chief firearms officer, to the issuance of the licence.

9. (1) Businesses — A business is eligible to hold a licence authorizing a particular activity only if every person who stands in a prescribed relationship to the business is eligible under sections 5 and 6 to hold a licence authorizing that activity or the acquisition of restricted firearms.

(2) Safety courses — A business other than a carrier is eligible to hold a licence only if

(a) a chief firearms officer determines that no individual who stands in a prescribed relationship to the business need be eligible to hold a licence under section 7; or

(b) the individuals who stand in a prescribed relationship to the business and who are determined by a chief firearms officer to be the appropriate individuals to satisfy the requirements of section 7 are eligible to hold a licence under that section.

(3) Employees — A business other than a carrier is eligible to hold a licence only if every employee of the business who, in the course of duties of employment, handles or would handle firearms, prohibited weapons, restricted weapons, prohibited devices or prohibited ammunition is the holder of a licence authorizing the holder to acquire restricted firearms.

(4) Exception — In subsection (3), "firearm" does not include a partially manufactured barrelled weapon that, in its unfinished state, is not a barrelled weapon

(a) from which any shot, bullet or other projectile can be discharged; and

(b) that is capable of causing serious bodily injury or death to a person.

(5) Exception — Subsection (1) does not apply in respect of a person who stands in a prescribed relationship to a business where a chief firearms officer determines that, in all the circumstances, the business should not be ineligible to hold a licence merely because of that person's ineligibility.

(6) **Exception for museums** — Subsection (3) does not apply in respect of an employee of a museum

(a) who, in the course of duties of employment, handles or would handle only firearms that are designed or intended to exactly resemble, or to resemble with near precision, antique firearms, and who has been trained to handle or use such a firearm; or

(b) who is designated, by name, by a provincial minister.

10. **International and interprovincial carriers** — Sections 5, 6 and 9 apply in respect of a carrier whose business includes the transportation of firearms, prohibited weapons, restricted weapons, prohibited devices or prohibited ammunition from one province to any other province, or beyond the limits of a province, as if each reference in those sections to a chief firearms officer were a reference to the Registrar.

Special Cases — Prohibited Firearms, Weapons, Devices and Ammunition

11. (1) **Prohibited firearms, weapons, devices and ammunition — businesses** — A business that is otherwise eligible to hold a licence is not eligible to hold a licence authorizing the business to possess prohibited firearms, prohibited weapons, prohibited devices or prohibited ammunition except as provided in this section.

(2) **Prescribed purposes** — A business other than a carrier is eligible to hold a licence authorizing the business to possess prohibited firearms, prohibited weapons, prohibited devices or prohibited ammunition if the business needs to possess them for a prescribed purpose.

(3) **Carriers** — A carrier is eligible to hold a licence authorizing the carrier to possess prohibited firearms, prohibited weapons, prohibited devices or prohibited ammunition.

12. (1) **Prohibited firearms — individuals** — An individual who is otherwise eligible to hold a licence is not eligible to hold a licence authorizing the individual to possess prohibited firearms except as provided in this section.

(2) **Grandfathered individuals — pre-January 1, 1978 automatic firearms** — An individual is eligible to hold a licence authorizing the individual to possess automatic firearms that, on the commencement day, were registered as restricted weapons under the former Act if the individual

(a) on January 1, 1978 possessed one or more automatic firearms;

(b) on the commencement day held a registration certificate under the former Act for one or more automatic firearms; and

(c) beginning on the commencement day was continuously the holder of a registration certificate for one or more automatic firearms.

(3) **Grandfathered individuals — pre-August 1, 1992 converted automatic firearms** — An individual is eligible to hold a licence authorizing the individual to possess automatic firearms that have been altered to discharge only one

projectile during one pressure of the trigger and that, on the commencement day, were registered as restricted weapons under the former Act if the individual

(a) on August 1, 1992 possessed one or more automatic firearms

(i) that had been so altered, and

(ii) for which on October 1, 1992 a registration certificate under the former Act had been issued or applied for;

(b) on the commencement day held a registration certificate under the former Act for one or more automatic firearms that had been so altered; and

(c) beginning on the commencement day was continuously the holder of a registration certificate for one or more automatic firearms that have been so altered.

(4) Grandfathered individuals — Prohibited Weapons Order, No. 12 —

An individual is eligible to hold a licence authorizing the individual to possess firearms that were declared to be prohibited weapons under the former Act by the *Prohibited Weapons Order, No. 12*, made by Order in Council P.C. 1992-1690 of July 23, 1992 and registered as SOR/92-471 and that, on October 1, 1992, either were registered as restricted weapons under the former Act or were the subject of an application for a registration certificate under the former Act if the individual

(a) before July 27, 1992 possessed one or more firearms that were so declared;

(b) on the commencement day held a registration certificate under the former Act for one or more firearms that were so declared; and

(c) beginning on the commencement day was continuously the holder of a registration certificate for one or more firearms that were so declared.

(5) Grandfathered individuals — Prohibited Weapons Order, No. 13 —

An individual is eligible to hold a licence authorizing the individual to possess firearms that were declared to be prohibited weapons under the former Act by the *Prohibited Weapons Order, No. 13*, made by Order in Council P.C. 1994-1974 of November 29, 1994 and registered as SOR/94-741 and that, on January 1, 1995, either were registered as restricted weapons under the former Act or were the subject of an application for a registration certificate under the former Act if the individual

(a) before January 1, 1995 possessed one or more firearms that were so declared;

(b) on the commencement day held a registration certificate under the former Act for one or more firearms that were so declared; and

(c) beginning on the commencement day was continuously the holder of a registration certificate for one or more firearms that were so declared.

(6) Grandfathered individuals — pre-February 14, 1995 handguns — A

particular individual is eligible to hold a licence authorizing the particular individual to possess handguns that have a barrel equal to or less than 105 mm in length or that are designed or adapted to discharge a 25 or 32 calibre cartridge and for which on February 14, 1995 a registration certificate under the former Act had been issued to or applied for by that or another individual if the particular individual

(a) on February 14, 1995

(i) held a registration certificate under the former Act for one or more of those handguns, or

(ii) had applied for a registration certificate that was subsequently issued under the former Act for one or more of those handguns;

(b) on the commencement day held a registration certificate under the former Act for one or more of those handguns; and

(c) beginning on the commencement day was continuously the holder of a registration certificate for one or more of those handguns.

(7) **Next of kin of grandfathered individuals — pre-February 14, 1995 handguns** — A particular individual is eligible to hold a licence authorizing the particular individual to possess a particular handgun referred to in subsection (6) that was manufactured before 1946 if the particular individual is the spouse or a brother, sister, child or grandchild of an individual who was eligible under this or that subsection to hold a licence authorizing the individual to possess the particular handgun.

(8) **Grandfathered individuals — regulations re prohibited firearms** — An individual is, in the prescribed circumstances, eligible to hold a licence authorizing the individual to possess firearms prescribed by a provision of regulations made by the Governor in Council under section 117.15 of the *Criminal Code* to be prohibited firearms if the individual

(a) on the day on which the provision comes into force possesses one or more of those firearms; and

(b) beginning on

(i) the day on which that provision comes into force, or

(ii) in the case of an individual who on that day did not hold but had applied for a registration certificate for one or more of those firearms, the day on which the registration certificate was issued

was continuously the holder of a registration certificate for one or more of those firearms.

Registration Certificates

13. **Registration certificate** — A person is not eligible to hold a registration certificate for a firearm unless the person holds a licence authorizing the person to possess that kind of firearm.

14. **Serial number** — A registration certificate may be issued only for a firearm

(a) that bears a serial number sufficient to distinguish it from other firearms; or

(b) that is described in the prescribed manner.

15. **Exempted firearms** — A registration certificate may not be issued for a firearm that is owned by Her Majesty in right of Canada or a province or by a police force.

16. (1) **Only one person per registration certificate** — A registration certificate for a firearm may be issued to only one person.

(2) **Exception** — Subsection (1) does not apply in the case of a firearm for which a registration certificate referred to in section 127 was issued to more than one person.

Authorized Transportation of Firearms

17. Places where prohibited and restricted firearms may be possessed — Subject to sections 18 to 20, a prohibited firearm or restricted firearm the holder of the registration certificate for which is an individual may be possessed only at the dwelling-house of the individual, as indicated on the registration certificate, or at a place authorized by a chief firearms officer.

18. Transporting and using prohibited firearms — An individual who holds a licence authorizing the individual to possess prohibited firearms may be authorized to transport a particular prohibited firearm between two or more specified places

(a) in the case of a handgun referred to in subsection 12(6) (pre-February 14, 1995 handguns), for use in target practice, or a target shooting competition, under specified conditions or under the auspices of a shooting club or shooting range that is approved under section 29; or

(b) if the individual

(i) changes residence,

(ii) wishes to transport the firearm to a peace officer, firearms officer or chief firearms officer for registration or disposal in accordance with this Act or Part III of the *Criminal Code*,

(iii) wishes to transport the firearm for repair, storage, sale, exportation or appraisal, or

(iv) wishes to transport the firearm to a gun show.

19. (1) Transporting and using restricted firearms — An individual who holds a licence authorizing the individual to possess restricted firearms may be authorized to transport a particular restricted firearm between two or more specified places for any good and sufficient reason, including, without restricting the generality of the foregoing,

(a) for use in target practice, or a target shooting competition, under specified conditions or under the auspices of a shooting club or shooting range that is approved under section 29; or

(b) if the individual

(i) changes residence,

(ii) wishes to transport the firearm to a peace officer, firearms officer or chief firearms officer for registration or disposal in accordance with this Act or Part III of the *Criminal Code*,

(iii) wishes to transport the firearm for repair, storage, sale, exportation or appraisal, or

(iv) wishes to transport the firearm to a gun show.

(2) Non-residents — A non-resident may be authorized to transport a particular restricted firearm between specified places in accordance with section 35.

20. Carrying restricted firearms and pre-February 14, 1995 handguns — An individual who holds a licence authorizing the individual to possess restricted firearms or handguns referred to in subsection 12(6) (pre-February 14, 1995 handguns) may be authorized to possess a particular restricted firearm or handgun at a place other than the place at which it is authorized to be possessed if the individual needs the particular restricted firearm or handgun

(a) to protect the life of that individual or of other individuals; or

(b) for use in connection with his or her lawful profession or occupation.

Authorized Transfers and Lending

General Provisions

21. Definition of "transfer" — For the purposes of sections 22 to 32, "transfer" means sell, barter or give.

22. Mental disorder, etc. — A person may transfer or lend a firearm to an individual only if the person has no reason to believe that the individual

(a) has a mental illness that makes it desirable, in the interests of the safety of that individual or any other person, that the individual not possess a firearm; or

(b) is impaired by alcohol or a drug.

Authorized Transfers

23. Authorization to transfer firearms — A person may transfer a firearm if, at the time of the transfer,

(a) the transferee produces to the person a document that purports to be a licence authorizing the transferee to acquire and possess that kind of firearm;

(b) the person

(i) has no reason to believe that the transferee is not authorized by the document to acquire and possess that kind of firearm, and

(ii) informs a chief firearms officer of the transfer and obtains the authorization of the chief firearms officer for the transfer;

(c) the transferee holds a licence authorizing the transferee to acquire and possess that kind of firearm;

(d) a new registration certificate for the firearm is issued in accordance with this Act; and

(e) the prescribed conditions are complied with.

24. (1) Authorization to transfer prohibited weapons, devices and ammunition — Subject to section 26, a person may transfer a prohibited weapon, prohibited device or prohibited ammunition only to a business.

(2) Conditions — A person may transfer a prohibited weapon, prohibited device, ammunition or prohibited ammunition to a business only if

(a) the business holds a licence authorizing the business to acquire and possess prohibited weapons, prohibited devices, ammunition or prohibited ammunition, as the case may be;

(b) the business produces to the person a document that purports to be a licence authorizing the business to acquire and possess prohibited weapons, prohibited devices, ammunition or prohibited ammunition, as the case may be;

24(2)(c), (d)

(c) the person

(i) has no reason to believe that the business is not authorized by the document to acquire and possess prohibited weapons, prohibited devices, ammunition or prohibited ammunition, as the case may be, and

(ii) informs a chief firearms officer of the transfer and obtains the authorization of the chief firearms officer for the transfer; and

(d) the prescribed conditions are complied with.

25. Authorization to transfer ammunition to individuals — A person may transfer ammunition that is not prohibited ammunition to an individual only if the individual

(a) until January 1, 2001, holds a licence authorizing him or her to possess firearms or a prescribed document; or

(b) after January 1, 2001, holds a licence authorizing him or her to possess firearms.

26. (1) Authorization to transfer firearms to the Crown and to the police — A person may transfer a firearm to Her Majesty in right of Canada or a province or to a police force if the person informs the Registrar of the transfer and complies with the prescribed conditions.

(2) Authorization to transfer prohibited weapons, etc., to the Crown and to the police — A person may transfer a prohibited weapon, restricted weapon, prohibited device, ammunition or prohibited ammunition to Her Majesty in right of Canada or a province or to a police force if the person informs a chief firearms officer of the transfer and complies with the prescribed conditions.

27. Chief firearms officer — On being informed of a proposed transfer of a firearm under section 23, of a proposed transfer of a firearm, prohibited weapon, prohibited device, ammunition or prohibited ammunition to a business under section 24 or of a proposed importation of a firearm that is not a prohibited firearm by an individual under paragraph 40(1)(c), a chief firearms officer shall

(a) verify

(i) whether the transferee or individual holds a licence,

(ii) whether the transferee or individual is still eligible to hold that licence, and

(iii) whether the licence authorizes the transferee or individual to acquire that kind of firearm or to acquire prohibited weapons, prohibited devices, ammunition or prohibited ammunition, as the case may be;

(b) in the case of

(i) a proposed transfer of a restricted firearm or a handgun referred to in subsection 12(6) (pre-February 14, 1995 handguns), or

(ii) a proposed importation of a restricted firearm,

verify the purpose for which the transferee or individual wishes to acquire the restricted firearm or handgun and determine whether the particular restricted firearm or handgun is appropriate for that purpose;

(c) decide whether to approve the transfer or importation and inform the Registrar of that decision; and

(d) take the prescribed measures.

28. Permitted purposes — A chief firearms officer may approve the transfer to an individual of a restricted firearm or a handgun referred to in subsection 12(6) (pre-February 14, 1995 handguns) or the importation by an individual of a restricted firearm under paragraph 40(1)(c) only if the chief firearms officer is satisfied

(a) that the individual needs the restricted firearm or handgun

(i) to protect the life of that individual or of other individuals, or

(ii) for use in connection with his or her lawful profession or occupation; or

(b) that the purpose for which the individual wishes to acquire the restricted firearm or handgun is

(i) for use in target practice, or a target shooting competition, under conditions specified in an authorization to transport or under the auspices of a shooting club or shooting range that is approved under section 29, or

(ii) to form part of a gun collection of the individual, in the case of an individual who satisfies the criteria described in section 30.

29.

Unproclaimed subsection — 29(1)

29. (1) Shooting clubs and shooting ranges — No person shall operate a shooting club or shooting range except under an approval of the provincial minister for the province in which the premises of the shooting club or shooting range are located.

(2) **Approval** — A provincial minister may approve a shooting club or shooting range for the purposes of this Act if

(a) the shooting club or shooting range complies with the regulations made under paragraph 117(e); and

(b) the premises of the shooting club or shooting range are located in that province.

(3) **Revocation** — A provincial minister who approves a shooting club or shooting range for the purposes of this Act may revoke the approval for any good and sufficient reason including, without limiting the generality of the foregoing, where the shooting club or shooting range contravenes a regulation made under paragraph 117(e).

(4) **Delegation** — A chief firearms officer who is authorized in writing by a provincial minister may perform such duties and functions of the provincial minister under this section as are specified in the authorization.

(5) **Notice of refusal to approve or revocation** — Where a provincial minister decides to refuse to approve or to revoke an approval of a shooting club or shooting range for the purposes of this Act, the provincial minister shall give notice of the decision to the shooting club or shooting range.

(6) **Material to accompany notice** — A notice given under subsection (5) must include reasons for the decision disclosing the nature of the information relied on for the decision and must be accompanied by a copy of sections 74 to 81.

(7) Non-disclosure of information — A provincial minister need not disclose any information the disclosure of which could, in the opinion of the provincial minister, endanger the safety of any person.

30. Gun collectors — The criteria referred to in subparagraph 28(b)(ii) are that the individual

(a) has knowledge of the historical, technological or scientific characteristics that relate or distinguish the restricted firearms or handguns that he or she possesses;

(b) has consented to the periodic inspection, conducted in a reasonable manner, of the premises in which the restricted firearms or handguns are to be kept; and

(c) has complied with such other requirements as are prescribed respecting knowledge, secure storage and the keeping of records in respect of restricted firearms or handguns.

31. (1) Registrar — On being informed of a proposed transfer of a firearm, the Registrar may

(a) issue a new registration certificate for the firearm in accordance with this Act; and

(b) revoke any registration certificate for the firearm held by the transferor.

(2) Transfers of firearms to the Crown and to the police — On being informed of a transfer of a firearm to Her Majesty in right of Canada or a province or to a police force, the Registrar shall revoke any registration certificate for the firearm.

32. Mail-order transfers of firearms — A person may transfer a firearm by mail only if

(a) the verifications, notifications, issuances and authorizations referred to in sections 21 to 28, 30, 31, 40 to 43 and 46 to 52 take place within a reasonable period before the transfer in the prescribed manner;

Unproclaimed paragraph — 32(b)

(b) the firearm is delivered by a person designated by a chief firearms officer and the person ensures that the transferee holds a licence authorizing the transferee to acquire that kind of firearm; and

(c) the prescribed conditions are complied with.

Authorized Lending

33. Authorization to lend — Subject to section 34, a person may lend a firearm only if

(a) the person

(i) has reasonable grounds to believe that the borrower holds a licence authorizing the borrower to possess that kind of firearm, and

(ii) lends the borrower the registration certificate for the firearm, except in the case of a borrower who uses the firearm to hunt or trap in order to sustain himself or herself or his or her family; or

(b) the borrower uses the firearm under the direct and immediate supervision of the person in the same manner in which the person may lawfully use it.

34. Authorization to lend firearms, etc., to the Crown and to the police — A person may lend a firearm, prohibited weapon, restricted weapon, prohibited device, ammunition or prohibited ammunition to Her Majesty in right of Canada or a province or to a police force if

(a) in the case of a firearm, the transferor lends the borrower the registration certificate for the firearm; and

(b) the prescribed conditions are complied with.

Authorized Exportation and Importation

Individuals

35. (1) Authorization for non-residents who do not hold a licence to import firearms that are not prohibited firearms — A non-resident who does not hold a licence may import a firearm that is not prohibited firearm if, at the time of the importation,

(a) the non-resident

(i) is eighteen years old or older,

Unproclaimed clause — 35(1)(a)(ii)

(ii) declares the firearm to a customs officer in the prescribed manner and, in the case of a declaration in writing, completes the prescribed form containing the prescribed information, and

(iii) in the case of a restricted firearm, produces an authorization to transport the restricted firearm; and

Unproclaimed clause — 35(1)(b)

(b) a customs officer confirms in the prescribed manner the declaration referred to in subparagraph (a)(ii) and the authorization to transport referred to in subparagraph (a)(iii).

Unproclaimed subsections — 35(2)-(4)

(2) Non-compliances — Where a firearm is declared at a customs office to a customs officer but the requirements of subparagraphs (1)(a)(ii) and (iii) are not complied with, the customs officer may authorize the firearm to be exported from that customs office or may detain the firearm and give the non-resident a reasonable time to comply with those requirements.

(3) Disposal of firearm — Where those requirements are not complied with within a reasonable time and the firearm is not exported, the firearm shall be disposed of in the prescribed manner.

(4) Non-compliance — Where a firearm that is neither a prohibited firearm nor a restricted firearm is declared at a customs office to a customs officer and

(a) the non-resident has not truthfully completed the prescribed form, or

(b) the customs officer has reasonable grounds to believe that it is desirable, in the interests of the safety of the non-resident or any other person, that the declaration not be confirmed, the customs officer may refuse to confirm the declaration and may authorize the firearm to be exported from that customs office.

Unproclaimed section — 36

36. (1) Temporary licence and registration certificate — A declaration that is confirmed under paragraph 35(1)(b) has the same effect after the importation of the firearm as a licence authorizing the non-resident to possess only that firearm and as a registration certificate for the firearm until the expiration of sixty days after the importation or, in the case of a restricted firearm, until the earlier of

  (a) the expiration of those sixty days, and

  (b) the expiration of the authorization to transport.

(2) Renewal — A chief firearms officer may renew the confirmation of a declaration for one or more periods of sixty days.

(3) Electronic or other means — For greater certainty, an application for a renewal of the confirmation of a declaration may be made by telephone or other electronic means or by mail and a chief firearms officer may renew that confirmation by electronic means or by mail.

Unproclaimed section — 37

37. (1) Authorization for non-residents who do not hold a licence to export firearms that are not prohibited firearms — A non-resident who does not hold a licence may export a firearm that is not a prohibited firearm and that was imported by the non-resident in accordance with section 35 if, at the time of the exportation,

  (a) the non-resident

    (i) declares the firearm to a customs officer, and

    (ii) produces to a customs officer in the prescribed manner the declaration and, where applicable, the authorization to transport that were confirmed in accordance with that section; and

  (b) a customs officer confirms the declaration referred to in subparagraph (a)(i) in the prescribed manner.

(2) Non-compliance — Where a firearm is declared to a customs officer but the requirements of subparagraph (1)(a)(ii) are not complied with, the customs officer may detain the firearm and, with the approval of a chief firearms officer, give the non-resident a reasonable time to comply with those requirements.

(3) Disposal of firearm — Where those requirements are not complied with within a reasonable time, the firearm shall be disposed of in the prescribed manner.

Unproclaimed section — 38

38. (1) Authorization for individuals who hold a licence to export firearms — An individual who holds a licence may export a firearm if, at the time of the exportation,

(a) the individual

(i) declares the firearm to a customs officer in the prescribed manner and, in the case of a declaration in writing, completes the prescribed form containing the prescribed information, and

(ii) produces his or her licence and the registration certificate for the firearm and, in the case of a prohibited firearm or restricted firearm, an authorization to transport the firearm; and

(b) a customs officer confirms the documents referred to in subparagraphs (a)(i) and (ii) in the prescribed manner.

(2) Non-compliance — Where a firearm is declared to a customs officer but the requirements of subparagraph (1)(a)(ii) are not complied with, the customs officer may detain the firearm.

(3) Disposal of firearm — A firearm that is detained under subsection (2) may be disposed of in the prescribed manner.

Unproclaimed section — 39

39. Authorization for individuals to export replica firearms — An individual may export a replica firearm if he or she declares the replica firearm to a customs officer in the prescribed manner.

Unproclaimed section — 40

40. (1) Authorization for individuals who hold a licence to import firearms — An individual who holds a licence may import a firearm if, at the time of the importation,

(a) the individual declares the firearm to a customs officer in the prescribed manner;

(b) in the case of a firearm that was exported in accordance with section 38, the individual produces the declaration confirmed in accordance with that section and, in the case of a prohibited firearm or restricted firearm, an authorization to transport the prohibited firearm or restricted firearm;

(c) in the case of a firearm that is not a prohibited firearm and for which a registration certificate has not been issued,

(i) the individual completes the prescribed form containing the prescribed information, if the declaration referred to in paragraph (a) is in writing,

(ii) the individual holds a licence authorizing him or her to acquire and possess that kind of firearm,

(iii) a customs officer informs a chief firearms officer of the importation and the chief firearms officer approves the importation in accordance with section 27, and

　　　　(iv) in the case of a restricted firearm, the individual produces an authorization to transport the restricted firearm; and

　　(d) a customs officer confirms the documents referred to in paragraph (b) or (c) in the prescribed manner.

(2) **Non-compliance** — Where a firearm is declared at a customs office to a customs officer but the requirements of paragraph (1)(b) or (c) are not complied with, the customs officer may authorize the firearm to be exported from that customs office or may detain the firearm and give the individual a reasonable time to comply with those requirements.

(3) **Disposal of firearm** — Where those requirements are not complied with within a reasonable time and the firearm is not exported, the firearm shall be disposed of in the prescribed manner.

(4) **Importation of prohibited firearms** — An individual who holds a licence may import a prohibited firearm only if he or she previously exported the prohibited firearm in accordance with section 38.

(5) **Prohibited firearm** — Where a prohibited firearm is declared at a customs office to a customs officer and the prohibited firearm was not previously exported in accordance with section 38, the customs officer may authorize the prohibited firearm to be exported from that customs office.

(6) **Disposal** — Prohibited firearms that are not immediately exported under subsection (5) are forfeited to Her Majesty in right of Canada and shall be disposed of in the prescribed manner.

Unproclaimed section — 41

41. Temporary registration certificate — A declaration that is confirmed in accordance with paragraph 40(1)(d) has the same effect as a registration certificate for the firearm for the period for which the confirmation is expressed to be effective.

Unproclaimed section — 42

42. Notification of Registrar — A customs officer shall inform the Registrar without delay of the exportation or importation of a firearm by an individual.

Unproclaimed sections — 43-53

Businesses

43. Authorization for businesses to import or export — A business may export or import a firearm, prohibited weapon, restricted weapon, prohibited device, component or part designed exclusively for use in the manufacture of or assembly into an automatic firearm or prohibited ammunition only if the business holds an authorization to export or an authorization to import.

44. Authorization to export — An authorization to export goods described in section 43 may be issued to a business only if the business that applies for such an authorization

　　(a) in the case of a firearm, holds the registration certificate for the firearm;

(b) in the case of a prohibited firearm, prohibited weapon, prohibited device, component or part designed exclusively for use in the manufacture of or assembly into an automatic firearm or prohibited ammunition, identifies it in the prescribed manner and specifies the prescribed purpose for the exportation;

(c) holds a licence authorizing it to possess those goods, except where those goods are to be shipped in transit through Canada by a business that does not carry on business in Canada;

(d) indicates the destination of those goods;

(e) provides the Registrar with the prescribed information and any other information reasonably required by the Registrar.

45. (1) Authorization to be produced — A business that holds an authorization to export goods described in section 43 must produce the authorization to a customs officer at the time of the exportation.

(2) Customs officer — A customs officer may confirm an authorization to export.

(3) Non-compliance — Where an authorization to export is not confirmed, a customs officer may detain goods described in section 43.

(4) Disposal — A good that is detained under subsection (3) my be disposed of in the prescribed manner.

46. Authorization to import — An authorization to import goods described in section 43 may be issued to a business only if the business that applies for such an authorization

(a) holds a licence authorizing it to acquire and possess those goods, except where those goods are to be shipped in transit through Canada by a business that does not carry on business in Canada;

(b) identifies those goods in the prescribed manner;

(c) in the case of either a firearm that is not a prohibited firearm or a restricted weapon, specifies the purpose for the importation;

(d) in the case of a prohibited firearm, prohibited weapon, prohibited device, component or part designed exclusively for use in the manufacture of or assembly into an automatic firearm or prohibited ammunition, specifies the prescribed purpose for the importation;

(e) indicates the destination in Canada of those goods; and

(f) provides the Registrar with the prescribed information and any other information reasonably required by the Registrar.

47. (1) Authorization to be produced — A business that holds an authorization to import goods described in section 43 must produce the authorization at a customs office to a customs officer at the time of the importation.

(2) Customs officer — A customs officer may confirm an authorization to import.

(3) Non-compliance — Where an authorization to import is not confirmed, a customs officer may authorize goods described in section 43 to be exported from that customs office, in which case the goods may be exported without any other authorization.

(4) Disposal — Goods that are not exported under subsection (3) within ten days are forfeited to Her Majesty in right of Canada and shall be disposed of in the prescribed manner.

48. Temporary registration certificate — An authorization to import a firearm that is confirmed in accordance with subsection 47(2) has the same effect as a registration certificate for the firearm for the period for which the confirmation is expressed to be effective.

49. Separate authorization — Each exportation or importation of goods described in section 43 requires a separate authorization to export or authorization to import.

50. Notification of Registrar — A customs officer shall inform the Registrar without delay of the exportation or importation of goods described in section 43 by a business.

51. Notification of Minister responsible for the Export and Import Permits Act — The Registrar shall inform the member of the Queen's Privy Council for Canada who is designated by the Governor in Council as the Minister for the purposes of the *Export and Import Permits Act* of every application by a business for an authorization to export or authorization to import.

52. Only at designated customs offices — No business shall export or import goods described in section 43 except at a customs office designated for that purpose by the Minister of National Revenue.

53. No in-transit shipments of prohibited firearms, weapons, devices and ammunition — No business shall import a prohibited firearm, prohibited weapon prohibited device or prohibited ammunition that is to be shipped in transit through Canada and exported.

Licences, Registration Certificates and Authorizations

Applications

54. (1) Applications — A licence, registration certificate or authorization may be issued only on application made in the prescribed form containing the prescribed information and accompanied by payment of the prescribed fees.

(2) To whom made — An application for a licence, registration certificate or authorization must be made to

(a) a chief firearms officer, in the case of a licence, an authorization to carry or an authorization to transport; or

(b) the Registrar, in the case of a registration certificate, an authorization to export or an authorization to import.

(3) Pre-commencement restricted firearms and handguns — An individual who, on the commencement day, possesses one or more restricted firearms or one or more handguns referred to in subsection 12(6) (pre-February 14, 1995 handguns) must specify, in any application for a licence authorizing the individual to possess restricted firearms or handguns that are so referred to,

(a) except in the case of a firearm described in paragraph (b), for which purpose described in section 28 the individual wishes to continue to possess restricted firearms or handguns that are so referred to; and

(b) for which of those firearms was a registration certificate under the former Act issued because they were relics, were of value as a curiosity or rarity or were valued as a memento, remembrance or souvenir.

55. (1) Further information — A chief firearms officer or the Registrar may require an applicant for a licence or authorization to submit such information, in addition to that included in the application, as may reasonably be regarded as relevant for the purpose of determining whether the applicant is eligible to hold the licence or authorization.

(2) Investigation — Without restricting the scope of the inquiries that may be made with respect to an application for a licence, a chief firearms officer may conduct an investigation of the applicant, which may consist of interviews with neighbours, community workers, social workers, individuals who work or live with the applicant, spouse, former spouse, dependants or whomever in the opinion of the chief firearms officer may provide information pertaining to whether the applicant is eligible under section 5 to hold a licence.

Issuance

56. (1) Licences — A chief firearms officer is responsible for issuing licences.

(2) Only one licence per individual — Only one licence may be issued to any one individual.

(3) Separate licence for each location — A business other than a carrier requires a separate licence for each place where the business is carried on.

57. Authorizations to carry or transport — A chief firearms officer is responsible for issuing authorizations to carry and authorizations to transport.

58. (1) Conditions — A chief firearms officer who issues a licence, an authorization to carry or an authorization to transport may attach any reasonable condition to it that the chief firearms officer considers desirable in the particular circumstances and in the interests of the safety of the holder or any other person.

(2) Minors — Before attaching a condition to a licence that is to be issued to an individual who is less than eighteen years old and who is not eligible to hold a licence under subsection 8(2) (minors hunting as a way of life), a chief firearms officer must consult with a parent or person who has custody of the individual.

(3) Minors — Before issuing a licence to an individual who is less than eighteen years old and who is not eligible to hold a licence under subsection 8(2) (minors hunting as a way of life), a chief firearms officer shall have a parent or person who has custody of the individual sign the licence, including any conditions attached to it.

59. Different registered owner — An individual who holds an authorization to carry or authorization to transport need not be the person to whom the registration certificate for the particular prohibited firearm or restricted firearm was issued.

60. Registration certificates and authorizations to export or import — The Registrar is responsible for issuing registration certificates for firearms and assigning firearms identification numbers to them and for issuing authorizations to export and authorizations to import.

61. (1) Form — A licence or registration certificate must be in the prescribed form and include the prescribed information and any conditions attached to it.

(2) Form of authorizations — An authorization to carry, authorization to transport, authorization to export or authorization to import may be in the prescribed form and include the prescribed information, including any conditions attached to it.

(3) Condition attached to licence — An authorization to carry or authorization to transport may take the form of a condition attached to a licence.

(4) Businesses — A licence that is issued to a business must specify each particular activity that the licence authorizes in relation to prohibited firearms, restricted firearms, firearms that are neither prohibited firearms nor restricted firearms, crossbows, prohibited weapons, restricted weapons, prohibited devices, ammunition or prohibited ammunition.

62. Not transferable — Licences, registration certificates, authorizations to carry, authorizations to transport, authorizations to export and authorizations to import are not transferable.

63. (1) Geographical extent — Subject to subsection (2), licences, registration certificates, authorizations to transport, authorizations to export and authorizations to import are valid throughout Canada.

(2) Intraprovincial carriers — A licence that is issued to carrier, other than a carrier described in section 73, is not valid outside the province in which it is issued.

(3) Authorizations to carry — Authorizations to carry are not valid outside the province in which they are issued.

Term

64. (1) Term of licences — A licence that is issued to an individual who is eighteen years old or older expires on the earlier of

    (a) five years after the birthday of the holder next following the day on which it is issued, and

    (b) the expiration of the period for which it is expressed to be issued.

(2) Minors — A licence that is issued to an individual who is less than eighteen years old expires on the earlier of

    (a) the day on which the holder attains the age of eighteen years, and

    (b) the expiration of the period for which it is expressed to be issued.

(3) **Businesses other than museums** — A licence that is issued to a business other than a museum expires on the earlier of

(a) one year after the day on which it is issued, and

(b) the expiration of the period for which it is expressed to be issued.

(4) **Museums** — A licence that is issued to a museum expires on the earlier of

(a) three years after the day on which it is issued, and

(b) the expiration of the period for which it is expressed to be issued.

65. (1) **Term of authorizations** — Subject to subsections (2) to (4), an authorization expires on the expiration of the period for which it is expressed to be issued.

(2) **Authorizations to transport** — Subject to subsection (3), an authorization to transport that takes the form of a condition attached to a licence expires on the earlier of

(a) the expiration of the period for which the condition is expressed to be attached, and

(b) the expiration of the licence.

(3) **Authorizations to transport** — An authorization to transport a restricted firearm or a handgun referred to in subsection 12(6) (pre-February 14, 1995 handguns) for use in target practice, or a target shooting competition, under specified conditions or under the auspices of a shooting club or shooting range that is approved under section 29 expires

(a) in the case of an authorization to transport that takes the form of a condition attached to a licence, on the earlier of

(i) the expiration of the period for which the condition is expressed to be attached, which period may not be less than one year or more than three years, and

(ii) the expiration of the licence; and

(b) in the case of an authorization to transport that does not take the form of a condition attached to a licence, on the expiration of the period for which the authorization is expressed to be issued, which period may not be less than one year or more than three years.

(4) **Authorizations to carry** — An authorization to carry expires

(a) in the case of an authorization to carry that takes the form of a condition attached to a licence, on the earlier of

(i) the expiration of the period for which the condition is expressed to be attached, which period may not be more than two years, and

(ii) the expiration of the licence; and

(b) in the case of an authorization to carry that does not take the form of a condition attached to a licence, on the expiration of the period for which the authorization is expressed to be issued, which period may not be more than two years.

66. **Term of registration certificates** — A registration certificate for a firearm expires where

(a) the holder of the registration certificate ceases to be the owner of the firearm; or

1483

(b) the firearm ceases to be a firearm.

67. (1) Renewal — A chief firearms officer may renew a licence, authorization to carry or authorization to transport in the same manner and in the same circumstances in which a licence, authorization to carry or authorization to transport may be issued.

(2) Restricted firearms and pre-February 14, 1995 handguns — On renewing a licence authorizing an individual to possess restricted firearms or handguns referred to in subsection 12(6) (pre-February 14, 1995 handguns), a chief firearms officer shall decide whether any of those firearms or handguns that the individual possesses are being used for

(a) the purpose described in section 28 for which the individual acquired the restricted firearms or handguns; or

(b) in the case of any of those firearms or handguns that were possessed by the individual on the commencement day, the purpose described in that section that was specified by the individual in the licence application.

(3) Registrar — A chief firearms officer who decides that any restricted firearms or any handguns referred to in subsection 12(6) (pre-February 14, 1995 handguns) that are possessed by an individual are not being used for that purpose shall

(a) give notice of that decision in the prescribed form to the individual; and

(b) inform the Registrar of that decision.

(4) Relics — Subsections (2) and (3) do not apply to a firearm

(a) that is a relic, is of value as a curiosity or rarity or is valued as a memento, remembrance or souvenir,

(b) that was specified in the licence application as being a firearm for which a registration certificate under the former Act was issued because the firearm was a relic, was of value as a curiosity or rarity or was valued as a memento, remembrance or souvenir;

(c) for which a registration certificate under the former Act was issued because the firearm was a relic, was of value as a curiosity or rarity or was valued as a memento, remembrance or souvenir; and

(d) in respect of which an individual, on the commencement day, held a registration certificate under the former Act.

(5) Material to accompany notice — A notice given under paragraph (3)(a) must include the reasons for the decision and be accompanied by a copy of sections 74 to 81.

Refusal to Issue and Revocation

68. Licences and authorizations — A chief firearms officer shall refuse to issue a licence if the applicant is not eligible to hold one and may refuse to issue an authorization to carry or authorization to transport for any good and sufficient reason.

69. Registration certificates — The Registrar may refuse to issue a registration certificate, authorization to export or authorization to import for any good and sufficient reason including, in the case of an application for a registration certificate, where the applicant is not eligible to hold a registration certificate.

70. (1) **Revocation of licence or authorization** — A chief firearms officer who issues a licence, authorization to carry or authorization to transport may revoke it for any good and sufficient reason including, without limiting the generality of the foregoing,

    (a) where the holder of the licence or authorization

        (i) is no longer or never was eligible to hold the licence or authorization,

        (ii) contravenes any condition attached to the licence or authorization, or

        (iii) has been convicted or discharged under section 736 of the *Criminal Code* of an offence referred to in paragraph 5(2)(a); or

    (b) where, in the case of a business, a person who stands in a prescribed relationship to the business has been convicted or discharged under section 736 of the *Criminal Code* of any such offence.

(2) **Registrar** — The Registrar may revoke an authorization to export or authorization to import for any good and sufficient reason.

71. (1) **Revocation of registration certificate** — The Registrar

    (a) may revoke a registration certificate for any good and sufficient reason; and

    (b) shall revoke a registration certificate for a firearm held by an individual where the Registrar is informed by a chief firearms officer under section 67 that the firearm is not being used for

        (i) the purpose for which the individual acquired it, or

        (ii) in the case of a firearm possessed by the individual on the commencement day, the purpose specified by the individual in the licence application.

(2) **Automatic revocation of registration certificate** — A registration certificate for a prohibited firearm referred to in subsection 12(3) (pre-August 1, 1992 converted automatic firearms) is automatically revoked on the change of any alteration in the prohibited firearm that was described in the application for the registration certificate.

72. (1) **Notice of refusal to issue or revocation** — Where a chief firearms officer decides to refuse to issue or to revoke a licence or authorization to transport or the Registrar decides to refuse to issue or to revoke a registration certificate, authorization to export or authorization to import, the chief firearms officer or Registrar shall give notice of the decision in the prescribed form to the applicant for or holder of the licence, registration certificate or authorization.

(2) **Material to accompany notice** — A notice given under subsection (1) must include reasons for the decision disclosing the nature of the information relied on for the decision and must be accompanied by a copy of sections 74 to 81.

(3) **Non-disclosure of information** — A chief firearms officer or the Registrar need not disclose any information the disclosure of which could, in the opinion of the chief firearms officer or the Registrar, endanger the safety of any person.

(4) **Disposal of firearms** — A notice given under subsection (1) in respect of a licence must specify a reasonable period during which the applicant for or holder of the licence may deliver to a peace officer or a firearms officer or a chief firearms officer or otherwise lawfully dispose of any firearm, prohibited weapon, restricted weapon, prohibited device or prohibited ammunition that the applicant for or holder of the licence

possesses and during which sections **91, 92** and **94** of the *Criminal Code* do not apply to the applicant or holder.

(5) **Idem** — A notice given under subsection (1) in respect of a registration certificate must specify a reasonable period during which the applicant for or holder of the registration certificate may deliver to a peace officer or a firearms officer or a chief firearms officer or otherwise lawfully dispose of the firearm to which the registration certificate relates and during which sections **91, 92** and **94** of the *Criminal Code* and section 112 of this Act do not apply to the applicant or holder.

(6) **Reference** — If the applicant for or holder of the licence or registration certificate refers the refusal to issue it or revocation of it to a provincial court judge under section 74, the reasonable period of time does not begin until after the reference is finally disposed of.

International and Interprovincial Carriers

73. Application — Sections 54 to 72 apply in respect of a carrier whose business includes the transportation of firearms, prohibited weapons, restricted weapons, prohibited devices or prohibited ammunition from one province to any other province, or beyond the limits of a province, as if each reference in those sections to a chief firearms officer were a reference to the Registrar.

References to Provincial Court Judge

74. (1) Reference to judge of refusal to issue or revocation, etc. — Subject to subsection (2), where

(a) a chief firearms officer or the Registrar refuses to issue or revokes a licence, registration certificate, authorization to transport, authorization to export or authorization to import,

(b) a chief firearms officer decides under section 67 that a firearm possessed by an individual who holds a licence is not being used for

(i) the purpose for which the individual acquired the firearm, or

(ii) in the case of a firearm possessed by an individual on the commencement day, the purpose specified by the individual in the licence application, or

(c) a provincial minister refuses to approve or revokes the approval of a shooting club or shooting range for the purposes of this Act,

the applicant for or holder of the licence, registration certificate, authorization or approval may refer the matter to a provincial court judge in the territorial division in which the applicant or holder resides.

(2) **Limitation period** — An applicant or holder may only refer a matter to a provincial court judge under subsection (1) within thirty days after receiving notice of the decision of the chief firearms officer, Registrar or provincial minister under section 29, 67 or 72 or within such further time as is allowed by a provincial court judge, whether before or after the expiration of those thirty days.

75. (1) Hearing of reference — On receipt of a reference under section 74, the provincial court judge shall fix a date for the hearing of the reference and direct that notice of the hearing be given to the chief firearms officer, Registrar or provincial minister and to the applicant for or holder of the licence, registration certificate, authorization or approval, in such manner as the provincial court judge may specify.

(2) **Evidence** — At the hearing of the reference, the provincial court judge shall hear all relevant evidence presented by or on behalf of the chief firearms officer, Registrar or provincial minister and the applicant or holder.

(3) **Burden of proof** — At the hearing of the reference, the burden of proof is on the applicant or holder to satisfy the provincial court judge that the refusal to issue or revocation of the licence, registration certificate or authorization, the decision or the refusal to approve or revocation of the approval was not justified.

(4) **Where hearing may proceed ex parte** — A provincial court judge may proceed *ex parte* to hear and determine a reference in the absence of the applicant or holder in the same circumstances as those in which a summary conviction court may, under Part XXVII of the *Criminal Code*, proceed with a trial in the absence of the defendant.

76. Decision by provincial court judge — On the hearing of a reference, the provincial court judge may, by order,

    (a) confirm the decision of the chief firearms officer, Registrar or provincial minister,

    (b) direct the chief firearms officer or Registrar to issue a licence, registration certificate or authorization or direct the provincial minister to approve a club or shooting range; or

    (c) cancel the revocation of the licence, registration certificate, authorization or approval or the decision of the chief firearms officer under section 67.

Appeals to Superior Court and Court of Appeal

76.1 Nunavut — With respect to Nunavut, the following definitions apply for the purposes of sections 77 to 81.

"provincial court judge" means a judge of the Nunavut Court of Justice.

"superior court" means a judge of the Court of Appeal of Nunavut.

1999, c. 3, s. 64

77. (1) Appeal to superior court — Subject to section 78, where a provincial court judge makes an order under paragraph 76(a), the applicant for or holder of the licence, registration certificate, authorization or approval, as the case may be, may appeal to the superior court against the order.

(2) **Appeal by Attorney General** — Subject to section 78, where a provincial court judge makes an order under paragraph 76(b) or (c),

    (a) the Attorney General of Canada may appeal to the superior court against the order, if the order is directed to a chief firearms officer who was designated by the federal Minister, to the Registrar or to the federal Minister; or

    (b) the attorney general of the province may appeal to the superior court against the order, in the case of any other order made under paragraph 76(b) or (c).

78. (1) Notice of appeal — An appellant who proposes to appeal an order made under section 76 to the superior court must give notice of appeal not later than thirty days after the order is made.

(2) Extension of time — The superior court may, either before or after the expiration of those thirty days, extend the time within which notice of appeal may be given.

(3) Contents of notice — A notice of appeal must set out the grounds of appeal, together with such further material as the superior court may require.

(4) Service of notice — A copy of any notice of appeal filed with the superior court under subsection (1) and of any further material required to be filed with it shall be served within fourteen days after the filing of the notice, unless before or after the expiration of those fourteen days further time is allowed by the superior court, on

(a) the Attorney General of Canada, in the case of an appeal of an order made under paragraph 76(a) confirming a decision of a chief firearms officer who was designated by the federal Minister, of the Registrar or of the federal Minister;

(b) the attorney general of the province, in the case of an appeal against any other order made under paragraph 76(a);

(c) the applicant for or holder of the licence, registration certificate, authorization or approval, in the case of an appeal against an order made under paragraph 76(b) or (c); and

(d) any other person specified by the superior court.

79. (1) Disposition of appeal — On the hearing of an appeal, the superior court may

(a) dismiss the appeal; or

(b) allow the appeal and, in the case of an appeal against an order made under paragraph 76(a),

(i) direct the chief firearms officer or Registrar to issue a licence, registration certificate or authorization or direct the provincial minister to approve a shooting club or shooting range, or

(ii) cancel the revocation of the licence, registration certificate, authorization or approval or the decision of the chief firearms officer under section 67.

(2) Burden on applicant — A superior court shall dispose of an appeal against an order made under paragraph 76(a) by dismissing it, unless the appellant establishes to the satisfaction of the court that a disposition referred to in paragraph (1)(b) is justified.

80. Appeal to court of appeal — An appeal to the court of appeal may, with leave of that court or of a judge of that court, be taken against a decision of a superior court under section 79 on any ground that involves a question of law alone.

81. Application of Part XXVII of the Criminal Code — Part XXVII of the *Criminal Code*, except sections 785 to 812, 816 to 819 and 829 to 838, applies in respect of an appeal under this Act, with such modifications as the circumstances require and as if each reference in that Part to the appeal court were a reference to the superior court.

Canadian Firearms Registration System

Registrar of Firearms

82. Appointment of Registrar of Firearms — The Commissioner of the Royal Canadian Mounted Police shall, after consulting with the federal Minister and the Solicitor General of Canada, appoint an individual as the Registrar of Firearms.

Records of the Registrar

83. (1) Canadian Firearms Registry — The Registrar shall establish and maintain a registry, to be known as the Canadian Firearms Registry, in which shall be kept a record of

(a) every licence, registration certificate and authorization that is issued or revoked by the Registrar;

(b) every application for a licence, registration certificate or authorization that is refused by the Registrar;

(c) every transfer of a firearm of which the Registrar is informed under section 26 or 27;

(d) every exportation from or importation into Canada of a firearm of which the Registrar is informed under section 42 or 50;

(e) every loss, finding, theft or destruction of a firearm of which the Registrar is informed under section 88; and

(f) such other matters as may be prescribed.

(2) Operation — The Registrar is responsible for the day-to-day operation of the Canadian Firearms Registry.

84. Destruction of records — The Registrar may destroy records kept in the Canadian Firearms Registry at such times and in such circumstances as may be prescribed.

85. (1) Other records of Registrar — The Registrar shall establish and maintain a record of

(a) firearms acquired or possessed by the following persons and used by them in the course of their duties or for the purposes of their employment, namely,

(i) peace officers,

(ii) persons training to become police officers or peace officers under the control and supervision of

(A) a police force, or

(B) a police academy or similar institution designated by the federal Minister or the lieutenant governor in council of a province,

(iii) persons or members of a class of persons employed in the public service of Canada or by the government of a province or municipality who are prescribed by the regulations made by the Governor in Council under Part III of the *Criminal Code* to be public officers, and

(iv) chief firearms officers and firearms officers; and

(b) firearms acquired or possessed by individuals on behalf of, and under the authority of, a police force or a department of the Government of Canada or of a province.

(2) **Reporting of acquisitions and transfers** — A person referred to in subsection (1) who acquires or transfers a firearm shall have the Registrar informed of the acquisition or transfer.

(3) **Destruction of records** — The Registrar may destroy any record referred to in subsection (1) at such times and in such circumstances as may be prescribed.

86. **Records to be transferred** — The records kept in the registry maintained pursuant to section 114 of the former Act that relate to registration certificates shall be transferred to the Registrar.

Records of Chief Firearms Officers

87. (1) **Records of chief firearms officers** — A chief firearms officer shall keep a record of

(a) every licence and authorization that is issued or revoked by the chief firearms officer;

(b) every application for a licence or authorization that is refused by the chief firearms officer;

(c) every prohibition order of which the chief firearms officer is informed under section 89; and

(d) such other matters as may be prescribed.

(2) **Destruction of records** — A chief firearms officer may destroy any record referred to in subsection (1) at such times and in such circumstances as may be prescribed.

88. **Reporting of loss, finding, theft and destruction of firearms** — A chief firearms officer to whom the loss, finding, theft or destruction of a firearm is reported shall have the Registrar informed without delay of the loss, finding, theft or destruction.

Reporting of Prohibition Orders

89. **Reporting of prohibition orders** — Every court, judge or justice that makes, varies or revokes a prohibition order shall have a chief firearms officer informed without delay of the prohibition order or its variation or revocation.

Access to Records

90. **Right of access** — The Registrar has a right of access to records kept by a chief firearms officer under section 87 and a chief firearms officer has a right of access to records kept by the Registrar under section 83 or 85 and to records kept by other chief firearms officers under section 87.

Electronic Filing

91. (1) Electronic filing — Subject to the regulations, notices and documents that are sent to or issued by the Registrar pursuant to this or any other Act of Parliament may be sent or issued in electronic or other form in any manner specified by the Registrar.

(2) **Time of receipt** — For the purposes of this Act and Part III of the *Criminal Code*, a notice or document that is sent or issued in accordance with subsection (1) is deemed to have been received at the time and date provided by the regulations.

92. (1) Records of Registrar — Records required by section 83 or 85 to be kept by the Registrar may

(a) be in bound or loose-leaf form or in photographic film form; or

(b) be entered or recorded by any system of mechanical or electronic data processing or by any other information storage device that is capable of reproducing any required information in intelligible written or printed form within a reasonable time.

(2) **Storage of documents or information in electronic or other form** — Subject to the regulations, a document or information received by the Registrar under this Act in electronic or other form may be entered or recorded by any information storage device, including any system of mechanical or electronic data processing, that is capable of reproducing stored documents or information in intelligible written or printed form within a reasonable time.

(3) **Probative value** — Where the Registrar maintains a record of a document otherwise than in written or printed form, an extract from that record that is certified by the Registrar has the same probative value as the document would have had if it had been proved in the ordinary way.

Reports

93. (1) Report to Solicitor General — The Registrar shall, as soon as possible after the end of each calendar year and at such other times as the Solicitor General of Canada may, in writing, request, submit to the Solicitor General a report, in such form and including such information as the Solicitor General may direct, with regard to the administration of this Act.

(2) **Laid before Parliament** — The Solicitor General of Canada shall have each report laid before each House of Parliament on any of the first fifteen days on which that House is sitting after the Solicitor General receives it.

94. Information to be submitted to Registrar — A chief firearms officer shall submit the prescribed information with regard to the administration of this Act at the prescribed time and in the prescribed form for the purpose of enabling the Registrar to compile the reports referred to in section 93.

General

Agreements with Provinces

95. Agreements with provinces — The federal Minister may, with the approval of the Governor in Council, enter into agreements with the governments of the provinces

    (a) providing for payment of compensation by Canada to the provinces in respect of administrative costs actually incurred by the provinces in relation to processing licences, registration certificates and authorizations and applications for licences, registration certificates and authorizations and the operation of the Canadian Firearms Registration System; and

    (b) notwithstanding subsections 17(1) and (4) of the *Financial Administration Act*, authorizing the governments of the provinces to withhold those costs, in accordance with the terms and conditions of the agreement, from fees under paragraph 117(p) collected or received by the governments of the provinces.

Other Matters

96. Other obligations not affected — The issuance of a licence, registration certificate or authorization under this Act does not affect the obligation of any person to comply with any other Act of Parliament or any regulation made under an Act of Parliament respecting firearms or other weapons.

97. (1) Exemptions — Subject to subsection (2), a provincial minister may exempt from the application in that province of any provision of this Act or the regulations or Part III of the *Criminal Code*, for any period not exceeding one year, the employees, in respect of any thing done by them in the course of or for the purpose of their duties or employment, of any business that holds a licence authorizing the business to acquire prohibited firearms, prohibited weapons, prohibited devices or prohibited ammunition.

(2) Public safety — Subsection (1) does not apply where it is not desirable, in the interests of the safety of any person, that the employees of the business be so exempted.

(3) Conditions — A provincial minister may attach to an exemption any reasonable condition that the provincial minister considers desirable in the particular circumstances and in the interests of the safety of any person.

Delegation

98. Authorized chief firearms officer may perform functions of provincial minister — A chief firearms officer of a province who is authorized in writing by a provincial minister may perform the function of the provincial minister of designating firearms officers for the province.

99. (1) Designated officers may perform functions of chief firearms officers — Subject to subsections (2) and (3), a firearms officer who is designated in writing by a chief firearms officer may perform such duties and functions of the chief firearms officer under this Act or Part III of the *Criminal Code* as are specified in the designation.

(2) **Exception** — A licence that is issued to a business authorizing the business to acquire prohibited firearms, prohibited weapons, prohibited devices or prohibited ammunition must be issued by a chief firearms officer personally.

(3) **Exception** — An authorization to carry must be issued by a chief firearms officer personally.

100. Designated officers may perform functions of Registrar — A person who is designated in writing by the Registrar for the purpose of this section may perform such duties and functions of the Registrar under this Act or Part III of the *Criminal Code* as are specified in the designation.

Inspection

101. Definition of "inspector" — In sections 102 to 105, "inspector" means a firearms officer and includes, in respect of a province, a member of a class of individuals designated by the provincial minister.

102. (1) Inspection — Subject to section 104, for the purpose of ensuring compliance with this Act and the regulations, an inspector may at any reasonable time enter and inspect any place where the inspector believes on reasonable grounds a business is being carried on or there is a record of a business, any place in which the inspector believes on reasonable grounds there is a gun collection or a record in relation to a gun collection or any place in which the inspector believes on reasonable grounds there is a prohibited firearm or there are more than 10 firearms and may

(a) open any container that the inspector believes on reasonable grounds contains a firearm or other thing in respect of which this Act or the regulations apply;

(b) examine any firearm and examine any other thing that the inspector finds and take samples of it;

(c) conduct any tests or analyses or take any measurements; and

(d) require any person to produce for examination or copying any records, books of account or other documents that the inspector believes on reasonable grounds contain information that is relevant to the enforcement of this Act or the regulations.

(2) **Operation of data processing systems and copying equipment** — In carrying out an inspection of a place under subsection (1), an inspector may

(a) use or cause to be used any data processing system at the place to examine any data contained in or available to the system;

(b) reproduce any record or cause it to be reproduced from the data in the form of a print-out or other intelligible output and remove the print-out or other output for examination or copying; and

(c) use or cause to be used any copying equipment at the place to make copies of any record, book of account or other document.

(3) **Use of force** — In carrying out an inspection of a place under subsection (1), an inspector may not use force.

(4) **Receipt for things taken** — An inspector who takes any thing while carrying out an inspection of a place under subsection (1) must give to the owner or occupant of the place at the time that the thing is taken a receipt for the thing that describes the

thing with reasonable precision, including, in the case of a firearm, the serial number if available of the firearm.

(5) **Definition of "business"** — For greater certainty, in this section, "business" has the meaning assigned by subsection 2(1).

103. **Duty to assist inspectors** — The owner or person in charge of a place that is inspected by an inspector under section 102 and every person found in the place shall

(a) give the inspector all reasonable assistance to enable him or her to carry out the inspection and exercise any power conferred by section 102; and

(b) provide the inspector with any information relevant to the enforcement of this Act or the regulations that he or she may reasonably require.

104. (1) **Inspection of dwelling-house** — An inspector may not enter a dwelling-house under section 102 except

(a) on reasonable notice to the owner or occupant, except where a business is being carried on in the dwelling-house; and

(b) with the consent of the occupant or under a warrant.

(2) **Authority to issue warrant** — A justice who on *ex parte* application is satisfied by information on oath

(a) that the conditions for entry described in section 102 exist in relation to a dwelling-house,

(b) that entry to the dwelling-house is necessary for any purpose relating to the enforcement of this Act or the regulations, and

(c) that entry to the dwelling-house has been refused or that there are reasonable grounds for believing that entry will be refused

may issue a warrant authorizing the inspector named in it to enter that dwelling-house subject to any conditions that may be specified in the warrant.

(3) **Areas that may be inspected** — For greater certainty, an inspector who is carrying out an inspection of a dwelling-house may enter and inspect only

(a) that part of a room of the dwelling-house in which the inspector believes on reasonable grounds there is a firearm, prohibited weapon, restricted weapon, prohibited device, prohibited ammunition, a record in relation to a gun collection or all or part of a device or other thing required by a regulation made under paragraph 117(h) respecting the storage of firearms and restricted weapons; and

(b) in addition, in the case of a dwelling-house where the inspector believes on reasonable grounds a business is being carried on, that part of a room in which the inspector believes on reasonable grounds there is ammunition or a record of the business.

105. **Demand to produce firearm** — An inspector who believes on reasonable grounds that a person possesses a firearm may, by demand made to that person, require that person, within a reasonable time after the demand is made, to produce the firearm in the manner specified by the inspector for the purpose of verifying the serial number or other identifying features of the firearm and of ensuring that the person is the holder of the registration certificate for the firearm.

Offences

106. (1) **False statements to procure licences, etc.** — Every person commits an offence who, for the purpose of procuring a licence, registration certificate or authorization for that person or any other person, knowingly makes a statement orally or in writing that is false or misleading or knowingly fails to disclose any information that is relevant to the application for the licence, registration certificate or authorization.

(2) **False statements to procure customs confirmations** — Every person commits an offence who, for the purpose of procuring the confirmation by a customs officer of a document under this Act for that person or any other person, knowingly makes a statement orally or in writing that is false or misleading or knowingly fails to disclose any information that is relevant to the document.

(3) **Definition of "statement"** — In this section, "statement" means an assertion of fact, opinion, belief or knowledge, whether material or not and whether admissible or not.

107. **Tampering with licences, etc.** — Every person commits an offence who, without lawful excuse the proof of which lies on the person, alters, defaces or falsifies

(a) a licence, registration certificate or authorization; or

(b) a confirmation by a customs officer of a document under this Act.

108. **Unauthorized possession of ammunition** — Every business commits an offence that possesses ammunition, unless the business holds a licence under which it may possess ammunition.

109. **Punishment** — Every person who commits an offence under section 106, 107 or 108, who contravenes subsection 29(1) or who contravenes a regulation made under paragraph 117(d), (e), (f), (g), (i), (j), (l), (m) or (n) the contravention of which has been made an offence under paragraph 117(o)

(a) is guilty of an indictable offence and liable to imprisonment for a term not exceeding five years; or

(b) is guilty of an offence punishable on summary conviction.

110. **Contravention of conditions of licences, etc.** — Every person commits an offence who, without lawful excuse, contravenes a condition of a licence, registration certificate or authorization held by the person.

111. **Punishment** — Every person who commits an offence under section 110 or who does not comply with section 103

(a) is guilty of an indictable offence and liable to imprisonment for a term not exceeding two years; or

(b) is guilty of an offence punishable on summary conviction.

112. (1) **Failure to register certain firearms** — Subject to subsections (2) and (3), every person commits an offence who, not having previously committed an offence under this subsection or subsection 91(1) or 92(1) of the *Criminal Code*, possesses a firearm that is neither a prohibited firearm nor a restricted firearm without being the holder of a registration certificate for the firearm.

(2) **Exceptions** — Subsection (1) does not apply to

(a) a person who possesses a firearm while the person is under the direct and immediate supervision of a person who may lawfully possess it, for the purpose of using it in a manner in which the supervising person may lawfully use it;

(b) a person who comes into possession of a firearm by operation of law and who, within a reasonable period after acquiring possession of it, lawfully disposes of it or obtains a registration certificate for it; or

(c) a person who possesses a firearm and who is not the holder of a registration certificate for the firearm if the person

(i) has borrowed the firearm,

(ii) is the holder of a licence under which the person may possess it, and

(iii) is in possession of the firearm to hunt or trap in order to sustain himself or herself or his or her family.

(3) **Transitional** — Every person who, at any particular time between the commencement day and the later of January 1, 1998 and such other date as is prescribed, possesses a firearm that, as of that particular time, is neither a prohibited firearm nor a restricted firearm is deemed for the purposes of subsection (1) to be, until January 1, 2003 or such other earlier date as is prescribed, the holder of a registration certificate for the firearm.

(4) **Onus on the defendant** — Where, in any proceedings for an offence under this section, any question arises as to whether a person is the holder of a registration certificate, the onus is on the defendant to prove that the person is the holder of the registration certificate.

113. Non-compliance with demand to produce firearm — Every person commits an offence who, without reasonable excuse, does not comply with a demand made to the person by an inspector under section 105.

114. Failure to deliver up revoked licence, etc. — Every person commits an offence who, being the holder of a licence, registration certificate or authorization that is revoked, does not deliver it up to a peace officer or firearms officer without delay after the revocation.

115. Punishment — Every person who commits an offence under section 112, 113 or 114 is guilty of an offence punishable on summary conviction.

116. Attorney General of Canada may act — Any proceedings in respect of an offence under this Act may be commenced at the instance of the Government of Canada and conducted by or on behalf of that government.

Regulations

117. Regulations — The Governor in Council may make regulations

(a) regulating the issuance of licences, registration certificates and authorizations, including regulations respecting the purposes for which they may be issued under any provision of this Act and prescribing the circumstances in which persons are or are not eligible to hold licences;

(b) regulating the revocation of licences, registration certificates and authorizations;

(c) prescribing the circumstances in which an individual does or does not need firearms

(i) to protect the life of that individual or of other individuals, or

(ii) for use in connection with his or her lawful profession or occupation;

(d) regulating the use of firearms in target practice or target shooting competitions;

(e) regulating

(i) the establishment and operation of shooting clubs and shooting ranges,

(ii) the activities that may be carried on at shooting clubs and shooting ranges,

(iii) the possession and use of firearms at shooting clubs and shooting ranges, and

(iv) the keeping and destruction of records in relation to shooting clubs and shooting ranges and members of those clubs and ranges;

(f) regulating the establishment and maintenance of gun collections and the acquisition and disposal or disposition of firearms that form part or are to form part of a gun collection;

(g) regulating the operation of gun shows, the activities that may be carried on at gun shows and the possession and use of firearms at gun shows;

(h) regulating the storage, handling, transportation, shipping, display, advertising and mail-order sale of firearms and restricted weapons and defining the expression "mail-order sale" for the purposes of this Act;

(i) regulating the storage, handling, transportation shipping, possession for a prescribed purpose, transfer, exportation or importation of

(i) prohibited firearms, prohibited weapons, restricted weapons, prohibited devices and prohibited ammunition, or

(ii) components or parts of prohibited firearms, prohibited weapons, restricted weapons, prohibited devices and prohibited ammunition;

(j) regulating the possession and use of restricted weapons;

(k) for authorizing

(i) the possession at any place,

(ii) the manufacture or transfer, whether or not for consideration, or offer to manufacture or transfer, whether or not for consideration, or

(iii) the importation or exportation

of firearms, prohibited weapons, restricted weapons, prohibited devices, ammunition, prohibited ammunition and components and parts designed exclusively for use in the manufacture of or assembly into automatic firearms;

(l) regulating the storage, handling, transportation, shipping, acquisition, possession, transfer, exportation, importation, use and disposal or disposition of firearms, prohibited weapons, restricted weapons, prohibited devices, prohibited ammunition and explosive substances

(i) by the following persons in the course of their duties or for the purposes of their employment, namely,

(A) peace officers,

(B) persons training to become police officers or peace officers under the control and supervision of a police force or a police academy or similar institution designated by the federal Minister or the lieutenant governor in council of a province,

(C) persons or members of a class of persons employed in the public service of Canada or by the government of a province or municipality who are prescribed by the regulations made by the Governor in Council under Part III of the *Criminal Code* to be public officers, and

(D) chief firearms officers and firearms officers, and

(ii) by individuals on behalf of, and under the authority of, a police force or a department of the Government of Canada or of a province;

(m) regulating the keeping and destruction of records in relation to firearms, prohibited weapons, restricted weapons, prohibited devices and prohibited ammunition;

(n) regulating the keeping and destruction of records by businesses in relation to ammunition;

(o) creating offences consisting of contraventions of the regulations made under paragraph (d), (e), (f), (g), (i), (j), (l), (m) or (n);

(p) prescribing the fees that are to be paid to Her Majesty in right of Canada for licences, registration certificates, authorizations, approvals of transfers and importations of firearms and confirmations by customs officers of documents under this Act;

(q) waiving or reducing the fees payable under paragraph (p) in such circumstances as may be specified in the regulations;

(r) prescribing the charges that are to be paid to Her Majesty in right of Canada in respect of costs incurred by Her Majesty in right of Canada in storing goods that are detained by customs officers or in disposing of goods;

(s) respecting the operation of the Canadian Firearms Registry;

(t) regulating the sending or issuance of notices and documents in electronic or other form, including

(i) the notices and documents that may be sent or issued in electronic or other form,

(ii) the persons or classes of persons by whom they may be sent or issued,

(iii) their signature in electronic or other form or their execution, adoption or authorization in a manner that pursuant to the regulations is to have the same effect for the purposes of this Act as their signature, and

(iv) the time and date when they are deemed to be received;

(u) respecting the manner in which any provision of this Act or the regulations applies to any of the aboriginal peoples of Canada, and adapting any such provision for the purposes of that application;

(v) repealing

(i) section 4 of the *Cartridge Magazine Control Regulations*, made by Order in Council P.C. 1992-1660 of July 16, 1992 and registered as SOR/92-460, and the heading before it,

(ii) the *Designated Areas Firearms Order*, C.R.C., chapter 430,

(iii) section 4 of the *Firearms Acquisition Certificate Regulations*, made by Order in Council P.C. 1992-1663 of July 16, 1992 and registered as SOR/92-461, and the heading before it,

(iv) section 7 of the *Genuine Gun Collector Regulations*, made by Order in Council P.C. 1992-1661 of July 16, 1992 and registered as SOR/92-435, and the heading before it,

(v) sections 8 and 13 of the *Prohibited Weapons Control Regulations*, made by Order in Council P.C. 1991-1925 of October 3, 1991 and registered as SOR/91-572, and the headings before them,

(vi) the *Restricted Weapon Registration Certificate for Classes of Persons other than Individuals Regulations*, made by Order in Council P.C. 1993-766 of April 20, 1993 and registered as SOR/93-200, and

(vii) sections 7, 15 and 17 of the *Restricted Weapons and Firearms Control Regulations*, made by Order in Council P.C. 1978-2572 of August 16, 1978 and registered as SOR/78-670, and the headings before them; and

(w) prescribing anything that by any provision of this Act is to be prescribed by regulation.

118. (1) Laying of proposed regulations — Subject to subsection (2), the federal Minister shall have each proposed regulation laid before each House of Parliament.

(2) Idem — Where a proposed regulation is laid pursuant to subsection (1), it shall be laid before each House of Parliament on the same day.

(3) Report by committee — Each proposed regulation that is laid before a House of Parliament shall, on the day it is laid, be referred by that House to an appropriate committee of that House, as determined by the rules of that House, and the committee may conduct inquiries or public hearings with respect to the proposed regulation and report its findings to that House.

(4) Making of regulations — A proposed regulation that has been laid pursuant to subsection (1) may be made

(a) on the expiration of thirty sitting days after it was laid; or

(b) where, with respect to each House of Parliament,

(i) the committee reports to the House, or

(ii) the committee decides not to conduct inquiries or public hearings.

(5) Definition of "sitting day" — For the purpose of this section, "sitting day" means a day on which either House of Parliament sits.

119. (1) Exception — No proposed regulation that has been laid pursuant to section 118 need again be laid under that section, whether or not it has been altered.

(2) Exception — minor changes — A regulation made under section 117 may be made without being laid before either House of Parliament if the federal Minister is of the opinion that the changes made by the regulation to an existing regulation are so immaterial or insubstantial that section 118 should not be applicable in the circumstances.

(3) **Exception — urgency** — A regulation made under paragraph 117(i), (l), (m), (n), (o), (q), (s) or (t) may be made without being laid before either House of Parliament if the federal Minister is of the opinion that the making of the regulation is so urgent that section 118 should not be applicable in the circumstances.

(4) **Notice of opinion** — Where the federal Minister forms the opinion described in subsection (2) or (3), he or she shall have a statement of the reasons why he or she formed that opinion laid before each House of Parliament.

(5) **Exception — prescribed dates** — A regulation may be made under paragraph 117(w) prescribing a date for the purposes of the application of any provision of this Act without being laid before either House of Parliament.

(6) **Part III of the Criminal Code** — For greater certainty, a regulation may be made under Part III of the *Criminal Code* without being laid before either House of Parliament.

Transitional Provisions

Licences

120. (1) **Firearms acquisition certificates** — A firearms acquisition certificate is deemed to be a licence if it

    (a) was issued under section 110 or 111 of the former Act;

    (b) had not been revoked before the commencement day; and

    (c) was valid pursuant to subsection 106(11) of the former Act, or pursuant to that subsection as applied by subsection 107(1) of the former Act, on the commencement day.

(2) **Authorizations** — A firearms acquisition certificate that is deemed to be a licence authorizes the holder

    (a) to acquire and possess any firearms other than prohibited firearms that are acquired by the holder on or after the commencement day and before the expiration or revocation of the firearms acquisition certificate;

    (b) in the case of an individual referred to in subsection 12(2), (3), (4), (5), (6) or (8), to acquire and possess any prohibited firearms referred to in that subsection that are acquired by the holder on or after the commencement day; and

    (c) in the case of a particular individual who is eligible under subsection 12(7) to hold a licence authorizing the particular individual to possess a handgun referred to in subsection 12(6) (pre-February 14, 1995 handguns) in the circumstances described in subsection 12(7), to acquire and possess such a handgun in those circumstances, if the particular handgun is acquired by the particular individual on or after the commencement day.

(3) **Expiration** — A firearms acquisition certificate that is deemed to be a licence expires on the earlier of

    (a) five years after the day on which it was issued, and

(b) the issuance of a licence to the holder of the firearms acquisition certificate.

(4) Lost, stolen and destroyed firearms acquisition certificates — Where a firearms acquisition certificate that is deemed to be a licence is lost, stolen or destroyed before its expiration under subsection (3), a person who has authority under this Act to issue a licence may issue a replacement firearms acquisition certificate that has the same effect as the one that was lost, stolen or destroyed.

121. (1) Minors' permits — A permit is deemed to be a licence if it

(a) was issued under subsection 110(6) or (7) of the former Act to a person who was under the age of eighteen years;

(b) had not been revoked before the commencement day; and

(c) remained in force pursuant to subsection 110(8) of the former Act on the commencement day.

(2) Authorizations — A permit that is deemed to be a licence authorizes the holder to possess firearms that are neither prohibited firearms nor restricted firearms.

(3) Geographical extent — A permit that is deemed to be a licence is valid only in the province in which it was issued, unless the permit was endorsed pursuant to subsection 110(10) of the former Act as being valid within the provinces indicated in the permit, in which case it remains valid within those provinces.

(4) Expiration — A permit that is deemed to be a licence expires on the earliest of

(a) the expiration of the period for which it was expressed to be issued,

(b) the day on which the person to whom it was issued attains the age of eighteen years, and

(c) five years after the birthday of the person next following the day on which it was issued, if that fifth anniversary occurs on or after the commencement day.

122. (1) Museum approvals — An approval of a museum, other than a museum established by the Chief of the Defence Staff, is deemed to be a licence if the approval

(a) was granted under subsection 105(1) of the former Act; and

(b) had not been revoked before the commencement day.

(2) Expiration — An approval of a museum that is deemed to be a licence expires on the earlier of

(a) the expiration of the period for which the approval was expressed to be granted, and

(b) three years after the commencement day.

123. (1) Permits to carry on business — A permit to carry on a business described in paragraph 105(1)(a) or (b) or subparagraph 105(2)(b)(i) of the former Act is deemed to be a licence if it

(a) was

(i) issued under subsection 110(5) of the former Act, or

(ii) continued under subsection 6(2) of the *Criminal Law Amendment Act, 1968–69*, chapter 38 of the Statutes of Canada, 1968–69, or subsection 48(1) of the *Criminal Law Amendment Act, 1977*, chapter 53 of the Statutes of Canada, 1976–77;

(b) had not been revoked before the commencement day;

(c) had not ceased to be in force or have any effect on October 30, 1992 under section 34 of *An Act to amend the Criminal Code and the Customs Tariff in consequence thereof*, chapter 40 of the Statutes of Canada, 1991; and

(d) remained in force pursuant to subsection 110(5) of the former Act on the commencement day.

(2) **Expiration** — A permit that is deemed to be a licence expires on the earlier of

(a) the expiration of the period for which the permit was expressed to be issued, and

(b) one year after the commencement day.

124. Geographical extent — A permit or an approval of a museum that is deemed to be a licence under section 122 or 123 is valid only for the location of the business or museum for which it was issued.

125. (1) Industrial purpose designations — A designation of a person is deemed to be a licence if it

(a) was made under subsection 90(3.1) or paragraph 95(3)(b) of the former Act; and

(b) had not been revoked before the commencement day.

(2) **Geographical extent** — A designation of a person that is deemed to be a licence is valid only in the province in which it was made.

(3) **Expiration** — A designation of a person that is deemed to be a licence expires on the earliest of

(a) the expiration of the period for which it was expressed to be made,

(b) one year after the commencement day, and

(c) in the case of a designation of a person who holds a permit that is deemed to be a licence under section 123, the expiration of the permit.

126. Pending applications — Every application that was pending on the commencement day for a document that would be a document referred to in any of sections 120 to 125 had it been issued before the commencement day shall be dealt with and disposed of under and in accordance with the former Act, except that

(a) a licence shall be issued instead of issuing a firearms acquisition certificate or a permit or making an approval or designation; and

(b) only a person who has authority under this Act to issue a licence may finally dispose of the application.

Registration Certificates

127. (1) Registration certificates — A registration certificate is deemed to be a registration certificate issued under section 60 if it

(a) was

(i) issued under subsection 109(7) of the former Act, or

(ii) continued under subsection 6(2) of the *Criminal Law Amendment Act, 1968–69*, chapter 38 of the Statutes of Canada, 1968–69, or subsection 48(2) of the *Criminal Law Amendment Act, 1977*, chapter 53 of the Statutes of Canada, 1976–77; and

(b) had not been revoked before the commencement day.

(2) **Expiration** — A registration certificate that is deemed to be a registration certificate issued under section 60 expires on the earlier of

(a) its expiration under section 66, and

(b) December 31, 2002, or such other date as is prescribed.

128. Pending applications — Every application for a registration certificate that was pending on the commencement day shall be dealt with and disposed of under and in accordance with the former Act, except that only a person who has authority under this Act to issue a registration certificate may finally dispose of the application.

Authorized Transportation of Firearms

129. (1) Permit to carry — A permit authorizing a person to possess a particular prohibited firearm or restricted firearm is deemed to be an authorization to carry or authorization to transport if it

(a) was

(i) issued under subsection 110(1) of the former Act, or

(ii) continued under subsection 6(2) of the *Criminal Law Amendment Act, 1968–69*, chapter 38 of the Statutes of Canada, 1968–69, or subsection 48(1) of the *Criminal Law Amendment Act, 1977*, chapter 53 of the Statutes of Canada, 1976–77;

(b) had not been revoked before the commencement day; and

(c) remained in force pursuant to subsection 110(1) of the former Act on the commencement day.

(2) **Geographical extent** — A permit that is deemed to be an authorization to carry or authorization to transport is valid only in the province in which the permit was issued, unless it was endorsed pursuant to subsection 110(10) of the former Act as being valid within the provinces indicated in the permit, in which case it remains valid within those provinces.

(3) **Expiration** — A permit that is deemed to be an authorization to carry or authorization to transport expires on the earlier of

(a) the expiration of the period for which it was expressed to be issued, and

(b) two years after the commencement day.

130. Temporary permit to carry — A permit authorizing a person who does not reside in Canada to possess and carry a particular prohibited firearm or restricted firearm is deemed to be an authorization to transport if it

(a) was issued under subsection 110(2.1) of the former Act;

(b) had not been revoked before the commencement day; and

(c) remained in force pursuant to that subsection on the commencement day.

131. Permit to transport or convey — A permit authorizing a person to transport or to convey to a local registrar of firearms a particular prohibited firearm or restricted firearm is deemed to be an authorization to transport if it

    (a) was

        (i) issued under subsection 110(3) or (4) of the former Act, or

        (ii) continued under subsection 6(2) of the *Criminal Law Amendment Act, 1968–69*, chapter 38 of the Statutes of Canada, 1968–69, or subsection 48(1) of the *Criminal Law Amendment Act, 1977*, chapter 53 of the Statutes of Canada, 1976–77;

    (b) had not been revoked before the commencement day; and

    (c) remained in force pursuant to subsection 110(3) or (4) of the former Act on the commencement day.

132. Expiration — A permit that is deemed to be an authorization to transport under section 130 or 131 expires on the expiration of the period for which the permit was expressed to be issued.

133. Pending applications — Every application that was pending on the commencement day for a document that would be a document referred to in any of sections 129 to 131 had it been issued before the commencement day shall be dealt with and disposed of under and in accordance with the former Act, except that

    (a) an authorization to carry or authorization to transport shall be issued or a condition shall be attached to a licence instead of issuing a permit; and

    (b) only a person who has authority under this Act to issue an authorization to carry or authorization to transport may finally dispose of the application.

134. (1) Shooting club approvals — An approval of a shooting club is deemed to be an approval granted under this Act if the approval

    (a) was granted under subparagraph 109(3)(c)(iii) or paragraph 110(2)(c) of the former Act; and

    (b) had not been revoked before the commencement day.

(2) Expiration — An approval of a shooting club that is deemed to be an approval granted under this Act expires on the earlier of

    (a) the expiration of the period for which it was expressed to be granted, and

    (b) one year after the commencement day.

135. Temporary storage permit — Every permit authorizing a person to temporarily store a particular prohibited firearm or restricted firearm

    (a) that was issued under subsection 110(3.1) of the former Act,

    (b) that had not been revoked before the commencement day, and

    (c) that remained in force pursuant to subsection 110(3.3) of the former Act on the commencement day

continues in force until the expiration of the period for which it was expressd to be issued, unless the permit is revoked by a chief firearms officer for any good and sufficient reason.

Conditional Amendments to this Act

136. Conditional amendment re Bill C-7 — If Bill C-7, introduced during the first session of the thirty-fifth Parliament and entitled *An Act respecting the control of certain drugs, their precursors and other substances and to amend certain other Acts and repeal the Narcotic Control Act in consequence thereof*, is assented to, then, on the later of the day on which sections 6 and 7 of that Act come into force and the day on which this Act is assented to, subparagraph 5(2)(a)(iv) of this Act is replaced by the following:

(iv) an offence relating to a contravention of subsection 6(1) or (2) or 7(1) or (2) of the *Controlled Drugs and Substances Act*;

137. Conditional amendments re Bill C-41 — If Bill C-41, introduced in the first session of the thirty-fifth Parliament and entitled *An Act to amend the Criminal Code (sentencing) and other Acts is consequence thereof*, is assented to, then, on the later of the day on which section 730 of the *Criminal Code*, as enacted by section 6 of that Act, comes into force and the day on which this Act is assented to, the following provisions of this Act are amended by replacing the expression "section 736 of the *Criminal Code*" with the expression "section 730 of the *Criminal Code*":

(a) paragraph 5(2)(a); and

(b) paragraphs 70(1)(a) and (b).

Editor's Note

[NOTE: ss. 138-192 deal with consequential amendments to other related acts. Amendments are included in the affected acts.]

193. Coming into force — Subject to subsection (2), this Act or any of its provisions or any provision of any other Act enacted or amended by this Act, other than sections 136, 137 and 174, shall come into force on a day or days to be fixed by order of the Governor in Council.

194. Coming into force if no order made — If no order bringing this Act or any of its provisions or any provision of any other Act enacted or amended by this Act is made before January 1, 2003, this Act, other than sections 136, 137 and 174, comes into force on that date.

INTERPRETATION ACT

An Act respecting the interpretation of statutes and regulations

R.S.C. 1985, c. I-21, as am. R.S.C. 1985, c. 11 (1st Supp.), s. 2; R.S.C. 1985, c. 27 (1st Supp.), s. 203; R.S.C. 1985, c. 27 (2nd Supp.), s. 10; 1990, c. 17, s. 26; 1992, c. 1, ss. 87–91; 1992, c. 47, s. 79; 1992, c. 51, s. 56; 1993, c. 28, s. 78 (Sched. III, item 82) [Amended 1998, c. 15, s. 28; 1999, c. 3, (Sched., item 18).]; 1993, c. 34, s. 88; 1993, c. 38, s. 87; 1995, c. 39, s. 174; 1996, c. 31, ss. 86–87; 1997, c. 39, s. 4; 1998, c. 30, s. 15(i); 1999, c. 3, s. 71.

Short Title

1. Short title — This Act may be cited as the *Interpretation Act*.

R.S., c. I-23, s. 1.

Interpretation

2. (1) Definitions — In this Act,

"Act"means an Act of Parliament;

"enact" includes to issue, make or establish;

"enactment" means an Act or regulation or any portion of an Act or regulation;

"public officer" includes any person in the public service of Canada who is authorized by or under an enactment to do or enforce the doing of an act or thing or to exercise a power, or on whom a duty is imposed by or under an enactment;

"regulation" includes an order, regulation, rule, rule of court, form, tariff of costs or fees, letters patent, commission, warrant, proclamation, by-law, resolution or other instrument issued, made or established

    (a) in the execution of a power conferred by or under the authority of an Act, or

    (b) by or under the authority of the Governor in Council;

"repeal" includes revoke or cancel.

(2) Expired and replaced enactment — For the purposes of this Act, an enactment that has been replaced, has expired, lapsed or has otherwise ceased to have effect is deemed to have been repealed.

R.S., c. I-23, s. 2;1993, c. 34, s. 88.

Application

3. (1) Application — Every provision of this Act applies, unless a contrary intention appears, to every enactment, whether enacted before or after the commencement of this Act.

(2) **Application to this Act** — The provisions of this Act apply to the interpretation of this Act.

(3) **Rules of construction not excluded** — Nothing in this Act excludes the application to an enactment of a rule of construction applicable to that enactment and not inconsistent with this Act.

R.S., c. I-23, s. 3.

Enacting Clause of Acts

4. (1) **Enacting clause** — The enacting clause of an Act may be in the following form:

"Her Majesty, by and with the advice and consent of the Senate and House of Commons of Canada, enacts as follows:".

(2) **Order of clauses** — The enacting clause of an Act shall follow the preamble, if any, and the various provisions within the purview or body of the Act shall follow in a concise and enunciative form.

R.S., c. I-23, s. 4.

Operation

Royal Assent

5. (1) **Royal Assent** — The Clerk of the Parliaments shall endorse on every Act, immediately after its title, the day, month and year when the Act was assented to in Her Majesty's name and the endorsement shall be a part of the Act.

(2) **Date of commencement** — If no date of commencement is provided for in an Act, the date of commencement of that Act is the date of assent to the Act.

(3) **Commencement provision** — Where an Act contains a provision that the Act or any portion thereof is to come into force on a day later than the date of assent to the Act, that provision is deemed to have come into force on the date of assent to the Act.

(4) **Commencement when no date fixed** — Where an Act provides that certain provisions thereof are to come or are deemed to have come into force on a day other than the date of assent to the Act, the remaining provisions of the Act are deemed to have come into force on the date of assent to the Act.

R.S., c. I-23, s. 5.

Day Fixed for Commencement or Repeal

6. (1) **Operation when date fixed for commencement or repeal** — Where an enactment is expressed to come into force on a particular day, it shall be construed as coming into force on the expiration of the previous day, and where an enactment is expressed to expire, lapse or otherwise cease to have effect on a particular day, it shall be construed as ceasing to have effect upon the commencement of the following day.

(2) When no date fixed — Every enactment that is not expressed to come into force on a particular day shall be construed as coming into force

    (a) in the case of an Act, on the expiration of the day immediately before the day the Act was assented to in Her Majesty's name; and

    (b) in the case of a regulation, on the expiration of the day immediately before the day the regulation was registered pursuant to section 6 of the *Statutory Instruments Act* or, if the regulation is of a class that is exempted from the application of subsection 5(1) of that Act, on the expiration of the day immediately before the day the regulation was made.

(3) Judicial notice — Judicial notice shall be taken of a day for the coming into force of an enactment that is fixed by a regulation that has been published in the *Canada Gazette*.

R.S., c. I-23, s. 6; c. 29 (2d Supp.), s. 1;1992, c. 1, s. 87.

Regulation Prior to Commencement

7. Preliminary proceedings — Where an enactment is not in force and it contains provisions conferring power to make regulations or do any other thing, that power may, for the purpose of making the enactment effective on its commencement, be exercised at any time before its commencement, but a regulation so made or a thing so done has no effect until the commencement of the enactment except in so far as may be necessary to make the enactment effective on its commencement.

R.S., c. I-23, s. 7.

Territorial Operation

8. (1) Territorial operation — Every enactment applies to the whole of Canada, unless a contrary intention is expressed in the enactment.

(2) Amending enactment — Where an enactment that does not apply to the whole of Canada is amended, no provision in the amending enactment applies to any part of Canada to which the amended enactment does not apply, unless it is provided in the amending enactment that it applies to that part of Canada or to the whole of Canada.

(2.1) Exclusive economic zone of Canada — Every enactment that applies in respect of exploring or exploiting, conserving or managing natural resources, whether living or non-living, applies, in addition to its application to Canada, to the exclusive economic zone of Canada, unless a contrary intention is expressed in the enactment.

(2.2) Continental shelf of Canada — Every enactment that applies in respect of exploring or exploiting natural resources that are

    (a) mineral or other non-living resources of the seabed or subsoil, or

    (b) living organisms belonging to sedentary species, that is to say, organisms that, at the harvestable stage, either are immobile on or under the seabed or are unable to move except in constant physical contact with the seabed or subsoil

applies, in addition to its application to Canada, to the continental shelf of Canada, unless a contrary intention is expressed in the enactment.

(3) Extra-territorial operation — Every Act now in force enacted prior to December 11, 1931 that expressly or by necessary or reasonable implication was intended, as to the whole or any part thereof, to have extra-territorial operation shall be construed as if, at the date of its enactment the Parliament of Canada had full power to make laws having extra-territorial operation as provided by the *Statute of Westminster, 1931.*

R.S., c. I-23, s. 8.1996, c. 31, s. 86

Rules of Construction

Private Acts

9. Provisions in private Acts — No provision in a private Act affects the rights of any person, except only as therein mentioned or referred to.

R.S., c. I-23, s. 9.

Law Always Speaking

10. Law always speaking — The law shall be considered as always speaking, and where a matter or thing is expressed in the present tense, it shall be applied to the circumstances as they arise, so that effect may be given to the enactment according to its true spirit, intent and meaning.

R.S., c. I-23, s. 10.

Imperative and Permissive Construction

11. "Shall" and "may" — The expression "shall" is to be construed as imperative and the expression "may" as permissive.

R.S., c. I-23, s. 28.

Enactments Remedial

12. Enactments deemed remedial — Every enactment shall be deemed remedial, and shall be given such fair, large and liberal construction and interpretation as best ensures the attainment of its objects.

R.S., c. I-23, s. 11.

Preambles and Marginal Notes

13. Preamble — The preamble of an enactment shall be read as a part of the enactment intended to assist in explaining its purport and object.

R.S., c. I-23, s. 12.

14. Marginal notes and historical references — Marginal notes and references to former enactments that appear after the end of a section or other division in an enactment form no part of the enactment, but are inserted for convenience of reference only.

R.S., c. I-23, s. 13.

Application of Interpretation Provisions

15. (1) Application of definitions and interpretation rules — Definitions or rules of interpretation in an enactment apply to all of the provisions of the enactment, including the provisions that contain those definitions or rules of interpretation.

(2) **Interpretation sections subject to exceptions** — Where an enactment contains an interpretation section or provision, it shall be read and construed

(a) as being applicable only if a contrary intention does not appear, and

(b) as being applicable to all other enactments relating to the same subject-matter unless a contrary intention appears.

R.S., c. I-23, s. 14.

16. **Words in regulations** — Where an enactment confers power to make regulations, expressions used in the regulations have the same respective meanings as in the enactment conferring the power.

R.S., c. I-23, s. 15.

Her Majesty

17. **Her Majesty not bound or affected unless stated** — No enactment is binding on Her Majesty or affects Her Majesty or Her Majesty's rights or prerogatives in any manner, except only as therein mentioned or referred to in the enactment.

Proclamations

18. (1) **Proclamation** — Where an enactment authorizes the issue of a proclamation, the proclamation shall be understood to be a proclamation of the Governor in Council.

(2) **Proclamation to be issued on advice** — Where the Governor General is authorized to issue a proclamation, the proclamation shall be understood to be a proclamation issued under an order of the Governor in Council, but it is not necessary to mention in the proclamation that it is issued under such an order.

(3) **Effective day of proclamations** — A proclamation that is issued under an order of the Governor in Council may purport to have been issued on the day of the order or on any subsequent day and, if so, takes effect on that day.

R.S., c. I-23, s. 17;1992, c. 1, s. 88.

Oaths

19. (1) **Administration of oaths** — Where by an enactment or by a rule of the Senate or House of Commons, evidence under oath is authorized or required to be taken, or an oath is authorized or directed to be made, taken or administered, the oath may be administered, and a certificate of its having been made, taken or administered may be given by

(a) any person authorized by the enactment or rule to take the evidence; or

(b) a judge of any court, a notary public, a justice of the peace, or a commissioner for taking affidavits, having authority or jurisdiction within the place where the oath is administered.

(2) **Where justice of peace empowered** — Where power is conferred upon a justice of the peace to administer an oath or solemn affirmation or to take an affidavit or declaration, the power may be exercised by a notary public or a commissioner for taking oaths.

R.S., c. I-23, s. 18.

Reports to Parliament

20. Reports to Parliament — Where an Act requires a report or other document to be laid before Parliament and, in compliance with the Act, a particular report or document has been laid before Parliament at a session thereof, nothing in the Act shall be construed as requiring the same report or document to be laid before Parliament at any subsequent session.

R.S., c. I-23, s. 19.

Corporations

21. (1) Powers vested in corporations — Words establishing a corporation shall be construed

    (a) as vesting in the corporation power to sue and be sued, to contract and be contracted with by its corporate name, to have a common seal and to alter or change it at pleasure, to have perpetual succession, to acquire and hold personal property for the purposes for which the corporation is established and to alienate that property at pleasure;

    (b) in the case of a corporation having a name consisting of an English and a French form or a combined English and French form, as vesting in the corporation power to use either the English or the French form of its name or both forms and to show on its seal both the English and French forms of its name or have two seals, one showing the English and the other showing the French form of its name;

    (c) as vesting in a majority of the members of the corporation the power to bind the others by their acts; and

    (d) as exempting from personal liability for its debts, obligations or acts such individual members of the corporation who do not contravene the provisions of the enactment establishing the corporation.

(2) Corporate name — Where an enactment establishes a corporation and in each of the English and French versions of the enactment the name of the corporation is in the form only of the language of that version, the name of the corporation shall consist of the form of its name in each of the versions of the enactment.

(3) Banking business — No corporation is deemed to be authorized to carry on the business of banking unless that power is expressly conferred on it by the enactment establishing the corporation.

R.S., c. I-23, s. 20.

Majority and Quorum

22. (1) Majorities — Where an enactment requires or authorizes more than two persons to do an act or thing, a majority of them may do it.

(2) Quorum of board, court, commission, etc — Where an enactment establishes a board, court, commission or other body consisting of three or more members, in this section called an "association",

    (a) at a meeting of the association, a number of members of the association equal to,

        (i) if the number of members provided for by the enactment is a fixed number, at least one-half of the number of members, and

(ii) if the number of members provided for by the enactment is not a fixed number but is within a range having a maximum or minimum, at least one-half of the number of members in office if that number is within the range,

constitutes a quorum;

(b) an act or thing done by a majority of the members of the association present at a meeting, if the members present constitute a quorum, is deemed to have been done by the association; and

(c) a vacancy in the membership of the association does not invalidate the constitution of the association or impair the right of the members in office to act, if the number of members in office is not less than a quorum.

R.S., c. I-23, s. 21.

Appointment, Retirement and Powers of Officers

23. (1) Public officers hold office during pleasure — Every public officer appointed by or under the authority of an enactment or otherwise is deemed to have been appointed to hold office during pleasure only, unless it is otherwise expressed in the enactment, commission or instrument of appointment.

(2) Effective day of appointments — Where an appointment is made by instrument under the Great Seal, the instrument may purport to have been issued on or after the day its issue was authorized, and the day on which it so purports to have been issued is deemed to be the day on which the appointment takes effect.

(3) Appointment or engagement otherwise than under Great Seal — Where there is authority in an enactment to appoint a person to a position or to engage the services of a person, otherwise than by instrument under the Great Seal, the instrument of appointment or engagement may be expressed to be effective on or after the day on which that person commenced the performance of the duties of the position or commenced the performance of the services, and the day on which it is so expressed to be effective, unless that day is more than sixty days before the day on which the instrument is issued, is deemed to be the day on which the appointment or engagement takes effect.

(4) Remuneration — Where a person is appointed to an office, the appointing authority may fix, vary or terminate that person's remuneration.

(5) Commencement of appointments or retirements — Where a person is appointed to an office effective on a specified day, or where the appointment of a person is terminated effective on a specified day, the appointment or termination is deemed to have been effected immediately on the expiration of the previous day.

R.S., c. I-23, s. 22.

24. (1) Implied powers respecting public officers — Words authorizing the appointment of a public officer to hold office during pleasure include, in the discretion of the authority in whom the power of appointment is vested, the power to

(a) terminate the appointment or remove or suspend the public officer;

(b) re-appoint or reinstate the public officer; and

(c) appoint another person in the stead of, or to act in the stead of, the public officer.

(2) Powers of acting Minister, successor or deputy — Words directing or empowering a minister of the Crown to do an act or thing, regardless of whether the act or thing is administrative, legislative or judicial, or otherwise applying to that minister as the holder of the office, include

(a) a minister acting for that minister or, if the office is vacant, a minister designated to act in the office by or under the authority of an order in council;

(b) the successors of that minister in the office;

(c) his or their deputy;

(d) notwithstanding paragraph (c), a person appointed to serve, in the department or ministry of state over which the minister presides, in a capacity appropriate to the doing of the act or thing, or to the words so applying.

(3) Restriction as to public servants — Nothing in paragraph (2)(c) or (d) shall be construed as authorizing the exercise of any authority conferred on a minister to make a regulation as defined in the *Statutory Instruments Act*.

(4) Successors to and deputy of public officer — Words directing or empowering any other public officer, other than a minister of the Crown, to do any act or thing, or otherwise applying to the public officer by his name of office, include his successors in the office and his or their deputy.

(5) Powers of holder of public office — Where a power is conferred or a duty imposed on the holder of an office, the power may be exercised and the duty shall be performed by the person for the time being charged with the execution of the powers and duties of the office.

R.S., c. I-23, s. 23; c. 29 (2d Supp.), s. 1;1992, c. 1, ss. 89(1), (3), (4).

Evidence

25. (1) Documentary evidence — Where an enactment provides that a document is evidence of a fact without anything in the context to indicate that the document is conclusive evidence, then, in any judicial proceedings, the document is admissible in evidence and the fact is deemed to be established in the absence of any evidence to the contrary.

(2) Queen's Printer — Every copy of an enactment having printed thereon what purports to be the name or title of the Queen's Printer and Controller of Stationery or the Queen's Printer is deemed to be a copy purporting to be printed by the Queen's Printer for Canada.

R.S., c. I-23, s. 24.

Computation of Time

26. (1) Time limits and holidays — Where the time limited for the doing of a thing expires or falls on a holiday, the thing may be done on the day next following that is not a holiday.

R.S., c. I-23, s. 25.

27. (1) Clear days — Where there is a reference to a number of clear days or "at least" a number of days between two events, in calculating that number of days the days on which the events happen are excluded.

(2) **Not clear days** — Where there is a reference to a number of days, not expressed to be clear days, between two events, in calculating that number of days the day on which the first event happens is excluded and the day on which the second event happens is included.

(3) **Beginning and ending of prescribed periods** — Where a time is expressed to begin or end at, on or with a specified day, or to continue to or until a specified day, the time includes that day.

(4) **After specified day** — Where a time is expressed to begin after or to be from a specified day, the time does not include that day.

(5) **Within a time** — Where anything is to be done within a time after, from, of or before a specified day, the time does not include that day.

R.S., c. I-23, s. 25.

28. Calculation of a period of months after or before a specified day — Where there is a reference to a period of time consisting of a number of months after or before a specified day, the period is calculated by

   (a) counting forward or backward from the specified day the number of months, without including the month in which that day falls;

   (b) excluding the specified day; and

   (c) including in the last month counted under paragraph (a) the day that has the same calendar number as the specified day or, if that month has no day with that number, the last day of that month.

R.S., c. I-23, s. 25.

29. Time of the day — Where there is a reference to time expressed as a specified time of the day, the time is taken to mean standard time.

R.S., c. I-23, s. 2.

30. Time when specified age attained — A person is deemed not to have attained a specified number of years of age until the commencement of the anniversary, of the same number, of the day of that person's birth.

R.S., c. I-23, s. 25.

Miscellaneous Rules

31. (1) Reference to provincial court judge, etc — Where anything is required or authorized to be done by or before a judge, provincial court judge, justice of the peace or any functionary or officer, it shall be done by or before one whose jurisdiction or powers extend to the place where the thing is to be done.

(2) **Ancillary powers** — Where power is given to a person, officer or functionary to do or enforce the doing of any act or thing, all such powers as are necessary to enable the person, officer or functionary to do or enforce the doing of the act or thing are deemed to be also given.

(3) **Powers to be exercised as required** — Where a power is conferred or a duty imposed, the power may be exercised and the duty shall be performed from time to time as occasion requires.

(4) Power to repeal — Where a power is conferred to make regulations, the power shall be construed as including a power, exercisable in the same manner, and subject to the same consent and conditions, if any, to repeal, amend or vary the regulations and make others.

R.S., c. I-23, s. 26.

32. Forms — Where a form is prescribed, deviations from that form, not affecting the substance or calculated to mislead, do not invalidate the form used.

R.S., c. I-23, s. 26.

33. (1) Gender — Words importing female persons include male persons and corporations and words importing male persons include female persons and corporations.

(2) Number — Words in the singular include the plural, and words in the plural include the singular.

(3) Parts of speech and grammatical forms — Where a word is defined, other parts of speech and grammatical forms of the same word have corresponding meanings.

R.S., c. I-23, s. 26;1992, c. 1, s. 90.

Offences

34. (1) Indictable and summary conviction offences — Where an enactment creates an offence,

    (a) the offence is deemed to be an indictable offence if the enactment provides that the offender may be prosecuted for the offence by indictment;

    (b) the offence is deemed to be one for which the offender is punishable on summary conviction if there is nothing in the context to indicate that the offence is an indictable offence; and

    (c) if the offence is one for which the offender may be prosecuted by indictment or for which he is punishable on summary conviction, no person shall be considered to have been convicted of an indictable offence by reason only of having been convicted of the offence on summary conviction.

(2) Criminal Code to apply — All the provisions of the *Criminal Code* relating to indictable offences apply to indictable offences created by an enactment, and all the provisions of that Code relating to summary conviction offences apply to all other offences created by an enactment, except to the extent that the enactment otherwise provides.

(3) Documents similarly construed — In a commission, proclamation, warrant or other document relating to criminal law or procedure in criminal matters,

    (a) a reference to an offence for which the offender may be prosecuted by indictment shall be construed as a reference to an indictable offence; and

    (b) a reference to any other offence shall be construed as a reference to an offence for which the offender is punishable on summary conviction.

R.S., c. I-23, s. 27.

Powers to Enter Dwelling-houses to Carry out Arrests

34.1 Authorization to enter dwelling-house — Any person who may issue a warrant to arrest or apprehend a person under any Act of Parliament, other than the *Criminal Code*, has the same powers, subject to the same terms and conditions, as a judge or justice has under the *Criminal Code*

(a) to authorize the entry into a dwelling-house described in the warrant for the purpose of arresting or apprehending the person, if the person issuing the warrant is satisified by information on oath that there are reasonable grounds to believe that the person is or will be present in the dwelling-house; and

(b) to authorize the entry into the dwelling-house without prior announcement if the requirement of subsection 529.4(1) is met.

1997, c. 39, s. 4.

Definitions

35. (1) General definitions — In every enactment,

"Act", as meaning an Act of a legislature, includes an ordinance of the Yukon Territory or of the Northwest Territories and a law of the Legislature for Nunavut;

"bank" means a bank to which the *Bank Act* applies;

"British Commonwealth" or "British Commonwealth of Nations" has the same meaning as "Commonwealth";

"Canada", for greater certainty, includes the internal waters of Canada and the territorial sea of Canada;

"Canadian waters" includes the territorial sea of Canada and the internal waters of Canada;

"broadcasting" means any radiocommunication in which the transmissions are intended for direct reception by the general public;

"Clerk of the Privy Council" or "Clerk of the Queen's Privy Council" means the Clerk of the Privy Council and Secretary to the Cabinet;

"commencement", when used with reference to an enactment, means the time at which the enactment comes into force;

"Commonwealth" or "Commonwealth of Nations" means the association of countries named in the schedule;

"Commonwealth and dependent Territories" means the several Commonwealth countries and their colonies, possessions, dependencies, protectorates, protected states, condominiums and trust territories;

"contiguous zone",

(a) in relation to Canada, means the contiguous zone of Canada as determined under the *Oceans Act*, and

(b) in relation to any other state, means the contiguous zone of the other state as determined in accordance with international law and the domestic laws of that other state;

"continental shelf",

> (a) in relation to Canada, means the continental shelf of Canada as determined under the *Oceans Act*, and

> (b) in relation to any other state, means the continental shelf of the other state as determined in accordance with international law and the domestic laws of that other state;

"contravene" includes fail to comply with;

"corporation" does not include a partnership that is considered to be a separate legal entity under provincial law;

"county" includes two or more counties united for purposes to which the enactment relates;

"diplomatic or consular officer" includes an ambassador, envoy, minister, chargé d'affaires, counsellor, secretary, attaché, consul-general, consul, vice-consul, pro-consul, consular agent, acting consul-general, acting consul, acting vice-consul, acting consular agent, high commissioner, permanent delegate, adviser, acting high commissioner, and acting permanent delegate;

"exclusive economic zone",

> (a) in relation to Canada, means the exclusive economic zone of Canada as determined under the *Oceans Act* and includes the seabed and subsoil below that zone, and

> (b) in relation to any other state, means the exclusive economic zone of the other state as determined in accordance with international law and the domestic laws of that other state;

"Federal Court" means the Federal Court of Canada;

"Federal Court — Appeal Division" or "Federal Court of Appeal" means that division of the Federal Court of Canada called the Federal Court — Appeal Division or referred to as the Court of Appeal or Federal Court of Appeal by the *Federal Court Act*;

"Federal Court — Trial Division" means that division of the Federal Court of Canada so named by the *Federal Court Act*;

"Governor", "Governor General", or "Governor of Canada" means the Governor General of Canada, or other chief executive officer or administrator carrying on the Government of Canada on behalf and in the name of the Sovereign, by whatever title that officer is designated;

"Governor General in Council", or "Governor in Council" means the Governor General of Canada acting by and with the advice of, or by and with the advice and consent of, or in conjunction with the Queen's Privy Council for Canada;

"Great Seal" means the Great Seal of Canada;

"Her Majesty", "His Majesty", "The Queen", "The King", or "The Crown" means the Sovereign of the United Kingdom, Canada and Her other Realms and Territories, and Head of the Commonwealth;

"Her Majesty's Realm and Territories" means all realms and territories under the sovereignty of Her Majesty;

"herein" used in any section shall be understood to relate to the whole enactment, and not to that section only;

"holiday" means any of the following days, namely, Sunday; New Year's Day; Good Friday; Easter Monday; Christmas Day; the birthday or the day fixed by proclamation for the celebration of the birthday of the reigning Sovereign; Victoria Day; Canada Day; the first Monday in September, designated Labour Day; Remembrance Day; any day appointed by proclamation to be observed as a day of general prayer or mourning or day of public rejoicing or thanksgiving; and any of the following additional days, namely:

(a) in any province, any day appointed by proclamation of the lieutenant governor of the province to be observed as a public holiday or as a day of general prayer or mourning or day of public rejoicing or thanksgiving within the province, and any day that is a non-juridical day by virtue of an Act of the legislature of the province, and

(b) in any city, town, municipality or other organized district, any day appointed to be observed as a civic holiday by resolution of the council or other authority charged with the administration of the civic or municipal affairs of the city, town, municipality or district;

"internal waters",

(a) in relation to Canada, means the internal waters of Canada as determined under the *Oceans Act* and includes the airspace above and the bed and subsoil below those waters, and

(b) in relation to any other state, means the waters on the landward aside of the baselines of the territorial sea of the other state;

"legislative assembly", "legislative council" or "legislature", includes the Lieutenant Governor in Council and the Legislative Assembly of the Northwest Territories, as constituted before September 1, 1905, the Commissioner in Council of the Yukon Territory, the Commissioner in Council of the Northwest Territories, and the Legislature for Nunavut;

"lieutenant governor" means the lieutenant governor or other chief executive officer or administrator carrying on the government of the province indicated by the enactment, by whatever title that officer is designated, and, in relation to the Yukon Territory or the Northwest Territories or Nunavut, means the Commissioner thereof;

"lieutenant governor in council" means the lieutenant governor acting by and with the advice of, or by and with the advice and consent of, or in conjunction with the executive council of the province indicated by the enactment and, in relation to the Yukon Territory, the Northwest Territories or Nunavut, means the Commissioner thereof;

"local time", in relation to any place, means the time observed in that place for the regulation of business hours;

"military" shall be construed as relating to all or any part of the Canadian Forces;

"month" means a calendar month;

"oath" includes a solemn affirmation or declaration when the context applies to any person by whom and to any case in which a solemn affirmation or declaration may be made instead of an oath, and in the same cases the expression "sworn" includes the expression "affirmed" or "declared";

"**Parliament**" means the Parliament of Canada;

"**person**" or any word or expression descriptive of a person, includes a corporation;

"**proclamation**" means a proclamation under the Great Seal;

"**province**" means a province of Canada, and includes the Yukon Territory, the Northwest Territories and Nunavut;

"**radio**" or "**radiocommunication**" means any transmission, emission or reception of signs, signals, writing, images, sounds or intelligence of any nature by means of electromagnetic waves of frequencies lower than 3,000 GHz propagated in space without artificial guide;

"**regular force**" means the component of the Canadian Forces that is referred to in the *National Defence Act* as the regular force;

"**reserve force**" means the component of the Canadian Forces that is referred to in the *National Defence Act* as the reserve force;

"**security**" means sufficient security, and "**sureties**" means sufficient sureties, and when those words are used one person is sufficient therefor, unless otherwise expressly required;

"**standard time**", except as otherwise provided by any proclamation of the Governor in Council that may be issued for the purposes of this definition in relation to any province or territory or any part thereof, means

 (a) in relation to the Province of Newfoundland, Newfoundland standard time, being three hours and thirty minutes behind Greenwich time,

 (b) in relation to the Provinces of Nova Scotia, New Brunswick and Prince Edward Island, that part of the Province of Quebec lying east of the sixty-third meridian of west longitude, and that part of Nunavut lying east of the sixty-eighth meridian of west longitude, Atlantic standard time, being four hours behind Greenwich time,

 (c) in relation to that part of the Province of Quebec lying west of the sixty-third meridian of west longitude, that part of the Province of Ontario lying between the sixty-eighth and the ninetieth meridians of west longitude, Southampton Island and the islands adjacent to Southampton Island, and that part of Nunavut lying between the sixty-eighth and the eighty-fifth meridians of west longitude, eastern standard time, being five hours behind Greenwich time,

 (d) in relation to that part of the Province of Ontario lying west of the ninetieth meridian of west longitude, the Province of Manitoba, and that part of Nunavut, except Southampton Island and the islands adjacent to Southampton Island, lying between the eighty-fifth and the one hundred and second meridians of west longitude, central standard time, being six hours behind Greenwich time,

 (e) in relation to the Provinces of Saskatchewan and Alberta, the Northwest Territories and that part of Nunavut lying west of the one hundred and second meridian of west longitude, mountain standard time, being seven hours behind Greenwich time,

 (f) in relation to the Province of British Columbia, Pacific standard time, being eight hours behind Greenwich time, and

 (g) in relation to the Yukon Territory, Yukon standard time, being nine hours behind Greenwich time;

"statutory declaration" means a solemn declaration made pursuant to section 41 of the *Canada Evidence Act*;

"superior court" means

(a) in the Province of Prince Edward Island or Newfoundland, the Supreme Court,

(a.1) in the Province of Ontario, the Court of Appeal for Ontario and the Superior Court of Justice

(b) in the Province of Quebec, the Court of Appeal, and the Superior Court in and for the Province,

(c) in the Province of New Brunswick, Manitoba, Saskatchewan or Alberta, the Court of Appeal for the Province and the Court of Queen's Bench for the Province,

(d) in the Provinces of Nova Scotia and British Columbia, the Court of Appeal and the Supreme Court of the Province, and

(e) in the Yukon Territory or the Northwest Territories, the Supreme Court of the territory, and in Nunavut, the Nunavut Court of Justice;

"telecommunication" means the emission, transmission or reception of signs, signals, writing, images, sounds or intelligence of any nature by any wire, cable, radio, optical or other electromagnetic system, or by any similar technical system;

"territorial sea",

(a) in relation to Canada, means the territorial sea of Canada as determined under the *Oceans Act* and includes the airspace above and the seabed and subsoil below that sea, and

(b) in relation to any other state, means the territorial sea of the other state as determined in accordance with international law and the domestic laws of that other state;

"territory" means the Yukon Territory, the Northwest Territories and, after section 3 of the *Nunavut Act* comes into force, Nunavut.

"two justices" means two or more justices of the peace, assembled or acting together;

"United Kingdom" means the United Kingdom of Great Britain and Northern Ireland;

"United States" means the United States of America;

"writing", or any term of like import, includes words printed, typewritten, painted, engraved, lithographed, photographed, or represented or reproduced by any mode of representing or reproducing words in visible form.

(2) **Governor in Council may amend schedule** — The Governor in Council may, by order, amend the schedule by adding thereto the name of any country recognized by the order to be a member of the Commonwealth or deleting therefrom the name of any country recognized by the order to be no longer a member of the Commonwealth.

R.S., c. I-23, s. 28; c. 10 (2nd Supp.), s. 65; 1972, c. 17, s. 2; 1974–75–76, c. 16, s. 4; c. 19, s. 2; 1978–79, c. 11, s. 10; 1990, c. 17, s. 26; 1992, c. 1, s. 91; 1992, c. 47, s. 79; 1992, c. 51, s. 56; 1993, c. 28, s. 78 (Sched. III, item 82) [Amended by 1998, c. 15, s. 28; 1999, c. 3, (Sched., item 18).]; 1993, c. 38, s. 87; 1995, c. 39, s. 174; 1996, c. 31, s. 87; 1998, c. 30, s. 15(i); 1999, c. 3, s. 71.

36. Construction of "telegraph" — The expression "telegraph" and its derivatives, in an enactment or in an Act of the legislature of any province enacted before that province became part of Canada on any subject that is within the legislative powers of Parliament, are deemed not to include the word "telephone" or its derivatives.

R.S., c. I-23, s. 29.

37. (1) Construction of "year" — The expression "year" means any period of twelve consecutive months, except that a reference

(a) to a "calendar year" means a period of twelve consecutive months commencing on January 1;

(b) to a "financial year" or "fiscal year" means, in relation to money provided by Parliament, or the Consolidated Revenue Fund, or the accounts, taxes or finances of Canada, the period beginning on April 1 in one calendar year and ending on March 31 in the next calendar year; and

(c) by number to a Dominical year means the period of twelve consecutive months commencing on January 1 of that Dominical year.

(2) Governor in Council may define year — Where in an enactment relating to the affairs of Parliament or the Government of Canada there is a reference to a period of a year without anything in the context to indicate beyond doubt whether a financial or fiscal year, any period of twelve consecutive months or a period of twelve consecutive months commencing on January 1 is intended, the Governor in Council may prescribe which of those periods of twelve consecutive months shall constitute a year for the purposes of the enactment.

R.S., c. I-23, s. 31.

38. Common names — The name commonly applied to any country, place, body, corporation, society, officer, functionary, person, party or thing means the country, place, body, corporation, society, officer, functionary, person, party or thing to which the name is commonly applied, although the name is not the formal or extended designation thereof.

R.S., c. I-23, s. 30.

39. (1) Affirmative and negative resolutions — In every Act,

(a) the expression "subject to affirmative resolution of Parliament", when used in relation to any regulation, means that the regulation shall be laid before Parliament within fifteen days after it is made or, if Parliament is not then sitting, on any of the first fifteen days next thereafter that Parliament is sitting and shall not come into force unless and until it is affirmed by a resolution of both Houses of Parliament introduced and passed in accordance with the rules of those Houses;

(b) the expression "subject to affirmative resolution of the House of Commons", when used in relation to any regulation, means that the regulation shall be laid before the House of Commons within fifteen days after it is made or, if the House is not then sitting, on any of the first fifteen days next thereafter that the House is sitting and shall not come into force unless and until it is affirmed by a resolution of the House of Commons introduced and passed in accordance with the rules of that House;

(c) the expression "subject to negative resolution of Parliament", when used in relation to any regulation, means that the regulation shall be laid before Parliament within fifteen days after it is made or, if Parliament is not then sitting, on any of the first fifteen days next thereafter that Parliament is sitting and may be annulled by a resolution of both Houses of Parliament introduced and passed in accordance with the rules of those Houses; and

(d) the expression "subject to negative resolution of the House of Commons", when used in relation to any regulation, means that the regulation shall be laid before the House of Commons within fifteen days after it is made or, if the House is not then sitting, on any of the first fifteen days next thereafter that the House is sitting and may be annulled by a resolution of the House of Commons introduced and passed in accordance with the rules of that House.

(2) **Effect of negative resolution** — Where a regulation is annulled by a resolution of Parliament or of the House of Commons, it is deemed to have been revoked on the day the resolution is passed and any law that was revoked or amended by the making of that regulation is deemed to be revived on the day the resolution is passed but the validity of any action taken or not taken in compliance with a regulation so deemed to have been revoked shall not be affected by the resolution.

R.S., c. 29 (2d Supp.), s. 1.

References and Citations

40. (1) Citation of enactment — In an enactment or document,

(a) an Act may be cited by reference to its chapter number in the Revised Statutes, by reference to its chapter number in the volume of Acts for the year or regnal year in which it was enacted or by reference to its long title or short title, with or without reference to its chapter number; and

(b) a regulation may be cited by reference to its long title or short title, by reference to the Act under which it was made or by reference to the number or designation under which it was registered by the Clerk of the Privy Council.

(2) **Citation includes amendment** — A citation of or reference to an enactment is deemed to be a citation of or reference to the enactment as amended.

R.S., c. I-23, s. 32.

41. (1) Reference to two or more parts, etc — A reference in an enactment by number or letter to two or more parts, divisions, sections, subsections, paragraphs, subparagraphs, clauses, subclauses, schedules, appendices or forms shall be read as including the number or letter first mentioned and the number or letter last mentioned.

(2) **Reference in enactments to parts, etc** — A reference in an enactment to a part, division, section, schedule, appendix or form shall be read as a reference to a part, division, section, schedule, appendix or form of the enactment in which the reference occurs.

(3) **Reference in enactment to subsections, etc** — A reference in an enactment to a subsection, paragraph, subparagraph, clause or subclause shall be read as a reference to a subsection, paragraph, subparagraph, clause or subclause of the section, subsection, paragraph, subparagraph or clause, as the case may be, in which the reference occurs.

(4) **Reference to regulations** — A reference in an enactment to regulations shall be read as a reference to regulations made under the enactment in which the reference occurs.

(5) **Reference to another enactment** — A reference in an enactment by number or letter to any section, subsection, paragraph, subparagraph, clause, subclause or other division or line of another enactment shall be read as a reference to the section, subsection, paragraph, subparagraph, clause, subclause or other division or line of such other enactment as printed by authority of law.

R.S., c. I-23, s. 33.

Repeal and Amendment

42. (1) **Power of repeal or amendment reserved** — Every Act shall be construed as to reserve to Parliament the power of repealing or amending it, and of revoking, restricting or modifying any power, privilege or advantage thereby vested in or granted to any person.

(2) **Amendment or repeal at same session** — An Act may be amended or repealed by an Act passed in the same session of Parliament.

(3) **Amendment part of enactment** — An amending enactment, as far as consistent with the tenor thereof, shall be construed as part of the enactment that it amends.

R.S., c. I-23, s. 34.

43. Effect of repeal — Where an enactment is repealed in whole or in part, the repeal does not

(a) revive any enactment or anything not in force or existing at the time when the repeal takes effect,

(b) affect the previous operation of the enactment so repealed or anything duly done or suffered thereunder,

(c) affect any right, privilege, obligation or liability acquired, accrued, accruing or incurred under the enactment so repealed,

(d) affect any offence committed against or contravention of the provisions of the enactment so repealed, or any punishment, penalty or forfeiture incurred under the enactment so repealed, or

(e) affect any investigation, legal proceeding or remedy in respect of any right, privilege, obligation, or liability, referred to in paragraph (c) or in respect of any punishment, penalty or forfeiture or referred to in paragraph (d),

and an investigation, legal proceeding or remedy as described in paragraph (e) may be instituted, continued or enforced, and the punishment, penalty or forfeiture may be imposed as if the enactment had not been so repealed.

R.S., c. I-23, s. 35.

44. Repeal and substitution — Where an enactment, in this section called the "former enactment", is repealed and another enactment, in this section called the "new enactment", is substituted therefor,

(a) every person acting under the former enactment shall continue to act, as if appointed under the new enactment, until another person is appointed in the stead of that person;

(b) every bond and security given by a person appointed under the former enactment remains in force, and all books, papers, forms and things made or used under the former enactment shall continue to be used as before the repeal in so far as they are consistent with the new enactment;

(c) every proceeding taken under the former enactment shall be taken up and continued under and in conformity with the new enactment in so far as it may be done consistently with the new enactment;

(d) the procedure established by the new enactment shall be followed as far as it can be adapted thereto

(i) in the recovery or enforcement of fines, penalties and forfeitures imposed under the former enactment,

(ii) in the enforcement of rights, existing or accruing under the former enactment, and

(iii) in a proceeding in relation to matters that have happened before the repeal;

(e) when any punishment, penalty or forfeiture is reduced or mitigated by the new enactment, the punishment, penalty or forfeiture if imposed or adjudged after the repeal shall be reduced or mitigated accordingly;

(f) except to the extent that the provisions of the new enactment are not in substance the same as those of the former enactment, the new enactment shall not be held to operate as new law, but shall be construed and have effect as a consolidation and as declaratory of the law as contained in the former enactment;

(g) all regulations made under the repealed enactment remain in force and are deemed to have been made under the new enactment, in so far as they are not inconsistent with the new enactment, until they are repealed or others made in their stead; and

(h) any reference in an unrepealed enactment to the former enactment shall, with respect to a subsequent transaction, matter or thing, be read and construed as a reference to the provisions of the new enactment relating to the same subject-matter as the former enactment, but where there are no provisions in the new enactment relating to the same subject-matter, the former enactment shall be read as unrepealed in so far as is necessary to maintain or give effect to the unrepealed enactment.

R.S., c. I-23, s. 36.

Case Law

R. v. Puskas (1998), 16 C.R. (5th) 324, 125 C.C.C. (3d) 433 (S.C.C.) — Under s. 44(c) of the *Interpretation Act*, an appeal taken as of right under former s. 691(2) of the *Criminal Code* as it stood before its repeal and substitution, should be quashed since the new enactment gives no appeal as of right from decisions of provincial appellate courts ordering a new trial after an acquittal.

45. (1) Repeal does not imply enactment was in force — The repeal of an enactment in whole or in part shall not be deemed to be or to involve a declaration that the enactment was previously in force or was considered by Parliament or other body or person by whom the enactment was enacted to have been previously in force.

(2) Amendment does not imply change in law — The amendment of an enactment shall not be deemed to be or to involve a declaration that the law under that enactment was or was considered by Parliament or other body or person by whom the enactment was enacted to have been different from the law as it is under the enactment as amended.

(3) Repeal does not declare previous law — The repeal or amendment of an enactment in whole or in part shall not be deemed to be or to involve any declaration as to the previous state of the law.

(4) Judicial construction not adopted — A re-enactment, revision, consolidation or amendment of an enactment shall not be deemed to be or to involve an adoption of the construction that has by judicial decision or otherwise been placed on the language used in the enactment or on similar language.

R.S., c. I-23, s. 37.

Demise of Crown

46. **(1) Effect of demise** — Where there is a demise of the Crown,

(a) the demise does not affect the holding of any office under the Crown in right of Canada; and

(b) it is not necessary by reason of the demise that the holder of any such office again be appointed thereto or, having taken an oath of office or allegiance before the demise, again take that oath.

(2) Continuation of proceedings — No writ, action or other process or proceeding, civil or criminal, in or issuing out of any court established by an Act of the Parliament of Canada is, by reason of a demise of the Crown, determined, abated, discontinued or affected, but every such writ, action, process or proceeding remains in full force and may be enforced, carried on or otherwise proceeded with or completed as though there had been no such demise.

R.S., c. I-23, s. 39.

SCHEDULE
(Section 35)

Antigua and Barbuda

Australia

The Bahamas

Bangladesh

Barbados

Belize

Botswana

Brunei Darussalem

Canada

Cyprus

Dominica

Fiji

Gambia

Ghana

Grenada

Guyana

India

Jamaica

Kenya

Kiribati
Lesotho
Malawi
Malaysia
Maldives
Malta
Mauritius
Nauru
New Zealand
Nigeria
Pakistan
Papua New Guinea
St. Christopher and Nevis
St. Lucia
St. Vincent and the Grenadines
Seychelles
Sierra Leone
Singapore
Solomon Islands
Sri Lanka
Swaziland
Tanzania
Tonga
Trinidad and Tobago
Tuvalu
Uganda
United Kingdom
Vanuatu
Western Samoa
Zambia
Zimbabwe

R.S., c. I-23, Schedule; SI/72-93; SOR/74-287; SOR/77-394; SI/80-136; SOR/81-208; SOR/84-186; SOR/86-532; SOR/93-140.

YOUNG OFFENDERS ACT

An Act respecting young offenders

R.S.C. 1985, c. Y-1, as am. R.S.C. 1985, c. 27 (1st Supp.), ss. 187, 203; R.S.C. 1985, c. 24 (2d Supp.), ss. 1–44; R.S.C. 1985, c. 1 (3d Supp.), s. 12; R.S.C. 1985, c. 1 (4th supp.), ss. 38–45; 1991, c. 43, ss. 31–35; 1992, c. 1, s. 143; 1992, c. 11, ss. 1–13; 1992, c. 47, ss. 81–83; 1993, c. 28, s. 78 (Sched. III, item 144) [Amended 1998, c. 15, s. 41.]; 1993, c. 45, s. 15, 1994, c. 26, s. 76; 1995, c. 19, ss. 1–36; 1995, c. 22, ss. 16, 17 (Sched. III, item 10), 25; 1995, c. 27, s. 2; 1995, c. 39, s. 177–187, 189; 1996, c. 19, s. 93.1; 1999, c. 3, ss. 86–89.

See Table of Amendments for coming into force.

Short Title

1. Short title — This Act may be cited as the *Young Offenders Act.*

1980–81–82–83, c. 110, s. 1.

Interpretation

2. (1) Definitions — In this Act,

"**adult**" means a person who is neither a young person nor a child;

"**alternative measures**" means measures other than judicial proceedings under this Act used to deal with a young person alleged to have committed an offence;

"**child**" means a person who is or, in the absence of evidence to the contrary, appears to be under the age of twelve years;

"**disposition**" means a disposition made under any of sections 20, 20.1 and 28 to 32, and includes a confirmation or a variation of a disposition;

"**offence**" means an offence created by an Act of Parliament or by any regulation, rule, order, by-law or ordinance made thereunder, other than an ordinance of the Yukon Territory or the Northwest Territories or a law of the Legislature for Nunavut;

"**ordinary court**" means the court that would, but for this Act, have jurisdiction in respect of an offence alleged to have been committed;

"**parent**" includes, in respect of another person, any person who is under a legal duty to provide for that other person or any person who has, in law or in fact, the custody or control of that other person, but does not include a person who has the custody or control of that other person by reason only of proceedings under this Act;

"**predisposition report**" means a report on the personal and family history and present environment of a young person made in accordance with section 14;

"**progress report**" means a report made in accordance with section 28 on the performance of a young person against whom a disposition has been made;

"**provincial director**" means a person, a group or class of persons or a body appointed or designated by or pursuant to an Act of the legislature of a province or by the Lieutenant Governor in Council of a province or his delegate to perform in that province, either generally or in a specific case, any of the duties or functions of a provincial director under this Act;

"**review board**" means a review board established or designated by a province for the purposes of section 30;

"**young person**" means a person who is or, in the absence of evidence to the contrary, appears to be twelve years of age or more, but under eighteen years of age and, where the context requires, includes any person who is charged under this Act with having committed an offence while he was a young person or is found guilty of an offence under this Act;

"**youth court**" means a court established or designated by or under an Act of the legislature of a province, or designated by the Governor in Council or the Lieutenant Governor in Council of a province, as a youth court for the purposes of this Act;

"**youth court judge**" means a person appointed to be a judge of a youth court;

"**youth worker**" means a person appointed or designated, whether by title of youth worker or probation officer or by any other title, by or pursuant to an Act of the legislature of a province or by the Lieutenant Governor in Council of a province or his delegate, to perform, either generally or in a specific case, in that province any of the duties or functions of a youth worker under this Act.

(2) words and expressions — Unless otherwise provided, words and expressions used in this Act have the same meaning as in the *Criminal Code*.
1980–81–82–83, c. 110, s. 2; R.S. 1985, c. 24 (2nd Supp.), s. 1; 1993, c. 28, s. 78 (Schedule III, item 144) [Amended 1998, c. 15, s. 41]; 1995, c. 39, s. 177.

Case Law
Young Person

R. v. Z. (D.A.) (1992), 16 C.R. (4th) 133, 76 C.C.C. (3d) 97 (S.C.C.) — The definition of "young person" in s. 2 ought only to be extended to include a person over the age of eighteen where the context requires.

R. v. M. (R.E.) (1989), 46 C.C.C. (3d) 315 (B.C. S.C.) — For the purpose of jurisdiction of the youth court the important date is the date on which the offence is alleged to have occurred. An accused who fails to comply with a disposition of the youth court after he has become 18 is not a young person and should be proceeded against in adult court.

Youth Court

Reference re Young Offenders Act (Canada) (1991), (sub nom. *Reference re Young Offenders Act & Youth Court Judges)* 121 N.R. 81 (S.C.C.); affirming (1988), , 45 C.C.C. (3d) 264 (P.E.I. C.A.) — *See also: R. v. W. (D.A.)* (1991), 61 C.C.C. (3d) 574 (S.C.C.); affirming (1989), 49 C.C.C. (3d) 284 (N.S. C.A.); reversing (1988), 44 C.C.C. (3d) 138 (N.S. T.D.); *R. v. L. (B.L.)* (1991), 121 N.R. 114 (S.C.C.); affirming 90 N.S.R. (2d) 355 (C.A.) — Provincially appointed judges can preside over youth courts without offending s. 96 of the *Constitution Act, 1867*. The establishment of youth courts is within provincial legislative competence. youth court judges need not be appointed by the Governor General, but can be appointed by the Lieutenant Governor in Council. A Supreme Court judge can also be appointed a youth court judge by the Lieutenant Governor in Council.

Charter Considerations

R. v. C. (R.) (1987), 56 C.R. (3d) 185 (Ont. C.A.); leave to appeal refused (1987), 23 O.A.C. 397n (S.C.C.) — The practice of sending youths aged 16 and over for trial before youth court judges of the Provincial Court (Criminal Division) and those 15 years and younger before youth court judges of the Family Division does *not* offend *Charter* s. 15.

2.1 Powers, duties and functions of provincial directors — Any power, duty or function of a provincial director under this Act may be exercised or performed by any person authorized by the provincial director to do so and, if so exercised or performed, shall be deemed to have been exercised or performed by the provincial director.

R.S. 1985, c. 24 (2d Supp.), s. 2.

Declaration of Principle

3. (1) Policy for Canada with respect to young offenders — It is hereby recognized and declared that

(a) crime prevention is essential to the long-term protection of society and requires addressing the underlying causes of crime by young persons and developing multi-disciplinary approaches to identifying and effectively responding to children and young persons at risk of committing offending behaviour in the future;

(a.1) while young persons should not in all instances be held accountable in the same manner or suffer the same consequences for their behaviour as adults, young persons who commit offences should nonetheless bear responsibility for their contraventions;

(b) society must, although it has the responsibility to take reasonable measures to prevent criminal conduct by young persons, be afforded the necessary protection from illegal behaviour;

(c) young persons who commit offences require supervision, discipline and control, but, because of their state of dependency and level of development and maturity, they also have special needs and require guidance and assistance;

(c.1) the protection of society, which is a primary objective of the criminal law applicable to youth, is best served by rehabilitation, wherever possible, of young persons who commit offences, and rehabilitation is best achieved by addressing the needs and circumstances of a young person that are relevant to the young person's offending behaviour;

(d) where it is not inconsistent with the protection of society, taking no measures or taking measures other than judicial proceedings under this Act should be considered for dealing with young persons who have committed offences;

(e) young persons have rights and freedoms in their own right, including those stated in the *Canadian Charter of Rights and Freedoms* or in the *Canadian Bill of Rights*, and in particular a right to be heard in the course of, and to participate in, the processes that lead to decisions that affect them, and young persons should have special guarantees of their rights and freedoms;

(f) in the application of this Act, the rights and freedoms of young persons include a right to the least possible interference with freedom that is consistent with the protection of society, having regard to the needs of young persons and the interests of their families;

(g) young persons have the right, in every instance where they have rights or freedoms that may be affected by this Act, to be informed as to what those rights and freedoms are; and

(h) parents have responsibility for the care and supervision of their children, and, for that reason, young persons should be removed from parental supervision either partly or entirely only when measures that provide for continuing parental supervision are inappropriate.

(2) Act to be liberally construed — This Act shall be liberally construed to the end that young persons will be dealt with in accordance with the principles set out in subsection (1).

1980–81–82–83, c. 110, s. 3; 1995, c. 19, s. 1.

Case Law

General Principles

R. v. M. (J.J.) (1993), 20 C.R. (4th) 295, 81 C.C.C. (3d) 487 (S.C.C.) — Although s. 3(1) suggests that a traditional criminal law approach ought to be taken into account in sentencing young offenders, dispositions must be imposed on young offenders differently since their needs and requirements differ from those of adults.*Proportionality* has greater significance in sentencing adults than young offenders. For young offenders, a proper disposition requires consideration not only of the seriousness of the crime, but also all the other relevant factors. The *home situation* of the offender must always be taken into account, but must not be made the predominant factor. *General deterrence* must be considered, but is of lesser importance than in the case of an adult. It ought not to be unduly emphasized. The disposition imposed on an individual member of a group should be such as to deter other group members. The *annual review* procedures of s. 28 should also be considered.

R. v. G. (A.) (1998), 122 C.C.C. (3d) 183 (B.C. C.A.) — Misconduct and good conduct of a young offender *subsequent* to the offence for which s/he is being sentenced may be considered in determining the disposition to be made under the *Y.O.A.*

Authority to Dismiss Charges: S. 3(1)(d)

R. v. T. (V.) (1992), 12 C.R. (4th) 133, 71 C.C.C. (3d) 32 (S.C.C.) — The conjoint effect of s. 3(1)(d) and s. 19 *Y.O.A.* does *not* empower the youth court to dismiss a charge, notwithstanding proof of all its essential elements, where the court is of opinion that the behaviour ought *not* to attract the attention of the courts. Absent circumstances that, for example, would amount to an abuse of process, the decision whether charges ought to proceed is for the prosecutorial authorities, *not* the court.

Effect

R. v. M. (J.J.) (1993), 20 C.R. (4th) 295, 81 C.C.C. (3d) 487 (S.C.C.) — Section 3 is *not* merely a preamble, but ought to be given the force normally attributed to substantive provisions.

R. v. T. (V.) (1992), 12 C.R. (4th) 133, 71 C.C.C. (3d) 32 (S.C.C.) — Section 3(1) is not merely a preamble. Included in the body of the Act, it carries the same force as a substantive provision. Section 3(1)(d) does *not* impose a positive obligation on P to consider bringing no charges where that would be consistent with the philosophy underlying the Act, nor does it give a youth court jurisdiction to dismiss charges otherwise proved, merely on the ground that they ought not to have been laid.

Pre-disposition Custody

R. v. G. (C.) (1993), 79 C.C.C. (3d) 446 (Ont. C.A.) — It is only in exceptional cases that pre-disposition custody of a young offender is justified.

Alternative Measures

4. (1) Alternative measures — Alternative measures may be used to deal with a young person alleged to have committed an offence instead of judicial proceedings under this Act only if

    (a) the measures are part of a program of alternative measures authorized by the Attorney General or his delegate or authorized by a person, or a person within a class of persons, designated by the Lieutenant Governor in Council of a province;

    (b) the person who is considering whether to use such measures is satisfied that they would be appropriate, having regard to the needs of the young person and the interests of society;

    (c) the young person, having been informed of the alternative measures, fully and freely consents to participate therein;

(d) the young person has, before consenting to participate in the alternative measures, been advised of his right to be represented by counsel and been given a reasonable opportunity to consult with counsel;

(e) the young person accepts responsibility for the act or omission that forms the basis of the offence that he is alleged to have committed;

(f) there is, in the opinion of the Attorney General or his agent, sufficient evidence to proceed with the prosecution of the offence; and

(g) the prosecution of the offence is not in any way barred at law.

(2) **Restriction on use** — Alternative measures shall not be used to deal with a young person alleged to have committed an offence if the young person

(a) denies his participation or involvement in the commission of the offence; or

(b) expresses his wish to have any charge against him dealt with by the youth court.

(3) **Admissions not admissible in evidence** — No admission, confession or statement accepting responsibility for a given act or omission made by a young person alleged to have committed an offence as a condition of his being dealt with by alternative measures shall be admissible in evidence against him in any civil or criminal proceedings.

(4) **No bar to proceedings** — The use of alternative measures in respect of a young person alleged to have committed an offence is not a bar to proceedings against him under this Act, but

(a) where the youth court is satisfied on a balance of probabilities that the young person has totally complied with the terms and conditions of the alternative measures, the youth court shall dismiss any charge against him; and

(b) where the youth court is satisfied on a balance of probabilities that the young person has partially complied with the terms and conditions of the alternative measures, the youth court may dismiss any charge against him if, in the opinion of the court, the prosecution of the charge would, having regard to the circumstances, be unfair, and the youth court may consider the young person's performance with respect to the alternative measures before making a disposition under this Act.

(5) **Laying of information, etc** — Subject to subsection (4), nothing in this section shall be construed to prevent any person from laying an information, obtaining the issue or confirmation of any process or proceeding with the prosecution of any offence in accordance with law.

1980–81–82–83, c. 110, s. 4.

Case Law

Youth Court [See s. 2]

Charter Considerations

R. v. S. (G.) (1990), 77 C.R. (3d) 303, 57 C.C.C. (3d) 92 (S.C.C.); affirming (1988), 46 C.C.C. (3d) 332 (Ont. C.A.) — *See also: R. v. P. (J.)* (1990), 57 C.C.C. (3d) 190 (S.C.C.); reversing (1988), 31 O.A.C. 231 (C.A.), reversing (August 23, 1988), Doc. No. Toronto 805070 (Ont. Fam. Ct.); *R. v. T. (A.)* (1990), 57 C.C.C. (3d) 255 (S.C.C.) — As the implementation by the province of a programme of alternative measures for young offenders is optional, neither *Charter* s. 7 nor s. 15(1) are offended by the designation of admission criteria for such programme.

R. v. S. (S.) (1990), 77 C.R. (3d) 273, 57 C.C.C. (3d) 115 (S.C.C.); affirming (1988), 63 C.R. (3d) 64, 42 C.C.C. (3d) 41 (Ont. C.A.) — Section 4(1) is validly enacted pursuant to Parliament's power over criminal law and is not *ultra vires* Parliament. The decision of the Attorney General of Ontario not to authorize a programme of alternative measures does not contravene *Charter* s. 15(1). The decision is in accordance with the permissive terms of s. 4. Furthermore, in this case a distinction based upon province of residence is not a distinction based upon a personal characteristic and so it does not give rise to a violation of s. 15(1).

Jurisdiction

5. (1) Exclusive jurisdiction of youth court — Notwithstanding any other Act of Parliament but subject to the *National Defence Act* and section 16, a youth court has exclusive jurisdiction in respect of any offence alleged to have been committed by a person while he was a young person and any such person shall be dealt with as provided in this Act.

Proposed Amendment — 5(1)

(1) Exclusive jurisdiction of youth Court — Notwithstanding any other Act of Parliament but subject to the *Contraventions Act* and the *National Defence Act* and section 16, a youth court has exclusive jurisdiction in respect of any offence alleged to have been committed by a person while a young person and any such person shall be dealt with as provided in this Act.

1992, c. 47, s. 81. Not in force at date of publication.

(2) Period of limitation — No proceedings in respect of an offence shall be commenced under this Act after the expiration of the time limit set out in any other Act of Parliament or any regulation made thereunder for the institution of proceedings in respect of that offence.

(3) Proceedings continued when adult — Proceedings commenced under this Act against a young person may be continued, after he becomes an adult, in all respects as if he remained a young person.

(4) Powers of youth court judge — A youth court judge, for the purpose of carrying out the provisions of this Act, is a justice and a provincial court judge and has the jurisdiction and powers of a summary conviction court under the *Criminal Code*.

(5) Court of record — A youth court is a court of record.

1980–81–82–83, c. 110, s. 5; R.S. 1985, c. 27 (1st Supp.), s. 203; c. 24 (2d Supp.), s. 3.

Case Law
Determination of Jurisdiction

R. v. M. (R.E.) (1989), 46 C.C.C. (3d) 315 (B.C. S.C.) — For the purpose of jurisdiction of the youth court the important date is the date on which the offence is alleged to have occurred. An accused who fails to comply with a disposition of the youth court after he has become 18 is not a young person and should be proceeded against in adult court.

R. v. Merrick (1987), 37 C.C.C. (3d) 285 (Man. Q.B.) — An accused charged after his 18th birthday with breaching a recognizance entered into before he turned 18 must be proceeded against in adult court.

Averment in Information

R. v. C. (S.A.) (1989), 47 C.C.C. (3d) 76 (Alta. C.A.); leave to appeal refused (1989), 100 A.R. 160n (S.C.C.) — It is *not* necessary to allege in the information that the accused is a young person.

R. v. R. (1985), 49 C.R. (3d) 93, 23 C.C.C. (3d) 11 (B.C. C.A.) — Except where age is an element of the offence charged, it is *not* necessary to prove the age of the young person as part of P's case at trial. Jurisdiction can be established by inquiry of the youth court prior to trial.

R. v. D. (J.S.) (1986), 36 C.C.C. (3d) 94 (B.C. S.C.) — In the absence of an averment in the information that the person charged is a young person the youth court has no jurisdiction.

6. Certain proceedings may be taken before justices — Any proceeding that may be carried out before a justice under the *Criminal Code*, other than a plea, a trial or an adjudication, may be carried out before a justice in respect of an offence alleged to have been committed by a young person, and any process that may be issued by a justice under the *Criminal Code* may be issued by a justice in respect of an offence alleged to have been committed by a young person.

1980–81–82–83, c. 110, s. 6; R.S. 1985, c. 24 (2d Supp.), s. 4.

Detention Prior to Disposition

7. (1) Designated place of temporary detention — A young person who is

(a) arrested and detained prior to the making of a disposition in respect of the young person under section 20, or

(b) detained pursuant to a warrant issued under subsection 32(6)

shall, subject to subsection (4), be detained in a place of temporary detention designated as such by the Lieutenant Governor in Council of the appropriate province or his delegate or in a place within a class of such places so designated.

(1.1) Exception — A young person who is detained in a place of temporary detention pursuant to subsection (1) may, in the course of being transferred from that place to the court or from the court to that place, be held under the supervision and control of a peace officer.

(2) Detention separate from adults — A young person referred to in subsection (1) shall be held separate and apart from any adult who is detained or held in custody unless a youth court judge or a justice is satisfied that

(a) the young person cannot, having regard to his own safety or the safety of others, be detained in a place of detention for young persons; or

(b) no place of detention for young persons is available within a reasonable distance.

(3) Transfer by provincial director — A young person who is detained in custody in accordance with subsection (1) may, during the period of detention, be transferred by the provincial director from one place of temporary detention to another.

(4) Exception relating to temporary detention — Subsections (1) and (2) do not apply in respect of any temporary restraint of a young person under the supervision and control of a peace officer after arrest, but a young person who is so restrained shall be transferred to a place of temporary detention referred to in subsection (1) as soon as is reasonably practicable, and in no case later than the first reasonable opportunity after the appearance of the young person before a youth court judge or a justice pursuant to section 503 of the *Criminal Code*.

(5) Authorization of provincial authority for detention — In any province for which the Lieutenant Governor in Council has designated a person or a group of persons whose authorization is required, either in all circumstances or in circumstances specified by the Lieutenant Governor in Council, before a young person who has been arrested may be detained in accordance with this section, no young person shall be so detained unless the authorization is obtained.

(6) Determination by provincial authority of place of detention — In any province for which the Lieutenant Governor in Council has designated a person or a group of persons who may determine the place where a young person who has been arrested may be detained in accordance with this section, no young person may be so detained in a place other than the one so determined.

1980–81–82–83, c. 110, s. 7; R.S. 1985, c. 24 (2d Supp.), s. 5.

Case Law

F. v. R. (1985), 20 C.C.C. (3d) 56 (Ont. H.C.) — Once transferred to adult court, the young person may be detained in custody in a provincial jail and need *not* be kept separate from adult offenders.

7.1 (1) Placement of young person in care of responsible person — Where a youth court judge or a justice is satisfied that

    (a) a young person who has been arrested would, but for this subsection, be detained in custody,

    (b) a responsible person is willing and able to take care of and exercise control over the young person, and

    (c) the young person is willing to be placed in the care of that person,

the young person may be placed in the care of that person instead of being detained in custody.

(2) Condition of placement — A young person shall not be placed in the care of a person under subsection (1) unless

    (a) that person undertakes in writing to take care of and to be responsible for the attendance of the young person in court when required and to comply with such other conditions as the youth court judge or justice may specify; and

    (b) the young person undertakes in writing to comply with the arrangement and to comply with such other conditions as the youth court judge or justice may specify.

(3) Removing young person from care — Where a young person has been placed in the care of a person under subsection (1) and

    (a) that person is no longer willing or able to take care of or exercise control over the young person, or

    (b) it is, for any other reason, no longer appropriate that the young person be placed in the care of that person,

the young person, the person in whose care the young person has been placed or any other person may, by application in writing to a youth court judge or a justice, apply for an order under subsection (4).

(4) Order — Where a youth court judge or a justice is satisfied that a young person should not remain in the custody of the person in whose care he was placed under subsection (1), the youth court judge or justice shall

    (a) make an order relieving the person and the young person of the obligations undertaken pursuant to subsection (2); and

    (b) issue a warrant for the arrest of the young person.

(5) Effect of arrest — Where a young person is arrested pursuant to a warrant issued under paragraph (4)(*b*), the young person shall be taken before a youth court judge or justice forthwith and dealt with under section 515 of the *Criminal Code*.

R.S. 1985, c. 24 (2d Supp.), s. 5.

Case Law

R. v. K. (G.) (1985), 25 C.C.C. (3d) 177 (Ont. H.C.) — A judge reviewing a detention order may consider any option available to a youth court judge hearing the original release application, including placement of the young offender with a responsible person, as an alternative to detention.

7.2 Offence and punishment — Any person who wilfully fails to comply with section 7, or with an undertaking entered into pursuant to subsection 7.1(2), is guilty of an offence punishable on summary conviction.

R.S. 1985, c. 24 (2d Supp.), s. 5.

8. (1) [Repealed R.S. 1985, c. 24 (2d Supp.), s. 6.]

(2) Application to youth court — Where an order is made under section 515 of the *Criminal Code* in respect of a young person by a justice who is not a youth court judge, an application may, at any time after the order is made, be made to a youth court for the release from or detention in custody of the young person, as the case may be, and the youth court shall hear the matter as an original application.

(3) Notice to prosecutor — An application under subsection (2) for release from custody shall not be heard unless the young person has given the prosecutor at least two clear days notice in writing of the application.

(4) Notice to young person — An application under subsection (2) for detention in custody shall not be heard unless the prosecutor has given the young person at least two clear days notice in writing of the application.

(5) Waiver of notice — The requirement for a notice under subsection (3) or (4) may be waived by the prosecutor or by the young person or his counsel, as the case may be.

(6) Application for review under section 520 or 521 of Criminal Code — An application under section 520 or 521 of the *Criminal Code* for a review of an order made in respect of a young person by a youth court judge who is a judge of a superior, county or district court shall be made to a judge of the court of appeal.

(6.1) Nunavut — Despite subsection (6), an application under section 520 or 521 of the *Criminal Code* for a review of an order made in respect of a young person by a youth court judge who is a judge of the Nunavut Court of Justice shall be made to a judge of that court.

(7) Idem — No application may be made under section 520 or 521 of the *Criminal Code* for a review of an order made in respect of a young person by a justice who is not a youth court judge.

(8) Interim release by youth court judge only — Where a young person against whom proceedings have been taken under this Act is charged with an offence referred to in section 522 of the *Criminal Code*, a youth court judge, but no other court, judge or justice, may release the young person from custody under that section.

(9) Review by court of appeal — A decision made by a youth court judge under subsection (8) may be reviewed in accordance with section 680 of the *Criminal Code* and that section applies, with such modifications as the circumstances require, to any decision so made.

1980–81–82–83, c. 110, s. 8; R.S. 1985, c. 24 (2d Supp.), s. 6; 1999, c. 3, s. 86.

Notices to Parents

9. (1) Notice to parent in case of arrest — Subject to subsections (3) and (4), where a young person is arrested and detained in custody pending his appearance in court, the officer in charge at the time the young person is detained shall, as soon as possible, give or cause to be given, orally or in writing, to a parent of the young person notice of the arrest stating the place of detention and the reason for the arrest.

(2) Notice to parent in case of summons or appearance notice — Subject to subsections (3) and (4), where a summons or an appearance notice is issued in respect of a young person, the person who issued the summons or appearance notice, or, where a young person is released on giving his promise to appear or entering into a recognizance, the officer in charge, shall, as soon as possible, give or cause to be given, in writing, to a parent of the young person notice of the summons, appearance notice, promise to appear or recognizance.

Proposed Addition — (2.1)

(2.1) Notice to parent in case of ticket — Subject to subsections (3) and (4), a person who serves a ticket under the *Contraventions Act* on a young person, other than a ticket served for a contravention relating to parking a vehicle, shall, as soon as possible, give or cause to be given notice in writing of the ticket to a parent of the young person.

1992, c. 47, s. 82(1). Not in force at date of publication.

(3) Notice to relative or other adult — Where the whereabouts of the parents of a young person

    (a) who is arrested and detained in custody,

    (b) in respect of whom a summons or an appearance notice is issued, or

    (c) who is released on giving his promise to appear or entering into a recognizance

Proposed Addition — 9(3)(d)

    (d) on whom a ticket is served under the *Contraventions Act* other than a ticket served for a contravention relating to parking a vehicle,

1992, c. 47, s. 82(2). Not in force at date of publication.

are not known or it appears that no parent is available, a notice under this section may be given to an adult relative of the young person who is known to the young person and is likely to assist him or, if no such adult relative is available, to such other adult who is known to the young person and is likely to assist him as the person giving the notice considers appropriate.

(4) Notice to spouse — Where a young person described in paragraph (3)(*a*), (*b*) or (*c*) is married, a notice under this section may be given to the spouse of the young person instead of a parent.

Proposed Amendment — 9(4)

(4) Notice to spouse — A notice under this section may be given to the spouse of a young person described in paragraph (3)(*a*), (*b*), (*c*) or (*d*) instead of to a parent.

1992, c. 47, s. 82(g). Not in force at date of publication.

(5) Notice on direction of youth court judge or justice — Where doubt exists as to the person to whom a notice under this section should be given, a youth court judge or, where a youth court judge is, having regard to the circumstances, not reasonably available, a justice may give directions as to the person to whom the notice should be given, and a notice given in accordance with those directions is sufficient notice for the purposes of this section.

(6) **Contents of notice** — Any notice under this section shall, in addition to any other requirements under this section, include

(a) the name of the young person in respect of whom it is given;

(b) the charge against the young person and the time and place of appearance; and

Proposed Amendment — 9(6)(b)

(b) the charge against the young person and, except in the case of a notice of a ticket served under the *Contraventions Act*, the time and place of appearance; and

1992, c. 47, s. 82(4). Not in force at date of publication.

(c) a statement that the young person has the right to be represented by counsel.

Proposed Addition — 9(6.1)

(6.1) **Notice of ticket under Contraventions Act** — A notice under subsection (2.1) shall include a copy of the ticket.

1992, c. 47, s. 84(5). Not in force at date of publication.

(7) **Service of notice** — Subject to subsections (9) and (10), a notice under this section given in writing may be served personally or may be sent by mail.

(8) **Proceedings not invalid** — Subject to subsections (9) and (10), failure to give notice in accordance with this section does not affect the validity of proceedings under this Act.

(9) **Exception** — Failure to give notice under subsection (2) in accordance with this section in any case renders invalid any subsequent proceedings under this Act relating to the case unless

(a) a parent of the young person against whom proceedings are held attends court with the young person; or

(b) a youth court judge or a justice before whom proceedings are held against the young person

(i) adjourns the proceedings and orders that the notice be given in such manner and to such persons as the judge or justice directs, or

(ii) dispenses with the notice where the judge or justice is of the opinion that, having regard to the circumstances, the notice may be dispensed with.

(10) **Where a notice not served** — Where there has been a failure to give a notice under subsection (1) in accordance with this section and none of the persons to whom such notice may be given attends court with a young person, a youth court judge or a justice before whom proceedings are held against the young person may

Proposed Amendment — 9(10)

(10) **Where notice is not served** — Where there has been a failure to give a notice under subsection (1) or (2.1) in accordance with this section and none of the persons to whom the notice may be given attends court with the young person, a

1539

youth court judge or a justice before whom proceedings are held against the young person may

1992, c. 47, s. 86(6). Not in force at date of publication.

(a) adjourn the proceedings and order that the notice be given in such manner and to such person as he directs; or

(b) dispense with the notice where, in his opinion, having regard to the circumstances, notice may be dispensed with.

(11) [Repealed R.S. 1985, c. 24 (2d Supp.), s. 7(2).]

1980–81–82–83, c. 110, s. 9; R.S. 1985, c. 24 (2d Supp.), s. 7(1); 1991, c. 43, ss. 31(1), (2).

Case Law
Detention Pending Court Appearance

R. v. T. (R.W.) (1987), 28 C.C.C. (3d) 193 (N.S. C.A.) — Where a young offender is arrested and detained in order to comply with a breathalyzer demand, s. 9(1) does *not* apply and there is no obligation on the police to notify the parents prior to administering the breathalyzer test.

10. (1) Order requiring attendance of parent — Where a parent does not attend proceedings before a youth court in respect of a young person, the court may, if in its opinion the presence of the parent is necessary or in the best interest of the young person, by order in writing require the parent to attend at any stage of the proceedings.

Proposed Addition — 10(1.1)

(1.1) No order in ticket proceedings — Subsection (1) does not apply in proceedings commenced by filing a ticket under the *Contraventions Act*.

1992, c. 47, s. 83. Not in force at date of publication.

(2) Service of order — A copy of any order made under subsection (1) shall be served by a peace officer or by a person designated by a youth court by delivering it personally to the parent to whom it is directed, unless the youth court authorizes service by registered mail.

(3) Failure to attend — A parent who is ordered to attend a youth court pursuant to subsection (1) and who fails without reasonable excuse, the proof of which lies on that parent, to comply with the order

(a) is guilty of contempt of court;

(b) may be dealt with summarily by the court; and

(c) is liable to the punishment provided for in the *Criminal Code* for a summary conviction offence.

(4) Appeal — Section 10 of the *Criminal Code* applies where a person is convicted of contempt of court under subsection (3).

(5) Warrant to arrest parent — If a parent who is ordered to attend a youth court pursuant to subsection (1) does not attend at the time and place named in the order or fails to remain in attendance as required and it is proved that a copy of the order was served on the parent, a youth court may issue a warrant to compel the attendance of the parent.

(6) [Repealed R.S. 1985, c. 24 (2d Supp.), s. 8(2).]

1980–81–82–83, c. 110, s. 10; R.S. 1985, c. 24 (2d Supp.), s. 8(1).

Right to Counsel

11. (1) **Right to retain counsel** — A young person has the right to retain and instruct counsel without delay, and to exercise that right personally, at any stage of proceedings against the young person and prior to and during any consideration of whether, instead of commencing or continuing judicial proceedings against the young person under this Act, to use alternative measures to deal with the young person.

(2) **Arresting officer to advise young person of right to counsel** — Every young person who is arrested or detained shall, forthwith on his arrest or detention, be advised by the arresting officer or the officer in charge, as the case may be, of his right to be represented by counsel and shall be given an opportunity to obtain counsel.

(3) **Justice, youth court or review board to advise young person of right to counsel** — Where a young person is not represented by counsel

(a) at a hearing at which it will be determined whether to release the young person or detain him in custody prior to disposition of his case,

(b) at a hearing held pursuant to section 16,

(c) at his trial,

(c.1) at any proceedings held pursuant to subsection 26.1(1), 26.2(1) or 26.6(1),

(d) at a review of a disposition held before a youth court or a review board under this Act, or

(e) at a review of the level of custody pursuant to subsection 28.1(1),

the justice before whom, or the youth court or review board before which, the hearing, trial or review is held shall advise the young person of his right to be represented by counsel and shall give the young person a reasonable opportunity to obtain counsel.

(4) **Trial, hearing or review before youth court or review board** — Where a young person at his trial or at a hearing or review referred to in subsection (3) wishes to obtain counsel but is unable to do so, the youth court before which the hearing, trial or review is held or the review board before which the review is held

(a) shall, where there is a legal aid or assistance program available in the province where the hearing, trial or review is held, refer the young person to that program for the appointment of counsel; or

(b) where no legal aid or assistance program is available or the young person is unable to obtain counsel through such a program, may, and on the request of the young person shall, direct that the young person be represented by counsel.

(5) **Appointment of counsel** — Where a direction is made under paragraph (4)(*b*) in respect of a young person, the Attorney General of the province in which the direction is made shall appoint counsel, or cause counsel to be appointed, to represent the young person.

(6) **Release hearing before justice** — Where a young person at a hearing before a justice who is not a youth court judge at which it will be determined whether to release the young person or detain him in custody prior to disposition of his case wishes to obtain counsel but is unable to do so, the justice shall

(a) where there is a legal aid or assistance program available in the province where the hearing is held,

(i) refer the young person to that program for the appointment of counsel, or

(ii) **refer the matter to a youth court to be dealt with in accordance with paragraph 4(a), or (b); or**

(b) **where no legal aid or assistance program is available or the young person is unable to obtain counsel through such a program, refer the matter to a youth court to be dealt with in accordance with paragraph (4)(b).**

(7) **Young person may be assisted by adult** — Where a young person is not represented by counsel at his trial or at a hearing or review referred to in subsection (3), the justice before whom or the youth court or review board before which the proceedings are held may, on the request of the young person, allow the young person to be assisted by an adult whom the justice, court or review board considers to be suitable.

(8) **Counsel independent of parents** — In any case where it appears to a youth court judge or a justice that the interests of a young person and his parents are in conflict or that it would be in the best interest of the young person to be represented by his own counsel, the judge or justice shall ensure that the young person is represented by counsel independent of his parents.

(9) **Statement of right to counsel** — A statement that a young person has the right to be represented by counsel shall be included in

(a) **any appearance notice or summons issued to the young person;**

(b) **any warrant to arrest the young person;**

(c) **any promise to appear given by the young person;**

(d) **any recognizance entered into before an officer in charge by the young person;**

(e) **any notice given to the young person in relation to any proceedings held pursuant to subsection 26.1(1), 26.2(1) or 26.6(1); or**

(f) **any notice of a review of a disposition given to the young person.**

1980–81–82–83, c. 110, s. 11; R.S. 1985, c. 24 (2nd Supp.), s. 9; 1992, c. 11, s. 1; 1995, c. 19, s. 2.

Case Law

Right to Retain Counsel: S. 11(1)

R. v. W. (W.W.) (1985), 20 C.C.C. (3d) 214 (Man. C.A.) — In spite of the wording of s. 11(1), the appropriate practice is for the lawyer representing the young offender to receive instruction from a guardian, next friend or guardian *ad litem*, and not from the young offender.

R. v. O. (M.C.), (sub nom. *R. v. Frohman)* 56 C.R. (3d) 130, 35 C.C.C. (3d) 163 — A young offender detained by the police for a roadside breathalyzer test need not be advised of his right to retain and instruct counsel and be given an opportunity to do so, prior to taking the test.

Right to Counsel — Alternative Measures

W. (T.) v. R. (1986), 25 C.C.C. (3d) 89 (Sask. Q.B.) — Section 11(1) does not entitle a young person to an opportunity to be heard where P is considering alternative measures, it merely intends that he have the benefit of counsel in deciding whether to use alternative measures.

Appearance

12. (1) **Where young person appears** — A young person against whom an information is laid must first appear before a youth court judge or a justice, and the judge or justice shall

(a) **cause the information to be read to the young person;**

(b) **where the young person is not represented by counsel, inform the young person of the right to be so represented; and**

(c) where the young person is a young person referred to in subsection 16(1.01), inform the young person that the young person will be proceeded against in ordinary court in accordance with the law ordinarily applicable to an adult charged with the offence unless an application is made to the youth court by the young person, the young person's counsel or the Attorney General or an agent of the Attorney General to have the young person proceeded against in the youth court and an order is made to that effect.

(2) **Waiver** — A young person may waive the requirement under paragraph (1)(*a*) where the young person is represented by counsel.

(3) **Where young person not represented by counsel** — Where a young person is not represented in youth court by counsel, the youth court shall, before accepting a plea,

(a) satisfy itself that the young person understands the charge against him; and

(b) explain to the young person that he may plead guilty or not guilty to the charge.

(3.1) **Idem** — Where a young person is a young person referred to in subsection 16(1.01) and is not represented in youth court by counsel, the youth court shall satisfy itself that the young person understands

(a) the charge against the young person;

(b) the consequences of being proceeded against in ordinary court; and

(c) the young person's right to apply to be proceeded against in youth court.

(4) **Where youth court not satisfied** — Where the youth court is not satisfied that a young person understands the charge against the young person, as required under paragraph (3)(*a*), the court shall enter a plea of not guilty on behalf of the young person and shall proceed with the trial in accordance with subsection 19(2) or, with respect to proceedings in Nunavut, subsection 19.1(2)..

(5) **Idem** — Where the youth court is not satisfied that a young person understands the matters referred to in subsection (3.1), the court shall direct that the young person be represented by counsel.

1980–81–82–83, c. 110, s. 12; 1995, c. 19, s. 3; 1999, c. 3, s. 87.

Case Law

Requirement that Information be Read: S. 12(1)(a)

H. v. R. (1985), 21 C.C.C. (3d) 396 (B.C. S.C.) — The jurisdiction of the court requires strict compliance with s. 12(1). It is not sufficient that the substance of the charge is stated to the young offender on the first appearance. The loss of jurisdiction cannot be cured by a subsequent appearance.

R. v. J. (J.T.) (No. 2) (1987), 28 C.C.C. (3d) 62 (Man. Q.B.) — The failure of the court to cause the information to be read on the young offender's first appearance does *not* deprive it of jurisdiction to deal with the charge.

Medical and Psychological Reports

13. (1) **Medical or psychological examination** — A youth court may, at any stage of proceedings against a young person

(a) with the consent of the young person and the prosecutor, or

(b) on its own motion or on application of the young person or the prosecutor, where

(i) the court has reasonable grounds to believe that the young person may be suffering from a physical or mental illness or disorder, a psychological disorder, an emotional disturbance, a learning disability or a mental disability,

(ii) the young person's history indicates a pattern of repeated findings of guilt under this Act, or

(iii) the young person is alleged to have committed an offence involving serious personal injury,

and the court believes a medical, psychological or psychiatric report in respect of the young person is necessary for a purpose mentioned in paragraphs (2)(a) to (f),

by order require that the young person be assessed by a qualified person and require the person who conducts the examination to report the results thereof in writing to the court.

(2) **Purpose of assessment** — A youth court may make an order under subsection (1) in respect of a young person for the purpose of

(a) considering an application under section 16;

(b) making or reviewing a disposition under this Act, other than a disposition made under section 672.54 or 672.58 of the *Criminal Code*;

(c) considering an application under subsection 26.1(1);

(d) setting conditions under subsection 26.2(1);

(e) making an order subsection 26.6(2); or

(f) authorizing disclosure under subsection 38(1.5).

(3) **Presumption against custodial remand** — Subject to subsections (3.1) and (3.3), for the purpose of an assessment under this section, a youth court may remand a young person to such custody as it directs for a period not exceeding thirty days.

(3.1) **Report of qualified person in writing** — A young person shall not be remanded in custody pursuant to an order made by a youth court under subsection (1) unless

(a) the youth court is satisfied that on the evidence custody is necessary to conduct an assessment of the young person, or that on the evidence of a qualified person detention of the young person in custody is desirable to conduct the assessment of the young person and the young person consents to custody; or

(b) the young person is required to be detained in custody in respect of any other matter or by virtue of any provision of the *Criminal Code*.

(3.2) **Application to vary assessment order where circumstances change** — For the purposes of paragraph (3.1)(a), when the prosecutor and the young person agree, evidence of a qualified person may be received in the form of a report in writing.

(3.3) **Custody for assessment** — A youth court may, at any time while an order in respect of a young person made by the court under subsection (1) is in force, on cause being shown, vary the terms and conditions specified in that order in such manner as the court considers appropriate in the circumstances.

(4) Disclosure of report — Where a youth court receives a report made in respect of a young person pursuant to subsection (1),

    (a) the court shall, subject to subsection (6), cause a copy of the report to be given to

        (i) the young person,

        (ii) a parent of the young person, if the parent is in attendance at the proceedings against the young person,

        (iii) counsel, if any, representing the young person, and

        (iv) the prosecutor; and

    (b) the court may cause a copy of the report to be given to a parent of the young person not in attendance at the proceedings against the young person if the parent is, in the opinion of the court, taking an active interest in the proceedings.

(5) Cross-examination — Where a report is made in respect of a young person pursuant to subsection (1), the young person, his counsel or the adult assisting him pursuant to subsection 11(7) and the prosecutor shall, subject to subsection (6), on application to the youth court, be given an opportunity to cross-examine the person who made the report.

(6) Report to be withheld where disclosure unnecessary or prejudicial — A youth court shall withhold all or part of a report made in respect of a young person pursuant to subsection (1) from a private prosecutor, where disclosure of the report or part, in the opinion of the court, is not necessary for the prosecution of the case and might be prejudicial to the young person.

(7) Report to be withheld where disclosure dangerous to any person — A youth court shall withhold all or part of a report made in respect of a young person pursuant to subsection (1) from the young person's parents or a private prosecutor where the court is satisfied, on the basis of the report or evidence given in the absence of the young person, parents or private prosecutor by the person who made the report, that disclosure of all or part of the report would seriously impair the treatment or recovery of the young person, or would be likely to endanger the life or safety of, or result in serious psychological harm to, another person.

(8) Idem — Notwithstanding subsection (7), the youth court may release all or part of the report referred to in that subsection to the young person, the young person's parents or the private prosecutor where the interests of justice make disclosure essential in the court's opinion.

(9) Report to be part of record — A report made pursuant to subsection (1) shall form part of the record of the case in respect of which it was requested.

(10) Disclosure by qualified person — Notwithstanding any other provision of this Act, a qualified person who is of the opinion that a young person held in detention or committed to custody is likely to endanger his own life or safety or to endanger the life of, or cause bodily harm to, another person may immediately so advise any person who has the care and custody of the young person whether or not the same information is contained in a report made pursuant to subsection (1).

(11) Definition of "qualified person" — In this section, "qualified person" means a person duly qualified by provincial law to practice medicine or psychiatry or to carry out psychological examinations or assessments, as the circumstances require, or, where no such law exists, a person who is, in the opinion of the youth court, so qualified, and includes a person or a person within a class of persons designated by the Lieutenant Governor in Council of a province or his delegate.

(12) [Repealed R.S. 1985, c. 24 (2d Supp.), s. 10.]

1980–81–82–83, c. 110, s. 13; 1991, c. 43, ss. 32, 35(a); 1995, c. 19, s. 4.

Case Law

Successive Reports

R. v. C. (B.) (1986), 53 C.R. (3d) 376, 29 C.C.C. (3d) 434 (Ont. H.C.) — An order cannot be made under s. 13 unless there is an evidentiary basis for it. While there may be successive assessments ordered, a second assessment cannot be ordered over the objection of the young offender merely because the first assessment is perceived to be inadequate.

13.1 (1) Statements not admissible against young person — Subject to subsection (2), where a young person is assessed pursuant to an order made under subsection 13(1), no statement or reference to a statement made by the young person during the course and for the purposes of the assessment to the person who conducts the assessment or to anyone acting under that person's direction is admissible in evidence, without the consent of the young person, in any proceeding before a court, tribunal, body or person with jurisdiction to compel the production of evidence.

(2) Exceptions — A statement referred to in subsection (1) is admissible in evidence for the purposes of

(a) considering an application under section 16 in respect of the young person;

(b) determining whether the young person is unfit to stand trial;

(c) determining whether the balance of the mind of the young person was disturbed at the time of commission of the alleged offence, where the young person is a female person charged with an offence arising out of the death of her newly-born child;

(d) making or reviewing a disposition in respect of the young person;

(e) determining whether the young person was, at the time of the commission of an alleged offence, suffering from automatism or a mental disorder so as to be exempt from criminal responsibility by virtue of subsection 16(1) of the *Criminal Code*, if the accused puts his or her mental capacity for criminal intent into issue, or if the prosecutor raises the issue after verdict;

(f) challenging the credibility of a young person in any proceeding where the testimony of the young person is inconsistent in a material particular with a statement referred to in subsection (1) that the young person made previously;

(g) establishing the perjury of a young person who is charged with perjury in respect of a statement made in any proceeding;

(h) deciding an application for an order under subsection 26.1(1);

(i) setting the conditions under subsection 26.2(1);

(j) conducting a review under subsection 26.6(1); or

(k) deciding an application for a disclosure order under subsection 38(1.5).

1991, c. 43, s. 33; c. 43, s. 35(b); 1994, c. 26, s. 76; 1995, c. 19, s. 5.

Case Law: *R. v. Spanevello* (1998), 125 C.C.C. (3d) 97 (B.C. C.A.) — "Statement" in s. 13.1 means *all* statements made by a young offender during the course of the assessment. A psychiatrist's opinion of a co-accused's disposition for violence, based, in part, on statements made by the co-accused during a s. 13(1) *Y.O.A.* assessment, is a reference to a statement under s. 13.1 that is prohibited.

Application of Part XX.1 of the Criminal Code (Mental Disorder)

13.2 (1) Sections of Criminal Code applicable — Except to the extent that they are inconsistent with or excluded by this Act, section 16 and Part XX.1 of the *Criminal Code*, except sections 672.65 and 672.66, apply, with such modifications as the circumstances require, in respect of proceedings under this Act in relation to offences alleged to have been committed by young persons.

(2) Notice and copies to counsel and parents — For the purposes of subsection (1), wherever in Part XX.1 of the *Criminal Code* a reference is made to

(a) a copy to be sent or otherwise given to an accused or a party to the proceedings, the reference shall be read as including a reference to a copy to be sent or otherwise given to

(i) counsel, if any, representing the young person,

(ii) any parent of the young person who is in attendance at the proceedings against the young person, and

(iii) any parent of the young person who is, in the opinion of the youth court or Review Board, taking an active interest in the proceedings; and

(b) notice to be given to an accused or a party to proceedings, the reference shall be read as including a reference to notice to be given to counsel, if any, representing the young person and the parents of the young person.

(3) Proceedings not invalid — Subject to subsection (4), failure to give a notice referred to in paragraph (2)(*b*) to a parent of a young person does not affect the validity of proceedings under this Act.

(4) Exception — Failure to give a notice referred to in paragraph (2)(*b*) to a parent of a young person in any case renders invalid any subsequent proceedings under this Act relating to the case unless

(a) a parent of the young person attends at the court or Review Board with the young person; or

(b) a youth court judge or Review Board before whom proceedings are held against the young person

(i) adjourns the proceedings and orders that the notice be given in such manner and to such persons as the judge or Review Board directs, or

(ii) dispenses with the notice where the youth court or Review Board is of the opinion that, having regard to the circumstances, the notice may be dispensed with.

(5) No hospital order assessments — A youth court may not make an order under subsection 672.11 of the *Criminal Code* in respect of a young person for the purpose of assisting in the determination of an issue mentioned in paragraph 672.11(*e*) of that Act.

(6) Considerations of court or Review Board making a disposition — Before making or reviewing a disposition in respect of a young person under Part XX.1 of the *Criminal Code*, a youth court or Review Board shall consider the age and special needs of the young person and any representations or submissions made by the young person's parents.

(7) Cap applicable to young persons — Subject to subsection (9), for the purpose of applying subsection 672.64(3) of the *Criminal Code* to proceedings under this Act in relation to an offence alleged to have been committed by a young person, the applicable cap shall be the maximum period during which the young person would be subject to a disposition by the youth court if found guilty of the offence.

(8) Application to increase cap of unfit young person subject to transfer — Where an application is made under section 16 to proceed against a young person in ordinary court and the young person is found unfit to stand trial, the Attorney General or the agent of the Attorney General may, before the youth court makes or refuses to make an order under that section, apply to the court to increase the cap that shall apply to the young person.

(9) Consideration of youth court for increase in cap — The youth court, after giving the Attorney General and the counsel and parents of the young person in respect of whom an application is made under subsection (8) an opportunity to be heard, shall take into consideration

    (a) the seriousness of the alleged offence and the circumstances in which it was allegedly committed,

    (b) the age, maturity, character and background of the young person and any previous findings of guilty against the young person under any Act of Parliament,

    (c) the likelihood that the young person will cause significant harm to any person if released on expiration of the cap that applies to the young person pursuant to subsection (7), and

    (d) the respective caps that would apply to the young person under this Act and under the *Criminal Code*,

and the youth court shall, where satisfied that the application under section 16 would likely succeed if the young person were fit to stand trial, apply to the young person the cap that would apply to an adult for the same offence.

(10) Prima facie case to be made every year — For the purpose of applying subsection 672.33(1) of the *Criminal Code* to proceedings under this Act in relation to an offence alleged to have been committed by a young person, wherever in that subsection a reference is made to two years, there shall be substituted a reference to one year.

(11) Designation of hospitals for young persons — A reference in Part XX.1 of the *Criminal Code* to a hospital in a province shall be construed as a reference to a hospital designated by the Minister of Health of the province for the custody, treatment or assessment of young persons.

1991, c. 43, s. 33.

Pre-Disposition Report

14. (1) Pre-disposition report — Where a youth court deems it advisable before making a disposition under section 20 in respect of a young person who is found guilty of an offence it may, and where a youth court is required under this Act to consider a pre-disposition report before making an order or a disposition in respect of a young person it shall, require the provincial director to cause to be prepared a pre-disposition report in respect of the young person and to submit the report to the court.

(2) Contents of report — A pre-disposition report made in respect of a young person shall, subject to subsection (3), be in writing and shall include,

    (a) the results of an interview with

        (i) the young person,

        (ii) where reasonably possible, the parents of the young person and,

        (iii) where appropriate and reasonably possible, members of the young person's extended family;

    (b) the results of an interview with the victim in the case, where applicable and where reasonably possible;

    (c) such information as is applicable to the case including, where applicable,

        (i) the age, maturity, character, behaviour and attitude of the young person and his willingness to make amends,

        (ii) any plans put forward by the young person to change his conduct or to participate in activities or undertake measures to improve himself,

        (iii) the history of previous findings of delinquency under the *Juvenile Delinquents Act*, chapter J-3 of the Revised Statutes of Canada, 1970, or previous findings of guilt under this or any other Act of Parliament or any regulation made thereunder or under an Act of the legislature of a province or any regulation made thereunder or a by-law or ordinance of a municipality, the history of community or other services rendered to the young person with respect to those findings and the response of the young person to previous sentences or dispositions and to services rendered to him,

        (iv) the history of alternative measures used to deal with the young person and the response of the young person thereto,

        (v) the availability and appropriateness of community services and facilities for young persons and the willingness of the young person to avail himself or herself of those services or facilities,

        (vi) the relationship between the young person and the young person's parents and the degree of control and influence of the parents over the young person and, where appropriate and reasonably possible, the relationship between the young person and the young person's extended family and the degree of control and influence of the young person's extended family over the young person,

        (vii) the school attendance and performance record and the employment record of the young person; and

    (d) such information as the provincial director considers relevant, including any recommendation that the provincial director considers appropriate.

(3) Oral report with leave — Where a pre-disposition report cannot reasonably be committed to writing, it may, with leave of the youth court, be submitted orally in court.

(4) Report to form part of record — A pre-disposition report shall form part of the record of the case in respect of which it was requested.

(5) **Copies of pre-disposition report** — Where a pre-disposition report made in respect of a young person is submitted to a youth court in writing, the court

   (a) shall, subject to subsection (7), cause a copy of the report to be given to

      (i) the young person,

      (ii) a parent of the young person, if the parent is in attendance at the proceedings against the young person,

      (iii) counsel, if any, representing the young person, and

      (iv) the prosecutor; and

   (b) may cause a copy of the report to be given to a parent of the young person not in attendance at the proceedings against the young person if the parent is, in the opinion of the court, taking an active interest in the proceedings.

(6) **Cross-examination** — Where a pre-disposition report made in respect of a young person is submitted to a youth court, the young person, his counsel or the adult assisting him pursuant to subsection 11(7) and the prosecutor shall, subject to subsection (7), on application to the youth court, be given the opportunity to cross-examine the person who made the report.

(7) **Report may be withheld from private prosecutor** — Where a pre-disposition report made in respect of a young person is submitted to a youth court, the court may, where the prosecutor is a private prosecutor and disclosure of the report or any part thereof to the prosecutor might, in the opinion of the court, be prejudicial to the young person and is not, in the opinion of the court, necessary for the prosecution of the case against the young person,

   (a) withhold the report or part thereof from the prosecutor, if the report is submitted in writing; or

   (b) exclude the prosecutor from the court during the submission of the report or part thereof, if the report is submitted orally in court.

(8) **Report disclosed to other persons** — Where a pre-disposition report made in respect of a young person is submitted to a youth court, the court

   (a) shall, on request, cause a copy or a transcript of the report to be supplied to

      (i) any court that is dealing with matters relating to the young person, and

      (ii) any youth worker to whom the young person's case has been assigned; and

   (b) may, on request, cause a copy or a transcript of the report, or a part thereof, to be supplied to any person not otherwise authorized under this section to receive a copy or transcript of the report if, in the opinion of the court, the person has a valid interest in the proceedings.

(9) **Disclosure by the provincial director** — A provincial director who submits a pre-disposition report made in respect of a young person to a youth court may make the report, or any part thereof, available to any person in whose custody or under whose supervision the young person is placed or to any other person who is directly assisting in the care or treatment of the young person.

(10) **Inadmissibility of statements** — No statement made by a young person in the course of the preparation of a pre-disposition report in respect of the young person

is admissible in evidence against him in any civil or criminal proceedings except in proceedings under section 16 or 20 or sections 28 to 32.

1980–81–82–83, c. 110, s. 14; R.S. 1985, c. 24 (2d Supp.), s. 11; 1995, c. 19, s. 6.

Case Law

Contents: S. 14(2)

R. v. S. (R.C.) (1986), 27 C.C.C. (3d) 239 (N.B. C.A.); leave to appeal refused (1986), 69 N.B.R. (2d) 270n (S.C.C.) — A predisposition report which did not address the availability of community services and facilities for young persons failed to provide the information necessary to determine whether custody should be open or secure.

Disqualification of Judge

15. (1) Disqualification of judge — Subject to subsection (2), a youth court judge who, prior to an adjudication in respect of a young person charged with an offence, examines a pre-disposition report made in respect of the young person, or hears an application under section 16 in respect of the young person, in connection with that offence shall not in any capacity conduct or continue the trial of the young person for the offence and shall transfer the case to another judge to be dealt with according to law.

(2) Exception — A youth court judge may, in the circumstances referred to in subsection (1), with the consent of the young person and the prosecutor, conduct or continue the trial of the young person if the judge is satisfied that he has not been predisposed by information contained in the pre-disposition report or by representations made in respect of the application under section 16.

1980–81–82–83, c. 110, s. 15.

Transfer

16. (1) Transfer to ordinary court — Subject to subsection (1.01), at any time after an information is laid against a young person alleged to have, after attaining the age of fourteen years, committed an indictable offence other than an offence referred to in section 553 of the *Criminal Code* but prior to adjudication, a youth court shall, on application of the young person or the young person's counsel or the Attorney General or an agent of the Attorney General, determine, in accordance with subsection (1.1), whether the young person should be proceeded against in ordinary court.

(1.01) Trial in ordinary court for certain offences — Every young person against whom an information is laid who is alleged to have committed

(a) first degree murder or second degree murder within the meaning of section 231 of the *Criminal Code*,

(b) an offence under section 239 of the *Criminal Code* (attempt to commit murder),

(c) an offence under section 232 or 234 of the *Criminal Code* (manslaughter), or

(d) an offence under section 273 of the *Criminal Code* (aggravated sexual assault),

and who was sixteen or seventeen years of age at the time of the alleged commission of the offence shall be proceeded against in ordinary court in accordance with the law ordinarily applicable to an adult charged with the offence unless the youth court, on application by the young person, the young person's counsel or the Attorney General or an agent of the Attorney General, makes an order under subsection (1.04) or (1.05) or subparagraph (1.1)(a)(ii) that the young person should be proceeded against in youth court.

(1.02) Making of application — An application to the youth court under subsection (1.01) must be made orally, in the presence of the other party to the proceedings, or in writing, with a notice served on the other party to the proceedings.

(1.03) Where application is opposed — Where the other party to the proceedings referred to in subsection (1.02) files a notice of opposition to the application with the youth court within twenty-one days after the making of the oral application, or the service of the notice referred to in that subsection, as the case may be, the youth court shall, in accordance with subsection (1.1), determine whether the young person should be proceeded against in youth court.

(1.04) Where application is unopposed — Where the other party to the proceedings referred to in subsection (1.02) files a notice of non-opposition to the application with the youth court within the time referred to in subsection (1.03), the youth court shall order that the young person be proceeded against in youth court.

(1.05) Deeming — Where the other party to the proceedings referred to in subsection (1.02) does not file a notice referred to in subsection (1.03) or (1.04) within the time referred to in subsection (1.03), the youth court shall order that the young person be proceeded against in youth court.

(1.06) Time may be extended — The time referred to in subsections (1.03) to (1.05) may be extended by mutual agreement of the parties to the proceedings by filing a notice to that effect with the youth court.

(1.1) Order — In making the determination referred to in subsection (1) or (1.03), the youth court, after affording both parties and the parents of the young person an opportunity to be heard, shall consider the interest of society, which includes the objectives of affording protection to the public and rehabilitation of the young person, and determine whether those objectives can be reconciled by the youth being under the jurisdiction of the youth court, and

    (a) if the court is of the opinion that those objectives can be so reconciled, the court shall

        (i) in the case of an application under subsection (1), refuse to make an order that the young person be proceeded against in ordinary court, and

        (ii) in the case of an application under subsection (1.01), order that the young person be proceeded against in youth court; or

    (b) if the court is of the opinion that those objectives cannot be so reconciled, protection of the public shall be paramount and the court shall

        (i) in the case of an application under subsection (1), order that the young person be proceeded against in ordinary court in accordance with the law ordinarily applicable to an adult charged with the offence, and

        (ii) in the case of an application under subsection (1.01), refuse to make an order that the young person be proceeded against in youth court.

(1.11) Onus — Where an application is made under subsection (1) or (1.01), the onus of satisfying the youth court of the matters referred to in subsection (1.1) rests with the applicant.

(2) **Considerations by youth court** — In making the determination referred to in subsection (1) or (1.03) in respect of a young person, a youth court shall take into account

    (a) the seriousness of the alleged offence and the circumstances in which it was allegedly committed;

    (b) the age, maturity, character and background of the young person and any record or summary of previous findings of delinquency under the Juvenile Delinquents Act, chapter J-3 of the Revised Statutes of Canada, 1970, or previous findings of guilt under this Act or any other Act of Parliament or any regulation made thereunder;

    (c) the adequacy of this Act, and the adequacy of the Criminal Code or any other Act of Parliament that would apply in respect of the young person if an order were made under this section to meet the circumstances of the case;

    (d) the availability of treatment or correctional resources;

    (e) any representations made to the court by or on behalf of the young person or by the Attorney General or his agent; and

    (f) any other factors that the court considers relevant.

(3) **Pre-disposition reports** — In making the determination referred to in subsection (1) or (1.03) in respect of a young person, a youth court shall consider a pre-disposition report.

(4) **Where young person on transfer status** — Notwithstanding subsections (1) and (3), where an application is made under subsection (1) by the Attorney General or the Attorney General's agent in respect of an offence alleged to have been committed by a young person while the young person was being proceeded against in ordinary court pursuant to an order previously made under this section or serving a sentence as a result of proceedings in ordinary court, the youth court may make a further order under this section without a hearing and without considering a pre-disposition report.

(5) **Court to state reasons** — Where a youth court makes an order or refuses to make an order under this section, it shall state the reasons for its decision and the reasons shall form part of the record of the proceedings in the youth court.

(6) **No further applications for transfer** — Where a youth court refuses to make an order under this section in respect of an alleged offence, no further application may be made under this section in respect of that offence.

(7) **Effect of order** — Where an order is made under this section pursuant to an application under subsection (1), proceedings under this Act shall be discontinued and the young person against whom the proceedings are taken shall be taken before the ordinary court.

(7.1) **Idem** — Where an order is made under this section pursuant to an application under subsection (1.01), the proceedings against the young person shall be in the youth court.

(8) **Jurisdiction of ordinary court limited** — Where a young person is proceeded against in ordinary court in respect of an offence by reason of

    (a) subsection (1.01), where no application is made under that subsection,

    (b) an order made under subparagraph (1.1)(b)(i), or

    (c) the refusal under subparagraph (1.1)(b)(ii) to make an order, that the court has jurisdiction only in respect of that offence; or an offence included therein.

(9) Review of youth court decision — An order made in respect of a young person under this section or a refusal to make such an order shall, on application of the young person or the young person's counsel or the Attorney General or the Attorney General's agent made within thirty days after the decision of the youth court, be reviewed by the court of appeal, and that court may, in its discretion, confirm or reverse the decision of the youth court.

(10) Extension of time to make application — The court of appeal may, at any time, extend the time within which an application under subsection (9) may be made.

(11) Notice of application — A person who proposes to apply for a review under subsection (9) shall give notice of the application in such manner and within such period of time as may be directed by rules of court.

(12) Inadmissibility of statement — No statement made by a young person in the course of a hearing held under this section is admissible in evidence against the young person in any civil or criminal proceeding held subsequent to that hearing.

(13) [Repealed 1992, c. 11, s. 16(3).]

(14) [Repealed R.S. 1985, c. 24 (2d Supp.), s. 12.]

1980–81–82–83, c. 110, s. 16; 1992, c. 11, s. 2; 1995, c. 19, s. 8.

Case Law

Test for Transfer under s. 16(1)

R. v. L. (J.E.) (1989), 71 C.R. (3d) 306, 50 C.C.C. (3d) 385 (S.C.C.) — *See also*: *R. v. M. (S.H.)* (1989), 71 C.R. (3d) 257, 50 C.C.C. (3d) 503 (S.C.C.); affirming (1987), 35 C.C.C. (3d) 515 (Alta. C.A.) — While there is a burden on the party seeking transfer to persuade the court that transfer is appropriate having regard to the factors in s. 16(2), the onus should not be regarded as a heavy one. The question is whether the judge is satisfied after weighing and balancing all the relevant considerations that the case should be transferred to ordinary court.

R. v. L. (R.A.) (1995), 103 C.C.C. (3d) 151 (B.C. C.A.) — A transfer order is mandatory when objectives of protection of the public and rehabilitation of the accused cannot be reconciled. Where the objectives can be reconciled, protection of the public is not paramount and there is no residual disrection to order a transfer.

R. v. V. (D.) (1986), 31 C.C.C. (3d) 253 (Man. C.A.) — There is no onus on a young person to bring forth compelling reasons why he should not be transferred. The transfer can only be made where the circumstances bring the court to the conclusion it is in the interests of society, having regard to the needs of the young person, to make the transfer.

R. v. M. (C.J.) (1986), 23 C.C.C. (3d) 538 (Man. C.A.) — In the test for transfer there is a slight emphasis on the interest of society, having regard to the needs of the young person.

R. v. Breau (1987), 33 C.C.C. (3d) 354 (N.B. C.A.) — Section 16(1) demonstrates a clear emphasis in favour of the interest of society and it is error for the court on a transfer hearing to focus almost solely on the needs of the accused.

R. v. M. (M.J.) (1989), 47 C.C.C. (3d) 436 (N.S. C.A.); affirming (1988), 87 N.S.R. (2d) 93 (T.D.) — The court must be of the opinion that transfer is in the interest of society and in forming that opinion, the court must have regard to the needs of the young person. The interests of society include the rehabilitation of the young offender and the protection of society.

R. v. B. (N.) (1985), 21 C.C.C. (3d) 374 (Que. C.A.) — Transfer is *not* automatic under s. 16(1). The interest of society and the needs of the young person must be balanced.

Transfer in Murder Cases

R. v. S. (D.) (1998), 127 C.C.C. (3d) 162 (Sask. C.A.) — The fundamental issue on a transfer hearing under *Y.O.A.* s. 16 is jurisdiction, *not* the guilt or innocence of D.

R. v. W. (B.) (1997), 121 C.C.C. (3d) 419 (Ont. C.A.) — Where the protection of the public and rehabilitation of the young person may both be accomplished in youth court, a transfer application on a charge of second degree murder should succeed. Where both objectives cannot be accommodated, however, public protection requires trial in the ordinary court.

Factors to be Considered: Ss. 16(1.1), (2)

R. v. M. (S.H.) (1989), 71 C.R. (3d) 257, 50 C.C.C. (3d) 503 (S.C.C.); affirming (1987), 35 C.C.C. (3d) 515 (Alta. C.A.) — *See also: R. v. L. (J.E.)* (1989), 71 C.R. (3d) 306, 50 C.C.C. (3d) 385 (S.C.C.); affirming (December 16, 1987), Doc. No. Edmonton Appeal 8703-0504-A (Alta. C.A.) — The *Act* does *not* require that all factors in s. 16(2) be given equal weight, only that each be considered. Some factors will assume greater importance than others depending on the nature of the case and the viewpoint of the tribunal.

Re T. (E.) (1990), 53 C.C.C. (3d) 209 (B.C. C.A.); leave to appeal refused (1990), 107 N.R. 233n (S.C.C.) — When the provisions of both the Act and the *Criminal Code* are inadequate, the view most favourable to the young person should be adopted.

R. v. K. (C.J.) (1994), 88 C.C.C. (3d) 82 (Man. C.A.) — Where the youth court is unable to reconcile the protection of the public with the rehabilitation of the young person within the youth court system, priority must be given to protection of the public and the young person transferred to the ordinary courts. Where the rehabilitation of the young person can be accomplished within the youth court system and the protection of the public can be reconciled with it, the young person is entitled to the special provisions of the *Y.O.A.*

R. v. C. (R.M.) (1987), 33 C.C.C. (3d) 136 (Man. C.A.) — A transfer order should not be refused solely because the young offender has a mental illness which requires treatment.

R. v. M. (F.D.) (1987), 33 C.C.C. (3d) 116 (Man. C.A.) — The issue of insanity is to be determined at trial and is not an appropriate consideration on a transfer hearing.

R. v. K. (G.S.) (1985), 22 C.C.C. (3d) 99 (Man. C.A.) — The brutality of the circumstances of the offence and the planning and premeditation involved are weighty factors in considering transfer.

R. v. H. (W.) (1989), 69 C.R. (3d) 168, 47 C.C.C. (3d) 72 (Ont. C.A.) — Trial in youth court can serve the purpose of protection of the public and punishment and reformation of the offender.

R. v. F. (1985), 20 C.C.C. (3d) 334 (Ont. H.C.) — Section 16(2) is directory, not mandatory. The failure to consider one of the enumerated factors does not result in a loss of jurisdiction, but may be reversible error of law if the neglected factor is relevant.

Factors to be Considered: Ss. 16(1.1), (2)

R. v. S. (D.) (1998), 127 C.C.C. (3d) 162 (Sask. C.A.) — *Y.O.A.* s. 16 is the ideal vehicle to permit a youth court judge to decide the proper jurisdiction to hear the charges. Where P cannot particularize the time of offences, hence alleges a period of time including when D was a young offender as well as an adult, P should *commence* proceedings in *youth court* because some offences are alleged to have occurred when D was a young offender. P should then apply to the youth court judge for a transfer hearing under s. 16 to determine the proper forum for trial.

Procedure

R. v. W. (1986), 28 C.C.C. (3d) 510 (B.C. C.A.) — Where the young offender is a ward of the provincial child protection agency, its superintendent is a parent for the purpose of s. 16.

R. v. W. (1986), 28 C.C.C. (3d) 510 (B.C. C.A.) — A youth court judge who hears evidence of age and identity of the young offender in order to establish jurisdiction, and orders a predisposition report, does *not* become seized of the transfer application.

R. v. M. (F.D.) (1987), 33 C.C.C. (3d) 116 (Man. C.A.) — Where there is more than one accused, the transfer applications should be heard together or, if separate hearings are necessary, as successive applications to the same judge.

R. v. M. (F.D.) (1987), 33 C.C.C. (3d) 116 (Man. C.A.) — [Per Monnin C.J.M.] — It is improper to hold a preliminary inquiry while a review of the transfer order is pending.

R. v. R. (E.S.) (1985), 49 C.R. (3d) 88 (Man. C.A.) — Transfer must not always be ordered where the co-accused of a young offender is to be tried in adult court. It is only one factor to be taken into account.

R. v. J. (J.T.) (No. 1) (1986), 27 C.C.C. (3d) 574 (Man. Q.B.) — Once transferred to adult court, D may be proceeded against in accordance with the law ordinarily applicable to an adult charged with that offence and may be subject to a preferred indictment notwithstanding his discharge at the preliminary inquiry.

F. v. R. (1985), 20 C.C.C. (3d) 56 (Ont. H.C.) — Once transferred to adult court, the young person may be detained in custody in a provincial jail and need not be kept separate from adult offenders.

Evidentiary Issues

R. v. W. (1985), 22 C.C.C. (3d) 269 (B.C. S.C.) — Hearsay evidence is admissible on a transfer hearing although it should be treated with great caution.

R. v. M. (1985), 23 C.C.C. (3d) 538 (Man. C.A.) — The strict rules of evidence that apply at trial do not necessarily apply at a transfer hearing or review, but disputed facts must be proved in the ordinary way.

R. v. B. (N.) (1985), 21 C.C.C. (3d) 374 (Que. C.A.) — The burden of proof is on the party who brings the application for transfer [under s. 16(1)]. The transfer must not only be desirable, it must be necessary.

Review (General Principles)

R. v. M. (S.H.) (1989), 71 C.R. (3d) 257, 50 C.C.C. (3d) 503 (S.C.C.) — *See also*: *R. v. L. (J.E.)* (1989), 71 C.R. (3d) 306, 50 C.C.C. (3d) 385 (S.C.C.) — The reviewing court must base its review on the facts found by the youth court judge and give due deference to the youth court judge's evaluation of the evidence, then apply the factors set out in s. 16(2) to that evidence. In applying those factors, the reviewing court is not confined to asking whether the youth court erred, but should make an independent evaluation on the basis of the facts found by the youth court judge and arrive at an independent conclusion.

Review by Superior Court: S. 16(9)

R. v. F. (1985), 20 C.C.C. (3d) 334 (Ont. H.C.) — The power of review in s. 16(9) includes the power to quash and remit the matter back to youth court for a new hearing, such as where the youth court failed to consider a relevant factor.

Review by Court of Appeal: S. 16(10)

R. v. C. (R.M.) (1987), 33 C.C.C. (3d) 136 (Man. C.A.) — [Per Twaddle J.A.] — Leave should not be given merely because the Court of Appeal would have reached a different decision, but should be given only where the reviewing judge applied a wrong principle or misapprehended the facts, or a point of law is raised which the Court of Appeal should decide.

R. v. M. (D.) (1991), 61 C.C.C. (3d) 129 (Ont. C.A.) — The requirement for leave to review is not a mere formality and the applicant must meet a threshold requirement that leave be granted. Conflicting decisions in the courts below, together with the difficulty raised by the issue of transfer, may warrant the granting of leave.

Charter Considerations

R. v. M. (L.A.) (1987), 33 C.C.C. (3d) 364 (B.C. C.A.) — Section 16(1) does *not* offend *Charter* s. 7, 11(c) or 11(d).

R. v. W. (1985), 22 C.C.C. (3d) 269 (B.C. S.C.) — Section 16 does not offend *Charter* s. 15(1).

R. v. R. (J.D.) (1991), 44 O.A.C. 260 (C.A.); leave to appeal to S.C.C. refused (1991), 49 O.A.C. 317 (note) (S.C.C.) — The appropriate time to raise a s. 12 challenge in respect of a transfer order is before the sentencing judge at the conclusion of D's trial if he is convicted.

16.1 (1) Detention pending trial — young person under eighteen — Notwithstanding anything in this or any other Act of Parliament, where a young person who is under the age of eighteen is to be proceeded against in ordinary court by reason of

(a) subsection 16(1.01), where no application is made under that subsection,

(b) an order under subparagraph 16(1.1)(b)(i), or

(c) the refusal under subparagraph 16(1.1)(b)(ii) to make an order,

and the young person is to be in custody pending the proceedings in that court, the young person shall be held separate and apart from any adult who is detained or held in custody unless the youth court is satisfied, on application, that the young person, having regard to the best interests of the young person and the safety of others, cannot be detained in a place of detention for young persons.

(2) **Detention pending trial — young person over eighteen —** Notwithstanding anything in this or any other Act of Parliament, where a young person who is over the age of eighteen is to be proceeded against in ordinary court by reason of

(a) subsection 16(1.01), where no application is made under that subsection,

(b) an order under subparagraph 16(1.1)(b)(i), or

(c) the refusal under subparagraph 16(1.1)(b)(ii) to make an order,

and the young person is to be in custody pending the proceedings in that court, the young person shall be held in a place of detention for adults unless the youth court is satisfied, on application, that the young person, having regard to the best interests of the young person and the safety of others, should be detained in a place of custody for young persons.

(3) **Review —** On application, the youth court shall review the placement of a young person in detention pursuant to this section and, if satisfied, having regard to the best interests of the young person and the safety of others, and after having afforded the young person, the provincial director and a representative of a provincial department responsible for adult correctional facilities an opportunity to be heard, that the young person should remain in detention where the young person is or be transferred to youth or adult detention, as the case may be, the court may so order.

(4) **Who may make application —** An application referred to in this section may be made by the young person, the young person's parents, the provincial director, the Attorney General or the Attorney General's agent.

(5) **Notice —** Where an application referred to in this section is made, the applicant shall cause a notice of the application to be given

(a) where the applicant is the young person or one of the young person's parents, to the provincial director and the Attorney General;

(b) where the applicant is the Attorney General or the Attorney General's agent, to the young person, the young person's parents and the provincial director; and

(c) where the applicant is the provincial director, to the young person, the parents of the young person and the Attorney General.

(6) **Statement of rights —** A notice given under subsection (5) by the Attorney General or the provincial director shall include a statement that the young person has the opportunity to be heard and the right to be represented by counsel.

(7) **Limit — age 20 —** Notwithstanding anything in this section, no young person shall remain in custody in a place of detention for young persons under this section after the young person attains the age of twenty years.

1992, c. 11, s. 2(3); 1995, c. 19, s. 9.

16.2 (1) Placement on conviction by ordinary court — Notwithstanding anything in this or any other Act of Parliament, where a young person who is proceeded against in ordinary court by reason of subsection 16(1.01), where no application is made under that subsection, or by reason of an order under subparagraph 16(1.1)(b)(i) or the refusal under subparagraph 16(1.1)(b)(ii) to make an order, is convicted and sentenced to imprisonment, the court shall, after affording the young person, the parents of the young person, the Attorney General, the provincial director and representatives of the provincial and federal correctional systems an opportunity to be heard, order that the young person serve any portion of the imprisonment in

(a) a place of custody for young persons separate and apart from any adult who is detained or held in custody;

(b) a provincial correctional facility for adults; or

(c) where the sentence is for two years or more, a penitentiary.

(2) **Factors to be taken into account** — In making an order under subsection (1), the court shall take into account

(a) the safety of the young person;

(b) the safety of the public;

(c) the young person's accessibility to family;

(d) the safety of other young persons if the young person were to be held in custody in a place of custody for young persons;

(e) whether the young person would have a detrimental influence on other young persons if the young person were to be held in custody in a place of custody for young persons;

(f) the young person's level of maturity;

(g) the availability and suitability of treatment, educational and other resources that would be provided to the young person in a place of custody for young persons and in a place of custody for adults;

(h) the young person's prior experiences and behaviour while in detention or custody;

(i) the recommendations of the provincial director and representatives of the provincial and federal correctional facilities; and

(j) any other factor the court considers relevant.

(3) **Report necessary** — Prior to making an order under subsection (1), the court shall require that a report be prepared for the purpose of assisting the court.

(4) **Review** — On application, the court shall review the placement of a young person in detention pursuant to this section and, if satisfied that the circumstances that resulted in the initial order have changed materially, and after having afforded the young person, the provincial director and the representatives of the provincial and federal correctional systems an opportunity to be heard, the court may order that the young person be placed in

(a) a place of custody for young persons separate and apart from any adult who is detained or held in custody;

(b) a provincial correctional facility for adults, or

(c) where the sentence is for two years or more, a penitentiary.

(5) **Who may make application** — An application referred to in this section may be made by the young person, the young person's parents, the provincial director, a

representative of the provincial and federal correctional systems and the Attorney General.

(6) Notice — Where an application referred to in this section is made, the applicant shall cause a notice of the application to be given

(a) where the applicant is the young person or one of the young person's parents, to the provincial director, to representatives of the provincial and federal correction systems and to the Attorney General;

(b) where the applicant is the Attorney General or the Attorney General's agent, to the young person, the young person's parents and the provincial director and representatives of the provincial and federal correction systems; and

(c) where an applicant is the provincial director, to the young person, the parents of the young person, the Attorney General and representatives of the provincial and federal correction systems.

1992, c. 11, s. 2(3); 1995, c. 19, s. 10.

Note: Transitional Provision, S.C. 1992, c. 11, s. 18 provides:

18. Where a young person is alleged to have committed first degree murder or second degree murder within the meaning of section 231 of the Criminal Code before the coming into force of this Act and

(a) an application was made in respect of the young person under subsection 16(1) of the Young Offenders Act, as that subsection read immediately before the coming into force of this Act, but no decision under that subsection had been issued before the coming into force of this Act, or

(b) an application is made in respect of the young person under subsection 16(1) of the Young Offenders Act after the coming into force of this Act,

the provisions of the Young Offenders Act enacted by this Act shall apply to the young person as if the offence had occurred after the coming into force of this Act.

Case Law: *R. v. G.(T.T.)* (1997), 113 C.C.C. (3d) 254 (N.S. C.A.) — Section 16.2 of the *Y.O.A.* continues to apply after a young person has reached the age of eighteen years.

17. (1) Order restricting publication of information presented at transfer hearing — Where a youth court hears an application for a transfer under section 16, it shall

(a) where the young person is not represented by counsel, or

(b) on application made by or on behalf of the young person or the prosecutor, where the young person is represented by counsel,

make an order directing that any information respecting the offence presented at the hearing shall not be published in any newspaper or broadcast before such time as

(c) an order for a transfer is refused or set aside on review and the time for all reviews against the decision has expired or all proceedings in respect of any such review have been completed; or

(d) the trial is ended, if the case is transferred to ordinary court.

(2) Offence — Every one who fails to comply with an order made pursuant to subsection (1) is guilty of an offence punishable on summary conviction.

(3) Definition of "newspaper" — In this section, "newspaper" has the meaning set out in section 297 of the *Criminal Code*.

1980–81–82–83, c. 110, s. 17; 1995, c. 19, s. 11.

Transfer of Jurisdiction

18. Transfer of jurisdiction — Notwithstanding subsections 478(1) and (3) of the *Criminal Code*, where a young person is charged with an offence that is alleged to have been committed in one province, he may, if the Attorney General of the province where the offence is alleged to have been committed consents, appear before a youth court of any other province and,

    (a) where the young person signifies his consent to plead guilty and pleads guilty to that offence, the court shall, if it is satisfied that the facts support the charge, find the young person guilty of the offence alleged in the information; and

    (b) where the young person does not signify his consent to plead guilty and does not plead guilty, or where the court is not satisfied that the facts support the charge, the young person shall, if he was detained in custody prior to his appearance, be returned to custody and dealt with according to law.

1980–81–82–83, c. 110, s. 18.

Adjudication

19. (1) Where young person pleads guilty — Where a young person pleads guilty to an offence charged against him and the youth court is satisfied that the facts support the charge, the court shall find the young person guilty of the offence.

(2) Where young person pleads not guilty — Where a young person charged with an offence pleads not guilty to the offence or pleads guilty but the youth court is not satisfied that the facts support the charge, the court shall, subject to subsection (4), proceed with the trial and shall, after considering the matter, find the young person guilty or not guilty or make an order dismissing the charge, as the case may be.

(3) Application for transfer to ordinary court — The court shall not make a finding under this section in respect of a young person in respect of whom an application may be made under section 16 for an order that the young person be proceeded against in ordinary court unless it has inquired as to whether any of the parties to the proceedings wishes to make such an application, and, if any party so wishes, has given that party an opportunity to do so.

(4) Election — offence of murder — Notwithstanding section 5, where a young person is charged with having committed first degree murder or second degree murder within the meaning of section 231 of the *Criminal Code*, the youth court, before proceeding with the trial, shall ask the young person to elect to be tried by a youth court judge alone or by a judge of a superior court of criminal jurisdiction with a jury, and where a young person elects to be tried by a judge of a superior court of criminal jurisdiction with a jury, the young person shall be dealt with as provided in this Act.

(5) Where no election made — Notwithstanding section 5, where an election is not made under subsection (4), the young person shall be deemed to have elected to be tried by a judge of a superior court of criminal jurisdiction with a jury and dealt with as provided for in this Act.

(5.1) Preliminary inquiry — Where a young person elects or is deemed to have elected to be tried by a judge of a superior court of criminal jurisdiction with a jury, the youth court shall conduct a preliminary inquiry and if, on its conclusion, the young person is ordered to stand trial, the proceedings shall be before a judge of the superior court of criminal jurisdiction with a jury.

(5.2) Preliminary inquiry provisions of Criminal Code — A preliminary inquiry referred to in subsection (5.1) shall be conducted in accordance with the provisions of Part XVIII of the *Criminal Code*, except to the extent that they are inconsistent with this Act.

(6) Parts XIX and XX of the Criminal Code — Proceedings under this Act before a judge of a superior court of criminal jurisdiction with a jury shall be conducted, with such modifications as the circumstances require, in accordance with the provisions of Parts XIX and XX of the *Criminal Code*, except that

(a) the provisions of this Act respecting the protection of privacy and young persons prevail over the provisions of the *Criminal Code*; and

(b) the young person is entitled to be represented in court by counsel if the young person is removed from court pursuant to subsection 650(2) of the *Criminal Code*.

1980–81–82–83, c. 110, s. 19; R.S. 1985, c. 24 (2d Supp.), s. 13; 1995, c. 19, s. 12.

Case Law

Plea of Guilty: S. 19(1)

R. v. K. (1985), 18 C.C.C. (3d) 94 (N.S. C.A.) — Where, prior to acceptance of the young offender's plea, there was no statement of the facts supporting the charge, the conviction will be quashed on appeal.

Authority to Dismiss Charges: S. 19(2)

R. v. T. (V.) (1992), 12 C.R. (4th) 133, 71 C.C.C. (3d) 32 (S.C.C.) — The conjoint effect of s. 3(1)(d) and s. 19 *Y.O.A.* does *not* empower the youth court to dismiss a charge, notwithstanding proof of all its essential elements, where the court is of opinion that the behaviour ought not to attract the attention of the courts. Absent circumstances, that, for example, would amount to an abuse of process, the decision whether charges ought to proceed is for the prosecutorial authorities, *not* the court.

19.1 (1) If young person pleads guilty — Nunavut — If a young person pleads guilty to an offence charged against the young person and the youth court is satisfied that the facts support the charge, the court shall find the young person guilty of the offence.

(2) If young person pleads not guilty — Nunavut — If a young person charged with an offence pleads not guilty to the offence or pleads guilty but the youth court is not satisfied that the facts support the charge, the court shall, subject to subsection (4), proceed with the trial and shall, after considering the matter, find the young person guilty or not guilty or make an order dismissing the charge, as the case may be.

(3) Application for transfer to ordinary court — Nunavut — The court shall not make a finding under this section in respect of a young person in respect of whom an application may be made under section 16 for an order that the young person be proceeded against in ordinary court unless it has inquired as to whether any of the parties to the proceedings wishes to make such an application, and, if any party so wishes, has given that party an opportunity to do so.

(4) Election re offence of murder — Nunavut — If a young person is charged with having committed first degree murder or second degree murder within the meaning of section 231 of the *Criminal Code*, the youth court, before proceeding with the trial, shall ask the young person to elect

(a) to be tried by a judge of the Nunavut Court of Justice alone, acting as a youth court, or

(b) to have a preliminary inquiry and to be tried by a judge of the Nunavut Court of Justice, acting as a youth court, with a jury, and if a young person elects under paragraph (*a*) or (*b*), the young person shall be dealt with as provided in this Act.

(5) **If no election made — Nunavut —** Despite section 5, if an election is not made under subsection (4), the young person shall be deemed to have elected under paragraph (4)(*b*).

(6) **Preliminary inquiry — Nunavut —** If a young person elects or is deemed to have elected under paragraph (4)(*b*), a preliminary inquiry shall be held in the youth court and if, on its conclusion, the young person is ordered to stand trial, the proceedings shall be before a judge of the Nunavut Court of Justice, acting as a youth court, with a jury.

(7) **Preliminary inquiry provisions of *Criminal Code* — Nunavut —** A preliminary inquiry referred to in subsection (6) shall be conducted in accordance with the provisions of Part XVIII of the *Criminal Code*, except to the extent that they are inconsistent with this Act.

(8) **Parts XIX and XX of the *Criminal Code* — Nunavut —** Proceedings under this Act before a judge of the Nunavut Court of Justice, acting as a youth court, with a jury shall be conducted, with any modifications that the circumstances require, in accordance with the provisions of Parts XIX and XX of the *Criminal Code*, except that

 (a) the provisions of this Act respecting the protection of privacy of young persons prevail over the provisions of the *Criminal Code*; and

 (b) the young person is entitled to be represented in court by counsel if the young person is removed from court pursuant to subsection 650(2) of the *Criminal Code*.

(9) **Application to Nunavut —** This section, and not section 19, applies in respect of proceedings under this Act in Nunavut.

1999, c. 3, s. 88.

Dispositions

20. (1) **Dispositions that may be made —** Where a youth court finds a young person guilty of an offence, it shall consider any pre-disposition report required by the court, any representations made by the parties to the proceedings or their counsel or agents and by the parents of the young person and any other relevant information before the court, and the court shall then make any one of the following dispositions, other than the disposition referred to in paragraph (k.1), or any number thereof that are not inconsistent with each other, and where the offence is first degree murder or second degree murder within the meaning of section 231 of the *Criminal Code*, the court shall make the disposition referred to in paragraph (k.1) and may make such other disposition as the court considers appropriate:

 (a) by order direct that the young person be discharged absolutely, if the court considers it to be in the best interests of the young person and not contrary to the public interest;

 (a.1) by order direct that the young person be discharged on such conditions as the court considers appropriate;

 (b) impose on the young person a fine not exceeding one thousand dollars to be paid at such time and on such terms as the court may fix;

 (c) order the young person to pay to any other person at such time and on such terms as the court may fix an amount by way of compensation for loss of or damage to property, for loss of income or support or for special damages for personal injury arising from the commission of the offence where the value thereof is readily ascertainable, but no order shall be made for general damages;

(d) order the young person to make restitution to any other person of any property obtained by the young person as a result of the commission of the offence within such time as the court may fix, if the property is owned by that other person or was, at the time of the offence, in his lawful possession;

(e) if any property obtained as a result of the commission of the offence has been sold to an innocent purchaser, where restitution of the property to its owner or any other person has been made or ordered, order the young person to pay the purchaser, at such time and on such terms as the court may fix, an amount not exceeding the amount paid by the purchaser for the property;

(f) subject to section 21, order the young person to compensate any person in kind or by way of personal services at such time and on such terms as the court may fix for any loss, damage or injury suffered by that person in respect of which an order may be made under paragraph (c) or (e);

(g) subject to section 21, order the young person to perform a community service at such time and on such terms as the court may fix;

(h) subject to section 20.1, make any order of prohibition, seizure or forfeiture that may be imposed under any Act of Parliament or any regulation made thereunder where an accused is found guilty or convicted of that offence;

(i) [Repealed 1995, c. 19, s. 13(2)].

(j) place the young person on probation in accordance with section 23 for a specified period not exceeding two years;

(k) subject to sections 24 to 24.5, commit the young person to custody, to be served continuously or intermittently, for a specified period not exceeding

(i) two years from the date of committal, or

(ii) where the young person is found guilty of an offence for which the punishment provided by the *Criminal Code* or any other Act of Parliament is imprisonment for life, three years from the date of committal;

(k.1) order the young person to serve a disposition not to exceed

(i) in the case of first degree murder, ten years comprised of

(A) a committal to custody, to be served continuously, for a period that shall not, subject to subsection 26.1(1), exceed six years from the date of committal, and

(B) a placement under conditional supervision to be served in the community in accordance with section 26.2, and

(ii) in the case of second degree murder, seven years comprised of

(A) a committal to custody, to be served continuously, for a period that shall not, subject to subsection 26.1(1), exceed four years from the date of committal, and

(B) a placement under conditional supervision to be served in the community in accordance with section 26.2; and

(l) impose on the young person such other reasonable and ancillary conditions as it deems advisable and in the best interest of the young person and the public.

(2) **Coming into force of disposition** — A disposition made under this section shall come into force on the date on which it is made or on such later date as the youth court specifies therein.

(3) **Duration of disposition** — No disposition made under this section, other than an order made under paragraph (1)(*h*), (*k*) or (*k*.1), shall continue in force for more than two years and, where the youth court makes more than one disposition at the same time in respect of the same offence, the combined duration of the dispositions, except in respect of an order made under paragraph (1)(*h*), (*k*) or (*k*.1), shall not exceed two years.

(4) **Combined duration of dispositions** — Subject to subsection (4.1), where more than one disposition is made under this section in respect of a young person with respect to different offences, the continuous combined duration of those dispositions shall not exceed three years, except where one of those offences is first degree murder or second degree murder within the meaning of section 231 of the *Criminal Code*, in which case the continuous combined duration of those dispositions shall not exceed ten years in the case of first degree murder, or seven years in the case of second degree murder.

(4.1) **Duration of dispositions made at different times** — Where a disposition is made under this section in respect of an offence committed by a young person after the commencement of, but before the completion of, any dispositions made in respect of previous offences committed by the young person,

    (a) the duration of the disposition made in respect of the subsequent offence shall be determined in accordance with subsections (3) and (4);

    (b) the disposition may be served consecutively to the dispositions made in respect of the previous offences; and

    (c) the combined duration of all the dispositions may exceed three years, except where the offence is, or one of the previous offences was,

        (i) first degree murder within the meaning of section 231 of the *Criminal Code*, in which case the continuous combined duration of the dispositions may exceed ten years, or

        (ii) second degree murder within the meaning of section 231 of the *Criminal Code*, in which case the continuous combined duration of the dispositions may exceed seven years.

(4.2) **Custody first** — Subject to subsection (4.3), where a young person who is serving a disposition made under paragraph (1)(*k*.1) is ordered to custody in respect of an offence committed after the commencement of, but before the completion of, that disposition, the custody in respect of that subsequent offence shall be served before the young person is placed under conditional supervision.

(4.3) **Conditional supervision suspended** — Where a young person referred to in subsection (4.2) is under conditional supervision at the time the young person is ordered to custody in respect of a subsequent offence, the conditional supervision shall be suspended until the young person is released from custody.

(5) **Disposition continues when adult** — Subject to section 743.5 of the *Criminal Code*, a disposition made under this section shall continue in effect in accordance with the terms thereof, after the young person against whom it is made becomes an adult.

(6) Reasons for the disposition — Where a youth court makes a disposition under this section, it shall state its reasons therefor in the record of the case and shall

(a) provide or cause to be provided a copy of the disposition, and

(b) on request, provide or cause to be provided a transcript or copy of the reasons for the disposition

to the young person in respect of whom the disposition was made, the young person's counsel and parents, the provincial director, where the provincial director has an interest in the disposition, the prosecutor and, in the case of a custodial disposition made under paragraph (1)(*k*) or (*k*.1), the review board, if a review board has been established or designated.

(7) Limitation on punishment — No disposition shall be made in respect of a young person under this section that results in a punishment that is greater than the maximum punishment that would be applicable to an adult who has committed the same offence.

(8) Application of Part XXIII of *Criminal Code* — Part XXIII of the *Criminal Code* does not apply in respect of proceedings under this Act except for section 722, subsection 730(2) and sections 748, 748.1 and 749, which provisions apply with such modifications as the circumstances require.

(9) Section 787 of *Criminal Code* **does not apply** — Section 787 of the *Criminal Code* does not apply in respect of proceedings under this Act.

(10) Contents of probation order — The youth court shall specify in any probation order made under paragraph (1)(*j*) the period for which it is to remain in force.

(11) No order under section 161 of *Criminal Code* — Notwithstanding paragraph (1)(*h*), a youth court shall not make an order of prohibition under section 161 of the *Criminal Code* against a young person.

1980–81–82–83, c. 110, s. 20; R.S. 1985, c. 27 (1st Supp.), s. 187, Schedule; c. 24 (2d Supp.), s. 14; c. 1 (4th Supp.), s. 38; 1992, c. 11, s. 3; 1993, c. 45, s. 15; 1995, c. 19, s. 13; 1995, c. 22, ss. 16, 17, 25; 1995, c. 39, s. 178.

Case Law

General Principles

R. v. W. (C.W.) (1986), 51 C.R. (3d) 89, 25 C.C.C. (3d) 355 (Alta. C.A.) — *See also*: *R. v. K. (G.)* (1985), 21 C.C.C. (3d) 558 (Alta. C.A.); additional reasons at (1985), 21 C.C.C. (3d) 558 at 561 (C.A.) — General deterrence is a different element from the protection of society and has no place in the sentencing of young offenders. Individual deterrence and segregation of the offender from society are to be considered as means of the protection of society.

R. v. W. (M.Y.) (1986), 26 C.C.C. (3d) 328 (B.C. C.A.) — The protection of society involves consideration of general deterrence, but the overriding consideration in the case of young offenders is that within the limits of protecting society, it is necessary to attempt to rehabilitate the young offender.

R. v. L. (C.J.) (1987), 29 C.C.C. (3d) 123 (Nfld. C.A.) — The principle of general deterrence is of minor importance in sentencing a young first offender. Individual deterrence may be an appropriate consideration where it may be necessary for the protection of society.

R. v. B. (S.A.) (1990), 56 C.C.C. (3d) 317 (N.S. C.A.) — There is a danger in using the sentences imposed on adults as strict guide-lines for dispositions imposed on young offenders, as the latter are governed by the principles set out in s. 3.

R. v. K. (M.) (1996), 107 C.C.C. (3d) 149 (Ont. C.A.) — The maximum penalty available under the YOA is somewhat artificially-truncated so as to preserve the jurisdiction of the youth court. The narrow range of sentence compresses all serious cases at the top of the range, hence may permit its imposition for "worse cases", notwithstanding that they may not be the worst that could arise.

R. v. H. (R.) (1992), 77 C.C.C. (3d) 198 (Ont. C.A.) — A young offender convicted of an offence under *Code* s. 85 (using a firearm in the commission of an indictable offence) is *not* liable to the minimum punishment of imprisonment for one year prescribed by the section. The sentencing provisions of *Code* s. 85 have been superseded by *Y.O.A.* s. 20.

R. v. B. (M.) (1988), 36 C.C.C. (3d) 573 (Ont. C.A.) — A disposition disproportionate to the offence cannot be imposed merely because of the young offender's psychiatric problems.

R. v. O. (1986), 27 C.C.C. (3d) 376 (Ont. C.A.) — The protection of society subsumes general and specific deterrence. General deterrence has diminished importance in the case of a young offender.

R. v. F. (J.) (1985), 22 C.C.C. (3d) 555 (Ont. C.A.) — The protection of society must be reconciled with the needs of young persons and is not a principle which must inevitably be reflected in a severe disposition. Unless the seriousness of the offence militates otherwise, it is best effected by a disposition which emphasizes individual deterrence and rehabilitation.

R. v. I. (R.) (1985), 17 C.C.C. (3d) 523 (Ont. C.A.) — The principles of adult sentencing that there is a close correlation between the seriousness of the offence and the length of sentence, and that the first custodial term should be short, may or may not be appropriate in the case of young offenders. The Act represents a shift to more accountability by young offenders for their offences. A maximum custodial disposition should be imposed only for the most serious offences.

Community Service: S. 20(1)(g)

R. v. P. (K.R.) (1987), 40 C.C.C. (3d) 376 (B.C. C.A.) — It is *not* appropriate that a community service order be contained in a probation order as a term of probation.

Probation: S. 20(1)(j) [See also s. 23]

R. v. G. (W.) (1985), 23 C.C.C. (3d) 93 (B.C. C.A.) — *See also*: *R. v. D.* (1985), 18 C.C.C. (3d) 476 (N.S. C.A.) — There is no power under s. 20 to suspend sentence. The proper disposition is to place the young person on probation for a specified period.

Custodial Term: S. 20(1)(k)

R. v. W. (C.W.) (1986), 51 C.R. (3d) 89, 25 C.C.C. (3d) 355 (Alta. C.A.) — It is an error in principle to reduce the length of the custodial term to be imposed because of the prospect of transfer to an adult facility.

R. v. S. (R.C.) (1986), 27 C.C.C. (3d) 239 (N.B. C.A.) — *See also*: *R. v. K. (G.)* (1985), 21 C.C.C. (3d) 558 (Alta. C.A.); additional reasons at (1985), 21 C.C.C. (3d) 558 at 561 (C.A.) — Custody is to be ordered only after all else fails. The necessity for a custodial term is to be determined by balancing the gravity of the Act with the needs of the young person, and the traditional principles of sentencing are not to be considered.

R. v. C. (M.J.) (1985), 22 C.C.C. (3d) 95 (Sask. C.A.) — A custodial term may be increased on appeal to ensure the young offender's supervised treatment and training.

Maximum Custodial Term: S. 20(1)(k)

R. v. L. (A.) (1986), 26 C.C.C. (3d) 467 (B.C. C.A.) — The maximum custodial term is not reserved for the worst offence committed by the worst offender.

R. v. T. (K.D.) (1986), 28 C.C.C. (3d) 110 (N.S. C.A.) — *See also*: *R. v. H. (R.)* (1992), 77 C.C.C. (3d) 198 (Ont. C.A.) — The sentencing provisions of the *Criminal Code* have been superseded by s. 20 of the Act. Where the imposition of a minimum sentence prescribed under the *Code* would result in a young offender receiving a custodial sentence longer than three years, the *Code* provision does not apply.

When Disposition Takes Effect: S. 20(2)

R. v. R. (D.J.) (1992), 76 C.C.C. (3d) 88 (Man. C.A.) — Section 20(2) *Y.O.A.* authorizes the imposition of consecutive dispositions.

R. v. P. (J.R.) (1987), 36 C.C.C. (3d) 134 (N.S. C.A.) — The commencement of a custodial term may not be postponed until such time as the young offender becomes eligible for review, as a way of requiring a prolonged period of good behaviour on probation in order to avoid imprisonment.

R. v. T. (K.D.) (1986), 28 C.C.C. (3d) 110 (N.S. C.A.) — The commencement of a custodial disposition can be postponed to permit the young offender to serve it during the summer school break.

V. (T.) v. Ontario (A.G.) (1990), 51 C.C.C. (3d) 155 (Ont. H.C.) — Section 20(2) confers on the youth court a statutory discretion to impose consecutive dispositions, and the court may order that a custodial disposition imposed under the Act should take effect on the expiration of a term of imprisonment imposed in adult court.

R. v. G. (W.J.) (1986), 29 C.C.C. (3d) 430 (P.E.I. C.A.) — Section 20(2) does not empower a youth court to impose consecutive dispositions, which are specifically excluded by s. 20(8).

Duration: S. 20(3)

R. v. C. (C.) (1991), 60 C.C.C. (3d) 418 (Ont. C.A.) — Only offences for which a three-year custodial disposition may be made are exempted from the two-year maximum in s. 20(3). In all other cases the combined length of dispositions made at the same time with respect to the same offence cannot exceed two years.

Combined Duration: Ss. 20(4), (4.1)

R. v. C. (W.J.) (1988), 42 C.C.C. (3d) 253 (N.S. C.A.) — The court has no power to direct that a disposition be consecutive to a disposition previously imposed by another judge, unless the young offender was under the prior disposition at the time of commission of the offence for which he is subsequently sentenced.

R. v. H. (J.) (1992), 71 C.C.C. (3d) 309 (Ont. C.A.) — All custodial parts of consecutive dispositions are to be served before non-custodial dispositions become effective. A probation order takes effect only upon the expiration of the continuous, combined custody. In determining whether the combined duration of dispositions exceeds the three year maximum, the probationary period must be included in the calculation of the duration.

R. v. B. (J.) (1985), 24 C.C.C. (3d) 142 (Ont. C.A.) — Section 20(4) limits the total duration of dispositions to which a young offender can be subject to three years, taking into account the duration of dispositions to which he is then subject.

Consecutive Dispositions: Ss. 20(2), (4)

R. v. R. (D.J.) (1992), 76 C.C.C. (3d) 88 (Man. C.A.) — Section 20(2) *Y.O.A.* authorizes the imposition of consecutive dispositions.

R. v. B. (D.W.) (1991), 2 O.R. (3d) 790, 64 C.C.C. (3d) 164 (C.A.) — A youth court judge is entitled to make a disposition consecutive to a disposition imposed earlier by another youth court judge, even though the subsequent offence was not committed during the term of the earlier disposition.

R. v. B. (D.W.) (1991), 2 O.R. (3d) 790, 64 C.C.C. (3d) 164 (C.A.) — This subsection applies where the young offender commits an offence after the commencement of, but before the completion of, dispositions made in respect of previous offences.

Maximum Punishment Applicable to Adult: S. 20(7)

R. v. G.(T.T.) (1997), 113 C.C.C. (3d) 254 (N.S. C.A.) — The maximum penalty for first degree murder in the *young offenders' system* is five years less one day comprised of

i.   a maximum of three years in open or secure *custody* in a young offender facility; and thereafter,

ii.   two years less one day of *community supervision* which may be converted to custody in certain circumstances.

In the ordinary court system, a person under eighteen years of age convicted of murder will be sentenced to imprisonment for life without eligibility for parole for such period between five and ten years as is specified by the trial judge.

R. v. B. (S.A.) (1990), 56 C.C.C. (3d) 317 (N.S. C.A.) — The effect of s. 20(7) is that a young person should not receive a custodial disposition longer than the maximum punishment applicable to an adult.

R. v. B. (D.W.) (1991), 2 O.R. (3d) 790, 64 C.C.C. (3d) 164 (C.A.) — The phrase "maximum punishment" refers to the maximum sentence to which an adult would be exposed upon conviction of the offence.

Breach of Probation: S. 20(8)

R. v. C. (J.) (1986), 29 C.C.C. (3d) 382 (Ont. C.A.) — Section 20(8) of the Act renders *Code* s. 740 inapplicable to young persons, nor can the Crown prosecute a young offender under *Code* s. 127 for breaching a probation order imposed when he was an adult.

20.1 (1) Mandatory prohibition order — Notwithstanding subsection 20(1), where a young person is found guilty of an offence referred to in any of paragraphs 109(1)(a) to (d) of the *Criminal Code*, the youth court shall, in addition to making any disposition referred to in subjection 20(1), make an order prohibiting the young person from possessing any firearm, cross-bow, prohibited weapon, restricted weapon, prohibited device, ammunition, prohibited ammunition and explosive substance during the period specified in the order as determined in accordance with subsection (2).

(2) Duration of prohibition order — An order made under subsection (1) begins on the day on which the order is made and ends not earlier than two years after the young person's release from custody after being found guilty of the offence or, if the young person is not then in custody or subject to custody, after the time the young person is found guilty of or discharged from the offence.

(3) Discretionary prohibition order — Notwithstanding subsection 20(1), where a young person is found guilty of an offence referred to in paragraph 110(1)(a) or (b) of the *Criminal Code*, the youth court shall, in addition to making any disposition referred to in subsection 20(1), consider whether it is desirable, in the interests of the safety of the person or of any other person, to make an order prohibiting the person from possessing any firearm, cross-bow, prohibited weapon, restricted weapon, prohibited device, ammunition, prohibited ammunition or explosive substance, or all such things, and where the court decides that it is so desirable, the court shall so order.

(4) Duration of prohibition order — An order made under subsection (3) against a young person begins on the day on which the order is made and ends not later than two years after the young person's release from custody or, if the young person is not then in custody or subject to custody, after the time the young person is found guilty of or discharged from the offence.

(5) Definition of "release from imprisonment" — In paragraph (2)(a) and subsection (4), "release from custody" means a release from custody in accordance with this Act, other than a release from custody under subsection 35(1), and includes the commencement of conditional supervision or probation.

(6) Reasons for the prohibition order — Where a youth court makes an order under this section, it shall state its reasons for making the order in the record of the case and shall

    (a) provide or cause to be provided a copy of the order, and

    (b) on request, provide or cause to be provided a transcript or copy of the reasons for making the order

to the young person against whom the order was made, the young person's counsel and parents and the provincial director.

(7) Reasons — Where the youth court does not make an order under subsection (3), or where the youth court does make such an order but does not prohibit the possession of everything referred to in that subsection, the youth court shall include in the record a statement of the youth court's reasons.

(8) Application of Criminal Code — Sections 113 to 117 of the *Criminal Code* apply in respect of any order made under this section.

(9) Report — Before making any order referred to in section 113 of the *Criminal Code* in respect of a young person, the youth court may require the provincial director to cause to be prepared, and to submit to the youth court, a report on the young person.

1995, c. 39, s. 179.

21. (1) Where a fine or other payment is ordered — The youth court shall, in imposing a fine on a young person under paragraph 20(1)(*b*) or in making an order against a young person under paragraph 20(1)(*c*) or (*e*), have regard to the present and future means of the young person to pay.

(2) Fine option program — A young person against whom a fine is imposed under paragraph 20(1)(*b*) may discharge the fine in whole or in part by earning credits for work performed in a program established for that purpose

(a) by the Lieutenant Governor in Council of the province in which the fine was imposed; or

(b) by the Lieutenant Governor in Council of the province in which the young person resides, where an appropriate agreement is in effect between the government of that province and the government of the province in which the fine was imposed.

(3) Rates, crediting and other matters — A program referred to in subsection (2) shall determine the rate at which credits are earned and may provide for the manner of crediting any amounts earned against the fine and any other matters necessary for or incidental to carrying out the program.

(4) Representations respecting orders under paras. 20(1)(c) to (f) — In considering whether to make an order under paragraphs (20)(1)(*c*) to (*f*), the youth court may consider any representations made by the person who would be compensated or to whom restitution or payment would be made.

(5) Notice of orders under paras. 20(1)(c) to (f) — Where the youth court makes an order under paragraphs 20(1)(*c*) to (*f*), it shall cause notice of the terms of the order to be given to the person who is to be compensated or to whom restitution or payment is to be made.

(6) Consent of person to be compensated — No order can be made under paragraph 20(1)(*f*) unless the youth court has secured the consent of the person to be compensated.

(7) Order for compensation or community service — No order may be made under paragraph 20(1)(*f*) or (*g*) unless the youth court

(a) is satisfied that the young person against whom the order is made is a suitable candidate for such an order; and

(b) is satisfied that the order does not interfere with the normal hours of work or education of the young person.

(8) Duration of order for service — No order may be made under paragraph 20(1)(*f*) or (*g*) to perform personal or community services unless those services can be completed in two hundred and forty hours or less and within twelve months of the date of the order.

(9) Community service order — No order may be made under paragraph 20(1)(*g*) unless

(a) the community service to be performed is part of a program that is approved by the provincial director; or

(b) the youth court is satisfied that the person or organization for whom the community service is to be performed has agreed to its performance.

(10) Application for further time to complete disposition — A youth court may, on application by or on behalf of the young person in respect of whom a disposition has been made under paragraphs 20(1)(*b*) to (*g*), allow further time for the completion of the disposition subject to any regulations made pursuant to paragraph 67(*b*) and to any rules made by the youth court pursuant to subsection 68(1).

1980–81–82–83, c. 110, s. 21; R.S. 1985, c. 24 (2d Supp.), s. 15.

22. [Repealed 1995, c. 19, s. 14].

23. (1) Conditions that must appear in probation orders — The following conditions shall be included in a probation order made under paragraph 20(1)(*j*):

(a) that the young person bound by the probation order shall keep the peace and be of good behaviour; and

(b) that the young person appear before the youth court when required by the court to do so.

(c) [Repealed R.S. 1985, c. 24 (2d Supp.), s. 16(1).]

(2) Conditions that may appear in probation orders — A probation order made under paragraph 20(1)(*j*) may include such of the following conditions as the youth court considers appropriate in the circumstances of the case:

(a) that the young person bound by the probation order report to and be under the supervision of the provincial director or a person designated by the youth court;

(a.1) that the young person notify the clerk of the youth court, the provincial director or the youth worker assigned to his case of any change of address or any change in his place of employment, education or training;

(b) that the young person remain within the territorial jurisdiction of one or more courts named in the order;

(c) that the young person make reasonable efforts to obtain and maintain suitable employment;

(d) that the young person attend school or such other place of learning, training or recreation as is appropriate, if the court is satisfied that a suitable program is available for the young person at that place;

(e) that the young person reside with a parent, or such other adult as the court considers appropriate, who is willing to provide for the care and maintenance of the young person;

(f) that the young person reside in such place as the provincial director may specify; and

(g) that the young person comply with such other reasonable conditions set out in the order as the court considers desirable, including conditions for securing the good conduct of the young person and for preventing the commission by the young person of other offences.

(3) Communication of probation order to young person and parent — Where the youth court makes a probation order under paragraph 20(1)(j), it shall

(a) cause the order to be read by or to the young person bound by the probation order;

(b) explain or cause to be explained to the young person the purpose and effect of the order and ascertain that the young person understands it; and

(c) cause a copy of the order to be given to the young person and to a parent of the young person, if the parent is in attendance at the proceedings against the young person.

(4) Copy of probation order to parent — Where the youth court makes a probation order under paragraph 20(1)(j), it may cause a copy of the report to be given to a parent of the young person not in attendance at the proceedings against the young person if the parent is, in the opinion of the court, taking an active interest in the proceedings.

(5) Endorsement of order by young person — After a probation order has been read by or to a young person and explained to him pursuant to subsection (3), the young person shall endorse the order acknowledging that he has received a copy of the order and acknowledging the fact that it has been explained to him.

(6) Validity of probate order — The failure of a young person to endorse a probation order pursuant to subsection (5) does not affect the validity of the order.

(7) Commencement of probation order — A probation order made under paragraph 20(1)(j) comes into force

(a) on the date on which the order is made; or

(b) where the young person in respect of whom the order is made is committed to continuous custody, on the expiration of the period of custody.

(8) Notice to appear — A young person may be given notice to appear before the youth court pursuant to paragraph (1)(b) orally or in writing.

(9) Warrant to arrest young person — If a young person to whom a notice is given in writing to appear before the youth court pursuant to paragraph (1)(b) does not appear at the time and place named in the notice and it is proved that a copy of the notice was served on him, a youth court may issue a warrant to compel the appearance of the young person.

1980–81–82–83, c. 110, s. 23; R.S. 1985, c. 24 (2d Supp.), s. 16; c. 1 (4th Supp.), s. 39.

Case Law

Conditions: Ss. 23(1), (2)

R. v. G. (W.) (1985), 23 C.C.C. (3d) 93 (B.C. C.A.) — Where a period of probation is imposed, the court has no power to order the young person to reside at a particular facility, rather the court may require that the young person reside in such place as the provincial director or his designate may specify.

Commencement: S. 23(7)(a)

R. v. L. (T.S.) (1988), 46 C.C.C. (3d) 126 (N.S. C.A.) — There is no power to direct that multiple probation orders imposed upon a young offender run one after the other.

Communication of Probation Orders

R. v. M. (L.A.) (1994), 92 C.C.C. (3d) 562 (Ont. C.A.) — "Proceedings " in s. 23(3)(c) is not limited to the actual proceedings before the court clerk when completing the probation order. It extends to the proceedings as a whole against the young offender.

R. v. M. (L.A.) (1994), 92 C.C.C. (3d) 562 (Ont. C.A.) — To comply with s. 23 as a whole, the youth court must determine, prior to delegating its function to a court official, whether a parent is entitled to receive a copy of the probation order

i.   as a parent in attendance at the disposition proceedings; or,

ii.   as a parent taking an interest in the proceedings under s. 23(4), though not in attendance.

In delegating its duties, the court must properly inform the clerk of the requirement, whether mandatory or discretionary, to inform a parent under s. 23(3) and (4).

R. v. M. (L.A.) (1994), 92 C.C.C. (3d) 562 (Ont. C.A.) — The duties imposed by s. 23(3)(c) may be delegated to the clerk of the court.

R. v. M. (L.A.) (1994), 92 C.C.C. (3d) 562 (Ont. C.A.) — There is no curative provision in s. 23 for failure to comply with the mandatory duty of s. 23(3).

24. (1) Conditions for custody — The youth court shall not commit a young person to custody under paragraph 20(1)(*k*) unless the court considers a committal to custody to be necessary for the protection of society having regard to the seriousness of the offence and the circumstances in which it was committed and having regard to the needs and circumstances of the young person.

(1.1) Factors — In making a determination under subsection (1), the youth court shall take the following into account:

(a) that an order of custody shall not be used as a substitute for appropriate child protection, health and other social measures;

(b) that a young person who commits an offence that does not involve serious personal injury should be held accountable to the victim and to society through non-custodial dispositions whenever appropriate; and

(c) that custody shall only be imposed when all available alternatives to custody that are reasonable in the circumstances have been considered.

(2) Pre-disposition report — Subject to subsection (3), before making an order of committal to custody, the youth court shall consider a pre-disposition report.

(3) Report dispensed with — The youth court may, with the consent of the prosecutor and the young person or his counsel, dispense with the pre-disposition report required under subsection (2) if the youth court is satisfied, having regard to the circumstances, that the report is unnecessary or that it would not be in the best interests of the young person to require one.

(4) Reasons — Where the youth court makes a disposition in respect of a young person under paragraph 20(1)(k), the youth court shall state the reasons why any other disposition or dispositions under subsection 20(1), without the disposition under paragraph 20(1)(k), would not have been adequate.

R.S. 1985, c. 24 (2d Supp.), s. 17; 1995, c. 19, s. 15.

Case Law
General Principles

R. v. S. (R.C.) (1986), 27 C.C.C. (3d) 239 (N.B. C.A.) — *See also*: *R. v. K. (G.)* (1985), 21 C.C.C. (3d) 558 (Alta. C.A.); additional reasons at (1985), 21 C.C.C. (3d) 561 (Alta. C.A.) — Custody is to be ordered only after all else fails. The necessity for a custodial term is to be determined by balancing the gravity of the act with the needs of the young person. The traditional principles of sentencing are not to be considered.

24.1 (1) Definitions — In this section and sections 24.2, 24.3, 28 and 29, "open custody" means custody in

(a) a community residential centre, group home, child care institution, or forest or wilderness camp, or

(b) any other like place or facility

designated by the Lieutenant Governor in Council of a province or his delegate as a place of open custody for the purposes of this Act, and includes a place or facility within a class of such places or facilities so designated;

"secure custody" means custody in a place or facility designated by the Lieutenant Governor in Council of a province for the secure containment or restraint of young persons, and includes a place or facility within a class of such places or facilities so designated.

(2) **Youth court to specify type of custody** — Subject to subsection (3), where the youth court commits a young person to custody under paragraph 20(1)(k) or (k.1) or makes an order under subsection 26.1(1) or paragraph 26.6(2)(b), it shall specify in the order whether the custody is to be open custody or secure custody.

(3) **Provincial director to specify level of custody** — In a province in which the Lieutenant Governor in Council has designated the provincial director to determine the level of custody, the provincial director shall, where a young person is committed to custody under paragraph 20(1)(k) or (k.1) or an order is made under subsection 26.1(1) or paragraph 26.6(2)(b), specify whether the young person shall be placed in open custody or secure custody.

(4) **Factors** — In deciding whether a young person shall be placed in open custody or secure custody, the youth court or the provincial director shall take into account the following factors:

(a) that a young person should be placed in a level of custody involving the least degree of containment and restraint, having regard to

(i) the seriousness of the offence in respect of which the young person was committed to custody and the circumstances in which that offence was committed,

(ii) the needs and circumstances of the young person, including proximity to family, school, employment and support services,

(iii) the safety of other young persons in custody, and

(iv) the interests of society;

(b) that the level of custody should allow for the best possible match of programs to the young person's needs and behaviour, having regard to the findings of any assessment in respect of the young person;

(c) the likelihood of escape if the young person is placed in open custody; and

(d) the recommendations, if any, of the youth court or the provincial director, as the case may be.

1980–81–82–83, c. 110, s. 24; R.S. 1985, c. 24 (2d Supp.), s. 17; 1992, c. 11, s. 4; 1995, c. 19, s. 16.

Case Law

Secure Custody: S. 24.1(1)

R. v. M. (F.H.) (1984), 14 C.C.C. (3d) 227 (Man. Q.B.) — Where P fails to elect the manner of proceeding on a hybrid offence, it is deemed to have elected to proceed summarily. The maximum punishment which can be imposed is six months' custody.

R. v. H. (S.R.) (1990), 56 C.C.C. (3d) 46 (Ont. C.A.) — In deciding whether a young person should be committed to open or secure custody, the court is required to consider a number of factors, including whether secure custody is necessary to prevent escape, further misconduct or violence; the effect upon rehabilitation of the young person; and general and specific deterrence and the expression of society's abhorrence of certain crimes.

C. (D.J.) v. R. (1985), 47 C.R. (3d) 270, 21 C.C.C. (3d) 246 (P.E.I. C.A.) — Where P elects to proceed summarily on a hybrid offence and the young person is convicted, the conviction is for a summary conviction offence. The maximum punishment for which an adult would be liable is six months' imprisonment. The young person cannot be committed to secure custody.

24.2 (1) Place of custody — Subject to this section and sections 24.3 and 24.5, a young person who is committed to custody shall be placed in open custody or secure custody, as specified pursuant to subsection 24.1(2) or (3), at such place or facility as the provincial director may specify.

(2) Warrant of committal — Where a young person is committed to custody, the youth court shall issue or cause to be issued a warrant of committal.

(3) Exception — A young person who is committed to custody may, in the course of being transferred from custody to the court or from the court to custody, be held under the supervision and control of a peace officer or in such place of temporary detention referred to in subsection 7(1) as the provincial director may specify.

(4) Young person to be held separate from adults — Subject to this section and section 24.5, a young person who is committed to custody shall be held separate and apart from any adult who is detained or held in custody.

(5) Subsection 7(2) applies — Subsection 7(2) applies, with such modifications as the circumstances require, in respect of a person held in a place of temporary detention pursuant to subsection (3).

(6) Transfer — A young person who is committed to custody may, during the period of custody, be transferred by the provincial director from one place or facility of open custody to another or from one place or facility of secure custody to another.

(7) Transfer to open custody — youth court — No young person who is committed to secure custody pursuant to subsection 24.1(2) may be transferred to a place or facility of open custody except in accordance with sections 28 to 31.

(8) No transfer to secure custody — youth court — Subject to subsection (9), no young person who is committed to open custody pursuant to subsection 24.1(2) may be transferred to a place or facility of secure custody.

(9) Exception — transfer to secure custody — youth court — Where a young person is placed in open custody pursuant to subsection 24.1(2), the provincial director may transfer the young person from a place or facility of open custody to a place or facility of secure custody for a period not exceeding fifteen days if

(a) the young person escapes or attempts to escape lawful custody; or

(b) the transfer is, in the opinion of the provincial director, necessary for the safety of the young person or the safety of others in the place or facility of open custody.

(10) Transfer to open custody — provincial director — The provincial director may transfer a young person from a place or facility of secure custody to a place or facility of open custody when the provincial director is satisfied that the needs of the young person and the interests of society would be better served thereby.

(11) **Transfer to secure custody — provincial director** — The provincial director may transfer a young person from a place or facility of open custody to a place or facility of secure custody when the provincial director is satisfied that the needs of the young person and the interests of society would be better served thereby

(a) having considered the factors set out in subsection 24.1(4); and

(b) having determined that there has been a material change in circumstances since the young person was placed in open custody.

(12) **Notice** — The provincial director shall cause a notice in writing of the decision to transfer a young person under subsection (11) to be given to the young person and the young person's parents and set out in that notice the reasons for the transfer.

(13) **Where application for review is made** — Where an application for review under section 28.1 of a transfer under subsection (11) is made to a youth court,

(a) the provincial director shall cause such notice as may be directed by rules of court applicable to the youth court or, in the absence of such direction, at least five clear days notice of the review to be given in writing to the young person and the young person's parents; and

(b) the youth court shall forthwith, after the notice required under paragraph (a) is given, review the transfer.

(14) **Interim custody** — Where an application for review under section 28.1 of a transfer under subsection (11) is made to a youth court, the young person shall remain in a place or facility of secure custody until the review is heard by the youth court unless the provincial director directs otherwise.

1980–81–82–83, c. 110, s. 24; R.S. 1985, c. 24 (2d Supp.), s. 17; 1995, c. 19, s. 17.

24.3 (1) Consecutive dispositions of custody — Where a young person is committed to open custody and secure custody pursuant to subsection 24.1(2), any portions of which dispositions are to be served consecutively, the disposition of secure custody shall be served first without regard to the order in which the dispositions were imposed.

(2) **Concurrent dispositions of custody** — Where a young person is committed to open custody and secure custody pursuant to subsection 24.1(2), any portions of which dispositions are to be served concurrently, the concurrent portions of the dispositions shall be served in secure custody.

1980–81–82–83, c. 110, s. 24; R.S. 1985, c. 24 (2d Supp.), s. 17; 1995, c. 19, s. 18.

24.4 (1) Committal to custody deemed continuous — A young person who is committed to custody under paragraph 20(1)(k) shall be deemed to be committed to continuous custody unless the youth court specifies otherwise.

(2) **Availability of place of intermittent custody** — Before making an order of committal to intermittent custody under paragraph 20(1)(k), the youth court shall require the prosecutor to make available to the court for its consideration a report of the provincial director as to the availability of a place of custody in which an order of intermittent custody can be enforced and, where the report discloses that no such place of custody is available, the court shall not make the order.

1980–81–82–83, c. 110, s. 24; R.S. 1985, c. 24 (2d Supp.), s. 17.

24.5 (1) **Transfer to adult facility** — Where a young person is committed to custody under paragraph 20(1)(k) or (k.1) the youth court may, on application of the provincial director made at any time after the young person attains the age of eighteen years, after affording the young person an opportunity to be heard, authorize the provincial director to direct that the young person serve the disposition or the remaining portion thereof in a provincial correctional facility for adults, if the court considers it to be in the best interests of the young person or in the public interest, but in that event, the provisions of this Act shall continue to apply in respect of that person.

(2) **Where disposition and sentence concurrent** — Where a young person is committed to custody under paragraph 20(1)(k) or (k.1) and is concurrently under sentence of imprisonment imposed in ordinary court, the young person may, in the discretion of the provincial director, serve the disposition and sentence, or any portion thereof, in a place of custody for young persons, in a provincial correctional facility for adults or, where the unexpired portion of the sentence is two years or more, in a penitentiary.

1980–81–82–83, c. 110, s. 24; R.S. 1985, c. 24 (2nd Supp.), s. 17; 1992, c. 11, s. 5.

25. (1) **Transfer of disposition** — Where a disposition has been made under paragraphs 20(1)(b) to (g) or paragraph 20(1)(j) or (l) in respect of a young person and the young person or a parent with whom the young person resides is or becomes a resident of a territorial division outside the jurisdiction of the youth court that made the disposition, whether in the same or in another province, a youth court judge in the territorial division in which the disposition was made may, on the application of the Attorney General or an agent of the Attorney General or on the application of the young person or the young person's parent with the consent of the Attorney General or an agent of the Attorney General, transfer the disposition and such portion of the record of the case as is appropriate to a youth court in the other territorial division, and all subsequent proceedings relating to the case shall thereafter be carried out and enforced by that court.

(2) **No transfer outside province before appeal completed** — No disposition may be transferred from one province to another under this section until the time for an appeal against the disposition or the finding on which the disposition was based has expired or until all proceedings in respect of any such appeal have been completed.

(3) **Transfer to a province where person is adult** — Where an application is made under subsection (1) to transfer the disposition of a young person to a province in which the young person is an adult, a youth court judge may, with the consent of the Attorney General, transfer the disposition and the record of the case to the youth court in the province to which the transfer is sought, and the youth court to which the case is transferred shall have full jurisdiction in respect of the disposition as if that court had made the disposition, and the person shall be further dealt with in accordance with this Act.

1980–81–82–83, c. 110, s. 25; R.S. 1985, c. 24 (2d Supp.), s. 18; 1995, c. 19, s. 19.

25.1 (1) **Interprovincial arrangements for probation or custody** — Where a disposition has been made under paragraphs 20(1)(j) to (k.1) in respect of a young person, the disposition in one province may be dealt with in any other province pursuant to any agreement that may have been made between those provinces.

(2) **Youth court retains jurisdiction** — Subject to subsection (3), where a disposition made in respect of a young person is dealt with pursuant to this section in a prov-

ince other than that in which the disposition was made, the youth court of the province in which the disposition was made shall, for all purposes of this Act, retain exclusive jurisdiction over the young person as if the disposition were dealt with within that province, and any warrant or process issued in respect of the young person may be executed or served in any place in Canada outside the province where the disposition was made as if it were executed or served in that province.

(3) Waiver of jurisdiction — Where a disposition made in respect of a young person is dealt with pursuant to this section in a province other than that in which the disposition was made, the youth court of the province in which the disposition was made may, with the consent in writing of the Attorney General of that province or his delegate and the young person, waive its jurisdiction, for the purpose of any proceeding under this Act, to the youth court of the province in which the disposition is dealt with, in which case the youth court in the province in which the disposition is so dealt with shall have full jurisdiction in respect of the disposition as if that court had made the disposition.

R.S. 1985, c. 24 (2d Supp.), s. 19; 1992, c. 11, s. 6; 1995, c. 19, s. 20.

26. Failure to comply with disposition — A person who is subject to a disposition made under paragraphs 20(1)(*b*) to (*g*) or paragraph 20(1)(*j*) or (*l*) and who wilfully fails or refuses to comply with that order is guilty of an offence punishable on summary conviction.

R.S. 1985, c. 24 (2d Supp.), s. 19.

26.1 (1) Continuation of custody — Where a young person is held in custody pursuant to a disposition made under paragraph 20(1)(*k*.1) and an application is made to the youth court by the Attorney General, or the Attorney General's agent, within a reasonable time prior to the expiration of the period of custody, the provincial director of the province in which the young person is held in custody shall cause the young person to be brought before the youth court and the youth court may, after affording both parties and the parents of the young person an opportunity to be heard and if it is satisfied that there are reasonable grounds to believe that the young person is likely to commit an offence causing the death of or serious harm to another person prior to the expiration of the disposition the young person is then serving, order that the young person remain in custody for a period not exceeding the remainder of the disposition.

(1.1) Idem — Where the hearing for an application under subsection (1) cannot be completed before the expiration of the period of custody, the court may order that the young person remain in custody pending the determination of the application if the court is satisfied that the application was made in a reasonable time, having regard to all the circumstances, and that there are compelling reasons for keeping the young person in custody.

(2) Factors — For the purpose of determining an application under subsection (1), the youth court shall take into consideration any factor that is relevant to the case of the young person including, without limiting the generality of the foregoing,

  (a) evidence of a pattern of persistent violent behaviour and, in particular,

    (i) the number of offences committed by the young person that caused physical or psychological harm to any other person,

    (ii) the young person's difficulties in controlling violent impulses to the point of endangering the safety of any other person,

    (iii) the use of weapons in the commission of any offence,

1577

(iv) explicit threats of violence,

(v) behaviour of a brutal nature associated with the commission of any offence, and

(vi) a substantial degree of indifference on the part of the young person as to the reasonably foreseeable consequences, to other persons, of the young person's behaviour;

(b) psychiatric or psychological evidence that a physical or mental illness or disorder of the young person is of such a nature that the young person is likely to commit, prior to the expiration of the disposition the young person is then serving, an offence causing the death of or serious harm to another person;

(c) reliable information that satisfies the youth court that the young person is planning to commit, prior to the expiration of the disposition the young person is then serving, an offence causing the death of or serious harm to another person; and

(d) the availability of supervision programs in the community that would offer adequate protection to the public from the risk that the young person might otherwise present until the expiration of the disposition the young person is then serving.

(3) Youth court to order appearance of young person — Where a provincial director fails to cause a young person to be brought before the youth court under subsection (1), the youth court shall order the provincial director to cause the young person to be brought before the youth court forthwith.

(4) Report — For the purpose of determining an application under subsection (1), the youth court shall require the provincial director to cause to be prepared, and to submit to the youth court, a report setting out any information of which the provincial director is aware with respect to the factors referred to in subsection (2) that may be of assistance to the court.

(5) Written or oral report — A report referred to in subsection (4) shall be in writing unless it cannot reasonably be committed to writing, in which case it may, with leave of the youth court, be submitted orally in court.

(6) Provisions apply — Subsections 14(4) to (10) apply, with such modifications as the circumstances require, in respect of a report referred to in subsection (4).

(7) Notice of hearing — Where an application is made under subsection (1) in respect of a young person, the Attorney General or the Attorney General's agent shall cause such notice as may be directed by rules of court applicable to the youth court or, in the absence of such direction, at least five clear days notice of the hearing to be given in writing to the young person and the young person's parents and the provincial director.

(8) Statement of right to counsel — Any notice given to a parent under subsection (7) shall include a statement that the young person has the right to be represented by counsel.

(9) Service of notice — A notice under subsection (7) may be served personally or may be sent by registered mail.

(10) Where notice not given — Where notice under subsection (7) is not given in accordance with this section, the youth court may

(a) adjourn the hearing and order that the notice be given in such manner and to such person as it directs; or

(b) dispense with the giving of the notice where, in the opinion of the youth court, having regard to the circumstances, the giving of the notice may be dispensed with.

(11) Reasons — Where a youth court makes an order under subsection (1), it shall state its reasons for the order in the record of the case and shall

(a) provide or cause to be provided a copy of the order, and

(b) on request, provide or cause to be provided a transcript or copy of the reasons for the order

to the young person in respect of whom the order was made, the counsel and parents of the young person, the Attorney General or the Attorney General's agent, the provincial director and the review board, if any has been established or designated.

(12) Review provisions apply — Subsections 16(9) to (11) apply, with such modifications as the circumstances require, in respect of an order made, or the refusal to make an order, under subsection (1).

(13) Where application denied — Where an application under subsection (1) is denied, the court may, with the consent of the young person, the Attorney General and the provincial director, proceed as though the young person had been brought before the court as required under subsection 26.2(1).

1992, c. 11, s. 7.

26.2 (1) Conditional supervision — The provincial director of the province in which a young person is held in custody pursuant to a disposition made under paragraph 20(1)(k.1) or, where applicable, an order made under subsection 26.1(1), shall cause the young person to be brought before the youth court at least one month prior to the expiration of the period of custody and the court shall, after affording the young person an opportunity to be heard, by order, set the conditions of the young person's conditional supervision.

(2) Conditions to be included in order — In setting conditions for the purposes of subsection (1), the youth court shall include in the order the following conditions, namely, that the young person

(a) keep the peace and be of good behaviour;

(b) appear before the youth court when required by the court to do so;

(c) report to the provincial director immediately on release, and thereafter be under the supervision of the provincial director or a person designated by the youth court;

(d) inform the provincial director immediately on being arrested or questioned by the police;

(e) report to the police, or any named individual, as instructed by the provincial director;

(f) advise the provincial director of the young person's address of residence on release and after release report immediately to the clerk of the youth court or the provincial director any change

    (i) in that address,

    (ii) in the young person's normal occupation, including employment, vocational or educational training and volunteer work,

    (iii) in the young person's family or financial situation, and

    (iv) that may reasonably be expected to affect the young person's ability to comply with the conditions of the order;

(g) not own, possess or have the control of any weapon, ammunition, prohibited ammunition, prohibited device or explosive substance, except as authorized by the order; and

(h) comply with such reasonable instructions as the provincial director considers necessary in respect of any condition of the conditional supervision in order to prevent a breach of that condition or to protect society.

(3) Order conditions — In setting conditions for the purposes of subsection (1), the youth court may include in the order the following conditions, namely, that the young person

    (a) on release, travel directly to the young person's place of residence, or to such other place as is noted in the order.

    (b) make reasonable efforts to obtain and maintain suitable employment;

    (c) attend school or such other place of learning, training or recreation as is appropriate, if the court is satisfied that a suitable program is available for the young person at such a place;

    (d) reside with a parent, or such other adult as the court considers appropriate, who is willing to provide for the care and maintenance of the young person;

    (e) reside in such place as the provincial director may specify;

    (f) remain within the territorial jurisdiction of one or more courts named in the order; and

    (g) comply with such other reasonable conditions set out in the order as the court considers desirable, including conditions for securing the good conduct of the young person and for preventing the commission by the young person of other offences.

(4) Temporary conditions — Where a provincial director is required under subsection (1) to cause a young person to be brought before the youth court but cannot do so for reasons beyond the young person's control, the provincial director shall so advise the youth court and the court shall, by order, set such temporary conditions for the young person's conditional supervision as are appropriate in the circumstances.

(5) Conditions to be set at first opportunity — Where an order is made under subsection (4), the provincial director shall bring the young person before the youth court as soon thereafter as the circumstances permit and the court shall then set the conditions of the young person's conditional supervision.

(6) Report — For the purpose of setting conditions under this section, the youth court shall require the provincial director to cause to be prepared, and to submit to the youth court, a report setting out any information that may be of assistance to the court.

(7) Provisions apply — Subsections 26.1(3) and (5) to (10) apply, with such modifications as the circumstances require, in respect of any proceedings held pursuant to subsection (1).

(8) Idem — Subsections 16(9) to (11) and 23(3) to (9) apply, with such modifications as the circumstances require, in respect of an order made under subsection (1).

1992, c. 11, s. 7; 1995, c. 39, s. 180.

26.3 Suspension of Conditional Supervision — Where the provincial director has reasonable grounds to believe that a young person has breached or is about to breach a condition of an order made under subsection 26.2(1), the provincial director may, in writing,

(a) suspend the conditional supervision; and

(b) order that the young person be remanded to such place of custody as the provincial director considers appropriate until a review is conducted under section 26.5 and, if applicable, section 26.6.

1992, c. 11, s. 7.

26.4 (1) Apprehension — Where the conditional supervision of a young person is suspended under section 26.3, the provincial director may issue a warrant in writing, authorizing the apprehension of the young person and, until the young person is apprehended, the young person is deemed not to be continuing to serve the disposition the young person is then serving.

(2) Warrants — A warrant issued under subsection (1) shall be executed by any peace officer to whom it is given at any place in Canada and has the same force and effect in all parts of Canada as if it had been originally issued or subsequently endorsed by a provincial court judge or other lawful authority having jurisdiction in the place where it is executed.

(3) Peace officer may arrest — Where a peace officer believes on reasonable grounds that a warrant issued under subsection (1) is in force in respect of a young person, the peace officer may arrest the young person without the warrant at any place in Canada.

(4) Requirement to bring before provincial director — Where a young person is arrested pursuant to subsection (3) and detained, the peace officer making the arrest shall cause the young person to be brought before the provincial director or a person designated by the provincial director

(a) where the provincial director or the designated person is available within a period of twenty-four hours after the young person is arrested, without unreasonable delay and in any event within that period; and

(b) where the provincial director or the designated person is not available within the period referred to in paragraph (a), as soon as possible.

(5) Release on remand in custody — Where a young person is brought, pursuant to subsection (4), before the provincial director or a person designated by the provincial director, the provincial director or the designated person,

(a) if not satisfied that there are reasonable grounds to believe that the young person is the young person in respect of whom the warrant referred to in subsection (1) was issued, shall release the young person; or

1581

(b) if satisfied that there are reasonable grounds to believe that the young person is the young person in respect of whom the warrant referred to in subsection (1) was issued, may remand the young person in custody to await execution of the warrant, but if no warrant for the young person's arrest is executed within a period of six days after the time the young person is remanded in such custody, the person in whose custody the young person then is shall release the young person.

1992, c. 11, s. 7.

26.5 Review by provincial director — Forthwith after the remand to custody of a young person whose conditional supervision has been suspended under section 26.3, or forthwith after being informed of the arrest of such a young person, the provincial director shall review the case and, within forty-eight hours, cancel the suspension of the conditional supervision or refer the case to the youth court for a review under section 26.6.

1992, c. 11, s. 7.

26.6 (1) Review by youth court — Where the case of a young person is referred to the youth court under section 26.5, the provincial director shall, as soon as is practicable, cause the young person to be brought before the youth court, and the youth court shall, after affording the young person an opportunity to be heard,

(a) if the court is not satisfied on reasonable grounds that the young person has breached or was about to breach a condition of the conditional supervision, cancel the suspension of the conditional supervision; or

(b) if the court is satisfied on reasonable grounds that the young person has breached or was about to breach a condition of the conditional supervision, review the decision of the provincial director to suspend the conditional supervision and make an order under subsection (2).

(2) Order — On completion of a review under subsection (1), the youth court shall order

(a) the cancellation of the suspension of the conditional supervision, and where the court does so, the court may vary the conditions of the conditional supervision or impose new conditions; or

(b) the continuation of the suspension of the conditional supervision for such period of time, not to exceed the remainder of the disposition the young person is then serving, as the court considers appropriate, and where the court does so, the court shall order that the young person remain in custody.

(3) Reasons — Where a youth court makes an order under subsection (2), it shall state its reasons for the order in the record of the case and shall

(a) provide or cause to be provided a copy of the order, and

(b) on request, provide or cause to be provided a transcript or copy of the reasons for the order

to the young person in respect of whom the order was made, the counsel and parents of the young person, the Attorney General or the Attorney General's agent, the provincial director and the review board, if any has been established or designated.

(4) Provisions apply — Subsections 26.1(3) and (5) to (10) and 26.2(6) apply, with such modifications as the circumstances require, in respect of a review under this section.

(5) Idem — Subsections 16(9) to (11) apply, with such modifications as the circumstances require, in respect of an order made under subsection (2).

1992, c. 11, s. 7.

Case Law: *R. v. M. (R.E.)* (1989), 46 C.C.C. (3d) 315 (B.C. S.C.) — An accused who fails to comply with a disposition of the Youth Court after he has become 18 is not a young person and should be proceeded against in adult court.

Appeals

27. (1) Appeals for indictable offences — An appeal lies under this Act in respect of an indictable offence or an offence that the Attorney General or his agent elects to proceed with as an indictable offence in accordance with Part XXI of the *Criminal Code*, which Part applies with such modifications as the circumstances require.

(1.1) Appeals for summary conviction offences — An appeal lies under this Act in respect of an offence punishable on summary conviction or an offence that the Attorney General or his agent elects to proceed with as an offence punishable on summary conviction in accordance with Part XXVII of the *Criminal Code*, which Part applies with such modifications as the circumstances require.

(1.2) Appeals where offences are tried jointly — An appeal involving one or more indictable offences and one or more summary conviction offences that are tried jointly or in respect of which dispositions are jointly made lies under this Act in accordance with Part XXI of the *Criminal Code*, which applies with such modifications as the circumstances require.

(2) Deemed election — For the purpose of appeals under this Act, where no election is made in respect of an offence that may be prosecuted by indictment or proceeded with by way of summary conviction, the Attorney General or his agent shall be deemed to have elected to proceed with the offence as an offence punishable on summary conviction.

(3) Where the youth court is a superior court — In any province where the youth court is a superior court, an appeal under subsection (1.1) shall be made to the court of appeal of the province.

(3.1) Nunavut — Despite subsection (3), if the Nunavut Court of Justice is acting as a youth court, an appeal under subsection (1.1) shall be made to a judge of the Court of Appeal of Nunavut, and an appeal of that judge's decision shall be made to the Court of Appeal of Nunavut in accordance with section 839 of the *Criminal Code*.

(4) Where the youth court is a county or district court — In any province where the youth court is a county or district court, an appeal under subsection (1.1) shall be made to the superior court of the province.

(5) Appeal to the Supreme Court of Canada — No appeal lies pursuant to subsection (1) from a judgment of the court of appeal in respect of a finding of guilt or an order dismissing an information to the Supreme Court of Canada unless leave to appeal is granted by the Supreme Court of Canada within twenty-one days after the judgment of the court of appeal is pronounced or within such extended time as the Supreme Court of Canada or a judge thereof may, for special reasons, allow.

(6) No appeal from disposition on review — No appeal lies from a disposition under sections 28 to 32.

1980–81–82–83, c. 110, s. 27; R.S. 1985, c. 24 (2d Supp.), s. 20; 1995, c. 19, s. 21; 1999, c. 3, s. 89.

Case Law

Election: S. 27(2)

R. v. B. (M.) (1997), 119 C.C.C. (3d) 570 (B.C. C.A.) — Where P fails to formally elect mode of procedure in open court in a case where the information was laid outside the summary conviction limitation period, *semble*, P has chosen to proceed by indictment. (per Macfarlane and Southin JJ.A.)

An endorsement on the information concerning mode of procedure is an acceptable means of indicating an election of mode of procedure. (per Goldie J.A.)

R. v. J. (H.W.) (1992), 71 C.C.C. (3d) 516 (B.C. C.A.) — In general, P should elect the mode of procedure prior to D's entry of a plea.

R. v. W. (W.W.) (1985), 20 C.C.C. (3d) 214 (Man. C.A.) — Where no election is made with respect to a dual procedure offence, it is to be treated as a summary conviction offence.

Rights of Appeal

R. v. B. (I.) (1994), 93 C.C.C. (3d) 121 (Ont. C.A.) — P may appeal an order of a youth court judge staying proceedings upon an information on account of abuse of process, notwithstanding that no evidence has been adduced. A youth court judge is "a trial court" within *Code* s. 676(1)(c).

Appeals From Dispositions

R. v. C. (T.L.) (1994), 32 C.R. (4th) 243, 92 C.C.C. (3d) 444 (S.C.C.) — Section 27(5) precludes appeals by D or P as of right in matters involving the trial of young persons for indictable offences under the *Y.O.A.* Leave to appeal is required.

R. v. H. (S.R.) (1990), 56 C.C.C. (3d) 46 (Ont. C.A.) — The incorporation of *Code* Part XXI provides for appeals from dispositions and includes all aspects of a disposition, both the length of the custodial period and whether it is to be open or secure.

Review of Dispositions

28. (1) Automatic review of disposition involving custody — Where a young person is committed to custody pursuant to a disposition made in respect of an offence for a period exceeding one year, the provincial director of the province in which the young person is held in custody shall cause the young person to be brought before the youth court forthwith at the end of one year from the date of the most recent disposition made in respect of the offence, and the youth court shall review the disposition.

(2) Idem — Where a young person is committed to custody pursuant to dispositions made in respect of more than one offence for a total period exceeding one year, the provincial director of the province in which the young person is held in custody shall cause the young person to be brought before the youth court forthwith at the end of one year from the date of the earliest disposition made, and the youth court shall review the dispositions.

(3) Optional review of disposition involving custody — Where a young person is committed to custody pursuant to a disposition made under subsection 20(1) in respect of an offence, the provincial director may, on the provincial director's own initiative, and shall, on the request of the young person, the young person's parent or the Attorney General or an agent of the Attorney General, on any of the grounds set out in subsection (4), cause the young person to be brought before a youth court

(a) where the committal to custody is for a period not exceeding one year, once at any time after the expiration of the greater of

(i) thirty days after the date of the disposition made under subsection 20(1) in respect of the offence, and

(ii) one third of the period of the disposition made under subsection 20(1) in respect of the offence, and

(b) where the committal to custody is for a period exceeding one year, at any time after six months after the date of the most recent disposition made in respect of the offence,

or, with leave of a youth court judge, at any other time, and where a youth court is satisfied that there are grounds for the review under subsection (4), the court shall review the disposition.

(4) **Grounds for review under subsection (3)** — A disposition made in respect of a young person may be reviewed under subsection (3)

(a) on the ground that the young person has made sufficient progress to justify a change in disposition;

(b) on the ground that the circumstances that led to the committal to custody have changed materially;

(c) on the ground that new services or programs are available that were not available at the time of the disposition;

(c.1) on the ground that the opportunities for rehabilitation are now greater in the community; or

(d) on such other grounds as the youth court considers appropriate.

(5) **No review where appeal pending** — No review of a disposition in respect of which an appeal has been taken shall be made under this section until all proceedings in respect of any such appeal have been completed.

(6) **Youth court may order appearance of young person for review** — Where a provincial director is required under subsections (1) to (3) to cause a young person to be brought before the youth court and fails to do so, the youth court may, on application made by the young person, his parent or the Attorney General or his agent, or on its own motion, order the provincial director to cause the young person to be brought before the youth court.

(7) **Progress report** — The youth court shall, before reviewing under this section a disposition made in respect of a young person, require the provincial director to cause to be prepared, and to submit to the youth court, a progress report on the performance of the young person since the disposition took effect.

(8) **Additional information in progress report** — A person preparing a progress report in respect of a young person may include in the report such information relating to the personal and family history and present environment of the young person as he considers advisable.

(9) **Written or oral report** — A progress report shall be in writing unless it cannot reasonably be committed to writing, in which case it may, with leave of the youth court, be submitted orally in court.

(10) **Provisions of subsections 14(4) to (10) to apply** — The provisions of subsections 14(4) to (10) apply, with such modifications as the circumstances require, in respect of progress reports.

(11) **Notice of review from provincial director** — Where a disposition made in respect of a young person is to be reviewed under subsection (1) or (2), the provincial director shall cause such notice as may be directed by rules of court applicable to the

youth court or, in the absence of such direction, at least five clear days notice of the review to be given in writing to the young person, his parents and the Attorney General or his agent.

(12) Notice of review from person requesting it — Where a review of a disposition made in respect of a young person is requested under subsection (3), the person requesting the review shall cause such notice as may be directed by rules of court applicable to the youth court or, in the absence of such direction, at least five clear days notice of the review to be given in writing to the young person, his parents and the Attorney General or his agent.

(13) Statement of right to counsel — Any notice given to a parent under subsection (11) or (12) shall include a statement that the young person whose disposition is to be reviewed has the right to be represented by counsel.

(14) Service of notice — A notice under subsection (11) or (12) may be served personally or may be sent by registered mail.

(15) Notice may be waived — Any of the persons entitled to notice under subsection (11) or (12) may waive the right to that notice.

(16) Where notice not given — Where notice under subsection (11) or (12) is not given in accordance with this section, the youth court may

(a) adjourn the proceedings and order that the notice be given in such manner and to such person as it directs; or

(b) dispense with the notice where, in the opinion of the court, having regard to the circumstances, notice may be dispensed with.

(17) Decision of the youth court after review — Where a youth court reviews under this section a disposition made in respect of a young person, it may, after affording the young person, his parent, the Attorney General or his agent and the provincial director an opportunity to be heard, having regard to the needs of the young person and the interests of society,

(a) confirm the disposition;

(b) where the young person is in secure custody pursuant to subsection 24.1(2), by order direct that the young person be placed in open custody; or

(c) release the young person from custody and place the young person

(i) on probation in accordance with section 23 for a period not exceeding the remainder of the period for which the young person was committed to custody, or

(ii) under conditional supervision in accordance with the procedure set out in section 26.2, with such modifications as the circumstances require, for a period not exceeding the remainder of the disposition the young person is then serving.

(18) [Repealed R.S. 1985, c. 24 (2d Supp.), s. 21.]

1980–81–82–83, c. 110, s. 28; R.S. 1985, c. 24 (2d Supp.), s. 21; 1992, c. 11, s. 8; 1995, c. 19, s. 22.

Case Law: *R. v. M. (J.J.)* (1993), 20 C.R. (4th) 295, 81 C.C.C. (3d) 487 (S.C.C.) — The annual review procedure of s. 28:

i.   provides an incentive to young offenders to perform well and to improve their behaviour significantly and expeditiously;

ii.   gives the court an opportunity to assess the offenders again and to ensure that the appropriate treatment or assistance has been provided; and,

iii.   introduces an aspect of review and flexibility into sentencing procedure to reward improvement and assess deterioration.

28.1 (1) Application to court for review of level of custody — Where a young person is placed in secure custody pursuant to subsection 24.1(3) or transferred to secure custody pursuant to subsection 24.2(11), the youth court shall review the level of custody if an application therefor is made by the young person or the young person's parent.

(2) Report — The youth court shall, before conducting a review under this section, require the provincial director to cause to be prepared and to submit to the youth court, a report setting out the reasons for the placement or transfer.

(3) Provisions apply — The provisions of subsections 14(4) to (10) apply, with such modifications as the circumstances require, in respect of the report referred to in subsection (2), and the provisions of subsections 28(11) to (16) apply, with such modifications as the circumstances require, to every review under this section.

(4) Decision of the youth court — Where the youth court conducts a review under this section, it may, after affording the young person, the young person's parents and the provincial director an opportunity to be heard, confirm or alter the level of custody, having regard to the needs of the young person and the interests of society.

(5) Decision is final — A decision of the youth court on a review under this section in respect of any particular placement or transfer is, subject to any subsequent order made pursuant to a review under section 28 or 29, final.

1995, c. 19, s. 23.

29. (1) Recommendation of provincial director for transfer to open custody or for probation — Where a young person is held in custody pursuant to a disposition, the provincial director may, if he is satisfied that the needs of the young person and the interests of society would be better served thereby, cause notice in writing to be given to the young person, his parent and the Attorney General or his agent that he recommends that the young person

     (a) be transferred from a place or facility of secure custody to a place or facility of open custody, where the young person is held in a place or facility of secure custody pursuant to subsection 24.1(2), or

     (b) be released from custody and placed on probation or, where the young person is in custody pursuant to a disposition made under paragraph 20(1)(k.1), placed under conditional supervision.

and give a copy of the notice to the youth court.

(1.1) Contents of notice — The provincial director shall include in any notice given under subsection (1) the reasons for the recommendation and

     (a) in the case of a recommendation that the young person be placed on probation, the conditions that the provincial director would recommend be attached to a probation order; and

     (b) in the case of a recommendation that the young person be placed under conditional supervision, the conditions that the provincial director would recommend be set pursuant to section 26.2.

(2) Application to court for review of recommendation — Where notice of a recommendation is made under subsection (1) with respect to a disposition made in respect of a young person, the youth court shall, if an application for review is made by the young person, his parent or the Attorney General or his agent within ten days after service of the notice, forthwith review the disposition.

(3) Subsections 28(5), (7) to (10) and (12) to (17) apply — Subject to subsection (4), subsections 28(5), (7) to (10) and (12) to (17) apply, with such modifications as the circumstances require, in respect of reviews made under this section and any notice required under subsection 28(12) shall be given to the provincial director.

(4) Where no application for review made under subsection (2) — A youth court that receives a notice under subsection (1) shall, if no application for a review is made under subsection (2),

> (a) in the case of a recommendation that a young person be transferred from a place or facility of secure custody to a place or facility of open custody, order that the young person be so transferred;

> (b) in the case of a recommendation that a young person be released from custody and placed on probation, release the young person and place him on probation in accordance with section 23;

> (b.1) in the case of a recommendation that a young person be released from custody and placed under conditional supervision, release the young person and place the young person under conditional supervision in accordance with section 26.2, having regard to the recommendations of the provincial director; or

> (c) where the court deems it advisable, make no direction under this subsection;

and for greater certainty, an order or direction under this subsection may be made without a hearing.

(4.1) Conditions in probation order — Where the youth court places a young person on probation pursuant to paragraph (4)(*b*), the court shall include in the probation order such conditions referred to in section 23 as it considers advisable, having regard to the recommendations of the provincial director.

(4.2) Notice where no direction made — Where a youth court, pursuant to paragraph (4)(*c*), makes no direction under subsection (4), it shall forthwith cause a notice of its decision to be given to the provincial director.

(4.3) Provincial director may request review — Where the provincial director is given a notice under subsection (4.2), he may request a review under this section.

(5) Where the provincial director requests a review — Where the provincial director requests a review pursuant to subsection (4.3),

> (a) the provincial director shall cause such notice as may be directed by rules of court applicable to the youth court or, in the absence of such direction, at least five clear days notice of the review to be given in writing to the young person, his parents and the Attorney General or his agent; and

> (b) the youth court shall forthwith, after the notice required under paragraph (*a*) is given, review the disposition.

(6) [Repealed R.S. 1985, c. 24 (2d Supp.), s. 22.]

1980–81–82–83, c. 110, s. 29; R.S. 1985, c. 24 (2d Supp.), s. 22; c. 1 (4th Supp.), s. 40; 1992, c. 11, s. 9; 1995, c. 19, s. 24.

30. (1) **Review board** — Where a review board is established or designated by a province for the purposes of this section, that board shall, subject to this section, carry out in that province the duties and functions of a youth court under sections 28 and 29, other than releasing a young person from custody and placing the young person on probation or under conditional supervision.

(2) **Other duties of review board** — Subject to this Act, a review board may carry out any duties or functions that are assigned to it by the province that established or designated it.

(3) **Notice under section 29** — Where a review board is established or designated by a province for the purposes of this section, the provincial director shall at the same time as any notice is given under subsection 29(1) cause a copy of the notice to be given to the review board.

(4) **Notice of decision of review board** — A review board shall cause notice of any decision made by it in respect of a young person pursuant to section 28 or 29 to be given forthwith in writing to the young person, his parents, the Attorney General or his agent and the provincial director, and a copy of the notice to be given to the youth court.

(5) **Decision of review board to take effect where no review** — Subject to subsection (6), any decision of a review board under this section shall take effect ten days after the decision is made unless an application for review is made under section 31.

(6) **Decision respecting release from custody and probation** — Where a review board decides that a young person should be released from custody and placed on probation, it shall so recommend to the youth court and, if no application for a review of the decision is made under section 31, the youth court shall forthwith on the expiration of the ten day period referred to in subsection (5) release the young person from custody and place him on probation in accordance with section 23, and shall include in the probation order such conditions referred to in that section as the court considers advisable having regard to the recommendations of the review board.

(7) **Idem** — Where a review board decides that a young person should be released from custody and placed under conditional supervision, it shall so recommend to the youth court and, if no application for a review of the decision is made under section 31, the youth court shall forthwith, on the expiration of the ten day period referred to in subsection (5), release the young person from custody and place the young person under conditional supervision in accordance with section 26.2, and shall include in the order under that section such conditions as the court considers advisable, having regard to the recommendations of the review board.

        1980–81–82–83, c. 110, s. 30; R.S. 1985, c. 24 (2nd Supp.), s. 23; 1992, c. 11, s. 10.

31. (1) **Review by youth court** — Where the review board reviews a disposition under section 30, the youth court shall, on the application of the young person in respect of whom the review was made, his parents, the Attorney General or his agent or the provincial director, made within ten days after the decision of the review board is made, forthwith review the decision.

(2) **Subsections 28(5), (7) to (10) and (12) to (17) apply** — Subsections 28(5), (7) to (10) and (12) to (17) apply, with such modifications as the circumstances require,

in respect of reviews made under this section and any notice required under subsection 28(12) shall be given to the provincial director.

1980–81–82–83, c. 110, s. 31; R.S. 1985, c. 1 (4th Supp.), s. 41.

32. (1) Review of other dispositions — Where a youth court has made a disposition in respect of a young person, other than a disposition under paragraph 20(1)(*k*) or (*k.1*) or section 20.1, the youth court shall, on the application of the young person, the young person's parents, the Attorney General or the Attorney General's agent or the provincial director, made at any time after six months from the date of the disposition or, with leave of a youth court judge, at any earlier time, review the disposition if the court is satisfied that there are grounds for a review under subsection (2).

(2) Grounds for review — A review of a disposition may be made under this section

(a) on the ground that the circumstances that led to the disposition have changed materially;

(b) on the ground that the young person in respect of whom the review is to be made is unable to comply with or is experiencing serious difficulty in complying with the terms of the disposition;

(c) on the ground that the terms of the disposition are adversely affecting the opportunities available to the young person to obtain services, education or employment; or

(d) on such other grounds as the youth court considers appropriate.

(3) Progress report — The youth court may, before reviewing under this section a disposition made in respect of a young person, require the provincial director to cause to be prepared, and to submit to the youth court, a progress report on the performance of the young person since the disposition took effect.

(4) Subsections 28(8) to (10) apply — Subsections 28(8) to (10) apply, with such modifications as the circumstances require, in respect of any progress report required under subsection (3).

(5) Subsections 28(5) and (12) to (16) apply — Subsections 28(5) and (12) to (16) apply, with such modifications as the circumstances require, in respect of reviews made under this section and any notice required under subsection 28(12) shall be given to the provincial director.

(6) Compelling appearance of young person — The youth court may, by summons or warrant, compel a young person in respect of whom a review is to be made under this section to appear before the youth court for the purposes of the review.

(7) Decision of the youth court after review — Where a youth court reviews under this section a disposition made in respect of a young person, it may, after affording the young person, his parent, the Attorney General or his agent and the provincial director an opportunity to be heard,

(a) confirm the disposition;

(b) terminate the disposition and discharge the young person from any further obligation of the disposition; or

(c) vary the disposition or make such new disposition listed in section 20, other than a committal to custody, for such period of time, not exceeding the remainder of the period of the earlier disposition, as the court deems appropriate in the circumstances of the case.

(8) **New disposition not to be more onerous** — Subject to subsection (9), where a disposition made in respect of a young person is reviewed under this section, no disposition made under subsection (7) shall, without the consent of the young person, be more onerous than the remaining portion of the disposition reviewed.

(9) **Exception** — A youth court may under this section extend the time within which a disposition made under paragraphs 20(1)(*b*) to (*g*) is to be complied with by a young person where the court is satisfied that the young person requires more time to comply with the disposition, but in no case shall the extension be for a period of time that expires more than twelve months after the date the disposition would otherwise have expired.

(10), (11) [Repealed R.S. 1985, c. 24 (2d Supp.), s. 24.]

1980–81–82–83, c. 110, s. 32; R.S. 1985, c. 24 (2d Supp.), s. 24; 1992, c. 11, s. 11; 1995, c. 39, s. 181.

33. (1) **Review of order made under s. 20.1** — A youth court or other court may, on application, review an order made under section 20.1 at any time after the circumstances set out in subsection 45(1) are realized in respect of any record in relation to the offence that resulted in the order being made.

(2) **Grounds** — In conducting a review under this section, the youth court or other court shall take into account

(a) the nature and circumstances of the offence in respect of which the order was made; and

(b) the safety of the young person and of other persons.

(3) **Decision of review** — Where a youth court or other court conducts a review under this section, it may, after affording the young person, one of the young person's parents, the Attorney General or an agent of the Attorney General and the provincial director an opportunity to be heard,

(a) confirm the order;

(b) revoke the order; or

(c) vary the order as it considers appropriate in the circumstances of the case.

(4) **New order not to be more onerous** — No variation of an order made under paragraph 3(*c*) may be more onerous than the order being reviewed.

(5) **Application of provisions** — Subsections 32(3) to (5) apply, with such modifications as the circumstances require, in respect of a review under this section.

1995, c. 39, s. 182.

34. (1) **Sections 20 to 26 apply to dispositions on review** — Subject to sections 28 to 32, subsections 20(2) to (8) and sections 21 to 25.1 apply, with such modifications as the circumstances require, in respect of dispositions made under sections 28 to 32.

(2) **Orders are dispositions** — Orders under subsections 26.1(1) and 26.2(1) and paragraph 26.6(2)(*b*) are deemed to be dispositions for the purposes of section 28.

1980–81–82–83, c. 110, s. 34; R.S. 1985, c. 24 (2d Supp.), s. 25; 1992, c. 11, s. 12.

Temporary Release From Custody

35. (1) Temporary absence or day release — The provincial director of a province may, subject to any terms or conditions that he considers desirable, authorize a young person committed to custody in the province pursuant to a disposition made under this Act

(a) to be temporarily released for a period not exceeding fifteen days where, in his opinion, it is necessary or desirable that the young person be absent, with or without escort, for medical, compassionate or humanitarian reasons or for the purpose of rehabilitating the young person or re-integrating him into the community; or

(b) to be released from custody on such days and during such hours as he specifies in order that the young person may

(i) attend school or any other educational or training institution,

(ii) obtain or continue employment or perform domestic or other duties required by the young person's family,

(iii) participate in a program specified by him that, in his opinion, will enable the young person to better carry out his employment or improve his education or training, or

(iv) attend an out-patient treatment program or other program that provides services that are suitable to addressing the young person's needs.

(2) Limitation — A young person who is released from custody pursuant to subsection (1) shall be released only for such periods of time as are necessary to attain the purpose for which the young person is released.

(3) Revocation of authorization for release — The provincial director of a province may, at any time, revoke an authorization made under subsection (1).

(4) Arrest and return to custody — Where the provincial director revokes an authorization for a young person to be released from custody under subsection (3) or where a young person fails to comply with any term or condition of release from custody under this section, the young person may be arrested without warrant and returned to custody.

(5) Prohibition — A young person who has been committed to custody under this Act shall not be released from custody before the expiration of the period of his custody except in accordance with subsection (1) unless the release is ordered under sections 28 to 31 or otherwise according to law by a court of competent jurisdiction.

1980–81–82–83, c. 110, s. 35; R.S. 1985, c. 24 (2d Supp.), s. 26; c. 1 (4th Supp.), s. 42; 1995, c. 19, s. 25.

Effect of Termination of Disposition

36. (1) Effect of absolute discharge or termination of dispositions — Subject to section 12 of the *Canada Evidence Act*, where a young person is found guilty of an offence, and

(a) a youth court directs under paragraph 20(1)(a) that the young person be discharged absolutely, or

(b) all the dispositions made under subsection 20(1) in respect of the offence, and all terms of those dispositions, have ceased to have effect.

the young person shall be deemed not to have been found guilty or convicted of the offence except that,

(c) the young person may plead *autrefois convict* in respect of any subsequent charge relating to the offence;

(d) a youth court may consider the finding of guilt in considering an application for a transfer to ordinary court under section 16;

(e) any court or justice may consider the finding of guilt in considering an application for judicial interim release or in considering what dispositions to make or sentence to impose for any offence; and

(f) the National Parole Board or any provincial parole board may consider the finding of guilt in considering an application for parole or pardon.

(2) Disqualifications removed — For greater certainty and without restricting the generality of subsection (1), an absolute discharge under paragraph 20(1)(*a*) or the termination of all dispositions in respect of an offence for which a young person is found guilty removes any disqualification in respect of the offence to which the young person is subject pursuant to any Act of Parliament by reason of a conviction.

(3) Applications for employment — No application form for or relating to

(a) employment in any department, as defined in section 2 of the *Financial Administration Act*,

(b) employment by any Crown corporation as defined in section 83 of the *Financial Administration Act*,

(c) enrolment in the Canadian Forces, or

(d) employment on or in connection with the operation of any work, undertaking or business that is within the legislative authority of Parliament,

shall contain any question that by its terms requires the applicant to disclose that the applicant has been charged with or found guilty of an offence in respect of which the applicant has, under this Act, been discharged absolutely or has completed all the dispositions made under subsection 20(1).

(4) Punishment — Any person who uses or authorizes the use of an application form in contravention of subsection (3) is guilty of an offence punishable on summary conviction.

(5) Finding of guilt not a previous conviction — A finding of guilt under this Act is not a previous conviction for the purposes of any offence under any Act of Parliament for which a greater punishment is prescribed by reason of previous convictions.

1980–81–82–83, c. 110, s. 36; 1984, c. 31, s. 14;R.S. 1985, c. 24 (2d Supp.), s. 27; 1995, c. 19, s. 26; 1995, c. 39, ss. 183, 189.

Youth Workers

37. Duties of youth worker — The duties and functions of a youth worker in respect of a young person whose case has been assigned to him by the provincial director include

(a) where the young person is bound by a probation order that requires him to be under supervision, supervising the young person in complying with the conditions of the probation order or in carrying out any other disposition made together with it;

(a.1) where the young person is placed under conditional supervision pursuant to an order made under section 26.2, supervising the young person in complying with the conditions of the order;

(b) where the young person is found guilty of any offence, giving such assistance to him as he considers appropriate up to the time the young person is discharged or the disposition of his case terminates;

(c) attending court when he considers it advisable or when required by the youth court to be present;

(d) preparing, at the request of the provincial director, a pre-disposition report or a progress report; and

(e) performing such other duties and functions as the provincial director requires.
1980–81–82–83, c. 110, s. 37; R.S. 1985, c. 24 (2d Supp.), s. 28; 1992, c. 11, s. 13.

Protection of Privacy of Young Persons

38. (1) Identity not to be published — Subject to this section, no person shall publish by any means any report

(a) of an offence committed or alleged to have been committed by a young person, unless an order has been made under section 16 with respect thereto, or

(b) of any hearing, adjudication, disposition or appeal concerning a young person who committed or is alleged to have committed an offence

in which the name of the young person, a child or a young person who is a victim of the offence or a child or a young person who appeared as a witness in connection with the offence, or in which any information serving to identify the young person or child, is disclosed.

(1.1) Limitation — Subsection (1) does not apply in respect of the disclosure of information in the course of administration of justice including, for greater certainty, the disclosure of information for the purposes of the *Firearms Act* and Part III of the *Criminal Code*, where it is not the purpose of the disclosure to make the information known in the community.

(1.11) Preparation of reports — Subsection (1) does not apply in respect of the disclosure of information by the provincial director or a youth worker where the disclosure is necessary for procuring information that relates to the preparation of any report required by this Act.

(1.12) No subsequent disclosure — No person to whom information is disclosed pursuant to subsection (1.11) shall disclose that information to any other person unless the disclosure is necessary for the purpose of preparing the report for which the information was disclosed.

(1.13) Schools and others — Subsection (1) does not apply in respect of the disclosure of information to any professional or other person engaged in the supervision or care of a young person, including the representative of any school board or school or any other educational or training institution, by the provincial director, a youth worker, a peace officer or any other person engaged in the provision of services to young persons where the disclosure is necessary

(a) to ensure compliance by the young person with an authorization pursuant to section 35 or an order of any court concerning bail, probation or conditional supervision; or

(b) to ensure the safety of staff, students or other persons, as the case may be.

(1.14) No subsequent disclosure — No person to whom information is disclosed pursuant to subsection (1.13) shall disclose that information to any other person unless the disclosure is necessary for a purpose referred to in that subsection.

(1.15) Information to be kept separate — Any person to whom information is disclosed pursuant to subsections (1.13) and (1.14) shall

(a) keep the information separate from any other record of the young person to whom the information relates;

(b) subject to subsection (1.14), ensure that no other person has access to the information; and

(c) destroy the information when the information is no longer required for the purpose for which it was disclosed.

(1.2) Ex parte application for leave to publish — A youth court judge shall, on the *ex parte* application of a peace officer, make an order permitting any person to publish a report described in subsection (1) that contains the name of a young person, or information serving to identify a young person, who has committed or is alleged to have committed an indictable offence, if the judge is satisfied that

(a) there is reason to believe that the young person is dangerous to others; and

(b) publication of the report is necessary to assist in apprehending the young person.

(1.3) Order ceases to have effect — An order made under subsection (1.2) shall cease to have effect two days after it is made.

(1.4) Application for leave to publish — The youth court may, on the application of any person referred to in subsection (1), make an order permitting any person to publish a report in which the name of that person, or information serving to identify that person, would be disclosed, if the court is satisfied that the publication of the report would not be contrary to the best interests of that person.

(1.5) Disclosure with court order — The youth court may, on the application of the provincial director, the Attorney General or an agent of the Attorney General or a peace officer, make an order permitting the applicant to disclose to such person or persons as are specified by the court such information about a young person as is specified if the court is satisfied that the disclosure is necessary, having regard to the following:

(a) the young person has been found guilty of an offence involving serious personal injury;

(b) the young person poses a risk of serious harm to persons; and

(c) the disclosure of the information is relevant to the avoidance of that risk.

(1.6) Opportunity to be heard — Subject to subsection (1.7), before making an order under subsection (1.5), the youth court shall afford the young person, the young person's parents, the Attorney General or an agent of the Attorney General an opportunity to be heard.

(1.7) Ex parte application — An application under subsection (1.5) may be made *ex parte* by the Attorney General or an agent of the Attorney General where the youth court is satisfied that reasonable efforts have been made to locate the young person and that those efforts have not been successful.

(1.8) Time limit — No information may be disclosed pursuant to subsection (1.5) after the record to which the information relates ceases to be available for inspection under subsection 45(1).

(2) Contravention — Every one who contravenes subsection (1), (1.12), (1.14) or (1.15)

    (a) is guilty of an indictable offence and liable to imprisonment for a term not exceeding two years; or

    (b) is guilty of an offence punishable on summary conviction.

(3) Provincial court judge has absolute jurisdiction on indictment — Where an accused is charged with an offence under paragraph (2)(*a*), a provincial court judge has absolute jurisdiction to try the case and his jurisdiction does not depend on the consent of the accused.

1980–81–82–83, c. 110, s. 38; R.S. 1985, c. 27 (1st Supp.), s. 203; c. 24 (2d Supp.), s. 29; 1995, c. 19, s. 27; 1995, c. 39, s. 184.

Case Law

Publication Prohibition: Ss. 38(1)–(1.4)

R. v. S. (T.), (sub nom. *R. v. Canadian Broadcasting Corp.)* 94 C.C.C. (3d) 372, 34 C.R. (4th) 351 — Where P obtains a publication ban by order of a youth court judge presiding at the trial of a young offender, a third party news media entity could apply for *certiorari* to a judge of the superior court of criminal jurisdiction to review the decision of the trial judge. An appeal could have been taken from the decision on the *certiorari* application to the provincial court of appeal. No direct appeal could be taken from the order of the youth court judge to the provincial court of appeal.

N. (F.), Re (1998), 126 C.C.C. (3d) 114 (Nfld. C.A.) — The practice of a youth court to forward its court docket to school boards with *Y.O.A.* ss. 38(1.13) and (1.14).

Smith v. Clerk of Youth Court (1986), 31 C.C.C. (3d) 27 (Ont. U.F.C.) — A victim may publish the name of the young offender and the particulars of the offence in a civil proceeding against him.

R. v. Publications Photo-Police Inc. (1986), 52 C.R. (3d) 301, 31 C.C.C. (3d) 93 (Que. C.A.) — The publication prohibition does not apply where the young person who is the victim is deceased.

Charter Considerations

Southam Inc. v. R. (1984), 42 C.R. (3d) 336, 16 C.C.C. (3d) 262 (Ont. H.C.); affirmed (1986), 50 C.R. (3d) 241, 25 C.C.C. (3d) 119 (Ont. C.A.); leave to appeal refused (1986), 50 C.R. (3d) xxvn (S.C.C.) — Section 38(1) does not contain an absolute ban. The protection and rehabilitation of young people involved in the criminal justice system justifies the abrogation of fundamental freedom of expression, including freedom of the press, and s. 28(1) is a reasonable limitation.

39. (1) Exclusion from hearing — Subject to subsection (2), where a court or justice before whom proceedings are carried out under this Act is of the opinion

    (a) that any evidence or information presented to the court or justice would be seriously injurious or seriously prejudicial to

        (i) the young person who is being dealt with in the proceedings,

        (ii) a child or young person who is a witness in the proceedings,

(iii) a child or young person who is aggrieved by or the victim of the offence charged in the proceedings, or

(b) that it would be in the interest of public morals, the maintenance of order or the proper administration of justice to exclude any or all members of the public from the court room,

the court or justice may exclude any person from all or part of the proceedings if the court or justice deems that person's presence to be unnecessary to the conduct of the proceedings.

(2) Exception — Subject to section 650 of the *Criminal Code* and except where it is necessary for the purposes of subsection 13(6) of this Act, a court or justice may not, pursuant to subsection (1), exclude from proceedings under this Act

(a) the prosecutor;

(b) the young person who is being dealt with in the proceedings, his parent, his counsel or any adult assisting him pursuant to subsection 11(7);

(c) the provincial director or his agent;or

(d) the youth worker to whom the young person's case has been assigned.

(3) Exclusion after adjudication or during review — The youth court, after it has found a young person guilty of an offence, or the youth court or the review board, during a review of a disposition under sections 28 to 32, may, in its discretion, exclude from the court or from a hearing of the review board, as the case may be, any person other than

(a) the young person or his counsel,

(b) the provincial director or his agent,

(c) the youth worker to whom the young person's case has been assigned, and

(d) the Attorney General or his agent,

when any information is being presented to the court or the review board the knowledge of which might, in the opinion of the court or review board, be seriously injurious or seriously prejudicial to the young person.

(4) Exception — The exception set out in paragraph (3)(a) is subject to subsection 13(6) of this Act and section 650 of the *Criminal Code*.

1980–81–82–83, c. 110, s. 39; R.S. 1985, c. 24 (2d Supp.), s. 30.

Case Law

Exclusion Order

Southam Inc. v. R. (1984), 42 C.R. (3d) 336, 16 C.C.C. (3d) 262 (Ont. H.C.); affirmed on other grounds (1986), 50 C.R. (3d) 241, 25 C.C.C. (3d) 119 (Ont. C.A.); leave to appeal refused (1986), 50 C.R (3d) xxvn, 25 C.C.C. (3d) 119n (S.C.C.) — The youth court judge may exclude the public and press from the courtroom during the *voir dire* proceedings.

Charter Considerations

Southam Inc. v. R. (1984), 42 C.R. (3d) 336, 16 C.C.C. (3d) 262 (Ont. H.C.); affirmed (1986), 50 C.R. (3d) 241, 25 C.C.C. (3d) 119 (Ont. C.A.); leave to appeal refused (1986), 50 C.R. (3d) xxvn, 25 C.C.C. (3d) 119 (S.C.C.) — The interests of society in the protection and rehabilitation of young persons involved in youth court proceedings is of such superordinate importance that s. 39(1)(a) is a reasonable limitation on freedom of expression including freedom of the press.

Maintenance and Use of Records

Records that may be Kept

40. (1) Youth court, review board and other courts — A youth court, review board or any court dealing with matters arising out of proceedings under this Act may keep a record of any case arising under this Act that comes before it.

(2) Exception — For greater certainty, this section does not apply in respect of proceedings held in ordinary court pursuant to an order under section 16.

(3) Records of offences that result in order under s. 20.1 — Notwithstanding anything in this Act, where a young person is found guilty of an offence that results in an order under section 20.1 being made against the young person, the youth court may keep a record of the conviction and the order until the expiration of the order.

(4) Disclosure — Any record that is kept under subsection (3) may be disclosed only to establish the existence of the order in any offence involving a breach of the order.

1980–81–82–83, c. 110, s. 40; R.S. 1985, c. 24 (2d Supp.), s. 31; 1995, c. 39, s. 185.

41. (1) Records in central repository — A record of any offence that a young person has been charged with having committed may, where the offence is an offence in respect of which an adult may be subjected to any measurement, process or operation referred to in the *Identification of Criminals Act*, be kept in such central repository as the Commissioner of the Royal Canadian Mounted Police may, from time to time, designate for the purpose of keeping criminal history files or records on offenders or keeping records for the identification of offenders.

(2) Police force may provide record — Where a young person is charged with having committed an offence referred to in subsection (1), the police force responsible for the investigation of the offence may provide a record of the offence, including the original or a copy of any fingerprints, palmprints or photographs and any other measurement, process or operation referred to in the *Identification of Criminals Act* taken of, or applied in respect of, the young person by or on behalf of the police force, for inclusion in any central repository designated pursuant to subsection (1).

(3) Police force shall provide record — Where a young person is found guilty of an offence referred to in subsection (1), the police force responsible for the investigation of the offence shall provide a record of the offence, including the original or a copy of any fingerprints, palmprints or photographs and any other measurement, process or operation referred to in the *Identification of Criminals Act* taken of, or applied in respect of, the young person by or on behalf of the police force, for inclusion in any central repository designated pursuant to subsection (1).

1980–81–82–83, c. 110, s. 41; R.S. 1985, c. 24 (2d Supp.), s. 31; 1995, c. 19, s. 28.

42. Police records — A record relating to any offence alleged to have been committed by a young person, including the original or a copy of any fingerprints or photographs of the young person, may be kept by any police force responsible for, or participating in, the investigation of the offence.

(2)–(5) [Repealed R.S. 1985, c. 24 (2d Supp.), s. 31.]

1980–81–82–83, c. 110, s. 42; R.S. 1985, c. 24 (2d Supp.), s. 31.

43. (1) Government records — A department or agency of any government in Canada may keep records containing information obtained by the department or agency

(a) for the purposes of an investigation of an offence alleged to have been committed by a young person;

(b) for use in proceedings against a young person under this Act;

(c) for the purpose of administering a disposition;

(d) for the purpose of considering whether, instead of commencing or continuing judicial proceedings under this Act against a young person, to use alternative measures to deal with the young person; or

(e) as a result of the use of alternative measures to deal with a young person.

(2) Private records — Any person or organization may keep records containing information obtained by the person or organization

(a) as a result of the use of alternative measures to deal with a young person alleged to have committed an offence; or

(b) for the purpose of administering or participating in the administration of a disposition.

(3), (4) [Repealed R.S. 1985, c. 24 (2d Supp.), s. 32.]

1980–81–82–83, c. 110, s. 43.

Fingerprints and Photographs

44. (1) *Identification of Criminals Act* applies — Subject to this section, the *Identification of Criminals Act* applies in respect of young persons.

(2) Limitation — No fingerprints, palmprints or photograph or any other measurement, process or operation referred to in the *Identification of Criminals Act* shall be taken of, or applied in respect of, a young person who is charged with having committed an offence except in the circumstances in which an adult may, under that Act, be subjected to the measurements, processes and operations referred to in that Act.

(3)–(5) [Repealed R.S. 1985, c. 24 (2d Supp.), s. 33.]

1980–81–82–83, c. 110, s. 44; 1995, c. 19, s. 29.

Case Law

Fingerprinting for Hybrid Offences: S. 44(2)

H. (M.) v. R. (1984), 14 C.C.C. (3d) 210 (Alta. Q.B.); additional reasons at (1984), (sub nom. *H. (M.) v. R. (No. 2)*) 17 C.C.C. (3d) 443; affirmed (1985), 21 C.C.C. (3d) 384 (Alta. C.A.); leave to appeal granted (1985), 21 C.C.C. (3d) 384n (S.C.C.) — An offence which may be prosecuted by way of indictment under the *Criminal Code* is an indictable offence for the purpose of the *Identification of Criminals Act* and the fingerprinting provisions of the *Code*, where the offender is a young person.

Charter Considerations

H. (M.) v. R. (No. 2) (1984), 17 C.C.C. (3d) 443 (Alta. Q.B.); affirmed (1985), 21 C.C.C. (3d) 384 (Alta. C.A.); leave to appeal granted (1985), 21 C.C.C. (3d) 384n (S.C.C.) — Section 44 does not violate *Charter* ss. 7, 8, 9 or in general, 12. However, in an unusual case, the effect of the fingerprinting process on a specific young offender could bring it within s. 12.

Disclosure of Records

44.1 (1) Records made available — Subject to subsections (2), (2.1), any record that is kept pursuant to section 40 shall, and any record that is kept pursuant to sections 41 to 43 may, on request, be made available for inspection to

(a) the young person to whom the record relates;

(b) counsel acting on behalf of the young person, or any representative of that counsel;

(c) the Attorney General or his agent;

(d) a parent of the young person or any adult assisting the young person pursuant to subsection 11(7), during the course of any proceedings relating to the offence or alleged offence to which the record relates or during the term of any disposition made in respect of the offence;

(e) any judge, court or review board, for any purpose relating to proceedings relating to the young person under this Act or to proceedings in ordinary court in respect of offences committed or alleged to have been committed by the young person, whether as a young person or an adult;

(f) any peace officer,

(i) for the purpose of investigating any offence that the young person is suspected on reasonable grounds of having committed, or in respect of which the young person has been arrested or charged, whether as a young person or an adult,

(ii) for any purpose related to the administration of the case to which the record relates during the course of proceedings against the young person or the term of any disposition, or

(iii) for the purpose of investigating any offence that another person is suspected on reasonable grounds of having committed against the young person while the young person is, or was, serving a disposition, or

(iv) for any other law enforcement purpose;

(g) any member of a department or agency of a government in Canada, or any agent thereof, that is

(i) engaged in the administration of alternative measures in respect of the young person,

(ii) preparing a report in respect of the young person pursuant to this Act or for the purpose of assisting a court in sentencing the young person after he becomes an adult or is transferred to ordinary court pursuant to section 16,

(iii) engaged in the supervision or care of the young person, whether as a young person or an adult, or in the administration of a disposition or a sentence in respect of the young person, whether as a young person or an adult, or

(iv) considering an application for parole or pardon made by the young person after he becomes an adult;

(h) any person, or person within a class of persons, designated by the Governor in Council, or the Lieutenant Governor in Council of a province, for a purpose and to the extent specified by the Governor in Council or the Lieutenant Governor in Council, as the case may be;

(i) any person, for the purpose of determining whether to grant security clearances required by the Government of Canada or the government of a province or a municipality for purposes of employment or the performance of services;

(i.1) to any person for the purposes of the *Firearms Act*;

(j) any employee or agent of the Government of Canada, for statistical purposes pursuant to the *Statistics Act*; and

(k) any other person who is deemed, or any person within a class of persons that is deemed, by a youth court judge to have a valid interest in the record, to the extent directed by the judge, if the judge is satisfied that the disclosure is

(i) desirable in the public interest for research or statistical purposes, or

(ii) desirable in the interest of the proper administration of justice.

(2) **Exception** — Where a youth court has withheld the whole or a part of a report from any person pursuant to subsection 13(6) or 14(7), the report or part thereof shall not be made available to that person for inspection under subsection (1).

(2.1) **Records of forensic DNA analysis of bodily substances** — Notwithstanding subsections (1) and (5), any record that is kept pursuant to any of sections 40 to 43 and that is a record of the results of forensic DNA analysis of a bodily substance taken from a young person in execution of a warrant issued under section 487.05 of the *Criminal Code* may be made available for inspection under this section only under paragraphs (1)(a), (b), (c), (d), (e), (f), (h) or subparagraph (1)(k)(ii).

(3) **Introduction into evidence** — Nothing in paragraph (1)(*e*) authorizes the introduction into evidence of any part of a record that would not otherwise be admissible in evidence.

(4) **Disclosures for research or statistical purposes** — Where a record is made available for inspection to any person under paragraph (1)(*j*) or subparagraph (1)(*k*)(i), that person may subsequently disclose information contained in the record, but may not disclose the information in any form that would reasonably be expected to identify the young person to whom it relates.

(5) **Record made available to victim** — Any record that is kept pursuant to sections 40 to 43 may, on request, be made available for inspection to the victim of the offence to which the record relates.

(6) **Disclosure of information and copies of records** — Any person to whom a record is required or authorized to be made available for inspection under this section may be given any information contained in the record and may be given a copy of any part of the record.

R.S. 1985, c. 24 (2d Supp.), s. 34; 1992, c. 43, s. 34; 1995, c. 27, s. 2; 1995, c. 19, s. 30; 1995, c. 39, s. 186.

Case Law: *N. (F.), Re* (1998), 126 C.C.C. (3d) 114 (Nfld. C.A.) — A youth court document is *not* a *record* for the purposes of ss. 40-46. At all events, the document may be made available to school boards under s. 44.1(1)(k)(ii).

Smith v. Clerk of Youth Court (1986), 31 C.C.C. (3d) 27 (Ont. U.F.C.) — A person whose property has been damaged by a young offender and who wishes to bring civil proceedings against him is a victim and comes within s. 44.1(1)(k).

44.2 (1) Disclosure by peace officer during investigation — A peace officer may disclose to any person any information in a record kept pursuant to section 42 that it is necessary to disclose in the conduct of the investigation of an offence.

(2) Disclosure to insurance company — A peace officer may disclose to an insurance company information in any record that is kept pursuant to section 42 for the purpose of investigating any claim arising out of an offence committed or alleged to have been committed by the young person to whom the record relates.

R.S. 1985, c. 24 (2d Supp.), s. 34.

Non-Disclosure and Destruction of Records

45. (1) Non-disclosure — Subject to sections 45.01, 45.1 and 45.2, records kept pursuant to sections 40 to 43 may not be made available for inspection under section 44.1 or 44.2 in the following circumstances:

(a) where the young person to whom the record relates is charged with the offence to which the record relates and is acquitted otherwise than by reason of a verdict of not criminally responsible on account of mental disorder, on the expiration of two months after the expiration of the time allowed for the taking of an appeal or, where an appeal is taken on the expiration of three months after all proceedings in respect of the appeal have been completed;

(b) where the charge against the young person is dismissed for any reason other than acquittal or withdrawn, on the expiration of one year after the dismissal or withdrawal;

(c) where the charge against the young person is stayed, with no proceedings being taken against the young person for a period of one year, on the expiration of the one year;

(d) where alternative measures are used to deal with the young person, on the expiration of two years after the young person consents to participate in the alternative measures in accordance with paragraph 4(1)(c);

(d.1) where the young person is found guilty of the offence and the disposition is an absolute discharge, on the expiration of one year after the young person is found guilty;

(d.2) where the young person is found guilty of the offence and the disposition is a conditional discharge, on the expiration of three years after the young person is found guilty;

(e) subject to paragraph (g), where the young person is found guilty of the offence and it is a summary conviction offence, on the expiration of three years after all dispositions made in respect of that offence;

(f) subject to paragraph (g), where the young person is found guilty of the offence and it is an indictable offence, on the expiration of five years after all dispositions made in respect of that offence; and

(g) where, before the expiration of the period referred to in paragraph (e) or (f), the young person is, as a young person, found guilty of

(i) a subsequent summary conviction offence, on the expiration of three years after all dispositions made in respect of that offence have been completed, and

(ii) a subsequent indictable offence, five years after all dispositions made in respect of that offence have been completed.

[Note: 1995, c. 19, s. 31(4) states: Paragraphs 45(1)(d.1) to (e) of the Act, as enacted by subsection (2), apply in respect of a record relating to a finding of guilt made before the coming into force of that subsection only if the person to whom the record relates applies,

after the coming into force of that subsection, to the Royal Canadian Mounted Police to have those paragraphs apply. 1995, c. 19, s. 31(2) came into force on December 1, 1995.]

(2) **Destruction of record** — Subject to subsections (2.1) and (2.2), when the circumstances set out in subsection (1) are realized in respect of any record kept pursuant to section 41, the record shall be destroyed forthwith.

(2.1) **Transfer of records relating to serious offences** — Where a special records repository has been established pursuant to subsection 45.02(1), all records in the central repository referred to in subsection 41(1) that relate to

(a) a conviction for first degree murder or second degree murder within the meaning of section 231 of the *Criminal Code*,

(b) an offence referred to in the schedule, or

(c) an order made under section 20.1,

shall, when the circumstances set out in subsection (1) are realized in respect of the records, be transferred to that special records repository.

(2.2) **Transfer of fingerprints** — Where a special fingerprints repository has been established pursuant to subsection 45.03(1), all fingerprints and any information necessary to identify the person to whom the fingerprints belong that are in the central repository referred to in subsection 41(1) shall, when the circumstances set out in subsection (1) are realized in respect of the records, be transferred to that special fingerprints repository.

(2.3) **Meaning of "destroy"** — For the purposes of subsection (2), "destroy", in respect of a record, means

(a) to shred, burn or otherwise physically destroy the record, in the case of a record other than a record in electronic form; and

(b) to delete, write over or otherwise render the record inaccessible, in the case of a record in electronic form.

(3) **Other records may be destroyed** — Any record kept pursuant to sections 40 to 43 may, in the discretion of the person or body keeping the record, be destroyed at any time before or after the circumstances set out in subsection (1) are realized in respect of that record.

(4) **Young person deemed not to have committed offence** — A young person shall be deemed not to have committed any offence to which a record kept pursuant to sections 40 to 43 relates when the circumstances set out in paragraph (1)(*d*), (*e*) or (*f*) are realized in respect of that record.

(5) **Deemed election** — For the purposes of paragraphs (1)(*e*) and (*f*), where no election is made in respect of an offence that may be prosecuted by indictment or proceeded with by way of summary conviction, the Attorney General or his agent shall be deemed to have elected to proceed with the offence as an offence punishable on summary conviction.

(5.1) **Orders made under s. 20.1 not included** — For the purposes of this Act, orders made under section 20.1 shall not be taken into account in determining any time period referred to in subsection (1).

(6) **Application to delinquency** — This section applies, with such modifications as the circumstances require, in respect of records relating to the offence of delinquency

under the *Juvenile Delinquents Act*, chapter J-3 of the Revised Statutes of Canada, 1970, as it read immediately prior to April 2, 1984.

1980–81–82–83, c. 110, s. 45; R.S. 1985, c. 24 (2d Supp.), s. 35; 1992, c. 43, s. 34; 1995, c. 19, s. 31; 1995, c. 39, ss. 187, 189.

Retention of Records

45.01 Retention of records — Where, before the expiration of the period referred to in paragraph 45(1)(e) or (f) or subparagraph 45(1)(g)(i) or (ii), the young person is found guilty of a subsequent offence as an adult, records kept pursuant to sections 40 to 43 shall be available for inspection under section 44.1 or 44.2 and the provisions applicable to criminal records of adults shall apply.

1995, c. 19, s. 32.

Special Records Repository

45.02 (1) Special records repository — The Commissioner of the Royal Canadian Mounted Police may establish a special records repository for records transferred pursuant to subsection 45(2.1).

(2) Records relating to murder — A record that relates to a conviction for the offence of first degree murder or second degree murder within the meaning of section 231 of the *Criminal Code* or an offence referred to in any of paragraphs 16(1.01)(b) to (d) may be kept indefinitely in the special records repository.

(3) Records relating to other serious offences — A record that relates to a conviction for an offence referred to in the schedule shall be kept in the special records repository for a period of five years and shall be destroyed forthwith at the expiration of that five year period, unless the young person to whom the record relates is subsequently found guilty of any offence referred to in the schedule, in which case the record shall be dealt with as the record of an adult.

(4) Disclosure — A record kept in the special records repository shall be made available for inspection to the following persons at the following times or in the following circumstances:

(a) at any time, to the person to whom the record relates and to counsel acting on behalf of the young person, or any representative of that counsel;

(b) where the young person has subsequently been charged with the commission of first degree murder or second degree murder within the meaning of section 231 of the *Criminal Code* or an offence referred to in the schedule, to any peace officer for the purpose of investigating any offence that the young person is suspected of having committed, or in respect of which the young person has been arrested or charged, whether as a young person or as an adult;

(c) where the young person has subsequently been convicted of an offence referred to in the schedule,

(i) to the Attorney General or an agent of the Attorney General,

(ii) to a parent of the young person or any adult assisting the young person,

(iii) to any judge, court or review board, for any purpose relating to proceedings relating to the young person under this Act or to proceedings in ordinary court in respect of offences committed or alleged to have been committed by the young person, whether as a young person or as an adult, or

(iv) to any member of a department or agency of a government in Canada, or any agent thereof, that is

(A) engaged in the administration of alternative measures in respect of the young person,

(B) preparing a report in respect of the young person pursuant to this Act or for the purpose of assisting a court in sentencing the young person after the young person becomes an adult or is transferred to ordinary court pursuant to section 16,

(C) engaged in the supervision or care of the young person, whether as a young person or as an adult, or in the administration of a disposition or a sentence in respect of the young person, whether as a young person or as an adult, or

(D) considering an application for parole or pardon made by the young person after the young person becomes an adult;

(c.1) to establish the existence of the order in any offence involving a breach of the order;

(c.2) for the purposes of the *Firearms Act*;

(d) at any time, to any employee or agent of the Government of Canada, for statistical purposes pursuant to the *Statistics Act*; or

(e) at any time, to any other person who is deemed, or any person within a class of persons that is deemed, by a youth court judge to have a valid interest in the record, to the extent directed by the judge, if the judge is satisfied that the disclosure is desirable in the public interest for research or statistical purposes.

1995, c. 19, s. 32; 1995, c. 39, s. 189(d).

Special Fingerprints Repository

45.03 (1) Special fingerprints repository — The Commissioner of the Royal Canadian Mounted Police may establish a special fingerprints repository for fingerprints and any related information transferred pursuant to subsection 45(2.2).

(2) Disclosure for identification purposes — Fingerprints and any related information may be kept in the special fingerprints repository for a period of five years following the date of their receipt and, during that time, the name, date of birth and last known address of the young person to whom the fingerprints belong may be disclosed for identification purposes if a fingerprint identified as that of the young person is found during the investigation of a crime or during an attempt to identify a deceased person or a person suffering from amnesia.

(3) Destruction — Fingerprints and any related information in the special fingerprints repository shall be destroyed five years after the date of their receipt in the repository.

(3.1) Records of orders made under s. 20.1 — A record that relates to an order made under section 20.1 shall be kept in the special records repository until the expiration of the order and shall be destroyed forthwith at that time.

1995, c. 19, s. 32; 1995, c. 39, s. 189(c)

Disclosure in Special Circumstances

45.1 (1) Where records may be made available — Subject to subsection (1.1), a youth court judge may, on application by any person, order that any record to which subsection 45(1) applies, or any part thereof, be made available for inspection to that person or a copy of the record or part thereof be given to that person, if a youth court judge is satisfied that

(a) that person has a valid and substantial interest in the record or part thereof;

(b) it is necessary for the record, part thereof or copy thereof to be made available in the interest of the proper administration of justice; and

(c) disclosure of the record or part thereof or information is not prohibited under any other Act of Parliament or the legislature of a province.

(1.1) Records — Subsection (1) applies in respect of any record relating to a particular young person or to any record relating to a class of young persons where the identity of young persons in the class at the time of the making of the application referred to in that subsection cannot reasonably be ascertained and the disclosure of the record is necessary for the purpose of investigating any offence that a person is suspected on reasonable grounds of having committed against a young person while the young person is, or was, serving a disposition.

(2) Notice — Subject to subsection (2.1), an application under subsection (1) in respect of a record shall not be heard unless the person who makes the application has given the young person to whom the record relates and the person or body that has possession of the record at least five days notice in writing of the application and the young person and the person or body that has possession has had a reasonable opportunity to be heard.

(2.1) Where notice not required — A youth court judge may waive the requirement in subsection (2) to give notice to a young person where the youth court is of the opinion that

(a) to insist on the giving of the notice would frustrate the application; or

(b) reasonable efforts have not been successful in finding the young person.

(3) Use of record — In any order under subsection (1), the youth court judge shall set out the purposes for which the record may be used.

R.S. 1985, c. 24 (2d Supp.), s. 35; 1995, c. 19, s. 34.

45.2 Records in the custody, etc., of archivists — Where records originally kept pursuant to section 40, 42 or 43 are under the custody or control of the National Archivist of Canada or the archivist for any province, that person may disclose any information contained in the records to any other person if

(a) the Attorney General or his agent is satisfied that the disclosure is desirable in the public interest for research or statistical purposes; and

(b) the person to whom the information is disclosed undertakes not to disclose the information in any form that could reasonably be expected to identify the young person to whom it relates.

R.S. 1985, c. 24 (2d Supp.), s. 35; c. 1 (3d Supp.), s. 12.

46. (1) Prohibition against disclosure — Except as authorized or required by this Act, no record kept pursuant to sections 40 to 43 may be made available for inspection, and no copy, print or negative thereof or information contained therein may be given, to any person where to do so would serve to identify the young person to whom it relates as a young person dealt with under this Act.

(2) **Exception for employees** — No person who is employed in keeping or maintaining records referred to in subsection (1) is restricted from doing anything prohibited under subsection (1) with respect to any other person so employed.

(3) **Prohibition against use** — Subject to section 45.1, no record kept pursuant to sections 40 to 43, and no copy, print or negative thereof, may be used for any purpose that would serve to identify the young person to whom the record relates as a young person dealt with under this Act after the circumstances set out in subsection 45(1) are realized in respect of that record.

(4) **Offence** — Any person who fails to comply with this section or subsection 45(2)

    (a) is guilty of an indictable offence and liable to imprisonment for a term not exceeding two years; or

    (b) is guilty of an offence punishable on summary conviction.

(5) **Absolute jurisdiction of provincial court judge** — The jurisdiction of a provincial court judge to try an accused is absolute and does not depend on the consent of the accused where the accused is charged with an offence under paragraph (4)(*a*).
1980–81–82–83, c. 110, s. 46; R.S. 1985, c. 27 (1st Supp.), s. 203; c. 24 (2d Supp.), s. 36.

Contempt of Court

47. (1) **Contempt against youth court** — Every youth court has the same power, jurisdiction and authority to deal with and impose punishment for contempt against the court as may be exercised by the superior court of criminal jurisdiction of the province in which the court is situated.

(2) **Exclusive jurisdiction of youth court** — The youth court has exclusive jurisdiction in respect of every contempt of court committed by a young person against the youth court whether or not committed in the face of the court and every contempt of court committed by a young person against any other court otherwise than in the face of that court.

(3) **Concurrent jurisdiction of youth court** — The youth court has jurisdiction in respect of every contempt of court committed by a young person against any other court in the face of that court and every contempt of court committed by an adult against the youth court in the face of the youth court, but nothing in this subsection affects the power, jurisdiction or authority of any other court to deal with or impose punishment for contempt of court.

(4) **Dispositions** — Where a youth court or any other court finds a young person guilty of contempt of court, it may make any one of the dispositions set out in section 20, or any number thereof that are not inconsistent with each other, but no other disposition or sentence.

(5) **Section 708 of *Criminal Code* applies in respect of adults** — Section 708 of the *Criminal Code* applies in respect of proceedings under this section in youth court against adults, with such modifications as the circumstances require.

(6) **Appeals** — A finding of guilt under this section for contempt of court or a disposition or sentence made in respect thereof may be appealed as if the finding were a con-

viction or the disposition or sentence were a sentence in a prosecution by indictment in ordinary court.

1980–81–82–83, c. 110, s. 47.

Case Law: *MacMillan Bloedel Ltd. v. Simpson* (1994), 89 C.C.C. (3d) 217 (B.C. C.A.); additional reasons at *(*sub nom. *MacMillan Bloedel v. Krawczyk)* 43 B.C.A.C. 136 (B.C. C.A.); further additional reasons at (March 8, 1994), Doc. No. V02012 (B.C. C.A.) — Section 47(2) *Y.O.A.*, which purports to give the Youth Court exclusive jurisdiction with respect to contempt of court committed by a young person, is unconstitutional. The inherent powers of a superior court to use its contempt power to enforce its orders and maintain its authority is beyond the reach of Parliament and the Legislature.

Forfeiture of Recognizances

48. Applications for forfeiture of recognizances — Applications for the forfeiture of recognizances of young persons shall be made to the youth court.

1980–81–82–83, c. 110, s. 48.

49. (1) Proceedings in case of default — Where a recognizance binding a young person has been endorsed with a certificate pursuant to subsection 770(1) of the *Criminal Code*, a youth court judge shall,

(a) on the request of the Attorney General or his agent, fix a time and place for the hearing of an application for the forfeiture of the recognizance; and

(b) after fixing a time and place for the hearing, cause to be sent by registered mail, not less than ten days before the time so fixed, to each principal and surety named in the recognizance, directed to him at his latest known address, a notice requiring him to appear at the time and place fixed by the judge to show cause why the recognizance should not be forfeited.

(2) Order for forfeiture of recognizance — Where subsection (1) is complied with, the youth court judge may, after giving the parties an opportunity to be heard, in his discretion grant or refuse the application and make any order with respect to the forfeiture of the recognizance that he considers proper.

(3) Judgment debtors of the Crown — Where, pursuant to subsection (2), a youth court judge orders forfeiture of a recognizance, the principal and his sureties become judgment debtors of the Crown, each in the amount that the judge orders him to pay.

(4) Order may be filed — An order made under subsection (2) may be filed with the clerk of the superior court or, in the province of Quebec, the prothonotary and, where an order is filed, the clerk or the prothonotary shall issue a writ of *fieri facias* in Form 34 set out in the *Criminal Code* and deliver it to the sheriff of each of the territorial divisions in which any of the principal and his sureties resides, carries on business or has property.

(5) Where a deposit has been made — Where a deposit has been made by a person against whom an order for forfeiture of a recognizance has been made, no writ of *fieri facias* shall issue, but the amount of the deposit shall be transferred by the person who has custody of it to the person who is entitled by law to receive it.

(6) Subsections 770(2) and (4) of *Criminal Code* do not apply — Subsections 770(2) and (4) of the *Criminal Code* do not apply in respect of proceedings under this Act.

(7) Sections 772 and 773 of *Criminal Code* apply — Sections 772 and 773 of the *Criminal Code* apply in respect of writs of *fieri facias* issued pursuant to this section as if they were issued pursuant to section 771 of the *Criminal Code*.

1980–81–82–83, c. 110, s. 49.

Interference with Dispositions

50. (1) Inducing a young person, etc — Every one who

(a) induces or assists a young person to leave unlawfully a place of custody or other place in which the young person has been placed pursuant to a disposition,

(b) unlawfully removes a young person from a place referred to in paragraph (*a*),

(c) knowingly harbours or conceals a young person who has unlawfully left a place referred to in paragraph (*a*),

(d) wilfully induces or assists a young person to breach or disobey a term or condition of a disposition, or

(e) wilfully prevents or interferes with the performance by a young person of a term or condition of a disposition

is guilty of an indictable offence and liable to imprisonment for a term not exceeding two years or is guilty of an offence punishable on summary conviction.

(2) Absolute jurisdiction of provincial court judge — The jurisdiction of a provincial court judge to try an adult accused of an indictable offence under this section is absolute and does not depend on the consent of the accused.

1980–81–82–83, c. 110, s. 50; R.S. 1985, c. 27 (1st Supp.), s. 203; c. 24 (2d Supp.), s. 37.

Application of the *Criminal Code*

51. Application of *Criminal Code* — Except to the extent that they are inconsistent with or excluded by this Act, all the provisions of the *Criminal Code* apply, with such modifications as the circumstances require, in respect of offences alleged to have been committed by young persons.

1980–81–82–83, c. 110, s. 51.

Case Law: *R. v. T. (K.D.)* (1987), 28 C.C.C. (3d) 110 (N.S. C.A.) — Sentencing provisions of the *Criminal Code* which are inconsistent with provisions of the Act do not apply to young offenders.

Charter Considerations

R. v. L. (R.) (1986), 52 C.R. (3d) 209, 26 C.C.C. (3d) 417 (Ont. C.A.); reversing (1985), 47 C.R. (3d) 278 (Ont. Prov. Ct.) — Although s. 52 deprives a young offender tried in youth court of trial by jury, it does not offend *Charter* s. 11(f) or 15.

R. v. B. (S.) (1989), 50 C.C.C. (3d) 34 (Sask. C.A.) — Until a judge has been asked and refused to make a transfer order to adult court, it is premature for a young offender to argue that *Charter* s. 15 has been breached by the denial of a jury trial.

Procedure

52. (1) Part XXVII and summary conviction trial provisions of *Criminal Code* to apply — Subject to this section and except to the extent that they are inconsistent with this Act,

(a) the provisions of Part XXVII of the *Criminal Code*, and

(b) any other provisions of the *Criminal Code* that apply in respect of summary conviction offences and relate to trial proceedings

apply to proceedings under this Act

(c) in respect of a summary conviction offence, and

(d) in respect of an indictable offence as if it were defined in the enactment creating it as a summary conviction offence.

(2) **Indictable offences** — For greater certainty and notwithstanding subsection (1) or any other provision of this Act, an indictable offence committed by a young person is, for the purposes of this or any other Act, an indictable offence.

(3) **Attendance of young person** — Section 650 of the *Criminal Code* applies in respect of proceedings under this Act, whether the proceedings relate to an indictable offence or an offence punishable on summary conviction.

(4) **Limitation period** — In proceedings under this Act, subsection 786(2) of the *Criminal Code* does not apply in respect of an indictable offence.

(5) **Costs** — Section 809 of the *Criminal Code* does not apply in respect of proceedings under this Act.

1980–81–82–83, c. 110, s. 52.

53. Counts Charged in Information — Indictable offences and offences punishable on summary conviction may under this Act be charged in the same information and tried jointly.

1980–81–82–83, c. 110, s. 53.

54. (1) Issue of subpoena — Where a person is required to attend to give evidence before a youth court, the subpoena directed to that person may be issued by a youth court judge, whether or not the person whose attendance is required is within the same province as the youth court.

(2) **Service of subpoena** — A subpoena issued by a youth court and directed to a person who is not within the same province as the youth court shall be served personally on the person to whom it is directed.

1980–81–82–83, c. 110, s. 54.

55. Warrant — A warrant that is issued out of a youth court may be executed anywhere in Canada.

1980–81–82–83, c. 110, s. 55.

Evidence

56. (1) General law on admissibility of statements to apply — Subject to this section, the law relating to the admissibility of statements made by persons accused of committing offences applies in respect of young persons.

(2) **When statements are admissible** — No oral or written statement given by a young person to a peace officer or to any other person who is, in law, a person in authority on the arrest or detention of the young person or in circumstances where the peace officer or other person has reasonable grounds for believing that the young person has committed an offence is admissible against the young person unless

(a) the statement was voluntary;

(b) the person to whom the statement was given has, before the statement was made, clearly explained to the young person, in language appropriate to his age and understanding, that

    (i) the young person is under no obligation to give a statement,

    (ii) any statement given by him may be used as evidence in proceedings against him,

    (iii) the young person has the right to consult counsel and a parent or other person in accordance with paragraph (c), and

    (iv) any statement made by the young person is required to be made in the presence of counsel and any other person consulted in accordance with paragraph (c), if any, unless the young person desires otherwise;

(c) the young person has, before the statement was made, been given a reasonable opportunity to consult

    (i) with counsel, and

    (ii) a parent, or in the absence of a parent, an adult relative, or in the absence of a parent and an adult relative, any other appropriate adult chosen by the young person; and

(d) where the young person consults any person pursuant to paragraph (c), the young person has been given a reasonable opportunity to make the statement in the presence of that person.

(3) Exception in certain cases for oral statements — The requirements set out in paragraphs (2)(b), (c) and (d) do not apply in respect of oral statements where they are made spontaneously by the young person to a peace officer or other person in authority before that person has had a reasonable opportunity to comply with those requirements.

(4) Waiver of right to consult — A young person may waive the rights under paragraph (2)(c) or (d) but any such waiver shall be videotaped or be in writing, and where it is in writing it shall contain a statement signed by the young person that the young person has been apprised of the right being waived.

(5) Statements given under duress are inadmissible — A youth court judge may rule inadmissible in any proceedings under this Act a statement given by the young person in respect of whom the proceedings are taken if the young person satisfies the judge that the statement was given under duress imposed by any person who is not, in law, a person in authority.

(5.1) Misrepresentation of age — A youth court judge may in any proceedings under this Act rule admissible any statement or waiver by a young person where, at the time of the making of the statement or waiver,

(a) the young person held himself or herself to be eighteen years of age or older;

(b) the person to whom the statement or waiver was made conducted reasonable inquiries as to the age of the young person and had reasonable grounds for believing that the young person was eighteen years of age or older; and

(c) in all other circumstances the statement or waiver would otherwise be admissible.

(6) Parent, etc., not a person in authority — For the purpose of this section, an adult consulted pursuant to paragraph 56(2)(c) shall, in the absence of evidence to the contrary, be deemed not to be a person in authority.

1980–81–82–83, c. 110, s. 56; R.S. 1985, c. 24 (2d Supp.), s. 38; 1995, c. 19, s. 35.

Case Law

Applicability

R. v. Z. (D.A.) (1992), 16 C.R. (4th) 133, 76 C.C.C. (3d) 97 (S.C.C.) — *See also*: *R. v. J. (G.R.)* (1986), 26 C.C.C. (3d) 471 (Man. C.A.); leave to appeal to S.C.C. refused (1986), 72 N.R. 159n (S.C.C.) — Section 56(2) does *not* apply to an accused who is 18 years of age at the time of making a statement, since the accused is no longer a "young person" for the purposes of the subsection.

R. v. J. (J.T.) (1990), 59 C.C.C. (3d) 1 (S.C.C.) — No statement given by a young person to a person in authority is admissible without compliance with s. 56(2), even where the young person stands trial in adult court.

R. v. D.(C.M.) (1996), 113 C.C.C. (3d) 56 (Que. C.A.) — Section 56 must be interpreted in a manner consistent with the right to counsel. A young person must be told that s/he

i. *may consult both counsel* and a *parent*;

ii. is entitled to a *reasonable opportunity* to consult both; and

iii. may have *counsel* present, with or without a parent, whilst a statement is given.

The fact that a young person had previously been apprised of the right to retain and instruct counsel does *not* constitute compliance with *Y.O.A.* s. 56.

R. v. J. (J.T.) (1987), 33 C.C.C. (3d) 239 (Man. C.A.) — Section 56(2) does not distinguish between a statement taken from a young person as a witness and a statement taken from a young person as a suspect.

R. v. J. (J.) (1989), 43 C.C.C. (3d) 257 (Ont. C.A.) — Section 56(2) is not applicable where a statement is taken from a young person as a complainant. It comes into play only in the case of a young person accused of committing an offence.

R. v. A. (S.) (1998), 129 C.C.C. (3d) 548 (Que. C.A.) — Where police mistakenly believe that they are required to comply with *Y.O.A.* s. 56(2) in relation to D, the requirements of the section are *relevant* in deciding whether the statement should be admitted.

Voluntariness: S. 56(2)(a)

R. v. M. (S.) (1996), 106 C.C.C. (3d) 289 (Ont. C.A.) — The communication to a young offender by his/her mother of the erroneous opinion that he/she would be permitted to go home if he/she told the police everything does *not* render involuntary the statement subsequently given.

R. v. B. (A.) (1986), 50 C.R. (3d) 247, 26 C.C.C. (3d) 17 (Ont. C.A.); leave to appeal refused (1986), 26 C.C.C. (3d) 17n (S.C.C.) — Generally, a person in authority is someone engaged in the arrest, detention, examination or prosecution of D. Before a parent of a young offender can be considered a person in authority, there must be some close connection between the calling in of the authorities and the parental questioning of the young person.

Consultation with Counsel, Parent or Other Adult: S. 56(2)(b)

R. v. J. (J.T.) (1990), 59 C.C.C. (3d) 1 (S.C.C.) — On every occasion when a young person is questioned by the police, the police are duty-bound to comply with s. 56(2) and to advise him of this right to consult an adult and to have that person present during the questioning.When gestures and verbal responses are an integral part of a statement, they are inadmissible unless there has been compliance with s. 56(2).

R. v. S. (L.J.) (1995), 97 C.C.C. (3d) 20 (Alta. C.A.) — The right of s. 56(2)(c) is conjunctive. D has a right to access to both a parent and a lawyer.

R. v. W. (B.C.) (1986), 52 C.R. (3d) 201, 27 C.C.C. (3d) 481 (Man. C.A.) — The young person must be told he has the right to consult an adult and be given an actual opportunity to do so.

R. v. H. (1986), 22 C.C.C. (3d) 114 (Man. C.A.) — The police ought not take a statement from a young offender until a guardian is made aware of the situation and a decision made whether or not to retain counsel.

R. v. M. (S.) (1996), 106 C.C.C. (3d) 289 (Ont. C.A.) — Section 56(2) does not make it mandatory that a young person be advised of the potential for transfer to adult court.

R. v. R. (G.) (1987), 37 C.C.C. (3d) 574 (Ont. U.F.C.) — It is not sufficient to advise a young person of his right to consult with only one of a parent or counsel, rather he must be given the totality of his right.

Waiver: S. 56(4)

R. v. M. (M.A.) (1986), 32 C.C.C. (3d) 566 (B.C. C.A.) — Section 56(2) has not been complied with where the police officer merely reads the young offender a form setting out the choices and offers no explanation of them.

R. v. G. (1985), 20 C.C.C. (3d) 289 (B.C. C.A.) — The rights of the young person must be clearly explained to him in language appropriate to his age and understanding.

R. v. W. (B.C.) (1986), 52 C.R. (3d) 201, 27 C.C.C. (3d) 481 (Man. C.A.) — Before a young person can waive his right of consultation, he must understand what is being waived and the consequences of doing so, and the waiver must be in writing.

57. (1) Testimony of a parent — In any proceedings under this Act, the testimony of a parent as to the age of a person of whom he is a parent is admissible as evidence of the age of that person.

(2) Evidence of age by certificate or record — In any proceedings under this Act,

> **(a)** a birth or baptismal certificate or a copy thereof purporting to be certified under the hand of the person in whose custody those records are held is evidence of the age of the person named in the certificate or copy; and

> **(b)** an entry or record of an incorporated society that has had the control or care of the person alleged to have committed the offence in respect of which the proceedings are taken at or about the time the person came to Canada is evidence of the age of that person, if the entry or record was made before the time when the offence is alleged to have been committed.

(3) Other evidence — In the absence, before the youth court, of any certificate, copy, entry or record mentioned in subsection (2), or in corroboration of any such certificate, copy, entry or record, the youth court may receive and act on any other information relating to age that it considers reliable.

(4) When age may be inferred — In any proceedings under this Act, the youth court may draw inferences as to the age of a person from the person's appearance or from statements made by the person in direct examination or cross-examination.

1980–81–82–83, c. 110, s. 57.

58. (1) Admissions — A party to any proceedings under this Act may admit any relevant fact or matter for the purpose of dispensing with proof thereof, including any fact or matter the admissibility of which depends on a ruling of law or of mixed law and fact.

(2) Other party may adduce evidence — Nothing in this section precludes a party to a proceeding from adducing evidence to prove a fact or matter admitted by another party.

1980–81–82–83, c. 110, s. 58.

59. Material evidence — Any evidence material to proceedings under this Act that would not but for this section be admissible in evidence may, with the consent of the parties to the proceedings and where the young person is represented by counsel, be given in such proceedings.

1980–81–82–83, c. 110, s. 59.

60. Evidence of a child or young person — In any proceedings under this Act where the evidence of a child or a young person is taken, it shall be taken only after the youth court judge or the justice, as the case may be, has

　　(a) in all cases, if the witness is a child, and

　　(b) where he deems it necessary, if the witness is a young person,

instructed the child or young person as to the duty of the witness to speak the truth and the consequences of failing to do so.

(2), (3) [Repealed R.S. 1985, c. 24 (2d Supp.), s. 39.]

1980–81–82–83, c. 110, s. 60; R.S. 1985, c. 24 (2d Supp.), s. 39.

61. [Repealed R.S. 1985, c. 24 (2d Supp.), s. 40.]

62. (1) Proof of service — For the purposes of this Act, service of any document may be proved by oral evidence given under oath by, or by the affidavit or statutory declaration of, the person claiming to have personally served it or sent it by mail.

(2) Proof of signature and official character unnecessary — Where proof of service of any document is offered by affidavit or statutory declaration, it is not necessary to prove the signature or official character of the person making or taking the affidavit or declaration, if the official character of that person appears on the face thereof.

1980–81–82–83, c. 110, s. 62.

63. Seal not required — It is not necessary to the validity of any information, summons, warrant, minute, disposition, conviction, order or other process or document laid, issued, filed or entered in any proceedings under this Act that any seal be attached or affixed thereto.

1980–81–82–83, c. 110, s. 63.

Substitution of Judges

64. (1) Powers of substitute youth court judge — A youth court judge who acts in the place of another youth court judge pursuant to subsection 669.2(1) of the *Criminal Code* shall,

　　(a) if an adjudication has been made, proceed with the disposition of the case or make the order that, in the circumstances, is authorized by law; or

　　(b) if no adjudication has been made, recommence the trial as if no evidence had been taken.

(2) Transcript of evidence already given — Where a youth court judge recommences a trial under paragraph (1)(*b*), he may, if the parties consent, admit into evidence a transcript of any evidence already given in the case.

1980–81–82–83, c. 110, s. 64; R.S. 1985, c. 27 (1st Supp.), s. 187, Schedule V.

Functions of Clerks of Courts

65. Powers of clerks — In addition to any powers conferred on a clerk of a court by the *Criminal Code*, a clerk of the youth court may exercise such powers as are ordinarily exercised by a clerk of a court, and, in particular, may

(a) administer oaths or solemn affirmations in all matters relating to the business of the youth court; and

(b) in the absence of a youth court judge, exercise all the powers of a youth court judge relating to adjournment.

1980–81–82–83, c. 110, s. 65.

Forms, Regulations and Rules of Court

66. (1) Forms — The forms prescribed under section 67, varied to suit the case, or forms to the like effect, are valid and sufficient in the circumstances for which they are provided.

(2) Where forms not prescribed — In any case for which forms are not prescribed under section 67, the forms set out in Part XXVIII of the *Criminal Code*, with such modifications as the circumstances require, or other appropriate forms, may be used.

1980–81–82–83, c. 110, s. 66; R.S. 1985, c. 1 (4th Supp.), s. 43.

67. Regulations — The Governor in Council may make regulations

(a) prescribing forms that may be used for the purposes of this Act;

(b) establishing uniform rules of court for youth courts across Canada, including rules regulating the practice and procedure to be followed by youth courts; and

(c) generally for carrying out the purposes and provisions of this Act.

1980–81–82–83, c. 110, s. 67; R.S. 1985, c. 24 (2d Supp.), s. 41.

68. (1) Youth court may make rules — Every youth court for a province may, at any time with the concurrence of a majority of the judges thereof present at a meeting held for the purpose and subject to the approval of the Lieutenant Governor in Council, establish rules of court not inconsistent with this Act or any other Act of Parliament or with any regulations made pursuant to section 67 regulating proceedings within the jurisdiction of the youth court.

(2) Rules of court — Rules under subsection (1) may be made

(a) generally to regulate the duties of the officers of the youth court and any other matter considered expedient to attain the ends of justice and carry into effect the provisions of this Act;

(b) subject to any regulations made under paragraph 67(*b*), to regulate the practice and procedure in the youth court; and

(c) to prescribe forms to be used in the youth court where not otherwise provided for by or pursuant to this Act.

(3) Publication of rules — Rules of court that are made under the authority of this section shall be published in the appropriate provincial gazette.

1980–81–82–83, c. 110, s. 68.

Youth Justice Committees

69. Youth justice committees — The Attorney General of a province or such other Minister as the Lieutenant Governor in Council of the province may designate, or a delegate thereof, may establish one or more committees of citizens, to be known as youth justice committees, to assist without remuneration in any aspect of the administration of this Act or in any programs or services for young offenders and may specify the method of appointment of committee members and the functions of the committees.

1980–81–82–83, c. 110, s. 69.

Agreements With Provinces

70. Agreements with provinces — Any Minister of the Crown may, with the approval of the Governor in Council, enter into an agreement with the government of any province providing for payments by Canada to the province in respect of costs incurred by the province or a municipality for care of and services provided to young persons dealt with under this Act.

1980–81–82–83, c. 110, s. 70; R.S. 1985, c. 24 (2d Supp.), s. 42.

SCHEDULE — (SS. 45(2.1), 45.02(3) AND (4))

1. An offence under any of the following provisions of the *Criminal Code*:

    (a) paragraph 81(2)(a) (causing injury with intent);

    (b) subsection 85(1) (using firearm in commission of offences);

    (c) (section 151 (sexual interference);

    (d) section 152 (invitation to sexual touching);

    (e) section 153 (sexual exploitation);

    (f) section 155 (incest);

    (g) section 159 (anal intercourse);

    (h) section 170 (parent or guardian procuring sexual activity by child);

    (i) subsection 212(2) (living off the avails of prostitution by a child);

    (j) subsection 212(4) (obtaining sexual services of a child);

    (k) section 236 (manslaughter);

    (l) section 239 (attempt to commit murder);

    (m) section 267 (assault with a weapon or causing bodily harm);

    (n) section 268 (aggravated assault);

    (o) section 269 (unlawfully causing bodily harm);

    (p) section 271 (sexual assault);

    (q) section 272 (sexual assault with a weapon, threats to a third party or causing bodily harm);

    (r) section 273 (aggravated sexual assault);

    (s) section 279 (kidnapping);

    (t) section 344 (robbery);

    (u) section 433 (arson — disregard for human life);

    (v) section 434.1 (arson — own property);

(w) section 436 (arson by negligence); and

(x) paragraph 465(1)(a) (conspiracy to commit murder).

2. An offence under any of the following provisions of the *Criminal Code*, as they read immediately before July 1, 1990:

(a) section 433 (arson);

(b) section 434 (setting fire to other substance); and

(c) section 436 (setting fire by negligence).

3. An offence under any of the following provisions of the *Criminal Code*, chapter C-34 of the Revised Statutes of Canada, 1970, as they read immediately before January 4, 1983:

(a) section 144 (rape);

(b) section 145 (attempt to commit rape);

(c) section 149 (indecent assault on female);

(d) section 156 (indecent assault on male); and

(e) section 246 (assault with intent).

4. An offence under any of the following provisions of the *Controlled Drugs and Substances Act*:

(a) section 5 (trafficking); and

(b) section 6 (importing and exporting); and

(c) section 7 (production of substance).

1995, c. 19, s. 36; 1995, c. 39, s. 189(e); 1996, c. 19, s. 93.1.

INDEX

Criminal Code *CC*; Constitution Act *CA*; Controlled Drugs and Substances Act *CDA*; Canada Evidence Act *CEA*; Firearms Act *FA*; Food and Drugs Act *FDA*; Interpretation Act *IA*; Narcotic Control Act *NCA*; Young Offenders Act *YOA*

Index

Index